Women's Worlds

The McGraw-Hill Anthology
of Women's Writing

Edited by

Robyn Warhol-Down
University of Vermont

Diane Price Herndl
Iowa State University

Mary Lou Kete
University of Vermont

Lisa Schnell
University of Vermont

Rashmi Varma
University of Warwick

Beth Kowaleski Wallace
Boston College

**McGraw-Hill
Higher Education**

Boston   Burr Ridge, IL   Dubuque, IA   New York   San Francisco   St. Louis
Bangkok   Bogotá   Caracas   Kuala Lumpur   Lisbon   London   Madrid   Mexico City
Milan   Montreal   New Delhi   Santiago   Seoul   Singapore   Sydney   Taipei   Toronto

The McGraw-Hill Companies

McGraw-Hill
Higher Education

Published by McGraw-Hill, an imprint of The McGraw-Hill Companies, Inc., 1221 Avenue of the Americas, New York, NY 10020. Copyright © 2008. All rights reserved. No part of this publication may be reproduced or distributed in any form or by any means, or stored in a database or retrieval system, without the prior written consent of The McGraw-Hill Companies, Inc., including, but not limited to, in any network or other electronic storage or transmission, or broadcast for distance learning.

1 2 3 4 5 6 7 8 9 0 DOC/DOC 0 9 8 7

ISBN: 978-0-07-256402-0
MHID: 0-07-256402-4

Editor in Chief: *Michael Ryan*
Publisher: *Lisa Moore*
Executive Editor: *Lisa Pinto*
Executive Marketing Manager:
  Tamara Wederbrand
Senior Development Editor: *Jane Carter*
Development Editor: *Betty Chen*
Editorial Assistant: *Meredith Grant*
Production Editor: *Carey Eisner*
Manuscript Editor: *Joan Pendleton*
Lead Design Manager and Cover
  Designer: *Cassandra Chu*

Text Designer: *Linda Robertson*
Senior Photo Research Coordinator:
  Natalia Peschiera
Photo Researcher: *Romy Charlesworth*
Art Editor: *Ayelet Arbel*
Production Supervisor: *Tandra Jorgensen*
Permissions Editor: *Marty Moga*
Composition: 9.5/11.5 Sabon by
  Thompson Type
Printing: 24# *Vista Opaque, R. R.*
  Donnelley & Sons

Cover: (clockwise from top right) *Four Praying Nuns*, by Friedrich Herlin, Photo: Erich Lessing/Art Resource, NY; *Godey's Fashions for January 1868*, Image by © Cynthia Hart Designer/Corbis; *A West Indian Flower Girl and Two Other Free Women of Colour*, by Agostino Brunias. © Yale Center for British Art, Paul Mellon Collection, USA/The Bridgeman Art Library; © Boris Roessler/dpa/Corbis.

Credits: The credits section for this book begins on page 2009 and is considered an extension of the copyright page.

Library of Congress Cataloging-in-Publication Data
Women's worlds : the McGraw-Hill anthology of women's writing / [edited by] Robyn Warhol.—1st ed.
    p. cm.
  Includes bibliographical references and index.
  ISBN-13: 978-0-07-256402-0 (alk. paper)
  ISBN-10: 0-07-256402-4 (alk. paper)
  1. English literature—Women authors. 2. American literature—Women authors. 3. Commonwealth literature (English)—Women authors. 4. Women—Literary collections. I. Warhol, Robyn R.
PR1110.W6W67 2008
820.8'09287—dc22

               2007043260

The Internet addresses listed in the text were accurate at the time of publication. The inclusion of a Web site does not indicate an endorsement by the authors or McGraw-Hill, and McGraw-Hill does not guarantee the accuracy of the information presented at these sites.

www.mhhe.com

About This Book

Women's Worlds: The McGraw-Hill Anthology of Women's Writing encompasses literature by women from seven centuries of writing in English. The works included are by women of different social backgrounds from all countries in the English-speaking world. Edited by a dynamic group of scholars with expertise in literature and women's studies, the anthology offers works by over two hundred women writers in traditional genres such as novels, stories, poems, essays, and plays, as well as nontraditional ones such as diary entries, letters, hymns, travelogues, blues lyrics, recipes, speeches, essays in literary and cultural criticism, and even an excerpt from a graphic memoir. The text offers all this in one volume and just over two thousand pages.

LITERATURE IN A CULTURAL STUDIES CONTEXT

To help students find their bearings in an often unfamiliar cultural landscape, *Women's Worlds* offers informative century introductions and timelines; both help students place the works in a broader social, material, cultural, and historical context. Historical maps open each century section to depict the world as it looked to authors writing in English during the period and showing how the English-speaking world expanded over the centuries. Headnotes for each author provide details about the writer's life and work that can illuminate the selections. The selections themselves are carefully footnoted, providing glosses of unfamiliar vocabulary and cultural-historical references (while avoiding interpreting the readings). An exciting innovation in anthology writing, Cultural Coordinates essays spotlight details of everyday life that writers assumed readers would understand but that have become unfamiliar over time and across locations. Illustrations—drawings, needlework productions, historical photographs, advertisements, and works of fine art—enrich the cultural context.

GLOBAL SCOPE

In addition to writers from England and the United States, the book includes classic and new voices from Africa, Asia, Australia, New Zealand, Canada, Scotland, Ireland, and the Caribbean to reflect the worldwide spread of English through colonization and emigration. In the later-nineteenth- and twentieth-century sections the anthology shifts the focus to writers from outside the United Kingdom and the United States, as well as to British and American women writers of color, moving away from the Anglo-American–focused model of traditional women's studies. The table of contents lists the writers' nationalities, so readers can place them; and an index that lists writers by region appears on the Web site (www .mhhe.com/warhol1) for readers interested in examining a range of voices from the same geographic area.

COMPLETE WORKS

Included in their entirety are many longer works, such as Aphra Behn's *The Rover*, Susanna Rowson's *Charlotte Temple*, Mary Prince's *The History of Mary Prince*, Rebecca Harding Davis's *Life in the Iron-Mills*, Christina Rossetti's "Goblin Market," Kate Chopin's *The Awakening*, and Susan Glaspell's *Trifles*.

THE LIBRARY OF WOMEN'S LITERATURE

To offer a manageable and affordable anthology while giving instructors a greater choice in the complete works they wish to assign, McGraw-Hill offers instructors who adopt the anthology the opportunity to package works from the Library of Women's Literature with the anthology at a discount. The Library of Women's Literature includes *Pride and Prejudice* (Jane Austen), *Jane Eyre* (Charlotte Brontë), *Little Women* (Louisa May Alcott), *The House of Mirth* (Edith Wharton), *Mrs. Dalloway* (Virginia Woolf), *Wide Sargasso Sea* (Jean Rhys), *The Handmaid's Tale* (Margaret Atwood), *A Raisin in the Sun* (Lorraine Hansberry), *Beloved* (Toni Morrison), *The House on Mango Street* (Sandra Cisneros), *Lucy* (Jamaica Kincaid), *Cracking India* (Bapsi Sidwa), *Second Class Citizen* (Buchi Emecheta), *The Namesake* (Jhumpa Lahiri), and *Playing in the Light* (Zoe Wicomb). *Women's Worlds* contains a biographical headnote for each writer in the Library of Women's Literature, helping instructors place them in the context of the anthology.

ONLINE RESOURCES

Additional resources for study and research, including a thorough bibliography and a list of authors by region, are available on the Online Learning Center for *Women's Worlds* (www.mhhe.com/warhol1). Using McGraw-Hill's Primis Online (www.primisonline.com), instructors can supplement the anthology with selections from McGraw-Hill's extensive literature database. The database includes works such as Aphra Behn's *Oroonoko*, Elizabeth Cady Stanton's essay "You Should Have Been a Boy," and poems by Elizabeth Bishop. Also available are chapters from many of McGraw-Hill's most popular textbooks in women's studies, such as Grewal-Kaplan's *An Introduction to Women's Studies: Gender in a Transnational World*, Second Edition; Lindemann's *An Invitation to Feminist Ethics*; and Woloch's *Women and the American Experience*, Fourth Edition.

Advance Praise for *Women's Worlds*

[*Women's Worlds*] offers its readers an exciting array of cross-cultural women writers, as well as a strategy of organization, pedagogical apparatus, and culture-studies approach that uniquely positions it among anthologies of women writers.
  —Jamie Barlowe, University of Toledo

[The Cultural Coordinates essays] promise to bridge the gap between what students see as the "stuff" we talk about in class and the ways they experience gender, culture, and social practices everyday. . . . The editors' inclusion both of information regarding the production and reception of the texts in the biographical headnotes and of the historical maps are . . . exciting innovations.
  —Cara Cilano, University of North Carolina at Wilmington

. . . The option to order additional novels [from the Library of Women's Literature] is particularly attractive to me, as I could continue to use the text and alter it each semester to keep material fresh and explore different themes.
  —Kathleen Helal, Southwestern University

A versatile, culturally-oriented text that would be successful in a variety of different courses on literature by women. Great choice!
  —Amy Levin, Northern Illinois University

A user-friendly collection of women's writing in English since the fourteenth century. The inclusion of cultural context helps to provide a broader base of knowledge about a wide range of women's experiences over the centuries. Strong inclusions by diverse women writers from a wide range of backgrounds and identities—you ought to take a look at it!
  —Jane Olmsted, Western Kentucky University

[The headnotes in *Women's Worlds*] are scholarly but also readable, suitable for undergraduates.
  —Stephanie Vandrick, University of San Francisco

This anthology takes its cultural studies seriously. Its international scope and innovative topics for [Cultural Coordinates essays] make it the only anthology of its kind.
  —Pamela Matthews, Texas A&M

[The Cultural Coordinates essays] are fascinating and valuable.
  —Ann Norton, Saint Anselm College

[*Women's Worlds*] is a text that represents women's writings across time and space, historically and geographically.
  —Jeana DelRosso, College of Notre Dame of Maryland

This looks like a more global, inclusive text than has been available before.
  —Gwen Argersinger, Mesa Community College at Red Mountain

To all the women writers who are not represented in this volume

Contents

Cultural Coordinates: Household Space   66

Cultural Coordinates: Scolds   79

Cultural Coordinates: Women's Community in Childbirth Rooms   87

Cultural Coordinates: Women's Spiritual Diaries   111

Cultural Coordinates: Prostitution   363

Cultural Coordinates: Breast-feeding and the Wet Nurse   383

Cultural Coordinates: The Tea Table   416

The Nineteenth Century 451

The Twentieth and Twenty–first Centuries   1181

Cultural Coordinates: A History of the Bra   1216

Cultural Coordinates: Chinese American Women and Immigration   1236

Cultural Coordinates: The Memsahib   1256

African American Women's Blues   1397

Cultural Coordinates: A Blues Life—Billie Holiday   1404

Cultural Coordinates: Anti-Lynching Campaigns   1419

Cultural Coordinates: Margaret Sanger, Abortion, and Birth Control   1435

Cultural Coordinates: The Pill   1642

Cultural Coordinates: Partitioning Women   1694

Cultural Coordinates: Cutting Women   1785

Cultural Coordinates: Sistren Theatre Collective   1808

List of Illustrations

General Introduction

"*A woman's place is in the home.*" For centuries most English speakers took this truism for granted. The home was supposed to be the woman's world, where she took care of her husband and children, decorated and cleaned the house, and supervised the religious and moral training of her family. But not all women inhabited that world. For reasons of need and desire, many have worked outside the home—in the fields, in the homes of others, in shops and factories, and in offices—to support themselves and their families and to generate wealth for others, and that home has been located around the world, from Australia to Zimbabwe. Over the centuries women fitting many descriptions have been living in what Barbara Johnson called "a world of difference," not just in countries around the globe, but inside Great Britain and the United States. This anthology invites readers into the rich variety of women's worlds, located wherever women have spoken English since the time English started being spoken. *Women's Worlds* offers a map of those worlds, as it surveys what anglophone women around the earth have had to say and how they have said it in writing from 1400 to the present.

Women's Worlds presents a new history of women's literature, organized to acknowledge the worldwide spread of the English language. This volume treats women's writing from places other than Great Britain and the United States, not as an outside addition to women's literary traditions in English, but as central to those traditions. As a result, writings by authors from India, Africa, Australia, and New Zealand, for example, are more numerous here than in comparable anthologies, and works by writers of mixed heritage (African American, Asian American, Afro-Caribbean, Anglo-Indian) take up a greater proportion of our selections than in similar volumes. This volume presents the female authors who make up the canon of what Elaine Showalter called "A Literature of Our Own," while adding works from every century by working-class women, immigrant women, native women, and lesbians who are not always part of that unofficial but generally accepted list of "important" literary works. By keeping the selections at a teachable length, we have increased the number as well as the diversity of authors available for surveys of women's literature.

Material Differences in Women's Worlds

To a middle-class British woman living in the nineteenth century, the invention of the sewing machine, with the dramatic changes in the production of clothing it brought, had a more vivid impact on her life than did the accession of Queen Victoria to the English throne, the progress of the Crimean War, or the specifics of political ideology that accompanied the romantic movement. Traditional periodization based on such political, military, and intellectual events elides the experience of women, especially those writing in social classes, nations, and racialized

xli

situations outside the dominant culture. For these reasons, in *Women's Worlds* the editorial apparatus—the century introductions, headnotes, Cultural Coordinates essays, and timelines—emphasizes material history. *Women's Worlds* illuminates aspects of women's lives that differ not only from our experience of the contemporary world but also from the worlds of women living in places and in racial, ethnic, sex, and class groups beyond our own.

The most innovative aspect of the anthology's editorial apparatus is the Cultural Coordinates feature. These brief essays provide insight into specific examples of material culture in women's lives over the past six hundred years, illuminating details from the anthologized selections or the lives of the writers and explaining what these details meant to the woman who mentions them. To understand what it meant to be a "scold" in early modern England or what it felt like to wear a hoop petticoat in the eighteenth century or what moved women in India to weave and wear the *khadi* as a sign of their resistance to the British Empire is to understand in a new, fuller way the piece of writing that includes this reference. We call these brief essays "Cultural Coordinates" to refer to the locations on a map specified by latitude and longitude: if you can give someone your coordinates, you can tell them exactly where you are, without naming any particular part of the world as your point of reference. Where are you located, for example, if you think of Asia as "the East"? From Europe, Asia may be east, but from Australia, Asia is north; from North America's West Coast it is west; and from China or India it is right where you are standing.

The century introductions and headnotes that frame the selections emphasize the lives of women writers, the conditions in which they lived and wrote, and the reception their work received. We have written these introductions and headnotes to reflect current trends in feminist literary and cultural theory as well as our many years' teaching experience. Each headnote tells the story of a woman's life, emphasizing the material constraints and opportunities her circumstances offered her. Similarly, the century introductions stress developments in everyday life throughout the anglophone world.

Differences within the English-Speaking World

The maps that open each section in this anthology remind readers of the importance of perspective in conceiving of the world. They also emphasize how important place is—the laws and language, social structure, and material conditions of a particular location—in forming one's perspective. The map that introduces the 1400–1700 section reflects England's perspective on its place in the world in 1540, when the map was drawn. It shows England—on its side!—suspended between a tiny strip of France (a threat to English power since before the Norman conquest in 1066) and Ireland (England's first colony, subdued through force and anglicization). Not surprisingly, France appears above England and Ireland below it, representing England's perspective on its own relationship to the two places. Before exploration and empire, this *was* the English-speaking world: a mere 5 to 7 million people on one island in the North Atlantic. For the period when English was spoken in England only, the women writers in this volume represent diverse social circumstances, from nuns like Julian of Norwich and Margery Kempe to aristocrats like Queen Elizabeth I and Lady Mary Wroth to Jane Sharpe, a midwife, and Anne Askew, a woman held in London's notorious Newgate prison.

Through British colonialism, the English language started to spread beyond the British Isles in the early seventeenth century, as English speakers began to claim territory in New England and Virginia, as well as in India and West Africa. The map at the beginning of the eighteenth-century section is centered on the Atlantic Ocean. During the seventeenth and eighteenth centuries, large numbers of English speakers moved from England and Ireland to North America, and English began to dominate the native languages—Algonquin, Arapaho, Ojibwa, among hundreds of others—and to push out the French (to the north) and Spanish (to the south) of earlier colonizers. Women were writing in places far afield from their British origins: in the late seventeenth century Mary Rowlandson, born in England, wrote about being captured and held hostage by a northeastern Native American tribe, and Janet Schaw, a Scotswoman, narrated her journey to Antigua, to give just two examples. At about the same time, enslaved Africans imported to work Caribbean and American plantations brought versions of English they learned on shipboard from their captors and fellow slaves. Here racial diversity enters the tradition of women's writing in English, as Phillis Wheatley—brought as a little girl from Africa to be a slave in the United States—became a great though unsung poet, and Mary Prince—born a slave in Bermuda—wrote her autobiography after escaping her owners and finding sanctuary in England.

The "map" included in this volume to represent the nineteenth century is actually an engraving of four women—Muses, to judge by their classical garments and props—examining a globe that is dwarfed by their size and substance. The woman who points to the globe is light-skinned with Anglo features, while the three Muses she instructs appear to be women of color wearing the hairstyles of Victorian ladies. The way these women overshadow the globe is not to imply that women in any sense dominated the nineteenth-century anglophone world, but the Anglo Muse does represent the British Empire's view of itself as the educating and "civilizing" force that was meant to remake the entire world in England's image. The period of British control of India (the "Raj"), which began as a trading venture in 1600 and ended when India and Pakistan regained independence in 1947, established English as the official language of government and education in India for 182 years. By the end of the nineteenth century, Indian-born women, such as Pandita Ramabai Saraswati, were writing in English to speak back to their colonizers, explaining the conditions of women's lives from their own point of view. Other English-speaking women who traveled the world during the nineteenth century—like Anna Leonowens of *The King and I* fame or Mary Kingsley, an explorer and anthropologist who wrote of her expeditions to western Africa—add their voices to those of better-known female authors such as Jane Austen, the Brontës, Emily Dickinson, Harriet Beecher Stowe, and George Eliot.

"The Antipodes"—as the British called Australia and New Zealand, thus placing themselves and those countries at opposite ends of the earth—also drew English speakers. Starting in 1788, British prisoners were transported to penal colonies in Australia; by the middle of the nineteenth century, sheep and wheat farms there attracted British immigrants as settlers, displacing the long-established Aboriginal culture and language. The first English colonists, like Mary Talbot, wrote of being forcibly relocated to what she saw as the other end of the world; later colonists, like Catherine Helen Spence and Rosa Praed, of making a middle-class life in the region. In Canada, Susanna Moodie wrote in a similar vein about living on the frontiers of Anglo culture. During that same period the British also began colonizing South Africa, where their language competed with Afrikaans, the language spoken by descendants of Dutch colonists, as well as the languages of indigenous peoples, such as Zulu and Xhosa. English became the official language of South Africa in 1822 and remained so until 1925. By 1840, colonists had also begun replacing the Maori culture by making English the dominant language in New Zealand, and English began spreading in East Africa, as well. This anglicization of Africa and New Zealand made possible the work in English of twentieth-century writers like Grace Ogot and Keri Hulme.

By the beginning of the twenty-first century, approximately 341 million of the world's people were native speakers of English. That makes English the third most common language, after Mandarin Chinese (spoken by more than twice as many people as English) and Hindi (with about 25 million more native speakers than English). In the year 2000, there were at least 104 countries in the world with significant numbers of native speakers of English, close to twice as many as the next most far-flung language, French, which is widely spoken in 53 countries. Because it followed the history of British and American imperialism; because it has become the international language of science and technology, not to mention popular culture; because it functions—much as Latin did centuries ago—as the common language of academic scholarship, travel, and diplomacy; English is now spoken and written not just in the United Kingdom and the United States, but in Canada, the Caribbean, Africa (particularly in the West, East, and South), South Asia (including India, Pakistan, and Sri Lanka), East Asia (mainly in Singapore, Malaysia, and the Philippines), Australia, New Zealand, and various South Pacific islands. In all of these locations—and the many other places English has gone that are not mentioned in this brief overview—native languages and competing colonial tongues inflected English, but it is still English, recognizable as a distinct language. And in all of these places, women have written English texts.

A WORLD OF WOMEN'S WRITING

This anthology brings together the creative efforts of women writing in English all over the world, placing them alongside many classics written by British and American women. Those classics include works that have been part of the mainstream literary canon (or at least on the margins of it) since their first publication, works such as Anne Bradstreet's and Emily Dickinson's poems, the stories of Edith Wharton and Willa Cather, the poetry of Gwendolyn Brooks, and Toni Morrison's fiction. We also include newly minted classics, works that have achieved canonical status since the feminist literary critical revolution of the 1970s and 1980s. Writers like Aphra Behn, Phillis Wheatley, Frances Burney, Susanna Rowson, Sojourner Truth, Harriet Jacobs, Harriet Beecher Stowe, Christina Rossetti, Kate Chopin, and Zora Neale Hurston were all but unknown in literature courses before the 1980s, absent from anthologies and syllabi alike. After the impact of feminist scholarship in the late twentieth century, they are now staples, even in courses that do not focus exclusively on women writers. This volume also includes works that may become classics, when the study of English literature branches out to include works from around the globe created in conversation—and often in conflict—with the Anglo-American classics. For instance, Annie Besant, Sui Sin Far, Cornelia Sorabji, Zitkala Sa, and Mourning Dove present a new historical context in which to read their contemporaries, Gertrude Stein and Virginia Woolf.

Because much of what women write goes beyond the traditional literary genres of fiction, poetry, and drama, we also include pieces of philosophy and feminist theory, not just by Mary Wollstonecraft and Margaret Fuller, but by such recent writers as Paula Gunn Allen, who speaks from a Native American perspective; bell hooks, whose point of view is African American; and Gloria Anzaldúa, who focuses on Latina experience. We include letters and selections from autobiographies, from the seventeenth-century memoirs of Lady Anne Halkett and the correspondence of eighteenth-century First Lady Abigail Adams to the slave narratives of Mary Prince, Harriet Jacobs, and Hannah Crafts to memoirs by such twentieth-century women as Jean Rhys (on her life in the Caribbean), or Julia Alvarez (on her Dominican American childhood). We include domestic handbooks, featuring recipes and household advice from Isabella Beeton, the Martha Stewart of the nineteenth century; hymns, both patriotic and devotional; lyrics written by blues artists; and a selection from the newest genre of women's writing in print, the graphic memoir (a selection from cartoonist Alison Bechdel's *Fun Home*).

We have avoided excerpts wherever possible, reprinting as many texts in their totality as we could. Among the long works we include in full are the novels *Charlotte Temple* (Susanna Rowson), *Life in the Iron-Mills* (Rebecca Harding Davis), and *The Awakening* (Kate Chopin); the plays *The Rover* (Aphra Behn) and *Trifles* (Susan Glaspell); the autobiography *The History of Mary Prince*; and the narrative poem *Goblin Market* (Christina Rossetti). Each complete long work in the volume represents an important genre for women writers of its period; taken together, they provide a survey of women's ways of representing their worlds over six centuries.

Including too many complete works makes for an anthology that is mammoth (and expensive). It also limits instructors' choice: Few instructors would ask students to supplement their 4,000-page anthology with additional novels. To offer an anthology of a manageable length at an affordable price, while giving instructors a greater choice in the complete works they wish to assign, *Women's Worlds* offers instructors who adopt the anthology the opportunity to package novels from McGraw-Hill's Library of Women's Literature with the anthology at a discount. The Library of Women's Literature includes *Pride and Prejudice* (Jane Austen); *Jane Eyre* (Charlotte Brontë); *Little Women* (Louisa May Alcott); *The House of Mirth* (Edith Wharton); *Mrs. Dalloway* (Virginia Woolf); *Wide Sargasso Sea* (Jean Rhys); *A Raisin in the Sun* (Lorraine Hansberry); *The Handmaid's Tale* (Margaret Atwood); *Beloved* (Toni Morrison); *The House on Mango Street* (Sandra Cisneros); *Lucy* (Jamaica Kincaid); *Cracking India* (Bapsi Sidwa); *Second Class Citizen* (Buchi Emecheta); *The Namesake* (Jhumpa Lahiri); and *Playing in the Light* (Zoë Wicomb). *Women's Worlds* contains a biographical headnote for each writer in the Library of Women's Literature, helping instructors place them in the context of the anthology.

Of course, no anthology seeking to cover six hundred years of women's writing in English can be exhaustive, even when supplemented by novels from Austen to Wicomb. Always there will be selections for which we could not obtain permission or selections whose permissions costs proved prohibitive, and there will be well-loved, familiar texts whose style or themes have been omitted because they duplicate those of another selection in the volume. Our goal thus has been to provide an ample selection of familiar texts and to supplement them with works from the Library of Women's Literature, while offering authors whose historical period, race, genre, sexuality, or nationality distinguishes their work from the mainstream.

PRINCIPLES OF ORGANIZATION

The anthology is organized chronologically, listing authors in the order in which they were born. When an author's life spans a century break, she appears in the century in which she produced the writing selected for this volume. We have avoided following the traditional periodization of British and American literature or even the recent critical challenges to those traditions, so there is no section called "Renaissance" or "Early Modern" literature, for example; nor is the nineteenth-century section broken into the dyad of "Romanticism" and "Victorian Literature" or the arbitrary "Nineteenth Century" and "Turn-of-the-Century" divisions. Instead, *Women's Worlds* is strictly chronological.

Each author's name and dates appear in the table of contents along with her nation of origin and—when appropriate—the nation(s) where she later lived and wrote. Authors are not grouped by nationality for two reasons: first, such division might suggest that women from a given nation share a common experience, when differences of race, class, and era are in fact profound; and second, the volume is arranged to provide readers with a sense of the simultaneity of profoundly different lives and modes of expression across women's worlds. What all these women writers do share, besides their sex, is the English language.

EDITING OF TEXTS

Wherever possible, we have chosen texts in the public domain; when necessary for clarity or readers' ease, we have modernized spelling and punctuation. When current scholarly editions of medieval and early modern texts have been used, they are noted in the permissions section, which appears at the end of the volume. Those texts still under copyright have been reprinted, with permission, from their most recent editions. At the end of each selection, we include the date of first publication at right and, where clearly established, the date of composition at left. Except those of the selection authors, footnotes are original with this volume. They are intended to assist twenty-first-century students in understanding archaic vocabulary, references to literary works and historical events, and details of material culture. The editors have rigorously avoided writing footnotes aimed at guiding a reader's interpretation of the text. Beyond the most basic information about geography and parentage, headnotes contain biographical details pertinent to the selection as well as some background on the production and reception of the text. At every stage of the anthology's production, we have done our best to maintain the strictest accuracy of dates, historical details, and textual editing.

ACKNOWLEDGMENTS

At each stage of development, a process that extended over several years, we relied on the thoughtful reactions of experienced teachers for guidance. Those who provided us with advice include the following:

Gwen Argersinger, Mesa Community College at Red Mountain, Mesa, AZ
Lori Askeland, Wittenberg University, Springfield, OH
Linda Austin, Glendale Community College, Glendale, AZ
Suzanne Bailey, Trent University, Peterborough, Ontario, Canada
Jamie Barlowe, University of Toldeo, Toledo, OH

Tamara Ponzo Brattoli, Joliet Junior College, Joliet, IL
Mary Bucklin, Northern Kentucky University, Highland Heights, KY
Elvira Casal, Middle Tennessee State University, Murfreesboro, TN
Nancy Chick, University of Wisconsin Colleges—Barron County, Rice Lake, WI
Cara Cilano, UNC—Wilmington, Wilmington, NC
Christine A. Colon, Wheaton College, Norton, MA
Elizabeth Cooper, Virginia Commonwealth University, Richmond, VA
Deanna Davis, College of the Canyons, Santa Clarita, CA
Mary De Jong, Pennsylvania State University, State College, PA
Lois Roma-Deeley, Paradise Valley Community College, Phoenix, AZ
Jeanna Del Rosso, College of Notre Dame of Maryland, Baltimore, MD
J. F. Diehl, University of California—Davis, Davis, CA
Sydney C. Dietrich, Bellevue Community College, Bellevue, WA
Mary Dockray-Miller, Lesley College, Cambridge, MA
Lise Esdaile, City University of New York—Lehman College, The Bronx,
  New York
Sonia Feder-Lewis, Saint Mary's University of Minnesota, Minneapolis, MN
Joanne Gates, Jacksonville State University, Jacksonville, AL
Jennifer Gehrman, Fort Lewis College, Durango, CO
Patricia Genz, College of Southern Maryland—La Plata, La Plata, MD
Margaret Graham, Iowa State University, Ames, IA
Ruth Haber, Worcester State College, Worcester, MA
Gail Hardaway, Mesa Community College, Mesa, AZ
Kathleen M. Helal, Southwestern University, Georgetown, TX
Shannon Hengen, Laurentian University, Sudbury, Ontario, Canada
Catherine Henze, University of Wisconsin—Green Bay, Green Bay, WI
Catherine Hoyser, Saint Joseph College, Hartford, CT
Sheila Hughes, University of Dayton, Dayton, OH
Kathryn R. Kent, Williams College, Williamstown, MA
Marsha Kruger, University of Nebraska—Omaha, Omaha, NE
Ellen Lansky, Inver Hills Community College, Inver Grove Heights, MN
Elaine Lawless, University of Missouri, Columbia, MO
Michelle Le Beau, University of New Mexico, Albuquerque, NM
Amy Levin, Northern Illinois University, Dekalb, IL
Jennifer Maier, Seattle Pacific University, Seattle, WA
Irma Maini, New Jersey City University, Jersey City, NJ
Karen B. Mann, Western Illinois University, Macomb, IL
Pamela R. Matthews, Texas A&M University, College Station, TX
Johnnie Clemens May, Glendale Community College, Glendale, AZ
Marcia P. McGowan, Eastern Connecticut State University, Willimantic, CT
Diane McPherson, Ithaca College, Ithaca, NY
Jennifer Mooney, Virginia Tech, Blacksburg, VA
Sarah R. Morrison, Morehead State University, Morehead, KY
Betty Moss, University of South Florida, Tampa, FL
Rachel Nash, Thompson Rivers University, Kamloops, British Columbia, Canada
Ann Norton, Saint Anselm College, Manchester, NH
Kathleen Oliver, University of South Florida, Tampa, FL
Jane Olmsted, Western Kentucky University, Bowling Green, KY
Delilah Orr, Fort Lewis College, Durango, CO

Brenda J. Powell, University of St. Thomas, St. Paul, MN
Cathy Preston, University of Colorado—Boulder, Boulder, CO
Katherine Romack, University of West Florida, Pensacola, FL
Barbara Rico, Loyola Marymount University, Los Angeles, CA
Robin A. Roberts, Louisiana State University, Baton Rouge, LA
Teri Delos Santos, Daytona Beach Community College, Daytona Beach, FL
Jane E. Schultz, Indiana University/Purdue University—Indianapolis,
  Indianapolis, IN
Bonnie Scott, San Diego State University, San Diego, CA
Ann Shapiro, Farmingdale State University of NY, Farmingdale, NY
Nancy St. Clair, Simpson College, Indianola, IA
Sheryl St. Germain, Iowa State University, Ames, IA
Lorena Stookey, University of Nevada, Reno, NV
Cynthia Taylor, University of Southern Colorado, Pueblo, CO
Annette Van Dyke, University of Springfield, Springfield, IL
Stephanie Vandrick, University of San Francisco, San Francisco, CA
Mary Katherine Wainwright, Manatee Community College—Bradenton,
  Bradenton, FL
Karen Weekes, Pennsylvania State University—Abington, Abington, PA
Carolyn Whitson, Metropolitan State College, St. Paul, MN
Celestine Woo, Fort Lewis College, Durango, CO

Each reviewer provided thoughtful advice that we have used to guide the book's creation, and to each we offer our sincere thanks. The final responsibility for the volume, of course, remains our own.

We each offer thanks to colleagues, students, friends, and family without whom this book and our lives would be much less rich:

Robyn Warhol-Down gratefully thanks Katherine Layton, Kathy Fitzgerald, and Peter Frechette, who are the most supportive of support staffs; the many UVM English work-study students who have copied, cut, and taped hundreds of pages over the past six years; Mercy Hyde, Helena Michie, and Bea Bookchin, the friends who put every little crisis into perspective; and Seth Warhol-Streeter and Richard Down, the loving family who make all things easier.

Diane Price Herndl would like to thank Iowa State University's English department for a research release that helped provide time to work on this book; to effusively thank Carl Herndl for extensive moral support and occasional perspective; and to thank Frances Adeline RuYi Price-Herndl for inspiration.

It has been wonderful to collaborate on this project with so many smart women, so Mary Lou Kete wants to extend her thanks to each of the co-editors but especially to Robyn Warhol-Down who had the unenviable task of riding herd on such an unruly group. She would also like to thank her ever-patient husband, John Howe, and her lovely daughter, Madeline, for their cheerful support of her and this project.

To her co-editors, Lisa Schnell gives her thanks for making a lengthy process also a deeply enriching one. She also thanks Emma and Ian, and especially her husband Andrew, whose love, companionship, and unqualified support are the keys that "set free whatever is in the brain."

Rashmi Varma would like to thank Robyn Warhol-Down for inviting her on this journey; her co-authors and Jane Carter for helping her along; Supriya Nair for suggesting names of some of the most amazing women writers from the

Caribbean; her students for their unending enthusiasm for women's writing; her partner Subir for being there constantly and lovingly; her family and friends for their affection and support; and her sister Ratna for her love of reading. Finally, her mother, for everything.

Beth Kowaleski Wallace thanks her family, and especially her husband Jim for his patience with her thousand queries about computer matters. She also thanks her Boston College students, who move and inspire her daily.

Finally, all the editors extend our heartfelt thanks to our student assistants: Jessica Barrett, Fade Brown, Chris Hrenko, John Landry, Krista Bera, Sara Burnett, Benjamin Beck, and Cate Racek. We thank Tatiana Abatemarco and Betty Chen for doing speedy and expert work on the bibliography. Our editorial assistant, Will Alexander—ever reliable, energetic, and gallant under pressure—gave crucial help with annotations and manuscript preparation, for which we are forever grateful. For finding a name for our focus boxes, we owe Liz Fenton one brilliant idea. We extend appreciation to Sarah Toubourg as well as George and Barbara Perkins for advice on our original conception of the book. Thanks are also due to Joan Pendleton, our copyeditor, and everyone at McGraw-Hill who worked on this book, including Lisa Pinto, Betty Chen, Meredith Grant, Marty Moga, Carcy Eisner, Romy Charlesworth, Natalia Peschiera, Cassandra Chu, Ayelet Arbel, Tandra Jorgensen, Nicole Netherton, Anne Stameshkin, Sarah Caldwell, Aaron Zook, and Tamara Wederbrand. And where would this anthology be without Lisa Moore and Jane Carter? They have poured their hearts—not to mention their expertise—into making *Women's Worlds* the book that it is. For their devotion to the project and their love of women's writing, we give thanks.

Robyn Warhol-Down
Diane Price Herndl
Mary Lou Kete
Lisa Schnell
Rashmi Varma
Beth Kowaleski Wallace

Map of England from *Geographia Universalis* (1540 edition) by Ptolemy.

The Fourteenth through Seventeenth Centuries

Until fairly recently, the best-known woman writing in English before 1700 was Judith Shakespeare, a fictional character created by Virginia Woolf in her long essay *A Room of One's Own* (1928, excerpted here on pp. 1342–50). Woolf, finding no evidence at all of women writers before the eighteenth century but feeling certain that there must have been suppressed poets among women in the years leading to 1700, imagines Judith as William Shakespeare's "wonderfully gifted sister" (p. 1332), who, thwarted in her pursuit of a literary career by a society that has no room for a woman writer and suffering from "the heat and violence of the poet's heart when caught and tangled in a woman's body," kills herself, having never penned a word.

Perhaps our first impulse on perusing the substantial number of entries for women prior to the eighteenth century in this anthology's table of contents is to be relieved that Woolf was wrong. In the years since *A Room of One's Own* was published, and particularly at the end of the twentieth century and into the twenty-first, what seems like an entire literary culture of women's writing in English has been unearthed. The collection in this anthology alone—and they represent only a tiny selection of the early women's writing we now have access to—include poems, devotional literature, autobiographies, diaries, advice books, philosophical essays, a medical manual, and a play. Where were these documents in 1928? Some had been misplaced, but most had simply been forgotten, buried and uncatalogued in manuscript archives, early book collections, and private libraries. How much has been lost we will never know, but certainly more women were writing in the early centuries of the past millennium than even the most thorough bibliography will show. And although far too many of those women died prematurely—in childbirth, from the plague, from infections that would now easily be cured by antibiotics—very few of them appear to have been suicides. (The saddest irony is that Virginia Woolf herself, a woman with one of the most successful literary careers in the first half of the twentieth century, put rocks in her pockets and walked into the River Ouse near her home in the south of England in 1941.)

But Woolf was also right: "The woman who was born with the gift of poetry in the sixteenth century," she wrote, "was an unhappy woman, a woman at strife against herself. All the conditions of her life, all her own instincts, were hostile to the state of mind which is needed to set free whatever is in the brain" (p. 1346). Even with much more historical evidence available to us—especially a much more thorough understanding of the material conditions of women's lives in this period—it is indeed true, almost without exception, that the woman writer was often a woman who, though she may have been happy in many ways, was also at strife with herself and with the society she inhabited.

A Historical Overview, 1300–1700

"By no possible means," says Woolf, iterating in 1928 what is one of the primary assumptions of this twenty-first-century anthology, "could middle-class women with nothing but brains and character at their commands have taken part in any one of the great movements which, brought together, constitute the historian's view of the past." While a very few women, as monarchs or aristocrats, did take part in (in the case of Elizabeth I, preside over) some of the political events that are the historical markers of this period, most of the women represented in these pages would be all but invisible to the historian. (Indeed, Woolf couldn't find them at all in the library at the University of Oxford). That is not to say, however, that women were not deeply affected by, often deeply implicated in, the changes

wrought by the great movements and events of the period 1300–1700. The Protestant Reformation is surely the defining "great movement" of these years. It is also a movement that affected and involved women in significant ways.

One of the major political events in the period occurred in 1309, when Pope Clement V moved the papacy from Rome to Avignon after a power struggle between the Roman church and the increasingly powerful French church. This transfer of power led to social upheaval that was exacerbated by the bubonic plague, or Black Death, which ravaged Europe, killing one-third to one-half the population and prompting a massive reorganization of the economy and, by extension, the entire society. Peasants and other rural workers, responding to the critical shortage of labor, moved in droves to the cities, where they found economic op-

The Black Death. Since the bubonic plague (or Black Death) killed roughly one-third the population of Europe as it swept across the continent in the fourteenth century, it is no surprise that the art of the period is rife with graphic images of death. (*Man Dying of the Plague*, fourteenth or fifteenth century, from an illustrated collection of English religious texts compiled by a Carthusian monk in Yorkshire in the fifteenth century. British, Library, London)

portunity in the form of wage-earning jobs. The capital that began to accumulate in the urban centers in turn led to increased trade and industry, with heightened competition both within and between countries and an increasing centralization of power in the hands of the monarchs, who sought to suppress unrest and control the burgeoning wealth of their citizens through taxation. (The Peasants' Revolt of 1381 was the first uprising in England of common people against the oppressive taxation of the English monarchs.) Western Europe, which had been characterized by internationalism and allegiance to the Holy Roman Church, became nationalistic in its interests.

As always, social upheaval was accompanied by intellectual change, the desire for economic freedom leading to the desire for greater intellectual freedom. The years leading to the Protestant Reformation represent, in some sense, a "perfect storm": the social, political, and intellectual upheaval occasioned by the population catastrophe of the Black Death found a collaborator in the newly invented printing press, and unrest over the authority of the Roman church spread through western Europe. In 1517, Martin Luther pinned his Ninety-five Theses, or protests, to a church door in the German city of Wittenberg, and Protestantism was born. In the Catholic Church, priests alone, taking their theological authority from the pope, could interpret scripture and administer the sacraments necessary for salvation. Luther and other reformers urged a return to the theological notion, advanced by the fifth-century St. Augustine, of salvation through "faith alone." Luther's Ninety-five Theses challenged Roman Catholic authority, hierarchy, and theology, insisting on the Bible as the sole theological authority and championing the individualization of faith. According to the Protestant reformers, salvation was a matter solely between the penitent and God.

The Reformation found its way to England through some of the chief reformers, including, most notably, John Wyclif (c. 1330–1384), a priest and Oxford scholar. (Margery Kempe, whose fourteenth-century autobiography is excerpted on pp. 29–33, was often associated with the followers of Wyclif, known as Lollards.) It wasn't fully resident in England, however, until Henry VIII, driven by political necessity in the early 1530s to dissolve his marriage to Katherine of Aragon (who was unable to provide him with a male heir), officially split with Rome and, in 1534, issued an Act of Supremacy that repudiated papal authority and declared the king to be the supreme head of the church in England.

Act of Supremacy or no, this was hardly the end of the story in England; in some ways it was just the beginning. Catholic opposition to Protestantism continued well into the sixteenth century, but of even more consequence was the growing group of Protestants who wished even further theological reform. The Puritans, as this group came to be called, objected to all the vestiges of Catholicism in the Church of England, including the rituals and prayers of the Book of Common Prayer. They also became increasingly organized around their opposition to the clericalism of the Church of England, which they saw as rivaling the political and theological hierarchies of the Catholic Church. That opposition culminated, in the 1640s, in the Puritan Revolution, or English Civil War, which deposed the monarch and invested authority in Parliament. Oliver Cromwell and his Parliament were in power only until 1660, but by the time the monarchy was restored under Charles II (the son of the executed Charles I, who had been in exile throughout the period now known as the Interregnum), a republican sensibility had taken hold in England.

Puritan zealotry spilled off the island of England as well and traveled west to the eastern seaboard of North America. Since the establishment of the Jamestown Colony by the entrepreneurial Virginia Company in 1607, there had been an English presence in North America, the "New World" as it was known. In 1620, however, a group of English Puritans who had been living in exile in the Netherlands since about 1605 but who were desperate to maintain their language and cultural identity landed north of Virginia at Plymouth and established an English Protestant presence in what came to be known as the Massachusetts Bay Colony.

WOMEN'S PLACE IN SOCIETY: THE DISPOSSESSED

To talk about women as if they were a single monolithic group would be wrong in any era but especially in the period 1300–1700, when the lives of everyone in society—women, men, children—were defined by the restrictions and distinctions of social class. The women of this period can be divided into six general categories:

1. The wives and daughters of artisans and laborers: shoemakers and tailors; general farm laborers like ploughmen and shepherds (peasants); workers in the construction trades—masons, carpenters, thatchers (roofers)
2. The wives and daughters of middle-class workers: mercers, tanners, butchers, farmers, and yeomen (servants of high standing in noble or aristocratic households); wealthy merchants in the cities
3. Wives and daughters of the gentry and nobility
4. Royalty
5. Widows
6. Nuns

But they did share some experiences: they would have been defined in terms of their relationships to men (as wives and daughters), as men were defined in terms of their work or their wealth, both of which were largely inherited. Also, although the class differences among women resulted in almost immeasurable disparity between the highest and the lowest classes, most women in the English-speaking world, which included England and, after the establishment of the Jamestown Settlement in 1607, eastern North America, would have been married, many as soon as they were able to bear children, around age thirteen or fourteen. (The exception was, before the sixteenth century, women who entered convents.) And all women, despite dramatic material differences, would have inhabited a world in which women were subordinate to men.

In the period 1300–1700, all the social, political, and religious institutions of the time were based upon a hierarchy headed by the monarch; all male subjects of the state were subordinate to the monarch, wives were subordinate to their husbands, children to their parents, and servants to their masters. Both men and women would have been reminded of this hierarchy every week during church services because it was believed to be ordained by God. Despite the enormous changes that swept across Europe from the fourteenth to the end of the seventeenth century—the Black Death, the development of the printing press, the rise of Protestantism, the spread of literacy, and the discovery and population of North America—and despite the fact that those changes did sometimes affect women's lives dramatically, the ideological structure of English-speaking society did not

Results of early marriage. Early marriage increased the risk of death during childbirth; high rates of infant mortality would have meant that the woman depicted here was very lucky. (*Afternoon Meal,* seventeenth century, by Louis Le Nain, National Gallery, London)

budge. Even when women were educated, as they increasingly were in the seventeenth century, the educational goal was chiefly to prepare them for life as a wife and a mother. Very few women would have put their education to other use. (That almost all the women represented in these pages put their educations to use by writing skews our sense of how exceptional that activity was.)

The Upper Classes and the Doctrine of Coverture

As is the case in almost every culture, the institution of law, particularly as it defined marriage, had a great deal to do with the way in which women were perceived in the English-speaking world. The law defined marriage through the *doctrine of coverture,* a legal doctrine which asserted that husband and wife were one person at law. While to twenty-first-century ears that may have an egalitarian ring to it, the doctrine of coverture meant that a married woman (known in the law as a *feme covert*) had no legal rights to anything, including her own body. The author T. E., in *The Lawes Resolutions of Women's Rights* (1632), wrote that every woman is, in effect, "an infant," lacking power "even in that which is more her own." A woman, says T. E. in the same text, "glittereth but in the riches of her husband, as the moone hath no light, but it is the sunnes."

There were no exceptions to the doctrine of coverture. Even queens were subject to its restrictions, which is almost certainly why Queen Elizabeth I, who

Queen Elizabeth, with Armada (in Stormy and Calm Seas) in the Background. (Collection of the Duke of Bedford, Woburn Abbey, Bedfordshire)

reigned successfully and prosperously over England from 1558 to 1603, chose—somewhat scandalously—never to marry. Indeed, in his memorial tribute to Queen Elizabeth after her death in 1603, Francis Bacon, a prominent philosopher and statesman (who himself never married), wrote, "The reigns of women are commonly obscured by marriage; their praises and actions passing to the credit of their husbands; whereas those that continue unmarried have their glory entire and proper to themselves."

The doctrine of coverture, which prevailed through the seventeenth century, has everything to do with the hierarchical view of life that places the monarch, together with God, at the top of the hierarchy and women only slightly above children and servants at the bottom. Related to the hierarchical view of the world is the political philosophy known as the divine right of kings, which began to crumble in England in the early seventeenth century and met its final demise in the middle of that century when a civil war was fought over the nature of monarchical authority. The Monarchists (or Royalists), those who supported a model of government that insisted on the absolute and divinely sanctioned authority of the monarch, lost both the war and their king—Charles I, who was beheaded in 1649—to the Parliamentarians (or Puritans), led by Oliver Cromwell. Cromwell and those who supported the Parliamentary cause had demanded a more republican style of government in which significant authority would be bestowed upon the quasi-democratic institution of the Parliament. Cromwell, as Lord Protector, and his

Parliament were in power only until 1660, but by the time the monarchy was restored under Charles II, a republican sensibility had taken hold in England.

By the end of the seventeenth century, the political philosophy known as the divine right of kings had been replaced by the social contract theories of the philosopher John Locke (1632–1704). Put simply, Locke argued in his *Two Treatises on Government* that all people belong equally to God and that they contract together to form a civil government in order, mainly, to protect their property (including the property of their own bodies). Given that the influence of Locke's social contract theory was profound and widespread in the English-speaking world by the end of the seventeenth century, one might also expect that the legal definition of the relationship between a husband and a wife would have changed as well. Yet despite Locke's own reliance on the model of the contractually related family in his writing, the theory of social contract as it was adopted by the government in England toward the end of the seventeenth century was not extended to the legal relationship between a husband and a wife. Coverture, as it had always been defined and interpreted, was still enforced.

The question of how upper-class women were affected by coverture takes us back to the issue of women's experience of marriage. Since the doctrine of coverture decrees that the husband has the sole right to all of his wife's property, including her body, all women gave up their rights over their bodies when they married. For all married women, then, the possibility of domestic abuse loomed large. And, indeed, there is plenty of evidence to suggest that wife abuse was widespread and completely condoned. The practice of "cucking," or ducking a woman in a fetid pond (see p. 79), for instance, was a fully authorized (even encouraged) form of spousal abuse practiced mostly among the lower orders.

But coverture, aimed as it was at consolidating and protecting wealth, had the most profound effect on the lives of noble and royal women. For a girl from a noble family, marriage was a political proposition. Betrothed often from the cradle, the daughters of the nobility appear to have had very little say over whom they married. At stake was the consolidation of property and power. Marriage among the nobility was only rarely a love match; instead, it was, like a merger, a mutually advantageous business deal between two powerful families. Coverture protected those consolidated assets by legally nullifying the possibility of female inheritance, which, on marriage, would draw wealth away from the birth family.

This is not to suggest, however, that all the daughters of wealthy men accepted courtship and marriage on these terms. Two selections included here, by seventeenth-century diarists Anne Halkett (pp. 97–100) and Mary Rich (pp. 103–10), vividly narrate the emotional and physical hardships they endured as very young women over the issue of marriage because they would not accede readily to their families' demands. In both cases, and at very young ages, the women were in love with men who were deemed unsuitable for marriage. Neither of these men were from "ignoble" families, but both were younger sons, which meant, according to the principle of primogeniture (by which the whole of the property of a noble family descended to the eldest son), that they would not bring with them into marriage the property wealth of their families. In the case of Halkett, she was simply prohibited from having any contact at all with her lover, Thomas Howard, the young man in question, a proscription with which she was eventually forced to comply when Howard was sent to France by his father. Rich, although only fourteen years old, simply refused to marry the man her father had chosen for her and was banished to a remote family estate. She continued in secret to see Charles Rich, the younger son with whom she was in love; eventually her siblings were able to intercede on her behalf, and her father grudgingly conceded both to the marriage and to an enormous dowry. (She was the daughter of one of the most powerful—certainly the wealthiest—man in the British Isles.)

The practice of coverture extended beyond the death of the husband or father as well, for although widows were left a "jointure," a portion of the estate designated for their provision, that property was not theirs to dispose of upon their deaths. In fact, from the thirteenth century onward, lawyers argued that, since wives and daughters could not own anything, they could not even make a will. In the middle of the sixteenth century, under Henry VIII, the law was changed to allow women to make a will with the consent of their husbands, but even then women were not allowed to decide independently what to do with their wealth. In some cases, most notably that of Anne Clifford, whose early-seventeenth-century diary chronicles her struggles (pp. 74–78), men went to great lengths to ensure that women did not have access to family wealth after the husband's or father's demise. At issue for Clifford was the enormous estate that should have been, in the language of early modern law, "entailed upon the heir of the body": Anne Clifford was the only surviving child of her parents' marriage; by law, therefore, she should have inherited all the Clifford land regardless of her gender. Despite the law, however, her father had willed his entire estate—minus his widow's jointure and an allowance for his daughter—to his brother.

The Middle and Laboring Classes: The Golden Age of Economic Independence?

Anne Clifford's lifelong legal battle for the Clifford estates is a reflection of the enormously complex body of law pertaining to women with property during the entire period, a body of law that, together with the principle of coverture, reveals an overwhelming anxiety about female independence—economic and otherwise. But it is necessary to take class status into account, for the kinds of anxieties circulating around women like Anne Clifford were specific to women from the propertied classes. The doctrine of coverture was applied to all married women, but it would clearly not find the same applications in the marriages of middle- and laboring-class women. The imperative to consolidate wealth and produce heirs simply did not exist for people who would never own land. A woman of the lower and middle classes, therefore, rarely married in her early or mid-teens and was much more likely to marry a man with whom she shared genuine affection. Furthermore, after the Black Death swept through England between 1348 and 1351, killing a third to a half of the population and bringing with it an economic crisis of almost incalculable proportions, the material lives of women from the lower and middle classes improved in ways that barely touched the noble classes. Historians have described the hundred years from about 1370 to 1470 as a kind of golden age for women of the middle and lower classes. With the urgent demand for labor, particularly in urban centers, women entered the workforce (and various lines of work) in unprecedented numbers and enjoyed for the first time the possibility of economic independence. Women worked side by side with men at almost all the manual labor jobs that had previously been reserved for men only, and they were paid their own wages.

Calling it a golden age, however, is clearly an overstatement. Economic independence, after all, requires more than just payment for goods and services; it also requires a living wage as well as the ability to control one's own finances. In general, women were paid just a fraction of what a man doing the same job would have been paid. Furthermore, under the doctrine of coverture (which was not suspended when a woman worked outside her household), the wages a married woman brought home were the property of her husband. A woman who made a decent living as a weaver, for instance, might have a husband who drank away all her profits, and she would have absolutely no legal recourse if he did. Still, while it is important not to romanticize the lives of lower- and middle-class women in the period, it remains true that the possibility of a relatively equal relationship with a spouse was, in theory at least, much more possible among women of the lower classes than it was for women in the upper classes.

A Modicum of Independence: Widows

Single women—known legally in England as *feme sole*—were rare in the period 1400–1700 (outside of convents), although there are some examples of unmarried women achieving economic independence in the period, particularly toward the end of the seventeenth century, when women were allowed to have stage careers (see pp. 200–201). But there were women who were neither married nor single, who occupied a kind of gray zone, and who managed to live quite independently. Those women were widows of prosperous merchants and the upper classes who could live comfortably on their jointures. There is plenty of evidence that men were anxiously aware of the kind of twilight zone widows occupied with respect to patriarchal authority. Shakespeare's *A Midsummer Night's Dream* (1605), for instance, contains two mentions of widows (or dowagers) in the very first scene of the play. In the first mention, Theseus, one of the play's primary male characters, complains that he has to wait until the next new moon to marry his betrothed, Hippolyta. "How slow this old moon wanes!" he complains. "She lingers my desires, like to a stepdame [stepmother] or dowager / Long withering out a young man's revenue." The moon, in other words, delays the fulfillment of his desires, just like a widow, whose fine living off her jointure eats into the inheritance of her son. Several lines later in the scene, the two young lovers, Hermia and Lysander, are plotting their escape from the oppressive Athenian court where Hermia's father has exercised his patriarchal authority and, under Athenian law, threatened to execute his daughter if she doesn't marry the young man—Demetrius—he has chosen for her. In the face of this threat, Lysander suggests the couple flee to the home of his "widow aunt, a dowager / Of great revenue." The implication here is that, from her place outside patriarchal constraints, even outside the law, the widow can provide the lovers with a refuge. She thus truly seems to possess a kind of political power not open to other women. It was almost certainly for this reason that Aphra Behn (pp. 125–99), the most extraordinarily independent of the early women writers represented in this anthology, chose to remain a widow after losing her husband (about whom nothing at all is known) very early in her marriage.

A Society of Women: Nuns

Before the dissolution of the monasteries in 1535–40, nunneries offered a refuge of prayer and purpose for pious young women who discerned in themselves a religious calling. Being a nun was the only career available for women in this period; it offered a purposeful life that did not involve marriage (either because the women

Four Praying Nuns, from a fifteenth-century altarpiece by Friedrich Herlin. (Stadtmuseum, Noerdlingen, Germany)

wished not to marry or were thought, by their families, to be unmarriageable). But convents also functioned as a kind of prison, a place for families to house difficult daughters. They were also a kind of boarding school for superfluous or troublesome daughters—as is suggested in Aphra Behn's *The Rover* (pp. 127–99) by the character of Hellena, who has been brought up in a convent and is expected to take vows but who "loves mischief strangely" (1.1.23).

Nunneries were not open to women of all classes. The first convents were founded by kings and the nobility for women of those classes; and while the number of nuns from the nobility declined over the years, they did continue to be recruited from the upper-middle and middle classes. Typically, they were the daughters of rural gentry and the urban elite—wealthy merchants and artisans.

Despite the example in this volume of the fourteenth-century nun and mystic Julian of Norwich (pp. 23–28), who spent all her time in solitary meditation, religious study, and prayer and who was, herself, an important theologian, the vast majority of nuns lived lives that were surprisingly ordinary. Like women outside the convent, they were expected to behave in unscandalous ways, and while technically cloistered, most nuns in fact had quite a bit of contact with the outside world: they taught in convent schools and tended the poor. If a nun was a prioress, she was also expected to manage the "household" of the nunnery. In terms of daily activities and governance, in other words, the lives of nuns mirrored those of married women from the middling classes.

One of the first official policies that Henry VIII enacted after breaking with Rome was the policy known as the dissolution of the monasteries. From 1535 to 1540, all the monasteries and convents in England were dissolved. With them disappeared the only opportunity for women of the middle classes to do something outside of marriage.

It is impossible to measure the impact of dissolution on English women, though it is tempting to think that it had relatively little effect: after all, there were only about 1,900 women in 150 nunneries in the whole of England at the time of the dissolution. But the disappearance of one of the only ways—perhaps the only way—in which women could live in a collective environment was surely not insignificant to the culture as a whole. The convent represented society's endorsement of the idea of women living communally. Once the convents were gone, so was the idea of women experiencing life in communion with other women. And, indeed, a great deal of the patriarchal energy of the next 150 years was expended in the discouragement of women's meeting and "gossiping" (see p. 88).

Protestantism, too, seems complicit in this individualization of women, for the very changes that were potentially liberating for women—namely, Protestantism's emphasis on the individual's encounter with God through reading scripture, which stimulated an explosion in literacy—also encouraged a kind of prayerful introspection that contained and controlled women's daily lives. The number of women's spiritual diaries from the period attests both to the fact that the Reformation was a "preeminently literary event," as the literary critic Jennifer Summit calls it, even for women, *and* to the fact that the emphasis on solitary reflection and study quieted and cloaked the increasingly audible and visible lives of women in the years following the Black Death.

OWNING THEIR WORDS: WOMEN'S WRITING, 1300–1700

Female dependence is in many ways the defining feature of the period for women. In a society where value was determined almost entirely by what one owned, the doctrine of coverture was a way of refusing women status as full members of the society, even though they were charged with the responsibility of peopling that society with the men who would become its members.

There are powerful ways of reading women's dissatisfaction with their status in this period. Consider, for instance, the conduct manual, one of the most popular genres of printed books in the period. These little books offered advice both on how women should behave and on how, in turn, their fathers and husbands should enforce those behaviors. The conduct books of the period insist on female "shrewishness," on women's bad temper and sharp tongue. It seems worth speculating that such seemingly universal shrewish behavior may have had to do with the unrelenting concerns women had about their property, or rather their lack of it. And when the definition of property extends to include one's own body, "shrewish" behavior among wives seems not surprising at all.

Notably, many of the works by women that express, implicitly or explicitly, a desire for some form of ownership do so through the language of mourning. It is one of the profound ironies of early women's writing that so often their desires—for power, for property, for access to education, for the liberty to speak their minds freely—are expressed only on the threshold of loss and death. It is as if they are allowed to declare themselves as people only at the moment—or in anticipation of the moment—in which they will cease to exist as a person.

The mother's legacy book, written for children to have after or in case of the mother's death, also reflects the desire to produce something of her *own*. Legacy books of Dorothy Leigh (pp. 81–83) and Elizabeth Jocelin (pp. 83–86), for instance, movingly reveal a woman's wish to lay claim in some way to her children (the father's property, by law), even from beyond the grave. These books are a kind of will, a willing of deeply personal intellectual property.

Isabella Whitney is even more explicit about her wish to lay claim in her long poem "The Manner of Her Will" (pp. 44–52). Her circumstances having left her with virtually no material possessions, Whitney constructs an elaborate fantasy in which she both designs and bequeaths the entire city of London. It is a fantasy, among other things, of vast, hyperbolic ownership.

Aemilia Lanyer's "The Description of Cooke-ham" (pp. 60–65) is perhaps the most deeply layered articulation of a woman's desire for ownership in this section of the anthology. Not only does Lanyer critique the social restrictions that kept her, a woman of the middle classes, from genuine friendships with women of the ruling class and all the privileges associated with nobility, but also the very ruling-class women to whom she dedicates the poem and who are, with Lanyer, forced to leave the country house of the poem are Margaret Cumberland and her daughter Anne Clifford, the same Anne Clifford who was embroiled in a lifelong legal battle for her family estates.

Much later in the seventeenth century, the young poet Anne Killigrew (p. 202) wrote a poem of outrage in which she protests the attribution of her poetry to another (pp. 203–7). And Aphra Behn's play *The Rover*, like the diary entries of Anne Halkett and Mary Rich, insists on a woman's right to choose her own marriage partner—choice itself being the most powerful fantasy of ownership for women.

Female expressions of worldly self-interest were viewed with suspicion and, often, overt hostility. A woman who expressed any interest at all in the material world beyond her family was labeled a whore or worse. Hence, the majority of the writing we have by women between 1300 and 1700 is devotional. Prayer and pious meditation were, in fact, encouraged, having their origin not in the woman's own position in the world but rather in the will and power of the great Father of them all, God. Yet women's experience and expression of religious devotion in this period is anything but simple.

Devotion was quite notably a female enterprise throughout the period, beginning with nuns who had been avid consumers of devotional manuals and who seem to have fostered a kind of female literary subculture. Certainly, Thomas Bentley, an English editor, defined it as one in 1582 when he put together the earliest published collection of English women's texts, the *Monument of Matrons,* a massive three-volume collection of prayers and meditations by, for, or about women. The *Monument,* which would have been an enormously expensive book, was clearly aimed at a very wealthy audience of women; and, indeed, every indication

Title page of Thomas Bentley's *Monument of Matrons (The Lampe of Virginitie),* 1582.

is that women in the upper classes spent a lot of time practicing devotion. For women like Mary Rich, whose diary is excerpted in this anthology (pp. 104–10), every day was almost entirely devoted to piety in its many forms: praying, reading scripture, meditating, keeping a spiritual diary. Rich and other women of the upper classes had much leisure time to fill up with pious practice, but even middle- and lower-class women incorporated much prayer and meditation into their days, getting up early to pray or singing psalms while they worked in the household. And in some cases, the practice of piety could lead to the temporary suspension of class division between women. Mary Rich, for instance, often shared pious concerns with her neighbor, the middle-class wife of a clergyman.

It is quite notable that, even among educated women, piety did not include the study of theology; the flowering of devotional literature written by and for women in the years following the break with Rome was clearly focused on the *experience* of religion, not on study. While this gave women many more opportunities to write and even publish (though often their writings were published posthumously by their families), it also had the effect of claiming a literary identity for women that was further cemented by its being incorporated into the identity of England as a whole. The English Reformation, after all, had represented not just a split with Rome but a break with the European continent altogether. Until 1534 and the break with Rome, England, though an island, had been a much more European nation; after 1534 the cultural work of claiming a distinct English identity began. Female piety became a part of that identity, and the pious woman writer became, as Bentley's anthology explicitly suggests, a kind of monument of English literary history. England increasingly came to define itself as a country of pious women and intellectual, practical men.

That identity followed women into the New World as well. When, in 1620, a group of Puritans, fearing religious persecution for their Reformist beliefs (most notably, their repudiation of the Church of England's Book of Common Prayer) and imagining a place where they could practice their religion in complete freedom, left England for America, they also took with them a commitment to experiential female piety that is reflected in the writings of both Anne Bradstreet (pp. 89–95) and Mary Rowlandson (pp. 119–25), two of the early American colonists who are represented in this anthology.

The hardships of life in the Massachusetts Bay Colony, together with the isolation and oppressiveness of, among other things, the insistence on female piety, came to a terrifying head in 1692 with the Salem witch trials. Between June and September of that year, nineteen people—thirteen of them women—were hanged on Gallows Hill near Salem Village. Although the causes of this event are far too complex to be articulated here, it is clear that at least part of what fueled the hysteria around the witch trials was a general anxiety about unconventional female behavior. Bridget Bishop, the first woman to be brought to trial and hanged as a witch, was, for instance, an outspoken woman with a blatant disregard for the demanding standards of female piety in the Puritan colony: she managed two popular taverns, she dressed flamboyantly, and she fought with her husbands.

Like the Black Death, the Civil War in England that was fought between 1642 and 1651 brought about enormous social change. In a war that was fought as much on the page as it was on the battlefield, traditional forms of female piety began to be challenged. The writings of Margaret Fell Fox, a selection of which are included here (pp. 95–97), are an example of the much more public, much more outspoken form female piety took during and after the Civil War. And it

Arrest warrant for Elizabeth Proctor and Sarah Cloyce, April 8, 1692. In the arrest warrant, Proctor and Cloyce are accused of "high suspition of Sundry acts of Witchcraft."

seems clear that the appearance of that more outspoken woman on the page opened the door to women like Margaret Cavendish, who, upon returning to England after being in exile during the 1640s, became the first English woman to write explicitly for publication and who wrote not about piety but about natural philosophy (science).

Thus, by the end of the seventeenth century, it is possible for Aphra Behn, living independently as a widow, to make a living as a writer and for her writing to be concerned not with piety at all but with politics and sexual intrigue. Behn was hardly typical, even in the 1680s, and she was the target of harsh disparagement throughout her career. Yet she did have a successful literary career, something that had been completely impossible even fifty years before. Sadly, the weight of patriarchal culture made it in certain ways unthinkable even after, so that when Virginia Woolf tried to imagine a seventeenth-century female literary career, she thought not of Behn but instead of the fictional, suicidal Judith Shakespeare.

If woman is a construction built up of her interactions with material culture, then it is impossible to avoid defining her in the period 1300–1700 in terms of patriarchy. The women of the fourteenth through seventeenth centuries whose writing follows both attest to the pervasive, material reality of patriarchy in their lives and—in sometimes subtle, sometimes explicit, ways—press up against it, exerting their wills and intelligence in the attempt to possess themselves, their thoughts and words, on their own terms in their lives as they lived them or wished to live them. That they could rarely free themselves from the everyday structures that dominated them makes them no less important, no less courageous, no less fundamental to a full understanding of the period than any of the men who were living and writing alongside them. These are the women Virginia Woolf was looking for; we feel certain she would have been happy to call them her sisters.

HISTORY		LITERATURE
Pope Clement V moves papacy to Avignon in France, beginning the 78-year "Babylonian Captivity"	**1309**	
Irish housewife Alice Kyteler is accused of witchcraft. Her first three husbands died, leaving her and three sons heirs. She is excommunicated and flees to England. Her servant is burned at the stake	**1324**	
The Hundred Years' War begins	**1337**	
The Black Death, or bubonic plague, reaches Florence and spreads to France and England. It will kill two-thirds of the population in some parts of Europe	**1348**	
The Great Schism divides the Catholic Church by setting up rival papacies in Rome and Avignon	**1378**	
The Peasants' Revolt is the first popular uprising in England against oppressive taxes	**1381**	
John Wyclif translates the Bible into English	**1382**	
	1387– **1400**	Geoffrey Chaucer *Canterbury Tales*
	1393	Julian of Norwich *Revelations of Divine Love*
Joan of Arc leads 4,000 men to liberate Orléans after receiving visions that France must be saved by a virgin	**1429**	
Joan is captured by the English and no attempt is made by Charles VII to save her	**1430**	
Joan is convicted and burned at the stake	**1431**	
	1433	Margery Kempe *The Book of Margery Kempe*
African slaves sold in Lisbon, initiating the slave trade, which will transport more than 20 million African men and women over the next 460 years to Europe and the New World	**1441**	
Hundred Years' War ends	**1453**	
The Gutenberg Bible is published at Mainz by Johann Gutenberg and marks one of the earliest uses of printing from movable type in Europe	**1456**	

HISTORY		LITERATURE
The Spanish Inquisition begins	1470	
Queen Isabella offers her jewelry as security to finance Christopher Columbus's voyage to the New World	1492	
Henry VIII begins his infamous reign	1509	
Spaniards import African slaves to Cuba following the deaths of most of the natives Parliament licenses 37 London women to practice surgery	1511	
Martin Luther posts his 95 Theses on a cathedral door in Wittenberg, Germany, and ignites the Protestant Reformation	1517	
Hernán Cortés sails from Cuba to conquer New Spain	1519	
Henry VIII divorces his first wife, Katherine of Aragon, after she fails to bear him male heirs	1527	
Henry VIII founds Church of England, marking an official separation from the Catholic Church in Rome	1534	
All monasteries and convents in England are dissolved, 1535–40	1535	
Henry VIII dies. His only son, Edward VI (son of Jane Seymour, Henry's third wife—of six) ascends to the English throne	1547	Anne Askew *The Latter Examination*
Lady Jane Grey named by the dying Edward VI as heiress to the English throne and proclaimed queen on July 9 but loses the throne 9 days later to Mary Tudor, Mary I, Edward's half-sister	1553	
Mary weds Prince Philip of Spain and begins persecuting Protestants	1555	
Elizabeth I succeeds as queen and reestablishes Protestantism. Peace and prosperity, the rise of the English navy, and a wealth of literature and arts mark her 45-year reign, known as the "Elizabethan"	1558	
Mary Stuart, known as Mary, Queen of Scots, begins her reign in Scotland	1561	

HISTORY		LITERATURE
Witchcraft becomes a capital offense in England	1562	
The Council of Trent reforms the Roman Catholic Church and begins the Counter-Reformation English Statute of Artificer sets women's wages at one-third to one-half that of men, though in many cases women work an equal number of hours and perform similar tasks	1563	
William Shakespeare, poet and playwright, is born	1564	
	1569	Elizabeth I "The Dread of Future Foes"
	1573	Isabella Whitney *A Sweet Nosegay*
Sir Walter Raleigh names the state of Virginia after Elizabeth I, the "virgin queen"	1584	
Virginia Dare is the first child of English parents born in America	1587	
The Spanish Armada of 132 vessels is defeated by the English navy	1588	Elizabeth I "A Song Made by Her Majesty"
Rev. William Lee of Cambridge invents the knitting machine, the stocking frame, capable of producing 1,000 stitches a minute	1589	
	1596	Edmund Spenser *The Faerie Queene*
	1602	Mary Sidney Herbert, Countess of Pembroke "A Dialogue between Two Shepherds"
Queen Elizabeth I dies and is succeeded by the Stuart son of Mary, Queen of Scots, James I. He reigns over a united kingdom with Anne of Denmark	1603	
Jamestown, Virginia, is founded According to legend, Pocahontas saves the life of Captain John Smith	1607	
	1608	Lady Margaret Cunningham's diary
The authorized King James version of the Bible is published for the Church of England	1611	Aemilia Lanyer *Salve Deus Rex Judaeorum*
	1616	Dorothy Leigh *The Mothers Blessing* Lady Anne Clifford's diary

HISTORY		LITERATURE
Three African women and 17 men are carried aboard a Dutch frigate at Jamestown to provide the nascent Virginia colony its first slaves Ninety young women arrive at Jamestown from England to marry settlers, who pay 120 lb. of tobacco for each of their brides	1619	
The *Mayflower* arrives off Cape Cod, bringing 100 pilgrims and 2 born on the voyage from England.	1620	
	1621	Lady Mary Wroth "Pamphilia to Amphilanthus"
	1623	William Shakespeare *First Folio* (posthumous)
	1624	Elizabeth Brooke Jocelin *The Mothers Legacie, to Her Unborne Childe*
James I dies and is succeeded by Charles I, who is beheaded by the English Puritans in 1649	1625	
English legal manual for women states that wife beating is still a husband's legal right	1632	
Astronomer and scientist Galileo Galilei is put on trial in Rome for "heresy" for defending the Copernican theory that the earth revolves around the sun	1633	John Donne *Songs and Sonnets*
Harvard University begins root as a seminary in the Massachusetts Bay Colony	1636	
Colonial American religious leader Anne Hutchinson and her husband gain territory in the Rhode Island colony after she was tried for sedition for advocating for women to have a voice in church affairs English clergyman John Harvard dies after one year in the Massachusetts Bay Colony and leaves his library and half of his estate to the seminary Colonist Ann Radcliffe contributes funds, and by 1650 Harvard will establish a 4-year program	1638	
Massachusetts is the first colony to recognize slavery as legal	1641	

JULIAN OF NORWICH
c. 1342–c. 1416

Very little is known about Julian's life beyond what little she tells us in the *Revelation of Divine Love* (c. 1373/1393). She was an anchoress—a religious recluse—who lived in a small, spare cell attached to St. Julian, one of the numerous churches of Norwich, a wealthy English city in the fourteenth century, second in population only to London. Supported almost entirely by alms, or the charity of the inhabitants of Norwich, Julian (who, like most anchoresses of her time, took the name of the patron saint of the church that housed her) would have spent her time in solitary meditation, religious study, and prayer.

At the age of thirty, Julian suffered an illness so critical that she was given last rites. Julian claimed that the illness was granted to her after she prayed to receive the three graces of God: the recollection of Christ's Passion; bodily sickness (so that she might feel pity for Christ's suffering); and God's gift of three wounds. Indeed, the illness ended miraculously after Julian experienced a series of visions, which she recorded as having taken place on May 13, 1373. Julian's account of the sixteen revelations occurs in both a short and a long version, the short version probably recorded soon after their reception and the longer version, demonstrating an expanded knowledge of classical and contemporary theological works, probably composed later and after considerable study.

The *Revelation of Divine Love* (also sometimes called *A Book of Showings*) secured Julian's place as a mystic in fourteenth-century England and established her as the first person, male or female, to write theology in the English vernacular. But the *Revelation* is also remarkable for its insistence on a God who is loving and compassionate—the adjective she attaches to God most often is "homely," by which she means comfortable and intimate as home. To Julian, God is both father *and* mother: "I am he, the power and goodness of fatherhood; I am he, the wisdom and the lovingness of motherhood."

The first excerpt below, from the longer, more theologically detailed version of the *Revelation,* contains her powerful exploration of the Trinity—God, Christ, Holy Spirit—that understands Christ as "Mother." The passage represents a particular achievement, for the Trinity was theological territory that even the most learned theologians had found daunting. The effectiveness of her theology comes, in part, from her ability to illustrate seemingly impenetrable mysteries with the everyday object. The exquisite passage on the hazelnut, included here, is an example of this kind of transformation.

Together with Margery Kempe, Julian of Norwich was recognized and respected as one of the most pious women of the late medieval period (fourteenth and fifteenth centuries) in England. The *Revelation* and the circumstances surrounding its composition have a great deal to do with that reputation.

From Revelation of Divine Love

3

The illness thus obtained from God

When I was half way through my thirty-first year God sent me an illness which prostrated me for three days and nights. On the fourth night I received the last rites of Holy Church as it was thought I could not survive till day. After this I lingered two more days and nights, and on the third night I was quite convinced that I was passing away—as indeed were those about me.

Since I was still young I thought it a great pity to die—not that there was anything on earth I wanted to live for, or on the other hand any pain that I was afraid of, for I trusted God and his mercy. But were I to live I might come to love God more and better, and so ultimately to know and love him more in the bliss of heaven. Yet compared with that eternal bliss the length of my earthly life was so insignificant and short that it seemed to me to be nothing. And so I thought, "Good Lord, let my ceasing to live be to your glory!" Reason and suffering alike told me I was going to die, so I surrendered my will wholeheartedly to the will of God.

Thus I endured till day. By then my body was dead from the waist downwards, so far as I could tell. I asked if I might be helped and supported to sit up, so that my heart could be more freely at God's disposal, and that I might think of him while my life lasted.

My parish priest was sent for to be at my end, and by the time he came my eyes were fixed, and I could no longer speak. He set the cross before my face and said, "I have brought you the image of your Maker and Saviour. Look at it, and be strengthened."

I thought indeed that what I was doing was good enough, for my eyes were fixed heavenwards where by the mercy of God I trusted to go. But I agreed none the less to fix my eyes on the face of the crucifix if I could. And this I was able to do. I thought that perhaps I could look straight ahead longer than I could look up.

Then my sight began to fail, and the room became dark about me, as if it were night, except for the image of the cross which somehow was lighted up; but how was beyond my comprehension. Apart from the cross everything else seemed horrible as if it were occupied by fiends.

Then the rest of my body began to die, and I could hardly feel a thing. As my breathing became shorter and shorter I knew for certain that I was passing away.

Suddenly all my pain was taken away, and I was as fit and well as I had ever been; and this was especially true of the lower part of my body. I was amazed at this sudden change, for I thought it must have been a special miracle of God, and not something natural. And though I felt so much more comfortable I still did not think I was going to survive. Not that this experience was any real comfort to me, for I was thinking I would much rather have been delivered from this world!

Then it came suddenly to mind that I should ask for the second wound[1] of our Lord's gracious gift, that I might in my own body fully experience and under-

---

1. In the first chapter of the short text of the *Revelation,* Julian explains that she was influenced by the legend of St. Cecelia, who was said to have received three literal sword wounds in her neck from which she died slowly and painfully. Julian, thus, asks God for three wounds of her own: the wound of contrition, the wound of compassion, and the wound of an "earnest longing for God." This second wound, then, is the wound of compassion she has asked for.

stand his blessed passion. I wanted his pain to be my pain: a true compassion producing a longing for God. I was not wanting a physical vision or revelation of God, but such compassion as a soul would naturally have for our Lord Jesus, who for love became a mortal man. Therefore I desired to suffer with him.

* * *

5

God is all that is good, and gently enfolds us; in comparison with almighty God creation is nothing; man can have no rest until he totally denies himself and everything else for love of God

It was at this time that our Lord showed me spiritually how intimately he loves us. I saw that he is everything that we know to be good and helpful. In his love he clothes us, enfolds and embraces us; that tender love completely surrounds us, never to leave us. As I saw it he is everything that is good.

And he showed me more, a little thing, the size of a hazelnut, on the palm of my hand, round like a ball. I looked at it thoughtfully and wondered, "What is this?" And the answer came, "It is all that is made." I marvelled that it continued to exist and did not suddenly disintegrate; it was so small. And again my mind supplied the answer, "It exists, both now and for ever, because God loves it." In short, everything owes its existence to the love of God.

In this "little thing" I saw three truths. The first is that God made it; the second is that God loves it; and the third is that God sustains it. But what he is who is in truth Maker, Keeper, and Lover I cannot tell, for until I am essentially united with him I can never have full rest or real happiness; in other words, until I am so joined to him that there is absolutely nothing between my God and me. We have got to realize the littleness of creation and to see it for the nothing that it is before we can love and possess God who is uncreated. This is the reason why we have no ease of heart or soul, for we are seeking our rest in trivial things which cannot satisfy, and not seeking to know God, almighty, all-wise, all-good. He is true rest. It is his will that we should know him, and his pleasure that we should rest in him. Nothing less will satisfy us. No soul can rest until it is detached from all creation. When it is deliberately so detached for love of him who is all, then only can it experience spiritual rest.

God showed me too the pleasure it gives him when a simple soul comes to him, openly, sincerely and genuinely. It seems to me as I ponder this revelation that when the Holy Spirit touches the soul it longs for God rather like this; "God, of your goodness give me yourself, for you are sufficient for me. I cannot properly ask anything less, to be worthy of you. If I were to ask less, I should always be in want. In you alone do I have all."

Such words are dear indeed to the soul, and very close to the will and goodness of God. For his goodness enfolds every one of his creatures and all his blessed works, eternally and surpassingly. For he himself is eternity, and has made us for himself alone, has restored us by his blessed passion, and keeps us in his blessed love. And all because he is goodness.

* * *

59

In the elect, wickedness is transformed into blessedness by the work of mercy and grace; God's way is to set good against evil by Jesus, our Mother in grace; the most virtuous soul is the most humble; all virtues are grounded in God

All this blessedness is ours through mercy and grace. We would never have had it or known it if goodness (that is, God) had not been opposed.[2] It is because of this that we enjoy this bliss. Wickedness was allowed to rise up against goodness, and the goodness of mercy and grace rose up against wickedness and then turned it all into goodness and honour, at least as far as those who are to be saved are concerned. For it is the way of God to set good against evil. So Jesus Christ who sets good against evil is our real Mother. We owe our being to him—and this is the essence of motherhood!—and all the delightful, loving protection which ever follows. God is as really our Mother as he is our Father. He showed this throughout, and particularly when he said that sweet word, "It is I." In other words, "It is I who am the strength and goodness of Fatherhood; I who am the wisdom of Motherhood; I who am light and grace and blessed love; I who am Trinity;[3] I who am Unity; I who am the sovereign goodness of every single thing; I who enable you to love; I who enable you to long. It is I, the eternal satisfaction of every genuine desire."

For the soul is at its best, its most noble and honourable, when it is most lowly, and humble, and gentle. Springing from this fundamental source and as part of our natural endowment, are all the virtues of our sensual nature, aided and abetted as they are by mercy and grace. Without such assistance we should be in a poor way!

Our great Father, God almighty, who is Being, knew and loved us from eternity. Through his knowledge, and in the marvellous depths of his charity, together with the foresight and wisdom of the whole blessed Trinity, he willed that the Second Person should become our Mother, Brother, and Saviour. Hence it follows that God is as truly our Mother as he is our Father. Our Father decides, our Mother works, our good Lord, the Holy Spirit, strengthens. So we ought to love our God in whom we have our own being, reverently thanking him, and praising him for creating us, earnestly beseeching our Mother for mercy and pity, and our Lord, the Spirit, for help and grace. For in these three is contained our life: nature, mercy, grace. From these we get our humility, gentleness, patience and pity. From them too we get our hatred of sin and wickedness—it is the function of virtue to hate these.

So we see that Jesus is the true Mother of our nature, for he made us. He is our Mother, too, by grace, because he took our created nature upon himself. All the lovely deeds and tender services that beloved motherhood implies are appropriate to the Second Person. In him the godly will is always safe and sound, both in nature and grace, because of his own fundamental goodness. I came to realize that there were three ways of looking at God's motherhood: the first is based on the fact that our nature is *made*; the second is found in the assumption of that nature—there begins the motherhood of grace; the third is the motherhood of work which flows out over all by that same grace—the length and breadth and height and depth of it is everlasting. And so is his love.

---

2. That is, if God had not been opposed by Satan, who, according to church doctrine, seduced Adam and Eve into wickedness.

3. The idea of a God who is three in one; typically, God the Father, Jesus Christ (the Son), and the Holy Spirit.

60

*We are brought back and fulfilled by the mercy and grace of our sweet, kind,
and ever-loving Mother Jesus; the attributes of motherhood; Jesus, our
true Mother, feeds us not with milk but with himself, opening his side to us,
and calling out all our love*

But now I must say a little more about this "overflowing" as I understand its
meaning:[4] how we have been brought back again by the motherhood of mercy
and grace to that natural condition which was ours originally when we were made
through the motherhood of natural love—which love, indeed, has never left us.

Our Mother by nature and grace—for he would become our Mother in everything—laid the foundation of his work in the Virgin's[5] womb with great and gentle condescension. (This was shown in the first revelation when I received a mental
picture of the Virgin's genuine simplicity at the time she conceived.) In other
words, it was in this lowly place that God most high, the supreme wisdom of all,
adorned and arrayed himself with our poor flesh, ready to function and serve as
Mother in all things.

A mother's is the most intimate, willing, and dependable of all services, because it is the truest of all. None has been able to fulfil it properly but Christ, and
he alone can. We know that our own mother's bearing of us was a bearing to pain
and death, but what does Jesus, our true Mother, do? Why, he, All-love, bears us
to joy and eternal life! Blessings on him! Thus he carries us within himself in love.
And he is in labour until the time has fully come for him to suffer the sharpest
pangs and most appalling pain possible—and in the end he dies. And not even
when this is over, and we ourselves have been born to eternal bliss, is his marvellous love completely satisfied. This he shows in that overwhelming word of
love, "If I could possibly have suffered more, indeed I would have done so."[6]

He might die no more, but that does not stop him working, for he needs to
feed us . . . it is an obligation of his dear, motherly, love. The human mother will
suckle her child with her own milk, but our beloved Mother, Jesus, feeds us with
himself, and, with the most tender courtesy, does it by means of the Blessed Sacrament,[7] the precious food of all true life. And he keeps us going through his mercy
and grace by all the sacraments. This is what he meant when he said, "It is I whom
Holy Church preaches and teaches."[8] In other words, "All the health and life of
sacraments, all the virtue and grace of my word, all the goodness laid up for you
in Holy Church—it is I." The human mother may put her child tenderly to her
breast, but our tender Mother Jesus simply leads us into his blessed breast through
his open side, and there gives us a glimpse of the Godhead and heavenly joy—the
inner certainty of eternal bliss. The tenth revelation showed this, and said as much
with that word, "See how I love you," as looking into his side he rejoiced.

This fine and lovely word *Mother* is so sweet and so much its own that it cannot properly be used of any but him, and of her who is his own true Mother—and
ours. In essence *motherhood* means love and kindness, wisdom, knowledge, goodness. Though in comparison with our spiritual birth our physical birth is a small,

4. She here refers back to the overflowing "motherhood of work" at the end of the previous chapter.
5. Mary, the mother of Jesus.
6. These words were revealed to Julian in the
ninth revelation.

7. The bread and wine consumed during the Eucharist, in Catholic theology said to become the
body and blood of Christ.
8. Words revealed in the twelfth revelation.

unimportant, straightforward sort of thing, it still remains that it is only through his working that it can be done at all by his creatures. A kind, loving mother who understands and knows the needs of her child will look after it tenderly just because it is the nature of a mother to do so. As the child grows older she changes her methods—but not her love. Older still, she allows the child to be punished so that its faults are corrected and its virtues and graces developed. This way of doing things, with much else that is right and good, is our Lord at work in those who are doing them. Thus he is our Mother in nature, working by his grace in our lower part, for the sake of the higher. It is his will that we should know this, for he wants all our love to be fastened on himself. Like this I could see that our indebtedness, under God, to fatherhood and motherhood—whether it be human or divine—is fully met in truly loving God. And this blessed love Christ himself produces in us. This was shown in all the revelations, and especially in those splendid words that he uttered, "It is I whom you love."[9]

c. 1373   c. 1393

➤◄ MARGERY KEMPE ►◄
c. 1373–c. 1438

Almost everything we know about Margery Kempe comes from her *Book* (an excerpt appears below), the first written autobiography in English. She was born in the prosperous port town of Lynn on the west coast of England into a prominent middle-class family: her father, John Brunham, was a local member of Parliament and was five times the mayor of Lynn. In 1393, at the age of twenty, she married John Kempe, a Lynn businessman who, though not as eminent as her father, was prosperous in his own right. Over the next twenty years, she bore fourteen children, although it was the birth of the first that seems most to have affected her. Suffering after months of debilitating morning sickness and the pain of labor, convinced that she was dying, she experienced an ecstatic conversion complete with visions of devils breathing fire and a redemptive conversation with Christ (the chapter narrating this incident is excerpted here). It was still many years before she devoted herself entirely to God, however; and although the *Book* does not narrate these years in detail, we get a wonderful thumbnail sketch of a strong-willed woman preoccupied with fashion and material acquisition who is also remarkably entrepreneurial, having for a time a successful brewing business and then a less successful stint as a miller. In fact, it was only after the sudden and seemingly inexplicable failure of both these business ventures that Margery finally surrendered to what she perceived to be God's will. Notably, although she bore thirteen more children in the approximately twenty years between her first ecstatic experience and this turning point, she mentions them scarcely ever in the *Book* and not at all in the section that narrates those twenty years.

The life Margery narrates after her full surrender to God would be extraordinary in any time; it is particularly remarkable for the fourteenth century. After securing a vow from her husband to cease sexual relations—a negotiation in the

---

9. Words revealed in the twelfth revelation.

truest sense of the word, for he finally concedes only after she agrees to pay his debts (see the second excerpt, from Chapter 11, below)—she begins a life as a kind of itinerant mystic, traveling throughout Britain and the Continent (some of her most intense visions occur in Rome). Her ministry is marked by uncontrollable fits of weeping that she calls her "cryings," visions that appear to be direct conversations with Christ, and a surprising outspokenness, even with important male clerics, about the need for total faith in God. (Chapter 46, the third and final excerpt below, narrates just such an incident.) During her travels, she met Julian of Norwich, a mystic to whom she is often compared (see pp. 23–28), although the two could scarcely be more different—Julian choosing a monastic life removed entirely from the world and Margery, though deeply spiritual, embracing a life that is perhaps best characterized by its worldliness.

The issue of authorship in the case of Margery Kempe is not entirely straightforward. Like most of her contemporaries (including men), Margery was almost certainly illiterate. She appears to have dictated most of her *Book*, therefore, to a priest who may have been nervous about the orthodoxy of Margery's beliefs and "cleaned up" certain sections to bring them more into line with official church doctrine. Still, most readers are struck by the singularly frank and vital voice that emanates from this volume, a vitality that is on full display in the excerpt that follows.

From The Book of Margery Kempe

Chapter 1

[MARGERY'S FIRST VISION]

When this creature was twenty years of age, or somewhat more, she was married to a worshipful burgess and was with child within a short time, as nature would have it. And after she had conceived, she was troubled with severe attacks of sickness until the child was born. And then, what with the labour-pains she had in childbirth and the sickness that had gone before, she despaired of her life, believing she might not live. Then she sent for her confessor, for she had a thing on her conscience which she had never revealed before that time in all her life. For she was continually hindered by her enemy—the devil—always saying to her while she was in good health that she didn't need to confess but to do penance by herself alone, and all should be forgiven, for God is merciful enough. And therefore this creature often did great penance in fasting on bread and water, and performed other acts of charity with devout prayers, but she would not reveal that one thing in confession.

And when she was at any time sick or troubled, the devil said in her mind that she should be damned, for she was not shriven[1] of that fault. Therefore, after her child was born, and not believing she would live, she sent for her confessor, as said before, fully wishing to be shriven of her whole lifetime, as near as she could. And when she came to the point of saying that thing which she had so long concealed, her confessor was a little too hasty and began sharply to reprove her before she had fully said what she meant, and so she would say no more in spite of anything he might do. And soon after, because of the dread she had of damnation on the one hand, and his sharp reproving of her on the other, this creature went

---

1. Had not confessed her sins to a priest.

out of her mind and was amazingly disturbed and tormented with spirits for half a year, eight weeks and odd days.

And in this time she saw, as she thought, devils opening their mouths all alight with burning flames of fire, as if they would have swallowed her in, sometimes pawing at her, sometimes threatening her, sometimes pulling her and hauling her about both night and day during the said time. And also the devils called out to her with great threats, and bade her that she should forsake her Christian faith and belief, and deny her God, his mother, and all the saints in heaven, her good works and all good virtues, her father, her mother, and all her friends. And so she did. She slandered her husband, her friends, and her own self. She spoke many sharp and reproving words; she recognized no virtue nor goodness; she desired all wickedness; just as the spirits tempted her to say and do, so she said and did. She would have killed herself many a time as they stirred her to, and would have been damned with them in hell, and in witness of this she bit her own hand so violently that the mark could be seen for the rest of her life. And also she pitilessly tore the skin on her body near her heart with her nails, for she had no other implement, and she would have done something worse, except that she was tied up and forcibly restrained both day and night so that she could not do as she wanted.

And when she had long been troubled by these and many other temptations, so that people thought she should never have escaped from them alive, then one time as she lay by herself and her keepers were not with her, our merciful Lord Christ Jesus—ever to be trusted, worshipped be his name, never forsaking his servant in time of need—appeared to his creature who had forsaken him, in the likeness of a man, the most seemly, most beauteous, and most amiable that ever might be seen with man's eye, clad in a mantle of purple silk, sitting upon her bedside, looking upon her with so blessed a countenance that she was strengthened in all her spirits, and he said to her these words: "Daughter, why have you forsaken me, and I never forsook you?"

And as soon as he had said these words, she saw truly how the air opened as bright as any lightning, and he ascended up into the air, not hastily and quickly, but beautifully and gradually, so that she could clearly behold him in the air until it closed up again.

And presently the creature grew as calm in her wits and her reason as she ever was before, and asked her husband, as soon as he came to her, if she could have the keys of the buttery to get her food and drink as she had done before. Her maids and her keepers advised him that he should not deliver up any keys to her, for they said she would only give away such goods as there were, because she did not know what she was saying, as they believed.

Nevertheless, her husband, who always had tenderness and compassion for her, ordered that they should give her the keys. And she took food and drink as her bodily strength would allow her, and she once again recognized her friends and her household, and everybody else who came to her in order to see how our Lord Jesus Christ had worked his grace in her—blessed may he be, who is ever near in tribulation. When people think he is far away from them he is very near through his grace. Afterwards this creature performed all her responsibilities wisely and soberly enough, except that she did not truly know our Lord's power to draw us to him.

* * *

Chapter 11

[MARGERY REACHES A SETTLEMENT WITH HER HUSBAND]

It happened one Friday, Midsummer Eve,[2] in very hot weather—as this creature was coming from York carrying a bottle of beer in her hand, and her husband a cake tucked inside his clothes against his chest—that her husband asked his wife this question: "Margery, if there came a man with a sword who would strike off my head unless I made love with you as I used to do before, tell me on your conscience—for you say you will not lie—whether you would allow my head to be cut off, or else allow me to make love with you again, as I did at one time?"

"Alas, sir," she said, "why are you raising this matter, when we have been chaste for these past eight weeks?"

"Because I want to know the truth of your heart."

And then she said with great sorrow, "Truly, I would rather see you being killed, than that we should turn back to our uncleanness."

And he replied, "You are no good wife."

And then she asked her husband what was the reason that he had not made love to her for the last eight weeks, since she lay with him every night in his bed. And he said that he was made so afraid when he would have touched her, that he dared do no more.

"Now, good sir, mend your ways and ask God's mercy, for I told you nearly three years ago that you would suddenly be slain[3]—and this is now the third year, and I hope yet that I shall have my wish. Good sir, I pray you to grant what I shall ask, and I shall pray for you to be saved through the mercy of our Lord Jesus Christ, and you shall have more reward in heaven than if you wore a hair-shirt or wore a coat of mail[4] as a penance. I pray you, allow me to make a vow of chastity at whichever bishop's hand that God wills."

"No," he said, "I won't allow you to do that, because now I can make love to you without mortal sin, and then I wouldn't be able to."

Then she replied, "If it be the will of the Holy Ghost to fulfil what I have said, I pray God that you may consent to this; and if it be not the will of the Holy Ghost, I pray God that you never consent."

Then they went on towards Bridlington and the weather was extremely hot, this creature all the time having great sorrow and great fear for her chastity. And as they came by a cross her husband sat down under the cross, calling his wife to him and saying these words to her: "Margery, grant me my desire, and I shall grant you your desire. My first desire is that we shall still lie together in one bed as we have done before; the second, that you shall pay my debts before you go to Jerusalem; and the third that you shall eat and drink with me on Fridays as you used to do."

"No, sir," she said, "I will never agree to break my Friday fast as long as I live."

"Well," he said, "then I'm going to have sex with you again."

She begged him to allow her to say her prayers, and he kindly allowed it. Then she knelt down beside a cross in the field and prayed in this way, with a great abundance of tears: "Lord God, you know all things. You know what sorrow I have had to be chaste for you in my body all these three years, and now I might have my will

2. Probably sometime around June 23, 1413.
3. That his desire for sex would disappear.

4. Armor composed of interlaced rings of chain work.

and I dare not, for love of you. For if I were to break that custom of fasting from meat and drink on Fridays which you commanded me, I should now have my desire. But, blessed Lord, you know I will not go against your will, and great is my sorrow now unless I find comfort in you. Now, blessed Jesus, make your will known to my unworthy self, so that I may afterwards follow and fulfil it with all my might."

And then our Lord Jesus Christ with great sweetness spoke to this creature, commanding her to go again to her husband and pray him to grant her what she desired: "And he shall have what he desires. For, my beloved daughter, this was the reason why I ordered you to fast, so that you should the sooner obtain your desire, and now it is granted to you. I no longer wish you to fast, and therefore I command you in the name of Jesus to eat and drink as your husband does."

Then this creature thanked our Lord Jesus Christ for his grace and his goodness, and afterwards got up and went to her husband, saying to him, "Sir, if you please, you shall grant me my desire, and you shall have your desire. Grant me that you will not come into my bed, and I grant you that I will pay your debts before I go to Jerusalem. And make my body free to God, so that you never make any claim on me requesting any conjugal debt after this day as long as you live—and I shall eat and drink on Fridays at your bidding."

Then her husband replied to her, "May your body be as freely available to God as it has been to me."

This creature thanked God greatly, rejoicing that she had her desire, praying her husband that they should say three paternosters in worship of the Trinity for the great grace that had been granted them. And so they did, kneeling under a cross, and afterwards they ate and drank together in great gladness of spirit. This was on a Friday, on Midsummer's Eve.

Then they went on to Bridlington and also to many other places, and spoke with God's servants, both anchorites and recluses, and many other of our Lord's lovers, with many worthy clerics, doctors and bachelors of divinity as well, in many different places. And to various people amongst them this creature revealed her feelings and her contemplations, as she was commanded to do, to find out if there were any deception in her feelings.

* * *

Chapter 46

[MARGERY'S ENCOUNTER WITH THE MAYOR OF LEICESTER]

Afterwards she went on to Leicester[5] with a good man, Thomas Marchale, of whom is written before. And there she came into a fine church where she beheld a crucifix, which was piteously portrayed and lamentable to behold, and through beholding of which, the Passion of our Lord entered her mind, whereupon she began to melt and utterly dissolve with tears of pity and compassion. Then the fire of love kindled so quickly in her heart that she could not keep it secret for, whether she liked it or not, it caused her to break out in a loud voice and cry astonishingly, and weep and sob very terribly, so that many men and women wondered at her because of it.

When it was overcome,[6] and she was going out of the church door, a man took her by the sleeve and said, "Woman, why are you weeping so bitterly?"

"Sir," she said, "it is not to be told to you."

5. A city in the Midlands (middle part of England).   6. When her crying fit had abated.

And so she and the good man, Thomas Marchale, went on and found lodgings for themselves and ate a meal there. When they had eaten, she asked Thomas Marchale to write a letter and send it to her husband, so that he might fetch her home. And while the letter was being written, the innkeeper came up to her room in great haste and took away her bag, and ordered her to come quickly and speak with the Mayor. And so she did. Then the Mayor asked her from which part of the country she came, and whose daughter she was.

"Sir," she said, "I am from Lynn in Norfolk, the daughter of a good man of the same Lynn, who has been five times mayor of that worshipful borough, and also an alderman for many years; and I have a good man, also a burgess of the said town of Lynn, for my husband."

"Ah," said the Mayor, "St Katherine told of what kindred she came, and yet you are not alike, for you are a false strumpet, a false Lollard,[7] and a false deceiver of the people, and therefore I shall have you in prison."

And she replied, "I am as ready, sir, to go to prison for God's love, as you are ready to go to church."

When the Mayor had rebuked her for a long time and said many evil and horrible words to her, and she—by the grace of Jesus—had reasonably answered him in everything that he could say, then he commanded the gaoler's man to lead her to prison. The gaoler's man, having compassion for her with weeping tears, said to the Mayor, "Sir, I have no place to put her in, unless I put her in among men."

Then she—moved with compassion for the man who had compassion for her, praying for grace and mercy to that man as to her own soul—said to the Mayor, "I beg you, sir, not to put me among men, so that I may keep my chastity, and my bond of wedlock to my husband, as I am bound to do."

And then the gaoler himself said to the Mayor, "Sir, I will undertake to keep this woman in my own safekeeping until you want to see her again."

Then there was a man from Boston,[8] who said to the good wife where she was lodging, "Truly," he said, "in Boston this woman is held to be a holy woman and a blessed woman."

Then the gaoler took her into his custody, and led her home to his own house and put her into a fine room, locking the door with a key, and ordering his wife to keep the key safe. Nevertheless, he let her go to church when she wished, and let her eat at his own table, and made her very welcome for our Lord's love—thanks be to Almighty God for it.

c. 1433

◄ ANNE ASKEW ►
c. 1521–1546

Anne Askew was born into a land-owning, politically prominent family in Lincolnshire (in the east of England). Her father, Sir William Askew, was a knight who, although he seems to have regarded his daughters (Anne was the second of two girls) mainly as a kind of commodity, nonetheless saw to it that they were

---

7. A follower of John Wyclif, fourteenth-century reformer of the Catholic Church in England and considered by many to be a heretic.

8. A town on the southeast coast of England.

educated. How widely Anne was educated is not known, but her writings indicate that she was intensely invested and fairly well read in the Christian religious issues of her day. In 1540, Anne was forced by her father to marry Thomas Kyme, the man to whom her sister, Martha, had been engaged when she died. The marriage, intended from the beginning to benefit Sir William's financial situation (a significant dowry was due from the wealthy Kyme family), was a profoundly unhappy one. The Catholic Kyme, unable to abide a wife who had chosen to become a Protestant, turned Anne out of the house relatively soon in the marriage, although not until she had borne two children. The fate of the children is unknown; it is quite possible that they did not survive infancy. If they did, Anne abandoned them to travel to London, where she sought a divorce on the grounds that her husband had no legal claim to her because he was an "unbeliever." By "unbeliever," she meant that her husband was Catholic in a country that, after Henry VIII's break with Rome in 1533–34, had declared itself Protestant. She did not succeed in her suit, England remaining, at least until the late sixteenth century, very Catholic despite Henry's decision. She nonetheless never lived again with Kyme, nor, in fact, did she ever leave London.

In London, Askew found support in Henry VIII's sixth wife—the only one to survive him—Katherine Parr. In fact, it may have been the queen's own growing influence in matters of Protestant reform that led to the persecution of the outspoken Askew. Perhaps seeking to incriminate Parr by her association with Askew, perhaps at the instigation of Kyme and his family, conservative members of Henry's court arrested Askew in June 1545 and interrogated her about her religious views. When no witnesses showed up to testify against her at her arraignment, she was released. A year later she was arrested again, arraigned again, sentenced to death, and then horribly tortured in the Tower of London (presumably to force her to implicate the queen—something she never did) before her execution by burning.

Askew's two *Examinations* narrate her interrogations after both arrests as well as the torture she was subjected to after the second; it is the second, or latter, examination that is included below. The *Examinations* also include letters she wrote while in prison, her confession of faith, a prayer before her death, and an original ballad, which is also printed below. Her writing reveals a remarkably independent woman of tremendous courage, considerable intellectual acumen, and enormous religious faith.

The Ballad Which Anne Askew Made and Sang When She Was in Newgate[1]

> Like as the armed knight
> Appointed to the field,
> With this world will I fight
> And faith shall be my shield.
>
> Faith is that weapon strong   5
> Which will not fail at need,

---

1. A prison in London.

My foes therefore among
Therewith will I proceed.

As it is had in strength
And force of Christ's way,
It will prevail at length
Though all the devils say nay.

Faith in the fathers old
Obtained righteousness;[2]
Which makes me very bold
To fear no world's distress.

I now rejoice in heart
And hope bid me do so;
For Christ will take my part
And ease me of my woe.

Thou sayst lord, who so knock
To them wilt thou attend;[3]
Undo therefore the lock
And thy strong power send.

More enemies now I have
Than hairs upon my head;
Let them not me deprave
But fight thy in my stead.

On thee my care I cast
For all their cruel spite;
I set not by their haste[4]
For thou art my delight.

I am not she that list[5]
My anchor to let fall
For every drizzling mist
My ship substantial.

Not oft use I to write
In prose or yet in rhyme;
Yet will I show one sight
That I saw in my time.

I saw a royal throne
Where Justice should have sit,
But in her stead was one
Of moody[6] cruel wit.

10

15

20

25

30

35

40

2. The faith of the biblical patriarchs (Abraham, Jacob, Moses, etc.) established their righteousness.
3. See Matthew 7:7: "Ask, and it will be given to you; search, and you will find; know, and the door will be opened for you."
4. Place no importance on their importuning.
5. Lets.
6. Angry.

Absorbed was righteousness   45
As of the raging flood;[7]
Satan in his excess
Sucked up the guiltless blood.

Then thought I, Jesus lord
When thou shalt judge us all,   50
Hard is it to record
On these men what will fall.

Yet lord I thee desire
For that they do to me,
Let not them taste the hire[8]   55
Of their iniquity.

                                                        1546

From The Latter Examination

The Sum of My Examination afore the King's[9] Council at Greenwich

Your request, as concerning my prison fellows, I am not able to satisfy because I heard not their examinations. But the effect of mine was this: I, being before the council, was asked of Master Kyme.[1] I answered that my lord Chancellor[2] knew already my mind in that matter. They with that answer were not contented, but said it was the King's pleasure that I should open the matter to them. I answered them plainly that I would not so do, but if it were the King's pleasure to hear me, I would show him the truth. Then they said it as not meet[3] for the King with me to be troubled. I answered that Solomon was reckoned the wisest king that ever lived, yet misliked not he to hear two poor common women,[4] much more his Grace a simple woman and his faithful subject. So, in conclusion, I made them none other answer in that matter.

Then my lord Chancellor asked me of my opinion in the sacrament.[5] My answer was this: "I believe that so oft as I, in a Christian congregation, do receive the bread in remembrance of Christ's death, and with thanksgiving according to his holy instruction, I receive therewith the fruits also of his most glorious pas-

---

7. Refers to the story of the Flood in Genesis 7, in which an angry God causes it to rain for forty days and forty nights, flooding and thereby destroying the entire earth and saving only Noah, his family, and the animals Noah leads onto the ark (boat) God commands him to make.
8. Reward.
9. The king referred to in the title is Henry VIII.
1. Her husband, whom she was trying unsuccessfully to divorce.
2. She refers to Thomas Wriothesley, Lord Chancellor of England.
3. Fit.
4. See 1 Kings 3:16–28: two prostitutes come to see King Solomon to resolve a dispute. Both women, who live in the same house, have recently

given birth, but one of the infants has died. Both women now claim the surviving baby as their own. Solomon asks that a sword be brought out and that the surviving child be divided in two and given to the two women. The first woman pleads with Solomon to give the living boy to the other woman; the other urges Solomon to divide the child. Solomon knew from the women's responses that the real mother of the boy was the first woman.
5. The issue here is whether Askew believes the communion wafer to be literally or figuratively the body of Christ. Roman Catholic doctrine insists on the former, known as the doctrine of transubstantiation.

sion." The Bishop of Winchester[6] bade me make a direct answer. I said I would not sing a new song to the lord in a strange land.[7] Then the bishop said I spake in parables. I answered, it was best for him, "for if I show the open truth", quoth I, "ye will not accept it". Then he said I was a parrot. I told him again I was ready to suffer all things at his hands, not only his rebukes but all that should follow besides, yea, and that gladly. Then had I divers rebukes of the council because I would not express my mind in all things as they would have me. But they were not in the meantime unanswered for all that (which now to rehearse were too much), for I was with them there above five hours. Then the clerk of the council conveyed me from thence to my Lady Garnish.[8]

The next day I was brought again before the council. Then would they needs know of me what I said to the sacrament. I answered that I already had said that I could say. Then, after divers words, they bade me go by. Then came my Lord Lisle, my Lord of Essex, and the Bishop of Winchester,[9] requiring me earnestly that I should confess the sacrament to be flesh, blood, and bone. Then said I to my Lord Parr and my Lord Lisle that it was great shame for them to counsel contrary to their knowledge. Whereunto, in few words, they did say that they would gladly all things were well.

Then the bishop said he would speak with me familiarly. I said, "So did Judas when he unfriendly betrayed Christ". Then desired the bishop to speak with me alone. But that I refused. He asked me why. I said that in the mouth of two or three witnesses every matter should stand, after Christ's and Paul's doctrine (Matthew 18 and 2 Corinthians 13).[1]

Then my lord Chancellor began to examine me again of the sacrament. Then I asked him how long he would halt on both sides. Then would he needs know where I found that. I said in the scripture (3 Kings 18).[2] Then he went his way.

Then the bishop said I should be burnt. I answered that I had searched all the scriptures yet could I never find there that either Christ or his apostles put any creature to death. "Well, well", said I, "God will laugh your threatenings to scorn" (Psalm 2).[3] Then was I commanded to stand aside.

Then came Master Paget[4] to me with many glorious words, and desired me to speak my mind to him. "I might," he said, "deny it again if need were." I said that I would not deny the truth. He asked me how I could avoid the very words of Christ, "Take, eat, this is my body which shall be broken for you". I answered that Christ's meaning was there, as in these other places of scripture: "I am the door" (John 10), "I am the vine" (John 15), "Behold the Lamb of God" (John 1), "The rock-stone was Christ" (1 Corinthians 10), and such other like. "Ye may

6. Stephen Gardiner, the Bishop of Winchester.
7. See Psalm 137:4: "How could we sing the Lord's song in a foreign land?"
8. There is no record of Lady Garnish; presumably she was a Protestant noblewoman with whom Askew had found refuge.
9. John Dudley, Viscount Lisle, and William Parr, Earl of Essex, prominent noblemen who were close to Henry VIII (William Parr was the brother of Katherine Parr, Henry's wife at the time) and sympathetic to Askew's situation and her views.
1. In Matthew 18:16, Jesus says that when a member of the church is being disciplined, "take

one or two others along with you, so that every work may be confirmed by the evidence of two or three witnesses." Likewise, in 2 Corinthians 13:1, Paul says, "Any charge must be sustained by the evidence of two or three witnesses."
2. 3 Kings 18:21 (from the Douay-Rheims Bible): "And Elias coming to all the people, said: How long do you halt between two sides? If the Lord be God, follow him: but if Baal, then follow him. And the people did not answer him a word."
3. Psalm 2:4: "He who sits in the heavens laughs; / the Lord has them in derision."
4. Sir William Paget, secretary of state to Henry VIII.

not here", said I, "take Christ for the material thing that he is signified by, for then ye will make him a very door, a vine, a lamb, and a stone, clean contrary to the Holy Ghost's meaning. All these indeed do signify Christ, like as the bread doth his body in that place. And though he did say there, 'Take, eat this in remembrance of me', yet did he not bid them hang up that bread in a box, and make it a god, or bow to it."

Then he compared it unto the king, and said that the more his majesty's honour is set forth, the more commendable it is. Then said I, that it was an abominable shame unto him to make no better of the eternal word of God than of his slenderly conceived fantasy. A far other meaning[5] requireth God therein than man's idle wit can devise, whose doctrine is but lies without his heavenly verity. Then he asked me if I would commune with some wiser man. "That offer", I said, "I would not refuse." Then he told the council. And so went I to my lady's again.

Then came to me Dr Coxe and Dr Robinson.[6] In conclusion, we could not agree. Then they made me a bill[7] of the sacrament, willing me to set my hand thereunto, but I would not. Then on the sunday I was sore sick,[8] thinking no less than to die. Therefore I desired to speak with Latimer.[9] It would no[t] be. Then was I sent to Newgate[1] in my extremity of sickness, for in all my life afore was I never in such pain. Thus the Lord strengthen you in the truth. Pray, pray, pray.

1547

---

5. Deeper meaning.
6. The prominent conservative theologian Richard Coxe and presumably another theologian named Robinson.
7. Prepared statement.

8. Refers cryptically to her torture on the rack.
9. The prominent Protestant reformer Hugh Latimer, Bishop of Gloucester.
1. London prison.

CULTURAL COORDINATES
Needlework

In 1640, the anonymous author of the *Woman's Sharp Revenge* wrote, "lest we should be made able to vindicate our own injuries, we are set only to the Needle, to prick our fingers, or else to the Wheel to spin a fair thread for our own undoing, or perchance to some more dirty and debased drudgery." Needlework, or embroidery, practiced by women across all class boundaries, was prescribed not as an art—though, indeed, the pieces that are preserved from the early modern period are astonishing in their artfulness—but, as the passage above complains, as an expression of femininity that was also a form of control. Eyes lowered, head bent, shoulders hunched over their work, women were producing their own invisibility as they produced their needlework. Indeed, a great deal of the prescriptive literature for women from the period exhorts women to devote themselves to their needlework in order to avoid the dangers of idleness, dangers that included reading and, especially, writing.

There were ways, however, that individual women covertly expressed things other than submissiveness with their needlework. The Princess Elizabeth—later to become Queen Elizabeth I—for instance, translated Marguerite de Navarre's

Elizabeth I's embroidered cover of *The Miroir or Glass of the Synnefull Soul.*

39

Miroir de l'âme pècheresse as *The Miroir or Glasse of the Synneful Soule* in 1548. She presented the volume to her educated stepmother, Katherine Parr, bound in a cover that she had elaborately embroidered. By doing so, Elizabeth subtly insisted that writing and needlework are related, not opposed, activities.

Much more consequential was the needlework of Elizabeth's famous cousin, Mary, Queen of Scots, which is subversive, in this case, in the minds of the very people who might have been encouraging the feminine pursuit in the first place. Known as a particularly gifted needleworker, Mary embroidered the middle panel of a large tapestry known as the Oxburgh Hanging, one of the few pieces from the period that is still extant (and hanging in the Victoria and Albert Museum in London), between the years 1569 and 1571, while she was imprisoned in the Tower of London on suspicion of treason. The emblem depicts two fruit trees and a hand extending from the sky holding a pruning hook. Above the scene is a scroll with a Latin inscription: *Virescit Vulnere Virtus* (courage grows strong at a wound). A copy of the emblem was found in the possession of Thomas, Duke of Norfolk, and was produced at his trial for treason as evidence of the threat he, and by association Mary, posed to Queen Elizabeth. He was executed for treason in 1571. Mary's own conviction—she was executed in London in 1587—was secured partly because of the evidence of other "emblems" she had embroidered that were thought to be seditious: an emblem of a grafted tree with bands holding the graft and the words *Per Vincula cresco* (through bands I grow) and an emblem of a palm tree pressed down and accompanied by the words *Ponderibus virtus innata resistit* (against weights does inbred virtue strive). It would seem that even these seemingly private cultural productions, so tied to the everyday expression of subjection and silence on the part of women, could ironically betray the ways in which women, and female authority in particular, were increasingly part of the public imagination in the early modern period.

1533–1603

Elizabeth Tudor was the daughter of Henry VIII and Anne Boleyn, Henry's second wife. Boleyn was executed in 1536 for failing to produce the male heir that Henry desired. Following what could only have been a deeply traumatic childhood and adolescence, her status in the king's household constantly in flux throughout Henry's four subsequent marriages and his break with the Roman church, Elizabeth found herself under what was effectively house arrest during the four-year reign (1554–58) of her half sister Mary. When Elizabeth herself ascended the throne in 1558, her status was no less imperiled. Having been declared illegitimate by Pope Clement VII after her father married a third time, Elizabeth's decision to remain unmarried throughout her life raised questions about her legitimacy as ruler. Yet that same decision may well have guaranteed the famously autonomous authority she managed to secure during her long and successful reign. It was perhaps because she refused to surrender her autonomy, to align herself with one group or another through marriage, that she was able to steer a course between the powerful Catholic factions within the English court who wished to realign English power with the Roman church and the extreme Protestant (Puritan) position that urged a complete purging of all things Catholic in the English church. The middle way, or *via media,* that Elizabeth was able to imagine and promote as a potent form of English nationalism eventually took hold theologically after her death and became Anglicanism in the first part of the seventeenth century.

Her refusal to marry was also, of course, an acknowledgment of the gender politics of the time. Had she married and borne children, she would have been declaring herself fully feminine, a gendered position seen as distinctly inferior to masculinity in the period. By remaining unmarried, she was able to distance herself somewhat from some of the gendered assumptions that might have interfered with her authority (indeed, she referred to herself as having the "body but of a weak and feeble woman; but . . . the heart and stomach of a king" in a famous speech she gave to the troops at Tilbury in 1588). Yet as canny as she seems to have been about gender and authority, she was not at all interested in promoting sexual equality beyond her own situation; she was not, in other words, a "feminist."

Like many of her closest advisors, Elizabeth wrote occasional poetry, and the two poems reproduced below reveal her preoccupations with power and authority. "The Dread of Future Woes" was almost certainly composed around 1569 and appears to be concerned with the arrival in England of Elizabeth's cousin, the Catholic Mary, Queen of Scots, a claimant to the throne. "A Song Made by Her Majesty" celebrates the 1588 English triumph over the Spanish Armada. The reference to the fiery pillar and cloud, an allusion to the biblical book of Exodus, sets up the connection of Elizabeth with Moses, the first great national leader of the Israelites.

The Dread of Future Foes[1]

The dread of future foes exiles my present joy,
And wit[2] me warns to shun such snares as threaten mine annoy;
For falsehood not doth flow, and subjects' faith doth ebb,
Which should not be if reason ruled or wisdom wove the web.
But clouds of joys untried, doth cloak aspiring minds,   5
Which turn to rage of late report, by changed course of minds
The tops of hope suppose, the root of rue shall be,
And fruitless of the grafted guile as shortly ye shall see.
The dazzled eyes with pride, with great ambition blinds.
Shall be unsealed by worthy wights,[3] whose foresight falsehood finds.   10
The daughter of debate, that discord aye[4] doth sow,
Shall reap no gain where former rule, still peace hath taught to know.
No foreign banished wight, shall anchor in this port;
Our realm brooks no seditious sects, let them elsewhere resort.
My rusty sword through rest, shall first his edge employ   15
To poll the tops[5] that seeks such change or gapes for further joy.

                                                          1569

A Song Made by Her Majesty

Sung in December after the scattering of the Spanish Navy[6]

Look and bow down thine ear, O Lord;
From thy bright sphere behold and see
Thy handmaid[7] and thy handy work
Amongst thy priests offering to thee
Zeal for incense reaching the skies;   5
My self and scepter sacrifice.

My soul ascend this holy place;
Ascribe him strength and sing his praise,
For he refraineth perjurers' spirit
And hath done wonders in my days.   10
He made the winds and waters rise
To scatter all mine enemies.[8]

This Joseph's Lord[9] and Israel's God,
The fiery pillar and day's cloud[1]

1. The poem likely refers to Elizabeth's Catholic
cousin, Mary, Queen of Scots, who fled England in
1568 and whose ambitions to the throne Elizabeth
feared.
2. Intelligence.
3. Persons.
4. Daughter of debate: Mary, Queen of Scots;
aye: always.
5. Prune the tops of trees.
6. Refers to the surprising defeat of the Spanish
Armada by the English fleet in 1588.
7. A female personal attendant or servant, often
used in reference to the Virgin Mary (handmaid

of the Lord).
8. Refers to the circumstances under which the
Armada was defeated but also alludes to the miracles God performed for the Israelites (the dividing of the Red Sea) when they escaped from
Pharaoh's Egypt under the guidance of Moses.
9. Refers to the biblical patriarch Joseph from the
book of Genesis.
1. After Moses leads the Israelites out of Egypt,
across the Red Sea, the "Lord went in front of
them in a pillar of cloud by day, to lead them
along the way, and in a pillar of fire by night, to
give them light" (Exodus 13:21).

That saved his saints from wicked men,   15
And drenched[2] the honor of the proud,
And hath preserved in tender love
The spirit of his turtle dove.

1588

ISABELLA WHITNEY
c. 1540s–c. 1578

There is no birth date or death date for Isabella Whitney; indeed, almost nothing is known about her other than the few details that can be gleaned from her published writings. She was likely born in the 1540s, probably to a middle-class family, as some of her writings refer to her serving in the household of a "virtuous lady"; such service positions were consistent with a middle-class background. She was probably the sister of Geoffrey Whitney, the author of a successful emblem book, *A Choice of Emblems* (1586) and someone to whom she refers in several of her poems. She refers, also in her poetry, to another brother, Brooke, and to two sisters (unnamed), also in service. Though she was probably born in the country, she appears to have lived most of her adult life in London, a city she writes of with great fondness and vividness in "The Manner of Her Will," the poem that is included below. There is no record of her marrying or having children, though it is quite possible that she did both.

Her works include an early verse letter written to an inconstant lover (1567) and a collection of advice poems and epistolary verse called *A Sweet Nosegay, or Pleasant Posy,* published in 1573. That collection concluded with "The Manner of Her Will." *A Sweet Nosegay* appears to have been written—if we believe the biographical information contained in it to be nonfictional—after she had been let go by her employer and had subsequently fallen ill. The poetry, nonetheless, is playful, almost breezy, and it is all secular. That fact alone makes Whitney truly exceptional at a time when the only acceptable literary pursuits for women were devotions or translations, often of religious texts. But it is just as exceptional that she published the *Nosegay* during her lifetime with the apparent hope of making money from its publication. This would make her the first professional woman poet writing in English. Like other women who found their way into print via the paradoxically enabling condition of imminent (or certain) death or illness, Whitney seems to exploit this opening by complaining of an illness and by concluding the collection with the playful "Will" (this is one of the reasons we have for doubting the veracity of the biographical information in the collection). Legacies were, of course (as we shall see with both Dorothy Leigh, pp. 81–83, and Elizabeth Jocelin, pp. 83–86, in the first part of the seventeenth century), one of the ways women were allowed to express desires and ideas that would normally have led to censure. But as well as offering a window into Whitney's mental world, "The Manner of Her Will" is also a vivid portrait of sixteenth-century London, a virtual guided tour of a city on the threshold of modernity.

2. Drowned.

Map of London (1593), by John Norden.

The Manner of Her Will, and What She Left to London and to All Those in It, at Her Departing

I whole in body and in mind,
But very weak in purse,
Do make and write my testament
For fear it will be worse.
And first I wholly do commend   5
My soul and body eke[1]
To God the Father and the Son,
So long as I can speak.
And after speech, my soul to him
And body to the grave,   10
Till time that all shall rise again
Their judgement for to have.
And then I hope they both shall meet
To dwell for aye[2] in joy,
Whereas[3] I trust to see my friends   15
Released from all annoy.
Thus have you heard touching my soul
And body, what I mean;

1. Also.   3. When.
2. Ever.

I trust you all will witness bear
    I have a steadfast brain.   20

And now let me dispose such things
    As I shall leave behind,
That those which shall receive the same
    May know my willing mind.
I first of all to London leave,   25
    Because I there was bred,
Brave buildings rare, of churches store,
    And Paules to the head.[4]
Between the same, fair streets there be
    And people goodly store;   30
Because their keeping craveth cost,
    I yet will leave him[5] more.
First for their food, I butchers leave,
    That every day shall kill;
By Thames you shall have brewers store   35
    And bakers at your will.
And such as orders do observe
    And eat fish thrice a week,[6]
I leave two streets full fraught therewith;
    They need not far to seek.   40
Watling Street and Canwick Street[7]
    I full of woollen leave,
And linen store in Friday Street,
    If they me not deceive.
And those which are of calling such   45
    That costlier they require,
I mercers[8] leave, with silk so rich
    As any would desire.
In Cheap,[9] of them they store shall find,
    And likewise in that street,   50
I goldsmiths leave with jewels such
    As are for ladies meet,[1]
And plate to furnish cupboards with
    Full brave[2] there shall you find,
With purl[3] of silver and of gold   55
    To satisfy your mind;

4. Paules: St. Paul's Cathedral in the City of London—the building was destroyed during the Great Fire of London in 1666 and replaced by a church designed by Sir Christopher Wren; to the head: to its top.
5. The City of London.
6. In 1563, in an attempt to build up its navy by strengthening the fishing industry, the English government passed an act that forbade people to eat any meat other than fish three days a week.

7. Streets known for their cloth merchants.
8. Merchants specializing in drapery, velvet, and silks.
9. Cheapside, an area that runs east from St. Paul's, that housed, among other things, Goldsmiths' Row.
1. Suitable.
2. Splendid.
3. Thread or cord of twisted gold or silver wire that was used for embroidery.

With hoods, bongraces,[4] hats or caps
    Such store are in that street
As, if on t'one side you should miss,
    The t'other serves you feat.[5]   60
For nets[6] of every kind of sort
    I leave within the Pawn,[7]
French ruffs, high purls, gorgets, and sleeves
    Of any kind of lawn.[8]
For purse or knives, for comb or glass,   65
    Or any needful knack,[9]
I by the Stocks[1] have left a boy
    Will ask you what you lack.
I hose do leave in Birchin Lane[2]
    Of any kind of size,   70
For women stitched, for men both trunks[3]
    And those of Gascoyne guise.[4]
Boots, shoes, or pantables good store
    St. Martin's[5] hath for you;
In Cornwall,[6] there I leave you beds   75
    And all that longs thereto.
For women shall you tailors have,
    By Bow[7] the chiefest dwell;
In every lane you some shall find
    Can do indifferent[8] well.   80
And for the men few streets or lanes
    But body-makers[9] be,
And such as make the sweeping cloaks
    With guards[1] beneath the knee.
Artillery at Temple Bar   85
    And dags at Tower Hill;[2]
Swords and bucklers of the best
    Are nigh the Fleet until.[3]

Now when thy folk are fed and clad
    With such as I have named,   90

4. A sunshade worn on the front of women's bonnets or caps.
5. Well.
6. Hairnets, worn under hats.
7. Covered arcade on Lombard Street that sold many kinds of fabrics.
8. Ruffs, purls, and gorgets: different kinds of collars or wimples that covered the neck and breast; lawn: linen.
9. Glass: mirror; knack: trinket.
1. A market in the center of the City of London.
2. Hose: stockings; Birchin Lane: a north-running street known for its drapers and secondhand clothes shops.
3. Stitched: embroidered; trunks: hose worn above the knee.

4. Wide, baggy hose.
5. Pantables: slippers, indoor shoes; St. Martin's: a shop known for its inexpensive boots and clothes.
6. Perhaps a printer's error for Cornhill, where there was a large market.
7. Probably refers to the Church of St. Mary le Bow.
8. Tolerably.
9. Tailors.
1. Decorative borders.
2. Temple Bar: the gate marking the boundary between the City of London and Westminster; dags: large pistols; Tower Hill: refers to the Tower of London.
3. Close to Fleet Street.

For dainty mouths and stomachs weak
    Some junkets[4] must be framed.
Wherefore I 'pothecaries leave,
    With banquets[5] in their shop,
Physicians also for the sick,   95
    Diseases for to stop.
Some roisters still must bide in thee
    And such as cut it out,[6]
That with the guiltless quarrel will
    To let their blood about.   100
For them I cunning[7] surgeons leave,
    Some plasters to apply,
That ruffians may not still be hanged
    Nor quiet persons die.
For salt, oatmeal, candles, soap,   105
    Or what you else do want,
In many places shops are full;
    I left you nothing scant.[8]
If they that keep what I you leave
    Ask money when they sell it,   110
At Mint there is such store it is
    Unpossible to tell[9] it.
At Steelyard[1] store of wines there be
    Your dulled minds to glad,
And handsome men that must not wed   115
    Except they leave their trade.[2]
They oft shall seek for proper girls
    (And some perhaps shall find),
That needs compels or lucre[3] lures
    To satisfy their mind.   120
And near the same I houses leave
    For people to repair[4]
To bathe themselves, so to prevent
    Infection of the air.
On Saturdays I wish that those   125
    Which all the week do drug[5]
Shall thither trudge to trim them up
    On Sundays to look smug.[6]
If any other thing be lacked
    In thee, I wish them look,   130

4. Dainty pastries.
5. 'Pothecaries: apothecaries, who sold spices, drugs, and perishable food; banquets: in this context refers to a dessert course.
6. Roisters: loud bullies; cut it out: show off.
7. Skilled.
8. Lacking.
9. Mint: located in the Tower of London; tell: count.
1. Also known as Stillyard, chiefly occupied by north German merchants who sold, among other things, strong German wine.
2. According to the Statute of Artificers (1563), apprentices, who would normally begin work at age fourteen, were to remain unmarried for seven years.
3. Money.
4. Go to frequently.
5. Drudge.
6. Neat, trim.

For there it is (I little brought
　　But nothing from thee took).
Now for the people in thee left,
　　I have done as I may,
And that the poor, when I am gone,   135
　　Have cause for me to pray,
I will to prisons portions leave
　　(What though but very small),
Yet that they may remember me,
　　Occasion be it shall.   140
And first the Counter they shall have,
　　Lest they should go to wrack,
Some coggers[7] and some honest men
　　That sergeants draw aback.
And such as friends will not them bail,   145
　　Whose coin is very thin,
For them I leave a certain Hole[8]
　　And little ease within.
The Newgate once a month shall have
　　A sessions[9] for his share,   150
Lest, being heaped,[1] infection might
　　Procure a further care.
And at those sessions some shall 'scape
　　With burning[2] near the thumb,
And afterward to beg their fees[3]   155
　　Till they have got the sum.
And such whose deeds deserveth death,
　　And twelve have found the same,
They shall be drawn up Holborn hill[4]
　　To come to further shame.   160
Well, yet to such I leave a nag
　　Shall soon their sorrows cease,
For he shall either break their necks
　　Or gallop from the press.[5]
The Fleet[6] not in their circuit is,   165
　　Yet if I give him nought,
It might procure his curse ere I
　　Unto the ground be brought.

---

7. Counter: the name given to debtors' prisons; wrack: ruin; coggers: cheats.
8. The bottom floor of a Counter, where prisoners held baskets through the grates to beg food from passersby.
9. Newgate: a prison located northwest of St. Paul's for those guilty of criminal offenses or offenses against the state; sessions: a judicial trial.
1. Crowded.
2. Branding, a common punishment for petty thieves.
3. Convicts could procure a license to beg in order to raise the money needed to pay their fines.
4. Condemned prisoners from Newgate were typically paraded up Holborn Hill on their way to execution by hanging.
5. Break their necks: i.e., by leading them to the gallows; press: crowd (hangings were popular spectator events).
6. Prison near Ludgate Hill.

Wherefore I leave some Papist[7] old
    To underprop his roof,   170
And to the poor within the same,
    A box[8] for their behoof.
What makes you standers-by to smile
    And laugh so in your sleeve?
I think it is because that I   175
    To Ludgate[9] nothing give.
I am not now in case[1] to lie,
    Here is no place of jest;
I did reserve that for myself
    If I my health possessed   180
And ever came in credit so
    A debtor for to be.
When days of payment did approach,
    I thither meant to flee,
To shroud myself amongst the rest   185
    That choose to die in debt.
Rather than any creditor
    Should money from them get
(Yet 'cause I feel myself so weak
    That none me credit dare),   190
I here revoke and do it leave
    Some bankrupts to his share.
To all the bookbinders by Paul's,[2]
    Because I like their art,
They every week shall money have   195
    When they from books depart.
Amongst them all my printer[3] must
    Have somewhat to his share;
I will my friends these books to buy
    Of him, with other ware.   200
For maidens poor, I widowers rich
    Do leave, that oft shall dote,
And by that means shall marry them
    To set the girls afloat.
And wealthy widows will I leave   205
    To help young gentlemen,
Which when you have, in any case,
    Be courteous to them then,
And see their plate and jewels eke
    May not be marred with rust,[4]   210
Nor let their bags too long be full,

---

7. Roman Catholic; Catholics were fined heavily for not attending services of the Protestant Church of England.
8. Alms box.
9. Prison for debtors west of St. Paul's.
1. In a position to.

2. St. Paul's Churchyard was known for its book-sellers.
3. Whitney's printer was Richard Jones, who printed works by other women writers of the period as well.
4. Tarnish.

For fear that they do burst.
To every gate under the walls
    That compass thee about,
I fruit-wives[5] leave to entertain   215
    Such as come in and out.
To Smithfield[6] I must something leave,
    My parents there did dwell;
So careless for to be of it
    None would account it well.   220
Wherefore it thrice a week shall have
    Of horse and neat[7] good store,
And in his spital,[8] blind and lame
    To dwell for evermore.
And Bedlam[9] must not be forgot,   225
    For that was oft my walk;
I people there too many leave
    That out of tune do talk.
At Bridewell there shall beadles be,[1]
    And matrons that shall still   230
See chalk well chopped, and spinning plied,
    And turning of the mill.
For such as cannot quiet be
    But strive for house or land,
At th'Inns of Court[2] I lawyers leave   235
    To take their cause in hand.
And also leave I at each Inn
    Of Court or Chancery,
Of gentlemen, a youthful rut[3]
    Full of activity;   240
For whom I store of books have left
    At each bookbinder's stall,
And part of all that London hath
    To furnish them withal.
And when they are with study cloyed,[4]   245
    To recreate their mind,
Of tennis courts, of dancing schools
    And fence,[5] they store shall find.
And every Sunday at the least,
    I leave, to make them sport,   250

5. Fruit sellers.
6. An area northwest, beyond the walls of the City of London, known for its horse market and as being the place where witches and heretics were burned at the stake, especially during the reign of Queen Mary in the mid-1550s.
7. Oxen.
8. Hospital of St. Bartholomew.
9. Hospital of St. Mary of Bethlehem, an insane asylum.
1. Bridewell: a former palace within the City of London that eventually became a prison for women; beadles: officers or guards.
2. The four sets of buildings in London belonging to the four legal societies that trained young men to be lawyers.
3. Literally, a company of deer in which the stag is in "rut," his annually occurring period of sexual excitement.
4. Satiated.
5. Fencing.

> In divers places players,[6] that
>   Of wonders shall report.
>
> Now London have I for thy sake
>   Within thee and without,
> As comes into my memory,   255
>   Dispersed round about
> Such needful things as they should have
>   Here left now unto thee;
> When I am gone, with conscience
>   Let them dispersed be.   260
> And though I nothing named have
>   To bury me withal,[7]
> Consider that above the ground
>   Annoyance be I shall.
> And let me have a shrouding sheet[8]   265
>   To cover me from shame,
> And in oblivion bury me
>   And never more me name.
> Ringings[9] nor other ceremonies
>   Use you not for cost,   270
> Nor at my burial make no feast;
>   Your money were but lost.
> Rejoice in God that I am gone
>   Out of this vale so vile,
> And that, of each thing left such store   275
>   As may your wants exile,
> I make thee[1] sole executor
>   Because I loved thee best,
> And thee I put in trust to give
>   The goods unto the rest.   280
> Because thou shalt a helper need
>   In this so great a charge,
> I wish good fortune be thy guide, lest
>   Thou shouldst run at large.
> The happy days and quiet times   285
>   They both her[2] servants be,
> Which well will serve to fetch and bring
>   Such things as need to thee.
> Wherefore, good London, not refuse
>   For helper her to take.   290
> Thus being weak and weary both
>   An end here will I make.
> To all that ask what end I made

6. Actors (acting at one of the many playhouses that lay just outside the City walls on the south bank of the Thames River).
7. For burial costs.
8. Winding sheet for wrapping corpses prior to burial.
9. Bell ringings.
1. London.
2. Good fortune.

And how I went away,
Thou answer may'st like those which here   295
    No longer tarry may.
And unto all that wish me well
    Or rue that I am gone,
Do me commend and bid them cease
    My absence for to moan.   300
And tell them further, if they would
    My presence still have had,
They should have sought to mend my luck
    Which ever was too bad.
So fare thou well a thousand times,   305
    God shield thee from thy foe;
And still make thee victorious
    Of those that seek thy woe.
And though I am persuade that I
    Shall never more thee see,   310
Yet to the last I shall not cease
    To wish much good to thee.
This 20 of October, I,
    In Anno Domini
A thousand five hundred seventy three,   315
    (As almanacs descry),[3]
Did write this will with mine own hand
    And it to London gave
In witness of the standers-by;
    Whose names (if you will have)   320
Paper, Pen, and Standish[4] were
    At that same present by,
With Time who promised to reveal
    So fast as she could hie[5]
The same, lest of my nearer kin   325
    From anything should vary.
So finally I make an end;
    No longer can I tarry.

                                                1573

◄ MARY SIDNEY HERBERT, ►
COUNTESS OF PEMBROKE
1561–1621

Born at Tickenhill Palace to a prominent aristocratic family, Mary Sidney, the fifth
of seven children, had an immensely privileged childhood that included an exceptional education for a girl of her time: she was taught not only French and Italian but also Latin, Hebrew, and Greek (languages usually reserved for boys'

3. Describe.   5. Hasten.
4. Inkstand.

education). Part of her education, or aristocratic training, included two years (1575–1577) as a lady-in-waiting to Queen Elizabeth, after which, at the age of sixteen, she was married to Henry Herbert, the second Earl of Pembroke; they had four children. Together with her older brother Philip, a sometime favorite of Queen Elizabeth's and one of the greatest English poets of the sixteenth century (although his role in the Elizabethan court was chiefly as a statesman), she shared a great love of literature and literary endeavor. And, indeed, Wilton House, the majestic seat of the earls of Pembroke where the countess lived for twenty-four years with her husband, became a kind of intellectuals' retreat during her time there, with many important poets, including her brother, benefiting from her generous patronage to write in residence. Her husband died in 1601, and afterward she lived an almost entirely private life, mainly in London, until her death.

As well as being one of the most celebrated literary patrons of the sixteenth century, the countess was herself also a writer of considerable skill and, it seems, ambition. In fact, more than almost any other woman writer during her lifetime (and for some years thereafter), Mary Sidney can be said to have fashioned a successful literary reputation. (Aemilia Lanyer would dedicate her *Salve Deus Rex Judaeorum* to Sidney in recognition of that reputation.) While, like many other literarily ambitious women of the time, Sidney was bound by the constraints of propriety to limit her literary production mainly to the translation of religious works, she broke through those constraints by translating works, such as Robert Garnier's *Antoine,* that were not particularly religious in nature. And although her most accomplished work is a complete translation of the biblical psalms that she began with her brother Philip shortly before he died in 1586, the translation is so imaginative and the versification so original that it seems almost to achieve artistic success equal to that of the original Hebrew text. Sidney's *Psalms* was widely circulated in manuscript during the seventeenth century and had a significant influence on the versification of poets like John Donne, George Herbert, and Ben Jonson.

"A Dialogue between Two Shepherds, Thenot and Piers, in Praise of Astraea" is one of the few fully original poems that Mary Sidney appears to have penned. Written ostensibly in anticipation of a visit by Queen Elizabeth (Astraea) to Wilton House (a visit that never, in fact, occurred), it playfully rehearses, as only someone who thought herself fully a poet would, two contending positions on language and poetry: one (Thenot's), that language can capture the divine essence of Astraea; the other (Piers's), that language is completely incapable of presenting eternal truth and that poetry is, therefore, a lie.

A Dialogue between Two Shepherds, Thenot and Piers, in Praise of Astraea[1]

THENOT I sing divine Astraea's praise,
O Muses![2]—Help my wits to raise
And heave my verses higher.

---

1. Thenot and Piers: conventional names for shepherds. Thenot here represents those who believe that poetry can express divine goodness and truth; Piers, spokesman for Protestant (later, Puritan) values, argues that language is inherently fallible and cannot represent eternal truths, that

poetry is a form of lying. Astraea: the virgin goddess of justice, a name often used in the period to refer to Elizabeth I.
2. The nine goddesses from classical Greek and Roman mythology whose role it is to inspire poets and musicians.

PIERS Thou needst the truth but plainly tell,
    Which much I doubt thou canst not well,   5
    Thou art so oft a liar.

THENOT If in my song no more I show
    Than heav'n, and earth, and sea do know,
    Then truly I have spoken.
PIERS Sufficeth not no more to name,   10
    But being no less, the like, the same,
    Else laws of truth be broken.

THENOT Then say, she is so good, so fair,
    With all the earth she may compare,
    Not Momus'[3] self denying.   15
PIERS Compare may think where likeness holds,[4]
    Nought like to her the earth enfolds—
    I looked to find you lying.

THENOT Astraea sees with wisdom's sight,
    Astraea works by virtue's might,   20
    And jointly both do stay in her.
PIERS Nay, take from them her hand, her mind;
    The one is lame, the other blind.
    Shall still your lying stain her?

THENOT Soon as Astraea shows her face,   25
    Straight every ill avoids the place,
    And every good aboundeth.
PIERS Nay, long before her face doth show,
    The last doth come, the first doth go.
    How loud this lie resoundeth!   30

THENOT Astraea is our chiefest joy,
    Our chiefest guard against annoy,[5]
    Our chiefest wealth, our treasure.
PIERS Where chiefest are, three others be,
    To us none else but only she.   35
    When wilt thou speak in measure?

THENOT Astraea may be justly said
    A field in flow'ry robe arrayed,
    In season freshly springing.
PIERS That spring endures but shortest time,   40
    This never leaves Astraea's clime.
    Thou liest, instead of singing.

THENOT As heavenly light that guides the day,
    Right so doth thine each lovely ray
    That from Astraea flyeth.   45

3. Greek god of satire.
4. Comparisons are only effective in representing   literal similarities.
    5. Trouble.

PIERS Nay, darkness oft that light enclouds,
  Astraea's beams no darkness shrouds.
  How loudly Thenot lieth!

THENOT Astraea rightly term I may
  A manly palm, a maiden bay,   50
  Her verdure[6] never dying.
PIERS Palm oft is crooked, bay is low,
  She still upright, still high doth grow.
  Good Thenot leave thy lying.

THENOT Then Piers, of friendship, tell me why 55
  My meaning true, my words should lie,
  And strive in vain to raise her?
PIERS Words from conceit[7] do only rise,
  Above conceit her honour flies;
  But[8] silence, nought can praise her. 60

            1602

◆► AEMILIA LANYER ►◆
1569–1645

Aemilia Lanyer was born Aemilia Bassani. The second daughter of Baptista Bassani and Margaret Johnson, Lanyer was, though not of the ruling class, brought up in the court of Queen Elizabeth I: her father was one of the queen's musicians. Like many of the court musicians of his time, Bassani was Italian—he was described in his will as "a native of Venice"—and almost certainly Jewish. England was not at all a hospitable place for Jews in the sixteenth century—between two thousand and three thousand Jews had been expelled from England in 1290, and there was no significant Jewish presence in the country again until the end of the seventeenth century—but the queen's musicians seem to have been considered an exception to the official policy of intolerance.

  What is known of Lanyer's early adult life is derived almost exclusively from the casebooks of the somewhat notorious astrologer Simon Forman, whom Lanyer appears to have consulted several times in 1597. From Forman's notes, we can glean that before she was twenty, Lanyer became the mistress of Elizabeth's Lord Chamberlain, Henry Hunsdon. He "maintained her in great pomp," according to Forman, but rather unceremoniously dispensed with her when she became pregnant with his child: she was hastily married to Alfonso Lanyer, another of the queen's musicians, in 1592. She had a son, Henry, and a daughter, Odillya, who lived only nine months.

  Much of Lanyer's adult life seems to have been concerned with getting and keeping an income: Forman reports a kind of desperation to rid herself of debt, and much of the last part of her life was taken up with issues of litigation regarding a patent that her husband had been issued in 1604 but that came under dispute

---

6. Greenness of a flourishing plant.   8. With the exception of.
7. An invented, affected style or thought.

after his death in 1613. She founded a school in 1617, which she maintained for two years despite a bitter legal dispute with the landlord over rent and building repairs. When Lanyer died at St. James Clerkenwell, she was listed as a "pensioner," a term used to denote someone who had a regular stipend, often from a patron. Some scholars suggest that she received steady support from a patron in the last years of her life, although the identity of that patron remains a mystery.

The selections that follow are from Lanyer's remarkable 1611 volume of poetry, *Salve Deus Rex Judaeorum (Hail, God, King of the Jews)*. The volume consists of several verse dedications to noblewomen, the prose epistle "To the Virtuous Reader" (included here), the long titular poem (a portion of which appears below) that takes as its ostensible subject the Passion of Christ, and, finally, "The Description of Cooke-ham," the final poem in the volume. It is difficult to know whether the relationships with noblewomen that Lanyer claims in the volume—and particularly the friendship with Margaret Clifford and her daughter Anne that she describes in "Cooke-ham"—actually existed or whether they are a kind of nostalgic reinvention of the privileged, but fleeting, life she lived at court when she was Hunsdon's mistress. (No mention of Lanyer, for instance, appears in the diaries of Anne Clifford.) Yet whether her relationship with the Cliffords was real or imagined, Lanyer's moving and sometimes sharp-edged elegy to Cookeham and the privileged life described in the poem reveals the huge gulf that existed between women of different social degree in the early seventeenth century, a gulf that could not be bridged by friendship.

She published *Salve Deus:* it is entered into the Stationers' Register, the government office that licensed all publications, late in 1610 (although its actual publication date would be 1611); and the book's title page tells us that the books were "Printed by Valentine Simmes for Richard Bonian, and are to be sold at his Shop in Paules Churchyard." Yet only eight copies of the book survive, and some of them were specially produced as "presentation copies," books printed specifically for one person. The rarity of the books has led some scholars to speculate that it was pulled from the marketplace shortly after its publication. Did the fact that the author was a woman of the decidedly middle classes offend someone of influence? Did something in the book cause the offense? We will probably never know, but we are indeed lucky that all the copies of this remarkable book were not destroyed.

From **Salve Deus Rex Judaeorum**[1]

To the Virtuous Reader

Often have I heard that it is the property of some women not only to emulate[2] the virtues and perfections of the rest, but also by all their powers of ill-speaking to eclipse the brightness of their deserved fame; now contrary to this custom, which men I hope unjustly lay to their charge, I have written this small volume or little book, for the general use of all virtuous ladies and gentlewomen of this kingdom; and in commendation of some particular persons of our own sex, such as for the most part are so well known to myself and others, that I dare undertake fame dares not to call any better. And this have I done to make known to the world that all women deserve not to be blamed, though some forgetting they are women them-

1. Hail, God, King of the Jews.   2. Rival, vie with.

selves, and in danger to be condemned by the words of their own mouths, fall into so great an error, as to speak unadvisedly against the rest of their sex; which if it be true, I am persuaded they can show their own imperfection in nothing more; and therefore could wish (for their own ease, modesties and credit) they would refer such points of folly to be practised by evil-disposed men, who forgetting they were born of women, nourished of women, and that if it were not by the means of women, they would be quite extinguished out of the world, and a final end of them all, do like vipers deface the wombs wherein they were bred, only to give way and utterance to their want of discretion and goodness. Such as these, were they that dishonoured Christ, his apostles and prophets, putting them to shameful deaths. Therefore we are not to regard any imputations, that they undeservedly lay upon us, no otherwise than to make use of them to our own benefits, as spurs to virtue, making us fly all occasions that may colour their unjust speeches to pass current.[3] Especially considering that they have tempted even the patience of God himself, who gave power to wise and virtuous women to bring down their pride and arrogance. As was cruel Cesarius by the discreet counsel of noble Deborah, judge and prophetess of Israel, and resolution of Jael, wife of Heber the Kenite; wicked Haman, by the divine prayers and prudent proceedings of beautiful Hester; blasphemous Holofernes, by the invincible courage, rare wisdom, and confident carriage of Judith; and the unjust judges, by the innocence of chaste Susanna; with infinite others, which for brevity's sake I will omit.[4] As also in respect it pleased our Lord and Saviour Jesus Christ, without the assistance of man, being free from original and all other sins, from the time of his conception till the hour of his death, to be begotten of a woman, born of a woman, nourished of a woman, obedient to a woman; and that he healed women, pardoned women, comforted women, yea, even when he was in his greatest agony and bloody sweat, going to be crucified, and also in the last hour of his death, took care to dispose of a woman; after his resurrection, appeared first to a woman, sent a woman to declare his most glorious resurrection to the rest of his disciples.[5] Many other examples I could allege of diverse faithful and virtuous women, who have in all ages not only been confessors, but also endured most cruel martyrdom for their faith in Jesus Christ. All which is sufficient to enforce all good Christians and honourable-minded men to speak reverently of our sex, and especially of all virtuous and good women. To the modest censures of both which I refer these my imperfect endeavours, knowing that according to their own excellent dispositions they will rather cherish, nourish, and increase the least spark of virtue where they find it, by their favourable and best interpretations, than quench it by wrong constructions. To whom I wish with all increase of virtue, and desire their best opinions.

1611

3. That is, pass as viable and authentic currency.
4. Cesarius: probably Sisera, an enemy of the Judge Deborah (see Judges 4); Sisera was put to death by Jael (wife of Heber), who lured him into her tent and then pounded a tent spike through his temples as he slept (see Judges 4); Haman: an enemy of the Jews who is hanged by Queen Esther (see Esther 5–7); Holofernes: decapitated by Judith, who thus saves her town from Nebuchadnezzar's army (see the Apocryphal Book of Judith

8–13); unjust judges: Susanna was falsely accused of sleeping with two men whose advances she had, in fact, rejected; the prophet Daniel revealed the truth and the men were put to death (see the Apocryphal History of Daniel and Susanna).
5. Jesus on the cross asks a disciple to care for his mother (see John 19); he also appears first after the crucifixion to Mary Magdalene, whom he asks to go announce his resurrection to his disciples (see John 20:11–18).

Eve's Apology in Defence of Women[6]

Now Pontius Pilate[7] is to judge the cause[8]
Of faultless Jesus, who before him stands,
Who neither hath offended prince nor laws
Although he now be brought in woeful bands;[9]
O nobel governor, make thou yet a pause;   5
Do not in innocent blood imbrue[1] thy hands,
But hear the words of thy most worthy wife
Who sends to thee to beg her savior's life.[2]

Let barb'rous cruelty far depart from thee,
And in true justice take affliction's part;   10
Open thine eyes, that thou the truth may'st see;
Do not the thing that goes against thy heart;
Condemn not him that must thy savior be,
But view his holy life, his good desert.[3]
Let not us women glory in men's fall   15
Who had power given to over-rule us all.[4]

Till now your indiscretion[5] sets us free,
And makes our former fault[6] much less appear;
Our mother Eve, who tasted of the tree,
Giving to Adam what she held most dear,   20
Was simply good, and had no power to see;
The after-coming harm did not appear;
The subtle[7] serpent that our sex betrayed,
Before our fall so sure a plot had laid.

That undiscerning ignorance perceived   25
No guile, or craft that was by him intended;
For had she known of what we were bereaved,[8]
To his request she had not condescended.
But she (poor soul) by cunning was deceived,
No hurt therein her harmless heart intended;   30
For she alleged[9] God's word, which he[1] denies,
That they should die, but even as gods, be wise.

6. The title Lanyer gave to this section of the titular poem from *Salve Deus Rex Judaeorum* in the
margin of the volume.
7. The Roman governor of Jerusalem who agreed
to put Jesus to death.
8. Case.
9. Restraints.
1. Stain, defile.
2. In Matthew 27:19 the unnamed wife of Pilate
begs her husband to have nothing to do with Jesus
because of a dream she has had (no details of
which are revealed); the words that follow in
Lanyer's poem are spoken in the voice of Pilate's
wife.
3. Worthiness.
4. Let not us women . . . over-rule us all: a refer-

ence to Adam's (man's) dominion over all, and
man's fall from that dominion in Pilate's sentencing of Christ to death.
5. Lack of judgment in sentencing Christ to death.
6. Eve's fall to temptation in eating the forbidden
fruit of the Tree of Knowledge and sharing that
fruit with Adam, only to be condemned by God
(see Genesis 3).
7. Crafty.
8. Deprived, bereft (of the innocence of the Garden of Eden, from which they were expelled).
9. Declared.
1. Refers perhaps to the serpent, or to Adam,
though neither character issues a denial in the biblical text.

But surely Adam cannot be excused;
Her fault though great, yet he was most to blame;
What weakness offered, strength might have refused,   35
Being lord of all, the greater was his shame;
Although the serpent's craft had her abused,
God's holy word ought all his actions frame,[2]
For he was lord and king of all the earth,
Before poor Eve had either life or breath.[3]   40

Who being framed by God's eternal hand
The perfect'st man that ever breathed on earth;
And from God's mouth received that strait[4] command,
The breach whereof he knew was present[5] death;
Yea, having power to rule both sea and land,   45
Yet with one apple won to lose that breath
Which God had breathed in his beauteous face,
Bringing us all in danger and disgrace.

And then to lay the fault on patience[6] back,
That we (poor women) must endure it all;   50
We know right well he did discretion lack,
Being not persuaded thereunto at all.
If Eve did err, it was for knowledge sake;
The fruit being fair persuaded him to fall;
No subtle serpent's falsehood did betray him,   55
If he would eat it, who had power to stay[7] him?

Not Eve, whose fault was only too much love,
Which made her give this present to her dear,
That what she tasted he likewise might prove,[8]
Whereby his knowledge might become more clear.   60
He never sought her weakness to reprove,
With those sharp words which he of God did hear;[9]
Yet men will boast of knowledge, which he took
From Eve's fair hand, as from a learned book.

If any evil did in her remain,   65
Being made of him, he was the ground of all;
If one of many worlds[1] could lay a stain
Upon our sex, and work so great a fall

2. Shape.
3. Genesis 2:7–22 tells the story of the creation of man (known as Adam): God forms him first from the "dust of the ground," and only after creating the garden in which he puts the man, and all the animals, creates "a helper as his partner" by putting the man to sleep, extracting one of his ribs, and making it into "woman."
4. Strict.
5. Immediate.
6. Eve's.

7. Stop.
8. To make a trial of something by tasting it.
9. In Genesis 2:16–17, before the creation of woman, God tells Adam, "You may freely eat of every tree in the garden; but of the tree of the knowledge of good and evil you shall not eat, for in the day that you eat of it you shall die."
1. Seems to refer to women, perhaps adapting the seventeenth-century commonplace that man is a little world.

To wretched man, by Satan's subtle train,[2]
What will so foul a fault amongst you all?   70
Her weakness did the serpent's words obey
But you in malice God's dear son betray.

Whom, if unjustly you condemn to die,
Her sin was small, to what you do commit;
All mortal sins[3] that do for vengeance cry   75
Are not to be compared unto it;
If many worlds would altogether try
By all their sins the wrath of God to get,
This sin of yours surmounts them all as far
As doth the sun another little star.[4]   80

Then let us have our liberty again,
And challenge[5] to yourselves no sov'reignty;
You came not in the world without our pain,
Make that a bar[6] against your cruelty.
Your fault being greater, why should you disdain   85
Our being your equals, free from tyranny?
If one weak woman simply did offend,
This sin of yours hath no excuse nor end.

To which (poore soules) we never gave consent,
Witnesse thy wife (O *Pilate*) speakes for all;   90
Who did but dreame, and yet a message sent,
That thou should'st have nothing to doe at all
With that just man,[7] which, if thy heart relent,
Why wilt thou be a reprobate with *Saul*?[8]
To seeke the death of him that is so good,   95
For thy soules health to shed his dearest blood.

1611

The Description of Cooke-ham[9]

Farewell (sweet Cooke-ham) where I first obtained
Grace from that grace where perfect grace[1] remained;
And where the muses[2] gave their full consent,

2. Satan: tradition, not the biblical story, identifies the serpent as Satan; train: line of reasoning.
3. Deadly sins.
4. According to the Ptolemaic system, the sun was thought to be larger than all the other stars in the universe.
5. Claim, demand as a right.
6. Barrier.
7. Christ.
8. Reprobate: a person rejected by God; Saul: in the book of 1 Samuel, Saul, the first king of Israel, seeks the death of David (who will become Israel's second king and who is often seen as a precursor of Jesus) and is for those acts and others completely abandoned by God (see 1 Samuel 9–31).

9. The poem is addressed to Margaret Russell, Countess of Cumberland; Cookeham was a manor leased to the countess's brother, a place where she lived occasionally with her daughter, Anne, until about 1605.
1. "Grace" is being used three ways here: in its first appearance in the line, the word refers to the favor or goodwill the poet receives from her benefactress; in its second appearance, the word refers to the Countess of Cumberland herself as though she were grace incarnate; in the third appearance, the word refers to God's grace or blessing.
2. The nine goddesses from classical Greek and Roman mythology who inspire poets and musicians.

I should have power the virtuous to content;
Where princely palace willed me to indite[3]   5
The sacred story of the soul's delight.
Farwell (sweet place) where virtue then did rest,
And all delights did harbour in her breast;
Never shall my sad eyes again behold
Those pleasures which my thoughts did then unfold;   10
Yet you (great lady) mistress of that place,
From whose desires did spring this work of grace,
Vouchsafe[4] to think upon these pleasures past
As fleeting, wordly joys that could not last,
Or as dim shadows of celestial pleasures,   15
Which are desired above all earthly treasures.
Oh how (methought) against[5] you thither came
Each part did seem some new delight to frame!
The house received all ornaments to grace it,
And would endure no foulness to deface it.   20
The walks put on their summer liveries,[6]
And all things else did hold like similes:
The trees with leaves, with fruits, with flowers clad,
Embraced each other, seeming to be glad,
Turning themselves to beauteous canopies   25
To shade the bright sun from your brighter eyes;
The crystal streams with silver spangles graced,
While by the glorious sun they were embraced;
The little birds in chirping notes did sing,
To entertain both you and that sweet spring;   30
And Philomela with her sundry lays,[7]
Both you and that delightful place did praise.
Oh, how methought each plant, each flower, each tree
Set forth their beauties then to welcome thee;
The very hills right humbly did descend,   35
When you to tread upon them did intend.
And as you set your feet, they still did rise,
Glad that they could receive so rich a prize.
The gentle winds did take delight to be
Among those woods that were so graced by thee   40
And in sad murmur uttered pleasing sound,
That pleasure in that place might more abound;
The swelling banks delivered all their pride,
When such a phoenix[8] once they had espied.
Each arbour, bank, each seat, each stately tree   45
Thought themselves honoured in supporting thee.
The pretty birds would oft come to attend thee,

3. Write, record.
4. Allow yourself.
5. In welcome of your coming.
6. Uniforms.
7. Philomela: from classical mythology, the woman
who was transformed into a nightingale; lays: songs.
8. Mythical bird of resurrection that rises from its own ashes; here a reference to the countess.

Yet fly away for fear they should offend thee;
The little creatures in the burrow by
Would come abroad to sport them in your eye;   50
Yet fearful of the bow in your fair hand
Would run away when you did make a stand.
Now let me come unto that stately tree,
Wherein such goodly prospects you did see;
That oak that did in height his fellows pass,   55
As much as lofty trees, low-growing grass;
Much like a comely cedar, straight and tall,
Whose beauteous stature far exceeded all;
How often did you visit this fair tree,
Which seeming joyful in receiving thee,   60
Would like a palm tree spread his arms abroad,
Desirous that you there should make abode;
Whose fair green leaves much like a comely veil
Defended Phoebus[9] when he would assail;
Whose pleasing boughs did lend a cool fresh air,   65
Joying[1] his happiness when you were there;
Where being seated, you might plainly see
Hills, vales and woods, as if on bended knee
They had appeared, your honour to salute,
Or to prefer some strange unlooked-for suit;[2]   70
All interlaced with brooks and crystal springs,
A prospect fit to please the eyes of kings;
And thirteen shires[3] appear all in your sight,
Europe could not afford much more delight.
What was there then but gave you all content,   75
While you the time in meditation spent,
Of their creator's power, which there you saw
In all his creatures held a perfect law,
And in their beauties did you plain descry[4]
His beauty, wisdom, grace, love, majesty.   80
In these sweet woods how often did you walk
With Christ and his apostles there to talk;
Placing his holy writ in some fair tree,
To meditate what you therein did see;
With Moses you did mount his holy hill,[5]   85
To know his pleasure and perform his will.
With lovely David[6] you did often sing,
His holy hymns to heaven's eternal king.
And in sweet music did your soul delight,
To sound his praises, morning, noon and night.   90

9. Shielded the countess from Phoebus Apollo,
the sun god of Greek myth.
1. Rejoicing in.
2. Prefer: advance or promote; suit: request.
3. Counties; emphasizes the immense view from
Cooke-ham.

4. Declare.
5. Refers to Mount Sinai, where Moses received
the Ten Commandments (see Exodus 19–20).
6. King David, Biblical psalmist and musician (see
1 Samuel 16:14–23).

With blessed Joseph[7] you did often feed
Your pined[8] brethren when they stood in need.
And that sweet lady sprung from Clifford's race,[9]
Of noble Bedford's blood, fair stem of grace,
To honourable Dorset now espoused,   95
In whose fair breast true virtue then was housed;
Oh what delight did my weak spirits find
In those pure parts of her well-framed mind;
And yet it grieves me that I cannot be
Near unto her, whose virtues did agree   100
With those fair ornaments of outward beauty,
Which did enforce from all both love and duty.
Unconstant fortune, thou art most to blame,
Who casts us down into so low a frame,
Where our great friends we cannot daily see,   105
So great a difference is there in degree.[1]
Many are placed in those orbs of state,
Parters[2] in honour, so ordained by fate,
Nearer in show, yet farther off in love,
In which the lowest always are above.   110
But whither am I carried in conceit?[3]
My wit too weak to conster[4] of the great.
Why not? although we are but born of earth,
We may behold the heavens, despising death;
And loving heaven that is so far above,   115
May in the end vouchsafe us entire love.
Therefore sweet memory, do thou retain
Those pleasures past, which will not turn again;
Remember beauteous Dorset's[5] summer sports,
So far from being touched by ill reports;   120
Wherein myself did always bear a part,
While reverend love presented my true heart;
Those recreations let me bear in mind,
Which her sweet youth and noble thoughts did find;
Whereof deprived, I evermore must grieve,   125
Hating blind fortune, careless to relieve.[6]
And you, sweet Cooke-ham, whom these ladies leave,
I now must tell the grief you did conceive

7. Joseph, after having been sold by ten of his brothers into slavery but eventually coming to prominence in Egypt as a chief overseer for Pharaoh, saves those same brothers from famine by, without their knowledge of his true identity, allowing them to take grain from his own storehouse back to Canaan (see Genesis 37–45).
8. Wasted by hunger.
9. Refers to the Countess's only child, her daughter Anne Clifford, who was the product of two prominent aristocratic families: her father's—the Cliffords—and her mother's—the Bedfords. She became a part of yet another prominent family when she married Richard Sackville, the Earl of Dorset.
1. "Frame" (in line 104 above) and "degree" both refer to social class.
2. Separated by rank.
3. Notion, ideas.
4. Construe, understand.
5. Refers to Anne.
6. Fortune does not care to relieve the poet of her grief.

At their departure; when they went away,
How everything retained a sad dismay;   130
Nay long before, when once an inkling came,
Methought each thing did unto sorrow frame;[7]
The trees that were so glorious in our view,
Forsook both flowers and fruit, when once they knew
Of your depart, their very leaves did wither,   135
Changing their colours as they grew together.
But when they saw this had no power to stay you,
They often wept, though speechless, could not pray[8] you;
Letting their tears in your fair bosoms fall,
As if they said: "Why will ye leave us all?"   140
This being vain, they cast their leaves away,
Hoping that pity would have made you stay;
Their frozen tops, like age's hoary hairs,
Shows their disasters, languishing in fears;
A swarthy rivelled rine[9] all overspread   145
Their dying bodies, half-alive, half-dead.
But your occasions[1] called you so away,
That nothing there had power to make you stay;
Yet did I see a noble, grateful mind,
Requiting[2] each according to their kind;   150
Forgetting not to turn and take your leave
Of these sad creatures, powerless to receive
Your favour, when with grief you did depart,
Placing their former pleasures in your heart;
Giving great charge to noble memory,   155
There to preserve their love continually;
But specially the love of that fair tree,
That first and last you did vouchsafe to see;
In which it pleased you oft to take the air,
With noble Dorset, then a virgin fair;[3]   160
Where many a learned book was read and scanned;
To this fair tree, taking me by the hand,
You did repeat the pleasures which had passed,
Seeming to grieve they could no longer last.
And with a chaste, yet loving kiss took leave,   165
Of which sweet kiss I did it soon bereave;[4]
Scorning a senseless creature should possess
So rare a favour, so great happiness.
No other kiss it could receive from me,

7. Give shape to sorrow.
8. Make request of.
9. Dark, rough bark.
1. Seems to refer to the fact that after her husband's death in 1605, Margaret Clifford lived primarily in her properties in the north of England, which had come to her through her birth family,
the Bedfords.
2. Rewarding.
3. Refers to Anne Clifford before she was married (in 1609).
4. Deprive, presumably by kissing the tree in the same spot as Margaret Clifford.

For fear to give back what it took of thee;   170
So I ungrateful creature did deceive[5] it,
Of that which you vouchsafed in love to leave it.
And though it oft had giv'n me much content,
Yet this great wrong I never could repent;
But of the happiest made it most forlorn,   175
To show that nothing's free from fortune's scorn,
While all the rest with this most beauteous tree,
Made their sad consort[6] sorrow's harmony.
The flowers that on the banks and walks did grow,
Crept in the ground, the grass did weep for woe.   180
The winds and waters seemed to chide together,
Because you went away, they knew not whither.
And those sweet brooks that ran so fair and clear,
With grief and trouble wrinkled did appear.
Those pretty birds that wonted[7] were to sing,   185
Now neither sing, nor chirp, nor use their wing;
But with their tender feet on some bare spray,
Warble forth sorrow, and their own dismay.
Fair Philomela leaves her mournful ditty,
Drowned in dead sleep, yet can procure no pity;   190
Each arbour, bank, each seat, each stately tree
Looks bare and desolate now, for want[8] of thee;
Turning green tresses into frosty grey,
While in cold grief they wither all away.
The sun grew weak, his beams no comfort gave,   195
While all green things did make the earth their grave;
Each briar, each bramble, when you went away,
Caught fast your clothes, thinking to make you stay;
Delightful Echo,[9] wonted to reply
To our last words, did now for sorrow die;   200
The house cast off each garment that might grace it,
Putting on dust and cobwebs to deface it.
All desolation then there did appear,
When you were going whom they held so dear.
This last farewell to Cooke-ham here I give;   205
When I am dead thy name in this may live,
Wherein I have performed her noble hest,[1]
Whose virtues lodge in my unworthy breast,
And ever shall, so long as life remains,
Tying my heart to her by those rich chains.[2]   210

1611

5. Trick it out of.
6. Company; "consort" also refers to a musical group (hence, sorrow's harmony).
7. Accustomed.
8. Lack.
9. In classical mythology a wood nymph who, deprived of the power to speak first (and hence, who can only echo another's words), dies of unrequited love.
1. Command, behest.
2. Chains of virtue.

CULTURAL COORDINATES
Household Space

The Cookeham of Aemilia Lanyer's seventeenth-century poem, built well before the poem was written, shared some of the spatial characteristics of the
aristocratic great houses of the late medieval period (the fourteenth and fifteenth
centuries). These houses would actually have been closer to what we today think
of as castles. In this period, aristocratic society was dominated by a kind of local
militarism, with lords supporting small armies to defend their own territory
against attack and to lend military support to the kingdom (or perhaps to overthrow it). The economy (feudal in nature) revolved around feeding and clothing
members of the lord's estate. And although women would have been involved in
this work, they were not considered part of the "household"; that designation referred only to the male members of the lord's retinue.

The architecture of the great house reflected this masculinist social structure.
The interior space was dominated by the huge central hall, which would have been
used mainly by the lord and his household—younger sons, the male members of
families of the lesser gentry, and the large servant class, which was almost entirely
male. While the women of the lesser gentry (mothers, wives, daughters, daugh-
ters-in-law) would have joined the men in the great hall for meals and, indeed, while the lady of the house would have had a particular visibility in the
hall, women would otherwise have been relegated to their own rooms in the
wings off the hall, which were often accessible only by narrow,

. . . [T]he . . . great houses of the late medieval period . . . reflected this masculinist social structure.

crooked hallways (designed to confine the smoke and smells from the great hall's
hearth). The stuffy interior rooms where the women spent most of their time were
tiny in comparison to the hall, accommodating probably only two or three of
them at a time. Their world was private and sheltered, in stark contrast to the rich
communal life of the lord's household.

Life in the aristocratic household began to change, however, during the Elizabethan era (1558–1603), a period of English history marked by a growing national economy and stable government. Diversification of the economy meant that
aristocratic younger sons and the lesser gentry (with their families) could move off
the great estates to find their own fortunes, particularly in London, where commercial activity flourished. The lords of the households themselves were often
away for long periods overseeing lucrative business interests, and their wives took
on more and more responsibility for the management of the estate. Thus, the great
houses came to be dominated by women; not only were they now more numerous
and more visible, but they also wielded a great deal more authority.

Over time, these changes in the social structure of households were reflected
in the physical structure of the great house. The great central hall (surrounded by
the now much more segregated working and living spaces of the servant class)
became a foyer, a display gallery, or a suite reserved for the master of the house.

The upper floors were divided into smaller, more comfortable rooms for individual family members (in keeping with the period's greater attention to family privacy), and more intimate spaces for entertaining—spaces shared by both men and women—were introduced. By the end of the seventeenth century, the male-dominated great hall had all but disappeared, and in its place appeared female-dominated parlors and drawing rooms.

c. 1580–c. 1622

Margaret Cunningham was born in Scotland, the daughter of Margaret Campbell and James Cunningham, Earl of Glencairn. In 1598, she was married to Sir James Hamilton of Crawfordjohn, a man she refers to in her diary as "unkind, cruel, and malicious." She appears to have left him permanently—or he her—in 1608, after the birth of their fifth child. After Hamilton's death, the date of which is unknown, she married Sir James Maxwell of Calderwood and was reported to have had a loving marriage with him, bearing six more children before her death sometime around 1622.

Her diary, which frankly chronicles her abuse at the hands of her first husband, was almost certainly written as a private document, perhaps serving a therapeutic role in her difficult life. Nevertheless, it seems to have circulated throughout the seventeenth and perhaps eighteenth century in original form and in copies reproduced by other hands. The diary was published in Edinburgh in 1827 after two copies were discovered: one was in the possession of a relation of Lady Margaret's, and one was owned by the popular novelist Sir Walter Scott.

We include this excerpt from Cunningham's remarkable diary as a window on the life of a woman, typical of her age and social class, who, because she had no fortune of her own and no legal recourse to divorce, was completely at the mercy of an abusive husband.

From A Part of the Life of Lady Margaret Cuninghame, Daughter of the Earl of Glencairn, That She Had with Her First Husband, the Master of Evandale

The Just and True Account Thereof, as It Was at First Written with Her Own Hand

[AN ACCOUNT OF DOMESTIC ABUSE]

I was married upon the 24th of January 1598, and I remained with my Lord my father three years, without receiving anything of my husband's living, but was furnished by my Lord my father in * * * all things needful.

In February 1601, I rode home to Evandale, and was boarded in a hostler house,[1] while[2] the next May following, and then I rode again to my Lord my father, being great with bairn:[3] and I bore with his Lordship my eldest son James, on the 4th of July, and I remained with his Lordship till the next February. Then I rode home to Evandale again, and was boarded in a hostler house six weeks, and then they would furnish me no longer, because they got evil payment. So then I was destitute, and I requested my goodfather and my goodmother[4] to deal with my husband to give me some reasonable money to live upon. * * *

In May 1602, my husband conceived a great anger against me (he being in fancy with Jean Boyd), and he would not come into the house I was in. I took

---

1. Inn.
2. Until.

3. Great with child, pregnant.
4. Godfather and godmother.

sickness, and lay bed fast six weeks. I requested my Lady his mother to deal with him in my favors, but he would neither speak to me nor give whereupon to sustain myself; so being altogether destitute, I was forced to advertise[5] my parents, and my Lady my mother sent my sister Mrs. Sussana to Evandale to me, and desired me to come with her to Finlaystone.[6]

My sister dealt earnestly with my husband in my favors. He gave her fair words and made her many fair promises, but performed none of them. So in July 1602, I was compelled to ride with her in a very disordered estate, as my Lord my father, and my Lady my mother, can bear record; for my gown had never been renewed since my coming from them. So they furnished me with clothes, and I remained with them till the next harvest, when my Lord Marquess of Hamilton caused my husband come to Finlaystone with his Lordship, which he did at his Lordship's request, and remained two or three nights, and was reconciled with me, and promised that he should send for me, and bring me home again to him; but that day that he was to ride away with my Lord Marquess, my Lord and my Lady, my parents, accused him before my Lord Marquess (who was then his young chief, my Lord, his Lordship's father being yet alive) why he had used me so rigorously without cause; and because they spoke sharply to him before my Lord his chief, his anger was renewed again toward me, and so he * * * would not let me come home to him at that time; so I remained still with my Lord my father till the next Mertimesse;[7] and then, after many fair letters of request that I wrote to him, he suffered me to come home at the Mertimesse, and I was boarded in a hostler house fifteen weeks.

In March 1603 my husband caused me ride up to Crawford-John, to save his mains[8] there, * * * and remained there twenty days, boarded in a hostler house. Then I came to Evandale again, and ate in my Lady my goodmother's house eight weeks. Then my husband caused me to ride again to Crawford-John, where I remained eight weeks, very ill furnished by a hostler, who was unable to furnish me without good payment; and he was informed by the parson of Crawford-John, that he would never get payment. Therefore he would furnish me no longer, which I wrote ofttimes to Evandale to my husband, but I received no answer; so having nothing there to live upon, I was forced to come to Evandale again, being great with bairn. * * *

In April 1604, my husband came home out of France; at his coming, he came to Finlaystone to me and promised to behave himself more lovingly to me nor he had done in time past, which, indeed, he did for the space of a quarter of a year, for within a month after he came home, he took me home to Evandale, where I remained with him, very lovingly used by him, for he was reformed and behaved himself both holily and civilly, so that he and I dwelt together very contentedly; howbeit, in the meantime, he had little of living to the fore, for all he took with him to France was spent, except a little quantity thereof, wherewith he caused John Stodhart, his servant, buy provision to his house, and contained himself very modestly and quietly the space of eight weeks; but alas, he continued no longer in that estate, for then he boarded himself and me, and all his family, in his servant John Hamilton's house, in which time he made filthy defection from God, and turned to all his wonted iniquities, so that he was in a worse estate nor ever I knew him before; and * * * he neglected his duty towards God, he kept no duty to me, but became altogether unkind,

5. Inform.
6. The seat of the Glencairn family.
7. November 11, the feast day of St. Martin.
8. The (mainly) Scottish term for the farm at-

tached to a mansion house, over which Cunningham's husband apparently needs to reassert his possession (or "save").

cruel, and malicious, as appeared plainly by his carriage towards me, which was openly seen in all the country, to his great shame. He would not suffer my gentlewoman to remain with me, who was known to be a very godly and discreet woman, one of his own name, Abigail Hamilton, father's sister to the Laird of Stenhouse; he gave credit to misreports of her and me both, and cruelly, in the night, put both her and me forth of his house naked, and would not suffer us to put on our clothes, but said he would strike both our backs in two with a sword. * * *

c. 1608

━━━━━━•❯━◄ LADY MARY WROTH ►━•❮━━━━━━
c. 1586–c. 1651

Mary Wroth was born Mary Sidney, the eldest daughter of Sir Robert Sidney and Lady Barbara Gamage, and part of one of the most prominent aristocratic families of the period. Her uncle, Sir Philip Sidney, and aunt, Mary Sidney Herbert, Countess of Pembroke (see pp. 52–55), were among the most celebrated poets and patrons, respectively, of the sixteenth century. So it is no surprise at all that, given her class position and her literary heritage, Mary Wroth should have been very well educated, particularly in English and Continental literary forms. She was married at age eighteen to Sir Robert Wroth, a man ten years her senior and a close friend of the newly crowned King James I. Although it was not a happy marriage, her notoriously profligate husband preferring hunting and other countryside sports to the arts, she did enjoy a time in London in the elite circle of female friends with whom James's queen, Anne, surrounded herself. She even participated in Ben Jonson's 1605 court entertainment, *The Masque of Blackness* (a highly stylized production including dancing, singing, pantomime, and dialogue written for the king and queen).

Two major sets of circumstances, however, conspired to alienate her from court circles after her initial popularity in London. One was the death of her husband in 1614, one month after the birth of their only child, James. Wroth left her £1,200 a year and an enormous debt of £23,000. (In terms of today's purchasing power, that would be an income of about $300,000 a year and debts of $5.5 million.) She would struggle for the rest of her life to settle her husband's debt. When her son died in 1616, her financial situation worsened: the estate, which he had inherited on his father's death, reverted to the ownership of her husband's uncle, along with the small income the estate provided. Her financial insolvency would have made it difficult for her to maintain a courtly lifestyle: dressing appropriately, traveling to the great houses of others, and maintaining an expensive town house would have been far beyond her means. More ruinous was the scandalous fallout of her long-standing affair with her first cousin, William Herbert, Earl of Pembroke (son to Mary Sidney Herbert and himself married), a scandal that deepened when she bore him two illegitimate children, William and Catherine, sometime after 1614. Even during the reign of more licentious kings—and James I was *not* licentious—such a scandal would render a woman *persona non grata*: no one would invite her to gatherings or attend those to which she had been invited.

While she was married (she never remarried), Mary Wroth's literary ambitions seem to have benefited from her Sidney connection. Poems of hers that circulated in manuscript were praised by some of the most prominent poets of the day, including Ben Jonson and William Drummond. However, after her disgrace, when she published her *Urania* (1621), a vast work of prose fiction that includes numerous songs and poems and an entire sonnet sequence, she found her capital as a Sidney in short supply. Although the *Urania* is, by almost any standard, a remarkable literary achievement, she was accused by Lord Edward Denny, whose family had experienced its own lurid court scandal early in the century, of libelous representation of his family in her narrative. Turning her heritage as a Sidney back on itself, Denny advised her to follow the example of her "virtuous and learned aunt," Mary Sidney Herbert, and confine her literary ambitions to religious translation. Despite Mary Wroth's having written a spirited letter defending her work to the Duke of Buckingham, answering Denny's charges line by line, *Urania* was immediately withdrawn from public circulation.

Mary Wroth lived the rest of her life in virtual solitude (not unlike her aunt) and financial hardship on her family's estate, Penshurst, where she wrote a sequel to *Urania* that was never published.

Selections from *Pamphilia to Amphilanthus,* the sequence of 103 sonnets and songs that Mary Wroth appended to *Urania,* are included below. The sequence is notable both for its use of the conventions of the sonnet sequence (as they had been invented by the Italian poet Petrarch and popularized in England by Philip Sidney in his *Astrophil and Stella* at the end of the sixteenth century) and for its divergence from those same conventions. Typically, a sonnet sequence involves a male lover yearning for the attentions of a beautiful but oblivious, or inconstant, woman. Wroth's sonnet sequence is written almost entirely in the voice of a passionate woman whose sexual and emotional desires are frustrated by her cruel and inconstant male lover.

From Pamphilia to Amphilanthus[1]

1

When night's black mantle could most darkness prove,[2]
    And sleep, death's image, did my senses hire[3]
    From knowledge of myself, then thoughts did move
    Swifter than those most swiftness need require:

In sleep, a chariot drawn by winged desire   5
    I saw: where sat bright Venus, Queen of Love,
    And at her feet her son,[4] still adding fire
    To burning hearts, which she did hold above,

But one heart flaming more than all the rest
    The goddess held, and put it to my breast,   10
    "Dear son, now shoot," said she, "thus must we win;"

1. Pamphilia, which means "all loving," and Amphilanthus, which means "lover of two," are the protagonists of Wroth's prose romance *Urania;* the sonnet sequence titled "Pamphilia to Amphilanthus," from which the selections below are drawn, was appended to *Urania.*
2. Create.
3. Engage or bribe.
4. Cupid.

He her obeyed, and martyred my poor heart.
  I, waking, hoped as dreams it would depart
  Yet since: O me: a lover I have been.

* * *

13

Cloyed[5] with the torments of a tedious night
  I wish for day; which come, I hope for joy:
  When cross I find new tortures to destroy
  My woe-killed heart, first hurt by mischief's might,

Then cry for night, and once more day takes flight   5
  And brightness gone; what rest should here enjoy
  Usurped is; Hate will her force employ;[6]
  Night cannot grief entomb though black as spite.

My thoughts are sad; her face[7] as sad doth seem:
  My pains are long; her hours tedious are: 10
  My grief is great, and endless is my care:
  Her face, her force, and all of woe's esteem:

Then welcome night, and farewell flatt'ring day
  Which all hopes breed, and yet our joys delay.

* * *

15

Dear famish[8] not what you yourself gave food;
  Destroy not what your glory is to save;
  Kill not that soul to which your spirit gave;
  In pity, not disdain, your triumph stood;

An easy thing it is to shed the blood   5
  Of one who, at your will, yields to the grave;
  But more you may true worth by mercy crave[9]
  When you preserve, not spoil, but nourish good;

Your sight is all the food I do desire;
  Then sacrifice me not in hidden fire,   10
  Or stop the breath which did your praises move:

Think but how easy 'tis a sight to give;
  Nay ev'n desert,[1] since by it I do live,
  I but chameleon-like[2] would live, and love.

16

Am I thus conquered: Have I lost the powers
  That to withstand, which joys[3] to ruin me?

---

5. Encumbered.
6. Use.
7. The face of the personified night.
8. Starve.
9. True: prove; crave: beg earnestly.

1. Deserved.
2. The lizardlike chameleon was thought to live
on air because of its inanimate appearance.
3. Takes joy in.

Must I be still while it my strength devours
And captive leads me prisoner, bound, unfree?

Love first shall leave men's fancies to them free,[4]   5
Desire shall quench love's flames, spring hate sweet showers,
Love shall loose all his darts, have sight, and see
His shame, and wishings hinder happy hours;

Why should we not Love's purblind[5] charms resist?
Must we be servile, doing what he list?[6]   10
No, seek some host to harbour thee: I fly

Thy babish[7] tricks, and freedom do profess;
But O my hurt, makes my lost heart confess
I love, and must: So farewell liberty.

* * *

22

Come darkest night, becoming sorrow best;
Light; leave thy light; fit for a lightsome[8] soul;
Darkness doth truly suit with me oppressed
Whom absence' power doth from mirth control:[9]

The very trees with hanging heads condole   5
Sweet summer's parting, and of leaves distressed
In dying colours make a grief-full role;
So much (alas) to sorrow are they pressed.

Thus of dead leaves her farewell carpet's made:
Their fall, their branches, all their mournings prove;   10
With leafless, naked bodies, whose hues vade[1]
From hopeful green, to wither in their love,

If trees and leaves, for absence, mourners be
No marvel that I grieve, who like want see.[2]

* * *

25

Like to the Indians, scorched with the sun,[3]
The sun which they do as their god adore
So am I used by Love, for ever more
I worship him, less favours have I won,

Better are they who thus to blackness run,   5
And so can only whiteness' want deplore[4]

---

4. Love first . . . them free: In other words, before
I surrender to love, all the impossibilities that follow will have to happen.
5. Totally blind.
6. Desires.
7. Childish.
8. "Light" is being used three different ways here:
as the first word of the line it refers to the personified day; in its second appearance it refers to ac-

tual light, or the sun; "lightsome" means unen-
cumbered by pain or sorrow.
9. Whom absence . . . control: absence wrests
control away from mirth, or happiness.
1. Fade.
2. Like want see: who see similar absence.
3. It was unfashionable to be suntanned in
seventeenth-century England.
4. Want: lack; deplore: regret.

Than I who pale and white am with grief's store,
Nor can have hope, but to see hopes undone;

Besides their sacrifice received's in sight
  Of their chose saint:[5] mine hid as worthless rite;   10
  Grant me to see where I my offerings give,

Then let me wear the mark of Cupid's might
  In heart as they in skin of Phoebus' light[6]
  Not ceasing off'rings to Love while I live.

1621

LADY ANNE CLIFFORD
1590–1676

Anne Clifford, born at Skipton Castle in the north of England, was the only surviving child of George Clifford, third Earl of Cumberland, and Lady Margaret Russell. Although her father forbade her to learn any foreign languages, she was nonetheless very well educated in English texts by her tutor, the well-known poet Samuel Daniel. She was very close to her mother, a pious, well-educated woman to whom Aemilia Lanyer (see pp. 55–65) dedicated her *Salve Deus Rex Judaeorum* and whose unhappy marriage to Anne's father seems both to have brought mother and daughter close and to have sadly influenced Anne's own marital history.

Anne was married in 1609 to her first husband, Richard Sackville, later Earl of Dorset, a man whose "profuseness in consuming his estate," as she writes in her *Diary*, was the source of constant and often maliciously tinged contention throughout their marriage. With Sackville, she had five children, three of whom (all sons) died in infancy. Sackville died in 1624, and six years later Anne married Philip Herbert, fourth Earl of Pembroke, who, her diaries tell us, was also unable to put marital companionship before monetary concerns, his focus being the £5,000 dowry (worth over $1 million today) of one of Anne's daughters from her first marriage, whom Herbert wished to marry to one of his sons. Anne's refusal to allow the marriage was a source of bitter contention between the two, and by 1643, they were living in separate houses. Herbert died in 1650.

Perhaps because of her difficult marriages, Anne Clifford's adult life was almost entirely dominated by a legal dispute over property that began in 1605 at her father's death and that was not resolved until 1643. By virtue of original legal documents dating from the early fourteenth century, documents that made it clear that the Clifford family title and estates should be passed through the family by direct heirs, male *or* female, Anne should have inherited the extensive Clifford lands and estates north of London upon the death of her father. Her father, however, willed the entire estate to his brother Francis and his succeeding male heirs. Under her father's will, the only condition under which Anne could inherit the estate would have involved the complete failure of the male Clifford line. The courts upheld George Clifford's will throughout the eleven years Anne's mother sued to recover

---

5. Chosen saint (the saint is not specified).
6. They wear the mark of the sun's (Phoebus Apollo's) strength on their skin; i.e., they are suntanned.

her daughter's inheritance and for the twenty-seven years following the death of her mother that Anne persisted in the legal suit. Indeed, part of the battle Anne waged was with her first husband, who repeatedly and aggressively attempted to persuade Anne to sign away her rights to the Clifford estate in return for a cash settlement (which would have paid off his gambling debts). Anne's steadfast refusal to settle despite enormous pressure from some very powerful men (including King James) eventually paid off; and when Francis Clifford's son Henry died in 1643 with no male heirs, she finally became Baroness Clifford. She took possession of her property in 1649, after the Civil War, and spent the remainder of her life serving as a kind of governor of her vast estate, lovingly restoring the many buildings, establishing houses of charity for widows, endowing schools and hospitals, organizing a tenancy system, and convening local courts of justice.

She also chronicled her family's history during the last twenty-seven years of her life, and three of the four autobiographical manuscripts she penned were written during this time. Those last three diaries chronicle the period 1630–1676 and, in large part, narrate the story of a woman who eventually triumphs in a legal dispute over an estate to which she had always been entitled and which she lovingly restores after inheriting it. The first volume, sometimes called the *Knole Diary* after the estate where Lady Anne lived during her marriage to Sackville and where the diary was written, also is concerned with the legal dispute but is considerably less triumphant in tone, having been written during the years 1616–1619. The excerpts below are from the earlier diary and contain descriptions of her difficult marriage and the news of her mother's death. They allow a window into the life of an aristocratic woman and are remarkable in revealing both her strength of will and her courage as well as an attention to a kind of literary quality: the diary has a fine sense of pacing and plot even with all its quotidian details.

From The Diary of Lady Anne Clifford (1616–19)

February 1616

[MEETING WITH THE ARCHBISHOP OF CANTERBURY]

All the time I stayed in the country I was sometimes merry and sometimes sad, as I had news from London.

Upon the 8th day of February I came to London, my Lord Bishop of St David's[1] riding with me in the coach and Mary Neville. This time I was sent for up by my lord about the composition[2] with my uncle of Cumberland. * * *

Upon the 16th my Lady Grantham and Mrs Newton came to see me—the next day, she told me, the Archbishop of Canterbury would come to [see] me, and

---

1. Mentioned in the excerpt from February are several friends, acquaintances, and family members of Anne Clifford's. In order, they are Bishop of St. David's (Wales): Richard Milbourne; Mary Neville: probably one of the daughters of Mary Sackville (the sister of Richard Sackville—Anne Clifford's husband) and Henry Neville; uncle of Cumberland: Francis Clifford, fourth Earl of Cumberland, brother of Anne's deceased father, George Clifford; Lady Grantham: the wife of Sir Thomas Grantham of Lincoln; Mrs. Newton: no

information available; Archbishop of Canterbury: George Abbot; my cousin Russell: Francis Russell, son of William Russell, her mother's brother; Lady Wotton: a first cousin of Anne's through her father's sister Frances; my Lord William Howard: Richard Sackville's uncle; my Lord Roos: William Cecil, Baron Ros or Roos; my brother Sackville: Edward Sackville, younger brother of Richard Sackville.
2. The settling with her uncle of her claim to the Clifford family lands with a cash settlement.

she persuaded me very earnestly to agree to this business,[3] which I took as a great argument of her love. My cousin Russell came to me the same day and chid me and told me of all my faults and errors in this business—he made me weep bitterly; then I spoke a prayer of Owen's[4] and went to see my Lady Wotton at Whitehall, where we walked five or six turns but spoke nothing of this business, though her heart and mine were full of it—from hence I went to the Abbey at Westminster where I saw the Queen of Scots,[5] her tomb and all the other tombs, and came home by water, where I took an extreme cold.

Upon the 17th my Lord Archbishop of Canterbury, my Lord William Howard, my Lord Roos, my cousin Russell, my brother Sackville, and a great company of men of note were all in the gallery at Dorset House,[6] where the Archbishop took me aside and talked with me privately one hour and half, and persuaded me both by divine and human means to set my hand to their arguments. But my answer to his lordship was that I would do nothing till my lady[7] and I had conferred together. Much persuasion was used by him and all the company, sometimes terrifying me and sometimes flattering me, but at length it was concluded that I should have leave to go to my mother and send an answer by the 22nd of March next, whether I will agree to the business or not, and to this prayer my Lord of Canterbury and the rest of the lords have set their hands.

Next day was a marvellous day to me through the mercy of God, for it was generally thought that I must either have sealed to the arguments or else have parted with my lord.[8] * * *

March 1616

[A REFUSAL TO CAPITULATE]

* * * Upon the 20th in the morning my Lord William Howard[9] with his son, my cousin William Howard, and Mr John Dudley came hither to take the answer of my mother and myself, which was a direct denial to stand to the judges' award. The same day came Sir Timothy Whittington hither, who did all he could do to mitigate the anger between my Lord William Howard and my mother, so as at last we parted all good friends, and it was agreed upon my men and horses should stay, and we should go up to London together after Easter. * * *

April 1616

[FROM LONDON TO KNOLE]

* * * Upon the 11th I came from London to Knole where I had but a cold welcome from my lord. My lady Margaret met me in the outermost gate and my lord came to me in the drawing chamber.

---

3. The potential settlement with her uncle.
4. Prayer of Owen's or ower's; the manuscript is not clear and neither is the provenance.
5. Elizabeth I's Catholic cousin Mary (great-granddaughter of Henry VII), who made claims to the English throne during Elizabeth's reign and was executed in 1587.
6. The London estate of Richard Sackville, Earl of Dorset.
7. Her mother, Margaret, Dowager Countess of Cumberland.
8. Anne Clifford refers to her husband, Richard Sackville, as "my lord" throughout the diary.
9. The following people are mentioned in this excerpt from March 1616: Lord Dudley: possibly one of the illegitimate children of Edward Sutton, Lord Dudley, a distant relation to the Clifford family; Sir Timothy Whittington: not identified in any other way.

Upon the 12th I told my lord how I had left those writings which the judges and my lord would have me sign and seal behind with my mother.

Upon the 13th my lord and Thomas Glenham[1] went up to London.

Upon the 17th came Tom Woodyatt from London, but brought me no news of my going up, which I daily look for.

Upon the 18th Baskett came hither and brought me a letter from my lord to let me know this was the last time of asking me whether I would set my hand to this award of the judges.

Upon the 19th I returned my lord for answer that I would not stand to the award of the judges, what misery soever it cost me. This morning the Bishop of St David's and my little child were brought to speak to me. * * *

May 1616

[HER MOTHER DIES]

* * * Upon the 2nd came Mr Legge[2] and told divers of the servants that my lord would come down and see me once more, which would be the last time that I should see him again.

Upon the 3rd came Baskett down from London and brought me a letter from my lord, by which I might see it was his pleasure that the child should go the next day to London, which at the first was somewhat grievous to me, but when I considered that it would both make my lord more angry with me and be worse for the child, I resolved to let her go. After, I had sent for Mr Legge and talked with him about that and other matters, and wept bitterly. * * *

Upon the 8th I dispatched a letter to my mother.

Upon the 9th I received a letter from Mr Bellasis, how extreme ill my mother had been, and in the afternoon came Humphrey Godding's son with letters that my mother was exceeding ill, and as they thought, in some danger of death—so as I sent Rivers presently to London with letters to be sent to her, and certain cordials and conserves.[3] At night was brought me a letter from my lord to let me know his determination was, the child should go live at Horsley, and not come hither any more, so as this was a very grievous and sorrowful day to me.

Upon the 10th Rivers came from London and brought me word from Lord William that she was not in such danger as I feared.

All this time my lord was in London, where he had all and infinite great resort coming to him. He went much abroad to cocking,[4] to bowling alleys, to plays and horse races, and [was] commended by all the world. I stayed in the country, having many times a sorrowful and heavy heart, and being condemned by most

---

1. The following people are mentioned in this excerpt from April 1616: Thomas Glenham: no reliable information available; Tom Woodyatt: Thomas Woodgate, yeoman of the great chamber at Dorset House; Baskett: Peter Basket, another servant who was Gentleman of the Horse.
2. The following are mentioned in this excerpt from May 1616: Mr. Legge: Edward Legge, a steward; Mr. Bellasis, Humphrey Godding's son, and Rivers: none of whom are identified but all of whom may have been servants of hers or her mother's; Lord William: William Howard (see

February exerpt above); Cecily Neville: probably a sister of Mary Neville's (see February excerpt above); Mr. Marsh: an otherwise unidentified servant; Mr. Davis: a servant; Mr. Amherst: elsewhere in the diary referred to as a preacher; my Lady Somerset: see note 7 below; Kendal: another servant.
3. Medicines and beverages believed to invigorate the heart and stimulate circulation.
4. Resort: large numbers of people coming to visit; cocking: cockfighting.

folks because I would not consent to the agreement, so as I may truly say, I am like an owl in the desert.[5] * * *

Upon the 15th my lord came down from London and my cousin Cecily Neville; my lord lying in Leslie Chamber and I in my own. * * *

Upon the 18th, being Saturday, in the morning my lord and I having much talk about these businesses, we agreed that Mr Marsh should go presently down to my mother and that by him I should write a letter to persuade her to give over her jointure[6] presently to my lord, and that he would give her yearly as much it was worth. * * *

Upon the 22nd Mr Davis came down from London and brought me word that my mother was very well recovered of her dangerous sickness; by him I writ a letter to my lord that Mr Amherst and Mr Davy might confer together about my jointure to free it from the payment of debts and all other incumbrances.

Upon the 24th my Lady Somerset was arraigned and condemned at Westminster Hall, where she confessed her fault and asked the King's mercy, and was much pitied by all beholders.[7] * * *

Upon the 29th Kendal came and brought me the heavy news of my mother's death, which I held as the greatest and most lamentable cross that could have befallen me. Also he brought her will along with him, wherein she appointed her body should be buried in the parish church of Alnwick, which was a double grief to me when I considered her body should be carried away and not interred at Skipton; so as I took that as a sign that I should be dispossessed of the inheritance of my forefathers.

1616

5. Psalm 102:4–6: "For my days pass away like smoke, / and my bones burn like a furnace. / My heart is stricken like grass; / I am too wasted to eat my bread. / Because of my loud groaning my bones cling to my skin. / I am like an owl of the wilderness, / like a little owl of the waste places."
6. Land that it was agreed upon she would inherit upon the death of her husband.

7. Refers to a court intrigue in which Frances Howard, cousin to Anne Clifford's husband, had been accused with her second husband, Robert Carr, Earl of Somerset (whom she had divorced her first husband to marry), of having fatally poisoned Carr's secretary, Thomas Overbury, who had objected strenuously and publicly to the marriage.

CULTURAL COORDINATES
Scolds

The word *scold* in early modern England referred to a woman who verbally resisted her husband's rule—or more publicly flouted male rule. Women, particularly middle-class women, accused of being scolds were often physically punished in humiliatingly public ways. Cucking, for instance, was a common punishment, reserved for scolds in sixteenth- and early-seventeenth-century England. A cucking was an almost carnival-like event. Women were first carted through the town or village on a two-wheeled contraption associated with dung collection. Often they were accompanied by a grotesque version of a marching band, a ragtag group of "musicians" blowing horns and beating drums, making sounds that were meant to imitate farting noises. The woman was then strapped to a chair called a "cucking stool" (or ducking stool) and then, in front of a loud, contemptuous crowd, was dunked—fully submerged—three or four times in a fetid pond or river.

Literature of the early seventeenth century also is full of allusions to the "scold's bridle," an instrument of torture that was used to punish women found guilty of verbal or sexual transgression. (Interestingly, the two were closely linked in the period, female outspokenness and sexual promiscuity referred to almost interchangeably in the conduct literature of the time.) The bridles were hinged metal headpieces; attached was a metal piece that would extend up to three inches into the woman's mouth so that her tongue was pressed down, effectively muting her

Woman on a Ducking Stool, Accused of Witchcraft (no date). (Woodcut, Stapleton Collection/ Bridgeman Art Library International)

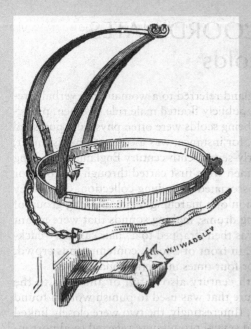

A Scold's Bridle (no date), Stockport, England. (From *Old-Time Punishments* by William Andrews, 1890)

and often inducing extreme gagging if she tried to speak at all. In a late-seventeenth-century sermon titled "On the Government of the Tongue," Thomas Watson chillingly refers to the taming of the tongue that the scold's bridle was meant to accomplish: "The Tongue, though it be a little Member, yet it hath a World of Sin in it. The Tongue is an unruly Evil. We put *Bitts* in Horses mouths and rule them; but the Tongue is an unbridled Thing. It is hard to find a Curbing-bitt to rule the Tongue."

Both the category of the scold and the instruments of shame used to tame her seem to have disappeared after 1660. The reasons for this are not completely understood, but they are almost certainly linked to the slightly changed status of women in England after the Restoration.

Active c. 1616

Very little biographical information exists about Dorothy Leigh outside of the book she wrote for her three sons, parts of which are excerpted below. *The Mothers Blessing* appears to have been written after the death of Leigh's husband and, if we take the letter to her sons at face value, shortly before her own death, a death she seems to be anticipating.

One of the things that makes this advice manual significant is that it was published at a time when very few women could have had works appear in print. As with Elizabeth Jocelin (whose own legacy book is excerpted later—see pp. 83–86), the circumstances of approaching death would seem to have annulled the typical prohibitions against female public expression. Certainly, while Leigh's advice manual does seem to follow some of the prescriptions for female public speech—most of the advice is devotional in nature—it is also quite obviously a woman instructing not only her children but most notably the English public in religion; and, as Margaret Fell Fox testifies later in the century, that was not an area typically open to women in this period. Yet Leigh's book was enormously popular: it was reissued nineteen times between 1616 and 1640. Some of its appeal may have had to do with Leigh's careful challenge to conventional ideas about marriage. Although she does not overturn the dominant idea of female obedience to the husband, she does shift the emphasis to a more companionate model of marriage, a model that became much more popular during the latter half of the seventeenth century.

From The Mothers Blessing

OR The Godly Counsaile of a Gentlewoman Not Long Since Deceased, Left Behind Her for Her Children

TO MY BELOVED SONS, GEORGE, JOHN, AND WILLIAM LEIGH,
ALL THINGS PERTAINING TO LIFE AND GODLINESS

My children, God having taken your father out of this vale of tears[1] to his everlasting mercy in Christ, myself not only knowing what a care he had in his lifetime that you should be brought up godlily, but also at his death being charged in his will by the love and duty which I bore him, to see you well instructed and brought up in knowledge, I could not choose but seek (according as I was by duty bound) to fulfill his will in all things, desiring no greater comfort in the world than to see you grow in godliness, that so you might meet your father in heaven, where I am sure he is, myself being a witness of his faith in Christ. And seeing myself going out of the world, and you but coming in, I know not how to perform this duty so well, as to leave you these few lines, which will show you as well the great desire your father had both of your spiritual and temporal good, as the care I had to fulfill his will in this, knowing it was the last duty I should perform unto him. * * *

---

1. An expression of piety common from about the early sixteenth century that refers to life on earth as a time of suffering that is left behind when the human soul goes to a better place in heaven.

Chapter 2
the first cause of writing is a motherly affection

But lest you should marvel, my children, why I do not, according to the usual custom of women, exhort you by word and admonitions rather than by writing (a thing so unusual among us, and especially in such a time when there be so many godly books in the world that they mould in some men's studies while their masters are marred because they will not meditate upon them, as many men's garments moth-eat in their chests while their Christian brethren quake with cold in the street for want of covering), know therefore that it was the motherly affection that I bare unto you all which made me now (as it often hath done heretofore) forget myself in regard of you. Neither care I what you or any shall think of me if among many words I may write but one sentence which may make you labour for the spiritual food of the soul, which must be gathered every day out of the word,[2] as the children of Israel gathered manna[3] in the wilderness. By the which you may see it is a labour. But what labour? A pleasant labour, a profitable labour, a labour without the which the soul cannot live. For as the children of Israel must needs starve except they gathered every day in the wilderness and fed of it, so must your souls, except you gather the spiritual manna out of the word every day and feed of it continually. * * * Whereas if you desire any food for your souls that is not in the written word of God, your souls die with it even in your hearts and mouths. Even as they that desired other food, died with it in their mouths, were it never so dainty, so shall you, and there is no recovery for you.

* * *

Chapter 13
it is great folly for a man to mislike his own choice

Methinks I never saw a man show a more senseless simplicity[4] than in misliking his own choice, when God hath given a man almost a world of women to choose him a wife in. If a man hath not wit enough to choose him one whom he can love to the end, yet methinks he should have discretion to cover his own folly. But if he want discretion, methinks he should have policy,[5] which never fails a man to dissemble his own simplicity in this case. If he want wit, discretion, and policy, he is unfit to marry any woman. Do not a woman that wrong as to take her from her friends that love her and after a while to begin to hate her. If she have no friends, yet thou knowest not but that she may have a husband that may love her. If thou canst not love her to the end, leave her to him that can. Methinks my son could not offend me in any thing, if he served God, except he chose a wife that he could not love to the end. I need not say if he served God, for if he served God he would obey God, and then he would choose a godly wife and live lovingly and godlily with her, and not do as some man who taketh a woman to make her a companion and fellow, and after he hath her, he makes her a servant and drudge. If she be thy wife, she is always too good to be thy servant, and worthy to be thy fellow. If thou wilt have a good wife, thou must go before her in all goodness and show her a

2. Bible.
3. In Exodus 16, manna is described as a miraculous type of food that God supplies to Moses and the Israelites in the wilderness after they escape
from slavery in Egypt.
4. Foolishness.
5. The skill to manage his wife such that she obeys him.

pattern of all good virtues by thy godly and discreet life, and especially in patience, according to the counsel of the Holy Ghost: "Bear with the woman, as with the weaker vessel."[6] Here God showeth that it is her imperfection that honoureth thee, and that it is thy perfection that maketh thee to bear with her. Follow the counsel of God, therefore, and bear with her. God willed a man to leave father and mother for his wife. This showeth what an excellent love God did appoint to be between man and wife. In truth I cannot by any means set down the excellency of that love. But this I assure you, that if you get wives that be godly, and you love them, you shall not need to forsake me. Whereas if you have wives that you love not, I am sure I will forsake you. Do not yourselves that wrong as to marry a woman that you cannot love. Show not so much childishness in your sex as to say you loved her once, and now your mind is changed. If thou canst not love her for the goodness that is in her, yet let the grace that is in thyself move thee to do it. And so I leave thee to the Lord, whom I pray to guide both thee and her with his grace, and grant that you may choose godlily, and live happily, and die comfortably through faith in Jesus Christ.

* * *

1616

━━━◅ ELIZABETH BROOKE JOCELIN ▻◦━━━
c. 1595–1622

An only child, Elizabeth Brooke was abandoned by her father, Nicholas Brooke, and left to the care of her mother, Joan Chaderton, and maternal grandfather when she was still an infant. This was in some ways fortuitous for the precocious girl, for her grandfather, Bishop William Chaderton—who brought Elizabeth up alone after her mother died in 1602—was an extremely learned man (bishop of Lincoln and the master of Queen's College, Cambridge) who believed emphatically in the education of his granddaughter. Thus, she grew up encouraged in the serious study of religion, languages, history, and art.

Elizabeth had been married to Turrell Jocelin for six years when, in 1622, she became pregnant with their first child. Worried that she would not survive the birth of the child, Elizabeth, who had been encouraged in the study of divinity by her husband, immediately began writing *The Mothers Legacie,* a book of (mainly) religious instruction for her unborn child. Her daughter, Theodora, was born on October 12, 1622, and Elizabeth, her prenatal fears proving sadly prophetic, died nine days later.

The excerpt below is the letter Elizabeth wrote to her husband and attached to her book as a sort of preface. It is particularly notable both for its articulation of the deeply gendered set of expectations she has for her unborn child and for the related tension it reveals between Elizabeth's obvious, and learned, eloquence and her suspicion of even her own learning.

6. See 1 Peter 3:7.

From The Mothers Legacie, to Her Unborne Childe

Epistle Dedicatory
to My Truly Loving and Most Dearly Loved Husband, Turrell Jocelin.

Mine own dear love, I no sooner conceived an hope that I should be made a mother by thee, but with it entered the consideration of a mother's duty, and shortly after followed the apprehension of danger that might prevent me from executing that care I so exceedingly desired, I mean in religious training our child. And in truth, death appearing in this shape was doubly terrible unto me. First in respect of the painfulness of that kind of death, an[d] next of the loss my little one should have in wanting me. But I thank God these fears were cured with the remembrance that all things work together for the best to those that love God, and a certain assurance that he will give me patience according to my pain.

Yet still I thought there was some good office I might do for my child more than only to bring it forth (though it should please God to take me). When I considered our frailty, our apt inclination to sin, the devil's subtlety, and the world's deceitfulness from these, how much I desired to admonish it! But still it came into my mind that death might deprive me of time if I should neglect the present. I knew not what to do. I thought of writing, but then mine own weakness appeared so manifestly that I was ashamed and durst not undertake it. But when I could find no other means to express my motherly zeal, I encouraged myself with these reasons:

First, that I wrote to a child, and though I were but a woman, yet to a child's judgement what I understood might serve for a foundation to better learning.

Again, I considered it was to my own,[1] not to the world, and my love to my own might excuse my errors.

And lastly but chiefly, I comforted myself that my intent was good, and that I was well assured God was the prosperer of good purposes.

Thus resolved, I writ this ensuing letter to our little one, to whom I could not find a fitter hand to convey it than thine own, which mayest with authority see the performance of this my little legacy, of which my child is executor.

And, dear love, as thou must be the overseer, for God's sake, when it shall fail in duty to God or to the world, do not let thy fondness wink at such folly but severely correct it. And that thy trouble may be little when it comes to years, I pray thee be careful when it is young. First, to provide it a religious nurse—no matter for her complexion.[2] As near as may be, choose a house[3] where it may not learn to swear or speak scurrilous words. I know I may be thought too scrupulous in this, but I am sure thou shalt find it a hard matter to break a child of that it learns so young. It will be a great while ere it will be thought old enough to be beaten for evil words, and by that time it will be so perfect that blows will not mend it. And when some charitable body reproves or corrects it for these faults, let nobody pity it with the loss of the mother, for truly I should use it no better.

Next, good sweetheart, keep it not from school, but let it learn betimes. If it be a son, I doubt not but thou wilt dedicate it to the Lord as his minister, if he will please of his mercy to give him grace and capacity for that great work. If it be a

---

1. Own family.
2. Temperament.
3. Families in this period who could afford to do

so often sent infants out to wet nurses to be breast-fed.

daughter, I hope my mother Brooke[4] (if thou desirest her) will take it among hers and let them learn one lesson. I desire her bringing up may be learning the Bible, as my sisters do, good housewifery, writing, and good work; other learning a woman needs not. Though I admire it in those whom God hath blessed with discretion, yet I desire it not much in my own, having seen that sometimes women have greater portions of learning than wisdom, which is of no better use to them than a main-sail to a fly-boat,[5] which runs it under water. But where learning and wisdom meet in a virtuous-disposed woman, she is the fittest closet[6] for all goodness. She is like a well-balanced ship that may bear all her sail. She is—indeed I should but shame myself if I should go about to praise her more.

But my dear, though she have all this in her, she will hardly make a poor man's wife. Yet I will leave it to thy will. If thou desirest a learned daughter, I pray God give her a wise and religious heart that she may use it to his glory, thy comfort, and her own salvation.

But howsoever thou disposest of her education, I pray thee labour by all means to teach her true humility, though I much desire it may be as humble if it be a son as a daughter. Yet in a daughter I more fear that vice, pride, being now rather accounted a virtue in our sex worthy praise than a vice fit for reproof. Parents read lectures of it to their children, how necessary it is, and they have principles that must not be disputed against. As first: "Look how much you esteem yourself, others will esteem of you". Again: "What you give to others, you derogate from yourself". And many more of these kind. I have heard men accounted wise that have maintained this kind of pride under the name of generous knowing or understanding themselves. But I am sure that he that truly knows himself shall know so much evil by himself, that he shall have small reason to think himself better than another man.

Dearest, I am so fearful to bring thee a proud, high-minded child that, though I know thy care will need no spur, yet I cannot but desire thee to double thy watchfulness over this vice; it is such a crafty, devilish, insinuating sin, it will enter little children in the likeness of wit, with which their parents are delighted, and that is sweet nourishment to it.

I pray thee, dear heart, delight not to have a bold child: modesty and humility are the sweetest groundworks of all virtue. Let not thy servants give it any other title than the Christian name, till it have discretion to understand how to respect others. And I pray thee be not profuse in the expense of clothes for it. Methinks it is a vain delight in parents to bestow that cost upon one child which would serve two or three. If they have them not of their own, *pauper ubique iacet.*[7]

Thus, dear, thou seest my belief. If thou canst teach thy little one humility, it must needs make thee a glad father.

But I know thou wonderest by this time what the cause should be that, we two continually unclasping our hearts one to another, I should reserve this to write. When thou thinkest thus, dear, remember how grievous it was to thee but to hear me say, "I may die", and thou wilt confess this would have been an unpleasing discourse to thee, and thou knowest I never durst displease thee willingly,

---

4. Probably refers to her old nurse, as her mother had died when Elizabeth was a child.
5. Main-sail: the principal sail on a large boat or ship; fly-boat: a very small boat.
6. Private space.

7. Literally, "the poor man lies low everywhere"; in effect, it means that if one has no children—or more money than one needs to raise one's children—give the money to those who truly need it.

so much I love thee. All I now desire is that the unexpectedness of it make it not more grievous to thee. But I know thou art a Christian, and therefore will not doubt thy patience.

And though I thus write to thee as heartily desiring to be religiously prepared to die, yet, my dear, I despair not of life, nay, I hope and daily pray for it, if so God will be pleased. Nor shall I think this labour lost though I do live; for I will make it my own looking-glass wherein to see when I am too severe, when too re- miss, and (in my child's fault through this glass) to discern mine own error. And I hope God will so give me his grace that I shall more skilfully act than apprehend a mother's duty.

My dear, thou knowest me so well, I shall not need to tell thee I have written honest thoughts in a disordered fashion, not observing method. For thou knowest how short I am of learning and natural endowments to take such a course in writ- ing. Or if that strong affection of thine have hid my weakness from thy sight, I now profess seriously my own ignorance; and though I did not, this following treatise would betray it. But I send it only to the eyes of a most loving husband, and a child exceedingly beloved, to whom I hope it will not be altogether unprofitable.

Thus humbly desiring God to give thee all comfort in this life and happiness in the life to come, I leave thee and thine to his most gracious protection.

Thine inviolable,
Eliza.

1624

CULTURAL COORDINATES
Women's Community
in Childbirth Rooms

In 1579 the physician John Jones asked, apparently with some aggravation, "Who ought to be at the birth?" His own answer was "a few rather of godly, expert and learned women . . . than a rude multitude given either to folly, banqueting or bravery, as in the towns of the east country is too much used." Jones was referring to a practice that was common all over England, not just in the east: the approximately six weeks after childbirth known as the lying-in. During her time as the "woman in the straw" (so called because of the straw mattress that would be bloodied by childbirth), a woman in childbed was the center of social attention in her community, specifically and exclusively women's attention. If it was not exactly the riotous banquet Jones protests above, it was certainly a communal affair, a bonding of women that included family and neighbors, often across

Women and Midwife Gathered around the Childbed (1682).

social classes, a kind of protracted party that, for those above the poorest classes, included abundant food and drink provided for and sometimes (but not always) by the guests. Indeed, in the early modern period, the social dimension of childbirth assumed almost as much importance as its biological purpose.

The semantic history of the word *gossip,* in fact, testifies both to the importance of the lying-in for women and to the perceived threat the custom posed to a patriarchally organized society. The *Oxford English Dictionary* tells us that, in its original incarnation, the word *gossip* referred to the "god-sibb" or the "one who has contracted spiritual affinity with another by acting as a sponsor at a baptism." A gossip, during the first half of the sixteenth century, was a godparent—either male or female. By 1590, however, the word was used mainly to refer to the female friends who were invited to be present at a birth and, according once again to the *Oxford English Dictionary,* more notably (and more commonly), "a person, mostly a woman, of light and trifling character, especially one who delights in idle talk; a newsmonger, a tattler." In other words, the meaning of the word had devolved from "spiritual affinity" to "idle chatter." This devolution is reflected in the *Ten Pleasures of Marriage* (1682), in which A. Marsh (thought by some to be a pseudonym for Aphra Behn), in response to several warnings like the one above about the dangers of the lying-in, says, "for gossips to meet . . . at lying in and not to talk, you may as well dam up the arches of London Bridge as stop their mouths at such a time. 'Tis a time when women, like parliament men, have a privilege to talk petty treason against their husbands."

ANNE BRADSTREET

1612–1672

Born to Thomas and Dorothy Dudley, the second of six children, Anne Bradstreet grew up on the country estate of the Earl of Lincoln, where her father was the steward, or manager, of the estate. Privately educated by tutors, she had extensive access to the libraries of her father and the earl (both Puritans who were very supportive of women's education).

In 1628 she married Simon Bradstreet, the son of a Puritan minister who had been part of the earl's household since the age of fourteen. Two years later, the young couple and Bradstreet's parents boarded the *Arbella,* one of the first ships to bring English Puritans to the new American colonies. After a difficult three-month crossing, and suffering from a debilitating illness that caused temporary paralysis, Bradstreet arrived at a colony very different from the privileged environment in which she had grown up; certainly, her life would never again be without hardship. Frequently in poor health, Bradstreet would nevertheless bear eight children in America. She would also survive long periods of loneliness without her husband, who, as judge and legislator, later royal councilor and governor, was frequently required to be away from home.

Bradstreet wrote most of the poems that appear in the first edition of *The Tenth Muse* (from which most of the poems below are taken) during the years 1635–45 while she lived in the town of Ipswich, about thirty miles north of Boston. She dedicated the volume to her father, who had taken great interest in her education and who had clearly appreciated his daughter's considerable intelligence. The poems are consciously literary, many of them directly influenced by the religious poetry of the French poet Guillaume Du Bartas and by the courtly, formal poetry of the sixteenth-century English poets Philip Sidney and Edmund Spenser.

Although the volume was self-consciously literary, it would appear that Bradstreet did not mean for it ever to be published. It was her brother-in-law, John Woodbridge, who took the volume to England in 1650 and had it published without her knowledge. The book attracted considerable attention, partly because it was written by a woman, partly because it was the first book to be published by anyone living in the American colonies. In the introduction, Woodbridge seems aware of the risks of a woman appearing in print: he takes care to reassure readers that the poems are "the work of a woman, honored and esteemed where she lives, for her gracious demeanor, her eminent parts, her pious conversation, her courteous disposition, her exact diligence in her place, and discreet managing of her family occasions." Nevertheless, and despite the volume's warm reception, Bradstreet was upset that the poems had been published as they were and revised them significantly for a second edition. Bradstreet's later poetry is much more personal in nature, a reflection of her life in New England, her love for her family (a great deal of it tinged by loss and sadness), and her ambivalence about the harshness of Puritan theology, particularly as it was articulated in the American colonies.

Ill for most of her life, Bradstreet finally succumbed to tuberculosis at the age of sixty.

From The Tenth Muse Lately Sprung Up in America

The Prologue[1]

1

To sing of wars, of captains, and of kings,
Of cities founded, commonwealths begun,
For my mean[2] pen, are too superior things,
And how they all, or each, their dates have run:
Let poets, and historians set these forth,   5
My obscure verse, shall not so dim their worth.

2

But when my wond'ring eyes, and envious heart,
Great Bartas'[3] sugared lines do but read o'er;
Fool, I do grudge, the Muses[4] did not part
'Twixt him and me, that over-fluent store;   10
A Bartas can do what a Bartas will,
But simple I, according to my skill.

3

From schoolboy's tongue, no rhetoric we expect,
Nor yet a sweet consort,[5] from broken strings,
Nor perfect beauty, where's a main defect,   15
My foolish, broken, blemished Muse so sings;
And this to mend, alas, no art is able,
'Cause nature made it so irreparable.

4

Nor can I, like that fluent sweet tongued Greek[6]
Who lisped at first, speak afterwards more plain.   20
By art, he gladly found what he did seek,
A full requital of his striving pain:
Art can do much, but this maxim's most sure,
A weak or wounded brain admits no cure.

5

I am obnoxious to each carping tongue,   25
Who says, my hand a needle better fits,
A poet's pen, all scorn, I should thus wrong;

1. This poem was the prologue to *The Tenth Muse Lately Sprung Up in America* (published in London in 1650).
2. Poor, inferior in ability.
3. Guillaume de Salluste Du Bartas (1544–90), French Protestant poet, author of *La sepmaine* (1578) and *La seconde sepmaine* (1584) (translated by Joshua Sylvester in 1621 as *Divine Weeks and Works*). *La sepmaine* and its sequel were epic poems chronicling Christian history.
4. The nine goddesses from classical Greek and Roman mythology who inspire poets and musicians.
5. Concert.
6. Demosthenes (c. 384–322 BCE), an Athenian orator who was said to have overcome a speech defect by speaking with pebbles in his mouth.

For such despite[7] they cast on female wits:
If what I do prove well, it won't advance,
They'll say it's stol'n, or else, it was by chance.   30

6

But sure the antique Greeks were far more mild,
Else of our sex, why feigned[8] they those nine,
And poesy made, Calliope's[9] own child,
So 'mongst the rest, they placed the arts divine:
But this weak knot they will full soon untie,   35
The Greeks did nought but play the fool and lie.

7

Let Greeks be Greeks, and women what they are,
Men have precedency, and still excel,
It is but vain, unjustly to wage war,
Men can do best, and women know it well;   40
Preeminence in each, and all is yours,
Yet grant some small acknowledgment of ours.

8

And oh, ye high flown quills,[1] that soar the skies,
And ever with your prey, still catch your praise,
If e'er you deign[2] these lowly lines, your eyes   45
Give wholesome parsley wreath, I ask no bays:[3]
This mean and unrefined ore of mine,
Will make your glistering gold but more to shine.

c. 1642   1650

The Author to Her Book[4]

Thou ill-formed offspring of my feeble brain,
Who after birth did'st by my side remain,
Till snatched from thence by friends, less wise than true
Who thee abroad, exposed to public view,
Made thee in rags, halting to th' press to trudge,   5
Where errors were not lessened (all may judge).
At thy return my blushing was not small,
My rambling brat (in print) should mother call,
I cast thee by as one unfit for light,
Thy visage was so irksome in my sight;   10

---

7. Scorn.
8. Imagined.
9. The muse of the heroic epic.
1. Feathers that were formed into pens by shaping and splitting the lower end of the barrel; here it seems to be used metaphorically to refer to great poets.
2. Condescend to accept.
3. In ancient Greece, the leaves of the bay laurel were woven together to create a wreath of reward and recognition for a great poet.
4. This poem describes Bradstreet's feelings when her brother-in-law took her manuscript of poems back to England, where, despite her insistence that she did not write the poems for publication, it was published in 1650 as *The Tenth Muse*. This poem was probably written in 1666 for a revised edition of the book.

Yet being mine own, at length affection would
Thy blemishes amend, if so I could:
I washed thy face, but more defects I saw,
And rubbing off a spot, still made a flaw.
I stretched thy joints to make thee even feet,   15
Yet still thou run'st more hobbling than is meet,[5]
In better dress to trim thee was my mind,[6]
But nought save homespun cloth, i' th' house I find.
In this array, 'mongst vulgars mayst thou roam,
In critics' hands, beware thou dost not come;   20
And take thy way where yet thou art not known,
If for thy father asked, say, thou hadst none:
And for thy mother, she alas is poor,
Which caused her thus to send thee out of door.

c. 1666   1678

Before the Birth of One of Her Children[7]

All things within this fading world hath end,
Adversity doth still our joys attend;
No ties so strong, no friends so dear and sweet,
But with death's parting blow is sure to meet.
The sentence past is most irrevocable,   5
A common thing, yet oh inevitable;
How soon, my Dear, death may my steps attend,
How soon'st may be thy lot to lose thy friend,
We both are ignorant, yet love bids me
These farewell lines to recommend to thee,   10
That when that knot's untied that made us one,
I may seem thine, who in effect am none.
And if I see not half my days that's due,
What nature would, God grant to yours and you;
The many faults that well you know I have,   15
Let be interr'd in my oblivion's grave;
If any worth or virtue were in me,
Let that live freshly in thy memory
And when thou feel'st no grief, as I no harms,
Yet love thy dead, who long lay in thine arms: 20
And when thy loss shall be repaid with gains
Look to my little babes my dear remains.
And if thou love they self, or loved'st me
These O protect from step dame's[8] injury.
And if chance to thine eyes shall bring this verse,   25
With some sad sighs honor my absent hearse;

5. Proper.
6. Intention.
7. This poem, found among Bradstreet's papers

after her death and not dated, is addressed to her
husband.
8. Stepmother's.

And kiss this paper for thy love's dear sake,
Who with salt tears this last farewell did take.

c. 1635   1678

In Memory of My Dear Grandchild
Elizabeth Bradstreet
Who Deceased August, 1665
Being a Year and Half Old[9]

Farewell dear babe, my heart's too much content
Farewell sweet babe, the pleasure of mine eye,
Farewell fair flower that for a space was lent,
Then ta'en away unto eternity.
Blest babe why should I once bewail thy fate,   5
Or sigh thy days so soon were terminate;
Sith[1] thou art settled in an everlasting state.

By nature trees do rot when they are grown.
And plums and apples thoroughly ripe do fall,
And corn and grass are in their season mown,   10
And time brings down what is both strong and tall.
But plants new set to be eradicate,
And buds new blown, to have so short a date,
Is by his hand alone that guides nature and fate.

c. 1665   1678

Some Verses upon the Burning of Our House, July 10th, 1666

In silent night when rest I took
For sorrow near I did not look,
I wakened was with thund'ring noise
And piteous shrieks of dreadful voice.
That fearful sound of "fire" and "fire,"   5
Let no man know is my desire.
I starting up the light did spy,
And to my God my heart did cry
To strengthen me in my distress
And not to leave me succourless.   10
Then coming out beheld a space
The flame consume my dwelling place,
And when I could no longer look
I blest his name that gave and took,[2]
That laid my goods now in the dust   15
Yea so it was, and so 'twas just.
It was his own, it was not mine
Far be it that I should repine,
He might of all justly bereft,

---

9. The eldest child of Bradstreet's son Samuel.
1. Since.
2. "The Lord gave, and the Lord hath taken

away, blessed be the name of the Lord" (Job
1:20–21).

But yet sufficient for us left.   20
When by the ruins oft I passed
My sorrowing eyes aside did cast
And here and there the places spy
Where oft I sat and long did lie,
Here stood that trunk, and there that chest   25
There lay that store I counted best.
My pleasant things in ashes lie
And them behold no more shall I.
Under the roof no guest shall sit,
Nor at thy table eat a bit.   30
No pleasant tale shall e'er be told
Nor things recounted done of old.
No candle e'er shall shine in thee
Nor bridegroom's voice e'er heard shall be.
In silence ever shalt thou lie   35
Adieu, Adieu, all's vanity.[3]
Then straight I 'gin my heart to chide,
And did thy wealth on earth abide,
Didst fix thy hope on mouldering dust.
The arm of flesh didst make thy trust?[4]   40
Raise up thy thoughts above the sky
That dunghill mists away may fly.
Thou hast a house on high erect
Framed by that mighty Architect,
With glory richly furnished   45
Stands permanent though this be fled.
It's purchased and paid for too
By him who has enough to do.
A price so vast as is unknown
Yet by his gift is made thine own.   50
There's wealth enough I need no more,
Farewell my pelf,[5] farewell my store.

1666   1678

To My Dear and Loving Husband

If ever two were one, then surely we.
If ever man were loved by wife, then thee;
If ever wife was happy in a man,
Compare with me ye women if you can.
I prize thy love more than whole mines of gold,   5
Or all the riches that the East doth hold.
My love is such that rivers cannot quench,
Nor ought but love from thee, give recompense.

3. "Vanity of vanities, saith the Preacher, vanity of vanities, all is vanity" (Ecclesiastes 1:2).
4. "With him is an arm of flesh, but with us is the Lord our God to help us and to fight our battles.
And the people rested themselves upon the words of Hezekiah King of Judah" (2 Chronicles 32:8).
5. Worthless property.

Thy love is such I can no way repay,
The heavens reward thee manifold I pray.   10
Then while we live, in love let's so persevere,
That when we live no more, we may live ever.

1678

◄ MARGARET FELL FOX ►
1614–1702

Margaret Fell Fox was born Margaret Askew in Lancashire, the daughter of the wealthy, landed John Askew. At eighteen, she married Judge Thomas Fell and together they had nine children—eight daughters and a son. Margaret was a deeply pious woman who, like the courageous and outspoken Anne Askew to whom she was related, believed fervently in women's right to freedom of conscience and expression. It was probably her commitment to those ideas that drew her to the Society of Friends, or Quakers, a Protestant nonconformist sect, a group of believers who had split away from the state-sponsored Church of England for theological reasons. Indeed, the founder of the Society of Friends, George Fox, a reportedly spellbinding preacher who had written in support of female education, visited the Fell estate, Swarthmore Hall, in 1652; shortly after that visit, Margaret and at least two of her daughters, Sarah and Isabel (who themselves later made lasting contributions to the Quaker movement), converted to Quakerism.

Often referred to now as the "Mother of Quakerism," Margaret actively advocated on behalf of imprisoned Quakers (who had been implicated in the execution of Charles I), writing Oliver Cromwell, the Lord Protector, four times between 1655 and 1657 asking for his intervention on their behalf. After Thomas Fell died in 1658, she became increasingly active in the political life of the Society, writing numerous tracts, letters, and pamphlets, some to the newly restored King Charles II urging an end to the religious persecution of Quakers. She was herself arrested in 1663 for holding Society meetings in her home and was imprisoned at Lancaster Castle from 1664 to 1668 for refusing to take an oath of allegiance to the Crown. During this time she wrote her most famous tract, *Women's Speaking Justified* (1667), from which the excerpt that follows is taken.

In 1669, she married George Fox. She was imprisoned again in 1670, once again for holding illegal meetings at Swarthmore Hall, and was released under a patent, a state pardon, in 1671. She herself persuaded Charles II to release Fox from prison in 1674, a testament to her considerable rhetorical power and influence. On April 23, 1702, eleven years after the death of her second husband, she died at Swarthmore Hall.

Margaret Fell Fox was not the first to defend a woman's right to preach. In the 1650s, women from other nonconformist religious sects had argued radically for the same right in response to a rash of pamphlets in the 1640s that had savagely derided a group of women preachers in the west of England. But *Women's Speaking Justified* was a longer, more measured response to the subject; and its careful, biblically based rebuttal to the standard arguments against women preachers gave it an authority that the earlier pamphlets had failed to secure. Like Aemilia Lanyer's "Eve's Apology in Defence of Eve" (though with much less poetic license), *Women's Speaking* revisits the Genesis story of Adam and Eve, reinterpreting in this case the relationship between the woman and the serpent after the Fall. It also argues more broadly that, because God conceives of the church as a woman, those who speak against women's right to preach speak against God.

From Women's Speaking Justified, Proved and Allowed Of by the Scriptures

[THE CHURCH OF CHRIST IS A WOMAN]

Whereas it hath been an objection in the minds of many, and several times hath been objected by the clergy, or ministers, and others, against women's speaking in the church; and so consequently may be taken, that they are condemned for meddling in the things of God, the ground of which objection is taken from the Apostle's[1] words, which he wrote in his first Epistle to the Corinthians, chap. 14, vers. 34, 35. And also what he wrote to Timothy in the first Epistle, chap. 2, vers. 11, 12.[2] But how far they wrong the Apostle's intentions in these scriptures, we shall show clearly when we come to them in their course and order. But first let me lay down how God himself hath manifested his will and mind concerning women, and unto women.

And first, when God created man in his own image, in the image of God created he them, male and female, and God blessed them, and God said unto them, "Be fruitful, and multiply." And God said, "Behold, I have given you of every herb," etc. (Gen. 1). Here God joins them together in his own image and makes no such distinctions and differences as men do; for though they be weak, he is strong; and as he said to the Apostle, his grace is sufficient, and his strength is made manifest in weakness (2 Cor. 12:9). And such hath the Lord chosen, even the weak things of the world to confound the things which are mighty; and things which are despised hath God chosen, to bring to naught things that are (1 Cor. 1). And God hath put no such difference between the male and female as men would make.

It is true, the serpent that was more subtle than any other beast of the field came unto the woman with his temptations, and with a lie, his subtilty discerning her to be more inclinable to hearken to him, when he said, "If ye eat, your eyes shall be opened." And the woman saw that the fruit was good to make one wise; there the temptation got into her, and she did eat, and gave to her husband, and he did eat also, and so they were both tempted into the transgression and disobedience; and therefore God said unto Adam, when that he hid himself when he heard his voice, "Hast thou eaten of the tree which I commanded thee that thou shouldest not eat?" And Adam said, "The woman which thou gavest me, she gave me of the tree, and I did eat." And the Lord said unto the woman, "What is this that thou hast done?" And the woman said, "The serpent beguiled me, and I did eat." Here the woman spoke the truth unto the Lord. See what the Lord said, verse 15, after he had pronounced sentence on the serpent: "I will put enmity between thee and the woman, and between thy seed and her seed; it shall bruise thy head, and thou shalt bruise his heel" (Gen. 3).

---

1. Paul's.
2. In 1 Corinthians 14:34–35, Paul says, "As in the churches of the saints, women should be silent in the churches. For they are not permitted to speak, but should be subordinate, as the law also says. If there is anything they desire to know, let them ask their husbands at home. For it is shameful for a woman to speak in church." Similarly, in his first letter to Timothy (2:11–12), Paul says, "Let a woman learn in silence with full submission. I permit no woman to teach or to have authority over a man; she is to keep silent."

Let this Word of the Lord, which was from the beginning, stop the mouths of all that oppose women's speaking in the power of the Lord; for he hath put enmity between the woman and the serpent; and if the seed of the woman speak not, the seed of the serpent speaks, for God hath put enmity between the two seeds, and it is manifest, that those that speak against the woman and her seeds speaking, speak out of the enmity of the old serpent's seeds; and God hath fulfilled his word and his promise, "When the fullness of time was come, he hath sent forth his Son, made of a woman, made under the law, that we might receive the adoption of sons" (Gal. 4:4, 5).

Moreover, the Lord is pleased, when he mentions his church, to call her by the name of woman, by his prophets, saying, "I have called thee as a woman forsaken, and grieved in spirit, and as a wife of youth" (Isaiah 54). Again, "How long wilt thou go about, thou backsliding daughter? For the Lord hath created a new thing in the earth, a woman shall compass a man" (Jer. 31:22). And David, when he was speaking of Christ and his church, said, "The King's daughter is all glorious within, her clothing is of wrought gold; she shall be brought unto the king; with gladness and rejoicing shall they be brought; they shall enter into the king's palace" (Psalm 45). And also King Solomon in his Song, where it speaks of Christ and his church, where she is complaining and calling for Christ, says, "If thou knowest not, O thou fairest among women, go thy way by the footsteps of the flock" (Cant. 1:8; 5:9).[3] And John, when he saw the wonder that was in heaven, he saw "a woman clothed with the sun, and the moon under her feet, and upon her head a crown of twelve stars; and there appeared another wonder in heaven, a great red dragon stood ready to devour her child." Here the enmity appears that God put between the woman and the dragon (Rev. 12).

Thus much may prove that the church of Christ is a woman, and those that speak against the woman's speaking, speak against the church of Christ, and the Seed of the woman, which Seed is Christ; that is to say, those that speak against the power of the Lord and the spirit of the Lord speaking in a woman, simply by reason of her sex, or because she is a woman, not regarding the Seed, and Spirit, and Power that speaks in her, such speak against Christ and his church and are of the seed of the serpent, wherein lodgeth the enmity. And as God the Father made no such difference in the first creation, nor never since between the male and the female, but always out of his mercy and loving-kindness had regard unto the weak, so also, his Son, Christ Jesus, confirms the same thing. When the Pharisees came to him and asked him if it were lawful for a man to put away his wife, he answered and said unto them, "Have you not read, that he that made them in the beginning made them male and female," and said, "For this cause shall a man leave father and mother and shall cleave unto his wife, and they twain shall be one flesh, wherefore they are no more twain but one flesh. What therefore God hath joined together, let no man put asunder" (Matt. 19).

1667

⮞ LADY ANNE HALKETT ⮜

1622–1699

Born in London to Scottish parents employed in the court of James I, Anne Halkett, the youngest of four children, grew up in the center of Stuart court culture. Her

---

3. Song of Solomon.

mother, Jane Drummond Murray, was a member of the Scottish gentry and a deeply religious woman who was, during Anne's childhood, the governess to the children of Charles I. Anne's father died when she was three months old, and her mother employed various tutors to teach Anne and her older sister Jane to write, to speak French, to play the lute, and to do various kinds of needlework. Chiefly, however, they received religious instruction from their mother.

A great deal is known about Halkett's adult life thanks to her autobiographical *Memoirs* (c. 1667) and the tremendous body of work known as the *Meditations,* twenty-one manuscript volumes composed between 1644 and the 1690s. As well as revealing her to be a genuinely pious woman, the writings also paint a picture of a passionate Royalist who was active in preserving Charles I's family in the early days of the Civil War. Most famously, she was involved in the escape of the young Duke of York, the second son of Charles I, from St. James's Palace in 1648. She and the Royalist spy Colonel Joseph Bampfield (her romantic interest) procured female clothing for the duke and helped him to reach the ship that took him to safety on the Continent. Halkett herself, afraid that she would be imprisoned for her exploits, was also forced to flee London for Scotland in 1650.

Halkett's political exploits are entangled throughout the *Memoirs* with her romantic adventures and misadventures. An example is found in the excerpt below, a description of the end of her complicated involvement at age twenty-two with Thomas Howard, the Mr. H. of the excerpt. Howard was a second son and therefore had no family fortune to bring to a marriage; this disqualified him from marriageability in the eyes of Halkett's mother. As the excerpt reveals, the affair very nearly tore mother and daughter apart. A second tumultuous, much more lengthy relationship, with Bampfield, whom she had agreed to marry unaware that his first wife was still alive, ended finally with her betrothal to Sir James Halkett, a widower, in 1656. By all accounts, and despite the sadness they suffered in losing several children to late miscarriage or infant death, her marriage to Halkett was a satisfying one. James Halkett died in 1670; Anne remained a widow, dedicating the rest of her life to charitable work and religious devotion.

As well as providing insight into the emotional world of a young woman torn between family obligation and romantic love, the excerpt reveals Halkett's engaging prose style, which seems to anticipate the narrative developments of the eighteenth and nineteenth centuries, particularly the novels of writers like Jane Austen and the Brontë sisters. Notably, part of what distinguishes her style is a sense of audience. This is particularly interesting given that Halkett does not appear to have written even for a côterie of friends and family; her manuscripts seem not to have circulated at all. Yet the manuscript volumes are set up like the printed volumes of her day: she includes titles, tables of contents, page numbers, and marginal glosses, as though she was preparing them for posthumous publication.

From Memoirs

[HER MOTHER THREATENS TO DISOWN HER]

The next morning early my Lord H.[1] went away, and took with him his son and daughter, and left me to the severities of my offended mother, whom nothing could pacify. After she had called for me, and said as many bitter things as passion could

---

1. Lord Howard, with whose son Thomas (the
Mr. H. referred to below) Halkett had an unsuc-   cessful romantic liaison in 1644.

dictate upon such a subject, she discharged me to see him, and did solemnly vow that if she should hear I did see Mr. H. she would turn me out of her doors, and never own me again. All I said to that part was that it should be against my will if ever she heard of it. Upon Tuesday my Lord H. writ to my mother that he had determined to send his son to France, and that upon Thursday after he was to begin his journey; but all he desired before he went was to have liberty to see me, which he thought was a satisfaction could not be denied him, and therefore desired my mother's consent to it; which she gave upon the condition that he should only come in and take his leave of me, but not to have any converse but what she should be a witness of herself. This would not at all please Mr. H., and therefore seemed to lay the desire of it aside. In the meantime my chamber and liberty of lying alone was taken from me, and my sister's woman was to be my guardian, who watched sufficiently so that I had not the least opportunity either day or night to be without her.

Upon Thursday morning early my mother sent a man of my sister's * * *—this Moses was sent to my Lord H. with a letter to inquire if his son were gone. I must here relate a little odd encounter which aggravated my misfortune. There came no return till night, and, having got liberty to walk in the hall, my mother sent a child of my sister's and bid him walk with me, and keep me company. I had not been there a quarter of an hour but my maid Miriam came to me and told me she was walking at the back gate and Mr. H. came to her and sent her to desire me to come there and speak but two or three words with him, for he had sworn not to go away without seeing me, nor would he come in to see my mother, for he had left London that morning very early and had rode up and down that part of the country only till it was the gloom of the evening to have the more privacy in coming to see me. I bid her go back and tell him I durst not see him because of my mother's oath and her discharge. While she was pressing me to run to the gate, and I was near to take the start, the child cried out, "O, my aunt is going"; which stopped me, and I sent her away to tell the reason why I could not come. I still stayed walking in the hall till she returned, wondering she stayed so long.

When she came, she was hardly able to speak, and with great disorder said, "I believe you are the most unfortunate person living, for I think Mr. H. is killed." Anyone that hath ever known what gratitude was, may imagine how these words disordered me; but impatient to know how (I was resolved to hazard my mother's displeasure rather than not see him), she told me that while she was telling him my answer there came a fellow with a great club behind him and struck him down dead, and others had seized upon Mr. T. (who formerly had been his governor, and was now entrusted to see him safe on shipboard) and his man. The reason of this was from what there was too many sad examples of at that time when the division was betwixt the king and Parliament, for to betray a master or a friend was looked upon as doing God good service. My brother-in-law Sir Henry Newton had been long from home in attendance on the king, for whose service he had raised a troop of horses upon his own expense, and had upon all occasions testified his loyalty, for which all his estate was sequestered,[2] and with much difficulty my sister got liberty to live in her own house, and had the fifth part to live upon, which was obtained with importunity. There was one of my brother's tenants called Musgrove, who was a very great rogue, who farmed my brother's land of the Parliament, and

2. Confiscated by the Puritan Parliament.

was employed by them as a spy to discover any of the Cavaliers[3] that should come within his knowledge: he, observing three gentlemen upon good horses scouting about all day and keeping at a distance from the high way, apprehends it was my brother who had come privately home to see my sister, and resolves to watch when he came near the house, and had followed so close as to come behind and give Mr. H. that stroke, thinking it had been my brother Newton, and ceased upon his governor and servant (the post boy being left at some distance with the horses).

In the midst of this disorder Moses came there, and Miriam having told what the occasion of it was, he told Musgrove it was my Lord H.'s son he had used so; upon which he and his complices went immediately away, and Moses and Mr. H.'s man carried him into an alehouse hard by[4] and laid him on a bed, where he lay some time before he came to himself.

c. 1667

◄ MARGARET LUCAS CAVENDISH, ► DUCHESS OF NEWCASTLE
1623–1674

The youngest of eight children, Margaret Lucas Cavendish was raised by her mother (her father died shortly after she was born) in a household that has sometimes been called eccentric, an adjective that shows up frequently in discussions of Cavendish. In fact, her taste for extravagant, even theatrical, dress, encouraged by her mother, aided in her gaining a reputation for madness. Her intellectual taste likely also had some part in the forging of that unwarranted reputation. In an age when women were encouraged mainly in the pursuit of piety, Margaret Cavendish read and wrote widely in natural philosophy (science).

She began her adult life, however, not as a writer, but as a maid of honor for Queen Henrietta Maria, Catholic consort to Charles I and sister of Louis XIII of France. Her original ambitions were courtly; in 1645, during the Civil War, she followed the queen to exile in France, where she met another prominent exiled aristocrat, the wealthy and widowed William Cavendish, Duke of Newcastle, nearly thirty years her senior, whom she married shortly thereafter. Cavendish was a man of expensive habits and extravagant taste; he also had a desire for recognition and fame, a desire shared by his young wife. In Paris, they were at the center of a group of intellectuals, including the philosophers Thomas Hobbes, René Descartes, and Pierre Gassendi; this informal salon society was called the "Newcastle Circle." Margaret came to value intellectual recognition over court recognition and, encouraged by her supportive husband, took her first book, *Poems and Fancies*, to press in London in 1653. When the couple returned to England permanently after the Restoration in 1660, Margaret Cavendish retired entirely from court life in order to pursue her intellectual interests in science—interests that had been kindled during the exile in Paris through the Newcastle Circle.

After she and her husband returned to England, the Duke's fortunes diminished rapidly with his political disappointment over his exclusion from the court's inner

---

3. A name given to seventeenth-century Royalists, those sympathetic to Charles II.   4. Close by.

circle. Margaret seems to have revenged herself by pouring herself into her writings. The first woman writer in England to write mainly for publication, Cavendish presented her *Philosophical and Physical Opinions* to both Cambridge and Oxford universities, hoping for recognition. In 1667 she got some of the recognition she desired when, after fierce debate among its membership, the Royal Society of London invited Cavendish to visit the prestigious scientific institution to observe as Robert Boyle and Robert Hooke, two of the most prominent scientists of the seventeenth century, conducted experiments on the weighing of air, among other things.

Clearly one of the first writers in English we can call a feminist, or protofeminist, Cavendish returns again and again in her writings to the power struggle between the sexes. Both pieces that follow are representative of her feminism; in both she draws attention to the fact that she is a woman and explains or complains about how this influences her work. Her notoriously complex grammar—long sentences that twist and wind, piling clause upon clause—is a vivid illustration of Cavendish's ambition and her irrepressible appetite for knowledge.

Margaret Cavendish died in London at age fifty-one of an illness that was exacerbated by self-inflicted experiments with prescriptions, purgings, and bloodlettings. She is buried in Westminster Abbey.

From The Philosophical and Physical Opinions

To the Two Universities

[EPISTLE: TO THE MOST FAMOUSLY LEARNED]

Most famously learned,
I here present the sum of my works, not that I think wise schoolmen, and industrious, laborious students should value my book for any worth, but to receive it without a scorn, for the good encouragement of our sex, lest in time we should grow irrational as idiots, by the dejectedness of our spirits, through the careless neglects, and despisements of the masculine sex to the effeminate, thinking it impossible we should have either learning or understanding, wit or judgement, as if we had not rational souls as well as men, and we out of a custom of dejectedness think so too, which makes us quit all industry towards profitable knowledge being employed only in low, and petty employments, which takes away not only our abilities towards arts, but higher capacities in speculations, so as we are become like worms that only live in the dull earth of ignorance, winding ourselves sometimes out, by the help of some refreshing rain of good educations which seldom is given us; for we are kept like birds in cages to hop up and down in our houses, not suffered to fly abroad to see the several changes of fortune, and the various humors, ordained and created by nature; thus wanting[1] the experiences of nature, we must needs want the understanding and knowledge and so consequently prudence, and invention of men: thus by an opinion, which I hope is but an erroneous one in men, we are shut out of all power, and authority by reason we are never employed either in civil nor martial affairs, our counsels are despised and laughed at, the best of our actions are trodden down with scorn, by the overweaning[2] conceit men have of themselves and through a despisement of us.

---

1. Lacking.   2. Arrogant.

But I considering with myself, that if a right judgement, and a true understanding, and a respectful civility live anywhere, it must be in learned universities, where nature is best known, where truth is oftenest found, where civility is most practised, and if I find not a resentment[3] here, I am very confident I shall find it nowhere, neither shall I think I deserve it, if you approve not of me, but if I deserve not praise, I am sure to receive so much courtship from this sage society, as to bury me in silence; thus I may have a quiet grave, since not worthy a famous memory; but to lie entombed under the dust of an university will be honour enough for me, and more than if I were worshipped by the vulgar as a deity. Wherefore if your wisdoms cannot give me the bays,[4] let your charity strew me with cypress;[5] and who knows but after my honourable burial, I may have a glorious resurrection in following ages, since time brings strange and unusual things to pass, I mean unusual to men, though not in nature: and I hope this action of mine, is not unnatural, though unusual for a woman to present a book to the university, nor impudence, for the action is honest, although it seem vainglorious,[6] but if it be, I am to be pardoned, since there is little difference between man and beast, but what ambition and glory makes.

1655

From Philosophical Letters: or, Modest Reflections[7]

XXXVI [Other Creatures May Be as Wise as Men]

Madam,

That all other animals, besides man, want reason, your author endeavours to prove in his *Discourse of Method*,[8] where his chief argument is, that other animals cannot express their mind, thoughts or conceptions, either by speech or any other signs, as man can do: For, says he, "it is not for want of the organs belonging to the framing of words, as we may observe in parrots and pies,[9] which are apt enough to express words they are taught, but understand nothing of them." My answer is, that one man expressing his mind by speech or words to another, doth not declare by it his excellency and supremacy above all other creatures, but for the most part more folly, for a talking man is not so wise as a contemplating man. But by reason other creatures cannot speak or discourse with each other as men, or make certain signs, whereby to express themselves as dumb and deaf men do, should we conclude they have neither knowledge, sense, reason, or intelligence? Certainly, this is a very weak argument; for one part of a man's body, as one hand, is not less sensible[1] than the other, nor the heel less sensible than the heart, nor the leg less sensible than the head, but each part hath its sense and reason, and so consequently its sensitive and rational knowledge; and although they cannot talk or give intelligence to each other by speech, nevertheless each hath its own peculiar and particular knowledge, just as each particular man has his own

3. Appreciation or understanding.
4. In ancient Greece, the leaves of the bay laurel were woven together to create a wreath to reward and recognize a great poet.
5. Cypress, a conifer, is traditionally associated with mourning.
6. Having unwarranted pride in one's accomplishments.
7. In the preface to her *Philosophical Letters*

(1664), Margaret Cavendish explains that the purpose of the letters is to debate the opinions of various "famous and learned authors." She uses the epistolary form to do so because, she says, it was "the easiest way for me to write."
8. French philosopher René Descartes (1596–1650) published his *Discourse on Method* in 1637.
9. Magpies.
1. Capable of feeling or perceiving.

particular knowledge, for one man's knowledge is not another man's knowledge; and if there be such a peculiar and particular knowledge in every several part of one animal creature, as man, well may there be such in creatures of different kinds and sorts: But this particular knowledge belonging to each creature, doth not prove that there is no intelligence at all betwixt them, no more than the want of human knowledge doth prove the want of reason; for reason is the rational part of matter, and makes perception, observation, and intelligence different in every creature, and every sort of creatures, according to their proper natures, but perception, observation and intelligence do not make reason, reason being the cause, and they the effects. Wherefore though other creatures have not the speech, nor mathematical rules and demonstrations, with other arts and sciences, as men; yet may their perceptions and observations be as wise as men's, and they may have as much intelligence and commerce betwixt each other, after their own manner and way, as men have after theirs: To which I leave them, and man to his conceited prerogative and excellence, resting,

Madam,

Your faithful Friend,
and Servant.
1664

◄ MARY BOYLE RICH ►
1624–1678

Mary Boyle was born in County Cork, Ireland, into a large Anglo-Irish family. Her father, Sir Richard Boyle, first Earl of Cork, became, despite humble beginnings in Kent, one of the richest men in the world after building a kind of colonial empire in southwestern Ireland. Mary was his seventh daughter, one of fifteen children born to his second wife, Catherine Fenton, the single child of a wealthy aristocratic family. She died when Mary was almost three, and Mary and her sister Margaret were raised by the wife of Sir Randall Clayton in another prominent Anglo-Irish family. At the age of fourteen, Mary refused to marry the wealthy young man her father had chosen for her; she was, instead, in love with Charles Rich, the second son of Robert, third Earl of Warwick. Angry at what he called her "unruliness," her father banished her to a family estate in England, near Hampton Court. Rich, however, continued to visit her in secret, and the two were married in 1641 when Mary was sixteen years old. After the intervention of her siblings, her father finally relented and gave her a substantial dowry of £7,000 per year (the purchasing power of this sum would be $1.5 million today). In fact, Charles Rich did become the fourth Earl of Warwick—and Mary the Countess of Warwick—because his older brother died without heirs. The diary entry that is excerpted here narrates and reflects on these singular events some twenty-five years after the events occurred.

The entry also has a clearly providential tone to it, a reflection of the spiritual conversion Rich experienced in 1647, a conversion that, given the Puritan emphasis on pious self-examination, led her to write the diary from 1666 to 1677. She died at age fifty-four after an adult life that seems to have been devoted mainly to meditation, prayer, and works of charity.

From **Diary**

[EVENTS OF 1624–43, INCLUDING A COMPLICATED ROMANTIC AFFAIR]

I was born November the 8th, 1625, at Yohall, in Ireland; my father was Richard Boyle Earl of Cork, my mother was Katheren Fentone. My father was second son to Mr. Roger Boyle, my mother was only daughter to Sir Jefrey Fentone.

My father, from being a younger brother of a younger brother, who was only a private gentleman of Herefordshire, was by his mother's care, after his father's death, bred by her at Cambridge, and afterwards at the inns of court, and from thence, by the good providence of God, brought into Ireland, where when he landed he was master of but twenty-seven pounds and three shillings in the world, and afterwards God so prospered him there that he had in that country about twenty thousand pound a-year coming in, and was made Lord Treasurer of Ireland, and one of the two Lord Justices of the government of that kingdom.

My wise, and as I have been informed pious, mother died when I was about three years old; and some time after, by the tender care of my indulgent father, that I might be carefully and piously educated, I was sent by him to a prudent and virtuous lady, my Lady Claytone, who never having had any child of her own, grew to make so much of me as if she had been an own mother to me, and took great care to have me soberly educated. Under her government I remained at Mallow, a town in Munster, till I was, I think, about eleven years old, and then my father called me from thence (much to my dissatisfaction), for I was very fond of that, to me, kind mother. Soon after my father removed, with his family, into England, and dwelt in Dorsetshire, at a house he had purchased there; which was called Stalbridge; and there, when I was about thirteen or fourteen years of age, came down to me one Mr. Hambletone, son to my Lord Clandeboyes, who was afterwards earl of Clanbrasell, and would fain have had me for his wife. My father and his had, some years before, concluded a match between us, if we liked when we saw one another, and that I was of years of consent; and now he being returned out of France, was by his father's command to come to my father's, where he received from him a very kind and obliging welcome, looking upon him as his son-in-law, and designing suddenly that we should be married, and gave him leave to make his address, with a command to me to receive him as one designed to be my husband. Mr. Hambletone (possibly to obey his father) did design gaining me by a very handsome address, which he made to me, and if he did not to a very high degree dissemble, I was not displeasing to him, for he professed a great passion for me. The professions he made me of his kindness were very unacceptable to me, and though I had by him very highly advantageous offers made me, for point of fortune (for his estate, that was settled upon him, was counted seven or eight thousand pound a-year), yet by all his kindness to me nor that I could be brought to endure to think of having him, though my father pressed me extremely to it; my aversion for him was extraordinary, though I could give my father no satisfactory account why it was so.

This continued between us for a long time, my father showing a very high displeasure at me for it, but though I was in much trouble about it, yet I could never be brought either by fair or foul means to it; so as my father was at last forced to break it off, to my father's unspeakable trouble, and to my unspeakable satisfaction, for hardly in any of the troubles of my life did I feel a more sensible[1] uneasi-

1. Considerable, acute.

ness than when that business was transacting. Afterwards I apparently saw a good providence of God in not letting me close with it, for within a year after my absolute refusing him he was, by the rebellion of Ireland, impoverished so that he lost for a great while his whole estate, the rebels being in possession of it; which I should have liked very ill, for if I had married him it must have been for his estate's sake, not his own, his person being highly disagreeable to me.

After this match was off, my father removed to London, and lived at a house of Sir Thomas Staford's. When we were once settled there, my father, living extraordinarily high, drew a very great resort[2] thither, and the report that he would give me a very great fortune made him have for me many very great and considerable offers, both of persons of great birth and fortune; but I still continued to have an aversion to marriage, living so much at my ease that I was unwilling to change my condition, and never could bring myself to close with any offered match, but still begged my father to refuse all the most advantageous proffers, though I was by him much pressed to settle myself.

About this time my fourth brother, Mr. Francis Boyle then (afterwards Lord Shannon), was by my father married to Mrs. Elizabeth Kilegrew, daughter to my Lady Staford; and my brother being then judged to be too young to live with his wife,[3] was a day or two after the celebrating the marriage (which was done before the King and Queen) at Whitehall[4] (she being then a maid of honor to the Queen) sent into France to travel, and his wife then brought home to our house, where she and I became chamber-fellows,[5] and constant bedfellows; and there then grew so great a kindness between us, that she soon had a great and ruling power with me; and by her having so brought me to be very vain and foolish, enticing me to spend (as she did) her time in seeing and reading plays and romances, and in exquisite and curious dressing.

When she was well settled in our family (but much more so in my heart) she had many of the young gallants[6] that she was acquainted with at Court that came to visit her at the Savoy (where we lived); amongst others there came one Mr. Charles Rich, second son to Robert Earl of Warwick, who was a very cheerful, and handsome, well-bred, and fashioned person, and being good company was very acceptable to us all, and so became very intimate in our house, visiting us almost every day. He was then in love with a maid of honor to the Queen, one Mrs. Hareson, that had been chamber-fellow to my sister-in-law whilst she lived at Court, and that brought on the acquaintance between him and my sister. He continued to be much with us, for about five or six months, till my brother Broghil then (afterwards Earl of Orrery), grew also to be passionately in love with the same Mrs. Hareson. My brother then having a quarrel with Mr. Thomas Howard, second son to the Earl of Berkshire, about Mrs. Hareson (with whom he also was in love), Mr. Rich brought my brother a challenge from Mr. Howard, and was second to him against my brother when they fought, which they did without any great hurt of any side, being parted. This action made Mr. Rich judge it not civil to come to our house, and so for some time forbore doing it, but at last my brother's match with Mrs. Hareson being unhandsomely (on her side) broken off, when they were so near being married as the wedding clothes were to be made, and she after married

2. Group of people.
3. Francis Boyle was fifteen when he was married to the sixteen-year-old Elizabeth Killegrew.
4. Main London residence of the English mon-

archs from 1530 until 1698.
5. Roommates.
6. Men of fashion and pleasure.

Mr. Thomas Howard (to my father's very great satisfaction, who always was averse to it, though to comply with my brother's passion he consented to it).

My brother being thus happily disengaged from that amour, brought again Mr. Rich to our family, and soon after he grew again as great among us, as if he had never done that disobliging action to us. By this time, upon what account I know not, he began to withdraw his visits to Mrs. Hareson (for that name she continued to have not being married to Mr. Howard in a good considerable time after), and his heart too; and in being encouraged in his resolution by my sister Boyle, began to think of making an address to me, she promising him all the assistance her power with me could give him to gain my affection, though she knew by attempting it she should lose my father's and all my family, that she believed would never be brought to consent to my having any younger brother,[7] my father's kindness to me making him, as she well knew, resolved to match me to a great fortune. At last, one day she began to acquaint me with Mr. Rich's, as she said, great passion for me; at which I was at the first much surprised, both at his having it for me, and at her telling it to me, knowing how much she hazarded by it, if I should acquaint my father with it. I confess I did not find his declaration of his kindness disagreeable to me, but the consideration of his being but a younger brother made me sadly apprehend my father's displeasure if I should embrace any such offer, and so resolved, at that time, to give her no answer, but seemed to disbelieve his loving me at the rate she informed me he did, though I had for some time taken notice of his loving me, though I never thought he designed trying to gain me.

After this first declaration of his esteem for me by my sister, he became a most diligent gallant to me, seeking by a most humble and respectful address to gain my heart, applying himself, when there was no other beholders in the room but my sister, to me; but if any other person came in he took no more than ordinary notice of me; but to disguise his design addressed himself much to her; and though his doing so was not well liked in our family, yet there was nothing said to him about their dislike of it; and by this way his design became unsuspected, and thus we lived for some months, in which time, by his more than ordinary humble behavior to me, he did insensibly[8] steal away my heart, and got a greater possession of it than I knew he had. My sister, when he was forced to be absent for fear of observing eyes, would so plead for him, that it worked, too, very much upon me. When I began to find, myself, that my kindness for him grew and increased so much, that though I had in the time of his private address to me, many great and advantageous offers made me by my father, and that I could not with any patience endure to hear of any of them, I began with some seriousness to consider what I was engaging myself in by my kindness for Mr. Rich, for my father, I knew, would never endure me, and besides I considered my mind was too high,[9] and I too expensively brought up to bring myself to live contentedly with Mr. Rich's fortune, who would never have, when his father was dead, above thirteen or fourteen (at the most) hundred pounds a-year. Upon these considerations I was convinced that it was time for me to give him a flat and final denial; and with this, as I thought, fixed resolution, I have laid me down in my bed to beg my sister never to name him to me more for a husband, and to tell him from me, that I desired him never

---

7. Because of the laws of primogeniture, only the eldest brother would inherit the family fortune; subsequent sons typically joined the church or the military.
8. Imperceptibly.
9. Well educated.

more to think of me, for I was resolved not to anger my father: but when I was upon a readiness to open my mouth to utter these words, my great kindness for him stopped it, and made me rise always without doing it, though I frequently resolved it; which convinced to me the great and full possession he had of my heart, which made me begin to give him more hopes of gaining me than before I had done, by anything but my inducing him to come to me after he had declared to me his design in doing so, which he well knew I would never endure from any other person that had offered themselves to me.

Thus we lived for some considerable time, my duty and my reason having frequent combats within me with my passion, which at last was always victorious, though my fear of my father's displeasure frighted me from directly owning[1] it to Mr. Rich; till my sister Boyle's taking sick of the measles (and by my lying with when she had them, though I thought at first it might be the smallpox, I got them of her), my kindness being then so great for her, that though of all diseases the smallpox was that I most apprehended,[2] yet from her I did not anything, and would have continued with her all her illness, had I not by my father's absolute command been separated into another room from her; but it was too late, for I had got from her the infection, and presently fell most dangerously ill of the measles too, and before they came out I was removed into another house, because my sister Dungarvan, in whose house I was, in Long Acre, was expecting daily to be delivered,[3] and was apprehensive of that distemper. Mr. Rich then was much concerned for me, and he was most obligingly careful of me; which as it did to a great degree heighten my passion for him, so it did also begin to make my family, and before suspecting friends, to see that they were by a false disguise of his kindness to my sister abused, and that he had for me, and I for him a respect which they feared was too far gone.

This made my old Lady Staford, mother to my sister Boyle (who was a cunning old woman, and who had been herself too much and too long versed in amours), begin to conclude the truth, and absolutely to believe that her daughter was the great actor in this business, and that her being confidant with us, would ruin her with my father; and therefore having some power with him, to prevent the inconveniences that would come to her daughter, resolved to acquaint my father with Mr. Rich's visiting me when I had the measles, and of his continuing to do so at the Savoy,—whither I was, after my recovery, by my father's order, removed, and where by reason of my being newly recovered of an infectious disease, I was free from any visits. After she had with great rage chid her daughter, and threatened her that she would acquaint my father with it (to keep me, as she said, from ruining myself), she accordingly, in a great heat and passion, did that very night do it. My sister presently acquainted both Mr. Rich and me with her mother's resolution, and when she had Mr. Rich alone, told him if he did not that very night prevail with me to declare my kindness for him and to give him some assurance of my resolution to have him, I would certainly the next day by my father be secured from his ever speaking to me, and so he would quite lose me. This discourse did make him resolve to do what she counseled him to; and that very night, when I was ill and laid upon my bed, she giving him an opportunity of being alone with me, and by her care keeping anybody from disturbing us; he had with

1. Admitting.
2. Feared.
3. Have a baby.

me about two hours' discourse, upon his knees, by my bedside, wherein he did so handsomely express his passion (he was pleased to say he had for me), and his fear of being by my father's command separated from me, that together with as many promises as any person in the world could make, of his endeavoring to make up to me the smallness of his fortune by the kindness he would have still to me, if I consented to be his wife; that though I can truly say, that when he kneeled down by me I was far from having resolved to own[4] I would have him, yet his discourse so far prevailed that I consented to give him, as he desired, leave to let his father mention it to mine; and promised him that, let him make his father say what he pleased, I would own it.

Thus we parted, this evening, after I had given away myself to him, and if I had not done so that night, I had been, by my father's separating us, kept from doing it, at least for a long time; for in the morning my father, upon what the night before had been told him by my Lady Staford, came early to me, and with a very frowning and displeasing look, bid me go (as I had before asked to do) into the country to air myself, at a little house near Hampton Court, which Mrs. Katheren Kilegrew, sister to my sister Boyle, then had; and told me that he was informed that I had young men who visited me, and commanded me if any did so, where I was now going, I should not see them. This he said in general, but named not Mr. Rich in particular, which I was glad of; and so after my father had dismissed me, with this unkind look (and I thought severe command), I was presently, by my brother Broghil, in his coach, conveyed to a very little house at Hampton, which was at that time though much more agreeable to me than the greatest and most stately one could be, because it did remove me from my father some distance, which I thought best for me, till his fury was in some measure over, which I much apprehended. That very day I removed into the country, my Lord Goreing, afterwards Earl of Norwich, was by my Lord of Warwick and my Lord of Holland's appointment chose to be the first person that should motion[5] the match to my father, and acquaint him with my esteem for Mr. Rich; he was chose by them, and approved of by me to do it, because his son having married one of my sisters, there was a great friendship between them, and he had a more than ordinary power with my father with what he was designed to do: but though he did it very well, my father was so troubled at it that he wept, and would by no means suffer him to go on.

The next day, as I remember, my Lord of Warwick and my Lord of Holland visited him, and mentioned it with great kindness to him; he used them with much respect, but told them he hoped his daughter would be advised by him, and he could not but still hope she would not give herself away without his consent, and therefore he was resolved to send to me to know what I said the next morning, which accordingly he did; and the persons he fixed upon to do it by were two of my brothers,—my eldest brother, Dungarvan, and my then third brother, Broghil, who came early down to me (but I was before informed by Mr. Rich of their coming), yet for all that I was disordered at their sight, knowing about what they came; but the extraordinary great kindness I had for Mr. Rich made me resolve to endure anything for his sake, and therefore when I had by my brothers been informed that they were, by my father's command, sent to examine me, what was between Mr. Rich and I, and threatened, in my father's name, if I did not renounce

---

4. Admit.   5. Mention.

ever having anything more to do with him, I made this resolute, but ill and horribly disobedient answer, that I did acknowledge a very great and particular kindness for Mr. Rich, and desired them, with my humble duty to my father, to assure him that I would not marry him without his consent, but that I was resolved not to marry any other person in the world; and that I hoped my father would be pleased to consent to my having Mr. Rich, to whom, I was sure, he could have no other objection, but that he was a younger brother; for he was descended from a very great and honorable family, and was in the opinion of all (as well as mine) a very deserving person, and I desired my father would be pleased to consider, I only should suffer by the smallness of his fortune, which I very contentedly chose to do, and should judge myself to be much more happy with his small one, than with the greatest without him.

After my two brothers saw I was unmovable in my resolution, say what they could to me, they returned highly unsatisfied from me to my father; who, when he had it once owned from my own mouth, that I would have him, or nobody, he was extraordinarily displeased with me, and forbid my daring to appear before him. But after some time he was persuaded, by the great esteem he had for my Lord of Warwick and my Lord of Holland, to yield to treat with them, and was at last brought, though not to give me my before designed portion, yet to give me seven thousand pounds, and was brought to see and be civil to Mr. Rich, who was a constant visitor of me at Hampton, almost daily; but he was the only person I saw, for my own family came not at me: and thus I continued there for about ten weeks, when I was at last, by my Lord of Warwick and my Lord Goreing led into my father's chamber, and there, upon my knees, humbly begged his pardon, which after he had, with great justice, severely chid me, he bid me rise, and was by my Lord of Warwick's and my Lord Goreing's intercession reconciled to me, and told me I should suddenly be married. But though he designed I should be so at London, with Mr. Rich and my friends at it, yet being a great enemy always to a public marriage, I was, by that fear, and Mr. Rich's earnest solicitation, prevailed with, without my father's knowledge, to be privately married at a little village near Hampton Court, on the 21st July 1641, called Shepertone; which when my father knew he was again something displeased at me for it, but after I had begged his pardon, and assured him I did it only to avoid a public wedding, which he knew I had always declared against, his great indulgence to me made him forgive me that fault also, and within few days after I was carried down to Lees, my Lord of Warwick's house in the country, but none of our friends accompanied me, but my dear sister Ranelagh, who great goodness made her forgive me, and stay with me some time at Lees, where I received as kind a welcome as was possible from that family, but particularly from my good father-in-law.

Here let me admire at the goodness of God, that by His good providence to me, when I by my marriage thought of nothing but having a person for whom I had a great passion, and never sought God in it, but by marrying my husband flatly disobeyed His command, which was given me in His sacred oracles, of obeying my father; yet was pleased by His unmerited goodness to me to bring me, by my marriage, into a noble and, which is much more, a religious family; where religion was both practiced and encouraged; and where there were daily many eminent and excellent divines, who preached in the chapel most edifyingly and awakeningly to us. Besides a famous household chaplain, my father-in-law had Doctor Gawden there, afterwards Lord Bishop of Worcester. I could not, as young as I was when I came to the family, being but fifteen years old, and as much as between the 8th of November and 21st of July, but admire at the excellent order there was in the family, and the great care that was had that God should be most solemnly worshiped and owned in that great family, both by the lord and lady of it. My mother-in-law was not my husband's own mother, she (Hatton) being dead, after she had brought her husband many fine children, and the greatest estate any woman had done for many years to a family. And my lord after her decease was married again to a rich woman, one Alderman Holiday's widow, of the City, who because she was a citizen[6] was not so much respected in the family as in my opinion she deserved to be; for she was one that assuredly feared God; but she was at my first coming to Lees removed to her daughter Hungerford's, near the Bath, where she was resolved to stay till she was by some person she credited, informed whether my humor were such as would make her to live comfortably with me; for by reason of some former disputes with my first Lady Rich (a daughter of Earl Devonshire), that had been between them, she was almost come to a resolution of never more living with any daughter-in-law. But my Lady Roberts, that was my lord's sister, and a very pious woman, was pleased to assure her I would be dutiful to her, and at last did prevail with her to come down to Lees, where I then was, and I was so fortunate as I gained so much of her kindness, that for about five years that I lived constantly with her I did never displease her, or ever had any unkindness from her, but found her as obliging to me as if she had been my own mother, and she would always profess she loved me at that rate, and I did when God called her away mourn much for my losing her.

After her death my Lord of Warwick married again, to the Countess of Sussex (widow of Thomas Savil, Earl of Sussex), with whom I had, too, the great happiness of living as lovingly as it was possible for an own mother and daughter to live, for about eleven years, in some of which time I went on in a vain kind of life, only studying to please my husband and the family I was matched into; but, alas, too much neglected the studying to please God, and to save my immortal soul; yet in this time of my vanity conscience would often speak to me, but yet I went on, regardless, though I was allured by God with many mercies, and had afflictions too.

In the first year I was married, God was pleased to give me a safe delivery of a girl, which I lay in with at Warwick House. And soon after the second year, I was brought abed of a boy, in September 28th, 1643. The girl was named Elizabeth, and the boy Charles. The girl God was pleased to take from me by death, when she was not a year and a quarter old. For which I was much afflicted; but my husband as passionately so as ever I saw him; he being most extraordinarily fond of her. When I lay in with my son, the ill news of my father's death was brought to my husband; but by his care of me, it was concealed from me till I was up again; and then it was told me first by my mother-in-law. I was much afflicted, and grieved at the loss of one of the best and kindest of fathers in the world: but I being young and inconsiderate, grief did not stick long with me.

c. 1666

---

6. Inhabitant of the City.

CULTURAL COORDINATES
Women's Spiritual Diaries

The sixteenth-century Reformation in England—the shift from Catholicism to a Protestant-based spirituality that stressed reading the Bible and Christian introspection—resulted in more widespread literacy and a new form of self-expression among middle-class women: the spiritual diary. Indeed, there is much evidence to suggest that by the mid–seventeenth century, diary keeping, especially among gentry and upper-middle-class women (where female literacy was common) was a well-established practice. Almost always, women's diaries were not published during the diarist's lifetime but were brought forward by a husband or another male relation after the woman had died.

The spiritual diary could and did include memoir, meditations, prayers, catalogues and narratives of special favors and providences from God, family and community records, and miscellanea. And while many women did focus almost completely on their spiritual lives in their diaries, meditating on biblical verses and reflecting on worship services and common prayers, others found solace for difficult parental or filial relationships, unhappy marriages, or, as was so often the case, the loss of infants and children. Several historians have speculated that the early modern family was characterized by an emotional distance made necessary by the high rates of infant, child, and maternal mortality and exacerbated by the lack of contact between upper-class parents and their children, who were typically suckled by wet nurses and cared for by nursemaids and nannies. Indeed, there was remarkably little public declaration of grief for dead offspring. Women's diaries, however, even the diaries of aristocratic women, often tell a different story. In particular, entries in which women memorialize their dead children reveal a depth of personal grief and sadness that can hardly be described as distant. It may well have been that verbal displays of grief, especially for children who had died, were untenable in a society that

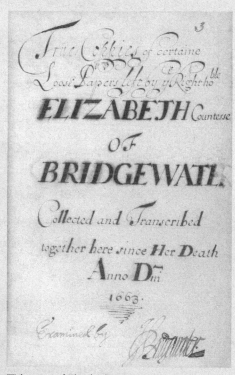

Title page of Elizabeth Egerton's *Loose Papers* (1663).

was characterized by so much loss and daily hardship. Certainly, the diary entries of Elizabeth Egerton (p. 113), who memorializes a beloved young daughter who died of smallpox, are so raw with heartbreak that it seems that the diary was one of the few places where a woman was truly free to express that emotion.

Yet, for all the moments of pure emotion, the spiritual diaries of the period also helped women impose a kind of narrative coherency on the incidents and accidents of their lives. Elizabeth Bury, a diarist of the late seventeenth century, reported that she "would often say, That were it not for her *diary*, she should neither know what she *was*, or what she *did*." That early novels like Daniel Defoe's *Robinson Crusoe* (first published in 1719) would adopt the form of the spiritual diary is evidence of the immense influence published spiritual diaries exerted, not only on the literary tastes of the period and the evolution of the novel form, but also on the way that ordinary women made meaningful their everyday lives.

◄ ELIZABETH CAVENDISH EGERTON ►
1626–1663

Elizabeth Cavendish Egerton, the second daughter of William Cavendish and Elizabeth Basset Howard, grew up in one of the wealthiest families in pre–Civil War England. Her early life seems to have been intellectually, socially, and emotionally comfortable and nurturing. Her father in particular seems to have encouraged in all five of his surviving children (five others died in infancy) a taste for extravagant country living and a courtly (as opposed to a pious) sort of literary sensibility. That sensibility was evident in his choice of a second wife: two years after the death of Elizabeth's mother in 1643, he married the young Margaret Lucas, who, as Margaret Cavendish, went on to a much more notorious literary career than her stepdaughter had (see pp. 100–103). However, Margaret Cavendish did not likely have a great effect on Egerton's own literary sensibilities. By 1645, at the age of nineteen, Elizabeth had already been married for four years to John Egerton, a member of one of the most literarily sophisticated aristocratic families of the seventeenth century.

Interestingly, Elizabeth's literary production turned from pastorals and light entertainments to more serious pious subjects after her marriage, perhaps at the encouragement of her affectionate but authoritative husband or perhaps because, for one so young and so privileged, she had experienced a remarkable amount of adversity: the extended siege of her father's estate during the Civil War, the arrest and imprisonment of her husband, and the deaths of three children. The piece included below, a heartbreaking reflection on the death of one of those children, is from her *Loose Papers,* a collection of private writings that made up Egerton's spiritual diary and that were collected (though not published) by her husband after her death. The piece, though brief, provides a candid glimpse into the pain that accompanied what was a sadly frequent occurrence in the period: the death of a child. Egerton's own life was short—she died at thirty-seven after giving birth to her ninth child.

From Loose Papers
When I Lost My Dear Girl Kate

My sorrow is great, I confess I am much grieved for the loss of my dear girl Katy, who was as fine a child as could be. She was but a year and ten months old, when, by the fatal disease of the small pox, it was God's pleasure to take her from me, who spoke any thing one bid her, and would call for any thing at dinner, and make her mind known at any time, and was kind to all, even to strangers, and had no anger in her. All thought she loved them, her brothers and sister loved her with a fond love. She was so good, she never slept, nor played, at sermon, or prayers. She had received the Sacrament of Baptism, which washed her from her original sin, and she lived holily. She took delight in nothing but me, if she had seen me; if absent, ever had me in her words, desiring to come to me. Never was there so fond a child of a mother, but she now is not in this world, which grieves my heart, even my soul. But I must submit, and give God my thanks, that he once was pleased to bestow so great a blessing as that sweet child upon me.

1660

KATHERINE FOWLER PHILIPS
1631–1664

Katherine Fowler Philips was born in London to a middle-class family and educated, beginning at the age of eight, at Mrs. Salmon's School for Girls in Hackney, a school where she learned to speak several languages and developed a taste for classical literature. Her father, a merchant, died when Katherine was eleven, and four years later her mother was remarried to Sir Richard Philips, whose son Hector by his first marriage became Katherine's husband in 1648: Katherine was sixteen; her husband was fifty-four.

Despite their age difference it was, by all accounts, a happy union. They had two children: Hector, who died shortly after his birth, and Katherine. They officially resided in Cardigan, on the coast of Wales, but Katherine divided her time between Wales and London. With the encouragement of her husband, she began to write and translate poetry in 1650. Like many other poets of the time, Philips wrote not for publication but for a kind of correspondence circle of friends and acquaintances, some of whom were very well connected. Her reputation grew partly through the correspondence circle she formed, known as the Society of Friendship, which was made up primarily of women, all of whom took pseudonyms from classical literature (Philips, for instance, called herself Orinda).

Fully half of Philips's poetry is dedicated to one particular member of the society, Anne Owen, who took the name of Lucasia. Considerable speculation exists as to the nature of the relationship between the two women; it was, if not sexual, certainly what we would call a "romantic" friendship. But Philips remarked that the love between women was pure, uncorrupted by the sexual. And indeed, intimate, sustaining, Platonic friendships were not at all uncommon among women in the seventeenth century.

Although Philips died of smallpox at thirty-three, her literary output was nonetheless quite remarkable. She wrote 120 original poems and translated 5 poems and 1 play (Corneille's *Pompey*) from the French; a translation of Corneille's play *Horace* was partially complete when she died. *Pompey* was, in fact, performed in London and Dublin to great acclaim a year before her death, making her the first woman to have her work performed on a London stage. The first authorized collection of her poetry (seventy-four poems were published in 1664 without her consent) was published posthumously in 1667.

The selections included here, all original poems (and all but the first published in the 1667 collection), reveal Philips's serious engagement in the tumultuous politics of the mid–seventeenth century (she, unlike her husband, was a supporter of the monarchy); her private grief over the death of her infant son; and the witty, playful poems to her female friends for which she is now best known.

A Married State

A married state affords but little ease:
The best of husbands are so hard to please.
This in wives' careful faces you may spell,[1]
Though they dissemble their misfortunes well.

---

1. Decipher.

A virgin state is crowned with much content,   5
It's always happy as it's innocent.

No blustering husbands to create your fears,
No pangs of childbirth to extort your tears,
No children's cries for to offend your ears,
Few worldly crosses to distract your prayers.   10
Thus are you freed from all the cares that do
Attend on matrimony and a husband too.
Therefore, madam, be advised by me:
Turn, turn apostate to love's levity.
Suppress wild nature if she dare rebel,   15
There's no such thing as leading apes in hell.[2]

c. 1646

Upon the Double Murder of K. Charles I
in Answer to a Libelous Copy of Rimes
by Vavasour Powell[3]

I think not on the state, nor am concerned
Which way soever the great helm is turned:
But as that son whose father's danger nigh
Did force his native dumbness, and untie
The fettered organs; so this is a cause   5
That will excuse the breach of nature's laws.
Silence were now a sin, nay passion now
Wise men themselves for merit would allow.
What noble eye could see (and careless pass)
The dying lion[4] kicked by every ass?   10
Has Charles so *broke God's laws,* he must not have
A quiet crown, nor yet a quiet grave?
Tombs have been sanctuaries; thieves lie there
Secure from all their penalty and fear.
Great Charles his double misery was this,   15
Unfaithful friends, ignoble enemies.
Had any heathen been this prince's foe,
He would have wept to see him injured so.
His title was his crime, they'd reason good
To quarrel at the right they had withstood.   20
He broke God's laws, and therefore he must die;

2. A proverb originating in the sixteenth century; in his *Paradoxes and Problems,* the seventeenth-century poet and churchman John Donne explains the proverb in the following way: "An Ape is a ridiculous and unprofitable Beast, whose flesh is not good for meat, nor its back for burden, nor is it commodious to keep an house; and perchance for the unprofitableness of this Beast did this proverb come up; For surely nothing is more unprofitable in the Commonwealth of *Nature,* than they that die old maids, because they refuse to be used to that end for which they were only made."

3. Powell was a member of a sect known as the Fifth Monarchists, begun in the 1650s, that regarded the beheading of Charles I in 1649 as a necessary prelude to the second coming of Christ. Powell had written an anti-monarchical poem about the dead Charles.

4. The Stuart monarch Charles I was often represented as a lion—reflecting the dominant image on the Stuart coat of arms.

And what shall then become of thee and I?
Slander must follow treason; but yet stay,
Take not our reason with our king away.
Though you have seized upon all our defence,   25
Yet do not sequester[5] our common sense.
Christ will be King, but I ne'er understood
His subjects built his kingdom up with blood,
Except their own; or that he would dispense
With his commands, though for his own defence.   30
Oh! to what height of horror are they come
Who dare pull down a crown, tear up a tomb?

c. 1649   1667

On the Death of My First and Dearest Child, Hector Philips[6]

1

Twice forty months of wedlock I did stay,
Then had my vows crowned with a lovely boy,
And yet in forty days[7] he dropped away,
O swift vicissitude of human joy.

2

I did but see him and he disappeared,   5
I did but pluck the rosebud and it fell,
A sorrow unforeseen and scarcely feared,
For ill can mortals their afflictions spell.[8]

3

And now (sweet babe) what can my trembling heart
Suggest to right my doleful fate or thee,   10
Tears are my muse and sorrow all my art,
So piercing groans must be thy elegy.

4

Thus whilst no eye is witness of my moan,
I grieve thy loss (Ah boy too dear to live)
And let the unconcerned world alone,   15
Who neither will, nor can refreshment give.

5

An off'ring too for thy sad tomb I have,
Too just a tribute to thy early hearse,
Receive these gasping numbers[9] to thy grave,
The last of thy unhappy mother's verse.   20

1655   1667

---

5. Confiscate.
6. The subtitle in the manuscript version of this poem reads, "born the 23d of April, and died the 2d of May 1655."

7. Within forty days.
8. Ill: unskillfully; spell: guess or suspect.
9. Poetic meter.

Friendship's Mystery,
To My Dearest Lucasia[1]

1

Come, my Lucasia, since we see
   That miracles men's faith do move,
By wonder and by prodigy[2]
   To the dull angry world let's prove
   There's a religion in our love.   5

2

For though we were designed[3] t'agree,
   That fate no liberty destroys,
But our election is as free
   As angels, who with greedy choice
   Are yet determined to their joys.   10

3

Our hearts are doubled by the loss,
   Here mixture is addition grown;
We both diffuse, and both engross:[4]
   And we whose minds are so much one,
   Never, yet ever are alone.   15

4

We court our own captivity
   Than thrones more great and innocent:
'Twere banishment to be set free,
   Since we wear fetters whose intent
   Not bondage is, but ornament.   20

5

Divided joys are tedious found,
   And griefs united easier grow:
We are ourselves but by rebound,
   And all our titles shuffled so,
   Both princes, and both subjects too.   25

6

Our hearts are mutual victims laid,
   While they (such power in friendship lies)
Are altars, priests, and off'rings made:
   And each heart which thus kindly[5] dies,
   Grows deathless by the sacrifice.   30

1655   1667

1. Lucasia was the name given to Philips's friend
Anne Owen in 1651 when she was officially admitted to the "Society of Friendship."
2. An amazing thing.

3. Destined.
4. Diffuse: extend; engross: absorb.
5. Readily.

To My Excellent Lucasia,
On Our Friendship

I did not live until this time
  Crowned my felicity,
When I could say without a crime,[6]
  I am not thine, but thee.

This carcass breathed, and walked, and slept,   5
  So that the world believed
There was a soul the motions kept;
  But they were all deceived.

For as a watch by art is wound
  To motion, such was mine: 10
But never had Orinda[7] found
  A soul till she found thine;

Which now inspires,[8] cures and supplies,
  And guides my darkened breast:
For thou art all that I can prize,   15
  My joy, my life, my rest.

No bridegroom's nor crown-conqueror's mirth
  To mine compared can be:
They have but pieces of this earth,
  I've all the world in thee.   20

Then let our flames still light and shine,
  And no false fear control,
As innocent as our design,
  Immortal as our soul.

                                        1667

Orinda to Lucasia

Observe the weary birds ere night be done,
How they would fain[9] call up the tardy sun,
  With feathers hung with dew,
  And trembling voices too.
They court their glorious planet to appear,   5
That they may find recruits of spirits there.
The drooping flowers hang their heads,
And languish down into their beds:
While brooks more bold and fierce than they,
  Wanting those beams, from whence   10

---

6. Without committing a crime (i.e., without   8. Breathes life into.
lying).   9. Gladly, rejoicingly.
7. Philips's name in the "Society of Friendship."

All things must drink influence,[1]
Openly murmur and demand the day.

2

Thou my Lucasia art far more to me,
Than he[2] to all the underworld can be;
    From thee I've heat and light,
    Thy absence makes my night.   15
But ah! my friend, it now grows very long,
The sadness weighty, and the darkness strong:
    My tears (its dew) dwell on my cheeks,
    And still my heart thy dawning seeks,   20
And to thee mournfully it cries,

    That if too long I wait,
    Ev'n thou mayst come too late,
And not restore my life, but close my eyes.

1667

MARY ROWLANDSON
c. 1637–1711

Mary Rowlandson was born Mary White in England to parents who immigrated to the Massachusetts Bay Colony in 1639. She married Joseph Rowlandson in the town of Lancaster in 1656; he was ordained as a Puritan minister in 1660. Between 1657 and 1670 they had four children, one of whom died in infancy. In 1676, while her husband was on his way to Boston to raise troops to protect Lancaster from Indian attack, Rowlandson and her three children were taken captive by a group of Wampanoag Indians who burned the town of Lancaster to the ground. The narrative of her three-month captivity with the Wampanoags in the forests of Massachusetts and New Hampshire, during which her youngest child, wounded in the initial attack on Lancaster, died, tells the story of a resourceful woman surviving nearly insurmountable odds. It also speaks of a religion in which God ordains such hardship so as to "make us the more to acknowledge his hand and to see that our help is always in him."

Its original title *(The Soveraignty & Goodness of God, Together with the Faithfulness of His Promises Displayed; Being a Narrative of the Captivity and Restauration of Mrs. Mary Rowlandson, Commended by her to all that Desire to Know the Lord's Doings to, and Dealings with Her. Especially to her Dear Children and Relations)* reveals its focus on Puritan religious doctrine. Indeed, the story of Rowlandson's captivity was first narrated to the public in a sermon delivered by her husband in 1678 (three days after which he died suddenly). Rowlandson's narrative of her captivity became a best seller and was the literary model for the numerous captivity narratives that followed. Rowlandson, who married Samuel Talcott in 1679, died in Wethersfield, Connecticut, at seventy-four.

1. An ethereal fluid thought to flow from the
stars and to affect all things.   2. The sun.

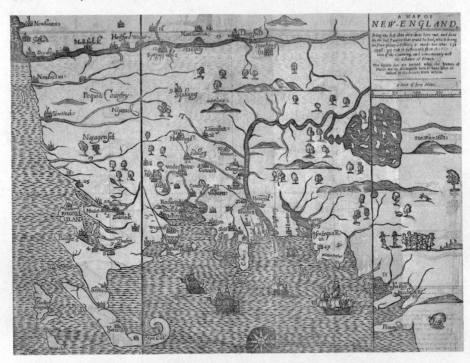

Map of New-England (1677), a wood engraving from William Hubbard's *A Narrative of Troubles with the Indians in New England.* (British Library)

From A Narrative of the Captivity and Restoration of Mrs. Mary Rowlandson

The First Remove

On the tenth of February 1675, Came the Indians with great numbers upon Lancaster:[1] Their first coming was about Sun-rising; hearing the noise of some Guns, we looked out; several Houses were burning, and the Smoke ascending to Heaven. Their were five persons taken in one house, the Father, and the Mother and a sucking Child, they knockt on the head; the other two they took and carried away alive. Their were two others, who being out of their Garison upon some occasion were set upon; one was knockt on the head, the other escaped: Another their was who running along was shot and wounded, and fell down; he begged of them his life, promising them Money (as they told me) but they would not hearken to him but knockt him in head, and stript him naked, and split open his Bowels. Another seeing many of the Indians about his Barn, ventured and went out, but was quickly shot down. There were three others belonging to the same Garison who were killed; the Indians getting up upon the roof of the Barn, had advantage to shoot down upon them over their Fortification. Thus these murtherous wretches went on, burning, and destroying before them.

---

1. A frontier town in what would become Massachusetts.

At length they came and beset our own house, and quickly it was the dolefullest day that ever mine eyes saw. The House stood upon the edg of a hill; some of the Indians got behind the hill, others into the Barn, and others behind any thing that could shelter them; from all which places they shot against the House, so that the Bullets seemed to fly like hail; and quickly they wounded one man among us, then another, and then a third. About two hours (according to my observation, in that amazing time) they had been about the house before they prevailed to fire it (which they did with Flax and Hemp, which they brought out of the Barn, and there being no defence about the House, only two Flankers[2] at two opposite corners and one of them not finished) they fired it once and one ventured out and quenched it, but they quickly fired it again, and that took. Now is the dreadfull hour come, that I have often heard of (in time of War, as it was the case of others) but now mine eyes see it. Some in our house were fighting for their lives, others wallowing in their blood, the House on fire over our heads, and the bloody Heathen ready to knock us on the head, if we stirred out. Now might we hear Mothers and Children crying out for themselves, and one another, Lord, What shall we do? Then I took my Children (and one of my sisters, hers) to go forth and leave the house: but as soon as we came to the dore and appeared, the Indians shot so thick that the bullets rattled against the House, as if one had taken an handfull of stones and threw them, so that we were fain to give back.[3] We had six stout Dogs belonging to our Garrison, but none of them would stir, though another time, if any Indian had come to the door, they were ready to fly upon him and tear him down. The Lord hereby would make us the more to acknowledge his hand, and to see that our help is always in him. But out we must go, the fire increasing, and coming along behind us, roaring, and the Indians gaping before us with their Guns, Spears and Hatchets to devour us. No sooner were we out of the House, but my Brother in Law (being before wounded, in defending the house, in or near the throat) fell down dead, wherat the Indians scornfully shouted, and hallowed, and were presently upon him, stripping off his cloaths, the bulletts flying thick, one went through my side, and the same (as would seem) through the bowels and hand of my dear Child in my arms. One of my elder Sisters Children, named William, had then his Leg broken, which the Indians perceiving, they knockt him on head. Thus were we butchered by those merciless Heathen, standing amazed, with the blood running down to our heels. My eldest Sister being yet in the House, and seeing those wofull sights, the Infidels haling Mothers one way, and Children another, and some wallowing in their blood: and her elder Son telling her that her Son William was dead, and my self was wounded, she said, And, Lord, let me dy with them; which was no sooner said, but she was struck with a Bullet, and fell down dead over the threshold. I hope she is reaping the fruit of her good labours, being faithfull to the service of God in her place. In her younger years she lay under much trouble upon spiritual accounts, till it pleased God to make that precious Scripture take hold of her heart, 2 Cor. 12. 9. *And he said unto me, my Grace is sufficient for thee.* More then twenty years after I have heard her tell how sweet and comfortable that place was to her. But to return: The Indians laid hold of us, pulling me one way, and the Children another, and said, Come go along with us; I told them they would kill me: they answered, If I were willing to go along with them, they would not hurt me.

---

2. A fortification of the house that projects out-   3. Obliged to retreat.
ward to defend another part of the house.

Oh the dolefull sight that now was to behold at this House! *Come, behold the works of the Lord, what dissolations he has made in the Earth.*[4] Of thirty seven persons who were in this one House, none escaped either present death, or a bitter captivity, save only one, who might say as he, Job 1. 15, *And I only am escaped alone to tell the News.* There were twelve killed, some shot, some stab'd with their Spears, some knock'd down with their Hatchets. When we are in prosperity, Oh the little that we think of such dreadfull sights, and to see our dear Friends, and Relations ly bleeding out their heart-blood upon the ground. There was one who was chopt into the head with a Hatchet, and stript naked, and yet was crawling up and down. It is a solemn sight to see so many Christians lying in their blood, some here, and some there, like a company of Sheep torn by Wolves, All of them stript naked by a company of hell-hounds, roaring, singing, ranting and insulting, as if they would have torn our very hearts out; yet the Lord by his Almighty power preserved a number of us from death, for there were twenty-four of us taken alive and carried Captive.

I had often before this said, that if the Indians should come, I should chuse rather to be killed by them then taken alive but when it came to the tryal my mind changed; their glittering weapons so daunted my spirit, that I chose rather to go along with those (as I may say) ravenous Beasts, then that moment to end my dayes; and that I may the better declare what happened to me during that grievous Captivity, I shall particularly speak of the severall Removes we had up and down the Wilderness.   * * *

The Third Remove

The morning being come, they prepared to go on their way. One of the Indians got up upon a horse, and they set me up behind him, with my poor sick Babe in my lap. A very wearisome and tedious day I had of it; what with my own wound, and my Childs being so exceeding sick, and in a lamentable condition with her wound. It may be easily judged what a poor feeble condition we were in, there being not the least crumb of refreshing that came within either of our mouths, from Wednesday night to Saturday night, except only a little cold water. This day in the afternoon, about an hour by Sun, we came to the place where they intended, *viz.* an Indian Town, called Wenimesset, Norward of Quabaug.[5] When we were come, Oh the number of Pagans (now merciless enemies) that there came about me, that I may say as David, Psal. 27. 13, *I had fainted, unless I had believed*, etc. The next day was the Sabbath: I then remembered how careless I had been of Gods holy time, how many Sabbaths I had lost and mispent, and how evily I had walked in God's sight; which lay so close unto my spirit, that it was easie for me to see how righteous it was with God to cut off the thread of my life, and cast me out of his presence for ever. Yet the Lord still shewed mercy to me, and upheld me; and as he wounded me with one hand, so he healed me with the other. This day there came to me one Robbert Pepper (a man belonging to Roxbury) who was taken in Captain Beers his Fight,[6] and had been now a considerable time with

---

4. See Psalm 46:8.
5. Near Brookfield, Massachusetts.
6. Captain Richard Beers was leading a party of would-be reinforcements to the Northfield garrison when he was attacked by Indians. Robert Pepper was the only soldier taken alive.

the Indians; and up with them almost as far as Albany, to see king Philip,[7] as he told me, and was now very lately come into these parts. Hearing, I say, that I was in this Indian Town, he obtained leave to come and see me. He told me, he himself was wounded in the leg at Captain Beers his Fight; and was not able some time to go, but as they carried him, and as he took Oaken leaves and laid to his wound, and through the blessing of God he was able to travel again. Then I took Oaken leaves and laid to my side, and with the blessing of God it cured me also; yet before the cure was wrought, I may say, as it is in Psal. 38. 5, 6. *My wounds stink and are corrupt, I am troubled, I am bowed down greatly, I go mourning all the day long.* I sat much alone with a poor wounded Child in my lap, which moaned night and day, having nothing to revive the body, or cheer the spirits of her, but in stead of that, sometimes one Indian would come and tell me one hour, that your Master will knock your Child in the head, and then a second, and then a third, your Master will quickly knock your Child in the head.

This was the comfort I had from them, miserable comforters are ye all, as he said.[8] Thus nine dayes I sat upon my knees, with my Babe in my lap, till my flesh was raw again; my Child being even ready to depart this sorrowfull world, they bade me carry it out to another Wigwam (I suppose because they would not be troubled with such spectacles) Whither I went with a very heavy heart, and down I sat with the picture of death in my lap. About two houres in the night, my sweet Babe like a Lambe departed this life, on Feb. 18, 1675. It being about six yeares, and five months old. It was nine dayes from the first wounding, in this miserable condition, without any refreshing of one nature or other, except a little cold water. I cannot, but take notice, how at another time I could not bear to be in the room where any dead person was, but now the case is changed; I must and could ly down by my dead Babe, side by side all the night after. I have thought since of the wonderfull goodness of God to me, in preserving me in the use of my reason and senses, in that distressed time, that I did not use wicked and violent means to end my own miserable life. In the morning, when they understood that my child was dead they sent for me home to my Masters Wigwam: (by my Master in this writing, must be understood Quanopin, who was a Saggamore,[9] and married King Phillips wives Sister; not that he first took me, but I was sold to him by another Narrhaganset Indian, who took me when first I came out of the Garison). I went to take up my dead child in my arms to carry it with me, but they bid me let it alone: there was no resisting, but goe I must and leave it. When I had been at my masters wigwam, I took the first opportunity I could get, to go look after my dead child; when I came I askt them what they had done with it? then they told me it was upon the hill: then they went and shewed me where it was, where I saw the ground was newly digged, and there they told me they had buried it: There I left that Child in the Wilderness, and must commit it, and my self also in this Wilderness-condition, to him who is above all. God having taken away this dear Child, I went to see my daughter Mary, who was at this same Indian Town, at a Wigwam not very far off, though we had little liberty or opportunity to see one another. She was about ten years old, and taken from the door at first by a Praying Ind and afterward sold for a gun. When I came in sight, she would fall a weeping;

7. The Wampanoag chief Metacomet, known as King Philip by the Plymouth colonists, had taken up winter quarters near Albany, New York, 1675–76.

8. Job 16:2.

9. Indian chief.

at which they were provoked, and would not let me come near her, but bade me be gone; which was a heart-cutting word to me. I had one Child dead, another in the Wilderness, I knew not where, the third they would not let me come near to: Me (as he said) *have ye bereaved of my Children, Joseph is not, and Simeon is not, and ye will take Benjamin also, all these things are against me.*[1] I could not sit still in this condition, but kept walking from one place to another. And as I was going along, my heart was even overwhelm'd with the thoughts of my condition, and that I should have Children, and a Nation which I knew not ruled over them. Whereupon I earnestly entreated the Lord, that he would consider my low estate, and shew me a token for good, and if it were his blessed will, some sign and hope of some relief. And indeed quickly the Lord answered, in some measure, my poor prayers: for as I was going up and down mourning and lamenting my condition, my Son came to me, and asked me how I did; I had not seen him before, since the destruction of the Town, and I knew not where he was, till I was informed by himself, that he was amongst a smaller percel of Indians, whose place was about six miles off; with tears in his eyes, he asked me whether his Sister Sarah was dead; and told me he had seen his Sister Mary; and prayed me, that I would not be troubled in reference to himself. * * *

The Twentieth Remove

* * * I can remember the time, when I used to sleep quietly without workings in my thoughts, whole nights together, but now it is other wayes with me. When all are fast about me, and no eye open, but his who ever waketh, my thoughts are upon things past, upon the awfull dispensation of the Lord towards us; upon his wonderfull power and might, in carrying of us through so many difficulties, in returning us in safety, and suffering none to hurt us. I remember in the night season, how the other day I was in the midst of thousands of enemies, and nothing but death before me: It is then hard work to perswade my self, that ever I should be satisfied with bread again. But now we are fed with the finest of the Wheat, and, as I may say, With honey out of the rock:[2] In stead of the Husk, we have the fatted Calf: The thoughts of these things in the particulars of them, and of the love and goodness of God towards us, make it true of me, what David said of himself, Psal. 6. 6. *I watered my Couch with my tears.* Oh! the wonderfull power of God that mine eyes have seen, affording matter enough for my thoughts to run in, that when others are sleeping mine eyes are weeping.

I have seen the extrem vanity of this World: One hour I have been in health, and wealth, wanting[3] nothing: But the next hour in sickness and wounds, and death, having nothing but sorrow and affliction.

Before I knew what affliction meant, I was ready sometimes to wish for it. When I lived in prosperity, having the comforts of the World about me, my relations by me, my Heart chearfull, and taking little care for any thing; and yet seeing many, whom I preferred before my self, under many tryals and afflictions, in sickness, weakness, poverty, losses, crosses, and cares of the World, I should be sometimes jealous least I should have my portion in this life, and that Scripture would come to my mind, Heb. 12. 6. *For whom the Lord loveth he chasteneth, and scourgeth every Son whom he receiveth.* But now I see the Lord had his time

---

1. Genesis 42:36.
2. Psalm 81:16.

3. Lacking.

to scourge and chasten me. The portion of some is to have their afflictions by drops, now one drop and then another; but the dregs of the Cup, the Wine of astonishment, like a sweeping rain that leaveth no food, did the Lord prepare to be my portion. Affliction I wanted, and affliction I had, full measure (I thought) pressed down and running over; yet I see, when God calls a Person to any thing, and through never so many difficulties, yet he is fully able to carry them through and make them see, and say they have been gainers thereby. And I hope I can say in some measure, As David did, *It is good for me that I have been afflicted.*[4] The Lord hath shewed me the vanity of these outward things. That they are the Vanity of vanities, and vexation of spirit;[5] that they are but a shadow, a blast, a bubble, and things of no continuance. That we must rely on God himself, and our whole dependance must be upon him. If trouble from smaller matters begin to arise in me, I have something at hand to check my self with, and say, why am I troubled? It was but the other day that if I had had the world, I would have given it for my freedom, or to have been a Servant to a Christian. I have learned to look beyond present and smaller troubles, and to be quieted under them, as Moses said, Exod. 14. 13. *Stand still and see the salvation of the Lord.*

Finis.

1682

◄ APHRA BEHN ►
c. 1640–1689

Despite the fact that Aphra Behn led one of the most public lives of any woman in seventeenth-century England, almost no reliable information exists as to the circumstances of her birth or her early life. Her biographers, however, have for the most part favored a line of specula-
tion that arises from the jottings of two of Behn's contemporaries, the poet Anne Finch and the eccentric Colonel Thomas Culpepper. Finch noted in the margin of one of her manuscript poems that Behn was the daughter of a barber from Wye; Culpepper indicated in one of his manuscript jottings that Behn was born at Canterbury and that her mother was Culpepper's wet nurse. Taken together, the speculation goes, Behn was born Aphra Johnson sometime around 1640 (perhaps as late as 1649) to Bartholomew Johnson

Earliest surviving image of Aphra Behn, an engraving from the frontispiece to the 1696 edition of her *Histories and Novels.*

---

4. Psalm 119:71.   5. Vanity . . . spirit: Ecclesiastes 1:4.

and his wife, Frances Denham, and, though her own mother was probably mainly illiterate, was educated with (or perhaps by) the Culpepper children and their aristocratic relatives in that household.

In the early 1660s, under circumstances that are not entirely clear (as is true of much of Behn's life), Behn appears to have visited two British colonies in the Americas: Virginia, in North America, and Surinam, on the northern coast of South America. (Behn's 1689 play *The Widow Ranter* and her important 1688 novella about an African slave, *Oroonoko*, reflect a very specific knowledge of both Virginia and Surinam, respectively.) Upon returning to England in about 1664, she married a merchant of Dutch extraction named Behn; he died a year later and she never remarried. About 1667 she was recruited as a spy for King Charles II and lived for a time in Antwerp, gaining information about Dutch military and political activity from William Scot, who had been in Surinam at the same time as Behn and who was rumored to have been her lover there. Despite her service to the king, Behn came back to London in 1668 in debt to several creditors in Antwerp; she was sent to debtors' prison for a short time that year.

In 1670, Behn's first play, *The Forc'd Marriage*, was produced in London to considerable acclaim and not insignificant profit for its playwright. How she became a playwright is unclear, though several scholars suggest that she was introduced to the theater by Thomas Killigrew, uncle of the poet Anne Killigrew, who owned one of the two theaters in London at the time and who had been one of the officials of Charles II's government with whom Behn had corresponded while in Antwerp. She may have turned to the stage, at least in part, as a result of her distressing experience of penury. Theaters that had been closed under the Puritan government of the Protectorate reopened with the restoration of the monarchy in 1660, and the renewed popularity of the theater meant that considerable fortunes were being made, particularly by theater owners and playwrights. Behn did, at any rate, spend the rest of her life as a publishing playwright, translator, poet, and novelist, the first woman in England to make her living from her pen.

Although Behn is known now mainly for her prose work (particularly the novella *Oroonoko*, an immensely sympathetic portrait of a noble African slave in the British colony of Surinam and a book that is sometimes referred to as the first American novel), she was in her own time known primarily as a playwright. *The Rover*, which appears here, was Behn's most successful play (although she did not at first claim authorship of it). As well as being an extremely fine example of Restoration comedy in general (with its hilarious cases of mistaken identity and its quick and witty dialogue), it wonderfully portrays the material that made Behn at once enormously popular and decidedly scandalous during the late seventeenth century—the dramatization of female (and male) sexual desire and behavior. John Dryden, England's most famous poet at the time, criticized Behn for "writing loosely, and giving . . . some Scandal to the Modesty of her Sex." She was also popular for her obvious sympathies to the Royalist cause, the theaters having always been particularly associated with the monarchy. *The Rover* is also a fine example of the political edginess—conservative edginess—that characterizes Behn's career as well as Restoration drama in general.

The 1680s were a period of intense political upheaval under the Catholic James II and an aggressive Protestant-controlled Parliament. Behn's livelihood would have been severely curtailed—the theaters were virtually shut down after 1680—and her own deeply held monarchist, and probably also Catholic, beliefs would have been deeply challenged. She died in 1689 still independent, but impoverished and profoundly disillusioned with the end of what she saw as the social and political "golden age" of the Restoration.

The
Rover

PROLOGUE

Wits, like physicians, never can agree,
When of a different society.
And Rabel's Drops[1] were never more cried down
By all the learned doctors of the town,
Than a new play whose author is unknown.   5
Nor can those doctors with more malice sue
(And powerful purses) the dissenting few,
Than those with an insulting price do rail
At all who are not of their own cabal.
    If a young poet hit your humour right,   10
You judge him then out of revenge and spite.
So amongst men there are ridiculous elves,
Who monkeys hate for being too like themselves.
So that the reason of the grand debate,
Why wit so oft is damned, when good plays take,   15
Is that you censure as you love, or hate.
    Thus like a learned conclave poets sit,
Catholic[2] judges both of sense and wit,
And damn or save, as they themselves think fit.
Yet those who to others faults are so severe,   20
Are not so perfect but themselves may err.
Some write correct indeed, but then the whole
(Bating[3] their own dull stuff i'th' play) is stole;
As bees do suck from flowers their honey dew,
So they rob others striving to please you.   25
Some write their characters gentle[4] and fine,
But then they do so toil for every line,
That what to you does easy seem, and plain,
Is the hard issue of their labouring brain.
And some th'effects of all their pains we see,   30
Is but to mimic good extempore.[5]
Others by long converse about the town,
Have wit enough to write a lewd lampoon,
But their chief skill lies in a bawdy song.
In short, the only wit that's now in fashion,   35
Is but the gleanings of good conversation.
As for the author of this coming play,
I asked him[6] what he thought fit I should say
In thanks for your good company today:

1. A marketed medicinal product.
2. Universal.
3. Lessening.
4. Well born.

5. Speech given without preparation.
6. The first edition of *The Rover* was published anonymously.

He called me fool, and said it was well known
You came not here for our sakes, but your own.   40
New plays are stuffed with wits, and with debauches,
That crowd and sweat like cits, in May-Day coaches.[7]

Written by a Person of Quality.[8]

THE ACTORS' NAMES.

Mr. Jevon	Don Antonio,	The Viceroy's son.
Mr. Medbourne	Don Pedro,	A noble Spaniard, his friend.
Mr. Betterton	Belvile,	An English colonel in love with Florinda.
Mr. Smith	Willmore,	The ROVER.[9]
Mr. Crosby	Frederick,	An English gentleman and friend to Belvile and Blunt.
Mr. Underhill	Blunt,	An English country gentleman.
Mr. Richards	Stephano,	Servant to Don Pedro.
Mr. Percival	Phillippo,	Lucetta's gallant.[1]
Mr. John Lee	Sancho,	Pimp to Lucetta.
	Biskey, and Sabastian,	Two bravoes[2] to Angellica
	Officers and Soldiers.	
	Diego Page to Don Antonio.	
	Boy	

Women.

Mrs. Betterton	Florinda,	Sister to Don Pedro.
Mrs. Barry	Hellena,	A gay young woman designed for a nun, and sister to Florinda
Mrs. Hughes	Valeria,	A kinswoman to Florinda.
Mrs. Quin	Angellica Bianca,	A famous courtesan.
Mrs. Leigh	Moretta,	Her woman.
Mrs. Norris	Callis,	Governess to Florinda and Hellena.
Mrs. Gillow	Lucetta,	A jilting wench.[3]
	Servants,	
	Other Masqueraders,	
	Men and Women.	

The Scene: NAPLES, in Carnival[4] time.

7. Cits: derogatory term used by the upper classes to refer to merchants and tradespeople living in the City of London; May-Day coaches: it was customary to ride around London's Hyde Park in horse-drawn coaches on May 1 (May Day).
8. The writer of the Prologue is unknown; prologues and epilogues to Restoration plays were traditionally written (often anonymously) by someone other than the playwright.
9. Wanderer.

1. Man of fashion and pleasure, a lover.
2. Bodyguards.
3. A harlot, sometimes simply called a "jilt."
4. Naples: the play is set in the Italian city of Naples but it is rife with references to Spain and Spanish culture partly because the text on which the play is based, Thomas Killigrew's *Thomaso*, was set in Spain; Carnival: the festival preceding Lent in which people dress in costume.

The
Rover

OR, The Banished Cavaliers.[5]

ACT THE FIRST.

Scene the First. A Chamber.

Enter FLORINDA and HELLENA.

FLORINDA. What an impertinent thing is a young girl bred in a nunnery! How full of questions! Prithee[6] no more Hellena; I have told thee more than thou understand'st already.

HELLENA. The more's my grief. I would fain[7] know as much as you, which makes me so inquisitive; nor is't enough I know you're a lover, unless you tell me too, who 'tis you sigh for.

FLORINDA. When you're a lover, I'll think you fit for a secret of that nature.

HELLENA. 'Tis true, I never was a lover yet—but I begin to have a shrewd guess what it is to be so, and fancy it very pretty to sigh, and sing, and blush, and wish, and dream, and wish, and long and wish to see the man, and when I do, look pale and tremble; just as you did when my brother brought home the fine English colonel to see you—what do you call him, Don Belvile?

FLORINDA. Fie, Hellena.

HELLENA. That blush betrays you—I am sure 'tis so—or is it Don Antonio the viceroy's son? Or perhaps the rich old Don Vincentio whom my father designs you for a husband? Why do you blush again?

FLORINDA. With indignation, and how near soever my father thinks I am to marrying that hated object, I shall let him see I understand better what's due to my beauty, birth and fortune, and more to my soul, than to obey those unjust commands.

HELLENA. Now hang me if I don't love thee for that dear disobedience. I love mischief strangely, as most of our sex do, who are come to love nothing else—but tell me dear Florinda, don't you love that fine Anglese?[8] For I vow, next to loving him myself, 'twill please me most that you do so, for he is so gay and so handsome.

FLORINDA. Hellena, a maid designed for a nun ought not to be so curious in a discourse of love.

HELLENA. And dost thou think that ever I'll be a nun? Or at least till I'm so old, I'm fit for nothing else—faith no, sister; and because I hope he has some mad companion or other that will spoil my devotion, nay I'm resolved to provide myself this carnival, if there be e'er a handsome proper fellow of my humour above ground, though I ask first.

FLORINDA. Prithee be not so wild.

HELLENA. Now you have provided yourself of a man, you take no care for poor me—prithee tell me, what dost thou see about me that is unfit for love— have I not a world of youth? A humour gay? A beauty passable? A vigour desirable? Well shaped? Clean limbed? Sweet breathed? And sense enough to know how all these ought to be employed to the best advantage? Yes, I do and will; therefore lay aside your hopes of my fortune by my being a devote,[9] and tell me

---

5. Supporters of the English monarchy during the English Civil War.
6. Please.
7. Gladly.
8. Englishman.
9. Nun.

how you came acquainted with this Belvile, for I perceive you knew him before he came to Naples.

FLORINDA. Yes, I knew him at the siege of Pamplona;[1] he was then a colonel of French horse, who when the town was ransacked, nobly treated my brother and myself, preserving us from all insolences; and I must own[2] (besides great obligations) I have I know not what that pleads kindly for him about my heart, and will suffer no other to enter—but see, my brother.

Enter DON PEDRO, STEPHANO *with a masquing habit,*[3] *and* CALLIS.

PEDRO. Good morrow sister—pray, when saw you your lover Don Vincentio?

FLORINDA. I know not, sir—Callis, when was he here? For I consider it so little, I know not when it was.

PEDRO. I have a command from my father here to tell you you ought not to despise him, a man of so vast a fortune and such a passion for you—Stephano, my things.

Puts on his masquing habit.

FLORINDA. A passion for me, 'tis more than e'er I saw, or he had a desire should be known—I hate Vincentio, sir, and I would not have a man so dear to me as my brother follow the ill customs of our country, and make a slave of his sister—and sir, my father's will I'm sure you may divert.

PEDRO. I know not how dear I am to you, but I wish only to be ranked in your esteem equal with the English Colonel Belvile—why do you frown and blush? Is there any guilt belongs to the name of that cavalier?

FLORINDA. I'll not deny I value Belvile. When I was exposed to such dangers as the licensed lust of common soldiers threatened, when rage and conquest flew through the city—then Belvile, this criminal for my sake, threw himself into all dangers to save my honour, and will you not allow him my esteem?

PEDRO. Yes, pay him what you will in honour—but you must consider Don Vincentio's fortune, and the jointure[4] he'll make you.

FLORINDA. Let him consider my youth, beauty and fortune, which ought not to be thrown away on his age and jointure.

PEDRO. 'Tis true, he's not so young and fine a gentleman as that Belvile—but what jewels will that cavalier present you with? Those of his eyes and heart?

HELLENA. And are not those better than any Don Vincentio has brought from the Indies?

PEDRO. Why, how now! Has your nunnery breeding taught you to understand the value of hearts and eyes?

HELLENA. Better than to believe Vincentio's deserve value from any woman—he may perhaps increase her bags,[5] but not her family.

PEDRO. This is fine—go—up to your devotion; you are not designed for the conversation of lovers.

HELLENA. [*Aside.*] Nor saints yet a while, I hope.

1. A town in northern Spain over which France and Spain fought for many years because of its strategic geographical importance in guarding the entrance to a pass through the Pyrenees to France.
2. Admit.
3. Costume.
4. Estate or monetary settlement left to a wife after the death of her husband.
5. Wealth.

—Is't not enough you make a nun of me, but you must cast my sister away too, exposing her to a worse confinement than a religious life?

PEDRO. The girl's mad—it is a confinement to be carried into the country, to an ancient villa belonging to the family of the Vincentios these five hundred years, and have no other prospect than that pleasing one of seeing all her own that meets her eyes—a fine air, large fields, and gardens where she may walk and gather flowers.

HELLENA. When, by moonlight? For I am sure she dares not encounter with the heat of the sun; that were a task only for Don Vincentio and his Indian breeding, who loves it in the dog days[6]—and if these be her daily divertisements,[7] what are those of the night? To lie in a wide moth-eaten bed chamber, with furniture in fashion in the reign of King Sancho the First; the bed, that which his forefathers lived and died in.

PEDRO. Very well.

HELLENA. This apartment (new furbished and fitted out for the young wife) he (out of freedom) makes his dressing room, and being a frugal and jealous coxcomb,[8] instead of a valet to uncase his feeble carcass, he desires you to do that office—signs of favour I'll assure you, and such as you must not hope for, unless your woman be out of the way.

PEDRO. Have you done yet?

HELLENA. That honour being past, the giant stretches itself, yawns and sighs a belch or two, loud as a musket, throws himself into bed, and expects you in his foul sheets, and ere you can get yourself undressed, calls you with a snore or two—and are not these fine blessings to a young lady?

PEDRO. Have you done yet?

HELLENA. And this man you must kiss; nay you must kiss none but him, too—and nuzzle through his beard to find his lips. And this you must submit to for threescore years,[9] and all for a jointure.

PEDRO. For all your character of Don Vincentio, she is as like to marry him as she was before.

HELLENA. Marry Don Vincentio! Hang me, such a wedlock would be worse than adultery with another man. I had rather see her in the Hotel de Dieu,[1] to waste her youth there in vows and be a handmaid to lazars[2] and cripples, than to lose it in such a marriage.

PEDRO. You have considered, sister, that Belvile has no fortune to bring you to—banished his country, despised at home, and pitied abroad.

HELLENA. What then? The viceroy's son is better than that old Sir Fifty. Don Vincentio! Don Indian! He thinks he's trading to Gambo[3] still and would barter himself (that bell and bauble) for your youth and fortune.

PEDRO. Callis, take her hence, and lock her up all this Carnival, and at Lent she shall begin her everlasting penance in a monastery.

HELLENA. I care not; I had rather be a nun than be obliged to marry as you would have me, if I were designed for't.

PEDRO. Do not fear the blessing of that choice—you shall be a nun.

HELLENA. Shall I so? You may chance to be mistaken in my way of devotion—a nun! Yes, I am like to make a fine nun! I have an excellent humour for a grate.[4]

---

6. Hottest days of summer.
7. Diversions (French).
8. Vain, conceited man.
9. Sixty.

1. Hospital run by nuns for the destitute.
2. Diseased people.
3. Gambia, a country on the coast of Africa.
4. Bars in the door of a convent.

[*Aside.*] I'll have a saint of my own to pray to shortly, if I like any that dares venture on me.

PEDRO. Callis, make it your business to watch this wild cat. As for you Florinda, I've only tried you all this while and urged my father's will; but mine is that you would love Antonio. He is brave and young, and all that can complete the happiness of a gallant maid. This absence of my father will give us opportunity to free you from Vincentio by marrying here, which you must do tomorrow.

FLORINDA. Tomorrow!

PEDRO. Tomorrow, or 'twill be too late—'tis not my friendship to Antonio which makes me urge this, but love to thee and hatred to Vincentio—therefore, resolve upon tomorrow.

FLORINDA. Sir, I shall strive to do as shall become your sister.

PEDRO. I'll both believe and trust you. Adieu.

Exeunt PEDRO *and* STEPHANO.

HELLENA. As becomes his sister! That is to be as resolved your way, as he is his—

HELLENA *goes to* CALLIS.

FLORINDA. I ne'er till now perceived my ruin near.
I've no defence against Antonio's love,
For he has all the advantages of nature,
The moving arguments of youth and fortune.

HELLENA. But hark you, Callis, you will not be so cruel to lock me up indeed, will you?

CALLIS. I must obey the commands I have—besides, do you consider what a life you are going to lead?

HELLENA. Yes, Callis, that of a nun; and till then I'll be indebted a world of prayers to you if you'll let me now see what I never did, the divertisements of a carnival.

CALLIS. What, go in masquerade? 'Twill be a fine farewell to the world, I take it—pray, what would you do there?

HELLENA. That which all the world does, as I am told—be as mad as the rest and take all innocent freedoms. Sister, you'll go too, will you not? Come, prithee be not sad. We'll outwit twenty brothers if you'll be ruled by me—come, put off this dull humour with your clothes, and assume one as gay, and as fantastic, as the dress my cousin Valeria and I have provided, and let's ramble.

FLORINDA. Callis, will you give us leave to go?

CALLIS. [*Aside.*] I have a youthful itch of going myself.—Madam, if I thought your brother might not know it, and I might wait on you; for by my troth I'll not trust young girls alone.

FLORINDA. Thou see'st my brother's gone already, and thou shalt attend, and watch us.

Enter STEPHANO.

STEPHANO. Madam, the habits[5] are come, and your cousin Valeria is dressed, and stays[6] for you.

5. Costumes.   6. Waits.

FLORINDA. 'Tis well. I'll write a note, and if I chance to see Belvile, and want an opportunity to speak to him, that shall let him know what I've resolved in favour of him.

HELLENA. Come, let's in and dress us.

Exeunt.

Scene II
A Long Street

Enter BELVILE *melancholy,* BLUNT *and* FREDERICK.

FREDERICK. Why what the devil ails the colonel? In a time when all the world is gay, to look like mere Lent thus? Had'st thou been long enough in Naples to have been in love, I should have sworn some such judgment had befallen thee.

BELVILE. No, I have made no new amours since I came to Naples.

FREDERICK. You have left none behind you in Paris?

BELVILE. Neither.

FREDERICK. I cannot divine the cause then, unless the old cause, the want of money.

BLUNT. And another old cause, the want of a wench—would not that revive you?

BELVILE. You are mistaken, Ned.

BLUNT. Nay, 'sheartlikins,[7] then thou'rt past cure.

FREDERICK. I have found it out; thou hast renewed thy acquaintance with the lady that cost thee so many sighs at the siege of Pamplona—pox on't, what d'ye call her—her brother's a noble Spaniard—nephew to the dead general—Florinda—ay Florinda—and will nothing serve thy turn but that damned virtuous woman? Whom on my conscience thou lovest in spite too, because thou seest little or no possibility of gaining her.

BELVILE. Thou art mistaken. I have interest enough in that lovely virgin's heart to make me proud and vain, were it not abated by the severity of a brother, who perceiving my happiness—

FREDERICK. Has civilly forbid thee the house?

BELVILE. 'Tis so; to make way for a powerful rival, the viceroy's son, who has the advantage of me in being a man of fortune, a Spaniard, and her brother's friend; which gives him liberty to make his court,[8] whilst I have recourse only to letters and distant looks from her window, which are as soft and kind as those which heaven sends down on penitents.

BLUNT. Heyday! 'Sheartlikins, simile! By this light, the man is quite spoiled. Fred, what the devil are we made of that we cannot be thus concerned for a wench? 'Sheartlikins, our cupids are like the cooks of the camp, they can roast or boil a woman, but they have none of the fine tricks to set 'em off, no hogoes[9] to make the sauce pleasant and the stomach sharp.

FREDERICK. I dare swear I have had a hundred as young, kind and handsome as this Florinda; and dogs eat me, if they were not as troublesome to me i'the morning as they were welcome o'er night.

---

7. An oath meaning God's little heart.
8. Court her in person.

9. Spicy condiments.

BLUNT. And yet I warrant he would not touch another woman if he might have her for nothing.

BELVILE. That's thy joy, a cheap whore.

BLUNT. Why 'sheartlikins, I love a frank soul—when did you ever hear of an honest woman that took a man's money? I warrant 'em good ones—but gentlemen, you may be free, you have been kept so poor with Parliaments and Protectors,[1] that the little stock you have is not worth preserving—but I thank my stars, I had more grace than to forfeit my estate by cavaliering.[2]

BELVILE. Methinks only following the court,[3] should be sufficient to entitle 'em to that.

BLUNT. 'Sheartlikins, they know I follow it to do it no good, unless they pick a hole in my coat for lending you money now and then, which is a greater crime to my conscience, gentlemen, than to the Commonwealth.[4]

Enter WILLMORE.

WILLMORE. Ha! Dear Belvile! Noble colonel!

BELVILE. Willmore! Welcome ashore, my dear rover! What happy wind blew us this good fortune?

WILLMORE. Let me salute[5] my dear Frederick and then command me. How is't, honest lad?

FREDERICK. Faith, sir, the old complement, infinitely the better to see my dear mad Willmore again. Prithee, why camest thou ashore? And where's the Prince?[6]

WILLMORE. He's well, and reigns still lord of the watery element. I must aboard again within a day or two, and my business ashore was only to enjoy myself a little this carnival.

BELVILE. Pray know our new friend, sir; he's but bashful, a raw traveller, but honest, stout and one of us.

Embraces BLUNT.

WILLMORE. That you esteem him gives him an interest here.

BLUNT. Your servant, sir.

WILLMORE. But well—faith, I'm glad to meet you again in a warm climate, where the kind sun has its god-like power still over the wine and women—love and mirth are my business in Naples, and if I mistake not the place, here's an excellent market for chapmen[7] of my humour.

BELVILE. See, here be those kind merchants of love you look for.

Enter several MEN *in masquing habits, some playing on music, others dancing after;* WOMEN *dressed like courtesans, with papers pinned on their breasts, and baskets of flowers in their hands.*

BLUNT. 'Sheartlikins, what have we here?

FREDERICK. Now the game begins.

1. The title Oliver Cromwell took during the time of Parliamentary rule after the Civil War.
2. Refers to the cavaliers, supporters of the monarchy, who left England during the Civil War and had their estates confiscated, or sequestered.
3. The court of the exiled Prince Charles, later

Charles II.
4. Name for England during the years of parliamentary rule.
5. Greet with a kiss.
6. Prince Charles.
7. Merchants.

WILLMORE. Fine pretty creatures! May a stranger have leave to look and love? What's here—[*Reads the papers.*] "Roses for every month"?

BLUNT. "Roses for every month"? What means that?

BELVILE. They are, or would have you think, they're courtesans, who here in Naples, are to be hired by the month.

WILLMORE. Kind and obliging to inform us—pray, where do these roses grow? I would fain plant some of 'em in a bed of mine.

WOMEN. Beware such roses, sir.

WILLMORE. A pox of fear; I'll be baked with thee between a pair of sheets, and that's thy proper still,[8] so I might but strew such roses over me, and under me—fair one, would you would give me leave to gather at your bush this idle month; I would go near to make some body smell of it all the year after.

BELVILE. And thou hast need of such a remedy, for thou stink'st of tar and rope's ends, like a dock or pest-house.[9]

The WOMAN *puts herself into the hands of a* MAN *and exeunt.*

WILLMORE. Nay, nay, you shall not leave me so.

BELVILE. By all means use no violence here.

WILLMORE. Death! Just as I was going to be damnably in love, to have her led off! I could pluck that rose out of his hand, and even kiss the bed the bush grew in.

FREDERICK. No friend to love like a long voyage at sea.

BLUNT. Except a nunnery, Frederick.

WILLMORE. Death! But will they not be kind? Quickly be kind? Thou know'st I'm no tame fighter, but a rampant lion of the forest.

Advance from the farther end of the scenes two MEN *dressed all over with horns[1] of several sorts, making grimaces at one another, with papers pinned on their backs.*

BELVILE. Oh the fantastical rogues, how they're dressed! 'Tis a satire against the whole sex.

WILLMORE. Is this a fruit that grows in this warm country?

BELVILE. Yes, 'tis pretty to see these Italians start, swell and stab at the word "cuckold," and yet stumble at horns on every threshold.

WILLMORE. See what's on their back—[*Reads*] "Flowers of every night." Ah, rogue! And more sweet than "Roses of every month"! This is a gardener of Adam's own breeding.

They dance.

BELVILE. What think you of those grave people? Is a wake in Essex[2] half so mad or extravagant?

WILLMORE. I like their sober grave way; 'tis a kind of legal authorized fornication, where the men are not chid[3] for't, nor the women despised, as amongst our dull English even the monsieurs want that part of good manners.

---

8. Refers to the process by which rose petals are distilled to make rosewater.
9. Hospital for plague victims.
1. The signs of a cuckold—a man whose wife sleeps with another man.
2. A town in England.
3. Scolded, rebuked.

BELVILE. But here in Italy a monsieur is the humblest, best-bred gentleman—duels are so baffled by bravoes, that an age shows not one but between a Frenchman and a hangman, who is as much too hard for him on the pazza,[4] as they are for a Dutchman on the New Bridge—but see, another crew.

Enter FLORINDA, HELLENA *and* VALERIA, *dressed like gypsies;* CALLIS *and* STEPHANO; LUCETTA, PHILIPO *and* SANCHO *in masquerade.*

HELLENA. Sister, there's your Englishman, and with him a handsome proper fellow—I'll to him, and instead of telling him his fortune, try my own.

WILLMORE. Gypsies, on my life—sure these will prattle if a man cross their hands.[5]

Goes to HELLENA.

Dear, pretty (and I hope) young devil, will you tell an amorous stranger what luck he's like to have?

HELLENA. Have a care how you venture with me, sir, lest I pick your pocket, which will more vex your English humour than an Italian fortune will please you.

WILLMORE. How the devil cam'st thou to know my country and humour?

HELLENA. The first I guess by a certain forward impudence, which does not displease me at this time; and the loss of your money will vex you because I hope you have but very little to lose.

WILLMORE. Egad child, thou'rt i'th'right; it is so little, I dare not offer it thee for a kindness—but cannot you divine what other things of more value I have about me, that I would more willingly part with?

HELLENA. Indeed no, that's the business of a witch, and I am but a gypsy yet. Yet without looking in your hand, I have a parlous[6] guess 'tis some foolish heart you mean, an inconstant English heart, as little worth stealing as your purse.

WILLMORE. Nay, then thou dost deal with the devil, that's certain—thou hast guessed as right as if thou had'st been one of that number it has languished for. I find you'll be better acquainted with it, nor can you take it in a better time; for I am come from the sea, child, and Venus not being propitious to me in her own element,[7] I have a world of love in store—would you would be good-natured and take some on't off my hands.

HELLENA. Why—I could be inclined that way—but for a foolish vow I am going to make—to die a maid.

WILLMORE. Then thou art damned without redemption, and as I am a good Christian, I ought in charity to divert so wicked a design—therefore prithee, dear creature, let me know quickly when and where I shall begin to set a helping hand to so good a work.

HELLENA. If you should prevail with my tender heart (as I begin to fear you will, for you have horrible loving eyes) there will be difficulty in't, that you'll hardly undergo for my sake.

---

4. Pazza: plaza, town square; Dutchman on the New Bridge: refers to the French defeat of the Dutch in 1673 at Nieuwerbrug (New Bridge).
5. With silver.

6. Perilous.
7. Venus, the Roman goddess of love, was born from the sea.

WILLMORE. Faith child, I have been bred in dangers, and wear a sword that has been employed in a worse cause than for a handsome kind woman—name the danger—let it be anything but a long siege—and I'll undertake it.

HELLENA. Can you storm?[8]

WILLMORE. Oh most furiously.

HELLENA. What think you of a nunnery wall? For he that wins me must gain that first.

WILLMORE. A nun! Oh how I love thee for't! There's no sinner like a young saint—nay, now there's no denying me, the old law[9] had no curse (to a woman) like dying a maid; witness Jepthah's daughter.[1]

HELLENA. A very good text this, if well handled, and I perceive, Father Captain, you would impose no severe penance on her who were inclined to console herself, before she took orders.

WILLMORE. If she be young and handsome.

HELLENA. Ay, there's it—but if she be not—

WILLMORE. By this hand, child, I have an implicit faith, and dare venture on thee with all faults—besides, 'tis more meritorious to leave the world when thou hast tasted and proved the pleasure on't. Then, 'twill be a virtue in thee, which now will be pure ignorance.

HELLENA. I perceive, good Father Captain, you design only to make me fit for heaven—but if on the contrary, you should quite divert me from it and bring me back to the world again, I should have a new man to seek, I find; and what a grief that will be—for when I begin, I fancy I shall love like anything. I never tried yet.

WILLMORE. Egad and that's kind—prithee dear creature, give me credit for a heart, for faith I'm a very honest fellow. Oh, I long to come first to the banquet of love! And such a swinging[2] appetite I bring—oh, I'm impatient—thy lodging, sweetheart, thy lodging, or I'm a dead man!

HELLENA. Why must we be either guilty of fornication or murder if we converse with you men—and is there no difference between leave to love me, and leave to lie with me?

WILLMORE. Faith, child, they were made to go together.

LUCETTA. Are you sure this is the man?

Pointing to BLUNT.

SANCHO. When did I mistake your game?

LUCETTA. This is a stranger, I know by his gazing; if he be brisk, he'll venture to follow me, and then, if I understand my trade, he's mine. He's English too, and they say that's a sort of good-natured loving people, and have generally so kind an opinion of themselves, that a woman of any wit may flatter 'em into any sort of fool she pleases.

She often passes by BLUNT *and gazes on him;*
he struts and cocks, and walks and gazes on her.

8. Make an assault on.
9. Old Testament.
1. In Judges 11, Jephthah, an Israelite Judge, makes a vow to God saying that if he is allowed to defeat the Ammonites, he will offer as a burnt sacrifice whoever comes out of his house to greet him when he returns from battle. His young daughter, who is unnamed in the story, is the first to greet the victorious Jephthah, who then must fulfill his vow.
2. Immense.

BLUNT. 'Tis so—she is taken—I have beauties which my false glass[3] at home did not discover.

FLORINDA. This woman watches me so, I shall get no opportunity to discover myself to him, and so miss the intent of my coming—but as I was saying, sir— [*Looking in his hand*] by this line you should be a lover.

BELVILE. I thought how right you guessed, all men are in love, or pretend to be so—come and let me go, I'm weary of this fooling.

Walks away.

FLORINDA. I will not, till you have confessed whether the passion that you have vowed Florinda be true or false.

She holds him, he strives to get from her. He turns quick towards her.

BELVILE. Florinda!
FLORINDA. Softly.
BELVILE. Thou hast named one will fix me here for ever.
FLORINDA. She'll be disappointed then, who expects you this night at the garden gate, and if you fail not, as—let me see the other hand—you will go near to do—she vows to die or make you happy.

Looks on CALLIS, *who observes 'em.*

BELVILE. What canst thou mean?
FLORINDA. That which I say—farewell.

Offers to go.

BELVILE. Oh charming sybil, stay, complete that joy which as it is will turn into distraction! Where must I be? At the garden gate? I know it—at night you say? I'll sooner forfeit heaven than disobey.

Enter DON PEDRO *and other* MASQUERS, *and pass over the stage.*

CALLIS. Madam, your brother's here.
FLORINDA. Take this to instruct you farther.

Gives him a letter, and goes off.

FREDERICK. Have a care, sir, what you promise; this may be a trap laid by her brother to ruin you.

BELVILE. Do not disturb my happiness with doubts.

Opens the letter.

WILLMORE. My dear pretty creature, a thousand blessings on thee! Still in this habit you say? And after dinner at this place?

HELLENA. Yes, if you will swear to keep your heart, and not bestow it between this and that.

WILLMORE. By all the little gods of love, I swear I'll leave it with you, and if you run away with it, those deities of justice will revenge me.

3. Mirror.

Exeunt all the WOMEN.

FREDERICK. Do you know the hand?[4]

BELVILE. 'Tis Florinda's.

All blessings fall upon the virtuous maid.

FREDERICK. Nay, no idolatry; a sober sacrifice I'll allow you.

BELVILE. Oh friends, the welcomest news! The softest letter! Nay, you shall all see it! And could you now be serious, I might be made the happiest man the sun shines on!

WILLMORE. The reason of this mighty joy?

BELVILE. See how kindly she invites me to deliver her from the threatened violence of her brother—will you not assist me?

WILLMORE. I know not what thou mean'st, but I'll make one at any mischief where a woman's concerned—but she'll be grateful to us for the favour, will she not?

BELVILE. How mean you?

WILLMORE. How should I mean? Thou know'st there's but one way for a woman to oblige me.

BELVILE. Do not profane—the maid is nicely virtuous.

WILLMORE. Who, pox, then she's fit for nothing but a husband, let her e'en go, colonel.

FREDERICK. Peace, she's the colonel's mistress, sir.

WILLMORE. Let her be the devil; if she be thy mistress, I'll serve her—name the way.

BELVILE. Read here this postscript.

Gives him a letter.

WILLMORE. [*Reads.*] "At ten at night—at the garden gate—of which, if I cannot get the key, I will contrive a way over the wall—come attended with a friend or two." Kind heart, if we three cannot weave a string to let her down a garden wall, 'twere pity but the hangman wove one for us all.

FREDERICK. Let her alone for that. Your woman's wit, your fair kind woman, will out-trick a broker or a Jew, and contrive like a Jesuit in chains—but see, Ned Blunt is stolen out after the lure of a damsel.

Exeunt BLUNT *and* LUCETTA.

BELVILE. So he'll scarce find his way home again, unless we get him cried by the bellman[5] in the market-place, and 'twould sound prettily—a lost English boy of thirty.

FREDERICK. I hope 'tis some common crafty sinner, one that will fit him;[6] it may be she'll sell him for Peru,[7] the rogue's sturdy and would work well in a mine; at least I hope she'll dress him for our mirth, cheat him of all, then have him well-favouredly banged[8] and turned out naked at midnight.

WILLMORE. Prithee, what humour is he of that you wish him so well?

BELVILE. Why of an English elder brother's humour, educated in a nursery, with a maid to tend him till fifteen, and lies with his grandmother till he's of age;

---

4. Handwriting.
5. Town crier.
6. Suit him (serve him right).

7. As a slave for service in Peru's mines.
8. Thrashed.

one that knows no pleasure beyond riding to the next fair, or going up to London with his right worshipful father in Parliament-time, wearing gay clothes, or making honourable love to his lady mother's laundry-maid; gets drunk at a hunting-match, and ten to one then gives some proofs of his prowess. A pox upon him, he's our banker and has all our cash about him; and if he fail, we are all broke.

FREDERICK. Oh let him alone for that matter, he's of a damned stingy quality; that will secure our stock. I know not in what danger it were indeed if the jilt should pretend she's in love with him, for 'tis a kind believing coxcomb; otherwise if he part with more than a piece of eight[9]—geld him; for which offer he may chance to be beaten, if she be a whore of the first rank.

BELVILE. Nay, the rogue will not be easily beaten, he's stout[1] enough. Perhaps if they talk beyond his capacity he may chance to exercise his courage upon some of them, else I'm sure they'll find it as difficult to beat as to please him.

WILLMORE. 'Tis a lucky devil to light upon so kind a wench!

FREDERICK. Thou had'st a great deal of talk with thy little gypsy; could'st thou do no good upon her? For mine was hard-hearted.

WILLMORE. Hang her, she was some damned honest person of quality, I'm sure, she was so very free and witty. If her face be but answerable to her wit and humour, I would be bound to constancy this month to gain her—in the meantime, have you made no kind acquaintance since you came to town? You do not use to be honest so long, gentlemen.

FREDERICK. Faith, love has kept us honest; we have been all fired with a beauty newly come to town, the famous Paduana,[2] Angellica Bianca.

WILLMORE. What, the mistress of the dead Spanish general?

BELVILE. Yes, she's now the only adored beauty of all the youth in Naples, who put on all their charms to appear lovely in her sight, their coaches, liveries, and themselves, all gay as on a monarch's birthday, to attract the eyes of this fair charmer, while she has the pleasure to behold all languish for her that see her.

FREDERICK. 'Tis pretty to see with how much love the men regard her, and how much envy the women.

WILLMORE. What gallant has she?

BELVILE. None, she's exposed to sale, and four days in the week she's yours—for so much a month.

WILLMORE. The very thought of it quenches all manner of fire in me—yet prithee let's see her.

BELVILE. Let's first to dinner, and after that we'll pass the day as you please—but at night ye must all be at my devotion.[3]

WILLMORE. I will not fail you.

ACT II

Scene I. The Long Street

Enter BELVILE *and* FREDERICK *in masquing habits, and* WILLMORE *in his own clothes, with a vizard[4] in his hand.*

---

9. Piece of eight: Spanish silver dollar (peso) so called because it was worth eight reals and marked with a figure eight. In the late seventeenth century, it was the leading currency in world trade, much like the U.S. dollar is today.

1. Fierce.
2. Woman from Padua, a town in northern Italy.
3. At my service.
4. Mask.

WILLMORE. But why thus disguised and muzzled?

BELVILE. Because whatever extravagances we commit in these faces, our own may not be obliged to answer 'em.

WILLMORE. I should have changed my eternal buff[5] too; but no matter, my little gipsy would not have found me out then, for if she should change hers, it is impossible I should know her, unless I should hear her prattle. A pox on't, I cannot get her out of my head; pray heaven, if ever I do see her again, she prove damnably ugly, that I may fortify myself against her tongue.

BELVILE. Have a care of love, for o'my conscience she was not of a quality to give thee any hopes.

WILLMORE. Pox on 'em, why do they draw a man in then? She has played with my heart so, that 'twill never lie still till I have met with some kind wench that will play the game out with me—oh, for my arms full of soft, white, kind—woman—such as I fancy Angellica.

BELVILE. This is her house, if you were but in stock to get admittance. They have not dined yet; I perceive the picture is not out.

Enter BLUNT.

WILLMORE. I long to see the shadow of the fair substance; a man may gaze on that for nothing.

BLUNT. Colonel, thy hand—and thine, Fred. I have been an ass; a deluded fool, a very coxcomb from my birth till this hour, and heartily repent my little faith.

BELVILE. What the devil's the matter with thee, Ned?

BLUNT. Oh such a mistress Fred, such a girl!

WILLMORE. Ha! where?

FREDERICK. Ay, where!

BLUNT. So fond, so amorous, so toying and so fine! And all for sheer love, ye rogue! Oh how she looked and kissed! And soothed my heart from my bosom—I cannot think I was awake, and yet methinks I see and feel her charms still—Fred, try if she have not left the taste of her balmy kisses upon my lips.

Kisses him.

BELVILE. Ha! Ha! Ha!

WILLMORE. Death, man, where is she?

BLUNT. What a dog was I to stay in dull England so long. How have I laughed at the colonel when he sighed for love! But now the little archer[6] has revenged him! And by this one dart, I can guess at all his joys, which then I took for fancies, mere dreams and fables. Well, I'm resolved to sell all in Essex, and plant here for ever.

BELVILE. What a blessing 'tis thou hast a mistress thou dar'st boast of, for I know thy humour is rather to have a proclaimed clap[7] than a secret amour.

WILLMORE. Dost know her name?

BLUNT. Her name? No, 'sheartlikins, what care I for names? She's fair! Young! Brisk and kind, even to ravishment! And what a pox care I for knowing her by any other title?

WILLMORE. Didst give her anything?

BLUNT. Give her! Ha, ha, ha! Why she's a person of quality—that's a good one, give her! 'Sheartlikins, dost think such creatures are to be bought? Or are we

---

5. A durable, yellowish leather used in soldiers' coats.

6. Cupid.

7. Gonorrhea.

provided for such a purchase? Give her, quoth ye? Why, she presented me with this bracelet for the toy of a diamond I used to wear. No, gentlemen, Ned Blunt is not everybody. She expects me again tonight.

WILLMORE. Egad, that's well; we'll all go.

BLUNT. Not a soul. No, gentlemen, you are wits; I am a dull country rogue, I.

FREDERICK. Well, sir, for all your person of quality, I shall be very glad to understand your purse be secure; 'tis our whole estate at present, which we are loath to hazard in one bottom,[8] come, sir, unlade.

BLUNT. Take the necessary trifle useless now to me, that am beloved by such a gentlewoman—'sheartlikins, money! Here, take mine too.

FREDERICK. No, keep that to be cozened,[9] that we may laugh.

WILLMORE. Cozened—death! Would I could meet with one that would cozen me of all the love I could spare tonight.

FREDERICK. Pox, 'tis some common whore, upon my life.

BLUNT. A whore! Yes, with such clothes! Such jewels! Such a house! Such furniture, and so attended! A whore!

BELVILE. Why yes, sir, they are whores, though they'll neither entertain you with drinking, swearing, or bawdry; are whores in all those gay clothes and right jewels; are whores with those great houses richly furnished with velvet beds, store of plate,[1] handsome attendance and fine coaches; are whores, and errant ones.

WILLMORE. Pox on't, where do these fine whores live?

BELVILE. Where no rogues in office ycleped[2] constables dare give 'em laws, nor the wine-inspired bullies of the town break their windows; yet they are whores, though this Essex calf[3] believe 'em persons of quality.

BLUNT. 'Sheartlikins, y'are all fools; there are things about this Essex calf that shall take with the ladies, beyond all your wit and parts—this shape and size, gentlemen, are not to be despised—my waist, too, tolerably long, with other inviting signs, that shall be nameless.

WILLMORE. Egad, I believe he may have met with some person of quality that may be kind to him.

BELVILE. Dost thou perceive any such tempting things about him, that should make a fine woman, and of quality, pick him out from all mankind to throw away her youth and beauty upon, nay and her dear heart too! No, no, Angellica has raised the price too high.

WILLMORE. May she languish for mankind till she die, and be damned for that one sin alone.

Enter two BRAVOES, *and hang up a great picture of* ANGELLICA's *against the balcony, and two little ones at each side of the door.*

BELVILE. See there, the fair sign to the inn where a man may lodge that's fool enough to give her price.

WILLMORE *gazes on the picture.*

BLUNT. 'Sheartlikins, gentlemen, what's this!

BELVILE. A famous courtesan, that's to be sold.

---

8. Cargo ship.
9. Cheated.
1. Silver-plated household items (tableware, utensils, ornaments).

2. Called.
3. Native of Essex (Essex was famous for its calves).

BLUNT. How? To be sold! Nay then, I have nothing to say to her—sold! What impudence is practiced in this country? With what order and decency whoring's established here by virtue of the Inquisition.[4] Come, let's begone, I'm sure we're no chapmen for this commodity.

FREDERICK. Thou art none, I'm sure, unless thou could'st have her in thy bed at a price of a coach in the street.

WILLMORE. How wondrous fair she is. A thousand crowns[5] a month—by heaven, as many kingdoms were too little; a plague of this poverty—of which I ne'er complain but when it hinders my approach to beauty which virtue ne'er could purchase.

Turns from the picture.

BLUNT. What's this? [*Reads.*]
A thousand crowns a month!
'Sheartlikins, here's a sum! Sure 'tis a mistake.
—Hark you friend, does she take or give so much by the month?

FREDERICK. A thousand crowns! Why 'tis a portion for the Infanta.[6]

BLUNT. Harkee, friends, won't she trust?[7]

BRAVO. This is a trade, sir, that cannot live by credit.

Enter DON PEDRO *in masquerade, followed by* STEPHANO.

BELVILE. See, here's more company; let's walk off a while.

Exeunt ENGLISH. PEDRO *reads.*

Enter ANGELLICA *and* MORETTA *in the balcony, and draw a silk curtain.*

PEDRO. Fetch me a thousand crowns, I never wished to buy this beauty at an easier rate.[8]

Passes off.

ANGELLICA. Prithee what said those fellows to thee?

BRAVO. Madam, the first were admirers of beauty only, but no purchasers; they were merry with your price and picture, laughed at the sum, and so passed off.

ANGELLICA. No matter, I'm not displeased with their rallying; their wonder feeds my vanity, and he that wishes but to buy gives me more pride than he that gives my price can make my pleasure.

BRAVO. Madam, the last I knew through all his disguises to be Don Pedro, nephew to the general, and who was with him in Pamplona.

ANGELLICA. Don Pedro! My old gallant's nephew. When his uncle died he left him a vast sum of money; it is he who was so in love with me at Padua, and who used to make the general so jealous.

MORETTA. Is this he that used to prance before our window, and take such care to show himself an amorous ass? If I am not mistaken, he is the likeliest man to give your price.

4. The Spanish Inquisition, a court instituted in Spain in 1478 with the aim of enforcing (often brutally) certain legal restrictions on non-Catholics, primarily Jews and Muslims.
5. A gold coin worth about a dollar in today's currency.
6. A dowry for the daughter of the Spanish king.
7. Harkee: listen; trust: give credit for services rendered.
8. Lower price.

ANGELLICA. The man is brave and generous, but of an humour so uneasy and inconstant, that the victory over his heart is as soon lost as won, a slave that can add little to the triumph of the conqueror. But inconstancy's the sin of all mankind; therefore I'm resolved that nothing but gold shall charm my heart.

MORETTA. I'm glad on't; 'tis only interest that women of our profession ought to consider, though I wonder what has kept you from that general disease of our sex so long, I mean that of being in love.

ANGELLICA. A kind but sullen star under which I had the happiness to be born. Yet I have had no time for love; the bravest and noblest of mankind have purchased my favours at so dear a rate as if no coin but gold were current with our trade—but here's Don Pedro again, fetch me my lute—for 'tis for him or Don Antonio the viceroy's son, that I have spread my nets.

Enter at one door DON PEDRO, STEPHANO; DON ANTONIO *and* DIEGO PAGE
at the other door, with PEOPLE *following him in masquerade,
anticly[9] attired, some with music; they both go up to the picture.*

ANTONIO. A thousand crowns! Had not the painter flattered her, I should not think it dear.[1]

PEDRO. Flattered her! By heav'n, he cannot; I have seen the original, nor is there one charm here more than adorns her face and eyes; all this soft and sweet, with a certain languishing air, that no artist can represent.

ANTONIO. What I heard of her beauty before had fired my soul, but this confirmation of it has blown it to a flame.

PEDRO. Ha!

PAGE. Sir, I have known you throw away a thousand crowns on a worse face, and though y'are near your marriage, you may venture a little love here. Florinda will not miss it.

PEDRO. [*Aside.*] Ha! Florinda! Sure 'tis Antonio.

ANTONIO. Florinda! Name not those distant joys; there's not one thought of her will check my passion here.

PEDRO. Florinda scorned! And all my hopes defeated of the possession of Angellica.

A noise of a lute above. ANTONIO *gazes up.*

Her injuries, by heaven, he shall not boast of.

Song to a lute above.

SONG.

When Damon first began to love
He languished in a soft desire,
And knew not how the gods to move,
To lessen or increase his fire.
For Caelia in her charming eyes
Wore all love's sweets, and all his cruelties.   5

9. Absurdly.   1. Expensive.

II.

But as beneath a shade he lay,
Weaving of flow'rs for Caelia's hair,
She chanced to lead her flock that way,
And saw the arm'rous shepherd there.   10
She gazed around upon the place,
And saw the grove (resembling night)
To all the joys of love invite,
Whilst guilty smiles and blushes dressed her face.
At this the bashful youth all transport grew,   15
And with kind force he taught the virgin how
To yield what all his sighs could never do.

ANGELLICA *throws open the curtains and bows to* ANTONIO,
who pulls off his vizard and bows and blows up kisses.

PEDRO *unseen looks in's face.*

ANTONIO. By Heav'n she's charming fair!

PEDRO. 'Tis he; the false Antonio!

ANTONIO. [*To the bravo.*] Friend, where must I pay my offering of love?
My thousand crowns I mean.

PEDRO. That offering I have designed to make.
And yours will come too late.

ANTONIO. Prithee begone, I shall grow angry else.
And then thou art not safe.

PEDRO. My anger may be fatal, sir, as yours,
And he that enters here may prove this truth.

ANTONIO. I know not who thou art, but I am sure thou'rt worth my killing,
for aiming at Angellica.

They draw and fight. Enter WILLMORE *and* BLUNT *who draw and part 'em.*

BLUNT. 'Sheartlikins, here's fine doings.

WILLMORE. Tilting[2] for the wench, I'm sure—nay, gad, if that would win her,
I have as good a sword as the best of ye. Put up—put up, and take another time
and place, for this is designed for lovers only.

They all put up.

PEDRO. We are prevented; dare you meet me tomorrow on the Molo?[3]
For I've a title to a better quarrel,
That of Florinda, in whose credulous heart
Thou'st made an int'rest and destroyed my hopes.

ANTONIO. Dare!
I'll meet thee there as early as the day.

PEDRO. We will come thus disguised that whosoever chance to get the better,
he may escape unknown.

ANTONIO. It shall be so.

---

2. Fighting.   3. Pier.

Exeunt PEDRO *and* STEPHANO.

Who should this rival be? Unless the English colonel, of whom I've often heard Don Pedro speak; it must be he, and time he were removed, who lays claim to all my happiness.

WILLMORE *having gazed all this while on the picture, pulls down a little one.*

WILLMORE. This posture's loose and negligent,
The sight on't would beget a warm desire
In souls whom impotence and age had chilled.
This must along with me.

BRAVO. What means this rudeness, sir? Restore the picture.

ANTONIO. Ha! Rudeness committed to the fair Angellica! Restore the picture, sir—

WILLMORE. Indeed I will not, sir.

ANTONIO. By heaven, but you shall.

WILLMORE. Nay, do not show your sword; if you do, by this dear beauty—
I will show mine too.

ANTONIO. What right can you pretend to't?

WILLMORE. That of possession, which I will maintain—you perhaps have a thousand crowns to give for the original.

ANTONIO. No matter, sir, you shall restore the picture.

ANGELLICA *and* MORETTA *above.*

ANGELLICA. Oh Moretta! What's the matter?

ANTONIO. Or leave your life behind.

WILLMORE. Death! you lie—I will do neither.

They fight; the Spaniards join with ANTONIO; BLUNT *laying on like mad.*

ANGELLICA. Hold, I command you, if for me you fight.

They leave off and bow.

WILLMORE. How heavenly fair she is! Ah, plague of her price.

ANGELLICA. You sir, in buff, you that appear a soldier, that first began this insolence—

WILLMORE. 'Tis true, I did so, if you call it insolence for a man to preserve himself. I saw your charming picture and was wounded; quite through my soul each pointed beauty ran, and, wanting a thousand crowns to procure my remedy, I laid this little picture to my bosom—which if you cannot allow me, I'll resign.

ANGELLICA. No, you may keep the trifle.

ANTONIO. You shall first ask me leave, and this.

Fight again as before.

Enter BELVILE *and* FREDERICK *who join with the* ENGLISH.

ANGELLICA. Hold! Will you ruin me? Biskey—Sebastian—part 'em.

The SPANIARDS *are beaten off.*

MORETTA. Oh madam, we're undone. A pox upon that rude fellow, he's set on to ruin us; we shall never see good days till all these fighting poor rogues are sent to the galleys.[4]

Enter BELVILE, BLUNT, FREDERICK, *and* WILLMORE *with's shirt bloody.*

BLUNT. 'Sheartlikins, beat me at this sport, and I'll ne'er wear sword more.

BELVILE. The devil's in thee for a mad fellow; thou art always one at an unlucky adventure—come, let's begone whilst we're safe, and remember these are Spaniards, a sort of people that know how to revenge an affront.

FREDERICK. [*To* WILLMORE.] You bleed! I hope you are not wounded.

WILLMORE. Not much—a plague on your dons; if they fight no better they'll ne'er recover Flanders.[5] What the devil was't to them that I took down the picture?

BLUNT. Took it! 'Sheartlikins, we'll have the great one too; 'tis ours by conquest. Prithee help me up and I'll pull it down—

ANGELLICA. Stay sir, and ere you affront me farther, let me know how you durst commit this outrage—to you I speak, sir, for you appear a gentleman.

WILLMORE. To me, madam—gentlemen, your servant.

BELVILE *stays*[6] *him.*

BELVILE. Is the devil in thee? Dost know the danger of entering the house of an incensed courtesan?

WILLMORE. I thank you for your care—but there are other matters in hand, there are, though we have no great temptation. Death! Let me go.

FREDERICK. Yes, to your lodging if you will, but not in here. Damn these gay harlots—by this hand I'll have as sound and handsome a whore for a patacoon[7]—death, man, she'll murder thee.

WILLMORE. Oh! Fear me not, shall I not venture where a beauty calls? A lovely charming beauty! For fear of danger! When by Heaven there's none so great as to long for her whilst I want money to purchase her.

FREDERICK. Therefore 'tis loss of time unless you had the thousand crowns to pay.

WILLMORE. It may be she may give a favour; at least I shall have the pleasure of saluting her when I enter, and when I depart.

BELVILE. Pox, she'll as soon lie with thee as kiss thee, and sooner stab than do either—you shall not go.

ANGELLICA. Fear not sir, all I have to wound with is my eyes.

BLUNT. Let him go. 'Sheartlikins, I believe the gentlewoman means well.

BELVILE. Well, take thy fortune; we'll expect you in the next street—farewell, fool—farewell—

WILLMORE. Bye colonel—

Goes in.

FREDERICK. The rogue's stark mad for a wench.

Exeunt.

4. Punishment, from the fact that galleys (low ships) were propelled by oarsmen who were usually criminals.
5. Dons: Spaniards; ne'er recover Flanders: part of the Spanish Netherlands for more than half of the seventeenth century but ceded to France in 1659 as part of Spain's ongoing wars with France (and other European countries).
6. Stops.
7. Spanish coin.

Scene II. A fine Chamber.

Enter WILLMORE, ANGELLICA *and* MORETTA.

ANGELLICA. Insolent sir, how durst you pull down my picture?

WILLMORE. Rather, how durst you set it up, to tempt poor amorous mortals with so much excellence, which I find you have but too well consulted by the unmerciful price you set upon't. Is all this heaven of beauty shown to move despair in those that cannot buy? And can you think th'effects of that despair should be less extravagant than I have shown?

ANGELLICA. I sent for you to ask my pardon sir, not to aggravate your crime— I thought I should have seen you at my feet imploring it.

WILLMORE. You are deceived; I came to rail at you, and rail such truths too, as shall let you see the vanity of that pride which taught you how to set such price on sin. For such it is, whilst that which is love's due is meanly bartered for.

ANGELLICA. Ha! ha! ha! Alas, good captain, what pity 'tis your edifying doctrine will do no good upon me—Moretta! Fetch the gentleman a glass, and let him survey himself, to see what charms he has— [*Aside in a soft tone.*] and guess my business.

MORETTA. He knows himself of old; I believe those breeches and he have been acquainted ever since he was beaten at Worcester.[8]

ANGELLICA. Nay, do not abuse the poor creature—

MORETTA. Good weather-beaten corporal, will you march off? We have no need of your doctrine, though you have of our charity, but at present we have no scraps, we can afford no kindness for God's sake; in fine, sirrah, the price is too high i'th'mouth[9] for you, therefore troop, I say.

WILLMORE. Here, good forewoman of the shop, serve me, and I'll be gone.

MORETTA. Keep it to pay your laundress, your linen stinks of the gunroom; for here's no selling by retail.

WILLMORE. Thou hast sold plenty of thy stale ware at a cheap rate.

MORETTA. Ay, the more silly kind heart I, but this is an age wherein beauty is at higher rates. In fine, you know the price of this.

WILLMORE. I grant you 'tis here—set down a thousand crowns a month— pray, how much may come to my share for a pistole? Bawd, take your black lead[1] and sum it up, that I may have a pistole's worth of this vain gay thing, and I'll trouble you no more.

MORETTA. Pox on him, he'll fret me to death—abominable fellow, I tell thee, we only sell by the whole piece.

WILLMORE. 'Tis very hard, the whole cargo or nothing. Faith, madam, my stock will not reach it; I cannot be your chapman[2]—yet I have countrymen in town, merchants of love like me; I'll see if they'll put in for a share. We cannot lose much by it, and what we have no use for, we'll sell upon the Friday's mart at "Who gives more?" I am studying, madam, how to purchase you, though at present I am unprovided of money.

---

8. The Battle of Worcester, in 1651, was the final defeat of the English Prince Charles by the parliamentary forces.
9. Above one's rank.

1. Pistole: a gold coin; bawd: a woman who keeps a house of prostitution; black lead: pencil.
2. Merchant.

ANGELLICA. [*Aside.*] Sure, this from any other man would anger me—nor
shall he know the conquest he has made
—Poor angry man, how I despise this railing.

WILLMORE. Yes, I am poor—but I am a gentleman,
And one that scorns this baseness which you practice;
Poor as I am, I would not sell myself,
No, not to gain your charming high prized person.
Though I admire you strangely for your beauty,
Yet I contemn[3] your mind.
And yet I would at any rate enjoy you
At your own rate—but cannot. See here
The only sum I can command on earth;
I know not where to eat when this is gone.
Yet such a slave I am to love and beauty
This last reserve I'll sacrifice to enjoy you.
Nay, do not frown, I know you're to be bought,
And would be bought by me, by me,
For a mean trifling sum if I could pay it down;
Which happy knowledge I will still repeat,
And lay it to my heart; it has a virtue in't,
And soon will cure those wounds your eyes have made.
And yet—there's something so divincly powerful there—
Nay, I will gaze—to let you see my strength.

Holds her, looks on her, and pauses and sighs.

By heav'n, bright creature—I would not for the world
Thy fame were half so fair as is thy face.

Turns her away from him.

ANGELLICA. [*Aside.*] His words go through me to the very soul.
—If you have nothing else to say to me—

WILLMORE. Yes, you shall hear how infamous you are—
For which I do not hate thee—
But that secures my heart, and all the flames it feels
Are but so many lusts—
I know it by their sudden bold intrusion.
The fire's impatient and betrays, 'tis false—
For had it been the purer flame of love,
I should have pined and languished at your feet,
Ere found the impudence to have discovered it.
I now dare stand your scorn, and your denial.

MORETTA. Sure she's bewitched, that she can stand thus tamely and hear his
saucy railing—sirrah, will you be gone?

ANGELLICA. [*To* MORETTA.] How dare you take this liberty? Withdraw.
—Pray tell me, sir, are not you guilty of the same mercenary crime? When a lady
is proposed to you for a wife, you never ask how fair, discreet, or virtuous she is,

3. Have contempt for.

but what's her fortune—which if but small, you cry, "She will not do my business" and basely leave her, though she languish for you—say, is not this as poor?

WILLMORE. It is a barbarous custom, which I will scorn to defend in our sex, and do despise in yours.

ANGELLICA. Thou'rt a brave fellow! Put up thy[4] gold, and know,
That were thy fortune as large as thy soul,
Thou should'st not buy my love,
Couldst thou forget those mean effects of vanity
Which set me out to sale, and, as a lover, prize my yielding joys.
Canst thou believe they'll be entirely thine,
Without considering they were mercenary?

WILLMORE. I cannot tell, I must bethink me first. [Aside.]—Ha—death, I'm going to believe her.

ANGELLICA. Prithee confirm that faith—or if thou canst not—flatter me a little, 'twill please me from thy mouth.

WILLMORE. [Aside.] Curse on thy charming tongue! Dost thou return
My feigned contempt with so much subtlety?
—Thou'st found the easiest way into my heart,
Though I yet know that all thou say'st is false.

Turning from her in rage.

ANGELLICA. By all that's good, 'tis real;
I never loved before, though oft a mistress.
Shall my first vows be slighted?

WILLMORE. [Aside.] What can she mean?

ANGELLICA. [In an angry tone.] I find you cannot credit me.

WILLMORE. I know you take me for an errant ass,
An ass that may be soothed into belief
And then be used at pleasure;
But madam, I have been so often cheated
By perjured soft deluding hypocrites,
That I've no faith left for the cozening sex;
Especially for women of your trade.

ANGELLICA. The low esteem you have of me, perhaps
May bring my heart again:
For I have pride, that yet surmounts my love.

She turns with pride; he holds her.

WILLMORE. Throw off this pride, this enemy to bliss,
And show the pow'r of love; 'tis with those arms
I can be only vanquished, made a slave.

ANGELLICA. Is all my mighty expectation vanished?
No, I will not hear thee talk—thou hast a charm
In every word that draws my heart away.
And all the thousand trophies I designed
Thou hast undone—why art thou soft?
Thy looks are bravely rough, and meant for war.

4. Put away.

Could'st thou not storm on still?
I then perhaps had been as free as thou.

WILLMORE. [*Aside.*] Death, how she throws her fire about my soul!
—Take heed, fair creature, how you raise my hopes,
Which once assumed pretends to all dominion.
There's not a joy thou hast in store,
I shall not then command.
For which I'll pay thee back my soul, my life!
Come, let's begin th'account this happy minute!

ANGELLICA. And will you pay me then the price I ask?

WILLMORE. Oh, why dost thou draw me from an awful worship,
By showing thou art no divinity?
Conceal the fiend, and show me the angel!
Keep me but ignorant, and I'll be devout
And pay my vows for ever at this shrine.

Kneels and kisses her hand.

ANGELLICA. The pay I mean, is but thy love for mine.
Can you give that?

WILLMORE. Entirely—come, let's withdraw! Where I'll renew my vows—and
breathe 'em with such ardour thou shalt not doubt my zeal.

ANGELLICA. Thou has a pow'r too strong to be resisted.

Exeunt WILLMORE *and* ANGELLICA.

MORETTA. Now my curse go with you—is all our project fallen to this? To
love the only enemy to our trade? Nay, to love such a shameroon,[5] a very beggar,
nay a pirate beggar, whose business is to rifle, and be gone, a no-purchase, no-pay
tatterdemalion and English picaroon.[6] A rogue that fights for daily drink, and
takes a pride in being loyally lousy[7]—oh, I could curse now, if I durst. This is the
fate of most whores.
Trophies, which from believing fops we win,
Are spoils to those who cozen us again.

ACT III.

Scene I. A Street.

Enter FLORINDA, VALERIA, HELLENA, *in antic different dresses from what they
were in before.* CALLIS *attending.*

FLORINDA. I wonder what should make my brother in so ill a humour? I hope
he has not found out our ramble this morning.

HELLENA. No, if he had, we should have heard on't at both ears, and have
been mewed[8] up this afternoon; which I would not for the world should have happened—hey ho, I'm as sad as a lover's lute.

VALERIA. Well, methinks we have learnt this trade of gypsies as readily as if
we have been bred upon the road to Loreto;[9] and yet I did so fumble when I told

---

5. A fake or phony.
6. Tatterdemalion: a ragamuffin; picaroon: pirate, thief.
7. To have lice.
8. Caged.
9. A city in Italy famous as a place of pilgrimage.

the stranger his fortune, that I was afraid I should have told my own and yours by mistake—but methinks Hellena has been very serious ever since.

FLORINDA. I would give my garters she were in love, to be revenged upon her for abusing me—how is't, Hellena?

HELLENA. Ah—would I had never seen my mad monsieur—and yet for all your laughing, I am not in love—and yet this small acquaintance, o' my conscience, will never out of my head.

VALERIA. Ha, ha, ha—I laugh to think how thou art fitted with a lover, a fellow that I warrant loves every new face he sees.

HELLENA. Hum—he has not kept his word with me here—and may be taken up—that thought is not very pleasant to me—what the deuce should this be now, that I feel?

VALERIA. What is't like?

HELLENA. Nay, the lord knows—but if I should be hanged, I cannot choose but be angry and afraid when I think that mad fellow should be in love with any body but me—what to think of myself, I know not—would I could meet with some true damned gypsy, that I might know my fortune.

VALERIA. Know it! Why there's nothing so easy; thou wilt love this wandering inconstant till thou find'st thyself hanged about his neck, and then be as mad to get free again.

FLORINDA. Yes, Valeria, we shall see her bestride his baggage horse, and follow him to the campaign.

HELLENA. So, so, now you are provided for there's no care taken of poor me—but since you have set my heart a-wishing—I am resolved to know for what; I will not die of the pip,[1] so I will not.

FLORINDA. Art thou mad to talk so? Who will like thee well enough to have thee, that hears what a mad wench thou art?

HELLENA. Like me! I don't intend every he that likes me shall have me, but he that I like; I should have stayed in the nunnery still, if I had liked my lady Abbess as well as she liked me—no, I came thence not (as my wise brother imagines) to take an eternal farewell of the world, but to love and to be beloved, and I will be beloved, or I'll get one of your men, so I will.

VALERIA. Am I put into the number of lovers?

HELLENA. You? Why coz, I know thou'rt too good-natured to leave us in any design; thou would venture a cast, though thou comest off a loser, especially with such a gamester. I observe your man, and your willing ear incline that way; and if you are not a lover, 'tis an art soon learnt—that I find.

Sighs.

FLORINDA. I wonder how you learnt to love so easily; I had a thousand charms to meet my eyes and ears ere I could yield, and 'twas the knowledge of Belvile's merit, not the surprising person, took my soul—thou art too rash, to give a heart at first sight.

HELLENA. Hang your considering lover; I never thought beyond the fancy that 'twas a very pretty, idle, silly kind of pleasure to pass one's time with, to write little soft nonsensical billets,[2] and with great difficulty and danger receive answers in which I shall have my beauty praised, my wit admired, (though little or none) and

1. Depression, despondency.   2. Billets-doux (French), love notes.

have the vanity and power to know I am desirable; then I have the more inclination that way, because I am to be a nun, and so shall not be suspected to have any such earthly thoughts about me—but when I walk thus—and sigh thus—they'll think my mind's upon my monastery, and cry how happy 'tis she's so resolved. But not a word of man.

FLORINDA. What a mad creature's this?

HELLENA. I'll warrant, if my brother hears either of you sigh, he cries (gravely)—I fear you have the indiscretion to be in love, but take heed of the honour of our house, and your own unspotted fame, and so he conjures on till he has laid the soft-winged god in your hearts, or broke the bird's nest—but see, here comes your lover, but where's my inconstant? Let's step aside, and we may learn something.

Go aside.

Enter BELVILE, FREDERICK *and* BLUNT.

BELVILE. What means this! The picture's taken in.

BLUNT. It may be the wench is good-natured, and will be kind gratis. Your friend's a proper handsome fellow.

BELVILE. I rather think she has cut his throat and is fled: I am mad he should throw himself into dangers—pox on't, I shall want him too at night—let's knock and ask for him.

HELLENA. My heart goes a-pit a-pat, for fear 'tis my man they talk of.

Knock; MORETTA *above.*

MORETTA. What would you have!

BELVILE. Tell the stranger that entered here about two hours ago that his friends stay here for him.

MORETTA. A curse upon him for Moretta; would he were at the devil—but he's coming to you.

Enter WILLMORE.

HELLENA. Ay, ay, 'tis he! Oh how this vexes me.

BELVILE. And how and how dear lad, has fortune smiled? Are we to break her windows? Or raise up altars to her, hah?

WILLMORE. Does not my fortune sit triumphant on my brow? Dost not see the little wanton god there all gay and smiling? Have I not an air about my face and eyes that distinguish me from the crowd of common lovers? By heaven, Cupid's quiver has not half so many darts as her eyes! Oh, such a bona roba! To sleep in her arms is lying in fresco,[3] all perfumed air about me.

HELLENA. [*Aside.*] Here's fine encouragement for me to fool on.

WILLMORE. Harkee, where didst thou purchase that rich Canary we drank today! Tell me, that I may adore the spigot and sacrifice to the butt![4] The juice was divine into which I must dip my rosary, and then bless all things that I would have bold or fortunate.

BELVILE. Well sir, let's go take a bottle, and hear the story of your success.

3. Bona roba: courtesan; fresco: fresh air.   wine cask.
4. Canary: wine from the Canary Islands; butt:

FREDERICK. Would not French wine do better?

WILLMORE. Damn the hungry balderdash, cheerful sack[5] has a generous virtue in't inspiring a successful confidence; gives eloquence to the tongue, and vigour to the soul, and has in a few hours completed all my hopes and wishes! There's nothing left to raise a new desire in me—come let's be gay and wanton—and gentlemen, study, study what you want, for here are friends that will supply gentlemen—hark! What a charming sound they make—'tis he and she gold whilst here, and shall beget new pleasures every moment.

BLUNT. But harkee sir, you are not married, are you?

WILLMORE. All the honey of matrimony, but none of the sting, friend.

BLUNT. 'Sheartlikins, thou'rt a fortunate rogue!

WILLMORE. I am so sir, let these—inform you! Ha, how sweetly they chime! Pox of poverty, it makes a man a slave, makes wit and honour sneak, my soul grew lean and rusty for want of credit.

BLUNT. 'Sheartlikins, this I like well, it looks like my lucky bargain! Oh how I long for the approach of my squire, that is to conduct me to her house again. Why—here's two provided for.

FREDERICK. By this light y'are happy men.

BLUNT. Fortune is pleased to smile on us, gentlemen—to smile on us.

Enter SANCHO *and pulls down* BLUNT *by the sleeve.*

SANCHO. Sir, my lady expects you—

They go aside.

She has remov'd all that might oppose your will and pleasure—and is impatient till you come.

BLUNT. Sir, I'll attend you—oh, the happiest rogue! I'll take no leave, lest they either dog me, or stay me.

Exit with SANCHO.

BELVILE. But then the little gypsy is forgot?

WILLMORE. A mischief on thee for putting her into my thoughts. I had quite forgot her else, and this night's debauch had drunk her quite down.

HELLENA. Had it so, good captain!

Claps him on the back.

WILLMORE. [*Aside.*] Hah! I hope she did not hear me.

HELLENA. What, afraid of such a champion?

WILLMORE. Oh! you're a fine lady of your word, are you not? To make a man languish a whole day—

HELLENA. In tedious search of me.

WILLMORE. Egad child, thou'rt in the right; had'st thou seen what a melancholy dog I been ever since I was a lover, how I have walked the streets like a Capuchin[6] with my hands in my sleeves—faith, sweetheart, thou would'st pity me.

HELLENA. [*Aside.*] Now if I should be hanged I can't be angry with him, he dissembles so heartily

5. Balderdash: jumbled mixture of alcoholic beverages; sack: white wine from Spain and the Canary Islands.

6. A friar of the order of St. Francis.

—alas, good captain, what pains you have taken—now were I ungrateful not to reward so true a servant.

WILLMORE. Poor soul! That's kindly said; I see thou barest a conscience—come then, for a beginning show me thy dear face.

HELLENA. I'm afraid, my small acquaintance, you have been staying that swinging stomach you boasted this morning; I then remember my little collation[7] would have gone down with you, without the sauce of a handsome face—is your stomach so queasy now?

WILLMORE. Faith, long fasting, child, spoils a man's appetite—yet if you durst treat, I could so lay about me still—

HELLENA. And would you fall to, before a priest says grace?

WILLMORE. Oh fie, fie, what an old, out of fashioned thing hast thou named? Thou could'st not dash me more out of countenance should'st thou show me an ugly face.

Whilst he is seemingly courting HELLENA, *enter* ANGELLICA, MORETTA, BISKEY *and* SEBASTIAN, *all in masquerade;* ANGELLICA *sees* WILLMORE *and stares.*

ANGELLICA. Heavens 'tis he! And passionately fond to see another woman.

MORETTA. What could you less expect from such a swaggerer?

ANGELLICA. Expect! As much as I paid him, a heart entire
Which I had pride enough to think when ere I gave,
It would have raised the man above the vulgar,
Made him all soul, and that all soft and constant.

HELLENA. You see, captain, how willing I am to be friends with you, till time and ill luck make us lovers, and ask you the question first, rather than put your modesty to the blush by asking me (for alas!) I know you captains are such strict men, and such severe observers of your vows to chastity, that 'twill be hard to prevail with your tender conscience to marry a young willing maid.

WILLMORE. Do not abuse me, for fear I should take thee at thy word, and marry thee indeed, which I'm sure will be revenge sufficient.

HELLENA. O' my conscience, that will be our destiny, because we are both of one humour; I am as inconstant as you, for I have considered, captain, that a handsome woman has a great deal to do whilst her face is good, for then is our harvest-time to gather friends; and should I in these days of my youth catch a fit of foolish constancy, I were undone; 'tis loitering by daylight in our great journey. Therefore, I declare I'll allow but one year for love, one year for indifference, and one year for hate—and then—go hang yourself—for I profess myself the gay, the kind, and the inconstant—the devil's in't if this won't please you.

WILLMORE. Oh most damnably—I have a heart with a hole quite through it too; no prison mine to keep a mistress in.

ANGELLICA. [*Aside.*] Perjured man! How I believe thee now.

HELLENA. Well, I see our business as well as humours are alike; yours to cozen as many maids as will trust you, and I as many men as have faith—see if I have not as desperate a lying look as you can have for the heart of you.

Pulls off her vizard: he starts.

—How do you like it, captain?

7. Light meal.

WILLMORE. Like it! By heaven, I never saw so much beauty! Oh the charms of those sprightly black eyes! That strangely fair face, full of smiles and dimples! Those soft round melting cherry lips! And small even white teeth! Not to be expressed, but silently adored! Oh, one look more! And strike me dumb, or I shall repeat nothing else till I'm mad.

He seems to court her to pull off her vizard: she refuses.

ANGELLICA. I can endure no more—nor is it fit to interrupt him, for if I do, my jealousy has so destroyed my reason, I shall undo him—therefore I'll retire—[*To one of her bravoes.*] and you, Sebastian, follow that woman, and learn who 'tis; [*To the other bravo.*] while you tell the fugitive, I would speak to him instantly.

Exit.

This while FLORINDA *is talking to* BELVILE, *who stands sullenly.*
FREDERICK *courting* VALERIA.

VALERIA. Prithee, dear stranger, be not so sullen, for though you have lost your love, you see my friend frankly offers you hers to play with in the meantime.
BELVILE. Faith, madam, I am sorry I can't play at her game.
FREDERICK. Pray leave your intercession, and mind your own affair. They'll better agree apart; he's a modest sigher in company, but alone no woman scapes him.
FLORINDA. Sure he does but rally—yet if it should be true—I'll tempt him farther. Believe me, noble stranger, I'm no common mistress, and for a little proof on't wear this jewel—nay, take it, sir, 'tis right, and bills of exchange[8] may sometimes miscarry.
BELVILE. Madam, why am I chose out of all mankind to be the object of your bounty?
VALERIA. There's another civil question asked.
FREDERICK. Pox of's modesty, it spoils his own markets and hinders mine.
FLORINDA. Sir, from my window, I have often seen you, and women of my quality have so few opportunities for love, that we ought to lose none.
FREDERICK. Ay, this is something! Here's a woman! When shall I be blessed with so much kindness from your fair mouth?
[*Aside to* BELVILE]—Take the jewel, fool.
BELVILE. You tempt me strangely, madam, every way—
FLORINDA. [*Aside.*] So, if I find him false, my whole repose is gone.
BELVILE. And but for a vow I've made to a very fair lady, this goodness has subdued me.
FREDERICK. Pox on't, be kind, in pity to me be kind, for I am to thrive here but as you treat her friend.
HELLENA. Tell me what you did in yonder house, and I'll unmask.
WILLMORE. Yonder house—oh—I went to—a—to—why, there's a friend of mine lives there.
HELLENA. What, a she, or a he friend?
WILLMORE. A man, upon honour! A man—a she friend—no, no, madam, you have done my business I thank you.

---

8. Written promises of future payment.

HELLENA. And was't your man friend that had more darts in's eyes than Cupid carries in's whole budget[9] of arrows?

WILLMORE. So—

HELLENA. Ah, such a bona roba! To be in her arms is lying in fresco, all perfumed air about me—was this your man friend too?

WILLMORE. So—

HELLENA. That gave you the he and the she gold, that begets young pleasures?

WILLMORE. Well, well, madam, then you see there are ladies in the world that will not be cruel—there are, madam, there are—

HELLENA. And there be men too, as fine, wild, inconstant fellows as yourself, there be, captain, there be, if you go to that now—therefore I'm resolved—

WILLMORE. Oh!

HELLENA. To see your face no more—

WILLMORE. Oh!

HELLENA. Till tomorrow.

WILLMORE. Egad, you frighted me.

HELLENA. Nor then neither, unless you'll swear never to see that lady more.

WILLMORE. See her!—Why, never to think of womankind again.

HELLENA. Kneel—and swear—

Kneels, she gives him her hand.

WILLMORE. I do, never to think—to see—to love—nor lie—with any but thy self.

HELLENA. Kiss the book.

WILLMORE. Oh, most religiously.

Kisses her hand.

HELLENA. Now what a wicked creature am I, to damn a proper fellow.

CALLIS. [*To* FLORINDA.] Madam, I'll stay no longer, 'tis e'en dark.

FLORINDA. However sir, I'll leave this with you—that when I'm gone, you may repent the opportunity you have lost by your modesty.

Gives him the jewel which is her picture, and exits. He gazes after her.

WILLMORE. 'Twill be an age till tomorrow—and till then I will most impatiently expect you. Adieu, my dear pretty angel.

Exeunt all the WOMEN.

BELVILE. Ha! Florinda's picture—'twas she herself—what a dull dog was I! I would have given the world for one minute's discourse with her.

FREDERICK. This comes of your modesty! Ah, pox o' your vow, 'twas ten to one, but we had lost the jewel by't.

BELVILE. Willmore! The blessed'st opportunity lost! Florinda! Friends! Florinda!

WILLMORE. Ah rogue! Such black eyes! Such a face! Such a mouth! Such teeth! And so much wit!

BELVILE. All, all, and a thousand charms besides.

WILLMORE. Why, dost thou know her?

9. Leather bag.

BELVILE. Know her! Ay, ay, and a pox take me with all my heart for being modest.

WILLMORE. But harkee, friend of mine, are you my rival? And have I been only beating the bush all this while?

BELVILE. I understand thee not—I'm mad—see here—

Shows the picture.

WILLMORE. Ha! Whose picture's this? 'Tis a fine wench!

FREDERICK. The colonel's mistress, sir.

WILLMORE. Oh, oh, here—I thought't had been another prize—come, come, a bottle will set thee right again.

Gives the picture back.

BELVILE. I am content to try, and by that time 'twill be late enough for our design.

WILLMORE. Agreed.
Love does all day the soul's great empire keep
But wine at night lulls the soft god asleep.

Exeunt.

Scene II.
Lucetta's House.

Enter BLUNT and LUCETTA with a light.

LUCETTA. Now we are safe and free; no fears of the coming home of my old jealous husband, which made me a little thoughtful[1] when you came in first—but now love is all the business of my soul.

BLUNT. [*Aside*] I am transported! Pox on't, that I had but some fine things to say to her, such as lovers use—I was a fool not to learn of Frederick a little by heart before I came—something I must say—
—'Sheartlikins, sweet soul! I am not used to compliment, but I'm an honest gentleman, and thy humble servant.

LUCETTA. I have nothing to pay for so great a favour, but such a love as cannot but be great, since at first sight of that sweet face and shape, it made me your absolute captive.

BLUNT. Kind heart! How prettily she talks! [*Aside.*] Egad, I'll show her husband a Spanish trick; send him out of the world and marry her. She's damnably in love with me, and will ne'er mind settlements,[2] and so there's that saved.

LUCETTA. Well sir, I'll go and undress me, and be with you instantly.

BLUNT. Make haste then, for 'sheartlikins, dear soul, thou canst not guess at the pain of a longing lover, when his joys are drawn within the compass of a few minutes.

LUCETTA. You speak my sense, and I'll make haste to prove it.

Exit.

1. Anxious.
2. Financial arrangements that are part of a mar-   riage contract, a kind of prenuptial agreement.

BLUNT. 'Tis a rare girl! And this one night's enjoyment with her will be worth all the days I ever passed in Essex. Would she would go with me into England; though to say truth, there's plenty of whores already. But a pox on 'em, they are such mercenary—prodigal whores, that they want such a one as this that's free and generous to give 'em good examples. Why, what a house she has, how rich and fine!

Enter SANCHO.

SANCHO. Sir, my lady has sent me to conduct you to her chamber.

BLUNT. Sir, I shall be proud to follow—here's one of her servants too! 'Sheartlikins, by this garb and gravity, he might be a justice of peace in Essex, and is but a pimp here.

Exeunt.

Scene III

The scene changes to a chamber with an alcove bed in't, a table, etc.
LUCETTA *in bed. Enter* SANCHO *and* BLUNT, *who takes
the candle of* SANCHO *at the door.*

SANCHO. Sir, my commission reaches no farther.

BLUNT. Sir, I'll excuse your compliment—what, in bed my sweet mistress?

LUCETTA. You see, I still outdo you in kindness.

BLUNT. And thou shalt see what haste I'll make to quit scores—oh, the luckiest rogue!

He undresses himself.

LUCETTA. Should you be false or cruel now!

BLUNT. False! 'Sheartlikins, what dost thou take me for? A Jew? An insensible heathen? A pox of thy old jealous husband; an[3] he were dead, egad, sweet soul, it should be none of my fault if I did not marry thee.

LUCETTA. It never should be mine.

BLUNT. Good soul! I'm the fortunatest dog!

LUCETTA. Are you not undressed yet?

BLUNT. As much as my impatience will permit.

Goes toward the bed in his shirt, drawers, etc.

LUCETTA. Hold, sir, put out the light, it may betray us else.

BLUNT. Anything, I need no other light but that of thine eyes! 'Sheartlikins, there I think I had it.

Puts out the candle, the bed descends,[4] he gropes about to find it.

—Why—why—where am I got? What, not yet? Where are you sweetest? Ah, the rogue's silent now—a pretty love-trick this—how she'll laugh at me anon! You need not, my dear rogue! You need not! I'm all on fire already—come, come, now call me in pity. Sure I'm enchanted! I have been round the chamber, and can find neither woman, nor bed—I locked the door, I'm sure she cannot go that way—or if she could, the bed could not.

3. If.   4. The bed disappears through a trapdoor.

Enough, enough, my pretty wanton, do not carry the jest too far—[*Lights on a trap,*[5] *and is let down.*] Ha, betrayed! Dogs! Rogues! Pimps! Help! Help!

Enter LUCETTA, PHILLIPPO, *and* SANCHO *with a light.*

PHILLIPPO. Ha, ha, ha, he's dispatched finely.

LUCETTA. Now, sir, had I been coy, we had missed of this booty.

PHILLIPPO. Nay, when I saw't was a substantial fool, I was mollified; but when you dote upon a serenading coxcomb, upon a face, fine clothes, and a lute, it makes me rage.

LUCETTA. You know I was never guilty of that folly, my dear Phillippo, but with yourself—but come, let's see what we have got by this.

PHILLIPPO. A rich coat! Sword and hat—these breeches, too, are well lined— see here, a gold watch! A purse—ha! Gold! At least two hundred pistoles! A bunch of diamond rings! And one with the family arms! A gold box—with a medal of his king! And his lady mother's picture! These were sacred relics, believe me. See, the waistband of his breeches have a mine of gold! Old Queen Bess's, we have a quarrel to her ever since eighty-eight, and may therefore justify the theft; the Inquisition might have committed it.[6]

LUCETTA. See, a bracelet of bowed[7] gold! These his sisters tied about his arm at parting—but well—for all this, I fear his being a stranger may make a noise and hinder our trade with them hereafter.

PHILLIPPO. That's our security; he is not only a stranger to us, but to the country too—the common shore[8] into which he is descended, thou knowst conducts him into another street, which this light will hinder him from ever finding again— he knows neither your name, nor that of the street where your house is, nay nor the way to his own lodgings.

LUCETTA. And art not thou an unmerciful rogue! Not to afford him one night for all this? I should not have been such a Jew.

PHILLIPPO. Blame me not, Lucetta, to keep as much of thee as I can to myself—come, that thought makes me wanton! Let's to bed! Sancho, lock up these. This is the fleece which fools do bear
Designed for witty men to shear.

Exeunt.

Scene IV

The scene changes and discovers BLUNT,
creeping out of a common shore, his face, etc. all dirty.

BLUNT. Oh lord!

Climbing up.

I am got out at last, and (which is a miracle) without a clue[9]—and now to damning and cursing—but if that would ease me, where shall I begin? With my fortune, myself, or the quean that cozened me? What a dog was I to believe in woman! Oh

5. Trapdoor.
6. Queen Bess: Elizabeth I of England; since eighty-eight: in 1688 the English navy defeated the Spanish Armada as it advanced toward England.
7. Bent, curved.
8. Sewer.
9. Ball of thread used as a guide to exit a maze.

coxcomb! Ignorant conceited coxcomb! To fancy she could be enamoured with my person! At first sight enamoured! Oh, I'm a cursed puppy! 'Tis plain, "fool" was writ upon my forehead! She perceived it—saw the Essex calf there—for what allurements could there be in this countenance, which I can endure, because I'm acquainted with it—oh, dull silly dog! To be thus soothed into a cozening! Had I been drunk, I might fondly have credited the young quean:[1] But as I was in my right wits, to be thus cheated confirms it I am a dull, believing, English country fop—but my comrades! Death and the devil! There's the worst of all—then a ballad will be sung tomorrow on the prado,[2] to a lousy tune of "The Enchanted 'Squire, and the Annihilated Damsel"—but Frederick, that rogue, and the colonel, will abuse me beyond all Christian patience—had she left me my clothes, I have a bill of exchange at home would have saved my credit—but now all hope is taken from me—well, I'll home (if I can find the way) with this consolation, that I am not the first kind, believing coxcomb; but there are, gallants, many such good natures amongst ye.

And though you've better arts to hide your follies,
Adsheartlikins y'are all as errant cullies.[3]

Exit.

Scene V, the Garden in the Night

Enter FLORINDA *in an undress,[4] with a key and a little box.*

FLORINDA. Well, thus far I'm on my way to happiness. I have got myself free from Callis; my brother too, I find by yonder light, is got into his cabinet,[5] and thinks not of me; I have by good fortune got the key of the garden back-door. I'll open it to prevent Belvile's knocking—a little noise will now alarm my brother. Now am I as fearful as a young thief.

Unlocks the door.

Hark—what noise is that? Oh, 'twas the wind that played amongst the boughs—Belvile stays long, methinks—it's time—stay—for fear of a surprise. I'll hide these jewels in yonder jessamin.[6]

She goes to lay down the box.

Enter WILLMORE *drunk.*

WILLMORE. What the devil is become of these fellows, Belvile and Frederick? They promised to stay at the next corner for me, but who the devil knows the corner of a full moon—now—whereabouts am I? Hah—what have we here, a garden! A very convenient place to sleep in—hah—what has God sent us here! A female! By this light a woman! I'm a dog if it be not a very wench!

FLORINDA. He's come! Hah—who's there?

WILLMORE. Sweet soul! Let me salute thy shoe-string.

FLORINDA. 'Tis not my Belvile—good heavens! I know him not—who are you, and from whence come you?

1. Prostitute.
2. Field or lawn (Spanish).
3. Fools.
4. House dress.
5. Small private room.
6. Jasmine.

WILLMORE. Prithee—prithee child—not so many questions—let it suffice I am here, child—come, come kiss me.

FLORINDA. Good gods! What luck is mine?

WILLMORE. Only good luck, child, parlous[7] good luck—come hither—'tis a delicate shining wench—by this hand she's perfumed, and smells like any nosegay—prithee, dear soul, let's not play the fool, and lose time—precious time—for as gad shall save me, I'm as honest a fellow as breathes, though I'm a little disguised[8] at present—come I say. Why, thou may'st be free with me, I'll be very secret. I'll not boast who 'twas obliged me, not I—for hang me if I know thy name.

FLORINDA. Heavens! What a filthy beast is this?

WILLMORE. I am so, and thou ought'st the sooner to lie with me for that reason—for look you child, there will be no sin in't, because 'twas neither designed nor premeditated. 'Tis pure accident on both sides—that's a certain thing now. Indeed should I make love to you, and you vow fidelity—and swear and lie till you believed and yielded—that were to make it wilful fornication, the crying sin of the nation. Thou art therefore (as thou art a good Christian) obliged in conscience to deny me nothing. Now—come be kind without any more idle prating.

FLORINDA. Oh I am ruined—wicked man, unhand me.

WILLMORE. Wicked! Egad child, a judge, were he young and vigorous and saw those eyes of thine, would know 'twas they gave the first blow—the first provocation—come prithee, let's lose no time, I say—this is a fine convenient place.

FLORINDA. Sir, let me go, I conjure you, or I'll call out.

WILLMORE. Ay, ay, you were best to call witness to see how finely you treat me—do—

FLORINDA. I'll cry murder, rape, or anything if you do not instantly let me go.

WILLMORE. A rape! Come, come, you lie, you baggage, you lie. What, I'll warrant you would fain have the world believe now that you are not so forward as I. No, not you. Why, at this time of night, was your cobweb door set open, dear spider—but to catch flies? Hah—come—or I shall be damnably angry. Why, what a coil[9] is here—

FLORINDA. Sir, can you think—

WILLMORE. That you would do't for nothing—oh, oh, I find what you would be at—look here's a pistole for you—here's a work indeed—here—take it I say—

FLORINDA. For heavens sake, sir, as you're a gentleman—

WILLMORE. So—now—now—she would be wheedling me for more—what, you will not take it then—you are resolved you will not—come—come take it or I'll put it up again—for look ye, I never give more. Why how now, mistress, are you so high i'th'mouth a pistole won't down with you—hah—why, what a works here—in good time—come, no struggling to be gone—but an[1] y'are good at a dumb wrestle I'm for ye—look ye—I'm for ye—

She struggles with him.

Enter BELVILE *and* FREDERICK.

BELVILE. The door is open. A pox of this mad fellow; I'm angry that we've lost him; I durst have sworn he had followed us.

---

7. Extremely.
8. Drunk.

9. Noisy disturbance
1. If.

FREDERICK. But you were so hasty, colonel to be gone.

FLORINDA. Help! Help! Murder! Help—oh, I am ruined.

BELVILE. Ha! Sure that's Florinda's voice.

Comes up to them.

A man! Villain, let go that lady!

A noise. WILLMORE *turns and draws,* FREDERICK *interposes.*

FLORINDA. Belvile! Heavens! My brother too is coming, and 'twill be impossible to escape—Belvile, I conjure you to walk under my chamber window, from whence I'll give you some instructions what to do—this rude man has undone us.

Exit.

WILLMORE. Belvile!

Enter PEDRO, STEPHANO, *and other* SERVANTS *with lights.*

PEDRO. I'm betrayed! Run, Stephano, and see if Florinda be safe.

Exit STEPHANO.

So, whoe'er they be, all is not well. I'll to Florinda's chamber.

They fight and PEDRO's *party beats 'em out. Going out, meets* STEPHANO.

STEPHANO. You need not, sir; the poor lady's fast asleep and thinks no harm. I would not wake her sir, for fear of frighting her with your danger.

PEDRO. I'm glad she's there—rascals, how came the garden door open?

STEPHANO. That question comes too late, sir; some of my fellow servants masquerading, I'll warrant.

PEDRO. Masquerading! A lewd custom to debauch our youth—there's something more in this then, I imagine.

Exeunt.

Scene VI

Scene changes to the street.

Enter BELVILE *in rage,* FREDERICK *holding him, and* WILLMORE *melancholy.*

WILLMORE. Why, how the devil should I know Florinda?

BELVILE. A plague of your ignorance! If it had not been Florinda, must you be a beast? A brute? A senseless swine?

WILLMORE. Well, sir, you see I am endued[2] with patience—I can bear—though egad, y'are very free with me, methinks. I was in good hopes the quarrel would have been on my side, for so uncivilly interrupting me.

BELVILE. Peace, brute! Whilst thou'rt safe—oh, I'm distracted.

2. Equipped.

WILLMORE. Nay, nay, I'm an unlucky dog, that's certain.

BELVILE. Ah, curse upon the star that ruled my birth! Or whatsoever other influence that makes me still so wretched.

WILLMORE. Thou break'st my heart with these complaints. There is no star in fault, no influence but sack, the cursed sack I drunk.

FREDERICK. Why how the devil came you so drunk?

WILLMORE. Why how the devil came you so sober?

BELVILE. A curse upon his thin skull, he was always before hand that way.

FREDERICK. Prithee, dear colonel, forgive him, he's sorry for his fault.

BELVILE. He's always so after he has done a mischief—a plague on all such brutes.

WILLMORE. By this light, I took her for an errant harlot.

BELVILE. Damn your debauched opinion! Tell me sot, had'st thou so much sense and light about thee to distinguish her woman, and could'st not see something about her face and person, to strike an awful reverence into thy soul?

WILLMORE. Faith no, I considered her as mere a woman as I could wish.

BELVILE. 'Sdeath, I have no patience—draw, or I'll kill you.

WILLMORE. Let that alone till tomorrow, and if I set not all right again, use your pleasure.

BELVILE. Tomorrow! Damn it.
The spiteful light will lead me to no happiness.
Tomorrow is Antonio's, and perhaps
Guides him to my undoing—oh, that I could meet
This rival! This pow'rful fortunate!

WILLMORE. What then?

BELVILE. Let thy own reason, or my rage, instruct thee.

WILLMORE. I shall be finely informed then, no doubt; hear me, colonel—hear me—show me the man and I'll do his business.

BELVILE. I know him no more than thou, or if I did I should not need thy aid.

WILLMORE. This, you say, is Angellica's house. I promised the kind baggage to lie with her tonight.

Offers to go in.

Enter ANTONIO *and his* PAGE. ANTONIO *knocks on the hilt of's sword.*

ANTONIO. You paid the thousand crowns I directed?

PAGE. To the lady's old woman, sir, I did.

WILLMORE. Who the devil have we here!

BELVILE. I'll now plant myself under Florinda's window, and if I find no comfort there, I'll die.

Exeunt BELVILE *and* FREDERICK.

Enter MORETTA.

MORETTA. Page!

PAGE. Here's my lord.

WILLMORE. How is this! A picaroon going to board my frigate? Here's one chase gun for you.

Drawing his sword, justles³ ANTONIO *who turns and draws.*
They fight, ANTONIO *falls.*

MORETTA. Oh bless us! We're all undone!

Runs in and shuts the door.

PAGE. Help! Murder!

BELVILE *returns at the noise of the fighting.*

BELVILE. Ha! The mad rogue's engaged in some unlucky adventure again.

Enter two or three MASQUERADERS.

MASQUERADERS. Ha! A man killed!
WILLMORE. How! A man killed! Then I'll go home to sleep.

Puts up and reels out. Exeunt MASQUERADERS *another way.*

BELVILE. Who should it be! Pray heaven the rogue is safe, for all my quarrel
to him.

As BELVILE *is groping about, enter an* OFFICER *and six* SOLDIERS.

SOLDIER. Who's there?
OFFICER. So here's one dispatched—secure the murderer.

SOLDIERS *seize on* BELVILE.

BELVILE. Do not mistake my charity for murder!
I came to his assistance.
OFFICER. That shall be tried, sir—St. Jago,⁴ swords drawn in carnival time!

Goes to ANTONIO.

ANTONIO. Thy hand, prithee.
OFFICER. Ha! Don Antonio! Look well to the villain there. How is it, sir?
ANTONIO. I'm hurt.
BELVILE. Has my humanity made me a criminal?
OFFICER. Away with him.
BELVILE. What a cursed chance is this?

Exeunt SOLDIERS *with* BELVILE.

ANTONIO. [*To the* OFFICER.] This is the man that has set upon me twice—carry
him to my apartment, till you have farther orders from me.

Exit ANTONIO *led.*

_____

3. Jostles.   4. St. James.

ACT IV.

Scene I. A fine room.

Discovers BELVILE as by dark alone.

BELVILE. When shall I be weary of railing on fortune, who is resolved never to turn with smiles upon me? Two such defeats in one night—none but the devil and that mad rogue could have contrived to have plagued me with. I am here a prisoner—but where—heaven knows—and if there be murder done, I can soon decide the fate of a stranger in a nation without mercy. Yet this is nothing to the torture my soul bows with when I think of losing my fair, my dear, Florinda—hark—my door opens—a light—a man—and seems of quality—armed too! Now shall I die like a dog without defence.

Enter ANTONIO *in a nightgown with a light; his arm in a scarf, and a sword under his arm. He sets the candle on the table.*

ANTONIO. Sir, I come to know what injuries I have done you that could provoke you to so mean an action as to attack me basely, without allowing time for my defence?

BELVILE. Sir, for a man in my circumstances to plead innocence would look like fear—but view me well, and you will find no marks of coward on me; nor anything that betrays that brutality you accuse me with.

ANTONIO. In vain, sir, you impose upon my sense.
You are not only he who drew on me last night,
But yesterday before the same house, that of Angellica.
Yet there is something in your face and mien
That makes me wish I were mistaken.

BELVILE. I own I fought today in the defence of a friend of mine, with whom you (if you're the same) and your party were first engaged.
Perhaps you think this crime enough to kill me,
But if you do, I cannot fear you'll do it basely.

ANTONIO. No, sir, I'll make you fit for a defence with this.

Gives him the sword.

BELVILE. This gallantry surprises me—nor know I how to use this present, sir, against a man so brave.

ANTONIO. You shall not need.
For know, I come to snatch you from a danger
That is decreed against you;
Perhaps your life, or long imprisonment;
And 'twas with so much courage you offended,
I cannot see you punished.

BELVILE. How shall I pay this generosity?

ANTONIO. It had been safer to have killed another
Than have attempted me.
To show your danger, sir, I'll let you know my quality;
And 'tis the viceroy's son whom you have wounded.

BELVILE. [*Aside.*] The viceroy's son!
Death and confusion! Was this plague reserved

To complete all the rest? Obliged by him!
The man of all the world I would destroy.

    ANTONIO. You seem disordered, sir.

    BELVILE. Yes, trust me sir, I am, and 'tis with pain
That man receives such bounties,
Who wants the pow'r to pay 'em back again.

    ANTONIO. To gallant spirits 'tis indeed uneasy;
But you may quickly overpay me, sir.

    BELVILE. Then I am well.
[*Aside.*] Kind heav'n, but set us even,
That I may fight with him and keep my honour safe.
—Oh, I'm impatient, sir, to be discounting the mighty debt I owe you; command
me quickly—

    ANTONIO. I have a quarrel with a rival, sir,
About the maid we love.

BELVILE. [*Aside.*] Death, 'tis Florinda he means—
That thought destroys my reason,
And I shall kill him—

    ANTONIO. My rival, sir,
Is one has all the virtues man can boast of.

    BELVILE. [*Aside.*] Death! Who should this be?

    ANTONIO. He challenged me to meet him on the Molo
As soon as day appeared; but last night's quarrel
Has made my arm unfit to guide a sword.

    BELVILE. I apprehend[5] you, sir; you'd have me kill the man
That lays a claim to the maid you speak of.
I'll do't—I'll fly to do't!

    ANTONIO. Sir, do you know her?

    BELVILE. No, sir, but 'tis enough she is admired by you.

    ANTONIO. Sir, I shall rob you of the glory on't,
For you must fight under my name and dress.

    BELVILE. That opinion must be strangely obliging that makes
You think I can personate the brave Antonio,
Whom I can but strive to imitate.

    ANTONIO. You say too much to my advantage.
Come, sir, the day appears that calls you forth.
Within, sir, is the habit.

Exit ANTONIO.

    BELVILE. Fantastic fortune, thou deceitful light,
That cheats the wearied traveller by night,
Though on a precipice each step you tread,
I am resolved to follow where you lead.

Exit.

5. Understand.

Scene II, The Molo.

Enter FLORINDA *and* CALLIS *in masks with* STEPHANO.

FLORINDA. [*Aside.*] I'm dying with my fears; Belvile's not coming as I expected under my window, makes me believe that all those fears are true.
—Canst thou not tell with whom my brother fights?

STEPHANO. No, madam, they were both in masquerade. I was by when they challenged one another, and they had decided the quarrel then, but were prevented by some cavaliers, which made 'em put it off till now—but I am sure 'tis about you they fight.

FLORINDA. [*Aside.*] Nay, then 'tis with Belvile, for what other lover have I that dares fight for me, except Antonio? And he is too much in favour with my brother. If it be he, for whom shall I direct my prayers to heaven?

STEPHANO. Madam, I must leave you, for if my master see me, I shall be hanged for being your conductor. I escaped narrowly for the excuse I made for you last night i'th'garden.

FLORINDA. And I'll reward thee for't—prithee no more.

Exit STEPHANO.

Enter DON PEDRO *in his masquing habit.*

PEDRO. Antonio's late today; the place will fill, and we may be prevented.

Walks about.

FLORINDA. [*Aside.*] "Antonio"—sure I heard amiss.

PEDRO. But who will not excuse a happy lover
When soft fair arms confine the yielding neck,
And the kind whisper languishingly breathes,
"Must you begone so soon?"
Sure I had dwelt for ever on her bosom.
But stay, he's here.

Enter BELVILE *dressed in* ANTONIO's *clothes.*

FLORINDA. 'Tis not Belvile; half my fears are vanisht.

PEDRO. Antonio!

BELVILE. [*Aside.*] This must be he.
—You're early, sir—I do not use to be outdone this way.

PEDRO. The wretched, sir, are watchful, and 'tis enough
You've the advantage of me in Angellica.

BELVILE. [*Aside.*] Angellica! Or I've mistook my man or else Antonio.
Can he forget his interest in Florinda,
And fight for common prize?

PEDRO. Come, sir, you know our terms—

BELVILE. [*Aside.*] By heav'n not I.
—No talking, I am ready, sir.

Offers to fight, FLORINDA *runs in.*

FLORINDA. [*To* BELVILE.] Oh hold! Whoe'er you be, I do conjure you hold!
If you strike here—I die.

PEDRO. Florinda!

BELVILE. Florinda imploring for my rival!

PEDRO. Away, this kindness is unreasonable.

Puts her by; they fight; she runs in just as BELVILE *disarms* PEDRO.

FLORINDA. Who are you, sir, that dares deny my prayers?

BELVILE. Thy prayers destroy him; if thou would'st preserve him,
Do that thou'rt unacquainted with and curse him.

She holds him.

FLORINDA. By all you hold most dear, by her you love,
I do conjure you, touch him not.

BELVILE. By her I love!
See—I obey—and at your feet resign
The useless trophy of my victory.

Lays his sword at her feet.

PEDRO. Antonio, you've done enough to prove you love Florinda.

BELVILE. Love Florinda!
Does heav'n love adoration, prayer or penitence! Love her! Here, sir—your sword
again.

Snatches up the sword and gives it him.

Upon this truth I'll fight my life away.

PEDRO. No, you've redeemed my sister, and my friendship!

He gives him FLORINDA *and pulls off his vizard to show his face
and puts it on again.*

BELVILE. Don Pedro!

PEDRO. Can you resign your claims to other women,
And give your heart entirely to Florinda?

BELVILE. Entire as dying saints' confessions are.
I can delay my happiness no longer.
This minute let me make Florinda mine!

PEDRO. This minute let it be—no time so proper.
This night my father will arrive from Rome,
And possibly may hinder what we purpose!

FLORINDA. Oh heavens! This minute!

Enter MASQUERADERS *and pass over.*

BELVILE. Oh, do not ruin me!

PEDRO. The place begins to fill, and that we may not be observed, do you walk
off to St. Peter's church, where I will meet you, and conclude your happiness.

BELVILE. I'll meet you there.

[*Aside.*]—If there be no more saints' churches in Naples.

FLORINDA. Oh, stay sir, and recall your hasty doom!
Alas, I have not yet prepared my heart
To entertain so strange a guest.

PEDRO. Away, this silly modesty is assumed too late.

BELVILE. Heaven, madam! What do you do?

FLORINDA. Do! Despise the man that lays a tyrant's claim
To what he ought to conquer by submission.

BELVILE. You do not know me—move a little this way.

Draws her aside.

FLORINDA. Yes, you may force me even to the altar,
But not the holy man that offers there
Shall force me to be thine.

PEDRO talks to CALLIS this while.

BELVILE. Oh do not lose so blest an opportunity—
See—'tis your Belvile—not Antonio,
Whom your mistaken scorn and anger ruins.

Pulls off his vizard.

FLORINDA. Belvile!
Where was my soul it could not meet thy voice
And take this knowledge in?

As they are talking, enter WILLMORE, finely dressed, and FREDERICK.

WILLMORE. No intelligence, no news of Belvile yet—well, I am the most unlucky rascal in nature—ha—am I deceived? Or is it he? Look Fred—'tis he—my
dear Belvile!

Runs and embraces him. BELVILE's vizard falls out on's hand.

BELVILE. Hell and confusion seize thee!

PEDRO. Ha! Belvile! I beg your pardon sir.

Takes FLORINDA from him.

BELVILE. Nay, touch her not. She's mine by conquest, sir;
I won her by my sword.

WILLMORE. Did'st thou so—and egad, child, we'll keep her by the sword.

Draws on PEDRO. BELVILE goes between.

BELVILE. Stand off!
Thou'rt so profanely lewd, so curst by heaven,
All quarrels thou espousest must be fatal.

WILLMORE. Nay, an you be so hot, my valour's coy, and shall be courted when
you want it next.

Puts up his sword.

BELVILE. [*To* PEDRO.] You know I ought to claim a victor's right.
But you're the brother to divine Florinda,
To whom I'm such a slave—to purchase her,
I durst not hurt the man she holds so dear.

PEDRO. 'Twas by Antonio's, not by Belvile's sword

This question should have been decided, sir.
I must confess, much to your bravery's due,
Both now, and when I met you last in arms.
But I am nicely punctual in my word,
As men of honour ought, and beg your pardon.
For this mistake another time shall clear.

Aside to FLORINDA *as they are going out.*

This was some plot between you and Belvile.
But I'll prevent you.

BELVILE *looks after her and begins to walk up and down in rage.*

WILLMORE. Do not be modest now and lose the woman, but if we shall fetch her back so—

BELVILE. Do not speak to me—

WILLMORE. Not speak to you—egad, I'll speak to you, and will be answered, too.

BELVILE. Will you, sir—

WILLMORE. I know I've done some mischief, but I'm so dull a puppy, that I'm the son of a whore if I know how, or where—prithee inform my understanding—

BELVILE. Leave me, I say, and leave me instantly.

WILLMORE. I will not leave you in this humour, nor till I know my crime.

BELVILE. Death, I'll tell you sir—

Draws and runs at WILLMORE. *He runs out,* BELVILE *after him;*
FREDERICK *interposes.*

Enter ANGELLICA, MORETTA *and* SEBASTIAN.

ANGELLICA. Ha—Sebastian—
Is not that Willmore? Haste—haste and bring him back.

FREDERICK. The colonel's mad—I never saw him thus before. I'll after 'em lest he do some mischief, for I am sure Willmore will not draw on him.

Exit.

ANGELLICA. I am all rage! My first desires defeated!
For one for aught he knows that has no
Other merit than her quality,
Her being Don Pedro's sister—he loves her!
I know 'tis so—dull, dull, insensible—
He will not see me now though oft invited,
And broke his word last night—false perjured man!
He that but yesterday fought for my favours,
And would have made his life a sacrifice
To've gained one night with me,
Must now be hired and courted to my arms.

MORETTA. I told you what would come on't, but Moretta's an old doting fool. Why did you give him five hundred crowns, but to set himself out for other lovers? You should have kept him poor if you had meant to have had any good from him.

ANGELLICA. Oh, name not such mean trifles—had I given him all
My youth has earned from sin,
I had not lost a thought, nor sigh upon't.
But I have given him my eternal rest,
My whole repose, my future joys, my heart!
My virgin heart, Moretta! Oh, 'tis gone!
    MORETTA. Curse on him, here he comes;
How fine she has made him too.

Enter WILLMORE *and* SEBASTIAN; ANGELLICA *turns and walks away.*

WILLMORE. How now, turned shadow!
Fly when I pursue and follow when I fly!

Sings.

Stay, gentle shadow of my dove
And tell me ere I go,
Whether the substance may not prove
A fleeting thing like you.

There's a soft kind look remaining yet.

As she turns she looks on him.

ANGELLICA. Well sir, you may be gay; all happiness, all joys, pursue you still.
Fortune's your slave, and gives you every hour choice of new hearts and beauties,
till you are cloyed with the repeated bliss which others vainly languish for.
[*Aside.*] But know, false man, that I shall be revenged.

Turns away in rage.

WILLMORE. So, gad, there are of those faint-hearted lovers, whom such a
sharp lesson next their hearts would make as impotent as fourscore. Pox o' this
whining. My business is to laugh and love. A pox on't—I hate your sullen lover.
A man shall lose as much time to put you in humour now, as would serve to gain
a new woman.
    ANGELLICA. I scorn to cool that fire I cannot raise,
Or do the drudgery of your virtuous mistress.
    WILLMORE. A virtuous mistress! Death, what a thing thou hast found out for
me. Why, what the devil should I do with a virtuous woman? A sort of ill-natured
creatures, that take a pride to torment a lover. Virtue is but an infirmity in woman,
a disease that renders even the handsome ungrateful; whilst the ill-favoured, for
want of solicitations and address, only fancy themselves so. I have lain with a
woman of quality, who has all the while been railing at whores.
    ANGELLICA. I will not answer for your mistress's virtue,
Though she be young enough to know no guilt;
And I could wish you would persuade my heart
'Twas the two hundred thousand crowns you courted.
    WILLMORE. Two hundred thousand crowns! What story's this? What trick?
What woman? Ha!
    ANGELLICA. How strange you make it; have you forgot the creature you en-
tertained on the piazza last night?

WILLMORE. [*Aside.*] Ha! My gypsy worth two hundred thousand crowns? Oh, how I long to be with her—pox, I knew she was of quality.

ANGELLICA. False man! I see my ruin in thy face.
How many vows you breathed upon my bosom,
Never to be unjust—have you forgot so soon?

WILLMORE. Faith no, I was just coming to repeat 'em—but here's a humour indeed would make a man a saint. [*Aside.*]—Would she would be angry enough to leave me, and command me not to wait on her.

Enter HELLENA *dressed in man's clothes.*

HELLENA. [*Aside.*] This must be Angellica! I know it by her mumping[6] matron here. Ay, ay, 'tis she! My mad captain's with her too, for all his swearing—how this unconstant humour makes me love him!
—Pray, good grave gentlewoman, is not this Angellica?

MORETTA. My too young sir, it is—[*Aside.*] I hope 'tis one from Don Antonio.

Goes to ANGELLICA.

HELLENA. [*Aside.*] Well, something I'll do to vex him for this.

ANGELLICA. I will not speak with him; am I in humour to receive a lover?

WILLMORE. Not speak with him! Why I'll be gone and wait your idler minutes—can I show less obedience to the thing I love so fondly?

Offers to go.

ANGELLICA. A fine excuse this! Stay—

WILLMORE. And hinder your advantage! Should I repay your bounties so ungratefully?

ANGELLICA. Come hither, boy—that I may let you see
How much above the advantages you name
I prize one minute's joy with you.

WILLMORE. Oh, you destroy me with this endearment.

Impatient to be gone.

Death! How shall I get away? Madam, 'twill not be fit I should be seen with you—besides, it will not be convenient—and I've a friend—that's dangerously sick.

ANGELLICA. I see you're impatient—yet you shall stay.

WILLMORE. [*Aside, and walks about impatiently.*] And miss my assignation with my gypsy.

HELLENA. Madam,

MORETTA *brings* HELLENA, *who addresses herself to* ANGELLICA.

You'll hardly pardon my intrusion
When you shall know my business,
And I'm too young to tell my tale with art;
But there must be a wondrous store of goodness,
Where so much beauty dwells.

ANGELLICA. A pretty advocate, whoever sent thee.

6. Mumbling, sullen.

Prithee proceed—[*To* WILLMORE, *who is stealing off.*]—nay, sir, you shall not go.

WILLMORE. [*Aside,*] Then I shall lose my dear gypsy for ever—pox on't, she stays me out of spite.

HELLENA. I am related to a lady, madam,
Young, rich, and nobly born, but has the fate
To be in love with a young English gentleman.
Strangely she loves him, at first sight she loved him,
But did adore him when she heard him speak;
For he, she said, had charms in every word,
That failed not to surprise, to wound and conquer.

WILLMORE. [*Aside.*] Ha! Egad, I hope this concerns me.

ANGELLICA. [*Aside.*] 'Tis my false man, he means—would he were gone.
This praise will raise his pride, and ruin me—[*To* WILLMORE] Well
Since you are so impatient to be gone
I will release you, sir.

WILLMORE. [*Aside.*] Nay, then, I'm sure 'twas me he spoke of; this cannot be the effects of kindness in her.
—No, madam, I've considered better on't, and will not give you cause of jealousy.

ANGELLICA. But, sir, I've—business, that—

WILLMORE. This shall not do; I know 'tis but to try me.

ANGELLICA. Well, to your story, boy—[*Aside.*] though 'twill undo me.

HELLENA. With this addition to his other beauties,
He won her unresisting tender heart.
He vowed, and sighed, and swore he loved her dearly;
And she believed the cunning flatterer,
And thought herself the happiest maid alive.
Today was the appointed time by both
To consummate their bliss,
The virgin, altar, and the priest were dressed
And whilst she languished for th'expected bridegroom,
She heard he paid his broken vows to you.

WILLMORE. So, this is some dear rogue that's in love with me, and this way lets me know it; or if it be not me, he means someone whose place I may supply.

ANGELLICA. Now I perceive
The cause of thy impatience to be gone,
And all the business of this glorious dress.

WILLMORE. Damn the young prater,[7] I know not what he means.

HELLENA. Madam,
In your fair eyes I read too much concern,
To tell my farther business.

ANGELLICA. Prithee, sweet youth, talk on, thou mayest perhaps
Raise here a storm that may undo my passion,
And then I'll grant thee anything.

HELLENA. Madam, 'tis to entreat you (oh unreasonable),
You would not see this stranger;
For if you do, she vows you are undone,

---

7. One who talks foolishly (prates).

Though nature never made a man so excellent,
And sure he'ad been a god, but for inconstancy.

    WILLMORE. [*Aside.*] Ah, rogue, how finely he's instructed!
—'Tis plain; some woman that has seen me *en passant*.[8]

    ANGELLICA. Oh, I shall burst with jealousy! Do you know the man you
speak of?

    HELLENA. Yes, madam, he used to be in buff and scarlet.

    ANGELLICA. [*To* WILLMORE.] Thou, false as hell, what canst thou say to this?

    WILLMORE. By heaven—

    ANGELLICA. Hold, do not damn thyself—

    HELLENA. Nor hope to be believed.

He walks about, they follow.

    ANGELLICA. Oh perjured man!
Is't thus you pay my generous passion back?

    HELLENA. Why would you, sir, abuse my lady's faith?

    ANGELLICA. And use me so unhumanely.

    HELLENA. A maid so young, so innocent—

    WILLMORE. Ah, young devil.

    ANGELLICA. Dost thou know thy life is in my power?

    HELLENA. Or think my lady cannot be revenged?

    WILLMORE [*Aside.*] So, so, the storm comes finely on.

    ANGELLICA. Now thou art silent, guilt has struck thee dumb.
Oh, hadst thou still been so, I'd lived in safety.

She turns away and weeps.

    WILLMORE. [*Aside to* HELLENA; *looks toward* ANGELLICA *to watch her turning
and as she comes towards them he meets her.*] Sweetheart, the lady's name and
house—quickly, I'm impatient to be with her.

    HELLENA. [*Aside.*] So, now is he for another woman.

    WILLMORE. The impudentest young thing in nature,
I cannot persuade him out of his error, madam.

    ANGELLICA. I know he's in the right—yet thou'st a tongue
That would persuade him to deny his faith.

In rage walks away.

    WILLMORE. Her name, her name, dear boy—

Said softly to HELLENA.

    HELLENA. Have you forgot it, sir?

    WILLMORE. [*Aside.*] Oh, I perceive he's not to know I am a stranger to this lady.
—Yes, yes, I do know—but I have forgot the—

ANGELLICA *turns.*

—By heaven such early confidence I never saw.

    ANGELLICA. Did I not charge you with this mistress, sir?

8. In passing (French).

Which you denied, though I beheld your perjury.
This little generosity of thine, has rendered back my heart.

Walks away.

WILLMORE. So, you have made sweet work here, my little mischief; look your
lady be kind and good-natured now, or I shall have but a cursed bargain on't.

ANGELLICA *turns toward them.*

—The rogue's bred up to mischief;
Art thou so great a fool to credit him?

ANGELLICA. Yes, I do, and you in vain impose upon me.
Come hither, boy—is not this he you spake of?

HELLENA. I think—it is; I cannot swear, but I vow he has just such another
lying lover's look.

HELLENA *looks in his face, he gazes on her.*

WILLMORE. Hah! Do not I know that face—
[*Aside.*] By heaven, my little gypsy; what a dull dog was I,
Had I but looked that way I'd known her.
Are all my hopes of a new woman banished?
—Egad, if I do not fit[9] thee for this, hang me.
—Madam, I have found out the plot.

HELLENA. [*Aside.*] Oh lord, what does he say? Am I discovered now?

WILLMORE. Do you see this young spark here?

HELLENA. [*Aside.*] He'll tell her who I am.

WILLMORE. Who do you think this is?

HELLENA. [*Aside.*] Ay, ay, he does know me—
Nay, dear captain! I am undone if you discover me.

WILLMORE. Nay, nay, no cogging;[1] she shall know what a precious mistress I have.

HELLENA. Will you be such a devil?

WILLMORE. [*Aside.*] Nay, nay, I'll teach you to spoil sport you will not make.
—This small ambassador comes not from a person of quality as you imagine, and
he says, but from a very errant gypsy, the talkingest, pratingest, cantingest little
animal thou ever saw'st.

ANGELLICA. What news you tell me, that's the thing I mean.

HELLENA. [*Aside.*] Would I were well off the place; if ever I go a captain-
hunting again—

WILLMORE. Mean that thing? That gypsy thing? Thou may'st as well be jealous of thy monkey or parrot, as of her; a German motion[2] were worth a dozen of
her, and a dream were a better enjoyment, a creature of a constitution fitter for
heaven than man.

HELLENA. [*Aside.*] Though I'm sure he lies, yet this vexes me.

ANGELLICA. You are mistaken, she's a Spanish woman
Made up of no such dull materials.

WILLMORE. Materials, egad an thee be made of any that will either dispense
or admit of love, I'll be bound to continence.

HELLENA. [*Aside to him.*] Unreasonable man, do you think so?

9. Pay back.   2. Puppet.
1. Begging.

WILLMORE. You may return, my little brazen head, and tell your lady that till she be handsome enough to be beloved, or I dull enough to be religious, there will be small hopes of me.

ANGELLICA. Did you not promise then to marry her?

WILLMORE. Not I, by heaven.

ANGELLICA. You cannot undeceive my fears and torments, till you have vowed you will not marry her.

HELLENA. [*Aside.*] If he swears that, he'll be revenged on me indeed for all my rogueries.

ANGELLICA. I know what arguments you'll bring up against me—fortune, and honour—

WILLMORE. Honour, I tell you, I hate it in your sex, and those that fancy themselves possessed of that foppery are the most impertinently troublesome of all womankind, and will transgress nine commandments to keep one, and to satisfy your jealousy, I swear.

HELLENA. [*Aside to him.*] Oh, no swearing, dear captain.

WILLMORE. If it were possible I should ever be inclined to marry, it should be some kind young sinner, one that has generosity enough to give a favour handsomely to one that can ask it discreetly, one that has wit enough to manage an intrigue of love—oh, how civil such a wench is, to a man that does her the honour to marry her.

ANGELLICA. By heaven, there's no faith in anything he says.

Enter SEBASTIAN.

SEBASTIAN. Madam, Don Antonio—

ANGELLICA. Come hither.

HELLENA. [*Aside.*] Ha! Antonio! He may be coming hither and he'll certainly discover me; I'll therefore retire without a ceremony.

Exit HELLENA.

ANGELLICA. I'll see him; get my coach ready.

SEBASTIAN. It waits you, madam.

WILLMORE. This is lucky. What, madam, now I may be gone and leave you to the enjoyment of my rival?

ANGELLICA. Dull man, that can'st not see how ill, how poor,
That false dissimulation looks—begone,
And never let me see thy cozening face again,
Lest I relapse and kill thee.

WILLMORE. Yes, you can spare me now—farewell, till you're in better humour—I'm glad of this release—
[*Aside*] Now for my gypsy:
For though to worse we change, yet still we find
New joys, new charms, in a new miss that's kind.

Exit WILLMORE.

ANGELLICA. He's gone, and in this ague[3] of my soul,
The shivering fit returns;

3. Violent fever.

Oh, with what willing haste he took his leave,
As if the longed-for minute were arrived
Of some blest assignation.
In vain I have consulted all my charms,
In vain this beauty prized, in vain believed
My eyes could kindle any lasting fires.
I had forgot my name, my infamy,
And the reproach that honour lays on those
That dare pretend a sober passion here.
Nice reputation, though it leave behind
More virtues than inhabit where that dwells,
Yet that once gone, those virtues shine no more.
Then since I am not fit to be beloved,
I am resolved to think on a revenge
On him that soothed me thus to my undoing.

Exeunt.

Scene III: A Street.

Enter FLORINDA *and* VALERIA *in habits different from that
they have been seen in.*

FLORINDA. We're happily escaped, and yet I tremble still.

VALERIA. Lover, and fear! Why, I am but half an one, and yet I have courage for any attempt. Would Hellena were here, I would fain have had her as deep in this mischief as we; she'll fare but ill else, I doubt.

FLORINDA. She pretended a visit to the Augustine nuns,[4] but I believe some other design carried her out; pray heaven we light on her. Prithee what did'st do with Callis?

VALERIA. When I saw no reason would do good on her, I followed her into the wardrobe,[5] and as she was looking for something in a great chest, I toppled her in by the heels, snatched the key of the apartment where you were confined, locked her in, and left her bawling for help.

FLORINDA. 'Tis well you resolve to follow my fortunes, for thou darest never appear at home again after such an action.

VALERIA. That's according as the young stranger and I shall agree. But to our business—I delivered your letter, your note to Belvile, when I got out under pretence of going to mass. I found him at his lodging, and believe me it came seasonably, for never was a man in so desperate a condition. I told him of your resolution of making your escape today if your brother would be absent long enough to permit you; if not, to die rather than be Antonio's.

FLORINDA. Thou should'st have told him I was confined to my chamber upon my brother's suspicion that the business on the Molo was a plot laid between him and I.

VALERIA. I said all this, and told him your brother was now gone to his devotions, and he resolves to visit every church till he find him; and not only undeceive him in that, but caress him so as shall delay his return home.

---

4. Nuns of the order of St. Augustine.   5. Dressing room.

FLORINDA. Oh heavens! He's here, and Belvile with him too.

They put on their vizards.

Enter DON PEDRO, BELVILE, WILLMORE; BELVILE *and* DON PEDRO
seeming in serious discourse.

VALERIA. Walk boldly by them, and I'll come at distance, lest he suspect us.

She walks by them, and looks back on them.

WILLMORE. Hah! A woman, and of an excellent mien.

PEDRO. She throws a kind look back on you.

WILLMORE. Death, 'tis a likely wench, and that kind look shall not be cast away—I'll follow her.

BELVILE. Prithee do not.

WILLMORE. Do not; by heavens, to the antipodes[6] with such an invitation.

She goes out, and WILLMORE *follows her.*

BELVILE. 'Tis a mad fellow for a wench.

Enter FREDERICK.

FREDERICK. Oh colonel, such news!

BELVILE. Prithee, what?

FREDERICK. News that will make you laugh in spite of fortune.

BELVILE. What, Blunt has had some damned trick put upon him—cheated, banged or clapped?[7]

FREDERICK. Cheated sir, rarely cheated of all but his shirt and drawers. The unconscionable whore, too, turned him out before consummation, so that traversing the streets at midnight, the watch found him in this fresco, and conducted him home. By heaven, 'tis such a sight, and yet I durst as well been hanged as laugh at him or pity him; he beats all that do but ask him a question, and is in such an humour.

PEDRO. Who is't has met with this ill usage, sir?

BELVILE. A friend of ours whom you must see for mirth's sake. [*Aside.*] I'll employ him to give Florinda time for an escape.

PEDRO. What is he?

BELVILE. A young countryman of ours, one that has been educated at so plentiful a rate, he yet ne'er knew the want of money, and 'twill be a great jest to see how simply he'll look without it. For my part, I'll lend him none, and the rogue know not how to put on a borrowing face, and ask first; I'll let him see how good 'tis to play our parts while I play his—prithee Frederick, do you go home and keep him in that posture till we come.

Exeunt.

Enter FLORINDA *from the farther end of the scene, looking behind her.*

FLORINDA. I am followed still—hah—my brother too, advancing this way. Good heavens, defend me from being seen by him.

6. Other side of the earth.   clap"—venereal disease).
7. Hit, slapped (with the connotation also of "the

She goes off.

Enter WILLMORE, *and after him* VALERIA, *at a little distance.*

WILLMORE. Ah! There she sails! she looks back as she were willing to be boarded. I'll warrant her prize.[8]

He goes out, VALERIA *following.*

Enter HELLENA, *just as he goes out, with a* PAGE.

HELLENA. Hah, is not that my captain that has a woman in chase? 'Tis not Angellica. Boy, follow those people at a distance, and bring me an account where they go in—I'll find his haunts, and plague him everywhere—ha—my brother—

Exit PAGE; BELVILE, WILLMORE, PEDRO *cross the stage;* HELLENA *runs off.*

Scene IV

Scene changes to another street. Enter FLORINDA.

FLORINDA. What shall I do, my brother now pursues me;
Will no kind power protect me from his tyranny?
Hah, here's a door open; I'll venture in, since nothing can be worse than to fall into his hands. My life and honour are at stake, and my necessity has no choice.

She goes in.
Enter VALERIA *and* HELLENA'S PAGE *peeping after* FLORINDA.

PAGE. Here she went in; I shall remember this house.

Exit BOY.

VALERIA. This is Belvile's lodging; she's gone in as readily as if she knew it—hah—here's that mad fellow again. I dare not venture in—I'll watch my opportunity.

Goes aside.
Enter WILLMORE, *gazing about him.*

WILLMORE. I have lost her hereabouts. Pox on't, she must not scape me so.

Goes out.

Scene V

Scene changes to BLUNT'S *chamber; discovers him sitting on a couch
in his shirt and drawers, reading.*

BLUNT. So, now my mind's a little at peace, since I have resolved revenge—a pox on this tailor though, for not bringing home the clothes I bespoke,[9] and a pox of all poor cavaliers; a man can never keep a spare suit for 'em; and I shall have these rogues come in and find me naked, and then I'm undone. But I'm resolved to arm myself—the rascals shall not insult over me too much.

Puts on an old rusty sword, and buff belt.

---

8. Willmore, a privateer, refers to the practice of taking captured ships—or "prizes"—as property.

9. Ordered to be made.

Now, how like a morris dancer[1] I am equipped—a fine lady-like whore to cheat me thus, without affording me a kindness for my money. A pox light on her, I shall never be reconciled to the sex more; she has made me as faithless as a physician, as uncharitable as a churchman, and as ill-natured as a poet. Oh, how I'll use all womankind hereafter! What would I give to have one of 'em within my reach now! Any mortal thing in petticoats, kind fortune, lend me, and I'll forgive thy last night's malice. Here's a cursed book too (a warning to all young travellers) that can instruct me how to prevent such mischiefs now 'tis too late; well, 'tis a rare convenient thing to read a little now and then, as well as hawk and hunt.

Sits down again and reads.

Enter to him FLORINDA.

FLORINDA. This house is haunted sure; 'tis well furnished and no living thing inhabits it—hah—a man; heavens, how he's attired! Sure 'tis some rope-dancer,[2] or fencing-master; I tremble now for fear, and yet I must venture now to speak to him. Sir, if I may not interrupt your meditations—

He starts up and gazes.

BLUNT. Hah—what's here! Are my wishes granted? And is not that a she creature? 'Sheartlikins, 'tis! What wretched thing art thou—hah!

FLORINDA. Charitable sir, you've told yourself already what I am, a very wretched maid, forced by a strange unlucky accident to seek safety here,
And must be ruined, if you do not grant it.

BLUNT. Ruined! Is there any ruin so inevitable as that which now threatens thee? Dost thou know, miserable woman, into what den of mischiefs thou art fallen? What abyss of confusion—hah! Dost not see something in my looks that frights thy guilty soul, and makes thee wish to change that shape of woman for any humble animal or devil? For those were safer for thee, and less mischievous.

FLORINDA. Alas, what mean you, sir? I must confess, your looks have something in 'em makes me fear, but I beseech you, as you seem a gentleman, pity a harmless virgin that takes your house for sanctuary.

BLUNT. Talk on, talk on, and weep too, till my faith return. Do, flatter me out of my senses again—a harmless virgin with a pox, as much one as t'other, 'sheartlikins. Why, what the devil, can I not be safe in my house for you, not in my chamber, nay, even being naked too cannot secure me; this is an impudence greater than has invaded me yet—come, no resistance.

Pulls her rudely.

FLORINDA. Dare you be so cruel?

BLUNT. Cruel? 'Sheartlikins, as a galley slave, or a Spanish whore. Cruel? Yes; I will kiss and beat thee all over, kiss and see thee all over; thou shalt lie with me too, not that I care for the enjoyment, but to let thee see I have ta'en deliberated malice to thee, and will be revenged on one whore for the sins of another. I will smile and deceive thee, flatter thee, and beat thee, kiss and swear and lie to thee,

---

1. A participant in a traditional kind of English country dancing; morris dancers wore loose, light clothing and bells and sometimes carried swords.

2. A performer, who also would have worn loose clothing, who did tricks on a tight or slack rope.

embrace thee and rob thee, as she did me; fawn on thee and strip thee stark naked; then hang thee out at my window by the heels, with a paper of scurvy verses fastened to thy breast, in praise of damnable women—come, come along.

FLORINDA. Alas, sir, must I be sacrificed for the crimes of the most infamous of my sex? I never understood the sins you name.

BLUNT. Do, persuade the fool you love him, or that one of you can be just or honest; tell me I was not an easy coxcomb, or any strange impossible tale. It will be believed sooner than by false showers[3] or protestations. A generation of damned hypocrites to flatter my very clothes from my back! Dissembling witches! Are these the returns you make an honest gentleman, that trusts, believes, and loves you—but if I be not even with you—come along—or I shall—

Pulls her again.

Enter FREDERICK.

FREDERICK. Hah! What's here to do?

BLUNT. 'Sheartlikins, Frederick. I am glad thou art come to be a witness of my dire revenge.

FREDERICK. What's this, a person of quality too, who is upon the ramble to supply the defects of some grave impotent husband?

BLUNT. No, this has another pretence; some very unfortunate accident brought her hither, to save a life pursued by I know not who, or why, and forced to take sanctuary here at Fool's Haven. 'Sheartlikins, to me of all mankind for protection? Is the ass to be cajoled again, think ye? No, young one, no prayers or tears shall mitigate my rage; therefore prepare for both my pleasures of enjoyment and revenge, for I am resolved to make up my loss here on thy body; I'll take it out in kindness and in beating.

FREDERICK. Now, mistress of mine, what do you think of this?

FLORINDA. I think he will not—dares not—be so barbarous.

FREDERICK. Have a care, Blunt, she fetched a deep sigh; she is enamoured with thy shirt and drawers. She'll strip thee even of that, there are of her calling such unconscionable baggages, and such dextrous thieves, they'll flay a man and he shall ne'er miss his skin till he feels the cold. There was a countryman of ours robbed of a row of teeth whilst he was a-sleeping, which the jilt made him buy again when he waked—you see, lady, how little reason we have to trust you.

BLUNT. 'Sheartlikins, why this is most abominable.

FLORINDA. Some such devils there may be, but by all that's holy, I am none such; I entered here to save a life in danger.

BLUNT. For no goodness, I'll warrant her.

FREDERICK. Faith, damsel, you had e'en confessed the plain truth, for we are fellows not to be caught twice in the same trap. Look on that wreck, a tight vessel when he set out of haven, well trimmed and laden, and see how a female picaroon of this island of rogues has shattered him, and canst thou hope for any mercy?

BLUNT. No, no, gentlewoman, come along; 'sheartlikins, we must be better acquainted—we'll both lie with her, and then let me alone to bang her.

FREDERICK. I'm ready to serve you in matters of revenge that has a double pleasure in't.

---

3. As in one who shows.

BLUNT. Well said. You hear, little one, how you are condemned by public vote to the bed within; there's no resisting your destiny, sweetheart.

Pulls her.

FLORINDA. Stay, sir; I have seen you with Belvile, an English cavalier; for his sake use me kindly; you know him, sir.

BLUNT. Belvile, why yes, sweeting, we do know Belvile, and wish he were with us now; he's a cormorant at whore and bacon; he'd have a limb or two of thee, my virgin pullet,[4] but 'tis no matter, we'll leave him the bones to pick.

FLORINDA. Sir, if you have any esteem for that Belvile, I conjure you to treat me with more gentleness; he'll thank you for the justice.

FREDERICK. Harkee, Blunt, I doubt[5] we are mistaken in this matter.

FLORINDA. Sir, if you find me not worth Belvile's care, use me as you please, and that you may think I merit better treatment than you threaten—pray take this present—

Gives him a ring; he looks on it.

BLUNT. Hum—a diamond! Why 'tis a wonderful virtue now that lies in this ring, a mollifying virtue; 'sheartlikins, there's more persuasive rhetoric in't than all her sex can utter.

FREDERICK. I begin to suspect something; and 'twould anger us vilely to be trussed up for a rape upon a maid of quality, when we only believe we ruffle a harlot.

BLUNT. Thou art a credulous fellow, but 'sheartlikins I have no faith yet; why my saint prattled as parlously as this does, she gave me a bracelet too, a devil on her, but I sent my man to sell it today for necessaries, and it proved as counterfeit as her vows of love.

FREDERICK. However, let it reprieve her till we see Belvile.

BLUNT. That's hard, yet I will grant it.

Enter a SERVANT.

SERVANT. Oh, sir, the colonel is just come in with his new friend and a Spaniard of quality, and talks of having you to dinner with 'em.

BLUNT. 'Sheartlikins, I'm undone—I would not see 'em for the world. Harkee, Frederick, lock up the wench in your chamber.

FREDERICK. Fear nothing, madam; whate'er he threatens, you are safe whilst in my hands.

Exeunt FREDERICK *and* FLORINDA.

BLUNT. And, sirrah, upon your life, say—I am not at home—or that I'm asleep—or—or anything—away—I'll prevent their coming this way.

ACT V.

Scene I. Blunt's Chamber.

After a great knocking as at his chamber door, enter BLUNT *softly crossing the stage, in his shirt and drawers as before.*

---

4. Cormorant: marine bird known for its vora-   5. Fear.
cious appetite; pullet: a young chicken.

Call within.

VOICES. Ned, Ned Blunt, Ned Blunt.

BLUNT. The rogues are up in arms. 'Sheartlikins, this villainous Frederick has betrayed me; they have heard of my blessed fortune.

Knocking within.

VOICES. Ned Blunt, Ned, Ned—

BELVILE. [*within.*] Why he's dead, sir, without dispute dead, he has not been seen today; let's break open the door—here—boy—

BLUNT. Ha, break open the door. 'Sheartlikins, that mad fellow will be as good as his word.

BELVILE. [*within.*] Boy, bring something to force the door.

A great noise within, at the door again.

BLUNT. So, now must I speak in my own defence; I'll try what rhetoric will do—hold—hold; what do you mean gentlemen, what do you mean?

BELVILE. [*within.*] Oh rogue, art alive; prithee open the door and convince us.

BLUNT. Yes, I am alive gentlemen—but at present a little busy.

BELVILE. [*within.*] How, Blunt grown man of business? Come, come, open and let's see this miracle.

BLUNT. No, no, no, no, gentlemen, 'tis no great business—but—I am—at—my devotion—'sheartlikins, will you not allow a man time to pray?

BELVILE. [*within.*] Turned religious! A greater wonder than the first, therefore open quickly, or we shall unhinge, we shall.

BLUNT. This won't do—why harkee, colonel, to tell you the plain truth, I am about a necessary affair of life—I have a wench with me—you apprehend me? The devil's in't if they be so uncivil as to disturb me now.

WILLMORE. [*within.*] How, a wench! Nay then, we must enter and partake no resistance—unless it be your lady of quality, and then we'll keep our distance.

BLUNT. So, the business is out.

WILLMORE. [*within.*] Come, come, lend's more hands to the door—now heave altogether—so, well done, my boys—

Breaks open the door.

Enter BELVILE, WILLMORE, FREDERICK, PEDRO *and* BOY.
BLUNT *looks simply, they all laugh at him, he lays his hand on his sword,*
and comes up to WILLMORE.

BLUNT. Harkee sir, laugh out your laugh quickly, d'ye hear, and begone. I shall spoil your sport else, 'sheartlikins sir, I shall—the jest has been carried on too long. [*Aside.*] Oh—a plague upon my tailor.

WILLMORE. 'Sdeath, how the whore has dressed him. Faith, sir, I'm sorry.

BLUNT. Are you so, sir; keep't to yourself then, sir, I advise you, d'ye hear, for I can as little endure your pity as his mirth.

Lays his hand on's sword.

BELVILE. Indeed, Willmore, thou wert a little too rough with Ned Blunt's mistress. Call a person of quality whore? And one so young, so handsome, and so eloquent—ha, ha, he.

BLUNT. Harkee sir, you know me, and know I can be angry; have a care—for, 'sheartlikins, I can fight too—I can, sir—do you mark me—no more—

BELVILE. Why so peevish, good Ned; some disappointments I'll warrant—what? Did the jealous count her husband return just in the nick?

BLUNT. Or the devil sir—d'ye laugh—

They laugh.

Look ye settle me a good sober countenance, and that quickly too, or you shall know Ned Blunt is not—

BELVILE. Not everybody, we know that.

BLUNT. Not an ass to be laughed at, sir.

WILLMORE. Unconscionable sinner, to bring a lover so near his happiness, a vigorous, passionate lover, and then not only cheat him of his movables,[6] but his very desires too.

BELVILE. Ah! Sir, a mistress is a trifle with Blunt. He'll have a dozen the next time he looks abroad. His eyes have charms not to be resisted; there needs no more than to expose that taking person to the view of the fair, and he leads 'em all in triumph.

PEDRO. Sir, though I'm a stranger to you, I am ashamed at the rudeness of my nation; and could you learn who did it, would assist you to make an example of 'em.

BLUNT. Why ay, there's one speaks sense now, and han'somely; and let me tell you, gentlemen, I should not have showed myself like a Jack Pudding,[7] thus to have made you mirth, but that I have revenge within my power. For know, I have got into my possession a female who had better have fallen under any curse than the ruin I design her; 'sheartlikins, she assaulted me here in my own lodgings, and had doubtless committed a rape upon me, had not this sword defended me.

FREDERICK. I know not that, but o'my conscience, thou had ravished her, had she not redeemed herself with a ring—let's see't, Blunt.

BLUNT shows the ring.

BELVILE. The ring I gave Florinda, when we exchanged our vows—harkee Blunt—

Goes to whisper to him.

WILLMORE. No whispering, good colonel, there's a woman in the case; no whispering.

BELVILE. Harkee fool, be advised, and conceal both the ring and the story for your reputation's sake. Do not let people know what despised cullies[8] we English are, to be cheated and abused by one whore, and another rather bribe thee than be kind to thee is an infamy to our nation.

WILLMORE. Come, come, where's the wench? We'll see her, let her be what she will; we'll see her.

PEDRO. Ay, ay, let us see her. I can soon discover whether she be of quality, or for your diversion.

BLUNT. She's in Fred's custody.

WILLMORE. Come, come, the key.

---

6. Property.   8. Dupes.
7. Clown or buffoon.

To FREDERICK *who gives him the key; they are going.*

BELVILE. Death, what shall I do   Stay gentlemen—yet if I hinder 'em, I shall discover all—hold—let's go at once—give me the key.

WILLMORE. Nay, hold there colonel; I'll go first.

FREDERICK. Nay, no dispute; Ned and I have the propriety of her.

WILLMORE. Damn propriety—then we'll draw cuts—[BELVILE *goes to whisper to* WILLMORE.] nay, no corruption, good colonel. Come, the longest sword carries her—

They all draw, forgetting DON PEDRO, *being as a Spaniard, had the longest.*[9]

BLUNT. I yield up my interest to you, gentlemen, and that will be revenge sufficient.

WILLMORE. [*To* PEDRO.] The wench is yours—
[*Aside.*] Pox of his Toledo;[1] I had forgot that.

FREDERICK. Come sir, I'll conduct you to the lady.

Exeunt FREDERICK *and* PEDRO.

BELVILE. [*Aside.*] To hinder him will certainly discover her—
—Dost know, dull beast, what mischief thou hast done?

WILLMORE *walking up and down out of humour.*

WILLMORE. Ay, ay, to trust our fortune to lots, a devil on't; 'twas madness, that's the truth on't.

BELVILE. Oh intolerable sot—

Enter FLORINDA *running masked,* PEDRO *after her;*
WILLMORE *gazing round her.*

FLORINDA. [*Aside.*] Good heaven, defend me from discovery.

PEDRO. 'Tis but in vain to fly me, you're fallen to my lot.

BELVILE. Sure she's undiscovered yet, but now I fear there is no way to bring her off.

WILLMORE. Why, what a pox; is not this my woman, the same I followed but now?

PEDRO *talking to* FLORINDA, *who walks up and down.*

PEDRO. As if I did not know ye, and your business here.

FLORINDA. [*Aside.*] Good heaven, I fear he does indeed—

PEDRO. Come, pray be kind; I know you meant to be so when you entered here, for these are proper gentlemen.

WILLMORE. But sir— perhaps the lady will not be imposed upon. She'll choose her man.

PEDRO. I am better bred, than not to leave her choice free.

Enter VALERIA, *and is surprised at sight of* DON PEDRO.

VALERIA. [*Aside.*] Don Pedro here! There's no avoiding him.

FLORINDA. [*Aside.*] Valeria! Then I'm undone—

9. The Spanish fashion was for particularly long   1. A Spanish city famous for its fine steel.
swords.

VALERIA. Oh! Have I found you, sir—

To PEDRO, *running to him.*

—the strangest accident—if I had breath—to tell it.

PEDRO. Speak—is Florinda safe? Hellena well?

VALERIA. Ay, ay sir—Florinda—is safe—from any fears of you.

PEDRO. Why, where's Florinda? Speak—

VALERIA. Ay, where indeed sir, I wish I could inform you—but to hold you no longer in doubt—

FLORINDA. [*Aside.*] Oh, what will she say—

VALERIA. She's fled away in the habit—of one of her pages, sir—but Callis thinks you may retrieve her yet. If you make haste away, she'll tell you, sir, the rest—[*Aside.*] if you can find her out.

PEDRO. Dishonourable girl, she has undone my aim. Sir—you see my necessity of leaving you, and hope you'll pardon it; my sister, I know, will make her flight to you; and if she do, I shall expect she should be rendered back.

BELVILE. I shall consult my love and honour, sir.

Exit PEDRO.

FLORINDA. [*To* VALERIA.] My dear preserver, let me embrace thee.

WILLMORE. What the devil's all this?

BLUNT. Mystery by this light.

VALERIA. Come, come, make haste and get yourselves married quickly, for your brother will return again.

BELVILE. I'm so surprised with fears and joys, so amazed to find you here in safety, I can scarce persuade my heart into a faith of what I see.

WILLMORE. Harkee colonel, is this that mistress who has cost you so many sighs, and me so many quarrels with you?

BELVILE. It is—[*To* FLORINDA.] Pray give him the honour of your hand.

WILLMORE. Thus it must be received then.

Kneels and kisses her hand.

And with it give your pardon, too.

FLORINDA. The friend to Belvile may command me anything.

WILLMORE. [*Aside.*] Death, would I might; 'tis a surprising beauty.

BELVILE. Boy, run and fetch a father[2] instantly.

Exit BOY.

FREDERICK. So, now do I stand like a dog, and have not a syllable to plead my own cause with; by this hand, madam, I was never thoroughly confounded before, nor shall I ever more dare look up with confidence, till you are pleased to pardon me.

FLORINDA. Sir, I'll be reconciled to you on one condition, that you'll follow the example of your friend, in marrying a maid that does not hate you, and whose fortune (I believe) will not be unwelcome to you.

FREDERICK. Madam, had I no inclinations that way, I should obey your kind commands.

2. Priest.

BELVILE. Who, Frederick marry? He has so few inclinations for womankind, that had he been possessed of paradise he might have continued there to this day, if no crime but love could have disinherited him.

FREDERICK. Oh, I do not use to boast of my intrigues.

BELVILE. Boast, why thou dost nothing but boast; and I dare swear, wert thou as innocent from the sin of the grape, as thou art from the apple, thou might'st yet claim that right in Eden which our first parents lost by too much loving.

FREDERICK. I wish this lady would think me so modest a man.

VALERIA. She would be sorry then, and not like you half as well, and I should be loath to break my word with you, which was, that if your friend and mine agreed, it should be a match between you and I.

She gives him her hand.

FREDERICK. Bear witness, colonel, 'tis a bargain.

Kisses her hand.

BLUNT. [*To* FLORINDA.] I have a pardon to beg too, but 'sheartlikins, I am so out of countenance that I'm a dog if I can say anything to purpose.

FLORINDA. Sir, I heartily forgive you all.

BLUNT. That's nobly said, sweet lady—Belvile, prithee present her her ring again; for I find I have not courage to approach her myself.

Gives him the ring; he gives it to FLORINDA.

Enter BOY.

BOY. Sir, I have brought the father that you sent for.

BELVILE. 'Tis well, and now my dear Florinda, let's fly to complete that mighty joy we have so long wished and sighed for. Come Frederick—you'll follow?

FREDERICK. Your example, sir, 'twas ever my ambition in war, and must be so in love.

WILLMORE. And must not I see this juggling knot tied?

BELVILE. No, thou shalt do us better service, and be our guard, lest Don Pedro's sudden return interrupt the ceremony.

WILLMORE. Content—I'll secure this pass.

Exeunt BELVILE, FLORINDA, FREDERICK *and* VALERIA.

Enter BOY.

BOY. [*To* WILLMORE.] Sir, there's a lady without would speak to you.

WILLMORE. Conduct her in, I dare not quit my post.

BOY. And sir, your tailor waits you in your chamber.

BLUNT. Some comfort yet, I shall not dance naked at the wedding.

Exeunt BLUNT *and* BOY.

Enter again the BOY, *conducting in* ANGELLICA *in a masquing habit and a vizard.* WILLMORE *runs to her.*

WILLMORE. This can be none but my pretty gypsy—oh, I see you can follow as well as fly. Come, confess thyself the most malicious devil in nature; you think you have done my business with Angellica—

ANGELLICA. Stand off, base villain—

She draws a pistol, and holds it to his breast.

WILLMORE. Hah, 'tis not she; who art thou? And what's thy business?
ANGELLICA. One thou hast injured, and who comes to kill thee for't.
WILLMORE. What the devil canst thou mean?
ANGELLICA. By all my hopes to kill thee—

Holds still the pistol to his breast, he going back, she following still.

WILLMORE. Prithee, on what acquaintance? For I know thee not.
ANGELLICA. Behold this face—so lost to thy remembrance,
And then call all thy sins about thy soul,

Pulls off her vizard.

And let 'em die with thee.
WILLMORE. Angellica!
ANGELLICA. Yes, traitor,
Does not thy guilty blood run shivering through thy veins?
Hast thou no horror at this sight that tells thee
Thou hast not long to boast thy shameful conquest?
WILLMORE. Faith, no, child; my blood keeps its old ebbs and flows still, and
that usual heat too, that could oblige thee with a kindness, had I but opportunity.
ANGELLICA. Devil! Dost wanton with my pain—have at thy heart.
WILLMORE. Hold, dear virago![3] Hold thy hand a little; I am not now at leisure
to be killed—hold and hear me—
[*Aside*]—Death, I think she's in earnest.
ANGELLICA. [*Aside, turning from him.*] Oh, if I take not heed,
My coward heart will leave me to his mercy.
—What have you, sir, to say? But should I hear thee,
Thou'dst talk away all that is brave about me:

Follows him with the pistol to his breast.

And I have vowed thy death, by all that's sacred.
WILLMORE. Why, then there's an end of a proper handsome fellow,
That might 'a' lived to have done good service yet;
That's all I can say to't.
ANGELLICA. [*Pausingly.*] Yet—I would give thee—time for—penitence.
WILLMORE. Faith child, I thank God I have ever took
Care to lead a good sober, hopeful life, and am of a religion
That teaches me to believe I shall depart in peace.
ANGELLICA. So will the devil! Tell me,
How many poor believing fools thou hast undone?
How many hearts thou hast betrayed to ruin?
Yet these are little mischiefs to the ills
Thou'st taught mine to commit: thou'st taught it love.
WILLMORE. Egad, 'twas shrewdly hurt the while.
ANGELLICA. Love, that has robbed it of its unconcern
Of all that pride that taught me how to value it.
And in its room

---

3. Strong or angry woman.

A mean submissive passion was conveyed,
That made me humbly bow, which I ne'er did
To any thing but heaven.
Thou, perjured man, didst this, and with thy oaths,
Which on thy knees, thou didst devoutly make,
Softened my yielding heart—and then, I was a slave—
Yet still had been content to've worn my chains,
Worn 'em with vanity and joy for ever,
Hadst thou not broke those vows that put them on.
'Twas then I was undone.

All this while follows him with the pistol to his breast.

WILLMORE. Broke my vows! Why, where hast thou lived?
Amongst the gods? For I never heard of mortal man
That has not broke a thousand vows.
    ANGELLICA. Oh impudence!
    WILLMORE. Angellica! That beauty has been too long tempting
Not to have made a thousand lovers languish,
Who in the amorous fever no doubt have sworn
Like me; did they all die in that faith? Still adoring?
I do not think they did.
    ANGELLICA. No, faithless man; had I repaid their vows, as I did thine,
I would have killed the ingrateful that had abandoned me.
    WILLMORE. This old general has quite spoiled thee; nothing makes a woman
so vain as being flattered. Your old lover ever supplies the defects of age, with in-
tolerable dotage, vast charge, and that which you call constancy; and attributing
this to your own merits, you domineer, and throw your favours in's teeth, up-
braiding him still with the defects of age, and cuckold him as often as he deceives
your expectations. But the gay, young, brisk lover that brings his equal fires, and
can give you dart for dart, will be as nice as you sometimes.
    ANGELLICA. All this thou'st made me know, for which I hate thee.
Had I remained in innocent security,
I should have thought all men were born my slaves,
And worn my pow'r like lightning in my eyes,
To have destroyed at pleasure when offended.
But when love held the mirror, the undeceiving glass
Reflected all the weakness of my soul, and made me know
My richest treasure being lost, my honour,
All the remaining spoil could not be worth
The conqueror's care or value.
Oh how I fell, like a long worshipped idol
Discovering all the cheat.
Would not the incense and rich sacrifice
Which blind devotion offered at my altars,
Have fall'n to thee?
Why wouldst thou then destroy my fancied pow'r?
    WILLMORE. By heaven thou'rt brave, and I admire thee strangely.
I wish I were that dull, that constant thing
Which thou wouldst have, and nature never meant me.

I must, like cheerful birds, sing in all groves,
And perch on every bough,
Billing[4] the next kind she that flies to meet me;
Yet after all could build my nest with thee,
Thither repairing when I'd loved my round,
And still reserve a tributary flame.
To gain your credit, I'll pay you back your charity,
And be obliged for nothing but for love.

Offers her a purse of gold.

ANGELLICA. Oh that thou wert in earnest!
So mean a thought of me,
Would turn my rage to scorn, and I should pity thee,
And give thee leave to live;
Which for the public safety of our sex,
And my own private injuries, I dare not do,
Prepare—

Follows still, as before.

I will no more be tempted with replies.
WILLMORE. Sure—
ANGELLICA. Another word will damn thee! I've heard thee talk too long.

She follows him with the pistol ready to shoot; he retires still amazed.

Enter DON ANTONIO, *his arm in a scarf, and lays hold on the pistol.*

ANTONIO. Hah! Angellica!
ANGELLICA. Antonio! What devil brought thee hither?
ANTONIO. Love and curiosity, seeing your coach at door.
Let me disarm you of this unbecoming instrument of death—

Takes away the pistol.

Amongst the number of your slaves, was there not one worthy the honour to have fought your quarrel?
—Who are you sir, that are so very wretched
To merit death from her?
WILLMORE. One, sir, that could have made a better end of an amorous quarrel without you, than with you.
ANTONIO. Sure 'tis some rival—hah—the very man took down her picture yesterday—the very same that set on me last night—blest opportunity—

Offers to shoot him.

ANGELLICA. Hold, you're mistaken sir.
ANTONIO. By heaven, the very same!
Sir, what pretensions have you to this lady?
WILLMORE. Sir, I do not use to be examined, and am ill at all disputes but this—

Draws; ANTONIO *offers to shoot.*

4. Stroking, caressing.

ANGELLICA. [*To* WILLMORE.] Oh hold! You see he's armed with certain death,
—And you Antonio, I command you hold,
By all the passion you've so lately vowed me.

Enter DON PEDRO, *sees* ANTONIO *and stays.*

PEDRO. [*Aside.*] Hah, Antonio! And Angellica!
ANTONIO. When I refuse obedience to your will,
May you destroy me with your mortal hate.
By all that's holy I adore you so,
That even my rival, who has charms enough
To make him fall a victim to my jealousy
Shall live, nay and have leave to love on still.
PEDRO. [*Aside.*] What's this I hear?
ANGELLICA. Ah thus! 'Twas thus he talked, and I believed.

Pointing to WILLMORE.

Antonio, yesterday,
I'd not have sold my interest in his heart
For all the sword has won and lost in battle.
But now to show my utmost of contempt,
I give thee life—which if thou wouldst preserve,
Live where my eyes may never see thee more,
Live to undo someone whose soul may prove
So bravely constant to revenge my love.

Goes out, ANTONIO *follows, but* PEDRO *pulls him back.*

PEDRO. Antonio—stay.
ANTONIO. Don Pedro—
PEDRO. What coward fear was that prevented thee
From meeting me this morning on the Molo?
ANTONIO. Meet thee?
PEDRO. Yes me; I was the man that dared thee to't.
ANTONIO. Hast thou so often seen me fight in war,
To find no better cause to excuse my absence?
I sent my sword and one to do thee right,
Finding myself uncapable to use a sword.
PEDRO. But 'twas Florinda's quarrel we fought,
And you, to show how little you esteemed her,
Sent me your rival, giving him your interest.
But I have found the cause of this affront,
And when I meet you fit for the dispute,
I'll tell you my resentment.
ANTONIO. I shall be ready, sir, ere long, to do you reason.

Exit ANTONIO.

PEDRO. If I could find Florinda now whilst my anger's high, I think I should
be kind, and give her to Belvile in revenge.
WILLMORE. Faith, sir, I know not what you would do, but I believe the priest
within has been so kind.

PEDRO. How! My sister married?

WILLMORE. I hope by this time he is, and bedded too, or he has not my longings about him.

PEDRO. Dares he do this! Does he not fear my power?

WILLMORE. Faith, not at all. If you will go in, and thank him for the favour he has done your sister, so; if not, sir, my power's greater in this house than yours. I have a damned surly crew here, that will keep you till the next tide, and then clap you on board for prize; my ship lies but a league off the Molo, and we shall show your donship a damned tramontana[5] rover's trick.

Enter BELVILE.

BELVILE. This rogue's in some new mischief—hah, Pedro returned!

PEDRO. Colonel Belvile, I hear you have married my sister?

BELVILE. You have heard the truth then, sir.

PEDRO. Have I so; then, sir, I wish you joy.

BELVILE. How!

PEDRO. By this embrace I do, and I am glad on't.

BELVILE. Are you in earnest?

PEDRO. By our long friendship and my obligations to thee, I am,
The sudden change I'll give you reasons for anon.
Come lead me to my sister,
That she may know I now approve her choice.

Exeunt BELVILE *with* PEDRO. WILLMORE *goes to follow them.*
Enter HELLENA *as before in* BOY's *clothes, and pulls him back.*

WILLMORE. Ha! My gypsy— now a thousand blessings on thee for this kindness. Egad child, I was e'en in despair of ever seeing thee again; my friends are all provided for within, each man his kind woman.

HELLENA. Ha! I thought they had served me some such trick!

WILLMORE. And I was e'en resolved to go aboard, and condemn myself to my lone cabin, and the thoughts of thee.

HELLENA. And could you have left me behind, would you have been so ill natured?

WILLMORE. Why, 'twould have broke my heart, child—but since we are met again, I defy foul weather to part us.

HELLENA. And would you be a faithful friend now, if a maid should trust you?

WILLMORE. For a friend I cannot promise; thou art of a form so excellent, a face and humour too good for cold dull friendship. I am parlously afraid of being in love, child, and you have not forgot how severely you have used me?

HELLENA. That's all one; such usage you must still look for, to find out all your haunts, to rail at you to all that love you, till I have made you love only me in your own defence, because nobody else will love you.

WILLMORE. But hast thou no better quality to recommend thyself by?

HELLENA. Faith, none, captain—why, 'twill be the greater charity to take me for thy mistress. I am alone, child, a kind of orphan lover, and why I should die a maid, and in a captain's hands too, I do not understand.

5. Literally, a person from the other side of the mountain, a term that refers to foreigners.

WILLMORE. Egad, I was never clawed away with broadsides[6] from any female before. Thou has one virtue I adore, good nature. I hate a coy demure mistress, she's as troublesome as a colt; I'll break none. No, give me a mad mistress when mewed,[7] and in flying, one I dare trust upon the wing, that whilst she's kind will come to the lure.

HELLENA. Nay, as kind as you will, good captain, whilst it lasts, but let's lose no time.

WILLMORE. My time's as precious to me as thine can be; therefore dear creature, since we are so well agreed, let's retire to my chamber, and if ever thou wert treated with such savoury love! Come—my bed's prepared for such a guest, all clean and sweet as thy fair self. I love to steal a dish and a bottle with a friend, and hate long graces—come let's retire and fall to.

HELLENA. 'Tis but getting my consent, and the business is soon done. Let but old gaffer Hymen[8] and his priest say amen to't, and I dare lay my mother's daughter by as proper a fellow as your father's son, without fear or blushing.

WILLMORE. Hold, hold, no bug words,[9] child; priest and Hymen? Prithee add a hangman to 'em to make up the consort—no, no, we'll have no vows but love, child, nor witness but the lover; the kind deity enjoins naught but love and enjoy! Hymen and priest wait still upon portion, and jointure;[1] love and beauty have their own ceremonies. Marriage is as certain a bane to love as lending money is to friendship. I'll neither ask nor give a vow—though I could be content to turn gypsy, and become a left-handed bridegroom[2] to have the pleasure of working that great miracle of making a maid a mother, if you durst venture; 'tis upse[3] gypsy that, and if I miss, I'll lose my labour.

HELLENA. And if you do not lose, what shall I get? A cradle full of noise and mischief, with a pack of repentance at my back? Can you teach me to weave incle[4] to pass my time with? 'Tis upse gypsy that too.

WILLMORE. I can teach thee to weave a true love's knot better.

HELLENA. So can my dog.

WILLMORE. Well, I see we are both upon our guards, and I see there's no way to conquer good nature, but by yielding—here—give me thy hand—one kiss and I am thine—

HELLENA. One kiss! How like my page he speaks; I am resolved you shall have none, for asking such a sneaking sum. He that will be satisfied with one kiss, will never die of that longing. Good friend single kiss, is all your talking come to this? A kiss, a caudle![5] Farewell captain single kiss.

Going out; he stays her.

WILLMORE. Nay, if we part so, let me die like a bird upon a bough, at the sheriff's charge. By heaven, both the Indies shall not buy thee from me. I adore thy hu-

---

6. A single sheet of paper, customarily printed with ballads. (Hellena's references to an orphan lover and a captain are both references to ballads.)
7. Confined in a cage; refers to hawks and the practice of hawking, in which a hawk is sent to hunt other birds and then encouraged to return with a lure.
8. Gaffer: old man; Hymen: the god of marriage.

9. Frightening words.
1. Portion: money a woman brings with her to a marriage; jointure: provision for the support of a wife after the death of her husband.
2. Without a legal marriage.
3. In the fashion or manner of.
4. Linen thread.
5. Thin porridge given to invalids.

mour and will marry thee, and we are so of one humour, it must be a bargain—give me thy hand—

Kisses her hand.

And now let the blind ones[6] (love and fortune) do their worst.

HELLENA. Why, god-a-mercy, captain!

WILLMORE. But harkee—the bargain is now made; but is it not fit we should know each other's names, that when we have reason to curse one another hereafter (and people ask me who 'tis I give to the devil) I may at least be able to tell what family you came of.

HELLENA. Good reason, captain; and where I have cause (as I doubt not but I shall have plentiful) that I may know at whom to throw my—blessings—I beseech ye your name.

WILLMORE. I am called Robert the Constant.

HELLENA. A very fine name; pray was it your falconer[7] or butler that christened you? Do they not use to whistle when they call you?

WILLMORE. I hope you have a better, that a man may name without crossing himself; you are merry with mine.

HELLENA. I am called Hellena the Inconstant.

Enter PEDRO, BELVILE, FLORINDA, FREDERICK, VALERIA.

PEDRO. Hah! Hellena!

FLORINDA. Hellena!

HELLENA. The very same—hah, my brother! Now captain, show your love and courage; stand to your arms, and defend me bravely, or I am lost for ever.

PEDRO. What's this I hear! False girl, how came you hither and what's your business? Speak.

Goes roughly to her.

WILLMORE. Hold off sir, you have leave to parley[8] only.

Puts himself between.

HELLENA. I had e'en as good tell it, as you guess it; faith, brother, my business is the same with all living creatures of my age, to love, and be beloved, and here's the man.

PEDRO. Perfidious maid, hast thou deceived me too? Deceived thy self and heaven?

HELLENA. 'Tis time enough to make my peace with that. Be you but kind; let me alone with heaven.

PEDRO. Belvile, I did not expect this false play from you; was't not enough you'd gain Florinda (which I pardoned) but your lewd friends too must be enriched with the spoils of a noble family?

BELVILE. Faith sir, I am as much surprised at this as you can be. Yet sir, my friends are gentlemen, and ought to be esteemed for their misfortunes, since they

---

6. Both Cupid (love) and Fortune are traditionally depicted as blind.

7. Keeper of hawks.

8. Speak.

have the glory to suffer with the best of men[9] and kings; 'tis true, he's a rover of fortune, yet a prince aboard his little wooden world.

PEDRO. What's this to the maintenance of a woman of her birth and quality?

WILLMORE. Faith, sir, I can boast of nothing but a sword which does me right where'er I come, and has defended a worse cause than a woman's; and since I loved her before I either knew her birth or name, I must pursue my resolution, and marry her.

PEDRO. And is all your holy intent of becoming a nun debauched into a desire of man?

HELLENA. Why—I have considered the matter, brother, and find the three hundred thousand crowns my uncle left me (and you cannot keep from me) will be better laid out in love than in religion, and turn to as good an account. Let most voices carry it, for heaven or the captain?

ALL CRY. A captain! A captain!

HELLENA. Look ye sir, 'tis a clear case.

PEDRO. [Aside.] Oh I am mad—if I refuse, my life's in danger— —Come—there's one motive induces me—take her—I shall now be free from fears of her honour; guard it you now, if you can; I have been a slave to't long enough.

Gives her to him.

WILLMORE. Faith sir, I am of a nation that are of opinion a woman's honour is not worth guarding when she has a mind to part with it.

HELLENA. Well said, captain.

PEDRO. [To VALERIA.] This was your plot, mistress, but I hope you have married one that will revenge my quarrel to you—

VALERIA. There's no altering destiny, sir.

PEDRO. Sooner than a woman's will; therefore I forgive you all—and wish you may get my father's pardon as easily, which I fear.

Enter BLUNT *dressed in a Spanish habit, looking very ridiculously; his* MAN *adjusting his band.[1]*

MAN. 'Tis very well, sir—

BLUNT. Well sir, 'sheartlikins, I tell you 'tis damnable ill, sir—a Spanish habit, good lord! Could the devil and my tailor devise no other punishment for me, but the mode of a nation I abominate?

BELVILE. What's the matter, Ned?

BLUNT. Pray view me round, and judge—

Turns round.

BELVILE. I must confess thou art a kind of an odd figure.

BLUNT. In a Spanish habit with a vengeance! I had rather be in the inquisition for Judaism, than in this doublet and breeches; a pillory[2] were an easy collar to this, three handfuls high; and these shoes too, are worse than the stocks, with the

---

9. Prince Charles, later Charles II.
1. Neckband.
2. Like the stocks, a device used for punishment,

in which a man was held between two wooden boards, with holes for his head and hands, and exposed publicly for ridicule and insult.

sole an inch shorter than my foot. In fine, gentlemen, methinks I look altogether like a bag of bays[3] stuffed full of fool's flesh.

BELVILE. Methinks 'tis well, and makes thee look e'en cavalier; come, sir, settle your face, and salute our friends. Lady—

BLUNT. Ha! Say'st thou so my little rover—

To HELLENA.

Lady—(if you be one), give me leave to kiss your hand, and tell you, 'sheartlikins, for all I look so, I am your humble servant—a pox of my Spanish habit.

Music is heard to play. Enter BOY.

WILLMORE. Hark—what's this?

BOY. Sir, as the custom is, the gay people in masquerade who make every man's house their own are coming up.

Enter several MEN *and* WOMEN *in masquing habits with music; they put themselves in order and dance.*

BLUNT. [*To the masquers.*] 'Sheartlikins, would 'twere lawful to pull off their false faces, that I might see if my doxy[4] were not among'st 'em.

BELVILE. Ladies and gentlemen, since you are come so *a propos,*[5] you must take a small collation with us.

WILLMORE. Whilst we'll to the good man within, who stays to give us a cast of his office.

To HELLENA.

—Have you no trembling at the near approach?

HELLENA. No more than you have in an engagement or a tempest.

WILLMORE. Egad thou'rt a brave girl, and I admire thy love and courage.
Lead on, no other dangers they can dread,
Who venture in the storms o'th' marriage bed.

Exeunt.

EPILOGUE

The banished cavaliers! A roving blade![6]
A Popish carnival! A masquerade!
The devil's in't if this will please the nation,
In these our blessed times of reformation,
When conventicling[7] is so much in fashion.   5
And yet—
That mutinous tribe less factions do beget,
Than your continual differing in wit;
Your judgement's (as your passion's) a disease:
Nor muse nor miss your appetite can please;   10

3. Used for cooking.
4. Prostitute.
5. Opportunely (French).

6. Swordsman.
7. Participating in a religious conventicle, a secret meeting of religious nonconformists or Dissenters.

You're grown as nice as queasy consciences,
Whose each convulsion, when the spirit moves,
Damns every thing that maggot[8] disapproves.
With canting rule you would the stage refine,
And to dull method all our sense confine.   15
With th' insolence of commonwealths you rule,
Where each gay fop, and politic grave fool
On monarch wit impose, without control.
As for the last, who seldom sees a play,
Unless it be the old Blackfriars[9] way,   20
Shaking his empty noddle o'er bamboo,[1]
He cries, "Good faith, these plays will never do.
Ah, sir, in my young days, what lofty wit,
What high strained scenes of fighting there were writ:
These are slight airy toys. But tell me, pray,   25
What has the House of Commons done today?"
Then shows his politics, to let you see,
Of state affairs he'll judge as notably,
As he can do of wit and poetry.
The younger sparks,[2] who hither do resort,   30
Cry,
"Pox o' your gentle things, give us more sport;
Damn me, I'm sure 'twill never please the court."
Such fops are never pleased unless the play
Be stuffed with fools as brisk and dull as they.   35
Such might the half-crown[3] spare, and in a glass
At home behold a more accomplished ass,
Where they may set their cravats, wigs and faces,
And practice all their buffoonry grimaces.
See how this huff becomes, this damny, stare—   40
Which they at home may act, because they dare,
But—must with prudent caution do elsewhere.
Oh that our Nokes, or Tony Lee,[4] could show
A fop but half so much to th'life as you.

Post-Script

This play had been sooner in print, but for a report about the town (made by some either very malicious or very ignorant) that 'twas *Thomaso*[5] altered, which made the booksellers fear some trouble from the proprietor of that admirable play, which indeed has wit enough to stock a poet, and is not to be pieced[6] or mended by any but the excellent author himself. That I have stolen some hints from it, may be a proof that I valued it more than to pretend to alter it, had I had the dexterity of some poets, who are not more expert in stealing than in the art of con-

---

8. A whimsical notion or idea.
9. A private theater popular in the early seventeenth century but closed in 1642.
1. Cane.
2. Foppish young men.
3. A coin that today would be worth about fifty

cents.
4. James Nokes: comic actor (d. 1696); Anthony Leigh, comic actor (d. 1692).
5. A play by Thomas Killigrew, published in 1663.
6. Patched.

cealing, and who even that way outdo the Spartan boys. I might have appropriated all to myself, but I, vainly proud of my judgment, hang out the sign of Angellica (the only stolen object) to give notice where a great part of the wit dwelt; though if the Play of the Novella[7] were as well worth remembering as *Thomaso,* they might (bating the name) have as well said, I took it from thence. I will only say the plot and business (not to boast on't) is my own; as for the words and characters, I leave the reader to judge and compare 'em with *Thomaso,* to whom I recommend the great entertainment of reading it, though had this succeeded ill, I should have had no need of imploring that justice from the critics who are naturally so kind to any that pretend to usurp their dominion, especially of our sex, they would doubtless have give me the whole honour on't. Therefore I will only say in English what the famous Virgil does in Latin; I made verses, and others have the fame.

FINIS.

1677

7. *The Novella* (1632), a play by Richard Brome.

CULTURAL COORDINATES
Restoration Actresses

Although there is some evidence that women appeared in public entertainments like medieval mystery plays as early as the fifteenth century, women in England were not regularly employed in commercial theater until the theaters reopened in 1660. (They had been closed by the Puritan parliamentary government in 1642.) During the first heyday of commercial theater in England—the late sixteenth and early seventeenth centuries—Puritan critics had harshly attacked the theater as immoral, a threat to female virtue: "Do they not," asked the Puritan Philip Stubbes, referring to playhouses, "induce whoredom and uncleanness and nay, are they not rather plain devourers of maidenly virginity and chastity?" The parts for women in Shakespeare's day and afterward were written for talented boys.

When the monarchy was restored under Charles II and the theaters were reopened, women were allowed onstage. (The court of Charles II was notable for its appreciation—some might even say exploitation—of female beauty and sexual availability.) No woman of means, however, would have dreamed of a stage career—the conflation of "actress" with "whore" had receded only a very little since the early seventeenth century. Yet prostitutes would simply not have been well enough educated to memorize their lines or imitate an upper-class woman. Typically, then, actresses were women from families that had come down in the world, daughters of tradesmen, or the illegitimate children of aristocratic men. Until the prospect of an acting career arose, most of these young women would have found employment in domestic service, but the job of an actress promised better pay and a more glamorous life. Thus to many independent-minded women it was irresistible.

The most popular actress of the Restoration was Elizabeth Barry (1658–1713), whose powerful performances both inspired pity and aroused the erotic

Portrait of Elizabeth Barry, 1658–1713 (1792), an engraving by Charles Knight after a portrait by Sir Godfrey Kneller. (National Portrait Gallery, London)

Portrait of Nell Gwyn (c. 1680), by Simon Verelst. (National Portrait Gallery, London)

Anne Bracegirdle (late 17th century), mezzotint, artist unknown. (National Portrait Gallery, London)

sensibilities of her audiences. Barry bore two children illegitimately—one fathered by the sexually notorious Earl of Rochester (1647–80), another by the playwright George Etherege (1635–90)—but remained single, retiring from the stage in 1709. She and other actresses of her generation, women like the longtime mistress of Charles II, Nell Gwyn (1650–87), and Anne Bracegirdle (1671–1748), quickly became the single most popular element of the London theater scene, so popular that by the 1680s plays were being written around them. Yet despite the fact that a theater company's financial success often rested on the popularity of its actresses, even the most successful of actresses was paid just a portion of what her male counterparts were paid, and no actress was ever allowed to become a theater manager.

ANNE KILLIGREW
c. 1660–1685

Born in London to a well-educated and well-connected Royalist family, Anne Killigrew grew up in the court of Charles II. Her father, Henry Killigrew, was a prominent cleric who held a position, before the Civil War, which brought a Puritan Parliament to power, as a prebend, or canon, at Westminster Abbey. Although he was removed from that position during the Civil War, he maintained contact with the Stuart monarchy, serving as chaplain to James, the Duke of York (later James II). After the Restoration in 1660, he was restored to his position in Westminster, and his daughter moved in court circles with him and other family members (most notably her uncles Thomas and William Killigrew, who were both prominent playwrights). Along with the poet Anne Finch, her contemporary, Killigrew served as maid of honor to Mary of Modena, the wife of the Duke of York.

Demonstrating prodigious artistic talent, she was an admired portraitist and painted portraits of both the Duke and Duchess of York as well as herself. She was also known in court circles for her poetry, which circulated in manuscript, a common practice among upper-class and aristocratic poets. Anne's dedication to the values of Mary of Modena, who stressed female virtue and wit, when the court of Charles II seems to have valued women solely for their beauty, passivity, and sexual availability, are revealed in her poems. So are her considerable frustrations as a young and accomplished poet whose work was attributed to others (see "Upon the Saying That My Verses Were Made by Another").

Anne Killigrew died of smallpox at the age of twenty-five. Her poems were published by her father a few months after her death and were accompanied by a famous ode to her memory commissioned by her father and written by the English poet John Dryden.

A Farewell to Worldly Joys

Farewell ye unsubstantial joys,
Ye gilded nothings, gaudy toys,
Too long ye have my soul misled,
Too long with airy diet fed:
But now my heart ye shall no more   5
Deceive, as you have heretofore:
For when I hear such Sirens sing,
Like Ithaca's forewarned king,[1]
With prudent resolution I
Will so my will and fancy tie,   10

---

1. In Greek mythology, the Sirens are island-dwelling creatures with the head of a female and the body of a bird who sing so beautifully that sailors are lured to their destruction on the rocks surrounding the Sirens' island. Odysseus, warned about the Sirens on his way home from the Trojan War, has his sailors strap him to his mast so that he can hear the Sirens' song but not steer into the rocks.

That stronger to the mast not he,
Than I to reason bound will be:
And though your witchcrafts strike my ear,
Unhurt, like him, your charms I'll hear.

1686

Upon the Saying That My Verses Were Made by Another

Next heaven my vows to thee (O sacred Muse!)
I offered up, nor didst thou them refuse.

   O Queen of Verse, said I, if thou'lt inspire,
And warm my soul with thy poetic fire,
No love of gold shall share with thee my heart,   5
Or yet ambition in my breast have part,
More rich, more noble I will ever hold
The muse's laurel,[2] than a crown of gold.
An undivided sacrifice I'll lay
Upon thine altar, soul and body pay;   10
Thou shalt my pleasure, my employment be,
My all I'll make a holocaust[3] to thee.

   The deity that ever does attend
Prayers so sincere, to mine did condescend.
I writ, and the judicious praised my pen: 15
Could any doubt ensuing glory then?
What pleasing raptures filled my ravished senses?
How strong, how sweet, fame, was thy influence?
And thine, false hope, that to my flattered sight
Didst glories represent so near, and bright?   20
By thee deceived, methought, each verdant tree,
Apollo's transformed Daphne seemed to be;[4]
And every fresher branch, and every bough
Appeared as garlands to impale my brow.
The learned in love say, thus the winged boy[5]   25
Does first approach, dressed up in welcome joy;
At first he to the cheated lover's sight
Nought represents, but rapture and delight,
Alluring hopes, soft fears, which stronger bind
Their hearts, than when they more assurance find.   30

   Emboldened thus, to fame I did commit,
(By some few hands) my most unlucky wit.
But, ah, the sad effects that from it came!
What ought t'have brought me honour, brought me shame!

---

2. In ancient Greece, the leaves of the bay laurel were woven together to create a wreath to recognize a great poet.
3. A burnt offering.

4. In Greek mythology, Daphne is transformed into a bay laurel to escape the unwelcome advances of Apollo, god of poetry and music.
5. Cupid.

Like Aesop's painted jay I seemed to all,[6]   35
Adorned in plumes, I not my own could call:
Rifled like her, each one my feathers tore,
And, as they thought, unto the owner bore.
My laurels thus another's brow adorned,
My numbers[7] they admired, but me they scorned: 40
Another's brow, that had so rich a store
Of sacred wreaths, that circled it before;
Where mine quite lost, (like a small stream that ran
Into a vast and boundless ocean)
Was swallowed up, with what it joined and drowned,   45
And that abyss yet no accession found.

   Orinda (Albion's[8] and her sex's grace)
Owed not her glory to a beauteous face,
It was her radiant soul that shone within,
Which struck a lustre through her outward skin;   50
That did her lips and cheeks with roses dye,
Advanced her height, and sparkled in her eye.
Nor did her sex at all obstruct her fame,
But higher 'mong the stars it fixed her name;
What she did write, not only all allowed,   55
But every laurel, to her laurel, bowed!

   Th'envious age, only to me alone,
Will not allow, what I do write, my own,
But let 'em rage, and 'gainst a maid conspire,
So deathless numbers from my tuneful lyre   60
Do ever flow; so Phoebus[9] I by thee
Divinely inspired and possessed may be;
I willingly accept Cassandra's[1] fate,
To speak the truth, although believed too late.

                                       1686

The Discontent

I

Here take no care, take here no care, my Muse,
   Nor ought of art or labour use:
   But let thy lines rude and unpolished go,
Nor equal be their feet, nor numerous let them flow.
   The ruggeder my measures run when read,   5
They'll livelier paint th'unequal paths fond mortals tread.

6. In Aesop's fable of the painted jay (translated
into English in 1693), the bird ornaments itself in
the colorful feathers of other birds and declares itself the best of all birds on the basis of its costume.
7. Metered lines; verse.
8. Orinda: the pseudonym of the poet Katherine

Philips (1631–64; see pp. 114–19); Albion: England.
9. Apollo.
1. In Greek mythology, Cassandra was given the
gift of prophecy by Apollo, who, when his advances were rebuffed, turned the gift into a curse
such that none of her prophecies would be believed.

Who when they're tempted by the smooth ascents,
    Which flattering hope presents,
Briskly they climb, and great things undertake;
But fatal voyages, alas, they make: 10
    For 'tis not long before their feet,
    Inextricable mazes meet,
    Perplexing doubts obstruct their way,
    Mountains withstand them of dismay;
Or to the brink of black despair them lead,   15
    Where's nought their ruin to impede,
In vain for aid they then to reason call,
Their senses dazzle, and their heads turn round,
    The sight does all their powers confound,
And headlong down the horrid precipice they fall: 20
    Where storms of sighs forever blow,
    Where rapid streams of tears do flow,
    Which drown them in a briny flood.
My Muse pronounce aloud, there's nothing good,
    Nought that the world can show,   25
    Nought that it can bestow.

II

Not boundless heaps of its admired clay,
    Ah, too successful to betray,
    When spread in our frail virtue's way:
For few do run with so resolved a pace,   30
That for the golden apple will not lose the race.[2]
    And yet not all the gold the vain would spend,
        Or greedy avarice would wish to save;
    Which on the earth refulgent beams doth send,
        Or in the sea has found a grave,   35
    Joined in one mass, can bribe sufficient be,
    The body from a stern disease to free,
        Or purchase for the mind's relief
One moment's sweet repose, when restless made by grief,
But what may laughter, more than pity, move: 40
When some the price of what they dearest love
Are masters of, and hold it in their hand,
To part with it their hearts they can't command:
But chose to miss, what missed does them torment,
And that to hug, affords them no content.   45
Wise fools, to do them right, we these must hold,
Who love depose, and homage pay to gold.

---

2. In Greek mythology, the fleet-footed Atalanta refused to marry anyone who could not beat her in a foot race. Hippomenes, who got three golden apples from Aphrodite (goddess of love), threw them during the race, diverting Atalanta (who could not resist the gold) and winning the race.

III

Nor yet, if rightly understood,
Does grandeur carry more of good;
To be o'th'number of the great enrolled,   50
A scepter o'er a mighty realm to hold.
    For what is this?
    If I judge not amiss.
But all th'afflicted of a land to take,
And of one single family to make?   55
    The wronged, the poor, th'oppressed, the sad,
    The ruined, malcontent, and mad?
    Which a great part of every empire frame,
    And interest in the common father claim.
    Again what is't, but always to abide   60
    A gazing crowd? Upon a stage to spend
    A life that's vain, or evil without end?
And which is yet nor safely held, nor laid aside?
And then, if lesser titles carry less of care,
Yet none but fools ambitious are to share   65
Such a mock-good, of which 'tis said, 'tis best,
When of the least of it men are possessed.

IV

But, O, the laurelled fool! that dotes on fame,
Whose hope's applause, whose fear's to want a name;
    Who can accept for pay   70
    Of what he does, what others say;
Exposes now to hostile arms his breast,
To toilsome study then betrays his rest;
    Now to his soul denies a just content,
    Then forces on it what it does resent;   75
    And all for praise of fools: for such are those,
    Which most of the admiring crowd compose.
    O famished soul, which such thin food can feed!
    O wretched labour crowned with such a meed![3]
    Too loud, O Fame! thy trumpet is too shrill,   80
        To lull a mind to rest,
        Or calm a stormy breast,
    Which asks a music soft and still.
    'Twas not Amalek's vanquished cry,
    Nor Israel's shout of victory,   85
        That could in Saul the rising passion lay,
'Twas the soft strains of David's lyre the evil spirit chased away.[4]

---

3. Reward.
4. In 1 Samuel 15 and 16, Saul, the first king of
Israel, is sick at heart over his abandonment by
God despite Israel's defeat of the Amalekites. Only
the harp playing of David can ease Saul's mind:

"And it came to pass, when the evil spirit from
God was upon Saul, that David took an harp, and
played with his hand: so Saul was refreshed, and
was well, and the evil spirit departed from him"
(1 Samuel 16:23).

V

But friendship fain[5] would yet itself defend,
    And mighty things it does pretend,
To be of this sad journey, life, the bait,
The sweet reflection of our toilsome state.   90
But though true friendship a rich cordial be,
    Alas, by most 'tis so allayed,[6]
        Its good so mixed with ill we see,
        That dross for gold is often paid.   95
And for one grain of friendship that is found,
Falsehood and interest do the mass compound,
Or coldness, worse than steel, the loyal heart doth wound.
    Love in no two was ever yet the same,
    No happy two e'er felt an equal flame.   100

VI

Is there that earth by human foot ne'er pressed?
That air which never yet by human breast
Respired, did life supply?
    Oh, thither let me fly!
    Where from the world at such a distance set,   105
All that's past, present, and to come I may forget:
The lover's sighs, and the afflicted's tears,
What e'er may wound my eyes or ears.
    The grating noise of private jars,
    The horrid sound of public wars,   110
    Of babbling fame the idle stories,
    The short-lived triumph's noisy glories,
    The curious nets the subtle weave,
    The word, the look that may deceive.
No mundane care shall more affect my breast,   115
    My profound peace shake or molest:
But stupor, like to death, my senses bind,
    That so I may anticipate the rest,
    Which only in my grave I hope to find.

                                                            1686

◄ ANNE FINCH ►

1661–1720

Anne Finch was the third child of the Royalist William Kingsmill and Anne Haslewood. Five months after her birth, her father died. Her mother remarried, turned
control of the Kingsmill estates over to her new husband, Sir Thomas Ogle, and
died not long after. As a result, Anne and her sister were sent to live with their paternal grandmother, Lady Kingsmill. A strong and independent woman, Lady

---

5. Willingly.   6. Mixed, corrupted.

Kingsmill successfully sued the Kingsmill estate for the funds needed to support and educate her two granddaughters, who received an excellent education for the time: they studied the Bible, the classics, history, poetry, and drama; and they learned French and some Italian. When Lady Kingsmill died in 1672, the two girls were reunited with their brother, who had been under the care of their mother's brother, William Haslewood, a man who also had progressive ideas about female education. In 1682, Anne went to court to become maid of honor to Mary of Modena, wife of James, the Duke of York (later James II). There she met Heneage Finch, who held a position similar to hers under the Duke of York. Despite Anne's reluctance, Finch persuaded her to marry him in 1684, and they began what was by all accounts a happy marriage.

The Finches' devotion to court life in general and to James II in particular (who became king in 1685) was disrupted in 1688 when James, distrusted for his Roman Catholicism, was overthrown in the so-called Glorious Revolution (an arrangement that put a Protestant monarch on the throne and instituted a constitutional monarchy). Heneage Finch, under suspicion for refusing to take an oath of allegiance to the new monarchs (Mary, Protestant daughter to James, and her husband, the Dutch William of Orange), was briefly arrested in 1690 in London and later that year reunited with Anne at Eastwell, the estate of his nephew, the Duke of Winchilsea. Although a difficult time emotionally for the couple, the years at Eastwell were also productive years for Anne, who received encouragement for her writing from both her husband (who also transcribed and compiled her poems) and her nephew, a patron of the arts. The poems from this period reflect Anne's appreciation of her friends and the beautiful countryside, but they also reveal her struggle with depression over her exile from court life and her doubts about her poetic talent.

The Finches returned permanently to London in 1710 and resumed life at court. (James II's daughter Anne had assumed the throne in 1702.) There, in the last years of her life, Anne Finch found friends and admirers in two of the most prominent writers of the day, Alexander Pope and Jonathan Swift. In 1713, her first and only volume of poetry was published. *Miscellany Poems, on Several Occasions* contained eighty-six poems and a play that was never performed. In 1714, the Stuart line was once again displaced from the throne with the accession of the Hanovers, and in 1715 the Jacobite rebellion—a Scottish rallying around the Stuart monarchy—was put down. These events once again imperiled the Finches. In 1715 Anne Finch became severely ill and wrote mainly religious poetry for the rest of her life. She died in London at age fifty-nine.

A Letter to Daphnis[1]

This to the crown and blessing of my life,
The much loved husband of a happy wife;
To him whose constant passion found the art
To win a stubborn and ungrateful heart,
And to the world by tenderest proof discovers   5
They err, who say that husbands can't be lovers.

---

1. In Greek mythology, the inventor of pastoral poetry; in Longus's *Daphnis and Chloe*, the shep- herd and shepherdess find mutual love and a happy life together.

With such return of passion as is due,
Daphnis I love, Daphnis my thoughts pursue;
Daphnis, my hopes and joys are bounded all in you.
Even I, for Daphnis' and my promise' sake,   10
What I in women censure, undertake.
But this from love, not vanity proceeds;
You know who writes, and I who 'tis that reads.
Judge not my passion by my want of skill:
Many love well, though they express it ill;   15
And I your censure could with pleasure bear,
Would you but soon return, and speak it here.

1685   1713

The Introduction

Did I my lines intend for public view,
How many censures would their faults pursue!
Some would, because such words they do affect,
Cry they're insipid, empty, incorrect.
And many have attained, dull and untaught,   5
The name of wit, only by finding fault.
True judges might condemn their want[2] of wit;
And all might say, they're by a woman writ.
Alas! a woman that attempts the pen,
Such an intruder on the rights of men,   10
Such a presumptuous creature is esteemed,
The fault can by no virtue be redeemed.
They tell us we mistake our sex and way;
Good breeding, fashion, dancing, dressing, play,
Are the accomplishments we should desire;   15
To write, or read, or think or to enquire,
Would cloud our beauty, and exhaust our time,
And interrupt the conquests of our prime;
While the dull manage of a servile house[3]
Is held by some our utmost art and use.   20
    Sure, 'twas not ever thus, nor are we told
Fables, of women that excelled of old;
To whom, by the diffusive hand of heaven,
Some share of wit and poetry was given.
On that glad day, on which the Ark[4] returned,   25
The holy pledge, for which the land had mourned,
The joyful tribes attend it on the way,
The Levites do the sacred charge convey,
Whilst various instruments before it play;
Here, holy virgins in the concert join,   30
The louder notes to soften and refine,

2. Lack.
3. Management of the servants in a house.

4. The chest in which were carried the Ten Commandments.

And with alternate verse complete the hymn divine.[5]
   Lo! the young poet,[6] after God's own heart,
By him inspired and taught the Muses' art,
Returned from conquest a bright chorus meets,   35
That sing his slain ten thousand in the streets.
In such loud numbers they his acts declare,
Proclaim the wonders of his early war,
That Saul upon the vast applause does frown,
And feel its mighty thunder shake the crown.   40
What can the threatened judgment now prolong?
Half of the kingdom is already gone:[7]
The fairest half, whose judgment guides the rest,
Have David's empire o'er their hearts confessed.

   A woman here leads fainting Israel on,   45
She fights, she wins, she triumphs with a song,
Devout, majestic, for the subject fit,
And far above her arms exalts her wit,
Then to the peaceful, shady palm withdraws,
And rules the rescued nation with her laws.[8]   50

   How are we fallen! fallen by mistaken rules,
And Education's, more than Nature's fools;
Debarred from all improvements of the mind,
And to be dull, expected and designed,
And if some one would soar above the rest,   55
With warmer fancy, and ambition pressed,
So strong the opposing faction still appears,
The hopes to thrive can ne'er outweigh the fears.
Be cautioned, then, my Muse, and still retired;
Nor be despised, aiming to be admired;   60
Conscious of wants, still with contracted wing,
To some few friends, and to thy sorrows sing.
For groves of laurel[9] thou wert never meant:
Be dark enough thy shades, and be thou there content.

1689   1713

Ardelia to Melancholy[1]

At last, my old, inveterate foe,
No opposition shalt thou know.
Since I, by struggling, can obtain
Nothing, but increase of pain
I will at last no more do so,   5
Though I confess I have applied

---

5. A reiteration of the events in 1 Chronicles 15 and 16.
6. The biblical King David.
7. A reiteration of the events in 1 Samuel 18:6–9.
8. The biblical Judge Deborah—see Judges 4 and 5.
9. Poets in ancient Greece were crowned with wreaths of laurel (or bay) leaves in ceremonies of reward and recognition.
1. Meaning "zealous" in Latin, Ardelia was Finch's literary name for herself; melancholy: depression.

Sweet mirth, and music, and have tried
A thousand other arts beside,
To drive thee from my darkened breast,
Thou, who has banished all my rest.   10
But though sometimes a short reprieve they gave,
Unable they, and far too weak, to save;
All arts to quell, did but augment thy force,
As rivers checked, break with a wilder course.

Friendship I to my heart have laid,   15
Friendship, the applauded sovereign aid,
And thought that charm so strong would prove,
As to compel thee to remove;
And to myself I boasting said,
Now I a conqueror sure shall be,   20
The end of all my conflicts see,
And noble triumph wait on me;
My dusky, sullen foe will sure
Ne'er this united charge endure.
But, leaning on his reed, ev'n whilst I spoke,   25
It pierced my hand, and into pieces broke.
Still some new object, or new interest came
And loosed the bonds, and quite dissolved the claim.

These failing, I invoke a Muse,
And poetry would often use   30
To guard me from thy tyrant power;
And to oppose thee every hour
New troops of fancies did I choose.
Alas! in vain, for all agree
To yield me captive up to thee,   35
And heaven alone can set me free.
Thou through my life wilt with me go,
And make the passage sad, and slow.
All that could e'er thy ill-got rule invade,
Their useless arms before thy feet have laid;   40
The fort is thine, now ruined all within,
Whilst by decays without, thy conquest too is seen.

c. 1690   1713

To the Nightingale

Exert thy voice, sweet harbinger of spring!
  This moment is thy time to sing,
  This moment I attend to praise,
And set my numbers to thy lays.[2]
    Free as thine shall be my song;   5
    As thy music, short, or long.

2. Numbers: poetic meter; lays: songs.

Poets, wild as thee, were born,
    Pleasing best when unconfined,
    When to please is least designed,
Soothing but their cares to rest;   10
    Cares do still their thoughts molest,
    And still th' unhappy poet's breast,
Like thine, when best he sings, is placed against a thorn.[3]
She begins, Let all be still!
    Muse, thy promise now fulfill!   15
Sweet, oh! sweet, still sweeter yet
Can thy words such accents fit,
Canst thou syllables refine,
Melt a sense that shall retain
Still some spirit of the brain,   20
Till with sounds like these it join.[4]
    'Twill not be! then change thy note;
    Let division[5] shake thy throat.
Hark! Division now she tries;
Yet as far the Muse outflies.   25
    Cease then, prithee, cease thy tune;
    Trifler, wilt thou sing till *June?*
Till thy business all lies waste,
And the time of building's past!
    Thus we poets that have speech,   30
    Unlike what thy forests teach,
    If a fluent vein be shown
    That's transcendent to our own,
Criticize, reform, or preach,
Or censure what we cannot reach.   35

c. 1702   1713

The Apology

'Tis true, I write; and tell me by what rule
I am alone forbid to play the fool,
To follow through the groves a wandering muse
And feigned ideas for my pleasures choose?
Why should it in my pen be held a fault,   5
Whilst Myra[6] paints her face, to paint a thought?
Whilst Lamia to the manly bumper[7] flies,
And borrowed spirits sparkle in her eyes,
Why should it be in me a thing so vain
To heat with poetry my colder brain?   10

---

3. European folk wisdom held that the nocturnal nightingale sang with its chest pressed against a thorn to keep it awake.
4. Allusion to the creation of an alloy by refining and mixing ore—here the two parts are sound and sense.
5. A variation on a melody.
6. Myra, Lamia, and Flavia are all Latin names, denoting here real or fictional notorious women.
7. Wineglass or cup filled to the brim.

But I write ill, and therefore should forbear.
Does Flavia cease now at her fortieth year
In every place to let that face be seen
Which all the town rejected at fifteen?
Each woman has her weakness; mine indeed   15
Is still to write, though hopeless to succeed.
Nor to the men is this so easy found;
Even in most works with which the wits abound
(So weak are all since our first breach with Heaven)
There's less to be applauded than forgiven.   20

c. 1703   1713

A Nocturnal Reverie

In such a night, when every louder wind
Is to its distant cavern safe confined;
And only gentle zephyr[8] fans his wings,
And lonely Philomel,[9] still waking, sings;
Or from some tree, famed for the owl's delight,   5
She, hollowing clear, directs the wanderer right;
In such a night, when passing clouds give place,
Or thinly veil the heaven's mysterious face;
When in some river, overhung with green,
The waving moon and trembling leaves are seen;   10
When freshened grass now bears itself upright,
And makes cool banks to pleasing rest invite,
Whence springs the woodbine[1] and the bramble-rose,
And where the sleepy cowslip sheltered grows;
Whilst now a paler hue the foxglove takes,   15
Yet chequers still with red the dusky brakes:[2]
When scattered glow-worms, but in twilight fine,
Show trivial beauties watch their hour to shine;
When odours, which declined repelling day,
Through temperate air uninterrupted stray;   20
When darkened groves their softest shadows wear,
And falling waters we distinctly hear;
When through the gloom more venerable shows
Some ancient fabric, awful in repose,
While sunburnt hills their swarthy looks conceal,   25
And swelling haycocks[3] thicken up the vale:
When the loosed horse now, as his pasture leads,
Comes slowly grazing through the adjoining meads,
Whose stealing pace, and lengthened shade we fear,

---

8. God of the west wind.
9. From an ancient Greek legend, the daughter of an Athenian king who was metamorphosed into a nightingale after her brother-in-law raped her and cut out her tongue.
1. Woodbine, bramble-rose, cowslip, and fox-

glove are all wildflowers.
2. Splashes the color red from the berries of the wild service tree among thickets, or clumps, of bushes.
3. A cone-shaped heap of hay.

Till torn-up forage[4] in his teeth we hear: 30
When nibbling sheep at large pursue their food,
And unmolested kine[5] rechew the cud;
When curlews[6] cry beneath the village walls,
And to her straggling brood the partridge calls;
Their short-lived jubilee the creatures keep,   35
Which but endures while tyrant man does sleep:
When a sedate content the spirit feels,
And no fierce light disturbs, whilst it reveals;
But silent musings urge the mind to seek
Something, too high for syllables to speak;   40
Till the free soul to a composedness charmed,
Finding the elements of rage disarmed,
O'er all below a solemn quiet grown,
Joys in the inferior world, and thinks it like her own:
In such a night let me abroad remain,   45
Till morning breaks, and all's confused again;
Our cares, our toils, our clamours are renewed,
Or pleasures, seldom reached, pursued.

c. 1710   1713

---

4. Food for horses and cattle.   6. A bird with a long, slender bill.
5. Cows.

CULTURAL COORDINATES
Menstruation and Misogyny

The emphasis on fluids and "humors" in the excerpt from Jane Sharp's *Midwives Book* (pp. 217–19)reflects the persistence, even in the late seventeenth century (almost fifty years after William Harvey's discovery of the circulation of blood), of Galenic medical theory. Galen, a Greek physician and philosopher from the third century, believed that illness was always caused by an internal imbalance of one or more of the four "humors," the fluids produced by the liver at different stages of the digestive process. Each of the four fluids—blood, phlegm, choler, and black bile—was associated with an element and the qualities of that element: blood was associated with air— hot and wet; phlegm with fire—hot and dry; choler with the earth—cold and dry; black bile with water—cold and wet.

> *Mother-fits were thought to be caused . . . by vapors from the womb rising to the brain.*

The warmer elements, thought to be superior, were associated with masculinity; and, indeed, Galenism may have been particularly enduring because of the "natural" explanation it provided for female inferiority.

From the beginning, Galen's theories had been used to support arguments that insisted on female subordination. Menstruation, and particularly its absence or excess, figures highly in these discussions. Physicians in the seventeenth century and earlier, for instance, refer to "greensickness," which was associated with the absence of menstruation in young women. In fact, it may most often have been caused by a poor diet, but physicians often dismissed it as an easily cured sexual dysfunction: "It is easily cured by Marriage in young Virgins." More troubling to the medical establishment were what Jane Sharp refers to in the excerpt as "fits of the mother," the mother, in this case, being the womb. Mother-fits were thought to be caused either by the suppression of menstruation or by an excess of blood flow and were characterized by extreme melancholy, peculiar behavior, even suicidal thoughts, all of which were said to be caused by vapors from the womb rising to the brain. Sometimes a change in diet was recommended, but the preferred treatment for mother-fits, particularly when the main physical symptom was the absence of menstruation, was, as with greensickness, marital sexual activity: "A good Husband will administer the Cure!" It was exactly this kind of "medical" thinking that led the sixteenth-century Dutch physician Lemnius, a prominent Galenic thinker, to counsel fathers to see to the timely marriage of their daughters, because "that Sex is frail and subject to ruine."

Sadly, the sexual inferiority that Galenic science appeared to endorse blossomed in this period into full-blown misogyny in popular lore about menstruation: menstrual blood was considered polluting to men; it was thought to flay the penis on contact and was considered a powerful component of love potions, which men feared unwittingly ingesting in food prepared by women.

Active 1671

The only biographical details we know of the midwife Jane Sharp, the first English-woman to write a book on childbirth and gynecology, are those she gives us in her *Midwives Book* (1671), an excerpt from which follows. We know, for instance, that she had been a midwife for "over 30 years" when she wrote her manual; we know that she was well read in medical textbooks and that she paid to have some trans-lated from French, Dutch, and Italian, a venture that would have cost her a signifi-cant amount of money. At the time of her writing, public opinion was shifting away from support for midwifery, opponents of the practice citing a high infant mortality rate among midwife-assisted births and lack of proper medical training among mid-wives. Sharp's purpose in writing *The Midwives Book* was to address those edu-cational lapses in the hope of keeping birthing practices in the hands of women.

In the excerpt that follows, it is interesting to note Sharp's insistence on a nonspecialized vocabulary and, despite her woman-centered agenda, her compar-isons of women's reproductive organs with the male "yard," or penis. This may be mainly because, although Sharp claims thirty years of experience as a midwife (and although her text displays a kind of wisdom and a sense of humor that might point to her hands-on experience with pregnant women), her text relies heavily on popular midwifery texts of the period written by men, Nicholas Culpeper's *Direc-tory for Midwives* (1651) chief among them. (Notably, men were rarely, if ever, present in child-birthing rooms.) Like many medical books of the time, the ex-

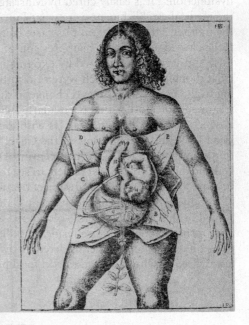

The Figure Explained:

Being a Dissection of the Womb, with the usual manner how the Child lies therein near the time of its Birth.

B B. The inner parts of the *Chorion* extended and branched out.

C. The *Amnios* extended.

D D. The Membrane of the Womb extended and branched.

E. The Fleshy substance call'd the *Cake* or *Placenta*, which nourishes the Infant, it is full of Vessels.

The Vessels appointed for the Navel string.

G. The Navel string carrying nourishment from the *Placenta* to the Navel.

H H H. The manner how the Infant lieth in the Womb near the time of its Birth.

The Navel string how it enters into the Navel.

Frontispiece from Jane Sharp's *Midwives Book* (1671).

cerpt below is at times exceedingly accurate in its descriptions of anatomy and bodily function, and at other times almost hilariously wrong (as in the explanation toward the end of the excerpt that "when women with child are in copulation with men, they do give seed forth, but that seed comes not from the bottom, as some think, but by the neck of the womb").

From **The Midwives Book**

Jane Sharp, Practitioner in the Art of Midwifery above Thirty Years

OF THE FASHION AND GREATNESS OF THE WOMB, AND OF THE PARTS IT IS MADE OF

The womb is of the form of a pear, round toward the bottom and large, but narrow by degrees to the neck; the roundness of it makes it fit to contain much, and it is therefore less subject to be hurt. When women are with child the bottom is broad like a bladder, and the neck narrow; but where they are not with child, the bottom is no broader than the neck. Some women's wombs are larger than others, according to the age, stature, and burden that they bear; maid's wombs are small and less than their bladders; but women's are greater, especially after they have once had a child, and so it will continue. It stretcheth after they have conceived, and the larger it extends the thicker it grows.

It hath parts of two kinds: the simple parts it is made of are membranes, veins, nerves, and arteries.

The compound parts are four: the mouth, the bottom, the neck, and the lap or lips. The membranes are two as I said, one outward and the other inward, that it may open and shut at pleasure; the outward membrane is sinewy, and the thickest of all the membranes that come from the peritoneum;[1] it is strong and doubled, and clothes the womb to make it more strong, and grows to it on both sides. The inward membrane is double also, but can scarce be seen but in exulcerations[2] of the womb. When the woman conceives, it is thick and soft, but it grows thicker daily, and is thickest when the time of birth is. Fibers of all kinds run between these membranes to draw and keep the seed, and to thrust forth the burden,[3] and the flesh of the womb is chiefly made up of fleshy fibers.

The three sorts of fibers for seed do plainly appear after women have gone long with child; those that draw the seed are inward, and are not many. Because the seed is most cast into the womb by the yard,[4] the thwart fibers are strongest, and most, and they are in the middle, but the fibers that lie transverse are strong also, and lie outward, because it is great force that is required in time of delivery.

The veins and arteries that pass through the membranes of the womb come from divers places, for two veins and two arteries come from the seed vessels, and two veins and two arteries from the vessels in the lower belly, and run upward, that from all the body, both from above and under, blood of all sorts might be conveyed, to bring nourishment for the womb, and for the infant in it; also they serve as scavengers to purge out the terms[5] every month. The twigs of the vein that is in the lower belly mingle in the womb with the branches of the seed veins, and the mouths of them reach into the hollow of the womb, and they are called

---

1. The membrane that lines the walls of the abdominal cavity and the undersurface of the diaphragm.
2. Ulcers.

3. Fetus.
4. Penis.
5. Menstrual period.

cups; through these comes more blood always than the infant needs, that the child may never want[6] nutriment in the womb, and there may be some to spare when the time comes for the child to be born; but after the birth, this blood comes not hither but goes to the breasts to make milk; but at all other times it is cast out monthly what is superfluous, and if it be not, it corrupts and causeth fits of the mother; yet they come more often from the seed corrupted and staying there than they do from blood.

It is not only blood is voided by the terms, but multitude of humors[7] and excrements, and these purgations last sometimes three or four days, sometimes a week, and young folk have them when the moon changeth, but women in years at the full of the moon; which is to be observed, that we may know when to give remedies to maids whose terms come not down, for we must do it in the time when the moon is new or ready to change, and to elder women about the time that nature uses to send them forth, because a physician is but a helper to nature, and if he observe not nature's rules, he will sooner kill than cure.

The sinews of the womb are small but many, and interwoven like network, which makes it quick of feeling; they come to the upper part of the bottom from the branches of the nerves of the sixth conjugation, which go to the root of the ribs, and to the lower part of the bottom, and to the neck of the womb from the marrow of loins and the great bone. Thus they by their quick feeling cause pleasure in copulation and expulsion of what offends the part; they are most plentiful at the bottom of the womb, to quicken and strengthen it in attracting and embracing the seed of man.

There is but one continued passage from the top or lap to the bottom of the womb; yet some divide it into four parts; namely into 1. The upper part, or bottom, for that lieth uppermost in the body. 2. The mouth or inward orifice of the neck. 3. The neck. 4. The outward lap, lips, or privity.

The chief part of these, which is properly the womb or matrix, is the bottom; here is the infant conceived, kept, formed and fed until the rational soul be infused from above, and the child born. The broader part or bottom is set above the share-bone[8] that may be dilated as the child grows; the outside is smooth and overlaid with a watery moisture: there is a corner on each side above, and when women are not with child, the seed is poured out into these, for the carrying vessels for seed are planted into them. They are to make more room for the child, and at first it is so small that the parents' seed fills it full, for it embraceth it, be it never so little, as close as 'tis possible: the bottom is full of pores, but they are but the mouths of the cups by which the blood in childbearing comes out of the veins of the womb into the cavity. The corners of the womb's bottom are wrinkled; the bottom is softer than the neck of it, yet harder than the lap and more thick. From the lower part of the bottom comes a piece an inch long like the nut of the man's yard, but small as one's little finger, and a pin's point will but enter into it, but it is rough to keep the seed from recoiling after it is once attracted, for when the parts are overslippery the humors are peccant,[9] and those women are barren. Hip-

6. Lack.
7. According to Galenic medical theory, a person's physical and mental qualities and dispositions were determined by the composition of the body's four chief fluids, or humors—blood, phlegm, choler, and melancholy (or black choler).
8. Pubic bone.
9. Unhealthy.

pocrates saith, that sometimes part of the kall[1] falls between the bladder and the womb and makes women fruitless.

This part may well be reckoned for[2] another part of the womb, for it lieth between the beginning of the bottom and the mouth, and there is a clear passage in it. The womb hath two mouths, the inward mouth and the outward; by the inward mouth the bottom opens directly into the neck, this mouth lieth overthwart like the mouth of a plaice,[3] or the passage of the nut of the yard; the whole orifice with the slit transverse is like the Greek letter theta θ: it is so little and narrow that the seed once in can scarce come back, nor any offensive thing enter into the hollow of the womb. The mouth lieth directly against the bottom, for the seed goeth in a straight line from the neck to the bottom.

The womb is always shut but in time of generation, and then the bottom draws in the seed, and it presently shuts so close that no needle, as I saith, can find an entrance, and thus it continues till the time of delivery, unless some ill accident, or disease force it to open; for when women with child are in copulation with men, they do give seed forth, but that seed comes not from the bottom, as some think, but by the neck of the womb. It must open when a child is born so wide as to give passage for it by degrees, because the neck of the womb is of a compact thick substance, and thicker when the birth is nigh; wherefore there cleaves to it a body like glue, and by that means the mouth opens safely without danger of being torn or broken; and as often as the passage is open, it comes away like a round crown, and midwives call it the rose, the garland, or the crown. If this mouth be too often and unreasonably opened by too frequent coition, or in overmoist bodies, or by the whites,[4] it makes women barren, and therefore whores have seldom any children; it is the same reason if it grow too hard or thick or fat, also the cancer and the scirrhus,[5] two diseases incurable, which happen but seldom till the courses fail, are bred here.

Thus I have as briefly and as plainly as I could, laid down a description of the parts of generation of both sexes, purposely omitting hard names, that I might have no cause to enlarge my work, by giving you the meaning of them where there is no need, unless it be for such persons who desire rather to know words than things.

1671

1. Hippocrates: famous Greek physician born about 4600 BCE; kall: amniotic sac.
2. Considered as.
3. A flatfish.
4. Vaginal mucous.
5. A hard tumor, usually cancerous.

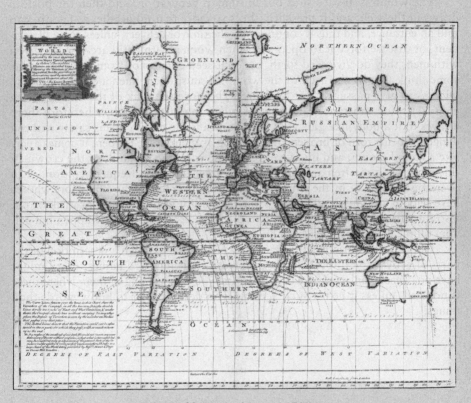

A New and Accurate Map of the World. (Emanuel Bowen, 1744)

The Eighteenth Century

In Chapter 4 of her novel *Orlando*, Virginia Woolf imagines her heroine pouring tea for a group of prominent eighteenth-century literary men, among them Alexander Pope, Joseph Addison, and Jonathan Swift. As Orlando hands the cups around, she thinks "how women of all ages to come will envy me." But she soon changes her mind when she discovers that the large intellects of the literary men fail to make them kind, charitable, or tolerant. Moreover, Orlando finds their company facetious and condescending toward women. Gradually, she realizes that she hates tea and loathes her illustrious company. She inadvertently insults Pope by letting a sugar cube fall with a great plop into his tea. He and the others depart, and Orlando, now cross-dressed in a magnificent black velvet suit richly trimmed with Venetian lace, leaves her tea table for a nighttime stroll around the streets of London.

Woolf offers an unromantic account of the eighteenth-century literary scene from the female perspective. Writing tongue in cheek, she imagines how a vibrant period of literary history failed to engage the energy, talent, and intellect of women. In the past few decades, feminist literary critics, as well as social and cultural historians, have similarly taken up the challenge of understanding the eighteenth century from a female perspective. Their efforts have resulted in an eighteenth-century canon vastly different from the one familiar to Woolf and her peers. No doubt the eighteenth century is still recognized as the literary period belonging to Swift and Pope, but it is now known as much more—namely, as a key period of transition in women's history, in which modern definitions of femininity emerged and during which women's lives were significantly transformed in social, political, and economic terms.

We also know now that women did not only pour the tea. They also engaged in a wide range of social, cultural, and political activities; and they played a vital part in eighteenth-century literary culture, producing poetry and prose writings of all kinds, from novels, romances, and plays to memoirs to didactic works on morality and philosophical treatises on women's rights. In response to feminist recovery work, the eighteenth-century canon now includes the writings of women who lived in a vast range of social circumstances, from an aristocrat who traveled with her husband and children to Turkey in the declining days of the Ottoman Empire (pp. 239–48) to a formerly enslaved African whose story was problematically transcribed by an abolitionist (pp. 418–38), from an agricultural laborer who describes the difficulties of balancing a life of exhausting physical labor with the demands of a household (pp. 269–75) to the wife of an American president who weighed in on matters of state policy despite the gaps in her own education (pp. 280–84).

THE EIGHTEENTH CENTURY: AN OVERVIEW

The discovery and insertion of such writing by women into the eighteenth-century canon challenges the preexisting definition of a century that has been known under several rubrics. Traditionally the eighteenth century has been identified as "the Age of Enlightenment," a period characterized by its chief political and philosophical movements, among them scientific rationalism (the belief that the world can be known and understood through the intelligent use of the mind and the senses) and humanism (a philosophy privileging the power and capabilities of the human being). Literary historians commonly divide the century into two halves. The first half is known as the neoclassical, or Augustan, period because it self-consciously modeled itself after the stable and peaceful period of the first Roman emperor, Augustus Caesar (63 BCE–14 CE), a time that produced the poets Virgil, Horace, and Ovid. The second half is called either the Age of Johnson—in homage to Dr. Samuel Johnson (1709–84), the period's preeminent literary figure—or the Age of Revolution, since both the American Revolution (1775–83) and the French Revolution (1789–99) occurred during this period.

Cultural historians also organize the century around its monarchical succession: after a period of transition, encompassing the reigns of William and Mary (1689–1702) and Queen Anne (1702–14), England reestablished Protestantism as the state religion. Parliament banished the Catholic, or Stuart, line from the throne and brought George I (1714–27)—a man who did not even speak English—over from Hanover, Germany, to ensure the Protestant line of succession. George I inaugurated the long "Georgian," or "Hanoverian," period. His reign was followed by that of his son George II (1727–60), who, like his father, had little interest in ruling the country. Then followed George III (1760–1820), famously king during the American Revolution.

The eighteenth century is also known as a time of important economic transition, when political power shifted away from an elite and privileged class whose wealth came largely from the land they owned to an ascendant group whose money came from other sources, chief among them trade. Many historians tell the story of an ongoing struggle between the Tories (the landed, more traditional and conservative group, whose sympathies often lay with the Catholic, or Stuart, line) and the Whigs (the moneyed, more urban and liberal group, who invested in the power of Parliament) to control England's destiny. In this version of history, the Whigs are commonly assumed to have become dominant, as the century saw the power of the king diminish and the power of Parliament increase. It was also during the eighteenth century that England became Great Britain: under the Act of Union in 1707, the parliaments of England and Scotland merged. Then, just after the close of the century in 1801, the Irish parliament was also merged into that of the United Kingdom, giving birth to the British flag, or Union Jack, as we know it today, with its distinctive amalgamation of the crosses of St. George, St. Andrew, and St. Patrick.

Rank and Social Position in the Eighteenth Century

Most historians date the birth of a class system, one based on groups of individuals sharing similar economic interests, to the nineteenth century. Thus, throughout the eighteenth century, English society continued to be arranged according to a strict hierarchy that depended on birth. Family and kinship ties determined one's social position, and possibilities for social mobility were limited.

According to Daniel Defoe (1660–1731), author of *Moll Flanders, Robinson Crusoe,* and *The Complete English Gentleman,* there were seven ranks in English society:

1. The great, who live profusely
2. The rich, who live plentifully

3. The middle sort, who live well
4. The working trades, who labor hard but feel no want
5. The country people, farmers, etc. who fare indifferently
6. The poor, who fare hard
7. The miserable, that really pinch and suffer want

Yet the ranks were economically uneven. Most of England's resources were concentrated in the hands of a very few elite families, and vast disparities existed in economic circumstances between other ranks. For instance, a laborer, or member of Defoe's "working trades," might have earned as little as £10 a year (£1 having 100 to 250 times as much buying power as today's dollar); in contrast, a nobleman might enjoy an income of £10,000 a year.

At the very top of the social ladder was a very small, elite class of nobility (dukes, marquesses, earls, viscounts, barons, and their immediate relations), a mere two or three hundred families, most of whom held titles that had been bestowed upon their families generations ago by the monarch. Under them were the gentry, people with "good" bloodlines and breeding, who might own land but not hold a title. By one estimate, in 1700 there were approximately 15,000 families in the gentry, with incomes ranging from £300 to £1,500 per year. Below the gentry was the lesser gentry, people even less well-connected, though still considered among the upper ranks of society.

For the nobility, the gentry, and even the lesser gentry (the top two levels of Defoe's stratification), wealth came primarily from the land—in other words, an estate. Some estates were enormous, encompassing thousands of acres, with natural resources like forests, fields, streams, and even whole villages with their shops, cottages, schools, and churches. Income from agriculture (growing grain and raising cattle), rents from cottages and other buildings, and revenues from timber and minerals found on the estates often produced vast sums for the owner, who lived off the labor of others. Indeed, at this level, it was a point of pride that one never had to work, although estates tended to do best when the owner took an active interest in managing his property.

The English practice of primogeniture (passing the entire estate on to the oldest son, rather than dividing the property evenly among family members) kept the estates intact and their owners powerful. Younger sons provided for themselves by obtaining a university education and becoming clergymen (a career that could be quite lucrative if one were ambitious, since parishes provided annual salaries, or "livings"); because families controlled the livings of churches on their property, finding a position for the well-connected was not difficult. Alternatively, they could buy themselves positions as military officers and advance through the ranks similarly by means of their connections.

Daughters were shut out of this system, although some female members of the aristocracy still stood to inherit large sums and others had sizeable dowries and jointures (provisions made for them after their husband's death). Once married under English law, however, a woman was a *feme covert*—a woman under the legal protection and control of her husband (pp. 7–10). As such, she could not, for instance, manage her own property, enter into contracts, or even take custody of her children if the couple separated or divorced.

Throughout the century, the lines between ranks remained somewhat fluid, as Frances Burney illustrates in *Evelina* (pp. 322–39): we follow Burney's heroine as she moves from the elite world of noblemen like Lord Orville, who in turn keeps company with members of the gentry like Mrs. Mirvan, to the more humble surroundings of her cousins, the Branghtons, who keep a silversmith's shop in east London. As typical members of the middle rank, the Branghtons are represented as living not off the land or the labor of others but off the capital they produce themselves. While Burney does not appear comfortable with the idea of "working" people, her representation captures the truth of an emerging class of people that included not only merchants, craftsmen, and manufacturers, but also lawyers and doctors—in short, anyone who had received training in order to make his living.

Below them was a vast group of laboring poor, who often survived only by piecing together a variety of jobs, from weaving to agricultural labor, from coal mining to sweeping the street. At this level of society, women took whatever jobs they could, often competing with men but being paid less. Large numbers of the laboring poor also often entered into domestic service. However, even domestic service had its hierarchy, with male servants who wore uniforms or livery above the female servants in both prestige and earning power. Similarly, a lady's maid, who knew about the care of her mistress's hair and clothing, outranked a scullery maid, who carried the slops and did other dirty work. Lowest of all the servants was the charwoman, or the woman hired by the day to do the heaviest and filthiest housework. Mary Collier, herself a laborer, describes the experiences of this rank of life (pp. 269–75).

Still, even the meanest employment was better than no work at all, and the hardest lot fell to a class of paupers who had no recourse but begging or crime. Indeed, strict vagrancy laws made it illegal for the impoverished to travel beyond the parish of their birth in search of aid, even when the situation there was hopeless, so the itinerant homeless were more likely to be prosecuted than assisted. Those driven to theft were treated mercilessly if caught: by 1795 over two hundred crimes, including burglary, robbery, and shoplifting, were felonies that could be punished by hanging. Although only 30–40 percent were hanged, from 1718 on many were transported, first to the colonies in North America (until the outbreak of war in 1776) and later (from 1787) to Australia. Women convicted of a crime could "plead their bellies"—that is, claim to be pregnant; in those cases, they were reprieved until after the birth of the child and often permanently, as the state did not want to be saddled with the expense of caring for the child.

By the beginning of the next century, the strict stratification of English society began to wane, as it became increasingly possible to make a fortune independently: trade and manufacturing became more lucrative, and new families of fortune gradually made their way through marriage into the upper ranks. Slowly the stigma associated with the idea of working for a living diminished. At the same time, new doctrines, articulated by men like French philosopher Jean-Jacques Rousseau (1712–78), promulgated the "natural rights of men" and spread revolutionary ideas about social equality, such as those articulated in the American Declaration of Independence (1776). Still, these new doctrines were narrow in their application, written only with the interests of propertied white men in mind. They did not apply to poor men, enslaved people, or women, who still found themselves subordinated to male authority and disenfranchised from the political system.

Colonialism, Slavery, and Mercantile Capitalism

In recent decades, some historians have sought to counter a traditional understanding of the Age of Enlightenment by focusing on the dark underside of this period—

namely, the fact that much of its vast economic expansion depended heavily on colonial expansion, or the sending of British ships to North America, the Caribbean, the East Indies, and the South Seas in the hopes of expanding English markets and of retrieving valuable commodities to be sold at home. Colonial expansion often meant the exploitation of resident populations, such as the Native American Indians. It entailed as well the spread of English culture, language, and customs. Many of the women authors in this collection, although they belong to disparate communities around the globe, write in English and not the original language of their indigenous countries because of colonial activity first occurring in the eighteenth century.

Initially, the English competed with the Portuguese, Spanish, and French for control of resources and a piece of the lucrative slave trade; but as a result of the Treaty of Utrecht in 1713, they received a monopoly on the shipment of enslaved Africans. Thus, colonial expansion resulted in the highly lucrative triangle trade, a three-part trade route bringing manufactured goods from English ports to the coast of Africa, where they were traded for the millions who were enslaved there, selling those enslaved peoples to the plantation owners of the Caribbean and North America, and carrying back to English markets the luxury goods like sugar and tobacco produced by slave labor. Several historians currently argue that virtually no one in the British Isles was untouched by this sinister exchange, as most English citizens—whether they retained holdings in the Royal African Company, manufactured goods to be sold in Africa, served in the British navy, or participated in the innumerable services and industries that sprang up around slave trade, including banking and insurance—were the beneficiaries of this morally reprehensible enterprise.

With the expansion of mercantile capitalism in the eighteenth century, the lifestyle of most Britons changed dramatically, as a range of consumer goods, including inexpensive textiles and china, were imported for home markets. Tea and sugar became household staples, while English manufacturers, responding to new consumer demands, produced many enticing goods, from mirrors and clocks to furniture and carriages. A new pastime—shopping—came

A West Indian Flower Girl and Two Other Free Women of Colour (c. 1769) by Agostino Brunias. (Yale Center for British Art, Paul Mellon Collection)

into existence, as modern retail practices, including the use of glass windows, better indoor lighting, and salesmanship, were introduced (see pp. 340–41). At the center of this consumer revolution was the figure of "woman," whom male writers simultaneously eulogized and demonized. On the one hand, woman's supposedly voracious appetite for "things" inspired fleets of British ships to obtain commodities from foreign shores, thereby stimulating the British economy. The whole world could be brought home for woman's benefit. Or, as Joseph Addison enthused in his periodical publication *The Tatler* (1716),

> I consider woman as a beautiful, romantic animal, that may be adorned with furs and feathers, pearls and diamonds, ores and silks. The lynx shall cast its skin at her feet to make her a tippet, the peacock, parrot, and swan shall pay for contributions to her muff; the sea shall be searched for shells, and the rocks for gems, and every part of nature furnish out its share towards the embellishment of a creature that is the most consummate work of it.

On the other hand, however, Jonathan Swift, among others, complained that woman's boundless appetite for exotic goods like tea and sugar made the local economy beholden to foreign suppliers while depleting national coffers. Neither portrait of "woman" was, of course, accurate: there is nothing to support the idea that women are naturally more prone to consumerism than men. Rather, both depictions suggest how men projected desires and anxieties onto women.

WOMEN'S PLACE IN SOCIETY: THE RISE OF THE NEW DOMESTIC WOMAN

This dual construction of "woman" raises the larger question of female identity in the eighteenth century: who was this creature known as woman? To ask this question is to acknowledge that female identity—then as now—was largely a concept produced through extensive discussions, debates, and writings. Many of our current assumptions about what it means to be a woman would not have applied at the end of the seventeenth century, and women did not yet necessarily recognize themselves as a group sharing a common identity. Before 1700, someone born female was more likely to group herself in terms of her political or religious affiliation, her rank, or her kin than in terms of her gender. Thus, for instance, she might have called herself a "Royalist" or a Catholic or a member of the Cavendish family, without necessarily identifying with other women outside these groups. By the end of the century, this was to change, as a collective identity gradually emerged. This new identity subordinated all other differences to the fact of biological difference. In a sense, we can say that modern "woman" as she is known today in western Europe was born in the eighteenth century.

Creating the New Domestic Woman

The first step in the birth of modern womanhood was the gradual acceptance of the two-sex model. Before the end of the eighteenth century, when people envisioned what it meant to be a man or a woman, they almost always resorted to a one-sex model based on the work of the Roman physician Claudius Galenus, or Galen (129–210 CE). Galen believed that male and female genitals were the same, with one important difference: the male organs were on the outside of the body, whereas the female were on the inside. In other words, the vagina was an interior penis, the ovaries were interior testes, the uterus an interior scrotum, and so on.

Because Galen believed that women's internalized genitalia generated less "vital heat," he argued that women were farther from perfection than men. Galen further believed that reproduction occurred in the heat generated from the two bodies in close contact and that both partners needed to achieve orgasm in order to heat and fuse the seeds.

It was not until the eighteenth century that the separate organs of the two sexes were given their distinct names and recognized as functioning differently. Also, around 1750 scientists began to use a female skeleton, one with a distinctly female bone structure. Newer scientific methods of observation, analysis, and experimentation gradually supported the idea that there were two very different human sexes. The two-sex model clearly put "woman" in a differ-

Study of a Lady (c. 1785–90) by Thomas Gainsborough. (The Pierpont Morgan Library, New York, NY)

ent category from "man," as female sexuality was now understood in different—and often more prescriptive—ways. For instance, female orgasm was no longer believed essential to conception, and "normal" women were now deemed sexually passive and without sexual desires of their own. Corresponding to this movement toward the two-sex model was a widespread cultural effort to define and codify "femininity" and "masculinity." Elaborate new codes of behavior arose, many of them designed to protect the second, "weaker" sex and to address physiological differences that had been previously less regarded.

By the end of the eighteenth century, regardless of religion, rank, or politics, most women would have identified themselves as members of the female sex, sharing a physiology and possessing a characteristic set of emotions, attitudes, and behaviors in common with other women. Conduct manuals and educational treatises stipulated the terms for a female identity and defined the concept of the "proper lady." These popular books and written materials, almost always produced by men, aimed to create an ideal of femininity. According to this ideal, women were

A

FATHER'S LEGACY

to

HIS DAUGHTERS.

By the late Dr. JOHN GREGORY, of Edinburgh.

Manchester,

Printed and sold at the Office of G. Nicholson, 9, Spring-gardens.

Sold also by T. Knott, 47, Lombard-street;

and Champante & Whitrow, Jewry-street, London.

Anno 1797.

Frontispiece from John Gregory's *A Father's Legacy to His Daughters* (1774).

supposed to contribute to a British economy no longer through their labor but through their supervisory capacities as wives and mothers. The "new domestic woman," as Nancy Armstrong has called her, was above all supposed to be an efficient, industrious, and frugal housewife. Most likely a member of the middle rank, the ideal woman was to distinguish herself from a now-old-fashioned generation of upper-rank or aristocratic women. These women had traditionally represented their power through an ornamental display of themselves—through their spectacular fashions, for instance, or through their elaborate household furnishings. The new domestic woman, in contrast, was discreet, self-effacing to the point of near invisibility in public. She was also extremely modest and chaste.

Among the most famous conduct books contributing to the creation of this ideal was that of Dr. John Gregory, titled *A Father's Legacy to His Daughters* (1774). A few excerpts from his often reprinted and massively circulated publication give the flavor of the paternalistic advice that was often given to women and suggest the parameters within which women were supposed to live. Dr. Gregory begins his book in typical fashion by avowing a disinterested dedication to the well-being of his female addressee: "You will hear, at least for once in your lives, the genuine sentiments of a man who has no interest in flattering or deceiving you." He lays out the simple "facts" of a woman's life—for instance, that she "cannot plunge into business, or dissipate [herself] in pleasure and riot, as men too often do, when under the pressure of misfortunes." Dr. Gregory's advice extends from dress, which must be neat and not draw attention, to company, which should not include the intimate friendship of married women. (He does not explain why.) He counsels against wit, deeming it "the most dangerous talent you can possess" and advocates for female modesty, "which I think so essential in your sex, will naturally dispose you to be rather silent in company, especially a large one." Even diet comes under his purview:

> There is a species of refinement in luxury, just beginning to prevail among the gentlemen of this country, to which our ladies are yet as great strangers as any women on earth; I hope, for the honor of the sex, they may ever continue so; I mean the luxury of eating. It is a despicable selfish vice in men, but in your sex is beyond expression indelicate and disgusting.

Should a woman enjoy good health, "she must never make a boast of it, but enjoy it in grateful silence."

Although it may now be difficult to believe that any woman would take such condescending and oppressive advice to heart, it is worth recognizing what Dr. Gregory offered along with his prescriptive behaviors, namely, the guarantee of unqualified paternal love and affection, a "disinterested" commitment to a woman's well-being, and protection from one's own supposedly worst impulses. In a context where women may have felt themselves vulnerable and believed themselves at the mercy of their own supposedly volatile female temperaments, it may well have seemed comforting to discover the rules that promised survival in a patriarchal society. Still, the transformation of "proper" womanhood from the beginning of the eighteenth century to the end was quite remarkable, as we can see from the following anecdote.

In his memoir, the famous novelist Sir Walter Scott (1771–1832) records how he was approached by his great-aunt, who requested a copy of Aphra Behn's novels, written during the Restoration (1660–88) and expressing a libertine attitude toward women's sexuality (see pp. 125–27). Before reluctantly sending her the novels, he marked the package "private and confidential." His great-aunt returned the novels, counseling that they be burned because of their salacious content. "Is it not a very odd thing," she reportedly said to Scott, "that I, an old woman of eighty and upwards, sitting alone, feel myself ashamed to read a book, which sixty years ago, I have heard read aloud for the amusement of large circles, consisting of the first and foremost creditable society in London?" Although Scott approvingly notes "the gradual improvement of the national taste and delicacy" bringing about the change, modern readers are likely to wonder about a social climate in which grown women could no longer read novels with sexual content without experiencing acute embarrassment.

Educating the New Domestic Woman

Throughout the eighteenth century, the school curriculum for girls matched the circumscribed sense of their potential. In the words of Hannah More (pp. 287–310), parents were counseled to teach their daughters that "this world is not a stage for the display of superficial or even of shining talents, but for the strict and sober exercise of fortitude, temperance, meekness, faith, diligence, and self-denial." The purpose of a girl's education was to create a satisfied and fulfilled wife and mother, as even the radical writer Mary Wollstonecraft (pp. 365–82) agreed. To be sure, a mother's role as religious and educational guide necessitated literacy, so that by 1800 most women of the middle rank could read and write. Women gained a basic education either at home, under their mother's tuition, or in small schools often run by elderly women. Later, a young woman of the middle ranks or above might attend a lady's "academy," comparable to a finishing school today. A basic curriculum would have included some arithmetic, especially the kind of computation necessary for household accounts, some geography, some history, and perhaps some French or Italian. The arts were also thought appropriate, so music (especially playing the piano or singing), painting watercolors, drawing, and dancing were also taught. A range of needlework skills filled out the program.

But women's curriculum was not supposed to include anything that challenged the intellect or stimulated the imagination. Hannah More decreed French and German novels too provocative, for instance, and she warned against philosophy. Mathematics would have been considered too masculine. Also pronounced inappropriate was the study of Latin and Greek, subjects that had been mastered by some aristocratic women in an earlier period. Although the seventeenth-century scholar Bathsua Makin (1660–75) had once militated for wider access for gentlewomen to the "ancient languages," now they were consigned to the all-male public schools (or, in the United States, preparatory schools) and universities, which denied access to women until the nineteenth century.

Thus, while literacy rates among women increased dramatically during the eighteenth century, the scope of women's education narrowed from a time when very few aristocratic women had been better schooled in a more intellectually rigorous curriculum. This earlier group of elite women had freely roamed their fathers' or brothers' libraries, sometimes with access to the same subjects as their brothers. Frequently proud of their accomplishments, they were not afraid to display their competence. For instance, Lady Mary Wortley Montagu (pp. 239–48), having learned French and Latin from her father's extensive library, went on to read widely in a range of literary, aesthetic, and historical topics. Later, she studied Arabic as well. Similarly, the Bluestockings (pp. 285–86) were an extraordinary generation of women: born before 1730, they demonstrated high intellectual achievement.

However, by the end of the century, such erudition was rejected by someone like Frances Burney (pp. 313–39), the daughter of a prominent organist and music scholar. Indeed, Burney is said to have turned down Dr. Johnson's offer to teach her Latin because she feared the subject was too masculine. Unlike Lady Mary Wortley Montagu, Burney was taught to shun the public eye, to hide what she knew, and to practice discretion. In her novels, Burney depicts intellectually strong, well-educated, and outspoken female characters who draw attention to themselves—like Mrs. Selwyn in *Evelina* (1778)—as troubling role models for her young heroines. The "learned lady" gradually became a risible stereotype not only on the page but also on the stage.

For women at the bottom of the social hierarchy—those who worked in domestic service or as farm laborers—even access to basic literacy would have been a struggle. In the days before free public schooling, few parents would have been able to afford the school fees. Books, even through membership in a lending library, were expensive. And long, grueling days, often stretching from sunrise to sunset, left little time or energy for those women struggling to educate themselves. Nonetheless, a few laboring women, among them Mary Leapor (pp. 251–58), Mary Collier (pp. 269–75), Janet Little (pp. 384–86), and Elizabeth Hands (pp. 438–42), not only became literate but also found the opportunity to publish descriptions of everyday life from their perspectives. Their poems fill out the story of women in the eighteenth century by reminding us how relatively few eighteenth-century women actually enjoyed the kind of leisured, gentrified lifestyle in which an education could occur.

Women growing up far from England were also educated somewhat differently, though not necessarily better. Abigail Adams (pp. 280–84), for instance, though destined to become the wife of the second president of the newly formed United States of America, was not allowed the formal education she craved. In the new republic, with its higher overall rates of literacy, attitudes about educating women beyond a minimal level progressed very little. Largely self-taught (though with the help of her grandmother), Adams found an intellectual outlet in her letters, where she signed herself Portia, after Shakespeare's learned character in *The Merchant of Venice*. Despite her errors in spelling and grammar, Adams managed to articulate clearly her opinions on a range of familial, social, and political topics. Yet even Adams's limited education would have been unfathomable for the many enslaved African women who found themselves working on the plantations in North America and the Caribbean. With very rare exception, basic literacy was out of their reach, meaning that their lives remain almost entirely unchronicled in print. The poems of Phillis Wheatley (pp. 342–46) and the testimony of Mary Prince (pp. 418–38), as transcribed by the abolitionists, stand in for the unwritten stories of innumerable enslaved women.

Portrait of Abigail Adams.

Labor and the New Domestic Woman

Those familiar with the eighteenth-century literary canon most likely assume that women did not work outside the home during this period. But works like *Clarissa* (1747–48) by

Portrait of Phillis Wheatley, from *Revue des Colonies.*

Samuel Richardson (1689–1761) or even *Evelina* by Frances Burney (pp. 322–39) tell only a small part of the story, as very few women had the resources of these heroines. Throughout the 1700s, most women would have been pressed to contribute to their family's income. Yet the situation for women who needed to make a living worsened over the century. Historian Deborah Valenze chronicles the various means of economic survival that were taken away from the poorest women. For instance, the practice of enclosure, or of consolidating small agricultural holdings into larger ones, transforming common fields into privately held farms, denied women the right to put any livestock they were lucky enough to own to pasture. Similarly, ancient gleaning rights, which had allowed women and children to gather what remained on a field after the wheat had been bound up and carried off, were terminated. Even gathering "snapwood," or little bits of wood and twigs to use as firewood, became illegal once farm lands were enclosed. In these and other ways, women at the bottom of the social ladder found it harder and harder to scrape together a living.

At the same time, various lucrative employment opportunities for women of the middle and lower ranks diminished. Where women had once ruled the dairies, supervising and participating in the making of cheese and butter, male managers gradually took charge, claiming greater expertise based on "rational" and scientific methodologies. Around the same time, spinning moved out of the home and into the factory, so that women could no longer work and care for their children simultaneously. Other possibilities for gainful employment for working women also diminished: Although their foremothers had had access to a range of trades, including enterprises like pewter making and beer brewing, girls were increasingly discouraged from taking on apprenticeships that were now deemed appropriate only for boys. By the end of the century, only two apprenticeships—mantua making (dressmaking) and millinery (hat making) were regularly open to girls, and both of these were thought to carry some risks, as they placed women in the public eye and therefore made them vulnerable to male sexual advances.

Rival milliners (1772), engraved by Robert Laurie after a painting by J. Collett.

Gradually, the idea that the male breadwinner should be the head of the household gained ascendancy. Regardless of the economic reality of her husband's earning power, a proper lady was not supposed to contribute to her family's coffers through labor outside the home. By the beginning of the nineteenth century, public opinion no longer supported or praised women whose labor produced wealth. Instead, women were restricted to bearing and raising children and to running the household.

Conduct books and medical manuals helped to spread the idea that women were happiest at home. They also promoted breast-feeding and the idea of sustained, intimate contact between mother and child (p. 383). This is not to say that motherhood or running a household was necessarily unfulfilling or unsatisfactory, as many women took pride in their domestic activities and found a sense of accomplishment through their families. Still, the idea that a woman might work outside the home and successfully raise a family died away in the eighteenth century and would not reappear until the twentieth century.

Beyond the New Domesticity: Women Travelers

Although an emerging domestic ideology consigned female activity to the home, many eighteenth-century women still traveled the globe for a number of reasons and under a range of conditions. One category of female traveler included all those whose economic circumstances made it difficult for them to stay home in the British Isles. For example, sometimes sailors' wives traveled on board ship, preferring a life at sea with their husbands over life on land, frequently without their spouses' wages to support them (pp. 267–68). Other women went with their husbands to colonial outposts in India or North America when better financial opportunities presented themselves. Eliza Fay (pp. 348–58), for instance, made the first of her four trips to India with her husband, who had been called to practice law there; she took her subsequent trips alone, having each time a plan to make her fortune.

In addition, the slave trade uprooted large numbers of African women: it wrenched the enslaved from their homelands and subjected them to the notorious "Middle Passage" across the Atlantic Ocean, during which they experienced horrific cruelties. Eventually, it placed those who survived along the coast of North America or in the Caribbean, as with Mary Prince (pp. 418–38), or occasionally for periods of time in England, as was the case for Phillis Wheatley (pp. 342–46), for instance. But the slave trade also made travelers out of women like Janet Schaw (pp. 262–66), who traveled from Scotland to the West Indies with her brother, manager of a plantation whose owners made their living off slave labor. Anna Falconbridge (pp. 442–49), most likely the first white woman to describe a voyage to Africa, lived with her abolitionist husband on the west coast of Africa in 1791 in a settlement for free black refugees, mostly ex-slaves who had fought for the British during the Revolutionary War.

For those with intellectual curiosity—like Lady Mary Wortley Montagu (pp. 239–48), the wife of an English diplomat to Turkey—travel was often an opportunity to learn about the other societies they visited and to embrace different cultural practices. Among others, Mary Wollstonecraft embraced her travels to revolutionary France, and later Scandinavia, as an opportunity for study and intellectual reflection. The writings of eighteenth-century women travelers, while testifying to early forms of global connection, also remind us that women did not necessarily live quietly at home during the eighteenth century.

WOMEN AND THE LITERARY SCENE, 1700–1799

Although Virginia Woolf imagines an eighteenth-century literary culture that consigned women to the tea table, we now recognize that the situation was far more complex. Before 1730, women published innumerable writings of a theological nature. By the late eighteenth century, women were contributing to all genres of writing and literature and gaining wider recognition. They wrote journalism: for example, Eliza Haywood (pp. 248–51), who began her career as a novelist, created *The Female Spectator* (1744–46), the first periodical for women actually edited by a woman. Frances Brooke (?–1789), publishing under the name Mary Singleton, produced a periodical called *The Old Maid* (1755–56). Later Sarah Trimmer (1741–1810) produced the *Family Magazine* (1788–89). Trimmer also wrote didactic stories for children, publishing them as *Fabulous Histories* (1786). Hannah More, Mary Wollstonecraft, Anna Laetitia Barbauld (pp. 275–80), and Maria Edgeworth (pp. 386–402) also wrote popular and successful literature for children.

Other literary women gained their fame by translating: Elizabeth Carter (1742–1817), for instance, produced a well-respected translation of the stoic Roman philosopher Epictetus (55 to 135 CE). Still others wrote histories, the most famous of which was *History of England from the Accession of James I to the Elevation of the House of Hanover*, by Catherine Sawbridge Macaulay (1731–91), published in eight volumes from 1763 to 1783 (see pp. 285–86).

Women writers also made notable contributions to the field of poetry. To take just one example, during her lifetime Anna Seward was nationally celebrated as "the Swan of Litchfield" (Litchfield being her place of residence). She published widely-read poems on current topics of national importance, including a "Monody on Major Andre," a poem about a British solider who was hung for espionage during the American War of Independence (1781) and an elegy on Captain Cook (1780). She is also known for her collection *Original Sonnets on Various Subjects* (1799). As her biography suggests, though many women poets did write on domestic topics, others readily engaged with historical and political subjects and attempted to position themselves as public voices.

Women writers also made extraordinary contributions to the emerging genre of the novel, as is now commonly acknowledged. Literary historian Cheryl Turner has counted at least 446 works of prose fiction by women published in Britain from 1696 to 1796. This number does not include anonymously published novels that may also have been written by women, or those written collaboratively. Notable female novelists from the period include Eliza Haywood (1693?–1756), whose fictions include *The History of Miss Betsy Thoughtless* (1751); Sarah Fielding (1710–68), sister to writer Henry Fielding and author of *The Adventures of David Simple* (1744); Charlotte Lennox (1720–1804), who wrote a parody of Cervantes titled *The Female Quixote* (1752); Anne Radcliffe (1764–1823), an innovator of the gothic novel, as seen in *The Mysteries of Udolpho* (1794) and *The Italian* (1797); and Frances Burney (1752–1840), whose novel *Evelina* (1778) is excerpted here.

Eighteenth-century women also wrote for the stage: no fewer than fifty women writers had at least one play produced during the eighteenth century. One female playwright, Susanna Centlivre (1667?–1723) wrote nineteen plays between 1700 and 1724. Another, Hannah Cowley (1743–1809), though still underrated today, was prolific and very well recognized during her lifetime. In the period from 1776 to 1794, she wrote a total of thirteen plays, all of which—except one—were produced at Drury Lane or Covent Garden, prominent London theaters. The subjects of these plays range widely, from the nature of the military man in the service of the British army in *Which Is the Man?* (1782) to "white slavery" in a Turkish harem in *A Day in Turkey, or the Russian Slaves* (1792). Her most famous play, *The Belle's Stratagem*, was performed 118 times between 1780 and 1800; it was the fourth most popularly performed piece during this period.

Still, because of the persistent idea that the stage was too indecorous an atmosphere for women, drama remained the most difficult genre for women, as Frances Burney's biography suggests. Attracted by the stage early on, she wrote a theatrical comedy called *The Witlings* (1778–80). But her father suppressed the play—even though playwright and producer Richard Brinsley Sheridan had agreed to produce it—because Charles Burney thought the stage too public a venue for his daughter. Yet throughout her lifetime, Burney often returned to drama, eventually writing ten plays in all. Only one of them—*Edwy and Elgiva* (1795)—was produced during her lifetime, and all went unpublished until the late twentieth century.

Though in *Orlando* Virginia Woolf imagines a literary scene that failed to make room for women's contribution, this survey suggests the contrary: many eighteenth-century women participated in the world of letters, and they were not necessarily restricted to one set of topics or one agenda. Indeed, though many wrote on "female" topics, such as motherhood, family, or domestic life, many others addressed themselves to a much wider range of topics, including such themes as nascent democracy, imperial expansion, the grueling toll of physical labor, abolition, and the national political scene. Nor did women writers of the period necessarily agree politically, divided as they sometimes were by rank or socioeconomic circumstance.

To hear the full expression of women's lives in the eighteenth century, it is necessary to balance one voice against the next, to contrast the viewpoints of those, like Lady Mary Wortley Montagu, who experienced relative wealth and privilege with those, like Mary Leapor, who saw life from another perspective. It helps as well to place the words of those who stayed at home alongside those who traveled more widely: How do the local insights of the rooted Dorothy Wordsworth (pp. 402–7) compare with the international observations of the roving Eliza Fay? How does the abolitionist emotion of Mary Birkett (pp. 407–15) emerge alongside the pro-slavery sentiment of Anna Falconbridge? How do Hannah More, Abigail Adams, and Mary Wollstonecraft compare on the topic of women's mission? Where are the important differences in their viewpoints? Only by reading widely across geographic, political, and class lines can we begin to understand the full complexity of women's lives in the eighteenth century.

HISTORY		LITERATURE
Queen Anne ascends to the English throne	**1702**	
First daily newspaper in England is founded—the *Daily Courant*		
First daily newspaper in the American colonies is founded— *The News-Letter* (Boston)	**1704**	Jonathan Swift *Tale of a Tub*
The parliaments of England and Scotland are united	**1707**	
	1713	Anne Finch *Miscellany Poems, on Several Occasions*
George I, from Germany, takes the throne and becomes first of four Hanoverian kings	**1714**	Alexander Pope *Rape of the Lock*
Lady Mary Wortley Montagu leaves for Turkey with her ambassador husband	**1716**	
	1719	Daniel Defoe *Robinson Crusoe*
	1722	Daniel Defoe *Moll Flanders*
George II becomes king	**1727**	
First Great Awakening—an intense religious revival among North American Protestants	**1730s– 40s**	
	1732	Benjamin Franklin *Poor Richard's Almanack*
	1733–34	Alexander Pope *An Essay on Man*
Britain repeals statutes against witchcraft	**1736**	
	1739	Mary Collier "The Woman's Labour"
	1740	Samuel Richardson *Pamela*
	1741	Jonathan Edwards *Sinners in the Hands of an Angry God*
	1744–46	*The Female Spectator* edited by Eliza Haywood
	1747	Samuel Richardson *Clarissa*
Marriage Act, also called Lord Hardwicke's Act, requires formal ceremony and consent of parents for matrimony, thereby abolishing common-law marriage	**1748**	
	1751	Mary Leapor *Crumble-Hall*

HISTORY   LITERATURE

HISTORY	Year	LITERATURE
French and Indian Wars: territorial struggles over North American lands between English and French, using Indian allies and proxies	1754–63	
	1755	Samuel Johnson *Dictionary*
George III ascends the throne, where he will remain until 1820	1760	
Phillis Wheatley is captured, most likely in Senegal	1761	
James Hargreaves invents the spinning jenny, an invention that will lead to the employment of young women in cotton mills	1764	
James Watt invents the steam engine	1769	
The Boston Massacre leaves three dead, two mortally wounded, and six injured	1770	
Lord Mansfield's ruling on the Somerset Case declares there is no legal backing for slavery in England (although slavery persists in the rest of the British Isles until 1834)	1772	
On her way to the West Indies, Janet Schaw sees ships en route to North America, where troops will fight in the battles of Lexington and Concord	1775	
American War of Independence	1775–83	
Declaration of Independence is signed at Philadelphia	1776	
	1778	Frances Burney *Evelina*
North American "Molly Pitcher" is famed for carrying water to tired and wounded soldiers and taking over the cannon of her husband, who is overcome by heat Eliza Fay leaves with her husband for India	1779	
Having returned to the family estate in Ireland, Maria Edgeworth begins writing stories for children	1782	
Edmund Cartwright invents the power loom	1785	
Mary Prince is born into slavery in Bermuda	1788	
Impeachment trials of Warren Hastings, colonial administrator in India; he is ultimately acquitted	1788–94	

HISTORY		LITERATURE
French Revolution	1789–99	
Anna Maria Falconbridge travels to Sierra Leone with her abolitionist husband Mary Talbot, prisoner transported to Australia, writes a letter that is published in England, making her the first Australian woman writer in English	1791	Mary Birkett "A Poem on the African Slave Trade"
	1792	Mary Wollstonecraft *A Vindication of the Rights of Woman*
Reign of Terror in France: a period of brutal repression resulting in many executions	1793–94	
	1794	Ann Radcliffe *The Mysteries of Udolpho* Susanna Rowson's *Charlotte Temple* becomes America's first best seller
	1795	Tom Paine *The Age of Reason* Anna Laetitia Barbauld writes "The Wrongs of Woman" (not published until 1825) Maria Edgeworth *Letters for Literary Ladies*
Abigail Adams becomes first lady when her husband John is inaugurated	1796	
Dorothy Wordsworth moves to Alfoxden with her brother William	1797	
	1798	William Wordsworth *Lyrical Ballads*
	1799	Hannah More *Strictures on a Modern System of Female Education*

LADY MARY WORTLEY MONTAGU
1689–1762

According to one often-told story, in 1697, the future Lady Mary's father brought his young daughter, resplendent in her finery, into the famous Kit-Kat Club in London, so that the eminent politicians gathered there could celebrate her as the "toast of the year." This story suggests the power and the rank of the Montagu family, and it forecasts the celebrity Lady Mary would experience all of her life. Born Mary Pierrepont, she gained her inalienable title when her father became an earl in 1690. After the death of her mother in 1693, she spent her early years at the lush estate of her paternal grandmother near Salisbury. Then, when her grandmother died, she went to live with her father, a move that gave her access to his extraordinary library.

Like other upper-rank ladies of her generation, Lady Mary largely educated herself. She read widely in English and French and secretly taught herself Latin. Edward Wortley Montagu, a wealthy and well-educated young politician, found her attractive and courted her. However, at a time when marriages entailed important property considerations, Montagu and Lady Mary's father could not agree on a marriage settlement, and the couple eloped. Their marriage was never happy, however. Montagu was a distant husband, even after the birth of their son, Edward, in 1713. When her husband was elected to Parliament the next year, Lady Mary moved to London and began her life at the center of a vibrant social and intellectual circle that included the poet Alexander Pope, with whom she established an especially close bond, as well as Joseph Addison and Richard Steele, editors and authors of *The Spectator*, and Henry Fielding, the novelist and playwright, whose career she promoted. Although she was writing widely—often in a satiric vein—she did not publish, but rather circulated her works among her circle of friends and acquaintances, as was common for writers during that time.

In 1715, she contracted smallpox. The disease left her scarred: her skin was deeply pitted and she lost her eyebrows, leaving her husband "inconsolable" for the setback his wife's disfigurement caused his career. In 1716, Edward Montagu was appointed ambassador to Turkey, and the family left for what was supposed to be a long sojourn. While in Turkey, Lady Mary had her son inoculated against the disease that had disfigured her—long before the practice of vaccination was established or accepted in England. She also studied Arabic poetry and absorbed much about Turkish society and culture. Her daughter, Mary (who later became Lady Bute), was born in Turkey in 1718. In the same year Edward Montagu was prematurely recalled for reasons that are still uncertain, and Lady Mary returned to London's literary circles. Soon after, she quarreled with Pope over an unknown issue. (Some speculate she rejected his sexual advances.) In a nasty war of words in "Epistle II: To a Lady" (lines 24–28), Pope memorialized her as slovenly, an unproven characterization that dogs her to this day.

In 1736, at age forty-seven, she became enamored of the bisexual writer and philosopher Francesco Algarotti. She followed him to Italy and only returned to England in 1762 (a year after her husband's death) as her daughter's advocate in a legal struggle over her husband's will that had been initiated by her son, by then a notorious gambler. The outcome of the case meant that Lady Mary received only £1,200 per year (about $300,000 today)—a small allowance relative to her husband's estate of over £800,000 (over $200 million today). (The bulk of the estate went to Lady Mary's daughter.) Lady Mary died in 1762 of breast cancer. Although she had written her *Turkish Embassy Letters* for a public audience, they were not published until 1763, under circumstances still subject to debate and against the wishes of her daughter, who was embarrassed by her mother's notoriety.

The following two letters suggest Lady Mary's liveliness and openness as a visitor to Turkey. In the first, she pays a visit to a Turkish bath, where she both gazes at and becomes the object of curiosity for the Turkish women. The second letter describes, in vivid, rich, and sensual detail, her visits to two women: one who had once been the consort of the Turkish emperor and another a friend who inhabits a harem. Both settings offer us the opportunity to compare Lady Mary's status as a privileged Englishwoman to that of elite, eighteenth-century women from a very different religion, culture, and society.

From **Turkish Embassy Letters**

Letter XXVII

[A VISIT TO A TURKISH BATH]

To Lady—,[1]   Adrianople,[2] 1 April 1717

I am now got into a new world, where everything I see appears to me a change of scene, and I write to your ladyship with some content of mind, hoping at least that you will find the charm of novelty in my letters, and no longer reproach me that I tell you nothing extraordinary. I won't trouble you with a relation of our tedious journey, but I must not omit what I saw remarkable at Sofia, one of the most beautiful towns in the Turkish empire, and famous for its hot baths, that are resorted to both for diversion and health. I stopped here one day on purpose to see them. Designing to go incognito I hired a Turkish coach. These voitures[3] are not at all like ours, but much more convenient for the country, the heat being so great that glasses would be very troublesome. They are made a good deal in the manner of the Dutch coaches, having wooden lattices painted and gilded, the inside being also painted with baskets and nosegays of flowers, intermixed commonly with little poetical mottos. They are covered all over with scarlet cloth, lined with silk, and very often richly embroidered and fringed. This covering entirely hides the persons in them, but may be thrown back at pleasure and the ladies peep through the lattices. They hold four people very conveniently, seated on cushions, but not raised.

In one of these covered waggons, I went to the bagnio[4] about ten o'clock. It was already full of women. It is built of stone in the shape of a dome, with no windows but in the roof, which gives light enough. There was five of these domes

1. The addressee of the letter remains unknown.
2. Adrianople, now known as Edirne, is in western Turkey. It was the capital of the Ottoman Empire, 1365–1453.
3. Carriages.
4. Bathhouse.

joined together, the outmost being less than the rest and serving only as a hall, where the portress stood at the door. Ladies of quality generally give this woman the value of a crown or ten shillings and I did not forget that ceremony. The next room is a very large one paved with marble, and all round it raised two sofas of marble one above another. There were four fountains of cold water in this room, falling first into marble basins, and then running on the floor in little channels made for that purpose, which carried the streams into the next room, something less than this, with the same sort of marble sofas, but so hot with steams of sulphur proceeding from the baths joining to it, 'twas impossible to stay there with one's clothes on. The two other domes were the hot baths, one of which had cocks of cold water turning into it to temper it to what degree of warmth the bathers have a mind to.

I was in my travelling habit, which is a rid-

Lady M-y W-r-t-l-y M-nt-g-e
The Female Traveller
In the Turkish   Drefs.

Let Men who glory in their better sense,
Read, hear, and learn Humility from hence;
No more let them Superior Wisdom boast,
They can but epual M-nt-g-e at most.

Lady Mary Wortley Montagu, the Female Traveller, in Dr. J. Doran's *A Lady of the Last Century* (1873).

ing dress, and certainly appeared very extraordinary to them. Yet there was not one of them that showed the least surprise or impertinent curiosity, but received me with all the obliging civility possible. I know no European court where the ladies would have behaved themselves in so polite a manner to a stranger. I believe, in the whole, there were two hundred women, and yet none of those disdainful smiles or satirical whispers that never fail in our assemblies when anybody appears that is not dressed exactly in fashion. They repeated over and over to me; "Güzelle, pek güzelle", which is nothing but "charming, very charming".

The first sofas were covered with cushions and rich carpets, on which sat the ladies, and on the second their slaves behind them, but without any distinction of rank by their dress, all being in the state of nature, that is, in plain English, stark naked, without any beauty or defect concealed. Yet there was not the least wanton smile or immodest gesture amongst them. They walked and moved with the same majestic grace which Milton describes of our general mother.[5] There were many amongst them as exactly proportioned as ever any goddess was drawn by the pencil of Guido or Titian, and most of their skins shiningly white, only adorned by their beautiful hair divided into many tresses, hanging on their shoulders, braided either with pearl or ribbon, perfectly representing the figures of the Graces.[6]

I was here convinced of the truth of a reflection I had often made, that if it was the fashion to go naked, the face would be hardly observed. I perceived that the ladies with finest skins and most delicate shapes had the greatest share of my admiration, though their faces were sometimes less beautiful than those of their companions. To tell you the truth, I had wickedness enough to wish secretly that Mr Gervase[7] could have been there invisible. I fancy it would have very much improved his art to see so many fine women naked, in different postures, some in conversation, some working, others drinking coffee or sherbet, and many negligently lying on their cushions while their slaves (generally pretty girls of seventeen or eighteen) were employed in braiding their hair in several pretty manners. In short, 'tis the women's coffee house, where all the news of the town is told, scandal invented etc. They generally take this diversion once a week, and stay there at least four or five hours, without getting cold by immediate coming out of the hot bath into the cool room, which was very surprising to me. The lady that seemed the most considerable amongst them entreated me to sit by her and would fain have undressed me for the bath. I excused myself with some difficulty, they being however all so earnest in persuading me, I was a last forced to open my shirt, and show them my stays,[8] which satisfied them very well, for I saw they believed I was so locked up in that machine, that it was not in my own power to open it, which contrivance they attributed to my husband. I was charmed by their civility and beauty, and should have been very glad to pass more time with them, but Mr Wortley resolving to pursue his journey the next morning early I was in haste to see the ruins of Justinian's church,[9] which did not afford me so agreeable a prospect as I had left, being little more than a heap of stones.

Adieu, madam, I am sure I have now entertained you with an account of such a sight as you never saw in your life, and what no book of travels could inform you of, as 'tis no less than death for a man to be found in one of these places.

5. In Book 4 of *Paradise Lost* (1667), poet John Milton describes Eve as created "For softness she and sweet attractive grace" (line 297). In Book 8, Milton writes of Eve, "Grace was in all her steps, heaven in her eye / In every gesture dignity and love" (lines 488–89).
6. Italian Renaissance painters Reni Guido (1575–1642) and Tiziano Vecellio, or Titian (1485–1576). As the daughters of Zeus and attendants to Aphrodite, the three graces were the goddesses of beauty and charm.
7. Gervase, or Charles Jervas (1675?–1739), Irish portrait painter.
8. Bones that lined a corset to keep the shape of the bodice.
9. Built on the ruins of an ancient temple to Apollo, the church was first completed in the fourth century but repeatedly destroyed—by fire and earthquakes—and rebuilt.

Letter XLI

[SULTANA HAFISE]

To Lady Mar,[1]   Pera, Constantinople, 10 March 1718
I have not writ to you, dear sister, these many months; a great piece of self-denial, but I know not where to direct or what part of the world you were in. I have received no letter from you since your short note of April last in which you tell me that you are on the point of leaving England and promise me a direction for the place you stay in, but I have in vain expected it till now, and now I only learn from the Gazette that you are returned, which induces me to venture this letter to your house at London. I had rather ten of my letters should be lost than you imagine I don't write and I think 'tis hard fortune if one in ten don't reach you. However, I am resolved to keep the copies as testimonies of my inclination to give you, to the utmost of my power, all the diverting part of my travels while you are exempt from all the fatigues and inconveniencies.

In the first place I wish you joy of your niece, for I was brought to bed of a daughter five weeks ago. I don't mention this as one of my diverting adventures, though I must own that it is not half so mortifying here as in England, there being as much difference as there is between a little cold in the head, which sometimes happens here, and the consumptive coughs so common in London. Nobody keeps their house a month for lying in,[2] and I am not so fond of any of our customs to retain them when they are not necessary. I returned my visits at three weeks end, and about four days ago crossed the sea which divides this place from Constantinople to make a new one, where I had the good fortune to pick up many curiosities.

I went to see the Sultana Hafise, favourite of the last Emperor Mustafa,[3] who, you know (or perhaps you don't know) was deposed by his brother the reigning Sultan, and died a few weeks after, being poisoned, as it was generally believed. This lady was immediately after his death saluted with an absolute order to leave the seraglio[4] and choose herself a husband from the great men at the Port. I suppose you imagine her overjoyed at this proposal. Quite contrary. These women, who are called and esteem themselves queens, look upon this liberty as the greatest disgrace and affront that can happen to them. She threw herself at the Sultan's feet and begged him to poniard[5] her rather than use his brother's widow with that contempt. She represented to him in agonies of sorrow that she was privileged from this misfortune by having brought five princes into the Ottoman family, but all the boys being dead and only one girl surviving this excuse was not received and she compelled to make her choice. She chose Bekir Effendi, then Secretary of State,[6] and above fourscore year old, to convince the world that she firmly intended to keep the vow she had made of never suffering a second husband to

---

1. The husband of Lady Mary's sister, the Countess of Mar, was implicated in a failed plot to dethrone George I and to place James III, of the Stuart line, in power. As a result, the family was exiled to France and the Earl of Mar imprisoned. During this period, Lady Mar was given permission to visit England several times, for example, when her father petitioned on her behalf to regain her forfeited estate in 1720.
2. Also called confinement, the practice called for

a woman to stay home after childbirth—traditionally for forty days after the birth of a daughter and for thirty days after the birth of a son.
3. Born in 1683, Sultana Hafise was the consort, or spouse, of Emperor (or Sultan) Mustafa II, deposed in 1703.
4. Harem.
5. To knife or stab her.
6. General term of respect given to a scholar or a man of letters.

approach her bed, and since she must honour some subject so far as to be called his wife she would choose him as a mark of her gratitude, since it was he that had presented her at the age of ten year old to her lost lord. But she has never permitted him to pay her one visit, though it is now fifteen year she has been in his house, where she passes her time in uninterrupted mourning with a constancy very little known in Christendom, especially in a widow of twenty-one, for she is now but thirty-six. She has no black eunuchs[7] for her guard, her husband being obliged to respect her as a queen and not enquire at all into what is done in her apartment, where I was led into a large room, with a sofa the whole length of it, adorned with white marble pillars like a ruelle,[8] covered with a pale blue figured velvet on a silver ground, with cushions of the same, where I was desired to repose till the Sultana appeared, who had contrived this manner of reception to avoid rising up at my entrance, though she made me an inclination of her head when I rose up to her. I was very glad to observe a lady that had been distinguished by the favour of an emperor to whom beauties were every day presented from all parts of the world. But she did not seem to me to have ever been half so beautiful as the fair Fatima[9] I saw at Adrianople, though she had the remains of a fine face more decayed by sorrow than time.

But her dress was something so surprisingly rich I cannot forbear describing it to you. She wore a vest called *dolaman,* and which differs from a caftan by longer sleeves and folding over at the bottom. It was of purple cloth straight to her shape and thick set, on each side down to her feet and round the sleeves, with pearls of the best water, of the same size as their buttons commonly are. You must not suppose I mean as large as those of my Lord—but about the bigness of a pea; and to these buttons large loops of diamonds in the form of those gold loops so common upon birthday coats.[1] This habit was tied at the waist with two large tassels of smaller pearl and round the arms embroidered with large diamonds; her shift fastened at the bosom with a great diamond shaped like a lozenge, her girdle as broad as the broadest English riband entirely covered with diamonds. Round her neck she wore three chains which reached to her knees, one of large pearl at the bottom of which hung a fine coloured emerald as big as a turkey egg, another consisting of two hundred emeralds close joined together, of the most lively green, perfectly matched, every one as large as a half crown piece and as thick as three crown pieces,[2] and another of emeralds perfectly round. But her earrings eclipsed all the rest. They were two diamonds shaped exactly like pears, as large as a big hazelnut. Round her talpack[3] she had four strings of pearl, the whitest and most perfect in the world, at least enough to make four necklaces every one as large as the Duchess of Marlborough's, and of the same size, fastened with two roses consisting of a large ruby for the middle stone and round them twenty drops of clean diamonds to each. Besides this, her headdress was covered with bodkins of emeralds and diamonds. She wore large diamond bracelets and had five rings on her fin-

---

7. Castrated men, or eunuchs, were commonly used as attendants or guards in the seraglio.
8. Boudoir.
9. Princess Fatima was the wife of Ali Pasha, the Grand Vizier (a high Muslim executive officer in the Ottoman Empire). She married her husband's successor after her husband's death.

1. Very fancy coats worn to court to celebrate a king's birthday.
2. Each gem was approximately one and three-eighths inches in diameter and three-eighths of an inch thick.
3. Headdress.

gers, all single diamonds, except Mr Pitt's[4] the largest I ever saw in my life. 'Tis for the jewellers to compute the value of these things, but according to the common estimation of jewels in our part of the world, her whole dress must be worth above £100,000 sterling.[5] This I am very sure of, that no European queen has half the quantity and the Empress's jewels,[6] though very fine, would look very mean near hers.

She gave me a dinner of fifty dishes of meat, which, after their fashion, was placed on the table but one at a time, and was extremely tedious, but the magnificence of her table answered very well to that of her dress. The knives were of gold, the hafts set with diamonds, but the piece of luxury that grieved my eyes was the table cloth and napkins, which were all tiffany,[7] embroidered with silks and gold in the finest manner in natural flowers. It was with the utmost regret that I made use of these costly napkins, as finely wrought as the finest handkerchiefs that ever came out of this country. You may be sure that they were entirely spoilt before dinner was over. The sherbet, which is the liquor they drink at meals, was served in china bowls, but the covers and salvers massy gold. After dinner water was brought in a gold basin and towels of the same kind of the napkins, which I very unwillingly wiped my hands upon, and coffee was served in china with gold soûcoupes.[8]

The Sultana seemed in very good humour and talked to me with the utmost civility. I did not omit this opportunity of learning all that I possibly could of the seraglio, which is so entirely unknown amongst us. She assured me that the story of the Sultan's throwing a handkerchief is altogether fabulous and the manner upon that occasion no other but that he send the Kuslir Aga to signify to the lady the honour he intends her.[9] She is immediately complimented upon it by the others and led to the bath where she is perfumed and dressed in the most magnificent and becoming manner. The Emperor precedes his visit by a royal present and then comes into her apartment. Neither is there any such thing as her creeping in at the bed's feet. She said that the first he make choice of was always after the first in rank and not the mother of the eldest son, as other writers would make us believe. Sometimes the Sultan diverts himself in the company of all his ladies, who stand in a circle round him, and she confessed that they were ready to die with jealousy and envy of the happy she that he distinguished by any appearance of preference. But this seemed to me neither better nor worse than the circles in most courts where the glance of the monarch is watched and every smile waited for with impatience and envied by those that cannot obtain it.

She never mentioned the Sultan without tears in her eyes, yet she seemed very fond of the discourse. My past happiness (said she) appears a dream to me, yet I cannot forget that I was beloved by the greatest and most lovely of mankind. I was chose from all the rest to make all his campaigns with him. I would not

4. The infamous diamond was bought in India under suspicious circumstances and owned by Governor Pitt, grandfather of William Pitt, the first Earl of Chatham and prime minister (1757–61, 1766–68).

5. Although monetary conversions can be problematic, at the time this selection was written £1 was worth about $260 today. So £100,000 was an enormous sum in eighteenth-century Britain, equivalent to over $26 million today.

6. Most likely a reference to the jewels of Wil-

helmine Amalie (1673–1742), Empress of the Holy Roman Empire, whom Lady Mary had encountered in 1716.

7. A sheer silk gauze.

8. Saucers.

9. In this paragraph describing the customs of the seraglio, Lady Mary refutes the idea, commonly held at the time, that the Sultan would throw down his handkerchief as a sign that he had chosen a woman with whom to have sex.

survive him if I was not passionately fond of the princess, my daughter, yet all my tenderness for her was hardly enough to make me preserve my life when I lost him. I passed a whole twelvemonth without seeing the light. Time has softened my despair, yet I now pass some days every week in tears devoted to the memory of my Sultan. There was no affectation in these words. It was easy to see she was in a deep melancholy, though her good humour made her willing to divert me.

She asked me to walk in her garden and one of her slaves immediately brought her a pelisse[1] of rich brocade lined with sables. I waited on her into the garden, which had nothing in it remarkable but the fountains, and from thence she showed me all her apartments. In her bedchamber her toilet[2] was displayed, consisting of two looking glasses, the frames covered with pearls, and her night *talpak* set with bodkins of jewels, and near it three vests of fine sables, every one of which is at least worth 1000 dollars, £200 English money.[3] I don't doubt these rich habits were purposely placed in sight, but they seemed negligently thrown on the sofa. When I took my leave of her I was complimented with perfumes as at the Grand Vizier's and presented with a very fine embroidered handkerchief. Her slaves were to the number of thirty, besides ten little ones, the eldest not above seven year old. These were the most beautiful girls I ever saw, all richly dressed, and I observed that the Sultana took a great deal of pleasure in these lovely children, which is a vast expense, for there is not a handsome girl of that age to be bought under £100 sterling.[4] They wore little garlands of flowers, and their own hair braided, which was all their headdress, but their habits all of gold stuffs. These served her coffee kneeling, brought water when she washed, etc. 'Tis a great part of the business of the older slaves to take care of these girls, to learn them to embroider and serve them as carefully as if they were children of the family.

Now do I fancy that you imagine I have entertained you all this while with a relation that has, at least, received many embellishments from my hand. This is but too like, says you, the Arabian tales;[5] these embroidered napkins, and a jewel as large as a turkey's egg! You forget, dear sister, those very tales were writ by an author of this country and, excepting the enchantments, are a real representation of the manners here. We travellers are in very hard circumstances. If we say nothing but what has been said before us we are dull and we have observed nothing. If we tell anything new, we are laughed at as fabulous and romantic, not allowing for the difference of ranks, which afford difference of company, more curiosity, or the changes of customs that happen every twenty year in every country. But people judge of travellers exactly with the same candour, good nature and impartiality they judge of their neighbours upon all occasions. For my part, if I live to return amongst you I am so well acquainted with the morals of all my dear friends and acquaintance that I am resolved to tell them nothing at all, to avoid the imputation, which their charity would certainly incline them to, of my telling too much. But I depend upon your knowing me enough to believe whatever I seriously assert for truth, though I give you leave to be surprised at an account so new to you. But

---

1. A lightweight cloak.
2. Dressing table.
3. Roughly the equivalent of $52,000 today.
4. During Lady Mary's lifetime, pirates from ports like Tunis and Tripoli frequently captured white European men and women and sold them into slavery in Arab countries. Though she ac-

knowledges their expense, Lady Mary may be unduly sanguine about the conditions of servitude described here.
5. *The Arabian Nights,* also known as *A Thousand and One Nights,* is a collection of ancient Persian, Indian, and Arab folktales that first appeared in translation in Europe in 1704.

what would you say if I told you that I have been in a harem where the winter apartment was wainscoted with inlaid work of mother of pearl, ivory of different colours and olive wood, exactly like the little boxes you have seen brought out of this country; and those rooms designed for summer, the walls all crusted with japan china, the roofs gilt and the floors spread with the finest Persian carpets. Yet there is nothing more true, such is the palace of my lovely friend, the fair Fatima, who I was acquainted with at Adrianople. I went to visit her yesterday and, if possible, she appeared to me handsomer than before. She met me at the door of her chamber and, giving me her hand with the best grace in the world: "You Christain ladies," said she with a smile that made her as handsome as an angel, "have the reputation of inconstancy, and I did not expect, whatever goodness you expressed for me at Adrianople, that I should ever see you again; but I am now convinced that I have really the happiness of pleasing you, and if you knew how I speak of you amongst our ladies you would be assured that you do me justice if you think me your friend." She placed me in the corner of the sofa and I spent the afternoon in her conversation with the greatest pleasure in the world.

The Sultana Hafise is what one would naturally expect to find a Turkish lady; willing to oblige, but not knowing how to go about it, and 'tis easy to see in her manner that she has lived excluded from the world. But Fatima has all the politeness and good breeding of a court, with an air that inspires at once respect and tenderness; and now I understand her language I find her wit as engaging as her beauty. She is very curious after the manners of other countries and has not that partiality for her own so common to little minds. A Greek that I carried with me who had never seen her before (nor could have been admitted now if she had not been in my train) showed that surprise at her beauty and manner which is unavoidable at the first sight, and said to me in Italian: "This is no Turkish lady; she is certainly some Christian." Fatima guessed she spoke of her and asked what she said. I would not have told, thinking she would have been no better pleased with the compliment than one of our court beauties to be told she had the air of a Turk. But the Greek lady told it her and she smiled, saying: "It is not the first time I have heard so. My mother was a Poloneze taken at the Siege of Camieniec,[6] and my father used to rally me, saying he believed his Christian wife had found some Christian gallant, for I had not the air of a Turkish girl." I assured her that if all the Turkish ladies were like her, it was absolutely necessary to confine them from public view for the repose of mankind, and proceeded to tell her what a noise such a face as hers would make in London or Paris. "I can't believe you", replied she agreeably; "if beauty was so much valued in your country as you say they would never have suffered you to leave it."[7]

Perhaps, dear sister, you laugh at my vanity in repeating this compliment, but I only do it as I think it very well turned and give it you as an instance of the spirit of her conversation. Her house was magnificently furnished and very well fancied, her winter rooms being furnished with figured velvet on gold grounds, and those for summer with fine Indian quilting embroidered with gold. The houses of the great Turkish ladies are kept clean with as much nicety as those in Holland. This

6. A Poloneze is a woman of Polish origin. Her mother must have been taken captive when Mehmed IV, the sultan of the Ottoman Empire, conquered the Polish fortress of Kamieneic in 1672.

7. A compliment—Lady Mary was disfigured by smallpox.

was situated in a high part of the town, and from the windows of her summer apartment we had the prospect of the sea and the islands and the Asian mountains. My letter is insensibly grown so long, I am ashamed of it. This is a very bad symptom. 'Tis well if I don't degenerate into a downright story teller. It may be our proverb that knowledge is no burden may be true to oneself, but knowing too much is very apt to make us troublesome to other people.

◄ ELIZA HAYWOOD ►
c. 1693–1756

One of Eliza Haywood's contemporaries described her as "evidently a lively, unconventional, opinionated gadabout fond of the company of similar She-romps, who exchanged verses and specimen letters with the lesser celebrities of the literary world." This description neither credits her remarkable range of literary output nor recognizes her powerful initiative to triumph as a writer.

Details of Haywood's early life are largely unknown. She was probably born in London to Elizabeth and Robert Fowler, who may have been a hosier or shopkeeper. Though we have no record of her schooling, she appears to have been well educated, especially in French language and literature. She was married, likely unhappily, to a clergyman named Valentine Haywood, and she appears to have had two illegitimate children. She started acting in Dublin at the Smock Alley Theatre in 1714, continuing in London until the Licensing Act of 1737 closed the theaters.

Driven by financial necessity to make her living by her pen, Haywood wrote prodigiously, turning out plays, best-selling novels, political pamphlets, periodicals, conduct books, poetry, and translations. One critic counts sixty-one works of fiction, including thirty-eight romances written between 1720 and 1730. Most controversial were Haywood's scandalous satires—writings in which she often called out the vice and folly of her thinly disguised characters. In one satire, *Memoirs of a Certain Island Adjacent to Utopia* (1725), she appended a key denoting the true identities of her characters, who were indicated only by their initials in the text. She similarly revealed the real-life objects of her satire attack in *The Secret History of the Present Intrigues of the Court of Caramania* (1727). Haywood also courted her audience through scandalous "amatory" fictions focusing on love and seduction.

At midcentury, she changed tone and published her moralistic novel *The History of Miss Betsy Thoughtless* (1751). By then, though, Haywood had a reputation for raciness, exacerbated by Alexander Pope's scurrilous attack on her literary work. In *The Dunciad* (1728/1743), he described her as a "Juno [Roman goddess] of majestic size / With cow-like udders, and with ox-like eyes." Jonathan Swift also maligned her as "a stupid, infamous scribbling woman." After apologizing to her audience for an illness that kept her from writing, she died on February 25, 1756.

The following selection is from *The Female Spectator* (1744–46)—known as the first woman's periodical written by a woman. In this periodical, Haywood covered topics ranging from the conduct of military men to the dangers of masquerades, from the state of the theater to the distinction between good manners and good breeding. Here Haywood's male persona bemoans the familial and social disruption caused by women drinking tea. White expressing a legitimate concern about the expense of tea, he taps into a larger social preoccupation with the ill effects of "luxury" on women.

[The Dangers of Tea]

To the Female Spectator.

Madam,

As I look upon you to be a Person who knows the World perfectly well, and has the Happiness of your own Sex very much at Heart, I wonder you have never yet thought fit to throw out some Admonitions concerning the immoderate Use of Tea; which however innocent it may seem to those that practise it, is a kind of Debauchery no less expensive, and perhaps even more pernicious in its Consequences, than those which the Men, who are not professed Rakes,[1] are generally accused of.

This, at first Sight, may be looked upon as too bold an Assertion, but, on a nearer Examination, I am perswaded will be found no more than reasonable, and will undertake to prove that the Tea-Table, as manag'd in some Families, costs more to support than would maintain two Children at Nurse.[2]—Yet is this by much the least Part of the Evil;—it is the utter Destruction of all Œconomy,—the Bane of good Housewifry,—and the Source of Idleness, by engrossing those Hours which ought to be employed in an honest and prudent Endeavour to add to, or preserve what Fortune, or former Industry has bestowed.—Were the Folly of wasting Time and Money in this manner confined only to the Great, who have enough of both to spare, it would not so much call for public Reproof; but all Degrees[3] of Women are infected with it, and a Wife now looks upon her Tea-Chest, Table, and its Implements, to be as much her Right by Marriage as her Wedding-Ring.

Tho' you cannot, Madam, be insensible that the trading Part of the Nation must suffer greatly on this score, especially those who keep Shops, I beg you will give me Leave to mention some few Particulars of the Hardships we Husbands of that Class are obliged to bear.

The first Thing the too genteel Wife does after opening her Eyes in the Morning, is to ring the Bell for her Maid, and ask if the Tea Kettle boils.—If any Accident has happened to delay this important Affair, the House is sure to eccho with Reproaches; but if there is no Disappointment in the Case, the Petticoats and Bed-Gown are hastily thrown over the Shoulders, Madam repairs to her easy Chair, sits down before her Table in Querpo[4] with all her Equipage[5] about her, and sips, and pauses, and then sips again, while the Maid attends assiduous to replenish, as often as call'd for, the drain'd Vehicle of that precious Liquor.

An Hour is the least can be allowed to Breakfast, after which the Maid carries all the Utensils down to the Kitchen, and sits down to the Remains of the Tea (or it is probable some fresh she has found Opportunity to purloin) with the same State as her Mistress, takes as much time, and would think herself highly injur'd should any one call her away, or attempt to interrupt her in it: So that, between both, the whole Morning is elapsed, and it is as much as the poor Husband can do to get a Bit of Dinner ready by two or three o'Clock.

---

1. Men of questionable morals.
2. The practice of paying women to breast-feed small children.
3. Classes.
4. In a state of less than full dress.
5. Equipment.

Dinner above and below[6] is no sooner over, than the Tea-Table must be again set forth:—Some friendly Neighbour comes in to chat away an Hour:—Two are no Company, and the Maid being very busy in cutting Bread and Butter, one 'Prentice[7] is called out of the Shop to run this Way and fetch Mrs. Such-a-one, and another that Way to fetch Mrs. Such-a-one, so that the Husband must be his own Man,[8] and if two Customers chance to come at the same Time, he frequently loses one for want of Hands to serve them.

It often happens, that when the Tea-drinking Company have almost finished their Regale,[9] and the Table is going to be removed, a fresh Visitor arrives, who must have fresh Tea made for her; after her another, who is always treated with the same Compliment; a third, perhaps a fourth, or more, till the Room is quite full, and the Entertainment prolonged a considerable Time after the Candles are lighted, when the Days are of a moderate Length.

This is sufficient to shew the Loss of Time both as to the Mistress and Servants, and how much the Regularity of the Tea-Table occasions a Want of Regularity in every Thing beside; but, Madam, there is yet another, and more mischievous Effect attends the Drinking too much of this *Indian* Herb.[1]

What I mean is too notorious a Fact not to be easily guessed at; but lest it should be misconstrued by any of your Readers, I shall venture to explain it.

Tea, whether of the *Green* or *Bohea*[2] kind, when taken to Excess, occasions a Dejection of Spirits and Flatulency, which lays the Drinkers of it under a kind of Necessity of having recourse to more animating Liquors.—The most temperate and sober of the Sex find themselves obliged to drink Wine pretty freely after it: None of them now-a-days pretend to entertain with the one without the other; and the Bottle and Glass are as sure an Appendix to the Tea-Table as the Slop-Bason.[3]

Happy are those who can content themselves with a Refreshment, which, tho' not to be had in any Perfection in *England,* is yet infinitely less destructive to the human System than some others too frequently substituted in its Place, when it is found too weak to answer the End proposed by taking it.

Brandy, Rum, and other Spirituous Liquors, being of a more exhillerating Nature, at least for the present, are become a usual Supplement to Tea, and, I am sorry to say, by their frequent Use grow so familiar to the Palate, that their intoxicating Qualities are no longer formidable, and the Vapours, Cholic, a bad Digestion, or some other Complaint, serves as an Excuse for drinking them in a more plentiful degree, than the best Constitution can for any length of Time support.

Hence ensue innumerable Maladies, Doctor's Fees, Apothecary's Bills, *Bath, Tunbridge,* the *Spa,*[4] and all that can destroy the wretched Husband's Peace, or impoverish him in his Fortune.

The more is his Affection for a Wife who takes so little Care of his Interest and Happiness, and of her own Health and Reputation, the more will his Affliction be; and the less will she be able to forgive herself, when brought by a too late and sad Experience to a right way of Thinking.

---

6. Downstairs, where the servants eat.
7. Apprentice.
8. Footman.
9. Party.
1. Imported Indian tea.

2. Black tea.
3. Container for used tea leaves and cold tea.
4. Bath and Tunbridge Wells were fashionable spas where people went to drink or bathe in waters thought to have medicinal properties.

That you will therefore use your Endeavours that so great an Enemy to the Felicity of the meaner sort of People may be banished from their Houses, is the unanimous Desire of all Husbands, and most humbly petition'd for by him who is,

With the greatest Admiration of your Writings,

Madam,

Your most humble, and

Fryday-Street,
Nov. 2, 1744.

Most obedient Servant,

John Careful.[5]

◄ MARY LEAPOR ►
1722–1746

A recent addition to the eighteenth-century canon, Mary ("Molly") Leapor depicts the experiences of women who labored in domestic service. The daughter of a Northamptonshire gardener, she learned to read and write at a free school in Brackley. Before her mother's death (c. 1742), Leapor worked as a cook's helper. (One of her employers later complained that she "scribbled" while the meat scorched.) After her mother died, Leapor returned home to keep house for her father, where she had time to pursue her art.

In her poetry, Leapor aimed to emulate the well-known poet Alexander Pope by writing in heroic couplets (rhymed pairs of lines in iambic pentameter that usually complete one thought) and by using a full range of classical allusions. Her poems were already circulating in manuscript when Bridget Freemantle, the daughter of Leapor's local rector, became her friend and patron. Freemantle raised money for Leapor in the form of a subscription for her poetry, but before she could make the gift, Leapor caught the measles and died at age twenty-four. A volume of poems by Leapor called *Poems on Several Occasions* was published posthumously in 1748 (reprinted 1751).

The subject of her poetry is not typical of the Augustan period. In "Crumble-Hall" Leapor takes us on the servant's tour of the Great House, showing us its back stairways, its storeroom, its attic, and its kitchen. In "An Essay on Woman," she bemoans the many social constructions inhibiting women, while in "The Headache," she offers us a playful assessment of the physical ailments that beset herself and a friend.

Crumble-Hall

When Friends or Fortune frown on *Mira*'s Lay,[1]
Or gloomy Vapours hide the Lamp of Day;
With low'ring Forehead, and with aching Limbs,
Oppressed with Head-ache, and eternal Whims,
Sad *Mira* vows to quit the darling Crime: 5
Yet takes her Farewell, and repents, in Rhyme.

---

5. A fictional persona assumed by Haywood.
1. "Crumble" satirically suggests the ancient con-

dition of the estate. "Mira" is Leapor's name for herself.

     But see (more charming than *Armida*'s Wiles)
     The Sun returns, and *Artemisia*[2] smiles:
     Then in a trice the Resolutions fly;
     And who so frolic as the Muse and I?   10
     We sing once more, obedient to her Call;
     Once more we sing; and 'tis of *Crumble-Hall;*
     That *Crumble-Hall,* whose hospitable Door
     Has fed the Stranger, and relieved the Poor;
     Whose *Gothic* Towers, and whose rusty Spires,   15
     Were known of old to Knights, and hungry Squires.
     There powdered Beef, and Warden-Pies, were found,
     And Pudden dwelt within her spacious Bound:[3]
     Pork, Peas, and Bacon (good old *English* Fare!),
     With tainted[4] Ven'son, and with hunted Hare,   20
     With humming Beer her Vats were wont to flow,
     And ruddy *Nectar* in her Vaults to glow.
     Here came the Wights, who battled for Renown,
     The sable Friar, and the russet Clown:[5]
     The loaded Tables and sent a sav'ry Gale.   25
     And the brown bowls were crowned with simp'ring Ale;[6]
     While the Guests ravaged on the smoking Store,
     Till their stretched Girdles would contain no more.

     Of this rude Palace might a Poet sing
     From cold *December* to returning Spring;   30
     Tell how the Building spreads on either hand,
     And two grim Giants[7] o'er the Portals stand;
     Whose grisled Beards are neither combed nor shorn,
     But look severe, and horribly adorn.

     Then step within—there stands a goodly Row   35
     Of oaken Pillars—where a gallant Show
     Of mimic Pears and carved Pom'granates twine,
     With the plump Clusters of the spreading Vine.
     Strange Forms above, present themselves to View;
     Some mouths that grin, some smile, and some that spew.   40
     Here a soft Maid or Infant seems to cry:
     Here stares a Tyrant, with distorted Eye:
     The Roof—no *Cyclops* e'er could reach so high:
     Not *Polypheme,*[8] though, formed for dreadful Harms,

---

2. Armida: referent unknown; Artemisia: Leapor's name for Bridget Freemantle, the local rector's daughter and Leapor's friend and benefactor.
3. Powdered: preserved; warden: a type of pear; pudden: pudding.
4. Not spoiled, but strongly scented.
5. Wights: valiant individuals; sable friar: a religious man dressed in dark robes; russet clown: a rustic person clothed in homespun, reddish brown cloth.

6. Simpering: simmering.
7. Carved wooden figures of knights who have their helmets, with grills, or bars over the mouthpiece, pulled down over their faces.
8. Polyphemos is the Cyclops (a one-eyed Giant) whom Odysseus outwits in Homer's *Odyssey,* Book 9. Leapor's point is that the decorative carvings are so high up that it is very hard to reach them in order to dust them properly.

The Top could measure with extended Arms.   45
Here the pleased Spider plants her peaceful Loom:
Here weaves secure, nor dreads the hated Broom.
But at the Head (and furbished once a Year)
The Herald's mystic Compliments appear:
Round the fierce Dragon *Honi Soit* twines,[9]   50
And Royal *Edward* o'er the Chimney shines.

   Safely the Mice through yon dark Passage run,
Where the dim Windows ne'er admit the Sun.
Along each Wall the Stranger blindly feels;
And (trembling) dreads a Spectre at his heels.   55

   The sav'ry Kitchen much Attention calls:
Westphalia Hams adorn the sable Walls:[1]
The Fires blaze; the greasy Pavements fry;
And steaming Odours from the Kettles fly.

   See! yon brown Parlour on the Left appears,   60
For nothing famous, but its leathern Chairs,
Whose shining Nails like polished Armour glow,
And the dull Clock beats audible and slow.
But on the Right we spy a Room more fair:
The Form—'tis neither long, nor round, nor square;   65
The Walls how lofty, and the Floor how wide,
We leave for learned *Quadrus*[2] to decide.
Gay *China* Bowls o'er the broad Chimney shine,
Whose long Description would be too sublime:
And much might of the Tapestry be sung: 70
But we're content to say, The Parlour's hung.

   We count the Stairs, and to the Right ascend,
Where on the Walls the gorgeous Colours blend.
There doughty *George* bestrides the goodly Steed;
The Dragon's slaughtered, and the Virgin freed: 75
And there (but lately rescued from their Fears)
The Nymph and serious *Ptolemy* appears:
Their awkward Limbs unwieldy are displayed;
And, like a Milk-wench, glares the royal Maid.[3]

   From hence we turn to more familiar Rooms;   80
Whose Hangings ne'er were wrought in *Grecian* Looms:
Yet the soft Stools, and eke the lazy Chairs,
To sleep invite the Weary, and the Fair.

9. *Honi soit qui mal y pense,* a common Latin
motto that translates as "evil to him who thinks
evil"; Royal Edward: a portrait of King Edward III
(reigned 1327–77).
1. Black from years of cooking smoke.
2. Quadras: name for a hypothetical mathematical scholar.

3. Description of paintings adorning the walls: St.
George, according to legend, slew a dragon to become the patron saint of England; Ptolemy, a first-
century Egyptian astronomer and mathematician,
with a nymph; and a member of royalty masquerading as a milkmaid.

Shall we proceed?—Yes, if you'll break the Wall:
If not, return, and tread once more the Hall.   85
Up ten Stone Steps now please to drag your Toes,
And a brick Passage will succeed to those.
Here the strong Doors were aptly framed to hold
Sir *Wary*'s Person, and Sir *Wary*'s Gold.
Here *Biron*[4] sleeps, with Books encircled round;   90
And him you'd guess a Student most profound,
Not so—in Form the dusty Volumes stand:
There's few that wear the Mark of *Biron*'s Hand.

Would you go further?—Stay a little then:
Back through the Passage—down the Steps again;   95
Through yon dark Room—Be careful how you tread
Up these steep Stairs—or you may break your Head.
These Rooms are furnished amiably, and full:
Old Shoes, and Sheep-ticks bred in Stacks of Wool;
Grey *Dobbin*'s Gears, and Drenching-Horns enow;   100
Wheel-spokes—the Irons of a tattered Plough.[5]

No further—Yes, a little higher, pray:
At yon small Door you'll find the Beams of Day,
While the hot Leads[6] return the scorching Ray.
Here a gay Prospect meets the ravished Eye: 105
Meads, Fields, and Groves, in beauteous Order lie.
From hence the Muse precipitant is hurled,
And drags down *Mira* to the nether World.

Thus far the Palace—Yet there still remain
Unsung the Gardens and the menial Train.[7]   110
Its Groves anon—its People first we sing:
Hear, *Artemisia,* hear the Song we bring.
Sophronia[8] first in Verse shall learn to chime,
And keep her Station, though in *Mira*'s Rhyme;
Sophronia sage! whose learned Knuckles know   115
To form round Cheese-cakes of the pliant Dough;
To bruise the Curd, and through her Fingers squeeze
Ambrosial Butter with the tempered Cheese:
Sweet Tarts and Pudden, too, her Skill declare;
And the soft Jellies, hid from baneful Air.   120

* * *

Now to those Meads let frolic Fancy rove,
Where o'er yon Waters nods a pendant Grove;
In whose clear Waves the pictured Boughs are seen,
With fairer Blossoms, and a brighter Green.

4. Leapor's name for a privileged inhabitant of
the estate, someone who uses the library as a place
for a nap, not as a place for learning.
5. The contents of the storeroom, including a
"drenching horn," used to give medicine to a
horse, and pieces of an old plow.

6. The roof is made of lead. Leapor is at the very
top of the house.
7. The people who work on the estate.
8. Not identified, but appears to be a housekeeper, or perhaps a relative.

Soft flow'ry Banks the spreading Lakes divide: 125
Sharp-pointed Flags adorn each tender Side.
See! the pleased Swans along the Surface play;
Where yon cool Willows meet the scorching Ray,
When fierce *Orion*[9] gives too warm a Day.

    But, hark! what Scream the wond'ring Ear invades!   130
The *Dryads*[1] howling for their threatened Shades:
Round the dear Grove each Nymph distracted flies
(Though not discovered but with Poet's Eyes):
And shall those Shades, where *Philomela*'s Strain[2]
Has oft to Slumber lulled the hapless Swain;   135
Where Turtles[3] used to clap their silken Wings;
Whose rev'rend Oaks have known a hundred Springs;
Shall these ignobly from their Roots be torn,
And perish shameful, as the abject Thorn;
While the slow Car[4] bears off their aged Limbs,   140
To clear the Way for Slopes, and modern Whims;
Where banished Nature leaves a barren Gloom,
And awkward Art Supplies the vacant Room?
Yet (or the Muse for Vengeance calls in vain)
The injured Nymphs shall haunt the ravaged Plain: 145
Strange Sounds and Forms shall tease the gloomy Green;
And Fairy-Elves by *Urs'la*[5] shall be seen:
Their new-built Parlour shall with Echoes ring:
And in their Hall shall doleful Crickets sing.

    Then cease, *Diracto,*[6] stay thy desp'rate Hand;   150
And let the Grove, if not the Parlour, stand.

                                1748/1751

An Essay on Woman[7]

    Woman, a pleasing but a short-lived Flow'r,
Too soft for Business and too weak for Power:
A Wife in Bondage, or neglected Maid;
Despised, if ugly; if she's fair, Betrayed.
'Tis Wealth alone inspires every Grace,   5
And calls the Raptures to her plenteous Face.
What Numbers for those charming Features pine,
If blooming Acres round her Temples twine!

9. A reference to the midsummer constellation (Orion), one of whose stars, Sirius, is thought to usher in the dog days of summer.
1. Wood nymphs.
2. In Greek mythology, Philomela was turned into a nightingale.
3. Turtle doves.
4. The narrator laments that the very old trees are being cut down and carted off in order to build on to the house, in accordance with trendy new architectural schemes.

5. Urs'la: a servant referred to by name in an omitted part of the poem.
6. Diracto: stock name for landscaper who would "improve" the estate by cutting down its ancient woods.
7. The female names in this poem—Pamphilia, Sylvia, Simplicius, and Cordia—are all made up to signify general types of women, rather than real people. "Mira," however (line 50), is Leapor's code name for herself.

Her Lip the Strawberry, and her Eyes more bright
Than sparkling Venus in a frosty Night;   10
Pale Lillies fade and, when the Fair appears,
Snow turns a Negro and dissolves in Tears,
And, where the Charmer treads her magic Toe,
On *English* ground *Arabian* odours grow,
Till mighty Hymen[8] lifts his sceptred Rod,   15
And sinks her Glories with a fatal Nod,
Dissolves her Triumphs, sweeps her Charms away,
And turns the Goddess to her native Clay.
    But, *Artemisia,* let your Servant sing
What small Advantage Wealth and Beauties bring.   20
Who would be Wise, that knew *Pamphilia*'s fate?
Or who be Fair, and joined to *Sylvia*'s mate?
Sylvia, whose Cheeks are fresh as early Day,
As Evening mild, and sweet as spicy May:
And yet that Face her partial Husband tires,   25
And those bright Eyes, that all the World admires.
Pamphilia's Wit who does not strive to shun,
Like Death's Infection or a Dog-day's Sun?
The Damsels view her with malignant Eyes,
The Men are vexed to find a Nymph so Wise: 30
And Wisdom only serves to make her know
The keen Sensation of superior Woe.
The secret Whisper and the list'ning Ear,
The scornful Eyebrow and the hated Sneer,
The giddy Censures of her babbling Kind,   35
With thousand Ills that grate a gentle Mind,
By her are tasted in the first Degree,
Though overlooked by *Simplicius* and me.
Does thirst of Gold a Virgin's Heart inspire,
Instilled by Nature or a careful Sire?   40
Then let her quit Extravagance and Play,
The brisk Companion and expensive Tea,
To feast with *Cordia* in her filthy Sty
On stewed Potatoes or on a mouldy Pie;
Whose eager Eyes stare ghastly at the Poor,   45
And fright the Beggars from her hated Door;
In greasy Clouts she wraps her smoky Chin,[9]
And holds that Pride's a never-pardoned Sin.
    If this be Wealth, no matter where it falls;
But save, ye Muses, save your *Mira*'s walls: 50
Still give me pleasing Indolence and Ease,
A Fire to warm me and a Friend to please.
    Since, whether sunk in Avarice or Pride,
A wanton Virgin or a starving Bride,

---

8. Hymen is the god of marriage in Greek   9. Clouts: rags.
mythology.

Or wond'ring Crowds attend her charming Tongue,   55
Or, deemed an Idiot, ever speaks the Wrong;
Though Nature armed us for the growing Ill
With fraudful Cunning and a headstrong Will;
Yet, with ten thousand Follies to her Charge,
Unhappy Woman's but a Slave at large.   60

                                            1748/1751

The Headache. To Aurelia[1]

Aurelia, when your zeal makes known
Each woman's failing but your own,
How charming Silvia's teeth decay,
And Celia's hair is turning grey;
Yet Celia gay has sparkling eyes,   5
But (to your comfort) is not wise:
Methinks you take a world of pains
To tell us Celia has no brains.

Now you wise folk, who make such a pother
About the wit of one another,   10
With pleasure would your brains resign,
Did all your noddles ache like mine.

Not cuckolds half my anguish know,
When budding horns begin to grow;
Nor battered skull of wrestling Dick,   15
Who late was drubbed at single-stick;[2]
Nor wretches that in fevers fry,
Not Sappho when her cap's awry,
E'er felt such torturing pangs as I;
Not forehead of Sir Jeffrey Strife,   20
When smiling Cynthio kissed his wife.

Not lovesick Marcia's languid eyes,
Who for her simpering Corin dies,
So sleepy look or dimly shine,
As these dejected eyes of mine: 25
Not Claudia's brow such wrinkles made
At sight of Cynthia's new brocade.

Just so, Aurelia, you complain
Of vapours, rheums, and gouty pain;
Yet I am patient, so should you,   30
For cramps and headaches are our due:
We suffer justly for our crimes,
For scandal you, and I for rhymes;

---

1. Aurelia has not been identified, though she
seems to be a friend. The other names in the poem,
including Silvia, Celia, Sappho, Marcia, and Cynthia, appear to be stock names that do not refer to
particular people.
2. A kind of fighting or fencing.

Yet we (as hardened wretches do)
Still the enchanting vice pursue;   35
Our reformation ne'er begin,
But fondly hug the darling sin.

  Yet there's a might difference too
Between the fate of me and you;
Though you with tottering age shall bow,   40
And wrinkles scar your lovely brow,
Your busy tongue may still proclaim
The faults of every sinful dame:
You still may prattle nor give o'er,
When wretched I must sin no more.   45
The sprightly Nine must leave me then,[3]
This trembling hand resign its pen:
No matron every sweetly sung,
Apollo only courts the young.[4]
Then who would not (Aurelia, pray)   50
Enjoy his favours while they may?
Nor cramps nor headaches shall prevail:
I'll still write on, and you shall rail.

                                                    1748/1751

◄ MERCY OTIS WARREN ►
1728–1814

Poet, dramatist, and historian of the American Revolution, Mercy Otis Warren
was a firsthand witness to the colonial struggle for independence and the establishment of the American republic. The descendant of a Mayflower family, she
was born in Barnstable, Massachusetts, the third child of James and Mary Allyne
Otis. Warren received almost the same lessons as her brother James, who was
being prepared to attend Harvard. (Greek and Latin were thought to be too masculine for girls, so she read the classics in translation.) In 1754, she wed James
Warren, inaugurating a long and happy marriage. The couple had five sons, three
of whom predeceased her. Warren's husband was active in Revolutionary politics,
and their social circle included John and Abigail Adams, with whom they were intimate friends (though differing political opinions later separated them), and
George and Martha Washington. She also enjoyed meeting the English historian
Catherine Macaulay, who visited the United States in 1784–85 (see p. 286).

  After her brother James received a debilitating beating from a group of British
customs officials in the British Coffee House in 1769, Warren began her own ca-

---

3. Nine: in Greek mythology, the nine Muses, or   4. Apollo: Greek god and patron of music and
goddesses representing the arts.   poetry associated with the nine Muses.

reer as a political writer. Because it would have been considered inappropriate for a woman to produce such materials, she did not sign her name to most of these writings, but she produced dramatic sketches attacking British leadership in the colonies, writings that became an important part of colonial propaganda. She also wrote poems and political tracts, in which she urged women to boycott British luxury goods and to jettison their imported tea. In addition, she wrote a total of five plays, all intended to be read, since Boston had no theater at that time. Warren publicly acknowledged authorship of only one play, *The Group,* a thinly veiled attack on colonial leadership that was inspired by the Boston Tea Party. She also published a volume titled *Poems, Dramatic and Miscellaneous* in 1790. In her later years, she completed her three-volume *History of the Rise, Progress, and Termination of American Revolution* (1805). She died of an unrecorded illness and was buried in Plymouth, Massachusetts, not far from her birthplace.

The following selection, written as the preface to her *History,* preserves Warren's original punctuation. In this selection we hear Warren subtly chafing against the restraints put on her as a woman. Regardless of the obstacles she faces, she remains confident in her abilities and committed to her task as a historian. After all, because of her important friends and personal involvement with the American Revolution, she had, she writes, "the best means of information."

An Address to the Inhabitants of the United States

At a period when every manly arm was occupied, and every trait of talent or activity engaged, either in the cabinet or the field, apprehensive, that amidst the sudden convulsions, crowded scenes, and rapid changes, that flowed in quick succession, many circumstances might escape the more busy and active members of society, I have been induced to improve the leisure Providence had lent, to record as they passed, in the following pages, the new and unexperienced events exhibited in a land previously blessed with peace, liberty simplicity, and virtue.

* * *

Connected by nature, friendship, and every social tie, with many of the first patriots, and most influential characters on the continent; in the habits of confidential and epistolary intercourse[1] with several gentlemen employed abroad in the most distinguished stations, and with others since elevated to the highest grades of rank and distinction, I had the best means of information, through a long period that the colonies were in suspense, waiting the operation of foreign courts, and the success of their own enterprising spirit.

The solemnity that covered every countenance, when contemplating the sword uplifted, and the horrors of civil war rushing to habitations not inured to scenes of rapine[2] and misery; even to the quiet cottage, where only concord and affection had reigned; stimulated to observation a mind that had not yielded to the assertion, that all political attentions lay out of the road of female life.

It is true there are certain appropriate duties assigned to each sex; and doubtless it is the more peculiar province of masculine strength, not only to repel the bold invader of the rights of his country and of mankind, but in the nervous style

---

1. Correspondence by letters.   2. Plunder.

of manly eloquence, to describe the blood-stained field, and relate the story of slaughtered armies.

Sensible of this, the trembling heart has recoiled at the magnitude of the undertaking, and the hand often shrunk back from the task; yet, recollecting that every domestic enjoyment depends on the unimpaired possession of civil and religious liberty, that a concern for the welfare of society ought equally to glow in every human breast, the work was not relinquished. The most interesting circumstances were collected, active characters portrayed, the principles of the times developed, and the changes marked; nor need it cause a blush to acknowledge, a detail was preserved with a view of transmitting it to the rising youth of my country, some of them in infancy, others in the European world, while the most interesting events lowered over their native land.

* * *

Several years have elapsed since the historical tracts, now with diffidence submitted to the public, have been arranged in their present order. Local circumstances, the decline of health, temporary deprivations of sight, the death of the most amiable of children,[3] "the shaft flew thrice, and thrice my peace was slain," have sometimes prompted to throw by the pen in despair. I draw a veil over the woe-fraught scenes that have pierced my own heart. "While the soul was melting inwardly, it has endeavoured to support outwardly, with decency and dignity, those accidents which admit of no redress, and to exert that spirit that enables to get the better of those that do."[4]

Not indifferent to the opinion of the world, nor servilely courting its smiles, no further apology is offered for the attempt, though many may be necessary, for the incomplete execution of a design, that had rectitude for its basis, and a beneficent regard for the civil and religious rights of mankind, for its motive.

The liberal-minded will peruse with candor, rather than criticise with severity; nor will they think it necessary, that any apology should be offered, for sometimes introducing characters nearly connected with the author of the following annals; as they were early and zealously attached to the public cause, uniform in their principles, and constantly active in the great scenes that produced the revolution, and obtained independence for their country, truth precludes that reserve which might have been proper on less important occasions, and forbids to pass over in silence the names of such as expired before the conflict was finished, or have since retired from public scenes. The historian has never laid aside the tenderness of the sex or the friend; at the same time, she has endeavoured, on all occasions, that the strictest veracity should govern her heart, and the most exact impartiality be the guide of her pen.

* * *

Before this address to my countrymen is closed, I beg leave to observe, that as a new century has dawned upon us, the mind is naturally led to contemplate the great events that have run parallel with, and have just closed the last. From the

---

3. Warren often had trouble with her eyes; she lost three sons: Charles died in 1785, Winslow was killed in battle against the Miami Indians in 1791, and George, her youngest, died in 1800.

4. The first quote is from Edward Young (1683–1765), author of *Night Thoughts* (Night 1, line 212). The second quote remains unidentified.

revolutionary spirit of the times, the vast improvements in science, arts, and agriculture, the boldness of genius that marks the age, the investigation of new theories, and the changes in the political, civil, and religious characters of men, succeeding generations have reason to expect still more astonishing exhibitions in the next. In the mean time, Providence has clearly pointed out the duties of the present generation, particularly the paths which Americans ought to tread. The United States form a young republic, a confederacy which ought ever to be cemented by a union of interest and affection, under the influence of those principles which obtained their independence. These have indeed, at certain periods, appeared to be in the wane; but let them never be eradicated, by the jarring interests of parties, jealousies of the sister states, or the ambition of individuals! It has been observed, by a writer of celebrity,[5] that "that people, government, and constitution is the freest, which makes the best provision for the enacting of expedient and salutary laws." May this truth be evinced to all ages, by the wise and salutary laws that shall be enacted in the federal legislature of America!

May the hands of the executive of their own choice, be strengthened more by the unanimity and affection of the people, than by the dread of penal inflictions, or any restraints that might repress free inquiry, relative to the principles of their own government, and the conduct of its administrators! The world is now viewing America, as experimenting a new system of government, a FEDERAL REBUBLIC, including a territory to which the Kingdom of Great Britain and Ireland bear little proportion. The practicability of supporting such a system, has been doubted by some; if she succeeds, it will refute the assertion, that none but small states are adapted to republican government; if she does not , and the union should be dissolved, some ambitious son of Columbia,[6] or some foreign adventurer, allured by the prize, may wade to empire through seas of blood, or the friends of monarchy may see a number of petty despots, stretching their sceptres over the disjointed parts of the continent. Thus by the mandate of a single sovereign, the degraded subjects of one state, under the bannerets of royalty, may be dragged to sheathe their swords in the bosoms of the inhabitants of another.[7]

The state of the public mind, appears at present to be prepared to weigh these reflections with solemnity, and to receive with pleasure an effort to trace the origin of the American revolution, to review the characters that effected it, and to justify the principles of the defection and final separation from the parent state. With an expanded heart, beating with high hopes of the continued freedom and prosperity of America, the writer indulges a modest expectation, that the following pages will be perused with kindness and candor: this she claims, both in consideration of her sex, the uprightness of her intentions, and the fervency of her wishes for the happiness of all the human race.

Mercy Warren
1805

---

5. William Paley, "Moral Philosophy," from *The Principles of Moral and Political Philosophy* (London, 1775), Book 6, Chapter 6, p. 448.
6. The United States.

7. Warren refers to an anxiety, common during her time, that the United States would split into separate countries, which would adopt different political systems and fight against each other.

JANET SCHAW

1734–c. 1801

We owe our knowledge of Janet Schaw to the accidental discovery in 1904 of her journal by a researcher working in the British Library. Schaw was born in a suburb of Edinburgh, Scotland, but we can only surmise that she was born around 1734–39 because she was thirty-five or forty at the time she wrote her journal. We know that she came from an old Scottish family of note, that she was one of six children, and that Sir Walter Scott was one of her relatives. Everything else about her must be pieced together from her writings.

In sections of the journal not included here, Schaw describes her travels from Scotland to the West Indies with her brother Alexander, who is about to relocate there. Also traveling with them are three children of a prominent resident of North Carolina, who are returning from school in Scotland, as well as Schaw's maid and an East Indian servant named Robert. While crossing the Atlantic, Schaw discovers, living below the deck, a group of very poor emigrants who have been driven from their crofts, or farms, in the Orkney Islands off Scotland's northern coast. After some initial disgust over their unhygienic and impoverished conditions, Schaw takes an interest in and even befriends a few of the emigrants. One of her more remarkable entries mentions an encounter with a British ship transporting soldiers to New England; those soldiers would later fight in the American Revolutionary battles at Lexington and Concord, though Schaw could not have known what would follow.

Her journal from the West Indies, a section of which is included here, begins in December 1774, a time when islands like Antigua and St. Christopher yielded lucrative crops of sugarcane, enabling Scots like Schaw's brother to lead wealthy, gracious plantation lives. In early 1775, Schaw traveled from the West Indies to North Carolina. In autumn 1775, she left for Lisbon. Nothing more is known about her after she returned to Edinburgh in 1776.

Schaw's journal offers intimate, firsthand perspectives on everyday life, both at sea and in the British colonies in the West, among a class of privileged Scots. It describes a life of graciousness and hospitality and betrays her many religious, social, and racial prejudices. In the two letters that follow—the first describing Antiguan society, the second the Olovaze sugar plantation in Saint Christopher—Schaw appears astoundingly oblivious to the suffering of the enslaved Africans, which was likely all around her. Schaw's perspective, while shocking to today's reader, was fairly typical of her age and class, which benefited mightily from the institution of slavery. The British slave trade was outlawed in 1807 and abolished throughout the British empire in 1833, but the movement for the abolition of the slave trade did not begin in earnest until the 1780s, after the Schaws' return to Edinburgh.

From The Journal of a Lady of Quality: Being a Narrative of a Journey from Scotland to the West Indies

[Society in Antigua]

* * *

As I am now about to leave them, you, no doubt, will expect me, to give my opinion as fully on the Inhabitants, as I have done on their Island and manners, but I am afraid you will suspect me of partiality, and were I to speak of Individuals, perhaps you might have reason, but as to the characters in general I can promise to write without prejudice, and if I only tell truth, they have nothing to fear from my pen. I think the men the most agreeable creatures I ever met with, frank, open, generous, and I dare say brave; even in advanced life they retain the Vivacity and Spirit of Youth; they are in general handsome, and all of them have that sort of air, that will ever attend a man of fashion. Their address is at once soft and manly; they have a kind of gallantry in their manner, which exceeds mere politeness, and in some countries, we know, would be easily mistaken for something more interesting than civility, yet you must not suppose this the politeness of French manners, merely words of course. No, what they say, they really mean; their whole intention is to make you happy, and this they endeavour to do without any other view or motive than what they are prompted to by the natural goodness of their own natures. In short, my friend, the woman that *brings a heart here* will have little sensibility if she carry it away.

I hear you ask me, if there is no alloy to this fine character, no reverse to this beautiful picture. Alas! my friend, tho' children of the Sun, they are mortals, and as such must have their share of failings, the most conspicuous of which is, the indulgence they give themselves in their licentious and even unnatural amours, which appears too plainly from the crouds of Mulattoes, which you meet in the streets, houses and indeed every where; a crime that seems to have gained sanction from custom, tho' attended with the greatest inconveniences not only to Individuals, but to the publick in general. The young black wenches lay themselves out for white lovers, in which they are but too successful. This prevents their marrying with their natural mates, and hence a spurious and degenerate breed, neither so fit for the field, nor indeed any work, as the true bred Negro. Besides these wenches become licentious and insolent past all bearing, and as even a mulattoe child interrupts their pleasures and is troublesome, they have certain herbs and medicines, that free them from such an incumbrance, but which seldom fails to cut short their own lives, as well as that of their offspring. By this many of them perish every year. I would have gladly drawn a veil over this part of a character, which in every thing else is most estimable.

As to the women, they are in general the most amiable creatures in the world, and either I have been remarkably fortunate in my acquaintance, or they are more than commonly sensible, even those who have never been off the Island are amazingly intelligent and able to converse with you on any subject. They make excellent wives, fond attentive mothers and the best house wives I have ever met with. Those of the first fortune and fashion keep their own keys and look after every thing within doors; the domestick Economy is entirely left to them; as the husband finds enough to do abroad. A fine house, an elegant table, handsome carriage, and a croud of mulattoe servants are what they all seem very fond of. The sun appears to affect the sexes very differently. While the men are gay, luxurious and amorous, the women are modest, genteel, reserved and temperate. This last virtue they have indeed in the extreme; they drink nothing stronger in general than Sherbet, and never eat above one or two things at table, and these the lightest and plainest. The truth is, I can observe no indulgence they allow themselves in, not so much as in scandal, and if I stay long in this country, I will lose the very idea of that innocent amusement; for since I resided amongst them, I have never heard one woman say a wrong thing of another. This is so unnatural, that I suppose you will (good naturedly) call it cunning; but if it is so, it is the most commendable cunning I ever met with, as nothing can give them a better appearance in the eyes of a stranger.

[A Visit to Olovaze]

* * *

Crouds of company are here every day, whose visits we shall return. My brother and Mr Hamilton[1] are mutually pleased with each other, and are never asunder; he goes down with him every morning to town and is as much at home as you can imagine, and intimate with every body. The great sugar-works of the plantations are just by, and I have viewed them with much attention. Mr Hughes, the Overseer, who is a worthy obliging young man a great friend of Mr Hamilton's, has been so good as shew me the whole grand operation, which fabricates one of the prettiest branches of the British trade. But I shall first finish the Olovaze and then take a tour with you thro' the Island, and give you every thing that pleases myself. But writing here, my friend, I assure you is no easy task; for besides the heat which is great, I grudge every moment that takes me from the company of my friends. We live in constant fear of the arrival of our ship, which will hurry us away, and we have not less than twenty invitations, and we dance every night for several hours, from which no person is exempted. All dance from fifteen to four score, and we are to have a fine ball here a few days hence, where the whole Island are to be.

I had a walk this morning, that you would hardly believe me able to have taken, as it was no less than two miles, and up hill. This was truly a British frolick, and what no creole[2] would ever dream of. The ascent however is not steep, and we set off several hours before the sun rose to a high plantation where breakfast was provided for us. The first part of the way was thro' cane pieces, which are just now in their greatest glory; but tho' they excluded the sun, they also prevented the breeze from giving us air, and we were a good deal incommoded, till we reached what is first called the mountain, which is one of the greatest beauties in nature, and I will take this opportunity to describe it. Properly speaking the whole Island forms its base, as the ascent begins from the sea and rises from all sides to the top. It is covered with canes for about the third of the way up, then with myrtles, tamarinds, oranges and fruits of various kinds. Above that is a great variety of trees, whose verdure is not inferior to those in Britain, and I am told the climate there approaches to cold; and that further up, the air is so cold, that those who have tried it, were instantly seized with plurisies, and this I can easily believe, for as we were a good deal warmed with walking, the sudden change was very perceptible, and I was shivering with cold all the time we were at breakfast.

I could not however forbear lengthening my walk, by taking a more particular survey of the mountain. My brother and I accordingly walked a good way up alongst one of the streams of water which comes down from it. It was at present only a scanty rill, but by the appearance of its bed, is at times a large fall. It divides the mountain for a good way up, and resembles one of our highland burns; its source as well as the burns being on the top. But how different is the appearance of its banks, where every thing most beautiful in nature is mixed in delightful

1. The Hamiltons, who owned a sugar plantation named Olovaze on the island of St. Christopher, had invited Janet Schaw and her brother to be their guests.
2. Someone of European or Latin American descent who was born in the West Indies.

confusion. Oranges, limes, shadocks, cherries, citron, papa trees[3] are all at once covered with flowers and fruit; besides a profusion of vines and flowers out of Number we also saw cotton in plenty, which here is a shrub, as is Coffee. But they are generally raised in cultivated plantations, for tho' they are all indigenous, they are much the better of culture. I formerly said that the seasons were united, which is the case all over the Islands, and just now they are planting, reaping and bruising, in which I include distilling.[4] But tho' perhaps there is no such rich land in the world as in this Island, they use manure in great abundance, and would be as glad of the rakes of Edinburgh streets as the Lothian farmers.[5] No planter is above attending to this grand article, which is hoarded up with the utmost care, and I every where saw large dunghills of compound manure, composed of the ashes from the boiling kettle, the bruised canes, the spilt leaves of the cane, the cleaning of the houses and dung of the stables. These are turned up and kept till proper for use, and no infant cane is placed in its pit without a very sufficient quantity of this to bed and nurse it up.

The Negroes who are all in troops are sorted so as to match each other in size and strength. Every ten Negroes have a driver, who walks behind them, holding in his hand a short whip and a long one. You will too easily guess the use of these weapons; a circumstance of all others the most horrid. They are naked, male and female, down to the girdle, and you constantly observe where the application has been made. But however dreadful this must appear to a humane European, I will do the creoles the justice to say, they would be as averse to it as we are, could it be avoided, which has often been tried to no purpose. When one comes to be better acquainted with the nature of the Negroes, the horrour of it must wear off. It is the suffering of the human mind that constitutes the greatest misery of punishment, but with them it is merely corporeal. As to the brutes it inflicts no wound on their mind, whose Natures seem made to bear it, and whose sufferings are not attended with shame or pain beyond the present moment. When they are regularly Ranged, each has a little basket, which he carries up the hill filled with the manure and returns with a load of canes to the Mill. They go up at a trot, and return at a gallop, and did you not know the cruel necessity of this alertness, you would believe them the merriest people in the world.

Since I am on the chapter of Negroes feelings, I must tell you that I was some days ago in town, when a number for market came from on board a ship. They stood up to be looked at with perfect unconcern. The husband was to be divided from the wife, the infant from the mother; but the most perfect indifference ran thro' the whole. They were laughing and jumping, making faces at each other, and not caring a single farthing for their fate. This is not however without exception; and it behoves the planter to consider the country from whence he purchases his slaves; as those from one coast are mere brutes and fit only for the labour of the field, while those from another are bad field Negroes, but faithful handy house-servants. There are others who seem entirely formed for the mechanick arts, and these of all others are the most valuable; but want of attention to this has been the ruin of many plantations. Strange as it may seem, they are very nervous and subject

3. Papaya.
4. Bruising and distilling are steps in sugar making—crushing the stalks to obtain the cane's juices and drying the liquid to make granulated sugar. Also refers to the process of making molasses into rum ("distilling").

5. A reference to the "recycling" of manure from the Edinburgh city streets to the farms in the surrounding countryside.

to fits of madness. This is looked on as witchcraft by themselves, and there is a seer on every plantation to whom they have recourse when taken ill. They are also very subject to dropsies, by which they[6] lose many of their boilers, who are always the best slaves on the plantation.

To remedy this evil, as much as possible, the boiling houses are very high and lofty, covered with shelving boards that admit the air freely as well as give vent to the steam. When one considers the heat that must be produced by four or five kettles which contain not less than a Hogshead apiece, and which requires a strong clear fire to boil the sugar to its proper consistence, it is very wonderful how they contrive to render them so sufferable as they are. Lady Isabella, Miss Rutherfurd and myself were in one of them last night above an hour, when they were boiling to their height, and were very little incommoded by the heat, and much entertained by being shown the process of this great work from the first throwing the canes into the mill to the casking the sugar and rum. But as Mr Hughes is so good as to promise to make it out for me in writing, I will not attempt to give a description from myself from a few slight observations of a business that requires years of study to be come perfect in. My Lady had another design, besides satisfying my curiosity in this visit to the boiling house. There were several of the boilers condemned to the lash, and seeing her face is pardon. Their gratitude on this occasion was the only instance of sensibility that I have observed in them. Their crime was the neglect of their own health which is indeed the greatest fault they can commit.

* * *

1774   1921

___

6. The planters.

CULTURAL COORDINATES
At Sea

During the eighteenth century, women found themselves on British naval ships under several circumstances, according to historian Suzanne Stark in *Female Tars: Women aboard Ship in the Age of Sail* (1996). First, warrant officers—non-commissioned officers in the employ of a particular ship, including the ship's boatswain, gunner, carpenter, cooper, sailmaker, and cook—all brought their wives to live with them on board. These women chose life at sea with their children over life on shore, where they could not depend on consistent financial support from their partners, who were away for long periods of time. The families lived in small canvas-sided cabins, with little privacy or comfort. It was not uncommon for the women to give birth during battle, since the noise and vibrations of the big guns could induce labor.

Petty officers and a few seamen also brought their wives on board, but their presence was not officially acknowledged; these women had to share their husbands' hammocks and rations. In battle, these wives helped to tend to the wounded, and they carried gunpowder from the magazine. We have no record of what happened to them if they became widowed.

On the lower decks, many ships also housed numbers of prostitutes. Their presence was officially forbidden yet tolerated as a means of keeping seamen who had been impressed (or forced) into the navy from going ashore and deserting. These women had little or no means of contraception and venereal disease was rampant. Their

Hannah Snell disguised herself in male clothing in order to enlist in the British Marines. (National Portrait Gallery, London)

nutrition, like that of the sailors, would have been substandard, and they would have been highly susceptible to disease. Life below the decks of a royal ship would have been chaotic, with crowds of dancing, drinking, and sometimes fornicating men and women sharing space with children and animals.

Other women found employment on hospital ships, serving as nurses and launderers. These women were paid and given provisions. It also appears that a few women occasionally disguised themselves as men in order to join the Royal Marines. Most likely these cross-dressed sailors were motivated by economic interests, or perhaps by the opportunity to escape from restrictive social conditions.

After 1815, the number of women on board British ships began to decrease, due to new regulations, new attitudes toward women, and better conditions on board militating against desertion. Not until 1933 were women integrated into the Royal Navy as full-fledged sailors.

MARY COLLIER
Active 1739–1760

The woman who wrote the remarkable poem that appears here is virtually un-known: described as a washerwoman in the first advertisement of her works, she left no trace of her birth, family, marital status, or death. In defense of Mary Collier's (at that time) outrageous act of daring to publish her works, she wrote, "I think it no Reproach to the Author, whose life is so toilsome, and her Wages inconsiderable, to confess honestly, that the view of her putting a small Sum of Money in her Pocket, as well as the Reader's Entertainment, had its Share of Influence upon this Publication."

The circumstances that generated this poem are as follows: In 1730, a "laboring-class" poet named Stephen Duck—a man who had formerly worked as an agricultural laborer—wrote a poem depicting the difficulty, drudgery, and tedium of his labor. He described as well the inimical relations between the "Master" and the workingmen. But in his poem he also attacked workingwomen, claiming that they sat around and chattered while the men did real work. In her eloquent, passionate, and detailed response, Collier points out the many blind spots in Duck's poem, in particular, how he fails to acknowledge that women not only work in the fields but also tend to the children (even through the night), make the meals, and do all the housework. She further describes how, during the winter, when there is no work in the fields, women go "a charing"—that is, they hire themselves out to do the low-est, most arduous kinds of household labor, labor done not even by the live-in ser-vants. Her description of the blood trickling down her wrists and fingers (lines 185–86) is probably not an exaggeration: before the invention of modern deter-gents, soaps and other cleaning products were highly caustic and certainly injuri-ous to hands already damaged from agricultural labor. Thus, Collier's poem provides us with a rare opportunity to hear the articulate voice of an eighteenth-century workingwoman, someone whose labor was almost entirely invisible to the upper classes, but who nonetheless made their gracious lifestyle possible.

The Woman's Labour

An Epistle to Mr. Stephen Duck; In Answer to his
late Poem, called
The Thresher's Labour . . .
By May Collier, Now a *Washer-Woman,*
at Petersfield in Hampshire

Immortal Bard! thou Favourite of the Nine!
Enriched by Peers, advanced by Caroline![1]
Deign to look down on One that's poor and low,
Remembering you yourself was lately so;
Accept these Lines: Alas! what can you have   5

---

1. A reference to Stephen Duck, whose celebrity as "the Thresher Poet" was acknowledged by many people in high places, including Queen Car-oline (1683–1737), consort to King George II of England; the "Nine" refers to the Muses, patron goddesses of the arts in Greek mythology.

From her, who ever was, and's still a Slave?
No Learning ever was bestowed on me;
My Life was always spent in Drudgery:
And not alone; alas! with Grief I find,
It is the Portion of poor Woman-kind.   10
Oft have I thought as on my Bed I lay,
Eased from the tiresome Labours of the Day,
Our first Extraction from a Mass refined,
Could never be for Slavery designed;
Till Time and Custom by degrees destroyed   15
That happy State our sex at first enjoyed.
When Men had used their utmost Care and Toil,
Their Recompense was but a Female Smile;
When they by Arts or Arms were rendered Great,
They laid their Trophies at a Woman's Feet;   20
They, in those Days, unto our Sex did bring
Their Hearts, their All, a Free-will Offering;
And as from us their Being they derive,
They back again should all due Homage give.
    Jove once descending from the Clouds, did drop   25
In Show'rs of Gold on lovely *Danae*'s Lap;[2]
The sweet-tongued Poets, in those generous Days,
Unto our Shrine still offered up their Lays:
But now, alas! that Golden Age is past,
We are the Objects of your Scorn at last.   30
And you, great Duck, upon whose happy Brow
The Muses seem to fix the Garland now,
In your late *Poem* boldly did declare
Alcides' Labours can't with yours compare;[3]
And of your annual Task have much to say,   35
Of threshing, Reaping, Mowing Corn and Hay;
Boasting your daily Toil, and nightly Dream,
But can't conclude your never-dying Theme,
And let our hapless Sex in Silence lie
Forgotten, and in dark Oblivion die;   40
But on our abject State you throw your Scorn,
And Women wrong, your Verses to adorn.
You of Hay-making speak a Word or two,
As if our Sex but little Work could do:
This makes the honest Farmer smiling say,   45
He'll seek for Women still to make his Hay;
For if his Back be turned, their Work they mind
As well as men, as far as he can find.
For my own Part, I many a *Summer*'s Day

---

2. In classical mythology, Jove (or Zeus) transformed himself into a shower of gold in order to
gain access to Danae, whose father had barricaded
her in her room.

3. Alcides (Hercules): Duck had compared his
agricultural labor to the labor of this Greek hero,
famed for his strength and fortitude.

Have spent in throwing, turning, making Hay; 50
But ne'er could see, what you have lately found,
Our Wages paid for sitting on the Ground.
'Tis true, that when our Morning's Work is done,
And all our Grass exposed unto the Sun,
While that his scorching Beams do on it shine, 55
As well as you, we have a Time to dine:
I hope, that since we freely toil and sweat
To earn our Bread, you'll give us Time to eat.
That over, soon we must get up again,
And nimbly turn our Hay upon the Plain; 60
Nay, rake and prow it in, the Case is clear;
Or how should Cocks in equal Rows appear?[4]
But if you'd have what you have wrote believed.
I find, that you to hear us talk are grieved:
In this, I hope, you do not speak your Mind, 65
For none but *Turks,* that ever could I find,
Have Mutes to serve them, or did e'er deny
Their Slaves, at Work, to chat it merrily.
Since you have Liberty to speak your Mind,
And are to talk, as well as we, inclined, 70
Why should you thus repine, because that we,
Like you, enjoy that pleasing Liberty?
What! would you lord it quite, and take away
The only Privilege our Sex enjoy?
    When Evening does approach, we homeward hie, 75
And our domestic Toils incessant ply:
Against your coming Home prepare to get
Our Work all done, our House in order set;
"Bacon" and "Dumpling" in the Pot we boil,
Our Beds we make, our Swine we feed the while; 80
Then wait at Door to see you coming Home,
And set the Table out against you come:
Early next Morning we on you attend;
Our Children dress and feed, their Clothes we mend;
And in the Field our daily Task renew, 85
Soon as the rising Sun has dried the Dew.
    When Harvest comes, into the Field we go,
And help to reap the Wheat as well as you;
Or else we go the Ears of Corn to glean;
No Labour scorning, be it e'er so mean; 90
But in the Work we freely bear a Part,
And what we can, perform with all our Heart.
To get a Living we so willing are,
Our tender Babes into the Field we bear,
And wrap them in our Clothes to keep them warm, 95
While round about we gather up the Corn;

---

4. Prow: plough; cocks: haystacks.

And often unto them our Course do bend,
To keep them safe, that nothing them offend:
Our children that are able, bear a Share
In gleaning Corn, such is our frugal care.   100
When Night comes on, unto our Home we go,
Our Corn we carry, and our Infant too;
Weary, alas! but 'tis not worth our while
Once to complain, or rest at every Stile;[5]
We must make haste, for when we Home are come,   105
Alas! we find our Work but just begun;
So many Things for our Attendance call,
Had we ten Hands, we could employ them all.
Our Children put to Bed, with greatest Care
We all Things for your coming Home prepare: 110
You sup, and go to Bed without delay,
And rest yourselves till the ensuing Day;
While we, alas! but little Sleep can have,
Because our froward[6] Children cry and rave;
Yet, without fail, soon as Day-light doth spring,   115
We in the Field again our Work begin,
And there, with all our Strength, our Toil renew,
Till *Titan*'s[7] golden Rays have dried the Dew;
Then home we go unto our Children dear,
Dress, feed, and bring them to the Field with care.   120
Were this your Case, you justly might complain
That Day nor Night you are secure from Pain;
Those mighty Troubles which perplex your Mind,
(*Thistles* before, and *Females* come behind)
Would vanish soon, and quickly disappear,   125
Were you, like us, encumbered thus with Care.
What you would have of us we do not know:
We oft' take up the Corn that you do mow;
We cut the Pease, and always ready are
In every Work to take our Proper Share;   130
And from the Time that Harvest doth begin,
Until the Corn be cut and carried in,
Our Toil and Labour's daily so extreme,
That we have hardly ever *Time to dream*.
      The Harvest ended, Respite none we find;   135
The hardest of our Toil is still behind:
Hard labour we most cheerfully pursue,
And out, abroad, a Charing[8] often go:
Of which I now will briefly tell in part,
What fully to declare is past my Art;   140

---

5. Steps for climbing over a wall separating fields.
6. Peevish.
7. In Greek mythology, the Titans were deities who were overthrown by Zeus and the Olympian gods.
8. Temporary cleaning jobs, usually scrubbing and other heavy toil not done by the servants who live in the house.

So many Hardships daily we go through,
I boldly say, the like *you* never knew.
    When bright *Orion* glitters in the Skies
In *Winter* Nights, then early we must rise;
The Weather ne'er so bad, Wind, Rain, or Snow.   145
Our Work appointed, we must rise and go;
While you on easy Beds may lie and sleep,
Till Light does through your Chamber-windows peep.
When to the House we come where we should go,
How to get in, alas! we do not know: 150
The Maid quite tir'd with Work the Day before,
O'ercome with Sleep; we standing at the Door
Oppressed with Cold, and often call in vain,
Ere to our Work we can Admittance gain:
But when from Wind and Weather we get in,   155
Briskly with Courage we our Work begin;
Heaps of fine Linen we before us view,
Whereon to lay our Strength and Patience too;
Cambrics and Muslins, which our ladies wear,
Laces and Edgings, costly, fine, and rare,   160
Which must be washed with utmost Skill and care;
With Holland Shirts,[9] Ruffles and Fringes too,
Fashions which our Fore-fathers never knew.
For several Hours here we work and slave,
Before we can one Glimpse of Day-light have;   165
We labour hard before the Morning's past,
Because we fear the Time runs on too fast.
    At length bright *Sol* illuminates the Skies,
And summons drowsy Mortals to arise;
Then comes our Mistress to us without fail,   170
And in her Hand, *perhaps,* a Mug of Ale
To cheer our Hearts, and also to inform
Herself, what Work is done that very Morn;
Lays her Command upon us, that we mind
Her Linen well, nor "leave the Dirt behind":   175
Not this alone, but also to take care
We don't her Cambrics nor her Ruffles tear;
And *these* most strictly does of us require,
"To save her Soap, and sparing be of Fire";
Tells us her Charge is great, nay furthermore,   180
Her Clothes are fewer than the Time before.
Now we drive on, resolved our Strength to try,
And what we can, we do most willingly;
Until with Heat and Work, 'tis often known
Not only Sweat, but Blood runs trickling down   185
Our Wrists and Fingers; still our Work demands
The constant Action of our lab'ring Hands.

9. Shirts made from fine Dutch linen.

Now Night comes on, from whence you have Relief,
But that, alas! does but increase our Grief;
With heavy Hearts we often view the Sun,   190
Fearing he'll set before our Work is done;
For either in the Morning, or at Night,
We piece[1] the *Summer*'s Day with Candle-light.
Though we all Day with Care our Work attend,
Such is our Fate, we know not when 'twill end: 195
When Evening's come, you Homeward take your Way,
We, till our Work is done, are forced to stay;
And after all our Toil and Labour past,
Six-pence or Eight-pence[2] pays us off at last;
For all our Pains, no Prospect can we see   200
Attend us, but *Old Age* and *Poverty*.
The *Washing* is not all we have to do:
We oft change Work for Work as well as you.
Our Mistress of her Pewter doth complain,
And 'tis our Part to make it clean again.   205
This Work, though very hard and tiresome too,
Is not the worst we hapless Females do:
When Night comes on, and we quite weary are,
We scarce can count what falls unto our Share;
Pots, Kettles, Sauce-pans, Skillets, we may see,   210
Skimmers and Ladles, and such Trumpery,
Brought in to make complete our Slavery,
Though early in the Morning 'tis begun,
'Tis often very late before we've done;
Alas! our Labours never know an End;   215
On Brass and Iron we our Strength must spend;
Our tender Hands and Fingers scratch and tear:
All this, and more, with Patience we must bear.
Coloured with Dirt and Filth we now appear;
Your threshing "sooty Peas" will not come near.   220
All the Perfections Woman once could boast,
Are quite obscured, and altogether lost.
Once more our Mistress sends to let us know
She wants our Help, because the Beer runs low:
Then in much haste for Brewing we prepare,   225
The Vessels clean, and scald with greatest care;
Often at Midnight, from our Bed we rise
At other Times, ev'n *that* will not suffice;
Our Work at Evening oft we do begin,
And ere we've done, the Night comes on again.   230

1. Prolong.
2. Although monetary conversions can be problematic, at the time this selection was written, a
pence would have been equivalent to $1 today, so
Collier's pay is $6 to $8.

Water we pump, the Copper we must fill,
Or tend the Fire; for if we e'er stand still,
Like you, when threshing, we a Watch must keep,
Our Wort[3] boils over if we dare to sleep.
  But to rehearse all Labour is in vain,   235
Of which we very justly might complain:
For us, you see, but little Rest is found;
Our Toil increases as the Year runs round.
While you to *Sisyphus* yourselves compare,
With *Danaus' Daughters* we may claim a Share;[4]   240
For while *he* labours against the Hill,
Bottomless Tubs of Water *they* must fill.
  So the industrious Bees do hourly strive
To bring their Loads of Honey to the Hive;
Their sordid[5] Owners always reap the Gains,   245
And poorly recompense their Toil and Pains.

                                                               1739

⊷ ANNA LAETITIA AIKIN BARBAULD ⊶
1743–1825

Anna Laetitia Aikin was born in a Leicestershire village about one hundred miles north of London. Her parents were Presbyterian; her father was a minister in the Church of Scotland and a schoolteacher. While educated primarily by her mother, Barbauld also learned some Greek and Latin from her father. Because of her family's status as Dissenters—nonconformists who rejected the beliefs and practices of the Church of England and were therefore subject to discrimination—Barbauld grew up in a separate society, one nonetheless containing many notable intellectual and political figures, including lifelong friend Joseph Priestley, the famous scientist and the discoverer of oxygen. In 1758 her family moved to Leeds, where her father became a tutor at Warrington Academy.

Barbauld's younger brother John Aikin first encouraged her to write and publish, and he included six of her early poems in his *Essays on Song Writing* in 1771. The first collection of Barbauld's poetry appeared in 1773. The book was very successful, seeing four editions in the first year alone. In 1774 she married Rochemont Barbauld, a descendant of French Huguenot refugees. Together, the couple opened a boys' school in 1775. Having no children of their own, they adopted her brother John's third son, Charles. Barbauld wrote *Devotional Pieces* (1775), *Lessons for Children* (1787–1788), and other works to fill a gap in materials available for teaching young pupils like Charles and the students at their school. They closed the

---

3. A cabbagelike plant.
4. In Greek mythology, Sisyphus was condemned to roll a heavy rock up a hill for all eternity;

Danaus's daughters were condemned to filling innumerable, perpetually leaking tubs of water.
5. Covetous.

school in 1785 and began a year's travel in Europe. Barbauld began to write progressive social and political criticism, taking up such controversial topics as the abolition of the slave trade, freedom of religion, revolutionary politics, and the 1793 war against the French Republic. That she wrote about such politicized subjects meant that Barbauld was frequently publicly criticized.

As her literary career took off, the mental health of her husband deteriorated. In 1808 Rochemont tried to stab her. She escaped by jumping through a window into the garden. Later that year, he drowned himself after eluding the keepers in charge of his care. Despite this domestic tumult, Barbauld remained focused on her work. In 1804 she had begun her career as an editor, publishing six volumes of novelist Samuel Richardson's correspondence. In 1810 she edited fifty volumes of *The British Novelists,* a work for which she wrote many biographical essays and critical reviews and in which she featured the work of many women authors. She also wrote a controversial poem titled "Eighteen Hundred and Eleven," a trenchant critique of the ongoing war between England and France and a prescient prediction that English power would ultimately diminish and be surpassed.

The following selections convey the scope of Barbauld's distinctive political and social vision, a unique combination of political radicalism and social conservatism on the subject of women's rights. "The Rights of Woman" positions her in a dialogue with Mary Wollstonecraft, who had attacked one of Barbauld's poems in *A Vindication of the Rights of Woman.* "To a Little Invisible Being" provides a poignant meditation on the prenatal experience, ironically from a woman who never had a child herself. Lastly, "Washing-Day" takes up the most mundane of household tasks—laundry. Yet, through its deft manipulation of imagery and allusion, the poem situates the domestic task within the wider world of history and politics.

The Rights of Woman

Yes, injured Woman! rise, assert thy right!
Woman! too long degraded, scorned, oppressed;
O born to rule in partial Law's despite,
Resume thy native empire o'er the breast!

Go forth arrayed in panoply divine,   5
That angel pureness which admits no stain;
Go, bid proud Man his boasted rule resign
And kiss the golden sceptre of thy reign.

Go, gird thyself with grace, collect thy store
Of bright artillery glancing from afar;   10
Soft melting tones thy thundering cannon's roar,
Blushes and fears thy magazine of war.

Thy rights are empire; urge no meaner claim,—
Felt, not defined, and if debated, lost;
Like sacred mysteries, which withheld from fame,   15
Shunning discussion, are revered the most.

Try all that wit and art suggest to bend
Of thy imperial foe the stubborn knee;

Make treacherous Man thy subject, not thy friend;
Thou mayst command, but never canst be free.   20

Awe the licentious and restrain the rude;
Soften the sullen, clear the cloudy brow:
Be, more than princes' gifts, thy favours sued;—
She hazards all, who will the least allow.

But hope not, courted idol of mankind,   25
On this proud eminence secure to stay;
Subduing and subdued, thou soon shalt find
Thy coldness soften, and thy pride give way.

Then, then, abandon each ambitious thought;
Conquest or rule thy heart shall feebly move,   30
In Nature's school, by her soft maxims taught
That separate rights are lost in mutual love.

1795   1825

To a Little Invisible Being Who Is Expected Soon to Become Visible

Germ of new life, whose powers expanding slow
For many a moon their full perfection wait—
Haste, precious pledge of happy love, to go
Auspicious borne through life's mysterious gate.

What powers lie folded in thy curious frame—   5
Senses from objects locked, and mind from thought!
How little canst thou guess thy lofty claim
To grasp at all the worlds the Almighty wrought!

And see, the genial season's warmth to share,
Fresh younglings shoot, and opening roses glow!
Swarms of new life exulting fill the air—   10
Haste, infant bud of being, haste to blow!

For thee the nurse prepares her lulling songs,
The eager matrons count the lingering day;
But far the most thy anxious parent longs   15
On thy soft cheek a mother's kiss to lay.

She only asks to lay her burden down,
That her glad arms that burden may resume;
And nature's sharpest pangs her wishes crown,
That free thee living from thy living tomb.   20

She longs to fold to her maternal breast
Part of herself, yet to herself unknown;
To see and to salute the stranger guest,
Fed with her life through many a tedious moon.

Come, reap thy rich inheritance of love!   25
Bask in the fondness of a Mother's eye!

Nor wit nor eloquence her heart shall move
Like the first accents of thy feeble cry.

Haste, little captive, burst thy prison doors!
Launch on the living world, and spring to light!   30
Nature for thee displays her various stores,
Opens her thousand inlets of delight.

If charmèd verse or muttered prayers had power
With favouring spells to speed thee on thy way,
Anxious I'd bid my beads each passing hour,   35
Till thy wished smile thy mother's pangs o'erpay.

1795   1825

Washing-Day

The Muses[1] are turned gossips; they have lost
The buskined step,[2] and clear high-sounding phrase,
Language of gods. Come then, domestic Muse,
In slipshod measure loosely prattling on
Of farm or orchard, pleasant curds and cream,   5
Or drowning flies, or shoe lost in the mire
By little whimpering boy, with rueful face;
Come, Muse, and sing the dreaded Washing-Day.
Ye who beneath the yoke of wedlock bend,
With bowèd soul, full well ye ken the day   10
Which week, smooth sliding after week, brings on
Too soon;—for to that day nor peace belongs
Nor comfort;—ere the first grey streak of dawn,
The red-armed washers come and chase repose.
Nor pleasant smile, nor quaint device of mirth,   15
E'er visited that day: the very cat,
From the wet kitchen scared, and reeking hearth,
Visits the parlour,—an unwonted guest.
The silent breakfast-meal is soon dispatched;
Uninterrupted, save by anxious looks   20
Cast at the lowering sky, if sky should lower.
From that last evil, O preserve us, heavens!
For should the skies pour down, adieu to all
Remains of quiet: then expect to hear
Of sad disasters—dirt and gravel stains   25
Hard to efface, and loaded lines at once
Snapped short—and linen-horse by dog thrown down,
And all the petty miseries of life.
Saints have been calm while stretched upon the rack,

1. Greek goddesses who presided over the arts   2. Wearing big boots, like the actors in a Greek
and science.   tragedy.

And Guatimozin[3] smiled on burning coals;   30
But never yet did housewife notable
Greet with a smile a rainy washing-day.
—But grant the welkin[4] fair, require not thou
Who call'st thyself perchance the master there,
Or study swept, or nicely dusted coat,   35
Or usual 'tendance;—ask not, indiscreet,
Thy stockings mended, though the yawning rents
Gape wide as Erebus,[5] nor hope to find
Some snug recess impervious: shouldst thou try
The 'customed garden walks, thin eye shall rue   40
The budding fragrance of thy tender shrubs,
Myrtle or rose, all crushed beneath the weight
Of coarse-checked apron—with impatient hand
Twitched off when showers impend: or crossing lines
Shall mar thy musings, as the wet cold sheet   45
Flaps in thy face abrupt. Woe to the friend
Whose evil stars have urged him forth to claim
On such a day the hospitable rites!
Looks, blank at best, and stinted courtesy,
Shall he receive. Vainly he feeds his hopes   50
With dinner of roast chicken, savoury pie,
Or tart or pudding:—pudding he nor tart
That day shall eat; nor, though the husband try,
Mending what can't be helped, to kindle mirth
From cheer deficient, shall his consort's brow   55
Clear up propitious:—the unlucky guest
In silence dines, and early slinks away.
I well remember, when a child, the awe
This day struck into me; for then the maids,
I scarce knew why, looked cross, and drove me from them: 60
Nor soft caress could I obtain, nor hope
Usual indulgencies; jelly or creams,
Relic of costly suppers, and set by
For me their petted one; or buttered toast,
When butter was forbid; or thrilling tale   65
Of ghost, or witch, or murder—so I went
And sheltered me beside the parlour fire:
There my dear grandmother, eldest of forms,
Tended the little ones, and watched from harm,
Anxiously fond, though oft her spectacles   70
With elfin cunning hid, and oft the pins
Drawn from her ravelled stocking, might have soured
One less indulgent.—

3. Another name for Cuauhtémoc (c. 1502–25), the last emperor of the Aztecs. Cuauhtémoc was tortured (by having his feet held to a fire) and executed by the Spanish forces led by Hernán Cortés (1485–1547).

4. Sky or air.
5. Son of Chaos and personification of darkness; here used to mean Hades, the netherworld of classical Greece.

At intervals my mother's voice was heard,
Urging dispatch: briskly the work went on,   75
All hands employed to wash, to rinse, to wring,
To fold, and starch, and clap, and iron, and plait.
Then would I sit me down, and ponder much
Why washings were. Sometimes through hollow bowl
Of pipe amused we blew, and sent aloft   80
The floating bubbles; little dreaming then
To see, Montgolfier,[6] thy silken ball
Ride buoyant through the clouds—so near approach
The sports of children and the toils of men.
Earth, air, and sky, and ocean, hath its bubbles,   85
And verse is one of them—this most of all.

   1797

◄ ABIGAIL ADAMS ►
1744–1818

Our second First Lady, Abigail Adams was a talented and prolific letter writer in an age when women had few opportunities to educate themselves as writers. Adams was the second of three daughters born to Congregational minister William Smith and his wife, Elizabeth Quincy. Her family had descended from Puritan settlers. Much to her regret, she received no formal education—though her grandmother appears to have facilitated her schooling. Adams met her future husband, John Adams, when she was fifteen and he was twenty-three. Initially, her family resisted the courtship because John was below the Smiths in social class, but he very soon proved his worth, and the couple married in 1764.

Active in colonial politics, John Adams was one of the signers of the Declaration of Independence and later became the second president of the United States. John was very often absent from the family for long periods of time, at first because of the American Revolution and First Continental Congress, and later because of his work in European diplomacy and politics. His absence left Abigail to raise four children, three sons and a daughter, and to manage the family farm in Massachusetts on her own. Their eldest son, John Quincy Adams, later became the sixth American president.

During her husband's absence, Abigail wrote numerous letters—as many as three hundred in all. Her topics are wide-ranging, from the state of her family's affairs to the injustice of slavery. She often signed the letters as Portia, after the Roman matron and the character in Shakespeare's *The Merchant of Venice* (c. 1594). By 1784, John had been abroad for six years, except for one three-month interval. That year Abigail traveled to Paris to join her husband. When John was appointed ambassador to London, they moved to England and remained there until 1788. John Adams served as vice president under George Washington for two terms (1788 and 1792), during which time the couple lived in New York City (then the nation's capital). When John became president in 1796, the couple

---

6. Montgolfier launched the first hot air balloon in France in 1783.

lived first in Philadelphia, the second national capital, and then finally in newly founded Washington, D.C. After John's political obligations ended, the couple retired to Quincy, Massachusetts, where Abigail Adams died at 74 of typhoid fever.

In the following letters, one to her cousin and two others to her husband, Adams comments on the nature of women's experience in the new republic. She reminds the men, especially her husband, to consider the female perspective and to consider the importance of female education. Despite the many spelling errors resulting from her own lack of formal education (which we have preserved here), she writes with great clarity and insight.

From The Adams Family Correspondence

[The Nature of Woman's Experience]

ABIGAIL ADAMS TO ISAAC SMITH JR.[1]

Dear Sir   Braintree April the 20 1771
I write you, not from the Noisy Buisy Town,[2] but from my humble Cottage in Braintree, where I arrived last Saturday and here again am to take up my abode.

> "Where Contemplation p[l]umes her rufled Wings
> And the free Soul look's down to pitty Kings."[3]

Suffer me to snatch you a few moments from all the Hurry and tumult of London and in immagination place you by me that I may ask you ten thousand Questions, and bear with me Sir, tis the only recompence you can make for the loss of your Company.

From my Infancy I have always felt a great inclination to visit the Mother Country[4] as tis call'd and had nature formed me of the other Sex, I should certainly have been a rover. And altho this desire has greatly diminished owing partly I believe to maturer years, but more to the unnatural treatment which this our poor America has received from her, I yet retain a curiosity to know what ever is valuable in her. I thank you Sir for the particular account you have already favoured me with, but you always took pleasure in being communicatively good.

Women you know Sir are considered as Domestick Beings, and altho they inherit an Eaquel Share of curiosity with the other Sex, yet but few are hardy eno' to venture abroad, and explore the amaizing variety of distant Lands. The Natural tenderness and Delicacy of our Constitutions, added to the many Dangers we are subject too from your Sex, renders it almost imposible for a Single Lady to travel without injury to her character. And those who have a protecter in an Husband, have generally speaking obstacles suffcent to prevent their Roving, and instead of visiting other Countries; are obliged to content themselves with seeing but a very small part of their own. To your Sex we are most of us indebted for all the knowledg we acquire of Distant lands. As to a Knowledg of Humane Nature, I believe it may as easily be obtained in this Country, as in England, France or Spain. Education alone I conceive Constitutes the difference in Manners. Tis natural

---

1. Abigail's cousin.
2. Boston, about fifteen miles north of Braintree.
3. A paraphrase of John Milton's *Comus* (1634), lines 375–78: "And Wisdom's self / Oft seeks to

sweet retired solitude, / Where with her best nurse Contemplation / She plumes her feathers and lets grow her wings"
4. England.

I believe for every person to have a partiality for their own Country. Dont you think this little Spot of ours better calculated for happiness than any other you have yet seen or read of. Would you exchange it for England, France, Spain or Ittally? Are not the people here more upon an Eaquality in point of knowledg and of circumstances—there being none so immensly rich as to Lord it over us, neither any so abjectly poor as to suffer for the necessaries of life provided they will use the means. It has heretofore been our boasted priviledg that we could sit under our own vine and Apple trees in peace enjoying the fruits of *our own labour*—but alass! the much dreaded change Heaven avert. Shall we ever wish to change Countries; to change conditions with the Affricans and the Laplanders for sure it were better never to have known the blessings of Liberty than to have enjoyed it, and then to have it ravished from us.

But where do I ramble? I only ask your ear a few moments longer. The Americans have been called a very religious people, would to Heaven they were so in earnest, but whatever they may have been I am affraid tis now only a negitive virtue, and that they are only a less vicious people. However I can quote Mr. Whitefield[5] as an authority that what has been said of us is not without foundation. The last Sermon I heard him preach, he told us that he had been a very great traveller, yet he had never seen so much of the real appearence of Religion in any Country, as in America, and from your discription I immagine you join with him in Sentiment. I think Dr. Sherbear in his remarks upon the english Nation has some such observation as this.[6] In London Religion seems to be periodical, like an ague which only returns once in Seven Days, and then attacks the inhabitants with the cold fit only, the burning never succeeds in this Country. Since which it seems they have found means to rid themselves intirely of the ague.—As to news I have none to tell you, nor any thing remarkable to entertain you with. But you Sir have every day new Scenes opening to you, and you will greatly oblige me by a recital of whatever you find worthy notice. I have a great desire to be made acquainted with Mrs. Maccaulays own history.[7] One of my own Sex so eminent in a tract so uncommon naturally raises my curiosity and all I could ever learn relative to her, is this that she is a widdow Lady and Sister to Mr. Sawbridge. I have a curiosity to know her Education, and what first prompted her to engage in a Study never before Exibited to the publick by one of her own Sex and Country, tho now to the honour of both so admirably performed by her. As you are now upon the Spot, and have been entroduced to her acquaintance, you will I hope be able to satisfie me with some account, in doing which you will confer an oblagation upon your assured Friend,

Abigail Adams

[*"Remember the Ladies"*]

ABIGAIL ADAMS TO JOHN ADAMS

Braintree March 31 1776

I wish you would ever write me a Letter half as long as I write you; and tell me if you may where your Fleet are gone? What sort of Defence Virginia can make

5. George Whitefield (1714–70)—pronounced "Whitfield"—an English preacher and leader of the Methodist movement.
6. Dr. John Shebbeare (1709–88) had published

Letters on the English Nation in 1755.
7. Catherine Macaulay (1731–91) wrote an eight-volume work titled *A History of England* (see p. 286).

against our common Enemy? Whether it is so situated as to make an able Defence? Are not the Gentery Lords and the common people vassals, are they not like the uncivilized Natives Brittain represents us to be? I hope their Riffel Men who have shewen themselves very savage and even Blood thirsty; are not a specimen of the Generality of the people.

I am willing to allow the Colony great merrit for having produced a Washington but they have been shamefully duped by a Dunmore.[8]

I have sometimes been ready to think that the passion for Liberty cannot be Eaquelly Strong in the Breasts of those who have been accustomed to deprive their fellow Creatures of theirs. Of this I am certain that it is not founded upon that generous and christian principal of doing to others as we would that others should do unto us.

Do not you want to see Boston; I am fearfull of the small pox, or I should have been in before this time. I got Mr. Crane[9] to go to our House and see what state it was in. I find it has been occupied by one of the Doctors of a Regiment, very dirty, but no other damage has been done to it. The few things which were left in it are all gone. Cranch[1] has the key which he never deliverd up. I have wrote to him for it and am determined to get it cleand as soon as possible and shut it up. I look upon it a new acquisition of property, a property which one month ago I did not value at a single Shilling, and could with pleasure have seen it in flames.

The Town in General is left in a better state than we expected, more oweing to a percipitate flight than any Regard to the inhabitants, tho some individuals discoverd a sense of honour and justice and have left the rent of the Houses in which they were, for the owners and the furniture unhurt, or if damaged sufficent to make it good.

Others have committed abominable Ravages. The Mansion House of your President is safe and the furniture unhurt whilst both the House and Furniture of the Solisiter General have fallen a prey to their own merciless party.[2] Surely the very Fiends feel a Reverential awe for Virtue and patriotism, whilst they Detest the paricide and traitor.

I feel very differently at the approach of spring to what I did a month ago. We knew not then whether we could plant or sow with safety, whether when we had toild we could reap the fruits of our own industery, whether we could rest in our own Cottages, or whether we should not be driven from the sea coasts to seek shelter in the wilderness, but now we feel as if we might sit under our own vine and eat the good of the land.

I feel a gaieti de Coar[3] to which before I was a stranger. I think the Sun looks brighter, the Birds sing more melodiously, and Nature puts on a more chearfull countanance. We feel a temporary peace, and the poor fugitives are returning to their deserted habitations.

Tho we felicitate ourselves, we sympathize with those who are trembling least the Lot of Boston should be theirs. But they cannot be in similar circumstances unless pusilanimity and cowardise should take possession of them. They have time

8. John Murray, fourth Earl of Dunmore (1732–1809), was the British governor of Virginia, 1771–75.
9. The family's agent; British troops were quartered in residents' homes, and following the Boston Tea Party in 1773, Boston was under martial law.

1. Probably a misprint for Crane.
2. John Hancock (1737–93), president of the Second Continental Congress and first governor of Massachusetts; Samuel Quincy (1735–89), the loyalist solicitor general of Massachusetts.
3. *Gaieté de coeur,* or lightness of heart, happiness (French).

and warning given them to see the Evil and shun it. I long to hear that you have declared an independancy—and by the way in the new Code of Laws which I suppose it will be necessary for you to make I desire you would Remember the Ladies, and be more generous and favourable to them than your ancestors. Do not put such unlimited power into the hands of the Husbands. Remember all Men would be tyrants if they could. If perticuliar care and attention is not paid to the Laidies we are determined to foment a Rebelion, and will not hold ourselves bound by any Laws in which we have no voice, or Representation.

That your Sex are Naturally Tyrannical is a Truth so thoroughly established as to admit of no dispute, but such of you as wish to be happy willingly give up the harsh title of Master for the more tender and endearing one of Friend. Why then, not put it out of the power of the vicious and the Lawless to use us with cruelty and indignity with impunity. Men of Sense in all Ages abhor those customs which treat us only as the vassals of your Sex. Regard us then as Beings placed by providence under your protection and in immitation of the Supreem Being make use of that power only for our happiness.

[Education in the New Republic]

ABIGAIL ADAMS TO JOHN ADAMS

August 14 1776

* * *

You remark upon the deficiency of Education in your Countrymen. It never I believe was in a worse state, at least for many years. The Colledge is not in the state one could wish, the Schollars complain that their professor in Philosophy is taken of by publick Buisness to their great detriment. In this Town I never saw so great a neglect of Education. The poorer sort of children are wholly neglected, and left to range the Streets without Schools, without Buisness, given up to all Evil. The Town is not as formerly divided into Wards. There is either too much Buisness left upon the hands of a few, or too little care to do it. We daily see the Necessity of a regular Government. * * *

If you complain of neglect of Education in sons, What shall I say with regard to daughters, who every day experience the want of it. With regard to the Education of my own children, I find myself soon out of my debth, and destitute and deficient in every part of Education.

I most sincerely wish that some more liberal plan might be laid and executed for the Benefit of the rising Generation, and that our new constitution may be distinguished for Learning and Virtue. If we mean to have Heroes, Statesmen and Philosophers, we should have learned women. The world perhaps would laugh at me, and accuse me of vanity, But you I know have a mind too enlarged and liberal to disregard the Sentiment. If much depends as is allowed upon the early Education of youth and the first principals which are instilld take the deepest root, great benifit must arise from litirary accomplishments in women.

* * *

CULTURAL COORDINATES
Bluestockings

Over the course of the eighteenth century, an increasing number of middle-rank women had access to an education. However, the new fashion for women's instruction did not resemble the aristocratic practice in which women plundered their fathers' libraries to read—and learn—as much as possible. Instead, middle-rank women found themselves consigned to schools in which an acceptable curriculum entailed music, drawing, dancing, and minimal geography, history, and arithmetic. This superficial approach denied them a true intellectual challenge. Despite this trend, the Bluestockings, a generation of middle-rank women born for the most part before 1730, remained committed to a rigorous life of the mind. They valued a vibrant social life centered on conversation, and they remained proud of their scholarly accomplishments, despite growing prejudice against "learned ladies."

Nine Living Muses of Great Britain: Portraits in the Characters of the Muses in the Temple of Apollo (1778) by Richard Samuel. From left to right: (standing) Hannah More, Elizabeth Montagu, Catherine Macaulay, Elizabeth Carter, Anna Laetitia Barbauld; (seated) Elizabeth Griffith, Angelica Lauffman, Elizabeth Linley, and Charlotte Lenox.

The pejorative phrase "blue stocking" came from a visitor to one of their London gatherings, Benjamin Stillingfleet, who wore blue worsted stockings because he could not afford more fashionable black silk ones. Neither a coherent society nor a club with clear membership rules, the Bluestockings were instead a loose circle of women with similar interests and politics. Many never married, instead dedicating themselves to philanthropic activities in addition to their intellectual work. The chief members of the society were Elizabeth Vesy (1715?–91), known for her skills as a hostess; Frances Glanville Boscawen (1719–1805), wife of the famous admiral; Mary Granville Delaney (1700–1788), renowned for her botanically precise flower collages and needlework; and Hester Mulso Chapone (1727–1801), author of educational treatises. In addition, the group included Elizabeth Montagu (1720–1800), a cousin of Lady Mary Wortley Montagu (pp. 239–48). A brilliant conversationalist, Montagu was known as "Queen of the Blues," and she often hosted many prominent men of the time, including Dr. Samuel Johnson, the celebrated literary figure and lexicographer; the philosopher Edmund Burke; the actor David Garrick; and the artist Sir Joshua Reynolds. Montagu was also the author of "An Essay on the Writings and Genius of Shakespeare" (1769). Elizabeth Carter (1716–1806), who knew Latin, Greek, Hebrew, and French, among other languages, and who translated Epictetus in 1758, was another member of the society, as was Carter's intimate friend and correspondent Catherine Talbot (1721–70). Catherine Macaulay (1731–91), who wrote an eight-volume History of England (1763–83), also held a salon that focused on national and international politics. And when Hannah More came to London in 1775, she too frequented Bluestocking circles. More later commemorated her scintillating experiences among the Blues in two poems, "Sensibility" (1782) and "Bas Bleu, or Conversation" (1787).

As the century progressed, the influence of the Blues on a younger generation of women waned. Having been introduced to their society, the novelist Frances Burney viewed the older generation of women with awe, but she also worried that she would be ostracized for over-intellectualism. In her novel Camilla (1796), Burney depicts her disfigured heroine Eugenia as the target of a misdirected, pedantic family tutor, who insists on teaching her the "masculine" subject of Latin, much to her detriment. Burney's attitude suggests a renewed cautiousness toward women's education at the end of the eighteenth century. Thus, despite their irrefutable contribution to an English life of letters, the Bluestockings were not able to counteract the societal trend toward lowered intellectual expectations for women.

Among scholars of women's literature, the response to Hannah More's life and career has been divided. On the one hand, More was a prolific and successful playwright, poet, essayist, tract writer, and novelist, whose accomplishments are bound to attract feminist attention. Having powerful political and social connections, she was profoundly influential in the debate over educating women and the "lower orders." Above all, she was an articulate advocate for middle-rank women, whose agency she deemed crucial for a reformed Britain. On the other hand, however, many of More's positions run counter to feminist politics. She urged women to shun the public spotlight, counseling them not only to avoid all public forums but also to restrict their reading. According to More, women gained little from reading fiction (especially French novels), German tragedies, or travel literature. In other words, More wanted women to ignore genres that stimulated the imagination or that encouraged them to imagine a life beyond the domestic sphere. Her educational treatises recommend that women learn modesty, reserve, and restraint. In addition, More's advocacy of the poor depends upon firm and immutable class distinctions, as well as an attitude toward the poor that some have found condescending for its insistence on staying in one's place. An opponent of both the French Revolution and widespread democracy, More fit a conservative political profile, even while many readers find radical aspects to her work.

Unlike the life she prescribed for other women, More's own biography encompassed a range of public activities and challenges. Born February 2, 1745, she was the fourth of five sisters. Her father was a schoolmaster who recognized her precocity early on. He tutored her in Latin but drew the line at mathematics, a subject thought inappropriate for women. With her sisters, More opened a famous girls' school in Bristol. From 1767 to 1773, More was engaged to William Turner, a man twenty years her senior. When he terminated the engagement for unknown reasons, he gave More £200 (over $35,000 today in purchasing power) as compensation. More never married.

She wrote her first drama, *A Search after Happiness,* for the girls in the school in 1773. Later that year, More left Bristol for London, where she wrote poetry and cultivated friendships with a number of notable men, including Dr. Samuel Johnson, actor David Garrick, philosopher Edmund Burke, and writer Horace Walpole. She also cultivated acquaintances with many of the Bluestockings—a coterie of older intellectual women known for their significant literary accomplishments (see pp. 285–86). She herself had some success as a playwright, presenting *The Inflexible Captive* (1774), *Percy* (1778), and *Fatal Falsehood* (1779).

In 1784 More left London and returned to the environs of Bristol to build a cottage she named Cowslip Green. Later she moved to Clifton, eventually dying there in 1833. After a visit from Evangelical leader William Wilberforce, who asked for her help with the poor, she pledged herself to the improvement and education of the lower orders, opening a charity school near Cheddar in 1789. But her greatest influence came in the form of the *Cheap Repository Tracts,* a large collection of short tales and poems with didactic messages. While some scholars praise the tracts for their realistic detail concerning the lives of the poor and their skillful manipulation of generic conventions, others deplore the fact that they were written to pacify the lower classes. Over two million tracts were circulated, though we do not know who read them.

In 1799, More published her most influential work for women: *Strictures on the Modern System of Female Education*. Her interests in female education can also be seen in her own novel (written to counteract other "negative" fictions), *Coelebs in Search of a Wife* (1808). While women's education remained a pressing issue for More, the abolitionist cause also absorbed her attention. Her anti-slavery poem "The Black Slave Trade" was published in 1788. More followed her poem with a short essay on the dangers of the fashionable world in 1805. In "The White Slave Trade," we see the coalescence of several of More's central preoccupations—the conditions of enslaved Africans, the female "marriage market," and the negative impact of fashion on women. Whether her satiric assertion that women are the "slaves" of fashion is effective is open to debate.

The Black Slave Trade

If Heaven has into being deign'd to call
Thy light, O LIBERTY! to shine on all;
Bright intellectual Sun! why does thy ray
To earth distribute only partial day?
Since no resisting cause from *spirit* flows   5
Thy universal presence to oppose;
No obstacles by Nature's hand imprest,
Thy subtle and ethereal beams arrest;
Not sway'd by *matter* is thy course benign,
Or more direct or more oblique to shine;   10
Nor motion's laws can speed thy active course,
Nor strong repulsion's pow'rs obstruct thy force;
Since there is no convexity in MIND,
Why are thy genial rays to parts confin'd?
While the chill North with thy bright beam is blest,   15
Why should fell darkness half the South invest?
Was it decreed, fair Freedom! at thy birth,
That thou shou'd'st ne'er irradiate *all* the earth?
While Britain basks in thy full blaze of light,
Why lies sad Afric quench'd in total night?   20
        Thee only, *sober* Goddess! I attest,
In smiles chastis'd, and decent graces drest;
To thee alone, pure daughter of the skies,
The hallow'd incense of the Bard shou'd rise!
Not that mad Liberty, in whose wild praise   25
Too oft he trims his prostituted bays;
Not that unlicens'd monster of the crowd,
Whose roar terrific bursts in peals so loud,
Deaf'ning the ear of Peace; fierce Faction's tool,
Of rash Sedition born, and mad Misrule;   30
Whose stubborn mouth, rejecting Reason's rein,

No strength can govern, and no skill restrain;
Whose magic cries the frantic vulgar draw
To spurn at Order, and to outrage Law;
To tread on grave Authority and Pow'r,   35
And shake the work of ages in an hour:
Convuls'd her voice, and pestilent her breath,
She raves of mercy, while she deals out death:
Each blast is fate; she darts from either hand
Red conflagration o'er th' astonish'd land;   40
Clamouring for peace, she rends the air with noise,
And to reform a part, the whole destroys.
Reviles oppression only to oppress,
And, in the act of murder, breathes redress.
Such have we seen on Freedom's genuine coast,   45
Bellowing for blessings which were never lost,
'Tis past, and Reason rules the lucid hour,
And beauteous ORDER re-assumes his power:
Lord of the bright ascendant may he reign,
Till perfect Peace eternal sway maintain!   50
    O, plaintive Southerne[1] whose impassion'd page
Can melt the soul to grief, or rouse to rage!
Now, when congenial themes engage the Muse,
She burns to emulate thy generous views;
Her failing efforts mock her fond desires,   55
She shares thy feelings, not partakes thy fires.
Strange pow'r of song! the strain that warms the heart
Seems the same inspiration to impart;
Touch'd by th' extrinsic energy alone,
We think the flame which melts us is our own;   60
Deceiv'd, for genius we mistake delight,
Charm'd as we read, we fancy we can write.
    Tho' not to me, sweet Bard, thy pow'rs belong,
The cause I plead shall sanctify my song.
The Muse awakes no artificial fire,   65
For Truth rejects what Fancy wou'd inspire:
Here Art wou'd weave her gayest flow'rs in vain,
The bright invention Nature wou'd disdain.
For no fictitious ills these numbers flow,
But living anguish, and substantial woe;   70
No individual griefs my bosom melt,
For millions feel what Oronoko felt:
Fir'd by no single wrongs, the countless host
I mourn, by rapine dragg'd from Afric's coast.
    Perish th' illiberal thought which wou'd debase   75
The native genius of the sable race!
Perish the proud philosophy, which sought

1. Thomas Southerne (1660–1746), author of a   story of Oroonoko, a royal African taken into
popular eighteenth-century tragedy based on the   slavery (originally told by Aphra Behn, pp. 125–27).

To rob them of the pow'rs of equal thought!
What! does th' immortal principle within
Change with the casual colour of a skin?   80
Does matter govern spirit? or is MIND
Degraded by the form to which 'tis join'd?
 No: they have heads to think, and hearts to feel,
And souls to act, with firm, tho' erring zeal;
For they have keen affections, soft desires,   85
Love strong as death, and active patriot fires:
All the rude energy, the fervid flame
Of high-soul'd passion, and ingenuous shame:
Strong, but luxuriant virtues, boldly shoot
From the wild vigour of a savage root.   90
 Nor weak their sense of honour's proud control,
For pride is virtue in a Pagan soul;
A sense of worth, a conscience of desert,
A high, unbroken haughtiness of heart;
And thou wast born where no recording page   95
Plucks the fair deed from Time's devouring rage.
Had Fortune plac'd thee on some happier coast,
Where *polish'd* Pagans souls heroic boast,
To thee, who sought'st a voluntary grave,
Th' uninjur'd honours of thy name to save,   100
Whose generous arm thy barbarous Master spar'd,
Altars had smok'd, and temples had been rear'd.
 Whene'er to Afric's shores I turn my eyes,
Horrors of deepest, deadliest guilt arise;
I see, by more than Fancy's mirror shewn,   105
The burning village, and the blazing town:
See the dire victim torn from social life,
See the scar'd infant, hear the shrieking wife!
She, wretch forlorn! is dragg'd by hostile hands,
To distant tyrants sold, in distant lands!   110
Transmitted miseries, and successive chains,
The sole sad heritage her child obtains!
E'en this last wretched boon their foes deny,
To weep together, or together die.
By felon hands, by one relentless stroke,   115
See the fond vital links of Nature broke!
The fibres twisting round a parent's heart,
Torn from their grasp, and bleeding as they part.
 Hold, murderers, hold! nor aggravate distress;
Respect the passions you yourselves possess;   120
Ev'n you, of ruffian heart, and ruthless hand,
Love your own offspring, love your native land:
Ev'n you, with fond impatient feelings burn,
Tho' free as air, tho' certain of return.
Then, if to you, who voluntary roam,   125
So dear the memory of your distant home,

O think how absence the lov'd scene endears
To him, whose food is groans, whose drink is tears;
Think on the wretch whose aggravated pains
To exile misery adds, to misery chains.   130
If warm *your* heart, to British feelings true,
As dear his land to him as yours to you;
And Liberty, in you a hallow'd flame,
Burns, unextinguish'd, in his breast the same.
Then leave him holy Freedom's cheering smile,   135
The heav'n-taught fondness for the parent soil;
Revere affections mingled with our frame,
In every nature, every clime the same;
In all, these feelings equal sway maintain;
In all, the love of HOME and FREEDOM reign: 140
And Tempe's vale, and parch'd Angola's sand,[2]
One equal fondness of their sons command.
Th' unconquer'd Savage laughs at pain and toil,
Basking in Freedom's beams which gild his native soil.
    Does thirst of empire, does desire of fame,   145
(For these are specious crimes,) our rage inflame?
No: sordid lust of gold their fate controls,
The basest appetite of basest souls;
Gold, better gain'd by what their ripening sky,
Their fertile fields, their arts, and mines supply.   150
    What wrongs, what injuries does Oppression plead,
To smooth the crime and sanctify the deed?
What strange offence, what aggravated sin?
They stand convicted—of a darker skin!
Barbarians, hold! th' opprobrious commerce spare,   155
Respect HIS sacred image which they bear.
Tho' dark and and savage, ignorant and blind,
They claim the common privilege of *kind;*
Let Malice strip them of each other plea,
They still are men, and men shou'd still be free.   160
Insulted Reason loaths th' inverted trade—
Loaths, as she views the human purchase made;
The outrag'd Goddess, with abhorrent eyes,
Sees MAN the traffic, SOULS the merchandize!
Man, whom fair Commerce taught with judging eye,   165
And liberal hand, to barter or to buy,
Indignant Nature blushes to behold,
Degraded Man himself, truck'd, barter'd, sold;
Of ev'ry native privilege bereft,
Yet curs'd with ev'ry wounded feeling left.   170
Hard lot! each brutal suff'ring to sustain,
Yet keep the sense acute of human pain.

2. The valley of Tempe runs between Mount   southwestern Africa.
Olympus and Mount Ossa in Greece; Angola is in

Plead not, in reason's palpable abuse,
Their sense of feeling callous and obtuse:
From heads to hearts lies Nature's plain appeal,   175
Tho' few can reason, all mankind can feel.
Tho' wit may boast a livelier dread of shame,
A loftier sense of wrong refinement claim;
Tho' polish'd manners may fresh wants invent,
And nice distinctions nicer souls torment;   180
Tho' these on finer spirits heavier fall,
Yet natural evils are the same to all.
Tho' wounds there are which reason's force may heal,
There needs no logic sure to make us feel.
The nerve, howe'er untutor'd, can sustain   185
A sharp, unutterable sense of pain;
As exquisitely fashion'd in a slave,
As where unequal fate a sceptre gave.
Sense is as keen where Gambia's waters glide,
As where proud Tiber rolls his classic tide.[3]   190
Tho' verse or rhetoric point the feeling line,
They do not whet sensation, but define.
That self-same stuff which erst proud empires sway'd,
Of which the conquerors of the world were made.
Capricious fate of men! that very pride   195
In Afric scourg'd, in Rome was deify'd.
   No Muse, O Qua-shi![4] shall thy deeds relate,
No statue snatch thee from oblivious fate!
For thou wast born where never gentle Muse
On Valour's grave the flow'rs of Genius strews;   200
Did ever wretch less feel the galling chain,
When Zeno prov'd there was no ill in pain?
In vain the sage to smooth its horror tries;
Spartans and Helots see with different eyes;[5]
Their miseries philosophic quirks deride,   205
Slaves groan in pangs disown'd by Stoic pride.
   When the fierce Sun darts vertical his beams,
And thirst and hunger mix their wild extremes;
When the sharp iron wounds his inmost soul,
And his strain'd eyes in burning anguish roll;   210
Will the parch'd Negro own, ere he expire,
No pain in hunger, and no heat in fire?
   For him, when agony his frame destroys,
What hope of present fame or future joys?

---

3. The river Gambia runs from northern Guinea through the country of Gambia to the Atlantic; the Tiber runs from the Apennine mountain range in Tuscany through Rome to the Mediterranean.
4. Reference to a story in Ramsay's *Treatment of African Slaves* (1784) in which a slave named Qua-shi committed suicide rather than allow himself to be punished; the Muses were goddesses of the arts in Greek mythology.
5. Zeno: Greek Stoic philosopher (333–264 BCE), who argued that we best attain tranquility through an indifference to pain and pleasure; Spartans: members of a militaristic city-state in ancient Greece who practiced rigorous self-discipline; Helots: the Spartans' serfs.

For *that* have Heroes shorten'd nature's date;   215
For *this* have Martyrs gladly met their fate;
But him, forlorn, no Hero's pride sustains,
No Martyr's blissful visions sooth his pains;
Sullen, he mingles with his kindred dust,
For he has learn'd to dread the Christian's trust;   220
To him what mercy can that GOD display,
Whose servants murder, and whose sons betray?
Savage! thy venial error I deplore,
They are *not* Christians who infest thy shore.
    O thou sad spirit, whose preposterous yoke   225
The great deliverer Death, at length, has broke!
Releas'd from misery, and escap'd from care,
Go, meet that mercy man deny'd thee here.
In thy dark home, sure refuge of th' oppress'd,
The wicked vex not, and the weary rest.   230
And, if some notions, vague and undefin'd,
Of future terrors have assail'd thy mind;
If such thy masters have presum'd to teach,
As terrors only they are prone to preach;
(For shou'd they paint eternal Mercy's reign,   235
Where were th' oppressor's rod, the captive's chain?)
If, then, thy troubled soul has learn'd to dread
The dark unknown thy trembling footsteps tread;
On HIM, who made thee what thou art, depend;
HE, who withholds the means, accepts the end.   240
Thy mental night thy Saviour will not blame,
He dy'd for those who never heard his name.
Not *thine* the reckoning dire of LIGHT abus'd,
KNOWLEDGE disgrac'd, and LIBERTY misus'd;
On *thee* no awful judge incens'd shall sit   245
For parts perverted, and dishonour'd wit.
Where ignorance will be found the safest plea,
How many learn'd and wise shall envy *thee!*
    And thou, WHITE SAVAGE! whether lust of gold
Or lust of conquest rule thee uncontroll'd!   250
Hero, or robber!—by whatever name
Thou plead thy impious claim to wealth or fame;
Whether inferior mischiefs be thy boast,
A tyrant trader rifling *Congo's* coast:
Or bolder carnage track thy crimson way,   255
Kings dispossess'd, and provinces thy prey;
Whether thou pant to tame earth's distant bound;
All Cortez murder'd, all Columbus found;[6]
O'er plunder'd realms to reign, detested Lord,

6. Reference to Hernán Cortés (1485–1547), Spanish explorer and conqueror of Mexico noted for his ruthlessness; the atrocities of Christopher Columbus (1451–1506) against the indigenous peoples he encountered were not widely known in the eighteenth century.

Make millions wretched, and thyself abhorr'd:—   260
Whether Cartouche in forests break the law,
Or bolder Cæsar keep the world in awe;[7]
In Reason's eye, in Wisdom's fair account,
Your sum of glory boasts a like amount;
The means may differ, but the end's the same;   265
Conquest is pillage with a nobler name.
Who makes the sum of human blessings less,
Or sinks the stock of general happiness,
Tho' erring fame may grace, tho' false renown
His life may blazon or his memory crown;   270
Yet the last audit shall reverse the cause;
And God shall vindicate his broken laws.

   Had those advent'rous spirits who explore
Thro' ocean's trackless wastes, the far-sought shore;
Whether of wealth insatiate, or of pow'r,   275
Conquerors who waste, or ruffians who devour;
Had these possess'd, O COOK![8] thy gentle mind,
Thy love of arts, thy love of human kind;
Had these pursued thy mild and liberal plan,
DISCOVERERS had not been a curse to man!   280
Then, bless'd Philanthropy! thy social hands
Had link'd dissever'd worlds in brothers' bands;
Careless, if colour, or if clime divide;
Then, lov'd and loving, man had liv'd, and died.
Then with pernicious skill we had not known   285
To bring their vices back and leave our own.

   The purest wreaths which hang on glory's shrine,
For empires founded, peaceful PENN![9] are thine;
No blood-stain'd laurels crown'd thy virtuous toil,
No slaughter'd natives drench'd thy fair-earn'd soil.   290

   Still thy meek spirit in thy flock survives,
Consistent still, *their* doctrines rule their lives,
Thy followers only have effac'd the shame
Inscrib'd by SLAVERY on the Christian name.

   Shall Britian, where the soul of Freedom reigns,   295
Forge chains for others she herself disdains?
Forbid it, Heaven! O let the nations know
The liberty she tastes she will bestow;
Not to herself the glorious gift confin'd,
She spreads the blessing wide as human kind;   300
And, scorning narrow views of time and place,
Bids all be free in earth's extended space.

---

7. Cartouche: notorious eighteenth-century French highwayman (1693–1721); Caesar: a generic title for the ruler of the ancient Roman Empire.
8. Captain James Cook (1728–79), English explorer who traveled throughout the South Pacific and explored the Antarctic Ocean.
9. William Penn (1644–1718), English Quaker who founded Pennsylvania; although a few Quakers were involved in the slave trade, many more were involved in the abolitionist cause.

What page of human annals can record
A deed so bright as human rights restor'd?
O may that god-like deed, that shining page,   305
Redeem OUR fame, and consecrate OUR age!
And let this glory mark our favour'd shore,
To curb FALSE FREEDOM and the TRUE restore!
   And see, the cherub MERCY from above,
Descending softly, quits the sphere of love!   310
On Britain's Isle she sheds her heavenly dew;
And breathes her spirit o'er th' enlighten'd few;
From soul to soul the generous influence steals,
Till every breast the soft contagion feels.
She speeds, exulting, to the burning shore,   315
With the best message Angel ever bore;
Hark! 'tis the note which spoke a Saviour's birth,
Glory to God on high, and peace on Earth!
She vindicates the Pow'r in Heaven ador'd,
She stills the clank of chains, and sheathes the sword;   320
She cheers the mourner, and with soothing hands
From bursting hearts unbinds th' Oppressor's bands;
Restores the lustre of the Christian name,
And clears the foulest blot that dimm'd its fame.
   As the mild Spirit hovers o'er the coast,   325
A fresher hue the wither'd landscapes boast;
Her healing smiles the ruin'd scenes repair,
And blasted Nature wears a joyous air;
While she proclaims thro' all their spicy groves,
"Henceforth your fruits, your labours, and your loves,   330
"All that your Sires possess'd, or you have sown,
"Sacred from plunder—all is now YOUR OWN."
   And now, her high commission from above,
Stamp'd with the holy characters of love,
The meek-ey'd spirit waving in her hand,   335
Breathes manumission[1] o'er the rescu'd land;
She tears the banner stain'd with blood and tears,
And, LIBERTY! thy shining standard rears!
As the bright ensign's glory she displays,
See pale OPPRESSION faints beneath the blaze!   340
The giant dies! no more his frown appals,
The chain, untouch'd, drops off; the fetter falls.
Astonish'd echo tells the vocal shore,
Oppression's fall'n, and Slavery is no more!
The dusky myriads crowd the sultry plain,   345
And hail that MERCY long invok'd in vain.
Victorious Pow'r! she bursts their two-fold bands,
And FAITH and FREEDOM spring from Britain's hands,

---

1. Release from slavery.

And THOU! great source of Nature and of Grace,
Who of one blood didst form the human race: 350
Look down in mercy in thy chosen time,
With equal eye on Afric's suff'ring clime:
Disperse her shades of intellectual night,
Repeat thy high behest—LET THERE BE LIGHT!
Bring each benighted soul, great GOD, to Thee.   355
And with thy wide Salvation make them free!

1788

From Strictures on the Modern System of Female Education

Chapter 1

AN ADDRESS TO WOMEN OF RANK AND FORTUNE

Among the talents for the application of which women of the higher class will be peculiarly accountable, there is one, the importance of which they can scarcely rate too highly. This talent is influence * * * and when one considers the variety of mischiefs which an ill-directed influence has been known to produce, one is led to reflect with the most sanguine hope on the beneficial effects to be expected from the same powerful force when exerted in its true direction.

The general state of civilized society depends more than those are aware, who are not accustomed to scrutinize into the springs of human action, on the prevailing sentiments and habits of women, and on the nature and degree of the estimation in which they are held. Even those who admit the power of female elegance on the manners of men, do not always attend to the influence of female principles on their character. In the former case, indeed, women are apt to be sufficiently conscious of their power, and not backward in turning it to account. But there are nobler objects to be effected by the exertion of their powers; and unfortunately, ladies, who are often unreasonably confident where they ought to be diffident, are sometimes capriciously diffident just when they ought to feel where their true importance lies; and, feeling, to exert it. To use their boasted power over mankind to no higher purpose than the gratification of vanity or the indulgence of pleasure, is the degrading triumph of those fair victims to luxury, caprice, and despotism, whom the laws and the religion of the voluptuous prophet of Arabia exclude from light, and liberty, and knowledge; and it is humbling to reflect, that in those countries in which fondness for the mere persons of women is carried to the highest excess, *they are slaves;* and that their moral and intellectual degradation increases in direct proportion to the adoration which is paid to mere external charms.[2]

But I turn to the bright reverse of this mortifying scene; to a country where our sex enjoys the blessings of liberal instruction, of reasonable laws, of a pure re-

2. More refers to the belief that Muslim women were more oppressed than their Western counterparts. ("The voluptuous prophet of Arabia" refers to Muhammad.) Though it is true that, under Islam, women were sometimes kept in harems, scholars currently contest the assumption of lowered status for Muslim women. For an account of women's lives in Muslim Turkey at the end of the seventeenth century, see the selection from Lady Mary Wortley Montagu's *Turkish Embassy Letters* (p. 240).

ligion, and all the endearing pleasures of an equal, social, virtuous, and delightful intercourse: I turn to them with a confident hope, that women, thus richly endowed with the bounties of Providence, will not content themselves with polishing, when they are able to reform; with entertaining, when they may awaken; and with captivating for a day, when they may bring into action powers of which the effects may be commensurate with eternity.

In this moment of alarm and peril, I would call on them with a "warning voice," which should stir up every latent principle in their minds, and kindle every slumbering energy in their hearts; I would call on them to come forward, and contribute their full and fair proportion towards the saving of their country. But I would call on them to come forward, without departing from the refinement of their character, without derogating from the dignity of their rank, without blemishing the delicacy of their sex: I would call them to the best and most appropriate exertion of their power, to raise the depressed tone of public morals, to awaken the drowsy spirit of religious principle, and to re-animate the dormant powers of active piety. They know too well how imperiously they give the law to manners, and with how despotic a sway they fix the standard of fashion. But this is not enough; this is a low mark, a prize not worthy of their high and holy calling. For, on the use which women of the superior class may be disposed to make of that power delegated to them by the courtesy of custom, by the honest gallantry of the heart, by the imperious controul of virtuous affections, by the habits of civilized states, by the usages of polished society; on the use, I say, which they shall hereafter make of this influence, will depend, in no low degree, the well-being of those states, and the virtue and happiness, nay perhaps the very existence of that society.

At this period, when our country can only hope to stand by opposing a bold and noble *unanimity* to the most tremendous confederacies against religion and order, and governments, which the world ever saw; what an accession would it bring to the public strength, could we prevail on beauty, and rank, and talents, and virtue, confederating their several powers, to come forward with a patriotism at once firm and feminine for the general good! I am not sounding an alarm to female warriors, or exciting female politicians: I hardly know which of the two is the most disgusting and unnatural character. Propriety is to a woman what the great Roman orator says action is to an orator; it is the first, the second, the third requisite.[3] A woman may be knowing, active, witty, and amusing; but without propriety she cannot be amiable. Propriety is the centre in which all the lines of duty and of agreeableness meet. It is to character what proportion is to figure, and grace to attitude. It does not depend on any one perfection; but it is the result of general excellence. It shews itself by a regular, orderly, undeviating course; and never starts from its sober orbit into any splendid eccentricities; for it would be ashamed of such praise as it might extort by any aberrations from its proper path. It renounces all commendation but what is characteristic; and I would make it the criterion of true taste, right principle, and genuine feeling, in a woman, whether she would be less touched with all the flattery of romantic and exaggerated panegyric, than with that beautiful picture of correct and elegant propriety, which Milton draws of our first mother, when he delineates

3. It was a Greek, not Roman, orator who made this comment, as recorded by Plutarch in his chapter on Demosthenes in *The Lives of Noble Grecians and Romans.*

"Those thousand decencies which daily flow
From all her words and actions"[4]

Even the influence of religion is to be exercised with discretion. A female Polemic wanders almost as far from the limits prescribed to her sex, as a female Machiavel or warlike Thalestris.[5] Fierceness and bigotry have made almost as few converts as the sword, and both are peculiarly ungraceful in a female. * * *

I am persuaded, if many a one, who is now disseminating unintended mischief, under the dangerous notion that there is no harm in any thing short of positive vice; and under the false colours of that indolent humility, "What good can I do?" could be brought to see in its collected force the annual aggregate of the random evil she is daily doing, by constantly throwing a *little* casual weight into the wrong scale, by mere inconsiderate and unguarded chat, she would start from her self complacent dream. If she could conceive how much she may be diminishing the good impressions of *young* men; and if she could imagine how little amiable levity or irreligion make her appear in the eyes of those who are older and abler, (however loose their own principles may be,) she would correct herself in the first instance, from pure good nature; and in the second, from worldly prudence and mere self-love. But on how much higher ground would she restrain herself, if she habitually took into account the important doctrine of consequences; and if she reflected that the lesser but more habitual corruptions make up by their number, what they may seem to come short of by their weight; then perhaps she would find that among the higher class of women, *inconsideration* is adding more to the daily quantity of evil than almost all the more ostensible causes put together.

There is an instrument of inconceivable force, when it is employed against the interests of christianity. It is not reasoning, for that may be answered; it is not learning, for luckily the infidel is not seldom ignorant; it is not invective, for we leave so coarse an engine to the hands of the vulgar; it is not evidence, for happily we have that all on our side. It is RIDICULE, the most deadly weapon in the whole arsenal of impiety, and which becomes an almost unerring shaft, when directed by a fair and fashionable hand. No maxim has been more readily adopted, or is more intrinsically false, than that which the fascinating eloquence of a noble sceptic of the last age contrived to render so popular, that "ridicule is the test of truth."[6] It is no test of truth itself; but of their firmness who assert the cause of truth, it is indeed a severe test. This light, keen, missile weapon, the irresolute, unconfirmed Christian, will find it harder to withstand, than the whole heavy artillery of infidelity united.

* * *

That cold compound of irony, irreligion, selfishness, and sneer, which make up what the French (from whom we borrow the thing as well as the word) so well express by the term *persiflage*, has of late years made an incredible progress in blasting the opening buds of piety in young persons of fashion. A cold pleasantry, a temporary cant word, the jargon of the day, for the "great vulgar" have their jargon, blight the first promise of seriousness. The ladies of *ton*[7] have certain

4. From John Milton's epic, *Paradise Lost,* 7:1238–39
5. Niccolo Machiavelli (1469–1527), Italian political philosopher and author of *The Prince* (1532); Thalestris: Amazon queen who, according to legend, approached Alexander the Great and asked him to father her child. (He declined.)

6. According to More editor Robert Hole, More quotes an aphorism attributed to Anthony Ashley Cooper (1621–1713), the third Earl of Shaftesbury and author of *Characteristics of Men, Manners, Opinions, Times* (1711; revised 1714).
7. Fashionable society (French).

watch-words, which may be detected as indications of this spirit. The clergy are spoken of under the contemptuous appellation of *The Parsons*. Some ludicrous association is infallibly combined with every idea of religion. If a warm-hearted youth has ventured to name with enthusiasm some eminently pious character, his glowing ardour is extinguished with a laugh; and a drawling declaration that the person in question is really a mighty *harmless* good creature, is uttered in a tone which leads the youth secretly to vow, that whatever else he may be, he will never be a good harmless creature.

Nor is ridicule more dangerous to true piety than to true taste. An age which values itself on parody, burlesque, irony, and caricature, produces little that is sublime, either in genius or in virtue; but they *amuse,* and we live in an age which *must* be amused, though genius, feeling, truth, and principle, be the sacrifice. Nothing chills the ardours of devotion like a frigid sarcasm; and, in the season of youth, the mind should be kept particularly clear of all light associations. * * *

There was a time when a variety of epithets were thought necessary to express various kinds of excellence, and when the different qualities of the mind were distinguished by appropriate and discriminating terms; when the words venerable, learned, sagacious, profound, acute, pious, ingenious, elegant, agreeable, wise or witty, were used as specific marks of distinct characters. But the legislators of fashion have of late years thought proper to comprise all merit in one established epithet, and it must be confessed to be a very desirable one as far as it goes. This epithet is exclusively and indiscriminately applied wherever commendation is intended. The word *pleasant* now serves to combine and express all moral and intellectual excellence. Every individual, from the gravest professors of the gravest profession, down to the trifler who is of no profession at all, must earn the epithet of *pleasant,* or must be contented to be nothing; but must be consigned over to ridicule, under the vulgar and inexpressive cant word of a *bore.* This is the mortifying designation of many a respectable man, who, though of much worth and much ability, cannot perhaps clearly make out his letters patent to the title of *pleasant.* But, according to this modern classification, there is no intermediate state, but all are comprised within the ample bounds of one or other of these two terms.

We ought to be more on our guard against this spirit of ridicule, because, whatever may be the character of the present day, its faults do not spring from the redundancies of great qualities, or the overflowings of extravagant virtues. It is well if more correct views of life, a more regular administration of laws, and a more settled state of society, have helped to restrain the excesses of the heroic ages, when love and war were considered as the great and sole business of human life. Yet, if that period was marked by a romantic extravagance, and the present by an indolent selfishness, our superiority is not so triumphantly decisive, as, in the vanity of our hearts, we may be ready to imagine.

I do not wish to bring back the frantic reign of chivalry, nor to reinstate women in that fantastic empire in which they then sat enthroned in the hearts, or rather in the imaginations of men. Common sense is an excellent material of universal application, which the sagacity of latter ages has seized upon, and rationally applied to the business of common life. But let us not forget, in the insolence of acknowledged superiority, that it was religion and chastity, operating on the romantic spirit of those times, which established the despotic sway of woman; and though she now no longer looks down on her adoring votaries, from the pedestal to which an absurd idolatry had lifted her, yet let her remember that it is the same religion and chastity which once raised her to such an elevation, that must still furnish the noblest energies of her character.

While we lawfully ridicule the absurdities which we have abandoned, let us not plume ourselves on that spirit of novelty which glories in the opposite extreme. If the manners of the period in question were affected, and if the gallantry was unnatural, yet the tone of virtue was high; and let us remember that constancy, purity, and honour, are not ridiculous in themselves, though they may unluckily be associated with qualities which are so; and women of delicacy would do well to reflect, when descanting on those exploded manners, how far it be decorous to deride with too broad a laugh, attachments which could subsist on remote gratifications; or grossly to ridicule the taste which led the admirer to sacrifice pleasure to respect, and inclination to honour; to sneer at that purity which made self-denial a proof of affection, to call in question the sound understanding of him who preferred the fame[8] of his mistress to his own indulgence.

One cannot but be struck with the wonderful contrast exhibited to our view, when we contemplate the manners of the two periods in question. In the former,[9] all the flower of Europe smit with a delirious gallantry; all that was young and noble, and brave and great, with a fanatic frenzy and preposterous contempt of danger, traversed seas, and scaled mountains, and compassed a large portion of the globe, at the expence of ease, and fortune, and life, for the unprofitable project of rescuing, by force of arms, from the hands of infidels, the sepulchre of that Saviour, whom, *in the other period,* their posterity would think it the height of fanaticism so much as to name in good company: whose altars they desert, whose temples they neglect; and though in more than one country at least they still call themselves by his name, yet too many consider it rather as a political than a religious distinction; to many, it is to be feared, contemn his precepts; still more are ashamed of his doctrines, and not a few reject his sacrifice.

But in an age when inversion is the order of the day, the modern idea of improvement does not consist in altering, but extirpating. We do not reform, but subvert. We do not correct old systems, but demolish them, fancying that when every thing shall be new it will be perfect. Not to have been wrong, but to have been at all, is the crime. Excellence is no longer considered as an experimental thing which is to grow gradually out of observation and practice, and to be improved by the accumulating additions brought by the wisdom of successive ages. *Our* wisdom is not a child perfected by gradual growth, but a goddess which starts at once, full grown, mature, armed cap-a-pee, from the heads of our modern thunderers.[1] Or rather, if I may change the illusion, a perfect system is *now* expected inevitably to spring at once, like the fabled bird of Arabia, from the ashes of its parent, and can receive its birth no other way but by the destruction if its predecessor.[2]

Instead of clearing away what is redundant, pruning what is cumbersome, supplying what is defective, and amending what is wrong, we adopt the indefinite rage for radical reform of Jack, who, in altering Lord Peter's coat, shewed his zeal

8. Reputation.
9. A reference to the Middle Ages and to the Crusades—a series of wars waged by several European nations to wrest control of Christ's tomb from the region's Muslim inhabitants; the Crusades occurred between the eleventh and the fourteenth centuries.
1. More alludes both to *Hamlet* (1.2.209), in which the ghost of Hamlet's father is described as

"Armed at points exactly, cap-a-pe" (that is, head to foot), and to the story of Athena, Greek goddess of wisdom, who is described as having sprung fully developed from the head of Zeus, the primary deity in the Greek pantheon and associated with thunder.
2. A reference to the phoenix, a mythological bird that would rise anew from the ashes of its self-immolation.

by crying out, "Tear away, brother Martin, for the love of heaven; never mind, so you do but tear away."[3]

This tearing system has unquestionably rent away some valuable parts of that strong, rich, native stuff which formed the antient texture of British manners. That we have gained much I am persuaded; that we have lost nothing I dare not therefore affirm. And though it fairly exhibits a mark of our improved judgment to ridicule the fantastic notions of love and honour in the heroic ages; let us not rejoice that that spirit of generosity in sentiment, and of ardour in piety, the exuberancies of which were then so inconvenient, are now sunk as unreasonably low. That revolution of manners which the unparalleled wit and genius of Don Quixote[4] so happily effected, by abolishing extravagances the most absurd and pernicious, was so far imperfect, that the virtues which he never meant to expose, fell into disrepute with the absurdities which he did; and it is become the turn of the present taste to attach in no small degree that which is ridiculous to that which is heroic. Some modern works of wit have assisted in bringing piety and some of the noblest virtues into contempt, by studiously associating them with oddity, childish simplicity, and ignorance of the world: and unnecessary pains have been taken to extinguish that zeal and ardour, which, however liable to excess and error, are yet the spring of whatever is great and excellent in the human character. The novel of Cervantes is incomparable; the Tartuffe of Moliere is unequalled;[5] but true generosity and true religion will never lose any thing of their intrinsic value, because knight-errantry and hypocrisy are legitimate objects for satire.

But to return from this too long digression, to the subject of female influence. Those who have not watched the united operation of vanity and feeling on a youthful mind, will not conceive how much less formidable the ridicule of all his own sex will be to a very young man, than that of those women to whom he has been taught to look up as the arbitresses of elegance. Such an one, I doubt not, might be able to work himself up, by the force of genuine christian principle, to such a pitch of true heroism, as to refuse a challenge,[6] (and it requires more real courage to refuse a challenge than to accept one,) who would yet be in danger of relapsing into the dreadful pusillanimity of the world, when he is told that no woman of fashion will hereafter look on him but with contempt. While we have cleared away the rubbish of the Gothic ages, it were to be wished we had not retained the most criminal of all their institutions. Why chivalry should indicate a madman, while its leading object, the *single combat,* should designate a gentleman, has not yet been explained. Nay the original motive is lost, while the sinful practice is continued; for the fighter of the duel no longer *pretends* to be a glorious redresser of the wrongs of strangers; no longer considers himself as piously appealing to heaven for the justice of his cause; but from the slavish fear of unmerited reproach, often selfishly hazards the happiness of his nearest connections,

3. Reference to *Tale of a Tub* (1704), an allegory by Irish satirist Jonathan Swift in which brothers Jack and Martin (representing two different branches of Protestantism) struggle to alter a coat (representing Christian doctrine) that had been previously altered by Peter (representing the Catholic Church).
4. *Don Quixote* (1605–15), by Miguel de Cervantes Saavedra (1547–1616), relates the comic adventures of the Spanish gentleman of the title whose overzealous devotion to romances leads him to believe he is a knight-errant on a mission to revive the age of chivalry.
5. A comedy by French playwright Molière (Jean-Baptiste Poquelin) (1622–73) that ridicules religious hypocrisy.
6. A challenge to duel; dueling, while against the law in late-eighteenth-century England (anyone who killed another in a duel was considered to have committed murder), was still fashionable.

and always comes forth in direct defiance of an acknowledged command of the Almighty. Perhaps there are few occasions on which female influence might be exerted to a higher purpose than in this, in which laws and conscience have hitherto effected so little; but while the duellist (who perhaps becomes a duellist only because he was first a seducer) is welcomed with smiles; the more hardy youth, who, not because he fears man but God, declines a challenge; who is resolved to brave disgrace rather than commit sin, would be treated with cool contempt by those very persons to whose esteem he might reasonably look, as one of the rewards of his true and substantial fortitude.

But how shall it be reconciled with the decisions of principle, that delicate women should receive with complacency the successful libertine, who has been detected by the wretched father or the injured husband in a criminal commerce, the discovery of which has too justly banished the unhappy partner of his crime from virtuous society? Nay, if he happens to be very handsome, or very brave, or very fashionable, is there not sometimes a kind of dishonourable competition for his favour? But, whether his popularity be derived from birth, or parts, or person, or (what is often a substitute for all) from his having made his way into *good company,* women of distinction sully the sanctity of virtue by the too visible pleasure they sometimes express at the attentions of a popular libertine, whose voluble small talk they admire, and whose sprightly nothings they quote, and whom perhaps their very favour tends to prevent from becoming a better character, because he finds himself more acceptable as he is.

* * *

In animadverting farther on the reigning evils which the times more particularly demand that women of rank and influence should repress, Christianity calls upon them to bear their decided testimony against every thing which is notoriously contributing to the public corruption. It calls upon them to banish from their dressing-rooms, (and oh, that their influence could banish from the libraries of their sons and husbands!) that sober and unsuspected mass of mischief, which, by assuming the plausible names of Science, of Philosophy, of Arts, of Belles Lettres, is gradually administering death to the principles of those who would be on their guard, had the poison been labelled with its own pernicious title. Avowed attacks upon revelation are more easily resisted, because the malignity is advertised. But who suspects the destruction which lurks under the harmless or instructive names of *General History, Natural History, Travels, Voyages, Lives, Encyclopedias, Criticism, and Romance?* Who will deny that many of these works contain much admirable matter; brilliant passages, important facts, just descriptions, faithful pictures of nature, and valuable illustrations of science? But while "the dead fly lies at the bottom," the whole will exhale a corrupt and pestilential stench.

Novels, which used chiefly to be dangerous in one respect, are now become mischievous in a thousand. They are continually shifting their ground, and enlarging their sphere, and are daily becoming vehicles of wider mischief. Sometimes they concentrate their force, and are at once employed to diffuse destructive politics, deplorable profligacy, and impudent infidelity. Rousseau was the first popular dispenser of this complicated drug, in which the deleterious infusion was strong, and the effect proportionably fatal.[7] For he does not attempt to seduce the

7. More attacks Swiss-French moralist, political philosopher, and author Jean-Jacques Rousseau (1712–78), who claimed that human beings are naturally good but may become depraved through the pernicious influence of society.

affections but through the medium of the principles. He does not paint an innocent woman, ruined, repenting, and restored; but with a far more mischievous refinement, he annihilates the value of chastity, and with pernicious subtlety attempts to make his heroine appear almost more amiable without it. He exhibits a virtuous woman, the victim not of temptation but of reason, not of vice but of sentiment, not of passion but of conviction; and strikes at the very root of honour by elevating a crime into a principle. With a metaphysical sophistry the most plausible, he debauches the heart of woman, by cherishing her vanity in the erection of a system of male virtues, to which, with a lofty dereliction of those that are her more peculiar and characteristic praise, he tempts her to aspire; powerfully insinuating, that to this splendid system chastity does not necessarily belong: thus corrupting the judgment and bewildering the understanding, as the most effectual way to inflame the imagination and deprave the heart.

The rare mischief of this author consists in his power of seducing by falsehood those who love truth, but whose minds are still wavering, and whose principles are not yet formed. He allures the warm-hearted to embrace vice, not because they prefer vice, but because he gives to vice so natural an air of virtue: and ardent and enthusiastic youth, too confidently trusting in their integrity and in their teacher, will be undone, while they fancy they are indulging in the noblest feelings of their nature. Many authors will more infallibly complete the ruin of the loose and ill-disposed; but perhaps (if I may change the figure) there never was a net of such exquisite art and inextricable workmanship, spread to entangle innocence and ensnare inexperience, as the writings of Rousseau: and, unhappily, the victim does not even struggle in the toils, because part of the delusion consists in imagining that he is set at liberty.

Some of our recent popular publications have adopted all the mischiefs of this school, and the principal evil arising from them is, that the virtues they exhibit are almost more dangerous than the vices. The chief materials out of which these delusive systems are framed, are characters who practise superfluous acts of generosity, while they are trampling on obvious and commanded duties; who combine sentiments of honour with actions the most flagitious;[8] a high-tone of self-confidence, with a perpetual breach of self-denial: pathetic apostrophes to the passions, but no attempt to resist them. They teach that no duty exists which is not prompted by feeling: that impulse is the main spring of virtuous actions, while laws and principles are only unjust restraints; the former imposed by arbitrary men, the latter by the absurd prejudices of timorous and unenlightened conscience. In some of the most splendid of these characters, compassion is erected into the throne of justice, and justice degraded into the rank of plebeian virtues. Creditors are defrauded, while money due to them is lavished in dazzling acts of charity to some object that affected their senses; which fits of charity are made the sponge of every sin, and the substitute of every virtue: the whole indirectly tending to intimate how very *benevolent people are who are not Christians*. From many of these compositions, indeed, Christianity is systematically, and always virtually excluded; for the law and the prophets and the gospel *can* make no part of a scheme in which this world is looked upon as all in all; in which poverty and misery are considered as evils arising solely from human governments, and not from the dispensations of God: this poverty is represented as the greatest of evils, and the restraints which tend to keep the poor honest, as the most flagrant injustice. The gospel can have

8. Heinous, extremely wicked.

nothing to do with a system in which sin is reduced to a little human imperfection, and Old Bailey[9] crimes are softened down into a few engaging weaknesses; and in which the turpitude of all the vices a man himself commits, is done away by his *candour* in tolerating all the vices committed by others.

But the most fatal part of the system to that class whom I am addressing is, that even in those works which do not go all the lengths of treating marriage as an unjust infringement on liberty, and a tyrannical deduction from general happiness; yet it commonly happens that the hero or heroine, who has practically violated the letter of the seventh commandment,[1] and continues to live in the allowed violation of its spirit, is painted as so amiable and so benevolent, so tender or so brave; and the temptation is represented as so *irresistible,* (for all these philosophers are fatalists,) the predominant and cherished sin is so filtered and purged of its pollutions, and is so sheltered and surrounded, and relieved with shining qualities, that the innocent and impressible young reader is brought to lose all horror of the awful crime in question, in the complacency she feels for the engaging virtues of the criminal.

* * *

Let not those to whom these pages are addressed deceive themselves, by supposing this to be a fable; and let them inquire most seriously whether I speak the truth, when I assert that the attacks of infidelity in Great Britain are at this moment principally directed against the female breast. Conscious of the influence of women in civil society, conscious of the effect which female infidelity produced in France, they attribute the ill success of their attempts in this country to their having been hitherto chiefly addressed to the male sex. They are now sedulously labouring to destroy the religious principles of women, and in too many instances they have fatally succeeded. For this purpose not only novels and romances have been made the vehicles of vice and infidelity, but the same allurement has been held out to the women of our country, which was employed by the original tempter to our first parent—Knowledge. Listen to the precepts of the new German enlighteners, and you need no longer remain in that situation in which Providence has placed you! Follow their examples, and you shall be permitted to indulge in all those gratifications which custom, not religion, has too far overlooked in the male sex!

We have hitherto spoken only of the German *writings;*[2] but because there are multitudes who never read, equal pains have been taken to promote the same object through the medium of the stage: and this weapon is, of all others, that against which it is at the present moment, the most important to warn my countrywomen. As a specimen of the German drama, it may not be unseasonable to offer a few remarks on the admired play of the *Stranger.*[3] In this piece the character of an adulteress, which, in all periods of the world, ancient as well as modern, in all countries heathen as well as Christian, has hitherto been held in detestation, and has never been introduced but to be reprobated, is for the first time presented to our view in the most pleasing and fascinating colours. The heroine is a woman who forsook a

9. Central criminal court located in London.
1. Exodus 20:14: "Thou shalt not commit adultery."
2. In the preceding section, More attacks German authors, especially Friedrich von Schiller (1759–

1805), historian, poet, and playwright, who wrote *The Robbers* (1781), a play condemning tyranny.
3. A comedy by German playwright August von Kotzebue (1761–1819), translated into English in 1798.

husband, the most affectionate and the most amiable, and lived for some time in the most criminal commerce with her seducer. Repenting at length of her crime, she buries herself in retirement. The talents of the poet during the whole piece are exerted in attempting to render this woman the object, not only of the compassion and forgiveness, but of the esteem and affection, of the audience. The injured husband, convinced of his wife's repentance, forms a resolution, which every man of true feeling and christian piety will probably approve. He forgives her offence, and promises her through life his advice, protection, and fortune, together with every thing which can alleviate the misery of her situation, but refuses to replace her in the situation of his wife. But this is not sufficient for the *German* author. His efforts are employed, and it is to be feared but too successfully, in making the audience consider the husband as an unrelenting savage, while they are led by the art of the poet anxiously to wish to see an adulteress restored to that rank of women who have not violated the most solemn covenant that can be made with man, nor disobeyed one of the most positive laws which has been enjoined by God.

About the same time that this first attempt at representing an adulteress in an exemplary light was made by a German dramatist, which forms an æra[4] in manners; a direct vindication of adultery was for the first time attempted by a *woman*, a professed admirer and imitator of the German suicide Werter. The Female Werter, as she is styled by her biographer, asserts, in a work, intitled "The Wrongs of Woman," that adultery is justifiable, and that the restrictions placed on it by the laws of England constitute part of the *wrongs of woman.*[5]

But let us take comfort. These fervid pictures are not yet generally realised. These atrocious principles are not yet adopted into common practice. Though corruptions seem to be pouring in upon us from every quarter, yet there is still left among us a discriminating judgement. Clear and strongly marked distinctions between right and wrong still subsist * * * thanks to the surviving efficacy of a holy religion, to the operation of virtuous laws, and to the energy and unshaken integrity with which these laws are *now* administered, and still more perhaps to a standard of morals which continues in force, when the principles which sanctioned it are no more; this crime, in the female sex at least, is still held in just abhorrence; if it be practised, it is not honourable; if it be committed, it is not justified; we do not yet affect to palliate its turpitude; as yet it hides its abhorred head in lurking privacy; and reprobation hitherto follows its publicity.

But on YOUR exerting your influence, with just application and increasing energy, may, in no small degree, depend whether this corruption shall still continue to be resisted. For, from admiring to adopting, the step is short, and the progress rapid; and it is in the moral as in the natural world, the motion, in the case of minds as well as of bodies, is accelerated on a nearer approach to the centre to which they are tending.

* * *

4. Era.

5. A reference to *The Sorrows of Young Werther* (1774) by Wolfgang von Goethe, in which the young protagonist kills himself after being rejected by the woman he loves. Biographer William Godwin used this phrase to describe Mary Wollstonecraft, author of *The Wrongs of Woman, or Maria* (1798). In that novel, the main character, whose husband has taken away her child and locked her in a madhouse, argues against laws that render women the property of their husbands. (See Wollstonecraft, pp. 365–82.)

There are certain women of good fashion who practise irregularities not consistent with the strictness of virtue; while their good sense and knowledge of the world make them at the same time keenly alive to the value of reputation. They want to retain their indulgences, without quite forfeiting their credit; but finding their fame fast declining, they artfully cling, by flattery and marked attentions, to a few persons of more than ordinary character; and thus, till they are driven to let go their hold, continue to prop a falling fame.

On the other hand, there are not wanting women of distinction, of very correct general conduct, and of no ordinary sense and virtue, who, confiding with a high mind on what they too confidently call *the integrity of their own hearts;* anxious of deserving a good fame on the one hand, by a life free from reproach, yet secretly too desirous on the other of securing a worldly and fashionable reputation; while their general associates are persons of honour, and their general resort places of safety; yet allow themselves to be occasionally present at the midnight orgies of revelry and gaming, in houses of no honourable estimation; and thus help to keep up characters, which, without their sustaining hand, would sink to their just level of reprobation and contempt. While they are holding out this plank to a drowning reputation, rather, it is to be feared, to shew their own strength than to assist another's weakness, they value themselves, perhaps, on not partaking of the worst parts of the amusements which may be carrying on; but they sanction them by their presence; they lend their countenance to corruptions they should abhor, and their example to the young and inexperienced, who are looking about for some such sanction to justify them in what they were before inclined to do, but were too timid to have done without the protection of such unsullied names. Thus these respectable characters, without looking to the general consequences of their indiscretion, are thoughtlessly employed in breaking down, as it were, the broad fence, which should ever separate two very different sorts of society, and are becoming a kind of unnatural link between vice and virtue.

But the great object to which YOU, who are, or may be mothers, are more especially called, is the education of your children. If we are responsible for the use of influence in the case of those over whom we have no definite right; in the case of our children we are responsible for the exercise of acknowledged *power:* a power wide in its extent, indefinite in its effects, and inestimable in its importance. On YOU, depend in no small degree the principles of the whole rising generation. To your direction the daughters are almost exclusively committed; and to a certain age, to you also is consigned the mighty privilege of forming the hearts and minds of your infant sons.

* * *

1799

The White Slave Trade

Whereas many members of both houses of parliament have long been indefatigably labouring to bring in a bill for the amelioration of the condition of slaves in our foreign plantations, as well as for the abolition of the trade itself; by which trade multitudes of fresh slaves are annually made: and whereas it is presumed that the profound attention of these grave legislators to this great foreign evil prevents their attending to domestic grievances of the same nature; it is, therefore, humbly proposed, that whilst these benevolent senators are thus meritoriously labouring for the deliverance of our black brethren, the printer will, as in duty bound, insert these loose hints of a bill for the abolition of slavery at home; a slavery which, in some few instances, as it is to be feared, may be found to involve the wives, daughters, aunts, nieces, cousins, and grandmothers even of these very zealous African abolitionists themselves.

In our West India plantations the lot of slaves is of all descriptions; here, it is uniform. There, there are diversities of masters; if some are cruel, others are kind; and the worst are mortal: here, there is one, arbitrary, universal tyrant, and like the lama of Thibet he never dies.[6] FASHION is his name. Here, indeed, the original subjection is voluntary, but, once engaged, the subsequent servility of the slaves keeps pace with the tyranny of the despot. They hug their chains, and because they are gilt and shining, this prevents them, not from feeling, but from acknowledging that they are heavy. With astonishing fortitude they carry them about, not only without repining, but as their glory and distinction. A few females are every where to be found who have manfully resisted the tyrant, but *they are people whom nobody knows;* as the free people are the minority, and as, in this one instance, the minority are peaceable persons, no one envies them an exemption from chains, and their freedom is considered only as a proof of their insignificance.

I propose to take up the question on the two notorious grounds of *inhumanity* and *impolicy;*[7] and first of the first, as our good old divines say. Here are great multitudes of beautiful white creatures, forced away, like their prototypes in Africa, from all the endearing connections of domestic life, separated from their husbands, dragged from their children, 'till these last are old enough to be also engaged as slaves in the same labour: nay, in some respects, their condition is worse than that of their African brethren; for, if they are less restricted in the article of food, they are more abridged in that of rest. It is well known that in some of our foreign plantations, under mild masters, the slaves have, in one instance, more indulgence than the English despot here allows them. Some of them have at least the Sunday to themselves, in which they may either serve God, or attend to their own families. Here, the tyrant allows of no such alleviation. So far from it, his rigour peculiarly assigns the sabbath for acts of superior fatigue and exertion, such as long journeys, crowded markets, &c. And whereas, in our foreign plantations, slaves too frequently do the work of horses in the system of domestic slavery, horses partake of the labour of the slave without diminishing his sufferings; many hundreds being regularly condemned, after the labours of the day are closed, to transport the slaves to the scene of their nightly labours, which scene shifts so often, that there is scarcely an interval of rest; so that the poor animals are exposed the greater part of the night to all the rigors of a northern winter.

Again—if the African slaves go nearly naked, their burning clime prevents the want of covering from being one of their greatest hardships: whereas, though the female slaves of London and Westminster were aforetime comfortably cloathed,

---

6. Here More betrays a common eighteenth-century bias by speaking facetiously about the Dalai Lama, the traditional political and spiritual leader of the Tibetan people, who was considered by his followers to be immortal; they believed he would be reincarnated on his death, and this new Dalai Lama would be sought out by monks to assume the throne.

7. Not according to good policy, not expedient.

and were allowed by the despot to accommodate their dress to the season, wearing the lightest raiment in the hottest weather, and thick silks trimmed with skins of beasts in cold and frost; now nakedness is of all seasons, and many of the most delicate females are allowed so little clothing as to give pain to the humane beholder. In the most rigorous seasons, they are so exposed as to endanger their own health, and shock the feelings of others.

The younger slaves are condemned to violent bodily labour, from midnight to sunrise. For this public service they are many years preparing by a severe drill under a great variety and succession of posture-masters. More compassion, indeed, seems to be shown to the more aged slaves, who are nightly allowed to sit, and do their work at a multitude of tables[8] provided for that purpose. Some of these employments are quiet enough, well suited to weakness and imbecility, and just serve to keep the slaves out of harm's way; but at other tables, the labour of the slave is most severe; and though you cannot perceive their fetters, yet they must undoubtedly be firmly chained to the spot, as appears by their inability to quit it; for by their long continuance in the same attitude one can hardly suppose them to be at liberty.

But if their bodies labour less than those of the more active slaves, they seem to suffer the severest agitations of mind; their colour often changes, their lips tremble, and their voice faulters; and no wonder, for sometimes all they have in the world is at stake, and depends on the next slight motion of the hand. In one respect the comparison between the African, and this part of the London slave trade fails: the former, though incompatible with the *spirit* of our laws, yet is not, alas! carried on in direct opposition to the *letter* of them; whereas these tables, at which some of the English slaves are so cruelly exercised, have the cannon of an act of parliament planted directly in their face; and the oddity of the thing is, that the act is not, as in most other cases, made by one set of people and broken by another, but in many instances the law-maker is the law-breaker.[9]

Many of these elderly female slaves excuse their constant attendance in the public markets, (for it is thought that, at a certain age, they might be emancipated if they wished it,) by asserting the necessity of their attendance, 'till their daughters are disposed of. They are often heard to lament the hardship of this slavery, and to anticipate the final period of their labours; but it is observable, that not only when their daughters, but even their grand-daughters, are taken off their hands, they still continue, from the mere force of habit, and when they are past their labour, to hover about the markets.

A multitude of fine fresh young slaves are annually imported at the age of seventeen or eighteen; or, according to the phrase of the despot, *they come out.*[1] This despot so completely takes them in as to make these lovely young creatures believe that the assigned period at which they lose the gaiety and independence of their former free life is, in fact, the day of their emancipation.

I come now to the question of *impolicy.* This white slavery, like the black, is evidently an injury to fair and lawful commerce, for the time spent in training and overworking these fair slaves might be better employed in promoting the more profitable articles of health, beauty, simplicity, modesty, and industry; articles

8. Card tables.
9. Playing cards for money was widespread but illegal nevertheless.

1. Make a formal entry into society and thereby announce their readiness for marriage.

which many think would fetch a higher price, and by which traffic, both the slave and the slave-owner would be mutually benefitted.

Those who take up this question on this ground maintain also that it does not answer to the slave holders; for that the markets are so glutted that there is less chance of a good bargain, in the best sense of the word, where there are so many competitors, and where there is so little opportunity of discriminating, than if the young slaves were disposed of by private contract; in which the respective value of each individual could be more exactly ascertained.

In the article of policy also, the slaves themselves are not only great losers; youth and beauty, by this promiscuous huddling of slaves together, failing to attract attention; but moreover youth and beauty are so soon impaired by hard labour, foul air, and late hours, that those who are not early disposed of, on the novelty of a first appearance, soon become withered, and are apt to lie a good while upon hands.

One strong argument brought to prove the impolicy of the African slave trade is, that it is a most improvident waste of the human species. What devastation is made in the human frame among our white slaves, by working over hours, by loss of sleep, want of clothing, fetid atmospheres, being crammed in the holds of smaller ships without their proper proportion of inches—what havoc, I say, is made by all those, and many other causes, let all the various baths and watering places, to which these poor exhausted slaves are sent every summer to recruit, after the working season[2] is over, declare.

Some candid members have hoped for a *gradual* abolition, concluding that if no interference took place, the evil was become so great, it must needs be cured by its very excess; the event, however, has proved so far otherwise, that the grievance is actually grown worse and worse.

And whereas, aforetime, the slaves were comfortably covered, and were not obliged to labour through the *whole* night, nor to labour *every* night, nor to labour at several places in the *same* night; and whereas, aforetime, the hold in which they were confined was not obliged to receive more slaves than it could contain; it is now a notorious fact, that their cloathing is stripped off in the severest weather; that their labours are protected 'till the morning; and that since the late great increase of trade, three hundred panting slaves are often crammed into an area which cannot conveniently accommodate more than fourscore, to the great damage of the healths and lives of his majesty's fair and faithful subjects.

From all the above causes it is evident, that the white slave trade has increased, is increasing, and ought to be diminished.

'Till, therefore, there be some hope that a complete abolition may be effected, the following regulations are humbly proposed.

Regulation 1st. That no slave be allowed to spend more than three hours in preparing her chains, beads, and other implements for the nightly labour.

2d. That no slave be allowed to paint her person of more than two colours for any market.

3d. That each slave be at least allowed sufficient covering for the purposes of decency, if not for those of health and comfort.

2. The "season" began when Parliament resumed sessions in mid- to late winter and continued until August 12, the beginning of grouse season.

4th. That no slave be put under more than four posture masters, in order to teach her such attitudes and exercises as shall enable her to fetch more money in the markets.

5th. That no slave be carried to more than three markets on the same night.

6th. That no trader be allowed to press more slaves into one hold than three times as many as it will contain.

7th. That the same regard to comfort, which has led the black factor to allow the African slaves a ton to a man, be extended to the white slaves, not allowing them less than one chair to five slaves.[3]

8th. That no white negro driver or horses be allowed to stand in the street more than five hours in a dry night, or four in a rainy one.

9th. That every elderly female slave, as soon as her youngest grandchild is fairly disposed of, be permitted to retire from her more public labours, without any fine or loss of character, or any other punishment from the despot.

To conclude:—the black slave trade has been taken up by its opposers, not only on the ground of *inhumanity* and *impolicy,* but on that of *religion* also. On the first two points alone have I ventured to examine the question of the white slave trade. It would be a folly to enquire into it on this last principle; it can admit no such discussion, as in this view it could not stand its ground for a single moment; for if that principle were allowed to operate, mitigations, nearly approaching to abolition, must inevitably and immediately take place.

An Enemy to all Slavery
1805

---

3. A reference to Dolben's Act (1788), a law intended to improve conditions for enslaved Africans on board ships crossing the Atlantic. This law set requirements for the weight of the slave cargo in relation to the tonnage of the ship.

CULTURAL COORDINATES
The Hoop-Petticoat

From its introduction around 1708 to its demise around 1780, the hoop-petticoat generated a great deal of negative commentary from its male critics. Despite its drawbacks, women might have adopted this extravagant fashion because its large shape enhanced mobility, thwarted prying male eyes, and created a protective circle around the female body.

Hooped skirts—previously called farthingales—had been worn previously in Spain and France. However, the hoop-petticoat seems to have been born in England. The hoop itself was made of whalebone or cane. It took the shape, at various times, of a dome, a bell, a drum, or a tub. Up to twenty-four yards of fabric were draped over this structure. For the wearer, the hoop had the advantage of lifting the heavy fabric away from a woman's legs, thus allowing for better ventilation and enhancing mobility.

But the hoop-petticoat was unpopular with male critics because it distorted the shape of the female body. Joseph Addison, writing in *The Spectator*, complained that the hoop-petticoat imitated a pregnancy and gave the false impression that a woman was out walking "so near her time." He also complained that the hoop made it difficult to distinguish the mother from the daughter, or the "breeder" from

The hoop-petticoat, c. 1740.

the "non-breeder." Conveniently, real pregnancies could be disguised beneath the hoop's form, allowing women to thwart public perception of their bodies.

In addition, the large circumference of the hoop took up a lot of public space and demanded that room be made for the wearer. At the same time, the hoop-petticoat created a protective area into which men were not supposed to intrude. Their clothing thus allowed women to demarcate their space and keep men at a safe distance.

Of course, the fashion was not without its difficulties: passing through narrow spaces, getting into and out of carriages, going up and down narrow staircases, or even sitting down was awkward. In addition, in the days of open fireplaces, the skirt was a fire hazard.

By the end of the eighteenth century, the hoop-petticoat had fallen out of fashion, replaced by a slimmer and sleeker silhouette. It reappeared as the crinoline in the nineteenth century.

FRANCES BURNEY (D'ARBLAY)
1752–1840

On June 13, 2002—the 250th anniversary of Frances Burney's birth—a window commemorating her work was dedicated at Westminster Abbey. Today, Burney is recognized as a brilliant satirist, a gifted writer of diaries and journals, a talented dramatist (although only one of her plays was produced during her lifetime), and an accomplished novelist who influenced later generations of women writers.

Burney—sometimes nicknamed Fanny—was born in Norfolk, in the east of England, the third child of Esther Sleepe Burney and Dr. Charles Burney, an organist and prominent musical historian. Several members of her family were distinguished: her brother James had a notable career in the navy, serving under the command of Captain James Cook during his second expedition to the South Pole. Her brother Charles was a respected theologian who became chaplain to King George III. Her sister Susan (Susanna) Burney Phillips—to whom Burney remained exceptionally close until her sister died in 1800—was a talented amateur musician whose letters have recently been published.

Burney's mother died in 1762, and in 1767 her father married Elizabeth Allen, a widow with three children. In 1770, after more than two years of separate residence, the two families moved in together at Queen Square, London. Burney's early diaries record the tensions present in the enlarged household. Her stepmother appears to have disapproved of Frances's habit of "scribbling." Nonetheless, the Burneys lived in the middle of a vibrant circle, with many famous musicians and singers as frequent guests. The family enjoyed as well the many social opportunities of the day, including frequent trips to the opera, the theater, and the famous pleasure gardens (described wittily in Burney's *Evelina*, pp. 322–39).

Burney's father later wrote of her intellectual beginnings that "she was wholly unnoticed in the nursery for any talents or quickness of study." However, although she received no formal education, by age twelve, she was reading widely in her father's library. By age fifteen, she had completed a manuscript titled "The History of Caroline Evelyn," which she subsequently burned for reasons not recorded. By age sixteen, she had begun a diary, which she continued to keep throughout her life. Then, in 1778, her literary career began in earnest with the publication of her first and best-known novel, *Evelina, or the History of a Young Lady's Entrance into the World*. Burney had written this work in secret, and she did not reveal its authorship to her father until after it appeared in print. The book was an immediate success. Pleased with his daughter's accomplishment, Charles Burney introduced her to Mr. and Mrs. Thrale, a socially prominent couple, and to Dr. Johnson, the most famous literary figure of the day. Next, Burney wrote a play, *The Witlings,* satirizing the pretensions of scholarly women. But the object of her attack—probably the famous Bluestocking Mrs. Montagu (see pp. 285–86)—may have been too apparent. This, coupled with Burney's father's disapproval of the public nature of the stage, discouraged her from writing plays for a time. Then, in 1782, Burney published a second novel, *Cecilia; or, Memoirs of an Heiress,* also a success, despite the fact that Burney published hurriedly, without time for revision.

In 1786, Burney's father convinced her to accept a royal invitation to be Second Keeper of the Robes to Queen Charlotte (consort to King George III). Although her family was very pleased with her prestigious position, Burney found the situation grueling and stressful. On duty every day from 7 a.m. to midnight or later, she attended to her royal mistress—often standing at attention without food or drink for long hours—and managed her elaborate gowns. But Burney had little interest in court fashion and less interest in its tedious intrigues, and the position left her little time or energy for her own writing. Still, she managed to keep vibrant journals during the time she spent there, and she also wrote several blank verse tragedies, including *Edwy and Elgiva,* which was begun in 1788 and produced for one night at the Drury Lane Theatre in 1795. In 1790, as a result of the conditions of court life, Burney became ill, and she convinced her family that she needed to leave her position. Upon her departure, Queen Charlotte granted her a pension of £100 per year (worth about $18,000 in today's money).

Free from the pressures of court, in 1793 Burney met and fell in love with a French émigré, an assistant general to the royalist Marquis de Lafayette, who had fled to England during the French Revolution. Although her father did not approve of the match, Burney married Alexandre d'Arblay twice—in a Protestant ceremony on July 28 and in a Catholic ceremony on July 30. Their son, Alexander, was born in 1794. Her husband began work on their home with money advanced on Burney's third novel, *Camilla; or, A Picture of Youth,* in 1796. Eventually, she received £2,000 from sales of the work—a considerable sum of money in those days (over $250,000 in today's money). In 1801, she also completed three comedies, *Love and Fashion, A Busy Day, or an Arrival from India,* and *The Woman Hater,* though none was performed onstage.

In 1802, Burney traveled to the Continent, following her husband, who had gone to France in hopes of recovering lost rights and property. When England declared war on France in 1803, she found herself unable to return home. When she was finally able to go back to England in 1812, her husband stayed behind. Then, in 1814, Burney lost her home, called Camilla Cottage, when it was discovered that the d'Arblays had no deed to the land on which it was built. To help support her family, Burney published her fourth novel, *The Wanderer; or, Female Difficulties* (1814), making another £2,000. By 1815 her husband had joined the royalist troops opposing Napoleon. Burney traveled to Belgium, where, after a series of harrowing events, she was finally reunited with her husband, who had fought in the Battle of Waterloo. Her husband died in England in 1818; her son, who became a clergyman, predeceased her in 1837. When Burney died in 1840, she was buried next to her husband and son in Bath.

Throughout her life, Burney gave an impression of shyness, quietness, and reserve, but she also demonstrated remarkable fortitude: she traversed war-torn France, underwent a radical mastectomy—without anesthesia—and nearly drowned when trapped in a seaside cavern at high tide. She was conventional enough to estrange herself from her friend, Mrs. Thale when the latter was remarried to an Italian music teacher named Gabriel Piozzi, a match considered beneath her socially. (They later reconciled.) On the other hand, Burney had a lifelong correspondence with the famous castrato Gaspar Pacchierotti, for whom she expressed a deep understanding and sympathy. Although often conventional in manner and behavior and heavily influenced by strong, intellectual men, including her father, Burney possessed a keenly perceptive and critical eye. Similarly, Burney's writings resist easy classification. She frequently exposes a patriarchal system that unduly constrains women without adequately protecting them from a potentially dangerous world.

The selections that appear here convey Burney's skill at re-creating voices, starting with her own: the first selection is drawn from her early diaries and shows us the lively, colloquial, and intimate voice of an eighteenth-century teenager. The second (also from her diaries) places Burney, now famous as the author of *Evelina,* in the middle of a fashionable literary scene and displays her evolving talent for re-creating the nuances and idiosyncrasies of personality. The third selection, a letter written in 1785 while Burney was at court, describes in ironic yet excruciating detail her experience with the discipline imposed on the female body in royal service. The final selection is an excerpt from her epistolary novel *Evelina,* which gives us the exhilarated, breathless narration of a young woman experiencing firsthand both the pleasures and the perils of her first trip to London.

From The Early Journals and Letters of Fanny Burney

[*A Young Writer's Diary*]

Poland Street,[1] London, March 27th [1768]

To have some account of my thoughts, manners, acquaintance & actions, when the Hour arrives in which time is more nimble than memory, is the reason which induces me to keep a Journal: a Journal in which I must confess my *every* thought, must open my whole Heart! But a thing of [this] kind ought to be addressed to somebody—I must imagion myself to be talking—talking to the most intimate of friends—to one in whom I should take delight in confiding, & remorse in concealment: but who must this friend be?—to make choice of one to whom I can but *half* rely, would be to frustrate entirely the intention of my plan. The only one I could wholly, totally confide in, lives in the same House with me, & not only never *has,* but never *will,* leave me one secret *to* tell her.[2] To whom, then, *must* I dedicate my wonderful, surprising & interesting adventures?—to *whom* [dare] I reveal my private opinion of my nearest Relations? the secret thoughts of my dearest friends? my own hopes, fears, reflections & dislikes?—Nobody!

To Nobody, then, will I write my Journal! since To Nobody can I be wholly unreserved—to Nobody can I reveal every thought, every wish of my Heart, with the most unlimited confidence, the most unremitting sincerity to the end of my Life! For what chance, what accident can end my connections with Nobody? No secret *can* I conceal from No—body, & to No—body can I be *ever* unreserved. Disagreement cannot stop our affection, Time itself has no power to end our friendship. The love, the esteem I entertain for Nobody, No-body's self has not power to destroy. From Nobody I have nothing to fear, secrets sacred to friendship, Nobody will not reveal, when the affair is doubtful, Nobody will not look towards the side least favourable—.

I will suppose you, then, to be my best friend; tho' God forbid you ever should! my dearest companion—& a romantick Girl, for mere oddity may perhaps be more

---

1. Burney's first address in London, in the fashionable Westminster area of London.
2. A reference to Burney's sister Susanna, to whom she was especially close. Despite the fact that she is writing to "Nobody," Burney seems to be writing with Susanna in mind.

sincere—more *tender*—than if you were a friend propria personæ[3]—in as much as imagination often exceeds reality. In your Breast my errors may create pity without exciting contempt; may raise your compassion, without eradicating your love.

From this moment, then, my dear Girl—but why, permit me to ask, must a *female* be made Nobody? Ah! my dear, what were this world good for, *were* Nobody a female? And now I have done with *perambulation.*

◦—◦—◦

From Diary and Letters of Madame d'Arblay

[The Publication of Evelina]

* * *

[1778]

Well, I cannot but rejoice that I published the Book,[4] little as I ever imagined how it would fare; but, hitherto, it has occasioned me no small diversion,—& *nothing* of the disagreeable sort,—but I often think a change *will* happen, for I am by no means so sanguine as to suppose such success will be uninterrupted. Indeed, in the midst of the greatest satisfaction that I feel, an inward *something* which I cannot account for, prepares me to expect a reverse! for the more the Book is drawn into notice, the more exposed it becomes to criticism & annotations.

June 23d [1778]

O not yet,—not yet, at least, is come the reverse! I have had a visit from my beloved, my kindest Father—& he came determined to complete my recovery by his goodness. I was *almost* afraid—& *quite* ashamed to be alone with him—but he soon sent for me to his little Gallery Cabinet—& then, with a significant smile that told me what was coming, & made me glow to my very forehead with anxious expectation, he said "I have read your Book, Fanny—but you need not blush at it.—it is full of merit—it is really extraordinary.—" I fell upon his Neck with heart-beating emotion, & he folded me in his arms so tenderly that I sobbed upon his shoulder—so delighted was I with his precious approbation. But I soon recovered to a gayer pleasure, more like his own: though the length of my illness, joined to severe mental suffering from a Family calamity which had occurred at that period,[5] had really made me too weak for a joy mixt with such excess of amazement. I had written my little Book simply for my amusement; I printed it, by the means first of my Brother, Charles, next of my Cousin, Edward Burney, merely for a frolic, to see how a production of my own would figure in that Author like form: but as I had never read any thing I had written to any human being but my sisters, I had taken it for granted that They, only, could be partial enough to endure my compositions. My unlooked for success surprized, therefore, my Father as much as my self—

* * *

---

3. "For one's self" or "on one's own behalf" (Latin).
4. *Evelina.*

5. The calamity to which Burney refers remains unidentified.

Aug[st] 26th [1778]

My opportunities for writing grow less & less, & my materials more & more:—yet I am unwilling, for a thousand reasons, to give over my attempt,—& the *first* is, the Debt I owe my dearest Susan,[6] who so kindly feeds *me,* whenever *I* am hungry, & *she* has abundance. But really, after Breakfast, I have scarce a moment that I can spare all Day.

Mrs. Thrale[7] I like more and more—And I am sure so would you!—for of all the people I have ever seen, since I came *into this gay & gaudy world,* I never before saw the person who so strongly resembles our dear Father!—I find the likeness perpetually; she has the same natural liveliness, the same general benevolence,—the same rare union of *gaity* & of *feeling* in her Disposition. And so kind is she to *me,* that *I know not what for to do!* She told me, at first, that I should have *all* my mornings to myself;—And therefore I have actually *studied* to avoid her, lest I should be in her way; but, since the first morning, she *seeks* me,—sits with me while I Dress, saunters with me in the park, or compares Notes over Books in the Library; there is an immediate communication from her Dressing Room to my Bed Room, & when she is up stairs, she flings open the Doors, & enters into Conversation.—And her Conversation is *delightful;* it is so entertaining, so gay, so enlivening, when she is in spirits; & so intelligent & instructive when she is otherwise, that I almost as much wish to record all *she* says, as all Dr. Johnson says. I have told her repeatedly how much I was afraid of her,—but that fear is now quite worn away; she is so perfectly natural & unassuming, & she is so *infinitely* kind to me, that fear, now, would be folly.

You know I told you I was determined not to Court Miss Thrale,—well, we are now wonderous intimate, for *she* Courts me:—I am sure I *owe* her favour to Evelina, which she has quite by Heart, & quotes eternally; & not a Creature comes to the House, but she *names* them from that Book. Indeed, with all her Coldness, distance & gravity, I find she loves a *titter* as much as any Girl, & when I am [*inclined*] to run on in a Rhodomantading[8] manner, she Laughs till she can't stand. I was quite *astonished,* to find how *merrily* she is, at Times, disposed.

Aug[st]

Proceed—no!—go back, my muse, to Thursday.

Dr. Johnson came Home to Dinner.

In the Evening, he was as lively & full of wit & sport as I have ever seen him,—& Mrs. Thrale & I had him quite to ourselves, for Mr. Thrale came in from giving an Election Dinner[9] to which he sent 2 Bucks & 6 pine apples so tired, that he niether opened his *Eyes* nor *mouth,* but fell fast asleep. Indeed, after Tea, he generally does.

Dr. Johnson was very communicative concerning his present work of the Lives of the Poets;—*Dryden* is now in the Press; & he told us he had been just writing a Dissertation upon Hudibras.[1]

---

6. Burney's sister Susanna.
7. Hester Thrale (1741–1821), Welsh diarist and socialite; close friend of Dr. Samuel Johnson (1709–84), the famous lexicographer and literary figure.
8. Blustering or boasting.
9. As a member of Parliament, Thrale entertained constituents from time to time between elections.

1. *Lives of the Poets* (1779–81), Johnson's last work. The volume that includes English poet John Dryden (1631–1700) is the first of the ten that make up this work. *Hudibras* (1660–80), a popular poem by English poet and satirist Samuel Butler (1612–80).

He gave us an account of *Mrs. Lenox*: her Female Quixote is very justly admired here; indeed, *I* think *all* her Novels far the best of any *Living* Author,—but Mrs. Thrale says that though her *Books* are generally approved, Nobody likes *her*. I find *she*, among others, waited on Dr. Johnson, upon her commencing writer: & he told us that, at her request, he carried her to *Richardson*: "Poor Charlotte Lenox! continued he;—when we came to the House, she desired *me* to leave her, 'for, says she, I am under great restraint in your presence, but if you leave me *alone* with Richardson, I'll give you a very good account of him:' however, I fear poor Charlotte was disappointed, for she gave me no account at all!"[2]

He then told us of 2 little productions of our Mr. Harris, which we read;— they are very short, & very clever: one is called *Fashion*, the other *Much ado*, & they both of them full of sportive humour, that I had not suspected to belong to Mr. Harris [the learned Grammarian].[3]

Some Time after, turning suddenly to me, he said "Miss Burney, what sort of Reading do you delight in?—History?—Travels?—Poetry?—or Romances?—"

"O Sir! cried I, I dread being Catechised by *You*!—I dare not make *any* answer, for I am sure whatever I should say would be wrong!—"

"*Whatever* you should say?—how's that?"

"Why not whatever I *should*,—but whatever I *could* say."

He Laughed, &, to my great relief, spared me any further questions upon the subject. Indeed, I was very happy I had the presence of mind to *evade* him as I did, for I am sure the examination which would have followed, had I made any direct answer, would have turned out sorely to my discredit.

"Do you remember, Sir, said Mrs. Thrale, how you tormented poor Miss Brown about reading?"

"She might soon be tormented, Madam, answered he, for I am not yet quite clear she knows what a Book is."

"O for shame! cried Mrs. Thrale; she reads not only English, but French & Italian. She was in Italy a great while."

"Pho,—exclaimed he,—*Italian* indeed!—Do you think she knows as much Italian as Rose Fuller does English?"

"Well, well, said Mrs. Thrale, Rose Fuller is a very good young man, for all he has not much command of Language; & though he is silly enough, yet I like him *very well*, for there is no manner of harm in him."

Then she told me, that he once said "Dr. Johnson's conversation is so instructive, that I'll ask him a question. 'Pray, Sir, what is *Palmyra*? I have often heard of it but never knew what it was.' 'Palmyra, Sir? said the Doctor; why it is a Hill in *Ireland*, situated in a Bog, & has Palm Trees at the Top, whence it is called *Palmmire*.'" And whether or not he *swallowed* this account, they know not yet.[4]

"But Miss Brown, continued she, is by no means such a simpleton as Mr. Johnson supposes her to be; she is not very *deep*, indeed, but she is a sweet, & a

---

2. Charlotte Lennox (1717–1804), author of *The Female Quixote* (1752), a novel based on Cervantes' *Don Quixote* that parodies the comic adventures of its heroine, a naïve country girl whose head has been turned by Romantic tales; Samuel Richardson (1689–1761), author of the highly

moralistic epistolary novels *Pamela* (1740) and *Clarissa* (1747–48).
3. Burney herself inserted the bracket; Mr. Harris's identity is otherwise unknown.
4. Johnson is, in typical fashion, teasing: Palmyra is an ancient city in Syria.

very ingenuous Girl, & nobody admired Miss Stretfield[5] more;—Miss Stretfield was *universally* admired, for her Learning, her beauty, & her manners; & poor Fanny Brown was so far from being hurt at her superiority, when they were here together, that she almost *adored* her, & was always pointing out her excellence. But she made a more foolish speech to Mr. Johnson than she would have done to any body else, because she was so frightened & embarrassed that she knew not *what* she said. He asked her some Question about *reading*, & she did, to be sure, make a very silly answer,—but she was so perplexed & bewildered, that she hardly knew where she was, & so she said the *beginning* of a Book was as good as the *End*, or the *End* was as good as the *beginning*, or some such stuff;—& Dr. Johnson told her of it so often, saying well, my dear, *which* part of a Book do you like best *now?*—that poor Fanny Brown burst into Tears!—"

"I am sure *I* should have compassion for her, cried I, for Nobody would be more likely to have blundered out such, or any such speech, from fright & terror."

"*You?* cried Dr. Johnson,—no; *you* are another Thing; she who could draw Smiths & Branghtons,[6] is quite another Thing."

O Susy,—how happy for such a poor sheepish wretch as I am among strangers *whom* I *fear*, is this *prevention* in my favour.

Mrs. Thrale then told some other stories of his degrading opinion of *us poor Fair sex;—* I mean in *general*, though, for in *particular*, he does them noble justice. Among others, was a Mrs. Somebody who spent a Day here once, & of whom he asked "*Can she Read?*" "Yes, to be sure; answered Mrs. Thrale, we have been reading together this Afternoon." "And what Book did you get for her?"—"Why what happened to lie in the way,—Hogarth's analysis of Beauty."—"Hogarth's analysis of Beauty!—for God's sake what made you chuse that?" "Why, Sir, what would you have had me take!" "What she could have understood, Cow hide,[7] or Cinderella!"—

"O, Dr. Johnson! cried I,—'tis not *for Nothing* you are feared!"

"O you're a Rogue! cried he, Laughing, & they would fear *you* if they knew you!"

"That they would! said Mrs. Thrale, but she's so shy they don't suspect her. Miss Pitches[8] gave her an account of all her *Dress*, to entertain her, t'other Night!—to be sure she was very *lucky* to fix on *Miss Burney* for such conversation!—But I have been telling her she *must* write a Comedy;—I am sure nobody could do it better,—is it not true, Mr. Johnson?"

I would fain have stopt her,—but she was not to be stopt,—& ran on saying *such* fine things!—though we had almost a *struggle* together:—& she said, at last, "Well, authors may say what they will of *modesty & modesty*—but I believe Miss Burney is *really* modest about her Book, for her Colour comes & goes every Time it is mentioned."

I then rose to look for a Book which we had been talking of, & Dr. Johnson said most civil things of me *the while*,—but I did not distinctly hear them. However, when I returned to my seat, he said he wished Richardson had been alive,

---

5. According to Burney scholar Lars Troide, Sophia Streatfield (1754–1835) was a mutual friend of Burney's and Mrs. Thrale's who was known for her scholarship and beauty.

6. Lower-rank characters in *Evelina*.

7. Hogarth's analysis of Beauty: a treatise on aesthetics by the English painter and printmaker

William Hogarth (1697–1764); Cow hide: a popular children's tale.

8. Burney editor Lars Troide identifies Sophia Pitches (1761–79) as the daughter of a brandy merchant, who may have died as a result of mercury poisoning from her toxic makeup.

"And then, he added, you should have been Introduced to him,—though, I don't know, niether;—Richardson would have been afraid of her!"

"O yes!—that's a likely matter!" quoth I.

"It's very true, continued he; Richardson would have been really *afraid* of her;—there is merit in Evelina which he could not have borne.—No, it would not have done!—unless, indeed, she would have flattered him prodigiously.—Harry Fielding,[9] too, would have been afraid of her,—there is nothing so delicately finished in *all* Harry Fielding's Works, as in Evelina; (Then, shaking his Head at me, he exclaimed) O, you little *Character-monger,* you!"

Mrs. Thrale then returned to her charge, & again urged me about a Comedy,—& again I tried to silence her,—& we had a *fine fight* together;—till she called upon Dr. Johnson to *back* her,—"Why, Madam, said he, Laughing,—she *is* Writing one!—What a rout is here, indeed!—She is writing one up stairs all the Time.—Who ever knew when she began Evelina?

"True, true Oh King![1] thought I.

"Well, that *will* be a sly trick! cried Mrs. Thrale;—however, you know best, I believe, about That, as well as about every other Thing."

Friday [Aug. 28th],—was a very *full* Day.—

In the morning, we began talking of "Irene,"[2] & Mrs. Thrale made Dr. Johnson read some Passages which I had been remarking as uncommonly applicable to the present Times. And he read several speeches, & told us he had not ever Read so much of it before since it was first printed.

"Why there is no making you read a play, said Mrs. Thrale, either of your own, or any other Person. What trouble had I to make you hear Murphy's "Know your own Mind."[3] "*Read rapidly, read rapidly!* you cried, & then took out your Watch to see how long I was about it!—Well, we won't serve *Miss Burney* so, Sir;—when we have *her* Comedy we will do it all justice."

Murphy, it seems, is a very great favourite here; he has been acquainted intimately with Mr. Thrale from both their *Boyhoods,* & Mrs. Thrale is very partial to him. She told me, therefore, *in a merry way,* that though she wished me to excell *Cumberland,* & all other Dramatic writers,—yet she would not wish me better than her old Friend Murphy.—I begged her, however, to be perfectly easy, & *assured* her I *would take care* not to Eclipse him!

Soon after Dr. Johnson began Laughing very Heartily to himself, & when upon repeated entreaty, he confessed the subject of his mirth, what should it be but an idea that had struck him that I should write *Stretham, a Farce*—Lord, how I laughed, & he carried on the notion, & said I should have *them all* in it & give a touch of the Pitches & Tattersalls![4]

"O if she does! cried Mrs. Thrale, if she *inserts* us in a *Comedy*—we'll serve her trick for trick—she is a young Authoress, & very delicate,—say it will be hard if we can't frighten her into order."

9. Henry Fielding (1710–54) was the author of, among other works, *Joseph Andrews* (1742), a parody of Richardson's *Pamela,* and *Tom Jones* (1749), a comic novel recounting the adventures of the novel's eponymous hero.

1. A reference to Daniel 3:24, the response of his counselors to King Nebuchadnezzar's puzzlement when victims of his ire miraculously escaped a

fiery death; apparently a comment on Johnson's perspicacity.

2. A 1754 play by Dr. Johnson.

3. A comedy produced at Covent Garden Theatre in 1777 by Arthur Murphy (1727–1805).

4. Families well known for eccentricity; see also note 8, p. 319.

Many more things were said, all of the most high seasoned flattery,—but I have not Time to write them.

* * *

From The Early Journals and Letters of Fanny Burney

[*Life in the Court of George III*]

Windsor,[5] Dec. 17th, 1785.

My dearest Hetty[6]

I am sorry I could not more immediately write; but I really have not had a moment since your last.

Now I know what you next want is, to hear accounts of kings, queens, and such royal personages. O ho! Do you so? Well.

Shall I tell you a few matters of fact?—or, had you rather a few matters of etiquette? Oh, matters of etiquette, you cry! for matters of fact are short and stupid, and anybody can tell, and everybody is tired with them.

Very well, take your own choice.

To begin, then, with the beginning.

You know I told you, in my last, my various difficulties, what sort of preferment to turn my thoughts to, and concluded with just starting a young budding notion of decision, by suggesting that a handsome pension for nothing at all would be as well as working night and day for a salary.

This blossom of an idea, the more I dwelt upon, the more I liked. Thinking served it for a hot-house and it came out into full blow as I ruminated upon my pillow. Delighted that thus all my contradictory and wayward fancies were overcome, and my mind was peaceably settled what to wish and to demand, I gave over all further meditation upon choice of elevation, and had nothing more to do but to make my election known.

My next business, therefore, was to be presented. This could be no difficulty; my coming hither had been their own desire, and they had earnestly pressed its execution. I had only to prepare myself for the rencounter.

You would never believe—you, who, distant from courts and courtiers, know nothing of their ways—the many things to be studied, for appearing with a proper propriety before crowned heads. Heads without crowns are quite other sort of rotundas.

Now, then, to the etiquette. I inquired into every particular, that no error might be committed. And as there is no saying what may happen in this mortal life, I shall give you those instructions I have received myself, that, should you find yourself in the royal presence, you may know how to comport yourself.

Directions for coughing, sneezing, or moving, before the King and Queen.

In the first place, you must not cough. If you find a cough tickling in your throat, you must arrest it from making any sound; if you find yourself choking with the forbearance, you must choke—but not cough.

---

5. Windsor Castle, a royal residence located about twenty-five miles west of London.   6. Nickname for Esther, Burney's older sister (1749–1832).

In the second place, you must not sneeze. If you have a vehement cold, you must take no notice of it; if your nose membranes feel a great irritation, you must hold your breath; if a sneeze still insists upon making its way, you must oppose it, by keeping your teeth grinding together; if the violence of the repulse breaks some blood-vessel, you must break the blood-vessel—but not sneeze.

In the third place, you must not, upon any account, stir either hand or foot. If, by chance, a black pin[7] runs into your head, you must not take it out. If the pain is very great, you must be sure to bear it without wincing; if it brings the tears into your eyes, you must not wipe them off; if they give you a tingling by running down your cheeks, you must look as if nothing was the matter. If the blood should gush from your head by means of the black pin, you must let it gush; if you are uneasy to think of making such a blurred appearance, you must be uneasy, but you must say nothing about it. If, however, the agony is very great, you may, privately, bite the inside of your cheek, or of your lips, for a little relief; taking care, meanwhile, to do it so cautiously as to make no apparent dent outwardly. And, with that precaution, if you even gnaw a piece out, it will not be minded, only be sure either to swallow it, or commit it to a corner of the inside of your mouth till they are gone—for you must not spit.

I have many other directions, but no more paper; I will endeavour, however, to have them ready for you in time. Perhaps, meanwhile, you will be glad to know if I have myself had opportunity to put in practice these receipts?

How can I answer in this little space? My love to Mr. B.[8] and the little ones, and remember me kindly to cousin Edward, and believe me, my dearest Esther,

Most affectionately yours,
F. B.

From Evelina, or the History of a Young Lady's Entrance into the World
Letter X [Evelina Arrives in London]

EVELINA TO THE REV. MR. VILLARS.[9]

Queen-Ann-Street, London, Saturday April 2.

This moment arrived. Just going to Drury-Lane theatre. The celebrated Mr. Garrick performs Ranger.[1] I am quite in extacy. So is Miss Mirvan. How fortunate, that he should happen to play! We would not let Mrs. Mirvan rest till she consented to go; her chief objection was to our dress, for we have had no time to Lon-

<hr>

7. A pin helping to hold up a very tall, somewhat precarious, and elaborate hairstyle then in fashion has shifted and is now sticking into the wearer's scalp.
8. Charles Rousseau Burney, cousin to Frances and Hetty—and Hetty's husband.
9. Letters I–IX reveal that Evelina has been raised in the country by the Reverend Villars, who has allowed her to visit London for the first time with

family friends Captain and Mrs. Mirvan and their daughter Miss Mirvan.
1. David Garrick (1717–79), an enormously popular dramatist, actor, and theater manager of the period, was cast as Ranger in *The Suspicious Husband* (1759) by Ben Hoadley. In her comment below, Evelina (or perhaps Burney) misremembers the play, as Clarinda does not dance with Ranger.

donize ourselves; but we teized her into compliance, and so we are to sit in some obscure place, that she may not be seen. As to me, I should be alike unknown in the most conspicuous or most private part of the house.

I can write no more now. I have hardly time to breathe—only just this, the houses and streets are not quite so superb as I expected. However, I have seen nothing yet, so I ought not to judge.

Well, adieu, my dearest Sir, for the present; I could not forbear writing a few words instantly on my arrival; though I suppose my letter of thanks for your consent is still on the road.

Saturday Night.

O my dear Sir, in what raptures am I returned! Well may Mr. Garrick be so celebrated, so universally admired—I had not any idea of so great a performer.

Such ease! such vivacity in his manner! such grace in his motions! such fire and meaning in his eyes!—I could hardly believe he had studied a written part, for every word seemed to be uttered from the impulse of the moment.

His action—at once so graceful and so free!—his voice—so clear, so melodious, yet so wonderfully various in its tones—such animation!—every look *speaks*!

I would have given the world to have had the whole play acted over again. And when he danced—O how I envied Clarinda! I almost wished to have jumped on the stage and joined them.

I am afraid you will think me mad, so I won't say any more; yet I really believe Mr. Garrick would make you mad too, if you could see him. I intend to ask Mrs. Mirvan to go to the play every night while we stay in town. She is extremely kind to me, and Maria, her charming daughter, is the sweetest girl in the world.

I shall write to you every evening all that passes in the day, and that in the same manner as, if I could see, I should tell you.

Sunday.

This morning we went to Portland chapel, and afterwards we walked in the Mall of St. James's Park, which by no means answered my expectations: it is a long straight walk, of dirty gravel, very uneasy to the feet; and at each end, instead of an open prospect, nothing is to be seen but houses built of brick. When Mrs. Mirvan pointed out the *Palace* to me—I think I was never much more surprised.[2]

However, the walk was very agreeable to us; every body looked gay, and seemed pleased, and the ladies were so much dressed, that Miss Mirvan and I could do nothing but look at them. Mrs. Mirvan met several of her friends. No wonder, for I never saw so many people assembled together before. I looked about for some of *my* acquaintance, but in vain, for I saw not one person that I knew, which is very odd, for all the world seemed there.

Mrs. Mirvan says we are not to walk in the Park again next Sunday, even if we should be in town, because there is better company in Kensington Gardens. But really if you had seen how much every body was dressed, you would not think that possible.

2. In the company of Mrs. and Miss Mirvan, Evelina visits a series of fashionable tourist sites, several of which, including St. Paul's Cathedral ("Portland Chapel"), St. James Park, "the Palace" (or the "Queen's House," later renovated and expanded into Buckingham Palace), and Kensington Gardens, remain popular today.

Monday.

We are to go this evening to a private ball, given by Mrs. Stanley, a very fashionable lady of Mrs. Mirvan's acquaintance.

We have been *a shopping*, as Mrs. Mirvan calls it, all this morning, to buy silks, caps, gauzes, and so forth.

The shops are really very entertaining, especially the mercers;[3] there seem to be six or seven men belonging to each shop, and every one took care, by bowing and smirking, to be noticed; we were conducted from one to another, and carried from room to room, with so much ceremony, that at first I was almost afraid to go on.

I thought I should never have chosen a silk, for they produced so many I knew not which to fix upon, and they recommended them all so strongly, that I fancy they thought I only wanted persuasion to buy every thing they shewed me. And, indeed, they took so much trouble, that I was almost ashamed I could not.

At the milliners,[4] the ladies we met were so much dressed, that I should rather have imagined they were making visits than purchases. But what most diverted me was, that we were more frequently served by men than by women; and such men! so finical, so affected! they seemed to understand every part of a woman's dress better than we do ourselves; and they recommended caps and ribbands with an air of so much importance, that I wished to ask them how long they had left off wearing them.

The dispatch with which they work in these great shops is amazing, for they have promised me a compleat suit of linen[5] against the evening.

I have just had my hair dressed.[6] You can't think how oddly my head feels; full of powder and black pins, and a great *cushion* on the top of it. I believe you would hardly know me, for my face looks quite different to what it did before my hair was dressed. When I shall be able to make use of a comb for myself I cannot tell, for my hair is so much entangled, *frizled* they call it, that I fear it will be very difficult.

I am half afraid of this ball to-night, for, you know, I have never danced but at school; however, Miss Mirvan says there is nothing in it. Yet I wish it was over.

Adieu, my dear Sir; pray excuse the wretched stuff I write, perhaps I may improve by being in this town, and then my letters will be less unworthy your reading. Mean time I am,

Your dutiful and affectionate,
though unpolished,
Evelina.

Poor Miss Mirvan cannot wear one of the caps she made, because they dress her hair too large for them.

Letter XI [*Evelina at the Ball*]

Queen-Ann-Street, April 5, Tuesday Morning.
I have a vast deal to say, and shall give all this morning to my pen. As to my plan of writing every evening the adventures of the day, I find it impracticable; for the

---

3. A fabric shop, where customers would choose fabrics to be made into articles of clothing.
4. A shop selling hats.
5. An ensemble, an outfit.
6. See note 7, p. 322.

diversions here are so very late, that if I begin my letters after them, I could not go to bed at all.

We past a most extraordinary evening. A *private* ball this was called, so I expected to have seen about four or five couple; but Lord! my dear Sir, I believe I saw half the world! Two very large rooms were full of company; in one, were cards for the elderly ladies, and in the other, were the dancers. My mamma Mirvan, for she always calls me her child, said she would sit with Maria and me till we were provided with partners, and then join the card-players.

The gentlemen, as they passed and re-passed, looked as if they thought we were quite at their disposal, and only waiting for the honour of their commands; and they sauntered about, in a careless indolent manner, as if with a view to keep us in suspense. I don't speak of this in regard to Miss Mirvan and myself only, but to the ladies in general; and I thought it so provoking, that I determined, in my own mind, that, far from humouring such airs, I would rather not dance at all, than with any one who should seem to think me ready to accept the first partner who would condescend to take me.

Not long after, a young man, who had for some time looked at us with a kind of negligent impertinence, advanced, on tip-toe, towards me; he had a set smile on his face, and his dress was so foppish, that I really believe he even wished to be stared at; and yet he was very ugly.

Bowing almost to the ground, with a sort of swing, and waving his hand with the greatest conceit, after a short and silly pause, he said, "Madam—may I presume?"—and stopt, offering to take my hand. I drew it back, but could scarce forbear laughing. "Allow me, Madam," (continued he, affectedly breaking off every half moment) "the honour and happiness—if I am not so unhappy as to address you too late—to have the happiness and honour——"

Again he would have taken my hand, but, bowing my head, I begged to be excused, and turned to Miss Mirvan to conceal my laughter. He then desired to know if I had already engaged myself to some more fortunate man? I said No, and that I believed I should not dance at all. He would keep himself, he told me, disengaged, in hopes I should relent; and then, uttering some ridiculous speeches of sorrow and disappointment, though his face still wore the same invariable smile, he retreated.

It so happened, as we have since recollected, that during this little dialogue, Mrs. Mirvan was conversing with the lady of the house. And very soon after another gentleman, who seemed about six and-twenty years old, gayly, but not foppishly, dressed, and indeed extremely handsome, with an air of mixed politeness and gallantry, desired to know if I was engaged, or would honour him with my hand. So he was pleased to say, though I am sure I know not what honour he could receive from me; but these sort of expressions, I find, are used as words of course, without any distinction of persons, or study of propriety.

Well, I bowed, and I am sure I coloured; for indeed I was frightened at the thoughts of dancing before so many people, all strangers, and, which was worse, *with* a stranger; however, that was unavoidable, for though I looked round the room several times, I could not see one person that I knew. And so, he took my hand, and led me to join in the dance.

The minuets were over before we arrived, for we were kept late by the milliner's making us wait for our things.

He seemed very desirous of entering into conversation with me; but I was seized with such a panic, that I could hardly speak a word, and nothing but the shame of so soon changing my mind, prevented my returning to my seat, and declining to dance at all.

He appeared to be surprised at my terror, which I believe was but too apparent: however, he asked no questions, though I fear he must think it very strange; for I did not choose to tell him it was owing to my never before dancing but with a schoolgirl.

His conversation was sensible and spirited; his air and address were open and noble; his manners gentle, attentive, and infinitely engaging; his person is all elegance, and his countenance, the most animated and expressive I have ever seen.

In a short time we were joined by Miss Mirvan, who stood next couple to us. But how was I startled, when she whispered me that my partner was a nobleman! This gave me a new alarm; how will he be provoked, thought I, when he finds what a simple rustic he has honoured with his choice! one whose ignorance of the world makes her perpetually fear doing something wrong!

That he should be so much my superior every way, quite disconcerted me; and you will suppose my spirits were not much raised, when I heard a lady, in passing us, say, "This is the most difficult dance I ever saw."

"O dear, then," cried Maria to her partner, "with your leave, I'll sit down till the next."

"So will I too, then," cried I, "for I am sure I can hardly stand."

"But you must speak to your partner first," answered she; for he had turned aside to talk with some gentlemen. However, I had not sufficient courage to address him, and so away we all three tript, and seated ourselves at another end of the room.

But, unfortunately for me, Miss Mirvan soon after suffered herself to be prevailed upon to attempt the dance; and just as she rose to go, she cried, "My dear, yonder is your partner, Lord Orville, walking about the room in search of you."

"Don't leave me then, dear girl!" cried I; but she was obliged to go. And now I was more uneasy than ever; I would have given the world to have seen Mrs. Mirvan, and begged of her to make my apologies; for what, thought I, can I possibly say to him in excuse for running away? he must either conclude me a fool, or half mad; for any one brought up in the great world, and accustomed to its ways, can have no idea of such sort of fears as mine.

My confusion encreased when I observed that he was every where seeking me, with apparent perplexity and surprise; but when, at last, I saw him move towards the place where I sat, I was ready to sink with shame and distress. I found it absolutely impossible to keep my seat, because I could not think of a word to say for myself, and so I rose, and walked hastily towards the card-room, resolving to stay with Mrs. Mirvan the rest of the evening, and not to dance at all. But before I could find her, Lord Orville saw and approached me.

He begged to know if I was not well? You may easily imagine how much I was embarrassed. I made no answer, but hung my head, like a fool, and looked on my fan.

He then, with an air the most respectfully serious, asked if he had been so unhappy as to offend me?

"No, indeed!" cried I: and, in hopes of changing the discourse, and preventing his further inquiries, I desired to know if he had seen the young lady who had been conversing with me?

No;—but would I honour him with any commands to her?

"O by no means!"

Was there any other person with whom I wished to speak?

I said *no*, before I knew I had answered at all.

Should he have the pleasure of bringing me any refreshment?

I bowed, almost involuntarily. And away he flew.

I was quite ashamed of being so troublesome, and so much *above* myself as these seeming airs made me appear; but indeed I was too much confused to think or act with any consistency.

If he had not been swift as lightning, I don't know whether I should not have stolen away again; but he returned in a moment. When I had drunk a glass of lemonade, he hoped, he said, that I would again honour him with my hand, as a new dance was just begun. I had not the presence of mind to say a single word, and so I let him once more lead me to the place I had left.

Shocked to find how silly, how childish a part I had acted, my former fears of dancing before such a company, and with such a partner, returned more forcibly than ever. I suppose he perceived my uneasiness, for he intreated me to sit down again, if dancing was disagreeable to me. But I was quite satisfied with the folly I had already shewn, and therefore declined his offer, tho' I was really scarce able to stand.

Under such conscious disadvantages, you may easily imagine, my dear Sir, how ill I acquitted myself. But, though I both expected and deserved to find him very much mortified and displeased at his ill fortune in the choice he had made, yet, to my very great relief, he appeared to be even contented, and very much assisted and encouraged me. These people in high life have too much presence of mind, I believe, to *seem* disconcerted, or out of humour, however they may feel: for had I been the person of the most consequence in the room, I could not have met with more attention and respect.

When the dance was over, seeing me still very much flurried, he led me to a seat, saying that he would not suffer me to fatigue myself from politeness.

And then, if my capacity, or even if my spirits had been better, in how animated a conversation might I have been engaged! It was then I saw that the rank of Lord Orville was his least recommendation, his understanding and his manners being far more distinguished. His remarks upon the company in general were so apt, so just, so lively, I am almost surprised myself that they did not re-animate me; but indeed I was too well convinced of the ridiculous part I had myself played before so nice an observer, to be able to enjoy his pleasantry: so self-compassion gave me feeling for others. Yet I had not the courage to attempt either to defend them, or to rally in my turn, but listened to him in silent embarrassment.

When he found this, he changed the subject, and talked of public places, and public performers; but he soon discovered that I was totally ignorant of them.

He then, very ingeniously, turned the discourse to the amusements and occupations of the country.

It now struck me, that he was resolved to try whether or not I was capable of talking upon *any* subject. This put so great a constraint upon my thoughts, that I was unable to go further than a monosyllable, and not even so far, when I could possibly avoid it.

We were sitting in this manner, he conversing with all gaiety, I looking down with all foolishness, when that fop who had first asked me to a dance, with a most ridiculous solemnity, approached, and after a profound bow or two, said, "I humbly beg pardon, Madam,—and of you too, my Lord,—for breaking in upon such agreeable conversation—which must, doubtless, be much more delectable—than what I have the honour to offer—but—"

I interrupted him—I blush for my folly,—with laughing; yet I could not help it, for, added to the man's stately foppishness, (and he actually took snuff[7] between every three words) when I looked round at Lord Orville, I saw such extreme surprise in his face,—the cause of which appeared so absurd, that I could not for my life preserve my gravity.

I had not laughed before from the time I had left Miss Mirvan, and I had much better have cried then; Lord Orville actually stared at me; the beau, I know not his name, looked quite enraged. "Refrain—Madam," (said he, with an important air,) "a few moments refrain!—I have but a sentence to trouble you with.—May I know to what accident I must attribute not having the honour of your hand?"

"Accident, Sir!" repeated I, much astonished.

"Yes, accident, Madam—for surely,—I must take the liberty to observe—pardon me, Madam,—it ought to be no common one—that should tempt a lady—so young a one too,—to be guilty of ill manners."

A confused idea now for the first time entered my head, of something I had heard of the rules of an assembly; but I was never at one before,—I have only danced at school,—and so giddy and heedless I was, that I had not once considered the impropriety of refusing one partner, and afterwards accepting another. I was thunderstruck at the recollection: but, while these thoughts were rushing into my head, Lord Orville, with some warmth, said, "This lady, Sir, is incapable of meriting such an accusation!"

The creature—for I am very angry with him—made a low bow, and, with a grin the most malicious I ever saw, "My Lord," said he, "far be it from me to *accuse* the lady, for having the discernment to distinguish and prefer—the superior attractions of your Lordship."

Again he bowed, and walked off.

Was ever any thing so provoking? I was ready to die with shame. "What a coxcomb!" exclaimed Lord Orville; while I, without knowing what I did, rose hastily, and moving off, "I can't imagine," cried I, "where Mrs. Mirvan has hid herself!"

"Give me leave to see," answered he. I bowed and sat down again, not daring to meet his eyes; for what must he think of me, between my blunder, and the supposed preference?

He returned in a moment, and told me that Mrs. Mirvan was at cards, but would be glad to see me; and I went immediately. There was but one chair vacant, so, to my great relief, Lord Orville presently left us. I then told Mrs. Mirvan my disasters, and she good-naturedly blamed herself for not having better instructed me, but said she had taken it for granted that I must know such common customs. However, the man may, I think, be satisfied with his pretty speech, and carry his resentment no farther.

In a short time, Lord Orville returned. I consented, with the best grace I could, to go down another dance, for I had had time to recollect myself, and therefore resolved to use some exertion, and, if possible, appear less a fool than I had hith-

---

7. Finely powdered tobacco inhaled through the nose.

erto done; for it occurred to me that, insignificant as I was, compared to a man of his rank and figure, yet, since he had been so unfortunate as to make choice of me for a partner, why I should endeavour to make the best of it.

The dance, however, was short, and he spoke very little; so I had no opportunity of putting my resolution in practice. He was satisfied, I suppose, with his former successless efforts to draw me out: or, rather, I fancied, he had been inquiring *who I was*. This again disconcerted me, and the spirits I had determined to exert, again failed me. Tired, ashamed, and mortified, I begged to sit down till we returned home, which I did soon after. Lord Orville did me the honour to hand me to the coach, talking all the way of the honour *I* had done *him!* O these fashionable people!

Well, my dear Sir, was it not a strange evening? I could not help being thus particular, because, to me, every thing is so new. But it is now time to conclude. I am, with all love and duty,

Your
Evelina.

Letter XII [*A Trip to Ranelagh*]

Tuesday, April 5.

There is to be no end to the troubles of last night. I have this moment, between persuasion and laughter, gathered from Maria the most curious dialogue that ever I heard. You will, at first, be startled at my vanity; but, my dear Sir, have patience!

It must have passed while I was sitting with Mrs. Mirvan in the card-room. Maria was taking some refreshment, and saw Lord Orville advancing for the same purpose himself; but he did not know her, though she immediately recollected him. Presently after, a very gay-looking man, stepping hastily up to him, cried, "Why, my Lord, what have you done with your lovely partner?"

"*Nothing!*" answered Lord Orville, with a smile and a shrug.

"By Jove," cried the man, "she is the most beautiful creature I ever saw in my life!"

Lord Orville, as he well might, laughed, but answered, "Yes, a pretty modest-looking girl."

"O my Lord!" cried the madman, "she is an angel!"

"A *silent* one," returned he.

"Why ay, my Lord, how stands she as to that? She looks all intelligence and expression."

"A poor weak girl!" answered Lord Orville, shaking his head.

"By Jove," cried the other, "I am glad to hear it!"

At that moment, the same odious creature who had been my former tormentor, joined them. Addressing Lord Orville with great respect, he said, "I beg pardon, my Lord,—if I was—as I fear might be the case—rather too severe in my censure of the lady who is honoured with your protection—but, my Lord, ill-breeding is apt to provoke a man."

"Ill-breeding!" cried my unknown champion, "impossible! that elegant face can never be so vile a mask!"

"O Sir, as to that," answered he, "you must allow *me* to judge; for though I pay all deference to your opinion—in other things,—yet I hope you will grant—

and I appeal to your Lordship also—that I am not totally despicable as a judge of good or ill manners."

"I was so wholly ignorant," said Lord Orville gravely, "of the provocation you might have had, that I could not but be surprised at your singular resentment."

"It was far from my intention," answered he, "to offend your Lordship; but really, for a person who is a nobody, to give herself such airs,—I own I could not command my passions. For, my Lord, though I have made diligent enquiry—I cannot learn who she is."

"By what I can make out," cried my defender, "she must be a country parson's daughter."

"He! he! he! very good, 'pon honour!" cried the fop,—"well, so I could have sworn by her manners."

And then, delighted at his own wit, he laughed, and went away, as I suppose, to repeat it.

"But what the deuce is all this?" demanded the other.

"Why a very foolish affair," answered Lord Orville; "your Helen first refused this coxcomb, and then—danced with me. This is all I can gather of it."

"O Orville," returned he, "you are a happy man!—But, *ill-bred?*—I can never believe it! And she looks too sensible to be *ignorant.*"

"Whether ignorant or mischievous, I will not pretend to determine, but certain it is, she attended to all *I* could say to her, though I have really fatigued myself with fruitless endeavours to entertain her, with the most immoveable gravity; but no sooner did Lovel begin his complaint, than she was seized with a fit of laughing, first affronting the poor beau, and then enjoying his mortification."

"Ha! ha! ha! why there's some *genius* in that, my Lord, though perhaps rather—*rustick.*"

Here Maria was called to dance, and so heard no more.

Now tell me, my dear Sir, did you ever know any thing more provoking? *"A poor weak girl!" "ignorant or mischievous!"* What mortifying words! I am resolved, however, that I will never again be tempted to go to an assembly. I wish I had been in Dorsetshire.

Well, after this, you will not be surprised that Lord Orville contented himself with an enquiry after our healths this morning, by his servant, without troubling himself to call; as Miss Mirvan had told me he would: but perhaps it may be only a country custom.

I would not live here for the world. I care not how soon we leave town. London soon grows tiresome. I wish the Captain[8] would come. Mrs. Mirvan talks of the opera for this evening; however, I am very indifferent about it.

Wednesday morning.

Well, my dear Sir, I have been pleased against my will, I could almost say, for I must own I went out in very ill-humour, which I think you cannot wonder at: but the music and the singing were charming; they soothed me into a pleasure the most grateful, the best suited to my present disposition in the world. I hope to persuade Mrs. Mirvan to go again on Saturday. I wish the opera was every night. It is, of all entertainments, the sweetest, and most delightful. Some of the songs

8. Captain Mirvan, Mrs. Mirvan's husband.

seemed to melt my very soul. It was what they call a *serious* opera, as the *comic* first singer was ill.

To-night we go to Ranelagh.[9] If any of those three gentlemen who conversed so freely about me should be there—but I won't think of it.

Thursday morning.

Well, my dear Sir, we went to Ranelagh. It is a charming place, and the brilliancy of the lights, on my first entrance, made me almost think I was in some inchanted castle, or fairy palace, for all looked like magic to me.

The very first person I saw was Lord Orville. I felt so confused!—but he did not see me. After tea, Mrs. Mirvan being tired, Maria and I walked round the room alone. Then again we saw him, standing by the orchestra. We, too, stopt to hear a singer. He bowed to me; I courtesied, and I am sure I coloured. We soon walked on, not liking our situation: however, he did not follow us; and when we passed by the orchestra again, he was gone. Afterwards, in the course of the evening, we met him several times; but he was always with some party, and never spoke to us, tho' whenever he chanced to meet my eyes, he condescended to bow.

I cannot but be hurt at the opinion he entertains of me. It is true, my own behaviour incurred it—yet he is himself the most agreeable and, seemingly, the most amiable man in the world, and therefore it is, that I am grieved to be thought ill of by him: for of whose esteem ought we to be ambitious, if not of those who most merit our own?—But it is too late to reflect upon this now. Well, I can't help it;—However, I think I have done with assemblies!

This morning was destined for *seeing sights,* auctions, curious shops,[1] and so forth; but my head ached, and I was not in a humour to be amused, and so I made them go without me, though very unwillingly. They are all kindness.

And now I am sorry I did not accompany them, for I know not what to do with myself. I had resolved not to go to the play to-night; but I believe I shall. In short, I hardly care whether I do or not.

I thought I had done wrong! Mrs. Mirvan and Maria have been half the town over, and so entertained!—while I, like a fool, stayed at home to do nothing. And, at an auction in Pall-mall, who should they meet but Lord Orville! He sat next to Mrs. Mirvan, and they talked a great deal together: but she gave me no account of the conversation.

I may never have such another opportunity of seeing London; I am quite sorry that I was not of the party; but I deserve this mortification, for having indulged my ill-humour.

Thursday night.

We are just returned from the play, which was King Lear, and has made me very sad. We did not see any body we knew.

Well, adieu, it is too late to write more.

---

9. A pleasure garden, in which, for the price of admission, visitors could view works of art, listen to concerts, take tea, see natural spectacles like waterfalls ("cascades"), watch pyrotechnic displays, or simply be part of the fashionable crowd. The outer fringes of such gardens were notorious as places for illicit rendezvous.

1. Curiosity shops selling novelty or decorative items.

Friday.

Captain Mirvan is arrived. I have not spirits to give an account of his introduction, for he has really shocked me. I do not like him. He seems to be surly, vulgar, and disagreeable.

Almost the same moment that Maria was presented to him, he began some rude jests upon the bad shape of her nose, and called her a tall, ill-formed thing. She bore it with the utmost good humour; but that kind and sweet-tempered woman, Mrs. Mirvan, deserved a better lot. I am amazed she would marry him.

For my own part, I have been so shy, that I have hardly spoken to him, or he to me. I cannot imagine why the family was so rejoiced at his return. If he had spent his whole life abroad, I should have supposed they might rather have been thankful than sorrowful. However, I hope they do not think so ill of him as I do. At least, I am sure they have too much prudence to make it known.

Saturday night.

We have been to the opera, and I am still more pleased than I was on Tuesday. I could have thought myself in paradise, but for the continual talking of the company around me. We sat in the pit,[2] where every body was dressed in so high a style, that, if I had been less delighted with the performance, my eyes would have found me sufficient entertainment from looking at the ladies.

I was very glad I did not sit next the Captain, for he could not bear the music, or singers, and was extremely gross in his observations on both. When the opera was over, we went into a place called the coffee-room, where ladies as well as gentlemen assemble. There are all sorts of refreshments, and the company walk about, and *chat* with the same ease and freedom as in a private room.

On Monday we go to a ridotto,[3] and on Wednesday we return to Howard Grove. The Captain says he won't stay here to be *smoked with filth* any longer; but, having been seven years *smoked with a burning sun,* he will retire to the country, and sink into a *fair-weather chap.*

Adieu, my dear Sir.

Letter XV [A Dangerous Walk in Vauxhall]

Holborn, June 17th.

Yesterday Mr. Smith carried his point, of making a party for Vauxhall, consisting of Madame Duval, M. Du Bois, all the Branghtons, Mr. Brown,[4] himself,—and me!—for I find all endeavours vain to escape any thing which these people desire I should not.

There were twenty disputes previous to our setting out; first, as to the *time* of our going: Mr. Branghton, his son, and young Brown, were for six o'clock; and all the ladies and Mr. Smith were for eight;—the latter, however, conquered.

2. The seating area just in front of the stage, which had recently become the fashionable place to sit.

3. Ridotto: a public performance consisting of music and dancing; Howard Grove: the Mirvans' home.

4. Evelina is now under the care of her vulgar grandmother Madam Duval, her grandmother's French beau Monsieur Du Bois, her shopkeeper-cousins the Branghtons, and their friend Mr. Brown; like Ranelagh, Vauxhall was a pleasure garden (see note 9, page 331).

Then, as to the *way* we should go; some were for a boat, others for a coach, and Mr. Branghton himself was for walking: but the boat, at length, was decided upon. Indeed this was the only part of the expedition that was agreeable to me, for the Thames was delightfully pleasant.

The Garden is very pretty, but too formal; I should have been better pleased, had it consisted less of strait walks, where

Grove nods at grove, each alley has its brother.[5]

The trees, the numerous lights, and the company in the circle round the orchestra make a most brilliant and gay appearance; and, had I been with a party less disagreeable to me, I should have thought it a place formed for animation and pleasure. There was a concert, in the course of which, a hautbois[6] concerto was so charmingly played, that I could have thought myself upon enchanted ground, had I had spirits more gentle to associate with. The hautboy in the open air is heavenly.

Mr. Smith endeavoured to attach himself to me, with such officious assiduity, and impertinent freedom, that he quite sickened me. Indeed, M. Du Bois was the only man of the party to whom, voluntarily, I ever addressed myself. He is civil and respectful, and I have found nobody else so since I left Howard Grove. His English is very bad, but I prefer it to speaking French myself, which I dare not venture to do. I converse with him frequently, both to disengage myself from others, and to oblige Madame Duval, who is always pleased when he is attended to.

As we were walking about the orchestra, I heard a bell ring, and, in a moment, Mr. Smith, flying up to me, caught my hand, and, with a motion too quick to be resisted, ran away with me many yards before I had breath to ask his meaning, though I struggled as well as I could to get from him. At last, however, I insisted upon stopping; "Stopping, Ma'am!" cried he, "why, we must run on, or we shall lose the cascade!"

And then again, he hurried me away, mixing with a crowd of people, all running with so much velocity, that I could not imagine what had raised such an alarm. We were soon followed by the rest of the party; and my surprise and ignorance proved a source of diversion to them all, which was not exhausted the whole evening. Young Branghton, in particular, laughed till he could hardly stand.

The scene of the cascade I thought extremely pretty, and the general effect striking and lively.

But this was not the only surprise which was to divert them at my expence; for they led me about the garden, purposely to enjoy my first sight of various other deceptions.

About ten o'clock, Mr. Smith having chosen a *box* in a very conspicuous place, we all went to supper. Much fault was found with every thing that was ordered, though not a morsel of any thing was left; and the dearness of the provisions, with conjectures upon what profit was made by them, supplied discourse during the whole meal.

When wine and cyder were brought, Mr. Smith said, "Now let's enjoy ourselves; now is the time, or never. Well, Ma'am, and how do you like Vauxhall?"

---

5. A slight misquotation of line 117 in Alexander Pope's poem "Epistle IV: To Richard Boyle, Earl of Burlington": "Grove nods at grove, and each   alley has *a* brother."
6. Oboe.

"Like it!" cried young Branghton, "why, how can she help liking it? she has never seen such a place before, that I'll answer for."

"For my part," said Miss Branghton, "I like it because it is not vulgar."

"This must have been a fine treat for you, Miss," said Mr. Branghton; "why, I suppose you was never so happy in all your life before?"

I endeavoured to express my satisfaction with some pleasure, yet I believe they were much amazed at my coldness.

"Miss ought to stay in town till the last night," said young Branghton, "and then, it's my belief, she'd say something to it! Why, Lord, it's the best night of any; there's always a riot,—and there the folks run about,—and then there's such squealing and squalling!—and there all the lamps are broke,—and the women run skimper scamper;—I declare I would not take five guineas to miss the last night!"

I was very glad when they all grew tired of sitting, and called for the waiter to pay the bill. The Miss Branghtons said they would walk on, while the gentlemen settled the account, and asked me to accompany them; which, however, I declined.

"You girls may do as you please," said Madame Duval, "but as to me, I promise you, I sha'n't go no where without the gentlemen."

"No more, I suppose, will my *Cousin*," said Miss Branghton, looking reproachfully towards Mr. Smith.

This reflection, which I feared would flatter his vanity, made me, most unfortunately, request Madame Duval's permission to attend them. She granted it, and away we went, having promised to meet in the room.

To the room therefore, I would immediately have gone: but the sisters agreed that they would first have a *little pleasure*, and they tittered, and talked so loud, that they attracted universal notice.

"Lord, Polly," said the eldest, "suppose we were to take a turn in the dark walks!"[7]

"Ay, do," answered she, "and then we'll hide ourselves, and then Mr. Brown will think we are lost."

I remonstrated very warmly against this plan, telling them that it would endanger our missing the rest of the party all the evening.

"O dear," cried Miss Branghton, "I thought how uneasy Miss would be, without a beau!"

This impertinence I did not think worth answering; and, quite by compulsion, I followed them down a long alley, in which there was hardly any light.

By the time we came near the end, a large party of gentlemen, apparently very riotous, and who were hallowing, leaning on one another, and laughing immoderately, seemed to rush suddenly from behind some trees, and, meeting us face to face, put their arms at their sides, and formed a kind of circle, which first stopped our proceeding, and then our retreating, for we were presently entirely inclosed. The Miss Branghtons screamed aloud, and I was frightened exceedingly: our screams were answered with bursts of laughter, and, for some minutes, we were kept prisoners, till, at last, one of them, rudely, seizing hold of me, said I was a pretty little creature.

Terrified to death, I struggled with such vehemence to disengage myself from him, that I succeeded, in spite of his efforts to detain me; and immediately, and with a swiftness which fear only could have given me, I flew rather than ran up

7. Walks bounded by shrubbery, notorious as illicit meeting places.

the walk, hoping to secure my safety by returning to the lights and company we had so foolishly left: but, before I could possibly accomplish my purpose, I was met by another party of men, one of whom placed himself so directly in my way, calling out, "Whither so fast, my love?"—that I could only have proceeded, by running into his arms.

In a moment, both my hands, by different persons, were caught hold of; and one of them, in a most familiar manner, desired, when I ran next, to accompany me in a race; while the rest of the party stood still and laughed.

I was almost distracted with terror, and so breathless with running, that I could not speak, till another advancing, said, I was as handsome as an angel, and desired to be of the party. I then just articulated, "For Heaven's sake, Gentlemen, let me pass!"

Another, then, rushing suddenly forward, exclaimed, "Heaven and earth! what voice is that?—"

"The voice of the prettiest little actress I have seen this age," answered one of my persecutors.

"No,—no,—no,—" I *panted* out, "I am no actress,—pray let me go,—pray let me pass—."

"By all that's sacred," cried the same voice, which I then knew for Sir Clement Willoughby's,[8] "'tis herself!"

"Sir Clement Willoughby!" cried I. "O Sir, assist—assist me—or I shall die with terror!—"

"Gentlemen," cried he, disengaging them all from me in an instant, "pray leave this lady to me."

Loud laughs proceeded from every mouth, and two or three said, "*Willoughby has all the luck!*" But one of them, in a passionate manner, vowed he would not give me up, for that he had the first right to me, and would support it.

"You are mistaken," said Sir Clement, "this lady is—I will explain myself to you another time; but, I assure you, you are all mistaken."

And then, taking my willing hand, he led me off, amidst the loud acclamations, laughter, and gross merriment of his impertinent companions.

As soon as we had escaped from them, Sir Clement, with a voice of surprise, exclaimed, "My dearest creature, what wonder, what strange revolution, has brought you to such a spot as this?"

Ashamed of my situation, and extremely mortified to be thus recognized by him, I was for some time silent, and when he repeated his question, only stammered out, "I have,—I hardly know how,—lost myself from my party.—"

He caught my hand, and eagerly pressing it, in a passionate voice, said, "O that I had sooner met with thee!"

Surprised at a freedom so unexpected, I angrily broke from him, saying, "Is this the protection you give me, Sir Clement?"

And then I saw, what the perturbation of my mind had prevented my sooner noticing, that he had led me, though I know not how, into another of the dark alleys, instead of the place whither I meant to go.

"Good God!" I cried, "where am I?—What way are you going?—"

---

8. A dissipated member of the upper class, Sir Clement Willoughby has been dogging Evelina throughout the novel, making unwanted advances and even threatening her with physical assault in a carriage.

"Where," answered he, "we shall be least observed."

Astonished at this speech, I stopped short, and declared I would go no further.

"And why not, my angel?" again endeavouring to take my hand.

My heart beat with resentment; I pushed him away from me with all my strength, and demanded how he dared treat me with such insolence?

"Insolence!" repeated he.

"Yes, Sir Clement, *insolence;* from you, who know me, I had a claim for protection,—not to such treatment as this."

"By heaven," cried he with warmth, "you distract me,—why, tell me,—why do I see you here?—Is this a place for Miss Anville?—these dark walks!—no party!—no companion!—by all that's good, I can scarce believe my senses!"

Extremely offended at this speech, I turned angrily from him, and, not deigning to make any answer, walked on towards that part of the garden whence I perceived the lights and company.

He followed me; but we were both some time silent.

"So you will not explain to me your situation?" said he, at length.

"No, Sir," answered I, disdainfully.

"Nor yet—suffer me to make my own interpretation?—"

I could not bear this strange manner of speaking; it made my very soul shudder,—and I burst into tears.

He flew to me, and actually flung himself at my feet, as if regardless who might see him, saying, "O Miss Anville—loveliest of women—forgive my—my—I beseech you forgive me;—if I have offended,—if I have hurt you—I could kill myself at the thought!—"

"No matter, Sir, no matter," cried I, "if I can but find my friends,—I will never speak to—never see you again!"

"Good God!—good Heaven!—my dearest life, what is it I have done?—what is it I have said?—"

"You best know, Sir *what* and *why,*—but don't hold me here,—let *me* be gone; and do *you!*"

"Not till you forgive me!—I cannot part with you in anger."

"For shame, for shame, Sir!" cried I indignantly, "do you suppose I am to be thus compelled?—do you take advantage of the absence of my friends, to affront me?"

"No, Madam," cried he, rising, "I would sooner forfeit my life than act so mean a part. But you have flung me into amazement unspeakable, and you will not condescend to listen to my request of giving me some explanation."

"The manner, Sir," said I, "in which you spoke that request, made, and will make me scorn to answer it."

"Scorn!—I will own to you, I expected not such displeasure from Miss Anville."

"Perhaps, Sir, if you had, you would less voluntarily have merited it."

"My dearest life, surely it must be known to you, that the man does not breathe, who adores you so passionately, so fervently, so tenderly as I do!—why then will you delight in perplexing me?—in keeping me in suspense—in torturing me with doubt?—"

"I, Sir, delight in perplexing you!—You are much mistaken.—Your suspence, your doubts, your perplexities,—are of your own creating; and believe me, Sir, they may *offend,* but they can never *delight* me:—but, as you have yourself raised, you must yourself satisfy them."

"Good God!—that such haughtiness and such sweetness can inhabit the same mansion!"

I made no answer, but quickening my pace, I walked on silently and sullenly; till this most impetuous of men, snatching my hand, which he grasped with violence, besought me to forgive him, with such earnestness of supplication, that, merely to escape his importunities, I was forced to speak, and, in some measure, to grant the pardon he requested: though it was accorded with a very ill grace: but, indeed, I knew not how to resist the humility of his entreaties: yet never shall I recollect the occasion he gave me of displeasure, without feeling it renewed.

We now soon arrived in the midst of the general crowd, and my own safety being then insured, I grew extremely uneasy for the Miss Branghtons, whose danger, however imprudently incurred by their own folly, I too well knew how to tremble for. To this consideration all my pride of heart yielded, and I determined to seek my party with the utmost speed; though not without a sigh did I recollect the fruitless attempt I had made, after the opera, of concealing from this man my unfortunate connections, which I was now obliged to make known.

I hastened, therefore, to the room, with a view of sending young Branghton to the aid of his sisters. In a very short time, I perceived Madame Duval, and the rest, looking at one of the paintings. I must own to you, honestly, my dear Sir, that an involuntary repugnance seized me, at presenting such a set to Sir Clement,—he, who had been used to see me in parties so different!—My pace slackened as I approached them,—but they presently perceived me.

"Ah, Mademoiselle!" cried M. Du Bois, "Que je suis charmé de vous voir!"[9]

"Pray, Miss," cried Mr. Brown, "where's Miss Polly?"

"Why, Miss, you've been a long while gone," said Mr. Branghton; "we thought you'd been lost. But what have you done with your cousins?"

I hesitated,—for Sir Clement regarded me with a look of wonder.

"Pardi," cried Madame Duval, "I sha'n't let you leave me again in a hurry. Why, here we've been in such a fright!—and, all the while, I suppose you've been thinking nothing about the matter."

"Well," said young Branghton, "as long as Miss is come back, I don't mind, for as to Bid and Poll, they can take care of themselves. But the best joke is, Mr. Smith is gone all about a looking for you."

These speeches were made almost all in a breath: but when, at last, they waited for an answer, I told them, that in walking up one of the long alleys, we had been frightened and separated.

"The long alleys!" repeated Mr. Branghton, "and, pray, what had you to do in the long alleys? why, to be sure, you must all of you have had a mind to be affronted!"

This speech was not more impertinent to me, than surprising to Sir Clement, who regarded all the party with evident astonishment. However, I told young Branghton that no time ought to be lost, for that his sisters might require his immediate protection.

"But how will they get it?" cried this brutal brother; "if they've a mind to behave in such a manner as that, they ought to protect themselves; and so they may for me."

"Well," said the simple Mr. Brown, "whether you go or no, I think I may as well see after Miss Polly."

9. "How charmed I am to see you!" (French).

The father, then, interfering, insisted that his son should accompany him; and away they went.

It was now that Madame Duval first perceived Sir Clement; to whom turning with a look of great displeasure, she angrily said, "*Ma foi,*[1] so you are comed here, of all the people in the world!—I wonder, child, you would let such a—such a *person* as that keep company with you."

"I am very sorry, Madam," said Sir Clement, in a tone of surprise, "if I have been so unfortunate as to offend you; but I believe you will not regret the honour I now have of attending Miss Anville, when you hear that I have been so happy as to do her some service."

Just as Madame Duval, with her usual *Ma foi,* was beginning to reply, the attention of Sir Clement was wholly drawn from her, by the appearance of Mr. Smith, who coming suddenly behind me, and freely putting his hands on my shoulders, cried, "O ho, my little runaway, have I found you at last? I have been scampering all over the gardens for you, for I was determined to find you, if you were above ground.—But how could you be so cruel as to leave us?"

I turned round to him, and looked with a degree of contempt that I hoped would have quieted him; but he had not the sense to understand me; and, attempting to take my hand, he added, "Such a demure looking lady as you are, who'd have thought of your leading one such a dance?—Come now, don't be so coy,—only think what a trouble I have had in running after you!"

"The trouble, Sir," said I, "was of your own choice,—not mine." And I walked round to the other side of Madame Duval.

Perhaps I was too proud,—but I could not endure that Sir Clement, whose eyes followed him with looks of the most surprised curiosity, should witness his unwelcome familiarity.

Upon my removal, he came up to me, and, in a low voice, said, "You are not, then, with the Mirvans?"

"No, Sir."

"And pray—may I ask,—have you left them long?"

"No, Sir."

"How unfortunate I am!—but yesterday I sent to acquaint the Captain I should reach the Grove by to-morrow noon! However, I shall get away as fast as possible. Shall you be long in town?"

"I believe not, Sir."

"And then, when you leave it.—which way—will you allow me to ask, which way you shall travel?"

"Indeed,—I don't know."

"Not know!—But do you return to the Mirvans any more?"

"I—I can't tell, Sir."

And then, I addressed myself to Madame Duval, with such a pretended earnestness, that he was obliged to be silent.

As he cannot but observe the great change in my situation, which he knows not how to account for, there is something in all these questions, and this unrestrained curiosity, that I did not expect from a man, who when he pleases can be so well-bred, as Sir Clement Willoughby. He seems disposed to think that the alteration in my companions authorises an alteration in his manners. It is true, he

---

1. "Really!" (French). (Literally, "My faith!")

has always treated me with uncommon freedom, but never before with so disrespectful an abruptness. This observation, which he has given me cause to make, of his *changing with the tide,* has sunk him more in my opinion, than any other part of his conduct.

Yet I could almost have laughed, when I looked at Mr. Smith, who no sooner saw me addressed by Sir Clement, than, retreating aloof from the company, he seemed to lose at once all his happy self-sufficiency and conceit; looking now at the baronet, now at himself, surveying, with sorrowful eyes, his dress, struck with his air, his gestures, his easy gaiety; he gazed at him with envious admiration, and seemed himself, with conscious inferiority, to shrink into nothing.

1778

CULTURAL COORDINATES
Shopping

In Frances Burney's novel *Evelina* (1778), the eponymous heroine writes home to tell how she has just participated in a relatively new pastime: "We have been *a shopping,* as Mrs. Mirvan calls it, all this morning, to buy silks, caps, gauzes, and so forth." Although shops had been around in some form for a long time, the earliest mention of the verb "to shop" dates only to 1764. The modern activity of "shopping" awaited changes in the physical space of retail and in the modern definition of buyers and sellers.

In the first part of the early modern period (1500–1750), most selling and buying occurred outdoors, at fairs or markets. Then, a shop was a room in a house lining a marketplace. Customers, coming and going freely, stood in the street and did business across a counter in the doorway. By the end of the seventeenth century, however, buyers began to move inside the shop. Around the same time, the shop became a separate and distinct space for selling: whereas the shop had once been an extension of the seller's workshop and dwelling, prosperous shopkeepers now began to live elsewhere, separating their business from their home life. Not until the early nineteenth century, with the invention of plate glass and better indoor lighting (to enhance the visibility of goods), did shops come to resemble those we would recognize today.

The Wedgwood and Byerley showroom was one of the most famous of the eighteenth-century shops, advertising and selling the newly popular Wedgwood china. (From Ackermann's *Repository of the Arts.* Courtesy of the Yale Center for British Art, Paul Mellon Collection)

In the late eighteenth century, modern "shopping" emerged as the pursuit of luxury items like tea, tobacco, and sugar, but soon shops offered a wide range of goods made available through the first "consumer revolution"—items like furniture, clocks, textiles, and fashion accessories. One of the most famous of the eighteenth-century shops advertised and sold newly popular Wedgwood china on a massive scale. In the early days of shopping, no prices were fixed on commodities. Buyers and sellers scrutinized each other closely. The seller tried to read what the buyer might be willing and able to pay, and the buyer tried to ascertain whether the negotiated price represented a good bargain. Modern retail practices were born out of a host of tradesmen's manuals and directories, written during the early eighteenth century by men like Daniel Defoe (author of *Robinson Crusoe,* 1719, and *Moll Flanders,* 1722). Such manuals defined and codified modes of behavior for seller and buyer alike. In the eighteenth century, tradesmen came to understand the art of selling as a psychological transaction in which a merchant (most often understood as a "masculinized" individual regardless of gender) aimed to master the customer (who was construed as a "feminized" persona). The intimate space of the shop—like other domestic interiors—facilitated a vocabulary of seduction. The result was the idea of the consumer as a compliant female subject to the manipulation of the male merchant, who would elicit and control her desires.

However, these were only the theories behind the shopping experience. Contemporary literature from the period—from periodical essays in *The Spectator* by Addison and Steele to the novel *Camilla* (1796) by Frances Burney—shows us how some women resisted the rhetoric of seduction and how they undermined the merchants' expectations. They continued to pick and choose carefully among the merchandise, resisting the retailers' efforts at control and sometimes exercising their agency by not buying anything at all.

c. 1754–1784

Most likely born in Senegal, Phillis Wheatley was captured in 1761 and sold into slavery. Because she was shedding her front teeth at the time, biographers surmise she was probably about seven years old. John Wheatley, a wealthy Boston tailor, bought her as a house servant for his wife, Susanna, and named the child after the slave ship that had brought her to America. The Wheatleys gave Phillis access to an education that was extremely rare for a woman and rarer still for a slave, including the study of history, geography, and astronomy. Wheatley's reading list included classical writers like Horace, Virgil, and Ovid, both in translation and in the original Latin. She also mastered works by British writers like Milton, Pope, and Gray, as well as the Bible. In 1767, she published her first poem titled "On Messrs. Hussey and Coffin" in the Newport, Rhode Island, *Mercury*. This was followed by several more poems published as broadsides and distributed on the streets, including an elegy on the death of evangelical preacher George Whitefield (1771). Wheatley's most famous poem, "On Being Brought from Africa to America," though perhaps written in 1768, was not published until 1773. Despite her growing local fame, doubts concerning the authenticity of Wheatley's work persisted, and she had difficulty finding sufficient numbers of subscribers to publish her first volume of poems.

Then, in 1773, she accompanied the Wheatleys to England. There, Selina Hastings, the Countess of Huntingdon, whom Whitefield had served as chaplain, supported Wheatley and made arrangements to publish her poems. *Poems on Various Subjects, Religious and Moral* appeared in 1773, and thereafter Wheatley became known as the "Sable Muse." She met many famous people, including the Lord Mayor of London, who gave her a copy of Milton's *Paradise Lost* (1667) and the American printer, inventor, and politician Benjamin Franklin. She also won the praise of the French Enlightenment philosopher Voltaire (1694–1778). When she came back from England with her published book, Wheatley was granted her freedom.

Around 1774, she began a famous correspondence on the injustice of slavery with Mohegan minister Samson Occum. After the Revolutionary War broke out in 1775, she wrote to George Washington to express support and to send him her poem "To His Excellency General Washington." Washington wrote back to thank her and helped to get the work published in the Virginia *Gazette* in March 1776.

She continued to live with the Wheatleys until 1778, when she married John Peters, a free black man who appears to have been a grocer. Her first two children died in infancy. After the birth of her third child, in 1784, Peters abandoned her. Both she and the child died soon afterward and were buried in an unmarked grave. Wheatley was about thirty. She had intended to dedicate a second book of poems to Benjamin Franklin, but she failed to get the necessary number of subscribers. Although her poems have generated considerable discussion on the subject of whether Wheatley conveys an "authentic" black voice, scholar Henry Louis Gates Jr. concludes, "If Wheatley stood for anything, of course, it was the creed that culture did, or could, belong equally to everyone."

The following selections suggest the scope of Wheatley's interests—from religious and political leadership in "On the Death of the Rev. Mr. George Whitefield" and "To His Excellency General Washington" to African American artistic expression in "To S. M. a Young African Painter, on Seeing His Works."

On Being Brought from Africa to America

> 'Twas mercy brought me from my *Pagan* land,
> Taught my benighted soul to understand
> That there's a God, that there's a *Saviour* too:
> Once I redemption neither sought nor knew.
> Some view our sable race with scornful eye.   5
> "Their colour is a diabolic die."
> Remember, *Christians*, *Negros*, black as *Cain*,
> May be refin'd and join th' angelic train.

1768   1773

On the Death of the Rev. Mr. George Whitefield[1]

> Hail, happy saint, on thine immortal throne,
> Possest of glory, life, and bliss unkown;
> We hear no more the music of thy tongue,
> Thy wonted auditories cease to throng.
> Thy sermons in unequall'd accents flow'd,   5
> And ev'ry bosom with devotion glow'd;
> Thou didst in strains of eloquence refin'd
> Inflame the heart, and captivate the mind.
> Unhappy we the setting sun deplore,
> So glorious once, but ah! it shines no more.   10
>
> Behold the prophet in his tow'ring flight!
> He leaves the earth for heav'n's unmeasur'd height,
> And worlds unknown receive him from our sight.
> There *Whitefield* wings with rapid course his way,
> And sails to *Zion* through vast seas of day.   15
> Thy pray'rs, great saint, and thine incessant cries
> Have pierc'd the bosom of thy native skies.
> Thou moon hast seen, and all the stars of light,
> How he has wrestled with his God by night.
> He pray'd that grace in ev'ry heart might dwell,   20
> He long'd to see *America* excel;
> He charg'd its youth that ev'ry grace divine
> Should with full lustre in their conduct shine;
> That Saviour, which his soul did first receive,
> The greatest gift that ev'n a God can give,   25
> He freely offer'd to the num'rous throng,
> That on his lips with list'ning pleasure hung.

1. George Whitefield (1714–70)—pronounced "Whitfield"—an English preacher and leader of the Methodist movement. He traveled to America seven times, where he participated in a religious revivalist movement called The Great Awakening (1730s–1740s).

"Take him, ye wretched, for your only good,
Take him ye starving sinners, for your food;
Ye thirsty, come to this life-giving stream,   30
Ye preachers, take him for your joyful theme;
Take him my dear *Americans,* he said,
Be your complaints on his kind bosom laid:
Take him, ye *Africans,* he longs for you,
Impartial Saviour is his title due: 35
Wash'd in the fountain of redeeming blood,
You shall be sons, and kings, and priests to God."

Great *Countess,*[2] we *Americans* revere
Thy name, and mingle in thy grief sincere;
New England deeply feels, the *Orphans* mourn,   40
Their more than father will no more return.

But, though arrested by the hand of death,
Whitefield no more exerts his lab'ring breath,
Yet let us view him in th' eternal skies,
Let ev'ry heart to this bright vision rise;   45
While the tomb safe retains its sacred trust,
Till life divine re-animates his dust.

                                                                        1770

To S. M.[3] a Young African Painter, on Seeing His Works

To show the lab'ring bosom's deep intent,
And thought in living characters to paint,
When first thy pencil did those beauties give,
And breathing figures learnt from thee to live,
How did those prospects give my soul delight,   5
A new creation rushing on my sight?
Still, wond'rous youth! each noble path pursue,
On deathless glories fix thine ardent view:
Still may the painter's and the poet's fire
To aid thy pencil, and thy verse conspire!   10
And may the charms of each seraphic theme
Conduct thy footsteps to immortal fame!
High to the blissful wonders of the skies
Elate thy soul, and raise thy wishful eyes.
Thrice happy, when exalted to survey   15
That splendid city, crown'd with endless day,
Whose twice six gates on radiant hinges ring:
Celestial *Salem*[4] blooms in endless spring.

Calm and serene thy moments glide along,
And may the muse inspire each future song!   20
Still, with the sweets of contemplation bless'd,

---

2. The Countess of Huntingdon, to whom Mr.   3. Scipio Moorehead, a servant.
Whitefield had been chaplain [Wheatley's note].   4. Signifying a place of peace.

May peace with balmy wings your soul invest!
But when these shades of time are chas'd away,
And darkness ends in everlasting day,
On what seraphic pinions shall we move,   25
And view the landscapes in the realms above?
There shall thy tongue in heav'nly murmurs flow,
And there my muse with heav'nly transport glow:
No more to tell of *Damon's*[5] tender sighs,
Or rising radiance of *Aurora's* eyes,[6]   30
For nobler themes demand a nobler strain,
And purer language on th' ethereal plain.
Cease, gentle muse! the solemn gloom of night
Now seals the fair creation from my sight.

                                                          1773

To His Excellency General Washington

Celestial choir! enthron'd in realms of light
Columbia's[7] scenes of glorious toils I write.
While freedom's cause her anxious breast alarms,
She flashes dreadful in refulgent arms.
See mother earth her offspring's fate bemoan,   5
And nations gaze at scenes before unknown!
See the bright beams of heaven's revolving light
Involved in sorrows and the veil of night!

The goddess comes, she moves divinely fair,
Olive and laurel binds her golden hair:
Wherever shines this native of the skies,   10
Unnumber'd charms and recent graces rise.

Muse! bow propitious while my pen relates
How pour her armies through a thousand gates:
As when Eolus[8] heaven's fair face deforms,   15
Enwrapp'd in tempest and a night of storms;
Astonish'd ocean feels the wild uproar,
The refluent surges beat the sounding shore;
Or thick as leaves in Autumn's golden reign,
Such, and so many, moves the warrior's train.   20
In bright array they seek the work of war,
Where high unfurl'd the ensign waves in air.
Shall I to Washington their praise recite?
Enough thou know'st them in the fields of fight.
Thee, first in place and honours,—we demand   25
The grace and glory of thy martial band.
Fam'd for thy valour, for thy virtues more,
Hear every tongue thy guardian aid implore!

5. A character in Greek legend who pledged his
life for his friend Pythias.
6. Goddess of the dawn in Roman mythology.

7. America's.
8. God of the winds in Roman mythology.

One century scarce perform'd its destin'd round,
When Gallic[9] powers Columbia's fury found;   30
And so may you, whoever dares disgrace
The land of freedom's heaven-defended race!
Fix'd are the eyes of nations on the scales,
For in their hopes Columbia's arm prevails.
Anon Britannia droops the pensive head,   35
While round increase the rising hills of dead.
Ah! cruel blindness to Columbia's state!
Lament thy thirst of boundless power too late.

　　Proceed, great chief, with virtue on thy side,
Thy ev'ry action let the goddess guide.   40
A crown, a mansion, and a throne that shine,
With gold unfading, WASHINGTON! be thine.

                                                                1775

➤◄ JANE CAVE ►◄
Active c. 1786

The facts of Jane Cave's life remain unrecorded, but her poems represent a typical strain of women's verse from the end of the eighteenth century. The subjects of her poems are largely such familial and everyday events as births, visits and departures of family members, and the mundane events of her neighborhood. Cave published a single volume of verse in 1783: *Poems on Various Subjects, Entertaining, Elegiac, and Religious*. This volume had a large subscription list—suggesting a wide circle of acquaintances willing to pay for her work—and was eventually published in four editions.

　　In the first of the two poems included here, "Written by Desire of a Lady" (1783), Cave satirizes the behavior of an angry kitchen maid who has apparently taken out her unhappiness on the other members of the staff. The comical tone, which pretends facetiously to align itself with a servant's perspective, emerges at the expense of the kitchen maid. (The kitchen maid's perspective on the matter might be glimpsed by reading this poem in contrast with Mary Collier's "The Woman's Labor," p. 269.) The second poem, "Written a Few Hours before the Birth of a Child" (1786), belongs to the genre of childbed poems. The speaker's final wish—that, should she die, her child die too—reminds us that childbirth remained highly perilous for women during this period.

Written by Desire of a Lady, on an Angry, Petulant Kitchen-Maid

Good Mistress Dishclout,[1] what's the matter?
Why here the spoon—and there the platter?
What demon causes all this lowering,
Black as the pot you oft are scouring?

---

9. French; a reference to the French and Indian Wars.　　1. Dishrag.

Hot as the fire you daily light, 5
Your speech with low invectives blight,
While rage impregnates every vein,
And dyes the face one crimson stain.
    Sure, someone has a word misplaced,
Or looked not equal to your taste; 10
Or, is this just the time you've chose
Your great acquirements to disclose,
Display the graces of your tongue,
Show with what eloquence 'tis hung,
as "dog, rogue, scoundrel, scrub", what not, 15
And twenty more I've quite forgot;
Which prove to a demonstration
You've had a liberal education?
Such titles must enchant the ear,
And make the bounteous donor dear; 20
But while these bounties are dispensing,
I wish I'd learned the art of fencing,
Lest, while at John you aim to throw,
My nob should chance to catch the blow;
Then I should get a broken pate, 25
And marks of violence I hate.
    Good Mistress Dishclout, condescend
To hear the counsel of a friend:
When next you are disposed to brawl,
Pray let the scullery hear it all, 30
And learn to know your fittest place
Is with the dishes and the grease;
And, when you are inclined to battle,
Engage the skimmer, spit, or kettle,
Or any other kitchen guest, 35
Which you in wisdom might think best.

1783

Written a Few Hours before the Birth of a Child

My God, prepare me for that hour
   When most thy aid I want;
Uphold me by thy mighty power,
   Nor let my spirits faint.

I ask not life, I ask not ease, 5
   But patience to submit
To what shall best thy goodness please,
   Then come what thou seest fit.

Come pain, or agony, or death,
   If such the will divine; 10
With joy shall I give up my breath,
   If resignation's mine.

>   One wish to name I'd humbly dare,
>   If death thy pleasure be;
>   O may the harmless babe I bear   15
>   Haply expire with me.

                                                         1786

◄ ELIZA FAY ►
1756–1816

When the novelist E. M. Forster condescendingly wrote that Eliza Fay's "mental equipment was that of an intelligent lady's maid," he did her a profound injustice. Despite her adverse circumstances, Fay embodies a sharp wit and deep powers of perception. History obscures her origins—even her birth name is unknown—but she was probably born in Blackheath, near London. Because of her familiarity with nautical experience, some guess that her father may have been a sailor. Her uneven knowledge of geography suggests that she may not have had access to a formal education, though she appears to have been able to read French, Italian, and Portuguese. We also know that her husband, Anthony Fay, was of Irish descent and the only son of a gentleman.

Over the course of her lifetime, Fay took four trips to India; all appear to have been motivated by hopes of financial gain. She took her first trip (1779–82) with her husband, who had been called to practice law as an advocate for the Supreme Court of Calcutta. His motive for traveling to India with his new wife was probably to make a reputation for himself, since the Indian subcontinent was, in the days of colonial expansion, the preferred destination for those whose career opportunities were otherwise limited in England. Their remarkable journey—recorded in Fay's *Original Letters from India* (1817)—took the couple to France (then at war with England), across the Alps to Italy and onto a boat to Egypt, across the desert by caravan (in the days before the Suez Canal, a very perilous trip, as bandits frequently preyed on travelers), and finally onto a ship bound for Bombay.

Fay's journal from that period records their arduous journey as well as a range of extraordinary experiences, among them her harrowing fifteen weeks as a prisoner of a local Indian governor, held in a fort located off the coast of Calicut, in southern India. During their first Indian sojourn, the Fays' marriage broke up—perhaps because Anthony had fathered an illegitimate child. Anthony went bankrupt, the couple separated, and Eliza Fay returned to England in 1782. In 1784 she returned to India alone to establish a dressmaker's shop, but it went bankrupt in 1788; and she returned home in 1794, leaving us no record of how she spent the intervening years in India. We do know that in 1794 she invested in a boat that exploded, thereby losing her money again. In 1796 she spent six months in India, hoping to make money off a cargo of muslins to be exported to the United States, but the muslins were ruined by water damage on the boat. Her last trip to India occurred in 1816, when she was sixty years old; she died there and was buried in a nameless Calcutta cemetery, leaving extensive debts behind her.

Fay's talents lie in her keen ability to observe manners and social and cultural nuances in a range of social settings. In the following letters, describing first eighteenth-century Madras and then Calcutta, she writes with a refreshing honesty. Although she is rarely impartial, she nonetheless offers us an accurate view of how an eighteenth-century Englishwoman would have struggled to convey and comprehend the profound cultural differences she encountered in colonial India.

From Original Letters from India
Letter XIV [Madras]

Madras, 13th April. [1780]

My Dear Friends,

Agreeably to my promise I take up the pen to give you some account of this settlement, which has proved to me a pleasant resting-place after the many hardships and distresses it has lately been my lot to encounter; and where in the kind attentions and agreeable society of some of my own sex, I have found myself soothed and consoled for the long want of that comfort; while my health has in general reaped great advantages from the same source.

There is something uncommonly striking and grand in this town, and its whole appearance charms you from novelty, as well as beauty. Many of the houses and public buildings are very extensive and elegant—they are covered with a sort of shell-lime which takes a polish like marble, and produces a wonderful effect.—I could have fancied myself transported into Italy, so magnificently are they decorated, yet with the utmost taste. People here say that the *chunam* as it is called, loses its properties when transported to Bengal, where the dampness of the atmosphere,

Life in colonial India. (*The Honorable William Monson and His Wife, Ann Debonnaire,* c. 1786, by Arthur William Devis)

prevents it from receiving that exquisite polish so much admired by all who visit Madras. This may very likely be the case.

The free exercise of all religions being allowed; the different sects seem to vie with each other in ornamenting their places of worship, which are in general well built, and from their great variety, and novel forms afford much gratification, particularly when viewed from the country, as the beautiful groups of trees intermingle their tall forms and majestic foliage, with the white chunam and rising spires, communicating such harmony softness and elegance to the scene, as to be altogether delightful; and rather resembling the images that float on the imagination after reading fairy tales, or the Arabian nights entertainment, than any thing in real life; in fact Madras *is* what I conceived Grand Cairo to be, before I was so unlucky as to be undeceived. This idea is still further heightened by the intermixture of inhabitants; by seeing Asiatic splendour, combined with European taste exhibited around you on every side, under the forms of flowing drapery, stately palanquins,[1] elegant carriages, innumerable servants, and all the pomp and circumstance of luxurious ease, and unbounded wealth. It is true this glittering surface is here, and there tinged with the sombre hue that more or less colours every condition of life;—you behold Europeans, languishing under various complaints which they call incidental to the climate, an assertion it would ill become a stranger like myself to controvert, but respecting which I am a little sceptical; because I see very plainly that the same mode of living, would produce the same effects, even "in the hardy regions of the North." You may likewise perceive that human nature has its faults and follies every where, and that *black* rogues are to the full as common as white ones, but in my opinion more impudent. On your arrival you are pestered with Dubashees, and servants of all kinds who crouch to you as if they were already your slaves, but who will cheat you in every possible way; though in fact there is no living without one of the former to manage your affairs as a kind of steward, and you may deem yourself very fortunate if you procure one in this land of pillagers, who will let nobody cheat you but himself. I wish these people would not vex one by their tricks; for there is something in the mild countenances and gentle manners of the Hindoos that interests me exceedingly.

* * *

We have made several excursions in the neighbourhood of Madras which is every where delightful, the whole vicinity being ornamented with gentlemen's houses built in a shewy style of architecture, and covered with that beautiful chunam. As they are almost surrounded by trees, when you see one of these superb dwellings incompassed by a grove, a distant view of Madras with the sea and shipping, so disposed as to form a perfect landscape, it is beyond comparison the most charming picture I ever beheld or could have imagined. Wonder not at my enthusiasm; so long shut up from every pleasing object, it is natural that my feelings should be powerfully excited when such are presented to me.

Nothing is more terrible at Madras than the surf which as I hinted before, is not only alarming but dangerous. They have here two kinds of boats to guard against this great evil, but yet, notwithstanding every care, many lives are lost. One of these conveyances called the Massulah boat, is large, but remarkably light, and the planks of which it is constructed are actually sewed together by the fibres of the Cocoa-nut. It is well calculated to stem the violence of the surf but for greater safety it requires to be attended by the other, called a Catamaran, which is

---

1. An enclosed chair supported by two poles carried on the shoulders by four men.

merely composed of bamboos fastened together and paddled by one man. Two or three of these attend the Massulah boat, and in case of its being overset usually pick up the drowning passengers. The dexterity with which they manage these things is inconceivable;—but no dexterity can entirely ward off the danger. The beach is remarkably fine.

The ladies here are very fashionable I assure you: I found several novelties in dress since I quitted England, which a good deal surprised me, as I had no idea that fashions travelled so fast. It is customary to take the air in carriages every evening in the environs of Madras: for excursions in the country these are commonly used; but in town they have Palanquins carried by four bearers, which I prefer. They are often beautifully ornamented, and appear in character with the country, and with the languid air of those who use them, which, though very different from any thing I have been accustomed to admire in a woman as you well know, yet is not unpleasing in a country the charms of which are heightened by exhibiting a view of society entirely new to me.

*   *   *

The Black town is that part of Madras, which was formerly inhabited wholly by the natives, but of late many Europeans have taken houses there, rents being considerably lower than in Fort St. George, which is a very strong Garrison, built by the English, and where since have been constructed many fine houses, &c.— this is considered of course a more fashionable place to reside in. Between the Black town and the Fort, lies Choultry Plain which being covered entirely with a whitish sand, reflects such a dazzling light, and intolerable heat, as to render it a terrible annoyance especially to strangers. Mr. Fay has been exceedingly pressed to take up his abode here, and really many substantial inducements have been held out to him; but as his views have been all directed to Calcutta, where knowledge and talents are most likely to meet encouragement he cannot be persuaded to remain. Besides, a capital objection is, that no Supreme Court being as yet established he could be only admitted to practise as an attorney, no advocates being allowed in the Mayors Court: so that his rank as a Barrister would avail nothing here: I most cordially acquiesce in this determination. But I must suspend my scribbling; Mr. P——is waiting to take me to St. Thomas's Mount.[2]

Letter XV [Calcutta]

[Calcutta, 22 May 1780]

*   *   *

Calcutta, you know is on the Hoogly, a branch of the Ganges, and as you enter Garden-reach which extends about nine miles below the town, the most interesting views that can possibly be imagined greet the eye. The banks of the river are as one may say absolutely studded with elegant mansions, called here as at Madras, garden-houses. These houses are surrounded by groves and lawns, which descend to the waters edge, and present a constant succession of whatever can delight the eye, or bespeak wealth and elegance in the owners. The noble appearance of the river also, which is much wider than the Thames at London bridge, together with the amazing variety of vessels continually passing on its surface, add to the beauty of the scene. Some of these are so whimsically constructed as to

2. Mr. Popham: an acquaintance Fay met in Madras whom Fay describes as eccentric and visionary; St. Thomas's Mount: the purported loca-   tion of the apostle Thomas's murder (c. 68 CE) on a rocky hill in southwestern Madras.

charm by their novelty. I was much pleased with the snake boat in particular. Budgerows somewhat resembling our city barges, are very common,—many of these are spacious enough to accommodate a large family. Besides these the different kinds of pleasure boats intermixed with mercantile vessels, and ships of war, render the whole a magnificent and beautiful moving picture; at once exhilarating the heart, and charming the senses: for every object of sight is viewed through a medium that heightens its attraction in this brilliant climate.

The town of Calcutta reaches along the eastern bank of the Hoogly; as you come up past Fort William and the Esplanade it has a beautiful appearance. Esplanade-row, as it is called, which fronts the Fort, seems to be composed of palaces; the whole range, except what is taken up by the Government and Council houses, is occupied by the principal gentlemen in the settlement—no person being allowed to reside in Fort William, but such as are attached to the Army, gives it greatly the advantage over Fort St. George, which is so incumbered with buildings of one kind or other, that it has more the look of a town than of a military Garrison. Our Fort is also so well kept and every thing in such excellent order, that it is quite a curiosity to see it—all the slopes, banks, and ramparts, are covered with the richest verdure, which completes the enchantment of the scene. Indeed the general aspect of the country is astonishing; notwithstanding the extreme heat (the thermometer seldom standing below ninety in the afternoon) I never saw a more vivid green than adorns the surrounding fields—not that parched miserable look our lands have during the summer heats;—large fissures opening in the earth, as if all vegetation were suspended; in fact the copious dews which fall at night, restore moisture to the ground, and cause a short thick grass to spring up, which makes the finest food imaginable for the cattle. Bengal mutton, always good, is at this period excellent—I must not forget to tell you that there is a very good race ground at a short distance from Calcutta, which is a place of fashionable resort, for morning and evening airings.

* * *

I am ever most affectionately your's,

E. F.

Letter XVI

Calcutta, 29th August [1780]

My Dear Friends,

* * *

I am happy to say that our house is a very comfortable one, but we are surrounded by a set of thieves. In England, if servants are dishonest we punish them, or turn them away in disgrace, and their fate proves, it may be hoped, a warning to others; but these wretches have no sense of shame. I will give you an instance or two of their conduct, that you may perceive how enviably I am situated. My Khansaman (or house steward) brought in a charge of a gallon of milk and thirteen eggs, for making scarcely a pint and half of custard; this was so barefaced a cheat, that I refused to allow it, on which he gave me warning. I sent for another, and, after I had hired him, "now said I, take notice friend, I have enquired into the market price of every article that enters my house and will submit to no imposition; you must therefore agree to deliver in a just account to me every morning"—what reply do you think he made? why he demanded double wages; you may be sure I dismissed him, and have since forgiven the first but not till he had *salaamed* to my foot, that is placed his right hand under my foot,—this is the most abject token of submission (alas! how much better should I like a little common honesty.) I know him to be a rogue, and so are they all, but as he understands me now, he will perhaps be induced to use rather more moderation in his attempts to defraud.—At first he used to charge me with twelve ounces of butter a day, for each person; now he grants that the consumption is only four ounces. As if these people were aware that I am writing about them, they have very obligingly furnished me with another anecdote. It seems my comprodore (or market man) is gone away; he says poor servants have no profit by staying with *me;* at other gentlemen's houses he always made a rupee a day at least! besides his wages; but here if he only charges an anna or two more, it is sure to be taken off—So you see what a terrible creature I am! I dare say you never gave me credit for being so close.—I find I was imposed on, in taking a comprodore at all; the Khansaman ought to do that business. Judge whether I have not sufficient employment among these harpies? feeling as I do the necessity of a reasonable economy. It is astonishing, and would be amusing if one did not suffer by it, to see the various arts they will practice to keep a few annas in their hands, for though the lawful interest of money is but 12 per Cent (enough you will say), yet twenty four is given by the shopkeepers, who will lend or borrow the smallest sums for a single day, and ascertain the precise interest to the greatest exactitude, having the advantage of cowrees, 5,120 of which go to make one rupee. The foolish custom which subsists here of keeping Banians,[3] gives rise to a thousand deceptions, as no one pays or receives money but through the medium of these people who have their profit on every thing that comes into the house.

In order to give you an idea of my household expenses and the price of living here, I must inform you that, our house costs only 200 rupees per month, because it is not in a part of the town much esteemed; otherwise we must pay 3 or 400 rupees;[4] we are now seeking for a better situation. We were very frequently told in England you know, that the heat in Bengal destroyed the appetite, I must own that I never yet saw any proof of that; on the contrary I cannot help thinking that I never saw an equal quantity of victuals consumed. We dine too at two o'clock, in the very heat of the day. At this moment Mr. F—— is looking out with an hawk's eye, for his dinner; and though still much of an invalid, I have no doubt of being able to pick a bit myself. I will give you our bill of fare, and the general prices of things. A soup, a roast fowl, curry and rice, a mutton pie, a fore quarter of lamb, a rice pudding, tarts, very good cheese, fresh churned butter, fine bread, excellent Madeira[5] (that is expensive but eatables are very cheap,)—a whole sheep costs but two rupees: a lamb one rupee, six good fowls or ducks ditto—twelve pigeons ditto—twelve pounds of bread ditto—two pounds butter ditto; and a joint of veal ditto—good cheese two months ago sold at the enormous price of three or four rupees per pound, but now you may buy it for one and a half—English claret sells at this time for sixty rupees a dozen. There's a price for you! I need not say that much of it will not be seen at our table; now and then we are forced to produce it,

3. Native interpreter, negotiator, and broker for European merchants in India.

4. The value of a rupee against the British pound sterling in 1780 is difficult to ascertain; a rupee in the early eighteenth century was worth about one-tenth of a pound, and a pound in 1710 would have been worth over $200 in today's money. But exchange rates could have varied considerably between the first part of the century and 1780, when this letter was written.

5. Fortified wine.

but very seldom. I assure you much caution is requisite to avoid running deeply in debt—the facility of obtaining credit is beyond what I could have imagined; the Europe shop keepers are always ready to send in goods; and the Banians are so anxious to get into employment, that they out bid each other. One says "master better take me, I will advance five thousand rupees"—another offers seven, and perhaps a third ten thousand: a Company's servant particularly will always find numbers ready to support his extravagance. It is not uncommon to see *writers* within a few months after their arrivals dashing away on the course *four in hand:*[6] allowing for the inconsiderateness of youth, is it surprising if many become deeply embarrassed?—Several have been pointed out to me, who in the course of two or three years, have involved themselves almost beyond hope of redemption. The interest of money here being twelve per Cent, and the Banian taking care to secure bonds for whatever he advances, making up the account yearly and adding the sum due for interest, his thoughtless *master,* (as he calls him, but in fact his slave) soon finds his debt doubled, and dares not complain unless he has the means of release which alas! are denied him.

I should have told you before that Mr. F—— was admitted an advocate in the Supreme Court, on the 16th June,—has been engaged in several causes, wherein he acquitted himself to general satisfaction and is at present as busy as can be desired. Every one seems willing to encourage him and if he continue but his own friend, all will, I feel persuaded, go well with us, and we shall collect our share of gold mohurs,[7] as well as our neighbours.—I like to see the briefs come in well enough. The fees are much higher here than in England, so you will say "they ought" and I perfectly agree with you.

* * *

19th December.

Mr. Fay has met with a gentleman here, a Dr. Jackson who comes from the same part of Ireland, and knows many of his connections; they soon became intimate. Dr. J—— is physician to the Company, and in very high practice besides; I have been visited by the whole family. The eldest son a fine noble looking young man, is a Lieutenant in the Army, and has lately married a very pretty little woman, who came out in the same ship under the protection of his mother; as did Miss Chantry a most amiable and interesting young Lady, who now resides with them. They have not been long arrived. The Doctor's Lady is a native of Jamaica and like those "children of the sun,"[8] frank and hospitable to a degree—fond of social parties in the old style "where the song and merry jest circulate round the festive board" particularly after supper. Dinner parties they seldom give; but I have been present at several elsewhere since the commencement of the cold season. The dinner hour as I mentioned before is two, and it is customary to sit a long while at table; particularly during the cold season; for people here are mighty fond of grills and stews, which they season themselves, and generally make very hot. The Burdwan stew takes a deal of time; it is composed of every thing at table, fish, flesh and fowl;—somewhat like the Spanish Olla Podrida,[9]—Many suppose that unless prepared in a silver saucepan it cannot be good; on this point I must

---

6. A vehicle with four horses driven by one person.
7. Gold coin worth fifteen rupees.
8. From Edward Young (1683–1765), *The Re-*

venge, 5.2.268–69: "Souls made of fire, and children of the sun, / With whom revenge is virtue."
9. A spicy meat and vegetable stew.

not presume to give an opinion, being satisfied with plain food; and never tasting any of these incentives to luxurious indulgence. During dinner a good deal of wine is drank, but a very little after the cloth is removed; except in Bachelors parties, as they are called; for the custom of reposing, if not of sleeping after dinner is so general that the streets of Calcutta are from four to five in the afternoon almost as empty of Europeans as if it were midnight—Next come the evening airings to the Course, every one goes, though sure of being half suffocated with dust. On returning from thence, tea is served, and universally drank here, even during the extreme heats. After tea, either cards or music fill up the space, 'till ten, when supper is generally announced. Five card loo is the usual game and they play a rupee a fish limited to ten. This will strike you as being enormously high but it is thought nothing of here. Tré dille and Whist are much in fashion but ladies seldom join in the latter; for though the stakes are moderate, bets frequently run high among the gentlemen which renders those anxious who sit down for amusement, lest others should lose by their blunders.[1]

Formal visits are paid in the evening; they are generally very short, as perhaps each lady has a dozen to make and a party waiting for her at home besides. Gentlemen also call to offer their respects and if asked to put down their hat, it is considered as an invitation to supper. Many a hat have I seen vainly dangling in its owner's hand for half an hour, who at last has been compelled to withdraw without any one's offering to relieve him from the burthen.

Great preparations are making for the Christmas, and New year's public balls;—of course you will not expect me to write much till they are over; nor to own the truth am I in spirits, having great reason to be dissatisfied with Mr. Fay's conduct. Instead of cultivating the intimacy of those who might be serviceable or paying the necessary attention to persons in power; I can scarcely ever prevail on him to accompany me even to Dr. Jackson's who is generally visited by the first people; but he cannot endure being subjected to the forms of society. * * * I will now close this letter in the hope of having better accounts to give you in my next.

Your's affectionately
E. F.

Letter XX

Calcutta, 28 August, 1781

My Dear Sister—

* * *

I now propose, having full leisure to give you some account of the East Indian customs and ceremonies, such as I have been able to collect, but it must be considered as a mere sketch, to point your further researches. And first for that horrible custom of widows burning themselves with the dead bodies of their husbands; the fact is indubitable, but I have never had an opportunity of witnessing the various incidental ceremonies, nor have I ever seen any European who had been present at them. I cannot suppose that the usage originated in the superior tenderness, and

1. Five card loo, tré dille, and whist are all card games in which the players wager to take "tricks" alone or with their partners by trumping cards thrown down by the other players; in five card loo, players must take at least one trick or contribute to the pot—this "contribution" is probably what is referred to as a "fish."

ardent attachment of Indian wives towards their spouses, since the same tenderness and ardour would doubtless extend to his offspring and prevent them from exposing the innocent survivors to the miseries attendant on an orphan state, and they would see clearly that to live and cherish these pledges of affection would be the most rational and natural way of shewing their regard for both husband and children. I apprehend that as personal fondness can have no part here at all, since all matches are made between the parents of the parties who are betrothed to each other at too early a period for choice to be consulted, this practice is entirely a political scheme intended to insure the care and good offices of wives to their husbands, who have not failed in most countries to invent a sufficient number of rules to render the weaker sex totally subservient to their authority. I cannot avoid smiling when I hear gentlemen bring forward the conduct of the Hindoo women, as a test of superior character, since I am well aware that so much are we the slaves of habit *every where* that were it necessary for a woman's reputation to burn herself in England, many a one who has *accepted* a husband merely for the sake of an establishment, who has lived with him without affection; perhaps thwarted his views, dissipated his fortune and rendered his life uncomfortable to its close, would yet mount the funeral pile with all imaginable decency and die with heroic fortitude. The most specious sacrifices are not always the greatest, she who wages war with a naturally petulant temper, who practises a rigid self-denial, endures without complaining the unkindness, infidelity, extravagance, meanness or scorn, of the man to whom she has given a tender and confiding heart, and for whose happiness and well being in life all the powers of her mind are engaged;—is ten times more of a heroine than the slave of bigotry and superstition, who affects to scorn the life demanded of her by the laws of her country or at least that country's custom; and many such we have in England, and I doubt not in India likewise: so indeed we ought, have we not a religion infinitely more pure than that of India? The Hindoos, or gentoos are divided into four castes or tribes called the Brahmin, the Khutree, the Buesho, and the Shodor: their rank in the land, declines gradually to the last named, and if any of them commit an offence which deprives them of the privileges that belong to their respective castes, they become Parias, which may therefore be called a filthy tribe formed as it were of the refuse of the rest. Those are indeed considered the very dregs of the people, and supply all the lowest offices of human life. They all profess what is called the religion of Brahma, from the caste which bears his name all the priests are chosen, who are treated in every respect with distinguished honour and reverence. Their religious Code is contained in a book called the Veda, which only the Brahmins are allowed to read; it is written in a dead language called the Sanscrit. They worship three Deities, Brahma, the creator, Vistnoo the preserver, and Sheevah the destroyer. But they profess to believe them only the representations or types of the great spirit Brahma (the Supreme God) whom they also call the spirit of wisdom, and the principle of Truth: none but Hindoos are allowed to enter temples, but I am told the Idols worshipped there are of the very ugliest forms that imagination can conceive; and to whom Pope's description of the heathen deities may, in other respects, be strictly applied.

"Gods changeful, partial, passionate unjust.
Whose attributes *are* rage, revenge, or lust."[2]

2. Alexander Pope (1688–1744), *An Essay on Man,* Epistle 3:256–57.

I lament to add to such wretched objects as these, numbers of the deluded natives are devoted in the strongest and most absolute manner possible. A certain sect named Pundarams live in continual beggary; extreme hunger alone induces them to ask for food, which when granted, they only take just what will preserve life, and spend all their days in singing songs in praise of Sheevah; another sect add a tabor, and hollow brass rings about their ancles to increase the noise with which they extol *their* deity. I consider both these as a species of monks but believe the holy fathers fall far short of the Jogees and Seniases of India, in their religious austerities. These not only endure all possible privations with apparent indifference, but invent for themselves various kinds of tortures which they carry to an astonishing length; such as keeping their hands clenched 'till the nails grow into them,—standing on one foot for days and even weeks together—and hiring people to support their hands in a perpendicular position.

Their expiatory punishments are some of them dreadful. I myself saw a man running in the streets with a piece of iron thrust through his tongue which was bleeding profusely. On the Churruk Poojah (swinging feast) hundreds I have heard, are suspended at an amazing height by means of hooks, firmly fixed in the flesh of the back, to which sometimes a cloth is added round the body to afford the miserable victim a chance of escape, should the hook give way. I, by accident, (for voluntarily nothing should have tempted me to witness such a spectacle) saw one of these wretches, who was whirling round with surprizing rapidity, and at that distance scarcely appeared to retain the semblance of a human form. They firmly expect by this infliction to obtain pardon of all their offences, and should death be the consequence, they go straight to heaven—thus changing the horrid state of privation and misery in which they exist here, for one of bliss: if such be their real persuasion, who can condemn the result.

Indeed under other circumstances it is found that, notwithstanding their apparent gentleness and timidity, the Hindoos will meet death with intrepid firmness—they are also invincibly obstinate, and will *die* rather than concede a point: of this a very painful instance has lately occurred.—A Hindoo beggar of the Brahmin caste went to the house of a very rich man, but of an inferior tribe, requesting alms; he was either rejected, or considered himself inadequately relieved, and refused to quit the place. As his lying before the door and thus obstructing the passage was unpleasant, one of the servants first intreated, then insisted on his retiring, and in speaking pushed him gently away; he chose to call this push a blow, and cried aloud for redress, declaring that he would never stir from the spot 'till he had obtained justice against the man: who now endeavoured to sooth him but in vain; like a true Hindoo he sat down, and never moved again, but thirty-eight hours afterwards expired, demanding justice with his latest breath; being well aware that in the event of this, the master would have an enormous fine to pay, which accordingly happened. I am assured that such evidences of the surprizing indifference to life, the inflexible stubbornness, and vindictive dispositions of these people are by no means rare; it seems extraordinary though, that sentiments and feelings apparently so contrary to each other should operate on the same minds; seeing them so quiet and supine, so (if it may be so expressed) only half alive, as they generally shew themselves, one is prepared for their sinking, without an effort to avert any impending danger; but that they should at the same time nourish so violent and active a passion as revenge, and brave even death so intrepidly as they often do in pursuit of it, is very singular:—but enough of these silly enthusiasts.

I had lately the opportunity of witnessing the marriage procession of a rich Hindoo. The bride (as I was told) sat in the same palanquin with the bridegroom, which was splendidly ornamented;—they were accompanied by all the relations on both sides, dressed in the most superb manner;—some on horse back, some in palanquins, and several on elephants;—bands of dancing girls and musicians I understood preceded them;—and in the evening there were fireworks at the bride's father's house and the appearance of much feasting &c. but no Europeans were present. This wedding was of a nature by no means uncommon here; a rich man had an only daughter, and he bargained to dispose of her, or rather to take for her a husband out of a poor man's family, but of his own *Caste*: for this is indispensable. In this case the bridegroom is brought home to his father-in-law's house and becomes a member of the family; so that although the law prohibits a man from giving a dowry with his daughter, yet you see he does it in effect, since he gives a house to a man who wants one; gives in fact, a fortune but saddled with an encumbrance;—perhaps in a few years the old man may die, and the young one having fulfilled the wishes of his parents, and provided for his own wants, may employ some of his female relations to look round among the poorer families of his caste for a pretty girl, whom he will take as a second wife, tho' the first always retains the pre-eminence, and governs the house; nor can the husband devote more of his time to one than the other,—the law compelling him to live with them alternately, you may be sure the account is strictly kept. My Banian Dattaram Chuckerbutty has been married between twenty and thirty years, without taking a second lady, and he boasts of being much happier with his old wife (as he calls her) than the generality of his friends are amidst the charms of variety. For my own part, I have not a doubt but he is in the right.

The Hindoo ladies are never seen abroad; when they go out their carriages are closely covered with curtains, so that one has little chance of satisfying curiosity. I once saw two apparently very beautiful women: they use so much art however, as renders it difficult to judge what claim they *really* have to that appellation—Their whole time is taken up in decorating their persons:—the hair—eye-lids—eye-brows—teeth—hands and nails, all undergo certain processes to render them more completely fascinating; nor can one seriously blame their having recourse to these, or the like artifices—the motive being to secure the affections of a husband, or to counteract the plans of a rival.

* * *

Your's most affectionately
E. F.

MARY DARBY ROBINSON
1758–1800

Once the notorious mistress of the Prince Regent (later King George IV), Mary Darby Robinson outlived her social celebrity to garner well-deserved respect for her abundant literary production, including six volumes of poetry, eight novels, and two plays, all produced between 1775 and 1800.

Born in Bristol, England, Robinson grew up in a family of seven plagued by financial difficulties. As a child, Robinson was educated at Hannah More's school in Bristol and later in Chelsea, where she learned several languages. Her father, a merchant named John Darby, had left for Newfoundland in 1760 to set up a whaling station, and his long absence put a strain on the family's resources. When his wife, Hester Seys Darby, opened a school in his absence and put the teenage Mary to work as a language tutor, he took objection and forced Robinson to stop working in her mother's school. Robinson then attended a finishing school at Marylebone, where she met the famous actor David Garrick, with whom she became friends.

In April 1774, at age fourteen, she married Thomas Robinson, a law clerk who had apparently exaggerated his financial prospects. Eventually her husband's profligacy forced the family to flee to Wales to escape his creditors. Robinson's daughter Mary Elizabeth was born on November 18, 1774, when Robinson was only fifteen. After her husband was arrested for debt in 1775, the family lived together in jail for ten months. There, Robinson published a volume of poems with the assistance of the Duchess of Devonshire.

To help the family's finances, Robinson's husband encouraged her to take to the stage. She was engaged at the Drury Lane Theatre, where she played Juliet and Cordelia to Garrick's Lear. Her career lasted for four seasons, during which time she experienced the death of her second child. In 1779, the future king of England saw her playing Perdita—a character in Shakespeare's *A Winter's Tale*—and fell instantly in love with her. Robinson became a celebrity. With her marriage over, she became the prince's mistress on the promise of £20,000 (equivalent to about $4 million today) when he came of age. But the prince lost interest in Robinson, and the promise was broken, though she did receive some money in exchange for the prince's letters, as well as a small annuity. Hounded by the press, she was forced to quit the stage.

After several other unsuccessful relationships, Robinson met an army officer back from the American Revolutionary War, Colonel Banastre Tarleton. When his debts forced him to flee to Europe, Robinson followed, but she suffered a miscarriage that left her partially paralyzed.

By 1788 Robinson was back in England, now with her daughter. She began to contribute poetical exchanges to newspapers, including *The World* and *The Oracle*. During this period she wrote prodigiously, producing several volumes of poetry, novels (including *Angelina*, 1796, and *The Natural Daughter*, 1799), and an essay, published pseudonymously, titled "A Letter to the Women of England, on the Injustice of Mental Insubordination" (1799). She also helped Tarleton write a history of the American Revolution in 1788. From 1799 to 1800 she was a paid contributor to a newspaper called the *Morning Post*. In the first four months of 1800, she published forty-five poems. She was also befriended by the English Romantic poet Samuel Taylor Coleridge (1772–1834), who admired her work and sent her a manuscript copy of his poem "Kubla Khan" (written 1797; published 1816). Robinson left an unfinished autobiography when she died.

In 1801, her daughter edited her memoirs, in which she promised "to show the exposed situation of an unprotected beauty . . . exposed to the gaze of libertine rank and fashion, under the mere nominal guardianship of a neglectful and profligate husband." The following two poems demonstrate the keen powers of perception that allowed Robinson to convey the intimate details of daily life, as seen from the streets, and to deliver trenchant, yet subtle, social critique.

London's Summer Morning

Who has not waked to list the busy sounds
Of summer's morning, in the sultry smoke
Of noisy London? On the pavement hot
The sooty chimney-boy, with dingy face
And tattered covering, shrilly bawls his trade,   5
Rousing the sleepy housemaid. At the door
The milk-pail rattles, and the tinkling bell
Proclaims the dustman's[1] office; while the street
Is lost in clouds impervious. Now begins
The din of hackney-coaches,[2] waggons, carts;   10
While tinmen's shops, and noisy trunk-makers,
Knife-grinders, coopers, squeaking cork-cutters,
Fruit-barrows, and the hunger-giving cries
Of vegetable-vendors, fill the air.
Now every shop displays its varied trade,   15
And the fresh-sprinkled pavement cools the feet
Of early walkers. At the private door
The ruddy housemaid twirls the busy mop,
Annoying the smart 'prentice, or neat girl,
Tripping with band-box[3] lightly. Now the sun   20
Darts burning splendour on the glittering pane,
Save where the canvas awning throws a shade
On the gay merchandise. Now, spruce and trim,
In shops (where beauty smiles with industry)
Sits the smart damsel; while the passenger   25
Peeps through the window, watching every charm.
Now pastry dainties catch the eye minute
Of humming insects, while the limy snare[4]
Waits to enthral them. Now the lamp-lighter
Mounts the tall ladder, nimbly vent'rous,   30
To trim the half-filled lamps, while at his feet
The pot-boy[5] yells discordant! All along
The sultry pavement, the old-clothes-man cries
In tone monotonous, and sidelong views
The area for his traffic: now the bag   35
Is slyly opened, and the half-worn suit
(Sometimes the pilfered treasure of the base
Domestic spoiler), for one half its worth,
Sinks in the green abyss. The porter now
Bears his huge load along the burning way;   40
And the poor poet wakes from busy dreams,
To paint the summer morning.

1794   1806

---

1. British term for garbage collector.   holding small articles of clothing.
2. A four-wheeled coach, seating six, available for   4. A fly trap filled with lime, a sticky substance
hire.   made from the bark of the holly tree.
3. A light box of cardboard or wood used for   5. Servant at an Inn or public house.

January, 1795

Pavement slippery, people sneezing,
Lords in ermine, beggars freezing;
Titled gluttons dainties carving,
Genius in a garret starving.

Lofty mansions, warm and spacious;   5
Courtiers cringing and voracious;
Misers scarce the wretched heeding;
Gallant soldiers fighting, bleeding.

Wives who laugh at passive spouses;
Theatres, and meeting-houses;   10
Balls, where simpering misses languish;
Hospitals, and groans of anguish.

Arts and sciences bewailing;
Commerce drooping, credit failing;
Placemen[6] mocking subjects loyal;   15
Separations, weddings royal.

Authors who can't earn a dinner;
Many a subtle rogue a winner;
Fugitives for shelter seeking;
Misers hoarding, tradesmen breaking.[7]   20

Taste and talents quite deserted;
All the laws of truth perverted;
Arrogance o'er merit soaring;
Merit silently deploring.

Ladies gambling night and morning;   25
Fools the works of genius scorning;
Ancient dames for girls mistaken,
Youthful damsels quite forsaken.

Some in luxury delighting;
More in talking than in fighting;   30
Lovers old, and beaux decrepid;
Lordlings empty and insipid.

Poets, painters, and musicians;
Lawyers, doctors, politicians:
Pamphlets, newspapers, and odes,   35
Seeking fame by different roads.

Gallant souls with empty purses,
Generals only fit for nurses;

---

6. Derogatory term for someone who, regardless   7. Going bankrupt.
of qualification, holds or aspires to political office.

School-boys, smit with martial spirit,
Taking place of veteran merit.   40

Honest men who can't get places,
Knaves who show unblushing faces;
Ruin hastened, peace retarded;
Candour spurned, and art[8] rewarded.

1795   1806

8. Artifice.

CULTURAL COORDINATES
Prostitution

O ver the course of the eighteenth century, English women experienced a loss of economic independence. Where laboring women had once had access to apprenticeships in a range of trades, from baking to pewter making, by midcentury only two trades were thought appropriate for young women—mantua making (dressmaking) and millinery (hat making). Even these trades were not considered entirely appropriate, as both put young girls in public places where they could be easily "corrupted." In addition, other livelihoods, like dairying, once the exclusive domain of women, were increasingly taken over by male managers, who argued that men were better suited to implement scientific improvements. By the end of the century, it would have been difficult for any lower- or middle-rank family to provide an independent means of economic survival for their daughters except through marriage to a man with solid prospects.

Working-class girls who did not marry and had no family to support them were left with few options for earning their bread besides prostitution. Historical evidence suggests that most prostitutes were poor women in their late teens or early twenties from outside London. Some of them may have been orphaned or

A Young Woman on the Road to Ruin; plate 1, The Harlot's Progress (1732) by William Hogarth.

abandoned by their parents. Others might have come to the city in search of work as domestic servants and fallen into prostitution when they were unable to find a position. A few might have turned to prostitution after the death of their spouses. Most prostitutes worked not in brothels (also called "stews") but outside, plying their trade in the streets, in public gardens (see *Evelina*, pp. 322–39), in public houses, or in bathhouses.

While there were a few highly successful prostitutes—like Mrs. Hays, who ran a society brothel and was said to be worth £20,000 (several million dollars today) when she retired—for the most part, prostitution was poorly paid and dangerous. It brought with it a high risk of venereal disease, incurable at the time and often treated with mercury, to deleterious effect. Prostitutes also ran the risk of being arrested for vagrancy or disorderly conduct. But many prostitutes were well integrated into the poor communities in which they lived. And often prostitution was a temporary occupation, lasting only a short time until another line of work could be procured.

Although some male writers—like Bernard Mandeville—argued that prostitutes were physically different from other women and therefore suited to their work, by midcentury a more sympathetic climate was emerging, as a movement directed at the reform of prostitutes began to take shape. While some social critics advocated the containment or punishment of prostitutes, who were to be disciplined into repentance, more progressive reformers recognized that women would need alternative ways of making a living if they were to leave prostitution behind.

◄ MARY WOLLSTONECRAFT ►

1759-1797

A woman of fierce intellect, Mary Wollstonecraft struggled passionately all her life against a range of social and political injustices, many of which she observed first-hand. She was born in Spitalfields, London, the second of seven children. Her grandfather had been a weaver who made enough money to raise his son, Edward, into gentility. But Edward failed as a gentleman farmer and became an alcoholic and an abusive husband and father, who frequently moved his wife—born Elizabeth Dickson—and his children from place to place in an attempt to survive financially.

Between the ages of nine and fifteen, Wollstonecraft attended a local school in Beverley, Yorkshire. In 1775, the family moved back to London, where she educated herself through free lectures, the library, and periodicals available in the coffee shop. It was in this period that she met Fanny Blood, with whom she developed a deep friendship. At the age of nineteen, she took her first job, as a companion to a wealthy widow in Bath. Although generally unhappy with a position requiring inordinate attention to dress and other superficialities, Wollstonecraft was able to observe keenly the higher ranks of English society through this role. Her observations would later inform her critique of social and political inequality. She returned home in 1781 to tend to her dying mother, in spite of her feeling that her mother had always favored the oldest son at the expense of the other children. While assuming financial responsibility for her own sisters, Wollstonecraft also took over the care of her friend Fanny Blood and her relations. In 1784, together with Fanny, she convinced her younger sister Eliza, who was stuck in an abusive marriage and in the throes of a deep post-partum depression, to run away from her husband with her baby.

Together with Eliza, Wollstonecraft and Fanny Blood opened a girls' school in Newington Green, near London, in 1784. They affiliated themselves with a nearby community of Dissenters—nonconformists who rejected the beliefs and practices of the Church of England—and met Dr. Richard Price, an author and ardent supporter of the French Revolution. But in 1785 Fanny left for Portugal to be with her lover Hugh Skeys. Following her friend, Wollstonecraft arrived in Lisbon just in time to witness Fanny's death in childbirth. By 1786, the school was experiencing a financial crisis, which Wollstonecraft tried to remedy by writing *Thoughts on the Education of Daughters* (1787). In the end, however, the little money she earned on the publication did not save the school but instead was used to help the remaining members of the Blood family.

On the closing of her school, Wollstonecraft briefly acted as a governess to the daughters of the aristocratic Lady Kingsborough. She was dismissed, however, when Lady Kingsborough felt that her daughters had become too attached to Wollstonecraft. While employed as a governess, Wollstonecraft wrote her first fiction, *Mary* (later published in 1788), based on the life of Fanny Blood.

In 1787, Wollstonecraft went to work for publisher Joseph Johnson. Her tasks included translating, reading, reviewing, and editing. Through Johnson, she met notable radical figures of the day, including Thomas Paine (1737–1809), an apologist for the American Revolution; Henry Fuseli (1741–1825), a German-Swiss painter; William Blake (1757–1827), an engraver and poet; William Godwin

(1756–1836), a political theorist; and Thomas Holcroft (1745–1809), a novelist and playwright. In 1790, she published *A Vindication of the Rights of Men*, in which she argued against the idea of privately held property and for the principles of liberty. Publication of her most famous work, *A Vindication of the Rights of Woman*, followed in 1792.

While the publication of the two *Vindication*s assured her high reputation as a notable public intellectual, her private life continued to be in turmoil. Expressing an unrequited love for married painter Henry Fuseli, she offered to join his family (an action as shocking and unusual then as it would be now), but Fuseli's wife sent her away. After this rejection, in 1792, she left England for France, where she immediately became caught up in the violent political strife of the Revolution. In response to her firsthand view of the Revolution, she wrote *An Historical and Moral View of the Origin and Progress of the French Revolution* in 1794. While in France, Wollstonecraft met and fell in love with the American speculator Gilbert Imlay, by whom she became pregnant. She gave birth to Fanny Imlay in 1794.

On her return to England in 1795, Wollstonecraft tried unsuccessfully to poison herself when she discovered that Imlay had been unfaithful to her. Imlay responded by sending her, her nursemaid, and her daughter to Scandinavia to represent his legal and business interests. Wollstonecraft's semipublic work, *Letters Written during a Short Residence in Sweden, Norway, and Demark*, was written during this period.

Upon her return to London, Wollstonecraft tried to kill herself once again after hearing of Imlay's further infidelity—this time, by jumping off Putney Bridge into the Thames—but she was rescued unconscious. She finally left Imlay in 1796 and reignited her earlier friendship with the rationalist thinker William Godwin, a man who understood both her intellectual interests and her emotional needs. Becoming pregnant a second time, Wollstonecraft privately married Godwin in 1797, despite the fact that both were known to be opposed to marriage. After their marriage, the couple lived independently in separate households. Their marriage was cut tragically short when Wollstonecraft died eleven days after giving birth to her daughter Mary—who later became Mary Shelley, the author of *Frankenstein*—from a prolonged fever caused by her infected placenta. A memoir of her life written by her husband, William Godwin, was published in 1798.

The following selections from *A Vindication of the Rights of Woman* bring into clear relief two of Wollstonecraft's most important arguments: first, that an unequal distribution of wealth corrupts everyone, not only the poor who struggle with their own destitution, but also the wealthy who are weakened by their luxuries and deprived of opportunities for meaningful labor; second, that women are disadvantaged by a philosophical and educational tradition that depicts them as "weak" creatures incapable of rational thought and that denies them the opportunity to contribute fully to society.

From A Vindication of the Rights of Woman with Strictures on Political and Moral Subjects

Author's Introduction

After considering the historic page, and viewing the living world with anxious solicitude, the most melancholy emotions of sorrowful indignation have depressed my spirits, and I have sighed when obliged to confess that either Nature has made a great difference between man and man, or that the civilization which has hitherto taken place in the world has been very partial. I have turned over various books written on the subject of education, and patiently observed the conduct of parents and the management of schools; but what has been the result?—a profound conviction that the neglected education of my fellow-creatures is the grand source of the misery I deplore, and that women, in particular, are rendered weak and wretched by a variety of concurring causes, originating from one hasty conclusion. The conduct and manners of women, in fact, evidently prove that their minds are not in a healthy state; for, like the flowers which are planted in too rich a soil, strength and usefulness are sacrificed to beauty; and the flaunting leaves, after having pleased a fastidious eye, fade, disregarded on the stalk, long before the season when they ought to have arrived at maturity. One cause of this barren blooming I attribute to a false system of education, gathered from the books written on this subject by men who, considering females rather as women than human creatures, have been more anxious to make them alluring mistresses than affectionate wives and rational mothers; and the understanding of the sex has been so bubbled by this specious homage, that the civilized women of the present century, with a few exceptions, are only anxious to inspire love, when they ought to cherish a nobler ambition, and by their abilities and virtues exact respect.

In a treatise, therefore, on female rights and manners, the works which have been particularly written for their improvement must not be overlooked, especially when it is asserted, in direct terms, that the minds of women are enfeebled by false refinement; that the books of instruction, written by men of genius, have had the same tendency as more frivolous productions; and that, in the true style of Mahometanism, they are treated as a kind of subordinate beings,[1] and not as a part of the human species, when improvable reason is allowed to be the dignified distinction which raises men above the brute creation, and puts a natural sceptre in a feeble hand.

Yet, because I am a woman, I would not lead my readers to suppose that I mean violently to agitate the contested question respecting the quality or inferiority of the sex; but as the subject lies in my way, and I cannot pass it over without subjecting the main tendency of my reasoning to misconstruction, I shall stop a moment to deliver, in a few words, my opinion. In the government of the physical world it is observable that the female in point of strength is, in general, inferior to the male. This is the law of Nature; and it does not appear to be suspended or abrogated in favour of woman. A degree of physical superiority cannot, therefore, be denied, and it is a noble prerogative! But not content with this natural pre-eminence, men endeavour to sink us still lower, merely to render us alluring objects for a moment; and women, intoxicated by the adoration which men, under the influence of their senses, pay them, do not seek to obtain a durable interest in their hearts, or to become the friends of the fellow-creatures who find amusement in their society.

I am aware of an obvious inference. From every quarter have I heard exclamations against masculine women, but where are they to be found? If by this appellation men mean to inveigh against their ardour in hunting, shooting, and gaming, I shall most cordially join in the cry; but if it be against the imitation of manly virtues, or, more properly speaking, the attainment of those talents and

---

1. Like most of her contemporaries, Wollstonecraft mistakenly believed that the Koran, the holy text of Islam, holds women in very low regard, even considering them soulless and disallowing them access to heaven.

virtues, the exercise of which ennobles the human character, and which raises females in the scale of animal being, when they are comprehensively termed mankind, all those who view them with a philosophic eye must, I should think, wish with me, that they may every day grow more and more masculine.

This discussion naturally divides the subject. I shall first consider women in the grand light of human creatures, who, in common with men, are placed on this earth to unfold their faculties; and afterwards I shall more particularly point out their peculiar designation.

I wish also to steer clear of an error which many respectable writers have fallen into; for the instruction which has hitherto been addressed to women, has rather been applicable to *ladies*, if the little indirect advice that is scattered through "Sandford and Merton"[2] be excepted; but, addressing my sex in a firmer tone, I pay particular attention to those in the middle class, because they appear to be in the most natural state.[3] Perhaps the seeds of false refinement, immorality, and vanity, have ever been shed by the great. Weak, artificial beings, raised above the common wants and affections of their race, in a premature unnatural manner, undermine the very foundation of virtue, and spread corruption through the whole mass of society! As a class of mankind they have the strongest claim to pity; the education of the rich tends to render them vain and helpless, and the unfolding mind is not strengthened by the practice of those duties which dignify the human character. They only live to amuse themselves, and by the same law which in Nature invariably produces certain effects, they soon only afford barren amusement.

But as I purpose taking a separate view of the different ranks of society, and of the moral character of women in each, this hint is for the present sufficient; and I have only alluded to the subject because it appears to me to be the very essence of an introduction to give a cursory account of the contents of the work it introduces.

My own sex, I hope, will excuse me, if I treat them like rational creatures, instead of flattering their *fascinating* graces, and viewing them as if they were in a state of perpetual childhood, unable to stand alone. I earnestly wish to point out in what true dignity and human happiness consists. I wish to persuade women to endeavour to acquire strength, both of mind and body, and to convince them that the soft phrases, susceptibility of heart, delicacy of sentiment, and refinement of taste, are almost synonymous with epithets of weakness, and that those beings who are only the objects of pity, and that kind of love which has been termed its sister, will soon become objects of contempt.

Dismissing, then, those pretty feminine phrases, which the men condescendingly use to soften our slavish dependence, and despising that weak elegancy of mind, exquisite sensibility, and sweet docility of manners, supposed to be the sexual characteristics of the weaker vessel, I wish to show that elegance is inferior to virtue, that the first object of laudable ambition is to obtain a character as a human being, regardless of the distinction of sex, and that secondary views should be brought to this simple touchstone.

This is a rough sketch of my plan; and should I express my conviction with the energetic emotions that I feel whenever I think of the subject, the dictates of

---

2. A moralistic three-volume children's story, *The History of Sandford and Merton* (1786–89) by Thomas Day, in which two children—the spoiled and wealthy Tommy Merton and the impover- ished and honorable Harry Sandford—learn many valuable life lessons.

3. That is, uncorrupted by property or great wealth.

experience and reflection will be felt by some of my readers. Animated by this important object, I shall disdain to cull my phrases or polish my style. I aim at being useful, and sincerity will render me unaffected; for wishing rather to persuade by the force of my arguments than dazzle by the elegance of my language, I shall not waste my time in rounding periods,[4] or in fabricating the turgid bombast of artificial feelings, which, coming from the head, never reach the heart. I shall be employed about things, not words! and, anxious to render my sex more respectable members of society, I shall try to avoid that flowery diction which has slided from essays into novels, and from novels into familiar letters and conversations.

These pretty superlatives, dropping glibly from the tongue, vitiate the taste, and create a kind of sickly delicacy that turns away from simple unadorned truth; and a deluge of false sentiments and overstretched feelings, stifling the natural emotions of the heart, render the domestic pleasures insipid, that ought to sweeten the exercise of those severe duties, which educate a rational and immortal being for a nobler field of action.

The education of women has of late been more attended to than formerly; yet they are still reckoned a frivolous sex, and ridiculed or pitied by the writers who endeavour by satire or instruction to improve them. It is acknowledged that they spend many of the first years of their lives in acquiring a smattering of accomplishments; meanwhile strength of body and mind are sacrificed to libertine notions of beauty, to the desire of establishing themselves—the only way women can rise in the world—by marriage. And this desire making mere animals of them, when they marry they act as such children may be expected to act—they dress, they paint, and nickname God's creatures.[5] Surely these weak beings are only fit for a seraglio![6] Can they be expected to govern a family with judgement, or take care of the poor babes whom they bring into the world?

If, then, it can be fairly deduced from the present conduct of the sex, from the prevalent fondness for pleasure which takes place of ambition and those nobler passions that open and enlarge the soul, that the instruction which women have hitherto received has only tended, with the constitution of civil society, to render them insignificant objects of desire—mere propagators of fools!—if it can be proved that in aiming to accomplish them, without cultivating their understandings, they are taken out of their sphere of duties, and made ridiculous and useless when the short-lived bloom of beauty is over,[7] I presume that *rational* men will excuse me for endeavouring to persuade them to become more masculine and respectable.

Indeed the word masculine is only a bugbear;[8] there is little reason to fear that women will acquire too much courage or fortitude, for their apparent inferiority with respect to bodily strength must render them in some degree dependent on men in the various relations of life; but why should it be increased by prejudices that give a sex to virtue, and confound simple truths with sensual reveries?

Women are, in fact, so much degraded by mistaken notions of female excellence, that I do not mean to add a paradox when I assert that this artificial weakness produces a propensity to tyrannize, and gives birth to cunning, the natural

---

4. Writing perfectly balanced sentences.
5. Echoing Hamlet's criticism of Ophelia's female behavior: "You jig, you amble, and you lisp and nickname God's creatures, and make your wantonness your ignorance" (3.1.146).
6. Harem.

7. A lively writer (I cannot recollect his name) asks what business women turned of forty have to do in the world? (Wollstonecraft's note).
8. A boogeyman, something imaginary that incites fear.

opponent of strength, which leads them to play off those contemptible infantine airs that undermine esteem even whilst they excite desire. Let men become more chaste and modest, and if women do not grow wiser in the same ratio it will be clear that they have weaker understandings. It seems scarcely necessary to say that I now speak of the sex in general. Many individuals have more sense than their male relatives; and, as nothing preponderates where there is a constant struggle for an equilibrium without[9] it has naturally more gravity, some women govern their husbands without degrading themselves, because intellect will always govern.

Chapter 2
The Prevailing Opinion of a Sexual Character Discussed

To account for, and excuse the tyranny of man, many ingenious arguments have been brought forward to prove, that the two sexes, in the acquirement of virtue, ought to aim at attaining a very different character; or, to speak explicitly, women are not allowed to have sufficient strength of mind to acquire what really deserves the name of virtue. Yet it should seem, allowing them to have souls, that there is but one way appointed by Providence to lead *mankind* to either virtue or happiness.

If then women are not a swarm of ephemeron[1] triflers, why should they be kept in ignorance under the specious name of innocence? Men complain, and with reason, of the follies and caprices of our sex, when they do not keenly satirise our headstrong passions and grovelling vices. Behold, I should answer, the natural effect of ignorance! The mind will ever be unstable that has only prejudices to rest on, and the current will run with destructive fury when there are no barriers to break its force. Women are told from their infancy, and taught by the example of their mothers, that a little knowledge of human weakness, justly termed cunning, softness of temper, *outward* obedience, and a scrupulous attention to a puerile kind of propriety, will obtain for them the protection of man; and should they be beautiful, everything else is needless, for at least twenty years of their lives.

Thus Milton describes our first frail mother; though when he tells us that women are formed for softness and sweet attractive grace,[2] I cannot comprehend his meaning, unless, in the true Mahometan strain, he meant to deprive us of souls,[3] and insinuate that we were beings only designed by sweet attractive grace, and docile blind obedience, to gratify the senses of man when he can no longer soar on the wing of contemplation.

How grossly do they insult us who thus advise us only to render ourselves gentle, domestic brutes! For instance, the winning softness so warmly and frequently recommended, that governs by obeying. What childish expressions, and how insignificant is the being—can it be an immortal one?—who will condescend to govern by such sinister methods? "Certainly," says Lord Bacon, "man is of kin to the beasts by his body; and if he be not of kin to God by his spirit, he is a base and ignoble creature!"[4] Men, indeed, appear to me to act in a very unphilosophical manner, when they try to secure the good conduct of women by attempting to keep them always in a state of childhood. Rousseau was more consistent when he

---

9. Unless.
1. A mayfly, an insect whose life is one day long; that is, short-lived persons.
2. From *Paradise Lost* (1667) by the English poet John Milton (1608–74), describing Adam and

Eve: "For contemplation he and valor form'd, / For softness she and sweet attractive grace; / He for God only, she for God in him" (4.297–99).
3. See note 1, page 367.
4. Francis Bacon, Essay 16, "Of Atheism" (1601).

wished to stop the progress of reason in both sexes, for if men eat of the tree of knowledge, women will come in for a taste; but, from the imperfect cultivation which their understandings now receive, they only attain a knowledge of evil.[5]

Children, I grant, should be innocent; but when the epithet is applied to men, or women, it is but a civil[6] term for weakness. For if it be allowed that women were destined by Providence to acquire human virtues, and, by the exercise of their understandings, that stability of character which is the firmest ground to rest our future hopes upon, they must be permitted to turn to the fountain of light, and not forced to shape their course by the twinkling of a mere satellite. Milton, I grant, was of a very different opinion; for he only bends to the indefeasible right of beauty, though it would be difficult to render two passages which I now mean to contrast, consistent. But into similar inconsistencies are great men often led by their senses:

> To whom thus Eve with *perfect beauty* adorn'd.
> My author and disposer, what thou bid'st
> *Unargued* I obey; so God ordains;
> God is *thy law, thou mine:* to know no more
> Is woman's *happiest* knowledge and her *praise.*[7]   5

These are exactly the arguments that I have used to children; but I have added, your reason is now gaining strength, and, till it arrives at some degree of maturity, you must look up to me for advice,—then you ought to *think,* and only rely on God.

Yet in the following lines Milton seems to coincide with me, when he makes Adam thus expostulate with his Maker:

> Hast Thou not made me here Thy substitute,
> And these inferior far beneath me set?
> Among *unequals* what society
> Can sort, what harmony or true delight?
> Which must be mutual, in proportion due   5
> Given and received; but in *disparity*
> The one intense, the other still remiss
> Cannot well suit with either, but soon prove
> Tedious alike; of *fellowship* I speak
> Such as I seek, fit to participate   10
> All rational delight—[8]

In treating therefore of the manners of women, let us, disregarding sensual arguments, trace what we should endeavour to make them in order to co-operate, if the expression be not too bold, with the Supreme Being.

By individual education, I mean, for the sense of the word is not precisely defined, such an attention to a child as will slowly sharpen the senses, from the temper, regulate the passions as they begin to ferment, and set the understanding to work before the body arrives at maturity; so that the man may only have to proceed, not to begin, the important task of learning to think and reason.

5. The Swiss philosopher Jean-Jacques Rousseau (1712–54), in his book *Emile* (1762), advocates a liberal education for Emile, but not for Sophie, Emile's wife.
6. Polite, euphemistic.

7. *Paradise Lost,* 4.634–38 (Wollstonecraft's italics).
8. *Paradise Lost,* 8.381–92 (Wollstonecraft's italics).

To prevent any misconstruction, I must add, that I do not believe that a private education can work the wonders which some sanguine writers have attributed to it. Men and women must be educated, in a great degree, by the opinions and manners of the society they live in. In every age there has been a stream of popular opinion that has carried all before it, and given a family character, as it were, to the century. It may then fairly be inferred, that, till society be differently constituted, much cannot be expected from education. It is, however, sufficient for my present purpose to assert that, whatever effect circumstances have on the abilities, every being may become virtuous by the exercise of its own reason; for if but one being was created with vicious inclinations, that is positively bad, what can save us from atheism? or if we worship a God, is not that God a devil?

Consequently, the most perfect education, in my opinion, is such an exercise of the understanding as is best calculated to strengthen the body and form the heart. Or, in other words, to enable the individual to attain such habits of virtue as will render it independent. In fact, it is a farce to call any being virtuous whose virtues do not result from the exercise of its own reason. This was Rousseau's opinion respecting men; I extend it to women, and confidently assert that they have been drawn out of their sphere by false refinement, and not by an endeavour to acquire masculine qualities. Still the regal homage which they receive is so intoxicating, that until the manners of the times are changed, and formed on more reasonable principles, it may be impossible to convince them that the illegitimate power which they obtain by degrading themselves is a curse, and that they must return to nature and equality if they wish to secure the placid satisfaction that unsophisticated affections impart. But for this epoch we must wait—wait perhaps till kings and nobles, enlightened by reason, and, preferring the real dignity of man to childish state, throw off their gaudy hereditary trappings; and if then women do not resign the arbitrary power of beauty—they will prove that they have *less* mind than man.

* * *

But to view the subject in another point of view. Do passive indolent women make the best wives? Confining our discussion to the present moment of existence, let us see how such weak creatures perform their part? Do the women who, by the attainment of a few superficial accomplishments, have strengthened the prevailing prejudice, merely contribute to the happiness of their husbands? Do they display their charms merely to amuse them? And have women who have early imbibed notions of passive obedience, sufficient character to manage a family or educate children? So far from it, that, after surveying the history of woman, I cannot help agreeing with the severest satirist, considering the sex as the weakest as well as the most oppressed half of the species. What does history disclose but marks of inferiority, and how few women have emancipated themselves from the galling yoke of sovereign man? So few that the exceptions remind me of an ingenious conjecture respecting Newton—that he was probably a being of superior order accidentally caged in a human body.[9] Following the same train of thinking, I have been led to imagine that the few extraordinary women who have rushed in

9. An allusion to "An Essay on Man" (2.31–34) by Alexander Pope (1688–1744): "Superior beings when of late they saw / A mortal Man unfold all Nature's law, / Admir'd such wisdom in an earthly shape, / And shewed Newton as we shew an Ape." The Newton referred to here is Sir Isaac Newton (1643–1727), English mathematician and physicist.

eccentrical directions out of the orbit prescribed to their sex, were *male* spirits, confined by mistake in female frames. But if it be not philosophical to think of sex when the soul is mentioned, the inferiority must depend on the organs; or the heavenly fire, which is to ferment the clay, is not given in equal portions.

But avoiding, as I have hitherto done, any direct comparison of the two sexes collectively, or frankly acknowledging the inferiority of woman, according to the present appearance of things, I shall only insist that men have increased that inferiority till women are almost sunk below the standard of rational creatures. Let their faculties have room to unfold, and their virtues to gain strength, and then determine where the whole sex must stand in the intellectual scale. Yet let it be remembered that for a small number of distinguished women I do not ask a place.

It is difficult for us purblind mortals to say to what height human discoveries and improvements may arrive, when the gloom of despotism subsides, which makes us stumble at every step; but, when morality shall be settled on a more solid basis, then, without being gifted with a prophetic spirit, I will venture to predict that woman will be either the friend or slave of man. We shall not, as at present, doubt whether she is a moral agent, or the link which unites man with brutes.[1] But should it then appear that like the brutes they were principally created for the use of man, he will let them patiently bite the bridle, and not mock them with empty praise; or, should their rationality be proved, he will not impede their improvement merely to gratify his sensual appetites. He will not, with all the graces of rhetoric, advise them to submit implicitly their understanding to the guidance of man. He will not, when he treats of the education of women, assert that they ought never to have the free use of reason, nor would he recommend cunning and dissimulation to beings who are acquiring, in like manner as himself, the virtues of humanity.

Surely there can be but one rule of right, if morality has an eternal foundation, and whoever sacrifices virtue, strictly so called, to present convenience, or whose *duty* it is to act in such a manner, lives only for the passing day, and cannot be an accountable creature.

The poet then should have dropped his sneer when he says:

> If weak women go astray,
> The stars are more in fault than they.[2]

For that they are bound by the adamantine chain of destiny is most certain, if it be proved that they are never to exercise their own reason, never to be independent, never to rise above opinion, or to feel the dignity of a rational will that only bows to God, and often forgets that the universe contains any being but itself and the model of perfection to which its ardent gaze is turned, to adore attributes that, softened into virtues, may be imitated in kind, though the degree overwhelms the enraptured mind.

If, I say, for I would not impress by declamation when Reason offers her sober light, if they be really capable of acting like rational creatures, let them not be treated like slaves; or, like the brutes who are dependent on the reason of man,

---

1. A reference to the Great Chain of Being, a hypothetical golden chain stretching from God in heaven to the world of inanimate objects, with everyone and everything assigned its place in the hierarchy; on the chain, women would have been placed below men, but above all other animals.
2. A slight misquote of "Hans Caravel" (1718) by Matthew Prior (1664–1721): "if weak Women went astray, / Their Stars were more in Fault than They" (lines 10–12).

when they associate with him; but cultivate their minds, give them the salutary sublime curb of principle, and let them attain conscious dignity by feeling themselves only dependent on God. Teach them, in common with man, to submit to necessity, instead of giving, to render them more pleasing, a sex to morals.

Further, should experience prove that they cannot attain the same degree of strength of mind, perseverance, and fortitude, let their virtues be the same in kind, though they may vainly struggle for the same degree; and the superiority of man will be equally clear, if not clearer; and truth, as it is a simple principle, which admits of no modification, would be common to both. Nay the order of society, as it is at present regulated, would not be inverted, for woman would then only have the rank that reason assigned her, and arts could not be practised to bring the balance even, much less to turn it.

These may be termed Utopian dreams. Thanks to that Being who impressed them on my soul, and gave me sufficient strength of mind to dare to exert my own reason, till, becoming dependent only on Him for the support of my virtue, I view, with indignation, the mistaken notions that enslave my sex.

I love man as my fellow; but his sceptre, real or usurped, extends not to me, unless the reason of an individual demands my homage; and even then the submission is to reason, and not to man. In fact, the conduct of an accountable being must be regulated by the operations of its own reason; or on what foundation rests the throne of God?

It appears to me necessary to dwell on these obvious truths, because females have been insulated, as it were; and while they have been stripped of the virtues that should clothe humanity, they have been decked with artificial graces that enable them to exercise a short-lived tyranny. Love, in their bosoms, taking place of every nobler passion, their sole ambition is to be fair, to raise emotion instead of inspiring respect; and this ignoble desire, like the servility in absolute monarchies, destroys all strength of character. Liberty is the mother of virtue, and if women be, by their very constitution, slaves, and not allowed to breathe the sharp invigorating air of freedom, they must ever languish like exotics, and be reckoned beautiful flaws in nature. Let it also be remembered, that they are the only flaw.

As to the argument respecting the subjection in which the sex has ever been held, it retorts on man. The many have always been enthralled by the few; and monsters, who scarcely have shown any discernment of human excellence, have tyrannized over thousands of their fellow-creatures. Why have men of superior endowments submitted to such degredation? For, is it not universally acknowledged that kings, viewed collectively, have ever been inferior, in abilities and virtue, to the same number of men taken from the common mass of mankind—yet have they not, and are they not still treated with a degree of reverence that is an insult to reason? China is not the only country where a living man has been made a God.[3] *Men* have submitted to superior strength to enjoy with impunity the pleasure of the moment; *women* have only done the same, and therefore till it is proved that the courtier, who servilely resigns the birthright of a man, is not a moral agent, it cannot be demonstrated that woman is essentially inferior to man because she has always been subjugated.

---

3. Referring to the Chinese practice of ancestor worship.

Brutal force has hitherto governed the world, and that the science of politics is in its infancy, is evident from philosophers scrupling to give the knowledge most useful to man that determinate distinction.

I shall not pursue this argument any further than to establish an obvious inference, that as sound politics diffuse liberty, mankind, including woman, will become more wise and virtuous.

Chapter 9
Of the Pernicious Effects Which Arise from the Unnatural Distinctions Established in Society

From the respect paid to property flow, as from a poisoned fountain, most of the evils and vices which render this world such a dreary scene to the contemplative mind. For it is in the most polished society that noisome reptiles and venomous serpents lurk under the rank herbage;[4] and there is voluptuousness pampered by the still sultry air, which relaxes every good disposition before it ripens into virtue.

One class presses on another, for all are aiming to procure respect on account of their property; and property once gained will procure the respect due only to talents and virtue. Men neglect the duties incumbent on man, yet are treated like demigods. Religion is also separated from morality by a ceremonial veil, yet men wonder that the world is almost, literally speaking, a den of sharpers or oppressors.

There is a homely proverb, which speaks a shrewd truth, that whoever the devil finds idle he will employ. And what but habitual idleness can hereditary wealth and title produce? For man is so constituted that he can only attain a proper use of his faculties by exercising them, and will not exercise them unless necessity of some kind first set the wheels in motion. Virtue likewise can only be acquired by the discharge of relative duties; but the importance of these sacred duties will scarcely be felt by the being who is cajoled out of his humanity by the flattery of sycophants. There must be more equality established in society, or morality will never gain ground, and this virtuous equality will not rest firmly even when founded on a rock, if one-half of mankind be chained to its bottom by fate, for they will be continually undermining it through ignorance or pride.

It is vain to expect virtue from women till they are in some degree independent of men; nay, it is vain to expect that strength of natural affection which would make them good wives and mothers. Whilst they are absolutely dependent on their husbands they will be cunning, mean, and selfish; and the men who can be gratified by the fawning fondness of spaniel-like affection have not much delicacy, for love is not to be bought; in any sense of the words, its silken wings are instantly shrivelled up when anything beside a return in kind is sought. Yet whilst wealth enervates men, and women live, as it were, by their personal charms, how can we expect them to discharge those ennobling duties which equally require exertion and self-denial? Hereditary property sophisticates[5] the mind, and the unfortunate victims to it—if I may so express myself—swathed from their birth, seldom exert the locomotive faculty or body of mind, and thus viewing everything through one medium, and that a false one, they are unable to discern in what true merit and happiness consist. False, indeed, must be the light when the drapery of situation hides the man, and makes him stalk in masquerade, dragging from one scene of

---

4. Grass on which livestock graze.   5. Corrupts.

dissipation to another the nerveless limbs that hang with stupid listlessness, and rolling round the vacant eye, which plainly tells us that there is no mind at home.

I mean therefore to infer that the society is not properly organized which does not compel men and women to discharge their respective duties by making it the only way to acquire that countenance from their fellow-creatures, which every human being wishes some way to attain. The respect consequently which is paid to wealth and mere personal charms is a true north-east blast that blights the tender blossoms of affection and virtue. Nature has wisely attached affections to duties to sweeten toil, and to give that vigour to the exertions of reason which only the heart can give. But the affection which is put on merely because it is the appropriated insignia of a certain character, when its duties are not fulfilled, is one of the empty compliments which vice and folly are obliged to pay to virtue and the real nature of things.

To illustrate my opinion, I need only observe that when a woman is admired for her beauty, and suffers herself to be so far intoxicated by the admiration she receives as to neglect to discharge the indispensable duty of a mother, she sins against herself by neglecting to cultivate an affection that would equally tend to make her useful and happy. True happiness—I mean all the contentment and virtuous satisfaction that can be snatched in this imperfect state—must arise from well-regulated affections, and an affection includes a duty. Men are not aware of the misery they cause, and the vicious weakness they cherish, by only inciting women to render themselves pleasing; they do not consider that they thus make natural and artificial duties clash by sacrificing the comfort and respectability of a woman's life to voluptuous notions of beauty when in nature they all harmonize.

Cold would be the heart of a husband, were he not rendered unnatural by early debauchery, who did not feel more delight at seeing his child suckled by its mother[6] than the most artful wanton tricks could ever raise, yet this natural way of cementing the matrimonial tie, and twisting esteem with fonder recollections, wealth leads women to spurn. To preserve their beauty, and wear the flowery crown of the day, which gives them a kind of right to reign for a short time over the sex, they neglect to stamp impressions on their husbands' hearts that would be remembered with more tenderness when the snow on the head began to chill the bosom than even their virgin charms. The maternal solicitude of a reasonable affectionate woman is very interesting, and the chastened dignity with which a mother returns the caresses that she and her child receive from a father who has been fulfilling the serious duties of his station is not only a respectable, but a beautiful sight. So singular, indeed, are my feelings—and I have endeavoured not to catch factitious ones—that after having been fatigued with the sight of insipid grandeur and the slavish ceremonies that with cumbrous pomp supplied the place of domestic affections, I have turned to some other scene to relieve my eye by resting it on the refreshing green everywhere scattered by Nature. I have then viewed with pleasure a woman nursing her children, and discharging the duties of her station with perhaps merely a servant-maid to take off her hands the servile part of the household business. I have seen her prepare herself and children, with only the luxury of cleanliness, to receive her husband, who, returning weary home in the evening, found smiling babes and a clean hearth. My heart has loitered in the

6. During Wollstonecraft's time, breast-feeding one's own children, rather than sending them to a wet nurse, would have only recently become standard practice; see p. 383.

midst of the group, and has even throbbed with sympathetic emotion when the scraping of the well-known foot has raised a pleasing tumult.

Whilst my benevolence has been gratified by contemplating this artless picture, I have thought that a couple of this description, equally necessary and independent of each other, because each fulfilled the respective duties of their station, possessed all that life could give. Raised sufficiently above abject poverty not to be obliged to weigh the consequence of every farthing they spend, and having sufficient to prevent their attending to a frigid system of economy which narrows both heart and mind, I declare, so vulgar are my conceptions, that I know not what is wanted to render this the happiest as well as the most respectable situation in the world, but a taste for literature, to throw a little variety and interest into social converse, and some superfluous money to give to the needy and to buy books. For it is not pleasant when the heart is opened by compassion, and the head active in arranging plans of usefulness, to have a prim urchin continually twitching back the elbow to prevent the hand from drawing out an almost empty purse, whispering at the same time some prudential maxim about the priority of justice.

Destructive, however, as riches and inherited honours are to the human character, women are more debased and cramped, if possible, by them than men, because men may still in some degree unfold their faculties by becoming soldiers and statesmen.

As soldiers, I grant they can now only gather for the most part vain-glorious laurels, whilst they adjust to a hair the European balance, taking especial care that no bleak northern nook or sound incline the beam. But the days of true heroism are over, when a citizen fought for his country like a Fabricius or a Washington, and then returned to his farm to let his virtuous fervour run in a more placid, but not a less salutary, stream.[7] No, our British heroes are oftener sent from the gaming-table than from the plough; and their passions have been rather inflamed by hanging with dumb suspense on the turn of a die, than sublimated by panting after the adventurous march of virtue in the historic page.

* * *

But, to have done with these episodical observations, let me return to the more specious slavery which chains the very soul of woman, keeping her for ever under the bondage of ignorance.

The preposterous distinctions of rank, which render civilization a curse, by dividing the world between voluptuous tyrants and cunning envious dependents, corrupt, almost equally, every class of people, because respectability is not attached to the discharge of the relative duties of life, but to the station, and when the duties are not fulfilled the affections cannot gain sufficient strength to fortify the virtue of which they are the natural reward. Still there are some loopholes out of which a man may creep, and dare to think and act for himself; but for a woman it is an herculean task,[8] because she has difficulties peculiar to her sex to overcome, which require almost superhuman powers.

A truly benevolent legislator always endeavours to make it the interest of each individual to be virtuous; and thus private virtue becoming the cement of public happiness, an orderly whole is consolidated by the tendency of all the parts towards a common centre. But the private or public virtue of woman is very problematical,

---

7. A Roman general from the third century BCE known for being incorruptible.
8. Referring to the Greek myth of Hercules, who performed twelve superhuman tasks as penance for murders he committed while temporarily deranged.

for Rousseau,[9] and a numerous list of male writers, insist that she should all her life be subjected to a severe restraint, that of propriety. Why subject her to propriety—blind propriety—if she be capable of acting from a nobler spring, if she be an heir of immortality? Is sugar always to be produced by vital blood? Is one half of the human species, like the poor African slaves, to be subjected to prejudices that brutalize them, when principles would be a surer guard, only to sweeten the cup of man?[1] Is not this indirectly to deny woman reason? for a gift is a mockery, if it be unfit for use.

Women are, in common with men, rendered weak and luxurious by the relaxing pleasures which wealth procures; but added to this they are made slaves to their persons, and must render them alluring that man may lend them his reason to guide their tottering steps aright. Or should they be ambitious, they must govern their tyrants by sinister tricks, for without rights there cannot be any incumbent duties. The laws respecting woman, which I mean to discuss in a future part, make an absurd unit of a man and his wife; and then, by the easy transition of only considering him as responsible, she is reduced to a mere cipher.[2]

The being who discharges the duties of its station is independent; and, speaking of women at large, their first duty is to find themselves as rational creatures, and the next, in point of importance, as citizens, is that, which includes so many, of a mother. The rank in life which dispenses with their fulfilling this duty, necessarily degrades them by making them mere dolls. Or should they turn to something more important than merely fitting drapery upon a smooth block, their minds are only occupied by some soft platonic attachment; or the actual management of an intrigue may keep their thoughts in motion; for when they neglect domestic duties, they have it not in their power to take the field, and march and counter-march like soldiers, or wrangle in the senate to keep their faculties from rusting.

I know that, as a proof of the inferiority of the sex, Rousseau has exultingly exclaimed, How can they leave the nursery for the camp![3] And the camp has by some moralists been proved the school of the most heroic virtues; though I think it would puzzle a keen casuist to prove the reasonableness of the greater number of wars that have dubbed heroes. I do not mean to consider this question critically; because, having frequently viewed these freaks of ambition as the first natural mode of civilization, when the ground must be torn up, and the woods cleared by fire and sword, I do not choose to call them pests; but surely the present system of war has little connection with virtue of any denomination, being rather the school of *finesse* and effeminacy than of fortitude.

Yet, if defensive war, the only justifiable war, in the present advanced state of society, where virtue can show its face and ripen amidst the rigours which purify the air on the mountain's top, were alone to be adopted as just and glorious, the true heroism of antiquity might again animate female bosoms. But fair and softly, gentle reader, male or female, do not alarm thyself, for though I have compared the character of a modern soldier with that of a civilized woman, I am not going to ad-

9. Swiss philosopher (1712–54); see also note 5, p. 371.
1. A reference to the abolitionist sentiment that to drink tea sweetened with sugar, which was produced by slave labor, was tantamount to drinking the slave's blood; see "A Poem on the African Slave Trade," p. 408, by Mary Birkett.

2. A reference to coverture, the English law that placed a woman (*feme covert*) under the protection of her husband.
3. The eponymous character of Rousseau's *Emile* (1762) asks: "Can [a woman] be a nursing woman today and a soldier tomorrow?" (Book 5).

vise them to turn their distaff[4] into a musket, though I sincerely wish to see the bayonet converted into a pruning-hook. I only re-created an imagination, fatigued by contemplating the vices and follies which all proceed from a feculent stream of wealth that has muddied the pure rills of natural affection, by supposing that society will some time or other be so constituted, that man must necessarily fulfil the duties of a citizen, or be despised, and that while he was employed in any of the departments of civil life, his wife, also an active citizen, should be equally intent to manage her family, educate her children, and assist her neighbours.

But to render her really virtuous and useful, she must not, if she discharge her civil duties, want individually the protection of civil laws; she must not be dependent on her husband's bounty for her subsistence during his life, or support after his death; for how can a being be generous who has nothing of its own? or virtuous who is not free? The wife, in the present state of things, who is faithful to her husband, and neither suckles nor educates her children, scarcely deserves the name of a wife, and has no right to that of a citizen. But take away natural rights, and duties become null.

Women then must be considered as only the wanton solace of men, when they become so weak in mind and body that they cannot exert themselves unless to pursue some frothy pleasure, or to invent some frivolous fashion. What can be a more melancholy sight to a thinking mind, than to look into the numerous carriages that drive helter-skelter about this metropolis in a morning full of pale-faced creatures who are flying from themselves! I have often wished, with Dr Johnson, to place some of them in a little shop with half a dozen children looking up to their languid countenances for support.[5] I am much mistaken, if some latent vigour would not soon give health and spirit to their eyes, and some lines drawn by the exercise of reason on the blank cheeks, which before were only undulated by dimples, might restore lost dignity to the character, or rather enable it to attain the true dignity of its nature. Virtue is not to be acquired even by speculation, much less by the negative supineness that wealth naturally generates.

Besides, when poverty is more disgraceful than even vice, is not morality cut to the quick? Still to avoid misconstruction, though I consider that women in the common walks of life are called to fulfil the duties of wives and mothers, by religion and reason, I cannot help lamenting that women of a superior cast have not a road open by which they can pursue more extensive plans of usefulness and independence. I may excite laughter, by dropping a hint, which I mean to pursue, some future time, for I really think that women ought to have representatives, instead of being arbitrarily governed without having any direct share allowed them in the deliberations of government.[6]

But, as the whole system of representation is now, in this country, only a convenient handle for despotism, they need not complain, for they are as well represented as a numerous class of hard-working mechanics, who pay for the support of royalty when they can scarcely stop their children's mouths with bread. How are they represented whose very sweat supports the splendid stud of an heir-apparent, or varnishes the chariot of some female favourite who looks down on shame? Taxes

4. A staff on the spinning wheel that holds the flax or wool.
5. A reference to Dr. Samuel Johnson's essay in number 85 of *The Rambler,* "The Mischiefs of Total Idleness" (January 8, 1751).

6. Not until 1918 did some British women—heads of households over the age of thirty—win the right to vote; full suffrage for women in Britain was not legislated until 1928.

on the very necessaries of life, enable an endless tribe of idle princes and princesses to pass with stupid pomp before a gaping crowd, who almost worship the very parade which costs them so dear. This is mere gothic grandeur, something like the barbarous useless parade of having sentinels on horseback at Whitehall,[7] which I could never view without a mixture of contempt and indignation.

How strangely must the mind be sophisticated when this sort of state impresses it! But, till these monuments of folly are levelled by virtue, similar follies will leaven the whole mass. For the same character, in some degree, will prevail in the aggregate of society; and the refinements of luxury, or the vicious repinings of envious poverty, will equally banish virtue from society, considered as the characteristic of that society, or only allow it to appear as one of the stripes of the harlequin coat,[8] worn by the civilized man.

In the superior ranks of life, every duty is done by deputies, as if duties could ever be waived, and the vain pleasures which consequent idleness forces the rich to pursue, appear so enticing to the next rank, that the numerous scramblers for wealth sacrifice everything to tread on their heels. The most sacred trusts are then considered as sinecures, because they were procured by interest, and only sought to enable a man to keep *good company*. Women, in particular, all want to be ladies. Which is simply to have nothing to do, but listlessly to go they scarcely care where, for they cannot tell what.

But what have women to do in society? I may be asked, but to loiter with easy grace; surely you would not condemn them all to suckle fools and chronicle small beer![9] No. Women might certainly study the art of healing and be physicians as well as nurses. And midwifery, decency seems to allot to them though I am afraid the word midwife, in our dictionaries, will soon give place to *accoucheur*,[1] and one proof of the former delicacy of the sex can be effaced from the language.

They might also study politics, and settle their benevolence on the broadest basis; for the reading of history will scarcely be more useful than the perusal of romances, if read as mere biography; if the character of the times, the political improvements, arts, etc., be not observed. In short, if it be not considered as the history of man; and not of particular men, who filled a niche in the temple of fame, and dropped into the black rolling stream of time, that silently sweeps all before it into the shapeless void called—eternity.—For shape, can it be called, "that shape hath none"?[2]

Business of various kinds, they might likewise pursue, if they were educated in a more orderly manner, which might save many from common and legal prostitution. Women would not then marry for a support, as men accept of places under Government, and neglect the implied duties; nor would an attempt to earn their own subsistence, a most laudable one! sink them almost to the level of those poor abandoned creatures who live by prostitution. For are not milliners and mantua-

7. A major thoroughfare between Parliament and Trafalgar Square in London, where even today the horse guards in their colorful uniforms parade.
8. Harlequin, a character in the Italian commedia dell'arte, traditionally wore an outfit of black and white interlocking diamond shapes; here, the reference is to an intrinsic versus a superficial characteristic.

9. From *Othello*, 2.1.160.
1. Male obstetrician (French).
2. *Paradise Lost*, 2.666–68, a passage that describes Death as "the other shape, / If shape it might be call'd that had none / Distinguishable in member, joint, or limb."

makers reckoned the next class?[3] The few employments open to women, so far, from being liberal, are menial; and when a superior education enables them to take charge of the education of children as governesses, they are not treated like the tutors of sons, though even clerical tutors are not always treated in a manner calculated to render them respectable in the eyes of their pupils, to say nothing of the private comfort of the individual. But as women educated like gentlewomen, are never designed for the humiliating situation which necessity sometimes forces them to fill; these situations are considered in the light of a degradation; and they know little of the human heart, who need to be told, that nothing so painfully sharpens sensibility as such a fall in life.[4]

Some of these women might be restrained from marrying by a proper spirit of delicacy, and others may not have had it in their power to escape in this pitiful way from servitude; is not that Government then very defective, and very unmindful of the happiness of one-half of its members, that does not provide for honest, independent women, by encouraging them to fill respectable stations? But in order to render their private virtue a public benefit, they must have a civil existence in the State, married or single; else we shall continually see some worthy woman, whose sensibility has been rendered painfully acute by undeserved contempt, droop like "the lily broken down by a plowshare".[5]

It is a melancholy truth; yet such is the blessed effect of civilization! the most respectable women are the most oppressed; and, unless they have understandings far superior to the common run of understandings, taking in both sexes, they must, from being treated like contemptible beings, become contemptible. How many women thus waste life away the prey of discontent, who might have practised as physicians, regulated a farm, managed a shop, and stood erect, supported by their own industry, instead of hanging their heads surcharged with the dew of sensibility, that consumes the beauty to which it at first gave lustre; nay, I doubt whether pity and love are so near akin as poets feign, for I have seldom seen much compassion excited by the helplessness of females, unless they were fair; then, perhaps, pity was the soft handmaid of love, or the harbinger of lust.

How much more respectable is the woman who earns her own bread by fulfilling any duty, than the most accomplished beauty!—beauty did I say!—so sensible am I of the beauty of moral loveliness, or the harmonious propriety that attunes the passions of a well-regulated mind, that I blush at making the comparison; yet I sigh to think how few women aim at attaining this respectability by withdrawing from the giddy whirl of pleasure, or the indolent calm that stupefies the good sort of women it sucks in.

Proud of their weakness, however, they must always be protected, guarded from care, and all the rough toils that dignify the mind. If this be the fiat of fate, if they will make themselves insignificant and contemptible, sweetly to waste "life away", let them not expect to be valued when their beauty fades, for it is the fate

3. Millinery (hat making) and mantua making (dressmaking) were the only two trades into which respectable, middle-rank women could be apprenticed at the end of the eighteenth century, though women who worked at these trades were considered little better than prostitutes because they placed themselves in public view; see p. 363.

4. Wollstonecraft herself had worked as a governess in 1786.
5. From the political work *Telemachus* (1699) by François Fenelon (1651–1715), in which Idomeneus must kill his own son to obey the gods; the son is described "as a beautiful lily of the field."

of the fairest flowers to be admired and pulled to pieces by the careless hand that plucked them. In how many ways do I wish, from the purest benevolence, to impress this truth on my sex; yet I fear that they will not listen to a truth that dear bought experience has brought home to many an agitated bosom, nor willingly resign the privileges of rank and sex for the privileges of humanity, to which those have no claim who do not discharge its duties.

Those writers are particularly useful, in my opinion, who make man feel for man, independent of the station he fills, or the drapery of factitious sentiments. I then would fain convince reasonable men of the importance of some of my remarks; and prevail on them to weigh dispassionately the whole tenor of my observations. I appeal to their understandings; and, as a fellow-creature, claim, in the name of my sex, some interest in their hearts. I entreat them to assist to emancipate their companion, to make her a *helpmeet* for them.

Would men but generously snap our chains, and be content with rational fellowship instead of slavish obedience, they would find us more observant daughters, more affectionate sisters, more faithful wives, more reasonable mothers—in a word, better citizens. We should then love them with true affection, because we should learn to respect ourselves; and the peace of mind of a worthy man would not be interrupted by the idle vanity of his wife, nor the babes sent to nestle in a strange bosom, having never found a home in their mother's.

1792

CULTURAL COORDINATES
Breast-Feeding and the Wet Nurse

At the beginning of the eighteenth century, most women of means did not nurse their own children. Instead, all women from the upper ranks—and indeed anyone with enough money—hired a wet nurse, a woman paid to breast-feed babies, sometimes more than one child at a time. Wet nurses usually came from a much lower rank than the children they nursed. Although certainly many carefully nurtured—and perhaps even grew to love—the children in their care, some were motivated only by money. Because the wet nurse might be inadequately nourished, unevenly attentive, or, in the worst case, beset by alcoholism, being put out to nurse could be risky for the baby. Some opponents to the practice expressed the erroneous fear that a child imbibed the nurse's character along with her milk.

Responding to concerns about the health of the children, as well as other issues, the eighteenth century saw a massive public relations campaign urging mothers to breast-feed their own babies. Innumerable medical treatises, such as *An Essay upon Nursing and the Management of Children, from Their Birth to Three Years of Age* (1749) by William Cadogan, pamphlets, and conduct books spread the idea that breast-feeding was best for mother and child alike. Certainly there were advantages to maternal breast-feeding, among them closer contact and bonding between mother and child and the ability to control the baby's nutrition.

But there was another side to the movement: breast-feeding also required a woman to keep the rigorous schedule of feedings demanded by a baby. Thus, it restricted her to the home and inhibited her ability to be socially active. Some medical manuals even insisted that the mother nurse the baby in the father's presence, making breast-feeding a central part of a new ideology of womanhood that placed a woman within a clear-cut domestic hierarchy. In this new ideology, a woman was to find fulfillment first and foremost as a wife and mother.

> *At the beginning of the eighteenth century . . . all women from the upper ranks . . . hired a wet nurse. . . .*

In its worst manifestations, the cult of maternal breast-feeding became socially coercive for its assertion that *all* women, regardless of individual situation, inclination, or even physical condition, needed to conform to a new maternal standard.

Thus, though it is now commonly assumed that breast-feeding is always better (an assumption shared by Mary Wollstonecraft in her essay *A Vindication of the Rights of Woman*), there may have been good reasons why not all women embraced the idea of maternal breast-feeding: the mother's health or other physical factors might have prevented an adequate supply of milk, and some women may have preferred to preserve their relative autonomy from a rigorous schedule.

It wasn't until the nineteenth century, when rubber products became widely available, that baby bottles with rubber nipples provided another option for nourishing infants. Then, in 1867, Henri Nestlé invented baby formula to assist a mother who was physically unable to breast-feed her child. At that point, women finally gained another option to nursing their own babies or sending them to someone else for breast-feeding.

1759–1813

Known as "the Scotch milkmaid," Janet Little was the daughter of a hired farm laborer, George Little, of Dumfries, Scotland. After a basic education, during which she showed early inclinations toward writing, she worked first as a servant to a local clergyman, the Reverend Johnstone, and then as a chambermaid to Mrs. Frances Dunlop, a friend and correspondent to Robert Burns, "the ploughman poet" known for his vibrant verse, often written in Scottish dialect that expressed themes from the lives of the Scottish laboring class.

Sometime after 1786, Little left Dunlop House, first taking employment as a child's nurse and then obtaining a position as superintendent of the dairy at Loudoun Castle in Galston. She published her first volume of poems in 1772, dedicating the collection to twelve-year-old Flora Mure Campbell, Countess of Loudoun, who bought twelve copies. In all, the book raised 700 subscriptions. Throughout this period, Little actively sought favor from and friendship with Robert Burns, believing that he would identify with her position as a laboring-class poet. She even went to visit him once but failed to see him because he was in bed with a broken arm. Overall, however, Little's relationship to Burns was conflicted: although she found his treatment of lower-rank poverty to be compassionate and sympathetic, she disagreed with his sometimes condescending attitudes toward women.

Little made £50 on the publication of her poems, which was, for that time, a large sum. (It would be worth about $10,000 in today's money.) Eventually she married John Richmond, a laborer at the castle, who was eighteen years her senior and a widower with five children. She died in 1813 after experiencing "a cramp in the stomach."

At a historic moment when the distinctness of Scottish culture was being assimilated into a British national identity, Little remains an important female voice invested in the values of her country and her heritage, despite all the obstacles placed in her way because of her class and gender. The following poem, written in Scottish dialect, should be read out loud to hear how Little uses wit and humor to defend herself against devastating class prejudice.

Given to a Lady Who Asked Me to Write a Poem

"In royal Anna's[1] golden days,
Hard was the task to gain the bays:[2]
Hard was it then the hill to climb;
Some broke a neck, some lost a limb.
The votaries for poetic fame   5
Got aff decrepit, blind an' lame:
Except that little fellow Pope,[3]
Few ever then got near its top:

1. Queen Anne (1665–1714), reigned 1702–14.
2. The wreath of laurels worn by the poet as a mark of honor.
3. Poet Alexander Pope (1688–1744) was handicapped and of short stature.

An' Homer's crutches he may thank,[4]
Or down the brae he'd got a clank.[5]   10

"Swift, Thomson, Addison, an' Young[6]
Made Pindus[7] echo to their tongue,
In hopes to please a learned age;
But Doctor Johnson,[8] in a rage,
Unto posterity did show   15
Their blunders great, their beauties few.
But now he's dead, we weel may ken;[9]
For ilka dunce maun hae a pen,[1]
To write in hamely, uncouth rhymes;
An' yet forsooth they please the times.   20

"A ploughman chiel, Rab Burns his name,[2]
Pretends to write; an' thinks nae shame
To souse[3] his sonnets on the court;
An' what is strange, they praise him for't.
Even folks, wha're of the highest station,   25
Ca' him the glory of our nation.

"But what is more surprising still,
A milkmaid must tak up her quill;
An' she will write, shame fa' the rabble!
That think to please wi' ilka bawble.   30
They may thank heaven auld Sam's asleep:
For could he ance but get a peep,
He, wi' a vengeance wad them sen'
A' headlong to the dunces' den.

"Yet Burns, I'm tauld, can write wi' ease,   35
An' a' denominations please;
Can wi' uncommon glee impart
A usefu' lesson to the heart;
Can ilka latent thought expose,
An' Nature trace whare'er she goes: 40
Of politics can talk wi' skill,
Nor dare the critics blame his quill.

"But then a rustic country quean
To write—was e'er the like o't seen?

---

4. Homer (active c. 1100 BC) was a blind poet who is thought to be the author of epic poems *The Iliad* and *The Odyssey*.
5. Brae: hillside; clank: referring to a noise (made by falling) stronger than a clink and duller than a clang.
6. Eminent literary figures of the time: Jonathan Swift (1667–1745), author of *Gulliver's Travels*; James Thompson (1700–1748), author of "Rule Britannia"; Joseph Addison (1672–1719), editor of *The Spectator*; and Edward Young (1683–

1765), author of *Night Thoughts*.
7. Mountain home of the muses.
8. Dr. Samuel Johnson (1709–84), famed lexicographer and essayist; also referred to below in line 31.
9. Well may know.
1. Ilka: every; maun: must.
2. Chiel: lad; Rab: Robert Burns (1759–96), the great Scottish national poet.
3. Pour.

A milkmaid poem-books to print: 45
Mair fit she wad her dairy tent;
Or labour at her spinning-wheel,
An' do her wark baith swift an' weel.
Frae[4] that she may some profit share,
But winna[5] frae her rhyming ware.   50
Does she, poor silly thing, pretend
The manners of our age to mend?
Mad as we are, we're wise enough
Still to despise sic paultry stuff.

  "May she wha writes, of wit get mair,   55
An' a' that read an ample share
Of candour every fault to screen,
That in her doggerel scrawls are seen."

  All this and more, a critic said;
I heard and slunk behind the shade: 60
So much I dread their cruel spite,
My hand still trembles when I write.

                                                   1792

◄ MARIA EDGEWORTH ►
1767–1849

Maria Edgeworth, a prolific novelist and essayist, wrote extensively on education, the nature of domesticity, and political life in Ireland. All of her writings express a belief in a necessary, guiding force, often represented in her works as a father figure or a benevolent landlord or master. Edgeworth's faith in such a guiding force has made her works controversial: on the one hand, her writings consistently express faith and optimism in rational education, the idea that all people can learn what is best for them; on the other hand, even her most rational schemes recognize traditional hierarchies requiring, for instance, that men move in the wider world, while women remain within the domestic sphere as wives and mothers. In addition, Edgeworth's investment in the policies of the Anglo-Irish Ascendancy—a class of English Protestant families to whom English rulers gave confiscated Irish Catholic estates—has made her work the subject of interest for Irish studies scholars, who debate her vision of Irish politics and history.

  Edgeworth was born in Oxfordshire, England, the child of Anna Maria Elers and Richard Lovell Edgeworth, a member of the Anglo-Irish gentry whose family had had an estate in Ireland since 1619. Her father was a powerful intellectual figure, an educational theorist, an inventor, and a member of the Lunar Society, a group of prominent scientists and industrialists that included naturalist Erasmus Darwin (1731–1802), chemist James Keir (1735–1820), and Josiah Wedgwood (1730–95), who created the pottery industry still known today. Richard, who

---

4. For.   5. Won't.

deeply inspired his daughter and sometimes served as her collaborator, would eventually marry four times and father twenty-two children.

After Maria's mother died in 1773, Richard remarried and moved to the family estate, Edgeworthstown, located northwest of Dublin, Ireland. By 1777 the family had returned to Hertfordshire, England, perhaps because the estate had not flourished or perhaps because Richard wished to be closer to his intellectual companions. When his second wife died, Richard married for the third time—this time the sister of his second wife—and Maria was sent to a new school, Mrs. Devis's Academy for Young Ladies. In 1782, the family returned again to Ireland, and, with her father's encouragement, Edgeworth began to write moralistic stories for children. Her three-volume work *The Parent's Assistant for Children: or Stories for Children* (1796) was one of the first works to depict children's lives realistically, and it has been credited with ushering in the modern genre of children's literature. Then, in 1798, Edgeworth collaborated with her father on the three-volume *Practical Education,* a pedagogical treatise in which reason is promoted as the guiding principle in child rearing.

By 1798, Richard's third wife had died, and he then remarried once again. That same year, political turmoil drove the Edgeworths from their estate, as militants for a separate, independent, and republican Ireland rebelled across the country. After the rebellion abated, the Edgeworths traveled to England and then, in 1802, to the Continent. There Maria received—and turned down—a proposal from Swedish diplomat Chevalier Edlecranz, whom Edgeworth felt she did not know well enough to consider marrying. Concerned that Napoleonic France was preparing for war, the Edgeworths returned to England in 1803 and made their way back to Ireland. Further travels followed: to England in 1819 and to Scotland in 1823, where Edgeworth met the novelist Sir Walter Scott, who was an admirer of her work. After her father died in 1817, Maria finished and published his memoirs. She took over management of the family estate from her brother in 1826, later observing firsthand the tragedy of the Irish potato famine of 1845. She died at Edgeworthstown at the age of eighty-one.

Edgeworth's prodigious output included *Moral Tales for Young People* in five volumes (1801); *Popular Tales* in three volumes (1804); and eight novels collected as *Tales of Fashionable Life* (1809 and 1812). Additional, multivolume novels include *Lenora* (1806), *Patronage* (1814), *Harrington* (1817), and *Ormond* (1817). Her last novel, *Helen,* was published in 1834. In *Northanger Abbey,* Jane Austen attests to Edgeworth's very high reputation among her contemporaries. Austen cites *Belinda* (1801) in particular, a novel that has recently received a great deal of interest and critical scrutiny for its vivid characters, among them the eccentric, cross-dressing Harriot Freke, who espouses a problematic feminism, and the dissipated Lady Delacour, an errant mother with a mysterious wound in her breast. Edgeworth remains most famous, however, for *Castle Rackrent* (1800), a novel about the several generations of a family on an Irish estate.

Excerpted from *Letters for Literary Ladies* (1795), the "Letters of Julia and Caroline" is a short, moralistic tale written in the form of a correspondence between two friends—the romantic, passionate, and undisciplined Julia and the philosophic, rational, and self-regulating Caroline. Edgeworth's deployment of this dichotomy brings into clear relief the options presented to women in British culture at this time and provides the paradigm for Jane Austen's more nuanced plot in *Sense and Sensibility.*

From Letters for Literary Ladies

Letters of Julia and Caroline

No penance can absolve their guilty fame,
Nor tears, that wash out guilt, can wash out shame.

—PRIOR[1]

LETTER I

Julia to Caroline

In vain, dear Caroline, you urge me to *think;* I profess only to *feel.*

"*Reflect upon my own feelings!* Analyse my notions of happiness! explain to you my system!"—My system! But I have no system: *that* is the very difference between us. My notions of happiness cannot be resolved into simple, fixed principles. Nor dare I even attempt to analyse them; the subtle essence would escape in the process: just punishment to the alchymist[2] in morality!

You, Caroline, are of a more sedate, contemplative character. Philosophy becomes the rigid mistress of your life, enchanting enthusiasm the companion of mine. Suppose she lead me now and then in pursuit of a meteor; am not I happy in the chase? When one illusion vanishes, another shall appear, and, still leading me forward towards an horizon that retreats as I advance, the happy prospect of futurity shall vanish only with my existence.

"Reflect upon my feelings!"—Dear Caroline, is it not enough that I do feel?— All that I dread is that *apathy* which philosophers call tranquillity. You tell me that by continually *indulging,* I shall weaken my natural sensibility;—are not all the faculties of the soul improved, refined by exercise? and why shall *this* be excepted from the general law?

But I must not, you tell me, indulge my taste for romance and poetry, lest I waste that sympathy on *fiction* which *reality* so much better deserves. My dear friend, let us cherish the precious propensity to pity! no matter what the object; sympathy with fiction or reality arises from the same disposition.

When the sigh of compassion rises in my bosom, when the spontaneous tear starts from my eye, what frigid moralist shall "stop the genial current of the soul"? shall say to the tide of passion, *So far shalt thou go, and no farther?*—Shall man presume to circumscribe that which Providence has left unbounded?

But oh, Caroline! if our feelings as well as our days are numbered; if, by the immutable law of nature, apathy be the sleep of passion, and languor the necessary consequence of exertion; if indeed the pleasures of life are so ill proportioned to its duration, oh, may that duration be shortened to me!—Kind Heaven, let not my soul die before my body!

Yes, if at this instant my guardian genius were to appear before me, and offering me the choice of my future destiny; on the one hand, the even temper, the poised judgment, the stoical serenity of philosophy; on the other, the eager genius, the exquisite sensibility of enthusiasm: if the genius said to me, "Choose"—the lot

---

1. From "Henry and Emma, a Poem, Upon the Model of The Nut-brown Maid. To Cloe" (1718) by Matthew Prior (1664–1721); in the poem, while Henry tests Emma with a series of verbal challenges, the ever-faithful Emma proclaims her unwavering love.

2. Alchemist, someone who practices alchemy, or the medieval "science" of turning common metals into gold.

of the one is great pleasure, and great pain—great virtues, and great defects—ardent hope, and severe disappointment—ecstasy, and despair:—the lot of the other is calm happiness unmixed with violent grief—virtue without heroism—respect without admiration—and a length of life, in which to every moment is allotted its proper portion of felicity:—Gracious genius! I should exclaim, if half my existence must be the sacrifice, take it; *enthusiasm is my choice*.

Such, my dear friend, would be my choice were I a man; as a woman, how much more readily should I determine!

What has woman to do with philosophy? The graces flourish not under her empire; a woman's part in life is to please, and Providence has assigned to her *success*, all the pride and pleasure of her being.

Then leave us our weakness, leave us our follies; they are our best arms:—

> Leave us to trifle with more grace and ease,
> Whom folly pleases and whose follies please.[3]

The moment grave sense and solid merit appear, adieu the bewitching caprice, the *"lively nonsense"*, the exquisite, yet childish susceptibility which charms, interests, captivates.—Believe me, our *amiable defects* win more than our noblest virtues. Love requires sympathy, and sympathy is seldom connected with a sense of superiority. I envy none their *"painful pre-eminence."*[4] Alas! whether it be deformity or excellence which makes us say with Richard the Third,

I am myself alone![5]

it comes to much the same thing. Then let us, Caroline, content ourselves to gain in love, what we lose in esteem.

Man is to be held only by the *slightest* chains; with the idea that he can break them at pleasure, he submits to them in sport; but his pride revolts against the power to which his *reason* tells him he ought to submit. What then can woman gain by reason? Can she prove by argument that she is amiable? or demonstrate that she is an angel?

Vain was the industry of the artist, who, to produce the image of perfect beauty, selected from the fairest faces their most faultless features. Equally vain must be the efforts of the philosopher, who would excite the idea of mental perfection, by combining an assemblage of party-coloured virtues.

Such, I had almost said, is my *system*, but I mean my *sentiments*. I am not accurate enough to compose a *system*. After all, how vain are systems, and theories, and reasonings!

We may *declaim*, but what do we really know? All is uncertainty—human prudence does nothing—fortune every thing: I leave every thing therefore to fortune; *you* leave nothing. Such is the difference between us,—and which shall be the happiest, time alone can decide.

Farewell, dear Caroline; I love you better than I thought I could love a philosopher.

Your ever affectionate
Julia.

3. From *Imitations of Horace* by English poet Alexander Pope (1688–1744), 2.2.326–27.
4. From the tragedy *Cato* (1713) by English playwright and essayist Joseph Addison (1672–1719), 3.5.
5. A rough paraphrase of Shakespeare's *Richard III*: "What do I fear? myself? there's none else by. / Richard loves Richard; that is, I am I" (5.3.136–37).

Caroline's answer to Julia

At the hazard of ceasing to be *"charming"*, *"interesting"*, *"captivating"*, I must, dear Julia, venture to reason with you, to examine your favourite doctrine of *"amiable defects"*, and, if possible, to dissipate that unjust dread of perfection which you seem to have continually before your eyes.

It is the sole object of a woman's life, you say, to *please*. Her amiable defects *please* more than her noblest virtues, her follies more than her wisdom, her caprice more than her temper, and *something*, a nameless something, which no art can imitate and no science can teach, more than all.

Art, you say, spoils the graces, and corrupts the heart of woman; and at best can produce only a cold model of perfection; which though perhaps strictly conformable to *rule,* can never touch the soul, or please the unprejudiced taste, like one simple stroke of genuine nature.

I have often observed, dear Julia, that an inaccurate use of words produces such a strange confusion in all reasoning, that in the heat of debate, the combatants, unable to distinguish their friends from their foes, fall promiscuously on both. A skilful disputant knows well how to take advantage of this confusion, and sometimes endeavours to create it. I do not know whether I am to suspect you of such a design; but I must guard against it.

You have with great address availed yourself of the *two* ideas connected with the word *art:* first, as opposed to simplicity, it implies artifice; and next, as opposed to ignorance, it comprehends all the improvements of science, which leading us to search for general causes, rewards us with a dominion over their dependent effects:—that which instructs how to pursue the objects which we may have in view with the greatest probability of success. All men who act from general principles are so far philosophers. Their objects may be, when attained, insufficient to their happiness, or they may not previously have known all the necessary means to obtain them: but they must not therefore complain, if they do not meet with success which they have no reason to expect.

Parrhasius,[6] in collecting the most admired excellences from various models, to produce perfection, concluded, from general principles that mankind would be pleased again with what had once excited their admiration.—So far he was a philosopher: but he was disappointed of success:—yes, for he was ignorant of the cause necessary to produce it. The separate features might be perfect, but they were unsuited to each other, and in their forced union he could not give to the whole countenance symmetry and an appropriate expression.

There was, as you say, a *something* wanting, which his science had not taught him. He should then have set himself to examine what that *something* was, and how it was to be obtained. His want of success arose from the *insufficiency,* not the *fallacy,* of theory. Your object, dear Julia, we will suppose is "to please". If general observation and experience have taught you, that slight accomplishments and a trivial character succeed more certainly in obtaining this end, than higher worth and sense, you act from principle in rejecting the one and aiming at the other. You have discovered, or think you have discovered, the secret causes which

---

6. An ancient Greek painter, active circa 400 BCE.

produce the desired effect, and you employ them. Do not call this *instinct* or *nature;* this also, though you scorn it, is *philosophy.*

But when you come soberly to reflect, you have a feeling in your mind, that reason and cool judgment disapprove of the part you are acting.

Let us, however, distinguish between disapprobation of the *object,* and the means.

Averse as enthusiasm is from the retrograde motion of analysis, let me, my dear friend, lead you one step backward.

Why do you wish to please? I except at present from the question, the desire to please, arising from a passion which requires a reciprocal return. Confined as *this* wish must be in a woman's heart to one object alone, when you say, Julia *that the admiration of others* will be absolutely necessary to your happiness, I must suppose you mean to express only a *general* desire to please?

Then under this limitation—let me ask you again, why do you wish to please?

Do not let a word stop you. The word *vanity* conveys to us a disagreeable idea. There seems something *selfish* in the sentiment—that all the pleasure we feel in pleasing others arises from the gratification it affords to our own *vanity.*

We refine, and explain, and never can bring ourselves fairly to make a confession, which we are sensible must lower us in the opinion of others, and consequently mortify the very *vanity* we would conceal. So strangely then do we deceive ourselves as to deny the existence of a motive, which at the instant prompts the denial. But let us, dear Julia, exchange the word *vanity* for a less odious word, self-complacency; let us acknowledge that we wish to please, because the success raises our self-complacency. If you ask why raising our self-approbation gives us pleasure, I must answer, that I do not know. Yet I see and feel that it does; I observe that the voice of numbers is capable of raising the highest transport or the most fatal despair. The eye of man seems to possess a fascinating power over his fellow-creatures, to raise the blush of shame, or the glow of pride.

I look around me, and I see riches, titles, dignities, pursued with such eagerness by thousands, only as the signs of distinction. Nay, are not all these things sacrificed the moment they cease to be distinctions? The moment the prize of glory is to be won by other means, do not millions sacrifice their fortunes, their peace, their health, their lives, for *fame?* Then amongst the highest pleasures of human beings I must place self-approbation. With this belief, let us endeavour to secure it in the greatest extent, and to the longest duration.

Then Julia, the wish to please becomes only a secondary motive, subordinate to the desire I have to secure my own self-complacency. We will examine how far they are connected.

In reflecting upon my own mind, I observe that I am flattered by the opinion of others, in proportion to the opinion I have previously formed of their judgment; or I perceive that the opinion of numbers, merely as numbers, has power to give me great pleasure or great pain. I would unite both these pleasures if I could, but in general I cannot—they are incompatible. The opinion of the vulgar crowd and the enlightened individual, the applause of the highest and the lowest of mankind, cannot be obtained by the same means.

Another question then arises,—whom shall we wish to please? We must choose, and be decided in the choice.

You say that you are proud; I am prouder.—You will be content with indiscriminate admiration—nothing will content me but what is *select.* As long as I have the use of my reason—as long as my heart can feel the delightful sense of a "well-earned praise", I will fix my eye on the highest pitch of excellence, and steadily endeavour to attain it.

Conscious of her worth, and daring to assert it, I would have a woman early in life know that she is capable of filling the heart of a man of sense and merit; that she is worthy to be his companion and friend. With all the energy of her soul, with all the powers of her understanding, I would have a woman endeavour to please those whom she esteems and loves.

She runs a risk, you will say, of never meeting her equal. Hearts and understandings of a superior order are seldom met with in the world; or when met with, it may not be a particular good fortune to win them.—True; but if ever she *wins*, she will *keep* them; and the prize appears to me well worth the pains and difficulty of attaining.

I, Julia, admire and feel enthusiasm; but I would have philosophy directed to the highest objects. I dread apathy as much as you can; and I would endeavour to prevent it, not by sacrificing half my existence, but by enjoying the whole with moderation.

You ask, why exercise does not increase sensibility, and why sympathy with imaginary distress will not also increase the disposition to sympathize with what is real?—Because pity should, I think, always be associated with the active desire to relieve. If it be suffered to become a *passive sensation*, it is a *useless weakness*, not a virtue. The species of reading you speak of must be hurtful, even in this respect, to the mind, as it indulges all the luxury of woe in sympathy with fictitious distress, without requiring the exertion which reality demands: besides, universal experience proves to us that habit, so far from increasing sensibility, absolutely destroys it, by familiarizing it with objects of compassion.

Let me, my dear friend, appeal even to your own experience in the very instance you mention. Is there any pathetic writer in the world who could move you as much at the "twentieth reading as at the first"?[7] Speak naturally, and at the third or fourth reading, you would probably say, It is very pathetic, but I have read it before—I liked it better the first time; that is to say, it *did* touch me once—I know it *ought* to touch me now, but it *does not*. Beware of this! Do not let life become *as tedious as a twice-told tale*.[8]

Farewell, dear Julia: this is the answer of fact against eloquence, philosophy against enthusiasm. You appeal from my understanding to my heart—I appeal from the heart to the understanding of my judge; and ten years hence the decision perhaps will be in my favour.

Yours sincerely,
Caroline.

LETTER III

Caroline to Julia
On her intended marriage

Indeed, my dear Julia, I hardly know how to venture to give you my advice upon a subject which ought to depend so much upon your own taste and feelings. My

7. In an original footnote, Edgeworth attributed this quotation to Scottish philosopher David Hume (1711–76).

8. A quote from Shakespeare's *King John:* "There's nothing in this world can make me joy. / Life is as tedious as a twice-told tale" (3.4.107–8).

opinion and my wishes I could readily tell you: the idea of seeing you united and attached to my brother is certainly the most agreeable to me; but I am to divest myself of the partiality of a sister, and to consider my brother and Lord V——[9] as equal candidates for your preference—equal, I mean, in your regard; for you say that "Your heart is not yet decided in its choice.—If that oracle would declare itself in intelligible terms, you would not hesitate a moment to obey its dictates." But, my dear Julia, is there not another, a *safer*, I do not say a *better* oracle, to be consulted—your reason? Whilst the "doubtful beam still nods from side to side", you may with a steady hand weigh your own motives, and determine what things will be essential to your happiness, and what *price* you will pay for them; for

> Each pleasure has its *price;* and they who pay
> Too much of pain, but squander life away.[1]

Do me the justice to believe that I do not quote these lines of Dryden as being the finest poetry he ever wrote; for poets, you know, as Waller wittily observed, never succeed so well in truth as in fiction.[2]

Since we cannot in life expect to realize all our wishes, we must distinguish those which claim the rank of wants. We must separate the fanciful from the real, or at least make the one subservient to the other.

It is of the utmost importance to you, more particularly, to take every precaution before you decide for life, because disappointment and restraint afterwards would be insupportable to your temper.

You have often declared to me, my dear friend, that your love of poetry, and of all the refinements of literary and romantic pursuits, is so intimately "interwoven in your mind, that nothing could separate them, without destroying the whole fabric".

Your tastes, you say, are fixed; if they are so, you must be doubly careful to ensure their gratification. If you cannot make *them* subservient to external circumstances, you should certainly, if it be in your power, choose a situation in which circumstances will be subservient to them. If you are convinced that you could not adopt the tastes of another, it will be absolutely necessary for your happiness to live with one whose tastes are similar to your own.

The belief in that sympathy of souls, which the poets suppose declares itself between two people at first sight, is perhaps as absurd as the late fashionable belief in animal magnetism:[3] but there is a sympathy which, if it be not the foundation, may be called the cement of affection. Two people could not, I should think, retain any lasting affection for each other, without a mutual sympathy in taste and in their diurnal occupations and domestic pleasures. This, you will allow, my dear Julia, even in a fuller extent than I do. Now, my brother's tastes, character, and habits of life, are so very different from Lord V——'s, that I scarcely know how you can compare them; at least before you can decide which of the two would make you the happiest in life, you must determine what kind of life you may wish to lead; for my brother, though he might make you very happy in domestic life, would not make the Countess of V—— happy; nor would Lord V—— make Mrs. Percy happy. They must be two different women, with different habits, and different wishes; so that you must

---

9. The anonymous aristocrat with whom Julia is considering marriage.
1. From "An Essay upon Satire" (1679) by English poet John Dryden (1631–1700), lines 176–77.

2. English poet Edmund Waller (1605–87).
3. Eighteenth-century term for mesmerism, an early form of hypnotism.

divide yourself, my dear Julia, like Araspes,[4] into two selves; I do not say into a bad and a good self; choose some other epithets to distinguish them, but distinct they must be: so let them now declare and decide their pretensions; and let the victor have not only the honours of a triumph, but all the prerogatives of victory. Let the subdued be subdued for life—let the victor take every precaution which policy can dictate, to prevent the possibility of future contests with the vanquished.

But without talking poetry to you, my dear friend, let me seriously recommend it to you to examine your own mind carefully; and if you find that public diversions and public admiration, dissipation, and all the pleasures of riches and high rank, are really and truly essential to your happiness, direct your choice accordingly. Marry Lord V——: he has a large fortune, extensive connexions, and an exalted station; his own taste for show and expense, his family pride, and personal vanity, will all tend to the end you propose. Your house, table, equipages,[5] may be all in the highest style of magnificence. Lord V——'s easiness of temper, and fondness for you, will readily give you that entire ascendancy over his pleasures, which your abilities give you over his understanding. He will not control your wishes; you may gratify them to the utmost bounds of his fortune, and perhaps beyond those bounds; you may have entire command at home and abroad. If these are your objects, Julia, take them; they are in your power. But remember, you must take them with their necessary concomitants—the restraints upon your time, upon the choice of your friends and your company, which high life imposes; the *ennui*[6] subsequent to dissipation; the mortifications of rivalship in beauty, wit, rank, and magnificence; the trouble of managing a large fortune, and the chance of involving your affairs and your family in difficulty and distress; these and a thousand more evils you must submit to. You must renounce all the pleasures of the heart and of the imagination; you must give up the idea of cultivating literary taste; you must not expect from your husband friendship and confidence, or any of the delicacies of affection:—you govern him, he cannot therefore be your equal; you may be a fond mother, but you cannot educate your children; you will neither have the time nor the power to do it; you must trust them to a governess. In the selection of your friends, and in the enjoyment of their company and conversation you will be still more restrained: in short, you must give up the pleasures of domestic life; for that is not in this case the life you have chosen. But you will exclaim against me for supposing you capable of making such a choice—such sacrifices!—I am sure, *next to my brother,* I am the last person in the world who would wish you to make them.

You have another choice, my dear Julia: domestic life is offered to you by one who has every wish and every power to make it agreeable to you; by one whose tastes resemble your own; who would be a judge and a fond admirer of all your perfections. You would have perpetual motives to cultivate every talent, and to exert every power of pleasing for his sake—for *his* sake, whose penetration no improvement would escape, and whose affection would be susceptible of every proof of yours. Am I drawing too flattering a picture?—A sister's hand may draw a partial likeness, but still it will be a likeness. At all events, my dear Julia, you would be certain of the mode of life you would lead with my brother. The regulation of your time and occupations would be your own. In the education of your family, you would meet with no interruptions or restraint. You would have no governess

4. A character in *Cyrus the Great* by Herodotus and Xenophon, who restrained himself from raping Panthea, whom he had taken captive.

5. A carriage and its related equipment.
6. Boredom (French).

to counteract, no strangers to intrude; you might follow your own judgment, or yield to the judgment of one who would never require you to submit to his opinion, but to his reasons.

All the pleasures of friendship you would enjoy in your own family in the highest perfection, and you would have for your sister the friend of your infancy,

Caroline.

LETTER IV

Caroline to Lady V——
Upon her intended separation from her husband

You need not fear, my dear Lady V——, that I should triumph in the accomplishment of my prophecies; or that I should reproach you for having preferred your own opinion to my advice. Believe me, my dear Julia, I am your friend, nor would the name of sister have increased my friendship.

Five years have made then so great a change in your feelings and views of life, that a few days ago, when my letter to you on your marriage accidentally fell into your hands, *"you were struck with a species of astonishment at your choice, and you burst into tears in an agony of despair, on reading the wretched doom foretold to the wife of Lord V——. A doom,"* you add, *"which I feel hourly accomplishing, and which I see no possibility of averting, but by a separation from a husband, with whom, I now think, it was madness to unite myself."* Your opinion I must already know upon this subject, *"as the same arguments which should have prevented me from making such a choice, ought now to determine me to abjure it."*

You say, dear Julia, that my letter struck you with despair.—Despair is either madness or folly; it obtains, it deserves nothing from mankind but pity; and pity, though it be akin to love, has yet a secret affinity to contempt. In strong minds, despair is an acute disease; the prelude to great exertion. In weak minds, it is a chronic distemper, followed by incurable indolence. Let the crisis be favourable, and resume your wonted energy. Instead of suffering the imagination to dwell with unavailing sorrow on the past, let us turn our attention towards the future. When an evil is irremediable, let us acknowledge it to be such, and bear it:—there is no power to which we submit so certainly as to necessity. With our hopes, our wishes cease. Imagination has a contracting, as well as an expansive faculty. The prisoner, who, deprived of all that we conceive to constitute the pleasures of life, could interest or occupy himself with the labours of a spider, was certainly a philosopher. He enjoyed all the means of happiness that were left in his power.

I know, my dear Lady V——, that words have little effect over grief; and I do not, I assure you, mean to insult you with the parade of stoic philosophy. But consider, your error is not perhaps so great as you imagine. Certainly, they who at the beginning of life can with a steady eye look through the long perspective of distant years, who can in one view comprise all the different objects of happiness and misery, who can compare accurately, and justly estimate their respective degrees of importance; and who, after having formed such a calculation, are capable of acting uniformly, in consequence of their own conviction, are the *wisest,* and, as far as prudence can influence our fortune, the *happiest* of human beings. Next to this favoured class are those who can perceive and repair their own errors; who can stop at any given period to take a new view of life. If unfortunate circumstances have denied you a place in the first rank, you may, dear Julia, secure yourself a station in the second. Is not the conduct of a woman, after her marriage, of infinitely more importance than her previous choice, whatever it may have been? Then now consider what yours should be.

You say that it is easier to *break* a chain than to *stretch* it; but remember that when broken, your part of the chain, Julia, will still remain with you, and fetter and disgrace you through life. Why should a woman be so circumspect in her choice? Is it not because when once made she must abide by it? "She sets her life upon the cast, and she must stand the hazard of the die."[7] From domestic uneasiness a man has a thousand resources: in middling life, the tavern, in high life, the gaming-table, suspends the anxiety of thought. Dissipation, ambition, business, the occupation of a profession, change of place, change of company, afford him agreeable and honourable relief from domestic chagrin. If his home become tiresome, he leaves it; if his wife become disagreeable to him, he leaves her, and in leaving her loses *only* a wife. But what resource has a woman?—Precluded from all the occupations common to the other sex, she loses even those peculiar to her own. She has no remedy, from the company of a man she dislikes, but a separation; and this remedy, desperate as it is, is allowed only to a certain class of women in society; to those whose fortune affords them the means of subsistence, and whose friends have secured to them a separate maintenance. A peeress then, probably, can leave her husband if she wish it; a peasant's wife cannot; she depends upon the character and privileges of a wife for actual subsistence. Her domestic care, if not her affection, is secured to her husband; and it is just that it should. He sacrifices his liberty, his labour, his ingenuity, his time, for the support and protection of his wife; and in proportion to his protection is his power.

In higher life, where the sacrifices of both parties in the original union are more equal, the evils of a separation are more nearly balanced. But even here, the wife who has hazarded least, suffers the most by the dissolution of the partnership; she loses a great part of her fortune, and of the conveniences and luxuries of life. She loses her home, her rank in society. She loses both the repellant and the attractive power of a mistress of a family. "Her occupation is gone."[8] She becomes a wanderer. Whilst her youth and beauty last, she may enjoy that species of delirium, caused by public admiration; fortunate if habit does not destroy the power of this charm, before the season of its duration expire. It was said to be the wish of a celebrated modern beauty, "that she might not survive her nine-and-twentieth birth-day". I have often heard this wish quoted for its extravagance; but I always admired it for its good sense. The lady foresaw the inevitable doom of her declining years. Her apprehensions for the future embittered even her enjoyment of the present; and she had resolution enough to offer to take "a bond of fate"[9] to sacrifice one-half of her life, to secure the pleasure of the other.

But, dear Lady V——, probably this wish was made at some distance from the destined period of its accomplishment. On the eve of her nine-and-twentieth birth-day, the lady perhaps might have felt inclined to retract her prayer. At least we should provide for the cowardice which might seize the female mind at such an instant. Even the most wretched life has power to attach us; none can be more wretched than the old age of a dissipated beauty:—unless, Lady V——, it be that of a woman, who, to all her evils has the addition of remorse, for having abjured

---

7. An appropriation of Richard's lines from Shakespeare's *Richard III*: "Slave, I have set my life upon a cast, / And I will stand the hazard of the die" (4.7.9–10).

8. A rephrasing from Shakespeare's *Othello*: "Farewell! Othello's occupation gone" (3.3.362).

9. Shakespeare's *Macbeth* (4.1.95) after Macbeth sees the apparition of a bloody child.

her duties and abandoned her family. Such is the situation of a woman who separates from her husband. Reduced to go the same insipid round of public amusements, yet more restrained than an unmarried beauty in youth, yet more miserable in age, the superiority of her genius and the sensibility of her heart become her greatest evils. She, indeed, must pray for indifference. Avoided by all her family connexions, hated and despised where she might have been loved and respected, solitary in the midst of society, she feels herself deserted at the time of life when she most wants social comfort and assistance.

Dear Julia, whilst it is yet in your power secure to yourself a happier fate; retire to the bosom of your own family; prepare for yourself a new society; perform the duties, and you shall soon enjoy the pleasures of domestic life; educate your children; whilst they are young, it shall be your occupation; as they grow up, it shall be your glory. Let me anticipate your future success, when they shall appear such as you can make them; when the world shall ask "who educated these amiable young women? Who formed their character? Who cultivated the talents of this promising young man? Why does this whole family live together in such perfect union?" With one voice, dear Julia, your children shall name their mother; she who in the bloom of youth checked herself in the career of dissipation, and turned all the ability and energy of her mind to their education.

Such will be your future fame. In the mean time, before you have formed for yourself companions in your own family, you will want a society suited to your taste. "Disgusted as you have been with frivolous company, you say that you wish to draw around you a society of literary and estimable friends, whose conversation and talents shall delight you, and who at the same time that they are excited to display their own abilities, shall be a judge of yours."

But, dear Lady V——, the possibility of your forming such a society must depend on your having a home to receive, a character and consequence in life to invite and attach friends. The opinion of numbers is necessary to excite the ambition of individuals. To be a female Mecænas[1] you must have power to confer favours, as well as judgment to discern merit.

What castles in the air are built by the synthetic wand of imagination, which vanish when exposed to the analysis of reason!

Then, Julia, supposing that Lord V——, as your husband, becomes a negative quantity as to your happiness, yet he will acquire another species of value as the master of your family and the father of your children; as a person who supports your public consequence, and your private self-complacency. Yes, dear Lady V——, he will increase your self-complacency; for do you not think, that when your husband sees his children prosper under your care, his family united under your management—whilst he feels your merit at home, and hears your praises abroad, do you not think he will himself learn to respect and love you? You say that *"he is not a judge of female excellence; that he has no real taste; that vanity is his ruling passion."* Then if his judgment be dependent on the opinions of others, he will be the more easily led by the public voice, and you will command the suffrages of the public. If he has not taste enough to approve, he will have vanity enough to be proud of you; and a vain man insensibly begins to love that of which he is proud. Why does Lord V—— love his buildings, his paintings, his equipages? It is not for their intrinsic value; but because they are means of distinction to him. Let his wife

---

1. Gaius Maecenas (c. 70–8 BCE), Roman diplomat and minor poet.

become a greater distinction to him, and on the same principles he will prefer her. Set an example, then, dear Lady V——, of domestic virtue; your talents shall make it admired, your rank shall make it conspicuous. You are ambitious, Julia, you love praise; you have been used to it; you cannot live happily without it.

Praise is a mental luxury, which becomes from habit absolutely necessary to our existence; and in purchasing it we must pay the price set upon it by society. The more curious, the more avaricious we become of this "aerial coin", the more it is our interest to preserve its currency and increase its value. You, my dear Julia, in particular, who have amassed so much of it, should not cry down its price, for your own sake!—Do not then say in a fit of disgust, that "you are grown too wise now to value applause."

If during youth, your appetite for applause was indiscriminate, and indulged to excess, you are now more difficult in your choice, and are become an *epicure* in your *taste* for praise.

Adieu, my dear Julia; I hope still to see you as happy in domestic life as

Your ever affectionate
and sincere friend,
Caroline.

LETTER V

Caroline to Lady V——
On her conduct after her separation from her husband

A delicacy, of which I now begin to repent, has of late prevented me from writing to you. I am afraid I shall be abrupt, but it is necessary to be explicit. Your conduct, ever since your separation from your husband, has been anxiously watched from a variety of motives, by his family and your own;—it has been blamed. Reflect upon your own mind, and examine with what justice.

Last summer, when I was with you, I observed a change in your conversation, and the whole turn of your thoughts. I perceived an unusual impatience of restraint; a confusion in your ideas when you began to reason,—an eloquence in your language when you began to declaim, which convinced me that from some secret cause the powers of your reason had been declining, and those of your imagination rapidly increasing; the boundaries of right and wrong seemed to be no longer marked in your mind. Neither the rational hope of happiness, nor a sense of duty governed you; but some unknown, wayward power seemed to have taken possession of your understanding, and to have thrown every thing into confusion. You appeared peculiarly averse to philosophy: let me recall your own words to you; you asked "of what use philosophy could be to beings who had no free will, and how the ideas of just punishment and involuntary crime could be reconciled?"

Your understanding involved itself in metaphysical absurdity. In conversing upon literary subjects one evening, in speaking of the striking difference between the conduct and the understanding of the great Lord Bacon, you said, that "It by no means surprised you; that to an enlarged mind, accustomed to consider the universe as one vast *whole*, the conduct of that little animated atom, that inconsiderable part *self*, must be too insignificant to fix or merit attention.[2] It was nothing," you said, "in the general mass of vice and virtue, happiness and misery." I

---

2. Francis Bacon (1561–1620), a renowned scientist and politician whose public career ended after he was found guilty of accepting a bribe while a judge.

believe I answered, "that it might be *nothing* compared to the great *whole,* but it was *every thing* to the individual." Such were your opinions in theory; you must know enough of the human heart to perceive their tendency when reduced to practice. Speculative opinions, I know, have little influence over the practice of those who *act* much and think little; but I should conceive their power to be considerable over the conduct of those who have much time for reflection and little necessity for action. In one case the habit of action governs the thoughts upon any sudden emergency; in the other, the thoughts govern the actions. The truth or falsehood then of speculative opinions is of much greater consequence to our sex than to the other; as we live a life of reflection, they of action.

Retrace, then, dear Julia, in your mind the course of your thoughts for some time past; discover the cause of this revolution in your opinions; judge yourself; and remember, that in the *mind* as well as in the body, the highest pitch of disease is often attended with an unconsciousness of its existence. If, then, Lady V——, upon receiving my letter, you should feel averse to this self-examination, or if you should imagine it to be useless, I no longer advise, I command you to quit your present abode; come to me: fly from the danger, and be safe.

Dear Julia, I must assume this peremptory tone: if you are angry, I must disregard your anger; it is the anger of disease, the anger of one who is roused from that sleep which would end in death.

I respect the equality of friendship; but this equality permits, nay requires, the temporary ascendancy I assume. In real friendship, the judgment, the genius, the prudence of each party become the common property of both. Even if they are equals, they may not be so *always.* Those transient fits of passion, to which the best and wisest are liable, may deprive even the superior of the advantage of their reason. She then has still in her friend an *impartial,* though perhaps an inferior judgment; each becomes the guardian of the other, as their mutual safety may require.

Heaven seems to have granted this double chance of virtue and happiness, as the peculiar reward of friendship.

Use it, then, my dear friend; accept the assistance you could so well return. Obey me; I shall judge of you by your resolution at this crisis: on it depends your fate, and my friendship.

Your sincere
and affectionate
Caroline.

LETTER VI

Caroline to Lady V——
Just before she went to France

The time is now come, Lady V——, when I must bid you an eternal adieu. With what deep regret, I need not, Julia, I cannot tell you.

I burned your letter the moment I had read it. Your past confidence I never will betray; but I must renounce all future intercourse with you. I am a sister, a wife, a mother; all these connexions forbid me to be longer your friend. In misfortune, in sickness, or in poverty, I never would have forsaken you; but infamy I cannot share. I would have gone, I went, to the brink of the precipice to save you; with all my force I held you back; but in vain. But why do I vindicate my conduct to you now? Accustomed as I have always been to think your approbation necessary to my happiness, I forgot that henceforward your opinion is to be nothing to me, or mine to you.

Oh, Julia! the idea, the certainty, that you must, if you live, be in a few years, in a few months, perhaps, reduced to absolute want, in a foreign country—without a friend—a protector, the fate of women who have fallen from a state as high as yours, the names of L——, of G——, the horror I feel at joining your name to theirs, impels me to make one more attempt to save you.

Companion of my earliest years! friend of my youth! my beloved Julia! by the happy innocent hours we have spent together, by the love you had for me, by the respect you bear to the memory of your mother, by the agony with which your father will hear of the loss of his daughter, by all that has power to touch your mind—I conjure you, I implore you to pause!—Farewell!

Caroline.

LETTER VII

Caroline to Lord V——
Written a few months after the date of the preceding letter

My Lord,
Though I am too sensible that all connexion between my unfortunate friend and her family must for some time have been dissolved, I venture now to address myself to your lordship.

On Wednesday last, about half after six o'clock in the evening, the following note was brought to me. It had been written with such a trembling hand that it was scarcely legible; but I knew the writing too well.

"If you ever loved me, Caroline, read this—do not tear it the moment you see the name of Julia: she has suffered—she is humbled. I left France with the hope of seeing you once more, but now I am so near you, my courage fails, and my heart sinks within me. I have no friend upon earth—I deserve none; yet I cannot help wishing to see, once more before I die, the friend of my youth, to thank her with my last breath.

"But, dear Caroline, if I must not see you, write to me, if possible, one line of consolation.

"Tell me, is my father living—do you know any thing of my children?—I dare not ask for my husband. Adieu! I am so weak that I can scarcely write—I hope I shall soon be no more. Farewell!

"Julia."

I immediately determined to follow the bearer of this letter. Julia was waiting for my answer at a small inn in a neighbouring village, at a few miles' distance. It was night when I got there: every thing was silent—all the houses were shut up, excepting one, in which we saw two or three lights glimmering through the window—this was the inn: as your lordship may imagine, it was a very miserable place. The mistress of the house seemed to be touched with pity for the stranger: she opened the door of a small room, where she said the poor lady was resting; and retired as I entered.

Upon a low matted seat beside the fire sat Lady V——; she was in black; her knees were crossed, and her white but emaciated arms flung on one side over her lap; her hands were clasped together, and her eyes fixed upon the fire: she seemed neither to hear nor see any thing round her, but, totally absorbed in her own reflections, to have sunk into insensibility. I dreaded to rouse her from this state of torpor; and I believe I stood for some moments motionless: at last I moved softly towards her—she turned her head—started up—a scarlet blush overspread her face—she grew livid again instantly, gave a faint shriek, and sunk senseless into my arms.

When she returned to herself, and found her head lying upon my shoulder, and heard my voice soothing her with all the expressions of kindness I could think of, she smiled with a look of gratitude, which I never shall forget. Like one who had been long unused to kindness, she seemed ready to pour forth all the fondness of her heart: but, as if recollecting herself better, she immediately checked her feelings—withdrew her hand from mine—thanked me—said she was quite well again—cast down her eyes, and her manner changed from tenderness to timidity. She seemed to think that she had lost all right to sympathy, and received even the common offices of humanity with surprise: her high spirit, I saw, was quite broken.

I think I never felt such sorrow as I did in contemplating Julia at this instant: she who stood before me, sinking under the sense of inferiority, I knew to be my equal—my superior; yet by fatal imprudence, by one rash step, all her great, and good, and amiable qualities were irretrievably lost to the world and to herself.

When I thought that she was a little recovered, I begged of her, if she was not too much fatigued, to let me carry her home. At these words she looked at me with surprise. Her eyes filled with tears; but without making any other reply, she suffered me to draw her arm within mine, and attempted to follow me. I did not know how feeble she was till she began to walk; it was with the utmost difficulty I supported her to the door; and by the assistance of the people of the house she was lifted into the carriage: we went very slowly. When the carriage stopped she was seized with an universal tremor; she started when the man knocked at the door, and seemed to dread its being opened. The appearance of light and the sound of cheerful voices struck her with horror.

I could not myself help being shocked with the contrast between the dreadful situation of my friend, and the happiness of the family to which I was returning.

"Oh!" said she, "what are these voices?—Whither are you taking me?—For Heaven's sake do not let any body see me!"

I assured her that she should go directly to her own apartment, and that no human being should approach her without her express permission.

Alas! it happened at this very moment that all my children came running with the utmost gaiety into the hall to meet us, and the very circumstance which I had been so anxious to prevent happened—little Julia was amongst them. The gaiety of the children suddenly ceased the moment they saw Lady V—— coming up the steps—they were struck with her melancholy air and countenance: she, leaning upon my arm, with her eyes fixed upon the ground, let me lead her in, and sunk upon the first chair she came to. I made a sign to the children to retire; but the moment they began to move, Lady V—— looked up—saw her daughter—and now for the first time burst into tears. The little girl did not recollect her poor mother till she heard the sound of her voice; and then she threw her arms round her neck, crying, "Is that you, mamma?"—and all the children immediately crowded round and asked, "if this was the same Lady V—— who used to play with them"?

It is impossible to describe the effect these simple questions had on Julia: a variety of emotions seemed struggling in her countenance; she rose and made an attempt to break from the children, but could not—she had not strength to support herself. We carried her away and put her to bed; she took no notice of any body, nor did she even seem to know that I was with her: I thought she was insensible, but as I drew the curtains I heard her give a deep sigh.

I left her, and carried away her little girl, who had followed us up stairs and begged to stay with her mother; but I was apprehensive that the sight of her might renew her agitation.

After I was gone, they told me that she was perfectly still, with her eyes closed; and I stayed away some time in hopes that she might sleep: however, about midnight she sent to beg to speak to me: she was very ill—she beckoned to me to sit down by her bedside—every one left the room; and when Julia saw herself alone with me, she took my hand, and in a low but calm voice she said, "I have not many hours to live—my heart is broken—I wished to see you, to thank you whilst it was yet in my power." She pressed my hand to her trembling lips: "Your kindness," added she, "touches me more than all the rest; but how ashamed you must be of such a friend! Oh, Caroline! to die a disgrace to all who ever loved me!"

The tears trickled down her face, and choked her utterance: she wiped them away hastily. "But it is not now a time," said she, "to think of myself—can I see my daughter?" The little girl was asleep: she was awakened, and I brought her to her mother. Julia raised herself in her bed, and summoning up all her strength, "My dearest friend!" said she, putting her child's hand into mine, "when I am gone, be a mother to this child—let her know my whole history, let nothing be concealed from her. Poor girl! you will live to blush at your mother's name." She paused and leaned back: I was going to take the child away, but she held out her arms again for her, and kissed her several times. "Farewell!" said she; "I shall never see you again." The little girl burst into tears. Julia wished to say something more—she raised herself again—at last she uttered these words with energy:— "My love, *be good and happy*"; she then sunk down on the pillow quite exhausted—she never spoke afterwards: I took her hand—it was cold—her pulse scarcely beat—her eyes rolled without meaning—in a few moments she expired.

Painful as it has been to me to recall the circumstances of her death to my imagination, I have given your lordship this exact and detailed account of my unfortunate friend's behaviour in her last moments. Whatever may have been her errors, her soul never became callous from vice. The sense of her own ill conduct, was undoubtedly the immediate cause of her illness, and the remorse which had long preyed upon her mind, at length brought her to the grave—

I have the honour to be,
My lord, &c.
Caroline.

1787   1795

►◄ DOROTHY WORDSWORTH ►◄
1771–1855

A perceptive and talented writer of journals and poetry not produced for publication, Dorothy Wordsworth spent most of her life in relative isolation, living with her brother, the poet William Wordsworth (1770–1850), for whom she cared and to whom she freely offered her ideas. Only within the past few decades have her works become the object of feminist study in their own right. They are now considered a telling reminder of what it meant to be a woman writer in the early nineteenth century.

Dorothy Wordsworth was the third of five children and the only daughter born to Ann Cookson and John Wordsworth. Her mother died when she was six, and her father, an attorney, died without a will when she was twelve, leaving his children in a precarious financial state. She went to live with relatives, including her uncle and grandparents. This meant she was separated from her brothers, to whom she was very attached. Little is known about her early education. She appears to have been largely self-taught and widely read. We know that she was often able to keep up intellectually with her university-educated brothers.

In 1795, her father's will was settled favorably, and, much to her happiness, she was able to move in with her brother William. At first they lived in Dorset, then moved on to Alfoxden in Somerset in 1797. In 1798–99 she traveled to Germany with William and poet Samuel Taylor Coleridge (1772–1834). When they returned, the brother and sister moved to the town of Grasmere in the Lake District, a picturesque part of northwest England. There they lived first at Dove Cottage—which remains open as a museum today—and later at nearby Rydal Mount. It was at Alfoxden that Dorothy Wordsworth started keeping her now-famous journal, which her brother sometimes mined for ideas for his poems. For example, William's poem titled "I wandered lonely as a cloud" was created directly out of the imagery in Dorothy's journal entry for April 15, 1802. We also know that she appears in William's poem "Lines Composed a Few Miles above Tintern Abbey" as his "dearest Friend," in whom he catches "the language of his former heart."

When William married his sister's close friend, Mary Hutchinson, in 1802, Dorothy was so upset, as she records in her journal entry for that day, included here, that she could not bring herself to attend the wedding. Over time she continued to live with her sister-in-law, her brother, and their children, and she grew to accept and become an important part of the expanded family. She was very ill during the last twenty years of her life. She is believed to have suffered from arteriosclerosis from around 1835 on, and she also suffered from mental problems, perhaps as a result of vitamin deficiency. Dorothy Wordsworth died in Rydal Mount in 1855.

Wordsworth's journals provide intimate, detailed, and astute observations of rural life in early-nineteenth-century England. She gives us access to the rhythm of her day, with its endless housework, as well as the deep pleasures experienced in the natural world. We also sense the texture of the period—the many homeless families, for example, who roamed the district, or the small circle of acquaintances known to the Wordsworths. Lastly, the evidence of Dorothy Wordsworth's literary talents leads to reflections on the circumstances that kept her from achieving the literary stature achieved by her brother.

From The Grasmere Journals

[A Brother's Departure, May 14, 1800]

May 14 1800.
Wm and John[1] set off into Yorkshire after dinner at ½ past 2 o'clock, cold pork in their pockets. I left them at the turning of the Low-wood bay under the trees. My

---

1. Wm (William), the famous Romantic poet, and John were Dorothy's brothers.

heart was so full that I could hardly speak to W. when I gave him a farewell kiss. I sate a long time upon a stone at the margin of the lake, and after a flood of tears my heart was easier. The lake looked to me I knew not why dull and melancholy, and the weltering on the shores seemed a heavy sound. I walked as long as I could amongst the stones of the shore. The wood rich in flowers. A beautiful yellow, palish yellow flower, that looked thick round and double, and smelt very sweet— I supposed it was a ranunculus[2]—Crowfoot, the grassy-leaved Rabbit-toothed white flower, strawberries, geranium—scentless violet, anemones two kinds, orchises, primroses. The heckberry[3] very beautiful, the crab coming out as a low shrub. Met a blind man, driving a very large beautiful Bull and a cow—he walked with two sticks. Came home by Clappersgate.[4] The valley very green, many sweet views up to Rydale head when I could juggle away the fine houses, but they disturbed me even more than when I have been happier. One beautiful view of the Bridge,[5] without Sir Michael's. Sate down very often, though it was cold. I resolved to write a journal of the time till W. and J. return, and I set about keeping my resolve because I will not quarrel with myself, and because I shall give Wm Pleasure by it when he comes home again. At Rydale a woman of the village, stout and well dressed, begged a halfpenny—she had never she said done it before, but these hard times——Arrived at home with a bad head-ach, set some slips of privett.[6] The evening cold, had a fire—my face now flame-coloured. It is nine o'clock, I shall soon go to bed. A young woman begged at the door—she had come from Manchester on Sunday morn with two shillings and a slip of paper which she supposed a Bank note—it was a cheat. She had buried her husband and three children within a year and a half—all in one grave—burying very dear—paupers all put in one place—20 shillings paid for as much ground as will bury a man—a stone to be put over it or the right will be lost—11/6 each time the ground is opened. Oh! that I had a letter from William![7]

[Daffodils, April 1802]

Tuesday 13th April.

I had slept ill and was not well and obliged to go to bed in the afternoon—Mrs C. waked me from sleep with a letter from Coleridge. After tea I went down to see the Bank and walked along the Lake side to the field where Mr Smith thought of building his house. The air was become still the lake was of a bright slate colour, the hills darkening. The Bays shot into the low fading shores. Sheep resting all things quiet. When I returned Jane met me—*William* was come. The surprize shot through me. He looked well but he was tired and went soon to bed after a dish of Tea.

Wednesday 14th.

William did not rise till dinner time. I walked with Mrs C. I was ill out of spirits— disheartened. Wm and I took a long walk in the Rain.

2. A buttercup.
3. A type of cherry tree.
4. Like so many of the specific place-names mentioned in her journal—among them Eversmere, Kirkstone, and Rydale—this name marks a precise location in the Lake District.
5. She is able to see Pelter Bridge in Rydal, without seeing the residence of Sir Michael le Fleming,

a local member of the upper ranks.
6. Arranged some cutting from a type of shrub.
7. Eleven shillings, six pence are charged for opening the gravesite in order to deposit another deceased member of the family. Although monetary conversions can be problematic, 11s 6d at the time this selection was written would be about $55 today.

Thursday 15th.
It was a threatening misty morning—but mild. We set off after dinner from Euse-
mere. Mrs Clarkson went a short way with us but turned back. The wind was
furious and we thought we must have returned. We first rested in the large Boat-
house, then under a furze Bush opposite Mr Clarkson's. Saw the plough going in
the field. The wind seized our breath the lake was rough. There was a Boat by itself
floating in the middle of the Bay below Water Millock. We rested again in the Water
Millock Lane. The hawthorns are black and green, the birches here and there green-
ish but there is yet more of purple to be seen on the Twigs. We got over into a field
to avoid some cows—people working, a few primroses by the roadside, wood-sor-
rel flower, the anemone, scentless violets, strawberries, and that starry yellow
flower which Mrs C. calls pile wort. When we were in the woods beyond Gowbar-
row park we saw a few daffodils close to the water side. We fancied that the lake
had floated the seeds ashore and that the little colony had so sprung up. But as we
went along there were more and yet more and at last under the boughs of the trees,
we saw that there was a long belt of them along the shore, about the breadth of a
country turnpike road. I never saw daffodils so beautiful they grew among the
mossy stones about and about them, some rested their heads upon these stones as
on a pillow for weariness and the rest tossed and reeled and danced and seemed as
if they verily laughed with the wind that blew upon them over the lake, they looked
so gay ever glancing ever changing. This wind blew directly over the lake to them.
There was here and there a little knot and a few stragglers a few yards higher up
but they were so few as not to disturb the simplicity and unity and life of that one
busy highway.[8] We rested again and again. The Bays were stormy, and we heard
the waves at different distances and in the middle of the water like the sea.

[*Good Friday, April 16, 1802*]

Friday 16th April.
When I undrew my curtains in the morning, I was much affected by the beauty of
the prospect and the change. The sun shone, the wind had passed away, the hills
looked chearful, the river was very bright as it flowed into the lake. The Church
rises up behind a little knot of Rocks, the steeple not so high as an ordinary 3 story
house. Bees, in a row in the garden under the wall. After Wm had shaved we set
forward. The valley is at first broken by little rocky woody knolls that make retiring places, fairy valleys in the vale, the river winds along under these hills travelling not in a bustle but not slowly to the lake. We saw a fisherman in the flat
meadow on the other side of the water. He came towards us and threw his line
over the two arched Bridge. It is a Bridge of a heavy construction, almost bending
inwards in the middle, but it is grey and there is a look of ancientry in the architecture of it that pleased me. As we go on the vale opens out more into one vale
with somewhat of a cradle Bed. Cottages with groups of trees on the side of the
hills. We passed a pair of twin Children 2 years old—Sate on the next bridge which

8. Compare lines 1–14 of the poem "I Wandered
Lonely as a Cloud" (1804) by William Wordsworth: I wandered lonely as a cloud / That floats
on high o'er vales and hills, / When all at once I
saw a crowd, / A host, of golden daffodils; / Beside the lake, beneath the trees, / Fluttering and
dancing in the breeze. / Continuous as the stars
that shine / And twinkle on the milky way, / They
stretched in never-ending line / Along the margin
of a bay: / Ten thousand saw I at a glance, / Tossing their heads in sprightly dance. / The waves beside them danced; but they / Out-did the sparkling
waves in glee.

we crossed a single arch. We rested again upon the Turf and looked at the same Bridge. We observed arches in the water occasioned by the large stones sending it down in two streams. A Sheep came plunging through the river, stumbled up the Bank and passed close to us, it had been frightened by an insignificant little Dog on the other side, its fleece dropped a glittering shower under its belly. Primroses by the roadside, pile wort that shone like stars of gold in the Sun, violets, strawberries, retired and half buried among the grass. When we came to the foot of Brothers water I left William sitting on the Bridge and went along the path on the right side of the Lake through the wood. I was delighted with what I saw. The water under the boughs of the bare old trees, the simplicity of the mountains and the exquisite beauty of the path. There was one grey cottage. I repeated the Glowworm[9] as I walked along. I hung over the gate, and thought I could have stayed for ever. When I returned I found William writing a poem descriptive of the sights and sounds we saw and heard.[1] There was the gentle flowing of the stream, the glittering lively lake; green fields without a living creature to be seen on them, behind us, a flat pasture with 42 cattle feeding to our left the road leading to the hamlet, no smoke there, the sun shone on the bare roofs. The people were at work ploughing, harrowing and sowing—lasses spreading dung, a dog's barking now and then, cocks crowing, birds twittering, the snow in patches at the top of the highest hills, yellow palms, purple and green twigs on the Birches, ashes with their glittering spikes quite bare. The hawthorn a bright green with black stems under the oak. The moss of the oak glossy. We then went on, passed two sisters at work, *they first passed us*, one with two pitch forks in her hand. The other had a spade. We had some talk with them. They laughed aloud after we were gone perhaps half in wantonness, half boldness. William finished his poem before we got to the foot of Kirkstone. There were hundreds of cattle in the vale. There we ate our dinner. The walk up Kirkstone was very interesting. The Becks among the rocks were all alive. Wm showed me the little mossy streamlet which he had before loved when he saw its bright green track in the snow. The view above Ambleside, very beautiful. There we sate and looked down on the green vale. We watched the crows at a little distance from us become white as silver as they flew in the sunshine, and when they went still further they looked like shapes of water passing over the green fields. The whitening of Ambleside Church is a great deduction from the beauty of it seen from this point. We called at the Luffs, the Boddingtons there did not go in and went round by the fields. I pulled off my stockings intending to wade the Beck but I was obliged to put them on and we climbed over the wall at the Bridge. The post passed us. No letters! Rydale Lake was in its own evening brightness, the Islands and points distinct. Jane Ashburner came up to us when we were sitting upon the wall. We rode in her cart to Tom Dawson's. All well. The garden looked pretty in the half moonlight-half daylight. As we went up the vale of Brothers Water more and more cattle feeding 100 of them.

[*William Marries, September 24, 1802*]

24th September.
Mary first met us in the avenue. She looked so fat and well that we were made very happy by the sight of her. Then came Sara, and last of all Joanna. Tom was

---

9. A poem by her brother, published in 1807 under the title "Among all lovely things my love had been."

1. "The Cock Is Crowing," published as "Written in March, while resting on the bridge at the foot of Brother's Water" (1807).

forking corn standing upon the corn cart. We dressed ourselves immediately and got tea—the garden looked gay with asters and sweet peas. I looked at everything with tranquillity and happiness—was ill on Saturday and on Sunday and continued to be during most of the time of our stay. Jack and George came on Friday Evening 1st October. On Saturday 2nd we rode to Hackness, William Jack George and Sara single, I behind Tom. On Sunday 3rd Mary and Sara were busy packing. On Monday 4th October 1802, my Brother William was married to Mary Hutchinson. I slept a good deal of the night and rose fresh and well in the morning. At a little after 8 o'clock I saw them go down the avenue towards the Church. William had parted from me upstairs. I gave him the wedding ring—with how deep a blessing! I took it from my forefinger where I had worn it the whole of the night before—he slipped it again onto my finger and blessed me fervently. When they were absent my dear little Sara prepared the breakfast. I kept myself as quiet as I could, but when I saw the two men running up the walk, coming to tell us it was over, I could stand it no longer and threw myself on the bed where I lay in stillness, neither hearing or seeing any thing, till Sara came upstairs to me and said "They are coming". This forced me from the bed where I lay and I moved I knew not how straight forward, faster than my strength could carry me till I met my beloved William and fell upon his bosom. He and John Hutchinson led me to the house and there I stayed to welcome my dear Mary. As soon as we had breakfasted we departed.[2] It rained when we set off. Poor Mary was much agitated when she parted from her Brothers and Sisters and her home. Nothing particular occurred till we reached Kirby.

MARY BIRKETT
1774–1817

Mary Birkett published her remarkable anti-slavery poem in 1791, when she was only seventeen. Born into a Quaker family, she was the daughter of a tallow chandler and soap boiler. The family lived in Liverpool, England, until Birkett was ten, and then moved to Dublin, Ireland. We have no evidence of how she was educated, though she likely went to a Quaker school. In 1801, she married her cousin Nathaniel Card, a merchant. The couple had eight children, one of whom, a son, hand-copied and bound Birkett's writings. Throughout her lifetime, Birkett was very active in the Irish Quaker community. She retired due to ill health and died in 1817, probably from liver failure. She published only one other work during her lifetime, an elegy on another member of her Quaker community.

Birkett's "Poem on the African Slave Trade" creates an immediate, almost visceral link between the drinking of tea, sweetened with sugar grown in the West Indies, and the horrific lives of the enslaved Africans who produced it. She was not the first to make this connection: in 1791, the Quaker William Fox published a famous pamphlet equating the consumption of sugar to the consumption of slaves' flesh. His publication launched the first successful orchestrated consumer boycott, as nearly 300,000 people—many of them women—abstained from West Indian sugar as a protest against slavery. In her poem, Birkett effectively argues against a racist ideology that denied enslaved Africans their humanity and demonstrates the

2. Dorothy returned to Grasmere with the newlyweds.

inhumane and illegal nature of the trade. If her portrait of an African man in his native setting is sentimentalized, she brings home a clear message nonetheless: women as consumers have a moral obligation to think about the origins of the products they enjoy. In addition, if her polemic seems couched in imperial terms, she still takes seriously the idea that commerce must be carried out to benefit everyone equally. Birkett also wrote a second part to this poem, in which she took up the theme of the rights of man and compared English and Irish attitudes toward slavery.

A Poem on the African Slave Trade

Oppression! thou, whose hard and cruel chain,
Entails on all thy victims woe and pain;
Who gives with tyrant force and scorpion whip,
The cup of mis'ry to a Negro's lip;
Marks with stern frown thy wide, unhallow'd reign,   5
And broods with gloomy wing o'er Afric's injur'd plain!
Thy voice which spreads pale desolation round,
While trembling myriads groan beneath the sound,
Thy voice more rude than Boreas'[1] chilling breath,
Calls thousands forth to feel a living death!   10
Which in hoarse thunders bids injustice rise!
While oft beneath the strokes the suff'rer dies:
Yes! thy infernal voice impels my song,
And o'er my soul its crude ideas throng;
A sorrowing sympathy surrounds my heart,   15
And mild compassion bleeds in every part.
Mov'd at the dire distress my brethren know
My mind in vain participates their woe;
In vain for them I raise the fervent sigh;
Ah! still they bleed!—they languish!—still they die!   20

How little think the giddy and the gay
While sipping o'er the sweets of charming tea,
How oft with grief they pierce the manly breast,
How oft their lux'ry robs the wretch of rest,
And that to gain the plant we idly waste   25
Th' *extreme of human mis'ry* they must taste!

Yes! 'tis no lying fable I relate,
Th' *extreme of human mis'ry* is their fate!
Let sordid traders call it what they will,
Men must be men, possest with feelings still;   30
And little boots[2] a white or sable skin,
To prove a fair inhabitant within.

There are, oh! scandal to the Christian name,
Who fierce of blood, and lost to sense of shame,

---

1. The Greek god of the north wind.   2. Profits.

Dare lave their impious hands in human gore,   35
And barter living souls for lust of ore;
More rav'nous than the foulest beasts of prey,
They but from Nature's powerful cravings slay;
More cruel than the thief, whose murd'rous knife
At once deprives the trembling wretch of life: 40
Him poverty, perchance, taught first to stray,
And strongly urg'd her too prevailing plea;
Yet him the justice of our laws condemn:
Beasts we destroy, but seldom think of them.
Strange paradox! we view with shrinking eye,   45
The murd'rer's crime, and bid him justly die;
But when our traders[3] snatch a thousand lives,
No pain, no punishment on them derives;
The guilt's diminish'd, as increas'd its size,
And they are clear—at least in mortal eyes.   50

   Tell me, ye friends of slav'ry's shameful cause,
Where shall I find the records—where the laws,
Which give to man indubitable power
To sell his brother, and the spoil devour?
And whence do we th' infernal doctrine hold,   55
To sell th' image of our God for gold?

   To our first parents when th' Almighty Cause
Reveal'd his holy will—his hallow'd laws;
When from his lips the wondrous accents broke,
And mortals listen'd while the Godhead spoke;   60
In that mysterious moment did he say?—
"Man shall his fellow ravage, sell, and slay;
"And one unhappy race shall always be
"Slave to another's pamper'd luxury."

   There are, I know, who think and *more* who say,   65
That not so injur'd—so opprest are they;
That under masters *just* they earn their bread,
And plenty crowns the board at which they're fed.
Ah, sophist, vain thy subtle reas'ning's aim!
Look at the Negro's sun-burnt, grief-worn frame!   70
Examine well each limb, each nerve, each bone,
Each artery—and then observe *thy own;*
The beating pulse, the heart that throbs within,
All, (save the sable tincture of his skin,)
Say, Christians, do they not resemble you?   75
If so, their feelings and sensations too:
One moment now with you his burthen rest,
Then tell me, is he happy—is he blest?

3. Slave traders.

Lo! where on Afric's shore the sable youth,
Feels each degree of honor, love, and truth;   80
(Though he ne'er heard the gospel's joyful sound,
Nor call'd on Jesus in his natal ground;
Reproach him not, oh, follower of thy Lord,
Who never knew the blessing of his word;
Think on thy own forefathers savage lore,   85
He keeps his inward guide, and dost thou more?)
Rear'd in the lap of innocence and ease,
Him simple Nature's genuine bounties please.
For him no palace rears its costly head,
Contented with an humble turf built shed;   90
On him no fawning lacqueys[4] proudly wait,
In all the pamper'd insolence of state;
No harmless lives, his taste to gratify,
Opprest with various torture slowly die.
And if his manners suit the savage name,   95
Uneducated man is every where the same.

There in that plain, when freedom was his guest,
And social love glow'd in his faithful breast;
Then when his soul youth's joyous feelings knew,
And manhood, ripening manhood, rose to view;   100
He to his parents eye perhaps appears,
The only staff of their declining years;
And he with ceaseless love and anxious care,
Does oft for them the hunted food prepare:
Perchance soft passion does his bosom move,   105
And his fond nymph returns his constant love;
Perhaps his offspring hail their honour'd sire,
And each to gain the envy'd kiss aspire:
On him a pleasing weight of cares attend,
As father, husband, brother, son or friend: 110
Haply the hour when their supply he fought,
His soul with ev'ry warm affection fraught,
As o'er the plain he chac'd his wonted prey,
And hope deceitful cheer'd the toilsome way;
When homeward now the lifeless prize he brought,   115
Already greets his cot[5] his rapid thought;
Him *Christian* traders see, his path surround,
In vain his feet pursue their nimble bound;
He's seiz'd and dragg'd along—in vain he cries,
Starts, stamps the ground—now groans, now weeps, now sighs; 120
And fill'd with all the agony of grief,
Raves with despair—now supplicates relief:
In vain he strives their pity to command,
The ruffians hear, but will not understand;

4. Servants.   5. Cottage.

Deaf to th' heart-rending groan, the plaintive sigh,   125
They view his misery with a stoic eye,
And to the vessel haul the wretch along
In chains to mingle with the suffering throng.

   Oh thou! whom more than all he loves beside,
Friend of his heart! his chaste and faithful bride!   130
What was thy anguish on that fatal day
Which bore thy spouse from Afric far away!
In vain for him thou heap'st the cheerful fire;
In vain thy little ones demand their sire;
In vain thou chid'st his long delay!——go, mourn,   135
For never must the youth thou lov'st return!

   Lo, now the winds embrace the swelling sail,
And the full bark[6] salutes the rising gale;
While now the desolated shore they leave,
And for Jamaica cut the briny wave.   140
While o'er the foaming sea their course they steal,
Think what the Negroes suffer!—what they feel!
Opprest with sickness, close confin'd they lie,
No kind, no sympathizing friend is nigh:
Grim Death his jaws insatiate shews around,   145
And bleeding Mem'ry opes the recent wound.
Thrice happy they who feel his icy hand!
No more they dread their tyrant's stern command;
No more expos'd to insult and to pain,
They drag along the hard and cruel chain;   150
But their freed souls approach the throne of grace,
To meet the proud oppressor face to face.

   Oh, tyrants, what will then your anguish be,
When God and men shall your injustice see!
And trust me that important day will come,   155
Which fixes your irrevocable doom,
When all your basely murder'd slaves shall rise,
And publish all your crimes throughout the skies.

   Here cease, oh Muse! nor dare the secret tell,
The dread event, which but with God must dwell.   160

   Now turn our eye to India's[7] sultry shore,
And tell, oh! tell me, are their sorrows o'er?

   The bark arrives, with those who yet remain,
They drag to land the feebly-tott'ring train:
Their squalid look, and meagre form declare   165
The soul opprest with sickness, grief and care.
I pass the complicated scenes of woe

6. Sailing ship.   7. The West Indies.

Which these sad vassals of our lux'ry know:
Their sickness, fatt'ning, shameful market, past,
And now for life the dreadful die is cast.   170

Grant a mild master kindly treats them well,
(Few such there are—and they who know can tell);
Grant that those masters plenteous meals prepare,
(Though well 'tis known their food is scant and bare);
Yet then, even then, can comfort on them wait,   175
Depress'd, degraded to a servile state?
And they once chieftains in their native land,
Shackled, in chains, and trembling at command;
Naked, expos'd to Phœbus'[8] piercing beams,
And yok'd (as horse or oxen) to the teams;   180
Dead to remorse, the overseer stands by,
And oft does he the sounding lash apply.
So Pharaoh's task-masters of yore opprest
Old Jacob's seed[9]—and thus the flock distrest.

Now dead to hope they see resistance vain,   185
They in their manly breasts conceal their pain;
A silent grief to furious rage succeeds,
And by resentment stung—their whole soul bleeds.
Firm in despair their hands refuse the yoke,
We call them stubborn—and apply the stroke;   190
Their reeking backs the dire correction shew,
Yet they unmov'd, nor fear nor tremor know;
Their strength heroic claims a nobler name,
And shews not their's—but their oppressor's shame.
Say not, that if not humbled they rebel;   195
Tyrant! the cause, the guilt with thee must dwell;
For when they view the authors of their woe,
No wonder if fierce passion aims the blow!
They all their blasted hopes and comforts see,
Condemn'd to linger life in misery.   200

What son of thine, oh Albion,[1] would bow down,
Would tremble at the upstart planter's frown?
What son of thine, oh Albion, thus opprest,
Nor feel revenge inflame his haughty breast?
                              * * *

"Must we abandon then, Camillus[2] cries,   205
"The wealth abundant which in Afric lies?

8. The sun's.
9. A reference to Joseph, son of Jacob in the Old Testament, who was sold into slavery in Egypt by his brothers. According to the book of Genesis, Joseph later became a political figure in Egypt and moved the Israelites there from Canaan during a famine; after Joseph's death, the Egyptians became suspicious of the large number of Israelites living among them, and the pharaoh enslaved and put "the flock" to work.
1. England.
2. Generic name for someone responding to Birkett's argument.

"Shall our fam'd commerce languish and decay,
"And we no more send fleets for slaves away?"

No, wise Camillus, search her fertile land,
Let the mild rays of commerce there expand;   210
Her plains abound in ore, in fruits her soil,
And the rich plain scarce needs the ploughman's toil;
Thy vessels crown'd with olive branches send,
And make each injur'd African thy friend:
So tides of wealth by peace and justice got,   215
Oh, philanthropic heart! will be thy lot.

Plant there our colonies, and to their soul,
Declare the God who form'd this boundless whole;
Improve their manners—teach them how to live,
To them the useful lore of science give;   220
So shall with us their praise and glory rest,
And we in blessing be supremely blest;
For 'tis a duty which we surely owe,
We to the Romans were what to us Afric now.[3]

Hibernian fair,[4] who own compassion's sway,   225
Scorn not a younger sister's artless lay;
To you the Muse would raise her daring song,
For Mercy's softest beams to you belong;
To you the sympathetic sigh is known,
And Charity's sweet lustre—all your own;   230
To you gali'd Mis'ry seldom pleads in vain,
Oh, let us rise and burst the Negro's chain!
Yes, sisters, yes, to us the task belongs,
'Tis we increase or mitigate their wrongs.
If we the produce of their toils refuse,   235
If we no more the blood-stain'd lux'ry choose;
If from our lips we push the plant away
For which the liberties of thousands pay,
Of thousands once as blest, and born as free,
And nurs'd with care, (tho' not so soft,) as we;   240
If in benev'lence *firm*, we this can dare,
And in our brethrens sufferings hold no share,
In no small part their long-borne pangs will cease,
And we to souls unborn may whisper peace.

Sisters! another theme, did fancy chuse,   245
Far from your view had shrunk my blushing Muse;
And still from you conceal'd my trembling form,
But here—I must, I dare, I will be warm—

---

3. The Roman army invaded Britain in 43 CE and   4. An Irishwoman, Birkett's intended audience.
pulled out the last of their forces in 410 CE.

Shall we who dwell in pleasure, peace and ease,
Shall we who but in meekness, mildness please,   250
Shall we surrounded by each dear delight,
To sooth the heart, or gratify the sight,
Say, shall for us the sable sufferers sigh?
Say, shall for us so many victims die?
Shall still for us the sable maid bewail?   255
Shall still the doating parents fondness fail?
Shall groans for ever ring thro' Afric's grove,
Of deep distress and disappointed love?

Oh, how would thorns of care enthral each breast,
How would it rob the passing hours of rest,   260
If from our arms our nearest kindred torn,
And we for ever doom'd their loss to mourn?

No, let Ierne's[5] gentle daughters prove
The kindling force of sympathetic love;
Now shew their virtues, by humane indeed,   265
And plead for those "who have no power to plead."

Say not that small's the sphere in which we move,
And our attempts would vain and fruitless prove;
Not so—we hold *a most important share,*
In all the evils—all the wrongs they bear;   270
And tho' their woes *entire* we can't remove,
We may th' *increasing* mis'ries which they prove,
Push far away the plant for which they die,
And in this one small thing our taste deny;
We must, we ought, 'tis Justice points the way;   275
Mercy and Charity loudly call—"obey."

Can you refuse to soothe, methinks they cry,
The heart of sorrow, or bid cease the sigh?
Can you whom plenty, wealth and peace surround,
Who in society's mild joys abound?   280
Commerce to you does its choice stores impart,
With all the gifts of Nature and of Art;
For you gay Flora[6] animates the scene,
And spreads with vast parterres the smiling green;
Her mingled pow'rs and varied charms unite,   285
And does each sense—not satiate but delight;
On you brown Ceres[7] sheds her richest powers,
Pomona's[8] fruits nectareous—all are yours;
For you Hygeia,[9] maid of blooming mien,
With joy rebounding, fills the mirthful scene;   290
Can you whose hearts these heav'n-crown'd blessings feel,

5. Ireland's.
6. The Roman goddess of spring, flowers, and fertility.
7. The Roman goddess of agriculture.
8. The Roman goddess of fruit trees.
9. The Greek goddess of health.

Refuse one sacrifice their wounds to heal?
A plant of which 'tis lux'ry gives the use,
Which our sad brethrens slav'ry does produce!
No, daughters of Ierne, you will give   295
This self-denying proof and bid them *live!*

    See where Religion's holy banners rise,
And to your view presents immortal skies!
List, for methinks I hear the Matron say,
Can you whose hearts confess my hallow'd sway;   300
Can you before my altar bow the knee,
And yet refuse to set a brother free?
In humble faith you hope for heaven's high crown,
Yet press with grief so many spirits down:
"Preserve us, Lord, from evil," can you pray,   305
Yet wilfully pursue the evil way?
And how can you his blessing think to prove,
Whose first, best law is *universal love?*
Man was his fav'rite work—he form'd him free;
His fav'rite work whate'er his colour be: 310
And far more dark's the sinful soul within,
Than the poor harmless Negro's sable skin.

* * *

    Oh! may that Power whose wondrous wisdom wrought
Myriads of worlds, with beauteous order fraught,
Whose fingers gave to heav'n's wide arch its bound,   315
And scatter'd those fair orbs which glitter round;
Who bade the moon to shine each night—each day
The sun to cheer us by his vital ray;
At whose command the rolling thunders rise,
And livid lightnings flash through blazing skies,   320
Whose word creative peopled earth with charms,
Whose grace preserves us and whose bounty warms:
May the mild dictates of his love impart
The path of virtue to each wand'ring heart!
Before him flee the mists of error blind,   325
And Truth's whole force irradiates all the mind.

    So when Aurora[1] through the gates of night,
Leads forth the ruddy blaze of opening light,
Bursts o'er the horizon with golden fire,
And bids the hovering shades of night expire;   330
Her foot-steps chase the sable clouds away,
And usher in the glorious light of day.

1791

---

1. The Roman goddess of dawn.

CULTURAL COORDINATES
The Tea Table

While the eighteen-century coffeehouse remained the sphere of men, the tea table was increasingly the locus for the "new domestic woman." When an eighteenth-century gentlewoman sat down at her tea table, she was the center of attention: All eyes focused on the bend of her wrist, how she held the spoon, and the manner in which she poured the tea. Such carefully choreographed gestures conveyed her status, breeding, and qualities as a lady. With intensified demands on her attention as mother and wife, this new domestic woman had the tasks of regulating her household and supervising her family's economy. At the tea table, she symbolically displayed her self-control and domestic discipline as wife and mother. Although tea service might prescribe a lady's movements, it did not restrict her speech; thus, the tea table remained a place important for female conversation (which critics often dismissed as gossip) and camaraderie.

The gentlewoman at the tea table was also participating in the earliest stages of a global economy. The tea itself was the product of English colonial expansion. The beverage became enormously popular after 1662, when Charles II married the Portuguese princess Catherine of Braganza, whose dowry included the right to

A Family of Three at Tea by Richard Collins, c. 1727.

trade freely with India, making tea an everyday commodity by the eighteenth century. The handleless china bowl for drinking tea, whether made domestically by Wedgwood or manufactured in China to English specifications, demonstrated how the foreign and exotic had been brought home, transformed, and appropriated as a part of British culture. The sugar sweetening the tea would have been slave-produced in the Caribbean.

As some women became aware of the inhumane conditions by which the sugar that sweetened their tea was produced, they chose to join the abolitionists and boycott sugar in an effort to shut down the African slave trade. As early as the end of the eighteenth century, women saw the connection between everyday products and world politics and participated in an early form of consumer activism.

Although the tea table was an important locus for female gentility, sociability, and even politics, not all women were thought to belong there. For laboring women, tea remained an expensive luxury. Because they were needed to serve as wet nurses or to work as servants and agricultural workers, they were warned not to imitate the enforced idleness or the self-display of the gentlewoman at the tea table.

✦◄ MARY PRINCE ►✦
1788–c.1833

Mary Prince was born a slave in 1788 on a farm in Brackish Pond, Bermuda. Her parents were owned by Charles Myners: her father, given the Christian name Prince, was a sawyer (or woodcutter) and her mother a house servant. Upon Myners's death in 1788, the infant Mary was sold to Captain John Williams and his wife, Sarah, for whom she was a slave for her first twelve years. After Sarah's death in 1798, Prince was leased to work for a nearby family, and she was sold to Captain John Ingham and Mary Spencer Ingham. Captain Ingham was an especially brutal master who often physically abused his slaves.

Prince was next sold, in 1806, to a man known only as Mr. D. She was relocated to the Turks Islands, southeast of the Bahamas. After an arduous sea journey, during which she almost starved, she was put to work panning salt, an especially grueling form of labor that involved standing in salt water for long periods of time. Mr. D repeatedly and cruelly beat her and also probably sexually abused her. In 1818, Mr. D sold her as a nursemaid, housekeeper, and washerwoman to John Wood, a merchant from the Bahamas who was moving to Antigua. Under the taxing conditions of her labor, she often endured bouts of severe illness, including rheumatism, which left her unable to work.

In Antigua, Prince began to attend the Moravian Church, where she learned to read. In December 1826, she married widower Daniel James, a freeman, carpenter, and barrel maker, at Spring Gardens, St. Johns. For this act, the Woods horsewhipped her. Prince eventually saved enough money to buy her freedom by selling coffee, yams, and other provisions to ships' captains, but the Woods refused to let her do so.

In 1828, the Woods had Prince accompany them on a trip to London, where she eventually ran away and found shelter at the Moravian Mission House. Thomas Pringle, secretary to the Anti-Slavery Society, hired her as a domestic servant and encouraged her to tell her story to Susan Strickland, who wrote it down. *The History of Mary Prince, a West Indian Slave: Related by Herself* was published in London and Edinburgh in 1831. When a magazine article contested the authenticity of Prince's story, Pringle sued the magazine on Prince's behalf and won. Later, her former masters, the Woods, sued Prince for injury to their character, and they lost. Because Prince would have had to return to slavery had she left England, her biographers believe that she remained in England for the rest of her life, probably working as a servant. The date and details of her death remain unknown.

The strong abolitionist influence on Prince in the narrative raises questions concerning what she was—and was not—free to articulate about her experiences. Her likely sexual exploitation, for instance, is never explicitly discussed because it would have been too shocking for her audience, while other aspects of her existence may have been overly emphasized to support an abolitionist viewpoint. Nonetheless, Prince powerfully communicates her determination to wrest control over her own life, no matter how oppressive her circumstances. Prince's *History* is reprinted here in its entirety.

The History of Mary Prince, a West Indian Slave
Related by Herself

I was born at Brackish-Pond, in Bermuda, on a farm belonging to Mr. Charles Myners. My mother was a household slave; and my father, whose name was Prince, was a sawyer[1] belonging to Mr. Trimmingham, a ship-builder at Crow-Lane. When I was an infant, old Mr. Myners died, and there was a division of the slaves and other property among the family. I was bought along with my mother by old Captain Darrel, and given to his grandchild, little Miss Betsey Williams. Captain Williams, Mr. Darrel's son-in-law, was master of a vessel which traded to several places in America and the West Indies, and he was seldom at home long together.

Mrs. Williams was a kind-hearted good woman, and she treated all her slaves well. She had only one daughter, Miss Betsey, for whom I was purchased, and who was about my own age. I was made quite a pet of by Miss Betsey, and loved her very much. She used to lead me about by the hand, and call me her little nigger. This was the happiest period of my life; for I was too young to understand rightly my condition as a slave, and too thoughtless and full of spirits to look forward to the days of toil and sorrow.

My mother was a household slave in the same family. I was under her own care, and my little brothers and sisters were my play-fellows and companions. My mother had several fine children after she came to Mrs. Williams,—three girls and two boys. The tasks given out to us children were light, and we used to play together with Miss Betsey, with as much freedom almost as if she had been our sister.

My master, however, was a very harsh, selfish man; and we always dreaded his return from sea. His wife was herself much afraid of him; and, during his stay at home, seldom dared to shew her usual kindness to the slaves. He often left her, in the most distressed circumstances, to reside in other female society, at some place in the West Indies of which I have forgot the name. My poor mistress bore his ill-treatment with great patience, and all her slaves loved and pitied her. I was truly attached to her, and, next to my own mother, loved her better than any creature in the world. My obedience to her commands was cheerfully given: it sprung solely from the affection I felt for her, and not from fear of the power which the white people's law had given her over me.

I had scarcely reached my twelfth year when my mistress became too poor to keep so many of us at home; and she hired me out to Mrs. Pruden, a lady who lived about five miles off, in the adjoining parish, in a large house near the sea. I cried bitterly at parting with my dear mistress and Miss Betsey, and when I kissed my mother and brothers and sisters, I thought my young heart would break, it pained me so. But there was no help; I was forced to go. Good Mrs. Williams comforted me by saying that I should still be near the home I was about to quit, and might come over and see her and my kindred whenever I could obtain leave of absence from Mrs. Pruden. A few hours after this I was taken to a strange house, and found myself among strange people. This separation seemed a sore trial to me then; but oh! 'twas light, light to the trials I have since endured!—'twas nothing—nothing to be mentioned with them; but I was a child then, and it was according to my strength.

1. Woodcutter.

I knew that Mrs. Williams could no longer maintain me; that she was fain to part with me for my food and clothing; and I tried to submit myself to the change. My new mistress was a passionate woman; but yet she did not treat me very unkindly. I do not remember her striking me but once, and that was for going to see Mrs. Williams when I heard she was sick, and staying longer than she had given me leave to do. All my employment at this time was nursing a sweet baby, little Master Daniel; and I grew so fond of my nursling that it was my greatest delight to walk out with him by the sea-shore, accompanied by his brother and sister, Miss Fanny and Master James.—Dear Miss Fanny! She was a sweet, kind young lady, and so fond of me that she wished me to learn all that she knew herself; and her method of teaching me was as follows:—Directly she had said her lessons to her grandmamma, she used to come running to me, and make me repeat them one by one after her; and in a few months I was able not only to say my letters but to spell many small words. But this happy state was not to last long. Those days were too pleasant to last. My heart always softens when I think of them.

At this time Mrs. Williams died. I was told suddenly of her death, and my grief was so great that, forgetting I had the baby in my arms, I ran away directly to my poor mistress's house; but reached it only in time to see the corpse carried out. Oh, that was a day of sorrow—a heavy day! All the slaves cried. My mother cried and lamented her sore; and I (foolish creature!) vainly entreated them to bring my dear mistress back to life. I knew nothing rightly about death then, and it seemed a hard thing to bear. When I thought about my mistress I felt as if the world was all gone wrong; and for many days and weeks I could think of nothing else. I returned to Mrs. Pruden's; but my sorrow was too great to be comforted, for my own dear mistress was always in my mind. Whether in the house or abroad, my thoughts were always talking to me about her.

I staid at Mrs. Pruden's about three months after this; I was then sent back to Mr. Williams to be sold. Oh, that was a sad sad time! I recollect the day well. Mrs. Pruden came to me and said, "Mary, you will have to go home directly; your master is going to be married, and he means to sell you and two of your sisters to raise money for the wedding." Hearing this I burst out a crying,—though I was then far from being sensible of the full weight of my misfortune, or of the misery that waited for me. Besides, I did not like to leave Mrs. Pruden, and the dear baby, who had grown very fond of me. For some time I could scarcely believe that Mrs. Pruden was in earnest, till I received orders for my immediate return.—Dear Miss Fanny! how she cried at parting with me, whilst I kissed and hugged the baby, thinking I should never see him again. I left Mrs. Pruden's, and walked home with a heart full of sorrow. The idea of being sold away from my mother and Miss Betsey was so frightful, that I dared not trust myself to think about it. We had been bought of Mrs. Myners, as I have mentioned, by Miss Betsey's grandfather, and given to her, so that we were by right *her* property, and I never thought we should be separated or sold away from her.

When I reached the house, I went in directly to Miss Betsey. I found her in great distress; and she cried out as soon as she saw me, "Oh, Mary! my father is going to sell you all to raise money to marry that wicked woman. You are *my* slaves, and he has no right to sell you; but it is all to please her." She then told me that my mother was living with her father's sister at a house close by, and I went there to see her. It was a sorrowful meeting; and we lamented with a great and sore crying our unfortunate situation. "Here comes one of my poor piccaninnies!"[2] She said, the moment I came in, "one of the poor slave-brood who are to be sold to-morrow."

Oh dear! I cannot bear to think of that day,—it is too much.—It recalls the great grief that filled my heart, and the woeful thoughts that passed to and fro through my mind, whilst listening to the pitiful words of my poor mother, weeping for the loss of her children. I wish I could find words to tell you all I then felt and suffered. The great God above alone knows the thoughts of the poor slave's heart, and the bitter pains which follow such separations as these. All that we love taken away from us—oh, it is sad, sad! and sore to be borne!—I got no sleep that night for thinking of the morrow; and dear Miss Betsey was scarcely less distressed. She could not bear to part with her old playmates and she cried sore and would not be pacified.

The black morning at length came; it came too soon for my poor mother and us. Whilst she was putting on us the new osnaburgs in which we were to be sold, she said, in a sorrowful voice, (I shall never forget it!) "See, I am *shrouding* my poor children; what a task for a mother!"[3]—She then called Miss Betsey to take leave of us. "I am going to carry my little chickens to market," (these were her very words) "take your last look of them; may be you will see them no more." "Oh, my poor slaves! my own slaves!" said dear Miss Betsey, "you belong to me; and it grieves my heart to part with you."—Miss Betsey kissed us all, and, when she left us, my mother called the rest of the slaves to bid us good bye. One of them, a woman named Moll, came with her infant in her arms. "Ay!" said my mother, seeing her turn away and look at her child with the tears in her eyes, "your turn will come next." The slaves could say nothing to comfort us; they could only weep and lament with us. When I left my dear little brothers and the house in which I had been brought up, I thought my heart would burst.

Our mother, weeping as she went, called me away with the children Hannah and Dinah, and we took the road that led to Hamble Town, which we reached about four o'clock in the afternoon. We followed my mother to the market-place, where she placed us in a row against a large house, with our backs to the wall and our arms folded across our breasts. I, as the eldest, stood first, Hannah next to me, then Dinah; and our mother stood beside, crying over us. My heart throbbed with grief and terror so violently, that I pressed my hands quite tightly across my breast, but I could not keep it still, and it continued to leap as though it would burst out of my body. But who cared for that? Did one of the many bystanders, who were looking at us so carelessly, think of the pain that wrung the hearts of the Negro woman and her young ones? No, no! They were not all bad, I dare say, but slavery hardens white people's hearts towards the blacks; and many of them were not slow to make their remarks upon us aloud, without regard to our grief— though their light words fell like cayenne on the fresh wounds of our hearts. Oh those white people have small hearts who can only feel for themselves.

At length the vendue master, who was to offer us for sale like sheep or cattle, arrived, and asked my mother which was the eldest. She said nothing, but pointed to me. He took me by the hand, and led me out into the middle of the street, and, turning me slowly round, exposed me to the view of those who attended the vendue. I was soon surrounded by strange men, who examined and handled me in the

---

2. A term—now considered racist—for a black child.

3. Osnaburgs: coarse linen garments; shrouding: preparing, as if for burial.

same manner that a butcher would a calf or a lamb he was about to purchase, and who talked about my shape and size in like words—as if I could no more understand their meaning than the dumb beasts. I was then put up for sale. The bidding commenced at a few pounds, and gradually rose to fifty-seven,[4] when I was knocked down to the highest bidder; and the people who stood by said that I had fetched a great sum for so young a slave.

I then saw my sisters led forth, and sold to different owners; so that we had not the sad satisfaction of being partners in bondage. When the sale was over, my mother hugged and kissed us, and mourned over us, begging of us to keep up a good heart, and do our duty to our new masters. It was a sad parting; one went one way, one another, and our poor mammy went home with nothing.

My new master was a Captain I——, who lived at Spanish Point. After parting with my mother and sisters, I followed him to his store, and he gave me into the charge of his son, a lad about my own age, Master Benjy, who took me to my new home. I did not know where I was going, or what my new master would do with me. My heart was quite broken with grief, and my thoughts went back continually to those from whom I had been so suddenly parted. "Oh, my mother! my mother!" I kept saying to myself, "Oh, my mammy and my sisters and my brothers, shall I never see you again!"

Oh, the trials! the trials! they make the salt water come into my eyes when I think of the days in which I was afflicted—the times that are gone; when I mourned and grieved with a young heart for those whom I loved.

It was night when I reached my new home. The house was large, and built at the bottom of a very high hill; but I could not see much of it that night. I saw too much of it afterwards. The stones and the timber were the best things in it; they were not so hard as the hearts of the owners.

Before I entered the house, two slave women, hired from another owner, who were at work in the yard, spoke to me, and asked who I belonged to? I replied, "I am come to live here." "Poor child, poor child!" they both said; "you must keep a good heart, if you are to live here."—When I went in, I stood up crying in a corner. Mrs. I—— came and took off my hat, a little black silk hat Miss Pruden made for me, and said in a rough voice, "You are not come here to stand up in corners and cry, you are come here to work." She then put a child into my arms, and, tired as I was, I was forced instantly to take up my old occupation of a nurse.—I could not bear to look at my mistress, her countenance was so stern. She was a stout tall woman with a very dark complexion, and her brows were always drawn together into a frown. I thought of the words of the two slave women when I saw Mrs. I——, and heard the harsh sound of her voice.

The person I took the most notice of that night was a French Black called Hetty, whom my master took in privateering from another vessel, and made his slave. She was the most active woman I ever saw, and she was tasked to her utmost. A few minutes after my arrival she came in from milking the cows, and put the sweet-potatoes on for supper. She then fetched home the sheep, and penned them in the fold; drove home the cattle, and staked them about the pond side, fed and rubbed down my master's horse, and gave the hog and the fed cow their suppers; prepared the beds, and undressed the children, and laid them to sleep. I liked

---

4. Although monetary conversions can be problematic, at the time this selection was written, this would have been £38 in Britain, or nearly $6,000 today.

to look at her and watch all her doings, for her's was the only friendly face I had as yet seen, and I felt glad that she was there. She gave me my supper of potatoes and milk, and a blanket to sleep upon, which she spread for me in the passage before the door of Mrs. I——'s chamber.

I got a sad fright, that night. I was just going to sleep, when I heard a noise in my mistress's room; and she presently called out to inquire if some work was finished that she had ordered Hetty to do. "No, Ma'am, not yet," was Hetty's answer from below. On hearing this, my master started up from his bed, and just as he was, in his shirt, ran down stairs with a long cow-skin[5] in his hand. I heard immediately after, the cracking of the thong, and the house rang to the shrieks of poor Hetty, who kept crying out, "Oh, Massa! Massa! me dead. Massa! have mercy upon me—don't kill me outright."—This was a sad beginning for me. I sat up upon my blanket, trembling with terror, like a frightened hound, and thinking that my turn would come next. At length the house became still, and I forgot for a little while all my sorrows by falling fast asleep.

The next morning my mistress set about instructing me in my tasks. She taught me to do all sorts of household work; to wash and bake, pick cotton and wool, and wash floors, and cook. And she taught me (how can I ever forget it!) more things than these; she caused me to know the exact difference between the smart of the rope, the cart-whip, and the cow-skin, when applied to my naked body by her own cruel hand. And there was scarcely any punishment more dreadful than the blows I received on my face and head from her hard heavy fist. She was a fearful woman, and a savage mistress to her slaves.

There were two little slave boys in the house, on whom she vented her bad temper in a special manner. One of these children was a mulatto, called Cyrus, who had been bought while an infant in his mother's arms; the other, Jack, was an African from the coast of Guinea, whom a sailor had given or sold to my master. Seldom a day passed without these boys receiving the most severe treatment, and often for no fault at all. Both my master and mistress seemed to think that they had a right to ill-use them at their pleasure; and very often accompanied their commands with blows, whether the children were behaving well or ill. I have seen their flesh ragged and raw with licks.[6] —Lick—lick—they were never secure one moment from a blow, and their lives were passed in continual fear. My mistress was not contented with using the whip, but often pinched their cheeks and arms in the most cruel manner. My pity for these poor boys was soon transferred to myself; for I was licked, and flogged, and pinched by her pitiless fingers in the neck and arms, exactly as they were. To strip me naked—to hang me up by the wrists and lay my flesh open with the cow-skin, was an ordinary punishment for even a slight offence. My mistress often robbed me too of the hours that belong to sleep. She used to sit up very late, frequently even until morning; and I had then to stand at a bench and wash during the greater part of the night, or pick wool and cotton and often I have dropped down overcome by sleep and fatigue, till roused from a state of stupor by the whip, and forced to start up to my tasks.

Poor Hetty, my fellow slave, was very kind to me, and I used to call her my Aunt; but she led a most miserable life, and her death was hastened (at least the slaves all believed and said so,) by the dreadful chastisement she received from my master during her pregnancy. It happened as follows. One of the cows had dragged

5. Whip made of twisted hide.   6. Whippings.

the rope away from the stake to which Hetty had fastened it, and got loose. My master flew into a terrible passion, and ordered the poor creature to be stripped quite naked, notwithstanding her pregnancy, and to be tied up to a tree in the yard. He then flogged her as hard as he could lick, both with the whip and cow-skin, till she was all over streaming with blood. He rested, and then beat her again and again. Her shrieks were terrible. The consequence was that poor Hetty was brought to bed before her time, and was delivered after severe labour of a dead child. She appeared to recover after her confinement, so far that she was repeatedly flogged by both master and mistress afterwards; but her former strength never returned to her. Ere long her body and limbs swelled to a great size; and she lay on a mat in the kitchen, till the water burst out of her body and she died. All the slaves said that death was a good thing for poor Hetty; but I cried very much for her death. The manner of it filled me with horror. I could not bear to think about it; yet it was always present to my mind for many a day.

After Hetty died all her labours fell upon me, in addition to my own. I had now to milk eleven cows every morning before sunrise, sitting among the damp weeds; to take care of the cattle as well as the children; and to do the work of the house. There was no end to my toils—no end to my blows. I lay down at night and rose up in the morning in fear and sorrow; and often wished that like poor Hetty I could escape from this cruel bondage and be at rest in the grave. But the hand of that God whom then I knew not, was stretched over me; and I was mercifully preserved for better things. It was then, however, my heavy lot to weep, weep, weep, and that for years; to pass from one misery to another, and from one cruel master to a worse. But I must go on with the thread of my story.

One day a heavy squall of wind and rain came on suddenly, and my mistress sent me round the corner of the house to empty a large earthen jar. The jar was already cracked with an old deep crack that divided it in the middle, and in turning it upside down to empty it, it parted in my hand. I could not help the accident, but I was dreadfully frightened, looking forward to a severe punishment. I ran crying to my mistress, "O mistress, the jar has come in two." "You have broken it, have you?" she replied; "come directly here to me." I came trembling: she stripped and flogged me long and severely with the cow-skin; as long as she had strength to use the lash, for she did not give over till she was quite tired.—When my master came home at night, she told him of my fault; and oh, frightful! how he fell a swearing. After abusing me with every ill name he could think of, (too, too bad to speak in England,) and giving me several heavy blows with his hand, he said, "I shall come home to-morrow morning at twelve, on purpose to give you a round hundred." He kept his word—Oh sad for me! I cannot easily forget it. He tied me up upon a ladder, and gave me a hundred lashes with his own hand, and master Benjy stood by to count them for him. When he had licked me for some time he sat down to take breath; then after resting, he beat me again and again, until he was quite wearied, and so hot (for the weather was very sultry), that he sank back in his chair, almost like to faint. While my mistress went to bring him drink, there was a dreadful earthquake. Part of the roof fell down, and every thing in the house went—clatter, clatter, clatter. Oh I thought the end of all things near at hand; and I was so sore with the flogging, that I scarcely cared whether I lived or died. The earth was groaning and shaking; every thing tumbling about; and my mistress and the slaves were shrieking and crying out, "The earthquake! the earthquake!" It was an awful day for us all.

During the confusion I crawled away on my hands and knees, and laid myself down under the steps of the piazza, in front of the house. I was in a dreadful state—my body all blood and bruises, and I could not help moaning piteously. The other slaves, when they saw me, shook their heads and said, "Poor child! poor child"—I lay there till the morning, careless of what might happen, for life was very weak in me, and I wished more than ever to die. But when we are very young, death always seems a great way off, and it would not come that night to me. The next morning I was forced by my master to rise and go about my usual work, though my body and limbs were so stiff and sore, that I could not move without the greatest pain.—Nevertheless, even after all this severe punishment, I never heard the last of that jar; my mistress was always throwing it in my face.

Some little time after this, one of the cows got loose from the stake, and eat one of the sweet-potatoe slips. I was milking when my master found it out. He came to me, and without any more ado, stooped down, and taking off his heavy boot, he struck me such a severe blow in the small of my back, that I shrieked with agony, and thought I was killed; and I feel a weakness in that part to this day. The cow was frightened by his violence, and kicked down the pail and spilt the milk all about. My master knew that this accident was his own fault, but he was so enraged that he seemed glad of an excuse to go on with his ill usage. I cannot remember how many licks he gave me then, but he beat me till I was unable to stand, and till he himself was weary.

After this I ran away and went to my mother, who was living with Mr. Richard Darrel. My poor mother was both grieved and glad to see me; grieved because I had been so ill used, and glad because she had not seen me for a long, long while. She dared not receive me into the house, but she hid me up in a hole in the rocks near, and brought me food at night, after every body was asleep. My father, who lived at Crow-Lane, over the salt-water channel, at last heard of my being hid up in the cavern, and he came and took me back to my master. Oh I was loth, loth to go back; but as there was no remedy, I was obliged to submit.

When we got home, my poor father said to Capt. I——, "Sir, I am sorry that my child should be forced to run away from her owner; but the treatment she has received is enough to break her heart. The sight of her wounds has nearly broke mine.—I entreat you, for the love of God, to forgive her for running away, and that you will be a kind master to her in future." Capt. I—— said I was used as well as I deserved, and that I ought to be punished for running away. I then took courage and said that I could stand the floggings no longer; that I was weary of my life, and therefore I had run away to my mother; but mothers could only weep and mourn over their children, they could not save them from cruel masters—from the whip, the rope, and the cow-skin. He told me to hold my tongue and go about my work, or he would find a way to settle me. He did not, however, flog me that day.

For five years after this I remained in his house, and almost daily received the same harsh treatment. At length he put me on board a sloop, and to my great joy sent me away to Turk's Island.[7] I was not permitted to see my mother or father, or poor sisters and brothers, to say good bye, though going away to a strange land, and might never see them again. Oh the Buckra people[8] who keep slaves think that black people are like cattle, without natural affection. But my heart tells me it is far otherwise.

7. An island southeast of the Bahamas.   8. White people.

We were nearly four weeks on the voyage, which was unusually long. Sometimes we had a light breeze, sometimes a great calm, and the ship made no way; so that our provisions and water ran very low, and we were put upon short allowance. I should almost have been starved had it not been for the kindness of a black man called Anthony, and his wife, who had brought their own victuals, and shared them with me.

When we went ashore at the Grand Quay, the captain sent me to the house of my new master, Mr. D——, to whom Captain I—— had sold me. Grand Quay is a small town upon a sandbank; the houses low and built of wood. Such was my new master's. The first person I saw, on my arrival, was Mr. D——, a stout sulky looking man, who carried me through the hall to show me to his wife and children. Next day I was put up by the vendue master to know how much I was worth, and I was valued at one hundred pounds currency.

My new master was one of the owners or holders of the salt ponds, and he received a certain sum for every slave that worked upon his premises, whether they were young or old. This sum was allowed him out of the profits arising from the salt works. I was immediately sent to work in the salt water with the rest of the slaves. This work was perfectly new to me. I was given a half barrel and a shovel, and had to stand up to my knees in the water, from four o'clock in the morning till nine, when we were given some Indian corn boiled in water, which we were obliged to swallow as fast as we could for fear the rain should come on and melt the salt. We were then called again to our tasks, and worked through the heat of the day; the sun flaming upon our heads like fire, and raising salt blisters in those parts which were not completely covered. Our feet and legs, from standing in the salt water for so many hours, soon became full of dreadful boils, which eat down in some cases to the very bone, afflicting the sufferers with great torment. We came home at twelve; ate our corn soup, called *blawly,* as fast as we could, and went back to our employment till dark at night. We then shovelled up the salt in large heaps, and went down to the sea, where we washed the pickle from our limbs, and cleaned the barrows and shovels from the salt. When we returned to the house, our master gave us each our allowance of raw Indian corn, which we pounded in a mortar and boiled in water for our suppers.

We slept in a long shed, divided into narrow slips, like the stalls used for cattle. Boards fixed upon stakes driven into the ground, without mat or covering, were our only beds. On Sundays, after we had washed the salt bags, and done other work required of us, we went into the bush and cut the long soft grass, of which we made trusses for our legs and feet to rest upon, for they were so full of the salt boils that we could get no rest lying upon the bare boards.

Though we worked from morning till night, there was no satisfying Mr. D——. I hoped, when I left Capt. I——, that I should have been better off, but I found it was but going from one butcher to another. There was this difference between them: my former master used to beat me while raging and foaming with passion; Mr. D—— was usually quite calm. He would stand by and give orders for a slave to be cruelly whipped, and assist in the punishment, without moving a muscle of his face; walking about and taking snuff[9] with the greatest composure. Nothing could touch his hard heart—neither sighs, nor tears, nor prayers, nor streaming blood; he was deaf to our cries, and careless of our sufferings.—Mr. D—— has

---

9. Powdered tobacco inhaled through the nose.

often stripped me naked, hung me up by the wrists, and beat me with the cow-skin, with his own hand, till my body was raw with gashes. Yet there was nothing very remarkable in this; for it might serve as a sample of the common usage of the slaves on that horrible island.

Owing to the boils in my feet, I was unable to wheel the barrow fast through the sand, which got into the sores, and made me stumble at every step; and my master, having no pity for my sufferings from this cause, rendered them far more intolerable, by chastising me for not being able to move so fast as he wished me. Another of our employments was to row a little way off from the shore in a boat, and dive for large stones to build a wall round our master's house. This was very hard work; and the great waves breaking over us continually, made us often so giddy that we lost our footing, and were in danger of being drowned.

Ah, poor me!—my tasks were never ended. Sick or well, it was work—work—work!—After the diving season was over, we were sent to the South Creek, with large bills, to cut up mangoes to burn lime with.[1] Whilst one party of slaves were thus employed, another were sent to the other side of the island to break up coral out of the sea.

When we were ill, let our complaint be what it might, the only medicine given to us was a great bowl of hot salt water, with salt mixed with it, which made us very sick. If we could not keep up with the rest of the gang of slaves, we were put in the stocks, and severely flogged the next morning. Yet, not the less, our master expected, after we had thus been kept from our rest, and our limbs rendered stiff and sore with ill usage, that we should still go through the ordinary tasks of the day all the same.—Sometimes we had to work all night, measuring salt to load a vessel; or turning a machine to draw water out of the sea for the salt-making. Then we had no sleep—no rest—but were forced to work as fast as we could, and go on again all next day the same as usual. Work—work—work—Oh that Turk's Island was a horrible place! The people in England, I am sure, have never found out what is carried on there. Cruel, horrible place!

Mr. D—— had a slave called old Daniel, whom he used to treat in the most cruel manner. Poor Daniel was lame in the hip, and could not keep up with the rest of the slaves; and our master would order him to be stripped and laid down on the ground, and have him beaten with a rod of rough briar till his skin was quite red and raw. He would then call for a bucket of salt, and fling upon the raw flesh till the man writhed on the ground like a worm, and screamed aloud with agony. This poor man's wounds were never healed, and I have often seen them full of maggots, which increased his torments to an intolerable degree. He was an object of pity and terror to the whole gang of slaves, and in his wretched case we saw, each of us, our own lot, if we should live to be as old.

Oh the horrors of slavery!—How the thought of it pains my heart! But the truth ought to be told of it; and what my eyes have seen I think it is my duty to relate; for few people in England know what slavery is. I have been a slave—I have felt what a slave feels, and I know what a slave knows; and I would have all the good people in England to know it too, that they may break our chains, and set us free.

Mr. D—— had another slave called Ben. He being very hungry, stole a little rice one night after he came in from work, and cooked it for his supper. But his

---

1. A bill is a type of sword, here used to cut the
mango trees that will be mixed with alkaline soil   (lime) and burned.

master soon discovered the theft; locked him up all night; and kept him without food till one o'clock the next day. He then hung Ben up by his hands, and beat him from time to time till the slaves came in at night. We found the poor creature hung up when we came home; with a pool of blood beneath him, and our master still licking him. But this was not the worst. My master's son was in the habit of stealing the rice and rum. Ben had seen him do this, and thought he might do the same, and when master found out that Ben had stolen the rice and swore to punish him, he tried to excuse himself by saying that Master Dickey did the same thing every night. The lad denied it to his father, and was so angry with Ben for informing against him, that out of revenge he ran and got a bayonet, and whilst the poor wretch was suspended by his hands and writhing under his wounds, he run it quite through his foot. I was not by when he did it, but I saw the wound when I came home, and heard Ben tell the manner in which it was done.

I must say something more about this cruel son of a cruel father.—He had no heart—no fear of God; he had been brought up by a bad father in a bad path, and he delighted to follow in the same steps. There was a little old woman among the slaves called Sarah, who was nearly past work; and, Master Dickey being the overseer of the slaves just then, this poor creature, who was subject to several bodily infirmities, and was not quite right in her head, did not wheel the barrow fast enough to please him. He threw her down on the ground, and after beating her severely, he took her up in his arms and flung her among the prickly-pear bushes, which are all covered over with sharp venomous prickles. By this her naked flesh was so grievously wounded, that her body swelled and festered all over, and she died in a few days after. In telling my own sorrows, I cannot pass by those of my fellow-slaves—for when I think of my own griefs, I remember theirs.

I think it was about ten years I had worked in the salt ponds at Turk's Island, when my master left off business, and retired to a house he had in Bermuda, leaving his son to succeed him in the island. He took me with him to wait upon his daughters; and I was joyful, for I was sick, sick of Turk's Island, and my heart yearned to see my native place again, my mother, and my kindred.

I had seen my poor mother during the time I was a slave in Turk's Island. One Sunday morning I was on the beach with some of the slaves, and we saw a sloop[2] come in loaded with slaves to work in the salt water. We got a boat and went aboard. When I came upon the deck I asked the black people, "Is there any one here for me?" "Yes," they said, "your mother." I thought they said this in jest—I could scarcely believe them for joy; but when I saw my poor mammy my joy was turned to sorrow, for she had gone from her senses. "Mammy," I said, "is this you!" She did not know me. "Mammy," I said, "what's the matter?" She began to talk foolishly and said that she had been under the vessel's bottom. They had been overtaken by a violent storm at sea. My poor mother had never been on the sea before, and she was so ill, that she lost her senses, and it was long before she came quite to herself again. She had a sweet child with her—a little sister I had never seen, about four years of age, called Rebecca. I took her on shore with me, for I felt I should love her directly; and I kept her with me a week. Poor little thing! her's has been a sad life, and continues so to this day. My mother worked for some years on the island, but was taken back to Bermuda some time before my master carried me again thither.

---

2. A small, one-masted ship.

After I left Turk's Island, I was told by some negroes that came over from it, that the poor slaves had built up a place with boughs and leaves, where they might meet for prayers, but the white people pulled it down twice, and would not allow them even a shed for prayers. A flood came down soon after and washed away many houses, filled the place with sand, and overflowed the ponds: and I do think that this was for their wickedness; for the Buckra men there were very wicked. I saw and heard much that was very very bad at that place.

I was several years the slave of Mr. D—— after I returned to my native place. Here I worked in the grounds. My work was planting and hoeing sweet-potatoes, Indian corn, plaintains, bananas, cabbages, pumpkins, onions, &c. I did all the household work, and attended upon a horse and cow besides,—going also upon all errands. I had to curry the horse—to clean and feed him—and sometimes to ride him a little. I had more than enough to do—but still it was not so very bad as Turk's Island.

My old master often got drunk, and then he would get in a fury with his daughter, and beat her till she was not fit to be seen. I remember on one occasion, I had gone to fetch water, and when I was coming up the hill I heard a great screaming; I ran as fast as I could to the house, put down the water, and went into the chamber, where I found my master beating Miss D—— dreadfully. I strove with all my strength to get her away from him; for she was all black and blue with bruises. He had beat her with his fist, and almost killed her. The people gave me credit for getting her away. He turned round and began to lick me. Then I said, "Sir, this is not Turk's Island." I can't repeat his answer, the words were too wicked—too bad to say. He wanted to treat me the same in Bermuda as he had done in Turk's Island.

He had an ugly fashion of stripping himself quite naked and ordering me then to wash him in a tub of water. This was worse to me than all the licks. Sometimes when he called me to wash him I would not come, my eyes were so full of shame. He would then come to beat me. One time I had plates and knives in my hand, and I dropped both plates and knives, and some of the plates were broken. He struck me so severely for this, that at last I defended myself, for I thought it was high time to do so. I then told him I would not live longer with him, for he was a very inde-cent man—very spiteful, and too indecent; with no shame for his servants, no shame for his own flesh. So I went away to a neighbouring house and sat down and cried till the next morning, when I went home again, not knowing what else to do.

After that I was hired to work at Cedar Hills, and every Saturday night I paid the money to my master. I had plenty of work to do there—plenty of washing; but yet I made myself pretty comfortable. I earned two dollars and a quarter a week, which is twenty pence a day.[3]

During the time I worked there, I heard that Mr. John Wood was going to Antigua. I felt a great wish to go there, and I went to Mr. D——, and asked him to let me go in Mr. Wood's service. Mr. Wood did not then want to purchase me; it was my own fault that I came under him, I was so anxious to go. It was or-dained to be, I suppose; God led me there. The truth is, I did not wish to be any longer the slave of my indecent master.

Mr. Wood took me with him to Antigua, to the town of St. John's, where he lived. This was about fifteen years ago. He did not then know whether I was to be

3. Equivalent to about $9 in today's money.

sold; but Mrs. Wood found that I could work, and she wanted to buy me. Her husband then wrote to my master to inquire whether I was to be sold? Mr. D—— wrote in reply, "that I should not be sold to any one that would treat me ill." It was strange he should say this, when he had treated me so ill himself. So I was purchased by Mr. Wood for 300 dollars (or £100 Bermuda currency.)[4]

My work there was to attend the chambers and nurse the child, and to go down to the pond and wash clothes. But I soon fell ill of the rheumatism, and grew so very lame that I was forced to walk with a stick. I got the Saint Anthony's fire,[5] also, in my left leg, and became quite a cripple. No one cared much to come near me, and I was ill a long long time; for several months I could not lift the limb. I had to lie in a little old out-house, that was swarming with bugs and other vermin, which tormented me greatly; but I had no other place to lie in. I got the rheumatism by catching cold at the pond side, from washing in the fresh water; in the salt water I never got cold. The person who lived in next yard, (a Mrs. Greene,) could not bear to hear my cries and groans. She was kind, and used to send an old slave woman to help me, who sometimes brought me a little soup. When the doctor found I was so ill, he said I must be put into a bath of hot water. The old slave got the bark of some bush that was good for pains, which she boiled in the hot water, and every night she came and put me into the bath, and did what she could for me; I don't know what I should have done, or what would have become of me, had it not been for her.—My mistress, it is true, did send me a little food; but no one from our family came near me but the cook, who used to shove my food in at the door, and say, "Molly, Molly, there's your dinner." My mistress did not care to take any trouble about me; and if the Lord had not put it into the hearts of the neighbours to be kind to me, I must, I really think, have lain and died.

It was a long time before I got well enough to work in the house. Mrs. Wood, in the meanwhile, hired a mulatto woman to nurse the child; but she was such a fine lady she wanted to be mistress over me. I thought it very hard for a coloured woman to have rule over me because I was a slave and she was free. Her name was Martha Wilcox; she was a saucy woman, very saucy; and she went and complained of me, without cause, to my mistress, and made her angry with me. Mrs. Wood told me that if I did not mind what I was about, she would get my master to strip me and give me fifty lashes: "You have been used to the whip," she said, "and you shall have it here." This was the first time she threatened to have me flogged; and she gave me the threatening so strong of what she would have done to me, that I thought I should have fallen down at her feet, I was so vexed and hurt by her words. The mulatto woman was rejoiced to have power to keep me down. She was constantly making mischief; there was no living for the slaves—no peace after she came.

I was also sent by Mrs. Wood to be put in the Cage one night, and was next morning flogged, by the magistrate's order, at her desire; and this all for a quarrel I had about a pig with another slave woman. I was flogged on my naked back on this occasion; although I was in no fault after all; for old Justice Dyett, when we came before him, said that I was in the right, and ordered the pig to be given to me. This was about two or three years after I came to Antigua.

---

4. About £68, equal to about $7,200 in today's money.
5. Also known as ergotism, a disease caused by a

fungus that contaminates grains and causes a painful burning sensation in the limbs.

When we moved from the middle of the town to the Point, I used to be in the house and do all the work and mind the children, though still very ill with the rheumatism. Every week I had to wash two large bundles of clothes, as much as a boy could help me to lift; but I could give no satisfaction. My mistress was always abusing and fretting after me. It is not possible to tell all her ill language.—One day she followed me foot after foot scolding and rating me. I bore in silence a great deal of ill words: at last my heart was quite full, and I told her that she ought not to use me so;—that when I was ill I might have lain and died for what she cared; and no one would then come near me to nurse me, because they were afraid of my mistress. This was a great affront. She called her husband and told him what I had said. He flew into a passion: but did not beat me then; he only abused and swore at me; and then gave me a note and bade me go and look for an owner. Not that he meant to sell me; but he did this to please his wife and to frighten me. I went to Adam White, a cooper,[6] a free black who had money, and asked him to buy me. He went directly to Mr. Wood, but was informed that I was not to be sold. The next day my master whipped me.

Another time (about five years ago) my mistress got vexed with me because I fell sick and I could not keep on with my work. She complained to her husband, and he sent me off again to look for an owner. I went to a Mr. Burchell, showed him the note, and asked him to buy me for my own benefit; for I had saved about 100 dollars, and hoped with a little help, to purchase my freedom. He accordingly went to my master:—"Mr. Wood," he said, "Molly has brought me a note that she wants an owner. If you intend to sell her, I may as well buy her as another." My master put him off and said that he did not mean to sell me. I was very sorry at this, for I had no comfort with Mrs. Wood, and I wished greatly to get my freedom.

The way in which I made my money was this.—When my master and mistress went from home, as they sometimes did, and left me to take care of the house and premises, I had a good deal of time to myself and made the most of it. I took in washing, and sold coffee and yams and other provisions to the captains of ships. I did not sit still idling during the absence of my owners; for I wanted, by all honest means, to earn money to buy my freedom. Sometimes I bought a hog cheap on board ship, and sold it for double the money on shore; and I also earned a good deal by selling coffee. By this means I by degrees acquired a little cash. A gentleman also lent me some to help to buy my freedom—but when I could not get free he got it back again. His name was Captain Abbot.

My master and mistress went on one occasion into the country, to Date Hill, for a change of air, and carried me with them to take charge of the children, and to do the work of the house. While I was in the country, I saw how the field negroes are worked in Antigua. They are worked very hard and fed but scantily. They are called out to work before daybreak, and come home after dark; and then each has to heave his bundle of grass for the cattle in the pen. Then, on Sunday morning, each slave has to go out and gather a large bundle of grass; and, when they bring it home, they have all to sit at the manager's door and wait till he comes out: often have they to wait there till past eleven o'clock without any breakfast. After that, those that have yams or potatoes, or fire-wood to sell, hasten to market to buy a dog's worth[7] of salt fish, or pork, which is a great treat for them. Some of them buy a little pickle out of the shad barrels, which they call sauce, to

6. Barrel maker.   7. One seventy-second of a dollar.

season their yams and Indian corn. It is very wrong, I know, to work on Sunday or go to market; but will not God call the Buckra men to answer for this on the great day of judgment—since they will give the slaves no other day?

While we were at Date Hill Christmas came; and the slave woman who had the care of the place (which then belonged to Mr. Roberts the marshal), asked me to go with her to her husband's house, to a Methodist meeting for prayer, at a plantation called Winthorps. I went; and they were the first prayers I ever under-stood. One woman prayed; and then they all sung a hymn; then there was another prayer and another hymn; and then they all spoke by turns of their own griefs as sinners. The husband of the woman I went with was a black driver. His name was Henry. He confessed that he had treated the slaves very cruelly; but said that he was compelled to obey the orders of his master. He prayed them all to forgive him, and he prayed that God would forgive him. He said it was a horrid thing for a ranger[8] to have sometimes to beat his own wife or sister; but he must do so if ordered by his master.

I felt sorry for my sins also. I cried the whole night, but I was too much ashamed to speak. I prayed God to forgive me. This meeting had a great impres-sion on my mind, and led my spirit to the Moravian church; so that when I got back to town, I went and prayed to have my name put down in the Missionaries' book; and I followed the church earnestly every opportunity. I did not then tell my mistress about it; for I knew that she would not give me leave to go. But I felt I *must* go. Whenever I carried the children their lunch at school, I ran round and went to hear the teachers.

The Moravian ladies (Mrs. Richter, Mrs. Olufsen, and Mrs. Sauter) taught me to read in the class; and I got on very fast. In this class there were all sorts of people, old and young, grey headed folks and children; but most of them were free people. After we had done spelling, we tried to read in the Bible. After the reading was over, the missionary gave out a hymn for us to sing. I dearly loved to go to the church, it was so solemn. I never knew rightly that I had much sin till I went there. When I found out that I was a great sinner, I was very sorely grieved, and very much fright-ened. I used to pray God to pardon my sins for Christ's sake, and forgive me for every thing I had done amiss; and when I went home to my work, I always thought about what I had heard from the missionaries, and wished to be good that I might go to heaven. After a while I was admitted a candidate for the holy Communion.— I had been baptized long before this, in August 1817, by the Rev. Mr. Curtin, of the English Church, after I had been taught to repeat the Creed and the Lord's Prayer.[9] I wished at that time to attend a Sunday School taught by Mr. Curtin, but he would not receive me without a written note from my master, granting his permission. I did not ask my owner's permission, from the belief that it would be refused; so that I got no further instruction at that time from the English Church.

Some time after I began to attend the Moravian[1] Church, I met with Daniel James, afterwards my dear husband. He was a carpenter and cooper to his trade; an honest, hard-working, decent black man, and a widower. He had purchased his freedom of his mistress, old Mrs. Baker, with money he had earned whilst a

---

8. The black superintendent of the estate under the manager.
9. The English Church: the Anglican Church, the official church of England; Creed and the Lord's Prayer: the Apostle's Creed and the Lord's Prayer

(or the "Our Father"), traditional Christian prayers.
1. A Protestant denomination, founded in Bo-hemia in 1457; throughout the eighteenth century, its missionary activities were especially widespread.

slave. When he asked me to marry him, I took time to consider the matter over with myself, and would not say yes till he went to church with me and joined the Moravians. He was very industrious after he bought his freedom; and he had hired a comfortable house, and had convenient things about him. We were joined in marriage, about Christmas 1826, in the Moravian Chapel at Spring Gardens, by the Rev. Mr. Olufsen. We could not be married in the English Church. English marriage is not allowed to slaves; and no free man can marry a slave woman.

When Mr. Wood heard of my marriage, he flew into a great rage, and sent for Daniel, who was helping to build a house for his old mistress. Mr. Wood asked him who gave him a right to marry a slave of his? My husband said, "Sir, I am a free man, and thought I had a right to choose a wife; but if I had known Molly was not allowed to have a husband, I should not have asked her to marry me." Mrs. Wood was more vexed about my marriage than her husband. She could not forgive me for getting married, but stirred up Mr. Wood to flog me dreadfully with his horsewhip. I thought it very hard to be whipped at my time of life[2] for getting a husband—I told her so. She said that she would not have nigger men about the yards and premises, or allow a nigger man's clothes to be washed in the same tub where hers were washed. She was fearful, I think, that I should lose her time, in order to wash and do things for my husband: but I had then no time to wash for myself; I was obliged to put out my own clothes, though I was always at the wash-tub.

I had not much happiness in my marriage, owing to my being a slave. It made my husband sad to see me so ill-treated. Mrs. Wood was always abusing me about him. She did not lick me herself, but she got her husband to do it for her, whilst she fretted the flesh off my bones. Yet for all this she would not sell me. She sold five slaves whilst I was with her; but though she was always finding fault with me, she would not part with me. However, Mr. Wood afterwards allowed Daniel to have a place to live in our yard, which we were very thankful for.

After this, I fell ill again with the rheumatism, and was sick a long time; but whether sick or well, I had my work to do. About this time I asked my master and mistress to let me buy my own freedom. With the help of Mr. Burchell, I could have found the means to pay Mr. Wood; for it was agreed that I should afterwards serve Mr. Burchell a while, for the cash he was to advance for me. I was earnest in the request to my owners; but their hearts were hard—too hard to consent. Mrs. Wood was very angry—she grew quite outrageous—she called me a black devil, and asked me who had put freedom into my head. "To be free is very sweet," I said: but she took good care to keep me a slave. I saw her change colour, and I left the room.

About this time my master and mistress were going to England to put their son in school, and bring their daughters home; and they took me with them to take care of the child. I was willing to come to England: I thought that by going there I should probably get cured of my rheumatism, and should return with my master and mistress, quite well, to my husband. My husband was willing for me to come away, for he had heard that my master would free me,—and I also hoped this might prove true; but it was all a false report.

The steward of the ship was very kind to me. He and my husband were in the same class in the Moravian Church. I was thankful that he was so friendly, for my mistress was not kind to me on the passage; and she told me, when she was angry,

2. Prince would have been approximately thirty-eight.

that she did not intend to treat me any better in England than in the West Indies—that I need not expect it. And she was as good as her word.

When we drew near to England, the rheumatism seized all my limbs worse than ever, and my body was dreadfully swelled. When we landed at the Tower, I shewed my flesh to my mistress, but she took no great notice of it. We were obliged to stop at the tavern till my master got a house; and a day or two after, my mistress sent me down into the wash-house to learn to wash in the English way. In the West Indies we wash with cold water—in England with hot. I told my mistress I was afraid that putting my hands first into the hot water and then into the cold, would increase the pain in my limbs. The doctor had told my mistress long before I came from the West Indies, that I was a sickly body and the washing did not agree with me. But Mrs. Wood would not release me from the tub, so I was forced to do as I could. I grew worse, and could not stand to wash. I was then forced to sit down with the tub before me, and often through pain and weakness was reduced to kneel or to sit down on the floor, to finish my task. When I complained to my mistress of this, she only got into a passion as usual, and said washing in hot water could not hurt any one;—that I was lazy and insolent, and wanted to be free of my work; but that she would make me do it. I thought her very hard on me, and my heart rose up within me. However I kept still at that time, and went down again to wash the child's things; but the English washerwomen who were at work there, when they saw that I was so ill, had pity upon me and washed them for me.

After that, when we came up to live in Leigh Street, Mrs. Wood sorted out five bags of clothes which we had used at sea, and also such as had been worn since we came on shore, for me and the cook to wash. Elizabeth the cook told her, that she did not think that I was able to stand to the tub, and that she had better hire a woman. I also said myself, that I had come over to nurse the child, and that I was sorry I had come from Antigua, since mistress would work me so hard, without compassion for my rheumatism. Mr. and Mrs. Wood, when they heard this, rose up in a passion against me. They opened the door and bade me get out. But I was a stranger, and did not know one door in the street from another, and was unwilling to go away. They made a dreadful uproar, and from that day they constantly kept cursing and abusing me. I was obliged to wash, though I was very ill. Mrs. Wood, indeed once hired a washerwoman, but she was not well treated, and would come no more.

My master quarrelled with me another time, about one of our great washings, his wife having stirred him up to do so. He said he would compel me to do the whole of the washing given out to me, or if I again refused, he would take a short course with me: he would either send me down to the brig[3] in the river, to carry me back to Antigua, or he would turn me at once out of doors, and let me provide for myself. I said I would willingly go back, if he would let me purchase my own freedom. But this enraged him more than all the rest: he cursed and swore at me dreadfully, and said he would never sell my freedom—if I wished to be free, I was free in England, and I might go and try what freedom would do for me, and be d——d. My heart was very sore with this treatment, but I had to go on. I continued to do my work, and did all I could to give satisfaction, but all would not do.

Shortly after, the cook left them, and then matters went on ten times worse. I always washed the child's clothes without being commanded to do it, and any thing else that was wanted in the family; though still I was very sick—very sick indeed.

3. Ship.

When the great washing came round, which was every two months, my mistress got together again a great many heavy things, such as bed-ticks, bed-coverlets, &c. for me to wash. I told her I was too ill to wash such heavy things that day. She said, she supposed I thought myself a free woman, but I was not; and if I did not do it directly I should be instantly turned out of doors. I stood a long time before I could answer, for I did not know well what to do. I knew that I was free in England, but I did not know where to go, or how to get my living; and therefore, I did not like to leave the house. But Mr. Wood said he would send for a constable to thrust me out; and at last I took courage and resolved that I would not be longer thus treated, but would go and trust to Providence. This was the fourth time they had threatened to turn me out, and, go where I might, I was determined now to take them at their word; though I thought it very hard, after I had lived with them for thirteen years, and worked for them like a horse, to be driven out in this way, like a beggar. My only fault was being sick, and therefore unable to please my mistress, who thought she never could get work enough out of her slaves; and I told them so: but they only abused me and drove me out. This took place from two to three months, I think, after we came to England.

When I came away, I went to the man (one Mash) who used to black the shoes of the family, and asked his wife to get somebody to go with me to Hatton Garden to the Moravian Missionaries: these were the only persons I knew in England. The woman sent a young girl with me to the mission house, and I saw there a gentlemen called Mr. Moore. I told him my whole story, and how my owners had treated me, and asked him to take in my trunk with what few clothes I had. The missionaries were very kind to me—they were sorry for my destitute situation, and gave me leave to bring my things to be placed under their care. They were very good people, and they told me to come to the church.

When I went back to Mr. Wood's to get my trunk, I saw a lady, Mrs. Pell, who was on a visit to my mistress. When Mr. and Mrs. Wood heard me come in, they set this lady to stop me, finding that they had gone too far with me. Mrs. Pell came out to me, and said, "Are you really going to leave, Molly? Don't leave, but come into the country with me." I believe she said this because she thought Mrs. Wood would easily get me back again. I replied to her, "Ma'am, this is the fourth time my master and mistress have driven me out, or threatened to drive me—and I will give them no more occasion to bid me go. I was not willing to leave them, for I am a stranger in this country, but now I must go—I can stay no longer to be used." Mrs. Pell then went up stairs to my mistress, and told that I would go, and that she could not stop me. Mrs. Wood was very much hurt and frightened when she found I was determined to go out that day. She said, "If she goes the people will rob her, and then turn her adrift." She did not say this to me, but she spoke it loud enough for me to hear; that it might induce me not to go, I suppose. Mr. Wood also asked me where I was going to. I told him where I had been, and that I should never have gone away had I not been driven out by my owners. He had given me a written paper some time before, which said that I had come with them to England by my own desire; and that was true. It said also that I left them of my own free will, because I was a free woman in England; and that I was idle and would not do my work—which was not true. I gave this paper afterwards to a gentleman who inquired into my case.

I went into the kitchen and got my clothes out. The nurse and the servant girl were there, and I said to the man who was going to take out my trunk, "Stop, before you take up this trunk, and hear what I have to say before these people. I am going out of this house, as I was ordered; but I have done no wrong at all to my owners, neither here nor in the West Indies. I always worked very hard to please them, both by night and day; but there was no giving satisfaction, for my mistress could never be satisfied with reasonable service. I told my mistress I was sick, and yet she has ordered me out of doors. This is the fourth time; and now I am going out."

And so I came out, and went and carried my trunk to the Moravians. I then returned back to Mash the shoeblack's house, and begged his wife to take me in. I had a little West Indian money in my trunk; and they got it changed for me. This helped to support me for a little while. The man's wife was very kind to me. I was very sick, and she boiled nourishing things up for me. She also sent for a doctor to see me, and sent me medicine, which did me good, though I was ill for a long time with the rheumatic pains. I lived a good many months with these poor people, and they nursed me, and did all that lay in their power to serve me. The man was well acquainted with my situation, as he used to go to and fro to Mr. Wood's house to clean shoes and knives; and he and his wife were sorry for me.

About this time, a woman of the name of Hill told me of the Anti-Slavery Society, and went with me to their office, to inquire if they could do any thing to get me my freedom, and send me back to the West Indies. The gentlemen of the Society took me to a lawyer, who examined very strictly into my case; but told me that the laws of England could do nothing to make me free in Antigua. However they did all they could for me: they gave me a little money from time to time to keep me from want; and some of them went to Mr. Wood to try to persuade him to let me return a free woman to my husband; but though they offered him, as I have heard, a large sum for my freedom, he was sulky and obstinate, and would not consent to let me go free.

This was the first winter I spent in England, and I suffered much from the severe cold, and from the rheumatic pains, which still at times torment me. However, Providence was very good to me, and I got many friends—especially some Quaker ladies,[4] who hearing of my case, came and sought me out, and gave me good warm clothing and money. Thus I had great cause to bless God in my affliction.

When I got better I was anxious to get some work to do, as I was unwilling to eat the bread of idleness. Mrs. Mash, who was a laundress, recommended me to a lady for a charwoman.[5] She paid me very handsomely for what work I did, and I divided the money with Mrs. Mash; for though very poor, they gave me food when my own money was done, and never suffered me to want.

In the spring, I got into service with a lady, who saw me at the house where I sometimes worked as a charwoman. This lady's name was Mrs. Forsyth. She had been in the West Indies, and was accustomed to Blacks, and liked them. I was with her six months, and went with her to Margate. She treated me well, and gave me a good character when she left London.[6]

After Mrs. Forsyth went away, I was again out of place, and went to lodgings, for which I paid two shillings a week, and found coals and candle. After eleven weeks, the money I had saved in service was all gone, and I was forced to

---

4. Many Quakers—including Mary Birkett (p. 407)—involved themselves in the abolitionist cause.
5. Woman hired to do heavy household labor

(refer to Mary Collier, "The Woman's Labour," p. 269).
6. Margate: a seaside resort in Kent, England; character: a letter of reference.

go back to the Anti-Slavery office to ask a supply, till I could get another situation. I did not like to go back—I did not like to be idle. I would rather work for my living than get it for nothing. They were very good to give me a supply, but I felt shame at being obliged to apply for relief whilst I had strength to work.

At last I went into the service of Mr. and Mrs. Pringle,[7] where I have been ever since, and am as comfortable as I can be while separated from my dear husband, and away from my own country and all old friends and connections. My dear mistress teaches me daily to read the word of God, and takes great pains to make me understand it. I enjoy the great privilege of being enabled to attend church three times on the Sunday; and I have met with many kind friends since I have been here, both clergymen and others. The Rev. Mr. Young, who lives in the next house, has shown me much kindness, and taken much pains to instruct me, particularly while my master and mistress were absent in Scotland. Nor must I forget, among my friends, the Rev. Mr. Mortimer, the good clergyman of the parish, under whose ministry I have now sat for upwards of twelve months. I trust in God I have profited by what I have heard from him. He never keeps back the truth, and I think he has been the means of opening my eyes and ears much better to understand the word of God. Mr. Mortimer tells me that he cannot open the eyes of my heart, but that I must pray to God to change my heart, and make me to know the truth, and the truth will make me free.

I still live in the hope that God will find a way to give me my liberty, and give me back to my husband. I endeavour to keep down my fretting, and to leave all to Him, for he knows what is good for me better than I know myself. Yet, I must confess, I find it a hard and heavy task to do so.

I am often much vexed, and I feel great sorrow when I hear some people in this country say, that the slaves do not need better usage, and do not want to be free. They believe the foreign people, who deceive them, and say slaves are happy. I say, Not so. How can slaves be happy when they have the halter round their neck and the whip upon their back? and are disgraced and thought no more of than beasts?—and are separated from their mothers, and husbands, and children, and sisters, just as cattle are sold and separated? Is it happiness for a driver in the field to take down his wife or sister or child, and strip them, and whip them in such a disgraceful manner?—women that have had children exposed in the open field to shame! There is no modesty or decency shown by the owner to his slaves; men, women, and children are exposed alike. Since I have been here I have often wondered how English people can go out into the West Indies and act in such a beastly manner. But when they go to the West Indies, they forget God and all feeling of shame, I think, since they can see and do such things. They tie up slaves like hogs—moor[8] them up like cattle, and they lick them, so as hogs, or cattle, or horses never were flogged;—and yet they come home and say, and make some good people believe, that slaves don't want to get out of slavery. But they put a cloak about the truth. It is not so. All slaves want to be free—to be free is very sweet. I will say the truth to English people who may read this history that my good friend, Miss S——,[9] is now writing down for me. I have been a slave myself—I know what slaves feel—I can tell by myself what other slaves feel, and by what they have told me. The man that says slaves be quite happy in slavery—that

7. Abolitionists who eventually encouraged   8. To fasten or tie up.
Prince to tell her story for publication.   9. Susanna Strickland.

they don't want to be free—that man is either ignorant or a lying person. I never heard a slave say so. I never heard a Buckra man say so, till I heard tell of it in England. Such people ought to be ashamed of themselves. They can't do without slaves, they say. What's the reason they can't do without slaves as well as in England? No slaves here—no whips—no stocks—no punishment, except for wicked people. They hire servants in England; and if they don't like them, they send them away: they can't lick them. Let them work ever so hard in England, they are far better off than slaves. If they get a bad master, they give warning and go hire to another. They have their liberty. That's just what *we* want. We don't mind hard work, if we had proper treatment, and proper wages like English servants, and proper time given in the week to keep us from breaking the Sabbath. But they won't give it; they will have work—work—work, night and day, sick or well, till we are quite done up; and we must not speak up nor look amiss, however much we be abused. And then when we are quite done up, who cares for us, more than for a lame horse? This is slavery. I tell it to let English people know the truth; and I hope they will never leave off to pray God, and call loud to the great King of England, till all the poor blacks be given free, and slavery done up for evermore.

1831

⊷◄ ELIZABETH HANDS ►⊷
Active 1789

Elizabeth Hands once described herself as "born in obscurity and never emerging beyond the lower stations of life." Like Mary Collier and other women poets who labored for their living, she left behind very little biographical information. She was a servant to a Mr. Huddesford and his daughter, both of Allesly, England. By 1785, she had married a blacksmith at Bourton, a town near Rugby, site of the famous English boys' school. Some evidence indicates she had at least one child.

Before 1789, she published a few poems under a pseudonym in the *Coventry Mercury*, a local newspaper. Eventually, her work titled *The Death of Amnon: A Poem, with an Appendix Containing Pastorals and Other Poetical Pieces* won her the recognition of Philip Bracebridge Homer, an assistant master at the Rugby school, who showed her volume to the school's headmaster, Dr. Thomas James. Although the title poem was somewhat controversial because of its subject—a biblical story of an incestuous rape—Dr. James helped to raise a subscription that allowed for the work's publication in 1789.

In the following two poems, Hands utilizes clever linguistic strategies for conveying potentially explosive commentary on class relationships and, in particular, for conveying her resentment toward the patronizing attitudes of her "superiors." In "Written, Originally Extempore, . . ." Hands uses mock-heroic language to satirize local response to a cow on the loose in a small village. In "A Poem, on the Supposition, . . ." she captures the vacuity of an idle, leisured society that passes judgment on the published poetry of a servant maid. Hands subtly conveys the idea that the pronouncements of society are rooted in both class prejudice and ignorance. The poem allows us to listen in, along with the servant, who hears such demeaning statements without being able to answer back.

Written, Originally Extempore, on Seeing a Mad Heifer Run through the Village Where the Author Lives

When summer smiled, and birds on every spray
In joyous warblings tuned their vocal lay,
Nature on all sides showed a lovely scene,
And people's minds were, like the air, serene;
Sudden from th' herd we saw an heifer stray,   5
And to our peaceful village bend her way.
She spurns the ground with madness as she flies,
And clouds of dust, like autumn mists, arise;
Then bellows loud: the villagers, alarmed,
Come rushing forth, with various weapons armed;   10
Some run with pieces of old broken rakes,
And some from hedges pluck the rotten stakes;
Here one in haste, with hand-staff of his flail,[1]
And there another comes with half a rail;
Whips, without lashes, sturdy ploughboys bring,   15
While clods of dirt and pebbles others fling.
Voices tumultuous rend the listening ear:
"Stop her", one cries; another, "Turn her there":
But furiously she rushes by them all,
And some huzza,[2] and some to cursing fall.   20
A mother snatched her infant off the road,
Close to the spot of ground where next she trod;
Camilla, walking, trembled and turned pale,
See o'er her gentle heart what fears prevail!
At last the beast, unable to withstand   25
Such force united, leaped into a pond:
The water quickly cooled her maddened rage,
No more she'll fright our village, I presage.

1789

A Poem, on the Supposition of the Book Having Been Published and Read

The dinner was over, the tablecloth gone,
The bottles of wine and the glasses brought on,
The gentlemen filled up the sparkling glasses,
To drink to their king, to their country and lasses:
The ladies a glass or two only required,   5
To the drawing-room then in due order retired,
The gentlemen likewise that chose to drink tea;
And, after discussing the news of the day,
What wife was suspected, what daughter eloped,
What thief was detected, that 'twas to be hoped   10
The rascals would all be convicted, and roped;
What chambermaid kissed when her lady was out;

---

1. A tool used for threshing wheat by hand.   2. Shout in exultation, like "hooray."

Who won, and who lost, the last night at the rout;[3]
What lord gone to France, and what tradesman unpaid,
And who and who danced at the last masquerade;   15
What banker stopped payment with evil intention,
And twenty more things much too tedious to mention:
Miss Rhymer says, "Mrs. Routella, ma'am, pray
Have you seen the new book (that we talked of that day
At your house, you remember) of *Poems*, 'twas said   20
Produced by the pen of a poor servant-maid?"
      The company, silent, the answer expected;
Says Mrs. Routella, when she'd recollected:
"Why, ma'am, I have bought it for Charlotte; the child
Is so fond of a book, I'm afraid it is spoiled: 25
I thought to have read it myself, but forgat it;
In short, I have never had time to look at it.
Perhaps I may look it o'er some other day;
Is there anything in it worth reading, I pray?
For your nice attention there's nothing can 'scape."   30
She answered, "There's one piece, whose subject's a Rape."
"A Rape!", interrupted the Captain Bonair;
"A delicate theme for a female, I swear";
Then smirked at the ladies, they simpered all round,
Touched their lips with their fans—Mrs. Consequence frowned.   35
The simper subsided, for she, with her nods,
Awes these lower assemblies, as Jove awes the gods.
She smiled on Miss Rhymer, and bade her proceed—
Says she, "There are various subjects indeed:
With some little pleasure I read all the rest,   40
But the 'Murder of Amnon's'[4] the longest and best."
"Of Amnon, of Amnon, Miss Rhymer, who's he?
His name," says Miss Gaiety, "'s quite new to me."—
"'Tis a Scripture tale, ma'am—he's the son of King David,"[5]
Says a reverend old Rector. Quoth madam, "I have it;   45
A Scripture tale?—ay—I remember it—true;
Pray, is it i' th' Old Testament or the New?
If I thought I could readily find it, I'd borrow
My housekeeper's Bible, and read it tomorrow."
"'Tis in Samuel, ma'am," says the Rector:—Miss Gaiety   50
Bowed, and the Reverend blushed for the laity.
      "You've read it, I find," says Miss Harriot Anderson;
"Pray, sir, is it anything like *Sir Charles Grandison*?"[6]
"How you talk," says Miss Belle, "how should such a girl write
A novel, or anything else that's polite?   55
You'll know better in time, Miss."—She was but fifteen:

---

3. Fashionable assembly, presumably where gambling occurred.
4. A reference to Hands's own poem *The Death of Amnon* (1789).
5. As told in 2 Samuel 13, David's son Amnon fell in love with and raped his sister Tamar.
6. A seven-volume epistolary novel of 1753–54 by Samuel Richardson (1689–1761).

Her mamma was confused—with a little chagrin,
Says, "Where's your attention, child? did not you hear
Miss Rhymer say that it was poems, my dear?"
Says Sir Timothy Turtle, "My daughters ne'er look   60
In anything else but a cookery-book:
The properest study for women designed."
Says Mrs. Domestic, "I'm quite of your mind."
"Your haricots, ma'am, are the best I e'er eat,"
Says the Knight; "may I venture to beg a receipt?"[7]   65
"'Tis much at your service," says madam, and bowed,
Then fluttered her fan, of the compliment proud.
Says Lady Jane Rational, "The bill of fare
Is th' utmost extent of my cookery care:
Most servants can cook for the palate, I find,   70
But very few of them can cook for the mind."
      "Who," says Lady Pedigree, "can this girl be?
Perhaps she's descended from some family—".
"Of family, doubtless," says Captain Bonair;
"She's descended from Adam, I'd venture to swear."   75
Her Ladyship drew herself up in her chair,
And, twitching her fan-sticks, affected a sneer.
"I know something of her," says Mrs. Devoir;
"She lived with my friend, Jacky Faddle, Esq.
'Tis some time ago, though; her mistress said then   80
The girl was excessively fond of a pen;
I saw her, but never conversed with her, *though*:
One can't make acquaintance with servants, you know."
"'Tis pity the girl was not bred in high life,"
Says Mr. Fribello.—"Yes,—then," says his wife,   85
"She doubtless might have wrote something worth notice."
"'Tis pity," says one—says another, "and so 'tis."
"O law!", says young Seagram, "I've seen the book, now
I remember; there's something about a mad cow."[8]
"A mad cow!—ha, ha, ha, ha," returned half the room;   90
"What can y' expect better?", says Madam Du Bloom.
      They look at each other—a general pause—
And Miss Coquettilla adjusted her gauze.
The Rector reclined himself back in his chair,
And opened his snuff-box with indolent air: 95
"This book," says he (snift, snift), "has, in the beginning,"
(The ladies give audience to hear his opinion),
"Some pieces, I think, that are pretty correct:
A style elevated you cannot expect;
To some of her equals they may be a treasure,   100
And country lasses may read 'em with pleasure.
That 'Amnon', you can't call it poetry neither,

---

7. Haricots: string beans; receipt: recipe.   nally Extempore" (see p. 439).
8. Reference to Hands's poem "Written, Origi-

There's no flights of fancy, or imagery either;
You may style it prosaic, blank verse at the best;
Some pointed reflections, indeed, are expressed;   105
The narrative lines are exceedingly poor:
Her Jonadab[9] is a——". The drawing-room door
Was opened, the gentlemen came from below,
And gave the discourse a definitive blow.

                                                                   1789

────────────◄ ANNA MARIA FALCONBRIDGE ►────────────

Active 1790s

Although other white women had traveled to Africa before the 1790s, Anna Maria
Falconbridge was likely the first to describe her own visit. Born Anna Maria Hor-
wood in Bristol, England, she was the youngest of five children. Her father was a
watchmaker and goldsmith. In 1788, against the advice of those close to her, she
married Alexander Falconbridge, a ship's surgeon who had worked on four slave-
trading voyages. Disgusted by what he had experienced, he eagerly responded to
the call of the abolitionist Thomas Clarkson for evidence against the slave trade.
In 1788, Alexander published *An Account of the Slave Trade off the Coast of
Africa,* a tract supporting the abolitionist cause.

In 1791, Anna Maria accompanied Alexander to Sierra Leone, a settlement
on the west coast of Africa for free black refugees, mostly ex-slaves who had
fought for the British during the American Revolution. But the land on which the
settlement was created was controlled by King Naimbana of the Temme tribe and
other tribal leaders. Thus—as Anna records—the future of the settlement required
careful negotiations. Also working against the settlement were rainy weather, inadequate supplies, illness, and the hostility of slave traders in the area, as well as
infighting among members of the Sierra Leone Company, a commercial venture
seeking to make money off the colony. Alexander Falconbridge's task was to persuade King Naimbana and the Temme chiefs to let the settlement remain, as well
as to boost morale. Later in 1791, the Falconbridges briefly returned to England,
taking Naimbana's son with them to be educated abroad. They then returned to
Sierra Leone in 1792.

The Falconbridges' marriage was unhappy: Alexander appears to have been
an abusive husband who was also probably an alcoholic. When he died in December 1792, Anna stayed in Sierra Leone and married Isaac Du Bois, a British loyalist from a southern slave-owning family in America. In 1793, she and Du Bois
returned to England, via Jamaica, on a slaving ship. In her letters, Falconbridge
defends conditions on board the slave ship, describing them as orderly and humane. Although shocking to the modern reader, her comments are meant to indict
the bureaucratic bungling of hypocritical white philanthropists, men who professed to befriend free black colonists while mercilessly exploiting them. Falcon-

9. Nephew of David, who announces Amnon's   13:32–33.
death at the hand of Absalom in 2 Samuel

bridge also writes to respond to charges being leveled by company managers against her first and second husbands, as well as the black colonists themselves.

In the following selection, Falconbridge describes a visit she and Alexander took from their ship, which she calls her "floating prison," to Bance Island, located in the Sierra Leone estuary, twenty miles above modern Freetown. On Bance Island, where the enslaved were gathered before being put on ships, Falconbridge narrates her first impressions of King Naimbana and his court and gives a first-hand description of the delicate dance of diplomacy necessary for the future of the African colony. She provides as well a brief glimpse of a group of enslaved Africans awaiting transport across the Atlantic.

From Two Voyages to Sierra Leone

[A Trip to Bance Island[1]]

* * * I must tell you what passed the remainder of the day at Bance Island, and give as far as my ideas allow me, a description of this factory.

We sat down to dinner with the same party as the first day, consisting of about fifteen in number; this necessary ceremony ended, and towards the cool of the afternoon, I proposed walking for a while: Mr. Tilly and a Mr. Barber[2] offered to accompany and show me the island, which not being objected to, we set out.

Adam's Town was the first place they took me to; it is so called from a native of that name, who has the management of all the gramattos, or free black servants, but under the controul of the Agent.[3]

The whole town consists of a street with about twenty-five houses on each side:—on the right of all is Adam's house.

This building does not differ from the rest, except in size, being much more spacious than any other, and being barracaded with a mud wall;—all of them are composed of thatch, wood, and clay, something resembling our poor cottages, in many parts of England.

I went into several of them—saw nothing that did not discover the occupiers to be very clean and neat; in some was a block or two of wood, which served for chairs,—a few wooden bowls or trenchers, and perhaps a pewter bason and an iron pot completed the whole of their furniture.

In every house I was accosted by whoever we found at home, in the Timmany language Currea Yaa which signifies—How do you do mother?—the most respectful way they can address any person.

Leaving the town, we proceeded first to the burying ground for Europeans, and then to that for blacks;—the only distinction between them was a few orange trees, that shaded two grave stones at the former,—one in memory of a Mr. Knight, who had died here after residing fifteen years as Agent;—the other was on the supposed grave of a Captain Tittle, who was murdered by one Signor Domingo, a native chief, for (as Domingo asserts) being the cause of his son's death.

The circumstance leading to the murder, as well as the murder itself, has been represented to me nearly in the following words:

1. A trading station where enslaved Africans were gathered before being put on slave ships; Bance (also called Bunce) Island is now a notorious part of African history.

2. John Tilley, a slave trader; Barber remains unidentified.

3. A representative of the Sierra Leone company, for whom the settlement was a commercial venture.

"One day while the son of Domingo was employed by Captain Tittle, as a gramatto, or pull-away boy,[4] Tittle's hat by accident blew overboard, and he insisted that the boy should jump into the water and swim after it, as the only means of saving his hat.

"The boy obstinately refused, saying, he could not swim, and he should either be drowned, or the sharks would catch him; upon which Tittle pushed him into the water, and the poor boy was lost; but whether devoured by sharks, or suffocated by water, is immaterial, he was never heard of, or seen after.

"The father, though sorely grieved for his son's death, was willing to consider it accidental, and requested Tittle would supply him with a small quantity of rum to make a cry[5] of lamentation in their country custom.

"The Captain, by promise, acquiesced to the demand, and sent him a cask; but instead of spirits filled with emptyings from the *tubs*[6] of his slaves.

"As soon as Domingo discovered this insult and imposition, he informed Tittle he must either submit to the decision of a Palaver,[7] or he would put him to death if ever an opportunity offered; but Tittle laughed at these threats, and disregarding them, vauntingly threw himself into the way of Domingo—while the trick played upon him, and the loss of his son were fresh in his memory.

"The African, however, instead of being daunted at the sight of this head strong man, soon convinced him he was serious: he had Tittle seized, and after confining him some time in irons, without food, ordered him to be broken to death,[8] which was executed under the inspection of the injured father, and to the great joy and satisfaction of a multitude of spectators."

Not a sentence or hint of the affair is mentioned on the tombstone; the reason assigned for the omission, was a wish to obliterate the melancholy catastrophe, and a fear least the record might be the means of kindling animosities at a future day.

Now, although I cannot without horror contemplate on the untimely end of this man, yet he assuredly in some degree merited it, if the account I have heard and just now related to you, be true, which I have no reason to question; for he who unprovoked can wantonly rob a fellow creature of his life, deserves not life himself!

From the catacombs which lay at the south-east end, we walked to the opposite point of the island; it is no great distance, for the whole island is very little more than a fourth of a mile in length, and scarcely a mile and a half in circumference.

Several rocks lay at a small distance from the shore at this end; they are by the natives called the Devil's Rocks,—from the superstitious opinion that the *old Gentleman* resides either there or in the neighbourhood.

Sammo, King of the Bulloms, comes to this place once a year to make a sacrifice and peace-offering to his infernal Majesty.

From this King Messrs. Anderson's[9] hold all their possessions here, and I understand they pay him an annual tribute—but to what amount I cannot say.

The King comes in person to receive his dues, which are paid him in his canoe, for he never ventures to put his foot on shore, as his *Gree Greemen* or fortune-tellers have persuaded him the island will sink under him, if ever he lands.

I am told at one time he suffered himself to be dragged up to the Factory House in his boat, but no argument was strong enough to seduce him to disem-

4. Oarsman.
5. Similar to a wake, a ritual involving rum and tobacco.
6. Chamberpots.
7. An African court.
8. Starved to death.
9. John and Alexander Anderson, who owned the majority interest in Bance Island.

bark, for he did not consider he incurred the penalty his prophets denounced while he continued in his canoe; though he could not avoid shewing evident tokens of uneasiness, 'till he was safe afloat again.

We now returned to the Factory, or as it is otherwise called Bance Island house.

This building at a distance has a respectable and formidable appearance; nor is it much less so upon a nearer investigation: I suppose it is about one hundred feet in length, and thirty in breadth, and contains nine rooms, all on one floor, under which are commodious large cellars and store rooms; to the right is the kitchen, forge, &c. and to the left other necessary buildings, all of country stone, and surrounded with a prodigious thick lofty wall.

There was formerly a fortification in front of those houses, which was destroyed by a French frigate during the last war;[1] at present several pieces of cannon are planted in the same place, but without embrassures or breastwork;[2] behind the great house is the slave yard, and houses for accommodating the slaves.

Delicacy, perhaps, prevented the gentlemen from taking me to see them; but the room where we dined looks directly into the yard.

Involuntarily I stroled to one of the windows a little before dinner, without the smallest suspicion of what I was to see;—judge then what my astonishment and feelings were at the sight of between two and three hundred wretched victims, chained and parcelled out in circles, just satisfying the cravings of nature from a trough of rice placed in the centre of each circle.

Offended modesty rebuked me with a blush for not hurrying my eyes from such disgusting scenes; but whether fascinated by female curiosity, or whatever else, I could not withdraw myself for several minutes—while I remarked some whose hair was withering with age, reluctantly tasting their food—and others thoughtless from youth, greedily devouring all before them: be assured I avoided the prospects from this side of the house ever after.

Having prolonged the time 'till nine at night, we returned to our floating prison, and what with the assiduity of the master in removing many inconveniencies, my mind being more at ease, want of rest for two nights, and somewhat fatigued with the exercise of the day, I, thank God, slept charmingly, and the next morning we set sail for Robana,[3] where we arrived about ten o'clock: I think it is called nine miles from Bance Island.

We went on shore, and rather caught his *Majesty* by surprize, for he was quite in *dishabille;* and at our approach retired in great haste.

I observed a person pass me in a loose white frock and trowsers, *whom I would not have suspected for a King!* if he had not been pointed out to me.

Mr. Elliotte[4] and the *Queen* met us; and after introducing her Majesty and himself, we were then conducted to her house.

She behaved with much indifference,—told me in broken English that the *King* would come presently—he was gone to *peginninee* woman house to dress himself.[5]

After setting nigh half an hour, Naimbana made his appearance, and received us with seeming good will: he was dressed in a purple embroidered coat, white

1. Most likely one of many skirmishes between the French and English to control the key slave ports along the coast.
2. The cannon were not fortified or behind protective walls.
3. A town on an island approximately nine miles

away from Bance Island.
4. Elliott Griffith: the secretary, translator, and son-in-law of King Naimbana.
5. One of King Naimbana's wives, a member of the Peginniee tribe.

sattin waistcoast and breeches, *thread stockings,* and his left side emblazoned with a flaming star; his legs to be sure were *harliquined,* by a number of holes in the stockings, through which his black skin appeared.[6]

Compliments ended, Mr. Falconbridge acquainted him with his errand, by a repetition of what he wrote the day before: and complained much of King Jemmy's[7] injustice in driving the settlers away, and burning their town.

The King answered through Elliotte, (for he speaks but little English) that Jemmy was partly right—the people had brought it on themselves; they had taken part with some Americans, with whom Jemmy had a dispute, and through that means drew the ill will of this man upon them, who had behaved, considering their conduct as well as they merited; for he gave them three days notice before he burned their town, that they might remove themselves and all their effects away; that he (Naimbana) could not prudently re-establish them, except by consent of all the Chiefs—for which purpose he must call a court or palaver; but it would be seven or eight days before they could be collected; however he would send a summons to the different parties directly, and give Falconbridge timely advice when they were to meet.

Falconbridge perceived clearly nothing was to be effected without a palaver, and unless the King's interest was secured his views would be frustrated, and his endeavours ineffectual; but how this was to be done, or what expedient to adopt, he was at a loss for.

He considered it impolitic to purchase his patronage by heavy presents, least the other *great men* might expect the same; and he had it not in his power to purchase them all in the same way, as the scanty cargo of the Lapwing would not admit of it.

At length, trusting that the praise-worthy purposes he was aiming at, insured him the assistance of the King of Kings, he resolved to try what good words would do.

Having prefaced his arguments with a small donation of some rum, wine, a cheese, and a gold laced hat, which Naimbana seemed much pleased with.

Falconbridge began, by explaining what advantages would accrue to his *Majesty,* and all the inhabitants round about, by such an establishment as the St. George's Bay Company were desirous of making;—the good they wished to do— *their disinterestednes in point of obtaining wealth,* and concluded by expostulating on the injustice and imposition of dispossessing the late settlers of the grounds and houses they occupied, which had been honestly and honorably purchased by Captain Thompson of the Navy, in the name of our gracious Sovereign, his Britannic Majesty.

That it was unusual for Englishmen to forego fulfilling any engagements they made; and they held in detestation every person so disposed.

He then entreated the King would use all his might to prevent any unfavourable prejudices which a refusal to reinstate the Settlers, or to confirm the bargain made with Captain Thompson, might operate against him in the minds of his good friends the King of England and the St. George's Bay Company.

---

6. Thread stockings: knitted stockings; harlequined: as if decorated with contrasting colors, based on the coat of Harlequin, a character in the Italian commedia dell' drte.

7. A native local chieftain, who, before the Falconbridges' arrival, had set fire to an earlier settlement and dispersed the settlers.

The King said he liked the English in preference to all white men, tho' he considered every white man as a *rogue,* and consequently saw them with a jealous eye; yet, he believed the English were by far the honestest, and for that reason, notwithstanding he had received more favors from the French than the English, he liked the latter much best.

He was decidedly of opinion, that all contracts or agreements between man and man however disadvantageous to either party should be binding; but observed, he was *hastily drawn in* to dispose of land to Captain Thompson, *which in fact he had not a right to sell,* because says he, "this is a great country, and belongs to many people—where I live belongs to myself—and I can live where I like; nay, can appropriate any unhabited land within my dominions to what use I please; but it is necessary for me to obtain the consent of my people, or rather the head man of every town, before I sell any land to a white man, or allow strangers to come and live among us."

"*I should have done this you will say at first*—Granted—but as I disobliged my subjects by suffering your people to take possession of the land without their approbation, from which cause I was not able to protect them, unless I hazarded civil commotions in my country; and as they have been *turned away*—it is best now—they should be replaced by the unanimous voice of all interested.

"I am bound from what I have heretofore done, to give my utmost support; and if my people do not acquiesce, it shall not be my fault."

Here Falconbridge, interrupting the King, said—"The King of the English will not blame your people, but load yourself with the stigma; it is King *Naimbana* who is ostensible[8] to King *George*—and I hope King, you will not fall out with your good friend."

This being explained by *Mr. Secretary Elliotte,* his Majesty was some moments silent—when clasping Falconbridge in his arms, told him—"*I believe you and King George* are my good friends—do not fear, have a good heart, I will do as much as I can for you."

They then shook hands heartily, and Naimbana retired, I suppose to his *Pegininee woman's house,* but presently returned dressed in a suit of black velvet, except the stockings, which were the same as before.

I often had an inclination to offer my services to close the holes: but was fearful least my needle might blunder into his *Majesty*'s leg, and start the blood, for drawing the blood of an African King, I am informed, whether occasioned by accident or otherwise, is punished with death: the dread of this only prevented me.

We were now invited to walk and see the town, while dinner was preparing.

It consists of about twenty houses irregularly placed, built of the same materials, but in a superior way to those of Adam's town;—the whole of them are either occupied by the King's wives and servants, or appropriated as warehouses.

I saw several of his wives, but his *Pegininee* woman is a most beautiful young girl of about fourteen.

None of them are titled with the appellation of *Queen,* but the oldest, who I was introduced to, and by whom the King has several children; one of the daughter's, named Clara, is wife to Elliotte, and a son named Bartholomew, is now in France for his education.

8. Responsible.

In different parts of the town I observed some rags stuck on poles, at the foot of each were placed—perhaps a rusty cutlass, some pieces of broken glass, and a pewter bason, containing a liquid of some sort; these are called *Gree Grees*, and considered as antidotes against the Devil's vengeance.

I was thoughtlessly offering to examine one of them, when Mr. Elliotte requested me to desist, or I should give offence, they being held in a very sacred point of view.

We were now led to the garden, which was only furnished with African plants, such as pines, melons, pumpkins, cucumbers, &c. &c.

The King cut two beautiful pines and presented to me: he then shewed us a large new house, at present building for him, which is after the same form, and of the same materials with the rest of his town, but much larger.

In our walk we saw many of the King's slaves employed in preparing the palm-nut, to make oil from them: It may not be amiss here to give you some description of the tree which produce these nuts.

It is remarkable strait and of a gigantic height; the trunk is quite naked, having neither limb or bark, for the only branches grow immediately from the top, and incline their points somewhat towards the ground.

This is a valuable tree, the nut not only produces a quantity of oil, but is esteemed excellent food by the natives, who also extract a liquor from the tree, which they call palm wine.

This I am told is done by means of an incision in the upper part of the trunk, in which a pipe is entered to convey the liquor into bottles placed beneath.

I have tasted some of this wine, and do not think it unpleasant when fresh made; it has a sweetish taste, and much the look of whey, but foments in a few days, and grows sour—however I really think this liquor distilled would make a decent kind of spirit.

Having seen all the raree-shows of Robana town, we returned to the Queens house to dinner, which was shortly after put on a table covered with a plain calico cloth, and consisted of boiled and broiled fowls, rice, and some greens resembling our spinage.

But I should tell you, before dinner Naimbana again changed his dress for a scarlet robe embroidered with gold.

Naimbana, Elliotte, Falconbridge, and myself, only set down; the Queen stood behind the King eating an onion I gave her, a bite of which she now and then indulged her *Royal Consort* with: silver forks were placed on the King's plate, and mine, but no where else.

The King is rather above common height, but meagre withal; the features of his face resemble a European more than any black I have seen; his teeth are mostly decayed, and his hair, or rather wool, bespeaks old age, which I judge to be about eighty; he was seldom without a smile on his countenance, but I think his smiles were suspicious.

He gave great attention while Falconbridge was speaking, for though he does not speak our language, he understands a good deal of it; his answers were slow, and on the whole tolerably reasonable.

The Queen is of a middle stature, plump and jolly; her temper seems placid and accommodating; her teeth are bad, but I dare say she has otherwise been a good looking woman in her youthful days.

I suppose her now to be about forty-five or six, at which age women are considered old here.

She sat on the King's right hand, while he and Falconbridge were in conversation; and now and then would clap her hands, and cry out *Ya hoo*, which signifies, that's well or proper.

She was dressed in the country manner, but in a dignified stile, having several yards of striped taffety[9] wrapped around her waist, which served as a petticoat; another piece of the same was carelessly thrown over her shoulders in form of a scarf; her head was decorated with two silk handkerchiefs; her ears with rich gold ear-rings, and her neck with gaudy necklaces; *but she had neither shoes nor stockings on.*

Clara was dressed much after the same way, but her apparel was not quite of such good materials as the Queen's: Mr. Elliotte apologized after dinner, that for want of *sugar* they could not offer tea or coffee.

The tide serving, and approaching night obliged us to re-embark and return to this place.

On the whole I was much pleased with the occurrences of the day; indeed, methinks, I hear you saying, "Why the week mind of this giddy girl will be quite intoxicated with the courtesy and attention paid her by such great folks;" but believe me, to whatever height of self-consequence I may have been lifted by aerial fancies, overpowering sleep prevailed, and clouding all my greatness—I awoke next morning without the slightest remains of fancied importance.

1794

---

9. Or taffeta, a glossy, stiff fabric made of silk.

Women of the World (Courtesy Joni Seager).

The Nineteenth Century

In Virginia Woolf's *Orlando* (1928), the title character—a poet who is born as a boy in Renaissance England, turns into a woman at the dawn of the eighteenth century, and continues living as a female into the modern period—is startled by the changes she sees as the nineteenth century draws to a close. Peering out the window of her London home, she realizes it is "now, in the evening, that the change [is] most remarkable." She exclaims to herself:

> Look at the lights in the houses! At a touch, a whole room was lit; hundreds of rooms were lit. . . . One could see everything in the little square-shaped boxes; there was no privacy; none of those lingering shadows and odd corners that there used to be; none of those women in aprons carrying wobbly lamps which they put down carefully on this table and on that. At a touch, the whole room was bright. And the sky was bright all night long; and the pavements were bright; everything was bright. (Chapter 6)

Indeed, in 1800, as in 1700 or 1600, homes in Britain, the British colonies, and the new United States were full of "lingering shadows and odd corners" because people still lit their homes with candles. These "lingering shadows" made reading and writing difficult and even made cleaning dangerous—overturned candles and oil lamps could set whole houses ablaze. But over the course of the nineteenth century, lighting improved: whale-oil lamps replaced candles, gas fixtures replaced whale oil. As the nineteenth century came to a close, the electric lightbulb put an end to the dangers of "wobbly lamps" with their open flames even as they banished the privacy of romantic shadows.

THE NINETEENTH CENTURY: AN OVERVIEW

As Orlando witnessed, the nineteenth century was a period of especially dramatic change for the English-speaking world. The fundamental technologies of living (such as lighting) shifted profoundly, as did the political and economic nature of that world. The English-speaking world was both larger and smaller than even the most visionary thinkers of the eighteenth century could have imagined. In the 1790s, for example, Britain was still smarting over the loss of some of her American colonies during the Revolutionary War and worrying about the threats posed by France in the wake of its revolution. Britain was also expanding its control of the Indian subcontinent and its holdings in the West Indies (the islands of the Caribbean) and was only beginning to look to Africa, East Asia, and New South Wales (Australia) for colonial opportunities. The new United States of America consisted of only sixteen states on or close to the Atlantic seaboard that were mired in debt and at odds over internal organization. By the 1890s, however, the British crown's loss of thirteen tiny American colonies had been more than made up for by the massive expansion of British control over territories around the globe. "The sun never sets on the British Empire," the boastful motto of England under Queen Victoria (1819–1901), was literally true. Over the same period, the once-fragile United States of America had expanded across the North American

Paraffin oil lamps like the one hanging from the ceiling of the morning room at Linley Sambourne House, London (pictured here), were invented in 1850 and were a great improvement over the oil lamps that had dominated homes earlier in the century; the fuel was cheaper and fed into the wick more easily. While London streets were lit by gas by early in the nineteenth century, homeowners generally distrusted it, and it did not become popular until the Houses of Parliament installed gas lamps in 1859. Most lower-income households continued to be poorly lit as they relied on less expensive oil lamps, tallow candles, and natural light.

continent and had become, itself, a colonial power with holdings in the Pacific, in the Caribbean, and on the continent of Africa.

Although the nineteenth century was known as the Victorian era, after the British queen who reigned for two-thirds of it, the most distinctive feature of the English-speaking world at the time was that it was no longer the same as the British world. Just as developments in technology radically transformed the material conditions of many women, so did shifts in the political and economic parameters of the world change women's experience. English-speaking women participated in these shifts, representing themselves and their own interests as never before through the medium of the language.

Colonial Transformations

In 1800, the colonization of the non-European world by white English speakers was understood as a positive good by the colonizers. After all, most of the western European governments were competing (as they would continue to do through the early twentieth century) to expand their domains and their power. The relative status of the European nations to each other depended to a great degree upon their control of the wealth of non-European lands. Colonization also seemed to improve the lives of many Britons and Americans because colonies supplied the raw resources that could be turned into commodities, such as the machine-woven cloth that made life easier and more comfortable. These resources included cotton, iron, silk, and sugar but also human labor performed by slaves; the labor of slaves kept labor-intensive crops and labor-intensive extraction of minerals profitable. While colonialism offered various political and economic benefits, it was also understood and justified as bringing the benefits of Christianity, technology, and representative governance to people who were imagined as backward, benighted, and primitive.

From the beginning of English colonialism during the Renaissance, the male colonists who journeyed as investors, soldiers, missionaries, exiles, and settlers brought their wives, sisters, and servants. Because of the legal, economic, and social dependence of women on men, many pioneer and colonial women had little choice regarding where they would go and, sometimes, a greater ambivalence about the colonial venture. Yet much of the success of the venture depended on women rising to the challenges of making new homes and new lives in alien conditions. Mary Talbot's letters (p. 477) convey glimpses of what it was like to be one of the many women who were transported to New South Wales by the British government for the crime of being poor. Like Susanna Moodie (pp. 635–39), whose circumstances brought her to a frontier of the British world in the North American province of Canada, Talbot and many others grappled with both the

The Promised Land—the Grayson Family by William S. Jewett, 1850. An idealized portrait of an American pioneer family resting in a romantic landscape before moving forward into the frontier. The father relies on his gun as both a weapon and a prop, while his wife converts the wild rocks into a comfortable couch for herself and her child. (Daniel J. Terra Collection, Terra Foundation for American Art, Chicago, 1850)

threats and the promises of creating a new mode of life. The women who already lived in the areas colonized by the English-speaking nations found their lives even more transformed as, often, the traditional fabric of their society—its religious, political, and economic foundation—was destroyed or eviscerated to serve the interests of the colonial powers. By the end of the nineteenth century, the colonized, such as Pandita Ramabai Saraswati (pp. 1152–54) and Sarah Winnemucca Hopkins (p. 1033) were beginning to use English to challenge the positive view of colonialism. Sarah Winnemucca Hopkins's memoir, *Life among the Piutes: Their Wrongs and Claims* (pp. 1033–35), for example, details the experience of being subject to the supposedly beneficent effects of colonization that not only cost her people sovereign control of their land but also deprived them of the ability to maintain their cultural traditions.

English: The Common Denominator

As the geographic space controlled by the English-speaking nations expanded throughout the nineteenth century, so did the number and variety of English speakers. Largely through voluntary immigration from England, Ireland, and other European countries, the population of English speakers in Canada and the United States grew from about 16 million in 1800 to more than 106 million at the century's end. English was the official language in both Canada and the United States—successful immigrants soon mastered it. The former penal colonies of New South Wales (what we now call Australia and New Zealand), where 2 million, mostly indigenous, non–English-speaking people had lived in 1800, tripled in population one hundred years later through both forced and voluntary immigration from Britain and Ireland, even as the indigenous populations shrank under Britain's genocidal policies.

Throughout the British Empire and the United States and its territories, English was imposed on the conquered peoples. In North America, for example, the children of formerly sovereign First Nation peoples (such as the Paiute and Cherokee) were taken from their families into boarding schools designed to replace the language and cultural values of their families with the English language and American national values. (The twentieth century would see Britain following the same strategy in Australia and New Zealand.) In Ireland, as in Wales and Scotland, English rulers discouraged or even outlawed the speaking of Gaelic and native dialects of English. On the subcontinent of India, by the middle of the nineteenth century, the colonial government had established a system of schools designed to create a class of people able to serve and maintain British interests. From the nineteenth century onward, the English-speaking world could no longer be considered ethnically or culturally homogeneous.

As disparate as they are, what the writers in this volume share is the English language; a language they use to express the different ways to be a "woman in the nineteenth century." Following the publication of Dr. Samuel Johnson's *Dictionary* in 1755, English had begun to be more conventionalized and standardized than it had ever been before. Johnson's work was part of a trend toward fixing and "normalizing" standards of spelling and usage for writers of English. Inspired by the Enlightenment urge to order and clarify, Johnson had sought to derive and then to articulate a set of rational rules that would govern and clarify the grammar and spelling of English. Before this, spelling, for example, was generally more or less phonetic. In other words, writers would choose consonant and vowel combinations to reflect their sense of how a word sounded to them rather than choosing a spelling that conformed to some abstract rule of correctness. This meant that the way people spelled reflected, quite closely, the way they spoke. One's spelling, like one's accent or dialect, conveyed much about one's regional and class affiliations. But Johnson's *Dictionary* and similar efforts established norms that could be taught and learned. Being able to learn correct or "proper" written English did much to erase the often disabling distinctions of region, class, and gender as, increasingly, it became expected that written English would conform to an abstract standard.

Although the national origins of writers such as Elizabeth Gaskell (British; pp. 713–14) and Harriet Beecher Stowe (American; pp. 732–34) are easily apparent by the content and setting of their stories, as well as the colorfully transcribed dialects of their less-educated characters, there is little apparent difference between the accents or dialects of their respective narrators. Most often, nineteenth-century writers reserved nonstandard English spelling and usage to denote the difference and distance between the sensibility of certain characters and what the author considered "normal" sensibility. Normal sensibility and normal English became analogous, and nineteenth-century women writers were able to claim this normality for themselves, whether they were born to a life of privilege or a life of deprivation. Denotations of accent or dialect in the form of nonconventional spelling or grammar became markers of difference reserved for representations of slaves, children, the poor, or rural dwellers. Non-conventional English, or dialect, was used for comic or sentimental effect in the many different genres in which nineteenth-century women wrote.

The Rise of Nationalism

Women who wrote in English during the nineteenth century were a heterogeneous group—they lived all over the globe, they came from every different class position, and they held different opinions regarding the pressing political concerns of the day. The late eighteenth century, with its empire building and suppression of indigenous cultures, gave rise around the world to a new value. Nationalism is the devotion to the interests or culture of the nation above all else. This sense of being part of a nation, recognized or unrecognized, pushed Britons, Americans, and the peoples whose lands were colonized to ask themselves what it meant to be British, what it meant to be American, what it meant to be either or neither. American culture had begun as a colonial culture, but with the successful Revolution of 1776, it began to define itself, not against British identity but against colonial identity. To have a colonial identity meant to be defined negatively in terms established not by oneself but by those at the cultural center. By the 1830s, though one could dispute whether there was any writing produced in America worthy of being called literature, one couldn't dispute that there was something recognizable as an American identity. English-speaking writers in Canada and India, however, continued to wrestle with the problem of national identity. Thus, the nineteenth-century women writers in this section write from one of three possible cultural positions: British, American, and another that is less neatly named, for it includes the indigenous women of colonized areas, black women in the United States who were excluded from the rights and protections of white-skinned women, and white women from Britain and the United States whose life circumstances brought them to the edges of the British Empire.

For British women writers, those who were born and wrote primarily in and of England, the designation "Englishwoman" was often as unproblematic and invisible as the choice to write in English. But for American women and those women who lived and wrote in the reaches of the British Empire, questions of nationality and its relationship to language were more complicated. White women in the United States wrote and read English, but they thought of themselves, even as they helped to define what this term would mean, as "American." Although writers who would have thought of themselves as either British or American dominate this section, on women writers of the nineteenth century—indeed, they were almost the only women publishing in this period—we also include the writings of some women whose cultural position was more complicated. Women who were born into slavery (for example, Sojourner Truth, pp. 606–11; Harriet Jacobs, pp. 792–813; and Hannah Crafts, pp. 1013–21) or were members of the First Nations (such as Sarah Winnemucca Hopkins) used English to represent themselves in writing to an audience predisposed to deny that such women had selves to represent. Likewise, English-speaking women who lived most of their lives in the British colonies (Susanna Moodie, pp. 635–39; Catherine Helen Spence, pp. 910–14; Anna Leonowens, pp. 992–99; Rosa Praed, pp. 1135–42) also began to describe their experiences in a world defined by its dependence on and difference from England. Not even these women, who wrote from the margins of society, are easily classifiable under one rubric, for they speak from various positions in terms of race and class.

Economic Expansion

Colonization fed the explosive economic growth of England and the United States as they shifted from mercantilist economies to fully fledged capitalist economies during the nineteenth century. Mercantilism (an economic system in which the merchant class and the government worked together to regulate the production, import, export, and marketing of goods) had prevailed through the eighteenth century, until it seemed to limit rather than foster the economic health of Britain and America. The late eighteenth century saw the rise of a new economic system, industrial capitalism, which matured throughout the nineteenth century. In a capitalist economy, the measure of the wealth of nations became not how much money was held by a country and its citizens, but how much growth there was in the country's means to make money (or capital). The more factories a country had, the more resources it controlled, the more means to transport those resources it possessed, the more markets in which goods could circulate, the more cash in its citizens' hands, the better. Colonial expansion provided raw resources (such as cotton and sugar) to keep the mills going, new markets for the goods produced by the factories, and, most importantly, sources of cheap labor in the form of slaves (in the United States) or indentured workers (in the United States and British Empire). Under the laissez-faire (or free market) doctrines of industrial capitalism, regulations controlling who could sell what to whom were removed so that individuals and corporations could more easily make profits and reinvest those profits into the means to make more profits and thus increase the amount of overall wealth in a country even as it dispersed this wealth among a wider variety of people. By any measure, the economies of both Britain and the United States were exponentially larger at the end of the nineteenth century than they had been at the beginning. More people had more money and lived with greater ease. Capitalism underwrote Virginia Woolf's dream that any woman who wanted to be an artist should be able to support the luxury of a room of her own through canny investments in the stock market.

Many women writers during the nineteenth century, whether they profited from this system or not, explored the human cost of this economic growth. Harriet Jacobs, who escaped from slavery in the United States, described what it was like to be considered a piece of property whose value could be measured in dollars and cents (see pp. 814–15). Until 1865 (with the abolition of slavery in the United States), the raw cotton, sugarcane, and rubber sap that were transformed by British and New England mills into inexpensive cloth or useful rubber boots were often produced by slaves who were forced to labor for no wages. Even after the abolition of slavery, indenture and virtual slavery remained prevalent in the colonized regions and for some blacks in the United States. The inexpensive labor provided by colonialism also helped to keep down the wages of free workers in Britain and America, who frequently worked for wages that hardly provided for the basic necessities of life. As the British author Elizabeth Gaskell (pp. 713–14) recounts in "The Three Eras of Libbie Marsh" (pp. 714–32), working women struggled against the alienating conditions produced by the transformation of the economy from one based on agriculture and home production of goods into one based on factory production. Likewise, the American author Rebecca Harding Davis (p. 966) wrote the novella *Life in the Iron-Mills* (pp. 967–92), to explore the loss of human dignity demanded by the industries that made the trains and engines and the needles and pins that were improving the lives of others.

Technological Innovation

The technological innovations of the Industrial Revolution, which had begun in the eighteenth century changed almost every aspect of existence by the end of the nineteenth century. The English-speaking world was, to take just one example, smaller than ever after the rapid development of the steam-powered railways during the 1820s and 1830s. In 1800 it would have taken three weeks to travel over land from Philadelphia to Boston by horseback or carriage and six to eight weeks to travel by sailing ship from London to Boston. By 1900, thanks to the steam engine, one could travel from Philadelphia to Boston by steam-powered train in less than a day, and the six-week crossing of the Atlantic was shortened to two weeks. In 1800 a person would be lucky to travel fifteen rural miles in two hours by horse and cart. By 1900 the train would cover the same distance in twenty minutes and with less expense. By the end of the nineteenth century, travelers could take the train between Bombay, Calcutta, and Madras in India or from city to city within the states of Australia. In London, where foot and horse had for centuries been the only means of getting from one section to another, an underground rapid transit system was begun in the 1860s, and by the 1890s, the system had developed into the deep-tunneled electrical system that still runs today. In Boston in 1895, a subway was proposed to alleviate the gridlock caused by people, carts, and animals, and by 1897 a portion of the system was open to the public. (New York's subway system wasn't started until the early years of the twentieth century.) By 1900 the mobility of individual people was even further extended by the newly invented, human-powered bicycle and engine-powered automobile.

The decorative nature of this Victorian toilet (c. 1870s) highlights the status of the flush toilet as a luxury item through much of the nineteenth century. Chamber pots, which had to be emptied by hand and usually by the women of the household into open sewers or outhouses, continued to be common.

Advances in the technology of communication, such as the telegraph and telephone, also made the world seem smaller by reducing the time between sending a message and receiving an answer. Rather than depending on ships, stagecoaches, and postmen on foot to carry personal letters and official documents, by the middle of the nineteenth century, people could communicate important news, almost instantly, across vast distances via the telegraph. And, as the century closed, telephones were beginning to allow individuals to speak with one another without being in the same place. At the same speed with which the flip of an electric switch could light an entire room, one's voice could now travel through wires to be heard across increasing distances. For those wealthy enough to have telephones, doctors could be summoned without leaving the sickroom, gossip could be exchanged without leaving the house, and groceries could be ordered without leaving the kitchen.

Few aspects of the material conditions of women's work were unchanged by the end of the nineteenth century. The list of changes that transformed just the work of housekeeping is almost endless: wood and gas ranges with cooktops and ovens replaced open fireplaces; flush toilets replaced chamber pots, privies, and open sewers; steel-pointed fountain pens replaced goose or turkey quill pens (pp. 640–41); machine-woven cloth replaced hand-loomed cloth; machine sewing replaced much hand sewing (pp. 1039–40). Innovations such as metal fasteners and elastic fabrics were about to yield the physical liberation of the brassiere (pp. 1216–17), which would put an end to the constriction of the corset (pp. 543–44). The list could go on.

But it was developments in the technology of mechanical representation—printing and publishing—that most directly affected the ability of the women writers we feature in this section to continue to speak to us through literature. Revolutions in printing made access to a public audience easier than it had ever been before. Books, newspapers, and magazines became cheap and proliferated in such great numbers that women writers found an eager market for their work. Not only did this new mass medium allow even non-elite people to keep abreast of world events, but it also provided an opportunity for women to become editors or publishers as well as to become what our current mass media call "content providers" (see pp. 785–86).

Political Transformations

In *A Vindication of the Rights of Woman* (1792; pp. 366–82), even the visionary radical Mary Wollstonecraft (p. 365) seems somewhat anxious lest she "excite laughter" by imagining "that women ought to have representatives, instead of being arbitrarily governed without having any direct share allowed them in the deliberations of government." In other words, women's suffrage (the right to vote) had been almost unimaginable at the end of the eighteenth century. Wollstonecraft was not one to shy away from difficult stances, but even she realized how far her culture was from being able to sanction the two sentences that form the Nineteenth Amendment to the Constitution of the United States (1920): "The right of citizens of the United States to vote shall not be denied or abridged by the United States or by any State on account of sex. Congress shall have power to enforce this article by appropriate legislation."

The English-speaking world of the nineteenth century was marked by struggles to expand the number and kind of people who were able to represent themselves economically, politically, and artistically. At the beginning of the century, the right to vote in Britain was limited by religion, by sex, by age, and by the amount of property a man owned. In some U.S. states, race joined these limitations. The battle to extend suffrage to all men in Britain was fought in the courts, in Parliament, and on the streets throughout the century until 1884 when, finally, all British men won the right to vote and to stand for election. Although all adult white men in the United States had won the right to vote by 1830, American men of African and First Nations descent had to fight for even the most basic rights to "life, liberty, and the pursuit of happiness" until—and after—the abolition of slavery during the Civil War (1861–65).

Not surprisingly in a century so given to change, the nineteenth century was an era of reform, and women not only actively participated in but also led efforts to create a more perfect world. Although the anti-slavery movement had begun in Britain during the eighteenth century, the nineteenth century saw reform efforts expand to include almost all aspects of society, to better conform with new, more democratic principles. Many of these reform groups drew their first members from various Christian churches in Britain, its colonies, and the United States. In these groups women were able to take the lead in confronting obstacles to the perfection of individual souls and society without violating conventions

In the late-eighteenth century, the British abolitionist Josiah Wedgwood had designed a medallion featuring the figure of a naked man kneeling in chains and having the motto: "Am I Not a Man and Brother?" This image was revised in the 1830s to feature a woman slave. The new image and motto "Am I Not a Woman and a Sister?" became the logo of the American abolitionist movement in which women and the appeal to feminine sentiment played such an important role.

that relegated women to matters concerning hearth, home, and church. Angelina Grimké, for example, took her critique of the U.S. system of racial slavery directly to the Christian women of the South (pp. 643–50), asking them to use their moral authority as wives and mothers to persuade their husbands and sons to repudiate the soul-killing practice of holding humans in bondage. Although many men at that time considered slavery to be a matter of business and politics (and, therefore, outside the purview of women), activists such as Grimké and Sojourner Truth claimed authority to speak based on their status as Christians and as women. Women also took on issues such as intemperate drinking, prostitution, the condition of prisoners, the paganism of other cultures, and the lack of literacy and Christianity among domestic workers.

As women gained experience writing petitions, organizing fund-raising events, and hosting speakers, they also developed skills that belied dominant conventions regarding the ability of women to do work that had been considered the province of men. Women also began to see that many of the social problems that concerned them were related to systematic disequilibrium of the rights of women and men. Unlike men, no women in the English-speaking world could vote at the beginning of the nineteenth century; nor could they control their own money or, to a great extent, their own bodies. Temperance, the political movement to reduce the consumption of alcohol, tobacco, and opiates, was considered a woman's issue because wives and children were unable to protect themselves from intoxicated husbands and fathers. By midcentury some women involved in temperance and abolitionist movements began to see that only by granting women the right to economic self-reliance and political self-determination could women actually be able to protect themselves and their children. In 1848, Elizabeth Cady Stanton (pp. 816–23) and some other veterans of the ongoing abolitionist and temperance movements organized the first convention to consider the rights of women at Seneca Falls, New York, where they claimed for women the rights guaranteed to "all men" by the Declaration of Independence. Although it took seventy-two years of activism, American women finally gained the right to vote in 1920 (see pp. 824–25).

Other women, including Florence Nightingale (pp. 883–92), began to assert their rights to use their organizational skills and analytical acumen to solve problems (such as sanitation at a war front) less obviously concerned with the condition of women. Still others fought to provide access for women to college-level education so that they could begin to compete with men in the professions. The gains in economic and political rights were hard won, "slow a' comin'," and, as Virginia Woolf (pp. 1330–51) notes in *A Room of One's Own* (pp. 1342–50), hardly able to make up for centuries of forced inequality.

WOMEN'S PLACE IN SOCIETY: RE-IMAGINING WOMANHOOD

If class and race prejudice were difficult for men to overcome in a patriarchal society, it was even harder for women to overcome the misogynistic belief in feminine inferiority. Gender, like language, is often an invisible and so uninterrogated structure of experience. It is also a category outside of which women couldn't think about themselves. Despite the many differences among the women writers in this century, they shared a concern over how best to define what it meant, or could someday mean, to be a woman. Most agreed that the situation for women needed improvement and that the dominant assumptions of the inferiority of women had to be countered. But how?

In wrestling with this question, women writers of the nineteenth century worked within and against prevalent assumptions about the essential nature of masculinity and femininity. Many of the authors here, including Harriet Beecher Stowe and Elizabeth Barrett Browning (pp. 650–80), subscribed to some version of the most prevalent way of thinking about gender, which divided the world into two separate but equal spheres. The public, masculine, sphere was the realm of politics, action, and moneymaking. In this masculine sphere, aggression, selfishness, and predatory behavior were sanctioned and even considered necessary. The prerogative of the father was to make decisions for and to be obeyed by the family. The private, feminine, sphere of the home was a refuge devoted to reproduction, nurturance, and morality. In this domestic refuge, modesty, sympathy, and selflessness were imagined to be the norm. The prerogative of the mother was to use her moral authority to persuade the father to make good decisions on behalf of the family. The two spheres were imagined to be mutually dependent, one providing material resources and protection, the other providing moral and physical sustenance. Within this model, women were essentially—physically, morally, and intellectually—different from men. Different, not inferior. This very difference was the ground on which the claim for improving the condition of women—for example, extending certain legal and economic protections to her—could be based. Some other authors, such as Florence Nightingale, Sojourner Truth, and George Eliot (pp. 862–80), held a less common view that denied any essential difference between women and men. What might seem like essential differences, for authors such as these, were only the effects of acculturation and were, perhaps, superficial performances designed to protect or further one's own interests in a world where this could not be done in any other way.

Although some economic and political rights had been extended to them by the end of the nineteenth century, women were still primarily understood and valued as objects of sexual pleasure and as vehicles for the reproduction of men's privilege, power, and children. Gynecologists even posited theories about the connections between women's brains and their uteruses: many nineteenth-century people believed that if a woman used her mind too much, her uterus would shrink, thus impairing her fertility; conversely, women who had produced many babies could not be expected to have much intellectual power left. It is no coincidence that the most celebrated and "canonical" women writers of the nineteenth century (for instance, Jane Austen, pp. 545–51; Emily Dickinson, pp. 938–51; George Eliot) were childless.

To be sure, medical experts did not need to posit a brain-uterus connection to account for this, as the exhausting and time-consuming demands of running a large household in the upper and middle classes or putting food on the table in the working classes required most or all of the time women might have spent educating themselves or expressing themselves in literary genres. In a time when reliable birth control was nonexistent, sexual intercourse often resulted in pregnancy, and death in childbirth was common among women of all classes in the English-speaking world. Until the 1840s, when chloroform and ether were introduced, all childbirth was fully "natural," assisted by no painkillers stronger than alcohol or opiates. Middle- and upper-class women stayed at home during their "confinement," which might extend weeks or even months before and after a baby's birth; factory workers, seamstresses, and servants were expected to keep working while pregnant and, of course, received no compensation for work time lost to maternity or postpartum recovery (see pp. 543–44).

Icons of Femininity

The clothes one wore, the laws one was subject to, and the manners one practiced all reinforced the notion that women were special, different, deviant from a norm that was imagined as maculine. Nineteenth-century women had a varied set of icons, or models, of femininity against which to measure themselves. Early in the century a particularly important icon for women of the United States arose in the wake of the Revolution: the Republican Mother. Essential to the success of the nation by virtue of her role as educator, nurturer, and moral compass for the men of the republic, she was required to be educated and to have a developed sense of the nature and needs of representative government. Lydia Sigourney (pp. 564–66) and Lydia Maria Child (pp. 619–20) are just two of the many authors in this collection who both produced and appropriated this icon. The ideal of the Republican Mother justified publishing their work without violating conventions of gender that would have classified writing for publication as a transgressively masculine, because public, activity.

Another icon, the Angel in the House, hovered over women on both sides of the Atlantic and throughout the colonies. The selfless Angel in the House existed to solace the members of her family and, most importantly, to provide loving, moral guidance to the men of the household. She prevails in fictions by Elizabeth Gaskell and Susan Warner (p. 848) as well as in the poetry of Felicia Hemans (pp. 572–74).

The Libyan Sibyl, on the other hand, was a very different icon. Black, inscrutable, and yet a source of insight, the Libyan Sibyl stood for the wisdom of the oppressed "others"—the enslaved, the wage laborers, the servants—a wisdom that came not from books but from painful experience. An idealized representation of those who haunt the psyche of the privileged women of the nineteenth century (as Bertha Mason haunts Jane Eyre), the Libyan Sibyl elides the more complicated representations black women authors such as Sojourner Truth, Hannah Crafts, and Harriet Jacobs offered of themselves.

Late in the century yet another icon emerged: the New Woman. The New Woman eschewed the confines of the domestic sphere and instead pursued higher education, entered professions, and declared sovereignty in herself. Authors such as Kate Chopin (pp. 1048–49) and Charlotte Perkins Gilman (pp. 1157–58) explored the cost paid by women who tried to embody this ideal in a world still uneasy with the promise of equal rights. But others, such as Frances Harper (pp. 914–15) and Louisa May Alcott (pp. 999–1000), revel in the New Woman's promise of freedom and autonomy.

The most inescapable icon of femininity to loom over English-speaking women in the nineteenth century, however, was a real person: Queen Victoria (1819–1901), who gave her name to the Victorian era, which spans the century from her accession to the throne of the United Kingdom of Great Britain and Ireland in 1837 until her death in 1901. Victoria was one of the first women to recognize the power of controlling and manipulating her own image in a world dominated by mass communication. Photography, invented only two years after she became queen, allowed Victoria to control the iconic power of her image as no previous monarch had been able to do, and she immediately took advantage of the many personal and political opportunities it offered by carefully constructing the successive images of herself that circulated as freely as the currency that also bore her image. Presenting herself in a variety of pictures as queen and empress, but also as wife,

This dual portrait of Queen Victoria and her youngest daughter Beatrice (1857–1944) was taken three years after the death of her husband, Prince Albert (1819–61). Victoria would continue to dress in formal mourning clothes until her own death as a symbol of her enduring love and devotion to her late husband. This picture emphasizes one of the era's favorite images of Victoria as the widowed mother to an orphaned child.

One of many formal state photographs, this 1877 image celebrates the addition of the title of Empress of India to Victoria's many other titles. Every aspect of her dress, from crown to sash, symbolizes her role as the personal incarnation of Britain's political power.

mother, and widow, Victoria embodied many of the contradictory fantasies of and about women in the nineteenth century. In early images that were sold at reasonable prices by photo studios and stationers, the young, lovely queen can be seen sitting at the domestic hearth with her babies on her lap and an adoring husband gazing at her. In these early images the queen is crowned by a domestic harmony that, the image suggests, is as valuable and enviable as the golden circlet she wears in her official portraits. But the two images that came to dominate her era are of her as a permanently bereft widow and as ever more powerful Queen. In Victoria, domestic virtue and political virtue united in an unprecedented manner that became characteristic of her age.

WOMEN'S WRITING, 1800–1899

In the eighteenth century, more English-speaking women had entered print in a wider variety of genres than ever before due to an expansion of literacy rates and shifts in the economy that increased access to print culture. The nineteenth century saw women coming to dominate the fields of literary representation as an unprecedented number of them began to turn the power of poetry, fiction, and nonfiction toward examining and representing the world on their own terms. Building on the gains of the eighteenth century, women writers were able to claim the authority to be authors. And they did.

Women in the nineteenth century who wrote in English, whether for printed publication or private communication, would have shared some expectations for how their writing would be read. Unlike literary culture in the twentieth century, reading in the nineteenth century was not necessarily or even primarily a silent or private exercise but remained linked to public, oral performance. The Bible, of course, was frequently read aloud and listened to not only in church but also in the home, where it served as a source of entertainment as well as spiritual direction. A library in itself, the Bible provided examples of all sorts of genres (lyric poetry, epic narrative, parable, genealogy) for its listeners and readers. Certainly, as lighting improved and print became less expensive, the practice of private, silent reading became more common. But the recitation of poetry and the reading aloud of novels and nonfiction, such as sermons and travelogues, remained a common practice. In middle- and upper-class homes, such reading would take place in the parlor as part of family entertainments that might also include the performance of instrumental or vocal music. Among the working classes, reading often occurred by open windows or in doorways lit by natural light or in the workplace where artificial light was available. For example, the women employed by *Godey's Lady's Book* to hand-color the engraved illustrations would take turns reading popular fiction aloud to the group as they worked (see pp. 785–86). The consciousness of the aural quality, the way in which sounds work together, was an important consideration for authors who could count on their works being read aloud by an audience with a highly developed taste for listening to and performing literature.

What Women Wrote: Poetry, Fiction, and Nonfiction

Women became innovators in the development of the major literary genres associated with the nineteenth century as well as leaders in editing and publishing. As the editor of one of the most popular magazines in nineteenth-century America, Sarah Josepha Hale (see pp. 785–86) did much to shape American tastes with a policy that favored the publication of American and British women authors. Policies such as Hale's helped women begin to be able to earn enough money to contribute significantly to the support of themselves and their families. Poets, such Felicia Hemans (British) and Lydia Sigourney (American), were also central to this transformation of the literary world. Both poets also helped articulate and disseminate a new sense of what was beautiful in poetry—the aesthetic of romanticism. And the very popularity of their poetry allowed them to begin commanding significant fees for their works and helped make authorship a paying profession for both men and women.

While there is no genre in which women didn't publish during the nineteenth century, the major ones were poetry, prose fiction (the short story and the novel), and nonfiction. Twentieth-century literary historians would point to the short story and the novel as the most significant and characteristic genres of the nineteenth century because these expressed the sensibility of the middle class. But nineteenth-century readers and writers continued to give pride of place to poetry. Poetry was both the most prestigious and most respectable genre as well as the most widely practiced. As in previous centuries, many literate women, from the most elite (Queen Victoria) to the most obscure (pioneer women in the American West), wrote occasional verse. Poetry written on occasions of grief or special happiness might be shared within the domestic circle but wasn't intended for publication. Professional women authors wrote in a vast range of verse genres, from the highly subjective lyric to the long narrative poem to the anthem, song, and prayer (pp. 842–43). Since the conventions governing each of these genres had been established by male poets in preceding centuries, the poetry of nineteenth-century women shows what happens to literary forms when women use them to explore and express feminine concerns and perspectives.

Prose fiction at the beginning of the nineteenth century enjoyed nowhere near the prestige of poetry. The form of the novel itself (a long prose narrative having a contemporary setting and a plot unfolded by the actions, speech, and thoughts of characters) had just come into being in English during the eighteenth century. So at the start of the nineteenth century, the novel was a popular genre, but it had no claims to classical authority and was viewed with suspicion as a threat to the morals of its readers. Susanna Rowson's *Charlotte Temple* (pp. 479–542), for example, typifies the anxiety early-nineteenth-century readers and writers felt about the power of novels. After describing her heroine's first false step, Rowson writes,

> Now, my dear sober matron, (if a sober matron should deign to turn over these pages, before she trusts them to the eye of a darling daughter,) let me intreat you not to put on a grave face, and throw down the book in a passion and declare 'tis enough to turn the heads of half the girls in England; I do solemnly protest, my dear madam, I mean no more by what I have here advanced, than to ridicule those romantic girls, who foolishly imagine a red coat and silver epaulet constitute the fine gentleman. (p. 491)

By the middle of the nineteenth century, the novel had become a powerful and subtle tool for the depiction and exploration of culture, and it had risen considerably in esteem. Few critics in the 1870s would have failed to recognize the importance and seriousness of writers such as George Eliot and Harriet Beecher Stowe. In fact, the genre that had the most influence on the development of twentieth-century literature was the novel.

If the novel was a relatively new literary form in the nineteenth century, the short story was brand new, and women writers both pioneered it and excelled in it. As a genre, it developed out of the tale or sketch, an informal prose account aimed at representing the essence of a situation. American women writers, in particular, developed this form by intensifying the role of plot and the degree to which the elements cohere to tell a story with significant narrative impact. Often humorous, like Sedgwick's *"Cacoethes Scribendi"* (pp. 555–64), sentimental, like Elizabeth Gaskell's "The Three Eras of Libbie Marsh" (pp. 714–32), or sensational, like Louisa May Alcott's " A Double Tragedy" (pp. 1000–1013), the form was almost infinitely malleable. By the late nineteenth century, in the hands of authors such as Mary Wilkins Freeman (pp. 1142–52) and Sarah Orne Jewett (pp. 1041–48), the short story had become a powerful vehicle for rendering the relationship between environment and personality.

Novels pose a particular challenge for anthologies because of their length. In this anthology we have tried to provide a taste of the variety of kinds of novels women wrote by including complete texts of three very different short novels: Rowson's *Charlotte Temple* (pp. 479–542), Rebecca Harding Davis's *Life in the Iron-Mills* (pp. 967–92), and Kate Chopin's *The Awakening* (pp. 1049–1135). These complete examples are supplemented by excerpts from important novels of other types, such as the fantastic realism of Mary Shelley's *Frankenstein* (pp. 579–606), the domestic pathos of Susan Warner's *Wide, Wide World* (pp. 849–62), the political allegory of Stowe's *Uncle Tom's Cabin* (pp. 734–78), and the hybrid form of the autobiographical novel used by the fugitive slave Harriet Jacobs (pp. 792–813) to simultaneously reveal and conceal her story. We are also making available two nineteenth-century novels in our Library of Women's Literature: Jane Austen's *Pride and Prejudice* and Charlotte Brontë's *Jane Eyre*.

While poetry and prose fiction offered women writers creative vehicles for self-exploration and self-expression, it was in the nonfiction genres of the speech, the essay, the memoir, the self-help guide, and journalism that they most directly declared their various intentions for themselves and their world. One of the oldest literary jokes about women and representation comes from the medieval author Geoffrey Chaucer's *Canterbury Tales*. Chaucer's Wife of Bath points out the absurdity and bias of most attempts by male artists to answer the question What do women want? Male artists fail, according to Chaucer's Wife of Bath, because what they are really interested in depicting is what men want women to want. In the nineteenth century, women wanted many things, and they were not shy about expressing those desires. George Eliot, in her groundbreaking essay "Silly Novels by Lady Novelists" (pp. 864–80), offers a literary manifesto calling for women authors to liberate themselves and their art from the constraints of being ladylike. Writers as different from each other as Margaret Fuller and Florence Nightingale used the extended essay to analyze the situation for women in the nineteenth century. Their essays were often experimental, incorporating narrative and speculative elements within a personalized expository form that was closely connected to the autobiographical tradition of the personal memoir. Women wrote memoirs for many reasons but most frequently published those that reported on journeys from the comfortable space of home to exciting or frightening edges of the known world. Some like Anna Leonowens's *Romance of the Harem* (pp. 993–99) and Mary Kingsley's *Travels in West Africa* (pp. 1173–78), were part of a well-established tradition of women capitalizing on the sensation caused by the representation of a white woman in an exotic culture and the often erotic attractions and threats of that culture. Some, like Susanna Moodie's *Roughing It in the Bush* (pp. 637–39), recount the pioneer experiences of the colonial project of settling in a new home. Others, such as Sarah Winnemucca Hopkins's *Life among the Piutes* (pp. 1033–35), recount the opposite experience—that of having one's land and culture colonized. Still others, such as Sojourner Truth's *Narrative of Sojourner Truth* (pp. 607–8), are part of the American tradition of the slave narrative.

While it was not unconventional for women to write and publish essays or memoirs in this period, nineteenth-century women had few models of direct political expression besides those of Mary Wollstonecraft. However, the nineteenth century saw women driven by their concerns to reform society to represent their political desires and give advice directly through published letters, public reports, and political speeches. Lacking the authority to change the laws of their country, women such as Angelina Grimké and Lydia Child could only *appeal to*—that is, *ask*—their readers to consider changing their behavior regarding slaves and slavery. Despite all her knowledge and research, Harriet Martineau (pp. 613–14) could only *report on* conditions of the poor in England and *suggest* that those in authority consider and respond to her suggestions. The social sanctions against women trying to participate in politics directly were so strong that, even as late as 1848, women who had any interest in maintaining respectability were loath to present themselves on the podium. Even established anti-slavery activists such as Elizabeth Cady Stanton and Lucretia Mott felt the need to have one of their husbands convene the first Women's Right's Convention before taking the platform themselves. (James Mott appeared on the dais before either of the women; see pp. 824–25.) Despite these sanctions, women did, often with well-founded trepidation, give speeches on pressing issues such as slavery and women's rights. Women such as Cady Stanton and Sojourner Truth became famous as masters of this most political art, speaking on behalf not only of themselves but also of others.

This image depicts Lucretia Mott and Elizabeth Cady Stanton being escorted through a hostile crowd to the women's rights convention they had organized in Seneca Falls, New York, in 1848. The dangers faced by women political activists are highlighted by the noose in the hand of the male figure in the foreground of the picture.

Why Women Wrote: Art, Family, Society

Although there were some women writers in this period, such as Mary Shelley, Fanny Osgood (pp. 781–84), Emily Dickinson, and Christina Rossetti (pp. 951–66), who wrote for art's sake, most women writers of the nineteenth century wrote for the sake of others. As the biographical notes to any number of the women writers in this section will attest, many entered the world of publication under the duress of having to support their families. Others entered the literary marketplace in the effort to reform society. The broad shift in aesthetic, cultural, and political values that occurred at the cusp of the eighteenth and nineteenth centuries—romanticism—validated the two aspirations governing these apparently diverse aims of women writers in English. On the one hand, women writers attempted to represent, as never before, the qualities and nature of their own sensibilities. On the other hand, they strove to represent reality as accurately as possible in order not only to understand the world better but also to improve it.

Mary Wollstonecraft's hopes for her daughter, as for all women, are clearly expressed in her *Vindication of the Rights of Woman* (pp. 366–82), a revolutionary manifesto of eighteenth-century Enlightenment politics that dared to expand the rights of men to women. Her daughter, Mary Wollstonecraft Shelley, explored the costs and unexpected consequences of revolution in her own manifesto of romantic aesthetics, the novel *Frankenstein* (pp. 579–606). In contrast to the other tendencies of eighteenth-century culture that had sought to sort, classify, and reinforce boundaries as a way to increase human happiness, knowledge, and order, romanticism sought to challenge the validity of apparent boundaries. An international movement having a political as well as an aesthetic aspect, romanticism represented a revolutionary shift in values toward an embrace of radical individualism and the authority of subjective experience. Fundamentally optimistic, in politics as well as art, romantic thought challenged conventional boundaries between self and other, governed and government, subject and object (pp. 711–12). By 1798, William Wordsworth (1770–1850) and Samuel Taylor Coleridge (1772–1834) were able to outline this new sense of the beautiful in the preface to their sensational collection of poems, *Lyrical Ballads*. Beautiful literature was the product of a "spontaneous overflow of powerful feelings" and depended less on an artist's practiced mastery of literary skill than on inspiration.

In general, romanticism valued emotions and intuition over intellect and analysis as important ways of understanding the world. Romantic literature of whatever genre tended to represent strong emotions as it tried to elicit strong emotions from the reader. Some topics seemed, to romantic writers, better suited to this objective than others: the close observation of nature, for example, could occasion profoundly disturbing or consoling feelings in the poet and reader. The supernatural (the intrusion into experience of objects, perceptions, or events that obviously violate all known natural laws) was also attractive as an occasion to explore the relationship between imagination and reality. And, for the first time in literary history, ordinary people and things (like children or dogs or pillowcases) seemed worthy of poetic treatment because these too could occasion in the poet strong feelings of sympathy or even disgust. Romanticism validated as interesting, and even demanded as necessary, the expression of feminine subjectivity by women themselves as a means of moving art forward. Women under this aesthetic could be the creators of beauty as well as beautiful objects. In the first half of the nineteenth century, writers like Felicia Hemans, Lydia Sigourney, and Margaret Fuller encouraged women, denied formal educations and considered by their culture to be essentially more emotional, to take on the role of poet and even sage.

But women writers in the nineteenth century wrote not only to express themselves but also to have an impact on the world. The promise of their world was deeply marred by radical inequalities of wealth and status as glaring as the enslavement of human beings in order to produce the raw resources that were transformed by mills into valuable commodities or the paid employment of small children to drag cartloads of coal through passages too narrow for men or ponies to fuel the machines of the mills. By the middle of the century, authors such as Harriet Beecher Stowe, George Eliot, and Rebecca Harding Davis were developing ways to depict the material and psychological reality of ordinary people within the novel and the short story. This technique, known as realism, became the signature aesthetic of the late nineteenth century. Often, as in Davis's novel *Life in the Iron-Mills,* the object of this treatment is to call attention to the injustice of a situation that might otherwise be invisible to the reader. "Stop a moment. I am going to be honest" (p. 969), warns Davis at the beginning of her novel about the despair of those who work in the "dark, Satanic mills" (to quote poet William Blake) producing the iron demanded by the Industrial Revolution. What she is honest about is the smells, the colors, the sounds, and even the temperature of the environment within which her flawed and complicated characters exist. Davis combined realistic notation of dialect, elaborate description of the material environment, and careful depiction of the consciousness of a nonheroic protagonist with a plot in which the protagonist claims meaning and dignity through the creation of art. In Davis's fiction, as in Stowe's, the reader remains conscious of the window the narrator has opened. By the end of the century, realists such as Sarah Orne Jewett and Kate Chopin used this representational technique to bring the reader inside the narrative frame as they depicted the effect of the environment on the qualities and nature of their characters. These writers' works of fiction suggest both that the environment determines much of human possibility and that human possibility can be expanded by altering the environment. Women writers in the nineteenth century did much to alter the cultural environment that limited and constrained the ability of women to represent themselves.

Twentieth-century literary history was not kind to the writing of nineteenth-century women. Even as late as the 1980s, college courses in nineteenth-century literature might have included the poetry of Emily Dickinson if there was time and a novel by Jane Austen or George Eliot, but such courses would not have been likely to include all three and certainly not more women writers. Modernism (see pp. 1181–98), the dominant aesthetic of the early twentieth century, was uneasy with the literary and cultural legacy of the nineteenth century. Not least of the sources of this uneasiness was the historically anomalous position of women in nineteenth-century literary culture, which seemed to imply a feminization of the author. Modernist authors (both men and women) devised a role for themselves in opposition to that of their nineteenth-century predecessors, just as they invented an aesthetic that repudiated the aesthetics of the Victorian and Romantic eras. Virginia Woolf (pp. 1330–51) understood, as she put it, that women writers "think back through our mothers," and she devotes a good part of her book-length essay *A Room of One's Own* (1928; pp. 1342–50) to looking for those literary foremothers. But she is choosy. With the exception of Jane Austen, Charlotte Brontë, George Eliot, and Christina Rossetti, Woolf fails to recognize the women writers of the nineteenth century as having helped mother her own literary progeny. Through most of the twentieth century, literary historians crafted the story of their own modernist present by downplaying the importance of women writers to nineteenth-century literature in particular and to the history of literature in general. So successful were the modernists in this that many of the women writers we include in this section had to be rediscovered by a new generation of literary historians in the last quarter of the twentieth century. As contemporary African American novelist Alice Walker has put it, feminist scholars and women writers have been "in search of our mothers' gardens," working to uncover the art and craft of women's works long dismissed as something less than literature. Learning to recognize the artistry of gardens, quilts, and cookery—as well as the literary value of letters, diaries, hymns, orations, and sentimental fiction—is what has made anthologies like this one possible.

HISTORY		LITERATURE
Napoleonic Wars	**1799–1815**	
Ireland joins the union of England and Scotland to create the United Kingdom	**1801**	
Louisiana Purchase doubles the size of the United States	**1803**	
Haiti is declared first independent black republic Gas lighting invented	**1804**	
Lewis and Clark are helped by native guide Sacagawea, who is married to Toussaint Charbonneau; he won his bride in a gambling game when she was fourteen	**1805**	
First European women arrive in New Zealand Britain takes over South Africa, the "Cape Colony"	**1806**	Mary Robinson *Poetical Works*
The Abolition Act makes the slave trade illegal in Great Britain, though slavery itself is not abolished until 1834 New Jersey revokes women's right to vote that it had adopted in 1776	**1807**	
Sierra Leone becomes the administrative center for British West Africa (Ghana, Nigeria, Liberia, and Sierra Leone) Mary Kies becomes the first woman to receive a patent, for improving the process of weaving straw with silk or thread	**1809**	
The Regency period: Prince of Wales rules in place of his father, who has been deemed unfit; takes throne as George IV in 1830	**1811–20**	
English Quaker Elizabeth Fry begins working to improve conditions of women in the Newgate Prison, where inmates are not segregated by sex	**1813**	Jane Austen *Pride and Prejudice*
British attack the U.S. in the Battle of Bladensburg, 4 miles from Washington, D.C.; they burn much of the city, including public buildings and the executive mansion The steam locomotive is invented	**1814**	
	1818	Mary Shelley *Frankenstein* Jane Austen *Northanger Abbey* Sir Walter Scott *Ivanhoe*

HISTORY		LITERATURE
First boarding school for African American girls opens in Washington, D.C., under the direction of teacher Maria Becraft Elastic is invented for use in making clothes	**1820**	
British census records that for the first time women outnumber men and are longer lived	**1821**	
New York opens its first high school for girls, which soon closes	**1826**	
Matches are invented	**1827**	
African American Maria W. Stewart becomes the first woman in the U.S. to deliver a speech in public	**1831**	Mary Prince *The History of Mary Prince,* *a West Indian Slave*
Free women of color found the Female Anti-Slavery Society of Salem, Massachusetts The sewing machine is invented by Walter Hunt	**1832**	
The first coal-powered kitchen stove is invented Parliament orders abolition of slavery in all British colonies James Mott founds the American Anti-Slavery Society in Philadelphia, and his wife, Lucretia Mott, founds the Female Anti-Slavery Society	**1833**	
English literary study is introduced in India, decades before English literature is taught in British or American colleges	**1835**	
Georgia's Wesleyan College begins as Georgia Female College, the first higher-education institution chartered to grant degrees to women	**1836**	Angelina Grimké (Weld) *Appeal to the Christian Women* *of the South*
Queen Victoria ascends to the British throne Oberlin College opens and admits qualified African Americans and women; four women are admitted, making it the first coeducational U.S. college, but female students are required to wash clothes, clean rooms, and serve their fellow male students at meals Mount Holyoke Female Seminary opens as the first U.S. college for women	**1837**	

HISTORY		LITERATURE
Boston schoolgirl Mary Ashton Rice and five other women petition Harvard president Josiah Quincy for admittance to the university but are denied despite their qualifications The Cherokee Nation is forcibly removed from Georgia and North Carolina to Oklahoma on the "Trail of Tears"	**1838**	Sarah Moore Grimké "Letters on Equality of the Sexes and the Conditions of Women; Addressed to Mary Parker, President of the Boston Female Anti-Slavery Society"
Mississippi grants wives the right to hold property in the first U.S. married women's property law The daguerreotype, an early form of photograph, is invented	**1839**	
British Mines Act prohibits the employment of women, girls, and boys less than ten years of age; women and girls had been harnessed like horses to pull coal trucks	**1842**	
Sojourner Truth, who said she did not escape from slavery but "walked off, believing that to be all right," becomes a sojourner for woman's suffrage and abolitionist causes	**1843**	
Anesthesia is used for the first time for a tooth extraction in Massachusetts; chloroform and ether are used in Scotland to quell the pain of childbirth one year later	**1846**	
Republic of Liberia is established in West Africa by black U.S. settlers Parliament limits the work day for women and children in Great Britain to 10 hours	**1847**	Charlotte Brontë *Jane Eyre* Emily Brontë *Wuthering Heights*
	1847–48	William Makepeace Thackeray *Vanity Fair*
First Australian railroad established The First Women's Rights Convention opens at Seneca Falls under the leadership of Elizabeth Cady Stanton and Lucretia Mott New York passes Married Woman's Property Act, allowing women to own assets separately from their husbands	**1848**	
Isaac Merritt Singer invents the Singer sewing machine	**1850**	The first installments of *Uncle Tom's Cabin* by Harriet Beecher Stowe appear in the antislavery weekly *National Era* William Wordsworth *The Prelude* Alfred Lord Tennyson *In Memoriam* Nathaniel Hawthorne *The Scarlet Letter*

HISTORY		LITERATURE
First railroad is established in British-controlled India	**1851**	Herman Melville *Moby Dick* Further installments of *Uncle Tom's Cabin* reach record sales
	1852	*Uncle Tom's Cabin* published in book form: 120 U.S. editions published in a year Emily Dickinson begins writing poems, but never publishes them in her lifetime Susanna Moodie *Roughing It in the Bush*
Florence Nightingale travels from England to the Crimean Wars to improve sanitary conditions among the troops	**1854**	Henry David Thoreau *Walden*
	1855	Walt Whitman *Leaves of Grass*
Pasteurization of milk is invented	**1856**	Elizabeth Barrett Browning *Aurora Leigh*
First mutiny of the Indian army is crushed by British forces Divorce becomes available in England without requiring an act of Parliament; men can claim a wife's adultery, but women must show that men's adultery is aggravated by cruelty, incest, bestiality, or bigamy	**1857**	
The English crown takes over control of India from the Britain-based East India Company	**1858**	
Elizabeth Cady Stanton inherits $50,000 from her father and founds the National Woman's Suffrage Association	**1859**	Charles Darwin *On the Origin of Species*
Abraham Lincoln is elected South Carolina secedes from the Union The first flush toilet in England is installed	**1860**	
	1860–61	Charles Dickens serialization of *Great Expectations*
U.S. Civil War begins Vassar Female College is chartered by local brewer Matthew Vassar Suez Canal is built, linking Europe and Asia	**1861**	
U.S. women begin working in jobs left open by men serving in the war	**1862**	
President Lincoln delivers the Emancipation Proclamation The London underground railway opens	**1863**	

HISTORY		LITERATURE
Scottish Woman's Suffrage Society is formed Howard University for Negroes is founded by white Congregationalists for both men and women Parliament passes a law that a woman can be tried for participating in her own miscarriage, i.e. abortion	**1867**	Kark Marx *Das Kapital,* an analysis of capitalism
Last convicts are transported from England to Australia	**1868**	Louisa May Alcott *Little Women*
The College for Women (later renamed Girton College) opens at Cambridge, England, but does not gain full membership in the university until 1948 Transcontinental railroad is completed across the U.S.	**1869**	
Women gain full suffrage in the territory of Utah Last British imperial forces leave New Zealand	**1870**	
	1871–72	George Eliot (Mary Anne Evans) serialization of *Middlemarch*
Victoria Woodhull announces her candidacy for the U.S. presidency on the Equal Rights Party ticket with Frederick Douglass for vice president	**1872**	
The London School of Medicine for Women is founded by Elizabeth Blackwell and three other female physicians; women are not permitted to register at any British medical school until 1876	**1874**	
The University of Vermont admits the first women to Phi Beta Kappa The first American Indian boarding schools open with the purpose of removing Native American children from their cultures to accelerate their assimilation	**1875**	
Elizabeth Cady Stanton and Matilda Gage present "Declaration of Rights of the Women of the U.S." the acting vice president on the to centennial anniversary of the nation's founding The first all-ceramic flush toilet is exhibited at the Philadelphia World's Fair The telephone is invented	**1876**	

HISTORY   LITERATURE

HISTORY		LITERATURE
The first telephone switchboard begins operation in Boston; within a few years thousands of women will be employed as switchboard operators Queen Victoria becomes empress of India Silas Weir Mitchell publishes his rest cure for "nervous and anaemic women," who must remain in bed for up to two months; for the first month patients are not allowed to sit up, sew, write, or read	**1877**	
Congress gives women the right to argue before the U.S. Supreme Court	**1879**	
Toilet paper is invented in England	**1880**	
Clara Barton founds the American Association of the Red Cross Cambridge University admits women formally but grants certificates instead of degrees Spelman College is founded and will be the leading U.S. college for African American women	**1881**	
Parliament passes a second Married Woman's Property Act, allowing women to own property independently from their husbands	**1882**	Matthew Arnold *Culture and Anarchy*
	1883	Sarah Winnemucca Hopkins *Life among the Piutes*
Ireland's first female college graduates receive degrees Lewis Waterman patents the fountain pen	**1884**	
Bryn Mawr College for women is founded and offers the first graduate program for women Sharpshooter Annie Oakley rises to fame by starring in Buffalo Bill's Wild West Show	**1885**	
I. M. Singer Co. introduces the first electric sewing machine and begins selling it to sweatshop operators	**1887**	Ramabai Saraswati *The High Caste Hindu Woman,* the first book in English by a woman from India
The Daughters of the American Revolution (D.A.R.) is organized in Washington, D.C. The Battle of Wounded Knee ends any remaining Native American independence from the U.S. government	**1890**	

HISTORY		LITERATURE
	1891	Thomas Hardy *Tess of the D'Urbervilles*
New York City Woman Teachers' Association petitions the state legislature for equal pay; men receive on average $3,000 per year, while women average $1,700 per year New Zealand becomes the first country to grant women the vote, followed by Australia in 1894 English naturalist Mary Kingsley travels for the first time to West Africa The zipper is invented in the U.S.	**1893**	
The word *feminist* appears for the first time in the English literary weekly *Athenaeum,* to signify a woman who "has in her the capacity of fighting her way back to independence"	**1895**	
Idaho women gain suffrage through an amendment to the state constitution Sigmund Freud uses the term *psychoanalysis* for the first time	**1896**	
Queen Victoria celebrates her diamond jubilee, commemorating sixty years on the throne; she dies four years later	**1897**	
	1898	Charlotte Perkins Gilman *Women and Economics* attacks gender roles
	1899	Kate Chopin *The Awakening* sparks moral outrage and harsh criticism

CULTURAL COORDINATES
The First Australian Woman Writer

New South Wales, as the British called Australia in the eighteenth and nineteenth centuries, was home to Aborigines when the First Fleet arrived in 1788 from England. The white settlers were mainly convicts, sentenced to "transportation" to Australia by the British courts. Among the 780 transported convicts were 192 women, none of whom wrote accounts of the experience that have survived. In 1791, however, a working-class English woman named Mary Talbot, whose husband had been injured and was unable to work, was transported to Australia for stealing food for her family.

During every moment . . . we expected to perish, . . . and the groans and shrieks of so many unhappy wretches made the situation we were in truly distressing. . . .

Talbot wrote a letter during the voyage, which made its way into *The Dublin Chronicle* as an item of "foreign news." Her account of the trip, written in March 1791, became the first published piece of English prose by a woman in Australia. An excerpt follows:

> On the 25th and 26th along the coast, we had a violent storm, which lasted twenty-four hours. During every moment of its continuance we expected to perish, and were washed out of our beds between decks, while the sea-sickness and the groans and shrieks of so many unhappy wretches made the situation we were in truly distressing for there were 138 women and five children, two of the latter born after we sailed, and only one died on our passage hither, where we remain no longer than is necessary to repair the ship and take in water. Our captain hopes we shall arrive at Botany Bay in August, if it please God the weather should prove favourable.

Talbot had not been permitted to see her husband before leaving England. She was "greatly distressed by want of money" and frantic with worry about the children she had left behind. No other letters of hers have been found; evidently she died in Australia in 1792.

Dale Spender, an Australian feminist critic who has worked for decades to reconstruct the lost traditions of women writers of English, points out in *Writing a New World: Two Centuries of Australian Women Writers* (1988) that Mary Talbot's letter "alert[s] us to the vulnerability of her situation and the bleakness of her plight" (8). There was no reliable mail service to which Talbot could entrust her letter. Even more important, as Spender explains, is the fact that the Australian women's literary tradition in English does not have upper-class roots. "Among the *convict* women there were those who possessed the skill and obtained the means to write—and who were therefore in a position to make a contribution to the Australian literary heritage. While it is perfectly possible that the published letter of Mary Talbot had been polished and edited," Spender continues, "the fact that she could write, that she could convey a compelling impression of her circumstances—and that her letter can now be quoted as part of the literary tradition—cannot be disputed." With neither education, leisure, nor social status, Mary Talbot was a woman writer to remember.

Remembered primarily as the author of *Charlotte Temple* (1794), the first best-selling novel written by an American woman, Susanna Haswell Rowson could hardly have been more different from the hapless, tragic heroine of her master-piece of eighteenth-century sentimentalism. As a playwright, actress, manager, novelist, songwriter, and educator, Rowson defied stereotypes of female helplessness in her life as well as in her other literary works.

Born in Portsmouth, England, Susanna Haswell—whose mother, also named Susanna, died bearing her—came to the North American colonies as a young child with her father, William Haswell, and her American stepmother. They lived in Nantasket, Massachusetts, until the Revolutionary War, when her father's position in the British navy motivated their return to England in 1778. The first of Susanna's many jobs was to serve as governess to the Duchess of Devonshire, who encouraged her in 1786 to publish her first novel, *Victoria*. The novel's subtitle—*taken from real Life, and Calculated to Improve the Morals of the Female Sex, By impressing them with a just Sense of the Merits of Filial Piety*—describes much of Rowson's early work, with its fictive emphasis on "truth" and its didactic targeting of young women readers.

In 1786, Susanna married William Rowson, a hardware merchant and member of the Horse Guard, the mounted cavalry who guard the lives of the British royal family. Contrary to eighteenth-century middle-class expectations, William Rowson proved unable to support his wife and family. His hardware business failed and he never recovered financially. Eventually, Susanna was the sole supporter of her husband; her husband's sister and her children; her husband's illegitimate son; and two children she had adopted.

One way Rowson made money was by writing. During her early adult life in England, she produced a volume of poetry, *Poems on Various Subjects* (1788); a long critical poem, *A Trip to Parnassus; or The Judgement of Apollo on Dramatic Authors and Performers* (1788); two sets of short fictions, *The Inquisitor* (1788, 1793) and *Mentoria; or The Young Lady's Friend* (1791, 1794); and three novels, *The Test of Honour* (1789); *Charlotte, A Tale of Truth* (1794), more commonly known as *Charlotte Temple*; and *The Fille de Chambre* ("the chambermaid") (1794). Another source of income was the theater. Susanna and her husband joined a company of actors; after touring Britain, they came to the United States to the stage of the New Theater in Philadelphia. They remained in the United States for the rest of their careers. In addition to acting, Susanna wrote a musical play, *Slaves in Algiers; or A Struggle for Freedom* (1794), and over forty popular songs, including "America, Commerce, and Freedom," which was a hit in 1794.

In 1797, Rowson made the unlikely transition from stage actress (not a highly respectable profession at the time) to schoolmistress, when she opened the Young Ladies' Academy in Boston. The academy was a success, and Rowson remained at its helm until her retirement in 1822. In her role as teacher, she wrote numerous textbooks for young women's education, and she continued writing fiction. Her last novel, published posthumously in 1828, was *Charlotte's Daughter; or, the Three Orphans,* a sequel to *Charlotte Temple.*

Charlotte Temple remained popular throughout the nineteenth century, finding American audiences at all social and economic levels. In the tradition of Samuel Richardson's eighteenth-century British novel *Clarissa* (though less than one-tenth as long), *Charlotte Temple* recounts the trials of an innocent young woman seduced away from her loving parents' protection by a charming, unscrupulous man. It sets the pattern for countless nineteenth-century sentimental novels. Unlike the heroine of Hannah Webster Foster's American novel *The Coquette* (1797), Charlotte is no conscious rebel against the constraints of conventional marriage. She is only "weak," but her story exposes the powerful sexual double standard of the day. Addressed to young women, the novel makes a case for chastity and filial duty, regardless of personal desires; it argues that young women will pay a far higher price than their male counterparts if they lose their virginity outside marriage. Rowson's devoted fans read the novel as a "true" account of a young woman's sufferings. Admirers of the novel used to visit a grave at New York City's Trinity Churchyard that bore the inscription "Charlotte Temple" to weep over their favorite character's fate. Although the modern reader may be moved to chuckle at all the shrieking and fainting, all the "falling prostrate to the floor" (indeed, such action is reminiscent of *Love and Freindship,* the parody of sentimental fiction Jane Austen wrote as a teenager), Rowson's readers generally took Charlotte's experiences with high gravity. All but forgotten until it was resurrected by feminist scholars in the late twentieth century, the novel serves as a classic example of its genre.

Charlotte Temple

Preface

For the perusal of the young and thoughtless of the fair sex, this Tale of Truth is designed; and I could wish my fair readers to consider it as not merely the effusion of Fancy,[1] but as a reality. The circumstances on which I have founded this novel were related to me some little time since by an old lady who had personally known Charlotte, though she concealed the real names of the characters, and likewise the place where the unfortunate scenes were acted: yet as it was impossible to offer a relation to the public in such an imperfect state, I have thrown over the whole a slight veil of fiction, and substituted names and places according to my own fancy. The principal characters in this little tale are now consigned to the silent tomb: it can therefore hurt the feelings of no one; and may, I flatter myself, be of service to some who are so unfortunate as to have neither friends to advise, or understanding to direct them, through the various and unexpected evils that attend a young and unprotected woman in her first entrance into life.

While the tear of compassion still trembled in my eye for the fate of the unhappy Charlotte, I may have children of my own, said I, to whom this recital may be of use, and if to your own children, said Benevolence, why not to the many daughters of Misfortune who, deprived of natural friends, or spoilt by a mistaken education, are thrown on an unfeeling world without the least power to defend

---

1. Fantasy, imagination.

themselves from the snares not only of the other sex, but from the more dangerous arts of the profligate of their own.

Sensible as I am that a novel writer, at a time when such a variety of works are
ushered into the world under that name, stands but a poor chance for fame in the
annals of literature, but conscious that I wrote with a mind anxious for the happiness of that sex whose morals and conduct have so powerful an influence on
mankind in general; and convinced that I have not wrote a line that conveys a wrong
idea to the head or a corrupt wish to the heart, I shall rest satisfied in the purity of
my own intentions, and if I merit not applause, I feel that I dread not censure.

If the following tale should save one hapless fair one from the errors which
ruined poor Charlotte, or rescue from impending misery the heart of one anxious
parent, I shall feel a much higher gratification in reflecting on this trifling performance, than could possibly result from the applause which might attend the
most elegant finished piece of literature whose tendency might deprave the heart
or mislead the understanding.

Volume I

CHAPTER I
A BOARDING SCHOOL

"Are you for a walk," said Montraville to his companion, as they arose from
table; "are you for a walk? or shall we order the chaise and proceed to Portsmouth?"[2] Belcour preferred the former; and they sauntered out to view the town,
and to make remarks on the inhabitants, as they returned from church.

Montraville was a Lieutenant in the army: Belcour was his brother officer:
they had been to take leave of their friends previous to their departure for America, and were now returning to Portsmouth, where the troops waited orders for
embarkation. They had stopped at Chichester[3] to dine; and knowing they had sufficient time to reach the place of destination before dark, and yet allow them a
walk, had resolved, it being Sunday afternoon, to take a survey of the Chichester
ladies as they returned from their devotions.

They had gratified their curiosity, and were preparing to return to the inn
without honouring any of the belles with particular notice, when Madame Du
Pont, at the head of her school, descended from the church. Such an assemblage
of youth and innocence naturally attracted the young soldiers: they stopped; and,
as the little cavalcade passed, almost involuntarily pulled off their hats. A tall, elegant girl looked at Montraville and blushed: he instantly recollected the features
of Charlotte Temple, whom he had once seen and danced with at a ball at
Portsmouth. At that time he thought on her only as a very lovely child, she being
then only thirteen; but the improvement two years had made in her person, and
the blush of recollection which suffused her cheeks as she passed, awakened in his
bosom new and pleasing ideas. Vanity led him to think that pleasure at again beholding him might have occasioned the emotion he had witnessed, and the same
vanity led him to wish to see her again.

"She is the sweetest girl in the world," said he, as he entered the inn. Belcour
stared. "Did you not notice her?" continued Montraville: "she had on a blue bon-

2. Portsmouth: a seaport on the English Channel;
chaise: a light, open, two-wheeled carriage for one
or two passengers, usually hooded and drawn by

one horse.
3. A town about twenty miles northeast of
Portsmouth.

net, and with a pair of lovely eyes of the same colour, has contrived to make me feel devilish odd about the heart."

"Pho," said Belcour, "a musket ball from our friends, the Americans, may in less than two months make you feel worse."

"I never think of the future," replied Montraville; "but am determined to make the most of the present, and would willingly compound with any kind Familiar[4] who would inform me who the girl is, and how I might be likely to obtain an interview."

But no kind Familiar at that time appearing, and the chaise which they had ordered, driving up to the door, Montraville and his companion were obliged to take leave of Chichester and its fair inhabitant, and proceed on their journey.

But Charlotte had made too great an impression on his mind to be easily eradicated: having therefore spent three whole days in thinking on her and in endeavouring to form some plan for seeing her, he determined to set off for Chichester, and trust to chance either to favour or frustrate his designs. Arriving at the verge of the town, he dismounted, and sending the servant forward with the horses, proceeded toward the place, where, in the midst of an extensive pleasure ground, stood the mansion which contained the lovely Charlotte Temple. Montraville leaned on a broken gate, and looked earnestly at the house. The wall which surrounded it was high, and perhaps the Argus's who guarded the Hesperian fruit within,[5] were more watchful than those famed of old.

"'Tis a romantic attempt," said he; "and should I even succeed in seeing and conversing with her, it can be productive of no good: I must of necessity leave England in a few days, and probably may never return; why then should I endeavour to engage the affections of this lovely girl, only to leave her a prey to a thousand inquietudes, of which at present she has no idea? I will return to Portsmouth and think no more about her."

The evening now was closed; a serene stillness reigned; and the chaste Queen of Night[6] with her silver crescent faintly illuminated the hemisphere. The mind of Montraville was hushed into composure by the serenity of the surrounding objects. "I will think on her no more," said he, and turned with an intention to leave the place; but as he turned, he saw the gate which led to the pleasure grounds open, and two women come out, who walked arm-in-arm across the field.

"I will at least see who these are," said he. He overtook them, and giving them the compliments of the evening, begged leave to see them into the more frequented parts of the town: but how was he delighted, when, waiting for an answer, he discovered, under the concealment of a large bonnet, the face of Charlotte Temple.

He soon found means to ingratiate himself with her companion, who was a French teacher at the school, and, at parting, slipped a letter he had purposely written, into Charlotte's hand, and five guineas[7] into that of Mademoiselle, who promised she would endeavour to bring her young charge into the field again the next evening.

---

4. Make a bargain with a spirit, supposed to be the helper of a witch, usually taking the form of a small animal.
5. In Greek mythology, Argus was a hundred-eyed monster-guard; the Hesperides were far western islands where mythical golden apples grew.

6. The moon.
7. Gold coin worth £1, 1s, or 21 shillings; although monetary conversions are problematic, £1 in 1775 would be equivalent to about $180 today; 5 guineas would be worth more than $900 today.

CHAPTER II

DOMESTIC CONCERNS

Mr. Temple was the youngest son of a nobleman whose fortune was by no means adequate to the antiquity, grandeur, and I may add, pride of the family. He saw his elder brother made completely wretched by marrying a disagreeable woman, whose fortune helped to prop the sinking dignity of the house; and he beheld his sisters legally prostituted to old, decrepid men, whose titles gave them consequence in the eyes of the world, and whose affluence rendered them splendidly miserable. "I will not sacrifice internal happiness for outward shew," said he: "I will seek Content; and, if I find her in a cottage, will embrace her with as much cordiality as I should if seated on a throne."

Mr. Temple possessed a small estate of about five hundred pounds[8] a year; and with that he resolved to preserve independence, to marry where the feelings of his heart should direct him, and to confine his expenses within the limits of his income. He had a heart open to every generous feeling of humanity, and a hand ready to dispense to those who wanted[9] part of the blessings he enjoyed himself.

As he was universally known to be the friend of the unfortunate, his advice and bounty was frequently solicited; nor was it seldom that he sought out indigent merit, and raised it from obscurity, confining his own expenses within a very narrow compass.

"You are a benevolent fellow," said a young officer to him one day; "and I have a great mind to give you a fine subject to exercise the goodness of your heart upon."

"You cannot oblige me more," said Temple, "than to point out any way by which I can be serviceable to my fellow creatures."

"Come along then," said the young man, "we will go and visit a man who is not in so good a lodging as he deserves; and, were it not that he has an angel with him, who comforts and supports him, he must long since have sunk under his misfortunes." The young man's heart was too full to proceed; and Temple, unwilling to irritate his feelings by making further enquiries, followed him in silence, til they arrived at the Fleet[1] prison.

The officer enquired for Captain Eldridge: a person led them up several pair of dirty stairs, and pointing to a door which led to a miserable, small apartment, said that was the Captain's room, and retired.

The officer, whose name was Blakeney, tapped at the door, and was bid to enter by a voice melodiously soft. He opened the door, and discovered to Temple a scene which rivetted him to the spot with astonishment.

The apartment, though small, and bearing strong marks of poverty, was neat in the extreme. In an arm-chair, his head reclined upon his hand, his eyes fixed on a book which lay open before him, sat an aged man in a Lieutenant's uniform, which, though threadbare, would sooner call a blush of shame into the face of those who could neglect real merit, than cause the hectic[2] of confusion to glow on the cheeks of him who wore it.

Beside him sat a lovely creature busied in painting a fan mount.[3] She was fair as the lily, but sorrow had nipped the rose in her cheek before it was half blown.[4]

---

8. About $130,000 today, converting from the value of the pound in 1760.
9. Did not have.
1. One of the debtors' prisons in London.

2. Blush or flush
3. Piece of wood on which a fan would be mounted and framed.
4. Had bloomed.

Her eyes were blue; and her hair, which was light brown, was slightly confined under a plain muslin cap, tied round with a black ribbon; a white linen gown and plain lawn handkerchief composed the remainder of her dress;[5] and in this simple attire, she was more irresistibly charming to such a heart as Temple's, than she would have been, if adorned with all the splendor of a courtly belle.

When they entered, the old man arose from his seat, and shaking Blakeney by the hand with great cordiality, offered Temple his chair; and there being but three in the room, seated himself on the side of his little bed with evident composure.

"This is a strange place," said he to Temple, "to receive visitors of distinction in; but we must fit our feelings to our station. While I am not ashamed to own[6] the cause which brought me here, why should I blush at my situation? Our misfortunes are not our faults; and were it not for that poor girl—"

Here the philosopher was lost in the father. He rose hastily from his seat, and walking toward the window, wiped off a tear which he was afraid would tarnish the cheek of a sailor.

Temple cast his eye on Miss Eldridge: a pellucid drop had stolen from her eyes, and fallen upon a rose she was painting. It blotted and discoloured the flower. "'Tis emblematic,"[7] said he mentally: "the rose of youth and health soon fades when watered by the tear of affliction."

"My friend Blakeney," said he, addressing the old man, "told me I could be of service to you: be so kind then, dear Sir, as to point out some way in which I can relieve the anxiety of your heart and increase the pleasures of my own."

"My good young man," said Eldridge, "you know not what you offer. While deprived of my liberty I cannot be free from anxiety on my own account; but that is a trifling concern; my anxious thoughts extend to one more dear a thousand times than life: I am a poor weak old man, and must expect in a few years to sink into silence and oblivion; but when I am gone, who will protect that fair bud of innocence from the blasts of adversity, or from the cruel hand of insult and dishonour."

"Oh, my father!" cried Miss Eldridge, tenderly taking his hand, "be not anxious on that account; for daily are my prayers offered to heaven that our lives may terminate at the same instant, and one grave receive us both; for why should I live when deprived of my only friend."

Temple was moved even to tears. "You will both live many years," said he, "and I hope see much happiness. Cheerly, my friend, cheerly; these passing clouds of adversity will serve only to make the sunshine of prosperity more pleasing. But we are losing time: you might ere this have told me who were your creditors, what were their demands, and other particulars necessary to your liberation."

"My story is short," said Mr. Eldridge, "but there are some particulars which will wring my heart barely to remember; yet to one whose offers of friendship appear so open and disinterested, I will relate every circumstance that led to my present, painful situation. But my child," continued he, addressing his daughter, "let me prevail on you to take this opportunity, while my friends are with me, to enjoy the benefit of air and exercise. Go, my love; leave me now; to-morrow at your usual hour I will expect you."

Miss Eldridge impressed on his cheek the kiss of filial affection, and obeyed.

---

5. Muslin: simple cotton fabric; black ribbon: for mourning; white linen: more expensive than cotton but equally plain; lawn: sheer fabric.

6. Acknowledge.

7. Symbolic.

CHAPTER III
UNEXPECTED MISFORTUNES

"My life," said Mr. Eldridge, "till within these few years was marked by no particular circumstance deserving notice. I early embraced the life of a sailor, and have served my King with unremitted ardour for many years. At the age of twenty-five I married an amiable woman; one son, and the girl who just now left us, were the fruits of our union. My boy had genius and spirit. I straitened my little income to give him a liberal education, but the rapid progress he made in his studies amply compensated for the inconvenience. At the academy where he received his education he commenced an acquaintance with a Mr. Lewis, a young man of affluent fortune: as they grew up their intimacy ripened into friendship, and they became almost inseparable companions.

"George chose the profession of a soldier. I had neither friends or money to procure him a commission, and had wished him to embrace a nautical life: but this was repugnant to his wishes, and I ceased to urge him on the subject.

"The friendship subsisting between Lewis and my son was of such a nature as gave him free access to our family; and so specious was his manner that we hesitated not to state to him all our little difficulties in regard to George's future views. He listened to us with attention, and offered to advance any sum necessary for his first setting out.

"I embraced the offer, and gave him my note for the payment of it, but he would not suffer me to mention any stipulated time, as he said I might do it whenever most convenient to myself. About this time my dear Lucy returned from school, and I soon began to imagine Lewis looked at her with eyes of affection. I gave my child a caution to beware of him, and to look on her mother as her friend. She was unaffectedly artless;[3] and when, as I suspected, Lewis made professions of love, she confided in her parents, and assured us her heart was perfectly unbiassed in his favour, and she would chearfully submit to our direction.

"I took an early opportunity of questioning him concerning his intentions towards my child: he gave an equivocal answer, and I forbade him the house.

"The next day he sent and demanded payment of his money. It was not in my power to comply with the demand. I requested three days to endeavour to raise it, determining in that time to mortgage my half pay,[9] and live on a small annuity which my wife possessed, rather than be under an obligation to so worthless a man: but this short time was not allowed me; for that evening, as I was sitting down to supper, unsuspicious of danger, an officer entered, and tore me from the embraces of my family.

"My wife had been for some time in a declining state of health: ruin at once so unexpected and inevitable was a stroke she was not prepared to bear, and I saw her faint into the arms of our servant, as I left my own habitation for the comfortless walls of a prison. My poor Lucy, distracted with her fears for us both, sunk on the floor and endeavoured to detain me by her feeble efforts; but in vain; they forced open her arms; she shrieked, and fell prostrate. But pardon me. The horrors of that night unman me. I cannot proceed."

He rose from his seat, and walked several times across the room: at length, attaining more composure, he cried—"What a mere infant I am! Why, Sir, I never felt thus in the day of battle."

---

8. Lacking in guile.   9. Military pension.

"No," said Temple; "but the truly brave soul is tremblingly alive to the feelings of humanity."

"True," replied the old man, (something like satisfaction darting across his features) "and painful as these feelings are, I would not exchange them for that torpor which the stoic mistakes for philosophy. How many exquisite delights should I have passed by unnoticed, but for these keen sensations, this quick sense of happiness or misery? Then let us, my friend, take the cup of life as it is presented to us, tempered by the hand of a wise Providence; be thankful for the good, be patient under the evil, and presume not to enquire why the latter predominates."

"This is true philosophy," said Temple.

"'Tis the only way to reconcile ourselves to the cross events of life," replied he. "But I forget myself. I will not longer intrude on your patience, but proceed in my melancholy tale.

"The very evening that I was taken to prison, my son arrived from Ireland, where he had been some time with his regiment. From the distracted expressions of his mother and sister, he learnt by whom I had been arrested; and, late as it was, flew on the wings of wounded affection, to the house of his false friend, and earnestly enquired the cause of this cruel conduct. With all the calmness of a cool deliberate villain, he avowed his passion for Lucy; declared her situation in life would not permit him to marry her; but offered to release me immediately, and make any settlement on her, if George would persuade her to live, as he impiously termed it, a life of honour.[1]

"Fired at the insult offered to a man and a soldier, my boy struck the villain, and a challenge[2] ensued. He then went to a coffee-house in the neighbourhood and wrote a long affectionate letter to me, blaming himself severely for having introduced Lewis into the family, or permitted him to confer an obligation, which had brought inevitable ruin on us all. He begged me, whatever might be the event of the ensuing morning, not to suffer regret or unavailing sorrow for his fate, to encrease the anguish of my heart, which he greatly feared was already insupportable.

"This letter was delivered to me early in the morning. It would be vain to attempt describing my feelings on the perusal of it; suffice it to say, that a merciful Providence interposed, and I was for three weeks insensible to miseries almost beyond the strength of human nature to support.

"A fever and strong delirium seized me, and my life was despaired of. At length, nature, overpowered with fatigue, gave way to the salutary power of rest, and a quiet slumber of some hours restored me to reason, though the extreme weakness of my frame prevented my feeling my distress so acutely as I otherways should.

"The first object that struck me on awaking, was Lucy sitting by my bedside; her pale countenance and sable dress prevented my enquiries for poor George: for the letter I had received from him, was the first thing that occurred to my memory. By degrees the rest returned: I recollected being arrested, but could no ways account for being in this apartment, whither they had conveyed me during my illness.

"I was so weak as to be almost unable to speak. I pressed Lucy's hand, and looked earnestly round the apartment in search of another dear object.

"Where is your mother?" said I faintly.

---

1. He proposes to make Lucy his mistress and provide her with an income.   2. To a duel.

"The poor girl could not answer: she shook her head in expressive silence; and throwing herself on the bed, folded her arms about me, and burst into tears.

"What! both gone?" said I.

"Both," she replied, endeavouring to restrain her emotions: "but they are happy, no doubt."

Here Mr. Eldridge paused: the recollection of the scene was too painful to permit him to proceed.

CHAPTER IV
CHANGE OF FORTUNE

"It was some days," continued Mr. Eldridge, recovering himself, "before I could venture to enquire the particulars of what had happened during my illness: at length I assumed courage to ask my dear girl how long her mother and brother had been dead: she told me, that the morning after my arrest, George came home early to enquire after his mother's health, staid with them but a few minutes, seemed greatly agitated at parting, but gave them strict charge to keep up their spirits, and hope every thing would turn out for the best. In about two hours after, as they were sitting at breakfast, and endeavouring to strike out some plan to attain my liberty, they heard a loud rap at the door, which Lucy running to open, she met the bleeding body of her brother, borne in by two men who had lifted him from a litter, on which they had brought him from the place where he fought. Her poor mother, weakened by illness and the struggles of the preceding night, was not able to support this shock; gasping for breath, her looks wild and haggard, she reached the apartment where they had carried her dying son. She knelt by the bed side; and taking his cold hand, 'my poor boy,' said she, 'I will not be parted from thee: husband! son! both at once lost. Father of mercies, spare me!' She fell into a strong convulsion, and expired in about two hours. In the mean time, a surgeon had dressed George's wounds; but they were in such a situation as to bar the smallest hopes of recovery. He never was sensible from the time he was brought home, and died that evening in the arms of his sister.

"Late as it was when this event took place, my affectionate Lucy insisted on coming to me. 'What must he feel,' said she, 'at our apparent neglect, and how shall I inform him of the afflictions with which it has pleased heaven to visit us?'

"She left the care of the dear departed ones to some neighbours who had kindly come in to comfort and assist her; and on entering the house where I was confined, found me in the situation I have mentioned.

"How she supported herself in these trying moments, I know not: heaven, no doubt, was with her; and her anxiety to preserve the life of one parent in some measure abated her affliction for the loss of the other.

"My circumstances were greatly embarrassed,[3] my acquaintance few, and those few utterly unable to assist me. When my wife and son were committed to their kindred earth, my creditors seized my house and furniture, which not being sufficient to discharge all their demands, detainers[4] were lodged against me. No friend stepped forward to my relief; from the grave of her mother, my beloved Lucy followed an almost dying father to this melancholy place.

"Here we have been nearly a year and a half. My half-pay I have given up to satisfy my creditors, and my child supports me by her industry: sometimes by fine

---

3. He had financial problems.   4. Legal orders to keep him imprisoned.

needlework, sometimes by painting. She leaves me every night, and goes to a lodging near the bridge; but returns in the morning, to chear me with her smiles, and bless me by her duteous affection. A lady once offered her an asylum in her family; but she would not leave me. 'We are all the world to each other,' said she. 'I thank God, I have health and spirits to improve the talents with which nature has endowed me; and I trust if I employ them in the support of a beloved parent, I shall not be thought an unprofitable servant.[5] While he lives, I pray for strength to pursue my employment; and when it pleases heaven to take one of us, may it give the survivor resignation to bear the separation as we ought: till then I will never leave him.'"

"But where is this inhuman persecutor?" said Temple.

"He has been abroad ever since," replied the old man; "but he has left orders with his lawyer never to give up the note till the utmost farthing is paid."

"And how much is the amount of your debts in all?" said Temple.

"Five hundred pounds," he replied.

Temple started: it was more than he expected. "But something must be done," said he: "that sweet maid must not wear out her life in a prison. I will see you again to-morrow, my friend," said he, shaking Eldridge's hand: "keep up your spirits: light and shade are not more happily blended than are the pleasures and pains of life; and the horrors of the one serve only to increase the splendor of the other."

"You never lost a wife and son," said Eldridge.

"No," replied he, "but I can feel for those that have." Eldridge pressed his hand as they went toward the door, and they parted in silence.

When they got without the walls of the prison, Temple thanked his friend Blakeney for introducing him to so worthy a character; and telling him he had a particular engagement in the city, wished him a good evening.

"And what is to be done for this distressed man," said Temple, as he walked up Ludgate Hill.[6] "Would to heaven I had a fortune that would enable me instantly to discharge his debt: what exquisite transport, to see the expressive eyes of Lucy beaming at once with pleasure for her father's deliverance, and gratitude for her deliverer: but is not my fortune affluence," continued he, "nay superfluous wealth, when compared to the extreme indigence of Eldridge; and what have I done to deserve ease and plenty, while a brave worthy officer starves in a prison? Three hundred a year is surely sufficient for all my wants and wishes: at any rate Eldridge must be relieved."

When the heart has will, the hands can soon find means to execute a good action.

Temple was a young man, his feelings warm and impetuous; unacquainted with the world, his heart had not been rendered callous by being convinced of its fraud and hypocrisy. He pitied their sufferings, overlooked their faults, thought every bosom as generous as his own, and would chearfully have divided his last guinea with an unfortunate fellow creature.

No wonder, then, that such a man (without waiting a moment for the interference of Madam Prudence) should resolve to raise money sufficient for the relief of Eldridge, by mortgaging part of his fortune.

5. Luke 17:10. Cathedral is located.
6. Hill in the City of London where St. Paul's

We will not enquire too minutely into the cause which might actuate him in this instance: suffice it to say, he immediately put the plan in execution; and in three days from the time he first saw the unfortunate Lieutenant, he had the superlative felicity of seeing him at liberty, and receiving an ample reward in the tearful eye and half articulated thanks of the grateful Lucy.

"And pray, young man," said his father to him one morning, "what are your designs[7] in visiting thus constantly that old man and his daughter?"

Temple was at a loss for a reply: he had never asked himself the question: he hesitated; and his father continued—

"It was not till within these few days that I heard in what manner your acquaintance first commenced, and cannot suppose any thing but attachment to the daughter could carry you such imprudent lengths for the father: it certainly must be her art[8] that drew you in to mortgage part of your fortune."

"Art, Sir!" cried Temple eagerly. "Lucy Eldridge is as free from art as she is from every other error: she is—"

"Everything that is amiable and lovely," said his father, interrupting him ironically: "no doubt in your opinion she is a pattern of excellence for all her sex to follow; but come, Sir, pray tell me what are your designs towards this paragon. I hope you do not intend to complete your folly by marrying her."

"Were my fortune such as would support her according to her merit, I don't know a woman more formed to insure happiness in the married state."

"Then prithee, my dear lad," said his father, "since your rank and fortune are so much beneath what your *Princess* might expect, be so kind as to turn your eyes on Miss Weatherby; who, having only an estate of three thousand a year, is more upon a level with you, and whose father yesterday solicited the mighty honour of your alliance. I shall leave you to consider on this offer; and pray remember, that your union with Miss Weatherby will put it in your power to be more liberally the friend of Lucy Eldridge."

The old gentleman walked in a stately manner out of the room; and Temple stood almost petrified with astonishment, contempt, and rage.

CHAPTER V
SUCH THINGS ARE

Miss Weatherby was the only child of a wealthy man, almost idolized by her parents, flattered by her dependants, and never contradicted even by those who called themselves her friends: I cannot give a better description than by the following lines.

> The lovely maid whose form and face
> Nature has deck'd with ev'ry grace,
> But in whose breast no virtues glow,
> Whose heart ne'er felt another's woe,
> Whose hand ne'er smooth'd the bed of pain,   5
> Or eas'd the captive's galling chain;
> But like the tulip caught the eye,
> Born just to be admir'd and die;
> When gone, no one regrets its loss,
> Or scarce remembers that it was.   10

7. Plans, purposes.   8. Cunning.

Such was Miss Weatherby: her form lovely as nature could make it, but her mind uncultivated, her heart unfeeling, her passions impetuous, and her brain almost turned with flattery, dissipation, and pleasure; and such was the girl, whom a partial grandfather left independent mistress of the fortune before mentioned.

She had seen Temple frequently; and fancying she could never be happy without him, nor once imagining he could refuse a girl of her beauty and fortune, she prevailed on her fond father to offer the alliance to the old Earl of D——,[9] Mr. Temple's father.

The Earl had received the offer courteously: he thought it a great match for Henry; and was too fashionable a man to suppose a wife could be any impediment to the friendship he professed for Eldridge and his daughter.

Unfortunately for Temple, he thought quite otherwise: the conversation he had just had with his father, discovered to him the situation of his heart; and he found that the most affluent fortune would bring no increase of happiness unless Lucy Eldridge shared it with him; and the knowledge of the purity of her sentiments, and the integrity of his own heart, made him shudder at the idea his father had started, of marrying a woman for no other reason than because the affluence of her fortune would enable him to injure her by maintaining in splendor the woman to whom his heart was devoted: he therefore resolved to refuse Miss Weatherby, and be the event what it might, offer his heart and hand to Lucy Eldridge.

Full of this determination, he fought his father, declared his resolution, and was commanded never more to appear in his presence. Temple bowed; his heart was too full to permit him to speak; he left the house precipitately, and hastened to relate the cause of his sorrows to his good old friend and his amiable daughter.

In the mean time, the Earl, vexed to the soul that such a fortune should be lost, determined to offer himself a candidate for Miss Weatherby's favour.

What wonderful changes are wrought by that reigning power, ambition! the love-sick girl, when first she heard of Temple's refusal, wept, raved, tore her hair, and vowed to found a protestant nunnery with her fortune; and by commencing abbess, shut herself up from the sight of cruel ungrateful man for ever.

Her father was a man of the world: he suffered this first transport to subside, and then very deliberately unfolded to her the offers of the old Earl, expatiated on the many benefits arising from an elevated title, painted in glowing colours the surprise and vexation of Temple when he should see her figuring as a Countess and his mother-in-law,[1] and begged her to consider well before she made any rash vows.

The *distressed* fair one dried her tears, listened patiently, and at length declared she believed the surest method to revenge the slight put on her by the son, would be to accept the father: so said so done, and in a few days she became the Countess D——.

Temple heard the news with emotion: he had lost his father's favour by avowing his passion for Lucy, and he saw now there was no hope of regaining it: "but he shall not make me miserable," said he. "Lucy and I have no ambitious notions: we can live on three hundred a year for some little time, till the mortgage is paid off, and then we shall have sufficient not only for the comforts but many of the little elegancies of life. We will purchase a little cottage, my Lucy," said he, "and thither with your reverend father we will retire; we will forget there are such things

9. By literary convention, the blank masks a real name.   1. Stepmother.

as splendor, profusion, and dissipation: we will have some cows, and you shall be queen of the dairy; in a morning, while I look after my garden, you shall take a basket on your arm, and sally forth to feed your poultry; and as they flutter round you in token of humble gratitude, your father shall smoke his pipe in a woodbine alcove, and viewing the serenity of your countenance, feel such real pleasure dilate his own heart, as shall make him forget he had ever been unhappy."

Lucy smiled; and Temple saw it was a smile of approbation. He sought and found a cottage suited to his taste; thither, attended by Love and Hymen, the happy trio retired; where, during many years of uninterrupted felicity, they cast not a wish beyond the little boundaries of their own tenement.[2] Plenty, and her handmaid, Prudence, presided at their board, Hospitality stood at their gate, Peace smiled on each face, Content reigned in each heart, and Love and Health strewed roses on their pillows.

Such were the parents of Charlotte Temple, who was the only pledge of their mutual love, and who, at the earnest entreaty of a particular friend, was permitted to finish the education her mother had begun, at Madame Du Pont's school, where we first introduced her to the acquaintance of the reader.

CHAPTER VI

AN INTRIGUING TEACHER

Madame Du Pont was a woman every way calculated to take the care of young ladies, had that care entirely devolved on herself; but it was impossible to attend the education of a numerous school without proper assistants; and those assistants were not always the kind of people whose conversation and morals were exactly such as parents of delicacy and refinement would wish a daughter to copy. Among the teachers at Madame Du Pont's school, was Mademoiselle La Rue, who added to a pleasing person and insinuating address, a liberal education and the manners of a gentlewoman. She was recommended to the school by a lady whose humanity overstepped the bounds of discretion: for though she knew Miss La Rue had eloped from a convent with a young officer, and, on coming to England, had lived with several different men in open defiance of all moral and religious duties; yet, finding her reduced to the most abject want, and believing the penitence which she professed to be sincere, she took her into her own family, and from thence recommended her to Madame Du Pont, as thinking the situation more suitable for a woman of her abilities. But Mademoiselle possessed too much of the spirit of intrigue to remain long without adventures. At church, where she constantly appeared, her person attracted the attention of a young man who was upon a visit at a gentleman's seat in the neighbourhood: she had met him several times clandestinely; and being invited to come out that evening, and eat some fruit and pastry in a summer-house belonging to the gentleman he was visiting, and requested to bring some of the ladies with her, Charlotte being her favourite, was fixed on to accompany her.

The mind of youth eagerly catches at promised pleasure: pure and innocent by nature, it thinks not of the dangers lurking beneath those pleasures, till too late to avoid them: when Mademoiselle asked Charlotte to go with her, she mentioned the gentleman as a relation, and spoke in such high terms of the elegance of his

---

2. Love: Cupid; Hymen: the Greek god of marriage; tenement: property.

gardens, the sprightliness of his conversation, and the liberality with which he ever entertained his guests, that Charlotte thought only of the pleasure she should enjoy in the visit,—not on the imprudence of going without her governess's knowledge, or of the danger to which she exposed herself in visiting the house of a gay young man of fashion.

Madame Du Pont was gone out for the evening, and the rest of the ladies retired to rest, when Charlotte and the teacher stole out at the back gate, and in crossing the field, were accosted by Montraville, as mentioned in the first chapter.

Charlotte was disappointed in the pleasure she had promised herself from this visit. The levity of the gentlemen and the freedom of their conversation disgusted her. She was astonished at the liberties Mademoiselle permitted them to take; grew thoughtful and uneasy, and heartily wished herself at home again in her own chamber.

Perhaps one cause of that wish might be, an earnest desire to see the contents of the letter which had been put into her hand by Montraville.

Any reader who has the least knowledge of the world, will easily imagine the letter was made up of encomiums on her beauty, and vows of everlasting love and constancy; nor will he be surprised that a heart open to every gentle, generous sentiment, should feel itself warmed by gratitude for a man who professed to feel so much for her; nor is it improbable but her mind might revert to the agreeable person and martial appearance of Montraville.

In affairs of love, a young heart is never in more danger than when attempted by a handsome young soldier. A man of an indifferent appearance, will, when arrayed in a military habit, shew to advantage; but when beauty of person, elegance of manner, and an easy method of paying compliments, are united to the scarlet coat, smart cockade, and military sash, ah! well-a-day for the poor girl who gazes on him: she is in imminent danger; but if she listens to him with pleasure, 'tis all over with her, and from that moment she has neither eyes nor ears for any other object.

Now, my dear sober matron, (if a sober matron should deign to turn over these pages, before she trusts them to the eye of a darling daughter,) let me intreat you not to put on a grave face, and throw down the book in a passion and declare 'tis enough to turn the heads of half the girls in England; I do solemnly protest, my dear madam, I mean no more by what I have here advanced, than to ridicule those romantic girls, who foolishly imagine a red coat and silver epaulet constitute the fine gentleman; and should that fine gentleman make half a dozen fine speeches to them, they will imagine themselves so much in love as to fancy it a meritorious action to jump out of a two pair of stairs window, abandon their friends, and trust entirely to the honour of a man, who perhaps hardly knows the meaning of the word, and if he does, will be too much the modern man of refinement, to practice it in their favour.

Gracious heaven! when I think on the miseries that must rend the heart of a doating parent, when he sees the darling of his age at first seduced from his protection, and afterwards abandoned, by the very wretch whose promises of love decoyed her from the paternal roof—when he sees her poor and wretched, her bosom torn between remorse for her crime and love for her vile betrayer—when fancy paints to me the good old man stooping to raise the weeping penitent, while every tear from her eye is numbered by drops from his bleeding heart, my bosom glows with honest indignation, and I wish for power to extirpate those monsters of seduction from the earth.

Oh my dear girls—for to such only am I writing—listen not to the voice of love, unless sanctioned by paternal approbation: be assured, it is now past the days of romance: no woman can be run away with contrary to her own inclination: then kneel down each morning, and request kind heaven to keep you free from temptation, or, should it please to suffer you to be tried, pray for fortitude to resist the impulse of inclination when it runs counter to the precepts of religion and virtue.

CHAPTER VII
NATURAL SENSE OF PROPRIETY INHERENT IN THE FEMALE BOSOM

"I cannot think we have done exactly right in going out this evening, Mademoiselle," said Charlotte, seating herself when she entered her apartment: "nay, I am sure it was not right; for I expected to be very happy, but was sadly disappointed."

"It was your own fault, then," replied Mademoiselle: "for I am sure my cousin omitted nothing that could serve to render the evening agreeable."

"True," said Charlotte: "but I thought the gentlemen were very free in their manner: I wonder you would suffer them to behave as they did."

"Prithee, don't be such a foolish little prude," said the artful woman, affecting anger: "I invited you to go in hopes it would divert you, and be an agreeable change of scene; however, if your delicacy was hurt by the behaviour of the gentlemen, you need not go again; so there let it rest."

"I do not intend to go again," said Charlotte, gravely taking off her bonnet, and beginning to prepare for bed: "I am sure, if Madame Du Pont knew we had been out to-night, she would be very angry; and it is ten to one but she hears of it by some means or other."

"Nay, Miss," said La Rue, "perhaps your mighty sense of propriety may lead you to tell her yourself: and in order to avoid the censure you would incur, should she hear of it by accident, throw the blame on me: but I confess I deserve it: it will be a very kind return for that partiality which led me to prefer you before any of the rest of the ladies; but perhaps it will give you pleasure," continued she, letting fall some hypocritical tears, "to see me deprived of bread, and for an action which by the most rigid could only be esteemed an inadvertency, lose my place and character, and be driven again into the world, where I have already suffered all the evils attendant on poverty."

This was touching Charlotte in the most vulnerable part: she rose from her seat, and taking Mademoiselle's hand—"You know, my dear La Rue," said she, "I love you too well, to do anything that would injure you in my governess's opinion: I am only sorry we went out this evening."

"I don't believe it, Charlotte," said she, assuming a little vivacity; "for if you had not gone out, you would not have seen the gentleman who met us crossing the field; and I rather think you were pleased with his conversation."

"I had seen him once before," replied Charlotte, "and thought him an agreeable man; and you know one is always pleased to see a person with whom one has passed several chearful hours. "But," said she pausing, and drawing the letter from her pocket, while a gentle suffusion of vermillion tinged her neck and face, "he gave me this letter; what shall I do with it?"

"Read it, to be sure," returned Mademoiselle.

"I am afraid I ought not," said Charlotte: "my mother has often told me, I should never read a letter given me by a young man, without first giving it to her."

"Lord bless you, my dear girl," cried the teacher smiling, "have you a mind to be in leading strings all your life time. Prithee open the letter, read it, and judge for yourself; if you show it your mother, the consequence will be, you will be taken from school, and a strict guard kept over you; so you will stand no chance of ever seeing the smart young officer again."

"I should not like to leave school yet," replied Charlotte, "till I have attained a greater proficiency in my Italian and music. But you can, if you please, Mademoiselle, take the letter back to Montraville, and tell him I wish him well, but cannot, with any propriety, enter into a clandestine correspondence with him." She laid the letter on the table, and began to undress herself.

"Well," said La Rue, "I vow you are an unaccountable girl: have you no curiosity to see the inside now? for my part I could no more let a letter addressed to me lie unopened so long, than I could work miracles: he writes a good hand," continued she, turning the letter, to look at the superscription.[3]

"'Tis well enough," said Charlotte, drawing it towards her.

"He is a genteel young fellow," said La Rue carelessly, folding up her apron at the same time; "but I think he is marked with the small pox."[4]

"Oh you are greatly mistaken," said Charlotte eagerly; "he has a remarkable clear skin and fine complexion."

"His eyes, if I could judge by what I saw," said La Rue, "are grey and want expression."

"By no means," replied Charlotte; "they are the most expressive eyes I ever saw."

"Well, child, whether they are grey or black is of no consequence: you have determined not to read his letter; so it is likely you will never either see or hear from him again."

Charlotte took up the letter, and Mademoiselle continued—

"He is most probably going to America; and if ever you should hear any account of him, it may possibly be that he is killed; and though he loved you ever so fervently, though his last breath should be spent in a prayer for your happiness, it can be nothing to you: you can feel nothing for the fate of the man, whose letters you will not open, and whose sufferings you will not alleviate, by permitting him to think you would remember him when absent, and pray for his safety."

Charlotte still held the letter in her hand: her heart swelled at the conclusion of Mademoiselle's speech, and a tear dropped upon the wafer[5] that closed it.

"The wafer is not dry yet," said she, "and sure there can be no great harm—" She hesitated. La Rue was silent. "I may read it, Mademoiselle, and return it afterwards."

"Certainly," replied Mademoiselle.

"At any rate I am determined not to answer it," continued Charlotte, as she opened the letter.

Here let me stop to make one remark, and trust me my very heart aches while I write it; but certain I am, that when once a woman has stifled the sense of shame in her own bosom, when once she has lost sight of the basis on which reputation, honour, every thing that should be dear to the female heart, rests, she grows hardened in guilt, and will spare no pains to bring down innocence and beauty to the

3. Address.
4. A viral disease that was often fatal; survivors were likely to be scarred by the rash that is part of

the illness.
5. Type of sealing material for letters.

shocking level with herself: and this proceeds from that diabolical spirit of envy, which repines at seeing another in the full possession of that respect and esteem which she can no longer hope to enjoy.

Mademoiselle eyed the unsuspecting Charlotte, as she perused the letter, with a malignant pleasure. She saw, that the contents had awakened new emotions in her youthful bosom: she encouraged her hopes, calmed her fears, and before they parted for the night, it was determined that she should meet Montraville the ensuing evening.

CHAPTER VIII
DOMESTIC PLEASURES PLANNED

"I think, my dear," said Mrs. Temple, laying her hand on her husband's arm as they were walking together in the garden, "I think next Wednesday is Charlotte's birth day: now I have formed a little scheme in my own mind, to give her an agreeable surprise; and if you have no objection, we will send for her home on that day." Temple pressed his wife's hand in token of approbation, and she proceeded.—"You know the little alcove at the bottom of the garden, of which Charlotte is so fond? I have an inclination to deck this out in a fanciful manner, and invite all her little friends to partake of a collation of fruit, sweetmeats, and other things suitable to the general taste of young guests; and to make it more pleasing to Charlotte, she shall be mistress of the feast, and entertain her visitors in this alcove. I know she will be delighted; and to complete all, they shall have some music, and finish with a dance."

"A very fine plan, indeed," said Temple, smiling; "and you really suppose I will wink at your indulging the girl in this manner? You will quite spoil her, Lucy; indeed you will."

"She is the only child we have," said Mrs. Temple, the whole tenderness of a mother adding animation to her fine countenance; but it was withal tempered so sweetly with the meek affection and submissive duty of the wife, that as she paused expecting her husband's answer, he gazed at her tenderly, and found he was unable to refuse her request.

"She is a good girl," said Temple.

"She is, indeed," replied the fond mother exultingly, "a grateful, affectionate girl; and I am sure will never lose sight of the duty she owes her parents."

"If she does," said he, "she must forget the example set her by the best of mothers."

Mrs. Temple could not reply; but the delightful sensation that dilated her heart sparkled in her intelligent eyes and heightened the vermillion on her cheeks.

Of all the pleasures of which the human mind is sensible, there is none equal to that which warms and expands the bosom, when listening to commendations bestowed on us by a beloved object, and are conscious of having deserved them.

Ye giddy flutterers in the fantastic round of dissipation, who eagerly seek pleasure in the lofty dome, rich treat, and midnight revel—tell me, ye thoughtless daughters of folly, have ye ever found the phantom you have so long sought with such unremitted assiduity? Has she not always eluded your grasp, and when you have reached your hand to take the cup she extends to her deluded votaries, have you not found the long-expected draught strongly tinctured with the bitter dregs of disappointment? I know you have: I see it in the wan cheek, sunk eye, and air of chagrin, which ever mark the children of dissipation. Pleasure is a vain illusion; she draws you on to a thousand follies, errors, and I may say vices, and then leaves you to deplore your thoughtless credulity.

Look, my dear friends, at yonder lovely Virgin, arrayed in a white robe devoid of ornament; behold the meekness of her countenance, the modesty of her gait; her handmaids are *Humility, Filial Piety, Conjugal Affection, Industry,* and *Benevolence;* her name is *Content;* she holds in her hand the cup of true felicity, and when once you have formed an intimate acquaintance with these her attendants, nay you must admit them as your bosom friends and chief counsellors, then, whatever may be your situation in life, the meek eyed Virgin will immediately take up her abode with you.

Is poverty your portion?—she will lighten your labours, preside at your frugal board, and watch your quiet slumbers.

Is your state mediocrity?[6]—she will heighten every blessing you enjoy, by informing you how grateful you should be to that bountiful Providence who might have placed you in the most abject situation; and, by teaching you to weigh your blessings against your deserts, show you how much more you receive than you have a right to expect.

Are you possessed of affluence?—what an inexhaustible fund of happiness will she lay before you! To relieve the distressed, redress the injured, in short, to perform all the good works of peace and mercy.

Content, my dear friends, will blunt even the arrows of adversity, so that they cannot materially harm you. She will dwell in the humblest cottage; she will attend you even to a prison. Her parent is Religion; her sisters, Patience and Hope. She will pass with you through life, smoothing the rough paths and tread to earth those thorns which every one must meet with as they journey onward to the appointed goal. She will soften the pains of sickness, continue with you even in the cold gloomy hour of death, and, chearing you with the smiles of her heaven born sister, Hope, lead you triumphant to blissfull eternity.

I confess I have rambled strangely from my story: but what of that? if I have been so lucky as to find the road to happiness, why should I be such a niggard[7] as to omit so good an opportunity of pointing out the way to others. The very basis of true peace of mind is a benevolent wish to see all the world as happy as one's self; and from my soul do I pity the selfish churl, who, remembering the little bickerings of anger, envy, and fifty other disagreeables to which frail mortality is subject, would wish to revenge the affront which pride whispers him he has received. For my own part, I can safely declare, there is not a human being in the universe, whose prosperity I should not rejoice in, and to whose happiness I would not contribute to the utmost limit of my power: and may my offences be no more remembered in the day of general retribution, than as from my soul I forgive every offence or injury received from a fellow creature.

Merciful heaven! who would exchange the rapture of such a reflexion for all the gaudy tinsel which the world calls pleasure!

But to return.—Content dwelt in Mrs. Temple's bosom, and spread a charming animation over her countenance, as her husband led her in, to lay the plan she had formed (for the celebration of Charlotte's birth day,) before Mr. Eldridge.

---

6. In the middle.   7. Miser.

Various were the sensations which agitated the mind of Charlotte, during the day preceding the evening in which she was to meet Montraville. Several times did she almost resolve to go to her governess, show her the letter, and be guided by her advice: but Charlotte had taken one step in the ways of imprudence; and when that is once done, there are always innumerable obstacles to prevent the erring person returning to the path of rectitude: yet these obstacles, however forcible they may appear in general, exist chiefly in imagination.

Charlotte feared the anger of her governess: she loved her mother, and the very idea of incurring her displeasure, gave her the greatest uneasiness: but there was a more forcible reason still remaining: should she show the letter to Madame Du Pont, she must confess the means by which it came into her possession; and what would be the consequence? Mademoiselle would be turned out of doors.

"I must not be ungrateful," said she. "La Rue is very kind to me; besides I can, when I see Montraville, inform him of the impropriety of our continuing to see or correspond with each other, and request him to come no more to Chichester."

However prudent Charlotte might be in these resolutions, she certainly did not take a proper method to confirm herself in them. Several times in the course of the day, she indulged herself in reading over the letter, and each time she read it, the contents sunk deeper in her heart. As evening drew near, she caught herself frequently consulting her watch. "I wish this foolish meeting was over," said she, by way of apology to her own heart, "I wish it was over; for when I have seen him, and convinced him my resolution is not to be shaken, I shall feel my mind much easier."

The appointed hour arrived. Charlotte and Mademoiselle eluded the eye of vigilance; and Montraville, who had waited their coming with impatience, received them with rapturous and unbounded acknowledgments for their condescension:[8] he had wisely brought Belcour with him to entertain Mademoiselle, while he enjoyed an uninterrupted conversation with Charlotte.

Belcour was a man whose character might be comprised in a few words; and as he will make some figure in the ensuing pages, I shall here describe him. He possessed a genteel fortune, and had a liberal education; dissipated, thoughtless, and capricious, he paid little regard to the moral duties, and less to religious ones: eager in the pursuit of pleasure, he minded not the miseries he inflicted on others, provided his own wishes, however extravagant, were gratified. Self, darling self, was the idol he worshipped, and to that he would have sacrificed the interest and happiness of all mankind. Such was the friend of Montraville: will not the reader be ready to imagine, that the man who could regard such a character, must be actuated by the same feelings, follow the same pursuits, and be equally unworthy with the person to whom he thus gave his confidence?

But Montraville was a different character: generous in his disposition, liberal in his opinions, and good-natured almost to a fault; yet eager and impetuous in the pursuit of a favorite object, he staid not to reflect on the consequence which might follow the attainment of his wishes; with a mind ever open to conviction, had he been so fortunate as to possess a friend who would have pointed out the cruelty of endeavouring to gain the heart of an innocent artless girl, when he knew

---

8. Courtesy, friendliness, usually from a superior.

it was utterly impossible for him to marry her, and when the gratification of his passion would be unavoidable infamy and misery to her, and a cause of never-ceasing remorse to himself: had these dreadful consequences been placed before him in a proper light, the humanity of his nature would have urged him to give up the pursuit: but Belcour was not this friend; he rather encouraged the growing passion of Montraville; and being pleased with the vivacity of Mademoiselle, resolved to leave no argument untried, which he thought might prevail on her to be the companion of their intended voyage; and he made no doubt but her example, added to the rhetoric of Montraville, would persuade Charlotte to go with them.

Charlotte had, when she went out to meet Montraville, flattered herself that her resolution was not to be shaken, and that, conscious of the impropriety of her conduct in having a clandestine intercourse[9] with a stranger, she would never repeat the indiscretion.

But alas! poor Charlotte, she knew not the deceitfulness of her own heart, or she would have avoided the trial of her stability.

Montraville was tender, eloquent, ardent, and yet respectful. "Shall I not see you once more," said he, "before I leave England? will you not bless me by an assurance, that when we are divided by a vast expanse of sea I shall not be forgotten?"

Charlotte sighed.

"Why that sigh, my dear Charlotte? could I flatter myself that a fear for my safety, or a wish for my welfare occasioned it, how happy would it make me."

"I shall ever wish you well, Montraville," said she; "but we must meet no more."

"Oh say not so, my lovely girl: reflect, that when I leave my native land, perhaps a few short weeks may terminate my existence; the perils of the ocean—the dangers of war—"

"I can hear no more," said Charlotte in a tremulous voice. "I must leave you."

"Say you will see me once again."

"I dare not," said she.

"Only for one half hour to-morrow evening: 'tis my last request. I shall never trouble you again, Charlotte."

"I know not what to say," cried Charlotte, struggling to draw her hands from him: "let me leave you now."

"And you will come to-morrow," said Montraville.

"Perhaps I may," said she.

"Adieu then. I will live upon that hope till we meet again."

He kissed her hand. She sighed an adieu, and catching hold of Mademoiselle's arm, hastily entered the garden gate.

CHAPTER X

WHEN WE HAVE EXCITED CURIOSITY,
IT IS BUT AN ACT OF GOOD NATURE TO GRATIFY IT

Montraville was the youngest son of a gentleman of fortune, whose family being numerous, he was obliged to bring up his sons to genteel professions, by the exercise of which they might hope to raise themselves into notice.[1]

---

9. Conversation.   reputation.
1. To improve the family's social status and

"My daughters," said he, "have been educated like gentlewomen; and should I die before they are settled, they must have some provision made, to place them above the snares and temptations which vice ever holds out to the elegant, accomplished female, when oppressed by the frowns of poverty and the sting of dependance: my boys, with only moderate incomes, when placed in the church, at the bar, or in the field, may exert their talents, make themselves friends, and raise their fortunes on the basis of merit."

When Montraville chose the profession of arms, his father presented him with a commission, and made him a handsome provision for his private purse. "Now, my boy," said he, "go! seek glory in the field of battle. You have received from me all I shall ever have it in my power to bestow: it is certain I have interest to gain you promotion; but be assured that interest shall never be exerted, unless by your future conduct you deserve it. Remember, therefore, your success in life depends entirely on yourself. There is one thing I think it my duty to caution you against; the precipitancy with which young men frequently rush into matrimonial engagements, and by their thoughtlessness draw many a deserving woman into scenes of poverty and distress. A soldier has no business to think of a wife till his rank is such as to place him above the fear of bringing into the world a train of helpless innocents, heirs only to penury and affliction. If, indeed, a woman, whose fortune is sufficient to preserve you in that state of independence I would teach you to prize, should generously bestow herself on a young soldier, whose chief hope of future prosperity depended on his success in the field—if such a woman should offer—every barrier is removed, and I should rejoice in an union which would promise so much felicity. But mark me, boy, if, on the contrary, you rush into a precipitate union with a girl of little or no fortune, take the poor creature from a comfortable home and kind friends, and plunge her into all the evils a narrow income and increasing family can inflict, I will leave you to enjoy the blessed fruits of your rashness; for by all that is sacred, neither my interest or fortune shall ever be exerted in your favour. I am serious," continued he, "therefore imprint this conversation on your memory, and let it influence your future conduct. Your happiness will always be dear to me; and I wish to warn you of a rock on which the peace of many an honest fellow has been wrecked; for believe me, the difficulties and dangers of the longest winter campaign are much easier to be borne, than the pangs that would seize your heart, when you beheld the woman of your choice, the children of your affection, involved in penury and distress, and reflected that it was your own folly and precipitancy had been the prime cause of their sufferings."

As this conversation passed but a few hours before Montraville took leave of his father, it was deeply impressed on his mind: when, therefore, Belcour came with him to the place of assignation with Charlotte, he directed him to enquire of the French woman what were Miss Temple's expectations in regard to fortune.

Mademoiselle informed him, that though Charlotte's father possessed a genteel independence, it was by no means probable that he could give his daughter more than a thousand pounds; and in case she did not marry to his liking, it was possible he might not give her a single *sous;*[2] nor did it appear the least likely, that Mr. Temple would agree to her union with a young man on the point of embarking for the feat of war.

---

2. Penny (French).

Montraville therefore concluded it was impossible he should ever marry Charlotte Temple; and what end he proposed to himself by continuing the acquaintance he had commenced with her, he did not at that moment give himself time to enquire.

CHAPTER XI
CONFLICT OF LOVE AND DUTY

Almost a week was now gone, and Charlotte continued every evening to meet Montraville, and in her heart every meeting was resolved to be the last; but alas! when Montraville at parting would earnestly intreat one more interview, that treacherous heart betrayed her; and, forgetful of its resolution, pleaded the cause of the enemy so powerfully, that Charlotte was unable to resist. Another and another meeting succeeded; and so well did Montraville improve each opportunity, that the heedless girl at length confessed no idea could be so painful to her as that of never seeing him again.

"Then we will never be parted," said he.

"Ah, Montraville," replied Charlotte, forcing a smile, "how can it be avoided? My parents would never consent to our union; and even could they be brought to approve it, how should I bear to be separated from my kind, my beloved mother?"

"Then you love your parents more than you do me, Charlotte?"

"I hope I do," said she, blushing and looking down, "I hope my affection for them will ever keep me from infringing the laws of filial duty."

"Well, Charlotte," said Montraville gravely, and letting go her hand, "since that is the case, I find I have deceived myself with fallacious hopes. I had flattered my fond heart, that I was dearer to Charlotte than any thing in the world beside. I thought that you would for my sake have braved the dangers of the ocean, that you would, by your affection and smiles, have softened the hardships of war, and, had it been my fate to fall, that your tenderness would chear the hour of death, and smooth my passage to another world. But farewel, Charlotte! I see you never loved me. I shall now welcome the friendly ball that deprives me of the sense of my misery."

"Oh stay, unkind Montraville," cried she, catching hold of his arm, as he pretended to leave her, "stay, and to calm your fears, I will here protest that was it not for the fear of giving pain to the best of parents, and returning their kindness with ingratitude, I would follow you through every danger, and, in studying to promote your happiness, insure my own. But I cannot break my mother's heart, Montraville; I must not bring the grey hairs of my doating grand-father with sorrow to the grave, or make my beloved father perhaps curse the hour that gave me birth." She covered her face with her hands, and burst into tears.

"All these distressing scenes, my dear Charlotte," cried Montraville, "are merely the chimeras[3] of a disturbed fancy. Your parents might perhaps grieve at first; but when they heard from your own hand that you was with a man of honour, and that it was to insure your felicity by an union with him, to which you feared they would never have given their assent, that you left their protection, they will, be assured, forgive an error which love alone occasioned, and when we return from America, receive you with open arms and tears of joy."

Belcour and Mademoiselle heard this last speech, and conceiving it a proper time to throw in their advice and persuasions, approached Charlotte, and so well

---

3. Illusions.

seconded the entreaties of Montraville, that finding Mademoiselle intended going with Belcour, and feeling her own treacherous heart too much inclined to accompany them, the hapless Charlotte, in an evil hour, consented that the next evening they should bring a chaise to the end of the town, and that she would leave her friends, and throw herself entirely on the protection of Montraville. "But should you," said she, looking earnestly at him, her eyes full of tears, "should you, forgetful of your promises, and repenting the engagements you here voluntarily enter into, forsake and leave me on a foreign shore—"

"Judge not so meanly of me," said he. "The moment we reach our place of destination, Hymen shall sanctify our love; and when I shall forget your goodness, may heaven forget me."

"Ah," said Charlotte, leaning on Mademoiselle's arm as they walked up the garden together, "I have forgot all that I ought to have remembered, in consenting to this intended elopement."

"You are a strange girl," said Mademoiselle: "you never know your own mind two minutes at a time. Just now you declared Montraville's happiness was what you prized most in the world; and now I suppose you repent having insured that happiness by agreeing to accompany him abroad."

"Indeed I do repent," replied Charlotte, "from my soul: but while discretion points out the impropriety of my conduct, inclination urges me on to ruin."

"Ruin! fiddlestick!" said Mademoiselle; "am I not going with you? and do I feel any of these qualms?

"You do not renounce a tender father and mother," said Charlotte.

"But I hazard my dear reputation," replied Mademoiselle, bridling.

"True," replied Charlotte, "but you do not feel what I do." She then bade her good night: but sleep was a stranger to her eyes, and the tear of anguish watered her pillow.

CHAPTER XII

> *Nature's last, best gift:*
> *Creature in whom excell'd, whatever could*
> *To sight or thought be nam'd!*
> *Holy, divine! good, amiable, and sweet!*
> *How thou art fall'n!—*

When Charlotte left her restless bed, her languid eye and pale cheek discovered to Madame Du Pont the little repose she had tasted.

"My dear child," said the affectionate governess, "what is the cause of the languor so apparent in your frame? Are you not well?"

"Yes, my dear Madam, very well," replied Charlotte, attempting to smile, "but I know not how it was; I could not sleep last night, and my spirits are depressed this morning."

"Come chear up, my love," said the governess; "I believe I have brought a cordial to revive them. I have just received a letter from your good mama, and here is one for yourself."

Charlotte hastily took the letter: it contained these words—

"As to-morrow is the anniversary of the happy day that gave my beloved girl to the anxious wishes of a maternal heart, I have requested your governess to let you come home and spend it with us; and as I know you to be a good affectionate child, and make it your study to improve in those branches of education which you know will give most pleasure to your delighted parents, as a reward for your diligence and attention I have prepared an agreeable surprise for your reception. Your grand-father, eager to embrace the darling of his aged heart, will come in the chaise for you; so hold yourself in readiness to attend him by nine o'clock. Your dear father joins in every tender wish for your health and future felicity, which warms the heart of my dear Charlotte's affectionate mother,

L. Temple."

"Gracious heaven!" cried Charlotte, forgetting where she was, and raising her streaming eyes as in earnest supplication.

Madame Du Pont was surprised. "Why these tears, my love?" said she. "Why this seeming agitation? I thought the letter would have rejoiced, instead of distressing you."

"It does rejoice me," replied Charlotte, endeavouring at composure, "but I was praying for merit to deserve the unremitted attentions of the best of parents."

"You do right," said Madame Du Pont, "to ask the assistance of heaven that you may continue to deserve their love. Continue, my dear Charlotte, in the course you have ever pursued, and you will insure at once their happiness and your own."

"Oh!" cried Charlotte, as her governess left her, "I have forfeited both for ever! Yet let me reflect:—the irrevocable step is not yet taken: it is not too late to recede from the brink of a precipice, from which I can only behold the dark abyss of ruin, shame, and remorse!"

She arose from her seat, and flew to the apartment of La Rue. "Oh Mademoiselle!" said she, "I am snatched by a miracle from destruction! This letter has saved me: it has opened my eyes to the folly I was so near committing. I will not go, Mademoiselle; I will not wound the hearts of those dear parents who make my happiness the whole study of their lives."

"Well," said Mademoiselle, "do as you please, Miss; but pray understand that my resolution is taken, and it is not in your power to alter it. I shall meet the gentlemen at the appointed hour, and shall not be surprized at any outrage which Montraville may commit, when he finds himself disappointed. Indeed I should not be astonished, was he to come immediately here, and reproach you for your instability in the hearing of the whole school: and what will be the consequence? you will bear the odium of having formed the resolution of eloping, and every girl of spirit will laugh at your want of fortitude to put it in execution, while prudes and fools will load you with reproach and contempt. You will have lost the confidence of your parents, incurred their anger, and the scoffs of the world; and what fruit do you expect to reap from this piece of heroism, (for such no doubt you think it is?) you will have the pleasure to reflect, that you have deceived the man who adores you, and whom in your heart you prefer to all other men, and that you are separated from him for ever."

This eloquent harangue was given with such volubility, that Charlotte could not find an opportunity to interrupt her, or to offer a single word till the whole was finished, and then found her ideas so confused, that she knew not what to say.

At length she determined that she would go with Mademoiselle to the place of assignation, convince Montraville of the necessity of adhering to the resolution of remaining behind; assure him of her affection, and bid him adieu.

Charlotte formed this plan in her mind, and exulted in the certainty of its success. "How shall I rejoice," said she, "in this triumph of reason over inclination, and, when in the arms of my affectionate parents, lift up my soul in gratitude to heaven as I look back on the dangers I have escaped!"

The hour of assignation arrived: Mademoiselle put what money and valuables she possessed in her pocket, and advised Charlotte to do the same; but she refused; "my resolution is fixed," said she; "I will sacrifice love to duty."

Mademoiselle smiled internally; and they proceeded softly down the back stairs and out of the garden gate. Montraville and Belcour were ready to receive them.

"Now," said Montraville, taking Charlotte in his arms, "you are mine for ever."

"No," said she, withdrawing from his embrace, "I am come to take an everlasting farewel."

It would be useless to repeat the conversation that here ensued; suffice it to say, that Montraville used every argument that had formerly been successful, Charlotte's resolution began to waver, and he drew her almost imperceptibly towards the chaise.

"I cannot go," said she: "cease, dear Montraville, to persuade. I must not: religion, duty, forbid."

"Cruel Charlotte," said he, "if you disappoint my ardent hopes, by all that is sacred, this hand shall put a period to my existence. I cannot—will not live without you."

"Alas! my torn heart!" said Charlotte, "how shall I act?"

"Let me direct you," said Montraville, lifting her into the chaise.

"Oh! my dear forsaken parents!" cried Charlotte.

The chaise drove off. She shrieked, and fainted into the arms of her betrayer.

CHAPTER XIII
CRUEL DISAPPOINTMENT

"What pleasure," cried Mr. Eldridge, as he stepped into the chaise to go for his grand-daughter, "what pleasure expands the heart of an old man when he beholds the progeny of a beloved child growing up in every virtue that adorned the minds of her parents. I foolishly thought, some few years since, that every sense of joy was buried in the graves of my dear partner and my son; but my Lucy, by her filial affection, soothed my soul to peace, and this dear Charlotte has twined herself round my heart, and opened such new scenes of delight to my view, that I almost forget I have ever been unhappy."

When the chaise stopped, he alighted with the alacrity of youth; so much do the emotions of the soul influence the body.

It was half past eight o'clock; the ladies were assembled in the school room, and Madame Du Pont was preparing to offer the morning sacrifice of prayer and praise, when it was discovered, that Mademoiselle and Charlotte were missing.

"She is busy, no doubt," said the governess, "in preparing Charlotte for her little excursion; but pleasure should never make us forget our duty to our Creator. Go, one of you, and bid them both attend prayers."

The lady who went to summon them, soon returned, and informed the governess, that the room was locked, and that she had knocked repeatedly, but obtained no answer.

"Good heaven!" cried Madame Du Pont, "this is very strange:" and turning pale with terror, she went hastily to the door, and ordered it to be forced open. The apartment instantly discovered, that no person had been in it the preceding night, the beds appearing as though just made. The house was instantly a scene of confusion: the garden, the pleasure grounds were searched to no purpose, every apartment rang with the names of Miss Temple and Mademoiselle; but they were too distant to hear; and every face wore the marks of disappointment.

Mr. Eldridge was sitting in the parlour, eagerly expecting his grand-daughter to descend, ready equipped for her journey: he heard the confusion that reigned in the house; he heard the name of Charlotte frequently repeated. "What can be the matter?" said he, rising and opening the door: "I fear some accident has befallen my dear girl."

The governess entered. The visible agitation of her countenance discovered that something extraordinary had happened.

"Where is Charlotte?" said he, "Why does not my child come to welcome her doating parent?"

"Be composed, my dear Sir," said Madame Du Pont, "do not frighten yourself unnecessarily. She is not in the house at present; but as Mademoiselle is undoubtedly with her, she will speedily return in safety; and I hope they will both be able to account for this unseasonable absence in such a manner as shall remove our present uneasiness."

"Madam," cried the old man, with an angry look, "has my child been accustomed to go out without leave, with no other company or protector than that French woman. Pardon me, Madam, I mean no reflections on your country, but I never did like Mademoiselle La Rue; I think she was a very improper person to be entrusted with the care of such a girl as Charlotte Temple, or to be suffered to take her from under your immediate protection."

"You wrong me, Mr. Eldridge," replied she, "if you suppose I have ever permitted your grand-daughter to go out unless with the other ladies. I would to heaven I could form any probable conjecture concerning her absence this morning, but it is a mystery which her return can alone unravel."

Servants were now dispatched to every place where there was the least hope of hearing any tidings of the fugitives, but in vain. Dreadful were the hours of horrid suspense which Mr. Eldridge passed till twelve o'clock, when that suspense was reduced to a shocking certainty, and every spark of hope which till then they had indulged, was in a moment extinguished.

Mr. Eldridge was preparing, with a heavy heart, to return to his anxiously-expecting children, when Madame Du Pont received the following note without either name or date.

"Miss Temple is well, and wishes to relieve the anxiety of her parents, by letting them know she has voluntarily put herself under the protection of a man whose future study shall be to make her happy. Pursuit is needless; the measures taken to avoid discovery are too effectual to be eluded. When she thinks her friends are reconciled to this precipitate step, they may perhaps be informed of her place of residence. Mademoiselle is with her."

As Madame Du Pont read these cruel lines, she turned pale as ashes, her limbs trembled, and she was forced to call for a glass of water. She loved Charlotte truly; and when she reflected on the innocence and gentleness of her disposition, she concluded that it must have been the advice and machinations of La Rue, which led her to this imprudent action; she recollected her agitation at the receipt of her mother's letter, and saw in it the conflict of her mind.

"Does that letter relate to Charlotte?" said Mr. Eldridge, having waited some time in expectation of Madame Du Pont's speaking.

"It does," said she. "Charlotte is well, but cannot return to-day."

"Not return, Madam? where is she? who will detain her from her fond, expecting parents?"

"You distract me with these questions, Mr. Eldridge. Indeed I know not where she is, or who has seduced her from her duty."

The whole truth now rushed at once upon Mr. Eldridge's mind. "She has eloped then," said he. "My child is betrayed; the darling, the comfort of my aged heart, is lost. Oh would to heaven I had died but yesterday."

A violent gush of grief in some measure relieved him, and, after several vain attempts, he at length assumed sufficient composure to read the note.

"And how shall I return to my children?" said he: "how approach that mansion, so late the habitation of peace? Alas! my dear Lucy, how will you support these heart-rending tidings? or how shall I be enabled to console you, who need so much consolation myself?"

The old man returned to the chaise, but the light step and chearful countenance were no more; sorrow filled his heart, and guided his motions; he seated himself in the chaise, his venerable head reclined upon his bosom, his hands were folded, his eye fixed on vacancy, and the large drops of sorrow rolled silently down his cheeks. There was a mixture of anguish and resignation depicted in his countenance, as if he would say, henceforth who shall dare to boast his happiness, or even in idea contemplate his treasure, lest, in the very moment his heart is exulting in its own felicity, the object which constitutes that felicity should be torn from him.

CHAPTER XIV
MATERNAL SORROW

Slow and heavy passed the time while the carriage was conveying Mr. Eldridge home; and yet when he came in sight of the house, he wished a longer reprieve from the dreadful task of informing Mr. and Mrs. Temple of their daughter's elopement.

It is easy to judge the anxiety of these affectionate parents, when they found the return of their father delayed so much beyond the expected time. They were now met in the dining parlour, and several of the young people who had been invited were already arrived. Each different part of the company was employed in the same manner, looking out at the windows which faced the road. At length the long-expected chaise appeared. Mrs. Temple ran out to receive and welcome her darling: her young companions flocked round the door, each one eager to give her joy on the return of her birth-day. The door of the chaise was opened: Charlotte was not there. "Where is my child?" cried Mrs. Temple, in breathless agitation.

Mr. Eldridge could not answer: he took hold of his daughter's hand and led her into the house; and sinking on the first chair he came to, burst into tears, and sobbed aloud.

"She is dead," cried Mrs. Temple. "Oh my dear Charlotte!" and clasping her hands in an agony of distress, fell into strong hysterics.

Mr. Temple, who had stood speechless with surprize and fear, now ventured to enquire if indeed his Charlotte was no more. Mr. Eldridge led him into another apartment; and putting the fatal note into his hand, cried—"Bear it like a Christian," and turned from him, endeavouring to suppress his own too visible emotions.

It would be vain to attempt describing what Mr. Temple felt whilst he hastily ran over the dreadful lines: when he had finished, the paper dropt from his unnerved hand. "Gracious heaven!" said he, "could Charlotte act thus?" Neither tear nor sigh escaped him; and he sat the image of mute sorrow, till roused from his stupor by the repeated shrieks of Mrs. Temple. He rose hastily, and rushing into the apartment where she was, folded his arms about her, and saying—"Let us be patient, my dear Lucy," nature relieved his almost bursting heart by a friendly[4] gush of tears.

Should any one, presuming on his own philosophic temper, look with an eye of contempt on the man who could indulge a woman's weakness, let him remember that man was a father, and he will then pity the misery which wrung those drops from a noble, generous heart.

Mrs. Temple beginning to be a little more composed, but still imagining her child was dead, her husband, gently taking her hand, cried—"You are mistaken, my love. Charlotte is not dead."

"Then she is very ill, else why did she not come? But I will go to her: the chaise is still at the door: let me go instantly to the dear girl. If I was ill, she would fly to attend me, to alleviate my sufferings, and chear me with her love."

"Be calm, my dearest Lucy, and I will tell you all," said Mr. Temple. "You must not go, indeed you must not; it will be of no use."

"Temple," said she, assuming a look of firmness and composure, "tell me the truth I beseech you. I cannot bear this dreadful suspense. What misfortune has befallen my child? Let me know the worst, and I will endeavour to bear it as I ought."

"Lucy," replied Mr. Temple, "imagine your daughter alive, and in no danger of death: what misfortune would you then dread?"

"There is one misfortune which is worse than death. But I know my child too well to suspect—"

"Be not too confident, Lucy."

"Oh heavens!" said she, "what horrid images do you start: is it possible she should forget—"

"She has forgot us all, my love; she has preferred the love of a stranger to the affectionate protection of her friends."

"Not eloped?" cried she eagerly.

Mr. Temple was silent.

"You cannot contradict it," said she. "I see my fate in those tearful eyes. Oh Charlotte! Charlotte! how ill have you requited our tenderness! But, Father of Mercies," continued she, sinking on her knees, and raising her streaming eyes and clasped hands to heaven, "this once vouchsafe to hear a fond, a distracted mother's prayer. Oh let thy bounteous Providence watch over and protect the dear thoughtless girl, save her from the miseries which I fear will be her portion, and oh! of thine infinite mercy, make her not a mother, lest she should one day feel what I now suffer."

The last words faultered on her tongue, and she fell fainting into the arms of her husband, who had involuntarily dropped on his knees beside her.

4. Consoling, comforting.

A mother's anguish, when disappointed in her tenderest hopes, none but a mother can conceive. Yet, my dear young readers, I would have you read this scene with attention, and reflect that you may yourselves one day be mothers. Oh my friends, as you value your eternal happiness, wound not, by thoughtless ingratitude, the peace of the mother who bore you: remember the tenderness, the care, the unremitting anxiety with which she has attended to all your wants and wishes from earliest infancy to the present day; behold the mild ray of affectionate applause that beams from her eye on the performance of your duty: listen to her reproofs with silent attention; they proceed from a heart anxious for your future felicity: you must love her; nature, all-powerful nature, has planted the seeds of filial affection in your bosoms.

Then once more read over the sorrows of poor Mrs. Temple, and remember, the mother whom you so dearly love and venerate will feel the same, when you, forgetful of the respect due to your maker and yourself, forsake the paths of virtue for those of vice and folly.

CHAPTER XV

EMBARKATION

It was with the utmost difficulty that the united efforts of Mademoiselle and Montraville could support Charlotte's spirits during their short ride from Chichester to Portsmouth, where a boat waited to take them immediately on board the ship in which they were to embark for America.

As soon as she became tolerably composed, she entreated pen and ink to write to her parents. This she did in the most affecting, artless manner, entreating their pardon and blessing, and describing the dreadful situation of her mind, the conflict she suffered in endeavouring to conquer this unfortunate attachment, and concluded with saying, her only hope of future comfort consisted in the (perhaps delusive) idea she indulged, of being once more folded in their protecting arms, and hearing the words of peace and pardon from their lips.

The tears streamed incessantly while she was writing, and she was frequently obliged to lay down her pen: but when the task was completed, and she had committed the letter to the care of Montraville to be sent to the post office, she became more calm, and indulging the delightful hope of soon receiving an answer that would seal her pardon, she in some measure assumed her usual chearfulness.

But Montraville knew too well the consequences that must unavoidably ensue, should this letter reach Mr. Temple: he therefore wisely resolved to walk on the deck, tear it in pieces, and commit the fragments to the care of Neptune,[5] who might or might not, as it suited his convenience, convey them on shore.

All Charlotte's hopes and wishes were now concentred in one, namely that the fleet might be detained at Spithead[6] till she could receive a letter from her friends: but in this she was disappointed, for the second morning after she went on board, the signal was made, the fleet weighed anchor, and in a few hours (the wind being favourable) they bid adieu to the white cliffs of Albion.[7]

In the mean time every enquiry that could be thought of was made by Mr. and Mrs. Temple; for many days did they indulge the fond hope that she was

5. In Roman mythology, the god of the sea.
6. Part of the channel between Portsmouth (Hampshire) and the Isle of Wight.
7. England.

merely gone off to be married, and that when the indissoluble knot was once tied, she would return with the partner she had chosen, and entreat their blessing and forgiveness.

"And shall we not forgive her?" said Mr. Temple.

"Forgive her!" exclaimed the mother. "Oh yes, whatever be our errors, is she not our child? and though bowed to the earth even with shame and remorse, is it not our duty to raise the poor penitent, and whisper peace and comfort to her desponding soul? would she but return, with rapture would I fold her to my heart, and bury every remembrance of her faults in the dear embrace."

But still day after day passed on, and Charlotte did not appear, nor were any tidings to be heard of her: yet each rising morning was welcomed by some new hope—the evening brought with it disappointment. At length hope was no more; despair usurped her place; and the mansion which was once the mansion of peace, became the habitation of pale, dejected melancholy.

The chearful smile that was wont to adorn[8] the face of Mrs. Temple was fled, and had it not been for the support of unaffected piety, and a consciousness of having ever set before her child the fairest example, she must have sunk under this heavy affliction.

"Since," said she, "the severest scrutiny cannot charge me with any breach of duty to have deserved this severe chastisement, I will bow before the power who inflicts it with humble resignation to his will; nor shall the duty of a wife be totally absorbed in the feelings of the mother; I will endeavour to appear more chearful, and by appearing in some measure to have conquered my own sorrow, alleviate the sufferings of my husband, and rouse him from that torpor into which this misfortune has plunged him. My father too demands my care and attention: I must not, by a selfish indulgence of my own grief, forget the interest those two dear objects take in my happiness or misery: I will wear a smile on my face, though the thorn rankles in my heart; and if by so doing, I in the smallest degree contribute to restore their peace of mind, I shall be amply rewarded for the pain the concealment of my own feelings may occasion.

Thus argued this excellent woman: and in the execution of so laudable a resolution we shall leave her, to follow the fortunes of the hapless victim of imprudence and evil counsellors.

CHAPTER XVI

NECESSARY DIGRESSION

On board of the ship in which Charlotte and Mademoiselle were embarked, was an officer of large unincumbered fortune and elevated rank, and whom I shall call Crayton.

He was one of those men, who, having travelled in their youth, pretend to have contracted a peculiar fondness for every thing foreign, and to hold in contempt the productions of their own country; and this affected partiality extended even to the women.

With him therefore the blushing modesty and unaffected simplicity of Charlotte passed unnoticed; but the forward pertness of La Rue, the freedom of her

---

8. That usually adorned.

conversation, the elegance of her person, mixed with a certain engaging *je ne sais quoi*,[9] perfectly enchanted him.

The reader no doubt has already developed the character of La Rue: designing, artful, and selfish, she had accepted the devoirs[1] of Belcour because she was heartily weary of the retired life she led at the school, wished to be released from what she deemed a slavery, and to return to that vortex of folly and dissipation which had once plunged her into the deepest misery; but her plan she flattered herself was now better formed: she resolved to put herself under the protection of no man till she had first secured a settlement; but the clandestine manner in which she left Madame Du Pont's prevented her putting this plan in execution, though Belcour solemnly protested he would make her a handsome settlement the moment they arrived at Portsmouth. This he afterwards contrived to evade by a pretended hurry of business; La Rue readily conceiving he never meant to fulfill his promise, determined to change her battery, and attack the heart of Colonel Crayton. She soon discovered the partiality he entertained for her nation; and having imposed on him a feigned tale of distress, representing Belcour as a villain who had seduced her from her friends under promise of marriage, and afterwards betrayed her, pretending great remorse for the errors she had committed, and declaring whatever her affection for Belcour might have been, it was now entirely extinguished, and she wished for nothing more than an opportunity to leave a course of life which her soul abhorred; but she had no friends to apply to, they had all renounced her, and guilt and misery would undoubtedly be her future portion through life.

Crayton was possessed of many amiable qualities, though the peculiar trait in his character, which we have already mentioned, in a great measure threw a shade over them. He was beloved for his humanity and benevolence by all who knew him, but he was easy and unsuspicious himself, and became a dupe to the artifice of others.

He was, when very young, united to an amiable Parisian lady, and perhaps it was his affection for her that laid the foundation for the partiality he ever retained for the whole nation. He had by her one daughter, who entered into the world but a few hours before her mother left it. This lady was universally beloved and admired, being endowed with all the virtues of her mother, without the weakness of the father: she was married to Major Beauchamp, and was at this time in the same fleet with her father, attending her husband to New-York.

Crayton was melted by the affected contrition and distress of La Rue: he would converse with her for hours, read to her, play cards with her, listen to all her complaints, and promise to protect her to the utmost of his power. La Rue easily saw his character; her sole aim was to awaken a passion in his bosom that might turn out to her advantage, and in this aim she was but too successful, for before the voyage was finished, the infatuated Colonel gave her from under his hand a promise of marriage on their arrival at New-York, under forfeiture of five thousand pounds.[2]

And how did our poor Charlotte pass her time during a tedious and tempestuous passage? naturally delicate, the fatigue and sickness which she endured rendered her so weak as to be almost entirely confined to her bed: yet the kindness and attention of Montraville in some measure contributed to alleviate her suffer-

---

9. "I don't know what" (French). Refers to a quality not easily described.

1. Civility, attention.
2. Equivalent to almost $1 million today.

ings, and the hope of hearing from her friends soon after her arrival, kept up her spirits, and cheered many a gloomy hour.

But during the voyage a great revolution took place not only in the fortune of La Rue but in the bosom of Belcour: whilst in pursuit of his amour with Mademoiselle, he had attended little to the interesting, inobtrusive charms of Charlotte, but when, cloyed by possession, and disgusted with the art and dissimulation of one, he beheld the simplicity and gentleness of the other, the contrast became too striking not to fill him at once with surprise and admiration. He frequently conversed with Charlotte; he found her sensible, well informed, but diffident and unassuming. The languor which the fatigue of her body and perturbation of her mind spread over her delicate features, served only in his opinion to render her more lovely: he knew that Montraville did not design to marry her, and he formed a resolution to endeavour to gain her himself whenever Montraville should leave her.

Let not the reader imagine Belcour's designs were honourable. Alas! when once a woman has forgot the respect due to herself, by yielding to the solicitations of illicit love, they lose all their consequence, even in the eyes of the man whose art has betrayed them, and for whose sake they have sacrificed every valuable consideration.

> The heedless Fair, who stoops to guilty joys,
> A man may pity—but he must despise.

Nay, every libertine will think he has a right to insult her with his licentious passion; and should the unhappy creature shrink from the insolent overture, he will sneeringly taunt her with pretence of modesty.

CHAPTER XVII
A WEDDING

On the day before their arrival at New-York, after dinner, Crayton arose from his seat, and placing himself by Mademoiselle, thus addressed the company—

"As we are now nearly arrived at our destined port, I think it but my duty to inform you, my friends, that this lady," (taking her hand,) "has placed herself under my protection. I have seen and severely felt the anguish of her heart, and through every shade which cruelty or malice may throw over her, can discover the most amiable qualities. I thought it but necessary to mention my esteem for her before our disembarkation, as it is my fixed resolution, the morning after we land, to give her an undoubted title to my favour and protection by honourably uniting my fate to hers. I would wish every gentleman here therefore to remember that her honour henceforth is mine, and," continued he, looking at Belcour, "should any man presume to speak in the least disrespectfully of her, I shall not hesitate to pronounce him a scoundrel."

Belcour cast at him a smile of contempt, and bowing profoundly low, wished Mademoiselle much joy in the proposed union; and assuring the Colonel that he need not be in the least apprehensive of any one throwing the least odium on the character of his lady, shook him by the hand with ridiculous gravity, and left the cabin.

The truth was, he was glad to be rid of La Rue, and so he was but freed from her, he cared not who fell a victim to her infamous arts.

The inexperienced Charlotte was astonished at what she heard. She thought La Rue had, like herself, only been urged by the force of her attachment to Belcour, to quit her friends, and follow him to the feat of war: how wonderful then, that she should resolve to marry another man. It was certainly extremely wrong. It was indelicate. She mentioned her thoughts to Montraville. He laughed at her simplicity, called her a little ideot, and patting her on the cheek, said she knew nothing of the world. "If the world sanctifies such things, 'tis a very bad world I think," said Charlotte. "Why I always understood they were to have been married when they arrived at New-York. I am sure Mademoiselle told me Belcour promised to marry her."

"Well, and suppose he did?"

"Why, he should be obliged to keep his word I think."

"Well, but I suppose he has changed his mind," said Montraville, "and then you know the case is altered."

Charlotte looked at him attentively for a moment. A full sense of her own situation rushed upon her mind. She burst into tears, and remained silent. Montraville too well understood the cause of her tears. He kissed her cheek, and bidding her not make herself uneasy, unable to bear the silent but keen remonstrance, hastily left her.

The next morning by sun-rise they found themselves at anchor before the city of New-York. A boat was ordered to convey the ladies on shore. Crayton accompanied them; and they were shewn to a house of public entertainment. Scarcely were they seated when the door opened, and the Colonel found himself in the arms of his daughter, who had landed a few minutes before him. The first transport of meeting subsided, Crayton introduced his daughter to Mademoiselle La Rue, as an old friend of her mother's, (for the artful French woman had really made it appear to the credulous Colonel that she was in the same convent with his first wife, and, though much younger, had received many tokens of her esteem and regard.)

"If, Mademoiselle," said Mrs. Beauchamp, "you were the friend of my mother, you must be worthy the esteem of all good hearts."

"Mademoiselle will soon honour our family," said Crayton, "by supplying the place that valuable woman filled: and as you are married, my dear, I think you will not blame—"

"Hush, my dear Sir," replied Mrs. Beauchamp: "I know my duty too well to scrutinize your conduct. Be assured, my dear father, your happiness is mine. I shall rejoice in it, and sincerely love the person who contributes to it. But tell me," continued she, turning to Charlotte, "who is this lovely girl? Is she your sister, Mademoiselle?"

A blush, deep as the glow of the carnation, suffused the cheeks of Charlotte. "It is a young lady," replied the Colonel, "who came in the same vessel with us from England." He then drew his daughter aside, and told her in a whisper, Charlotte was the mistress of Montraville.

"What a pity!" said Mrs. Beauchamp softly, (casting a most compassionate glance at her.) "But surely her mind is not depraved. The goodness of her heart is depicted in her ingenuous countenance."

Charlotte caught the word pity. "And am I already fallen so low?" said she. A sigh escaped her, and a tear was ready to start, but Montraville appeared, and she checked the rising emotion. Mademoiselle went with the Colonel and his daughter to another apartment. Charlotte remained with Montraville and Belcour. The next morning the Colonel performed his promise, and La Rue became in due form Mrs. Crayton, exulted in her own good fortune, and dared to look with an eye of contempt on the unfortunate but far less guilty Charlotte.

END OF THE FIRST VOLUME.

Volume II

CHAPTER XVIII
REFLECTIONS

"And am I indeed fallen so low," said Charlotte, "as to be only pitied? Will the voice of approbation no more meet my ear? and shall I never again possess a friend, whose face will wear a smile of joy whenever I approach? Alas! how thoughtless, how dreadfully imprudent have I been! I know not which is most painful to endure, the sneer of contempt, or the glance of compassion, which is depicted in the various countenances of my own sex: they are both equally humiliating. Ah! my dear parents, could you now see the child of your affections, the daughter whom you so dearly loved, a poor solitary being, without society, here wearing out her heavy hours in deep regret and anguish of heart, no kind friend of her own sex to whom she can unbosom her griefs, no beloved mother, no woman of character will appear in my company, and low as your Charlotte is fallen, she cannot associate with infamy."

These were the painful reflections which occupied the mind of Charlotte. Montraville had placed her in a small house a few miles from New-York: he gave her one female attendant, and supplied her with what money she wanted; but business and pleasure so entirely occupied his time, that he had little to devote to the woman, whom he had brought from all her connections, and robbed of innocence. Sometimes, indeed, he would steal out at the close of evening, and pass a few hours with her; and then so much was she attached to him, that all her sorrows were forgotten while blest with his society: she would enjoy a walk by moonlight, or sit by him in a little arbour at the bottom of the garden, and play on the harp, accompanying it with her plaintive, harmonious voice. But often, very often, did he promise to renew his visits, and, forgetful of his promise, leave her to mourn her disappointment. What painful hours of expectation would she pass! She would sit at a window which looked toward a field he used to cross, counting the minutes, and straining her eyes to catch the first glimpse of his person, till blinded with tears of disappointment, she would lean her head on her hands, and give free vent to her sorrows: then catching at some new hope, she would again renew her watchful position, till the shades of evening enveloped every object in a dusky cloud: she would then renew her complaints, and, with a heart bursting with disappointed love and wounded sensibility, retire to a bed which remorse had strewed with thorns, and court in vain that comforter of weary nature (who seldom visits the unhappy) to come and steep her senses in oblivion.

Who can form an adequate idea of the sorrow that preyed upon the mind of Charlotte? The wife, whose breast glows with affection to her husband, and who in return meets only indifference, can but faintly conceive her anguish. Dreadfully painful is the situation of such a woman, but she has many comforts of which our poor Charlotte was deprived. The duteous, faithful wife, though treated with indifference, has one solid pleasure within her own bosom, she can reflect that she has not deserved neglect—that she has ever fulfilled the duties of her station with the strictest exactness; she may hope, by constant assiduity and unremitted attention, to recall her wanderer, and be doubly happy in his returning affection; she knows he cannot leave her to unite himself to another: he cannot cast her out to poverty and contempt; she looks around her, and sees the smile of friendly welcome, or the tear of affectionate consolation, on the face of every person whom she favours with her esteem; and from all these circumstances she gathers comfort: but the poor girl by thoughtless passion led astray, who, in parting with her honour, has forfeited the esteem of the very man to whom she has sacrificed every thing dear and valuable in life, feels his indifference in the fruit of her own folly, and laments her want of power to recall his lost affection; she knows there is no tie but honour, and that, in a man who has been guilty of seduction, is but very feeble: he may leave her in a moment to shame and want; he may marry and forsake her for ever; and should he, she has no redress, no friendly, soothing companion to pour into her wounded mind the balm of consolation, no benevolent hand to lead her back to the path of rectitude; she has disgraced her friends, forfeited the good opinion of the world, and undone herself; she feels herself a poor solitary being in the midst of surrounding multitudes; shame bows her to the earth, remorse tears her distracted mind, and guilt, poverty, and disease close the dreadful scene: she sinks unnoticed to oblivion. The finger of contempt may point out to some passing daughter of youthful mirth, the humble bed where lies this frail sister of mortality; and will she, in the unbounded gaiety of her heart, exult in her own unblemished fame, and triumph over the silent ashes of the dead? Oh no! has she a heart of sensibility, she will stop, and thus address the unhappy victim of folly—

"Thou had'st thy faults, but sure thy sufferings have expiated them: thy errors brought thee to an early grave; but thou wert a fellow-creature—thou hast been unhappy—then be those errors forgotten."

Then, as she stoops to pluck the noxious weed from off the sod, a tear will fall, and consecrate the spot to Charity.

For ever honoured be the sacred drop of humanity; the angel of mercy shall record its source, and the soul from whence it sprang shall be immortal.

My dear Madam, contract not your brow into a frown of disapprobation. I mean not to extenuate the faults of those unhappy women who fall victims to guilt and folly; but surely, when we reflect how many errors we are ourselves subject to, how many secret faults lie hid in the recesses of our hearts, which we should blush to have brought into open day (and yet those faults require the lenity and pity of a benevolent judge, or awful would be our prospect of futurity) I say, my dear Madam, when we consider this, we surely may pity the faults of others.

Believe me, many an unfortunate female, who has once strayed into the thorny paths of vice, would gladly return to virtue, was any generous friend to endeavour to raise and re-assure her; but alas! it cannot be, you say; the world would deride and scoff. Then let me tell you, Madam, 'tis a very unfeeling world, and does not deserve half the blessings which a bountiful Providence showers upon it.

Oh, thou benevolent giver of all good! how shall we erring mortals dare to look up to thy mercy in the great day of retribution, if we now uncharitably refuse to overlook the errors, or alleviate the miseries, of our fellow-creatures.

CHAPTER XIX
A MISTAKE DISCOVERED

Julia Franklin was the only child of a man of large property, who, at the age of eighteen, left her independent mistress of an unincumbered income of seven hundred a year;[3] she was a girl of a lively disposition, and humane, susceptible heart: she resided in New-York with an uncle, who loved her too well, and had too high an opinion of her prudence, to scrutinize her actions so much as would have been necessary with many young ladies, who were not blest with her discretion: she was, at the time Montraville arrived at New-York, the life of society, and the universal toast. Montraville was introduced to her by the following accident.

One night when he was upon guard, a dreadful fire broke out near Mr. Franklin's house, which, in a few hours, reduced that and several others to ashes; fortunately no lives were lost, and, by the assiduity of the soldiers, much valuable property was saved from the flames. In the midst of the confusion an old gentleman came up to Montraville, and, putting a small box into his hands, cried— "Keep it, my good Sir, till I come to you again;" and then rushing again into the thickest of the croud, Montraville saw him no more. He waited till the fire was quite extinguished and the mob dispersed; but in vain: the old gentleman did not appear to claim his property; and Montraville, fearing to make any enquiry, lest he should meet with impostors who might lay claim, without any legal right, to the box, carried it to his lodgings, and locked it up: he naturally imagined, that the person who committed it to his care knew him, and would, in a day or two, reclaim it; but several weeks passed on, and no enquiry being made, he began to be uneasy, and resolved to examine the contents of the box, and if they were, as he supposed, valuable, to spare no pains to discover, and restore them to the owner. Upon opening it, he found it contained jewels to a large amount, about two hundred pounds in money, and a miniature picture set for a bracelet. On examining the picture, he thought he had somewhere seen features very like it, but could not recollect where. A few days after, being at a public assembly, he saw Miss Franklin, and the likeness was too evident to be mistaken: he enquired among his brother officers if any of them knew her, and found one who was upon terms of intimacy in the family: "then introduce me to her immediately," said he, "for I am certain I can inform her of something which will give her peculiar pleasure."

He was immediately introduced, found she was the owner of the jewels, and was invited to breakfast the next morning in order to their restoration. This whole evening Montraville was honoured with Julia's hand; the lively sallies of her wit, the elegance of her manner, powerfully charmed him: he forgot Charlotte, and indulged himself in saying every thing that was polite and tender to Julia. But on retiring, recollection returned. "What am I about?" said he: "though I cannot marry Charlotte, I cannot be villain enough to forsake her, nor must I dare to trifle with the heart of Julia Franklin. I will return this box," said he, "which has been the source of so much uneasiness already, and in the evening pay a visit to my poor melancholy Charlotte, and endeavour to forget this fascinating Julia."

---

3. An income (with no debts) equal to nearly $130,000 a year today using the retail price index and converting from the pound's value in 1775.

He arose, dressed himself, and taking the picture out, "I will reserve this from the rest," said he, "and by presenting it to her when she thinks it is lost, enhance the value of the obligation." He repaired to Mr. Franklin's, and found Julia in the breakfast parlour alone.

"How happy am I, Madam," said he, "that being the fortunate instrument of saving these jewels has been the means of procuring me the acquaintance of so amiable a lady. There are the jewels and money all safe."

"But where is the picture, Sir?" said Julia.

"Here, Madam. I would not willingly part with it."

"It is the portrait of my mother," said she, taking it from him: "'tis all that remains." She pressed it to her lips, and a tear trembled in her eyes. Montraville glanced his eye on her grey night gown and black ribbon,[4] and his own feelings prevented a reply.

Julia Franklin was the very reverse of Charlotte Temple: she was tall, elegantly shaped, and possessed much of the air and manner of a woman of fashion; her complexion was a clear brown, enlivened with the glow of health, her eyes, full, black, and sparkling, darted their intelligent glances through long silken lashes; her hair was shining brown, and her features regular and striking; there was an air of innocent gaiety that played about her countenance, where good humour sat triumphant.

"I have been mistaken," said Montraville. "I imagined I loved Charlotte: but alas! I am now too late convinced my attachment to her was merely the impulse of the moment. I fear I have not only entailed lasting misery on that poor girl, but also thrown a barrier in the way of my own happiness, which it will be impossible to surmount. I feel I love Julia Franklin with ardour and sincerity; yet, when in her presence, I am sensible of my own inability to offer a heart worthy her acceptance, and remain silent."

Full of these painful thoughts, Montraville walked out to see Charlotte: she saw him approach, and ran out to meet him: she banished from her countenance the air of discontent which ever appeared when he was absent, and met him with a smile of joy.

"I thought you had forgot me, Montraville," said she, "and was very unhappy."

"I shall never forget you, Charlotte," he replied, pressing her hand.

The uncommon gravity of his countenance, and the brevity of his reply, alarmed her.

"You are not well," said she; "your hand is hot; your eyes are heavy; you are very ill."

"I am a villain," said he mentally, as he turned from her to hide his emotions.

"But come," continued she tenderly, "you shall go to bed, and I will sit by, and watch you; you will be better when you have slept."

Montraville was glad to retire, and by pretending sleep, hide the agitation of his mind from her penetrating eye. Charlotte watched by him till a late hour, and then, lying softly down by his side, sunk into a profound sleep, from whence she awoke not till late the next morning.

---

4. A robe; gray and black are the colors of mourning.

CHAPTER XX

Virtue never appears so amiable as when reaching forth her hand
to raise a fallen sister.

—CHAPTER OF ACCIDENTS[5]

When Charlotte awoke, she missed Montraville; but thinking he might have arisen early to enjoy the beauties of the morning, she was preparing to follow him, when casting her eye on the table, she saw a note, and opening it hastily, found these words—

"My dear Charlotte must not be surprised, if she does not see me again for some time: unavoidable business will prevent me that pleasure: be assured I am quite well this morning; and what your fond imagination magnified into illness, was nothing more than fatigue, which a few hours rest has entirely removed. Make yourself happy, and be certain of the unalterable friendship of

"Montraville."

"*Friendship!*" said Charlotte emphatically, as she finished the note, "is it come to this at last? Alas! poor, forsaken Charlotte, thy doom is now but too apparent. Montraville is no longer interested in thy happiness; and shame, remorse, and disappointed love will henceforth be thy only attendants."

Though these were the ideas that involuntarily rushed upon the mind of Charlotte as she perused the fatal note, yet after a few hours had elapsed, the syren[6] Hope again took possession of her bosom, and she flattered herself she could, on a second perusal, discover an air of tenderness in the few lines he had left, which at first had escaped her notice.

"He certainly cannot be so base as to leave me," said she, "and in stiling himself my friend does he not promise to protect me. I will not torment myself with these causeless fears; I will place a confidence in his honour; and sure he will not be so unjust as to abuse it."

Just as she had by this manner of reasoning brought her mind to some tolerable degree of composure, she was surprised by a visit from Belcour. The dejection visible in Charlotte's countenance, her swoln eyes and neglected attire, at once told him she was unhappy: he made no doubt but Montraville had, by his coldness, alarmed her suspicions, and was resolved, if possible, to rouse her to jealousy, urge her to reproach him, and by that means occasion a breach between them. "If I can once convince her that she has a rival," said he, "she will listen to my passion if it is only to revenge his slights." Belcour knew but little of the female heart; and what he did know was only of those of loose and dissolute lives. He had no idea that a woman might fall a victim to imprudence, and yet retain so strong a sense of honour, as to reject with horror and contempt every solicitation to a second fault. He never imagined that a gentle, generous female heart, once tenderly attached, when treated with unkindness might break, but would never harbour a thought of revenge.

5. Paraphrase of a line (2.5) from Sophia Lee's play *Chapter of Accidents* (1782).
6. Temptress, after partly human creatures in

Greek mythology who sang to lure sailors to their death.

His visit was not long, but before he went he fixed a scorpion in the heart of Charlotte, whose venom embittered every future hour of her life.

We will now return for a moment to Colonel Crayton. He had been three months married, and in that little time had discovered that the conduct of his lady was not so prudent as it ought to have been: but remonstrance was vain; her temper was violent; and to the Colonel's great misfortune he had conceived a sincere affection for her: she saw her own power, and, with the art of a Circe,[7] made every action appear to him in what light she pleased: his acquaintance laughed at his blindness, his friends pitied his infatuation, his amiable daughter, Mrs. Beauchamp, in secret deplored the loss of her father's affection, and grieved that he should be so entirely swayed by an artful, and, she much feared, infamous woman.

Mrs. Beauchamp was mild and engaging; she loved not the hurry and bustle of a city, and had prevailed on her husband to take a house a few miles from New-York. Chance led her into the same neighbourhood with Charlotte; their houses stood within a short space of each other, and their gardens joined: she had not been long in her new habitation before the figure of Charlotte struck her; she recollected her interesting features; she saw the melancholy so conspicuous in her countenance, and her heart bled at the reflection, that perhaps deprived of honour, friends, all that was valuable in life, she was doomed to linger out a wretched existence in a strange land, and sink broken-hearted into an untimely grave. "Would to heaven I could snatch her from so hard a fate," said she; "but the merciless world has barred the doors of compassion against a poor weak girl, who, perhaps, had she one kind friend to raise and reassure her, would gladly return to peace and virtue; nay, even the woman who dares to pity, and endeavour to recall a wandering sister, incurs the sneer of contempt and ridicule, for an action in which even angels are said to rejoice."

The longer Mrs. Beauchamp was a witness to the solitary life Charlotte led, the more she wished to speak to her, and often as she saw her cheeks wet with the tears of anguish, she would say—"Dear sufferer, how gladly would I pour into your heart the balm of consolation, were it not for the fear of derision."

But an accident soon happened which made her resolve to brave even the scoffs of the world, rather than not enjoy the heavenly satisfaction of comforting a desponding fellow-creature.

Mrs. Beauchamp was an early riser. She was one morning walking in the garden, leaning on her husband's arm, when the sound of a harp attracted their notice; they listened attentively, and heard a soft melodious voice distinctly sing the following stanzas:

> Thou glorious orb, supremely bright,
>   Just rising from the sea,
> To chear all nature with thy light,
>   What are thy beams to me?
> In vain thy glories bid me rise,   5
>   To hail the new-born day,
> Alas! my morning sacrifice
>   Is still to weep and pray.

7. In Greek mythology, a sorceress who lured the   them, and then turned them into pigs.
sailors in Homer's *Odyssey* to her island, seduced

For what are nature's charms combin'd,
     To one, whose weary breast   10
Can neither peace nor comfort find,
     Nor friend whereon to rest?
Oh! never! never! whilst I live
     Can my heart's anguish cease:
Come, friendly death, thy mandate give,   15
     And let me be at peace.

"'Tis poor Charlotte!" said Mrs. Beauchamp, the pellucid drop of humanity stealing down her cheek.

Captain Beauchamp was alarmed at her emotion. "What Charlotte?" said he; "do you know her?"

In the accent of a pitying angel did she disclose to her husband Charlotte's unhappy situation, and the frequent wish she had formed of being serviceable to her. "I fear," continued she, "the poor girl has been basely betrayed; and if I thought you would not blame me, I would pay her a visit, offer her my friendship, and endeavour to restore to her heart that peace she seems to have lost, and so pathetically laments. Who knows, my dear," laying her hand affectionately on his arm, "who knows but she has left some kind, affectionate parents to lament her errors, and would she return, they might with rapture receive the poor penitent, and wash away her faults in tears of joy. Oh! what a glorious reflexion would it be for me could I be the happy instrument of restoring her. Her heart may not be depraved, Beauchamp."

"Exalted woman!" cried Beauchamp, embracing her, "how dost thou rise every moment in my esteem. Follow the impulse of thy generous heart, my Emily. Let prudes and fools censure if they dare, and blame a sensibility they never felt; I will exultingly tell them that the heart that is truly virtuous is ever inclined to pity and forgive the errors of its fellow-creatures."

A beam of exulting joy played round the animated countenance of Mrs. Beauchamp, at these encomiums bestowed on her by a beloved husband, the most delightful sensations pervaded her heart, and, having breakfasted, she prepared to visit Charlotte.

CHAPTER XXI

Teach me to feel another's woe,
     To hide the fault I see,
That mercy I to others show,
     That mercy show to me.

—POPE[8]

When Mrs. Beauchamp was dressed, she began to feel embarrassed at the thought of beginning an acquaintance with Charlotte, and was distressed how to make the first visit. "I cannot go without some introduction," said she, "it will look so like impertinent curiosity." At length recollecting herself, she stepped into the garden,

---

8. From *The Universal Prayer* (1738), lines 37–40, by English poet Alexander Pope (1688–1744).

and gathering a few fine cucumbers, took them in her hand by way of apology for her visit.

A glow of conscious shame vermillioned Charlotte's face as Mrs. Beauchamp entered.

"You will pardon me, Madam," said she, "for not having before paid my respects to so amiable a neighbour; but we English people[9] always keep up that reserve which is the characteristic of our nation wherever we go. I have taken the liberty to bring you a few cucumbers, for I observed you had none in your garden."

Charlotte, though naturally polite and well-bred, was so confused she could hardly speak. Her kind visitor endeavoured to relieve her by not noticing her embarrassment. "I am come, Madam," continued she, "to request you will spend the day with me. I shall be alone; and, as we are both strangers in this country, we may hereafter be extremely happy in each other's friendship."

"Your friendship, Madam," said Charlotte blushing, "is an honour to all who are favoured with it. Little as I have seen of this part of the world, I am no stranger to Mrs. Beauchamp's goodness of heart and known humanity: but my friendship—" She paused, glanced her eye upon her own visible situation,[1] and, spite of her endeavours to suppress them, burst into tears.

Mrs. Beauchamp guessed the source from whence those tears flowed. "You seem unhappy, Madam," said she: "shall I be thought worthy your confidence? will you entrust me with the cause of your sorrow, and rest on my assurances to exert my utmost power to serve you." Charlotte returned a look of gratitude, but could not speak, and Mrs. Beauchamp continued—"My heart was interested in your behalf the first moment I saw you, and I only lament I had not made earlier overtures towards an acquaintance; but I flatter myself you will henceforth consider me as your friend."

"Oh Madam!" cried Charlotte, "I have forfeited the good opinion of all my friends; I have forsaken them, and undone myself."

"Come, come, my dear," said Mrs. Beauchamp, "you must not indulge these gloomy thoughts: you are not I hope so miserable as you imagine yourself: endeavour to be composed, and let me be favoured with your company at dinner, when, if you can bring yourself to think me your friend, and repose a confidence in me, I am ready to convince you it shall not be abused." She then arose, and bade her good morning.

At the dining hour Charlotte repaired to Mrs. Beauchamp's, and during dinner assumed as composed an aspect as possible; but when the cloth was removed,[2] she summoned all her resolution and determined to make Mrs. Beauchamp acquainted with every circumstance preceding her unfortunate elopement, and the earnest desire she had to quit a way of life so repugnant to her feelings.

With the benignant aspect of an angel of mercy did Mrs. Beauchamp listen to the artless tale: she was shocked to the soul to find how large a share La Rue had in the seduction of this amiable girl, and a tear fell, when she reflected so vile a woman was now the wife of her father. When Charlotte had finished, she gave her a little time to collect her scattered spirits, and then asked her if she had never written to her friends.

---

9. The American Revolution has not yet taken place.
1. Charlotte is pregnant and beginning to "show."

2. When the table was cleared (and the tablecloth removed).

"Oh yes, Madam," said she, "frequently: but I have broke their hearts: they are either dead or have cast me off for ever, for I have never received a single line from them."

"I rather suspect," said Mrs. Beauchamp, "they have never had your letters: but suppose you were to hear from them, and they were willing to receive you, would you then leave this cruel Montraville, and return to them?"

"Would I!" said Charlotte, clasping her hands; "would not the poor sailor, tost on a tempestuous ocean, threatened every moment with death, gladly return to the shore he had left to trust to its deceitful calmness? Oh, my dear Madam, I would return, though to do it I were obliged to walk barefoot over a burning desart, and beg a scanty pittance of each traveller to support my existence. I would endure it all chearfully, could I but once more see my dear, blessed mother, hear her pronounce my pardon, and bless me before I died; but alas! I shall never see her more; she has blotted the ungrateful Charlotte from her remembrance, and I shall sink to the grave loaded with her's and my father's curse."

Mrs. Beauchamp endeavoured to sooth her. "You shall write to them again," said she, "and I will see that the letter is sent by the first packet that sails for England; in the mean time keep up your spirits, and hope every thing, by daring to deserve it."

She then turned the conversation, and Charlotte having taken a cup of tea, wished her benevolent friend a good evening.

CHAPTER XXII

SORROWS OF THE HEART

When Charlotte got home she endeavoured to collect her thoughts, and took up a pen in order to address those dear parents, whom, spite of her errors, she still loved with the utmost tenderness, but vain was every effort to write with the least coherence; her tears fell so fast they almost blinded her; and as she proceeded to describe her unhappy situation, she became so agitated that she was obliged to give over the attempt and retire to bed, where, overcome with the fatigue her mind had undergone, she fell into a slumber which greatly refreshed her, and she arose in the morning with spirits more adequate to the painful task she had to perform, and, after several attempts, at length concluded the following letter to her mother—

To Mrs. Temple.

New-York.

"Will my once kind, my ever beloved mother, deign to receive a letter from her guilty, but repentant child? or has she, justly incensed at my ingratitude, driven the unhappy Charlotte from her remembrance? Alas! thou much injured mother! shouldst thou even disown me, I dare not complain, because I know I have deserved it: but yet, believe me, guilty as I am, and cruelly as I have disappointed the hopes of the fondest parents, that ever girl had, even in the moment when, forgetful of my duty, I fled from you and happiness, even then I loved you most, and my heart bled at the thought of what you would suffer. Oh! never, never! whilst I have existence, will the agony of that moment be erased from my memory. It seemed like the separation of soul and body. What can I plead in excuse for my conduct? alas! nothing! That I loved my seducer is but too true! yet powerful as that passion is when operating in a young heart glowing with sensibility, it never would have conquered my affection to you, my beloved parents, had I not been encouraged, nay, urged to take the fatally imprudent step, by one of my own sex, who, under the mask of friendship, drew me on to ruin. Yet think not your Charlotte was so lost as to voluntarily rush into a life of infamy; no, my dear mother, deceived by the specious appearance of my betrayer, and every suspicion lulled asleep by the most solemn promises of marriage, I thought not those promises would so easily be forgotten. I never once reflected that the man who could stoop to seduction, would not hesitate to forsake the wretched object of his passion, whenever his capricious heart grew weary of her tenderness. When we arrived at this place, I vainly expected him to fulfil his engagements, but was at last fatally convinced he had never intended to make me his wife, or if he had once thought of it, his mind was now altered. I scorned to claim from his humanity what I could not obtain from his love: I was conscious of having forfeited the only gem that could render me respectable in the eye of the world. I locked my sorrows in my own bosom, and bore my injuries in silence. But how shall I proceed? This man, this cruel Montraville, for whom I sacrificed honour, happiness, and the love of my friends, no longer looks on me with affection, but scorns the credulous girl whom his art has made miserable. Could you see me, my dear parents, without society, without friends, stung with remorse, and (I feel the burning blush of shame die my cheeks while I write it) tortured with the pangs of disappointed love; cut to the soul by the indifference of him, who, having deprived me of every other comfort, no longer thinks it worth his while to sooth the heart where he has planted the thorn of never-ceasing regret. My daily employment is to think of you and weep, to pray for your happiness and deplore my own folly: my nights are scarce more happy, for if by chance I close my weary eyes, and hope some small forgetfulness of sorrow, some little time to pass in sweet oblivion, fancy, still waking, wafts me home to you: I see your beloved forms, I kneel and hear the blessed words of peace and pardon. Extatic joy pervades my soul; I reach my arms to catch your dear embraces; the motion chases the illusive dream; I wake to real misery. At other times I see my father angry and frowning, point to horrid caves, where, on the cold damp ground, in the agonies of death, I see my dear mother and my revered grand-father. I strive to raise you; you push me from you, and shrieking cry—"Charlotte, thou hast murdered me!" Horror and despair tear every tortured nerve; I start, and leave my restless bed, weary and unrefreshed.

"Shocking as these reflexions are, I have yet one more dreadful than the rest. Mother, my dear mother! do not let me quite break your heart when I tell you, in a few months I shall bring into the world an innocent witness of my guilt. Oh my bleeding heart, I shall bring a poor little helpless creature, heir to infamy and shame.

"This alone has urged me once more to address you, to interest you in behalf of this poor unborn, and beg you to extend your protection to the child of your lost Charlotte; for my own part I have wrote so often, so frequently have pleaded for forgiveness, and entreated to be received once more beneath the paternal roof, that having received no answer, not even one line, I much fear you have cast me from you for ever.

"But sure you cannot refuse to protect my innocent infant: it partakes not of its mother's guilt. Oh my father, oh beloved mother, now do I feel the anguish I inflicted on your hearts recoiling with double force upon my own.

"If my child should be a girl (which heaven forbid) tell her the unhappy fate of her mother, and teach her to avoid my errors; if a boy, teach him to lament my miseries, but tell him not who inflicted them, lest in wishing to revenge his mother's injuries, he should wound the peace of his father.

"And now, dear friends of my soul, kind guardians of my infancy, farewell. I feel I never more must hope to see you; the anguish of my heart strikes at the strings of life, and in a short time I shall be at rest. Oh could I but receive your blessing and forgiveness before I died, it would smooth my passage to the peaceful grave, and be a blessed foretaste of a happy eternity. I beseech you, curse me not, my adored parents, but let a tear of pity and pardon fall to the memory of your lost

Charlotte.

CHAPTER XXIII
A MAN MAY SMILE, AND SMILE, AND BE A VILLAIN[3]

While Charlotte was enjoying some small degree of comfort in the consoling friendship of Mrs. Beauchamp, Montraville was advancing rapidly in his affection towards Miss Franklin. Julia was an amiable girl; she saw only the fair side of his character; she possessed an independent fortune, and resolved to be happy with the man of her heart, though his rank and fortune were by no means so exalted as she had a right to expect; she saw the passion which Montraville struggled to conceal; she wondered at his timidity, but imagined the distance fortune had placed between them occasioned his backwardness, and made every advance which strict prudence and a becoming modesty would permit. Montraville saw with pleasure he was not indifferent to her, but a spark of honour which animated his bosom would not suffer him to take advantage of her partiality.[4] He was well acquainted with Charlotte's situation, and he thought there would be a double cruelty in forsaking her at such a time; and to marry Miss Franklin, while honour, humanity, every sacred law, obliged him still to protect and support Charlotte, was a baseness which his soul shuddered at.

He communicated his uneasiness to Belcour: it was the very thing this pretended friend had wished. "And do you really," said he, laughing, "hesitate at marrying the lovely Julia, and becoming master of her fortune, because a little foolish, fond girl chose to leave her friends, and run away with you to America. Dear Montraville, act more like a man of sense; this whining, pining Charlotte, who occasions you so much uneasiness, would have eloped with somebody else if she had not with you."

"Would to heaven," said Montraville, "I had never seen her; my regard for her was but the momentary passion of desire, but I feel I shall love and revere Julia Franklin as long as I live; yet to leave poor Charlotte in her present situation would be cruel beyond description."

"Oh my good sentimental friend," said Belcour, "do you imagine no body has a right to provide for the brat but yourself."

Montraville started. "Sure," said he, "you cannot mean to insinuate that Charlotte is false."

"I don't insinuate it," said Belcour, "I know it."

Montraville turned pale as ashes. "Then there is no faith in woman," said he.

---

3. From William Shakespeare's *Hamlet* 1.5.105: "That one may smile, and smile, and be a villain."   4. He saw she had feelings for him; "suffer" means "allow."

"While I thought you attached to her," said Belcour with an air of indifference, "I never wished to make you uneasy by mentioning her perfidy, but as I know you love and are beloved by Miss Franklin, I was determined not to let these foolish scruples of honour step between you and happiness, or your tenderness for the peace of a perfidious girl prevent your uniting yourself to a woman of honour."

"Good heavens!" said Montraville, "what poignant reflections does a man endure who sees a lovely woman plunged in infamy, and is conscious he was her first seducer; but are you certain of what you say, Belcour?"

"So far," replied he, "that I myself have received advances from her which I would not take advantage of out of regard to you: but hang it, think no more about her. I dined at Franklin's to-day, and Julia bid me seek and bring you to tea: so come along, my lad, make good use of opportunity, and seize the gifts of fortune while they are within your reach."

Montraville was too much agitated to pass a happy evening even in the company of Julia Franklin: he determined to visit Charlotte early the next morning, tax her with her falsehood, and take an everlasting leave of her; but when the morning came, he was commanded on duty,[5] and for six weeks was prevented from putting his design in execution. At length he found an hour to spare, and walked out to spend it with Charlotte: it was near four o'clock in the afternoon when he arrived at her cottage; she was not in the parlour, and without calling the servant he walked up stairs, thinking to find her in her bed room. He opened the door, and the first object that met his eyes was Charlotte asleep on the bed, and Belcour by her side.

"Death and distraction," said he, stamping, "this is too much. Rise, villain, and defend yourself." Belcour sprang from the bed. The noise awoke Charlotte; terrified at the furious appearance of Montraville, and seeing Belcour with him in the chamber, she caught hold of his arm as he stood by the bed-side, and eagerly asked what was the matter.

"Treacherous, infamous girl," said he, "can you ask? How came he here?" pointing to Belcour.

"As heaven is my witness," replied she weeping, "I do not know. I have not seen him for these three weeks."

"Then you confess he sometimes visits you?"

"He came sometimes by your desire."

"'Tis false; I never desired him to come, and you know I did not: but mark me, Charlotte, from this instant our connexion is at an end. Let Belcour, or any other of your favoured lovers, take you and provide for you; I have done with you for ever."

He was then going to leave her; but starting wildly from the bed, she threw herself on her knees before him, protesting her innocence and entreating him not to leave her. "Oh Montraville," said she, "kill me, for pity's sake kill me, but do not doubt my fidelity. Do not leave me in this horrid situation; for the sake of your unborn child, oh! spurn not the wretched mother from you."

"Charlotte," said he, with a firm voice, "I shall take care that neither you nor your child want any thing in the approaching painful hour; but we meet no more." He then endeavoured to raise her from the ground; but in vain; she clung about his knees, entreating him to believe her innocent, and conjuring Belcour to clear up the dreadful mystery.

---

5. Ordered to report to his military assignment.

Belcour cast on Montraville a smile of contempt: it irritated him almost to madness; he broke from the feeble arms of the distressed girl; she shrieked and fell prostrate on the floor.

Montraville instantly left the house and returned hastily to the city.

CHAPTER XXIV
MYSTERY DEVELOPED

Unfortunately for Charlotte, about three weeks before this unhappy rencontre, Captain Beauchamp, being ordered to Rhode-Island, his lady[6] had accompanied him, so that Charlotte was deprived of her friendly advice and consoling society. The afternoon on which Montraville had visited her she had found herself languid and fatigued, and after making a very slight dinner had lain down to endeavour to recruit her exhausted spirits, and, contrary to her expectations, had fallen asleep. She had not long been lain down, when Belcour arrived, for he took every opportunity of visiting her, and striving to awaken her resentment against Montraville. He enquired of the servant where her mistress was, and being told she was asleep, took up a book to amuse himself: having sat a few minutes, he by chance cast his eyes towards the road, and saw Montraville approaching; he instantly conceived the diabolical scheme of ruining the unhappy Charlotte in his opinion for ever; he therefore stole softly up stairs, and laying himself by her side with the greatest precaution, for fear she should awake, was in that situation discovered by his credulous friend.

When Montraville spurned the weeping Charlotte from him, and left her almost distracted with terror and despair, Belcour raised her from the floor, and leading her down stairs, assumed the part of a tender, consoling friend; she listened to the arguments he advanced with apparent composure; but this was only the calm of a moment: the remembrance of Montraville's recent cruelty again rushed upon her mind: she pushed him from her with some violence, and crying— "Leave me, Sir, I beseech you leave me, for much I fear you have been the cause of my fidelity being suspected; go, leave me to the accumulated miseries my own imprudence has brought upon me."

She then left him with precipitation, and retiring to her own apartment, threw herself on the bed, and gave vent to an agony of grief which it is impossible to describe.

It now occurred to Belcour that she might possibly write to Montraville, and endeavour to convince him of her innocence: he was well aware of her pathetic remonstrances, and, sensible of the tenderness of Montraville's heart, resolved to prevent any letters ever reaching him: he therefore called the servant, and, by the powerful persuasion of a bribe, prevailed with her to promise whatever letters her mistress might write should be sent to him. He then left a polite, tender note for Charlotte, and returned to New-York. His first business was to seek Montraville, and endeavour to convince him that what had happened would ultimately tend to his happiness: he found him in his apartment, solitary, pensive, and wrapped in disagreeable reflexions.

"Why how now, whining, pining lover?" said he, clapping him on the shoulder. Montraville started; a momentary flush of resentment crossed his cheek, but instantly gave place to a death-like paleness, occasioned by painful remembrance—

6. Rencontre: meeting, often military (French); his lady: Mrs. Beauchamp.

remembrance awakened by that monitor, whom, though we may in vain endeavour, we can never entirely silence.

"Belcour," said he, "you have injured me in a tender point."

"Prithee, Jack," replied Belcour, "do not make a serious matter of it: how could I refuse the girl's advances? and thank heaven she is not your wife."

"True," said Montraville; "but she was innocent when I first knew her. It was I seduced her, Belcour. Had it not been for me, she had still been virtuous and happy in the affection and protection of her family."

"Pshaw," replied Belcour, laughing, "if you had not taken advantage of her easy nature, some other would, and where is the difference, pray?"

"I wish I had never seen her," cried he passionately, and starting from his seat. "Oh that cursed French woman," added he with vehemence, "had it not been for her, I might have been happy—" He paused.

"With Julia Franklin," said Belcour. The name, like a sudden spark of electric fire, seemed for a moment to suspend his faculties—for a moment he was transfixed; but recovering, he caught Belcour's hand, and cried—"Stop! stop! I beseech you, name not the lovely Julia and the wretched Montraville in the same breath. I am a seducer, a mean, ungenerous seducer of unsuspecting innocence. I dare not hope that purity like her's would stoop to unite itself with black, premeditated guilt: yet by heavens I swear, Belcour, I thought I loved the lost, abandoned Charlotte till I saw Julia—I thought I never could forsake her; but the heart is deceitful, and I now can plainly discriminate between the impulse of a youthful passion, and the pure flame of disinterested affection."

At that instant Julia Franklin passed the window, leaning on her uncle's arm. She curtseyed as she passed, and, with the bewitching smile of modest chearfulness, cried—"Do you bury yourselves in the house this fine evening, gents?" There was something in the voice! the manner! the look! that was altogether irresistible. "Perhaps she wishes my company," said Montraville mentally, as he snatched up his hat: "if I thought she loved me, I would confess my errors, and trust to her generosity to pity and pardon me." He soon overtook her, and offering her his arm, they sauntered to pleasant but unfrequented walks. Belcour drew Mr. Franklin on one side and entered into a political discourse: they walked faster than the young people, and Belcour by some means contrived entirely to lose sight of them. It was a fine evening in the beginning of autumn; the last remains of daylight faintly streaked the western sky, while the moon, with pale and virgin lustre in the room of gorgeous gold and purple, ornamented the canopy of heaven with silver, fleecy clouds, which now and then half hid her lovely face, and, by partly concealing, heightened every beauty; the zephyrs[7] whispered softly through the trees, which now began to shed their leafy honours; a solemn silence reigned: and to a happy mind an evening such as this would give serenity, and calm, unruffled pleasure; but to Montraville, while it soothed the turbulence of his passions, it brought increase of melancholy reflections. Julia was leaning on his arm: he took her hand in his, and pressing it tenderly, sighed deeply, but continued silent. Julia was embarrassed; she wished to break a silence so unaccountable, but was unable; she loved Montraville, she saw he was unhappy, and wished to know the cause of his uneasiness, but that innate modesty, which nature has implanted in the female breast, prevented her enquiring. "I am bad company, Miss Franklin," said he, at

---

7. Breezes.

last recollecting himself; "but I have met with something to-day that has greatly distressed me, and I cannot shake off the disagreeable impression it has made on my mind."

"I am sorry," she replied, "that you have any cause of inquietude. I am sure if you were as happy as you deserve, and as all your friends wish you—" She hesitated. "And might I," replied he with some animation, "presume to rank the amiable Julia in that number?"

"Certainly," said she, "the service you have rendered me, the knowledge of your worth, all combine to make me esteem you."

"Esteem, my lovely Julia," said he passionately, "is but a poor cold word. I would if I dared, if I thought I merited your attention—but no, I must not—honour forbids. I am beneath your notice, Julia, I am miserable and cannot hope to be otherwise."

"Alas!" said Julia, "I pity you."

"Oh thou condescending charmer," said he, "how that sweet word chears my sad heart. Indeed if you knew all, you would pity; but at the same time I fear you would despise me."

Just then they were again joined by Mr. Franklin and Belcour. It had interrupted an interesting discourse. They found it impossible to converse on indifferent subjects, and proceeded home in silence. At Mr. Franklin's door Montraville again pressed Julia's hand, and faintly articulating "good night," retired to his lodgings dispirited and wretched, from a consciousness that he deserved not the affection, with which he plainly saw he was honoured.

CHAPTER XXV
RECEPTION OF A LETTER

"And where now is our poor Charlotte?" said Mr. Temple one evening, as the cold blasts of autumn whistled rudely over the heath, and the yellow appearance of the distant wood, spoke the near approach of winter. In vain the chearful fire blazed on the hearth, in vain was he surrounded by all the comforts of life; the parent was still alive in his heart, and when he thought that perhaps his once darling child was ere this exposed to all the miseries of want in a distant land, without a friend to sooth and comfort her, without the benignant look of compassion to chear, or the angelic voice of pity to pour the balm of consolation on her wounded heart; when he thought of this, his whole soul dissolved in tenderness; and while he wiped the tear of anguish from the eye of his patient, uncomplaining Lucy, he struggled to suppress the sympathizing drop that started in his own.

"Oh, my poor girl," said Mrs. Temple, "how must she be altered, else surely she would have relieved our agonizing minds by one line to say she lived—to say she had not quite forgot the parents who almost idolized her."

"Gracious heaven," said Mr. Temple, starting from his seat, "who would wish to be a father, to experience the agonizing pangs inflicted on a parent's heart by the ingratitude of a child?" Mrs. Temple wept: her father took her hand; he would have said, "be comforted my child," but the words died on his tongue. The sad silence that ensued was interrupted by a loud rap at the door. In a moment a servant entered with a letter in his hand.

Mrs. Temple took it from him: she cast her eyes upon the superscription; she knew the writing. "'Tis Charlotte," said she, eagerly breaking the seal, "she has not quite forgot us." But before she had half gone through the contents, a sudden sickness seized her; she grew cold and giddy, and putting it into her husband's hand, she cried—"Read it: I cannot." Mr. Temple attempted to read it aloud, but frequently paused to give vent to his tears. "My poor deluded child," said he, when he had finished.

"Oh, shall we not forgive the dear penitent?" said Mrs. Temple. "We must, we will, my love; she is willing to return, and 'tis our duty to receive her."

"Father of mercy," said Mr. Eldridge, raising his clasped hands, "let me but live once more to see the dear wanderer restored to her afflicted parents, and take me from this world of sorrow whenever it seemeth best to thy wisdom."

"Yes, we will receive her," said Mr. Temple; "we will endeavour to heal her wounded spirit, and speak peace and comfort to her agitated soul. I will write to her to return immediately."

"Oh!" said Mrs. Temple, "I would if possible fly to her, support and chear the dear sufferer in the approaching hour of distress, and tell her how nearly penitence is allied to virtue. Cannot we go and conduct her home, my love?" continued she, laying her hand on his arm. "My father will surely forgive our absence if we go to bring home his darling."

"You cannot go, my Lucy," said Mr. Temple: "the delicacy of your frame would but poorly sustain the fatigue of a long voyage; but I will go and bring the gentle penitent to your arms: we may still see many years of happiness."

The struggle in the bosom of Mrs. Temple between maternal and conjugal tenderness was long and painful. At length the former triumphed, and she consented that her husband should set forward to New-York by the first opportunity: she wrote to her Charlotte in the tenderest, most consoling manner, and looked forward to the happy hour, when she should again embrace her, with the most animated hope.

CHAPTER XXVI

WHAT MIGHT BE EXPECTED

In the mean time the passion Montraville had conceived for Julia Franklin daily encreased, and he saw evidently how much he was beloved by that amiable girl: he was likewise strongly prepossessed with an idea of Charlotte's perfidy. What wonder then if he gave himself up to the delightful sensation which pervaded his bosom; and finding no obstacle arise to oppose his happiness, he solicited and obtained the hand of Julia. A few days before his marriage he thus addressed Belcour:

"Though Charlotte, by her abandoned conduct, has thrown herself from my protection, I still hold myself bound to support her till relieved from her present condition, and also to provide for the child. I do not intend to see her again, but I will place a sum of money in your hands, which will amply supply her with every convenience; but should she require more, let her have it, and I will see it repaid. I wish I could prevail on the poor deluded girl to return to her friends: she was an only child, and I make no doubt but that they would joyfully receive her; it would shock me greatly to see her henceforth leading a life of infamy, as I should always accuse myself of being the primary cause of all her errors. If she should chuse to remain under your protection, be kind to her, Belcour, I conjure you. Let not satiety prompt you to treat her in such a manner, as may drive her to actions which necessity might urge her to, while her better reason disapproved them: she shall never want a friend while I live, but I never more desire to behold her; her presence would be always painful to me, and a glance from her eye would call the blush of conscious guilt into my cheek.

"I will write a letter to her, which you may deliver when I am gone, as I shall go to St. Eustatia[8] the day after my union with Julia, who will accompany me."

Belcour promised to fulfil the request of his friend, though nothing was farther from his intentions, than the least design of delivering the letter, or making Charlotte acquainted with the provision Montraville had made for her; he was bent on the complete ruin of the unhappy girl, and supposed, by reducing her to an entire dependance on him, to bring her by degrees to consent to gratify his ungenerous passion.

The evening before the day appointed for the nuptials of Montraville and Julia, the former retired early to his apartment; and ruminating on the past scenes of his life, suffered the keenest remorse in the remembrance of Charlotte's seduction. "Poor girl," said he, "I will at least write and bid her adieu; I will too endeavour to awaken that love of virtue in her bosom which her unfortunate attachment to me has extinguished." He took up the pen and began to write, but words were denied him. How could he address the woman whom he had seduced, and whom, though he thought unworthy his tenderness, he was about to bid adieu for ever? How should he tell her that he was going to abjure her, to enter into the most indissoluble ties with another, and that he could not even own the infant which she bore as his child? Several letters were begun and destroyed: at length he completed the following:

To Charlotte.

"Though I have taken up my pen to address you, my poor injured girl, I feel I am inadequate to the task; yet, however painful the endeavour, I could not resolve upon leaving you for ever without one kind line to bid you adieu, to tell you how my heart bleeds at the remembrance of what you was, before you saw the hated Montraville. Even now imagination paints the scene, when, torn by contending passions, when, struggling between love and duty, you fainted in my arms, and I lifted you into the chaise: I see the agony of your mind, when, recovering, you found yourself on the road to Portsmouth: but how, my gentle girl, how could you, when so justly impressed with the value of virtue, how could you, when loving as I thought you loved me, yield to the solicitations of Belcour?

"Oh Charlotte, conscience tells me it was I, villain that I am, who first taught you the allurements of guilty pleasure; it was I who dragged you from the calm repose which innocence and virtue ever enjoy; and can I, dare I tell you, it was not love prompted to the horrid deed? No, thou dear, fallen angel, believe your repentant Montraville, when he tells you the man who truly loves will never betray the object of his affection. Adieu, Charlotte: could you still find charms in a life of unoffending innocence, return to your parents; you shall never want the means of support both for yourself and child. Oh! gracious heaven! may that child be entirely free from the vices of its father and the weakness of its mother.

"To-morrow—but no, I cannot tell you what to-morrow will produce; Belcour will inform you: he also has cash for you, which I beg you will ask for whenever you may want it. Once more adieu: believe me could I hear you was returned to your friends, and enjoying that tranquillity of which I have robbed you, I should be as completely happy as even you, in your fondest hours, could wish me, but till then a gloom will obscure the brightest prospects of

Montraville."

8. An island in the West Indies.

After he had sealed this letter he threw himself on the bed, and enjoyed a few hours repose. Early in the morning Belcour tapped at his door: he arose hastily, and prepared to meet his Julia at the altar.

"This is the letter to Charlotte," said he, giving it to Belcour: "take it to her when we are gone to Eustatia; and I conjure you, my dear friend, not to use any sophistical arguments to prevent her return to virtue; but should she incline that way, encourage her in the thought, and assist her to put her design in execution."

CHAPTER XXVII
PENSIVE SHE MOURN'D, AND HUNG HER LANGUID HEAD,
LIKE A FAIR LILY OVERCHARG'D WITH DEW.

Charlotte had now been left almost three months a prey to her own melancholy reflexions—sad companions indeed; nor did any one break in upon her solitude but Belcour, who once or twice called to enquire after her health, and tell her he had in vain endeavoured to bring Montraville to hear reason; and once, but only once, was her mind cheared by the receipt of an affectionate letter from Mrs. Beauchamp. Often had she wrote to her perfidious seducer, and with the most persuasive eloquence endeavoured to convince him of her innocence; but these letters were never suffered to reach the hands of Montraville, or they must, though on the very eve of marriage, have prevented his deserting the wretched girl. Real anguish of heart had in a great measure faded her charms, her cheeks were pale from want of rest, and her eyes, by frequent, indeed almost continued weeping, were sunk and heavy. Sometimes a gleam of hope would play about her heart when she thought of her parents—"They cannot surely," she would say, "refuse to forgive me; or should they deny their pardon to me, they will not hate my innocent infant on account of its mother's errors." How often did the poor mourner wish for the consoling presence of the benevolent Mrs. Beauchamp.

"If she were here," she would cry, "she would certainly comfort me, and sooth the distraction of my soul."

She was sitting one afternoon, wrapped in these melancholy reflexions, when she was interrupted by the entrance of Belcour. Great as the alteration was which incessant sorrow had made on her person, she was still interesting, still charming; and the unhallowed flame, which had urged Belcour to plant dissension between her and Montraville, still raged in his bosom: he was determined, if possible, to make her his mistress; nay, he had even conceived the diabolical scheme of taking her to New-York, and making her appear in every public place where it was likely she should meet Montraville, that he might be a witness to his unmanly triumph.

When he entered the room where Charlotte was sitting, he assumed the look of tender, consolatory friendship. "And how does my lovely Charlotte?" said he, taking her hand: "I fear you are not so well as I could wish."

"I am not well, Mr. Belcour," said she, "very far from it; but the pains and infirmities of the body I could easily bear, nay, submit to them with patience, were they not aggravated by the most insupportable anguish of my mind."

"You are not happy, Charlotte," said he, with a look of well-dissembled sorrow.

"Alas!" replied she mournfully, shaking her head, "how can I be happy, deserted and forsaken as I am, without a friend of my own sex to whom I can unburthen my full heart, nay, my fidelity suspected by the very man for whom I have sacrificed every thing valuable in life, for whom I have made myself a poor despised creature, an outcast from society, an object only of contempt and pity."

"You think too meanly of yourself, Miss Temple: there is no one who would dare to treat you with contempt: all who have the pleasure of knowing you must admire and esteem. You are lonely here, my dear girl; give me leave to conduct you to New-York, where the agreeable society of some ladies, to whom I will introduce you, will dispel these sad thoughts, and I shall again see returning chearfulness animate those lovely features."

"Oh never! never!" cried Charlotte, emphatically: "the virtuous part of my sex will scorn me, and I will never associate with infamy. No, Belcour, here let me hide my shame and sorrow, here let me spend my few remaining days in obscurity, unknown and unpitied, here let me die unlamented, and my name sink to oblivion." Here her tears stopped her utterance. Belcour was awed to silence: he dared not interrupt her; and after a moment's pause she proceeded—"I once had conceived the thought of going to New-York to seek out the still dear, though cruel, ungenerous Montraville, to throw myself at his feet, and entreat his compassion; heaven knows, not for myself; if I am no longer beloved, I will not be indebted to his pity to redress my injuries, but I would have knelt and entreated him not to forsake my poor unborn—" She could say no more; a crimson glow rushed over her cheeks, and covering her face with her hands, she sobbed aloud.

Something like humanity was awakened in Belcour's breast by this pathetic speech: he arose and walked towards the window; but the selfish passion which had taken possession of his heart, soon stifled these finer emotions; and he thought if Charlotte was once convinced she had no longer any dependance on Montraville, she would more readily throw herself on his protection. Determined, therefore, to inform her of all that had happened, he again resumed his seat; and finding she began to be more composed, enquired if she had ever heard from Montraville since the unfortunate rencontre in her bed chamber.

"Ah no," said she. "I fear I shall never hear from him again."

"I am greatly of your opinion," said Belcour, "for he has been for some time past greatly attached—"

At the word "attached" a death-like paleness overspread the countenance of Charlotte, but she applied to some hartshorn[9] which stood beside her, and Belcour proceeded.

"He has been for some time past greatly attached to one Miss Franklin, a pleasing lively girl, with a large fortune."

"She may be richer, may be handsomer," cried Charlotte, "but cannot love him so well. Oh may she beware of his art, and not trust him too far as I have done."

"He addresses her publicly," said he, "and it was rumoured they were to be married before he sailed for Eustatia, whither his company is ordered."

"Belcour," said Charlotte, seizing his hand, and gazing at him earnestly, while her pale lips trembled with convulsive agony, "tell me, and tell me truly, I beseech you, do you think he can be such a villain as to marry another woman, and leave me to die with want and misery in a strange land: tell me what you think; I can bear it very well; I will not shrink from this heaviest stroke of fate; I have deserved my afflictions, and I will endeavour to bear them as I ought."

"I fear," said Belcour, "he can be that villain."

9. A form of ammonia used as smelling salts; originally made from antlers—hence the name.

"Perhaps," cried she, eagerly interrupting him, "perhaps he is married already: come, let me know the worst," continued she with an affected look of composure: "you need not be afraid, I shall not send the fortunate lady a bowl of poison."

"Well then, my dear girl," said he, deceived by her appearance, "they were married on Thursday, and yesterday morning they sailed for Eustatia."

"Married—gone—say you?" cried she in a distracted accent, "what without a last farewell, without one thought on my unhappy situation! Oh Montraville, may God forgive your perfidy." She shrieked, and Belcour sprang forward just in time to prevent her falling to the floor.

Alarming faintings now succeeded each other, and she was conveyed to her bed, from whence she earnestly prayed she might never more arise. Belcour staid with her that night, and in the morning found her in a high fever. The fits she had been seized with had greatly terrified him; and confined as she now was to a bed of sickness, she was no longer an object of desire: it is true for several days he went constantly to see her, but her pale, emaciated appearance disgusted him: his visits became less frequent; he forgot the solemn charge given him by Montraville; he even forgot the money entrusted to his care; and, the burning blush of indignation and shame tinges my cheek while I write it, this disgrace to humanity and manhood at length forgot even the injured Charlotte; and, attracted by the blooming health of a farmer's daughter, whom he had seen in his frequent excursions to the country, he left the unhappy girl to sink unnoticed to the grave, a prey to sickness, grief, and penury; while he, having triumphed over the virtue of the artless cottager,[1] rioted in all the intemperance of luxury and lawless pleasure.

CHAPTER XXVII

A TRIFLING RETROSPECT

"Bless my heart," cries my young, volatile reader, "I shall never have patience to get through these volumes, there are so many ahs! and ohs! so much fainting, tears, and distress, I am sick to death of the subject." My dear, chearful, innocent girl, for innocent I will suppose you to be, or you would acutely feel the woes of Charlotte, did conscience say, thus might it have been with me, had not Providence interposed to snatch me from destruction: therefore, my lively, innocent girl, I must request your patience: I am writing a tale of truth. I mean to write it to the heart: but if perchance the heart is rendered impenetrable by unbounded prosperity, or a continuance in vice, I expect not my tale to please, nay, I even expect it will be thrown by with disgust. But softly, gentle fair one; I pray you throw it not aside till you have perused the whole; mayhap you may find something therein to repay you for the trouble. Methinks I see a sarcastic smile sit on your countenance.—"And what," cry you, "does the conceited[2] author suppose we can glean from these pages, if Charlotte is held up as an object of terror, to prevent us from falling into guilty errors? does not La Rue triumph in her shame, and by adding art to guilt, obtain the affection of a worthy man, and rise to a station where she is beheld with respect, and chearfully received into all companies. What then is the moral you would inculcate? Would you wish us to think that a deviation from virtue, if covered by art and hypocrisy, is not an object of detestation, but on the contrary shall raise us to fame and honour? while the hapless girl who falls a victim to her too great sensibility, shall be loaded with ignominy and shame?" No,

1. He has seduced the farmer's daughter—a naive   2. Whimsical.
country person.

my fair querist,[3] I mean no such thing. Remember the endeavours of the wicked are often suffered to prosper, that in the end their fall may be attended with more bitterness of heart; while the cup of affliction is poured out for wise and salutary ends, and they who are compelled to drain it even to the bitter dregs, often find comfort at the bottom; the tear of penitence blots their offences from the book of fate, and they rise from the heavy, painful trial, purified and fit for a mansion in the kingdom of eternity.

Yes, my young friends, the tear of compassion shall fall for the fate of Charlotte, while the name of La Rue shall be detested and despised. For Charlotte, the soul melts with sympathy; for La Rue, it feels nothing but horror and contempt. But perhaps your gay hearts would rather follow the fortunate Mrs. Crayton through the scenes of pleasure and dissipation in which she was engaged, than listen to the complaints and miseries of Charlotte. I will for once oblige you; I will for once follow her to midnight revels, balls, and scenes of gaiety, for in such was she constantly engaged.

I have said her person was lovely; let us add that she was surrounded by splendor and affluence, and he must know but little of the world who can wonder, (however faulty such a woman's conduct,) at her being followed by the men, and her company courted by the women: in short Mrs. Crayton was the universal favourite: she set the fashions, she was toasted by all the gentlemen, and copied by all the ladies.

Colonel Crayton was a domestic man. Could he be happy with such a woman? impossible! Remonstrance was vain: he might as well have preached to the winds, as endeavour to persuade her from any action, however ridiculous, on which she had set her mind: in short, after a little ineffectual struggle, he gave up the attempt, and left her to follow the bent of her own inclinations: what those were, I think the reader must have seen enough of her character to form a just idea. Among the number who paid their devotions at her shrine, she singled one, a young Ensign of mean birth, indifferent education,[4] and weak intellects. How such a man came into the army, we hardly know to account for, and how he afterwards rose to posts of honour is likewise strange and wonderful. But fortune is blind, and so are those too frequently who have the power of dispensing her favours: else why do we see fools and knaves at the very top of the wheel, while patient merit sinks to the extreme of the opposite abyss. But we may form a thousand conjectures on this subject, and yet never hit on the right. Let us therefore endeavour to deserve her smiles, and whether we succeed or not, we shall feel more innate satisfaction, than thousands of those who bask in the sunshine of her favour unworthily. But to return to Mrs. Crayton: this young man, whom I shall distinguish by the name of Corydon, was the reigning favourite of her heart. He escorted her to the play, danced with her at every ball, and when indisposition prevented her going out, it was he alone who was permitted to chear the gloomy solitude to which she was obliged to confine herself. Did she ever think of poor Charlotte?—if she did, my dear Miss, it was only to laugh at the poor girl's want of spirit in consenting to be moped up in the country, while Montraville was enjoying all the pleasures of a gay, dissipated city. When she heard of his marriage, she smiling said, so there's an end of Madam Charlotte's hopes. I wonder who will take her now, or what will become of the little affected prude?

3. Inquirer.
4. Of low social class and having a mediocre education.

But as you have lead to the subject, I think we may as well return to the distressed Charlotte, and not, like the unfeeling Mrs. Crayton, shut our hearts to the call of humanity.

CHAPTER XXIX

WE GO FORWARD AGAIN

The strength of Charlotte's constitution combatted against her disorder, and she began slowly to recover, though she still laboured under a violent depression of spirits: how must that depression be encreased, when, upon examining her little store, she found herself reduced to one solitary guinea, and that during her illness the attendance of an apothecary and nurse, together with many other unavoidable expences, had involved her in debt, from which she saw no method of extricating herself. As to the faint hope which she had entertained of hearing from and being relieved by her parents; it now entirely forsook her, for it was above four months since her letter was dispatched, and she had received no answer: she therefore imagined that her conduct had either entirely alienated their affection from her, or broken their hearts, and she must never more hope to receive their blessing.

Never did any human being wish for death with greater fervency or with juster cause; yet she had too just a sense of the duties of the Christian religion to attempt to put a period to her own existence. "I have but to be patient a little longer," she would cry, "and nature, fatigued and fainting, will throw off this heavy load of mortality, and I shall be released from all my sufferings."

It was one cold stormy day in the latter end of December, as Charlotte sat by a handful of fire, the low state of her finances not allowing her to replenish her stock of fuel, and prudence teaching her to be careful of what she had, when she was surprised by the entrance of a farmer's wife, who, without much ceremony, seated herself, and began this curious harangue.

"I'm come to see if as how you can pay your rent, because as how we hear Captain Montable is gone away, and it's fifty to one if he b'ant killed afore he comes back again; an then, Miss, or Ma'am, or whatever you may be, as I was saying to my husband, where are we to look for our money."

This was a stroke altogether unexpected by Charlotte: she knew so little of the ways of the world that she had never bestowed a thought on the payment for the rent of the house; she knew indeed that she owed a good deal, but this was never reckoned among the others: she was thunder-struck; she hardly knew what answer to make, yet it was absolutely necessary that she should say something; and judging of the gentleness of every female disposition by her own, she thought the best way to interest the woman in her favour would be to tell her candidly to what a situation she was reduced, and how little probability there was of her ever paying any body.

Alas poor Charlotte, how confined was her knowledge of human nature, or she would have been convinced that the only way to insure the friendship and assistance of your surrounding acquaintance is to convince them you do not require it, for when once the petrifying aspect of distress and penury appear, whose qualities, like Medusa's head, can change to stone all that look upon it; when once this Gorgon[5] claims acquaintance with us, the phantom of friendship, that before courted our notice, will vanish into unsubstantial air, and the whole world before us appear a barren waste. Pardon me, ye dear spirits of benevolence, whose be-

5. In Greek mythology, Medusa was one of three   place of hair) would turn a person to stone.
Gorgons; looking at her head (with its snakes in

nign smiles and chearful-giving hand have strewed sweet flowers on many a thorny path through which my wayward fate forced me to pass; think not, that, in condemning the unfeeling texture of the human heart, I forget the spring from whence flow all the comforts I enjoy: oh no! I look up to you as to bright constellations, gathering new splendours from the surrounding darkness; but ah! whilst I adore the benignant rays that cheared and illumined my heart, I mourn that their influence cannot extend to all the sons and daughters of affliction.

"Indeed, Madam," said poor Charlotte in a tremulous accent, "I am at a loss what to do. Montraville placed me here, and promised to defray all my expenses: but he has forgot his promise, he has forsaken me, and I have no friend who has either power or will to relieve me. Let me hope, as you see my unhappy situation, your charity—"

"Charity," cried the woman impatiently interrupting her, "charity indeed: why, Mistress, charity begins at home, and I have seven children at home, *honest, lawful* children, and it is my duty to keep them; and do you think I will give away my property to a nasty, impudent hussey, to maintain her and her bastard; an I was saying to my husband the other day what will this world come to; honest women are nothing now-a-days, while the harlotings are set up for fine ladies, and look upon us no more nor the dirt they walk upon: but let me tell you, my fine spoken Ma'am, I must have my money; so seeing as how you can't pay it, why you must troop, and leave all your fine gimcracks and fal der ralls behind you. I don't ask for no more nor my right, and nobody shall dare for to go for to hinder me of it."

"Oh heavens," cried Charlotte, clasping her hands, "what will become of me?"

"Come on ye!" retorted the unfeeling wretch: "why go to the barracks and work for a morsel of bread; wash and mend the soldiers cloaths, an cook their victuals, and not expect to live in idleness on honest people's means. Oh I wish I could see the day when all such cattle were obliged to work hard and eat little; it's only what they deserve."

"Father of mercy," cried Charlotte, "I acknowledge thy correction just; but prepare me, I beseech thee, for the portion of misery thou may'st please to lay upon me."

"Well," said the woman, "I shall go an tell my husband as how you can't pay; and so d'ye see, Ma'am, get ready to be packing away this very night, for you should not stay another night in this house, though I was sure you would lay in the street."

Charlotte bowed her head in silence; but the anguish of her heart was too great to permit her to articulate a single word.

CHAPTER XXX

And what is friendship but a name,
A charm that lulls to sleep,
A shade that follows wealth and fame,
But leaves the wretch to weep.[6]

When Charlotte was left to herself, she began to think what course she must take, or to whom she could apply, to prevent her perishing for want, or perhaps that very night falling a victim to the inclemency of the season. After many perplexed

6. From Oliver Goldsmith (1730?–1774), "The Hermit," lines 73–76, a poem included in his novel   *The Vicar of Wakefield* (1766).

thoughts, she at last determined to set out for New-York, and enquire out Mrs. Crayton, from whom she had no doubt but she should obtain immediate relief as soon as her distress was made known; she had no sooner formed this resolution than she resolved immediately to put it in execution: she therefore wrote the following little billet[7] to Mrs. Crayton, thinking if she should have company with her it would be better to send it in than to request to see her.

To Mrs. Crayton.

"Madam,

"When we left our native land, that dear, happy land which now contains all that is dear to the wretched Charlotte, our prospects were the same; we both, pardon me, Madam, if I say, we both too easily followed the impulse of our treacherous hearts, and trusted our happiness on a tempestuous ocean, where mine has been wrecked and lost for ever; you have been more fortunate—you are united to a man of honour and humanity, united by the most sacred ties, respected, esteemed, and admired, and surrounded by innumerable blessings of which I am bereaved, enjoying those pleasures which have fled my bosom never to return; alas! sorrow and deep regret have taken their place. Behold me, Madam, a poor forsaken wanderer, who has no where to lay her weary head, wherewith to supply the wants of nature, or to shield her from the inclemency of the weather. To you I sue, to you I look for pity and relief. I ask not to be received as an intimate or an equal; only for charity's sweet sake receive me into your hospitable mansion, allot me the meanest apartment in it, and let me breath out my soul in prayers for your happiness; I cannot, I feel I cannot long bear up under the accumulated woes that pour in upon me; but oh! my dear Madam, for the love of heaven suffer me not to expire in the street; and when I am at peace, as soon I shall be, extend your compassion to my helpless offspring, should it please heaven that it should survive its unhappy mother. A gleam of joy breaks in on my benighted soul while I reflect that you cannot, will not refuse your protection to the heart-broken.

Charlotte."

When Charlotte had finished this letter, late as it was in the afternoon, and though the snow began to fall very fast, she tied up a few necessaries which she had prepared against her expected confinement, and terrified lest she should be again exposed to the insults of her barbarous landlady, more dreadful to her wounded spirit than either storm or darkness, she set forward for New-York.

It may be asked by those, who, in a work of this kind, love to cavil at every trifling omission, whether Charlotte did not possess any valuable of which she could have disposed, and by that means have supported herself till Mrs. Beauchamp's return, when she would have been certain of receiving every tender attention which compassion and friendship could dictate: but let me entreat these wise, penetrating gentlemen to reflect, that when Charlotte left England, it was in such haste that there was no time to purchase any thing more than what was wanted for immediate use on the voyage, and after her arrival at New-York, Montraville's affection soon began to decline, so that her whole wardrobe consisted of only nec-

7. Note.

essaries, and as to baubles, with which fond lovers often load their mistresses, she possessed not one, except a plain gold locket of small value, which contained a lock of her mother's hair, and which the greatest extremity of want could not have forced her to part with.

I hope, Sir, your prejudices are now removed in regard to the probability of my story? Oh they are. Well then, with your leave, I will proceed.

The distance from the house which our suffering heroine occupied, to New-York, was not very great, yet the snow fell so fast, and the cold so intense, that, being unable from her situation to walk quick, she found herself almost sinking with cold and fatigue before she reached the town; her garments, which were merely suitable to the summer season, being an undress robe[8] of plain white muslin, were wet through, and a thin black cloak and bonnet, very improper habiliments for such a climate, but poorly defended her from the cold. In this situation she reached the city, and enquired of a foot soldier whom she met, the way to Colonel Crayton's.

"Bless you, my sweet lady," said the soldier with a voice and look of compassion, "I will shew you the way with all my heart; but if you are going to make a petition to Madam Crayton it is all to no purpose I assure you: if you please I will conduct you to Mr. Franklin's; though Miss Julia is married and gone now, yet the old gentleman is very good."

"Julia Franklin," said Charlotte; "is she not married to Montraville?"

"Yes," replied the solider, "and may God bless them, for a better officer never lived, he is so good to us all; and as to Miss Julia, all the poor folk almost worshipped her."

"Gracious heaven," cried Charlotte, "is Montraville unjust then to none but me."

The soldier now shewed her Colonel Crayton's door, and, with a beating heart, she knocked for admission.

CHAPTER XXXI
SUBJECT CONTINUED

When the door was opened, Charlotte, in a voice rendered scarcely articulate, through cold and the extreme agitation of her mind, demanded whether Mrs. Crayton was at home. The servant hesitated: he knew that his lady was engaged at a game of picquet[9] with her dear Corydon, nor could he think she would like to be disturbed by a person whose appearance spoke her of so little consequence as Charlotte; yet there was something in her countenance that rather interested him in her favour, and he said his lady was engaged, but if she had any particular message he would deliver it.

"Take up this letter," said Charlotte: "tell her the unhappy writer of it waits in her hall for an answer."

The tremulous accent, the tearful eye, must have moved any heart not composed of adamant. The man took the letter from the poor suppliant, and hastily ascended the stair case.

8. A kind of wrapper or casual dress to be worn   9. A card game.
at home.

"A letter, Madam," said he, presenting it to his lady: "an immediate answer is required."

Mrs. Crayton glanced her eye carelessly over the contents. "What stuff is this;" cried she haughtily; "have not I told you a thousand times that I will not be plagued with beggars, and petitions from people one knows nothing about? Go tell the woman I can't do any thing in it. I'm sorry, but one can't relieve every body."

The servant bowed, and heavily returned with this chilling message to Charlotte.

"Surely," said she, "Mrs. Crayton has not read my letter. Go, my good friend, pray go back to her; tell her it is Charlotte Temple who requests beneath her hospitable roof to find shelter from the inclemency of the season."

"Prithee, don't plague me, man," cried Mrs. Crayton impatiently, as the servant advanced something in behalf of the unhappy girl. "I tell you I don't know her."

"Not know me," cried Charlotte, rushing into the room, (for she had followed the man up stairs) "not know me, not remember the ruined Charlotte Temple, who, but for you, perhaps might still have been innocent, still have been happy. Oh! La Rue, this is beyond every thing I could have believed possible."

"Upon my honour, Miss," replied the unfeeling woman with the utmost effrontery, "this is a most unaccountable address: it is beyond my comprehension. John," continued she, turning to the servant, "the young woman is certainly out of her senses: do pray take her away, she terrifies me to death."

"Oh God," cried Charlotte, clasping her hands in an agony, "this is too much; what will become of me? but I will not leave you; they shall not tear me from you; here on my knees I conjure you to save me from perishing in the streets; if you really have forgot me, oh for charity's sweet sake this night let me be sheltered from the winter's piercing cold."

The kneeling figure of Charlotte in her affecting situation might have moved the heart of a stoic to compassion; but Mrs. Crayton remained inflexible. In vain did Charlotte recount the time they had known each other at Chichester, in vain mention their being in the same ship, in vain were the names of Montraville and Belcour mentioned. Mrs. Crayton could only say she was sorry for her imprudence, but could not think of having her own reputation endangered by encouraging a woman of that kind in her own house, besides she did not know what trouble and expense she might bring upon her husband by giving shelter to a woman in her situation.

"I can at least die here," said Charlotte, "I feel I cannot long survive this dreadful conflict. Father of mercy, here let me finish my existence." Her agonizing sensations overpowered her, and she fell senseless on the floor.

"Take her away," said Mrs. Crayton, "she will really frighten me into hysterics; take her away I say this instant."

"And where must I take the poor creature?" said the servant with a voice and look of compassion.

"Any where," cried she hastily, "only don't let me ever see her again. I declare she has flurried me so I shan't be myself again this fortnight."

John, assisted by his fellow-servant, raised and carried her down stairs. "Poor soul," said he, "you shall not lay in the street this night. I have a bed and a poor little hovel, where my wife and her little ones rest them, but they shall watch to night, and you shall be sheltered from danger." They placed her in a chair; and the benevolent man, assisted by one of his comrades, carried her to the place where his wife and children lived. A surgeon was sent for: he bled her,[1] she gave signs of returning life, and before the dawn gave birth to a female infant. After this event she lay for some hours in a kind of stupor; and if at any time she spoke, it was with a quickness and incoherence that plainly evinced the total deprivation of her reason.

CHAPTER XXXII

REASONS WHY AND WHEREFORE

The reader of sensibility may perhaps be astonished to find Mrs. Crayton could so positively deny any knowledge of Charlotte; it is therefore but just that her conduct should in some measure be accounted for. She had ever been fully sensible of the superiority of Charlotte's sense and virtue; she was conscious that she had never swerved from rectitude, had it not been for her bad precepts and worse example. These were things as yet unknown to her husband, and she wished not to have that part of her conduct exposed to him, as she had great reason to fear she had already lost considerable part of that power she once maintained over him. She trembled whilst Charlotte was in the house, lest the Colonel should return; she perfectly well remembered how much he seemed interested in her favour whilst on their passage from England, and made no doubt, but, should he see her in her present distress, he would offer her an asylum, and protect her to the utmost of his power. In that case she feared the unguarded nature of Charlotte might discover to the Colonel the part she had taken in the unhappy girl's elopement, and she well knew the contrast between her own and Charlotte's conduct would make the former appear in no very respectable light. Had she reflected properly, she would have afforded the poor girl protection; and by enjoining her silence, ensured it by acts of repeated kindness; but vice in general blinds its votaries, and they discover their real characters to the world when they are most studious to preserve appearances.

Just so it happened with Mrs. Crayton: her servants made no scruple of mentioning the cruel conduct of their lady to a poor distressed lunatic who claimed her protection; every one joined in reprobating her inhumanity; nay even Corydon thought she might at least have ordered her to be taken care of, but he dare not even hint it to her, for he lived but in her smiles, and drew from her lavish fondness large sums to support an extravagance to which the state of his own finances was very inadequate; it cannot therefore be supposed that he wished Mrs. Crayton to be very liberal in her bounty to the afflicted suppliant; yet vice had not so entirely seared over his heart, but the sorrows of Charlotte could find a vulnerable part.

Charlotte had now been three days with her humane preservers, but she was totally insensible of every thing: she raved incessantly for Montraville and her father: she was not conscious of being a mother, nor took the least notice of her child except to ask whose it was, and why it was not carried to its parents.

"Oh," said she one day, starting up on hearing the infant cry, "why, why will you keep that child here; I am sure you would not if you knew how hard it was for a mother to be parted from her infant: it is like tearing the cords of life asunder. Oh could you see the horrid sight which I now behold—there—there stands my dear mother, her poor bosom bleeding at every vein, her gentle, affectionate

---

1. Surgeon: doctor; bled her: it was still believed well into the nineteenth century that drawing blood could cure sickness.

heart torn in a thousand pieces, and all for the loss of a ruined, ungrateful child. Save me—save me—from her frown. I dare not—indeed I dare not speak to her."

Such were the dreadful images that haunted her distracted mind, and nature was sinking fast under the dreadful malady which medicine had no power to remove. The surgeon who attended her was a humane man; he exerted his utmost abilities to save her, but he saw she was in want of many necessaries and comforts, which the poverty of her hospitable host rendered him unable to provide: he therefore determined to make her situation known to some of the officers' ladies, and endeavour to make a collection for her relief.

When he returned home, after making this resolution, he found a message from Mrs. Beauchamp, who had just arrived from Rhode-Island, requesting he would call and see one of her children, who was very unwell. "I do not know," said he, as he was hastening to obey the summons, "I do not know a woman to whom I could apply with more hope of success than Mrs. Beauchamp. I will endeavour to interest her in this poor girl's behalf; she wants the soothing balm of friendly consolation: we may perhaps save her; we will try at least."

"And where is she," cried Mrs. Beauchamp when he had prescribed something for the child, and told his little pathetic tale, "where is she, Sir? we will go to her immediately. Heaven forbid that I should be deaf to the calls of humanity. Come we will go this instant." Then seizing the doctor's arm, they sought the habitation that contained the dying Charlotte.

CHAPTER XXXIII
WHICH PEOPLE VOID OF FEELING NEED NOT READ

When Mrs. Beauchamp entered the apartment of the poor sufferer, she started back with horror. On a wretched bed, without hangings and but poorly supplied with covering, lay the emaciated figure of what still retained the semblance of a lovely woman, though sickness had so altered her features that Mrs. Beauchamp had not the least recollection of her person. In one corner of the room stood a woman washing, and, shivering over a small fire, two healthy but half naked children; the infant was asleep beside its mother, and, on a chair by the bed side, stood a porrenger[2] and wooden spoon, containing a little gruel, and a tea-cup with about two spoonfuls of wine in it. Mrs. Beauchamp had never before beheld such a scene of poverty; she shuddered involuntarily, and exclaiming—"heaven preserve us!" leaned on the back of a chair ready to sink to the earth. The doctor repented having so precipitately brought her into this affecting scene; but there was no time for apologies: Charlotte caught the sound of her voice, and starting almost out of bed, exclaimed—"Angel of peace and mercy, art thou come to deliver me? Oh, I know you are, for whenever you was near me I felt eased of half my sorrows; but you don't know me, nor can I, with all the recollection I am mistress of, remember your name just now, but I know that benevolent countenance, and the softness of that voice which has so often comforted the wretched Charlotte."

Mrs. Beauchamp had, during the time Charlotte was speaking, seated herself on the bed and taken one of her hands; she looked at her attentively, and at the name of Charlotte she perfectly conceived the whole shocking affair. A faint sickness came over her. "Gracious heaven," said she, "is this possible?" and bursting into tears, she reclined the burning head of Charlotte on her own bosom; and

2. Porringer: a bowl with a handle.

folding her arms about her, wept over her in silence. "Oh," said Charlotte, "you are very good to weep thus for me: it is a long time since I shed a tear for myself: my head and heart are both on fire, but these tears of your's seem to cool and refresh it. Oh now I remember you said you would send a letter to my poor father: do you think he ever received it? or perhaps you have brought me an answer: why don't you speak, Madam? Does he say I may go home? Well he is very good; I shall soon be ready."

She then made an effort to get out of bed; but being prevented, her frenzy again returned, and she raved with the greatest wildness and incoherence. Mrs. Beauchamp, finding it was impossible for her to be removed, contented herself with ordering the apartment to be made more comfortable, and procuring a proper nurse for both mother and child; and having learnt the particulars of Charlotte's fruitless application to Mrs. Crayton from honest John, she amply rewarded him for his benevolence, and returned home with a heart oppressed with many painful sensations, but yet rendered easy by the reflexion that she had performed her duty towards a distressed fellow-creature.

Early the next morning she again visited Charlotte, and found her tolerably composed; she called her by name, thanked her for her goodness, and when her child was brought to her, pressed it in her arms, wept over it, and called it the offspring of disobedience. Mrs. Beauchamp was delighted to see her so much amended, and began to hope she might recover, and, spite of her former errors, become an useful and respectable member of society; but the arrival of the doctor put an end to these delusive hopes: he said nature was making her last effort, and a few hours would most probably consign the unhappy girl to her kindred dust.

Being asked how she found herself, she replied—"Why better, much better, doctor. I hope now I have but little more to suffer. I had last night a few hours sleep, and when I awoke recovered the full power of recollection. I am quite sensible of my weakness; I feel I have but little longer to combat with the shafts of affliction. I have an humble confidence in the mercy of him who died to save the world, and trust that my sufferings in this state of mortality, joined to my unfeigned repentance, through his mercy, have blotted my offences from the sight of my offended maker. I have but one care—my poor infant! Father of mercy," continued she, raising her eyes, "of thy infinite goodness, grant that the sins of the parent be not visited on the unoffending child. May those who taught me to despise thy laws be forgiven; lay not my offences to their charge, I beseech thee; and oh! shower the choicest of thy blessings on those whose pity has soothed the afflicted heart, and made easy even the bed of pain and sickness."

She was exhausted by this fervent address to the throne of mercy, and though her lips still moved her voice became inarticulate: she lay for some time as it were in a doze, and then recovering, faintly pressed Mrs. Beauchamp's hand, and requested that a clergyman might be sent for.

On his arrival she joined fervently in the pious office,[3] frequently mentioning her ingratitude to her parents as what lay most heavy at her heart. When she had performed the last solemn duty, and was preparing to lie down, a little bustle on the outside door occasioned Mrs. Beauchamp to open it, and enquire the cause. A man in appearance about forty, presented himself, and asked for Mrs. Beauchamp.

"That is my name, Sir," said she.

---

3. Pious office: the task of spiritually preparing herself for death.

"Oh then, my dear Madam," cried he, "tell me where I may find my poor, ruined, but repentant child."

Mrs. Beauchamp was surprised and affected; she knew not what to say; she foresaw the agony this interview would occasion Mr. Temple, who had just arrived in search of his Charlotte, and yet was sensible that the pardon and blessing of her father would soften even the agonies of death to the daughter.

She hesitated. "Tell me, Madam," cried he wildly, "tell me, I beseech thee, does she live? shall I see my darling once again? Perhaps she is in this house. Lead, lead me to her, that I may bless her, and then lie down and die."

The ardent manner in which he uttered these words occasioned him to raise his voice. It caught the ear of Charlotte: she knew the beloved sound: and uttering a loud shriek, she sprang forward as Mr. Temple entered the room. "My adored father." "My long lost child." Nature could support no more, and they both sunk lifeless[4] into the arms of the attendants.

Charlotte was again put into bed, and a few moments restored Mr. Temple: but to describe the agony of his sufferings is past the power of any one, who, though they may readily conceive, cannot delineate the dreadful scene. Every eye gave testimony of what each heart felt—but all were silent.

When Charlotte recovered, she found herself supported in her father's arms. She cast on him a most expressive look, but was unable to speak. A reviving cordial was administered. She then asked, in a low voice, for her child: it was brought to her: she put it in her father's arms. "Protect her," said she, "and bless your dying—"

Unable to finish the sentence, she sunk back on her pillow: her countenance was serenely composed; she regarded her father as he pressed the infant to his breast with a steadfast look; a sudden beam of joy passed across her languid features, she raised her eyes to heaven—and then closed them for ever.

CHAPTER XXXIV
RETRIBUTION

In the mean time Montraville having received orders to return to New-York, arrived, and having still some remains of compassionate tenderness for the woman whom he regarded as brought to shame by himself, he went out in search of Belcour, to enquire whether she was safe, and whether the child lived. He found him immersed in dissipation, and could gain no other intelligence than that Charlotte had left him, and that he knew not what was become of her.

"I cannot believe it possible," said Montraville, "that a mind once so pure as Charlotte Temple's, should so suddenly become the mansion of vice. Beware, Belcour," continued he, "beware if you have dared to behave either unjust or dishonourably to that poor girl, your life shall pay the forfeit:—I will revenge her cause."

He immediately went into the country, to the house where he had left Charlotte. It was desolate. After much enquiry he at length found the servant girl who had lived with her. From her he learnt the misery Charlotte had endured from the complicated evils of illness, poverty, and a broken heart, and that she had set out on foot for New-York, on a cold winter's evening; but she could inform him no further.

Tortured almost to madness by this shocking account, he returned to the city, but, before he reached it, the evening was drawing to a close. In entering the town he was obliged to pass several little huts, the residence of poor women who sup-

---

4. In a faint, unconscious.

ported themselves by washing the cloaths of the officers and soldiers. It was nearly dark: he heard from a neighbouring steeple a solemn toll that seemed to say some poor mortal was going to their last mansion: the sound struck on the heart of Montraville, and he involuntarily stopped, when, from one of the houses, he saw the appearance of a funeral. Almost unknowing what he did, he followed at a small distance; and as they let the coffin into the grave, he enquired of a soldier who stood by, and had just brushed off a tear that did honour to his heart, who it was that was just buried. "An please[5] your honour," said the man, "'tis a poor girl that was brought from her friends by a cruel man, who left her when she was big with child, and married another." Montraville stood motionless, and the man proceeded—"I met her myself not a fortnight since one night all wet and cold in the streets; she went to Madam Crayton's, but she would not take her in, and so the poor thing went raving mad." Montraville could bear no more; he struck his hands against his forehead with violence; and exclaiming "poor murdered Charlotte!" ran with precipitation towards the place where they were heaping the earth on her remains. "Hold, hold, one moment," said he. "Close not the grave of the injured Charlotte Temple till I have taken vengeance on her murderer."

"Rash young man," said Mr. Temple, "who art thou that thus disturbest the last mournful rites of the dead, and rudely breakest in upon the grief of an afflicted father."

"If thou art the father of Charlotte Temple," said he, gazing at him with mingled horror and amazement—"if thou art her father—I am Montraville." Then falling on his knees, he continued—"Here is my bosom. I bare it to receive the stroke I merit. Strike—strike now, and save me from the misery of reflexion."

"Alas!" said Mr. Temple, "if thou wert the seducer of my child, thy own reflexions be thy punishment. I wrest not the power from the hand of omnipotence. Look on that little heap of earth, there hast thou buried the only joy of a fond father. Look at it often; and may thy heart feel such true sorrow as shall merit the mercy of heaven." He turned from him; and Montraville starting up from the ground, where he had thrown himself, and at that instant remembering the perfidy of Belcour, flew like lightning to his lodgings. Belcour was intoxicated; Montraville impetuous: they fought, and the sword of the latter entered the heart of his adversary. He fell, and expired almost instantly. Montraville had received a slight wound; and overcome with the agitation of his mind and loss of blood, was carried in a state of insensibility to his distracted wife. A dangerous illness and obstinate delirium ensued, during which he raved incessantly for Charlotte: but a strong constitution, and the tender assiduities of Julia, in time overcame the disorder. He recovered; but to the end of his life was subject to severe fits of melancholy, and while he remained at New-York frequently retired to the church-yard, where he would weep over the grave, and regret the untimely fate of the lovely Charlotte Temple.

CHAPTER XXXV

CONCLUSION

Shortly after the interment of his daughter, Mr. Temple, with his dear little charge and her nurse, set forward for England. It would be impossible to do justice to the meeting scene between him, his Lucy, and her aged father. Every heart of sensibility can easily conceive their feelings. After the first tumult of grief was subsided,

---

5. If it please.

Mrs. Temple gave up the chief of her time to her grand-child, and as she grew up and improved, began to almost fancy she again possessed her Charlotte.

It was about ten years after these painful events, that Mr. and Mrs. Temple, having buried their father, were obliged to come to London on particular business, and brought the little Lucy with them. They had been walking one evening, when on their return they found a poor wretch sitting on the steps of the door. She attempted to rise as they approached, but from extreme weakness was unable, and after several fruitless efforts fell back in a fit. Mr. Temple was not one of those men who stand to consider whether by assisting an object in distress they shall not inconvenience themselves, but instigated by the impulse of a noble feeling heart, immediately ordered her to be carried into the house, and proper restoratives applied.

She soon recovered; and fixing her eyes on Mrs. Temple, cried—"You know not, Madam, what you do; you know not whom you are relieving, or you would curse me in the bitterness of your heart. Come not near me, Madam, I shall contaminate you. I am the viper that stung your peace. I am the woman who turned the poor Charlotte out to perish in the street. Heaven have mercy! I see her now," continued she looking at Lucy; "such, such was the fair bud of innocence that my vile arts blasted ere it was half blown."

It was in vain that Mr. and Mrs. Temple intreated her to be composed and to take some refreshment. She only drank half a glass of wine; and then told them that she had been separated from her husband seven years, the chief of which she had passed in riot, dissipation, and vice, till, overtaken by poverty and sickness, she had been reduced to part with every valuable, and thought only of ending her life in a prison; when a benevolent friend paid her debts and released her; but that her illness encreasing, she had no possible means of supporting herself, and her friends were weary of relieving her. "I have fasted," said she, "two days, and last night lay my aching head on the cold pavement: indeed it was but just that I should experience those miseries myself which I had unfeelingly inflicted on others."

Greatly as Mr. Temple had reason to detest Mrs. Crayton, he could not behold her in this distress without some emotions of pity. He gave her shelter that night beneath his hospitable roof, and the next day got her admission into an hospital; where having lingered a few weeks, she died, a striking example that vice, however prosperous in the beginning, in the end leads only to misery and shame.

1791?   1794

CULTURAL COORDINATES
The Corset, or,
Why Heroines Faint So Often

Charlotte Temple frequently "shrieks and falls senseless" onto the floor or into the arms of other people. While the sentimental heroine's heightened "sensibility," or emotional sensitivity, is one explanation for her continually slipping into unconsciousness, a tight-laced corset also might have contributed to her inability to breathe under stress.

Middle-class and upper-class English women wore corsets to enforce and emphasize a particular idea of the female form. Tight stays—stiff supports firmly laced together—dominated later-eighteenth-century fashion, fell out of favor at the turn of the century (when the high-waisted Empire dresses of Jane Austen's era allowed a more natural profile), and came back strong in the Victorian period, a time when gender roles were strictly differentiated in the public and private spheres. The visual difference between male and female bodies was made more obvious by the enhanced breasts, small waist, and broadened yet nearly invisible hips of the corseted figure.

Corsets evolved from stays in the 1820s and 1830s. Stiffened with metal or whalebone and made of cotton, satin, cashmere, silk, or leather lined with muslin, corsets were usually fastened with hooks in front and were tightened at the back with crisscrossed laces that tied at the bottom. Pregnant women wore corsets until they could no longer fasten them; after that, they could not appear in polite

Thomson's New Styles
Glove-Fitting Corset.

All Infringers of our Patents, or of our Copyright

in Names, Will be Prosecuted.

THE VENTILATING OR SUMMER CORSET.
Entirely NEW in Style and Perfect in Shape.
The **Curvilinear**, rich and elegant in finish.
Also, a lower cost "**Glove-Fitting**" than ever before offered; which, with our former regular qualities, make the assortment complete.
These justly celebrated PATENT GLOVE-FITTING CORSETS are constantly gaining favor in the United States as well as in foreign countries.
Always ask for **Thomson's** GENUINE GLOVE-FITTING, every Corset being Stamped.
THOMSON, LANGDON, & CO.,
Sole Patentees, 391 BROADWAY, N. Y.

An 1871 advertisement shows the tight-laced hourglass figure that dominated European and American fashion throughout the nineteenth century. This corset is designed for summer wear, a further reminder of how uncomfortable stylish ladies always had to be.

company until their "confinement" ended. Little girls began wearing simple corsets at the age of eight or ten.

From the 1840s to the 1890s, the ideal waist measurement for a fashionable woman ranged between seventeen and twenty-one inches. Although health and etiquette manuals warned against the dangers of lacing too tightly, young women would risk displacement of ribs and organs to achieve the physical ideal. Add to this that the definition of "exercise" for young women in the first half of the nineteenth century was walking demurely or riding horseback—side-saddle, of course—and the swooning heroine's inability to catch her breath is less remarkable.

Considering how quietly she lived, Jane Austen has become quite a celebrity since her death. A cult of personality, informally known as the "Janeites," developed in the past century among fans of her novels, and they meet in regular conferences of the Jane Austen Society to discuss details and recite well-loved passages from her six novels, as well as to hear scholars present new research on their idol. More recently, several popular movies and television miniseries have been based on her novels. While Janeites and movie fans tend to think of their favorite author as "gentle Jane," academic critics in the earlier part of the twentieth century considered Austen's tone one of "regulated hatred," as male critic D. W. Harding called it. At first chastised by feminist critics for letting each of her heroines "dwindle into a wife," Austen is now more frequently embraced for her feminist conception of intelligent, independent-minded heroines who do their best to find a suitable place for themselves in the oppressively patriarchal world of upper-middle-class England in the early nineteenth century.

Austen was born into that world on December 16, 1775, in Steventon, England. She was the seventh child (of eight) and the second daughter of a clergyman, George Austen, and his wife, Cassandra Leigh Austen, and she grew up in the rectory in that Hampshire village. Austen's early schooling included a brief stay at a boarding school and a longer attendance at another school in nearby Reading. As a woman, she had no access to university, but she rounded out her education by means of her father's excellent library. Throughout her life, Austen enjoyed close relations with her siblings, especially Henry and Cassandra—her only sister and most intimate friend—with whom she often corresponded when away from home. (Later, she appears to have been beloved by an extended circle of nieces and nephews.)

Austen was raised as a member of the "gentry," that class of well-born Englishmen just below the nobility. While the gentry did not inherit titles or hold impressive estates, a gentleman usually owned enough property to enable him to live at least partly on interest and rents. Because he did not need to earn all his living, a gentleman and his family enjoyed relative financial privilege. That said, Austen herself did not live an extraordinarily privileged life. While George Austen was alive, the Austen family lived in quiet simplicity among a wide circle of wealthier relatives and acquaintances. When her father died in 1805, leaving his wife and daughters an income of £210 per year (roughly the equivalent of $23,000 today), the Austen women often had to be helped by family and friends.

In 1801, Austen left Steventon and moved with her parents and Cassandra to Bath, a city with which she remains associated today, though she would not likely have taken much pleasure in the association: family lore recounts that she fainted when she heard the news that her father planned to move from the countryside she loved so well to the bustling, urban resort town. After her father died, she left Bath (with her mother and sister), eventually settling in a cottage on her brother Edward's estate in Chawton. (Edward had been adopted by wealthy childless relations and made their heir.) Edward's patronage made it possible for the widowed Mrs. Austen and her two unmarried daughters to live comfortably.

Jane Austen remained at Chawton for the rest of her life, except for brief visits to family members in London. She died in 1817, perhaps from Addison's disease, an endocrine disorder that was then incurable. Austen never married, though her biography (written by her nephew J. E. Austen-Leigh) mentions several love interests, including a clergyman who died and a younger man from whom she accepted a proposal, only to change her mind the next day. Biographers have long regretted her sister, Cassandra's, decision to destroy much of Jane's correspondence after her death, as the letters that remain—full of domestic detail and gossip—provide very little insight into Austen's personal relationships or romances.

Austen's writing career began at around age eleven, with her family members as audience and critics. Her earliest works (or *juvenilia*), including *Love and Freindship* (c. 1790; Austen's spelling) and *The History of England* (c. 1792), are spoofs of popular romance novels and of historical writing. In this period, she may also have written drafts of her first two published novels—*Sense and Sensibility* and *Pride and Prejudice*—in epistolary form, revealing the plot in letters exchanged among the characters as in Samuel Richardson's popular novels *Pamela* (1740) and *Clarissa* (1748).

As she grew interested in publishing, her father and brothers supported her efforts and carried out the transactions. At first she published her works anonymously—signed "by a Lady"—but her brothers' pride in her success soon led them to reveal her secret to the reading public. Her first attempt at publication in 1795 was unsuccessful. A second novel was bought but never published. Finally, *Sense and Sensibility* was published in 1811, followed by *Pride and Prejudice* (1813), *Mansfield Park* (1814), and *Emma* (1816). *Northanger Abbey* and *Persuasion* were published in 1818 after her death. We might find it difficult to imagine the literary canon without Austen, but in fact her reputation took a long time to establish itself. Despite favorable notice for her published works, Austen did not receive much public or critical acclaim until well into the twentieth century.

Of Jane Austen's six completed novels, *Northanger Abbey* (1818) is the one she spent the most years revising. Published posthumously, it is her most satirical work and her most explicit statement on literature. From the beginning, the narrator presents Catherine Moreland as an anti-heroine in an anti-romance, a perfectly ordinary middle-class girl from the English countryside whose life up to the age of fifteen has been utterly unremarkable. Given the chance to visit the fashionable English resort town Bath with her parents' friends Mr. and Mrs. Allen, Catherine—whose expectations about life, shaped by romance novels, have so far been disappointed—accepts with delight. Although the narrator repeatedly denies that Catherine is a heroine, Catherine thinks of herself as one and always interprets people and situations as if they were characters from her favorite books. Eventually her tendency to project romantic fantasies onto real people threatens to ruin her future happiness, but in the scene we have excerpted, she is still cheerfully oblivious to the differences between life and romantic fiction. The first young man she meets in Bath is Mr. Henry Tilney, a charming single clergyman introduced to her by the master of ceremonies at a public dance. Immediately Mr. Tilney becomes the hero of Catherine's imaginary novel. Throughout *Northanger Abbey* the narrator comments on ways in which Austen's novel departs from the conventions of the kind of romance fiction Catherine has in mind.

In her novels, Austen characteristically concentrated on "three or four families in a country village," as she wrote in a letter to a niece. These families were usually of the gentry, like her own, or occasionally somewhat higher. She also described her work (in a letter to a nephew) as "a small square two inches of ivory." But it would be a mistake to underestimate how well she uses this circumscribed subject matter to tease out much larger gender, social, and political themes. Her novels inevitably raise profound questions concerning women's social and economic lives, the English system of primogeniture (the practice of passing down the estate to the oldest son), the evolving nature of the English class structure, and even—as has been most recently argued—the relationship of England to the slave trade.

The novel *Pride and Prejudice*, 1813, appears in full in the Library of Women's Literature.

From Northanger Abbey

[Catherine and Isabella Become Friends]

CHAPTER 4

With more than usual eagerness did Catherine hasten to the Pumproom[1] the next day, secure within herself of seeing Mr Tilney there before the morning were over, and ready to meet him with a smile:—but no smile was demanded—Mr Tilney did not appear. Every creature in Bath, except himself, was to be seen in the room at different periods of the fashionable hours; crowds of people were every moment passing in and out, up the steps and down; people whom nobody cared about, and nobody wanted to see; and he only was absent. "What a delightful place Bath is," said Mrs Allen, as they sat down near the great clock,[2] after parading the room till they were tired; "and how pleasant it would be if we had any acquaintance here."

This sentiment had been uttered so often in vain, that Mrs Allen had no particular reason to hope it would be followed with more advantage now; but we are told to "despair of nothing we would attain," as "unwearied diligence our point would gain;"[3] and the unwearied diligence with which she had every day wished for the same thing was at length to have its just reward, for hardly had she been seated ten minutes before a lady of about her own age, who was sitting by her, and had been looking at her attentively for several minutes, addressed her with great complaisance in these words:—"I think, madam, I cannot be mistaken; it is a long time since I had the pleasure of seeing you, but is not your name Allen?" This question answered, as it readily was, the stranger pronounced her's to be Thorpe; and Mrs Allen immediately recognized the features of a former schoolfellow and intimate, whom she had seen only once since their respective marriages, and that many years ago. Their joy on this meeting was very great, as well it might, since they had been contented to know nothing of each other for the last fifteen years. Compliments on good looks now passed; and, after observing how time

1. In Bath, the public facility next to the ruins of Roman baths. Guests drank water pumped from the hot spring, believing it to be beneficial to health.
2. Famous eighteenth-century clockmaker Thomas Tompion built and presented to Bath a combination clock and sundial, displayed in the Pump Room.
3. A version of this couplet appeared in Thomas Dyche's *A Guide to the English Tongue* (1707), which contained sayings for children to copy and learn; according to scholar Deirdre Le Faye, a version closer to Austen's appears on a child's needlework sampler from 1794.

had slipped away since they were last together, how little they had thought of meeting in Bath, and what a pleasure it was to see an old friend, they proceeded to make inquiries and give intelligence as to their families, sisters, and cousins, talking both together, far more ready to give than to receive information, and each hearing very little of what the other said. Mrs Thorpe, however, had one great advantage as a talker, over Mrs Allen, in a family of children; and when she expatiated on the talents of her sons, and the beauty of her daughters,—when she related their different situations and views,—that John was at Oxford, Edward at Merchant Taylors',[4] and William at sea,—and all of them more beloved and respected in their different station than any other three beings ever were, Mrs Allen had no similar information to give, no similar triumphs to press on the unwilling and unbelieving ear of her friend, and was forced to sit and appear to listen to all these maternal effusions, consoling herself, however, with the discovery, which her keen eye soon made, that the lace on Mrs Thorpe's pelisse was not half so handsome as that on her own.

"Here come my dear girls," cried Mrs Thorpe, pointing at three smart looking females, who, arm in arm, were then moving towards her. "My dear Mrs Allen, I long to introduce them; they will be so delighted to see you: the tallest is Isabella, my eldest; is not she a fine young woman? The others are very much admired too, but I believe Isabella is the handsomest."

The Miss Thorpes were introduced; and Miss Morland, who had been for a short time forgotten, was introduced likewise. The name seemed to strike them all; and, after speaking to her with great civility, the eldest young lady observed aloud to the rest, "How excessively like her brother Miss Morland is!"

"The very picture of him indeed!" cried the mother—and "I should have known her any where for his sister!" was repeated by them all, two or three times over. For a moment Catherine was surprized; but Mrs Thorpe and her daughters had scarcely begun the history of their acquaintance with Mr James Morland, before she remembered that her eldest brother had lately formed an intimacy with a young man of his own college, of the name of Thorpe; and that he had spent the last week of the Christmas vacation with his family, near London.

The whole being explained, many obliging things were said by the Miss Thorpes of their wish of being better acquainted with her; of being considered as already friends, through the friendship of their brothers, &c. which Catherine heard with pleasure, and answered with all the pretty expressions she could command; and, as the first proof of amity, she was soon invited to accept an arm of the eldest Miss Thorpe, and take a turn with her about the room. Catherine was delighted with this extension of her Bath acquaintance, and almost forgot Mr Tilney while she talked to Miss Thorpe. Friendship is certainly the finest balm for the pangs of disappointed love.

Their conversation turned upon those subjects, of which the free discussion has generally much to do in perfecting a sudden intimacy between two young ladies; such as dress, balls, flirtations, and quizzes.[5] Miss Thorpe, however, being four years older than Miss Morland, and at least four years better informed, had a very decided advantage in discussing such points; she could compare the balls of

---

4. Founded in the sixteenth century, Merchant Taylors' School was one of the earliest public schools for boys established in London.

5. Individuals singled out from a crowd for ridicule.

Bath with those of Tunbridge;[6] its fashions with the fashions of London; could rectify the opinions of her new friend in many articles of tasteful attire; could discover a flirtation between any gentleman and lady who only smiled on each other; and point out a quiz through the thickness of a crowd. These powers received due admiration from Catherine, to whom they were entirely new; and the respect which they naturally inspired might have been too great for familiarity, had not the easy gaiety of Miss Thorpe's manners, and her frequent expressions of delight on this acquaintance with her, softened down every feeling of awe, and left nothing but tender affection. Their increasing attachment was not to be satisfied with half a dozen turns in the Pump-room, but required, when they all quitted it together, that Miss Thorpe should accompany Miss Morland to the very door of Mr Allen's house; and that they should there part with a most affectionate and lengthened shake of hands, after learning, to their mutual relief, that they should see each other across the theatre at night, and say their prayers in the same chapel the next morning. Catherine then ran directly up stairs, and watched Miss Thorpe's progress down the street from the drawing-room window; admired the graceful spirit of her walk, the fashionable air of her figure and dress; and felt grateful, as well she might, for the chance which had procured her such a friend.

Mrs Thorpe was a widow, and not a very rich one; she was a good-humoured, well-meaning woman, and a very indulgent mother. Her eldest daughter had great personal beauty, and the younger ones, by pretending to be as handsome as their sister, imitating her air, and dressing in the same style, did very well.

This brief account of the family is intended to supersede the necessity of a long and minute detail from Mrs Thorpe herself, of her past adventures and sufferings, which might otherwise be expected to occupy the three or four following chapters; in which the worthlessness of lords and attornies might be set forth, and conversations, which had passed twenty years before, be minutely repeated.

CHAPTER 5

Catherine was not so much engaged at the theatre that evening, in returning the nods and smiles of Miss Thorpe, though they certainly claimed much of her leisure, as to forget to look with an inquiring eye for Mr Tilney in every box which her eye could reach; but she looked in vain. Mr Tilney was no fonder of the play than the Pump-room. She hoped to be more fortunate the next day; and when her wishes for fine weather were answered by seeing a beautiful morning, she hardly felt a doubt of it; for a fine Sunday in Bath empties every house of its inhabitants, and all the world appears on such an occasion to walk about and tell their acquaintance what a charming day it is.

As soon as divine service was over, the Thorpes and Allens eagerly joined each other; and after staying long enough in the Pump-room to discover that the crowd was insupportable, and that there was not a genteel face to be seen, which everybody discovers every Sunday throughout the season, they hastened away to the Crescent,[7] to breathe the fresh air of better company. Here Catherine and Isabella, arm in arm, again tasted the sweets of friendship in an unreserved conversation;— they talked much, and with much enjoyment; but again was Catherine disappointed

6. Tunbridge Wells is another British spa town, offering balls, concerts, and theater for visitors' entertainment.

7. A popular destination for walks, the Royal Crescent is an arc of thirty townhouses arranged as a half-coliseum.

in her hope of re-seeing her partner. He was no where to be met with; every search for him was equally unsuccessful, in morning lounges or evening assemblies; neither at the upper nor lower rooms, at dressed or undressed balls,[8] was he perceivable; nor among the walkers, the horsemen, or the curricle-drivers[9] of the morning. His name was not in the Pump-room book,[1] and curiosity could do no more. He must be gone from Bath. Yet he had not mentioned that his stay would be so short! This sort of mysteriousness, which is always so becoming in a hero, threw a fresh grace in Catherine's imagination around his person and manners, and increased her anxiety to know more of him. From the Thorpes she could learn nothing, for they had been only two days in Bath before they met with Mrs Allen. It was a subject, however, in which she often indulged with her fair friend, from whom she received every possible encouragement to continue to think of him; and his impression on her fancy was not suffered therefore to weaken. Isabella was very sure that he must be a charming young man; and was equally sure that he must have been delighted with her dear Catherine, and would therefore shortly return. She liked him the better for being a clergyman, "for she must confess herself very partial to the profession;" and something like a sigh escaped her as she said it. Perhaps Catherine was wrong in not demanding the cause of that gentle emotion—but she was not experienced enough in the finesse of love, or the duties of friendship, to know when delicate raillery was properly called for, or when a confidence should be forced.

Mrs Allen was now quite happy—quite satisfied with Bath. She had found some acquaintance, had been so lucky too as to find in them the family of a most worthy old friend; and, as the completion of good fortune, had found these friends by no means so expensively dressed as herself. Her daily expressions were no longer, "I wish we had some acquaintance in Bath!" They were changed into— "How glad I am we have met with Mrs Thorpe!"—and she was as eager in promoting the intercourse of the two families, as her young charge and Isabella themselves could be; never satisfied with the day unless she spent the chief of it by the side of Mrs Thorpe, in what they called conversation, but in which there was scarcely ever any exchange of opinion, and not often any resemblance of subject, for Mrs Thorpe talked chiefly of her children, and Mrs Allen of her gowns.

The progress of the friendship between Catherine and Isabella was quick as its beginning had been warm, and they passed so rapidly through every gradation of increasing tenderness, that there was shortly no fresh proof of it to be given to their friends or themselves. They called each other by their Christian name, were always arm in arm when they walked, pinned up each other's train for the dance, and were not to be divided in the set;[2] and if a rainy morning deprived them of other enjoyments, they were still resolute in meeting in defiance of wet and dirt, and shut themselves up, to read novels together. Yes, novels;—for I will not adopt that ungenerous and impolitic custom so common with novel writers, of degrading by their contemptuous censure the very performances, to the number of which

8. The Upper Rooms and Lower Rooms contained reception and concert halls; a dressed ball required formal attire, while one could wear less elaborate clothing to an undressed ball.
9. Curricle: a small, two-person carriage with two large wheels drawn by a pair of horses, popular among dashing young men.
1. Guests signed in at the Pump Room each day

they visited.
2. Their close friendship is signaled by their saying "Catherine" and "Isabella," not "Miss"; their helping each other fasten up the long backs of their skirts at dances; and their insisting during balls on being always next to each other in the line of dancers.

they are themselves adding—joining with their greatest enemies in bestowing the harshest epithets on such works, and scarcely ever permitting them to be read by their own heroine, who, if she accidentally take up a novel, is sure to turn over its insipid pages with disgust. Alas! If the heroine of one novel be not patronized by the heroine of another, from whom can she expect protection and regard? I cannot approve of it. Let us leave it to the Reviewers to abuse such effusions of fancy at their leisure, and over every new novel to talk in threadbare strains of the trash with which the press now groans. Let us not desert one another; we are an injured body. Although our productions have afforded more extensive and unaffected pleasure than those of any other literary corporation in the world, no species of composition has been so much decried. From pride, ignorance, or fashion, our foes are almost as many as our readers. And while the abilities of the nine-hundredth abridger of the History of England,[3] or of the man who collects and publishes in a volume some dozen lines of Milton, Pope, and Prior, with a paper from the Spectator, and a chapter from Sterne,[4] are eulogized by a thousand pens,—there seems almost a general wish of decrying the capacity and undervaluing the labour of the novelist, and of slighting the performances which have only genius, wit, and taste to recommend them. "I am no novel reader—I seldom look into novels—Do not imagine that I often read novels—It is really very well for a novel."—Such is the common cant.—"And what are you reading, Miss—?" "Oh! it is only a novel!" replies the young lady; while she lays down her book with affected indifference, or momentary shame.—"It is only Cecilia, or Camilla, or Belinda;"[5] or, in short, only some work in which the greatest powers of the mind are displayed, in which the most thorough knowledge of human nature, the happiest delineation of its varieties, the liveliest effusions of wit and humour, are conveyed to the world in the best chosen language. Now, had the same young lady been engaged with a volume of the Spectator, instead of such a work, how proudly would she have produced the book, and told its name; though the chances must be against her being occupied by any part of that voluminous publication, of which either the matter or manner would not disgust a young person of taste: the substance of its papers so often consisting in the statement of improbable circumstances, unnatural characters, and topics of conversation, which no longer concern any one living; and their language, too, frequently so coarse as to give no very favourable idea of the age that could endure it.

1818

3. Contemporary novels were popular culture; more respectable reading included The History of England (1771) by Oliver Goldsmith, abridged in 1774; or excerpts from John Milton, the author of Paradise Lost (1667); or eighteenth-century poets Alexander Pope and Matthew Prior.
4. Laurence Sterne serialized his novel Tristram

Shandy between 1759 and 1767; Joseph Addison and Richard Steele published The Spectator daily in 1711–12, reporting on social and literary news 100 years before Austen's time.
5. Recent novels by women: Frances Burney's Cecilia (1782) and Camilla (1796), and Maria Edgeworth's Belinda (1801).

CULTURAL COORDINATES
Cassandra's Sketch and "Gentle Jane"

Twenty-first-century readers who pay close attention to the voice that narrates Jane Austen's novels might wonder where the image of "gentle Jane"—as many of her nineteenth- and twentieth-century fans have called her—came from. The narrator of *Persuasion*, for instance, refers to Mrs. Musgrove's "large fat sighings over the destiny of a son, whom alive nobody had cared for." Admitting in an aside that "personal size and mental sorrow have certainly no necessary proportions," the narrator concludes that "fair or not fair, there are unbecoming conjunctions, which reason will patronize in vain,—which taste cannot tolerate,—which ridicule will seize." Witty (note the parallel structure of the final sentence), critical, even cruel: surely a "gentle Jane" would not speak this way about a mother's grief over her dead son. Nevertheless, Austen's narrator does speak this way, in *Persuasion* and in her other novels, which suggests that Janeites were responding to something other than Austen's texts when they thought about their favorite author.

"Gentle Jane" is, as feminist critic Margaret Kirkham has argued, a construction of the Victorian era, based partly on her nephew J. E. Austen-Leigh's highly idealized memoir of his aunt (1871) and partly on Victorian cultural anxieties about the potentially subversive power of critical, intellectual women. Kirkham has contrasted the only portrait made of Austen during her lifetime, a sketch by her sister, Cassandra, with a revised version of the portrait that was commissioned in 1869 by Austen-Leigh for the first edition of his memoir. Following conven-

(Left) Austen's sister, Cassandra's, drawing made during Austen's lifetime; (right) the 1869 steel engraving made to illustrate J. E. Austen-Leigh's memoir.

tions of beauty, fashion, and social class, the Victorian portraitist, "Mr. Andrews of Maidenhead," transforms Cassandra's sister into "gentle Jane."

In Cassandra's drawing, Austen sits with arms folded decisively and mouth turned downward into a perhaps amused, perhaps impatient or annoyed expression. Dark shadows under the eyes emphasize the sharpness of her gaze, which is mirrored by an angular jaw and chin. Her unruly hair pokes out from an informal cap, as if she has been interrupted in a household task to sit for this portrait. She perches on a kitchen chair, and looks ready to spring into action at any moment.

In Mr. Andrews's revision of the portrait, everything about Austen is softer, more passive. Her cheeks and chin are fuller, giving her a more youthful look; her rosebud mouth turns up in a pleasant half-smile. Her eyes, enlarged, dominate her face as would a child's. The hairstyle has not changed, but the cap is now demurely trimmed with frills, as are the sleeves and neckline of the dress. Her arms are invisible, and her hands appear to be calmly folded in her lap. The energy, assertiveness, maturity, and intelligence caught in Cassandra's original are smoothed down and rounded out, constructing a Jane Austen who better fits the Victorian norm of respectable femininity. This was the image of Austen most familiar to readers from 1870 until the last quarter of the twentieth century, when feminist critics began reading her novels more closely and recognizing in them the spirit of Cassandra's sketch.

CATHARINE MARIA SEDGWICK
1789–1867

Born in the same year that George Washington became the first president of the new United States of America, Catharine Maria Sedgwick became one of the founders of a distinctly American literature. Sedgwick was uniquely prepared for this role by her early life in western Massachusetts in a family whose members were intimately involved with the workings of the new nation. Her father, Theodore, served six terms in the U.S. Congress representing Massachusetts; her mother came from a family that would eventually include three presidents of Yale University. But her father's position entailed long absences from the family, and her mother was so disabled by the birth of ten children in nine years that she was only a weak presence in her own home. Even so, Sedgwick did have close relationships with her brothers and their families. She also benefited from the presence of a strong, nurturing adult, former slave Elizabeth Freeman, who served as the Sedgwicks' housekeeper. Freeman, whose legal suit for freedom initiated the abolition of slavery in Massachusetts, did as much as Congressman Sedgwick to initiate Sedgwick into an awareness of the challenges and promises of life in the new nation.

Sedgwick remained a single woman at a time when nine out of ten American women married. Eschewing a fixed residence of her own, she traveled frequently and became a connoisseur and critic of different attempts at "the domestic ideal." Sedgwick's popularity as a writer allowed her the means to travel not only within the United States and its territories but also to Europe.

As with her contemporaries Lydia Sigourney, Lydia Maria Child, and James Fenimore Cooper, Sedgwick's desire to support herself through her writing meant she had to invent her own role as a professional author. This required, most importantly, that she sell what she wrote, and Sedgwick did so by providing a literary commodity that spoke to the needs of a divergent audience. A prolific author, Sedgwick experimented with the full range of prose genres—novels, short stories, sketches, advice manuals, travelogues, religious tracts—but she was and is best known for her novels and short stories.

Sedgwick's topics, like her genre choices, are eclectic and democratic. Her protagonists tend to be the underdogs of society: the old maid, the young girl, the sailor, the Native American, the Catholic. (At its beginnings, the United States was largely Protestant.) Her most famous novel, *Hope Leslie* (1827), for example, is a historical romance set in colonial times featuring a Native American woman as the heroine. Her long and short fictions share a realistic style; they attend to the meaningful details that distinguish the cultures of particular times and places. Many of her works deploy gentle humor even as they offer almost anthropological accounts of American life. The story included here, "Cacoethes Scribendi" (1830), is affectionately ironic in its depiction of life for women in a New England village that was suffering a decline in economic and social vitality as the American frontiers opened up new opportunities for men.

Cacoethes Scribendi[1]

Glory and gain the industrious tribe provoke.[2]

—POPE

The little secluded and quiet village of H.[3] lies at no great distance from our "literary emporium." It was never remarked or remarkable for anything, save one mournful preeminence, to those who sojourned within its borders—it was duller even than common villages. The young men of the better class all emigrated. The most daring spirits adventured on the sea. Some went to Boston; some to the south; and some to the west; and left a community of women who lived like nuns, with the advantage of more liberty and fresh air, but without the consolation and excitement of a religious vow. Literally, there was not a single young gentleman in the village—nothing in manly shape to which these desperate circumstances could give the form and quality and use of a beau. Some dashing city blades, who once strayed from the turnpike to this sequestered spot, averred that the girls stared at them as if, like Miranda,[4] they would have exclaimed—

> "What is't? a spirit?
> Lord, how it looks about! Believe me, sir,
> It carries a brave form:—But 'tis a spirit."

A peculiar fatality hung over this devoted place. If death seized on either head of a family, he was sure to take the husband; every woman in H. was a widow or maiden; and it is a sad fact, that when the holiest office of the church[5] was celebrated, they were compelled to borrow deacons from an adjacent village. But, incredible as it may be, there was no great diminution of happiness in consequence of the absence of the nobler sex. Mothers were occupied with their children and housewifery, and the young ladies read their books with as much interest as if they had lovers to discuss them with, and worked their frills and capes[6] as diligently, and wore them as complacently, as if they were to be seen by manly eyes. Never were there pleasanter gatherings or parties (for that was the word even in their nomenclature) than those of the young girls of H. There was no mincing—no affectation—no hope of passing for what they were not—no envy of the pretty and fortunate—no insolent triumph over the plain and demure and neglected,—but all was good will and good humour. They were a pretty circle of girls—a garland of bright fresh flowers. Never were there more sparkling glances,—never sweeter smiles—nor more of them. Their present was all health and cheerfulness; and their future, not the gloomy perspective of dreary singleness, for somewhere in the passage of life they were sure to be mated. Most of the young men who had abandoned their native soil, as soon as

---

1. "Compulsion to write"; *cacoethes* is a Latinization of the Greek *kakoethes,* from *kakos* ("bad") and *ethos* ("habit"), connoting urge, itch, compulsion, mania.
2. From *The Dunciad* (1728; 2.33) by English poet Alexander Pope (1688–1744).
3. Use of the initial was a literary convention to suggest that the story was set in a real place.

4. Blade: a dashing young man; turnpike: a form of tollgate, also the roads with such gates; Miranda: character in Shakespeare's *The Tempest* (c. 1610), who speaks the lines (1.2.574–76) that follow.
5. Last rites.
6. They sewed elaborate, decorative, and fashionable details on their clothing.

they found themselves *getting along,* loyally returned to lay their fortunes at the feet of the companions of their childhood.

The girls made occasional visits to Boston, and occasional journeys to various parts of the country, for they were all enterprising and independent, and had the characteristic New England avidity for seizing a "privilege;" and in these various ways, to borrow a phrase of their good grandames, "a door was opened for them," and in due time they fulfilled the destiny of women.

We spoke strictly, and à la lettre,[7] when we said that in the village of H. there was not a single *beau.*[8] But on the outskirts of the town, at a pleasant farm, embracing hill and valley, upland and meadow land; in a neat house, looking to the south, with true economy of sunshine and comfort, and overlooking the prettiest winding stream that ever sent up its sparkling beauty to the eye, and flanked on the north by a rich maple grove, beautiful in spring and summer, and glorious in autumn, and the kindest defense in winter;—on this farm and in this house dwelt a youth, to fame unknown, but known and loved by every inhabitant of H., old and young, grave and gay, lively and severe. Ralph Hepburn was one of nature's favourites. He had a figure that would have adorned courts and cities; and a face that adorned human nature, for it was full of good humour, kind-heartedness, spirit, and intelligence; and driving the plough or wielding the scythe, his cheek flushed with manly and profitable exercise, he looked as if he had been moulded in a poet's fancy—as farmers look in Georgics and Pastorals.[9] His gifts were by no means all external. He wrote verses in every album in the village, and very pretty album verses they were, and numerous too—for the number of albums was equivalent to the whole female population. He was admirable at pencil sketches; and once with a little paint, the refuse of a house painting, he achieved an admirable portrait of his grandmother and her cat. There was, to be sure, a striking likeness between the two figures, but he was limited to the same colours for both; and besides, it was not out of nature, for the old lady and her cat had purred together in the chimney corner, till their physiognomies bore an obvious resemblance to each other. Ralph had a talent for music too. His voice was the sweetest of all the Sunday choir, and one would have fancied, from the bright eyes that were turned on him from the long line and double lines of treble and counter singers, that Ralph Hepburn was a note book, or that the girls listened with their eyes as well as their ears. Ralph did not restrict himself to psalmody. He had an ear so exquisitely susceptible to the "touches of sweet harmony,"[1] that he discovered, by the stroke of his axe, the musical capacities of certain species of wood, and he made himself a violin of chestnut, and drew strains from it, that if they could not create a soul under the ribs of death, could make the prettiest feet and the lightest hearts dance, an achievement far more to Ralph's taste than the aforesaid miracle. In short, it seemed as if nature, in her love of compensation, had showered on Ralph all the gifts that are usually diffused through a community of beaux. Yet Ralph was no prodigy; none of his talents were in excess, but all in moderate degree. No genius was ever so good humoured, so useful, so practical; and though, in his small and modest way, a Crichton,[2] he was not, like most universal geniuses, good for noth-

---

7. Literally.
8. Available, handsome young man.
9. Literary works that evoke agricultural or rural life; *The Georgics* were written by the Roman poet Virgil about 29 BCE, and pastoral works

focus on shepherds and shepherdesses.
1. From Shakespeare's play *The Merchant of Venice* (c. 1596; 5.1.65).
2. James Crichton (1560–82), a brilliant and learned Scottish adventurer and man of letters.

ing for any particular office in life. His farm was not a pattern farm—a prize farm for an agricultural society, but in wonderful order considering—his miscellaneous pursuits. He was the delight of his grandfather for his sagacity in hunting bees— the old man's favourite, in truth his only pursuit. He was so skilled in woodcraft that the report of his gun was as certain a signal of death as the tolling of a church bell. The fish always caught at his bait. He manufactured half his farming utensils, improved upon old inventions, and struck out some new ones; tamed partridges—the most untameable of all the feathered tribe; domesticated squirrels; rivalled Scheherazade[3] herself in telling stories, strange and long—the latter quality being essential at a country fireside; and, in short, Ralph made a perpetual holiday of a life of labour.

Every girl in the village street knew when Ralph's wagon or sleigh traversed it; indeed, there was scarcely a house to which the horses did not, as if by instinct, turn up while their master greeted its fair tenants. This state of affairs had continued for two winters and two summers since Ralph came to his majority and, by the death of his father, to the sole proprietorship of the "Hepburn farm,"—the name his patrimonial acres had obtained from the singular circumstance (in our *moving* country) of their having remained in the same family for four generations. Never was the matrimonial destiny of a young lord, or heir just come to his estate, more thoroughly canvassed than young Hepburn's by mothers, aunts, daughters, and nieces. But Ralph, perhaps from sheer good heartedness, seemed reluctant to give to one the heart that diffused rays of sunshine through the whole village.

With all decent people he eschewed the doctrines of a certain erratic female lecturer on the odious monopoly of marriage, yet Ralph, like a tender hearted judge, hesitated to place on a single brow the crown matrimonial which so many deserved, and which, though Ralph was far enough from a coxcomb, he could not but see so many coveted.

Whether our hero perceived that his mind was becoming elated or distracted with this general favour, or that he observed a dawning of rivalry among the fair competitors, or whatever was the cause, the fact was, that he by degrees circumscribed his visits, and finally concentrated them in the family of his aunt Courland.

Mrs Courland was a widow, and Ralph was the kindest of nephews to her, and the kindest of cousins to her children. To their mother he seemed their guardian angel. That the five lawless, daring little urchins did not drown themselves when they were swimming, nor shoot themselves when they were shooting, was, in her eyes, Ralph's merit; and then "he was so attentive to Alice, her only daughter—a brother could not be kinder." But who would not be kind to Alice? she was a sweet girl of seventeen, not beautiful, not handsome perhaps,—but pretty enough—with soft hazel eyes, a profusion of light brown hair, always in the neatest trim, and a mouth that could not but be lovely and loveable, for all kind and tender affections were playing about it. Though Alice was the only daughter of a doting mother, the only sister of five loving boys, the only niece of three single, fond aunts, and, last and greatest, the only cousin of our only beau, Ralph Hepburn, no girl of seventeen was ever more disinterested, unassuming, unostentatious, and unspoiled. Ralph and Alice had always lived on terms of cousinly affection—an affection of a neutral tint that they never thought of being shaded

---

3. The sultan's wife in *The Arabian Nights,* who foils his plan to behead her in the morning by nightly telling him stories that make him wish to keep her alive another day.

into the deep dye of a more tender passion. Ralph rendered her all cousinly offices. If he had twenty damsels to escort, not an uncommon case, he never forgot Alice. When he returned from any little excursion, he always brought some graceful offering to Alice.

He had lately paid a visit to Boston. It was at the season of the periodical inundation of annuals.[4] He brought two of the prettiest to Alice. Ah! little did she think they were to prove Pandora's box[5] to her. Poor simple girl! she sat down to read them, as if an annual were meant to be read, and she was honestly interested and charmed. Her mother observed her delight. "What have you there, Alice?" she asked. "Oh the prettiest story, mamma!—two such tried faithful lovers, and married at last! It ends beautifully: I hate love stories that don't end in marriage."

"And so do I, Alice," exclaimed Ralph, who entered at the moment, and for the first time Alice felt her cheeks tingle at his approach. He had brought a basket, containing a choice plant he had obtained for her, and she laid down the annual and went with him to the garden to see it set by his own hand.

Mrs Courland seized upon the annual with avidity. She had imbibed a literary taste in Boston, where the best and happiest years of her life were passed. She had some literary ambition too. She read the *North American Review*[6] from beginning to end, and she fancied no conversation could be sensible or improving that was not about books. But she had been effectually prevented, by the necessities of a narrow income, and by the unceasing wants of five teasing boys, from indulging her literary inclinations; for Mrs Courland, like all New England women, had been taught to consider domestic duties as the first temporal duties of her sex. She had recently seen some of the native productions with which the press is daily teeming, and which certainly have a tendency to dispel our early illusions about the craft of authorship. She had even felt some obscure intimations, within her secret soul, that she might herself become an author. The annual was destined to fix her fate. She opened it—the publisher had written the names of the authors of the anonymous pieces against their productions. Among them she found some of the familiar friends of her childhood and youth.

If, by a sudden gift of second sight, she had seen them enthroned as kings and queens, she would not have been more astonished. She turned to their pieces, and read them, as perchance no one else ever did, from beginning to end—faithfully. Not a sentence—a sentence! not a word was skipped. She paused to consider commas, colons, and dashes. All the art and magic of authorship were made level to her comprehension, and when she closed the book, she *felt a call* to become an author, and before she retired to bed she obeyed the call, as if it had been, in truth, a divinity stirring within her. In the morning she presented an article to *her* public, consisting of her own family and a few select friends. All applauded, and every voice, save one, was unanimous for publication—that one was Alice. She was a modest, prudent girl; she feared failure, and feared notoriety still more. Her mother laughed at her childish scruples. The piece was sent off, and in due time graced the pages of an annual. Mrs Courland's fate was now decided. She had, to use her own

---

4. Books printed annually, often called gift books. This is an "inside joke" because this story was first printed in an annual, the *Atlantic Souvenir*.
5. In Greek mythology, the god Zeus presented Pandora with a box that she was forbidden to open; when she did, all human suffering escaped.
6. Influential literary magazine founded in Boston in 1815.

phrase, started in the career of letters, and she was no Atalanta[7] to be seduced from her straight onward way. She was a social, sympathetic, good hearted creature too, and she could not bear to go forth in the golden field to reap alone.

She was, besides, a prudent woman, as most of her countrywomen are, and the little pecuniary equivalent for this delightful exercise of talents was not overlooked. Mrs Courland, as we have somewhere said, had three single sisters—worthy women they were—but nobody ever dreamed of their taking to authorship. She, however, held them all in sisterly estimation. Their talents were magnified as the talents of persons who live in a circumscribed sphere are apt to be, particularly if seen through the dilating medium of affection.

Miss Anne, the oldest, was fond of flowers, a successful cultivator, and a diligent student of the science of botany. All this taste and knowledge, Mrs Courland thought, might be turned to excellent account; and she persuaded Miss Anne to write a little book entitled "Familiar Dialogues on Botany." The second sister, Miss Ruth, had a turn for education ("bachelor's wives and maid's children are always well taught"), and Miss Ruth undertook a popular treatise on that subject. Miss Sally, the youngest, was the saint of the family, and she doubted about the propriety of a literary occupation, till her scruples were overcome by the fortunate suggestion that her coup d'essai[8] should be a Saturday night book entitled "Solemn Hours,"—and solemn hours they were to their unhappy readers. Mrs Courland next besieged her old mother. "You know, mamma," she said, "you have such a precious fund of anecdotes of the revolution and the French war, and you talk just like the "Annals of the Parish,"[9] and I am certain you can write a book fully as good."

"My child, you are distracted! I write a dreadful poor hand, and I never learned to spell—no girls did in my time."

"Spell! that is not of the least consequence—the printers correct the spelling."

But the honest old lady would not be tempted on the crusade, and her daughter consoled herself with the reflection that if she would not write, she was an admirable subject to be written about, and her diligent fingers worked off three distinct stories in which the old lady figured.

Mrs Courland's ambition, of course, embraced within its widening circle her favourite nephew Ralph. She had always thought him a genius, and genius in her estimation was the philosopher's stone. In his youth she had laboured to persuade his father to send him to Cambridge, but the old man uniformly replied that Ralph "was a smart lad on the farm, and steady, and by that he knew he was no genius." As Ralph's character was developed, and talent after talent broke forth, his aunt renewed her lamentations over his ignoble destiny. That Ralph was useful, good, and happy—the most difficult and rare results achieved in life—was nothing, so long as he was but a farmer in H. Once she did half persuade him to turn painter, but his good sense and filial duty triumphed over her eloquence, and suppressed the hankerings after distinction that are innate in every human breast, from the little ragged chimneysweep that hopes to be a *boss,* to the political aspirant whose bright goal is the presidential chair.

---

7. In Greek mythology, a beautiful maiden whose suitors have to beat her in a race to win her hand. She finally loses to Hippomenes when she stops to pick up golden apples he had dropped.
8. Experiment, first try (French).
9. Hypothetical name for a book on local history.

Now Mrs Courland fancied Ralph might climb the steep of fame without quitting his farm; occasional authorship was compatible with his vocation. But alas! she could not persuade Ralph to pluck the laurels that she saw ready grown to his hand. She was not offended, for she was the best natured woman in the world, but she heartily pitied him, and seldom mentioned his name without repeating that stanza of Gray's, inspired for the consolation of hopeless obscurity:

"Full many a gem of purest ray serene," etc.[1]

Poor Alice's sorrows we have reserved to the last, for they were heaviest. "Alice," her mother said, "was gifted; she was well educated, well informed; she was every thing necessary to be an author." But Alice resisted; and, though the gentlest, most complying of all good daughters, she would have resisted to the death— she would as soon have stood in a pillory as appeared in print. Her mother, Mrs Courland, was not an obstinate woman, and gave up in despair. But still our poor heroine was destined to be the victim off this *cacoethes scribendi;* for Mrs Courland divided the world into two classes, or rather parts—authors and subjects for authors; the one active, the other passive. At first blush one would have thought the village of H. rather a barren field for such a reaper as Mrs Courland, but her zeal and indefatigableness worked wonders. She converted the stern scholastic divine of H. into as much of a La Roche as she could describe; a tall wrinkled bony old woman, who reminded her of Meg Merrilies, sat for a witch; the school master for an Ichabod Crane;[2] a poor half witted boy was made to utter as much pathos and sentiment and wit as she could put into his lips; and a crazy vagrant was a God-send to her. Then every "wide spreading elm," "blasted pine," or "gnarled oak," flourished on her pages. The village church and school house stood there according to their actual dimensions. One old *pilgrim* house was as prolific as haunted tower or ruined abbey. It was surveyed outside, ransacked inside, and again made habitable for the reimbodied spirits of its founders.

The most kind hearted of women, Mrs Courland's interests came to be so at variance with the prosperity of the little community of H., that a sudden calamity, a death, a funeral, were fortunate events to her. To do her justice she felt them in a twofold capacity. She wept as a woman, and exulted as an author. The days of the calamities of authors have passed by. We have all wept over Otway and shivered at the thought of Tasso.[3] But times are changed. The lean sheaf is devouring the full one. A new class of sufferers has arisen, and there is nothing more touching in all the memoirs Mr D'Israeli[4] has collected, than the trials of poor Alice, tragicomic though they were. Mrs Courland's new passion ran most naturally in the worn channel of maternal affection. Her boys were too purely boys for her art—

---

1. Line 53 of "Elegy Written in a Country Court-yard" (1751) by English poet Thomas Gray (1716–71).
2. La Roche: a character created by Henry Mackenzie (1745–1831), a Scottish writer of sentimental fiction; Meg Merrilies: a character (a gypsy) in Scottish writer Sir Walter Scott's (1771–1832) *Guy Mannering* and also the subject of a poem by English poet John Keats (1795–1821); Ichabod Crane: character in *The Legend of Sleepy Hollow* by American writer Washington Irving (1783–1859).

3. Otway: English dramatist Thomas Otway (1652–85); Tasso: Italian poet (1544–95) who was known to have suffered severe mental illness. Goethe's play named *Torquato Tasso* documents the artist's struggle and celebrates him as a suffering artist.
4. Isaac D'Israeli (1766–1848) was a British writer and scholar. His 1814 *Quarrels of Authors: Or, Some Memoirs for Our Literary History Including Specimens of Controversy to the Reign of Elizabeth* focused on the personalities and interrelationships among authors.

but Alice, her sweet Alice, was preeminently lovely in the new light in which she now placed every object. Not an incident of her life but was inscribed on her mother's memory, and thence transferred to her pages, by way of precept, or example, or pathetic or ludicrous circumstance. She regretted now, for the first time, that Alice had no lover whom she might introduce among her dramatis personæ. Once her thoughts did glance on Ralph, but she had not quite merged the woman in the author; she knew instinctively that Alice would be particularly offended at being thus paired with Ralph. But Alice's *public life* was not limited to her mother's productions. She was the darling niece of her three aunts. She had studied botany with the eldest, and Miss Anne had recorded in her private diary all her favourite's clever remarks during their progress in the science. This diary was now a mine of gold to her, and faithfully worked up for a circulating medium. But, most trying of all to poor Alice, was the attitude in which she appeared in her aunt Sally's "solemn hours." Every aspiration of piety to which her young lips had given utterance was there *printed*. She felt as if she were condemned to say her prayers in the market place. Every act of kindness, every deed of charity, she had ever performed, were produced to the public. Alice would have been consoled if she had known how small that public was; but, as it was, she felt like a modest country girl when she first enters an apartment, hung on every side with mirrors, when, shrinking from observation, she sees in every direction her image multiplied and often distorted; for, notwithstanding Alice's dutiful respect for her good aunts, and her consciousness of their affectionate intentions, she could not but perceive that they were unskilled painters. She grew afraid to speak or to act, and from being the most artless, frank, and, at home, social little creature in the world, she became as silent and as stiff as a statue. And, in the circle of her young associates, her natural gaiety was constantly checked by their winks and smiles, and broader allusions to her multiplied portraits; for they had instantly recognized them through the thin veil of feigned names of persons and places. They called her a blue stocking[5] too; for they had the vulgar notion that every body must be tinged that lived under the same roof with an author. Our poor victim was afraid to speak of a book—worse than that, she was afraid to touch one, and the last Waverley novel actually lay in the house a month before she opened it. She avoided wearing even a blue ribbon, as fearfully as a forsaken damsel shuns the colour of green.[6]

It was during the height of this literary fever in the Courland family, that Ralph Hepburn, as has been mentioned, concentrated all his visiting there. He was of a compassionate disposition, and he knew Alice was, unless relieved by him, in solitary possession of their once social parlour, while her mother and aunts were driving their quills in their several apartments.

Oh! what a changed place was that parlour! Not the tower of Babel, after the builders had forsaken it, exhibited a sadder reverse; not a Lancaster school,[7] when the boys have left it, a more striking contrast. Mrs Courland and her sisters were all "talking women," and too generous to encroach on one another's rights and

---

5. Here, a pejorative term for a learned woman (see p. 285).
6. Waverley novel: the novel *Waverley* by Scottish writer Sir Walter Scott (1771–1832) is considered the first historical novel, and his historical novels as a group are referred to as the Waverley novels, initially because they were published anonymously; forsaken damsel: an old rhyme says

"Green is forsaken / And yellow is forsworn."
7. Tower of Babel: the people of Babel had to stop work on the tower they were building to heaven when God made them speak different languages (Genesis 11:1–9); Lancaster school: a school based on the educational theories of Joseph Lancaster (1778–1838), which had students teaching students, under adult supervision.

happiness. They had acquired the power to hear and speak simultaneously. Their parlour was the general gathering place, a sort of village exchange, where all the innocent gossips, old and young, met together. "There are tongues in trees,"[8] and surely there seemed to be tongues in the very walls of that vocal parlour. Every thing there had a social aspect. There was something agreeable and conversable in the litter of netting and knitting work, of sewing implements, and all the signs and shows of happy female occupation.

Now, all was as orderly as a town drawing room in company hours. Not a sound was heard there save Ralph's and Alice's voices, mingling in soft and suppressed murmurs, as if afraid of breaking the chain of their aunt's ideas, or, perchance, of too rudely jarring a tenderer chain. One evening, after tea, Mrs Courland remained with her daughter, instead of retiring, as usual, to her writing desk.—"Alice, my dear," said the good mother, "I have noticed for a few days past that you look out of spirits. You will listen to nothing I say on that subject; but if you would try it, my dear, if you would only try it, you would find there is nothing so tranquillizing as the occupation of writing."

"I shall never try it, mamma."

"You are afraid of being called a blue stocking. Ah! Ralph, how are you?"— Ralph entered at this moment—"Ralph, tell me honestly, do you not think it a weakness in Alice to be so afraid of blue stockings?"

"It would be a pity, aunt, to put blue stockings[9] on such pretty feet as Alice's."

Alice blushed and smiled, and her mother said—"Nonsense, Ralph; you should bear in mind the celebrated saying of the Edinburgh wit—"no matter how blue the stockings are, if the petticoats are long enough to hide them.'"[1]

"Hide Alice's feet! Oh aunt, worse and worse!"

"Better hide her feet, Ralph, than her talents—that is a sin for which both she and you will have to answer. Oh! you and Alice need not exchange such significant glances! You are doing yourselves and the public injustice, and you have no idea how easy writing is."

"Easy writing, but hard reading, aunt."

"That's false modesty, Ralph. If I had but your opportunities to collect materials"—Mrs Courland did not know that in literature, as in some species of manufacture, the most exquisite productions are wrought from the smallest quantity of raw material—"There's your journey to New York, Ralph," she continued, "you might have made three capital articles out of that. The revolutionary officer would have worked up for the 'Legendary;' the mysterious lady for the 'Token;' and the man in black for the 'Remember Me;'—all founded on fact, all romantic and pathetic."[2]

"But mamma," said Alice, expressing in words what Ralph's arch smile expressed almost as plainly, "you know the officer drank too much; and the mysterious lady turned out to be a runaway milliner; and the man in black—oh! what a theme for a pathetic story!—the man in black was a widower, on his way to Newhaven, where he was to select his third wife from three *recommended* candidates."

---

8. From *As You Like It* (2.1.16) by William Shakespeare.
9. A derisive term originally applied to certain eighteenth-century women with pronounced literary interests.

1. Edinburgh wits of the 1820s that were a regular feature of *Blackwood's Edinburgh Magazine*.
2. A combination of imaginary and real ("The Token") names for annuals or gift books.

"Pshaw! Alice: do you suppose it is necessary to tell things precisely as they are?"

"Alice is wrong, aunt, and you are right; and if she will open her writing desk for me, I will sit down this moment, and write a story—a true story—true from beginning to end; and if it moves you, my dear aunt, if it meets your approbation, my destiny is decided."

Mrs Courland was delighted; she had slain the giant, and she saw fame and fortune smiling on her favourite. She arranged the desk for him herself; she prepared a folio sheet of paper, folded the ominous margins; and was so absorbed in her bright visions, that she did not hear a little by-talk between Ralph and Alice, nor see the tell-tale flush on their cheeks, nor notice the perturbation with which Alice walked first to one window and then to another, and finally settled herself to that best of all sedatives—hemming a ruffle. Ralph chewed off the end of his quill, mended his pen twice, though his aunt assured him "printers did not mind the penmanship," and had achieved a single line when Mrs Courland's vigilant eye was averted by the entrance of her servant girl, who put a packet into her hands. She looked at the direction,[3] cut the string, broke the seals, and took out a periodical fresh from the publisher. She opened at the first article—a strangely mingled current of maternal pride and literary triumph rushed through her heart and brightened her face. She whispered to the servant a summons to all her sisters to the parlour, and an intimation, sufficiently intelligible to them, of her joyful reason for interrupting them.

Our readers will sympathize with her, and with Alice too, when we disclose to them the secret of her joy. The article in question was a clever composition written by our devoted Alice when she was at school. One of her fond aunts had preserved it, and aunts and mother had combined in the pious fraud if giving it to the public, unknown to Alice. They were perfectly aware of her determination never to be an author. But they fancied it was the mere timidity of an unfledged bird; and that when, by their innocent artifice, she found that her pinions could soar in a literary atmosphere, she would realize the sweet fluttering sensations they had experienced at their first flight. The good souls all hurried to the parlour, eager to witness the coup de théatre.[4] Miss Sally's pen stood emblematically erect in her turban;[5] Miss Ruth, in her haste, had overset her inkstand, and the drops were trickling down her white dressing, or, as she now called it, writing gown; and Miss Anne had a wild flower in her hand, as she hoped, of an undescribed species, which, in her joyful agitation, she most unluckily picked to pieces. All bit their lips to keep impatient congratulation from bursting forth. Ralph was so intent on his writing, and Alice on her hemming, that neither noticed the irruption; and Mrs Courland was obliged twice to speak to her daughter before she could draw her attention.

"Alice, look here—Alice, my dear."

"What is it, mamma? something new of yours?"

"No; guess again, Alice."

"Of one of my aunts, of course?"

---

3. Address.
4. A sudden or unexpected happening in a play.
5. Instead of a feather or a flower, she has stuck her ink pen in her turban. A turban was a pretentious and theatrical choice of headcovering.

"Neither, dear, neither. Come and look for yourself, and see if you can then tell whose it is."

Alice dutifully laid aside her work, approached and took the book. The moment her eye glanced on the fatal page, all her apathy vanished—deep crimson overspread her cheeks, brow, and neck. She burst into tears of irrepressible vexation, and threw the book into the blazing fire.

The gentle Alice! Never had she been guilty of such an ebullition of temper. Her poor dismayed aunts retreated; her mother looked at her in mute astonishment; and Ralph, struck with her emotion, started from the desk, and would have asked an explanation, but Alice exclaimed—"Don't say any thing about it, mamma—I cannot bear it now."

Mrs Courland knew instinctively that Ralph would sympathize entirely with Alice, and quite willing to avoid an éclaircissement,[6] she said—"Some other time, Ralph, I'll tell you the whole. Show me now what you have written. How have you begun?"

Ralph handed her the paper with a novice's trembling hand.

"Oh! how very little! and so scratched and interlined! but never mind—'c'est le premier pas qui coute.'"[7]

While making these general observations, the good mother was getting out and fixing her spectacles, and Alice and Ralph had retreated behind her. Alice rested her head on his shoulder, and Ralph's lips were not far from her ear. Whether he was soothing her ruffled spirit, or what he was doing, is not recorded. Mrs Courland read and re-read the sentence. She dropped a tear on it. She forgot her literary aspirations for Ralph and Alice—forgot she was herself an author—forgot every thing but the mother; and rising, embraced them both as her dear children, and expressed, in her raised and moistened eye, consent to their union, which Ralph had dutifully and prettily asked in that short and true story of his love for his sweet cousin Alice.

In due time the village of H. was animated with the celebration of Alice's nuptials: and when her mother and aunts saw her the happy mistress of the Hepburn farm, and the happiest of wives, they relinquished, without a sigh, the hope of ever seeing her an author.

1830

⸻•⸺ LYDIA HOWARD HUNTLEY SIGOURNEY ⸺•⸻
1791–1865

Born just three years after the ratification of the U.S. Constitution, Lydia Sigourney (née Huntley) rose from poverty to help define what it would mean to be a professional woman in the new nation. Although Sigourney was forgotten through most of the twentieth century, her role in the American romantic movement (p. 464) and in the establishment of authorship as a viable profession for Americans, especially American women, has been increasingly recognized. The poems

6. A clearing-up, a moment of enlightenment (French).

7. The first step is the hardest (French).

included here represent the most important strands of her work: as a theorist of the sentimental aspect of romanticism and as a humorous critic of gender roles.

Sigourney's life could easily have been the model for mid-nineteenth century sensational fiction. Her mother died when she was very young, and her father worked as a handyman for the wealthy Lathrop family of Hartford, Connecticut. It would have been expected that she grow up to be a laundress or, at best, the wife of a minor tradesman. However, Mrs. Lathrop recognized Sigourney's intelligence and provided her with the kind of private education generally reserved for elite boys. Like several of the remarkable women of the United States before the Civil War—Margaret Fuller, pp. 685–86 and Lydia Maria Child, pp. 619–20, for example—she was provided, by this unusual education, with the means both to critique her society and to attempt practical change. Lydia Huntley gave up her early careers as a poet and an educator upon her marriage in 1819 to the successful Hartford businessman Charles Sigourney. Or, at least, that is what Charles thought: during this period, Sigourney continued to write and publish anonymously without her husband's blessing. As was common in the lives of literary women from this era, Sigourney gained her husband's full support for her art only after his business collapsed during one of the frequent economic crashes of that time. When Sigourney publicly reentered the literary marketplace, the popularity of her poems and prose transformed it. Her contributions to magazines, gazettes, and newspapers commanded the highest prices in the business. If she was looked down on by other would-be "professional" authors such as Edgar Allan Poe, Nathaniel Hawthorne, and Herman Melville, they welcomed the increasing standard of wages for which she was partially responsible. Before her death in 1865, she had published sixty-four books of poetry, advice, and inspiration.

Although earlier women writers in Britain and the colonies hid their identities under carefully chosen, flowery aliases, Sigourney was given several cognomens, or nicknames, by her fans. She was "The Sweet Singer of Hartford" for those who wanted to celebrate her particular "Americanness," while she was "The American Hemans" (a reference to British poet Felicia Hemans, whose work Sigourney had promoted and published in the United States) for those who wanted to emphasize her place in the trans-Atlantic literary milieu. In a way that perhaps became paradigmatic for later American women artists, Sigourney manipulated models of gender roles to create and control images of herself as a paragon of genteel femininity. Despite the fact that she had been born into the working class and was the main breadwinner for her family, Sigourney became the advocate and arbiter of proper middle-class mores when the popular women's magazine *Godey's Lady's Book* (see pp. 785–86) solicited an engraving of her face to be used as an endorsement of genteel probity. Sigourney willingly agreed, for a suitable price.

Taken as a whole, Sigourney's work articulates a distinctly American poetic voice. Through her particular form of romanticism, called sentimentalism, Sigourney sought to expand the power of the domestic sphere over the public, political, and commercial spheres. Although she has been remembered primarily as a writer of the kind of mortuary and occasional verse that became the model for greeting card sentiments, Sigourney wrote in all the romantic and Victorian poetic genres, including dramatic monologues, long and short narratives, lyrics, and political anthems. She frequently treated explicitly political subjects of the day—Napoleon, the mistreatment of Native peoples, and U.S. policies of territorial expansion.

Sigourney, like Harriet Beecher Stowe, co-opted the public domain of politics by making it an extension of, not the opponent of, the home.

To a Shred of Linen

Would they swept cleaner!
                              Here's a littering shred
Of linen left behind—a vile reproach
To all good housewifery. Right glad am I
That no neat lady, train'd in ancient times
Of pudding-making, and of sampler-work,   5
And speckless sanctity of household care,
Hath happen'd here to spy thee. She, no doubt,
Keen looking through her spectacles, would say,
"This comes of reading books." Or some spruce beau,
Essenced and lily-handed, had he chanced   10
To scan thy slight superfices, 'twould be,
"This comes of writing poetry."—Well, well,
Come forth, offender!—hast thou aught to say?
Canst thou, by merry thought or quaint conceit,
Repay this risk that I have run for thee?   15
——Begin at alpha, and resolve thyself
Into thine elements. I see the stalk
And bright blue flower of flax, which erst o'erspread
That fertile land, where mighty Moses stretch'd
His rod miraculous.[1] I see thy bloom   20
Tinging, too scantly, these New England vales.
But, lo! the sturdy farmer lifts his flail
To crush thy bones unpitying, and his wife,
With kerchief'd head and eye brimfull of dust,
Thy fibrous nerves with hatchel-tooth[2] divides.   25
——I hear a voice of music—and behold!
The ruddy damsel singeth at her wheel,[3]
While by her side the rustic lover sits.
Perchance, his shrewd eye secretly doth count
The mass of skeins, which, hanging on the wall,   30
Increaseth day by day. Perchance his thought
(For men have deeper minds than women—sure!)
Is calculating what a thrifty wife
The maid will make; and how his dairy shelves
Shall groan beneath the weight of golden cheese,   35
Made by her dexterous hand, while many a keg
And pot of butter to the market borne,
May, transmigrated, on his back appear
In new thanksgiving coats.
                              Fain would I ask,
Mine own New England, for thy once loved wheel,   40

1. Egypt, where Moses used his rod to part the   3. A hand- or foot-driven machine for spinning
Red Sea in the Old Testament (Exodus 14:16–22).   thread or yarn.
2. A tool for combing flax, wool, hemp.

By sofa and piano quite displaced.
Why dost thou banish from thy parlour hearth
That old Hygeian harp, whose magic ruled
Dyspepsia, as the minstrel-shepherd's skill
Exorcised Saul's ennui?[4] There was no need,   45
In those good times of callisthenics, sure;
And there was less of gadding, and far more
Of home-born, heart-felt comfort, rooted strong
In industry, and bearing such rare fruit
As wealth might never purchase.
                       But come back,   50
Thou shred of linen. I did let thee drop
In my harangue, as wiser ones have lost
The thread of their discourse. What was thy lot
When the rough battery of the loom had stretch'd
And knit thy sinews, and the chemist sun   55
Thy brown complexion bleach'd?
                       Methinks I scan
Some idiosyncrasy that marks thee out
A defunct pillow-case. Did the trim guest,
To the best chamber usher'd e'er admire
The snowy whiteness of thy freshen'd youth,   60
Feeding thy vanity? or some sweet babe
Pour its pure dream of innocence on thee?
Say, hast thou listen'd to the sick one's moan,
When there was none to comfort?—or shrunk back
From the dire tossings of the proud man's brow?   65
Or gather'd from young beauty's restless sigh
A tale of untold love?
                     Still close and mute!—
Wilt tell no secrets, ha?—Well then, go down,
With all thy churl-kept hoard of curious lore,
In majesty and mystery, go down   70
Into the paper-mill, and from its jaws,
Stainless and smooth, emerge. Happy shall be
The renovation, if on thy fair page
Wisdom and truth their hallow'd lineaments
Trace for posterity. So shall thine end   75
Be better than thy birth, and worthier bard
Thine apotheosis immortalize.

                                        1849

Unspoken Language

Language is slow. The mastery of wants
Doth teach it to the infant, drop by drop,
As brooklets gather.

4. Hygeian: belonging to Hygeia, the goddess of health in Greek mythology; Saul's ennui: Old Testament story of the shepherd (and future king) David, who played the harp to calm King Saul's troubled mind (1 Samuel 16–22).

      Years of studious toil
Unfold its classic labyrinths to the boy;
Perchance its idioms and its sequences   5
May wear the shadow of the lifted rod,
And every rule of syntax leave its tear
For Memory's tablet.
        He who would acquire
The speech of many lands, must make the lamp
His friend at midnight, while his fellows sleep,   10
Bartering to dusty lexicons and tomes
The hour-glass of his life.
         Yet, there's a lore,
Simple and sure, that asks no discipline
Of weary years,—the language of the soul,
Told through the eye.
       The mother speaks it well   15
To the unfolding spirit of her babe,
The lover to the lady of his heart,
At the soft twilight hour, the parting soul
Unto the angels hovering o'er its couch,
With Heaven's high welcome.
         Oft the stammering lip 20
Marreth the perfect thought, and the dull ear
Doth err in its more tortuous embassy;
But the heart's lightning hath no obstacle;
Quick glances, like the thrilling wires, transfuse
The telegraphic thought.
        The wily tongue,   25
To achieve its purpose, may disguise itself,
Oft, 'neath a glozing mask;[5] and written speech
Invoke the pomp of numbers to enrich
Its dialect; but this ambassador
From soul to sense may wear the plainest suit,— 30
Ebon or hazel, azure-tint or gray,
It matters not: the signet-ring of truth
Doth give him credence.—
        Once, old Ocean raged;
And a vex'd ship, by maddening waves impell'd,
Rush'd on the breakers. Mid the wild turmoil   35
Of rock and wave, the trumpet-clang, and tramp
Of hurrying seamen, and the fearful shock
With which the all-astonish'd mind resigns
The hope of life, a mother with her babe
Sate in the cabin. He was all to her,   40
The sole companion of her watery way,
And nestling towards her bosom, raised his face
Upward to hers.

---

5. A flattering and misleading appearance.

Her raven hair fell down
In masses o'er her shoulders, while her eyes
Fix'd with such deep intensity, that his   45
Absorb'd their rays of thought, and seem'd to draw
The soul mature, with all its burdening cares,
Its wondrous knowledge, and mysterious strength,
Into his baby-bosom.
             Word nor sound
Pass'd 'tween that mother and her youngling child,—   50
Too young to syllable the simplest name,—
And yet, methought, they interchanged a vow
Calmly beneath the unfathomable deep
Together to go down, and that her arm
Should closely clasp him mid its coral caves.   55
The peril pass'd: but the deep eloquence
Of that communion might not be forgot.

A youth and maiden, on the banks of Tweed,[6]
Roved, mid the vernal flowers. At distance rose
The towers of Abbotsford,[7] among the trees,   60
Which he, the great magician, who at will
Could summon "spirits from the vasty deep,"
Had loved to plant.
             Methought of him they spake,
Disporting in the fields of old romance
With Ivanhoe, or the proud knight who fell   65
At Flodden-field.[8] Then, as the sun drew low,
They sate them down, where the fresh heather grew,
Listing, perchance, the descant of the birds,
Or ripple of the stream. The hazel eye
Of the young dweller 'neath the Eildon-Hills[9]   70
Perused the fair one's brow, till o'er it stole
A deeper colouring than the rose-leaf tinge.
—Speech there was none, nor gesture, yet the depth
Of some unutter'd dialect did seem
Well understood by them. And so they rose,   75
And went their way.
             There was a crowded kirk,
But not for Sabbath worship. With the train
Was more of mirth than might, perchance, beseem
Such sacred place. Wreaths too there were, and knots
Of marriage-favour, and a group that prest   80
Before the altar. And the trembling lip
Of that young white-robed bride, murmuring the vow

6. A river in Scotland.
7. An estate on the River Tweed owned by Sir Walter Scott.
8. Sir Walter Scott's 1819 novel *Ivanhoe* is set in the twelfth century and is often credited with ini-
tiating the nineteenth-century fascination with all things medieval.
9. A low mountain range near the border of England and Scotland

To love till death should part, interpreted
That strong and voiceless language of the eye
Upon the banks of Tweed.—
                        I had a friend   85
Beloved in halcyon days, whom stern disease
Smote ere her prime.
                    In curtain'd room she dwelt,
A lingerer, while each waning moon convey'd
Some treasured leaflet of our hope away.
The power that with the tissued lungs doth dwell,   90
Sweetly to wake the modulating lip,
Was broken,—but the violet-tinctured eye
Acquired new pathos.
                    When the life-tide crept
Cold through its channels, o'er her couch I bent.
There was no sound. But in the upraised glance   95
Her loving heart held converse, as with forms
Not of this outer world. Unearthly smiles
Gave earnest beauty to the pallid brow;
While ever and anon the emaciate hand
Spread its white fingers, as it fain would clasp   100
Some object hovering near.
                        The last faint tone
Was a fond sister's name, one o'er whose grave
The turf of years had gather'd. Was she there,—
That disembodied dear one? Did she give
The kiss of welcome to the occupant   105
Of her own infant cradle?
                        So 'twould seem.
But that fix'd eye no further answer deign'd,
Its earthly mission o'er. Henceforth it spake
The spirit-lore of immortality.

                                                           1849

Eve[1]

For the first time, a lovely scene
    Earth saw, and smiled,—
A gentle form with pallid mien
    Bending o'er a new-born child:
The pang, the anguish, and the wo   5
    That speech hath never told,
Fled, as the sun with noontide glow
    Dissolves the snow-wreath cold,
Leaving the bliss that none but mothers know;

1. In the Judeo-Christian tradition, Adam and
Eve are the first people created by God in the Gar-
den of Eden. The third and fourth chapters of
Genesis tell of their expulsion from Eden and the
fratricide of their first children, Cain and Abel.
The poem retells the events of Genesis 4.2 through
Genesis 4.16.

While he, the partner of her heaven-taught joy,   10
Knelt in adoring praise beside his beauteous boy.

    She, first of all our mortal race,
    Learn'd the ecstasy to trace
  The expanding form of infant grace
      From her own life-spring fed;   15
     To mark, each radiant hour,
Heaven's sculpture still more perfect growing,
      More full of power;
   The little foot's elastic tread,
  The rounded cheek, like rose-bud glowing,   20
  The fringed eye with gladness flowing,
    As the pure, blue fountains roll;
  And then those lisping sounds to hear,
  Unfolding to her thrilling ear
 The strange, mysterious, never-dying soul,   25
    And with delight intense
To watch the angel-smile of sleeping innocence.

   No more she mourn'd lost Eden's joy,[2]
    Or wept her cherish'd flowers,
     In their primeval bowers   30
    By wrecking tempests riven;
 The thorn and thistle of the exile's lot
     She heeded not,
So all-absorbing was her sweet employ
To rear the incipient man,[3] the gift her God had given.   35

   And when his boyhood bold
    A richer beauty caught,
  Her kindling glance of pleasure told
    The incense of her idol-thought:
  Not for the born of clay[4]   40
     Is pride's exulting thrill,
  Dark herald of the downward way,
     And ominous of ill.
 Even his cradled brother's[5] smile
  The haughty first-born jealously survey'd,   45
And envy mark'd the brow with hate and guile,
    In God's own image made.

    At the still twilight hour,
   When saddest images have power,
   Musing Eve her fears exprest:—   50
"He loves me not; no more with fondness free

---

2. In the Old Testament account of the creation
(Genesis 1–4), Adam and Eve were expelled from
the Garden of Eden after they were tempted and
disobeyed God.

3. Cain, Adam and Eve's first son.
4. Human; see Genesis 2:7, "The Lord God
formed the man from the dust of the ground."
5. Abel, Adam and Eve's second son.

His clear eye looks on me;
Dark passions rankle there, and moody hate
    Predicts some adverse fate.
        Ah! is this he, whose waking eye,   55
        Whose faint, imploring cry,
With new and unimagined rapture blest?
Alas! alas! the throes his life that bought,
Were naught to this wild agony of thought
    That racks my boding breast."   60

So mourn'd our mother, in her secret heart,
    With presage all too true;
And often from the midnight dream would start,
    Her forehead bathed in dew;
        But say, what harp shall dare,   65
    Unless by hand immortal strung,
        What pencil touch the hue,
        Of that intense despair
    Her inmost soul that wrung!
For Cain was wroth, and in the pastures green,   70
Where Abel led his flock, mid waters cool and sheen,
With fratricidal hand, that blameless shepherd slew.

Earth learn'd strong lessons in her morning prime,
    More strange than Chaos taught,
When o'er contending elements the darkest veil was wrought;   75
    The poison of the tempter's[6] glozing tongue,
        Man's disobedience and expulsion dire,
        The terror of the sword of fire[7]
        At Eden's portal hung,
    Inferior creatures filled with savage hate,   80
    No more at peace, no more subordinate;
Man's birth in agony, man's death by crime,
        The taste of life-blood, brother-spilt;
        But that red stain of guilt
Sent through her inmost heart such sickening pain,   85
    That in her path o'er ether's plain
She hid her head and mourn'd, amid the planet-train.

                                                                   1849

◄ FELICIA DOROTHEA BROWNE HEMANS ►
1793–1835

By the mid-1820s, Felicia Hemans had become one of the most successful and celebrated British poets of her generation. Hemans's poetry, like herself, was ambi-

---

6. Satan, who as a snake tempted Adam and Eve
to their disobedience.
7. After he expelled them from Eden, God placed

an angel with a flaming sword at the entrance of
the garden so no one could return.

tious, dramatic, complex, and experimental. A contemporary of John Keats, Percy and Mary Shelley (pp. 577–79), and Lord Byron, Hemans participated in the revolution in aesthetic and cultural values that has come to be known as romanticism (p. 468). She experimented in a variety of lyric forms, as well as narrative and dramatic verse. Hemans's poems depict the qualities and consequences of heightened states of feeling as she attempts to elicit strong emotional responses from her readers. Many of her poems take the exotic past as their subjects, but quite a few treat contemporary political and military events. Throughout her work, Hemans is concerned with the nature of heroism, and some of her best works celebrate the heroism of women under both ordinary and extraordinary conditions, for which she gained a reputation as the voice of the "true Victorian woman."

Hemans's apotheosis into an icon of Victorian femininity occurred despite the unconventional aspects of her biography. She was born in Liverpool, and for most of her life she lived in households where the fathers and husbands were absent or had little authority. Hemans's father, Mr. Browne, was an unsuccessful merchant who fled the thriving port of Liverpool, first with his family to rural Wales and later alone to Canada in pursuit of business. Hemans's mother, on the other hand, played a significant role not only in the early education and support of her daughter but also in Hemans's adult career as a poet and mother. Despite troubled finances, Hemans's mother maintained a household that included a large private library. She encouraged her daughter to read widely and to contemplate nature and taught her the modern European languages, as well as music, painting, and Latin. Hemans began writing poetry as a child and published her first poem in 1807, at age fourteen.

By nineteen, Felicia Browne had fallen in love with and married a dashing army captain, Alfred Hemans, who had returned seriously weakened from the Napoleonic Wars. Together they lived in Mrs. Browne's household and had five children before Captain Hemans's health forced him to leave the family to live in Italy. This matriarchal household provided Hemans with the time and resources needed to study and to pursue increasingly ambitious writing projects, which drew the attention of critics and publishers. After her mother died in 1827, the extended family lost its center, and Hemans's own health began to fail. Although she continued to produce poetry, it became more difficult to support herself and her family as she grew sicker. She died less than ten years after her mother, at the age of forty-two.

Hemans published over nine books of poetry, but the true source of her fame came from two new and popular publishing trends of the day: weekly and monthly magazines that were marketed to the middle class and yearly anthologies of popular literature (known as annuals or gift books). These annuals were often extravagantly produced but popularly priced, and they were commonly given as gifts among friends. No other author was as sought after as Hemans: in Britain, she could command almost any price for her verse. Her poems had up-to-date circulation throughout the British Empire because of these magazines and annuals, while in America, she became one of the first and best known of the romantic poets.

In the years after her early death, Hemans became ensconced within the Victorian sensibility in a way that obscured the complexity of her work beneath a reputation for conventionality. Throughout the English-speaking world, schoolchildren were taught to commit her poems, such as the ones printed here, to memory. On the one hand, her poems on martial and patriotic topics pervaded British culture as it solidified its status as an empire through military ventures around the globe. On the other hand, Hemans came to be considered the voice of the "true woman" whose learning and ability celebrated the domestic sphere.

England's Dead

Son of the ocean isle!
Where sleep your mighty dead?
Show me what high and stately pile
Is rear'd o'er Glory's bed.

Go, stranger! track the deep,   5
Free, free, the white sail spread!
Wave may not foam, nor wild wind sweep,
Where rest not England's dead.

On Egypt's burning plains,
By the pyramid o'ersway'd,   10
With fearful power the noon-day reigns,
And the palm-trees yield no shade.

But let the angry sun
From heaven look fiercely red,
Unfelt by those whose task is done!   15
There slumber England's dead.

The hurricane hath might
Along the Indian shore,
And far, by Ganges' banks at night,
Is heard the tiger's roar.   20

But let the sound roll on!
It hath no tone of dread,
For those that from their toils are gone;
—*There* slumber England's dead.

Loud rush the torrent-floods   25
The western wilds among,
And free, in green Columbia's[1] woods,
The hunter's bow is strung.

But let the floods rush on!
Let the arrow's flight be sped!   30
Why should *they* reck whose task is done?
There slumber England's dead!

The mountain-storms rise high
In the snowy Pyrenees,
And toss the pine-boughs through the sky,   35
Like rose-leaves on the breeze.

---

1. America's.

But let the storm rage on!
Let the forest-wreaths be shed!
For the Roncesvalles' field is won,
   There slumber England's dead.   40

On the frozen deep's repose
'Tis a dark and dreadful hour,
When round the ship the ice-fields close,
   To chain her with their power.

But let the ice drift on!   45
Let the cold-blue desert spread!
Their course with mast and flag is done,
   There slumber England's dead.

The warlike of the isles,
The men of field and wave!   50
Are not the rocks their funeral piles,
   The seas and shores their grave?

Go, stranger! track the deep,
Free, free the white sail spread!
Wave may not foam, nor wild wind sweep,   55
   Where rest not England's dead.

                   1822

Bring Flowers

Bring flowers, young flowers, for the festal board,
To wreathe the cup ere the wine is pour'd;
Bring flowers! they are springing in wood and vale,
Their breath floats out on the southern gale,
And the touch of the sunbeam hath waked the rose,   5
To deck the hall where the bright wine flows.

Bring flowers to strew in the conqueror's path—
He hath shaken thrones with his stormy wrath!
He comes with the spoils of nations back,
The vines lie crush'd in his chariot's track,   10
The turf looks red where he won the day—
Bring flowers to die in the conqueror's way!

Bring flowers to the captive's lonely cell,
They have tales of the joyous woods to tell;
Of the free blue streams, and the glowing sky,   15
And the bright world shut from his languid eye;
They will bear him a thought of the sunny hours,
And a dream of his youth—bring him flowers, wild flowers!

Bring flowers, fresh flowers, for the bride to wear!
They were born to blush in her shining hair.   20
She is leaving the home of her childhood's mirth,

She hath bid farewell to her father's hearth,
Her place is now by another's side—
Bring flowers for the locks of the fair young bride!

Bring flowers, pale flowers, o'er the bier to shed,   25
A crown for the brow of the early dead!
For this through its leaves hath the white rose burst,
For this in the woods was the violet nurs'd!
Though they smile in vain for what once was ours,
They are love's last gift—bring ye flowers, pale flowers!   30

Bring flowers to the shrine where we kneel in prayer,
They are nature's offering, their place is *there!*
They speak of hope to the fainting heart,
With a voice of promise they come and part,
They sleep in dust through the wintry hours,   35
They break forth in glory—bring flowers, bright flowers!

1824

Casabianca

The boy[2] stood on the burning deck
   Whence all but he had fled;
The flame that lit the battle's[3] wreck,
   Shone round him o'er the dead.

Yet beautiful and bright he stood,   5
   As born to rule the storm;
A creature of heroic blood,
   A proud, though child-like form.

The flames rolled on—he would not go,
   Without his Father's word;   10
That Father, faint in death below,
   His voice no longer heard.

He called aloud:—"Say, Father, say
   If yet my task is done?"
He knew not that the chieftain lay   15
   Unconscious of his son.

"Speak, Father!" once again he cried,
   "If I may yet be gone!
And"—but the booming shots replied,
   And fast the flames rolled on.   20

Upon his brow he felt their breath,
   And in his waving hair,
And looked from that lone post of death,
   In still, yet brave despair.

2. Giacomo Jocante Casabianca, son of the admiral of the French ship *Orient*; he remained at his post after all the guns had been abandoned.

3. The Battle of the Nile, Aboukir Bay, August 1, 1798, at which the British fleet, under Lord Nelson, defeated Napoleon's navy.

And shouted but once more aloud,   25
    "My Father! must I stay?"
While o'er him fast, through sail and shroud,
    The wreathing fires made way.

They wrapt the ship in splendour wild,
    They caught the flag on high,   30
And streamed above the gallant child,
    Like banners in the sky.

There came a burst of thunder sound—
    The boy—oh! where was he?
Ask of the winds that far around   35
    With fragments strewed the sea!—

With mast, and helm, and pennon fair,
    That well had borne their part—
But the noblest thing which perished there
    Was that young faithful heart!   40

                                                    1826

⊷◄ MARY SHELLEY ►⊶
1797–1851

The only child of two radical authors, Mary Shelley was born to write. Her mother, Mary Wollstonecraft (p. 365), wrote *A Vindication of the Rights of Woman* (1792), and her father, William Godwin, argued in tracts and novels for a society based on genuine political equality. Both parents were freethinkers who did not approve of the institution of marriage, and they caused great damage to Mary Wollstonecraft's social reputation by living together openly. When she became pregnant, Wollstonecraft decided it would disadvantage their child to be born "illegitimately," so the couple married in 1796, before the birth of their only child, Mary Wollstonecraft Godwin, in London in 1797. But just twelve days later her mother died of a postpartum infection. Mary Shelley was, then, one of the many nineteenth-century children who never knew her mother.

Though he grieved for his loss, Godwin remarried in 1801 to a neighbor with two out-of-wedlock children of her own. Mary Jane Clairmont, the stepmother, and her daughter, Jane (later Claire), and son, Charles, joined Mary and her mother's daughter by a previous liaison, Fanny, to form a blended family in William Godwin's household. Mary is said to have resented her stepmother's harsh manners and ability to draw her father's attention away from herself, but she maintained a close relationship with her father as well as a growing acquaintance with the work of her late mother. In early adolescence, Mary spent time away from home, ostensibly to seek a cure for eczema outbreaks, but perhaps also to ease tensions with her stepfamily. She spent a short time at a boarding school at age thirteen and later went to live with family friends in Scotland, where she was healthy and happy.

On returning to her father's London home, Mary met Percy Bysshe Shelley (1792–1822), a twenty-one-year-old poet who had recently broken off relations with his prosperous and titled father and had been "sent down" (expelled) from

Oxford University for coauthoring a tract called "The Necessity of Atheism." Shelley looked to William Godwin as an intellectual and political mentor and became Godwin's financial patron by borrowing against his own expected inheritance to help support Godwin's domestic expenses. Shelley and Mary, along with Mary's stepsister Claire, became closely acquainted, enjoying long walks and conversations together, even though Shelley was already married and had two children (he had eloped in 1811, when Harriet Westbrook, his wife, was sixteen years old). Mary and Shelley fell passionately in love, and they agreed to run away together to the Continent in 1814, taking Claire with them. As Mary was only sixteen, her father strenuously objected to this arrangement, but the trio traveled against his wishes for six months in Germany and Switzerland, where they saw the castle that would eventually serve as one of the locations for Mary Shelley's *Frankenstein*. When they returned to London, Mary's father would not even speak to them in the street, let alone allow them to rejoin his household, even though Mary was now visibly pregnant.

Mary's first child died at two weeks old. She and Shelley had struggled financially on their return to England, but in 1815, Shelley reached an agreement with his father which enabled him to support Mary as well as his estranged wife and to give William Godwin the money he had promised as patronage. Then, Shelley's first wife, Harriet, committed suicide in 1816, and Shelley and Mary married shortly after her death. Their marriage included periods of emotional estrangement as well as companionship and collaboration, and they had many friendships with other writers of the day. Mary's stepsister Claire Clairmont began an affair with George Gordon, Lord Byron, who was as famous for his promiscuity as he was for poetry. Byron and Shelley became friends, and the couples spent time together in Switzerland, where the idea for *Frankenstein* was born.

According to Mary Shelley's introduction to the novel, the friends were telling ghost stories one night, challenging one another to be as frightening as possible. Mary had no idea for a story until a "waking dream" later came to her, inspired by discussions of galvanism, or using electricity to reanimate dead creatures. A vision of a creature, patched together of dead parts and brought to life by scientific means, occurred to her—and terrified her. This became the kernel of her first novel, published in England in 1818, when Mary was twenty-one years old. Though many reviewers considered the material too shocking to be suitable for a woman writer, the novel found an audience and produced a myth that has persisted in Western culture ever since, revived on the London stage during Shelley's lifetime and later in films, parodies, cartoons, and countless allusions.

By the time she finished *Frankenstein*, Mary had given birth to two more children, but both died in Italy before they reached the age of four: her daughter died of dysentery and her son of malaria. She sought solace in her work, revising and copying her husband's poetry as well as composing novels and travel writings of her own. Their fourth child, Percy Florence Shelley, was born in Italy in 1819; he was eventually educated at Harrow and Cambridge and inherited his grandfather's title and estate. Mary miscarried during her final pregnancy: Percy was the only one of her five children who survived to adulthood.

In 1822, Shelley had been complaining of his wife's "coldness" to him when he went sailing in Italy with a friend during a bad storm, during which both men were drowned. Mary managed her grief by devoting much of her attention to publishing his later work and trying to produce a biography, which his father would not permit. She returned to England, where she continued writing novels—*Valperga* (1823), *The Last Man* (1826), *Lodore* (1835), and *Falkner* (1837)—and produced two volumes of biographies of "eminent literary and scientific men" of Europe. In 1839, she brought out an authoritative edition of Shelley's poems, as well as a volume of his essays and letters, annotated with comments about their life together. In the next year she began to feel the effects of what turned out to be a brain tumor. She died in London in 1851.

    Frankenstein has become a classic of Gothic fiction, with its ominous European settings, its exploration of the darker side of human psychology, and its elements of horror; it has also been hailed as an early work of science fiction. Like most of Mary Shelley's fiction, however, *Frankenstein* is fundamentally a philosophical novel. Women philosophers were rare in the first three decades of the nineteenth century, and novel writing gave a woman author access to a much broader audience than she could reach with essays and tracts. What makes *Frankenstein* unusual among philosophical novels is the way the two central figures—the overreaching scientist, whose hubris motivates him to emulate God by creating new life, and his creature, whose initial victimization leads to depravity and revenge—so vividly persist in the common imagination. *Frankenstein* is a "framed" novel, containing three embedded narratives. The book begins with the narrative of a fictional British explorer, Robert Walton, writing letters home about his travels in the far north. In his letters, Walton transcribes the account of a desperate Dr. Victor Frankenstein, whom he meets on the ice. Contained within Frankenstein's story is a long quotation, the creature's own narrative, which he has told to Frankenstein to explain his actions after leaving the lab where he was created. The selection reproduced here is the entirety of the monster's narrative, which ends with his creator's reactions to and reflections on his story.

From Frankenstein

[The Monster's Narrative]

CHAPTER 11
[THE MONSTER'S EARLY DAYS]

"It is with considerable difficulty that I remember the original era of my being; all the events of that period appear confused and indistinct. A strange multiplicity of sensations seized me, and I saw, felt, heard, and smelt at the same time; and it was, indeed, a long time before I learned to distinguish between the operations of my various senses. By degrees, I remember, a stronger light pressed upon my nerves, so that I was obliged to shut my eyes. Darkness then came over me and troubled me, but hardly had I felt this when, by opening my eyes, as I now suppose, the light poured in upon me again. I walked and, I believe, descended, but I presently found a great alteration in my sensations. Before, dark and opaque bodies had surrounded me, impervious to my touch or sight; but I now found that I could wander on at liberty, with no obstacles which I could not either surmount or avoid. The light became more and more oppressive to me, and the heat wearying me as I walked, I sought a place where I could receive shade. This was the forest near Ingolstadt;[1] and here I lay by the side of a brook resting from my fatigue, until I felt tormented

---

1. A university town in Bavaria, in southern Germany.

by hunger and thirst. This roused me from my nearly dormant state, and I ate some berries which I found hanging on the trees or lying on the ground. I slaked my thirst at the brook, and then lying down, was overcome by sleep.

"It was dark when I awoke; I felt cold also, and half frightened, as it were, instinctively, finding myself so desolate. Before I had quitted your apartment,[2] on a sensation of cold, I had covered myself with some clothes, but these were insufficient to secure me from the dews of night. I was a poor, helpless, miserable wretch; I knew, and could distinguish, nothing; but feeling pain invade me on all sides, I sat down and wept.

"Soon a gentle light stole over the heavens and gave me a sensation of pleasure. I started up and beheld a radiant form rise from among the trees.[3] I gazed with a kind of wonder. It moved slowly, but it enlightened my path, and I again went out in search of berries. I was still cold when under one of the trees I found a huge cloak, with which I covered myself, and sat down upon the ground. No distinct ideas occupied my mind; all was confused. I felt light, and hunger, and thirst, and darkness; innumerable sounds rang in my ears, and on all sides various scents saluted me; the only object that I could distinguish was the bright moon, and I fixed my eyes on that with pleasure.

"Several changes of day and night passed, and the orb of night had greatly lessened, when I began to distinguish my sensations from each other. I gradually saw plainly the clear stream that supplied me with drink and the trees that shaded me with their foliage. I was delighted when I first discovered that a pleasant sound, which often saluted my ears, proceeded from the throats of the little winged animals who had often intercepted the light from my eyes. I began also to observe, with greater accuracy, the forms that surrounded me, and to perceive the boundaries of the radiant roof of light which canopied me. Sometimes I tried to imitate the pleasant songs of the birds but was unable. Sometimes I wished to express my sensations in my own mode, but the uncouth and inarticulate sounds which broke from me frightened me into silence again.

"The moon had disappeared from the night, and again, with a lessened form, showed itself, while I still remained in the forest. My sensations had by this time become distinct, and my mind received every day additional ideas. My eyes became accustomed to the light and to perceive objects in their right forms; I distinguished the insect from the herb, and by degrees, one herb from another. I found that the sparrow uttered none but harsh notes, whilst those of the blackbird and thrush were sweet and enticing.

"One day, when I was oppressed by cold, I found a fire which had been left by some wandering beggars, and was overcome with delight at the warmth I experienced from it. In my joy I thrust my hand into the live embers, but quickly drew it out again with a cry of pain. How strange, I thought, that the same cause should produce such opposite effects! I examined the materials of the fire, and to my joy found it to be composed of wood. I quickly collected some branches, but they were wet and would not burn. I was pained at this and sat still watching the operation of the fire. The wet wood which I had placed near the heat dried and itself became inflamed. I reflected on this, and by touching the various branches, I dis-

2. The creature is addressing Victor Frankenstein, who had created him out of body parts in a laboratory, then abandoned the monster after bringing him to life.
3. The moon. [Mary Shelley's note]

covered the cause and busied myself in collecting a great quantity of wood, that I might dry it and have a plentiful supply of fire. When night came on and brought sleep with it, I was in the greatest fear lest my fire should be extinguished. I covered it carefully with dry wood and leaves and placed wet branches upon it; and then, spreading my cloak, I lay on the ground and sank into sleep.

"It was morning when I awoke, and my first care was to visit the fire. I uncovered it, and a gentle breeze quickly fanned it into a flame. I observed this also and contrived a fan of branches, which roused the embers when they were nearly extinguished. When night came again I found, with pleasure, that the fire gave light as well as heat and that the discovery of this element was useful to me in my food, for I found some of the offals[4] that the travellers had left had been roasted, and tasted much more savoury than the berries I gathered from the trees. I tried, therefore, to dress my food in the same manner, placing it on the live embers. I found that the berries were spoiled by this operation, and the nuts and roots much improved.

"Food, however, became scarce, and I often spent the whole day searching in vain for a few acorns to assuage the pangs of hunger. When I found this, I resolved to quit the place that I had hitherto inhabited, to seek for one where the few wants I experienced would be more easily satisfied. In this emigration I exceedingly lamented the loss of the fire which I had obtained through accident and knew not how to reproduce it. I gave several hours to the serious consideration of this difficulty, but I was obliged to relinquish all attempts to supply it, and wrapping myself up in my cloak, I struck across the wood towards the setting sun. I passed three days in these rambles and at length discovered the open country. A great fall of snow had taken place the night before, and the fields were of one uniform white; the appearance was disconsolate, and I found my feet chilled by the cold damp substance that covered the ground.

"It was about seven in the morning, and I longed to obtain food and shelter; at length I perceived a small hut, on a rising ground, which had doubtless been built for the convenience of some shepherd. This was a new sight to me, and I examined the structure with great curiosity. Finding the door open, I entered. An old man sat in it, near a fire, over which he was preparing his breakfast. He turned on hearing a noise, and perceiving me, shrieked loudly, and quitting the hut, ran across the fields with a speed of which his debilitated form hardly appeared capable. His appearance, different from any I had ever before seen, and his flight, somewhat surprized me. But I was enchanted by the appearance of the hut; here the snow and rain could not penetrate; the ground was dry; and it presented to me then as exquisite and divine a retreat as Pandaemonium appeared to the daemons of hell[5] after their sufferings in the lake of fire. I greedily devoured the remnants of the shepherd's breakfast, which consisted of bread, cheese, milk, and wine; the latter, however, I did not like. Then, overcome by fatigue, I lay down among some straw and fell asleep.

"It was noon when I awoke, and allured by the warmth of the sun, which shone brightly on the white ground, I determined to recommence my travels; and, depositing the remains of the peasant's breakfast in a wallet I found, I proceeded across the fields for several hours, until at sunset I arrived at a village.

4. Discarded food.
5. See *Paradise Lost* (1.670 and following), the

seventeenth-century epic poem (1667 and 1674) by John Milton (1608–14).

How miraculous did this appear! The huts, the neater cottages, and stately houses engaged my admiration by turns. The vegetables in the gardens, the milk and cheese that I saw placed at the windows of some of the cottages, allured my appetite. One of the best of these I entered, but I had hardly placed my foot within the door before the children shrieked, and one of the women fainted. The whole village was roused; some fled, some attacked me, until, grievously bruised by stones and many other kinds of missile weapons, I escaped to the open country and fearfully took refuge in a low hovel, quite bare, and making a wretched appearance after the palaces I had beheld in the village. This hovel, however, joined a cottage of a neat and pleasant appearance, but after my late dearly bought experience, I dared not enter it. My place of refuge was constructed of wood, but so low that I could with difficulty sit upright in it. No wood, however, was placed on the earth which formed the floor, but it was dry; and although the wind entered it by innumerable chinks, I found it an agreeable asylum from the snow and rain.

"Here, then, I retreated and lay down happy to have found a shelter, however miserable, from the inclemency of the season, and still more from the barbarity of man.

"As soon as morning dawned I crept from my kennel, that I might view the adjacent cottage and discover if I could remain in the habitation I had found. It was situated against the back of the cottage and surrounded on the sides which were exposed by a pig sty and a clear pool of water. One part was open, and by that I had crept in; but now I covered every crevice by which I might be perceived with stones and wood, yet in such a manner that I might move them on occasion to pass out; all the light I enjoyed came through the sty, and that was sufficient for me.

"Having thus arranged my dwelling and carpeted it with clean straw, I retired, for I saw the figure of a man at a distance, and I remembered too well my treatment the night before to trust myself in his power. I had first, however, provided for my sustenance for that day by a loaf of coarse bread, which I purloined, and a cup with which I could drink, more conveniently than from my hand, of the pure water which flowed by my retreat. The floor was a little raised, so that it was kept perfectly dry, and by its vicinity to the chimney of the cottage it was tolerably warm.

"Being thus provided, I resolved to reside in this hovel until something should occur which might alter my determination. It was indeed a paradise compared to the bleak forest, my former residence, the rain-dropping branches, and dank earth. I ate my breakfast with pleasure and was about to remove a plank to procure myself a little water when I heard a step, and looking through a small chink, I beheld a young creature, with a pail on her head, passing before my hovel. The girl was young and of gentle demeanour, unlike what I have since found cottages and farmhouse servants to be. Yet she was meanly dressed, a coarse blue petticoat and a linen jacket being her only garb; her fair hair was plaited but not adorned: she looked patient yet sad. I lost sight of her, and in about a quarter of an hour she returned bearing the pail, which was now partly filled with milk. As she walked along, seemingly incommoded by the burden, a young man met her, whose countenance expressed a deeper despondence. Uttering a few sounds with an air of melancholy, he took the pail from her head and bore it to the cottage himself. She followed, and they disappeared. Presently I saw the young man again, with some tools in his hand, cross the field behind the cottage; and the girl was also busied, sometimes in the house and sometimes in the yard.

"On examining my dwelling, I found that one of the windows of the cottage had formerly occupied a part of it, but the panes had been filled up with wood. In one of these was a small and almost imperceptible chink through which the eye could just penetrate. Through this crevice a small room was visible, white-washed and clean but very bare of furniture. In one corner, near a small fire, sat an old man, leaning his head on his hands in a disconsolate attitude. The young girl was occupied in arranging the cottage; but presently she took something out of a drawer, which employed her hands, and she sat down beside the old man, who, taking up an instrument, began to play and to produce sounds sweeter than the voice of the thrush or the nightingale. It was a lovely sight, even to me, poor wretch! who had never beheld aught beautiful before. The silver hair and benevolent countenance of the aged cottager won my reverence, while the gentle manners of the girl enticed my love. He played a sweet mournful air which I perceived drew tears from the eyes of his amiable companion, of which the old man took no notice, until she sobbed audibly; he then pronounced a few sounds, and the fair creature, leaving her work, knelt at his feet. He raised her and smiled with such kindness and affection that I felt sensations of a peculiar and over-powering nature; they were a mixture of pain and pleasure, such as I had never before experienced, either from hunger or cold, warmth or food; and I withdrew from the window, unable to bear these emotions.

"Soon after this the young man returned, bearing on his shoulders a load of wood. The girl met him at the door, helped to relieve him of his burden, and taking some of the fuel into the cottage, placed it on the fire; then she and the youth went apart into a nook of the cottage, and he showed her a large loaf and a piece of cheese. She seemed pleased and went into the garden for some roots and plants, which she placed in water, and then upon the fire. She afterwards continued her work, whilst the young man went into the garden and appeared busily employed in digging and pulling up roots. After he had been employed thus about an hour, the young woman joined him and they entered the cottage together.

"The old man had, in the mean time, been pensive, but on the appearance of his companions he assumed a more cheerful air, and they sat down to eat. The meal was quickly dispatched. The young woman was again occupied in arranging the cottage, the old man walked before the cottage in the sun for a few minutes, leaning on the arm of the youth. Nothing could exceed in beauty the contrast between these two excellent creatures. One was old, with silver hairs and a countenance beaming with benevolence and love; the younger was slight and graceful in his figure, and his features were moulded with the finest symmetry, yet his eyes and attitude expressed the utmost sadness and despondency. The old man returned to the cottage, and the youth, with tools different from those he had used in the morning, directed his steps across the fields.

"Night quickly shut in, but to my extreme wonder, I found that the cottagers had a means of prolonging light by the use of tapers, and was delighted to find that the setting of the sun did not put an end to the pleasure I experienced in watching my human neighbours. In the evening the young girl and her companion were employed in various occupations which I did not understand; and the old man again took up the instrument which produced the divine sounds that had enchanted me in the morning. So soon as he had finished, the youth began, not to play, but to utter sounds that were monotonous, and neither resembling the harmony of the old man's instrument nor the songs of the birds; I since found that he read aloud, but at that time I knew nothing of the science of words or letters.

"The family, after having been thus occupied for a short time, extinguished their lights and retired, as I conjectured, to rest."

Chapter 12

[THE MONSTER LEARNS LANGUAGE]

"I lay on my straw, but I could not sleep. I thought of the occurrences of the day. What chiefly struck me was the gentle manners of these people, and I longed to join them, but dared not. I remembered too well the treatment I had suffered the night before from the barbarous villagers, and resolved, whatever course of conduct I might hereafter think it right to pursue, that for the present I would remain quietly in my hovel, watching and endeavouring to discover the motives which influenced their actions.

"The cottagers arose the next morning before the sun. The young woman arranged the cottage and prepared the food, and the youth departed after the first meal.

"This day was passed in the same routine as that which preceded it. The young man was constantly employed out of doors, and the girl in various laborious occupations within. The old man, whom I soon perceived to be blind, employed his leisure hours on his instrument or in contemplation. Nothing could exceed the love and respect which the younger cottagers exhibited towards their venerable companion. They performed towards him every little office of affection and duty with gentleness, and he rewarded them by his benevolent smiles.

"They were not entirely happy. The young man and his companion often went apart and appeared to weep. I saw no cause for their unhappiness, but I was deeply affected by it. If such lovely creatures were miserable, it was less strange that I, an imperfect and solitary being, should be wretched. Yet why were these gentle beings unhappy? They possessed a delightful house (for such it was in my eyes) and every luxury; they had a fire to warm them when chill, and delicious viands when hungry; they were dressed in excellent clothes; and, still more, they enjoyed one another's company and speech, interchanging each day looks of affection and kindness. What did their tears imply? Did they really express pain? I was at first unable to solve these questions, but perpetual attention and time explained to me many appearances which were at first enigmatic.

"A considerable period elapsed before I discovered one of the causes of the uneasiness of this amiable family: it was poverty, and they suffered that evil in a very distressing degree. Their nourishment consisted entirely of the vegetables of their garden and the milk of one cow, which gave very little during the winter, when its masters could scarcely procure food to support it. They often, I believe, suffered the pangs of hunger very poignantly, especially the two younger cottagers, for several times they placed food before the old man when they reserved none for themselves.

"This trait of kindness moved me sensibly. I had been accustomed, during the night, to steal a part of their store for my own consumption, but when I found that in doing this I inflicted pain on the cottagers, I abstained and satisfied myself with berries, nuts, and roots which I gathered from a neighbouring wood.

"I discovered also another means through which I was enabled to assist their labours. I found that the youth spent a great part of each day in collecting wood for the family fire, and during the night I often took his tools, the use of which I quickly discovered, and brought home firing sufficient for the consumption of several days.

"I remember, the first time that I did this, the young woman, when she opened the door in the morning, appeared greatly astonished on seeing a great pile of wood on the outside. She uttered some words in a loud voice, and the youth joined her, who also expressed surprize. I observed, with pleasure, that he did not go to the forest that day, but spent it in repairing the cottage and cultivating the garden.

"By degrees I made a discovery of still greater moment. I found that these people possessed a method of communicating their experience and feelings to one another by articulate sounds. I perceived that the words they spoke sometimes produced pleasure or pain, smiles or sadness, in the minds and countenances of the hearers. This was indeed a godlike science, and I ardently desired to become acquainted with it. But I was baffled in every attempt I made for this purpose. Their pronunciation was quick, and the words they uttered, not having any apparent connection with visible objects, I was unable to discover any clue by which I could unravel the mystery of their reference. By great application, however, and after having remained during the space of several revolutions of the moon in my hovel, I discovered the names that were given to some of the most familiar objects of discourse; I learned and applied the words, 'fire,' 'milk,' 'bread,' and 'wood.' I learned also the names of the cottagers themselves. The youth and his companion had each of them several names, but the old man had only one, which was 'father.' The girl was called 'sister' or 'Agatha,' and the youth 'Felix,' 'brother,' or 'son.' I cannot describe the delight I felt when I learned the ideas appropriated to each of these sounds and was able to pronounce them. I distinguished several other words without being able as yet to understand or apply them, such as 'good,' 'dearest,' 'unhappy.'

"I spent the winter in this manner. The gentle manners and beauty of the cottagers greatly endeared them to me; when they were unhappy, I felt depressed; when they rejoiced, I sympathized in their joys. I saw few human beings besides them, and if any other happened to enter the cottage, their harsh manners and rude gait only enhanced to me the superior accomplishments of my friends. The old man, I could perceive, often endeavoured to encourage his children, as sometimes I found that he called them, to cast off their melancholy. He would talk in a cheerful accent, with an expression of goodness that bestowed pleasure even upon me. Agatha listened with respect, her eyes sometimes filled with tears, which she endeavoured to wipe away unperceived; but I generally found that her countenance and tone were more cheerful after having listened to the exhortations of her father. It was not thus with Felix. He was always the saddest of the group, and even to my unpractised senses, he appeared to have suffered more deeply than his friends. But if his countenance was more sorrowful, his voice was more cheerful than that of his sister, especially when he addressed the old man.

"I could mention innumerable instances which, although slight, marked the dispositions of these amiable cottagers. In the midst of poverty and want, Felix carried with pleasure to his sister the first little white flower that peeped out from beneath the snowy ground. Early in the morning, before she had risen, he cleared away the snow that obstructed her path to the milk-house, drew water from the well, and brought the wood from the out-house, where, to his perpetual astonishment, he found his store always replenished by an invisible hand. In the day, I believe, he worked sometimes for a neighbouring farmer, because he often went forth and did not return until dinner, yet brought no wood with him. At other times he worked in the garden, but as there was little to do in the frosty season, he read to the old man and Agatha.

"This reading had puzzled me extremely at first, but by degrees I discovered that he uttered many of the same sounds when he read as when he talked. I conjectured, therefore, that he found on the paper signs for speech which he understood, and I ardently longed to comprehend these also; but how was that possible when I did not even understand the sounds for which they stood as signs? I improved, however, sensibly in this science, but not sufficiently to follow up any kind of conversation, although I applied my whole mind to the endeavour: for I easily perceived that, although I eagerly longed to discover myself[6] to the cottagers, I ought not to make the attempt until I had first become master of their language, which knowledge might enable me to make them overlook the deformity of my figure; for with this also the contrast perpetually presented to my eyes had made me acquainted.

"I had admired the perfect forms of my cottagers—their grace, beauty, and delicate complexions; but how was I terrified when I viewed myself in a transparent pool! At first I started back, unable to believe that it was indeed I who was reflected in the mirror; and when I became fully convinced that I was in reality the monster that I am, I was filled with the bitterest sensations of despondence and mortification. Alas! I did not yet entirely know the fatal effects of this miserable deformity.

"As the sun became warmer and the light of day longer, the snow vanished, and I beheld the bare trees and the black earth. From this time Felix was more employed, and the heart-moving indications of impending famine disappeared. Their food, as I afterwards found, was coarse, but it was wholesome; and they procured a sufficiency of it. Several new kinds of plants sprang up in the garden, which they dressed; and these signs of comfort increased daily as the season advanced.

"The old man, leaning on his son, walked each day at noon, when it did not rain, as I found it was called when the heavens poured forth its water. This frequently took place, but a high wind quickly dried the earth, and the season became far more pleasant than it had been.

"My mode of life in my hovel was uniform. During the morning I attended the motions of the cottagers, and when they were dispersed in various occupations, I slept; the remainder of the day was spent in observing my friends. When they had retired to rest, if there was any moon or the night was star-light, I went into the woods and collected my own food and fuel for the cottage. When I returned, as often as it was necessary, I cleared their path from the snow and performed those offices that I had seen done by Felix. I afterwards found that these labours, performed by an invisible hand, greatly astonished them; and once or twice I hard them, on these occasions, utter the words 'good spirit,' 'wonderful,' but I did not then understand the signification of these terms.

"My thoughts now became more active, and I longed to discover the motives and feelings of these lovely creatures; I was inquisitive to know why Felix appeared so miserable and Agatha so sad. I thought (foolish wretch!) that it might be in my power to restore happiness to these deserving people. When I slept or was absent, the forms of the venerable blind father, the gentle Agatha, and the ex-

6. Reveal myself.

cellent Felix flitted before me. I looked upon them as superior beings who would
be the arbiters of my future destiny. I formed in my imagination a thousand pictures of presenting myself to them, and their reception of me. I imagined that they
would be disgusted, until, by my gentle demeanour and conciliating words, I
should first win their favour and afterwards their love.

"These thoughts exhilarated me and led me to apply with fresh ardour to the
acquiring the art of language. My organs were indeed harsh, but supple; and although my voice was very unlike the soft music of their tones, yet I pronounced
such words as I understood with tolerable ease. It was as the ass and the lap-dog;[7]
yet surely the gentle ass whose intentions were affectionate, although his manners
were rude, deserved better treatment than blows and execration.

"The pleasant showers and genial warmth of spring greatly altered the aspect
of the earth. Men, who before this change seemed to have been hid in caves, dispersed themselves and were employed in various arts of cultivation. The birds
sang in more cheerful notes, and the leaves began to bud forth on the trees. Happy,
happy earth! Fit habitation for gods, which, so short a time before, was bleak,
damp, and unwholesome. My spirits were elevated by the enchanting appearance
of nature; the past was blotted from my memory, the present was tranquil, and
the future gilded by bright rays of hope and anticipations of joy."

Chapter 13

[THE MONSTER BEGINS TO RECOGNIZE HIS DIFFERENCE]

"I now hasten to the more moving part of my story. I shall relate events that impressed me with feelings which, from what I had been, have made me what I am.

"Spring advanced rapidly; the weather became fine and the skies cloudless. It
surprized me that what before was desert and gloomy should now bloom with the
most beautiful flowers and verdure. My senses were gratified and refreshed by a
thousand scents of delight and a thousand sights of beauty.

"It was on one of these days, when my cottagers periodically rested from
labour—the old man played on his guitar, and the children listened to him—that I
observed the countenance of Felix was melancholy beyond expression; he sighed
frequently, and once his father paused in his music, and I conjectured by his manner that he enquired the cause of his son's sorrow. Felix replied in a cheerful accent,
and the old man was recommencing his music when some one tapped at the door.

"It was a lady on horseback, accompanied by a countryman as a guide. The
lady was dressed in a dark suit and covered with a thick black veil. Agatha asked
a question, to which the stranger only replied by pronouncing, in a sweet accent,
the name of Felix. Her voice was musical but unlike that of either of my friends.
On hearing this word, Felix came up hastily to the lady, who, when she saw him,
threw up her veil, and I beheld a countenance of angelic beauty and expression.
Her hair of a shining raven black, and curiously braided; her eyes were dark, but
gentle, although animated; her features of a regular proportion, and her complexion wondrously fair, each cheek tinged with a lovely pink.

"Felix seemed ravished with delight when he saw her, every trait of sorrow
vanished from his face, and it instantly expressed a degree of ecstatic joy, of which
I could hardly have believed it capable; his eyes sparkled, as his cheek flushed

7. Allusion to a fable by Jean de La Fontaine   a lapdog but gets beaten for the attempt.
(1621–95) in which a donkey tries to behave like

with pleasure; and at that moment I thought him as beautiful as the stranger. She appeared affected by different feelings; wiping a few tears from her lovely eyes, she held out her hand to Felix, who kissed it rapturously and called her, as well as I could distinguish, his sweet Arabian. She did not appear to understand him, but smiled. He assisted her to dismount, and dismissing her guide, conducted her into the cottage. Some conversation took place between him and his father, and the young stranger knelt at the old man's feet and would have kissed his hand, but he raised her and embraced her affectionately.

"I soon perceived that although the stranger uttered articulate sounds and appeared to have a language of her own, she was neither understood by, nor herself understood, the cottagers. They made many signs which I did not comprehend, but I saw that her presence diffused gladness through the cottage, dispelling their sorrow as the sun dissipates the morning mists. Felix seemed peculiarly happy and with smiles of delight welcomed his Arabian. Agatha, the ever-gentle Agatha, kissed the hands of the lovely stranger and pointing to her brother, made signs which appeared to me to mean that he had been sorrowful until she came. Some hours passed thus, while they, by their countenances, expressed joy, the cause of which I did not comprehend. Presently I found, by the frequent recurrence of some sound which the stranger repeated after them, that she was endeavouring to learn their language; and the idea instantly occurred to me that I should make use of the same instructions to the same end. The stranger learned about twenty words at the first lesson, most of them, indeed, were those which I had before understood, but I profited by the others.

"As night came on Agatha and the Arabian retired early. When they separated Felix kissed the hand of the stranger and said, 'Good night, sweet Safie.' He sat up much longer, conversing with his father, and by the frequent repetition of her name, I conjectured that their lovely guest was the subject of their conversation. I ardently desired to understand them, and bent every faculty towards that purpose, but found it utterly impossible.

"The next morning Felix went out to his work, and after the usual occupations of Agatha were finished, the Arabian sat at the feet of the old man, and taking his guitar, played some airs so entrancingly beautiful that they at once drew tears of sorrow and delight from my eyes. She sang, and her voice flowed in a rich cadence, swelling or dying away like a nightingale of the woods.

"When she had finished, she gave the guitar to Agatha, who at first declined it. She played a simple air, and her voice accompanied it in sweet accents, but unlike the wondrous strain of the stranger. The old man appeared enraptured and said some words which Agatha endeavoured to explain to Safie, and by which he appeared to wish to express that she bestowed on him the greatest delight by her music.

"The days now passed as peaceably as before, with the sole alteration that joy had taken place of sadness in the countenances of my friends. Safie was always gay and happy; she and I improved rapidly in the knowledge of language, so that in two months I began to comprehend most of the words uttered by my protectors.

"In the meanwhile also the black ground was covered with herbage, and the green banks interspersed with innumerable flowers, sweet to the scent and the eyes, stars of pale radiance among the moonlight woods; the sun became warmer, the nights clear and balmy; and my nocturnal rambles were an extreme pleasure to me, although they were considerably shortened by the late setting and early rising of the sun, for I never ventured abroad during daylight, fearful of meeting with the same treatment I had formerly endured in the first village which I entered.

"My days were spent in close attention, that I might more speedily master the language; and I may boast that I improved more rapidly than the Arabian, who understood very little and conversed in broken accents, whilst I comprehended and could imitate almost every word that was spoken.

"While I improved in speech, I also learned the science of letters as it was taught to the stranger, and this opened before me a wide field for wonder and delight.

"The book from which Felix instructed Safie was Volney's *Ruins of Empires*.[8] I should not have understood the purport of this book had not Felix, in reading it, given very minute explanations. He had chosen this work, he said, because the declamatory style was framed in imitation of the Eastern authors. Through this work, I obtained a cursory knowledge of history and a view of the several empires at present existing in the world; it gave me an insight into the manners, governments, and religions of the different nations of the earth. I heard of the slothful Asiatics, of the stupendous genius and mental activity of the Grecians, of the wars and wonderful virtue of the early Romans—of their subsequent degenerating—of the decline of that mighty empire, of chivalry, Christianity, and kings. I heard of the discovery of the American hemisphere and wept with Safie over the hapless fate of its original inhabitants.

"These wonderful narrations inspired me with strange feelings. Was man, indeed, at once so powerful, so virtuous, and magnificent, yet so vicious and base? He appeared at one time a mere scion of the evil principle and at another as all that can be conceived as noble and godlike. To be a great and virtuous man appeared the highest honour that can befall a sensitive being; to be base and vicious, as many on record have been, appeared the lowest degradation, a condition more abject than that of the blind mole or harmless worm. For a long time I could not conceive how one man could go forth to murder his fellow, or even why there were laws and governments; but when I heard details of vice and bloodshed, my wonder ceased and I turned away with disgust and loathing.

"Every conversation of the cottagers now opened new wonders to me. While I listened to the instructions which Felix bestowed upon the Arabian, the strange system of human society was explained to me. I heard of the division of property, of immense wealth and squalid poverty; of rank, descent, and noble blood.

"The words induced me to turn towards myself. I learned that the possessions most esteemed by your fellow creatures were high and unsullied descent united with riches. A man might be respected with only one of these advantages, but without either he was considered, except in very rare instances, as a vagabond and a slave, doomed to waste his powers for the profits of the chosen few. And what was I? Of my creation and creator I was absolutely ignorant, but I knew that I possessed no money, no friends, no kind of property. I was, besides, endued with a figure hideously deformed and loathsome; I was not even of the same nature as man. I was more agile than they and could subsist upon coarser diet; I bore the extremes of heat and cold with less injury to my frame; my stature far exceeded theirs. When I looked around I saw and heard of none like me. Was I, then, a monster, a blot upon the earth, from which all men fled and whom all men disowned?

8. A 1791 essay on the philosophy of history, by   boeuf, comte de Volney (1757–1820).
French scholar Constantin François de Chasse-

"I cannot describe to you the agony that these reflections inflicted upon me; I tried to dispel them, but sorrow only increased with knowledge. Oh, that I had forever remained in my native wood, nor known nor felt beyond the sensations of hunger, thirst, and heat!

"Of what a strange nature is knowledge! It clings to the mind, when it has once seized on it, like a lichen on the rock. I wished sometimes to shake off all thought and feeling, but I learned that there was but one means to overcome the sensation of pain, and that was death—a state which I feared yet did not understand. I admired virtue and good feelings and loved the gentle manners and amiable qualities of my cottagers, but I was shut out from intercourse with them, except through means which I obtained by stealth, when I was unseen and unknown, and which rather increased than satisfied the desire I had of becoming one among my fellows. The gentle words of Agatha and the animated smiles of the charming Arabian were not for me. The mild exhortations of the old man and the lively conversation of the loved Felix were not for me. Miserable, unhappy wretch!

"Other lessons were impressed upon me even more deeply. I heard of the difference of sexes, and the birth and growth of children; how the father doated on the smiles of the infant, and the lively sallies of the older child; how all the life and cares of the mother were wrapped up in the precious charge; how the mind of youth expanded and gained knowledge; of brother, sister, and all the various relationships which bind one human being to another in mutual bonds.

"But where were my friends and relations? No father had watched my infant days, no mother had blessed me with smiles and caresses; or if they had, all my past life was now a blot, a blind vacancy in which I distinguished nothing. From my earliest remembrance I had been as I then was in height and proportion. I had never yet seen a being resembling me or who claimed any intercourse with me. What was I? The question again recurred, to be answered only with groans.

"I will soon explain to what these feelings tended, but allow me now to return to the cottagers, whose story excited in me such various feelings of indignation, delight, and wonder, but which all terminated in additional love and reverence for my protectors (for so I loved, in an innocent, half-painful self-deceit, to call them)."

Chapter 14

[THE COTTAGERS' HISTORY]

"Some time elapsed before I learned the history of my friends. It was one which could not fail to impress itself deeply on my mind, unfolding as it did a number of circumstances, each interesting and wonderful to one so utterly inexperienced as I was.

"The name of the old man was De Lacey. He was descended from a good family in France, where he had lived for many years in affluence, respected by his superiors and beloved by his equals. His son was bred in the service of his country, and Agatha had ranked with ladies of the highest distinction. A few months before my arrival they had lived in a large and luxurious city called Paris, surrounded by friends and possessed of every enjoyment which virtue, refinement of intellect, or taste, accompanied by a moderate fortune, could afford.

"The father of Safie had been the cause of their ruin. He was a Turkish merchant and had inhabited Paris for many years, when, for some reason which I could not learn, he became obnoxious to the government. He was seized and cast into prison the very day that Safie arrived from Constantinople to join him. He was tried and condemned to death. The injustice of his sentence was very flagrant; all Paris was indignant; and it was judged that his religion and wealth rather than the crime alleged against him had been the cause of his condemnation.

"Felix had accidentally been present at the trial; his horror and indignation were uncontrollable when he heard the decision of the court. He made, at that moment, a solemn vow to deliver him and then looked around for the means. After many fruitless attempts to gain admittance to the prison, he found a strongly grated window in an unguarded part of the building, which lighted the dungeon of the unfortunate Muhammadan, who, loaded with chains, waited in despair the execution of the barbarous sentence. Felix visited the grate at night and made known to the prisoner his intentions in his favour. The Turk, amazed and delighted, endeavoured to kindle the zeal of his deliverer by promises of reward and wealth. Felix rejected his offers with contempt, yet when he saw the lovely Safie, who was allowed to visit her father and who, by her gestures, expressed her lively gratitude, the youth could not help owning to his own mind that the captive possessed a treasure which would fully reward his toil and hazard.

"The Turk quickly perceived the impression that his daughter had made on the heart of Felix and endeavoured to secure him more entirely in his interests by the promise of her hand in marriage so soon as he should be conveyed to a place of safety. Felix was too delicate to accept his offer, yet he looked forward to the probability of the event as to the consummation of his happiness.

"During the ensuing days, while the preparations were going forward for the escape of the merchant, the zeal of Felix was warmed by several letters that he received from this lovely girl, who found means to express her thoughts in the language of her lover by the aid of an old man, a servant of her father who understood French. She thanked him in the most ardent terms for his intended services towards her parent, and at the same time she gently deplored her own fate.

"I have copies of these letters; for I found means, during my residence in the hovel, to procure the implements of writing; and the letters were often in the hands of Felix or Agatha. Before I depart I will give them to you; they will prove the truth of my tale; but at present, as the sun is already far declined, I shall only have time to repeat the substance of them to you.

"Safie related that her mother was a Christian Arab, seized and made a slave by the Turks; recommended by her beauty, she had won the heart of the father of Safie, who married her. The young girl spoke in high and enthusiastic terms of her mother, who, born in freedom, spurned the bondage to which she was now reduced. She instructed her daughter in the tenets of her religion and taught her to aspire to higher powers of intellect and an independence of spirit forbidden to the female followers of Muhammad. This lady died, but her lessons were indelibly impressed on the mind of Safie, who sickened at the prospect of again returning to Asia and being immured within the walls of a harem, allowed only to occupy herself with infantile amusements, ill-suited to the temper of her soul, now accustomed to grand ideas and a noble emulation of virtue. The prospect of marrying a Christian and remaining in a country where women were allowed to take a rank in society was enchanting to her.

"The day for the execution of the Turk was fixed, but on the night previous to it he quitted his prison and before morning was distant many leagues from Paris. Felix had procured passports in the name of his father, sister, and himself. He had previously communicated his plan to the former, who aided the deceit by quitting his house, under the pretence of a journey and concealing himself, with his daughter, in an obscure part of Paris.

"Felix conducted the fugitives through France to Lyons and across Mont Cenis to Leghorn, where the merchant had decided to wait a favourable opportunity of passing into some part of the Turkish dominions.

"Safie resolved to remain with her father until the moment of his departure, before which time the Turk renewed his promise that she should be united to his deliverer; and Felix remained with them in expectation of that event; and in the mean time he enjoyed the society of the Arabian, who exhibited towards him the simplest and tenderest affection. They conversed with one another through the means of an interpreter, and sometimes with the interpretation of looks; and Safie sang to him the divine airs of her native country.

"The Turk allowed this intimacy to take place and encouraged the hopes of the youthful lovers, while in his heart he had formed far other plans. He loathed the idea that his daughter should be united to a Christian, but he feared the resentment of Felix if he should appear lukewarm, for he knew that he was still in the power of his deliverer if he should choose to betray him to the Italian state which they inhabited. He revolved a thousand plans by which he should be enabled to prolong the deceit until it might be no longer necessary, and secretly to take his daughter with him when he departed. His plans were facilitated by the news which arrived from Paris.

"The government of France were greatly enraged at the escape of their victim and spared no pains to detect and punish his deliverer. The plot of Felix was quickly discovered, and De Lacey and Agatha were thrown into prison. The news reached Felix and roused him from his dream of pleasure. His blind and aged father and his gentle sister lay in a noisome dungeon while he enjoyed the free air and the society of her whom he loved. This idea was torture to him. He quickly arranged with the Turk that if the latter should find a favourable opportunity for escape before Felix could return to Italy, Safie should remain as a boarder at a convent at Leghorn; and then, quitting the lovely Arabian, he hastened to Paris and delivered himself up to the vengeance of the law, hoping to free De Lacey and Agatha by this proceeding.

"He did not succeed. They remained confined for five months before the trial took place, the result of which deprived them of their fortune and condemned them to a perpetual exile from their native country.

"They found a miserable asylum in the cottage in Germany, where I discovered them. Felix soon learned that the treacherous Turk, for whom he and his family endured such unheard-of oppression, on discovering that his deliverer was thus reduced to poverty and ruin, became a traitor to good feeling and honour and had quitted Italy with his daughter, insultingly sending Felix a pittance of money to aid him, as he said, in some plan of future maintenance.

"Such were the events that preyed on the heart of Felix and rendered him, when I first saw him, the most miserable of his family. He could have endured poverty, and while this distress had been the meed of his virtue, he gloried in it; but the ingratitude of the Turk and the loss of his beloved Safie were misfortunes more bitter and irreparable. The arrival of the Arabian now infused new life into his soul.

"When the news reached Leghorn that Felix was deprived of his wealth and rank, the merchant commanded his daughter to think no more of her lover, but to prepare to return to her native country. The generous nature of Safie was outraged by this command; she attempted to expostulate with her father, but he left her angrily, reiterating his tyrannical mandate.

"A few days after, the Turk entered his daughter's apartment and told her hastily that he had reason to believe that his residence at Leghorn had been divulged and that he should speedily be delivered up to the French government; he had consequently hired a vessel to convey him to Constantinople, for which city he should sail in a few hours. He intended to leave his daughter under the care of a confidential servant, to follow at her leisure with the greater part of his property, which had not yet arrived at Leghorn.

"When alone, Safie resolved in her own mind the plan of conduct that it would become her to pursue in this emergency. A residence in Turkey was abhorrent to her; her religion and her feelings were alike averse to it. By some papers of her father which fell into her hands she heard of the exile of her lover and learnt the name of the spot where he then resided. She hesitated some time, but at length she formed her determination. Taking with her some jewels that belonged to her and a sum of money, she quitted Italy with an attendant, a native of Leghorn, but who understood the common language of Turkey, and departed for Germany.

"She arrived in safety at a town about twenty leagues from the cottage of De Lacey, when her attendant fell dangerously ill. Safie nursed her with the most devoted affection, but the poor girl died, and the Arabian was left alone, unacquainted with the language of the country and utterly ignorant of the customs of the world. She fell, however, into good hands. The Italian had mentioned the name of the spot for which they were bound, and after her death the woman of the house in which they had lived took care that Safie should arrive in safety at the cottage of her lover."

Chapter 15

[THE MONSTER READS THE CLASSICS AND MAKES A FRIEND]

"Such was the history of my beloved cottagers. It impressed me deeply. I learned, from the views of social life which it developed, to admire their virtues and to deprecate the vices of mankind.

"As yet I looked upon crime as a distant evil; benevolence and generosity were ever present before me, inciting within me a desire to become an actor in the busy scene where so many admirable qualities were called forth and displayed. But in giving an account of the progress of my intellect, I must not omit a circumstance which occurred in the beginning of the month of August of the same year.

"One night during my accustomed visit to the neighbouring wood where I collected my own food and brought home firing for my protectors, I found on the ground a leathern portmanteau containing several articles of dress and some books. I eagerly seized the prize and returned with it to my hovel. Fortunately the books were written in the language, the elements of which I had acquired at the cottage; they consisted of *Paradise Lost,* a volume of Plutarch's *Lives,* and the *Sorrows of Werter.*[9] The possession of these treasures gave me extreme delight; I

9. *Parallel Lives* (c. 100 CE), the series of biographies by Greek historian Plutarch (c. 46–127); *The Sorrows of Young Werther* (1774), a novel by German novelist, dramatist, and poet Johann Wolfgang von Goethe (1749–1832).

now continually studied and exercised my mind upon these histories, whilst my friends were employed in their ordinary occupations.

"I can hardly describe to you the effect of these books. They produced in me an infinity of new images and feelings, that sometimes raised me to ecstasy, but more frequently sunk me into the lowest dejection. In the *Sorrows of Werter,* besides the interest of its simple and affecting story, so many opinions are canvassed and so many lights thrown upon what had hitherto been to me obscure subjects that I found in it a never-ending source of speculation and astonishment. The gentle and domestic manners it described, combined with lofty sentiments and feelings, which had for their object something out of self, accorded well with my experience among my protectors and with the wants which were forever alive in my own bosom. But I thought Werter himself a more divine being than I had ever beheld or imagined; his character contained no pretension, but it sank deep. The disquisitions upon death and suicide were calculated to fill me with wonder. I did not pretend to enter into the merits of the case, yet I inclined towards the opinions of the hero, whose extinction I wept, without precisely understanding it.

"As I read, however, I applied much personally to my own feelings and condition. I found myself similar yet at the same time strangely unlike to the beings concerning whom I read and to whose conversation I was a listener. I sympathized with and partly understood them, but I was unformed in mind; I was dependent on none and related to none. 'The path of my departure was free,'[1] and there was none to lament my annihilation. My person was hideous and my stature gigantic. What did this mean? Who was I? What was I? Whence did I come? What was my destination? These questions continually recurred, but I was unable to solve them.

"The volume of Plutarch's *Lives* which I possessed contained the histories of the first founders of the ancient republics. This book had a far different effect upon me from the *Sorrows of Werter.* I learned from Werter's imaginations despondency and gloom, but Plutarch taught me high thoughts; he elevated me above the wretched sphere of my own reflections, to admire and love the heroes of past ages. Many things I read surpassed my understanding and experience. I had a very confused knowledge of kingdoms, wide extents of country, mighty rivers, and boundless seas. But I was perfectly unacquainted with towns and large assemblages of men. The cottage of my protectors had been the only school in which I had studied human nature, but this book developed new and mightier scenes of action. I read of men concerned in public affairs, governing or massacring their species. I felt the greatest ardour for virtue rise within me, and abhorrence for vice, as far as I understood the signification of those terms, relative as they were, as I applied them, to pleasure and pain alone. Induced by these feelings, I was of course led to admire peaceable lawgivers, Numa, Solon, and Lycurgus, in preference to Romulus and Theseus.[2] The patriarchal lives of my protectors caused these impressions to take a firm hold on my mind; perhaps, if my first introduction to humanity had been made by a young soldier, burning for glory and slaughter, I should have been imbued with different sensations.

"But *Paradise Lost* excited different and far deeper emotions. I read it, as I had read the other volumes which had fallen into my hands, as a true history. It moved every feeling of wonder and awe that the picture of an omnipotent God

---

1. Paraphrase of a line from Percy Shelley's poem "Mutability."

2. Rulers discussed in the *Lives* of Plutarch (46– c. 122 CE)

warring with his creatures was capable of exciting. I often referred the several situations, as their similarity struck me, to my own. Like Adam, I was apparently united by no link to any other being in existence; but his state was far different from mine in every other respect. He had come forth from the hands of God a perfect creature, happy and prosperous, guarded by the especial care of his Creator; he was allowed to converse with and acquire knowledge from beings of a superior nature, but I was wretched, helpless, and alone. Many times I considered Satan as the fitter emblem of my condition, for often, like him, when I viewed the bliss of my protectors, the bitter gall of envy rose within me.

"Another circumstance strengthened and confirmed these feelings. Soon after my arrival in the hovel I discovered some papers in the pocket of the dress which I had taken from your laboratory. At first I had neglected them, but now that I was able to decipher the characters in which they were written, I began to study them with diligence. It was your journal of the four months that preceded my creation. You minutely described in these papers every step you took in the progress of your work; this history was mingled with accounts of domestic occurrences. You doubtless recollect these papers. Here they are. Every thing is related in them which bears reference to my accursed origin; the whole detail of that series of disgusting circumstances which produced it is set in view; the minutest description of my odious and loathsome person is given, in language which painted your own horrors and rendered mine indelible. I sickened as I read. 'Hateful day when I received life!' I exclaimed in agony. 'Accursed creator! Why did you form a monster so hideous that even *you* turned from me in disgust? God, in pity, made man beautiful and alluring, after his own image; but my form is a filthy type of yours, more horrid even from the very resemblance. Satan had his companions, fellow devils, to admire and encourage him, but I am solitary and abhorred.'

"These were the reflections of my hours of despondency and solitude; but when I contemplated the virtues of the cottagers, their amiable and benevolent dispositions, I persuaded myself that when they should become acquainted with my admiration of their virtues they would compassionate me and overlook my personal deformity. Could they turn from their door one, however monstrous, who solicited their compassion and friendship? I resolved, at least, not to despair, but in every way to fit myself for an interview with them which would decide my fate. I postponed this attempt for some months longer, for the importance attached to its success inspired me with a dread lest I should fail. Besides, I found that my understanding improved so much with every day's experience that I was unwilling to commence this undertaking until a few more months should have added to my sagacity.

"Several changes, in the mean time, took place in the cottage. The presence of Safie diffused happiness among its inhabitants, and I also found that a greater degree of plenty reigned there. Felix and Agatha spent more time in amusement and conversation, and were assisted in their labours by servants. They did not appear rich, but they were contented and happy; their feelings were serene and peaceful, while mine became every day more tumultuous. Increase of knowledge only discovered to me more clearly what a wretched outcast I was. I cherished hope, it is true, but it vanished when I beheld my person reflected in water or my shadow in the moonshine, even as that frail image and that inconstant shade.

"I endeavoured to crush these fears and to fortify myself for the trial which in a few months I resolved to undergo; and sometimes I allowed my thoughts, unchecked by reason, to ramble in the fields of Paradise, and dared to fancy amiable and lovely creatures sympathizing with my feelings and cheering my gloom; their angelic countenances breathed smiles of consolation. But it was all a dream; no Eve soothed my sorrows nor shared my thoughts; I was alone. I remembered Adam's supplication to his Creator. But where was mine? He had abandoned me, and in the bitterness of my heart I cursed him.

"Autumn passed thus. I saw, with surprize and grief, the leaves decay and fall, and nature again assume the barren and bleak appearance it had worn when I first beheld the woods and the lovely moon. Yet I did not heed the bleakness of the weather; I was better fitted by my conformation for the endurance of cold than heat. But my chief delights were the sight of the flowers, the birds, and all the gay apparel of summer; when those deserted me, I turned with more attention towards the cottagers. Their happiness was not decreased by the absence of summer. They loved and sympathized with one another; and their joys, depending on each other, were not interrupted by the casualties that took place around them. The more I saw of them, the greater became my desire to claim their protection and kindness; my heart yearned to be known and loved by these amiable creatures; to see their sweet looks directed towards me with affection was the utmost limit of my ambition. I dared not think that they would turn them from me with disdain and horror. The poor that stopped at their door were never driven away. I asked, it is true, for greater treasures than a little food or rest: I required kindness and sympathy; but I did not believe myself unworthy of it.

"The winter advanced, and an entire revolution of the seasons had taken place since I awoke into life. My attention at this time was solely directed towards my plan of introducing myself into the cottage of my protectors. I revolved many projects, but that on which I finally fixed was to enter the dwelling when the blind old man should be alone. I had sagacity enough to discover that the unnatural hideousness of my person was the chief object of horror with those who had formerly beheld me. My voice, although harsh, had nothing terrible in it; I thought, therefore, that if in the absence of his children I could gain the good will and mediation of the old De Lacey, I might by his means be tolerated by my younger protectors.

"One day, when the sun shone on the red leaves that strewed the ground and diffused cheerfulness, although it denied warmth, Safie, Agatha, and Felix departed on a long country walk, and the old man, at his own desire, was left alone in the cottage. When his children had departed, he took up his guitar and played several mournful but sweet airs, more sweet and mournful than I had ever heard him play before. At first his countenance was illuminated with pleasure, but as he continued, thoughtfulness and sadness succeeded; at length, laying aside the instrument, he sat absorbed in reflection.

"My heart beat quick; this was the hour and moment of trial, which would decide my hopes or realize my fears. The servants were gone to a neighbouring fair. All was silent in and around the cottage; it was an excellent opportunity; yet, when I proceeded to execute my plan, my limbs failed me and I sank to the ground. Again I rose, and exerting all the firmness of which I was master, removed the planks which I had placed before my hovel to conceal my retreat. The fresh air revived me, and with renewed determination I approached the door of their cottage.

"I knocked. 'Who is there?' said the old man—'Come in.'

"I entered. 'Pardon this intrusion,' said I; 'I am a traveller in want of a little rest; you would greatly oblige me if you would allow me to remain a few minutes before the fire.'

" 'Enter,' said De Lacey, 'and I will try in what manner I can to relieve your wants; but, unfortunately, my children are from home, and as I am blind, I am afraid I shall find it difficult to procure food for you.'

" 'Do not trouble yourself, my kind host; I have food; it is warmth and rest only that I need.'

"I sat down, and a silence ensued. I knew that every minute was precious to me, yet I remained irresolute in what manner to commence the interview, when the old man addressed me. 'By your language, stranger, I suppose you are my countryman; are you French?'

" 'No; but I was educated by a French family and understand that language only. I am now going to claim the protection of some friends, whom I sincerely love, and of whose favour I have some hopes.'

" 'Are they Germans?'

" 'No, they are French. But let us change the subject. I am an unfortunate and deserted creature; I look around and I have no relation or friend upon earth. These amiable people to whom I go have never seen me and know little of me. I am full off fears, for if I fail there, I am an outcast in the world forever.'

" 'Do not despair. To be friendless is indeed to be unfortunate, but the hearts of men, when unprejudiced by any obvious self-interest, are full of brotherly love and charity. Rely, therefore, on your hopes; and if these friends are good and amiable, do not despair.'

" 'They are kind—they are the most excellent creatures in the world; but, unfortunately, they are prejudiced against me. I have good dispositions; my life has been hitherto harmless and in some degree beneficial; but a fatal prejudice clouds their eyes, and where they ought to see a feeling and kind friend, they behold only a detestable monster.'

" 'That is indeed unfortunate; but if you are really blameless, cannot you undeceive them?'

" 'I am about to undertake that task; and it is on that account that I feel so many overwhelming terrors. I tenderly love these friends; I have, unknown to them, been for many months in the habits of daily kindness towards them; but they believe that I wish to injure them, and it is that prejudice which I wish to overcome.'

" 'Where do these friends reside?'

" 'Near this spot.'

"The old man paused and then continued, 'If you will unreservedly confide to me the particulars of your tale, I perhaps may be of use in undeceiving them. I am blind and cannot judge of your countenance, but there is something in your words which persuades me that you are sincere. I am poor and an exile, but it will afford me true pleasure to be in any way serviceable to a human creature.'

" 'Excellent man! I thank you and accept your generous offer. You raise me from the dust by this kindness; and I trust that, by your aid, I shall not be driven from the society and sympathy of your fellow creatures.'

" 'Heaven forbid! Even if you were really criminal, for that can only drive you to desperation, and not instigate you to virtue. I also am unfortunate; I and my family have been condemned, although innocent; judge, therefore, if I do not feel for your misfortunes.'

" 'How can I thank you, my best and only benefactor? From your lips first have I heard the voice of kindness directed towards me; I shall be forever grateful;

and your present humanity assures me of success with those friends whom I am on the point of meeting.'

"'May I know the names and residence of those friends?'

"I paused. This, I thought, was the moment of decision, which was to rob me of or bestow happiness on me forever. I struggled vainly for firmness sufficient to answer him, but the effort destroyed all my remaining strength; I sank on the chair and sobbed aloud. At that moment I heard the steps of my younger protectors. I had not a moment to lose, but seizing the hand of the old man, I cried, 'Now is the time! Save and protect me! You and your family are the friends whom I seek. Do not you desert me in the hour of trial!'

"'Great God!' exclaimed the old man. 'Who are you?'

"At that instant the cottage door was opened, and Felix, Safie, and Agatha entered. Who can describe their horror and consternation on beholding me? Agatha fainted, and Safie, unable to attend to her friend, rushed out of the cottage. Felix darted forward, and with supernatural force tore me from his father, to whose knees I clung; in a transport of fury, he dashed me to the ground and struck me violently with a stick. I could have torn him limb from limb, as the lion rends the antelope. But my heart sank within me as with bitter sickness, and I refrained. I saw him on the point of repeating the blow, when, overcome by pain and anguish, I quitted the cottage, and in the general tumult escaped unperceived to my hovel."

Chapter 16

[THE MONSTER SEEKS HIS CREATOR]

"Cursed, cursed creator! Why did I live? Why, in that instant, did I not extinguish the spark of existence which you had so wantonly bestowed? I know not; despair had not yet taken possession of me; my feelings were those of rage and revenge. I could with pleasure have destroyed the cottage and its inhabitants and have glutted myself with their shrieks and misery.

"When night came I quitted my retreat and wandered in the wood; and now, no longer restrained by the fear of discovery, I gave vent to my anguish in fearful howlings. I was like a wild beast that had broken the toils, destroying the objects that obstructed me and ranging through the wood with a staglike swiftness. Oh! What a miserable night I passed! The cold stars shone in mockery, and the bare trees waved their branches above me; now and then the sweet voice of a bird burst forth amidst the universal stillness. All, save I, were at rest or in enjoyment; I, like the arch-fiend, bore a hell within me, and finding myself unsympathized with, wished to tear up the trees, spread havoc and destruction around me, and then to have sat down and enjoyed the ruin.

"But this was a luxury of sensation that could not endure; I became fatigued with excess of bodily exertion and sank on the damp grass in the sick impotence of despair. There was none among the myriads of men that existed who would pity or assist me; and should I feel kindness towards my enemies? No; from that moment I declared ever-lasting war against the species, and more than all against him who had formed me and sent me forth to this insupportable misery.

"The sun rose; I heard the voices of men and knew that it was impossible to return to my retreat during that day. Accordingly, I hid myself in some thick underwood, determining to devote the ensuing hours to reflection on my situation.

"The pleasant sunshine and the pure air of day restored me to some degree of tranquillity; and when I considered what had passed at the cottage, I could not help believing that I had been too hasty in my conclusions. I had certainly acted imprudently. It was apparent that my conversation had interested the father in my behalf, and I was a fool in having exposed my person to the horror of his children. I ought to have familiarized the old De Lacey to me, and by degrees to have discovered myself to the rest of his family, when they should have been prepared for my approach. But I did not believe my errors to be irretrievable, and after much consideration I resolved to return to the cottage, seek the old man, and by my representations win him to my party.

"These thoughts calmed me, and in the afternoon I sank into a profound sleep; but the fever of my blood did not allow me to be visited by peaceful dreams. The horrible scene of the preceding day was forever acting before my eyes; the females were flying and the enraged Felix tearing me from his father's feet. I awoke exhausted, and finding that it was already night, I crept forth from my hiding-place, and went in search of food.

"When my hunger was appeased, I directed my steps towards the well-known path that conducted to the cottage. All there was at peace. I crept into my hovel and remained in silent expectation of the accustomed hour when the family arose. That hour passed, the sun mounted high in the heavens, but the cottagers did not appear. I trembled violently, apprehending some dreadful misfortune. The inside of the cottage was dark, and I heard no motion; I cannot describe the agony of this suspense.

"Presently two countrymen passed by, but pausing near the cottage, they entered into conversation, using violent gesticulations; but I did not understand what they said, as they spoke the language of the country, which differed from that of my protectors. Soon after, however, Felix approached with another man; I was surprized, as I knew that he had not quitted the cottage that morning, and waited anxiously to discover from his discourse the meaning of these unusual appearances.

"'Do you consider,' said his companion to him, 'that you will be obliged to pay three months' rent and to lose the produce of your garden? I do not wish to take any unfair advantage, and I beg therefore that you will take some days to consider of your determination.'

"'It is utterly useless,' replied Felix; 'we can never again inhabit your cottage. The life of my father is in the greatest danger, owing to the dreadful circumstance that I have related. My wife and my sister will never recover from their horror. I intreat you not to reason with me any more. Take possession of your tenement and let me fly from this place.'

"Felix trembled violently as he said this. He and his companion entered the cottage, in which they remained for a few minutes, and then departed. I never saw any of the family of De Lacey more.

"I continued for the remainder of the day in my hovel in a state of utter and stupid despair. My protectors had departed and had broken the only link that held me to the world. For the first time the feelings of revenge and hatred filled my bosom, and I did not strive to control them, but allowing myself to be borne away by the stream, I bent my mind towards injury and death. When I thought of my friends, of the mild voice of De Lacey, the gentle eyes of Agatha, and the exquisite beauty of the Arabian, these thoughts vanished and a gush of tears somewhat soothed me. But again when I reflected that they had spurned and deserted me, anger returned, a rage of anger, and unable to injure anything human, I turned my fury towards inanimate objects. As night advanced I placed a variety of combustibles around the cottage, and after having destroyed every vestige of cultivation in the garden, I waited with forced impatience until the moon had sunk to commence my operations.

"As the night advanced, a fierce wind arose from the woods and quickly dispersed the clouds that had loitered in the heavens; the blast tore along like a mighty avalanche and produced a kind of insanity in my spirits that burst all bounds of reason and reflection. I lighted the dry branch of a tree and danced with fury around the devoted cottage, my eyes still fixed on the western horizon, the edge of which the moon nearly touched. A part of its orb was at length hid, and I waved my brand; it sank, and with a loud scream I fired the straw, and heath, and bushes, which I had collected. The wind fanned the fire, and the cottage was quickly enveloped by the flames, which clung to it and licked it with their forked and destroying tongues.

"As soon as I was convinced that no assistance could save any part of the habitation, I quitted the scene and sought for refuge in the woods.

"And now, with the world before me, whither should I bend my steps? I resolved to fly far from the scene of my misfortunes; but to me, hated and despised, every country must be equally horrible. At length the thought of you crossed my mind. I learned from your papers that you were my father, my creator; and to whom could I apply with more fitness than to him who had given me life? Among the lessons that Felix had bestowed upon Safie, geography had not been omitted; I had learned from these the relative situations of the different countries of the earth. You had mentioned Geneva as the name of your native town, and towards this place I resolved to proceed.

"But how was I to direct myself? I knew that I must travel in a southwesterly direction to reach my destination, but the sun was my only guide. I did not know the names of the towns that I was to pass through, nor could I ask information from a single human being; but I did not despair. From you only could I hope for succour, although towards you I felt no sentiment but that of hatred. Unfeeling, heartless creator! You had endowed me with perceptions and passions and then cast me abroad an object for the scorn and horror of mankind. But on you only had I any claim for pity and redress, and from you I determined to seek that justice which I vainly attempted to gain from any other being that wore the human form.

"My travels were long and the sufferings I endured intense. It was late in autumn when I quitted the district where I had so long resided. I travelled only at night, fearful of encountering the visage of a human being. Nature decayed around me, and the sun became heatless; rain and snow poured around me; mighty rivers were frozen; the surface of the earth was hard and chill, and bare, and I found no shelter. Oh, earth! How often did I imprecate curses on the cause of my being! The mildness of my nature had fled, and all within me was turned to gall and bitterness. The nearer I approached to your habitation, the more deeply did I feel the spirit of revenge enkindled in my heart. Snow fell, and the waters were hardened, but I rested not. A few incidents now and then directed me, and I possessed a map of the country; but I often wandered wide from my path. The agony of my feelings allowed me no respite; no incident occurred from which my rage and misery could not extract its food; but a circumstance that happened when I arrived on the confines of Switzerland, when the sun had recovered its warmth and the earth again began to look green, confirmed in an especial manner the bitterness and horror of my feelings.

"I generally rested during the day and travelled only when I was secured by night from the view of man. One morning, however, finding that my path lay through a deep wood, I ventured to continue my journey after the sun had risen; the day, which was one of the first of spring, cheered even me by the loveliness of its sunshine and the balminess of the air. I felt emotions of gentleness and pleasure, that had long appeared dead, revive within me. Half surprized by the novelty of these sensations, I allowed myself to be borne away by them, and forgetting my solitude and deformity dared to be happy. Soft tears again bedewed my cheeks, and I even raised my humid eyes with thankfulness towards the blessed sun, which bestowed such joy upon me.

"I continued to wind among the paths of the wood, until I came to its boundary which was skirted by a deep and rapid river, into which many of the trees bent their branches, now budding with the fresh spring. Here I paused, not exactly knowing what path to pursue, when I heard the sound of voices, that induced me to conceal myself under the shade of a cypress. I was scarcely hid when a young girl came running towards the spot where I was concealed, laughing, as if she ran from some one in sport. She continued her course along the precipitous sides of the river, when suddenly her foot slipped, and she fell into the rapid stream. I rushed from my hiding-place and with extreme labour from the force of the current, saved her and dragged her to shore. She was senseless, and I endeavoured by every means in my power to restore animation, when I was suddenly interrupted by the approach of a rustic, who was probably the person from whom she had playfully fled. On seeing me, he darted towards me, and tearing the girl from my arms, hastened towards the deeper parts of the wood. I followed speedily, I hardly knew why; but when the man saw me draw near, he aimed a gun, which he carried, at my body, and fired. I sank to the ground, and my injurer, with increased swiftness, escaped into the wood.

"This was then the reward of my benevolence! I had saved a human being from destruction, and as a recompense I now writhed under the miserable pain of a wound which shattered the flesh and bone. The feelings of kindness and gentleness which I had entertained but a few moments before gave place to hellish rage and gnashing of teeth. Inflamed by pain, I vowed eternal hatred and vengeance to all mankind. But the agony of my wound overcame me; my pulses paused, and I fainted.

"For some weeks I led a miserable life in the woods, endeavouring to cure the wound which I had received. The ball had entered my shoulder, and I knew not whether it had remained there or passed through; at any rate I had no means of extracting it. My sufferings were augmented also by the oppressive sense of the injustice and ingratitude of their infliction. My daily vows rose for revenge—a deep and deadly revenge, such as would alone compensate for the outrages and anguish I had endured.

"After some weeks my wound healed, and I continued my journey. The labours I endured were no longer to be alleviated by the bright sun or gentle breezes of spring; all joy was but a mockery which insulted my desolate state and made me feel more painfully that I was not made for the enjoyment of pleasure.

"But my toils now drew near a close, and in two months from this time I reached the environs of Geneva.

"It was evening when I arrived, and I retired to a hiding-place among the fields that surround it to meditate in what manner I should apply to you. I was oppressed by fatigue and hunger and far too unhappy to enjoy the gentle breezes of evening or the prospect of the sun setting behind the stupendous mountains of Jura.

"At this time a slight sleep relieved me from the pain of reflection, which was disturbed by the approach of a beautiful child, who came running into the recess I had chosen, with all the sportiveness of infancy. Suddenly, as I gazed on him, an idea seized me that this little creature was unprejudiced and had lived too short a time to have imbibed a horror of deformity. If, therefore, I could seize him and educate him as my companion and friend, I should not be so desolate in this peopled earth.

"Urged by this impulse, I seized on the boy as he passed and drew him towards me. As soon as he beheld my form, he placed his hands before his eyes and uttered a shrill scream; I drew his hand forcibly from his face and said, 'Child, what is the meaning of this? I do not intend to hurt you; listen to me.'

"He struggled violently. 'Let me go,' he cried; 'monster! Ugly wretch! You wish to eat me and tear me to pieces. You are an ogre. Let me go, or I will tell my papa.'

"'Boy, you will never see your father again; you must come with me.'

"'Hideous monster! Let me go. My papa is a syndic—he is M. Frankenstein[3]— he will punish you. You dare not keep me.'

"'Frankenstein! You belong then to my enemy—to him towards whom I have sworn eternal revenge; you shall be my first victim.'

"The child still struggled and loaded me with epithets which carried despair to my heart; I grasped his throat to silence him, and in a moment he lay dead at my feet.

"I gazed on my victim, and my heart swelled with exultation and hellish triumph; clapping my hands, I exclaimed, 'I too can create desolation; my enemy is not invulnerable; this death will carry despair to him, and a thousand other miseries shall torment and destroy him.'

"As I fixed my eyes on the child, I saw something glittering on his breast. I took it; it was a portrait of a most lovely woman. In spite of my malignity, it softened and attracted me. For a few moments I gazed with delight on her dark eyes, fringed by deep lashes, and her lovely lips; but presently my rage returned; I remembered that I was forever deprived of the delights that such beautiful creatures could bestow and that she whose resemblance I contemplated would, in regarding me, have changed that air of divine benignity to one expressive of disgust and affright.

"Can you wonder that such thoughts transported me with rage? I only wonder that at that moment, instead of venting my sensations in exclamations and agony, I did not rush among mankind and perish in the attempt to destroy them.

"While I was overcome by these feelings, I left the spot where I had committed the murder, and seeking a more secluded hiding-place, I entered a barn which had appeared to me to be empty. A woman was sleeping on some straw; she was young, not indeed so beautiful as her whose portrait I held, but of an agreeable aspect and blooming in the loveliness of youth and health. Here, I thought, is one of those whose joy-imparting smiles are bestowed on all but me. And then I bent over her and whispered, 'Awake, fairest, thy lover is near—he who would give his life but to obtain one look of affection from thine eyes; my beloved, awake!'

"The sleeper stirred; a thrill of terror ran through me. Should she indeed awake, and see me, and curse me, and denounce the murderer? Thus would she assuredly act if her darkened eyes opened and she beheld me. The thought was

3. Syndic: a senior state legislator; M. Franken-   brother).
stein: Victor's father (William is Victor's young

madness; it stirred the fiend within me—not I, but she, shall suffer; the murder I have committed because I am forever robbed of all that she could give me, she shall atone. The crime had its source in her; be hers the punishment! Thanks to the lessons of Felix and the sanguinary laws of man, I had learned now to work mischief. I bent over her and placed the portrait securely in one of the folds of her dress. She moved again, and I fled.

"For some days I haunted the spot where these scenes had taken place, sometimes wishing to see you, sometimes resolved to quit the world and its miseries forever. At length I wandered towards these mountains, and have ranged through their immense recesses, consumed by a burning passion which you alone can gratify. We may not part until you have promised to comply with my requisition. I am alone and miserable; man will not associate with me; but one as deformed and horrible as myself would not deny herself to me. My companion must be of the same species and have the same defects. This being you must create."

Chapter 17

[THE MONSTER'S DEMAND]

The being finished speaking and fixed his looks upon me in the expectation of a reply. But I was bewildered, perplexed, and unable to arrange my ideas sufficiently to understand the full extent of his proposition. He continued, "You must create a female for me with whom I can live in the interchange of those sympathies necessary for my being. This you alone can do, and I demand it of you as a right which you must not refuse to concede."

The latter part of his tale had kindled anew in me the anger that had died away while he narrated his peaceful life among the cottagers, and as he said this I could no longer suppress the rage that burned within me.

"I do refuse it," I replied; "and no torture shall ever extort a consent from me. You may render me the most miserable of men, but you shall never make me base in my own eyes. Shall I create another like yourself, whose joint wickedness might desolate the world? Begone! I have answered you; you may torture me, but I will never consent."

"You are in the wrong," replied the fiend; "and instead of threatening, I am content to reason with you. I am malicious because I am miserable. Am I not shunned and hated by all mankind? You, my creator, would tear me to pieces and triumph; remember that, and tell me why I should pity man more than he pities me? You would not call it murder if you could precipitate me into one of those ice-rifts and destroy my frame, the work of your own hands. Shall I respect man when he condemns me? Let him live with me in the interchange of kindness, and instead of injury I would bestow every benefit upon him with tears of gratitude at his acceptance. But that cannot be; the human senses are insurmountable barriers to our union. Yet mine shall not be the submission of abject slavery. I will revenge my injuries; if I cannot inspire love, I will cause fear, and chiefly towards you my arch-enemy, because my creator, do I swear inextinguishable hatred. Have a care; I will work at your destruction, nor finish until I desolate your heart, so that you shall curse the hour of your birth."

A fiendish rage animated him as he said this; his face was wrinkled into contortions too horrible for human eyes to behold; but presently he calmed himself and proceeded, "I intended to reason. This passion is detrimental to me, for you do not reflect that *you* are the cause of its excess. If any being felt emotions of benevolence towards me, I should return them a hundred and a hundredfold; for that one creature's sake I would make peace with the whole kind! But I now indulge in dreams of bliss that cannot be realized. What I ask of you is reasonable and moderate; I demand a creature of another sex, but as hideous as myself; the gratification is small, but it is all that I can receive, and it shall content me. It is true, we shall be monsters, cut off from all the world; but on that account we shall be more attached to one another. Our lives will not be happy, but they will be harmless and free from the misery I now feel. Oh! My creator, make me happy; let me feel gratitude towards you for one benefit! Let me see that I excite the sympathy of some existing thing; do not deny me my request!"

I was moved. I shuddered when I thought of the possible consequences of my consent, but I felt that there was some justice in his argument. His tale and the feelings he now expressed proved him to be a creature of fine sensations, and did I not as his maker owe him all the portion of happiness that it was in my power to bestow? He saw my change of feeling and continued, "If you consent, neither you nor any other human being shall ever see us again; I will go to the vast wilds of South America. My food is not that of man; I do not destroy the lamb and the kid to glut my appetite; acorns and berries afford me sufficient nourishment. My companion will be of the same nature as myself and will be content with the same fare. We shall make our bed of dried leaves; the sun will shine on us as on man and will ripen our food. The picture I present to you is peaceful and human, and you must feel that you could deny it only in the wantonness of power and cruelty. Pitiless as you have been towards me, I now see compassion in your eyes; let me seize the favourable moment and persuade you to promise what I so ardently desire."

"You propose," replied I, "to fly from the habitations of man, to dwell in those wilds where the beasts of the field will be your only companions. How can you, who long for the love and sympathy of man, persevere in this exile? You will return and again seek their kindness, and you will meet with their detestation; your evil passions will be renewed, and you will then have a companion to aid you in the task of destruction. This may not be; cease to argue the point, for I cannot consent."

"How inconstant are your feelings! But a moment ago you were moved by my representations, and why do you again harden yourself to my complaints? I swear to you, by the earth which I inhabit, and by you that made me, that with the companion you bestow I will quit the neighbourhood of man and dwell, as it may chance, in the most savage of places. My evil passions will have fled, for I shall meet with sympathy! My life will flow quietly away, and in my dying moments I shall not curse my maker."

His words had a strange effect upon me. I compassionated him and sometimes felt a wish to console him, but when I looked upon him, when I saw the filthy mass that moved and talked, my heart sickened and my feelings were altered to those of horror and hatred. I tried to stifle these sensations; I thought that as I could not sympathize with him, I had no right to withhold from him the small portion of happiness which was yet in my power to bestow.

"You swear," I said, "to be harmless; but have you not already shown a degree of malice that should reasonably make me distrust you? May not even this be a feint that will increase your triumph by affording a wider scope for your revenge?"

"How is this? I must not be trifled with, and I demand an answer. If I have no ties and no affections, hatred and vice must be my portion; the love of another will destroy the cause of my crimes, and I shall become a thing of whose existence every one will be ignorant. My vices are the children of a forced solitude that I abhor, and my virtues will necessarily arise when I live in communion with an equal. I shall feel the affections of a sensitive being and become linked to the chain of existence and events from which I am now excluded."

I paused some time to reflect on all he had related and the various arguments which he had employed. I thought of the promise of virtues which he had displayed on the opening of his existence and the subsequent blight of all kindly feeling by the loathing and scorn which his protectors had manifested towards him. His power and threats were not omitted in my calculations; a creature who could exist in the ice caves of the glaciers and hide himself from pursuit among the ridges of inaccessible precipices was a being possessing faculties it would be vain to cope with. After a long pause of reflection I concluded that the justice due both to him and my fellow creatures demanded of me that I should comply with his request. Turning to him, therefore, I said, "I consent to your demand, on your solemn oath to quit Europe forever, and every other place in the neighbourhood of man, as soon as I shall deliver into your hands a female who will accompany you in your exile."

"I swear," he cried, "by the sun, and by the blue sky of heaven, and by the fire of love that burns my heart, that if you grant my prayer, while they exist you shall never behold me again. Depart to your home and commence your labours; I shall watch their progress with unutterable anxiety; and fear not but that when you are ready I shall appear."

Saying this, he suddenly quitted me, fearful, perhaps, of any change in my sentiments. I saw him descend the mountain with greater speed than the flight of an eagle, and quickly lost among the undulations of the sea of ice.

His tale had occupied the whole day, and the sun was upon the verge of the horizon when he departed. I knew that I ought to hasten my descent towards the valley, as I should soon be encompassed in darkness; but my heart was heavy, and my steps slow. The labour of winding among the little paths of the mountain and fixing my feet firmly as I advanced, perplexed me, occupied as I was by the emotions which the occurrences of the day had produced. Night was far advanced when I came to the halfway resting-place and seated myself beside the fountain. The stars shone at intervals as the clouds passed from over them; the dark pines rose before me, and every here and there a broken tree lay on the ground; it was a scene of wonderful solemnity and stirred strange thoughts within me. I wept bitterly, and clasping my hands in agony, I exclaimed, "Oh! Stars and clouds and winds, ye are all about to mock me; if ye really pity me, crush sensation and memory; let me become as nought; but if not, depart, depart, and leave me in darkness."

These were wild and miserable thoughts, but I cannot describe to you how the eternal twinkling of the stars weighed upon me and how I listened to every blast of wind as if it were a dull ugly siroc[4] on its way to consume me.

Morning dawned before I arrived at the village of Chamonix;[5] I took no rest, but returned immediately to Geneva. Even in my own heart I could give no expression to my sensations—they weighed on me with a mountain's weight and their excess destroyed my agony beneath them. Thus I returned home, and entering the house, presented myself to the family. My haggard and wild appearance awoke

4. Sirocco, a hot, dusty, humid wind that begins in the Sahara and picks up moisture as it crosses the Mediterranean Sea.

5. Village in the Swiss Alps visited by the Shelleys in 1816.

intense alarm, but I answered no question, scarcely did I speak. I felt as if I were placed under a ban—as if I had no right to claim their sympathies—as if never more might I enjoy companionship with them. Yet even thus I loved them to adoration; and to save them, I resolved to dedicate myself to my most abhorred task. The prospect of such an occupation made every other circumstance of existence pass before me like a dream, and that thought only had to me the reality of life.

1818

►◄ SOJOURNER TRUTH ►◄
c. 1797–1883

The woman who named herself Sojourner Truth to express her dedication to sojourning in the land speaking God's truth, was born a slave in New York State, which had the largest slave population of any Northern colony. Her Dutch-speaking parents, Elizabeth and James, had already had at least ten children who had been sold away when Isabella, as Truth was known, and a younger brother were born. Although Truth was sold as a young girl, her parents conveyed to her a deep spirituality, a devotion to family, and a belief in the dignity of human life. Although it is unknown whether her parents had been stolen from Africa, they seem to have passed on to their daughter some African manners of speech and habits of spirituality. Sold three times before she was twelve, Truth endured hard labor, sexual abuse, and forced separation from her own children before her emancipation in 1827. Once legally free, Truth moved to New York City, where she worked as a paid domestic servant. America in the 1820s was experiencing a Great Awakening of interest in spiritual matters, and Truth, like many Americans, became deeply involved with Christian evangelism and other mystical cults that spoke to her intuitive belief in the perfectibility of all individuals. In 1843, Truth responded to what she felt was a call from God to preach against the sins of slavery and other social inequities. For the rest of her life, Truth spoke against slavery and for universal human rights, including the rights of women to have direct political and economic representation.

And people listened. Though Truth was illiterate ("I cannot read a book, but I can read the people"), her power as a speaker was remarkable even in an era known for celebrated orators. Truth drew upon the Bible, which she had memorized, as a frame of reference, into which she wove parables from her own life and critiques of the belief systems that maintained the oppression of the powerless. After listening to her seemingly spontaneous, and often humorous, speeches Truth's auditors struggled to capture their essence in print. Several accounts, for example, exist of a speech that has come to be known as the "Ar'n't I a Woman" speech, which Truth gave at the 1851 Women's Rights Convention in Akron, Ohio. The two included here transcribe white listeners' memories of an event whose power exceeded the capacities of the written word. One version, originally written down by the feminist activist Frances Dana Gage (p. 680) in the 1860s, became part of the formal history of the women's suffrage movement when Gage included it in her contribution to *History of Woman Suffrage,* edited and published by Elizabeth Cady Stanton, Susan B. Anthony, and Matilda Joslyn Gage in 1881; the other is an 1851 newspaper report from the *Anti-Slavery Bugle.* Truth's power as a storyteller is also conveyed in a mediated form through her *Narrative* of *Sojourner Truth* (1850), which she dictated to a white secretary, Olive Gilbert. (An excerpt appears below.) Truth sold copies of the *Narrative* along with several carefully posed photographs of herself (see p. 612) to audiences on her preaching tours. By selling "the shadow to support the substance," Truth financed her life-long crusade against the systems that held the "shadows" of sex or skin color to be more important than the substance of a person's character.

From The Narrative of Sojourner Truth

Her Birth and Parentage

The subject of this biography, SOJOURNER TRUTH, as she now calls herself—but whose name, originally, was Isabella—was born, as near as she can now calculate, between the years 1797 and 1800. She was the daughter of James and Betsey, slaves of one Colonel Ardinburgh, Hurley, Ulster County, New York.

Colonel Ardinburgh belonged to that class of people called Low Dutch.[1]

Of her first master, she can give no account, as she must have been a mere infant when he died; and she, with her parents and some ten or twelve other fellow human chattels, became the legal property of his son, Charles Ardinburgh. She distinctly remembers hearing her father and mother say, that their lot was a fortunate one, as Master Charles was the best of the family,—being, comparatively speaking, a kind master to his slaves.

James and Betsey having, by their faithfulness, docility, and respectful behavior, won his particular regard, received from him particular favors—among which was a lot of land, lying back on the slope of a mountain, where, by improving the pleasant evenings and Sundays, they managed to raise a little tobacco, corn, or flax; which they exchanged for extras, in the articles of food or clothing for themselves and children. She has no remembrance that Saturday afternoon was ever added to their own time, as it is by *some* masters in the Southern States.

Accommodations

Among Isabella's earliest recollections was the removal of her master, Charles Ardinburgh, into his new house, which he had built for a hotel, soon after the decease of his father. A cellar, under this hotel, was assigned to his slaves, as their sleeping apartment,—all the slaves he possessed, of both sexes, sleeping (as is quite common in a state of slavery) in the same room. She carries in her mind, to this day, a vivid picture of this dismal chamber; its only lights consisting of a few panes of glass, through which she thinks the sun never shone, but with thrice reflected rays; and the space between the loose boards of the floor, and the uneven earth below, was often filled with mud and water, the uncomfortable splashings of which were as annoying as its noxious vapors must have been chilling and fatal to health. She shudders, even now, as she goes back in memory, and revisits this cellar, and sees its inmates, of both sexes and all ages, sleeping on those damp boards, like the horse, with a little straw and a blanket; and she wonders not at the rheumatisms, and fever-sores, and palsies, that distorted the limbs and racked the bodies of those fellow-slaves in after-life. Still, she does not attribute this cruelty—for cruelty it certainly is, to be so unmindful of the health and comfort of any being,

---

1. Descendants of German-speaking settlers who emigrated to Pennsylvania prior to the Revolu- tionary War.

leaving entirely out of sight his more important part, his everlasting interests,—so much to any innate or constitutional cruelty of the master, as to that gigantic inconsistency, that inherited habit among slaveholders, of expecting a willing and intelligent obedience from the slave, because he is a MAN—at the same time every thing belonging to the soul-harrowing system does its best to crush the last vestige of a man within him; and when it *is* crushed, and often before, he is denied the comforts of life, on the plea that he knows neither the want nor the use of them, and because he is considered to be little more or little *less* than a beast.

Her Brothers and Sisters

Isabella's father was very tall and straight, when young, which gave him the name of "Bomefree"—low Dutch for tree—at least, this is SOJOURNER's pronunciation of it—and by this name he usually went. The most familiar appellation of her mother was "Mau-mau Bett." She was the mother of some ten or twelve children; though Sojourner is far from knowing the exact number of her brothers and sisters; she being the youngest, save one, and all older than herself having been sold before her remembrance. She was privileged to behold six of them while she remained a slave.

Of the two that immediately preceded her in age, a boy of five years, and a girl of three, who were sold when she was an infant, she heard much; and she wishes that all who could fain believe that slave parents have not natural affection for their offspring could have listened as *she* did, while Bomefree and Mau-mau Bett,— their dark cellar lighted by a blazing pineknot,[2]—would sit for hours, recalling and recounting every endearing, as well as harrowing circumstance that taxed memory could supply, from the histories of those dear departed ones, of whom they had been robbed, and for whom their hearts still bled. Among the rest, they would relate how the little boy, on the last morning he was with them, arose with the birds, kindled a fire, calling for his Mau-mau to "come, for all was now ready for her"— little dreaming of the dreadful separation which was so near at hand, but of which his parents had an uncertain, but all the more cruel foreboding. There was snow on the ground, at the time of which we are speaking; and a large old-fashioned sleigh was seen to drive up to the door of the late Col. Ardinburgh. This event was noticed with childish pleasure by the unsuspicious boy; but when he was taken and put into the sleigh, and saw his little sister actually shut and locked into the sleigh-box, his eyes were at once opened to their intentions; and, like a frightened deer, he sprang from the sleigh, and running into the house, concealed himself under a bed. But this availed him little. He was reconveyed to the sleigh, and separated for ever from those whom God had constituted his natural guardians and protectors, and who should have found him, in return, a stay and a staff to them in their declining years. But I make no comments on facts like these, knowing that the heart of every slave parent will make its own comments, involuntarily and correctly, as soon as each heart shall make the case its own. Those who are not parents will draw their conclusions from the promptings of humanity and philanthropy:—these, enlightened by reason and revelation, are also unerring.

1850

---

2. Poor people would light small pine branches to provide limited and dangerous light in their homes or to serve as torches.

[Sojourner Truth's "Ar'n't I a Woman" Speech, as Reported in the Anti-Slavery Bugle]

One of the most unique and interesting speeches of the Convention[3] was made by Sojourner Truth, an emancipated slave. It is impossible to transfer it to paper, or convey any adequate idea of the effect it produced upon the audience. Those only can appreciate it who saw her powerful form, her whole-souled, earnest gesture, and listened to her strong and truthful tones. She came forward to the platform and addressing the President said with great simplicity: "May I say a few words?" Receiving an affirmative answer, she proceeded:

I want to say a few words about this matter. I am a woman's rights. I have as much muscle as any man, and can do as much work as any man. I have plowed and reaped and husked and chopped and mowed, and can any man do more than that? I have heard much about the sexes being equal. I can carry as much as any man, and can eat as much too, if I can get it. I am as strong as any man that is now. As for intellect, all I can say is, if woman have a pint, and man a quart—why can't she have her little pint full? You need not be afraid to give us our rights for fear we will take too much,—for we can't take more than our pint'll hold. The poor men seem to be all in confusion, and don't know what to do. Why children, if you have woman's rights, give it to her and you will feel better. You will have your own rights, and they won't be so much trouble. I can't read, but I can hear. I have heard the bible and have learned that Eve caused man to sin. Well, if woman upset the world, do give her a chance to set it right side up again. The Lady has spoken about Jesus, how he never spurned woman from him, and she was right. When Lazarus died, Mary and Martha came to him with faith and love and besought him to raise their brother. And Jesus wept and Lazarus came forth.[4] And how came Jesus into the world? Through God who created him and a woman who bore him. Man, where is your part? But the women are coming up blessed be God and a few of the men are coming up with them. But man is in a tight place, the poor slave is on him, woman is coming on him, he is surely between a hawk and a buzzard.

1851

[Sojourner Truth's "Ar'n't I a Woman" Speech, as Recorded in Reminiscences of Frances D. Gage]

The leaders of the movement trembled on seeing a tall, gaunt black woman in a gray dress and white turban, surmounted with an uncouth sun-bonnet, march deliberately into the church, walk with the air of a queen up the aisle, and take her seat upon the pulpit steps. A buzz of disapprobation was heard all over the house, and there fell on the listening ear, "An abolition affair!" "Woman's rights and niggers!" "I told you so!" "Go it, darkey!"

I chanced on that occasion to wear my first laurels in public life as president of the meeting. At my request order was restored, and the business of the Convention

3. The 1851 Women's Rights Convention in Akron, Ohio.   4. John 11:20–44.

went on. Morning, afternoon, and evening exercises came and went. Through all these sessions old Sojourner, quiet and reticent as the "Lybian Statue,"[5] sat crouched against the wall on the corner of the pulpit stairs, her sun-bonnet shading her eyes, her elbows on her knees, her chin resting upon her broad, hard palms. At intermission she was busy selling the "Life of Sojourner Truth," a narrative of her own strange and adventurous life. Again and again, timorous and trembling ones came to me and said, with earnestness, "Don't let her speak, Mrs. Gage, it will ruin us. Every newspaper in the land will have our cause mixed up with abolition and niggers, and we shall be utterly denounced." My only answer was, "We shall see when the time comes."

The second day the work waxed warm. Methodist, Baptist, Episcopal, Presbyterian, and Universalist ministers came in to hear and discuss the resolutions presented. One claimed superior rights and privileges for man, on the ground of "superior intellect"; another, because of the "manhood of Christ; if God had desired the equality of woman, He would have given some token of His will through the birth, life, and death of the Saviour." Another gave us a theological view of the "sin of our first mother."

There were very few women in those days who dared to "speak in meeting", and the august teachers of the people were seemingly getting the better of us, while the boys in the galleries, and the sneerers among the pews, were hugely enjoying the discomfiture, as they supposed, of the "strong-minded." Some of the tender-skinned friends were on the point of losing dignity, and the atmosphere betokened a storm. When, slowly from her seat in the corner rose Sojourner Truth, who, till now, had scarcely lifted her head. "Don't let her speak!" gasped half a dozen in my ear. She moved slowly and solemnly to the front, laid her old bonnet at her feet, and turned her great speaking eyes to me. There was a hissing sound of disapprobation above and below. I rose and announced "Sojourner Truth," and begged the audience to keep silence for a few moments.

The tumult subsided at once, and every eye was fixed on this almost Amazon[6] form, which stood nearly six feet high, head erect, and eyes piercing the upper air like one in a dream. At her first word there was a profound hush. She spoke in deep tones, which, though not loud, reached every ear in the house, and away through the throng at the doors and windows.

"Wall, chilern, whar dar is so much racket dar must be somethin' out o' kilter. I tink dat 'twixt de niggers of de Souf and de womin at de Norf, all talkin' 'bout rights, de white men will be in a fix pretty soon. But what's all dis here talkin' 'bout?

"Dat man ober dar say dat womin needs to be helped into carriages, and lifted ober ditches, and to hab de best place everywhar. Nobody eber helps me into carriages, or ober mud-puddles, or gibs me any best place!" And raising herself to her full height, and her voice to a pitch like rolling thunder, she asked, "And a'n't I a woman? Look at me! Look at my arm! (and she bared her right arm to the shoulder, showing her tremendous muscular power). I have ploughed, and planted, and gathered into barns, and no man could head me! And a'n't I a woman? I could work as much and eat as much as a man—when I could get it—and bear de lash

---

5. "The Libyan Sibyl" (1868) is a sculpture by William Wetmore Story of a female figure sitting with chin in hand and elbow on knee, inspired by Truth.
6. A mythical female warrior.

as well! And a'n't I a woman? I have borne thirteen chilern, and seen 'em mos' all sold off to slavery, and when I cried out with my mother's grief, none but Jesus heard me! And a'n't I a woman?

"Den dey talks 'bout dis ting in de head; what dis dey call it?" ("Intellect," whispered some one near.) "Dat's it, honey. What's dat got to do wid womin's rights or nigger's rights? If my cup won't hold but a pint, and yourn holds a quart, wouldn't ye be mean not to let me have my little half-measure full?" And she pointed her significant finger, and sent a keen glance at the minister who had made the argument. The cheering was long and loud.

"Den dat little man in black dar, he say women can't have as much rights as men, 'cause Christ wan't a woman! Whar did your Christ come from?" Rolling thunder couldn't have stilled that crowd, as did those deep, wonderful tones, as she stood there with outstretched arms and eyes of fire. Raising her voice still louder, she repeated, "Whar did your Christ come from? From God and a woman! Man had nothin' to do wid Him." Oh, what a rebuke that was to that little man.

Turning again to another objector, she took up the defense of Mother Eve. I can not follow her through it all. It was pointed, and witty, and solemn; eliciting at almost every sentence deafening applause; and she ended by asserting: "If de fust woman God ever made was strong enough to turn de world upside down all alone, dese women togedder (and she glanced her eye over the platform) ought to be able to turn it back, and get it right side up again! And now dey is asking to do it, de men better let 'em." Long-continued cheering greeted this. "'Bleeged[7] to ye for hearin' on me, and now ole Sojourner han't got nothin' more to say."

Amid roars of applause, she returned to her corner, leaving more than one of us with streaming eyes, and hearts beating with gratitude. She had taken us up in her strong arms and carried us safely over the slough of difficulty turning the whole tide in our favor. I have never in my life seen anything like the magical influence that subdued the mobbish spirit of the day, and turned the sneers and jeers of an excited crowd into notes of respect and admiration. Hundreds rushed up to shake hands with her, and congratulate the glorious old mother, and bid her God-speed on her mission of "testifyin' agin concerning the wickedness of this 'ere people."

1881

---

7. (Much) obliged.

CULTURAL COORDINATES
Cartes de Visite

During the mid-1850s, developments in the new field of photography made it possible to capture images inexpensively and permanently on paper through the use of albumen print technology. For the first time, it was possible for people of ordinary means to possess portraits of themselves. A French photographer had started a fad that would last through the end of the century by mounting small prints on heavy card stock that was cut into a convenient carrying size. Marketed as *cartes de visite*, these cards with images almost immediately replaced conventional visiting cards, which consisted only of a printed name. By 1863, *cartes de visite* had become so popular as collector's items that American poet Oliver Wendell Holmes said that "card portraits, as everybody knows, have become the social currency, the 'green-back' of civilization."

Men and women collected the *cartes de visite* not only of people they knew but also of famous people. Photography studios and stationery stores would sell *cartes de visite* of prominent people and landscapes, which became popular gifts that could be mailed and easily circulated among friends. Politicians and lecturers in America began to capitalize on the public's desire for photographs by selling *cartes de visite* of themselves following their appearances. As a prominent, even famous, person, Sojourner Truth was not alone in having numerous portraits of herself taken and made into *cartes de visite*. As she traveled throughout the country, she would sell these "shadows" following her lectures along with copies of her *Narrative*, to "support the substance"—the woman herself.

I SELL THE SHADOW TO SUPPORT THE SUBSTANCE.
SOJOURNER TRUTH.

Sojourner Truth's 1864 *carte de visite:* "I sell the Shadow to support the Substance."

HARRIET MARTINEAU
1802–1876

A prolific and popular writer, Harriet Martineau has been called "the first sociologist." Known in her day as a "radical" political theorist, essayist, and novelist, she was as strong a proponent of women's rights as she was a critic of slavery. Her essays and works of fiction illustrate her concept of how governmental economic policies affect relations among the classes in English and American society. Often controversial among her contemporaries, her writings circulated widely.

Martineau was born into an upper-middle-class family of Unitarians, a Protestant denomination that emphasizes individual freedom of belief and liberal social action; her father, Thomas M. Martineau, was a cloth manufacturer who, with his wife, Elizabeth, had eight children. Martineau was the sixth child, and her busy parents considered her "delicate" and difficult. At a young age she began to suffer from nervous and digestive problems that would last throughout her lifetime; she also began losing her hearing during childhood and became increasingly deaf with age. She went to a day school in her hometown of Norwich, England, and also attended boarding school in Bristol. Too hard of hearing to become a teacher, Martineau began writing to support her family when her father's business collapsed. Martineau lived long and productively as a single woman. Despite the recurring pain of an ovarian cyst that formed in 1839 and led eventually to her death, she continued writing until the end.

Some of Martineau's earliest writings, beginning in 1823, were essays about women's education, in which she argued that the discrepancies between men's and women's positions in society stemmed from the differences in their schooling. She also wrote as an insider about women's experiences in *Life in the Sickroom* (1844), from the points of view of both patient and caregiver. Her first fame came with *Illustrations of Political Economy* (1832–34), a series of tales supporting capitalism and its prospects, she believed, to enable individuals to succeed through their abilities and energy, not their families' social status. In *Poor Laws and Paupers Illustrated* (1833), she continued her political project. These four sad stories show what she saw as the unfairness of Great Britain's Poor Law, under which indigent people received public support; Martineau argued that this law unfairly burdened the middle classes and reduced the incentive for the working poor to continue their labor. Her economic views would be considered staunchly conservative today, but for the middle of the nineteenth century, they were radically new.

Despite recurrent illness, Martineau traveled to the United States and wrote *Society in America* (1837), an extended analysis of the living conditions for Americans under their system of government. Though most of what she published in her lifetime came out in periodicals or as pamphlets, Martineau also wrote novels, including *Deerbrook* (1839), a story of women's struggle to aspire to professions beyond the domestic sphere, and *The Hour and the Man* (1841), a fictional account of a black revolutionary in Haiti.

"Morals of Slavery," which appears here, is a chapter from *Society in America*. In this selection, her views on women and on slavery come into the foreground. Martineau exemplifies the typical educated British woman's abhorrence of American slavery, citing the corroding effects the institution has on the morality of white Southerners, particularly women. Throughout the book, Martineau quotes from conversations she had with Americans to illustrate her arguments, effectively combining her personal encounters with eloquently analytical prose.

From Morals of Slavery

It may be said that it is doing an injustice to cite extreme cases of vice as indications of the state of society.[1] I do not think so, as long as such cases are so common as to strike the observation of a mere passing stranger; to say nothing of their incompatibility with a decent and orderly fulfilment of the social relations. Let us, however, see what is the very best state of things. Let us take the words and deeds of some of the most religious, refined, and amiable members of society. It was this aspect of affairs which grieved me more, if possible, than the stormier one which I have presented. The coarsening and hardening of mind and manners among the best; the blunting of the moral sense among the most conscientious, gave me more pain than the stabbing, poisoning, and burning. A few examples which will need no comment, will suffice.

Two ladies, the distinguishing ornaments of a very superior society in the south, are truly unhappy about slavery, and opened their hearts freely to me upon the grief which it caused them,—the perfect curse which they found it. They need no enlightening on this, nor any stimulus to acquit themselves as well as their unhappy circumstances allow. They one day pressed me for a declaration of what I should do in their situation. I replied that I would give up everything, go away with my slaves, settle them, and stay by them in some free place. I had said, among other things, that I dare not stay there,—on my own account,—from moral considerations. "What, not if you had no slaves?" "No." "Why?" "I could not trust myself to live where I must constantly witness the exercise of irresponsible power." They made no reply at the moment: but each found occasion to tell me, some days afterwards, that she had been struck to the heart by these words: the consideration I mentioned having never occurred to her before!

Madame Lalaurie,[2] the person who was mobbed at New Orleans, on account of her fiendish cruelty to her slaves,—a cruelty so excessive as to compel the belief that she was mentally deranged, though her derangement could have taken such a direction nowhere but in a slave country;—this person was described to me as having been "very pleasant to whites."

A common question put to me by amiable ladies was, "Do not you find the slaves generally very happy?" They never seemed to have been asked, or to have asked themselves, the question with which I replied:—"Would you be happy with their means?"

One sultry morning, I was sitting with a friend, who was giving me all manner of information about her husband's slaves, both in the field and house; how she fed and clothed them; what indulgences they were allowed; what their respective capabilities were; and so forth. While we were talking, one of the house-slaves passed us. I observed that she appeared superior to all the rest; to which my friend assented. "She is A.'s wife?" said I. "We call her A.'s wife, but she has never been

1. The previous section of *Society in America* detailed stories of physical violence against slaves.
2. Delphine LaLaurie (c. 1775–1842), who re-

portedly had imprisoned and tortured slaves in the attic of her New Orleans mansion.

married to him. A. and she came to my husband, five years ago, and asked him to let them marry: but he could not allow it, because he had not made up his mind whether to sell A.; and he hates parting husband and wife." "How many children have they?" "Four." "And they are not married yet?" "No; my husband has never been able to let them marry. He certainly will not sell her: and he has not determined yet whether he shall sell A."

Another friend told me the following story. B. was the best slave in her husband's possession. B. fell in love with C., a pretty girl, on a neighbouring estate, who was purchased to be B.'s wife. C.'s temper was jealous and violent; and she was always fancying that B. showed attention to other girls. Her master warned her to keep her temper, or she should be sent away. One day, when the master was dining out, B. came to him, trembling, and related that C. had, in a fit of jealousy, aimed a blow at his head with an axe, and nearly struck him. The master went home, and told C. that her temper could no longer be borne with, and she must go. He offered her the choice of being sold to a trader, and carried to New Orleans, or of being sent to field labour on a distant plantation. She preferred being sold to the trader; who broke his promise of taking her to New Orleans, and disposed of her to a neighbouring proprietor. C. kept watch over her husband, declaring that she would be the death of any girl whom B. might take to wife. "And so," said my informant, "poor B. was obliged to walk about in single blessedness for some time; till, last summer, happily, C. died."—"Is it possible," said I, "that you pair and part these people like brutes?"[3]—The lady looked surprised, and asked what else could be done.

One day at dinner, when two slaves were standing behind our chairs, the lady of the house was telling me a ludicrous story, in which a former slave of hers was one of the personages, serving as a butt on the question of complexion. She seemed to recollect that slaves were listening; for she put in, "D. was an excellent boy," (the term for male slaves of every age.) "We respected him very highly as an excellent boy. We respected him almost as much as if he had been a white. But, &c.———"[4]

A southern lady, of fair reputation for refinement and cultivation, told the following story in the hearing of a company, among whom were some friends of mine. She spoke with obvious unconsciousness that she was saying anything remarkable: indeed such unconsciousness was proved by her telling the story at all. She had possessed a very pretty mulatto girl, of whom she declared herself fond. A young man came to stay at her house, and fell in love with the girl. "She came to me," said the lady, "for protection; which I gave her." The young man went away, but after some weeks, returned, saying he was so much in love with the girl that he could not live without her. "I pitied the young man," concluded the lady; "so I sold the girl to him for 1,500 dollars."

I repeatedly heard the preaching of a remarkably liberal man, of a free and kindly spirit, in the south. His last sermon, extempore, was from the text "Cast all your care upon him, for He careth for you."[5] The preacher told us, among other things, that God cares for all,—for the meanest as well as the mightiest. "He cares for that coloured person, said he, pointing to the gallery where the people of colour sit,—"he cares for that coloured person as well as for the wisest and best of you whites." This was the most wanton insult I had ever seen offered to a human being;

---

3. Animals.
4. &c.———: etcetera and so forth; Martineau

declines to repeat the end of the lady's speech.
5. 1 Peter 5:7.

and it was with difficulty that I refrained from walking out of the church. Yet no one present to whom I afterwards spoke of it seemed able to comprehend the wrong. "Well!" said they: "does not God care for the coloured people?"

Of course, in a society where things like these are said and done by its choicest members, there is a prevalent unconsciousness of the existing wrong. The daily and hourly plea is of good intentions towards the slaves; of innocence under the aspersions of foreigners. They are as sincere in the belief that they are injured as their visitors are cordial in their detestation of the morals of slavery. Such unconsciousness of the milder degrees of impurity and injustice as enables ladies and clergymen of the highest character to speak and act as I have related, is a sufficient evidence of the prevalent grossness of morals. One remarkable indication of such blindness was the almost universal mention of the state of the Irish[6] to me, as a worse case than American slavery. I never attempted, of course, to vindicate the state of Ireland: but I was surprised to find no one able, till put in the way, to see the distinction between political misgovernment and personal slavery: between exasperating a people by political insult, and possessing them, like brutes, for pecuniary profit. The unconsciousness of guilt is the worst of symptoms, where there are means of light to be had. I shall have to speak hereafter of the state of religion throughout the country. It is enough here to say that if, with the law of liberty and the gospel of peace and purity within their hands, the inhabitants of the south are unconscious of the low state of the morals of society, such blindness proves nothing so much as how far that which is highest and purest may be confounded with what is lowest and foulest, when once the fatal attempt has been entered upon to make them co-exist. From their co-existence, one further step may be taken; and in the south has been taken; the making the high and pure a sanction for the low and foul. Of this, more herafter.

The degradation of the women is so obvious a consequence of the evils disclosed above, that the painful subject need not be enlarged on. By the degradation of women, I do not mean to imply any doubt of the purity of their manners. There are reasons, plain enough to the observer, why their manners should be even peculiarly pure. They are all married young, from their being out-numbered by the other sex: and there is ever present an unfortunate servile class of their own sex to serve the purposes of licentiousness, so as to leave them untempted. Their degradation arises, not from their own conduct, but from that of all other parties about them. Where the generality of men carry secrets which their wives must be the last to know; where the busiest and more engrossing concerns of life must wear one aspect to the one sex, and another to the other, there is an end to all wholesome confidence and sympathy, and woman sinks to be the ornament of her husband's house, the domestic manager of his establishment, instead of being his all-sufficient friend. I am speaking not only of what I suppose must necessarily be; but of what I have actually seen. I have seen, with heart-sorrow, the kind politeness, the gallantry, so insufficient to the loving heart, with which the wives of the south are treated by their husbands. I have seen the horror of a woman's having to work,— to exert the faculties which her Maker gave her;—the eagerness to ensure her unearned ease and rest; the deepest insult which can be offered to an intelligent and conscientious woman. I know the tone of conversation which is adopted towards

6. The famine that devastated Ireland began in 1840; in the 1830s Irish peasants suffered economic oppression by English landlords.

women; different in its topics and its style from that which any man would dream of offering to any other man. I have heard the boast of the chivalrous consideration in which women are held throughout their woman's paradise; and seen something of the anguish of crushed pride, of the conflict of bitter feelings with which such boasts have been listened to by those whose aspirations teach them the hollowness of the system. The gentlemen are all the while unaware that women are not treated in the best possible manner among them: and they will remain thus blind as long as licentious intercourse with the lowest of the sex unfits them for appreciating the highest. Whenever their society shall take rank according to moral rather than physical considerations; whenever they shall rise to crave sympathy in the real objects of existence; whenever they shall begin to inquire what human life is, and wherefore, and to reverence it accordingly, they will humble themselves in shame for their abuse of the right of the strongest; for those very arrangements and observances which now constitute their boast. A lady who, brought up elsewhere to use her own faculties, and employ them on such objects as she thinks proper, and who has more knowledge and more wisdom than perhaps any gentleman of her acquaintance, told me of the disgust with which she submits to the conversation which is addressed to her, under the idea of being fit for her; and how she solaces herself at home, after such provocation, with the silent sympathy of books. A father of promising young daughters, whom he sees likely to be crushed by the system, told me in a tone of voice which I shall never forget, that women there might as well be turned into the street, for anything they are fit for. There are reasonable hopes that his children may prove an exception. One gentleman who declares himself much interested in the whole subject, expresses his horror of the employment of women in the northern States, for useful purposes.[7] He told me that the same force of circumstances which, in the region he inhabits, makes men independent, increases the dependence of women, and will go on to increase it. Society is there, he declared, "always advancing towards orientalism."[8] "There are but two ways in which woman can be exercised to the extent of her powers; by genius and by calamity, either of which may strengthen her to burst her conventional restraints. The first is too rare a circumstance to afford any basis for speculation: and may Heaven avert the last!" O, may Heaven hasten it! would be the cry of many hearts, if these be indeed the conditions of woman's fulfilling the purposes of her being. There are, I believe, some who would scarcely tremble to see their houses in flames, to hear the coming tornado, to feel the threatening earthquake, if these be indeed the messengers who must open their prison doors, and give their heaven-born spirits the range of the universe. God has given to them the universe, as to others: man has caged them in one corner of it, and dreads their escape from their cage, while man does that which he would not have woman hear of. He puts genius out of sight, and deprecates calamity. He has not, however, calculated all the forces in nature. If he had, he would hardly venture to hold either negroes or women as property, or to trust to the absence of genius and calamity.

One remarkable warning has been vouchsafed to him. A woman of strong mind, whose strenuous endeavours to soften the woes of slavery to her own dependents, failed to satisfy her conscience and relieve her human affections, has shaken the blood-slaked dust from her feet, and gone to live where every man can

---

7. Women were employed in factories in the North.   8. Decadence.

call himself his own: and not only to live, but to work there, and to pledge herself to death, if necessary, for the overthrow of the system which she abhors in proportion to her familiarity with it. Whether we are to call her Genius or Calamity, or by her own honoured name of Angelina Grimke,[9] certain it is that she is rousing into life and energy many women who were unconscious of genius, and unvisited by calamity, but who carry honest and strong human hearts. This lady may ere long be found to have materially checked the "advance towards orientalism."

Of course, the children suffer, perhaps the most fatally of all, under the slave system. What can be expected from little boys who are brought up to consider physical courage the highest attribute of manhood; pride of section and of caste its loftiest grace; the slavery of a part of society essential to the freedom of the rest; justice of less account than generosity; and humiliation in the eyes of men the most intolerable of evils? What is to be expected of little girls who boast of having got a negro flogged for being impertinent to them, and who are surprised at the "ungentlemanly" conduct of a master who maims his slave? Such lessons are not always taught expressly. Sometimes the reverse is expressly taught. But this is what the children in a slave country necessarily learn from what passes around them; just as the plainest girls in a school grow up to think personal beauty the most important of all endowments, in spite of daily assurances that the charms of the mind are all that are worth regarding.

The children of slave countries learn more and worse still. It is nearly impossible to keep them from close intercourse[1] with the slaves; and the attempt is rarely made. The generality of slaves are as gross as the total absence of domestic sanctity might be expected to render them. They do not dream of any reserves with children. The consequences are inevitable. The woes of mothers from this cause are such that, if this "peculiar domestic institution" were confided to their charge, I believe they would accomplish its overthrow with an energy and wisdom that would look more like inspiration than orientalism. Among the incalculable forces in nature is the grief of mothers weeping for the corruption of their children.

One of the absolutely inevitable results of slavery is a disregard of human rights; an inability even to comprehend them. Probably the southern gentry, who declare that the presence of slavery enhances the love of freedom; that freedom can be duly estimated only where a particular class can appropriate all social privileges; that, to use the words of one of them, "they know too much of slavery to be slaves themselves," are sincere enough in such declarations; and if so, it follows that they do not know what freedom is. They may have the benefit of the alternative,—of not knowing what freedom is, and being sincere; or of knowing what freedom is, and not being sincere. I am disposed to think that the first is the more common case.

One reason for my thinking so is, that I usually found in conversation in the south, that the idea of human rights was—sufficient subsistence in return for labour. This was assumed as the definition of human rights on which we were to argue the case of the slave. When I tried the definition by the golden rule,[2] I found that even that straight, simple rule had become singularly bent in the hands of those who profess to acknowledge and apply it. A clergyman preached from the

9. Angelina Grimké Weld (1805–79), an early Southern abolitionist (see p. 642).
1. Socializing, conversation.

2. "Do unto others as you would have them do unto you."

pulpit the following application of it, which is echoed unhesitatingly by the most religious of the slaveholders:—"Treat your slaves as you would wish to be treated if you were a slave yourself." I verily believe that hundreds, or thousands, do not see that this is not an honest application of the rule; so blinded are they by custom to the fact that the negro is a man and a brother. * * *

1837

━━━━◄ LYDIA MARIA CHILD ►━━━━
1802–1880

Lydia Maria Child's parents, Susannah and David Francis, no doubt would have approved of the course of their daughter's career even if they could not have predicted it. After all, they had brought her up to embody a particularly public-minded and politically responsible sense of womanhood. Her father was a baker and an abolitionist in the Boston suburb of Medford, Massachusetts, who believed in the education of daughters as well as in religious and racial tolerance. Thus prepared to participate in a life devoted to the reform and improvement of American society, Lydia married a man whose politics and bravery she admired, lawyer David Child.

Like her friends and rivals Lydia Sigourney and Catharine Sedgwick, Child had already become a famous and beloved figure in the American literary scene before her marriage. Ten years earlier she had published the daring yet well-received historical fiction *Hobomok* (1824); the story was set in colonial New England and treated native peoples sympathetically. Building on her success, Child actively articulated what her contemporaries saw as an "American" cultural voice. She published early self-help books such as *The Frugal Housewife* (1829) and *The Mother's Book* (1831); began publishing *History of the Condition of Women* (1835); and, most importantly, started the first children's periodical, *The Juvenile Miscellany* (1826). Her success as an author allowed her to support her family and finance the political activism of her husband. Mrs. Child (as she was known) was considered a model of American womanhood: self-sacrificing, domestic, and subservient, yet politically engaged.

In 1833, with the publication of *An Appeal in Favor of That Class of Americans Called Africans,* a section of which is included here, Child's life changed forever. As the first book-length anti-slavery work published in America, it systematically examined and undermined the claims upon which racial slavery rested and went beyond the accepted boundaries of reform. Child unflinchingly analyzed the costs to both blacks and whites of slavery; she unmasked the complicity of Northerners in the slave system; and, most importantly, she called for the immediate abolition of slavery on legal and moral grounds. Mrs. Child had gone from a pillar of decency to a radical threat to the American status quo. She lost her family's main source of income when subscriptions to her *Juvenile Miscellany* dried up, and the magazines that had previously published her work, such as *Godey's Lady's Book* (see pp. 785–86), declined to continue to do so. However, *An Appeal* did not ruin Child's career as an author; on the contrary, it transformed her into one of the most influential figures of the nineteenth century. A younger generation of New England reform activists used the intellectual and rhetorical weapons

Child provided to continue their struggle against the institution of slavery. Child wholly devoted herself and her talents to the reform movements of abolition, native peoples' rights, women's rights, and, after the Civil War, freedmen's rights.

By 1841, Child had moved to New York City, where she became an editor of the newspaper *The National Anti-slavery Standard* and began a series of articles on New York life that she would later publish as *Letters from New York* (1843). These letters, one of which is included here, range in topic from the landscape to capital punishment to the critical "woman question" (whether women should have equal rights with men) and are written as an old friend would address the reader. Though never as financially secure from her writing as she might have hoped, Child was revered in reform circles for her intelligence and integrity as an author and editor. She facilitated the careers of many younger women, such as Harriet Jacobs (pp. 792–813), who might never have published *Incidents in the Life of a Slave Girl* (1861) without Child's encouragement and editorial help.

Child's last major works, a novel called *A Romance of the Republic* (1867) and an anthology called *The Freedman's Book* (1865), typified her activist relationship to literature. In the novel, Child uses the speculative possibilities of fiction to offer interracial marriage as the antidote to America's racism, while in *The Freedman's Book* she offers essays, poems, and fictions by and about black people in a text designed to help freed slaves attain literacy.

From An Appeal in Favor of That Class of Americans Called Africans

We have offended, Oh! my countrymen!
We have offended very grievously,
And been most tyrannous. From east to west
A groan of accusation pierces Heaven!
The wretched plead against us; multitudes,
Countless and vehement, the sons of God,
Our brethren!

—COLERIDGE[1]

Preface

Reader, I beseech you not to throw down this volume as soon as you have glanced at the title. Read it, if your prejudices will allow, for the very truth's sake:—If I have the most trifling claims upon your good will, for an hour's amusement to yourself, or benefit to your children, read it for *my* sake:—Read it, if it be merely to find fresh occasion to sneer at the vulgarity of the cause:—Read it, from sheer curiosity to see what a woman (who had much better attend to her household concerns) will say upon such a subject:—Read it, on *any* terms, and my purpose will be gained.

The subject I have chosen admits of no encomiums on my country; but as I generally make it an object to supply what is most needed, this circumstance is unimportant; the market is so glutted with flattery, that a little truth may be acceptable, were it only for its rarity.

I am fully aware of the unpopularity of the task I have undertaken; but though I *expect* ridicule and censure, I cannot *fear* them.

1. Lines 41–47 of "Fears in Solitude" (1798) by English poet Samuel Taylor Coleridge (1772–1834).

A few years hence, the opinion of the world will be a matter in which I have not even the most transient interest; but this book will be abroad on its mission of humanity, long after the hand that wrote it is mingling with the dust.

Should it be the means of advancing, even one single hour, the inevitable progress of truth and justice, I would not exchange the consciousness for all Rothchild's wealth, or Sir Walter's fame.[2]

Chapter I
Brief History of Negro Slavery—Its Inevitable Effect upon All Concerned in It.

The lot is wretched, the condition sad,
Whether a pining discontent survive,
And thirst for change; or habit hath subdued
The soul depressed; dejected—even to love
Of her dull tasks and close captivity.

—WORDSWORTH[3]

My ear is pained,
My soul is sick with every day's report
Of wrong and outrage, with which this earth is filled.
There is no flesh in man's obdurate heart,
It does not feel for man.

—COWPER[4]

While the Portuguese were exploring Africa, in 1442, Prince Henry ordered Anthony Gonsalez to carry back certain Moorish[5] prisoners, whom he had seized two years before near Cape Bajador: this order was obeyed, and Gonsalez received from the Moors in exchange for the captives, ten negroes, and a quantity of gold dust. Unluckily, this wicked speculation proved profitable, and other Portuguese were induced to embark in it.

In 1492, the West India islands were discovered by Columbus. The Spaniards, dazzled with the acquisition of a new world and eager to come into possession of their wealth, compelled the natives of Hispaniola to dig in the mines. The native Indians died rapidly, in consequence of hard work and cruel treatment; and thus a new market was opened for the negro slaves captured by the Portuguese. They were accordingly introduced as early as 1503. Those who bought and those who sold were alike prepared to trample on the rights of their fellow beings, by that most demoralizing of all influences, the accursed love of gold.

Cardinal Ximenes, while he administered the government, before the accession of Charles the Fifth,[6] was petitioned to allow a regular commerce in African

---

2. Rothchild: German family of bankers who established branches of banks throughout Europe in the eighteenth century; Sir Walter: Sir Walter Scott (1771–1832), British writer of ballads and historical novels.
3. From "The Excursion" (1814) by British poet William Wordsworth (1770–1850).
4. From "The Time-Piece" (1785) by British poet William Cowper (1731–1800).
5. Prince Henry of Portugal (1394–1460), also

called Prince Henry the Navigator, was known for his patronage of expeditions to the west coast of Africa; Moorish: referring to the Moors, Muslim inhabitants of northwestern Africa.
6. Cardinal Ximenes: Francisco Cardinal Jiménez de Cisneros (1436–1517), Spanish cardinal and Grand Inquisitor who forced the Moors to convert to Christianity; Charles the Fifth: Charles V (1500–1558), Holy Roman Emperor (1519–56) and the first king of Spain.

negroes. But he rejected the proposal with promptitude and firmness, alike honorable to his head and heart. This earliest friend of the Africans, living in a comparatively unenlightened age, has peculiar claims upon our gratitude and reverence. In 1517, Charles the Fifth granted a patent for an annual supply of four thousand negroes to the Spanish islands. He probably soon became aware of the horrible, and ever-increasing evils, attendant upon this traffic; for twenty-five years after he emancipated every negro in his dominions. But when he resigned his crown and retired to a monastery, the colonists resumed their shameless tyranny.

Captain Hawkins,[7] afterward Sir John Hawkins, was the first Englishman, who disgraced himself and his country by this abominable trade. Assisted by some rich people in London, he fitted out three ships, and sailed to the African coast, where he burned and plundered the towns, and carried off three hundred of the defenceless inhabitants to Hispaniola.

Elizabeth[8] afterwards authorized a similar adventure with one of her own vessels. "She expressed her concern lest any of the Africans should be carried off without their free consent; declaring that such a thing would be detestable, and call down the vengeance of Heaven upon the undertakers." For this reason, it has been supposed that the Queen was deceived—that she imagined the negroes were transported to the Spanish colonies as voluntary laborers. But history gives us slight reasons to judge Elizabeth so favorably. It was her system always to preserve an *appearance* of justice and virtue. She was a shrewd, far-sighted politician; and had in perfection the clear head and cold heart calculated to form that character. Whatever she might believe of the trade at its beginning, she was too deeply read in human nature, not to foresee the inevitable consequence of placing power in the hands of avarice.

A Roman priest persuaded Louis the Thirteenth[9] to sanction slavery for the sake of converting the negroes to Christianity; and thus this bloody iniquity, disguised with gown, hood, and rosary, entered the fair dominions of France. To be violently wrested from his home, and condemned to toil without hope, by Christians, to whom he had done no wrong, was, methinks, a very odd beginning to the poor negro's course of religious instruction!

When this evil had once begun, it, of course, gathered strength rapidly; for all the bad passions of human nature were eagerly enlisted in its cause. The British formed settlements in North America, and in the West Indies; and these were stocked with slaves. From 1680 to 1786 *two million, one hundred and thirty thousand* negroes were imported into the British colonies!

In almost all great evils there is some redeeming feature—*some* good results, even where it is not intended: pride and vanity, utterly selfish and wrong in themselves, often throw money into the hands of the poor, and thus tend to excite industry and ingenuity, while they produce comfort. But slavery is *all* evil—within and without—root and branch,—bud, blossom and fruit!

In order to show how dark it is in every aspect—how invariably injurious both to nations and individuals,—I will select a few facts from the mass of evidence now before me.

7. Sir John Hawkins (1532–95), the first Englishman to capture people in Sierra Leone and sell them as slaves to Spanish settlers.
8. Elizabeth I (1533–1603), Queen of England from 1558 until her death.
9. Louis XIII (1601–43), king of France from 1610 until his death.

In the first place, its effects upon *Africa* have been most disastrous. All along the coast, intercourse with Europeans has deprived the inhabitants of their primitive simplicity, without substituting in its place the order, refinement, and correctness of principle, attendant upon true civilization. The soil of Africa is rich in native productions, and honorable commerce might have been a blessing to her, to Europe, and to America; but instead of that, a trade has been substituted, which operates like a withering curse, upon all concerned in it.

There are green and sheltered valleys in Africa,—broad and beautiful rivers,— and vegetation in its loveliest and most magnificent forms.—But no comfortable houses, no thriving farms, no cultivated gardens;—for it is not safe to possess permanent property, where each little state is surrounded by warlike neighbors, continually sending out their armed bands in search of slaves. The white man offers his most tempting articles of merchandize to the negro, as a price for the flesh and blood of his enemy; and if we, with all our boasted knowledge and religion, are seduced by money to do such grievous wrong to those who have never offended us, what can we expect of men just emerging from the limited wants of savage life, too uncivilized to have formed any habits of steady industry, yet earnestly coveting the productions they know not how to earn? The inevitable consequence is, that war is made throughout that unhappy continent, not only upon the slightest pretences, but often without any pretext at all. Villages are set on fire, and those who fly from the flames rush upon the spears of the enemy. Private kidnapping is likewise carried on to a great extent; for he who can catch a neighbor's child is sure to find a ready purchaser; and it sometimes happens that the captor and his living merchandize are both seized by the white slave-trader. Houses are broken open in the night, and defenceless women and children carried away into captivity. If boys, in the unsuspecting innocence of youth, come near the white man's ships, to sell vegetables or fruit, they are ruthlessly seized and carried to slavery in a distant land. Even the laws are perverted to this shameful purpose. If a chief wants European commodities, he accuses a parent of witchcraft; the victim is tried by the ordeal of poisoned water; and if he sicken at the draught, the king claims a right to punish him by selling his whole family. In African legislation, almost all crimes are punished with slavery; and, thanks to the white man's rapacity, there is always a very powerful motive for finding the culprit guilty. He must be a very good king indeed, that judges his subjects impartially, when he is sure of making money by doing otherwise!

The king of Dahomy,[1] and other despotic princes, do not scruple to seize their own people and sell them, without provocation, whenever they happen to want anything, which slave-ships can furnish. If a chief has conscience enough to object to such proceedings, he is excited by presents of gun-powder and brandy. One of these men, who could not resist the persuasions of the slave traders while he was intoxicated, was conscience-stricken when he recovered his senses, and bitterly reproached his *Christian* seducers. One negro king, debarred by his religion from the use of spirituous liquors, and therefore less dangerously tempted than others, abolished the slave trade throughout his dominions, and exerted himself to encourage honest industry; but his people must have been as sheep among wolves.

1. An African kingdom in what is now Benin. King Agadja, who ruled Dahomey (1708–32), and his successors profited enormously from selling captive African soldiers and their own citizens into slavery.

Relentless bigotry brings its aid to darken the horrors of the scene. The Mo-hammedans deem it right to subject the heathen tribes to perpetual bondage. The Moors and Arabs think Alla and the Prophet have given them an undisputed right to the poor Caffre,[2] his wife, his children, and his goods. But mark how the slave-trade deepens even the fearful gloom of bigotry! These Mohammedans are by no means zealous to enlighten their Pagan neighbors—they do not wish them to come to a knowledge of what they consider the true religion—lest they should forfeit the only ground, on which they can even pretend to the right of driving them by thousands to the markets of Kano and Tripoli.[3]

This is precisely like our own conduct. We say the negroes are so ignorant that they must be slaves; and we insist upon keeping them ignorant, lest we spoil them for slaves. The same spirit that dictates this logic to the Arab, teaches it to the European and the American:—Call it what you please—it is certainly neither of heaven nor of earth.

When the slave ships are lying on the coast of Africa, canoes well armed are sent into the inland country, and after a few weeks they return with hundreds of negroes, tied fast with ropes. Sometimes the white men lurk among the bushes, and seize the wretched beings who incautiously venture from their homes; sometimes they paint their skins as black as their hearts, and by this deception suddenly sur-prise the unsuspecting natives; at other times the victims are decoyed on board the vessel, under some kind pretence or other, and then lashed to the mast, or chained in the hold. Is it not very natural for the Africans to say "devilish white"?

All along the shores of this devoted country, terror and distrust prevail. The natives never venture out without arms, when a vessel is in sight, and skulk through their own fields, as if watched by a panther. All their worst passions are called into full exercise, and all their kindlier feelings smothered. Treachery, fraud and vio-lence desolate the country, rend asunder the dearest relations, and pollute the very fountains of justice. The history of the negro, whether national or domestic, is writ-ten in blood. Had half the skill and strength employed in the slave-trade been en-gaged in honorable commerce, the native princes would long ago have directed their energies toward clearing the country, destroying wild beasts, and introducing the arts and refinements of civilized life. Under such influences, Africa might be-come an earthly paradise;—the white man's avarice has made it a den of wolves.

Having thus glanced at the miserable effects of this system on the condition of Africa, we will now follow the poor *slave* through his wretched wanderings, in order to give some idea of his physical suffering, his mental, and moral degradation.

Husbands are torn from their wives, children from their parents, while the air is filled with the shrieks and lamentations of the bereaved. Sometimes they are brought from a remote country; obliged to wander over mountains and through deserts; chained together in herds; driven by the whip; scorched by a tropical sun; compelled to carry heavy bales of merchandize; suffering with hunger and thirst; worn down with fatigue; and often leaving their bones to whiten in the desert. A large troop of slaves, taken by the Sultan of Fezzan,[4] died in the desert for want of food. In some places, travellers meet with fifty or sixty skeletons in a day, of which the largest proportion were no doubt slaves, on their way to European markets. Sometimes the poor creatures refuse to go a step further, and even the lacerating

2. Kaffir, a black African.   Tripoli is in Libya.
3. African cities; Kano is in modern-day Nigeria;   4. A region of what is now the country of Libya.

whip cannot goad them on; in such cases, they become the prey of wild beasts, more merciful than white men.

Those who arrive at the sea-coast, are in a state of desperation and despair. Their purchasers are so well aware of this, and so fearful of the consequences, that they set sail in the night, lest the negroes should know when they depart from their native shores.

And here the scene becomes almost too harrowing to dwell upon. But we must not allow our nerves to be more tender than our consciences. The poor wretches are stowed by hundreds, like bales of goods, between the low decks, where filth and putrid air produce disease, madness, and suicide. Unless they die in *great* numbers, the slave captain does not even concern himself enough to fret; his live stock cost nothing, and he is sure of such a high price for what remains at the end of the voyage, that he can afford to lose a good many.

The following account is given by Dr Walsh, who accompanied Viscount Strangford, as chaplain, on his embassy to Brazil.[5] The vessel in which he sailed chased a slave ship; for to the honor of England be it said, she has asked and obtained permission from other governments to treat as pirates such of their subjects as are discovered carrying on this guilty trade north of the equator. Doctor Walsh was an eye witness of the scene he describes; and the evidence given, at various times, before the British House of Commons, proves that the frightful picture is by no means exaggerated.

"The vessel had taken in, on the coast of Africa, three hundred and thirtysix males, and two hundred and twentysix females, making in all five hundred and sixtytwo; she had been out seventeen days, during which she had thrown overboard fiftyfive. They were all inclosed under grated hatchways, between decks. The space was so low, and they were stowed so close together, that there was no possibility of lying down, or changing their position, night or day. The greater part of them were shut out from light and air; and this when the thermometer, exposed to the open sky, was standing, in the shade on our deck, at eightynine degrees.

"The space between decks was divided into two compartments, three feet three inches high. Two hundred and twentysix women and girls were thrust into one space two hundred and eightyeight feet square; and three hundred and thirtysix men and boys were crammed into another space eight hundred feet square; giving the whole an average of twentythree inches; and to each of the women not more than thirteen inches; though several of them were in a state of health, which peculiarly demanded pity.—As they were shipped on account of different individuals, they were branded like sheep, with the owner's marks of different forms; which, as the mate informed me with perfect indifference, had been burnt in with red-hot iron. Over the hatch-way stood a ferocious looking fellow, the slave-driver of the ship, with a scourge of many-twisted thongs in his hand; whenever he heard the slightest noise from below, he shook it over them, and seemed eager to exercise it.

"As soon as the poor creatures saw us looking down at them, their melancholy visages brightened up. They perceived something of sympathy and kindness in our looks, to which they had not been accustomed; and feeling instinctively that we were friends, they immediately began to shout and clap their hands. The women were particularly excited. They all held up their arms, and when we bent

5. An abolitionist who accompanied Viscount Strangford (Percy Clinton Sydney Smythe), 1780– 1855, represented the Court of St. James in Brazil in 1828.

down and shook hands with them, they could not contain their delight; they endeavored to scramble upon their knees, stretching up to kiss our hands, and we understood they knew we had come to liberate them. Some, however, hung down their heads in apparently hopeless dejection; some were greatly emaciated; and some, particularly children, seemed dying. The heat of these horrid places was so great, and the odor so offensive, that it was quite impossible to enter them, even had there been room.

"The officers insisted that the poor, suffering creatures should be admitted on deck to get air and water. This was opposed by the mate of the slaver, who (from a feeling that they deserved it,) declared they should be all murdered. The officers, however, persisted, and the poor beings were all turned out together. It is impossible to conceive the effect of this eruption—five hundred and seventeen fellow-creatures, of all ages and sexes; some children, some adults, some old men and women, all entirely destitute of clothing, scrambling out together to taste the luxury of a little fresh air and water. They came swarming up, like bees from a hive, till the whole deck was crowded to suffocation from stem to stern; so that it was impossible to imagine where they could all have come from, or how they could have been stowed away. On looking into the places where they had been crammed, there were found some children next the sides of the ship, in the places most remote from light and air; they were lying nearly in a torpid state, after the rest had turned out. The little creatures seemed indifferent as to life or death; and when they were carried on deck, many of them could not stand. After enjoying for a short time the unusual luxury of air, some water was brought; it was then that the extent of their sufferings was exposed in a fearful manner. They all rushed like maniacs towards it. No entreaties, or threats, or blows, could restrain them; they shrieked, and struggled, and fought with one another, for a drop of this precious liquid, as if they grew rabid at the sight of it. There is nothing from which slaves in the mid-passage suffer so much as want of water. It is sometimes usual to take out casks filled with sea-water as ballast, and when the slaves are received on board, to start the casks, and re-fill them with fresh. On one occasion, a ship from Bahia[6] neglected to change the contents of their casks, and on the mid-passage found, to their horror, that they were filled with nothing but salt water. All the slaves on board perished! We could judge of the extent of their sufferings from the afflicting sight we now saw. When the poor creatures were ordered down again, several of them came, and pressed their heads against our knees, with looks of the greatest anguish, with the prospect of returning to the horrid place of suffering below."

Alas! the slave-captain proved by his papers that he confined his traffic strictly to the south of the Line, where it was yet lawful; perhaps his papers were forged; but the English officers were afraid to violate an article of the treaty, which their government had made with Brazil. Thus does cunning wickedness defeat benevolence and justice in this world! Dr Walsh continues: "With infinite regret, therefore, we were obliged to restore his papers to the captain, and permit him to proceed, after nine hours' detention and close investigation. It was dark when we separated, and the last parting sounds we heard from the unhallowed ship, were the cries and shrieks of the slaves, suffering under some bodily infliction."

6. Salvador da Bahia, a state in Brazil.

I suppose the English officers acted politically right; but not for the world's wealth, would I have acted politically right, under such circumstances!

Arrived at the place of destination, the condition of the slave is scarcely less deplorable. They are advertised with cattle; chained in droves, and driven to market with a whip; and sold at auction, with the beasts of the field. They are treated like brutes, and all the influences around them conspire to make them brutes.

"Some are employed as domestic slaves, when and how the owner pleases; by day or by night, on Sunday or other days, in any measure or degree, with any remuneration or with none, with what kind or quantity of food the owner of the human beast may choose. Male or female, young or old, weak or strong, may be punished with or without reason, as caprice or passion may prompt. When the drudge does not suit, he may be sold for some inferior purpose, like a horse that has seen his best days, till like a worn-out beast he dies, unpitied and forgotten! Kept in ignorance of the holy precepts and divine consolations of Christianity, he remains a Pagan in a Christian land, without even an object of idolatrous worship—'having no hope, and without God in the world.'"

From the moment the slave is kidnapped, to the last hour he draws his miserable breath, the white man's influence directly cherishes ignorance, fraud, treachery, theft, licentiousness, revenge, hatred and murder. It cannot be denied that human nature thus operated upon, *must* necessarily yield, more or less, to all these evils.—And thus do we dare to treat beings, who, like ourselves, are heirs of immortality!

And now let us briefly inquire into the influence of slavery on the *white man's* character; for in this evil there is a mighty re-action. "Such is the constitution of things, that we cannot inflict an injury without suffering from it ourselves: he, who blesses another, benefits himself but he who sins against his fellow creature, does his own soul a grievous wrong." The effect produced upon *slave captains* is absolutely frightful. Those who wish to realize it in all its awful extent, may find abundant information in Clarkson's History of Slavery;[7] the authenticity of the facts there given cannot be doubted; for setting aside the perfect honesty of Clarkson's character, these facts were principally accepted as evidence before the British Parliament, where there was a very strong party of slave owners desirous to prove them false.

Indeed when we reflect upon the subject, it cannot excite surprise that slave-captains become as hard hearted and fierce as tigers. The very first step in their business is a deliberate invasion of the rights of others; its pursuit combines every form of violence, bloodshed, tyranny and anguish; they are accustomed to consider their victims as cattle, or blocks of wood; and they are invested with perfectly despotic powers.

There is a great waste of life among white seamen employed in this traffic, in consequence of the severe punishment they receive, and diseases originating in the unwholesome atmosphere on board. Clarkson, after a long and patient investigation, came to the conclusion that two slave voyages to Africa, would destroy more seamen than eightythree to Newfoundland; and there is this difference to be observed, that the loss in one trade is generally occasioned by weather or accident, in the other by cruelty or disease. The instances are exceedingly numerous of sailors on board slave-ships, that have died under the lash or in consequence of it. Some of

7. *History of the Rise, Progress and Accomplishment of the Abolition of the African Slave Trade,* a book by Thomas Clarkson (1760–1846), British abolitionist.

the particulars are so painful that it has made me sicken to read them; and I therefore forbear to repeat them. Of the Alexander's crew, in 1785, no less than eleven deserted at Bonny, on the African coast, because life had become insupportable. They chose all that could be endured from a most inhospitable climate, and the violence of the natives, rather than remain in their own ship. Nine others died on the voyage, and the rest were exceedingly abused. This state of things was so universal that seamen were notoriously averse to enter the hateful business. In order to obtain them it became necessary to resort to force or deception. (Behold how many branches there are to the tree of crime!) Decoyed to houses where night after night was spent in dancing, rioting and drunkenness, the thoughtless fellows gave themselves up to the merriment of the scene, and in a moment of intoxication the fatal bargain was sealed. Encouraged to spend more than they owned, a jail or the slave-ship became the only alternatives. The superiority of wages was likewise a strong inducement; but this was a cheat. The wages of the sailors were half paid in the currency of the country where the vessel carried her slaves; and thus they were actually lower than in other trades, while they were nominally higher.

In such an employment the morals of the seamen of course became corrupt, like their masters; and every species of fraud was thought allowable to deceive the ignorant Africans, by means of false weights, false measures, adulterated commodities, and the like.

Of the cruelties on board slave-ships, I will mention but a few instances; though a large volume might be filled with such detestable anecdotes perfectly well authenticated.

"A child on board a slave-ship, of about ten months old, took sulk and would not eat; the captain flogged it with a cat-o'-nine tails; swearing that he would make it eat, or kill it. From this, and other ill-treatment, the limbs swelled. He then ordered some water to be made hot to abate the swelling. But even his tender mercies were cruel. The cook, on putting his hand into the water, said it was too hot. Upon this the captain swore at him, and ordered the feet to be put in. This was done. The nails and skin came off. Oiled cloths were then put around them. The child was at length tied to a heavy log. Two or three days afterwards, the captain caught it up again, and repeated that he would make it eat, or kill it. He immediately flogged it again, and in a quarter of an hour it died. And after the babe was dead, whom should the barbarian select to throw it overboard, but the wretched mother! In vain she tried to avoid the office. He beat her, till he made her take up the child and carry it to the side of the vessel. She then dropped it into the sea, turning her head the other way, that she might not see it."

"In 1780, a slave-trader, detained by contrary winds on the American coast, and in distress, selected one hundred and thirtytwo of his sick slaves, and threw them into the sea, tied together in pairs, that they might not escape by swimming. He hoped the Insurance Company would indemnify him for his loss; and in the lawsuit, to which this gave birth, he observed that 'negroes cannot be considered in any other light than as beasts of burden; and to lighten a vessel it is permitted to throw overboard its least valuable effects.'

"Some of the unhappy slaves escaped from those who attempted to tie them, and jumped into the sea. One of them was saved by means of a cord thrown by the sailors of another vessel; and the monster who murdered his innocent companions had the audacity to claim him as his property. The judges, either from shame, or a sense of justice, refused his demand."

Some people speculate in what are called refuse slaves; i.e. the poor diseased ones. Many of them die in the piazzas of the auctioneers; and sometimes, in the agonies of death, they are sold as low as a dollar.

Even this is better than to be unprotected on the wide ocean in the power of such wild beasts as I have described. It may seem incredible to some that human nature is capable of so much depravity. But the confessions of pirates show how habitual scenes of blood and violence harden the heart of man; and history abundantly proves that despotic power produces a fearful species of moral insanity. The wanton cruelties of Nero, Caligula, Domitian, and many of the officers of the Inquisition, seem like the frantic acts of madmen.

The public has, however, a sense of justice, which can never be entirely perverted. Since the time when Clarkson, Wilberforce and Fox[8] made the horrors of the slave trade understood, the slave captain, or slave jockey is spontaneously and almost universally regarded with dislike and horror. Even in the slave-holding States it is deemed disreputable to associate with a professed slave-trader, though few perhaps would think it any harm to bargain with him. This public feeling makes itself felt so strongly, that men engaged in what is called the African traffic, kept it a secret, if they could, even before the laws made it hazardous.

No man of the least principle could for a moment think of engaging in such enterprises; and if he have any feeling, it is soon destroyed by familiarity with scenes of guilt and anguish. The result is, that the slave-trade is a monopoly in the hands of the very wicked; and this is one reason why it has always been profitable.

Yet even the slave *trade* has had its champions—of course among those who had money invested in it. Politicians have boldly said that it was a profitable branch of commerce, and ought not to be discontinued on account of the idle dreams of benevolent enthusiasts. They have argued before the House of Commons, that others would enslave the negroes, if the English gave it up—as if it were allowable for one man to commit a crime because another was likely to do it! They tell how merciful it is to bring the Africans away from the despotism and wars, which desolate their own continent; but they do not add that the white man is himself the cause of these wars, nor do they prove our right to judge for another man where he will be the happiest. If the Turks, or the Algerines[9] saw fit to exercise this right, they might carry away captive all the occupants of our prisons and penitentiaries.

Some of the advocates of this traffic maintained that the voyage from Africa to the slave-market, called the Middle Passage, was an exceedingly comfortable portion of existence. One went so far as to declare it "the happiest part of a negro's life." They aver that the Africans, on their way to slavery, are so merry, that they dance and sing. But upon a careful examination of witnesses, it was found that their singing consisted of dirge-like lamentations for their native land. One of the captains threatened to flog a woman, because the mournfulness of her song was too painful to him. After meals they jumped up in their irons for exercise. This was considered so necessary for their health, that they were whipped, if they refused to do it. And this was their dancing! "I," said one of the witnesses, "was employed to dance the men, while another person danced the women."

8. Wilberforce: William Wilberforce (1759–1833), a member of the British parliament who founded the Society for the Abolition of Slavery; Fox: Charles James Fox (1749–1806), Whig member of Parliament and abolitionist.
9. Algerians.

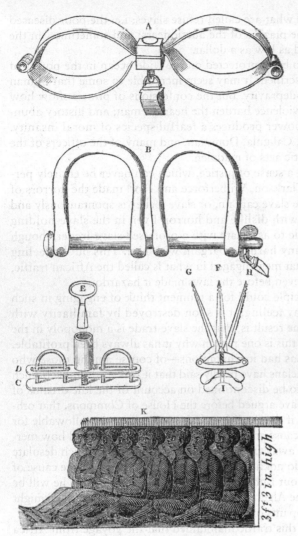

These pretences, ridiculous as they appear, are worth about as much as any of the arguments that can be brought forward in defence of any part of the slave system.

The engraving [included here] will help to give a vivid idea of the Elysium enjoyed by negroes, during the Middle Passage. Fig. A represents the iron hand-cuffs, which fasten the slaves together by means of a little bolt with a padlock.

B represents the iron shackles by which the ancle of one is made fast to the ancle of his next companion. Yet even thus secured, they do often jump into the sea, and wave their hands in triumph at the approach of death. E is a thumb-screw. The thumbs are put into two round holes at the top; by turning a key a bar rises from C to D by means of a screw; and the pressure becomes very painful. By turning it further, the blood is made to start; and by taking away the key as at E, the tortured person is left in agony, without the means of helping himself, or being helped by others. This is applied in case of obstinacy, at the discretion of the captain. I, F, is a speculum oris. The dotted lines represent it when shut; the black lines when open. It opens at G, H, by a screw below with a knob at the end of it. This instrument was used by surgeons to wrench open the mouth in case of lock-jaw. It is used in slave-ships to compel the negroes to take food; because a loss to the owners would follow their persevering attempts to die. K represents the manner of stowing in a slave-ship.

According to Clarkson's estimate, about two and a half out of a hundred of human beings die annually, in the ordinary course of nature, including infants and the aged: but in an African voyage, where few babes and no old people are admitted, so that those shipped are at the firmest period of life, the annual mortality is fortythree in a hundred. In vessels that sail from Bonny, Benin, and the Calabars,[1]

---

1. West African ports that were centers of slave trade.

whence a large proportion of slaves are brought, this mortality is so much increased by various causes, that eightysix in a hundred die yearly. He adds, "It is a destruction, which if general but for ten years, would depopulate the world, and extinguish the human race."

1833

From Letters from New-York

Letter XXXIV [Women's Rights]

January, 1843.

You ask what are my opinions about "Women's Rights." I confess, a strong distaste to the subject, as it has been generally treated. On no other theme, probably, has there been uttered so much of false, mawkish sentiment, shallow philosophy, and sputtering, farthing-candle[2] wit. If the style of its advocates has often been offensive to taste, and unacceptable to reason, assuredly that of its opponents have been still more so. College boys have amused themselves with writing dreams, in which they saw women in hotels, with their feet hoisted, and chairs tilted back, or growling and bickering at each other in legislative halls, or fighting at the polls, with eyes blackened by fisticuffs. But it never seems to have occurred to these facetious writers, that the proceedings which appear so ludicrous and improper in *women,* are also ridiculous and disgraceful in *men.* It were well that *men* should learn not to hoist their feet above their heads, and tilt their chairs backward, not to growl and snap in the halls of legislation, or give each other black eyes at the polls.

Maria Edgeworth[3] says, "We are disgusted when we see a woman's mind overwhelmed with a torrent of learning; that the tide of literature has passed over it should be betrayed only by its fertility." This is beautiful and true; but is it not likewise applicable to man? The truly great never seek to display themselves. If they carry their heads high above the crowd, it is only made manifest to others by accidental revelations of their extended vision. "Human duties and proprieties do not lie so very far apart," said Harriet Martineau;[4] "if they did, there would be two gospels, and two teachers, one for man, and another for woman."

It would seem, indeed, as if men were willing to give women the exclusive benefit of gospel-teaching. "*Women* should be gentle," say the advocates of subordination; but when Christ said, "Blessed are the meek,"[5] did he preach to women only? "*Girls* should be modest," is the language of common teaching, continually uttered in words and customs. Would it not be an improvement for men, also, to be scrupulously pure in manners, conversation, and life? Books addressed to young married people abound with advice to the *wife,* to control her temper, and never to utter wearisome complaints, or vexatious words, when the husband comes home fretful or unreasonable, from his out-of-door conflicts with

---

2. Worthless.
3. British writer (1767–1849) noted for her realistic novels (see p. 386).
4. British writer (1802–76). This quote is from

her *Illustrations of Political Economy* (1832–34) (see pp. 613–14).
5. Matthew 5:5.

632   Lydia Maria Child

the world. Would not the advice be as excellent and appropriate, if the husband were advised to conquer *his* fretfulness, and forbear *his* complaints, in consideration of his wife's ill-health, fatiguing cares, and the thousand disheartening influences of domestic routine? In short, whatsoever can be named as loveliest, best, and most graceful in woman, would likewise be good and graceful in man. You will perhaps remind me of courage. If you use the word in its highest signification, I answer that woman, above others, has abundant need of it, in her pilgrimage; and the true woman wears it with a quiet grace. If you mean mere animal courage, *that* is not mentioned in the Sermon on the Mount,[6] among those qualities which enable us to inherit the earth, or become the children of God. That the feminine ideal approaches much nearer to the gospel standard, than the prevalent idea of manhood, is shown by the universal tendency to represent the Saviour and his most beloved disciple with mild, meek expression, and feminine beauty. None speak of the bravery, the might, or the intellect of Jesus; but the devil is always imagined as a being of acute intellect, political cunning, and the fiercest courage. These universal and instinctive tendencies of the human mind reveal much.

That the present position of women in society is the result of physical force, is obvious enough; whosoever doubts it, let her reflect why she is afraid to go out in the evening without the protection of a man. What constitutes the danger of aggression? Superior physical strength, uncontrolled by the moral sentiments. If physical strength were in complete subjection to moral influence, there would be no need of outward protection. That animal instinct and brute force now govern the world, is painfully apparent in the condition of women everywhere; from the Morduan Tartars, whose ceremony of marriage consists in placing the bride on a mat, and consigning her to the bridegroom, with the words, "Here, wolf, take thy lamb,"—to the German remark, that "stiff ale, stinging tobacco, and a girl in her smart dress, are the best things." The same thing, softened by the refinements of civilization, peeps out in Stephen's remark, that "woman never looks so interesting, as when leaning on the arm of a soldier:" and in Hazlitt's complaint that "it is not easy to keep up a conversation with women in company. It is thought a piece of rudeness to differ from them; it is not quite fair to ask them a *reason* for what they say."[7]

This sort of politeness to women is what men call gallantry; an odious word to every sensible woman, because she sees that it is merely the flimsy veil which foppery throws over sensuality, to conceal its grossness. So far is it from indicating sincere esteem and affection for women, that the profligacy of a nation may, in general, be fairly measured by its gallantry. This taking away *rights,* and *condescending* to grant *privileges,* is an old trick of the physical force principle; and with the immense majority, who only look on the surface of things, this mask effectually disguises an ugliness, which would otherwise be abhorred. The most inveterate slaveholders are probably those who take most pride in dressing their household servants handsomely, and who would be most ashamed to have the name of being *unnecessarily* cruel. And profligates,[8] who form the lowest and most sensual estimate of women, are the very ones to treat them with an excess of outward deference.

---

6. A sermon Jesus gives in the New Testament book of Matthew, part of which lists the qualities of those who are blessed (Matthew 5:3–12).

7. William Hazlitt (1778–1830), British reporter, essayist, and author.
8. Dissolutes.

There are few books, which I can read through, without feeling insulted as a woman; but this insult is almost universally conveyed through that which was intended for praise. Just imagine, for a moment, what impression it would make on men, if women authors should write about *their* "rosy lips," and "melting eyes," and "voluptuous forms," as they write about *us!* That women in general do not feel this kind of flattery to be an insult, I readily admit; for, in the first place, they do not perceive the gross chattel-principle, of which it is the utterance; moreover, they have, from long habit, become accustomed to consider themselves as household conveniences, or gilded toys. Hence, they consider it feminine and pretty to abjure all such use of their faculties, as would make them co-workers with man in the advancement of those great principles, on which the progress of society depends. "There is perhaps no *animal*," says Hannah More,[9] "so much indebted to subordination, for its good behaviour, as woman." Alas, for the animal age, in which such utterance could be tolerated by public sentiment!

Martha More, sister of Hannah, describing a very impressive scene at the funeral of one of her Charity School teachers, says: "The spirit within seemed struggling to speak, and I was in a sort of agony; but I recollected that I had heard, somewhere, a woman must not speak in the *church*. Oh, had she been buried in the church *yard*, a messenger from Mr. Pitt[1] himself should not have restrained me; for I seemed to have received a message from a higher Master within."

This application of theological teaching carries its own commentary.

I have said enough to show that I consider prevalent opinions and customs highly unfavourable to the moral and intellectual development of women: and I need not say, that, in proportion to their true culture, women will be more useful and happy, and domestic life more perfected. True culture, in them, as in men, consists in the full and free development of individual character, regulated by their *own* perceptions of what is true, and their *own* love of what is good.

This individual responsibility is rarely acknowledged, even by the most refined, as necessary to the spiritual progress of women. I once heard a very beautiful lecture from R. W. Emerson[2] on Being and Seeming. In the course of many remarks, as true as they were graceful, he urged women to *be*, rather than *seem*. He told them that all their laboured education of forms, strict observance of genteel etiquette, tasteful arrangement of the toilette, &c. all this *seeming* would not *gain hearts* like *being* truly what God made them; that earnest simplicity, the sincerity of nature, would kindle the eye, light up the countenance, and give an inexpressible charm to the plainest features.

The advice was excellent, but the motive, by which it was urged, brought a flush of indignation over my face. *Men* were exhorted to *be*, rather than to *seem*, that they might fulfil the sacred mission for which their souls were embodied; that they might, in God's freedom, grow up into the full stature of spiritual manhood; but *women* were urged to simplicity and truthfulness, that they might become more *pleasing*.

Are we not all immortal beings? Is not each one responsible for himself and herself? There is no measuring the mischief done by the prevailing tendency to teach women to be virtuous as a duty to *man*, rather than to *God*—for the sake of

<hr />

9. English religious writer and philanthropist (1745–1833); see p. 287.
1. William Pitt the Younger (1759–1806), prime minister of England from 1783 until his death.
2. Ralph Waldo Emerson (1803–82), American writer and leader of the transcendental movement.

pleasing the creature, rather than the Creator. "*God* is thy law, *thou* mine," said Eve to Adam. May Milton[3] be forgiven for sending that thought "out into everlasting time" in such a jewelled setting. What weakness, vanity, frivolity, infirmity of moral purpose, sinful flexibility of principle—in a word, what soul-stifling, has been the result of thus putting man in the place of God!

But while I see plainly that society is on a false foundation, and that prevailing views concerning women indicate the want of wisdom and purity, which they serve to perpetuate—still, I must acknowledge that much of the talk about Women's Rights offends both my reason and my taste. I am not of those who maintain there is no sex in souls; nor do I like the results deducible from that doctrine. Kinmont,[4] in his admirable book, called the Natural History of Man, speaking of the warlike courage of the ancient German women, and of their being respectfully consulted on important public affairs, says: "You ask me if I consider all this right, and deserving of approbation? or that women were here engaged in their appropriate tasks? I answer, yes; it is just *as* right that they should take this interest in the honour of their country, as the other sex. Of course, I do not think that women were *made* for war and battle; neither do I believe that *men* were. But since the fashion of the times had made it so, and settled it that war was a necessary element of greatness, and that no safety was to be procured without it, I argue that it shows a healthful state of feeling in other respects, that the feelings of both sexes were *equally* enlisted in the cause; that there was no *division* in the house, or the State; and that the serious pursuits and objects of the one were also the serious pursuits and objects of the other."

The nearer society approaches to divine order, the less separation will there be in the characters, duties, and pursuits of men and women. Women will not become less gentle and graceful, but men will become more so. Women will not neglect the care and education of their children, but men will find themselves ennobled and refined by sharing those duties with them; and will receive, in return, co-operation and sympathy in the discharge of various other duties, now deemed inappropriate to women. The more women become rational companions, partners in business and in thought, as well as in affection and amusement, the more highly will men appreciate *home*—that blessed word, which opens to the human heart the most perfect glimpse of Heaven, and helps to carry it thither, as on an angel's wings.

> "Domestic bliss,
> That can, the world eluding, be itself
> A world enjoyed; that wants no witnesses
> But its own sharers, and approving heaven;
> That, like a flower deep hid in rocky cleft,
> Smiles, though 'tis looking only at the sky."[5]

Alas, for these days of Astor houses, and Tremonts, and Albions! where families exchange comfort for costliness, fireside retirement for flirtation and flaunting, and the simple, healthful, cozy meal, for gravies and gout, dainties and dyspepsia. There is no characteristic of my countrymen which I regret so deeply, as their slight degree of adhesiveness to home. Closely intertwined with this in-

---

3. John Milton (1608–74), English poet best known for his epic *Paradise Lost*, from which Eve's quote is taken (4.637).

4. American scholar Alexander Kinmont (1799–1838); his *Natural History of Man* was published in 1839.

stinct, is the religion of a nation. The Home and the Church bear a near relation to each other. The French have no such word as home in their language, and I believe they are the least reverential and religious of all the Christian nations. A Frenchman had been in the habit of visiting a lady constantly for several years, and being alarmed at a report that she was sought in marriage, he was asked why he did not marry her himself. "*Marry* her!" exclaimed he; "Good heavens! *where should I spend my evenings?*" The idea of domestic happiness was altogether a foreign idea to his soul, like a word that conveyed no meaning. Religious sentiment in France leads the same roving life as the domestic affections; breakfasting at one restaurateur's, and supping at another's. When some wag in Boston reported that Louis Philippe had sent over for Dr. Channing to manufacture a religion for the French people, the witty significance of the joke was generally appreciated.[5]

There is a deep spiritual reason why all that relates to the domestic affections should ever be found in close proximity with religious faith. The age of chivalry was likewise one of unquestioning veneration, which led to the crusade for the holy sepulchre.[6] The French Revolution,[7] which tore down churches, and voted that there was no God, likewise annulled marriage; and the doctrine that there is no sex in souls has usually been urged by those of infidel tendencies. Carlyle says: "But what feeling it was in the ancient, devout, deep soul, which of marriage made a *sacrament,* this, of all things in the world, is what Diderot will think of for æons without discovering; unless, perhaps, it were to increase the *vestry fees.*"[8]

The conviction that woman's present position in society is a false one, and therefore re-acts disastrously on the happiness and improvement of man, is pressing, by slow degrees, on the common consciousness, through all the obstacles of bigotry, sensuality, and selfishness. As man approaches to the truest life, he will perceive more and more that there is no separation or discord in their mutual duties. They will be one; but it will be as affection and thought are one; the treble and bass of the same harmonious tune.

1843

◄ SUSANNA MOODIE ►
1803–1885

Although Susanna Moodie's book of collected autobiographical sketches, *Roughing It in the Bush* (1852), has become a classic of Canadian literature, Moodie always spoke and wrote of herself as an Englishwoman rather than a Canadian. Born in Suffolk and raised in a Tudor mansion that her parents, Elizabeth and

---

5. Louis Philippe: the last king of France (1773–1850); reigned 1830–48. Dr. Channing: William Ellery Channing (1780–1842), a Unitarian minister associated with the transcendentalist movement in America.
6. Between the eleventh and thirteenth centuries Catholic Europe undertook several military campaigns to gain control of the lands where Jesus of Nazareth had lived and died. The holy sepulchre is considered the tomb where Jesus' followers had buried his body before his resurrection.
7. 1789–99.
8. Carlyle: Scottish-born essayist and historian Thomas Carlyle (1795–1881); Diderot: French philosopher, writer, and prominent figure of the Enlightenment Denis Diderot (1713–84).

Thomas Strickland, bought after her father retired from his career as a docks manager in London, Susanna Strickland lived with them until she was almost thirty years old. Her parents raised Moodie and her five older sisters in this prosperous setting, encouraging them to read what they pleased from their father's extensive library. Well read in the English classics, Moodie decided at a young age that she wanted to distinguish herself in the London literary scene.

Though London was far from her Suffolk home, Moodie was able through her father's connections to begin publishing poems and sketches as early as 1827. One of these literary connections, Thomas Pringle, was also the secretary of the British Anti-Slavery Society. Strongly opposed to slavery and recently converted (against her family's wishes) from the Anglican faith to the more activist Nonconformist version of Christianity, Susanna served as amanuensis for the autobiographies of two former slaves, Mary Prince and Ashton Warner, to whom Pringle had introduced her.

Pringle also introduced her to her future husband, Lieutenant J. W. Dunbar Moodie. Having recently returned to England from South Africa when he met Susanna, Moodie was looking for a wife. After some hesitation due to the possibility of his moving again to South Africa, Susanna married him in 1831. That same year, along with contributing to literary and ladies' journals, she published a book of her own poetry, *Enthusiasm, and Other Poems.* Reluctantly, she emigrated to Upper Canada with her husband in 1832 to claim lands the British government had granted him for military service.

While doing the work of a pioneer wife and mother on their Canadian farm, Moodie continued to write. *Roughing It in the Bush* (1852) is a collection of (slightly fictionalized) autobiographical sketches that she contributed to *The Literary Garland,* a prestigious journal published in Montreal. In form it resembles *Backwoods of Canada* (1836), written by Susanna's sister, Catharine Parr Traill, who, having emigrated with her husband to rural Ontario in 1832, became another major figure in Canadian literature. In addition, Moodie wrote novels set in Canada, always contrasting Canadian (and Yankee) manners with the values she had brought from England.

Moodie's voice found a prominent place in the literary imaginations of Canadian authors throughout the twentieth century. She figures in *At My Heart's Core* (1950), a play by Robertson Davies; a novel called *Small Ceremonies* (1976) by Carol Shields; and a book of poems and a novel by Margaret Atwood (pp. 1773–79), *The Journals of Susanna Moodie* (1970) and *Alias Grace* (1996).

In *Roughing It in the Bush,* Moodie finds humor and pathos in the stories of the people she meets in rural Canada, often making herself the butt of her narrative jokes. Moodie writes of how she came to love the land and the people in Canada and includes sketches of a "crazy" hunter who had once attempted suicide and is trying alone to raise his disabled son; an analysis of the ways working-class servants' attitudes toward their employers change when they move from England to Canada; and the tale of how Moodie and her children saved the family's possessions from a burning house. The selection included here is Moodie's story of the first night she is left alone in her Canadian home, when Brian, a solitary hunter, brings her some news. Typically for Moodie, her self-deprecating humor offsets the real terror she felt in confronting the possibility that her husband might not return to their home in the bush.

From Roughing It in the Bush

[The Adventures of One Night]

My recollections of Brian seem more particularly to concentrate in the adventures of one night, when I happened to be left alone, for the first time since my arrival in Canada. I cannot now imagine how I could have been such a fool as to give way for four-and-twenty hours to such childish fears; but so it was, and I will not disguise my weakness from my indulgent reader.

Moodie[1] had bought a very fine cow of a black man, named Mollineux, for which he was to give twenty-seven dollars. The man lived twelve miles back in the woods; and one fine, frosty spring day—(don't smile at the term frosty, thus connected with the genial season of the year; the term is perfectly correct when applied to the Canadian spring, which, until the middle of May, is the most dismal season of the year)—he and John Monaghan[2] took a rope, and the dog, and sallied forth to fetch the cow home. Moodie said that they should be back by six o'clock in the evening, and charged me to have something cooked for supper when they returned, as he doubted not their long walk in the sharp air would give them a good appetite. This was during the time that I was without a servant, and living in old Mrs. ——'s[3] shanty.

The day was so bright and clear, and Katie was so full of frolic and play, rolling upon the floor, or toddling from chair to chair, that the day passed on without my feeling remarkably lonely. At length the evening drew nigh, and I began to expect my husband's return, and to think of the supper that I was to prepare for his reception. The red heifer that we had bought of Layton, came lowing to the door to be milked; but I did not know how to milk in those days, and, besides this, I was terribly afraid of cattle. Yet, as I knew that milk would be required for the tea, I ran across the meadow to Mrs. Joe, and begged that one of her girls would be so kind as to milk for me. My request was greeted with a rude burst of laughter from the whole set.

"If you can't milk," said Mrs. Joe, "it's high time you should learn. My girls are above being helps."

"I would not ask you but as a great favour; I am afraid of cows."

"*Afraid of cows!* Lord bless the woman! A farmer's wife, and afraid of cows!"

Here followed another laugh at my expense; and, indignant at the refusal of my first and last request, when they had all borrowed so much from me, I shut the inhospitable door, and returned home.

After many ineffectual attempts, I succeeded at last, and bore my half-pail of milk in triumph to the house. Yes! I felt prouder of that milk than many an author of the best thing he ever wrote, whether in verse or prose; and it was doubly sweet when I considered that I had procured it without being under any obligation to my ill-natured neighbours. I had learned a useful lesson of independence, to which in after-years I had often again to refer.

1. Following upper-middle-class nineteenth-century convention, Moodie refers to her husband by his last name.
2. Monaghan, like Layton and "Mrs. Joe," are

neighbors; Katie is Moodie's daughter.
3. By literary convention, the blank masks a real name.

I fed little Katie and put her to bed, made the hot cakes for tea, boiled the potatoes, and laid the ham, cut in nice slices, in the pan, ready to cook the moment I saw the men enter the meadow, and arranged the little room with scrupulous care and neatness. A glorious fire was blazing on the hearth, and everything was ready for their supper; and I began to look out anxiously for their arrival.

The night had closed in cold and foggy, and I could no longer distinguish any object at more than a few yards from the door. Bringing in as much wood as I thought would last me for several hours, I closed the door; and for the first time in my life I found myself at night in a house entirely alone. Then I began to ask myself a thousand torturing questions as to the reason of their unusual absence. Had they lost their way in the woods? Could they have fallen in with wolves (one of my early bugbears)? Could any fatal accident have befallen them? I started up, opened the door, held my breath, and listened. The little brook lifted up its voice in loud, hoarse wailing, or mocked, in its babbling to the stones, the sound of human voices. As it became later, my fears increased in proportion. I grew too superstitious and nervous to keep the door open. I not only closed it, but dragged a heavy box in front, for bolt there was none. Several ill-looking men had, during the day, asked their way to Toronto. I felt alarmed lest such rude wayfarers should come to-night and demand a lodging, and find me alone and unprotected. Once I thought of running across to Mrs. Joe, and asking her to let one of the girls stay with me until Moodie returned; but the way in which I had been repulsed in the evening prevented me from making a second appeal to their charity.

Hour after hour wore away, and the crowing of the cocks proclaimed midnight, and yet they came not. I had burnt out all my wood, and I dared not open the door to fetch in more. The candle was expiring in the socket, and I had not courage to go up into the loft and procure another before it went finally out. Cold, heart-weary, and faint, I sat and cried. Every now and then the furious barking of the dogs at the neighbouring farms, and the loud cackling of the geese upon our own, made me hope that they were coming; and then I listened till the beating of my own heart excluded all other sounds. Oh, that unwearied brook! how it sobbed and moaned like a fretful child;—what unreal terrors and fanciful illusions my too active mind conjured up, whilst listening to its mysterious tones!

Just as the moon rose, the howling of a pack of wolves, from the great swamp in our rear, filled the whole air. Their yells were answered by the barking of all the dogs in the vicinity, and the geese, unwilling to be behind-hand in the general confusion, set up the most discordant screams. I had often heard, and even been amused, during the winter, particularly on thaw nights, with hearing the howls of these formidable wild beasts; but I had never before heard them alone, and when one dear to me was abroad amid their haunts. They were directly in the track that Moodie and Monaghan must have taken; and I now made no doubt that they had been attacked and killed on their return through the woods with the cow, and I wept and sobbed until the cold grey dawn peered in upon me through the small dim windows. I have passed many a long cheerless night, when my dear husband was away from me during the rebellion,[4] and I was left in my forest home with five little children, and only an old Irish woman to draw and cut wood for my

4. In late 1837 and early 1838, Moodie's husband served as captain of a militia assigned to defend the British colony against "rebels" from the United States.

fire, and attend to the wants of the family, but that was the saddest and longest night I ever remember.

Just as the day broke, my friends the wolves set up a parting benediction, so loud, and wild, and near to the house, that I was afraid lest they should break through the frail windows, or come down the low, wide chimney, and rob me of my child. But their detestable howls died away in the distance, and the bright sun rose up and dispersed the wild horrors of the night, and I looked once more timidly around me. The sight of the table spread, and the uneaten supper, renewed my grief, for I could not divest myself of the idea that Moodie was dead. I opened the door, and stepped forth into the pure air of the early day. A solemn and beautiful repose still hung like a veil over the face of Nature. The mists of night still rested upon the majestic woods, and not a sound but the flowing of the waters went up in the vast stillness. The earth had not yet raised her matin[5] hymn to the throne of the Creator. Sad at heart, and weary and worn in spirit, I went down to the spring and washed my face and head, and drank a deep draught of its icy waters. On returning to the house, I met, near the door, old Brian the hunter, with a large fox dangling across his shoulder, and the dogs following at his heels.

"Good God! Mrs. Moodie, what is the matter? You are early abroad this morning, and look dreadful ill. Is anything wrong at home? Is the baby or your husband sick?"

"Oh!" I cried, bursting into tears, "I fear he is killed by the wolves."

The man stared at me, as if he doubted the evidence of his senses, and well he might; but this one idea had taken such strong possession of my mind that I could admit no other. I then told him, as well as I could find words, the cause of my alarm, to which he listened very kindly and patiently.

"Set your heart at rest; your husband is safe. It is a long journey on foot to Mollineux, to one unacquainted with a blazed path in a bush road. They have staid all night at the black man's shanty, and you will see them back at noon."

I shook my head and continued to weep.

"Well, now, in order to satisfy you, I will saddle my mare, and ride over to the nigger's, and bring you word as fast as I can."

I thanked him sincerely for his kindness, and returned, in somewhat better spirits, to the house. At ten o'clock my good messenger returned with the glad tidings that all was well.

The day before, when half the journey had been accomplished, John Monaghan let go the rope by which he led the cow, and she had broken away through to the woods, and returned to her old master; and when they again reached his place, night had set in, and they were obliged to wait until the return of day. Moodie laughed heartily at all my fears; but indeed I found them no joke.

1852

5. Early morning.

CULTURAL COORDINATES
How *Did* They Do It?
The Mechanics of Writing

Susanna Moodie (pp. 635–36), like more than a few of the authors in the nine-teenth century, suffered from what Catharine Maria Sedgwick (p. 554) called *cacoethes scribendi*—the unbearable urge to write. For those on the fringes of em-pire, like Moodie, that was particularly challenging. But even for those at its heart, writing was a complex undertaking. Until the mid–nineteenth century, authors wrote mainly with quill pens. (Quills are strong flight feathers, usually from geese or turkeys.) The nib was made so that it would take up a small amount of ink and release it smoothly in response to varying degrees of pressure from the writer's hand. An early-nineteenth-century writer needed to know at least how to mend and maintain a quill nib, if not how to produce an entire pen. By the mid-1800s the quill nib began to be replaced by manufactured steel nibs; they still required skill to use but didn't have to be mended.

In addition to a pen, a writer also needed a supply of paper. Until after the Civil War, paper was made mostly from recycled rags and was expensive, so the frugal would save scraps of paper from publications, letters, or bills on which to write a draft. Only the very rich or improvident composed on quality paper, which was reserved for fair copies intended for someone other than the writer to see. The cost of paper (and postage) encouraged let-ter writers to "cross" their pages: After writing on a sheet of paper from top to bottom, the author would turn the sheet 90 degrees and, writing be-tween the existing words, cover the sheet from top to bottom again.

In cities, the well-to-do could buy ink in pow-dered or liquid form from druggists or stationers; in rural areas or frugal households, ink was pro-duced at home from both imported and domestic ingredients, such as oak galls and iron filings. Small amounts could then be decanted into por-table containers, or ink-wells. Inkwells were never

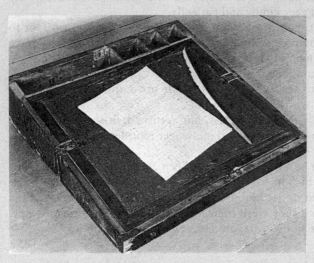

The portable writing desk. The desk shown here belonged to Narcissa Whitman, who journeyed across North America to the Oregon Territory in the 1840s. Closed, the small desk (no more than eight by eleven by four inches) provides a slanted, velvet-covered writing surface. Inside are compartments for paper; along the top, compartments for pen-wipe, ink, and sand. Whitman's desk is much like the one Mrs. Montgomery fits out for her daughter, Ellen, in Susan Warner's *Wide, Wide World* (pp. 849–62).

watertight, so they were made as small as possible to minimize mess. A writer had to master exactly how to dip the pen into the ink—a good penwoman using quality ink and a decent pen might be able to write up to twenty words before re-dipping her pen. Recipes and penmanship manuals suggest that even the best penwomen faced ink that evaporated or congealed too quickly, filling up the slits in the pen nib and causing unsightly blots on the paper.

Writing, even under the best conditions, was messy. Writers would use a pen-wipe, to remove excess ink from the outside of the quill. To absorb wet ink, they would sprinkle (and reuse) fine sand on the finished pages or lay a piece of absorbent paper or cloth on the page. Many women would also wear a special sleeve to cover their wrist and forearm so that the ink would not stain their skin or clothes.

In the 1870s, inventors began patenting pens that could contain their own ink supply. These self-filling, or "fountain," pens liberated writers from the mess of dipping but still required frequent tending. Not until the mid–twentieth century, with the invention of the ballpoint pen and the production of affordable type-writers, did writing become a less messy (though no less difficult) affair.

ANGELINA GRIMKÉ (WELD)
1805–1879

Angelina Emily Grimké began her career as an abolitionist and women's rights activist with a letter to radical abolitionist William Lloyd Garrison, who published it without her permission in 1835. Her letter was an impassioned response to reports of the mobbing of anti-slavery women in Boston. In it, Grimké, the privileged daughter of wealthy slaveholders, embraced the call to resist slavery. This wasn't all that unexpected. After all, her feelings about slavery had already led to a painful separation from her parents, Mary and John Grimké of South Carolina, as she followed her older sister's example and moved to Philadelphia, where she had become a Quaker. Her impulsive letter to Garrison reads like a prospectus for the work Grimké and her sister, Sarah, would pursue over the next few years on the lecture circuit and in print.

In 1836, Grimké issued an *Appeal to Christian Women of the South,* which appears here. Counseling them on how to avoid further complicity in what she presented as the personal and national sin of slavery, her *Appeal* attempts to undercut the various rationales of racial slavery on moral and Christian grounds. It is a paradigmatic example of the early-nineteenth-century belief in the efficacy of "moral suasion." Moral suasion was the belief that all people are naturally good as well as rational and, therefore, will choose to follow the best moral course if given a choice. For Grimké and her intended audience, Christianity and morality were inextricably linked; thus, she exposed the ways in which pro-slavery advocates had corrupted interpretations of the Bible in their efforts to disguise the inequities of an essentially venal practice. Admitting that the disenfranchisement of women apparently limits them, Grimké reminds her readers of the not inconsiderable power they nevertheless have. Most radically, Grimké urges her readers to break the law if necessary in order to obey what she sees as the higher and explicitly Christian law to resist slavery. The publication of the *Appeal* enraged readers in the Southern states. Even some in the reformist camp, like Harriet Beecher Stowe's sister, Catharine, felt Grimké had gone too far in urging her female readership to rebel not only against slavery but implicitly against the claims of patriarchy. Pro-slavery advocates used Grimké's pamphlet to underscore that the threat of abolitionism wasn't just to the economic basis of their wealth but also to the patriarchal basis of their entire way of life.

For the next several years, until 1838, when she married fellow activist Theodore Weld, Grimké and her sister, Sarah, played increasingly public roles in the abolitionist movement. Despite their genteel upbringing, Angela and Sarah Grimké became the first women to lecture to a "promiscuous audience" (that is, an audience composed of both men and women), when they addressed the New York Anti-Slavery Society in 1836. The three essays Grimké published in the few years between the publication of her impulsive letter to Garrison and her marriage to Weld established the framework for an explicitly Christian critique of slavery that would be deployed with increasing effectiveness for the next twenty years, until the abolition of slavery in the United States. Grimké and her sister, Sarah, continued their activist work away from the public stage until their deaths in 1879 and 1873, respectively.

From **Appeal to the Christian Women of the South**

*Then Mordecai commanded to answer Esther, Think not within thyself
that thou shalt escape in the king's house more than all the Jews. For if
thou altogether holdest thy peace at this time, then shall there enlargement
and deliverance arise to the Jews from another place: but thou and thy
father's house shall be destroyed: and who knoweth whether thou art
come to the kingdom for such a time as this. And Esther bade them return
Mordecai this answer:—and so will I go in unto the king, which is not
according to law, and if I perish, I perish.*

—ESTHER IV. 13–16.

Respected Friends,

It is because I feel a deep and tender interest in your present and eternal welfare that I am willing thus publicly to address you. Some of you have loved me as a relative, and some have felt bound to me in Christian sympathy, and Gospel fellowship; and even when compelled by a strong sense of duty, to break those outward bonds of union which bound us together as members of the same community, and members of the same religious denomination, you were generous enough to give me credit, for sincerity as a Christian, though you believed I had been most strangely deceived. I thanked you then for your kindness, and I ask you *now,* for the sake of former confidence, and former friendship, to read the following pages in the spirit of calm investigation and fervent prayer. It is because you have known me, that I write thus unto you.

But there are other Christian women scattered over the Southern States, a very large number of whom have never seen me, and never heard my name, and who feel *no* interest whatever in *me.* But I feel an interest in *you,* as branches of the same vine from whose root I daily draw the principle of spiritual vitality—Yes! Sisters in Christ I feel an interest in *you,* and often has the secret prayer arisen on your behalf, Lord "open thou their eyes that they may see wondrous things out of thy Law"[1]—It is then, because I *do feel* and *do pray* for you, that I thus address you upon a subject about which of all others, perhaps you would rather not hear any thing; but, "would to God ye could bear with me a little in my folly, and indeed bear with me, for I am jealous over you with godly jealousy."[2] Be not afraid then to read my appeal; it is *not* written in the heat of passion or prejudice, but in that solemn calmness which is the result of conviction and duty. It is true, I am going to tell you unwelcome truths, but I mean to speak those *truths in love,* and remember Solomon says, "faithful are the *wounds* of a friend."[3] I do not believe the time has yet come when *Christian women* "will not endure sound doctrine," even on the subject of Slavery, if it is spoken to them in tenderness and love, therefore I now address *you.*

To all of you then, known or unknown, relatives or strangers, (for you are all *one* in Christ,) I would speak. I have felt for you at this time, when unwelcome light is pouring in upon the world on the subject of slavery; light which even Christians would exclude, if they could, from our country, or at any rate from the southern portion of it, saying, as its rays strike the rock bound coasts of New England and scatter their warmth and radiance over her hills and valleys, and from thence

1. Psalm 119:18.
2. 2 Corinthians 11:1.
3. Proverbs 24:6.

travel onward over the Palisades of the Hudson, and down the soft flowing waters of the Delaware and gild the waves of the Potomac, "hitherto shalt thou come and no further;" I know that even professors of His name who has been emphatically called the "Light of the world" would, if they could, build a wall of adamant around the Southern States whose top might reach unto heaven, in order to shut out the light which is bounding from mountain to mountain and from the hills to the plains and valleys beneath, through the vast extent of our Northern States. But believe me, when I tell you, their attempts will be as utterly fruitless as were the efforts of the builders of Babel;[4] and why? Because moral, like natural light, is so extremely subtle in its nature as to overleap all human barriers, and laugh at the puny efforts of man to control it. All the excuses and palliations of this system must inevitably be swept away, just as other "refuges of lies" have been, by the irresistible torrent of a rectified public opinion. "The *supporters* of the slave system," says Jonathan Dymond in his admirable work on the Principles of Morality, "will *hereafter* be regarded with the *same* public feeling, as he who was an advocate for the slave trade *now is*." It will be, and that very soon, clearly perceived and fully acknowledged by all the virtuous and the candid, that in *principle* it is as sinful to hold a human being in bondage who has been born in Carolina, as one who has been born in Africa. All that sophistry of argument which has been employed to prove, that although it is sinful to send to Africa to procure men and women as slaves, who have never been in slavery, that still, it is not sinful to keep those in bondage who have come down by inheritance, will be utterly overthrown. We must come back to the good old doctrine of our forefathers[5] who declared to the world, "this self evident truth that *all* men are created equal, and that they have certain *inalienable* rights among which are life, *liberty,* and the pursuit of happiness." It is even a greater absurdity to suppose a man can be legally born a slave under *our free Republican* Government, than under the petty despotisms of barbarian Africa. If then, we have no right to enslave an African, surely we can have none to enslave an American; if it is a self evident truth that *all* men, every where and of every color are born equal, and have an *inalienable right to liberty,* then it is equally true that *no* man can be born a slave, and no man can ever *rightfully* be reduced to *involuntary* bondage and held as a slave, however fair may be the claim of his master or mistress through wills and title-deeds.

* * *

But perhaps you will be ready to query, why appeal to *women* on this subject? *We* do not make the laws which perpetuate slavery. *No* legislative power is vested in *us; we* can do nothing to overthrow the system, even if we wished to do so. To this I reply, I know you do not make the laws, but I also know that *you are the wives and mothers, the sisters and daughters of those who do;* and if you really suppose *you* can do nothing to overthrow slavery, you are greatly mistaken. You can do much in every way: four things I will name. 1st. You can read on this subject. 2d. You can pray over this subject. 3d. You can speak on this subject. 4th. You can *act* on this subject. I have not placed reading before praying because I regard it more important, but because, in order to pray aright, we must understand what we are praying for; it is only then we can "pray with the understanding and the spirit also."

* * *

4. Genesis 10–11 tells of the arrogant construc-   by God.
tion of the Tower of Babel and its destruction   5. The Declaration of Independence.

But why, my dear friends, have I thus been endeavoring to lead you through the history of more than three thousand years, and to point you to that great cloud of witnesses who have gone before, "from works to rewards?" Have I been seeking to magnify the sufferings, and exalt the character of woman, that she "might have praise of men?" No! no! my object has been to arouse *you*, as the wives and mothers, the daughters and sisters, of the South, to a sense of your duty as *women*, and as Christian women, on that great subject, which has already shaken our country, from the St. Lawrence and the lakes, to the Gulf of Mexico, and from the Mississippi to the shores of the Atlantic; *and will continue mightily to shake it*, until the polluted temple of slavery fall and crumble into ruin. I would say unto each one of you, "what meanest thou, O sleeper! arise and call upon thy God, if so be that God will think upon us that we perish not."[6] Perceive you not that dark cloud of vengeance which hangs over our boasting Republic? Saw you not the lightnings of Heaven's wrath, in the flame which leaped from the Indian's torch to the roof of yonder dwelling, and lighted with its horrid glare the darkness of midnight? Heard you not the thunders of Divine anger, as the distant roar of the cannon came rolling onward, from the Texian country, where Protestant American Rebels are fighting with Mexican Republicans—for what? For the re-establishment of *slavery*; yes! of American slavery in the bosom of a Catholic Republic, where that system of robbery, violence, and wrong, had been legally abolished for twelve years. Yes! citizens of the United States, after plundering Mexico of her land, are now engaged in deadly conflict, for the privilege of fastening chains, and collars, and manacles—upon whom? upon the subjects of some foreign prince? No! upon native born American Republican citizens, although the fathers of these very men declared to the whole world, while struggling to free themselves from the three penny taxes of an English king, that they believed it to be a *self-evident* truth that *all men* were created equal, and had an *unalienable right to liberty*.

Well may the poet exclaim in bitter sarcasm,

> "The fustian flag that proudly waves
> In solemn mockery o'er *a land of slaves*."[7]

Can you not, my friends, understand the signs of the times; do you not see the sword of retributive justice hanging over the South, or are you still slumbering at your posts?—Are there no Shiphrahs, no Puahs[8] among you, who will dare in Christian firmness and Christian meekness, to refuse to obey the *wicked laws* which require *woman to enslave, to degrade and to brutalize woman?* Are there no Miriams, who would rejoice to lead out the captive daughters of the Southern States to liberty and light? Are there no Huldahs[9] there who will dare to *speak the truth* concerning the sins of the people and those judgments, which it requires no prophet's eye to see, must follow if repentance is not speedily sought? Is there no Esther[1]

6. Jonah 1:6.

7. These lines conclude a jeremiad published by the abolitionist J. Miller M'Kim on March 3, 1838. M'Kim, like the Grimké sisters, was active in the Philadelphia anti-slavery circles. Grimké's use of these lines shows they were circulating before M'Kim's publication of them.

8. Shiphrahs: one of two midwives in the Book of Exodus, 1:15; Puahs: one of two midwives in the Book of Exodus, 1:15.

9. Miriam: Aaron's sister; a prophetess (Exodus 15:20); Hulda: a prophetess who foretells the destruction of Jerusalem (2 Kings 22:14–20; 2 Chronicles 34:22–28).

1. The Book of Esther tells the story of an orphaned Jewish girl who lives in Babylon under the Persian Empire in a time when the Jews are an oppressed and scattered people. Esther marries the king and defies convention to protect her people.

among you who will plead for the poor devoted slave? Read the history of this Persian queen, it is full of instruction; she at first refused to plead for the Jews; but, hear the words of Mordecai, "Think not within thyself, that *thou* shalt escape in the king's house more than all the Jews, for *if thou altogether holdest thy peace at this time,* then shall there enlargement and deliverance arise to the Jews from another place: but *thou and thy father's house shall be destroyed.*"[2] Listen, too, to her magnanimous reply to this powerful appeal; "*I will* go in unto the king, which is *not* according to law, and if I perish, I perish." Yes! if there were but *one* Esther at the South, she *might* save her country from ruin; but let the Christian women there arise, as the Christian women of Great Britain did, in the majesty of moral power, and that salvation is certain. Let them embody themselves in societies, and send petitions up to their different legislatures, entreating their husbands, fathers, brothers and sons, to abolish the institution of slavery; no longer to subject *woman* to the scourge and the chain, to mental darkness and moral degradation; no longer to tear husbands from their wives, and children from their parents; no longer to make men, women, and children, work *without wages;* no longer to make their lives bitter in hard bondage; no longer to reduce *American citizens* to the abject condition of *slaves,* of "chattels personal;" no longer to barter the *image of God* in human shambles for corruptible things such as silver and gold.

The *women of the South can overthrow* this horrible system of oppression and cruelty, licentiousness and wrong. Such appeals to your legislatures would be irresistible, for there is something in the heart of man which *will bend under moral suasion.* There is a swift witness for truth in his bosom, which *will respond to truth* when it is uttered with calmness and dignity. If you could obtain but six signatures to such a petition in only one state, I would say, send up that petition, and be not in the least discouraged by the scoffs and jeers of the heartless, or the resolution of the house to lay it on the table. It will be a great thing if the subject can be introduced into your legislatures in any way, even by *women,* and *they* will be the most likely to introduce it there in the best possible manner, as a matter of *morals* and *religion,* not of expediency or politics. You may petition, too, the different ecclesiastical bodies of the slave states. Slavery must be attacked with the whole power of truth and the sword of the spirit. You must take it up on *Christian* ground, and fight against it with Christian weapons, whilst your feet are shod with the preparation of the gospel of peace. And *you are now* loudly called upon by the cries of the widow and the orphan, to arise and gird yourselves for this great moral conflict, with the whole armour of righteousness upon the right hand and on the left.

There is every encouragement for you to labor and pray, my friends, because the abolition of slavery as well as its existence, has been the theme of prophecy. "Ethiopia (says the Psalmist) shall stretch forth her hands unto God."[3] And is she not now doing so? Are not the Christian negroes of the south lifting their hands in prayer for deliverance, just as the Israelites did when their redemption was drawing nigh?[4] Are they not sighing and crying by reason of the hard bondage? And think you, that He, of whom it was said, "and God heard their groaning, and their cry came up unto him by reason of the hard bondage," think you that his ear is heavy that he cannot *now* hear the cries of his suffering children? Or that He who raised up a Moses, an Aaron, and a Miriam, to bring them up out of the land

2. Esther 4:14.   4. Exodus 2.
3. Psalm 68:31.

of Egypt from the house of bondage, cannot now, with a high hand and a stretched out arm, rid the poor negroes out of the hands of their masters? Surely you believe that his arm is *not* shortened that he cannot save. And would not such a work of mercy redound to his glory? But another string of the harp of prophecy vibrates to the song of deliverance: "But they shall sit every man under his vine, and under his fig-tree, and *none shall make them afraid;* for the mouth of the Lord of Hosts hath spoken it."[5] The *slave* never can do this as long as he is a *slave;* whilst he is a "chattel personal" he can own *no* property; but the time *is to come* when *every* man is to sit under *his own* vine and *his own* fig-tree, and no domineering driver, or irresponsible master, or irascible mistress, shall make him afraid of the chain or the whip. Hear, too, the sweet tones of another string: "Many shall run to and fro, and *knowledge* shall be increased."[6] Slavery is an insurmountable barrier to the increase of knowledge in every community where it exists; *slavery, then, must be abolished before* this prediction can be fulfilled. The last chord I shall touch, will be this, "They shall *not* hurt nor destroy in all my holy mountain."[7]

Slavery, then, must be overthrown before the prophecies can be accomplished, but how are they to be fulfiled? Will the wheels of the millennial car be rolled onward by miraculous power? No! God designs to confer this holy privilege upon *man;* it is through *his* instrumentality that the great and glorious work of reforming the world is to be done. And see you not how the mighty engine of *moral power* is dragging in its rear the Bible and peace societies, anti-slavery and temperance, sabbath schools, moral reform, and missions? or to adopt another figure, do not these seven philanthropic associations compose the beautiful tints in that bow of promise which spans the arch of our moral heaven? Who does not believe, that if these societies were broken up, their constitutions burnt, and the vast machinery with which they are laboring to regenerate mankind was stopped, that the black clouds of vengeance would soon burst over our world, and every city would witness the fate of the devoted cities of the plain? Each one of these societies is walking abroad through the earth scattering the seeds of truth over the wide field of our world, not with the hundred hands of a Briareus,[8] but with a hundred thousand.

Another encouragement for you to labor, my friends, is, that you will have the prayers and co-operation of English and Northern philanthropists. You will never bend your knees in supplication at the throne of grace for the overthrow of slavery, without meeting there the spirits of other Christians, who will mingle their voices with yours, as the morning or evening sacrifice ascends to God. Yes, the spirit of prayer and of supplication has been poured out upon many, many hearts; there are wrestling Jacobs who will not let go of the prophetic promises of deliverance for the captive, and the opening of prison doors to them that are bound. There are Pauls[9] who are saying, in reference to this subject, "Lord, what wilt thou have me to do?" There are Marys sitting in the house now, who are ready to arise and go forth in this work as soon as the message is brought, "the master is come and calleth for thee." And there are Marthas, too, who have already gone out to meet Jesus, as he bends his footsteps to their brother's grave, and weeps, *not* over the

---

5. Micah 4:4.
6. Daniel 12:4.
7. Isaiah 11:9.
8. In Greek mythology, one of three 100-armed, 50-headed Hecatoncheires (from the Greek words for "hundred" and "hands"), the sons of the deities Uranus and Gaea. The gods called him Briareus; mortals called him Aegaeon.
9. Jacob, a prophet, wrestles with an angel (Genesis 25); with the reference to Paul, Grimké shifts her frame of reference from the Old Testament to the Gospel, or New Testament.

lifeless body of Lazarus[1] bound hand and foot in grave-clothes, but over the politically and intellectually lifeless slave, bound hand and foot in the iron chains of oppression and ignorance. Some may be ready to say, as Martha did, who seemed to expect nothing but sympathy from Jesus, "Lord, by this time he stinketh, for he hath been dead four days." She thought it useless to remove the stone and expose the loathsome body of her brother; she could not believe that so great a miracle could be wrought, as to raise *that putrefied body* into life; but "Jesus said, take *ye* away the stone;" and when *they* had taken away the stone where the dead was laid, and uncovered the body of Lazarus, then it was that "Jesus lifted up his eyes and said, Father, I thank thee that thou hast heard me," &c. "And when he had thus spoken, he cried with a loud voice, Lazarus, come forth." Yes, some may be ready to say of the colored race, how can *they* ever be raised politically and intellectually, they have been dead four hundred years? But *we* have *nothing* to do with *how* this is to be done; *our business* is to take away the stone which has covered up the dead body of our brother, to expose the putrid carcass, to show *how* that body has been bound with the grave-clothes of heathen ignorance, and his face with the napkin of prejudice, and having done all it was our duty to do, to stand by the negro's grave, in humble faith and holy hope, waiting to hear the life-giving command of "Lazarus, come forth." This is just what Anti-Slavery Societies are doing; they are taking away the stone from the mouth of the tomb of slavery, where lies the putrid carcass of our brother. They want the pure light of heaven to shine into that dark and gloomy cave; they want all men to see *how* that dead body has been bound, *how* that face has been wrapped in the *napkin of prejudice;* and shall they wait beside that grave in vain? Is not Jesus still the resurrection and the life?[2] Did He come to proclaim liberty to the captive, and the opening of prison doors to them that are bound, in vain? Did He promise to give beauty for ashes, the oil of joy for mourning, and the garment of praise for the spirit of heaviness unto them that mourn in Zion,[3] and will He refuse to beautify the mind, anoint the head, and throw around the captive negro the mantle of praise for that spirit of heaviness which has so long bound him down to the ground? Or shall we not rather say with the prophet, "the zeal of the Lord of Hosts *will* perform this?" Yes, his promises are sure, and amen in Christ Jesus, that he will assemble her that halteth, and gather her that is driven out, and her that is afflicted.

But I will now say a few words on the subject of Abolitionism. Doubtless you have all heard Anti-Slavery Societies denounced as insurrectionary and mischievous, fanatical and dangerous. It has been said they publish the most abominable untruths, and that they are endeavoring to excite rebellions at the South. Have you believed these reports, my friends? have *you* also been deceived by these false assertions? Listen to me, then, whilst I endeavor to wipe from the fair character of Abolitionism such unfounded accusations. You know that *I* am a Southerner; you know that my dearest relatives are now in a slave State. Can you for a moment believe I would prove so recreant to the feelings of a daughter and a sister, as to join a society which was seeking to overthrow slavery by falsehood, bloodshed, and murder? I appeal to you who have known and loved me in days that are passed, can *you*

---

1. Mary and Martha are women disciples of Christ. In John 11:41–44, Lazarus, the brother of Mary and Martha, has died and the grief of the sisters affects Him so strongly that He restores Lazarus to life.
2. John 11:24–26.
3. A term for the land of Israel and more generally the chosen people of God.

believe it? No! my friends. As a Carolinian, I was peculiarly jealous of any movements on this subject; and before I would join an Anti-Slavery Society, I took the precaution of becoming acquainted with some of the leading Abolitionists, of reading their publications and attending their meetings, at which I heard addresses both from colored and white men; and it was not until I was fully convinced that their principles were *entirely pacific,* and their efforts *only moral,* that I gave my name as a member to the Female Anti-Slavery Society of Philadelphia. Since that time, I have regularly taken the Liberator,[4] and read many Anti-Slavery pamphlets and papers and books, and can assure you I *never* have seen a single insurrectionary paragraph, and never read any account of cruelty which I could not believe. Southerners may deny the truth of these accounts, but why do they not *prove* them to be false. Their violent expressions of horror at such accounts being believed, *may* deceive some, but they cannot deceive *me,* for I lived too long in the midst of slavery, not to know what slavery is. When *I* speak of this system, "I speak that I do know," and I am not at all afraid to assert, that Anti-Slavery publications have *not* overdrawn the monstrous features of slavery at all. And many a Southerner *knows* this as well as I do. A lady in North Carolina remarked to a friend of mine, about eighteen months since, "Northerners know nothing at all about slavery; they think it is perpetual bondage only; but of the *depth of degradation* that word involves, they have no conception; if they had, *they would never cease* their efforts until so *horrible* a system was overthrown." She did not know how faithfully some Northern men and Northern women had studied this subject; how diligently they had searched out the cause of "him who had none to help him," and how fearlessly they had told the story of the negro's wrongs. Yes, Northerners know *every* thing about slavery now. This monster of iniquity has been unveiled to the world, her frightful features unmasked, and soon, very soon will she be regarded with no more complacency by the American republic than is the idol of Juggernaut, rolling its bloody wheels over the crushed bodies of its prostrate victims.

But you will probably ask, if Anti-Slavery societies are not insurrectionary, why do Northerners tell us they are? Why, I would ask you in return, did Northern senators and Northern representatives give their votes, at the last sitting of congress, to the admission of Arkansas Territory as a state? Take those men, one by one, and ask them in their parlours, do you *approve of slavery?* ask them on *Northern* ground, where they will speak the truth, and I doubt not *every man* of them will tell you, *no!* Why then, I ask, did *they* give their votes to enlarge the mouth of that grave which has already destroyed its tens of thousands? All our enemies tell *us* they are as much anti-slavery as we are. Yes, my friends, thousands who are helping you to bind the fetters of slavery on the negro, despise you in their hearts for doing it; they rejoice that such an institution has not been entailed upon them. Why then, I would ask, do *they* lend you their help? I will tell you, "they love *the praise of men more* than the praise of God." The Abolition cause has not yet become so popular as to induce them to believe, that by advocating it in congress, they shall sit still more securely in their seats there and like the *chief rulers* in the days of our Saviour, though *many* believed on him, yet they did *not* confess him, lest they should *be put out of the synagogue;* John xii, 42, 43.[5] Or

---

4. An abolitionist newspaper distributed from January 1831 to January 1866, published in Boston by William Lloyd Garrison. It was considered so inflammatory that several states made it a crime to distribute it.

5. Roman governor of Judaea during the life of Jesus of Nazareth. See Matthew 27, Mark 15, Luke 23, John 18:28–40, Acts 3:13.

perhaps like Pilate, thinking they could prevail nothing, and fearing a tumult, they determined to release Barabbas[6] and surrender the just man, the poor innocent slave to be stripped of his rights and scourged. In vain will such men try to wash their hands, and say, with the Roman governor, "I am innocent of the blood of this just person."[7] Northern American statesmen are no more innocent of the crime of slavery, than Pilate was of the murder of Jesus, or Saul of that of Stephen.[8] These are high charges, but I appeal to *their hearts;* I appeal to public opinion ten years from now. Slavery then is a national sin.

* * *

Sisters in Christ, I have done. As a Southerner, I have felt it was my duty to address you. I have endeavoured to set before you the exceeding sinfulness of slavery, and to point you to the example of those noble women who have been raised up in the church to effect great revolutions, and to suffer for the truth's sake. I have appealed to your sympathies as women, to your sense of duty as *Christian women.* I have attempted to vindicate the Abolitionists, to prove the entire safety of immediate Emancipation, and to plead the cause of the poor and oppressed. I have done—I have sowed the seeds of truth, but I well know, that even if an Apollos[9] were to follow in my steps to water them, "*God only* can give the increase." To Him then who is able to prosper the work of his servant's hand, I commend this Appeal in fervent prayer, that as he "hath *chosen the weak things of the world,* to confound the things which are mighty,"[1] so He may cause His blessing, to descend and carry conviction to the hearts of many Lydias through these speaking pages. Farewell—Count me not your "enemy because I have told you the truth,"[2] but believe me in unfeigned affection,

Your sympathizing Friend,
Angelina E. Grimké.
1836

◄ ELIZABETH BARRETT BROWNING ►
1806–1861

Aurora Leigh, the eponymous heroine of Elizabeth Barrett Browning's epic poem, resembles her creator in many ways. Like her author, Aurora is a brilliant, ambitious poet who breaks with social convention while arguing passionately that women's art should be taken as seriously as men's. But Aurora complains bitterly, in the passage excerpted here from the novel-length poem, about the useless feminine education she received as a girl; Barrett Browning could not make the same complaint, as she begged for and received a classical education at her brother's side in her wealthy father's home. Elizabeth Barrett Browning was born the eldest daughter of Edward Moulton-Barrett—an Englishman born in Jamaica, where his

---

6. Barabbas: a prisoner released by Pilate in honor of Passover. See Matthew 27:16–26, Mark 15:7–15, Luke 23:18–25, John 18:40.
7. Matthew 27:23–25.
8. Acts 6:8–10 tells of the death of the first Christian martyr; Saul is named as one of those who stoned Stephen to death following his condemnation by the Jewish priests.
9. In Greek mythology, the patron god of Delphi, poets, music, and persuasion.
1. 1 Corinthians 1:27.
2. Acts 16:1.

family's fortune arose from sugar plantations worked by slaves—and Mary Graham-Clarke. Barrett grew up in her father's twenty-bedroom mansion in the English countryside, along with eleven siblings, ten of whom survived infancy. As a child, she enjoyed economic and educational privileges that were rare among women of the Victorian era, including her classical education.

By the age of twelve, Barrett was reading Homer in the original Greek (while also learning Latin and French); studying philosophers, including Mary Wollstonecraft, one of her favorites; and both reading the English literary classics and writing poetry and plays of her own. She began publishing poems at age fourteen; this early work reflects her avid interests in history, politics, and philosophy and demonstrates her belief that poetry should not be a vehicle for romantic fantasy but instead should engage with controversial issues in the real world. She was eventually to write poems supporting women's rights, the abolition of slavery, and the reform of working conditions in factories, especially for children.

In 1821, at the age of fifteen, Barrett became chronically ill with an affliction that has never been definitively diagnosed. A slight woman, she was never very physically active, but her prolonged illness made her a semi-invalid throughout her adult life. No doubt the Victorian treatments for mysterious female ailments— including enforced bedrest and laudanum, a highly addictive mixture of opium and alcohol—did nothing to improve her strength. Despite her doctors' ban on reading and writing, Barrett continued to study and to produce poetry.

In 1832, her father suffered economic misfortunes that forced the family to sell their country home; they moved briefly to the seacoast and eventually settled in a spacious apartment at 50 Wimpole Street in London. Her indisposition, not to mention her shyness, prevented her from mixing with the literary celebrities of the city, though she carried on extensive correspondences with some fellow writers. (She was to become famous enough herself to have been mentioned as a possible successor to William Wordsworth as poet laureate, but Alfred, Lord Tennyson won the post instead.) One of her correspondents was native Londoner Robert Browning, a poet of meager means but prodigious talent. His poems were, and still are, considered among the most intellectually challenging works of the Victorian period; he is best known for his "dramatic monologues" (such as "My Last Duchess"; 1842) and for his verse-novel, The Ring and the Book (1868–69). An admirer of Barrett's poems and six years her junior, he tried and failed to meet her in 1842 but wrote her a very effective fan letter in 1845. His appreciation for her poetry broke through her customary reserve, and she received him for regular visits in her father's home over the course of that year. These visits quickly became courtship. During this year Barrett wrote Sonnets from the Portuguese (1850), the only one of her major works that has been consistently popular for the past 150 years. The poems adapt the traditionally masculine sonnet form to do something English sonnets had rarely, if ever, done before: speak of a woman's love for a man in the first person, from her perspective. The sonnets are original, though Barrett's title implies she translated them. Their content is personal, and Barrett was not interested in anonymous publication; hence, this little artifice was meant to shield the poet's privacy.

Barrett had concealed her deepening relationship with Browning from her father, who harbored an eccentric and implacable prejudice against marriage. He refused to give permission for any of his eleven adult children to marry, evidently giving no explanation for this unusual action. Though she loved and respected her father, Barrett could not accept this ban: she and Browning were secretly married in a civil ceremony in 1846 and left England for Italy. In Florence, she miscarried twice before giving birth in 1849 to her only child, a son named Robert Wiedeman Barrett Browning, called "Pen." A house called Casa Guidi in Florence was to remain the family's home, though the Brownings made extended visits to France and England. Barrett Browning died in Florence in 1861 of a lung ailment just five years after publishing her masterpiece, *Aurora Leigh* (1856).

Aurora Leigh is the only work of its kind among women's writing in English. It is an epic poem, on the scale of John Milton's *Paradise Lost*, which chronicled the creation and fall of man, or William Wordsworth's *Prelude*, which narrated the lifelong development of the male romantic poet's consciousness. Epic poetry in English is written in unrhymed iambic pentameter; the form itself suggests a monumentally important subject. Barrett Browning broke from convention by making the subject of her epic poem the development of a woman poet's consciousness. The poem is a novel in verse, telling the story of the life and loves of Aurora, as well as detailing her theories of poetry. While Aurora is not Elizabeth, the poet's ardent feminism comes through in her heroine's words and actions. The excerpt included here is taken from the beginning of the poem, which explains how the orphaned Aurora, age thirteen, came to leave her native Italy to live with her straitlaced, conventional British aunt. The spirit of feminist protest established in this section carries through all nine books of the poem, showing that the spirit of Mary Wollstonecraft (p. 365) was very much alive in Barrett Browning.

From Sonnets from the Portuguese

XIV

> If thou must love me, let it be for nought
> Except for love's sake only. Do not say
> "I love her for her smile . . . her look . . . her way
> Of speaking gently, . . . for a trick of thought
> That falls in well with mine, and certes[1] brought   5
> A sense of pleasant ease on such a day"—
> For these things in themselves, Belovèd, may
> Be changed, or change for thee,—and love, so wrought,
> May be unwrought so. Neither love me for
> Thine own dear pity's wiping my cheeks dry,—   10
> A creature might forget to weep who bore
> Thy comfort long, and lose thy love thereby.
> But love me for love's sake, that evermore
> Thou mayst love on through love's eternity.

XLIII

> How do I love thee? Let me count the ways.
> I love thee to the depth and breadth and height
> My soul can reach, when feeling out of sight

---

1. Certainly (archaic).

For the ends of Being and ideal Grace.
I love thee to the level of everyday's   5
Most quiet need, by sun and candlelight.
I love thee freely, as men strive for Right;
I love thee purely, as they turn from Praise.
I love thee with the passion put to use[2]
In my old griefs, and with my childhood's faith.   10
I love thee with a love I seemed to lose
With my lost saints,—I love thee with the breath,
Smiles, tears, of all my life!—and, if God choose,
I shall but love thee better after death.

1850

From Aurora Leigh

Book I [Aurora's Education]

Of writing many books there is no end;
And I who have written much in prose and verse
For others' uses, will write now for mine—
Will write my story for my better self
As when you paint your portrait for a friend,   5
Who keeps it in a drawer and looks at it
Long after he has ceased to love you, just
To hold together what he was and is.

I, writing thus, am still what men call young;
I have not so far left the coasts of life   10
To travel inland, that I cannot hear
That murmur of the outer Infinite
Which unweaned babies smile at in their sleep
When wondered at for smiling; not so far,
But still I catch my mother at her post   15
Beside the nursery-door, with finger up,
"Hush, hush—here's too much noise!" while her sweet eyes
Leap forward, taking part against her word
In the child's riot. Still I sit and feel
My father's slow hand, when she had left us both,   20
Stroke out my childish curls across his knee,
And hear Assunta's[3] daily jest (she knew
He liked it better than a better jest)
Inquire how many golden scudi[4] went
To make such ringlets. O my father's hand,   25
Stroke heavily, heavily the poor hair down,
Draw, press the child's head closer to thy knee!
I'm still too young, too young, to sit alone.

2. That is, where passion had earlier been chan-
neled into grief, it now became love.

3. Aurora's nanny.
4. Italian coins.

I write. My mother was a Florentine,
Whose rare blue eyes were shut from seeing me   30
When scarcely I was four years old, my life
A poor spark snatched up from a failing lamp
Which went out therefore. She was weak and frail;
She could not bear the joy of giving life,
The mother's rapture slew her. If her kiss   35
Had left a longer weight upon my lips
It might have steadied the uneasy breath,
And reconciled and fraternised my soul
With the new order.[5] As it was, indeed,
I felt a mother-want about the world,   40
And still went seeking, like a bleating lamb
Left out at night in shutting up the fold[6]—
As restless as a nest-deserted bird
Grown chill through something being away, though what
It knows not. I, Aurora Leigh, was born   45
To make my father sadder, and myself
Not overjoyous, truly. Women know
The way to rear up children (to be just),
They know a simple, merry, tender knack
Of tying sashes, fitting baby-shoes,   50
And stringing pretty words that make no sense,
And kissing full sense into empty words,
Which things are corals[7] to cut life upon,
Although such trifles: children learn by such,
Love's holy earnest in a pretty play   55
And get not over-early solemnised,
But seeing, as in a rose-bush, Love's Divine
Which burns and hurts not—not a single bloom,
Become aware and unafraid of Love.
Such good do mothers. Fathers love as well   60
—Mine did, I know—but still with heavier brains,
And wills more consciously responsible,
And not as wisely, since less foolishly;
So mothers have God's licence to be missed.

My father was an austere Englishman,   65
Who, after a dry life-time spent at home
In college-learning, law, and parish talk,
Was flooded with a passion unaware,
His whole provisioned and complacent past
Drowned out from him that moment. As he stood   70
In Florence, where he had come to spend a month
And note the secret of Da Vinci's drains,[8]
He musing somewhat absently perhaps

5. That is, her new condition of having no mother.
6. Sheep pen.
7. Teething rings for babies, made of polished coral.

8. Leonardo da Vinci (1452–1519), engineer and artist, designed a drainage system for the city of Florence.

Some English question . . . whether men should pay
The unpopular but necessary tax[9]   75
With left or right hand—in the alien sun
In that great square of the Santissima[1]
There drifted past him (scarcely marked enough
To move his comfortable island scorn)[2]
A train of priestly banners, cross and psalm,   80
The white-veiled rose-crowned maidens holding up
Tall tapers, weighty for such wrists, aslant
To the blue luminous tremor of the air,
And letting drop the white wax as they went
To eat the bishop's wafer at the church;[3]   85
From which long trail of chanting priests and girls,
A face flashed like a cymbal on his face
And shook with silent clangour brain and heart,
Transfiguring him to music. Thus, even thus,
He too received his sacramental gift   90
With eucharistic[4] meanings; for he loved.

And thus beloved, she died. I've heard it said
That but to see him in the first surprise
Of widower and father, nursing me,
Unmothered little child of four years old,   95
His large man's hands afraid to touch my curls,
As if the gold would tarnish—his grave lips
Contriving such a miserable smile
As if he knew needs must, or I should die,
And yet 'twas hard—would almost make the stones   100
Cry out for pity. There's a verse he set
In Santa Croce to her memory—
"Weep for an infant too young to weep much
When death removed this mother"—stops the mirth
Today on women's faces when they walk   105
With rosy children hanging on their gowns,
Under the cloister to escape the sun
That scorches in the piazza. After which
He left our Florence and made haste to hide
Himself, his prattling child, and silent grief,   110
Among the mountains above Pelago;[5]
Because unmothered babes, he thought, had need
Of mother nature more than others use,
And Pan's white goats, with udders warm and full[6]
Of mystic contemplations, come to feed   115
Poor milkless lips of orphans like his own—
Such scholar-scraps he talked, I've heard from friends,

9. Probably an allusion to the British income tax.
1. A public square in front of the Church of Santissima Annunziata in Florence.
2. As an Englishman, he is prejudiced against
Catholicism.
3. To take communion. The wafer of bread is

"the body of Christ."
4. Eucharist: the ritual of communion.
5. Village near Florence.
6. Pan is the Greek god of herdsmen and often
affiliated with goats.

For even prosaic men who wear grief long
Will get to wear it as a hat aside
With a flower stuck in't. Father, then, and child,   120
We lived among the mountains many years,
God's silence on the outside of the house,
And we who did not speak too loud within,
And old Assunta to make up the fire,
Crossing herself whene'er a sudden flame   125
Which lightened from the firewood, made alive
That picture of my mother on the wall.

The painter drew it after she was dead,
And when the face was finished, throat and hands,
Her cameriera[7] carried him, in hate   130
Of the English-fashioned shroud, the last brocade
She dressed in at the Pitti;[8] "he should paint
No sadder thing than that," she swore, "to wrong
Her poor signora." Therefore very strange
The effect was. I, a little child, would crouch   135
For hours upon the floor with knees drawn up,
And gaze across them, half in terror, half
In adoration, at the picture there—
That swan-like supernatural white life
Just sailing upward from the red stiff silk   140
Which seemed to have no part in it nor power
To keep it from quite breaking out of bounds.
For hours I sat and stared. Assunta's awe
And my poor father's melancholy eyes
Still pointed that way. That way went my thoughts   145
When wandering beyond sight. And as I grew
In years, I mixed, confused, unconsciously,
Whatever I last read or heard or dreamed,
Abhorrent, admirable, beautiful,
Pathetical, or ghastly, or grotesque,   150
With still that face . . . which did not therefore change,
But kept the mystic level of all forms,
Hates, fears, and admirations, was by turns
Ghost, fiend, and angel, fairy, witch, and sprite,
A dauntless Muse who eyes a dreadful Fate,   155
A loving Psyche who loses sight of Love,
A still Medusa[9] with mild milky brows
All curdled and all clothed upon with snakes
Whose slime falls fast as sweat will; or anon
Our Lady of the Passion, stabbed with swords[1]   160

7. Ladies' maid.
8. A palace in Florence.
9. Muse: Greek goddess of arts who inspired poets and artists; Psyche: in Greek myth, a beautiful woman and lover of Cupid (Love), who abandoned

her when she looked at him directly; Medusa: mythological monster with snakes for hair.
1. The Virgin Mary, who grieved at the suffering of her son Jesus.

Where the Babe sucked; or Lamia[2] in her first
Moonlighted pallor, ere she shrunk and blinked
And shuddering wriggled down to the unclean;
Or my own mother, leaving her last smile
In her last kiss upon the baby-mouth   165
My father pushed down on the bed for that—
Or my dead mother, without smile or kiss,
Buried at Florence. All which images,
Concentred on the picture, glassed themselves
Before my meditative childhood, as   170
The incoherencies of change and death
Are represented fully, mixed and merged,
In the smooth fair mystery of perpetual Life.

And while I stared away my childish wits
Upon my mother's picture (ah, poor child!),   175
My father, who through love had suddenly
Thrown off the old conventions, broken loose
From chin-bands of the soul, like Lazarus,[3]
Yet had no time to learn to talk and walk
Or grow anew familiar with the sun—   180
Who had reached to freedom, not to action, lived,
But lived as one entranced, with thoughts, not aims—
Whom love had unmade from a common man
But not completed to an uncommon man—
My father taught me what he had learnt the best   185
Before he died and left me—grief and love.
And, seeing we had books among the hills,
Strong words of counselling souls confederate
With vocal pines and waters—out of books
He taught me all the ignorance of men,   190
And how God laughs in heaven when any man
Says "Here I'm learned; this, I understand;
In that, I am never caught at fault or doubt."
He sent the schools to school, demonstrating
A fool will pass for such through one mistake,   195
While a philosopher will pass for such,
Through said mistakes being ventured in the gross
And heaped up to a system.
                            I am like,
They tell me, my dear father. Broader brows
Howbeit, upon a slenderer undergrowth   200
Of delicate features—paler, near as grave;
But then my mother's smile breaks up the whole,
And makes it better sometimes than itself.

2. In a poem of the same name (1819) by John
Keats (1795–1821), Lamia is a beautiful woman
who turns into a snake.

3. Chin-bands: used to hold corpses' mouths
closed; Lazarus: a friend whom Jesus resurrects
(John 11:41–44).

So, nine full years, our days were hid with God
Among his mountains: I was just thirteen,   205
Still growing like the plants from unseen roots
In tongue-tied Springs—and suddenly awoke
To full life and life's needs and agonies
With an intense, strong, struggling heart beside
A stone-dead father. Life, struck sharp on death,   210
Makes awful lightning. His last word was, "Love—"
"Love, my child, love, love!" (then he had done with grief)
"Love, my child." Ere I answered he was gone,
And none was left to love in all the world.

There, ended childhood. What succeeded next   215
I recollect as, after fevers, men
Thread back the passage of delirium,
Missing the turn still, baffled by the door;
Smooth endless days, notched here and there with knives;
A weary, wormy darkness, spurred i' the flank   220
With flame, that it should eat and end itself
Like some tormented scorpion. Then at last
I do remember clearly, how there came
A stranger with authority, not right
(I thought not), who commanded, caught me up   225
From old Assunta's neck; how, with a shriek,
She let me go—while I, with ears too full
Of my father's silence to shriek back a word,
In all a child's astonishment at grief
Stared at the wharf-edge where she stood and moaned,   230
My poor Assunta, where she stood and moaned!
The white walls, the blue hills, my Italy,
Drawn backward from the shuddering steamer-deck,
Like one in anger drawing back her skirts
Which suppliants catch it. Then the bitter sea   235
Inexorably pushed between us both,
And sweeping up the ship with my despair
Threw us out as a pasture to the stars.

Ten nights and days we voyaged on the deep;
Ten nights and days without the common face   240
Of any day or night; the moon and sun
Cut off from the green reconciling earth,
To starve into a blind ferocity
And glare unnatural; the very sky
(Dropping its bell-net down upon the sea   245
As if no human heart should 'scape alive)
Bedraggled with the desolating salt,
Until it seemed no more that holy heaven
To which my father went. All new and strange;
The universe turned stranger, for a child.   250

Then, land!—then, England! oh, the frosty cliffs
Looked cold upon me. Could I find a home
Among those mean red houses through the fog?
And when I heard my father's language first
From alien lips which had no kiss for mine   255
I wept aloud, then laughed, then wept, then wept,
And some one near me said the child was mad
Through much sea-sickness. The train swept us on.
Was this my father's England? the great isle?
The ground seemed cut up from the fellowship   260
Of verdure, field from field, as man from man;
The skies themselves looked low and positive,
As almost you could touch them with a hand,
And dared to do it they were so far off
From God's celestial crystals; all things blurred   265
And dull and vague. Did Shakespeare and his mates
Absorb the light here?—not a hill or stone
With heart to strike a radiant colour up
Or active outline on the indifferent air.

I think I see my father's sister stand   270
Upon the hall-step of her country-house
To give me welcome. She stood straight and calm,
Her somewhat narrow forehead braided tight
As if for taming accidental thoughts
From possible pulses; brown hair pricked with gray   275
By frigid use of life (she was not old
Although my father's elder by a year);
A nose drawn sharply, yet in delicate lines;
A close mild mouth, a little soured about
The ends, through speaking unrequited loves   280
Or peradventure⁴ niggardly half-truths;
Eyes of no colour—once they might have smiled,
But never, never have forgot themselves
In smiling; cheeks, in which was yet a rose
Of perished summers, like a rose in a book,   285
Kept more for ruth⁵ than pleasure—if past bloom,
Past fading also.
                       She had lived, we'll say,
A harmless life, she called a virtuous life,
A quiet life, which was not life at all
(But that, she had not lived enough to know),   290
Between the vicar and the county squires,
The lord-lieutenant looking down sometimes
From the empyrean⁶ to assure their souls

4. Perhaps (archaic).   6. The highest part of heaven.
5. Pity.

Against chance vulgarisms, and, in the abyss
The apothecary, looked on once a year   295
To prove their soundness of humility.
The poor-club[7] exercised her Christian gifts
Of knitting stockings, stitching petticoats,
Because we are of one flesh after all
And need one flannel (with a proper sense   300
Of difference in the quality)—and still
The book-club, guarded from your modern trick
Of shaking dangerous questions from the crease,
Preserved her intellectual. She had lived
A sort of cage-bird life,[8] born in a cage,   305
Accounting that to leap from perch to perch
Was act and joy enough for any bird.
Dear heaven, how silly are the things that live
In thickets, and eat berries!
                     I, alas,
A wild bird scarcely fledged, was brought to her cage,   310
And she was there to meet me. Very kind.
Bring the clean water, give out the fresh seed.

She stood upon the steps to welcome me,
Calm, in black garb. I clung about her neck—
Young babes, who catch at every shred of wool   315
To draw the new light closer, catch and cling
Less blindly. In my ears, my father's word
Hummed ignorantly, as the sea in shells,
"Love, love, my child!" She, black there with my grief,
Might feel my love—she was his sister once,   320
I clung to her. A moment she seemed moved,
Kissed me with cold lips, suffered me to cling,
And drew me feebly through the hall into
The room she sat in.
                     There, with some strange spasm
Of pain and passion, she wrung loose my hands   325
Imperiously, and held me at arm's length,
And with two gray-steel naked-bladed eyes
Searched through my face—ay, stabbed it through and through,
Through brows and cheeks and chin, as if to find
A wicked murderer in my innocent face,   330
If not here, there perhaps. Then, drawing breath,
She struggled for her ordinary calm
And missed it rather—told me not to shrink,
As if she had told me not to lie or swear—
"She loved my father and would love me too   335
As long as I deserved it." Very kind.

---

7. Ladies' private charitable organization.   for women's oppression.
8. Allusion to Mary Wollstonecraft's metaphor

I understood her meaning afterward;
She thought to find my mother in my face,
And questioned it for that. For she, my aunt,
Had loved my father truly, as she could,   340
And hated, with the gall of gentle souls,
My Tuscan[9] mother who had fooled away
A wise man from wise courses, a good man
From obvious duties, and, depriving her,
His sister, of the household precedence,   345
Had wronged his tenants, robbed his native land,
And made him mad, alike by life and death,
In love and sorrow. She had pored for years
What sort of woman could be suitable
To her sort of hate, to entertain it with,   350
And so, her very curiosity
Became hate too, and all the idealism
She ever used in life, was used for hate,
Till hate, so nourished, did exceed at last
The love from which it grew, in strength and heat,   355
And wrinkled her smooth conscience with a sense
Of disputable virtue (say not, sin)
When Christian doctrine was enforced at church.

And thus my father's sister was to me
My mother's hater. From that day, she did   360
Her duty to me (I appreciate it
In her own word as spoken to herself),
Her duty, in large measure, well pressed out,
But measured always. She was generous, bland,
More courteous than was tender, gave me still   365
The first place—as if fearful that God's saints
Would look down suddenly and say, "Herein
You missed a point, I think, through lack of love."
Alas, a mother never is afraid
Of speaking angrily to any child,   370
Since love, she knows, is justified of love.

And I, I was a good child on the whole,
A meek and manageable child. Why not?
I did not live, to have the faults of life:
There seemed more true life in my father's grave   375
Than in all England. Since *that* threw me off
Who fain would cleave (his latest will, they say,
Consigned me to his land), I only thought
Of lying quiet there where I was thrown
Like seaweed on the rocks, and suffering her   380
To prick me to a pattern with her pin
Fibre from fibre, delicate leaf from leaf,

9. Florence is in the region of Italy called Tuscany.

And dry out from my drowned anatomy
The last sea-salt left in me.
                    So it was.
I broke the copious curls upon my head   385
In braids, because she liked smooth-ordered hair.
I left off saying my sweet Tuscan words
Which still at any stirring of the heart
Came up to float across the English phrase
As lilies (*Bene* or *Che che*),[1] because   390
She liked my father's child to speak his tongue.
I learnt the collects and the catechism,[2]
The creeds, from Athanasius back to Nice,
The Articles,[3] the Tracts *against* the times[4]
(By no means Buonaventure's "Prick of Love"),[5]   395
And various popular synopses of
Inhuman doctrines never taught by John,
Because she liked instructed piety.
I learnt my complement of classic French
(Kept pure of Balzac and neologism)[6]   400
And German also, since she liked a range
Of liberal education—tongues, not books.
I learnt a little algebra, a little
Of the mathematics—brushed with extreme flounce
The circle of the sciences, because   405
She misliked women who are frivolous.
I learnt the royal genealogies
Of Oviedo,[7] the internal laws
Of the Burmese empire—by how many feet
Mount Chimborazo outsoars Tenerife,   410
What navigable river joins itself
To Lara, and what census of the year five
Was taken at Klagenfurt—because she liked
A general insight into useful facts.
I learnt much music—such as would have been   415
As quite impossible in Johnson's day

1. Italian exclamations, the first meaning "Well!" and the other "What, what?"
2. Collects: short, standardized prayers; catechism: set questions and answers summarizing Christian belief.
3. Statements elaborating the Christian idea of the Trinity (Father, Son, and Holy Spirit). Athanasius was a first-century bishop of Alexandria to whom the first creed is attributed; it was replaced in the fourth century by the Nicene Creed. The Articles of Faith, thirty-nine in all, written in the sixteenth century, summarize the beliefs of the Church of England.
4. "Tracts for the Times" were published 1833–41 by the Oxford Movement, who sought to bring the Church of England closer to Catholicism in its beliefs and rituals.
5. St. Bonaventure advocated a love-based Christianity in the thirteenth century.
6. Honoré de Balzac (1799–1850): a controversial realist French novelist; neologisms: newly coined words.
7. Oviedo: a province of Spain; Burma: an independent South Asian kingdom at war with imperial England in the 1820s and again in 1852; Chimborazo is a volcano in Ecuador, Tenerife one of the seven Canary islands off the coast of Africa; Lara: a rural Australian town; Klagenfurt: a city in Austria.

As still it might be wished[8]—fine sleights of hand
And unimagined fingering, shuffling off
The hearer's soul through hurricanes of notes
To a noisy Tophet;[9] and I drew . . . costumes   420
From French engravings, nereids[1] neatly draped
(With smirks of simmering godship)—I washed in[2]
Landscapes from nature (rather say, washed out).
I danced the polka and Cellarius,[3]
Spun glass, stuffed birds, and modelled flowers in wax,   425
Because she liked accomplishments in girls.
I read a score of books on womanhood
To prove, if women do not think at all,
They may teach thinking (to a maiden-aunt
Or else the author)—books that boldly assert   430
Their right of comprehending husband's talk
When not too deep, and even of answering
With pretty "may it please you," or "so it is"—
Their rapid insight and fine aptitude,
Particular worth and general missionariness,   435
As long as they keep quiet by the fire
And never say "no" when the world says "ay,"
For that is fatal—their angelic reach
Of virtue, chiefly used to sit and darn,
And fatten household sinners—their, in brief,   440
Potential faculty in everything
Of abdicating power in it: she owned
She liked a woman to be womanly,
And English women, she thanked God and sighed
(Some people always sigh in thanking God),   445
Were models to the universe. And last
I learnt cross-stitch, because she did not like
To see me wear the night with empty hands
A-doing nothing. So, my shepherdess
Was something after all (the pastoral[4] saints   450
Be praised for't), leaning lovelorn with pink eyes
To match her shoes, when I mistook the silks;
Her head uncrushed by that round weight of hat
So strangely similar to the tortoise-shell
Which slew the tragic poet.[5]
                    By the way,   455
The works of women are symbolical.
We sew, sew, prick our fingers, dull our sight,

8. An allusion to a joke attributed to British writer and critic Samuel Johnson (1709–84) about a violin performance: "Difficult do you call it, Sir? I wish it were impossible."
9. Hell.
1. Sea nymphs in Greek mythology.
2. Washed in: filled in drawings with watercolor.

3. A waltz.
4. Having to do with a romanticized notion of country life.
5. The Greek tragedian Aeschylus (525–456 BCE) is supposed to have died when an eagle accidentally dropped a tortoise on his head.

Producing what? A pair of slippers, sir,
To put on when you're weary—or a stool
To stumble over and vex you . . . "curse that stool!"   460
Or else at best, a cushion, where you lean
And sleep, and dream of something we are not
But would be for your sake. Alas, alas!
This hurts most, this—that, after all, we are paid
The worth of our work, perhaps.

                              In looking down   465
Those years of education (to return)
I wonder if Brinvilliers[6] suffered more
In the water-torture . . . flood succeeding flood
To drench the incapable throat and split the veins . . .
Than I did. Certain of your feebler souls   470
Go out[7] in such a process; many pine
To a sick, inodorous light; my own endured:
I had relations in the Unseen, and drew
The elemental nutriment and heat
From nature, as earth feels the sun at nights,   475
Or as a babe sucks surely in the dark.
I kept the life thrust on me, on the outside
Of the inner life with all its ample room
For heart and lungs, for will and intellect,
Inviolable by conventions. God,   480
I thank thee for that grace of thine!

                              At first
I felt no life which was not patience—did
The thing she bade me, without heed to a thing
Beyond it, sat in just the chair she placed,
With back against the window, to exclude   485
The sight of the great lime-tree on the lawn,
Which seemed to have come on purpose from the woods
To bring the house a message—ay, and walked
Demurely in her carpeted low rooms,
As if I should not, hearkening my own steps,   490
Misdoubt I was alive. I read her books,
Was civil to her cousin, Romney Leigh,
Gave ear to her vicar, tea to her visitors,
And heard them whisper, when I changed a cup
(I blushed for joy at that)—"The Italian child,   495
For all her blue eyes and her quiet ways,
Thrives ill in England: she is paler yet
Than when we came the last time; she will die."

"Will die." My cousin, Romney Leigh, blushed too,
With sudden anger, and approaching me   500

6. A seventeenth-century French noblewoman,   water down her throat, her torturers executed her
the Marquise de Brinvilliers, who was tortured for   by beheading.
allegedly plotting murder. After forcing gallons of   7. Are extinguished; die.

Said low between his teeth, "You're wicked now?
You wish to die and leave the world a-dusk
For others, with your naughty light blown out?"
I looked into his face defyingly;
He might have known that, being what I was,   505
'Twas natural to like to get away
As far as dead folk can: and then indeed
Some people make no trouble when they die.
He turned and went abruptly, slammed the door
And shut his dog out.

Romney, Romney Leigh.   510

I have not named my cousin hitherto,
And yet I used him as a sort of friend;
My elder by few years, but cold and shy
And absent . . . tender, when he thought of it,
Which scarcely was imperative, grave betimes,   515
As well as early master of Leigh Hall,[8]
Whereof the nightmare sat upon his youth
Repressing all its seasonable delights
And agonising with a ghastly sense
Of universal hideous want and wrong   520
To incriminate possession. When he came
From college to the country, very oft
He crossed the hill on visits to my aunt,
With gifts of blue grapes from the hothouses,
A book in one hand—mere statistics (if   525
I chanced to lift the cover), count of all
The goats whose beards grow sprouting down toward hell
Against God's separative judgment-hour.[9]
And she, she almost loved him—even allowed
That sometimes he should seem to sigh my way;   530
It made him easier to be pitiful,
And sighing was his gift. So, undisturbed
At whiles she let him shut my music up
And push my needles down, and lead me out
To see in that south angle of the house   535
The figs grow black as if by a Tuscan rock,
On some light pretext. She would turn her head
At other moments, go to fetch a thing,
And leave me breath enough to speak with him,
For his sake; it was simple.

Sometimes too   540

He would have saved me utterly, it seemed,
He stood and looked so.

---

8. Romney's inherited estate.
9. Matthew 25:32–33, 41: "And before him shall be gathered all nations: and he shall separate them one from another, as a shepherd divideth [his] sheep from the goats: / And he shall set the sheep on his right hand, but the goats on the left. . . . / Then shall he say also unto them on the left hand, Depart from me, ye cursed, into everlasting fire, prepared for the devil and his angels."

Once, he stood so near
He dropped a sudden hand upon my head
Bent down on woman's work, as soft as rain—
But then I rose and shook it off as fire,   545
The stranger's touch that took my father's place
Yet dared seemed soft.
              I used him for a friend
Before I ever knew him for a friend.
'Twas better, 'twas worse also, afterward:
We came so close, we saw our differences   550
Too intimately. Always Romney Leigh
Was looking for the worms, I for the gods.
A godlike nature his; the gods look down,
Incurious of themselves; and certainly
'Tis well I should remember, how, those days,   555
I was a worm too, and he looked on me.

A little by his act perhaps, yet more
By something in me, surely not my will,
I did not die. But slowly, as one in swoon,
To whom life creeps back in the form of death,   560
With a sense of separation, a blind pain
Of blank obstruction, and a roar i' the ears
Of visionary chariots which retreat
As earth grows clearer . . . slowly, by degrees,
I woke, rose up . . . where was I? in the world;   565
For uses therefore I must count worth while.

I had a little chamber in the house,
As green as any privet-hedge[1] a bird
Might choose to build in, though the nest itself
Could show but dead-brown sticks and straws; the walls   570
Were green, the carpet was pure green, the straight
Small bed was curtained greenly, and the folds
Hung green about the window which let in
The outdoor world with all its greenery.
You could not push your head out and escape   575
A dash of dawn-dew from the honeysuckle,
But so you were baptised into the grace
And privilege of seeing . . .
                First, the lime
(I had enough there, of the lime, be sure—
My morning-dream was often hummed away   580
By the bees in it); past the lime, the lawn,
Which, after sweeping broadly round the house,
Went trickling through the shrubberies in a stream
Of tender turf, and wore and lost itself
Among the acacias, over which you saw   585

---

1. Hedge surrounding a property.

The irregular line of elms by the deep lane
Which stopped the grounds and dammed the overflow
Of arbutus and laurel. Out of sight
The lane was; sunk so deep, no foreign tramp
Nor drover of wild ponies out of Wales   590
Could guess if lady's hall or tenant's lodge
Dispensed such odours—though his stick well-crooked
Might reach the lowest trail of blossoming briar
Which dipped upon the wall. Behind the elms,
And through their tops, you saw the folded hills   595
Striped up and down with hedges (burly oaks
Projecting from the line to show themselves),
Through which my cousin Romney's chimneys smoked
As still as when a silent mouth in frost
Breathes, showing where the woodlands hid Leigh Hall;   600
While, far above, a jut of table-land,
A promontory without water, stretched—
You could not catch it if the days were thick,
Or took it for a cloud; but, otherwise,
The vigorous sun would catch it up at eve   605
And use it for an anvil till he had filled
The shelves of heaven with burning thunderbolts,
Protesting against night and darkness: then,
When all his setting trouble was resolved
To a trance of passive glory, you might see   610
In apparition on the golden sky
(Alas, my Giotto's background!)[2] the sheep run
Along the fine clear outline, small as mice
That run along a witch's scarlet thread.

Not a grand nature. Not my chestnut-woods   615
Of Vallombrosa,[3] cleaving by the spurs
To the precipices. Not my headlong leaps
Of waters, that cry out for joy or fear
In leaping through the palpitating pines,
Like a white soul tossed out to eternity   620
With thrills of time upon it. Not indeed
My multitudinous mountains, sitting in
The magic circle, with the mutual touch
Electric, panting from their full deep hearts
Beneath the influent heavens, and waiting for   625
Communion and commission. Italy
Is one thing, England one.
                              On English ground
You understand the letter—ere the fall
How Adam lived in a garden. All the fields

2. The thirteenth-century Italian painter Giotto   ground color.
di Bondone (1267–1337) favored gold as a back-   3. A valley in Tuscany.

Are tied up fast with hedges, nosegay-like;   630
The hills are crumpled plains, the plains parterres,
The trees, round, woolly, ready to be clipped,
And if you seek for any wilderness
You find, at best, a park. A nature tamed
And grown domestic like a barn-door fowl,   635
Which does not awe you with its claws and beak
Nor tempt you to an eyrie too high up,
But which, in cackling, sets you thinking of
Your eggs tomorrow at breakfast, in the pause
Of finer meditation.
                            Rather say,   640
A sweet familiar nature, stealing in
As a dog might, or child, to touch your hand
Or pluck your gown, and humbly mind you so
Of presence and affection, excellent
For inner uses, from the things without.   645

I could not be unthankful, I who was
Entreated thus and holpen.[4] In the room
I speak of, ere the house was well awake,
And also after it was well asleep,
I sat alone, and drew the blessing in   650
Of all that nature. With a gradual step,
A stir among the leaves, a breath, a ray,
It came in softly, while the angels made
A place for it beside me. The moon came,
And swept my chamber clean of foolish thoughts.   655
The sun came, saying, "Shall I lift this light
Against the lime-tree, and you will not look?
I make the birds sing—listen! but, for you,
God never hears your voice, excepting when
You lie upon the bed at nights and weep."   660

Then, something moved me. Then, I wakened up
More slowly than I verily write now,
But wholly, at last, I wakened, opened wide
The window and my soul, and let the airs
And outdoor sights sweep gradual gospels in,   665
Regenerating what I was. O Life,
How oft we throw it off and think—"Enough,
Enough of life in so much!—here's a cause
For rupture; herein we must break with Life,
Or be ourselves unworthy; here we are wronged,   670
Maimed, spoiled for aspiration: farewell Life!"
And so, as froward[5] babes, we hide our eyes
And think all ended.—Then, Life calls to us
In some transformed, apocalyptic voice,

4. Helped.   5. Disobedient or contrary.

Above us, or below us, or around: 675
Perhaps we name it Nature's voice, or Love's,
Tricking ourselves, because we are more ashamed
To own our compensations than our griefs:
Still, Life's voice!—still, we make our peace with Life.

And I, so young then, was not sullen. Soon   680
I used to get up early, just to sit
And watch the morning quicken in the gray,
And hear the silence open like a flower
Leaf after leaf—and stroke with listless hand
The woodbine through the window, till at last   685
I came to do it with a sort of love,
At foolish unaware: whereat I smiled—
A melancholy smile, to catch myself
Smiling for joy.
                    Capacity for joy
Admits temptation. It seemed, next, worth while   690
To dodge the sharp sword set against my life;
To slip downstairs through all the sleepy house,
As mute as any dream there, and escape
As a soul from the body, out of doors,
Glide through the shrubberies, drop into the lane,   695
And wander on the hills an hour or two,
Then back again before the house should stir.
Or else I sat on in my chamber green,
And lived my life, and thought my thoughts, and prayed
My prayers without the vicar,[6] read my books,   700
Without considering whether they were fit
To do me good. Mark, there. We get no good
By being ungenerous, even to a book,
And calculating profits—so much help
By so much reading. It is rather when   705
We gloriously forget ourselves and plunge
Soul-forward, headlong, into a book's profound,
Impassioned for its beauty and salt of truth—
'Tis then we get the right good from a book.

I read much. What my father taught before   710
From many a volume, Love re-emphasised
Upon the self-same pages: Theophrast
Grew tender with the memory of his eyes,
And Aelian made mine wet.[7] The trick of Greek
And Latin, he had taught me, as he would   715
Have taught me wrestling or the game of fives[8]
If such he had known—most like a shipwrecked man

---

6. Minister in the Church of England.
7. Theophrast: Theophrastus, Greek philosopher,
fourth century BCE; Aelian: Claudius Aelianus,

third-century Roman teacher who wrote in Greek.
8. Handball.

Who heaps his single platter with goats' cheese
And scarlet berries; or like any man
Who loves but one, and so gives all at once,   720
Because he has it, rather than because
He counts it worthy. Thus, my father gave;
And thus, as did the women formerly
By young Achilles, when they pinned a veil
Across the boy's audacious front,[9] and swept   725
With tuneful laughs the silver-fretted rocks,
He wrapped his little daughter in his large
Man's doublet, careless did it fit or no.

But, after I had read for memory,
I read for hope. The path my father's foot   730
Had trod me out (which suddenly broke off
What time he dropped the wallet of the flesh
And passed), alone I carried on, and set
My child-heart 'gainst the thorny underwood,
To reach the grassy shelter of the trees.   735
Ah babe i' the wood, without a brother-babe!
My own self-pity, like the red-breast bird,
Flies back to cover all that past with leaves.[1]

Sublimest danger, over which none weeps,
When any young wayfaring soul goes forth   740
Alone, unconscious of the perilous road,
The day-sun dazzling in his limpid eyes,
To thrust his own way, he an alien, through
The world of books! Ah, you!—you think it fine,
You clap hands—"A fair day!"—you cheer him on,   745
As if the worst, could happen, were to rest
Too long beside a fountain. Yet, behold,
Behold!—the world of books is still the world,
And worldlings in it are less merciful
And more puissant. For the wicked there   750
Are winged like angels; every knife that strikes
Is edged from elemental fire to assail
A spiritual life; the beautiful seems right
By force of beauty, and the feeble wrong
Because of weakness; power is justified   755
Though armed against Saint Michael;[2] many a crown
Covers bald foreheads. In the book-world, true,
There's no lack, neither, of God's saints and kings,
That shake the ashes of the grave aside
From their calm locks and undiscomfited   760

9. In Greek mythology, Achilles' mother dressed
her son in women's clothing and hid him among
the daughters of King Lycomedes to prevent his
going to war.
1. In the popular ballad of the time "The Chil-

dren in the Wood," two orphans are abandoned
in the forest by an uncle who wants their inheritance; when they die, a robin covers them up with
leaves.
2. A powerful archangel.

Look steadfast truths against Time's changing mask.
True, many a prophet teaches in the roads;
True, many a seer pulls down the flaming heavens
Upon his own head in strong martyrdom
In order to light men a moment's space.   765
But stay!—who judges?—who distinguishes
'Twixt Saul and Nahash justly, at first sight,
And leaves King Saul precisely at the sin,
To serve King David? who discerns at once
The sound of the trumpets, when the trumpets blow   770
For Alaric as well as Charlemagne?[3]
Who judges wizards, and can tell true seers
From conjurors? the child, there? Would you leave
That child to wander in a battle-field
And push his innocent smile against the guns;   775
Or even in a catacomb—his torch
Grown ragged in the fluttering air, and all
The dark a-mutter round him? not a child.

I read books bad and good—some bad and good
At once (good aims not always make good books: 780
Well-tempered spades turn up ill-smelling soils
In digging vineyards even); books that prove
God's being so definitely, that man's doubt
Grows self-defined the other side the line,
Made atheist by suggestion; moral books,   785
Exasperating to license; genial books,
Discounting from the human dignity;
And merry books, which set you weeping when
The sun shines—ay, and melancholy books,
Which make you laugh that any one should weep   790
In this disjointed life for one wrong more.

The world of books is still the world, I write,
And both worlds have God's providence, thank God,
To keep and hearten: with some struggle, indeed,
Among the breakers, some hard swimming through   795
The deeps—I lost breath in my soul sometimes
And cried, "God save me if there's any God,"
But, even so, God saved me; and, being dashed
From error on to error, every turn
Still brought me nearer to the central truth.   800

I thought so. All this anguish in the thick
Of men's opinions . . . press and counter-press,
Now up, now down, now underfoot, and now
Emergent . . . all the best of it, perhaps,

---

3. Old Testament story in which King Saul of Israel defeats the Ammonite King Nahash (1 Samuel
11:1–11) and is jealous of his successor, King
David; Alaric: a fourth-century Visigoth conqueror; Charlemagne: ninth-century founder of
the Holy Roman Empire.

But throws you back upon a noble trust   805
And use of your own instinct—merely proves
Pure reason stronger than bare inference
At strongest. Try it—fix against heaven's wall
The scaling-ladders of school logic—mount
Step by step!—sight goes faster; that still ray   810
Which strikes out from you, how, you cannot tell,
And why, you know not (did you eliminate,
That such as you indeed should analyse?),
Goes straight and fast as light, and high as God.

The cygnet finds the water, but the man   815
Is born in ignorance of his element
And feels out blind at first, disorganised
By sin i' the blood[4]—his spirit-insight dulled
And crossed by his sensations. Presently
He feels it quicken in the dark sometimes,   820
When, mark, be reverent, be obedient,
For such dumb motions of imperfect life
Are oracles of vital Deity
Attesting the Hereafter. Let who says
"The soul's a clean white paper," rather say,   825
A palimpsest, a prophet's holograph
Defiled, erased and covered by a monk's—
The apocalypse, by a Longus! poring on
Which obscene text, we may discern perhaps
Some fair, fine trace of what was written once,   830
Some upstroke of an alpha and omega
Expressing the old scripture.[5]

                    Books, books, books!
I had found the secret of a garret-room
Piled high with cases in my father's name,
Piled high, packed large—where, creeping in and out   835
Among the giant fossils of my past,
Like some small nimble mouse between the ribs
Of a mastodon,[6] I nibbled here and there
At this or that box, pulling through the gap,
In heats of terror, haste, victorious joy,   840
The first book first. And how I felt it beat
Under my pillow, in the morning's dark,
An hour before the sun would let me read!

---

4. Original sin, inherited by all humans from
Adam and Eve.
5. "A clean white paper": allusion to the proposition generally attributed to the English philosopher John Locke (1632–1704) that at birth the
mind is a *tabula rasa* (Latin), or blank slate, to be
written upon by experience; palimpsest: a manuscript erased and written over; holograph: a hand

written text; Longus: third-century author of
Daphnis and Chloë, a sexually explicit romance;
alpha and omega: the first and last letters of the
Greek alphabet, often used to express the eternal
qualities of God.
6. Elephant-like creatures that went extinct about
10,000 years ago.

My books! At last because the time was ripe,
I chanced upon the poets.
As the earth   845
Plunges in fury, when the internal fires
Have reached and pricked her heart, and, throwing flat
The marts and temples, the triumphal gates
And towers of observation, clears herself
To elemental freedom—thus, my soul,   850
At poetry's divine first finger-touch,
Let go conventions and sprang up surprised,
Convicted of the great eternities
Before two worlds.
What's this, Aurora Leigh,
You write so of the poets, and not laugh?   855
Those virtuous liars, dreamers after dark,
Exaggerators of the sun and moon,
And soothsayers in a tea-cup?[7]
I write so
Of the only truth-tellers now left to God,
The only speakers of essential truth,   860
Opposed to relative, comparative,
And temporal truths; the only holders by
His sun-skirts, through conventional gray glooms;
The only teachers who instruct mankind
From just a shadow on a charnel-wall[8]   865
To find man's veritable stature out
Erect, sublime—the measure of a man,
And that's the measure of an angel, says
The apostle.[9] Ay, and while your common men
Lay telegraphs, gauge railroads, reign, reap, dine,   870
And dust the flaunty carpets of the world
For kings to walk on, or our president,
The poet suddenly will catch them up
With his voice like a thunder—"This is soul,
This is life, this word is being said in heaven,   875
Here's God down on us! what are you about?"
How all those workers start amid their work,
Look round, look up, and feel, a moment's space,
That carpet-dusting, though a pretty trade,
Is not the imperative labour after all.   880

My own best poets, am I one with you,
That thus I love you—or but one through love?

---

7. Those who claim to read the future in the tea
leaves left behind in a cup.
8. A reference to Plato's Allegory of the Cave
(*The Republic*, Book 7), in which Socrates compares most people's understanding of the good to
the understanding of the world that prisoners
would have if chained in a cave and able to per-

ceive actions in the world only indirectly, as shadows cast on the cave's wall.
9. See Revelation 21:17: "And he measured the
wall thereof, an hundred and forty and four cu-
bits, according to the measure of a man, that is, of
the angel."

Does all this smell of thyme about my feet
Conclude my visit to your holy hill
In personal presence, or but testify   885
The rustling of your vesture through my dreams
With influent odours? When my joy and pain,
My thought and aspiration, like the stops
Of pipe or flute, are absolutely dumb
Unless melodious, do you play on me   890
My pipers—and if, sooth, you did not blow,
Would no sound come? or is the music mine,
As a man's voice or breath is called his own,
Inbreathed by the Life-breather? There's a doubt
For cloudy seasons!

            But the sun was high   895
When first I felt my pulses set themselves
For concord; when the rhythmic turbulence
Of blood and brain swept outward upon words,
As wind upon the alders, blanching them
By turning up their under-natures till   900
They trembled in dilation. O delight
And triumph of the poet, who would say
A man's mere "yes," a woman's common "no,"
A little human hope of that or this,
And says the word so that it burns you through   905
With a special revelation, shakes the heart
Of all the men and women in the world,
As if one came back from the dead and spoke,
With eyes too happy, a familiar thing
Become divine i' the utterance! while for him   910
The poet, speaker, he expands with joy;
The palpitating angel in his flesh
Thrills inly with consenting fellowship
To those innumerous spirits who sun themselves
Outside of time.

           O life, O poetry   915
—Which means life in life! cognisant of life
Beyond this blood-beat, passionate for truth
Beyond these senses!—poetry, my life,
My eagle, with both grappling feet still hot
From Zeus's thunder, who has ravished me   920
Away from all the shepherds, sheep, and dogs,
And set me in the Olympian roar and round
Of luminous faces for a cup-bearer,
To keep the mouths of all the godheads moist
For everlasting laughters—I myself   925
Half drunk across the beaker with their eyes!
How those gods look!
              Enough so, Ganymede,[1]

---

1. Cup-bearer brought to Olympus by Zeus to serve Hera ("Heré"), his wife.

We shall not bear above a round or two.
We drop the golden cup at Heré's foot
And swoon back to the earth—and find ourselves   930
Face-down among the pine-cones, cold with dew,
While the dogs bark, and many a shepherd scoffs,
"What's come now to the youth?" Such ups and downs
Have poets.
                    Am I such indeed? The name
Is royal, and to sign it like a queen,   935
Is what I dare not—though some royal blood
Would seem to tingle in me now and then,
With sense of power and ache—with imposthumes[2]
And manias usual to the race. Howbeit
I dare not: 'tis too easy to go mad   940
And ape a Bourbon[3] in a crown of straws;
The thing's too common.
                    Many fervent souls
Strike rhyme on rhyme, who would strike steel on steel
If steel had offered, in a restless heat
Of doing something. Many tender souls   945
Have strung their losses on a rhyming thread,
As children, cowslips: the more pains they take,
The work more withers. Young men, ay, and maids,
Too often sow their wild oats in tame verse,
Before they sit down under their own vine   950
And live for use. Alas, near all the birds
Will sing at dawn—and yet we do not take
The chaffering swallow for the holy lark.

In those days, though, I never analysed,
Not even myself. Analysis comes late.   955
You catch a sight of Nature, earliest,
In full front sun-face, and your eyelids wink
And drop before the wonder of't; you miss
The form, through seeing the light. I lived, those days,
And wrote because I lived—unlicensed else;   960
My heart beat in my brain. Life's violent flood
Abolished bounds—and, which my neighbour's field,
Which mine, what mattered? it is thus in youth!
We play at leap-frog over the god Term;[4]
The love within us and the love without   965
Are mixed, confounded; if we are loved or love,
We scarce distinguish: thus, with other power;
Being acted on and acting seem the same:
In that first onrush of life's chariot-wheels,
We know not if the forests move or we.   970

2. Cysts or abscesses.   4. In Roman mythology, the god of boundaries.
3. Heirs to the thrones of France and Spain.

And so, like most young poets, in a flush
Of individual life I poured myself
Along the veins of others, and achieved
Mere lifeless imitations of live verse,
And made the living answer for the dead,   975
Profaning nature. "Touch not, do not taste,
Nor handle"—we're too legal, who write young:
We beat the phorminx[5] till we hurt our thumbs,
As if still ignorarnt of counterpoint;
We call the Muse—"O Muse, benignant Muse"—   980
As if we had seen her purple-braided head,
With the eyes in it, start between the boughs
As often as a stag's. What make-believe,
With so much earnest! what effete results
From virile efforts! what cold wire-drawn odes,   985
From such white heats!—bucolics, where the cows
Would scare the writer if they splashed the mud
In lashing off the flies—didactics, driven
Against the heels of what the master said;
And counterfeiting epics, shrill with trumps   990
A babe might blow between two straining cheeks
Of bubbled rose, to make his mother laugh;
And elegiac griefs, and songs of love,
Like cast-off nosegays picked up on the road,
The worse for being warm: all these things, writ   995
On happy mornings, with a morning heart,
That leaps for love, is active for resolve,
Weak for art only. Oft, the ancient forms
Will thrill, indeed, in carrying the young blood.
The wine-skins, now and then, a little warped,   1000
Will crack even, as the new wine gurgles in.
Spare the old bottles!—spill not the new wine.[6]

By Keats's soul, the man who never stepped
In gradual progress like another man,
But, turning grandly on his central self,   1005
Ensphered himself in twenty perfect years
And died, not young (the life of a long life
Distilled to a mere drop, falling like a tear
Upon the world's cold cheek to make it burn
For ever);[7] by that strong excepted soul,   1010
I count it strange and hard to understand
That nearly all young poets should write old,
That Pope was sexagenary at sixteen,
And beardless Byron academical,[8]

5. Stringed instrument from ancient Greece.   at twenty-six.
6. An allusion to Matthew 9:17.   8. English poets Alexander Pope (1688–1744)
7. The English poet John Keats (1795–1821) died   and George Gordon, Lord Byron (1788–1824).

And so with others. It may be perhaps   1015
Such have not settled long and deep enough
In trance, to attain to clairvoyance—and still
The memory mixes with the vision, spoils,
And works it turbid.
                    Or perhaps, again,
In order to discover the Muse-Sphinx,[9]   1020
The melancholy desert must sweep round,
Behind you as before.—
                    For me, I wrote
False poems, like the rest, and thought them true
Because myself was true in writing them.
I peradventure have writ true ones since   1025
With less complacence.
                    But I could not hide
My quickening inner life from those at watch.
They saw a light at a window now and then,
They had not set there: who had set it there?
My father's sister started when she caught   1030
My soul agaze in my eyes. She could not say
I had no business with a sort of soul,
But plainly she objected—and demurred
That souls were dangerous things to carry straight
Through all the spilt saltpetre[1] of the world.   1035

She said sometimes, "Aurora, have you done
Your task this morning? have you read that book?
And are you ready for the crochet here?"—
As if she said, "I know there's something wrong;
I know I have not ground you down enough   1040
To flatten and bake you to a wholesome crust
For household uses and proprieties,
Before the rain has got into my barn
And set the grains a-sprouting. What, you're green
With outdoor impudence? you almost grow?"   1045
To which I answered, "Would she hear my task,
And verify my abstract of the book?
Or should I sit down to the crochet work?
Was such her pleasure?" Then I sat and teased
The patient needle till it spilt the thread,   1050
Which oozed off from it in meandering lace
From hour to hour. I was not, therefore, sad;
My soul was singing at a work apart

---

9. Muse: one of nine Greek goddesses who preside over the arts and sciences; sphinx: in Greek
myth, a monster with a woman's head and lion's
body that posed a riddle to passersby and killed
them when they could not answer.
1. Potassium or sodium nitrate, an ingredient in
gunpowder.

Behind the wall of sense, as safe from harm
As sings the lark when sucked up out of sight   1055
In vortices of glory and blue air.

And so, through forced work and spontaneous work,
The inner life informed the outer life,
Reduced the irregular blood to a settled rhythm,
Made cool the forehead with fresh-sprinkling dreams,   1060
And, rounding to the spheric soul the thin,
Pined body, struck a colour up the cheeks
Though somewhat faint. I clenched by brows across
My blue eyes greatening in the looking-glass,
And said, "We'll live, Aurora! we'll be strong.   1065
The dogs are on us—but we will not die."

Whoever lives true life, will love true love.
I learnt to love that England. Very oft,
Before the day was born, or otherwise
Through secret windings of the afternoons,   1070
I threw my hunters off and plunged myself
Among the deep hills, as a hunted stag
Will take the waters, shivering with the fear
And passion of the course. And when at last
Escaped, so many a green slope built on slope   1075
Betwixt me and the enemy's house behind,
I dared to rest, or wander, in a rest
Made sweeter for the step upon the grass,
And view the ground's most gentle dimplement
(As if God's finger touched but did not press   1080
In making England), such an up and down
Of verdure—nothing too much up or down,
A ripple of land; such little hills, the sky
Can stoop to tenderly and the wheatfields climb;
Such nooks of valleys lined with orchises,[2]   1085
Fed full of noises by invisible streams;
And open pastures where you scarcely tell
White daisies from white dew—at intervals
The mythic oaks and elm-trees standing out
Self-poised upon their prodigy of shade—   1090
I thought my father's land was worthy too
Of being my Shakespeare's.
                         Very oft alone,
Unlicensed; not infrequently with leave
To walk the third with Romney and his friend
The rising painter, Vincent Carrington,   1095

---

2. Orchids.

Whom men judge hardly as bee-bonneted,[3]
Because he holds that, paint a body well,
You paint a soul by implication, like
The grand first Master. Pleasant walks! for if
He said, "When I was last in Italy,"   1100
It sounded as an instrument that's played
Too far off for the tune—and yet it's fine
To listen.
        Often we walked only two
If cousin Romney pleased to walk with me.
We read, or talked, or quarrelled, as it chanced.   1105
We were not lovers, nor even friends well matched:
Say rather, scholars upon different tracks,
And thinkers disagreed, he, overfull
Of what is, and I, haply, overbold
For what might be.
           But then the thrushes sang,   1110
And shook my pulses and the elms' new leaves;
At which I turned, and held my finger up,
And bade him mark that, howsoe'er the world
Went ill, as he related, certainly
The thrushes still sang in it. At the word   1115
His brow would soften—and he bore with me
In melancholy patience, not unkind,
While breaking into voluble ecstasy
I flattered all the beauteous country round,
As poets use, the skies, the clouds, the fields,   1120
The happy violets hiding from the roads
The primroses run down to, carrying gold;
The tangled hedgerows, where the cows push out
Impatient horns and tolerant churning mouths
'Twixt dripping ash-boughs—hedgerows all alive   1125
With birds and gnats and large white butterflies
Which look as if the May-flower had caught life
And palpitated forth upon the wind;
Hills, vales, woods, netted in a silver mist,
Farms, granges, doubled up among the hills;   1130
And cattle grazing in the watered vales,
And cottage-chimneys smoking from the woods,
And cottage-gardens smelling everywhere,
Confused with smells of orchards. "See," I said,
"And see! is God not with us on earth?   1135
And shall we put Him down by aught we do?
Who says there's nothing for the poor and vile
Save poverty and wickedness? behold!"

---

3. To "have a bee in one's bonnet" is to have an eccentric whim.

And ankle-deep in English grass I leaped
And clapped my hands, and called all very fair.   1140

In the beginning when God called all good,
Even then was evil near us, it is writ;
But we indeed who call things good and fair,
The evil is upon us while we speak;
Deliver us from evil, let us pray.[4]   1145

* * *

1856

◄ FRANCES DANA GAGE ►

1808–1880

Born in Ohio when it was still the wild frontier, Frances Gage (née Barker) inherited much of the bravery of her pioneer parents, whose concern with social issues led them actively to resist slavery. This bravery led their daughter to take a leading role in the anti-slavery and women's rights movements of her time, despite the family obligations associated with raising the eight children she had with her lawyer husband, James Gage. Although she did not have the benefit of an elite education, Gage was an effective speaker, journalist, and fiction writer who was able to address the concerns of rural women and enlist them in the intertwined reform issues of the day.

Violating gender conventions, Gage worked with others in 1850 to have Ohio remove the words *male* and *white* from the state constitution. She included in her "Reminiscences" of 1881 a famous account of the speech Sojourner Truth gave at the 1851 Women's Rights Convention, which Gage had helped organize (pp. 824–25). The memoir was published in *History of Woman Suffrage*, volume 1, edited by Elizabeth Cady Stanton, Susan B. Anthony, and Matilda Joslyn Gage (1881), which was a collection of first person accounts of the early years of the struggle for equal rights in America. Throughout her life, Gage spoke, wrote, and inspired resistance to the policies that oppressed women.

In addition to fighting for the vote for women, Gage took up the issue of temperance, a reform advocating abstinence from alcohol. Temperance was considered a woman's issue because alcohol abuse often led to the physical abuse of women and children in the household. Gage viewed her temperance stories as a way to ameliorate the condition of women and children until the right of self-representation (and the liberation it would bring) could be achieved. The temperance selection included here uses fiction to warn readers against the costs of alcohol to themselves and society and uses the conversational style for which Gage would become known.

---

4. Allusion to the creation narrative in Genesis (1:31) and the Lord's Prayer (Matthew 6:13).

Tales of Truth, No. 1

"Will you please, ma'am, to let my mother have some milk?" said a pale-faced, slender little girl, of about ten years.

"Which will you have, Jenny, sweet or sour, this morning?"

"Mother said it was no difference which, we can eat either; and mother says beggars must not be choosers."

"How is your mother, now, Jenny—any better than she was last week?"

"Yes, I guess she is. She has been out washing every day this week—though she says her breast hurts her all the time."

"She ought to keep quiet till her breast gets well. You tell her, Jenny, that I said so; if she don't she will be entirely laid up, and then she will lose more than she gains by hurrying out."

"So Mrs. Keys said to her the other day.—But mother said it was no use for people to talk so—she could not lie by; if she did she must starve, for she had not got her winter's wood, or flour, or meal, nor any shoes for Kate or Edward. The day that she went out first after she was sick, she cried hard before she started. We had not a mite of bread in the house, and mother said she was afraid she should get clear down again—but what could she do?"

"True enough," said Mrs. Marcy, musing, after Jenny was gone, "what can she do? How heartless it is for us to tell one like Mary Harris to keep still; how wrong it is too, to do it, without we open our hands to help her hard needs. No, she cannot rest and get well, with her children crying for food; and we, reveling in luxury, forget her poverty, her sorrow and her pain, till she is forced to do what we heartlessly, coldly tell her she must not do."

"Mother," said Helen, "what made Mrs. Harris so poor?"

"Listen, and I will tell you—and you, George, may give heed, for it is a talk that may teach you a deep and impressive lesson. Yes, my son, though you feel strong in the fresh vigor of your manhood to resist evil, you may still be overtaken; and when I saw you yesterday smoking that cigar, and laughing over it in your glee, I felt a sad presentiment creeping into my heart. Yes, George, this thought stung me like the bite of an adder—MY BOY, TOO, MAY FALL! But to my story."

Mary Cadwallader was, twelve years ago, one of the brightest and smartest girls in L.[1] Her father was a farmer and well to do; and Mary was better educated than the common run of farmer's daughters. She was not taught what the world calls accomplishments; but she was accomplished in the principles of honest industry, careful frugality, and earnest truth, which, if we can have but the one, are far better than the outward garnishings of genteel life. Mary was considered a great beauty; but beauty did not spoil her heart, though it worked out for her a sad and fearful destiny.

In one of her visits to the village, she met Edward Harris—then a young lawyer just commencing practice. He was considered far above mediocrity, for talent and manliness, and every one thought when he offered himself to Mary, that he was almost stooping from his high elevation; for he might have married among

---

1. The abbreviation is a literary convention to indicate a real place.

the gay, the wealthy, and fashionable. But he chose Mary. Her father gave her a good setting out, and Mr. Harris' prosperous business enabled them to live pleasantly and comfortable, and bid fair to soon provide for them an ample independence. Mary seemed as happy as her good heart deserved to be, and all went on quietly and peaceable for two or three years. But Edward was often from home, and in his association with "gentlemen of the Bar"—men, educated, intelligent, and influential—men to whom the young and less favored mentally look up as patterns—he learned to be a drinker of ardent spirits,—*genteelly,* at first—and when Mary cautiously and kindly remonstrated, and spoke of danger, he laughed rudely at her fears, and pointed to Judge G., who took his dram half-a-dozen times a day, and had done so for twenty years without hurting him. Oh! ye moderate drinkers—ye who stand in high places in society, how fearful is your responsibility! How many thousand noble souls ye have led to perdition! how many thousand hearts ye have broken! how many thousand wives ye have widowed! how many thousand children ye have beggared and orphaned! Oh, George! trust not thy own strength. Where one man has self-control and self-denial to tamper with the accursed stimulant, and yet be saved, thousands fail.

But as I was saying, Edward laughed at the fears of his gentle wife; but too soon, Oh, all too soon, her fears were realized. The bloated countenance, the dull eye, the morose temper, told the stricken wife their fearful tale.—Things grew worse and worse. Clients forsook him, and business left his hands. His unkindness almost prompted Mary to leave him and try to take care of herself. She consulted with a few friends, upon whose counsel she felt she could rely; but they told her the old tale of woman's patient kindness and endearing love, bade her be gentle, smiling—aye, and *loving,*—as if woman could love and fondle the man who with every passing hour is giving himself up to his hellish appetites, and becoming in thought, word, and deed—a *fiend.* But they bade her be kind, and try it awhile longer. If she left him he would be totally lost—she was his wife, and she must not violate her marriage vow. He was not so bad yet as Mr. Jones, who often beat his wife, and took her hard earnings to buy his liquor.—Besides, Edward would never let her have any peace—he was a lawyer and would try to get the children—every body would blame her, &c., &c.[2] With such arguments was she kept at his side, while every feeling of her soul revolted at the idea of living with a drunkard. Edward Harris had broken, in the sight of God and man, *his* marriage vow. The compact entered into, *he* had made null and void. He did neither *love, cherish* nor *protect,* nor did he, "*leaving all others, cleave only unto her.*" Religiously, sacredly had she lived up to every requirement of duty, while he recklessly, boldly set every duty aside; and yet the world said she must live with him—live, bear, and suffer on. And she did live and suffer on for two years more, and then a pair of twins— two little girls—were added to her heart trials. This was what she had dreaded— that she should, by living with him, add to the number of those whom his hourly self-indulgence was bringing down to wretchedness and woe. Had she yielded to the suggestions of her heart, there would have been but two to have born the name of "drunken Harris' children."

About the time her babes were born his house, and all his effects that the law would allow to be taken, went through the sheriff's hands at public auction, and

---

2. *Et cetera,* or "and so forth" (Latin).

the proceeds into the pockets of the tavern keeper of the village—a very *good man*—so the world said, for he was a member of the most popular church, never drank a drop himself, gave largely to benevolent societies, and was *very liberal to the poor.*

Mary and her four children, (the oldest our little Jenny, not five years old,) were obliged, while she was yet weak, to move into a hovel in the outskirts of the town; and Edward, driven to desperation, drank more freely than ever. He pawned his own clothes for drink, and finally stole away some trinkets, which had been Mary's in her better days, and sold them for one-half their value. With this money he got liquor, and for days lay drunk around the bar-room doors. In this state he was laid on a sled and brought home to his poor, despairing wife. She, pale, trembling, with her wailing infants not yet four weeks old, received him—aye, received him—what can I say more? A fit of delirium tremens[3] followed, and the poor, suffering woman seemed to have strength given her to live and bear, still—to nurse him and comfort him, for his horrid agony stirred her sympathies to their lowest depths. You will wonder where Mary's father was all this time. He was dead—the brothers had sold the homestead, and with their widowed mother and sister gone to the far west; leaving Mary four years before, prosperous and happy. The small estate, though it made a comfortable living for them while the managing, energetic father lived, made but a small stipend when divided among eight children. They had not prospered, and were not in condition to help Mary.

By degrees Edward Harris recovered from his dreadful disease, but too weak to go out and obtain again the poisonous draught, and for once in years, he became duly sober. Conscience seemed to be awakened as he gained strength. He seemed to feel, more and more acutely, his terrible situation. He knew his name and fame bore a brand that in his old haunts could never be expunged; and he urged Mary to pack up their few effects and go with him to a new country. He promised her, faithfully and solemnly, to reform, and become a good father and husband. Mary consented; and by selling everything that would bring money, and by the assistance of a few friends who loved her, she gathered together enough to pay their way upon a steamer's deck to a far-off western village.—Edward kept sober till they arrived there; and here they were set down by the captain without one dollar. They found a vacant room, into which they moved, and Edward, with a humbled pride and an aching heart, went to hunt work, that they might again live. He found a job of sawing wood, and at night took home three-quarters of a dollar. Mary fixed up their straw bed in the corner of the room, and made things just as comfortable as possible, and then she went out, feeble as she was, to hunt work also. This she soon found, in the shape of washing. By borrowing a tub, a kettle, and some other things, which her lady-like manners and her pleasant pale face insured to her for the asking, she, too, had earned fifty cents ere nightfall; and as they gathered round the poor, broken hearth, and ate the scant, but wholesome meal of their own earning, Mary's heart swelled with hope—aye, earnest hope, that the husband of her early love, the father of her children, might yet be a man; and she laid her head upon his shoulder and wept tears of hopeful joy.

A little meal, and a little flour were procured, and with the surplus of their day's labor, Mary bought a wash-tub; and as their house was on the bank of the

---

3. The uncontrollable hallucinations and tremors that characterize serious alcohol poisoning.

stream, where water was handy, and she could still have the kettle a few days, she went on with her work rejoicing. For a week all went well. Edward's fine manners and education attracted attention, and his resolution to help himself, made others willing to help him. Many little comforts were furnished, and Mary's renewed hopes seemed to give renewed strength. But, at the expiration of a week, all her bright prospects banished! Edward came home one evening evidently excited with liquor, and told her that he had found permanent business—that the tavern-keeper of the village had offered him the place of bar keeper, till he could get acquainted and set up his profession again. Mary warned, begged, prayed, but all in vain. He had already tasted, and the demon was within. Down, down, down he went. Mary toiled, toiled, toiled, as he went down. She was a good sewer, but she knew that she could not support herself at that slow work, neither would it secure her health.—Everybody pitied, everybody loved her that knew her. But she was too proud—loved independence too well, to beg.

At length the scarlet-fever swept through the neighborhood, and her little twins, now two years old, died. Mary clasped her hands in mute anguish over the little, unadorned coffin that held them both, and hardly knew, amid her soul's deep tortures, whether to weep or rejoice that they were taken from life's sufferings. Subdued and chastened, was her sorrow over that humble mound in the rural churchyard, compared with the soul-sickening conviction that another was soon to be added to share her trials—another, whose ushering into life would deprive her of the power of ministering to the wants of those who had only a mother's care to shield them.—Edward Harris was often found drunk in the muddy streets, rooted about by the hogs, and picked up by some one more humane than his fellows, and brought home to his own wretched door, to get sober on his own wretched bed, and to pour out his hideous curses and imprecations in the ears of his own wretched wife and children.

Mary's fifth child was born, and kind neighbors (for where are there not kind neighbors?) helped her through her day of trial; and she was soon well enough to resume her labors, little by little. Two years more—two terrible wearisome years, passed over her with no change for the better in Edward. At length, one stormy, dreary, cold spring morning, he was found, half-way between his home and the tavern—DEAD. He had fallen, on his way the night before, with his face in a pool of water, and was too drunk to get out; and there he had strangled—his face to the earth, and the ice frozen about his head. Oh! horrible death! But yet, was it more horrible than his life? No, nothing can be more horrible than the life of a drunkard!

This happened two years ago. Since then Mary has got into a better cabin, and still works and washes round for those who need her, because she can thus earn more than in any other way. Little Jenny and Edward do go to school, and she takes her baby with her to her work.—She was doing pretty well till she took that cold a few days ago, and her sickness exhausted her little means.

Now you know, my children, how Mrs. Harris came to be so poor. George, you are just entering life with a fair prospect before you. But not fairer or clearer is your sky, than was Edward Harris' when he married Mary Cadwallader. Had there been no fashionable drinking—had there been no licensed bar-rooms—had there been no strong, proud men to have winked at his first steppings aside from duty, he might now be standing among the great, the wealthy, and the good. His wife would not have been a washerwoman, toiling with an aching breast and heart, nor his children begging at this neighbor's door for a little milk. George, my child, BEWARE!

1852

◄► MARGARET FULLER ►◄
1810–1850

Born in Cambridgeport, Massachusetts, not far from Boston, Margaret Fuller's short life was dominated by idealist ambitions for both herself and the American nation. She played a key role in the several related movements reacting against the materialism and provincial conformity that dominated her culture. Fuller was rigorously educated by her father to exceed Harvard's entrance standards at a time when only men could attain admission. When she had the chance to direct her own education, Fuller turned to the writings of European romantic authors, such as Johann Goethe and Madame de Staël, who were challenging themselves and their readers to transcend apparent limitations and realize the potential within themselves. Fuller, unlike most contemporary American women authors, preferred to write in nonfiction genres: the philosophical essay, literary review, travelogue, newspaper article, and historical account. She is best known for her extensive defense of a woman's right "as a nature to grow, as an intellect to discern, as a soul to live freely, and unimpeded to unfold such powers as were given her when we left our common home" in her revolutionary treatise *Woman in the Nineteenth Century* (1845), a section of which is included here. But her shorter works, published in newspapers and periodicals, offered romantic critiques of subjects from literary criticism to the taming of the American frontier.

Although she was ambivalent about her father's pedagogical methods (which had all but deprived her of a childhood and ruined her health), the classical education he provided to her and her own native intelligence allowed her not only to converse but also to collaborate with leading cultural critics such as Ralph Waldo Emerson. With Emerson, Fuller founded *The Dial,* a journal devoted to publishing the works of the loose set of cultural radicals known as the transcendentalists. Fuller lived most of her life as part of this vibrant intellectual community. Her importance to this group has been ascribed to her brilliant powers of conversation that owed as much to her willingness to listen as to her ability to talk. In her conversation, of which we have only secondhand accounts, Fuller displayed the power of the kind of dialectical thinking that she calls for in "A Short Essay on Critics" (1840) and which pervades her longer works. Fuller had begun writing for publication after her father's death left her without adequate financial resources. She also began teaching and, most importantly, leading a series of formal "conversations," or seminars, with groups of women who wished to address what they and Fuller believed were the inadequacies of the conventional education of women.

In her thirties, Fuller, who had lived most of her life in New England, traveled through what was then the western frontier of the United States. Her life changed when she returned and published her "poetic impression of the country at large" in *Summer on the Lakes* (1844), excerpted here, which gained a national audience.

Soon afterward, she moved to New York to become a journalist for the *New York Tribune,* the editor of which, Horace Greeley, asked her to travel to Europe as one of the first foreign correspondents. Her dispatches provided an American point of view of the republican revolutions that were springing up throughout Europe in the late 1840s. While in Rome covering the brief career of the Roman Republic, Fuller fell in love with and eventually married Giovanni Angelo, marchese d'Ossoli, with whom she had a son, Angelo Eugene, in 1848. Fuller documented the brief history of the Roman Republic in a book-length study, which was lost when she and her family drowned on the return trip to New England in 1850.

From **Summer on the Lakes**

SUMMER ON THE LAKES

Summer days of busy leisure,
Long summer days of dear-bought pleasure,
You have done your teaching well;
Had the scholar means to tell
How grew the vine of bitter-sweet,   5
What made the path for truant feet,
Winter nights would quickly pass,
Gazing on the magic glass
O'er which the new-world shadows pass;
But, in fault of wizard spell,   10
Moderns their tale can only tell
In dull words, with a poor reed
Breaking at each time of need.
But those to whom a hint suffices
Mottoes find for all devices,   15
See the knights behind their shields,
Through dried grasses, blooming fields.

TO A FRIEND

Some dried grass-tufts from the wide flowery plain,
A muscle[1] shell from the lone fairy shore,
Some antlers from tall woods which never more
To the wild deer a safe retreat can yield,
An' eagle's feather which adorned a Brave,   5
Well-nigh the last of his despairing band,
For such slight gifts wilt thou extend thy hand
When weary hours a brief refreshment crave?
I give you what I can, not what I would,
If my small drinking-cup would hold a flood,   10
As Scandinavia sung those must contain
With which the giants gods may entertain;
In our dwarf day we drain few drops, and soon must thirst again.

---

1. Mussel shell.

Chapter 1 [*Gateway to the West: Niagara Falls*]

Niagara, June 10, 1843.

Since you are to share with me such foot-notes as may be made on the pages of my life during this summer's wanderings, I should not be quite silent as to this magnificent prologue to the, as yet, unknown drama. Yet I, like others, have little to say where the spectacle is, for once, great enough to fill the whole life, and supersede thought, giving us only its own presence. "It is good to be here," is the best as the simplest expression that occurs to the mind.

We have been here eight days, and I am quite willing to go away. So great a sight soon satisfies, making us content with itself, and with what is less than itself. Our desires, once realized, haunt us again less readily. Having "lived one day" we would depart, and become worthy to live another.

We have not been fortunate in weather, for there cannot be too much, or too warm sunlight for this scene, and the skies have been lowering, with cold, unkind winds. My nerves, too much braced up by such an atmosphere, do not well bear the continual stress of sight and sound. For here there is no escape from the weight of a perpetual creation; all other forms and motions come and go, the tide rises and recedes, the wind, at its mightiest, moves in gales and gusts, but here is really an incessant, an indefatigable motion. Awake or asleep, there is no escape, still this rushing round you and through you. It is in this way I have most felt the grandeur—somewhat eternal, if not infinite.

At times a secondary music rises; the cataract seems to seize its own rhythm and sing it over again, so that the ear and soul are roused by a double vibration. This is some effect of the wind, causing echoes to the thundering anthem. It is very sublime, giving the effect of a spiritual repetition through all the spheres.

When I first came I felt nothing but a quiet satisfaction. I found that drawings, the panorama, &c. had given me a clear notion of the position and proportions of all objects here; I knew where to look for everything, and everything looked as I thought it would.

Long ago, I was looking from a hill-side with a friend at one of the finest sunsets that ever enriched this world. A little cow-boy, trudging along, wondered what we could be gazing at. After spying about some time, he found it could only be the sunset, and looking, too, a moment, he said approvingly "that sun looks well enough;" a speech worthy of Shakespeare's Cloten, or the infant Mercury,[2] up to everything from the cradle, as you please to take it.

Even such a familiarity, worthy of Jonathan,[3] our national hero, in a prince's palace, or "stumping" as he boasts to have done, "up the Vatican stairs, into the Pope's presence, in my old boots," I felt here; it looks really *well enough*, I felt, and was inclined, as you suggested, to give my approbation as to the one object in the world that would not disappoint.

But all great expression, which, on a superficial survey, seems so easy as well as so simple, furnishes, after a while, to the faithful observer its own standard by which to appreciate it. Daily these proportions widened and towered more and more upon my sight, and I got, at last, a proper foreground for these sublime distances. Before

2. Cloten: a young and scheming prince in Shakespeare's play *Cymbeline* (c. 1609); Mercury: the Roman god of trade and commerce who proves himself an accomplished thief and trickster while still an infant.

3. Generic term for an American man from the country.

coming away, I think I really saw the full wonder of the scene. After awhile it so drew me into itself as to inspire an undefined dread, such as I never knew before, such as may be felt when death is about to usher us into a new existence. The perpetual trampling of the waters seized my senses. I felt that no other sound, however near, could be heard, and would start and look behind me for a foe. I realized the identity of that mood of nature in which these waters were poured down with such absorbing force, with that in which the Indian was shaped on the same soil. For continually upon my mind came, unsought and unwelcome, images, such as never haunted it before, of naked savages stealing behind me with uplifted tomahawks; again and again this illusion recurred, and even after I had thought it over, and tried to shake it off, I could not help starting and looking behind me.

As picture, the Falls can only be seen from the British side.[4] There they are seen in their veils, and at sufficient distance to appreciate the magical effects of these, and the light and shade. From the boat, as you cross, the effects and contrasts are more melodramatic. On the road back from the whirlpool, we saw them as a reduced picture with delight. But what I liked best was to sit on Table Rock,[5] close to the great fall. There all power of observing details, all separate consciousness, was quite lost.

Once, just as I had seated myself there, a man came to take his first look. He walked close up to the fall, and, after looking at it a moment, with an air as if thinking how he could best appropriate it to his own use, he spat into it.

This trait seemed wholly worthy of an age whose love of *utility* is such that the Prince Puckler Muskau[6] suggests the probability of men coming to put the bodies of their dead parents in the fields to fertilize them, and of a country such as Dickens has described;[7] but these will not, I hope, be seen on the historic page to be truly the age or truly the America. A little leaven is leavening the whole mass for other bread.

The whirlpool I like very much. It is seen to advantage after the great falls; it is so sternly solemn. The river cannot look more imperturbable, almost sullen in its marble green, than it does just below the great fall; but the slight circles that mark the hidden vortex, seem to whisper mysteries the thundering voice above could not proclaim,—a meaning as untold as ever.

It is fearful, too, to know, as you look, that whatever has been swallowed by the cataract, is like to rise suddenly to light here, whether up-rooted tree, or body of man or bird.

The rapids enchanted me far beyond what I expected; they are so swift that they cease to seem so; you can think only of their beauty. The fountain beyond the Moss Islands, I discovered for myself, and thought it for some time an accidental beauty which it would not do to leave, lest I might never see it again. After I found it permanent, I returned many times to watch the play of its crest. In the little waterfall beyond, nature seems, as she often does, to have made a study for some larger design. She delights in this,—a sketch within a sketch, a dream within a dream. Wherever we see it, the lines of the great buttress in the fragment of stone, the hues of the waterfall, copied in the flowers that star its bordering mosses, we

---

4. Niagara Falls can be seen from New York or Canada (i.e., the British side).
5. A large rock formation.
6. Hermann Ludwig Heinrich von Pückler-Muskau (1785–1871), a German nobleman, military officer, author, and landscape designer.
7. Popular British novelist Charles Dickens (1812–70), whose sentimental novels dominated the literary landscape of the nineteenth century.

are delighted; for all the lineaments become fluent, and we mould the scene in congenial thought with its genius.

People complain of the buildings at Niagara, and fear to see it further deformed. I cannot sympathize with such an apprehension: the spectacle is capable to swallow up all such objects; they are not seen in the great whole, more than an earthworm in a wide field.

The beautiful wood on Goat Island is full of flowers; many of the fairest love to do homage here. The Wake Robin and May Apple are in bloom now; the former, white, pink, green, purple, copying the rainbow of the fall, and fit to make a garland for its presiding deity when he walks the land, for they are of imperial size, and shaped like stones for a diadem. Of the May Apple, I did not raise one green tent without finding a flower beneath.

And now farewell, Niagara. I have seen thee, and I think all who come here must in some sort see thee; thou art not to be got rid of as easily as the stars. I will be here again beneath some flooding July moon and sun. Owing to the absence of light, I have seen the rainbow only two or three times by day; the lunar bow[8] not at all. However, the imperial presence needs not its crown, though illustrated by it. 1844

A Short Essay on Critics

An essay on Criticism were a serious matter; for, though this age be emphatically critical, the writer would still find it necessary to investigate the laws of criticism as a science, to settle its conditions as an art. Essays entitled critical are epistles addressed to the public through which the mind of the recluse relieves itself of its impressions. Of these the only law is, "Speak the best word that is in thee." Or they are regular articles, got up to order by the literary hack writer, for the literary mart, and the only law is to make them plausible. There is not yet deliberate recognition of a standard of criticism, though we hope the always strengthening league of the republic of letters must ere long settle laws on which its Amphictyonic council[9] may act. Meanwhile let us not venture to write on criticism, but by classifying the critics imply our hopes, and thereby our thoughts.

First, there are the subjective class, (to make use of a convenient term, introduced by our German benefactors). These are persons to whom writing is no sacred, no reverend employment. They are not driven to consider, not forced upon investigation by the fact, that they are deliberately giving their thoughts an independent existence, and that it may live to others when dead to them. They know no agonies of conscientious research, no timidities of self-respect. They see no Ideal beyond the present hour, which makes its mood an uncertain tenure. How things affect them now they know; let the future, let the whole take care of itself. They state their impressions as they rise, of other men's spoken, written, or acted thoughts. They never dream of going out of themselves to seek the motive, to trace

8. A nighttime rainbow. Niagara Falls is famous   9. Councils organized to protect and maintain
for this rare phenomenon.   temples and religious festivals in ancient Greece.

the law of another nature. They never dream that there are statures which cannot be measured from their point of view. They love, they like, or they hate; the book is detestable, immoral, absurd, or admirable, noble, of a most approved scope;— these statements they make with authority, as those who bear the evangel of pure taste and accurate judgment, and need be tried before no human synod.[1] To them it seems that their present position commands the universe.

Thus the essays on the works of others, which are called criticisms, are often, in fact, mere records of impressions. To judge of their value you must know where the man was brought up, under what influences,—his nation, his church, his family even. He himself has never attempted to estimate the value of these circumstances, and find a law or raise a standard above all circumstances, permanent against all influence. He is content to be the creature of his place, and to represent it by his spoken and written word. He takes the same ground with the savage, who does not hesitate to say of the product of a civilization on which he could not stand, "It is bad," or "It is good."

The value of such comments is merely reflex. They characterize the critic. They give an idea of certain influences on a certain act of men in a certain time or place. Their absolute, essential value is nothing. The long review, the eloquent article by the man of the nineteenth century are of no value by themselves considered, but only as samples of their kind. The writers were content to tell what they felt, to praise or to denounce without needing to convince us or themselves. They sought not the divine truths of philosophy, and she proffers them not, if unsought.

Then there are the apprehensive. These can go out of themselves and enter fully into a foreign existence. They breathe its life; they live in its law; they tell what it meant, and why it so expressed its meaning. They reproduce the work of which they speak, and make it better known to us in so far as two statements are better than one. There are beautiful specimens in this kind. They are pleasing to us as bearing witness of the genial sympathies of nature. They have the ready grace of love with somewhat of the dignity of disinterested friendship. They sometimes give more pleasure than the original production of which they treat, as melodies will sometimes ring sweetlier in the echo. Besides there is a peculiar pleasure in a true response; it is the assurance of equipoise in the universe. These, if not true critics, come nearer the standard than the subjective class, and the value of their work is ideal as well as historical.

Then there are the comprehensive, who must also be apprehensive. They enter into the nature of another being and judge his work by its own law. But having done so, having ascertained his design and the degree of his success in fulfilling it, thus measuring his judgment, his energy, and skill, they do also know how to put that aim in its place, and how to estimate its relations. And this the critic can only do who perceives the analogies of the universe, and how they are regulated by an absolute, invariable principle. He can see how far that work expresses this principle as well as how far it is excellent in its details. Sustained by a principle, such as can be girt within no rule, no formula, he can walk around the work, he can stand above it, he can uplift it, and try its weight. Finally he is worthy to judge it.

Critics are poets cut down, says some one by way of jeer; but, in truth, they are men with the poetical temperament to apprehend, with the philosophical tendency to investigate. The maker is divine; the critic sees this divine, but brings it

---

1. Assembly or council, usually an administrative council of a Christian church.

down to humanity by the analytic process. The critic is the historian who records the order of creation. In vain for the maker, who knows without learning it, but not in vain for the mind of his race.

The critic is beneath the maker, but is his needed friend. What tongue could speak but to an intelligent ear, and every noble work demands its critic. The richer the work, the more severe would be its critic; the larger its scope, the more comprehensive must be his power of scrutiny. The critic is not a base caviller, but the younger brother of genius. Next to invention is the power of interpreting invention; next to beauty the power of appreciating beauty.

And of making others appreciate it; for the universe is a scale of infinite gradation, and below the very highest, every step is explanation down to the lowest. Religion, in the two modulations of poetry and music, descends through an infinity of waves to the lowest abysses of human nature. Nature is the literature and art of the divine mind; human literature and art the criticism on that; and they, too, find their criticism within their own sphere.

The critic, then, should be not merely a poet, not merely a philosopher, not merely an observer, but tempered of all three. If he criticize the poem, he must want nothing of what constitutes the poet, except the power of creating forms and speaking in music. He must have as good an eye and as fine a sense; but if he had as fine an organ for expression also, he would make the poem instead of judging it. He must be inspired by the philosopher's spirit of inquiry and need of generalization, but he must not be constrained by the hard cemented masonry of method to which philosophers are prone. And he must have the organic acuteness of the observer, with a love of ideal perfection, which forbids him to be content with mere beauty of details in the work or the comment upon the work.

There are persons who maintain, that there is no legitimate criticism, except the reproductive; that we have only to say what the work is or is to us, never what it is not. But the moment we look for a principle, we feel the need of a criterion, of a standard; and then we say what the work is *not*, as well as what it *is*; and this is as healthy though not as grateful and gracious an operation of the mind as the other. We do not seek to degrade but to classify an object by stating what it is not. We detach the part from the whole, lest it stand between us and the whole. When we have ascertained in what degree it manifests the whole we may safely restore it to its place, and love or admire it there ever after.

The use of criticism in periodical writing is to sift, not to stamp a work. Yet should they not be "sieves and drainers for the use of luxurious readers," but for the use of earnest inquirers, giving voice and being to their objections, as well as stimulus to their sympathies. But the critic must not be an infallible adviser to his reader. He must not tell him what books are not worth reading, or what must be thought of them when read, but what he read in them. Wo to that coterie where some critic sits despotic, intrenched behind the infallible "We." Wo to that oracle who has infused such soft sleepiness, such a gentle dulness into his atmosphere, that when he opes his lips no dog will bark. It is this attempt at dictatorship in the reviewers, and the indolent acquiescence of their readers, that has brought them into disrepute. With such fairness did they make out their statements, with such dignity did they utter their verdicts, that the poor reader grew all too submissive. He learned his lesson with such docility, that the greater part of what will be said at any public or private meeting can be foretold by any one who has read the leading periodical works for twenty years back. Scholars sneer at and would fain dispense with them altogether; and the public, grown lazy and helpless by this constant use of props and stays, can now scarce brace itself even to get through a magazine article, but reads in the daily paper laid beside the breakfast plate a short notice of the last number of the long established and popular review, and thereupon passes its judgment and is content.

Then the partisan spirit of many of these journals has made it unsafe to rely upon them as guide-books and expurgatory indexes. They could not be content merely to stimulate and suggest thought, they have at last become powerless to supersede it.

From these causes and causes like these, the journals have lost much of their influence. There is a languid feeling about them, an inclination to suspect the justice of their verdicts, the value of their criticisms. But their golden age cannot be quite past. They afford too convenient a vehicle for the transmission of knowledge; they are too natural a feature of our time to have done all their work yet. Surely they may be redeemed from their abuses, they may be turned to their true uses. But how?

It were easy to say what they should *not* do. They should not have an object to carry or a cause to advocate, which obliges them either to reject all writings which wear the distinctive traits of individual life, or to file away what does not suit them, till the essay, made true to their design, is made false to the mind of the writer. An external consistency is thus produced, at the expense of all salient thought, all genuine emotion of life, in short, and living influences. Their purpose may be of value, but by such means was no valuable purpose ever furthered long. There are those, who have with the best intention pursued this system of trimming and adaptation, and thought it well and best to

> *"Deceive their country for their country's good."*

But their country cannot long be so governed. It misses the pure, the full tone of truth; it perceives that the voice is modulated to coax, to persuade, and it turns from the judicious man of the world, calculating the effect to be produced by each of his smooth sentences to some earnest voice which is uttering thoughts, crude, rash, ill-arranged it may be, but true to one human breast, and uttered in full faith, that the God of Truth will guide them aright.

And here, it seems to me, has been the greatest mistake in the conduct of these journals. A smooth monotony has been attained, an uniformity of tone, so that from the title of a journal you can infer the tenor of all its chapters. But nature is ever various, ever new, and so should be her daughters, art and literature. We do not want merely a polite response to what we thought before, but by the freshness of thought in other minds to have new thought awakened in our own. We do not want stores of information only, but to be roused to digest these into knowledge. Able and experienced men write for us, and we would know what they think, as they think it not for us but for themselves. We would live with them, rather than be taught by them how to live; we would catch the contagion of their mental activity, rather than have them direct us how to regulate our own. In books, in reviews, in the senate, in the pulpit, we wish to meet thinking men, not schoolmasters or pleaders. We wish that they should do full justice to their own view, but also that they should be frank with us, and, if now our superiors, treat us as if we might some time rise to be their equals. It is this true manliness, this firmness in his own position, and this power of appreciating the position of others, that alone can make the critic our companion and friend. We would converse with him, secure that he will tell us all his thought, and speak as man to man. But if he adapts his work to us, if he stifles what is distinctively his, if he shows himself either arrogant or mean, or, above all, if he wants faith in the healthy action of free thought, and the safety of pure motive, we will not talk with him, for we cannot confide in him. We will go to the critic who trusts Genius and trusts us, who knows that all good writing must be spontaneous, and who will write out the bill of fare for the public as he read it for himself,—

> "Forgetting vulgar rules, with spirit free
> To judge each author by his own intent,
> Nor think one standard for all minds is meant."

Such an one will not disturb us with personalities, with sectarian prejudices, or an undue vehemence in favor of petty plans or temporary objects. Neither will he disgust us by smooth obsequious flatteries and an inexpressive, lifeless gentleness. He will be free and make free from the mechanical and distorting influences we hear complained of on every side. He will teach us to love wisely what we before loved well, for he knows the difference between censoriousness and discernment, infatuation and reverence; and, while delighting in the genial melodies of Pan,[2] can perceive, should Apollo[3] bring his lyre into audience, that there may be strains more divine than those of his native groves.

1845

⟨•⟩

From **Woman in the Nineteenth Century**

Preface

The following essay is a reproduction, modified and expanded, of an article published in "The Dial, Boston, July, 1843," under the title of "The Great Lawsuit. Man versus Men: Woman versus Women."

This article excited a good deal of sympathy, and still more interest. It is in compliance with wishes expressed from many quarters, that it is prepared for publication in its present form.

Objections having been made to the former title, as not sufficiently easy to be understood, the present has been substituted as expressive of the main purpose of the essay; though, by myself, the other is preferred, partly for the reason others do not like it, *i. e.,* that it requires some thought to see what it means, and might thus prepare the reader to meet me on my own ground. Beside, it offers a larger scope, and is, in that way, more just to my desire. I meant, by that title, to intimate the fact that, while it is the destiny of Man, in the course of the Ages, to ascertain and fulfil the law of his being, so that his life shall be seen, as a whole, to be that of an angel or messenger, the action of prejudices and passions, which attend, in the day, the growth of the individual, is continually obstructing the holy work that is

---

2. Greek god of shepherds and rustic music, known for making wild and pleasant music with his "pan-pipes."

3. Greek god of medicine, healing, and music, he plays the lyre—a harplike instrument of sophistication and beauty.

to make the earth a part of heaven. By Man I mean both man and woman: these are the two halves of one thought. I lay no especial stress on the welfare of either. I believe that the development of the one cannot be effected without that of the other. My highest wish is that this truth should be distinctly and rationally apprehended, and the conditions of life and freedom recognized as the same for the daughters and the sons of time; twin exponents of a divine thought.

I solicit a sincere and patient attention from those who open the following pages at all. I solicit of women that they will lay it to heart to ascertain what is for them the liberty of law. It is for this, and not for any, the largest, extension of partial privileges that I seek. I ask them, if interested by these suggestions, to search their own experience and intuitions for better, and fill up with fit materials the trenches that hedge them in. From men I ask a noble and earnest attention to any thing that can be offered on this great and still obscure subject, such as I have met from many with whom I stand in private relations.

And may truth, unpolluted by prejudice, vanity, or selfishness, be granted daily more and more, as the due inheritance, and only valuable conquest for us all!

November, 1844.

[*Woman, Present and Future*]

Frailty, thy name is WOMAN.[4]
The Earth waits for her Queen.

The connection between these quotations may not be obvious, but it is strict. Yet would any contradict us, if we made them applicable to the other side, and began also

Frailty, thy name is MAN.
The Earth waits for its King.

Yet man, if not yet fully installed in his powers, has given much earnest of his claims. Frail he is indeed, how frail! how impure! Yet often has the vein of gold displayed itself amid the baser ores, and Man has appeared before us in princely promise worthy of his future.

If, oftentimes, we see the prodigal son[5] feeding on the husks in the fair field no more his own, anon, we raise the eyelids, heavy from bitter tears, to behold in him the radiant apparition of genius and love, demanding not less than the all of goodness, power and beauty. We see that in him the largest claim finds a due foundation. That claim is for no partial sway, no exclusive possession. He cannot be satisfied with any one gift of life, any one department of knowledge or telescopic peep at the heavens. He feels himself called to understand and aid nature, that she may, through his intelligence, be raised and interpreted; to be a student of, and servant to, the universe-spirit; and king of his planet, that as an angelic minister, he may bring it into conscious harmony with the law of that spirit.

In clear triumphant moments, many times, has rung through the spheres the prophecy of his jubilee, and those moments, though past in time, have been translated into eternity by thought; the bright signs they left hang in the heavens, as

---

4. *Hamlet* (1.2.146).   5. A parable from the Gospel (Luke 15:11–32).

single stars or constellations, and, already, a thickly sown radiance consoles the wanderer in the darkest night. Other heroes since Hercules[6] have fulfilled the zodiac of beneficent labors, and then given up their mortal part to the fire without a murmur, while no God dared deny that they should have their reward

> *Siquis tamen, Hercule, siquis*
> *Forte Deo doliturus erit, data præmia nollet,*
> *Sed meruise dari sciet, invitus que probabit,*
> *Assensere Dei.*[7]

Sages and lawgivers have bent their whole nature to the search for truth, and thought themselves happy if they could buy, with the sacrifice of all temporal ease and pleasure, one seed for the future Eden. Poets and priests have strung the lyre with the heartstrings, poured out their best blood upon the altar, which, reared anew from age to age shall at last sustain the flame pure enough to rise to highest heaven. Shall we not name with as deep a benediction those who, if not so immediately, or so consciously, in connection with the eternal truth, yet, led and fashioned by a divine instinct, serve no less to develope and interpret the open secret of love passing into life, energy creating for the purpose of happiness; the artist whose hand, drawn by a pre-existent harmony to a certain medium, moulds it to forms of life more highly and completely organized than are seen elsewhere, and, by carrying out the intention of nature, reveals her meaning to those who are not yet wise enough to divine it; the philosopher who listens steadily for laws and causes, and from those obvious, infers those yet unknown; the historian who, in faith that all events must have their reason and their aim, records them, and thus fills archives from which the youth of prophets may be fed. The man of science dissects the statements, tests the facts, and demonstrates order, even where he cannot its purpose.

Lives, too, which bear none of these names, have yielded tones of no less significance. The candlestick set in a low place has given light as faithfully, where it was needed, as that upon the hill. In close alleys, in dismal nooks, the Word has been read as distinctly, as when shown by angels to holy men in the dark prison. Those who till a spot of earth scarcely larger than is wanted for a grave, have deserved that the sun should shine upon its sod till violets answer.

So great has been, from time to time, the promise, that, in all ages, men have said the gods themselves came down to dwell with them; that the All-Creating wandered on the earth to taste, in a limited nature, the sweetness of virtue; that the All-Sustaining incarnated himself to guard, in space and time, the destinies of this world; that heavenly genius dwelt among the shepherds, to sing to them and teach them how to sing. Indeed

> *Der stets den Hirten gnadig sich bewies.*

"He has constantly shown himself favorable to shepherds."

---

6. Zodiac of beneficent labors: the mythological Greek hero Hercules performed twelve labors as penance for murder, and there are twelve signs in the zodiac; mortal part to the fire: Hercules' story ends with his cremation.
7. *Metamorphosis* by Ovid (43 BCE–17 CE); "The Death and Transformation of Hercules"

(9.256–59): "If anyone / Should grieve that Hercules becomes a god / Should be unwilling that he have this honor / Well, let him grieve, and let him grunt, and let him, / Even against his will, own it was proper" [Latin: translation by Rolfe Humphries, 1954].

And the dwellers in green pastures and natural students of the stars were selected to hail, first among men, the holy child, whose life and death were to present the type of excellence, which has sustained the heart of so large a portion of mankind in these later generations.

Such marks have been made by the footsteps of *man*, (still alas! to be spoken of as the *ideal* man,) wherever he has passed through the wilderness of *men*, and whenever the pigmies stepped in one of those they felt dilate within the breast somewhat that promised nobler stature and purer blood. They were impelled to forsake their evil ways of decrepit scepticism, and covetousness of corruptible possessions. Conviction flowed in upon them. They, too, raised the cry; God is living, now, to-day; and all beings are brothers, for they are his children. Simple words enough, yet which only angelic nature, can use or hear in their full free sense.

These were the triumphant moments, but soon the lower nature took its turn, and the era of a truly human life was postponed.

Thus is man still a stranger to his inheritance, still a pleader, still a pilgrim. Yet his happiness is secure in the end. And now, no more a glimmering consciousness, but assurance begins to be felt and spoken, that the highest ideal man can form of his own powers, is that which he is destined to attain. Whatever the soul knows how to seek, it cannot fail to obtain. This is the law and the prophets. Knock and it shall be opened, seek and ye shall find. It is demonstrated; it is a maxim. Man no longer paints his proper nature in some form and says, "Prometheus[8] had it; it is God-like;" but "Man must have it; it is human." However disputed by many, however ignorantly used, or falsified by those who do receive it, the fact of an universal, unceasing revelation has been too clearly stated in words to be lost sight of in thought, and sermons preached from the text, "Be ye perfect," are the only sermons of a pervasive and deep-searching influence.

But, among those who meditate upon this text, there is a great difference of view, as to the way in which perfection shall be sought.

Through the intellect, say some. Gather from every growth of life its seed of thought; look behind every symbol for its law; if thou canst *see* clearly, the rest will follow.

Through the life, say others. Do the best thou knowest to-day. Shrink not from frequent error in this gradual fragmentary state. Follow thy light for as much as it will show thee, be faithful as far as thou canst, in hope that faith presently will lead to sight. Help others, without blaming their need of thy help. Love much and be forgiven.

It needs not intellect, needs not experience, says a third. If you took the true way, your destiny would be accomplished in a purer and more natural order. You would not learn through facts of thought or action, but express through them the certainties of wisdom. In quietness yield thy soul to the causal soul. Do not disturb thy apprenticeship by premature effort; neither check the tide of instruction by methods of thy own. Be still, seek not, but wait in obedience. Thy commission will be given.

Could we indeed say what we want, could we give a description of the child that is lost, he would be found. As soon as the soul can affirm clearly that a certain demonstration is wanted, it is at hand. When the Jewish prophet described

---

8. In Greek mythology, Prometheus gave the gift of fire to humankind.

the Lamb,[9] as the expression of what was required by the coming era, the time drew nigh. But we say not, see not as yet, clearly, what we would. Those who call for a more triumphant expression of love, a love that cannot be crucified, show not a perfect sense of what has already been given. Love has already been expressed, that made all things new, that gave the worm its place and ministry as well as the eagle; a love to which it was alike to descend into the depths of hell, or to sit at the right hand of the Father.[1]

Yet, no doubt, a new manifestation is at hand, a new hour in the day of man. We cannot expect to see any one sample of completed being, when the mass of men still lie engaged in the sod, or use the freedom of their limbs only with wolfish energy. The tree cannot come to flower till its root be free from the cankering worm, and its whole growth open to air and light. While any one is base, none can be entirely free and noble. Yet something new shall presently be shown of the life of man, for hearts crave, if minds do not know how to ask it.

Among the strains of prophecy, the following, by an earnest mind of a foreign land, written some thirty years ago, is not yet outgrown; and it has the merit of being a positive appeal from the heart, instead of a critical declaration what man should *not* do.

"The ministry of man implies, that he must be filled from the divine fountains which are being engendered through all eternity, so that, at the mere name of his master, he may be able to cast all his enemies into the abyss; that he may deliver all parts of nature from the barriers that imprison them; that he may purge the terrestrial atmosphere from the poisons that infect it; that he may preserve the bodies of men from the corrupt influences that surround, and the maladies that afflict them; still more, that he may keep their souls pure from the malignant insinuations which pollute, and the gloomy images that obscure them; that he may restore its serenity to the Word, which false words of men fill with mourning and sadness; that he may satisfy the desires of the angels, who await from him the development of the marvels of nature; that, in fine, his world may be filled with God, as eternity is."[2]

Another attempt we will give, by an obscure observer of our own day and country, to draw some lines of the desired image. It was suggested by seeing the design of Crawford's Orpheus,[3] and connecting with the circumstance of the American, in his garret at Rome, making choice of this subject, that of Americans here at home, showing such ambition to represent the character, by calling their prose and verse "Orphic sayings"—"Orphics." We wish we could add that they have shown that musical apprehension of the progress of nature through her ascending gradations which entitled them so to do, but their attempts are frigid, though sometimes grand; in their strain we are not warmed by the fire which fertilized the soil of Greece.

Orpheus[4] was a law-giver by theocratic commission. He understood nature, and made her forms move to his music. He told her secrets in the form of hymns, nature as seen in the mind of God. His soul went forth toward all beings, yet could remain sternly faithful to a chosen type of excellence. Seeking what he loved, he

---

9. Isaiah 53.
1. Matthew 25:34.
2. From French mystic Louis-Claude de Saint-Martin's *The Ministry of Man and Spirit* (1802).
3. Thomas Crawford's *Orpheus and Cerberus*

(1843) was the first sculpture of a male nude to be put on public display in the United States.
4. The mythic Greek musician who travels among the dead to rescue his wife, Eurydice, who had been killed on their wedding day.

feared not death nor hell, neither could any shape of dread daunt his faith in the power of the celestial harmony that filled his soul.

It seemed significant of the state of things in this country, that the sculptor should have represented the seer at the moment when he was obliged with his hand to shade his eyes.

> *Each Orpheus must to the depths descend,*
> *For only thus the Poet can be wise,*
> *Must make the sad Persephone his friend,*
> *And buried love to second life arise;*
> *Again his love must lose through too much love,*
> *Must lose his life by living life too true,*
> *For what he sought below is passed above,*
> *Already done is all that he would do;*
> *Must tune all being with his single lyre,*
> *Must melt all rocks free from their primal pain,*
> *Must search all nature with his one soul's fire,*
> *Must bind anew all forms in heavenly chain.*
> *If he already sees what he must do,*
> *Well may he shade his eyes from the far-shining view.*[5]

A better comment could not be made on what is required to perfect man, and place him in that superior position for which he was designed, than by the interpretation of Bacon[6] upon the legends of the Syren coast. When the wise Ulysses passed, says he, he caused his mariners to stop their ears with wax, knowing there was in them no power to resist the lure of that voluptuous song.[7] But he, the much experienced man, who wished to be experienced in all, and use all to the service of wisdom, desired to hear the song that he might understand its meaning. Yet, distrusting his own power to be firm in his better purpose, he caused himself to be bound to the mast, that he might be kept secure against his own weakness. But Orpheus passed unfettered, so absorbed in singing hymns to the gods that he could not even hear those sounds of degrading enchantment.

Meanwhile not a few believe, and men themselves have expressed the opinion, that the time is come when Eurydice is to call for an Orpheus, rather than Orpheus for Eurydice: that the idea of Man, however imperfectly brought out, has been far more so than that of Woman, that she, the other half of the same thought, the other chamber of the heart of life, needs now to take her turn in the full pulsation, and that improvement in the daughters will best aid in the reformation of the sons of this age.

It should be remarked that, as the principle of liberty is better understood, and more nobly interpreted, a broader protest is made in behalf of Woman. As men become aware that few men have had a fair chance, they are inclined to say that no women have had a fair chance. The French Revolution,[8] that strangely disguised angel, bore witness in favor of woman, but interpreted her claims no less ignorantly than those of man. Its idea of happiness did not rise beyond out-

---

5. These verses are apparently by Fuller.
6. English writer and philosopher Francis Bacon (1561–1626) wrote *Wisdom of the Ancients* (1610).
7. Ulysses (Roman name: Odysseus) encounters the Sirens, women whose irresistible song lures

sailors to their deaths, in Book 12 of Homer's *Odyssey*.
8. The republican revolution in France against the Bourbons (1789–99).

ward enjoyment, unobstructed by the tyranny of others. The title it gave was citoyen, citoyenne, and it is not unimportant to woman that even this species of equality was awarded her. Before, she could be condemned to perish on the scaffold for treason, not as a citizen, but as a subject.[9] The right with which this title then invested a human being, was that of bloodshed and license. The Goddess of Liberty was impure. As we read the poem addressed to her not long since, by Beranger,[1] we can scarcely refrain from tears as painful as the tears of blood that flowed when "such crimes were committed in her name." Yes! man, born to purify and animate the unintelligent and the cold, can, in his madness, degrade and pollute no less the fair and the chaste. Yet truth was prophesied in the ravings of that hideous fever, caused by long ignorance and abuse. Europe is conning a valued lesson from the blood-stained page. The same tendencies, farther unfolded, will bear good fruit in this country.

Yet, by men in this country, as by the Jews, when Moses was leading them to the promised land, every thing has been done that inherited depravity could do, to hinder the promise of heaven from its fulfilment. The cross here as elsewhere, has been planted only to be blasphemed by cruelty and fraud. The name of the Prince of Peace[2] has been profaned by all kinds of injustice toward the Gentile whom he said he came to save. But I need not speak of what has been done towards the red man, the black man. Those deeds are the scoff of the world; and they have been accompanied by such pious words that the gentlest would not dare to intercede with "Father, forgive them, for they know not what they do."[3]

Here, as elsewhere, the gain of creation consists always in the growth of individual minds, which live and aspire, as flowers bloom and birds sing, in the midst of morasses; and in the continual development of that thought, the thought of human destiny, which is given to eternity adequately to express, and which ages of failure only seemingly impede. Only seemingly, and whatever seems to the contrary, this country is as surely destined to elucidate a great moral law, as Europe was to promote the mental culture of man.

Though the national independence be blurred by the servility of individuals, though freedom and equality have been proclaimed only to leave room for a monstrous display of slave-dealing and slave-keeping; though the free American so often feels himself free, like the Roman, only to pamper his appetites and his indolence through the misery of his fellow beings, still it is not in vain, that the verbal statement has been made, "All men are born free and equal." There it stands, a golden certainty wherewith to encourage the good, to shame the bad. The new world may be called clearly to perceive that it incurs the utmost penalty, if it reject or oppress the sorrowful brother. And, if men are deaf, the angels hear. But men cannot be deaf. It is inevitable that an external freedom, an independence of the encroachments of other men, such as has been achieved for the nation, should be so also for every member of it. That which has once been clearly conceived in the intelligence cannot fail sooner or later to be acted out. It has become a law as irrevocable as that of the Medes[4] in their ancient dominion; men will privately sin against it, but the law, as expressed by a leading mind of the age,

---

9. Second-class citizen.
1. Pierre-Jean de Béranger (1780–1857), a French revolutionary songwriter.
2. Jesus.

3. Luke 23:34.
4. An Indo-Iranian people who established an empire in the sixth century BCE.

> *Tutti fatti a sembianza d'un Solo,*
> *Figli tutti d'un solo riscatto,*
> *In qual'ora, in qual parte del suolo*
> *Trascorriamo quest' aura vital,*
> *Siam fratelli, siam stretti ad un patto:*
> *Maladetto colui che lo infrange,*
> *Che s'innalza sul fiacco che piange*
> *Che contrista uno spirto immortal.*[5]

> *All made in the likeness of the One,*
>   *All children of one ransom,*
> *In whatever hour, in whatever part of the soil,*
>   *We draw this vital air,*
> *We are brothers; we must be bound by one compact,*
>   *Accursed he who infringes it,*
> *Who raises himself upon the weak who weep,*
> *Who saddens an immortal spirit.*

This law cannot fail of universal recognition. Accursed be he who willingly saddens an immortal spirit, doomed to infamy in later, wiser ages, doomed in future stages of his own being to deadly penance, only short of death. Accursed be he who sins in ignorance, if that ignorance be caused by sloth.

We sicken no less at the pomp than the strife of words. We feel that never were lungs so puffed with the wind of declamation, on moral and religious subjects, as now. We are tempted to implore these "word-heroes," these word-Catos, word-Christs, to beware of cant above all things; to remember that hypocrisy is the most hopeless as well as the meanest of crimes, and that those must surely be polluted by it, who do not reserve a part of their morality and religion for private use. Landor[6] says that he cannot have a great deal of mind who cannot afford to let the larger part of it lie fallow, and what is true of genius is not less so of virtue. The tongue is a valuable member, but should appropriate but a small part of the vital juices that are needful all over the body. We feel that the mind may "grow black and rancid in the smoke" even "of altars." We start up from the harangue to go into our closet and shut the door. There inquires the spirit, "Is this rhetoric the bloom of healthy blood or a false pigment artfully laid on?" And yet again we know where is so much smoke, must be some fire; with so much talk about virtue and freedom, must be mingled some desire for them; that it cannot be in vain that such have become the common topics of conversation among men, rather than schemes for tyranny and plunder, that the very newspapers see it best to proclaim themselves Pilgrims, Puritans, Heralds of Holiness. The king that maintains so costly a retinue cannot be a mere boast, or Carabbas fiction. We have waited here long in the dust; we are tired and hungry, but the triumphal procession must appear at last.

Of all its banners, none has been more steadily upheld, and under none have more valor and willingness for real sacrifices been shown, than that of the champions of the enslaved African. And this band it is, which, partly from a natural following out of principles, partly because many women have been prominent in that cause, makes, just now, the warmest appeal in behalf of woman.

---

5. From *Il Conte de Carmagnola* by Italian poet Alessandro Manzoni (1785–1873).

6. English poet Walter Savage Landor (1775–1864).

Though there has been a growing liberality on this subject, yet society at large is not so prepared for the demands of this party, but that they are and will be for some time, coldly regarded as the Jacobins[7] of their day.

"Is it not enough," cries the irritated trader, "that you have done all you could to break up the national union, and thus destroy the prosperity of our country, but now you must be trying to break up family union, to take my wife away from the cradle and the kitchen hearth to vote at polls, and preach from a pulpit? Of course, if she does such things, she cannot attend to those of her own sphere. She is happy enough as she is. She has more leisure than I have, every means of improvement, every indulgence."

"Have you asked her whether she was satisfied with these *indulgences?*"

"No, but I know she is. She is too amiable to wish what would make me unhappy, and too judicious to wish to step beyond the sphere of her sex. I will never consent to have our peace disturbed by any such discussions."

"'Consent—you?' it is not consent from you that is in question, it is assent from your wife."

"Am not I the head of my house?"

"You are not the head of your wife. God has given her a mind of her own."

"I am the head and she the heart."

"God grant you play true to one another then. I suppose I am to be grateful that you did not say she was only the hand. If the head represses no natural pulse of the heart, there can be no question as to your giving your consent. Both will be of one accord, and there needs but to present any question to get a full and true answer. There is no need of precaution, of indulgence, or consent. But our doubt is whether the heart does consent with the head, or only obeys its decrees with a passiveness that precludes the exercise of its natural powers, or a repugnance that turns sweet qualities to bitter, or a doubt that lays waste the fair occasions of life. It is to ascertain the truth, that we propose some liberating measures."

Thus vaguely are these questions proposed and discussed at present. But their being proposed at all implies much thought and suggests more. Many women are considering within themselves, what they need that they have not, and what they can have, if they find they need it. Many men are considering whether women are capable of being and having more than they are and have, *and,* whether, if so, it will be best to consent to improvement in their condition.

This morning, I open the Boston "Daily Mail," and find in its "poet's corner," a translation of Schiller's "Dignity of Woman."[8] In the advertisement of a book on America, I see in the table of contents this sequence, "Republican Institutions. American Slavery. American Ladies."

I open the "*Deutsche Schnellpost,*" published in New-York, and find at the head of a column, *Juden- und Frauen-emancipation in Ungarn.* Emancipation of Jews and Women in Hungary.

The past year has seen action in the Rhode-Island legislature, to secure married women rights over their own property, where men showed that a very little examination of the subject could teach them much; an article in the Democratic Review on the same subject more largely considered, written by a woman, impelled, it is said, by glaring wrong to a distinguished friend having shown the

---

7. A French political club during the revolutionary era espousing anti-government ideas.

8. "Shall I degrade the dignity of woman, / The

masterpiece of the Almighty's hand, / To charm the evening of a reveller?" from German poet Friedrich Schiller's (1759–1805) *Don Carlos,* 2.8 (1787).

defects in the existing laws, and the state of opinion from which they spring; and an answer from the revered old man, J. Q. Adams, in some respects the Phocion[9] of his time, to an address made him by some ladies. To this last I shall again advert in another place.

These symptoms of the times have come under my view quite accidentally: one who seeks, may, each month or week, collect more.

The numerous party, whose opinions are already labelled and adjusted too much to their mind to admit of any new light, strive, by lectures on some model-woman of bride-like beauty and gentleness, by writing and lending little treatises, intended to mark out with precision the limits of woman's sphere, and woman's mission, to prevent other than the rightful shepherd from climbing the wall, or the flock from using any chance to go astray.

Without enrolling ourselves at once on either side, let us look upon the subject from the best point of view which to-day offers. No better, it is to be feared, than a high house-top. A high hill-top, or at least a cathedral spire, would be desirable.

It may well be an Anti-Slavery party that pleads for woman, if we consider merely that she does not hold property on equal terms with men; so that, if a husband dies without making a will, the wife, instead of taking at once his place as head of the family, inherits only a part of his fortune, often brought him by herself, as if she were a child, or ward only, not an equal partner.

We will not speak of the innumerable instances in which profligate and idle men live upon the earnings of industrious wives; or if the wives leave them, and take with them the children, to perform the double duty of mother and father, follow from place to place, and threaten to rob them of the children, if deprived of the rights of a husband, as they call them, planting themselves in their poor lodgings, frightening them into paying tribute by taking from them the children, running into debt at the expense of these otherwise so overtasked helots. Such instances count up by scores within my own memory. I have seen the husband who had stained himself by a long course of low vice, till his wife was wearied from her heroic forgiveness, by finding that his treachery made it useless, and that if she would provide bread for herself and her children, she must be separate from his ill fame. I have known this man come to install himself in the chamber of a woman who loathed him and say she should never take food without his company. I have known these men steal their children whom they knew they had no means to maintain, take them into dissolute company, expose them to bodily danger, to frighten the poor woman, to whom, it seems, the fact that she alone had borne the pangs of their birth, and nourished their infancy, does not give an equal right to them. I do believe that this mode of kidnapping, and it is frequent enough in all classes of society, will be by the next age viewed as it is by Heaven now, and that the man who avails himself of the shelter of men's laws to steal from a mother her own children, or arrogate any superior right in them, save that of superior virtue, will bear the stigma he deserves, in common with him who steals grown men from their mother land, their hopes, and their homes.

I said, we will not speak of this now, yet I have spoken, for the subject makes me feel too much. I could give instances that would startle the most vulgar and

9. J. Q. Adams: John Quincy Adams, sixth president of the United States and later a congressman who supported the anti-slavery movement and defended the rights of women to speak in the political arena. Phocion: Athenian statesman and general (c. 402–c. 317 BCE) who often expressed unpopular viewpoints.

callous, but I will not, for the public opinion of their own sex is already against such men, and where cases of extreme tyranny are made known, there is private action in the wife's favor. But she ought not to need this, nor, I think, can she long. Men must soon see that, on their own ground, that woman is the weaker party, she ought to have legal protection, which would make such oppression impossible. But I would not deal with "atrocious instances" except in the way of illustration, neither demand from men a partial redress in some one matter, but go to the root of the whole. If principles could be established, particulars would adjust themselves aright. Ascertain the true destiny of woman, give her legitimate hopes, and a standard within herself; marriage and all other relations would by degrees be harmonized with these.

But to return to the historical progress of this matter. Knowing that there exists in the minds of men a tone of feeling towards women as towards slaves, such as is expressed in the common phrase, "Tell that to women and children," that the infinite soul can only work through them in already ascertained limits; that the gift of reason, man's highest prerogative, is allotted to them in much lower degree; that they must be kept from mischief and melancholy by being constantly engaged in active labor, which is to be furnished and directed by those better able to think, &c. &c.; we need not multiply instances, for who can review the experience of last week without recalling words which imply, whether in jest or earnest, these views or views like these; knowing this, can we wonder that many reformers think that measures are not likely to be taken in behalf of women, unless their wishes could be publicly represented by women?

That can never be necessary, cry the other side. All men are privately influenced by women; each has his wife, sister, or female friends, and is too much biased by these relations to fail of representing their interests, and, if this is not enough, let them propose and enforce their wishes with the pen. The beauty of home would be destroyed, the delicacy of the sex be violated, the dignity of halls of legislation degraded by an attempt to introduce them there. Such duties are inconsistent with those of a mother; and then we have ludicrous pictures of ladies in hysterics at the polls, and senate chambers filled with cradles.

But if, in reply, we admit as truth that woman seems destined by nature rather for the inner circle, we must add that the arrangements of civilized life have not been, as yet, such as to secure it to her. Her circle, if the duller, is not the quieter. If kept from "excitement," she is not from drudgery. Not only the Indian squaw carries the burdens of the camp, but the favorites of Louis the Fourteenth[1] accompany him in his journeys, and the washerwoman stands at her tub and carries home her work at all seasons, and in all states of health. Those who think the physical circumstances of woman would make a part in the affairs of national government unsuitable, are by no means those who think it impossible for the negresses to endure field work, even during pregnancy, or the sempstresses to go through their killing labors.

As to the use of the pen, there was quite as much opposition to woman's possessing herself of that help to free agency, as there is now to her seizing on the rostrum or the desk; and she is likely to draw, from a permission to plead her cause that way, opposite inferences to what might be wished by those who now grant it.

As to the possibility of her filling with grace and dignity, any such position, we should think those who had seen the great actresses, and heard the Quaker

---

1. Women in favor with Louis XIV (1638–1715), the king of France.

preachers of modern times, would not doubt, that woman can express publicly the fulness of thought and creation, without losing any of the peculiar beauty of her sex. What can pollute and tarnish is to act thus from any motive except that something needs to be said or done. Women could take part in the processions, the songs, the dances of old religion; no one fancied their delicacy was impaired by appearing in public for such a cause.

As to her home, she is not likely to leave it more than she now does for balls, theatres, meetings for promoting missions, revival meetings, and others to which she flies, in hope of an animation for her existence, commensurate with what she sees enjoyed by men. Governors of ladies' fairs[2] are no less engrossed by such a change, than the Governor of the state by his; presidents of Washingtonian societies no less away from home than presidents of conventions. If men look straitly to it, they will find that, unless their lives are domestic, those of the women will not be. A house is no home unless it contain food and fire for the mind as well as for the body. The female Greek, of our day, is as much in the street as the male to cry, What news? We doubt not it was the same in Athens of old. The women, shut out from the market place, made up for it at the religious festivals. For human beings are not so constituted that they can live without expansion. If they do not get it one way, they must another, or perish.

As to men's representing women fairly at present, while we hear from men who owe to their wives not only all that is comfortable or graceful, but all that is wise in the arrangement of their lives, the frequent remark, "You cannot reason with a woman," when from those of delicacy, nobleness, and poetic culture, the contemptuous phrase "women and children," and that in no light sally of the hour, but in works intended to give a permanent statement of the best experiences, when not one man, in the million, shall I say? no, not in the hundred million, can rise above the belief that woman was made *for man*, when such traits as these are daily forced upon the attention, can we feel that man will always do justice to the interests of woman? Can we think that he takes a sufficiently discerning and religious view of her office and destiny, *ever* to do her justice, except when prompted by sentiment, accidentally or transiently, that is, for the sentiment will vary according to the relations in which he is placed. The lover, the poet, the artist, are likely to view her nobly. The father and the philosopher have some chance of liberality; the man of the world, the legislator for expediency, none.

Under these circumstances, without attaching importance, in themselves, to the changes demanded by the champions of woman, we hail them as signs of the times. We would have every arbitrary barrier thrown down. We would have every path laid open to woman as freely as to man. Were this done and a slight temporary fermentation allowed to subside, we should see crystallizations more pure and of more various beauty. We believe the divine energy would pervade nature to a degree unknown in the history of former ages, and that no discordant collision, but a ravishing harmony of the spheres would ensue.

Yet, then and only then, will mankind be ripe for this, when inward and outward freedom for woman as much as for man shall be acknowledged as a right, not yielded as a concession. As the friend of the negro assumes that one man cannot by right, hold another in bondage, so should the friend of woman assume that

2. Nineteenth-century women often organized fund-raising sales for reform movements.

man cannot, by right, lay even well-meant restrictions on woman. If the negro be a soul, if the woman be a soul, appareled in flesh, to one Master only are they accountable. There is but one law for souls, and if there is to be an interpreter of it, he must come not as man, or son of man, but as son of God.

Were thought and feeling once so far elevated that man should esteem himself the brother and friend, but nowise the lord and tutor of woman, were he really bound with her in equal worship, arrangements as to function and employment would be of no consequence. What woman needs is not as a woman to act or rule, but as a nature to grow, as an intellect to discern, as a soul to live freely and unimpeded, to unfold such powers as were given her when we left our common home. If fewer talents were given her, yet if allowed the free and full employment of these, so that she may render back to the giver his own with usury, she will not complain; nay I dare to say she will bless and rejoice in her earthly birth-place, her earthly lot. Let us consider what obstructions impede this good era, and what signs give reason to hope that it draws near.

I was talking on this subject with Miranda,[3] a woman, who, if any in the world could, might speak without heat and bitterness of the position of her sex. Her father was a man who cherished no sentimental reverence for woman, but a firm belief in the equality of the sexes. She was his eldest child, and came to him at an age when he needed a companion. From the time she could speak and go alone, he addressed her not as a plaything, but as a living mind. Among the few verses he ever wrote was a copy addressed to this child, when the first locks were cut from her head, and the reverence expressed on this occasion for that cherished head, he never belied. It was to him the temple of immortal intellect. He respected his child, however, too much to be an indulgent parent. He called on her for clear judgment, for courage, for honor and fidelity; in short, for such virtues as he knew. In so far as he possessed the keys to the wonders of this universe, he allowed free use of them to her, and by the incentive of a high expectation, he forbade, as far as possible, that she should let the privilege lie idle.

Thus this child was early led to feel herself a child of the spirit. She took her place easily, not only in the world of organized being, but in the world of mind. A dignified sense of self-dependence was given as all her portion, and she found it a sure anchor. Herself securely anchored, her relations with others were established with equal security. She was fortunate in a total absence of those charms which might have drawn to her bewildering flatteries, and in a strong electric nature, which repelled those who did not belong to her, and attracted those who did. With men and women her relations were noble, affectionate without passion, intellectual without coldness. The world was free to her, and she lived freely in it. Outward adversity came, and inward conflict, but that faith and self-respect had early been awakened which must always lead at last, to an outward serenity and an inward peace.

Of Miranda I had always thought as an example, that the restraints upon the sex were insuperable only to those who think them so, or who noisily strive to break them. She had taken a course of her own, and no man stood in her way. Many of her acts had been unusual, but excited no uproar. Few helped, but none checked her, and the many men, who knew her mind and her life, showed to her

---

3. Miranda's background, as described here, closely resembles Fuller's.

confidence, as to a brother, gentleness as to a sister. And not only refined, but very coarse men approved and aided one in whom they saw resolution and clearness of design. Her mind was often the leading one, always effective.

When I talked with her upon these matters, and had said very much what I have written, she smilingly replied: "and yet we must admit that I have been fortunate, and this should not be. My good father's early trust gave the first bias, and the rest followed of course. It is true that I have had less outward aid, in after years, than most women, but that is of little consequence. Religion was early awakened in my soul, a sense that what the soul is capable to ask it must attain, and that, though I might be aided and instructed by others, I must depend on myself as the only constant friend. This self dependence, which was honored in me, is deprecated as a fault in most women. They are taught to learn their rule from without, not to unfold it from within.

"This is the fault of man, who is still vain, and wishes to be more important to woman than, by right, he should be."

"Men have not shown this disposition toward you," I said.

"No! because the position I early was enabled to take was one of self-reliance. And were all women as sure of their wants as I was, the result would be the same. But they are so overloaded with precepts by guardians, who think that nothing is so much to be dreaded for a woman as originality of thought or character, that their minds are impeded by doubts till they lose their chance of fair free proportions. The difficulty is to get them to the point from which they shall naturally develope self-respect, and learn self-help.

"Once I thought that men would help to forward this state of things more than I do now. I saw so many of them wretched in the connections they had formed in weakness and vanity. They seemed so glad to esteem women whenever they could.

"The soft arms of affection," said one of the most discerning spirits, "will not suffice for me, unless on them I see the steel bracelets of strength."

But early I perceived that men never, in any extreme of despair, wished to be women. On the contrary they were ever ready to taunt one another at any sign of weakness, with,

Art thou not like the women, who—

The passage ends various ways, according to the occasion and rhetoric of the speaker. When they admired any woman they were inclined to speak of her as "above her sex." Silently I observed this, and feared it argued a rooted scepticism, which for ages had been fastening on the heart, and which only an age of miracles could eradicate. Ever I have been treated with great sincerity; and I look upon it as a signal instance of this, that an intimate friend of the other sex said, in a fervent moment, that I "deserved in some star to be a man." He was much surprised when I disclosed my view of my position and hopes, when I declared my faith that the feminine side, the side of love, of beauty, of holiness, was now to have its full chance, and that, if either were better, it was better now to be a woman, for even the slightest achievement of good was furthering an especial work of our time. He smiled incredulous. "She makes the best she can of it," thought he. "Let Jews believe the pride of Jewry, but I am of the better sort, and know better."

Another used as highest praise, in speaking of a character in literature, the words "a manly woman."

So in the noble passage of Ben Jonson:

> *I meant the day-star should not brighter ride,*
> *Nor shed like influence from its lucent seat;*
> *I meant she should be courteous, facile, sweet,*
> *Free from that solemn vice of greatness, pride;*
> *I meant each softest virtue there should meet,*
> *Fit in that softer bosom to abide,*
> *Only a learned and a* manly *soul,*
> *I purposed her, that should with even powers,*
> *The rock, the spindle, and the shears control*
> *Of destiny, and spin her own free hours.*[4]

"Methinks," said I, "you are too fastidious in objecting to this. Jonson in using the word 'manly' only meant to heighten the picture of this, the true, the intelligent fate, with one of the deeper colors." "And yet," said she, "so invariable is the use of this word where a heroic quality is to be described, and I feel so sure that persistence and courage are the most womanly no less than the most manly qualities, that I would exchange these words for others of a larger sense at the risk of marring the fine tissue of the verse. Read, 'a heavenward and instructed soul,' and I should be satisfied. Let it not be said, wherever there is energy or creative genius, 'She has a masculine mind.'"

This by no means argues a willing want of generosity toward woman. Man is as generous toward her, as he knows how to be.

Wherever she has herself arisen in national or private history, and nobly shone forth in any form of excellence, men have received her, not only willingly, but with triumph. Their encomiums indeed, are always, in some sense, mortifying; they show too much surprise. Can this be you? he cries to the transfigured Cinderella; well I should never have thought it, but I am very glad. We will tell every one that you have "*surpassed your sex.*"

In every-day life the feelings of the many are stained with vanity. Each wishes to be lord in a little world, to be superior at least over one; and he does not feel strong enough to retain a life-long ascendancy over a strong nature. Only a Theseus could conquer before he wed the Amazonian Queen. Hercules wished rather to rest with Dejanira, and received the poisoned robe, as a fit guerdon.[5] The tale should be interpreted to all those who seek repose with the weak.

But not only is man vain and fond of power, but the same want of development, which thus affects him morally, prevents his intellectually discerning the destiny of woman. The boy wants no woman, but only a girl to play ball with him, and mark his pocket handkerchief.

Thus, in Schiller's Dignity of Woman, beautiful as the poem is, there is no "grave and perfect man," but only a great boy to be softened and restrained by the influence of girls. Poets, the elder brothers of their race, have usually seen farther; but what can you expect of every-day men, if Schiller was not more prophetic as to what women must be? Even with Richter, one foremost thought about a wife was that she would "cook him something good." But as this is a delicate subject,

---

4. Lines 7–16 from "On Lucy, Countess of Bedford" (1616) by English poet Ben Jonson (1572–1637).

5. In Greek myth, Theseus fights and weds Hippolyta, queen of the Amazons.

and we are in constant danger of being accused of slighting what are called "the functions," let me say in behalf of Miranda and myself, that we have high respect for those who cook something good, who create and preserve fair order in houses, and prepare therein the shining raiment for worthy inmates, worthy guests. Only these "functions" must not be a drudgery, or enforced necessity, but a part of life. Let Ulysses drive the beeves home while Penelope[6] there piles up the fragrant loaves; they are both well employed if these be done in thought and love, willingly. But Penelope is no more meant for a baker or weaver solely, than Ulysses for a cattle-herd.

The sexes should not only correspond to and appreciate, but prophesy to one another. In individual instances this happens. Two persons love in one another the future good which they aid one another to unfold. This is imperfectly or rarely done in the general life. Man has gone but little way; now he is waiting to see whether woman can keep step with him, but instead of calling out, like a good brother, "you can do it, if you only think so," or impersonally; "any one can do what he tries to do;" he often discourages with school-boy brag: "Girls can't do that; girls can't play ball." But let any one defy their taunts, break through and be brave and secure, they rend the air with shouts.

This fluctuation was obvious in a narrative I have lately seen, the story of the life of Countess Emily Plater,[7] the heroine of the last revolution in Poland. The dignity, the purity, the concentrated resolve, the calm, deep enthusiasm, which yet could, when occasion called, sparkle up a holy, an indignant fire, make of this young maiden the figure I want for my frontispiece. Her portrait is to be seen in the book, a gentle shadow of her soul. Short was the career—like the maid of Orleans,[8] she only did enough to verify her credentials, and then passed from a scene on which she was, probably, a premature apparition.

When the young girl joined the army where the report of her exploits had preceded her, she was received in a manner that marks the usual state of feeling. Some of the officers were disappointed at her quiet manners; that she had not the air and tone of a stage-heroine. They thought she could not have acted heroically unless in buskins; had no idea that such deeds only showed the habit of her mind. Others talked of the delicacy of her sex, advised her to withdraw from perils and dangers, and had no comprehension of the feelings within her breast that made this impossible. The gentle irony of her reply to these self-constituted tutors, (not one of whom showed himself her equal in conduct or reason,) is as good as her indignant reproof at a later period to the general, whose perfidy ruined all.

But though, to the mass of these men, she was an embarrassment and a puzzle, the nobler sort viewed her with a tender enthusiasm worthy of her. "Her name," said her biographer, "is known throughout Europe. I paint her character that she may be as widely loved."

With pride, he shows her freedom from all personal affections; that, though tender and gentle in an uncommon degree, there was no room for a private love in her consecrated life. She inspired those who knew her with a simple energy of feeling like her own. We have seen, they felt, a woman worthy the name, capable of all sweet affections, capable of stern virtue.

6. In Homer's *Odyssey*, Penelope is the faithful wife of Odysseus (Ulysses).
7. Countess Emily Plater (1806–31).

8. Joan of Arc (1412–31), French saint who led troops into battle against the English in the Battle of Orléans.

It is a fact worthy of remark, that all these revolutions in favor of liberty have produced female champions that share the same traits, but Emily alone has found a biographer. Only a near friend could have performed for her this task, for the flower was reared in feminine seclusion, and the few and simple traits of her history before her appearance in the field could only have been known to the domestic circle. Her biographer has gathered them up with a brotherly devotion.

No! man is not willingly ungenerous. He wants faith and love, because he is not yet himself an elevated being. He cries, with sneering skepticism, Give us a sign. But if the sign appears, his eyes glisten, and he offers not merely approval, but homage.

The severe nation which taught that the happiness of the race was forfeited through the fault of a woman, and showed its thought of what sort of regard man owed her, by making him accuse her on the first question to his God; who gave her to the patriarch as a handmaid, and by the Mosaical law, bound her to allegiance like a serf; even they greeted, with solemn rapture, all great and holy women as heroines, prophetesses, judges in Israel; and if they made Eve listen to the serpent, gave Mary as a bride to the Holy Spirit. In other nations it has been the same down to our day. To the woman who could conquer, a triumph was awarded. And not only those whose strength was recommended to the heart by association with goodness and beauty, but those who were bad, if they were steadfast and strong, had their claims allowed. In any age a Semiramis, an Elizabeth of England, a Catharine of Russia[9] makes her place good, whether in a large or small circle. How has a little wit, a little genius, been celebrated in a woman! What an intellectual triumph was that of the lonely Aspasia,[1] and how heartily acknowledged! She, indeed, met a Pericles. But what annalist, the rudest of men, the most plebeian of husbands, will spare from his page one of the few anecdotes of Roman women—Sappho! Eloisa![2] The names are of threadbare celebrity. Indeed they were not more suitably met in their own time than the Countess Colonel Plater on her first joining the army. They had much to mourn, and their great impulses did not find due scope. But with time enough, space enough, their kindred appear on the scene. Across the ages, forms lean, trying to touch the hem of their retreating robes. The youth here by my side cannot be weary of the fragments from the life of Sappho. He will not believe they are not addressed to himself, or that he to whom they were addressed could be ungrateful. A recluse of high powers devotes himself to understand and explain the thought of Eloisa; he asserts her vast superiority in soul and genius to her master; he curses the fate that cast his lot in another age than hers. He could have understood her: he would have been to her a friend, such as Abelard never could. And this one woman he could have loved and reverenced, and she, alas! lay cold in her grave hundreds of years ago. His sorrow is truly pathetic. These responses that come too late to give joy are as tragic as any thing we know, and yet the tears of later ages glitter as they fall on Tasso's prison bars. And we know how elevating to the captive is the security that somewhere an intelligence must answer to his.

9. Semiramis: an Assyrian queen of legend; Elizabeth I (1533–1603), queen of England, 1558–1603; Catherine the Great (1729–96), czarina of Russia, 1762–96.
1. Aspasia (469–406 BCE), famously intellectual courtesan, lover of the Athenian statesman Peri-

cles and hostess to philosophers such as Socrates.
2. Sappho: a female Greek poet of the seventh century BCE; Eloisa: French philosopher, writer, and religious figure (1098?–1164), who was the lover and wife of French philosopher Peter Abelard.

The man habitually most narrow towards women will be flushed, as by the worst assault on Christianity, if you say it has made no improvement in her condition. Indeed, those most opposed to new acts in her favor, are jealous of the reputation of those which have been done.

We will not speak of the enthusiasm excited by actresses, improvisatrici,[3] female singers, for here mingles the charm of beauty and grace; but female authors, even learned women, if not insufferably ugly and slovenly, from the Italian professor's daughter, who taught behind the curtain, down to Mrs. Carter and Madame Dacier, are sure of an admiring audience, and what is far better, chance to use what they have learned, and to learn more, if they can once get a platform on which to stand.

But how to get this platform, or how to make it of reasonably easy access is the difficulty. Plants of great vigor will almost always struggle into blossom, despite impediments. But there should be encouragement, and a free genial atmosphere for those of more timid sort, fair play for each in its own kind. Some are like the little, delicate flowers which love to hide in the dripping mosses, by the sides of mountain torrents, or in the shade of tall trees. But others require an open field, a rich and loosened soil, or they never show their proper hues.

It may be said that man does not have his fair play either; his energies are repressed and distorted by the interposition of artificial obstacles. Ay, but he himself has put them there; they have grown out of his own imperfections. If there *is* a misfortune in woman's lot, it is in obstacles being interposed by men, which do *not* mark her state; and, if they express her past ignorance, do not her present needs. As every man is of woman born, she has slow but sure means of redress, yet the sooner a general justness of thought makes smooth the path, the better.

1845

3. Women performance artists.

CULTURAL COORDINATES
Niagara Falls

It is not surprising that Margaret Fuller began her "poetic description of the country at large," *Summer on the Lakes* (1844), with her impression of Niagara Falls. Through most of the eighteenth century, the falls had served as an icon for a romantic conception of the American continent: immense and unknowable, beautiful and horrible. By Fuller's time it had become one of America's first tourist attractions.

One of the largest-volume waterfalls in the world, Niagara Falls exists on the border between Canada and the United States. French explorers Jacques Cartier (in the mid-1500s) and Samuel de Champlain (in the early 1600s) had heard of the falls from the native peoples they met in their explorations. What they heard seemed unbelievable—even to men who had spent so much time pursuing new worlds. In 1678, however, a European finally saw the falls: Brother Louis Hennepin traveled in 1678 with Jesuit missionaries who explored the Great Lakes and, eventually, the Mississippi River. The first engraving of Niagara Falls was published in Hennepin's *Nouvelle Decouverte* (1657), and the image immediately entered the imaginations of the French intellectuals and philosophers of the eighteenth century. Numerous depictions of Niagara Falls, inspired by this engraving, circulated in France and Europe. For most of the eighteenth century, the mystery of Niagara Falls was heightened by the fact that the Iroquois were able to prevent European settlement of this area.

Known before the nineteenth century only through writings and drawings, the falls were understood to be so big, so loud, so deep, so full of rocks, mist, and rainbows that an observer could not help but experience the most intense physical and emotional sensations. In the nineteenth century, Americans and Europeans

Niagara (1857) by Frederic Edwin Church (1826–1900). For many Americans, Niagara Falls symbolized the splendor and power of nature unsullied by humanity, which was quickly being lost through industrialization. Painters from the Hudson River school, like Church, tried to capture the sublimity of nature before it was lost. (Oil on canvas 42½ × 90½ inches, Corcoran Gallery of Art, Washington, D.C., Museum Purchase, Gallery Fund 76.15)

made a point of experiencing Niagara's power themselves. Prominent visitors to the falls included Vice President Aaron Burr's daughter Theodosia and her husband, who made a wedding tour to the falls in 1801; Jerome Bonaparte, brother of Napoleon, and his bride, did likewise in 1804 in search of direct experience of the romantic sublime   .

There were few American poets of the first half of the nineteenth century who did not treat Niagara Falls or one of its associated legends in verse. For those who experienced it in person in the early nineteenth century, as Margaret Fuller did in the 1840s, Niagara Falls promised a confrontation with nature and beauty that was otherwise impossible. By the end of the nineteenth century, however, the falls had become a parody of themselves: no longer an experience of the romantic sublime, the falls had become a vacation destination for romantic couples seeking comfortable pleasure and a source of power for factories and cities.

ELIZABETH GASKELL
1810–1865

Despite critics' long-standing habit of calling her "Mrs. Gaskell," as her contemporary readers had done, Elizabeth Gaskell solidly established herself as a professional author in the mid–nineteenth century, making a significant contribution to the genres of realistic fiction and the social-problem novel.

Gaskell was born in London, to William and Elizabeth Holland Stevenson, who had moved there from Scotland en route—they hoped—to India, where her father was to act as assistant to a new governor-general. Elizabeth's father had been trained as a Unitarian minister, but he had repudiated the career if not the faith. The family was in London only a few months before Elizabeth was born, and in that time they learned the appointment of the governor-general had fallen through. Stevenson then stayed and acquired a civil service post in London.

Her mother died when Elizabeth was only thirteen months old, having weathered the deaths of six of her eight children in early childhood. Elizabeth's only surviving sibling was her oldest brother, John, a sailor with whom she carried on an affectionate correspondence until he was lost at sea on a voyage to India when Elizabeth was eighteen years old.

After her mother's death, Elizabeth was raised by Mrs. Lumb, her maternal aunt, in a small town called Knutsford not far from the factory city of Manchester. Her aunt's twenty-one-year-old daughter, who had never been able to walk because of a back injury she sustained as an infant, initially intended to adopt Gaskell—she had the financial means and the willingness to adopt her young cousin—but she died unexpectedly before she was able to do so, leaving Elizabeth in the comparatively impoverished hands of her aunt. Her childhood was nevertheless happy, spent among loving relations in comfortable countryside settings. She attended a boarding school between the ages of eleven and sixteen, learning the usual accomplishments of a middle-class young lady, such as drawing, music, needlework, and French. As a young woman, Gaskell spent time in London with her father and his second wife, where she studied Italian and Latin under her father's tutelage. After his death in 1831, she traveled to Manchester. There she met the Reverend William Gaskell, a Unitarian minister with a background in the classics and a passion for social work. They married when she was twenty-two, beginning a lifelong collaboration of teaching, writing, and work among the laboring classes of Manchester. Gaskell spent thirty-three years in Manchester, coming to know firsthand the lives and neighborhoods of a broad range of working people struggling to survive the "Hungry Forties," a period of desperation for Irish peasants suffering the potato famine and for England's rural and industrial poor.

Like her mother, she also knew firsthand the all-too-common pain of losing children to early deaths: she gave birth to seven children, but three of them died in infancy. These experiences were to underpin the sympathetic stance she takes in her fiction toward characters who suffer loss. She mentioned her grief over her infant son William's death as one of the motivations for writing her first novel, *Mary Barton* (1848).

Mary Barton concentrates on the lives of young working-class women in Manchester and other industrial towns. Depicting domestic life among both the working poor and the factory owners, the novel lays out sympathetically the rea sons for unrest among the workers while holding that "masters," too, have reasons to grieve. *Mary Barton* was a popular success, making Gaskell a literary celebrity in England. *Cranford* (1853), her second novel, sketches life among gossipy women in a country town and is based on the Knutsford of her youth. This novel was also very popular, but her third, *Ruth* (1853), caused a scandal. *Ruth* tells of a young woman who is seduced by a prosperous man, giving a sympathetic account of what it meant for a working-class woman to "fall." Moralistic readers were outraged by the novel, and Gaskell's reputation for respectability suffered for a time. Her later novels, especially *North and South* (1855), which appeared first in serial installments in one of Charles Dickens's magazines, were more kindly received. Her *Life of Charlotte Brontë* (1857), written shortly after the writer's death, was also a success, having grown out of a mutually admiring friendship that developed between Gaskell and Brontë in the last years of Brontë's life. Gaskell was in the course of writing *Wives and Daughters* (serialized 1864–66) when she died unexpectedly of heart failure in 1865, surrounded by her beloved daughters and their families at a tea party at home. She is said to have died in cheerful midsentence, showing no signs of distress.

"The Three Eras of Libbie Marsh," which appears here, connects life in Manchester, holidays in the surrounding countryside, and Gaskell's interest in working-class women with a figure who recalls the disabled cousin she never knew. Like her other social-problem fiction, the story promotes personal relationships as solutions for intractable economic problems. Gaskell's story is an example of nineteenth-century sentimentalism, given her focus on a long-suffering crippled child, the pet that brings him joy, and the Christian forbearance that leads her heroine to reach out to the child's unhappy mother in her loneliness. For nineteenth-century authors, the possible endings for young female protagonists were very limited: usually a heroine either gets married or she dies. Gaskell meets the challenge of this convention by imagining an alternate future for Libbie Marsh.

The Three Eras of Libbie Marsh

St Valentine's Day

Last November but one there was a flitting[1] in our neighbourhood; hardly a flitting after all, for it was only a single person changing her place of abode, from one lodging to another; and instead of a comfortable cartload of drawers, and baskets, and dressers, and beds, with old king clock at the top of all, there was only one large wooden chest to be carried after the girl, who moved slowly and heavily along the streets, listless and depressed more from the state of her mind than of her body. It was Libbie Marsh, who had been obliged to quit her room in Dunn Street, because the acquaintances, with whom she had been living there, were leaving Manchester. She tried to think herself fortunate in having met with lodgings rather more out of the town, and with those who were known to be respectable; she did indeed try to be contented, but in spite of her reason, the old

1. When households move from one rental space to another.

feeling of desolation came over her, as she was now about to be again thrown entirely among strangers.

No. 2, ——[2] Court, Albemarle Street, was reached at last; and the pace, slow as it was, slackened, as she drew near the spot where she was to be left by the man who carried her box; for trivial as his acquaintance with her was, he was not quite a stranger, as every one else was, peering out of their open doors, and satisfying themselves it was only "Dixon's new lodger."

Dixon's house was the last on the left hand side of the court. A high dead brick wall connected it with its opposite neighbour. All the dwellings were of the same monotonous pattern, and one side of the court looked at its exact likeness opposite, as if it were seeing itself in a looking-glass.

Dixon's house was shut up, and the key left next door; but the woman in whose care it was knew that Libbie was expected, and came forwards to say a few explanatory words, to unlock the door, and stir the dull-grey ashes which were lazily burning in the grate, and then she returned to her own house; leaving poor Libbie standing alone with her great big chest on the middle of the house-place floor, with no one to say a word, (even a commonplace remark would have been better than that dull silence), that could help her to repel the fast-coming tears.

Dixon and his wife, and their eldest girl, worked in factories and were absent all day from their house; the youngest child, (also a little girl), was boarded out for the week days at the neighbour's where the door-key was deposited; but, although busy making dirt-pies at the entrance to the court when Libbie came in, she was too young to care much about her parents' new lodger. Libbie knew she was to sleep with the elder girl in the front bed-room; but, as you may fancy, it seemed a liberty even to go up stairs to take off her things, when no one was at home to marshal the way up the ladder-like steps. So she could only take off her bonnet, and sit down, and gaze at the now blazing fire, and think sadly on the past, and on the lonely creature she was in this wide world.

Father and mother gone; her little brother long since dead; (he would have been more than nineteen, had he been alive, but she only thought of him as the darling baby); her only friends (to call friends) living far away at their new home; her employers,—kind enough people in their way, but too rapidly twirling round on this bustling earth to have leisure to think of the little work-woman, excepting when they wanted gowns turned, carpets mended, or household linen darned; and hardly even the natural, though hidden hope, of a young girl's heart, to cheer her on with bright visions of a home of her own at some future day, where, loving and beloved, she might fulfil a woman's dearest duties.

For Libbie was very plain, as she had known so long, that the consciousness of it had ceased to mortify her. You can hardly live in Manchester without having some idea of your personal appearance. The factory lads and lasses take good care of that, and if you meet them at the hours when they are pouring out of the mills, you are sure to hear a good number of truths, some of them combined with such a spirit of impudent fun, that you can scarcely keep from laughing even at the joke against yourself. Libbie had often and often been greeted by such questions as "How long is it since you were a beauty?" "What would you take a day to stand in a field to scare away the birds?" etc., for her to linger under any delusion as to her looks.

2. Literary convention uses the blank to mask a real address.

While she was thus musing, and quietly crying over the pictures her fancy conjured up, the Dixons came dropping in, and surprised her with wet cheeks and quivering lips.

She almost wished to have the stillness again she had felt so oppressive an hour ago, they talked and laughed so loudly and so much, and bustled about so noisily over every thing they did. Dixon took hold of one iron handle of her box, and helped her to bump it up stairs; while his daughter Anne followed to see the unpacking, and what sort of clothes "little sewing-body had gotten." Mrs Dixon rattled out the tea-things, and put the kettle on; fetched home her youngest child, which added to the commotion. Then she called Anne down stairs and sent her off for this thing, and that. Eggs to put to the cream, it was so thin. Ham to give a relish to the bread and butter. Some new bread (hot, if she could get it). Libbie heard all these orders given at full pitch of Mrs Dixon's voice, and wondered at their extravagance, so different to the habits of the place where she had last lodged. But they were fine spinners in the receipt of good wages; and confined all day to an atmosphere ranging from 75 to 80 degrees; they had lost all natural healthy appetite for simple food, and having no higher tastes, found their greatest enjoyment in their luxurious meals.

When tea was ready, Libbie was called down stairs with a rough but hearty invitation to share their meal; she sat mutely at the corner of the tea-table, while they went on with their own conversation about people and things she knew nothing about; till at length she ventured to ask for a candle to go and finish her unpacking before bed-time, as she had to go out sewing for several succeeding days. But once in the comparative peace of her bed-room her energy failed her, and she contented herself with locking her Noah's ark of a chest, and put out her candle, and went to sit by the window and gaze out at the night heavens; for ever and ever the "blue sky that bends over all,"[3] sheds down a feeling of sympathy with the sorrowful at the solemn hours, when the ceaseless stars are seen to pace its depths.

By and by her eye fell down to gazing at the corresponding window to her own on the opposite side of the court. It was lighted, but the blind was drawn down. Upon the blind she saw, at first unconsciously, the constant weary motion of a little, spectral shadow; a child's hand and arm,—no more; long, thin fingers hanging listlessly down from the wrist, while the arm moved up and down, as if keeping time to the heavy pulses of dull pain. She could not help hoping that sleep would soon come to still that incessant, feeble motion; and now and then it did cease, as if the little creature had dropped into a slumber from very weariness; but presently the arm jerked up with the fingers clenched, as if with a sudden start of agony. When Anne came up to bed, Libbie was still sitting watching the shadow; and she directly asked to whom it belonged.

"It will be Margaret Hall's lad. Last summer when it was so hot, there was no biding[4] with the window shut at nights; and their'n were open too; and many's the time he waked me up with his moans. They say he's been better sin' cold weather came."

"Is he always so bad? Whatten ails him?" asked Libbie.

"Summut's amiss wi' his back-bone, folks say; he's better and worse like. He's a nice little chap enough; and his mother's not that bad either; only my mother and her had words, so now we don't speak."

3. From the song "The Blue Sky," by British jour-   4. It was unbearable.
nalist and poet Charles Mackay (1814–99).

Libbie went on watching, and when she next spoke to ask who and what his mother was, Anne Dixon was fast asleep.

Time passed away, and, as usual, unveiled the hidden things.

Libbie found out that Margaret Hall was a widow, who earned her living as a washerwoman; that this little suffering lad was her only child, her dearly beloved. That while she scolded pretty nearly every body else "till her name was up"[5] in the neighbourhood for a termagant, to him she was evidently most tender and gentle. He lay alone on his little bed near the window through the day, while she was away, toiling for a livelihood. But when Libbie had plain sewing to do at her lodgings instead of going out to sew, she used to watch from her bed-room window for the time when the shadows opposite, by their mute gestures, told that the mother had returned to bend over her child; to smooth his pillow, to alter his position, to get him his nightly cup of tea. And often in the night Libbie could not help rising gently from bed to see if the little arm was waving up and down, as was his accustomed habit when sleepless from pain.

Libbie had a good deal of sewing to do at home that winter, and whenever it was not so cold as to numb her fingers, she took it up stairs in order to watch the little lad in her few odd moments of pause. On his better days he could sit up enough to peep out of his window, and she found he liked to look at her. Presently she ventured to nod to him across the court, and his faint smile, and ready nod back again, showed that this gave him pleasure. I think she would have been encouraged by this smile to proceed to a speaking acquaintance, if it had not been for his terrible mother, to whom it seemed to be irritation enough to know that Libbie was a lodger at the Dixons', for her to talk *at* her whenever they encountered each other, and to live evidently in wait for some good opportunity of abuse.

With her constant interest in him, Libbie soon discovered his great want of an object on which to occupy his thoughts, and which might distract his attention, when alone through the long day, from the pain he endured. He was very fond of flowers. It was November when she had first removed to her lodgings, but it had been very mild weather and a few flowers yet lingered in the gardens, which the country-people gathered into nosegays, and brought on market days into Manchester. His mother had bought him a bunch of Michaelmas daisies[6] the very day that Libbie had become a neighbour, and she watched their history. He put them first in an old tea-pot, of which the spout was broken off, and the lid lost; and he daily replenished the tea-pot from the jug of water his mother left near him to quench his feverish thirst. By and by one or two out of the constellation of lilac stars faded, and then the time he had hitherto spent in admiring (almost caressing) them, was devoted to cutting off those flowers whose decay marred the beauty of his nosegay. It took him half the morning with his feeble languid motions, and his cumbrous old scissors, to trim up his diminishing darlings. Then at last he seemed to think he had better preserve the few that remained by drying them; so they were carefully put between the leaves of the old Bible; and then whenever a better day came, when he had strength enough to lift the ponderous book, he used to open its pages to look at his flower friends. In winter he could have no more living flowers to tend.

5. Evidently a regional phrase.
6. Asters, a late-blooming perennial associated   with the Feast of St. Michael, September 29.

Libbie thought and thought, till at last an idea flashed upon her mind that often made a happy smile steal over her face as she stitched away, and which cheered her through that solitary winter—for solitary it continued to be, although the Dixons were very good sort of people; never pressed her for payment if she had had but little work that week; never grudged her a share of their extravagant meals, which were far more luxurious than she could have met with any where else for her previously agreed payment in case of working at home; and they would fain have taught her to drink rum in her tea, assuring her that she should have it for nothing, and welcome. But they were too loud, too prosperous, too much absorbed in themselves to take off Libbie's feeling of solitariness; not half as much as did the little face by day, and the shadow by night, of him with whom she had never yet exchanged a word.

Her idea was this: her mother came from the east of England, where, as perhaps you know, they have the pretty custom of sending presents on St Valentine's day, with the donor's name unknown, and of course that mystery constitutes half the enjoyment. The 14th of February was Libbie's birthday too; and many a year in the happy days of old had her mother delighted to surprise her with some little gift, of which she more than half guessed the giver, although each Valentine's day the manner of its arrival was varied. Since then, the 14th of February had been the dreariest day of all the year, because the most haunted by memory of departed happiness. But now, this year, if she could not have the old gladness of heart herself, she would try and brighten the life of another. She would save, and she would screw, but she would buy a canary and a cage for that poor little laddie opposite, who wore out his monotonous life with so few pleasures, and so much pain.

I doubt I may not tell you here of the anxieties, and the fears, of the hopes, and the self-sacrifices,—all perhaps small in tangible effect as the widow's mite,[7] yet not the less marked by the viewless angels who go about continually among us,—which varied Libbie's life before she accomplished her purpose. It is enough to say, it was accomplished. The very day before the 14th she found time to go with her half-guinea[8] to a barber's, who lived near Albemarle Street, and who was famous for his stock of singing birds. There are enthusiasts about all sorts of things, both good and bad; and many of the weavers in Manchester know and care more about birds that any one would easily credit. Stubborn, silent, reserved men on many things, you have only to touch on the subject of birds to light up their faces with brightness. They will tell you who won the prizes at the last canary show, where the prize birds may be seen; and give you all the details of those funny though pretty and interesting mimicries of great people's cattle shows. Among these amateurs, Emanuel Morris the barber was an oracle.

He took Libbie into his little back room, used for private shaving of modest men, who did not care to be exhibited in the front shop, decked out in the full glories of lather; and which was hung round with birds in rude wicker cages, with the exception of those who had won prizes, and were consequently honoured with gilt wire prisons. The longer and thinner the body of the bird was, the more admiration it received as far as its external beauty went; and when in addition to this chance the colour was deep and clear, and its notes strong and varied, the more did Emanuel dwell upon their perfections. But these were all prize birds; and on inquiry Libbie heard, with a little sinking at her heart, that their price ran from one to two guineas.

"I'm not over-particular as to shape and colour," said she. "I should like a good singer, that's all."

She dropped a little in Emanuel's estimation. However, he showed her his good singers, but all were above Libbie's means.

"After all, I don't think I care so much about the singing very loud, it's but a noise after all; and sometimes noises fidgets folks."

"They must be nesh[9] folk as is put out with the singing o' birds," replied Emanuel, rather affronted.

"It's for one who is poorly," said Libbie, deprecatingly.

"Well," said he, as if considering the matter, "folk that are cranky often take more to them as shows 'em love, than to them who is clever and gifted. Happen yo'd rather have this'n," opening a cage-door, and calling to a dull-coloured bird, sitting moped up in a corner, "Here! Jupiter, Jupiter!"

The bird smoothed its feathers in an instant, and uttering a little note of delight, flew to Emanuel, putting its beak to his lips as if kissing him, and then perching on his head, it began a gurgling warble of pleasure, not by any means so varied or so clear as the song of the others, but which pleased Libbie more (for she was always one to find out she liked the gooseberries that were accessible, better than the grapes which were beyond her reach). The price, too, was just right; so she gladly took possession of the cage, and hid it under her cloak, preparatory to carrying it home. Emanuel meanwhile was giving her directions as to its food, with all the minuteness of one loving his subject.

"Will it soon get to know any one?" asked she.

"Give him two days only, and you and he'll be as thick as him and me are now. You've only to open his door, and call him, and he'd follow you round the room; but he'd first kiss you, and then perch on your head. He only wants larning,[1] (which I've no time to give him), to do many another accomplishment."

"What's his name? I didn't rightly catch it."

"Jupiter; it's not common, but the town is o'errun with Bobbys and Dickys, and as my birds are thought a bit out o' the way, I like to have better names for 'em, so I just picked a few out o' my lad's school-books. It's just as ready, when you're used to it, to say Jupiter as Dicky."

"I could bring my tongue round to Peter better; would he answer to Peter?" asked Libbie, now on the point of departure.

"Happen he might; but I think he'd come readier to the three syllables."

On Valentine's day, Jupiter's cage was decked round with ivy leaves, making quite a pretty wreath on the wicker-work; and to one of them was pinned a slip of paper, with these words written in Libbie's best round hand:—

"From your faithful Valentine. Please take notice: His name is Peter, and he will come if you call him, after a bit."

But little work did Libbie do that afternoon, she was so engaged in watching for the messenger who was to bear her present to her little Valentine, and run away as soon as he had delivered up the canary, and explained for whom it was sent.

9. Finicky.   1. Learning, education.

At last he came, then there was a pause before the woman of the house was at leisure to take it up stairs. Then Libbie saw the little face flush into a bright colour, the feeble hands tremble with delighted eagerness, the head bent down to try and make out the writing, (beyond his power, poor lad, to read), the rapturous turning round of the cage in order to see the canary in every point of view, head, tail, wings and feet; an intention which Jupiter, in his uneasiness at being again among strangers, did not second, for he hopped round so as continually to present a full front to the boy. It was a source of never-wearying delight to the little fellow till daylight closed in; he evidently forgot to wonder who had sent it him, in his gladness at the possession of such a treasure; and when the shadow of his mother darkened on the blind, and the bird had been exhibited, Libbie saw her do what, with all her tenderness, seemed rarely to have entered into her thoughts—she bent down, and kissed her boy in a mother's sympathy with the joy of her child.

The canary was placed for the night between the little bed and window, and when Libbie rose once to take her accustomed peep, she saw the little arm put fondly round the cage, as if embracing his new treasure even in his sleep. How Jupiter slept that first night is quite another thing.

So ended the first day of Libbie's three eras in last year.

Whitsuntide[2]

The brightest, fullest daylight poured down into No. 2, ——Court, Albemarle Street, and the heat, even at the early hour of five, was almost as great as at the noontide on the June days of many years past.

The court seemed alive, and merry with voices and laughter. The bed-room windows were open wide, (and had been so all night on account of the heat), and every now and then you might see a head and a pair of shoulders, simply encased in shirt sleeves, popped out, and you might hear the inquiry passed from one to the other:—

"Well, Jack, and where art thou bound to?"

"Dunham!"

"Why what an old-fashioned chap thou be'st. Thy granddad afore thee went to Dunham; but thou wert always a slow coach. I'm off to Alderley,—me, and my missus."

"Aye, that's because there's only thee and thy missus; wait till thou hast gotten four childer like me, and thou'lt be glad enough to take 'em to Dunham, oud-fashioned way, for fourpence[3] a-piece."

"I'd still go to Alderley; I'd not be bothered with my childer; they should keep house at home."

A pair of hands (the person to whom they belonged invisible behind her husband) boxed his ears at this last speech, in a very spirited, although a playful manner, and the neighbours all laughed at the surprized look of the speaker, at this assault from an unseen foe; the man who had been holding the conversation with him, cried out,

"Sarved him right, Mrs Slater; he knows nought about it yet, but when he gets them, he'll be as loth to leave the babbies at home on a Whitsuntide, as any on us. We shall live to see him in Dunham park yet, wi' twins in his arms, and an-

2. The days around Whitsunday, also known as   3. Equivalent to about $2 today.
Pentecost, or the seventh Sunday after Easter.

other pair on 'em clutching at daddy's coat tails, let alone your share of young-sters, missus."

At this moment our friend Libbie appeared at her window, and Mrs Slater, who had taken her discomfited husband's place, called out,

"Elizabeth Marsh, where are Dixons and you bound to?"

"Dixons are not up yet; he said last night he'd take his holiday out in lying in bed. I'm going to th' old-fashioned place,—Dunham."

"Thou art never going by thyself, moping!"

"No! I'm going with Margaret Hall and her lad," replied Libbie, hastily with-drawing from the window in order to avoid hearing any remarks on the associates she had chosen for her day of pleasure—the scold of the neighbourhood, and her sickly, ailing child!

But Jupiter might have been a dove, and his ivy-leaves an olive-branch, for the peace he had brought, the happiness he had caused, to three individuals at least. For of course it could not long be a mystery who had sent little Frank Hall his Valentine; nor could his mother long maintain her hard manner towards one who had given her child a new pleasure. She was shy, and she was proud, and for some time she struggled against the natural desire of manifesting her gratitude; but one evening, when Libbie was returning home with a bundle of work half as large as herself, as she dragged herself along through the heated street she was overtaken by Margaret Hall, her burden gently pulled from her, and her way home shortened, and her weary spirits soothed and cheered by the outpourings of Mar-garet's heart; for her barrier of reserve once broken down, she had much to say, to thank her for days of amusement and happy employment for her lad, to speak of his gratitude, to tell of her hopes and fears—the hopes and fears which made up the dates of her life. From that time Libbie lost her awe of the termagant in inter-est for the mother, whose all was ventured in so frail a bark. From that time Lib-bie was a fast friend with both mother and son; planning mitigations to the sorrowful days of the latter, as eagerly as poor Margaret Hall, and with far more resources. His life had flickered up under the charm and the excitement of the last few months. He even seemed strong enough to undertake the journey to Dunham, which Libbie had arranged as a Whitsuntide treat, and for which she and his mother had been hoarding up for several weeks. The canal-boat left Knott-Mill[4] at six, and it was now past five; so Libbie let herself out very gently, and went across to her friends. She knocked at the door of their lodging room, and without waiting for an answer entered.

Franky's face was flushed, and he was trembling with excitement, partly from pleasure, but partly from some eager wish not yet granted.

"He wants sore to take Peter with him," said his mother, as if referring the matter to Libbie. The boy looked imploringly at her.

"He would so like it, I know. For one thing, he'd miss me sadly, and chirp for me all day long, he'd be so lonely. I could not be half so happy, a-thinking on him, left alone here by himself. Then Libbie, he's just like a Christian, so fond of flow-ers, and green leaves, and them sort of things. He chirrups to me so when mother brings me a pennyworth of wall-flowers to put round his cage. He would talk if he could, you know, but I can tell what he means quite as one as if he spoke. Do let Peter go, Libbie! I'll carry him in my own arms."

4. Now Deansgate in Manchester. Canal-boat rides are still available for amusement.

So Jupiter was allowed to be of the party. Now Libbie had overcome the great difficulty of conveying Franky to the boat by offering to "slay" for a coach, and the shouts and exclamations of the neighbours told them that their conveyance awaited them at the bottom of the court. His mother carried Franky, light in weight, though heavy in helplessness; and he would hold the cage, believing that he was thus redeeming his promise that Peter should be a trouble to no one. Libbie preceded to arrange the bundle containing their dinner, as a support in the corner of the coach. The neighbours came out with many blunt speeches, and more kindly wishes, and one or two of them would have relieved Margaret of her burden, if she would have allowed it. The presence of that little crippled fellow seemed to obliterate all the angry feelings which had existed between his mother and her neighbours, and which had formed the politics of that little court for many a day.

And now they were fairly off! Franky bit his lips in attempted endurance of the pain the motion caused him, but winced and shrunk, until they were fairly on a macadamized[5] thoroughfare, when he closed his eyes, and seemed desirous of a few minutes' rest. Libbie felt very shy, and very much afraid of being seen by her employers "set up in a coach;" and so she hid herself in a corner, and made herself as small as possible; while Mrs Hall had exactly the opposite feeling, and was delighted to stand up, stretching out of the window, and nodding to pretty nearly every one they met, or passed, on the footpaths; and they were not a few, for the streets were quite gay, even at that early hour, with parties going to this or that railway station; or to the boats which crowded the canals in this bright holiday week. And almost every one they met seemed to enter into Mrs Hall's exhilaration of feeling, and had a smile or a nod in return, At last she plumped down by Libbie and exclaimed,

"I never was in a coach but once afore, and that was when I was a going to be married. It's like heaven; and all done over with such beautiful gimp,[6] too," continued she, admiring the lining of the vehicle. Jupiter did not enjoy it so much.

As if the holiday time, the lovely weather, and the "sweet hour of prime"[7] had a genial influence, (as no doubt they have), everybody's heart seemed softened towards poor Franky. The driver lifted him out with the gentleness of strength, and bore him tenderly down to the boat; the people there made way, and gave him up the best seat in their power; or rather, I should call it a couch, for they saw he was weary, and insisted on his lying down—an attitude he would have been ashamed to assume without the protection of his mother and Libbie, who now appeared, bearing their tickets, and carrying Peter.

Away the boat went to make room for others; for every conveyance both by land and by water is in requisition in Whitsunweek to give the hard-worked crowds an opportunity of tasting the charms of the country. Even every standing place in the canal packets was occupied; and as they glided along, the banks were lined by people, who seemed to find it object enough to watch the boats go by, packed close and full with happy beings brimming with anticipation of a day's pleasure. The country through which they passed is as uninteresting as can well be imagined, but still it is country; and the screams of delight from the children, and the low laughs of pleasure from the parents, at every blossoming tree which trailed

5. Paved.
6. Trimming made of silk, wool, or cotton twisted around a cord.

7. Prime: from six to nine a.m. The line is from John Milton's *Paradise Lost* 5.170.

its wreaths against some cottage-wall, or at the tufts of late primroses which lingered in the cool depths of grass along the canal banks, the thorough relish of everything, as if dreading to let the least circumstance on this happy day pass over without its due appreciation, made the time seem all too short, although it took two hours to arrive at a place only eight miles distant from Manchester. Even Franky, with all his impatience to see Dunham woods, (which I think he confused with London, believing both to be paved with gold), enjoyed the easy motion of the boat as much, floating along, while pictures moved before him, that he regretted when the time came for landing among the soft green meadows that come sloping down to the dancing water's brim. His fellow passengers carried him to the park, and refused all payment; although his mother had laid by sixpence on purpose, as a recompense for this service.

"Oh, Libbie, how beautiful! Oh, mother, mother! Is the whole world out of Manchester as beautiful as this! I did not know trees were like this. Such green homes for birds! Look, Peter! would not you like to be there, up among those boughs? But I can't let you go, you know, because you're my little bird-brother, and I should be quite lost without you."

They spread a shawl upon the fine mossy turf at the root of a beech tree, which made a sort of natural couch, and there they laid him, and bade him rest in spite of the delight which made him believe himself capable of any exertion. Where he lay, (always holding Jupiter's cage, and often talking to him as to a play-fellow), he was on the verge of a green area shut in by magnificent trees, in all the glory of their early foliage before the summer heats have deepened their verdure into one rich monotonous tint. And hither came party after party; old men and maidens, young men and children—whole families trooped along after the guiding fathers, who bore the youngest in their arms, or astride upon their backs, while they turned round occasionally to the wives, with whom they shared some fond local remembrance. For years has Dunham park been the favourite resort of the Manchester workpeople; for more years than I can tell; probably ever since "The Duke,"[8] by his canals, opened out the system of cheap travelling. It is scenery, too, which presents such a complete contrast to the whirl and turmoil of Manchester; so thoroughly woodland, with its ancestral trees, (here and there lightning-blanched), its "verdurous walls," its grassy walks leading far away into some glade where you start at the rabbit, rustling among the last year's fern, and where the wood-pigeon's call seems the only fitting and accordant sound. Depend upon it, this complete sylvan repose, this accessible depth of quiet, this lapping the soul in green images of the country, forms the most complete contrast to a townsperson, and consequently has over such the greatest power to charm.

Presently Libbie found out she was very hungry. Now they were but provided with dinner, which was of course to be eaten as near twelve o'clock as might be; and Margaret Hall, in her prudence, asked a working man near, to tell her what o'clock it was?

"Nay!" said he; "I'll ne'er look at clock or watch to-day. I'll not spoil my pleasure by finding out how fast it's going away. If thou'rt hungry, eat. I make my own dinner hour, and I've eaten mine an hour ago."

8. Francis Egerton, third Duke of Bridgewater (1736–1803), was called the Canal Duke for de-   veloping inland waterways in Manchester.

So they had their veal pies, and then found out it was only about half-past ten o'clock, by so many pleasurable events had that morning been marked. But such was their buoyancy of spirits that they only enjoyed their mistake, and joined in the general laugh against the man who had eaten his dinner somewhere about nine. He laughed most heartily of all, till suddenly stopping, he said,

"I must not go on at this rate; laughing gives me such an appetite."

"Oh, if that's all," said a merry-looking man, lying at full length, and crushing the fresh scent out of the grass, while two or three little children tumbled over him, and crept about him, as kittens or puppies frolic with their parents; "if that's all, we'll have a subscription of eatables for them improvident folk as have eaten their dinner for their breakfast. Here's a sausage pasty and a handful of nuts for my share. Bring round a hat, Bob, and see what the company will give."

Bob carried out the joke, much to little Franky's amusement, and no one was so churlish as to refuse, although the contributions varied from a peppermint drop up to a veal-pie, and a sausage pasty.

"It's a thriving trade," said Bob, as he emptied his hatful of provisions on the grass by Libbie's side. "Besides, it's tip-top too to live on the public. Hark! what is that?"

The laughter and the chat were suddenly hushed, and mothers told their little ones to listen, as far away in the distance, now sinking and falling, now swelling and clear, came a ringing peal of children's voices, blended together in one of those psalm tunes which we are all of us familiar with, and which bring to mind the old, old days when we, as wondering children, were first led to worship "Our Father," by those beloved ones who have since gone to the more perfect worship. Holy was that distant choral praise even to the most thoughtless; and when it in fact was ended, in the instant's pause during which the ear awaited the repetition of the air, they caught the noon-tide hum and buz of the myriads of insects, who danced away their lives in that glorious day; they heard the swaying of the mighty woods in the soft, yet resistless breeze; and then again once more burst forth the merry jests and the shouts of childhood; and again the elder ones resumed their happy talk, as they lay or sat "under the greenwood tree." Fresh parties came dropping in; some loaded with wild flowers, almost with branches of hawthorn indeed; while one or two had made prize of the earliest dog-roses, and had cast away campion, stitchwort, ragged robin, all, to keep the lady of the hedges from being obscured or hidden among the commonalty.

One after another drew near to Franky, and looked on with interest as he lay, sorting the flowers given to him. Happy parents stood by, with their household bands around them in health and comeliness, and felt the sad prophecy of those shrivelled limbs, those wasted fingers, those lamp-like eyes, with their bright dark lustre. His mother was too eagerly watching his happiness to read the meaning of the grave looks, but Libbie saw them, and understood them, and a chill shudder went through her even on that day, as she thought on the future.

"Aye! I thought we should give you a start!"

A start they did give, with their terrible slap on Libbie's back, as she sat, idly grouping flowers, and following out her sorrowful thoughts. It was the Dixons! Instead of keeping their holiday by lying in bed, they and their children had roused themselves, and had come by the omnibus to the nearest point. For an instant the meeting was an awkward one on account of the feud between Margaret Hall and Mrs Dixon; but there was no long resisting of kindly Mother Nature's soothings at that holiday time, and in that lovely tranquil spot; or if they could have been unheeded, the sight of Franky would have awed every angry feeling into rest, so changed was he since the Dixons had last seen him; since he had been the Puck, or Robin-goodfellow[9] of the neighbourhood, whose marbles were always rolling themselves under people's feet, and whose top strings were always hanging in nooses to catch the unwary. Yes! he, the feeble, mild, almost girlish-looking lad, had once been a merry, happy rogue, and as such often cuffed by Mrs Dixon, the very Mrs Dixon who now stood gazing with the tears in her eyes. Could she, in sight of him, the changed, the fading, keep up a quarrel with his mother?

"How long hast thou been here?" asked Dixon.

"Welly on for all day," answered Libbie.

"Hast never been to see the deer, or the king and queen oaks? Lord! how stupid!"

His wife pinched his arm, to remind him of Franky's helpless condition, which of course tethered the otherwise willing feet.

But Dixon had a remedy. He called Bob, and one or two others, and each taking a corner of the strong plaid shawl, they slung Franky as in a hammock, and thus carried him merrily along down the wood-paths, over the soft grassy turf, while the glimmering shine and shadow fell on his upturned face. The women walked behind, talking, loitering along, always in sight of the hammock, now picking up some green treasure from the ground, now catching at the low-hanging branches of the horse-chestnut. The soul grew much on that day, and in those woods, and all unconsciously, as souls do grow. They followed Franky's hammock-bearers up a grassy knoll, on the top of which stood a group of pine-trees, whose stems looked like dark red gold in the sunbeams. They had taken Franky there to show him Manchester, far away in the blue plain, against which the woodland foreground cut with a soft clear line. Far, far away in the distance on that flat plain you might see the motionless cloud of smoke hanging over a great town; and that was Manchester, old, ugly, smoky Manchester! dear, busy, earnest, working, noble Manchester; where their children had been born, (and perhaps where some lay buried), where their homes were, where God had cast their lives, and told them to work out their destiny.

"Hurrah for oud smoke-jack!" cried Bob, putting Franky softly down on the grass, before he whirled his hat round, preparatory for a cheer. "Hurrah! hurrah!" from all the men.

"There's the rim of my hat lying like a quoit[1] yonder," observed Bob quietly, as he replaced his brimless hat on his head, with the gravity of a judge.

"Here's the Sunday-school childer a-coming to sit on this shady side, and have their buns and milk. Hark! they're singing the Infant School grace."[2]

They sat close at hand, so that Franky could hear the words they sang, in rings of children, making (in their gay summer prints, newly donned for that week) garlands of little faces, all happy and bright upon the green hill side. One little "Dot" of a girl came shyly near Franky, whom she had long been watching, and threw her half bun at his side, and then ran away and hid herself, in very shame at the boldness of her own sweet impulse. She kept peeping behind her screen at

9. A mischievous spirit in Shakespeare's *Midsummer Night's Dream* (c. 1595).
1. Discus made of stone or metal, thrown as an exercise in strength or skill.

2. Grace: sung prayer from the *Infant School and Nursery Hymn Book* (1829); infant school: small, local schools, for children ages four to seven.

Franky all the time; and he meanwhile was almost too much pleased and happy to eat: the world was so beautiful; and men, and women, and children, all so tender and kind; so softened, in fact, by the beauty of that earth; so unconsciously touched by the Spirit of Love which was the Creator of that lovely earth. But the day drew to an end; the heat declined; the birds once more began their warblings; the fresh scents again hung about plant, and tree, and grass, betokening the fragrant presence of the reviving dew; and—the boat time was near. As they trod the meadow path once more, they were joined by many a party they had encountered during the day, all abounding in happiness, all full of the day's adventures. Long-cherished quarrels had been forgotten, new friendships formed. Fresh tastes and higher delights had been imparted that day. We have all of us one look, now and then, called up by some noble or loving thought, (our highest on earth), which will be our likeness in Heaven. I can catch the glance on many a face; the glancing light of the cloud of glory from Heaven, "which is our home." That look was present on numbers of hard-worked, wrinkled countenances, as they turned backwards to cast a longing, lingering look at Dunham woods, fast deepening into the blackness of night, but whose memory was to haunt in greenness and freshness many a loom, and workshop, and factory, with images of peace and beauty.

That night, as Libbie lay awake, revolving the incidents of the day, she caught Franky's voice through the open windows. Instead of the frequent moan of pain, he was trying to recall the burden[3] of one of the children's hymns:—

> "Here we suffer grief and pain,
> Here we meet to part again,
> In Heaven we part no more.
> Oh! that will be joyful," etc.[4]

She recalled his question, his whispered question, to her in the happiest part of the day. He asked, "Libbie, is Dunham like Heaven? The people here are as kind as angels; and I don't want Heaven to be more beautiful than this place. If you and mother would but die with me, I should like to die, and live always there." She had checked him, for she had feared he was impious; but now the young child's craving for some definite idea of the land to which his inner wisdom told him he was hastening, had nothing in it wrong or even sorrowful, for

> "In Heaven we part no more."

Michaelmas[5]

The church clocks had struck three; the crowds of gentlemen returning to business after their early dinners had disappeared within offices and warehouses; the streets were comparatively clear and quiet, and ladies were venturing to sally forth for their afternoon's shopping, and their afternoon calls.

Slowly, slowly along the streets, elbowed by life at every turn, a little funeral wound its quiet way. Four men bore along a child's coffin; two women, with bowed heads, followed meekly.

3. Refrain.
4. Hymn by Thomas Bilby, in *The Infant School Teachers' Assistant* (1831), edited by Bilby and

R. B. Ridgway.
5. September 29, a Christian holy day and the beginning of a new school year.

I need not tell you whose coffin it was, or who were these two mourners. All was now over with little Frank Hall; his romps, his games, his sickening, his suffering, his death. All was now over, but the Resurrection and the Life![6]

His mother walked as in a stupor. Could it be that he was dead? If he had been less of an object to her thoughts, less of a motive for her labours, she could sooner have realized it. As it was, she followed his poor, cast-off, worn-out body, as if she were borne along by some oppressive dream. If he were really dead, how could *she* be alive?

Libbie's mind was far less stunned, and consequently far more active than Margaret Hall's. Visions, as in a phantasmagoria, came rapidly passing before her,—recollections of the time (which seemed now so long ago) when the shadow of the feebly-waving arm first caught her attention; of the bright, strangely isolated day at Durnham Park, where the world had seemed so full of enjoyment, and beauty, and life; of the long-continued heat, through which poor Franky had panted his strength away in the little close room, where there was no escaping the hot rays of the afternoon sun; of the long nights, when his mother and she had watched by his side, as he moaned continually, whether awake or asleep; of the fevered moaning slumber of exhaustion; of the pitiful little self-upbraidings for his own impatience of suffering, (only impatience to his own eyes,—most true and holy patience in the sight of others); and then the fading away of life, the loss of power, the increased unconsciousness, the lovely look of angelic peace which followed the dark shadow on the countenance,—where was he—what was he now?

And so they laid him in his grave; and heard the solemn funeral words; but far off, in the distance—as if not addressed to them.

Margaret Hall bent over the grave to catch one last glance—she had not spoken, or sobbed, or done aught but shiver now and then, since the morning; but now her weight bore more heavily on Libbie's arm, and without sigh or sound she fell, an unconscious heap on the piled-up gravel. They helped Libbie to bring her round; but long after her half-opened eyes and altered breathings showed that her senses were restored, she lay, speechless and motionless, without attempting to rise from her strange bed, as if earth now contained nothing worth even that trifling exertion.

At last Libbie and she left that holy consecrated spot, and bent their steps back to the only place more consecrated still; where he had rendered up his spirit; and where memories of him haunted each common, rude piece of furniture that their eyes fell upon. As the woman of the house opened the door, she pulled Libbie on one side, and said,

"Anne Dixon has been across to see you; she wants to have a word with you."

"I cannot go now," replied Libbie, as she pushed hastily along in order to enter the room (*his* room), at the same time with the childless mother. For, as she anticipated, the sight of that empty spot, the glance at the uncurtained open window, letting in the fresh air, and the broad rejoicing light of day, where all had so long been darkened and subdued, unlocked the waters of the fountain, and long and shrill were the cries for her boy, that the poor woman uttered.

"Oh! dear Mrs Hall," said Libbie, herself drenched in tears, "do not take on so badly; I'm sure it would grieve *him* sore, if he was alive,—and you know he

6. John 11:25: "Jesus said unto her, I am the resurrection, and the life: he that believeth in me,   though he were dead, yet shall he live."

is,—Bible tells us so; and may be he's here, watching how we go on without him, and hoping we don't fret over-much."

Mrs Hall's sobs grew worse, and more hysterical.

"Oh! listen!" said Libbie, once more struggling against her own increasing agitation. "Listen! there's Peter chirping as he always does when he's put about, frightened like; and you know, he that's gone could never abide to hear the canary chirp in that shrill way."

Margaret Hall did check herself, and curb her expression of agony, in order not to frighten the little creature he had loved; and as her outward grief subsided, Libbie took up the old large Bible, which fell open at the never-failing comfort of the 14th chapter of St John's Gospel.[7] How often those large family Bibles do fall open at that chapter! as if, unused in more joyous and prosperous times, the soul went home to its words of loving sympathy when weary and sorrowful, just as the little child seeks the tender comfort of its mother in all its griefs and cares.

And Margaret put back her wet, ruffled, grey hair from her heated, tear-stained, woeful face, and listened with such earnest eyes; trying to form some idea of the "Father's House," where her boy had gone to dwell.

They were interrupted by a low tap at the door. Libbie went.

"Anne Dixon has watched you home, and wants to have a word with you," said the woman of the house in a whisper. Libbie went back, and closed the book with a word of explanation to Margaret Hall, and then ran down stairs to learn the reason of Anne's anxiety to see her.

"Oh, Libbie!" she burst out with, and then checking herself, into the remembrance of Libbie's last solemn duty; "how's Margaret Hall? But of course, poor thing, she'll fret a bit at first; she'll be some time coming round, mother says, seeing it's as well that poor lad is taken; for he'd always ha' been a cripple, and a trouble to her—he was a fine lad once, too."

She had come full of another and a different subject; but the sight of Libbie's sad weeping face, and the quiet subdued tone of her manner, made her feel it awkward to begin on any other theme than the one which filled up her companion's mind. To her last speech, Libbie answered sorrowfully,

"No doubt, Anne, it's ordered for the best; but oh! don't call him, don't think he could ever ha' been a trouble to his mother, though he were a cripple. She loved him all the more for each thing she had to do for him,—I'm sure I did." Libbie cried a little behind her apron. Anne Dixon felt still more awkward at introducing her discordant subject.

"Well!—Flesh is grass,[8] Bible says!" and having fulfilled the etiquette of quoting a text if possible, if not, of making a moral observation on the fleeting nature of earthly things, she thought she was at liberty to pass on to her real errand.

"You must not go on moping yourself, Libbie Marsh. What I wanted special for to see you this afternoon, was to tell you, you must come to my wedding to-morrow. Nancy Dawson has fallen sick, and there's none I should like to have bridesmaid in her place so well as you."

"To-morrow! Oh, I cannot; indeed I cannot."

"Why not?"

<hr />

7. John 14:2–3: "In my father's house are many mansions. . . . I go to prepare a place for you. And . . . I will come again and receive you unto myself; that where I am, there ye may be also."

8. See Isaiah 40:6.

Libbie did not answer, and Anne Dixon grew impatient.

"Surely in the name o' goodness, you're never going to baulk yourself of a day's pleasure for the sake of yon little cripple that's dead and gone?"

"No,—it's not baulking myself of,—don't be angry, Anne Dixon, with me please, but I don't think it would be pleasure to me—I don't feel as if I could enjoy it; thank you all the same, but I did love that little lad very dearly,—I did," (sobbing a little), "and I can't forget him, and make merry so soon."

"Well, I never!" exclaimed Anne, almost angrily.

"Indeed, Anne, I feel your kindness, and you and Bob have my best wishes,—that's what you have,—but even if I went, I should be thinking all day of him, and of his poor, poor mother, and they say it's bad to think over-much on them that is dead, at a wedding!"

"Nonsense!" said Anne, "I'll take the risk of the ill-luck. After all, what is marrying? just a spree, Bob says. He often says he does not think I shall make him a good wife, for I know nought about house-matters wi' working in a factory; but he says he'd rather be uneasy wi' me, than easy wi' any one else. There's love for you! And I tell him I'd rather have him tipsy than any one else sober."

"Oh, Anne Dixon, hush! you don't know yet what it is to have a drunken husband! I have seen something of it; father used to get fuddled: and in the long run it killed mother, let alone—Oh, Anne, God above only knows what the wife of a drunken man has to bear. Don't tell," said she, lowering her voice, "but father killed our little baby in one of his bouts; mother never looked up again, nor father either, for that matter, only his was in a different way. Mother will have gotten to little Jeannie now, and they'll be so happy together,—and perhaps Franky too. Oh!" said she, recovering herself from her train of thought, "never say aught lightly of the wife's lot whose husband is given to drink."

"Dear! what a preachment! I tell you what, Libbie! you're as born an old maid as ever I saw. You'll never be married, to either drunken or sober."

Libbie's face went rather red, but without losing its meek expression.

"I know that as well as you can tell me. And more reason, therefore, that as God has seen fit to keep me out o' woman's natural work, I should try and find work for myself. I mean," said she, seeing Anne Dixon's puzzled look, "that as I know I'm never like for to have a home of my own, or a husband, who would look to me to make all straight, or children to watch over and care for, all which I take to be woman's natural work, I must not lose time in fretting and fidgeting after marriage, but just look about me for somewhat else to do. I can see many a one misses it in this. They will hanker after what is ne'er likely to be theirs, instead of facing it out, and settling down to be old maids; and as old maids, just looking round for the odd jobs God leaves in the world for such as old maids to do,—there's plenty of such work,—and there's the blessing of God on them as does it." Libbie was almost out of breath at this outpouring of what had long been her inner thoughts.

"That's all very true, I make no doubt, for them as is to be old maids; but as I'm not, (please God, to-morrow comes), you might have spared your breath to cool your porridge.[9] What I want to know is, whether you'll be bridesmaid to-morrow or not. Come now, do! it will do you good, after all your watching, and working, and slaving yourself for that poor Franky Hall."

---

9. A Lancashire saying.

"It was one of my odd jobs," said Libbie, smiling, though her eyes were brimming over with tears. "But, dear Anne," continued she, recovering herself, "I could not do it to-morrow; indeed I could not!"

"And I can't wait," said Anne Dixon, almost sulkily. "Bob and I put if off from to-day because of the funeral, and Bob had set his heart on its being on Michaelmas-day; and mother says the goose won't keep beyond to-morrow. Do come! father finds eatables, and Bob finds drink, and we shall be so jolly! And after we've been to church, we're to walk round the town in pairs; white satin ribbon in our bonnets, and refreshment at any public-house we like, Bob says. And after dinner, there's to be a dance. Don't be a fool; you can do no good by staying. Margaret Hall will have to go out washing, I'll be bound."

"Yes! she must go to Mrs Wilkinson's, and for that matter I must go working too. Mrs Williams has been after me to make her girl's winter things ready; only I could not leave Franky, he clung so to me."

"Then you won't be bridesmaid! Is that your last word?"

"It is; you must not be angry with me, Anne Dixon," said Libbie, deprecatingly. But Anne was gone without a reply.

With a heavy heart Libbie mounted the little staircase. For she felt how ungracious her refusal of Anne's kindness must appear to one, who understood so little the feelings which rendered her acceptance of it a moral impossibility.

On opening the door, she saw Margaret Hall, with the Bible open on the table before her. For she had puzzled out the place where Libbie was reading, and with her finger under the line, was spelling out the words of consolation, piecing the syllables together aloud, with the earnest anxiety of comprehension with which a child first learns to read. So Libbie took the stool by her side, before she was aware that any one had entered the room.

"What did she want you for?" asked Margaret. "But I can guess: she wanted you to be at th'wedding as is to come off this week, they say. Ay! they'll marry, and laugh, and dance, all as one as if my boy was alive," said she, bitterly; "well, he was neither kith nor kin of yours, so I maun[1] try and be thankful for what you've done for him, and not wonder at your forgetting him afore he's well settled in his grave."

"I never can forget him, and I'm not going to the wedding," said Libbie, gently, for she understood the mother's jealousy of her dead child's claims.

"I must go work at Mrs Williams's to-morrow," she said in explanation, for she was unwilling to boast of the tender fond regret which had been her principal motive for declining Anne's invitation.

"And I mun[2] go washing, just as if nothing had happened," sighed forth Mrs Hall. "And I mun come home at night, and find his place empty, and all still where I used to be sure of hearing his voice, ere ever I got up the stair. No one will ever call me mother again!"

She fell a crying pitifully, and Libbie could not speak for her own emotion for some time. But during this silence she put the key stone in the arch of thoughts she had been building up for many days; and when Margaret was again calm in her sorrow, Libbie said, "Mrs Hall, I should like—would you like me to come for to live here altogether?"

---

1. To manage to do.   2. Must.

Margaret Hall looked up with a sudden light on her countenance, which encouraged Libbie to go on.

"I could sleep with you, and pay half, you know; and we should be together in the evenings, and her as was home first would watch for the other,—and" (dropping her voice) "we could talk of him at nights, you know."

She was going on, but Mrs Hall interrupted her.

"Oh! Libbie Marsh! and can you really think of coming to live wi' me! I should like it above—But no! it must not be; you've no notion on what a creature I am at times. More like a mad one, when I'm in a rage; and I can't keep it down. I seem to get out of bed wrong side in the morning, and I must have my passion out with the first person I meet. Why, Libbie," said she, with a doleful look of agony on her face, "I even used to fly out on him, poor sick lad as he was, and you may judge how little I can keep it down frae that. No! you must not come. I must live alone now," sinking her voice into the low tones of despair. But Libbie's resolution was brave and strong:

"I'm not afraid," said she, smiling. "I know you better than you know yourself, Mrs Hall. I've seen you try of late to keep it down, when you've been boiling over, and I think you'll go on a-doing so. And at any rate, when you've had your fit out you're very kind; and I can forget if you have been a bit put out. But I'll try not to put you out. Do let me come; I think *he* would like us to keep together. I'll do my very best to make you comfortable."

"It's me! It's me as will be making your life miserable with my temper, or else, God knows how my heart clings to you. You and me is folk alone in the world, for we both loved one who is dead, and who had none else to love him. If you will live with me, Libbie, I'll try as I never did afore, to be gentle and quiet-tempered. Oh! will you try me, Libbie Marsh?"

So, out of the little grave, there sprang a hope and a resolution, which made life an object to each of the two.

When Elizabeth Marsh returned home the next evening from her day's labours, Anne (Dixon no longer) crossed over, all in her bridal finery, to endeavour to induce her to join the dance going on in her father's house.

"Dear Anne! this is good of you, a-thinking of me to-night," said Libbie, kissing her. "And though I cannot come, (I've promised Mrs Hall to be with her), I shall think on you, and trust you'll be happy; I have got a little needle-case,[3] I looked out for you,—stay, here it is—I wish it were more, only—"

"Only—I know what—you've been a-spending all your money in nice things for poor Franky. Thou'rt a real good 'un, Libbie, and I'll keep your needle-book to my dying day, that I will."

Seeing Anne in such a friendly mood emboldened Libbie to tell her of her change of place; of her intention of lodging henceforward with Margaret Hall.

"Thou never will! Why, father and mother are as fond of thee as can be,—they'll lower thy rent, if that's what it is; and thou know'st they never grudge thee bit or drop. And Margaret Hall of all folk to lodge wi'! She's such a Tartar![4] Sooner than not have a quarrel, she'd fight right hand against left. Thou'lt have no peace of thy life. What on earth can make you think of such a thing, Libbie Marsh?"

3. Small fabric folder for keeping sewing needles,   4. A fearsome or ferocious person.
often decorated in cross-stitch or embroidery.

"She'd be so lonely without me," pleaded Libbie. "I'm sure I could make her happier (even if she does scold me a bit now and then) then she'd be living alone. And I'm not afraid of her; and I mean to do my best not to vex her; and it will ease her heart, may be, to talk to me at times about Franky. I shall often see your father and mother, and I shall always thank them for their kindness to me. But they have you, and little Mary, and poor Mrs Hall has no one."

Anne could only repeat "Well! I never!" and hurry off to tell the news at home.

But Libbie was right. Maragret Hall is a different woman to the scold of the neighbourhood she once was; touched and softened by the two purifying angels, Sorrow and Love. And it is beautiful to see her affection, her reverence for Libbie Marsh. Her dead mother could hardly have cared for her more tenderly than does the hard-featured washerwoman, not long ago so fierce and unwomanly. Libbie herself has such peace shining on her countenance, as almost makes it beautiful, as she renders the services of a daughter to Franky's mother—no longer the desolate, lonely orphan, a stranger on the earth.

Do you ever read the moral concluding sentence of a story? I never do; but I once (in the year 1811, I think) heard of a deaf old lady living by herself, who did; and as she may have left some descendants with the same amiable peculiarity, I will put in for their benefit what I believe to be the secret of Libbie's piece of mind, the real reason why she no longer feels oppressed at her own loneliness in the world.

She has a purpose in life, and that purpose is a holy one.

1847

HARRIET BEECHER STOWE
1811–1896

Few writers affect their cultures to the extent that Harriet Beecher Stowe did with the publication of her two novels treating the subject of slavery, *Uncle Tom's Cabin* (1852) and *Dred: A Tale of the Dismal Swamp* (1856). Born in what was then the rural town of Litchfield, Connecticut, to a family embroiled in the religious controversies of her day, Stowe became a leader in the cultural vanguard of her times. She is, perhaps, best remembered for her contributions to the American anti-slavery movement, but her writing also contributed to the definition of three critical aspects of American identity: gender, spirituality, and social class. In addition, her novels and short stories, characterized by attention to local dialects and habits, participated in the international movement that would come to be known in the later nineteenth century as literary realism.

Stowe was an extraordinary child of an extraordinary family. Like all her siblings, she was bright, well educated, and destined by her parents to contribute to her world. Nevertheless, early-nineteenth-century gender conventions would have made it hard to predict that this seventh child of the Reverend Lyman Beecher and his wife Roxanna would be the best remembered among their children. After all, her father was deeply involved in fighting for the soul of American Protestantism, and her brothers carried on this fight in their individual ways as ordained ministers.

Stowe's childhood was marked by three tragedies: one was the loss of her mother; the others, her failure to experience the love and presence of Jesus Christ that is central to Calvinism and her father's disappointment at that failure. She suffered a dual sense of having lost her mother's love too soon and of being essentially unworthy of God's love and her father's. Stowe, like her sisters Isabelle and Catharine Beecher, was expected to play an auxiliary (though no less crucial) role as helpmeet to a "naturally" more important male minister. The sisters did fulfill these expectations but in ways that both illustrated and shaped changes in America over the course of the nineteenth century. Catharine cared for her twice-widowed father and never married; Isabelle and Harriet both married ministers; all three became prominent cultural activists. In 1832, at age twenty-one, Stowe moved with her family to the rough border city of Cincinnati, Ohio, where her father established the first Protestant divinity school west of the Mississippi—the Lane Theological Seminary. Four years later, she married the widowed Reverend Calvin Ellis Stowe, who was a minister and teacher at Lane. Later, Stowe followed her husband's career as a professor of Greek back to Connecticut and then to Maine. Eventually, Stowe's success as a writer allowed them to move to a fashionable neighborhood in Hartford, Connecticut, where Stowe would be close to her family until her death in 1896.

Stowe found the key to her political, religious, and aesthetic beliefs during her years as a young wife. Cincinnati, bordering free and slave states, provided her firsthand experience with former slaves. While the Stowes' middle-class status was assured, their monetary woes meant that much of the grueling labor of cooking and cleaning for a large family of young children fell to Stowe alone, since she could not afford to hire adequate household help. Her feelings of helplessness and despair were exacerbated when disease attacked her family. In both her voluminous personal correspondence and in her early experiments with published writings, Stowe articulated her conviction that the personal was the political and the spiritual. Much "that is in" *Uncle Tom's Cabin,* Stowe later wrote, "had its roots in the awful scenes and bitter sorrows of that summer" of 1847 when her sixth child died of cholera. Both *Uncle Tom's Cabin* and *Dred* depict the love and loss of children as the common denominator of humanity.

Stowe's life of obscure genteel poverty ended with the publication of her first full-length novel, *Uncle Tom's Cabin,* in 1852. First published as a serial in an abolitionist newspaper (the *National Era*), the novel sold over 300,000 copies in its first year (earning Stowe $10,000 in the first three months) and went on to be one of the most popular novels ever published in America and beyond. *Uncle Tom's Cabin* had an unprecedented relevance in the wake of the passing of the Fugitive Slave Law (1850), which required everyone to assist in returning escaped slaves to their "masters." This law brought the debate about slavery into parlors and kitchens across America. Two more anti-slavery books quickly followed: *The Key to "Uncle Tom's Cabin"* (1853) and *Dred: A Tale of the Great Dismal Swamp. The Key* is a nonfiction account of the sources from which Stowe crafted her novel; *Dred* is a novel that focuses on the high personal cost of the economic, legal, and moral morass of slavery. Stowe also wrote a series of four historical novels about New England, including *The Minister's Wooing* (1859), which depicts the spiritual struggles of ordinary people within highly particularized environments. These books laid the foundations for the "local color" and "realism" movements of the later nineteenth century. Stowe also wrote a variety of popular nonfiction books and articles, including a travelogue, a household manual, and biographies of biblical heroines.

Uncle Tom's Cabin, seven chapters of which we include here, features four analogous plots locked together by the character of Uncle Tom. Each of the plots describes the suffering of the protagonists under slavery and the particular efforts of these protagonists to achieve their freedom. The main narrative strategy of the novel is sentimental; that is, Stowe intends to produce strong feelings of pity and identification. These feelings are intended to break down apparent differences so that the more authentic bonds of similarities can be recognized. On the level of plot, for example, the protagonists span a continuum of color and condition from the white child, Eva, to the white yet older "young mas'r George," to the mulatto, Eliza, to the "coal black Tom." The strong analogies among the stories of these characters belie the differences upon which racialized slavery rests: white/black, free/slave, human/thing. More important, perhaps, is the way that Stowe tries to force the reader to recognize her similarities with the characters and her implicit participation in the evils of slavery. Stowe's explicitly didactic and political goal is to encourage her readers to become heroes, like her characters, in the national drama. Though a "serious" book, *Uncle Tom's Cabin* also showcases Stowe's humor and her ability to capture the essences of character in the minutiae of language, dress, and gesture. She is one of the first white writers to depict black characters subverting the power of whites by playing upon white prejudice.

The following chapters focus on Tom as he is sold "downriver" into increasingly degraded forms of slavery. Over the course of these chapters, Stowe depicts Tom's resistance to the dehumanization of slavery as a form of Christian heroism that is extreme but also exemplary. The action begins in the parlor of the Shelby plantation of Kentucky, where debt is forcing Mr. Shelby to sell his most valuable "hand," Tom, and the attractive boy, Harry, to a slave trader in order to avoid having to sell all the slaves and break up the household as a whole. It ends following Tom's death, back at the Shelby plantation, which the Shelby son, "young mas'r George," is reorganizing into a free labor farm to prevent the repetition of Tom's fate. In between, Stowe presents several different but analogous models of resistance, from the story of Eliza, who flees the Shelby plantation in order to save her son, to the story of Eva, who dies in an unsuccessful effort to persuade her parents to forgo slave ownership. Throughout the novel, Stowe insists on the connection between the black and white characters; the fictionalized setting and the culture of 1850s America; the narrator and the reader—connected by a shared humanity shaped by love of one's children.

From Uncle Tom's Cabin

Chapter I
In Which the Reader Is Introduced to a Man of Humanity

Late in the afternoon of a chilly day in February, two gentlemen were sitting alone over their wine, in a well-furnished dining parlor, in the town of P——[1] in Kentucky. There were no servants present, and the gentlemen, with chairs closely approaching, seemed to be discussing some subject with great earnestness.

For convenience' sake, we have said, hitherto, two *gentlemen*. One of the parties, however, when critically examined, did not seem, strictly speaking, to come under the species. He was a short thick-set man, with coarse commonplace features, and that swaggering air of pretension which marks a low man who is trying

---

1. By literary convention, the blank masks a real name.

to elbow his way upward in the world. He was much overdressed, in a gaudy vest of many colors, a blue neckerchief, bedropped gayly with yellow spots, and arranged with a flaunting tie, quite in keeping with the general air of the man. His hands, large and coarse, were plentifully bedecked with rings; and he wore a heavy gold watchchain, with a bundle of seals of portentous size, and a great variety of colors, attached to it,—which, in the ardor of conversation, he was in the habit of flourishing and jingling with evident satisfaction. His conversation was in free and easy defiance of Murray's Grammar,[2] and was garnished at convenient intervals with various profane expressions, which not even the desire to be graphic in our account shall induce us to transcribe.

His companion, Mr. Shelby, had the appearance of a gentleman; and the arrangements of the house, and the general air of the housekeeping, indicated easy, and even opulent, circumstances. As we before stated, the two were in the midst of an earnest conversation.

"That is the way I should arrange the matter," said Mr. Shelby.

"I can't make trade that way,—I positively can't, Mr. Shelby," said the other, holding up a glass of wine between his eye and the light.

"Why, the fact is, Haley, Tom is an uncommon fellow; he is certainly worth that sum anywhere,—steady, honest, capable, manages my whole farm like a clock."

"You mean honest, as niggers go," said Haley, helping himself to a glass of brandy.

"No; I mean, really, Tom is a good, steady, sensible, pious fellow. He got religion at a camp-meeting, four years ago; and I believe he really *did* get it. I've trusted him, since then, with everything I have,—money, house, horses,—and let him come and go round the country; and I always found him true and square in everything."

"Some folks don't believe there is pious niggers, Shelby," said Haley, with a candid flourish of his hand, "but *I do*. I had a fellow, now, in this yer last lot I took to Orleans,—'t was as good as a meetin', now, really, to hear that critter pray; and he was quite gentle and quiet like. He fetched me a good sum, too, for I bought him cheap of a man that was 'bliged to sell out; so I realized six hundred on him. Yes, I consider religion a valeyable thing in a nigger, when it's the genuine article, and no mistake."

"Well, Tom's got the real article, if ever a fellow had," rejoined the other. "Why, last fall, I let him go to Cincinnati alone, to do business for me, and bring home five hundred dollars. 'Tom,' says I to him, 'I trust you, because I think you're a Christian,—I know you wouldn't cheat.' Tom comes back, sure enough; I knew he would. Some low fellows, they say, said to him, 'Tom, why don't you make tracks for Canada?'[3] 'Ah, master trusted me, and I couldn't,'—they told me about it. I am sorry to part with Tom, I must say. You ought to let him cover the whole balance of the debt; and you would, Haley, if you had any conscience."

"Well, I've got just as much conscience as any man in business can afford to keep,—just a little, you know, to swear by, as 'twere," said the trader, jocularly; "and, then, I'm ready to do anything in reason to 'blige friends; but this yer, you

2. The most popular guide to English grammar in the United States.
3. Canada—a British province—was the most common destination for escaped slaves; British law by this time made both slavery and the slave trade illegal.

see, is a leetle too hard on a fellow,—a leetle too hard." The trader sighed contemplatively, and poured out some more brandy.

"Well then, Haley, how will you trade?" said Mr. Shelby, after an uneasy interval of silence.

"Well, haven't you a boy or gal that you could throw in with Tom?"

"Hum!—none that I could well spare; to tell the truth, it's only hard necessity makes me willing to sell at all. I don't like parting with any of my hands, that's a fact."

Here the door opened, and a small quadroon boy,[4] between four and five years of age, entered the room. There was something in his appearance remarkably beautiful and engaging. His black hair, fine as floss silk, hung in glossy curls about his round dimpled face, while a pair of large dark eyes, full of fire and softness, looked out from beneath the rich, long lashes, as he peered curiously into the apartment. A gay robe of scarlet and yellow plaid, carefully made and neatly fitted, set off to advantage the dark and rich style of his beauty; and a certain comic air of assurance, blended with bashfulness, showed that he had been not unused to being petted and noticed by his master.

"Hulloa, Jim Crow!"[5] said Mr. Shelby, whistling, and snapping a bunch of raisins towards him, "pick that up, now!"

The child scampered, with all his little strength, after the prize, while his master laughed.

"Come here, Jim Crow," said he. The child came up, and the master patted the curly head, and chucked him under the chin.

"Now, Jim, show this gentleman how you can dance and sing." The boy commenced one of those wild, grotesque songs common among the Negroes, in a rich, clear voice, accompanying his singing with many evolutions of the hands, feet, and whole body, all in perfect time to the music.

"Bravo!" said Haley, throwing him a quarter of an orange.

"Now, Jim, walk like old Uncle Cudjoe when he has the rheumatism," said his master.

Instantly the flexible limbs of the child assumed the appearance of deformity and distortion, as, with his back humped up, and his master's stick in his hand, he hobbled about the room, his childish face drawn into a doleful pucker, and spitting from right to left, in imitation of an old man.

Both gentlemen laughed uproariously.

"Now, Jim," said his master, "show us how old Elder Robbins leads the psalm." The boy drew his chubby face down to a formidable length, and commenced toning a psalm tune through his nose with imperturbable gravity.

"Hurrah! bravo! what a young un!" said Haley; "that chap's a case, I'll promise. Tell you what," said he, suddenly clapping his hand on Mr. Shelby's shoulder, "fling in that chap and I'll settle the business,—I will. Come, now, if that an't doing the thing up about the rightest!"

At this moment, the door was pushed gently open, and a young quadroon woman, apparently about twenty-five, entered the room.

There needed only a glance from the child to her, to identify her as its mother. There was the same rich, full, dark eye, with its long lashes; the same ripples of

---

4. Nineteenth-century Americans had an elaborate vocabulary to describe varying amounts of what they considered "black" versus "white"

blood. A "quadroon" is one-quarter black.
5. Generic and disrespectful term for African Americans.

silky black hair. The brown of her complexion gave way on the cheek to a perceptible flush, which deepened as she saw the gaze of the strange man fixed upon her
in bold and undisguised admiration. Her dress was of the neatest possible fit, and
set off to advantage her finely moulded shape; a delicately formed hand and a
trim foot and ankle were items of appearance that did not escape the quick eye of
the trader, well used to run up at a glance the points of a fine female article.

"Well, Eliza?" said her master, as she stopped and looked hesitatingly at him.

"I was looking for Harry, please, sir;" and the boy bounded toward her, showing his spoils, which he had gathered in the skirt of his robe.

"Well, take him away, then," said Mr. Shelby; and hastily she withdrew, carrying the child on her arm.

"By Jupiter," said the trader, turning to him in admiration, "there's an article,
now! You might make your fortune on that ar gal in Orleans, any day. I've seen
over a thousand, in my day, paid down for gals not a bit handsomer."

"I don't want to make my fortune on her," said Mr. Shelby, dryly; and, seeking to turn the conversation, he uncorked a bottle of fresh wine, and asked his
companion's opinion of it.

"Capital, sir,—first chop!" said the trader; then turning, and slapping his
hand familiarly on Shelby's shoulder, he added,—

"Come, how will you trade about the gal?—what shall I say for her—what'll
you take?"

"Mr. Haley, she is not to be sold," said Shelby. "My wife would not part with
her for her weight in gold."

"Ay, ay! women always say such things, cause they han't no sort of calculation. Just show 'em how many watches, feathers, and trinkets one's weight in gold
would buy, and that alters the case, I reckon."

"I tell you, Haley, this must not be spoken of; I say no, and I mean no," said
Shelby, decidedly.

"Well, you'll let me have the boy, though," said the trader; "you must own
I've come down pretty handsomely for him."

"What on earth can you want with the child?" said Shelby.

"Why, I've got a friend that's going into this yer branch of the business,—
wants to buy up handsome boys to raise for the market. Fancy articles entirely,—
sell for waiters, and so on, to rich 'uns, that can pay for handsome 'uns. It sets off
one of yer great places,—a real handsome boy to open door, wait, and tend. They
fetch a good sum; and this little devil is such a comical, musical concern, he's just
the article."

"I would rather not sell him," said Mr. Shelby, thoughtfully; "the fact is, sir,
I'm a humane man, and I hate to take the boy from his mother, sir."

"Oh, you do?—La! yes,—something of that ar natur. I understand, perfectly. It
is mighty onpleasant getting on with women, sometimes. I al'ays hates these yer
screechin' screamin' times. They are *mighty* onpleasant; but, as I manages business,
I generally avoids 'em, sir. Now, what if you get the girl off for a day, or a week, or
so; then the thing's done quietly,—all over before she comes home. Your wife might
get her some ear-rings, or a new gown, or some such truck, to make up with her."

"I'm afraid not."

"Lor bless ye, yes! These critters an't like white folks, you know; they gets over
things, only manage right. Now, they say," said Haley, assuming a candid and confidential air, "that this kind o' trade is hardening to the feelings; but I never found
it so. Fact is, I never could do things up the way some fellers manage the business.

I've seen 'em as would pull a woman's child out of her arms, and set him up to sell, and she screechin' like mad all the time;—very bad policy,—damages the article,— makes 'em quite unfit for service sometimes. I knew a real handsome gal once, in Orleans, as was entirely ruined by this sort o' handling. The fellow that was trading for her didn't want her baby; and she was one of your real high sort, when her blood was up. I tell you, she squeezed up her child in her arms, and talked, and went on real awful. It kinder makes my blood run cold to think on't; and when they carried off the child, and locked her up, she jest went ravin' mad, and died in a week. Clear waste, sir, of a thousand dollars, jest for want of management,— there's where 'tis. It's always best to do the humane thing, sir; that's been *my* experience." And the trader leaned back in his chair, and folded his arms, with an air of virtuous decision, apparently considering himself a second Wilberforce.[6]

The subject appeared to interest the gentleman deeply; for while Mr. Shelby was thoughtfully peeling an orange, Haley broke out afresh, with becoming diffidence, but as if actually driven by the force of truth to say a few words more.

"It don't look well, now, for a feller to be praisin' himself; but I say it jest because it's the truth. I believe I'm reckoned to bring in about the finest droves of niggers that is brought in,—at least, I've been told so; if I have once, I reckon I have a hundred times, all in good case,—fat and likely, and I lose as few as any man in the business. And I lays it all to my management, sir; and humanity, sir, I may say, is the great pillar of *my* management."

Mr. Shelby did not know what to say, and so he said, "Indeed!"

"Now, I've been laughed at for my notions, sir, and I've been talked to. They an't pop'lar, and they an't common; but I stuck to 'em, sir; I've stuck to 'em, and realized well on 'em; yes, sir, they have paid their passage, I may say," and the trader laughed at his joke.

There was something so piquant and original in these elucidations of humanity, that Mr. Shelby could not help laughing in company. Perhaps you laugh too, dear reader, but you know humanity comes out in a variety of strange forms nowadays, and there is no end to the odd things that humane people will say and do.

Mr. Shelby's laugh encouraged the trader to proceed.

"It's strange now, but I never could beat this into people's heads. Now, there was Tom Loker, my old partner, down in Natchez; he was a clever fellow, Tom was, only the very devil with niggers,—on principle 'twas, you see, for a better-hearted feller never broke bread; 'twas his *system*, sir. I used to talk to Tom. 'Why, Tom,' I used to say, 'when your gals takes on and cry, what's the use o' crackin' on 'em over the head, and knockin' on 'em round? It's ridiculous,' says I, 'and don't do no sort o' good. Why, I don't see no harm in their cryin',' says I; 'it's natur,' says I, 'and if natur can't blow off one way, it will another. Besides Tom,' says I, 'it jest spiles your gals; they get sickly and down in the mouth; and sometimes they gets ugly,—particular yallow[7] gals do,—and it's the devil and all gettin' on 'em broke in. Now,' says I, 'why can't you kinder coax 'em up, and speak 'em fair? Depend on it, Tom, a little humanity, thrown in along, goes a heap further than all your jawin' and crackin'; and it pays better,' says I, 'depend on 't.' But Tom couldn't get the hang on 't; and he spiled so many for me, that I had to break off with him, though he was a good-hearted fellow, and as fair a business hand as is goin'."

---

6. William Wilberforce (1759–1833), a member of Britain's Parliament who founded the Society   for the Abolition of Slavery.
7. Mixed-race person of light skin.

"And do you find your ways of managing do the business better than Tom's?" said Mr. Shelby.

"Why, yes, sir, I may say so. You see, when I any ways can, I takes a leetle care about the onpleasant parts, like selling young uns and that,—get the gals out of the way,—out of sight, out of mind, you know,—and when it's clean done, and can't be helped, they naturally gets used to it. 'Tan't,[8] you know, as if it was white folks, that's brought up in the way of 'spectin' to keep their children and wives, and all that. Niggers, you know, that's fetched up properly han't no kind of 'spectations of no kind; so all these things comes easier."

"I'm afraid mine are not properly brought up, then," said Mr. Shelby.

"S'pose not; you Kentucky folks spile your niggers. You mean well by 'em, but 'tan't no real kindness, arter all. Now, a nigger, you see, what's got to be hacked and tumbled round the world, and sold to Tom, and Dick, and the Lord knows who, 'tan't no kindness to be givin' on him notions and expectations, and bringin' on him up too well, for the rough and tumble comes all the harder on him arter. Now, I venture to say, your niggers would be quite chop-fallen in a place where some of your plantation niggers would be singing and whooping like all possessed. Every man, you know, Mr. Shelby, naturally thinks well of his own ways; and I think I treat niggers just about as well as it's ever worth while to treat 'em."

"It's a happy thing to be satisfied," said Mr. Shelby, with a slight shrug, and some perceptible feelings of a disagreeable nature.

"Well," said Haley, after they had both silently picked their nuts for a season, "what do you say?"

"I'll think the matter over, and talk with my wife," said Mr. Shelby. "Meantime, Haley, if you want the matter carried on in the quiet way you speak of, you'd best not let your business in this neighborhood be known. It will get out among my boys, and it will not be a particularly quiet business getting away any of my fellows, if they know it, I'll promise you."

"Oh, certainly, by all means, mum! of course. But I'll tell you, I'm in a devil of a hurry, and shall want to know, as soon as possible, what I may depend on," said he, rising and putting on his overcoat.

"Well, call up this evening, between six and seven, and you shall have my answer," said Mr. Shelby, and the trader bowed himself out of the apartment.

"I'd like to have been able to kick the fellow down the steps," said he to himself, as he saw the door fairly closed, "with his impudent assurance; but he knows how much he has me at advantage. If anybody had ever said to me that I should sell Tom down south to one of those rascally traders, I should have said, 'Is thy servant a dog, that he should do this thing?' And now it must come, for aught I see. And Eliza's child, too! I know that I shall have some fuss with wife about that; and, for that matter, about Tom, too. So much for being in debt,—heigh-ho! The fellow sees his advantage, and means to push it."

Perhaps the mildest form of the system of slavery is to be seen in the State of Kentucky. The general prevalence of agricultural pursuits of a quiet and gradual nature, not requiring those periodic seasons of hurry and pressure that are called for in the business of more southern districts, makes the task of the Negro a more healthful and reasonable one; while the master, content with a more gradual style of acquisition, has not those temptations to hardheartedness which always overcome frail

8. Contraction for "It is not" ('Tis not).

human nature when the prospect of sudden and rapid gain is weighed in the balance, with no heavier counterpoise than the interests of the helpless and unprotected.

Whoever visits some estates there, and witnesses the good-humored indulgence of some masters and mistresses, and the affectionate loyalty of some slaves, might be tempted to dream the oft-fabled poetic legend of a patriarchal institution, and all that; but over and above the scene there broods a portentous shadow,—the shadow of *law*. So long as the law considers all these human beings, with beating hearts and living affections, only as so many *things* belonging to a master,—so long as the failure, or misfortune, or imprudence, or death of the kindest owner may cause them any day to exchange a life of kind protection and indulgence for one of hopeless misery and toil,—so long it is impossible to make anything beautiful or desirable in the best-regulated administration of slavery.

Mr. Shelby was a fair average kind of man, good natured and kindly, and disposed to easy indulgence of those around him, and there had never been a lack of anything which might contribute to the physical comfort of the Negroes on his estate. He had, however, speculated largely and quite loosely; had involved himself deeply, and his notes to a large amount had come into the hands of Haley; and this small piece of information is the key to the preceding conversation.

Now it had so happened that, in approaching the door, Eliza had caught enough of the conversation to know that a trader was making offers to her master for somebody.

She would gladly have stopped at the door to listen, as she came out; but her mistress just then calling, she was obliged to hasten away.

Still she thought she heard the trader make an offer for her boy;—could she be mistaken? Her heart swelled and throbbed, and she involuntarily strained him so tight that the little fellow looked up into her face in astonishment.

"Eliza, girl, what ails you to-day?" said her mistress, when Eliza had upset the wash-pitcher, knocked down the work-stand, and finally was abstractedly offering her mistress a long nightgown in place of the silk dress she had ordered her to bring from the wardrobe.

Eliza started. "Oh, missis!" she said, raising her eyes; then, bursting into tears, she sat down in a chair, and began sobbing.

"Why, Eliza, child! what ails you?" said her mistress.

"Oh, Missis," said Eliza, "there's been a trader talking with Master in the parlor! I heard him."

"Well, silly child, suppose there has."

"Oh, Missis, *do* you suppose Mas'r would sell my Harry?" And the poor creature threw herself into a chair, and sobbed convulsively.

"Sell him! No, you foolish girl! you know your master never deals with those southern traders, and never means to sell any of his servants, as long as they behave well. Why, you silly child, who do you think would want to buy your Harry? Do you think all the world are set on him as you are, you goosie! Come, cheer up, and hook my dress. There now, put my back hair up in that pretty braid you learnt the other day, and don't go listening at doors any more."

"Well, but, missis, *you* never would give your consent—to—to"—

"Nonsense, child! to be sure I shouldn't. What do you talk so for? I would as soon have one of my own children sold. But really, Eliza, you are getting altogether too proud of that little fellow. A man can't put his nose into the door, but you think he must be coming to buy him."

Reassured by her mistress's confident tone, Eliza proceeded nimbly and adroitly with her toilet, laughing at her own fears, as she proceeded.

Mrs. Shelby was a woman of a high class, both intellectually and morally. To that natural magnanimity and generosity of mind which one often marks as characteristic of the women of Kentucky, she added high moral and religious sensibility and principle, carried out with great energy and ability into practical results. Her husband, who made no professions to any particular religious character, nevertheless, reverenced and respected the consistency of hers, and stood, perhaps, a little in awe of her opinion. Certain it was that he gave her unlimited scope in all her benevolent efforts for the comfort, instruction, and improvement of her servants, though he never took any decided part in them himself. In fact, if not exactly a believer in the doctrine of the efficacy of the extra good works of saints, he really seemed somehow or other to fancy that his wife had piety and benevolence enough for two,—to indulge a shadowy expectation of getting into heaven through her superabundance of qualities to which he made no particular pretension.

The heaviest load on his mind, after his conversation with the trader, lay in the foreseen necessity of breaking to his wife the arrangement contemplated,— meeting the importunities and opposition which he knew he should have reason to encounter.

Mrs. Shelby, being entirely ignorant of her husband's embarrassments, and knowing only the general kindliness of his temper, had been quite sincere in the entire incredulity with which she had met Eliza's suspicions. In fact, she dismissed the matter from her mind, without a second thought; and being occupied in preparations for an evening visit, it passed out of her thoughts entirely.

* * *

Chapter V
Showing the Feelings of Living Property on Changing Owners

Mr. and Mrs. Shelby had retired to their apartment for the night. He was lounging in a large easy chair, looking over some letters that had come in the afternoon mail, and she was standing before her mirror, brushing out the complicated braids and curls in which Eliza had arranged her hair; for, noticing her pale cheeks and haggard eyes, she had excused her attendance that night, and ordered her to bed. The employment, naturally enough, suggested her conversation with the girl in the morning; and, turning to her husband, she said, carelessly,—

"By the by, Arthur, who was that low-bred fellow that you lugged in to our dinner-table to-day?"

"Haley is his name," said Shelby, turning himself rather uneasily in his chair, and continuing with his eyes fixed on a letter.

"Haley! Who is he, and what may be his business here, pray?"

"Well, he's a man that I transacted some business with, last time I was at Natchez," said Mr. Shelby.

"And he presumed on it to make himself quite at home, and call and dine here, ay?"

"Why, I invited him; I had some accounts with him," said Shelby.

"Is he a Negro-trader?" said Mrs. Shelby, noticing a certain embarrassment in her husband's manner.

"Why, my dear, what put that into your head?" said Shelby, looking up.

"Nothing,—only Eliza came in here, after dinner, in a great worry, crying and taking on, and said you were talking with a trader, and that she heard him make an offer for her boy,—the ridiculous little goose!"

"She did, hey?" said Mr. Shelby, returning to his paper, which he seemed for a few moments quite intent upon, not perceiving that he was holding it bottom upwards.

"It will have to come out," said he, mentally; "as well now as ever."

"I told Eliza," said Mrs. Shelby, as she continued brushing her hair, "that she was a little fool for her pains, and that you never had anything to do with that sort of persons. Of course, I knew you never meant to sell any of our people,— least of all, to such a fellow."

"Well, Emily," said her husband, "so I have always felt and said; but the fact is that my business lies so that I cannot get on without. I shall have to sell some of my hands."

"To that creature? Impossible! Mr. Shelby, you cannot be serious."

"I'm sorry to say that I am," said Mr. Shelby. "I've agreed to sell Tom."

"What! our Tom?—that good, faithful creature!—been your faithful servant from a boy! Oh, Mr. Shelby!—and you have promised him his freedom, too,— you and I have spoken to him a hundred times of it. Well, I can believe anything now,—I can believe *now* that you could sell little Harry, poor Eliza's only child!" said Mrs. Shelby, in a tone between grief and indignation.

"Well, since you must know all, it is so. I have agreed to sell Tom and Harry both; and I don't know why I am to be rated, as if I were a monster, for doing what every one does every day."

"But why, of all others, choose these?" said Mrs. Shelby. "Why sell them, of all on the place, if you must sell at all?"

"Because they will bring the highest sum of any,—that's why. I could choose another, if you say so. The fellow made me a high bid on Eliza, if that would suit you any better," said Mr. Shelby.

"The wretch!" said Mrs. Shelby, vehemently.

"Well, I didn't listen to it, a moment,—out of regard to your feelings, I wouldn't,—so give me some credit."

"My dear," said Mrs. Shelby, recollecting herself, "forgive me. I have been hasty. I was surprised, and entirely unprepared for this;—but surely you will allow me to intercede for these poor creatures. Tom is a noble-hearted, faithful fellow, if he is black. I do believe, Mr. Shelby, that if he were put to it, he would lay down his life for you."

"I know it,—I dare say;—but what's the use of all this?—I can't help myself."

"Why not make a pecuniary sacrifice? I'm willing to bear my part of the inconvenience. Oh, Mr. Shelby, I have tried—tried most faithfully, as a Christian woman should—to do my duty to these poor, simple, dependent creatures. I have cared for them, instructed them, watched over them, and known all their little cares and joys, for years; and how can I ever hold up my head again among them, if, for the sake of a little paltry gain, we sell such a faithful, excellent, confiding creature as poor Tom, and tear from him in a moment all we have taught him to love and value? I have taught them the duties of the family, of parent and child, and husband and wife; and how can I bear to have this open acknowledgment that we care for no tie, no duty, no relation, however sacred, compared with money? I have talked with Eliza about her boy,—her duty to him as a Christian mother, to watch over him, pray for him, and bring him up in a Christian way; and now what can I say, if you tear him away, and sell him, soul and body, to a profane, unprincipled man, just to save a little money? I have told her that one soul is worth more than all the money in the world, and how will she believe me when she sees us turn round and sell her child?—sell him, perhaps, to certain ruin of body and soul!

"I'm sorry you feel so about it, Emily,—indeed I am," said Mr. Shelby; "and I respect your feelings, too, though I don't pretend to share them to their full extent; but I tell you now, solemnly, it's of no use,—I can't help myself. I didn't mean to tell you this, Emily, but in plain words, there is no choice between selling these two and selling everything. Either they must go, or *all* must. Haley has come into possession of a mortgage, which, if I don't clear off with him directly, will take everything before it. I've raked, and scraped, and borrowed, and all but begged,— and the price of these two was needed to make up the balance, and I had to give them up. Haley fancied the child; he agreed to settle the matter that way and no other. I was in his power, and *had* to do it. If you feel so to have them sold, would it be any better to have *all* sold?"

Mrs. Shelby stood like one stricken. Finally, turning to her toilet, she rested her face in her hands, and gave a sort of groan.

"This is God's curse on slavery!—a bitter, bitter, most accursed thing!—a curse to the master and a curse to the slave! I was a fool to think I could make anything good out of such a deadly evil. It is a sin to hold a slave under laws like ours,—I always felt it was,—I always thought so when I was a girl,—I thought so still more after I joined the church, but I thought I could gild it over,—I thought, by kindness, and care, and instruction, I could make the condition of mine better than freedom,—fool that I was!"

"Why, wife, you are getting to be an abolitionist, quite."

"Abolitionist! if they knew all I know about slavery they *might* talk! We don't need them to tell us; you know I never thought that slavery was right,—never felt willing to own slaves."

"Well, therein you differ from many wise and pious men," said Mr. Shelby. "You remember Mr. B's sermon, the other Sunday?"

"I don't want to hear such sermons; I never wish to hear Mr. B in our church again. Ministers can't help the evil, perhaps,—can't cure it, any more than we can,—but defend it!—it always went against my common sense. And I think you didn't think much of that sermon, either."

"Well," said Shelby, "I must say these ministers sometimes carry matters further than we poor sinners would exactly dare to do. We men of the world must wink pretty hard at various things, and get used to a deal that isn't the exact thing. But we don't quite fancy, when women and ministers come out broad and square, and go beyond us in matters of either modesty or morals, that's a fact. But now, my dear, I trust you see the necessity of the thing, and you see that I have done the very best that circumstances would allow."

"Oh, yes, yes!" said Mrs. Shelby, hurriedly and abstractedly fingering her gold watch,—"I haven't any jewelry of any amount," she added, thoughtfully; "but would not this watch do something?—it was an expensive one when it was bought. If I could only at least save Eliza's child, I would sacrifice anything I have."

"I'm sorry, very sorry, Emily," said Mr. Shelby, "I'm sorry that this takes hold of you so; but it will do no good. The fact is, Emily, the thing's done; the bills of sale are already signed, and in Haley's hands; and you must be thankful it is no worse. That man has had it in his power to ruin us all,—and now he is fairly off. If you knew the man as I do, you'd think that we had a narrow escape."

"Is he so hard, then?"

"Why, not a cruel man, exactly, but a man of leather,—a man alive to nothing but trade and profit,—cool, and unhesitating, and unrelenting, as death and the grave. He'd sell his own mother at a good percentage,—not wishing the old woman any harm, either."

"And this wretch owns that good, faithful Tom, and Eliza's child!"

"Well, my dear, the fact is that this goes rather hard with me; it's a thing I hate to think of. Haley wants to drive matters, and take possession to-morrow. I'm going to get out my horse bright and early, and be off. I can't see Tom, that's a fact; and you had better arrange to drive somewhere, and carry Eliza off. Let the thing be done when she is out of sight."

"No, no," said Mrs. Shelby; "I'll be in no sense accomplice or help in this cruel business. I'll go and see poor old Tom, God help him, in his distress! They shall see, at any rate, that their mistress can feel for and with them. As to Eliza, I dare not think about it. The Lord forgive us! What have we done, that this cruel necessity should come on us?"

There was one listener to this conversation whom Mr. and Mrs. Shelby little suspected.

Communicating with their apartment was a large closet, opening by a door into the outer passage. When Mrs. Shelby had dismissed Eliza for the night her feverish and excited mind had suggested the idea of this closet; and she had hidden herself there, and with her ear pressed close against the crack of the door, had lost not a word of the conversation.

When the voices died into silence, she rose and crept stealthily away. Pale, shivering, with rigid features and compressed lips, she looked an entirely altered being from the soft and timid creature she had been hitherto. She moved cautiously along the entry, paused one moment at her mistress's door and raised her hands in mute appeal to Heaven, and then turned and glided into her own room. It was a quiet, neat apartment, on the same floor with her mistress. There was the pleasant sunny window, where she had often sat singing at her sewing; there, a little case of books, and various little fancy articles, ranged by them, the gifts of Christmas holidays; there was her simple wardrobe in the closet and in the drawers:—here was, in short, her home; and, on the whole, a happy one it had been to her. But there, on the bed, lay her slumbering boy, his long curls falling negligently around his unconscious face, his rosy mouth half open, his little fat hands thrown out over the bedclothes, and a smile spread like a sunbeam over his whole face.

"Poor boy! poor fellow!" said Eliza; "they have sold you! but your mother will save you yet!"

No tear dropped over that pillow; in such straits as these the heart has no tears to give,—it drops only blood, bleeding itself away in silence. She took a piece of paper and a pencil, and wrote hastily,—

"Oh, Missis! dear Missis! don't think me ungrateful,—don't think hard of me, any way,—I heard all you and master said to-night. I am going to try to save my boy,—you will not blame me! God bless and reward you for all your kindness!"

Hastily folding and directing this, she went to a drawer and made up a little package of clothing for her boy, which she tied with a handkerchief firmly round her waist; and, so fond is a mother's remembrance, that, even in the terrors of that hour, she did not forget to put in the little package one or two of his favorite toys, reserving a gayly painted parrot to amuse him when she should be called on to awaken him. It was some trouble to arouse the little sleeper; but, after some effort, he sat up, and was playing with his bird, while his mother was putting on her bonnet and shawl.

"Where are you going, mother?" said he, as she drew near the bed, with his little coat and cap.

His mother drew near, and looked so earnestly into his eyes, that he at once divined that something unusual was the matter.

"Hush, Harry," she said; "mustn't speak loud, or they will hear us. A wicked man was coming to take little Harry away from his mother, and carry him 'way off in the dark; but mother won't let him,—she's going to put on her little boy's cap and coat, and run off with him, so the ugly man can't catch him."

Saying these words, she had tied and buttoned on the child's simple outfit, and, taking him in her arms, she whispered to him to be very still; and, opening a door in her room which led into the outer veranda, she glided noiselessly out.

It was a sparkling, frosty, starlight night, and the mother wrapped the shawl close round her child, as, perfectly quiet with vague terror, he clung round her neck.

Old Bruno, a great Newfoundland, who slept at the end of the porch, rose, with a low growl, as she came near. She gently spoke his name, and the animal, an old pet and playmate of hers, instantly, wagging his tail, prepared to follow her, though apparently revolving much, in his simple dog's head, what such an indiscreet midnight promenade might mean. Some dim ideas of imprudence or impropriety in the measure seemed to embarrass him considerably; for he often stopped, as Eliza glided forward, and looked wistfully, first at her and then at the house, and then, as if reassured by reflection, he pattered along after her again. A few minutes brought them to the window of Uncle Tom's cottage, and Eliza, stopping, tapped lightly on the window-pane.

The prayer-meeting at Uncle Tom's had, in the order of hymn-singing, been protracted to a very late hour; and, as Uncle Tom had indulged himself in a few lengthy solos afterwards, the consequence was, that, although it was now between twelve and one o'clock, he and his worthy helpmeet were not yet asleep.

"Good Lord! what's that?" said Aunt Chloe, starting up and hastily drawing the curtain. "My sakes alive, if it an't Lizy! Get on your clothes, old man, quick!— there's old Bruno, too, a-pawin' round; what on airth! I'm gwine to open the door."

And, suiting the action to the word, the door flew open, and the light of the tallow candle, which Tom had hastily lighted, fell on the haggard face and dark, wild eyes of the fugitive.

"Lord bless you!—I'm skeered to look at ye, Lizy! Are ye tuck sick, or what's come over ye?"

"I'm running away,—Uncle Tom and Aunt Chloe,—carrying off my child,— Master sold him!"

"Sold him?" echoed both, lifting up their hands in dismay.

"Yes, sold him!" said Eliza, firmly; "I crept into the closet by Mistress's door to-night, and I heard Master tell Missis that he had sold my Harry, and you, Uncle Tom, both, to a trader; and that he was going off this morning on his horse, and that the man was to take possession to-day."

Tom had stood, during this speech, with his hands raised, and his eyes dilated, like a man in a dream. Slowly and gradually, as its meaning came over him, he collapsed, rather than seated himself, on his old chair, and sunk his head down upon his knees.

"The good Lord have pity on us!" said Aunt Chloe. "Oh, it don't seem as if it was true! What has he done, that Mas'r should sell *him?*"

"He hasn't done anything,—it isn't for that. Master don't want to sell; and Missis,—she's always good. I heard her plead and beg for us; he told her 'twas no use; that he was in this man's debt, and that this man had got the power over him; and that if he didn't pay him off clear, it would end in his having to sell the place and all the people, and move off. Yes, I heard him say there was no choice between selling these two and selling all, the man was driving him so hard. Master said he was sorry; but oh, Missis,—you ought to have heard her talk! If she an't a Christian and an angel, there never was one. I'm a wicked girl to leave her so; but, then, I can't help it. She said, herself, one soul was worth more than the world; and this boy has a soul, and if I let him be carried off, who knows what'll become of it? It must be right; but, if it an't right, the Lord forgive me, for I can't help doing it!"

"Well, old man!" said Aunt Chloe, "why don't you go, too? Will you wait to be toted down river, where they kill niggers with hard work and starving? I'd a heap rather die than go there, any day! There's time for ye,—be off with Lizy,— you've got a pass to come and go any time. Come, bustle up, and I'll get your things together."

Tom slowly raised his head, and looked sorrowfully but quietly around, and said,—

"No, no,—I an't going. Let Eliza go,—it's her right! I wouldn't be the one to say no,—'tan't in *natur* for her to stay; but you heard what she said! If I must be sold, or all the people on the place, and everything go to rack, why, let me be sold. I s'pose I can b'ar it as well as any on 'em," he added, while something like a sob and a sigh shook his broad, rough chest convulsively. "Mas'r always found me on the spot,—he always will. I never have broke trust, nor used my pass no ways contrary to my word, and I never will. It's better for me alone to go, than to break up the place and sell all. Mas'r an't to blame, Chloe, and he'll take care of you and the poor"—

Here he turned to the rough trundle-bed full of little woolly heads, and broke fairly down. He leaned over the back of the chair, and covered his face with his large hands. Sobs, heavy, hoarse, and loud, shook the chair, and great tears fell through his fingers on the floor: just such tears, sir, as you dropped into the coffin where lay your first-born son; such tears, woman, as you shed when you heard the cries of your dying babe. For, sir, he was a man,—and you are but another man. And, woman, though dressed in silk and jewels, you are but a woman, and, in life's great straits and mighty griefs, ye feel but one sorrow!

"And now," said Eliza, as she stood in the door, "I saw my husband only this afternoon, and I little knew then what was to come. They have pushed him to the very last standing-place, and he told me, to-day, that he was going to run away. Do try, if you can, to get word to him. Tell him how I went, and why I went; and tell him I'm going to try and find Canada. You must give my love to him, and tell him, if I never see him again,"—she turned away, and stood with her back to them for a moment, and then added, in a husky voice, "tell him to be as good as he can, and try and meet me in the kingdom of heaven."

"Call Bruno in there," she added. "Shut the door on him, poor beast! He mustn't go with me!"

A few last words and tears, a few simple adieus and blessings, and, clasping her wondering and affrighted child in her arms, she glided noiselessly away.

* * *

Chapter VII
The Mother's Struggle

It is impossible to conceive of a human creature more wholly desolate and forlorn than Eliza, when she turned her footsteps from Uncle Tom's cabin.

Her husband's suffering and dangers, and the danger of her child, all blended in her mind, with a confused and stunning sense of the risk she was running, in leaving the only home she had ever known, and cutting loose from the protection of a friend whom she loved and revered. Then there was the parting from every familiar object,—the place where she had grown up, the trees under which she had played, the groves where she had walked many an evening in happier days, by the side of her young husband,—everything, as it lay in the clear, frosty starlight, seemed to speak reproachfully to her, and ask her whither she could go from a home like that?

But stronger than all was maternal love, wrought into a paroxysm of frenzy by the near approach of a fearful danger. Her boy was old enough to have walked by her side, and, in an indifferent case, she would only have led him by the hand; but now the bare thought of putting him out of her arms made her shudder, and she strained him to her bosom with a convulsive grasp, as she went rapidly forward.

The frosty ground creaked beneath her feet, and she trembled at the sound; every quaking leaf and fluttering shadow sent the blood backward to her heart, and quickened her footsteps. She wondered within herself at the strength that seemed to be come upon her; for she felt the weight of her boy as if it had been a feather, and every flutter of fear seemed to increase the supernatural power that bore her on, while from her pale lips burst forth, in frequent ejaculations, the prayer to a Friend above,—"Lord, help! Lord, save me!"

If it were *your* Harry, mother, or your Willie, that were going to be torn from you by a brutal trader, to-morrow morning,—if you had seen the man, and heard that the papers were signed and delivered, and you had only from twelve o'clock till morning to make good your escape,—how fast could *you* walk? How many miles could you make in those few brief hours, with the darling at your bosom,—the little sleepy head on your shoulder,—the small, soft arms trustingly holding on to your neck?

For the child slept. At first, the novelty and alarm kept him waking; but his mother so hurriedly repressed every breath or sound, and so assured him that if he were only still she would certainly save him, that he clung quietly round her neck, only asking, as he found himself sinking to sleep,—

"Mother, I don't need to keep awake, do I?"

"No, my darling; sleep, if you want to."

"But, mother, if I do get asleep, you won't let him get me?"

"No! so may God help me!" said his mother, with a paler cheek and a brighter light in her large, dark eyes.

"You're *sure,* an't you, mother?"

"Yes, sure!" said the mother, in a voice that startled herself; for it seemed to her to come from a spirit within, that was no part of her; and the boy dropped his little weary head on her shoulder and was soon asleep. How the touch of those warm arms, and gentle breathings that came in her neck, seemed to add fire and spirit to her movements. It seemed to her as if strength poured into her in electric streams, from every gentle touch and movement of the sleeping, confiding child. Sublime is the dominion of the mind over the body, that, for a time, can make flesh and nerve impregnable, and string the sinews like steel, so that the weak become so mighty.

The boundaries of the farm, the grove, the wood-lot, passed by her dizzily, as she walked on; and still she went, leaving one familiar object after another, slacking not, pausing not, till reddening daylight found her many a long mile from all traces of any familiar objects upon the open highway.

She had often been, with her mistress, to visit some connections, in the little village of T——, not far from the Ohio River, and knew the road well. To go thither, to escape across the Ohio River, were the first hurried outlines of her plan of escape; beyond that, she could only hope in God.

When horses and vehicles began to move along the highway, with that alert perception peculiar to a state of excitement, and which seems to be a sort of inspiration, she became aware that her headlong pace and distracted air might bring on her remark and suspicion. She therefore put the boy on the ground, and, adjusting her dress and bonnet, she walked on at as rapid a pace as she thought consistent with the preservation of appearances. In her little bundle she had provided a store of cakes and apples, which she used as expedients for quickening the speed of the child, rolling the apple some yards before them, when the boy would run with all his might after it; and this ruse, often repeated, carried them over many a half-mile.

After a while, they came to a thick patch of woodland, through which murmured a clear brook. As the child complained of hunger and thirst, she climbed over the fence with him; and, sitting down behind a large rock which concealed them from the road, she gave him a breakfast out of her little package. The boy wondered and grieved that she could not eat; and when, putting his arms round her neck, he tried to wedge some of his cake into her mouth, it seemed to her that the rising in her throat would choke her.

"No, no, Harry darling! mother can't eat till you are safe! We must go on,— on,—till we come to the river!" And she hurried again into the road, and again constrained herself to walk regularly and composedly forward.

She was many miles past any neighborhood where she was personally known. If she should chance to meet any who knew her, she reflected that the well-known kindness of the family would be of itself a blind to suspicion, as making it an unlikely supposition that she could be a fugitive. As she was also so white as not to be known as of colored lineage, without a critical survey, and her child was white also, it was much easier for her to pass on unsuspected.

On this presumption, she stopped at noon at a neat farmhouse, to rest herself, and buy some dinner for her child and self; for, as the danger decreased with the distance, the supernatural tension of the nervous system lessened, and she found herself both weary and hungry.

The good woman, kindly and gossiping, seemed rather pleased than otherwise with having somebody come in to talk with; and accepted, without examination, Eliza's statement that she "was going on a little piece, to spend a week with her friends,"—all which she hoped in her heart might prove strictly true.

An hour before sunset, she entered the village of T——, by the Ohio River, weary and footsore, but still strong in heart. Her first glance was at the river, which lay, like Jordan, between her and the Canaan of liberty[9] on the other side.

It was now early spring, and the river was swollen and turbulent; great cakes of floating ice were swinging heavily to and fro in the turbid waters. Owing to the peculiar form of the shore on the Kentucky side, the land bending far out into the water, the ice had been lodged and detained in great quantities, and the narrow channel which swept round the bend was full of ice, piled one cake over another, thus forming a temporary barrier to the descending ice, which lodged, and formed a great, undulating raft, filling up the whole river, and extending almost to the Kentucky shore.

Eliza stood, for a moment, contemplating this unfavorable aspect of things, which she saw at once must prevent the usual ferry-boat from running, and then turned into a small public house on the bank, to make a few inquiries.

The hostess, who was busy in various fizzing and stewing operations over the fire, preparatory to the evening meal, stopped, with a fork in her hand, as Eliza's sweet and plaintive voice arrested her.

"What is it?" she said.

"Isn't there any ferry or boat, that takes people over to B——, now?" she said.

"No, indeed!" said the woman; "the boats has stopped running."

Eliza's look of dismay and disappointment struck the woman, and she said, inquiringly,—

"May be you're wanting to get over?—anybody sick? Ye seem mighty anxious?"

"I've got a child that's very dangerous," said Eliza. "I never heard of it till last night, and I've walked quite a piece to-day, in hopes to get to the ferry."

"Well, now, that's onlucky," said the woman, whose motherly sympathies were much aroused; "I'm re'lly consarned for ye. Solomon!" she called, from the window, towards a small back building. A man, in leather apron and very dirty hands, appeared at the door.

"I say, Sol," said the woman, "is that ar man going to tote them bar'ls over to-night?"

"He said he should try, if 't was any way prudent," said the man.

"There's a man a piece down here, that's going over with some truck this evening, if he durs' to; he'll be in here to supper to-night, so you'd better set down and wait. That's a sweet little fellow," added the woman, offering him a cake.

But the child, wholly exhausted, cried with weariness.

"Poor fellow! he isn't used to walking, and I've hurried him on so," said Eliza.

"Well, take him into this room," said the woman, opening into a small bedroom, where stood a comfortable bed. Eliza laid the weary boy upon it, and held his hands in hers till he was fast asleep. For her there was no rest. As a fire in her bones, the thought of the pursuer urged her on; and she gazed with longing eyes on the sullen, surging waters that lay between her and liberty.

Here we must take our leave of her for the present, to follow the course of her pursuers.

Though Mrs. Shelby had promised that the dinner should be hurried on table, yet it was soon seen, as the thing has often been seen before, that it required more

---

9. The Ohio River is like the Jordan River, which   or the Promised Land of Exodus.
separated the Hebrews from the land of Canaan

than one to make a bargain. So, although the order was fairly given out in Haley's hearing, and carried to Aunt Chloe by at least half a dozen juvenile messengers, that dignitary only gave certain very gruff snorts, and tosses of her head, and went on with every operation in an unusually leisurely and circumstantial manner.

For some singular reason, an impression seemed to reign among the servants generally that Missis would not be particularly disobliged by delay; and it was wonderful what a number of counter accidents occurred constantly, to retard the course of things. One luckless wight contrived to upset the gravy; and then gravy had to be got up *de novo*,[1] with due care and formality, Aunt Chloe watching and stirring with dogged precision, answering shortly, to all suggestions of haste, that she "warn't a going to have raw gravy on the table, to help nobody's catchings." One tumbled down with the water, and had to go to the spring for more; and another precipitated the butter into the path of events; and there was from time to time giggling news brought into the kitchen that "Mas'r Haley was mighty oneasy, and that he couldn't sit in his cheer no ways, but was walkin' and stalkin' to the winders and through the porch."

"Sarves him right!" said Aunt Chloe, indignantly. "He'll get wus nor oneasy, one of these days, if he don't mend his ways. *His* master'll be sending for him, and then see how he'll look!"

"He'll go to torment and no mistake," said little Jake.

"He desarves it!" said Aunt Chloe, grimly; "he's broke a many, many, many hearts,—I tell ye all!" she said, stopping, with a fork uplifted in her hands;"it's like what Mas'r George reads in Ravelations,[2]—souls a callin' under the altar! and a callin' on the Lord for vengeance on sich!—and by and by the Lord he'll hear 'em,—so he will!"

Aunt Chloe, who was much revered in the kitchen, was listened to with open mouth; and, the dinner being now fairly sent in, the whole kitchen was at leisure to gossip with her and to listen to her remarks.

"Sich'll be burnt up forever, and no mistake; won't ther?" said Andy.

"I'd be glad to see it, I'll be boun'," said little Jake.

"Chil'en!" said a voice, that made them all start. It was Uncle Tom, who had come in, and stood listening to the conversation at the door.

"Chil'en!" he said. "I'm afeard you don't know what ye're sayin'. Forever is a *dre'ful* word, chil'en; it's awful to think on 't. You oughtenter wish that ar to any human crittur."

"We wouldn't to anybody but the soul-drivers," said Andy, "nobody can help wishing it to them, they's so awful wicked."

"Don't natur herself kinder cry out on 'em?" said Aunt Chloe. "Don't dey tear der suckin' baby right off his mother's breast, and sell him, and der little children as is crying and holding on by her clothes,—don't dey pull 'em off and sells 'em? Don't dey tear wife and husband apart?" said Aunt Chloe, beginning to cry, "when it's jest takin' the very life on 'em?—and all the while does they feel one bit,—don't dey drink and smoke, and take it oncommon easy? Lor', if the devil don't get them, what's he good for?" And Aunt Chloe covered her face with her checked apron, and began to sob in good earnest.

---

1. From scratch, anew.
2. The book of Revelation is one of the New Tes-
tament books containing a vision of the end of the world and the reward for good Christians.

"Pray for them that 'spitefully use you, the good book says," says Tom.

"Pray for 'em!" said Aunt Chloe; "Lor, it's too tough! I can't pray for 'em."

"It's natur, Chloe, and natur's strong," said Tom, "but the Lord's grace is stronger; besides, you oughter think what an awful state a poor crittur's soul's in that'll do them ar things,—you oughter thank God that you an't *like* him, Chloe. I'm sure I'd rather be sold, ten thousand times over, than to have all that ar poor crittur's got to answer for."

"So'd I, a heap," said Jake. "Lor, *shouldn't* we cotch it. Andy?"

Andy shrugged his shoulders, and gave an acquiescent whistle.

"I'm glad Mas'r didn't go off this morning, as he looked to," said Tom; "that ar hurt me more than sellin', it did. Mebbe it might have been natural for him, but 't would have come desp't hard on me, as has known him from a baby; but I've seen Mas'r, and I begin ter feel sort o' reconciled to the Lord's will now. Mas'r couldn't help hisself; he did right, but I'm feared things will be kinder goin' to rack, when I'm gone. Mas'r can't be spected to be a pryin' round everywhar, as I've done, a keepin' up all the ends. The boys all means well, but they's powerful car'less. That ar troubles me."

The bell here rang, and Tom was summoned to the parlor.

"Tom," said his master, kindly, "I want you to notice that I give this gentleman bonds to forfeit a thousand dollars if you are not on the spot when he wants you; he's going to-day to look after his other business, and you can have the day to yourself. Go anywhere you like, boy."

"Thank you, Mas'r," said Tom.

"And mind yerself," said the trader, "and don't come it over your master with any o' yer nigger tricks; for I'll take every cent out of him, if you an't thar. If he'd hear to me he wouldn't trust any on ye,—slippery as eels!"

"Mas'r," said Tom,—and he stood very straight,—"I was just eight years old when ole Missis put you into my arms, and you wasn't a year old. 'Thar,' says she, 'Tom, that's to be *your* young Mas'r; take good care on him,' says she. And now I jist ask you, Mas'r, have I ever broke word to you, or gone contrary to you, 'specially since I was a Christian?"

Mr. Shelby was fairly overcome, and the tears rose to his eyes.

"My good boy," said he, "the Lord knows you say but the truth; and if I was able to help it, all the world shouldn't buy you."

"And sure as I am a Christian woman," said Mrs. Shelby, "you shall be redeemed as soon as I can any way bring together means. Sir," she said to Haley, "take good account of whom you sell him to, and let me know."

"Lor, yes, for that matter," said the trader, "I may bring him up in a year, not much the wuss for wear, and trade him back."

"I'll trade with you then, and make it for your advantage," said Mrs. Shelby.

"Of course," said the trader, "all's equal with me; li'ves trade 'em up as down, so I does a good business. All I want is a livin', you know, ma'am; that's all any on us wants, I s'pose."

Mr. and Mrs. Shelby both felt annoyed and degraded by the familiar impudence of the trader, and yet both saw the absolute necessity of putting a constraint on their feelings. The more hopelessly sordid and insensible he appeared, the greater became Mrs. Shelby's dread of his succeeding in recapturing Eliza and her child, and of course the greater her motive for detaining him by every female artifice. She therefore graciously smiled, assented, chatted familiarly, and did all she could to make time pass imperceptibly.

At two o'clock Sam and Andy brought the horses up to the posts, apparently greatly refreshed and invigorated by the scamper of the morning.

Sam was there new oiled from dinner, with an abundance of zealous and ready officiousness. As Haley approached, he was boasting, in flourishing style, to Andy, of the evident and eminent success of the operation, now that he had "farly come to it."

"Your master, I s'pose, don't keep no dogs," said Haley, thoughtfully, as he prepared to mount.

"Heaps on 'em," said Sam, triumphantly; "thar's Bruno,—he's a roarer! and, besides that, 'bout every nigger of us keeps a pup of some natur or uther."

"Poh!" said Haley,—and he said something else, too, with regard to the said dogs, at which Sam muttered,—

"I don't see no use cussin' on 'em, no way."

"But your master don't keep no dogs (I pretty much know he don't) for trackin' out niggers."

Sam knew exactly what he meant, but he kept on a look of earnest and desperate simplicity.

"Our dogs all smells round consid'able sharp. I spect they's the kind, though they han't never had no practice. They's *far* dogs, though, at most anything, if you'd get 'em started. Here, Bruno," he called, whistling to the lumbering Newfoundland, who came pitching tumultuously toward them.

"You go hang!" said Haley, getting up. "Come, tumble up now."

Sam tumbled up accordingly, dexterously contriving to tickle Andy as he did so, which occasioned Andy to split out into a laugh, greatly to Haley's indignation, who made a cut at him with his riding-whip.

"I's 'stonished at yer, Andy," said Sam, with awful gravity. "This yer's a seris bisness, Andy. Yer mustn't be a makin' game. This yer an't no way to help Mas'r."

"I shall take the straight road to the river," said Haley, decidedly, after they had come to the boundaries of the estate. "I know the way of all of 'em,—they makes tracks for the underground."

"Sartin," said Sam, "dat's de idee. Mas'r Haley hits de thing right in de middle. Now, der's two roads to de river,—de dirt road and der pike,—which Mas'r means to take?"

Andy looked up innocently at Sam, surprised at hearing this new geographical fact, but instantly confirmed what he said by a vehement reiteration.

" 'Cause," said Sam, "I'd rather be 'clined to 'magine that Lizy'd take de dirt road, bein' it's the least travelled."

Haley, notwithstanding that he was a very old bird, and naturally inclined to be suspicious of chaff,[3] was rather brought up by this view of the case.

"If yer warn't both on yer such cussed liars, now!" he said, contemplatively, as he pondered a moment.

The pensive, reflective tone in which this was spoken appeared to amuse Andy prodigiously, and he drew a little behind, and shook so as apparently to run a

---

3. The unusable material left over after grain has been harvested.

great risk of falling off his horse, while Sam's face was immovably composed into the most doleful gravity.

"Course," said Sam, "Mas'r can do as he'd ruther; go de straight road, if Mas'r thinks best,—it's all one to us. Now, when I study 'pon it, I think the straight road de best, *decidedly*."

"She would naturally go a lonesome way," said Haley, thinking aloud, and not minding Sam's remark.

"Dar an't no sayin'," said Sam; "gals is pecular; they never does nothin' ye thinks they will; mose gen'lly the contrar. Gals is nat'lly made contrary; and so, if you thinks they've gone one road, it is sartin you'd better go t' other, and then you'll be sure to find 'em. Now, my private 'pinion is, Lizy took der dirt road; so I think we'd better take de straight one."

This profound generic view of the female sex did not seem to dispose Haley particularly to the straight road; and he announced decidedly that he should go the other, and asked Sam when they should come to it.

"A little piece ahead," said Sam, giving a wink to Andy with the eye which was on Andy's side of the head; and he added, gravely, "but I've studded on de matter, and I'm quite clar we ought not to go dat ar way. I nebber been over it no way. It's despit lonesome, and we might lose our way,—whar we'd come to, de Lord only knows."

"Nevertheless," said Haley, "I shall go that way."

"Now I think on 't, I think I hearn 'em tell that dat ar road was all fenced up and down by der creek, and thar, an't it, Andy?"

Andy wasn't certain; he'd only "hearn tell" about that road, but never been over it. In short, he was strictly noncommittal.

Haley, accustomed to strike the balance of probabilities between lies of greater or lesser magnitude, thought that it lay in favor of the dirt road aforesaid. The mention of the thing he thought he perceived was involuntary on Sam's part at first, and his confused attempts to dissuade him he set down to a desperate lying on second thoughts, as being unwilling to implicate Eliza.

When, therefore, Sam indicated the road, Haley plunged briskly into it, followed by Sam and Andy.

Now, the road, in fact, was an old one, that had formerly been a thoroughfare to the river, but abandoned for many years after the laying of the new pike. It was open for about an hour's ride, and after that it was cut across by various farms and fences. Sam knew this fact perfectly well,—indeed, the road had been so long closed up, that Andy had never heard of it. He therefore rode along with an air of dutiful submission, only groaning and vociferating occasionally that 'twas "desp't rough, and bad for Jerry's foot."

"Now, I jest give yer warning," said Haley, "I know yer; yer won't get me to turn off this yer road, with all yer fussin',—so you shet up!"

"Mas'r will go his own way!" said Sam, with rueful submission, at the same time winking most portentously to Andy, whose delight was now very near the explosive point.

Sam was in wonderful spirits,—professed to keep a very brisk lookout,—at one time exclaiming that he saw "a gal's bonnet" on the top of some distant eminence, or calling to Andy "if that thar wasn't 'Lizy' down in the hollow;" always making these exclamations in some rough or craggy part of the road, where the sudden quickening of speed was a special inconvenience to all parties concerned, and thus keeping Haley in a state of constant commotion.

After riding about an hour in this way, the whole party made a precipitate and tumultuous descent into a barnyard belonging to a large farming establishment. Not a soul was in sight, all the hands being employed in the fields; but, as the barn stood conspicuously and plainly square across the road, it was evident that their journey in that direction had reached a decided finale.

"Warn't dat ar what I telled Mas'r?" said Sam, with an air of injured innocence. "How does strange gentleman spect to know more about a country dan de natives born and raised?"

"You rascal!" said Haley, "you knew all about this."

"Didn't I tell yer I *know'd,* and yer wouldn't believe me? I telled Mas'r 'twas all shet up, and fenced up, and I didn't spect we could get through,—Andy heard me."

It was all too true to be disputed, and the unlucky man had to pocket his wrath with the best grace he was able, and all three faced to the right about, and took up their line of march for the highway.

In consequence of all the various delays, it was about three quarters of an hour after Eliza had laid her child to sleep in the village tavern that the party came riding into the same place. Eliza was standing by the window, looking out in another direction, when Sam's quick eye caught a glimpse of her. Haley and Andy were two yards behind. At this crisis, Sam contrived to have his hat blown off, and uttered a loud and characteristic ejaculation, which startled her at once; she drew suddenly back; the whole train swept by the window, round to the front door.

A thousand lives seemed to be concentrated in that one moment to Eliza. Her room opened by a side door to the river. She caught her child, and sprang down the steps towards it. The trader caught a full glimpse of her, just as she was disappearing down the bank, and throwing himself from his horse, and calling loudly on Sam and Andy, he was after her like a hound after a deer. In that dizzy moment her feet to her scarce seemed to touch the ground, and a moment brought her to the water's edge. Right on behind her they came; and, nerved with strength such as God gives only to the desperate, with one wild cry and flying leap, she vaulted sheer over the turbid current by the shore, on to the raft of ice beyond. It was a desperate leap,—impossible to anything but madness and despair; and Haley, Sam, and Andy instinctively cried out, and lifted up their hands, as she did it.

The huge green fragment of ice on which she alighted pitched and creaked as her weight came on it, but she stayed there not a moment. With wild cries and desperate energy she leaped to another and still another cake;—stumbling,—leaping,—slipping,—springing upwards again! Her shoes are gone,—her stockings cut from her feet,—while blood marked every step; but she saw nothing, felt nothing, till dimly, as in a dream, she saw the Ohio side, and a man helping her up the bank.

"Yer a brave gal, now, whoever ye ar!" said the man, with an oath.[4]

Eliza recognized the voice and face of a man who owned a farm not far from her old home.

"Oh Mr. Symmes!—save me,—do save me,—do hide me!" said Eliza.

"Why, what's this?" said the man. "Why, if 't an't Shelby's gal!"

---

4. A swear word.

"My child!—this boy!—he'd sold him! There is his Mas'r," said she, pointing to the Kentucky shore. "Oh, Mr. Symmes, you've got a little boy!"

"So I have," said the man, as he roughly, but kindly, drew her up the steep bank. "Besides, you're a right brave gal. I like grit, wherever I see it."

When they had gained the top of the bank, the man paused. "I'd be glad to do something for ye," said he; "but then there's nowhar I could take ye. The best I can do is to tell ye to go *thar*," said he, pointing to a large white house which stood by itself off the main street of the village. "Go thar; they're kind folks. Thar's no kind o' danger but they'll help you,—they're up to all that sort o' thing."

"The Lord bless you!" said Eliza earnestly.

"No 'casion, no 'casion in the world," said the man. "What I've done's of no 'count."

"And oh, surely, sir, you won't tell any one!"

"Go to thunder, gal! What do you take a feller for? In course not," said the man. "Come, now, go along like a likely, sensible gal, as you are. You've arnt your liberty, and you shall have it, for all me."

The woman folded her child to her bosom, and walked firmly and swiftly away. The man stood and looked after her.

"Shelby, now, mebbe won't think this yer the most neighborly thing in the world; but what's a feller to do? If he catches one of my gals in the same fix, he's welcome to pay back. Somehow I never could see no kind o' crittur a strivin' and pantin', and trying to clar theirselves, with the dogs arter 'em, and go agin 'em. Besides, I don't see no kind of 'casion for me to be hunter and catcher for other folks, neither."

So spoke this poor, heathenish Kentuckian, who had not been instructed in his constitutional relations, and consequently was betrayed into acting in a sort of Christianized manner, which, if he had been better situated and more enlightened, he would not have been left to do.

Haley had stood a perfectly amazed spectator of the scene, till Eliza had disappeared up the bank, when he turned a blank, inquiring look on Sam and Andy.

"That ar was a tolable fair stroke of business," said Sam.

"The gal's got seven devils in her, I believe!" said Haley. "How like a wildcat she jumped!"

"Wal, now," said Sam, scratching his head, "I hope Mas'r'll scuse us tryin' dat ar road. Don't think I feel spry enough for dat ar, no way!" and Sam gave a hoarse chuckle.

"*You* laugh!" said the trader, with a growl.

"Lord bless you, Mas'r, I couldn't help it, now," said Sam, giving way to the long pent-up delight of his soul. "She looked so curi's a leapin' and springin'—ice a crackin'—and only to hear her,—plump! ker chunk! ker splash! Spring! Lord! how she goes it!" and Sam and Andy laughed till the tears rolled down their cheeks.

"I'll make yer laugh t' other side yer mouths!" said the trader, laying about their heads with his riding-whip.

Both ducked, and ran shouting up the bank, and were on their horses before he was up.

"Good evening, Mas'r!" said Sam, with much gravity. "I bery much spect Missis be anxious 'bout Jerry. Mas'r Haley won't want us no longer. Missis wouldn't hear of our ridin' the critters over Lizy's bridge to-night" and with a facetious poke into Andy's ribs, he started off, followed by the latter, at full speed,—their shouts of laughter coming faintly on the wind.

* * *

Chapter XIV
Evangeline

"*A young star! which shone
O'er life,—too sweet an image for such glass!
A lovely being, scarcely formed or moulded;
A rose with all its sweetest leaves yet folded.*"[5]

The Mississippi! How, as by an enchanted wand, have its scenes been changed, since Chateaubriand[6] wrote his prose-poetic description of it, as a river of mighty, unbroken solitudes, rolling amid undreamed wonders of vegetable and animal existence.

But, as in an hour, this river of dreams and wild romance has emerged to a reality scarcely less visionary and splendid. What other river of the world bears on its bosom to the ocean the wealth and enterprise of such another country?—a country whose products embrace all between the tropics and the poles! Those turbid waters, hurrying, foaming, tearing along, an apt resemblance of that headlong tide of business which is poured along its wave by a race more vehement and energetic than any the world ever saw. Ah! would that they did not also bear along a more fearful freight,—the tears of the oppressed, the sighs of the helpless, the bitter prayers of poor, ignorant hearts to an unknown God,—unknown, unseen, and silent, but who will yet "come out of his place to save all the poor of the earth!"

The slanting light of the setting sun quivers on the sea-like expanse of the river; the shivery canes, and the tall, dark cypress, hung with wreaths of dark, funereal moss, glow in the golden ray, as the heavily laden steamboat marches onward.

Piled with cotton-bales, from many a plantation, up over deck and sides, till she seems in the distance a square, massive block of gray, she moves heavily onward to the nearing mart. We must look some time among its crowded decks before we shall find again our humble friend Tom. High on the upper deck, in a little nook among the everywhere predominant cotton-bales, at last we may find him.

Partly from confidence inspired by Mr. Shelby's representations, and partly from the remarkably inoffensive and quiet character of the man, Tom had insensibly won his way far into the confidence of such a man as Haley.

At first he had watched him narrowly through the day, and never allowed him to sleep at night unfettered; but the uncomplaining patience and apparent contentment of Tom's manner led him gradually to discontinue these restraints, and for some time Tom had enjoyed a sort of parole of honor, being permitted to come and go freely where he pleased on the boat.

Ever quiet and obliging, and more than ready to lend a hand in every emergency which occurred among the workmen below, he had won the good opinion of all the hands, and spent many hours in helping them with as hearty a good-will as ever he worked on a Kentucky farm.

---

5. Lines from *Don Juan* (1819–24) by English poet George Gordon, Lord Byron (1788–1824).
6. François-René, vicomte de Chateaubriand (1768–1848), visited America during the 1790s and wrote about what he saw in a romantic manner.

When there seemed to be nothing for him to do, he would climb to a nook among the cotton-bales of the upper deck, and busy himself in studying over his Bible,—and it is there we see him now.

For a hundred or more miles above New Orleans, the river is higher than the surrounding country, and rolls its tremendous volume between massive levees twenty feet in height. The traveller from the deck of the steamer, as from some floating castle top, overlooks the whole country for miles and miles around. Tom, therefore, had spread out full before him, in plantation after plantation, a map of the life to which he was approaching.

He saw the distant slaves at their toil; he saw afar their villages of huts gleaming out in long rows on many a plantation, distant from the stately mansions and pleasure-grounds of the master;—and as the moving picture passed on, his poor, foolish heart would be turning backward to the Kentucky farm, with its old shadowy beeches,—to the master's house, with its wide, cool halls, and, near by, the little cabin, overgrown with the multiflora and bignonia. There he seemed to see familiar faces of comrades, who had grown up with him from infancy; he saw his busy wife, bustling in her preparations for his evening meal; he heard the merry laugh of his boys at their play, and the chirrup of the baby at his knee; and then, with a start, all faded, and he saw again the cane-brakes and cypresses and gliding plantations, and heard again the creaking and groaning of the machinery, all telling him too plainly that all that phase of life had gone by forever.

In such a case, you write to your wife, and send messages to your children; but Tom could not write,—the mail for him had no existence, and the gulf of separation was unbridged by even a friendly word or signal.

Is it strange, then, that some tears fall on the pages of his Bible, as he lays it on the cotton-bale, and, with patient finger, threading his slow way from word to word, traces out its promises? Having learned late in life, Tom was but a slow reader, and passed on laboriously from verse to verse. Fortunate for him was it that the book he was intent on was one which slow reading cannot injure,—nay, one whose words, like ingots of gold, seem often to need to be weighed separately, that the mind may take in their priceless value. Let us follow him a moment, as, pointing to each word, and pronouncing each half aloud, he reads,—

"Let—not—your—heart—be—troubled. In—my—Father's—house—are—many—mansions. I—go—to—prepare—a—place—for—you."[7]

Cicero,[8] when he buried his darling and only daughter, had a heart as full of honest grief as poor Tom's,—perhaps no fuller, for both were only men;—but Cicero could pause over no such sublime words of hope, and look to no such future reunion; and if he *had* seen them, ten to one he would not have believed,—he must fill his head first with a thousand questions of authenticity of manuscript, and correctness of translation. But, to poor Tom, there it lay, just what he needed, so evidently true and divine that the possibility of a question never entered his simple head. It must be true; for, if not true, how could he live?

As for Tom's Bible, though it had no annotations and helps in margin from learned commentators, still it had been embellished with certain way-marks and guide-boards of Tom's own invention, and which helped him more than the most learned expositions could have done. It had been his custom to get the Bible read

7. John 14:2.
8. Marcus Tullio Cicero (106 BCE–43 BCE), a   Roman statesman whose grief for his daughter almost destroyed him.

to him by his master's children, in particular by young Master George; and, as they read, he would designate, by bold, strong marks and dashes, with pen and ink, the passages which more particularly gratified his ear or affected his heart. His Bible was thus marked through, from one end to the other, with a variety of styles and designations; so he could in a moment seize upon his favorite passages, without the labor of spelling out what lay between them—and while it lay there before him, every passage breathing of some old home scene, and recalling some past enjoyment, his Bible seemed to him all of this life that remained, as well as the promise of a future one.

Among the passengers on the boat was a young gentleman of fortune and family, resident in New Orleans, who bore the name of St. Clare. He had with him a daughter between five and six years of age, together with a lady who seemed to claim relationship to both, and to have the little one especially under her charge.

Tom had often caught glimpses of this little girl,—for she was one of those busy, tripping creatures, that can be no more contained in one place than a sunbeam or a summer breeze,—nor was she one that, once seen, could be easily forgotten.

Her form was the perfection of childish beauty, without its usual chubbiness and squareness of outline. There was about it an undulating and aerial grace, such as one might dream of for some mythic and allegorical being. Her face was re-markable, less for its perfect beauty of feature than for a singular and dreamy earnestness of expression, which made the ideal start when they looked at her, and by which the dullest and most literal were impressed, without exactly know-ing why. The shape of her head and the turn of her neck and bust were peculiarly noble, and the long golden-brown hair that floated like a cloud around it, the deep spiritual gravity of her violet blue eyes, shaded by heavy fringes of golden brown,—all marked her out from other children, and made every one turn and look after her, as she glided hither and thither on the boat. Nevertheless, the little one was not what you would have called either a grave child or a sad one. On the contrary, an airy and innocent playfulness seemed to flicker like the shadow of summer leaves over her childish face, and around her buoyant figure. She was al-ways in motion, always with a half-smile on her rosy mouth, flying hither and thither, with an undulating and cloud-like tread, singing to herself as she moved, as in a happy dream. Her father and female guardian were incessantly busy in pursuit of her,—but, when caught, she melted from them again like a summer cloud; and as no word of chiding or reproof ever fell on her ear for whatever she chose to do, she pursued her own way all over the boat. Always dressed in white, she seemed to move like a shadow through all sorts of places, without contracting spot or stain; and there was not a corner or nook, above or below, where those fairy footsteps had not glided, and that visionary, golden head, with its deep blue eyes, fleeted along.

The fireman, as he looked up from his sweaty toil, sometimes found those eyes looking wonderingly into the raging depths of the furnace, and fearfully and pityingly at him, as if she thought him in some dreadful danger. Anon the steers-man at the wheel paused and smiled, as the picture-like head gleamed through the window of the round-house, and in a moment was gone again. A thousand times a day rough voices blessed her, and smiles of unwonted softness stole over hard faces, as she passed; and when she tripped fearlessly over dangerous places, rough, sooty hands were stretched involuntarily out to save her, and smooth her path.

Tom, who had the soft, impressible nature of his kindly race, ever yearning toward the simple and childlike, watched the little creature with daily increasing interest. To him she seemed something almost divine; and whenever her golden head and deep blue eyes peered out upon him from behind some dusky cotton-bale, or looked down upon him over some ridge of packages, he half believed that he saw one of the angels stepped out of his New Testament.

Often and often she walked mournfully round the place where Haley's gang of men and women sat in their chains. She would glide in among them, and look at them with an air of perplexed and sorrowful earnestness; and sometimes she would lift their chains with her slender hands, and then sigh woefully, as she glided away. Several times she appeared suddenly among them, with her hands full of candy, nuts, and oranges, which she would distribute joyfully to them, and then be gone again.

Tom watched the little lady a great deal, before he ventured on any overtures towards acquaintanceship. He knew an abundance of simple acts to propitiate and invite the approaches of the little people, and he resolved to play his part right skilfully. He could cut cunning little baskets out of cherry-stones, could make grotesque faces on hickory-nuts, or odd-jumping figures out of elder-pith, and he was a very Pan in the manufacture of whistles of all sizes and sorts. His pockets were full of miscellaneous articles of attraction, which he had hoarded in days of old for his master's children, and which he now produced, with commendable prudence and economy, one by one, as overtures for acquaintance and friendship.

The little one was shy, for all her busy interest in everything going on, and it was not easy to tame her. For a while, she would perch like a canary-bird on some box or package near Tom, while busy in the little arts aforenamed, and take from him, with a kind of grave bashfulness, the little articles he offered. But at last they got on quite confidential terms.

"What's little missy's name?" said Tom, at last, when he thought matters were ripe to push such an inquiry.

"Evangeline St. Clare," said the little one, "though papa and everybody else call me Eva. Now, what's your name?"

"My name's Tom; the little chil'en used to call me Uncle Tom, way back thar in Kentuck."

"Then I mean to call you Uncle Tom, because, you see, I like you," said Eva. "So, Uncle Tom, where are you going?"

"I don't know, Miss Eva."

"Don't know?" said Eva.

"No. I am going to be sold to somebody. I don't know who."

"My papa can buy you," said Eva, quickly; "and if he buys you, you will have good times. I mean to ask him to, this very day!"

"Thank you, my little lady," said Tom.

The boat here stopped at a small landing to take in wood, and Eva, hearing her father's voice, bounded nimbly away. Tom rose up, and went forward to offer his service in wooding, and soon was busy among the hands.

Eva and her father were standing together by the railings to see the boat start from the landing-place, the wheel had made two or three revolutions in the water, when, by some sudden movement, the little one suddenly lost her balance, and fell sheer over the side of the boat into the water. Her father, scarce knowing what he did, was plunging in after her, but was held back by some behind him, who saw that more efficient aid had followed his child.

Tom was standing just under her on the lower deck, as she fell. He saw her strike the water, and sink, and was after her in a moment. A broad-chested, strong-armed fellow, it was nothing for him to keep afloat in the water, till, in a moment or two, the child rose to the surface, and he caught her in his arms, and, swimming with her to the boat-side, handed her up, all dripping, to the grasp of hundreds of hands, which, as if they had all belonged to one man, were stretched eagerly out to receive her. A few moments more, and her father bore her, dripping and senseless, to the ladies' cabin, where, as is usual in cases of the kind, there ensued a very well-meaning and kind-hearted strife among the female occupants generally, as to who should do the most things to make a disturbance, and to hinder her recovery in every way possible.

It was a sultry, close day, the next day, as the steamer drew near to New Orleans. A general bustle of expectation and preparation was spread through the boat; in the cabin, one and another were gathering their things together, and arranging them, preparatory to going ashore. The steward and chambermaid, and all, were busily engaged in cleaning, furbishing, and arranging the splendid boat, preparatory to a grand *entrée*.

On the lower deck sat our friend Tom, with his arms folded, and anxiously, from time to time, turning his eyes towards a group on the other side of the boat.

There stood the fair Evangeline, a little paler than the day before, but otherwise exhibiting no traces of the accident which had befallen her. A graceful, elegantly formed young man stood by her, carelessly leaning one elbow on a bale of cotton, while a large pocket-book lay open before him. It was quite evident, at a glance, that the gentleman was Eva's father. There was the same noble cast of head, the same large blue eyes, the same golden-brown hair; yet the expression was wholly different. In the large, clear, blue eyes, though in form and color exactly similar, there was wanting that misty, dreamy depth of expression; all was clear, bold, and bright, but with a light wholly of this world: the beautifully cut mouth had a proud and somewhat sarcastic expression, while an air of free-and-easy superiority sat not ungracefully in every turn and movement of his fine form. He was listening, with a good-humored, negligent air, half comic, half contemptuous, to Haley, who was very volubly expatiating on the quality of the article for which they were bargaining.

"All the moral and Christian virtues bound in black morocco, complete!" he said, when Haley had finished. "Well, now, my good fellow, what's the damage, as they say in Kentucky; in short, what's to be paid out for this business? How much are you going to cheat me, now? Out with it!"

"Wal," said Haley, "if I should say thirteen hundred dollars[9] for that ar fellow, I shouldn't but just save myself; I shouldn't now, re'ly."

"Poor fellow!" said the young man, fixing his keen, mocking, blue eye on him; "but I suppose you'd let me have him for that, out of a particular regard for me."

"Wal, the young lady here seems to be sot on him, and nat'lly enough."

"Oh, certainly, there's a call on your benevolence, my friend. Now, as a matter of Christian charity, how cheap could you afford to let him go, to oblige a young lady that's particular sot on him?"

"Wal, now, just think on't," said the trader; "just look at them limbs,—broad-chested, strong as a horse. Look at his head; them high forrads allays shows calcu-

---

9. Although monetary conversions can be problematic, the value of $1 when this selection was written was equivalent to about $27. Haley was asking for the equivalent of about $35,000 today.

latin' niggers, that'll do any kind o' thing. I've marked that ar. Now, a nigger of that ar heft and build is worth considerable, just, as you may say, for his body, sup-posin' he's stupid; but come to put in his calculatin' faculties, and them which I can show he has oncommon, why, of course, it makes him come higher. Why, that ar fellow managed his master's whole farm. He has a strornary talent for business."

"Bad, bad, very bad; knows altogether too much!" said the young man, with the same mocking smile playing about his mouth. "Never will do, in the world. Your smart fellows are always running off, stealing horses, and raising the devil generally. I think you'll have to take off a couple of hundred for his smartness."

"Wal, there might be something in that ar, if it warn't for his character; but I can show recommends from his master and others, to prove he is one of your real pious,—the most humble, prayin', pious crittur ye ever did see. Why, he's been called a preacher in them parts he came from."

"And I might use him for a family chaplain, possibly," added the young man, dryly. "That's quite an idea. Religion is a remarkably scarce article at our house."

"You're joking, now."

"How do you know I am? Didn't you just warrant him for a preacher? Has he been examined by any synod or council? Come, hand over your papers."

If the trader had not been sure, by a certain good-humored twinkle in the large, blue eye, that all this banter was sure, in the long run, to turn out a cash concern, he might have been somewhat out of patience; as it was, he laid down a greasy pocket-book on the cotton-bales, and began anxiously studying over cer-tain papers in it, the young man standing by, the while, looking down on him with an air of careless, easy drollery.

"Papa, do buy him! it's no matter what you pay," whispered Eva, softly, get-ting up on a package, and putting her arm around her father's neck. "You have money enough, I know. I want him."

"What for, pussy? Are you going to use him for a rattle-box, or a rocking-horse, or what?"

"I want to make him happy."

"An original reason, certainly."

Here the trader handed up a certificate, signed by Mr. Shelby, which the young man took with the tips of his long fingers, and glanced over carelessly.

"A gentlemanly hand," he said, "and well spelt, too. Well, now, but I'm not sure, after all, about this religion," said he, the old wicked expression returning to his eye; "the country is almost ruined with pious white people: such pious politi-cians as we have just before elections,—such pious goings on in all departments of church and state, that a fellow does not know who'll cheat him next. I don't know, either, about religion's being up in the market, just now. I have not looked in the papers lately, to see how it sells. How many hundred dollars, now, do you put on for this religion?"

"You like to be a jokin', now," said the trader; "but, then, there's *sense* under all that ar. I know there's differences in religion. Some kinds is mis'rable: there's your meetin' pious; there's your singin', roarin' pious; them ar an't no account, in black or white;—but these raily is; and I've seen it in niggers as often as any, your rail softly, quiet stiddy, honest, pious, that the hull world couldn't tempt 'em to do nothing that they thinks is wrong; and ye see in this letter what Tom's old master says about him."

"Now," said the young man, stooping gravely over his book of bills, "if you can assure me that I really can buy *this* kind of pious, and that it will be set down to my account in the book up above, as something belonging to me, I wouldn't care if I did go a little extra for it. How d' ye say?"

"Wal, raily, I can't do that," said the trader. "I'm a thinkin' that every man'll have to hang on his own hook, in them ar quarters."[1]

"Rather hard on a fellow that pays extra on religion, and can't trade with it in the state where he wants it most, an't it, now?" said the young man, who had been making out a roll of bills while he was speaking. "There, count your money, old boy!" he added, as he handed the roll to the trader.

"All right," said Haley, his face beaming with delight; and pulling out an old inkhorn,[2] he proceeded to fill out a bill of sale, which, in a few moments, he handed to the young man.

"I wonder, now, if I was divided up and inventoried," said the latter, as he ran over the paper, "how much I might bring. Say so much for the shape of my head, so much for a high forehead, so much for arms, and hands, and legs, and then so much for education, learning, talent, honesty, religion! Bless me! there would be small charge on that last, I'm thinking. But come, Eva," he said; and taking the hand of his daughter, he stepped across the boat, and carelessly putting the tip of his finger under Tom's chin, said, good-humoredly, "Look up, Tom, and see how you like your new master."

Tom looked up. It was not in nature to look into that gay, young, handsome face, without a feeling of pleasure; and Tom felt the tears start in his eyes as he said, heartily, "God bless you, Mas'r!"

"Well, I hope he will. What's your name? Tom? Quite as likely to do it for your asking as mine, from all accounts. Can you drive horses, Tom?"

"I've been allays used to horses," said Tom. "Mas'r Shelby raised heaps on 'em."

"Well, I think I shall put you in coachy, on condition that you won't be drunk more than once a week, unless in cases of emergency, Tom."

Tom looked surprised, and rather hurt, and said, "I never drink, Mas'r."

"I've heard that story before, Tom; but then we'll see. It will be a special accommodation to all concerned, if you don't. Never mind, my boy," he added, good-humoredly, seeing Tom still looked grave; "I don't doubt you mean to do well."

"I sartin' do, Mas'r," said Tom.

"And you shall have good times," said Eva. "Papa is very good to everybody, only he always will laugh at them."

"Papa is much obliged to you for his recommendation," said St. Clare, laughing, as he turned on his heel and walked away.

* * *

Chapter XXII
"The Grass Withereth—the Flower Fadeth."[3]

Life passes, with us all, a day at a time; so it passed with our friend Tom, till two years were gone. Though parted from all his soul held dear, and though often yearning for what lay beyond, still was he never positively and consciously miserable; for, so well is the harp of human feeling strung, that nothing but a crash that breaks every string can wholly mar its harmony; and, on looking back to seasons which in review appear to us as those of deprivation and trial, we can remember

1. Like butchered animals.   3. Isaiah 40:6–9.
2. A portable inkwell made of an animal's horn.

that each hour as it glided, brought its diversions and alleviations, so that, though not happy wholly, we were not, either, wholly miserable.

Tom read, in his only literary cabinet, of one who had "learned in whatsoever state he was, therewith to be content." It seemed to him good and reasonable doctrine, and accorded well with the settled and thoughtful habit which he had acquired from the reading of that same book.

His letter homeward * * * was in due time answered by Master George, in a good, round, school-boy hand, that Tom said might be read "most acrost the room." It contained various refreshing items of home intelligence, with which our reader is fully acquainted; stated how Aunt Chloe had been hired out to a confectioner in Louisville, where her skill in the pastry line was gaining wonderful sums of money, all of which, Tom was informed, was to be laid up to go to make up the sum of his redemption money; Mose and Pete were thriving, and the baby was trotting all about the house, under the care of Sally and the family generally.

Tom's cabin was shut up for the present; but George expatiated brilliantly on ornaments and additions to be made to it when Tom came back.

The rest of this letter gave a list of George's school studies, each one headed by a flourishing capital; and also told the names of four new colts that appeared on the premises since Tom left; and stated, in the same connection, that father and mother were well. The style of the letter was decidedly concise and terse; but Tom thought it the most wonderful specimen of composition that had appeared in modern times. He was never tired of looking at it, and even held a council with Eva on the expediency of getting it framed, to hang up in his room. Nothing but the difficulty of arranging it so that both sides of the page would show at once stood in the way of this undertaking.

The friendship between Tom and Eva had grown with the child's growth. It would be hard to say what place she held in the soft, impressible heart of her faithful attendant. He loved her as something frail and earthly, yet almost worshipped her as something heavenly and divine. He gazed on her as the Italian sailor gazes on his image of the child Jesus,—with a mixture of reverence and tenderness; and to humor her graceful fancies, and meet those thousand simple wants which invest childhood like a many-colored rainbow, was Tom's chief delight. In the market, at morning, his eyes were always on the flower-stalls for rare bouquets for her, and the choicest peach or orange was slipped into his pocket to give to her when he came back; and the sight that pleased him most was her sunny head looking out the gate for his distant approach, and her childish question,—"Well, Uncle Tom, what have you got for me today?"

Nor was Eva less zealous in kind offices, in return. Though a child, she was a beautiful reader;—a fine musical ear, a quick poetic fancy, and an instinctive sympathy with what is grand and noble, made her such a reader of the Bible as Tom had never before heard. At first, she read to please her humble friend; but soon her own earnest nature threw out its tendrils, and wound itself around the majestic book; and Eva loved it, because it woke in her strange yearnings, and strong, dim emotions, such as impassioned, imaginative children love to feel.

The parts that pleased her most were the Revelation and the Prophecies,— parts whose dim and wondrous imagery, and fervent language, impressed her the more, that she questioned vainly of their meaning; and she and her simple friend, the old child and the young one, felt just alike about it. All that they knew was, that they spoke of a glory to be revealed,—a wondrous something yet to come, wherein their soul rejoiced, yet knew not why; and though it be not so in the physical, yet in moral science that which cannot be understood is not always profitless. For the soul awakes, a trembling stranger, between two dim eternities,—the eternal past, the eternal future. The light shines only on a small space around her; therefore, she needs must yearn towards the unknown; and the voices and shadowy movings which come to her from out the cloudy pillar of inspiration have each one echoes and answers in her own expecting nature. It's mystic imageries are so many talismans and gems inscribed with unknown hieroglyphics; she folds them in her bosom, and expects to read them when she passes beyond the veil.

At this time in our story, the whole St. Clare establishment is, for the time being, removed to their villa on Lake Pontchartrain.[4] The heats of summer had driven all who were able to leave the sultry and unhealthy city, to seek the shores of the lake, and its cool sea-breezes.

St. Clare's villa was an East-Indian cottage, surrounded by light verandas of bamboo-work, and opening on all sides into gardens and pleasure-grounds. The common sitting-room opened on to a large garden, fragrant with every picturesque plant and flower of the tropics, where winding paths ran down to the very shores of the lake, whose silvery sheet of water lay there, rising and falling in the sunbeams,—a picture never for an hour the same, yet every hour more beautiful.

It is now one of those intensely golden sunsets which kindles the whole horizon into one blaze of glory, and makes the water another sky. The lake lay in rosy or golden streaks, save where white-winged vessels glided hither and thither, like so many spirits, and little golden stars twinkled through the glow, and looked down at themselves as they trembled in the water.

Tom and Eva were seated on a little mossy seat, in an arbor, at the foot of the garden. It was Sunday evening, and Eva's Bible lay open on her knee. She read,—"And I saw a sea of glass, mingled with fire."[5]

"Tom," said Eva, suddenly stopping, and pointing to the lake, "there 't is."

"What, Miss Eva?"

"Don't you see,—there?" said the child, pointing to the glassy water, which, as it rose and fell, reflected the golden glow of the sky. "There's a 'sea of glass, mingled with fire.'"

"True enough, Miss Eva," said Tom; and Tom sang:—

> "Oh, had I the wings of the morning,
>   I'd fly away to Canaan's shore;
> Bright angels should convey me home,
>   To the new Jerusalem."[6]

"Where do you suppose new Jerusalem is, Uncle Tom?" said Eva.

"Oh, up in the clouds, Miss Eva."

"Then I think I see it," said Eva. "Look in those clouds!—they look like great gates of pearl; and you can see beyond them,—far, far off,—it's all gold. Tom, sing about 'spirits bright.'"

Tom sung the words of a well-known Methodist hymn,—

---

4. A large lake close to New Orleans.
5. Revelaton 15:1–3: "And I saw as it were a sea of glass mingled with fire: and them that had gotten the victory over the beast and over his image, and over his mark, and over the number of his name, stand on the sea of glass, having the harps of God."
6. A popular Methodist hymn.

> "I see a band of spirits bright,
> That taste the glories there;
> They all are robed in spotless white,
> And conquering palms they bear."[7]

"Uncle Tom, I've seen *them,*" said Eva.

Tom had no doubt of it at all; it did not surprise him in the least. If Eva had told him she had been to heaven, he would have thought it entirely probable.

"They come to me sometimes in my sleep, those spirits;" and Eva's eyes grew dreamy, and she hummed, in a low voice,—

> "They are all robed in spotless, white,
> And conquering palms they bear."

"Uncle Tom," said Eva, "I'm going there."

"Where, Miss Eva?"

The child rose, and pointed her little hand to the sky; the glow of evening lit her golden hair and flushed cheek with a kind of unearthly radiance, and her eyes were bent earnestly on the skies.

"I'm going *there,*" she said, "to the spirits bright, Tom. *I'm going before long.*"

The faithful old heart felt a sudden thrust; and Tom thought how often he had noticed, within six months, that Eva's little hands had grown thinner, and her skin more transparent, and her breath shorter; and how, when she ran or played in the garden, as she once could for hours, she became soon so tired and languid. He had heard Miss Ophelia[8] speak often of a cough, that all her medicaments could not cure; and even now that fervent cheek and little hand were burning with hectic fever; and yet the thought that Eva's words suggested had never come to him till now.

Has there ever been a child like Eva? Yes, there have been; but their names are always on gravestones, and their sweet smiles, their heavenly eyes, their singular words and ways, are among the buried treasures of yearning hearts. In how many families do you hear the legend that all the goodness and graces of the living are nothing to the peculiar charms of one who *is not!* It is as if Heaven had an especial band of angels, whose office it was to sojourn for a season here, and endear to them the wayward human heart, that they might bear it upward with them in their homeward flight. When you see that deep, spiritual light in the eye,—when the little soul reveals itself in words sweeter and wiser than the ordinary words of children,—hope not to retain that child; for the seal of heaven is on it, and the light of immortality looks out from its eyes.

Even so, beloved Eva! fair star of thy dwelling! Thou art passing away; but they that love thee dearest know it not.

The colloquy between Tom and Eva was interrupted by a hasty call from Miss Ophelia.

"Eva—Eva!—why, child, the dew is falling; you mustn't be out there!"

Eva and Tom hastened in.

Miss Ophelia was old, and skilled in the tactics of nursing. She was from New England, and knew well the first guileful footsteps of that soft, insidious disease,

---

7. Another popular hymn. Both of these allude to   8. Eva's aunt.
the book of Revelation.

which sweeps away so many of the fairest and loveliest, and, before one fibre of life seems broken, seals them irrevocably for death.

She had noted the slight, dry cough, the daily brightening cheek; nor could the lustre of the eye, and the airy buoyancy born of fever, deceive her.

She tried to communicate her fears to St. Clare; but he threw back her suggestions with a restless petulance, unlike his usual careless good-humor.

"Don't be croaking, cousin,—I hate it!" he would say; "don't you see that the child is only growing? Children always lose strength when they grow fast."

"But she has that cough!"

"Oh, nonsense of that cough!—it is not anything. She has taken a little cold, perhaps."

"Well, that was just the way Eliza Jane was taken, and Ellen and Maria Sanders."

"Oh, stop these hobgoblin nurse-legends. You old hands get so wise, that a child cannot cough, or sneeze, but you see desperation and ruin at hand. Only take care of the child, keep her from the night air, and don't let her play too hard, and she'll do well enough."

So St. Clare said; but he grew nervous and restless. He watched Eva feverishly day by day, as might be told by the frequency with which he repeated over that "the child was quite well,"—that there wasn't anything in that cough,—it was only some little stomach affection, such as children often had. But he kept by her more than before, took her oftener to ride with him, brought home every few days some receipt or strengthening mixture,—"not," he said, "that the child *needed* it, but then it would not do her any harm."

If it must be told, the thing that struck a deeper pang to his heart than anything else was the daily increasing maturity of the child's mind and feelings. While still retaining all a child's fanciful graces, yet she often dropped, unconsciously, words of such a reach of thought, and strange unworldly wisdom, that they seemed to be an inspiration. At such times, St. Clare would feel a sudden thrill, and clasp her in his arms, as if that fond clasp could save her; and his heart rose up with wild determination to keep her, never to let her go.

The child's whole heart and soul seemed absorbed in works of love and kindness. Impulsively generous she had always been; but there was a touching and womanly thoughtfulness about her now, that every one noticed. She still loved to play with Topsy,[9] and the various colored children; but she now seemed rather a spectator than an actor of their plays, and she would sit for half an hour at a time, laughing at the odd tricks of Topsy,—and then a shadow would seem to pass across her face, her eyes grew misty, and her thoughts were afar.

"Mamma," she said, suddenly, to her mother, one day, "why don't we teach our servants to read?"

"What a question, child! People never do."

"Why don't they?" said Eva.

"Because it is no use for them to read. It don't help them to work any better, and they are not made for anything else."

"But they ought to read the Bible, mamma, to learn God's will."

"Oh, they can get that read to them all *they* need."

---

9. A little slave girl owned by Miss Ophelia, who is loved only by Eva.

"It seems to me, mamma, the Bible is for every one to read themselves. They need it a great many times when there is nobody to read it."

"Eva, you are an odd child," said her mother.

"Miss Ophelia has taught Topsy to read," continued Eva.

"Yes, and you see how much good it does. Topsy is the worst creature I ever saw!"

"Here's poor Mammy!" said Eva. "She does love the Bible so much, and wishes so she could read! And what will she do when I can't read to her?"

Marie[1] was busy turning over the contents of a drawer, as she answered,—

Well, of course, by and by, Eva, you will have other things to think of, besides reading the Bible round to servants. Not but that is very proper; I've done it myself, when I had health. But when you come to be dressing and going into company, you won't have time. See here!" she added, "these jewels I'm going to give you when you come out. I wore them to my first ball. I can tell you, Eva, I made a sensation."

Eva took the jewel-case, and lifted from it a diamond necklace. Her large, thoughtful eyes rested on them, but it was plain her thoughts were elsewhere.

"How sober you look, child!" said Marie.

"Are these worth a great deal of money, mamma?"

"To be sure, they are. Father sent to France for them. They are worth a small fortune."

"I wish I had them," said Eva, "to do what I pleased with!"

"What would you do with them?"

"I'd sell them, and buy a place in the free states, and take all our people there, and hire teachers, to teach them to read and write."

Eva was cut short by her mother's laughing.

"Set up a boarding-school! Wouldn't you teach them to play on the piano, and paint on velvet?"[2]

"I'd teach them to read their own Bible, and write their own letters, and read letters that are written to them," said Eva, steadily. "I know, mamma, it does come very hard on them, that they can't do these things. Tom feels it,—Mammy does,— a great many of them do. I think it's wrong."

"Come, come, Eva; you are only a child! You don't know anything about these things," said Marie; "besides, your talking makes my head ache."

Marie always had a headache on hand for any conversation that did not exactly suit her.

Eva stole away; but after that, she assiduously gave Mammy reading lessons.

* * *

Chapter XXXII
Dark Places

*"The dark places of the earth are full
of the habitations of cruelty."*[3]

Trailing wearily behind a rude wagon, and over a ruder road, Tom and his associates faced onward.

---

1. Eva's mother.   3. Psalm 74:20.
2. Decorative arts for young ladies.

In the wagon was seated Simon Legree;[4] and the two women, still fettered together, were stowed away with some baggage in the back part of it; and the whole company were seeking Legree's plantation, which lay a good distance off.

It was a wild, forsaken road, now winding through dreary pine barrens, where the wind whispered mournfully, and now over log causeways, through long cypress swamps, the doleful trees rising out of the slimy, spongy ground, hung with long wreaths of funereal black moss, while ever and anon the loathsome form of the moccasin snake might be seen sliding among broken stumps and shattered branches that lay here and there, rotting in the water.

It is disconsolate enough, this riding, to the stranger, who, with well-filled pocket and well-appointed horse, threads the lonely way on some errand of business; but wilder, drearier, to the man enthralled, whom every weary step bears further from all that man loves and prays for.

So one should have thought, that witnessed the sunken and dejected expression on those dark faces; the wistful, patient weariness with which those sad eyes rested on object after object that passed them in their sad journey.

Simon rode on, however, apparently well pleased, occasionally pulling away at a flask of spirit, which he kept in his pocket.

"I say, *you!*" he said, as he turned back and caught a glance at the dispirited faces behind him. "Strike up a song, boys,—come!"

The men looked at each other, and the *"come"* was repeated, with a smart crack of the whip which the driver carried in his hands. Tom began a Methodist hymn,—

> "Jerusalem, my happy home,
> Name ever dear to me!
> When shall my sorrows have an end,
> Thy joys when shall"—[5]

"Shut up, you black cuss!" roared Legree; "did ye think I wanted any o' yer infernal old Methodism? I say, tune up, now, something real rowdy,—quick!"

One of the other men struck up one of those unmeaning songs, common among the slaves.

> "Mas'r see'd me cotch a coon,
> High boys, high!
> He laughed to split,—d' ye see the moon,
> Ho! ho! ho! boys, ho!
> Ho! yo! hi—e! oh!"[6]

The singer appeared to make up the song to his own pleasure, generally hitting on rhyme, without much attempt at reason; and all the party took up the chorus, at intervals,—

> "Ho! ho! ho! boys, ho!
> High—e—oh! high—e—oh!"[7]

---

4. Following Eva's death, her father also dies. Tom has been sold to the brutal Simon Legree, who operates a factory-like plantation.
5. An eighteenth-century version of a sixteenth-century hymn.
6. African American work song.
7. African American work song.

It was sung very boisterously, and with a forced attempt at merriment; but no wail of despair, no words of impassioned prayer, could have had such a depth of woe in them as the wild notes of the chorus. As if the poor, dumb heart, threatened,—prisoned,—took refuge in that inarticulate sanctuary of music, and found there a language in which to breathe its prayer to God! There was a prayer in it, which Simon could not hear. He only heard the boys singing noisily, and was well pleased; he was making them "keep up their spirits."

"Well, my little dear," said he, turning to Emmeline,[8] and laying his hand on her shoulder, "we're almost home!"

When Legree scolded and stormed, Emmeline was terrified; but when he laid his hand on her, and spoke as he now did, she felt as if she had rather he would strike her. The expression of his eyes made her soul sick, and her flesh creep. Involuntarily she clung closer to the mulatto woman by her side, as if she were her mother.

"You didn't ever wear ear-rings," he said, taking hold of her small ear with his coarse fingers.

"No, Mas'r!" said Emmeline, trembling and looking down.

"Well, I'll give you a pair, when we get home, if you're a good girl. You needn't be so frightened; I don't mean to make you work very hard. You'll have fine times with me, and live like a lady,—only be a good girl."

Legree had been drinking to that degree that he was inclining to be very gracious; and it was about this time that the inclosures of the plantation rose to view. The estate had formerly belonged to a gentleman of opulence and taste, who had bestowed some considerable attention to the adornment of his grounds. Having died insolvent, it had been purchased, at a bargain, by Legree, who used it, as he did everything else, merely as an implement for money-making. The place had that ragged, forlorn appearance, which is always produced by the evidence that the care of the former owner has been left to go to utter decay.

What was once a smooth-shaven lawn before the house, dotted here and there with ornamental shrubs, was now covered with frowsy tangled grass, with horse-posts set up, here and there, in it, where the turf was stamped away, and the ground littered with broken pails, cobs of corn, and other slovenly remains. Here and there, a mildewed jessamine or honey-suckle hung raggedly from some ornamental support, which had been pushed to one side by being used as a horse-post. What once was a large garden was now all grown over with weeds, through which, here and there, some solitary exotic reared its forsaken head. What had been a conservatory had now no window-sashes, and on the mouldering shelves stood some dry, forsaken flower-pots, with sticks in them, whose dried leaves showed they had once been plants.

The wagon rolled up a weedy gravel walk, under a noble avenue of China-trees, whose graceful forms and ever-springing foliage seemed to be the only things there that neglect could not daunt or alter,—like noble spirits, so deeply rooted in goodness, as to flourish and grow stronger amid discouragement and decay.

The house had been large and handsome. It was built in a manner common at the south; a wide veranda of two stories running round every part of the house, into which every outer door opened, the lower tier being supported by brick pillars.

---

8. Legree has bought a young girl to be his sexual slave.

But the place looked desolate and uncomfortable; some windows stopped up with boards, some with shattered panes, and shutters hanging by a single hinge,—all telling of coarse neglect and discomfort.

Bits of board, straw, old decayed barrels and boxes, garnished the ground in all directions; and three or four ferocious-looking dogs, roused by the sound of the wagon-wheels, came tearing out, and were with difficulty restrained from laying hold of Tom and his companions, by the effort of the ragged servants who came after them.

"Ye see what ye'd get!" said Legree, caressing the dogs with grim satisfaction, and turning to Tom and his companions. "Ye see what ye'd get, if ye try to run off. These yer dogs has been raised to track niggers; and they'd jest as soon chaw one on ye up as to eat their supper. So, mind yerself! How now, Sambo!" he said, to a ragged fellow, without any brim to his hat, who was officious in his attentions. "How have things been going?"

"Fust-rate, Mas'r."

"Quimbo," said Legree to another, who was making zealous demonstrations to attract his attention, "ye minded what I telled ye?"

"Guess I did, didn't I?"

These two colored men were the two principal hands on the plantation. Legree had trained them in savageness and brutality as systematically as he had his bull-dogs; and, by long practice in hardness and cruelty, brought their whole nature to about the same range of capacities. It is a common remark, and one that is thought to militate strongly against the character of the race; that the Negro overseer is always more tyrannical and cruel than the white one. This is simply saying that the Negro mind has been more crushed and debased than the white. It is no more true of this race than of every oppressed race, the world over. The slave is always a tyrant, if he can get a chance to be one.

Legree, like some potentates we read of in history, governed his plantation by a sort of resolution of forces. Sambo and Quimbo cordially hated each other; the plantation hands, one and all, cordially hated them; and by playing off one against another, he was pretty sure, through one or the other of the three parties, to get informed of whatever was on foot in the place.

Nobody can live entirely without social intercourse; and Legree encouraged his two black satellites to a kind of coarse familiarity with him,—a familiarity, however, at any moment liable to get one or the other of them into trouble; for, on the slightest provocation, one of them always stood ready, at a nod, to be a minister of his vengeance on the other.

As they stood there now by Legree, they seemed an apt illustration of the fact that brutal men are lower even than animals. Their coarse, dark, heavy features; their great eyes, rolling enviously on each other; their barbarous, gutteral, half-brute intonation; their dilapidated garments fluttering in the wind,—were all in admirable keeping with the vile and unwholesome character of everything about the place.

"Here, you Sambo," said Legree, "take these yer boys down to the quarters; and here's a gal I've got for *you*," said he, as he separated the mulatto woman from Emmeline, and pushed her towards him;—"I promised to bring you one, you know."

The woman gave a sudden start, and, drawing back, said suddenly,—

"Oh, Mas'r! I left my old man in New Orleans."

"What of that, you———; won't you want one here? None o' yer words,—go 'long!" said Legree, raising his whip.

"Come, mistress," he said to Emmeline, "you go in here with me."

A dark, wild face was seen, for a moment, to glance at the window of the house; and, as Legree opened the door, a female voice said something, in a quick, imperative tone. Tom, who was looking, with anxious interest, after Emmeline, as she went in, noticed this, and heard Legree answer, angrily, "You may hold your tongue! I'll do as I please, for all you!"

Tom heard no more; for he was soon following Sambo to the quarters. The quarters was a little sort of street of rude shanties, in a row, in a part of the plantation, far off from the house. They had a forlorn, brutal, forsaken air. Tom's heart sunk when he saw them. He had been comforting himself with the thought of a cottage, rude, indeed, but one which he might make neat and quiet, and where he might have a shelf for his Bible, and a place to be alone out of his laboring hours. He looked into several; they were mere rude shells, destitute of any species of furniture, except a heap of straw, foul with dirt, spread confusedly over the floor, which was merely the bare ground, trodden hard by the tramping of innumerable feet.

"Which of these will be mine?" said he, to Sambo, submissively.

"Dunno; ken turn in here, I s'pose," said Sambo; "spects thar's room for another thar; thar's a pretty smart heap o' niggers to each on 'em now; sure, I dunno what I's to do with more."

It was late in the evening when the weary occupants of the shanties came flocking home,—men and women, in soiled and tattered garments, surly and uncomfortable, and in no mood to look pleasantly on new-comers. The small village was alive with no inviting sounds; hoarse, gutteral voices contending at the handmills where their morsel of hard corn was yet to be ground into meal, to fit it for the cake that was to constitute their only supper. From the earliest dawn of the day, they had been in the fields, pressed to work under the driving lash of the overseers; for it was now in the very heat and hurry of the season, and no means was left untried to press every one up to the top of their capabilities. "True," says the negligent lounger; "picking cotton isn't hard work." Isn't it? And it isn't much inconvenience, either, to have one drop of water fall on your head; yet the worst torture of the inquisition is produced by drop after drop, drop after drop, falling moment after moment, with monotonous succession, on the same spot; and work, in itself not hard, becomes so, by being pressed, hour after hour, with unvarying, unrelenting sameness, with not even the consciousness of free-will to take from its tediousness. Tom looked in vain among the gang, as they poured along, for companionable faces. He saw only sullen, scowling, imbruted men, and feeble, discouraged women, or women that were not women,—the strong pushing away the weak,—the gross, unrestricted animal selfishness of human beings, of whom nothing good was expected and desired; and who, treated in every way like brutes, had sunk as nearly to their level as it was possible for human beings to do. To a late hour in the night the sound of the grinding was protracted; for the mills were few in number compared with the grinders, and the weary and feeble ones were driven back by the strong, and came on last in their turn.

"Ho yo!" said Sambo, coming to the mulatto woman, and throwing down a bag of corn before her; "what a cuss yo' name?"

"Lucy," said the woman.

"Wal, Lucy, yo' my woman now. Yo' grind dis yer corn, and get *my* supper baked, ye har?"

"I an't your woman, and I won't be!" said the woman, with the sharp, sudden courage of despair; "you go 'long!"

"I'll kick yo', then!" said Sambo, raising his foot threateningly.

"Ye may kill me, if ye choose,—the sooner the better! Wish't I was dead!" said she.

"I say, Sambo, you go to spilin the hands, I'll tell Mas'r o' you," said Quimbo, who was busy at the mill, from which he had viciously driven two or three tired women, who were waiting to grind their corn.

"And I'll tell him ye won't let the women come to the mills, yo' old nigger!" said Sambo. "Yo' jes keep to yo' own row."

Tom was hungry with his day's journey, and almost faint for want of food.

"Thar, yo'!" said Quimbo, throwing down a coarse bag, which contained a peck of corn; "thar, nigger, grab, take car' on't,—yo' won't get no more, *dis* yer week."

Tom waited till a late hour, to get a place at the mills; and then, moved by the utter weariness of two women, whom he saw trying to grind their corn there, he ground for them, put together the decaying brands of the fire where many had baked cakes before them, and then went about getting his own supper. It was a new kind of work there,—a deed of charity, small as it was; but it woke an answering touch in their hearts,—an expression of womanly kindness came over their hard faces; they mixed his cake for him, and tended its baking; and Tom sat down by the light of the fire, and drew out his Bible,—for he had need of comfort.

"What's that?" said one of the women.

"A Bible," said Tom.

"Good Lord! han't seen un since I was in Kentuck."

"Was you raised in Kentuck?" said Tom, with interest.

"Yes, and well raised, too; never spected to come to dis yer!" said the woman, sighing.

"What's dat ar book, any way?" said the other woman.

"Why, the Bible."

"Laws a me! what's dat?" said the woman.

"Do tell! you never hearn on 't?" said the other woman. "I used to har Missis a readin' on 't, sometimes, in Kentucky; but, laws o' me! we don't har nothin' here but crackin' and swarin'."

"Read a piece, anyways!" said the first woman, curiously, seeing Tom attentively poring over it.

Tom read,—"Come unto Me, all ye that labor and are heavy laden, and I will give you rest."[9]

"Them's good words enough," said the woman; "who says 'em?"

"The Lord," said Tom.

"I jest wish I know'd whar to find him," said the woman. "I would go; 'pears like I never should get rested again. My flesh is fairly sore, and I tremble all over, every day, and Sambo's allers a jawin' at me, 'cause I doesn't pick faster; and nights it's most midnight 'fore I can get my supper; and den 'pears like I don't turn over

9. Matthew 11:28.

and shut my eyes, 'fore I hear de horn blow to get up, and at it agin in de mornin'. If I knew whar de Lord was, I'd tell him."

"He's here, he's everywhere," said Tom.

"Lor, you an't gwine to make me believe dat ar! I know de Lord an't here," said the woman; " 't an't no use talking, though. I's jest gwine to camp down, and sleep while I ken."

The women went off to their cabins, and Tom sat alone, by the smouldering fire, that flickered up redly in his face.

The silver, fair-browed moon rose in the purple sky, and looked down, calm and silent, as God looks on the scene of misery and oppression,—looked calmly on the lone black man, as he sat, with his arms folded, and his Bible on his knee.

"Is God HERE?" Ah, how is it possible for the untaught heart to keep its faith, unswerving, in the face of dire misrule, and palpable, unrebuked injustice? In that simple heart waged a fierce conflict: the crushing sense of wrong, the foreshadowing of a whole life of future misery, the wreck of all past hopes, mournfully tossing in the soul's sight, like dead corpses of wife, and child, and friend, rising from the dark wave, and surging in the face of the half-drowned mariner! Ah, was it easy *here* to believe and hold fast the great password of Christian faith, "that God IS, and is the REWARDER of them that diligently seek him"?

Tom rose, disconsolate, and stumbled into the cabin that had been allotted to him. The floor was already strewn with weary sleepers, and the foul air of the place almost repelled him, but the heavy night-dews were chill, and his limbs weary, and, wrapping about him a tattered blanket, which formed his only bed-clothing, he stretched himself in the straw and fell asleep.

In dreams, a gentle voice came over his ear; he was sitting on the mossy seat in the garden by Lake Pontchartrain, and Eva, with her serious eyes bent downward, was reading to him from the Bible; and he heard her read,—

"When thou passest through the waters, I will be with thee, and the rivers they shall not overflow thee; when thou walkest through the fire, thou shalt not be burned, neither shall the flame kindle upon thee; for I am the Lord thy God, the Holy One of Israel, thy Saviour."[1]

Gradually the words seemed to melt and fade, as in a divine music; the child raised her deep eyes, and fixed them lovingly on him, and rays of warmth and comfort seemed to go from them to his heart; and, as if wafted on the music, she seemed to rise on shining wings, from which flakes and spangles of gold fell off like stars, and she was gone.

Tom woke. Was it a dream? Let it pass for one. But who shall say that that sweet young spirit, which in life so yearned to comfort and console the distressed, was forbidden of God to assume this ministry after death?

> "It is a beautiful belief,
> That ever round our head
> Are hovering, on angel wings,
> The spirits of the dead."[2]

* * *

1. Isaiah 43:2.   Presence," 1830.
2. James H. Perkins (1810–31), "The Spiritual

Chapter XL
The Martyr

"Deem not the just by Heaven forgot!
Though life its common gifts deny,—
Though, with a crushed and bleeding heart,
And spurned of man, he goes to die!
For God hath marked each sorrowing day,   5
And numbered every bitter tear;
And heaven's long years of bliss shall pay
For all his children suffer here."

—BRYANT[3].

The longest way must have its close,—the gloomiest night will wear on to a morning. An eternal, inexorable lapse of moments is ever hurrying the day of the evil to an eternal night, and the night of the just to an eternal day. We have walked with our humble friend thus far in the valley of slavery; first through flowery fields of ease and indulgence, then through heart-breaking separations from all that man holds dear. Again, we have waited with him in a sunny island, where generous hands concealed his chains with flowers; and, lastly, we have followed him when the last ray of earthly hope went out in night, and seen how, in the blackness of earthly darkness, the firmament of the unseen has blazed with stars of new and significant lustre.

The morning star now stands over the tops of the mountains, and gales and breezes, not of earth, show that the gates of day are unclosing.

The escape of Cassy and Emmeline[4] irritated the before surly temper of Legree to the last degree; and his fury, as was to be expected, fell upon the defenceless head of Tom. When he hurriedly announced the tidings among his hands, there was a sudden light in Tom's eye, a sudden upraising of his hands, that did not escape him. He saw that he did not join the muster of the pursuers. He thought of forcing him to do it; but having had, of old, experience of his inflexibility when commanded to take part in any deed of inhumanity, he would not, in his hurry, stop to enter into any conflict with him.

Tom, therefore, remained behind, with a few who had learned of him to pray, and offered up prayers for the escape of the fugitives.

When Legree returned, baffled and disappointed, all the long-working hatred of his soul towards his slave began to gather in a deadly and desperate form. Had not this man braved him,—steadily, powerfully, resistlessly,—ever since he bought him? Was there not a spirit in him which, silent as it was, burned on him like the fires of perdition?

"I *hate* him!" said Legree, that night, as he sat up in his bed; "I *hate* him! And isn't he MINE? Can't I do what I like with him? Who's to hinder, I wonder?" And Legree clenched his fist, and shook it, as if he had something in his hands that he could rend in pieces.

But, then, Tom was a faithful, valuable servant; and, although Legree hated him the more for that, yet the consideration was still somewhat of a restraint to him.

---

3. American poet William Cullen Bryant (1794–1878); the poem is unknown.

4. Cassy, the woman Emmeline is meant to replace, has been held as a sex slave by Legree.

The next morning, he determined to say nothing, as yet; to assemble a party, from some neighboring plantations, with dogs and guns; to surround the swamp, and go about the hunt systematically. If it succeeded, well and good; if not, he would summon Tom before him, and—his teeth clenched and his blood boiled—*then* he would break that fellow down, or—there was a dire inward whisper, to which his soul assented.

Ye say that the *interest* of the master is a sufficient safeguard for the slave. In the fury of man's mad will, he will wittingly, and with open eye, sell his own soul to the devil to gain his ends; and will he be more careful of his neighbor's body?

"Well," said Cassy, the next day, from the garret, as she reconnoitred through the knot-hole, "the hunt's going to begin again, to-day!"

Three or four mounted horsemen were curvetting about, on the space front of the house; and one or two leashes of strange dogs were struggling with the Negroes who held them, baying and barking at each other.

The men are, two of them, overseers of plantations in the vicinity; and others were some of Legree's associates at the tavern-bar of a neighboring city, who had come for the interest of the sport. A more hard-favored set, perhaps, could not be imagined. Legree was serving brandy, profusely, round among them, as also among the Negroes, who had been detailed from the various plantations for this service; for it was an object to make every service of this kind, among the Negroes, as much of a holiday as possible.

Cassy placed her ear at the knot-hole; and, as the morning air blew directly towards the house, she could overhear a good deal of the conversation. A grave sneer overcast the dark, severe gravity of her face, as she listened, and heard them divide out the ground, discuss the rival merits of the dogs, give orders about firing, and the treatment of each, in case of capture.

Cassy drew back; and, clasping her hands, looked upward, and said, "Oh great Almighty God! we are *all* sinners, but what have *we* done, more than all the rest of the world, that we should be treated so?"

There was a terrible earnestness in her face and voice, as she spoke.

"If it wasn't for *you*, child," she said, looking at Emmeline, "I'd *go* out to them; and I'd thank any one of them that *would* shoot me down; for what use will freedom be to me? Can it give me back my children, or make me what I used to be?"

Emmeline, in her childlike simplicity, was half afraid of the dark moods of Cassy. She looked perplexed, but made no answer. She only took her hand, with a gentle, caressing movement.

"Don't!" said Cassy, trying to draw it away; "you'll get me to loving you; and I never mean to love anything, again!"

"Poor Cassy!" said Emmeline, "don't feel so! If the Lord gives us liberty, perhaps he'll give you back your daughter; at any rate, I'll be like a daughter to you. I know I'll never see my poor old mother again! I shall love you, Cassy, whether you love me or not!"

The gentle, childlike spirit conquered. Cassy sat down by her, put her arm around her neck, stroked her soft, brown hair and Emmeline then wondered at the beauty of her magnificent eyes, now soft with tears.

"Oh, Em!" said Cassy, "I've hungered for my children, and thirsted for them, and my eyes fail with longing for them! Here! here!" she said, striking her breast, "it's all desolate, all empty! If God would give me back my children, then I could pray."

"You must trust him, Cassy," said Emmeline; "he is our Father!"

"His wrath is upon us," said Cassy; "he has turned away in anger."

"No, Cassy! He will be good to us! Let us hope in him," said Emmeline,—"I always have had hope."

The hunt was long, animated, and thorough, but unsuccessful; and with grave, ironic exultation, Cassy looked down on Legree, as, weary and dispirited, he alighted from his horse.

"Now, Quimbo," said Legree, as he stretched himself down in the sitting-room, "you jest go and walk that Tom up here, right away! The old cuss is at the bottom of this yer whole matter; and I'll have it out of his old black hide, or I'll know the reason why."

Sambo and Quimbo, both, though hating each other, were joined in one mind by a no less cordial hatred of Tom. Legree had told them, at first, that he had bought him for a general overseer, in his absence; and this had begun an ill will, on their part, which had increased, in their debased and servile natures, as they saw him becoming obnoxious to their master's displeasure. Quimbo, therefore, departed, with a will, to execute his orders.

Tom heard the message with a forewarning heart; for he knew all the plan of the fugitives' escape, and the place of their present concealment; he knew the deadly character of the man he had to deal with; and his despotic power. But he felt strong in God to meet death, rather than betray the helpless.

He set his basket down by the row, and, looking up, said, "Into thy hands I commend my spirit! Thou hast redeemed me, O Lord God of truth!"[5] and then quietly yielded himself to the rough, brutal grasp with which Quimbo seized him.

"Ay, ay!" said the giant, as he dragged him along; "ye'll cotch it, now! I'll boun' Mas'r's back's up *high*! No sneaking out, now! Tell ye, ye'll get it, and no mistake! See how ye'll look, now, helpin' Mas'r's niggers to run away! See what ye'll get!"

The savage words none of them reached that ear!—a higher voice there was saying, "Fear not them that kill the body, and, after that, have no more that they can do."[6] Nerve and bone of that poor man's body vibrated to those words, as if touched by the finger of God; and he felt the strength of a thousand souls in one. As he passed along, the trees and bushes, the huts of his servitude, the whole scene of his degradation, seemed to whirl by him as the landscape by the rushing car. His soul throbbed,—his home was in sight,—and the hour of release seemed at hand.

"Well, Tom!" said Legree, walking up, and seizing him grimly by the collar of his coat, and speaking through his teeth, in a paroxysm of determined rage, "do you know I've made up my mind to KILL you?"

"It's very likely, Mas'r," said Tom, calmly.

"I *have*," said Legree, with grim, terrible calmness, "*done—just—that—thing*, Tom, unless you'll tell me what you know about these yer gals!"

Tom stood silent.

"D'ye hear?" said Legree, stamping, with a roar like that of an incensed lion. "Speak!"

"*I han't got nothing to tell, Mas'r*," said Tom, with a slow, firm, deliberate utterance.

5. The last words of Christ, Luke 23:46.   6. Matthew 10:28.

"Do you dare to tell me, ye old black Christian, ye don't *know?*" said Legree. Tom was silent.

"Speak!" thundered Legree, striking him furiously. "Do you know anything?"

"I know, Mas'r; but I can't tell anything. *I can die!*"

Legree drew in a long breath; and, suppressing his rage, took Tom by the arm, and, approaching his face almost to his, said in a terrible voice, "Hark 'e Tom!— ye think, 'cause I've let you off before, I don't mean what I say; but, this time, I've *made up my mind,* and counted the cost. You've always stood it out agin me: now, I'll *conquer ye or kill ye!*—one or t' other. I'll count every drop of blood there is in you, and take 'em, one by one, till ye give up!"

Tom looked up to his master, and answered, "Mas'r, if you was sick, or in trouble, or dying, and I could save ye, I'd *give* ye my heart's blood; and, if taking every drop of blood in this poor old body would save your precious soul, I'd give 'em freely, as the Lord gave his for me. Oh, Mas'r! don't bring this great sin on your soul! It will hurt you more than 't will me! Do the worst you can, my troubles'll be over soon; but, if ye don't repent, yours won't *never* end!"

Like a strange snatch of heavenly music, heard in the lull of a tempest, this burst of feeling made a moment's blank pause. Legree stood aghast, and looked at Tom; and there was such a silence that the tick of the old clock could be heard, measuring, with silent touch, the last moments of mercy and probation to that hardened heart.

It was but a moment. There was one hesitating pause,—one irresolute, relenting thrill,—and the spirit of evil came back, with sevenfold vehemence; and Legree, foaming with rage, smote his victim to the ground.

Scenes of blood and cruelty are shocking to our ear and heart. What man has nerve to do, man has not nerve to hear. What brother-man and brother-Christian must suffer, cannot be told us, even in our secret chamber, it so harrows up the soul! And yet, oh, my country! these things are done under the shadow of thy laws! O Christ! thy church sees them, almost in silence!

But, of old, there was One whose suffering changed an instrument of torture, degradation, and shame, into a symbol of glory, honor, and immortal life; and, where his spirit is, neither degrading stripes, nor blood, nor insults, can make the Christian's last struggle less than glorious.[7]

Was he alone, that long night, whose brave, loving spirit was bearing up, in that old shed, against buffeting and brutal stripes?

Nay! There stood by him ONE,—seen by him alone,—"like unto the Son of God."

The tempter stood by him, too,—blinded by furious, despotic will,—every moment pressing him to shun that agony by the betrayal of the innocent. But the brave, true heart was firm on the Eternal Rock. Like his Master, he knew that, if he saved others, himself he could not save; not could utmost extremity wring from him words, save of prayer and holy trust.

"He's most gone, Mas'r," said Sambo, touched, in spite of himself, by the patience of his victim.

"Pay away, till he gives up! Give it to him!—give it to him!" shouted Legree. "I'll take every drop of blood he has, unless he confesses!"

---

7. The Christian Gospels tell that Jesus suffered degrading torture and the most humiliating form of execution.

Tom opened his eyes, and looked upon his master. "Ye poor miserable crittur!" he said, "there an't no more ye can do! I forgive ye, with all my soul!" and he fainted entirely away.

"I b'lieve, my soul, he's done for, finally," said Legree, stepping forward, to look at him "Yes, he is! Well, his mouth's shut up, at last,—that's one comfort!"

Yes, Legree; but who shall shut up that voice in thy soul? that soul, past repentance, past prayer, past hope, in whom the fire that never shall be quenched is already burning!

Yet Tom was not quite gone. His wondrous words and pious prayers had struck upon the hearts of the imbruted blacks, who had been the instruments of cruelty upon him; and, the instant Legree withdrew, they took him down, and, in their ignorance, sought to call him back to life,—as if *that* were any favor to him.

"Sartin, we's been doin' a dreful wicked thing!" said Sambo; "hopes Mas'r'll have to 'count for it, and not we."

They washed his wounds,—they provided a rude bed, of some refuse cotton, for him to lie down on; and one of them, stealing up to the house, begged a drink of brandy of Legree, pretending that he was tired, and wanted it for himself. He brought it back and poured it down Tom's throat.

"Oh, Tom!" said Quimbo, "we's been awful wicked to ye!"

"I forgive ye, with all my heart!" said Tom, faintly.

"Oh, Tom! do tell us who is *Jesus*, anyhow?" said Sambo,—"Jesus, that's been a standin' by you so, all this night?—Who is he?"

The word roused the failing, fainting spirit. He poured forth a few energetic sentences of that wondrous One,—his life, his death, his everlasting presence, and power to save.

They wept,—both the two savage men.

"Why didn't I never hear this before?" said Sambo; "but I do believe!—I can't help it! Lord Jesus, have mercy on us!"

"Poor critturs!" said Tom, "I'd be willin' to bar all I have, if it'll only bring ye to Christ! O Lord! give me these two more souls, I pray!"

That prayer was answered.

* * *

1852

CULTURAL COORDINATES
The Realism of Stereotypes

Modern readers often respond negatively to the tendency of nineteenth-century poets and fiction writers to deploy stereotypical characters. Harriet Beecher Stowe's Tom (see pp. 734–78) and Frances Harper's Eliza (see pp. 915–17) seem formulaic and oversimplified. In addition, such characters seem to conform to and reinforce prejudices, whether positive or negative, about entire groups of people. More than anything else, as a narrative technique, stereotyping seems old-fashioned and anti-realistic.

But in the mid–nineteenth century, the term *stereotype* referred to the most advanced technology of visual reproduction of the day. The beauty of the stereotype was that it was able to create the illusion of three-dimensional reality from a two-dimensional image. Like the *carte de visite* (p. 612), the stereotype depended first upon innovations in photography that made possible the inexpensive reproduction of images on paper. But stereotyping also depended upon developments in the field of optics (the study of vision and lenses). To make a stereoview, the photographer would take two pictures of the same image from slightly different perspectives. These two images would be mounted side by side on a card and placed in a viewer that had specialized lenses. When a person looked through the machine, the lenses tricked the eye, merging the two images into one. This new image gave the illusion of three-dimensionality that was unique to this new medium. If you have ever looked through a toy View-Master, you've experienced a modern stereotype.

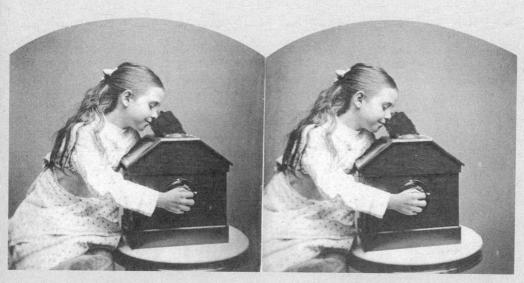

A stereotype. In the nineteenth century, a stereotype was a photograph that appeared three-dimensional when viewed through a stereograph machine, like that through which the little girl here is looking.

In the stereoview here, a girl is shown looking through an elaborate, parlor version of a stereotype viewer. More common were inexpensive, handheld versions. If she were looking at this stereoview of herself, she would note the way the stereotype image in the viewer seemed to reveal more details—and reveal them more vividly—than would either of the images as seen outside the viewer.

The peculiar vividness of the stereotype image comes from the repetition of images that vary from one another only slightly. In effect, the stereographer creates a formulaic version of whatever is being represented that exceeds the dictates of "realism" in a way that provided entertainment to audiences in the era preceding electronic media.

FRANCES (FANNY) LOCKE OSGOOD
1811–1850

Although Fanny Osgood died of tuberculosis before she was forty, her popular poetry epitomized the literary values that were coming to dominate mid-nineteenth-century America. Musical and sentimental, her poetry explored the erotic bonds holding relationships together. Osgood was especially fascinated by the filial relationships between parents and their children, on the one hand, and the sexual dynamics between men and women, on the other.

Born in Boston and raised in one of its suburbs, Osgood spent her early years as the indulged daughter of a happy and comfortable family. Osgood's father, Joseph Locke, was successful enough as a merchant to provide a comfortable home where the literary ambitions of his children could be nurtured. Two of Osgood's older siblings, Anna Maria Wells and Andrew Locke, also became published poets. Osgood herself began writing verse as a child, and by the time she was fourteen, she had gained the attention of Lydia Maria Child (pp. 619–20), who began publishing Osgood's work in *Juvenile Miscellany*, the children's monthly periodical she edited. At twenty-three, Osgood met and married the portrait painter Samuel Stillman Osgood, with whom she traveled to England. While in England, Samuel Osgood pursued his career as a society painter, and he and Fanny—both attractive, young Americans—were welcomed by the literary and artistic elite of London. Returning to America, the Osgoods settled in New York City, where they became associated with a literary coterie that included, most famously, Edgar Allan Poe, but the writers Margaret Fuller (pp. 685–86), Fanny Fern (pp. 787–88), Grace Greenwood, and Anne Lynch, as well as the publishers N. P. Willis, Rufus Griswold, and Horace Greeley, were also part of Osgood's larger community. While Fanny's ability and fame as a poet grew throughout these years, Samuel's career faltered, and their marriage suffered strain. Samuel followed the lure of the 1849 gold rush to California but returned just before his wife died.

Like many of her contemporaries, Osgood benefited from the proliferation of publishing opportunities during the 1840s. Her poems were much sought after, not only by editors of the more established periodicals like *Godey's Lady's Book* (see pp. 785–86), but also by the publishers of literary gift books and newspapers throughout the country. These popular venues were more profitable and generated more fame for poets than books of collected poems did, though Osgood did publish at least eleven collections of verse between 1838 and 1849. Best appreciated during her own time as a writer of "poetry of the affections," Osgood wrote verse celebrating a range of emotional states while pushing the possibilities of the sentimental lyric to its limits.

Ellen Learning to Walk

My beautiful trembler! how wildly she shrinks!
    And how wistful she looks while she lingers!
Papa is extremely uncivil, she thinks,—
    She but pleaded for one of his fingers!

What eloquent pleading! the hand reaching out,   5
    As if doubting so strange a refusal;
While her blue eyes say plainly, "What is he about
    That he does not assist me as usual?"

Come on, my pet Ellen! we won't let you slip,—
    Unclasp those soft arms from his knee, love;   10
I see a faint smile round that exquisite lip,
    A smile half reproach and half glee, love.

So! that's my brave baby! one foot falters forward,
    Half doubtful the other steals by it!
What, shrinking again! why, you shy little coward!   15
    'Twon't kill you to walk a bit!—try it!

There! steady, my darling! huzza![1] I have caught her!
    I clasp her, caress'd and caressing!
And she hides her bright face, as if what we had taught her
    Were something to blush for—the blessing!   20

Now back again! Bravo! that shout of delight,
    How it thrills to the hearts that adore her!
Joy, joy for her mother! and blest be the night
    When her little light feet first upbore her!

                                                            1838

The Little Hand

We wandered sadly round the room,—
    We missed the voice's play,
That warbled through our hours of gloom,
    And charmed the cloud away;—

We missed the footstep, loved and light,—   5
    The tiny, twining hand,—
The quick, arch smile, so wildly bright,—
    The brow, with beauty bland!

We wandered sadly round the room,—
    No relic could we find,   10
No toy of hers, to soothe our gloom,—
    She left not one behind!

But look! there is a misty trace,
    Faint, undefined and broken,
Of fingers, on the mirror's face—   15
    A dear, though simple token!

A cherub hand!—the child we loved
    Had left its impress there,
When first, by young Ambition moved,
    She climbed the easy-chair;—   20

1. Hurray! or Hurrah!

She saw her own sweet self, and tried
  To touch what seemed to be
So near, so beautiful! and cried,—
  "Why! there's another me!"

Dear hand! though from the mirror's face   25
  Thy form did soon depart,
I wore its welcome, tender trace,
  Long after, in my heart!

                                                        1838

He Bade Me Be Happy

He bade me "Be happy," he whisper'd "Forget me;"
  He vow'd my affection was cherish'd in vain.
"Be happy!" "Forget me!" I would, if he'd let me—
  Why will he keep coming to say so again?

He came—it was not the first time, by a dozen—   5
  To take, as he said, "an eternal adieu;"
He went, and, for comfort, I turn'd to—my cousin,
  When back stalk'd the torment his vows to renew.

"You must love me no longer!" he said but this morning.
  "I love you no longer!" I meekly replied.   10
"Is this my reward?" he cried; "falsehood and scorning
  "From her who was ever my idol, my pride!"

                                                        1850

Forgive and Forget

"Forgive—forget! I own the wrong!"
  You fondly sigh'd when last I met you;
The task is neither hard nor long—
  I *do* forgive—I *will* forget you!

                                                        1850

A Reply

To One Who Said, Write from Your Heart

  Ah! woman still
  Must veil the shrine,
Where feeling feeds the fire divine,
  Nor sing at will,
  Untaught by art,   5
The music prison'd in her heart!

  Still gay the note
  And light the day,
The woodbird warbles on the spray,
  Afar to float;   10

But homeward flown,
Within his next, how changed the tone!

Oh! none can know,
Who have not heard
The music-soul that thrills the bird,   15
The carol low,
As coo of dove
He warbles to his woodland love!

The world would say
'Twas vain and wild,   20
Th'impassion'd lay of Nature's child;
And Feeling, so
Should veil the shrine,
Where softly glows her fires divine!

1850

CULTURAL COORDINATES
The Invention of the Ladies' Magazine: *Godey's Lady's Book*

The nineteenth century experienced an explosion of periodicals—daily, weekly, monthly, and quarterly—addressed to various audiences. One of the most popular in the United States was *Godey's Lady's Book* (1830–98), which sought to provide American women with original fiction and poetry and to provide advice on fashion, health, and family.

The most successful American women's magazine of its day—at its high point of circulation in 1860, it sold over 150,000 copies—*Godey's Lady's Book* was edited by Louis Godey (1806–77) for the first six years of its existence, but it began to gain popularity only after Godey bought Boston's *Ladies' Magazine* and hired its editor, Sarah Josepha Hale (1788–1879). Hale's innovation, and what helped make *Godey's Lady's Book* so popular, was to provide her readers with compelling original material written mainly by American authors, both men and women. (In the 1830s and 1840s, many magazines simply reprinted material published elsewhere.) She commissioned fiction and poetry from many of America's most important authors, including Lydia Sigourney (pp. 564–66), Harriet Beecher Stowe (pp. 732–34), Nathaniel Hawthorne, Edgar Allan Poe, Henry Wadsworth

A fashion plate from *Godey's Lady's Book,* January 1868. In the nineteenth century, ladies relied on colored engravings like these to keep abreast of current fashions.

Longfellow, and Ralph Waldo Emerson. The nonfiction selections focused on health, fashion, and domestic economy, avoiding topics like politics and religion. The format and editorial conventions that Hale established continue to be evident in the women's magazines of the twenty-first century, including the depictions of the latest and most extravagant fashions of Europe and Britain (in hand-colored engravings rather than color photographs).

Godey's Lady's Book was one of the most important exponents of what has been called the "cult of true womanhood." Its proponents believed that women should devote themselves to the concerns of the domestic sphere, keeping themselves free from the taint of business and politics in order to better serve as a moral compass for their husbands, sons, and brothers. Hale, herself one of the first successful businesswomen in American history, believed ardently in improving the status of women in America, not by expanding the franchise, but by increasing the reverence in which women were held. Although Hale consciously fostered employment opportunities for women, to her the ideal woman was a mother. Hale, who began writing for publication and then editing only after the death of her husband, believed that the true woman could and should enter the world of commerce only to fulfill her first responsibility—the nurturance of her children.

Godey's Lady's Book began to lose circulation in the 1880s and finally ceased publication in 1898. It had to face more competition from other women's magazines that had followed its lead in publishing original material only, and it lost its two guiding forces: in 1877, Hale retired and Godey sold the magazine; he died later the same year.

Fanny Fern (Sara Payson Willis Parton)

►◄ FANNY FERN (SARA PAYSON WILLIS PARTON) ►◄
1811–1872

Fanny Fern was the pen name of the novelist and journalist Sara Payson Willis Parton. The name pays subversive homage not only to the publishing conventions of earlier generations, in which ladies modestly protected their reputations by publishing under a learned alias, but also to contemporary gender expectations that aligned proper femininity with flowery nature. As both a novelist and a journalist, Fanny Fern deployed a witty yet critical pen in an effort to expose the hypocrisy of mid-nineteenth-century America. Her special subject was the condition of women: in particular, the condition of women who had to work for a living under a political system in which they had no right to vote and, hence, no ability to redress the inequities of their situation.

Fanny Fern was born Sara Payson Willis in 1811 into the large family of Nathaniel and Hannah Willis. Hers was a family deeply involved with the evolving and increasingly important business of periodical publication. Her father, Nathaniel Sr., had founded the first religious newspaper in America and later founded the first children's newspaper. Two of her brothers, Nathaniel Jr. and Richard, were also editors and publishers of periodicals. Fern's early life was dominated by her father's strict adherence to the Presbyterian Church, but she was unable to feel committed to its tenets. She attended Catharine Beecher's Female Seminary in Hartford, Connecticut, where she did not become a more pious Christian but did begin her career as a writer.

Fern married three times. The happiness of her first marriage was followed by the despair of complete economic ruin upon the early death of this husband. Always a keen observer, Fern came to know firsthand the cost of systemic gender inequities when, liable for her first husband's debts yet unable to make enough money to support her children, she became dependent on the grudging support of her father and father-in-law. Fern's famous first novel, *Ruth Hall* (1855), is based upon these experiences and depicts the quandary of American middle-class women who were brought up, as Americans, to value self-reliance but who were denied, as women, the ability to be self-reliant. Fern's second marriage ended, scandalously, in divorce after she left this violently abusive husband. It was at this point that Sarah Payson Willis Eldrige Farrington began submitting articles to newspapers and magazines under the alias Fanny Fern. Fern's last marriage was to James Parton, a longtime friend who agreed to a prenuptial agreement, rare in those days, relinquishing his legal right to her earnings.

Both of Fern's novels, *Ruth Hall* and *Rose Clark* (1856), are feminist stories centered on strong women protagonists who are negotiating milieus similar to those of the author herself. But Fern was most famous in her own time as a journalist. The late 1840s had seen women such as Margaret Fuller (pp. 685–86), Elizabeth Oakes-Smith, and Lydia Maria Child (pp. 619–20) begin to contribute nonfiction articles and essays to newspapers. In 1855, Fern became the highest-paid journalist in America when she was hired as a columnist by the *New York Ledger*. Like those of her predecessors, Fern's main topics were social inequities. But unlike these trailblazers, the persona of Fanny Fern addressed the inequities of her society in the conversational voice of a female observer who has a knack for cutting through the self-serving hypocrisies of her era. Fern takes a rhetorical stance that allows her to address her reader as an equal who will understand and share her ironic appreciation of absurdities. While Fern's allegiances are always with the oppressed, her combination of self-deprecating humor and biting satire made her often unconventional views accessible to a broad audience.

Hints to Young Wives

Shouldn't I like to make a bon-fire of all the "Hints to Young Wives," "Married Woman's Friend,"[1] etc., and throw in the authors after them? I have a little neighbor who believes all they tell her is gospel truth, and lives up to it. The minute she sees her husband coming up the street, she makes for the door, as if she hadn't another minute to live, stands in the entry with her teeth chattering in her head till he gets all his coats and mufflers, and overshoes, and what-do-you-call-'ems off, then chases round (like a cat in a fit) after the boot-jack; warms his slippers and puts 'em on, and dislocates her wrist carving at the table for fear it will tire him.

Poor little innocent fool! she imagines that's the way to preserve his affection. Preserve a fiddlestick! The consequence is, he's sick of the sight of her; snubs her when she asks him a question, and after he has eaten her good dinners takes himself off as soon as possible, bearing in mind the old proverb "that too much of a good thing is good for nothing." Now the truth is just this, and I wish all the women on earth had but one ear in common, so that I could put this little bit of gospel into it:—Just so long as a man isn't quite as sure as if he knew for certain, whether nothing on earth could ever disturb your affection for him, he is your humble servant, but the very second he finds out (or thinks he does) that he has possession of every inch of your heart, and no neutral territory—he will turn on his heel and march off whistling "Yankee Doodle!"

Now it's no use to take your pocket handkerchief and go snivelling round the house with a pink nose and red eyes; not a bit of it! If you have made the interesting discovery that you were married for a sort of upper servant or housekeeper, just *fill that place and no other*, keep your temper, keep all his strings and buttons and straps on; and then keep him at a distance as a housekeeper should—"them's my sentiments!" I have seen one or two men in my life who could bear to be loved (as a woman with a soul knows how), without being spoiled by it, or converted into a tyrant—but they are rare birds, and should be caught, stuffed and handed over to Barnum![2] Now as the ministers say, "I'll close with an interesting little incident that came under my observation."

Mr. Fern came home one day when I had such a crucifying headache that I couldn't have told whether I was married or single, and threw an old coat into my lap to mend. Well, I tied a wet bandage over my forehead, "left all flying," and sat down to it—he might as well have asked me to make a *new* one; however I new lined the sleeves, mended the buttonholes, sewed on new buttons down the front, and all over the coat tails—when finally it occurred to me (I believe it was a suggestion of Satan,) that the *pocket* might need mending; so I turned it inside out, and *what do you think I found? A love-letter from him to my dress-maker!!*

1. The mid–nineteenth century saw an explosion of self-help books directed toward women.

2. Phineas Taylor Barnum (1810–91) founded a famous circus.

I dropped the coat, I dropped the work-basket, I dropped the buttons, I dropped the baby (it was a *female,* and I thought it just as well to put her out of future misery) and then I hopped up into a chair front of the looking-glass, and remarked to the young woman I saw there, "*F-a-n-n-y F-e-r-n! if you—are—ever—such—a—confounded fool again*"—*and I wasn't.*

1852

———◆———

Mrs. Stowe's Uncle Tom

"*Mrs. Stowe's* Uncle Tom *is too graphic ever to have been written by a* woman."

—*EXCHANGE.*

"Too graphic to be written by a woman?" D'ye hear that, Mrs. Stowe? or has English thunder stopped your American ears? Oh, I can tell you, Mrs. "Tom Cabin," that you've got to pay "for the bridge that has carried you over." Do you suppose that you can quietly take the wind out of everybody's sails, the way you have, without having harpoons, and lampoons, and all sorts of *miss*—iles thrown after you? No indeed; every distanced scribbler is perfectly frantic; they stoutly protest your book shows no genius, which fact is unfortunately corroborated by the difficulty your publishers find in disposing of it; they are transported with rage in proportion as *you* are *translated.* Everybody whose cat ever ran through your great grandfather's entry "knows all about you," and how long it took you to cut your first "wisdom tooth." Then all the bitter sectarian enemies your wide awake brothers have evoked, and who are afraid to measure lances with them, huddle into a corner to revenge by "making mouths" at their sister!

Certainly; what right had you to get an "invitation to Scotland" free gratis? or to have "Apsley House" placed at your disposal, as soon as your orthodox toes touched English ground?[3] or to have "a silver salver" presented to you? or to have lords and ladies, and dukes and duchesses paying homage to you? or in short to raise such a little young tornado to sweep through the four quarters of the globe? *You?* nothing but a woman—an *American* woman! and a *Beecher* at that! It is perfectly insufferable—one genius in a family is enough. There's your old patriarch father—God bless him!—there's material enough in him to make a dozen ordinary men, to say nothing of "Henry Ward"[4] who's not so great an idiot as he might be! You see you had no "call," Mrs. Tom Cabin, to drop your babies and darning-needle to immortalize your name.

Well, I hope your feminine shoulders are broad enough and strong enough to bear all the abuse your presumption will call down upon you. All the men in your family, your husband included, belong to "the cloth,"[5] and consequently can't practice pistol shooting; there's where your enemies have you, you little simpleton! that's the only objection I have to Mr. Fern's "taking orders," for I've quite a penchant for ministers.

3. Stowe took a celebratory tour of England in 1853–54, where she was hailed as a leader of the anti-slavery movement and as the representative American author.

4. Henry Ward Beecher (1813–87) was the most famous of the Beecher children besides Harriet.
5. A minister.

I trust you are convinced by this time that "Uncle Tom's Cabin" is a "flash in the pan." I'm sorry you have lost so much money by it, but it will go to show you, that women should have their ambition bounded by a gridiron, and a darning needle. If you had not meddled with your husband's *divine* inkstand for such a *dark* purpose, nobody would have said you was "40 years old and looked like an Irish woman;" and between you and me and the vestry door, I don't believe they've done with you yet; for I see that every steamer tosses fresh laurels on your ortho- dox head, from foreign shores, and foreign powers. Poor *unfortunate* Mrs. Tom Cabin! Ain't you to be pitied.

1853

Shall Women Vote?

The principal objection made by conservatives to their doing so, is on the score of their being thrown into rowdy company of both sexes. Admitting this necessity (though, by the way, I don't do it! because if incompetent men-voters are ruled out, it would follow incompetent women should be also), I cannot sufficiently ad- mire the objection; when a good-looking woman, wife or sister, whom husbands and brothers allow, without a demur, to walk our public thoroughfares unat- tended, can scarcely do it without being jostled, and ogled at street corners, by squads of gamblers, and often times followed whole blocks, and even spoken to by well-dressed villains; when these ladies often have their toes and elbows nudged by them in omnibusses and cars, or an impertinent hand dropped on their shoul- der or waist as if by accident. When two ladies, though leaning on the arm of a gentleman, cannot return from the Opera late at night, to a ferry-boat, without being insulted by the wretched of their own sex, or the rascals who make them such. I admire that, when a husband thinks it quite the thing for his wife to ex- plore all sorts of localities, in search of articles needed for family consumption, because "he has not time to attend to it." I like that, when he coolly permits his wife and daughters to waltz at public places, with the chance male acquaintance of a week or a day. I admire that, when his serenity is undisturbed, though Tom, Dick and Harry, tear the crinoline from their backs, in the struggle to secure seats for an hour's enjoyment of the latest nine-day, New York wonder.

Pshaw! all such talk is humbug, as the men themselves very well know. We are always "dear—delicate fragile creatures," who should be immediately gagged with this sugar plum whenever we talk about that of which it is their interest to keep us ignorant. It won't do, gentlemen; the sugar-plum game is well nigh "played out." *Women will assuredly vote some day;* meanwhile the majority of them will "keep up a considerable of a thinking." The whole truth about the male creatures' dislike to it, is embodied in a remark of "Mr. Tulliver's,"[6] in a late admirable work. This gentleman, with more honesty than is usual with the sex, having ad- mitted that from out a bunch of sisters, he selected his milk-and-water wife *"be- cause he was not going to be told the right of things by his own fireside!"* I take particular pleasure in passing this sentiment round, because editors who have

---

6. Allusion to George Eliot's novel of 1860, *The Mill on the Floss*.

quoted largely and approvingly from this book, somehow or other, have never seemed to see *this* passage!

1860

The Working Girls of New York

Nowhere more than in New York does the contest between squalor and splendor so sharply present itself. This is the first reflection of the observing stranger who walks its streets. Particularly is this noticeable with regard to its women. Jostling on the same pavement with the dainty fashionist is the care-worn working-girl. Looking at both these women, the question arises, which lives the more miserable life—she whom the world styles "fortunate," whose husband belongs to three clubs, and whose only meal with his family is an occasional breakfast, from year's end to year's end; who is as much a stranger to his own children as to the reader; whose young son of seventeen has already a detective on his track employed by his father to ascertain where and how he spends his nights and his father's money; swift retribution for that father who finds food, raiment, shelter, equipages for his household; but love, sympathy, companionship—never? Or she—this other woman—with a heart quite as hungry and unappeased, who also faces day by day the same appalling question: *Is this all life has for me?*

A great book is yet unwritten about women. Michelet[7] has aired his wax-doll theories regarding them. The defender of "woman's rights" has given us her views. Authors and authoresses of little, and big repute, have expressed themselves on this subject, and none of them as yet have begun to grasp it: men—because they lack spirituality, rightly and justly to interpret women; women—because they dare not, or will not tell us that which most interests us to know. Who shall write this bold, frank, truthful book remains to be seen. Meanwhile woman's millennium[8] is yet a great way off; and while it slowly progresses, conservatism and indifference gaze through their spectacles at the seething elements of to-day, and wonder "what ails all our women?"

Let me tell you what ails the working-girls. While yet your breakfast is progressing, and your toilet unmade, comes forth through Chatham Street and the Bowery,[9] a long procession of them by twos and threes to their daily labor. Their breakfast, so called, has been hastily swallowed in a tenement house, where two of them share, in a small room, the same miserable bed. Of its quality you may better judge, when you know that each of these girls pays but three dollars a week for board, to the working man and his wife where they lodge.

The room they occupy is close and unventilated, with no accommodations for personal cleanliness, and so near to the little Flinegans that their Celtic[1] night-cries are distinctly heard. They have risen unrefreshed, as a matter of course, and their ill-cooked breakfast does not mend the matter. They emerge from the doorway

---

7. The French historian Jules Michelet (1798–1874).
8. The achievement of a new era for women.

9. Streets in New York City.
1. Many underpaid servants and working-class laborers were recent Irish immigrants.

where their passage is obstructed by "nanny goats"[2] and ragged children rooting together in the dirt, and pass out into the street. They shiver as the sharp wind of early morning strikes their temples. There is no look of youth on their faces; hard lines appear there. Their brows are knit; their eyes are sunken; their dress is flimsy, and foolish, and tawdry; always a hat, and feather or soiled artificial flower upon it; the hair dressed with an abortive attempt at style; a soiled petticoat; a greasy dress, a well-worn sacque[3] or shawl, and a gilt breast-pin and earrings.

Now follow them to the large, black-looking building, where several hundred of them are manufacturing hoop-skirts. If you are a woman you have worn plenty; but you little thought what passed in the heads of these girls as their busy fingers glazed the wire, or prepared the spools for covering them, or secured the tapes which held them in their places. *You* could not stay five minutes in that room, where the noise of the machinery used is so deafening, that only by the motion of the lips could you comprehend a person speaking.

Five minutes! Why, these young creatures bear it, from seven in the morning till six in the evening; week after week, month after month, with only half an hour at midday to eat their dinner of a slice of bread and butter or an apple, which they usually eat in the building, some of them having come a long distance. As I said, the roar of machinery in that room is like the roar of Niagara.[4] Observe them as you enter. Not one lifts her head. They might as well be machines, for any interest or curiosity they show, save always to know *what o'clock it is*. Pitiful! pitiful, you almost sob to yourself, as you look at these young girls. *Young?* Alas! it is only in years that they are young.

1868

◄── HARRIET JACOBS ──►
1813–1897

In 1842, Harriet Jacobs escaped slavery in Edenton, North Carolina, and began a new life in New York City. Her fictionalized autobiography, *Incidents in the Life of a Slave Girl* (1861), describes the complex and paradoxical culture of the slave-holding states, where bonds of violence, affection, sexual desire, and kinship made growing up especially perplexing and dangerous. In New York, having attained emancipation for herself and her children, Jacobs began working to realize what she called "the dream of my life," which was to sit with her children in a home of her own. For almost twenty years she worked as a paid domestic servant in the home of the publisher and editor N. P. Willis, who was the brother of Fanny Fern (pp. 787–88). Working for the Willises brought Jacobs in contact with many prominent people in the literary, activist, and abolitionist circles of the day. In the mid-1850s, Jacobs determined to make a contribution to the anti-slavery effort by publishing her story, even though she initially doubted her own ability to express

2. Goats, chickens, pigs, and horses were not uncommon in nineteenth-century American cities.

3. A loose dress.
4. Niagara Falls was famous for its sublime noise.

it. After a discouraging interaction with Harriet Beecher Stowe (pp. 732–34), who wanted to make use of Jacobs's story for her own purposes, Jacobs completed her manuscript in 1858. With the help and encouragement of Lydia Maria Child (pp. 619–20), Jacobs's book was published in 1862 to acclaim from both the African American and the white reform presses. During the Civil War and immediately after, Jacobs devoted herself to the cause of helping freed slaves make the transition to paid labor. With the exception of letters and reports, Jacobs did not write after the publication of *Incidents*. She lived the last thirty years of her life with her daughter Louisa in Cambridge, Massachusetts, and later, in Washington, D.C., where she remained active in the struggle for political and social rights of blacks in post-Reconstruction America. Jacobs ran boardinghouses as a way to support herself, making home and hearth available to an extended network of family and friends.

In many ways, Jacobs's *Incidents in the Life of a Slave Girl* is a typical American slave narrative. Jacobs's story begins with the discovery of what it means to be a slave, then presents examples of the personal suffering endured by the protagonist, and ends with an account of the struggle for physical—if not legal—freedom. But Jacobs's *Incidents* differs significantly from the slave narrative in the degree to which the story is shaped by the nineteenth-century traditions of the novels of domestic life and those of seduction. Jacobs, the freed slave, doesn't tell her own story; instead, Jacobs creates a fictional narrator, Linda Brent, to tell a story based on the events of Jacobs's life. As a first-person narrator and protagonist, Brent is not an isolated individual fighting against slavery, but a person involved in complicated webs of relationships as a daughter, mother, sister, and lover. For Jacobs, as for her heroine Linda Brent, these relationships crossed the lines of black and white, slave and free. The explicitly literary modes of sentimentality helped Jacobs to make sense of and render some of the more disturbing aspects of her life as a woman under slavery, including a woman slave's sexual oppression by her "master," as well as a woman slave's use of her own sexuality to resist this oppression. We sympathize with Brent because we realize that her being a slave dooms her to the status of a "fallen woman" regardless of her own moral values. But we also can see how the novelistic aspects of this autobiography help Jacobs present her alter ego as a heroine not merely because she has overcome the injustice of slavery but more importantly because she is a good mother in spite of her hardships.

From Incidents in the Life of a Slave Girl

Written by Herself

"Northerners know nothing at all about Slavery. They think it is perpetual bondage only. They have no conception of the depth of degradation involved in the word, SLAVERY; if they had, they would never cease their efforts until so horrible a system was overthrown."

—A WOMAN OF NORTH CAROLINA.

"Rise up, ye women that are at ease! Hear my voice, ye careless daughters! Give ear unto my speech."

—ISAIAH 32:9.

Preface by the Author

Reader, be assured this narrative is no fiction. I am aware that some of my adventures may seem incredible; but they are, nevertheless, strictly true. I have not exaggerated the wrongs inflicted by Slavery; on the contrary, my descriptions fall far short of the facts. I have concealed the names of places, and given persons fictitious names. I had no motive for secrecy on my own account, but I deemed it kind and considerate towards others to pursue this course.

I wish I were more competent to the task I have undertaken. But I trust my readers will excuse deficiencies in consideration of circumstances. I was born and reared in Slavery; and I remained in a Slave State twenty-seven years. Since I have been at the North, it has been necessary for me to work diligently for my own support, and the education of my children. This has not left me much leisure to make up for the loss of early opportunities to improve myself; and it has compelled me to write these pages at irregular intervals, whenever I could snatch an hour from household duties.

When I first arrived in Philadelphia, Bishop Paine[1] advised me to publish a sketch of my life, but I told him I was altogether incompetent to such an undertaking. Though I have improved my mind somewhat since that time, I still remain of the same opinion; but I trust my motives will excuse what might otherwise seem presumptuous. I have not written my experiences in order to attract attention to myself; on the contrary, it would have been more pleasant to me to have been silent about my own history. Neither do I care to excite sympathy for my own sufferings. But I do earnestly desire to arouse the women of the North to a realizing sense of the condition of two millions of women at the South, still in bondage, suffering what I suffered, and most of them far worse. I want to add my testimony to that of abler pens to convince the people of the Free States what Slavery really is. Only by experience can any one realize how deep, and dark, and foul is that pit of abominations. May the blessing of God rest on this imperfect effort in behalf of my persecuted people!

Linda Brent[2]

Introduction by the Editor

The author of the following autobiography is personally known to me, and her conversation and manners inspire me with confidence. During the last seventeen years, she has lived the greater part of the time with a distinguished family in New York, and has so deported herself as to be highly esteemed by them. This fact is sufficient, without further credentials of her character. I believe those who know her will not be disposed to doubt her veracity, though some incidents in her story are more romantic than fiction.

At her request, I have revised her manuscript; but such changes as I have made have been mainly for purposes of condensation and orderly arrangement. I have not added any thing to the incidents, or changed the import of her very pertinent remarks. With trifling exceptions, both the ideas and the language are her own. I pruned excrescences a little, but otherwise I had no reason for changing her lively

---

1. Daniel Payne (1811–93), bishop in the African   2. Jacobs's pen name.
Methodist Episcopal Church.

and dramatic way of telling her own story. The names of both persons and places are known to me; but for good reasons I suppress them.

It will naturally excite surprise that a woman reared in Slavery should be able to write so well. But circumstances will explain this. In the first place, nature endowed her with quick perceptions. Secondly, the mistress, with whom she lived till she was twelve years old, was a kind, considerate friend, who taught her to read and spell. Thirdly, she was placed in favorable circumstances after she came to the North; having frequent intercourse with intelligent persons, who felt a friendly interest in her welfare, and were disposed to give her opportunities for self-improvement.

I am well aware that many will accuse me of indecorum for presenting these pages to the public; for the experiences of this intelligent and much-injured woman belong to a class which some call delicate subjects, and others indelicate. This peculiar phase of Slavery has generally been kept veiled; but the public ought to be made acquainted with its monstrous features, and I willingly take the responsibility of presenting them with the veil withdrawn. I do this for the sake of my sisters in bondage, who are suffering wrongs so foul, that our ears are too delicate to listen to them. I do it with the hope of arousing conscientious and reflecting women at the North to a sense of their duty in the exertion of moral influence on the question of Slavery, on all possible occasions. I do it with the hope that every man who reads this narrative will swear solemnly before God that, so far as he has power to prevent it, no fugitive from Slavery shall ever be sent back to suffer in that loathsome den of corruption and cruelty.[3]

L. Maria Child[4]

I
Childhood

I was born a slave; but I never knew it till six years of happy childhood had passed away. My father was a carpenter, and considered so intelligent and skilful in his trade, that, when buildings out of the common line were to be erected, he was sent for from long distances, to be head workman. On condition of paying his mistress two hundred dollars a year, and supporting himself, he was allowed to work at his trade, and manage his own affairs. His strongest wish was to purchase his children; but, though he several times offered his hard earnings for that purpose, he never succeeded. In complexion my parents were a light shade of brownish yellow, and were termed mulattoes. They lived together in a comfortable home; and, though we were all slaves, I was so fondly shielded that I never dreamed I was a piece of merchandise, trusted to them for safe keeping, and liable to be demanded of them at any moment. I had one brother, William, who was two years younger than myself—a bright, affectionate child. I had also a great treasure in my maternal grandmother, who was a remarkable woman in many respects. She was the daughter of a planter in South Carolina, who, at his death, left her mother and his three children free, with money to go to St. Augustine, where they had relatives. It was during the Revolutionary War; and they were captured on their passage, carried back, and sold to different purchasers. Such was the story my grandmother used to tell me; but I do not remember all the particulars. She was a

---

3. The Fugitive Slave Act (1850) required citizens in all states, slave and free, to assist in returning escaped slaves to their "master."

4. American writer and abolitionist (1802–80); see pp. 619–35.

little girl when she was captured and sold to the keeper of a large hotel. I have often heard her tell how hard she fared during childhood. But as she grew older she evinced so much intelligence, and was so faithful, that her master and mistress could not helping seeing it was for their interest to take care of such a valuable piece of property. She became an indispensable personage in the household, officiating in all capacities, from cook and wet nurse to seamstress. She was much praised for her cooking; and her nice crackers became so famous in the neighborhood that many people were desirous of obtaining them. In consequence of numerous requests of this kind, she asked permission of her mistress to bake crackers at night, after all the household work was done; and she obtained leave to do it, provided she would clothe herself and her children from the profits. Upon these terms, after working hard all day for her mistress, she began her midnight bakings, assisted by her two oldest children. The business proved profitable; and each year she laid by a little, which was saved for a fund to purchase her children. Her master died, and the property was divided among his heirs. The widow had her dower in the hotel, which she continued to keep open. My grandmother remained in her service as a slave; but her children were divided among her master's children. As she had five, Benjamin, the youngest one, was sold, in order that each heir might have an equal portion of dollars and cents. There was so little difference in our ages that he seemed more like my brother than my uncle. He was a bright, handsome lad, nearly white; for he inherited the complexion my grandmother had derived from Anglo-Saxon ancestors. Though only ten years old, seven hundred and twenty dollars were paid for him. His sale was a terrible blow to my grandmother; but she was naturally hopeful, and she went to work with renewed energy, trusting in time to be able to purchase some of her children. She had laid up three hundred dollars, which her mistress one day begged as a loan, promising to pay her soon. The reader probably knows that no promise or writing given to a slave is legally binding; for, according to Southern laws, a slave, *being* property, can *hold* no property. When my grandmother lent her hard earnings to her mistress, she trusted solely to her honor. The honor of a slaveholder to a slave!

To this good grandmother I was indebted for many comforts. My brother Willie and I often received portions of the crackers, cakes, and preserves, she made to sell; and after we ceased to be children we were indebted to her for many more important services.

Such were the unusually fortunate circumstances of my early childhood. When I was six years old, my mother died; and then, for the first time, I learned, by the talk about me, that I was a slave. My mother's mistress was the daughter of my grandmother's mistress. She was the foster sister of my mother; they were both nourished at my grandmother's breast. In fact, my mother had been weaned at three months old, that the babe of the mistress might obtain sufficient food. They played together as children; and, when they became women, my mother was a most faithful servant to her whiter foster sister. On her deathbed her mistress promised that her children should never suffer for any thing; and during her lifetime she kept her word. They all spoke kindly of my dead mother, who had been a slave merely in name, but in nature was noble and womanly. I grieved for her, and my young mind was troubled with the thought who would now take care of me and my little brother. I was told that my home was now to be with her mistress; and I found it a happy one. No toilsome or disagreeable duties were imposed upon me. My mistress was so kind to me that I was always glad to do her bidding, and proud to labor for her as much as my young years would permit. I would sit by her side for hours, sewing diligently, with a heart as free from care as that of any free-born white child. When she thought I was tired, she would send me out to run and jump; and away I bounded, to gather berries or flowers to decorate her room. Those were happy days—too happy to last. The slave child had no thought for the morrow; but there came that blight, which too surely waits on every human being born to be a chattel.

When I was nearly twelve years old, my kind mistress sickened and died. As I saw the cheek grow paler, and the eye more glassy, how earnestly I prayed in my heart that she might live! I loved her; for she had been almost like a mother to me. My prayers were not answered. She died, and they buried her in the little church-yard, where, day after day, my tears fell upon her grave.

I was sent to spend a week with my grandmother. I was now old enough to begin to think of the future; and again and again I asked myself what they would do with me. I felt sure I should never find another mistress so kind as the one who was gone. She had promised my dying mother that her children should never suf-fer for any thing; and when I remembered that, and recalled her many proofs of attachment to me, I could not help having some hopes that she had left me free. My friends were almost certain it would be so. They thought she would be sure to do it, on account of my mother's love and faithful service. But, alas! we all know that the memory of a faithful slave does not avail much to save her children from the auction block.

After a brief period of suspense, the will of my mistress was read, and we learned that she had bequeathed me to her sister's daughter, a child of five years old. So vanished our hopes. My mistress had taught me the precepts of God's Word: "Thou shalt love thy neighbor as thyself." "Whatsoever ye would that men should do unto you, do ye even so unto them."[5] But I was her slave, and I sup-pose she did not recognize me as her neighbor. I would give much to blot out from my memory that one great wrong. As a child, I loved my mistress; and, looking back on the happy days I spent with her, I try to think with less bitterness of this act of injustice. While I was with her, she taught me to read and spell; and for this privilege, which so rarely falls to the lot of a slave, I bless her memory.

She possessed but few slaves; and at her death those were all distributed among her relatives. Five of them were my grandmother's children, and had shared the same milk that nourished her mother's children. Notwithstanding my grand-mother's long and faithful service to her owners, not one of her children escaped the auction block. These God-breathing machines are no more, in the sight of their masters, than the cotton they plant, or the horses they tend.

II
The New Master and Mistress

Dr. Flint, a physician in the neighborhood, had married the sister of my mistress, and I was now the property of their little daughter. It was not without murmuring that I prepared for my new home; and what added to my unhappiness, was the fact that my brother William was purchased by the same family. My father, by his nature, as well as by the habit of transacting business as a skilful mechanic, had more of the feelings of a freeman than is common among slaves. My brother was

5. Matthew 19:19; 7:12.

a spirited boy; and being brought up under such influences, he early detested the name of master and mistress. One day, when his father and his mistress both happened to call him at the same time, he hesitated between the two; being perplexed to know which had the strongest claim upon his obedience. He finally concluded to go to his mistress. When my father reproved him for it, he said, "You both called me, and I didn't know which I ought to go to first."

"You are *my* child," replied our father, "and when I call you, you should come immediately, if you have to pass through fire and water."

Poor Willie! He was now to learn his first lesson of obedience to a master. Grandmother tried to cheer us with hopeful words, and they found an echo in the credulous hearts of youth.

When we entered our new home we encountered cold looks, cold words, and cold treatment. We were glad when the night came. On my narrow bed I moaned and wept, I felt so desolate and alone.

I had been there nearly a year, when a dear little friend of mine was buried. I heard her mother sob, as the clods fell on the coffin of her only child, and I turned away from the grave, feeling thankful that I still had something left to love. I met my grandmother, who said, "Come with me, Linda;" and from her tone I knew that something sad had happened. She led me apart from the people, and then said, "My child, your father is dead." Dead! How could I believe it? He had died so suddenly I had not even heard that he was sick. I went home with my grandmother. My heart rebelled against God, who had taken from me mother, father, mistress, and friend. The good grandmother tried to comfort me. "Who knows the ways of God?" said she. "Perhaps they have been kindly taken from the evil days to come." Years afterwards I often thought of this. She promised to be a mother to her grandchildren, so far as she might be permitted to do so; and strengthened by her love, I returned to my master's. I thought I should be allowed to go to my father's house the next morning; but I was ordered to go for flowers, that my mistress's house might be decorated for an evening party. I spent the day gathering flowers and weaving them into festoons, while the dead body of my father was lying within a mile of me. What cared my owners for that? he was merely a piece of property. Moreover, they thought he had spoiled his children, by teaching them to feel that they were human beings. This was blasphemous doctrine for a slave to teach; presumptuous in him, and dangerous to the masters.

The next day I followed his remains to a humble grave beside that of my dear mother. There were those who knew my father's worth, and respected his memory.

My home now seemed more dreary than ever. The laugh of the little slave-children sounded harsh and cruel. It was selfish to feel so about the joy of others. My brother moved about with a very grave face. I tried to comfort him, by saying, "Take courage, Willie; brighter days will come by and by."

"You don't know any thing about it, Linda," he replied. "We shall have to stay here all our days; we shall never be free."

I argued that we were growing older and stronger, and that perhaps we might, before long, be allowed to hire our own time, and then we could earn money to buy our freedom. William declared this was much easier to say than to do; moreover, he did not intend to *buy* his freedom. We held daily controversies upon this subject.

Little attention was paid to the slaves' meals in Dr. Flint's house. If they could catch a bit of food while it was going, well and good. I gave myself no trouble on that score, for on my various errands I passed my grandmother's house, where there was always something to spare for me. I was frequently threatened with punishment if I stopped there; and my grandmother, to avoid detaining me, often stood at the gate with something for my breakfast or dinner. I was indebted to *her* for all my comforts, spiritual or temporal. It was *her* labor that supplied my scanty wardrobe. I have a vivid recollection of the linsey-woolsey[6] dress given me every winter by Mrs. Flint. How I hated it! It was one of the badges of slavery.

While my grandmother was thus helping to support me from her hard earnings, the three hundred dollars she had lent her mistress were never repaid. When her mistress died, her son-in-law, Dr. Flint, was appointed executor. When grandmother applied to him for payment, he said the estate was insolvent, and the law prohibited payment. It did not, however, prohibit him from retaining the silver candelabra, which had been purchased with that money. I presume they will be handed down in the family, from generation to generation.

My grandmother's mistress had always promised her that, at her death, she should be free; and it was said that in her will she made good the promise. But when the estate was settled, Dr. Flint told the faithful old servant that, under existing circumstances, it was necessary she should be sold.

On the appointed day, the customary advertisement was posted up, proclaiming that there would be a "public sale of negroes, horses, &c." Dr. Flint called to tell my grandmother that he was unwilling to wound her feelings by putting her up at auction, and that he would prefer to dispose of her at private sale. My grandmother saw through his hypocrisy; she understood very well that he was ashamed of the job. She was a very spirited woman, and if he was base enough to sell her, when her mistress intended she should be free, she was determined the public should know it. She had for a long time supplied many families with crackers and preserves; consequently, "Aunt Marthy," as she was called, was generally known, and every body who knew her respected her intelligence and good character. Her long and faithful service in the family was also well known, and the intention of her mistress to leave her free. When the day of the sale came, she took her place among the chattels, and at the first call she sprang upon the auction-block. Many voices called out, "Shame! Shame! Who is going to sell *you*, aunt Marthy? Don't stand there! That is no place for *you*." Without saying a word, she quietly awaited her fate. No one bid for her. At last, a feeble voice said, "Fifty dollars." It came from a maiden lady, seventy years old, the sister of my grandmother's deceased mistress. She had lived forty years under the same roof with my grandmother; she knew how faithfully she had served her owners, and how cruelly she had been defrauded of her rights; and she resolved to protect her. The auctioneer waited for a higher bid; but her wishes were respected; no one bid above her. She could neither read nor write; and when the bill of sale was made out, she signed it with a cross. But what consequence was that, when she had a big heart overflowing with human kindness? She gave the old servant her freedom.

At that time, my grandmother was just fifty years old. Laborious years had passed since then; and now my brother and I were slaves to the man who had defrauded her of her money, and tried to defraud her of her freedom. One of my mother's sisters, called Aunt Nancy, was also a slave in his family. She was a kind, good aunt to me; and supplied the place of both housekeeper and waiting maid to her mistress. She was, in fact, at the beginning and end of every thing.

6. A rough fabric woven from linen and wool.

Mrs. Flint, like many southern women, was totally deficient in energy. She had not strength to superintend her household affairs; but her nerves were so strong, that she could sit in her easy chair and see a woman whipped, till the blood trickled from every stroke of the lash. She was a member of the church; but partaking of the Lord's supper[7] did not seem to put her in a Christian frame of mind. If dinner was not served at the exact time on that particular Sunday, she would station herself in the kitchen, and wait till it was dished, and then spit in all the kettles and pans that had been used for cooking. She did this to prevent the cook and her children from eking out their meagre fare with the remains of the gravy and other scrapings. The slaves could get nothing to eat except what she chose to give them. Provisions were weighed out by the pound and ounce, three times a day. I can assure you she gave them no chance to eat wheat bread from her flour barrel. She knew how many biscuits a quart of flour would make, and exactly what size they ought to be.

Dr. Flint was an epicure. The cook never sent a dinner to his table without fear and trembling; for if there happened to be a dish not to his liking, he would either order her to be whipped, or compel her to eat every mouthful of it in his presence. The poor, hungry creature might not have objected to eating it; but she did object to having her master cram it down her throat till she choked.

They had a pet dog, that was a nuisance in the house. The cook was ordered to make some Indian mush[8] for him. He refused to eat, and when his head was held over it, the froth flowed from his mouth into the basin. He died a few minutes after. When Dr. Flint came in, he said the mush had not been well cooked, and that was the reason the animal would not eat it. He sent for the cook, and compelled her to eat it. He thought that the woman's stomach was stronger than the dog's; but her sufferings afterwards proved that he was mistaken. This poor woman endured many cruelties from her master and mistress; sometimes she was locked up, away from her nursing baby, for a whole day and night.

When I had been in the family a few weeks, one of the plantation slaves was brought to town, by order of his master. It was near night when he arrived, and Dr. Flint ordered him to be taken to the work house, and tied up to the joist, so that his feet would just escape the ground. In that situation he was to wait till the doctor had taken his tea. I shall never forget that night. Never before, in my life, had I heard hundreds of blows fall, in succession, on a human being. His piteous groans, and his "O, pray don't, massa," rang in my ear for months afterwards. There were many conjectures as to the cause of this terrible punishment. Some said master accused him of stealing corn; others said the slave had quarrelled with his wife, in presence of the overseer, and had accused his master of being the father of her child. They were both black, and the child was very fair.

I went into the work house next morning, and saw the cowhide still wet with blood, and the boards all covered with gore. The poor man lived, and continued to quarrel with his wife. A few months afterwards Dr. Flint handed them both over to a slave-trader. The guilty man put their value into his pocket, and had the satisfaction of knowing that they were out of sight and hearing. When the mother was delivered into the trader's hands, she said, "You *promised* to treat me well."

7. Taking Communion in a Christian religious   8. Cornmeal cooked in water; hasty pudding.
service.

To which he replied, "You have let your tongue run too far; damn you!" She had forgotten that it was a crime for a slave to tell who was the father of her child.

From others than the master persecution also comes in such cases. I once saw a young slave girl dying soon after the birth of a child nearly white. In her agony she cried out, "O Lord, come and take me!" Her mistress stood by, and mocked at her like an incarnate fiend. "You suffer, do you?" she exclaimed. "I am glad of it. You deserve it all, and more too."

The girl's mother said, "The baby is dead, thank God; and I hope my poor child will soon be in heaven, too."

"Heaven!" retorted the mistress. "There is no such place for the like of her and her bastard."

The poor mother turned away, sobbing. Her dying daughter called her, feebly, and as she bent over her, I heard her say, "Don't grieve so, mother; God knows all about it; and HE will have mercy upon me."

Her sufferings, afterwards, became so intense, that her mistress felt unable to stay; but when she left the room, the scornful smile was still on her lips. Seven children called her mother. The poor black woman had but the one child, whose eyes she saw closing in death, while she thanked God for taking her away from the greater bitterness of life.

* * *

V

The Trials of Girlhood

During the first years of my service in Dr. Flint's family, I was accustomed to share some indulgences with the children of my mistress. Though this seemed to me no more than right, I was grateful for it, and tried to merit the kindness by the faithful discharge of my duties. But I now entered on my fifteenth year—a sad epoch in the life of a slave girl. My master began to whisper foul words in my ear. Young as I was, I could not remain ignorant of their import. I tried to treat them with indifference or contempt. The master's age, my extreme youth, and the fear that his conduct would be reported to my grandmother, made him bear this treatment for many months. He was a crafty man, and resorted to many means to accomplish his purposes. Sometimes he had stormy, terrific ways, that made his victims tremble; sometimes he assumed a gentleness that he thought must surely subdue. Of the two, I preferred his stormy moods, although they left me trembling. He tried his utmost to corrupt the pure principles my grandmother had instilled. He peopled my young mind with unclean images, such as only a vile monster could think of. I turned from him with disgust and hatred. But he was my master. I was compelled to live under the same roof with him—where I saw a man forty years my senior daily violating the most sacred commandments of nature. He told me I was his property; that I must be subject to his will in all things. My soul revolted against the mean tyranny. But where could I turn for protection? No matter whether the slave girl be as black as ebony or as fair as her mistress. In either case, there is no shadow of law to protect her from insult, from violence, or even from death; all these are inflicted by fiends who bear the shape of men. The mistress, who ought to protect the helpless victim, has no other feelings towards her but those of jealousy and rage. The degradation, the wrongs, the vices, that grow out of slavery, are more than I can describe. They are greater than you would willingly believe. Surely, if you credited one half the truths that are told you concerning the helpless millions suffering in this cruel bondage, you at the north would not help to tighten the yoke. You surely would refuse to do for the master, on your own soil, the mean and cruel work which trained bloodhounds and the lowest class of whites do for him at the south.

Every where the years bring to all enough of sin and sorrow; but in slavery the very dawn of life is darkened by these shadows. Even the little child, who is accustomed to wait on her mistress and her children, will learn, before she is twelve years old, why it is that her mistress hates such and such a one among the slaves. Perhaps the child's own mother is among those hated ones. She listens to violent outbreaks of jealous passion, and cannot help understanding what is the cause. She will become prematurely knowing in evil things. Soon she will learn to tremble when she hears her master's footfall. She will be compelled to realize that she is no longer a child. If God has bestowed beauty upon her, it will prove her greatest curse. That which commands admiration in the white woman only hastens the degradation of the female slave. I know that some are too much brutalized by slavery to feel the humiliation of their position; but many slaves feel it most acutely, and shrink from the memory of it. I cannot tell how much I suffered in the presence of these wrongs, nor how I am still pained by the retrospect. My master met me at every turn, reminding me that I belonged to him, and swearing by heaven and earth that he would compel me to submit to him. If I went out for a breath of fresh air, after a day of unwearied toil, his footsteps dogged me. If I knelt by my mother's grave, his dark shadow fell on me even there. The light heart which nature had given me became heavy with sad forebodings. The other slaves in my master's house noticed the change. Many of them pitied me; but none dared to ask the cause. They had no need to inquire. They knew too well the guilty practices under that roof; and they were aware that to speak of them was an offence that never went unpunished.

I longed for some one to confide in. I would have given the world to have laid my head on my grandmother's faithful bosom, and told her all my troubles. But Dr. Flint swore he would kill me, if I was not as silent as the grave. Then, although my grandmother was all in all to me, I feared her as well as loved her. I had been accustomed to look up to her with a respect bordering upon awe. I was very young, and felt shamefaced about telling her such impure things, especially as I knew her to be very strict on such subjects. Moreover, she was a woman of a high spirit. She was usually very quiet in her demeanor; but if her indignation was once roused, it was not very easily quelled. I had been told that she once chased a white gentleman with a loaded pistol, because he insulted one of her daughters. I dreaded the consequences of a violent outbreak; and both pride and fear kept me silent. But though I did not confide in my grandmother, and even evaded her vigilant watchfulness and inquiry, her presence in the neighborhood was some protection to me. Though she had been a slave, Dr. Flint was afraid of her. He dreaded her scorching rebukes. Moreover, she was known and patronized by many people; and he did not wish to have his villainy made public. It was lucky for me that I did not live on a distant plantation, but in a town not so large that the inhabitants were ignorant of each other's affairs. Bad as are the laws and customs in a slaveholding community, the doctor, as a professional man, deemed it prudent to keep up some outward show of decency.

O, what days and nights of fear and sorrow that man caused me! Reader, it is not to awaken sympathy for myself that I am telling you truthfully what I suffered in slavery. I do it to kindle a flame of compassion in your hearts for my sisters who are still in bondage, suffering as I once suffered.

I once saw two beautiful children playing together. One was a fair white child; the other was her slave, and also her sister. When I saw them embracing each other, and heard their joyous laughter, I turned sadly away from the lovely sight. I foresaw the inevitable blight that would fall on the little slave's heart. I knew how soon her laughter would be changed to sighs. The fair child grew up to be a still fairer woman. From childhood to womanhood her pathway was blooming with flowers, and overarched by a sunny sky. Scarcely one day of her life had been clouded when the sun rose on her happy bridal morning.

How had those years dealt with her slave sister, the little playmate of her childhood? She, also, was very beautiful; but the flowers and sunshine of love were not for her. She drank the cup of sin, and shame, and misery, whereof her persecuted race are compelled to drink.

In view of these things, why are ye silent, ye free men and women of the north? Why do your tongues falter in maintenance of the right? Would that I had more ability! But my heart is so full, and my pen is so weak! There are noble men and women who plead for us, striving to help those who cannot help themselves. God bless them! God give them strength and courage to go on! God bless those, every where, who are laboring to advance the cause of humanity!

* * *

X
A Perilous Passage in the Slave Girl's Life

* * * Dr. Flint contrived a new plan. He seemed to have an idea that my fear of my mistress was his greatest obstacle. In the blandest tones, he told me that he was going to build a small house for me, in a secluded place, four miles away from the town. I shuddered; but I was constrained to listen, while he talked of his intention to give me a home of my own, and to make a lady of me. Hitherto, I had escaped my dreaded fate, by being in the midst of people. My grandmother had already had high words with my master about me. She had told him pretty plainly what she thought of his character, and there was considerable gossip in the neighborhood about our affairs, to which the open-mouthed jealousy of Mrs. Flint contributed not a little. When my master said he was going to build a house for me, and that he could do it with little trouble and expense, I was in hopes something would happen to frustrate his scheme; but I soon heard that the house was actually begun. I vowed before my Maker that I would never enter it. I had rather toil on the plantation from dawn till dark; I had rather live and die in jail, than drag on, from day to day, through such a living death. I was determined that the master, whom I so hated and loathed, who had blighted the prospects of my youth, and made my life a desert, should not, after my long struggle with him, succeed at last in trampling his victim under his feet. I would do any thing, every thing, for the sake of defeating him. What *could* I do? I thought and thought, till I became desperate, and made a plunge into the abyss.

And now, reader, I come to a period in my unhappy life, which I would gladly forget if I could. The remembrance fills me with sorrow and shame. It pains me to tell you of it; but I have promised to tell you the truth, and I will do it honestly, let it cost me what it may. I will not try to screen myself behind the plea of compulsion from a master; for it was not so. Neither can I plead ignorance or thoughtlessness. For years, my master had done his utmost to pollute my mind with foul images, and to destroy the pure principles inculcated by my grandmother, and the good mistress of my childhood. The influences of slavery had had the same effect on me that they had on other young girls; they had made me prematurely knowing, concerning the evil ways of the world. I knew what I did, and I did it with deliberate calculation.

But, O, ye happy women, whose purity has been sheltered from childhood, who have been free to choose the objects of your affection, whose homes are protected by law, do not judge the poor desolate slave girl too severely! If slavery had been abolished, I, also, could have married the man of my choice; I could have had a home shielded by the laws; and I should have been spared the painful task of confessing what I am now about to relate; but all my prospects had been blighted by slavery. I wanted to keep myself pure; and, under the most adverse circumstances, I tried hard to preserve my self-respect; but I was struggling alone in the powerful grasp of the demon Slavery; and the monster proved too strong for me. I felt as if I was forsaken by God and man; as if all my efforts must be frustrated; and I became reckless in my despair.

I have told you that Dr. Flint's persecutions and his wife's jealousy had given rise to some gossip in the neighborhood. Among others, it chanced that a white unmarried gentleman had obtained some knowledge of the circumstances in which I was placed. He knew my grandmother, and often spoke to me in the street. He became interested for me, and asked questions about my master, which I answered in part. He expressed a great deal of sympathy, and a wish to aid me. He constantly sought opportunities to see me, and wrote to me frequently. I was a poor slave girl, only fifteen years old.

So much attention from a superior person was, of course, flattering; for human nature is the same in all. I also felt grateful for his sympathy, and encouraged by his kind words. It seemed to me a great thing to have such a friend. By degrees, a more tender feeling crept into my heart. He was an educated and eloquent gentleman; too eloquent, alas, for the poor slave girl who trusted in him. Of course I saw whither all this was tending. I knew the impassable gulf between us; but to be an object of interest to a man who is not married, and who is not her master, is agreeable to the pride and feelings of a slave, if her miserable situation has left her any pride or sentiment. It seems less degrading to give one's self, than to submit to compulsion. There is something akin to freedom in having a lover who has no control over you, except that which he gains by kindness and attachment. A master may treat you as rudely as he pleases, and you dare not speak; moreover, the wrong does not seem so great with an unmarried man, as with one who has a wife to be made unhappy. There may be sophistry in all this; but the condition of a slave confuses all principles of morality, and, in fact, renders the practise of them impossible.

When I found that my master had actually begun to build the lonely cottage, other feelings mixed with those I have described. Revenge, and calculations of interest, were added to flattered vanity and sincere gratitude for kindness. I knew nothing would enrage Dr. Flint so much as to know that I favored another; and it was something to triumph over my tyrant even in that small way. I thought he would revenge himself by selling me, and I was sure my friend, Mr. Sands, would buy me. He was a man of more generosity and feeling than my master, and I thought my freedom could be easily obtained from him. The crisis of my fate now came so near that I was desperate. I shuddered to think of being the mother of children that should be owned by my old tyrant. I knew that as soon as a new fancy took him, his victims were sold far off to get rid of them; especially if they had children. I had seen several women sold, with his babies at the breast. He never allowed his offspring by slaves to remain long in sight of himself and his wife. Of a man who was not my master I could ask to have my children well supported; and in this case, I felt confident I should obtain the boon. I also felt quite sure that they would be made free. With all these thoughts revolving in my mind, and seeing no other way of escaping the doom I so much dreaded, I made a headlong plunge. Pity me, and pardon me, O virtuous reader! You never knew what it is to be a slave; to be entirely unprotected by law or custom; to have the laws reduce you to the condition of a chattel, entirely subject to the will of another. You never exhausted your ingenuity in avoiding the snares, and eluding the power of a hated tyrant; you never shuddered at the sound of his footsteps, and trembled within hearing of his voice. I know I did wrong. No one can feel it more sensibly than I do. The painful and humiliating memory will haunt me to my dying day. Still, in looking back, calmly, on the events of my life, I feel that the slave woman ought not to be judged by the same standard as others.

The months passed on. I had many unhappy hours. I secretly mourned over the sorrow I was bringing on my grandmother, who had so tried to shield me from harm. I knew that I was the greatest comfort of her old age, and that it was a source of pride to her that I had not degraded myself, like most of the slaves. I wanted to confess to her that I was no longer worthy of her love; but I could not utter the dreaded words.

As for Dr. Flint, I had a feeling of satisfaction and triumph in the thought of telling *him*. From time to time he told me of his intended arrangements, and I was silent. At last, he came and told me the cottage was completed, and ordered me to go to it. I told him I would never enter it. He said, "I have heard enough of such talk as that. You shall go, if you are carried by force; and you shall remain there."

I replied, "I will never go there. In a few months I shall be a mother."

He stood and looked at me in dumb amazement, and left the house without a word. I thought I should be happy in my triumph over him. But now that the truth was out, and my relatives would hear of it, I felt wretched. Humble as were their circumstances, they had pride in my good character. Now, how could I look them in the face? My self-respect was gone! I had resolved that I would be virtuous, though I was a slave. I had said, "Let the storm beat! I will brave it till I die." And now, how humiliated I felt!

I went to my grandmother. My lips moved to make confession, but the words stuck in my throat. I sat down in the shade of a tree at her door and began to sew. I think she saw something unusual was the matter with me. The mother of slaves is very watchful. She knows there is no security for her children. After they have entered their teens she lives in daily expectation of trouble. This leads to many questions. If the girl is of a sensitive nature, timidity keeps her from answering truthfully, and this well-meant course has a tendency to drive her from maternal counsels. Presently, in came my mistress, like a mad woman, and accused me concerning her husband. My grandmother, whose suspicions had been previously awakened, believed what she said. She exclaimed, "O Linda! has it come to this? I had rather see you dead than to see you as you now are. You are a disgrace to your dead mother." She tore from my fingers my mother's wedding ring and her

silver thimble. "Go away!" she exclaimed, "and never come to my house, again."
Her reproaches fell so hot and heavy, that they left me no chance to answer. Bitter
tears, such as the eyes never shed but once, were my only answer. I rose from my
seat, but fell back again, sobbing. She did not speak to me; but the tears were running down her furrowed cheeks, and they scorched me like fire. She had always
been so kind to me! *So* kind! How I longed to throw myself at her feet, and tell
her all the truth! But she had ordered me to go, and never to come there again.
After a few minutes, I mustered strength, and started to obey her. With what feelings did I now close that little gate, which I used to open with such an eager hand
in my childhood! It closed upon me with a sound I never head before.

Where could I go? I was afraid to return to my master's. I walked on recklessly, not caring where I went, or what would become of me. When I had gone
four or five miles, fatigue compelled me to stop. I sat down on the stump of an old
tree. The stars were shining through the boughs above me. How they mocked me,
with their bright, calm light! The hours passed by, and as I sat there alone a chilli-
ness and deadly sickness came over me. I sank on the ground. My mind was full
of horrid thoughts. I prayed to die; but the prayer was not answered. At last, with
great effort I roused myself, and walked some distance further, to the house of a
woman who had been a friend of my mother. When I told her why I was there,
she spoke soothingly to me; but I could not be comforted. I thought I could bear
my shame if I could only be reconciled to my grandmother. I longed to open my
heart to her. I thought if she could know the real state of the case, and all I had
been bearing for years, she would perhaps judge me less harshly. My friend advised me to send for her. I did so; but days of agonizing suspense passed before
she came. Had she utterly forsaken me? No. She came at last. I knelt before her,
and told her the things that had poisoned my life; how long I had been persecuted;
that I saw no way of escape; and in an hour of extremity I had become desperate.
She listened in silence. I told her I would bear any thing and do any thing, if in
time I had hopes of obtaining her forgiveness. I begged of her to pity me, for my
dead mother's sake. And she did pity me. She did not say, "I forgive you;" but she
looked at me lovingly, with her eyes full of tears. She laid her old hand gently on
my head, and murmured, "Poor child! Poor child!"

* * *

XXI
The Loophole of Retreat

[AFTER HAVING TWO CHILDREN, LINDA BRENT DECIDES SHE MUST ESCAPE SLAVERY
FOR HER SAKE AND HER CHILDREN'S]

A small shed had been added to my grandmother's house years ago. Some boards
were laid across the joists at the top, and between these boards and the roof was a
very small garret, never occupied by any thing but rats and mice. It was a pent
roof,[9] covered with nothing but shingles, according to the southern custom for
such buildings. The garret was only nine feet long and seven wide. The highest
part was three feet high, and sloped down abruptly to the loose board floor. There
was no admission for either light or air. My uncle Phillip, who was a carpenter,
had very skilfully made a concealed trap-door, which communicated with the

9. A shallow, peaked roof.

storeroom. He had been doing this while I was waiting in the swamp.[1] The store-room opened upon a piazza. To this hole I was conveyed as soon as I entered the house. The air was stifling; the darkness total. A bed had been spread on the floor. I could sleep quite comfortably on one side; but the slope was so sudden that I could not turn on the other without hitting the roof. The rats and mice ran over my bed; but I was weary, and I slept such sleep as the wretched may, when a tempest has passed over them. Morning came. I knew it only by the noises I heard; for in my small den day and night were all the same. I suffered for air even more than for light. But I was not comfortless. I heard the voices of my children. There was joy and there was sadness in the sound. It made my tears flow. How I longed to speak to them! I was eager to look on their faces; but there was no hole, no crack, through which I could peep. This continued darkness was oppressive. It seemed horrible to sit or lie in a cramped position day after day, without one gleam of light. Yet I would have chosen this, rather than my lot as a slave, though white people considered it an easy one; and it was so compared with the fate of others. I was never cruelly over-worked; I was never lacerated with the whip from head to foot; I was never so beaten and bruised that I could not turn from one side to the other; I never had my heel-strings[2] cut to prevent my running away; I was never chained to a log and forced to drag it about, while I toiled in the fields from morning till night; I was never branded with hot iron, or torn by bloodhounds. On the contrary, I had always been kindly treated, and tenderly cared for, until I came into the hands of Dr. Flint. I had never wished for freedom till then. But though my life in slavery was comparatively devoid of hardships, God pity the woman who is compelled to lead such a life!

My food was passed up to me through the trap-door my uncle had contrived; and my grandmother, my uncle Phillip, and aunt Nancy would seize such opportunities as they could, to mount up there and chat with me at the opening. But of course this was not safe in the daytime. It must all be done in darkness. It was impossible for me to move in an erect position, but I crawled about my den for exercise. One day I hit my head against something, and found it was a gimlet. My uncle had left it sticking there when he made the trap-door. I was as rejoiced as Robinson Crusoe[3] could have been at finding such a treasure. It put a lucky thought into my head. I said to myself, "Now I will have some light. Now I will see my children." I did not dare to begin my work during the daytime, for fear of attracting attention. But I groped round; and having found the side next the street, where I could frequently see my children, I stuck the gimlet in and waited for evening. I bored three rows of holes, one above another; then I bored out the interstices between. I thus succeeded in making one hole about an inch long and an inch broad. I sat by it till late into the night, to enjoy the little whiff of air that floated in. In the morning I watched for my children. The first person I saw in the street was Dr. Flint. I had a shuddering, superstitious feeling that it was a bad omen. Several familiar faces passed by. At last I heard the merry laugh of children, and presently two sweet little faces were looking up at me, as though they knew I

---

1. Linda has been temporarily hiding in a local swamp.
2. Achilles tendon.
3. A character in the novel of the same name

(1719) by English writer and spy Daniel Defoe (1660?–1731); Robinson Crusoe spends twenty-eight years on a desert island before being rescued.

was there, and were conscious of the joy they imparted. How I longed to *tell* them I was there!

My condition was now a little improved. But for weeks I was tormented by hundreds of little red insects, fine as a needle's point, that pierced through my skin, and produced an intolerable burning. The good grandmother gave me herb teas and cooling medicines, and finally I got rid of them. The heat of my den was intense, for nothing but thin shingles protected me from the scorching summer's sun. But I had my consolations. Through my peeping-hole I could watch the children, and when they were near enough, I could hear their talk. Aunt Nancy brought me all the news she could hear at Dr. Flint's. From her I learned that the doctor had written to New York to a colored woman, who had been born and raised in our neighborhood, and had breathed his contaminating atmosphere. He offered her a reward if she could find out any thing about me. I know not what was the nature of her reply; but he soon after started for New York in haste, saying to his family that he had business of importance to transact. I peeped at him as he passed on his way to the steamboat. It was a satisfaction to have miles of land and water between us, even for a little while; and it was a still greater satisfaction to know that he believed me to be in the Free States. My little den seemed less dreary than it had done. He returned, as he did from his former journey to New York, without obtaining any satisfactory information. When he passed our house next morning, Benny was standing at the gate. He had heard them say that he had gone to find me, and he called out, "Dr. Flint, did you bring my mother home? I want to see her." The doctor stamped his foot at him in a rage, and exclaimed, "Get out of the way, you little damned rascal! If you don't, I'll cut off your head."

Benny ran terrified into the house, saying, "You can't put me in jail again. I don't belong to you now." It was well that the wind carried the words away from the doctor's ear. I told my grandmother of it, when we had our next conference at the trap-door; and begged of her not to allow the children to be impertinent to the irascible old man.

Autumn came, with a pleasant abatement of heat. My eyes had become accustomed to the dim light, and by holding my book or work in a certain position near the aperture I contrived to read and sew. That was a great relief to the tedious monotony of my life. But when winter came, the cold penetrated through the thin shingle roof, and I was dreadfully chilled. The winters there are not so long, or so severe, as in northern latitudes; but the houses are not built to shelter from cold, and my little den was peculiarly comfortless. The kind grandmother brought me bed-clothes and warm drinks. Often I was obliged to lie in bed all day to keep comfortable; but with all my precautions, my shoulders and feet were frostbitten. O, those long, gloomy days, with no object for my eye to rest upon, and no thoughts to occupy my mind, except the dreary past and the uncertain future! I was thankful when there came a day sufficiently mild for me to wrap myself up and sit at the loophole to watch the passers by. Southerners have the habit of stopping and talking in the streets, and I heard many conversations not intended to meet my ears. I heard slave-hunters planning how to catch some poor fugitive. Several times I heard allusions to Dr. Flint, myself, and the history of my children, who, perhaps, were playing near the gate. One would say, "I wouldn't move my little finger to catch her, as old Flint's property." Another would say, "I'll catch *any* nigger for the reward. A man ought to have what belongs to him, if he *is* a damned brute." The opinion was often expressed that I was in the Free

States. Very rarely did any one suggest that I might be in the vicinity. Had the least suspicion rested on my grandmother's house, it would have been burned to the ground. But it was the last place they thought of. Yet there was no place, where slavery existed, that could have afforded me so good a place of concealment.

Dr. Flint and his family repeatedly tried to coax and bribe my children to tell something they had heard said about me. One day the doctor took them into a shop, and offered them some bright little silver pieces and gay handkerchiefs if they would tell where their mother was. Ellen shrank away from him, and would not speak; but Benny spoke up, and said, "Dr. Flint, I don't know where my mother is. I guess she's in New York; and when you go there again, I wish you'd ask her to come home, for I want to see her; but if you put her in jail, or tell her you'll cut her head off, I'll tell her to go right back."

* * *

XLI
Free at Last

Mrs. Bruce,[4] and every member of her family, were exceedingly kind to me. I was thankful for the blessings of my lot, yet I could not always wear a cheerful countenance. I was doing harm to no one; on the contrary, I was doing all the good I could in my small way; yet I could never go out to breathe God's free air without trepidation at my heart.[5] This seemed hard; and I could not think it was a right state of things in any civilized country.

From time to time I received news from my good old grandmother. She could not write; but she employed others to write for her. The following is an extract from one of her last letters:—

"Dear Daughter: I cannot hope to see you again on earth; but I pray to God to unite us above, where pain will no more rack this feeble body of mine; where sorrow and parting from my children will be no more.[6] God has promised these things if we are faithful unto the end. My age and feeble health deprive me of going to church now; but God is with me here at home. Thank your brother for his kindness. Give much love to him, and tell him to remember the Creator in the days of his youth,[7] and strive to meet me in the Father's kingdom. Love to Ellen and Benjamin. Don't neglect him. Tell him for me, to be a good boy. Strive, my child, to train them for God's children. May he protect and provide for you, is the prayer of your loving old mother."

These letters both cheered and saddened me. I was always glad to have tidings from the kind, faithful old friend of my unhappy youth; but her messages of love made my heart yearn to see her before she died, and I mourned over the fact that it was impossible. Some months after I returned from my flight to New England,[8] I received a letter from her, in which she wrote, "Dr. Flint is dead. He has left a distressed family. Poor old man! I hope he made his peace with God."

I remembered how he had defrauded my grandmother of the hard earnings she had loaned; how he had tried to cheat her out of the freedom her mistress had promised her, and how he had persecuted her children; and I thought to myself that she was a better Christian than I was, if she could entirely forgive him. I cannot

---

4. Brent has escaped to the North, dressed as a man. She is employed by the Bruce family.
5. With the Fugitive Slave Act (1850), she is not safe, even in the North.
6. A rewording of Revelation 21:4.
7. Ecclesiastes 12:1.
8. Linda has had to leave New York City to hide temporarily from slave catchers.

say, with truth, that the news of my old master's death softened my feelings towards him. There are wrongs which even the grave does not bury. The man was odious to me while he lived, and his memory is odious now.

His departure from this world did not diminish my danger. He had threatened my grandmother that his heirs should hold me in slavery after he was gone; that I never should be free so long as a child of his survived. As for Mrs. Flint, I had seen her in deeper afflictions than I supposed the loss of her husband would be, for she had buried several children; yet I never saw any signs of softening in her heart. The doctor had died in embarrassed circumstances, and had little to will to his heirs, except such property as he was unable to grasp. I was well aware what I had to expect from the family of Flints; and my fears were confirmed by a letter from the south, warning me to be on my guard, because Mrs. Flint openly declared that her daughter could not afford to lose so valuable a slave as I was.

I kept close watch of the newspapers for arrivals; but one Saturday night, being much occupied, I forgot to examine the Evening Express as usual. I went down into the parlor for it, early in the morning, and found the boy about to kindle a fire with it. I took it from him and examined the list of arrivals. Reader, if you have never been a slave, you cannot imagine the acute sensation of suffering at my heart, when I read the names of Mr. and Mrs. Dodge, at a hotel in Courtland Street. It was a third-rate hotel, and that circumstance convinced me of the truth of what I had heard, that they were short of funds and had need of my value, as *they* valued me; and that was by dollars and cents. I hastened with the paper to Mrs. Bruce. Her heart and hand were always open to every one in distress, and she always warmly sympathized with mine. It was impossible to tell how near the enemy was. He might have passed and repassed the house while we were sleeping. He might at that moment be waiting to pounce upon me if I ventured out of doors. I had never seen the husband of my young mistress, and therefore I could not distinguish him from any other stranger. A carriage was hastily ordered; and, closely veiled, I followed Mrs. Bruce, taking the baby again with me into exile. After various turnings and crossings, and returnings, the carriage stopped at the house of one of Mrs. Bruce's friends, where I was kindly received. Mrs. Bruce returned immediately, to instruct the domestics what to say if any one came to inquire for me.

It was lucky for me that the evening paper was not burned up before I had a chance to examine the list of arrivals. It was not long after Mrs. Bruce's return to her house, before several people came to inquire for me. One inquired for me, another asked for my daughter Ellen, and another said he had a letter from my grandmother, which he was requested to deliver in person.

They were told, "She *has* lived here, but she has left."

"How long ago?"

"I don't know, sir."

"Do you know where she went?"

"I do not, sir." And the door was closed.

This Mr. Dodge, who claimed me as his property, was originally a Yankee pedler in the south; then he became a merchant, and finally a slaveholder. He managed to get introduced into what was called the first society, and married Miss Emily Flint. A quarrel arose between him and her brother, and the brother cowhided him. This led to a family feud, and he proposed to remove to Virginia. Dr. Flint left him no property, and his own means had become circumscribed, while a wife and children depended upon him for support. Under these circumstances, it was very natural that he should make an effort to put me into his pocket.

I had a colored friend, a man from my native place, in whom I had the most implicit confidence. I sent for him, and told him that Mr. and Mrs. Dodge had arrived in New York. I proposed that he should call upon them to make inquiries about his friends at the south, with whom Dr. Flint's family were well acquainted. He thought there was no impropriety in his doing so, and he consented. He went to the hotel, and knocked at the door of Mr. Dodge's room, which was opened by the gentleman himself, who gruffly inquired, "What brought you here? How came you to know I was in the city?"

"Your arrival was published in the evening papers, sir; and I called to ask Mrs. Dodge about my friends at home. I didn't suppose it would give any offence."

"Where's that negro girl, that belongs to my wife?"

"What girl, sir?"

"You know well enough. I mean Linda, that ran away from Dr. Flint's plantation, some years ago. I dare say you've seen her, and know where she is."

"Yes, sir, I've seen her, and know where she is. She is out of your reach, sir."

"Tell me where she is, or bring her to me, and I will give her a chance to buy her freedom."

"I don't think it would be of any use, sir. I have heard her say she would go to the ends of the earth, rather than pay any man or woman for her freedom, because she thinks she has a right to it. Besides, she couldn't do it, if she would, for she has spent her earnings to educate her children."

This made Mr. Dodge very angry, and some high words passed between them. My friend was afraid to come where I was; but in the course of the day I received a note from him. I supposed they had not come from the south, in the winter, for a pleasure excursion; and now the nature of their business was very plain.

Mrs. Bruce came to me and entreated me to leave the city the next morning. She said her house was watched, and it was possible that some clew to me might be obtained. I refused to take her advice. She pleaded with an earnest tenderness, that ought to have moved me; but I was in a bitter, disheartened mood. I was weary of flying from pillar to post. I had been chased during half my life, and it seemed as if the chase was never to end. There I sat, in that great city, guiltless of crime, yet not daring to worship God in any of the churches. I heard the bells ringing for afternoon service, and, with contemptuous sarcasm, I said, "Will the preachers take for their text, 'Proclaim liberty to the captive, and the opening of prison doors to them that are bound'?[9] or will they preach from the text, "Do unto others as ye would they should do unto you'?" Oppressed Poles and Hungarians could find a safe refuge in that city; John Mitchell[1] was free to proclaim in the City Hall his desire for "a plantation well stocked with slaves;" but there I sat, an oppressed American, not daring to show my face. God forgive the black and bitter thoughts I indulged on that Sabbath day! The Scripture says, "Oppression makes even a wise man mad;"[2] and I was not wise.

I had been told that Mr. Dodge said his wife had never signed away her right to my children, and if he could not get me, he would take them. This it was, more than any thing else, that roused such a tempest in my soul. Benjamin was with his

9. Isaiah 61:1.   (1815–75).
1. Irish journalist and proponent of slavery   2. Ecclesiastes 7:7.

uncle William in California, but my innocent young daughter had come to spend a vacation with me. I thought of what I had suffered in slavery at her age, and my heart was like a tiger's when a hunter tries to seize her young.

Dear Mrs. Bruce! I seem to see the expression of her face, as the turned away discouraged by my obstinate mood. Finding her expostulations unavailing, she sent Ellen to entreat me. When ten o'clock in the evening arrived and Ellen had not returned, this watchful and unwearied friend became anxious. She came to us in a carriage, bringing a well-filled trunk for my journey—trusting that by this time I would listen to reason. I yielded to her, as I ought to have done before.

The next day, baby and I set out in a heavy snow storm, bound for New England again. I received letters from the City of Iniquity,[3] addressed to me under an assumed name. In a few days one came from Mrs. Bruce, informing me that my new master was still searching for me, and that she intended to put an end to this persecution by buying my freedom. I felt grateful for the kindness that prompted this offer, but the idea was not so pleasant to me as might have been expected. The more my mind had become enlightened, the more difficult it was for me to consider myself an article of property; and to pay money to those who had so grievously oppressed me seemed like taking from my sufferings the glory of triumph. I wrote to Mrs. Bruce, thanking her, but saying that being sold from one owner to another seemed too much like slavery; that such a great obligation could not be easily cancelled; and that I preferred to go to my brother in California.

Without my knowledge, Mrs. Bruce employed a gentleman in New York to enter into negotiations with Mr. Dodge. He proposed to pay three hundred dollars down, if Mr. Dodge would sell me, and enter into obligations to relinquish all claim to me or my children forever after. He who called himself my master said he scorned so small an offer for such a valuable servant. The gentleman replied, "You can do as you choose, sir. If you reject this offer you will never get any thing; for the woman has friends who will convey her and her children out of the country."

Mr. Dodge concluded that "half a loaf was better than no bread," and he agreed to the proffered terms. By the next mail I received this brief letter from Mrs. Bruce: "I am rejoiced to tell you that the money for your freedom has been paid to Mr. Dodge. Come home to-morrow. I long to see you and my sweet babe."

My brain reeled as I read these lines. A gentleman near me said, "It's true; I have seen the bill of sale." "The bill of sale!" Those words struck me like a blow. So I was *sold* at last! A human being *sold* in the free city of New York! The bill of sale is on record, and future generations will learn from it that women were articles of traffic in New York, late in the nineteenth century of the Christian religion. It may hereafter prove a useful document to antiquaries, who are seeking to measure the progress of civilization in the United States. I well know the value of that bit of paper; but much as I love freedom, I do not like to look upon it. I am deeply grateful to the generous friend who procured it, but I despise the miscreant who demanded payment for what never rightfully belonged to him or his.

I had objected to having my freedom bought, yet I must confess that when it was done I felt as if a heavy load had been lifted from my weary shoulders. When I rode home in the cars I was no longer afraid to unveil my face and look at people as they passed. I should have been glad to have met Daniel Dodge himself; to

3. New York City.

have had him seen me and known me, that he might have mourned over the unto-ward circumstances which compelled him to sell me for three hundred dollars.

When I reached home, the arms of my benefactress were thrown round me, and our tears mingled. As soon as she could speak, she said, "O Linda, I'm *so* glad it's all over! You wrote to me as if you thought you were going to be trans-ferred from one owner to another. But I did not buy you for your services. I should have done just the same, if you had been going to sail for California tomorrow. I should, at least, have the satisfaction of knowing that you left me a free woman."

My heart was exceedingly full. I remembered how my poor father had tried to buy me, when I was a small child, and how he had been disappointed. I hoped his spirit was rejoicing over me now. I remembered how my good old grandmother had laid up her earnings to purchase me in later years, and how often her plans had been frustrated. How that faithful, loving old heart would leap for joy, if she could look on me and my children now that we were free! My relatives had been foiled in all their efforts, but God had raised me up a friend among strangers, who had bestowed on me the precious, long-desired boon. Friend! It is a common word, often lightly used. Like other good and beautiful things, it may be tarnished by careless handling; but when I speak of Mrs. Bruce as my friend, the word is sacred.

My grandmother lived to rejoice in my freedom; but not long after, a letter came with a black seal. She had gone "where the wicked cease from troubling, and the weary are at rest."[4]

Time passed on, and a paper came to me from the south, containing an obitu-ary notice of my uncle Phillip. It was the only case I ever knew of such an honor conferred upon a colored person. It was written by one of his friends, and con-tained these words: "Now that death has laid him low, they call him a good man and a useful citizen; but what are eulogies to the black man, when the world has faded from his vision? It does not require man's praise to obtain rest in God's kingdom." So they called a colored man a *citizen!* Strange words to be uttered in that region!

Reader, my story ends with freedom; not in the usual way, with marriage. I and my children are now free! We are as free from the power of slaveholders as are the white people of the north; and though that, according to my ideas, is not saying a great deal, it is a vast improvement in *my* condition. The dream of my life is not yet realized. I do not sit with my children in a home of my own. I still long for a hearthstone of my own, however humble. I wish it for my children's sake far more than for my own. But God so orders circumstances as to keep me with my friend Mrs. Bruce. Love, duty, gratitude, also bind me to her side. It is a privilege to serve her who pities my oppressed people, and who has bestowed the inestimable boon of freedom on me and my children.

It has been painful to me, in many ways, to recall the dreary years I passed in bondage. I would gladly forget them if I could. Yet the retrospection is not alto-gether without solace; for with those gloomy recollections come tender memories of my good old grandmother, like light, fleecy clouds floating over a dark and troubled sea.

1858   1862

4. Job 3:17.

CULTURAL COORDINATES
Reward for the Capture
of Harriet Jacobs

When James Norcom, who thought of himself as the owner of Harriet Jacobs, wanted to retrieve his "property," he turned to the mass media of the day—the newspapers—to offer a reward. For quite a reasonable rate, Norcom placed this ad in papers serving the urban areas where Harriet Jacobs might have sought shelter. The one reproduced here was printed in the July 4, 1835, edition of the Norfolk, Virginia, daily newspaper, the *American Beacon*.

Norcom's ad follows well-established conventions: it begins with the amount of the reward, it presents a description of the "property," it explains the acts that will be rewarded (that is, capture and retention or delivery, information, or execution), and it provides information for how to get in touch with Norcom. Like all ads for fugitive slaves, this one provides insight into the internal paradoxes of America's culture of slavery. Norcom describes his "Servant Girl Harriet," much as he would describe an animal, perhaps a favorite horse, noting her skin color, height, body type, and temperament—attributes that he, and his readers, would perceive as significant. But even in this description, Norcom undercuts his own claim that Harriet isa piece of property by briefly indicating the ways she is likely to express her belief that she owns herself. She might, for example, comb her hair in a particular way, she might indulge her taste in fine clothes, and she might be planning to "transport herself to the North."

$100 REWARD

WILL be given for the apprehension and delivery of my Servant Girl HARRIET. She is a light mulatto, 21 years of age, about 5 feet 4 inches high, of a thick and corpulent habit, having on her head a thick covering of black hair that curls naturally, but which can be easily combed straight. She speaks easily and fluently, and has an agreeable carriage and address. Being a good seamstress, she has been accustomed to dress well, has a variety of very fine clothes, made in the prevailing fashion, and will probably appear, if abroad, tricked out in gay and fashionable finery. As this girl absconded from the plantation of my son without any known cause or provocation, it is probable she designs to transport herself to the North.

The above reward, with all reasonable charges, will be given for apprehending her, or securing her in any prison or jail within the U. States.

All persons are hereby forewarned against harboring or entertaining her, or being in any way instrumental in her escape, under the most rigorous penalties of the law.
                                        JAMES NORCOM.
Edenton, N. C. June 30   tra2w

Advertisement from the Norfolk, Virginia, *American Beacon* for the return of Harriet Jacobs to her "owner," James Norcom.

The idiosyncrasies of Norcom's ad are also tell-

814

ing. Norcom's offer of $100 (about $2,300 today) was exceptionally large, bespeaking both the intensity of his desire to recover his "property" and his frustration with his failure, so far, to find her. The last paragraph of the ad, which is not conventional, suggests his suspicion that Jacobs is being helped by others as it threatens any who might be "harboring or entertaining her" with the "most rigorous penalties of the law." (In 1850 Congress passed the Fugitive Slave Act, making it a crime to help or house runaway slaves.) Norcom's ad was not successful, though it and others like it caused Jacobs to live in fear for much of her life. Its details helped modern scholars to establish the links between Harriet Jacobs and her alter ego, Linda Brent.

Eighteen years before the United States would pass the Nineteenth Amendment to its Constitution, granting women the right to vote, a very ill and elderly Elizabeth Cady Stanton asked her daughters to help her dress. She then stood at a table for seven or eight minutes as if making a speech. Two hours later, after falling asleep, she died. It seems that even on her deathbed, Cady Stanton was unwilling to give up the fight for civil and political rights for which she had worked steadily since her marriage in 1840. Best known as the prime mover of the American women's suffrage movement because of her co-sponsorship of the Seneca Falls convention of 1848 (see pp. 824–25), Cady Stanton and the other attendees wrote the "Declaration of Sentiments" (1848), included here, which parallel the Declaration of Independence to argue for equal financial, social, and political rights for women. A tireless activist, Cady Stanton went on to become one of the most important feminist and liberal thinkers of the nineteenth century. Although she wrote in several nonfiction genres, Cady Stanton was best known as a skillful orator in an age when speechmaking was a highly valued art.

Born to a wealthy and politically conservative family in Johnstown, New York, Elizabeth Cady was not immune to the spirit of reform that swept America during her teenage years. Her father, a prominent judge, had indulged her intellect and spirit by educating her as he would have his sons (had they lived) to assist in his law office. He nevertheless begrudged the fact that she was female and therefore could never aspire to being a lawyer. When her cousins introduced her to the cause of abolition, Cady Stanton used her legal training to see slavery, as she would women's rights, as a systemic problem to be attacked rationally. She drew inspiration from the liberal philosophers of the eighteenth century who had provided the philosophical underpinnings of the American Revolution. Her cousins also introduced her to the man who would be her husband and the father of her seven children. Henry Stanton was already a prominent abolitionist, lecturer, and activist. The Stantons spent their honeymoon in England, in order to attend the World Anti-Slavery Convention of 1840; there, Cady Stanton was outraged when the organizers refused to seat women delegates on the grounds of propriety. From that time on, she became a radical proponent of women's rights. Along with other women who were active in the reform movements of the day, she organized conventions for those interested in working toward expansion of suffrage to women. For the rest of her life, with her longtime colleague and collaborator Susan B. Anthony, Cady Stanton organized national and state campaigns, gave speeches, and raised funds for the wide set of reform issues that touched the lives of American women.

For Cady Stanton, as for most thinkers in the liberal tradition, the basis of all just relationships is the self-possessed individual. As a suffragist, she articulated a belief, not only in the ability, but also in the necessity of women's legal control over their inalienable assets (their bodies and minds) and their alienable ones (their money, labor, and property). The only way to ensure this control, Cady Stanton argued, is for women to have the right to participate directly in the making of law. Although she was forward looking in terms of women's rights, the limits to her radicalism can be seen in the biases she expresses in "The Solitude of Self," a speech she gave before the U.S. Senate Committee on Women's Suffrage on January 18, 1892.

Declaration of Sentiments[1]

When, in the course of human events, it becomes necessary for one portion of the family of man to assume among the people of the earth a position different from that which they have hitherto occupied, but one to which the laws of nature and of nature's God entitle them, a decent respect to the opinions of mankind requires that they should declare the causes that impel them to such a course.

We hold these truths to be self-evident: that all men and women are created equal; that they are endowed by their Creator with certain inalienable rights; that among these are life, liberty, and the pursuit of happiness; that to secure these rights governments are instituted, deriving their just powers from the consent of the governed. Whenever any form of government becomes destructive of these ends, it is the right of those who suffer from it to refuse allegiance to it, and to insist upon the institution of a new government, laying its foundation on such principles, and organizing its powers in such form, as to them shall seem most likely to effect their safety and happiness. Prudence, indeed, will dictate that governments long established should not be changed for light and transient causes; and accordingly all experience hath shown that mankind are more disposed to suffer, while evils are sufferable, than to right themselves by abolishing the forms to which they were accustomed. But when a long train of abuses and usurpations, pursuing invariably the same object evinces a design to reduce them under absolute despotism, it is their duty to throw off such government, and to provide new guards for their future security. Such has been the patient sufferance of the women under this government, and such is now the necessity which constrains them to demand the equal station to which they are entitled.

The history of mankind is a history of repeated injuries and usurpations on the part of man toward woman, having in direct object the establishment of an absolute tyranny over her. To prove this, let facts be submitted to a candid world.

He has never permitted her to exercise her inalienable right to the elective franchise.

He has compelled her to submit to laws, in the formation of which she had no voice.

He has withheld from her rights which are given to the most ignorant and degraded men—both natives and foreigners.

Having deprived her of this first right of a citizen, the elective franchise, thereby leaving her without representation in the halls of legislation, he has oppressed her on all sides.

He has made her, if married, in the eye of the law, civilly dead.

He has taken from her all right in property, even to the wages she earns.

He has made her, morally, an irresponsible being, as she can commit many crimes with impunity, provided they be done in the presence of her husband. In

---

1. This document was signed in 1848 by sixty-eight women and thirty-two men, all delegates to the first women's rights convention in Seneca Falls, New York, now known to historians as the 1848 Women's Rights Convention. It was published in reform newspapers and reprinted in *History of Woman Suffrage* (1881–1922), co-edited by Stanton, Susan B. Anthony, Matilda Joslyn Gage, and Ida Husted Harper.

the covenant of marriage she is compelled to promise obedience to her husband, he becoming, to all intents and purposes, her master—the law giving him power to deprive her of her liberty, and to administer chastisement.

He has so framed the laws of divorce, as to what shall be the proper causes, and in case of separation, to whom the guardianship of the children shall be given, as to be wholly regardless of the happiness of women—the law, in all cases, going upon a false supposition of the supremacy of man, and giving all power into his hands.

After depriving her of all rights as a married woman, if single, and the owner of property, he has taxed her to support a government which recognizes her only when her property can be made profitable to it.

He has monopolized nearly all the profitable employments, and from those she is permitted to follow, she receives but a scanty remuneration. He closes against her all the avenues to wealth and distinction which he considers most honorable to himself. As a teacher of theology, medicine, or law, she is not known.

He has denied her the facilities for obtaining a thorough education, all colleges being closed against her.

He allows her in Church, as well as State, but a subordinate position, claiming Apostolic authority[2] for her exclusion from the ministry, and, with some exceptions, from any public participation in the affairs of the Church.

He has created a false public sentiment by giving to the world a different code of morals for men and women, by which moral delinquencies which exclude women from society, are not only tolerated, but deemed of little account in man.

He has usurped the prerogative of Jehovah[3] himself, claiming it as his right to assign for her a sphere of action, when that belongs to her conscience and to her God.

He has endeavored, in every way that he could, to destroy her confidence in her own powers, to lessen her self-respect, and to make her willing to lead a dependent and abject life.

Now, in view of this entire disfranchisement of one-half the people of this country, their social and religious degradation—in view of the unjust laws above mentioned, and because women do feel themselves aggrieved, oppressed, and fraudulently deprived of their most sacred rights, we insist that they have immediate admission to all the rights and privileges which belong to them as citizens of the United States.

In entering upon the great work before us, we anticipate no small amount of misconception, misrepresentation, and ridicule; but we shall use every instrumentality within our power to effect our object. We shall employ agents, circulate tracts, petition the State and National legislatures, and endeavor to enlist the pulpit and the press in our behalf. We hope this Convention will be followed by a series of Conventions embracing every part of the country.
1848

The Solitude of Self

The point I wish plainly to bring before you on this occasion is the individuality of each human soul; our Protestant idea, the right of individual conscience and

2. Christian doctrine had long excluded women from positions of authority because none of the twelve apostles were women.
3. A name for God.

judgement; our republican idea, individual citizenship. In discussing the rights of woman, we are to consider, first, what belongs to her as an individual, in a world of her own, the arbiter of her own destiny, an imaginary Robinson Crusoe, with her woman, Friday, on a solitary island.[4] Her rights under such circumstances are to use all her faculties for her own safety and happiness.

Secondly, if we consider her as a citizen, as a member of a great nation, she must have the same rights as all other members, according to the fundamental principles of our Government.

Thirdly, viewed as a woman, an equal factor in civilization, her rights and duties are still the same—individual happiness and development.

Fourthly, it is only the incidental relations of life, such as mother, wife, sister, daughter, which may involve some special duties and training.

* * *

The strongest reason for giving woman all the opportunities for higher education, for the full development of her faculties, her forces of mind and body; for giving her the most enlarged freedom of thought and action; a complete emancipation from all forms of bondage, of custom, dependence, superstition; from all the crippling influences of fear—is the solitude and personal responsibility of her own individual life. The strongest reason why we ask for woman a voice in the government under which she lives; in the religion she is asked to believe; equality in social life, where she is the chief factor; a place in the trades and professions, where she may earn her bread, is because of her birthright to self-sovereignty; because, as an individual, she must rely on herself. No matter how much women prefer to lean, to be protected and supported, nor how much men desire to have them do so, they must make the voyage of life alone, and for safety in an emergency, they must know something of the laws of navigation. To guide our own craft, we must be captain, pilot, engineer; with chart and compass to stand at the wheel; to watch the winds and waves, and know when to take in the sail, and to read the signs in the firmament over all. It matters not whether the solitary voyager is man or woman; nature; having endowed them equally, leaves them to their own skill and judgment in the hour of danger, and, if not equal to the occasion, alike they perish.

To appreciate the importance of fitting every human soul for independent action, think for a moment of the immeasurable solitude of self. We come into the world alone, unlike all who have gone before us, we leave it alone, under circumstances peculiar to ourselves. No mortal ever has been, no mortal ever will be like the soul just launched on the sea of life. There can never again be just such a combination of prenatal influences; never again just such environments as make up the infancy, youth and manhood of this one. Nature never repeats herself, and the possibilities of one human soul will never be found in another. No one has ever found two blades of ribbon grass alike, and no one will ever find two human beings alike. Seeing, then, what must be the infinite diversity in human character, we can in a measure appreciate the loss to a nation when any large class of the people is uneducated and unrepresented in the government.

We ask for the complete development of every individual, first, for his own benefit and happiness. In fitting out an army, we give each soldier his own knapsack, arms, powder, his blanket, cup, knife, fork and spoon. We provide alike for all their individual necessities; then each man bears his own burden.

4. In *Robinson Crusoe* (1719), by English writer   are both male characters.
Daniel Defoe (1660?–1731), Crusoe and Friday

Again, we ask complete individual development for the general good; for the consensus of the competent on the whole round of human interests, on all questions of national life; and here each man must bear his share of the general burden. It is sad to see how soon friendless children are left to bear their own burdens, before they can analyze their feelings; before they can even tell their joys and sorrows, they are thrown on their own resources. The great lesson that nature seems to teach us at all ages is self-dependence, self-protection, self-support. * * *

In youth our most bitter disappointments, our brightest hopes and ambitions, are known only to ourselves. Even our friendship and love we never fully share with another; there is something of every passion, in every situation, we conceal. Even so in our triumphs and our defeats. * * *

We ask no sympathy from others in the anxiety and agony of a broken friendship or shattered love. When death sunders our nearest ties, alone we sit in the shadows of our affliction. Alike amid the greatest triumphs and darkest tragedies of life, we walk alone. On the divine heights of human attainment, eulogized and worshipped as a hero or saint, we stand alone. In ignorance, poverty and vice, as a pauper or criminal, alone we starve or steal; alone we suffer the sneers and rebuffs of our fellows; alone we are hunted and hounded through dark courts and alleys, in by-ways and high-ways; alone we stand in the judgment seat; alone in the prison cell we lament our crimes and misfortunes; alone we expiate them on the gallows. In hours like these we realize the awful solitude of individual life, its pains, its penalties, its responsibilities; hours in which the youngest and most helpless are thrown on their own resources for guidance and consolation. Seeing, then, that life must ever be a march and a battle, that each soldier must be equipped for his own protection, it is the height of cruelty to rob the individual of a single natural right.

To throw obstacles in the way of a complete education is like putting out the eyes; to deny the rights of property is like cutting off the hands. To refuse political equality is to rob the ostracized of all self-respect; of credit in the market place; of recompense in the world of work, of a voice in choosing those who make and administer the law, a choice in the jury before whom they are tried, and in the judge who decides their punishment. [Think of] * * * woman's position! Robbed of her natural rights, handicapped by law and custom at every turn, yet compelled to fight her own battles, and in the emergencies of life to fall back on herself for protection.

* * *

The young wife and mother, at the head of some establishment, with a kind husband to shield her from the adverse winds of life, with wealth, fortune and position, has a certain harbor of safety, secure against the ordinary ills of life. But to manage a household, have a desirable influence in society, keep her friends and the affections of her husband, train her children and servants well, she must have rare common sense, wisdom, diplomacy, and a knowledge of human nature. To do all this, she needs the cardinal virtues and the strong points of character that the most successful statesman possesses. An uneducated woman trained to dependence, with no resources in herself, must make a failure of any position in life. But society says women do not need a knowledge of the world, the liberal training that experience in public life must give, all the advantages of collegiate education; but when for the lack of all this, the woman's happiness is wrecked, alone she bears her humiliation; and the solitude of the weak and the ignorant is indeed pitiable. In the wild chase for the prizes of life, they are ground to powder.

In age, when the pleasures of youth are passed, children grown up, married and gone, the hurry and bustle of life in a measure over, when the hands are weary of active service, when the old arm chair and the fireside are the chosen resorts, then men and women alike must fall back on their own resources. If they cannot find companionship in books, if they have no interest in the vital questions of the hour, no interest in watching the consummation of reforms with which they might have been identified, they soon pass into their dotage. The more fully the faculties of the mind are developed and kept in use, the longer the period of vigor and active interest in all around us continues. If, from a life-long participation in public affairs, a woman feels responsible for the laws regulating our system of education, the discipline of our jails and prisons, the sanitary condition of our private homes, public buildings and thoroughfares, an interest in commerce, finance, our foreign relations, in any or all these questions, her solitude will at least be respectable, and she will not be driven to gossip or scandal for entertainment.

The chief reason for opening to every soul the doors to the whole round of human duties and pleasures is the individual development thus attained, the resources thus provided under all circumstances to mitigate the solitude that at times must come to everyone.

* * *

Inasmuch, then, as woman shares equally the joys and sorrows of time and eternity, is it not the height of presumption in man to propose to represent her at the ballot box and the throne of grace, to do her voting in the state, her praying in the church, and to assume the position of high priest at the family altar?

Nothing strengthens the judgment and quickens the conscience like individual responsibility. Nothing adds such dignity to character as the recognition of one's self-sovereignty; the right to an equal place, everywhere conceded—a place earned by personal merit, not an artificial attainment by inheritance, wealth, family and position. Conceding, then, that the responsibilities of life rest equally on man and woman, that their destiny is the same, they need the same preparation for time and eternity. The talk of sheltering woman from the fierce storms of life is the sheerest mockery, for they beat on her from every point of the compass, just as they do on man, and with more fatal results, for he has been trained to protect himself, to resist, and to conquer. Such are the facts in human experience, the responsibilities of individual sovereignty. Rich and poor, intelligent and ignorant, wise and foolish, virtuous and vicious, man and woman; it is ever the same, each soul must depend wholly on itself.

Whatever the theories may be of woman's dependence on man, in the supreme moments of her life, he cannot bear her burdens. Alone she goes to the gates of death to give life to every man that is born into the world; no one can share her fears, no one can mitigate her pangs; and if her sorrow is greater than she can bear, alone she passes beyond the gates into the vast unknown.

From the mountain-tops of Judea long ago, a heavenly voice bade his disciples, "Bear ye one another's burdens"; but humanity has not yet risen to that point of self-sacrifice; and if ever so willing, how few the burdens are that one soul can bear for another!

* * *

So it ever must be in the conflicting scenes of life, in the long, weary march, each one walks alone. We may have many friends, love, kindness, sympathy and charity, to smooth our pathway in everyday life, but in the tragedies and triumphs of human experience, each mortal stands alone.

But when all artificial trammels are removed, and women are recognized as individuals, responsible for their own environments, thoroughly educated for all positions in life they may be called to fill; with all the resources in themselves that liberal thought and broad culture can give; guided by their own conscience and judgment, trained to self-protection, by a healthy development of the muscular system, and skill in the use of weapons and defence; and stimulated to self-support by a knowledge of the business world and the pleasure that pecuniary independence must ever give; when women are trained in this way, they will in a measure be fitted for those hours of solitude that come alike to all, whether prepared or otherwise. As in our extremity we must depend on ourselves, the dictates of wisdom point to complete individual development.

In talking of education, how shallow the argument that each class must be educated for the special work it proposes to do, and that all those faculties not needed in this special work must lie dormant and utterly wither for want of use, when, perhaps, these will be the very faculties needed in life's greatest emergencies! Some say, "Where is the use of drilling girls in the languages, the sciences, in law, medicine, theology. As wives, mothers, housekeepers, cooks, they need a different curriculum from boys who are to fill all positions. The chief cooks in our great hotels and ocean steamers are men. In our large cities, men run the bakeries; they make our bread, cake and pies. They manage the laundries; they are now considered our best milliners and dressmakers. Because some men fill these departments of usefulness, shall we regulate the curriculum in Harvard and Yale to their present necessities? If not, why this talk in our best colleges of a curriculum for girls who are crowding into the trades and professions, teachers in all our public schools, rapidly filling many lucrative and honorable positions in life?"

* * *

Women are already the equals of men in the whole realm of thought, in art, science, literature and government.

* * *

The poetry and novels of the century are theirs, and they have touched the keynote of reform, in religion, politics and social life. They fill the editor's and professor's chair, plead at the bar of justice,[5] walk the wards of the hospital, speak from the pulpit and the platform. Such is the type of womanhood that an enlightened public sentiment welcomes to-day, and such the triumph of the facts of life over the false theories of the past.

Is it, then, consistent to hold the developed woman of this day within the same narrow political limits as the dame with the spinning wheel and knitting needle occupied in the past? No, no! Machinery has taken the labors of woman as well as man on its tireless shoulders; the loom and the spinning wheel are but dreams of the past; the pen, the brush, the easel, the chisel, have taken their places, while the hopes and ambitions of women are essentially changed.

We see reason sufficient in the outer conditions of human beings for individual liberty and development, but when we consider the self-dependence of every human

5. Lawyers.

soul, we see the need of courage, judgment and the exercise of every faculty of mind and body, strengthened and developed by use, in woman as well as man.

Whatever may be said of man's protecting power in ordinary conditions, amid all the terrible disasters by land and sea, in the supreme moments of danger, alone woman must ever meet the horrors of the situation. The Angel of Death even makes no royal pathway for her. Man's love and sympathy enter only into the sunshine of our lives. In that solemn solitude of self, that links us with the immeasurable and the eternal, each soul lives alone forever. A recent writer says: "I remember once, in crossing the Atlantic, to have gone upon the deck of the ship at midnight, when a dense black cloud enveloped the sky, and the great deep was roaring madly under the lashes of demoniac winds. My feeling was not of danger or fear (which is a base surrender of the immortal soul) but of utter desolation and loneliness; a little speck of life shut in by a tremendous darkness." * * *

And yet, there is a solitude which each and every one of us has always carried with him, more inaccessible than the ice-cold mountains, more profound than the midnight sea; the solitude of self. Our inner being which we call ourself, no eye nor touch of man or angel has ever pierced. It is more hidden than the caves of the gnome; the sacred adytum of the oracle; the hidden chamber of Eleusinian mystery, for to it only omniscience is permitted to enter.[6]

Such is individual life. Who, I ask you, can take, dare take on himself the rights, the duties, the responsibilities of another human soul?

1892

---

6. Adytum: the secret, inner sanctum of a temple, where oracles would deliver prophecies; Eleusin-ian mysteries: referring to the ancient Greeks' worship of the goddess Demeter in Eleusis.

CULTURAL COORDINATES
The Seneca Falls Convention, July 19–20, 1848

Eight years after Elizabeth Cady Stanton (pp. 816–23) and Lucretia Mott met in London at the World Anti-Slavery Convention, they met again in the parlor of a mutual acquaintance in western New York State. Cady Stanton and Mott had been disgusted by the treatment of women by the organizers of the convention, who had denied seats to women activists. Women were welcome to raise and donate money, and otherwise sacrifice for the cause, but they were not welcome to participate in matters of policy. Like many in the abolition movement, Cady Stanton and Mott had each already begun to see analogies between the condition of blacks and free white women in America. Both the oppressive degradation of blacks to the status of property and the oppressive protection of women posed critical challenges to the premises of the nation as expressed in the Declaration of Independence. Cady Stanton and Mott decided to organize a convention devoted to examining the condition of women in America and proposing some solutions.

When they met again in July 1848, Mott and Cady Stanton arranged to hold the convention in the Wesleyan Chapel in Seneca Falls and placed a small ad in local newspapers. They had no great hope of high attendance, since it was the height of haying season, so they were surprised when over 260 women and almost

A contemporary depiction of Elizabeth Cady Stanton reading the "Declaration of Sentiments" at the 1848 Women's Rights Convention in Seneca Falls, New York. (Library of Congress, Division of Prints and Photographs, Washington, D.C.)

40 men convened. Neither Mott nor Cady Stanton had ever addressed a crowd before; neither felt up to running the extensive meeting. With James Mott presiding, Mott and Cady Stanton took to the stage to lead the discussion about the "Declaration of Sentiments." The most radical of all the resolutions offered during the convention was the ninth: that it was the duty of women to secure the vote for themselves. Mott felt the proposition was so shocking that it would make them look ridiculous; Cady Stanton's own husband, the radical abolitionist Henry Stanton, threatened to walk out if it was read. Cady Stanton, however, prevailed, and the ninth resolution was passed by the convention after much debate.

One of the youngest signers of the declaration at Seneca Falls was Charlotte Woodward, a factory girl from Waterloo, New York. She explained in her memoirs that she did not "believe there was any community anywhere in which the souls of some women were not beating their wings in rebellion": "Every fiber of my being rebelled, although silently, for all the hours that I sat and sewed gloves for a miserable pittance which, after it was earned, could never be mine. I wanted to work, but I wanted to choose my task and I wanted to collect my wages." Of the three hundred or so who attended, Woodward was the only one alive in 1920 to see the passage of the Nineteenth Amendment to the United States Constitution: "The right of citizens of the United States to vote shall not be denied or abridged by the United States or by any State on account of sex. Congress shall have power to enforce this article by appropriate legislation."

Charlotte Brontë's life was full of personal losses and disappointments, and—only thirty-nine when she died—she had a short literary career. However, the novels she wrote in her thirties have become standards of the feminist canon, and her most famous, *Jane Eyre* (1847), was a best seller in its day and remains a classic of British fiction.

Brontë was the oldest child to survive into her twenties in a Yorkshire family that had once had five daughters and a son. She and her siblings were raised in Haworth, a small town where her father, Reverend Patrick Brontë, was perpetual curate of the Haworth parish church, drawing a minimal salary for the pastoral care of the Church of England members in his neighborhood and for weekly sermons. Having grown up a laborer's son in Ireland, Patrick Brontë was unusual in his day for having attended university on a scholarship, thus rising from his working-class origins to the middle-class profession of Anglican minister. Although never especially prosperous, he was an active and influential participant in local politics and theological debates. The mother of the Brontë children, Maria Branwell Brontë, died when Charlotte was five years old; and Maria's sister, Elizabeth Branwell, moved in to help care for the children.

The Reverend Brontë and his sister-in-law undertook the early education of the six children at home. The young Brontës were voracious readers with vivid imaginations. They read the English classics and the newspapers and journals their father subscribed to, and they carried on lively debates about historical and current events. They also wrote miniature magazines in imitation of the literary and political periodicals they enjoyed reading. With her brother, Branwell (next in age), Charlotte invented a fantasy world, Angria, for which they created elaborate, detailed histories (complete with tragic queens, dark warriors, and epic battles) in high-romance style, sometimes encrypting them in her and Branwell's own secret script. (Her younger sisters, Emily and Anne, collaborated to create Gondal, a parallel fantasy world; large portions of both these tales have been published as the Brontës' juvenilia, or childhood writings, and the characters of Gondal and Angria are often the speakers in the Brontë sisters' poems.)

The Brontë children's community was interrupted in 1824, when Charlotte, her two older sisters (Maria and Elizabeth), and her younger sister Emily were sent to the Clergy Daughters' School at Cowan Bridge, a charitable boarding school for impoverished clergymen's daughters. This school was the inspiration for Lowood School in *Jane Eyre,* with its bad food, unhealthy surroundings, and dreary living conditions. Maria and Elizabeth became seriously ill there—as does Helen Burns in *Jane Eyre*—probably from typhoid fever (which is spread through contaminated food and water) and perhaps also from tuberculosis (which flourished in cold, damp nineteenth-century England). They died at home the next year. Their father then brought Charlotte and Emily home, and Charlotte did not attend school again until she was fifteen, when she was awarded a scholarship by friends and founders of Miss Wooler's school at Roe Head. She so distinguished herself as a student that she was asked to become a teacher in her second year. Although Miss Wooler did her best to support her, Charlotte was miserable in her new role. Her writings from Roe Head show her struggles with the tedious routine of teaching unmotivated and unappreciative students; they also continue to chronicle the lively imaginary history of Angria, which she elaborated, off and on, throughout her teenage years, and which contrasted starkly with the world she actually inhabited.

At twenty-two, Charlotte left Miss Wooler's school and returned home to advertise her services as a governess. At twenty-three, she took a position, but she remained at the job only two and a half months. She took another position two years later but remained at that post for just ten months. As difficult as teaching school had been, her life as a governess was even harder: the governess in an upper-class household was a woman with an elite education who lived a servant's lifestyle. She had very low wages, almost no free time, and the duties of a child care worker as well as an academic tutor. Brontë did not thrive under these conditions.

Faced with the necessity of supporting themselves, Charlotte and Emily conceived a plan for opening their own school. They needed stronger foreign language skills to succeed with this plan, so—with financial backing from their Aunt Elizabeth Branwell—they went in 1842 to Brussels to study at the Pensionnat Heger, a boarding school for upper-middle-class Belgian girls run by Constantín Heger and his wife, Zoe. Emily soon returned home, but Charlotte repeated her success at Roe Head and was quickly elevated to a teaching position at the *Pensionnat* under her mentor, Heger. Charlotte stayed in Brussels for two years, becoming fluent in French and gaining teaching experience. Her time at the *Pensionnat* is related—and heavily fictionalized—in her last novel, *Villette* (1853). She was passionately attached to the married Heger, but their correspondence after her return to Yorkshire suggests that he neither shared the intensity of her feeling nor took advantage of it.

Once again at home in Yorkshire, Charlotte realized with some bitterness that the plan for a school was not workable, as the sisters were not able to attract any students. However, she discovered that Emily and Anne had been writing poetry that departed in subject matter from their Gondal stories, focusing on themes of domesticity, nature, and religious faith. Adding these to poems of her own, Charlotte arranged to publish a collection, *Poems by Currer, Ellis, and Acton Bell* (1846). The sisters chose gender-neutral pseudonyms to protect their much-valued privacy and to avoid the inevitable critical dismissal of "poetesses." The book sold only two copies. Undeterred, the sisters agreed to begin working on novels. Charlotte's first attempt, *The Professor* (1857), did not find a publisher until after her death, but the second novel she wrote, *Jane Eyre*, was an instant success. The story of the plain, independent orphan-governess who wins the heart of her "master" but follows her own conscience set a pattern for romance heroines throughout the twentieth century.

Charlotte's subsequent novels were neither as popular nor as critically successful as *Jane Eyre,* but Brontë nonetheless became a literary celebrity. She traveled to London to meet novelists she admired, including William Makepeace Thackeray, her favorite writer, and Elizabeth Gaskell, who became a close friend and wrote the first full-length biography of Brontë.

Between September 1848 and May 1849, Brontë faced terrible losses: her brother, Branwell, who had tried but failed to become a writer or painter, died at age thirty-one of a combinaton of tuberculosis, advanced alcoholism, and opium addiction. Then Emily, quite unexpectedly at age thirty, died just four months later, most likely from tuberculosis as well. To recover her health and spirits, Charlotte took Anne, who was also suffering from tuberculosis, to the seaside, where Anne died in May at only twenty-nine.

Left alone to grieve with her aging and nearly blind father, Charlotte was remarkably productive, publishing *Shirley* in the fall of 1849, following Anne's death. *Shirley* is a social-problem novel outlining conflicts between factory owners and workers in northern England, but it also focuses on the marital prospects of Caroline Helstone and her cousin Shirley Keeldar, an independent, powerful, and charming young woman who insists she is not interested in marriage. Shirley is supposed to have been modeled on Emily Brontë, as Charlotte imagined Emily would have been had she lived.

In 1854, Brontë married her father's longtime assistant, Arthur Bell Nichols. For several years he had been in love with her and, while she had been friendly with him, she had always rebuffed his advances. But after five years alone with her ailing father, she decided to marry Nichols; she was thirty-eight. Their short time together was happy, but Brontë became pregnant and died in less than nine months from dehydration attributed to severe morning sickness. Before her death, she completed *Villette* (1853), a semi-autobiographical novel about a young woman who goes to teach English in a boarding school located in a fictionalized Brussels. Lucy Snowe, the novel's heroine, stands out among nineteenth-century female narrators for her intelligence, defiance, evasiveness, and independence. Both *Jane Eyre* and *Villette* are justly celebrated as feminist classics.

Until the late 1970s, *Jane Eyre* had always been a popular book, but it was not a favorite among scholars. The "second wave" of feminism in the last quarter of the twentieth century brought new enthusiasm to the study of *Jane Eyre*. Jane's quest for an independent identity, her resistance against prescribed female roles, her passionate rebelliousness against patriarchal authority, her conflicted relationships with other women, and her self-presentation as the author of her own story inspired praise from feminist critics. The novel provided the source for the title of the groundbreaking feminist study *The Madwoman in the Attic* by Sandra Gilbert and Susan Gubar, first published in 1979. By the 1990s, race-centered and post-colonialist criticism had drawn attention to ways in which *Jane Eyre*, while it celebrates one woman's triumphant individualism, also presents non-Anglo women as "the other," having no subjectivity of their own. The ending—which we will not give away here—has inspired as much frustration as satisfaction among readers.

"We wove a web in childhood," the section of Charlotte Brontë's journals included here, begins wistfully as a memoir of her years collaborating with Branwell, Emily, and Anne in creating their fantasy worlds, Angria and Gondal. Quickly the poem transitions into a scene in Angria, eventually becoming a passage of romantic prose narrative. The abrupt ending of the journal entry is a reminder of the contrast between the "web woven in childhood" and the here-and-now of Brontë's young adult life.

[We wove a web in childhood]

We wove a web in childhood
    A web of sunny air
We dug a spring in infancy
    Of water pure and fair

We sowed in youth a mustard seed   5
We cut an almond rod
We are now grown up to riper age
Are they withered in the sod

Are they blighted failed and faded
   Are they mouldered back to clay   10
For life is darkly shaded
And Its joys fleet fast away

Faded! the web is still of air
But now its folds are spread
And from its tints of crimson clear   15
How deep a glow is shed
The light of an Italian sky
Where clouds of sunset lingering lie
Is not more ruby-red

But the spring was under a mossy stone   20
   Its jet may gush no more
Heark! sceptic bid thy doubts be gone
Is that a feeble roar
Rushing around thee lo! the tides
Of waves where armed fleets may ride   25
Sinking and swelling frowns & smiles
  An ocean with a thousand Isles
And scarce a glimpse of shore

The mustard-seed on distant land
Bends down a mighty tree   30
The dry unbudding almond-wand
   Has touched eternity

There came a second miracle
Such as on Aaron's sceptre fell[1]
And sapless grew like life from heath   35
Bud bloom & fruit in mingling wreath
All twined the shrivelled off-shoot round
As flowers lie on the lone grave-mound.

Dream that stole o'er us in the time
When life was in its vernal clime   40
Dream that still faster o'er us steals
As the mild star of spring declining
The advent of that day reveals
That glows in Sirius' fiery shining[2]
Oh! as thou swellest and as the scenes   45
Cover this cold world's darkest features
Stronger each change my spirit weans
To bow before thy god-like creatures

---

1. Aaron's rod, a staff that miraculously buds,   2. The Dog Star, the brightest star in the night
producing flowers and almonds (Numbers 17:8).   sky.

When I sat 'neath a strange roof-tree.[3]
With nought I knew or loved around me   50
Oh how my heart shrank back to thee
Then I felt how fast thy ties had bound me

That hour that bleak hour when the day
Closed in the cold autumnal gloaming
When the clouds hung so bleak & drear & grey   55
And a bitter wind through their folds was roaming

There shone no fire on the cheerless hearth
In the chamber there gleam'd no taper's twinkle
Within neither sight nor sound of mirth
Without but the blast & the sleet's chill sprinkle   60

Then sadly I longed for my own dear home
For a sight of the old familliar faces
I drew near the casement & sat in its gloom
And looked forth on the tempests desolate traces

Ever anon that wolfish breeze   65
The dead leaves & sere from their boughs was shaking
And I gazed on the hills through the leafless trees
And felt as if my heart was breaking

Where was I e'er an hour had past
Still list'ning to that dreary blast   70
Still in that mirthless lifeless room
Cramped chilled & deadened by its gloom

No! thanks to that bright darling dream
Its power had shot one kindling gleam
Its voice had sent one wakening cry   75
And bade me lay my sorrows by
And called me earnestly to come
And borne me to my moorland home
I heard no more the senseless sound
Of task & chat that hummed around   80
I saw no more that grisly night
Closing the day's sepulchral light

The vision's spell had deepened o'er me
Its lands its scenes were spread before me
In one short hour a hundred homes   85
Had roofed me with their lordly domes
And I had sat by fires whose light
Flashed wide o're halls of regal height
And I had seen those come & go
Whose forms gave radiance to the glow   90
And I had heard the matted floor

3. Horizontal ridge-pole holding up a roof.

Of ante-room & corridor
Shake to some half-remembered tread
Whose haughty firmness woke even dread
As through the curtained portal strode   95
Some spurred & fur-wrapped Demi-God
Whose ride through that tempestuous night
Had added somewhat of a frown
To brow's that shadowed eyes of light
Fit to flash fire from Scythian crown   100
Till sweet salute from lady gay
Chased that unconscious scowl away
And then the savage fur-cap doffed
The Georgian mantle laid aside
The satrap[4] stretched on cushion soft   105
His lov'd & chosen by his side
That hand that in its horseman's glove
Looked fit for nought but bridle rein
Caressesses now its lady-love
With fingers white that shew no stain   110
They got in hot & jarring strife
When hate or honour warred with life
Nought redder than the roseate ring
That glitters fit for Eastern King

In one proud household where the sound   115
Of life & stir rang highest round
Hall within hall burned starry bright
And light gave birth to richer light
Grandly its social tone seemed strung
Wildly its keen excitement rung   120
And hundreds mid its splendors free
Moved with unfettered liberty
Not gathered to a lordly feast
But each a self-invited Guest
It was the kingly custom there   125
That each at will the house should share

I saw the master not alone
He crossed me in a vast saloon
Just seen, then sudden vanishing
As laughingly he joined the ring   130
That closed around a dazzling fire
& listened to a trembling lyre
He was in light & licensed mood
Fierce gaiety had warmed his blood
Kindled his dark & brilliant eye   135
And toned his lips full melody

---

4. Scythian: ancient Greek name for an Iranian
(Persian) tribe of horseback-riding nomads; Georgian mantle: a military cloak; satrap: a governor
of a province in Persia.

I saw him take a little child
That stretched its arms & called his name
It was his own & half he smiled
As the small eager creature came   140
Nestling upon his stately breast
And its fair curls & forehead laying
To what but formed a fevered nest
Its father's cheek where curls were straying
Thicker and darker on a bloom   145
Whose hectic brightness[5] boded doom

He kissed it and a deeper blush
Rose to the already crimson flush
And a wild sadness flung its grace
Over his grand & Roman face.   150
The little heedless lovely thing
Lulled on the bosom of a king
Its fingers 'mid his thick locks twining
Pleased with their rich & wreathed shining
Dreamed not what thoughts his soul were haunting   155
Nor why his heart so high was panting

I went out in a summer night
My path lay o'er a lonesome waste
Slumbring & still in clear moon-light
A noble road was o'er it traced   160
Far as the eye of man could see
No shade upon its surface stirred
All slept in mute tranquillity
Unbroke by step or wind or word

That waste had been a battle-plain   165
Head-stones were reared in the waving fern
There they had buried the gallant slain
That dust to its own dust might return

And one black marble monument
Rose where the heather was rank & deep   170
Its base was hid with the bracken & bent[6]
Its sides were bare to the night-winds sweep

A Victory carved in polished stone
Her trumpet to her cold lips held
And strange it seemed as she stood alone   175
That not a single note was blown
That not a whisper swelled

---

5. Flushed cheeks were associated with tuberculosis, then called consumption, for which there
was no cure.

6. Bracken: a type of fern; bent: a kind of grass
used in lawns.

It was Camalia's[7] ancient field
I knew the desert well
For traced around a sculptured shield   180
These words the summer moon revealed
    "Here brave Macarthy fell!
The men of Keswick[8] leading on
There first their best their noblest one
    He did his duty well"   185

I now heard the far clatter of hoofs on the hard & milk-white road, the great high-way that turns in a bend from Free-Town And stretches on to the West, two horse-men rode slowly up in the moon light & leaving the path struck deep into the moor galloping through heather to their Chargers breasts.

"Hah!" said one of them as he flung himself from his steed & walked for-ward to the monument "Hah Edward here's my Kinsman's tomb, now for the bugle sound! he must have his requiem or he will trouble me—the bell tolled for him in Alderwood on the eve of the conflict, I heard it myself & though then but a very little child I remember well how my mother trembled as she sat in the Drawing-room of the manor house & listened while that unaccountable & super-natural sound was booming so horribly through the woods. Edward begin"

Never shall I Charlotte Brontë forget what a voice of wild & wailing music Now came thrillingly to my mind's almost to my body's ear, nor how distinctly I sitting in the schoolroom at Roe-head[9] saw the Duke of Zamorna leaning against that obelisk with the mute marble Victory above him, the fern waving at his feet his black horse turned loose grazing among the heather, the moonlight so mild & so exquisitely tranquil sleeping upon that vast & vacant road & the African sky quivering & shaking with stars expanded above all. I was quite gone I had really utterly forgot where I was and all the gloom & cheerlessness of my situation. I felt myself breathing quick & short as I beheld the Duke lifting up his sable crest which undulated as the plume of a hearse[1] waves to the wind & knew that that music which seems as mournfully triumphant as the Scriptural verse

> "Oh Grave where is thy sting Oh Death where
> is thy victory"[2]

was exciting him & quickening his ever rapid pulse.

"Miss Brontë what are you thinking about?" said a voice that dissipated all the charm & Miss Lister thrust her little rough black head into my face. "Sic tran-sit" &c.

December 19, 1835   1991

The novel _Jane Eyre_, 1847, appears in full in the Library of Women's Literature.

---

7. A location in "The Green Dwarf," a piece of Charlotte Brontë's juvenilia.
8. A market town in Cumberland, in the north of England.
9. Girls' boarding school where Brontë was em-ployed as a teacher.

1. Black feather decorating the top of a wagon for carrying coffins or the head of the horse that draws the wagon.
2. A misquotation of 1 Corinthians 15:55: "O death, where is thy sting? O grave, where is thy victory?"

CULTURAL COORDINATES
Phrenology

In describing characters' appearances and behavior, Charlotte Brontë often adhered to the principles of phrenology, a pseudoscientific study of the brain popular in nineteenth-century Europe. Phrenology holds that the brain is divided into segments in which specific sentiments and propensities reside. Phrenologists diagrammed the head to show the locations of the organs of *amativeness* (sexual love), *philoprogenitiveness* (love of children), *concentrativeness* (desire for permanence of place), *adhesiveness* (attachment), *combativeness* (courage), *destructiveness* (desire to destroy "noxious objects"), *secretiveness* (discretion), *acquisitiveness* (desire to possess), and *constructiveness* (desire to build). Each of these propensities—according to George Combe, whose 1828 book *The Constitution of Man Considered* was very popular in England, could work for the good of the individual and society or, if overdeveloped or distorted, could cause vice and corruption. This was also true of the organs housing the "sentiments": self-esteem, love of approbation (approval), caution, benevolence, veneration (the ability to worship), firmness, conscientiousness, hope, wonder, ideality (love of the beautiful), wit (sense of humor), and imitation. Other segments of the brain were associated with the senses and other intellectual capacities that modern medicine would attribute to brain function, though not in the same locations.

Phrenologists studied the shape of the head, attributing personality differences to the bumps, swellings, and recessions of the forehead

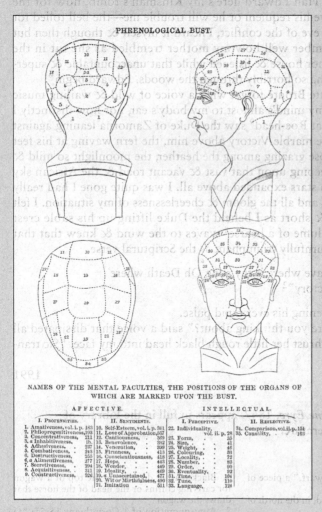

PHRENOLOGICAL BUST.

NAMES OF THE MENTAL FACULTIES, THE POSITIONS OF THE ORGANS OF WHICH ARE MARKED UPON THE BUST.

AFFECTIVE.		INTELLECTUAL.	
I. PROPENSITIES.	**II. SENTIMENTS.**	**I. PERCEPTIVE.**	**II. REFLECTIVE.**
1. Amativeness, vol.i.p. 183	10. Self-Esteem, vol.i.p. 341	22. Individuality, vol. ii. p. 28	34. Comparison, vol.ii.p. 154
2. Philoprogenitiveness,193	11. Love of Approbation,357	23. Form, 35	35. Causality, 163
3. Concentrativeness, 211	12. Cautiousness, 369	24. Size, 41	
3 a Inhabitiveness, ib.	13. Benevolence, 382	25. Weight, 46	
4. Adhesiveness, 237	14. Veneration, 399	26. Colouring, 53	
5. Combativeness, 243	15. Firmness, 413	27. Locality, 72	
6. Destructiveness, 255	16. Conscientiousness, 418	28. Number, 83	
6 a Alimentiveness, 277	17. Hope, 443	29. Order, 90	
7. Secretiveness, 294	18. Wonder, 449	30. Eventuality, 92	
8. Acquisitiveness, 311	19. Ideality, 469	31. Time, 104	
9. Constructiveness, 326	19. a Unascertained, 477	32. Tune, 110	
	20. Wit or Mirthfulness, 490	33. Language, 124	
	21. Imitation, 511		

Frontispiece to the 1853 edition of George Combe's *System of Phrenology*. (British Library)

and top of the skull. For Combe, a high, broad forehead denoted intelligence, nobility, morality, and strong religious feeling. A forehead sloping backward, by contrast, meant a deficiency in benevolence, veneration, conscientiousness, and intellectual capacity. Phrenology therefore saw character as inborn, physiology as fate. "Many marriages are unhappy in consequence of an instinctive discord between the modes of feeling and thinking of the husband and wife," Combe remarks, "the cause of which they themselves cannot explain. The mental differences will be found to arise from different configurations and qualities of the brain. Thus, if the husband be deficient in the organ of Conscientiousness, and the wife possess it in a high degree, she will be secretly disgusted with the dishonesty and inherent falsehood of his character" (*Embodied Selves*, ed. J. B. Taylor and S. Shuttleworth, Oxford: Oxford UP, 1998, 39). Combe recommends that potential spouses look carefully at their chosen partners' heads before committing themselves.

1818–1848

Only thirty years old when she died, Emily Brontë spent all but a few months of her life at Haworth parsonage, her family home on the Yorkshire moors in the far north of England. She had intense relationships with her clergyman father, Patrick; her ne'er-do-well brother, Branwell; and her four sisters Maria, Elizabeth, Charlotte, and Anne, as well as a few close friendships with women; but as a rule she neither socialized nor traveled. As her sister Charlotte put it, "Stronger than a man, simpler than a child, her nature stood alone." Emily Brontë's choice of lifestyle enabled her to achieve unparalleled focus and concentration on her creative work. In her short lifetime, she produced a body of important poetry as well as the novel *Wuthering Heights* (1847), acknowledged since the early twentieth century as a masterpiece of British fiction.

Brontë's childhood was marred by severe family losses: she was only three years old when her mother (Maria Branwell Brontë) died, leaving her and her siblings in the care of her maternal aunt (Elizabeth Branwell) and her father. When Emily was five, she went with her three older sisters, Maria, Elizabeth, and Charlotte, to the Clergy Daughters' School at Cowan Bridge, a charitable boarding school for poor clergymen's daughters. A disastrously unhealthy place, the school was racked with infection that the living conditions did little to ameliorate. Brontë's two oldest sisters, Maria and Elizabeth, contracted typhoid fever and possibly tuberculosis there in 1824; they died within the year, and their father brought Emily and Charlotte home immediately to safeguard their health.

At Haworth parsonage, Emily was a central participant in the constant reading, writing, debating, and fantasizing that occupied the surviving siblings' days. Brontë shared her family's passion for literature, history, and current events; she was also deeply interested in the people of her neighborhood, whom she observed intently, if from a distance. Together, she and her younger sister, Anne, created Gondal, a literary fantasy land about which they wrote and told stories, incorporating high drama, tragedy, romance, and comedy from the literature they loved. (Branwell and Charlotte created their own fantasy land, called Angria.) Emily and Anne kept Gondal alive in fiction and verse well into their twenties. (Selections from the Gondal and Angria stories, classified as juvenilia, or childhood writings, were published in the twentieth century.)

Reluctant to leave home for extended periods, Brontë had no enthusiasm for the role of governess that she and her sisters were expected to assume to support themselves. In her teens, she briefly joined Charlotte at the boarding school where Charlotte was teaching but got too homesick to stay. At age eighteen she tried teaching in a school herself but left, exhausted by long hours and difficult students, after only six months. Six years later, she traveled with Charlotte to Brussels, where she was to improve her French with a view to the sisters' opening a school of their own in Yorkshire. Her sojourn in Brussels lasted only a few months and was not a happy time—the bourgeois Belgian girls at the school remarked on her distant manners and her old-fashioned dress. Socially and geographically, Brontë was very much out of place. After returning from Belgium, she remained at Haworth parsonage, taking on the role of her father's housekeeper when her aunt died in 1842. She spent her days reading, drawing, walking, writing poetry, and doing housework.

In 1846, Charlotte returned from Brussels, and the sisters reluctantly acknowledged that they did not have the personal or financial resources to run a school. During this time, though, Charlotte came across poems that Emily and Anne had written in her absence and decided to publish a collection of the three's poetry. A deeply private person, Brontë was at first furious that her work would be made public, but eventually she reconciled herself to the idea. With Charlotte and Anne she concocted the pseudonyms that would appear on all of their publications: Currer, Ellis, and Acton Bell. The presumed masculinity of the names was a shield for the sisters' privacy as well as a conventional solution for female authors who did not wish to be judged by their gender. Portraying Emily's personality in the heroine of her novel *Shirley* (1849), Charlotte suggests that a gender-neutral name suited Emily's unconventional character. Both Emily and Shirley were physically tough: both are described as having cauterized a dog bite on their arms themselves with a hot iron. *Poems by Currer, Ellis, and Acton Bell* was published in 1846 but received few reviews and fewer readers. It sold only two copies, and the sisters soon shifted their efforts to writing novels.

Although Charlotte's first novel did not find a publisher, Emily's *Wuthering Heights* and Anne's *Agnes Grey* came out together in a three-volume set in 1847. Emily's first and only novel received savage reviews: her creations—Heathcliff and Catherine—have become icons of high romance in our era, but the gritty details, mixed characterizations, violent action, intense passions, and narrative experimentation that made *Wuthering Heights* famous in the twentieth century unnerved Victorian audiences. Emily's poetry continues many of the themes of nature and passion that come up in her novel. Many of her poems are dramatic monologues spoken by characters inhabiting Gondal, but some may be read as expressions of her own feelings.

Brontë died young and very rapidly, becoming ill with tuberculosis (then called "consumption") in 1848, just three months after nursing her brother, Branwell, who died at home after suffering from a combination of tuberculosis, advanced alcoholism, and opium addiction, and not long before her sister Anne, who also suffered from consumption. When she fell ill, Emily refused to consult a doctor, forcing herself to go through her daily housework until she was too weak to walk. According to family stories, Brontë's huge mastiff, Keeper, would not leave his post by her bedroom door, waiting indefinitely for her return even after she died. Private, even obscure, during her short life, Brontë stands now as one of the most celebrated of English authors.

A.G.A.[1]

To the Bluebell

Sacred watcher, wave thy bells!
Fair hill flower and woodland child!
Dear to me in deep green dells—
Dearest on the mountains wild.

1. The initials attribute the poem to Queen Augusta Geraldine Almeda, a character in the Gondal   stories.

Bluebell, even as all divine   5
I have seen my darling shine—
Bluebell, even as wan and frail—
I have seen my darling fail—
Thou hast found a voice for me,
And soothing words are breathed by thee.   10

Thus they murmur, "Summer's sun
Warms me till my life is done.
Would I rather choose to die
Under winter's ruthless sky?

"Glad I bloom and calm I fade;   15
Weeping twilight dews my bed;
Mourner, mourner, dry thy tears—
Sorrow comes with lengthened years!"

May 9, 1839   1910

Song

O between distress and pleasure
Fond affection cannot be;
Wretched hearts in vain would treasure
Friendship's joys when others flee.

Well I know thine eye would never   5
Smile, while mine grieved, willingly;
Yet I know thine eye for ever
Could not weep in sympathy.

Let us part, the time is over
When I thought and felt like thee;   10
I will be an Ocean rover,
I will sail the desert sea.

Isles there are beyond its billow:
Lands where woe may wander free;
And, beloved, thy midnight pillow   15
Will be soft unwatched by me.

Not on each returning morrow
When thy heart bounds ardently
Need'st thou then dissemble sorrow,
Marking my despondency.   20

Day by day some dreary token
Will forsake thy memory
Till at last all old links broken
I shall be a dream to thee.

October 15, 1839   1910

Love and Friendship

Love is like the wild rose-briar,
Friendship like the holly-tree—
The holly is dark when the rose-briar blooms
But which will bloom most constantly?

The wild rose-briar is sweet in spring,   5
Its summer blossoms scent the air;
Yet wait till winter comes again
And who will call the wild-briar fair?

Then scorn the silly rose-wreath now
And deck thee with the holly's sheen,   10
That when December blights thy brow
He still may leave thy garland green.

ca. 1841   1850

[Shall Earth no more inspire thee]

Shall Earth no more inspire thee,
Thou lonely dreamer now?
Since passion may not fire thee
Shall Nature cease to bow?

Thy mind is ever moving   5
In regions dark to thee;
Recall its useless roving—
Come back and dwell with me.

I know my mountain breezes
Enchant and soothe thee still—   10
I know my sunshine pleases
Despite thy wayward will.

When day with evening blending
Sinks from the summer sky,
I've seen thy spirit bending   15
In fond idolatry.

I've watched thee every hour;
I know my mighty sway,
I know my magic power
To drive thy griefs away.   20

Few hearts to mortals given
On earth so wildly pine;
Yet none would ask a Heaven
More like this Earth than thine.

Then let my winds caress thee;   25
Thy comrade let me be—

Since nought beside can bless thee,
Return and dwell with me.

May 16, 1841

A.S. TO G.S.[2]

[I do not weep, I would not weep]

I do not weep, I would not weep;
Our Mother needs no tears;
Dry thine eyes too, 'tis vain to keep
This causeless grief for years.

What though her brow be changed and cold,   5
Her sweet eyes closed for ever?
What though the stone—the darksome mould
Our mortal bodies sever?

What though her hand smoothe ne'er again
Those silken locks of thine—   10
Nor through long hours of future pain
Her kind face o'er thee shine?

Remember still she is not dead,
She sees us, Gerald,[3] now,
Laid where her angel spirit fled   15
'Mid heath and frozen snow.

And from that world of heavenly light
Will she not always bend,
To guide us in our lifetime's night
And guard us to the end?   20

Thou know'st she will, and well may'st mourn
That we are left below,
But not that she can ne'er return
To share our earthly woe.

December 19, 1841   1850

To Imagination

When weary with the long day's care,
And earthly change from pain to pain,
And lost, and ready to despair,
Thy kind voice calls me back again—
O my true friend, I am not lone   5
While thou canst speak with such a tone!

So hopeless is the world without,
The world within I doubly prize;

---

2. The poem is spoken by one Gondal character   3. Gerald, the poem's addressee.
to another.

Thy world where guile and hate and doubt
And cold suspicion never rise;   10
Where thou and I and Liberty
Have undisputed sovereignty.

What matters it that all around
Danger and grief and darkness lie,
If but within our bosom's bound   15
We hold a bright unsullied sky,
Warm with ten thousand mingled rays
Of suns that know no winter days?

Reason indeed may oft complain
For Nature's sad reality,   20
And tell the suffering heart how vain
Its cherished dreams must always be;
And Truth may rudely trample down
The flowers of Fancy newly blown.

But thou art ever there to bring   25
The hovering visions back and breathe
New glories o'er the blighted spring
And call a lovelier life from death,
And whisper with a voice divine
Of real worlds as bright as thine.   30

I trust not to thy phantom bliss,
Yet still in evening's quiet hour
With never-failing thankfulness
I welcome thee, benignant power,
Sure solacer of human cares   35
And brighter hope when hope despairs.

September 3, 1844   1846

[No coward soul is mine]

No coward soul is mine[4]
No trembler in the world's storm-troubled sphere
I see Heaven's glories shine
And Faith shines equal arming me from Fear

O God within my breast   5
Almighty ever-present Deity
Life, that in me hast rest
As I Undying Life, have power in Thee

Vain are the thousand creeds
That move men's hearts, unutterably vain,   10
Worthless as withered weeds
Or idlest froth amid the boundless main

4. The following are the last lines my sister Emily ever wrote. [Charlotte Brontë's note]

To waken doubt in one
Holding so fast by thy infinity
So surely anchored on   15
The steadfast rock of Immortality

With wide-embracing love
Thy spirit animates eternal years
Pervades and broods above,
Changes, sustains, dissolves, creates and rears   20

Though Earth and moon were gone
And suns and universes ceased to be
And thou wert left alone
Every Existence would exist in thee

There is not room for Death   25
Nor atom that his might could render void
Since thou art Being and Breath
And what thou art may never be destroyed.

Jan. 2, 1846   1850

◆ WOMEN COMPOSERS OF HYMNS ◆
1840–1899

Protestant family life in England and America during the nineteenth century involved religious rituals besides attending church on Sunday mornings. Many families "observed the Sabbath" after church by reading scripture or sermons silently
or aloud to the gathered household. Families also sang songs about God, Jesus,
the church, and faith that personalized their Christian message by placing "I" or
"we" in the subject position within their lyrics. These hymns were generally sung
at home until the last half of the nineteenth century, when they began to make
their way into church services alongside the previously familiar musical settings of
psalms and scriptural verses. Perhaps in part because of their domestic origin,
hymns were a popular form of expression among women poets of the period. The
selection here includes hymns that survive in twenty-first-century hymnals as a
record of women's contributions to the Christian liturgical tradition.

These hymns represent the range of subjects popular with nineteenth-century
women hymnodists: the individual's relationship with God, the contrasts between
this life and the next, and the links between nationalism and Christianity. In terms
of form, "Nearer, My God, to Thee" and the "Battle Hymn of the Republic" feature verses that all end with a repeated refrain, a good model for public singing
where many participants might not know all the lyrics or might not be able to
read them. The verse form of "O Beautiful for Spacious Skies"—four beats or
stresses, in the first and third lines, and three in the second and fourth—is a commonly employed structure in much nineteenth-century women's poetry, including
that of Emily Dickinson (pp. 938–51). Both "The Narrow Way" and "In the Bleak
Midwinter" were set to music by others for use as hymns. The hymnodists represented here include poets Christina Rossetti and Anne Brontë, canonized among

the most significant British women writers, as well as women whose only fame is attached to their popular hymns: Sarah Flower Adams, Julia Ward Howe, and Katharine Lee Bates.

◄ SARAH FLOWER ADAMS ►

1805–1848

Sarah Flower Adams was born in England to a father whose criticism of a bishop's political conduct landed him in prison for six months before he married her mother, a teacher. As a young woman, Sarah worked on the stage, appearing as Lady Macbeth in a London production in 1837. By the end of her life, she was writing more often than acting. Like her contemporaries the Brontë sisters, she died young of tuberculosis.

Nearer, My God, to Thee

Nearer, my God, to Thee, nearer to Thee!
E'en though it be a cross that raiseth me,
Still all my song shall be, nearer, my God, to Thee.
    Nearer, my God, to Thee,
    Nearer to Thee!   5
Though like the wanderer, the sun gone down,
Darkness be over me, my rest a stone.[1]
Yet in my dreams I'd be nearer, my God, to Thee.
    Nearer, my God, to Thee,
    Nearer to Thee!   10
There let the way appear, steps unto Heav'n;
All that Thou sendest me, in mercy given;
Angels to beckon me nearer, my God, to Thee.
    Nearer, my God, to Thee,
    Nearer to Thee!   15
Then, with my waking thoughts bright with Thy praise,
Out of my stony griefs Bethel[2] I'll raise;
So by my woes to be nearer, my God, to Thee.
    Nearer, my God, to Thee,
    Nearer to Thee!   20
Or, if on joyful wing cleaving the sky,
Sun, moon, and stars forgot, upward I'll fly,
Still all my song shall be, nearer, my God, to Thee.
    Nearer, my God, to Thee,
    Nearer to Thee!   25
There in my Father's home, safe and at rest,
There in my Savior's love, perfectly blest;
Age after age to be, nearer, my God, to Thee.

---

1. The speaker lies on the ground without bed or pillow.

2. "House of God," the site of Jacob's vision of a stairway or ladder to heaven (Genesis 28:10–19).

Nearer, my God, to Thee,
Nearer to Thee!   30

                                                                1841

◄ JULIA WARD HOWE ►

1819–1910

Julia Ward Howe (1819–1910) was a New Yorker who settled in Boston after her 1843 marriage to Dr. Samuel Howe. An avid supporter of the Union during the American Civil War, she wrote her famous "Battle Hymn of the Republic" in Virginia in 1861. She is supposed to have been inspired by hearing the soldiers sing "John Brown's Body," writing new words for that hymn, words that have been reprinted and sung continuously since their composition.

Battle Hymn of the Republic

Mine eyes have seen the glory of the coming of the Lord;
He is trampling down the vintage where the grapes of wrath are stored;[1]
He hath loosed the fateful lightning of His terrible swift sword;
His truth is marching on.
Glory! Glory! Hallelujah! Glory! Glory! Hallelujah!   5
Glory! Glory! Hallelujah! His truth is marching on.

I have seen Him in the watch fires of a hundred circling camps;
They have builded Him an altar in the evening dews and damps;
I can read His righteous sentence by the dim and flaring lamps;
His day is marching on.   10
Glory! Glory! Hallelujah! Glory! Glory! Hallelujah!
Glory! Glory! Hallelujah! His day is marching on.

I have read a fiery Gospel writ in burnished rows of steel;
"As ye deal with My condemners, so with you My grace shall deal";[2]
Let the Hero, born of woman, crush the serpent with His heel,[3]   15
Since God is marching on.
Glory! Glory! Hallelujah! Glory! Glory! Hallelujah!
Glory! Glory! Hallelujah! Since God is marching on.

He has sounded forth the trumpet that shall never call retreat;
He is sifting out the hearts of men before His judgment seat;   20
Oh, be swift, my soul, to answer Him! be jubilant, my feet;
Our God is marching on.
Glory! Glory! Hallelujah! Glory! Glory! Hallelujah!
Glory! Glory! Hallelujah! Our God is marching on.

---

1. Revelation 14:19: "And the angel thrust in his sickle into the earth, and gathered the vine of the earth, and cast it into the great winepress of the wrath of God."
2. Luke 6:37: "Judge not, and ye shall not be judged: condemn not, and ye shall not be condemned" (paraphrased).
3. Psalm 91:13: "You will tread on the lion and cobra. You will trample the young lion and the serpent underfoot."

In the beauty of the lilies Christ was born across the sea,   25
With a glory in His bosom that transfigures you and me:
As He died to make men holy, let us die to make men free;[4]
While God is marching on.
Glory! Glory! Hallelujah! Glory! Glory! Hallelujah!
Glory! Glory! Hallelujah! While God is marching on.   30

He is coming like the glory of the morning on the wave,
He is wisdom to the mighty, He is honor to the brave;
So the world shall be His footstool,[5] and the soul of wrong His slave,
Our God is marching on.
Glory! Glory! Hallelujah! Glory! Glory! Hallelujah!   35
Glory! Glory! Hallelujah! Our God is marching on.

                                                                              1862

ANNE BRONTË
1820–1849

Anne Bronte was the youngest sister of Charlotte and Emily Brontë (pp. 826–33 and 836–42). Like her sisters, she trained to work as a governess, but unlike them, she managed to endure the conditions of her position longer than a few months at a time. She published her early poems under a pseudonym with her sisters in *Poems by Currer, Ellis, and Acton Bell* (1846), but the book was not a success. While Charlotte and Emily were working on their first novels, *The Professor* (published posthumously, 1857) and *Wuthering Heights* (1848), respectively, Anne Brontë wrote *Agnes Grey* (1847), a protest novel about the plight of governesses employed in upper-middle-class households. She followed it up with *The Tenant of Wildfell Hall* (1848), a novel illustrating the oppression of women in marriages to abusive, alcoholic husbands. She died young, just a few months after her sister Emily, probably of tuberculosis.

The Narrow Way[1]

Believe not those who say
The upward path is smooth,
Lest thou shouldst stumble in the way,
And faint before the truth.

It is only the road   5
Unto the realms of joy;
But he who seeks that blest abode
Must all his powers employ.

Bright hopes and pure delights
Upon his course may beam,   10

---

4. This line is often rewritten as "let us *live* to make men free."
5. Acts 7:49: "Heaven is my throne, and the earth a footstool for my feet."

1. Matthew 7:14: "Strait is the gate, and narrow is the way, which leadeth unto life, and few there be that find it."

And there, amid the sternest heights,
The sweetest flowerets gleam.

On all her breezes borne,
Earth yields no scents like those;
But he that dares not grasp the thorn　　　　　15
Should never crave the rose.

Arm—arm thee for the fight!
Cast useless loads away;
Watch through the darkest hours of night,
Toil through the hottest day.　　　　　　20

Crush pride into the dust,
Or thou must needs be slack;
And trample down rebellious lust,
Or it will hold thee back.

Seek not thy honour here;　　　　　　25
Waive pleasure and renown;
The world's dread scoff undaunted bear,
And face its deadliest frown.

To labour and to love,
To pardon and endure,　　　　　　30
To life thy heart to God above,
And keep thy conscience pure;

Be this thy constant aim,
Thy hope, thy chief delight;
What matter who should whisper blame,　　　　　　35
Or who should scorn or slight?

What matter, if thy God approve,
And if, within thy breast,
Thou feel the comfort of His love,
The earnest of His rest?　　　　　　40

1848

⚫◄ CHRISTINA ROSSETTI ►⚫
1830–1894

Rossetti's biography, along with her poems, can be found on pp. 951–66.

In the Bleak Midwinter

In the bleak midwinter, frosty wind made moan,
Earth stood hard as iron, water like a stone;
Snow had fallen, snow on snow, snow on snow,
In the bleak midwinter, long ago.

Our God, heaven cannot hold Him, nor earth sustain;   5
Heaven and earth shall flee away when He comes to reign.
In the bleak midwinter a stable[1] place sufficed
The Lord God Almighty, Jesus Christ.

Enough for Him, Whom cherubim, worship night and day,
Breastful of milk, and a mangerful of hay;   10
Enough for Him, Whom angels fall before,
The ox and ass and camel which adore.[2]

Angels and archangels may have gathered there,
Cherubim and seraphim thronged the air;[3]
But His mother only, in her maiden bliss,[4]   15
Worshipped the beloved with a kiss.

What can I give Him, poor as I am?
If I were a shepherd, I would bring a lamb;
If I were a Wise Man, I would do my part;
Yet what can I give Him: give my heart.   20

1872

◄ KATHARINE LEE BATES ►
1859–1929

Like "Battle Hymn," "O Beautiful for Spacious Skies" is now sung as a patriotic
song. Its author, Katharine Lee Bates, the daughter of a Congregationalist minister, is the only nineteenth-century woman writer in this anthology who was a professional academic. A native of Massachusetts, she attended Wellesley College,
receiving her bachelor of arts in 1880. After teaching high school, she joined the
faculty of Wellesley in 1886 and taught there until four years before her death.
She wrote literary history as well as poetry and published almost two dozen books.
The inspiration for her famous hymn came from a visit to Colorado, where she
had a spiritual experience while gazing at Pike's Peak.

O Beautiful for Spacious Skies

O beautiful for spacious skies,
For amber waves of grain;
For purple mountain majesties
Above the fruited plain!
America! America!   5
God shed His grace on thee,
And crown thy good with brotherhood,
From sea to shining sea.

---

1. The manger, or feeding trough, in which the newborn Jesus slept.
2. Animals present at the birth of Jesus.
3. The two highest orders of angels in medieval Christian theology.
4. In the New Testament Mary, Jesus' mother, becomes pregnant without losing her virginity when the holy spirit enters her.

O beautiful for heroes proved
In liberating strife,   10
Who more than self their country loved,
And mercy more than life!
America! America!
May God thy gold refine,
Till all success be nobleness,   15
And every gain divine.

O beautiful for patriot dream
That sees beyond the years
Thine alabaster cities gleam,
Undimmed by human tears!   20
America! America!
God mend thine every flaw,
Confirm thy soul in self control,
Thy liberty in law.

1893   1899

<hr>

◄ SUSAN WARNER ►

1819–1885

For the first eighteen years of her life, Susan Warner enjoyed an almost fairy-tale existence as the petted daughter of a socially prominent and wealthy family. Although her beloved mother, Anna, died when she was nine, her father, Henry, and his sister, Fanny, saw that Warner and her younger sister, also named Anna, lacked for nothing. The mid-1830s saw Warner ready to take a leading place in the elite society of New York City until the catastrophic banking "crash" of 1837 erased Henry Warner's wealth. The family sold their New York City home and moved to an old farmhouse on Constitution Island in the Hudson River near West Point, which Henry had originally bought as a vacation property. None of the family was prepared for the isolation and hard work of rural life. Warner's father continued to lose money in lawsuits.

Like the protagonist of *The Wide, Wide World,* Warner had to struggle on multiple fronts to meet the challenges posed by her change in circumstance. One response was to embrace a demanding form of Presbyterian Christianity. By becoming a more pious Presbyterian, Warner was able to redefine her material deprivations as spiritual lessons. She and her sister became active in proselytizing—both in print and in person—their faith among the poor of New York City. Although brought up to be the pampered wives of rich men, Warner and her sister became the financial supports of their birth family. Anna's effort, the design and creation of a children's board game, was of limited success. But Warner's effort, the novel *The Wide, Wide World,* was startlingly successful when it was published in 1850 under the pen name Elizabeth Wetherell. Despite the money earned from this and Warner's next novel, *Queechy* (1852), Warner and her sister had to continue to publish and teach to support themselves and their family.

The Wide, Wide World epitomizes the American sentimental and domestic novel with its orphan-girl protagonist, Ellen Montgomery, who is seemingly unprepared to negotiate her world. This five-hundred-page novel details how Ellen masters the self-discipline she needs to submit to her fate. Warner's skill lies in her ability to render the psychological import of a child's making tea—just so—for the mother she only subconsciously knows is dying. In the initial chapters we include here, seemingly insignificant actions of everyday life are full of consequences for the protagonist.

From **The Wide, Wide World**

Chapter 1
[Ellen and Her Mother]

Enjoy the spring of love and youth,
To some good angel leave the rest,
For time will teach thee soon the truth,
"There are no birds in last year's nest."[1]

—LONGFELLOW.

"Mamma, what was that I heard papa saying to you this morning about his lawsuit?"

"I cannot tell you just now. Ellen, pick up that shawl, and spread it over me."

"Mamma!—are you cold in this warm room?"

"A little,—there, that will do. Now, my daughter, let me be quiet awhile—don't disturb me."

There was no one else in the room. Driven thus to her own resources, Ellen betook herself to the window and sought amusement there. The prospect without gave little promise of it. Rain was falling, and made the street and everything in it look dull and gloomy. The foot-passengers plashed through the water, and the horses and carriages plashed through the mud; gayety had forsaken the sidewalks, and equipages were few, and the people that were out were plainly there only because they could not help it. But yet Ellen, having seriously set herself to study everything that passed, presently became engaged in her occupation; and her thoughts travelling dreamily from one thing to another, she sat for a long time with her little face pressed against the window-frame, perfectly regardless of all but the moving world without.

Daylight gradually faded away, and the street wore a more and more gloomy aspect. The rain poured, and now only an occasional carriage or footstep disturbed the sound of its steady pattering. Yet still Ellen sat with her face glued to the window as if spellbound, gazing out at every dusky form that passed, as though it had some strange interest for her. At length, in the distance, light after light began to appear; presently Ellen could see the dim figure of the lamplighter crossing the street, from side to side, with his ladder; then he drew near enough for her to watch him as he hooked his ladder on the lamp-irons, ran up and lit the lamp, then shouldered the ladder and marched off quick, the light glancing on his wet oil-skin hat, rough great coat and lantern, and on the pavement and iron railings. The veriest moth could not have followed the light with more perseverance than did Ellen's eyes, till the lamplighter gradually disappeared from view, and the last lamp she could see was lit; and not till then did it occur to her that there was such a place as

1. Lines 21–24 of "It Is Not Always May" by   (1807–82).
American poet Henry Wadsworth Longfellow

in-doors. She took her face from the window. The room was dark and cheerless; and Ellen felt stiff and chilly. However, she made her way to the fire, and having found the poker, she applied it gently to the Liverpool coal[2] with such good effect that a bright ruddy blaze sprang up, and lighted the whole room. Ellen smiled at the result of her experiment. "That is something like," said she to herself; "who says I can't poke the fire? Now, let us see if I can't do something else. Do but see how those chairs are standing—one would think we had had a sewing-circle here—there, go back to your places,—that looks a little better; now these curtains must come down, and I may as well shut the shutters too; and now this table-cloth must be content to hang straight, and mamma's box and the books must lie in their places, and not all helter-skelter. Now, I wish mamma would wake up; I should think she might. I don't believe she is asleep either, she don't look as if she was."

Ellen was right in this; her mother's face did not wear the look of sleep, nor indeed of repose at all: the lips were compressed, and the brow not calm. To try, however, whether she was asleep or not, and with the half-acknowledged intent to rouse her at all events, Ellen knelt down by her side and laid her face close to her mother's on the pillow. But this failed to draw either word or sign. After a minute or two Ellen tried stroking her mother's cheek very gently; and this succeeded, for Mrs. Montgomery arrested the little hand as it passed her lips, and kissed it fondly two or three times.

"I haven't disturbed you, mamma, have I?" said Ellen.

Without replying, Mrs. Montgomery raised herself to a sitting posture, and lifting both hands to her face, pushed back the hair from her forehead and temples, with a gesture which Ellen knew meant that she was making up her mind to some disagreeable or painful effort. Then taking both Ellen's hands, as she still knelt before her, she gazed in her face with a look even more fond than usual, Ellen thought, but much sadder too; though Mrs. Montgomery's cheerfulness had always been of a serious kind.

"What question was that you were asking me awhile ago, my daughter?"

"I thought, mamma, I heard papa telling you this morning, or yesterday, that he had lost that lawsuit."

"You heard right, Ellen,—he has lost it," said Mrs. Montgomery, sadly.

"Are you sorry, mamma?—does it trouble you?"

"You know, my dear, that I am not apt to concern myself over-much about the gain or loss of money. I believe my Heavenly Father will give me what is good for me."

"Then, mamma, why are you troubled?"

"Because, my child, I cannot carry out this principle in other matters, and leave quietly my *all* in His hands."

"What is the matter, dear mother? What makes you look so?"

"This lawsuit, Ellen, has brought upon us more trouble than I ever thought a lawsuit could,—the loss of it, I mean."

"How, mamma?"

"It has caused an entire change of all our plans. Your father says he is too poor now to stay here any longer; and he has agreed to go soon on some government or military business to Europe."

"Well, mamma, that is bad; but he has been away a great deal before, and I am sure we were always very happy."

---

2. A high-quality coal.

"But, Ellen, he thinks now, and the doctor thinks too, that it is very important for my health that I should go with him."

"Does he, mamma?—and do you mean to go?"

"I am afraid I must, my dear child."

"Not, and leave *me*, mother?"

The imploring look of mingled astonishment, terror, and sorrow with which Ellen uttered these words, took from her mother all power of replying. It was not necessary; her little daughter understood only too well the silent answer of her eye. With a wild cry she flung her arms round her mother, and hiding her face in her lap, gave way to a violent burst of grief that seemed for a few moments as if it would rend soul and body in twain. For her passions were by nature very strong, and by education very imperfectly controlled; and time, "that rider that breaks youth,"[3] had not as yet tried his hand upon her. And Mrs. Montgomery, in spite of the fortitude and calmness to which she had steeled herself, bent down over her, and folding her arms about her, yielded to sorrow deeper still, and for a little while scarcely less violent in its expression than Ellen's own.

Alas! she had too good reason. She knew that the chance of her ever returning to shield the little creature who was nearest her heart from the future evils and snares of life was very, very small. She had at first absolutely refused to leave Ellen, when her husband proposed it: declaring that she would rather stay with her and die than take the chance of recovery at such a cost. But her physician assured her she could not live long without a change of climate; Captain Montgomery urged that it was better to submit to a temporary separation, than to cling obstinately to her child for a few months and then leave her for ever; said he must himself go speedily to France, and that now was her best opportunity; assuring her, however, that his circumstances would not permit him to take Ellen along, but that she would be secure of a happy home with his sister during her mother's absence; and to the pressure of argument Captain Montgomery added the weight of authority, insisting on her compliance. Conscience also asked Mrs. Montgomery whether she had a *right* to neglect any chance of life that was offered her; and at last she yielded to the combined influence of motives no one of which would have had power sufficient to move her, and, though with a secret consciousness it would be in vain, she consented to do as her friends wished. And it was for Ellen's sake she did it, after all.

Nothing but necessity had given her the courage to open the matter to her little daughter. She had foreseen and endeavored to prepare herself for Ellen's anguish; but nature was too strong for her, and they clasped each other in a convulsive embrace, while tears fell like rain.

It was some minutes before Mrs. Montgomery recollected herself, and then, though she struggled hard, she could not immediately regain her composure. But Ellen's deep sobs at length fairly alarmed her; she saw the necessity, for both their sakes, of putting a stop to this state of violent excitement; self-command was restored at once.

"Ellen! Ellen! listen to me," she said; "my child, this is not right. Remember, my darling, who it is that brings this sorrow upon us; though we *must* sorrow, we must not rebel."

3. From *Jacula Prudentum*, a collection of proverbs   published in 1651 after his death.
by English poet George Herbert (1593–1633),

Ellen sobbed more gently; but that and the mute pressure of her arms was her only answer.

"You will hurt both yourself and me, my daughter, if you cannot command yourself. Remember, dear Ellen, God sends no trouble upon his children but in love; and though we cannot see how, he will no doubt make all this work for our good."

"I know it, dear mother," sobbed Ellen, "but it's just as hard!"

Mrs. Montgomery's own heart answered so readily to the truth of Ellen's words that for the moment she could not speak.

"Try, my daughter," she said, after a pause,—"try to compose yourself. I am afraid you will make me worse, Ellen, if you cannot,—I am, indeed."

Ellen had plenty of faults, but amidst them all love to her mother was the strongest feeling her heart knew. It had power enough now to move her as nothing else could have done; and exerting all her self-command, of which she had sometimes a good deal, she *did* calm herself; ceased sobbing; wiped her eyes; arose from her crouching posture, and seating herself on the sofa by her mother, and laying her head on her bosom, she listened quietly to all the soothing words and cheering considerations with which Mrs. Montgomery endeavoured to lead her to take a more hopeful view of the subject. All she could urge, however, had but very partial success, though the conversation was prolonged far into the evening. Ellen said little, and did not weep any more; but in secret her heart refused consolation.

Long before this the servant had brought in the tea-things. Nobody regarded it at the time, but the little kettle hissing away on the fire now by chance attracted Ellen's attention, and she suddenly recollected her mother had had no tea. To make her mother's tea was Ellen's regular business. She treated it as a very grave affair, and loved it as one of the pleasantest in the course of the day. She used in the first place to make sure that the kettle really boiled; then she carefully poured some water into the tea-pot and rinsed it, both to make it clean and to make it hot; then she knew exactly how much tea to put into the tiny little tea-pot, which was just big enough to hold two cups of tea, and having poured a very little boiling water to it, she used to set it by the side of the fire while she made half a slice of toast. How careful Ellen was about that toast! The bread must not be cut too thick, nor too thin; the fire must, if possible, burn clear and bright, and she herself held the bread on a fork, just at the right distance from the coals to get nicely browned without burning. When this was done to her satisfaction (and if the first piece failed she would take another), she filled up the little tea-pot from the boiling kettle, and proceeded to make a cup of tea. She knew, and was very careful to put in, just the quantity of milk and sugar that her mother liked; and then she used to carry the tea and toast on a little tray to her mother's side, and very often held it there for her while she eat. All this Ellen did with the zeal that love gives, and though the same thing was to be gone over every night of the year, she was never wearied. It was a real pleasure; she had the greatest satisfaction in seeing that the little her mother could eat was prepared for her in the nicest possible manner; she knew her hands made it taste better; her mother often said so.

But this evening other thoughts had driven this important business quite out of poor Ellen's mind. Now, however, when her eyes fell upon the little kettle, she recollected her mother had not had her tea, and must want it very much; and silently slipping off the sofa, she set about getting it as usual. There was no doubt this time whether the kettle boiled or no; it had been hissing for an hour and more, calling as loud as it could to somebody to come and make the tea. So Ellen made it, and then began the toast. But she began to think, too, as she watched it, how few more times she would be able to do so,—how soon her pleasant tea-makings would be over,—and the desolate feeling of separation began to come upon her before the time. These thoughts were too much for poor Ellen; the thick tears gathered so fast she could not see what she was doing; and she had no more than just turned the slice of bread on the fork when the sickness of heart quite overcame her; she could not go on. Toast and fork and all dropped from her hand into the ashes; and rushing to her mother's side, who was now lying down again, and throwing herself upon her, she burst into another fit of sorrow; not so violent as the former, but with a touch of hopelessness in it which went yet more to her mother's heart. Passion in the first said, "I cannot;" despair now seemed to say, "I must."

But Mrs. Montgomery was too exhausted to either share or soothe Ellen's agitation. She lay in suffering silence; till after some time she said, faintly, "Ellen, my love, I cannot bear this much longer."

Ellen was immediately brought to herself by these words. She arose, sorry and ashamed that she should have given occasion for them; and tenderly kissing her mother, assured her most sincerely and resolutely that she would not do so again. In a few minutes she was calm enough to finish making the tea, and having toasted another piece of bread, she brought it to her mother. Mrs. Montgomery swallowed a cup of tea, but no toast could be eaten that night.

Both remained silent and quiet awhile after this, till the clock struck ten. "You had better go to bed, my daughter," said Mrs. Montgomery.

"I will, mamma."

"Do you think you can read me a little before you go?"

"Yes, indeed, mamma;" and Ellen brought the book. "Where shall I read?"

"The twenty-third psalm."

Ellen began it, and went through it steadily and slowly, though her voice quavered a little.

"'The Lord is my Shepherd; I shall not want.

"'He maketh me to lie down in green pastures: He leadeth me beside the still waters.

"'He restoreth my soul: He leadeth me in the paths of righteousness for his name's sake.

"'Yea, though I walk through the valley of the shadow of death, I will fear no evil: for Thou art with me; thy rod and thy staff they comfort me.

"'Thou preparest a table before me in the presence of mine enemies: Thou anointest my head with oil; my cup runneth over.

"'Surely goodness and mercy shall follow me all the days of my life: and I will dwell in the house of the Lord forever.'"[4]

Long before she had finished, Ellen's eyes were full, and her heart too. "If I only could feel these words as mamma does!" she said to herself. She did not dare look up till the traces of tears had passed away; then she saw that her mother was asleep. Those first sweet words had fallen like balm upon the sore heart; and mind and body had instantly found rest together.

4. Psalm 23:1–6.

Ellen breathed the lightest possible kiss upon her forehead, and stole quietly out of the room to her own little bed.

* * *

Chapter 3
[Ellen Goes Shopping]

Sweetheart, we shall be rich ere we depart,
If fairings come thus plentifully in.

—SHAKESPEARE.[5]

Ellen had to wait some time for the desired fine day. The equinoctial storms would have their way as usual, and Ellen thought they were longer than ever this year. But after many stormy days had tried her patience, there was at length a sudden change, both without and within doors. The clouds had done their work for that time, and fled away before a strong northerly wind, leaving the sky bright and fair. And Mrs. Montgomery's deceitful disease took a turn, and for a little space raised the hopes of her friends. All were rejoicing but two persons; Mrs. Montgomery was not deceived, neither was the doctor. The shopping project was kept a profound secret from him and from everybody except Ellen.

Ellen watched now for a favourable day. Every morning as soon as she rose she went to the window to see what was the look of the weather; and about a week after the change above noticed, she was greatly pleased one morning, on opening her window as usual, to find the air and sky promising all that could be desired. It was one of those beautiful days in the end of September, that sometimes herald October before it arrives,—cloudless, brilliant, and breathing balm. "This will do," said Ellen to herself, in great satisfaction. "I think this will do; I hope mamma will think so."

Hastily dressing herself, and a good deal excited already, she ran down-stairs; and after the morning salutations, examined her mother's looks with as much anxiety as she had just done those of the weather. All was satisfactory there also, and Ellen ate her breakfast with an excellent appetite; but she said not a word of the intended expedition till her father should be gone. She contented herself with strengthening her hopes by making constant fresh inspections of the weather and her mother's countenance alternately; and her eyes, returning from the window on one of these excursions and meeting her mother's face, saw a smile there which said all she wanted. Breakfast went on more vigorously than ever. But after breakfast it seemed to Ellen that her father never would go away. He took the newspaper, an uncommon thing for him, and pored over it most perseveringly, while Ellen was in a perfect fidget of impatience. Her mother, seeing the state she was in, and taking pity on her, sent her up-stairs to do some little matters of business in her own room. These Ellen despatched with all possible zeal and speed; and coming down again found her father gone and her mother alone. She flew to kiss her in the first place, and then make the inquiry, "Don't you think to-day will do, mamma?"

"As fine as possible, daughter; we could not have a better; but I must wait till the doctor has been here."

5. From William Shakespeare's (c. 1595) play *Love's Labours Lost* (5.2.1–2).

"Mamma," said Ellen, after a pause, making a great effort of self-denial, "I am afraid you oughtn't to go out to get these things for me. Pray don't, mamma, if you think it will do you harm. I would rather go without them; indeed I would."

"Never mind that, daughter," said Mrs. Montgomery, kissing her. "I am bent upon it; it would be quite as much of a disappointment to me as to you not to go. We have a lovely day for it, and we will take our time and walk slowly, and we haven't far to go, either. But I must let Dr. Green make his visit first."

To fill up the time till he came, Mrs. Montgomery employed Ellen in reading to her as usual. And this morning's reading Ellen long after remembered. Her mother directed her to several passages in different parts of the Bible that speak of heaven and its enjoyments; and though, when she began, her own little heart was full of excitement, in view of the day's plans, and beating with hope and pleasure, the sublime beauty of the words and thoughts, as she went on, awed her into quiet, and her mother's manner at length turned her attention entirely from herself. Mrs. Montgomery was lying on the sofa, and for the most part listened in silence, with her eyes closed, but sometimes saying a word or two that made Ellen feel how deep was the interest her mother had in the things she read of, and how pure and strong the pleasure she was even now taking in them; and sometimes there was a smile on her face that Ellen scarce liked to see; it gave her an indistinct feeling that her mother would not be long away from that heaven to which she seemed already to belong. Ellen had a sad consciousness, too, that she had no part with her mother in this matter. She could hardly go on. She came to that beautiful passage in the seventh of Revelation:

"And one of the elders answered, saying unto me, What are these which are arrayed in white robes? and whence came they? And I said unto him, Sir, thou knowest. And he said unto me, These are they which came out of great tribulation, and have washed their robes, and made them white in the blood of the Lamb. Therefore are they before the throne of God, and serve him day and night in his temple: and he that sitteth on the throne shall dwell among them. They shall hunger no more, neither thirst any more; neither shall the sun light on them, nor any heat. For the Lamb which is in the midst of the throne shall feed them, and shall lead them unto living fountains of waters: and God shall wipe away all tears from their eyes."[6]

With difficulty, and a husky voice, Ellen got through it. Lifting then her eyes to her mother's face, she saw again the same singular sweet smile. Ellen felt that she could not read another word; to her great relief the door opened, and Dr. Green came in. His appearance changed the whole course of her thoughts. All that was grave or painful fled quickly away; Ellen's head was immediately full again of what had filled it before she began to read.

As soon as the doctor had retired and was fairly out of hearing, "Now, mamma, shall we go?" said Ellen. "You needn't stir, mamma; I'll bring all your things to you, and put them on; may I, mamma? then you won't be a bit tired before you set out."

Her mother assented; and with a great deal of tenderness and a great deal of eagerness, Ellen put on her stockings and shoes, arranged her hair, and did all that she could toward changing her dress and putting on her bonnet and shawl; and greatly delighted she was when the business was accomplished.

6. Revelation 7:13–17.

"Now, mamma, you look like yourself; I haven't seen you look so well this great while. I'm so glad you're going out again," said Ellen, putting her arms round her; "I do believe it will do you good. Now, mamma, I'll go and get ready; I'll be very quick about it; you shan't have to wait long for me."

In a few minutes the two set forth from the house. The day was as fine as could be; there was no wind, there was no dust; the sun was not oppressive; and Mrs. Montgomery did feel refreshed and strengthened during the few steps they had to take to their first stopping-place.

It was a jeweller's store. Ellen had never been in one before in her life, and her first feeling on entering was of dazzled wonderment at the glittering splendours around; this was presently forgotten in curiosity to know what her mother could possibly want there. She soon discovered that she had come to sell and not to buy. Mrs. Montgomery drew a ring from her finger, and after a little chaffering parted with it to the owner of the store for eighty dollars,[7] being about three-quarters of its real value. The money was counted out, and she left the store.

"Mamma," said Ellen, in a low voice, "wasn't that grandmamma's ring, which I thought you loved so much?"

"Yes, I did love it, Ellen, but I love you better."

"Oh, mamma, I am very sorry!" said Ellen.

"You need not be sorry, daughter. Jewels in themselves are the merest nothings to me; and as for the rest, it doesn't matter; I can remember my mother without any help from a trinket."

There were tears, however, in Mrs. Montgomery's eyes, that showed the sacrifice had cost her something; and there were tears in Ellen's that told it was not thrown away upon her.

"I am sorry you should know of this," continued Mrs. Montgomery; "you should not if I could have helped it. But set your heart quite at rest, Ellen; I assure you this use of my ring gives me more pleasure on the whole than any other I could have made of it."

A grateful squeeze of her hand and glance into her face was Ellen's answer.

Mrs. Montgomery had applied to her husband for the funds necessary to fit Ellen comfortably for the time they should be absent; and in answer he had given her a sum barely sufficient for her mere clothing. Mrs. Montgomery knew him better than to ask for a further supply, but she resolved to have recourse to other means to do what she had determined upon. Now that she was about to leave her little daughter, and it might be forever, she had set her heart upon providing her with certain things which she thought important to her comfort and improvement, and which Ellen would go very long without if *she* did not give them to her, and *now*. Ellen had had very few presents in her life, and those always of the simplest and cheapest kind; her mother resolved that in the midst of the bitterness of this time she would give her one pleasure, if she could; it might be the last.

They stopped next at a bookstore. "Oh, what a delicious smell of new books!" said Ellen, as they entered. "Mamma, if it wasn't for one thing, I should say I never was so happy in my life."

Children's books, lying in tempting confusion near the door, immediately fastened Ellen's eyes and attention. She opened one, and was already deep in the in-

7. While monetary conversions can be problematic, the value of $1 in 1850 is over $26 today, so $80 would be worth more than $2,100.

terest of it, when the word *"Bibles"* struck her ear. Mrs. Montgomery was desiring the shopman to show her various kinds and sizes that she might choose from among them. Down went Ellen's book, and she flew to the place, where a dozen different Bibles were presently displayed. Ellen's wits were ready to forsake her. Such beautiful Bibles she had never seen; she pored in ecstasy over their varieties of type and binding, and was very evidently in love with them all.

"Now, Ellen," said Mrs. Montgomery, "look and choose; take your time, and see which you like best."

It was not likely that Ellen's "time" would be a short one. Her mother, seeing this, took a chair at a little distance to await patiently her decision; and while Ellen's eyes were riveted on the Bibles, her own very naturally were fixed upon her. In the excitement and eagerness of the moment, Ellen had thrown off her light bonnet, and with flushed cheek and sparkling eye, and a brow grave with unusual care, as though a nation's fate were deciding, she was weighing the comparative advantages of large, small, and middle-sized; black, blue, purple, and red; gilt and not gilt; clasp and no clasp. Everything but the Bibles before her Ellen had forgotten utterly; she was deep in what was to her the most important of business; she did not see the bystanders smile; she did not know there were any. To her mother's eye it was a most fair sight. Mrs. Montgomery gazed with rising emotions of pleasure and pain that struggled for the mastery, but pain at last got the better and rose very high. "How can I give thee up!" was the one thought of her heart. Unable to command herself, she rose and went to a distant part of the counter, where she seemed to be examining books; but tears, some of the bitterest she had ever shed, were falling thick upon the dusty floor, and she felt her heart like to break. Her little daughter at one end of the counter had forgotten there ever was such a thing as sorrow in the world; and she at the other was bowed beneath a weight of it that was nigh to crush her. But in her extremity she betook herself to that refuge she had never known to fail; it did not fail her now. She remembered the words Ellen had been reading to her but that very morning, and they came like the breath of heaven upon the fever of her soul. "Not my will, but thine be done."[8] She strove and prayed to say it, and not in vain; and after a little while she was able to return to her seat. She felt that she had been shaken by a tempest, but she was calmer now than before.

Ellen was just as she had left her, and apparently just as far from coming to any conclusion. Mrs. Montgomery was resolved to let her take her way. Presently Ellen came over from the counter with a large royal octavo Bible,[9] heavy enough to be a good lift for her. "Mamma," said she, laying it on her mother's lap and opening it, "what do you think of that? isn't that splendid?"

"A most beautiful page, indeed; is this your choice, Ellen?"

"Well, mamma, I don't know; what do you think?"

"I think it is rather inconveniently large and heavy for everyday use. It is quite a weight upon my lap. I shouldn't like to carry it in my hands long. You would want a little table on purpose to hold it."

"Well, that wouldn't do at all," said Ellen, laughing; "I believe you are right, mamma; I wonder I didn't think of it. I might have known that myself."

8. Luke 22:42.
9. A large book made from sheets folded to make   sixteen pages (eight "leaves").

She took it back; and there followed another careful examination of the whole stock; and then Ellen came to her mother with a beautiful miniature edition in two volumes, gilt and clasped, and very perfect in all respects, but of exceeding small print.

"I think I'll have this, mamma," said she; "isn't it a beauty? I could put it in my pocket, you know, and carry it anywhere with the greatest ease."

"It would have one great objection to me," said Mrs. Montgomery, "inasmuch as I cannot possibly see to read it."

"Cannot you, mamma! But I can read it perfectly."

"Well, my dear, take it; that is, if you will make up your mind to put on spectacles before your time."

"Spectacles, mamma! I hope I shall never wear spectacles."

"What do you propose to do when your sight fails, if you shall live so long?"

"Well, mamma,—if it comes to that,—but you don't advise me, then, to take this little beauty?"

"Judge for yourself; I think you are old enough."

"I know what you think, though, mamma, and I dare say you are right, too; I won't take it, though it's a pity. Well, I must look again."

Mrs. Montgomery came to her help, for it was plain Ellen had lost the power of judging amidst so many tempting objects. But she presently simplified the matter by putting aside all that were decidedly too large, or too small, or of too fine print. There remained three, of moderate size and sufficiently large type, but different binding. "Either of these I think will answer your purpose nicely," said Mrs. Montgomery.

"Then, mamma, if you please, I will have the red one. I like that best, because it will put me in mind of yours."

Mrs. Montgomery could find no fault with this reason. She paid for the red Bible, and directed it to be sent home. "Shan't I carry it, mamma?" said Ellen.

"No, you would find it in the way; we have several things to do yet."

"Have we, mamma? I thought we only came to get a Bible."

"That is enough for one day, I confess; I am a little afraid your head will be turned; but I must run the risk of it. I dare not lose the opportunity of this fine weather; I may not have such another. I wish to have the comfort of thinking, when I am away, that I have left you with everything necessary to the keeping up of good habits,—everything that will make them pleasant and easy. I wish you to be always neat, and tidy, and industrious; depending upon others as little as possible; and careful to improve yourself by every means, and especially by writing to me. I will leave you no excuse, Ellen, for failing in any of these duties. I trust you will not disappoint me in a single particular."

Ellen's heart was too full to speak; she again looked up tearfully and pressed her mother's hand.

"I do not expect to be disappointed, love," returned Mrs. Montgomery.

They now entered a large fancy store. "What are we to get here, mamma?" said Ellen.

"A box to put your pens and paper in," said her mother, smiling.

"Oh, to be sure," said Ellen; "I had almost forgotten that." She quite forgot it a minute after. It was the first time she had ever seen the inside of such a store; and the articles displayed on every side completely bewitched her. From one thing to another she went, admiring and wondering; in her wildest dreams she had never imagined such beautiful things. The store was fairy-land.

Mrs. Montgomery meanwhile attended to business. Having chosen a neat little japanned dressing-box,[1] perfectly plain, but well supplied with everything a child could want in that line, she called Ellen from the delightful journey of discovery she was making round the store, and asked her what she thought of it. "I think it's a little beauty," said Ellen; "but I never saw such a place for beautiful things."

"You think it will do, then?" said her mother.

"For me, mamma! You don't mean to give it to me? Oh, mother, how good you are! But I know what is the best way to thank you, and I'll do it. What a perfect little beauty! Mamma, I'm too happy."

"I hope not," said her mother, "for you know I haven't got you the box for your pens and paper yet."

"Well, mamma, I'll try and bear it," said Ellen, laughing. "But do get me the plainest little thing in the world, for you're giving me too much."

Mrs. Montgomery asked to look at writing-desks, and was shown to another part of the store for the purpose. "Mamma," said Ellen, in a low tone, as they went, "you're not going to get me a writing-desk?"

"Why, that is the best kind of box for holding writing materials," said her mother, smiling; "don't you think so?"

"I don't know what to say!" exclaimed Ellen. "I can't thank you, mamma; I haven't any words to do it. I think I shall go crazy."

She was truly overcome with the weight of happiness. Words failed her, and tears came instead.

From among a great many desks of all descriptions, Mrs. Montgomery with some difficulty succeeded in choosing one to her mind. It was of mahogany, not very large, but thoroughly well made and finished, and very convenient and perfect in its internal arrangements. Ellen was speechless; occasional looks at her mother, and deep sighs, were all she had now to offer. The desk was quite empty. "Ellen," said her mother, "do you remember the furniture of Miss Allen's desk,[2] that you were so pleased with a while ago."

"Perfectly, mamma; I know all that was in it."

"Well, then, you must prompt me if I forget anything. Your desk will be furnished with every thing really useful. Merely showy matters we can dispense with. Now, let us see.—Here is a great empty place that I think wants some paper to fill it. Show me some of different sizes, if you please."

The shopman obeyed, and Mrs. Montgomery stocked the desk well with letter paper, large and small. Ellen looked on in great satisfaction. "That will do nicely," she said;—"that large paper will be beautiful whenever I am writing to you, mamma, you know, and the other will do for other times when I haven't so much to say; though I am sure I don't know who there is in the world I should ever send letters to except you."

"If there is nobody now, perhaps there will be at some future time," replied her mother. "I hope I shall not always be your only correspondent. Now what next?"

"Envelopes, mamma?"

"To be sure; I had forgotten them. Envelopes of both sizes to match."

"Because, mamma, you know I might, and I certainly shall, want to write upon the fourth page of my letter, and I couldn't do it unless I had envelopes."

A sufficient stock of envelopes was laid in.

1 A box made of black lacquered wood.
2. See the Cultural Coordinates box "How Did

They Do It?: Narcissa Whitman's Writing Desk"
(pp. 640–41).

"Mamma," said Ellen, "what do you think of a little note-paper?"

"Who are the notes to be written to, Ellen?" said Mrs. Montgomery, smiling.

"You needn't smile, mamma; you know, as you said, if I don't now know, perhaps I shall by and by. Miss Allen's desk had note-paper; that made me think of it."

"So shall yours, daughter; while we are about it we will do the thing well. And your note-paper will keep quite safely in this nice little place provided for it, even if you should not want to use a sheet of it in half a dozen years."

"How nice that is!" said Ellen, admiringly.

"I suppose the note-paper must have envelopes too," said Mrs. Montgomery.

"To be sure, mamma; I suppose so," said Ellen, smiling; "Miss Allen's had."

"Well now we have got all the paper we want, I think," said Mrs. Montgomery; "the next thing is ink,—or an inkstand rather."

Different kinds were presented for her choice.

"Oh, mamma, that one won't do," said Ellen, anxiously; "you know the desk will be knocking about in a trunk, and the ink would run out, and spoil every thing. It should be one of those that shut tight. I don't see the right kind here."

The shopman brought one.

"There, mamma, do you see?" said Ellen; "it shuts with a spring, and nothing can possibly come out; do you see, mamma? You can turn it topsy turvy."

"I see you are quite right, daughter; it seems I should get on very ill without you to advise me. Fill the inkstand, if you please."

"Mamma, what shall I do when my ink is gone? that inkstand will hold but a little, you know."

"Your aunt will supply you, of course, my dear, when you are out."

"I'd rather take some of my own by half," said Ellen.

"You could not carry a bottle of ink in your desk without great danger to every thing else in it. It would not do to venture."

"We have excellent ink-powder," said the shopman, "in small packages, which can be very conveniently carried about. You see, ma'am, there is a compartment in the desk for such things; and the ink is very easily made at any time."

"Oh, that will do nicely," said Ellen, "that is just the thing."

"Now what is to go in this other square place opposite the inkstand?" said Mrs. Montgomery.

"That is the place for the box of lights, mamma."

"What sort of lights?"

"For sealing letters, mamma, you know. They are not like your wax taper at all; they are little wax matches, that burn just long enough to seal one or two letters; Miss Allen showed me how she used them. Hers were in a nice little box just like the inkstand on the outside; and there was a place to light the matches, and a place to set them in while they are burning. There, mamma, that's it," said Ellen, as the shopman brought forth the article which she was describing, "that's it, exactly; and that will just fit. Now, mamma, for the wax."

"You want to seal your letter before you have written it," said Mrs. Montgomery,—"we have not got the pens yet."

"That's true, mamma; let us have the pens. And some quills too, mamma?"

"Do you know how to make a pen, Ellen?"

"No, mamma, not yet; but I want to learn very much. Miss Pichegru says that every lady ought to know how to make her own pens."

"Miss Pichegru is very right; but I think you are rather too young to learn. However, we will try. Now here are steel points enough to last you a great while,—

and as many quills as it is needful you should cut up for one year at least;—we haven't a pen-handle yet."

"Here, mamma," said Ellen, holding out a plain ivory one,—"don't you like this? I think that it is prettier than these that are all cut and fussed, or those other gay ones either."

"I think so too, Ellen; the plainer the prettier. Now what comes next?"

"The knife, mamma, to make the pens," said Ellen, smiling.

"True, the knife. Let us see some of your best pen-knives. Now, Ellen, choose. That one won't do, my dear; it should have two blades,—a large as well as a small one. You know you want to mend a pencil sometimes."

"So I do, mamma, to be sure, you're very right; here's a nice one. Now, mamma, the wax."

"There is a box full; choose your own colours." Seeing it was likely to be a work of time, Mrs. Montgomery walked away to another part of the store. When she returned Ellen had made up an assortment of the oddest colours she could find.

"I won't have any red, mamma, it is so common," she said.

"I think it is the prettiest of all," said Mrs. Montgomery.

"Do you, mamma? then I will have a stick of red on purpose to seal to you with."

"And who do you intend shall have the benefit of the other colours?" inquired her mother.

"I declare, mamma," said Ellen, laughing; "I never thought of that; I am afraid they will have to go to you. You must not mind, mamma, if you get green and blue and yellow seals once in a while."

"I dare say I shall submit myself to it with a good grace," said Mrs. Montgomery. "But come, my dear, have we got all that we want? This desk has been very long in furnishing."

"You haven't given me a seal yet, mamma."

"Seals! There are a variety before you; see if you can find one that you like. By the way, you cannot seal a letter, can you?"

"Not yet, mamma," said Ellen, smiling again; "that is another of the things I have got to learn."

"Then I think you had better have some wafers[3] in the mean time."

While Ellen was picking out her seal, which took not a little time, Mrs. Montgomery laid in a good supply of wafers of all sorts; and then went on further to furnish the desk with an ivory leaf-cutter, a paper-folder, a pounce-box,[4] a ruler, and a neat little silver pencil; also, some drawing-pencils, India-rubber,[5] and sheets of drawing-paper. She took a sad pleasure in adding every thing she could think of that might be for Ellen's future use or advantage; but as with her own hands she placed in the desk one thing after another, the thought crossed her mind how Ellen would make drawings with those very pencils, on those very sheets of paper, which her eyes would never see! She turned away with a sigh, and receiving Ellen's seal from her hand, put that also in its place. Ellen had chosen one with her own name.

"Will you send these things at once?" said Mrs. Montgomery. "I particularly wish them at home as early in the day as possible."

3. Soft disks of wax for sealing letters. They did not require heat from a flame to work.
4. A small box to hold the fine sand one would sprinkle over one's writing to help it dry faster.
5. An eraser.

The man promised. Mrs. Montgomery paid the bill, and she and Ellen left the store.

They walked a little way in silence.

"I cannot thank you, mamma," said Ellen.

"It is not necessary, my dear child," said Mrs. Montgomery, returning the pressure of her hand; "I know all that you would say."

There was as much sorrow as joy at that moment in the heart of the joyfullest of the two.

"Where are we going now, mamma?" said Ellen again, after a while.

"I wished and intended to have gone to St. Clair and Fleury's to get you some merino[6] and other things; but we have been detained so long already that I think I had better go home. I feel somewhat tired."

"I am very sorry, dear mamma," said Ellen; "I am afraid I kept you too long about that desk."

"You did not keep me, daughter, any longer than I chose to be kept. But I think I will go home how, and take the chance of another fine day for the merino."

* * *

1850

◄ GEORGE ELIOT ►
1819–1880

Calling herself "Mary Anne Evans" as a child, "Mary Ann Evans" as a teenager, "Marian Evans" as a young woman, "Mrs. George Lewes" as an unmarried partner, and "Mrs. John Cross" as a later-life bride, the woman who wrote under the name George Eliot is acknowledged as one of the great authors of the English novel. Writing her first novel at the age of thirty-eight, she chose her pen name to shield her early writing from the scandal associated with her own name, as well as to sidetrack critics who might disregard her work if they knew it had been written by a woman. Unlike Currer and Ellis Bell, the almost forgotten pen names adopted by her fellow Victorians Charlotte and Emily Brontë, George Eliot's name has lived on with her works.

Mary Anne Evans was born the youngest of five surviving children of Robert Evans, a successful land agent for an estate near Coventry, England, and his second wife, Christiana. Eliot's closest friends in childhood were her sister Chrissey, who was five years older than she, and her brother Isaac, who was three years her senior. She later said that her relationships with her brother and father were the most important in her early life. Robert Evans was a political conservative, defending the rights of landowners and titled nobility, and he was a strong "Churchman," supporting the established Anglican Church against Evangelicalism (a scripture-based challenge to Anglican doctrines from within the church) and Dissenters (Protestants who broke with the Anglican Church to form their own, more ascetic, religious rituals). Eliot began attending boarding school with Chrissey at age five; while there, she began questioning her father's religious assumptions and assumed attitudes he strongly rejected as evangelical. She excelled at playing the

---

6. A high-quality fabric made from the wool of merino sheep.

piano, painting, arithmetic, and French, the typical curriculum of a girls' school of the period. Her mother, to whom she had not been close, died when Eliot was six-teen, and her sister's subsequent marriage gave Eliot the opportunity to become the mistress of her father's house. For the next seven years she kept house, visited the neighborhood poor, and studied German and Italian at home.

Influenced by brilliant and progressive friends, Eliot broke in her twenties with her father over their religious differences. She wrote a translation of David Friedrich Strauss's *Das Leben Jesu* ("The Life of Jesus"), a humanist biography of Jesus that treats him as a historical, not a divine figure, which she published in 1846. She also began working as a journalist, writing reviews and essays. After leaving her father's home, she spent some time in Geneva, Switzerland, then relo-cated to London in 1850, where she was to establish herself as a professional au-thor. Her review essay "Silly Novels by Lady Novelists" (1856), reprinted here, reflects her thinking about women's ways of writing as she prepared to become a novelist herself. In London she translated philosophical texts and became ac-quainted with the leading intellectuals of her day.

Among her London friends was George Henry Lewes, a brilliant man of let-ters and amateur naturalist who was married but separated from his wife. They had lived in a commune advocating free love, and his wife had borne children by another man under that arrangement. Because Lewes did not object at the time, the strict family laws of England did not allow him to use this infidelity as grounds for divorce. Thus, when Eliot and Lewes fell in love, they traveled together to Germany in 1854 to confirm their marriage, but it was never made legal in En-gland. As a result, Eliot was shunned by women in "respectable" society, and her brother Isaac refused to have any contact with her until her marriage to John Cross at the end of her life.

Lewes believed in Eliot's brilliance and urged her to write fiction. Strongly moral and full of original philosophical aphorisms as well as realistic detail, her first work of fiction, *Scenes from Clerical Life* (1857), attracted an audience under the name "George Eliot" before she was forced to break her anonymity with the publication of her second book, *Adam Bede* (1859). By that time, she was a com-mercially successful author, and she did not need to worry about her social repu-tation's effect on the reception of her work. She was, however, very sensitive to adverse criticism and asked Lewes to screen her reviews. Her next novel, *The Mill on the Floss* (1860), is strongly autobiographical, drawing especially on her early relationship with Isaac, whom she sorely missed. She also wrote an allegorical novel, *Silas Marner* (1861); a historical novel, *Romola* (1862–63); and a social-problem novel, *Felix Holt, the Radical* (1866), before she produced her acknowl-edged masterpiece, *Middlemarch* (1871–72). Written and published in nine serial parts, the novel creates the intricate social world of a provincial English town. The narrator gives special attention to an idealistic young upper-class woman, Dorothea Brooke, and to a scientifically oriented physician, Dr. Lydgate, but bal-ances their stories with sympathetic portrayals of scores of other characters, in-cluding those who make Dorothea's and Lydgate's lives most difficult. Eliot's final novel, *Daniel Deronda* (1876), is unusual among nineteenth-century novels for its sympathetic portrayal of Jewish characters, usually reduced to negative stereo-types in Victorian fiction.

Eliot and Lewes lived together in an idyllic country home they purchased in Surrey—just an hour away from London by train—until Lewes died in 1878. Their circle included Lewes's children and many of Eliot's literary admirers. One of these was John Walter Cross, a bachelor banker in his thirties who was much devoted to Eliot and her writing. During Lewes's lifetime, he was a constant visitor to their household, and after Lewes's death, Cross became Eliot's close companion and financial advisor. In 1880, when she was nearly sixty and he was forty, they married, prompting her brother Isaac to contact his sister after many years of estrangement. The Crosses took a honeymoon in Italy that retraced a trip Eliot had taken with Lewes; all seemed well until Cross, a depressive overwhelmed by the situation, jumped out of their hotel window into the Grand Canal in Venice and had to be fished out by gondoliers. The memory of this scene clouded their short time together. Eliot, whose health had not been strong, died later that year in London. After her death, Cross became her official biographer, spending the next forty years maintaining her estate and her literary reputation.

Eliot's essay "Silly Novels by Lady Novelists" (1856) has become a classic of feminist literary criticism. She presents a catalogue of the ridiculous situations and bad writing found in many popular women's novels of her day; her direct quotations are as laughable as the parodies Eliot makes of their plots. Eliot singles out for criticism examples of genres she would later tackle herself, such as stories about evangelical characters (*Scenes from Clerical Life*) and fiction set in long-past times (*Romola*). In the end, she contrasts the silly lady novelists with female authors she considers great, including Harriet Beecher Stowe (pp. 732–34), "Currer Bell" (Charlotte Brontë's pen name) (pp. 826–33), Harriet Martineau (pp. 613–14), and Elizabeth Gaskell (pp. 713–14). For Eliot, being female would be no excuse for writing bad fiction. Her essay establishes the ground on which her contemporary female novelists would stand.

Silly Novels by Lady Novelists

Silly novels by Lady Novelists are a genus with many species, determined by the particular quality of silliness that predominates in them—the frothy, the prosy, the pious, or the pedantic. But it is a mixture of all these—a composite order of feminine fatuity, that produces the largest class of such novels, which we shall distinguish as the *mind-and-millinery* species. The heroine is usually an heiress, probably a peeress in her own right, with perhaps a vicious baronet, an amiable duke, and an irresistible younger son of a marquis as lovers in the foreground,[1] a clergyman and a poet sighing for her in the middle distance, and a crowd of undefined adorers dimly indicated beyond. Her eyes and her wit are both dazzling; her nose and her morals are alike free from any tendency to irregularity; she has a superb *contralto* and a superb intellect; she is perfectly well-dressed and perfectly religious; she dances like a sylph, and reads the Bible in the original tongues. Or it may be that the heroine is not an heiress—that rank and wealth are the only things in which she is deficient; but she infallibly gets into high society, she has the triumph of refusing many matches and securing the best, and she wears some family jewels or other as a sort of crown of righteousness at the end. Rakish men either bite their lips in impotent confusion at her repartees, or are touched to penitence by her reproofs, which, on appropriate occasions, rise to a lofty strain of rhetoric; indeed, there is a

---

1. The English peerage, or nobility, hold titles (until 1876, hereditary) conferred by a monarch; the five ranks are, in order of precedence, duke, marquess (or marquis), earl, viscount, and baroness. (A baronet, although holding a hereditary title, is not part of the peerage.)

general propensity in her to make speeches, and to rhapsodize at some length when she retires to her bedroom. In her recorded conversations she is amazingly eloquent, and in her unrecorded conversations, amazingly witty. She is understood to have a depth of insight that looks through and through the shallow theories of philosophers, and her superior instincts are a sort of dial by which men have only to set their clocks and watches, and all will go well. The men play a very subordinate part by her side. You are consoled now and then by a hint that they have affairs,[2] which keeps you in mind that the working-day business of the world is somehow being carried on, but ostensibly the final cause of their existence is that they may accompany the heroine on her "starring" expedition through life. They see her at a ball, and are dazzled; at a flower-show, and they are fascinated; on a riding excursion, and they are witched by her noble horsemanship; at church, and they are awed by the sweet solemnity of her demeanour. She is the ideal woman in feelings, faculties, and flounces. For all this, she as often as not marries the wrong person to begin with, and she suffers terribly from the plots and intrigues of the vicious baronet; but even death has a soft place in his heart for such a paragon, and remedies all mistakes for her just at the right moment. The vicious baronet is sure to be killed in a duel, and the tedious husband dies in his bed requesting his wife, as a particular favour to him, to marry the man she loves best, and having already dispatched a note to the lover informing him of the comfortable arrangement. Before matters arrive at this desirable issue our feelings are tried by seeing the noble, lovely, and gifted heroine pass through many *mauvais moments*,[3] but we have the satisfaction of knowing that her sorrows are wept into embroidered pocket-handkerchiefs, that her fainting form reclines on the very best upholstery, and that whatever vicissitudes she may undergo, from being dashed out of her carriage to having her head shaved in a fever, she comes out of them all with a complexion more blooming and locks more redundant than ever.

We may remark, by the way, that we have been relieved from a serious scruple by discovering that silly novels by lady novelists rarely introduce us into any other than very lofty and fasionable society. We had imagined that destitute women turned novelists, as they turned governesses, because they had no other "lady-like" means of getting their bread. On this supposition, vacillating syntax and improbable incident had a certain pathos for us, like the extremely supererogatory pincushions and ill-devised nightcaps that are offered for sale by a blind man. We felt the commodity to be a nuisance, but we were glad to think that the money went to relieve the necessitous, and we pictured to ourselves lonely women struggling for a maintenance, or wives and daughters devoting themselves to the production of "copy"[4] out of pure heroism,—perhaps to pay their husband's debts, or to purchase luxuries for a sick father. Under these impressions we shrank from criticising a lady's novel: her English might be faulty, but, we said to ourselves, her motives are irreproachable; her imagination may be uninventive, but her patience is untiring. Empty writing was excused by an empty stomach, and twaddle was consecrated by tears. But no! This theory of ours, like many other pretty theories, has had to give way before observation. Women's silly novels, we are now convinced, are written under totally different circumstances. The fair writers have evidently never talked to a tradesman except from a carriage window;

2. Business or professional occupations.
3. Bad moments (French).

4. Text for a news article or book to be set in type and printed.

they have no notion of the working-classes except as "dependents"; they think five hundred a-year a miserable pittance; Belgravia[5] and "baronial halls" are their primary truths; and they have no idea of feeling interest in any man who is not at least a great landed proprietor, if not a prime minister. It is clear that they write in elegant boudoirs, with violet-coloured ink and a ruby pen; that they must be entirely indifferent to publishers' accounts, and inexperienced in every form of poverty except poverty of brains. It is true that we are constantly struck with the want of verisimilitude in their representations of the high society in which they seem to live; but then they betray no closer acquaintance with any other form of life. If their peers and peeresses are improbable, their literary men, tradespeople, and cottagers[6] are impossible; and their intellect seems to have the peculiar impartiality of reproducing both what they *have* seen and heard, and what they have *not* seen and heard, with equal unfaithfulness.

There are few women, we suppose, who have not seen something of children under five years of age, yet in "Compensation", a recent novel of the mind-and-millinery species, which calls itself a "story of real life", we have a child of four and a half years old talking in this Ossianic fashion.[7]

"Oh, I am so happy, dear gran'mamma;—I have seen,—I have seen such a delightful person: he is like everything beautiful,—like the smell of sweet flowers, and the view from Ben Lomond;[8]—or no, *better than that*—he is like what I think of and see when I am very, very happy; and he is really like mamma, too, when she sings; and his forehead is like *that distant sea*," she continued, pointing to the blue Mediterranean; "there seems no end—no end; or like the clusters of stars I like best to look at on a warm fine night. . . . Don't look so . . . your forehead is like Loch Lomond, when the wind is blowing and the sun is gone in; I like the sunshine best when the lake is smooth. . . . So now—I like it better than ever . . . it is more beautiful still from the dark cloud that has gone over it, *when the sun suddenly lights up all the colours of the forests and shining purple rocks, and it is all reflected in the waters below.*"

We are not surprised to learn that the mother of this infant phenomenon, who exhibits symptoms so alarmingly like those of adolescence repressed by gin, is herself a phœnix. We are assured, again and again, that she had a remarkably original mind, that she was a genius, and "conscious of her originality," and she was fortunate enough to have a lover who was also a genius, and a man of "most original mind."

This lover, we read, though "wonderfully similar" to her "in powers and capacity," was "infinitely superior to her in faith and development," and she saw in him the "'Agape'[9]—so rare to find—of which she had read and admired the meaning in her Greek Testament; having, *from her great facility in learning languages,* read the Scriptures in their original *tongues.*" Of course! Greek and Hebrew are mere play to a heroine; Sanscrit is no more than *a b c* to her; and she can talk with perfect correctness in any language except English. She is a polking polyglot, a Creuzer[1] in crinoline. Poor men! There are so few of you who know even Hebrew; you think it something to boast of if, like Bolingbroke, you only "under-

5. Dependents: workers on the family's estate or in their household; Belgravia: a fashionable London neighborhood.
6. Farm laborers who rent a house and a piece of land from an estate.
7. In the manner of Ossian, a poet and hero of

third-century Gaelic legend.
8. A mountain in the Scottish highlands overlooking Loch (Lake) Lomond.
9. Love that is wholly selfless and spiritual (Greek).
1. Georg Friedrich Creuzer (1771–1858), a German philosopher.

stand that sort of learning, and what is writ about it;"[2] and you are perhaps adoring women who can think slightingly of you in all the Semitic languages successively. But, then, as we are almost invariably told, that a heroine has a "beautifully small head," and as her intellect has probably been early invigorated by an attention to costume and deportment, we may conclude that she can pick up the Oriental tongues, to say nothing of their dialects, with the same aërial facility that the butterfly sips nectar. Besides, there can be no difficulty in conceiving the depth of the heroine's erudition, when that of the authoress is so evident.

In "Laura Gay," another novel of the same school, the heroine seems less at home in Greek and Hebrew, but she makes up for the deficiency by a quite playful familiarity with the Latin classics—with the "dear old Virgil," "the graceful Horace, the humane Cicero, and the pleasant Livy;"[3] indeed, it is such a matter of course with her to quote Latin, that she does it at a pic-nic in a very mixed company of ladies and gentlemen, having, we are told, "no conception that the nobler sex were capable of jealousy on this subject. And if, indeed," continues the biographer of Laura Gay, "the wisest and noblest portion of that sex were in the majority, no such sentiment would exist; but while Miss Wyndhams and Mr. Redfords abound, great sacrifices must be made to their existence." Such sacrifices, we presume, as abstaining from Latin quotations, of extremely moderate interest and applicability, which the wise and noble minority of the other sex would be quite as willing to dispense with as the foolish and ignoble majority. It is as little the custom of well-bred men as of well-bred women to quote Latin in mixed parties; they can contain their familiarity with "the humane Cicero" without allowing it to boil over in ordinary conversation, and even references to "the pleasant Livy" are not absolutely irrepressible. But Ciceronian Latin is the mildest form of Miss Gay's conversational power. Being on the Palatine[4] with a party of sightseers, she falls into the following vein of well-rounded remark: "Truth can only be pure objectively, for even in the creeds where it predominates, being subjective, and parcelled out into portions, each of these necessarily receives a hue of idiosyncrasy, that is, a taint of superstition more or less strong; while in such creeds as the Roman Catholic, ignorance, interest, the bias of ancient idolatries, and the force of authority, have gradually accumulated on the pure truth, and transformed it, at last, into a mass of superstition for the majority of its votaries; and how few are there, alas! whose zeal, courage, and intellectual energy are equal to the analysis of this accumulation, and to the discovery of the pearl of great price which lies hidden beneath this heap of rubbish." We have often met with women much more novel and profound in their observations than Laura Gay, but rarely with any so inopportunely long winded. A clerical lord, who is half in love with her, is alarmed by the daring remarks just quoted, and begins to suspect that she is inclined to free-thinking. But he is mistaken; when in a moment of sorrow he delicately begs leave to "recal to her memory, a depôt of strength and consolation under affliction, which, until we are hard pressed by the trials of life, we are too apt to forget," we learn that she really has "recurrence to that sacred depôt," together with

2. A remark supposed to have been made by eighteenth-century English poet Alexander Pope (1688–1744).
3. Publius Vergilius Maro (70 BCE–19 BCE), Roman epic poet, author of *The Aeneid;* Quintus Horatius Flaccus (65 BCE–8 BCE), Roman lyric

poet; Marcus Tullius Cicero (106 BCE–43 BCE), Roman orator; Titus Livius (c. 59 BCE–17 CE), Roman historian.
4. The highest of the seven hills upon which Rome is built.

the tea-pot. There is a certain flavour of orthodoxy mixed with the parade of fortunes and fine carriages in "Laura Gay", but it is an orthodoxy mitigated by study of "the humane Cicero," and by an "intellectual disposition to analyse."

"Compensation" is much more heavily dosed with doctrine, but then it has a treble amount of snobbish worldliness and absurd incident to tickle the palate of pious frivolity. Linda, the heroine, is still more speculative and spiritual than Laura Gay, but she has been "presented,"[5] and has more, and far grander, lovers; very wicked and fascinating women are introduced—even a French *lionne;*[6] and no expense is spared to get up as exciting a story as you will find in the most immoral novels. In fact, it is a wonderful *pot pourri* of Almack's, Scotch second-sight, Mr. Rogers's breakfasts,[7] Italian brigands, death-bed conversions, superior authoresses, Italian mistresses, and attempts at poisoning old ladies, the whole served up with a garnish of talk about "faith and development," and "most original minds." Even Miss Susan Barton, the superior authoress, whose pen moves in a "quick decided manner when she is composing," declines the finest opportunities of marriage; and though old enough to be Linda's mother (since we are told that she refused Linda's father), has her hand sought by a young earl, the heroine's rejected lover. Of course, genius and morality must be backed by eligible offers, or they would seem rather a dull affair; and piety, like other things, in order to be *comme il faut,*[8] must be in "society," and have admittance to the best circles.

"Rank and Beauty" is a more frothy and less religious variety of the mind-and-millinery species. The heroine, we are told, "if she inherited her father's pride of birth and her mother's beauty of person, had in herself a tone of enthusiastic feeling that perhaps belongs to her age even in the lowly born, but which is refined into the high spirit of wild romance only in the far descended, who feel that it is their best inheritance." This enthusiastic young lady, by dint of reading the newspaper to her father, falls in love with the *prime minister,* who, through the medium of leading articles and "the *resumé* of the debates," shines upon her imagination as a bright particular star, which has no parallax for her, living in the country as simple Miss Wyndham. But she forthwith becomes Baroness Umfraville in her own right, astonishes the world with her beauty and accomplishments when she bursts upon it from her mansion in Spring Gardens, and, as you foresee, will presently come into contact with the unseen *objet aimé.*[9] Perhaps the words "prime minister" suggest to you a wrinkled or obese sexagenarian; but pray dismiss the image. Lord Rupert Conway has been "called while still almost a youth to the first situation which a subject can hold in the *universe,*" and even leading articles and a *resumé* of the debates have not conjured up a dream that surpasses the fact.

The door opened again, and Lord Rupert Conway entered. Evelyn gave one glance. It was enough; she was not disappointed. It seemed as if a picture on which she had long gazed was suddenly instinct with life, and had stepped from its frame before her. His tall figure, the distinguished simplicity of his air—it was a living Vandyke,[1] a cavalier, one of his noble

5. Presented at St. James's court in London to the king and queen.
6. Lioness (French).
7. Almack's: assembly rooms open to fashionable men and women of the upper class; Scottish second-sight: premonition purportedly common among Scottish highlanders; Mr. Rogers's breakfasts: poet-banker Samuel Rogers (1763–1855)

hosted literary celebrities of the day, such as Charles Dickens and Sir Walter Scott, at his breakfasts and even more exclusive dinners.
8. In fashion (French).
9. Object of her affection (French).
1. Like a nobleman in a painting by Flemish artist Sir Anthony van Dyck (1599–1641).

cavalier ancestors, or one to whom her fancy had always likened him, who long of yore had, with an Umfraville, fought the Paynim[2] far beyond sea. Was this reality?

Very little like it, certainly.

By-and-by, it becomes evident that the ministerial heart is touched. Lady Umfraville is on a visit to the Queen at Windsor,[3] and,

The last evening of their stay, when they returned from riding, Mr. Wyndham took her and a large party to the top of the Keep, to see the view. She was leaning on the battlements, gazing from that "stately height" at the prospect beneath her, when Lord Rupert was by her side. "What an unrivalled view!" exclaimed she.

"Yes, it would have been wrong to go without having been up here. You are pleased with your visit?"

"Enchanted! A Queen to live and die under, to live and die for!"

"Ha!" cried he, with sudden emotion, and with a *eureka* expression of countenance, as if he had *indeed found a heart in unison with his own.*

The "*eureka* expression of countenance," you see at once to be prophetic of marriage at the end of the third volume; but before that desirable consummation, there are very complicated misunderstandings, arising chiefly from the vindictive plotting of Sir Luttrell Wycherley, who is a genius, a poet, and in every way a most remarkable character indeed. He is not only a romantic poet, but a hardened rake and a cynical wit; yet his deep passion for Lady Umfraville has so impoverished his epigrammatic talent, that he cuts an extremely poor figure in conversation. When she rejects him, he rushes into the shrubbery, and rolls himself in the dirt; and on recovering, devotes himself to the most diabolical and laborious schemes of vengeance, in the course of which he disguises himself as a quack physician, and enters into general practice, foreseeing that Evelyn will fall ill, and that he shall be called in to attend her. At last, when all his schemes are frustrated, he takes leave of her in a long letter, written, as you will perceive from the following passage, entirely in the style of an eminent literary man:

"Oh, lady, nursed in pomp and pleasure, will you ever cast one thought upon the miserable being who addresses you? Will you ever, as your gilded galley is floating down the unruffled stream of prosperity, will you ever, while lulled by the sweetest music—thine own praises,—hear the far-off sigh from that world to which I am going?"

On the whole, however, frothy as it is, we rather prefer "Rank and Beauty" to the other two novels we have mentioned. The dialogue is more natural and spirited; there is some frank ignorance, and no pedantry; and you are allowed to take the heroine's astounding intellect upon trust, without being called on to read her conversational refutations of sceptics and philosophers, or her rhetorical solutions of the mysteries of the universe.

Writers of the mind-and-millinery school are remarkably unanimous in their choice of diction. In their novels, there is usually a lady or gentleman who is more or less of a upas tree:[4] the lover has a manly breast; minds are redolent of various things; hearts are hollow; events are utilized; friends are consigned to the tomb; infancy is an engaging period; the sun is a luminary that goes to his western couch,

2. Archaic term for a Muslim.
3. Windsor Castle, one of the royal family's primary residences, in Berkshire County, west of London.

4. A tropical mulberry tree that grows in Africa, Asia, and the Philippines; it produces a poisonous latex resin.

or gathers the rain-drops into his refulgent bosom; life is a melancholy boon; Albion and Scotia[5] are conversational epithets. There is a striking resemblance, too, in the character of their moral comments, such, for instance, as that "It is a fact, no less true than melancholy, that all people, more or less, richer or poorer, are swayed by bad example;" that "Books, however trivial, contain some subjects from which useful information may be drawn;" that "Vice can too often borrow the language of virtue;" that "Merit and nobility of nature must exist, to be accepted, for clamour and pretension cannot impose upon those too well read in human nature to be easily deceived;" and that, "In order to forgive, we must have been injured." There is, doubtless, a class of readers to whom these remarks appear peculiarly pointed and pungent; for we often find them doubly and trebly scored with the pencil, and delicate hands giving in their determined adhesion to these hardy novelties by a distinct *tres vrai*,[6] emphasized by many notes of exclamation. The colloquial style of these novels is often marked by much ingenious inversion, and a careful avoidance of such cheap phraseology as can be heard every day. Angry young gentlemen exclaim—"'Tis ever thus, methinks;" and in the half-hour before dinner a young lady informs her next neighbour that the first day she read Shakspeare she "stole away into the park, and beneath the shadow of the greenwood tree, devoured with rapture the inspired page of the great magician." But the most remarkable efforts of the mind-and-millinery writers lie in their philosophic reflections. The authoress of "Laura Gay," for example, having married her hero and heroine, improves the event by observing that "if those sceptics, whose eyes have so long gazed on matter that they can no longer see aught else in man, could once enter with heart and soul into such bliss as this, they would come to say that the soul of man and the polypus[7] are not of common origin, or of the same texture." Lady novelists, it appears, can see something else besides matter; they are not limited to phenomena, but can relieve their eyesight by occasional glimpses of the *noumenon*,[8] and are, therefore, naturally better able than any one else to confound sceptics, even of that remarkable, but to us unknown school, which maintains that the soul of man is of the same texture as the polypus.

The most pitiable of all silly novels by lady novelists are what we may call the *oracular* species—novels intended to expound the writer's religious, philosophical, or moral theories. There seems to be a notion abroad among women, rather akin to the superstition that the speech and actions of idiots are inspired, and that the human being most entirely exhausted of common sense is the fittest vehicle of revelation. To judge from their writings, there are certain ladies who think that an amazing ignorance, both of science and of life, is the best possible qualification for forming an opinion on the knottiest moral and speculative questions. Apparently, their recipe for solving all such difficulties is something like this: Take a woman's head, stuff it with a smattering of philosophy and literature chopped small, and with false notions of society baked hard, let it hang over a desk a few hours every day, and serve up hot in feeble English, when not required. You will rarely meet with a lady novelist of the oracular class who is diffident of her ability to decide on theological questions,—who has any suspicion that she is not capable

---

5. England and Scotland.
6. Very true (French).
7. Obscure. Since the suffix "pus" can mean "foot," perhaps the reference is to the "polypod,"

an insect larva with many legs and feet.
8. Something perceived only by the intellect, not by the senses (Greek).

of discriminating with the nicest accuracy between the good and evil in all church parties,—who does not see precisely how it is that men have gone wrong hitherto,—and pity philosophers in general that they have not had the opportunity of consulting her. Great writers, who have modestly contented themselves with putting their experience into fiction, and have thought it quite a sufficient task to exhibit men and things as they are, she sighs over as deplorably deficient in the application of their powers. "They have solved no great questions"—and she is ready to remedy their omission by setting before you a complete theory of life and manual of divinity, in a love story, where ladies and gentlemen of good family go through genteel vicissitudes, to the utter confusion of Deists, Puseyites, and ultra-Protestants,[9] and to the perfect establishment of that particular view of Christianity which either condenses itself into a sentence of small caps, or explodes into a cluster of stars on the three hundred and thirtieth page. It is true, the ladies and gentlemen will probably seem to you remarkably little like any you have had the fortune or misfortune to meet with, for, as a general rule, the ability of a lady novelist to describe actual life and her fellow-men, is in inverse proportion to her confident eloquence about God and the other world, and the means by which she usually chooses to conduct you to true ideas of the invisible is a totally false picture of the visible.

As typical a novel of the oracular kind as we can hope to meet with, is "The Enigma: a Leaf from the Chronicles of the Wolchorley House." The "enigma" which this novel is to solve, is certainly one that demands powers no less gigantic than those of a lady novelist, being neither more nor less than the existence of evil. The problem is stated, and the answer dimly foreshadowed on the very first page. The spirited young lady, with raven hair, says, "All life is an inextricable confusion;" and the meek young lady, with auburn hair, looks at the picture of the Madonna which she is copying, and—"*There* seemed the solution of that mighty enigma." The style of this novel is quite as lofty as its purpose; indeed, some passages on which we have spent much patient study are quite beyond our reach, in spite of the illustrative aid of italics and small caps; and we must await further "development" in order to understand them. Of Ernest, the model young clergyman, who sets every one right on all occasions, we read, that "he held not of marriage in the marketable kind, after a social desecration;" that, on one eventful night, "sleep had not visited his divided heart, where tumultuated, in varied type and combination, the aggregate feelings of grief and joy;" and that, "for the *marketable* human article he had no toleration, be it of what sort, or set for what value it might, whether for worship or class, his upright soul abhorred it, whose ultimatum, the self-deceiver, was to him THE *great spiritual lie,* 'living in a vain show, deceiving and being deceived;' since he did not suppose the phylactery[1] and enlarged border on the garment to be *merely* a social trick." (The italics and small caps are the author's, and we hope they assist the reader's comprehension.) Of Sir Lionel, the model old gentleman, we are told that "the simple ideal of the middle age, apart from its anarchy and decadence, in him most truly seemed to live again, when the ties which knit men together were of heroic cast. The first-born colours of pristine faith and truth engraven on the common soul of man, and blent into the wide arch of brotherhood, where the primæval law of *order* grew and multiplied, each perfect after his kind, and mutually inter-dependent." You see clearly,

9. Various schisms among Victorian Protestants.   1. Case for a relic or charm.

of course, how colours are first engraven on a soul, and then blent into a wide arch, on which arch of colours—apparently a rainbow—the law of order grew and multiplied, each—apparently the arch and the law—perfect after his kind? If, after this, you can possibly want any further aid towards knowing what Sir Lionel was, we can tell you, that in his soul "the scientific combinations of thought could educe no fuller harmonies of the good and the true, than lay in the primæval pulses which floated as an atmosphere around it!" and that, when he was sealing a letter, "Lo! The responsive throb in that good man's bosom echoed back in simple truth the honest witness of a heart that condemned him not, as his eye, bedewed with love, rested, too, with something of ancestral pride, on the undimmed motto of the family—'LOIAUTÉ'."[2]

The slightest matters have their vulgarity fumigated out of them by the same elevated style. Commonplace people would say that a copy of Shakspeare lay on a drawing-room table; but the authoress of "The Enigma," bent on edifying periphrasis, tells you that there lay on the table, "that fund of human thought and feeling, which teaches the heart through the little name, 'Shakspeare.'" A watchman sees a light burning in an upper window rather longer than usual, and thinks that people are foolish to sit up late when they have an opportunity of going to bed; but, lest this fact should seem too low and common, it is presented to us in the following striking and metaphysical manner: "He marvelled—as man *will* think for others in a necessarily separate personality, consequently (though disallowing it) in false mental premise,—how differently *he* should act, how gladly *he* should prize the rest so lightly held of within." A footman—an ordinary Jeames, with large calves and aspirated vowels[3]—answers the door-bell, and the opportunity is seized to tell you that he was a "type of the large class of pampered menials, who follow the curse of Cain—'vagabonds' on the face of the earth, and whose estimate of the human class varies in the graduated scale of money and expenditure. . . . These, and such as these, O England, be the false lights of thy morbid civilization!" We have heard of various "false lights," from Dr. Cumming to Robert Owen, from Dr. Pusey to the Spirit-rappers,[4] but we never before heard of the false light that emanates from plush and powder.

In the same way very ordinary events of civilized life are exalted into the most awful crises, and ladies in full skirts and *manches à la Chinoise*,[5] conduct themselves not unlike the heroines of sanguinary melodramas. Mrs. Percy, a shallow woman of the world, wishes her son Horace to marry the auburn-haired Grace, she being an heiress; but he, after the manner of sons, falls in love with the ravenhaired Kate, the heiress's portionless cousin; and, moreover, Grace herself shows every symptom of perfect indifference to Horace. In such cases, sons are often sulky or fiery, mothers are alternately manœuvring and waspish, and the portionless young lady often lies awake at night and cries a good deal. We are getting used to these things now, just as we are used to eclipses of the moon, which no longer set us howling and beating tin kettles. We never heard of a lady in a fash-

2. *Loyauté*, or "loyalty" (French).
3. To add an "h" sound to the beginning of a word that starts with a vowel ("hever" for "ever"), a hallmark of working-class London.
4. Rev. John Cumming (1807–81), evangelical minister who preached anti-Catholicism; Robert Owen (1771–1858), mill owner, proponent of utopian socialism, a founder of New Harmony, a secular utopian community; Edward Pusey (1800–1882), Anglican minister and leader of the Oxford Movement promoting Roman Catholic practices within the Anglican church; Spirit-rappers: mediums who claim to communicate with the dead in séances (see pp. 881–82).
5. Literally "sleeves of the Chinese" (French), an upper-class fashion.

ionable "front" behaving like Mrs. Percy under these circumstances. Happening one day to see Horace talking to Grace at a window, without in the least knowing what they are talking about, or having the least reason to believe that Grace, who is mistress of the house and a person of dignity, would accept her son if he were to offer himself, she suddenly rushes up to them and clasps them both, saying, "with a flushed countenance and in an excited manner"—"This is indeed happiness; for, may I not call you so, Grace?—my Grace—my Horace's Grace!—my dear children!" Her son tells her she is mistaken, and that he is engaged to Kate, whereupon we have the following scene and tableau:

Gathering herself up to an unprecedented height,(!) her eyes lightning forth the fire of her anger:—

"Wretched boy!" she said, hoarsely and scornfully, and clenching her hand, "Take then the doom of your own choice! Bow down your miserable head and let a mother's—"

"Curse not!" spake a deep low voice from behind, and Mrs. Percy started, scared, as though she had seen a heavenly visitant appear, to break upon her in the midst of her sin.

Meantime, Horace had fallen on his knees at her feet, and hid his face in his hands.

Who, then, is she—who! Truly his "guardian spirit" hath stepped between him and the fearful words, which, however unmerited, must have hung as a pall over his future existence;—a spell which could not be unbound—which could not be unsaid.

Of an earthly paleness, but calm with the still, iron-bound calmness of death—the only calm one there,—Katherine stood; and her words smote on the ear in tones whose appallingly slow and separate intonation rung on the heart like the chill, isolated tolling of some fatal knell.

"He would have plighted me his faith, but I did not accept it; you cannot, therefore—you *dare* not curse him. And here," she continued, raising her hand to heaven, whither her large dark eyes also rose with a chastened glow, which, for the first time, *suffering* had lighted in those passionate orbs,—"here I promise, come weal, come woe, that Horace Wolchorley and I do never interchange vows without his mother's sanction—without his mother's blessing"!

Here, and throughout the story, we see that confusion of purpose which is so characteristic of silly novels written by women. It is a story of quite modern drawing-room society—a society in which polkas are played and Puseyism discussed; yet we have characters, and incidents, and traits of manner introduced, which are mere shreds from the most heterogeneous romances. We have a blind Irish harper "relic of the picturesque bards of yore," startling us at a Sunday-school festival of tea and cake in an English village; we have a crazy gipsy, in a scarlet cloak, singing snatches of romantic song, and revealing a secret on her deathbed which, with the testimony of a dwarfish miserly merchant, who salutes strangers with a curse and a devilish laugh, goes to prove that Ernest, the model young clergyman, is Kate's brother; and we have an ultra-virtuous Irish Barney, discovering that a document is forged, by comparing the date of the paper with the date of the alleged signature, although the same document has passed through a court of law, and occasioned a fatal decision. The "Hall" in which Sir Lionel lives is the venerable country-seat of an old family, and this, we suppose, sets the imagination of the authoress flying to donjons and battlements, where "lo! the warder blows his horn;" for, as the inhabitants are in their bedrooms on a night certainly within the recollection of Pleaceman[6] X., and a breeze springs up, which we are at first told was faint, and then that it made the old cedars bow their branches to the

6. Policeman, the spelling to suggest Irish pronunciation.

greensward, she falls into this mediæval vein of description (the italics are ours): "The banner *unfurled it* at the sound, and shook its guardian wing above, while the startled owl *flapped her* in the ivy; the firmament looking down through her 'argus eyes,'[7]—

Ministers of heaven's mute melodies.

And lo! two strokes tolled from out the warder tower, and 'Two o'clock' re-echoed its interpreter below."

Such stories as this of "The Enigma" remind us of the pictures clever children sometimes draw "out of their own head", where you will see a modern villa on the right, two knights in helmets fighting in the foreground, and a tiger grinning in a jungle on the left, the several objects being brought together because the artist thinks each pretty, and perhaps still more because he remembers seeing them in other pictures.

But we like the authoress much better on her mediæval stilts than on her oracular ones,—when she talks of the *Ich*[8] and of "subjective" and "objective", and lays down the exact line of Christian verity, between "right-hand excesses and left-hand declensions." Persons who deviate from this line are introduced with a patronizing air of charity. Of a certain Miss Inshquine she informs us, with all the lucidity of italics and small caps, that "*function,* not *form,* AS *the inevitable outer expression of the spirit in this tabernacled age,* weakly engrossed her." And *à propos* of Miss Mayjar, an evangelical lady who is a little too apt to talk of her visits to sick women and the state of their souls, we are told that the model clergyman is "not one to disallow, through the *super* crust, the undercurrent towards good in the *subject,* or the positive benefits, nevertheless, to the *object.*" We imagine the double-refined accent and protrusion of chin which are feebly represented by the italics in this lady's sentences! We abstain from quoting any of her oracular doctrinal passages, because they refer to matters too serious for our pages just now.

The epithet "silly" may seem impertinent, applied to a novel which indicates so much reading and intellectual activity as "The Enigma;" but we use this epithet advisedly. If, as the world has long agreed, a very great amount of instruction will not make a wise man, still less will a very mediocre amount of instruction make a wise woman. And the most mischievous form of feminine silliness is the literary form, because it tends to confirm the popular prejudice against the more solid education of women. When men see girls wasting their time in consultations about bonnets and ball dresses, and in giggling or sentimental love-confidences, or middle-aged women mismanaging their children, and solacing themselves with acrid gossip, they can hardly help saying, "For Heaven's sake, let girls be better educated; let them have some better objects of thought—some more solid occupations." But after a few hours' conversation with an oracular literary woman, or a few hours' reading of her books, they are likely enough to say, "After all, when a woman gets some knowledge, see what use she makes of it! Her knowledge remains acquisition, instead of passing into culture; instead of being subdued into modesty and simplicity by a larger acquaintance with thought and fact, she has a feverish consciousness of her attainments; she keeps a sort of mental pocket-mirror, and is continually looking in it at her own 'intellectuality'; she spoils the taste of one's muffin by questions of metaphysics; 'puts down' men at a dinner table with her

7. In Greek mythology, Argus was a hundred-eyed giant set to guard Io.   8. The self (German).

superior information; and seizes the opportunity of a *soirée* to catechise us on the vital question of the relation between mind and matter. And then, look at her writings! She mistakes vagueness for depth, bombast for eloquence, and affectation for originality; she struts on one page, rolls her eyes on another, grimaces in a third, and is hysterical in a fourth. She may have read many writings of great men, and a few writings of great women; but she is as unable to discern the difference between her own style and theirs as a Yorkshireman is to discern the difference between his own English and a Londoner's: rhodomontade is the native accent of her intellect.[9] No—the average nature of women is too shallow and feeble a soil to bear much tillage; it is only fit for the very lightest crops."

It is true that the men who come to such a decision on such very superficial and imperfect observation may not be among the wisest in the world; but we have not now to contest their opinion—we are only pointing out how it is unconsciously encouraged by many women who have volunteered themselves as representatives of the feminine intellect. We do not believe that a man was ever strengthened in such an opinion by associating with a woman of true culture, whose mind had absorbed her knowledge instead of being absorbed by it. A really cultured woman, like a really cultured man, is all the simpler and the less obtrusive for her knowledge; it has made her see herself and her opinions in something like just proportions; she does not make it a pedestal from which she flatters herself that she commands a complete view of men and things, but makes it a point of observation from which to form a right estimate of herself. She neither spouts poetry nor quotes Cicero on slight provocation; not because she thinks that a sacrifice must be made to the prejudices of men, but because that mode of exhibiting her memory and Latinity does not present itself to her as edifying or graceful. She does not write books to confound philosophers, perhaps because she is able to write books that delight them. In conversation she is the least formidable of women, because she understands you, without wanting to make you aware that you *can't* understand her. She does not give you information, which is the raw material of culture,—she gives you sympathy, which is its subtlest essence.

A more numerous class of silly novels than the oracular, (which are generally inspired by some form of High Church, or transcendental Christianity,) is what we may call the *white neck-cloth* species, which represent the tone of thought and feeling in the Evangelical party.[1] This species is a kind of genteel tract on a large scale, intended as a sort of medicinal sweetmeat for Low Church young ladies; an Evangelical substitute for the fashionable novel, as the May Meetings are a substitute for the Opera. Even Quaker children, one would think, can hardly have been denied the indulgence of a doll; but it must be a doll dressed in a drab gown and a coal-scuttle bonnet—not a wordly doll, in gauze and spangles. And there are no young ladies, we imagine,—unless they belong to the Church of the United Brethren, in which people are married without any love-making[2]—who can dispense with love stories. Thus, for Evangelical young ladies there are Evangelical

9. Inhabitants of Yorkshire, in northern England, traditionally speak a dialect of English influenced by the Scandinavian spoken by the Vikings and very difficult for a Londoner to understand; rhodomontade: boastful.
1. High Church: Anglican religious practice most akin to Roman Catholicism; white neck-cloth: the badge of office of the Anglican minister until the mid-nineteenth century, when the "Roman color" became widely adopted; Evangelical party: reformers within the Anglican Church seeking to de-emphasize ceremony and purge the church of vestiges of Roman Catholicism.
2. Courting or flirtatious conversation.

love stories, in which the vicissitudes of the tender passion are sanctified by saving views of Regeneration and the Atonement. These novels differ from the oracular ones, as a Low Churchwoman often differs from a High Churchwoman: they are a little less supercilious, and a great deal more ignorant, a little less correct in their syntax, and a great deal more vulgar.

The Orlando[3] of Evangelical literature is the young curate, looked at from the point of view of the middle class, where cambric bands are understood to have as thrilling an effect on the hearts of young ladies as epaulettes have in the classes above and below it. In the ordinary type of these novels, the hero is almost sure to be a young curate, frowned upon, perhaps, by worldly mammas, but carrying captive the hearts of their daughters, who can "never forget *that* sermon"; tender glances are seized from the pulpit stairs instead of the opera-box; *tête-à-têtes* are seasoned with quotations from Scripture, instead of quotations from the poets; and questions as to the state of the heroine's affections are mingled with anxieties as to the state of her soul. The young curate always has a background of well-dressed and wealthy, if not fashionable society;—for Evangelical silliness is as snobbish as any other kind of silliness; and the Evangelical lady novelist, while she explains to you the type of the scapegoat on one page, is ambitious on another to represent the manners and conversation of aristocratic people. Her pictures of fashionable society are often curious studies considered as efforts of the Evangelical imagination; but in one particular the novels of the White Neck-cloth School are meritoriously realistic,—their favourite hero, the Evangelical young curate is always rather an insipid personage.

The most recent novel of this species that we happen to have before us, is "The Old Grey Church." It is utterly tame and feeble; there is no one set of objects on which the writer seems to have a stronger grasp than on any other; and we should be entirely at a loss to conjecture among what phases of life her experience has been gained, but for certain vulgarisms of style which sufficiently indicate that she has had the advantage, though she has been unable to use it, of mingling chiefly with men and women whose manners and characters have not had all their bosses and angles rubbed down by refined conventionalism. It is less excusable in an Evangelical novelist, than in any other, gratuitously to seek her subjects among titles and carriages. The real drama of Evangelicalism—and it has abundance of fine drama for any one who has genius enough to discern and reproduce it—lies among the middle and lower classes; and are not Evangelical opinions understood to give an especial interest in the weak things of the earth, rather than in the mighty? Why then, cannot our Evangelical lady novelists show us the operation of their religious views among people (there really are many such in the world) who keep no carriage, "not so much as a brassbound gig,"[4] who even manage to eat their dinner without a silver fork, and in whose mouths the authoress's questionable English would be strictly consistent? Why can we not have pictures of religious life among the industrial classes in England, as interesting as Mrs. Stowe's pictures of religious life among the negroes.[5] Instead of this, pious ladies nauseate us with novels which remind us of what we sometimes see in a worldly

3. Orlando: the hero-warrior, also called Roland, in medieval and Renaissance epics; cambric bands: formal neckwear favored by Low Church ministers; epaulettes: shoulder ornaments on dress uniforms of military officers.

4. A two-wheeled carriage pulled by one horse.
5. George Eliot positively reviewed the novel *Dred* (1856) by Harriet Beecher Stowe (1811–96; see pp. 732–34) in the same issue of the *Westminster* containing this essay.

woman recently "converted"...
she invites clergymen instead o...
but she adopts a more sober choi... ond of a fine dinner table as before, but
trivial as before, but the triviality thinks as much of her dress as before,
"The Old Grey Church," we have is and patterns; her conversation is as
fashionable novel, and of course the vi... d with gospel instead of gossip. In
is worth while to give a sample of the sty... ort of Evangelical travesty of the
born rake—a style that in its profuse italics iguing baronet is not wanting. It
Miss Squeers.[6] In an evening visit to the ru... ersation attributed to this high-
young clergyman, has been withdrawing the h... he able innuendoes, is worthy of ... he Colosseum, Eustace, the
rest of the party, for the sake of a *tête-à-tête*. The Miss Lushington, from the
pique in this way: ... et is jealous, and vents his

There they are, and Miss Lushington, no doubt, quite safe; fo...
ance of Pope Eustace the First, who has, of course, been delivering under the holy guid-
ily on the wickedness of the heathens of yore, who, as tradition tells her an edifying hom-
loose the wild *beastises* on poor St. Paul!—Oh, no! by-the-bye, I believe this very place let
betraying my want of clergy, and that it was not at all St. Paul, nor was it her m wrong, and
ter, it would equally serve as a text to preach from, and from which to diverge to the degenerate *heathen* Christians of the present day, and all their naughty practices, and so end with
an exhortation to "come out from among them, and be separate;"—and I am sure, Miss
Lushington, you have most scrupulously conformed to that injunction this evening, for we
have seen nothing of you since our arrival. But every one seems agreed it has been a *charming party of pleasure*, and I am sure we all feel *much indebted* to Mr. Grey for having *suggested* it; and as he seems so capital a cicerone, I hope he will think of something else equally
agreeable to *all*.

This drivelling kind of dialogue, and equally drivelling narrative, which, like
a bad drawing, represents nothing, and barely indicates what is meant to be represented, runs through the book; and we have no doubt is considered by the amiable authoress to constitute an improving novel, which Christian mothers will do
well to put into the hands of their daughters. But everything is relative; we have
met with American vegetarians whose normal diet was dry meal, and who, when
their appetite wanted stimulating, tickled it with *wet* meal; and so, we can imagine that there are Evangelical circles in which "The Old Grey Church" is devoured
as a powerful and interesting fiction.

But, perhaps, the least readable of silly women's novels, are the *modern-
antique* species, which unfold to us the domestic life of Jannes and Jambres, the
private love affairs of Sennacherib, or the mental struggles and ultimate conversion of Demetrius the silversmith.[7] From most silly novels we can at least extract
a laugh; but those of the modern antique school have a ponderous, a leaden kind
of fatuity, under which we groan. What can be more demonstrative of the inability of literary women to measure their own powers, than their frequent assumption of a task which can only be justified by the rarest concurrence of acquirement
with genius? The finest effort to reanimate the past is of course only approxima-
tive—is always more or less an infusion of the modern spirit into the ancient form,

6. A character in *Nicholas Nickleby* (1838–39), a novel by Charles Dickens (1812–70), much given to brazen flirtations.
7. Jannes and Jambres: supposed names for Egyptian magicians who opposed Moses (2 Timo-

thy 3:8); Sennacherib: Assyrian king (762 BCE–745 BCE) who unsuccessfully attacked Jerusalem (2 Kings 18–19); Demetrius: Ephesian silversmith who quarreled with St. Paul (Acts 19:24).

> Was ihr den Geist der Zei... Geist,
> Das ist im Grund der H...
> In dem die Zeiten sich ...[8]

Admitting that genius which has fa... ...self with all the relics of an ancient period can sometimes, by the fo... ...mpathetic divination, restore the missing notes in the "music of hum... ...nd reconstruct the fragments into a whole which will really bring the ... ...st nearer to us, and interpret it to our duller apprehension,—this form... ...native power must always be among the very rarest, because it demand... ...ch accurate and minute knowledge as creative vigour. Yet we find ladie... it in a masquerade of ancient names; by putting rity more conspicuous, by ... mouths of Roman vestals or Egyptian princesses, their feeble sentimentalit... ...rical arguments to Jewish high-priests and Greek and attributing their... ...ample of this heavy imbecility is, "Adonijah, a Tale of philosophers. A rec... which forms part of a series, "uniting," we are told, "taste, the Jewish Dispe... ...nd principles." "Adonijah," we presume, exemplifies the tale of humour, and ...ples;" the taste and humour are to be found in other members of the "sound pr... series. ...old on the cover, that the incidents of this tale are "fraught with un...al interest," and the preface winds up thus: "To those who feel interested in the dispersed of Israel and Judea, these pages may afford, perhaps, information on an important subject, as well as amusement." Since the "important subject" on which this book is to afford information is not specified, it may possibly lie in some esoteric meaning to which we have no key; but if it has relation to the dispersed of Israel and Judea at any period of their history, we believe a tolerably well-informed school-girl already knows much more of it than she will find in this "Tale of the Jewish Dispersion." "Adonijah" is simply the feeblest kind of love story, supposed to be instructive, we presume, because the hero is a Jewish captive, and the heroine a Roman vestal; because they and their friends are converted to Christianity after the shortest and easiest method approved by the "Society for Promoting the Conversion of the Jews;" and because, instead of being written in plain language, it is adorned with that peculiar style of grandiloquence which is held by some lady novelists to give an antique colouring, and which we recognise at once in such phrases as these: "the splendid regnal talents undoubtedly possessed by the Emperor Nero"[1]—"the expiring scion of a lofty stem"—"the virtuous partner of his couch"—"ah, by Vesta!"—and "I tell thee, Roman." Among the quotations which serve at once for instruction and ornament on the cover of this volume, there is one from Miss Sinclair, which informs us that "Works of imagination are avowedly read by men of science, wisdom, and piety"; from which we suppose the reader is to gather the cheering inference that Dr. Daubeny, Mr. Mill, or Mr. Maurice,[2] may openly indulge himself with the perusal of "Adoni-

---

8. From *Faust* I, "Night," lines 577–79, by German novelist, poet, and playwright Johann Wolfgang von Goethe (1749–1832). "The so-called spirit of the age, you'll find, / In truth is but the gentlemen's own mind / In which the ages are reflected" (German; translation by Walter Arndt).
9. Line 91 from "Lines Composed a Few Miles above Tintern Abbey" (1798) by English poet William Wordsworth (1770–1850).
1. Nero: Roman emperor (37–68 CE; ruled 54–68 CE), whose excesses and purported murder of his mother earned him the title "Mad Emperor"; Vesta: Roman goddess of the hearth.
2. Dr. Daubeny: Charles Daubeny (1795–1867), English chemist and chair of botany at University of Oxford; Mr. Mill: John Stuart Mill (1806–73), English philosopher and proponent of utilitarianism; Mr. Maurice: Frederick Maurice (1805–72), English writer, editor, and, later, Anglican theologian.

jah", without being obliged to secrete it among the sofa cushions, or read it by snatches under the dinner table.

"Be not a baker if your head be made of butter," says a homely proverb, which, being interpreted, may mean, let no woman rush into print who is not prepared for the consequences. We are aware that our remarks are in a very different tone from that of the reviewers who, with a perennial recurrence of precisely similar emotions, only paralleled, we imagine, in the experience of monthly nurses, tell one lady novelist after another that they "hail" her productions "with delight." We are aware that the ladies at whom our criticism is pointed are accustomed to be told, in the choicest phraseology of puffery, that their pictures of life are brilliant, their characters well drawn, their style fascinating, and their sentiments lofty. But if they are inclined to resent our plainness of speech, we ask them to reflect for a moment on the chary praise, and often captious blame, which their panegyrists give to writers whose works are on the way to become classics. No sooner does a woman show that she has genius or effective talent, than she receives the tribute of being moderately praised and severely criticised. By a peculiar thermometric adjustment, when a woman's talent is at zero, journalistic approbation is at the boiling pitch; when she attains mediocrity, it is already at no more than summer heat; and if ever she reaches excellence, critical enthusiasm drops to the freezing point. Harriet Martineau, Currer Bell, and Mrs. Gaskell[3] have been treated as cavalierly as if they had been men. And every critic who forms a high estimate of the share women may ultimately take in literature, will, on principle, abstain from any exceptional indulgence towards the productions of literary women. For it must be plain to every one who looks impartially and extensively into feminine literature, that its greatest deficiencies are due hardly more to the want of intellectual power than to the want of those moral qualities that contribute to literary excellence—patient diligence, a sense of the responsibility involved in publication, and an appreciation of the sacredness of the writer's art. In the majority of women's books you see that kind of facility which springs from the absence of any high standard; that fertility in imbecile combination or feeble imitation which a little self-criticism would check and reduce to barrenness; just as with a total want of musical ear people will sing out of tune, while a degree more melodic sensibility would suffice to render them silent. The foolish vanity of wishing to appear in print, instead of being counter balanced by any consciousness of the intellectual or moral derogation implied in futile authorship, seems to be encouraged by the extremely false impression that to write *at all* is a proof of superiority in a woman. On this ground, we believe that the average intellect of women is unfairly represented by the mass of feminine literature, and that while the few women who write well are very far above the ordinary intellectual level of their sex, the many women who write ill are very far below it. So that, after all, the severer critics are fulfilling a chivalrous duty in depriving the mere fact of feminine authorship of any false prestige which may give it a delusive attraction, and in recommending women of mediocre faculties—as at least a negative service they can render their sex—to abstain from writing.

---

3. Harriet Martineau: English writer (1802–76)— see pp. 613–14; Currer Bell: pseudonym for English novelist Charlotte Brontë (1816–55)—see pp. 826–33; Mrs. Gaskell: English novelist Elizabeth Gaskell (1810–65)—see pp. 713–14.

The standing apology for women who become writers without any special qualification is, that society shuts them out from other spheres of occupation. Society is a very culpable entity, and has to answer for the manufacture of many unwholesome commodities, from bad pickles to bad poetry. But society, like "matter," and Her Majesty's Government, and other lofty abstractions, has its share of excessive blame as well as excessive praise. Where there is one woman who writes from necessity, we believe there are three women who write from vanity; and, besides, there is something so antiseptic in the mere healthy fact of working for one's bread, that the most trashy and rotten kind of feminine literature is not likely to have been produced under such circumstances. "In all labour there is profit;"[4] but ladies' silly novels, we imagine, are less the result of labour than of busy idleness.

Happily, we are not dependent on argument to prove that Fiction is a department of literature in which women can, after their kind, fully equal men. A cluster of great names, both living and dead, rush to our memories in evidence that women can produce novels not only fine, but among the very finest;—novels, too, that have a precious speciality, lying quite apart from masculine aptitudes and experience. No educational restrictions can shut women out from the materials of fiction, and there is no species of art which is so free from rigid requirements. Like crystalline masses, it may take any form, and yet be beautiful; we have only to pour in the right elements—genuine observation, humour, and passion. But it is precisely this absence of rigid requirement which constitutes the fatal seduction of novel-writing to incompetent women. Ladies are not wont to be very grossly deceived as to their power of playing on the piano; here certain positive difficulties of execution have to be conquered, and incompetence inevitably breaks down. Every art which has its absolute *technique* is, to a certain extent, guarded from the intrusions of mere left-handed imbecility. But in novel-writing there are no barriers for incapacity to stumble against, no external criteria to prevent a writer from mistaking foolish facility for mastery. And so we have again and again the old story of La Fontaine's ass, who puts his nose to the flute, and, finding that he elicits some sound, exclaims, "Moi, aussi, je joue de la flute;"[5]—a fable which we commend, at parting, to the consideration of any feminine reader who is in danger of adding to the number of "silly novels by lady novelists."

1856

---

4. Proverbs 14:23.
5. I can play the flute, too! (French). Thomas Pinney, the editor of Eliot's essays, could not locate

this story among the fables of Jean de la Fontaine (1621–95).

CULTURAL COORDINATES
Spirit Rappers and Spiritualism

George Eliot speaks of "false lights" in her essay "Silly Novels by Lady Novelists," referring to thinkers and movements of her day that had been proven to stray from the truth. Her list of suspected frauds included "the Spirit rappers," or mediums who said they could communicate with the dead. In 1856, when Eliot was writing, someone as well educated as she would have assumed that these mediums were surreptitiously producing the knocks, bumps, and groans they claimed were coming from the dead. Between 1848 and the 1860s, though, many did believe in spiritualism, a movement that had a particularly strong following among women.

Spirit rapping began in 1848 in upstate New York. Two teenage sisters frightened their parents, their neighbors, and evidently even themselves when they claimed they heard a continual, mysterious knocking in the family home every night. Margaret and Kate Fox told their parents about the knocking, and eventually everyone in their neighborhood had come to the house to hear for themselves the sounds they took to be emanating from a ghost. Those searching the house heard knocks, but no one could find their source. Using a "no knocks for 'no,' knocks for 'yes'" code, the family and spectators questioned the spirit and "learned" he was a peddler who had been murdered in the house and buried in the basement. Repeated attempts to dig in the spot that was supposed to have been the grave failed, as groundwater kept filling up the hole.

Shortly after this first incident, the Fox sisters moved to Rochester, New York, to live with another sister, Leah Fish. Fish became their public relations manager

A séance. Spiritualists (or mediums) claimed that knocking and rapping noises at séances were messages from beyond the grave, but skeptics attributed such tricks to the "spiritualists" themselves.

and agent, and by the end of 1848, all three were living on the proceeds of the younger girls' work as professional mediums. Inspired by the Foxes' success, other mediums began setting up séances, gatherings where the mediums purportedly communicated with dead celebrities or the loved ones of their clients. Throughout the 1850s, participants in a séance could witness such phenomena as visions, "spirit writing," where the medium writes messages under the spirit's power, and "trance-speaking," in which the medium passes on messages from the spirit world. Some mediums, like the Foxes, spelled out messages by calling out the letters of the alphabet and asking the spirit to knock when they had reached the correct letter. This knocking, or "rapping," gave the mediums their name.

Spirit rappers were widely condemned by scientists, clergymen, and magicians, all of whom had their own reasons for wishing to debunk the claims of this new "religion." Some theorized that the girls were producing the knocks by manipulating the joints of their toes or their knees, but no one publicly proved it. Later in life, one of the sisters admitted faking the knocking communications from the dead, but later still, she recanted, saying she had only denied the truth under pressure from her critics. As many as one million Americans during the 1850s reportedly believed the rappings to be genuine messages from beyond the grave.

Florence Nightingale—"the Lady with the Lamp," as she is called in "Santa Filomena," an 1857 poem by Henry Wadsworth Longfellow—survives in popular memory as an icon for "nurse." By the end of the twentieth century, nursing, like teaching, was considered a feminine profession, suitable to women. Both professions draw on skills that would seem to emulate women's supposedly innate ability to nurture the young and the sick. But when Nightingale was young, nursing was not yet a profession open to upper- or middle-class women. Indeed, women of her elevated social class generally expected to lead lives of leisure, reigning over households where low-paid servants did the actual work. When, in her twenties, Nightingale told her family that she wanted to leave home to train as a nurse, they reacted, she later wrote, "as if I had said I wanted to be a kitchenmaid." Most women who worked in the middle of the nineteenth century were, after all, domestics, unless they labored in factories, as dressmakers, or as milliners. Nightingale struggled with her parents for nine years before finally receiving permission to go, demonstrating the stubborn determination that would drive her working life.

Nightingale's life became a powerful example of what women could achieve—in her or any period—given the chance to work. The daughter of an English country gentleman, William Edward Nightingale, and Fanny Smith Nightingale, his wife, Florence Nightingale received unusually strong instruction at the family homes in Derbyshire and Hampshire, learning philosophy and the classical languages in addition to the usual feminine subjects of modern foreign languages, history, music, and needlework. As a child, she begged to be allowed to study mathematics; although her socialite mother considered math unsuitable for a girl, Nightingale eventually prevailed, receiving tutoring in the subject. Her youth was filled with frustration at the triviality of the life her family expected her to enjoy: she found dinner parties, embroidery, and superficial chat mind-numbing. She spent much of her time daydreaming, or falling into what she called a "trance," in which she imagined herself living more heroically. Nightingale always saw this habit as a moral failing, although she later acknowledged that it was the logical outcome of the limitations placed on a leisured woman's activities.

One pursuit open to upper-class ladies was charity work, such as visiting the sick and bringing food or clothing to the poor. Nightingale had little interest in amateur charity, but she began studying reports on sanitary conditions and medical practice in England and other European countries. She would rise early, fill her notebooks with information from the publications she could gather on the subject, then join her family for breakfast and the usual round of morning visits. In 1849, she received a marriage proposal from a man she loved, Richard Monckton Milnes, a wealthy poet and politician who supported liberal reforms. Anticipating the protest she would raise in *Cassandra* (1852) against the argument that women should not satisfy their own intellectual, passionate, and moral natures, Nightingale wrote in a note to a friend:

I have an intellectual nature which requires satisfaction and that would find it in him. I have a passionate nature which requires satisfaction and that would find it in him. I have a moral, an active nature which requires satisfaction and that would not find it in his life. Sometimes I think I will satisfy my passional nature at all events, because that will at least secure me from the evils of dreaming. But would it? I could be satisfied to spend a life with him in combining our different powers in some great object. I could not satisfy this nature by spending a life with him in making society and arranging domestic things. (Quoted in Cecil Woodham-Smith, *Florence Nightingale*, New York: McGraw Hill, 1951, p. 51)

She refused Milnes's offer of marriage and stayed at home for three more years; she wrote *Cassandra*, an unpublished essay denouncing women's subjugation to domestic duties, in 1851 and 1852. Finally, she enrolled for a three-month nurses' training course in Kaiserwerth, Germany. As part of her studies, she visited hospitals in Scotland, Ireland, and France. Her father settled on her an income of £500 a year (which would be equivalent to about $80,000 today), and she went to work and live alone as the unpaid superintendent of a small women's hospital in London.

In 1854, after Great Britain declared war on Russia in what was to become the Crimean War, Nightingale led a group of nurses to the Turkish front lines to gather information on medical and sanitary conditions in the British army. Widely reported in the London newspapers, her calls for reform made her a celebrity at home and established her image as the saintly lady nurse. Her public popularity suggests that her compatriots had begun to see that it was wrong to assume women could not work and remain respectable.

When she returned to London in 1856, she helped begin the Royal Commission on the Sanitary State of the Army and later worked to initiate a similar commission for the British army in India. In 1860, she gave her name to a school for nurses at St. Thomas's Hospital in London, and in 1861 she established a similar school for training midwives. Her book, *Notes on Nursing: What It Is and What It Is Not* (1860), was a best seller, selling 15,000 copies in its first month. Nightingale's own health collapsed on her return from the Crimea in 1857, and she worked from home as a medical reformer for the rest of her career, well into her eighties. Though she was not opposed to women's suffrage, she did not get involved in that movement, because she believed women faced material problems—such as limited property rights and professional opportunities—that were more pressing than the need to vote. In 1907, three years before her death, she won the Order of Merit, an honor bestowed by the Crown for distinguished service. Nightingale was the first woman ever to receive that honor.

When Nightingale wrote *Cassandra*, she could not have foreseen the impact her career would have. In her essay, she raged against the constraints her later activism would help to reduce for women. *Cassandra* is brief, only about twice as long as the sections we have reprinted here. It begins with the plaintive question, "Why have women passion, intellect, moral activity—these three—and a place in society where no one of the three can be exercised?" We have reproduced sections II, IV, and VII, on intellect, moral activity and marriage, and death, respectively. (Nightingale uses Emily Brontë's lines that serve as the epigraph to Section II as inspiration for her meditation in Section VII). The note of despair in the essay gives way, in its conclusion and in Nightingale's own life story, to the hope of a better future for women of action.

From Cassandra

II
[Intellect]

"Yet I would spare no pang,
Would wish no torture less,
The more that anguish racks,
The earlier it will bless."[1]

Give us back our suffering, we cry to Heaven in our hearts—suffering rather than indifferentism; for out of nothing comes nothing.[2] But out of suffering may come the cure. Better have pain than paralysis! A hundred struggle and drown in the breakers. One discovers the new world. But rather, ten times rather, die in the surf, heralding the way to that new world, than stand idly on the shore!

Passion, intellect, moral activity—these three have never been satisfied in woman. In this cold and oppressive conventional atmosphere, they cannot be satisfied. To say more on this subject would be to enter into the whole history of society, of the present state of civilization.

Look at that lizard—"It is not hot," he says, "I like it. The atmosphere which enervates you is life to me." The state of society which some complain of makes others happy. Why should these complain to those? *They* do not suffer. *They* would not understand it, any more than that lizard would comprehend the sufferings of a Shetland sheep.[3]

The progressive world is necessarily divided into two classes—those who take the best of what there is and enjoy it—those who wish for something better and try to create it. Without these two classes, the world would be badly off. They are the very conditions of progress, both the one and the other. Were there none who were discontented with what they have, the world would never reach anything better. And, through the other class, which is constantly taking the best of what the first is creating for them, a balance is secured, and that which is conquered is held fast. But with neither class must we quarrel for not possessing the privileges of the other. The laws of the nature of each make it impossible.

Is discontent a privilege?

Yes, it is a privilege to suffer for your race—a privilege not reserved to the Redeemer and the martyrs alone, but one enjoyed by numbers in every age.

The common-place lives of thousands; and in that is its only interest—its only merit as a history: vis., that it *is* the type of common sufferings—the story of one who has not the courage to resist nor to submit to the civilization of her time—is this.

Poetry and imagination begin life. A child will fall on its knees on the gravel walk at the sight of a pink hawthorn in full flower, when it is by itself, to praise God for it.

Then comes intellect. It wishes to satisfy the wants which intellect creates for it. But there is a physical, not moral, impossibility of supplying the wants of the

1. Lines spoken by a female prisoner in an 1845 fragment by Emily Brontë, beginning, "Silent is the House—all are laid asleep." Nightingale, evidently quoting from memory, changes the opening line, "Yet I would lose no sting, would wish no

torture less."
2. Shakespeare's *King Lear* (1.1.90): "Nothing will come of nothing."
3. Scottish sheep with heavy wool.

intellect in the state of civilization at which we have arrived. The stimulus, the training, the time, are all three wanting[4] to us; or, in other words, the means and inducements are not there.

Look at the poor lives which we lead. It is a wonder that we are so good as we are, not that we are so bad. In looking round we are struck with the power of the organizations we see, not with their want of power. Now and then, it is true, we are conscious that *there* is an inferior organization, but, in general, just the contrary. Mrs. A. has the imagination, the poetry of a Murillo,[5] and has sufficient power of execution to show that she might have had a great deal more. Why is she not a Murillo? From a material difficulty, not a mental one. If she has a knife and fork in her hands during three hours of the day, she cannot have a pencil or brush. Dinner is the great sacred ceremony of this day, the great sacrament. To be absent from dinner is equivalent to being ill. Nothing else will excuse us from it. Bodily incapacity is the only apology valid. If she has a pen and ink in her hands during other three hours, writing answers for the penny post;[6] again, she cannot have her pencil, and so *ad infinitum* through life. People have no type before them in their lives, neither fathers and mothers, nor the children themselves. They look at things in detail. They say, "It is very desirable that A., my daughter, should go to such a party, should know such a lady, should sit by such a person." It is true. But what standard have they before them? of the nature and destination of man? The very words are rejected as pedantic. But might they not, at least, have a type in their minds that such an one might be a discoverer through her intellect, such another through her art, a third through her moral power?

Women often try one branch of intellect after another in their youth, *e.g.,* mathematics. But that, least of all, is compatible with the life of "society." It is impossible to follow up anything systematically. Woman often long to enter some man's profession where they would find direction, competition (or rather opportunity of measuring the intellect with others), and, above all, time.

In those wise institutions, mixed as they are with many follies, which will last as long as the human race lasts, because they are adapted to the wants of the human race; those institutions which we call monasteries, and which, embracing much that is contrary to the laws of nature, are yet better adapted to the union of the life of action and that of thought than any other mode of life with which we are acquainted; in many such, four and a half hours, at least, are daily set aside for thought, rules are given for thought, training and opportunity afforded. Among us, there is *no* time appointed for this purpose, and the difficulty is that, in our social life, we must be always doubtful whether we ought not to be with somebody else or be doing something else.

Are men better off than women in this?

If one calls upon a friend in London and sees her son in the drawing-room, it strikes one as odd to find a young man sitting idling in his mother's drawing-room in the morning. For men, who are seen much in those haunts, there is no end of the epithets we have; "knights of the carpet," "drawing-room heroes," "ladies' men." But suppose we were to see a number of men in the morning sitting round a table in the drawing-room, looking at prints, doing worsted work,[7] and reading

---

4. Wants: desires; wanting: lacking.
5. Spanish painter of religious subjects Bartolomé Murillo (1618–82).
6. Regular mail delivery.
7. Needlepoint; also knitting and crochet.

little books, how we should laugh! A member of the House of Commons was once known to do worsted work. Of another man was said, "His only fault is that he is too good; he drives out with his mother every day in the carriage, and if he is asked anywhere he answers that he must dine with his mother, but, if she can spare him, he will come in to tea, and he does not come."

Now, why is it more ridiculous for a man than for a woman to do worsted work and drive out every day in the carriage? Why should we laugh if we were to see a parcel of men sitting round a drawing-room table in the morning, and think it all right if they were women?

Is man's time more valuable than woman's? or is the difference between man and woman this, that woman has confessedly nothing to do?

Women are never supposed to have any occupation of sufficient importance *not* to be interrupted, except "suckling their fools;"[8] and women themselves have accepted this, have written books to support it, and have trained themselves so as to consider whatever they do as *not* of such value to the world or to others, but that they can throw it up at the first "claim of social life." They have accustomed themselves to consider intellectual occupation as a merely selfish amusement, which it is their "duty" to give up for every trifler more selfish than themselves.

A young man (who was afterwards useful and known in his day and generation) when busy reading and sent for by his proud mother to shine in some morning visit, came; but, after it was over, he said, "Now, remember, this is not to happen again. I came that you might not think me sulky, but I shall not come again." But for a young woman to send such a message to her mother and sisters, how impertinent it would be! A woman of great administrative powers said that she never undertook anything which she "could not throw by at once, if necessary."

How do we explain then the many cases of women who have distinguished themselves in classics, mathematics, even in politics?

Widowhood, ill-health, or want of bread, these three explanations or excuses are supposed to justify a woman in taking up an occupation. In some cases, no doubt, an indomitable force of character will suffice without any of these three, but such are rare.

But see how society fritters away the intellects of those committed to her charge! It is said that society is necessary to sharpen the intellect. But what do we seek society for? It does sharpen the intellect, because it is a kind of *tour-de-force* to say something at a pinch—unprepared and uninterested with any subject, to improvise something under difficulties. But what "go we out for to seek?" To take the chance of some one having something to say which we want to hear? or of our finding something to say which *they* want to hear? You have a little to say, but not much. You often make a stipulation with some one else, "Come in ten minutes, for I shall not be able to find enough to spin out longer than that." You are not to talk of anything very interesting, for the essence of society is to prevent any long conversations and all *tête-à-têtes*. "Glissez, n'appuyez pas" is its very motto. The praise of a good "*maîtresse de maison*"[9] consists in this, that she allows no one person to be too much absorbed in, or too long about, a conversation. She always recalls them to their "duty." People do not go into the company of their

---

8. Nursing babies. In Shakespeare's *Othello* (2.1.159), the villainous Iago says women are "To suckle fools and chronicle small beer."

9. Glissez, n'appuyez pas: keep sliding, don't linger (French); *maîtresse de maison*: lady of the house (French).

fellow-creatures for what would seem a very sufficient reason, namely, that they have something to say to them, or something that they want to hear from them; but in the vague hope that they may find something to say.

Then as to solitary opportunities. Women never have half an hour in all their lives (excepting before or after anybody is up in the house) that they can call their own, without fear of offending or of hurting some one. Why do people sit up so late, or, more rarely, get up so early? Not because the day is not long enough, but because they have "no time in the day to themselves."

If we do attempt to do anything in company, what is the system of literary exercise which we pursue? Everybody reads aloud out of their own book or newspaper—or, every five minutes, something is said. And what is it to be "read aloud to?" The most miserable exercise of the human intellect. Or rather, is it any exercise at all? Is it like lying on one's back, with one's hands tied and having liquid poured down one's throat. Worse than that, because suffocation would immediately ensue and put a stop to this operation. But no suffocation would stop the other.

So much for the satisfaction of the intellect. Yet for a married woman in society, it is even worse. A married woman was heard to wish that she could break a limb that she might have a little time to herself. Many take advantage of the fear of "infection" to do the same.

It is a thing so accepted among women that they have nothing to do, that one woman has not the least scruple in saying to another, "I will come and spend the morning with you." And you would be thought quite surly and absurd, if you were to refuse it on the plea of occupation. Nay, it is thought a mark of amiability and affection, if you are "on such terms" that you can "come in" "any morning you please."

In a country house, if there is a large party of young people, "You will spend the morning with us," they say to the neighbours, "we will drive together in the afternoon," "tomorrow we will make an expedition, and we will spend the evening together." And this is thought friendly, and spending time in a pleasant manner. So women play through life. Yet time is the most valuable of all things. If they had come every morning and afternoon and robbed us of half-a-crown we should have had redress from the police. But it is laid down, that our time is of no value. If you offer a morning visit to a professional man, and say, "I will just stay an hour with you, if you will allow me, till so and so comes back to fetch me;" it costs him the earnings of an hour, and therefore he has a right to complain. But women have no right, because it is "*only* their time."

Women have no means given them, whereby they *can* resist the "claims of social life." They are taught from their infancy upwards that it is wrong, ill-tempered, and a misunderstanding of "a woman's mission" (with a great M.[1]) if they do not allow themselves *willingly* to be interrupted at all hours. If a woman has once put in a claim to be treated as a man by some work of science or art or literature, which she can *show* as the "fruit of her leisure," then she will be considered justified in *having* leisure (hardly, perhaps, even then). But if not, not. If she has nothing to show, she must resign herself to her fate.

* * *

1. Capital letter "M".

IV
[Moral Activity and Marriage]

Moral activity? There is scarcely such a thing possible! Everything is sketchy. The world does nothing but sketch. One Lady Bountiful sketches a school, but it never comes to a finished study; she can hardly work at it two weeks consecutively. Here and there a solitary individual, it is true, makes a really careful study,—as Mrs. Chisholm of emigration—as Miss Carpenter of reformatory discipline. But, in general, a "lady" has too many sketches on hand. She has a sketch of society, a sketch of her children's education, sketches of her "charities," sketches of her reading. She is like a painter who should have five pictures in his studio at once, and giving now a stroke to one, and now a stroke to another, till he had made the whole round, should continue this routine to the end.

All life is sketchy,—the poet's verse (compare Tennyson, Milnes, and Mrs. Browning with Milton or even Byron:[2] it is not the difference of genius which strikes one so much as the unfinished state of these modern sketches compared with the studies of the old masters),—the artist's picture, the author's composition—all are rough, imperfect, incomplete, even as works of art.

And how can it be otherwise? A "leader"[3] out of a newspaper, an article out of a review, five books read aloud in the course of an evening, such is our literature. What mind can stand three leading articles every morning as its food?

When shall we see a woman making a *study* of what she does? Married women cannot; for a man would think, if his wife undertook any great work with the intention of carrying it out,—of making anything but a sham of it—that she would "suckle his fools and chronicle his small beer" less well for it,—that he would not have so good a dinner—that she would destroy, as it is called, his domestic life.

The intercourse of man and woman—how frivolous, how unworthy it is! Can we call *that* the true vocation of woman—her high career? Look round at the marriages which you know. The true marriage—that noble union, by which a man and woman become together the one perfect being—probably does not exist at present upon earth.

It is not surprising that husbands and wives seem so little part of one another. It is surprising that there is so much love as there is. For there is no food for it. What does it live upon—what nourishes it? Husbands and wives never seem to have anything to say to one another. What do they talk about? Not about any great religious, social, political questions or feelings. They talk about who shall come to dinner, who is to live in this lodge and who in that, about the improvement of the place, or when they shall go to London. If there are children, they form a common subject of some nourishment. But, even then, the case is oftenest thus,—the husband is to think of how they are to get on in life; the wife of bringing them up at home.

But any real communion between husband and wife—any descending into the depths of their being, and drawing out thence what they find and comparing it— do we ever dream of such a thing? Yes, we may dream of it during the season of "passion;" but we shall not find it afterwards. We even *expect* it to go off, and lay

---

2. Nightingale contrasts Victorian poets Richard Monckton Milnes (1809–85, her suitor), Alfred, Lord Tennyson (1809–92), and Elizabeth Barrett Browning (1806–61) with John Milton (1608– 74), the author of *Paradise Lost* (1667), and George Gordon, Lord Byron (1788–1824), a romantic poet.
3. A front-page story.

our account that it will. If the husband has, by chance, gone into the depths of *his* being, and found anything there unorthodox, he, oftenest, conceals it carefully from his wife,—he is afraid of "unsettling her opinions."

What is the mystery of passion, spiritually speaking? For there *is* a passion of the Spirit. *Blind* passion, as it has most truly been called, seems to come on in man without his exactly knowing why, without his *at all* knowing why for *this* person rather than for *that,* and (whether it has been satisfied or unsatisfied) to go off again after a while, as it came, also without his knowing why.

The woman's passion is generally more lasting.

It is possible that this difference may be, because there is really more in man than in woman. There is nothing in her for him to have this intimate communion *with*. He cannot impart to her his religious beliefs, if he have any, because she would be "shocked." Religious men are and must be heretics now—for we must not pray, except in a "form" of words, made beforehand—or think of God but with a pre-arranged idea.

With the man's political ideas, if they extend beyond the merest party politics, she has no sympathy.

His social ideas, if they are "advanced," she will probably denounce without knowing why, as savouring of "socialism" (a convenient word, which covers a multitude of new ideas and offences). For woman is "by birth a Tory,"[4]—has been often said—by education a "Tory," we mean.

Woman has nothing but her affections,—and this makes her at once more loving and less loved.

But is it surprising that there should be so little real marriage, when we think what the process is which leads to marriage?

Under the eyes of an always present mother and sisters (of whom even the most refined and intellectual cannot abstain from a jest upon the subject, who think it their *duty* to be anxious, to watch every germ and bud of it) the acquaintance begins. It is fed—upon what?—the gossip of art, musical and pictorial, the party politics of the day, the chit-chat of society, and people marry or sometimes they don't marry, discouraged by the impossibility of knowing any more of one another than this will furnish.

They prefer to marry in *thought,* to hold imaginary conversations with one another in idea, rather than, on such a flimsy pretext of communion, to take the chance (*certainly* it cannot be) of having more to say to one another in marriage.

Men and women meet now *to be idle.* Is it extraordinary that they do not know each other, and that, in their mutual ignorance, they form no surer friendships? Did they meet to *do* something together, then indeed they might form some real tie.

But, as it is, *they* are not there, it is only a mask which is there—a mouthpiece of ready-made sentences about the "topics of the day;" and then people rail against men for choosing a woman "for her face"—why, what else do they see?

It is very well to say "be prudent, be careful, try to know each other." But how are you to know each other?

Unless a woman has lost all pride, how is it possible for her, under the eyes of all her family, to indulge in long exclusive conversations with a man? "Such a thing" must not take place till after her "engagement." And how is she to make an engagement, if "such a thing" has not taken place?

---

4. The more conservative of the two leading English political parties of the time, Whig and Tory.

Besides, young women at home have so little to occupy and to interest them— they have so little reason for *not* quitting their home, that a young and independent man cannot look at a girl without giving rise to "expectations," if not on her own part, on that of her family. Happy he, if he is not said to have been "trifling with her feelings," or "disappointing her hopes!" Under these circumstances, how can a man, who has any pride or any principle, become acquainted with a woman in such a manner as to *justify* them in marrying?

There are four ways in which people marry. First, accident or relationship has thrown them together in their childhood, and acquaintance has grown up naturally and unconsciously. Accordingly, in novels, it is generally cousins who marry; and *now* it seems the only natural thing—the only possible way of making an intimacy. And yet, we know that intermarriage between relations is in direct contravention of the laws of nature for the well-being of the race; witness the Quakers, the Spanish grandees, the royal races, the secluded valleys of mountainous countries, where madness, degeneration of race, defective organization and cretinism flourish and multiply.

The second way, and by far the most general, in which people marry, is this. A woman, thoroughly uninterested at home, and having formed a slight acquaintance with some accidental person, accepts him, if he "falls in love" with her, as it is technically called, and takes the chance. Hence the vulgar expression of marriage being a lottery, which it most truly is, for that the *right* two should come together has as many chances against it as there are blanks in any lottery.

The third way is, that some person is found sufficiently independent, sufficiently careless of the opinions of others, or sufficiently without modesty to speculate thus:—"It is worth while that I should become acquainted with so and so. I do not care what his or her opinion of me is, if, *after* having become acquainted, to do which can bear no other construction in people's eyes than a desire of marriage, I retreat." But there is this to be said, that it is doubtful whether, under this unnatural tension, which, to all susceptible characters, such a disregard of the opinions which they care for must be, a healthy or a natural feeling can grow up.

And now they are married—that is to say, two people have received the licence of a man in a white surplice. But they are no more man and wife for that than Louis XIV and the Infanta of Spain, married by proxy, were man and wife.[5] The woman who has sold herself for an establishment, in what is she superior to those we may not name?

Lastly, in a few rare, very rare, cases, such as circumstances, always provided in novels, but seldom to be met with in real life, present—whether the accident of parents' neglect, or of parents' unusual skill and wisdom, or of having no parents at all, which is generally the case in novels—or marrying out of the person's rank of life, by which the usual restraints are removed, and there is room and play left for attraction—or extraordinary events, isolation, misfortunes, which many wish for, even though their imaginations be not tainted by romance-reading; such alternatives as these give food and space for the development of character and mutual sympathies.

But a girl, if she has any pride, is so ashamed of having any thing she wishes to say out of the hearing of her own family, she thinks it must be something so very wrong, that it is ten to one, if she have the opportunity of saying it, that she will not.

5. Following the victory of France over Spain in 1658, Louis XIV, king of France, married Marie Thérèse, daughter of the Spanish king Philip IV.

And yet she is spending her life, perhaps, in dreaming of accidental means of unrestrained communion.

And then it is thought pretty to say that "Women have no passion." If passion is excitement in the daily social intercourse with men, women think about marriage much more than men do; it is the only event of their lives. It ought to be a sacred event, but surely not the only event of a woman's life, as it is now. Many women spend their lives in asking men to marry them, in a refined way. Yet it is true that women are seldom in love. How can they be?

How cruel are the revulsions which high-minded women suffer! There was one who loved, in connexion with great deeds, noble thoughts, devoted feelings. They met after an interval. It was at one of those crowded parties of Civilization which we call Society. His only careless passing remark was, "The buzz to-night is like a manufactory."[6] Yet he loved her.

* * *

VII
[The Dying Woman]

The dying woman to her mourners:—"Oh! if you knew how gladly I leave this life, how much more courage I feel to take the chance of another, than of anything I see before me in this, you would put on your wedding-clothes instead of mourning for me!"

"But," they say, "so much talent! so many gifts! such good which you might have done!"

"The world will be put back some little time by my death," she says; "you see I estimate my powers at least as highly as you can; but it is by the death which has taken place some years ago in me, not by the death which is about to take place now." And so is the world put back by the death of every one who has to sacrifice the development of his or her peculiar gifts (which were meant, not for selfish gratification, but for the improvement of that world) to conventionality.

"My people were like children playing on the shore of the eighteenth century. I was their hobby-horse, their plaything; and they drove me to and fro, dear souls! never weary of the play themselves, till I, who had grown to woman's estate and to the ideas of the nineteenth century, lay down exhausted, my mind closed to hope, my heart to strength.

"Free—free—oh! divine freedom, art thou come at last? Welcome, beautiful death!"

Let neither name nor date be placed on her grave, still less the expression of regret or of admiration; but simply the words, "I believe in God."

1852

MARY BOYKIN CHESNUT
1823–1886

Mary Chesnut spent much of the Civil War in Richmond, Virginia, then capital of the Confederate States of America. Unusually well educated, Chesnut understood the historical import of the moment in which she lived and devoted her consider-

6. Factory.

able literary skill to recording a personal account of what she thought would be the birth of a new nation. Chesnut used her diary as the source for a memoir she began to compose in the early 1880s but did not complete before her death. Although expurgated versions of her journal were published in the early twentieth century, the complete journal was not published until 1981. *Mary Chesnut's Civil War,* as edited by C. Vann Woodward, from which the following selections are drawn, interleaves the extant version of Chesnut's memoir with passages from the actual diary she kept during the war. The memoir vividly portrays life at the epicenter of a struggle for American identity through a variety of techniques that owe more to the tradition of the novel—such as heavy use of dialogue—than to the autobiography.

Chesnut was born in Stateburg, South Carolina, the oldest daughter of Mary and Stephen Miller. The Millers moved in the highest social and political circles in the South, as there were few positions of political significance that Stephen Miller did not, at some point, hold: U.S. congressman, U.S. senator, governor, and state senator. When Chesnut married James Chesnut Jr., she was barely seventeen. Like her father, James Chesnut was a slaveholder who held various elected offices that culminated in a seat in the U.S. Senate, which he gave up when the election of Abraham Lincoln seemed to foreclose any possibility of avoiding war. The Chesnuts had no children, and until the fall of Richmond, Chesnut's parlor attracted the most powerful figures associated with Southern interests. Despite her contact with the Southern elite, as her journal shows, Chesnut herself was in some ways ambivalent toward slavery, which she understood as a mixed blessing and threat to white women. But Chesnut's proximity to power, combined with her own astute analysis, provides us access to ideological factors behind the Civil War that went beyond states' rights.

As edited by the scholar C. Vann Woodward, the following selections meld material from the autobiographical memoir Chesnut was working on at the time of her death in the 1880s with more raw material found in the diary she kept during the 1860s. These recount two days within a week of the writing of the formal constitution of the Confederate States of America (February 9, 1861) and less than two months before the Confederate attack on Fort Sumter (April 12), which marked the beginning of the Civil War.

From Civil War Journal

[I wanted them to fight and stop talking]

February 18, 1861.

Conecuh. Ems.[1] I do not allow myself vain regrets or sad foreboding. This Southern Confederacy must be supported now by calm determination and cool brains. We have risked all, and we must play our best, for the stake is life or death. I shall always regret that I had not kept a journal during the two past delightful and eventful years. The delights having exhausted themselves in the latter part of 1860 and the events crowding in so that it takes away one's breath to think about it all. I daresay I might have recorded with some distinctness the daily shocks—"Earthquakes as usual" (Lady Sale).[2] But now it is to me one nightmare from the time I left Charleston for Florida, where I remained two anxious weeks amid hammocks

---

1. Conecuh: a county in South Carolina, where Chesnut's brother lived; Ems: apparently her name for her mother.

2. Florentia Wynch Sale, wife of a British general, who experienced with him Britain's first disastrous invasion of Afghanistan (1839–42).

and everglades, oppressed and miserable, and heard on the cars returning to the world that Lincoln was elected and our fate sealed. Saw at Fernandina a few men running up a wan Palmetto flag[3] and crying, South Carolina has seceded. Overjoyed at the tribute to South Carolina, I said, "So Florida sympathizes." I inquired the names of our *few* but undismayed supporters in Florida. Heard Gadsden, Holmes, Porcher, &c&c—names as inevitably South Carolina's as Moses or Lazarus are Jews'. When we arrived in Charleston, my room was immediately over a supper given by the city to a delegation from Savannah, and Colonel Bartow, the mayor of Savannah, was speaking in the hot, fervid, after-supper Southern style. They contrived to speak all night and to cheer &c. I remember liking one speech so much—*voice*, tone, temper, sentiments, and all. I sent to ask the name of the orator, and the answer came: "Mr. Alfred Huger." He may not have been the wisest or wittiest man there—but certainly when on his legs[4] he had the best of it that night. After such a night of impassioned Southern eloquence I traveled next day with (in the first place, a racking nervous headache and a morphine bottle, and also) Colonel Colcock, formerly member of Congress, and U.S. Judge Magrath, of whom likenesses were suspended, in the frightfullest signpost style of painting, across various thoroughfares in Charleston. The happy moment seized by the painter to depict him, while Magrath was in the act, most dramatically, of tearing off his robes of office in rage and disgust at Lincoln's election.

My father was a South Carolina nullifier, governor of the state at the time of the nullification row,[5] and then U.S. senator. So I was of necessity a rebel born. My husband's family being equally pledged to the Union party rather exasperated my zeal, as I heard taunts and sneers so constantly thrown out against the faith I had imbibed before I understood anything at all about it. If I do yet.

I remember feeling a nervous dread and horror of this break with so great a power as U.S.A., but I was ready and willing. South Carolina had been so rampant for years. She was the torment of herself and everybody else. Nobody could live in this state unless he were a fire-eater. Come what would, I wanted them to fight and stop talking. South Carolina—Bluffton, Rhetts, &c had exasperated and heated themselves into a fever that only bloodletting could ever cure—it was the inevitable remedy.

So I was a seceder,[6] *but* I dreaded the future. I bore in mind Pugh's letter, his description of what he saw in Mexico when he accompanied an invading army.[7] My companions had their own thoughts and misgivings, doubtless, but they breathed fire and defiance.

> Their bosoms they bared to the glorious strife
> And their oaths were recorded on high
> To prevail in the cause that was dearer than life
> Or crushed in its ruins to die.[8]

3 South Carolina's flag.
4. When giving a speech.
5. In 1832, South Carolina had voted to "nullify," or abrogate, the authority of the federal government of the United States to regulate certain aspects of interstate trade. This established South Carolina as a leader in the fight for the recognition of the superiority of the rights of individual states over the power of the federal government.
6. Devoted to the cause of the secession of some states from the United States.
7. In the Mexican-American War of 1846–48 the United States invaded Mexico.
8. Rewording of lines from Scottish poet Thomas Campbell's "Stanzas on the Threatened Invasion," 1803.

Consequently they were a deputation from Charleston, risen against tyrants to her representatives in Columbia, telling them they were too slow, to hurry up, dissolve the Union, or it would be worse for them. There was a fire in the rear of the hottest.

At Kingsville I met my husband. He had resigned his seat in the Senate U.S. and was on his way home. Had burned the ships behind him. No hope now—he was in bitter earnest.

I thought him right—but going back to Mulberry to live was indeed offering up my life on the altar of country. Secession was delayed—was very near destroyed. The members were rushing away from Columbia. That band of invincibles certainly feared smallpox. But they adjourned to Charleston, and the decree was rendered there. Camden was in unprecedented excitement. Minutemen arming, with immense blue cockades and red sashes, some with sword and gun, marching and drilling.

I spent Christmas at Combahee—a most beautiful country seat. Live oaks in all their glory, camellias as plentiful on the lawn as the hawthorn in an English hedge.

Mrs. Charles Lowndes was with us when the secession ordinance came. We sat staring in each other's faces. She spoke first. "As our days, so shall our strength be." I am truly glad I have seen those lovely Combahee places—they are so exposed, they will doubtless suffer from invasion.

We soon returned to Charleston. At Mrs. Gidiere's we had a set of very pleasant people. Our rage for news was unappeasable—and we had enough. One morning Mrs. Gidiere, coming home from market, announced Fort Sumter seized by the Yankee garrison. Pickens, our governor,[9] sleeping serenely.

One of the first things which depressed me was the kind of men put in office at this crisis, invariably some sleeping deadhead long forgotten or passed over. Young and active spirits ignored, places for worn-out politicians seemed the rule—when our only hope is to use *all* the talents God has given us. This thing continues. In every state, as each election comes on, they resolutely put aside everything but the inefficient. To go back to Pickens the 1st and South Carolina. Very few understood the consequences of that quiet move of Major Anderson.[1] At first it was looked on as a misfortune. Then, as we saw that it induced the seizure of U.S. forts in other states—we thought it a blessing in disguise. So far we were out in the cold alone. And our wise men say if the president had left us there to fret and fume awhile with a little wholesome neglect, we would have come *back* in time. Certainly nobody would have joined us. But Fort Sumter in Anderson's hands united the cotton states—and we are here in Montgomery to make a new Confederacy—a new government, constitution, &c&c.

I left them hard at it and came on a visit to my mother.

[*We have to meet tremendous odds*]

February 19, 1861.
I left the brand-new Confederacy making—or remodeling—its Constitution. Everybody wanted Mr. Davis[2] to be general in chief or president.

9. Francis Wilkinson Pickens (1805–69) was governor of South Carolina when the state seceded from the United States on January 9, 1861.
1. U.S. Army major (Robert Anderson) who led the U.S. forces holding Fort Sumter.
2. Jefferson Davis (1808–89) served as president of the Confederate States of America.

Keitt and Boyce and a party preferred Howell Cobb for president. And the fire-eaters per se wanted Barnwell Rhett.

Today at dinner, Stephen brought in the officers of the Montgomery Blues.[3]

"Very soiled Blues," they said, apologizing for their rough condition.

Poor fellows! they had been a month before Fort Pickens and not allowed to attack it. They said Colonel Chase built it and he was sure it was impregnable.

Colonel Lomax telegraphed to Governor Moore "if he might try, Chase or no Chase," and got for his answer no.

"And now," say the Blues, "we have worked like niggers—and when the fun and the fighting begins, they send us home and put regulars there."

They have an immense amount of powder along. The wheel of the car in which it was took fire. There was an escape for you!

We are packing a hamper of eatables for them. If they fight as they eat, they are Trojans indeed. Just now they are enjoying a quiet game of billiards.

Colonel Chase insulted them by blazing out a road behind them, in case of a sudden necessity for retreat.

It was not needed, for Stephen took one of his men with him to whom cannon was new. A double-barreled gun was his only experience in firearms. He saw the huge mouth of the cannon, and at the firing of the evening gun he dashed for home, straight as the crow flies, and was there by breakfast, cured forever of all weakness for soldiering. Fifty miles or more!

I am despondent once more. If I thought them in earnest because they put their best in front, *at first*—what now? We have to meet tremendous odds by pluck, activity, zeal, dash, endurance of the toughest, military instinct. We had to choose the born leaders of men, people who could attract love and trust. Everywhere political intrigue is as rife as in Washington.

Somebody likened it to the boys who could not catch up with the carriage, calling out to the coachman, "cut behind," to dislodge the luckier ones. At any rate, I hear it said, "Surely if they believed a war inevitable, very different would be their choice"—and that gives us some hope. Cecil's saying of Sir Walter Raleigh "I know he can labor terribly" is an electric touch.

Clarendon's portraits. These are idlers—they only talk. "Hampden, who was of an industry and vigilance not to be tired out or wearied by the most laborious, and of parts not to be imposed on by the most subtile and sharp, and of a personal courage equal to his best parts. Falkland, who was so severe an adorer of truth that he could as easily have given himself leave to steal as to dissemble."

Above all, let the men to save South Carolina be young and vigorous. While I was cudgeling my brain to say what kind of men we ought to choose, I fell on Clarendon, and it was easy to construct my man out of this material. What has been may be again. So it need not be a purely ideal type.

We keep each other in countenance and exasperate by emulation the frenzy of the time. The shield against the stinging of conscience is the universal practice of our contemporaries.[4]

—EMERSON

Aye—aye—sir—

---

3. The regimental name of a unit from Alabama.   *Seven Lectures* (1850).
4. Ralph W. Emerson's *Representative Men:*

Mr. Toombs told us a story of General Scott and himself a few days before I left Montgomery. He said he was dining in Washington with General Scott, who seasoned every dish and every glass of wine with the eternal refrain "Save the Union"—"The Union must be preserved."

Toombs remarked that he knew why the Union was so dear to the general and illustrated by a steamboat anecdote. An explosion, of course; and while the passengers were struggling in the water, a woman ran up and down the bank, crying, "Oh, save the redheaded man!" The redhead man was saved, and his preserver, after landing him, noticed with surprise how little interest in him the woman who had made such moving appeals seemed to feel. He asked her, "Why did you make that pathetic outcry?" "Oh, he owes me ten thousand dollars." "Now, general, the U.S.A. or the Union owes you seventeen thousand a year."

I can imagine the scorn of old Scott's face.

My husband writes in fine spirits, but the daily bulletins are very contradictory. Down here they did not like the president's message.[5]

1860s–1880s   1981

►►◄ HARRIET E. WILSON ►◄◄
1825?–1900?

Until very recently, the biography of the author of *Our Nig; or, Sketches from the Life of a Free Black, in a Two-Story White House, North, Showing That Slavery's Shadows Fall Even There. By "Our Nig"* was shorter than the title of her book. Her birth date, actual name, death date, and race were obscured by the author's own attempt to be anonymous and by her culture's tendency not to keep track of those who lived on its margins, such as women, blacks, and the poor. Since the republication of the book in the mid-1980s, scholars have pieced together the story of the first African American woman to write a novel. Indeed, *Our Nig* is more than a novel: it quilts together the popular genres of the first half of the nineteenth century into an autobiographical fiction that tells a distinctively American story of an individual's attempt to transcend the contingencies (such as poverty and skin color) that denied dignity to an individual in the complex culture of pre–Civil War New England.

The painstaking efforts of numerous scholarly sleuths have uncovered much about the seemingly obscure H. E. W. who published *Our Nig* in 1859. Harriet Wilson (née Adams) was born in 1825 in Milford, New Hampshire, to a black father who was a barrel hooper and a white mother who had been a washerwoman. Wilson's parents belonged to the large class of itinerant workers who, though largely invisible in writings of that day, performed much of the heavy work of a premechanized society for little pay and less respect. As Wilson depicts in *Our Nig,* such people were often just one illness or accident away from destitution. The children of the destitute, like the protagonist, Frado, in Wilson's novel, were often put to work as formally or informally indentured servants. An indentured servant, while not a slave for life, owed his or her labor for a set period in exchange for basic necessities such as room, board, and rudimentary education.

---

5. Confederate president Davis's inaugural address.

Wilson, abandoned by her widowed mother, was informally indentured to Mr. and Mrs. Hayward of Milford, New Hampshire, when she was six years old. *Our Nig* draws much of its force from the tragic irony that Milford in general and the Hayward family in particular were noted for their anti-slavery leanings. Although Wilson was able to leave service with the Haywards once she turned twenty-one to seek work for pay, the town records list her as a pauper. Like her parents, who "moved on" from Milford in a futile search for better work, Wilson moved to Massachusetts in search of better opportunities. During this time she married, had a child, was deserted by her husband, and was then widowed. Unable, due to poor health, to make enough money to support her child and herself, she moved back to New Hampshire and periodically lived on the county poor farm. *Our Nig* was just one of many attempts to achieve financial independence and self-sufficiency. Although her child died at age six before she succeeded, Wilson did escape the cycle of poverty in the mid-1860s by becoming a noted "medium" in spiritualist circles (see pp. 881–82). As a medium she claimed to facilitate communication between the material and spiritual worlds, offering emotional solace and physical healing to those who sought her help. Dr. Hattie E. Wilson, as she became known, was remarried in 1870 to an apothecary named John Robinson and continued to be active in the spiritualist movement as a celebrated speaker until her death.

Our Nig ends on a hopeful note. The narrator is hopeful that her "experiment" (the text of *Our Nig*) "shall aid me in maintaining myself and my child" and she is hopeful that she will be able to make money from marketing a hair dye. Most of all she expresses faith "in the value of useful books," which have taught her to feel "capable of elevation." The beginning of the book couldn't be more different. Each of the initial three chapters of *Our Nig*, presented here, details the overwhelming odds that Frado is up against: Frado is an heir "of parental disgrace and calumny"; she is abandoned by her mother; and she is of African American descent. These chapters also typify the narrative choices of Wilson, who draws on the New England captivity tale, the American slave narrative, the seduction novel, the domestic novel, and the sentimental lyric to depict the struggle to escape from the shadows of slavery that fall "even there" in a "white-house, north."

From **Our Nig;**

or,

Sketches from the Life of a Free Black

Preface

In offering to the public the following pages, the writer confesses her inability to minister to the refined and cultivated, the pleasure supplied by abler pens. It is not for such these crude narrations appear. Deserted by kindred, disabled by failing health, I am forced to some experiment which shall aid me in maintaining myself and child without extinguishing this feeble life. I would not from these motives even palliate slavery at the South, by disclosures of its appurtenances North. My mistress was wholly imbued with *southern* principles. I do not pretend to divulge every transaction in my own life, which the unprejudiced would declare unfavorable in comparison with treatment of legal bondmen; I have purposely omitted what would most provoke shame in our good anti-slavery friends at home.

My humble position and frank confession of errors will, I hope, shield me from severe criticism. Indeed, defects are so apparent it requires no skilful hand to expose them.

I sincerely appeal to my colored brethren universally for patronage, hoping they will not condemn this attempt of their sister to be erudite, but rally around me a faithful band of supporters and defenders.

H. E. W.

Chapter 1
Mag Smith, My Mother

> Oh, Grief beyond all other griefs, when fate
> First leaves the young heart lone and desolate
> In the wide world, without that only tie
> For which it loved to live or feared to die;
> Lorn as the hung-up lute, that ne'er hath spoken   5
> Since the sad day its master chord was broken!
>
> —MOORE.[1]

Lonely Mag Smith! See her as she walks with downcast eyes and heavy heart. It was not always thus. She *had* a loving, trusting heart. Early deprived of parental guardianship, far removed from relatives, she was left to guide her tiny boat over life's surges alone and inexperienced. As she merged into womanhood, unprotected, uncherished, uncared for, there fell on her ear the music of love, awakening an intensity of emotion long dormant. It whispered of an elevation before unaspired to; of ease and plenty her simple heart had never dreamed of as hers. She knew the voice of her charmer, so ravishing, sounded far above her. It seemed like an angel's, alluring her upward and onward. She thought she could ascend to him and become an equal. She surrendered to him a priceless gem, which he proudly garnered as a trophy, with those of other victims, and left her to her fate. The world seemed full of hateful deceivers and crushing arrogance. Conscious that the great bond of union to her former companions was severed, that the disdain of others would be insupportable, she determined to leave the few friends she possessed, and seek an asylum among strangers. Her offspring came unwelcomed, and before its nativity numbered weeks, it passed from earth, ascending to a purer and better life.

"God be thanked," ejaculated Mag, as she saw its breathing cease; "no one can taunt *her* with my ruin."

Blessed release! may we all respond. How many pure, innocent children not only inherit a wicked heart of their own, claiming life-long scrutiny and restraint, but are heirs also of parental disgrace and calumny, from which only long years of patient endurance in paths of rectitude can disencumber them.

Mag's new home was soon contaminated by the publicity of her fall; she had a feeling of degradation oppressing her; but she resolved to be circumspect, and

1. From "The Veiled Prophet of Khorassan"   Moore (1779–1852).
in *Lalla Rookh* (1817) by Irish poet Thomas

try to regain in a measure what she had lost. Then some foul tongue would jest of her shame, and averted looks and cold greetings disheartened her. She saw she could not bury in forgetfulness her misdeed, so she resolved to leave her home and seek another in the place she at first fled from.

Alas, how fearful are we to be first in extending a helping hand to those who stagger in the mires of infamy; to speak the first words of hope and warning to those emerging into the sunlight of morality! Who can tell what numbers, advancing just far enough to hear a cold welcome and join in the reserved converse of professed reformers, disappointed, disheartened, have chosen to dwell in unclean places, rather than encounter these "holier-than-thou" of the great brotherhood of man!

Such was Mag's experience; and disdaining to ask favor or friendship from a sneering world, she resolved to shut herself up in a hovel she had often passed in better days, and which she knew to be untenanted. She vowed to ask no favors of familiar faces; to die neglected and forgotten before she would be dependent on any. Removed from the village, she was seldom seen except as upon your introduction, gentle reader, with downcast visage, returning her work to her employer, and thus providing herself with the means of subsistence. In two years many hands craved the same avocation; foreigners who cheapened toil and clamored for a livelihood, competed with her, and she could not thus sustain herself. She was now above no drudgery. Occasionally old acquaintances called to be favored with help of some kind, which she was glad to bestow for the sake of the money it would bring her; but the association with them was such a painful reminder of bygones, she returned to her hut morose and revengeful, refusing all offers of a better home than she possessed. Thus she lived for years, hugging her wrongs, but making no effort to escape. She had never known plenty, scarcely competency; but the present was beyond comparison with those innocent years when the coronet of virtue was hers.

Every year her melancholy increased, her means diminished. At last no one seemed to notice her, save a kind-hearted African, who often called to inquire after her health and to see if she needed any fuel, he having the responsibility of furnishing that article, and she in return mending or making garments.

"How much you earn dis week, Mag?" asked he one Saturday evening.

"Little enough, Jim. Two or three days without any dinner. I washed for the Reeds, and did a small job for Mrs. Bellmont; that's all. I shall starve soon, unless I can get more to do. Folks seem as afraid to come here as if they expected to get some awful disease. I don't believe there is a person in the world but would be glad to have me dead and out of the way."

"No, no, Mag! don't talk so. You shan't starve so long as I have barrels to hoop. Peter Greene boards me cheap. I'll help you, if nobody else will."

A tear stood in Mag's faded eye. "I'm glad," she said, with a softer tone than before, "if there is *one* who isn't glad to see me suffer. I b'lieve all Singleton wants to see me punished, and feel as if they could tell when I've been punished long enough. It's a long day ahead they'll set it, I reckon."

After the usual supply of fuel was prepared, Jim returned home. Full of pity for Mag, he set about devising measures for her relief. "By golly!" said he to himself one day—for he had become so absorbed in Mag's interest that he had fallen into a habit of musing aloud—"By golly! I wish she'd *marry* me."

"Who?" shouted Pete Greene, suddenly starting from an unobserved corner of the rude shop.

"Where you come from, you sly nigger!" exclaimed Jim.

"Come, tell me, who is't?" said Pete; "Mag Smith, you want to marry?"

"Git out, Pete! And when you come in dis shop again, let a nigger know it. Don't steal in like a thief."

Pity and love know little severance. One attends the other. Jim acknowledged the presence of the former, and his efforts in Mag's behalf told also of a finer principle.

This sudden expedient which he had unintentionally disclosed, roused his thinking and inventive powers to study upon the best method of introducing the subject to Mag.

He belted his barrels, with many a scheme revolving in his mind, none of which quite satisfied him, or seemed, on the whole, expedient. He thought of the pleasing contrast between her fair face and his own dark skin; the smooth, straight hair, which he had once, in expression of pity, kindly stroked on her now wrinkled but once fair brow. There was a tempest gathering in his heart, and at last, to ease his pent-up passion, he exclaimed aloud, "By golly!" Recollecting his former exposure, he glanced around to see if Pete was in hearing again. Satisfied on this point, he continued: "She'd be as much of a prize to me as she'd fall short of coming up to the mark with white folks. I don't care for past things. I've done things 'fore now I's 'shamed of. She's good enough for me, any how."

One more glance about the premises to be sure Pete was away.

The next Saturday night brought Jim to the hovel again. The cold was fast coming to tarry its apportioned time. Mag was nearly despairing of meeting its rigor.

"How's the wood, Mag?" asked Jim.

"All gone; and no more to cut, any how," was the reply.

"Too bad!" Jim said. His truthful reply would have been, I'm glad.

"Anything to eat in the house?" continued he.

"No," replied Mag.

"Too bad!" again, orally, with the same *inward* gratulation as before.

"Well, Mag," said Jim, after a short pause, "you's down low enough. I don't see but I've got to take care of ye. 'Sposin' we marry!"

Mag raised her eyes, full of amazement, and uttered a sonorous "What?"

Jim felt abashed for a moment. He knew well what were her objections.

"You's had trial of white folks, any how. They run off and left ye, and now none of 'em come near ye to see if you's dead or alive. I's black outside, I know, but I's got a white heart inside. Which you rather have, a black heart in a white skin, or a white heart in a black one?"

"Oh, dear!" sighed Mag; "Nobody on earth cares for *me*—"

"I do," interrupted Jim.

"I can do but two things," said she, "beg my living, or get it from you."

"Take me, Mag. I can give you a better home than this, and not let you suffer so."

He prevailed; they married. You can philosophize, gentle reader, upon the impropriety of such unions, and preach dozens of sermons on the evils of amalgamation![2] Want is a more powerful philosopher and preacher. Poor Mag. She has

2. Early-nineteenth-century term for interracial marriage.

sundered another bond which held her to her fellows. She has descended another step down the ladder of infamy.

Chapter 2
My Father's Death

Misery! we have known each other,
Like a sister and a brother,
Living in the same lone home
Many years—we must live some
Hours or ages yet to come.   5

—SHELLEY.[3]

Jim, proud of his treasure,—a white wife,—tried hard to fulfil his promises; and furnished her with a more comfortable dwelling, diet, and apparel. It was comparatively a comfortable winter she passed after her marriage. When Jim could work, all went on well. Industrious, and fond of Mag, he was determined she should not regret her union to him. Time levied an additional charge upon him, in the form of two pretty mulattos, whose infantile pranks amply repaid the additional toil. A few years, and a severe cough and pain in his side compelled him to be an idler for weeks together, and Mag had thus a reminder of by-gones. She cared for him only as a means to subserve her own comfort; yet she nursed him faithfully and true to marriage vows till death released her. He became the victim of consumption.[4] He loved Mag to the last. So long as life continued, he stifled his sensibility to pain, and toiled for her sustenance long after he was able to do so.

A few expressive wishes for her welfare; a hope of better days for her; an anxiety lest they should not all go to the "good place;" brief advice about their children; a hope expressed that Mag would not be neglected as she used to be; the manifestation of Christian patience; these were *all* the legacy of miserable Mag. A feeling of cold desolation came over her, as she turned from the grave of one who had been truly faithful to her.

She was now expelled from companionship with white people; this last step— her union with a black—was the climax of repulsion.

Seth Shipley, a partner in Jim's business, wished her to remain in her present home; but she declined, and returned to her hovel again, with obstacles threefold more insurmountable than before. Seth accompanied her, giving her a weekly allowance which furnished most of the food necessary for the four inmates. After a time, work failed; their means were reduced.

How Mag toiled and suffered, yielding to fits of desperation, bursts of anger, and uttering curses too fearful to repeat. When both were supplied with work, they prospered; if idle, they were hungry together. In this way their interests became united; they planned for the future together. Mag had lived an outcast for years. She had ceased to feel the gushings of penitence; she had crushed the sharp agonies of an awakened conscience. She had no longings for a purer heart, a better life. Far easier to descend lower. She entered the darkness of perpetual infamy. She asked not the rite of civilization or Christianity. Her will made her the wife of Seth. Soon followed scenes familiar and trying.

---

3. From the poem "Invocation to Misery" (1832)   4. Nineteenth-century term for tuberculosis.
by English poet Percy Bysshe Shelley (1792–1822).

"It's no use," said Seth one day; "we must give the children away, and try to get work in some other place."

"Who'll take the black devils?" snarled Mag.

"They're none of mine," said Seth; "what you growling about?"

"Nobody will want any thing of mine, or yours either," she replied.

"We'll make 'em, p'r'aps," he said. "There's Frado's six years old, and pretty, if she is yours, and white folks'll say so. She'd be a prize somewhere," he continued, tipping his chair back against the wall, and placing his feet upon the rounds, as if he had much more to say when in the right position.

Frado, as they called one of Mag's children, was a beautiful mulatto, with long, curly black hair, and handsome, roguish eyes, sparkling with an exuberance of spirit almost beyond restraint.

Hearing her name mentioned, she looked up from her play, to see what Seth had to say of her.

"Wouldn't the Bellmonts take her?" asked Seth.

"Bellmonts?" shouted Mag. "His wife is a right she-devil! and if—"

"Hadn't they better be all together?" interrupted Seth, reminding her of a like epithet used in reference to her little ones.

Without seeming to notice him, she continued, "She can't keep a girl in the house over a week; and Mr. Bellmont wants to hire a boy to work for him, but he can't find one that will live in the house with her; she's so ugly, they can't."

"Well, we've got to make a move soon," answered Seth; "if you go with me, we shall go right off. Had you rather spare the other one?" asked Seth, after a short pause.

"One's as bad as t'other," replied Mag. "Frado is such a wild, frolicky thing, and means to do jest as she's a mind to; she won't go if she don't want to. I don't want to tell her she is to be given away."

"I will," said Seth. "Come here, Frado?"

The child seemed to have some dim foreshadowing of evil, and declined.

"Come here," he continued; "I want to tell you something."

She came reluctantly. He took her hand and said: "We're going to move, by-'m-bye; will you go?"

"No!" screamed she; and giving a sudden jerk which destroyed Seth's equilibrium, left him sprawling on the floor, while she escaped through the open door.

"She's a hard one," said Seth, brushing his patched coat sleeve. "I'd risk her at Bellmont's."

They discussed the expediency of a speedy departure. Seth would first seek employment, and then return for Mag. They would take with them what they could carry, and leave the rest with Pete Greene, and come for them when they were wanted. They were long in arranging affairs satisfactorily, and were not a little startled at the close of their conference to find Frado missing. They thought approaching night would bring her. Twilight passed into darkness, and she did not come. They thought she had understood their plans, and had, perhaps, permanently withdrawn. They could not rest without making some effort to ascertain her retreat. Seth went in pursuit, and returned without her. They rallied others when they discovered that another little colored girl was missing, a favorite playmate of Frado's. All effort proved unavailing. Mag felt sure her fears were realized, and that she might never see her again. Before her anxieties became realities, both were safely returned, and from them and their attendant they learned that they went to walk, and not minding the direction soon found themselves lost. They had climbed fences and walls, passed through thickets and marshes, and when night approached selected a thick cluster of shrubbery as a covert for the night. They were discovered by the person who now restored them, chatting of their prospects, Frado attempting to banish the childish fears of her companion. As they were some miles from home, they were kindly cared for until morning. Mag was relieved to know her child was not driven to desperation by their intentions to relieve themselves of her, and she was inclined to think severe restraint would be healthful.

The removal was all arranged; the few days necessary for such migrations passed quickly, and one bright summer morning they bade farewell to their Singleton hovel, and with budgets and bundles commenced their weary march. As they neared the village, they heard the merry shouts of children gathered around the schoolroom, awaiting the coming of their teacher.

"Halloo!" screamed one, "Black, white and yeller!" "Black, white and yeller,"[5] echoed a dozen voices.

It did not grate so harshly on poor Mag as once it would. She did not even turn her head to look at them. She had passed into an insensibility no childish taunt could penetrate, else she would have reproached herself as she passed familiar scenes, for extending the separation once so easily annihilated by steadfast integrity. Two miles beyond lived the Bellmonts, in a large, old fashioned, two-story white house, environed by fruitful acres, and embellished by shrubbery and shade trees. Years ago a youthful couple consecrated it as home; and after many little feet had worn paths to favorite fruit trees, and over its green hills, and mingled at last with brother man in the race which belongs neither to the swift or strong, the sire became gray-haired and decrepid, and went to his last repose. His aged consort soon followed him. The old homestead thus passed into the hands of a son, to whose wife Mag applied the epithet "she devil," as may be remembered. John, the son, had not in his family arrangements departed from the example of the father. The pastimes of his boyhood were ever freshly revived by witnessing the games of his own sons as they rallied about the same goal his youthful feet had often won; as well as by the amusements of his daughters in their imitations of maternal duties.

At the time we introduce them, however, John is wearing the badge of age. Most of his children were from home; some seeking employment; some were already settled in homes of their own. A maiden sister shared with him the estate on which he resided, and occupied a portion of the house.

Within sight of the house, Seth seated himself with his bundles and the child he had been leading, while Mag walked onward to the house leading Frado. A knock at the door brought Mrs. Bellmont, and Mag asked if she would be willing to let that child stop there while she went to the Reed's house to wash, and when she came back she would call and get her. It seemed a novel request, but she consented. Why the impetuous child entered the house, we cannot tell; the door closed, and Mag hastily departed. Frado waited for the close of day, which was to bring back her mother. Alas! it never came. It was the last time she ever saw or heard of her mother.

5. Yellow.

Chapter 3
A New Home for Me

Oh! did we but know of the shadows so nigh,
    The world would indeed be a prison of gloom;
All light would be quenched in youth's eloquent eye,
    And the prayer-lisping infant would ask for the tomb.

For if Hope be a star that may lead us astray,
    And "deceiveth the heart," as the aged ones preach;
Yet 'twas Mercy that gave it, to beacon our way,
    Though its halo illumes where it never can reach.

—ELIZA COOK.[6]

As the day closed and Mag did not appear, surmises were expressed by the family that she never intended to return. Mr. Bellmont was a kind, humane man, who would not grudge hospitality to the poorest wanderer, nor fail to sympathize with any sufferer, however humble. The child's desertion by her mother appealed to his sympathy, and he felt inclined to succor her. To do this in opposition to Mrs. Bellmont's wishes, would be like encountering a whirlwind charged with fire, daggers and spikes. She was not as susceptible of fine emotions as her spouse. Mag's opinion of her was not without foundation. She was self-willed, haughty, undisciplined, arbitrary and severe. In common parlance, she was a *scold*, a thorough one. Mr. B. remained silent during the consultation which follows, engaged in by mother, Mary and John, or Jack, as he was familiarly called.

"Send her to the County House,"[7] said Mary, in reply to the query what should be done with her, in a tone which indicated self-importance in the speaker. She was indeed the idol of her mother, and more nearly resembled her in disposition and manners than the others.

Jane, an invalid daughter, the eldest of those at home, was reclining on a sofa apparently uninterested.

"Keep her," said Jack. "She's real handsome and bright, and not very black, either."

"Yes," rejoined Mary; "that's just like you, Jack. She'll be of no use at all these three years, right under foot all the time."

"Poh! Miss Mary; if she should stay, it wouldn't be two days before you would be telling the girls about *our nig, our nig!*" retorted Jack.

"I don't want a nigger 'round *me*, do you, mother?" asked Mary.

"I don't mind the nigger in the child. I should like a dozen better than one," replied her mother. "If I could make her do my work in a few years, I would keep her. I have so much trouble with girls I hire, I am almost persuaded if I have one to train up in my way from a child, I shall be able to keep them awhile. I am tired of changing every few months."

"Where could she sleep?" asked Mary. "I don't want her near me."

"In the L chamber," answered the mother.

6. Eliza Cook (1817–89), a popular English poet, frequently published in newspapers and magazines associated with reform movements.

7. An institution for caring for the indigent by providing a home and source of work.

"How'll she get there?" asked Jack. "She'll be afraid to go through that dark passage, and she can't climb the ladder safely."

"She'll have to go there; it's good enough for a nigger," was the reply.

Jack was sent on horseback to ascertain if Mag was at her home. He returned with the testimony of Pete Greene that they were fairly departed, and that the child was intentionally thrust upon their family.

The imposition was not at all relished by Mrs. B., or the pert, haughty Mary, who had just glided into her teens.

"Show the child to bed, Jack," said his mother. "You seem most pleased with the little nigger, so you may introduce her to her room."

He went to the kitchen, and, taking Frado gently by the hand, told her he would put her in bed now; perhaps her mother would come the next night after her.

It was not yet quite dark, so they ascended the stairs without any light, passing through nicely furnished rooms, which were a source of great amazement to the child. He opened the door which connected with her room by a dark, unfinished passageway. "Don't bump your head," said Jack, and stepped before to open the door leading into her apartment,—an unfinished chamber over the kitchen, the roof slanting nearly to the floor, so that the bed could stand only in the middle of the room. A small half window furnished light and air. Jack returned to the sitting room with the remark that the child would soon outgrow those quarters.

"When she *does*, she'll outgrow the house," remarked the mother.

"What can she do to help you?" asked Mary. "She came just in the right time, didn't she? Just the very day after Bridget[8] left," continued she.

"I'll see what she can do in the morning," was the answer.

While this conversation was passing below, Frado lay, revolving in her little mind whether she would remain or not until her mother's return. She was of wilful, determined nature, a stranger to fear, and would not hesitate to wander away should she decide to. She remembered the conversation of her mother with Seth, the words "given away" which she heard used in reference to herself; and though she did not know their full import, she thought she should, by remaining, be in some relation to white people she was never favored with before. So she resolved to tarry, with the hope that mother would come and get her some time. The hot sun had penetrated her room, and it was long before a cooling breeze reduced the temperature so that she could sleep.

Frado was called early in the morning by her new mistress. Her first work was to feed the hens. She was shown how it was *always* to be done, and in no other way; any departure from this rule to be punished by whipping. She was then accompanied by Jack to drive the cows to pasture, so she might learn the way. Upon her return she was allowed to eat her breakfast, consisting of a bowl of skimmed milk, with brown bread crusts, which she was told to eat, standing, by the kitchen table, and must not be over ten minutes about it. Meanwhile the family were taking their morning meal in the dining-room. This over, she was placed on a cricket[9] to wash the common dishes; she was to be in waiting always to bring wood and chips, to run hither and thither from room to room.

A large amount of dish-washing for small hands followed dinner. Then the same after tea and going after the cows finished her first day's work. It was a new

---

8. A typical Irish name. The previous servant had been an Irishwoman.

9. Low stool.

discipline to the child. She found some attractions about the place, and she retired to rest at night more willing to remain. The same routine followed day after day, with slight variation; adding a little more work, and spicing the toil with "words that burn," and frequent blows on her head. These were great annoyances to Frado, and had she known where her mother was, she would have gone at once to her. She often greatly wearied, and silently wept over her sad fate. At first she wept aloud, which Mrs. Bellmont noticed by applying a raw-hide,[1] always at hand in the kitchen. It was a symptom of discontent and complaining which must be "nipped in the bud," she said.

Thus passed a year. No intelligence of Mag. It was now certain Frado was to become a permanent member of the family. Her labors were multiplied; she was quite indispensable, although but seven years old. She had never learned to read, never heard of a school until her residence in the family.

Mrs. Bellmont was in doubt about the utility of attempting to educate people of color, who were incapable of elevation. This subject occasioned a lengthy discussion in the family. Mr. Bellmont, Jane and Jack arguing for Frado's education; Mary and her mother objecting. At last Mr. Bellmont declared decisively that she *should* go to school. He was a man who seldom decided controversies at home. The word once spoken admitted of no appeal; so, notwithstanding Mary's objection that she would have to attend the same school she did, the word became law.

It was to be a new scene to Frado, and Jack had many queries and conjectures to answer. He was himself too far advanced to attend the summer school, which Frado regretted, having had too many opportunities of witnessing Miss Mary's temper to feel safe in her company alone.

The opening day of school came. Frado sauntered on far in the rear of Mary, who was ashamed to be seen "walking with a nigger." As soon as she appeared, with scanty clothing and bared feet, the children assembled, noisily published her approach: "See that nigger," shouted one. "Look! look!" cried another. "I won't play with her," said one little girl. "Nor I neither," replied another.

Mary evidently relished these sharp attacks, and saw a fair prospect of lowering Nig where, according to her views, she belonged. Poor Frado, chagrined and grieved, felt that her anticipations of pleasure at such a place were far from being realized. She was just deciding to return home, and never come there again, when the teacher appeared, and observing the downcast looks of the child, took her by the hand, and led her into the school-room. All followed, and, after the bustle of securing seats was over, Miss Marsh inquired if the children knew "any cause for the sorrow of that little girl?" pointing to Frado. It was soon all told. She then reminded them of their duties to the poor and friendless; their cowardice in attacking a young innocent child; referred them to one who looks not on outward appearances, but on the heart. "She looks like a good girl; I think *I* shall love her, so lay aside all prejudice, and vie with each other in shewing kindness and goodwill to one who seems different from you," were the closing remarks of the kind lady. Those kind words! The most agreeable sound which ever meets the ear of sorrowing, grieving childhood.

Example rendered her words efficacious. Day by day there was a manifest change of deportment towards "Nig." Her speeches often drew merriment from the children; no one could do more to enliven their favorite pastimes than Frado.

---

1. A whip made of untanned and therefore stiff leather.

Mary could not endure to see her thus noticed, yet knew not how to prevent it. She could not influence her schoolmates as she wished. She had not gained their affections by winning ways and yielding points of controversy. On the contrary, she was self-willed, domineering; every day reported "mad" by some of her companions. She availed herself of the only alternative, abuse and taunts, as they returned from school. This was not satisfactory; she wanted to use physical force "to subdue her," to "keep her down."

There was, on their way home, a field intersected by a stream over which a single plank was placed for a crossing. It occurred to Mary that it would be a punishment to Nig to compel her to cross over; so she dragged her to the edge, and told her authoritatively to go over. Nig hesitated, resisted. Mary placed herself behind the child, and, in the struggle to force her over, lost her footing and plunged into the stream. Some of the larger scholars being in sight, ran, and thus prevented Mary from drowning and Frado from falling. Nig scampered home fast as possible, and Mary went to the nearest house, dripping, to procure a change of garments. She came loitering home, half crying, exclaiming, "Nig pushed me into the stream!" She then related the particulars. Nig was called from the kitchen. Mary stood with anger flashing in her eyes. Mr. Bellmont sat quietly reading his paper. He had witnessed too many of Miss Mary's outbreaks to be startled. Mrs. Bellmont interrogated Nig.

"I didn't do it! I didn't do it!" answered Nig, passionately, and then related the occurrence truthfully.

The discrepancy greatly enraged Mrs. Bellmont. With loud accusations and angry gestures she approached the child. Turning to her husband, she asked, "Will you sit still, there, and hear that black nigger call Mary a liar?"

"How do we know but she has told the truth? I shall not punish her," he replied, and left the house, as he usually did when a tempest threatened to envelop him. No sooner was he out of sight than Mrs. B. and Mary commenced beating her inhumanly; then propping her mouth open with a piece of wood, shut her up in a dark room, without any supper. For employment, while the tempest raged within, Mr. Bellmont went for the cows, a task belonging to Frado, and thus unintentionally prolonged her pain. At dark Jack came in, and seeing Mary, accosted her with, "So you thought you'd vent your spite on Nig, did you? Why can't you let her alone? It was good enough for you to get a ducking, only you did not stay in half long enough."

"Stop!" said his mother. "You shall never talk so before me. You would have that little nigger trample on Mary, would you? She came home with a lie; it made Mary's story false."

"What was Mary's story?" asked Jack.

It was related.

"Now," said Jack, sallying into a chair, "the school-children happened to see it all, and they tell the same story Nig does. Which is most likely to be true, what a dozen agree they saw, or the contrary?"

"It was very strange you will believe what others say against your sister," retorted his mother, with flashing eye. "I think it is time your father subdued you."

"Father is a sensible man," argued Jack. "He would not wrong a dog. Where *is* Frado?" he continued.

"Mother gave her a good whipping and shut her up," replied Mary.

Just then Mr. Bellmont entered, and asked if Frado was "shut up yet."

The knowledge of her innocence, the perfidy of his sister, worked fearfully on Jack. He bounded from his chair, searched every room till he found the child; her mouth wedged apart, her face swollen, and full of pain.

How Jack pitied her! He relieved her jaws, brought her some supper, took her to her room, comforted her as well as he knew how, sat by her till she fell asleep, and then left for the sitting room. As he passed his mother, he remarked, "If that was the way Frado was to be treated, he hoped she would never wake again!" He then imparted her situation to his father, who seemed untouched, till a glance at Jack exposed a tearful eye. Jack went early to her next morning. She awoke sad, but refreshed. After breakfast Jack took her with him to the field, and kept her through the day. But it could not be so generally. She must return to school, to her household duties. He resolved to do what he could to protect her from Mary and his mother. He bought her a dog, which became a great favorite with both. The invalid, Jane, would gladly befriend her; but she had not the strength to brave the iron will of her mother. Kind words and affectionate glances were the only expressions of sympathy she could safely indulge in. The men employed on the farm were always glad to hear her prattle; she was a great favorite with them. Mrs. Bellmont allowed them the privilege of talking with her in the kitchen. She did not fear but she should have ample opportunity of subduing her when they were away. Three months of schooling, summer and winter, she enjoyed for three years. Her winter over-dress was a cast-off overcoat, once worn by Jack, and a sun-bonnet. It was a source of great merriment to the scholars, but Nig's retorts were so mirthful, and their satisfaction so evident in attributing the selection to "Old Granny Bellmont," that it was not painful to Nig or pleasurable to Mary. Her jollity was not to be quenched by whipping or scolding. In Mrs. Bellmont's presence she was under restraint; but in the kitchen, and among her schoolmates, the pent up fires burst forth. She was ever at some sly prank when unseen by her teacher, in school hours; not unfrequently some outburst of merriment, of which she was the original, was charged upon some innocent mate, and punishment inflicted which she merited. They enjoyed her antics so fully that any of them would suffer wrongfully to keep open the avenues of mirth. She would venture far beyond propriety, thus shielded and countenanced.

The teacher's desk was supplied with drawers, in which were stored his books and other *et ceteras* of the profession. The children observed Nig very busy there one morning before school, as they flitted in occasionally from their play outside. The master came; called the children to order; opened a drawer to take the book the occasion required; when out poured a volume of smoke. "Fire! fire!" screamed he, at the top of his voice. By this time he had become sufficiently acquainted with the peculiar odor, to know he was imposed upon. The scholars shouted with laughter to see the terror of the dupe, who, feeling abashed at the needless fright, made no very strict investigation, and Nig once more escaped punishment. She had provided herself with cigars, and puffing, puffing away at the crack of the drawer, had filled it with smoke, and then closed it tightly to deceive the teacher, and amuse the scholars. The interim of terms was filled up with a variety of duties new and peculiar. At home, no matter how powerful the heat when sent to rake hay or guard the grazing herd, she was never permitted to shield her skin from the sun. She was not many shades darker than Mary now; what a calamity it would be ever to hear the contrast spoken of. Mrs. Bellmont was determined the sun should have full power to darken the shade which nature had first bestowed upon her as best befitting.

1859

---◄••◄ CATHERINE HELEN SPENCE ►••►---

1825–1910

Born and educated in Scotland, Catherine Helen Spence emigrated with her parents (David and Helen Brodie Spence) to South Australia when she was fourteen years old. David Spence, a lawyer, had speculated disastrously in wheat and lost his family's fortune. Although her father's financial failure was the motive for the move to Adelaide—where the family spent seven very difficult months living in a tent—Spence came to love Australia and claimed it as her home.

Novelist, journalist, and activist, Spence never married. She distinguished herself by accomplishing a number of "firsts": *Clara Morison* (1854), her novelistic debut, was the first novel both set in Australia and written by a woman. Spence became Australia's first female candidate for political office, in 1897. She also wrote the first social studies textbook to be adopted by Australian schools, *The Laws We Live Under* (1880). Her relocation at a young age from Scotland offered her opportunities for independence and innovation that might have been more difficult to attain in Great Britain.

All her life, Spence wrote. She began her career as a governess in Australia at the age of seventeen, working in her limited spare time at her craft. Beginning in 1846, she taught in a school with her sister and wrote regularly for the local newspaper. Her journalism reflected her strong political and religious views. She was an avid supporter of women's rights and argued for female suffrage and women's economic equality with men. Although she had been raised in a fire-and-brimstone religious tradition, she became a Unitarian, finding in its more rationalist teachings a faith she could embrace. She preached in the Unitarian church at a time when female preachers were unheard of.

Published when Spence was twenty-nine, *Clara Morison: A Tale of South Australia during the Gold Fever* is a domestic romance, following the fortunes of a middle-class, nineteen-year-old orphan. Clara's uncle separates her from her sister and sends her "sixteen thousand miles off" to Australia to work as a governess. Unable to secure a position suited to her education and social class, Clara decides to take a job as a "maid of all work," disqualifying herself for social contact with colonists of "respectable" status. Although the novel follows a conventional marriage plot, it also offers an unusual example of a secondary female character who is content to remain unmarried. It was the first of six novels Spence was to complete, though two of them (*Gathered In*, 1881–82, published 1977; *Handfasted*, 1879, published 1984) could not be published during her lifetime because their overtly feminist content was too strong for her contemporaries. She was working on her autobiography when she died; her companion, Jeanne F. Young, completed and published it in 1910.

From Clara Morison

Chapter 8
At Service[1]

When young ladies in novels are set to any work to which they are unaccustomed, it is surprising how instantaneously they always get over all the difficulties before them. They row boats without feeling fatigued, they scale walls, they rein in restive horses, they can lift the most ponderous articles, though they are of the most delicate and fragile constitutions, and have never had such things to do in their lives.

It was not so with Clara, however. She found the work dreadfully hard, and by no means fascinating; and though she was willing and anxious even to painfulness, the memory that had tenaciously kept hold of hard names and dates, which her father had trusted to as to an encyclopædia, seemed utterly to fail her in recollecting when saucepans were to be put on and taken off, and every day brought the same puzzling uncertainty as to how plates and dishes were to be arranged at the breakfast and dinner-table, which Mrs. Bantam had more than once shown her, with a particular desire that she should do it exactly in the same way.

Then she was very awkward at lighting a fire, and would often let it go out black just when it was most wanted. The camp-oven[2] was a perfect heart-break to her, for she could never hit upon any medium between scorching heat and lukewarmness. Mrs. Bantam said that every new comer from England was awkward with the wood-fires and the camp-oven at first, so she excused her; but Clara knew that she should have been no better if the fires had been of coal, and the oven the newest invented patent cooking apparatus, but this opinion she prudently kept to herself.

She made a considerable smashing of crockery the first week; next week she scalded her arm pretty severely, and felt almost unable to move it for two days; the third week she was becoming more fit to be trusted, but yet she was conscious that if Mrs. Bantam had not been a paragon of good nature she would not have patience with her even for the month that she got no wages. And as for her work ever being done, she never could see over the top of it. Mrs. Bantam came into the kitchen every day to bring up arrears, and Clara with hopeless admiration saw her quietly put one thing after another out of her hands finished.

"I am afraid I shall never learn," said Clara to her mistress one day. "I am sorry I am so dreadfully stupid."

"I dare say you will learn in time, though you seem determined to take your time to it, Clara; but where in all the world can you have been brought up to be so helpless. I do not know a young *lady* in the colony so ignorant of all household matters.[3] The people next door, whom you see sometimes in the back yard, keep no servant, and do all their own work, but yet every body knows the Miss Elliots are ladies, though I do not visit them myself."

---

1. Clara has agreed to work at Mrs. Bantam's house for one month at no pay while her employer teaches her to do housework.
2. Cast-iron oven used for cooking in the Australian bush.
3. Mrs. Bantam does not know that Clara was raised in Scotland.

"I am heartily ashamed of my ignorance," said Clara, "but I was a spoilt child at home, and am suffering for it now. I fear you do not think me anxious to do right from the many failures I make."

"You are too anxious, I think, and get nervous. Keep yourself cooler in future, and you will do better."

Clara endeavoured to keep herself cooler during the last week of her month's probation, for she was very anxious to remain with Mrs. Bantam. It seemed to be a quiet place, and neither her master nor mistress was unreasonable. She was too busy to feel her solitary kitchen dull, and though she ached all over every morning from the exertions of the preceding day, that was preferable to the headache which Mrs. Handy's young gentlemen had inflicted upon her every evening.[4] She was subjected to no impertinence; the butcher and baker called her "Miss" when they came with their commodities; Mrs. Bantam did not send her out on many errands, and though waiting at table was a humiliating piece of work, there had been no strangers as yet to make her feel it deeply.

The month having expired, Mrs. Bantam was of opinion that though a very great deal was yet to be learned, some progress had been made; and offered Clara four shillings[5] a week to stay. "You are nothing of a servant," said she, "but you are civil and honest, so I will try you a little longer. If you would only learn to be methodical you would suit me."

Clara was grateful and happy, and sat down forthwith to write to her uncle, in order to give him a clear statement of the new position in which she was placed. She had not considered it advisable to write on the subject till the month of trial had expired. To Susan she would have written on the same day, but could not find time, and was forced to delay it till the next Sunday evening, when she entered into detail, describing her mode of life at Mrs. Handy's, her two unsuccessful attempts at getting a situation as governess, and her final settlement as maid of all work, with a very kind lady.

"Do not fancy that it is so very dreadful, my dear sister, or that I am completely miserable. I am determined to be happy if it is possible, and though now I feel the toil fatiguing, because I am new to bodily labour, in time I shall feel it nothing, and have leisure in the long winter evenings which are coming on to read and to write to you.

"The house I am living in is situated in a little garden; it is a real cottage of one story, which almost all the houses in Adelaide are, with only a trap ladder leading up to the little attic where I sleep. I have a fine view of the hills from my bed-room window, and now that the great heat has moderated I think the climate delightful. I still sleep with my window open that I may have enough of fresh air, and it is no uncommon thing in summer for people to leave all their doors and windows open through the night. I think that shows that the colony must be an honest place; but you must always bear in mind that this never has been a penal settlement.[6]

"I do not think you would fancy the trees here, at least taken separately. They are evergreens, and looked fresh when everything else was burnt up, but now the newly sprung grass makes them look rather lugubrious. They are somewhat

4. Clara previously had lived at Mrs. Handy's boardinghouse, where young men teased her with inappropriate jokes.

5. In British money of the time, worth about $25 today.

6. Other Australian cities were founded as penal colonies, where transported British prisoners served their sentences.

scraggy, and the bark is white on the greater proportion of the trees around the town, which gives them quite a ghostly appearance by moonlight. There are a few near the river Torrens[7] which look really pretty, and I have been told that in the bush there are much finer trees than in the neighbourhood of town. They say that South Australian wood, being of slow growth, and consequently very hard, makes the best fuel possible, but I find it no easy matter to kindle it, and am always getting splinters of it in my hands; but of course I shall learn to do better soon.

"I suppose that when you receive this you will be in London with my uncle and aunt to see the world, and to wonder at the Great Exhibition.[8] But, Susan, I am seeing life, and learning lessons which I hope I shall never forget; it is not merely the things I am learning to do, useful as they undoubtedly are, but the new thoughts and feelings which my present employments awaken, which will benefit me much. I have hitherto lived too much in books, and thought them all-important; now I see what things fill the minds of nine-tenths of my sex—daily duties, daily cares, daily sacrifices. I see now the line of demarcation which separates the employers from the employed; and if I ever, by any chance, should again have a servant under me, I shall surely understand her feelings, and be considerate and kind. How I reproach myself now for the unnecessary trouble I used to give our good faithful Peggy and Helen, and all through want of thought.

"So again I say, do not pity me much; feel for me a little, but rest assured that these little trials I meet with will do a great deal of good to

"Your most affectionate sister,
"Clara."

Mrs. Bantam at last found Clara useful. If she learned slowly it was surely; and at the end of three months she was really a tolerable servant—not a strong one, but industrious and tidy. She often speculated upon the girls next door. There were three of them. They must be Scotch, for they were always singing Scotch ballads, and they went to the Scotch Church.[9]

They were all very comely, if not positively pretty, and in spite of the work they had to do Clara would have known them to be ladies even if Mrs. Bantam had not told her so. Their two brothers went to business in the morning, and returned in the evening, and Clara would sometimes see one or two of the sisters meeting them at the gate, and bringing them into the house through the little garden. They had a piano, and used to play and sing in the evenings; sometimes Clara would go into the corner of Mrs. Bantam's yard to listen, or if she happened to be passing that way she would linger near the windows to catch the words of some familiar ditty. The young men used to dig in the garden, or sometimes chop wood in the yard in the mornings.

Clara had been once sent by Mrs. Bantam to borrow a log of wood, for they happened to be out of it; and she saw the eldest Miss Elliot busy washing out her kitchen. Clara was delighted to see it, but Miss Elliot did not like quite so much to be caught by the girl next door doing the most disagreeable piece of work in the house. However, she pulled down her sleeves, and showed Clara where to get the wood, saying that Mrs. Bantam was welcome to it.

7. The River Torrens rises near Adelaide and flows into Gulf St. Vincent in South Australia.
8. Also called the Crystal Palace, the 1851 Great Exhibition in London was the first world's fair, featuring industrial technologies from many nations.
9. The state religion of Scotland is Presbyterianism.

As Clara got more *au fait*[1] in the routine of her daily duties, she found the evenings long and wearisome. She thought that she ought to employ them in sewing for herself, for her wages were not high, and the clothes she had were not suitable to her employments; so she began her first attempt at dress-making on a dark-brown print, with unhappy looking white spots on it, which was to be a morning wrapper.[2] She did not know how to cut it rightly, and it turned out to be a deplorable misfit; and what between the gloomy colour of the thing itself, and the cheerless solitude in which she made it, the tears dropped often and fast over it. Stitch after stitch she put in, and thought of her old happy home—her father, her mother, her sister; of the want of some one to exchange an idea with; of the constraint of this continual reticence, till her heart felt ready to break. When the gown was really done, she brought down a blank book that she had got for a journal on board ship, but which she had written nothing upon there, and relieved her mind by expressing her thoughts.

"It is right that I have made this dress, but to make another in the same way would kill me, I think. I had better go in rags than have my heartstrings torn up like this. I must read, though I have no face to look up to when I lift my eyes from the book; I must write, though nobody but myself shall read it.

"I hope I may never meet Mr. Reginald[3] again; I feel that once we were equals, but that now, without any fault of mine, I am hopelessly his inferior."

Such were a very few of the thoughts which Clara committed to paper. She felt relieved by doing so, and then began to read something not very wise, or very deep, but amusing; for she did not want to over-think.

1854

◄ FRANCES E. W. HARPER ►
1825–1911

Frances Ellen Harper (née Watkins) was born to free parents in Baltimore, Maryland, at a time when the rights of free, urban blacks were becoming increasingly constrained and the conditions of enslaved blacks continued to deteriorate. Although orphaned by age three, she remained a part of her father's extended family of relatively prosperous artisans, educators, and tradesmen. In her early years, she not only received a thorough education at a school for free blacks run by her uncle, the Reverend William Watkins, but also learned how to support herself doing the hard, physical work of domestic labor. After leaving school, Harper worked as a domestic. But with the publication of *Forest Leaves* (c. 1845), she became a published poet before she left Baltimore to begin her career as an educator, author, and political activist in the free states. Her first job was as a teacher in a school run by the African Methodist Episcopal Church in Ohio. During her twen-

---

1. Complete in knowledge (French).
2. Housecoat or dressing gown.
3. An attractive gentleman Clara met at the boardinghouse.

ties, Harper became increasingly active in politics until, in 1853, she left teaching to devote herself to a dual career as a political activist and author devoted to extending the rights of citizenship to African Americans and women. At age thirty-five in 1860, she married a widower with three children and withdrew somewhat from politics to give birth to a daughter and help run their farm. When her husband died in 1864, Harper returned to the front lines of politics, where she remained until her death.

Harper was a prodigious author who published at least ten volumes of poetry, three novels, and numerous short stories, speeches, and newspaper columns. The selections included here show her expertise in three genres: the speech, the poem, and the short story. Harper presented her speech "Woman's Political Future" at the 1893 World's Fair in Chicago, where she was one of four African American women invited to address the World's Congress of Representative Women. In this masterful example of an American jeremiad, or political sermon, Harper examines with both confidence and concern the challenges women will face once they achieve the right to vote. Harper's use of ornate figures of speech and elaborate biblical and literary allusions is typical of nineteenth-century oratory.

In contrast, her poetry and short stories show a more conversational style. The short story "The Two Offers" (1859) was published in one of the first literary journals devoted to a black readership (*The Anglo-African Magazine*). It features many of the qualities of Harper's later fiction, including the creation of dramatic tableaus such as the ones that open and close the story. Although she experimented with various verse forms, her most famous poems are designed to be accessible to listeners as well as to readers. Often dramatic, Harper's poems confront the audience with situations that demand an emotional response while maintaining distance between the speaker and the audience. One of Harper's most frequently anthologized poems (and one of the poems included here) is "Eliza Harris." Published in 1853, around the time Harper herself was becoming politically radicalized, this poem is a response to and an elaboration of a key figure from Harriet Beecher Stowe's 1852 novel *Uncle Tom's Cabin* (see pp. 734–78). In the years following the Civil War, Harper's verse turned to other subjects, such as the proper use of black suffrage ("Aunt Chloe's Politics," 1872).

Eliza Harris

Like a fawn from the arrow, startled and wild,
A woman swept by us, bearing a child;
In her eye was the night of a settled despair,
And her brow was o'ershaded with anguish and care.

She was nearing the river—in reaching the brink,   5
She heeded no danger, she paused not to think!
For she is a mother—her child is a slave—
And she'll give him his freedom, or find him a grave!

It was a vision to haunt us, that innocent face—
So pale in its aspect, so fair in its grace;   10
As the tramp of the horse and the bay of the hound,
With the fetters that gall, were trailing the ground!

She was nerv'd by despair, and strengthened by woe,
As she leap'd o'er the chasms that yawn'd from below;
Death howl'd in the tempest, and rav'd in the blast,   15
But she heard not the sound till the danger was past.

Oh! how shall I speak of my proud country's shame?
Of the stains on her glory, how give them their name?
How say that her banner in mockery waves—
Her "star spangled banner"—o'er millions of slaves?   20

How say that the lawless may torture and chase
A woman whose crime is the hue of her face?
How the depths of the forest may echo around
With the shrieks of despair, and the bay of the hound?

With her step on the ice, and her arm on her child,   25
The danger was fearful, the pathway was wild;
But, aided by Heaven, she gained a free shore,
Where the friends of humanity open'd their door.

So fragile and lovely, so fearfully pale,
Like a lily that bends to the breath of the gale,   30
Save the heave of her breast, and the sway of her hair,
You'd have thought her a statue of fear and despair.

In agony close to her bosom she press'd
The life of her heart, the child of her breast:—
Oh! love from its tenderness gathering might,   35
Had strengthen'd her soul for the dangers of flight.

But she's free—yes, free from the land where the slave
From the hand of oppression must rest in the grave;
Where bondage and torture, where scourges and chains,
Have plac'd on our banner indelible stains.   40

Did a fever e'er burning through bosom and brain,
Send a lava-like flood through every vein,
Till it suddenly cooled 'neath a healing spell,
And you knew, oh! the joy! you knew you were well?

So felt this young mother, as a sense of the rest   45
Stole gently and sweetly o'er *her* weary breast,
As her boy looked up, and, wondering, smiled
On the mother whose love had freed her child.

The bloodhounds have miss'd the scent of her way;
The hunter is rifled and foil'd of his prey;   50
Fierce jargon and cursing, with clanking of chains,
Make sounds of strange discord on Liberty's plains.

With rapture love and fulness of bliss,
She plac'd on his brow a mother's fond kiss:—

Oh! poverty, danger and death she can brave,   55
For the child of her love is no longer a slave!

                                                                1853

The Slave Mother

Heard you that shriek? It rose
    So wildly on the air,
It seemed as if a burden'd heart
    Was breaking in despair.

Saw you those hands so sadly clasped—   5
    The bowed and feeble head—
The shuddering of that fragile form—
    That look of grief and dread?

Saw you the sad, imploring eye?
    Its every glance was pain,   10
As if a storm of agony
    Were sweeping through the brain.

She is a mother, pale with fear,
    Her boy clings to her side,
And in her kirtle[1] vainly tries   15
    His trembling form to hide.

He is not hers, although she bore
    For him a mother's pains;
He is not hers, although her blood
    Is coursing through his veins!   20

He is not hers, for cruel hands
    May rudely tear apart
The only wreath of household love
    That binds her breaking heart.

His love has been a joyous light   25
    That o'er her pathway smiled,
A fountain gushing ever new,
    Amid life's desert wild.

His lightest word has been a tone
    Of music round her heart,   30
Their lives a streamlet blent in one—
    Oh, Father! must they part?

They tear him from her circling arms,
    Her last and fond embrace.
Oh! never more may her sad eyes   35
    Gaze on his mournful face.

1. Loose skirt.

No marvel, then, these bitter shrieks
Disturb the listening air:
She is a mother, and her heart
Is breaking in despair.   40

1854

The Two Offers

"What is the matter with you, Laura, this morning? I have been watching you this hour, and in that time you have commenced a half dozen letters and torn them all up. What matter of such grave moment is puzzling your dear little head, that you do not know how to decide?"

"Well, it is an important matter: I have two offers for marriage, and I do not know which to choose."

"I should accept neither, or to say the least, not at present."

"Why not?"

"Because I think a woman who is undecided between two offers, has not love enough for either to make a choice; and in that very hesitation, indecision, she has a reason to pause and seriously reflect, lest her marriage, instead of being an affinity of souls or a union of hearts, should only be a mere matter of bargain and sale, or an affair of convenience and selfish interest."

"But I consider them both very good offers, just such as many a girl would gladly receive. But to tell you the truth, I do not think that I regard either as a woman should the man she chooses for her husband. But then if I refuse, there is the risk of being an old maid, and that is not to be thought of."

"Well, suppose there is, is that the most dreadful fate that can befall a woman? Is there not more intense wretchedness in an ill-assorted marriage—more utter loneliness in a loveless home, than in the lot of the old maid who accepts her earthly mission as a gift from God, and strives to walk the path of life with earnest and unfaltering steps?"

"Oh! what a little preacher you are. I really believe that you were cut out for an old maid; that when nature formed you, she put in a double portion of intellect to make up for a deficiency of love; and yet you are kind and affectionate. But I do not think that you know anything of the grand, overmastering passion, or the deep necessity of woman's heart for loving."

"Do you think so?" resumed the first speaker; and bending over her work she quietly applied herself to the knitting that had lain neglected by her side, during this brief conversation; but as she did so, a shallow flitted over her pale and intellectual brow, a mist gathered in her eyes, and a slight quivering of the lips, revealed a depth of feeling to which her companion was a stranger.

But before I proceed with my story, let me give you a slight history of the speakers. They were cousins, who had met life under different auspices. Laura Lagrange, was the only daughter of rich and indulgent parents, who had spared no pains to make her an accomplished lady. Her cousin, Janette Alston, was the child of parents, rich only in goodness and affection. Her father had been unfortunate in business, and dying before he could retrieve his fortunes, left his business in an embarrassed state. His widow was unacquainted with his business affairs, and when the estate was settled, hungry creditors had brought their claims and the lawyers had received their fees, she found herself homeless and almost penniless, and she who had been sheltered in the warm clasp of loving arms, found them too powerless to shield her from the pitiless pelting storms of adversity. Year after year she struggled with poverty and wrestled with want, till her toil-worn hands became too feeble to hold the shattered chords of existence, and her tear-dimmed eyes grew heavy with the slumber of death. Her daughter had watched over her with untiring devotion, had closed her eyes in death, and gone out into the busy, restless world, missing a precious tone from the voices of earth, a beloved step from the paths of life. Too self reliant to depend on the charity of relations, she endeavored to support herself by her own exertions, and she had succeeded. Her path for a while was marked with struggle and trial, but instead of uselessly repining, she met them bravely, and her life became not a thing of ease and indulgence, but of conquest, victory, and accomplishments. At the time when this conversation took place, the deep trials of her life had passed away. The achievements of her genius had won her a position in the literary world, where she shone as one of its bright particular stars. And with her fame came a competence of worldly means, which gave her leisure for improvement, and the riper development of her rare talents. And she, that pale intellectual woman, whose genius gave life and vivacity to the social circle, and whose presence threw a halo of beauty and grace around the charmed atmosphere in which she moved, had at one period of her life, known the mystic and solemn strength of an all-absorbing love. Years faded into the misty past, had seen the kindling of her eye, the quick flushing of her cheek, and the wild throbbing of her heart, at tones of a voice long since hushed to the stillness of death. Deeply, wildly, passionately, she had loved. Her whole life seemed like the pouring out of rich, warm and gushing affections. This love quickened her talents, inspired her genius, and threw over her life a tender and spiritual earnestness. And then came a fearful shock, a mournful waking from that "dream of beauty and delight." A shadow fell around her path; it came between her and the object of her heart's worship; first a few cold words, estrangement, and then a painful separation; the old story of woman's pride—digging the sepulchre of her happiness, and then a new-made grave, and her path over it to the spirit world; and thus faded out from that young heart her bright, brief and saddened dream of life. Faint and spirit-broken, she turned from the scenes associated with the memory of the loved and lost. She tried to break the chain of sad associations that bound her to the mournful past; and so, pressing back the bitter sobs from her almost breaking heart, like the dying dolphin, whose beauty is born of its death anguish, her genius gathered strength from suffering and wonderous power and brilliancy from the agony she hid within the desolate chambers of her soul. Men hailed her as one of earth's strangely gifted children, and wreathed the garlands of fame for her brow, when it was throbbing with a wild and fearful unrest. They breathed her name with applause, when through the lonely halls of her stricken spirit, was an earnest cry for peace, a deep yearning for sympathy and heart-support.

But life, with its stern realities, met her; its solemn responsibilities confronted her, and turning, with an earnest and shattered spirit, to life's duties and trials, she found a calmness and strength that she had only imagined in her dreams of poetry and song. We will now pass over a period of ten years, and cousins have met again. In that calm and lovely woman, in whose eyes is a depth of tenderness, tempering the flashes of her genius, whose looks and tones are full of sympathy and love, we recognize the once smitten and stricken Janette Alston. The bloom of her girlhood had given way to a higher type of spiritual beauty, as if some unseen hand had been polishing and refining the temple in which her lovely spirit found its habitation; and this had been the fact. Her inner life had grown beautiful, and it was this that was constantly developing the outer. Never, in the early flush of womanhood, when an absorbing love had lit up her eyes and glowed in her life, had she appeared so interesting as when, with a countenance which seemed overshadowed with a spiritual light, she bent over the death-bed of a young woman, just lingering at the shadowy gates of the unseen land.

"Has he come?" faintly but eagerly exclaimed the dying woman. "Oh! how I have longed for his coming, and even in death he forgets me."

"Oh, do not say so, dear Laura, some accident may have detained him," said Janette to her cousin; for on that bed, from whence she will never rise, lies the once-beautiful and light-hearted Laura Lagrange, the brightness of whose eyes has long since been dimmed with tears, and whose voice had become like a harp whose every chord is tuned to sadness—whose faintest thrill and loudest vibrations are but the variations of agony. A heavy hand was laid upon her once warm and bounding heart, and a voice came whispering through her soul, that she must die. But, to her, the tidings was a message of deliverance—a voice, hushing her wild sorrows to the calmness of resignation and hope. Life had grown so weary upon her head—the future looked so hopeless—she had no wish to tread again the track where thorns had pierced her feet, and clouds overcast her sky; and she hailed the coming of death's angel as the footsteps of a welcome friend. And yet, earth had one object so very dear to her weary heart. It was her absent and recreant husband; for, since that conversation, she had accepted one of her offers, and become a wife. But, before she married, she learned that great lesson of human experience and woman's life, to love the man who bowed at her shrine, a willing worshipper. He had a pleasing address, raven hair, flashing eyes, a voice of thrilling sweetness, and lips of persuasive eloquence; and being well versed in the ways of the world, he won his way to her heart, and she became his bride, and he was proud of his prize. Vain and superficial in his character, he looked upon marriage not as a divine sacrament for the soul's development and human progression, but as the title-deed that gave him possession of the woman he thought he loved. But alas for her, the laxity of his principles had rendered him unworthy of the deep and undying devotion of a pure-hearted woman; but, for awhile, he hid from her his true character, and she blindly loved him, and for a short period was happy in the consciousness of being beloved; though sometimes a vague unrest would fill her soul, when, overflowing with a sense of the good, the beautiful, and the true, she would turn to him, but find no response to the deep yearnings of her soul—no appreciation of life's highest realities—its solemn grandeur and significant importance. Their souls never met, and soon she found a void in her bosom, that his earth-born love could not fill. He did not satisfy the wants of her mental and moral nature—between him and her there was no affinity of minds, no intercommunion of souls.

Talk as you will of woman's deep capacity for loving, of the strength of her affectional nature. I do not deny it; but will the mere possession of any human love, fully satisfy all the demands of her whole being? You may paint her in poetry or fiction, as a frail vine, clinging to her brother man for support, and dying when deprived of it; and all this may sound well enough to please the imaginations of school-girls, or love-lorn maidens. But woman—the true woman—if you would render her happy, it needs more than the mere development of her affectional nature. Her conscience should be enlightened, her faith in the true and right established, and scope given to her Heaven-endowed and God-given faculties. The true aim of female education should be, not a development of one or two, but all the faculties of the human soul, because no perfect womanhood is developed by imperfect culture. Intense love is often akin to intense suffering, and to trust the whole wealth of a woman's nature on the frail bark[2] of human love, may often be like trusting a cargo of gold and precious gems, to a bark that has never battled with the storm, or buffetted the waves. Is it any wonder, then, that so many life-barks go down, paving the ocean of time with precious hearts and wasted hopes? that so many float around us, shattered and dismasted wrecks? that so many are stranded on the shoals of existence, mournful beacons and solemn warnings for the thoughtless, to whom marriage is a careless and hasty rushing together of the affections? Alas that an institution so fraught with good for humanity should be so perverted, and that state of life, which should be filled with happiness, become so replete with misery. And this was the fate of Laura Lagrange. For a brief period after her marriage her life seemed like a bright and beautiful dream, full of hope and radiant with joy. And then there came a change—he found other attractions that lay beyond the pale of home influences. The gambling saloon had power to win him from her side, he had lived in an element of unhealthy and unhallowed excitements, and the society of a loving wife, the pleasures of a well-regulated home, were enjoyments too tame for one who had vitiated his tastes by the pleasures of sin. There were charmed houses of vice, built upon dead men's loves, where, amid a flow of song, laughter, wine, and careless mirth, he would spend hour after hour, forgetting the cheek that was paling through his neglect, heedless of the tear-dimmed eyes, peering anxiously into the darkness, waiting, or watching his return.

The influence of old associations was upon him. In early life, home had been to him a place of ceilings and walls, not a true home, built upon goodness, love and truth. It was a place where velvet carpets hushed his tread, where images of loveliness and beauty invoked into being by painter's art and sculptor's skill, pleased the eye and gratified the taste, where magnificence surrounded his way and costly clothing adorned his person; but it was not the place for the true culture and right development of his soul. His father had been too much engrossed in making money, and his mother in spending it, in striving to maintain a fashionable position in society, and shining in the eyes of the world, to give the proper direction to the character of their wayward and impulsive son. His mother put beautiful robes upon his body, but left ugly scars upon his soul; she pampered his appetite, but starved his spirit. Every mother should be a true artist, who knows how to weave into her child's life images of grace and beauty, the true poet capable of writing on the soul of childhood the harmony of love and truth, and teaching it how to produce the grandest of all poems—the poetry of a true and noble life. But in his home, a love for the good, the true and right, had been sacrificed at the shrine of frivolity and fashion. That parental authority which should have been preserved as a string of precious pearls, unbroken and unscattered, was simply the administration of chance. At one time obedience was enforced by authority, at another time by flattery and promises, and just as often it was not enforced at all. His early associations were formed as chance directed, and from his want of

2. Boat, vessel.

home-training, his character received a bias, his life a shade, which ran through every avenue of his existence, and darkened all his future hours. Oh, if we would trace the history of all the crimes that have o'ershadowed this sin-shrouded and sorrow-darkened world of ours, how many might be seen arising from the wrong home influences, or the weakening of the home ties. Home should always be the best school for the affections, the birthplace of high resolves, and the altar upon which lofty aspirations are kindled, from whence the soul may go forth strengthened, to act its part aright in the great drama of life, with conscience enlightened, affections cultivated, and reason and judgment dominant. But alas for the young wife. Her husband had not been blessed with such a home. When he entered the arena of life, the voices from home did not linger around his path as angels of guidance about his steps; they were not like so many messages to invite him to deeds of high and holy worth. The memory of no sainted mother arose between him and deeds of darkness; the earnest prayers of no father arrested him in his downward course; and before a year of his married life had waned, his young wife had learned to wait and mourn his frequent and uncalled-for absence. More than once had she seen him come home from his midnight haunts, the bright intelligence of his eye displaced by the drunkard's stare, and his manly gait changed to the inebriate's stagger; and she was beginning to know the bitter agony that is compressed in the mournful words, a drunkard's wife. And then there came a bright but brief episode in her experience; the angel of life gave to her existence a deeper meaning and loftier significance: she sheltered in the warm clasp of her loving arms, a dear babe, a precious child, whose love filled every chamber of her heart, and felt the fount of maternal love gushing so new within her soul. That child was hers. How overshadowing was the love with which she bent over its helplessness, how much it helped to fill the void and chasms in her soul. How many lonely hours were beguiled by its winsome ways, its answering smiles and fond caresses. How exquisite and solemn was the feeling that thrilled her heart when she clasped the tiny hands together and taught her dear child to call God "Our Father."

What a blessing was that child. The father paused in his headlong career, awed by the strange beauty and precocious intellect of his child; and the mother's life had a better expression through her ministrations of love. And then there came hours of bitter anguish, shading the sunlight of her home and hushing the music of her heart. The angel of death bent over the couch of her child and beaconed it away. Closer and closer the mother strained her child to her wildly heaving breast, and struggled with the heavy hand that lay upon its heart. Love and agony contended with death, and the language of the mother's heart was,

> "Oh, Death, away! that innocent is mine;
>   I cannot spare him from my arms
> To lay him, Death, in thine.
>   I am a mother, Death; I gave that darling birth
> I could not bear his lifeless limbs   5
>   Should moulder in the earth."

But death was stronger than love and mightier than agony and won the child for the land of crystal founts and deathless flowers, and the poor, stricken mother sat down beneath the shadow of her mighty grief, feeling as if a great light had gone out from her soul, and that the sunshine had suddenly faded around her path. She turned in her deep anguish to the father of her child, the loved and cherished dead. For awhile his words were kind and tender, his heart seemed subdued, and his tenderness fell upon her worn and weary heart like rain on perishing flowers, or cooling waters to lips all parched with thirst and scorched with fever; but the change was evanescent, the influence of unhallowed associations and evil habits had vitiated and poisoned the springs of his existence. They had bound him in their meshes, and he lacked the moral strength to break his fetters, and stand erect in all the strength and dignity of a true manhood, making life's highest excellence his ideal, and striving to gain it.

And yet moments of deep contrition would sweep over him, when he would resolve to abandon the wine-cup forever, when he was ready to forswear the handling of another card, and he would try to break away from the associations that he felt were working his ruin; but when the hour of temptation came his strength was weakness, his earnest purposes were cobwebs, his well-meant resolutions ropes of sand, and thus passed year after year of the married life of Laura Lagrange. She tried to hide her agony from the public gaze, to smile when her heart was almost breaking. But year after year her voice grew fainter and sadder, her once light and bounding step grew slower and faltering. Year after year she wrestled with agony, and strove with despair, till the quick eyes of her brother read, in the paling of her cheek and the dimming eye, the secret anguish of her worn and weary spirit. On that wan, sad face, he saw the death-tokens, and he knew the dark wing of the mystic angel swept coldly around her path. "Laura," said her brother to her one day, "you are not well, and I think you need our mother's tender care and nursing. You are daily losing strength, and if you will go I will accompany you." At first, she hesitated, she shrank almost instinctively from presenting that pale sad face to the loved ones at home. That face was such a tell-tale; it told of heart-sickness, of hope deferred, and the mournful story of unrequited love. But then a deep yearning for home sympathy woke within her a passionate longing for love's kind words, for tenderness and heart-support, and she resolved to seek the home of her childhood, and lay her weary head upon her mother's bosom, to be folded again in her loving arms, to lay that poor, bruised and aching heart where it might beat and throb closely to the loved ones at home. A kind welcome awaited her. All that love and tenderness could devise was done to bring the bloom to her cheek and the light to her eye; but it was all in vain; her's was a disease that no medicine could cure, no earthly balm would heal. It was a slow wasting of the vital forces, the sickness of the soul. The unkindness and neglect of her husband, lay like a leaden weight upon her heart, and slowly oozed away its life-drops. And where was he that had won her love, and then cast it aside as a useless thing, who rifled her heart of its wealth and spread bitter ashes upon its broken altars? He was lingering away from her when the death-damps were gathering on her brow, when his name was trembling on her lips! lingering away when she was watching his coming, though the death films were gathering before her eyes, and earthly things were fading from her vision. "I think I hear him now," said the dying woman, "surely that is his step;" but the sound died away in the distance. Again she started from an uneasy slumber, "That is his voice! I am so glad he has come." Tears gathered in the eyes of the sad watchers by that dying bed, for they knew that she was deceived. He had not returned. For her sake they wished his coming. Slowly the hours waned away, and then came the sad, soul-sickening thought that she was forgotten, forgotten in the last hour of human need, forgotten when the spirit, about to be dissolved, paused for the last time on the threshold of existence, a weary watcher at the gates of death. "He has forgotten me," again she faintly murmured, and the last tears she would ever shed on earth sprung to her mournful eyes, and clasping her hands together in silent anguish, a few broken sentences issued from her pale and quivering lips. They were prayers for strength and earnest pleading for him who had desolated her young life, by turning its sunshine to shadows, its smiles to tears. "He has forgotten me," she murmured again, "but I can bear it, the bitterness of death is passed, and soon I hope to exchange the shadows of death for the brightness of eternity, the rugged paths of life for the golden streets of glory, and the care and turmoils of earth for the peace and rest of heaven." Her voice grew fainter and fainter, they saw the shadows that never deceive flit over her pale and faded face, and knew that the death angel waited to soothe their weary one to rest, to calm the throbbing of her bosom and cool the fever of her brain. And amid the silent hush of their grief the freed spirit, refined through suffering, and brought into divine harmony through the spirit of the living Christ, passed over the dark waters of death as on a bridge of light, over whose radiant arches hovering angels bent. They parted the dark locks from her marble brow, closed the waxen lids over the once bright and laughing eye, and left her to the dreamless slumber of the grave. Her cousin turned from that deathbed a sadder and wiser woman. She resolved more earnestly than ever to make the world better by her example, gladder by her presence, and to kindle the fires of her genius on the altars of universal love and truth. She had a higher and better object in all her writings than the mere acquisition of gold, or acquirement of fame. She felt that she had a high and holy mission on the battle-field of existence, that life was not given her to be frittered away in nonsense, or wasted away in trifling pursuits. She would willingly espouse an unpopular cause but not an unrighteous one. In her the down-trodden slave found an earnest advocate; the flying fugitive remembered her kindness as he stepped cautiously through our Republic, to gain his freedom in a monarchial land, having broken the chains on which the rust of centuries had gathered. Little children learned to name her with affection, the poor called her blessed, as she broke her bread to the pale lips of hunger. Her life was like a beautiful story, only it was clothed with the dignity of reality and invested with the sublimity of truth. True, she was an old maid, no husband brightened her life with his love, or shaded it with his neglect. No children nestling lovingly in her arms called her mother. No one appended Mrs. to her name; she was indeed an old maid, not vainly striving to keep up an appearance of girlishness, when departed was written on her youth. Not vainly pining at her loneliness and isolation: the world was full of warm, loving hearts, and her own beat in unison with them. Neither was she always sentimentally sighing for something to love, objects of affection were all around her, and the world was not so wealthy in love that it had no use for her's; in blessing others she made a life and benediction, and as old age descended peacefully and gently upon her, she had learned one of life's most precious lessons, that true happiness consists not so much in the fruition of our wishes as in the regulation of desires and the full development and right culture of our whole natures.

1859

Aunt Chloe's Politics

Of course, I don't know very much
　　About these politics,
But I think that some who run 'em
　　Do mighty ugly tricks.

I've seen 'em honey-fugle[3] round,　　　　　5
　　And talk so awful sweet,
That you'd think them full of kindness,
　　As an egg is full of meat.

Now I don't believe in looking
　　Honest people in the face,
And saying when you're doing wrong,　　10
　　That "I haven't sold my race."[4]

When we want to school our children,
　　If the money isn't there,
Whether black or white have took it,　　15
　　The loss we all must share.

And this buying up each other[5]
　　Is something worse than mean,
Though I thinks a heap of voting,
　　I go for voting clean.　　　　　　　20

1872

Woman's Political Future[6]

If before sin had cast its deepest shadows or sorrow had distilled its bitterest tears,
it was true that it was not good for man to be alone, it is no less true, since the
shadows have deepened and life's sorrows have increased, that the world has need
of all the spiritual aid that woman can give for the social advancement and moral
development of the human race. The tendency of the present age, with its restlessness, religious upheavals, failures, blunders, and crimes, is toward broader freedom, an increase of knowledge, the emancipation of thought, and a recognition of
the brotherhood of man; in this movement woman, as the companion of man,
must be a sharer. So close is the bond between man and woman that you can not
raise one without lifting the other. The world can not move without woman's
sharing in the movement, and to help give a right impetus to that movement is
woman's highest privilege.

　　If the fifteenth century discovered America to the Old World, the nineteenth
is discovering woman to herself. Little did Columbus imagine, when the New

3. Talk or act kindly in order to deceive.
4. Betrayed one's own people.
5. Buying someone's (usually a black person's)
vote.
6. Given as an address to World's Congress of
Representative Women at the 1893 World's Fair.

World broke upon his vision like a lovely gem in the coronet of the universe, the glorious possibilities of a land where the sun should be our engraver, the winged lightning our messenger, and steam our beast of burden. But as mind is more than matter, and the highest ideal always the true real, so to woman comes the opportunity to strive for richer and grander discoveries than ever gladdened the eye of the Genoese mariner.[7]

Not the opportunity of discovering new worlds, but that of filling this old world with fairer and higher aims than the greed of gold and the lust of power, is hers. Through weary, wasting years men have destroyed, dashed in pieces, and overthrown, but to-day we stand on the threshold of woman's era, and woman's work is grandly constructive. In her hand are possibilities whose use or abuse must tell upon the political life of the nation, and send their influence for good or evil across the track of unborn ages.

As the saffron tints and crimson flushes of morn herald the coming day, so the social and political advancement which woman has already gained bears the promise of the rising of the full-orbed sun of emancipation. The result will be not to make home less happy, but society more holy; yet I do not think the mere extension of the ballot a panacea for all the ills of our national life. What we need to-day is not simply more voters, but better voters. To-day there are red-handed men[8] in our republic, who walk unwhipped of justice, who richly deserve to exchange the ballot of the freeman for the wristlets[9] of the felon; brutal and cowardly men, who torture, burn, and lynch their fellow-men, men whose defenselessness should be their best defense and their weakness an ensign of protection. More than the changing of institutions we need the development of a national conscience, and the upbuilding of national character. Men may boast of the aristocracy of blood, may glory in the aristocracy of talent, and be proud of the aristocracy of wealth, but there is one aristocracy which must ever outrank them all, and that is the aristocracy of character; and it is the women of a country who help to mold its character, and to influence if not determine its destiny; and in the political future of our nation woman will not have done what she could if she does not endeavor to have our republic stand foremost among the nations of the earth, wearing sobriety as a crown and righteousness as a garment and a girdle. In coming into her political estate woman will find a mass of illiteracy to be dispelled. If knowledge is power, ignorance is also power. The power that educates wickedness may manipulate and dash against the pillars of any state when they are undermined and honeycombed by injustice.

I envy neither the heart nor the head of any legislator who has been born to an inheritance of privileges, who has behind him ages of education, dominion, civilization, and Christianity, if he stands opposed to the passage of a national education bill, whose purpose is to secure education to the children of those who were born under the shadow of institutions which made it a crime to read.

To-day women hold in their hands influence and opportunity, and with these they have already opened doors which have been closed to others. By opening doors of labor woman has become a rival claimant for at least some of the wealth monopolized by her stronger brother. In the home she is the priestess, in society the queen, in literature she is a power, in legislative halls law-makers have re-

7. Christopher Columbus.   9. Handcuffs.
8. Criminals.

sponded to her appeals, and for her sake have humanized and liberalized their laws. The press has felt the impress of her hand. In the pews of the church she constitutes the majority; the pulpit has welcomed her, and in the school she has the blessed privilege of teaching children and youth. To her is apparently coming the added responsibility of political power; and what she now possesses should only be the means of preparing her to use the coming power for the glory of God and the good of mankind; for power without righteousness is one of the most dangerous forces in the world.

Political life in our country has plowed in muddy channels, and needs the infusion of clearer and cleaner waters. I am not sure that women are naturally so much better than men that they will clear the stream by the virtue of their womanhood; it is not through sex but through character that the best influence of women upon the life of the nation must be exerted.

I do not believe in unrestricted and universal suffrage for either men or women. I believe in moral and educational tests. I do not believe that the most ignorant and brutal man is better prepared to add value to the strength and durability of the government than the most cultured, upright, and intelligent woman. I do not think that willful ignorance should swamp earnest intelligence at the ballot-box, nor that educated wickedness, violence, and fraud should cancel the votes of honest men. The unsteady hands of a drunkard can not cast the ballot of a free-man. The hands of lynchers are too red with blood to determine the political character of the government for even four short years. The ballot in the hands of woman means power added to influence. How well she will use that power I can not foretell. Great evils stare us in the face that need to be throttled by the combined power of an upright manhood and an enlightened womanhood; and I know that no nation can gain its full measure of enlightenment and happiness if one-half of it is free and the other half is fettered. China compressed the feet of her women[1] and thereby retarded the steps of her men. The elements of a nation's weakness must ever be found at the hearthstone.

More than the increase of wealth, the power of armies, and the strength of fleets is the need of good homes, of good fathers, and good mothers.

The life of a Roman citizen was in danger in ancient Palestine, and men had bound themselves with a vow that they would eat nothing until they had killed the Apostle Paul. Pagan Rome threw around that imperiled life a bulwark of living clay consisting of four hundred and seventy human hearts, and Paul was saved.[2] Surely the life of the humblest American citizen should be as well protected in America as that of a Roman citizen was in heathen Rome. A wrong done to the weak should be an insult to the strong. Woman coming into her kingdom will find enthroned three great evils, for whose overthrow she should be as strong in a love of justice and humanity as the warrior is in his might. She will find intemperance sending its flood of shame, and death, and sorrow to the homes of men, a fretting leprosy in our politics, and a blighting curse in our social life; the social evil sending to our streets women whose laughter is sadder than their tears, who slide from the paths of sin and shame to the friendly shelter of the grave; and lawlessness enacting in our republic deeds over which angels might weep, if heaven knows sympathy.

1. Foot binding among Chinese women began in the mid-tenth century CE; it was outlawed in 1911, but the practice continued in some rural areas until the mid-twentieth century.

2. The Roman government protected St. Paul, a Roman citizen, from those who disagreed with his teachings and wished him harm (Acts 23–26).

How can any woman send petitions to Russia against the horrors of Siberian prisons if, ages after the Inquisition has ceased to devise its tortures, she has not done all she could by influence, tongue, and pen to keep men from making bonfires of the bodies of real or supposed criminals?

O women of America! into your hands God has pressed one of the sublimest opportunities that ever came into the hands of the women of any race or people. It is yours to create a healthy public sentiment; to demand justice, simple justice, as the right of every race; to brand with everlasting infamy the lawless and brutal cowardice that lynches, burns, and tortures your own countrymen.

To grapple with the evils which threaten to undermine the strength of the nation and to lay magazines of powder under the cribs of future generations is no child's play.

Let the hearts of the women of the world respond to the song of the herald angels of peace on earth and good will to men.[3] Let them throb as one heart unified by the grand and holy purpose of uplifting the human race, and humanity will breathe freer, and the world grow brighter. With such a purpose Eden would spring up in our path, and Paradise be around our way.

1893

►◄ DINAH MULOCK CRAIK ►◄
1826–1887

During her lifetime, Dinah Mulock Craik was a prolific and popular novelist. Her work, however, has not become part of the new feminist canon, even though some of her contemporaries thought her as talented as Charlotte Brontë and George Eliot. Craik was undoubtedly a feminist, but she was at the same time a traditionalist. She argued passionately for such radical causes (in her time) as women's right to own property, to work to support themselves, to redeem themselves after giving birth out of wedlock, and to gain child custody in cases of divorce. At the same time, she saw the differences between men and women as intrinsic and immutable, their roles necessarily distinct.

Craik believed women should have opportunities to become economically self-sufficient, as she herself was forced to do at an unusually young age. Her father, Thomas Mulock, was a Nonconformist preacher whose erratic behavior and financial irresponsibility lost him his congregation and chapel in Stoke-on-Trent, in the northwest Midlands of England, when Craik was a child. Seriously impoverished, the family moved to Newcastle-under-Lyme, also in the Midlands, where Craik's mother, Dinah Mellard Mulock, opened a school. Craik, who had briefly attended a school herself and who loved to read, was helping her mother to teach by the age of thirteen. Then, in 1845, the family moved to London, Mrs. Mulock died, and Thomas Mulock inexplicably renounced his children, leaving Craik, age nineteen, and her two teenage brothers to support themselves.

Craik became a professional author at once, at first publishing poems, children's books, and stories, and eventually writing novels. Her first novel, *The*

3. An allusion to Luke 2:14 (". . . on earth peace, good will toward men") and to the popular Christmas carol "Hark! The Herald Angels Sing" (1739) by Charles Wesley, brother of John Wesley, who founded the Methodist Church and was an abolitionist.

Ogilvies (1849), about young women deciding whom to marry, came out in 1849; *John Halifax, Gentleman* (1856), the story of a self-made man, was her most popular and critically acclaimed novel. Riding her newfound fame, she wrote *A Woman's Thoughts about Women* in 1857. Here, we have reprinted the first chapter of this self-help manual, which contains advice to women on such topics as women servants, the mistress of the house, female friendships, and happiness. Like Florence Nightingale's *Cassandra*, written five years earlier though not yet published, Craik's text attacks the idea that middle- and upper-class women ought to be idle. Unlike Nightingale, however, Craik does not advocate women taking up professions; instead, she prescribes activities that are strictly domestic.

In 1865 she married George Lillie Craik, who soon became a partner at Macmillan publishers. Four years later, they adopted an abandoned baby from a parish workhouse, an unusual act in an era when people believed that children inherited their birth parents' bad qualities. Craik's duties as a wife and mother did not curtail her activity as a writer: she published the novel *A Noble Life* in 1866; in 1872 she published *The Adventures of a Brownie,* a children's book; in 1875 she published *The Little Lame Prince* (a children's book) and *Songs of Our Youth,* and in 1884 she published *An Unsentimental Journey through Cornwall.* In addition, she published articles and criticism throughout the period. She died in 1887 of a heart attack, during preparations for her daughter's wedding.

From A Woman's Thoughts about Women

Chapter 1
Something to Do

I premise that these thoughts do not concern married women, for whom there are always plenty to think, and who have generally quite enough to think of for themselves and those belonging to them. They have cast their lot for good or ill, have realised in greater or less degree the natural destiny of our sex. They must find out its comforts, cares, and responsibilities, and make the best of all. It is the single women, belonging to those supernumerary[1] ranks, which, political economists tell us, are yearly increasing, who most need thinking about.

First, in their early estate, when they have so much in their possession—youth, bloom, and health giving them that temporary influence over the other sex which may result, and is meant to result, in a permanent one. Secondly, when this sovereignty is passing away, the chance of marriage lessening, or wholly ended, or voluntarily set aside, and the individual making up her mind to that which, respect for Grandfather Adam and Grandmother Eve must compel us to admit, is an unnatural condition of being.

Why this undue proportion of single women should almost always result from over-civilisation, and whether, since society's advance is usually indicated by the advance, morally and intellectually, of its women—this progress, by raising women's ideal standard of the "holy estate,"[2] will not necessarily cause a decline in the very *un*holy estate which it is most frequently made—are questions too wide to be entered upon here. We have only to deal with facts—with a certain

1. Extra, exceeding the usual number. According to the 1851 British census, there were approximately 1.75 million single or widowed women in Great Britain, 400,000 more than there were single or widowed men.
2. Matrimony.

acknowledged state of things, perhaps incapable of remedy, but by no means incapable of amelioration.

But, granted these facts, and leaving to wiser heads the explanation of them—if indeed there be any—it seems advisable, or at least allowable, that any woman who has thought a good deal about the matter, should not fear to express in word—or deed, which is better,—any conclusions, which out of her own observation and experience she may have arrived at. And looking around upon the middle classes, which form the staple stock of the community, it appears to me that the chief canker at the root of women's lives is the want[3] of something to do.

Herein I refer, as this chapter must be understood especially to refer, not to those whom ill or good fortune—query, is it not often the latter?—has forced to earn their bread; but "to young ladies," who have never been brought up to do anything. Tom, Dick, and Harry, their brothers, has each had it knocked into him from school-days that he is to do something, to be somebody. Counting-house, shop, or college, afford him a clear future on which to concentrate all his energies and aims. He has got the grand pabulum[4] of the human soul—occupation. If any inherent want in his character, any unlucky combination of circumstances, nullifies this, what a poor creature the man becomes!—what a dawdling, moping, sitting-over-the-fire, thumb-twiddling, lazy, ill-tempered animal! And why? "Oh, poor fellow! 'tis because he has got nothing to do!"

Yet this is precisely the condition of women for a third, a half, often the whole of their existence.

That Providence ordained it so—made men to work, and women to be idle—is a doctrine that few will be bold enough to assert openly. Tacitly they do, when they preach up lovely uselessness, fascinating frivolity, delicious helplessness—all those polite impertinences and poetical degradations to which the foolish, lazy, or selfish of our sex are prone to incline an ear, but which any woman of common-sense must repudiate as insulting not only her womanhood but her Creator.

Equally blasphemous, and perhaps even more harmful, is the outcry about "the equality of the sexes;" the frantic attempt to force women, many of whom are either ignorant of or unequal for their own duties—into the position and duties of men. A pretty state of matters would ensue! Who that ever listened for two hours to the verbose confused inanities of a ladies' committee, would immediately go and give his vote for a female House of Commons?[5] or who, on the receipt of a lady's letter of business—I speak of the average—would henceforth desire to have our courts of justice stocked with matronly lawyers, and our colleges thronged by

"Sweet girl-graduates with their golden hair?"[6]

As for finance, in its various branches—if you pause to consider the extreme difficulty there always is in balancing Mrs Smith's housekeeping-book, or Miss Smith's quarterly allowance, I think, my dear Paternal Smith, you need not be much afraid lest this loud acclaim for "women's rights" should ever end in pushing you from your stools, in counting-house, college, or elsewhere.

No; equality of the sexes is not in the nature of things. Man and woman were made for, and not like one another. One only "right" we have to assert in com-

---

3. Lack.
4. Food.
5. The lower, elected, house of Britain's parliament.

6. From the prologue to The Princess (1847), a poem by Alfred, Lord Tennyson (1809–92).

mon with mankind—and that is as much in our own hands as theirs—the right of having something to do.

That both sexes were meant to labour, one "by the sweat of his brow," the other "in sorrow to bring forth"—and bring up—"children"[7]—cannot, I fancy, be questioned. Nor, when the gradual changes of the civilised world, or some special destiny, chosen or compelled, have prevented that first, highest, and in earlier times almost universal lot, does this accidental fate in any way abrogate the necessity, moral, physical, and mental, for a woman to have occupation in other forms.

But how few parents ever consider this? Tom, Dick, and Harry, aforesaid, leave school and plunge into life; "the girls" likewise finish their education, come home, and stay at home. That is enough. Nobody thinks it needful to waste a care upon them. Bless them, pretty dears, how sweet they are! papa's nosegay of beauty to adorn his drawing-room. He delights to give them all they can desire—clothes, amusements, society; he and mamma together take every domestic care off their hands; they have abundance of time and nothing to occupy it; plenty of money, and little use for it; pleasure without end, but not one definite object of interest or employment; flattery and flummery[8] enough, but no solid food whatever to satisfy mind or heart—if they happen to possess either—at the very emptiest and most craving season of both. They have literally nothing whatever to do, except to fall in love, which they accordingly do, the most of them, as fast as ever they can.

"Many think they are in love, when in fact they are only idle"[9]—is one of the truest sayings of that great wise bore, Imlac, in *Rasselas*, and it has been proved by many a shipwrecked life, of girls especially. This "falling in love" being usually a mere delusion of the fancy, and not the real thing at all, the object is generally unattainable or unworthy. Papa is displeased, mamma somewhat shocked and scandalised; it is a "foolish affair," and no matrimonial results ensue. There only ensues—what?

A long, dreary season, of pain, real or imaginary, yet not the less real because it is imaginary; of anger and mortification, of important struggle—against unjust parents, the girl believes, or, if romantically inclined, against cruel destiny. Gradually this mood wears out; she learns to regard "love" as folly, and turns her whole hope and aim to—matrimony! Matrimony in the abstract; not *the* man, but any man—any person who will snatch her out of the dulness of her life, and give her something really to live for, something to fill up the hopeless blank of idleness into which her days are gradually sinking.

Well, the man may come, or he may not. If the latter melancholy result occurs, the poor girl passes into her third stage of young-ladyhood, fritters or mopes away her existence, sullenly bears it, or dashes herself blindfold against its restrictions; is unhappy, and makes her family unhappy; perhaps herself cruelly conscious of all this, yet unable to find the true root of bitterness in her heart: not knowing exactly what she wants, yet aware of a morbid, perpetual want of something. What is it?

Alas! the boys only have had the benefit of that well-known juvenile apophthegm, that

7. Genesis 3:16, 19.
8. Literally, a gelatin dessert; figuratively, meaningless words.
9. Advice the philosopher Imlac gives the titular

hero in vol. 1, ch. 25, of the novella *The History of Rasselas* (1759), by English writer and lexicographer Samuel Johnson (1709–84).

"Satan finds some mischief still
For idle hands to do:"[1]

it has never crossed the parents' minds that the rhyme could apply to the delicate digital extremities of the daughters.

And so their whole energies are devoted to the massacre of old Time. They prick him to death with crochet and embroidery needles; strum him deaf with piano and harp playing—*not* music; cut him up with morning-visitors, or leave his carcass in ten-minute parcels at every "friend's" house they can think of. Finally, they dance him defunct at all sort of unnatural hours; and then, rejoicing in the excellent excuse, smother him in sleep for a third of the following day. Thus he dies, a slow, inoffensive, perfectly natural death; and they will never recognise his murder till, on the confines of this world, or from the unknown shores of the next, the question meets them: "What have you done with Time?"—Time, the only mortal gift bestowed equally on every living soul, and excepting the soul, the only mortal loss which is totally irretrievable.

Yet this great sin, this irredeemable loss, in many women arises from pure ignorance. Men are taught as a matter of business to recognise the value of time, to apportion and employ it: women rarely or never. The most of them have no definite appreciation of the article as a tangible divisible commodity at all. They would laugh at a mantua-maker[2] who cut up a dress-length into trimmings, and then expected to make out of two yards of silk a full skirt. Yet that the same laws of proportion should apply to time and its measurements—that you cannot dawdle away a whole forenoon, and then attempt to cram into the afternoon the entire business of the day—that every minute's unpunctuality constitutes a debt or a theft (lucky, indeed, if you yourself are the only party robbed or made creditor thereof!): these slight facts rarely seem to cross the feminine imagination.

It is not their fault; they have never been "accustomed to business." They hear that with men "time is money;" but it never strikes them that the same commodity, equally theirs, is to them not money, perhaps, but *life*—life in its highest form and noblest uses—life bestowed upon every human being, distinctly and individually, without reference to any other being, and for which every one of us, married or unmarried, woman as well as man, will assuredly be held accountable before God.

My young-lady friends, of from seventeen upwards, your time, and the use of it, is as essential to you as to any father or brother of you all. You are accountable for it just as much as he is. If you waste it, you waste not only your substance, but your very souls—not that which is your own, but your Maker's.

Ay, there the core of the matter lies. From the hour that honest Adam and Eve were put into the garden, not—as I once heard some sensible preacher observe— "not to be idle in it, but to dress it and to keep it," the Father of all has never put one man or one woman into this world without giving each something to do there, in it and for it: some visible, tangible work, to be left behind them when they die.

Young ladies, 'tis worth a grave thought—what, if called away at eighteen, twenty, or thirty, the most of you would leave behind you when you die? Much embroidery, doubtless; various pleasant, kindly, illegible letters; a moderate store

---

1. Satan . . . do: lines from the poem "Against   (1674–1748).
Idleness and Mischief" (1715) by Isaac Watts   2. Dressmaker.

of good deeds; and a cart-load of good intentions. Nothing else—save your name on a tombstone, or lingering for a few more years in family or friendly memory. "Poor dear—! what a nice lively girl she was!" For any benefit accruing through you to your generation, you might as well never have lived at all.

But "what am I to do with my life?" as once asked me one girl out of the numbers who begin to feel aware that, whether marrying or not, each possesses an individual life, to spend, to use, or to lose. And herein lies the momentous question.

The difference between man's vocation and woman's seems naturally to be this—one is abroad, the other at home: one external, the other internal: one active, the other passive. He has to go and seek out his path; hers usually lies close under her feet. Yet each is as distinct, as honourable, as difficult; and whatever custom may urge to the contrary—if the life is meant to be a worthy or a happy one—each must resolutely and unshrinkingly be trod. But—*how?*

A definite answer to this question is simply impossible. So diverse are characters, tastes, capabilities, and circumstances, that to lay down a distinct line of occupation for any six women of one's own acquaintance, would be the merest absurdity.

"Herein the patient must minister to herself."[3]

To few is the choice so easy, the field of duty so wide, that she need puzzle very long over what she ought to do. Generally—and this is the best and safest guide—she will find her work lying very near at hand: some desultory tastes to condense into regular studies, some faulty household quietly to remodel, some child to teach, or parent to watch over. All these being needless or unattainable, she may extend her service out of the home into the world, which perhaps never at any time so much needed the help of us women. And hardly one of its charities and duties can be done so thoroughly as by a wise and tender woman's hand.

Here occurs another of those plain rules which are the only guidance possible in the matter—a Bible rule, too—"*Whatsoever thy hand findeth to do, do it with thy might.*"[4] Question it not, philosophise not over it—do it!—only *do it!* Thoroughly and completely, never satisfied with less than perfectness. Be it ever so great or so small, from the founding of a village-school to the making of a collar—do it "with thy might;" and never lay it aside till it is done.

Each day's account ought to leave this balance—of something done. Something beyond mere pleasure, one's own or another's—though both are good and sweet in their way. Let the superstructure of life be enjoyment, but let its foundation be in solid work—daily, regular, conscientious work: in its essence and results as distinct as any "business" of men. What they expend for wealth and ambition, shall not we offer for duty and love—the love of our fellow-creatures, or, far higher, the love of God?

"Labour is worship," says the proverb: also—nay, necessarily so—labour is happiness. Only let us turn from the dreary, colourless lives of the women, old and young, who have nothing to do, to those of their sisters who are always busy doing something; who, believing and accepting the universal law, that pleasure is

3. Feminizing Shakespeare's *Macbeth*, 5.3.40.   4. Ecclesiastes 9:10.

the mere accident of our being, and work its natural and most holy necessity, have set themselves steadily to seek out and fulfil theirs.

These are they who are little spoken of in the world at large. I do not include among them those whose labour should spring from an irresistible impulse, and become an absolute vocation, or it is not worth following at all—namely, the professional women, writers, painters, musicians, and the like. I mean those women who lead active, intelligent, industrious lives: lives complete in themselves, and therefore not giving half the trouble to their friends that the idle and foolish virgins do[5]—no, not even in love-affairs. If love comes to them accidentally, (or rather providentially), and happily, so much the better!—they will not make the worse wives for having been busy maidens. But the "tender passion" is not to them the one grand necessity that it is to aimless lives; they are in no haste to wed: their time is duly filled up; and if never married, still the habitual faculty of usefulness gives them in themselves and with others that obvious value, that fixed standing in society, which will for ever prevent their being drifted away, like most old maids, down the current of the new generation, even as dead May-flies down a stream.

They have made for themselves a place in the world: the harsh, practical, yet not ill-meaning world, where all find their level soon or late, and where a frivolous young maid sunk into a helpless old one, can no more expect to keep her pristine position than a last year's leaf to flutter upon a spring bough. But an old maid who deserves well of this same world, by her ceaseless work therein, having won her position, keeps it to the end.

Not an ill position either, or unkindly; often higher and more honourable than that of many a mother of ten sons. In households, where "Auntie" is the universal referee, nurse, play-mate, comforter, and counsellor: in society, where "that nice Miss So-and-so," though neither clever, handsome, nor young, is yet such a person as can neither be omitted nor overlooked: in charitable works, where she is "such a practical body—always knows exactly what to do, and how to do it:" or perhaps, in her own house, solitary indeed, as every single woman's home must be, yet neither dull nor unhappy in itself, and the nucleus of cheerfulness and happiness to many another home besides.

She has not married. Under Heaven, her home, her life, her lot, are all of her own making. Bitter or sweet they may have been—it is not ours to meddle with them, but we can any day see their results. Wide or narrow as her circle of influence appears, she has exercised her power to the uttermost, and for good. Whether great or small her talents, she has not let one of them rust for want of use.[6] Whatever the current of her existence may have been, and in whatever circumstances it has placed her, she has voluntarily wasted no portion of it—not a year, not a month, not a day.

Published or unpublished, this woman's life is a goodly chronicle, the title-page of which you may read in her quiet countenance; her manner, settled, cheerful, and at ease; her unfailing interest in all things and all people. You will rarely find she thinks much about herself; she has never had time for it. And this her life-chronicle, which, out of its very fulness, has taught her that the more one does,

5. Reference to Matthew 25:1–13, the parable of the wise and foolish virgins.

6. Reference to Matthew 25:14–30, the parable of the talents (coins).

the more one finds to do—she will never flourish in your face, or the face of Heaven, as something uncommonly virtuous and extraordinary. She knows that, after all, she has simply done what it was her duty to do.

But—and when her place is vacant on earth, this will be said of her assuredly, both here and Otherwhere—"*She hath done what she could.*"[7]

1857

HELEN HUNT JACKSON
1830–1885

Helen Hunt Jackson (née Fiske) was born in the college town of Amherst in western Massachusetts in 1830. A poet, novelist, and essayist, Jackson embraced the possibilities of travel, publication, and reform. Her nonfiction exposé *A Century of Dishonor* (1881) and her novel *Ramona* (1884) criticize her government's treatment of the native peoples. Jackson's poetry was celebrated in the second half of the nineteenth century for successfully marrying traditional poetic forms with American topics. A popular poet, Jackson did much to disseminate transcendentalist values—the elevation of the spiritual over the material, reverence of nature, and the belief that one's values should derive from careful self-reflection—during the post–Civil War years.

Her father, a professor at Amherst College, and her mother both died of lung disease before Jackson was twenty, leaving Jackson financially well-off but with a lifelong anxiety about her health. Jackson married twice: first, in 1852, to Edward Hunt, who died during the Civil War; and second, in 1875, to William Jackson. Like most young women of her class, Jackson had learned as a schoolgirl to write conventional verse. After the deaths of her first husband and then of her last child in the mid–1860s, Jackson began to write poetry in earnest. Her talent was nurtured by Thomas Wentworth Higginson—war hero, women's rights activist, editor—who helped Jackson begin publishing and who remained her friend for life. However, it was when Jackson moved west—first to Colorado and later to California—that she found the two topics to which she would devote herself: vanishing nature and the plight of native peoples. Over the years, Jackson published under different names, including the pseudonym Saxe Holm and cognomens such as "Rip Van Winkle." She died in California in 1885.

My Tenants

I never had a title-deed
To my estate. But little heed
Eyes give to me, when I walk by
My fields, to see who occupy.

7. Mark 14:8.

Some clumsy men who lease and hire   5
And cut my trees to feed their fire,
Own all the land that I possess,
And tax my tenants to distress.

And if I say I had been first,
And, reaping, left for them the worst,   10
That they were beggars at the hands
Of dwellers on my royal lands,
With idle laugh of passing scorn
As unto words of madness born,
They would reply
            I do not care;   15
They cannot crowd the charméd air;
They cannot touch the bonds I hold
On all that they have bought and sold.
They can waylay my faithful bees,
Who, lulled to sleep, with fatal ease,   20
Are robbe[d]. Is one day's honey sweet
Thus snatched? All summer round my feet
In golden drifts from plumy wings,
In shining drops on fragrant things
Free gift, it came to me. My corn,   25
With burnished banners, morn by morn,
Comes out to meet and honor me;
The glittering ranks spread royally
Far as I walk. When hasty greed
Tramples it down for food and seed,   30
I, with a certain veiled delight,
Hear half the crop is lost by blight.

Letter of the law these may fulfil,
Plant where they like, slay what they will,
Count up their gains and make them great;   35
Nevertheless, the whole estate
Always belongs to me and mine.
We are the only royal line.
And though I have no title-deed
My tenants pay me royal heed   40
When our sweet fields I wander by
To see what strangers occupy.

                         1886

September

    The golden-rod is yellow;
      The corn is turning brown;
    The trees in apple orchards
      With fruit are bending down.

The gentian's bluest fringes   5
    Are curling in the sun;
In dusty pods the milkweed
    Its hidden silk has spun.

The sedges flaunt their harvest,
    In every meadow nook;   10
And asters by the brook-side
    Make asters in the brook,

From dewy lanes at morning
    The grapes' sweet odors rise;
At noon the roads all flutter   15
    With yellow butterflies.

By all these lovely tokens
    September days are here,
With summer's best of weather,
    And autumn's best of cheer.   20

But none of all this beauty
    Which floods the earth and air
Is unto me the secret
    Which makes September fair.

'T is a thing which I remember;   25
    To name it thrills me yet:
One day of one September
    I never can forget.

                        1886

The Victory of Patience

Armed of the gods! Divinest conqueror!
What soundless hosts are thine! Nor pomp, nor state,
Nor token, to betray where thou dost wait.
All Nature stands, for thee, ambassador;
Her forces all thy serfs, for peace or war.   5
Greatest and least alike, thou rul'st their fate,—
The avalanch chained until its century's date,
The mulberry leaf made robe for emperor![1]
Shall man alone thy law deny?—refuse
Thy healing for his blunders and his sins?   10
Oh, make us thine! Teach us who waits best sues;
Who longest waits of all most surely wins.
When Time is spent, Eternity begins.
To doubt, to chafe, to haste, doth God accuse.

                        1886

---

1. Silk (for emperors' robes) was spun by silkworms who fed on mulberry leaves.

Chance

These things wondering I saw beneath the sun:
That never yet the race was to the swift,
The fight unto the mightiest to lift,
Nor favors unto men whose skill had done
Great works, nor riches ever unto one
Wise man of understanding. All is drift
Of time and chance, and none may stay or sift
Or know the end of that which is begun.
Who waits until the wind shall silent keep,
Will never find the ready hour to sow.
Who watcheth clouds will have no time to reap.
At daydawn plant thy seed, and be not slow
At night God doth not slumber take nor sleep:
Which seed shall prosper thou shalt never know.[2]

1886

◄ EMILY DICKINSON ►
1830–1886

The daughter of a prominent New England family, Emily Dickinson was educated at home and in prestigious local schools. That she was a prolific letter and verse writer would not have been remarkable. Nor would it have been remarkable had she, like her childhood friend Helen Hunt Jackson (p. 935), become a published poet. What is remarkable is the degree to which Dickinson devoted herself to a lifetime project of exploring the power and limits of the lyric poem.

The outline of her biography suggests a conventional life. Her father, Edward Dickinson, was a lawyer and treasurer of Amherst College; he also served as a Massachusetts congressional representative. Her mother, Emily Norcross Dickinson, was herself highly educated. Never marrying, Dickinson took care of her father's household after the death of her mother. Traveling with him to Philadelphia and Washington, D.C., as his career dictated, but spending most of her life in the family home, Dickinson met many of the most prominent politicians and artists of her day. She had close ties with her sister, Lavinia; her brother, Austin, and his wife, Susan; and a close-knit circle of friends with whom she maintained an ongoing correspondence. She died, at age fifty-six, having published only a handful of poems.

If the lineaments of Dickinson's biography would depict her as a slightly exaggerated version of the "true woman" (homebound, pious, self-negating), her

---

2. A reference to Psalm 121:4: "Behold, he that keepeth Israel shall neither slumber nor sleep"; also a reference to Matthew 13:3–8: "Behold, a sower went forth to sow; and when he sowed, some fell by the wayside. . . . Some fell upon stony places. . . . And some fell among thorns. . . . But other fell into good ground, and brought forth fruit, some an hundredfold, some sixtyfold, some thirtyfold."

letters reveal a subversive mastery of her culture's norms and codes. She was unswayed by conventional Christianity as an avenue to spirituality, unswayed by the inherent heterosexist bias of contemporary gender norms, unswayed by conventional understandings of limits of language to express subjectivity. Dickinson used and exploded these norms through her own behavior. She seems to have been protecting her ability to devote herself to writing by hiding behind a screen of unimpeachable domesticity. This screen allowed her, for example, to decline active involvement in the distractions of small-town life so that she could cultivate her chosen relationships with a small set of friends and with language itself.

The extent of Dickinson's relationship with language was not known until after her death, when her sister, Lavinia, discovered the 814 poems Dickinson had copied neatly and sewn into booklets, the 333 poems that seemed ready for sewing, and a large set of rough copies of poems in process. Various people who had had a chance to read some of Dickinson's poems while she was alive had appreciated their worth. Helen Hunt Jackson, for example, repeatedly urged Dickinson to publish, as did another friend, Thomas Wentworth Higginson. A small selection of these poems was edited by Mabel Todd Loomis and T. W. Higginson and published in the 1890s in editions that regularized the punctuation, line, and rhymes of Dickinson's verse. In the 1950s, however, Thomas Johnson published a complete edition of her poems. Johnson's edition numbered the poems and tried to be as faithful as possible to Dickinson's handwritten versions. While twentieth-century poets generally eschewed the poetry of the century before, Dickinson's poems had an immediate and indelible effect on modern poets and readers, including Adrienne Rich (pp. 1558–88) and Sylvia Plath (pp. 1625–41).

Although Dickinson did group many of her poems, she did not give them titles. Today they are referred to by the numbers Johnson ascribed to them or by the first line of the poem. Her poems are visually distinctive due to her heavy use of dashes and unconventional capitalization. When read, they reveal an intense representation of a felt intensity of an expanded moment. They also reveal a "slanted" relationship to the poetry of her contemporaries in her treatment of the familiar topics of nature, spirituality, erotic desire, mourning, and the family. Like her rhymes and her meters, which are frequently "off" just enough to interrupt the complacency of the reader, poems such as number 258, "There's a certain Slant of light," direct the reader to pay attention to the "internal difference, / where the Meanings, are—."

6

Frequently the woods are pink—
Frequently are brown.
Frequently the hills undress
Behind my native town.
Oft a head is crested   5
I was wont to see—
And as oft a cranny
Where it used to be—
And the Earth—they tell me—
On its Axis turned!   10

Wonderful Rotation!
By but *twelve* performed!

c. 1858   c. 1891

14

One sister have I in our house,
And one, a hedge away.
There's only one recorded,
But both belong to me.

One came the road that I came—   5
And wore my last year's gown—
The other, as a bird her nest,
Builded our hearts among.

She did not sing as we did—
It was a different tune—   10
Herself to her a music
As Bumble bee of June.

Today is far from Childhood—
But up and down the hills
I held her hand the tighter—   15
Which shortened all the miles—

And still her hum
The years among,
Deceives the Butterfly;
Still in her Eye   20
The Violets lie
Mouldered this many May.

I spilt the dew—
But took the morn—
I chose this single star   25
From out the wide night's numbers—
Sue—forevermore!

1858   1914

216

Safe in their Alabaster Chambers—
Untouched by Morning—
And untouched by Noon—
Lie the meek members of the Resurrection—
Rafter of Satin—and Roof of Stone!   5

Grand go the Years—in the Crescent—above them—
Worlds scoop their Arcs—
And Firmaments—row—

Diadems—drop—and Doges—surrender—
Soundless as dots—on a Disc of Snow—   10

1861 version   1890

241

I like a look of Agony,
Because I know it's true—
Men do not sham Convulsion,
Nor simulate, a Throe—

The Eyes glaze once—and that is Death—   5
Impossible to feign
The Beads upon the Forehead
By homely Anguish strung.

c. 1861   1890

249

Wild Nights—Wild Nights!
Were I with thee
Wild Nights should be
Our luxury!

Futile—the Winds—   5
To a Heart in port—
Done with the Compass—
Done with the Chart!

Rowing in Eden—
Ah, the Sea!   10
Might I but moor —Tonight—
In Thee!

c. 1861   1891

252

I can wade Grief—
Whole Pools of it—
I'm used to that—
But the least push of Joy
Breaks up my feet—   5
And I tip—drunken—
Let no Pebble—smile—
'Twas the New Liquor—
That was all!

Power is only Pain—   10
Stranded, thro' Discipline,
Till Weights—will hang—
Give Balm—to Giants—
And they'll wilt, like Men—

Give Himmaleh —[1]   15
They'll Carry—Him!

c. 1861   1891

258

There's a certain Slant of light,
Winter Afternoons—
That oppresses, like the Heft
Of Cathedral Tunes—

Heavenly Hurt, it gives us—   5
We can find no scar,
But internal difference,
Where the Meanings, are—

None may teach it—Any—
'Tis the Seal Despair—   10
An imperial affliction
Sent us of the Air—

When it comes, the Landscape Listens—
Shadows—hold their breath—
When it goes, 'tis like the Distance   15
On the look of Death—

c. 1861   1891

280

I felt a Funeral, in my Brain,
And Mourners to and fro
Kept treading—treading—till it seemed
That Sense was breaking through—

And when they all were seated,   5
A Service, like a Drum—
Kept beating—beating—till I thought
My Mind was going numb—

And then I heard them lift a Box
And creak across my Soul   10
With those same Boots of Lead, again,
Then Space—began to toll,

As all the Heavens were a Bell,
And Being, but an Ear,
And I, and Silence, some strange Race   15
Wrecked, solitary, here—

And then a Plank in Reason, broke,
And I dropped down, and down—

1. The Himalaya Mountains, here personified.

And hit a World, at every plunge,
And Finished knowing—then—   20

c. 1861   1896

288

I'm Nobody! Who are you?
Are you—Nobody—Too?
Then there's a pair of us!
Don't tell! They'd advertise—you know!

How dreary—to be—Somebody!   5
How public—like a Frog—
To tell one's name—the livelong June—
To an admiring Bog!

c. 1861   1891

341

After great pain, a formal feeling comes—
The Nerves sit ceremonious, like Tombs—
The stiff Heart questions was it He, that bore,
And Yesterday, or Centuries before?

The Feet, mechanical, go round—   5
Of Ground, or Air, or Ought—
A Wooden way
Regardless grown,
A Quartz contentment, like a stone—

This is the Hour of Lead—   10
Remembered, if outlived,
As Freezing persons, recollect the Snow—
First—Chill—then Stupor—then the letting go—

c. 1862   1929

365

Dare you see a Soul *at the White Heat?*
Then crouch within the door—
Red—is the Fire's common tint—
But when the vivid Ore
Has vanquished Flame's conditions,   5
It quivers from the Forge
Without a color, but the light
Of unanointed Blaze.
Least Village has its Blacksmith
Whose Anvil's even ring   10
Stands symbol for the finer Forge
That soundless tugs—within—
Refining these impatient Ores

With Hammer, and with Blaze
Until the Designated Light   15
Repudiate the Forge—

c. 1862   1935

441

This is my letter to the World
That never wrote to Me—
The simple News that Nature told—
With tender Majesty

Her Message is committed   5
To Hands I cannot see—
For love of Her—Sweet—countrymen—
Judge tenderly—of Me

c. 1862   1890

444

It feels a shame to be Alive—
When Men so brave—are dead—
One envies the Distinguished Dust—
Permitted—such a Head—

The Stone—that tells defending Whom   5
This Spartan put away
What little of Him we—possessed
In Pawn for Liberty—

The price is great—Sublimely paid—
Do we deserve—a Thing
That lives—like Dollars—must be piled   10
Before we may obtain?

Are we that wait—sufficient worth—
That such Enormous Pearl
As life—dissolved be—for Us—   15
In Battle's—horrid Bowl?

It may be—a Renown to live—
I think the Man who die—
Those unsustained—Saviors—
Present Divinity—   20

1862   1929

579

I had been hungry, all the Years—
My Noon had Come—to dine—
I trembling drew the Table near—
And touched the Curious Wine—

'Twas this on Tables I had seen—   5
When turning, hungry, Home
I looked in Windows, for the Wealth
I could not hope—for Mine—

I did not know the ample Bread—
'Twas so unlike the Crumb   10
The Birds and I, had often shared
In Nature's—Dining Room—

The Plenty hurt me—'twas so new—
Myself felt ill—and odd—
As Berry—of a Mountain Bush—   15
Transplanted—to the Road—

Nor was I hungry—so I found
That Hunger—was a way
Of Persons outside Windows—
The Entering—takes away—   20

c. 1862   1891

656

The name—of it—is "Autumn"—
The hue—of it—is Blood—
An Artery—upon the Hill—
A Vein—along the Road—

Great Globules—in the Alleys—   5
And Oh, the Shower of Stain—
When Winds—upset the Basin—
And spill the Scarlet Rain—

It sprinkles Bonnets—far below—
It gathers ruddy Pools—   10
Then—eddies like a Rose—away—
Upon Vermilion Wheels—

1862   1892

709

Publication—is the Auction
Of the Mind of Man—
Poverty—be justifying
For so foul a thing

Possibly—but We—would rather   5
From Our Garret go
White—Unto the White Creator—
Than invest—Our Snow—

Thought belong to Him who gave it—
Then—to Him Who bear   10

Its Corporeal illustration—Sell
The Royal Air—

In the Parcel—Be the Merchant
Of the Heavenly Grace—
But reduce no Human Spirit   15
To Disgrace of Price—

c. 1863   1929

754

My Life had stood—a Loaded Gun—
In Corners—till a Day
The Owner passed—identified—
And carried Me away—

And now We roam in Sovereign Woods—   5
And now We hunt the Doe—
And every time I speak for Him—
The Mountains straight reply—

And do I smile, such cordial light
Upon the Valley glow—   10
It is as a Vesuvian face
Had let its pleasure through—

And when at Night—Our good Day done—
I guard My Master's Head—
'Tis better than the Eider-Duck's   15
Deep Pillow—to have shared—

To foe of His—I'm deadly foe—
None stir the second time—
On whom I lay a Yellow Eye—
Or an emphatic Thumb—   20

Though I than He—may longer live
He longer must—than I—
For I have but the power to kill,
Without—the power to die—

c. 1863   1929

812

A Light exists in Spring
Not present on the Year
At any other period—
When March is scarcely here

A Color stands abroad   5
On Solitary Fields

That Science cannot overtake
But Human Nature feels.

It waits upon the Lawn,
It shows the furthest Tree   10
Upon the furthest Slope you know
It almost speaks to you.

Then as Horizons step
Or Noons report away
Without the Formula of sound   15
It passes and we stay—

A quality of loss
Affecting our Content
As Trade had suddenly encroached
Upon a Sacrament.   20

c. 1864   1945

912

Peace is a fiction of our Faith—
The Bells a Winter Night
Bearing the Neighbor out of Sound
That never did alight.

c. 1864   1945

986

A narrow Fellow in the Grass
Occasionally rides—
You may have met Him—did you not
His notice sudden is—

The Grass divides as with a Comb—   5
A spotted shaft is seen—
And then it closes at your feet
And opens further on—

He likes a Boggy Acre
A Floor too cool for Corn—   10
Yet when a Boy, and Barefoot—
I more than once at Noon
Have passed, I thought, a Whip lash
Unbraiding in the Sun
When stooping to secure it   15
It wrinkled, and was gone—

Several of Nature's People
I know, and they know me—
I feel for them a transport
Of cordiality—   20

But never met this Fellow
Attended, or alone
Without a tighter breathing
And Zero at the Bone—

c. 1865   1866

1101

Between the form of Life and Life
The difference is as big
As Liquor at the Lip between
And Liquor in the Jug
The latter—excellent to keep—   5
But for ecstatic need
The corkless is superior—
I know for I have tried

c. 1866   1945

1129

Tell all the Truth but tell it slant—
Success in Circuit lies
Too bright for our infirm Delight
The Truth's superb surprise

As Lightning to the Children eased   5
With explanation kind
The Truth must dazzle gradually
Or every man be blind—

c. 1868   1945

1263

There is no Frigate like a Book
To take us Lands away
Nor any Coursers like a Page
Of prancing Poetry—
This Traverse may the poorest take   5
Without oppress of Toll—
How frugal is the Chariot
That bears the Human soul.

c. 1873   1894

1580

We shun it ere it comes,
Afraid of Joy,
Then sue it to delay
And lest it fly,
Beguile it more and more—   5
May not this be

Old Suitor Heaven,
Like our dismay at thee?

c. 1882   1894

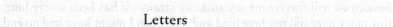

Letters

To Susan Gilbert (Dickinson)[2]

early June 1852

They are cleaning house today, Susie, and I've made a flying retreat to my own little chamber, where with affection, and you, I will spend this my precious hour, most of all the hours which dot my flying days, and the one so dear, that for it I barter everything, and as soon as it is gone, I am sighing for it again.

I cannot believe, dear Susie, that I have stayed without you almost a whole year long; sometimes the time seems short, and the thought of you as warm as if you had gone but yesterday, and again if years and years had trod their silent pathway, the time would seem less long. And now how soon I shall have you, shall hold you in my arms; you will forgive the tears, Susie, they are so glad to come that it is not in my heart to reprove them and send them home. I don't know why it is—but there's something in your name, now you are taken from me, which fills my heart so full, and my eye, too. It is not that the mention *grieves* me, no, Susie, but I think of each "sunnyside" where we have sat together, and lest there be no more, I guess is what makes the tears come. Mattie[3] was here last evening, and we sat on the front door stone, and talked about life and love, and whispered our childish fancies about such blissful things—the evening was gone so soon, and I walked home with Mattie beneath the silent moon, and wished for you, and Heaven. You did not come, Darling, but a bit of Heaven did, or so it *seemed* to us, as we walked side by side and wondered if that great blessedness which may be our's sometime, is granted now, to some. Those unions, my dear Susie, by which two lives are one, this sweet and strange adoption wherein we can but look, and are not yet admitted, how it can fill the heart, and make it gang wildly beating, how it will take *us* one day, and make us all it's own, and we shall not run away from it, but lie still and be happy!

You and I have been strangely silent upon this subject, Susie, we have often touched upon it, and as quickly fled away, as children shut their eyes when the sun is too bright for them. I have always hoped to know if you had no dear fancy, illumining all your life, no one of whom you murmured in the faithful ear of night—and at whose side in fancy, you walked the livelong day; and when you come home, Susie, we must speak of these things. How dull our lives must seem to the bride, and the plighted maiden, whose days are fed with gold, and who gathers pearls every evening; but to the *wife,* Susie, sometimes the *wife forgotten,* our lives perhaps seem dearer than all others in the world; you have seen flowers at morning, *satisfied* with the dew, and those same sweet flowers at noon with their heads bowed in anguish before the mighty sun; think you these thirsty blossoms will

2. Gilbert (1830–1913), a friend of Emily Dickinson's, married her brother Austin in 1856.   3. Susan Gilbert's sister Martha.

now need naught but—*dew?* No, they will cry for sunlight, and pine for the burning noon, tho' it scorches them, scathes them; they have got through with peace—they know that the man of noon, is *mightier* than the morning and their life is henceforth to him. Oh, Susie, it is dangerous, and it is all too dear, these simple trusting spirits, and the spirits mightier, which we cannot resist! It does so rend me, Susie, the thought of it when it comes, that I tremble lest at sometime I, too, am yielded up. Susie, you will forgive me my amatory strain—it has been a very long one, and if this saucy page did not here bind and fetter me, I might have had no end.

I have got the letter, Susie, dear little bud, and all—and the tears came again, that alone in this big world, I am not *quite* alone. Such tears are showers—friend, thro' which when smiles appear, the angels call them rainbows, and mimic them in Heaven.

And now in four weeks more—you are mine, *all* mine, except I *lend* you a little occasionally to Hattie[4] and Mattie, if they promise not to lose you, and to bring you back very soon. I shall not count the days. I shall not fill my cups with this expected happiness, for perhaps if I do, the angels, being thirsty, will drink them up—I shall only *hope,* my Susie, and *that* tremblingly, for hav'nt barques the fullest, stranded upon the shore?

God is good, Susie, I trust he will save you, I pray that in his good time we once more meet each other, but if this life holds not another meeting for us, remember also, Susie, that it had no *parting* more, wherever that hour finds us, for which we have hoped so long, we shall not be separated, neither death, nor the grave can part us, so that we only *love!*

Your Emilie—

Austin has come and gone; life is so still again; why must the storm have calms? I hav'nt seen Root this term, I guess Mattie and I, are not sufficient for him! When will you come again, in a week? Let it be a *swift* week!

Vinnie[5] sends much love, and Mother; and might I be so bold as to enclose a *remembrance?*[6]

To T. W. Higginson[7]

7 June 1862

Dear friend.

Your letter gave no Drunkenness, because I tasted Rum before—Domingo comes but once—yet I have had few pleasures so deep as your opinion, and if I tried to thank you, my tears would block my tongue—

My dying Tutor told me that he would like to live till I had been a poet, but Death was much of Mob as I could master—then—And when far afterward—a sudden light on Orchards, or a new fashion in the wind troubled my attention— I felt a palsy, here—the Verses just relieve—

Your second letter surprised me, and for a moment, swung—I had not supposed it. Your first—gave no dishonor, because the True—are not ashamed— I thanked you for your justice—but could not drop the Bells whose jingling cooled my Tramp—Perhaps the Balm, seemed better, because you bled me, first.

---

4. Susan Gilbert's sister Harriet Gilbert Cutler, who lived in Amherst.
5. Root: Abiah Root, a friend since youth; Vinnie: Dickinson's sister Lavinia.

6. A small gift, perhaps a poem.
7. Thomas Wentworth Higginson (1823–1911), Dickinson's friend and later an editor of her published poetry.

I smile when you suggest that I delay "to publish"—that being foreign to my thought, as Firmament to Fin—

If fame belonged to me, I could not escape her—if she did not, the longest day would pass me on the chase—and the approbation of my Dog, would forsake me—then—My Barefoot-Rank is better—

You think my gait "spasmodic"—I am in danger—Sir—

You think me "uncontrolled"—I have no Tribunal.

Would you have time to be the "friend" you should think I need? I have a little shape—it would not crowd your Desk—nor make much Racket as the Mouse, that dents your Galleries—

If I might bring you what I do—not so frequent to trouble you—and ask you if I told it clear—'twould be control, to me—

The Sailor cannot see the North—but knows the Needle can—

The "hand you stretch me in the Dark," I put mine in, and turn away—I have no Saxon, now—

> As if I asked a common Alms,
> And in my wondering hand
> A Stranger pressed a Kingdom,
> And I, bewildered, stand —
> As if I asked the Orient   5
> Had it for me a Morn—
> And it should lift it's purple Dikes,
> And shatter me with Dawn!

But, will you be my Preceptor, Mr Higginson?

Your friend
E Dickinson—

To T. W. Higginson

February 1885

Dear friend—

It is long since I asked and received your consent to accept the Book, should it be, and the ratification at last comes, a pleasure I feared to hope—

Biography first convinces us of the fleeing of the Biographied—

> Pass to thy Rendezvous of Light,
> Pangless except for us—
> Who slowly ford the Mystery
> Which thou hast leaped across!

Your Scholar—

CHRISTINA ROSSETTI

1830–1894

Christina Rossetti was born into a family of teachers, artists, and writers. Her Italian father, Gabriele Rossetti, who had come to England as a political refugee, held a university professorship in London and supplemented his small income with private language lessons. Her mother, Frances Polidori, worked as a day-governess when her husband's health began to fail, and her older sister, Maria, became a full-time governess. Rossetti, who had been a healthy and cheerful child but suffered from a mysterious illness and apparently from depression during her teenage years, was not to follow her sister's example. A poet from the age of eleven onward, she wrote continually throughout her life, rivaling the fame of her brother Dante Gabriel Rossetti, the poet and Pre-Raphaelite painter.

Rossetti was an earnest High Church Anglican. Although she practiced a form of the state-supported religion that closely resembled Catholicism in its rituals and theology, like most people in England at the time, she disapproved of Roman Catholicism. She became engaged in 1848 to James Collinson, a poet, painter, and an associate of her brother's. She had rejected his first proposal because he was a Roman Catholic, but he had converted to the Church of England, and she accepted his proposal when it came from an Anglican. In 1850 he reverted to Catholicism, however, and the engagement was broken off. A later relationship of long standing, with classical scholar Charles Bagot Caley, also did not lead to marriage; Rossetti cited his lack of Christian faith as the reason for refusing the proposal he made in 1866. Even so, her poems hum with consummated passion: in *A Room of One's Own* Virginia Woolf mentions Rossetti's "A Birthday" to illustrate "what women hummed at luncheon parties before the war," when relations between men and women were "musical, exciting."

In her youth, Rossetti published poems in the Pre-Raphaelite journal *The Germ,* using the pseudonym "Ellen Alleyn." The Pre-Raphaelite Brotherhood, or "PRB," was a group of writers and painters, co-founded by her famous brother, devoted to returning art to the more realistic style popular before Raphael, an Italian Renaissance painter born in 1483. As a woman in the Victorian era, Rossetti could not casually mingle with the all-male PRB, but in addition to contributing poetry to their journal, she also sat as a model for her brother's paintings.

Although Rossetti was remembered by her contemporaries (particularly in the biographical commentaries of her brother William, a critic, editor, and translator) as a quiet, calm, reserved, and even repressed woman, her poetic voice is vivid, passionate, and—in the case of her poem "Goblin Market"—anything but proper. "Goblin Market" was popular in its day but has since become even more important given the attention of feminist critics who have read it as an allegory of developing female sexuality. The poet herself insisted that it was only a "fairy tale." Her first published volume, *Goblin Market and Other Poems* (1862), made Rossetti famous, providing an audience for her subsequent books: *The Prince's Progress and Other Poems* (1866), *Sing-Song: A Nursery Rhyme Book* (1872), and *A Pageant and Other Poems* (1881). This last volume included a sonnet sequence, "Monna Innominata," which Rossetti described as a variation on Elizabeth Barrett Browning's *Sonnets from the Portuguese* (see pp. 652–53). Like Barrett Browning, Rossetti appropriated the male-dominated sonnet form to speak in the first person of a woman's love, but unlike Barrett Browning's sonnet cycle, Rossetti's told of sadness rather than joy. Much of her poetry is explicitly Christian, such as "A Better Resurrection" (1862), reprinted here. She also produced three volumes of devotional prose writings and a novel, *Maude: A Story for Girls* (1850/1897), published posthumously. She died of cancer in London, the city of her birth, in 1894.

A Birthday

My heart is like a singing bird
   Whose nest is in a watered shoot;
My heart is like an apple tree
   Whose boughs are bent with thickset fruit;
My heart is like a rainbow shell   5
   That paddles in a halcyon sea;
My heart is gladder than all these
   Because my love is come to me.

Raise me a dais of silk and down;
   Hang it with vair[1] and purple dyes;   10
Carve it in doves and pomegranates,
   And peacocks with a hundred eyes;
Work it in gold and silver grapes,
   In leaves and silver fleurs-de-lys,[2]
Because the birthday of my life   15
   Is come, my love is come to me.

1857   1862

A Better Resurrection

I have no wit, no words, no tears;
   My Heart within me like a stone
Is numbed too much for hopes or fears;
   Look right, look left, I dwell alone;
I lift mine eyes, but dimmed with grief   5
   No everlasting hills I see;
My life is in the falling leaf:
   O Jesus, quicken me.

My life is like a faded leaf,
   My harvest dwindled to a husk;   10
Truly my life is void and brief
   And tedious in the barren dusk;
My life is like a frozen thing,
   No bud nor greenness can I see:
Yet rise it shall—the sap of Spring;   15
   O Jesus, rise in me.

My life is like a broken bowl,
   A broken bowl that cannot hold
One drop of water for my soul
   Or cordial in the searching cold;   20
Cast in the fire the perished thing,
   Melt and remould it, till it be

---

1. A blue-and-white squirrel fur used on heraldic shields.   2. Work: embroider; fleurs-de-lys: a stylized iris, used in heraldry.

A royal cup for Him my King:
O Jesus, drink of me.

1862

Goblin Market

Morning and evening
Maids[3] heard the goblins cry:
"Come buy our orchard fruits,
Come buy, come buy:
Apples and quinces,   5
Lemons and oranges,
Plump unpecked cherries,
Melons and raspberries,
Bloom-down-cheeked peaches,
Swart-headed[4] mulberries,   10
Wild free-born cranberries,
Crab-apples, dewberries,
Pine-apples, blackberries,
Apricots, strawberries;—
All ripe together   15
In summer weather,—
Morns that pass by,
Fair eves that fly;
Come buy, come buy:
Our grapes fresh from the vine,   20
Pomegranates full and fine,
Dates and sharp bullaces,
Rare pears and greengages,
Damsons[5] and bilberries,
Taste them and try: 25
Currants and gooseberries,
Bright-fire-like barberries,
Figs to fill your mouth
Citrons from the South,
Sweet to tongue and sound to eye;   30
Come buy, come buy."

Evening by evening
Among the brookside rushes,
Laura bowed her head to hear,
Lizzie veiled her blushes: 35
Crouching close together
In the cooling weather,
With clasping arms and cautioning lips,
With tingling cheeks and finger tips.
"Lie close," Laura said,   40

3. Virginal young women.
4. Black.

5. Damson is a type of plum, as are bullaces and greengages.

Pricking up her golden head:
"We must not look at goblin men,
We must not buy their fruits:
Who knows upon what soil they fed
Their hungry thirsty roots?"   45
"Come buy," call the goblins
Hobbling down the glen.
"Oh," cried Lizzie, "Laura, Laura,
You should not peep at goblin men."
Lizzie covered up her eyes,   50
Covered close lest they should look;
Laura reared her glossy head,
And whispered like the restless brook:
"Look, Lizzie, look, Lizzie,
Down the glen tramp little men.   55
One hauls a basket,
One bears a plate,
One lugs a golden dish
Of many pounds weight.
How fair the vine must grow   60
Whose grapes are so luscious;
How warm the wind must blow
Thro' those fruit bushes."
"No," said Lizzie: "No, no, no;
Their offers should not charm us,   65
Their evil gifts would harm us."
She thrust a dimpled finger
In each ear, shut eyes and ran:
Curious Laura chose to linger
Wondering at each merchant man.   70
One had a cat's face,
One whisked a tail,
One tramped at a rat's pace,
One crawled like a snail,
One like a wombat prowled obtuse and furry,   75
One like a ratel[6] tumbled hurry skurry.
She heard a voice like voice of doves
Cooing all together:
They sounded kind and full of loves
In the pleasant weather.   80

Laura stretched her gleaming neck
Like a rush-imbedded swan,
Like a lily from the beck,[7]
Like a moonlit poplar branch,
Like a vessel at the launch   85
When its last restraint is gone.

6. Aggressive, short-legged, carnivorous mammal   7. Brook or small stream.
found in Asia and Africa.

Backwards up the mossy glen
Turned and trooped the goblin men,
With their shrill repeated cry,
"Come buy, come buy."   90
When they reached where Laura was
They stood stock still upon the moss,
Leering at each other,
Brother with queer brother;
Signalling each other,   95
Brother with sly brother.
One set his basket down,
One reared his plate;
One began to weave a crown
Of tendrils, leaves and rough nuts brown   100
(Men sell not such in any town);
One heaved the golden weight
Of dish and fruit to offer her:
"Come buy, come buy," was still their cry.
Laura stared but did not stir,   105
Longed but had no money:
The whisk-tailed merchant bade her taste
In tones as smooth as honey,
The cat-faced purr'd,
The rat-paced spoke a word   110
Of welcome, and the snail-paced even was heard;
One parrot-voiced and jolly
Cried "Pretty Goblin" still for "Pretty Polly;"—
One whistled like a bird.

But sweet-tooth Laura spoke in haste: 115
"Good folk, I have no coin;
To take were to purloin:
I have no copper in my purse,
I have no silver either,
And all my gold is on the furze[8]   120
That shakes in windy weather
Above the rusty heather."
"You have much gold upon your head,"
They answered all together:
"Buy from us with a golden curl."   125
She clipped a precious golden lock,
She dropped a tear more rare than pearl,
Then sucked their fruit globes fair or red:
Sweeter than honey from the rock.
Stronger than man-rejoicing wine,   130
Clearer than water flowed that juice;
She never tasted such before,

8. A spiny, yellow-flowered shrub.

How should it cloy with length of use?
She sucked and sucked and sucked the more
Fruits which that unknown orchard bore;   135
She sucked until her lips were sore;
Then flung the emptied rinds away
But gathered up one kernel-stone,
And knew not was it night or day
As she turned home alone.   140

Lizzie met her at the gate
Full of wise upbraidings:
"Dear, you should not stay so late,
Twilight is not good for maidens;
Should not loiter in the glen   145
In the haunts of goblin men.
Do you not remember Jeanie,
How she met them in the moonlight,
Took their gifts both choice and many,
Ate their fruits and wore their flowers   150
Plucked from bowers
Where summer ripens at all hours?
But ever in the noonlight
She pined and pined away;
Sought them by night and day,   155
Found them no more but dwindled and grew grey;
Then fell with the first snow,
While to this day no grass will grow
Where she lies low:
I planted daises there a year ago   160
That never blow.
You should not loiter so."
"Nay, hush," said Laura:
"Nay, hush, my sister:
I ate and ate my fill,   165
Yet my mouth waters still;
Tomorrow night I will
Buy more:" and kissed her:
"Have done with sorrow;
I'll bring you plums tomorrow   170
Fresh on their mother twigs,
Cherries worth getting;
You cannot think what figs
My teeth have met in,
What melons icy-cold   175
Piled on a dish of gold
Too huge for me to hold,
What peaches with a velvet nap,
Pellucid grapes without one seed:
Odorous indeed must be the mead   180

Whereon they grow, and pure the wave they drink
With lilies at the brink,
And sugar-sweet their sap."

Golden head by golden head,
Like two pigeons in one nest   185
Folded in each other's wings,
They lay down in their curtained bed:
Like two blossoms on one stem,
Like two flakes of new-fall'n snow,
Like two wands of ivory   190
Tipped with gold for awful⁹ kings.
Moon and stars gazed in at them,
Wind sang to them lullaby,
Lumbering owls forbore to fly,
Not a bat flapped to and fro   195
Round their rest:
Cheek to cheek and breast to breast
Locked together in one nest.

Early in the morning
When the first cock crowed his warning,   200
Neat like bees, as sweet and busy,
Laura rose with Lizzie:
Fetched in honey, milked the cows,
Aired and set to rights the house,
Kneaded cakes of whitest wheat,   205
Cakes for dainty mouths to eat,
Next churned butter, whipped up cream,
Fed their poultry, sat and sewed;
Talked as modest maidens should:
Lizzie with an open heart,   210
Laura in an absent dream,
One content, one sick in part;
One warbling for the mere bright day's delight,
One longing for the night.

At length slow evening came: 215
They went with pitchers to the reedy brook;
Lizzie most placid in her look,
Laura most like a leaping flame.
They drew the gurgling water from its deep;
Lizzie plucked purple and rich golden flags,   220
Then turning homewards said: "The sunset flushes
Those furthest loftiest crags;
Come, Laura, not another maiden lags,
No wilful squirrel wags,
The beasts and birds are fast asleep."   225

9. Awe-inspiring.

But Laura loitered still among the rushes
And said the bank was steep.

And said the hour was early still,
The dew not fall'n, the wind not chill:
Listening ever, but not catching   230
The customary cry,
"Come buy, come buy,"
With its iterated jingle
Of sugar-baited words:
Not for all her watching   235
Once discerning even one goblin
Racing, whisking, tumbling, hobbling;
Let alone the herds
That used to tramp along the glen,
In groups or single,   240
Of brisk fruit-merchant men.
Till Lizzie urged, "O Laura, come;
I hear the fruit-call but I dare not look:
You should not loiter longer at this brook·
Come with me home.   245
The stars rise, the moon bends her arc,
Each glowworm winks her spark,
Let us get home before the night grows dark:
For clouds may gather
Tho' this is summer weather,   250
Put out the lights and drench us thro';
Then if we lost our way what should we do?"

Laura turned cold as stone
To find her sister heard that cry alone,
That goblin cry,   255
"Come buy our fruits, come buy."
Must she then buy no more such dainty fruit?
Must she no more such succous pasture find,
Gone deaf and blind?
Her tree of life drooped from the root: 260
She said not one word in her heart's sore ache;
But peering thro' the dimness, nought discerning,
Trudged home, her pitcher dripping all the way;
So crept to bed, and lay
Silent till Lizzie slept;   265
Then sat up in a passionate yearning,
And gnashed her teeth for baulked desire, and wept
As if her heart would break.

Day after day, night after night,
Laura kept watch in vain   270
In sullen silence of exceeding pain.
She never caught again the goblin cry:

"Come buy, come buy;"—
She never spied the goblin men
Hawking their fruits along the glen: 275
But when the noon waxed bright
Her hair grew thin and gray;
She dwindled, as the fair full moon doth turn
To swift decay and burn
Her fire away.   280

One day remembering her kernel-stone
She set it by a wall that faced the south;
Dewed it with tears, hoped for a root,
Watched for a waxing shoot,
But there came none;   285
It never saw the sun,
It never felt the trickling moisture run:
While with sunk eyes and faded mouth
She dreamed of melons, as a traveller sees
False waves in desert drouth   290
With shade of leaf-crowned trees,
And burns the thirstier in the sandful breeze.

She no more swept the house,
Tended the fowls or cows,
Fetched honey, kneaded cakes of wheat,   295
Brought water from the brook:
But sat down listless in the chimney-nook
And would not eat.

Tender Lizzie could not bear
To watch her sister's cankerous[1] care   300
Yet not to share.
She night and morning
Caught the goblins' cry:
"Come buy our orchard fruits,
Come buy, come buy:"—   305
Beside the brook, along the glen,
She heard the tramp of goblin men,
The voice and stir
Poor Laura could not hear;
Longed to buy fruit to comfort her,   310
But feared to pay too dear.
She thought of Jeanie in her grave,
Who should have been a bride;
But who for joys brides hope to have
Fell sick and died   315
In her gay prime,
In earliest Winter time,

---

1. Corrupting, diseased.

With the first glazing rime,
With the first snow-fall of crisp Winter time.

Till Laura dwindling   320
Seemed knocking at Death's door:
Then Lizzie weighed no more
Better and worse;
But put a silver penny in her purse,
Kissed Laura, crossed the heath with clumps of furze   325
At twilight, halted by the brook:
And for the first time in her life
Began to listen and look.

Laughed every goblin
When they spied her peeping: 330
Came towards her hobbling,
Flying, running, leaping,
Puffing and blowing,
Chuckling, clapping, crowing,
Clucking and gobbling,   335
Mopping and mowing,
Full of airs and graces,
Pulling wry faces,
Demure grimaces,
Cat-like and rat-like,   340
Ratel- and wombat-like,
Snail-paced in a hurry,
Parrot-voiced and whistler,
Helter skelter, hurry skurry,
Chattering like magpies,   345
Fluttering like pigeons,
Gliding like fishes,—
Hugged her and kissed her,
Squeezed and caressed her:
Stretched up their dishes,   350
Panniers, and plates:
"Look at our apples
Russet and dun,
Bob at our cherries,
Bite at our peaches,   355
Citrons and dates,
Grapes for the asking,
Pears red with basking
Out in the sun,
Plums on their twigs;   360
Pluck them and suck them,
Pomegranates, figs."—

"Good folk," said Lizzie,
Mindful of Jeanie:
"Give me much and many:"—   365

Held out her apron,
Tossed them her penny.
"Nay, take a seat with us,
Honour and eat with us,"
They answered grinning: 370
"Our feast is but beginning.
Night yet is early,
Warm and dew-pearly,
Wakeful and starry:
Such fruits as these   375
No man can carry;
Half their bloom would fly,
Half their dew would dry,
Half their flavour would pass by.
Sit down and feast with us,   380
Be welcome guest with us,
Cheer you and rest with us."—
"Thank you," said Lizzie: "But one waits
At home alone for me:
So without further parleying,   385
If you will not sell me any
Of your fruits tho' much and many,
Give me back my silver penny
I tossed you for a fee."—
They began to scratch their pates,   390
No longer wagging, purring,
But visibly demurring,
Grunting and snarling.
One called her proud,
Cross-grained, uncivil;   395
Their tones waxed loud,
Their looks were evil.
Lashing their tails
They trod and hustled her,
Elbowed and jostled her,   400
Clawed with their nails,
Barking, mewing, hissing, mocking,
Tore her gown and soiled her stocking,
Twitched her hair out by the roots,
Stamped upon her tender feet,   405
Held her hands and squeezed their fruits
Against her mouth to make her eat.

White and golden Lizzie stood,
Like a lily in a flood,—
Like a rock of blue-veined stone   410
Lashed by tides obstreperously,—
Like a beacon left alone
In a hoary roaring sea,

Sending up a golden fire,—
Like a fruit-crowned orange-tree   415
White with blossoms honey-sweet
Sore beset by wasp and bee,—
Like a royal virgin town
Topped with gilded dome and spire
Close beleaguered by a fleet   420
Mad to tug her standard down.

One may lead a horse to water,
Twenty cannot make him drink.
Tho' the goblins cuffed and caught her,
Coaxed and fought her,   425
Bullied and besought her,
Scratched her, pinched her black as ink,
Kicked and knocked her,
Mauled and mocked her,
Lizzie uttered not a word;   430
Would not open lip from lip
Lest they should cram a mouthful in:
But laughed in heart to feel the drip
Of juice that syrupped all her face,
And lodged in dimples of her chin,   435
And streaked her neck which quaked like curd.
At last the evil people
Worn out by her resistance
Flung back her penny, kicked their fruit
Along whichever road they took,   440
Not leaving root or stone or shoot;
Some writhed into the ground,
Some dived into the brook
With ring and ripple,
Some scudded on the gale without a sound,   445
Some vanished in the distance.

In a smart, ache, tingle,
Lizzie went her way;
Knew not was it night or day;
Sprang up the bank, tore thro' the furze,   450
Threaded copse and dingle,
And heard her penny jingle
Bouncing in her purse,
Its bounce was music to her ear.
She ran and ran   455
As if she feared some goblin man
Dogged her with gibe or curse
Or something worse:
But not one goblin skurried after,
Nor was she pricked by fear;   460
The kind heart made her windy-paced

That urged her home quite out of breath with haste
And inward laughter.

She cried "Laura," up the garden,
"Did you miss me?   465
Come and kiss me.
Never mind my bruises,
Hug me, kiss me, suck my juices
Squeezed from goblin fruits for you,
Goblin pulp and goblin dew.   470
Eat me, drink me, love me;
Laura, make much of me:
For your sake I have braved the glen
And had to do with goblin merchant men."

Laura started from her chair,   475
Flung her arms up in the air,
Clutched her hair:
"Lizzie, Lizzie, have you tasted
For my sake the fruit forbidden?
Must your light like mine be hidden,   480
Your young life like mine be wasted,
Undone in mine undoing
And ruined in my ruin,
Thirsty, cankered, goblin-ridden?"—
She clung about her sister,   485
Kissed and kissed and kissed her:
Tears once again
Refreshed her shrunken eyes,
Dropping like rain
After long sultry drouth;   490
Shaking with aguish fear, and pain,
She kissed and kissed her with a hungry mouth.

Her lips began to scorch,
That juice was wormwood to her tongue,
She loathed the feast: 495
Writhing as one possessed she leaped and sung,
Rent all her robe, and wrung
Her hands in lamentable haste,
And beat her breast.
Her locks streamed like the torch   500
Borne by a racer at full speed,
Or like the mane of horses in their flight,
Or like an eagle when she stems² the light
Straight toward the sun,

2. Makes headway against, as does a ship against the tide.

Or like a caged thing freed,   505
Or like a flying flag when armies run.

Swift fire spread thro' her veins, knocked at her heart,
Met the fire smouldering there
And overbore its lesser flame;
She gorged on bitterness without a name: 510
Ah! fool, to choose such part
Of soul-consuming care!
Sense failed in the mortal strife:
Like the watch-tower of a town
Which an earthquake shatters down,   515
Like a lightning-stricken mast,
Like a wind-uprooted tree
Spun about,
Like a foam-topped waterspout
Cast down headlong in the sea,   520
She fell at last;
Pleasure past and anguish past,
Is it death or is it life?

Life out of death.
That night long Lizzie watched by her,   525
Counted her pulse's flagging stir,
Felt for her breath,
Held water to her lips, and cooled her face
With tears and fanning leaves:
But when the first birds chirped about their eaves,   530
And early reapers plodded to the place
Of golden sheaves,
And dew-wet grass
Bowed in the morning winds so brisk to pass,
And new buds with new day   535
Opened of cup-like lilies on the stream,
Laura awoke as from a dream,
Laughed in the innocent old way,
Hugged Lizzie but not twice or thrice;
Her gleaming locks showed not one thread of grey,   540
Her breath was sweet as May
And light danced in her eyes.

Days, weeks, months, years
Afterwards, when both were wives
With children of their own;   545
Their mother-hearts beset with fears,
Their lives bound up in tender lives;
Laura would call the little ones
And tell them of her early prime,
Those pleasant days long gone   550
Of not-returning time:

Would talk about the haunted glen,
The wicked, quaint fruit-merchant men,
Their fruits like honey to the throat
But poison in the blood;   555
(Men sell not such in any town:)
Would tell them how her sister stood
In deadly peril to do her good,
And win the fiery antidote:
Then joining hands to little hands   560
Would bid them cling together,
"For there is no friend like a sister
In calm or stormy weather;
To cheer one on the tedious way,
To fetch one if one goes astray,   565
To lift one if one totters down,
To strengthen whilst one stands."

1859   1862

In an Artist's Studio

One face looks out from all his canvases,[3]
    One selfsame figure sits or walks or leans:
    We found her hidden just behind those screens,
That mirror gave back all her loveliness.
A queen in opal or in ruby dress,   5
    A nameless girl in freshest summer-greens,
    A saint, an angel—every canvas means
The same one meaning, neither more nor less.
He feeds upon her face by day and night,
    And she with true kind eyes looks back on him,   10
Fair as the moon and joyful as the light:
    Not wan with waiting, not with sorrow dim;
Not as she is, but was when hope shone bright;
    Not as she is, but as she fills his dream.

1861   1896

————◦—◄ **REBECCA HARDING DAVIS** ►—◦————
1831–1910

Rebecca Harding Davis was born to a large and prosperous family in Washington,
Pennsylvania, but she became and remains famous for her depictions of the working poor. The granddaughter of a veteran of the American Revolution and the
daughter of an English immigrant who had made a fortune in industry, Harding
spent most of her childhood in the rapidly developing town of Wheeling, Virginia
(now West Virginia). She was educated at home before returning to Pennsylvania

3. The poet's brother, Dante Gabriel Rossetti,   times, eventually marrying her.
painted model Elizabeth Siddall (1834–62) many

to attend the Washington Female Seminary. Married at thirty-two to the lawyer Lemuel Clarke Davis, she was less financially secure during the second half of her life despite the success of her first novella, *Life in the Iron-Mills*, published to much acclaim by the *Atlantic Monthly* magazine in the spring of 1861. She continued to be a prolific writer, especially for the flourishing magazine trade, of stories concerned with contemporary social issues, but financial pressures often forced her to compromise the standards set by her earliest work.

Wheeling, where Davis returned after graduation from the seminary, was a crucible of the best and worst of pre–Civil War U.S. culture. Not far from Pittsburgh, the railroads made it a standard stop on the Lyceum circuit that brought writers, lecturers, and politicians. But as an early industrial city, Wheeling also provided firsthand evidence of the cost of capitalism borne by workers. *Life in the Iron-Mills* explores this cost with an unsparing attention to the physical and spiritual pain of unremitting, underpaid work in the iron mills, where ore was transformed into iron usable for the bridges, railroads, and buildings that formed the infrastructure of the new economy.

The same spring that saw the publication of *Life in the Iron-Mills* also saw Fort Sumter, South Carolina, fired upon by the self-declared Confederate States of America. This coincidence reminds us that the American Civil War was the product of stresses along numerous fault lines in American society including race, class, and economic systems. The western Virginia area in which Davis lived adhered to its cultural and economic allegiances with the Union to become a new state, West Virginia, distinct from the Confederate state of Virginia.

Like Harriet Beecher Stowe, Davis contributed to the later movement of literary realism with her lifelike depictions of dialect and uncompromising representations of the rough physicality of "life among the lowly." Although encouraged by her parents to view herself and others of her class as essentially different from immigrant laborers, Davis featured in *Life in the Iron-Mills* a character whose tragedy inheres in his thwarted desire to make art. The novella is an exposé of lives "vainly lived and lost" in order to make the modern comforts of the nineteenth century possible. It explores the strategic separation of the laboring and middle classes so that each class is unknowable to the other, with only the laborers paying the cost of this ignorance, and it takes up the question of whether and to what degree it is possible to be both an American and an artist. Davis participates in the examinations begun by earlier authors such as Margaret Fuller and continued by later authors such as Kate Chopin into what constitutes an appropriate subject for art in America. Like her protagonist Hugh Wolfe, who sculpts the waste products of ore smelting (korl) and ultimately his own body into objects of transcendent beauty, Davis suggests that the cost of art for America might be prohibitively expensive to the status quo.

Life in the Iron-Mills

> *"Is this the end?*
> *O Life, as futile, then, as frail!*
> *What hope of answer or redress?"* [1]

A cloudy day: do you know what that is in a town of iron-works? The sky sank down before dawn, muddy, flat, immovable. The air is thick, clammy with the

---

1. Line 1 is Davis's; lines 2–3 are from stanza 56   lish poet Alfred, Lord Tennyson (1809–83).
of "In Memoriam" (1850, lines 25–26) by Eng-

breath of crowded human beings. I open the window, and, looking out, can scarcely see through the rain the grocer's shop opposite, where a crowd of drunken Irishmen are puffing Lynchburg tobacco[2] in their pipes. I can detect the scent through all the foul smells ranging loose in the air.

The idiosyncracy of this town is smoke. It rolls sullenly in slow folds from the great chimneys of the iron-foundries, and settles down in black, slimy pools on the muddy streets. Smoke on the wharves, smoke on the dingy boats, on the yellow river,—clinging in a coating of greasy soot to the house-front, the two faded poplars, the faces of the passers-by. The long train of mules, dragging masses of pig-iron[3] through the narrow street, have a foul vapor hanging to their reeking sides. Here, inside, is a little broken figure of an angel pointing upward from the mantel-shelf; but even its wings are covered with smoke, clotted and black. Smoke everywhere! A dirty canary chirps desolately in a cage beside me. Its dream of green fields and sunshine is a very old dream—almost worn out, I think.

From the back-window I can see a narrow brick-yard sloping down to the river-side, strewed with rain-butts[4] and tubs. The river, dull and tawny-colored, (*la bella rivière!*)[5] drags itself sluggishly along, tired of the heavy weight of boats and coal-barges. What wonder? When I was a child, I used to fancy a look of weary, dumb appeal upon the face of the negro-like river slavishly bearing its burden day after day. Something of the same idle notion comes to me to-day, when from the street-window I look on the slow stream of human life creeping past, night and morning, to the great mills. Masses of men, with dull, besotted faces bent to the ground, sharpened here and there by pain or cunning; skin and muscle and flesh begrimed with smoke and ashes; stooping all night over boiling cauldrons of metal, laired by day in dens of drunkenness and infamy; breathing from infancy to death an air saturated with fog and grease and soot, vileness for soul and body. What do you make of a case like that, amateur psychologist? You call it an altogether serious thing to be alive: to these men it is a drunken jest, a joke,—horrible to angels perhaps, to them commonplace enough. My fancy about the river was an idle one: it is no type of such a life. What if it be stagnant and slimy here? It knows that beyond there waits for it odorous sunlight,—quaint old gardens, dusky with soft, green foliage of apple-trees, and flushing crimson with roses,—air, and fields, and mountains. The future of the Welsh puddler[6] passing just now is not so pleasant. To be stowed away, after his grimy work is done, in a hole in the muddy graveyard, and after that,—*not* air, nor green fields, nor curious roses.

Can you see how foggy the day is? As I stand here, idly tapping the window-pane, and looking out through the rain at the dirty back-yard and the coal-boats below, fragments of an old story float up before me,—a story of this oldhouse into which I happened to come to-day. You may think it a tiresome story enough, as foggy as the day, sharpened by no sudden flashes of pain or pleasure.—I know: only the outline of a dull life, that long since, with thousands of dull lives like its own, was vainly lived and lost: thousands of them,—massed, vile, slimy lives, like those of the torpid lizards in yonder stagnant water-butt.—Lost? There is a curious point for you to settle, my friend, who study psychology in a lazy, *dil-*

---

2. Cheap tobacco grown around Lynchburg, Virginia.
3. Iron melted in a blast furnace and poured into bar-shaped molds called pigs.
4. Casks for collecting rain.

5. The beautiful river! (French). The Ohio was already polluted in Davis's time.
6. A worker who "puddles" pig iron into wrought iron or steel by heating and stirring the molten metal.

ettante[7] way. Stop a moment. I am going to be honest. This is what I want you to do. I want you to hide your disgust, take no heed to your clean clothes, and come right down with me,—here, into the thickest of the fog and mud and foul effluvia. I want you to hear this story. There is a secret down here, in this nightmare fog, that has lain dumb for centuries: I want to make it a real thing to you. You, Egoist, or Pantheist, or Arminian,[8] busy in making straight paths for your feet on the hills, do not see it clearly,—this terrible question which men here have gone mad and died trying to answer. I dare not put this secret into words. I told you it was dumb. These men, going by with drunken faces and brains full of unawakened power, do not ask it of Society or of God. Their lives ask it; their deaths ask it. There is no reply. I will tell you plainly that I have a great hope; and I bring it to you to be tested. It is this: that this terrible dumb question is its own reply; that it is not the sentence of death we think it, but, from the very extremity of its darkness, the most solemn prophecy which the world has known of the Hope to come. I dare make my meaning no clearer, but will only tell my story. It will, perhaps, seem to you as foul and dark as this thick vapor about us, and as pregnant with death; but if your eyes are free as mine are to look deeper, no perfume-tinted dawn will be so fair with promise of the day that shall surely come.

My story is very simple,—only what I remember of the life of one of these men,—a furnace-tender in one of Kirby & John's rolling-mills,[9]—Hugh Wolfe. You know the mills? They took the great order for the Lower Virginia railroads there last winter; run usually with about a thousand men. I cannot tell why I choose the half-forgotten story of this Wolfe more than that of myriads of these furnace-hands. Perhaps because there is a secret underlying sympathy between that story and this day with its impure fog and thwarted sunshine,—or perhaps simply for the reason that this house is the one where the Wolfes lived. There were the father and son,—both hands, as I said, in one of Kirby & John's mills for making railroad-iron,—and Deborah, their cousin, a picker[1] in some of the cotton-mills. The house was rented then to half a dozen families. The Wolfes had two of the cellar-rooms. The old man, like many of the puddlers and feeders of the mills, was Welsh,—had spent half of his life in the Cornish tin-mines.[2] You may pick the Welsh emigrants, Cornish miners, out of the throng passing the windows, any day. They are a trifle more filthy; their muscles are not so brawny; they stoop more. When they are drunk, they neither yell, nor shout, nor stagger, but skulk along like beaten hounds. A pure, unmixed blood, I fancy: shows itself in the slight angular bodies and sharply-cut facial lines. It is nearly thirty years since the Wolfes lived here. Their lives were like those of their class: incessant labor, sleeping in kennel-like rooms, eating rank pork and molasses, drinking—God and the distillers only know what; with an occasional night in jail, to atone for some drunken excess. Is that all of their lives?—of the portion given to them and these their duplicates swarming the streets to-day?—nothing beneath?—all? So many a political

7. Amateurish.
8. Egoist: one who is self-interested; pantheist: one who believes God is present in everything and goes by many names; Arminians: Protestant Christians who reject the doctrine of predestination but embrace the doctrine of salvation by God's grace alone.

9. Factories where iron is rolled into sheets.
1. A worker who cleans cotton fibers or, here (as shown later), a worker who throws the shuttle of a loom.
2. Feeder: a worker who pours the molten metal into molds; Cornish tin-mines: mines in southwest England, just south of Wales.

reformer will tell you,—and many a private reformer too, who has gone among them with a heart tender with Christ's charity, and come out outraged, hardened.

One rainy night, about eleven o'clock, a crowd of half-clothed women stopped outside of the cellar-door. They were going home from the cotton-mill.

"Good-night, Deb," said one, a mulatto, steadying herself against the gas-post. She needed the post to steady her. So did more than one of them.

"Dah's a ball to Miss Potts' to-night. Ye'd best come."

"Inteet, Deb, if hur'll[3] come, hur'll hef fun," said a shrill Welsh voice in the crowd.

Two or three dirty hands were thrust out to catch the gown of the woman, who was groping for the latch of the door.

"No."

"No? Where's Kit Small, then?"

"Begorra![4] on the spools. Alleys behint, though we helped her, we dud. An wid ye! Let Deb alone! It's ondacent frettin' a quite body. Be the powers, an' we'll have a night of it! there'll be lashin's o' drink,—the Vargent[5] be blessed and praised for't!"

Then went on, the mulatto inclining for a moment to show fight, and drag the woman Wolfe off with them; but, being pacified, she staggered away.

Deborah groped her way into the cellar, and, after considerable stumbling, kindled a match, and lighted a tallow dip,[6] that sent a yellow glimmer over the room. It was low, damp,—the earthen floor covered with a green, slimy moss,—a fetid air smothering the breath. Old Wolfe lay asleep on a heap of straw, wrapped in a torn horse-blanket. He was a pale, meek little man, with a white face and red rabbit-eyes. The woman Deborah was like him; only her face was even more ghastly, her lips bluer, her eyes more watery. She wore a faded cotton gown and a slouching bonnet. When she walked, one could see that she was deformed, almost a hunchback. She trod softly, so as not to waken him, and went through into the room beyond. There she found by the half-extinguished fire an iron saucepan filled with cold boiled potatoes, which she put upon a broken chair with a pint-cup of ale. Placing the old candlestick beside this dainty repast, she untied her bonnet, which hung limp and wet over her face, and prepared to eat her supper. It was the first food that had touched her lips since morning. There was enough of it, however: there is not always. She was hungry,—one could see that easily enough,—and not drunk, as most of her companions would have been found at this hour. She did not drink, this woman,—her face told that, too,—nothing stronger than ale. Perhaps the weak, flaccid wretch had some stimulant in her pale life to keep her up,—some love or hope, it might be, or urgent need. When that stimulant was gone, she would take to whiskey. Man cannot live by work alone. While she was skinning the potatoes, and munching them, a noise behind her made her stop.

"Janey!" she called, lifting the candle and peering into the darkness. "Janey, are you there?"

A heap of ragged coats was heaved up, and the face of a young girl emerged, staring sleepily at the woman.

3. Pronoun in Welsh dialect used here to mean "you'll."
4. Begorra: Irish euphemism for "by God"; on the spools: working at the cotton mill.
5. lashin's: lots; Vargent: the Virgin Mary.
6. A string laid in a dish of inexpensive animal tallow and lit for light.

"Deborah," she said, at last, "I'm here the night."

"Yes, child. Hur's welcome," she said, quietly eating on.

The girl's face was haggard and sickly; her eyes were heavy with sleep and hunger: real Milesian[7] eyes they were, dark, delicate blue, glooming out from black shadows with a pitiful fright.

"I was alone," she said, timidly.

"Where's the father?" asked Deborah, holding out a potato, which the girl greedily seized.

"He's beyant,—wid Haley,—in the stone house." (Did you ever hear the word *jail* from an Irish mouth?) "I came here. Hugh told me never to stay me-lone."

"Hugh?"

"Yes."

A vexed frown crossed her face. The girl saw it, and added quickly,—

"I have not seen Hugh the day, Deb. The old man says his watch[8] lasts till the mornin'."

The woman sprang up, and hastily began to arrange some bread and flitch[9] in a tin pail, and to pour her own measure of ale into a bottle. Tying on her bonnet, she blew out the candle.

"Lay ye down, Janey dear," she said, gently, covering her with the old rags. "Hur can eat the potatoes, if hur's hungry."

"Where are ye goin', Deb? The rain's sharp."

"To the mill, with Hugh's supper."

"Let him bide till th' morn. Sit ye down."

"No, no,"—sharply pushing her off. "The boy'll starve."

She hurried from the cellar, while the child wearily coiled herself up for sleep. The rain was falling heavily, as the woman, pail in hand, emerged from the mouth of the alley, and turned down the narrow street, that stretched out, long and black, miles before her. Here and there a flicker of gas lighted an uncertain space of muddy footwalk and gutter; the long rows of houses, except an occasional lager-bier[1] shop, were closed; now and then she met a band of mill-hands skulking to or from their work.

Not many even of the inhabitants of a manufacturing town know the vast machinery of system by which the bodies of workmen are governed, that goes unceasingly from year to year. The hands of each mill are divided into watches that relieve each other as regularly as the sentinels of an army. By night and day the work goes on, the unsleeping engines groan and shriek, the fiery pools of metal boil and surge. Only for a day in the week, a half-courtesy to public censure, the fires are partially veiled; but as soon as the clock strikes midnight, the great furnaces break forth with renewed fury, the clamor begins with fresh, breathless vigor, the engines sob and shriek like "gods in pain."

As Deborah hurried down through the heavy rain, the noise of these thousand engines sounded through the sleep and shadow of the city like far-off thunder. The mill to which she was going lay on the river, a mile below the city-limits. It was far, and she was weak, aching from standing twelve hours at the spools. Yet

---

7. Irish, referring to descendants of Miledh, who, according to legend, came to Ireland from Spain around 1000 BCE.

8. Shift at work.
9. Bacon or salt pork.
1. Lager beer, originally brewed in Bavaria.

it was her almost nightly walk to take this man his supper, though at every square she sat down to rest, and she knew she should receive small word of thanks.

Perhaps, if she had possessed an artist's eye, the picturesque oddity of the scene might have made her step stagger less, and the path seem shorter; but to her the mills were only "summat deilish[2] to look at by night."

The road leading to the mills had been quarried from the solid rock, which rose abrupt and bare on one side of the cinder-covered road, while the river, sluggish and black, crept past on the other. The mills for rolling iron are simply immense tent-like roofs, covering acres of ground, open on every side. Beneath these roofs Deborah looked in on a city of fires, that burned hot and fiercely in the night. Fire in every horrible form: pits of flame waving in the wind; liquid metal-flames writhing in tortuous streams through the sand; wide caldrons filled with boiling fire, over which bent ghastly wretches stirring the strange brewing; and through all, crowds of half-clad men, looking like revengeful ghosts in the red light, hurried, throwing masses of glittering fire. It was like a street in Hell. Even Deborah muttered, as she crept through, "'T looks like t' Devil's place!" It did,— in more ways than one.

She found the man she was looking for, at last, heaping coal on a furnace. He had not time to eat his supper; so she went behind the furnace, and waited. Only a few men were with him, and they noticed her only by a "Hyur comes t' hunchback, Wolfe."

Deborah was stupid with sleep; her back pained her sharply; and her teeth chattered with cold, with the rain that soaked her clothes and dripped from her at every step. She stood, however, patiently holding the pail, and waiting.

"Hout, woman! ye look like a drowned cat. Come near to the fire,"—said one of the men, approaching to scrape away the ashes.

She shook her head. Wolfe had forgotten her. He turned, hearing the man, and came closer.

"I did no' think; gi' me my supper, woman."

She watched him eat with a painful eagerness. With a woman's quick instinct, she saw that he was not hungry,—was eating to please her. Her pale, watery eyes began to gather a strange light.

"Is't good, Hugh? T'ale was a bit sour, I feared."

"No, good enough." He hesitated a moment. "Ye're tired, poor lass! Bide here till I go. Lay down there on that heap of ash, and go to sleep."

He threw her an old coat for a pillow, and turned to his work. The heap was the refuse of the burnt iron, and was not a hard bed; the half-smothered warmth, too, penetrated her limbs, dulling their pain and cold shiver.

Miserable enough she looked, lying there on the ashes like a limp, dirty rag,— yet not an unfitting figure to crown the scene of hopeless discomfort and veiled crime: more fitting, if one looked deeper into the heart of things,—at her thwarted woman's form, her colorless life, her waking stupor that smothered pain and hunger,—even more fit to be a type of her class. Deeper yet if one could look, was there nothing worth reading in this wet, faded thing, half-covered with ashes? no story of a soul filled with groping passionate love, heroic unselfishness, fierce jealousy? of years of weary trying to please the one human being whom she loved, to gain one look of real heart-kindness from him? If anything like this were hidden

2. Something devilish.

beneath the pale, bleared eyes, and dull, washed-out-looking face, no one had ever taken the trouble to read its faint signs: not the half-clothed furnace-tender, Wolfe, certainly. Yet he was kind to her: it was his nature to be kind, even to the very rats that swarmed in the cellar: kind to her in just that same way. She knew that. And it might be that very knowledge had given to her face its apathy and vacancy more than her low, torpid life. One sees that dead, vacant look steal sometimes over the rarest, finest of women's faces,—in the very midst, it may be, of their warmest summer's day; and then one can guess at the secret of intolerable solitude that lies hid beneath the delicate laces and brilliant smile. There was no warmth, no brilliancy, no summer for this woman; so the stupor and vacancy had time to gnaw into her face perpetually. She was young, too, though no one guessed it; so the gnawing was the fiercer.

She lay quiet in the dark corner, listening, through the monotonous din and uncertain glare of the works, to the dull plash of the rain in the far distance,— shrinking back whenever the man Wolfe happened to look towards her. She knew, in spite of all his kindness, that there was that in her face and form which made him loathe the sight of her. She felt by instinct, although she could not comprehend it, the finer nature of the man, which made him among his fellow-workmen something unique, set apart. She knew, that, down under all the vileness and coarseness of his life, there was a groping passion for whatever was beautiful and pure,—that his soul sickened with disgust at her deformity, even when his words were kindest. Through this dull consciousness, which never left her, came, like a sting, the recollection of the little Irish girl she had left in the cellar. The recollection struck through even her stupid intellect with a vivid glow of beauty and grace. Little Janey, timid, helpless, clinging to Hugh as her only friend: that was the sharp thought, the bitter thought, that drove into the glazed eyes a fierce light of pain. You laugh at it? Are pain and jealousy less savage realities down here in this place I am taking you to than in your own house or your own heart,—your heart, which they clutch at sometimes? The note is the same, I fancy, be the octave high or low.

If you could go into this mill where Deborah lay, and drag out from the hearts of these men the terrible tragedy of their lives, taking it as a symptom of the disease of their class, no ghost Horror would terrify you more. A reality of soul-starvation, of living death, that meets you every day under the besotted faces on the street,—I can paint nothing of this, only give you the outside outlines of a night, a crisis in the life of one man: whatever muddy depth of soul-history lies beneath you can read according to the eyes God has given you.

Wolfe, while Deborah watched him as a spaniel its master, bent over the furnace with his iron pole, unconscious of her scrutiny, only stopping to receive orders. Physically, Nature had promised the man but little. He had already lost the strength and instinct vigor of a man, his muscles were thin, his nerves weak, his face (a meek, woman's face) haggard, yellow with consumption.[3] In the mill he was known as one of the girl men: "Molly Wolfe" was his *sobriquet*.[4] He was never seen in the cockpit, did not own a terrier,[5] drank but seldom; when he did, desperately. He fought sometimes, but was always thrashed, pommelled to a jelly. The man was game enough, when his blood was up: but he was no favorite in the

---

3. Tuberculosis—an incurable and common disease before penicillin.
4. Nickname (French).

5. Cockpit: ring for cockfighting, where roosters fought and gamblers bet on which would kill the other; terrier: hunting dog.

mill; he had the taint of school-learning on him,   not to a dangerous extent, only a quarter or so in the free-school[6] in fact, but enough to ruin him as a good hand in a fight.

For other reasons, too, he was not popular. Not one of themselves, they felt that, though outwardly as filthy and ash-covered; silent, with foreign thoughts and longings breaking out through his quietness in innumerable curious ways: this one, for instance. In the neighboring furnace-buildings lay great heaps of the refuse from the ore after the pig-metal is run. *Korl* we call it here: a light, porous substance, of a delicate, waxen, flesh-colored tinge. Out of the blocks of this korl, Wolfe, in his off-hours from the furnace, had a habit of chipping and moulding figures,—hideous, fantastic enough, but sometimes strangely beautiful: even the mill-men saw that, while they jeered at him. It was a curious fancy in the man, al-most a passion. The few hours for rest he spent hewing and hacking with his blunt knife, never speaking, until his watch came again,—working at one figure for months, and, when it was finished, breaking it to pieces perhaps, in a fit of disap-pointment. A morbid, gloomy man, untaught, unled, left to feed his soul in gross-ness and crime, and hard, grinding labor.

I want you to come down and look at this Wolfe, standing there among the lowest of his kind, and see him just as he is, that you may judge him justly when you hear the story of this night. I want you to look back, as he does every day, at his birth in vice, his starved infancy; to remember the heavy years he has groped through as boy and man,—the slow, heavy years of constant, hot work. So long ago he began, that he thinks sometimes he has worked there for ages. There is no hope that it will ever end. Think that God put into this man's soul a fierce thirst for beauty,—to know it, to create it; to *be*—something, he knows not what,—other than he is. There are moments when a passing cloud, the sun glinting on the purple thistles, a kindly smile, a child's face, will rouse him to a passion of pain,—when his nature starts up with a mad cry of rage against God, man, whoever it is that has forced this vile, slimy life upon him. With all this groping, this mad de-sire, a great blind intellect stumbling through wrong, a loving poet's heart, the man was by habit only a coarse, vulgar laborer, familiar with sights and words you would blush to name. Be just: when I tell you about this night, see him as he is. Be just,—not like man's law, which seizes on one isolated fact, but like God's judging angel, whose clear, sad eye saw all the countless cankering days of this man's life, all the countless nights, when, sick with starving, his soul fainted in him, before it judged him for this night, the saddest of all.

I called this night the crisis of his life. If it was, it stole on him unawares. These great turning-days of life cast no shadow before, slip by unconsciously. Only a trifle, a little turn of the rudder, and the ship goes to heaven or hell.

Wolfe, while Deborah watched him, dug into the furnace of melting iron with his pole, dully thinking only how many rails the lump would yield. It was late,—nearly Sunday morning; another hour, and the heavy work would be done,—only the furnaces to replenish and cover for the next day. The workmen were growing more noisy, shouting, as they had to do, to be heard over the deep clamor of the mills. Suddenly they grew less boisterous,—at the far end, entirely silent. Some-thing unusual had happened. After a moment, the silence came nearer; the men stopped their jeers and drunken choruses. Deborah, stupidly lifting up her head,

6. Public school.

saw the cause of the quiet. A group of five or six men were slowly approaching, stopping to examine each furnace as they came. Visitors often came to see the mills after night: except by growing less noisy, the men took no notice of them. The furnace where Wolfe worked was near the bounds of the works; they halted there hot and tired: a walk over one of these great foundries is no trifling task. The woman, drawing out of sight, turned over to sleep. Wolfe, seeing them stop, suddenly roused from his indifferent stupor, and watched them keenly. He knew some of them: the overseer, Clarke,—a son of Kirby, one of the mill-owners,—and a Doctor May, one of the town-physicians. The other two were strangers. Wolfe came closer. He seized eagerly every chance that brought him into contact with this mysterious class that shone down on him perpetually with the glamour of another order of being. What made the difference between them? That was the mystery of his life. He had a vague notion that perhaps to-night he could find it out. One of the strangers sat down on a pile of bricks, and beckoned young Kirby to his side.

"This *is* hot, with a vengeance. A match, please?"—lighting his cigar. "But the walk is worth the trouble. If it were not that you must have heard it so often, Kirby, I would tell you that your works look like Dante's Inferno."[7]

Kirby laughed.

"Yes. Yonder is Farinata[8] himself in the burning tomb,"—pointing to some figure in the shimmering shadows.

"Judging from some of the faces of your men," said the other, "they bid fair to try the reality of Dante's vision, some day."

Young Kirby looked curiously around, as if seeing the faces of his hands for the first time.

"They're bad enough, that's true. A desperate set, I fancy. Eh, Clarke?"

The overseer did not hear him. He was talking of net profits just then,—giving, in fact, a schedule of the annual business of the firm to a sharp peering little Yankee, who jotted down notes on a paper laid on the crown of his hat: a reporter for one of the city-papers, getting up a series of reviews of the leading manufactories. The other gentlemen had accompanied them merely for amusement. They were silent until the notes were finished, drying their feet at the furnaces, and sheltering their faces from the intolerable heat. At last the overseer concluded with—

"I believe that is a pretty fair estimate, Captain."

"Here, some of you men!" said Kirby, "bring up those boards. We may as well sit down, gentlemen, until the rain is over. It cannot last much longer at this rate."

"Pig-metal,"—mumbled the reporter,—"um!—coal facilities,—um!—hands employed, twelve hundred,—bitumen,[9]—um!—all right, I believe, Mr. Clarke;—sinking-fund,[1]—what did you say was your sinking-fund?"

"Twelve hundred hands?" said the stranger, the young man who had first spoken. "Do you control their votes, Kirby?"

"Control? No." The young man smiled complacently. "But my father brought seven hundred votes to the polls for his candidate last November. No force-work, you understand,—only a speech or two, a hint to form themselves into a society, and a bit of red and blue bunting to make them a flag. The Invincible Roughs,—I believe that is their name. I forget the motto: 'Our country's hope,' I think."

7. Dante Alighieri (1265–1321) is best known as the author of *The Divine Comedy,* an epic poem describing hell, purgatory, and heaven.
8. A heretic whom Dante meets burning in hell (canto 10).
9. Residue from distillation of petroleum, tar, or pitch.
1. Money set aside to pay off debts.

There was a laugh. The young man talking to Kirby sat with an amused light in his cool gray eye, surveying critically the half-clothed figures of the puddlers, and the slow swing of their brawny muscles. He was a stranger in the city,—spending a couple of months in the borders of a Slave State, to study the institutions of the South,—a brother-in-law of Kirby's,—Mitchell. He was an amateur gymnast,—hence his anatomical eye; a patron, in a *blasé* way, of the prize-ring; a man who sucked the essence out of a science or philosophy in an indifferent, gentlemanly way; who took Kant, Novalis, Humboldt,[2] for what they were worth in his own scales; accepting all, despising nothing, in heaven, earth, or hell, but one-idead men; with a temper yielding and brilliant as summer water, until his Self was touched, when it was ice, though brilliant still. Such men are not rare in the States.

As he knocked the ashes from his cigar, Wolfe caught with a quick pleasure the contour of the white hand, the blood-glow of a red ring he wore. His voice, too, and that of Kirby's, touched him like music,—low, even, with chording cadences. About this man Mitchell hung the impalpable atmosphere belonging to the thoroughbred gentleman. Wolfe, scraping away the ashes beside him, was conscious of it, did obeisance to it with his artist sense, unconscious that he did so.

The rain did not cease. Clarke and the reporter left the mills; the others, comfortably seated near the furnace, lingered, smoking and talking in a desultory way. Greek would not have been more unintelligible to the furnace-tenders, whose presence they soon forgot entirely. Kirby drew out a newspaper from his pocket and read aloud some article, which they discussed eagerly. At every sentence, Wolfe listened more and more like a dumb, hopeless animal, with a duller, more stolid look creeping over his face, glancing now and then at Mitchell, marking acutely every smallest sign of refinement, then back to himself, seeing as in a mirror his filthy body, his more stained soul.

Never! He had no words for such a thought, but he knew now, in all the sharpness of the bitter certainty, that between them there was a great gulf never to be passed.[3] Never!

The bell of the mills rang for midnight. Sunday morning had dawned. Whatever hidden message lay in the tolling bells floated past these men unknown. Yet it was there. Veiled in the solemn music ushering the risen Saviour was a key-note to solve the darkest secrets of a world gone wrong,—even this social riddle which the brain of the grimy puddler grappled with madly to-night.

The men began to withdraw the metal from the caldrons. The mills were deserted on Sundays, except by the hands who fed the fires, and those who had no lodgings and slept usually on the ash-heaps. The three strangers sat still during the next hour, watching the men cover the furnaces, laughing now and then at some jest of Kirby's.

"Do you know," said Mitchell, "I like this view of the works better than when the glare was fiercest? These heavy shadows and the amphitheatre of smothered fires are ghostly, unreal. One could fancy these red smouldering lights to be the half-shut eyes of wild beasts, and the spectral figures their victims in the den."

2. Immanuel Kant: German philosopher (1724–1804); Novalis: the pen name of Friedrich von Hardenberg (1762–1801), German novelist and poet; Baron Alexander von Humboldt (1769– 1859): German naturalist and explorer.
3. Echoes Luke 16:26, "Between us and you there is a great gulf fixed: so that they which would pass from hence to you cannot. . . ."

Kirby laughed. "You are fanciful. Come, let us get out of the den. The spectral figures, as you call them, are a little too real for me to fancy a close proximity in the darkness,—unarmed, too."

The others rose, buttoning their overcoats, and lighting cigars.

"Raining, still, said Doctor May, "and hard. Where did we leave the coach, Mitchell?"

"At the other side of the works.—Kirby, what's that?"

Mitchell started back, half-frightened, as, suddenly turning a corner, the white figure of a woman faced him in the darkness,—a woman, white, of giant proportions, crouching on the ground, her arms flung out in some wild gesture of warning.

"Stop! Make that fire burn there!" cried Kirby, stopping short.

The flame burst out, flashing the gaunt figure into bold relief.

Mitchell drew a long breath.

"I thought it was alive," he said, going up curiously.

The others followed.

"Not marble, eh?" asked Kirby, touching it.

One of the lower overseers stopped.

"Korl, Sir."

"Who did it?"

"Can't say. Some of the hands; chipped it out in off-hours."

"Chipped to some purpose, I should say. What a flesh-tint the stuff has! Do you see, Mitchell?"

"I see."

He had stepped aside where the light fell boldest on the figure, looking at it in silence. There was not one line of beauty or grace in it: a nude woman's form, muscular, grown coarse with labor, the powerful limbs instinct with some one poignant longing. One idea: there it was in the tense, rigid muscles, the clutching hands, the wild, eager face, like that of a starving wolf's. Kirby and Doctor May walked around it, critical, curious. Mitchell stood aloof, silent. The figure touched him strangely.

"Not badly done," said Doctor May. "Where did the fellow learn that sweep of the muscles in the arm and hand? Look at them! They are groping,—do you see?—clutching: the peculiar action of a man dying of thirst."

"They have ample facilities for studying anatomy," sneered Kirby, glancing at the half-naked figures.

"Look," continued the Doctor, "at this bony wrist, and the strained sinews of the instep! A working-woman,—the very type of her class."

"God forbid!" muttered Mitchell.

"Why?" demanded May. "What does the fellow intend by the figure? I cannot catch the meaning."

"Ask him," said the other, dryly. "There he stands,"—pointing to Wolfe, who stood with a group of men, leaning on his ash-rake.

The Doctor beckoned him with the affable smile which kind-hearted men put on, when talking to these people.

"Mr. Mitchell has picked you out as the man who did this,—I'm sure I don't know why. But what did you mean by it?"

"She be hungry."

Wolfe's eyes answered Mitchell, not the Doctor.

"Oh-h! But what a mistake you have made, my fine fellow! You have given no sign of starvation to the body. It is strong,—terribly strong. It has the mad, half-despairing gesture of drowning."

Wolfe stammered, glanced appealingly at Mitchell, who saw the soul of the thing, he knew. But the cool, probing eyes were turned on himself now,—mocking, cruel, relentless.

"Not hungry for meat," the furnace-tender said at last.

"What then? Whiskey?" jeered Kirby, with a coarse laugh.

Wolfe was silent a moment, thinking.

"I dunno," he said, with a bewildered look. "It mebbe. Summat to make her live, I think,—like you. Whiskey ull do it, in a way."

The young man laughed again. Mitchell flashed a look of disgust somewhere,—not at Wolfe.

"May," he broke out impatiently, "are you blind? Look at that woman's face! It asks questions of God, and says 'I have a right to know.' Good God, how hungry it is!"

They looked a moment; then May turned to the mill-owner:—

"Have you many such hands as this? What are you going to do with them? Keep them at puddling iron?"

Kirby shrugged his shoulders. Mitchell's look had irritated him.

"*Ce n'est pas mon affaire.*[4] I have no fancy for nursing infant geniuses. I suppose there are some stray gleams of mind and soul among these wretches. The Lord will take care of his own; or else they can work out their own salvation. I have heard you call our American system a ladder which any man can scale. Do you doubt it? Or perhaps you want to banish all social ladders, and put us all on a flat table-land,—eh, May?"

The Doctor looked vexed, puzzled. Some terrible problem lay hid in this woman's face, and troubled these men. Kirby waited for an answer, and, receiving none, went on, warming with his subject.

"I tell you, there's something wrong that no talk of '*Liberté*' or '*Egalité*'[5] will do away. If I had the making of men, these men who do the lowest part of the world's work should be machines,—nothing more,—hands. It would be kindness. God help them! What are taste, reason, to creatures who must live such lives as that?" He pointed to Deborah, sleeping on the ash-heap. "So many nerves to sting them to pain. What if God had put your brain, with all its agony of touch, into your fingers, and bid you work and strike with that?"

"You think you could govern the world better?" laughed the Doctor.

"I do not think at all."

"That is true philosophy. Drift with the stream, because you cannot dive deep enough to find bottom, eh?"

"Exactly," rejoined Kirby. "I do not think. I wash my hands of all social problems,—slavery, caste, white or black. My duty to my operatives has a narrow limit,—the pay-hour on Saturday night. Outside of that, if they cut korl, or cut each other's throats, (the more popular amusement of the two,) I am not responsible."

The Doctor sighed,—a good honest sigh, from the depths of his stomach.

"God help us! Who is responsible?"

---

4. It's not my concern (French).
5. "*Liberté, égalité, fraternité*" (liberty, equality,

fraternity) was the motto of the French Revolution.

"Not I, I tell you," said Kirby, testily. "What has the man who pays them money to do with their souls' concerns, more than the grocer or butcher who takes it?"

"And yet," said Mitchell's cynical voice, "look at her! How hungry she is!"

Kirby tapped his boot with his cane. No one spoke. Only the dumb face of the rough image looking into their faces with the awful question, "What shall we do to be saved?"[6] Only Wolfe's face, with its heavy weight of brain, its weak, uncertain mouth, its desperate eyes, out of which looked the soul of his class,—only Wolfe's face turned towards Kirby's. Mitchell laughed,—a cool, musical laugh.

"Money has spoken!" he said, seating himself lightly on a stone with the air of an amused spectator at a play. "Are you answered?"—turning to Wolfe his clear, magnetic face.

Bright and deep and cold as Arctic air, the soul of the man lay tranquil beneath. He looked at the furnace-tender as he had looked at a rare mosaic in the morning; only the man was the more amusing study of the two.

"Are you answered? Why, May, look at him! '*De profundis clamavi*.'[7] Or, to quote in English, 'Hungry and thirsty, his soul faints in him.' And so Money sends back its answer into the depths through you, Kirby! Very clear the answer, too!—I think I remember reading the same words somewhere:—washing your hands in Eau de Cologne, and saying, 'I am innocent of the blood of this man. See ye to it!' "[8]

Kirby flushed angrily.

"You quote Scripture freely."

"Do I not quote correctly? I think I remember another line, which may amend my meaning: 'Inasmuch as ye did it unto one of the least of these, ye did it unto me.' Deist?[9] Bless you, man, I was raised on the milk of the Word. Now, Doctor, the pocket of the world having uttered its voice, what has the heart to say? You are a philanthropist, in a small way,—*n'est ce pas?*[1] Here, boy, this gentleman can show you how to cut korl better,—or your destiny. Go on, May!"

"I think a mocking devil possesses you to-night," rejoined the Doctor, seriously.

He went to Wolfe and put his hand kindly on his arm. Something of a vague idea possessed the Doctor's brain that much good was to be done here by a friendly word or two: a latent genius to be warmed into life by a waited-for sunbeam. Here it was: he had brought it. So he went on complacently:—

"Do you know, boy, you have it in you to be a great sculptor, a great man?—do you understand?" (talking down to the capacity of his hearer: it is a way people have with children, and men like Wolfe,)—"to live a better, stronger life than I, or Mr. Kirby here? A man may make himself anything he chooses. God has given you stronger powers than many men,—me, for instance."

May stopped, heated, glowing with his own magnanimity. And it was magnanimous. The puddler had drunk in every word, looking through the Doctor's flurry, and generous heat, and self-approval, into his will, with those slow, absorbing eyes of his.

"Make yourself what you will. It is your right."

"I know," quietly. "Will you help me?"

Mitchell laughed again. The Doctor turned now, in a passion,—

6. Acts 16:30.
7. We shout out of the deep (Latin version of Psalm 130:1).
8. The words of Pontius Pilate, the Roman leader who allowed Christ to be crucified but would not accept responsibility; see Matthew 27:24.
9. Matthew 25:40; deists believe in God but believe he does not interfere in human affairs.
1. Isn't it so? (French).

"You know, Mitchell, I have not the means. You know, if I had, it is in my heart to take this boy and educate him for"—

"The glory of God, and the glory of John May."

May did not speak for a moment; then, controlled, he said,—

"Why should one be raised, when myriads are left?—I have not the money, boy," to Wolfe, shortly.

"Money?" He said it over slowly, as one repeats the guessed answer to a riddle, doubtfully. "That is it? Money?"

"Yes, money,—that is it," said Mitchell, rising, and drawing his furred coat about him. "You've found the cure for all the world's diseases.—Come, May, find your good-humor, and come home. This damp wind chills my very bones. Come and preach your Saint-Simonian[2] doctrines to-morrow to Kirby's hands. Let them have a clear idea of the rights of the soul, and I'll venture next week they'll strike for higher wages. That will be the end of it."

"Will you send the coach-driver to this side of the mills?" asked Kirby, turning to Wolfe.

He spoke kindly: it was his habit to do so. Deborah, seeing the puddler go, crept after him. The three men waited outside. Doctor May walked up and down, chafed. Suddenly he stopped.

"Go back, Mitchell! You say the pocket and the heart of the world speak without meaning to these people. What has its head to say? Taste, culture, refinement? Go!"

Mitchell was leaning against a brick wall. He turned his head indolently, and looked into the mills. There hung about the place a thick, unclean odor. The slightest motion of his hand marked that he perceived it, and his insufferable disgust. That was all. May said nothing, only quickened his angry tramp.

"Besides," added Mitchell, giving a corollary to his answer, "it would be of no use. I am not one of them."

"You do not mean"—said May, facing him.

"Yes, I mean just that. Reform is born of need, not pity. No vital movement of the people's has worked down, for good or evil; fermented, instead, carried up the heaving, cloggy mass. Think back through history, and you will know it. What will this lowest deep—thieves, Magdalens, negroes—do with the light filtered through ponderous Church creeds, Baconian theories, Goethe schemes?[3] Some day, out of their bitter need will be thrown up their own light-bringer,—their Jean Paul, their Cromwell, their Messiah."[4]

"Bah!" was the Doctor's inward criticism. However, in practice, he adopted the theory; for, when, night and morning, afterwards, he prayed that power might be given these degraded souls to rise, he glowed at heart, recognizing an accomplished duty.

Wolfe and the woman had stood in the shadow of the works as the coach drove off. The Doctor had held out his hand in a frank, generous way, telling him

2. Socialist, referring to French philosopher Claude-Henri de Rouvroy, comte de Saint-Simon (1760–1825).
3. Magdalens: prostitutes, referring to Mary Magdalene; Baconian theories: Sir Francis Bacon (1561–1626), English philosopher, statesman, and essayist; Goethe schemes: Johann Wolfgang von Goethe (1749–1832), German poet, playwright, and novelist. Both Bacon and Goethe were known for their esoteric social theories.
4. Jean Paul Marat (1743–1793), French politician, physician, and revolutionary; Oliver Cromwell (1599–1658), English leader who revolted against the British crown and became lord protector of England (1653–1658); the Messiah: the Christian savior.

to "take care of himself, and to remember it was his right to rise." Mitchell had simply touched his hat, as to an equal, with a quiet look of thorough recognition. Kirby had thrown Deborah some money, which she found, and clutched eagerly enough. They were gone now, all of them. The man sat down on the cinder-road, looking up into the murky sky.

"'T be late, Hugh. Wunnot hur come?"

He shook his head doggedly, and the woman crouched out of his sight against the wall. Do you remember rare moments when a sudden light flashed over yourself, your world, God? when you stood on a mountain-peak, seeing your life as it might have been, as it is? one quick instant, when custom lost its force and everyday usage? when your friend, wife, brother, stood in a new light? your soul was bared, and the grave,—a fore-taste of the nakedness of the Judgment-Day? So it came before him, his life, that night. The slow tides of pain he had borne gathered themselves up and surged against his soul. His squalid daily life, the brutal coarseness eating into his brain, as the ashes into his skin: before, these things had been a dull aching into his consciousness; to-night, they were reality. He gripped the filthy red shirt that clung, stiff with soot, about him, and tore it savagely from his arm. The flesh beneath was muddy with grease and ashes,—and the heart beneath that! And the soul? God knows.

Then flashed before his vivid poetic sense the man who had left him,—the pure face, the delicate, sinewy limbs, in harmony with all he knew of beauty or truth. In his cloudy fancy he had pictured a Something like this. He had found it in this Mitchell, even when he idly scoffed at his pain: a Man all-knowing, all-seeing, crowned by Nature, reigning,—the keen glance of his eye falling like a sceptre on other men. And yet his instinct taught him that he too—He! He looked at himself with sudden loathing, sick, wrung his hands with a cry, and then was silent. With all the phantoms of his heated, ignorant fancy, Wolfe had not been vague in his ambitions. They were practical, slowly built up before him out of his knowledge of what he could do. Through years he had day by day made this hope a real thing to himself,—a clear, projected figure of himself, as he might become.

Able to speak, to know what was best, to raise these men and women working at his side up with him: sometimes he forgot this defined hope in the frantic anguish to escape,—only to escape,—out of the wet, the pain, the ashes, somewhere, anywhere,—only for one moment of free air on a hill-side, to lie down and let his sick soul throb itself out in the sunshine. But to-night he panted for life. The savage strength of his nature was roused; his cry was fierce to God for justice.

"Look at me!" he said to Deborah, with a low, bitter laugh, striking his puny chest savagely. "What am I worth, Deb? Is it my fault that I am no better? My fault? My fault?"

He stopped, stung with a sudden remorse, seeing her hunchback shape writhing with sobs. For Deborah was crying thankless tears, according to the fashion of women.

"God forgi' me, woman! Things go harder wi' you nor me. It's a worse share."

He got up and helped her to rise; and they went doggedly down the muddy street, side by side.

"It's all wrong," he muttered, slowly,—"all wrong! I dunnot understan'. But it'll end some day."

"Come home, Hugh!" she said, coaxingly; for he had stopped, looking around bewildered.

"Home,—and back to the mill!" He went on saying this over to himself, as if he would mutter down every pain in this dull despair.

She followed him through the fog, her blue lips chattering with cold. They reached the cellar at last. Old Wolfe had been drinking since she went out, and had crept nearer the door. The girl Janey slept heavily in the corner. He went up to her, touching softly the worn white arm with his fingers. Some bitterer thought stung him, as he stood there. He wiped the drops from his forehead, and went into the room beyond, livid, trembling. A hope, trifling, perhaps, but very dear, had died just then out of the poor puddler's life, as he looked at the sleeping, innocent girl,—some plan for the future, in which she had borne a part. He gave it up that moment, then and forever. Only a trifle, perhaps, to us: his face grew a shade paler,—that was all. But, somehow, the man's soul, as God and the angels looked down on it, never was the same afterwards.

Deborah followed him into the inner room. She carried a candle, which she placed on the floor, closing the door after her. She had seen the look on his face, as he turned away: her own grew deadly. Yet, as she came up to him, her eyes glowed. He was seated on an old chest, quiet, holding his face in his hands.

"Hugh!" she said, softly.

He did not speak.

"Hugh, did hur hear what the man said,—him with the clear voice? Did hur hear? Money, money,—that it wud do all?"

He pushed her away,—gently, but he was worn out; her rasping tone fretted him.

"Hugh!"

The candle flared a pale yellow light over the cobwebbed brick walls, and the woman standing there. He looked at her. She was young, in deadly earnest; her faded eyes, and wet, ragged figure caught from their frantic eagerness a power akin to beauty.

"Hugh, it is true! Money ull do it! Oh, Hugh, boy, listen till me! He said it true! It is money!"

"I know. Go back! I do not want you here."

"Hugh, it is t' last time. I'll never worrit hur[5] again."

There were tears in her voice now, but she choked them back.

"Hear till me only to-night! If one of t' witch people wud come, them we heard of t' home, and gif hur all hur wants, what then? Say, Hugh!"

"What do you mean?"

"I mean money."

Her whisper shrilled through his brain.

"If one of t' witch dwarfs wud come from t' lane moors to-night, and gif hur money, to go out,—out, I say,—out, lad, where t' sun shines, and t' heath grows, and t' ladies walk in silken gownds, and God stays all t' time,—where t' man lives that talked to us to-night,—Hugh knows,—Hugh could walk there like a king!"

He thought the woman mad, tried to check her, but she went on, fierce in her eager haste.

"If *I* were t' witch dwarf, if I had t' money, wud hur thank me? Wud hur take me out o' this place wid hur and Janey? I wud not come into the gran' house hur wud build, to vex hur wid t' hunch,—only at night, when t' shadows were dark, stand far off to see hur."

5. Bother you (Welsh dialect).

Mad? Yes! Are many of us mad in this way?

"Poor Deb! poor Deb!" he said, soothingly.

"It is here," she said, suddenly jerking into his hand a small roll. "I took it! I did it! Me, me!—not hur! I shall be hanged, I shall be burnt in hell, if anybody knows I took it! Out of his pocket, as he leaned against t' bricks. Hur knows?"

She thrust it into his hand, and then, her errand done, began to gather chips together to make a fire, choking down hysteric sobs.

"Has it come to this?"

That was all he said. The Welsh Wolfe blood was honest. The roll was a small green pocket-book containing one or two gold pieces, and a check for an incredible amount, as it seemed to the poor puddler. He laid it down, hiding his face again in his hands.

"Hugh, don't be angry wud me! It's only poor Deb,—hur knows?"

He took the long skinny fingers kindly in his.

"Angry? God help me, no! Let me sleep. I am tired."

He threw himself heavily down on the wooden bench, stunned with pain and weariness. She brought some old rags to cover him.

It was late on Sunday evening before he awoke. I tell God's truth, when I say he had then no thought of keeping this money. Deborah had hid it in his pocket. He found it there. She watched him eagerly, as he took it out.

"I must gif it to him," he said, reading her face.

"Hur knows," she said with a bitter sigh of disappointment. "But it is hur right to keep it."

His right! The word struck him. Doctor May had used the same. He washed himself, and went out to find this man Mitchell. His right! Why did this chance word cling to him so obstinately? Do you hear the fierce devils whisper in his ear, as he went slowly down the darkening street?

The evening came on, slow and calm. He seated himself at the end of an alley leading into one of the larger streets. His brain was clear to-night, keen, intent, mastering. It would not start back, cowardly, from any hellish temptation, but meet it face to face. Therefore the great temptation of his life came to him veiled by no sophistry, but bold, defiant, owning its own vile name, trusting to one bold blow for victory.

He did not deceive himself. Theft! That was it. At first the word sickened him; then he grappled with it. Sitting there on a broken cart-wheel, the fading day, the noisy groups, the church-bells' tolling passed before him like a panorama,[6] while the sharp struggle went on within. This money! He took it out, and looked at it. If he gave it back, what then? He was going to be cool about it.

People going by to church saw only a sickly mill-boy watching them quietly at the alley's mouth. They did not know that he was mad, or they would not have gone by so quietly: mad with hunger; stretching out his hands to the world, that had given so much to them, for leave to live the life God meant him to live. His soul within him was smothering to death; he wanted so much, thought so much, and *knew*—nothing. There was nothing of which he was certain, except the mill and things there. Of God and heaven he had heard so little, that they were to him what fairy-land is to a child: something real, but not here; very far off. His brain,

6. Paintings, often of a landscape or scene, that were frequently unveiled a section at a time be- fore nineteenth-century audiences as a form of entertainment.

greedy, dwarfed, full of thwarted energy and unused powers, questioned these men and women going by, coldly, bitterly, that night. Was it not his right to live as they,—a pure life, a good, true-hearted life, full of beauty and kind words? He only wanted to know how to use the strength within him. His heart warmed, as he thought of it. He suffered[7] himself to think of it longer. If he took the money?

Then he saw himself as he might be, strong, helpful, kindly. The night crept on, as this one image slowly evolved itself from the crowd of other thoughts and stood triumphant. He looked at it. As he might be! What wonder, if it blinded him to delirium,—the madness that underlies all revolution, all progress, and all fall?

You laugh at the shallow temptation? You see the error underlying its argument so clearly,—that to him a true life was one of full development rather than self-restraint? that he was deaf to the higher tone in a cry of voluntary suffering for truth's sake than in the fullest flow of spontaneous harmony? I do not plead his cause. I only want to show you the mote in my brother's eye: then you can see clearly to take it out.[8]

The money,—there it lay on his knee, a little blotted slip of paper, nothing in itself; used to raise him out of the pit; something straight from God's hand. A thief! Well, what was it to be a thief? He met the question at last, face to face, wiping the clammy drops of sweat from his forehead. God made this money—the fresh air, too—for his children's use. He never made the difference between poor and rich. The Something who looked down on him that moment through the cool gray sky had a kindly face, he knew,—loved his children alike. Oh, he knew that!

There were times when the soft floods of color in the crimson and purple flames, or the clear depth of amber in the water below the bridge, had somehow given him a glimpse of another world than this,—of an infinite depth of beauty and of quiet somewhere,—somewhere,—a depth of quiet and rest and love. Looking up now, it became strangely real. The sun had sunk quite below the hills, but his last rays struck upward, touching the zenith. The fog had risen, and the town and river were steeped in its thick, gray, damp; but overhead, the sun-touched smoke-clouds opened like a cleft ocean,—shifting, rolling seas of crimson mist, waves of billowy silver veined with blood-scarlet, inner depths unfathomable of glancing light. Wolfe's artist-eye grew drunk with color. The gates of that other world! Fading, flashing before him now! What, in that world of Beauty, Content, and Right, were the petty laws, the mine and thine, of mill-owners and mill-hands?

A consciousness of power stirred within him. He stood up. A man,—he thought, stretching out his hands,—free to work, to live, to love! Free! His right! He folded the scrap of paper in his hand. As his nervous fingers took it in, limp and blotted, so his soul took in the mean temptation, lapped it in fancied rights, in dreams of improved existences, drifting and endless as the cloud-seas of color. Clutching it, as if the tightness of his hold would strengthen his sense of possession, he went aimlessly down the street. It was his watch at the mill. He need not go, need never go again, thank God!—shaking off the thought with unspeakable loathing.

Shall I go over the history of the hours of that night? how the man wandered from one to another of his old haunts, with a half-consciousness of bidding them

---

7. Allowed.

8. Jesus says in Matthew 7:3–4: "And why beholdest thou the mote that is in thy brother's eye, but considerest not the beam that is in thine own eye? Or how wilt thou say to thy brother, let me pull out the mote out of thine eye, and, behold, a beam is in thine own eye?"

farewell,—lanes and alleys and back-yards where the mill-hands lodged,—noting, with a new eagerness, the filth and drunkenness, the pig-pens, the ash-heaps covered with potato-skins, the bloated, pimpled women at the doors,—with a new disgust, a new sense of sudden triumph, and, under all, a new, vague dread, unknown before, smothered down, kept under, but still there? It left him but once during the night, when, for the second time in his life, he entered a church. It was a sombre Gothic pile, where the stained light lost itself in far-retreating arches; built to meet the requirements and sympathies of a far other class than Wolfe's. Yet it touched, moved him uncontrollably. The distances, the shadows, the still, marble figures, the mass of silent kneeling worshippers, the mysterious music, thrilled, lifted his soul with a wonderful pain. Wolfe forgot himself, forgot the new life he was going to live, the mean terror gnawing underneath. The voice of the speaker strengthened the charm; it was clear, feeling, full, strong. An old man, who had lived much, suffered much; whose brain was keenly alive, dominant; whose heart was summer-warm with charity. He taught it to-night. He held up Humanity in its grand total; showed the great world-cancer to his people. Who could show it better? He was a Christian reformer; he had studied the age thoroughly; his outlook at man had been free, world-wide, over all time. His faith stood sublime upon the Rock of Ages; his fiery zeal guided vast schemes by which the gospel was to be preached to all nations. How did he preach it to-night? In burning, light-laden words he painted the incarnate Life, Love, the universal Man: words that became reality in the lives of these people,—that lived again in beautiful words and actions, trifling, but heroic. Sin, as he defined it, was a real foe to them; their trials, temptations, were his. His words passed far over the furnace-tender's grasp, toned to suit another class of culture; they sounded in his ears a very pleasant song in an unknown tongue. He meant to cure this world-cancer with a steady eye that had never glared with hunger, and a hand that neither poverty nor strychnine-whiskey[9] had taught to shake. In this morbid, distorted heart of the Welsh puddler he had failed.

Wolfe rose at last, and turned from the church down the street. He looked up; the night had come on foggy, damp; the golden mists had vanished, and the sky lay dull and ash-colored. He wandered again aimlessly down the street, idly wondering what had become of the cloud-sea of crimson and scarlet. The trial-day of this man's life was over, and he had lost the victory. What followed was mere drifting circumstance,—a quicker walking over the path,—that was all. Do you want to hear the end of it? You wish me to make a tragic story out of it? Why, in the police-reports of the morning paper you can find a dozen such tragedies: hints of shipwrecks unlike any that ever befell on the high seas; hints that here a power was lost to heaven,—that there a soul went down where no tide can ebb or flow. Commonplace enough the hints are,—jocose sometimes, done up in rhyme.

Doctor May, a month after the night I have told you of, was reading to his wife at breakfast from this fourth column of the morning-paper: an unusual thing,—these police-reports not being, in general, choice reading for ladies; but it was only one item he read.

"Oh, my dear! You remember that man I told you of, that we saw at Kirby's mill?—that was arrested for robbing Mitchell? Here he is; just listen:—'Circuit Court. Judge Day. Hugh Wolfe, operative in Kirby & John's Loudon Mills.

9. A kind of alcohol made from the poison strychnine.

Charge, grand larceny. Sentence, nineteen years hard labor in penitentiary.'—Scoundrel! Serves him right! After all our kindness that night! Picking Mitchell's pocket at the very time!"

His wife said something about the ingratitude of that kind of people, and then they began to talk of something else.

Nineteen years! How easy that was to read! What a simple word for Judge Day to utter! Nineteen years! Half a lifetime![1]

Hugh Wolfe sat on the window-ledge of his cell, looking out. His ankles were ironed. Not usual in such cases; but he had made two desperate efforts to escape. "Well," as Haley, the jailer, said, "small blame to him! Nineteen years' imprisonment was not a pleasant thing to look forward to." Haley was very good-natured about it, though Wolfe had fought him savagely.

"When he was first caught," the jailer said afterwards, in telling the story, "before the trial, the fellow was cut down at once,—laid there on that pallet like a dead man, with his hands over his eyes. Never saw a man so cut down in my life. Time of the trial, too, came the queerest dodge of any customer I ever had. Would choose no lawyer. Judge gave him one, of course. Gibson it was. He tried to prove the fellow crazy; but it wouldn't go. Thing was plain as daylight: money found on him. 'Twas a hard sentence,—all the law allows; but it was for 'xample's sake. These mill-hands are getting' onbearable. When the sentence was read, he just looked up, and said the money was his by rights, and that all the world had gone wrong. That night, after the trial, a gentleman came to see him here, name of Mitchell,—him as he stole from. Talked to him for an hour. Thought he came for curiosity, like. After he was gone, thought Wolfe was remarkable quiet, and went into his cell. Found him very low; bed all bloody. Doctor said he had been bleeding at the lungs. He was as weak as a cat; yet, if ye'll b'lieve me, he tried to get a-past me and get out. I just carried him like a baby, and threw him on the pallet. Three days after, he tried it again: that time reached the wall. Lord help you! he fought like a tiger,—giv' some terrible blows. Fightin' for life, you see; for he can't live long, shut up in the stone crib down yonder. Got a death-cough now. 'T took two of us to bring him down that day; so I just put the irons on his feet. There he sits, in there. Goin' to-morrow, with a batch more of 'em. That woman, hunchback, tried with him,—you remember?—she's only got three years. 'Complice. But *she's* a woman, you know. He's been quiet ever since I put on irons: giv' up, I suppose. Looks white, sick-lookin'. It acts different on 'em, bein' sentenced. Most of 'em gets reckless, devilish-like. Some prays awful, and sings them vile songs of the mills, all in a breath. That woman, now, she's desper't'. Been beggin' to see Hugh, as she calls him, for three days. I'm a-goin' to let her in. She don't go with him. Here she is in this next cell. I'm a-goin' now to let her in."

He let her in. Wolfe did not see her. She crept into a corner of the cell, and stood watching him. He was scratching the iron bars of the window with a piece of tin which he had picked up, with an idle, uncertain, vacant stare, just as a child or idiot would do.

"Tryin' to get out, old boy?" laughed Haley. "Them irons will need a crowbar beside your tin, before you can open 'em."

Wolfe laughed, too, in a senseless way.

"I think I'll get out," he said.

1. Through 1900 the average life expectancy of Americans was less than forty-five years.

"I believe his brain's touched," said Haley, when he came out.

The puddler scraped away with the tin for half an hour. Still Deborah did not speak. At last she ventured nearer, and touched his arm.

"Blood?" she said, looking at some spots on his coat with a shudder.

He looked up at her. "Why, Deb!" he said, smiling,—such a bright, boyish smile, that it went to poor Deborah's heart directly, and she sobbed and cried out loud.

"Oh, Hugh, lad! Hugh! dunnot look at me, when it wur my fault! To think I brought hur to it! And I loved hur so! Oh, lad, I dud!"

The confession, even in this wretch, came with the woman's blush through the sharp cry.

He did not seem to hear her,—scraping away diligently at the bars with the bit of tin.

Was he going mad? She peered closely into his face. Something she saw there made her draw suddenly back,—something which Haley had not seen, that lay beneath the pinched, vacant look it had caught since the trial, or the curious gray shadow that rested on it. That gray shadow,—yes, she knew what that meant. She had often seen it creeping over women's faces for months, who died at last of slow hunger or consumption. That meant death, distant, lingering: but this—Whatever it was the woman saw, or thought she saw, used as she was to crime and misery, seemed to make her sick with a new horror. Forgetting her fear of him, she caught his shoulders, and looked keenly, steadily into his eyes.

"Hugh!" she cried, in a desperate whisper,—"oh, boy, not that! for God's sake, not *that!*"

The vacant laugh went off his face, and he answered her in a muttered word or two that drove her away. Yet the words were kindly enough. Sitting there on his pallet, she cried silently a hopeless sort of tears, but did not speak again. The man looked up furtively at her now and then. Whatever his own trouble was, her distress vexed him with a momentary sting.

It was market-day. The narrow window of the jail looked down directly on the carts and wagons drawn up in a long line, where they had unloaded. He could see, too, and hear distinctly the clink of money as it changed hands, the busy crowd of whites and blacks shoving, pushing one another, and the chaffering[2] and swearing at the stalls. Somehow, the sound, more than anything else had done, wakened him up,—made the whole real to him. He was done with the world and the business of it. He let the tin fall, and looked out, pressing his face close to the rusty bars. How they crowded and pushed! And he,—he should never walk that pavement again! There came Neff Sanders, one of the feeders at the mill, with a basket on his arm. Sure enough, Neff was married the other week. He whistled, hoping he would look up; but he did not. He wondered if Neff remembered he was there,—if any of the boys thought of him up there, and thought that he never was to go down that old cinder-road again. Never again! He had not quite understood it before; but now he did. Not for days or years, but never!—that was it.

How clear the light fell on that stall in front of the market! and how like a picture it was, the dark-green heaps of corn, and the crimson beets, and golden melons! There was another with game: how the light flickered on that pheasant's breast, with the purplish blood dripping over the brown feathers! He could see

2. Squabbling over prices.

the red shining of the drops, it was so near. In one minute he could be down there. It was just a step. So easy, as it seemed, so natural to go! Yet it could never be— not in all the thousands of years to come—that he should put his foot on that street again! He thought of himself with a sorrowful pity, as of some one else. There was a dog down in the market, walking after his master with such a stately, grave look!—only a dog, yet he could go backwards and forwards just as he pleased: he had good luck! Why, the very vilest cur, yelping there in the gutter, had not lived his life, had been free to act out whatever thought God had put into his brain; while he—No, he would not think of that! He tried to put the thought away, and to listen to a dispute between a countryman and a woman about some meat; but it would come back. He, what had he done to bear this?

Then came the sudden picture of what might have been, and now. He knew what it was to be in the penitentiary,—how it went with men there. He knew how in these long years he should slowly die, but not until soul and body had become corrupt and rotten,—how, when he came out, if he lived to come, even the lowest of the mill-hands would jeer him,—how his hands would be weak, and his brain senseless and stupid. He believed he was almost that now. He put his hand to his head, with a puzzled, weary look. It ached, his head, with thinking. He tried to quiet himself. It was only right, perhaps; he had done wrong. But was there right or wrong for such as he? What was right? And who had ever taught him? He thrust the whole matter away. A dark, cold quiet crept through his brain. It was all wrong; but let it be! It was nothing to him more than the others. Let it be!

The door grated, as Haley opened it.

"Come, my woman! Must lock up for t' night. Come, stir yerself!"

"Good-night, Deb," he said, carelessly.

She had not hoped he would say more; but the tired pain on her mouth just then was bitterer than death. She took his passive hand and kissed it.

"Hur'll never see Deb again!" she ventured, her lips growing colder and more bloodless.

What did she say that for? Did he not know it? Yet he would not be impatient with poor old Deb. She had trouble of her own, as well as he.

"No, never again," he said, trying to be cheerful.

She stood just a moment, looking at him. Do you laugh at her, standing there, with her hunchback, her rags, her bleared, withered face, and the great despised love tugging at her heart?

"Come, you!" called Haley, impatiently.

She did not move.

"Hugh!" she whispered.

It was to be her last word. What was it?

"Hugh, boy, not THAT!"

He did not answer. She wrung her hands, trying to be silent, looking in his face in an agony of entreaty. He smiled again, kindly.

"It is best, Deb. I cannot bear to be hurted any more."

"Hur knows," she said, humbly.

"Tell my father good-bye; and—and kiss little Janey."

She nodded, saying nothing, looked in his face again, and went out of the door. As she went, she staggered.

"Drinkin' to-day?" broke out Haley, pushing her before him. "Where the Devil did you get it? Here, in with ye!" and he shoved her into her cell, next to Wolfe's, and shut the door.

Along the wall of her cell there was a crack low down by the floor, through which she could see the light from Wolfe's. She had discovered it days before. She hurried in now, and, kneeling down by it, listened, hoping to hear some sound. Nothing but the rasping of the tin on the bars. He was at his old amusement again. Something in the noise jarred on her ear, for she shivered as she heard it. Hugh rasped away at the bars. A dull old bit of tin, not fit to cut korl with.

He looked out of the window again. People were leaving the market now. A tall mulatto girl, following her mistress, her basket on her head, crossed the street just below, and looked up. She was laughing; but, when she caught sight of the haggard face peering out through the bars, suddenly grew grave, and hurried by. A free, firm step, a clear-cut olive face, with a scarlet turban tied on one side, dark, shining eyes, and on the head the basket poised, filled with fruit and flowers, under which the scarlet turban and bright eyes looked out half-shadowed. The picture caught his eye. It was good to see a face like that. He would try to-morrow, and cut one like it. *To-morrow!* He threw down the tin, trembling, and covered his face with his hands. When he looked up again, the daylight was gone.

Deborah, crouching near by on the other side of the wall, heard no noise. He sat on the side of the low pallet, thinking. Whatever was the mystery which the woman had seen on his face, it came out now slowly, in the dark there, and became fixed,—a something never seen on his face before. The evening was darkening fast. The market had been over for an hour; the rumbling of the carts over the pavement grew more infrequent: he listened to each, as it passed, because he thought it was to be for the last time. For the same reason, it was, I suppose, that he strained his eyes to catch a glimpse of each passer-by, wondering who they were, what kind of homes they were going to, if they had children,—listening eagerly to every chance word in the street, as if—(God be merciful to the man! what strange fancy was this?)—as if he never should hear human voices again.

It was quite dark at last. The street was a lonely one. The last passenger, he thought, was gone. No,—there was a quick step: Joe Hill, lighting the lamps. Joe was a good old chap; never passed a fellow without some joke or other. He remembered once seeing the place where he lived with his wife. "Granny Hill" the boys called her. Bedridden she was; but so kind as Joe was to her! kept the room so clean!—and the old woman, when he was there, was laughing at "some of t' lad's foolishness." The step was far down the street; but he could see him place the ladder, run up, and light the gas. A longing seized him to be spoken to once more.

"Joe!" he called, out of the grating. "Good-bye, Joe!"

The old man stopped a moment, listening uncertainly; then hurried on. The prisoner thrust his hand out of the window, and called again, louder; but Joe was too far down the street. It was a little thing; but it hurt him,—this disappointment.

"Good-bye, Joe!" he called, sorrowfully enough.

"Be quiet!" said one of the jailers, passing the door, striking on it with his club. Oh, that was the last, was it?

There was an inexpressible bitterness on his face, as he lay down on the bed, taking the bit of tin, which he had rasped to a tolerable degree of sharpness, in his hand,—to play with, it may be. He bared his arms, looking intently at their corded veins and sinews. Deborah, listening in the next cell, heard a slight clicking sound, often repeated. She shut her lips tightly, that she might not scream; the cold drops of sweat broke over her, in her dumb agony.

"Hur knows best," she muttered at last, fiercely clutching the boards where she lay.

If she could have seen Wolfe, there was nothing about him to frighten her. He lay quite still, his arms outstretched, looking at the pearly stream of moonlight coming into the window. I think in that one hour that came then he lived back over all the years that had gone before. I think that all the low, vile life, all his wrongs, all his starved hopes, came then, and stung him with a farewell poison that made him sick unto death. He made neither moan nor cry, only turned his worn face now and then to the pure light, that seemed so far off, as one that said, "How long, O Lord? how long?"

The hour was over at last. The moon, passing over her nightly path, slowly came nearer, and threw the light across his bed on his feet. He watched it steadily, as it crept up, inch by inch, slowly. It seemed to him to carry with it a great silence. He had been so hot and tired there always in the mills! The years had been so fierce and cruel! There was coming now quiet and coolness and sleep. His tense limbs relaxed, and settled in a calm languor. The blood ran fainter and slow from his heart. He did not think now with a savage anger of what might be and was not; he was conscious only of deep stillness creeping over him. At first he saw a sea of faces: the mill-men,—women he had known, drunken and bloated,—Janeys timid and pitiful,—poor old Debs: then they floated together like a mist, and faded away, leaving only the clear, pearly moonlight.

Whether, as the pure light crept up the stretched-out figure, it brought with it calm and peace, who shall say? His dumb soul was alone with God in judgment. A Voice may have spoken for it from far-off Calvary, "Father, forgive them, for they know not what they do!"[3] Who dare say? Fainter and fainter the heart rose and fell, slower and slower the moon floated from behind a cloud, until, when at last its full tide of white splendor swept over the cell, it seemed to wrap and fold into a deeper stillness the dead figure that never should move again. Silence deeper than the Night! Nothing that moved, save the black, nauseous stream of blood dripping slowly from the pallet to the floor!

There was outcry and crowd enough in the cell the next day. The coroner and his jury, the local editors, Kirby himself, and boys with their hands thrust knowingly into their pockets and heads on one side, jammed into the corners. Coming and going all day. Only one woman. She came late, and outstayed them all. A Quaker, or Friend,[4] as they call themselves. I think this woman was known by that name in heaven. A homely body, coarsely dressed in gray and white. Deborah (for Haley had let her in) took notice of her. She watched them all—sitting on the end of the pallet, holding his head in her arms—with the ferocity of a watch-dog, if any of them touched the body. There was no meekness, no sorrow, in her face; the stuff out of which murderers are made, instead. All the time Haley and the woman were laying straight the limbs and cleaning the cell, Deborah sat still, keenly watching the Quaker's face. Of all the crowd there that day, this woman alone had not spoken to her,—only once or twice had put some cordial to her lips. After they all were gone, the woman, in the same still, gentle way, brought a vase of wood-leaves and berries, and placed it by the pallet, then opened the narrow window. The fresh air blew in, and swept the woody fragrance over the dead face. Deborah looked up with a quick wonder.

"Did hur know my boy wud like it? Did hur know Hugh?"

---

3. Luke 23:34, words Christ spoke from the cross.   4. A member of the Society of Friends.

"I know Hugh now."

The white fingers passed in a slow, pitiful way over the dead, worn face. There was a heavy shadow in the quiet eyes.

"Did hur know where they'll bury Hugh?" said Deborah in a shrill tone, catching her arm.

This had been the question hanging on her lips all day.

"In t' town-yard? Under t' mud and ash? T' lad'll smother, woman! He wur born on t' lane moor, where t' air is frick[5] and strong. Take hur out, for God's sake, take hur out where t' air blows!"

The Quaker hesitated, but only for a moment. She put her strong arm around Deborah and led her to the window.

"Thee sees the hills, friend, over the river? Thee sees how the light lies warm there, and the winds of God blow all the day? I live there,—where the blue smoke is, by the trees. Look at me." She turned Deborah's face to her own, clear and earnest. "Thee will believe me? I will take Hugh and bury him there to-morrow."

Deborah did not doubt her. As the evening wore on, she leaned against the iron bars, looking at the hills that rose far off, through the thick sodden clouds, like a bright, unattainable calm. As she looked, a shadow of their solemn repose fell on her face: its fierce discontent faded into a pitiful, humble quiet. Slow, solemn tears gathered in her eyes: the poor weak eyes turned so hopelessly to the place where Hugh was to rest, the grave heights looking higher and brighter and more solemn than ever before. The Quaker watched her keenly. She came to her at last, and touched her arm.

"When thee comes back," she said, in a low, sorrowful tone, like one who speaks from a strong heart deeply moved with remorse or pity, "thee shall begin thy life again,—there on the hills. I came too late; but not for thee,—by God's help, it may be."

Not too late. Three years after, the Quaker began her work. I end my story here. At evening-time it was light. There is no need to tire you with the long years of sunshine, and fresh air, and slow, patient Christ-love, needed to make healthy and hopeful this impure body and soul. There is a homely pine house, on one of these hills, whose windows overlook broad, wooded slopes and clover-crimsoned meadows,—niched into the very place where the light is warmest, the air freest. It is the Friends' meeting-house. Once a week they sit there, in their grave, earnest way, waiting for the Spirit of Love to speak, opening their simple hearts to receive His words. There is a woman, old, deformed, who takes a humble place among them: waiting like them: in her gray dress, her worn face, pure and meek, turned now and then to the sky. A woman much loved by these silent, restful people; more silent than they, more humble, more loving. Waiting: with her eyes turned to hills higher and purer than these on which she lives,—dim and far off now, but to be reached some day. There may be in her heart some latent hope to meet there the love denied her here,—that she shall find him whom she lost, and that then she will not be all-unworthy. Who blames her? Something is lost in the passage of every soul from one eternity to the other,—something pure and beautiful, which might have been and was not: a hope, a talent, a love, over which the soul mourns,

5. Fresh.

like Esau deprived of his birthright.[6] What blame to the meek Quaker, if she took her lost hope to make the hills of heaven more fair?

Nothing remains to tell that the poor Welsh puddler once lived, but this figure of the mill-woman cut in korl. I have it here in a corner of my library. I keep it hid behind a curtain,—it is such a rough, ungainly thing. Yet there are about it touches, grand sweeps of outline, that show a master's hand. Sometimes,—to-night, for instance,—the curtain is accidentally drawn back, and I see a bare arm stretched out imploringly in the darkness, and an eager, wolfish face watching mine: a wan, woful face, through which the spirit of the dead korl-cutter looks out, with its thwarted life, its mighty hunger, its unfinished work. Its pale, vague lips seem to tremble with a terrible question. "Is this the End?" they say,—"nothing beyond?—no more?" Why, you tell me you have seen that look in the eyes of dumb brutes,—horses dying under the lash. I know.

The deep of the night is passing while I write. The gas-light wakens from the shadows here and there the objects which lie scattered through the room: only faintly, though; for they belong to the open sunlight. As I glance at them, they each recall some task or pleasure of the coming day. A half-moulded child's head; Aphrodite;[7] a bough of forest-leaves; music; work; homely fragments, in which lie the secrets of all eternal truth and beauty. Prophetic all! Only this dumb, woful face seems to belong to and end with the night. I turn to look at it. Has the power of its desperate need commanded the darkness away? While the room is yet steeped in heavy shadow, a cool, gray light suddenly touches its head like a blessing, and its groping arm points through the broken cloud to the far East, where, in the flickering, nebulous crimson, God has set the promise of the Dawn.

1861

◄ ANNA LEONOWENS ►
1831–1914

The woman who called herself Anna Leonowens spent her life taking advantage of the opportunities offered by the hybrid energies of the British colonial frontiers. Best known as a teacher and lecturer, she wrote two highly novelistic travelogues of her experiences in India and Siam. Most famously, she served as governess at the court of Siam. Leonowens was a master of self-creation whose own account of her life is, in places, significantly at odds with the facts as indicated by official records. The biographical facts of her life suggest the kind of disruption and costs borne by the many non-elite Britons who did the work of the empire but did not profit immensely from it themselves.

Leonowens's origins were distinctly nongenteel. Her mother, Mary Ann, was born in India and married a noncommissioned officer, Sergeant Thomas Edwards, who died before Leonowens was born. Mary Ann Edwards quickly remarried a corporal who was soon demoted to private. Leonowens was sent, for at least some time, to Wales and England, but she returned to India at fifteen. Before marrying Thomas Leon Owens in 1849, she (scandalously) traveled the Middle East for

---

6. The eldest son of Isaac and Rebecca, who sold his birthright to his brother, Jacob; see Genesis 25:33–34.

7. Goddess of love in Greek mythology.

three years with an unmarried clergyman in his early thirties. Thomas Leon Owens was a clerk, a minor functionary in a business office. With him, Leonowens traveled from colonial outpost to colonial outpost looking, as people do on the frontiers, for the next good chance. They buried their first child in India, their second in Australia; Tom Owens himself died in Singapore in 1859. After his death, Leonowens combined her husband's names into a new surname, one that connoted "old" Welsh heritage.

Leonowens supported herself and her two remaining children by opening a school in Singapore for the children of British colonials. In 1862, Leonowens accepted a unique offer to become governess to the royal children of King Mongut of Siam, who charged her with teaching the English language and British culture to his many children and their mothers. After five years, Leonowens left the post, moved to the United States, and began publishing her reminiscences. In America, she became friends with Harriet Beecher Stowe (pp. 732–34) and Annie Fields, the wife of her American publisher. From the 1870s until her death, Leonowens supported herself by lecturing about her experiences in the East, as well as about (what were to her) the related subjects of slavery and women's rights. She later moved to Canada, living in several different provinces; she died there in 1914.

Renaming herself Anna Leonowens after the death of her husband was part of an effort to re-present herself, obscuring the dubious respectability of her immediate family and the indiscretions of her past. Her father and stepfather were refashioned in her reminiscences into commissioned officers, her mother into a sentimentalized widow, herself into a genteel and heroic lady. Her unchaperoned adventures with an older man became an educational tour with a minister and his wife. In *The English Governess at the Siamese Court* (1870) and in the lectures she gave in America and Canada, this conventionalized version of her story lent authority to Leonowens and was integral to establishing the narrative credibility of the storyteller. Both *The English Governess* and *The Romance of the Harem* (1873) are written in the tradition of Western orientalist fantasias by women that stretches back into the eighteenth century. In *The Romance of the Harem*, chapter 2 of which we present here, Leonowens presents a series of stories featuring women who subvert the foundations of life in the harem in small and large ways. Leonowens depicts herself simultaneously as a supporting character and the narrator who validates the struggles for self-determinacy she witnesses.

From **The Romance of the Harem**

Chapter 2
Tuptim: A Tragedy of the Harem

Those of my readers who may recur to my late work, "The English Governess at the Siamese Court," will find on the 265th page mention of "a young girl of fresh and striking beauty, and delightful piquancy of ways and expression, who, with a clumsy club, was pounding fragments of pottery—urns, vases, and goblets—for the foundation of the Watt (or Temple) Rajah Bah ditt Sang. Very artless and happy she seemed, and as free as she was lovely; but the instant she perceived that she had attracted the notice of the king,—who presided at the laying of the foundation of the temple, and flung gold and silver coins among the workwomen,— she sank down and hid her face in the earth, forgetting or disregarding the falling vessels that threatened to crush her; but the king merely diverted himself with inquiring her name and parentage, and some one answering for her, he turned away." This is all that is there said of her.

A week later I saw the girl again, as I was passing through the long enclosed corridor within the palace on my way to my school-room in the temple. She was lying prostrate on the marble pavement among the offerings which were placed there for the king's acceptance, and which he would inspect in his leisurely progress towards his breakfast-hall.

I never went that way without seeing something lying there,—bales of silk on silver trays, boxes of tea, calicoes, velvets, fans, priests' robes, precious spices, silver, gold, and curiosities of all kinds, in fact, almost anything and everything that money could purchase, or the most abject sycophancy could imagine as likely to gratify the despot. Every noble, prince, and merchant sought to obtain the royal favor by gifts thus presented, it being fully understood between the giver and receiver that whoever gave the most costly presents should receive the largest share of royal patronage and support. But the most precious things ever laid upon that pavement were the young hearts of women and children.

Two women were crouching on either side of the young girl, waiting for the entrance of the king, in order to present her to him. I was hardly surprised to see her there. I had grown accustomed to such sights. But I was surprised at the unusual interest she appeared to excite in the other women present, who were all whispering and talking together about her, and expressing their admiration of her beauty in the most extravagant language.

She was certainly very beautiful by nature, and those who sent her there had exhausted all the resources of art to complete, according to their notions, what nature had begun, and to render her a fitter offering for the king. Her lips were dyed a deep crimson by the use of betel;[1] her dark eyebrows were continued in indigo until they met on her brow; her eyelashes were stained with kohl; the tips of her fingers and her nails were made pink with henna; while enormous gold chains and rings bedizened her person. Already too much saddened by the frequency of such sights, I merely cast a passing glance upon her and went my way; but now, as I see in memory that tiny figure lying there, and the almost glorified form in which I beheld it for the last time, I cannot keep the tears from my eyes, nor still the aching of my heart.

About three months or so later we met again in the same place. I was passing through to the school-room, when I saw her joyously exhibiting to her companions a pomegranate which she held in her hand. It seemed to be the largest and finest fruit of the kind I had ever seen, and I stopped to get a closer view both of the girl and of the fruit, each perfect in its kind. I found, however, that the fruit was not real, only an imitation. It was a casket of pure gold, the lids of which were inlaid with rubies, which looked exactly like the seeds of the pomegranate when ripe. It was made to open and shut at the touch of a small spring, and was most exquisitely moulded into the shape and enamelled with the tints of pomegranate. It was her betel-box.

"Where did you get this box?" I inquired.

---

1. Juice from the kernel of the betel palm nut, which is frequently chewed in South Asia.

She turned to me with a child's smile upon her face, pointed to the lofty chamber of the king, and said, "My name, you know, is Tuptim" (Pomegranate). I understood the gift.

Afterwards I saw her frequently. On one occasion she was crying bitterly, while head wife, Thieng, was reproving her with unusual warmth for some fault. I interrupted Thieng to ask for some paper and ink for the school-room, but she paid no attention to my demands. Instead of complying with them at once, as usual, she inquired of me, "What shall I do with this Tuptim? She is very disobedient. Shall I whip her, or starve her till she minds?"

"Forgive her, and be good to her," I whispered in Thieng's ear.

"What!" said the offended lady in an angry tone, "when she does wrong all the time, and is so naughty and wilful? Why, when she is ordered to remain up stairs, she runs away, and hides herself in Maprang's or Simlah's rooms, and we are taken to task by his Majesty, who accuses us of jealousy and unkind treatment towards her. Then we have to search all the houses of the Choms (concubines) until we find her, either in hiding or asleep, and bring her to him. The moment she comes into his presence she goes down upon her knees, appearing so very bashful and innocent that he is enraptured at the sight, and declares that she is the most perfect, the most fascinating of women. But as soon as she can get away, she does the same thing again, only finding some new hiding-place, and so she makes an infinity of trouble. Now, she says she is ill, and cannot wait upon the king, while the physicians declare that there is nothing whatever the matter with her. I really don't know what to do or what to say, for I don't dare to tell the truth to the king, and I'm in constant fear that she will come to a bad end, if she doesn't follow my advice and make up her mind to bear her life here more patiently."

I pitied the poor girl, who really looked either sick or unhappy. Child as she was, there was a great deal of quiet dignity about her, as, with eyes filled with tears, she protested that she was utterly sick at heart, and could not go up stairs any more. I was sure that Thieng's sweeping reproof did not indicate any malice or real anger towards the girl, and, putting my arms around the elder lady, I succeeded in soothing her indignation, and at length obtained permission for Tuptim to be absent from duty for a few days. A grateful smile lit up the girl's tearful face as she crept away.

"That girl is too artless," said kind-hearted Thieng to me, as soon as the child was out of sight; "and she will not even try to like her life here. I pity her from my very heart, mam dear, but it would not do to show it. She would take advantage of my kindness, and keep away from the king altogether, as Marchand does; and in all such cases we head wives have to bear the brunt of the king's displeasure, and are thought to be jealous and intriguing, when the holy Buddh[2] in heaven knows that there is only kindness in our hearts."

Not long after the above conversation, Tuptim began to come to school. She wanted to learn to write her name in English, she said, and she came to me once or twice a week until she had acquired that accomplishment, which seemed to give her immense satisfaction. After she had done this, she asked me if I would write the name "Khoon P'hra Bâlât" for her in English. I wrote it for her at once, without asking her why she wanted it or whose name it was. I did not even know if it was

2. Buddha, Siddhartha Gautama, the founder of Buddhism and the guide who leads practitioners toward enlightenment. The official religion of Siam was Buddhism.

the name of a man or a woman, as the Siamese have no masculine and feminine terminations to their names and titles. She immediately began to trace the letters for herself, and I could see a world of tenderness in her large dreamy eyes as she copied and recopied the name in its English characters. I cannot rightly remember how often or how long she came to the school, for she was but one among many; but, whenever she found me engaged with the princes and princesses, she would sit for hours on the marble floor, and listen to our simple exercises of translating English into Siamese or Siamese into English, with increasing interest and delight expressed in her pure, guileless face. I do remember that she was never alone, but always accompanied by two or three young companions of about her own age, who were as listless and idle as she was absorbed and interested.

Perhaps this was the reason—with her extreme youth, for she was still but a child, and seemed even younger than she really was—why I never attempted to enter into conversation with her, or to learn anything about her history and her feelings. If I had done this, I might have succeeded in winning her confidence, and perhaps have been the means of reconciling her to her life in the palace. That I did not, will ever be a source of poignant regret to me.

One afternoon, as I was about leaving the palace after school, she came running up to me, took a scrap of paper from under her vest, and held it silently before my eyes, while I read what was written upon it. It was the name "Khoon P'hra Bâlât," carefully written in English characters, and she seemed delighted with the praise I bestowed on the writing.

"Whose name is it, Tuptim?" I asked.

She cast down her eyes and hesitated for a moment; then, raising them to mine, she replied: "It is the name of the favorite disciple of the high-priest, Chow Khoon San; he lives at the temple of Rajah Bah ditt Sang, and sometimes preaches to us in the palace."

The expression of deep reverence that animated her face as she spoke revealed to me a new phase in her character, and I felt strongly attracted towards her. I nevertheless left the palace without further conversation, but, on my way home, formed a vague resolution that I would endeavor to become better acquainted with her, and attempt to win her confidence.

My half-formed resolve was without result, however, since, for some reason unknown to me, she never came to the school-room again; and, as I did not chance to meet her on my visits to the palace, she soon passed from my thoughts, and I forgot all about her.

Some nine months, or perhaps a year, after my last encounter with Tuptim, I became conscious of a change in the demeanor of my elder pupils; they were abstracted, and appeared desirous to get away from their studies as soon as possible. It seemed as if there were some secret they had been ordered to conceal from my boy and me. My imagination immediately took the alarm, and I became possessed with the idea that some grave calamity was impending.

One day, when breaking up school for the afternoon, I heard one of the princes say to the others in Siamese: "Come, let's go and hunt for Tuptim."

"Why! where has she gone?"

As soon as I asked the question, Princess Ying Yonwalacks angrily seized him by the arm and hurried him away. I had no wish to inquire further. What I had heard was enough to excite my imagination afresh, and I hurried home full of anxiety about poor little Tuptim, thus suddenly brought back to my remembrance.

On the following evening, it being Sunday, one of my servants informed me that a slave-girl from the palace wished to speak with me in private. When she came in, her face seemed familiar, but I could not remember where I had seen her or whose slave she was. She crawled up close to my chair, and told me in a low voice that her mistress, Khoon Chow Tuptim, had sent her to me. "You know," she added, "that my mistress has been found."

"Found!" I exclaimed; "what do you mean?"

She repeated my question, and in great astonishment asked: "Why! did you not know that my mistress had disappeared from the palace; that his Majesty had offered a reward of twenty caties (about fifteen hundred dollars)[3] to any one who would bring any information about her; and that no trace of her could be discovered, though everybody had been searching for her far and near?"

"No, I have never heard a word about it. But how could she have got out of the palace, through the three rows of gates that are always bolted, and not be seen by the Amazons[4] on guard?"

"Alas! my lady, she did get out," replied the girl, who looked very wan and weary, whose eyes seemed to have been shedding tears for a long time, and who was on the point of breaking down again. She then went on to tell me that two priests had that morning discovered her mistress in the monastery attached to the temple of Rajah Bah ditt Sang, and had brought the information to the king, by whose order she had been arrested and imprisoned in one of the palace dungeons.

"But what good can I do, Phim?" I asked, sorrowfully.

"O mam dear, if you don't help her, she's lost, she'll be killed!" cried the girl, bursting into a passion of tears. "Oh! do, do go to the king, and ask him to forgive her. He'll grant her life to you. I'm sure he will. Oh! oh! what shall I do! I've nobody to go to but you, and there's nobody but you can help her!" And her tears and sobs were truly heart-rending.

I tried to soothe her. "Tell me, Phim," I said, "why did your mistress leave the palace, and who helped her to get away?"

The girl would not answer my question, but kept repeating, "Oh! do come and see her yourself! Do come and see her yourself! You can go to the palace after dark, and the gate-keepers will let you in. Nobody need know that you are going to see my dear mistress."

As there was no other method of quieting the poor girl, I finally made the promise, though I did not see what good my going could do, and was fully convinced that Phim had abetted Tuptim in her wrong-doing, whatever that might have been.

After the slave-girl had left me, I sat by my window and watched the stars as they came out, one by one, and shone with unusual splendor in the cloudless sky. It was a lovely night, and I felt the soothing influence of the Christian Sabbath even in that pagan land; but the one idea that took possession of my mind was: "Poor Little Tuptim, in that dreadful dungeon underground." Still, and notwithstanding my promise, I felt a strong reluctance to respond to the cry which had reached me from her, and wished that I had never heard it. I was tired of the palace, tired of witnessing wrongs I could not remedy, and half afraid, too, to enter that weird, mysterious prison-world after nightfall. So I sat still in dreamy

3. About $25,000 in today's dollars.   4. Female warriors.

uncertainty, till a warm hand was laid upon mine, and I turned my eyes from the stars above to the poor slave-girl's sad, tear-stained face at my feet.

"The gates are open for the prime-minister, mam dear," said she, in a low, pleading voice, "and you can get in now without any difficulty."

I rose at once, resolutely cast my cowardly fears behind me, told my boy where and why I was going, put twenty ticals[5] in my purse, wrapped my black cloak about me, and hurried towards the palace gate. Phim had run back at once, for fear of being shut out for the night. The women at the gates, who were all friendly to me, admitted me without question, and, as I passed, I dropped two ticals into the hand of the chief of the Amazons on guard, saying that I had been called into the palace on important business, and begging her to keep the inner gates open for my return.

"You must be sure and come back before it strikes eleven," said she, and I passed on. As soon as I entered the main street within the walls, the slave-girl joined me, and led the way, crouching and running along in the deep shadow of the houses, until we reached the gate of the prison in which Tuptim was immured, when she immediately disappeared.

The hall I entered was immense, with innumerable pillars, and a floor which seemed to be entirely made up of huge trap-doors, double barred and locked, while the lanterns by which it was dimly lighted were hung so high that they looked like distant stars. There were about a dozen Amazons on guard, some of whom were already stretched in sleep on their mats and leather pillows, their weapons lying within reach. The eyes of all the wakeful custodians of the prison were fixed upon me as I entered. A courteous return was made to my polite salutation, and Ma Ying Taphan—Great Mother of War—addressed me kindly, inquiring what was my object in coming there at that time of night. I told her that I had just heard of Tuptim's having got into trouble and being imprisoned, and had come to ascertain if I could be of any assistance to her.

"The child is in trouble, indeed," replied Ma Ying Taphan; "and has not only got herself into prison, but her two young friends, Maprang and Simlah, who are confined with her."

"Can I not help them in any way?" I asked.

"No," said the Amazon, gently, "I fear you cannot. Her guilt is too great, and she must take the consequences."

"What has she been doing?"

To this question I could get no answer; and after vainly attempting to persuade Ma Ying Taphan to tell me, I tried to induce her to let me go down and visit poor Tuptim. "Myde" (impossible), was the reply, "without an express order from the king. When you bring us that, we will let you in, but without it we cannot." And "myde" was the only answer I could get to my repeated and urgent entreaties. I sat there, hopelessly looking at the Amazons, who, in the dim light of the distant lanterns overhead, seemed to me to be changed from tender-hearted women, as they were, into fierce, vindictive executioners, and at the huge trap-door at our feet, beneath which the three children, as the Amazon had rightly called them, were imprisoned, but from which no sound, no cry, no indication of life escaped, until, tired and despairing, I rose and left the place.

---

5. A tical, composed of 15 grams of silver, would be worth about $6 in today's dollars.

As soon as I was out of the building I saw Phim, the slave-girl, crouching in the shadows on the opposite side of the street, and keeping pace with me as I went towards the palace gate. When I turned into another street she joined me, and I found that she had been hidden under the portico of the prison, and had heard all my conversation with the Amazons. Prostrating herself till her forehead touched my feet, she implored me, in the name of the P'hra Chow in heaven, not to forsake her dear mistress. "She is to be brought before the court in the outside hall of justice to-morrow," she said. "Oh! do come early. Perhaps you can persuade Koon Thow App to be merciful to her." And, with a sickening sense of my utter powerlessness, I promised to be present at the trial.

1873

►◄ LOUISA MAY ALCOTT ►◄

1832–1888

Few daughters have had more idealistic parents than Louisa May Alcott. Both of her parents, Bronson and Abigail, committed their own lives and the lives of their children to the pursuit of a perfection. In fact, her father was a central member of the loosely associated group of American romantics known as the transcendentalists. Bronson's particular focus was on reforming education so that the inner strengths and morality of children could be enhanced rather than stifled; he experimented with what this would mean in the education of his own daughters. As a child, Alcott was the intimate and student of radical transcendentalists such as Margaret Fuller (pp. 685–86), Henry David Thoreau, and Ralph Waldo Emerson. Although Alcott's own idealism was tempered by her experiences with her family, in the workplace, and during the Civil War, she remained an active proponent of progressive causes such as the rights of women and the rights of African Americans.

Although Bronson Alcott's idealism made it difficult for him to support his family, it forced his daughters, particularly Alcott, to embrace the transcendentalist ideal of self-reliance in their efforts to pay the bills and keep the close-knit family together. By her late teens, Alcott was contributing to the family income as a teacher, seamstress, and governess; she also had begun to write and publish for money. With the onset of the Civil War, Alcott joined the war effort as a nurse in Washington, D.C. The work was physically hard and the conditions were horrifying—the germ theory of disease had not yet been accepted, and anesthesia had only just been developed. Contracting typhoid fever, Alcott returned home to Concord, Massachusetts, but turned her experiences into the well-received book *Hospital Sketches* (1863), which provides insight into the reality of the war in which so many had so much invested.

Throughout her life, Alcott wrote for three very different audiences. Her work for children began in the 1850s with the publication of *Flower Fables* (1855). *Little Women* (1868), a sentimental novel loosely based upon her own family and written in the realistic mode, shares with her other children's work a devotion to the normalization of the more radical values of her father. Alcott also wrote fiction and nonfiction for adult audiences. Neither of her topical novels, *Moods* (1864) and *Work* (1873), achieved the popularity of her children's fiction. Alcott was also fascinated by the dark promises of romanticism, and she explored these in sensational fiction published in popular, inexpensive newspapers and periodicals such as *Frank Leslie's Illustrated Newspaper*. In these gothic tales, like the one we include here, "A Double Tragedy" (1865), Alcott explores the transgressive pleasures of cross-dressing, supernaturalism, and destructive desire.

A Double Tragedy: An Actor's Story

Chapter 1

Clotilde was in her element that night, for it was a Spanish play, requiring force and fire in its delineation, and she threw herself into her part with an *abandon* that made her seem a beautiful embodiment of power and passion. As for me I could not play ill, for when with her my acting was not art but nature, and I *was* the lover that I seemed. Before she came I made a business, not a pleasure, of my profession, and was content to fill my place, with no higher ambition than to earn my salary with as little effort as possible, to resign myself to the distasteful labor to which my poverty condemned me. She changed all that; for she saw the talent I neglected, she understood the want of motive that made me indifferent, she pitied me for the reverse of fortune that placed me where I was; by her influence and example she roused a manlier spirit in me, kindled every spark of talent I possessed, and incited me to win a success I had not cared to labor for till then.

She was the rage that season, for she came unheralded and almost unknown. Such was the power of beauty, genius, and character, that she made her way at once into public favor, and before the season was half over had become the reigning favorite. My position in the theatre threw us much together, and I had not played the lover to this beautiful woman many weeks before I found I was one in earnest. She soon knew it, and confessed that she returned my love; but when I spoke of marriage, she answered with a look and tone that haunted me long afterward.

"Not yet, Paul; something that concerns me alone must be settled first. I cannot marry till I have received the answer for which I am waiting; have faith in me till then, and be patient for my sake."

I did have faith and patience; but while I waited I wondered much and studied her carefully. Frank, generous, and deep-hearted, she won all who approached her; but I, being nearest and dearest, learned to know her best, and soon discovered that some past loss, some present anxiety or hidden care, oppressed and haunted her. A bitter spirit at times possessed her, followed by a heavy melancholy, or an almost fierce unrest, which nothing could dispel but some stormy drama, where she could vent her pent-up gloom or desperation in words and acts which seemed to have a double significance to her. I had vainly tried to find some cause or explanation of this one blemish in the nature which, to a lover's eyes, seemed almost perfect, but never had succeeded till the night of which I write.

The play was nearly over, the interest was at its height, and Clotilde's best scene was drawing to a close. She had just indignantly refused to betray a state secret which would endanger the life of her lover; and the Duke had just wrathfully vowed to denounce her to the Inquisition[1] if she did not yield, when I her lover, disguised as a monk, saw a strange and sudden change come over her. She should

---

1. The Spanish Inquisition, an attempt to weed out heretics from the Catholic church, but also frequently used to suppress other faiths; the Span- ish Inquisition was instituted in 1478 and formally disbanded in 1834, although it had lost much of its power by the late eighteenth century.

have trembled at a threat so full of terror, and have made one last appeal to the stern old man before she turned to defy and dare all things for her lover. But she seemed to have forgotten time, place, and character, for she stood gazing straight before her as if turned to stone. At first I thought it was some new presentiment of fear, for she seldom played a part twice alike, and left much to the inspiration of the moment. But an instant's scrutiny convinced me that this was not acting, for her face paled visibly, her eyes dilated as they looked beyond the Duke, her lips fell apart, and she looked like one suddenly confronted by a ghost. An inquiring glance from my companion showed me that he, too, was disturbed by her appearance, and fearing that she had over-exerted herself, I struck into the dialogue as if she had made her appeal. The sound of my voice seemed to recall her; she passed her hand across her eyes, drew a long breath, and looked about her. I thought she had recovered herself and was about to resume her part, but, to my great surprise, she only clung to me, saying in a shrill whisper, so full of despair, it chilled my blood—

"The answer, Paul, the answer: it has come!"

The words were inaudible to all but myself; but the look, the gesture were eloquent with terror, grief, and love; and taking it for a fine piece of acting, the audience applauded loud and long. The accustomed sound roused Clotilde, and during that noisy moment a hurried dialogue passed between us.

"What is it? Are you ill?" I whispered.

"He is here, Paul, alive; I saw him. Heaven help us both!"

"Who is here?"

"Hush! not now; there is no time to tell you."

"You are right; compose yourself; you must speak in a moment."

"What do I say? Help me, Paul; I have forgotten every thing but that man."

She looked as if bewildered; and I saw that some sudden shock had entirely unnerved her. But actors must have neither hearts nor nerves while on the stage. The applause was subsiding, and she must speak. Fortunately I remembered enough of her part to prompt her as she struggled through the little that remained; for, seeing her condition, Denon and I cut the scene remorselessly, and brought it to a close as soon as possible. The instant the curtain fell we were assailed with questions, but Clotilde answered none; and though hidden from her sight, still seemed to see the object that had wrought such an alarming change in her. I told them she was ill, took her to her dressing-room, and gave her into the hands of her maid, for I must appear again, and delay was impossible.

How I got through my part I cannot tell, for my thoughts were with Clotilde; but an actor learns to live a double life, so while Paul Lamar suffered torments of anxiety Don Felix fought a duel, killed his adversary, and was dragged to judgment. Involuntarily my eyes often wandered toward the spot where Clotilde's had seemed fixed. It was one of the stage-boxes, and at first I thought it empty, but presently I caught the glitter of a glass turned apparently on myself. As soon as possible I crossed the stage, and as I leaned haughtily upon my sword while the seconds adjusted the preliminaries, I searched the box with a keen glance. Nothing was visible, however, but a hand lying easily on the red cushion; a man's hand, white and shapely; on one finger shone a ring, evidently a woman's ornament, for it was a slender circlet of diamonds that flashed with every gesture.

"Some fop, doubtless; a man like that could never daunt Clotilde," I thought. And eager to discover if there was not another occupant in the box, I took a step nearer, and stared boldly into the soft gloom that filled it. A low derisive laugh came from behind the curtain as the hand gathered back as if to permit me to satisfy myself. The act showed me that a single person occupied the box, but also effectually concealed that person from my sight; and as I was recalled to my duty by a warning whisper from one of my comrades, the hand appeared to wave me a mocking adieu. Baffled and angry, I devoted myself to the affairs of Don Felix, wondering the while if Clotilde would be able to reappear, how she would bear herself, if that hidden man was the cause of her terror, and why? Even when immured in a dungeon, after my arrest, I beguiled the tedium of a long soliloquy with these questions, and executed a better stage-start than any I had ever practised, when at last she came to me, bringing liberty and love as my reward.

I had left her haggard, speechless, overwhelmed with some mysterious woe, she reappeared beautiful and brilliant, with a joy that seemed too lovely to be feigned. Never had she played so well; for some spirit, stronger than her own, seemed to possess and rule her royally. If I had ever doubted her love for me, I should have been assured of it that night, for she breathed into the fond words of her part a tenderness and grace that filled my heart to overflowing, and inspired me to play the grateful lover to the life. The last words came all too soon for me, and as she threw herself into my arms she turned her head as if to glance triumphantly at the defeated Duke, but I saw that again she looked beyond him, and with an indescribable expression of mingled pride, contempt, and defiance. A soft sound of applause from the mysterious occupant of that box answered the look, and the white hand sent a superb bouquet flying to her feet. I was about to lift and present it to her, but she checked me and crushed it under foot with an air of the haughtiest disdain. A laugh from behind the curtain greeted this demonstration, but it was scarcely observed by others; for that first bouquet seemed a signal for a rain of flowers, and these latter offerings she permitted me to gather up, receiving them with her most gracious smiles, her most graceful obeisances, as if to mark, for one observer at least, the difference of her regard for the givers. As I laid the last floral tribute in her arms I took a parting glance at the box, hoping to catch a glimpse of the unknown face. The curtains were thrown back and the door stood open, admitting a strong light from the vestibule, but the box was empty.

Then the green curtain fell, and Clotilde whispered, as she glanced from her full hands to the rejected bouquet—

"Bring that to my room; I must have it."

I obeyed, eager to be enlightened; but when we were alone she flung down her fragrant burden, snatched the stranger's gift, tore it apart, drew out a slip of paper, read it, dropped it, and walked to and fro, wringing her hands, like one in a paroxysm of despair. I seized the note and looked at it, but found no key to her distress in the enigmatical words—

"I shall be there. Come and bring your lover with you, else—"

There it abruptly ended; but the unfinished threat seemed the more menacing for its obscurity, and I indignantly demanded,

"Clotilde, who dares address you so? Where will this man be? You surely will not obey such a command? Tell me; I have a right to know."

"I cannot tell you, now; I dare not refuse him; he will be at Keen's; we *must* go. How will it end! How will it end!"

I remembered then that we were all to sup *en costume,* with a brother actor, who did not play that night. I was about to speak yet more urgently, when the entrance of her maid checked me. Clotilde composed herself by a strong effort—

"Go and prepare," she whispered; "have faith in me a little longer, and soon you shall know all."

There was something almost solemn in her tone; her eye met mine, imploringly, and her lips trembled as if her heart were full. That assured me at once; and with a reassuring word I hurried away to give a few touches to my costume, which just then was fitter for a dungeon than a feast. When I rejoined her there was no trace of past emotion; a soft color bloomed upon her cheek, her eyes were tearless and brilliant, her lips were dressed in smiles. Jewels shone on her white forehead, neck, and arms, flowers glowed in her bosom; and no charm that art or skill could lend to the rich dress or its lovely wearer, had been forgotten.

"What an actress!" I involuntarily exclaimed, as she came to meet me, looking almost as beautiful and gay as ever.

"It is well that I am one, else I should yield to my hard fate without a struggle. Paul, hitherto I have played for money, now I play for love; help me by being a calm spectator to-night, and whatever happens promise me that there shall be no violence."

I promised, for I was wax in her hands; and, more bewildered than ever, followed to the carriage, where a companion was impatiently awaiting us.

Chapter 2

We were late; and on arriving found all the other guests assembled. Three strangers appeared; and my attention was instantly fixed upon them, for the mysterious "he" was to be there. All three seemed gay, gallant, handsome men; all three turned admiring eyes upon Clotilde, all three were gloved. Therefore, as I had seen no face, my one clue, the ring, was lost. From Clotilde's face and manner I could learn nothing, for a smile seemed carved upon her lips, her drooping lashes half concealed her eyes, and her voice was too well trained to betray her by a traitorous tone. She received the greetings, compliments, and admiration of all alike, and I vainly looked and listened till supper was announced.

As I took my place beside her, I saw her shrink and shiver slightly, as if a chilly wind had blown over her, but before I could ask if she were cold a bland voice said,

"Will Mademoiselle Varian permit me to drink her health?"

It was one of the strangers; mechanically I offered her glass; but the next instant my hold tightened till the slender stem snapped, and the rosy bowl fell broken to the table, for on the handsome hand extended to fill it shone the ring.

"A bad omen, Mr. Lamar. I hope my attempt will succeed better," said St. John, as he filled another glass and handed it to Clotilde, who merely lifted it to her lips, and turned to enter into an animated conversation with the gentleman who sat on the other side. Some one addressed St. John, and I was glad of it; for now all my interest and attention was centered in him. Keenly, but covertly, I examined him, and soon felt that in spite of that foppish ornament he *was* a man to daunt a woman like Clotilde. Pride and passion, courage and indomitable will met and mingled in his face, though the obedient features wore whatever expression he imposed upon them. He was the handsomest, most elegant, but least attractive of the three, yet it was hard to say why. The others gave themselves freely to the enjoyment of a scene which evidently possessed the charm of novelty to them; but St. John unconsciously wore the half sad, half weary look that comes to those who have led lives of pleasure and found their emptiness. Although the wittiest, and most brilliant talker at the table, his gaiety seemed fitful, his manner absent at times. More than once I saw him knit his black brows as he met my eye, and more than once I caught a long look fixed on Clotilde,—a look full of the lordly admiration and pride which a master bestows upon a handsome slave. It made my blood boil, but I controlled myself, and was apparently absorbed in Miss Damareau, my neighbor.

We seemed as gay and care-free a company as ever made midnight merry; songs were sung, stories told, theatrical phrases added sparkle to the conversation, and the varied costumes gave an air of romance to the revel. The Grand Inquisitor still in his ghostly garb, and the stern old Duke were now the jolliest of the group; the page flirted violently with the princess; the rivals of the play were bosom-friends again, and the fair Donna Olivia had apparently forgotten her knightly lover, to listen to a modern gentleman.

Clotilde sat leaning back in a deep chair, eating nothing, but using her fan with the indescribable grace of a Spanish woman. She was very lovely, for the dress became her, and the black lace mantilla falling from her head to her shoulders, heightened her charms by half concealing them; and nothing could have been more genial and gracious than the air with which she listened and replied to the compliments of the youngest stranger, who sat beside her and was all devotion.

I forgot myself in observing her till something said by our opposite neighbors arrested both of us. Some one seemed to have been joking St. John about his ring, which was too brilliant an ornament to pass unobserved.

"Bad taste, I grant you," he said, laughing, "but it is a *gage d'amour*, and I wear it for a purpose."

"I fancied it was the latest Paris fashion," returned Keen. "And apropos to Paris, what is the latest gossip from the gay city?"

A slow smile rose to St. John's lips as he answered, after a moment's thought and a quick glance across the room.

"A little romance; shall I tell it to you? It is a love story, ladies, and not long."

A unanimous assent was given; and he began with a curious glitter in his eyes, a stealthy smile coming and going on his face as the words dropped slowly from his lips.

"It begins in the old way. A foolish young man fell in love with a Spanish girl much his inferior in rank, but beautiful enough to excuse his folly, for he married her. Then came a few months of bliss; but Madame grew jealous. Monsieur wearied of domestic tempests, and, after vain efforts to appease his fiery angel, he proposed a separation. Madame was obdurate, Monsieur rebelled; and in order to try the soothing effects of absence upon both, after settling her in a charming chateau, he slipped away, leaving no trace by which his route might be discovered."

"Well, how did the experiment succeed?" asked Keen. St. John shrugged his shoulders, emptied his glass, and answered tranquilly.

"Like most experiments that have women for their subjects, for the amiable creatures always devise some way of turning the tables, and defeating the best laid plans. Madame waited for her truant spouse till rumors of his death reached Paris, for he had met with mishaps, and sickness detained him long in an obscure place, so the rumors seemed confirmed by his silence, and Madame believed him dead. But instead of dutifully mourning him, this inexplicable woman shook the dust of the chateau off her feet and disappeared, leaving everything, even to her wedding ring, behind her."

"Bless me, how odd! what became of her?" exclaimed Miss Damareau, forgetting the dignity of the Princess in the curiosity of the woman.

"The very question her repentant husband asked when, returning from his long holiday, he found her gone. He searched the continent for her, but in vain; and for two years she left him to suffer the torments of suspense."

"As he had left her to suffer them while he went pleasuring. It was a light punishment for his offence."

Clotilde spoke; and the sarcastic tone for all its softness, made St. John wince, though no eye but mine observed the faint flush of shame or anger that passed across his face.

"Mademoiselle espouses the lady's cause, of course, and as a gallant man I should do likewise, but unfortunately my sympathies are strongly enlisted on the other side."

"Then you know the parties?" I said, impulsively, for my inward excitement was increasing rapidly, and I began to feel rather than to see the end of this mystery.

"I have seen them, and cannot blame the man for claiming his beautiful wife, when he found her," he answered, briefly.

"Then he did find her at last? Pray tell us how and when," cried Miss Damareau.

"She betrayed herself. It seems that Madame had returned to her old profession, and fallen in love with an actor; but being as virtuous as she was fair, she would not marry till she was assured beyond a doubt of her husband's death. Her engagements would not allow her to enquire in person, so she sent letters to various places asking for proofs of his demise; and as ill, or good fortune would have it, one of these letters fell into Monsieur's hands, giving him an excellent clue to her whereabouts, which he followed indefatigably till he found her."

"Poor little woman, I pity her! How did she receive Monsieur De Trop?" asked Keen.

"You shall know in good time. He found her in London playing at one of the great theatres, for she had talent, and had become a star. He saw her act for a night or two, made secret inquiries concerning her, and fell more in love with her than ever. Having tried almost every novelty under the sun he had a fancy to attempt something of the dramatic sort, so presented himself to Madame at a party."

"Heavens! what a scene there must have been," ejaculated Miss Damareau.

"On the contrary, there was no scene at all, for the man was not a Frenchman, and Madame was a fine actress. Much as he had admired her on the stage he was doubly charmed with her performance in private, for it was superb. They were among strangers, and she received him like one, playing her part with the utmost grace and self-control, for with a woman's quickness of perception, she divined his purpose, and knowing that her fate was in his hands, endeavored to propitiate him by complying with his caprice. Mademoiselle, allow me to send you some of these grapes, they are delicious."

As he leaned forward to present them he shot a glance at her that caused me to start up with a violence that nearly betrayed me. Fortunately the room was close, and saying something about the heat, I threw open a window, and let in a balmy gust of spring air that refreshed us all.

"How did they settle it, by duels and despair, or by repentance and reconciliation all round, in the regular French fashion?"

"I regret that I'm unable to tell you, for I left before the affair was arranged. I only know that Monsieur was more captivated than before, and quite ready to forgive and forget, and I suspect that Madame, seeing the folly of resistance, will submit with a good grace, and leave the stage to play 'The Honey Moon' for a second time in private with a husband who adores her. What is the Mademoiselle's opinion?"

She had listened, without either question or comment, her fan at rest, her hands motionless, her eyes downcast; so still it seemed as if she had hushed the breath upon her lips, so pale despite her rouge, that I wondered no one observed it, so intent and resolute that every feature seemed under control,—every look and gesture guarded. When St. John addressed her, she looked up with a smile as bland as his own, but fixed her eyes on him with an expression of undismayed defiance and supreme contempt that caused him to bite his lips with ill-concealed annoyance.

"My opinion?" she said, in her clear, cold voice, "I think that Madame, being a woman of spirit, would *not* endeavor to propitiate that man in any way except for her lover's sake, and having been once deserted would not subject herself to a second indignity of that sort while there was a law to protect her."

"Unfortunately there is no law for her, having once refused a separation. Even if there were, Monsieur is rich and powerful, she is poor and friendless; he loves her, and is a man who never permits himself to be thwarted by any obstacle; therefore, I am convinced it would be best for this adorable woman to submit without defiance or delay—and I do think she will," he added, significantly.

"They seem to forget the poor lover; what is to become of him?" asked Keen.

"*I* do not forget him;" and the hand that wore the ring closed with an ominous gesture, which I well understood. "Monsieur merely claims his own, and the other, being a man of sense and honor, will doubtless withdraw at once; and though 'desolated,' as the French say, will soon console himself with a new *inamorata*. If he is so unwise as to oppose Monsieur, who by the by is a dead shot, there is but one way in which both can receive satisfaction."

A significant emphasis on the last word pointed his meaning, and the smile that accompanied it almost goaded me to draw the sword I wore, and offer him that satisfaction on the spot. I felt the color rise to my forehead, and dared not look up, but leaning on the back of Clotilde's chair, I bent as if to speak to her.

"Bear it a little longer for my sake, Paul," she murmured, with a look of love and despair, that wrung my heart. Here some one spoke of a long rehearsal in the morning, and the lateness of the hour.

"A farewell toast before we part," said Keen. "Come, Lamar, give us a sentiment, after that whisper you ought to be inspired."

"I am. Let me give you—The love of liberty and the liberty of love."

"Good! That would suit the hero and heroine of St. John's story, for Monsieur wished much for his liberty, and, no doubt, Madame will for her love," said Denon, while the glasses were filled.

Then the toast was drunk with much merriment and the party broke up. While detained by one of the strangers, I saw St. John approach Clotilde, who stood alone by the window, and speak rapidly for several minutes. She listened with half-averted head, answered briefly, and wrapping the mantilla closely about her, swept away from him with her haughtiest mien. He watched for a moment, then followed, and before I could reach her, offered his arm to lead her to the carriage. She seemed about to refuse it, but something in the expression of his face restrained her; and accepting it, they went down together. The hall and little anteroom were dimly lighted, but as I slowly followed, I saw her snatch her hand away, when she thought they were alone; saw him draw her to him with an embrace as fond as it was irresistible; and turning her indignant face to his, kiss it ardently, as he said in a tone, both tender and imperious—

"Good night, my darling. I give you one more day, and then I claim you."

"Never!" she answered, almost fiercely, as he released her. And wishing me pleasant dreams, as he passed, went out into the night, gaily humming the burden of a song Clotilde had often sung to me.

The moment we were in the carriage all her self-control deserted her, and a tempest of despairing grief came over her. For a time, both words and caresses were unavailing, and I let her weep herself calm before I asked the hard question—

"Is all this true, Clotilde?"

"Yes, Paul, all true, except that he said nothing of the neglect, the cruelty, the insult that I bore before he left me. I was so young, so lonely, I was glad to be loved and cared for, and I believed that he would never change. I cannot tell you all I suffered, but I rejoiced when I thought death had freed me; I would keep nothing that reminded me of the bitter past, and went away to begin again, as if it had never been."

"Why delay telling me this? Why let me learn it in such a strange and sudden way?"

"Ah, forgive me! I am so proud I could not bear to tell you that any man had wearied of me and deserted me. I meant to tell you before our marriage, but the fear that St. John was alive haunted me, and till it was set at rest I would not speak. To-night there was no time, and I was forced to leave all to chance. He found pleasure in tormenting me through you, but would not speak out, because he is as proud as I, and does not wish to hear our story bandied from tongue to tongue."

"What did he say to you, Clotilde?"

"He begged me to submit and return to him, in spite of all that has passed; he warned me that if we attempted to escape it would be at the peril of your life, for he would most assuredly follow and find us, to whatever corner of the earth we might fly; and he will, for he is as relentless as death."

"What did he mean by giving you one day more?" I asked, grinding my teeth with impatient rage as I listened.

"He gave me one day to recover from my surprise, to prepare for my departure with him, and to bid you farewell."

"And will you, Clotilde?"

"No!" she replied, clenching her hands with a gesture of dogged resolution, while her eyes glittered in the darkness. "I never will submit; there must be some way of escape; I shall find it, and if I do not—I can die."

"Not yet, dearest; we will appeal to the law first; I have a friend whom I will consult to-morrow, and he may help us."

"I have no faith in law," she said, despairingly, "money and influence so often outweigh justice and mercy. I have no witnesses, no friends, no wealth to help me; he has all, and we shall only be defeated. I must devise some surer way. Let me think a little; a woman's wit is quick when her heart prompts it."

I let the poor soul flatter herself with vague hopes; but I saw no help for us except in flight, and that she would not consent to, lest it should endanger me. More than once I said savagely within myself, "I will kill him," and then shuddered at the counsels of the devil, so suddenly roused in my own breast. As if she divined my thought by instinct, Clotilde broke the heavy silence that followed her last words, by clinging to me with the imploring cry,

"Oh, Paul, shun him, else your fiery spirit will destroy you. He promised me he would not harm you unless we drove him to it. Be careful, for my sake, and if any one must suffer let it be miserable me."

I soothed her as I best could, and when our long, sad drive ended, bade her rest while I worked, for she would need all her strength on the morrow. Then I left her, to haunt the street all night long, guarding her door, and while I paced to and fro without, I watched her shadow come and go before the lighted window as she paced within, each racking our brains for some means of help till day broke.

Chapter 3

Early on the following morning I consulted my friend, but when I laid the case before him he gave me little hope of a happy issue should the attempt be made. A divorce was hardly possible, when an unscrupulous man like St. John was bent on opposing it; and though no decision could force her to remain with him, we should not be safe from his vengeance, even if we chose to dare everything and fly together. Long and earnestly we talked, but to little purpose, and I went to rehearsal with a heavy heart.

Clotilde was to have a benefit that night, and what a happy day I had fancied this would be; how carefully I had prepared for it; what delight I had anticipated in playing Romeo to her Juliet; and how eagerly I had longed for the time which now seemed to approach with such terrible rapidity, for each hour brought our parting nearer! On the stage I found Keen and his new friend amusing themselves with fencing, while waiting the arrival of some of the company. I was too miserable to be dangerous just then, and when St. John bowed to me with his most courteous air, I returned the greeting, though I could not speak to him. I think he saw my suffering, and enjoyed it with the satisfaction of a cruel nature, but he treated me with the courtesy of an equal, which new demonstration surprised me, till, through Denon, I discovered that having inquired much about me he had learned that I was a gentleman by birth and education, which fact accounted for the change in his demeanor. I roamed restlessly about the gloomy green room and stage, till Keen, dropping his foil, confessed himself outfenced and called to me.

"Come here, Lamar, and try a bout with St. John. You are the best fencer among us, so, for the honor of the company, come and do your best instead of playing Romeo before the time."

A sudden impulse prompted me to comply, and a few passes proved that I was the better swordsman of the two. This annoyed St. John, and though he complimented me with the rest, he would not own himself outdone, and we kept it up till both grew warm and excited. In the midst of an animated match between us, I observed that the button was off his foil, and a glance at his face assured me that he was aware of it, and almost at the instant he made a skilful thrust, and the point pierced my flesh. As I caught the foil from his hand and drew it out with an exclamation of pain, I saw a gleam of exultation pass across his face, and knew that his promise to Clotilde was but idle breath. My comrades surrounded me with anxious inquiries, and no one was more surprised and solicitous than St. John. The wound was trifling, for a picture of Clotilde had turned the thrust aside, else the force with which it was given might have rendered it fatal. I made light of it, but hated him with a redoubled hatred for the cold-blooded treachery that would have given to revenge the screen of accident.

The appearance of the ladies caused us to immediately ignore the mishap, and address ourselves to business. Clotilde came last, looking so pale it was not necessary for her to plead illness; but she went through her part with her usual fidelity, while her husband watched her with the masterful expression that nearly drove me wild. He haunted her like a shadow, and she listened to him with the desperate look of a hunted creature driven to bay. He might have softened her just resentment by a touch of generosity or compassion, and won a little gratitude, even though love was impossible; but he was blind, relentless, and goaded her beyond endurance, rousing in her fiery Spanish heart a dangerous spirit he could not control. The rehearsal was over at last, and I approached Clotilde with a look that mutely asked if I should leave her. St. John said something in a low voice, but she answered sternly, as she took my arm with a decided gesture.

"This day is mine; I will not be defrauded of an hour," and we went away together for our accustomed stroll in the sunny park.

A sad and memorable walk was that, for neither had any hope with which to cheer the other, and Clotilde grew gloomier as we talked. I told her of my fruitless consultation, also of the fencing match; at that her face darkened, and she said, below her breath, "I shall remember that."

We walked long together, and I promised plan after plan, all either unsafe or impracticable. She seemed to listen, but when I paused she answered with averted eyes—

"Leave it to me; I have a project; let me perfect it before I tell you. Now I must go and rest, for I have had no sleep, and I shall need all my strength for the tragedy to-night."

All that afternoon I roamed about the city, too restless for anything but constant motion, and evening found me ill prepared for my now doubly arduous duties. It was late when I reached the theatre, and I dressed hastily. My costume was new for the occasion, and not till it was on did I remember that I had neglected to try it since the finishing touches were given. A stitch or two would remedy the defects, and, hurrying up to the wardrobe room, a skilful pair of hands soon set me right. As I came down the winding-stairs that led from the lofty chamber to a dimly-lighted gallery below, St. John's voice arrested me, and pausing I saw that Keen was doing the honors of the theatre[2] in defiance of all rules. Just as they reached the stair-foot some one called to them, and throwing open a narrow door, he said to his companion—

"From here you get a fine view of the stage; steady yourself by the rope and look down. I'll be with you in a moment."

He ran into the dressing-room from whence the voice proceeded, and St. John stepped out upon a little platform, hastily built for the launching of an aeriel-car in some grand spectacle. Glad to escape meeting him, I was about to go on, when, from an obscure corner, a dark figure glided noiselessly to the door and leaned in. I caught a momentary glimpse of a white extended arm and the glitter of steel, then came a cry of mortal fear, a heavy fall; and flying swiftly down the gallery the figure disappeared. With one leap I reached the door, and looked in; the raft

---

2. Giving a tour of the theater.

hung broken, the platform was empty. At that instant Keen rushed out, demanding what had happened, and scarcely knowing what I said, I answered hurriedly,

"The rope broke and he fell."

Keen gave me a strange look, and dashed down stairs. I followed, to find myself in a horror-stricken crowd, gathered about the piteous object which a moment ago had been a living man. There was no need to call a surgeon, for that headlong fall had dashed out life in the drawing of a breath, and nothing remained to do but to take the poor body tenderly away to such friends as the newly-arrived stranger possessed. The contrast between the gay crowd rustling before the curtain and the dreadful scene transpiring behind it, was terrible; but the house was filling fast; there was no time for the indulgence of pity or curiosity, and soon no trace of the accident remained but the broken rope above, and an ominous damp spot on the newly-washed boards below. At a word of command from our energetic manager, actors and actresses were sent away to retouch their pale faces with carmine,[3] to restoring their startled nerves with any stimulant at hand, and to forget, if possible, the awesome sight just witnessed.

I returned to my dressing-room hoping Clotilde had heard nothing of this sad, and yet for us most fortunate accident, though all the while a vague dread haunted me, and I feared to see her. Mechanically completing my costume, I looked about me for the dagger with which poor Juliet was to stab herself, and found that it was gone. Trying to recollect where I put it, I remembered having it in my hand just before I went up to have my sword-belt altered; and fancying that I must have inadvertently taken it with me, I reluctantly retraced my steps. At the top of the stairs leading to that upper gallery a little white object caught my eye, and, taking it up, I found it to be a flower. If it had been a burning coal I should not have dropped it more hastily than I did when I recognized it was one of a cluster I had left in Clotilde's room because she loved them. They were a rare and delicate kind, no one but herself was likely to possess them in that place, nor was she likely to have given one away, for my gifts were kept with jealous care; yet how came it there? And as I asked myself the question, like an answer returned the remembrance of her face when she said, "I shall remember this." The darkly-shrouded form was a female figure, the white arm a woman's, and horrible as was the act, who but that sorely-tried and tempted creature would have committed it. For a moment my heart stood still, then I indignantly rejected the black thought, and thrusting the flower into my breast went on my way, trying to convince myself that the foreboding fear which oppressed me was caused by the agitating events of the last half hour. My weapon was not in the wardrobe-room; and as I returned, wondering what I had done with it, I saw Keen standing in the little doorway with a candle in his hand. He turned and asked what I was looking for. I told him, and explained why I was searching for it there.

"Here it is; I found it at the foot of these stairs. It is too sharp for a stage-dagger, and will do mischief unless you dull it," he said, adding, as he pointed to the broken rope, "Lamar, that was cut; I have examined it."

The light shone full in my face, and I knew that it changed, as did my voice, for I thought of Clotilde, and till that fear was at rest resolved to be dumb concerning what I had seen, but I could not repress a shudder as I said, hastily,

3. Red pigment, stage makeup.

"Don't suspect me of any deviltry, for heaven's sake. I've got to go on in fifteen minutes, and how can I play unless you let me forget this horrible business."

"Forget it then, if you can; I'll remind you of it to-morrow." And, with a significant nod, he walked away, leaving behind him a new trial to distract me. I ran to Clotilde's room, bent on relieving myself, if possible, of the suspicion that would return with redoubled pertinacity since the discovery of the dagger, which I was sure I had not dropped where it was found. When I tapped at her door, her voice, clear and sweet as ever, answered "Come!" and entering, I found her ready, but alone. Before I could open my lips she put up her hand as if to arrest the utterance of some dreadful intelligence.

"Don't speak of it; I have heard, and cannot bear a repetition of the horror. I must forget it till to-morrow, then—." There she stopped abruptly, for I produced the flower, asking as naturally as I could—

"Did you give this to any one?"

"No; why ask me that?" and she shrunk a little, as I bent to count the blossoms in the cluster on her breast. I gave her seven; now there were but six, and I fixed on her a look that betrayed my fear, and mutely demanded its confirmation or denial. Other eyes she might have evaded or defied, not mine; the traitorous blood dyed her face, then fading, left it colorless; her eyes wandered and fell, she clasped her hands imploringly, and threw herself at my feet, crying in a stifled voice,

"Paul, be merciful; that was our only hope, and the guilt is mine alone!"

But I started from her, exclaiming with mingled incredulity and horror—

"Was this the tragedy you meant? What devil devised and helped you execute a crime like this?"

"Hear me! I did not plan it, yet I longed to kill him, and all day the thought would haunt me. I have borne so much, I could bear no more, and he drove me to it. To-night the thought still clung to me, till I was half mad. I went to find you, hoping to escape it; you were gone, but on your table lay the dagger. As I took it in my hand I heard his voice, and forgot every thing except my wrongs and the great happiness one blow could bring us. I followed then, meaning to stab him in the dark; but when I saw him leaning where a safer stroke would destroy him, I gave it, and we are safe."

"Safe!" I echoed. "Do you know you left my dagger behind you? Keen found it; he suspects me, for I was near; and St. John has told him something of the cause I have to wish you free."

She sprung up, and seemed about to rush away to proclaim her guilt, but I restrained her desperate purpose, saying sternly—

"Control yourself and be cautious. I may be mistaken; but if either must suffer, let it be me. I can bear it best, even if it comes to the worst, for my life is worthless now."

"And I have made it so? Oh, Paul, can you never forgive me and forget my sin?"

"Never, Clotilde; it is too horrible."

I broke from her trembling hold, and covered up my face, for suddenly the woman whom I once loved had grown abhorrent to me. For many minutes neither spoke or stirred; my heart seemed dead within me, and what went on in that stormy soul I shall never know. Suddenly I was called, and as I turned to leave her, she seized both my hands in a despairing grasp, covered them with tender kisses, wet them with repentant tears, and clung to them in a paroxysm of love, remorse, and grief, till I was forced to go, leaving her alone with the memory of her sin.

That night I was like one in a terrible dream; every thing looked unreal, and like an automaton I played my part, for always before me I seemed to see that shattered body and to hear again that beloved voice confessing a black crime. Rumors of the accident had crept out, and damped the spirits of the audience, yet it was as well, perhaps, for it made them lenient to the short-comings of the actors, and lent another shadow to the mimic tragedy that slowly darkened to its close. Clotilde's unnatural composure would have been a marvel to me had I not been past surprise at any demonstration on her part. A wide gulf now lay between us, and it seemed impossible for me to cross it. The generous, tender woman whom I first loved, was still as beautiful and dear to me as ever, but as much lost as if death had parted us. The desperate, despairing creature I had learned to know within an hour, seemed like an embodiment of the murderous spirit which had haunted me that day, and though by heaven's mercy it had not conquered me, yet I now hated it with remorseful intensity. So strangely were the two images blended in my troubled mind that I could not separate them, and they exerted a mysterious influence over me. When with Clotilde she seemed all she had ever been, and I enacted the lover with a power I had never known before, feeling the while that it might be for the last time. When away from her the darker impression returned, and the wildest of the poet's words were not too strong to embody my own sorrow and despair. They told me long afterwards that never had the tragedy been better played, and I could believe it, for the hapless Italian lovers[4] never found better representatives than in us that night.

Worn out with suffering and excitement, I longed for solitude and silence with a desperate longing, and when Romeo murmured, "With a kiss I die," I fell beside the bier, wishing that I too was done with life. Lying there, I watched Clotilde, through the little that remained, and so truly, tenderly, did she render the pathetic scene that my heart softened; all the early love returned strong, and warm as ever, and I felt that I *could* forgive. As she knelt to draw my dagger, I whispered, warningly,

"Be careful, dear, it is very sharp."

"I know it," she answered with a shudder, then cried aloud.

"Oh happy dagger! this is thy sheath; there rust, and let me die."

Again I saw the white arm raised, the flash of steel as Juliet struck the blow that was to free her, and sinking down beside her lover, seemed to breathe her life away.

"I thank God it's over," I ejaculated, a few minutes later, as the curtain slowly fell. Clotilde did not answer, and feeling how cold the cheek that touched my own had grown, I thought she had given way at last.

"She has fainted; lift her, Denon, and let me rise," I cried, as Count Paris sprang up with a joke.

"Good God, she has hurt herself with that cursed dagger!" he exclaimed, as raising her he saw a red stain on the white draperies she wore.

I staggered to my feet, and laid her on the bier she had just left, but no mortal skill could heal that hurt, and Juliet's grave-clothes were her own. Deaf to the enthusiastic clamor that demanded our re-appearance, blind to the confusion and dismay about me, I leaned over her passionately, conjuring her to give me one word of pardon and farewell. As if my voice had power to detain her, even when death called, the dark eyes, full of remorseful love, met mine again, and feebly

4. Shakespeare's *Romeo and Juliet* is set in Verona, Italy.

drawing from her breast a paper, she motioned Keen to take it, murmuring in a tone that changed from solemn affirmation to the tenderest penitence,

"Larmar is innocent—I did it. This will prove it. Paul, I have tried to atone—oh, forgive me, and remember me for my love's sake."

I did forgive her; and she died, smiling on my breast. I did remember her through a long, lonely life, and never played again since the night of that DOUBLE TRAGEDY.

1865

The novel *Little Women,* 1868, appears in full in the Library of Women's Literature.

◄ HANNAH CRAFTS ►
Active 1850s

The handwritten title page to a manuscript titled *The Bondwoman's Narrative* identifies the author as Hannah Crafts, "A Fugitive Slave, Recently Escaped from North Carolina." The handwritten pages tell the story of her escape from slavery in a highly novelistic manner, featuring literary allusions, fictional rather than historical names, and literary devices that heighten the dramatic tension of the plot. There was no published version of this text before the twenty-first century; it existed only as a single, handwritten artifact until it came to light at an auction of rare books in February 2000. The scholar Henry Louis Gates Jr. edited and published it in 2002, and we include the preface and first chapter here.

The Bondwoman's Narrative is a complex sentimental novel having dual protagonists—the narrator (Hannah) and her mistress, who has been "passing" as a white woman—and many sensational fictions such as babies switched at birth, haunted trees, and young women who dress as boys. The narrator starts out ignorant and illiterate, alone and powerless in a world filled with the threat of sexual and physical abuse. But she ends her story ensconced as a beloved wife and teacher. Although attempts at linking the name of Hannah Crafts with a historical person have been unsuccessful, scholars have been able to determine that the manuscript was written in the 1850s and that many of the details of the book correspond closely to actual places and people. Ironically, many of the events recounted in *The Bondwoman's Narrative* are corroborated by the private diary of a famous pro-slavery politician from North Carolina named John Hill Wheeler. However, the text of *The Bondwoman's Narrative* weaves many close paraphrases and other obvious "borrowings" from popular nineteenth-century British and American novels into this otherwise verifiable story. The author of *The Bondwoman's Narrative,* scholars agree, was probably a light-skinned woman who had been enslaved to Wheeler during the 1840s.

Although this manuscript offers many interpretive puzzles, it also offers unprecedented insights. Unlike most other black-authored texts from the antebellum era, this manuscript has had no "help" from white editors, publishers, or printers. Raw as it is, this text grants rare insight into how a former slave might make sense of the life she led in what Harriet Wilson (pp. 897–910) would call "slavery's shadows."

From **The Bondwoman's Narrative**

Preface

In presenting this record of plain unvarnished facts to a generous public I feel a certain degree of diffidence and self-distrust. I ask myself for the hundredth time How will such a literary venture, coming from a sphere so humble be received? Have I succeeded in portraying any of the peculiar features of that institution whose curse rests over the fairest land the sun shines upon? Have I succeeded in showing how it blights the happiness of the white as well as the black race? Being the truth it makes no pretensions to romance, and relating events as they occurred it has no especial reference to a moral, but to those who regard truth as stranger than fiction it can be no less interesting on the former account, while others of pious and discerning minds can scarcely fail to recognise the hand of Providence in giving to the righteous the reward of their works, and to the wicked the fruit of their doings.

Chapter 1
In Childhood

Look not upon me because I am black; because the sun hath looked upon me.

—SONG OF SOLOMON[1]

It may be that I assume too much responsibility in attempting to write these pages. The world will probably say so, and I am aware of my deficiencies. I am neither clever, nor learned, nor talented. When a child they used to scold and find fault with me because they said I was dull and stupid. Perhaps under other circumstances and with more encouragement I might have appeared better; for I was shy and reserved and scarce dared open my lips to any one I had none of that quickness and animation which are so much admired in children, but rather a silent unobtrusive way of observing things and events, and wishing to understand them better than I could.

I was not brought up by any body in particular that I know of. I had no training, no cultivation. The birds of the air, or beasts of the feild are not freer from moral culture than I was. No one seemed to care for me till I was able to work, and then it was Hannah do this and Hannah do that, but I never complained as I found a sort of pleasure and something to divert my thoughts in employment. Of my relatives I knew nothing. No one ever spoke of my father or mother, but I soon learned what a curse was attached to my race, soon learned that the African blood in my veins would forever exclude me from the higher walks of life. That toil unremitted unpaid toil must be my lot and portion, without even the hope or expectation of any thing better. This seemed the harder to be borne, because my complexion was almost white, and the obnoxious descent could not be readily traced, though it gave a rotundity to my person, a wave and curl to my hair, and perhaps led me to fancy pictorial illustrations and flaming colors.

The busiest life has its leisure moments; it was so with mine. I had from the first an instinctive desire for knowledge and the means of mental improvement. Though neglected and a slave, I felt the immortal longings in me. In the absence of

---

1. Song of Solomon 1:6.

books and teachers and schools I determined to learn if not in a regular, approved, and scientific way. I was aware that this plan would meet with opposition, perhaps with punishment. My master never permitted his slaves to be taught. Education in his view tended to enlarge and expand their ideas; made them less subservient to their superiors, and besides that its blessings were destined to be conferred exclusively on the higher and nobler race. Indeed though he was generally easy and good-tempered, there was nothing liberal or democratic in his nature. Slaves were slaves to him, and nothing more. Practically he regarded them not as men and women, but in the same light as horses or other domestic animals. He ~~furnished~~[2] supplied their necessities of food and clothing from ~~the same~~ motives of policy, but scouted the ideas of equality and fraternity as preposterous and absurd. Of course I had nothing to expect from him, yet "where there's a will there's a way."

I was employed about the house, consequently my labors were much easier than those of the field servants, and I enjoyed intervals of repose and rest unknown to them. Then, too, I was a mere child and some hours of each day were allotted to play. On such occasions, and while the other children of the house were amusing themselves I would quietly steal away from their company to ponder over the pages of some old book or newspaper that chance had thrown in my way. Though I knew not the meaning of a single letter, and had not the means of finding out I loved to look at them and think that some day I should probably understand them all.

My dream was destined to be realized. One day while ~~I was~~ sitting on a little bank, beneath the shade of some large trees, at a short distance from my playmates, ~~when~~ an aged woman approached me. She was white, and looked venerable with her grey hair smoothly put back beneath a plain sun bonnet, and I recollected having seen her once or twice at my master's house whither she came to sell salves and ointments, and hearing it remarked that she was the wife of a sand digger and very poor.

She smiled benevolently and inquired why I concealed my book, and with child-like artlessness I told her all. How earnestly I desired knowledge, how our Master interdicted it, and how I was trying to teach myself. She stood for a few moments apparently buried in deep thought, but I interpreted her looks and actions favorably, and an idea struck me that perhaps she could read, and would become my teacher. She seemed to understand my wish before I expressed it.

"Child" she said "I was thinking of our Saviour's words to Peter where he commands the latter to 'feed his lambs.'[3] I will dispense to you such knowledge as I possess. Come to me each day. I will teach you to read in the hope and trust that you will thereby be made better in this world and that to come." Her demeanor like her words was very grave and solemn.

"Where do you live?" I inquired.

"In the little cottage just around the foot of the hill" she replied.

"I will come: Oh how eagerly, how joyfully" I answered "but if master finds it out his anger will be terrible; and then I have no means of paying you."

She smiled quietly, bade me fear nothing, and went her way. I returned home that evening with a light heart. Pleased, delighted, overwhelmed with my good

---

2. Strikethroughs indicate words that Crafts crossed out in her manuscript.   3. John 21:15.

fortune in prospective I felt like a being to whom a new world with all its mysteries and marvels was opening, and could scarcely repress my tears of joy and thankfulness. It sometimes seems that we require sympathy more in joy than sorrow; for the heart exultant, and overflowing with good nature longs to impart a portion of its happiness. Especialy is this the case with children. How it augments the importance of any little success to them that some one probably a mother will receive the intelligence with a show of delight and interest. But I had no mother, no friend.

The next day and the next I went out to gather blackberries, and took advantage of the fine opportunity to visit my worthy instructress and receive my first lesson. I was surprised at the smallness yet perfect neatness of her dwelling, at the quiet and orderly repose that reigned in through all its appointments; it was in such pleasing contrast to our great house with its bustle, confusion, and troops of servants of all ages and colors.

"Hannah, my dear, you are welcome" she said coming forward and extending her hand. "I rejoice to see you. I am, or rather was a northern woman, and consequently have no prejudices against your birth, or race, or condition, indeed I feel a warmer interest in your welfare than I should were you the daughter of a queen." I should have thanked her for so much kindness, and interest such expressions of motherly interest, but could find no words, and so sat silent and embarrassed.

I had heard of the North where the people were all free, and where the colored race had so many and such true friends, and was more delighted with her, and with the idea that I had found some of them than I could possibly have expressed in words.

At length while I was stumbling over the alphabet and trying to impress the different forms of the letters on my mind, an old man with a cane and silvered hair walked in, and coming close to me inquired "Is this the girl mother of whom you spoke, mother?" and when she answered in the affirmative he said many words of kindness and encouragement to me, and that though a slave I must be good and trust in God.

They were an aged couple, who for more than fifty years had occupied the same home, and who had shared together all the vicissitudes of life—its joys and sorrows, its hopes and fears. Wealth had been theirs, with all the appliances of luxury, and they became poor through a series of misfortunes. Yet as they had borne riches with virtuous moderation they conformed to poverty with subdued content, and readily exchanged the splendid mansion for the lowly cottage, and the merchant's desk and counting room for the fields of toil. Not that they were insensible to the benefits or advantages of riches, but they felt that life had something more—that the peace of God and their own consciences united to honor and intelligence were in themselves a fortune which the world neither gave nor could take away.

They had long before relinquished all selfish projects and ambitious aims. To be upright and honest, to incumber neither public nor private charity, and to contribute something to the happiness of others seemed to be the sum total of their present desires. Uncle Siah, as I learned to call him, had long been unable to work, except at some of the lighter branches of employment, or in cultivating the small garden which furnished their supply of excellent vegetables and likewise the simple herbs which imparted such healing properties to the salves and unguents that the kind old woman distributed around the neighborhood.

Educated at the north they both felt keenly on the subject of slavery and the degradation and ignorance it imposes on one portion of the human race. Yet all their conversation on this point was tempered with the utmost discretion and judgement, and though they could not be reconciled to the system they were disposed to stand still and wait in faith and hope for the salvation of the Lord.

In their morning and evening sacrifice of worship the poor slave was always remembered, and even their devout songs of praise were imbued with the same spirit. They loved to think and to speak of all mankind as brothers, the children of one great parent, and all bound to the same eternity.

Simple and retiring in their habits modest unostentatious and poor their virtues were almost wholly unknown. In that wearied and bent old man, who frequently went out in pleasant weather to sell baskets at the doors of the rich few recognised the possessor of sterling worth, and the candidate for immortality, yet his meek gentle smile, and loving words excited their sympathies and won their regard.

How I wished to be with them all the time—how I entreated them to buy me, but in vain. They had not the means.

It must not be supposed that learning to read was all they taught me, or that my visits to them were made with regularity. They gave me an insight to many things. They cultivated my moral nature. They led me to the foot of the Cross. Sometimes in the evening while the other slaves were enjoying the banjo and the dance I would steal away to hold sweet converse with them. Sometimes a morning walk with the other children, or an errand to a neighbor's would furnish the desired opportunity, and sometimes an interval of many days elapsed between my calls to their house.

At such times, however, I tried to remember the good things they had taught me, and to improve myself by gathering up such crumbs of knowledge as I could, and adding little by little to my stock of information. Of course my opportunities were limited, and I had much to make me miserable and discontented. The life of a slave at best is not a pleasant one, but I had formed a resolution to always look on the bright side of things, to be industrious, cheerful, and true-hearted, to do some good though in an humble way, and to win some love if I could. "I am a slave" thus my thoughts would run. "I can never be great, nor rich; I cannot hold an elevated position in society, but I can do my duty, and be kind in the sure and certain hope of an eternal reward."

By and by as I grew older, and was enabled to manifest my good intentions, not so much by words, as a manner of sympathy and consideration for every one, I was quite astonished to see how much I was trusted and confided in, how I was made the repository of secrets, and how the weak, the sick, and the suffering came to me for advice and assistance. Then the little slave children were almost entirely confided to my care. I hope that I was good and gentle to them; for I pitied their hard and cruel fate very much, and used to think that, notwithstanding all the labor and trouble they gave me, if I could so discharge my duty by them that in after years their memories would hover over this as the sunshiny period of their lives I should be amply repaid.

What a blessing it is that faith, and hope, and love are universal in their nature and operation—that poor as well as rich, bond[4] as well as free are susceptible to their pleasing influences, and contain within themselves a treasure of consolation for all the ills of life. These little children, slaves though they were, and doomed to a life of toil and drudgery, ignorant, and untutored, assimilated thus to

---

4. Enslaved, in bondage.

the highest and proudest in the land—thus evinced their equal origin, and immortal destiny.

How much love and confidence and affection I won it is impossible to describe. How the rude and boisterous became gentle and obliging, and how ready ~~they~~ all were to serve and obey me, not because I exacted the service or obedience, but because their own loving natures prompted them to reciprocate my love. How I longed to become their teacher, and open the door of knowledge to their minds by instructing them to read but it might not be. I could not have even hoped to escape detection ~~would have~~ and discovery would have entailed punishment on all.

Thus the seasons passed away. Summer insensibly melted into autumn, and autumn gave place to winter. I still visited Aunt Hetty, and enjoyed the benefits of her gracious counsels. Seated by the clear wood fire she was always busy in the preparation or repair of garments as perfect taste and economy dictated, or plying her bright knitting needles by the evening lamp, while her aged companion sat socially by her side.

One evening I was sitting with them, and reading from the book of God. Our intercourse[5] had remained so long undiscovered that I had almost ceased to fear disclosure. Probably I had grown less circumspect though not intentionally, or it might be that in conformity to the inscrutable ways of Providence the faith and strength of these aged servants of the Cross were to be tried by a more severe ordeal. Alas: Alas that I should have been the means.

The door suddenly opened without warning, and the overseer of my master's estate walked into the house. My horror, and grief, and astonishment were indescribable. I felt Oh how much more than I tell. He addressed me rudely, and bade me begone home on the instant. I durst not disobey, but retreating through the doorway I glanced back at the calm sedate countenances of the aged couple, who were all unmoved by the torrent of threats and invectives he poured out against them.

My Master was absent at the time, ~~over~~ the overseer could find no precedent for my case, and so I escaped the punishment I should otherwise have suffered. Not so with my venerable and venerated teachers. It was considered necessary to make an example of them, that others might be deterred from the like attempts. Years passed, however, before I learned their fate. The cruel overseer would not tell me whither he had removed them, but to all my inquiries he simply answered that he would take good care I never saw them again. My fancy painted them as immured in a dungeon for the crime of teaching a slave to read. Their cottage ~~of~~ home remained uninhabited for a time, and then strangers came and took possession of it. But Oh the difference to me. For days and weeks I was inconsolable, and how I hated and blamed myself as the cause of their misery. After a time the intensity of my feelings subsided, and I came to a more rational and consistent manner of thinking. I concluded that they were happy whatever might be their condition, and that only by doing right and being good I could make anything like an adequate return for all they had done and suffered for me.

Another year passed away. There was to be a change in our establishment, and the ancient mansion of Lindendale was to receive a mistress. Hitherto our master had been a bachelor. He was a portly man, middle-aged, and of aristocratic name and connexions. His estate had descended to him through many gen-

---

5. Interchange, relationship.

erations, and it was whispered though no one seemed to know, that he was bringing his beautiful bride to an impoverished house.

~~holidays and the time for warming fires to be kindled in the dusty chimneys~~
~~of southern chambers It was then that our master brought home his bride~~ The remembrance is fresh to me as that of yesterday. The holidays were passed, and we
had been promised another in honor of the occasion. But we were not animated
with the idea of that half so much as because something had occurred to break the
dull monotony of our existence; something that would give life, and zest, and interest, to one day at least; and something that would afford a theme for conversation and speculation. Then our preparations were quite wonderful, and the old
housekeeper nearly overdid herself in fidgetting and fretting and worrying while
dragging her unwieldly weight of flesh up and down the staircases, along the galleries and passages, and through the rooms where floors were undergoing the
process of being rubbed bright, carpets were being spread, curtains shaken out,
beds puffed and covered ~~and~~ furniture dusted and polished, and all things prepared as beseemed the dignity of the family and the fastidious taste of its expected
mistress. It was a grand time for me as now I had an opportunity of seeing the
house, and ascertaining what a fine old place it was. Heretofore all except certain
apartments had been interdicted to us, but now that the chambers were opened to
be aired and renovated no one could prevent us making good use of our eyes. And
we saw on all sides the appearance of wealth and splendor, and the appliances to
every luxury. What a variety of beautiful rooms, all splendid yet so different, and
seemingly inhabited by marble images of art, or human forms pictured on the
walls. What an array of costly furniture adorned the rich saloons and gorgeous
halls. We thought our master must be a very great man to have so much wealth at
his command, but it never occurred to us to inquire whose sweat and blood and
unpaid labor had contributed to produce it.

The evening previous to the expected arrival of the bridal party Mrs Bry the
housekeeper, announced the preparations to be complete and all things in readiness. Then she remembered that the windows of one apartment had been left open
for a freer admission of air. ~~It must be closed~~ They must be closed and barred and
the good old dame imposed that duty on me. "I am so excessively weary or I
would attend to it myself" she said giving me my directions "but I think that I can
rely on you not to touch or misplace anything or loiter in the rooms." I assured
her that she could and departed on my errand.

There is something inexpressibly dreary and solemn in passing through the
silent rooms of a large house, especially one whence many generations have passed
to the grave. Involuntarily you find yourself thinking of them, and wondering
how they looked in life, and how the rooms looked in their possession, and
whether or not they would recognise their former habitations if restored once
more to earth and them. Then all we have heard or fancied of spiritual existences
occur to us. There is the echo of a stealthy tread behind us. There is a shadow flitting past through the gloom. There is a sound, but it does not seem of mortality. A
supernatural thrill pervades your frame, and you feel the presence of mysterious
beings. It may be foolish and childish, but it is one of the unaccountable things instinctive to the human nature.

Thus I felt while treading the long galleries which led to the southern turret.
The apartment there was stately rather than splendid, and in other days before
the northern and eastern wing had been added to the building it had formed the

family drawing room, and was now from its retired situation the favorite resort of my master; when he became weary of noise and bustle and turmoil as he sometimes did. It was adorned with a long succession of family portraits ranged against the walls in due order of age and ancestral dignity. To these portraits Mrs Bry had informed me a strange legend was attached. It was said that Sir Clifford De Vincent, a nobleman of power and influence in the old world, having incurred the wrath of his sovereign, fled for safety to the shores of the Old Dominion,[6] and became the founder of my Master's paternal estate. ~~When the~~ When the house had been completed according to his directions, he ordered his portrait and that of his wife to be hung in the drawing room, and denounced a severe malediction against the person who should ever presume to remove them, and against any possessor of the mansion who being of his name and blood should neglect to follow his example. And well had his wishes been obeyed. Generation had succeeded generation, and a long line of De Vincents occupied the family residence, yet each ~~one~~ inheritor had contributed to the adornments of the drawing-room a faithful transcript of his person and lineaments, side by side with that of his Lady. The ceremonial of hanging up these portraits was usually made the occasion of a great festivity, in which hundreds of the neighboring gentry participated. But my master had seen fit to dissent from this custom, and his portrait unaccompanied by that of a Lady had been added to the number, though without the usual demonstration of mirth and rejoicing.

Memories of the dead give at any time a haunting air to a silent room. How much more this becomes the case when standing face to face with their pictured resemblances and looking into the stony eyes motionless and void of expression as those of an exhumed corpse. But even as I gazed the golden light of sunset penetrating through the open windows in an oblique direction set each rigid feature in a glow. Movements like those of life came over the line of stolid faces as the shadows of a linden played there. The stern old sire with sword and armorial bearings seems moodily to relax his haughty ~~brow~~ aspect. The countenance of another, a veteran in the old-time wars, assumes a gracious expression it never wore in life; and another appears to open and shut his lips continually though they emit no sound. Over the pale pure features of a bride descends a halo of glory; the long shining locks of a young mother waver and float over the child she holds; and the frozen cheek of an ancient dame seems beguiled into smiles and dimples.

Involuntarily I gazed as the fire of the sun died out, even untill the floor became dusky, and the shadows of the linden falling broader and deeper wrapped all in gloom. Hitherto I had not contemplated my Master's picture; for my thoughts had been with the dead, but now I looked for it, where it hung solitary, and thought how soon it would have a companion like the others, and what a new aspect would thereby be given to the apartment. But was it prophecy, or presentiment, or why was it that this idea was attended to my mind with something painful? That it seemed the first scene in some fearful tragedy; the foreboding of some great calamity; a curse of destiny that no circumstances could avert or soften. And why was it that as I mused the portrait of my master ~~changed~~ seemed to change from its usually kind and placid expression to one of wrath and gloom, that the calm brow should become wrinkled with passion, the lips turgid with malevolence—yet thus it was.

6. Nickname for Virginia.

Though filled with superstitious awe I was in no haste to leave the room; for there surrounded by mysterious associations I seemed suddenly to have grown old, to have entered a new world of thoughts, and feelings and sentiments. I was not a slave with these pictured memorials of the past. They could not enforce drudgery, or condemn me on account of my color to a life of servitude. As their companion I could think and speculate. In their presence my mind seemed to run riotous and exult in its freedom as a rational being, and one destined for something higher and better than this world can afford.

I closed the windows, for the night air had become sharp and piercing, and the linden creaked and swayed its branches to the fitful gusts. Then, there was a sharp voice at the door. It said "child what are you doing?" I turned round and answered "Looking at the pictures."

Mrs Bry alarmed at my prolonged absence had actually dragged her unweildly person thither to ascertain the cause.

"Looking at the pictures" she repeated "as if such an ignorant thing as you are would know any thing about them."

Ignorance, forsooth. Can ignorance quench the immortal mind or prevent its feeling at times the indications of its heavenly origin? Can it destroy that deep abiding appreciation of the beautiful that seems inherent to the human soul? Can it seal up the fountains of truth and all intuitive perception of life, death and eternity? I think not. Those to whom man ~~learns little nature~~ teaches little, nature like a wise and prudent mother teaches much.

* * *

c. 1850–1860   2002

◦◄ ISABELLA BEETON ►◦
1836–1865

For the second half of the nineteenth century, *Mrs. Beeton's Book of Household Management* (1861), by Isabella Beeton, served as the standard set of directions for middle-class British women who wanted to run their homes in the "proper" way. More than 1,100 pages long, the book gives specific directions for everything from carving a codfish to equipping a housemaid. A Victorian Martha Stewart (without the scandal), Beeton had a profound influence on British domestic life. Although the authoritative voice of "Mrs. Beeton" may have conjured an image of a well-brought-up middle-aged lady in an apron and cap, Beeton was only in her mid-twenties when she wrote her book, and the home she came from was very different from the ideal households her work prescribes.

Born Isabella Mary Mason, Beeton was the oldest of a blended family of twenty-one children—including Beeton's siblings from her mother's first marriage, as well as the stepsiblings and half-siblings from her mother's remarriage after her father's early death. She grew up in the grandstand at the horse-racing track where the derby was run every year in England: not in a house near the grandstand, but in the racing facility itself. Beeton's stepfather, Henry Dorling, was clerk of the racecourse at Epsom, a position affording him a good upper-middle-class living, but not enough to sustain a house for twenty-one children, their parents and grandmother, and the servants who cared for them all. The grandstand became a permanent nursery for the children, with cots and cribs set up in offices. Beeton helped her grandmother superintend the other children for most of the year, and they all went away as if on holiday during the weeks that the horse races were run. With living arrangements as unorthodox and chaotic as these, it is easy to see why the subject of household management might have appealed to young Beeton.

In her teens, Beeton attended boarding school, where she became a proficient pianist; she also studied for a time in Germany, mastering German, French, and— more unusually—the skills befitting a pastry chef. Intelligent and ambitious, she married Sam Beeton, an aspiring publisher of magazines and dictionaries, at age twenty. At once she became his collaborator, taking on writing and editorial duties for the women's magazine he produced, *Englishwoman's Domestic Magazine*. As a journalist, Beeton focused on practical solutions to everyday domestic problems, making the *Englishwoman's Domestic Magazine* a prototype for women's magazines in the next century.

Happily married, the Beetons began their life together with the losses of two children in early childhood to illness, one in infancy and the other at the age of three. During this period, Beeton began researching the enormous project that would become her *Book of Household Management*. She improved on previous cookbooks by listing ingredients at the beginning of each recipe and giving clear, precise directions for preparing every dish, from the most ordinary (baked custard or brown gravy) to the most elaborate (ragout of wild duck, carrot jam to imitate apricot preserve). In addition to hundreds of recipes, the book includes guides to entertaining guests, supervising servants, rearing children and nursing them through childhood diseases, and dealing with physicians and lawyers. The book became a tremendous success, continuing to sell strongly long after Beeton died of a postpartum infection contracted while giving birth to her second surviving child. She was twenty-eight years old.

The extracts included here from the *Book of Household Management* give a taste of the range of advice the volume contains: recipes, menus, and how-to's for managing servants. The recipes and menus are typical of what would now be seen as overcooking (fresh asparagus boiled for fifteen to eighteen minutes would turn to stringy mush) and overeating (even plain family meals in Beeton's book usually have three courses, and sugars and fats abound in Victorian dishes). The descriptions of the duties of the valet (personal servant to the master of the house) and the wet nurse (the servant who would breast-feed an infant when the mother could not) give insight into the strict distinctions of social class within the home, as well as the complex details involved in running a large household without modern conveniences. Beeton's taste for moralizing and for educating her readers is also evident in these extracts.

From Mrs. Beeton's Book of Household Management

[Sample Recipes]

Lark Pie (An Entrée)

971.[1] INGREDIENTS.—A few thin slices of beef, the same of bacon, 9 larks, flour; for stuffing, 1 teacupful of bread crumbs, ½ teaspoonful of minced lemon-

---

1. Entrée: served between fish and meat courses;   the chapters on household management.
each recipe is numbered, as are the paragraphs of

peel, 1 teaspoonful of minced parsley, 1 egg, salt and pepper to taste, 1 teaspoon-ful of chopped shalot, ½ pint of weak stock or water, puff-paste.[2]

Mode.—Make a stuffing of bread crumbs, minced lemon-peel, parsley, and the yolk of an egg, all of which should be well mixed together; roll the larks in flour, and stuff them. Line the bottom of a pie-dish with a few slices of beef and bacon; over these place the larks, and season with salt, pepper, minced parsley, and chopped shalot, in the above proportion. Pour in the stock or water, cover with crust, and bake for an hour in a moderate oven. During the time the pie is baking, shake it 2 or 3 times, to assist in thickening the gravy, and serve very hot.

Time.—1 hour. *Average cost,* 1s. 6d.[3] a dozen.

Sufficient for 5 or 6 persons.

Seasonable.—In full season in November.

Boiled Asparagus

1087. INGREDIENTS.—To each ½ gallon of water allow 1 heaped tablespoon-ful of salt; asparagus.

Mode.—Asparagus should be dressed as soon as possible after it is cut, al-though it may be kept for a day or two by putting the stalks into cold water; yet, to be good, like every other vegetable, it cannot be cooked too fresh. Scrape the white part of the stems, *beginning* from the *head,* and throw them into cold water; then tie them into bundles of about 20 each, keeping the heads all one way, and cut the stalks evenly, that they may all be the same length; put them into *boiling* water, with salt in the above proportion; keep them boiling quickly until tender, with the saucepan uncovered. When the asparagus is done, dish it upon toast, which should be dipped in the water it was cooked in, and leave the white ends outwards each way, with the points meeting in the middle. Serve with a tureen of melted butter.

Time.—15 to 18 minutes after the water boils.

Average cost, in full season, 2s. 6d.[4] the 100 heads.

Sufficient.—Allow about 50 heads for 4 or 5 persons.

Seasonable.—May be had, forced, from January, but cheapest in May, June, and July.

* * *

Christmas Plum-Pudding (*Very Good*)

1328. INGREDIENTS.—1½ lb. of raisins, ½ lb. of currants, ½ lb. of mixed peel, ¾ lb. of bread crumbs, ¾ lb. of suet, 8 eggs, 1 wineglassful of brandy.[5]

Mode.—Stone[6] and cut the raisins in halves, but do not chop them; wash, pick, and dry the currants, and mince the suet finely; cut the candied peel into thin slices, and grate down the bread into fine crumbs. When all these dry ingredients

---

2. Puff pastry, made of multiple layers of butter and dough, often used as a pie crust.

3. Before British currency was converted to the decimal system in 1971, a pound (£) was equal to 20 shillings (s.), a crown was equal to 5 shillings, a shilling was equal to 12 pence (d.), and a penny was equal to 4 farthings; although monetary conversions can be problematic, 1 shilling 6 pence at the time this selection was written would be the equivalent of about £4.73 or $8.82 in today's currency.

4. About £7.89 or $14.72 in today's dollars.

5. Mixed peel: the peels of citrus fruits cooked in a sugar syrup and then dried; suet: fat from cooking beef or sheep.

6. Remove the seeds; seedless grapes (and the raisins they make when dried) had not yet been bred.

are prepared, mix them well together; then moisten the mixture with the eggs, which should be well beaten, and the brandy; stir well, that everything may be very thoroughly blended, and *press* the pudding into a buttered mould; tie it down tightly with a floured cloth, and boil for 5 or 6 hours. It may be boiled in a cloth without a mould, and will require the same time allowed for cooking. As Christmas puddings are usually made a few days before they are required for table, when the pudding is taken out of the pot, hang it up immediately, and put a plate or saucer underneath to catch the water that may drain from it. The day it is to be eaten, plunge it into boiling water, and keep it boiling for at least 2 hours; then turn it out of the mould, and serve with brandy-sauce. On Christmas-day a sprig of holly is usually placed in the middle of the pudding, and about a wineglassful of brandy poured round it, which, at the moment of serving, is lighted, and the pudding thus brought to table encircled in flame.

Time.—5 or 6 hours the first time of boiling; 2 hours the day it is to be served.

Average cost, 4s.

Sufficient for a quart mould for 7 or 8 persons.

Seasonable on the 25th of December, and on various festive occasions till March.

Note.—Five or six of these puddings should be made at one time, as they will keep good for many weeks, and in cases where unexpected guests arrive, will be found an acceptable, and, as it only requires warming through, a quickly-prepared dish. Moulds of every shape and size are manufactured for these puddings, and may be purchased of Messrs. R. & J. Slack, 336, Strand.[7]

[Sample Bills of Fare]

Plain Family Dinners for January

1895. *Sunday.*—1. Boiled turbot and oyster sauce, potatoes. 2. Roast leg or griskin of pork, apple sauce, brocoli, potatoes. 3. Cabinet pudding, and damson tart made with preserved damsons.

1896. *Monday.*—1. The remains of turbot warmed in oyster sauce, potatoes. 2. Cold pork, stewed steak. 3. Open jam tart, which should have been made with the pieces of paste left from the damson tart; baked arrowroot pudding.

1897. *Tuesday.*—1. Boiled neck of mutton, carrots, mashed turnips, suet dumplings, and caper sauce: the broth should be served first, and a little rice or pearl barley should be boiled with it along with the meat. 2. Rolled jam pudding.

1898. *Wednesday.*—1. Roast rolled ribs of beef, greens, potatoes, and horse-radish sauce. 2. Bread-and-butter pudding, cheesecakes.

1899. *Thursday.*—1. Vegetable soup (the bones from the ribs of beef should be boiled down with this soup), cold beef, mashed potatoes. 2. Pheasants, gravy, bread sauce. 3. Macaroni.

1900. *Friday.*—1. Fried whitings or soles. 2. Boiled rabbit and onion sauce, minced beef, potatoes. 3. Currant dumplings.

1901. *Saturday.*—1. Rump-steak pudding or pie, greens, and potatoes. 2. Baked custard pudding and stewed apples.

---

7. A cooking shop in central London.

1902. *Sunday.*—1. Codfish and oyster sauce, potatoes. 2. Joint of roast mutton, either leg, haunch, or saddle; brocoli and potatoes, red-currant jelly. 3. Apple tart and custards, cheese.

1903. *Monday.*—1. The remains of codfish picked from the bone, and warmed through in the oyster sauce; if there is no sauce left, order a few oysters and make a little fresh; and do not let the fish boil, or it will be watery. 2. Curried rabbit, with boiled rice served separately, cold mutton, mashed potatoes. 3. Somersetshire dumplings with wine sauce.

1904. *Tuesday.*—1. Boiled fowls, parsley-and-butter; bacon garnished with Brussels sprouts, minced or hashed mutton. 2. Baroness pudding.

1905. *Wednesday.*—1. The remains of the fowls cut up into joints and fricasseed; joint of roast pork and apple sauce, and, if liked, sage-and-onion, served on a dish by itself; turnips and potatoes. 2. Lemon pudding, either baked or boiled.

1906. *Thursday.*—1. Cold pork and jugged hare, red-currant jelly, mashed potatoes. 2. Apple pudding.

1907. *Friday.*—1. Boiled beef, either the aitchbone or the silver side of the round; carrots, turnips, suet dumplings, and potatoes: if there is a marrow-bone, serve the marrow on toast at the same time. 2. Rice snowballs.

1908. *Saturday.*—1. Pea-soup made from liquor in which beef was boiled; cold beef, mashed potatoes. 2. Baked batter fruit pudding.

[Sample Sections from "Household Management"]

Duties of the Valet

2234. *Attendants on the Person.*—"No man is a hero to his valet," saith the proverb; and the corollary may run, "No lady is a heroine to her maid." The infirmities of humanity are, perhaps, too numerous and too equally distributed to stand the severe microscopic tests which attendants on the person have opportunities of applying. The valet and waiting-maid are placed near the persons of the master and mistress, receiving orders only from them, dressing them, accompanying them in all their journeys, the confidants and agents of their most unguarded moments, of their most secret habits, and of course subject to their commands,— even to their caprices; they themselves being subject to erring judgment, aggravated by an imperfect education. All that can be expected from such servants is polite manners, modest demeanour, and a respectful reserve, which are indispensable. To these, good sense, good temper, some self-denial, and consideration for the feelings of others, whether above or below them in the social scale, will be useful qualifications. Their duty leads them to wait on those who are, from sheer wealth, station, and education, more polished, and consequently more susceptible of annoyance; and any vulgar familiarity of manner is opposed to all their notions of self-respect. Quiet unobtrusive manners, therefore, and a delicate reserve in speaking of their employers, either in praise or blame, is as essential in their absence, as good manners and respectful conduct in their presence.

2235. Some of the duties of the valet we have just hinted at in treating of the duties of the footman[8] in a small family. His day commences by seeing that his master's dressing-room is in order; that the housemaid has swept and dusted it

---

8. A uniformed servant who answers the door and waits at table.

properly; that the fire is lighted and burns cheerfully; and some time before his master is expected, he will do well to throw up the sash to admit fresh air, closing it, however, in time to recover the temperature which he knows his master prefers. It is now his duty to place the body-linen on the horse[9] before the fire, to be aired properly; to lay the trousers intended to be worn, carefully brushed and cleaned, on the back of his master's chair; while the coat and waistcoat, carefully brushed and folded, and the collar cleaned, are laid in their place ready to put on when required. All the articles of the toilet[1] should be in their places, the razors properly set and stropped, and hot water ready for use.

2236. Gentlemen generally prefer performing the operation of shaving themselves, but a valet should be prepared to do it if required; and he should, besides, be a good hairdresser. Shaving over, he has to brush the hair, beard, and moustache, where that appendage is encouraged, arranging the whole simply and gracefully, according to the age and style of countenance. Every fortnight, or three weeks at the utmost, the hair should be cut, and the points of the whiskers trimmed as often as required. A good valet will now present the various articles of the toilet as they are wanted; afterwards, the body-linen, neck-tie, which he will put on, if required, and, afterwards, waistcoat, coat, and boots, in suitable order, and carefully brushed and polished.

2237. Having thus seen his master dressed, if he is about to go out, the valet will hand him his cane, gloves, and hat, the latter well brushed on the outside with a soft brush, and wiped inside with a clean handkerchief, respectfully attend him to the door, and open it for him, and receive his last orders for the day.

2238. He now proceeds to put everything in order in the dressing-room, cleans the combs and brushes, and brushes and folds up any clothes that may be left about the room, and puts them away in the drawers.

2239. Gentlemen are sometimes indifferent as to their clothes and appearance; it is the valet's duty, in this case, where his master permits it, to select from the wardrobe such things as are suitable for the occasion, so that he may appear with scrupulous neatness and cleanliness; that his linen and neck-tie, where that is white or coloured, are unsoiled; and where he is not accustomed to change them every day, that the cravat is turned, and even ironed, to remove the crease of the previous fold. The coat collar,—which where the hair is oily and worn long, is apt to get greasy—should also be examined; a careful valet will correct this by removing the spots day by day as they appear, first by moistening the grease-spots with a little rectified spirits of wine or spirits of hartshorn,[2] which has a renovating effect, and the smell of which soon disappears. The grease is dissolved and removed by gentle scraping. The grease removed, add a little more of the spirit, and rub with a piece of clean cloth; finish by adding a few drops more; rub it with the palm of the hand, in the direction of the grain of the cloth, and it will be clean and glossy as the rest of the garment.

2240. Polish for the boots is an important matter to the valet, and not always to be obtained good by purchase; never so good, perhaps, as he can make

9. Body linen: underwear; horse: the clothes horse, a movable rack.
1. Grooming equipment, such as comb and brush.

2. Spirits of wine: grain alcohol, ethanol; hartshorn: ammonia, formerly made from a deer (or "hart") antler.

for himself after the following recipes:—Take of ivory-black and treacle[3] each 4 oz., sulphuric acid 1 oz., best olive-oil 2 spoonfuls, best white-wine vinegar 3 half-pints: mix the ivory-black and treacle well in an earthen jar; then add the sulphuric acid, continuing to stir the mixture; next pour in the oil; and, lastly, add the vinegar, stirring it in by degrees, until thoroughly incorporated.

2241. Another polish is made by mixing 1 oz. each of pounded galls[4] and logwood-chips, and 3 lbs. of red French wine (ordinaire). Boil together till the liquid is reduced to half the quantity, and pour it off through a strainer. Now take ½ lb. each of pounded gum-arabic and lump-sugar, 1 oz. of green copperas,[5] and 3 lbs. of brandy. Dissolve the gum-arabic in the preceding decoction, and add the sugar and copperas: when all is dissolved and mixed together, stir in the brandy, mixing it smoothly. This mixture will yield 5 or 6 lbs. of a very superior polishing paste for boots and shoes.

2242. It is, perhaps, unnecessary to add, that having discharged all the commissions intrusted to him by his master, such as conveying notes or messages to friends, or the tradesmen, all of which he should punctually and promptly attend to, it is his duty to be in waiting when his master returns home to dress for dinner, or for any other occasion, and to have all things prepared for this second dressing. Previous to this, he brings under his notice the cards of visitors who may have called, delivers the messages he may have received for him, and otherwise acquits himself of the morning's commissions, and receives his orders for the remainder of the day. The routine of his evening duty is to have the dressing-room and study, where there is a separate one, arranged comfortably for his master, the fires lighted, candles prepared, dressing-gown and slippers in their place, and aired, and everything in order that is required for his master's comforts.

The Wet-Nurse

2435. We are aware that, according to the opinion of some ladies, there is no domestic theme, during a certain period of their married lives, more fraught with vexation and disquietude than that ever-fruitful source of annoyance, "the Nurse;" but, as we believe, there are thousands of excellent wives and mothers who pass through life without even a temporary embroglio in the kitchen, or suffering a state of moral hectic the whole time of a nurse's empire in the nursery or bedroom. Our own experience goes to prove, that although many unqualified persons palm themselves off on ladies as fully competent for the duties they so rashly and dishonestly undertake to perform, and thus expose themselves to ill-will and merited censure, there are still very many fully equal to the legitimate exercise of what they undertake; and if they do not in every case give entire satisfaction, some of the fault,—and sometimes a great deal of it,—may be honestly placed to the account of the ladies themselves, who, in many instances, are so impressed with the propriety of their own method of performing everything, as to insist upon the adoption of *their* system in preference to that of the nurse, whose plan is probably

3. Ivory-black: a fine, soft black pigment; treacle: molasses.
4. Black pigment derived from oak galls, or swellings of plant tissue, produced when wasp

eggs are laid on new leaves or twigs.
5. Gum-arabic: a gum produced by the acacia tree and used as a thickener; green copperas: iron sulfate used in making red pigment.

based on a comprehensive forethought, and rendered perfect in all its details by an ample experience.

2436. In all our remarks on this subject, we should remember with gentleness the order of society from which our nurses are drawn; and that those who make their duty a study, and are termed professional nurses, have much to endure from the caprice and egotism of their employers; while others are driven to the occupation from the laudable motive of feeding their own children, and who, in fulfilling that object, are too often both selfish and sensual, performing, without further interest than is consistent with their own advantage, the routine of customary duties.

2437. Properly speaking, there are two nurses,—the nurse for the mother and the nurse for the child, or, the monthly[6] and the wet nurse. Of the former we have already spoken, and will now proceed to describe the duties of the latter, and add some suggestions as to her age, physical health, and moral conduct, subjects of the utmost importance as far as the charge intrusted to her is concerned, and therefore demanding some special remarks.

2438. When from illness, suppression of the milk, accident, or some natural process, the mother is deprived of the pleasure of rearing her infant, it becomes necessary at once to look around for a fitting substitute, so that the child may not suffer, by any needless delay, a physical loss by the deprivation of its natural food. The first consideration should be as regards age, state of health, and temper.

2439. The age, if possible, should not be less than twenty or nor exceed thirty years, with the health sound in every respect, and the body free from all eruptive disease or local blemish. The best evidence of a sound state of health will be found in the woman's clear open countenance, the ruddy tone of the skin, the full, round, and elastic state of the breasts, and especially in the erectile, firm condition of the nipple, which, in all unhealthy states of the body, is pendulous, flabby, and relaxed; in which case, the milk is sure to be imperfect in its organization, and, consequently, deficient in its nutrient qualities. Appetite is another indication of health in the suckling nurse or mother; for it is impossible a woman can feed her child without having a corresponding appetite; and though inordinate craving for food is neither desirable nor necessary, a natural vigour should be experienced at mealtimes, and the food taken should be anticipated and enjoyed.

2440. Besides her health, the moral state of the nurse is to be taken into account, or that mental discipline or principle of conduct which would deter the nurse from at any time gratifying her own pleasures and appetites at the cost or suffering of her infant charge.

2441. The conscientiousness and good faith that would prevent a nurse so acting are, unfortunately, very rare; and many nurses, rather than forego the enjoyment of a favourite dish, though morally certain of the effect it will have on the child, will, on the first opportunity, feed with avidity on fried meats, cabbage, cucumbers, pickles,[7] or other crude and injurious aliments, in defiance of all orders

6. A woman hired to take care of the mother (and baby) during the month after a woman gave birth.

7. Foods believed to give an infant colic.

given, or confidence reposed in their word, good sense, and humanity. And when the infant is afterwards racked with pain, and a night of disquiet alarms the mother, the doctor is sent for, and the nurse, covering her dereliction by falsehood, the consequence of her gluttony is treated as a disease, and the poor infant is dosed for some days with medicines, that can do it but little if any good, and, in all probability, materially retard its physical development. The selfish nurse, in her ignorance, believes, too, that as long as she experiences no admonitory symptoms herself, the child cannot suffer; and satisfied that, whatever is the cause of its screams and plunges, neither she, nor what she had eaten, had anything to do with it, with this flattering assurance at her heart, she watches her opportunity, and has another luxurious feast off the proscribed dainties, till the increasing disturbance in the child's health, or treachery from the kitchen, opens the eyes of mother and doctor to the nurse's unprincipled conduct. In all such cases the infant should be spared the infliction of medicine, and, as a wholesome corrective to herself, and relief to her charge, a good sound dose administered to the nurse.

2442. Respecting the diet of the wet-nurse, the first point of importance is to fix early and definite hours for every meal; and the mother should see that no cause is ever allowed to interfere with their punctuality. The food itself should be light, easy of digestion, and simple. Boiled or roast meat, with bread and potatoes, with occasionally a piece of sago,[8] rice, or tapioca pudding, should constitute the dinner, the only meal that requires special comment; broths, green vegetables, and all acid or salt foods, must be avoided. Fresh fish, once or twice a week, may be taken; but it is hardly sufficiently nutritious to be often used as a meal. If the dinner is taken early,—at one o'clock,—there will be no occasion for luncheon, which too often, to the injury of the child, is made the cover for a first dinner. Half a pint of stout, with a Reading biscuit, at eleven o'clock, will be abundantly sufficient between breakfast at eight and a good dinner, with a pint of porter at one o'clock.[9] About eight o'clock in the evening, half a pint of stout, with another biscuit, may be taken; and for supper, at ten or half-past, a pint of porter, with a slice of toast or a small amount of bread and cheese, may conclude the feeding for the day.

2443. Animal food once in twenty-four hours is quite sufficient. All spirits, unless in extreme cases, should be avoided; and wine is still more seldom needed. With a due quantity of plain digestible food, and the proportion of stout and porter ordered, with early hours and regularity, the nurse will not only be strong and healthy herself, but fully capable of rearing a child in health and strength. There are two points all mothers, who are obliged to employ wet-nurses, should remember, and be on their guard against. The first is, never to allow a nurse to give medicine to the infant on her own authority: many have such an infatuated idea of the *healing excellence* of castor-oil,[1] that they would administer a dose of this disgusting grease twice a week, and think they had done a meritorious service to the child. The next point is, to watch carefully, lest, to insure a night's sleep for herself, she does not dose the infant with Godfrey's cordial, syrup of poppies, or some narcotic potion,[2] to insure tranquillity to the one and give the opportunity

8. A mild pudding made from the starch of sago palms.
9. Stout: dark, sweet ale; Reading biscuit: a cookie produced by Huntley and Palmer's Biscuits, in Reading, England; porter: a dark, heavy ale.
1. A laxative and emetic made from seeds of the tropical castor plant.
2. Alcohol or opium drinks to induce sleep.

of sleep to the other. The fact that scores of nurses keep secret bottles of these deadly syrups, for the purpose of stilling their charges, is notorious; and that many use them to a fearful extent, is sufficiently patent to all.

2444. It therefore behoves the mother, while obliged to trust to a nurse, to use her best discretion to guard her child from the unprincipled treatment of the person she must, to a certain extent, depend upon and trust; and to remember, in all cases, rather than resort to castor-oil or sedatives, to consult a medical man for her infant in preference to following the counsel of her nurse.

1861

CULTURAL COORDINATES
Level Measures

Middle- and upper-class women who were raised in households with full-time cooks often had great difficulty learning to navigate the kitchen. Today we might have limited sympathy for them: how hard can it be, after all, to read a recipe? Nineteenth-century cooking, however, required expertise and guesswork. To know how much of a given ingredient to add to a batter or a salad, the aspiring cook needed either to have seen someone else make the dish many times or to have studied cookery books written by experts.

The problem was that the experts' advice about measurements was inconsistent. Isabella Beeton (see pp. 1021–30) gives strict definitions for her measurements: she explains a tablespoonful ("By it is generally meant and understood a measure or bulk equal to that which would be produced by *half an ounce* of water"); a dessert-spoonful ("a measure or bulk equal to a *quarter of an ounce* of water"); and a teaspoonful ("equal in quantity to a *drachm* of water"). When she gets to a "drop," however, Beeton despairs of being exact: "This is the name of a vague kind of measure, and is so called on account of the liquid being *dropped* from the mouth of a bottle. Its quantity, however, will vary, either from the consistency of the liquid or the size and shape of the mouth of the bottle."

But measures of solid or semisolid substances, such as butter, were conceived metaphorically

THE

BOSTON COOKING-SCHOOL

COOK BOOK.

BY

FANNIE MERRITT FARMER,

PRINCIPAL OF THE BOSTON COOKING-SCHOOL.

BOSTON:
LITTLE, BROWN, AND COMPANY.
1896.

Fannie Farmer's *Boston Cooking-School Cook Book* (1896) was the first to replace measurements like "butter in the size of an egg" with measurements in terms of an 8-ounce cup, earning Farmer the title "Mother of the Level Measure."

and inexactly, even by Beeton: "A lump of butter the size of a walnut" or "butter in the size of an egg" is typical. Whether that egg should be small, medium, large, or extra large was up to the experience and observations of the cook. Grainy substances, such as flour or salt, were also measured in variable ways, including the "pinch" and the "handful." A "heaping" or a "rounded" teaspoonful might contain significantly different quantities, depending on how cooks interpreted the direction.

European-style cooking relied on using a kitchen scale to determine the weight of ingredients. American cooks looked to standardized measuring spoons and cups, which began to be available in the mid-1880s. Still, the rounded or heaping measure left quantities uncertain. Fannie Farmer, who had risen from being a student at the Boston Cooking-School to becoming its principal and a leading writer on cooking, invented the "level measure." She recommended using a knife to scrape off the excess from the top of a measuring spoon or cup and wrote foolproof recipes using these standard measures. According to Laura Shapiro (*Perfection Salad*, 1986), Farmer's unbending insistence on this technique earned her the title of "Mother of the Level Measure."

What Farmer's innovation meant for women was that a lengthy apprenticeship in the kitchen was no longer necessary for every woman who wanted to feed a household. Middle-class and upper-class women who had been raised to depend on kitchen servants could fend better for themselves. A woman who could read was now a woman who could cook.

SARAH WINNEMUCCA HOPKINS
c. 1844–1891

The woman who became known for attempts to mediate between the native peoples of the American West and the U.S. government was named Thocmetony, or Shell Flower, by her parents, Chief Winnemucca and Tuboitonie of the Numa people. Known to Americans as the Northern Paiutes, the Numa lived in the high deserts of what are now the American states of California, Nevada, and Oregon. By 1844, when Hopkins was born, the Numa way of life was already being threatened by the western emigration of European Americans. Hopkins's father advocated cultural consolidation and resistance, while her maternal grandfather, known as Captain Truckee, favored cooperation and assimilation as the best way to protect the lives and livelihoods of his people. As a child, Hopkins became fluent in English, Spanish, and several native languages as she moved among the contesting cultures of the American West. Married and divorced twice before her final marriage to European American Lewis Hopkins in 1881, Hopkins was devoted to ameliorating the condition of her people through several means. An astute political observer, she advised the Paiute leaders such as her father (and later, her cousin) in their attempts to protect the interests of their people in the face of increasing assaults. She also, at times, worked directly for the U.S. government and military as a guide and an advisor on "Indian affairs." Hopkins, though pragmatic, maintained a belief that mutual understanding would facilitate coexistence between the native peoples of the Americas and the United States. To this end, she established schools (with the help of philanthropists) to enable Paiute children to compete in a world dominated by the interests and power of the United States. She also created stage shows, in which she brought the humanity of Paiute life to a European American audience. Although photographs still exist of these shows, the texts have never been uncovered. Published in 1883, Hopkins's *Life among the Piutes* (1883) attempts to convey the paradoxes of the Paiute situation to a white audience in the form of a memoir or autobiography. We include the first chapter here, in which Hopkins describes the first time the Numa and white settlers crossed paths.

From Life among the Piutes

Chapter 1
First Meeting of Piutes and Whites

I was born somewhere near 1844, but am not sure of the precise time. I was a very small child when the first white people came into our country. They came like a lion, yes, like a roaring lion, and have continued so ever since, and I have never forgotten their first coming. My people were scattered at that time over nearly all the territory now known as Nevada. My grandfather was chief of the entire Piute nation, and was camped near Humboldt Lake, with a small portion of his tribe, when a party travelling eastward from California was seen coming. When the news was brought to my grandfather, he asked what they looked like?

When told that they had hair on their faces, and were white, he jumped up and clasped his hands together, and cried aloud,—

"My white brothers,—my long-looked for white brothers have come at last!"

He immediately gathered some of his leading men, and went to the place where the party had gone into camp. Arriving near them, he was commanded to halt in a manner that was readily understood without an interpreter. Grandpa at once made signs of friendship by throwing down his robe and throwing up his arms to show them he had no weapons; but in vain,—they kept him at a distance. He knew not what to do. He had expected so much pleasure in welcoming his white brothers to the best in the land, that after looking at them sorrowfully for a little while, he came away quite unhappy. But he would not give them up so easily. He took some of his most trustworthy men and followed them day after day, camping near them at night, and travelling in sight of them by day, hoping in this way to gain their confidence. But he was disappointed, poor dear old soul!

I can imagine his feelings, for I have drank deeply from the same cup. When I think of my past life, and the bitter trials I have endured, I can scarcely believe I live, and yet I do; and, with the help of Him who notes the sparrow's fall,[1] I mean to fight for my down-trodden race while life lasts.

Seeing they would not trust him, my grandfather left them, saying, "Perhaps they will come again next year." Then he summoned his whole people, and told them this tradition:—

"In the beginning of the world there were only four, two girls and two boys. Our forefather and mother were only two, and we are their children. You all know that a great while ago there was a happy family in this world. One girl and one boy were dark and the others were white. For a time they got along together without quarrelling, but soon they disagreed, and there was trouble. They were cross to one another and fought, and our parents were very much grieved. They prayed that their children might learn better, but it did not do any good; and afterwards the whole household was made so unhappy that the father and mother saw that they must separate their children; and then our father took the dark boy and girl, and the white boy and girl, and asked them, 'Why are you so cruel to each other?' They hung down their heads, and would not speak. They were ashamed. He said to them, 'Have I not been kind to you all, and given you everything your hearts wished for? You do not have to hunt and kill your own game to live upon. You see, my dear children, I have power to call whatsoever kind of game we want to eat; and I also have the power to separate my dear children, if they are not good to each other.' So he separated his children by a word. He said, 'Depart from each other, you cruel children;—go across the mighty ocean and do not seek each other's lives.'

"So the light girl and boy disappeared by that one word, and their parents saw them no more, and they were grieved, although they knew their children were happy. And by-and-by the dark children grew into a large nation; and we believe it is the one we belong to, and that the nation that sprung from the white children will some time send some one to meet us and heal all the old trouble. Now, the white people we saw a few days ago must certainly be our white brothers, and I want to welcome them. I want to love them as I love all of you. But they would not

---

1. See Matthew 10:28–30: "Are not two sparrows sold for a penny? Yet not one of them will fall to the ground apart from the will of your Father."

let me; they were afraid. But they will come again, and I want you one and all to promise that, should I not live to welcome them myself, you will not hurt a hair on their heads, but welcome them as I tried to do."

How good of him to try and heal the wound, and how vain were his efforts! My people had never seen a white man, and yet they existed, and were a strong race. The people promised as he wished, and they all went back to their work.

The next year came a great emigration, and camped near Humboldt Lake. The name of the man in charge of the trains was Captain Johnson, and they stayed three days to rest their horses, as they had a long journey before them without water. During their stay my grandfather and some of his people called upon them, and they all shook hands, and when our white brothers were going away they gave my grandfather a white tin plate. Oh, what a time they had over that beautiful gift,—it was so bright! They say that after they left, my grandfather called for all his people to come together, and he then showed them the beautiful gift which he had received from his white brothers. Everybody was so pleased; nothing like it was ever seen in our country before. My grandfather thought so much of it that he bored holes in it and fastened it on his head, and wore it as his hat. He held it in as much admiration as my white sisters hold their diamond rings or a sealskin jacket. So that winter they talked of nothing but their white brothers. The following spring there came great news down the Humboldt River, saying that there were some more of the white brothers coming, and there was something among them that was burning all in a blaze. My grandfather asked them what it was like. They told him it looked like a man; it had legs and hands and a head, but the head had quit burning, and it was left quite black. There was the greatest excitement among my people everywhere about the men in a blazing fire. They were excited because they did not know there were any people in the world but the two,—that is, the Indians and the whites; they thought that was all of us in the beginning of the world, and, of course, we did not know where the others had come from, and we don't know yet. Ha! ha! oh, what a laughable thing that was! It was two negroes wearing red shirts!

The third year more emigrants came.

* * *

1883

EMMA LAZARUS
1849–1887

Emma Lazarus began life as an indulged daughter of a wealthy New York City family. The Lazarus family had been established in New York since the mid–seventeenth century and was at the center of elite Jewish culture. Although they retained the religious practice of Judaism, the Lazaruses defined themselves primarily in national terms as Americans. The fourth of seven surviving children of Moses and Esther Lazarus, Lazarus was well educated at home in music, languages, and the other accomplishments of a society girl in the mid–nineteenth century. Never marrying, Lazarus seems to have devoted herself early on to becoming a published—and important—poet. Before succumbing to cancer at age thirty-eight, Lazarus had begun to receive serious critical attention not only for her poetry and translations but also for her powerful social criticism. One of the first Americans to argue for the establishment of a Jewish homeland in Palestine, Lazarus also helped to establish the New York Hebrew Technical Institute in response to the needs of the thousands of Jews fleeing persecution in Europe.

Lazarus's short career had two phases. The first began in her teenage years with her devotion to the practice of poetry. Her tastes at this time were for the romantic poets of Britain, Europe, and America. She sought guidance from such cultural eminences as transcendentalist writer and philosopher Ralph Waldo Emerson and Thomas Wentworth Higginson, friend and mentor to Emily Dickinson, (pp. 938–39). Both men deemed her work promising, and though besieged with similar requests, both advised her because they were impressed by her precocious talents. Lazarus also began to translate for publication the works of German romantic poets and philosophers. Her best poems from this period treat the topic of nature and express transcendentalist ideals.

Her second phase began in her late twenties and was characterized both by a conscious exploration of the nature of Jewish subjectivity and by a mastery of lyric form. Like her British contemporary Elizabeth Barrett Browning (pp. 650–52), Lazarus explored the artistic possibilities of the sonnet. Having been introduced to the works of medieval- and Renaissance-era Jewish poets, Lazarus began translating these poems for publication. Lazarus's own lyric practice, like that of the modernist poets of the next generation, was invigorated by the "metaphysical" energy of these non-romantic lyrics. While her poetry was already in dialogue with that of the contemporary American and British writers of midcentury, these translations allowed Lazarus to begin to see herself as part of a tradition that extended into the past, connecting her with her religious and ethnic heritage.

Nineteenth-century New York had seen an influx of Jews from Germany; her own mother's family had been immigrants. The last quarter of the century, however, saw Jews from Russia and Eastern Europe fleeing murderous pogroms and flooding New York. While Lazarus herself responded to the needs of the refugees with practical solutions, such as the founding of a technical institution, her poetry began to express her own negotiation of what it meant to be both an American and a Jew. Her most famous poem, "The New Colossus," was written to support the purchase of the pedestal for the Statue of Liberty. Against the strains of parochialism and xenophobia in American culture, Lazarus names America the "Mother of Exiles" who welcomes the "huddled masses yearning to breathe free."

In the Jewish Synagogue at Newport

Here, where the noises of the busy town,
    The ocean's plunge and roar can enter not,
We stand and gaze around with tearful awe,
    And muse upon the consecrated spot.

No signs of life are here: the very prayers   5
    Inscribed around are in a language dead;
The light of the "perpetual lamp" is spent
    That an undying radiance was to shed.[1]

---

1. A language dead: until the twentieth-century establishment of Israel, Hebrew was not used except in religious services; perpetual lamp: a lamp symbolizing God's presence is kept burning in front of the holy ark in which the sacred text of the Torah is kept within a synagogue.

What prayers were in this temple offered up,
　　Wrung from sad hearts that knew no joy on earth,　　　10
By these lone exiles of a thousand years,
　　From the fair sunrise land that gave them birth!

Now as we gaze, in this new world of light,
　　Upon this relic of the days of old,
The present vanishes, and tropic bloom　　　　　　　　15
　　And Eastern towns and temples we behold.

Again we see the patriarch with his flocks,
　　The purple seas, the hot blue sky o'erhead,
The slaves of Egypt,—omens, mysteries,—
　　Dark fleeing hosts by flaming angels led,[2]　　　　　20

A wondrous light upon a sky-kissed mount,
　　A man who reads Jehovah's written law,[3]
'Midst blinding glory and effulgence rare,
　　Unto a people prone with reverent awe.

The pride of luxury's barbaric pomp,　　　　　　　　　25
　　In the rich court of royal Solomon—
Alas! we wake: one scene alone remains,—
　　The exiles by the streams of Babylon.[4]

Our softened voices send us back again
　　But mournful echoes through the empty hall;　　　30
Our footsteps have a strange unnatural sound,
　　And with unwonted gentleness they fall.

The weary ones, the sad, the suffering,
　　All found their comfort in the holy place,
And children's gladness and men's gratitude　　　　　35
　　Took voice and mingled in the chant of praise.

The funeral and the marriage, now, alas!
　　We know not which is sadder to recall;
For youth and happiness have followed age,
　　And green grass lieth gently over all.　　　　　　　40

Nathless[5] the sacred shrine is holy yet,
　　With its lone floors where reverent feet once trod.
Take off your shoes as by the burning bush,[6]
　　Before the mystery of death and God.

1867　　　　　　　　　　　　　　　　　　　　　　　　1871

2. The book of Exodus tells how Moses, guided by God, liberates the Hebrews who had been held as slaves by the Egyptians and leads them to the promised land.
3. Moses is given the Ten Commandments by God upon Mount Sinai.
4. See Psalm 137: "By the rivers of Babylon we sat and wept when we remembered Zion."
5. Nevertheless.
6. See Exodus 3:1–6. While the Hebrews are still enslaved, God reveals himself to Moses in the form of a burning bush and promises to lead them out of slavery.

1492

Thou two-faced year, Mother of Change and Fate,
Didst weep when Spain cast forth with flaming sword,
The children of the prophets of the Lord,[7]
Prince, priest, and people, spurned by zealot hate.
Hounded from sea to sea, from state to state,   5
The West refused them, and the East abhorred.
No anchorage the known world could afford,
Close-locked was every port, barred every gate.
Then smiling, thou unveil'dst, O two-faced year,
A virgin world where doors of sunset part,   10
Saying, "Ho, all who weary, enter here!
There falls each ancient barrier that the art
Of race or creed or rank devised, to rear
Grim bulwarked hatred between heart and heart!"

c. 1883

The New Colossus[8]

Not like the brazen giant of Greek fame,
With conquering limbs astride from land to land;
Here at our sea-washed, sunset gates shall stand
A mighty woman with a torch, whose flame
Is the imprisoned lightning, and her name   5
Mother of Exiles. From her beacon-hand
Glows world-wide welcome; her mild eyes command
The air-bridged harbor that twin cities[9] frame.
"Keep, ancient lands, your storied pomp!" cries she
With silent lips. "Give me your tired, your poor,   10
Your huddled masses yearning to breathe free,
The wretched refuse of your teeming shore.
Send these, the homeless, tempest-tost to me,
I lift my lamp beside the golden door!"

1883

7. In 1492, Ferdinand and Isabella expelled all the Jews from Spain.
8. The Colossus, a giant statue of the sun god Helios, erected 282 BCE near the harbor in Rhodes; this sonnet was written to raise money for the erection of the Statue of Liberty's pedestal.
9. New York City and Brooklyn, a separate city until 1898.

CULTURAL COORDINATES
The Sewing Machine

Until the middle of the nineteenth century, all clothing was hand-sewn with a needle and thread. Wealthy families hired seamstresses or tailors; governesses and poor relations wore hand-me-downs from employers and family; servants and factory workers made simple clothes to wear at work; and middle-class women hand-stitched their own dresses (as well as everything else their families wore). If a family was strapped for money, a dress could be "turned," that is, turned inside out and remade to wear for a few more years. Secondhand clothes could be bought, but "ready-to-wear" women's clothes did not become widely available until after the development of the sewing machine between 1830 and 1851. Men and boys could find ready-made clothing by the 1850s, but it was not until the 1880s that women could buy dresses "off the rack."

Sewing was a time-intensive activity. Hand-stitching a simple dress in the early nineteenth century took at least ten hours; a gentleman's shirt required fourteen hours of labor. Accordingly, styles were not elaborate, and middle-class women did not have large wardrobes. They changed their (handmade) undergarments more frequently than they did their dresses. In Jane Austen's day, during the first two decades of the century, women's fashions emulated a classical Grecian style (the "Empire waist" dress, named for Napoleon's wife Josephine, who popularized it), with simple lines and few seams. By the 1850s, at the end of Charlotte Brontë's life, the profile of dresses had changed to include a voluminous skirt falling over a cagelike crinoline, marking out a space as much as six feet wide around a woman's ankles. Although mid-Victorian dress required enormous quantities of fabric, its construction was still comparatively simple.

(Left) "Here's youthful vigor and midnight oil consumed by a 'life of constant toil'"; (right) "Here's pleasant pastime brought to view of 'toil made easy' and attractive too." (c. 1860)

Sewing machines dramatically cut down the time required for making simple garments. In 1845, inventor Elias Howe publicly challenged five seamstresses to a race against his newly developed machine. Before any of the women had completed one seam, he had finished five. With the invention of the sewing machine, sewing was no longer done just at home; it was a public, mechanized activity. The notorious "sweat shops" (pp. 1357–58) of the late nineteenth century were one result of this shift in workplace.

For middle-class women who could afford to have the new machines at home, the invention might have promised more time to devote to other household tasks or even to such leisure activities as reading and exercise. Instead, dress styles became increasingly elaborate. By the 1880s, fashionable dresses were covered with shirring, ruffles, gathers, and flounces. These effects would have been practically impossible to achieve with hand-sewing; with machine-sewing, they were possible, but they increased the amount of time needed to make each dress. As with many "labor-saving" devices, rather than freeing up women's time, the sewing machine introduced a higher standard for household production.

1849–1909

By the time Theodora Sarah Orne Jewett was twenty, she was already attempting to publish short fiction in the prestigious literary magazines of her time. Her ostensible topic—the everyday dramas of life in coastal Maine—remained the same throughout her career, though her skill allowed her to focus with increasing clarity on the relationship between the outer environment and inner psychology. By the time Jewett died, she was recognized by her contemporaries as a master of literary realism and a leading exponent of the local color movement for her book-length narrative *The Country of the Pointed Firs* (1896), and her numerous influential short fictions, such as "A White Heron" of 1886, which we include here.

Jewett's parents, Theodore and Caroline, were both descended from families with deep roots in American colonial history as merchants, shipbuilders, ministers, and physicians. Jewett and her two sisters grew up with a sense of privileged belonging in the town of South Berwick, Maine, which, during their childhood, was undergoing a shift in its economy. The coastal towns of Maine had once played a vital role in the national economy as producers of ships and as brokers of goods from around the Atlantic and beyond. But by the time Jewett was born, the American economy had changed. Its centers of vitality were now the major cities—Boston, New York, Philadelphia, Baltimore—and its lifeblood was coming from the newly opened West. Many who had been born in places like Berwick moved away. The economy of the area became increasingly dominated by mills, where European immigrants worked, and by domestic tourism, which drew middle- and upper-class Americans to escape the heat of the cities during temporary stays in rural locales. Jewett's work captures the complicated nostalgia of Americans for a way of life they were glad to have escaped but which they nevertheless mourned.

Jewett's fiction drew on her experiences as a child whose parents encouraged her to learn by closely observing both the workings of the natural world and the lives of people. She frequently accompanied her father, a country doctor, as he traveled by horse-drawn buggy throughout the region. At one point Jewett even considered the then-daring step of becoming a physician herself. Although her poor health prohibited her from becoming a doctor, her narrative technique is informed by a rigorous empiricism, a habit of scientific observation and taxonomy, and a generous sympathy for her objects of observation. Inspired by reading *The Pearl of Orr's Island* (1862) by Harriet Beecher Stowe (pp. 732–34), Jewett devoted herself to depicting the inhabitants of Berwick and the environment that shaped them with the realism and dignity she felt they deserved.

From her twenties onward, Jewett lived part of the year in Boston, where she became a member of the literary circle that revolved around the publisher James T. Fields and his wife, Annie. Many of the members of this circle, like critic William Dean Howells and novelist Henry James, were also experimenting with literary realism. Never marrying, Jewett had intense and passionate friendships. The last twenty years of her life she spent with Annie Fields, who had been widowed in 1881. Together, they traveled frequently to Europe, the Caribbean, and Florida. Where Jewett had taken inspiration and had been mentored by her older contemporary Harriet Beecher Stowe, she inspired and mentored her own group of younger authors, such as Mary Wilkins Freeman (pp. 1142–43) and Willa Cather (pp. 1269–75).

A White Heron

I

The woods were already filled with shadows one June evening, just before eight o'clock, though a bright sunset still glimmered faintly among the trunks of the trees. A little girl was driving home her cow, a plodding, dilatory, provoking creature in her behavior, but a valued companion for all that. They were going away from whatever light there was, and striking deep into the woods, but their feet were familiar with the path, and it was no matter whether their eyes could see it or not.

There was hardly a night the summer through when the old cow could be found waiting at the pasture bars; on the contrary, it was her greatest pleasure to hide herself away among the huckleberry bushes, and though she wore a loud bell she had made the discovery that if one stood perfectly still it would not ring. So Sylvia had to hunt for her until she found her, and call Co'! Co'! with never an answering Moo, until her childish patience was quite spent. If the creature had not given good milk and plenty of it, the case would have seemed very different to her owners. Besides, Sylvia had all the time there was, and very little use to make of it. Sometimes in pleasant weather it was a consolation to look upon the cow's pranks as an intelligent attempt to play hide and seek, and as the child had no playmates she lent herself to this amusement with a good deal of zest. Though this chase had been so long that the wary animal herself had given an unusual signal of her whereabouts, Sylvia had only laughed when she came upon Mistress Moolly at the swampside, and urged her affectionately homeward with a twig of birch leaves. The old cow was not inclined to wander farther, she even turned in the right direction for once as they left the pasture, and stepped along the road at a good pace. She was quite ready to be milked now, and seldom stopped to browse. Sylvia wondered what her grandmother would say because they were so late. It was a great while since she had left home at half-past five o'clock, but everybody knew the difficulty of making this errand a short one. Mrs. Tilley had chased the hornéd torment too many summer evenings herself to blame any one else for lingering, and was only thankful as she waited that she had Sylvia, nowadays, to give such valuable assistance. The good woman suspected that Sylvia loitered occasionally on her own account; there never was such a child for straying about out-of-doors since the world was made! Everybody said that it was a good change for a little maid who had tried to grow for eight years in a crowded manufacturing town, but, as for Sylvia herself, it seemed as if she never had been alive at all before she came to live at the farm. She thought often with wistful compassion of a wretched geranium that belonged to a town neighbor.

"'Afraid of folks,'" old Mrs. Tilley said to herself, with a smile, after she had made the unlikely choice of Sylvia from her daughter's houseful of children, and was returning to the farm. "'Afraid of folks,' they said! I guess she won't be troubled no great[1] with 'em up to the old place!" When they reached the door of

---

1. Won't be much troubled.

the lonely house and stopped to unlock it, and the cat came to purr loudly, and rub against them, a deserted pussy, indeed, but fat with young robins, Sylvia whispered that this was a beautiful place to live in, and she never should wish to go home.

The companions followed the shady woodroad, the cow taking slow steps and the child very fast ones. The cow stopped long at the brook to drink, as if the pasture were not half a swamp, and Sylvia stood still and waited, letting her bare feet cool themselves in the shoal water, while the great twilight moths struck softly against her. She waded on through the brook as the cow moved away, and listened to the thrushes with a heart that beat fast with pleasure. There was a stirring in the great boughs overhead. They were full of little birds and beasts that seemed to be wide awake, and going about their world, or else saying good-night to each other in sleepy twitters. Sylvia herself felt sleepy as she walked along. However, it was not much farther to the house, and the air was soft and sweet. She was not often in the woods so late as this, and it made her feel as if she were a part of the gray shadows and the moving leaves. She was just thinking how long it seemed since she first came to the farm a year ago, and wondering if everything went on in the noisy town just the same as when she was there; the thought of the great red-faced boy who used to chase and frighten her made her hurry along the path to escape from the shadow of the trees.

Suddenly this little woods-girl is horror-stricken to hear a clear whistle not very far away. Not a bird's-whistle, which would have a sort of friendliness, but a boy's whistle, determined, and somewhat aggressive. Sylvia left the cow to whatever sad fate might await her, and stepped discreetly aside into the bushes, but she was just too late. The enemy had discovered her, and called out in a very cheerful and persuasive tone, "Halloa, little girl, how far is it to the road?" and trembling Sylvia answered almost inaudibly, "A good ways."

She did not dare to look boldly at the tall young man, who carried a gun over his shoulder, but she came out of her bush and again followed the cow, while he walked alongside.

"I have been hunting for some birds," the stranger said kindly, "and I have lost my way, and need a friend very much. Don't be afraid," he added gallantly. "Speak up and tell me what your name is, and whether you think I can spend the night at your house, and go out gunning early in the morning."

Sylvia was more alarmed than before. Would not her grandmother consider her much to blame? But who could have foreseen such an accident as this? It did not seem to be her fault, and she hung her head as if the stem of it were broken, but managed to answer "Sylvy," with much effort when her companion again asked her name.

Mrs. Tilley was standing in the doorway when the trio came into view. The cow gave a loud moo by way of explanation.

"Yes, you'd better speak up for yourself, you old trial! Where'd she tucked herself away this time, Sylvy?" But Sylvia kept an awed silence; she knew by instinct that her grandmother did not comprehend the gravity of the situation. She must be mistaking the stranger for one of the farmer-lads of the region.

The young man stood his gun beside the door, and dropped a lumpy game-bag beside it; then he bade Mrs. Tilley good-evening, and repeated his wayfarer's story, and asked if he could have a night's lodging.

"Put me anywhere you like," he said. "I must be off early in the morning, before day; but I am very hungry, indeed. You can give me some milk at any rate, that's plain."

"Dear sakes, yes," responded the hostess, whose long slumbering hospitality seemed to be easily awakened. "You might fare better if you went out to the main road a mile or so, but you're welcome to what we've got. I'll milk right off, and you make yourself at home. You can sleep on husks or feathers," she proffered graciously. "I raised them all myself. There's good pasturing for geese just below here towards the ma'sh. Now step round and set a plate for the gentleman, Sylvy!" And Sylvia promptly stepped. She was glad to have something to do, and she was hungry herself.

It was a surprise to find so clean and comfortable a little dwelling in this New England wilderness. The young man had known the horrors of its most primitive housekeeping, and the dreary squalor of that level of society which does not rebel at the companionship of hens. This was the best thrift of an old-fashioned farmstead, though on such a small scale that it seemed like a hermitage. He listened eagerly to the old woman's quaint talk, he watched Sylvia's pale face and shining gray eyes with ever growing enthusiasm, and insisted that this was the best supper he had eaten for a month, and afterward the new-made friends sat down in the door-way together while the moon came up.

Soon it would be berry-time, and Sylvia was a great help at picking. The cow was a good milker, though a plaguy thing to keep track of, the hostess gossiped frankly, adding presently that she had buried four children, so Sylvia's mother, and a son (who might be dead) in California were all the children she had left. "Dan, my boy, was a great hand to go gunning," she explained sadly. "I never wanted for pa'tridges or gray squer'ls while he was to home. He's been a great wand'rer, I expect, and he's no hand to write letters. There, I don't blame him, I'd ha' seen the world myself if it had been so I could."

"Sylvy takes after him," the grandmother continued affectionately, after a minute's pause. "There ain't a foot o' ground she don't know her way over, and the wild creaturs counts her one o' themselves. Squer'ls she'll tame to come an' feed right out o' her hands, and all sorts o' birds. Last winter she got the jaybirds to bangeing[2] here, and I believe she'd 'a' scanted herself of her own meals to have plenty to throw out amongst 'em, if I had n't kep' watch. Anything but crows, I tell her, I'm willin' to help support—though Dan he had a tamed one o' them that did seem to have reason same as folks. It was round here a good spell after he went away. Dan an' his father they did n't hitch,—but he never held up his head ag'in after Dan had dared him[3] an' gone off."

The guest did not notice this hint of family sorrows in his eager interest in something else.

"So Sylvy knows all about birds, does she?" he exclaimed, as he looked round at the little girl who sat, very demure but increasingly sleepy, in the moonlight. "I am making a collection of birds myself. I have been at it ever since I was a boy." (Mrs. Tilley smiled.) "There are two or three very rare ones I have been hunting for these five years. I mean to get them on my own ground if they can be found."

---

2. Jaybirds: slang term for blue jays, crows, or grackles; bangeing: hanging around, visiting.   3. Hitch: get along; dared him: defied him.

"Do you cage 'em up?" asked Mrs. Tilley doubtfully, in response to this enthusiastic announcement.

"Oh no, they're stuffed and preserved, dozens and dozens of them," said the ornithologist, "and I have shot or snared every one myself. I caught a glimpse of a white heron a few miles from here on Saturday, and I have followed it in this direction. They have never been found in this district at all. The little white heron, it is," and he turned again to look at Sylvia with the hope of discovering that the rare bird was one of her acquaintances.

But Sylvia was watching a hop-toad in the narrow footpath.

"You would know the heron if you saw it," the stranger continued eagerly. "A queer tall white bird with soft feathers and long thin legs. And it would have a nest perhaps in the top of a high tree, made of sticks, something like a hawk's nest."

Sylvia's heart gave a wild beat; she knew that strange white bird, and had once stolen softly near where it stood in some bright green swamp grass, away over at the other side of the woods. There was an open place where the sunshine always seemed strangely yellow and hot, where tall, nodding rushes grew, and her grandmother had warned her that she might sink in the soft black mud underneath and never be heard of more. Not far beyond were the salt marshes just this side the sea itself, which Sylvia wondered and dreamed much about, but never had seen, whose great voice could sometimes be heard above the noise of the woods on stormy nights.

"I can't think of anything I should like so much as to find that heron's nest," the handsome stranger was saying. "I would give ten dollars to anybody who could show it to me," he added desperately, "and I mean to spend my whole vacation hunting for it if need be. Perhaps it was only migrating, or had been chased out of its own region by some bird of prey."

Mrs. Tilley gave amazed attention to all this, but Sylvia still watched the toad, not divining, as she might have done at some calmer time, that the creature wished to get to its hole under the door-step, and was much hindered by the unusual spectators at that hour of the evening. No amount of thought, that night, could decide how many wished-for treasures the ten dollars, so lightly spoken of, would buy.

The next day the young sportsman hovered about the woods, and Sylvia kept him company, having lost her first fear of the friendly lad, who proved to be most kind and sympathetic. He told her many things about the birds and what they knew and where they lived and what they did with themselves. And he gave her a jack-knife, which she thought as great a treasure as if she were a desert-islander. All day long he did not once make her troubled or afraid except when he brought down some unsuspecting singing creature from its bough. Sylvia would have liked him vastly better without his gun; she could not understand why he killed the very birds he seemed to like so much. But as the day waned, Sylvia still watched the young man with loving admiration. She had never seen anybody so charming and delightful; the woman's heart, asleep in the child, was vaguely thrilled by a dream of love. Some premonition of that great power stirred and swayed these young creatures who traversed the solemn woodlands with soft-footed silent care. They stopped to listen to a bird's songs; they pressed forward again eagerly, parting the branches—speaking to each other rarely and in whispers; the young man going first and Sylvia following, fascinated, a few steps behind, with her gray eyes dark with excitement.

She grieved because the longed-for white heron was elusive, but she did not lead the guest, she only followed, and there was no such thing as speaking first. The sound of her own unquestioned voice would have terrified her—it was hard enough to answer yes or no when there was need of that. At last evening began to fall, and they drove the cow home together, and Sylvia smiled with pleasure when they came to the place where she heard the whistle and was afraid only the night before.

II

Half a mile from home, at the farther edge of the woods, where the land was highest, a great pine-tree stood, the last of its generation. Whether it was left for a boundary mark, or for what reason, no one could say; the wood-choppers who had felled its mates were dead and gone long ago, and a whole forest of sturdy trees, pines and oaks and maples, had grown again. But the stately head of this old pine towered above them all and made a landmark for sea and shore miles and miles away. Sylvia knew it well. She had always believed that whoever climbed to the top of it could see the ocean; and the little girl had often laid her hand on the great rough trunk and looked up wistfully at those dark boughs that the wind always stirred, no matter how hot and still the air might be below. Now she thought of the tree with a new excitement, for why, if one climbed it at break of day could not one see all the world, and easily discover from whence the white heron flew, and mark the place, and find the hidden nest?

What a spirit of adventure, what wild ambition! What fancied triumph and delight and glory for the later morning when she could make known the secret! It was almost too real and too great for the childish heart to bear.

All night the door of the little house stood open and the whippoorwills came and sang upon the very step. The young sportsman and his old hostess were sound asleep, but Sylvia's great design kept her broad awake and watching. She forgot to think of sleep. The short summer night seemed as long as the winter darkness, and at last when the whippoorwills ceased, and she was afraid the morning would after all come too soon, she stole out of the house and followed the pasture path through the woods, hastening toward the open ground beyond, listening with a sense of comfort and companionship to the drowsy twitter of a half-awakened bird, whose perch she had jarred in passing. Alas, if the great wave of human interest which flooded for the first time this dull little life should sweep away the satisfactions of an existence heart to heart with nature and the dumb life of the forest!

There was the huge tree asleep yet in the paling moonlight, and small and silly Sylvia began with utmost bravery to mount to the top of it, with tingling, eager blood coursing the channels of her whole frame, with her bare feet and fingers, that pinched and held like bird's claws to the monstrous ladder reaching up, up, almost to the sky itself. First she must mount the white oak tree that grew alongside, where she was almost lost among the dark branches and the green leaves heavy and wet with dew; a bird fluttered off its nest, and a red squirrel ran to and fro and scolded pettishly at the harmless housebreaker. Sylvia felt her way easily. She had often climbed there, and knew that higher still one of the oak's upper branches chafed against the pine trunk, just where its lower boughs were set close together. There, when she made the dangerous pass from one tree to the other, the great enterprise would really begin.

She crept out along the swaying oak limb at last, and took the daring step across into the old pine-tree. The way was harder than she thought; she must reach far and hold fast, the sharp dry twigs caught and held her and scratched her like angry talons, the pitch made her thin little fingers clumsy and stiff as she went round and round the tree's great stem, higher and higher upward. The sparrows and robins in the woods below were beginning to wake and twitter to the dawn, yet it seemed much lighter there aloft in the pine-tree, and the child knew she must hurry if her project were to be of any use.

The tree seemed to lengthen itself out as she went up, and to reach farther and farther upward. It was like a great main-mast to the voyaging earth; it must truly have been amazed that morning through all its ponderous frame as it felt this determined spark of human spirit wending its way from higher branch to branch. Who knows how steadily the least twigs held themselves to advantage this light, weak creature on her way! The old pine must have loved his new dependent. More than all the hawks, and bats, and moths, and even the sweet voiced thrushes, was the brave, beating heart of the solitary gray-eyed child. And the tree stood still and frowned away the winds that June morning while the dawn grew bright in the east.

Sylvia's face was like a pale star, if one had seen it from the ground, when the last thorny bough was past, and she stood trembling and tired but wholly triumphant, high in the treetop. Yes, there was the sea with the dawning sun making a golden dazzle over it, and toward that glorious east flew two hawks with slow-moving pinions. How low they looked in the air from that height when one had only seen them before far up, and dark against the blue sky. Their gray feathers were as soft as moths; they seemed only a little way from the tree, and Sylvia felt as if she too could go flying away among the clouds. Westward, the woodlands and farms reached miles and miles into the distance; here and there were church steeples, and white villages, truly it was a vast and awesome world!

The birds sang louder and louder. At last the sun came up bewilderingly bright. Sylvia could see the white sails of ships out at sea, and the clouds that were purple and rose-colored and yellow at first began to fade away. Where was the white heron's nest in the sea of green branches, and was this wonderful sight and pageant of the world the only reward for having climbed to such a giddy height? Now look down again, Sylvia, where the green marsh is set among the shining birches and dark hemlocks; there where you saw the white heron once you will see him again; look, look! a white spot of him like a single floating feather comes up from the dead hemlock and grows larger, and rises, and comes close at last, and goes by the landmark pine with steady sweep of wing and outstretched slender neck and crested head. And wait! wait! do not move a foot or a finger, little girl, do not send an arrow of light and consciousness from your two eager eyes, for the heron has perched on a pine bough not far beyond yours, and cries back to his mate on the nest and plumes his feathers for the new day!

The child gives a long sigh a minute later when a company of shouting cat-birds comes also to the tree, and vexed by their fluttering and lawlessness the solemn heron goes away. She knows his secret now, the wild, light, slender bird that floats and wavers, and goes back like an arrow presently to his home in the green world beneath. Then Sylvia, well satisfied, makes her perilous way down again, not daring to look far below the branch she stands on, ready to cry sometimes because her fingers ache and her lamed feet slip. Wondering over and over again what the stranger would say to her, and what he would think when she told him how to find his way straight to the heron's nest.

"Sylvy, Sylvy!" called the busy old grandmother again and again, but nobody answered, and the small husk bed was empty and Sylvia had disappeared.

The guest waked from a dream, and remembering his day's pleasure hurried to dress himself that might it sooner begin. He was sure from the way the shy little girl looked once or twice yesterday that she had at least seen the white heron, and now she must really be made to tell. Here she comes now, paler than ever, and her worn old frock is torn and tattered, and smeared with pine pitch. The grandmother and the sportsman stand in the door together and question her, and the splendid moment has come to speak of the dead hemlock-tree by the green marsh.

But Sylvia does not speak after all, though the old grandmother fretfully rebukes her, and the young man's kind, appealing eyes are looking straight in her own. He can make them rich with money; he has promised it, and they are poor now. He is so well worth making happy, and he waits to hear the story she can tell.

No, she must keep silence! What is it that suddenly forbids her and makes her dumb? Has she been nine years growing and now, when the great world for the first time puts out a hand to her, must she thrust it aside for a bird's sake? The murmur of the pine's green branches is in her hears, she remembers how the white heron came flying through the golden air and how they watched the sea and the morning together, and Sylvia cannot speak; she cannot tell the heron's secret and give its life away.

Dear loyalty, that suffered a sharp pang as the guest went away disappointed later in the day, that could have served and followed him and loved him as a dog loves! Many a night Sylvia heard the echo of his whistle haunting the pasture path as she came home with the loitering cow. She forgot even her sorrow at the sharp report of his gun and the sight of thrushes and sparrows dropping silent to the ground, their songs hushed and their pretty feathers stained and wet with blood. Were the birds better friends than their hunter might have been,—who can tell? Whatever treasures were lost to her, woodlands and summer-time, remember! Bring your gifts and graces and tell your secrets to this lonely country child!

1886

◄ KATE CHOPIN ►
1850–1904

Descended on one side from the Creole elite of St. Louis, Missouri, and on the other from a successful Irish immigrant, Kate Chopin (née O'Flaherty) was singularly situated to observe and preserve the "local colors" that were yielding to American homogenization through the end of the nineteenth century. Her father's early death in a railway accident rendered her family financially secure, leaving her mother, grandmother, and the nuns of the Academy of the Sacred Heart to raise Chopin. In 1870, Chopin left this woman-dominated world to marry a French-Creole cotton trader, Oscar Chopin, with whom she moved to Louisiana.

The Chopins had six children before Oscar's death in 1882. Following her husband's death, Chopin returned to her mother's home in St. Louis, where she became an avid student of the latest developments in philosophy, literature, and the natural sciences. By the late 1880s, when she began publishing, Chopin was bringing an almost scientific attention to characters and situations drawn from her experiences in Louisiana. Chopin focused this seemingly objective and nonmoralizing attention on such transgressive subjects as women's desires for sensual, intellectual, and emotional satisfaction outside the confines of marriage and motherhood. A stroke, in 1904, put an early end to Chopin's career.

Through most of the twentieth century, Chopin was remembered as a "local color" writer: nothing more than a minor "feminine" writer of realistic sketches of life on America's geographical and cultural margins. The novella included here, *The Awakening* (1899), belies this reputation. Chopin is now valued as an important American practitioner of literary "naturalism" and women's erotica. In *The Awakening*, Chopin depicts a woman's emerging sense of how trapped and unhappy she feels despite having material wealth, a husband, and children. The ambivalence of the plot's ending and absence of any clear moral pronouncements by the narrator outraged Chopin's early readers. More recent readers, however, have been intrigued by Chopin's compelling rendering of the sensual responses of a woman to her environment.

The Awakening

I

A green and yellow parrot, which hung in a cage outside the door, kept repeating over and over:

"*Allez vous-en! Allez vous-en! Sapristi!*[1] That's all right!"

He could speak a little Spanish, and also a language which nobody understood, unless it was the mocking-bird that hung on the other side of the door, whistling his fluty notes out upon the breeze with maddening persistence.

Mr. Pontellier, unable to read his newspaper with any degree of comfort, arose with an expression and an exclamation of disgust. He walked down the gallery and across the narrow "bridges" which connected the Lebrun cottages one with the other. He had been seated before the door of the main house. The parrot and the mocking-bird were the property of Madame Lebrun, and they had the right to make all the noise they wished. Mr. Pontellier had the privilege of quitting their society when they ceased to be entertaining.

He stopped before the door of his own cottage, which was the fourth one from the main building and next to the last. Seating himself in a wicker rocker which was there, he once more applied himself to the task of reading the newspaper. The day was Sunday; the paper was a day old. The Sunday papers had not yet reached Grand Isle.[2] He was already acquainted with the market reports, and he glanced restlessly over the editorials and bits of news which he had not had time to read before quitting New Orleans the day before.

Mr. Pontellier wore eye-glasses. He was a man of forty, of medium height and slender build; he stooped a little. His hair was brown and straight, parted on one side. His beard was neatly and closely trimmed.

1. Go away! Go away! For God's sake! (French).   2. Resort island south of New Orleans.

Once in a while he withdrew his glance from the newspaper and looked about him. There was more noise than ever over at the house. The main building was called "the house," to distinguish it from the cottages. The chattering and whistling birds were still at it. Two young girls, the Farival twins, were playing a duet from "Zampa"[3] upon the piano. Madame Lebrun was bustling in and out, giving orders in a high key to a yard-boy whenever she got inside the house, and directions in an equally high voice to a dining-room servant whenever she got outside. She was a fresh, pretty woman, clad always in white with elbow sleeves. Her starched skirts crinkled as she came and went. Farther down, before one of the cottages, a lady in black was walking demurely up and down, telling her beads. A good many persons of the *pension*[4] had gone over to the *Chênière Caminada* in Beaudelet's lugger to hear mass. Some young people were out under the water-oaks playing croquet. Mr. Pontellier's two children were there—sturdy little fellows of four and five. A quadroon[5] nurse followed them about with a far-away, meditative air.

Mr. Pontellier finally lit a cigar and began to smoke, letting the paper drag idly from his hand. He fixed his gaze upon a white sunshade[6] that was advancing at snail's pace from the beach. He could see it plainly between the gaunt trunks of the water-oaks and across the stretch of yellow camomile. The gulf looked far away melting hazily into the blue of the horizon. The sunshade continued to approach slowly. Beneath its pink-lined shelter were his wife, Mrs. Pontellier, and young Robert Lebrun. When they reached the cottage, the two seated themselves with some appearance of fatigue upon the step of the porch, facing each other, each leaning against a supporting post.

"What folly! to bathe[7] at such an hour in such heat!" exclaimed Mr. Pontellier. He himself had taken a plunge at daylight. That was why the morning seemed long to him.

"You are burnt beyond recognition," he added, looking at his wife as one looks at a valuable piece of personal property which has suffered some damage. She held up her hands, strong, shapely hands, and surveyed them critically, drawing up her lawn[8] sleeves above the wrists. Looking at them reminded her of her rings, which she had given to her husband before leaving for the beach. She silently reached out to him, and he, understanding, took the rings from his vest pocket and dropped them into her open palm. She slipped them upon her fingers; then clasping her knees, she looked across at Robert and began to laugh. The rings sparkled upon her fingers. He sent back an answering smile.

"What is it?" asked Pontellier, looking lazily and amused from one to the other. It was some utter nonsense; some adventure out there in the water, and they both tried to relate it at once. It did not seem half so amusing when told. They realized this, and so did Mr. Pontellier. He yawned and stretched himself. Then he got up, saying he had half a mind to go over to Klein's hotel and play a game of billiards.

"Come go along, Lebrun," he proposed to Robert. But Robert admitted quite frankly that he preferred to stay where he was and talk to Mrs. Pontellier.

---

3. Opera by French composer Ferdinand Hérold (1791–1833).
4. *Pension:* small hotel or boardinghouse; Chênière Caminada: a settlement near New Orleans in the coastal wetlands or bayous of Louisi-ana; lugger: a small boat.
5. A quarter African American.
6. Umbrella or parasol.
7. To go swimming.
8. Linen or cotton.

"Well, send him about his business when he bores you, Edna," instructed her husband as he prepared to leave.

"Here, take the umbrella," she exclaimed, holding it out to him. He accepted the sunshade, and lifting it over his head descended the steps and walked away.

"Coming back to dinner?" his wife called after him. He halted a moment and shrugged his shoulders. He felt in his vest pocket; there was a ten-dollar[9] bill there. He did not know; perhaps he would return for the early dinner and perhaps he would not. It all depended upon the company which he found over at Klein's and the size of "the game." He did not say this, but she understood it, and laughed, nodding good-by to him.

Both children wanted to follow their father when they saw him starting out. He kissed them and promised to bring them back bonbons and peanuts.

II

Mrs. Pontellier's eyes were quick and bright; they were a yellowish brown, about the color of her hair. She had a way of turning them swiftly upon an object and holding them there as if lost in some inward maze of contemplation or thought.

Her eyebrows were a shade darker than her hair. They were thick and almost horizontal, emphasizing the depth of her eyes. She was rather handsome than beautiful. Her face was captivating by reason of a certain frankness of expression and a contradictory subtle play of features. Her manner was engaging.

Robert rolled a cigarette. He smoked cigarettes because he could not afford cigars, he said. He had a cigar in his pocket which Mr. Pontellier had presented him with, and he was saving it for his after-dinner smoke.

This seemed quite proper and natural on his part. In coloring he was not unlike his companion. A clean-shaven face made the resemblance more pronounced than it would otherwise have been. There rested no shadow of care upon his open countenance. His eyes gathered in and reflected the light and languor of the summer day.

Mrs. Pontellier reached over for a palmleaf fan that lay on the porch and began to fan herself, while Robert sent between his lips light puffs from his cigarette. They chatted incessantly: about the things around them; their amusing adventure out in the water—it had again assumed its entertaining aspect; about the wind, the trees, the people who had gone to the *Chênière;* about the children playing croquet under the oaks, and the Farival twins, who were now performing the overture to "The Poet and Peasant."[1]

Robert talked a good deal about himself. He was very young, and did not know any better. Mrs. Pontellier talked a little about herself for the same reason. Each was interested in what the other said. Robert spoke of his intention to go to Mexico in the autumn, where fortune awaited him. He was always intending to go to Mexico, but some way never got there. Meanwhile he held on to his modest position in a mercantile house in New Orleans, where an equal familiarity with English, French and Spanish gave him no small value as a clerk and correspondent.

He was spending his summer vacation, as he always did, with his mother at Grand Isle. In former times, before Robert could remember, "the house" had been

9. Although monetary conversions can be problematic, $1 at the time this selection was written was worth about $25 today; $10 would be equivalent to about $250 today.
1. Operetta by Austrian composer Franz von Suppé (1819–95).

a summer luxury of the Lebruns. Now flanked by its dozen or more cottages, which were always filled with exclusive visitors from the "*Quartier Français,*"[2] it enabled Madame Lebrun to maintain the easy and comfortable existence which appeared to be her birthright.

Mrs. Pontellier talked about her father's Mississippi plantation and her girl-hood home in the old Kentucky blue-grass country. She was an American woman, with a small infusion of French which seemed to have been lost in dilution. She read a letter from her sister, who was away in the East, and who had engaged herself to be married. Robert was interested, and wanted to know what manner of girls the sisters were, what the father was like, and how long the mother had been dead.

When Mrs. Pontellier folded the letter it was time for her to dress for the early dinner.

"I see Léonce isn't coming back," she said, with a glance in the direction whence her husband had disappeared. Robert supposed he was not, as there were a good many New Orleans club men over at Klein's.

When Mrs. Pontellier left him to enter her room, the young man descended the steps and strolled over toward the croquet players, where, during the half-hour before dinner, he amused himself with the little Pontellier children, who were very fond of him.

III

It was eleven o'clock that night when Mr. Pontellier returned from Klein's hotel. He was in an excellent humor, in high spirits, and very talkative. His entrance awoke his wife, who was in bed and fast asleep when he came in. He talked to her while he undressed, telling her anecdotes and bits of news and gossip that he had gathered during the day. From his trousers pockets he took a fistful of crumpled bank notes and a good deal of silver coin, which he piled on the bureau indiscriminately with keys, knife, handkerchief, and whatever else happened to be in his pockets. She was overcome with sleep, and answered him with little half utterances.

He thought it very discouraging that his wife, who was the sole object of his existence, evinced so little interest in things which concerned him and valued so little his conversation.

Mr. Pontellier had forgotten the bonbons and peanuts for the boys. Notwith-standing he loved them very much, and went into the adjoining room where they slept to take a look at them and make sure that they were resting comfortably. The result of his investigation was far from satisfactory. He turned and shifted the youngsters about in bed. One of them began to kick and talk about a basket full of crabs.

Mr. Pontellier returned to his wife with the information that Raoul had a high fever and needed looking after. Then he lit a cigar and went and sat near the open door to smoke it.

Mrs. Pontellier was quite sure Raoul had no fever. He had gone to bed per-fectly well, she said, and nothing had ailed him all day. Mr. Pontellier was too well acquainted with fever symptoms to be mistaken. He assured her the child was consuming[3] at that moment in the next room.

---

2. The French Quarter of New Orleans, then a bastion of wealthy, well-established French families.

3. Suffering from fever.

He reproached his wife with her inattention, her habitual neglect of the children. If it was not a mother's place to look after children, whose on earth was it? He himself had his hands full with his brokerage business. He could not be in two places at once; making a living for his family on the street, and staying at home to see that no harm befell them. He talked in a monotonous, insistent way.

Mrs. Pontellier sprang out of bed and went into the next room. She soon came back and sat on the edge of the bed, leaning her head down on the pillow. She said nothing, and refused to answer her husband when he questioned her. When his cigar was smoked out he went to bed, and in half a minute he was fast asleep.

Mrs. Pontellier was by that time thoroughly awake. She began to cry a little, and wiped her eyes on the sleeve of her *peignoir*.[4] Blowing out the candle, which her husband had left burning, she slipped her bare feet into a pair of satin *mules*[5] at the foot of the bed and went out on the porch, where she sat down in the wicker chair and began to rock gently to and fro.

It was then past midnight. The cottages were all dark. A single faint light gleamed out from the hallway of the house. There was no sound abroad except the hooting of an old owl in the top of a water-oak, and the everlasting voice of the sea, that was not uplifted at that soft hour. It broke like a mournful lullaby upon the night.

The tears came so fast to Mrs. Pontellier's eyes that the damp sleeve of her *peignoir* no longer served to dry them. She was holding the back of her chair with one hand; her loose sleeve had slipped almost to the shoulder of her uplifted arm. Turning, she thrust her face, steaming and wet, into the bend of her arm, and she went on crying there, not caring any longer to dry her face, her eyes, her arms. She could not have told why she was crying. Such experiences as the foregoing were not uncommon in her married life. They seemed never before to have weighed much against the abundance of her husband's kindness and a uniform devotion which had come to be tacit and self-understood.

An indescribable oppression, which seemed to generate in some unfamiliar part of her consciousness, filled her whole being with a vague anguish. It was like a shadow, like a mist passing across her soul's summer day. It was strange and unfamiliar; it was a mood. She did not sit there inwardly upbraiding her husband, lamenting at Fate, which had directed her footsteps to the path which they had taken. She was just having a good cry all to herself. The mosquitoes made merry over her, biting her firm, round arms and nipping at her bare insteps.

The little stinging, buzzing imps succeeded in dispelling a mood which might have held her there in the darkness half a night longer.

The following morning Mr. Pontellier was up in good time to take the rockaway[6] which was to convey him to the steamer at the wharf. He was returning to the city to his business; and they would not see him again at the Island till the coming Saturday. He had regained his composure, which seemed to have been somewhat impaired the night before. He was eager to be gone, as he looked forward to a lively week in Carondelet Street.[7]

Mr. Pontellier gave his wife half the money which he had brought away from Klein's hotel the evening before. She liked money as well as most women, and accepted it with no little satisfaction.

4. Dressing gown.
5. Open-heeled slipper.

6. A light, four-wheeled carriage.
7. New Orleans's financial district.

"It will buy a handsome wedding present for Sister Janet!" she exclaimed, smoothing out the bills as she counted them one by one.

"Oh! we'll treat Sister Janet better than that, my dear," he laughed, as he prepared to kiss her good-by.

The boys were tumbling about, clinging to his legs, imploring that numerous things be brought back to them. Mr. Pontellier was a great favorite, and ladies, men, children, even nurses, were always on hand to say good-by to him. His wife stood smiling and waving, the boys shouting, as he disappeared in the old rockaway down the sandy road.

A few days later a box arrived for Mrs. Pontellier from New Orleans. It was from her husband. It was filled with *friandises,* with luscious and toothsome bits— the finest of fruits, *pâtés,*[8] a rare bottle or two, delicious syrups, and bonbons in abundance.

Mrs. Pontellier was always very generous with the contents of such a box; she was quite used to receiving them when away from home. The *pâtés* and fruit were brought to the dining-room; the bonbons were passed around. And the ladies, selecting with dainty and discriminating fingers and a little greedily, all declared that Mr. Pontellier was the best husband in the world. Mrs. Pontellier was forced to admit that she knew of none better.

IV

It would have been a difficult matter for Mr. Pontellier to define to his own satisfaction or any one else's wherein his wife failed in her duty toward their children. It was something which he felt rather than perceived, and he never voiced the feeling without subsequent regret and ample atonement.

If one of the little Pontellier boys took a tumble whilst at play, he was not apt to rush crying to his mother's arms for comfort; he would more likely pick himself up, wipe the water out of his eyes and the sand out of his mouth, and go on playing. Tots as they were, they pulled together and stood their ground in childish battles with doubled fists and uplifted voices, which usually prevailed against the other mother-tots. The quadroon nurse was looked upon as a huge encumbrance, only good to button up waists and panties and to brush and part hair; since it seemed to be a law of society that hair must be parted and brushed.

In short, Mrs. Pontellier was not a mother-woman. The mother-women seemed to prevail that summer at Grand Isle. It was easy to know them, fluttering about with extended, protecting wings when any harm, real or imaginary, threatened their precious brood. They were women who idolized their children, worshipped their husbands, and esteemed it a holy privilege to efface themselves as individuals and grow wings as ministering angels.

Many of them were delicious in the rôle; one of them was the embodiment of every womanly grace and charm. If her husband did not adore her, he was a brute, deserving of death by slow torture. Her name was Adèle Ratignolle. There are no words to describe her save the old ones that have served so often to picture the bygone heroine of romance and the fair lady of our dreams. There was nothing subtle or hidden about her charms; her beauty was all there, flaming and apparent: the spun-gold hair that comb nor confining pin could restrain; the blue eyes

8. *Friandises:* small delicacies; *pâtés:* meat paste.

that were like nothing but sapphires; two lips that pouted, that were so red one could only think of cherries or some other delicious crimson fruit in looking at them. She was growing a little stout, but it did not seem to detract an iota from the grace of every step, pose, gesture. One would not have wanted her white neck a mite less full or her beautiful arms more slender. Never were hands more exquisite than hers, and it was a joy to look at them when she threaded her needle or adjusted her gold thimble to her taper middle finger as she sewed away on the little night-drawers[9] or fashioned a bodice or a bib.

Madame Ratignolle was very fond of Mrs. Pontellier, and often she took her sewing and went over to sit with her in the afternoons. She was sitting there the afternoon of the day the box arrived from New Orleans. She had possession of the rocker, and she was busily engaged in sewing upon a diminutive pair of night drawers.

She had brought the pattern of the drawers for Mrs. Pontellier to cut out—a marvel of construction, fashioned to enclose a baby's body so effectually that only two small eyes might look out from the garment, like an Eskimo's. They were designed for winter wear, when treacherous drafts came down chimneys and insidious currents of deadly cold found their way through keyholes.

Mrs. Pontellier's mind was quite at rest concerning the present material needs of her children, and she could not see the use of anticipating and making winter night garments the subject of her summer meditations. But she did not want to appear unamiable and uninterested, so she had brought forth newspapers which she spread upon the floor of the gallery, and under Madame Ratignolle's directions she had cut a pattern of the impervious garment.

Robert was there, seated as he had been the Sunday before, and Mrs. Pontellier also occupied her former position on the upper step, leaning listlessly against the post. Beside her was a box of bonbons, which she held out at intervals to Madame Ratignolle.

That lady seemed at a loss to make a selection, but finally settled upon a stick of nugat, wondering if it were not too rich; whether it could possibly hurt her. Madame Ratignolle had been married seven years. About every two years she had a baby. At that time she had three babies, and was beginning to think of a fourth one. She was always talking about her "condition."[1] Her "condition" was in no way apparent, and no one would have known a thing about it but for her persistence in making it the subject of conversation.

Robert started to reassure her, asserting that he had known a lady who had subsisted upon nugat during the entire—but seeing the color mount into Mrs. Pontellier's face he checked himself and changed the subject.

Mrs. Pontellier, though she had married a Creole,[2] was not thoroughly at home in the society of Creoles; never before had she been thrown so intimately among them. There were only Creoles that summer at Lebrun's. They all knew each other, and felt like one large family, among whom existed the most amicable relations. A characteristic which distinguished them and which impressed Mrs. Pontellier most forcibly was their entire absence of prudery. Their freedom of expression was at first incomprehensible to her, though she had no difficulty in rec-

9. Taper: slender, tapered; nightdrawers: bloomers to wear in bed.
1. Being pregnant.
2. A French-speaker from urban Louisiana descended from the original French and Spanish settlers.

onciling it with a lofty chastity which in the Creole woman seems to be inborn and unmistakable.

Never would Edna Pontellier forget the shock with which she heard Madame Ratignolle relating to old Monsieur Farival the harrowing story of one of her *accouchements,*[3] withholding no intimate detail. She was growing accustomed to like shocks, but she could not keep the mounting color back from her cheeks. Oftener than once her coming had interrupted the droll story with which Robert was entertaining some amused group of married women.

A book had gone the rounds of the *pension.* When it came her turn to read it, she did so with profound astonishment. She felt moved to read the book in secret and solitude, though none of the others had done so—to hide it from view at the sound of approaching footsteps. It was openly criticised and freely discussed at table. Mrs. Pontellier gave over being astonished, and concluded that wonders would never cease.

V

They formed a congenial group sitting there that summer afternoon—Madame Ratignolle sewing away, often stopping to relate a story or incident with much expressive gesture of her perfect hands: Robert and Mrs. Pontellier sitting idle, exchanging occasional words, glances or smiles which indicated a certain advanced stage of intimacy and *camaraderie.*

He had lived in her shadow during the past month. No one thought anything of it. Many had predicted that Robert would devote himself to Mrs. Pontellier when he arrived. Since the age of fifteen, which was eleven years before, Robert each summer at Grand Isle had constituted himself the devoted attendant of some fair dame or damsel. Sometimes it was a young girl, again a widow; but as often as not it was some interesting married woman.

For two consecutive seasons he lived in the sunlight of Mademoiselle Duvigné's presence. But she died between summers; then Robert posed as an inconsolable, prostrating himself at the feet of Madame Ratignolle for whatever crumbs of sympathy and comfort she might be pleased to vouchsafe.

Mrs. Pontellier like to sit and gaze at her fair companion as she might look upon a faultless Madonna.

"Could any one fathom the cruelty beneath that fair exterior?" murmured Robert. "She knew that I adored her once, and she let me adore her. It was 'Robert, come; go; stand up; sit down; do this; do that; see if the baby sleeps; my thimble, please, that I left God knows where. Come and read Daudet[4] to me while I sew'"

"*Par exemple!*"[5] I never had to ask. You were always there under my feet, like a troublesome cat."

"You mean like an adoring dog. And just as soon as Ratignolle appeared on the scene, then it *was* like a dog. '*Passez! Adieu! Allez vous-en!*'"[6]

"Perhaps I feared to make Alphonse jealous," she interjoined, with excessive naïveté. That made them all laugh. The right hand jealous of the left! The heart

---

3. Childbirths.
4. French writer of short stories and novels Alphonse Daudet (1840–87).

5. My goodness (French).
6. Go on! Good-bye! Go away! (French).

jealous of the soul! But for that matter, the Creole husband is never jealous; with him the gangrene passion is one which has become dwarfed by disuse.

Meanwhile Robert, addressing Mrs. Pontellier, continued to tell of his one time hopeless passion for Madame Ratignolle; of sleepless nights, of consuming flames till the very sea sizzled when he took his daily plunge. While the lady at the needle kept up a little running, contemptuous comment:

"*Blagueur—farceur—gros bête, va!*"[7]

He never assumed this serio-comic tone when alone with Mrs. Pontellier. She never knew precisely what to make of it; at that moment it was impossible for her to guess how much of it was jest and what proportion was earnest. It was understood that he had often spoken words of love to Madame Ratignolle, without any thought of being taken seriously. Mrs. Pontellier was glad he had not assumed a similar rôle toward herself. It would have been unacceptable and annoying.

Mrs. Pontellier had brought her sketching materials, which she sometimes dabbled with in an unprofessional way. She liked the dabbling. She felt in it satisfaction of a kind which no other employment afforded her.

She had long wished to try herself on Madame Ratignolle. Never had that lady seemed a more tempting subject than at that moment, seated there like some sensuous Madonna, with the gleam of the fading day enriching her splendid color.

Robert crossed over and seated himself upon the step below Mrs. Pontellier, that he might watch her work. She handled her brushes with a certain ease and freedom which came, not from long and close acquaintance with them, but from a natural aptitude. Robert followed her work with close attention, giving forth little ejaculatory expressions of appreciation in French, which he addressed to Madame Ratignolle.

"*Mais ce n'est pas mal! Elle s'y connait, elle a de la force, oui.*"[8]

During his oblivious attention he once quietly rested his head against Mrs. Pontellier's arm. As gently she repulsed him. Once again he repeated the offense. She could not but believe it to be thoughtlessness on his part; yet that was no reason she should submit to it. She did not remonstrate, except again to repulse him quietly but firmly. He offered no apology.

The picture completed bore no resemblance to Madame Ratignolle. She was greatly disappointed to find that it did not look like her. But it was a fair enough piece of work, and in many respects satisfying.

Mrs. Pontellier evidently did not think so. After surveying the sketch critically she drew a broad smudge of paint across its surface, and crumpled the paper between her hands.

The youngsters came tumbling up the steps, the quadroon following at the respectful distance which they required her to observe. Mrs. Pontellier made them carry her paints and things into the house. She sought to detain them for a little talk and some pleasantry. But they were greatly in earnest. They had only come to investigate the contents of the bonbon box. They accepted without murmuring what she chose to give them, each holding out two chubby hands scoop-like, in the vain hope that they might be filled; and then away they went.

The sun was low in the west, and the breeze soft and languorous that came up from the south, charged with the seductive odor of the sea. Children, freshly

---

7. Joker—prankster—big beast, go! (French).   she has strength, doesn't she. (French).
8. But it's not too bad! She knows how to do it,

befurbelowed,[9] were gathering for their games under the oaks. Their voices were high and penetrating.

Madame Ratignolle folded her sewing, placing thimble, scissors and thread all neatly together in the roll, which she pinned securely. She complained of faintness. Mrs. Pontellier flew for the cologne water and a fan. She bathed Madame Ratignolle's face with cologne, while Robert plied the fan with unnecessary vigor.

The spell was soon over, and Mrs. Pontellier could not help wondering if there were not a little imagination responsible for its origin, for the rose tint had never faded from her friend's face.

She stood watching the fair woman walk down the long line of galleries with the grace and majesty which queens are sometimes supposed to possess. Her little ones ran to meet her. Two of them clung about her white skirts, the third she took from its nurse and with a thousand endearments bore it along in her own fond, encircling arms. Though, as everybody well knew, the doctor had forbidden her to lift so much as a pin!

"Are you going bathing?" asked Robert of Mrs. Pontellier. It was not so much a question as a reminder.

"Oh, no," she answered, with a tone of indecision. "I'm tired; I think not." Her glance wandered from his face away toward the Gulf, whose sonorous murmur reached her like a loving but imperative entreaty.

"Oh, come!" he insisted. "You mustn't miss your bath. Come on. The water must be delicious; it will not hurt you. Come."

He reached up for her big, rough straw hat that hung on a peg outside the door, and put it on her head. They descended the steps, and walked away together toward the beach. The sun was low in the west and the breeze was soft and warm.

VI

Edna Pontellier could not have told why, wishing to go to the beach with Robert, she should in the first place have declined, and in the second place have followed in obedience to one of the two contradictory impulses which impelled her.

A certain light was beginning to dawn dimly within her,—the light which, showing the way, forbids it.

At that early period it served but to bewilder her. It moved her to dreams, to thoughtfulness, to the shadowy anguish which had over-come her the midnight when she had abandoned herself to tears.

In short, Mrs. Pontellier was beginning to realize her position in the universe as a human being, and to recognize her relations as an individual to the world within and about her. This may seem like a ponderous weight of wisdom to descend upon the soul of a young woman of twenty-eight—perhaps more wisdom than the Holy Ghost is usually pleased to vouchsafe to any woman.

But the beginning of things, of a world especially, is necessarily vague, tangled, chaotic, and exceedingly disturbing. How few of us ever emerge from such beginning! How many souls perish in its tumult!

The voice of the sea is seductive; never ceasing, whispering, clamoring, murmuring, inviting the soul to wander for a spell in abysses of solitude; to lose itself in mazes of inward contemplation.

9. Dressed in ruffles and flounces, dressed up.

The voice of the sea speaks to the soul. The touch of the sea is sensuous, enfolding the body in its soft, close embrace.

VII

Mrs. Pontellier was not a woman given to confidences, a characteristic hitherto contrary to her nature. Even as a child she had lived her own small life all within herself. At a very early period she had apprehended instinctively the dual life—that outward existence which conforms, the inward life which questions.

That summer at Grand Isle she began to loose a little the mantle of reserve that had always enveloped her. There may have been—there must have been—influences, both subtle and apparent, working in their several ways to induce her to do this; but the most obvious was the influence of Adèle Ratignolle. The excessive physical charm of the Creole had first attracted her, for Edna had a sensuous susceptibility to beauty. Then the candor of the woman's whole existence, which everyone might read, and which formed so striking a contrast to her own habitual reserve—this might have furnished a link. Who can tell what metals the gods use in forging the subtle bond which we call sympathy, which we might as well call love.

The two women went away one morning to the beach together, arm in arm, under the huge white sunshade. Edna had prevailed upon Madame Ratignolle to leave the children behind, though she could not induce her to relinquish a diminutive roll of needlework, which Adèle begged to be allowed to slip into the depths of her pocket. In some unaccountable way they had escaped from Robert.

The walk to the beach was no inconsiderable one, consisting as it did of a long, sandy path, upon which a sporadic and tangled growth that bordered it on either side made frequent and unexpected inroads. There were acres of yellow camomile reaching out on either hand. Further away still, vegetable gardens abounded, with frequent small plantations of orange or lemon trees intervening. The dark green clusters glistened from afar in the sun.

The women were both of goodly height, Madame Ratignolle possessing the more feminine and matronly figure. The charm of Edna Pontellier's physique stole insensibly upon you. The lines of her body were long, clean and symmetrical; it was a body which occasionally fell into splendid poses; there was no suggestion of the trim, stereotyped fashion-plate about it. A casual and indiscriminating observer, in passing, might not cast a second glance upon the figure. But with more feeling and discernment he would have recognized the noble beauty of its modeling, and the graceful severity of poise and movement, which made Edna Pontellier different from the crowd.

She wore a cool muslin that morning—white, with a waving vertical line of brown running through it; also a white linen collar and the big straw hat which she had taken from the peg outside the door. The hat rested any way on her yellow-brown hair, that waved a little, was heavy, and clung close to her head.

Madame Ratignolle, more careful of her complexion, had twined a gauze veil about her head. She wore dogskin gloves, white gauntlets that protected her wrists. She was dressed in pure white, with a fluffiness of ruffles that became her. The draperies and fluttering things which she wore suited her rich, luxuriant beauty as a greater severity of line could not have done.

There were a number of bath-houses along the beach, of rough but solid construction, built with small, protecting galleries facing the water. Each house consisted of two compartments, and each family at Lebrun's possessed a compartment for itself, fitted out with all the essential paraphernalia of the bath and whatever other conveniences the owners might desire. The two women had no intention of bathing; they had just strolled down to the beach for a walk and to be alone and near the water. The Pontellier and Ratignolle compartments adjoined one another under the same roof.

Mrs. Pontellier had brought down her key through force of habit. Unlocking the door of her bath-room she went inside, and soon emerged, bringing a rug, which she spread upon the floor of the gallery, and two huge hair pillows covered with crash,[1] which she placed against the front of the building.

The two seated themselves there in the shade of the porch, side by side, with their backs against the pillows and their feet extended. Madame Ratignolle removed her veil, wiped her face with a rather delicate handkerchief, and fanned herself with the fan which she always carried suspended somewhere about her person by a long, narrow ribbon. Edna removed her collar and opened her dress at the throat. She took the fan from Madame Ratignolle and began to fan both herself and her companion. It was very warm, and for a while they did nothing but exchange remarks about the heat, the sun, the glare. But there was a breeze blowing, a choppy stiff wind that whipped the water into froth. It fluttered the skirts of the two women and kept them for a while engaged in adjusting, readjusting, tucking in, securing hair-pins and hat-pins. A few persons were sporting some distance away in the water. The beach was very still of human sound at that hour. The lady in black was reading her morning devotions on the porch of a neighboring bath-house. Two young lovers were exchanging their hearts' yearnings beneath the children's tent, which they had found unoccupied.

Edna Pontellier, casting her eyes about, had finally kept them at rest upon the sea. The day was clear and carried the gaze out as far as the blue sky went; there were a few white clouds suspended idly over the horizon. A lateen[2] sail was visible in the direction of Cat Island, and others to the south seemed almost motionless in the far distance.

"Of whom—of what are you thinking?" asked Adèle of her companion, whose countenance she had been watching with a little amused attention, arrested by the absorbed expression which seemed to have seized and fixed every feature into a statuesque repose.

"Nothing," returned Mrs. Pontellier, with a start, adding at once: "How stupid! But it seems to me it is the reply we make instinctively to such a question. Let me see," she went on, throwing back her head and narrowing her fine eyes till they shone like two vivid points of light. "Let me see. I was really not conscious of thinking of anything; but perhaps I can retrace my thoughts."

"Oh! never mind!" laughed Madame Ratignolle. "I am not quite so exacting. I will let you off this time. It is really too hot to think, especially to think about thinking."

"But for the fun of it," persisted Edna. "First of all, the sight of the water stretching so far away, those motionless sails against the blue sky, made a delicious picture that I just wanted to sit and look at. The hot wind beating in my face made me think—without any connection that I can trace—of a summer day

1. Rug: blanket; hair pillows: pillows stuffed with   2. A triangular, sloping sail.
horsehair; crash: a fabric woven of rough yarn.

in Kentucky, of a meadow that seemed as big as the ocean to the very little girl walking through the grass, which was higher than her waist. She threw out her arms as if swimming when she walked, beating the tall grass as one strikes out in the water. Oh, I see the connection now!"

"Where were you going that day in Kentucky, walking through the grass?"

"I don't remember now. I was just walking diagonally across a big field. My sun-bonnet obstructed the view. I could see only the stretch of green before me, and I felt as if I must walk on forever, without coming to the end of it. I don't remember whether I was frightened or pleased. I must have been entertained.

"Likely as not it was Sunday," she laughed; "and I was running away from prayers, from the Presbyterian service, read in a spirit of gloom by my father that chills me yet to think of."

"And have you been running away from prayers ever since, *ma chère*?"[3] asked Madame Ratignolle, amused.

"No! oh, no!" Edna hastened to say. "I was a little unthinking child in those days, just following a misleading impulse without question. On the contrary, during one period of my life religion took a firm hold upon me; after I was twelve and until—until—why, I suppose until now, though I never thought much about it—just driven along by habit. But do you know," she broke off, turning her quick eyes upon Madame Ratignolle and leaning forward a little so as to bring her face quite close to that of her companion, "sometimes I feel this summer as if I were walking through the green meadow again; idly, aimlessly, unthinking and unguided."

Madame Ratignolle laid her hand over that of Mrs. Pontellier, which was near her. Seeing that the hand was not withdrawn, she clasped it firmly and warmly. She even stroked it a little, fondly, with the other hand, murmuring in an undertone, "*Pauvre chérie*."[4]

The action was at first a little confusing to Edna, but she soon lent herself readily to the Creole's gentle caress. She was not accustomed to an outward and spoken expression of affection, either in herself or in others. She and her younger sister, Janet, had quarreled a good deal through force of unfortunate habit. Her older sister, Margaret, was matronly and dignified, probably from having assumed matronly and house-wifely responsibilities too early in life, their mother having died when they were quite young. Margaret was not effusive; she was practical. Edna had had an occasional girl friend, but whether accidentally or not, they seemed to have been all of one type—the self-contained. She never realized that the reserve of her own character had much, perhaps everything, to do with this. Her most intimate friend at school had been one of rather exceptional intellectual gifts, who wrote fine-sounding essays which Edna admired and strove to imitate; and with her she talked and glowed over the English classics, and sometimes held religious and political controversies.

Edna often wondered at one propensity which sometimes had inwardly disturbed her without causing any outward show or manifestation on her part. At a very early age—perhaps it was when she traversed the ocean of waving grass—she remembered that she had been passionately enamored of a dignified and sad-eyed cavalry officer who visited her father in Kentucky. She could not leave his presence when he was there, nor remove her eyes from his face which was something

---

3. My dear (French).   4. Poor darling (French).

like Napoleons's, with a lock of black hair falling across the forehead. But the cavalry officer melted imperceptibly out of her existence.

At another time her affections were deeply engaged by a young gentleman who visited a lady on a neighboring plantation. It was after they went to Mississippi to live. The young man was engaged to be married to the young lady, and they sometimes called upon Margaret, driving over of afternoons in a buggy. Edna was a little miss, just merging into her teens; and the realization that she herself was nothing, nothing, nothing to the engaged young man was a bitter affliction to her. But he, too, went the way of dreams.

She was a grown young woman when she was overtaken by what she supposed to be the climax of her fate. It was when the face and figure of a great tragedian began to haunt her imagination and stir her senses. The persistence of the infatuation lent it an aspect of genuineness. The hopelessness of it colored it with the lofty tones of a great passion.

The picture of the tragedian stood enframed upon her desk. Any one may possess the portrait of a tragedian without exciting suspicion or comment. (This was a sinister reflection which she cherished.) In the presence of others she expressed admiration for his exalted gifts, as she handed the photograph around and dwelt upon the fidelity of the likeness. When alone she sometimes picked it up and kissed the cold glass passionately.

Her marriage to Léonce Pontellier was purely an accident, in this respect resembling many other marriages which masquerade as the decrees of Fate. It was in the midst of her secret great passion that she met him. He fell in love, as men are in the habit of doing, and pressed his suit with an earnestness and an ardor which left nothing to be desired. He pleased her; his absolute devotion flattered her. She fancied there was a sympathy of thought and taste between them, in which fancy she was mistaken. Add to this the violent opposition of her father and her sister Margaret to her marriage with a Catholic, and we need seek no further for the motives which led her to accept Monsieur Pontellier for her husband.

The acme of bliss, which would have been a marriage with the tragedian, was not for her in this world. As the devoted wife of a man who worshiped her, she felt she would take her place with a certain dignity in the world of reality, closing the portals forever behind her upon the realm of romance and dreams.

But it was not long before the tragedian had gone to join the cavalry officer and the engaged young man and a few others; and Edna found herself face to face with the realities. She grew fond of her husband, realizing with some unaccountable satisfaction that no trace of passion or excessive and fictitious warmth colored her affection, thereby threatening its dissolution.

She was fond of her children in an uneven, impulsive way. She would sometimes gather them passionately to her heart; she would sometimes forget them. The year before they had spent part of the summer with their grandmother Pontellier in Iberville.[5] Feeling secure regarding their happiness and welfare, she did not miss them except with an occasional intense longing. Their absence was a sort of relief, though she did not admit this, even to herself. It seemed to free her of a responsibility which she had blindly assumed and for which Fate had not fitted her.

Edna did not reveal so much as all this to Madame Ratignolle that summer day when they sat with faces turned to the sea. But a good part of it escaped her.

5. A rural parish (or county) west of Baton Rouge, Louisiana.

She had put her head down on Madame Ratignolle's shoulder. She was flushed and felt intoxicated with the sound of her own voice and the unaccustomed taste of candor. It muddled her like wine, or like a first breath of freedom.

There was the sound of approaching voices. It was Robert, surrounded by a troop of children, searching for them. The two little Pontelliers were with him, and he carried Madame Ratignolle's little girl in his arms. There were other children beside, and two nursemaids followed, looking disagreeable and resigned.

The women at once rose and began to shake out their draperies and relax their muscles. Mrs. Pontellier threw the cushions and rug into the bath-house. The children all scampered off to the awning, and they stood there in a line, gazing upon the intruding lovers, still exchanging their vows and sighs. The lovers got up, with only a silent protest, and walked slowly away somewhere else.

The children possessed themselves of the tent, and Mrs. Pontellier went over to join them.

Madame Ratignolle begged Robert to accompany her to the house; she complained of cramp in her limbs and stiffness of the joints. She leaned draggingly upon his arm as they walked.

VIII

"Do me a favor, Robert," spoke the pretty woman at his side, almost as soon as she and Robert had started on their slow, homeward way. She looked up in his face, leaning on his arm beneath the encircling shadow of the umbrella which he had lifted.

"Granted; as many as you like," he returned, glancing down into her eyes that were full of thoughtfulness and some speculation.

"I only ask for one; let Mrs. Pontellier alone."

"*Tiens!*" he exclaimed, with a sudden, boyish laugh. "*Voilà que Madame Ratignolle est jealouse!*"[6]

"Nonsense! I'm in earnest; I mean what I say. Let Mrs. Pontellier alone."

"Why?" he asked; himself growing serious at his companion's solicitation.

"She is not one of us; she is not like us. She might make the unfortunate blunder of taking you seriously."

His face flushed with annoyance, and taking off his soft hat he began to beat it impatiently against his leg as he walked. "Why shouldn't she take me seriously?" he demanded sharply. "Am I a comedian, a clown, a jack-in-the-box? Why shouldn't she? You Creoles! I have no patience with you! Am I always to be regarded as a feature of an amusing programme? I hope Mrs. Pontellier does take me seriously. I hope she has discernment enough to find in me something besides the *blagueur*. If I thought there was any doubt—"

"Oh, enough, Robert!" she broke into his heated outburst. "You are not thinking of what you are saying. You speak with about as little reflection we might expect from one of those children down there playing in the sand. If your attentions to any married women here were ever offered with any intention of being convincing, you would not be the gentleman we all know you to be, and you would be unfit to associate with the wives and daughters of the people who trust you."

Madame Ratignolle had spoken what she believed to be the law and the gospel. The young man shrugged his shoulders impatiently.

6. Well! So Madame Ratignolle is jealous! (French).

"Oh! well! That isn't it," slamming his hat down vehemently upon his head. "You ought to feel that such things are not flattering to say to a fellow."

"Should our whole intercourse consist of an exchange of compliments? *Ma foi!*"[7]

"It isn't pleasant to have a woman tell you—" he went on, unheedingly, but breaking off suddenly: "Now if I were like Arobin—you remember Alcée Arobin and that story of the consul's wife at Biloxi?" And he related the story of Alcée Arobin and the consul's wife; and another about the tenor of the French Opera who received letters which should never have been written; and still other stories, grave and gay, till Mrs. Pontellier and her possible propensity for taking young men seriously was apparently forgotten.

Madame Ratignolle, when they had regained her cottage, went in to take the hour's rest which she considered helpful. Before leaving her, Robert begged her pardon for the impatience—he called it rudeness—with which he had received her well-meant caution.

"You made one mistake, Adèle," he said, with a light smile; "there is no earthly possibility of Mrs. Pontellier ever taking me seriously. You should have warned me against taking myself seriously. Your advice might then have carried some weight and given me subject for some reflection. *Au revoir.* But you look tired," he added, solicitously. "Would you like a cup of bouillon? Shall I stir you a toddy? Let me mix you a toddy with a drop of Angostura."[8]

She acceded to the suggestion of bouillon, which was grateful and acceptable. He went himself to the kitchen, which was a building apart from the cottages and lying to the rear of the house. And he himself brought her the golden-brown bouillon, in a dainty Sèvres[9] cup, with a flaky cracker or two on the saucer.

She thrust a bare, white arm from the curtain which shielded her open door, and received the cup from his hands. She told him he was a *bon garçon,*[1] and she meant it. Robert thanked her and turned away toward "the house."

The lovers were just entering the grounds of the *pension.* They were leaning toward each other as the water-oaks bent from the sea. There was not a particle of earth beneath their feet. Their heads might have been turned upside-down, so absolutely did they tread upon blue ether. The lady in black, creeping behind them, looked a trifle paler and more jaded than usual. There was no sign of Mrs. Pontellier and the children. Robert scanned the distance for any such apparition. They would doubtless remain away till the dinner hour. The young man ascended to his mother's room. It was situated at the top of the house, made up of odd angles and a queer, sloping ceiling. Two broad dormer windows looked out toward the Gulf, and as far across it as a man's eye might reach. The furnishings of the room were light, cool, and practical.

Madame Lebrun was busily engaged at the sewing-machine. A little black girl sat on the floor, and with her hands worked the treadle of the machine. The Creole woman does not take any chances which may be avoided of imperiling her health.

Robert went over and seated himself on the broad sill of one of the dormer windows. He took a book from his pocket and began energetically to read it, judging by the precision and frequency with which he turned the leaves. The sewing-machine made a resounding clatter in the room; it was of a ponderous, by-gone make. In the lulls, Robert and his mother exchanged bits of desultory conversation.

7. My word! (French).
8. *Au revoir:* until we meet again; Angostura: aromatic flavoring.
9. Fine French china.
1. Good fellow (French); also a play on "good waiter."

"Where is Mrs. Pontellier?"

"Down at the beach with the children."

"I promised to lend her the Goncourt.[2] Don't forget to take it down when you go; it's there on the bookshelf over the small table." Clattter, clatter, clatter, bang! for the next five or eight minutes.

"Where is Victor going with the rockaway?"

"The rockaway? Victor?"

"Yes; down there in front. He seems to be getting ready to drive away somewhere."

"Call him." Clatter, clatter!

Robert uttered a shrill, piercing whistle which might have been heard back at the wharf.

"He won't look up."

Madame Lebrun flew to the window. She called "Victor!" She waved a handkerchief and called again. The young fellow below got into the vehicle and started the horse off at a gallop.

Madame Lebrun went back to the machine, crimson with annoyance. Victor was the younger son and brother—a *tête montée*,[3] with a temper which invited violence and a will which no ax could break.

"Whenever you say the word I'm ready to thrash any amount of reason into him that he's able to hold."

"If your father had only lived!" Clatter, clatter, clatter, clatter, bang! It was a fixed belief with Madame Lebrun that the conduct of the universe and all things pertaining thereto would have been manifestly of a more intelligent and higher order had not Monsieur Lebrun been removed to other spheres during the early years of their married life.

"What do you hear from Montel?" Montel was a middle-aged gentleman whose vain ambition and desire for the past twenty years had been to fill the void which Monsieur Lebrun's taking off had left in the Lebrun household. Clatter, clatter, bang, clatter!

"I have a letter somewhere," looking in the machine drawer and finding the letter in the bottom of the work basket. "He says to tell you he will be in Vera Cruz[4] the beginning of next month"—clatter, clatter!—"and if you still have the intention of joining him"—bang! clatter, clatter, bang!

"Why didn't you tell me so before, mother? You know I wanted—" Clatter, clatter, clatter!

"Do you see Mrs. Pontellier starting back with the children? She will be in late to luncheon again. She never starts to get ready for luncheon till the last minute." Clatter, clatter! "Where are you going?"

"Where did you say the Goncourt was?"

IX

Every light in the hall was ablaze; every lamp turned as high as it could be without smoking the chimney or threatening explosion. The lamps were fixed at intervals against the wall, encircling the whole room. Some one had gathered orange and lemon branches and with these fashioned graceful festoons between. The dark

2. Novel by the French brothers Edmond (1822–96) and Jules (1830–70) de Goncourt.

3. Hotheaded.

4. City on Mexico's Gulf coast.

green of the branches stood out and glistened against the white muslin curtains which draped the windows, and which puffed, floated, and flapped at the capricious will of a stiff breeze that swept up from the Gulf.

It was Saturday night a few weeks after the intimate conversation held between Robert and Madame Ratignolle on their way from the beach. An unusual number of husbands, fathers, and friends had come down to stay over Sunday; and they were being suitably entertained by their families, with the material help of Madame Lebrun. The dining tables had all been removed to one end of the hall, and the chairs ranged about in rows and in clusters. Each little family group had had its say and exchanged its domestic gossip earlier in the evening. There was now an apparent disposition to relax; to widen the circle of confidences and give a more general tone to the conversation.

Many of the children had been permitted to sit up beyond their usual bedtime. A small band of them were lying on their stomachs on the floor looking at the colored sheets of the comic papers which Mr. Pontellier had brought down. The little Pontellier boys were permitting them to do so, and making their authority felt.

Music, dancing, and a recitation or two were the entertainments furnished, or rather, offered. But there was nothing systematic about the programme, no appearance of prearrangement nor even premeditation.

At an early hour in the evening the Farival twins were prevailed upon to play the piano. They were girls of fourteen, always clad in the Virgin's colors, blue and white, having been dedicated to the Blessed Virgin at their baptism. They played a duet from "Zampa," and at the earnest solicitation of every one present followed it with the overture to "The Poet and the Peasant."

"*Allez vous-en! Sapristi!*" shrieked the parrot outside the door. He was the only being present who possessed sufficient candor to admit that he was not listening to these gracious performances for the first time that summer. Old Monsieur Farival, grandfather of the twins, grew indignant over the interruption, and insisted upon having the bird removed and consigned to regions of darkness. Victor Lebrun objected; and his decrees were as immutable as those of Fate. The parrot fortunately offered no further interruption to the entertainment, the whole venom of his nature apparently having been cherished up and hurled against the twins in that one impetuous outburst.

Later a young brother and sister gave recitations, which every one present had heard many times at winter evening entertainments in the city.

A little girl performed a skirt dance in the center of the floor. The mother played her accompaniments and at the same time watched her daughter with greedy admiration and nervous apprehension. She need have had no apprehension. The child was mistress of the situation. She had been properly dressed for the occasion in black tulle and black silk tights. Her little neck and arms were bare, and her hair, artificially crimped, stood out like fluffy black plumes over her head. Her poses were full of grace, and her little back-shod toes twinkled as they shot out and upward with a rapidity and a suddenness which were bewildering.

But there was no reason why every one should not dance. Madame Ratignolle could not, so it was she who gaily consented to play for the others. She played very well, keeping excellent waltz time and infusing an expression into the strains which was indeed inspiring. She was keeping up her music on account of the children she said; because she and her husband both considered it a means of brightening the home and making it attractive.

Almost every one danced but the twins, who could not be induced to separate during the brief period when one or the other should be whirling around the room in the arms of a man. They might have danced together, but they did not think of it.

The children were sent to bed. Some went submissively; others with shrieks and protests as they were dragged away. They had been permitted to sit up till after the ice-cream, which naturally marked the limit of human indulgence.

The ice-cream was passed around with cake—gold and silver cake arranged on platters in alternate slices; it had been made and frozen during the afternoon back of the kitchen by two black women, under the supervision of Victor. It was pronounced a great success—excellent if it had only contained a little less vanilla or a little more sugar, if it had been frozen a degree harder, and if the salt might have been kept out of portions of it. Victor was proud of his achievement, and went about recommending it and urging every one to partake of it to excess.

After Mrs. Pontellier had danced twice with her husband, once with Robert, and once with Monsieur Ratignolle, who was thin and tall and swayed like a reed in the wind when he danced, she went out on the gallery and seated herself on the low window-sill, where she commanded a view of all that went on in the hall and could look out toward the Gulf. There was a soft effulgence in the east. The moon was coming up, and its mystic shimmer was casting a million lights across the distant, restless water.

"Would you like to hear Mademoiselle Reisz play?" asked Robert, coming out on the porch where she was. Of course Edna would like to hear Mademoiselle Reisz play; but she feared it would be useless to entreat her.

"I'll ask her," he said. "I'll tell her that you want to hear her. She likes you. She will come." He turned and hurried away to one of the far cottages, where Mademoiselle Reisz was shuffling away. She was dragging a chair in and out of her room, and at intervals objecting to the crying of a baby, which a nurse in the adjoining cottage was endeavoring to put to sleep. She was a disagreeable little woman, no longer young, who had quarreled with almost every one, owing to a temper which was self-assertive and a disposition to trample upon the rights of others. Robert prevailed upon her without any too great difficulty.

She entered the hall with him during a lull in the dance. She made an awkward, imperious little bow as she went in. She was a homely woman, with a small weazened face and body and eyes that glowed. She had absolutely no taste in dress, and wore a batch of rusty black lace with a bunch of artificial violets pinned to the side of her hair.

"Ask Mrs. Pontellier what she would like to hear me play," she requested of Robert. She sat perfectly still before the piano, not touching the keys, while Robert carried her message to Edna at the window. A general air of surprise and genuine satisfaction fell upon every one as they saw the pianist enter. There was a settling down, and a prevailing air of expectancy everywhere. Edna was a trifle embarrassed at being thus signaled out for the imperious little woman's favor. She would not dare to choose, and begged that Madmoiselle Reisz would please herself in selections.

Edna was what she herself called very fond of music. Musical strains, well rendered, had a way of evoking pictures in her mind. She sometimes liked to sit in the room of mornings when Madame Ratignolle played or practiced. One piece which that lady played Edna had entitled "Solitude." It was a short, plaintive, minor strain. The name of the piece was something else, but she called it "Solitude." When she heard it there came before her imagination the figure of a man standing beside a desolate rock on the seashore. He was naked. His attitude was one of hopeless resignation as he looked toward a distant bird winging its flight away from him.

Another piece called to her mind a dainty young woman clad in an Empire gown,[5] taking mincing dancing steps as she came down a long avenue between tall hedges. Again, another reminded her of children at play, and still another of nothing on earth but a demure lady stroking a cat.

The very first chords which Mademoiselle Reisz struck upon the piano sent a keen tremor down Mrs. Pontellier's spinal column. It was not the first time she had heard an artist at the piano. Perhaps it was the first time she was ready, perhaps the first time her being was tempered to take an impress of the abiding truth.

She waited for the material pictures which she thought would gather and blaze before her imagination. She waited in vain. She saw no pictures of solitude, of hope, of longing, or of despair. But the very passions themselves were aroused within her soul, swaying it, lashing it, as the waves daily beat upon her splendid body. She trembled, she was choking, and the tears blinded her.

Mademoiselle had finished. She arose, and bowing her stiff, lofty bow, she went away, stopping for neither thanks nor applause. As she passed along the gallery she patted Edna upon the shoulder.

"Well, how did you like my music?" she asked. The young woman was unable to answer; she pressed the hand of the pianist convulsively. Mademoiselle Reisz perceived her agitation and even her tears. She patted her again upon the shoulder as she said:

"You are the only one worth playing for. Those others? Bah!" and she went shuffling and sidling on down the gallery toward her room.

But she was mistaken about "those others." Her playing had aroused a fever of enthusiasm. "What passion!" "What an artist!" "I have always said no one could play Chopin like Mademoiselle Reisz!" "That last prelude! *Bon Dieu!*[6] It shakes a man!"

It was growing late, and there was a general disposition to disband. But someone, perhaps it was Robert, thought of a bath at that mystic hour and under that mystic moon.

X

At all events Robert proposed it, and there was not a dissenting voice. There was not one but was ready to follow when he led the way. He did not lead the way, however, he directed the way; and he himself loitered behind with the lovers, who had betrayed a disposition to linger and hold themselves apart. He walked between them, whether with malicious or mischievous intent was not wholly clear, even to himself.

The Pontelliers and Ratignolles walked ahead; the women leaning upon the arms of their husbands. Edna could hear Robert's voice behind them, and could sometimes hear what he said. She wondered why he did not join them. It was unlike him not to. Of late he had sometimes held away from her for an entire day, redoubling his devotion upon the next and the next, as though to make up for hours that had been lost. She missed him the days when some pretext served to

5. A high-waisted, low-cut, short-sleeved dress.   Chopin (1810–49); *Bon Dieu:* Good God! (French).
6. Chopin: Polish composer and pianist Frédéric

take him away from her, just as one misses the sun on a cloudy day without having thought much about the sun when it was shining.

The people walked in little groups toward the beach. They talked and laughed; some of them sang. There was a band playing down at Klein's hotel, and the strains reached them faintly, tempered by the distance. There were strange, rare odors abroad—a tangle of the sea smell and of weeds and damp, new-plowed earth, mingled with the heavy perfume of a field of white blossoms somewhere near. But the night sat light upon the sea and the land. There was no weight of darkness; there were no shadows. The white light of the moon had fallen upon the world like the mystery and the softness of sleep.

Most of them walked into the water as though into a native element. The sea was quiet now, and swelled lazily in broad billows that melted into one another and did not break except upon the beach in little foamy crests that coiled back like slow, white serpents.

Edna had attempted all summer to learn to swim. She had received instructions from both the men and women; in some instances from the children. Robert had pursued a system of lessons almost daily; and he was nearly at the point of discouragement in realizing the futility of his efforts. A certain ungovernable dread hung about her when in the water, unless there was a hand near by that might reach out and reassure her.

But that night she was like the little tottering, stumbling, clutching child, who of a sudden realizes its powers, and walks for the first time alone, boldly and with over-confidence. She could have shouted for joy. She did shout for joy, as with a sweeping stroke or two she lifted her body to the surface of the water.

A feeling of exultation overtook her, as if some power of significant import had been given her soul. She grew daring and reckless, overestimating her strength. She wanted to swim far out, where no woman had swum before.

Her unlooked-for achievement was the subject of wonder, applause, and admiration. Each one congratulated himself that his special teachings had accomplished this desired end.

"How easy it is!" she thought. "It is nothing," she said aloud: "why did I not discover before that it was nothing. Think of the time I have lost splashing about like a baby!" She would not join the groups in their sports and bouts, but intoxicated with her newly conquered power, she swam out alone.

She turned her face seaward to gather in an impression of space and solitude, which the vast expanse of water, meeting and melting with moonlit sky, conveyed to her excited fancy. As she swam she seemed to be reaching out for the unlimited in which to lose herself.

Once she turned and looked toward the shore, toward the people she had left there. She had not gone any great distance—that is, what would have been great distance for an experienced swimmer. But to her unaccustomed vision the stretch of water behind her assumed the aspect of a barrier which her unaided strength would never be able to overcome.

A quick vision of death smote her soul, and for a second of time appalled and enfeebled her senses. But by an effort she rallied her staggering faculties and managed to regain the land.

She made no mention of her encounter with death and her flash of terror, except to say to her husband, "I thought I should have perished out there alone."

"You were not so very far, my dear; I was watching you," he told her.

Edna went at once to the bath-house, and she had put on her dry clothes and was ready to return home before the others had left the water. She started to walk away alone. They all called to her and shouted to her. She waved a dissenting hand, and went on paying no further heed to their renewed cries which sought to detain her.

"Sometimes I am tempted to think that Mrs. Pontellier is capricious," said Madame Lebrun, who was amusing herself immensely and feared that Edna's abrupt departure might put an end to the pleasure.

"I know she is," assented Mr. Pointellier; "sometimes, not often."

Edna had not traversed a quarter of the distance on her way home before she was overtaken by Robert.

"Did you think I was afraid?" she asked him, without a shade of annoyance.

"No; I knew you weren't afraid."

"Then why did you come? Why didn't you stay out there with the others?"

"I never thought of it."

"Thought of what?"

"Of anything. What difference does it make?"

"I'm very tired," she uttered, complainingly.

"I know you are."

"You don't know anything about it. Why should you know? I never was so exhausted in my life. But it isn't unpleasant. A thousand emotions have swept through me to-night. I don't comprehend half of them. Don't mind what I'm saying; I am just thinking aloud. I wonder if I shall ever be stirred again as Mademoiselle Reisz's playing moved me to-night. I wonder if any night on earth will ever again be like this one. It is like a night in a dream. The people about me are like some uncanny, half-human beings. There must be spirits abroad to-night."

"There are," whispered Robert. "Didn't you know this was the twenty-eighth of August?

"The twenty-eighth of August?"

"Yes. On the twenty-eighth of August, at the hour of midnight, and if the moon is shining—the moon must be shining—a spirit that has haunted these shores for ages rises up from the Gulf. With its own penetrating vision the spirit seeks some one mortal worthy to hold him company, worthy of being exalted for a few hours into realms of the semi-celestials. His search has always hitherto been fruitless, and he has sunk back, disheartened, into the sea. But tonight he found Mrs. Pontellier. Perhaps he will never wholly release her from the spell. Perhaps she will never again suffer a poor, unworthy earthling to walk in the shadow of her divine presence."

"Don't banter me," she said, wounded at what appeared to be his flippancy. He did not mind the entreaty, but the tone with its delicate note of pathos was like a reproach. He could not explain; he could not tell her that he had penetrated her mood and understood. He said nothing except to offer her his arm, for, by her own admission, she was exhausted. She had been walking alone with her arms hanging limp, letting her white skirts trail along the dewy path. She took his arm, but she did not lean upon it. She let her hand lie listlessly, as though her thoughts were elsewhere—somewhere in advance of her body, and she was striving to overtake them.

Robert assisted her into the hammock which swung from the post before her door out to the trunk of a tree.

"Will you stay out here and wait for Mr. Pontellier?" he asked.

"I'll stay out here. Good-night."

"Shall I get you a pillow?"

"There's one here," she said, feeling about, for they were in the shadow.

"It must be soiled; the children have been tumbling it about."

"No matter." And having discovered the pillow, she adjusted it beneath her head. She extended herself in the hammock with a deep breath of relief. She was not a supercilious or an over-dainty woman. She was not much given to reclining in the hammock, and when she did so it was with no cat-like suggestion of voluptuous ease, but with a beneficent repose which seemed to invade her whole body.

"Shall I stay with you till Mr. Pontellier comes?" asked Robert, seating himself on the outer edge of one of the steps and taking hold of the hammock rope which was fastened to the post.

"If you wish. Don't swing the hammock. Will you get my white shawl which I left on the window-sill over at the house?"

"Are you chilly?"

"No; but I shall be presently."

"Presently?" he laughed. "Do you know what time it is? How long are you going to stay out here?"

"I don't know. Will you get the shawl?"

"Of course I will," he said rising. He went over to the house, walking along the grass. She watched his figure pass in and out of the strips of moonlight. It was past midnight. It was very quiet.

When he returned with the shawl she took it and kept it in her hand. She did not put it around her.

"Did you say I should stay till Mr. Pontellier came back?"

"I said you might if you wished to."

He seated himself again and rolled a cigarette, which he smoked in silence. Neither did Mrs. Pontellier speak. No multitude of words could have been more significant than those moments of silence, or more pregnant with the first-felt throbbings of desire.

When the voices of the bathers were heard approaching, Robert said good-night. She did not answer him. He thought she was asleep. Again she watched his figure pass in and out of the strips of moonlight as he walked away.

XI

"What are you doing out here, Edna? I thought I should find you in bed," said her husband, when he discovered her lying there. He had walked up with Madame Lebrun and left her at the house. His wife did not reply.

"Are you asleep?" he asked, bending down close to look at her.

"No." Her eyes gleamed bright and intense, with no sleepy shadows, as they looked into his.

"Do you know it is past one o'clock? Come on," and he mounted the steps and went into their room.

"Edna!" called Mr. Pontellier from within, after a few moments had gone by.

"Don't wait for me," she answered. He thrust his head through the door.

"You will take cold out there," he said, irritably. "What folly is this? Why don't you come in?"

"It isn't cold; I have my shawl."

"The mosquitoes will devour you."

"There are no mosquitoes."

She heard him moving about the room; every sound indicating impatience and irritation. Another time she would have gone in at his request. She would, through habit, have yielded to his desire; not with any sense of submission or obedience to his compelling wishes, but unthinkingly, as we walk, move, sit, stand, go through the daily treadmill of the life which has been portioned out to us.

"Edna, dear, are you not coming in soon?" he asked again, this time fondly, with a note of entreaty.

"No; I am going to stay out here."

"This is more than folly," he blurted out. "I can't permit you to stay out there all night. You must come in the house instantly."

With a writhing motion she settled herself more securely in the hammock. She perceived that her will had blazed up, stubborn and resistant. She could not at that moment have done other than denied and resisted. She wondered if her husband had ever spoken to her like that before, and if she had submitted to his command. Of course she had; she remembered that she had. But she could not realize why or how she should have yielded, feeling as she then did.

"Léonce, go to bed," she said. "I mean to stay out here. I don't wish to go in, and I don't intend to. Don't speak to me like that again; I shall not answer you."

Mr. Pontellier had prepared for bed, but he slipped on an extra garment. He opened a bottle of wine, of which he kept a small and select supply in a buffet of his own. He drank a glass of the wine and went out on the gallery and offered a glass to his wife. She did not wish any. He drew up the rocker, hoisted his slippered feet on the rail, and proceeded to smoke a cigar. He smoked two cigars; then he went inside and drank another glass of wine. Mrs. Pontellier again declined to accept a glass when it was offered to her. Mr. Pontellier once more seated himself with elevated feet, and after a reasonable interval of time smoked some more cigars.

Edna began to feel like one who awakens gradually out of a dream, a delicious, grotesque, impossible dream, to feel again the realities pressing into her soul. The physical need for sleep began to overtake her; the exuberance which had sustained and exalted her spirit left her helpless and yielding to the conditions which crowded her in.

The stillest hour of the night had come, the hour before dawn, when the world seems to hold its breath. The moon hung low, and had turned from silver to copper in the sleeping sky. The old owl no longer hooted, and the water-oaks had ceased to moan as they bent their heads.

Edna arose, cramped from lying so long and still in the hammock. She tottered up the steps, clutching feebly at the post before passing into the house.

"Are you coming in, Léonce?" she asked, turning her face toward her husband.

"Yes, dear," he answered, with a glance following a misty puff of smoke. "Just as soon as I have finished my cigar."

XII

She slept but a few hours. They were troubled and feverish hours, disturbed with dreams that were intangible, that eluded her, leaving only an impression upon her half-awakened senses of something unattainable. She was up and dressed in the cool of the early morning. The air was invigorating and steadied somewhat her faculties. However, she was not seeking refreshment or help from any source either external or from within. She was blindly following whatever impulse moved her, as if she had placed herself in alien hands for direction, and freed her soul of responsibility.

Most of the people at that early hour were still in bed and asleep. A few, who intended to go over to the *Chênière* for mass, were moving about. The lovers, who had laid their plans the night before, were already strolling toward the wharf. The lady in black with her Sunday prayer book, velvet and gold-clasped, and her Sunday silver beads, was following them at no great distance. Old Monsieur Farival was up, and was more than half inclined to do anything that suggested itself. He put on his big straw hat, and taking his umbrella from the stand in the hall, followed the lady in black, never overtaking her.

The little negro girl who worked Madame Lebrun's sewing-machine was sweeping the galleries with long, absent-minded strokes of the broom. Edna sent her up into the house to awaken Robert.

"Tell him I am going to the Chênière. The boat is ready, tell him to hurry."

He had soon joined her. She had never sent for him before. She had never asked for him. She had never seemed to want him before. She did not appear conscious that she had done anything unusual in commanding his presence. He was apparently equally unconscious of anything extraordinary in the situation. But his face was suffused with a quiet glow when he met her.

They went together back to the kitchen to drink coffee. There was no time to wait for any nicety of service. They stood outside the window and the cook passed them their coffee and a roll, which they drank and ate from the window-sill. Edna said it tasted good. She had not thought of coffee nor of anything. He told her he had often noticed that she lacked forethought.

"Wasn't it enough to think of going to the *Chênière* and waking you up?" she laughed. "Do I have to think of everything?—as Léonce says when he's in a bad humor. I don't blame him; he'd never be in a bad humor if it weren't for me."

They took a short cut across the sands. At a distance they could see the curious procession moving toward the wharf—the lovers, shoulder to shoulder, creeping; the lady in black, gaining steadily upon them; old Monsieur Farival, losing ground inch by inch, and a young barefooted Spanish girl, with a red kerchief on her head and a basket on her arm, bringing up the rear.

Robert knew the girl, and he talked to her a little in the boat. No one present understood what they said. Her name was Mariequita. She had a round, sly, piquant face and pretty black eyes. Her hands were small, and she kept them folded over the handle of her basket. Her feet were broad and coarse. She did not strive to hide them. Edna looked at her feet, and noticed the sand and slime between her brown toes.

Beaudelet grumbled because Mariequita was there, taking up so much room. In reality he was annoyed at having old Monsieur Farival, who considered himself the better sailor of the two. But he would not quarrel with so old a man as Monsieur Farival, so he quarreled with Mariequita. The girl was deprecatory at one moment, appealing to Robert. She was saucy the next, moving her head up and down, making "eyes" at Robert and making "mouths" at Beaudelet.

The lovers were all alone. They saw nothing, they heard nothing. The lady in black was counting her beads[7] for the third time. Old Monsieur Farival talked

7. Reciting a series of prayers and keeping track of them on her rosary beads.

incessantly of what he knew about handling a boat, and of what Beaudelet did not know on the same subject.

Edna liked it all. She looked Mariequita up and down, from her ugly brown toes to her pretty black eyes, and back again.

"Why does she look at me like that?" inquired the girl of Robert.

"Maybe she thinks you are pretty. Shall I ask her?"

"No. Is she your sweetheart?"

"She's a married lady, and has two children."

"Oh! well! Francisco ran away with Sylvano's wife, who had four children. They took all his money and one of the children and stole his boat."

"Shut up!"

"Does she understand?"

"Oh, hush!"

"Are those two married over there—leaning on each other?"

"Of course not," laughed Robert.

"Of course not," echoed Mariequita, with a serious, confirmatory bob of the head.

The sun was high up and beginning to bite. The swift breeze seemed to Edna to bury the sting of it into the pores of her face and hands. Robert held his umbrella over her.

As they went cutting sidewise through the water, the sails bellied taut, with the wind filling and overflowing them. Old Monsieur Farival laughed sardonically at something as he looked at the sails, and Beaudelet swore at the old man under his breath.

Sailing across the bay to the *Chênière Caminada*, Edna felt as if she were being borne away from some anchorage which had held her fast, whose chains had been loosening—had snapped the night before when the mystic spirit was abroad, leaving her free to drift whithersoever she chose to set her sails. Robert spoke to her incessantly; he no longer noticed Mariequita. The girl had shrimps in her bamboo basket. They were covered with Spanish moss. She beat the moss impatiently, and muttered to herself sullenly.

"Let us go to Grande Terre[8] to-morrow?" said Robert in a low voice.

"What shall we do there?"

"Climb up the hill to the old fort and look at the little wriggling gold snakes, and watch the lizards sun themselves."

She gazed away toward Grande Terre and thought she would like to be alone there with Robert, in the sun, listening to the ocean's roar and watching the slimy lizards writhe in and out among the ruins of the old fort.

"And the next day or the next we can sail to the Bayou Brulow,"[9] he went on.

"What shall we do there?"

"Anything—cast bait for fish."

"No; we'll go back to Grande Terre. Let the fish alone."

"We'll go wherever you like," he said. "I'll have Tonie come over and help me patch and trim my boat. We shall not need Beaudelet nor any one. Are you afraid of the pirogue?"[1]

"Oh, no."

---

8. A barrier island off coastal Louisiana.   of coastal Louisiana.
9. A village close by in the wetlands (or bayous)   1. Canoe.

"Then I'll take you some night in the pirogue when the moon shines. Maybe your Gulf spirit will whisper to you in which of these islands the treasures are hidden—direct you to the very spot, perhaps."

"And in a day we should be rich!" she laughed. "I'd give it all to you, the pirate gold and every bit of treasure we could dig up. I think you would know how to spend it. Pirate gold isn't a thing to be hoarded or utilized. It is something to squander and throw to the four winds, for the fun of seeing the golden specks fly."

"We'd share it, and scatter it together," he said. His face flushed.

They all went together up to the quaint little Gothic church of Our Lady of Lourdes, gleaming all brown and yellow with paint in the sun's glare.

Only Beaudelet remained behind, tinkering at his boat, and Mariequita walked away with her basket of shrimps, casting a look of childish ill-humor and reproach at Robert from the corner of her eye.

XIII

A feeling of oppression and drowsiness overcame Edna during the service. Her head began to ache, and the lights on the altar swayed before her eyes. Another time she might have made an effort to regain her composure; but her one thought was to quit the stifling atmosphere of the church and reach the open air. She arose, climbing over Robert's feet with a muttered apology. Old Monsieur Farival, flurried, curious, stood up, but upon seeing that Robert had followed Mrs. Pontellier, he sank back into his seat. He whispered an anxious inquiry of the lady in black, who did not notice him or reply, but kept her eyes fastened upon the pages of her velvet prayer-book.

"I felt giddy and almost overcome," Edna said, lifting her hands instinctively to her head and pushing her straw hat up from her forehead. "I couldn't have stayed through the service." They were outside in the shadow of the church. Robert was full of solicitude.

"It was folly to have thought of going in the first place, let alone staying. Come over to Madame Antoine's; you can rest there." He took her arm and led her away, looking anxiously and continuously down into her face.

How still it was, with only the voice of the sea whispering through the reeds that grew in the salt-water pools! The long line of little gray, weather-beaten houses nestled peacefully among the orange trees. It must always have been God's day on that low, drowsy island, Edna thought. They stopped, leaning over a jagged fence made of sea-drift, to ask for water. A youth, a mild-faced Acadian,[2] was drawing water from the cistern, which was nothing more than a rusty buoy, with an opening on one side, sunk in the ground. The water which the youth handed to them in a tin pail was not cold to taste, but it was cool to her heated face, and it greatly revived and refreshed her.

Madame Antoine's cot[3] was at the far end of the village. She welcomed them with all the native hospitality, as she would have opened her door to let the sunlight in. She was fat, and walked heavily and clumsily across the floor. She could speak no English, but when Robert made her understand that the lady who accompanied him was ill and desired to rest, she was all eagerness to make Edna feel at home and to dispose of her comfortably.

2. Descended from Louisiana's early French-   3. Cottage.
Canadian inhabitants, a Cajun.

The whole place was immaculately clean, and the big, four-posted bed, snow-white, invited one to repose. It stood in a small side room which looked out across a narrow grass plot toward the shed, where there was a disabled boat lying keel upward.

Madame Antoine had not gone to mass. Her son Tonie had, but she supposed he would soon be back, and she invited Robert to be seated and wait for him. But he went and sat outside the door and smoked. Madame Antoine busied herself in the large front room preparing dinner. She was boiling mullets[4] over a few red coals in the huge fireplace.

Edna, left alone in the little side room, loosened her clothes, removing the greater part of them. She bathed her face, her neck and arms in the basin that stood between the windows. She took off her shoes and stockings and stretched herself in the very center of the high, white bed. How luxurious it felt to rest thus in a strange, quaint bed, with its sweet country odor of laurel lingering about the sheets and mattress! She stretched her strong limbs that ached a little. She ran her fingers through her loosened hair for a while. She looked at her round arms as she held them straight up and rubbed them one after the other, observing closely, as if it were something she saw for the first time, the fine, firm quality and texture of her flesh. She clasped her hands easily above her head, and it was thus she fell asleep.

She slept lightly at first, half awake and drowsily attentive to the things about her. She could hear Madame Antoine's heavy, scraping tread as she walked back and forth on the sanded floor. Some chickens were clucking outside the windows, scratching for bits of gravel in the grass. Later she half heard the voices of Robert and Tonie talking under the shed. She did not stir. Even her eyelids rested numb and heavily over her sleepy eyes. The voices went on—Tonie's slow, Acadian drawl, Robert's quick, soft, smooth French. She understood French imperfectly unless directly addressed, and the voices were only part of the other drowsy, muf-fled sounds lulling her.

When Edna awoke it was with the conviction that she had slept long and soundly. The voices were hushed under the shed; Madame Antoine's step was no longer to be heard in the adjoining room. Even the chickens had gone elsewhere to scratch and cluck. The mosquito bar[5] was drawn over her; the old woman had come in while she slept and let down the bar. Edna arose quietly from the bed, and looking between the curtains of the window, she saw by the slanting rays of the sun that the afternoon was far advanced. Robert was out there under the shed, reclining in the shade against the sloping keel of the overturned boat. He was reading from a book. Tonie was no longer with him. She wondered what had be-come of the rest of the party. She peeped out at him two or three times as she stood washing herself in the little basin between the windows.

Madame Antoine had laid some coarse, clean towels upon a chair, and had placed a box of *poudre de riz*[6] within easy reach. Edna dabbed the powder upon her nose and cheeks as she looked at herself closely in the little distorted mirror which hung on the wall above the basin. Her eyes were bright and wide awake and her face glowed.

4. A small, spiny fish.
5. A frame to which mosquito netting was attached.

6. Rice powder.

When she had completed her toilet[7] she walked into the adjoining room. She was very hungry. No one was there. But there was a cloth spread upon the table that stood against the wall, and a cover was laid for one, with a crusty brown loaf and a bottle of wine beside the plate. Edna bit a piece from the brown loaf, tearing it with her strong, white teeth. She poured some of the wine into the glass and drank it down. Then she went softly out of doors, and plucking an orange from the low-hanging bough of a tree, threw it at Robert, who did not know she was awake and up.

And illumination broke over his whole face when he saw her and joined her under the orange tree.

"How many years have I slept?" she inquired. "The whole island seems changed. A new race of beings must have sprung up, leaving only you and me as past relics. How many ages ago did Madame Antoine and Tonie die? and when did our people from Grand Isle disappear from the earth?"

He familiarly adjusted a ruffle upon her shoulder.

"You have slept precisely one hundred years. I was left here to guard your slumbers; and for one hundred years I have been out under the shed reading a book. The only evil I couldn't prevent was to keep a broiled fowl from drying up."

"If it had turned to stone, still will I eat it," said Edna, moving with him into the house. "But really, what has become of Monsieur Farival and the others?"

"Gone hours ago. When they found that you were sleeping they thought it best not to awake you. Anyway, I wouldn't have let them. What was I here for?"

"I wonder if Léonce will be uneasy!" she speculated, as she seated herself at table.

"Of course not; he knows you are with me," Robert replied, as he busied himself among sundry pans and covered dishes which had been left standing on the hearth.

"Where are Madame Antoine and her son?" asked Edna.

"Gone to Vespers,[8] and to visit some friends, I believe. I am to take you back in Tonie's boat whenever you are ready to go."

He stirred the smoldering ashes till the broiled fowl began to sizzle afresh. He served her with no mean repast, dripping the coffee anew and sharing it with her. Madame Antoine had cooked little else than the mullets, but while Edna slept Robert had foraged the island. He was childishly gratified to discover her appetite, and to see the relish with which she ate the food which he had procured for her.

"Shall we go right away?" she asked, after draining her glass and brushing together the crumbs of the crusty loaf.

"The sun isn't as low as it will be in two hours," he answered.

"The sun will be gone in two hours."

"Well, let it go; who cares!"

They waited a good while under the orange trees, till Madame Antoine came back, panting, waddling, with a thousand apologies to explain her absence. Tonie did not dare to return. He was shy, and would not willingly face any woman except his mother.

It was very pleasant to stay there under the orange trees, while the sun dipped lower and lower, turning the western sky to flaming copper and gold. The shadows lengthened and crept out like stealthy, grotesque monsters across the grass.

7. Getting dressed. 8. Evening church service.

Edna and Robert both sat upon the ground—that is, he lay upon the ground beside her, occasionally picking at the hem of her muslin gown.

Madame Antoine seated her fat body, broad and squat, upon a bench beside the door. She had been talking all the afternoon, and had wound herself up to the story-telling pitch.

And what stories she told them! But twice in her life she had left the *Chênière Caminada,* and then for the briefest span. All her years she had squatted and waddled there upon the island, gathering legends of the Baratarians[9] and the sea. The night came on, with the moon to lighten it. Edna could hear the whispering voices of dead men and the click of muffled gold.

When she and Robert stepped into Tonie's boat, with the red lateen sail, misty spirit forms were prowling in the shadows and among the reeds, and upon the water were phantom ships, speeding to cover.

XIV

The youngest boy, Étienne, had been very naughty, Madame Ratignolle said, as she delivered him into the hands of his mother. He had been unwilling to go to bed and had made a scene; where upon she had taken charge of him and pacified him as well as she could. Raoul had been in bed and asleep for two hours.

The youngster was in his long white nightgown, that kept tripping him up as Madame Ratignolle led him along by the hand. With the other chubby fist he rubbed his eyes, which were heavy with sleep and ill humor. Edna took him in her arms, and seating herself in the rocker, began to coddle and caress him, calling him all manner of tender names, soothing him to sleep.

It was not more than nine o'clock. No one had yet gone to bed but the children.

Léonce had been very uneasy at first, Madame Ratignolle said, and had wanted to start at once for the *Chênière.* But Monsieur Farival had assured him that his wife was only overcome with sleep and fatigue, that Tonie would bring her safely back later in the day; and he had thus been dissuaded from crossing the bay. He had gone over to Klein's, looking up some cotton broker whom he wished to see in regard to securities, exchanges, stocks, bonds, or something of the sort, Madame Ratignolle did not remember what. He said he would not remain away late. She herself was suffering from heat and oppression, she said. She carried a bottle of salts and a large fan. She would not consent to remain with Edna, for Monsieur Ratignolle was alone, and he detested above all things to be left alone.

When Étienne had fallen asleep Edna bore him into the back room, and Robert went and lifted the mosquito bar that she might lay the child comfortably in his bed. The quadroon had vanished. When they emerged from the cottage Robert bade Edna good-night. "Do you know we have been together the whole livelong day, Robert—since early this morning?" she said at parting.

"All but the hundred years when you were sleeping. Good-night."

He pressed her hand and went away in the direction of the beach. He did not join any of the others, but walked alone toward the Gulf.

Edna stayed outside, awaiting her husband's return. She had no desire to sleep or to retire; nor did she feel like going over to sit with the Ratignolles, or to join Madame Lebrun and a group whose animated voices reached her as they sat in conversation before the house. She let her mind wander back over her stay at

---

9. Pirates who used Barataria Bay, northeast of Grande Isle, as a refuge.

Grand Isle; and she tried to discover wherein this summer had been different from any and every other summer of her life. She could only realize that she herself— her present self—was in some way different from the other self. That she was see- ing with different eyes and making the acquaintance of new conditions in herself that colored and changed her environment, she did not yet suspect.

She wondered why Robert had gone away and left her. It did not occur to her to think he might have grown tired of being with her the livelong day. She was not tired, and she felt that he was not. She regretted that he had gone. It was so much more natural to have him stay, when he was not absolutely required to leave her.

As Edna waited for her husband she sang low a little song that Robert had sung as they crossed the bay. It began with "Ah! *Si tu savais*,"[1] and every verse ended with "*si tu savais*."

Robert's voice was not pretentious. It was musical and true. The voice, the notes, the whole refrain haunted her memory.

XV

When Edna entered the dining-room one evening a little late, as was her habit, an unusually animated conversation seemed to be going on. Several persons were talking at once, and Victor's voice was predominating, even over that of his mother. Edna had returned late from her bath, had dressed in some haste, and her face was flushed. Her head, set off by the dainty white gown, suggested a rich, rare blossom. She took her seat at table between old Monsieur Farival and Madame Ratignolle.

As she seated herself and was about to begin to eat her soup, which had been served when she entered the room, several persons informed her simultaneously that Robert was going to Mexico. She laid her spoon down and looked about her bewildered. He had been with her, reading to her all the morning, and had never even mentioned such a place as Mexico. She had not seen him during the after- noon; she had heard some one say he was at the house, upstairs with his mother. This she had thought nothing of, though she was surprised when he did not join her later in the afternoon, when she went down to the beach.

She looked across at him, where he sat beside Madame Lebrun, who presided. Edna's face was a blank picture of bewilderment, which she never thought of dis- guising. He lifted his eyebrows with the pretext of a smile as he returned her glance. He looked embarrassed and uneasy.

"When is he going?" she asked of everybody in general, as if Robert were not there to answer for himself.

"To-night!" "This very evening!" "Did you ever!" "What possesses him!" some of the replies she gathered, uttered simultaneously in French and English.

"Impossible!" she exclaimed. "How can a person start off from Grand Isle to Mexico at a moment's notice, as if he were going over to Klein's or to the wharf or down to the beach?"

"I said all along I was going to Mexico; I've been saying so for years!" cried Robert, in an excited and irritable tone, with the air of a man defending himself against a swarm of stinging insects.

Madame Lebrun knocked on the table with her knife handle.

---

1. "Ah! If You Knew" (French), a song by Irish composer Michael William Balfe (1808–70).

"Please let Robert explain why he is going, and why he is going to-night," she called out. "Really, this table is getting to be more and more like Bedlam[2] every day, with everybody talking at once. Sometimes—I hope God will forgive me—but positively, sometimes I wish Victor would lose the power of speech."

Victor laughed sardonically as he thanked his mother for her holy wish, of which he failed to see the benefit to anybody, except that it might afford her a more ample opportunity and license to talk herself.

Monsieur Farival thought that Victor should have been taken out in mid-ocean in his earliest youth and drowned. Victor thought there would be more logic in thus disposing of old people with an established claim for making themselves universally obnoxious. Madame Lebrun grew a trifle hysterical; Robert called his brother some sharp, hard names.

"There's nothing much to explain, mother," he said; though he explained, nevertheless—looking chiefly at Edna—that he could only meet the gentleman whom he intended to join at Vera Cruz by taking such and such a steamer, which left New Orleans on such a day; that Beaudelet was going out with his lugger-load of vegetables that night, which gave him an opportunity of reaching the city and making his vessel in time.

"But when did you make up your mind to all this?" demanded Monsieur Farival.

"This afternoon," returned Robert, with a shade of annoyance.

"At what time this afternoon?" persisted the old gentleman, with nagging determination, as if he were cross-questioning a criminal in a court of justice.

"At four o'clock this afternoon, Monsieur Farival," Robert replied, in a high voice and with a lofty air, which reminded Edna of some gentleman on the stage.

She had forced herself to eat most of her soup, and now she was picking the flaky bits of a *court bouillon*[3] with her fork.

The lovers were profiting by the general conversation on Mexico to speak in whispers of matters which they rightly considered were interesting to no one but themselves. The lady in black had once received a pair of prayer-beads of curious workmanship from Mexico, with very special indulgence[4] attached to them, but she had never been able to ascertain whether the indulgence extended outside the Mexican border. Father Fochel of the Cathedral had attempted to explain it; but he had not done so to her satisfaction. And she begged that Robert would interest himself, and discover, if possible, whether she was entitled to the indulgence accompanying the remarkably curious Mexican prayer-beads.

Madame Ratignolle hoped that Robert would exercise extreme caution in dealing with the Mexicans, who, she considered, were a treacherous people, unscrupulous and revengeful. She trusted she did them no injustice in thus condemning them as a race. She had known personally but one Mexican, who made and sold excellent tamales, and whom she would have trusted implicitly, so soft-spoken was he. One day he was arrested for stabbing his wife. She never knew whether he had been hanged or not.

Victor had grown hilarious, and was attempting to tell an anecdote about a Mexican girl who served chocolate one winter in a restaurant in Dauphine Street. No one would listen to him but old Monsieur Farival, who went into convulsions over the droll story.

2. An asylum for the mentally ill in London.
3. Fish stew.

4. In Roman Catholicism, the remission of punishment for sin.

Edna wondered if they had all gone mad, to be talking and clamoring at that rate. She herself could think of nothing to say about Mexico or the Mexicans.

"At what time do you leave?" she asked Robert.

"At ten," he told her. "Beaudelet wants to wait for the moon."

"Are you all ready to go?"

"Quite ready. I shall only take a handbag, and shall pack my trunk in the city."

He turned to answer some question put to him by his mother and Edna, having finished her black coffee, left the table.

She went directly to her room. The little cottage was close and stuffy after leaving the outer air. But she did not mind; there appeared to be a hundred different things demanding her attention indoors. She began to set the toilet-stand to rights, grumbling at the negligence of the quadroon, who was in the adjoining room putting the children to bed. She gathered together stray garments that were hanging on the backs of chairs, and put each where it belonged in closet or bureau drawer. She changed her gown for a more comfortable and commodious wrapper. She rearranged her hair, combing and brushing it with unusual energy. Then she went in and assisted the quadroon in getting the boys to bed.

They were very playful and inclined to talk—to do anything but lie quiet and go to sleep. Edna sent the quadroon away to her supper and told her she need not return. Then she sat and told the children a story. Instead of soothing it excited them, and added to their wakefulness. She left them in heated argument, speculating about the conclusion of the tale which their mother promised to finish the following night.

The little black girl came in to say that Madame Lebrun would like to have Mrs. Pontellier go and sit with them over at the house till Mr. Robert went away. Edna returned answer that she had already undressed, that she did not feel quite well, but perhaps she would go over to the house later. She started to dress again, and got as far advanced as to remove her *peignoir.* But changing her mind once more she resumed the *peignoir,* and went outside and sat down before her door. She was overheated and irritable, and fanned herself energetically for a while. Madame Ratignolle came down to discover what was the matter.

"All that noise and confusion at the table must have upset me," replied Edna, "and moreover, I hate shocks and surprises. The idea of Robert starting off in such a ridiculously sudden and dramatic way! As if it were a matter of life and death! Never saying a word about it all morning when he was with me."

"Yes," agreed Madame Ratignolle. "I think it was showing us all—you especially—very little consideration. It wouldn't have surprised me in any of the others; those Lebruns are all given to heroics. But I must say I should never have expected such a thing from Robert. Are you not coming down? Come on, dear; it doesn't look friendly."

"No," said Edna, a little sullenly. "I can't go to the trouble of dressing again; I don't feel like it."

"You needn't dress; you look all right; fasten a belt around your waist. Just look at me!"

"No," persisted Edna; "but you go on. Madame Lebrun might be offended if we both stayed away."

Madame Ratignolle kissed Edna good-night, and went away, being in truth rather desirous of joining in the general and animated conversation which was still in progress concerning Mexico and the Mexicans.

Somewhat later Robert came up, carrying his hand-bag.

"Aren't you feeling well?" he asked.

"Oh, well enough. Are you going right away?"

He lit a match and looked at his watch. "In twenty minutes," he said. The sudden and brief flare of the match emphasized the darkness for a while. He sat down upon a stool which the children had left out on the porch.

"Get a chair," said Edna.

"This will do," he replied. He put on his soft hat and nervously took it off again, and wiping his face with his handkerchief, complained of the heat.

"Take the fan," said Edna, offering it to him.

"Oh, no! Thank you. It does no good; you have to stop fanning some time, and feel all the more uncomfortable afterward."

"That's one of the ridiculous things which men always say. I have never known one to speak otherwise of fanning. How long will you be gone?"

"Forever, perhaps. I don't know. It depends upon a good many things."

"Well, in case it shouldn't be forever, how long will it be?"

"I don't know."

"This seems to me perfectly preposterous and uncalled for. I don't like it. I don't understand your motive for silence and mystery, never saying a word to me about it this morning." He remained silent, not offering to defend himself. He only said, after a moment:

"Don't part from me in an ill-humor. I never knew you to be out of patience with me before."

"I don't want to part in any ill-humor," said she. "But can't you understand? I've grown used to seeing you, to having you with me all the time, and your action seems unfriendly, even unkind. You don't even offer an excuse for it. Why, I was planning to be together, thinking of how pleasant it would be to see you in the city next winter."

"So was I," he blurted. "Perhaps that's the—" He stood up suddenly and held out his hand. "Good-by, my dear Mrs. Pontellier; good-by. You won't—I hope you won't completely forget me." She clung to his hand, striving to detain him.

"Write to me when you get there, won't you, Robert?" she entreated.

"I will, thank you. Good-by."

How unlike Robert! The merest acquaintance would have said something more emphatic than "I will, thank you; good-by," to such a request.

He had evidently already taken leave of the people over at the house, for he descended the steps and went to join Beaudelet, who was out there with an oar across his shoulder waiting for Robert. They walked away in the darkness. She could only hear Beaudelet's voice; Robert had apparently not even spoken a word of greeting to his companion.

Edna bit her handkerchief convulsively, striving to hold back and to hide, even from herself as she would have hidden from another the emotion which was troubling—tearing—her. Her eyes were brimming with tears.

For the first time she recognized anew the symptoms of infatuation which she felt incipiently as a child, as a girl in her earliest teens, and later as a young woman. The recognition did not lessen the reality, the poignancy of the revelation by any suggestion or promise of instability. The past was nothing to her; offered no lesson which she was willing to heed. The future was a mystery which she never attempted to penetrate. The present alone was significant; was hers, to torture her as it was doing then with the biting conviction that she had lost that which she had held, that she had been denied that which her impassioned, newly awakened being demanded.

XVI

"Do you miss your friend greatly?" asked Mademoiselle Reisz one morning as she came creeping up behind Edna, who had just left her cottage on her way to the beach. She spent much of her time in the water since she had acquired finally the art of swimming. As their stay at Grand Isle drew near its close, she felt that she could not give too much time to a diversion which afforded her the only real pleasurable moments that she knew. When Mademoiselle Reisz came and touched her upon the shoulder and spoke to her, the woman seemed to echo the thought which was ever in Edna's mind; or, better, the feeling which constantly possessed her.

Robert's going had some way taken the brightness, the color, the meaning out of everything. The conditions of her life were in no way changed, but her whole existence was dulled, like a faded garment which seems to be no longer worth wearing. She sought him everywhere—in others whom she induced to talk about him. She went up in the mornings to Madame Lebrun's room, braving the clatter of the old sewing-machine. She sat there and chatted at intervals as Robert had done. She gazed around the room at the pictures and photographs hanging upon the wall, and discovered in some corner an old family album, which she examined with the keenest interest, appealing to Madame Lebrun for enlightenment concerning the many figures and faces which she discovered between its pages.

There was a picture of Madame Lebrun with Robert as a baby, seated in her lap, a round-faced infant with a fist in his mouth. The eyes alone in the baby suggested the man. And that was he also in kilts,[5] at the age of five, wearing long curls and holding a whip in his hand. It made Edna laugh, and she laughed, too, at the portrait in his first long trousers; while another interested her, taken when he left for college, looking thin, long-faced, with eyes full of fire, ambition and great intentions. But there was no recent picture, none which suggested the Robert who had gone away five days ago, leaving a void and wilderness behind him.

"Oh, Robert stopped having his pictures taken when he had to pay for them himself! He found wiser use for his money, he says," explained Madame Lebrun. She had a letter from him, written before he left New Orleans. Edna wished to see the letter, and Madame Lebrun told her to look for it either on the table or the dresser, or perhaps it was on the mantelpiece.

The letter was on the bookshelf. It possessed the greatest interest and attraction for Edna; the envelope, its size and shape, the postmark, the handwriting. She examined every detail of the outside before opening it. There were only a few lines, setting forth that he would leave the city that afternoon, that he had packed his trunk in good shape, that he was well, and sent her his love and begged to be affectionately remembered to all. There was no special message to Edna except a postscript saying that if Mrs. Pontellier desired to finish the book which he had been reading to her, his mother would find it in his room, among other books there on the table. Edna experienced a pang of jealousy because he had written to his mother rather than to her.

5. Through the early twentieth century, young children of both sexes wore dresslike clothing. Boys would then be put into shorts before being allowed to wear long pants.

Every one seemed to take for granted that she missed him. Even her husband, when he came down the Saturday following Robert's departure, expressed regret that he had gone.

"How do you get on without him, Edna?" he asked.

"It's very dull without him," she admitted. Mr. Pontellier had seen Robert in the city, and Edna asked him a dozen questions or more. Where had they met? On Carondelet Street, in the morning. They had gone "in" and had a drink and a cigar together. What had they talked about? Chiefly about his prospects in Mexico, which Mr. Pontellier thought were promising. How did he look? How did he seem—grave, or gay, or how? Quite cheerful, and wholly taken up with the idea of his trip, which Mr. Pontellier found altogether natural in a young fellow about to seek fortune and adventure in a strange, queer country.

Edna tapped her foot impatiently, and wondered why the children persisted in playing in the sun when they might be under the trees. She went down and led them out of the sun, scolding the quadroon for not being more attentive.

It did not strike her as in the least grotesque that she should be making of Robert the object of conversation and leading her husband to speak of him. The sentiment which she entertained for Robert in no way resembled that which she felt for her husband, or had ever felt, or ever expected to feel. She had all her life long been accustomed to harbor thoughts and emotions which never voiced themselves. They had never taken the form of struggles. They belonged to her and were her own, and she entertained the conviction that she had a right to them and that they concerned no one but herself. Edna had once told Madame Ratignolle that she would never sacrifice herself for her children, or for any one. Then had followed a rather heated argument; the two women did not appear to understand each other or to be talking the same language. Edna tried to appease her friend, to explain.

"I would give up the unessential; I would give my money. I would give my life for my children; but I wouldn't give myself. I can't make it more clear; it's only something which I am beginning to comprehend, which is revealing itself to me."

"I don't know what you would call the essential, or what you mean by the unessential," said Madame Ratignolle, cheerfully; "but a woman who would give her life for her children could do no more than that—your Bible tells you so. I'm sure I couldn't do more than that."

"Oh, yes you could!" laughed Edna.

She was not surprised at Mademoiselle Reisz's question the morning that lady, following her to the beach, tapped her on the shoulder and asked if she did not greatly miss her young friend.

"Oh, good morning, Mademoiselle; it is you? Why, of course I miss Robert. Are you going down to bathe?"

"Why should I go down to bathe at the very end of the season when I haven't been in the surf all summer?" replied the woman, disagreeably.

"I beg your pardon," offered Edna, in some embarrassment, for she should have remembered that Mademoiselle Reisz's avoidance of the water had furnished a theme for much pleasantry. Some among them thought it was on account of her false hair, or the dread of getting the violets wet, while others attributed it to the natural aversion for water sometimes believed to accompany the artistic temperament. Mademoiselle offered Edna some chocolates in a paper bag, which she took from her pocket, by way of showing that she bore no ill feeling. She habitually ate chocolates for their sustaining quality; they contained much nutriment in small compass, she said. They saved her from starvation, as Madame Lebrun's table was utterly impossible; and no one save so impertinent a woman as Madame Lebrun could think of offering such food to people and requiring them to pay for it.

"She must feel very lonely without her son," said Edna, desiring to change the subject. "Her favorite son, too. It must have been quite hard to let him go."

Mademoiselle laughed maliciously.

"Her favorite son! Oh dear! Who could have been imposing such a tale upon you? Aline Lebrun lives for Victor, and for Victor alone. She has spoiled him into the worthless creature he is. She worships him and the ground he walks on. Robert is very well in a way, to give up all the money he can earn to the family, and keep the barest pittance for himself. Favorite son, indeed! I miss the poor fellow myself, my dear. I liked to see him and to hear him about the place—the only Lebrun who is worth a pinch of salt. He comes to see me often in the city. I like to play to him. That Victor! hanging would be too good for him. It's a wonder Robert hasn't beaten him to death long ago."

"I thought he had great patience with his brother," offered Edna, glad to be talking about Robert, no matter what was said.

"Oh! he thrashed him well enough a year or two ago," said Mademoiselle. "It was about a Spanish girl, whom Victor considered that he had some sort of claim upon. He met Robert one day talking to the girl, or walking with her, or bathing with her, or carrying her basket—I don't remember what;—and he became so insulting and abusive that Robert gave him a thrashing on the spot that has kept him comparatively in order for a good while. It's about time he was getting another."

"Was her name Mariequita?" asked Edna.

"Mariequita—yes, that was it. Mariequita. I had forgotten. Oh, she's a sly one, and a bad one, that Mariequita!"

Edna looked down at Mademoiselle Reisz and wondered how she could have listened to her venom so long. For some reason she felt depressed, almost unhappy. She had not intended to go into the water; but she donned her bathing suit, and left Mademoiselle alone, seated under the shade of the children's tent. The water was growing cooler as the season advanced. Edna plunged and swam about with an abandon that thrilled and invigorated her. She remained a long time in the water, half hoping that Mademoiselle Reisz would not wait for her.

But Mademoiselle waited. She was very amiable during the walk back, and raved much over Edna's appearance in her bathing suit. She talked about music. She hoped that Edna would go to see her in the city, and wrote her address with the stub of a pencil on a piece of card which she found in her pocket.

"When do you leave?" asked Edna.

"Next Monday; and you?"

"The following week," answered Edna, adding, "It has been a pleasant summer, hasn't it, Mademoiselle?"

"Well," agreed Mademoiselle Reisz, with a shrug, "rather pleasant, if it hadn't been for the mosquitoes and the Farival twins."

XVII

The Pontelliers possessed a very charming home on Esplanade Street[6] in New Orleans. It was a large, double cottage, with a broad front veranda, whose round, fluted columns supported the sloping roof. The house was painted a dazzling

6. An exclusive address.

white; the outside shutters, or jalousies, were green. In the yard, which was kept scrupulously neat, were flowers and plants of every description which flourishes in South Louisiana. Within doors the appointments were perfect after the conventional type. The softest carpets and rugs covered the floors; rich and tasteful draperies hung at doors and windows. There were paintings, selected with judgment and discrimination, upon the walls. The cut glass, the silver, the heavy damask which daily appeared upon the table were the envy of many women whose husbands were less generous than Mr. Pontellier.

Mr. Pontellier was very fond of walking about his house examining its various appointments and details, to see that nothing was amiss. He greatly valued his possessions, chiefly because they were his, and derived genuine pleasure from contemplating a painting, a statuette, a rare lace curtain—no matter what—after he had bought it and placed it among his household goods.

On Tuesday afternoons—Tuesday being Mrs. Pontellier's reception day[7]— there was a constant stream of callers—women who came in carriages or in the street cars, or walked when the air was soft and distance permitted. A light-colored mulatto boy, in dress coat and bearing a diminutive silver tray for the reception of cards, admitted them. A maid, in white fluted cap, offered the callers liqueur, coffee, or chocolate, as they might desire. Mrs. Pontellier, attired in a handsome reception gown, remained in the drawing-room the entire afternoon receiving her visitors. Men sometimes called in the evening with their wives.

This had been the programme which Mrs. Pontellier had religiously followed since her marriage, six years before. Certain evenings during the week she and her husband attended the opera or sometimes the play.

Mr. Pontellier left his home in the mornings between nine and ten o'clock, and rarely returned before half-past six or seven in the evening—dinner being served at half-past seven.

He and his wife seated themselves at table on Tuesday evening, a few weeks after their return from Grand Isle. They were alone together. The boys were being put to bed; the patter of their bare, escaping feet could be heard occasionally, as well as the pursuing voice of the quadroon, lifted in mild protest and entreaty. Mrs. Pontellier did not wear her usual Tuesday reception gown; she was in ordinary house dress. Mr. Pontellier who was observant about such things, noticed it, as he served the soup and handed it to the boy in waiting.

"Tired out, Edna? Whom did you have? Many callers?" he asked. He tasted his soup and began to season it with pepper, salt, vinegar, mustard—everything within reach.

"There were a good many," replied Edna, who was eating her soup with evident satisfaction. "I found their cards[8] when I got home; I was out."

"Out!" exclaimed her husband, with something like genuine consternation in his voice as he laid down the vinegar cruet and looked at her through his glasses. "Why, what could have taken you out on Tuesday? What did you have to do?"

"Nothing. I simply felt like going out, and I went out."

"Well, I hope you left some suitable excuse," said her husband, somewhat appeased, as he added a dash of cayenne pepper to the soup.

"No, I left no excuse. I told Joe to say I was out, that was all."

7. The day when she would receive visitors who dropped in.

8. Cards that would be dropped off to acknowledge a visit (see p. 612).

"Why, my dear, I should think you'd understand by this time that people don't do such things; we've got to observe *les convenances*[9] if we ever expect to get on and keep up with procession. If you felt that you had to leave home this afternoon, you should have left some suitable explanation for your absence.

"This soup is really impossible; it's strange that woman hasn't learned yet to make a decent soup. Any free-lunch stand in town serves a better one. Was Mrs. Belthrop here?"

"Bring the tray with cards, Joe. I don't remember who was here."

The boy retired and returned after a moment, bringing the tiny silver tray, which was covered with ladies' visiting cards. He handed it to Mrs. Pontellier.

"Give it to Mr. Pontellier," she said.

Joe offered the tray to Mr. Pontellier, and removed the soup.

Mr. Pontellier scanned the names of his wife's callers, reading some of them aloud, with comments as he read.

" 'The Misses Delasidas.' I worked a big deal in futures[1] for their father this morning; nice girls; it's time they were getting married. 'Mrs. Belthrop.' I tell you what it is, Edna; you can't afford to snub Mrs. Belthrop. Why, Belthrop could buy and sell us ten times over. His business is worth a good, round sum to me. You'd better write her a note. 'Mrs. James Highcamp.' Hugh! the less you have to do with Mrs. Highcamp, the better. 'Madame Laforcé.' Came all the way from Carrolton,[2] too, poor old soul. 'Miss Wiggs,' 'Mrs. Eleanor Boltons.' " He pushed the cards aside.

"Mercy!" exclaimed Edna, who had been fuming. "Why are you taking the thing so seriously and making such a fuss over it?"

"I'm not making any fuss over it. But it's just such seeming trifles that we've got to take seriously; such things count."

The fish was scorched. Mr. Pontellier would not touch it. Edna said she did not mind a little scorched taste. The roast was in some way not to his fancy, and he did not like the manner in which the vegetables were served.

"It seems to me," he said, "we spend money enough in this house to procure at least one meal a day which a man could eat and retain his self-respect."

"You used to think the cook was a treasure," returned Edna, indifferently.

"Perhaps she was when she first came; but cooks are only human. They need looking after, like any other class of persons that you employ. Suppose I didn't look after the clerks in my office, just let them run things their own way; they'd soon make a nice mess of me and my business."

"Where are you going?" asked Edna, seeing that her husband arose from table without having eaten a morsel except a taste of the highly-seasoned soup.

"I'm going to get my dinner at the club. Good night." He went into the hall, took his hat and stick from the stand, and left the house.

She was somewhat familiar with such scenes. They had often made her very unhappy. On a few previous occasions she had been completely deprived of any desire to finish her dinner. Sometimes she had gone into the kitchen to administer a tardy rebuke to the cook. Once she went to her room and studied the cookbook during an entire evening, finally writing out a menu for the week, which left her

9. The conventions.
1. Items purchased at today's prices for delivery later; a type of speculation.

2. Then a village on the outskirts of New Orleans.

harassed with a feeling that, after all, she had accomplished no good that was worth the name.

But that evening Edna finished her dinner alone, with forced deliberation. Her face was flushed and her eyes flamed with some inward fire that lighted them. After finishing her dinner she went to her room, having instructed the boy to tell any other callers that she was indisposed.

It was a large, beautiful room, rich and picturesque in the soft, dim light which the maid had turned low. She went and stood at an open window and looked out upon the deep tangle of the garden below. All the mystery and witchery of the night seemed to have gathered there amid the perfumes and the dusky and tortuous outlines of flowers and foliage. She was seeking herself and finding herself in just such sweet, half-darkness which met her moods. But the voices were not soothing that came to her from the darkness and the sky above and the stars. They jeered and sounded mournful notes without promise, devoid even of hope. She turned back into the room and began to walk to and fro down its whole length, without stopping, without resting. She carried in her hands a thin handkerchief, which she tore into ribbons, rolled into a ball, and flung from her. Once she stopped, and taking off her wedding ring, flung it upon the carpet. When she saw it lying there, she stamped her heel upon it, striving to crush it. But her small boot heel did not make an indenture, not a mark upon the little glittering circlet.

In a sweeping passion she seized a glass vase from the table and flung it upon the tiles of the hearth. She wanted to destroy something. The crash and clatter were what she wanted to hear.

A maid, alarmed at the din of breaking glass, entered the room to discover what was the matter.

"A vase fell upon the hearth," said Edna. "Never mind; leave it till morning."

"Oh! you might get some of the glass in your feet, ma'am," insisted the young woman, picking up bits of the broken vase that were scattered upon the carpet. "And here's your ring, ma'am, under the chair."

Edna held out her hand, and taking the ring, slipped it upon her finger.

XVIII

The following morning Mr. Pontellier, upon leaving for his office, asked Edna if she would not meet him in town in order to look at some new fixtures for the library.

"I hardly think we need new fixtures, Léonce. Don't let us get anything new; you are too extravagant. I don't believe you ever think of saving or putting by."

"The way to become rich is to make money, my dear Edna, not to save it," he said. He regretted that she did not feel inclined to go with him and select new fixtures. He kissed her good-by, and told her she was not looking well and must take care of herself. She was unusually pale and very quiet.

She stood on the front veranda as he quitted the house, and absently picked a few sprays of jessamine that grew upon a trellis near by. She inhaled the odor of the blossoms and thrust them into the bosom of her white morning gown. The boys were dragging along the banquette a small "express wagon,"[3] which they had filled with block and sticks. The quadroon was following them with little

---

3. Jessamine: jasmine; banquette: a raised side-walk; express wagon: a child's toy, such as a red   Radio Flyer wagon.

quick steps, having assumed a fictitious animation and alacrity for the occasion. A fruit vender was crying his wares in the street.

Edna looked straight before her with a self-absorbed expression upon her face. She felt no interest in anything about her. The street, the children, the fruit vender, the flowers growing there under her eyes, were all part and parcel of an alien world which had suddenly become antagonistic.

She went back into the house. She had thought of speaking to the cook concerning her blunders of the previous night; but Mr. Pontellier had saved her that disagreeable mission, for which she was so poorly fitted. Mr. Pontellier's arguments were usually convincing with those whom he employed. He left home feeling quite sure that he and Edna would sit down that evening, and possibly a few subsequent evenings, to a dinner deserving of the name.

Edna spent an hour or two looking over some of her old sketches. She could see their shortcomings and defects, which were glaring in her eyes. She tried to work a little, but found she was not in the humor. Finally she gathered together a few of the sketches—those which she considered the least discreditable; and she carried them with her when, a little later, she dressed and left the house. She looked handsome and distinguished in her street gown. The tan of the seashore had left her face, and her forehead was smooth, white, and polished beneath her heavy, yellow-brown hair. There were a few freckles on her face, and a small, dark mole near the under lip and one on the temple, half-hidden in her hair.

As Edna walked along the street she was thinking of Robert. She was still under the spell of her infatuation. She had tried to forget him, realizing the inutility of remembering. But the thought of him was like an obsession, ever pressing itself upon her. It was not that she dwelt upon details of their acquaintance, or recalled in any special or peculiar way his personality; it was his being, his existence, which dominated her thought, fading sometimes as if it would melt into the mist of the forgotten, reviving again with an intensity which filled her with an incomprehensible longing.

Edna was on her way to Madame Ratignolle's. Their intimacy, begun at Grand Isle, had not declined, and they had seen each other with some frequency since their return to the city. The Ratignolles lived at no great distance from Edna's home, on the corner of a side street, where Monsieur Ratignolle owned and conducted a drug store which enjoyed a steady and prosperous trade. His father had been in the business before him, and Monsieur Ratignolle stood well in the community and bore an enviable reputation for integrity and clear-headedness. His family lived in commodious apartments over the store, having an entrance on the side within the *porte cochère*.[4] There was something which Edna thought very French, very foreign, about their whole manner of living. In the large and pleasant salon which extended across the width of the house, the Ratignolles entertained their friends once a fortnight with a *soirée musicale*,[5] sometimes diversified by card-playing. There was a friend who played upon the cello. One brought his flute and another his violin, while there were some who sang and a number who performed upon the piano with various degrees of taste and agility. The Ratignolles' *soirées musicales* were widely known, and it was considered a privilege to be invited to them.

4. A covered entranceway.　　　　　　　　5. An evening party with music.

Edna found her friend engaged in assorting the clothes which had returned that morning from the laundry. She at once abandoned her occupation upon seeing Edna, who had been ushered without ceremony into her presence.

"'Cité can do it as well as I; it is really her business," she explained to Edna, who apologized for interrupting her. And she summoned a young black woman, whom she instructed, in French, to be very careful in checking off the list which she handed her. She told her to notice particularly if a fine linen handkerchief of Monsieur Ratignolle's, which was missing last week, had been returned; and to be sure to set to one side such pieces as required mending and darning.

Then placing an arm around Edna's waist, she led her to the front of the house, to the salon, where it was cool and sweet with the odor of great roses that stood upon the hearth in jars.

Madame Ratignolle looked more beautiful than ever there at home, in a negligé which left her arms almost wholly bare and exposed the rich, melting curves of her white throat.

"Perhaps I shall be able to paint your picture some day," said Edna with a smile when they were seated. She produced the roll of sketches and started to unfold them. "I believe I ought to work again. I feel as if I wanted to be doing something. What do you think of them? Do you think it worth while to take it up again and study some more? I might study for a while with Laidpore."

She knew that Madame Ratignolle's opinion in such a matter would be next to valueless, that she herself had not alone decided, but determined; but she sought the words and praise and encouragement that would help her to put her heart into her venture.

"Your talent is immense, dear!"

"Nonsense!" protested Edna, well pleased.

"Immense, I tell you," persisted Madame Ratignolle, surveying the sketches one by one, at close range, then holding them at arm's length, narrowing her eyes, and dropping her head on one side. "Surely, this Bavarian peasant is worthy of framing; and this basket of apples! never have I seen anything more life-like. One might almost be tempted to reach out a hand and take one."

Edna could not control a feeling which bordered upon complacency at her friend's praise, even realizing, as she did, its true worth. She retained a few of the sketches, and gave all the rest to Madame Ratignolle, who appreciated the gift far beyond its value and proudly exhibited the pictures to her husband when he came up from the store a little later for his midday dinner.

Mr. Ratignolle was one of those men who are called the salt of the earth. His cheerfulness was unbounded, and it was matched by his goodness of heart, his broad charity, and common sense. He and his wife spoke English with an accent which was only discernible through its un-English emphasis and a certain carefulness and deliberation. Edna's husband spoke English with no accent whatever. The Ratignolles understood each other perfectly. If ever the fusion of two human beings into one has been accomplished on this sphere it was surely in their union.

As Edna seated herself at table with them she thought, "Better a dinner of herbs,"[6] though it did not take her long to discover that was no dinner of herbs, but a delicious repast, simple, choice, and in every way satisfying.

6. See Proverbs 15:17: "Better a dinner with herbs where love is, than a stalled ox and hatred therewith."

Monsieur Ratignolle was delighted to see her, though he found her looking not so well as at Grand Isle, and he advised a tonic. He talked a good deal on various topics, a little politics, some city news and neighborhood gossip. He spoke with an animation and earnestness that gave an exaggerated importance to every syllable he uttered. His wife was keenly interested in everything he said, laying down her fork the better to listen, chiming in, taking the words out of his mouth.

Edna felt depressed rather than soothed after leaving them. The little glimpse of domestic harmony which had been offered her, gave her no regret, no longing. It was not a condition of life which fitted her, and she could see in it but an appalling and hopeless ennui. She was moved by a kind of commiseration for Madame Ratignolle,—a pity for that colorless existence which never uplifted its possessor beyond the region of blind contentment, in which no moment of anguish ever visited her soul, in which she would never have the taste of life's delirium. Edna vaguely wondered what she meant by "life's delirium." It had crossed her thought like some unsought, extraneous impression.

XIX

Edna could not help but think that it was very foolish, very childish, to have stamped upon her wedding ring and smashed the crystal vase upon the tiles. She was visited by no more outbursts, moving her to such futile expedients. She began to do as she liked and to feel as she liked. She completely abandoned her Tuesdays at home, and did not return the visits of those who had called upon her. She made no ineffectual efforts to conduct her household *en bonne ménagère*,[7] going and coming as it suited her fancy, and, so far as she was able, lending herself to any passing caprice.

Mr. Pontellier had been a rather courteous husband so long as he met a certain tacit submissiveness in his wife. But her new and unexpected line of conduct completely bewildered him. It shocked him. Then her absolute disregard for her duties as a wife angered him. When Mr. Pontellier became rude, Edna grew insolent. She had resolved never to take another step backward.

"It seems to me the utmost folly for a woman at the head of a household, and the mother of children, to spend in an atelier[8] days which would be better employed contriving for the comfort of her family."

"I feel like painting," answered Edna. "Perhaps I shan't always feel like it."

"Then in God's name paint! but don't let the family go to the devil. There's Madame Ratignolle; because she keeps up her music, she doesn't let everything go to chaos. And she's more of a musician than you are a painter."

"She isn't a musician, and I'm not a painter. It isn't on account of painting that I let things go."

"On account of what, then?"

"Oh! I don't know. Let me alone; you bother me."

It sometimes entered Mr. Pontellier's mind to wonder if his wife were not growing a little unbalanced mentally. He could see plainly that she was not herself. That is, he could not see that she was becoming herself and daily casting aside that fictitious self which we assume like a garment with which to appear before the world.

---

7. As a good housewife.   8. An artist's studio.

Her husband let her alone as she requested, and went away to his office. Edna went up to her atelier—a bright room in the top of the house. She was working with great energy and interest, without accomplishing anything, however, which satisfied her even in the smallest degree. For a time she had the whole household enrolled in the service of art. The boys posed for her. They thought it amusing at first, but the occupation soon lost its attractiveness when they discovered that it was not a game arranged especially for their entertainment. The quadroon sat for hours before Edna's palette, patient as a savage, while the housemaid took charge of the children, and the drawing-room went undusted. But the house-maid, too, served her term as model when Edna perceived that the young woman's back and shoulders were molded on classic lines, and that her hair, loosened from its confining cap, became an inspiration. While Edna worked she sometimes sang low the little air, "*Ah! si tu savais!*"

It moved her with recollections. She could hear again the ripple of the water, the flapping sail. She could see the glint of the moon upon the bay, and could feel the soft, gusty beating of the hot south wind. A subtle current of desire passed through her body, weakening her hold upon the brushes and making her eyes burn.

There were days when she was very happy without knowing why. She was happy to be alive and breathing, when her whole being seemed to be one with the sunlight, the color, the odors, the luxuriant warmth of some perfect Southern day. She liked then to wander alone into strange and unfamiliar places. She discovered many a sunny, sleepy corner, fashioned to dream in. And she found it good to dream and to be alone and unmolested.

There were days when she was unhappy, she did not know why,—when it did not seem worth while to be glad or sorry, to be alive or dead; when life appeared to her like a grotesque pandemonium and humanity like worms struggling blindly toward inevitable annihilation. She could not work on such a day, nor weave fancies to stir her pulses and warm her blood.

XX

It was during such a mood that Edna hunted up Mademoiselle Reisz. She had not forgotten the rather disagreeable impression left upon her by their last interview; but she nevertheless felt a desire to see her—above all, to listen while she played upon the piano. Quite early in the afternoon she started upon her quest for the pianist. Unfortunately she had mislaid or lost Mademoiselle Reisz's card, and looking up her address in the city directory, she found that the woman lived on Bienville Street, some distance away. The directory which fell into her hands was a year or more old, however, and upon reaching the number indicated, Edna discovered that the house was occupied by a respectable family of mulattoes who had *chambres garnies*[9] to let. They had been living there for six months, and knew absolutely nothing of a Mademoiselle Reisz. In fact, they knew nothing of any of their neighbors; their lodgers were all people of the highest distinction, they assured Edna. She did not linger to discuss class distinctions with Madame Pouponne, but hastened to a neighboring grocery store, feeling sure that Mademoiselle would have left her address with the proprietor.

He knew Mademoiselle Reisz a good deal better than he wanted to know her, he informed his questioner. In truth, he did not want to know her at all, anything

9. Furnished rooms.

concerning her—the most disagreeable and unpopular woman who ever lived in Bienville Street. He thanked heaven she had left the neighborhood, and was equally thankful that he did not know where she had gone.

Edna's desire to see Mademoiselle Reisz had increased tenfold since these unlooked for obstacles had arisen to thwart it. She was wondering who could give her the information she sought, when it suddenly occurred to her that Madame Lebrun would be the one most likely to do so. She knew it was useless to ask Madame Ratignolle, who was on the most distant terms with the musician, and preferred to know nothing concerning her. She had once been almost as emphatic in expressing herself upon the subject as the corner grocer.

Edna knew that Madame Lebrun had returned to the city, for it was the middle of November. And she also knew where the Lebruns lived, on Chartres Street.

Their home from the outside looked like a prison, with iron bars before the door and lower windows. The iron bars were a relic of the old *régime*,[1] and no one had ever thought of dislodging them. At the side was a high fence enclosing the garden. A gate or door opening upon the street was locked. Edna rang the bell at this side garden gate, and stood upon the banquette, waiting to be admitted.

It was Victor who opened the gate for her. A black woman, wiping her hands upon her apron, was close at his heels. Before she saw them Edna could hear them in altercation, the woman—plainly an anomaly—claiming the right to be allowed to perform her duties, one of which was to answer the bell.

Victor was surprised and delighted to see Mrs. Pontellier, and he made no attempt to conceal either his astonishment or his delight. He was a dark-browed, good-looking youngster of nineteen, greatly resembling his mother, but with ten times her impetuosity. He instructed the black woman to go at once and inform Madame Lebrun that Mrs. Pontellier desired to see her. The woman grumbled a refusal to do part of her duty when she had not been permitted to do it all, and started back to her interrupted task of weeding the garden. Whereupon Victor administered a rebuke in the form of a volley of abuse, which owing to its rapidity and incoherence, was all but incomprehensible to Edna. Whatever it was, the rebuke was convincing, for the woman dropped her hoe and went mumbling into the house.

Edna did not wish to enter. It was very pleasant there on the side porch, where there were chairs, a wicker lounge, and a small table. She seated herself, for she was tired from her long tramp; and she began to rock gently and smooth out the folds of her silk parasol. Victor drew up his chair beside her. He at once explained that the black woman's offensive conduct was all due to imperfect training, as he was not there to take her in hand. He had only come up from the island the morning before, expected to return next day. He stayed all winter at the island; he lived there, and kept the place in order and got things ready for the summer visitors.

But a man needed occasional relaxation, he informed Mrs. Pontellier, and every now and again he drummed up a pretext to bring him to the city. My! but he had had a time of it the evening before! He wouldn't want his mother to know, and he began to talk in a whisper. He was scintillant with recollections. Of course, he couldn't think of telling Mrs. Pontellier all about it, she being a woman and not comprehending such things. But it all began with a girl peeping and smiling at

1. In the style of the Spanish, who controlled the region 1766–1803.

him through the shutters as he passed by. Oh! but she was a beauty! Certainly he smiled back, and went up and talked to her. Mrs. Pontellier did not know him if she supposed he was one to let an opportunity like that escape him. Despite herself, the youngster amused her. She must have betrayed in her look some degree of interest or entertainment. The boy grew more daring, and Mrs. Pontellier might have found herself, in a little while, listening to a highly colored story but for the timely appearance of Madame Lebrun.

That lady was still clad in white, according to her custom of the summer. Her eyes beamed an effusive welcome. Would not Mrs. Pontellier go inside? Would she partake of some refreshment? Why had she not been there before? How was that dear Mr. Pontellier and how were those sweet children? Had Mrs. Pontellier ever known such a warm November?

Victor went and reclined on the wicker lounge behind his mother's chair, where he commanded a view of Edna's face. He had taken her parasol from her hands while he spoke to her, and he now lifted it and twirled it above him as he lay on his back. When Madame Lebrun complained that it was so dull coming back to the city; that she saw so few people now; that even Victor, when he came up from the island for a day or two, had so much to occupy him and engage his time, then it was that the youth went into contortions on the lounge and winked mischievously at Edna. She somehow felt like a confederate in crime, and tried to look severe and disapproving.

There had been but two letters from Robert, with little in them they told her. Victor said it was really not worth while to go inside for the letters, when his mother entreated him to go in search of them. He remembered the contents, which in truth he rattled off very glibly when put to the test.

One letter was written from Vera Cruz and the other from the City of Mexico. He had met Montel, who was doing everything toward his advancement. So far, the financial situation was no improvement over the one he had left in New Orleans, but of course the prospects were vastly better. He wrote of the City of Mexico, the buildings, the people and their habits, the conditions of life which he found there. He sent his love to the family. He inclosed a check to his mother, and hoped she would affectionately remember him to all his friends. That was about the substance of the two letters. Edna felt that if there had been a message for her, she would have received it. The despondent frame of mind in which she had left home began again to overtake her, and she remembered that she wished to find Mademoiselle Reisz.

Madame Lebrun knew where Mademoiselle Reisz lived. She gave Edna the address, regretting that she would not consent to stay and spend the remainder of the afternoon, and pay a visit to Mademoiselle Reisz some other day. The afternoon was already well advanced.

Victor escorted her out upon the banquette, lifted her parasol, and held it over her while he walked to the car with her. He entreated her to bear in mind that the disclosures of the afternoon were strictly confidential. She laughed and bantered him a little, remembering too late that she should have been dignified and reserved.

"How handsome Mrs. Pontellier looked!" said Madame Lebrun to her son.

"Ravishing!" he admitted. "The city atmosphere has improved her. Some way she doesn't seem like the same woman."

XXI

Some people contended that the reason Mademoiselle Reisz always chose apartments up under the roof was to discourage the approach of beggars, peddlars and callers. There were plenty of windows in her little front room. They were for the most part dingy, but as they were nearly always open it did not make so much difference. They often admitted into the room a good deal of smoke and soot; but at the same time all the light and air that there was came through them. From her windows could be seen the crescent of the river, the masts of ships and the big chimneys of the Mississippi steamers. A magnificent piano crowded the apartment. In the next room she slept, and in the third and last she harbored a gasoline stove on which she cooked her meals when disinclined to descend to the neighboring restaurant. It was there also that she ate, keeping her belongings in a rare old buffet, dingy and battered from a hundred years of use.

When Edna knocked at Mademoiselle Reisz's front room door and entered, she discovered that person standing beside the window, engaged in mending or patching an old prunella gaiter.[2] The little musician laughed all over when she saw Edna. Her laugh consisted of a contortion of the face and all the muscles of the body. She seemed strikingly homely, standing there in the afternoon light. She still wore the shabby lace and the artificial bunch of violets on the side of her head.

"So you remembered me at last," said Mademoiselle. "I had said to myself, 'Ah, bah! she will never come.'"

"Did you want me to come?" asked Edna with a smile.

"I had not thought much about it," answered Mademoiselle. The two had seated themselves on a little bumpy sofa which stood against the wall. "I am glad, however, that you came. I have the water boiling back there, and was just about to make some coffee. You will drink a cup with me. And how is *la belle dame*?[3] Always handsome! always healthy! always contented!" She took Edna's hand between her strong wiry fingers, holding it loosely without warmth, and executing a sort of double theme upon the back and palm.

"Yes," she went on; "I sometimes thought: 'She will never come. She promised as those women in society always do, without meaning it. She will not come.' For I really don't believe you like me, Mrs. Pontellier."

"I don't know whether I like you or not," replied Edna, gazing down at the little woman with a quizzical look.

The candor of Mrs. Pontellier's admission greatly pleased Mademoiselle Reisz. She expressed her gratification by repairing forthwith to the region of the gasoline stove and rewarding her guest with the promised cup of coffee. The coffee and the biscuit accompanying it proved very acceptable to Edna, who had declined refreshment at Madame Lebrun's and was now beginning to feel hungry. Mademoiselle set the tray which she brought in upon a small table near at hand, and seated herself once again on the lumpy sofa.

"I have had a letter from your friend," she remarked, as she poured a little cream into Edna's cup and handed it to her.

"My friend?"

"Yes, your friend Robert. He wrote to me from the City of Mexico."

2. A legging made of strong cloth.   3. The beautiful lady.

"Wrote to *you?*" repeated Edna in amazement, stirring her coffee absently.

"Yes, to me. Why not? Don't stir all the warmth out of your coffee; drink it. Though the letter might as well have been sent to you; it was nothing but Mrs. Pontellier from beginning to end."

"Let me see it," requested the young woman, entreatingly.

"No; a letter concerns no one but the person who writes it and the one to whom it is written."

"Haven't you just said it concerned me from beginning to end?"

"It was written about you, not to you. 'Have you seen Mrs. Pontellier? How is she looking?' he asks. 'As Mrs. Pontellier says,' or 'as Mrs. Pontellier once said.' 'If Mrs. Pontellier should call upon you, play for her that Impromptu of Chopin's, my favorite. I heard it here a day or two ago, but not as you play it. I should like to know how it affects her,' and so on, as if he supposed we were constantly in each other's society."

"Let me see the letter."

"Oh, no."

"Have you answered it?"

"No."

"Let me see the letter."

"No, and again, no."

"Then play the Impromptu for me."

"It is growing late; what time do you have to be home?"

"Time doesn't concern me. Your question seems a little rude. Play the Impromptu."

"But you have told me nothing of yourself. What are you doing?"

"Painting!" laughed Edna. "I am becoming an artist. Think of it!"

"Ah! an artist! You have pretensions, Madame."

"Why pretensions? Do you think I could not become an artist?"

"I do not know you well enough to say. I do not know your talent or your temperament. To be an artist includes much; one must possess many gifts—absolute gifts—which have not been acquired by one's own effort. And, moreover, to succeed, the artist must possess the courageous soul."

"What do you mean by the courageous soul?"

"Courageous, *ma foi!* The brave soul. The soul that dares and defies."

"Show me the letter and play for me the Impromptu. You see that I have persistence. Does that quality count for anything in art?"

"It counts with a foolish old woman whom you have captivated," replied Mademoiselle, with her wriggling laugh.

The letter was right there at hand in the drawer of the little table upon which Edna had just placed her coffee cup. Mademoiselle opened the drawer and drew forth the letter, the topmost one. She placed it in Edna's hands, and without further comment arose and went to the piano.

Mademoiselle played a soft interlude. It was an improvisation. She sat low at the instrument, and the lines of her body settled into ungraceful curves and angles that gave it an appearance of deformity. Gradually and imperceptibly the interlude melted into the soft opening minor chords of the Chopin Impromptu.

Edna did not know when the impromptu began or ended. She sat in the sofa corner reading Robert's letter by the fading light. Mademoiselle had glided from the Chopin into the quivering love-notes of Isolde's song,[4] and back again to the Impromptu with its soulful and poignant longing.

The shadows deepened in the little room. The music grew strange and fantastic—turbulent, insistent, plaintive and soft with entreaty. The shadows grew deeper. The music filled the room. It floated out upon the night, over the housetops, the crescent of the river, losing itself in the silence of the upper air.

Edna was sobbing, just as she had wept one midnight at Grand Isle when strange, new voices awoke in her. She arose in some agitation to take her departure. "May I come again, Mademoiselle?" she asked at the threshold.

"Come whenever you feel like it. Be careful; the stairs and landings are dark; don't stumble."

Mademoiselle reëntered and lit a candle. Robert's letter was on the floor. She stooped and picked it up. It was crumpled and damp with tears. Mademoiselle smoothed the letter out, restored it to the envelope, and replaced it in the table drawer.

XXII

One morning on his way into town Mr. Pontellier stopped at the house of his old friend and family physician, Doctor Mandelet. The Doctor was a semi-retired physician, resting, as the saying is, upon his laurels. He bore a reputation for wisdom rather than skill—leaving the active practice of medicine to his assistants and younger contemporaries—and was much sought for in matters of consultation. A few families, united to him by bonds of friendship, he still attended when they required the services of a physician. The Pontelliers were among these.

Mr. Pontellier found the Doctor reading at the open window of his study. His house stood rather far back from the street, in the center of a delightful garden, so that it was quiet and peaceful at the old gentleman's study window. He was a great reader. He stared up disapprovingly over his eyeglasses as Mr. Pontellier entered, wondering who had the temerity to disturb him at that hour of the morning.

"Ah, Pontellier! Not sick, I hope. Come and have a seat. What news do you bring this morning?" He was quite portly, with a profusion of gray hair, and small blue eyes which age had robbed of much of their brightness but none of their penetration.

"Oh! I'm never sick, Doctor. You know that I come of tough fiber—of that old Creole race of Pontelliers that dry up and finally blow away. I come to consult—no, not precisely to consult—to talk to you about Edna. I don't know what ails her."

"Madame Pontellier not well?" marveled the Doctor. "Why I saw her—I think it was a week ago—walking along Canal Street,[5] the picture of health, it seemed to me."

"Yes, yes; she seems quite well," said Mr. Pontellier, leaning forward and whirling his stick between his two hands; "but she doesn't act well. She's odd, she's not like herself. I can't make her out, and I thought perhaps you'd help me."

"How does she act?" inquired the doctor.

4. Isolde's "Liebestod," the song she sings to her dead lover before she dies herself, from the opera *Tristan und Isolde* (1857–59) by German composer Richard Wagner (1813–83).
5. A main street in New Orleans.

"Well, it isn't easy to explain," said Mr. Pontellier, throwing himself back in his chair. "She lets the housekeeping go to the dickens."

"Well, well; women are not all alike, my dear Pontellier. We've got to consider—"

"I know that; I told you I couldn't explain. Her whole attitude—toward me and everybody and everything—has changed. You know I have a quick temper, but I don't want to quarrel or be rude to a woman, especially my wife; yet I'm driven to it, and feel like ten thousand devils after I've made a fool of myself. She's making it devilishly uncomfortable for me," he went on nervously. "She's got some sort of notion in her head concerning the eternal rights of women; and—you understand—we meet in the morning at the breakfast table."

The old gentleman lifted his shaggy eyebrows, protruded his thick nether lip, and tapped the arms of his chair with his cushioned finger-tips.

"What have you been doing to her, Pontellier?"

"Doing! *Parbleu!*"[6]

"Has she," asked the Doctor, with a smile, "has she been associating of late with a circle of pseudo-intellectual women—superspiritual superior beings? My wife has been telling me about them."

"That's the trouble," broke in Mr. Pontellier, "she hasn't been associating with any one. She has abandoned her Tuesdays at home, has thrown over all her acquaintances, and goes tramping about by herself, moping in the street-cars, getting in after dark. I tell you she's peculiar. I don't like it; I feel a little worried over it."

This was a new aspect for the Doctor. "Nothing hereditary?" he asked, seriously. "Nothing peculiar about her family antecedents, is there?"

"Oh, no, indeed! She comes of sound old Presbyterian Kentucky stock. The old gentleman, her father, I have heard, used to atone for his week-day sins with his Sunday devotions. I know for a fact, that his race horses literally ran away with the prettiest bit of Kentucky farming land I ever laid eyes upon. Margaret—you know Margaret—she has all the Presbyterianism undiluted. And the youngest is something of a vixen. By the way, she gets married in a couple of weeks from now."

"Send your wife up to the wedding," exclaimed the Doctor, foreseeing a happy solution. "Let her stay among her own people for a while; it will do her good."

"That's what I want her to do. She won't go to the marriage. She ways a wedding is one of the most lamentable spectacles on earth. Nice thing for a woman to say to her husband!" exclaimed Mr. Pontellier, fuming anew at the recollection.

"Pontellier," said the Doctor, after a moment's reflection, "let your wife alone for a while. Don't bother her, and don't let her bother you. Woman, my dear friend, is a very peculiar and delicate organism—a sensitive and highly organized woman, such as I know Mrs. Pontellier to be, is especially peculiar. It would require an inspired psychologist to deal successfully with them. And when ordinary fellows like you and me attempt to cope with their idiosyncrasies the result is bungling. Most women are moody and whimsical. This is some passing whim of your wife, due to some cause or causes which you and I needn't try to fathom. But it will pass happily over, especially if you let her alone. Send her around to see me."

"Oh! I couldn't do that; there'd be no reason for it," objected Mr. Pontellier.

"Then I'll go around and see her," said the Doctor. "I'll drop in to dinner some evening *en bon ami.*"[7]

---

6. By Jove! (French).

7. As a good friend (French).

"Do! by all means," urged Mr. Pontellier. "What evening will you come? Say Thursday. Will you come Thursday?" he asked, rising to take his leave.

"Very well; Thursday. My wife may possibly have some engagement for me Thursday. In case she has, I shall let you know. Otherwise, you may expect me."

Mr. Pontellier turned before leaving to say:

"I am going to New York on business very soon. I have a big scheme on hand, and want to be on the field proper to pull the ropes and handle the ribbons.[8] We'll let you in on the inside if you say so, Doctor," he laughed.

"No, I thank you, my dear sir," returned the Doctor. "I leave such ventures to you younger men with the fever of life still in your blood."

"What I wanted to say," continued Mr. Pontellier, with his hand on the knob; "I may have to be absent a good while. Would you advise me to take Edna along?"

"By all means, if she wishes to go. If not, leave her here. Don't contradict her. The mood will pass, I assure you. It may take a month, two, three months—possibly longer, but it will pass; have patience."

"Well, good-by, *à jeudi*,"[9] said Mr. Pontellier, as he let himself out.

The Doctor would have liked during the course of conversation to ask, "Is there any man in the case?" but he knew his Creole too well to make such a blunder as that.

He did not resume his book immediately, but sat for a while meditatively looking out into the garden.

XXIII

Edna's father was in the city, and had been with them several days. She was not very warmly or deeply attached to him, but they had certain tastes in common, and when together they were companionable. His coming was in the nature of a welcome disturbance; it seemed to furnish a new direction for her emotions.

He had come to purchase a wedding gift for his daughter, Janet, and an outfit for himself in which he might make a creditable appearance at her marriage. Mr. Pontellier had selected the bridal gift, as every one immediately connected with him always deferred to his taste in such matters. And his suggestions on the question of dress—which too often assumes the nature of a problem—were of inestimable value to his father-in-law. But for the past few days the old gentleman had been upon Edna's hands, and in his society she was becoming acquainted with a new set of sensations. He had been a colonel in the Confederate army, and still maintained, with the title, the military bearing which had always accompanied it. His hair and mustache were white and silky, emphasizing the rugged bronze of his face. He was tall and thin, and wore his coats padded, which gave a fictitious breadth and depth to his shoulders and chest. Edna and her father looked very distinguished together, and excited a good deal of notice during their perambulations. Upon his arrival she began by introducing him to her atelier and making a sketch of him. He took the whole matter very seriously. If her talent had been ten-fold greater than it was, it would not have surprised him, convinced as he was that he had bequeathed to all of his daughters the germs of a masterful capability, which only depended upon their own efforts to be directed toward successful achievement.

Before her pencil he sat rigid and unflinching, as he had faced the cannon's mouth in days gone by. He resented the intrusion of the children, who gaped with

8. Reins.   9. Until Thursday (French).

wondering eyes at him, sitting so stiff up there in their mother's bright atelier. When they drew near he motioned them away with an expressive action of the foot, loath to disturb the fixed lines of his countenance, his arms, or his rigid shoulders.

Edna, anxious to entertain him, invited Mademoiselle Reisz to meet him, having promised him a treat in her piano playing; but Mademoiselle declined the invitation. So together they attended a *soirée musicale* at the Ratignolles'. Monsieur and Madame Ratignolle made much of the Colonel, installing him as the guest of honor and engaging him at once to dine with them the following Sunday, or any day which he might select. Madame coquetted with him in the most captivating and naïve manner, with eyes, gestures, and a profusion of compliments, till the Colonel's old head felt thirty years younger on his padded shoulders. Edna marveled, not comprehending. She herself was almost devoid of coquetry.

There were one or two men whom she observed at the *soirée musicale;* but she would never have felt moved to any kittenish display to attract their notice—to any feline or feminine wiles to express herself toward them. Their personality attracted her in an agreeable way. Her fancy selected them, and she was glad when a lull in the music gave them an opportunity to meet her and talk with her. Often on the street the glance of strange eyes had lingered in her memory, and sometimes had disturbed her.

Mr. Pontellier did not attend these *soirées musicales.* He considered them *bourgeois,* and found more diversion at the club. To Madame Ratignolle he said the music dispensed at her *soirées* was "too heavy," too far beyond his untrained comprehension. His excuse flattered her. But she disapproved of Mr. Pontellier's club, and she was frank enough to tell Edna so.

"It's a pity Mr. Pontellier doesn't stay home more in the evenings. I think you would be more—well, if you don't mind my saying it—more united, if he did."

"Oh! dear no!" said Edna, with a blank look in her eyes. "What should I do if he stayed home? We wouldn't have anything to say to each other."

She had not much of anything to say to her father, for that matter; but he did not antagonize her. She discovered that he interested her, though she realized that he might not interest her long; and for the first time in her life she felt as if she were thoroughly acquainted with him. He kept her busy serving him and ministering to his wants. It amused her to do so. She would not permit a servant or one of the children to do anything for him which she might do herself. Her husband noticed, and thought it was the expression of a deep filial attachment which he had never suspected.

The Colonel drank numerous "toddies" during the course of the day, which left him, however, imperturbed. He was an expert at concocting strong drinks. He had even invented some, to which he had given fantastic names, and for whose manufacture he required diverse ingredients that it devolved upon Edna to procure for him.

When Doctor Mandelet dined with the Pontelliers on Thursday he could discern in Mrs. Pontellier no trace of that morbid condition which her husband had reported to him. She was excited and in a manner radiant. She and her father had been to the race course, and their thoughts when they seated themselves at table were still occupied with the events of the afternoon, and their talk was still of the track. The Doctor had not kept pace with turf affairs. He had certain recollections of racing in what he called "the good old times" when the Lecompte stables flour-

after dinner and read the evening papers together under the drop-light;[7] while the younger people went into the drawing-room near by and talked. Miss Highcamp played some selections from Grieg[8] upon the piano. She seemed to have apprehended all of the composer's coldness and none of his poetry. While Edna listened she could not help wondering if she had lost her taste for music.

When the time came for her to go home, Mr. Highcamp grunted a lame offer to escort her, looking down at his slippered feet with tactless concern. It was Arobin who took her home. The car ride was long, and it was late when they reached Esplanade Street. Arobin asked permission to enter for a second to light his cigarette—his match safe[9] was empty. He filled his match safe, but did not light his cigarette until he left her, after she had expressed her willingness to go to the races with him again.

Edna was neither tired nor sleepy. She was hungry again, for the Highcamp dinner, though of excellent quality, had lacked abundance. She rummaged in the larder and brought forth a slice of "Gruyère"[1] and some crackers. She opened a bottle of beer which she found in the ice-box. Edna felt extremely restless and excited. She vacantly hummed a fantastic tune as she poked at the wood embers on the hearth and munched a cracker.

She wanted something to happen—something, anything; she did not know what. She regretted that she had not made Arobin stay a half hour to talk over the horses with her. She counted the money she had won. But there was nothing else to do, so she went to bed, and tossed there for hours in a sort of monotonous agitation.

In the middle of the night she remembered that she had forgotten to write her regular letter to her husband; and she decided to do so next day and tell him about her afternoon at the Jockey Club. She lay wide awake composing a letter which was nothing like the one which she wrote the next day. When the maid awoke her in the morning Edna was dreaming of Mr. Highcamp playing the piano at the entrance of a music store on Canal Street, while his wife was saying to Alcée Arobin, as they boarded an Esplanade Street car:

"What a pity that so much talent has been neglected! but I must go."

When a few days later, Alcée Arobin again called for Edna in his drag, Mrs. Highcamp was not with him. He said they would pick her up. But as the lady had not been apprised of his intention of picking her up, she was not at home. The daughter was just leaving the house to attend the meeting of a branch Folk Lore Society, and regretted that she could not accompany them. Arobin appeared nonplused, and asked Edna if there were any one else she cared to ask.

She did not deem it worthwhile to go in search of any of the fashionable acquaintances from whom she had withdrawn herself. She thought of Madame Ratignolle, but knew that her fair friend did not leave the house, except to take a languid walk around the block with her husband after nightfall. Mademoiselle Reisz would have laughed at such a request from Edna. Madame Lebrun might have enjoyed the outing, but for some reason Edna did not want her. So they went alone, she and Arobin.

The afternoon was intensely interesting to her. The excitement came back upon her like a remittent fever. Her talk grew familiar and confidential. It was no

---

7. A light that is suspended from the ceiling.
8. Norwegian composer Edvard Grieg (1843–1907).
9. A box for matches.
1. A cheese from Switzerland.

labor to become intimate with Arobin. His manner invited easy confidence. The preliminary stage of becoming acquainted was one which he always endeavored to ignore when a pretty and engaging woman was concerned.

He stayed and dined with Edna. He stayed and sat beside the wood fire. They laughed and talked; and before it was time to go he was telling her how different life might have been if he had known her years before. With ingenuous frankness he spoke of what a wicked, ill-disciplined boy he had been, and impulsively drew up his cuff to exhibit upon his wrist the scar from a saber cut which he had received in a duel outside of Paris when he was nineteen. She touched his hand as she scanned the red cicatrice[2] on the inside of his white wrist. A quick impulse that was somewhat spasmodic impelled her fingers to close in a sort of clutch upon his hand. He felt the pressure of her pointed nails in the flesh of his palm.

She arose hastily and walked toward the mantel.

"The sight of a wound or scar always agitates and sickens me," she said. "I shouldn't have looked at it."

"I beg your pardon," he entreated, following her; "it never occurred to me that it might be repulsive."

He stood close to her, and the effrontery in his eyes repelled the old, vanishing self in her, yet drew all her awakening sensuousness. He saw enough in her face to impel him to take her hand and hold it while he said his lingering good night.

"Will you go to the races again?" he asked.

"No," she said. "I've had enough of the races. I don't want to lose all the money I've won, and I've got to work when the weather is bright, instead of—"

"Yes; work; to be sure. You promised to show me your work. What morning may I come up to your atelier? To-morrow?"

"No!"

"Day after?"

"No, no."

"Oh, please don't refuse me! I know something of such things, I might help you with a stray suggestion or two."

"No. Good night. Why don't you go after you have said good night? I don't like you," she went on in a high, excited pitch, attempting to draw away her hand. She felt that her words lacked dignity and sincerity, and she knew that he felt it.

"I'm sorry you don't like me. I'm sorry I offended you. How have I offended you? What have I done? Can't you forgive me?" And he bent and pressed his lips upon her hand as if he wished never more to withdraw them.

"Mr. Arobin," she complained, "I'm greatly upset by the excitement of the afternoon; I'm not myself. My manner must have misled you in some way. I wish you to go, please." She spoke in a monotonous, dull tone. He took his hat from the table, and stood with eyes turned from her, looking into the dying fire. For a moment or two he kept an impressive silence.

"Your manner has not misled me, Mrs. Pontellier," he said finally. "My own emotions have done that. I couldn't help it. When I'm near you, how could I help it? Don't think anything of it, don't bother, please. You see, I go when you command me. If you wish me to stay away, I shall do so. If you let me come back, I—oh! you will let me come back?"

2. Scar.

He cast one appealing glance at her, to which she made no response. Alcée Arobin's manner was so genuine that it often deceived even himself.

Edna did not care or think whether it were genuine or not. When she was alone she looked mechanically at the back of her hand which he had kissed so warmly. Then she leaned her head down on the mantelpiece. She felt somewhat like a woman who in a moment of passion is betrayed into an act of infidelity, and realizes the significance of the act without being wholly awakened from its glamour. The thought was passing vaguely through her mind, "what would he think?"

She did not mean her husband; she was thinking of Robert Lebrun. Her husband seemed to her now like a person whom she had married without love as an excuse.

She lit a candle and went up to her room. Alcée Arobin was absolutely nothing to her. Yet his presence, his manners, the warmth of his glances, and above all the touch of his lips upon her hand had acted like a narcotic upon her.

She slept a languorous sleep, interwoven with vanishing dreams.

XXVI

Alcée Arobin wrote Edna an elaborate note of apology, palpitant with sincerity. It embarrassed her; for in a cooler, quieter moment it appeared to her absurd that she should have taken his action so seriously, so dramatically. She felt sure that the significance of the whole occurrence had lain in her own self-consciousness. If she ignored his note it would give undue importance to a trivial affair. If she replied to it in a serious spirit it would still leave in his mind the impression that she had in a susceptible moment yielded to his influence. After all, it was no great matter to have one's hand kissed. She was provoked at his having written the apology. She answered in as light and bantering a spirit as she fancied it deserved, and said she would be glad to have him look in upon her at work whenever he felt the inclination and his business gave him the opportunity.

He responded at once by presenting himself at her home with all his disarming naïveté. And then there was scarcely a day which followed that she did not see him or was not reminded of him. He was prolific in pretexts. His attitude became one of good-humored subservience and tacit adoration. He was ready at all times to submit to her moods, which were as often kind as they were cold. She grew accustomed to him. They became intimate and friendly by imperceptible degrees, and then by leaps. He sometimes talked in a way that astonished her at first and brought the crimson into her face; in a way that pleased her at last, appealing to the animalism that stirred impatiently within her.

There was nothing which so quieted the turmoil of Edna's senses as a visit to Mademoiselle Reisz. It was then, in the presence of that personality which was offensive to her, that the woman, by her divine art, seemed to reach Edna's spirit and set it free.

It was misty, with heavy, lowering atmosphere, one afternoon, when Edna climbed the stairs to the pianist's apartments under the roof. Her clothes were dripping with moisture. She felt chilled and pinched as she entered the room. Mademoiselle was poking at a rusty stove that smoked a little and warmed the room indifferently. She was endeavoring to heat a pot of chocolate on the stove. The room looked cheerless and dingy to Edna as she entered. A bust of Beethoven, covered with a hood of dust, scowled at her from the mantelpiece.

"Ah! here comes the sunlight!" exclaimed Mademoiselle, rising from her knees before the stove. "Now it will be warm and bright enough; I can let the fire alone."

She closed the stove door with a bang, and approaching assisted in removing Edna's dripping mackintosh.

"You are cold; you look miserable. The chocolate will soon be hot. But would you rather have a taste of brandy? I have scarcely touched the bottle which you brought me for my cold." A piece of red flannel was wrapped around Mademoiselle's throat; a stiff neck compelled her to hold her head on one side.

"I will take some brandy," said Edna, shivering as she removed her gloves and overshoes. She drank the liquor from the glass as a man would have done. Then flinging herself upon the uncomfortable sofa she said, "Mademoiselle, I am going to move away from my house on Esplanade Street."

"Ah!" ejaculated the musician, neither surprised nor especially interested. Nothing ever seemed to astonish her very much. She was endeavoring to adjust the bunch of violets which had become loose from its fastening in her hair. Edna drew her down upon the sofa and taking a pin from her own hair, secured the shabby artificial flowers in their accustomed place.

"Aren't you astonished?"

"Passably. Where are you going? To New York? to Iberville? to your father in Mississippi? where?"

"Just two steps away," laughed Edna, "in a little four-room house around the corner. It looks so cozy, so inviting and restful, whenever I pass by; and it's for rent. I'm tired looking after that big house. It never seemed like mine, anyway—like home. It's too much trouble. I have to keep too many servants. I am tired bothering with them."

"That is not your true reason, *ma belle*.[3] There is no use in telling me lies. I don't know your reason, but you have not told me the truth." Edna did not protest or endeavor to justify herself.

"The house, the money that provides for it, are not mine. Isn't that enough reason?"

"They are your husband's," returned Mademoiselle, with a shrug and a malicious elevation of the eyebrows.

"Oh! I see there is no deceiving you. Then let me tell you: it is a caprice. I have a little money of my own from my mother's estate, which my father sends me by driblets. I won a large sum this winter on the races, and I am beginning to sell my sketches. Laidpore is more and more pleased with my work; he says it grows in force and individuality. I cannot judge of that myself, but I feel that I have gained in ease and confidence. However, as I said, I have sold a good many through Laidpore. I can live in the tiny house for little or nothing, with one servant. Old Celestine, who works occasionally for me, says she will come stay with me and do my work. I know I shall like it, like the feeling of freedom and independence."

"What does your husband say?"

"I have not told him yet. I only thought of it this morning. He will think I am demented, no doubt. Perhaps you think so."

Mademoiselle shook her head slowly. "Your reason is not yet clear to me," she said.

Neither was it quite clear to Edna herself; but it unfolded itself as she sat for a while in silence. Instinct had prompted her to put away her husband's bounty in

3. My beauty (French).

casting off her allegiance. She did not know how it would be when he returned. There would have to be an understanding, an explanation. Conditions would some way adjust themselves, she felt, but whatever came, she had resolved never again to belong to another than herself.

"I shall give a grand dinner before I leave the old house!" Edna exclaimed. You will have to come to it, Mademoiselle. I will give you everything that you like to eat and drink. We shall sing and laugh and be merry for once." And she uttered a sigh that came from the very depth of her being.

If Mademoiselle happened to have received a letter from Robert during the interval of Edna's visits, she would give her the letter unsolicited. And she would seat herself at the piano and play as her humor prompted her while the young woman read the letter.

The little stove was roaring; it was red-hot, and the chocolate in the tin sizzled and sputtered. Edna went forward and opened the stove door, and Mademoiselle rising took a letter from under the bust of Beethoven and handed it to Edna.

"Another! so soon!" she exclaimed, her eyes filled with delight. "Tell me, Mademoiselle, does he know that I see his letters?"

"Never in the world! He would be angry and would never write to me again if he thought so. Does he write to you? Never a line. Does he send you a message? Never a word. It is because he loves you, poor fool, and is trying to forget you, since you are not free to listen to him or to belong to him."

"Why do you show me his letters, then?"

"Haven't you begged for them? Can I refuse you anything? Oh! you cannot deceive me," and Mademoiselle approached her beloved instrument and began to play. Edna did not at once read the letter. She sat holding it in her hand, while the music penetrated her whole being like an effulgence, warming and brightening the dark places of her soul. It prepared her for joy and exultation.

"Oh!" she exclaimed, letting the letter fall to the floor. "Why did you not tell me?" She went and grasped Mademoiselle's hands up from the keys. "Oh! unkind! malicious! Why did you not tell me?"

"That he was coming back? No great news, *mu foi.* I wonder he did not come long ago."

"But when, when?" cried Edna, impatiently. "He does not say when."

"He says 'very soon.' You know as much about it as I do, it is all in the letter."

"But why? Why is he coming? Oh, if I thought—" and she snatched the letter from the floor and turned the pages this way and that way, looking for the reason, which was left untold.

"If I were young and in love with a man," said Mademoiselle, turning on the stool and pressing her wiry hands between her knees as she looked down at Edna, who sat on the floor holding the letter, "it seems to me he would have to be some *grand esprit,*[4] a man with lofty aims and ability to reach them; one who stood high enough to attract the notice of his fellow-men. It seems to me if I were young and in love I should never deem a man of ordinary caliber worthy of my devotion."

"Now it is you who are telling lies and seeking to deceive me, Mademoiselle; or else you have never been in love, and know nothing about it. Why," went on Edna, clasping her knees and looking up into Mademoiselle's twisted face, "do you suppose a woman knows why she loves? Does she select? Does she say to herself: 'Go to! Here is a distinguished statesman with presidential possibilities: I shall proceed

---

4. Great soul (French).

to fall in love with him.' Or, 'I shall set my heart upon this musician, whose fame is on every tongue?' Or, 'This financier, who controls the world's money markets?'"

"You are purposely misunderstanding me, *ma reine*.[5] Are you in love with Robert?"

"Yes," said Edna. It was the first time she had admitted it, and a glow overspread her face, blotching it with red spots.

"Why?" asked her companion. "Why do you love him when you ought not to?"

Edna, with a motion or two, dragged herself on her knees before Mademoiselle Reisz, who took the glowing face between her two hands.

"Why? Because his hair is brown and grows away from his temples; because he opens and shuts his eyes, and his nose is a little out of drawing; because he has two lips and a square chin, and a little finger which he can't straighten from having played baseball too energetically in his youth. Because——"

"Because you do, in short," laughed Mademoiselle. "What will you do when he comes back?" she asked.

"Do? Nothing, except feel glad and happy to be alive."

She was already glad and happy to be alive at the mere thought of his return. The murky, lowering sky, which had depressed her a few hours before, seemed bracing and invigorating as she splashed through the streets on her way home.

She stopped at a confectioner's and ordered a huge box of bonbons for the children in Iberville. She slipped a card in the box, on which she scribbled a tender message and sent an abundance of kisses.

Before dinner in the evening Edna wrote a charming letter to her husband, telling him of her intention to move for a while into the little house around the block, and to give a farewell dinner before leaving, regretting that he was not there to share it, to help her out with the menu and assist her in entertaining the guests. Her letter was brilliant and brimming with cheerfulness.

XXVII

"What is the matter with you?" asked Arobin that evening. "I never found you in such a happy mood." Edna was tired by that time, and was reclining on the lounge before the fire.

"Don't you know the weather prophet has told us we shall see the sun pretty soon?"

"Well, that ought to be reason enough," he acquiesced. "You wouldn't give me another if I sat here all night imploring you." He sat close to her on a low tabouret,[6] and as he spoke his fingers lightly touched the hair that fell a little over her forehead. She liked the touch of his fingers through her hair, and closed her eyes sensitively.

"One of these days," she said, "I'm going to pull myself together for a while and think—try to determine what character of a woman I am; for, candidly, I don't know. By all the codes which I am acquainted with, I am a devilishly wicked specimen of the sex. But some way I can't convince myself that I am. I must think about it."

"Don't. What's the use? Why should you bother thinking about it when I can tell you what manner of woman you are?" His fingers strayed occasionally down to her warm, smooth cheeks and firm chin, which was growing a little full and double.

5. My queen (French).   6. Stool.

"Oh, yes! You will tell me that I am adorable; everything that is captivating. Spare yourself the effort."

"No; I shan't tell you anything of the sort, though I shouldn't be lying if I did."

"Do you know Mademoiselle Reisz?" she asked irrelevantly.

"The pianist? I know her by sight. I've heard her play."

"She says queer things sometimes in a bantering way that you don't notice at the time and you feel yourself thinking about afterward."

"For instance?"

"Well, for instance, when I left her today, she put her arms around me and felt my shoulder blades, to see if my wings were strong, she said. 'The bird that would soar above the level plain of tradition and prejudice must have strong wings. It is a sad spectacle to see the weaklings bruised, exhausted, fluttering back to earth.'"

"Whither would you soar?"

"I'm not thinking of any extraordinary flights. I only half comprehend her."

"I've heard she's partially demented," said Arobin.

"She seems to me wonderfully sane," Edna replied.

"I'm told she's extremely disagreeable and unpleasant. Why have you introduced her at a moment when I desired to talk of you?"

"Oh! talk of me if you like," cried Edna, clasping her hands beneath her head; "but let me think of something else while you do."

"I'm jealous of your thoughts to-night. They're making you a little kinder than usual; but some way I feel as if they were wandering, as if they were not here with me." She only looked at him and smiled. His eyes were very near. He leaned upon the lounge with an arm extended across her, while the other hand still rested upon her hair. They continued silently to look into each other's eyes. When he leaned forward and kissed her, she clasped his head, holding his lips to hers.

It was the first kiss of her life to which her nature had really responded. It was a flaming torch that kindled desire.

XXVIII

Edna cried a little that night after Arobin left her. It was only one phase of the multitudinous emotions which had assailed her. There was with her an overwhelming feeling of irresponsibility. There was the shock of the unexpected and the unaccustomed. There was her husband's reproach looking at her from external existence. There was Robert's reproach making itself felt by a quicker, fiercer, more overpowering love, which had awakened within her toward him. Above all, there was understanding. She felt as if a mist had been lifted from her eyes, enabling her to look upon and comprehend the significance of life, that monster made up of beauty and brutality. But among the conflicting sensations which assailed her, there was neither shame nor remorse. There was a dull pang of regret because it was not the kiss of love which had inflamed her, because it was not love which had held this cup of life to her lips.

XXIX

Without even waiting for an answer from her husband regarding his opinion or wishes in the matter, Edna hastened her preparations for quitting her home on Esplanade Street and moving into the little house around the block. A feverish anxiety attended her every action in that direction. There was no moment of deliberation, no interval of repose between the thought and its fulfillment. Early upon the morning following those hours passed in Arobin's society, Edna set about securing her new abode and hurrying her arrangements for occupying it. Within the precincts of her home she felt like one who has entered and lingered within the portals of some forbidden temple in which a thousand muffled voices bade her begone.

Whatever was her own in the house, everything which she had acquired aside from her husband's bounty, she caused to be transported to the other house, supplying simple and meager deficiencies from her own resources.

Arobin found her with rolled sleeves, working in company with the housemaid when he looked in during the afternoon. She was splendid and robust, and had never appeared handsomer than in the old blue gown, with a red silk handkerchief knotted at random around her head to protect her hair from the dust. She was mounted upon a high step-ladder, unhooking a picture from the wall when he entered. He had found the front door open, and had followed his ring by walking in unceremoniously.

"Come down!" he said. "Do you want to kill yourself?" She greeted him with affected carelessness, and appeared absorbed in her occupation.

If he had expected to find her languishing, reproachful, or indulging in sentimental tears, he must have been greatly surprised.

He was no doubt prepared for any emergency, ready for any one of the foregoing attitudes, just as he bent himself easily and naturally to the situation which confronted him.

"Please come down," he insisted, holding the ladder and looking up at her.

"No," she answered; "Ellen is afraid to mount the ladder. Joe is working at the 'pigeon house'—that's the name Ellen gives it, because it's so small and looks like a pigeon house—and some one has to do this."

Arobin pulled off his coat, and expressed himself ready and willing to tempt fate in her place. Ellen brought him one of her dustcaps, and went into contortions of mirth, which she found it impossible to control, when she saw him put it on before the mirror as grotesquely as he could. Edna herself could not refrain from smiling when she fastened it at his request. So it was he who in turn mounted the ladder, unhooking pictures and curtains, and dislodging ornaments as Edna directed. When he had finished he took off his dustcap and went out to wash his hands.

Edna was sitting on the tabouret, idly brushing the tips of a feather duster along the carpet when he came in again.

"Is there anything more you will let me do?" he asked.

"That is all," she answered. "Ellen can manage the rest." She kept the young woman occupied in the drawing-room, unwilling to be left alone with Arobin.

"What about the dinner?" he asked; "the grand event, the *coup d'état*?"[7]

"It will be day after to-morrow. Why do you call it the " '*coup d'état*?' Oh! it will be very fine; all my best of everything—crystal, silver and gold. Sèvres, flowers, music, and champagne to swim in. I'll let Léonce pay the bills. I wonder what he'll say when he sees the bills."

"And you ask me why I call it a *coup d'état*?" Arobin had put on his coat, and he stood before her and asked if his cravat was plumb. She told him it was, looking no higher than the tip of his collar.

---

7. Government overthrow, final blow (French).

"When do you go to the 'pigeon house?'—with all due acknowledgement to Ellen."

"Day after to-morrow, after the dinner. I shall sleep there."

"Ellen, will you very kindly get me a glass of water?" asked Arobin. "The dust in the curtains, if you will pardon me for hinting such a thing, has parched my throat to a crisp."

"While Ellen gets the water," said Edna, rising, "I will say good-by and let you go. I must get rid of this grime, and I have a million things to do and think of."

"When shall I see you?" asked Arobin, seeking to detain her, the maid having left the room.

"At the dinner, of course. You are invited."

"Not before?—not to-night or to-morrow morning or to-morrow noon or night? or the day after morning or noon? Can't you see yourself, without my telling you, what an eternity it is?"

He had followed her into the hall and to the foot of the stairway, looking up at her as she mounted with her face half turned to him.

"Not an instant sooner," she said. But she laughed and looked at him with eyes that at once gave him courage to wait and made it torture to wait.

XXX

Though Edna had spoken of the dinner as a very grand affair, it was in truth a very small affair and very select, in so much as the invited were few and were selected with discrimination. She had counted upon an even dozen seating themselves at her round mahogany board, forgetting for the moment that Madame Ratignolle was to the last degree *souffrante*[8] and unpresentable, and not foreseeing that Madame Lebrun would send a thousand regrets at the last moment. So there were only ten, after all, which made a cozy, comfortable number.

There were Mr. and Mrs. Merriman, a pretty vivacious little woman in the thirties; her husband, a jovial fellow, something of a shallow-pate,[9] who laughed a good deal at other people's witticisms, and had thereby made himself extremely popular. Mrs. Highcamp had accompanied them. Of course, there was Alcée Arobin; and Mademoiselle Reisz had consented to come. Edna had sent her a fresh bunch of violets with black lace trimmings for her hair. Monsieur Ratignolle brought himself and his wife's excuses. Victor Lebrun, who happened to be in the city, bent upon relaxation, had accepted with alacrity. There was a Miss Mayblunt, no longer in her teens, who looked at the world through lorgnettes and with the keenest interest. It was thought and said that she was intellectual; it was suspected of her that she wrote under a *nom de guerre*.[1] She had come with a gentleman by the name of Gouvernail, connected with one of the daily papers, of whom nothing special could be said, except that he was observant and seemed quiet and inoffensive. Edna herself made the tenth, and at half-past eight they seated themselves at table, Arobin and Monsieur Ratignolle on either side of their hostess.

Mrs. Highcamp sat between Arobin and Victor Lebrun. Then came Mrs. Merriman, Mr. Gouvernail, Miss Mayblunt, Mr. Merriman, and Mademoiselle Reisz next to Monsieur Ratignolle.

8. Sickly.   1. Pen name.
9. Shallow, simple.

There was something extremely gorgeous about the appearance of the table, an effect of splendor conveyed by a cover of pale yellow satin under strips of lacework. There were wax candles in massive brass candelabra, burning softly under yellow silk shades; full, fragrant roses, yellow and red, abounded. There were silver and gold, as she had said there would be, and crystal which glittered like the gems which the women wore.

The ordinary stiff dining chairs had been discarded for the occasion and replaced by the most commodious and luxurious which could be collected throughout the house. Mademoiselle Reisz, being exceedingly diminutive, was elevated upon cushions, as small children are sometimes hoisted at table upon bulky volumes.

"Something new, Edna?" exclaimed Miss Mayblunt, with lorgnette directed toward a magnificent cluster of diamonds that sparkled, that almost sputtered, in Edna's hair, just over the center of her forehead.

"Quite new; 'brand' new, in fact; a present from my husband. It arrived this morning from New York. I may as well admit that this is my birthday, and that I am twenty-nine. In good time I expect you to drink my health. Meanwhile, I shall ask you to begin with this cocktail, composed—would you say 'composed?'" with an appeal to Miss Mayblunt—"composed by my father in honor of Sister Janet's wedding."

Before each guest stood a tiny glass that looked and sparkled like a garnet gem.

"Then, all things considered," spoke Arobin, "it might not be amiss to start out by drinking the Colonel's health in the cocktail which he composed, on the birthday of the most charming of women—the daughter whom he invented."

Mr. Merriman's laugh at this sally was such a genuine outburst and so contagious that it started the dinner with an agreeable swing that never slackened.

Miss Mayblunt begged to be allowed to keep her cocktail untouched before her, just to look at. The color was marvelous! She could compare it to nothing she had ever seen, and the garnet lights which it emitted were unspeakably rare. She pronounced the Colonel an artist, and stuck to it.

Monsieur Ratignolle was prepared to take things seriously; the *mets*, and *entre-mets*, the service, the decorations, even the people. He looked up from his pompono[2] and inquired of Arobin if he were related to the gentleman of that name who formed one of the firm of Laitner and Arobin, lawyers. The young man admitted that Laitner was a warm personal friend, who permitted Arobin's name to decorate the firm's letterheads and to appear upon a shingle that graced Perdido Street.

"There are so many inquisitive people and institutions abounding," said Arobin, "that one is really forced as a matter of convenience these days to assume the virtue of an occupation if he has it not."

Monsieur Ratignolle stared a little, and turned to ask Mademoiselle Reisz if she considered the symphony concerts up to the standard which had been set the previous winter. Mademoiselle Reisz answered Monsieur Ratignolle in French, which Edna thought a little rude, under the circumstances, but characteristic. Mademoiselle had only disagreeable things to say of the symphony concerts, and insulting remarks to make of all the musicians of New Orleans, singly and collectively. All her interest seemed to be centered upon the delicacies placed before her.

---

2. *Mets*: main course; *entre-mets*: side dishes;   pompano.
pompono: a fish from the Gulf of Mexico, the

Mr. Merriman said that Mr. Arobin's remark about inquisitive people reminded him of a man from Waco[3] the other day at the St. Charles Hotel—but as Mr. Merriman's stories were always lame and lacking point, his wife seldom permitted him to complete them. She interrupted him to ask if he remembered the name of the author whose book she had bought the week before to send to a friend in Geneva. She was talking "books" with Mr. Gouvernail and trying to draw from him his opinion upon current literary topics. Her husband told the story of the Waco man privately to Miss Mayblunt, who pretended to be greatly amused and to think it extremely clever.

Mrs. Highcamp hung with languid but unaffected interest upon the warm and impetuous volubility of her left-hand neighbor, Victor Lebrun. Her attention was never for a moment withdrawn from him after seating herself at table; and when he turned to Mrs. Merriman, who was prettier and more vivacious than Mrs. Highcamp, she waited with easy indifference for an opportunity to reclaim his attention. There was the occasional sound of music, of mandolins, sufficiently removed to be an agreeable accompaniment rather than an interruption to the conversation. Outside the soft, monotonous splash of a fountain could be heard; the sound penetrated into the room with the heavy odor of jessamine that came through the open windows.

The golden shimmer of Edna's satin gown spread in rich folds on either side of her. There was a soft fall of lace encircling her shoulders. It was the color of her skin, without the glow, the myriad living tints that one may sometimes discover in vibrant flesh. There was something in her attitude, in her whole appearance when she leaned her head against the high-backed chair and spread her arms, which suggested the regal woman, the one who rules, who looks on, who stands alone.

But as she sat there amid her guests, she felt the old ennui overtaking her; the hopelessness which so often assailed her, which came upon her like an obsession, like something extraneous, independent of volition. It was something which announced itself; a chill breath that seemed to issue from some vast cavern wherein discords wailed. There came over her the acute longing which always summoned into her spiritual vision the presence of the beloved one, overpowering her at once with a sense of the unattainable.

The moments glided on, while a feeling of good fellowship passed around the circle like a mystic cord, holding and binding these people together with jest and laughter. Monsieur Ratignolle was the first to break the pleasant charm. At ten o'clock he excused himself. Madame Ratignolle was waiting for him at home. She was *bien souffrante,* and she was filled with vague dread, which only her husband's presence could allay.

Mademoiselle Reisz arose with Monsieur Ratignolle, who offered to escort her to the car. She had eaten well; she had tasted the good rich wines, and they must have turned her head, for she bowed pleasantly to all as she withdrew from table. She kissed Edna upon the shoulder, and whispered: "*Bonne nuit, ma reine; soyez sage.*"[4] She had been a little bewildered upon rising, or rather, descending from her cushions, and Monsieur Ratignolle gallantly took her arm and led her away.

Mrs. Highcamp was weaving a garland of roses, yellow and red. When she had finished the garland, she laid it lightly upon Victor's black curls. He was reclining far back in the luxurious chair, holding a glass of champagne to the light.

---

3. Waco, Texas.   4. Goodnight, my queen; be wise (French).

As if a magician's wand had touched him, the garland of roses transformed him into a vision of Oriental beauty. His cheeks were the color of crushed grapes, and his dusky eyes glowed with a languishing fire.

"*Sapristi!*" exclaimed Arobin.

But Mrs. Highcamp had one more touch to add to the picture. She took from the back of her chair a white silken scarf, with which she had covered her shoulders in the early part of the evening. She draped it across the boy in graceful folds, and in a way to conceal his black, conventional evening dress. He did not seem to mind what she did to him, only smiled, showing a faint gleam of white teeth, while he continued to gaze with narrowing eyes at the light through his glass of champagne.

"Oh! to be able to paint in color rather than in words!" exclaimed Miss Mayblunt, losing herself in a rhapsodic dream as she looked at him.

"There was a graven image of Desire
Painted with red blood on a ground of gold"[5]

murmured Gouvernail, under his breath.

The effect of the wine upon Victor was, to change his accustomed volubility into silence. He seemed to have abandoned himself to a reverie, and to be seeing pleasing visions in the amber bead.

"Sing," entreated Mrs. Highcamp. "Won't you sing to us?"

"Let him alone," said Arobin.

"He's posing," offered Mr. Merriman; "let him have it out."

"I believe he's paralyzed," laughed Mrs. Merriman. And leaning over the youth's chair, she took the glass from his hand and held it to his lips. He sipped the wine slowly, and when he had drained the glass she laid it upon the table and wiped his lips with her little filmy handkerchief.

"Yes, I'll sing for you," he said, turning in his chair toward Mrs. Highcamp. He clasped his hands behind his head, and looking up at the ceiling began to hum a little, trying his voice like a musician tuning an instrument. Then, looking at Edna, he began to sing:

"Ah! si tu savais!"

"Stop!" she cried, "don't sing that. I don't want you to sing it," and she laid her glass so impetuously and blindly upon the table as to shatter it against a caraffe. The wine spilled over Arobin's legs and some of it trickled down upon Mrs. Highcamp's black gauze gown. Victor had lost all idea of courtesy, or else he thought his hostess was not in earnest, for he laughed and went on:

"Ah! si tu savais
Ce que tes yeux me dissent"—[6]

"Oh! you mustn't! you mustn't," exclaimed Edna, and pushing back her chair she got up, and going behind him placed her hand over his mouth. He kissed the soft palm that pressed upon his lips.

5. The opening of "A Cameo," a sonnet by the English poet Algernon Charles Swinburne (1837–1909).

6. "Ah, if you knew / What your eyes tell me" (French).

"No, no, I won't, Mrs. Pontellier. I didn't know you meant it," looking up at her with caressing eyes. The touch of his lips was like a pleasing sting to her hand. She lifted the garland of roses from his head and flung it across the room.

"Come, Victor; you've posed long enough. Give Mrs. Highcamp her scarf."

Mrs. Highcamp undraped the scarf from about him with her own hands. Miss Mayblunt and Mr. Gouvernail suddenly conceived the notion that it was time to say good night. And Mr. and Mrs. Merriman wondered how it could be so late.

Before parting from Victor, Mrs. Highcamp invited him to call upon her daughter, who she knew would be charmed to meet him and talk French and sing French songs with him. Victor expressed his desire and intention to call upon Miss Highcamp at the first opportunity which presented itself. He asked if Arobin were going his way. Arobin was not.

The mandolin players had long since stolen away. A profound stillness had fallen upon the broad, beautiful street. The voices of Edna's disbanding guests jarred like a discordant note upon the quiet harmony of the night.

XXXI

"Well?" questioned Arobin, who had remained with Edna after the others had departed.

"Well," she reiterated, and stood up, stretching her arms, and feeling the need to relax her muscles after having been so long seated.

"What next?" he asked.

"The servants are all gone. They left when the musicians did. I have dismissed them. The house has to be closed and locked, and I shall trot around to the pigeon house, and shall send Celestine over in the morning to straighten things up."

He looked around, and began to turn out some of the lights.

"What about upstairs?" he inquired.

"I think it is all right; but there may be a window or two unlatched. We had better look; you might take a candle and see. And bring me my wrap and hat on the foot of the bed in the middle room."

He went up with the light, and Edna began closing doors and windows. She hated to shut in the smoke and the fumes of the wine. Arobin found her cape and hat, which he brought down and helped her to put on.

When everything was secured and the lights put out, they left through the front door, Arobin locking it and taking the key, which he carried for Edna. He helped her down the steps.

"Will you have a spray of jessamine?" he asked, breaking off a few blossoms as he passed.

"No; I don't want anything."

She seemed disheartened, and had nothing to say. She took his arm, which he offered her, holding up the weight of her satin train with the other hand. She looked down, noticing the black line of his leg moving in and out so close to her against the yellow shimmer of her gown. There was the whistle of a railway train somewhere in the distance, and the midnight bells were ringing. They met no one in their short walk.

The "pigeon-house" stood behind a locked gate, and a shallow *parterre*[7] that had been somewhat neglected. There was a small front porch, upon which a long

7. A flower garden.

window and the front door opened. The door opened directly into the parlor; there was no side entry. Back in the yard was a room for servants, in which old Celestine had been ensconced.

Edna had left a lamp burning low upon the table. She had succeeded in making the room look habitable and homelike. There were some books on the table and a lounge near at hand. On the floor was a fresh matting, covered with a rug or two; and on the walls hung a few tasteful pictures. But the room was filled with flowers. These were a surprise to her. Arobin had sent them, and had had Celestine distribute them during Edna's absence. Her bedroom was adjoining, and across a small passage were the dining-room and kitchen.

Edna seated herself with every appearance of discomfort.

"Are you tired?" he asked.

"Yes, and chilled and miserable. I feel as if I had been wound up to a certain pitch—too tight—and something inside of me had snapped." She rested her head against the table upon her bare arm.

"You want to rest," he said, "and to be quiet. I'll go; I'll leave you and let you rest."

"Yes," she replied.

He stood up beside her and smoothed her hair with his soft magnetic hand. His touch conveyed to her a certain physical comfort. She could have fallen quietly asleep there if he had continued to pass his hand over her hair. He brushed the hair upward from the nape of her neck.

"I hope you will feel better and happier in the morning," he said. "You have tried to do too much in the past few days. The dinner was the last straw; you might have dispensed with it."

"Yes," she admitted; "it was stupid."

"No, it was delightful; but it has worn you out." His hand had strayed to her beautiful shoulders, and he could feel the response of her flesh to his touch. He seated himself beside her and kissed her lightly upon the shoulder.

"I thought you were going away," she said, in an uneven voice.

"I am, after I have said good night."

"Good night," she murmured.

He did not answer, except to continue to caress her. He did not say good night until she had become supple to his gentle, seductive entreaties.

XXXII

When Mr. Pontellier learned of his wife's intention to abandon her home and take up her residence elsewhere, he immediately wrote her a letter of unqualified disapproval and remonstrance. She had given reasons which he was unwilling to acknowledge as adequate. He hoped she had not acted upon her rash impulse; and he begged her to consider first, foremost, and above all else, what people would say. He was not dreaming of scandal when he uttered this warning; that was a thing which would never have entered into his mind to consider in connection with his wife's name or his own. He was simply thinking of his financial integrity. It might get noised about that the Pontelliers had met with reverses, and were forced to conduct their *ménage*[8] on a humbler scale than heretofore. It might do incalculable mischief to his business prospects.

8. Household.

But remembering Edna's whimsical turn of mind of late, and foreseeing that she had immediately acted upon her impetuous determination, he grasped the situation with his usual promptness and handled it with his well-known business tact and cleverness.

The same mail which brought to Edna his letter of disapproval carried instructions—the most minute instructions—to a well-known architect concerning the remodeling of his home, changes which he had long contemplated, and which he desired carried forward during his temporary absence.

Expert and reliable packers and movers were engaged to convey the furniture, carpets, pictures—everything movable, in short—to places of security. And in an incredibly short time the Pontellier house was turned over to the artisans. There was to be an addition—a small snuggery;[9] there was to be frescoing, and hardwood flooring was to be put into such rooms as had not yet been subjected to this improvement.

Furthermore, in one of the daily papers appeared a brief notice to the effect that Mr. and Mrs. Pontellier were contemplating a summer sojourn abroad, and that their handsome residence on Esplanade Street was undergoing sumptuous alterations, and would not be ready for occupancy until their return. Mr. Pontellier had saved appearances!

Edna admired the skill of his maneuver, and avoided any occasion to balk his intentions. When the situation as set forth by Mr. Pontellier was accepted and taken for granted, she was apparently satisfied that it should be so.

The pigeon-house pleased her. It at once assumed the intimate character of a home, while she herself invested it with a charm which it reflected like a warm glow. There was with her a feeling of having descended in the social scale, with a corresponding sense of having risen in the spiritual. Every step which she took toward relieving herself from obligations added to her strength and expansion as an individual. She began to look with her own eyes; to see and to apprehend the deeper undercurrents of life. No longer was she content to "feed upon opinion" when her own soul had invited her.

After a little while, a few days, in fact, Edna went up and spent a week with her children in Iberville. They were delicious February days, with all the summer's promises hovering in the air.

How glad she was to see the children! She wept for very pleasure when she felt their little arms clasping her; their hard, ruddy cheeks pressed against her own glowing cheeks. She looked into their faces with hungry eyes that could not be satisfied with looking. And what stories they had to tell their mother! About the pigs, the cows, the mules! About riding to the mill behind Gluglu; fishing back in the lake with their Uncle Jasper; picking pecans with Lidie's little black brood, and hauling chips in their express wagon. It was a thousand times more fun to haul real chips for old lame Susie's real fire than to drag painted blocks along the banquette on Esplanade Street!

She went with them herself to see the pigs and the cows, to look at the darkies laying the cane, to thrash the pecan trees, and catch fish in the back lake. She lived with them a whole week long, giving them all of herself, and gathering and filling herself with their young existence. They listened, breathless, when she told them the house in Esplanade Street was crowded with workmen, hammering, nailing,

9. Small, cozy room.

sawing, and filling the place with clatter. They wanted to know where their bed was; what had been done with their rocking-horse; and where did Joe sleep, and where had Ellen gone, and the cook? But, above all, they were fired with a desire to see the little house around the block. Was there any place to play? Were there any boys next door? Raoul, with pessimistic foreboding, was convinced that there were only girls next door. Where would they sleep, and where would papa sleep? She told them the fairies would fix it all right.

The old Madame was charmed with Edna's visit, and showered all manner of delicate attentions upon her. She was delighted to know that the Esplanade Street house was in a dismantled condition. It gave her the promise and pretext to keep the children indefinitely.

It was with a wrench and a pang that Edna left her children. She carried away with her the sound of their voices and the touch of their cheeks. All along the journey homeward their presence lingered with her like the memory of a delicious song. But by the time she had regained the city the song no longer echoed in her soul. She was again alone.

XXXIII

It happened sometimes when Edna went to see Mademoiselle Reisz that the little musician was absent, giving a lesson or making some small necessary household purchase. The key was always left in a secret hiding-place in the entry, which Edna knew. If Mademoiselle happened to be away, Edna would usually enter and wait for her return.

When she knocked at Mademoiselle Reisz's door one afternoon there was no response; so unlocking the door, as usual, she entered and found the apartment deserted, as she had expected. Her day had been quite filled up, and it was for a rest, for a refuge, and to talk about Robert, that she sought out her friend.

She had worked at her canvas—a young Italian character study—all the morning, completing the work without the model; but there had been many interruptions, some incident to her modest housekeeping, and others of a social nature.

Madame Ratignolle had dragged herself over, avoiding the too public thoroughfares, she said. She complained that Edna had neglected her much of late. Besides, she was consumed with curiosity to see the little house and the manner in which it was conducted. She wanted to hear all about the dinner party; Monsieur Ratignolle had left so early. What had happened after he left? The champagne and grapes which Edna sent over were *too* delicious. She had so little appetite; they had refreshed and toned her stomach. Where on earth was she going to put Mr. Pontellier in that little house, and the boys? And then she made Edna promise to go to her when her hour of trial overtook her.

"At any time—any time of the day or night, dear," Edna assured her.

Before leaving Madame Ratignolle said:

"In some way you seem to me like a child, Edna. You seem to act without a certain amount of reflection which is necessary in this life. That is the reason I want to say you mustn't mind if I advise you to be a little careful while you are living here alone. Why don't you have some one come and stay with you? Wouldn't Mademoiselle Reisz come?"

"No; she wouldn't wish to come, and I shouldn't want her always with me."

"Well, the reason—you know how evil-minded the world is—some one was talking of Alcée Arobin visiting you. Of course, it wouldn't matter if Mr. Arobin had not such a dreadful reputation. Monsieur Ratignolle was telling me that his attentions alone are considered enough to ruin a woman's name."

"Does he boast of his successes?" asked Edna, indifferently, squinting at her picture.

"No, I think not. I believe he is a decent fellow as far as that goes. But his character is so well known among the men. I shan't be able to come back and see you; it was very, very imprudent today."

"Mind the step!" cried Edna.

"Don't neglect me," entreated Madame Ratignolle; "and don't mind what I said about Arobin, or having some one to stay with you."

"Of course not," Edna laughed. "You may say anything you like to me." They kissed each other good-bye. Madame Ratignolle had not far to go, and Edna stood on the porch a while watching her walk down the street.

Then in the afternoon Mrs. Merriman and Mrs. Highcamp had made their "party call." Edna felt that they might have dispensed with the formality. They had also come to invite her to play *vingt-et-un*[1] one evening at Mrs. Merriman's. She was asked to go early, to dinner, and Mr. Merriman or Mr. Arobin would take her home. Edna accepted in a half-hearted way. She sometimes felt very tired of Mrs. Highcamp and Mrs. Merriman.

Late in the afternoon she sought refuge with Mademoiselle Reisz, and stayed there alone, waiting for her, feeling a kind of repose invade her with the very atmosphere of the shabby, unpretentious little room.

Edna sat at the window, which looked out over the house-tops and across the river. The window frame was filled with pots of flowers, and she sat and picked the dry leaves from a rose geranium. The day was warm, and the breeze which blew from the river was very pleasant. She removed her hat and laid it on the piano. She went on picking the leaves and digging around the plants with her hat pin. Once she thought she heard Mademoiselle Reisz approaching. But it was a young black girl, who came in, bringing a small bundle of laundry, which she deposited in the adjoining room, and went away.

Edna seated herself at the piano, and softly picked out with one hand the bars of a piece of music which lay open before her. A half-hour went by. There was the occasional sound of people going and coming in the lower hall. She was growing interested in her occupation of picking out the aria, when there was a second rap at the door. She vaguely wondered what these people did when they found Mademoiselle's door locked.

"Come in," she called, turning her face toward the door. And this time it was Robert Lebrun who presented himself. She attempted to rise; she could not have done so without betraying the agitation which mastered her at sight of him, so she fell back upon the stool, only exclaiming, "Why, Robert!"

He came and clasped her hand, seemingly without knowing what he was saying or doing.

"Mrs. Pontellier! How do you happen—oh! how well you look! Is Mademoiselle Reisz not here? I never expected to see you."

1. The card game blackjack.

"When did you come back?" asked Edna in an unsteady voice, wiping her face with her handkerchief. She seemed ill at ease on the piano stool, and he begged her to take the chair by the window. She did so, mechanically, while he seated himself on the stool.

"I returned day before yesterday," he answered, while he leaned his arm on the keys, bringing forth a crash of discordant sound.

"Day before yesterday!" she repeated, aloud, and went on thinking to herself, "day before yesterday," in a sort of an uncomprehending way. She had pictured him seeking her at the very first hour, and he had lived under the same sky since day before yesterday; while only by accident had he stumbled upon her. Mademoiselle must have lied when she said, "Poor fool, he loves you."

"Day before yesterday," she repeated, breaking off a spray of Mademoiselle's geranium; "then if you had not met me here to-day you wouldn't—when—that is, didn't you mean to come and see me?"

"Of course, I should have gone to see you. There have been so many things—" he turned the leaves of Mademoiselle's music nervously. "I started in at once yesterday with the old firm. After all there is as much chance for me here as there was there—that is, I might find it profitable some day. The Mexicans were not very congenial."

So he had come back because the Mexicans were not congenial; because business was as profitable here as there; because of any reason, and not because he cared to be near her. She remembered the day she sat on the floor, turning the pages of his letter, seeking the reason which was left untold.

She had not noticed how he looked—only feeling his presence; but she turned deliberately and observed him. After all, he had been absent but a few months, and was not changed. His hair—the color of hers—waved back from his temples in the same way as before. His skin was not more burned than it had been at Grand Isle. She found in his eyes, when he looked at her for one silent moment, the same tender caress, with an added warmth and entreaty which had not been there before—the same glance which had penetrated to the sleeping places of her soul and awakened them.

A hundred times Edna had pictured Robert's return, and imagined their first meeting. It was usually at her home, whither he had sought her out at once. She always fancied him expressing or betraying in some way his love for her. And here, the reality was that they sat ten feet apart, she at the window, crushing geranium leaves in her hand and smelling them, he twirling around on the piano stool, saying:

"I was very much surprised to hear of Mr. Pontellier's absence; it's a wonder Mademoiselle Reisz did not tell me; and your moving—mother told me yesterday. I should think you would have gone to New York with him, or to Iberville with the children, rather than be bothered here with housekeeping. And you are going abroad, too, I hear. We shan't have you at Grand Isle next summer; it won't seem—do you see much of Mademoiselle Reisz? She often spoke of you in the few letters she wrote."

"Do you remember that you promised to write to me when you went away?" A flush overspread his whole face.

"I couldn't believe that my letters would be of any interest to you."

"That is an excuse; it isn't the truth." Edna reached for her hat on the piano. She adjusted it, sticking the hat pin through the heavy coil of hair with some deliberation.

"Are you not going to wait for Mademoiselle Reisz?" asked Robert.

"No; I have found when she is absent this long, she is liable not to come back till late." She drew on her gloves, and Robert picked up his hat.

"Won't you wait for her?" asked Edna.

"Not if you think she will not be back till late," adding, as if suddenly aware of some discourtesy in his speech, "and I should miss the pleasure of walking home with you." Edna locked the door and put the key back in its hiding place.

They went together, picking their way across muddy streets and sidewalks encumbered with the cheap display of small tradesmen. Part of the distance they rode in the car, and after disembarking, passed the Pontellier mansion, which looked broken and half torn asunder. Robert had never known the house, and looked at it with interest.

"I never knew you in your home," he remarked.

"I am glad you did not."

"Why?" She did not answer. They went on around the corner, and it seemed as if her dreams were coming true after all, when he followed her into the little house.

"You must say and dine with me, Robert. You see I am all alone, and it is so long since I have seen you. There is so much I want to ask you."

She took off her hat and gloves. He stood irresolute, making some excuse about his mother who expected him; he even muttered something about an engagement. She struck a match and lit the lamp on the table; it was growing dusk. When he saw her face in the lamplight, looking pained, with all the soft lines gone out of it, he threw his hat aside and seated himself.

"Oh! you know I want to stay if you will let me!" he exclaimed. All the softness came back. She laughed, and went and put her hand on his shoulder.

"This is the first moment you have seemed like the old Robert. I'll go tell Celestine." She hurried away to tell Celestine to set an extra place. She even sent her off in search of some added delicacy which she had not thought of for herself. And she recommended great care in dripping the coffee and having the omelet done to a proper turn.

When she reëntered, Robert was turning over magazines, sketches, and things that lay upon the table in great disorder. He picked up a photograph, and exclaimed:

"Alcée Arobin! What on earth is his picture doing here?"

"I tried to make a sketch of his head one day," answered Edna, "and he thought the photograph might help me. It was at the other house. I thought it had been left there. I must have picked it up with my drawing materials."

"I should think you would give it back to him if you have finished with it."

"Oh! I have a great many such photographs. I never think of returning them. They don't amount to anything." Robert kept on looking at the picture.

"It seems to me—do you think his head worth drawing? Is he a friend of Mr. Pontellier's? You never said you knew him."

"He isn't a friend of Mr. Pontellier's; he's a friend of mine. I always knew him—that is, it is only of late that I know him pretty well. But I'd rather talk about you, and know what you have been seeing and doing and feeling out there in Mexico." Robert threw aside the picture.

"I've been seeing the waves and the white beach of Grand Isle; the quiet, grassy street of the Chênière; the old fort at Grande Terre. I've been working like a machine, and feeling like a lost soul. There was nothing interesting."

She leaned her head upon her hand to shade her eyes from the light.

"And what have you been seeing and doing and feeling all these days?" he asked.

"I've been seeing the waves and the white beach of Grande Isle; the quiet, grassy street of the *Chênière Caminada;* the old sunny fort at Grande Terre. I've been working with little more comprehension than a machine, and still feeling like a lost soul. There was nothing interesting."

"Mrs. Pontellier, you are cruel," he said, with feeling, closing his eyes and resting his head back in his chair. They remained in silence till old Celestine announced dinner.

XXXIV

The dining-room was very small. Edna's round mahogany would have almost filled it. As it was there was but a step or two from the little table in the kitchen, to the mantel, the small buffet, and the side door that opened out on the narrow brick-paved yard.

A certain degree of ceremony settled upon them with the announcement of dinner. There was no return to personalities. Robert related incidents of his sojourn in Mexico, and Edna talked of events likely to interest him, which had occurred during his absence. The dinner was of ordinary quality, except for the few delicacies which she had sent out to purchase. Old Celestine, with a bandana *tignon* twisted about her head,[2] hobbled in and out, taking a personal interest in everything; and she lingered occasionally to talk *patois* with Robert, whom she had known as a boy.

He went out to a neighboring cigar stand to purchase cigarette papers, and when he came back he found that Celestine had served the black coffee in the parlor.

"Perhaps I shouldn't have come back," he said. "When you are tired of me, tell me to go."

"You never tire me. You must have forgotten the hours and hours at Grand Isle in which we grew accustomed to each other and used to being together."

"I have forgotten nothing at Grand Isle," he said, not looking at her, but rolling a cigarette. His tobacco pouch, which he laid upon the table, was a fantastic embroidered silk affair, evidently the handiwork of a woman.

"You used to carry your tobacco in a rubber pouch," said Edna, picking up the pouch and examining the needlework.

"Yes; it was lost."

"Where did you buy this one? In Mexico?"

"It was given to me by a Vera Cruz girl; they are very generous," he replied, striking a match and lighting his cigarette.

"They are very handsome, I suppose, those Mexican women; very picturesque, with their black eyes and their lace scarfs."

"Some are; others are hideous. Just as you find women everywhere."

"What was she like—the one who gave you the pouch? You must have known her very well."

"She was very ordinary. She wasn't of the slightest importance. I knew her well enough."

"Did you visit at her house? Was it interesting? I should like to know and hear about the people you met, and the impressions they made on you."

2. A bandana wrapped around her head as a turban.

"There are some people who leave impressions not so lasting as the imprint of an oar upon the water."

"Was she such a one?"

"It would be ungenerous for me to admit that she was of that order and kind." He thrust the pouch back in his pocket, as if to put away the subject with the trifle which had brought it up.

Arobin dropped in with a message from Mrs. Merriman, to say that the card party was postponed on account of the illness of one of her children.

"How do you do, Arobin?" said Robert, rising from the obscurity.

"Oh! Lebrun. To be sure! I heard yesterday you were back. How did they treat you down in Mexico?"

"Fairly well."

"But not well enough to keep you there. Stunning girls, though, in Mexico. I thought I should never get away from Vera Cruz when I was down there a couple of years ago."

"Did they embroider slippers and tobacco pouches and hat bands and things for you?" asked Edna.

"Oh! my! no! I didn't get so deep in their regard. I fear they made more impression on me than I made on them."

"You were less fortunate than Robert, then."

"I am always less fortunate than Robert. Has he been imparting tender confidences?"

"I've been imposing myself long enough," said Robert, rising, and shaking hands with Edna. "Please convey my regards to Mr. Pontellier when you write."

He shook hands with Arobin and went away.

"Fine fellow, that Lebrun," said Arobin when Robert had gone. "I never heard you speak of him."

"I knew him last summer at Grand Isle," she replied. "Here is that photograph of yours. Don't you want it?"

"What do I want with it? Throw it away." She threw it back on the table.

"I'm not going to Mrs. Merriman's," she said. "If you see her, tell her so. But perhaps I had better write. I think I shall write now, and say that I am sorry her child is sick, and tell her not to count on me."

"It would be a good scheme," acquiesced Arobin. "I don't blame you; stupid lot!"

Edna opened the blotter, and having procured paper and pen, began to write a note. Arobin lit a cigar and read the evening paper, which he had in his pocket.

"What is the date?" she asked. He told her.

"Will you mail this for me when you go out?"

"Certainly." He read to her little bits out of the newspaper, while she straightened things on the table.

"What do you want to do?" he asked, throwing aside the paper. "Do you want to go for a walk or a drive or anything? It would be a fine night to drive."

"No; I don't want to do anything but just be quiet. You go away and amuse yourself. Don't stay."

"I'll go away if I must; but I shan't amuse myself. You know that I only live when I am near you."

He stood up to bid her good night.

"Is that one of the things you always say to women?"

"I have said it before, but I don't think I ever came so near meaning it," he answered with a smile. There were no warm lights in her eyes; only a dreamy, absent look.

"Good night. I adore you. Sleep well," he said, and he kissed her hand and went away.

She stayed alone in a kind of reverie—a sort of stupor. Step by step she lived over every instant of the time she had been with Robert after he had entered Mademoiselle Reisz's door. She recalled his words, his looks. How few and meager they had been for her hungry heart! A vision—a transcendently seductive vision of a Mexican girl arose before her. She writhed with a jealous pang. She wondered when he would come back. He had not said he would come back. She had been with him, had heard his voice and touched his hand. But some way he had seemed nearer to her off there in Mexico.

XXXV

The morning was full of sunlight and hope. Edna could see before her no denial—only the promise of excessive joy. She lay in bed awake, with bright eyes full of speculation. "He loves you, poor fool." If she could but get that conviction firmly fixed in her mind, what mattered about the rest? She felt she had been childish and unwise the night before in giving herself over to despondency. She recapitulated the motives which no doubt explained Robert's reserve. They were not insurmountable; they would not hold if he really loved her; they could not hold against her own passion, which he must come to realize in time. She pictured him going to his business that morning. She even saw how he was dressed; how he walked down one street, and turned the corner of another; saw him bending over his desk, talking to people who entered the office, going to his lunch, and perhaps watching for her on the street. He would come to her in the afternoon or evening, sit and roll his cigarette, talk a little, and go away as he had done the night before. But how delicious it would be to have him there with her! She would have no regrets, nor seek to penetrate his reserve if he still chose to wear it.

Edna ate her breakfast only half dressed. The maid brought her a delicious printed scrawl from Raoul, expressing his love, asking her to send him some bonbons, and telling her they had found that morning ten tiny white pigs all lying in a row beside Lidie's big white pig.

A letter also came from her husband, saying he hoped to be back early in March, and then they would get ready for that journey abroad which he had promised her so long, which he felt now fully able to afford; he felt able to travel as people should, without any thought of small economies—thanks to his recent speculations in Wall Street.

Much to her surprise she received a note from Arobin, written at midnight from the club. It was to say good morning to her, to hope that she had slept well, to assure her of his devotion, which he trusted she in some faintest manner returned.

All these letters were pleasing to her. She answered the children in a cheerful frame of mind, promising them bonbons, and congratulating them upon their happy find of the little pigs.

She answered her husband with friendly evasiveness,—not with any fixed design to mislead him, only because all sense of reality had gone out of her life, she had abandoned herself to Fate, and awaited the consequences with indifference.

To Arobin's note she made no reply. She put it under Celestine's stove-lid.

Edna worked several hours with much spirit. She saw no one but a picture dealer, who asked her if it were true that she was going abroad to study in Paris.

She said possibly she might, and he negotiated with her for some Parisian studies to reach him in time for the holiday trade in December.

Robert did not come that day. She was keenly disappointed. He did not come the following day, nor the next. Each morning she awoke with hope, and each night she was a prey to despondency. She was tempted to seek him out. But far from yielding to the impulse, she avoided any occasion which might throw her in his way. She did not go to Mademoiselle Reisz's nor pass by Madame Lebrun's, as she might have done if he had still been in Mexico.

When Arobin, one night, urged her to drive with him, she went—out to the lake, on the Shell Road.[3] His horses were full of mettle, and even a little unmanageable. She liked the rapid gait at which they spun along, and the quick, sharp sound of the horses' hoofs on the hard road. They did not stop anywhere to eat or to drink. Arobin was not needlessly imprudent. But they ate and they drank when they regained Edna's little dining-room—which was comparatively early in the evening.

It was late when he left her. It was getting to be more than a passing whim with Arobin to see her and be with her. He had detected the latent sensuality, which unfolded under his delicate sense of her nature's requirements like a torpid, torrid, sensitive blossom.

There was no despondency when she fell asleep that night; nor was there hope when she awoke in the morning.

XXXVI

There was a garden out in the suburbs; a small, leafy corner, with a few green tables under the orange trees. An old cat slept all day on the stone step in the sun, and an old *mulatresse*[4] slept her idle hours away in her chair at the open window, till some one happened to knock on one of the green tables. She had milk and cream cheese to sell, and bread and butter. There was no one who could make such excellent coffee or fry a chicken so golden brown as she.

The place was too modest to attract the attention of people of fashion, and so quiet as to have escaped the notice of those in search of pleasure and dissipation. Edna had discovered it accidentally one day when the high-board gate stood ajar. She caught sight of a little green table, blotched with the checkered sunlight that filtered through the quivering leaves overhead. Within she had found the slumbering *mulatresse,* the drowsy cat, and a glass of milk which reminded her of the milk she had tasted in Iberville.

She often stopped there during her perambulations; sometimes taking a book with her, and sitting an hour or two under the trees when she found the place deserted. Once or twice she took a quiet dinner there alone, having instructed Celestine beforehand to prepare no dinner at home. It was the last place in the city where she would have expected to meet any one she knew.

Still she was not astonished when, as she was partaking of a modest dinner late in the afternoon, looking into an open book, stroking the cat, which had made friends with her—she was not greatly astonished to see Robert come in at the tall garden gate.

---

3. A road along the shore of Lake Pontchartrain.   4. A mixed-race woman, a female mulatto.

"I am destined to see you only by accident," she said, shoving the cat off the chair beside her. He was surprised, ill at ease, almost embarrassed at meeting her thus so unexpectedly.

"Do you come here often?" he asked.

"I almost live here," she said.

"I used to drop in very often for a cup of Catiche's good coffee. This is the first time since I came back."

"She'll bring you a plate, and you will share my dinner. There's always enough for two—even three." Edna had intended to be indifferent and as reserved as he when she met him; she had reached the determination by a laborious train of reasoning, incident to one of her despondent moods. But her resolve melted when she saw him before her, seated there beside her in the little garden, as if a designing Providence had led him into her path.

"Why have you kept away from me, Robert?" she asked, closing the book that lay open upon the table.

"Why are you so personal, Mrs. Pontellier? Why do you force me to idiotic subterfuges?" he exclaimed with sudden warmth. "I suppose there's no use telling you I've been very busy, or that I've been sick, or that I've been to see you and not found you at home. Please let me off with any one of those excuses."

"You are the embodiment of selfishness," she said. "You save yourself something—I don't know what—but there is some selfish motive, and in sparing yourself you never consider for a moment what I think, or how I feel your neglect and indifference. I suppose this is what you would call unwomanly; but I have got into a habit of expressing myself. It doesn't matter to me, and you may think me unwomanly if you like."

"No; I only think you cruel, as I said the other day. Maybe not intentionally cruel; but you seem to be forcing me into disclosures which can result in nothing, as if you would have me bare a wound for the pleasure of looking at it, without the intention or power of healing it."

"I'm spoiling your dinner, Robert; never mind what I say. You haven't eaten a morsel."

"I only came in for a cup of coffee." His sensitive face was all disfigured with excitement.

"Isn't this a delightful place?" she remarked. "I am so glad it has never actually been discovered. It is so quiet, so sweet here. Do you notice there is scarcely a sound to be heard? It's so out of the way; and a good walk from the car. However, I don't mind walking. I always feel so sorry for women who don't like to walk; they miss so much—so many rare little glimpses of life; and we women learn so little of life on the whole.

"Catiche's coffee is always hot. I don't know how she manages it, here in the open air. Celestine's coffee gets cold bringing it from the kitchen to the dining-room. Three lumps! How can you drink it so sweet? Take some of the cress with your chop; it's so biting and crisp. Then there's the advantage of being able to smoke with your coffee out here. Now, in the city—aren't you going to smoke?"

"After a while," he said, laying a cigar on the table.

"Who gave it to you?" she asked.

"I bought it. I suppose I'm getting reckless; I bought a whole box." She was determined not to be personal again and make him uncomfortable.

The cat made friends with him, and climbed into his lap when he smoked his cigar. He stroked her silky fur, and talked a little about her. He looked at Edna's book, which he had read; and he told her the end, to save her the trouble of wading through it, he said.

Again he accompanied her back to her home; and it was after dusk when they reached the little "pigeon-house." She did not ask him to remain, which he was grateful for, as it permitted him to stay without the discomfort of blundering through an excuse which he had no intention of considering. He helped her to light the lamp; then she went into her room to take off her hat and to bathe her face and hands.

When she came back Robert was not examining the pictures and magazines as before; he sat off in the shadow, leaning his head back on the chair as if in a reverie. Edna lingered a moment beside the table, arranging the books there. Then she went across the room to where he sat. She bent over the arm of his chair and called his name.

"Robert," she said, "are you asleep?"

"No," he answered, looking up at her.

She leaned over and kissed him—a soft, cool, delicate kiss, whose voluptuous sting penetrated his whole being—then she moved away from him. He followed, and took her in his arms, just holding her close to him. She put her hand up to his face and pressed his cheek against her own. The action was full of love and tenderness. He sought her lips again. Then he drew her down upon the sofa beside him and held her hand in both of his.

"Now you know," he said, "now you know what I have been fighting against since last summer at Grand Isle; what drove me away and drove me back again."

"Why have you been fighting against it?" she asked. Her face glowed with soft lights.

"Why? Because you were not free; you were Léonce Pontellier's wife. I couldn't help loving you if you were ten times his wife, but so long as I went away from you and kept away I could help telling you so." She put her free hand up to his shoulder, and then against his cheek, rubbing it softly. He kissed her again. His face was warm and flushed.

"There in Mexico I was thinking of you all the time, and longing for you."

"But not writing to me," she interrupted.

"Something put into my head that you cared for me; and I lost my senses. I forgot everything but a wild dream of your some way becoming my wife."

"Your wife!"

"Religion, loyalty, everything would give way if only you cared."

"Then you must have forgotten that I was Léonce Pontellier's wife."

"Oh! I was demented, dreaming of wild, impossible things, recalling men who had set their wives free, we have heard of such things."

"Yes, we have heard of such things."

"I came back full of vague, mad intentions. And when I got here—"

"When you got here you never came near me!" She was still caressing his cheek.

"I realized what a cur I was to dream of such a thing, even if you had been willing."

She took his face between her hands and looked into it as if she would never withdraw her eyes more. She kissed him on the forehead, the eyes, the cheeks, and the lips.

"You have been a very, very foolish boy, wasting your time dreaming of impossible things when you speak of Mr. Pontellier setting me free! I am no longer one of Mr. Pontellier's possessions to dispose of or not. I give myself where I choose. If he were to say, 'Here, Robert, take her and be happy; she is yours,' I should laugh at you both."

His face grew a little white. "What do you mean?" he asked.

There was a knock at the door. Old Celestine came in to say that Madame Ratignolle's servant had come around the back way with a message that Madame had been taken sick and begged Mrs. Pontellier to go to her immediately.

"Yes, yes," said Edna, rising: "I promised. Tell her yes—to wait for me. I'll go back with her."

"Let me walk over with you," offered Robert.

"No", she said; "I will go with the servant." She went into her room to put on her hat, and when she came in again she sat once more upon the sofa beside him. He had not stirred. She put her arms about his neck.

"Good-by, my sweet Robert. Tell me good-by." He kissed her with a degree of passion which had not before entered into his caress, and strained her to him.

"I love you," she whispered, "only you; no one but you. It was you who awoke me last summer out of a life-long, stupid dream. Oh! you have made me so unhappy with your indifference. Oh! I have suffered, suffered! Now you are here we shall love each other, my Robert. We shall be everything to each other. Nothing else in the world is of any consequence. I must go to my friend; but you will wait for me? No matter how late; you will wait for me, Robert?"

"Don't go; don't go! Oh! Edna, stay with me," he pleaded. "Why should you go? Stay with me, stay with me."

"I shall come back as soon as I can; I shall find you here." She buried her face in his neck, and said good-by again. Her seductive voice, together with his great love for her, had enthralled his senses, had deprived him of every impulse but the longing to hold her and keep her.

XXXVII

Edna looked in at the drug store. Monsieur Ratignolle was putting up a mixture himself, very carefully, dropping a red liquid into a tiny glass. He was grateful to Edna for having come; her presence would be a comfort to his wife. Madame Ratignolle's sister, who had always been with her at such trying times, had not been able to come up from the plantation, and Adèle had been inconsolable until Mrs. Pontellier so kindly promised to come to her. The nurse had been with them at night for the past week, as she lived a great distance away. And Dr. Mandelet had been coming and going all the afternoon. They were then looking for him any moment.

Edna hastened upstairs by a private stairway that led from the rear of the store to the apartments above. The children were all sleeping in a back room. Madame Ratignolle was in the salon, whither she had strayed in her suffering impatience. She sat on the sofa, clad in an ample white *peignoir,* holding a handkerchief tight in her hand with a nervous clutch. Her face was drawn and pinched, her sweet blue eyes haggard and unnatural. All her beautiful hair had been drawn back and plaited. It lay in a long braid on the soft pillow, coiled like a golden serpent. The nurse, a comfortable looking *Griffe*[5] woman in white apron and cap, was urging her to return to her bedroom.

"There is no use, there is no use," she said at once to Edna. "We must get rid of Mandelet; he is getting too old and careless. He said he would be here at half-past seven; now it must be eight. See what time it is, Joséphine."

5. A woman three-quarters black.

The woman was possessed of a cheerful nature, and refused to take any situation too seriously, especially a situation with which she was so familiar. She urged Madame to have courage and patience. But Madame only set her teeth hard into her under lip, and Edna saw the sweat gather in beads on her white forehead. After a moment or two she uttered a profound sigh and wiped her face with the handkerchief rolled in a ball. She appeared exhausted. The nurse gave her a fresh handkerchief, sprinkled with cologne water.

"This is too much!" she cried. "Mandelet ought to be killed! Where is Alphonse? Is it possible I am to be abandoned like this—neglected by every one?"

"Neglected, indeed!" exclaimed the nurse. Wasn't she there? And here was Mrs. Pontellier leaving, no doubt, a pleasant evening at home to devote to her? And wasn't Monsieur Ratignolle coming that very instant through the hall? And Joséphine was quite sure she had heard Doctor Mandelet's coupé.[6] Yes, there it was, down at the door.

Adèle consented to go back to her room. She sat on the edge of a little low couch next to her bed.

Doctor Mandelet paid no attention to Madame Ratignolle's upbraidings. He was accustomed to them at such times, and was too well convinced of her loyalty to doubt it.

He was glad to see Edna, and wanted her to go with him into the salon and entertain him. But Madame Ratignolle would not consent that Edna should leave her for an instant. Between agonizing moments, she chatted a little, and said it took her mind off her sufferings.

Edna began to feel uneasy. She was seized with a vague dread. Her own like experiences seemed far away, unreal, and only half remembered. She recalled faintly an ecstasy of pain, the heavy odor of chloroform, a stupor which had deadened sensation, and an awakening to find a little new life to which she had given being, added to the great, unnumbered multitude of souls that come and go.

She began to wish she had not come; her presence was not necessary. She might have invented a pretext for staying away; she might even invent a pretext now for going. But Edna did not go. With an inward agony, with a flaming, outspoken revolt against the ways of Nature, she witnessed the scene of torture.

She was still stunned and speechless with emotion when later she leaned over her friend to kiss her and softly say good-by. Adèle, pressing her cheek, whispered in an exhausted voice: "Think of the children, Edna. Oh think of the children! Remember them!"

XXXVIII

Edna still felt dazed when she got outside in the open air. The Doctor's coupé had returned for him and stood before the *porte cochère*. She did not wish to enter the coupé, and told Doctor Mandelet she would walk; she was not afraid, and would go alone. He directed his carriage to meet him at Mrs. Pontellier's, and he started to walk home with her.

Up—away up, over the narrow street between the tall houses, the stars were blazing. The air was mild and caressing, but cool with the breath of spring and the night. They walked slowly, the Doctor with a heavy, measured tread and his hands

6. Two-passenger, closed carriage.

behind him; Edna, in an absent-minded way, as she had walked one night at Grand Isle, as if her thoughts had gone ahead of her and she was striving to overtake them.

"You shouldn't have been there, Mrs. Pontellier," he said. "That was no place for you. Adèle is full of whims at such times. There were a dozen women she might have had with her, unimpressionable women. I felt that it was cruel, cruel. You shouldn't have gone."

"Oh, well!" she answered, indifferently. "I don't know that it matters after all. One has to think of the children some time or other; the sooner the better."

"When is Léonce coming back?"

"Quite soon. Some time in March."

"And you are going abroad?"

"Perhaps—no, I am not going. I'm not going to be forced into doing things. I don't want to go abroad. I want to be let alone. Nobody has any right—except children, perhaps—and even then, it seems to me—or it did seem—" She felt that her speech was voicing the incoherency of her thoughts, and stopped abruptly.

"The trouble is," sighed the Doctor, grasping her meaning intuitively, "that youth is given up to illusions. It seems to be a provision of Nature; a decoy to secure mothers for the race. And Nature takes no account of moral consequences, of arbitrary conditions which we create, and which we feel obliged to maintain at any cost."

"Yes," she said. "The years that are gone seem like dreams—if one might go on sleeping and dreaming—but to wake up and find—oh! well! perhaps it is better to wake up after all, even to suffer, rather than to remain a dupe to illusions all one's life."

"It seems to me, my dear child," said the Doctor at parting, holding her hand, "you seem to me to be in trouble. I am not going to ask for your confidence. I will only say that if ever you feel moved to give it to me, perhaps I might help you. I know I would understand, and I tell you there are not many who would—not many, my dear."

"Some way I don't feel moved to speak of things that trouble me. Don't think I am ungrateful or that I don't appreciate your sympathy. There are periods of despondency and suffering which take possession of me. But I don't want anything but my own way. That is wanting a good deal, of course, when you have to trample upon the lives, the hearts, the prejudices of others—but no matter—still, I shouldn't want to trample upon the little lives. Oh! I don't know what I'm saying, Doctor. Good night. Don't blame me for anything."

"Yes, I will blame you if you don't come and see me soon. We will talk of things you never have dreamt of talking about before. It will do us both good. I don't want you to blame yourself, whatever comes. Good night, my child."

She let herself in at the gate, but instead of entering she sat upon the step of the porch. The night was quiet and soothing. All the tearing emotion of the last few hours seemed to fall away from her like a somber, uncomfortable garment, which she had but to loosen to be rid of. She went back to that hour before Adèle had sent for her; and her senses kindled afresh in thinking of Robert's words, the pressure of his arms, and the feeling of his lips upon her own. She could picture at that moment no greater bliss on earth than possession of the beloved one. His expression of love had already given him to her in part. When she thought that he was there at hand, waiting for her, she grew numb with the intoxication of expectancy. It was so late; he should be asleep perhaps. She would awaken him with a kiss. She hoped he would be asleep that she might arouse him with her caresses.

Still, she remembered Adèle's voice whispering, "Think of the children; think of them." She meant to think of them, that determination had driven into her soul like a death wound—but not to-night. To-morrow would be time to think of everything.

Robert was not waiting for her in the little parlor. He was nowhere at hand. The house was empty. But he had scrawled on a piece of paper that lay in the lamplight:

"I love you. Good-by—because I love you."

Edna grew faint when she read the words. She went and sat on the sofa. Then she stretched herself out there, never uttering a sound. She did not sleep. She did not go to bed. The lamp sputtered and went out. She was still awake in the morning, when Celestine unlocked the kitchen door and came in to light the fire.

XXXIX

Victor, with hammer and nails and scraps of scantling,[7] was patching a corner of one of the galleries. Mariequita sat near by, dangling her legs, watching him work, and handing him nails from the tool-box. The sun was beating down upon them. The girl had covered her head with her apron folded into a square pad. They had been talking for an hour or more. She was never tired of hearing Victor describe the dinner at Mrs. Pontellier's. He exaggerated every detail, making it appear a veritable Lucillean[8] feast. The flowers were in tubs, he said. The champagne was quaffed from huge golden goblets. Venus rising from the foam[9] could have presented no more entrancing a spectacle than Mrs. Pontellier, blazing with beauty and diamonds at the head of the board, while the other women were all of them youthful houris[1] possessed of incomparable charms.

She got it into her head that Victor was in love with Mrs. Pontellier, and he gave her evasive answers, framed so as to confirm her belief. She grew sullen and cried a little, threatening to go off and leave him to his fine ladies. There were a dozen men crazy about her at the *Chênière;* and since it was the fashion to be in love with married people, why she could run away any time she liked to New Orleans with Célina's husband.

Célina's husband was a fool, a coward, and a pig, and to prove it to her, Victor intended to hammer his head into a jelly the next time he encountered him. This assurance was very consoling to Mariequita. She dried her eyes, and grew cheerful at the prospect.

They were still talking of the dinner and the allurements of city life when Mrs. Pontellier herself slipped around the corner of the house. The two youngsters stayed dumb with amazement before what they considered to be an apparition. But it was really she in flesh and blood, looking tired and a little travel-stained.

"I walked up from the wharf," she said, "and heard the hammering. I supposed it was you, mending the porch. It's a good thing. I was always tripping over those loose planks last summer. How dreary and deserted everything looks!"

It took Victor some little time to comprehend that she had come in Beaudelet's lugger, that she had come alone, and for no purpose but to rest.

"There's nothing fixed up yet, you see. I'll give you my room; it's the only place."

"Any corner will do," she assured him.

7. Timber fragments.
8. Probably a misprint for *Lucullean,* of or respecting Roman general Licinius Lucullus (c. 180–102 BCE) notorious for his luxurious banquets.

9. Roman goddess of love and beauty, born from the foam of the sea.
1. Beautiful maidens inhabiting Muslim paradise.

"And if you can stand Philomel's cooking," he went on, "though I might try to get her mother while you are here. Do you think she would come?" turning to Mariequita.

Mariequita thought that perhaps Philomel's mother might come for a few days, and money enough.

Beholding Mrs. Pontellier make her appearance, the girl had at once suspected a lovers' rendezvous. But Victor's astonishment was so genuine, and Mrs. Pontellier's indifference so apparent, that the disturbing notion did not lodge long in her brain. She contemplated with the greatest interest this woman who gave the most sumptuous dinners in America, and who had all the men in New Orleans at her feet.

"What time will you have dinner?" asked Edna. "I'm very hungry; but don't get anything extra."

"I'll have it ready in little or no time," he said, bustling and packing away his tools. "You may go to my room to brush up and rest yourself. Mariequita will show you."

"Thank you," said Edna. "But, do you know, I have a notion to go down to the beach and take a good wash and even a little swim, before dinner?"

"The water is too cold!" they both exclaimed. "Don't think of it."

"Well, I might go down and try—dip my toes in. Why, it seems to me the sun is hot enough to have warmed the very depths of the ocean. Could you get me a couple of towels? I'd better go right away, so as to be back in time. It would be a little too chilly if I waited till this afternoon."

Mariequita ran over to Victor's room, and returned with some towels, which she gave to Edna.

"I hope you have fish for dinner," said Edna, as she started to walk away; "but don't do anything extra if you haven't."

"Run and find Philomel's mother," Victor instructed the girl. "I'll go to the kitchen and see what I can do. By Gimminy! Women have no consideration! She might have sent me word."

Edna walked on down to the beach rather mechanically, not noticing anything special except that the sun was hot. She was not dwelling upon any particular train of thought. She had done all the thinking which was necessary after Robert went away, when she lay awake upon the sofa till morning.

She had said over and over to herself: "To-day it is Arobin; tomorrow it will be some one else. It makes no difference to me, it doesn't matter about Léonce Pontellier—but Raoul and Étienne!" She understood now clearly what she had meant long ago when she said to Adèle Ratignolle that she would give up the unessential, but she would never sacrifice herself for her children.

Despondency had come upon her there in the wakeful night, and had never lifted. There was no one thing in the world that she desired. There was no human being whom she wanted near her except Robert; and she even realized that the day would come when he, too, and the thought of him would melt out of her existence, leaving her alone. The children appeared before her like antagonists who had overcome her; who had overpowered her and sought to drag her into the soul's slavery for the rest of her days. But she knew a way to elude them. She was not thinking of these things when she walked down to the beach.

The water of the Gulf stretched out before her gleaming with the million lights of the sun. The voice of the sea is seductive, never ceasing, whispering, clamoring, murmuring, inviting the soul to wander in abysses of solitude. All along the white beach, up and down, there was no living thing in sight. A bird with a broken wing was beating the air above, reeling, fluttering, circling disabled down, down to the water.

Edna had found her old bathing suit still hanging, faded, upon its accustomed peg.

She put it on, leaving her clothing in the bath-house. But when she was there beside the sea, absolutely alone, she cast the unpleasant, pricking garments from her, and for the first time in her life she stood naked in the open air, at the mercy of the sun, the breeze that beat upon her, and the waves that invited her.

How strange and awful it seemed to stand naked under the sky! how delicious! She felt like some new-born creature, opening its eyes in a familiar world that it had never known.

The foamy wavelets curled up to her white feet, and coiled like serpents about her ankles. She walked out. The water was chill, but she walked on. The water was deep, but she lifted her white body and reached out with a long, sweeping stroke. The touch of the sea is sensuous, enfolding the body in its soft, close embrace.

She went on and on. She remembered the night she swam far out, and recalled the terror that seized her at the fear of being unable to regain the shore. She did not look back now, but went on and on, thinking of the blue-grass meadow that she had traversed when a little child, believing that it had no beginning and no end.

Her arms and legs were growing tired.

She thought of Léonce and the children. They were a part of her life. But they need not have thought that they could possess her, body and soul. How Mademoiselle Reisz would have laughed, perhaps sneered, if she knew! "And you call yourself an artist! What pretensions, Madame! The artist must possess the courageous soul that dares and defies."

Exhaustion was pressing upon and over-powering her.

"Good-by—because, I love you." He did not know; he did not understand. He would never understand. Perhaps Doctor Mandelet would have understood if she had seen him—but it was too late; the shore was far behind her, and her strength was gone.

She looked into the distance, and the old terror flamed up for an instant, then sank again. Edna heard her father's voice and her sister Margaret's. She heard the barking of an old dog that was chained to the sycamore tree. The spurs of the cavalry officer clanged as he walked across the porch. There was the hum of bees, and the musky odor of pinks[2] filled the air.

1899

◄►◄ ROSA PRAED ►◄►

1851–1935

A prolific novelist and dramatist, Rosa Praed was the first woman born in Australia to have an international literary reputation. She was the daughter of Matilda Harpur and her husband, Thomas Murray-Prior, a politician and civil servant in Queensland. Educated at home and, for a brief time, at a school in Brisbane, she

2. Carnations.

shared her father's fascination with colonial politics. From an early age, she was at home in the "bush," playing with Aborigine children and learning from them their language and culture. Reading Elizabeth Gaskell's biography of Charlotte Brontë inspired her and her mother to start a magazine at home in 1866, in imitation of the Brontë children.

Although she began writing at age ten, she did not publish her first book until eight years after her marriage in 1872 to Arthur Campbell Praed. In stark contrast to the social life of Brisbane the twenty-five-year-old Praed had enjoyed, their three-year stay in an isolated outpost, where they were subjected to heat, insects, poor food, and loneliness, was unhappy. They then moved to England, where Praed was to live for the rest of her life. She drew on her early experience of Australia in roughly half of her more than forty novels, most of them romances.

Unlike many successful women authors of the nineteenth century, Praed had children, but all of them were to die in unhappy circumstances. She had three sons: one was killed in an automobile accident, one was gored by a rhinoceros, and one committed suicide. Her only daughter, who was born deaf, died in a mental institution. A firm believer in reincarnation, Praed thought that her family's sufferings were connected to her previous life as an ancient Roman priestess. She separated from her husband in 1899 and moved in with Nancy Harward, who became her longtime companion. Praed believed Harward was the reincarnation of a Roman slave, a story she elaborated in *Nyria* (1904) and *The Soul of Nyria* (1931), published after Harward's death in 1927. Praed's other occult interests included telepathic communication and astral bodies (the human body is said to have its "astral" counterpart in a nonphysical realm of existence).

Beginning with her first novel, *An Australian Heroine* (1880), Praed incorporated her knowledge of the Australian landscape, culture, and politics into her stories of romance and marriage. In her time her novels were considered "racy" because she wrote frankly about the pressure to marry and the unhappiness women experienced in failed marriages. The love triangles in her novels often force a young Australian woman to choose between an earnest, honest, but dull Australian and a more attractive but less reliable Englishman; the proper choice is not always clear. *Policy and Passion* (1881), the most popular of her novels, centers on the marital choices of the heroine, Honoria Longleat, but places her story in the context of the political challenges facing her native Queensland in the years after it separated from New South Wales. The particular issue at the beginning of this novel is whether a railroad should be built to connect remote stations with the cities and ports of Australia's east coast. Descriptions of the landscape and political conversations between men mix with the love story to make an unusual nineteenth-century woman's novel.

The passage from *Policy and Passion* excerpted here introduces two male characters, one of them a suitor to Honoria, and outlines the friendship they have developed in the bush. Praed's character the "Australian Explorer," named Dyson Maddox, exemplifies the colonialist attitude toward the land and people of Australia, even though he himself was born there. For the benefit of European and American readers, Praed's narrator describes the Australian landscapes and defines the colloquial speech in the scene. Praed also portrays racism toward Aborigines at the end of the passage, reflecting both Maddox's colonialist attitude and Praed's unself-consciousness about the racial politics of her homeland.

From Policy and Passion

An Australian Explorer

Some few days after the arrival of Barrington at Dyraaba, Mr. Dyson Maddox and his superintendent, Cornelius Cathcart, were riding over the ranges from Barramunda in the direction of Kooralbyn.[1] The two stations, with Dyraaba forming the point of a triangle between, lay about fifteen miles apart, a convenient distance to be pleaded as an excuse for remaining the night when alluring attractions offered themselves, and not too far to be retraced late in the day when circumstances rendered return desirable.

Of the two men, the superintendent, as requiring the shortest notice, may be described first. He was small and spare, with a loosely-built frame, upon which his clothes hung as upon a peg; a yellow face ornamented by a tiny flaxen imperial,[2] and narrow blue eyes. He was always shabbily dressed. At all times a restless imp seemed to possess his frame. When he walked, his body jerked convulsively; when he rode, his limbs twitched as though he were a victim to incipient St. Vitus's dance.[3] His tone was caustic, and he affected cynicism. He had been Maddox's companion for several years, first in certain exploring expeditions on the northern coast which the latter had conducted, and afterwards as manager of Barramunda.

Maddox had upon one occasion saved Cathcart's life in a flooded creek, and this circumstance was sufficient warrant for the strong, undemonstrative attachment that existed between two dissimilar natures. Of late, however, a slight constraint had arisen in their intercourse.[4] It was suspected by both, though not admitted by either, that this was due to Miss Longleat's influence.

Yet in what way was difficult to define. There could be no question of rivalry between the two men. Had there been, Cathcart would certainly have withdrawn in favour of his friend, while he would as certainly have cloaked his generosity under an appearance of snarling contempt. As it was, circumstances forbade him to think of matrimony. To aspire to the heiress of the Tarrangella Mine[5] would have been ridiculous presumption. Cathcart would not acknowledge to himself that Honoria attracted him; but that she constantly filled his mind was evident, and that there was a latent bitterness in his thoughts of her was equally certain.

Dyson Maddox was broad-shouldered and thick-set, with muscles like iron, and a skin mellowed by exposure to the colour of untanned leather. He had finely-hewn features, a determined mouth, and brown, level eyes. There was brusque daring in his glance, and much frank nobility in the sweep of his brow. He had a trick of frowning when preoccupied, which gave a morose expression to his face; but when the frown dispersed there was sweetness in his look. His hair curled in heavy locks, and his moustache and whiskers were carelessly trimmed, as though he were not accustomed to expend thought upon his toilette.[6]

1. Barrington and Dyson are both suitors to Honoria Longleat, an heiress whose beauty and accomplishments are famous throughout the region.
2. A pointed beard grown from the lower lip to the chin.
3. Epilepsy.
4. Communication.
5. Fictional tin mine owned by Honoria's father.
6. Personal grooming.

A typical Australian of the second generation,[7] unconventional, courageous, and energetic, lacking somewhat the graces of society, but rich in an air of native distinction, and in the chivalry which arises from intuitive good breeding. He was far removed from the thin-skinned, metaphysical breed, and had none of that aesthetic sentimentalism which is a development of Old-World civilisation. His passions were strong, but balanced by logical power and by the discipline of a hard life. He had a rare faculty for repressing emotion; was deliberate in action, and slow to receive new impressions. Though fairly cultivated, he had not followed intellectual pursuits more closely than the exigencies of a purely Australian career had demanded.

The master and the manager had been discoursing for some time upon bovine matters, when Maddox remarked, apropos of an arrangement for selling fat cattle during the winter: "It is possible that I may not be much at Barramunda after the opening of Parliament. I am thinking of taking a more active part in politics this session."

"So I imagined. Of course you have been offered the post of Minister for Lands. It seems the pet ambition nowadays to make one's self into a target for scurrilous attacks."

"You take an unfortunate view of the question," replied Dyson. "Why should political distinction be an unworthy aim here? There must be interested motives underlying all party strife; they come nearer the surface in a small community. I have always wished to be in the Cabinet, but there are reasons which make me hesitate to accept the position. I must, however, let the Premier know my decision this evening."

"But beforehand you must make yourself certain of your ground with Miss Longleat. I understand. This is the reason of your détour by Kooralbyn. I hope she will be there, and that you may catch her in a listening mood. That is the worst of having to do with capricious persons; there is no calculating their humours. Well, if you are successful in your suit, be good enough to apprise me as early as possible of the fact, so that I may clear out of Barramunda without delay."

"You have always said that you would leave Barramunda when I married. Why should you do so? No one should interfere with you in the Bachelors' Quarters."

"Not even the Bachelors' Quarters would be sacred to Mrs. Maddox," answered Cathcart, shortly. "Thank you, but there is not room at Barramunda for Miss Longleat and for me. I shall take up country out west, or go to Fiji, which seems the refuge for unfortunates just now."

"I have sometimes fancied," said Dyson in a hesitating manner, though he spoke with deliberate emphasis, "that you were attracted by Miss Longleat. The thought has troubled me, although I have no actual grounds for entertaining it. I only guess at your feelings. You know my wishes. Come, hadn't we better have the matter out?"

"Make your mind easy," said Cathcart. "I am too good a servant to poach on my master's preserves.[8] I may be a fool, but I am not such a drivelling idiot as to suppose that Miss Longleat would think of me as a husband. An admirer is an-

---

7. This implies that his grandparents were transported as convicts from England to a penal colony in Australia, but later in the passage we learn his grandfather came as a government appointee of Queen Victoria.

8. A poacher hunts illegally on privately owned land.

other thing; a chimneysweep may be at liberty to worship a goddess. I dare say that she is piqued because I have not thrown myself at her feet; but I have some self-respect. That girl puzzles me. I cannot make up my mind whether I dislike or pity her most."

"Tell me your reasons for disliking her," said Maddox.

"She is always posing for effect. There is nothing genuine about her except her greediness for sensation. She is an actress who believes in her parts. She is cold-blooded and passionate together. She is intolerably selfish; she has everything to make her happy, and she is morbidly discontented. She despises her father who adores her. She is not womanly. Then her frankness is extraordinary. She is essentially a New-World product. No European young woman could combine so much boldness with an innocence which one is obliged to take for granted. Excuse me if I offend your susceptibilities; you asked my opinion."

"Go on," said Maddox. "Now, why do you pity her?"

"She is absolutely solitary; she has neither women friends nor relations. As long as she cultivates fastidiousness, there can be no sympathy between her and her father. She has been badly brought up. What result could one expect from a Sydney boarding-school? And I think that there is a certain nobility in her nature. She will be either good or bad. She is discontented with herself. If she were wise she would marry you, but I do not think she will—just yet. Our roads separate here. I am going to meet Brown at Jaff's Peak Camp."

"You'll not come on to Kooralbyn, then?"

"No; there are the weaners[9] to be looked after, and the long-tailed strawberry cow to be brought in. And I am not unselfish enough to play bodkin."[1]

Cathcart turned his horse, and with a curt good-bye galloped away through the trees, till he had disappeared over the brow of the hill. Maddox rode on through the silent forest, descending the range and skirting the creek, where the tall cedars, laden with the golden berries of autumn, cast their shadows over the tracks.

Dyson Maddox's grandfather had come out to Australia holding a Crown appointment in New South Wales. The office under a responsible Government had descended to the son, who, in his turn, had died suddenly before Dyson had attained his majority. Thus it will be seen that the lad was a true native of the soil. He inherited from his father an easy competence,[2] and having neither brothers, sisters, nor near relations, had no claims upon his purse. But he was not content to plod on in conventional fashion; he must needs carve his fortune in his own manner. It was his ambition to become one of the pioneers of Australian civilisation. He had made several more or less successful attempts to penetrate into the interior, and a few years before the present date had equipped and commanded an exploring expedition, which, with a dauntless energy seldom equalled in the annals of Australia, had fought its way through the heart of Leichardt's Land[3] to a point on the extreme northern coast, hitherto only accessible by sea.

At the risk of starvation, and of murder by the hostile tribes, whose territories had never before been invaded by white men, the little band, with Dyson Maddox at its head, pushed on towards the northern peninsula. Halfway the horses perished from eating poisonous berries in a scrub; provisions failed, and sickness

9. Young animals newly removed from their
mothers.
1. Obscure: dagger or stiletto.

2. Sufficient income to live comfortably.
3. Praed's fictitious name for Queensland.

thinned the number. Nevertheless, the brave men pursued their way on foot, through forest and desert, subject to night attacks and to daily peril of native ambuscades, till they reached the remote seaboard township of Gundaroo, a port commanding the northern waters, and a touching-place for mail-steamers of sufficient importance to render the establishment of land communication with the southern districts a matter of concern to the Leichardt's Land Government.

In the course of this expedition Maddox's left arm had been disabled by the thrust of a black's[4] spear, hurled during a midnight surprise of his camp. He was almost a cripple when he reached Gundaroo. A few months later he knew that he could no longer draw his trigger with certainty of effect, or rely upon his physical strength to aid him in combating the dangers and difficulties which beset the path of an explorer.

Thirst after unknown country had been the ruling motive of his life. The miner who digs in the expectation of striking a priceless nugget knows no keener excitement than that which Dyson experienced at the first glimpse of some broad river or fertile rolling plain, never before gazed upon by any but barbarian eyes, but which, by his discovery, might in future ages become the home of thousands of his race.

The abstract side of existence had few claims upon him, yet he was not without enthusiasm of an inspiring, practical kind, and was strongly imbued with the notion that he who places fresh territory at the service of his country has a no less exalted mission than the scientific investigator, the mechanical discoverer, or the pathological inquirer.

Now this wound, inflicted by the ignominious weapon of an aboriginal, had changed the whole current of his existence. He could no longer lead the life of perilous adventure which had held for him so great a charm. His health had been injured by exposure and privation, and those anxious six months, during which death had stared him in the face, had visibly whitened his hair and perceptibly reduced his vigour.

He had left Leichardt's Town full of animal health and reckless bravery; he reached Gundaroo broken-down, subdued, and prematurely aged, his ambition checked in the very hour of fulfilment. There was nothing for him but to return south, and to embrace a tranquil, bucolic career, seasoned by the mild excitement of politics.

But when, after his purchase of Barramunda, he paid his first visit to Kooralbyn, and saw again Honoria Longleat, whom he had known as a child, now fresh from school, and radiant in the first consciousness of power and the bloom of early womanhood, he almost ceased to regret the life he had quitted. A vague, delicious dream, which had sweetened his wanderings, took defined shape, and imparted a new zest to existence. Frank, daring, original, with the touch of passionate sensibility that he himself lacked, he felt that she was the one woman who could make his happiness.

But he was cautious and deliberate, and did not snatch the prize when it was, perhaps, within his reach. Honoria had her ambitious dreams of a life of colour and excitement. Sometimes he seemed to her cold and commonplace, sometimes unrefined. She began to mix in the world and to taste the sweets of coquetry. She

---

4. An Aborigine's.

accustomed herself to associate elegance of manners with an European education. As a slave or an adoring mentor, Dyson pleased her well enough, but she was almost convinced that he would not be a husband to her liking. Yet she was not happy when he absented himself from her society. She paid deference to his opinion: by turns she piqued and enthralled him, offended if he refused to dance attendance in her train, despising him for patient endurance of her whims. So matters stood, but Honoria was not aware that he had given her a certain length of tether, and had determined to suffer these alternations of hope and despair no longer.

After an hour's riding Maddox crossed the river for the last time, and entered an extensive plain, commonly called "the racecourse," that lay between the creek and the hill upon which Kooralbyn was built. Now he passed through the slip-rails and was admitted into the home-paddock. Behind him rose the mountains, sloping in a series of wooded ranges to the plain. Herds of cattle and horses browsed upon the rich pasture, which was dotted with clumps of trees and bordered by a fringe of green that marked the course of the river.

The head-station of Kooralbyn consisted of a cluster of cottages built upon the hump of a low hill that overlooked the racecourse. Three of these buildings were placed in a garden enclosed by a high fence, of which one portion was overgrown with passion-fruit, while the remainder supported a hedge of cactus. Round each was a wide verandah, partly trellised with vines, and festooned by bougainvillea, snowy stephanotis, and the orange, bell-shaped flowers of the begonia. The two smaller cottages, in one of which dwelt Mr. Ferris[5] and his family, while the other was the kitchen of the establishment, were connected by covered passages with the larger house occupied by Mr. Longleat and his two daughters. Outside the enclosure stood the Bachelors' Quarters, set apart for the accommodation of passing strangers, and for the use of gentlemen stockmen, and *new chums*,[6] of which, upon a large Australian station, there are often several.

The garden sloped in vine-covered walks towards the plain. At its foot lay a small silvery lagoon, with lilies, white and delicate mauve, floating upon its surface. Beyond, in the distance, rose the amphitheatre of hills, some purple and shadowy, some grey and barren, prominent among them the Koorong Crag, to which Barrington's attention had been directed during his ride to Dyraaba.

The stockyards and outhouses were situated at some little distance from the cluster of cottages.

An avenue of bunyas,[7] still in their youth, led from the stables to the back-entrance to the garden. Maddox rode straight hither, dismounted, and called:

"Hi, Cobra Ball!"

A black-boy, grinning from ear to ear, woolly-haired and red-lipped, approached at the summons, and took Maddox's horse.

"Ba'al Massa want em'yarraman again today?"[8] he asked, in the curious vernacular common to half-civilised natives.

"Yes," replied Dyson; "this fellow go along a Kooya to-night. Keep him in the yard."

---

5. Old man, a failed artist, employed by Honoria's father as storekeeper on his estate.
6. Newly arrived immigrant (originally referred to convicts exiled to Australia).

7. An evergreen tree native to Australia.
8. Being interpreted, runs thus: "Does the master want the horse again to-day?" [Author's note.]

"Youi," said Cobra Ball. "Missee Honoria along a humpey. Missa Longleat ba'al at Kooralbyn; that fellow gone along a Leichardt's Town."[9]

* * *

1881

◄ MARY E. WILKINS FREEMAN ►
1852–1930

In 1852, when Mary E. Wilkins Freeman was born, the rural mill towns of western New England that would be the setting of her novels and stories were poised for a significant change in fortune. The Civil War would accelerate the drain on manpower and prosperity from New England that had already begun with the opening up of the West. Freeman, who published much of her best-known work before her marriage under the name of Mary Wilkins, explored the nature of the experience for those left behind. Although she practiced a variety of genres in her attempt to capture the color of local experience, she found the short story most suited to her topics. Building on groundwork laid by Harriet Beecher Stowe (pp. 732–34), Nathaniel Hawthorne, and Herman Melville, Freeman experimented with and tested the expressive capacities of this form.

Freeman's early family life, in Randolph, Massachusetts, and Brattleboro, Vermont, was characterized by the kind of struggles with poverty and isolation featured in her stories. Like many New Englanders, Freeman's father struggled to make a living, first as a builder and later as a storekeeper. Nevertheless, he and his wife provided their daughter with affection and supported her artistic ambitions. Freeman lived with them until their deaths, when she was in her early thirties, during which time she began to publish fiction in magazines. After the death of her parents, she returned to Randolph and moved in with the family of a childhood friend, Mary Wales, with whom she lived for the next twenty years. These years were fruitful: during this period Freeman published much of the work for which she is best known, including *A Humble Romance and Other Stories* (1887) and *A New England Nun and Other Stories* (1891).

In 1901, after much indecision, she married a wealthy New Jersey doctor, Charles Freeman, but the marriage was marred by his drug abuse and alcoholism. They were legally separated.

Soon after Freeman began publishing, her work started to receive accolades and was highly sought after by popular magazines of the day; in 1926 she won the Howells Medal for Fiction and was elected to the National Institute for Arts and Letters. Freeman's protagonists are almost all women of strongly marked individuality. This individuality, which often is at odds with social conventions, is the product of, the response to, the seldom nurturing environment of rural poverty and patriarchal oppression. Although committed to exploring and commemorating the subjective exigencies of a particular landscape, Freeman's work repudiates nostalgia in favour of precision and honesty. Her narrative technique exemplifies the literary realism that so many late-nineteenth-century Western authors and crit-

---

9. "Yes. Miss Honoria is at the house. Mr. Longleat is not at Kooralbyn." [Author's note.]

ics espoused, yet her depiction of the felt experiences of women under particular environmental constraints has led her to be classified and often dismissed as a minor "local color" or regionalist writer. "A Poetess," which we include here, was first published in *Harper's Monthly* in 1890. Like many of her stories, it explores issues of gender and class while precisely rendering the nuances of language and manners within a small New England town.

A Poetess

The garden-patch at the right of the house was all a gay spangle with sweet-peas and red-flowering beans, and flanked with feathery asparagus. A woman in blue was moving about there. Another woman, in a black bonnet, stood at the front door of the house. She knocked and waited. She could not see from where she stood the blue-clad woman in the garden. The house was very close to the road, from which a tall evergreen hedge separated it, and the view to the side was in a measure cut off.

The front door was open; the woman had to reach to knock on it, as it swung into the entry. She was a small woman and quite young, with a bright alertness about her which had almost the effect of prettiness. It was to her what greenness and crispness are to a plant. She poked her little face forward, and her sharp pretty eyes took in the entry and a room at the left, of which the door stood open. The entry was small and square and unfurnished, except for a well-rubbed old card-table against the back wall. The room was full of green light from the tall hedge, and bristling with grasses and flowers and asparagus stalks.

"Betsey, you there?" called the woman. When she spoke, a yellow canary, whose cage hung beside the front door, began to chirp and twitter.

"Betsey, you there?" the woman called again. The bird's chirps came in a quick volley; then he began to trill and sing.

"She ain't there," said the woman. She turned and went out of the yard through the gap in the hedge; then she looked around. She caught sight of the blue figure in the garden. "There she is," said she.

She went around the house to the garden. She wore a gay cashmere-patterned calico dress with her mourning bonnet, and she held it carefully away from the dewy grass and vines.

The other woman did not notice her until she was close to her and said, "Good-mornin', Betsey." Then she started and turned around.

"Why, Mis' Caxton! That you?" said she.

"Yes. I've been standin' at your door for the last half-hour. I was jest goin' away when I caught sight of you out here."

In spite of her brisk speech her manner was subdued. She drew down the corners of her mouth sadly.

"I declare I'm dreadful sorry you had to stan' there so long!" said the other woman.

She set a pan partly filled with beans on the ground, wiped her hands, which were damp and green from the wet vines, on her apron, then extended her right one with a solemn and sympathetic air.

"It don't make much odds, Betsey," replied Mrs. Caxton. "I ain't got much to take up my time nowadays." She sighed heavily as she shook hands, and the other echoed her.

"We'll go right in now. I'm dreadful sorry you stood there so long," said Betsey.

"You'd better finish pickin' your beans."

"No; I wa'n't goin' to pick any more. I was jest goin' in."

"I declare, Betsey Dole, I shouldn't think you'd got enough for a cat!" said Mrs. Caxton, eying the pan.

"I've got pretty near all there is. I guess I've got more flowerin' beans than eatin' ones, anyway."

"I should think you had," said Mrs. Caxton, surveying the row of bean-poles topped with swarms of delicate red flowers. "I should think they were pretty near all flowerin' ones. Had any peas?"

"I didn't have more'n three or four messes. I guess I planted sweet-peas mostly. I don't know hardly how I happened to."

"Had any summer squash?"

"Two or three. There's some more set, if they ever get ripe. I planted some gourds. I think they look real pretty on the kitchen shelf in the winter."

"I should think you'd got a sage bed big enough for the whole town."

"Well, I have got a pretty good-sized one. I always liked them blue sage-blows. You'd better hold up your dress real careful goin' through here, Mis' Caxton, or you'll get it wet."

The two women picked their way through the dewy grass, around a corner of the hedge, and Betsey ushered her visitor into the house.

"Set right down in the rockin-chair," said she. "I'll jest carry these beans out into the kitchen."

"I should think you'd better get another pan and string 'em, or you won't get 'em done for dinner."

"Well, mebbe I will, if you'll excuse it, Mis' Caxton. The beans had ought to boil quite a while; they're pretty old."

Betsey went into the kitchen and returned with a pan and an old knife. She seated herself opposite Mrs. Caxton, and began to string and cut the beans.

"If I was in your place I shouldn't feel as if I'd got enough to boil a kettle for," said Mrs. Caxton, eying the beans. "I should 'most have thought when you didn't have any more room for a garden than you've got that you'd planted more real beans and peas instead of so many flowerin' ones. I'd rather have a good mess of green peas boiled with a piece of salt pork than all the sweet-peas you could give me. I like flowers well enough, but I never set up for a butterfly, an' I want something else to live on." She looked at Betsey with pensive superiority.

Betsey was near-sighted; she had to bend low over the beans in order to string them. She was fifty years old, but she wore her streaky light hair in curls like a young girl. The curls hung over her faded cheeks and almost concealed them. Once in a while she flung them back with a childish gesture which sat strangely upon her.

"I dare say you're in the right of it," she said, meekly.

"I know I am. You folks that write poetry wouldn't have a single thing to eat growin' if they were left alone. And that brings to mind what I come for. I've been thinkin' about it ever since—our—little Willie—left us." Mrs. Caxton's manner was suddenly full of shamefaced dramatic fervor, her eyes reddened with tears.

Betsey looked up inquiringly, throwing back her curls. Her face took on unconsciously lines of grief so like the other woman's that she looked like her for the minute.

"I thought maybe," Mrs. Caxton went on, tremulously, "you'd be willin' to—write a few lines."

"Of course I will, Mis' Caxton. I'll be glad to, if I can do 'em to suit you," Betsey said, tearfully.

"I thought jest a few—lines. You could mention how—handsome he was, and good, and I never had to punish him but once in his life, and how pleased he was with his little new suit, and what a sufferer he was, and—how we hope he is at rest—in a better land."

"I'll try, Mis' Caxton, I'll try," sobbed Betsey. The two women wept together for a few minutes.

"It seems as if—I couldn't have it so sometimes," Mrs. Caxton said, brokenly. "I keep thinkin' he's in the other—room. Every time I go back home when I've been away it's like—losin' him again. Oh, it don't seem as if I could go home and not find him there—it don't, it don't! Oh, you don't know anything about it, Betsey. You never had any children!"

"I don't s'pose I do, Mis' Caxton; I don't s'pose I do."

Presently Mrs. Caxton wiped her eyes. "I've been thinkin'," said she, keeping her mouth steady with an effort, "that it would be real pretty to have—some lines printed on some sheets of white paper with a neat black border. I'd like to send some to my folks, and one to the Perkinses in Brigham, and there's a good many others I thought would value 'em."

"I'll do jest the best I can, Mis' Caxton, an' be glad to. It's little enough anybody can do at such times."

Mrs. Caxton broke out weeping again. "Oh, it's true, it's true, Betsey!" she sobbed. "Nobody can do anything, and nothin' amounts to anything—poetry or anything else—when he's *gone*. Nothin' can bring him back. Oh, what shall I do, what shall I do?"

Mrs. Caxton dried her tears again, and arose to take leave. "Well, I must be goin', or Wilson won't have any dinner," she said, with an effort at self-control.

"Well, I'll do jest the best I can with the poetry," said Betsey. "I'll write it this afternoon." She had set down her pan of beans and was standing beside Mrs. Caxton. She reached up and straightened her black bonnet, which had slipped backward.

"I've got to get a pin," said Mrs. Caxton, tearfully. "I can't keep it anywheres. It drags right off my head, the veil is so heavy."

Betsey went to the door with her visitor. "It's dreadful dusty, ain't it?" she remarked, in that sad, contemptuous tone with which one speaks of discomforts in the presence of affliction.

"Terrible," replied Mrs. Caxton. "I wouldn't wear my black dress in it nohow; a black bonnet is bad enough. This dress is 'most too good. It's enough to spoil everything. Well, I'm much obliged to you, Betsey, for bein' willin' to do that."

"I'll do jest the best I can, Mis' Caxton."

After Betsey had watched her visitor out of the yard she returned to the sitting-room and took up the pan of beans. She looked doubtfully at the handful of beans all nicely strung and cut up. "I declare I don't know what to do," said she. "Seems as if I should kind of relish these, but it's goin' to take some time to cook 'em, tendin' the fire an' everything, an' I'd ought to go to work on that poetry. Then, there's another thing, if I have 'em to-day, I can't to-morrow. Mebbe I shall take more comfort thinkin' about 'em. I guess I'll leave 'em over till to-morrow."

Betsey carried the pan of beans out into the kitchen and set them away in the pantry. She stood scrutinizing the shelves like a veritable Mother Hubbard.[1] There was a plate containing three or four potatoes and a slice of cold boiled pork, and a spoonful of red jelly in a tumbler; that was all the food in sight. Betsey stooped and lifted the lid from an earthen jar on the floor. She took out two slices of bread. "There!" said she. "I'll have this bread and that jelly this noon, an' to-night I'll have a kind of dinner-supper with them potatoes warmed up with the pork. An' then I can sit right down an' go to work on that poetry."

It was scarcely eleven o'clock, and not time for dinner. Betsey returned to the sitting-room, got an old black portfolio and pen and ink out of the chimney cup-board, and seated herself to work. She meditated, and wrote one line, then another. Now and then she read aloud what she had written with a solemn intonation. She sat there thinking and writing, and the time went on. The twelve-o'clock bell rang, but she never noticed it; she had quite forgotten the bread and jelly. The long curls drooped over her cheeks; her thin yellow hand, cramped around the pen, moved slowly and fitfully over the paper. The light in the room was dim and green, like the light in an arbor, from the tall hedge before the windows. Great plumy bunches of asparagus waved over the tops of the looking-glass; a framed sampler,[2] a steel engraving of a female head taken from some old magazine, and sheaves of dried grasses hung on or were fastened to the walls; vases and tumblers of flowers stood on the shelf and table. The air was heavy and sweet.

Betsey in this room, bending over her portfolio, looked like the very genius[3] of gentle, old-fashioned, sentimental poetry. It seemed as if one, given the prem-ises of herself and the room, could easily deduce what she would write, and read without seeing those lines wherein flowers rhymed sweetly with vernal bowers, home with beyond the tomb, and heaven with even.

The summer afternoon wore on. It grew warmer and closer; the air was full of the rasping babble of insects, with the cicadas shrilling over them; now and then a team passed, and a dust cloud floated over the top of the hedge; the canary at the door chirped and trilled, and Betsey wrote poor little Willie Caxton's obitu-ary poetry.

Tears stood in her pale blue eyes; occasionally they rolled down her cheeks, and she wiped them away. She kept her handkerchief in her lap with her portfolio. When she looked away from the paper she seemed to see two childish forms in the room—one purely human, a boy clad in his little girl petticoats, with a fair chubby face; the other in a little straight white night-gown, with long, shining wings, and the same face. Betsey had not enough imagination to change the face. Little Willie Caxton's angel was still himself to her, although decked in the paraphernalia of the resurrection.

"I s'pose I can't feel about it nor write about it anything the way I could if I'd had any children of my own an' lost 'em. I s'pose it *would* have come home to me different," Betsey murmured once, sniffing. A soft color flamed up under her curls at the thought. For a second the room seemed all aslant with white wings, and smiling with the faces of children that had never been. Betsey straightened herself

1. A reference to a nursery rhyme: "Old Mother Hubbard went to her cupboard to fetch her poor doggie a bone. When she got there, The cupboard was bare, So her poor doggie had none."

2. A piece of needlework showing examples of embroidery stitches.
3. Guardian spirit.

as if she were trying to be dignified to her inner consciousness. "That's one trouble I've been clear of, anyhow," said she; "an' I guess I can enter into her feelin's considerable."

She glanced at a great pink shell on the shelf, and remembered how she had often given it to the dead child to play with when he had been in with his mother, and how he had put it to his ear to hear the sea.

"Dear little fellow!" she sobbed, and sat awhile with her handkerchief at her face.

Betsey wrote her poem upon backs of old letters and odd scraps of paper. She found it difficult to procure enough paper for fair copies of her poems when composed; she was forced to be very economical with the first draft. Her portfolio was piled with a loose litter of written papers when she at length arose and stretched her stiff limbs. It was near sunset; men with dinner-pails were tramping past the gate, going home from their work.

Betsey laid the portfolio on the table. "There! I've wrote sixteen verses," said she, "an' I guess I've got everything in. I guess she'll think that's enough. I can copy it off nice to-morrow. I can't see to-night to do it, anyhow."

There were red spots on Betsey's cheeks; her knees were unsteady when she walked. She went into the kitchen and made a fire, and set on the tea-kettle. "I guess I won't warm up them potatoes to-night," said she; "I'll have the bread an' jelly, an' save 'em for breakfast. Somehow I don't seem to feel so much like 'em as I did, an' fried potatoes is apt to lay heavy at night."

When the kettle boiled, Betsey drank her cup of tea and soaked her slice of bread in it; then she put away her cup and saucer and plate, and went out to water her garden. The weather was so dry and hot it had to be watered every night. Betsey had to carry the water from a neighbor's well; her own was dry. Back and forth she went in the deepening twilight, her slender body strained to one side with the heavy water-pail, until the garden-mould looked dark and wet. Then she took in the canary-bird, locked up her house, and soon her light went out. Often on these summer nights Betsey went to bed without lighting a lamp at all. There was no moon, but it was a beautiful starlight night. She lay awake nearly all night, thinking of her poem. She altered several lines in her mind.

She arose early, made herself a cup of tea, and warmed over the potatoes, then sat down to copy the poem. She wrote it out on both sides of note-paper, in a neat, cramped hand. It was the middle of the afternoon before it was finished. She had been obliged to stop work and cook the beans for dinner, although she begrudged the time. When the poem was fairly copied, she rolled it neatly and tied it with a bit of black ribbon; then she made herself ready to carry it to Mrs. Caxton's.

It was a hot afternoon. Betsey went down the street in her thinnest dress—an old delaine,[4] with delicate bunches of faded flowers on a faded green ground. There was a narrow green belt ribbon around her long waist. She wore a green barège bonnet, stiffened with rattans,[5] scooping over her face, with her curls pushed forward over her thin cheeks in two bunches, and she carried a small green parasol with a jointed handle. Her costume was obsolete, even in the little country village where she lived. She had worn it every summer for the last twenty years. She made no more change in her attire than the old perennials in her garden. She

4. A light woolen fabric, usually black.
5. A bonnet made from sheer silk or cotton and

made rigid with stays made from rattan, the material from which wicker furniture is constructed.

had no money with which to buy new clothes, and the old satisfied her. She had come to regard them as being as unalterably a part of herself as her body.

Betsey went on, setting her slim, cloth-gaitered feet daintily in the hot sand of the road. She carried her roll of poetry in a black-mitted hand. She walked rather slowly. She was not very strong; there was a limp feeling in her knees; her face, under the green shade of her bonnet, was pale and moist with the heat.

She was glad to reach Mrs. Caxton's and sit down in her parlor, damp and cool and dark as twilight, for the blinds and curtains had been drawn all day. Not a breath of the fervid out-door air had penetrated it.

"Come right in this way; it's cooler than the sittin'-room," Mrs. Caxton said; and Betsey sank into the haircloth rocker[6] and waved a palm-leaf fan.

Mrs. Caxton sat close to the window in the dim light, and read the poem. She took out her handkerchief and wiped her eyes as she read. "It's beautiful, beautiful," she said, tearfully, when she had finished. "It's jest as comfortin' as it can be, and you worked that in about his new suit so nice. I feel real obliged to you, Betsey, and you shall have one of the printed ones when they're done. I'm goin' to see to it right off."

Betsey flushed and smiled. It was to her as if her poem had been approved and accepted by one of the great magazines. She had the pride and self-wonderment of recognized genius. She went home buoyantly, under the wilting sun, after her call was done. When she reached home there was no one to whom she could tell her triumph, but the hot spicy breath of the evergreen hedge and the fervent sweetness of the sweet-peas seemed to greet her like the voices of friends.

She could scarcely wait for the printed poem. Mrs. Caxton brought it, and she inspected it, neatly printed in its black border. She was quite overcome with innocent pride.

"Well, I don't know but it does read pretty well," said she.

"It's beautiful," said Mrs. Caxton, fervently. "Mr. White said he never read anything any more touchin', when I carried it to him to print. I think folks are goin' to think a good deal of havin' it. I've had two dozen printed."

It was to Betsey like a large edition of a book. She had written obituary poems before, but never one had been printed in this sumptuous fashion. "I declare I think it would look pretty framed!" said she.

"Well, I don't know but it would," said Mrs. Caxton. "Anybody might have a neat little black frame, and it would look real appropriate."

"I wonder how much it would cost?" said Betsey.

After Mrs. Caxton had gone, she sat long, staring admiringly at the poem, and speculating as to the cost of a frame. "There ain't no use; I can't have it nohow, not if it don't cost more'n a quarter of a dollar," said she.

Then she put the poem away and got her supper. Nobody knew how frugal Betsey Dole's suppers and breakfasts and dinners were. Nearly all her food in the summer came from the scanty vegetables which flourished between the flowers in her garden. She ate scarcely more than her canary-bird, and sang as assiduously. Her income was almost infinitesimal: the interest at a low per cent. of a tiny sum in the village savings-bank, the remnant of her father's little hoard after his funeral expenses had been paid. Betsey had lived upon it for twenty years, and considered herself well-to-do. She had never received a cent for her poems; she had

6. A rocking chair with a seat cushion covered in a tough fabric woven from horsehair.

not thought of such a thing as possible. The appearance of this last in such shape was worth more to her than its words represented in as many dollars.

Betsey kept the poem pinned on the wall under the looking-glass; if any one came in, she tried with delicate hints to call attention to it. It was two weeks after she received it that the downfall of her innocent pride came.

One afternoon Mrs. Caxton called. It was raining hard. Betsey could scarcely believe it was she when she went to the door and found her standing there.

"Why, Mis' Caxton!" said she. "Ain't you wet to your skin?"

"Yes, I guess I be, pretty near. I s'pose I hadn't ought to come 'way down here in such a soak; but I went into Sarah Rogers's a minute after dinner, and something she said made me so mad, I made up my mind I'd come down here and tell you about it if I got drowned." Mrs. Caxton was out of breath; rain-drops trickled from her hair over her face; she stood in the door and shut her umbrella with a vicious shake to scatter the water from it. "I don't know what you're goin' to do with this," said she; "it's drippin'."

"I'll take it out an' put it in the kitchen sink."

"Well, I'll take off my shawl here too, and you can hang it out in the kitchen. I spread this shawl out. I thought it would keep the rain off me some. I know one thing, I'm goin' to have a waterproof[7] if I live."

When the two women were seated in the sitting-room, Mrs. Caxton was quiet for a moment. There was a hesitating look on her face, fresh with the moist wind, with strands of wet hair clinging to the temples.

"I don't know as I had ought to tell you," she said, doubtfully.

"Why hadn't you ought to?"

"Well, I don't care; I'm goin' to, anyhow. I think you'd ought to know, an' it ain't so bad for you as it is for me. It don't begin to be. I put considerable money into 'em. I think Mr. White was pretty high, myself."

Betsey looked scared. "What is it?" she asked, in a weak voice.

"*Sarah Rogers says that the minister told her Ida that that poetry you wrote was jest as poor as it could be, an' it was in dreadful bad taste to have it printed an' sent round that way. What do you think of that?*"

Betsey did not reply. She sat looking at Mrs. Caxton as a victim whom the first blow had not killed might look at her executioner. Her face was like a pale wedge of ice between her curls.

Mrs. Caxton went on. "Yes, she said that right to my face, word for word. An' there was something else. She said the minister said that you had never wrote anything that could be called poetry, an' it was a dreadful waste of time. I don't s'pose he thought 'twas comin' back to you. You know he goes with Ida Rogers, an' I s'pose he said it to her kind of confidential when she showed him the poetry. There! I gave Sarah Rogers one of them nice printed ones, an' she acted glad enough to have it. Bad taste! H'm! If anybody wants to say anything against that beautiful poetry, printed with that nice black border, they can. I don't care if it's the minister, or who it is. I don't care if he does write poetry himself, an' has had some printed in a magazine. Maybe his ain't quite so fine as he thinks 'tis. Maybe them magazine folks jest took his for lack of something better. I'd like to have you send that poetry there. Bad taste! I jest got right up. 'Sarah Rogers,' says I, 'I hope

<hr>

7. Raincoat.

you won't never do anything yourself in any worse taste.' I trembled so I could hardly speak, and I made up my mind I'd come right straight over here."

Mrs. Caxton went on and on. Betsey sat listening, and saying nothing. She looked ghastly. Just before Mrs. Caxton went home she noticed it. "Why, Betsey Dole," she cried, "you look as white as a sheet. You ain't takin' it to heart as much as all that comes to, I hope. Goodness, I wish I hadn't told you!"

"I'd a good deal ruther you told me," replied Betsey, with a certain dignity. She looked at Mrs. Caxton. Her back was as stiff as if she were bound to a stake.

"Well, I thought you would," said Mrs. Caxton, uneasily; "and you're dreadful silly if you take it to heart, Betsey, that's all I've got to say. Goodness, I guess I don't, and it's full as hard on me as 'tis on you!"

Mrs. Caxton arose to go. Betsey brought her shawl and umbrella from the kitchen, and helped her off. Mrs. Caxton turned on the door-step and looked back at Betsey's white face. "Now don't go to thinkin' about it any more," said she. "I ain't goin' to. It ain't worth mindin'. Everybody knows what Sarah Rogers is. Good-by."

"Good-by, Mis' Caxton," said Betsey. She went back into the sitting-room. It was a cold rain, and the room was gloomy and chilly. She stood looking out of the window, watching the rain pelt on the hedge. The bird-cage hung at the other window. The bird watched her with his head on one side; then he begun to chirp.

Suddenly Betsey faced about and began talking. It was not as if she were talking to herself; it seemed as if she recognized some other presence in the room. "I'd like to know if it's fair," said she. "I'd like to know if you think it's fair. Had I ought to have been born with the wantin' to write poetry if I couldn't write it—had I? Had I ought to have been let to write all my life, an' not know before there wa'n't any use in it? Would it be fair if that canary-bird there, that ain't never done anything but sing, should turn out not to be singin'? Would it, I'd like to know? S'pose them sweet-peas shouldn't be smellin' the right way? I ain't been dealt with as fair as they have, I'd like to know if I have."

The bird trilled and trilled. It was as if the golden down on his throat bubbled. Betsey went across the room to a cupboard beside the chimney. On the shelves were neatly stacked newspapers and little white rolls of writing-paper. Betsey began clearing the shelves. She took out the newspapers first, got the scissors, and cut a poem neatly out of the corner of each. Then she took up the clipped poems and the white rolls in her apron, and carried them into the kitchen. She cleaned out the stove carefully, removing every trace of ashes; then she put in the papers, and set them on fire. She stood watching them as their edges curled and blackened, then leaped into flame. Her face twisted as if the fire were curling over it also. Other women might have burned their lovers' letters in agony of heart. Betsey had never had any lover, but she was burning all the love-letters that had passed between her and life. When the flames died out she got a blue china sugar-bowl from the pantry and dipped the ashes into it with one of her thin silver tea-spoons; then she put on the cover and set it away in the sitting-room cupboard.

The bird, who had been silent while she was out, began chirping again. Betsey went back to the pantry and got a lump of sugar, which she stuck between the cage wires. She looked at the clock on the kitchen shelf as she went by. It was after six. "I guess I don't want any supper to-night," she muttered.

She sat down by the window again. The bird pecked at his sugar. Betsey shivered and coughed. She had coughed more or less for years. People said she had the old-fashioned consumption.[8] She sat at the window until it was quite dark; then she went to bed in her little bedroom out of the sitting-room. She shivered so she could not hold herself upright crossing the room. She coughed a great deal in the night.

Betsey was always an early riser. She was up at five the next morning. The sun shone, but it was very cold for the season. The leaves showed white in a north wind, and the flowers looked brighter than usual, though they were bent with the rain of the day before. Betsey went out in the garden to straighten her sweet-peas.

Coming back, a neighbor passing in the street eyed her curiously. "Why, Betsey, you sick?" said she.

"No; I'm kinder chilly, that's all," replied Betsey.

But the woman went home and reported that Betsey Dole looked dreadfully, and she didn't believe she'd ever see another summer.

It was now late August. Before October it was quite generally recognized that Betsey Dole's life was nearly over. She had no relatives, and hired nurses were rare in this little village. Mrs. Caxton came voluntarily and took care of her, only going home to prepare her husband's meals. Betsey's bed was moved into the sitting room, and the neighbors came every day to see her, and brought little delicacies. Betsey had talked very little all her life; she talked less now, and there was a reticence about her which somewhat intimidated the other women. They would look pityingly and solemnly at her, and whisper in the entry when they went out.

Betsey never complained; but she kept asking if the minister had got home. He had been called away by his mother's illness, and returned only a week before Betsey died.

He came over at once to see her. Mrs. Caxton ushered him in one afternoon.

"Here's Mr. Lang come to see you, Betsey," said she, in the tone she would have used towards a little child. She placed the rocking-chair for the minister, and was about to seat herself, when Betsey spoke:

"Would you mind goin' out in the kitchen jest a few minutes, Mis' Caxton?" said she.

Mrs. Caxton arose, and went out with an embarrassed trot. Then there was silence. The minister was a young man—a country boy who had worked his way through a country college. He was gaunt and awkward, but sturdy in his loose clothes. He had a homely, impetuous face, with a good forehead.

He looked at Betsey's gentle, wasted face, sunken in the pillow, framed by its clusters of curls; finally he began to speak in the stilted fashion, yet with a certain force by reason of his unpolished honesty, about her spiritual welfare. Betsey listened quietly; now and then she assented. She had been a church member for years. It seemed now to the young man that this elderly maiden, drawing near the end of her simple, innocent life, had indeed her lamp, which no strong winds of temptation had ever met, well trimmed and burning.[9]

When he paused, Betsey spoke. "Will you go to the cupboard side of the chimney and bring me the blue sugar-bowl on the top shelf?" said she, feebly.

The young man stared at her a minute; then he went to the cupboard, and brought the sugar-bowl to her. He held it, and Betsey took off the lid with her weak hand. "Do you see what's in there?" said she.

"It looks like ashes."

8. Tuberculosis.
9. A metaphor for keeping oneself prepared to meet the Lord, as the Hebrew priests in Leviticus and Aaron in Exodus were directed to.

"It's—the ashes of all—the poetry I—ever wrote."

"Why, what made you burn it, Miss Dole?"

"I found out it wa'n't worth nothin'."

The minister looked at her in a bewildered way. He began to question if she were not wandering in her mind. He did not once suspect his own connection with the matter.

Betsey fastened her eager, sunken eyes upon his face. "What I want to know is—if you'll 'tend to—havin' this—buried with me."

The minister recoiled. He thought to himself that she certainly was wandering.

"No, I ain't out of my head," said Betsey. "I know what I'm sayin'. Maybe it's queer soundin', but it's a notion I've took. If you'll—'tend to it, I shall be—much obliged. I don't know anybody else I can ask."

"Well, I'll attend to it, if you wish me to, Miss Dole," said the minister, in a serious, perplexed manner. She replaced the lid on the sugar-bowl, and left it in his hands.

"Well, I shall be much obliged if you will 'tend to it; an' now there's something else," said she.

"What is it, Miss Dole?"

She hesitated a moment. "You write poetry, don't you?"

The minister colored. "Why, yes; a little sometimes."

"It's good poetry, ain't it? They printed some in a magazine."

The minister laughed confusedly. "Well, Miss Dole. I don't know how good poetry it may be, but they did print some in a magazine."

Betsey lay looking at him. "I never wrote none that was—good," she whispered, presently; "but I've been thinkin'—if you would jest write a few—lines about me—afterward— I've been thinkin' that—mebbe my—dyin' was goin' to make me—a good subject for—poetry, if I never wrote none. If you would jest write a few lines."

The minister stood holding the sugar-bowl; he was quite pale with bewilderment and sympathy. "I'll—do the best I can, Miss Dole," he stammered.

"I'll be much obliged," said Betsey, as if the sense of grateful obligation was immortal like herself. She smiled, and the sweetness of the smile was as evident through the drawn lines of her mouth as the old red in the leaves of a withered rose. The sun was setting; a red beam flashed softly over the top of the hedge and lay along the opposite wall; then the bird in his cage began to chirp. He chirped faster and faster until he trilled into a triumphant song.

1890

►◄ PANDITA RAMABAI SARASWATI ►◄
1858–1922

Nineteenth-century India was dominated by the reform agendas of British colonialists and Indian nationalists, with both groups preoccupied with what came to be known as the "woman question," which in India asked not only "What do women want?" but also "How can Indian women be saved from backwardness and oppression?" It is in that context that Ramabai Saraswati developed a distinctive voice and perspective. She championed Hindu women's struggles against the social conservatism of both British colonialists and orthodox, high-caste Hindus and also supported women's roles as writers and teachers.

Saraswati was the daughter of Anant Shastri Dongre, a renowned scholar and teacher who had resisted Hindu orthodoxy by educating his wife and daughters. As a consequence of this and other unorthodox practices, Saraswati's parents were ostracized from traditional Hindu society. They earned a living, starting when Saraswati was nine, by traveling through pilgrimage centers, reciting the *Puranas*, collections of religious tales from ancient times, and giving lectures that provided progressive interpretations of religious texts. But the remuneration was meager, and her parents and older sister died of starvation during the famine of 1874–77.

After their deaths, Saraswati and her brother continued this itinerant life, covering 2,000 miles on foot and often experiencing hunger and exhaustion. Like their parents before them, they earned a sparse living from recitations and lectures. Upon their arrival in the city of Calcutta, though, Saraswati publicly lectured in Sanskrit and debated well-known theologians on scriptural interpretation. For these accomplishments, she was given the title Pandita ("learned woman").

While Saraswati was hailed as a celebrity in Calcutta, her personal life was struck by a series of additional tragedies. In 1880, her brother died. She subsequently married his friend Bipin Behari Das, a choice that led to their ostracism, as he was of a lower caste. Then her husband died of cholera in early 1882, just nineteen months after their marriage and not long after the birth of their daughter, Manorama.

Saraswati's Hindu faith had dwindled over her hard life; it was further eroded by the harsh treatment that Hindu society meted out to widows who did not commit *sati,* or ritual suicide. In 1882, she returned to western India to form the Arya Mahila Samaj, a Hindu reformist group for women; she lectured on the status of women within Hinduism, testified on the question of women's education before the Hunter Commission, which had been set up to study the state of education in India, and expressed her strong opposition to colonial government policy. Through all this work Saraswati emerged as a strong advocate for secular, ethical education and for improving the material conditions of women teachers and doctors.

In 1883, Saraswati traveled to England, the trip paid for by the proceeds from her book *Stroo dharma neeti (Morals for Women)*. Later that year, she converted to Christianity, a decision that caused a sensation among her supporters, who now saw her as a traitor. The missionaries, on the other hand, embraced this high-caste woman convert with great enthusiasm. But even in her Christianity, Saraswati was a dissident, remaining to the end a fervent believer in a progressive and secular faith. From England Saraswati traveled to the United States, where she raised money for a widow's home that she planned to set up on her return to India. In the United States, she published *The High Caste Hindu Woman* (1887), a book she dedicated to her mother. Although Saraswati derided the racism she saw all around her in the United States, she also saw the country as a beacon of democracy for the colonized world. America returned the admiration: the first printing of her book sold out in a matter of months.

In 1889, Saraswati returned to India and founded Sharda Sadan, a home for widows. Nationalists attacked or deserted her for trying to convert residents of the home, but she carried on her work, remaining a staunch opponent of both Hindu orthodoxy and British colonial policy on women. In 1907, she published her autobiography, *My Testimony.*

Saraswati was among the few Indian women of her time who supported herself through such work as writing, translating, and public speaking. She is rightly credited as a precursor of modern Indian feminism. Perhaps growing up as a wanderer enabled her to resist social convention and to imagine a different way of being for the generations of women to come. In the following extract from *The High Caste Hindu Woman*, for example, Saraswati decries the practice of *suttee* (*sati*), or widow burning, common even in British-controlled nineteenth-century India.

From The High Caste Hindu Woman
Chapter 5
[*Suttee*]

We now come to the worst and most dreaded period of a high-caste woman's life. Throughout India, widowhood is regarded as the punishment for a horrible crime or crimes committed by the woman in her former existence upon earth.[1] The period of punishment may be greater or less, according to the nature of the crime. Disobedience and disloyalty to the husband, or murdering him in an earlier existence are the chief crimes punished in the present birth by widowhood.

If the widow be a mother of sons, she is not usually a pitiable object; although she is certainly looked upon as a sinner, yet social abuse and hatred are greatly diminished in virtue of the fact that she is a mother of the superior beings. Next in rank to her stands an ancient widow, because a virtuous, aged widow who has bravely withstood the thousand temptations and persecutions of her lot commands an involuntary respect from all people, to which may be added the honor given to old age quite independent of the individual. The widow-mother of girls is treated indifferently and sometimes with genuine hatred, especially so, when her daughters have not been given in marriage in her husband's life-time. But it is the child-widow or a childless young widow upon whom in an especial manner falls the abuse and hatred of the community as the greatest criminal upon whom Heaven's judgment has been pronounced.

In ancient times when the code of Manu was yet in the dark future and when the priesthood had not yet mutilated the original reading of a Vedic text concerning widows, a custom of re-marriage was in existence.[2]

Its history may be briefly stated:—The rite of child-marriage left many a girl a widow before she knew what marriage was, and her husband having died sonless had no right to enter into heaven and enjoy immortality, for "the father throws his debts on the son and obtains immortality if he sees the face of a living son. It is declared in the Vedas, endless are the worlds of those who have sons; there is no place for the man who is destitute of male offspring."[3] The greatest curse that could be pronounced on enemies, was "may our enemies be destitute of offspring."

In order that these young husbands might attain the abodes of the blessed, the ancient sages invented the custom of "appointment" by which as among the Jews, the Hindu Aryans raised up seed for the deceased husband. The husband's brother,

---

1. Hindus believe in reincarnation.
2. The code of Manu: the Manusmriti (c. 200 CE), a foundational text and encyclopedia of Hindu law and ancient Indian society ascribed to

the sage Manu; Vedic text: the Vedas, the earliest Hindu scriptures, believed to be divinely revealed.
3. From the Vedas, Book 17, 84:1–2.

cousin or other kinsman successively was "appointed" and duly authorized to raise up offspring to the dead. The desired issue having been obtained any intercourse between the appointed persons was thenceforth considered illegal and sinful.

The woman still remained the widow of her deceased husband, and her children by the appointment were considered his heirs. Later on, this custom of "appointment" was gradually discouraged in spite of the Vedic text already quoted "there is no place for the man who is destitute of male offspring."

The duties of a widow are thus described in the code of Manu:—

"At her pleasure let her emaciate her body by living on pure flowers, roots and fruit; but she must never even mention the name of another man after her husband has died."

"Until death let her be patient of hardships, self-controlled, and chaste, and strive to fulfil that most excellent duty which is prescribed for wives who have one husband only." —Manu v., 157, 158.

". . . . Nor is a second husband anywhere prescribed for virtuous women."—Manu v., 162.

"A virtuous wife who after the death of her husband constantly remains chaste, reaches heaven, . . ."—Manu v., 160.

"In reward of such conduct, a female who controls her thoughts, speech, and actions, gains in this life highest renown, and in the next world a place near her husband."[4]—Manu v., 166.

The following are the rules for a widower:—

"A twice-born man, versed in the sacred law, shall burn a wife of equal caste who conducts herself thus and dies before him, with the sacred fires used for the Agnihotra, and with the sacrificial implements."[5]

"Having thus at the funeral, given the sacred fires to his wife who dies before him, he may marry again, and again kindle the (nuptial) fires."

". . . . And having taken a wife, he must dwell in his own house during the second period of his life."—Manu v., 167–169.

The self immolation of widows on their deceased husband's pyre was evidently a custom invented by the priesthood after the code of Manu was compiled. The laws taught in the schools of Apastamba, Asvalayana and others older than Manu do not mention it, neither does the code of Manu. The code of Vishnu which is comparatively recent, says, that a woman "after the death of her husband should either lead a virtuous life or ascend the funeral pile of her husband."—Vishnu xxv., 2.

It is very difficult to ascertain the motives of those who invented the terrible custom of the so-called Suttee, which was regarded as a sublimely meritorious act. As Manu the greatest authority next to the Vedas did not sanction this sacrifice, the priests saw the necessity of producing some text which would overcome the natural fears of the widow as well as silence the critic who should refuse to allow such a horrid rite without strong authority. So the priests said there was a text in the Rig-veda[6] which according to their own rendering reads thus:—

4. "It should be borne in mind that according to the popular belief that there is no other heaven to a woman than the seat or mansion of her husband, where she shares the heavenly bliss with him in the next world if she be faithful to him in the thought, word and deed. The only place where she can be independent of him is in hell." [Saraswati's note.]

5. Twice-born man: an upper-caste man; Agnihotra: a ritual prayer to Agni, the god of fire.

6. The earliest of the Vedas.

"Om! let these women, not to be widowed, good wives, adorned with collyrium, holding clarified butter, consign themselves to the fire! Immortal, not childless, not husbandless, well adorned with gems, let them pass into the fire whose original element is water."

Here was an authority greater than that of Manu or of any other law giver, which could not be disobeyed. The priests and their allies, pictured heaven in the most beautiful colors and described various enjoyments so vividly that the poor widow became madly impatient to get to the blessed place in company with her departed husband. Not only was the woman assured of her getting into heaven by this sublime act, but also that by this great sacrifice she would secure salvation to herself and husband, and to their families to the seventh generation. Be they ever so sinful, they would surely attain the highest bliss in heaven, and prosperity on earth. Who would not sacrifice herself if she were sure of such a result to herself and her loved ones? Besides this, she was conscious of the miseries and degradation to which she would be subjected now that she had survived her husband. The momentary agony of suffocation in the flames was nothing compared to her lot as a widow. She gladly consented and voluntarily offered herself to please the gods and men. The rite of Suttee is thus described:—

"The widow bathed, put on new and bright garments, and, holding Kusha grass in her left hand, sipped water from her right palm, scattered some tila grains, and then, looking eastward, quietly said, 'Om! on this day I, such and such a one, of such a family, die in the fire, that I may meet Arundhati, and reside in Svarga; that the years of my sojourn there may be as many as the hairs upon my husband, many scores multiplied; that I may enjoy with him the facilities of heaven, and bless my maternal and paternal ancestors, and those of my lord's line; that praised by Apsarasas, I may go far through the fourteen regions of Indra; that pardon may be given to my lord's sins whether he have ever killed a Brahman, broken the laws of gratitude and truth, or slain his friend.[7] Now I do ascend this funeral pile of my husband, and I call upon you, guardians of the eight regions of the world, of sun, moon, air, of the fire, the ether, the earth and the water, and my own soul. Yama, King of Death, and you, Day, Night and Twilight, witness that I die for my beloved, by his side upon his funeral pile.' Is it wonderful that the passage of the Sati to her couch of flame was like a public festival, that the sick and sorrowful prayed her to touch them with her little, fearless, conquering hand, that criminals were let loose if she looked upon them, that the horse which carried her was never used again for earthly service?" (E. Arnold.)

The act was supposed to be altogether a voluntary one, and no doubt it was so in many cases. Some died for the love stronger than death which they cherished for their husbands. Some died not because they had been happy in this world, but because they believed with all their heart that they should be made happy hereafter. Some to obtain great renown, for tombstones and monuments were erected to those who thus died, and afterwards the names were inscribed on the long list of family gods; others again, to escape the thousand temptations, and sins and miseries which they knew would fall to their lot as widows. Those who from pure ambition or from momentary impulse, declared their intentions thus to die, very often shrank from the fearful altar; no sooner did they feel the heat of the flames than they tried to leap down and escape the terrible fate; but it was too late. They had taken the solemn oath which must never be broken, priests and other men were at hand to force them to remount the pyre. In Bengal, where this custom was most in practice,

---

7. Arundhati: goddesses in the Hindu pantheon; Svarga: heaven; Apsarasas: divine female messengers; Indra: regions ruled by Indra, Hindu god of war; Brahman: the highest, priestly caste in Hindu society.

countless, fearful tragedies of this description occurred even after British rule was long established there. Christian missionaries petitioned the government to abolish this inhuman custom, but they were told that the social and religious customs of the people constituted no part of the business of the government, and that their rule in India might be endangered by such interference. The custom went on unmolested until the first quarter of the present century, when a man from among the Hindus, Raja Ram Mohun Roy, set his face against it, and declared that it was not sanctioned by the Veda as the priests claimed. He wrote many books on this subject, showing the wickedness of the act, and with the noble co-operation of a few friends, he succeeded at last in getting the government to abolish it. Lord William Bentinck, when Governor-general of India, had the moral courage to enact the famous law of 1829, prohibiting the Suttee rite within British domains, and holding as criminals, subject to capital punishment, those who countenanced it. But it was not until 1844 that the law had any effect upon orthodox Hindu minds.

That the text quoted from the Veda was mistranslated, and a part of it forged, could have been easily shown had all Brahmans known the meaning of the Veda. The Vedic language is the oldest form of Sanskrit, and greatly differs from the later form. Many know the Vedas by heart and repeat them without a mistake, but few indeed, are those that know the meaning of the texts they repeat. "The Rig-veda," says Max Muller,[8] "so far from enforcing the burning of widows, shows clearly that this custom was not sanctioned during the earliest period of Indian history. According to the hymns of the Rig-veda, and the Vedic ceremonial contained in the Grihya-sutras, the wife accompanies the corpse of her husband to the funeral pile, but she is there addressed with a verse taken from the Rig-veda, and ordered to leave her husband and to return to the world of the living."

1887

————•►◄ CHARLOTTE PERKINS GILMAN ►◄•————
1860–1935

Charlotte Perkins Gilman was more familiar to her contemporaries as an editor, publisher, and economist devoted to improving the condition of women than as a fiction writer. In 1898, for example, she published a book-length essay, *Women and Economics,* that systematically attacked what she would later call "androcentric culture," which not only oppressed women as individuals and as a group but also threatened the very possibility of human progress. In 1909, she founded *The Forerunner,* an explicitly feminist literary magazine in which most of her fiction (including her 1915 utopian fiction *Herland*) was originally published. Gilman drew upon her understanding of contemporary theories of social Darwinism as well as socialism and nationalism to fashion a feminist critique of American culture. At the heart of this critique was an understanding that capitalist patriarchy depended on a sexual division of labor that undervalued the work of women. Women, Gilman argued, were reduced to the status of commodities whose function and value depended, in turn, upon their role as consumers of other commodities.

8. Nineteenth-century German philologist and orientalist who helped establish India as a major   field of academic study.

Born in Hartford, Connecticut, Gilman had one brother and was related to Harriet Beecher Stowe (pp. 732–34) through her father, Frederick Beecher Perkins. Stowe, along with other women of the extended Beecher clan, made Hartford home and served as an inspiration to Gilman for what a woman could do that countered the depressing example offered by her own mother. Soon after Gilman was born, her father abandoned his wife, Mary, and their children. Perkins continued to play a role in his daughter's life, but his leaving devastated Mary, who never recovered financially or emotionally. Gilman was largely self-educated, but early on she supported herself by teaching and creating designs for the new market for commercial greeting cards. Coming of age in an era that found women entering professions, Gilman had decided on a career as a professional artist and began training herself. Despite this ambition, in 1884 Gilman married Charles Walter Stetson, an artist from Providence, Rhode Island. Following the birth of a daughter, Gilman suffered from severe postpartum depression. She was treated by Dr. S. Weir Mitchell, who used techniques he had developed for Civil War veterans suffering from nervous collapse (or what we would now call post-traumatic stress syndrome). Mitchell's "rest cure" (see pp. 1170–71) was designed to remove all sources of irritation to the nerves while allowing the body to rebuild its strength. Mitchell also prescribed devotion to domestic work and to child rearing as long-term solutions to depression, the root cause of which, he believed, was inappropriate ambition. Gilman's attempt to follow this advice, however, almost led to complete "mental ruin" in the form of despair and suicide. In response, Gilman divorced Stetson and, most shockingly to her contemporaries, relinquished control of her child to him and his new wife before moving to California. "The Yellow Wallpaper," published in 1892 in the *New England Magazine* and included here, is a fictionalized exposé of Mitchell's rest cure.

For the rest of her life, Gilman lived in California, where she began the systematic study of the "woman question" that informed her lectures, political activism, and fiction. In 1900, Gilman married George Houghton Gilman, with whom she lived until his death in 1934. The next year, following a diagnosis of breast cancer, Gilman took her own life.

The Yellow Wallpaper

It is very seldom that mere ordinary people like John and myself secure ancestral halls for the summer.

A colonial mansion, a hereditary estate, I would say a haunted house, and reach the height of romantic felicity—but that would be asking too much of fate!

Still I will proudly declare that there is something queer about it.

Else, why should it be let so cheaply? And why have stood so long untenanted?

John laughs at me, of course, but one expects that in marriage.

John is practical in the extreme. He has no patience with faith, an intense horror of superstition, and he scoffs openly at any talk of things not to be felt and seen and put down in figures.

John is a physician, and *perhaps*—(I would not say it to a living soul, of course, but this is dead paper and a great relief to my mind)—*perhaps* that is one reason I do not get well faster.

You see he does not believe I am sick!

And what can one do?

If a physician of high standing, and one's own husband, assures friends and relatives that there is really nothing the matter with one but temporary nervous depression—a slight hysterical[1] tendency—what is one to do?

My brother is also a physician, and also of high standing, and he says the same thing.

So I take phosphates or phosphites—whichever it is, and tonics, and journeys, and air, and exercise, and am absolutely forbidden to "work" until I am well again.

Personally, I disagree with their ideas.

Personally, I believe that congenial work, with excitement and change, would do me good.

But what is one to do?

I did write for a while in spite of them; but it *does* exhaust me a good deal—having to be so sly about it, or else meet with heavy opposition.

I sometimes fancy that in my condition if I had less opposition and more society and stimulus—but John says the very worst thing I can do is to think about my condition, and I confess it always makes me feel bad.

So I will let it alone and talk about the house.

The most beautiful place! It is quite alone, standing well back from the road, quite three miles from the village. It makes me think of English places that you read about, for there are hedges and walls and gates that lock, and lots of separate little houses for the gardeners and people.

There is a *delicious* garden! I never saw such a garden—large and shady, full of box-bordered paths, and lined with long grape-covered arbors with seats under them.

There were greenhouses, too, but they are all broken now.

There was some legal trouble, I believe, something about the heirs and co-heirs; anyhow, the place has been empty for years.

That spoils my ghostliness, I am afraid, but I don't care—there is something strange about the house—I can feel it.

I even said so to John one moonlight evening, but he said what I felt was a *draught*, and shut the window.

I get unreasonably angry with John sometimes. I'm sure I never used to be so sensitive. I think it is due to this nervous condition.

But John says if I feel so, I shall neglect proper self-control; so I take pains to control myself—before him, at least, and that makes me very tired.

I don't like our room a bit. I wanted one downstairs that opened on the piazza and had roses all over the window, and such pretty old-fashioned chintz hangings! But John would not hear of it.

He said there was only one window and not room for two beds, and no near room for him if he took another.

He is very careful and loving, and hardly lets me stir without special direction.

I have a schedule prescription for each hour in the day; he takes all care from me, and so I feel basely ungrateful not to value it more.

He said we came here solely on my account, that I was to have perfect rest and all the air I could get. "Your exercise depends on your strength, my dear,"

1. *Hysteria*, derived from the Greek *hysterikos* ("of the womb"), was the nineteenth-century di-agnosis for anxiety and depression, which were believed to be related to the uterus.

said he, "and your food somewhat on your appetite; but air you can absorb all the time." So we took the nursery at the top of the house.

It is a big, airy room, the whole floor nearly, with windows that look all ways, and air and sunshine galore. It was nursery first and then playroom and gymnasium, I should judge; for the windows are barred for little children, and there are rings and things in the walls.

The paint and paper look as if a boys' school had used it. It is stripped off— the paper—in great patches all around the head of my bed, about as far as I can reach, and in a great place on the other side of the room low down. I never saw a worse paper in my life.

One of those sprawling flamboyant patterns committing every artistic sin.

It is dull enough to confuse the eye in following, pronounced enough to constantly irritate and provoke study, and when you follow the lame uncertain curves for a little distance they suddenly commit suicide—plunge off at outrageous angles, destroy themselves in unheard of contradictions.

The color is repellant, almost revolting; a smouldering unclean yellow, strangely faded by the slow-turning sunlight.

It is a dull yet lurid orange in some places, a sickly sulphur tint in others.

No wonder the children hated it! I should hate it myself if I had to live in this room long.

There comes John, and I must put this away,—he hates to have me write a word.

* * * * * *

We have been here two weeks, and I haven't felt like writing before, since that first day.

I am sitting by the window now, up in this atrocious nursery, and there is nothing to hinder my writing as much as I please, save lack of strength.

John is away all day, and even some nights when his cases are serious.

I am glad my case is not serious!

But these nervous troubles are dreadfully depressing.

John does not know how much I really suffer. He knows there is no *reason* to suffer, and that satisfies him.

Of course it is only nervousness. It does weigh on me so not to do my duty in any way!

I meant to be such a help to John, such a real rest and comfort, and here I am a comparative burden already!

Nobody would believe what an effort it is to do what little I am able,—to dress and entertain, and order things.

It is fortunate Mary is so good with the baby. Such a dear baby!

And yet I *cannot* be with him, it makes me so nervous.

I suppose John never was nervous in his life. He laughs at me so about this wall-paper!

At first he meant to repaper the room, but afterwards he said that I was letting it get the better of me, and that nothing was worse for a nervous patient than to give way to such fancies.

He said that after the wall-paper was changed it would be the heavy bedstead, and then the barred windows, and then that gate at the head of the stairs, and so on.

"You know the place is doing you good," he said, "and really, dear, I don't care to renovate the house just for a three months' rental."

"Then do let us go downstairs," I said, "there are such pretty rooms there."

Then he took me in his arms and called me a blessed little goose, and said he would go down cellar, if I wished, and have it whitewashed into the bargain.

But he is right enough about the beds and windows and things.

It is an airy and comfortable room as any one need wish, and, of course, I would not be so silly as to make him uncomfortable just for a whim.

I'm really getting quite fond of the big room, all but that horrid paper.

Out of one window I can see the garden, those mysterious deep-shaded arbors, the riotous old-fashioned flowers, and bushes and gnarly trees.

Out of another I get a lovely view of the bay and a little private wharf belonging to the estate. There is a beautiful shaded lane that runs down there from the house. I always fancy I see people walking in these numerous paths and arbors, but John has cautioned me not to give way to fancy in the least. He says that with my imaginative power and habit of story-making, a nervous weakness like mine is sure to lead to all manner of excited fancies, and that I ought to use my will and good sense to check the tendency. So I try.

I think sometimes that if I were only well enough to write a little it would relieve the press of ideas and rest me.

But I find I get pretty tired when I try.

It is so discouraging not to have any advice and companionship about my work. When I get really well, John says we will ask Cousin Henry and Julia down for a long visit; but he says he would as soon put fireworks in my pillow-case as to let me have those stimulating people about now.

I wish I could get well faster.

But I must not think about that. This paper looks to me as if it *knew* what a vicious influence it had!

There is a recurrent spot where the pattern lolls like a broken neck and two bulbous eyes stare at you upside down.

I get positively angry with the impertinence of it and the everlastingness. Up and down and sideways they crawl, and those absurd, unblinking eyes are everywhere. There is one place where two breadths didn't match, and the eyes go all up and down the line, one a little higher than the other.

I never saw so much expression in an inanimate thing before, and we all know how much expression they have! I used to lie awake as a child and get more entertainment and terror out of blank walls and plain furniture than most children could find in a toy-store.

I remember what a kindly wink the knobs of our big, old bureau used to have, and there was one chair that always seemed like a strong friend.

I used to feel that if any of the other things looked too fierce I could always hop into that chair and be safe.

The furniture in this room is no worse than inharmonious, however, for we had to bring it all from downstairs. I suppose when this was used as a playroom they had to take the nursery things out, and no wonder! I never saw such ravages as the children have made here.

The wall-paper, as I said before, is torn off in spots, and it sticketh closer than a brother—they must have had perseverance as well as hatred.

Then the floor is scratched and gouged and splintered, the plaster itself is dug out here and there, and this great heavy bed which is all we found in the room, looks as if it had been through the wars.

But I don't mind it a bit—only the paper.

There comes John's sister. Such a dear girl as she is, and so careful of me! I must not let her find me writing.

She is a perfect and enthusiastic housekeeper, and hopes for no better profession. I verily believe she thinks it is the writing which made me sick!

But I can write when she is out, and see her a long way off from these windows.

There is one that commands the road, a lovely shaded winding road, and one that just looks off over the country. A lovely country, too, full of great elms and velvet meadows.

This wallpaper has a kind of sub-pattern in a different shade, a particularly irritating one, for you can only see it in certain lights, and not clearly then.

But in the places where it isn't faded and where the sun is just so—I can see a strange, provoking, formless sort of figure, that seems to skulk about behind that silly and conspicuous front design.

There's sister on the stairs!

* * * * * * *

Well, the Fourth of July is over! The people are all gone and I am tired out. John thought it might do me good to see a little company, so we just had mother and Nellie and the children down for a week.

Of course I didn't do a thing. Jennie sees to everything now.

But it tired me all the same.

John says if I don't pick up faster he shall send me to Weir Mitchell[2] in the fall.

But I don't want to go there at all. I had a friend who was in his hands once, and she says he is just like John and my brother, only more so!

Besides, it is such an undertaking to go so far.

I don't feel as if it was worth while to turn my hand over for anything, and I'm getting dreadfully fretful and querulous.

I cry at nothing, and cry most of the time.

Of course I don't when John is here, or anybody else, but when I am alone.

And I am alone a good deal just now. John is kept in town very often by serious cases, and Jennie is good and lets me alone when I want her to.

So I walk a little in the garden or down that lovely lane, sit on the porch under the roses, and lie down up here a good deal.

I'm getting really fond of the room in spite of the wallpaper. Perhaps *because* of the wallpaper.

It dwells in my mind so!

I lie here on this great immovable bed—it is nailed down, I believe—and follow that pattern about by the hour. It is as good as gymnastics, I assure you. I start, we'll say, at the bottom, down in the corner over there where it has not been touched, and I determine for the thousandth time that I *will* follow that pointless pattern to some sort of a conclusion.

I know a little of the principle of design, and I know this thing was not arranged on any laws of radiation, or alternation, or repetition, or symmetry, or anything else that I ever heard of.

It is repeated, of course, by the breadths, but not otherwise.

---

2. Dr. Silas Weir Mitchell (1829–1914), specialist in neurology and originator of the "rest cure," de- scribed in his work *Fat and Blood* (1877).

Looked at in one way each breadth stands alone, the bloated curves and flourishes—a kind of "debased Romanesque" with *delirium tremens*[3]—go waddling up and down in isolated columns of fatuity.

But, on the other hand, they connect diagonally, and the sprawling outlines run off in great slanting waves of optic horror, like a lot of wallowing seaweeds in full chase.

The whole thing goes horizontally, too, at least it seems so, and I exhaust myself in trying to distinguish the order of its going in that direction.

They have used a horizontal breadth for a frieze,[4] and that adds wonderfully to the confusion.

There is one end of the room where it is almost intact, and there, when the crosslights fade and the low sun shines directly upon it, I can almost fancy radiation after all,—the interminable grotesques seem to form around a common centre and rush off in headlong plunges of equal distraction.

It makes me tired to follow it. I will take a nap I guess.

* * * * * *

I don't know why I should write this.

I don't want to.

I don't feel able.

And I know John would think it absurd. But I *must* say what I feel and think in some way—it is such a relief!

But the effort is getting to be greater than the relief.

Half the time now I am awfully lazy, and lie down ever so much.

John says I mustn't lose my strength, and has me take cod liver oil and lots of tonics and things, to say nothing of ale and wine and rare meat.

Dear John! He loves me very dearly, and hates to have me sick. I tried to have a real earnest reasonable talk with him the other day, and tell him how I wish he would let me go and make a visit to Cousin Henry and Julia.

But he said I wasn't able to go, nor able to stand it after I got there; and I did not make out a very good case for myself, for I was crying before I had finished.

It is getting to be a great effort for me to think straight. Just this nervous weakness I suppose.

And dear John gathered me up in his arms, and just carried me upstairs and laid me on the bed, and sat by me and read to me till it tired my head.

He said I was his darling and his comfort and all he had, and that I must take care of myself for his sake, and keep well.

He says no one but myself can help me out of it, that I must use my will and self-control and not let any silly fancies run away with me.

There's one comfort, the baby is well and happy, and does not have to occupy this nursery with the horrid wallpaper.

If we had not used it, that blessed child would have! What a fortunate escape! Why, I wouldn't have a child of mine, an impressionable little thing, live in such a room for worlds.

I never thought of it before, but it is lucky that John kept me here after all, I can stand it so much easier than a baby, you see.

3. Romanesque: an architectural style characterized by heavy masonry and rounded arches; delirium tremens: tremors and hallucinations characteristic of alcohol withdrawal.
4. Border.

Of course I never mention it to them any more—I am too wise,—but I keep watch of it all the same.

There are things in that paper that nobody knows but me, or ever will.

Behind that outside pattern the dim shapes get clearer every day.

It is always the same shape, only very numerous.

And it is like a woman stooping down and creeping about behind that pattern. I don't like it a bit. I wonder—I begin to think—I wish John would take me away from here!

* * * * * * * *

It is so hard to talk to John about my case, because he is so wise, and because he loves me so.

But I tried it last night.

It was moonlight. The moon shines in all around just as the sun does.

I hate to see it sometimes, it creeps so slowly, and always comes in by one window or another.

John was asleep and I hated to waken him, so I kept still and watched the moonlight on that undulating wallpaper till I felt creepy.

The faint figure behind seemed to shake the pattern, just as if she wanted to get out.

I got up softly and went to feel and see if the paper *did* move, and when I came back John was awake.

"What is it, little girl?" he said. "Don't go walking about like that—you'll get cold."

I thought it was a good time to talk, so I told him that I really was not gaining here, and that I wished he would take me away.

"Why, darling!" said he, "our lease will be up in three weeks, and I can't see how to leave before.

"The repairs are not done at home, and I cannot possibly leave town just now. Of course if you were in any danger, I could and would, but you really are better, dear, whether you can see it or not. I am a doctor, dear, and I know. You are gaining flesh and color, your appetite is better, I feel really much easier about you."

"I don't weigh a bit more," said I, "nor as much; and my appetite may be better in the evening when you are here, but it is worse in the morning when you are away!"

"Bless her little heart!" said he with a big hug, "she shall be as sick as she pleases! But now let's improve the shining hours[5] by going to sleep, and talk about it in the morning!"

"And you won't go away?" I asked gloomily.

"Why, how can I, dear? It is only three weeks more and then we will take a nice little trip of a few days while Jennie is getting the house ready. Really dear you are better!"

"Better in body perhaps—" I began, and stopped short, for he sat up straight and looked at me with such a stern, reproachful look that I could not say another word.

"My darling," said he, "I beg of you, for my sake and for our child's sake, as well as for your own, that you will never for one instant let that idea enter your

---

5. From "Against Idleness and Mischief" by English hymnodist Isaac Watts (1674–1748); the poem, which begins "How doth the little busy Bee / Improve each shining hour" (lines 1–2), was published in *Divine Songs in Easy Language for the Use of Children* (1715).

mind! There is nothing so dangerous, so fascinating, to a temperament like yours. It is a false and foolish fancy. Can you not trust me as a physician when I tell you so?"

So of course I said no more on that score, and we went to sleep before long. He thought I was asleep first, but I wasn't, and lay there for hours trying to decide whether that front pattern and the back pattern really did move together or separately.

* * * * * * *

On a pattern like this, by daylight, there is a lack of sequence, a defiance of law, that is a constant irritant to a normal mind.

The color is hideous enough, and unreliable enough, and infuriating enough, but the pattern is torturing.

You think you have mastered it, but just as you get well underway in following, it turns a back-somersault and there you are. It slaps you in the face, knocks you down, and tramples upon you. It is like a bad dream.

The outside pattern is a florid arabesque,[6] reminding one of a fungus. If you can imagine a toadstool in joints, an interminable string of toadstools, budding and sprouting in endless convolutions—why, that is something like it.

That is, sometimes!

There is one marked peculiarity about this paper, a thing nobody seems to notice but myself, and that is that it changes as the light changes.

When the sun shoots in through the east window—I always watch for that first long, straight ray—it changes so quickly that I never can quite believe it.

That is why I watch it always.

By moonlight—the moon shines in all night when there is a moon—I wouldn't know it was the same paper.

At night in any kind of light, in twilight, candlelight, lamplight, and worst of all by moonlight, it becomes bars! The outside pattern I mean, and the woman behind it is as plain as can be.

I didn't realize for a long time what the thing was that showed behind, that dim sub-pattern, but now I am quite sure it is a woman.

By daylight she is subdued, quiet. I fancy it is the pattern that keeps her so still. It is so puzzling. It keeps me quiet by the hour.

I lie down ever so much now. John says it is good for me, and to sleep all I can.

Indeed he started the habit by making me lie down for an hour after each meal.

It is a very bad habit I am convinced, for you see I don't sleep.

And that cultivates deceit, for I don't tell them I'm awake—O no!

The fact is I am getting a little afraid of John.

He seems very queer sometimes, and even Jennie has an inexplicable look.

It strikes me occasionally, just as a scientific hypothesis,—that perhaps it is the paper!

I have watched John when he did not know I was looking, and come into the room suddenly on the most innocent excuses, and I've caught him several times *looking at the paper!* And Jennie too. I caught Jennie with her hand on it once.

She didn't know I was in the room, and when I asked her in a quiet, a very quiet voice, with the most restrained manner possible, what she was doing with the paper—she turned around as if she had been caught stealing, and looked quite angry—asked me why I should frighten her so!

6. An intricate design style that includes flowers, fruits, animals, and abstract patterns.

Then she said that the paper stained everything it touched, that she had found yellow smooches on all my clothes and John's, and she wished we would be more careful!

Did not that sound innocent? But I know she was studying that pattern, and I am determined that nobody shall find it out but myself!

Life is very much more exciting now than it used to be. You see I have something more to expect, to look forward to, to watch. I really do eat better, and am more quiet than I was.

John is so pleased to see me improve! He laughed a little the other day, and said I seemed to be flourishing in spite of my wall-paper.

I turned it off with a laugh. I had no intention of telling him it was *because* of the wall-paper—he would make fun of me. He might even want to take me away.

I don't want to leave now until I have found it out. There is a week more, and I think that will be enough.

* * * * * *

I'm feeling ever so much better! I don't sleep much at night, for it is so interesting to watch developments; but I sleep a good deal in the daytime.

In the daytime it is tiresome and perplexing.

There are always new shoots on the fungus, and new shades of yellow all over it. I cannot keep count of them, though I have tried conscientiously.

It is the strangest yellow, that wall-paper! It makes me think of all the yellow things I ever saw—not beautiful ones like buttercups, but old foul, bad yellow things.

But there is something else about that paper—the smell! I noticed it the moment we came into the room, but with so much air and sun it was not bad. Now we have had a week of fog and rain, and whether the windows are open or not, the smell is here.

It creeps all over the house.

I find it hovering in the dining-room, skulking in the parlor, hiding in the hall, lying in wait for me on the stairs.

It gets into my hair.

Even when I go to ride, if I turn my head suddenly and surprise it—there is that smell!

Such a peculiar odor, too! I have spent hours in trying to analyze it, to find what it smelled like.

It is not bad—at first, and very gentle, but quite the subtlest, most enduring odor I ever met.

In this damp weather it is awful, I wake up in the night and find it hanging over me.

It used to disturb me at first. I thought seriously of burning the house—to reach the smell.

But now I am used to it. The only thing I can think of that it is like is the *color* of the paper! A yellow smell.

There is a very funny mark on this wall, low down, near the mop-board. A streak that runs round the room. It goes behind every piece of furniture, except the bed, a long, straight, even *smooch*, as if it had been rubbed over and over.

I wonder how it was done and who did it, and what they did it for. Round and round and round—round and round and round—it makes me dizzy!

* * * * * *

I really have discovered something at last.

Through watching so much at night, when it changes so, I have finally found out.

The front pattern *does* move—and no wonder! The woman behind shakes it!

Sometimes I think there are a great many women behind, and sometimes only one, and she crawls around fast, and her crawling shakes it all over.

Then in the very bright spots she keeps still, and in the very shady spots she just takes hold of the bars and shakes them hard.

And she is all the time trying to climb through. But nobody could climb through that pattern—it strangles so; I think that is why it has so many heads.

They get through, and then the pattern strangles them off and turns them upside down, and makes their eyes white!

If those heads were covered or taken off it would not be half so bad.

* * * * * *

I think that woman gets out in the daytime!

And I'll tell you why—privately—I've seen her!

I can see her out of every one of my windows!

It is the same woman, I know, for she is always creeping, and most women do not creep by daylight.

I see her in that long shaded lane, creeping up and down. I see her in those dark grape arbors, creeping all around the garden.

I see her on that long road under the trees, creeping along, and when a carriage comes she hides under the blackberry vines.

I don't blame her a bit. It must be very humiliating to be caught creeping by daylight!

I always lock the door when I creep by daylight. I can't do it at night, for I know John would suspect something at once.

And John is so queer now, that I don't want to irritate him. I wish he would take another room! Besides, I don't want anybody to get that woman out at night but myself.

I often wonder if I could see her out of all the windows at once.

But, turn as fast as I can, I can only see out of one at one time.

And though I always see her, she *may* be able to creep faster than I can turn!

I have watched her sometimes away off in the open country, creeping as fast as a cloud shadow in a high wind.

* * * * * *

If only that top pattern could be gotten off from the under one! I mean to try it, little by little.

I have found out another funny thing, but I shan't tell it this time! It does not do to trust people too much.

There are only two more days to get this paper off, and I believe John is beginning to notice. I don't like the look in his eyes.

And I heard him ask Jennie a lot of professional questions about me. She had a very good report to give.

She said I slept a good deal in the daytime.

John knows I don't sleep very well at night, for all I'm so quiet!

He asked me all sorts of questions, too, and pretended to be very loving and kind.

As if I couldn't see through him!

Still, I don't wonder he acts so, sleeping under this paper for three months.

It only interests me, but I feel sure John and Jennie are secretly affected by it.

* * * * * *

Hurrah! This is the last day, but it is enough. John to stay in town over night, and won't be out until this evening.

Jennie wanted to sleep with me—the sly thing! But I told her I should undoubtedly rest better for a night all alone.

That was clever, for really I wasn't alone a bit! As soon as it was moonlight and that poor thing began to crawl and shake the pattern, I got up and ran to help her.

I pulled and she shook, I shook and she pulled, and before morning we had peeled off yards of that paper.

A strip about as high as my head and half around the room.

And then when the sun came and that awful pattern began to laugh at me, I declared I would finish it to-day!

We go away to-morrow, and they are moving all my furniture down again to leave things as they were before.

Jennie looked at the wall in amazement, but I told her merrily that I did it out of pure spite at the vicious thing.

She laughed and said she wouldn't mind doing it herself, but I must not get tired. How she betrayed herself that time!

But I am here, and no person touches this paper but me,—not *alive!*

She tried to get me out of the room—it was too patent! But I said it was so quiet and empty and clean now that I believed I would lie down again and sleep all I could; and not to wake me even for dinner—I would call when I woke.

So now she is gone, and the servants are gone, and the things are gone, and there is nothing left but that great bedstead nailed down, with the canvas mattress we found on it.

We shall sleep downstairs to-night, and take the boat home to-morrow.

I quite enjoy the room, now it is bare again.

How those children did tear about here!

This bedstead is fairly gnawed!

But I must get to work.

I have locked the door and thrown the key down into the front path.

I don't want to go out, and I don't want to have anybody come in, till John comes.

I want to astonish him.

I've got a rope up here that even Jennie did not find. If that woman does get out, and tries to get away, I can tie her!

But I forgot I could not reach far without anything to stand on!

This bed will *not* move.

I tried to lift and push it until I was lame, and then I got so angry I bit off a little piece at one corner—but it hurt my teeth.

Then I peeled off all the paper I could reach standing on the floor. It sticks horribly and the pattern just enjoys it! All those strangled heads and bulbous eyes and waddling fungus growths just shriek with derision!

I am getting angry enough to do something desperate. To jump out of the window would be admirable exercise, but the bars are too strong even to try.

Besides I wouldn't do it. Of course not. I know well enough that a step like that is improper and might be misconstrued.

I don't like to *look* out of the windows even—there are so many of those creeping women, and they creep so fast.

I wonder if they all come out of that wall-paper as I did?

But I am securely fastened now by my well-hidden rope—you don't get *me* out in the road there!

I suppose I shall have to get back behind the pattern when it comes night, and that is hard!

It is so pleasant to be out in this great room and creep around as I please!

I don't want to go outside. I won't, even if Jennie asks me to.

For outside you have to creep on the ground, and everything is green instead of yellow.

But here I can creep smoothly on the floor, and my shoulder just fits in that long smooch around the wall, so I cannot lose my way.

Why there's John at the door!

It is no use, young man, you can't open it!

How he does call and pound!

Now he's crying for an axe.

It would be a shame to break down that beautiful door!

"John dear!" said I in the gentlest voice, "the key is down by the front steps, under a plantain leaf!"

That silenced him for a few moments.

Then he said—very quietly indeed, "Open the door, my darling!"

"I can't," said I. "The key is down by the front door under a plantain leaf!"

And then I said it again, several times, very gently and slowly, and said it so often that he had to go and see, and he got it of course, and came in. He stopped short by the door.

"What is the matter?" he cried. "For God's sake, what are you doing?"

I kept on creeping just the same, but I looked at him over my shoulder.

"I've got out at last," said I, "in spite of you and Jane.[7] And I've pulled off most of the paper, so you can't put me back!"

Now why should that man have fainted? But he did, and right across my path by the wall, so that I had to creep over him every time!

1892

---

7. "Jennie" is a diminutive for "Jane."

CULTURAL COORDINATES
Nervousness and the Rest Cure

John, the physician husband in Charlotte Perkins Gilman's "The Yellow Wall-paper" (pp. 1158–69), "assures friends and relatives that there is really nothing the matter with [the narrator] but temporary nervous depression—a slight hysterical tendency" and threatens that if she does not get better, he'll "send [her] to Weir Mitchell in the fall." When someone from the nineteenth century describes nervous depression, though, do they mean the same thing we do? And why might Weir Mitchell be such a threat?

The second half of the nineteenth century saw an unprecedented increase in the diagnosis of "nervous" illnesses, grouped in a general category called "nervousness." One physician writing in *McClure's Magazine* in 1893 called nervousness the "national disease of America,"

Men were advised to treat their nervousness with . . . physical activity. . . . Women . . . were given the rest cure.

but the phenomenon was widespread in Britain as well. While almost any symptom could be a sign of the disease (from tenderness of the scalp and forgetfulness to insomnia, headaches, or yawning), it was a class-based diagnosis. Upper- and middle-class people were diagnosed as nervous; workers, immigrants, and people of color were considered either lazy or corrupt. And while the diagnosis was not entirely gender based, the treatment was. Men were advised to treat their nervousness with increased physical activity. In fact, we may owe the United States' National Park system to the fact that when Theodore Roosevelt was diagnosed as nervous he was sent out west to ride, camp, and canoe in the wilderness. He found the treatment so congenial and successful that he began a program to preserve wild places. Women, on the other hand, were given the rest cure.

As its name suggests, the rest cure involved a long period of bed rest. While at first this may sound ideal to a busy twenty-first-century woman, consider the real parameters of the cure as it was usually practiced: six weeks in bed with no physical activity at all (women were sometimes even sponge-bathed and encouraged to use bedpans so that they literally never left their beds), no reading, no visitors, no crafts, no music; one would then be fed a diet rich in milk and milk fat. If this sounds to you like a routine for a newborn infant, you are right (and this is part of Gilman's point in setting her story in a nursery), and many recent critics have suggested that it was part of an ideology that infantilized women and encouraged passivity.

The theory of women's nervousness was that they were overexerting themselves: if we think about running a household without electricity or running water and with many children and servants to supervise, that may seem reasonable; but that was not the kind of overexertion physicians were worried about. In the nineteenth century, physicians believed that women's bodies were designed for only one thing: bearing and raising children. They believed that any attempt to do other things—especially intellectual things like studying, reading, or trying to have a career—would bring on nervousness. The rest cure was designed to stop women's involvement with "unfeminine" pursuits by restoring them to a "natural" feminine passivity. While it may not surprise us that such a "cure" would have the devastating effects that Gilman shows us, what is surprising is how popular and effective the cure was for many nineteenth-century women.

Silas Weir Mitchell (1829–1914) was known as one of the chief inventors and practitioners of the rest cure, and he was Charlotte Perkins Gilman's doctor. (He also later became a well-known novelist.) To his credit, when confronted by Gilman, he modified his rest cure to allow a limited amount of reading and writing; when he supervised the rest cure that Edith Wharton (pp. 1218–28) went through, she was allowed a certain amount of time every day to write. In fact, she later credited her rest cure with helping her begin her career as a writer, and for the rest of her life she spent her mornings writing in bed.

◄ MARY KINGSLEY ►

1862–1900

Ethnographer, travel writer, and scientist, Mary Kingsley was the daughter of Mary Bailey and Dr. George Kingsley. Her father explored the South Seas and the American West as personal physician to traveling English aristocrats. Dr. Kingsley's family did not travel with him, but they benefited from his wide knowledge of the world. Although she never attended school, Kingsley acquired a remarkable education in her father's library, studying cultural anthropology, chemistry, entomology (the study of insects), ichthyology (the study of fish), and physics, and enjoying eighteenth- and nineteenth-century novels (with Charles Dickens and Mark Twain her special favorites). Born in Islington, in the county of Surrey, England, and living for much of her youth in Kent, Kingsley moved with her family at age twenty-four to Cambridge, England, where her brother had enrolled at the university. Her parents' drawing room there became a classroom where she learned from the scholars and intellectuals who visited.

Kingsley developed a strong enthusiasm for all branches of natural history, including ethnology (the comparative study of cultures) and field biology. It was not unusual for Victorian gentlemen to be "naturalists," observing and sketching plants and animals and their habitats, particularly those that had not yet been catalogued. Some, such as George Eliot's partner George Henry Lewes, combined this avocation with gentlemanly professions such as authorship. For a young woman to become a serious naturalist, though, was rare.

Kingsley's family background was literary as well as scientific: the novelists Charles and Henry Kingsley were her uncles. But she did not begin her adult life with literary ambitions. Originally, she planned to become a physician like her father. She went to Paris in 1888 to study and travel but returned home to Cambridge in 1891 to take care of her ailing parents. When both parents died in 1892, she began to plan her first trip to West Africa.

In 1893, Cambridge University helped finance this first trip, on which Kingsley was to sketch and collect specimens of unknown beetles and freshwater fish along the Congo River. In 1894–95, she took a second trip, making notes this time about the laws and customs of the Fan, Adooma, and Ajumba people she encountered. She traveled in true British style, insisting on proper dress and footwear, even when she was paddling canoes through rapids or slogging, neck-deep, through swamps. Her first book, *Travels in West Africa* (1897), described her second trip in detail, including giving minute descriptions of landscapes and sketches of particularly tricky passages in the rivers. She reported that her African guides and assistants were impressed with her growing prowess in navigating the rapids.

On returning to England, Kingsley was often invited to speak publicly about her travels. After writing her first book, she completed two more, *West African Studies* (1899) and *The Story of West Africa* (1899), a history of the region. A supporter of imperial colonization, she disapproved of the practice of ruling African communities from abroad and argued that drawing on local laws and installing indigenous leaders would be a more effective way for Britain to govern its colonies. She traveled once more to Africa in 1900 to nurse British soldiers wounded in the Boer War (1899–1902) against white South Africans of Dutch extraction. There she developed a fatal fever and died after working in the hospital for only two months.

Travels in West Africa, a section of which we include here, is a long and entertaining book, consisting of an illustrated travelogue and extensive appendices containing Kingsley's scientific and ethnographic findings. She introduces many characters encountered along the way, using dialogue and wryly ironic storytelling to bring them to life. Much like her favorites, Dickens and Twain, she employs exaggeration and self-deprecation to comical effect. She clearly enjoyed the friendships she gained in Africa, and though she certainly condescends to many of the Africans she describes, she expresses respect for many others. Her humor and independence, as well as her careful attention to local customs, are the great strengths of her book.

From Travels in West Africa

[A West African River and a Canoe]

About 4 a.m. in the moonlight we started to drop down river on the tail of the land breeze, and as I observed Obanjo[1] wanted to sleep I offered to steer. After putting me through an examination in practical seamanship, and passing me, he gladly accepted my offer, handed over the tiller which stuck out across my bamboo staging,[2] and went and curled himself up, falling sound asleep among the crew in less time than it takes to write. On the other nights we spent on this voyage I had no need to offer to steer; he handed over charge to me as a matter of course, and as I prefer night to day in Africa, I enjoyed it. Indeed, much as I have enjoyed life in Africa, I do not think I ever enjoyed it to the full as I did on those nights dropping down the Rembwé. The great, black, winding river with a pathway in its midst of frosted silver where the moonlight struck it: on each side the ink-black mangrove walls, and above them the band of star and moonlit heavens that the walls of mangrove allowed one to see. Forward rose the form of our sail, idealised from bed-sheetdom to glory,[3] and the little red glow of our cooking fire gave a single note of warm colour to the cold light of the moon. Three or four times during the second night, while I was steering along by the south bank, I found the mangrove wall thinner, and standing up, looked through the network of their roots and stems on to what seemed like plains, acres upon acres in extent, of polished silver—more specimens of those awful slime lagoons, one of which, before we reached Ndorko, had so very nearly collected me. I watched them, as we leisurely stole past, with a sort of fascination. On the second night, towards the dawn, I had the great joy of seeing Mount Okoneto, away to the S.W., first showing moonlit, and then taking the colours of the dawn before they reached us down below. Ah me! give me a West African river and a canoe for sheer good pleasure. Drawbacks, you say? Well, yes, but where are there not drawbacks? The only drawbacks on those Rembwé nights were the series of horrid frights I got by steering

1. Also known as Captain Johnson, Obanjo took Kingsley and her African guides through a hard passage in the river in his large cargo canoe. He called himself a "bush and river trader."
2. Rough scaffolding across the interior end of the boat, where Kingsley set up a "reclining couch" for herself.
3. The main sail of Obanjo's boat is an old, torn quilt.

on to tree shadows and thinking they were mud banks, or trees themselves, so black and solid did they seem. I never roused the watch fortunately, but got her off the shadow gallantly single-handed every time, and called myself a fool instead of getting called one. My nautical friends carp at me for getting on shadows, but I beg them to consider before they judge me, whether they have ever steered at night down a river quite unknown to them an unhandy canoe, with a bed-sheet sail, by the light of the moon. And what with my having a theory of my own regarding the proper way to take a vessel round a corner, and what with having to keep the wind in the bed-sheet where the bed-sheet would hold it, it's a wonder to me I did not cast that vessel away, or go and damage Africa.

By daylight the Rembwé scenery was certainly not so lovely, and might be slept through without a pang. It had monotony, without having enough of it to amount to grandeur. Every now and again we came to villages, each of which was situated on a heap of clay and sandy soil, presumably the end of a spit of land running out into the mangrove swamp fringing the river. Every village we saw we went alongside and had a chat with, and tried to look up cargo in the proper way.[4] One village in particular did we have a lively time at. Obanjo had a wife and home there, likewise a large herd of goats, some of which he was desirous of taking down with us to sell at Gaboon.[5] It was a pleasant-looking village, with a clean yellow beach which most of the houses faced. But it had ramifications in the interior. I being very lazy, did not go ashore, but watched the pantomime from the bamboo staging. The whole flock of goats enter at right end of stage, and tear violently across the scene, disappearing at left. Two minutes elapse. Obanjo and his gallant crew enter at right hand of stage, leg it like lamplighters[6] across front, and disappear at left. Fearful pow-wow behind the scenes. Five minutes elapse. Enter goats at right as before, followed by Obanjo and company as before, and so on *da capo*.[7] It was more like a fight I once saw between the armies of Macbeth and Macduff than anything I have seen before or since; only our Rembwé play was better put on, more supers,[8] and noise, and all that sort of thing, you know. It was a spirited performance I assure you and I and the inhabitants of the village, not personally interested in goat-catching, assumed the *rôle* of audience and cheered it to the echo. While engaged in shouting "Encore" to the third round, I received a considerable shock by hearing a well-modulated evidently educated voice saying in most perfect English:

"Most diverting spectacle, madam, is it not?"

Now you do not expect to hear things called "diverting spectacles" on the Rembwé; so I turned round and saw standing on the bank against which our canoe was moored, what appeared to me to be an English gentleman who had from some misfortune gone black all over and lost his trousers and been compelled to replace them with a highly ornamental table-cloth. The rest of his wardrobe was in exquisite condition, with the usual white jean coat, white shirt and collar, very neat tie, and felt hat affected by white gentlemen out here. Taking a large and powerful cigar from his lips with one hand, he raised his hat gracefully with the other and said:

"Pray excuse me, madam."

4. Part of Obanjo's business is to ship cargo among villages along the river.
5. Northern portion of the French Congo.
6. To run, as would stagehands lighting lamps onstage.

7. From the beginning (Italian; a musical term).
8. A "super," or supernumerary, is an actor employed in a walk-on part; Macduff and Macbeth do battle in Act 5 of Shakespeare's *Macbeth*.

I said, "Oh, please go on smoking."

"May I?" he said, offering me a cigar-case.

"Oh, no thank you," I replied.

"Many ladies do now," he said, and asked me whether I "preferred Liverpool, London, or Paris."

I said, "Paris; but there were nice things in both the other cities."

"Indeed that is so," he said; "they have got many very decent works of art in the St. George's Hall."

I agreed, but said I thought the National Gallery[9] preferable because there you got such fine representative series of works of the early Italian schools. I felt I had got to rise to this man whoever he was, somehow, and having regained my nerve, I was coming up hand over hand to the level of his culture when Obanjo and the crew arrived, carrying goats. Obanjo dropped his goat summarily into the hold, and took off his hat with his very best bow to my new acquaintance, who acknowledged the salute with a delicious air of condescension.

"Introduce me," said the gentleman.

"I cannot," said Obanjo.

"I regret, madam," said the gentleman, "I have not brought my card-case with me. One little expects in such a remote region to require one; my name is Prince Makaga."[1]

I said I was similarly card-caseless for reasons identical with his own, but gave him my name and address, and Obanjo, having got all aboard, including a member of the crew, fetched by the leg, shoved off, and with many bows we and the black gentleman parted. As soon as we were out of earshot from shore "Who is he, Obanjo?" said I. Obanjo laughed, and said he was a M'pongwe[2] gentleman who had at one time been agent for one of the big European firms at Gaboon, and had been several times to Europe. Thinking that he could make more money on his own account, he had left the firm and started trading all round this district. At first he made a great deal of money, but a lot of his trust had recently gone bad, and he was doubtless up here now looking after some such matter. Obanjo evidently thought him too much of a lavender-kid-glove gentleman to deal with bush trade, and held it was the usual way; a man got spoilt by going to Europe. I quite agree with him on general lines, but Prince Makaga had a fine polish on him without the obvious conceit usually found in men who have been home.[3]

We had another cheerful little incident that afternoon. While we were going along softly, softly as was our wont, in the broiling heat, I wishing I had an umbrella—for sitting on that bamboo stage with no sort of protection from the sun was hot work after the forest shade I had had previously—two small boys in two small canoes shot out from the bank and paddled hard to us and jumped on board. After a few minutes' conversation with Obanjo one of them carefully sank his

9. St. George's Hall: an elegant assembly hall built in the mid–nineteenth century in Liverpool; The National Gallery: a famous art museum in London.

1. "Makaga, an honourable name, which only one man, and he the bravest and best hunter in the tribe, may bear. The office of the Makaga is to lead all desperate affairs—for instance, if any one has murdered one of his fellow-villagers, and the murderer's town refuses to give him up (which is almost always the case, they thinking it is a shame to surrender any one who has taken refuge with them), then it is the business of the Makaga to take the best men of his village, and lead them to the assault of that which protects the murderer, and destroy it with its inhabitants."—Du Chaillu's Explorations and Adventures in Equatorial Africa, 1861, p. 393. [Kingsley's note.]

2. A settled Bantu group in Gaboon.

3. That is, to England.

canoe; the other just turned his adrift and they joined our crew. I saw they were Fans,[4] as indeed nearly all the crew were, but I did not think much of the affair. Our tender, the small canoe, had been sent out as usual with the big black man and another A. B. to fish; it being one of our industries to fish hard all the time with that big net. The fish caught, sometimes a bushel or two at a time, almost all grey mullet, were then brought alongside, split open, and cleaned. We then had all round as many of them for supper as we wanted, the rest we hung on strings over our fire, more or less insufficiently smoking them to prevent decomposition, it being Obanjo's intention to sell them when he made his next trip up the 'Como; for the latter being less rich in fish than the Rembwé they would command a good price there. We always had our eye on things like this, being, I proudly remark, none of your gilded floating hotel of a ferry-boat like those Cunard or White Star liners[5] are, but just a good trader that was not ashamed to pay, and not afraid of work.

Well, just after we had leisurely entered a new reach of the river, round the corner after us, propelled at a phenomenal pace, came our fishing canoe, which we had left behind to haul in the net and then rejoin us. The occupants, particularly the big black A. B., were shouting something in terror stricken accents. "What?" says Obanjo springing to his feet. "The Fan! the Fan!" shouted the canoe men as they shot towards us like agitated chickens making for their hen. In another moment they were alongside and tumbling over our gunwale into the bottom of the vessel still crying "The Fan! The Fan! The Fan!" Obanjo then by means of energetic questioning externally applied, and accompanied by florid language that cast a rose pink glow, smelling of sulphur, round us, elicited the information that about 40,000 Fans, armed with knives and guns, were coming down the Rembwé with intent to kill and slay us, and might be expected to arrive within the next half wink. On hearing this, the whole of our gallant crew took up masterly recumbent positions in the bottom of our vessel and turned gray round the lips. But Obanjo rose to the situation like ten lions. "Take the rudder," he shouted to me, "take her into the middle of the stream and keep the sail full." It occurred to me that perhaps a position underneath the bamboo staging might be more healthy than one on the top of it, exposed to every microbe of a bit of old iron and what not and a half that according to native testimony would shortly be frisking through the atmosphere from those Fan guns; and moreover I had not forgotten having been previously shot in a somewhat similar situation, though in better company. However I did not say anything; neither, between ourselves, did I somehow believe in those Fans. So regardless of danger, I grasped the helm, and sent our gallant craft flying before the breeze down the bosom of the great wild river (that's the proper way to put it, but in the interests of science it may be translated into crawling towards the middle). Meanwhile Obanjo performed prodigies of valour all over the place. He triced up[6] the mainsail, stirred up his faint-hearted crew, and got out the sweeps,[7] i.e. one old oar and four paddles, and with this assistance we solemnly trudged away from danger at a pace that nothing slower than a Thames dumb barge,[8] going against stream, could possibly overhaul. Still we did not feel safe, and I suggested to Ngouta[9] he should rise up and help; but he

4. Members of a West African tribe.
5. British companies operating ocean liners.
6. Nautical term for "to pull up sharply."
7. Long, heavy oar for rowing a barge or vessel.

8. A barge used as a pier on the English river Thames.
9. One of Kingsley's guides.

declined, stating he was a married man. Obanjo cheering the paddlers with inspir-
iting words sprang with the agility of a leopard on to the bamboo staging aft,
standing there with his gun ready loaded and cocked to face the coming foe, looking like a statue put up to himself at the public expense. The worst of this was,
however, that while Obanjo's face was to the coming foe, his back was to the crew,
and they forthwith commenced to re-subside into the bottom of the boat, paddles
and all. I, as second in command, on seeing this, said a few blood-stirring words
to them, and Obanjo sent a few more of great power at them over his shoulder,
and so we kept the paddles going.

Presently from round the corner shot a Fan canoe. It contained a lady in the
bows, weeping and wringing her hands, while another lady sympathetically howling, paddled it. Obanjo in lurid language requested to be informed why they were
following us. The lady in the bows said, "My son! my son!" and in a second more
three other canoes shot round the corner full of men with guns. Now this looked
like business, so Obanjo and I looked round to urge our crew to greater exertions
and saw, to our disgust, that the gallant band had successfully subsided into the
bottom of the boat while we had been eying the foe. Obanjo gave me a recipe for
getting the sweeps out again. I did not follow it, but got the job done, for Obanjo
could not take his eye and gun off the leading canoe and the canoes having crept
up to within some twenty yards of us, poured out their simple tale of woe.

It seemed that one of those miscreant boys was a runaway from a Fan village.
He had been desirous, with the usual enterprise of young Fans, of seeing the great
world that he knew lay down at the mouth of the river, *i.e.* Libreville Gaboon. He
had pleaded with his parents for leave to go down and engage in work there, but
the said parents holding the tenderness of his youth unfitted to combat with Coast
Town life and temptation, refused this request, and so the young rascal had run
away without leave and with a canoe, and was surmised to have joined the well-
known Obanjo. Obanjo owned he had (more armed canoes were coming round
the corner), and said if the mother would come and fetch her boy she could have
him. He for his part would not have dreamed of taking him if he had known his
relations disapproved. Every one seemed much relieved, except the *causa belli*.[1]
The Fans did not ask about two boys and providentially we gave the lady the right
one. He went reluctantly. I feel pretty nearly sure he foresaw more kassengo than
fatted calf[2] for him on his return home. When the Fan canoes were well back
round the corner again, we had a fine hunt for the other boy, and finally unearthed
him from under the bamboo staging. When we got him out he told the same tale.
He also was a runaway who wanted to see the world, and taking the opportunity
of the majority of the people of his village being away hunting, he had slipped off
one night in a canoe, and dropped down river to the village of the boy who had
just been reclaimed. The two boys had fraternised, and come on the rest of their
way together, lying waiting, hidden up a creek, for Obanjo, who they knew was
coming down river; and having successfully got picked up by him, they thought
they were safe. But after this affair boy number two judged there was no more
safety yet, and that his family would be down after him very shortly; for he said he
was a more valuable and important boy than his late companion, but his family

---

1. Causes or pretexts for war (Latin); that is, the
boy.
2. Kassengo: an instrument used for punishment

among the Fan; fatted calf: refers to the celebration of the return of the prodigal son in Luke
15:11–32.

were an uncommon savage set. We felt not the least anxiety to make their acquaintance, so clapped heels on our gallant craft and kept the paddles going, and as no more Fans were in sight our crew kept at work bravely. While Obanjo, now in a boisterous state of mind, and flushed with victory, said things to them about the way they had collapsed when those two women in a canoe came round that corner, that must have blistered their feelings, but they never winced. They laughed at the joke against themselves merrily. The other boy's family we never saw and so took him safely to Gaboon, where Obanjo got him a good place.[3]

Really how much danger there was proportionate to the large amount of fear on our boat I cannot tell you. It never struck me there was any, but on the other hand the crew and Obanjo evidently thought it was a bad place; and my white face would have been no protection, for the Fans would not have suspected a white of being on such a canoe and might have fired on us if they had been unduly irritated and not treated by Obanjo with that fine compound of bully and blarney[4] that he is such a master of.

Whatever may have been the true nature of the affair, however, it had one good effect, it got us out of the Rembwé into the Gaboon, and although at the time this seemed a doubtful blessing, it made for progress.

* * *

1897

---

3. A job.

4. Bully: admirability; blarney: harmless nonsense, flattery.

Spheres of Influence (2001) by Joyce Kozloff. (Acrylic on canvas, 96 × 192 inches. Courtesy D. C. Moore Gallery, New York City)

The Twentieth and Twenty-first Centuries

In *Three Guineas* (1938), published a year before the outbreak of World War II, Virginia Woolf imagines a hypothetical "Outsiders' Society" for daughters of educated men who would work for "justice and equality and liberty for all men and women" by opposing all forms of war. Woolf asks, "What does 'our country' mean to me an outsider?" She concludes that a clear look at English history and culture will tell this outsider that "her sex and class has very little to thank England for in the past; not much to thank England for in the present . . . [and that] the security of her person in the future is highly dubious." Reviewing the ways that England is not a country for women—in her time women did not own much property, were not genuinely protected by laws, and were not even able to keep citizenship if they married a foreigner—Woolf concludes that her outsider would say " '[I]n fact, as a woman, I have no country. As a woman I want no country. As a woman, my country is the whole world.' " In imagining a woman without a country, Woolf's narrative creates space both to claim the whole world and at the same time to lament the ways in which women are disempowered at home.

Now consider a scene from another text, from a novel written several decades after Woolf wrote those words. In Jamaica Kincaid's *Lucy* (1990), a young girl at Queen Victoria Girls' School in Antigua, in the Caribbean, recites a famous poem. The poem is William Wordsworth's "Daffodils" (1804):

> I wandered lonely as a cloud
> That floats on high o'er vales and hills
> When all at once I saw a crowd
> A host, of golden daffodils . . .

In praise of her excellent recitation of the poem, her teachers tell Lucy "how proud the poet, now long dead, would have been to hear his words ringing out of [her] mouth." For Lucy, who has never seen a daffodil in the Caribbean, this praise feels like a curse. She takes a vow "to erase from [her] mind, line by line, every word of that poem." But the daffodils do not disappear so easily; they reappear to haunt her at night and threaten to crush her into oblivion. Lucy's internalization of a poem that is part of her colonial education, of re-citing a powerful canonicity, is represented here as a nightmare. The will to erase and forget this colonial legacy becomes both an act of anti-colonial resistance and one of a traumatic repetition.

The two instances from Woolf and Kincaid can be read as allegories of women writing globally in English in the twentieth and twenty-first centuries. While Woolf suggests that many European women were left feeling "without a country" because of the legacy of sexist disenfranchisement and masculinist warmongering, Kincaid illuminates how that legacy is also colonizing and racist. In both instances, the writers struggle to find ways to write their own experiences into existence. These literary moments allow us to reframe women's literature from a global perspective.

That Woolf is writing from England and Kincaid from the Caribbean and the United States reminds us of the interlocking geographies Europe shares with its "others," including the black Atlantic diaspora that followed the Middle Passage, the exportation of Africans as slaves.

THE TWENTIETH AND TWENTY-FIRST CENTURIES: AN OVERVIEW

If the nineteenth century was marked by the consolidation of the ideology of separate spheres for men (public) and women (private), as well as the struggles to make literary and political venues open for women in the industrializing West, the twentieth century would see the dismantling of many of the seemingly settled ideas about gender and society, just as it would witness the constitution of an entirely new set of relations between nations and the world. Some key events in the twentieth and twenty-first centuries—the catastrophic world wars; the Russian Revolution of 1917; the rise and consolidation of totalitarian and fascist movements in Europe; the anti-colonial movements in Africa, the Caribbean, and Asia; the cold war that polarized the world into capitalist and communist spheres of influence; the civil rights and anti–Vietnam War movements in the United States, as well as the anti-apartheid movement in South Africa—look very different from women's perspectives. Within anti-colonial movements, women saw their struggles as being waged not just against an external colonial power but also against native patriarchal structures. For women, the struggle for national independence was inseparable from the struggle for gender equality. In Europe, as young men were sent off to the battlefronts during World War I (1914–18) and World War II (1939–45), women found themselves coming out of their homes to work in ammunition factories, hospitals, and other public venues. The end of World War I was also marked by an intensification of the suffragist movement, so that shortly after the war ended, women in Britain and the United States won the right to vote.

Two World War II–era aircraft production workers.

Ironically, the end of the world wars also gave way to a resurgent conservatism toward gender roles, even as the public sphere had opened up to women as never before, ushering in an era of freedom and experimentation with different lifestyles and identities. The years between the world wars were marked by upheavals in women's positions; women had the vote and began to live freer lives as "flappers"—women who were more physically and socially active than their mothers' generation had been—but the economic disaster of the Depression also forced many women out of the workforce as employers gave preference to "heads of household." During World War II, women again went to work in offices and factories to support the war effort, but when the war ended, and men returned, women again were pushed out of public employment. The cult of the housewife gained momentum in the 1950s, as new technological developments and postwar affluence in the United States gave rise to the image of the happy suburban homemaker surrounded by her vacuum cleaner and washer-dryer, waiting for her husband and children to come home. In *The Feminine Mystique* (1963), the feminist writer Betty Friedan unraveled the underlying ideology behind the happy housewife myth and its reliance on strict gender roles. In reality, Friedan argued, these white, middle-class, suburban women were alienated and disempowered from fulfilling their real potential as human beings. In France, the feminist philosopher Simone de Beauvoir wrote in *The Second Sex* (1949) about the ways in which women had been incorporated as the oppressed Other of man and thus been subjected to psychological and social domination.

The 1960s was the decade of rebellion against entrenched gender roles and race-based social divisions. While black leaders such as Martin Luther King Jr. and Malcolm X have become emblematic as civil rights heroes, black women such as Rosa Parks and Fanny Lou Hamer were important forces behind the civil rights movement as instigators, activists, and intellectuals. Coming on the heels of decolonization in Africa, Asia, and the Caribbean, the late 1960s were marked by anti–Vietnam War protests, university sit-ins, and strikes by students and young people all over the world who were no longer willing to be part of a racist and sexist system. Nineteen sixty-eight was not only the year in which Martin Luther King Jr. was assassinated; it was also the year in which hundreds of students in New York marched against Dow Chemical, manufacturers of napalm, the deadly chemical being used by the United States military in Vietnam. Other protests rocked the streets of Chicago, Paris, Mexico City, London and elsewhere. When the United States invaded Cambodia, student uprisings at Kent State University, Ohio, were met by brutal repression; on May 4, 1970, members of the Ohio National Guard opened fire on campus, killing four students.

Black writers such as Angela Davis were key to a new theory of the inseparability of race, class, and gender as principles of social domination, ideas that Davis published in *Women, Race, and Class* (1981). Working-class Chicana women and lesbians of all races were also challenging the middle-class basis of the mainstream women's movement of the earlier decades, even as the birth control pill liberated women of all classes from their fate as perpetual child-bearers (see pp. 1642–43). In Africa, Asia, and the Caribbean, women came out into the streets as part of anti-colonial and nationalist movements and challenged the Western, colonial stereotype of the colonized woman as a passive victim. Newly independent states in the postcolonial world saw women in leadership positions, and women's rights became an integral part of new constitutions. When the United Nations declared 1975 to be International Women's Year, it became clear that even international organizations had to give official recognition to women's issues, especially in terms of economic development, health, and education, as well as women's legal rights of inheritance, divorce, child custody, and protection against rape, sexual harassment, and domestic abuse.

Globally, women also played a key role in challenging the cold war mentality that was fuelling a deadly arms race. In the 1980s, women of the Greenham Commons in the United Kingdom set up peace camps at the sites of cruise missile establishments and famously opposed the nuclear proliferation that was deemed to be the inevitable fate of humanity. In the closing decades of the twentieth century and the opening of the twenty-first, women writers and activists from all over the world have staked a claim to the earth's environment, articulating a vision for justice and sustainability for all humanity. The movement toward global women's empowerment was the chief mission of the 1995 United Nations World Conference on Women in Beijing, China. At that conference, women from around the world met to discuss activist strategies, to affirm the ways in which women's rights are human rights, and to demand that governments everywhere recognize the basic need for gender equality.

On the other hand, late-twentieth-century world politics can be seen to reveal an effort to reinstate and concentrate power yet again. The cold war, for instance, could be understood as an attempt to align the world into just two camps—a Western European/American capitalist axis set up against an Eastern European/Asian communist one, each hoping for ultimate world domination. Simultaneously, as more nation-states in Africa and Asia began to win their political independence, transnational corporations consolidated their monopoly positions on the world economy, and international economic organizations such as the World Bank and the International Monetary Fund implemented Structural Adjustment Programs on debt-ridden countries to bring them in line with the global capitalist system dominated by the United States and Western Europe. Economic alliances and organizations, such as the North American Free Trade Agreement and the World Trade Organization, are taking precedence over older political alliances and often at a cost to the poor, the women, and the marginalized within nation-states.

By the close of the twentieth century, both gender and nation would be reconfigured separately and in relation to each other within the context of globalization (an economic and cultural process that links up disparate spheres) and new imperialisms (expansion of Euro-American power after World War II). The twentieth century can be read as a reaction against the colonization of the world by Europe and North America during the nineteenth century: events such as World Wars I and II; the struggles of India and of African and Caribbean nations against colonial powers; and the Korean, Vietnam, and Iraq wars are all manifestations of people seeking to resist the consolidation of power in just a few wealthy countries. We could similarly read the civil rights movement, various women's movements, and the anti-apartheid movement as efforts to challenge power structures that recognized only one type of person—usually a white man—as a legitimate citizen.

Today, the idea of a "global village" encompasses not only communication technologies such as the Internet and satellite television but also trade and a pervasive economic faith in the logic of free markets. Look at the labels in your clothing or at the "Made in" tags on anything you have bought recently, and it will become clear how much our world is now economically interdependent. But when we realize how often factories around the world, in the Philippines, Vietnam, and Sri Lanka, to name just a few places—where our sneakers and shirts are made—are staffed by women who are paid less than enough to feed and clothe themselves, much less their families, and are not allowed to unionize, we only just begin to grasp the profound way in which the new imperialism works: the wealth and prosperity of some in the first world are built on the backs of women in the third world.

There are other ways in which the world is starting to contract. At the beginning of the twentieth century, people were amazed at how much their world had shrunk. The telegraph and telephone, mass-circulation newspapers and magazines had revolutionized communications. The train and the steamship, the subway and the automobile had made travel faster, cheaper, and more convenient than ever before. One could hear news from around the world in just a few hours and travel to new continents in just days. By the end of the twentieth century, wireless telephones and computers, worldwide airline routes, and transnational corporations that move flexibly across national borders have made the idea of the world as a "global village" a cliché.

Such technological transformations have speeded up the rate at which people move, whether as refugees fleeing civil wars and famines, as migrants (legal or illegal) in search of work, as political exiles from authoritarian and dangerous regimes, as multinational corporate executives on business, or as tourists trying to consume the dizzyingly varied sights and sounds of the world. This dispersal of people and ideas has eroded organic, homogeneous communities and led to increased border patrols, visa restrictions, and security measures to circumscribe who can travel where and how. This paradox is particularly salient for women, many of whom now cross borders as refugees of political or domestic conflicts, as rural migrants looking for better-paying jobs in the city, as domestic servants for the global elites, and as sex workers—some by choice and some trafficked in the international sex trade.

GLOBAL ENGLISHES: THE SPREAD OF ENGLISH IN THE TWENTIETH AND TWENTY-FIRST CENTURIES

One of the most striking characteristics of the twentieth and twenty-first centuries is the fact that English has become a genuinely global language. This is in no small part due to the spread of the British Empire through the nineteenth and twentieth centuries and the consolidation of the military, economic, cultural, and political influence of the United States as a world superpower in the twentieth century. The multibillion-dollar Hollywood film industry beams images of American cinema idols speaking in American English all over the world. In the early years of the twenty-first century, about 20 percent of the world's population speaks English competently, and that number continues to grow. In India alone, it is estimated that at least 10 percent of the population (over 1 million people) is familiar with some form of English. In countries with many language groups (such as Nigeria, South Africa, and India), English is used widely as the language of science, business, and government and is often a passport to economic security.

At the beginning of the twentieth century, the dictionaries and grammars developed in the eighteenth and nineteenth centuries were being used in increasingly democratic educational settings and contributed to the standardization of English across all sectors of the culture. In Great Britain and North America, education was becoming more widely available not only to middle-class white women but also to working-class people and the less privileged members of society. While vast inequalities in education did—and still do—exist, in the twentieth century education came to be considered a right. For instance, in 1954, the U.S. Supreme Court, in *Brown v. the Board of Education,* overturned the 1895 *Plessy v. Ferguson* decision that had allowed so-called separate but equal public education for children. While the *Plessy* decision did assert that all children were entitled to an education, it allowed for (some might even argue promulgated) racial differences in the quality of that education; the "equal" in "separate but equal" was not genuine. *Brown,* in principle at least, rejected the idea that differences in education could be tied to race.

We should bear in mind, though, that what might seem to some a boon may seem to others an act of oppression. American Indian children and aboriginal children in Australia were often forced to attend English-language schools and harshly punished if they continued to use their own tribes' languages (see pp. 1309–10 and pp. 1303–5). Around the world, colonized peoples were taught that their own histories and languages were "primitive" and undeveloped. As far back as the nineteenth century, the English lawyer and politician Thomas Macaulay had written in "Minute of 2nd February 1835 on Indian Education" that "a single shelf of a good European library was worth the whole native literature of India and Arabia." In her 1989 book, *Masks of Conquest,* the literary critic Gauri Viswanathan argued that English education in colonies such as India provided one of the "masks of conquest" of British colonialism—it was used to justify not only the superiority of English as a language and as a marker of civilization and culture, but also colonial rule itself.

While we can trace the history of the phenomenon of English as a global language to the history of British and American imperialisms, during which English was typically imposed upon native and colonized populations, we also need to note that the native middle classes and elites were sometimes eager to partake of this education. For these privileged classes, English would become the means to achieve high social status and gain access to elite professions. For women in particular, learning English was sometimes a dangerous and sometimes a necessary task. The colonizers' language was understood as properly belonging to the public world, from which women had to be shielded. An English-speaking native woman in the colonies, particularly one who read and wrote in English, signified an embrace of modernity and freedom from the shackles of tradition and domesticity. Many writers included in this volume, such as Rokeya Sakhawat Hossain (pp. 1316–24), learned English at the cost of challenging a tradition that decreed women's learning to be limited to indigenous languages; others, like Cornelia Sorabji (pp. 1238–50) and Sarojini Naidu (pp. 1313–16), came from elite, Westernized families where an English education was seen as opening the doors to a wider world. Indeed, like their male counterparts, many of these women, including Naidu and Attia Hosain (pp. 1461–64) absorbed the most liberal and radical ideas of Western literary and philosophical traditions and deployed them toward nationalist causes. Yet many middle-class women in the colonies who did read English were often exposed to the Victorian romances and domesticity manuals that perpetuated conservative Western notions of women's proper sphere as the home. Women readers in the colonies reading European and American women's magazines, romantic novels, and the classics of English literature were offered images of an ideal womanhood that were both alien and alienating to social conditions in the colonies. Some American Indian women used their schooling in English and in the American political tradition to work for the freedom of their people; for instance, Zitkala Sa (pp. 1303–8) founded the National Council of American Indians to promote pan-tribal American Indian rights and wrote many books and political papers on the mistreatment and mismanagement of American Indian issues.

Over the course of the twentieth century and into the twenty-first, English has been broken up, scattered, appropriated, and domesticated. The erstwhile language of the oppressor now reverberates in the street languages of Mumbai and Nairobi and in the ghetto accents of Jamaica and southern Africa. At the beginning of the twenty-first century, people from around the world are claiming their own versions of English. More diverse "Englishes" are joining the global conversation as English becomes a language that is not simply British or American, but African, Asian, and Caribbean as well. Even within the United States and Britain, we can see different groups arguing for the right to represent their differences in their speech and written words. Black American writers like Toni Morrison (pp. 1598–1617) and ethnic minority writers in Britain like Grace Nichols (pp. 1870–73) have exemplified through their work that English is no longer the preserve of a racially and economically homogeneous national group; and Chicana writers like Gloria Anzaldúa (pp. 1737–47) reveal that the borders of the English language are fractured and hybrid.

The globalization of English necessitates a major transformation in the way we think of the terrain of English literature. The twentieth century afforded us literatures in English from the Caribbean, from east, west, and southern Africa, from the Indian subcontinent, and from countries of the Pacific Rim, in addition to the Anglo-American literary traditions that most students of English literature are familiar with. While some names might be totally unfamiliar to readers, keep in mind that they might be household names elsewhere. Marjorie Macgoye (pp. 1536–44) is read by thousands of high school students in Kenya, and Nayantara Sahgal (pp. 1518–29) is one of the most important literary figures in India writing in English, even as younger writers like Anita Desai (pp. 1669–74) bask in the glory of a globalizing market for Indian writing. As you read this anthology, you will encounter women's diverse literary traditions in relation to, rather than in isolation from, one another or in terms of rigid national, ethnic, and even linguistic boundaries.

WOMEN'S PLACE IN THE TWENTIETH AND TWENTY-FIRST CENTURIES: WOMEN IN MOVEMENT

At the start of the twentieth century, only women in New Zealand had the right to vote. In many of the nationalist struggles against colonial rule, such as in India and Nigeria, women won the right to vote with national independence. And while by the century's end the United States had not yet had a woman president or vice president, many other countries represented in this anthology, including India, Britain, Pakistan, Canada, Haiti, Liberia, and New Zealand, have had women serve as prime ministers. Around the world women organize politically in parties, trade unions, social movements, and grassroots organizations, work in professions, and participate in the global economy and global media. Although inequalities among women both within and between nations are profound, and though women are still nowhere in the world the political, economic, or social equals of men, women have nonetheless gained significant roles in every sphere of life.

Feminisms in the United States and Britain

While learning about the history of the feminist movements in the United States and Britain, students are often introduced to feminist theorist Elaine Showalter's description of these movements as coming in three "waves": the first from the mid–nineteenth century until women got the vote in the 1920s; the second from the late 1950s until the late 1970s, when feminism reemerged as (largely) a movement of middle-class white women who were interested in economic and social equality, and in which feminism imagined "woman" to be an unproblematic category; and the third from the 1970s until the present, in which feminists embraced the understanding that "woman" is not a category that neatly describes similar cases of oppression and that differences of race, ethnicity, sexuality, class, and nationality intersect with issues of gender to create very different kinds of social and cultural oppressions. However, the three-wave model oversimplifies the development of the feminist movement over the past two centuries. As early as the mid–nineteenth century, and certainly into the early twentieth, African American women like Sojourner Truth and Ida B. Wells were already looking at the differences that race can make in being a feminist (see pp. 606–7, 1419–20). And women writers like Sui Sin Far (pp. 1228–35), Cornelia Sorabji (pp. 1238–50), Anzia Yezierska (pp. 1351–56), Zitkala Sa (pp. 1303–8), and Zora Neale Hurston (pp. 1405–14) were exploring the differences that class, ethnicity, and race made to the experience of being a woman. Showalter's model reflects some real differences in the ways that the different moments in British and American feminist movements have imagined their political demands, but when we look at feminism as a worldwide phenomenon, the "three waves" metaphor does not always hold up.

Early feminists believed that full political enfranchisement—having the right to vote and to hold political office—would make social inequalities disappear. Many women therefore worked ferociously to gain the vote. In the United Kingdom, under the leadership of Emmeline Pankhurst (1858–1928), the president and founder of the Women's Social and Political Union (1903), women organized marches and protests; undertook acts of civil disobedience; went on hunger strikes (during which many were brutally force-fed); and engaged in violent acts of vandalism, arson, and bombings (including the bombing of Westminster Abbey). Like their sisters in the United Kingdom, women in the United States organized rallies and marches, founded newspapers, and worked both within and outside political channels to gain the right to vote, though there was less violence associated with the American movement. There were, though, tensions in American campaigns to achieve the vote for women (which began in the nineteenth century and came to fruition in the twentieth). They were sometimes fraught with racism, and organizations set up to work for the vote often fractured along color lines; when African American men, but not women of any race, were granted the vote by the Fifteenth Amendment in 1870, many white women were outraged. When, during the early twentieth century, organizations devoted to getting the vote for women did not fight equally to ensure that African American men were not denied their rights to vote, many people were alienated from the movement. Even in issues of gender, the organizations did not always agree; the National Woman Suffrage Association took a more aggressive line than did the American Woman Suffrage Association, though the two merged in 1890 to become the National American Woman Suffrage Association (NAWSA).

In 1900, Carrie Chapman Catt (1859–1947) took over the reins of the national women's suffrage campaign, and the leadership of NAWSA, from Susan B. Anthony (1820–1906). Meanwhile, Alice Paul (1885–1977), inspired by Emmeline Pankhurst's efforts in the United Kingdom, found NAWSA too conservative and formed the more radical National Woman's Party. The NWP began very visible campaigns of marches, including one that attracted thousands of protesters to Woodrow Wilson's first inauguration in 1913, and the first picketing of the White House. When the picketers were arrested for obstructing traffic, they staged a hunger strike that helped put pressure on President Wilson. Women's participation in the public sphere during World War I—especially their contributions in factories and offices—finally persuaded Wilson to back women's suffrage.

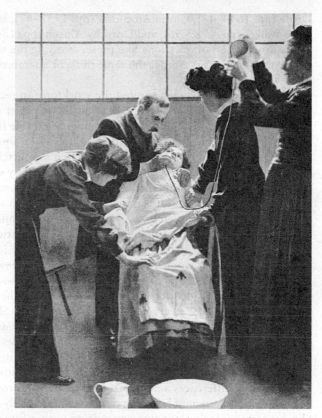

Suffragist being force-fed.

The suffragists had believed that when women had the vote, their position in society would improve; they would be accorded more dignity and would have more educational and work opportunities. When that did not happen after more than thirty years, women began to demand that attention be paid to gendered differences: Why were men paid more than women? Why were there such educational disparities in the 1950s? Why were women expected to take care of children and domestic duties, even if they also worked outside the home? Why were women's bodies objectified, when both men and women are sexual beings? From these questions, a new feminist movement was born (what is sometimes called the "second wave" of feminism), marked in the United States by the formation of NOW (the National Organization for Women), efforts to enact the Equal Rights Amendment (passed by the Senate in 1972, but never ratified), and a new consciousness of discrimination in hiring practices, social policies, and cultural norms. Many feminists in the 1960s and 1970s hoped to build a global sisterhood of women, but it soon became clear that not all women were treated the same or faced the same oppressions. Are lesbians objectified in the same way as heterosexual women? How can a woman of color be a "sister" to the white woman who either ignores the issue of racial oppression or, worse, is actively involved in exploiting other women? Should we take seriously the problems of the middle-class woman who is worried about a glass ceiling at work when poor women cannot find adequate child care or job training to get out of poverty? The women's rights movement of the mid–twentieth century came of age during the years of the civil rights movement and the gay rights movement; and their goals, while often congruent, were sometimes at odds. Women of color and lesbians often found themselves torn between different ideals and different goals. When the feminist movement began to take seriously the differences between women, the "third wave" of feminism was born. Women writers, including Adrienne Rich (pp. 1558–60), Audre

Lorde (pp. 1644–48), Gloria Anzaldúa (pp. 1737–47), bell hooks (pp. 1893–99), Alice Walker (pp. 1789–96), and Dorothy Allison (pp. 1847–51), have been central to the articulation of questions like these, stressing the ways that *woman* is not a simple term that always means the same thing or guarantees political solidarity with other women.

As middle-class women entered the workforce in record numbers throughout the century, it also became less clear what the feminist movement needed to address most critically. Are questions of gender separable from questions of sex and class? Most contemporary feminists would answer "no" and point to the ways that oppressions overlap and intersect. When a politician goes on a rant about "welfare mothers," such rhetoric is marked not only by sexist ideas about women but also by classist ideas about the poor and (more covertly) by racist ideas about African American women. It is impossible to sort out a single "oppression" when a Latina lesbian is subjected to workplace harassment and discrimination or when a woman wearing a veil is singled out for "extra questioning" when crossing an international border. By the end of the century, in the industrialized first world, such questions about women's material well-being had taken their place alongside an even more fundamental one: Does the descriptor *woman* make sense as a primary designation of identity? Debates rage over whether sexual difference really matters, over what the term *woman* might encompass: Should it include transsexuals? intersexuals? Should it be a biological category at all? The more we learn about biology, genetics, and hormonal variations, the less clear it is that rigid sexual differences exist. For instance, biologist Ann Fausto-Sterling argues in books like *Myths of Gender* and *Sexing the Body* that the more we learn about genetic and hormonal differences among people, the more appropriate it may be to reconsider our whole system of believing that "men" are really different from "women." She suggests replacing our two-sex system with a five-sex system. As feminists began to confront these kinds of questions, the analyses of gender oppression became more complex, but they also began to fragment. For many young women, it can seem as though gender oppression is over and that feminism is outdated. And yet, at the end of the twentieth century (1998), nearly one-third of American women reported being sexually or physically abused by their husbands or boyfriends; at the beginning of the twenty-first (2005), one in six American women—but only one in thirty-three men—has been sexually assaulted.

Feminisms in the Postcolonial World

If we look outside the Western world, feminist movements have traversed somewhat different paths. For women in India, where there is a growing gap in the ratio of males to females and female fetuses are aborted in disproportionate numbers (the latest numbers show that for every 1,000 boys born, only 800 girls are born), biology and culture present a lethal mix of gender oppression. In many African nations, women are expected to carry water and firewood for many miles and then to do without food so that their husbands and children can eat. In some countries that have adopted an authoritarian version of Muslim law, women are killed for having been raped or for insisting on getting an education.

In the United States and Europe, the first- and second-wave feminist movements have been seen as key to the evocation of women's freedoms in the twentieth century. The struggles for women's rights in colonial India and Africa are more complex. In the third world, women's movements have shaped, as much as they were shaped by, relations of power between men and women, among women, and among races, classes, and nationalities. The experiences and histories of imperialism, slavery, colonization, and other modes of exploitation have contributed to third world women's challenging the universalism imposed upon the term *women*. Through their writings and political movements, women from the third world have shown us how history and geography shape women's experiences of their bodies, their everyday lives, and the larger structures within which they are located. Thus, Jamaica Kincaid (pp. 1853–60) presents a devastating account of the landscape of her home, and the American poet and essayist Adrienne Rich draws our attention to the importance of the "politics of location." In doing so, both writers stress the importance not only of a person's personal history but also of her situation within a nation's history and her life experiences—whether of privilege or of oppression—in how she is able to see the world. Thus, every selection in this section of the anthology is presented in terms of the politics of location of the writer and her literary world, even as we invite you to read her work as comprising interlocking and interwoven cartographies of struggle.

Women's movements in much of the third world were incubated in the catastrophic encounter with colonialism and its version of modernity. In the nineteenth century, colonial officers, missionaries, and native reformers had sought to improve the condition of native women, who were seen as victims of blind tradition and regressive patriarchy. But the twentieth century saw women taking their fates into their own hands. It heralded an era of women's active participation within nationalist and anti-colonialist movements in India, Nigeria, Kenya, and elsewhere. No longer were native women, to be seen as passive objects of white men's attempts to save them from native men and patriarchal control within the home. Many middle-class and elite women began to form women's associations such as the Women's Indian Association, founded in 1914 and organizing conferences and working to promote better labor conditions, health care, and literacy among women from all strata of society. In South Africa, the Native and Coloured Women's Association was formed in 1912 to campaign against the racist "pass laws" and was followed by the formation of the African National Congress Women's League in 1943. In India, activists like Rokeya Sakhawat Hossain (pp. 1316–24) worked to establish girls' and women's schools even among traditional and conservative social groups and sparked reforms within caste and religious groupings. In Nigeria, women set up a range of social and political groups that supported and sustained the movement for independence. Early-twentieth-century women activists and writers such as Annie Besant (pp. 1212–15) and Margaret Cousins (pp. 1311–13) were inspired by the freedom struggle in India, and particularly by the moral courage and strength of Indian women. These European women became among the most eloquent advocates of the possibilities of feminist solidarity across racial difference. On the other hand, Katherine Mayo (pp. 1250–55), an American journalist who traveled to India, could see things only through imperialist eyes—for her, Indian women were backward, passive, and docile, doomed to a life of oppression. These examples illustrate the simultaneous complicity and resistance of Western women in the colonial enterprise, even as native and indigenous women were becoming an indispensable part of anti-colonial nationalist movements.

Post-independence struggles ushered in a new era of women's activism in the third world. Where national sovereignty had been achieved, women had to remain vigilant that their specific demands for autonomy not be elided in the process of nation formation. Women demanded the right to equal citizenship, to equal wages, to protection from state and domestic violence, and to social welfare measures such as health care, child care, and education. The law became an important site of struggle, as women's movements demanded that older laws, both customary and colonial, on rape, marriage, divorce, and property rights be remade according to the principles of gender equality. Questions of women's well-being also impinged heavily on processes of economic development within postcolonial national projects. Issues such as environmental sustainability, poverty reduction programs, and employment guarantee schemes would succeed only if women's work, both within the household and outside it, was factored in. While middle-class women were and still are fighting for equal wages within the workplace globally, the majority of the world's work is carried out by women working in the households, fields, and factories of Africa, Latin America, and Asia.

At the turn of the twenty-first century women are facing new challenges globally. Under pressure from their own corrupt elites and from organizations such as the World Bank and the International Monetary Fund, third world nations have increasingly privatized social services, public spaces, and family life in ways that affect women disproportionately (see p. 1808). A recent report by the World Health Organization on gender inequality and labor details the ways in which women all over the world are endangered by unsafe workplaces; by unfair, gendered labor practices; by social and economic situations that force them into sex work; and by policies that put them (and their fetuses) at risk. In reaction to these forces of global capitalism, right-wing religious ideologies (Christian, Jewish, Muslim, and Hindu) are fighting to control women's bodies by limiting abortion rights in the

Carrying water in drought-ravaged India.

United States or by requiring women to wear the veil elsewhere (see pp. 1325–26). The global spread of AIDS, the deepening of poverty in Africa, and transnational sex trafficking are making the lives of women in the poorest nations ever more precarious. The waning of the utopian hopes of nationalist resistance and their usurpation by the new imperialisms of the twenty-first century, characterized by the "war on terror" and the governmental promotion of profit-making over welfare in every sphere—from the realm of the body, sexuality, and imagination to places of work and worship—create daunting challenges for women in movement.

The twentieth- and twenty-first-century selections in this anthology take the long history of British and American colonialism, with their apparatuses of economic exploitation and political dominance, as key to the formation of literary cultures—the production of books, women's access to education, what women wrote and thought about in the twentieth century, and what they are yet to imagine in the following decades of the twenty-first. Women's works from many segments of political and popular culture—blues lyrics (pp. 1397–98), working-class drama by the Sistren Collective (p. 1808), narratives of lesbian and working-class pride (pp. 1847–51)—are interwoven in this anthology with what might readily be recognized as women's "literature." Cultural work and literary production both show that women writers have resisted, and continue to resist, domination in its multifarious forms and to work for a more just and humane world.

WOMEN'S WRITING, 1900 TO THE PRESENT: THE SHAPE AND LIMITATIONS OF MODERNISM AND POSTMODERNISM

Many of the profound changes in ways of thinking during the twentieth century were driven by writers, especially women writers, who came into their own as professionals, as citizens, and as commentators in this period. Nineteenth-century women writers were often reluctant to enter the public scene and often did so only on behalf of others (pp. 463–67). Twentieth-century women became writers for more diverse reasons: certainly the trend to write on behalf of others (both to support families and to advocate for others) continues, but more and more women find themselves motivated to write on their own behalf. These women write not only to present their life experiences to a wider world but also to claim for themselves the role of artist and writer and thereby to call into question not only the designation "woman" or "writer" but also labels like "Englishwoman" or "American," for instance, that earlier generations found obvious. Not all women writers, of course, would claim the label of "feminist" or wish to be remembered as a "woman writer" rather than simply as an "author"; for instance, Elizabeth Bishop (1911–79), an important poet who would otherwise be included in an anthology like this, left strict instructions in her will that her work never be included in an anthology of women's writing.

"Modernism" and Challenges to Tradition

Typically, introductions to the literature of the twentieth century divide that literature into movements labeled modernism and postmodernism. While these labels are not wholly satisfactory when looking at women's writing in English globally (as they are embedded within a specifically European American history), they are useful as a starting point. Modernism as a literary movement is closely aligned with changes in other artistic forms, including music, the visual arts, and dance.

La Toilette (1891) by Mary Cassatt.

Not surprisingly, an artistic movement that was spawned during an era of great technological change and political upheaval is noted for its questioning of traditions, especially of traditional forms. In dance, artists like Isadora Duncan (1877–1927), Martha Graham (1894–1991), and Ruth St. Denis (1878–1968) moved from traditional ballet to freer and looser movement, with more emphasis on personal expression. In painting, the movement began with impressionism in the late nineteenth century, emphasizing form, light, and the act of perception over carefully finished canvases that privileged traditional artistic techniques; soon, artists began to experiment with paintings that either were not representational at all or attempted to represent the world in different dimensions or scale. Mary Cassatt's impressionist painting *La Toilette* (1891) breaks with mid-nineteenth-century conventions of portraiture, both in its emphasis on the humble subject (a woman at her bath rather than posing formally alone or with her husband and children) and also in its simplicity of line and color; it makes use of a Japanese style, new to American painting at that time. Georgia O'Keeffe's *A Street* (1926) is more "modern" than Cassatt's; it still represents the world, but it does so by emphasizing scale to the point of distortion, offering a new way of seeing. These two paintings represent modernism in art, with its increasing challenges to traditions of representation.

In literature, writers began to chafe at the restrictions of realism (which strives to achieve verisimilitude in representing the world as it truly seems) and began instead to try to represent internal states and to convey the act of perception. Gertrude Stein (pp. 1275–84) and Virginia Woolf (pp. 1330–51), for example, experimented with how one might represent the world: Stein used language like a musician, aiming to approximate feeling through sound and rhythm as much as through the meaning of the words. Woolf entered a character's mind (using the technique of stream of consciousness, which she pioneered) in order to convey experience as it is really felt, without the ostensible framework of a coherent narrative. Modernist writers in general were ambivalent about the past and often took up experimental techniques in both narrative and poetry. Such writers, especially when writing after World War I, felt both alienated from the orthodoxies of patriotic sentiment and social mores and overwhelmed by a loss of certainty and an established social order. For women writers, this experience was sometimes liberating, sometimes painful; Edna St. Vincent Millay (pp. 1421–24), for example, broke with poetic traditions by writing both of sexuality unfettered by convention and of the injustices resulting from political upheaval, and H.D. (pp. 1363–73) faced the devastation of World War II but attempted to create a new mythology out of the loss.

A Street (1926) by Georgia O'Keeffe.

Modernism also saw the rise of women writers of color in the United States and elsewhere. As African Americans began moving to cities in great numbers during the early twentieth century, artists found themselves working in communities where artistic expression was encouraged. Writers like Nella Larsen (pp. 1414–18) and Zora Neale Hurston (pp. 1405–14) were part of a world in which writers, musicians, dancers, and actors associated with intellectuals, journalists, activists, and politicians and debated whether African American art was part of or separate from American art. The Harlem Renaissance—a flowering of jazz, the blues, and many different experiments with form in literature—generated works that share one thing in common: they all represent African Americans from a new perspective of respect, taking African American lives and history as central and important.

For many women writers, modernism seemed revolutionary as it marked a break from stultifying tradition. But modernism also had a conservative dimension; its dominant style was markedly masculinist, embodied by figures such as Ezra Pound (1885–1972), James Joyce (1882–1941), and T. S. Eliot (1888–1965) and in artistic movements such as futurism (which despised the past and advocated speed, technology, and violence) and surrealism (which questioned the value of rationality, explored the unconscious, and advocated irrationality and randomness). Modernism also spawned a culture of elitism: at its center was a coterie culture of male artists. This world was made visible by the writer Jean Rhys (pp. 1382–89), the daughter of a white, plantation-owning family in the Caribbean who arrived in London as a sixteen-year-old girl. Deprived of family backing and never quite fitting into mainstream English society, Rhys revealed in her writings both her struggle to be taken seriously within high modernism's literary circles and her experience of the dark underside of European modernity, with her stories of prostitutes, chorus girls, and women eking out a marginal existence in Europe's capitals of avant-garde modernism. Critics are still unsure how to classify her work.

Feminist art and literary critics also point to the ways in which Western, male modernist artists and writers appropriated figures from indigenous cultures—African masks in paintings by Pablo Picasso (1881–1973), the Tahitian women in paintings by Paul Gauguin (1848–1903), the Indian and African landscapes as emblems of desolation ("the horror, the horror") in the writings of Joseph Conrad (1857–1924) and E. M. Forster (1879–1970)—in order to rejuvenate their own artistic capacities and those of their cultures and civilizations. The ultimate objection to these iterations of modernism is that the representation of foreign objects, exotic places, and strange women in modernist art typically deprives women of agency and voice. Jamaica Kincaid depicts this in *Lucy;* traditional histories of modernism focusing on art from the male-centered, dominant culture tend to treat women—especially women of color—as mere objects rather than as subjects or practitioners of modernist art and literature.

Of course, many women writers embraced the linguistic experimentation of modernism, finding the self-conscious focus on language and its relationship to culture liberating. The painting by Amrita Sher Gil, an Indian modernist painter, illustrates the mixing of European and Indian elements. The canonical examples of Virginia Woolf and Gertrude Stein show only part of this picture. For many African

The Swing (1940) by Amrita Sher Gil.

women writers, their experiments with modernism entailed a deep engagement with African oral traditions of music, poetry, and performance. Grace Ogot (pp. 1589–98) uses Luo myth in a modern setting, and Ama Ata Aidoo (pp. 1747–59) draws on the art of storytelling that she learned from her grandmother. Caribbean women writers such as Grace Nichols (pp. 1870–73) and Merle Collins (pp. 1868–70) weave the multilayered myths and spirit worlds of the Caribbean through their work. South Asian writers, such as Meena Alexander (pp. 1882–87) and Sara Suleri (pp. 1911–23), and Egyptian writer Ahdaf Soueif (pp. 1873–82) work with multiple languages and cultures to express a distinctive polyglot sensibility that is characteristic of modernism.

Many third world women, who write in the context of decolonization and nation building, embrace realism as a mode of writing socially engaged literature, or what Beryl Gilroy (pp. 1510–16) termed "fact-fiction." For these writers, literature is central to the struggle against social injustice. Realism enables them to represent the everyday, mundane aspects of women's lives in both the domestic and public spheres. Still, they felt no hesitation about jettisoning older modes of representation, modes that assumed a stable and fixed reality, as well as writing back to the canonical texts of modernism. The novella *Our Sister Killjoy* by Ama Ata Aidoo can be read as a response to Joseph Conrad's *Heart of Darkness,* a novel that is endlessly recited as exposing the hopelessness and savagery of Africa; in Aidoo's version, a young African woman travels to the heart of Europe, only to find it spiritually barren and desolate.

Postmodernism and the Challenge to Representation

Some critics do not consider postmodernism a genuinely different movement from modernism, since in many ways its emphases on historical discontinuity, alienation, and individualism and its rejection of traditional forms continue the work of modernism. But most modernist works, even as they reject traditional forms, still create meaningful patterns, develop intricate systems of symbolism, and build their own structured universe. In its most recognizable expression, postmodernism tends to deny any meaning at all, emphasizing instead a world where things do not make sense and where structures tend to be random and fragmented or nonsensical. While this accurately portrays some women's writing during the postmodern era (sometimes described as beginning after 1945, sometimes in the mid-1960s), it does not account for much of the writing done by women in the late twentieth century. Certainly, women writers often use fragmentation and disconnection as both form and theme in their work, as in the poetry of Diane Wakoski (pp. 1674–78), but more often, they draw connections among seemingly disconnected things. For instance, in many writers' work, small, private moments that in previous generations would have seemed too unimportant for serious literary consideration come to be symbolic of larger, even global, political issues. In Toni Morrison's story "Recitatif" (pp. 1599–1612), for example, chance meetings between two women over a number of years come to represent a whole history of racism and classism in America. In a poem like Sylvia Plath's "Daddy" (pp. 1636–38), a father's abuse becomes analogous to the murderous fascism of Nazi Germany.

The postmodernist period is in many ways the era when women writers, especially women writing from previously marginalized positions, have come into their own. One of the chief strands of postmodernism, poststructuralism, consciously emphasizes the value of decentering knowledge, of looking at the margins for what has traditionally been excluded. In the postmodern period, we see the emergence of women writers from countries once colonized by American, British, and other European countries and from oppressed groups in the United States and Britain—people of color, gay and lesbian people, working-class people. Such writing sometimes conforms to postmodernist ideas of fragmentation and alienation and often includes moments that one might describe as "magical realism" (including within an otherwise mundane reality elements of the miraculous or inexplicable); Ana Castillo's *The Mixquiahuala Letters,* for example, is marked by its mixture of the mundane and the fantastic as well as by its randomness (the "novel" suggests several different orders in which you might read the numbered letters).

Often, though, women's postmodernist writing is marked by a reluctance to hold to a single view of "truth." In her Nobel acceptance speech, Toni Morrison (pp. 1612–17) describes an old storyteller who refuses to give her audience an easy answer, because to do so would nail down language and make it into a dead—and murderous—thing. Instead, she argues, language can be life-giving: "Word-work is sublime . . . because it is generative; it makes meaning that secures our difference, our human difference—the way in which we are like no other life" (p. 1615). Women writers in the postmodern era have imagined such a generative language that refuses to close off possibilities: Gloria Anzaldúa (pp. 1737–47) revitalizes English with infusions of other languages; Marilyn Chin imagines connections between her Chinese and American ancestries (pp. 1944–48). Jhumpa Lahiri makes self-conscious use of the ways memory works in order to question and problematize history and our connection to it. In "When Mr. Pirzada Came to Dine" (pp. 1984–94), the narrator recalls a moment from her childhood in a Boston suburb to tell the story of larger political events on the Indian subcontinent.

Mapping the Present

When selecting readings for inclusion, editors of anthologies make claims about what needs to be read. The proliferation of works by women writers from around the globe in English in the twentieth century was both our challenge and our incentive. Because we were working without the hindsight of several centuries (or even decades in some cases), the main issue was how to map the present literary landscape of women's writing for our readers. To be sure, no previous century has experienced the globalization of English that the twentieth century witnessed. As a result, we could feel thousands of writers calling on us to include them. After all, few anthologies of postcolonial literature exist, let alone anthologies of postcolonial literature by women or anthologies of literature by working-class women, black women, lesbians. Collections of works by women writers who also wrote songs or performed other arts are also not easily accessible. In this anthology, we wanted genuinely to recognize the myriad "worlds" of women's writing, in all their complexity. Every bit of common ground that allows us to recognize a global sisterhood is also contested terrain that positions us in competition or as working toward different ends.

Woolf's image of women as having "no country" of their own and Kincaid's rejection of the inherited literary legacies of colonialism help us begin to read critically outside and beyond existing frames of period and nation but also call for a genuine global solidarity among women, not based on sameness or an uncritical celebration of difference, but emerging out of attentive readings of women drawing their own literary, cultural, and political maps of an ever-changing world.

HISTORY		LITERATURE
First Pan-African Congress, London	**1900**	Theodore Dreiser *Sister Carrie* Ida B. Wells *Mob Rule in New Orleans* Zitkala Sa "Impressions of an Indian Childhood"
Australian Commonwealth is created; Queen Victoria dies after a 64-year reign and is succeeded by her son, Edward VII British women textile workers present a suffrage petition to Parliament	**1901**	Booker T. Washington's *Up from Slavery*
U.S. feminists mourn death of Elizabeth Cady Stanton Parliament passes the Midwives' Act, requiring medical licensing of midwives; midwifery declines significantly in Britain	**1902**	
The Great Train Robbery (first commercial film) is produced Women's Social and Political Union, a militant group fighting for women's suffrage, is founded Wright brothers' first successful powered flight Marie Curie becomes first female recipient of Nobel Peace Prize, which she wins with her husband and Henri Becquerel; Madame Curie wins the prize again in 1911 on her own	**1903**	
Ida Tarbell exposes the oil monopoly of John D. Rockefeller in her book *History of the Standard Oil Company*	**1904**	Sigmund Freud *Psychopathology of Everyday Life*
The Women's Vote Bill fails in Parliament; English suffragists led by Emmeline Pankhurst resort to sensationalist methods such as bombing, hunger strikes, and window smashing to stimulate national awareness	**1905**	Mary Boykin Chesnut *A Diary from Dixie* Edith Wharton *House of Mirth* Willa Cather "A Wagner Matinee"
Finland becomes first European nation to grant women right to vote	**1906**	
New Zealand Dominion is declared Florence Nightingale is the first woman awarded the British Order of Merit	**1907**	
Model T Ford is unveiled Emmeline Pankhurst and her daughter Christabel storm Parliament with 100,000 suffragists; two dozen are arrested; Parliament responds by prohibiting women from entering its doors	**1908**	

HISTORY		LITERATURE
Forced feeding of women suffragists (UK) begins Union of South Africa is declared by act of Parliament (UK) National Association for the Advancement of Colored People (NAACP) is founded in New York	**1909**	Cicely Hamilton *Marriage as a Trade* Gertrude Stein *Three Lives*
300 women protest outside Parliament against Prime Minister Asquith's refusal to sign the Conciliation Bill, allowing married women to vote in the general election; over 100 women are arrested and many complain of assault by police Madame C. J. Walker Co. moves into its Indianapolis headquarters; Walker will become first self-made African American woman millionaire through sale of hair-straightening product marketed to black women	**1910**	*How the Vote Was Won,* a play by Cicely Hamilton and Christopher St. John, is performed; U.S. women don't win the vote until 1921 Emma Goldman *The Traffic in Women*
The first International Women's Day is proclaimed; California grants women right to vote; Missouri becomes first state to provide public aid to mothers of dependent children	**1911**	Olive Schreiner *Woman and Labor*
Michigan, Kansas, Oregon, and Arizona grant women the right to vote; Massachusetts passes first minimum wage law for women and children The *Titanic* sinks in its maiden voyage and the "unsinkable Molly Brown" rises to fame for her heroism in rescuing 23 other women	**1912**	Sui Sin Far *Mrs. Spring Fragrance*
Lloyd George's house is burned down by members of the Women's Social and Political Union for withdrawing support for women's suffrage Emily Davison is killed when she throws herself under King George V's horse at Epson Derby to protest continued denial of vote to women	**1913**	Sir Almoth Wright *The Unexpurgated Case against Woman's Suffrage* Willa Cather *O Pioneers!*
Panama Canal is opened Assassination of Austria's archduke Ferdinand and his wife at Sarajevo, Bosnia, initiates World War I First national Mother's Day	**1914**	Gertrude Stein *Tender Buttons*
Ireland's Easter Rising Margaret Sanger (later founder of N.Y. Birth Control League) is jailed for 30 days for opening first birth control clinic (Brooklyn) Jeannette Rankin is elected first female member of Congress	**1916**	Susan Glaspell *Trifles*

HISTORY		LITERATURE

Russian Revolution begins
Congress declares war on Germany
New York grants women right to vote
Annie Besant delivers speech
  "The Case for India" before the
  32nd Indian National Congress
	1917	

World War I ends
House of Representatives passes
  resolution for a U.S. Woman Suffrage
  Amendment, but Senate rejects it
British women over age 30 get
  the vote
	1918	Willa Cather
		  My Ántonia

Spanish flu pandemic kills up to 100 million worldwide	**1918–19**	
Bell System introduces dial telephones, eliminating need for switchboard operators, who are mostly women	**1919**	Virginia Woolf "Kew Gardens"

19th Amendment for Woman's
  Suffrage passes both houses of
  Congress; Wisconsin becomes first
  state to ratify it, with Illinois and
  Michigan close behind
League of Women Voters is founded
	1920	Edith Wharton
		  Age of Innocence; awarded
		  Pulitzer Prize in 1921
		Alice Dunbar-Nelson
		  "I Sit and Sew"

	1921	Marianne Moore
		  Poems
		Zitkala Sa
		  American Indian Stories

Mussolini takes power in Italy	**1922**	T. S. Eliot *The Waste Land*

National Woman's Party endorses
an Equal Rights Amendment at
convention in Seneca Falls
	1923	Ellen Glasgow
		  "Jordan's End"
		Alberta Hunter
		  "You Gotta Reap What You Sow"
		Katherine Anne Porter
		  "Virgin Violeta"
		Virginia Woolf
		  "Mrs. Dalloway on Bond Street"
		Edna St. Vincent Millay wins
		  Pulitzer Prize

Texas elects first female governor,
Miriam "Ma" Ferguson, after
impeachment of her husband,
the former governor
	1925	Virginia Woolf
		  Mrs. Dalloway
		"Ma" Rainey
		  "Louisiana Hoodoo Blues"
		Ellen Glasgow
		  Barren Ground

	1925–26	Adolf Hitler *Mein Kampf*
Hirohito becomes emperor of Japan	**1926**	Zora Neale Hurston, "Sweat"

Joseph Stalin takes power
in Soviet Union
	1927	Virginia Woolf
		  To the Lighthouse
		Mourning Dove
		  Cogewea, the Half-Blood
		Bessie Smith
		  "Preachin' the Blues"

HISTORY		LITERATURE
Women in the UK get the vote on equal terms with men Amelia Earhart rises to fame as first woman to make trans-Atlantic crossing in flight co-piloted with two men	**1928**	Susan Glaspell *Brook Evans* Nella Larsen *Quicksand* Bessie Smith "Poor Man's Blues" "Ma" Rainey "Prove it on me Blues"
U.S. stock market crashes	**1929**	Virginia Woolf *A Room of One's Own* Nella Larsen *Passing*
Great Depression	**1929–39**	
United Airlines hires first flight attendants to aid anxious fliers and stipulates they must not be taller than 5 feet 4 inches or weigh more than 115 lb	**1930**	Nella Larsen "Sanctuary"
In Scottsboro, Alabama, 9 African American men are convicted of raping 2 white women despite dubious evidence; state court sentences them to death, but Supreme Court commutes sentences to life imprisonment.	**1931**	Susan Glaspell wins Pulitzer Prize for *Alison's House* Edna St. Vincent Millay *Fatal Interview* Willa Muir *Imagined Corners*
Amelia Earhart completes first solo transatlantic flight by a woman Franklin Delano Roosevelt (FDR) elected U.S. president	**1932**	Dorothy Parker "Lady with a Lamp"
Adolf Hitler becomes chancellor of Germany FDR nominates first female cabinet secretary, Frances Perkins	**1933**	Gertrude Stein *Autobiography of Alice B. Toklas*
China's "Long March," led by Mao Tse-tung, begins	**1934**	Lillian Hellman *The Children's Hour*
Mary McLeod Bethune founds National Council of Negro Women. FDR signs Social Security Act	**1935**	
Spanish Civil War erupts Eleanor Roosevelt becomes first president's wife to write own syndicated column Tampax Inc. introduces first cotton tampon	**1936**	Edith Wharton "Roman Fever" Margaret Mitchell *Gone with the Wind*
Amelia Earhart disappears in Pacific while attempting around-the-world flight	**1937**	Zora Neale Hurston, *Their Eyes Were Watching God*
Munich Pact signed	**1938**	Henry Miller *Tropic of Capricorn*
Hitler invades Czechoslovakia; Hitler-Stalin Pact signed; World War II begins as Germany invades Poland	**1939**	James Joyce *Finnegan's Wake* John Steinbeck *Grapes of Wrath*
Pearl Harbor is attacked; U.S. enters World War II	**1941**	

HISTORY		LITERATURE
Gandhi launches Quit India Movement, directed against British rule Anne Frank begins diary while in hiding with her family and others Women's Army Auxiliary Corps (WAAC) places women in noncombatant positions at home to free men for battle duty	**1942**	
	1943	Jean-Paul Sartre *Being and Nothingness* Eudora Welty *The Wide Net* Virginia Woolf "A Haunted House"
Anne Frank and others are betrayed; Anne and her sister are sent first to Auschwitz and then to Bergen-Belsen, where they die of typhus a few weeks before camp is liberated	**1944**	H.D. *The Walls Do Not Fall*
Yalta Conference: Churchill and Roosevelt cede eastern Europe to Stalin Atomic bombs are dropped on Hiroshima and Nagasaki; World War II ends Many U.S. women lose their jobs as men return from war, but number of working women is still higher than before the war Indonesia, freed from Dutch rule, declares itself a republic Fifth Pan-African Congress takes place in England and declares the "right of all colonial peoples to control their own destiny" International Monetary Fund (IMF) and World Bank are founded	**1945**	H.D. *Tribute to the Angels* Gwendolyn Brooks *A Street in Bronzeville*
First Indochina War, to expel French from Vietnam	**1946–54**	H.D. *The Flowering of the Rod*
House Un-American Affairs Committee investigations lead to blacklisting of Hollywood writers, directors, and actors for refusing to name Communists India gains independence and is partitioned into 2 countries: India and Pakistan U.N. announces plan for partition of Palestine, granting large amount of land to the minority Jewish population to form Israel	**1947**	Expurgated edition of Anne Frank's diary published
Gandhi is assassinated in India Afrikaner Nationalist Party comes to power in South Africa and implements policy of apartheid U.N. adopts Universal Declaration of Human Rights	**1948**	Norman Mailer *Naked and the Dead*

HISTORY		LITERATURE
Communist forces gain victory in China under the leadership of Mao Tse-tung	**1949**	Simone de Beauvoir *The Second Sex* Hisaye Yamamoto "Seventeen Syllables"
Korean War begins China invades Tibet U.S. military advisors are first sent to Vietnam to assist French colonial troops	**1950**	Doris Lessing *The Grass Is Singing* Gwendolyn Brooks wins Pulitzer Prize for *Annie Allen*
I Love Lucy airs on television	**1951**	Marianne Moore wins Pulitzer Prize and National Book Award for *Collected Poems*
Queen Elizabeth II ascends British throne General Dwight D. Eisenhower is elected U.S. president	**1952**	Samuel Beckett *Waiting for Godot*
Joseph Stalin dies suddenly Julius and Ethel Rosenberg are executed for treason.	**1953**	Gertrude Stein "Patriarchal Poetry"
Brown v. Board of Education outlaws separate educational institutions for black and white students in U.S. public schools Algerian war of independence begins *Father Knows Best* airs on television	**1954**	
Bandung Conference of independent Asian and African states is held Rosa Parks begins Montgomery, Alabama, bus boycott by refusing to give up her seat to a white man	**1955**	Vladimir Nabokov *Lolita*
First African American woman (Autherine Juanita Lucy) attends graduate classes at University of Alabama–Tuscaloosa; school suspends her for her safety in face of riots; U.S. District Court forces university to readmit her but she is later expelled for claiming university complicit with the white mob Egyptian president Nasser nationalizes Suez Canal; Israel invades Egypt with support from Great Britain and France Morocco, Tunisia, and Sudan gain independence	**1956**	Allen Ginsberg *Howl* Carlos Bulosan *America Is in the Heart* Naguib Mahfouz *Cairo Trilogy* Sam Selvon *Lonely Londoners* John Osborne *Look Back in Anger*
Ghana gains independence *Leave It to Beaver* airs on television	**1957**	Jack Kerouac *On the Road* Isak Dinesen *Seven Gothic Tales*
	1958	Chinua Achebe *Things Fall Apart*
Fidel Castro assumes power in Cuba after overthrow of Batista regime Famine in China kills 30–40 million Billie Holiday dies of cirrhosis of the liver	**1959**	Lorraine Hansberry's *A Raisin in the Sun* debuts on Broadway; wins New York Drama Critics' Circle Award for best play and is nominated for 35 Tony Awards

HISTORY		LITERATURE

Nigeria gains independence
Oral birth control pills introduced in
    United States
Students for Democratic Society (SDS),
    a student activist group, is founded
	1960	Sylvia Plath
		    The Colossus and Other Poems

Oral birth control pills are introduced
in Great Britain
	1961	Tillie Olsen
		    Tell Me a Riddle
		Frantz Fanon
		    The Wretched of the Earth

Algeria gains independence
Marilyn Monroe dies of an overdose
    of Nembutal, a sleeping pill
SDS issues Port Huron Statement
	1962	Doris Lessing
		    The Golden Notebook
		Katherine Anne Porter
		    Ship of Fools

Four African American schoolgirls
    are killed and 19 injured in racist
    bombing of Birmingham Baptist
    Church during Sunday services;
    race riots erupt throughout Alabama
Martin Luther King Jr. delivers his
    "I Have a Dream" speech during civil
    rights march on Washington, D.C.
John F. Kennedy is assassinated; Vice
    President Lyndon Johnson takes
    office
Kenya gains independence
Congress votes to guarantee women
    equal pay for equal work in the
    Equal Pay Act, but it proves difficult
    to enforce
	1963	Sylvia Plath
		    The Bell Jar
		Betty Friedan
		    The Feminine Mystique
		Adrienne Rich
		    Snapshots of a Daughter-in-Law

President Johnson declares his war
    on poverty
U.S. Civil Rights Act is passed
	1964	Lorraine Hansberry
		    *The Sign in Sidney Brustein's
		    Window*

Malcolm X is assassinated
Military coups in Indonesia and Congo
United States reactivates Food Stamps
    Program, which had been terminated
    in 1943
Over 180,000 U.S. soldiers on the
    ground in Vietnam
	1965	Sylvia Plath
		    Ariel
		Tillie Olsen
		    "Silences"

Black Panther Party, a black nationalist
    organization, is founded
First Tri-Continental Conference is
    held in Havana, Cuba
Grace Slick joins psychedelic rock
    group the Jefferson Airplane
NOW (National Organization for
    Women) is founded by Betty Friedan
	1966	Jean Rhys
		    Wide Sargasso Sea
		Louise Bennett Coverley
		    Jamaica Labrish

Civil war erupts in Nigeria
Ernesto ("Che") Guevara is captured
    by Bolivian Rangers supported
    by CIA
Abortion Act legalizes abortion in
    Great Britain
Folk singer Joan Baez is arrested for
    singing anti-war songs and serves
    45 days
	1967	Gabriel Garcia Marquez
		    One Hundred Years of Solitude
		Audre Lorde
		    The First Cities

HISTORY		LITERATURE
Martin Luther King Jr. is assassinated; Robert F. Kennedy is assassinated Protesters against Miss America pageant throw bras and girdles into a trash can to protest the pageant and the treatment of women as sexual objects Shirley Chisholm is elected to Congress from New York's 12th District for the first of her seven terms; first African American woman elected to Congress Richard M. Nixon is elected U.S. president	**1968**	Eldridge Cleaver *Soul on Ice*
Students for a Democratic Society (SDS) is dissolved Apollo 11 astronauts Neil Armstrong and "Buzz" Aldrin walk on the moon	**1969**	Anais Nin *Delta of Venus* Kate Millett *Sexual Politics*
Beatles break up Students shot by Ohio National Guard at Kent State University, Ohio, during protest; 4 killed; nationwide student strikes follow Janis Joplin, blues-rock singer, dies of a heroin overdose Socialist Salvador Allende elected in Chile	**1970**	Toni Morrison *The Bluest Eye* Germaine Greer *The Female Eunuch* Maya Angelou *I Know Why the Caged Bird Sings* Philip Roth *Portnoy's Complaint* Ama Ata Aidoo *No Sweetness Here*
Idi Amin comes to power in Uganda 26th Amendment lowers U.S. voting age from 21 to 18 Civil war in Pakistan leads to formation of Bangladesh	**1971**	
Equal Rights Amendment is approved by both houses of Congress Representative Shirley Chisholm becomes first African American woman to run for president Barbara Jordan becomes first African American woman elected to Congress from a southern state; serves three terms in House of Representatives for Texas	**1972**	Adrienne Rich *Diving into the Wreck*
U.S. forces withdraw from Vietnam Salvador Allende is assassinated as General Pinochet seizes power in Chile Organization of Petroleum Exporting Countries (OPEC) increases oil prices and reduces production, causing worldwide oil crisis *Roe v. Wade* strikes down all state laws prohibiting abortion during the first trimester	**1973**	Erica Jong *Fear of Flying* Bessie Head *A Question of Power* Alice Walker "Everyday Use" Eudora Welty wins Pulitzer Prize for *The Optimist's Daughter* Toni Morrison *Sula*

HISTORY		LITERATURE

Nixon resigns in face of Watergate scandal
Union activist and whistle blower Karen Silkwood is killed—foul play is suspected
	1974	Doris Lessing
		   Memoirs of a Survivor
		Toni Morrison
		   Sula

South Vietnam falls to Communist North
Indian president Ahmed, in consultation with Prime Minister Indira Gandhi, declares state of emergency in India and suspends civil rights
Indonesia occupies East Timor
	1975	Nawal el Saadawi
		   Woman at Point Zero
		Ruth Prawer Jhabvala
		   Heat and Dust

Soweto township uprisings begin in South Africa
First home computers produced (Apple II followed in 1977 and the IBM Home Computer in 1981)
	1976	Adrienne Rich
		   Of Woman Born
		Maxine Hong Kingston
		   The Woman Warrior

Anti-apartheid activist Steve Biko dies in police custody in South Africa
General Zia comes to power in Pakistan, following a coup
Indiana becomes 35th and last state (to date) to ratify U.S. Equal Rights Amendment
	1977	Marilyn French
		   The Women's Room
		Ngugi wa Thiong'o
		   Petals of Blood
		Toni Morrison
		   Song of Solomon
		Leslie Marmon Silko
		   Ceremony

Soviet Union backs coup in Afghanistan	**1978**	Tillie Olsen
		   Silences
		Adrienne Rich
		   Dream of a Common Language

Margaret Thatcher becomes Great Britain's first woman prime minister Iranian Revolution ousts Shah Mohammad Reza Pahlavi; Ayatollah Khomeini takes power; American hostages are taken and held for over a year when U.S. embassy in Tehran is stormed by Iranian students	**1979**	Buchi Emecheta *The Joys of Motherhood*

Ronald Reagan is elected president
John Lennon is shot to death outside his apartment building, the Dakota, by Mark Chapman
	1980	Salman Rushdie
		   Midnight's Children
		Audre Lorde
		   The Cancer Journals
		Maxine Hong Kingston
		   China Men

	1981	Toni Morrison
		   Tar Baby
		Cherríe Moraga and Gloria Anzaldúa
		   This Bridge Called My Back
		Sylvia Plath posthumously wins Pulitzer Prize for *Collected Poems*

Argentina invades Falklands Islands (British territory), leading to Falklands War Israel invades Lebanon, culminating in Sabra and Shatila massacres.	**1982**	Alice Walker *The Color Purple*

HISTORY		LITERATURE
The film *Silkwood*, starring Meryl Streep and Cher, airs	**1983**	Sandra Cisneros *House on Mango Street* Octavia Butler "Speech Sounds" Cherríe Moraga *Loving in the War Years* Toni Morrison "Recitatíf"
Democratic Representative Geraldine Ferraro from New York becomes first woman to win vice presidential nomination Indian prime minister Indira Gandhi is assassinated by bodyguard	**1984**	Rigoberta Menchu *I, Rigoberta Menchu* Louise Erdrich *Love Medicine* and *Jacklight*
	1985	Margaret Atwood *The Handmaid's Tale* Helena Maria Viramontes *The Moths*
	1986	Ana Castillo *The Mixquiahuala Letters* Marjorie Macgoye *Coming to Birth* Art Spiegelman *Maus* Denise Chavez *Last of the Menu Girls* Meridel Lesueur "Rites of Ancient Ripening"
First intifada (uprising) against Israeli occupation breaks out in Palestine; lasts six years	**1987**	Michelle Cliff *No Telephone to Heaven* Toni Morrison *Beloved* Gloria Anzaldúa *Borderlands/La Frontera*
George H. W. Bush is elected president Benazir Bhutto, first woman prime minister of Pakistan, is elected	**1988**	Tsitsi Dangarembga *Nervous Conditions* Louise Erdrich *Tracks*
Tiananmen Square student uprising in Beijing is brutally put down Berlin Wall falls, signaling collapse of the Soviet Union; communist states of eastern Europe gain independence Civil rights activist Aung San Suu Kyi is arrested by military dictatorship in Burma United States invades Panama	**1989**	Cynthia Ozick *The Shawl* Sandra Cisneros *The House on Mango Street*
Nelson Mandela is released after 28 years in prison in South Africa Women earn an average of $0.67 per $1.00 earned by men doing comparable work Americans with Disabilities Act is passed.	**1990**	Jamaica Kincaid *Lucy* Jessica Hagedorn *Dogeaters*

HISTORY		LITERATURE

The film *Thelma and Louise,* starring Geena Davis and Susan Sarandon, airs
First Gulf War launched, in which U.S.-led coalition forces attack Iraq for its invasion of Kuwait
U.S. activists demanding more breast cancer research found the National Breast Cancer Coalition
Coup in Haiti overthrows Jean Bertrand Aristide
	1991	Bapsi Sidhwa
		    Cracking India (originally published 1988 as *Ice Candy Man*)
		Sandra Cisneros
		    Woman Hollering Creek
		Nadine Gordimer of South Africa wins Nobel Prize for Literature
		Linda Hogan
		    Red Clay
		Leslie Marmon Silko
		    Almanac of the Dead

Peace treaty is signed between Mozambique and South African–backed forces, after a war in which over 1 million are killed
Bill Clinton is elected U.S. president
	1992	Marilyn Hacker
		    "Cancer Winter"
		Toni Morrison
		    Playing in the Dark and *Jazz*
		Dorothy Allison
		    Bastard Out of Carolina

President Bill Clinton marks the 20th anniversary of *Roe v. Wade* by reversing abortion restrictions imposed by Reagan and Bush administrations
The FDA approves the first female condom; though less effective than the male condom, it offers women more control
U.N. peacekeeping troops intervene in Bosnia to stop "ethnic cleansing" of Muslims by Serbian Christians
Eritrea gains independence from Ethiopia
	1993	Bharati Mukherjee
		    The Holder of the World
		Toni Morrison awarded the Nobel Prize for Literature
		Pat Mora
		    Nepantla
		Linda Hogan
		    The Book of Medicines

Nelson Mandela is inaugurated as president of South Africa
Republicans take control of both houses of Congress for the first time in 40 years
Peasant uprising in Chiapas, Mexico
Death toll of Rwandan civil war reaches 1 million people
	1994	Denise Chavez
		    Face of an Angel
		Marilyn Chin
		    The Phoenix Gone, the Terrace Empty

Federal office building in Oklahoma City bombed by U.S. terrorist Timothy McVeigh, killing 168 people, many of them children Nigerian dictatorship executes writer Ken Saro-Wiwa	**1995**	Helena Maria Viramontes *Under the Feet of Jesus*
President Bill Clinton is reelected, defeating Senator Robert Dole of Kansas Taliban gains power in Afghanistan	**1996**	Nancy Mairs *Waist-High in the World*
British scientist clones first mammal, a sheep named Dolly Hong Kong is restored to Chinese rule after more than 150 years as British colony Diana, Princess of Wales, dies in Paris car crash	**1997**	Arundhati Roy *The God of Small Things*

HISTORY		LITERATURE

Peace agreement between Catholics and Protestants in Northern Ireland is reached
Suharto dictatorship is overthrown in Indonesia after 32 years
Paula Jones's sexual-harassment lawsuit against President Clinton is dismissed
President Clinton is impeached by the House of Representatives for attempted cover-up of his affair with Monica Lewinsky; Clinton is acquitted by the Senate in 1999
	1998	Barbara Kingsolver
		   The Poisonwood Bible
		Yvonne Vera
		   Butterfly Burning
		Toni Morrison
		   Paradise

Indonesia begins withdrawal from East Timor
Massacre at Columbine High School, Littleton, Colorado; 15 are killed and 23 wounded
Earthquake devastates Turkey, killing 17,000
	1999	Eli Clare
		   Exile and Pride
		Leslie Marmon Silko
		   Gardens in the Dunes

Second intifada (uprising) breaks out in Palestine
George W. Bush becomes U.S. president when Democratic candidate Albert Gore concedes, following Republican-dominated Supreme Court's decision that a hand recount of Florida ballots shall not continue
	2000	Zadie Smith
		   White Teeth
		Helena Maria Viramontes
		   Their Dogs Came With Them

Al Qaeda members fly jets into World Trade Towers and the Pentagon and a fourth plane is downed over Pennsylvania, killing 2,819; U.S. attacks Taliban and al Qaeda in Afghanistan	**2001**	Denise Chavez
		   Loving Pedro Infante
		Louise Erdrich
		   Miracles at Little No Horse
		Harilyn Rousso
		   Strong, Proud Sisters!

Lula de Silva takes office in Brazil after Workers' Party wins general elections	**2002**	Anne Finger
		   Past Due
		Sandra Cisneros
		   Caramelo

President George W. Bush orders troops into Iraq	**2003**	Jhumpa Lahiri
		   The Namesake
		Lucy Grealy
		   Autobiography of a Face
		Toni Morrison
		   Love

Iraqi insurgency ramps up and sectarian violence in Iraq explodes, with kidnappings and killings of civilians rampant	**2003–**	
George W. Bush wins a second term	**2004**	

	2005	Simi Linton
		   My Body Politic
		Harriet McBryde Johnson
		   Too Late to Die Young

HISTORY		LITERATURE
Democrats retake both houses of U.S. Congress	**2006**	Zoe Wicomb *Playing in the Light* Alison Bechdel *Fun Home: A Tragic-Comic*
Protestants and Catholics in Northern Ireland agree to share power U.S. Supreme Court makes an abortion procedure (called "partial birth" by opponents) illegal British prime minister Tony Blair steps down	**2007**	Indian-born author Kiran Desai wins Booker Prize for novel *The Inheritance of Loss* Nigerian-born author Chimamanda Ngozi Adichie wins Orange Prize for women's literature for novel *Half of a Yellow Sun* Doris Lessing wins the Nobel Prize for Literature

ANNIE BESANT

1847–1933

Annie Besant, born in London of Irish parents, was a freethinker, educator, Theosophist, and supporter of home rule for Ireland and India. Besant's early life was a struggle. She lost her father, Dr. William Wood, when she was only five years old. Her mother, Emily Morris, persuaded a friend, Ellen Marryat, to take the girl under her wing and educate her. In 1866, at the age of nineteen, Besant met and married the Reverend Frank Besant, a vicar in Lincolnshire. Over the next four years, she gave birth to two children, but it was an unhappy marriage because her political liberalism clashed with the conservatism of her husband. Besant had also by now begun to question her religious beliefs. When she refused to attend communion, Frank Besant requested a legal separation, and in 1873, Besant left with her daughter to live in London. Unable to divorce, she remained married but lived apart from her husband until her death.

Besant made a final break with Christianity when in 1874 she joined the Secular Society. In 1889, she also became a member of the Fabian Society, a noted socialist organization founded by Sidney and Beatrice Webb. The society's members included the playwright George Bernard Shaw, with whom Besant forged a close friendship, and the suffragist Emmeline Pankhurst. She contributed to the influential collection *Fabian Essays* (1889), edited by Shaw. She also worked closely with Charles Bradlaugh, leader of the secular movement in Britain, with whom she edited the radical *National Reformer.* Besant wrote articles on such issues as marriage and women's rights. She also published (with Bradlaugh) a book advocating birth control, titled *The Laws of Population* (1887), described by *The Times* of London as "an indecent, lewd, filthy, bawdy and obscene book." A pamphlet she wrote with Charles Bradlaugh, *Why I Do Not Believe in God* (1887) was widely distributed by the secularists.

In 1888, Besant started her own newspaper, called *The Link,* and published the article "White Slavery in London," which drew attention to the dangerous conditions faced by women who worked at Bryant and May, a match factory in the city's East End. She then helped organize a strike of the female workforce at the factory. In 1889, Besant was elected to the London School Board, where she advocated large-scale reform of local schools, including the provision of free meals and health checkups for poor children.

While engaged in social and political reform, Besant also struggled for an alternative truth to that offered by orthodox religions. In the 1890s, she became interested in Theosophy, a religious movement founded by Madame Blavatsky in 1875. Theosophy was based on the Hindu ideas of karma (belief in ethical consequences generated by a person's actions) and reincarnation, with nirvana (salvation) as the eventual aim. She helped to spread Theosophical beliefs around the world, most notably in India, where she went to live in 1893. From there, she continued to support women's suffrage, a cause she had been committed to in England, arguing the case in letters to British newspapers. She also maintained her interest in education, founding the Central Hindu College for Boys at Benares (now Varanasi) in 1898.

While in India, Besant joined the struggle for Indian home rule, and during World War I, she was imprisoned by the British authorities. Undeterred, she founded the Indian Home Rule League in 1916 and became its president. In 1917, she was also elected president of the Indian National Congress. She declared in 1918 in her paper *New India:* "I love the Indian people as I love none other . . . , my heart and my mind . . . have long been laid on the altar of the Motherland." She died in India in 1933.

The following piece, excerpted from her pamphlet *A Nation's Rights* (1918), makes the case for individual liberty as a natural right. Written in the context of British colonial rule in India and the infringement of civil liberties during World War I, Besant's plea for a free India as part of the global community was visionary.

From **A Nation's Rights**

[*The Foundation of Rights*]

* * *

The first thing that we have to make clear to Great Britain is that we are determined to have Home Rule,[1] and that the Nation's Right to Freedom is based on eternal principles. It is the passing fashion of reactionaries to ridicule "Natural Rights," and some foolish person declared the other day that to talk of "Natural Rights," was as out of date as the presence of a dinotherium.[2] That is, of course, the Prussian doctrine.[3] A man has no Rights, *a fortiori*[4] a Nation has none. A man's so-called rights are privileges given to him and taken away from him by laws made by the "State"—the governing body as apart from the Nation. To the State he belongs, and the State may do with him as it wills. He has no valid appeal to Justice, to Equity, to what has been called "Natural Law." As to the State, it is above law, and its only justification is Power. It *may* do whatever it *can* do, and its action is determined by the limitations of its Power, Duty being for it, in any real sense, nonexistent. The position is logically defensible, provided that the State is recognised as the highest authority, the source of all law, the determiner of the duty of the citizen so as to ensure its own highest good, Supreme Power upon earth. Hence the ideal of imposing on all peoples its own Kultur,[5] of becoming the sole arbiter of right and wrong, of crushing all who resist it. A universal absolute despotism, conferring derived subordinate powers on its agents, and recognising naught beyond itself—such is the Prussian Ideal, well symbolised by "the mailed fist." There is no logical resting place between this theory of the supreme lordship of the State and that which recognises man as a spiritual Intelligence, an embodiment of a fragment of the Self Universal, unfolding the capacities and qualities inherent in that fragment of the Divine Nature. The right to grow by unfoldment of these is an exercise of the freedom which abides in that Nature. It is not bestowed

1. Self-determination.
2. Natural rights: the belief that some rights, such as life, liberty, free speech, and so on, are so basic that the state is unjustified in abrogating them; dinotherium: a prehistoric, elephant-like mammal.
3. Written during World War I, in which Britain, France, Italy, Russia, and the United States battled

Germany (or Prussia) and the Austro-Hungarian Empire.
4. "All the more so" or "for a more certain reason" (Latin), a form of argument.
5. A German term meaning something between "culture" and "civilization."

by any human law, by any State or any Nation; it is divine; when God gives a portion of Himself to be a human Spirit, He gives part of His own Nature, eternally free. This is the foundation of Natural Rights, the various exercises of freedom being rooted in this, inhering in this. Man is free because he is divine. When many men gather into a community, a tribe, a Nation, they may make what laws they will to regulate their inter-relations to their mutual advantage; these are mutable, may be passed and repealed, depend on circumstances and on the stage of evolution reached. None of these touch the inherent right of each individual to be himself; if, owing to his low stage of growth, he asserts his claim to be himself by injuring another, then may the inter-related body of individuals exclude him from their society, or, if he remain in it, put him under such restraints as shall prevent the recurrence of the injury. The sharing in the One Life is the foundation of all social unions, small or large, the bedrock on which Society is founded. As the Oneness is recognised, harmony reigns; as it is disregarded, discord and unhappiness prevail.

Between these two fundamental Ideals, that of Force and that of Oneness, between that of Might and that of Right, there is no logical resting place, though there are many transitory stages. Since in a Nation a portion of the Divine Nature is embodied, the Spirit of the Nation, the Right of a Nation to Liberty is a Natural Right.

APPLICATION TO INDIA

Those who agree with the general proposition as to the Natural Right of a Nation to Liberty, laid down above, will be prepared to follow, or at least to consider, the application of that fundamental principle to the particular case of India. It strikes at the root of all the favourite "arguments" of the Anglo-Indians[6] and their Indian parasites as to unfitness, necessity for electorates on English models as approved by them, welfare of the masses as ensured by the Bureaucracy, inefficiency, lack of expert knowledge, divisions, and the rest. These and similar propositions are, as we have often stated, excuses for continued injustice and not arguments. They are all irrelevant, because they do not touch the main proposition, and are merely "red herrings drawn across the track."

We admit that so long as a Nation is drugged into lethargy by ignorance, by weariness, by cowardice, or by any other cause, its Natural Right remains in abeyance because unclaimed, and any other Nation which is strong enough to conquer it may hold it while the lethargy endures. The conquering Nation is not, in the present lack of international morality, open to special censure; it usurps an illegitimate authority, and pursues its own advantage without regard to the rights of its neighbour; but as the neighbour does not assert his rights, the intruder cannot be blamed, save on the ground of a morality too advanced for the present stage of the world's evolution. The rough assertion of superior power or superior craft and the subjugation of the weaker and the simpler is one of the methods of evolution dominating the sub-human kingdoms of nature; and while man is merely a two-legged animal, with the human qualities latent or subordinate, wars, invasions, conquests, are all in the game. In the long run they work for progress, alike for conquerors and conquered—mostly for the latter—and when the conquerors are demoralised beyond recovery by their triumph, their ill-gotten power is swept away—as we see now happening in the case of Germany, morally ruined by her

6. The English in India.

evil triumphs over Denmark, Austria and France.[7] She qualified herself for the villain's part in the great drama, for becoming the embodiment of autocracy, of strength without compassion, of power divorced from duty, and her end is destruction. She will be the great object-lesson of the twentieth century, and over her will sound out the funeral dirge as over her ancient prototype: "Babylon the Great is fallen, is fallen."[8] The lesson of the Christian religion, given for the shaping of western civilisation, was the evolution of strength, alike in the individual and in the Nation, and then *the yoking of that strength to Service*. Germany has learnt the first part, but not the second; hence must her strength be broken, and the Nation must learn the second part of the lesson, to turn the splendid qualities evolved by the first part to the service, and not the subjugation, of the world.

* * *

* * * The fierce outbreak of the Sepoy Rebellion[9] showed that a large part of the Indian People resented the subjugation of their ancient land.

With the help of Indian swords, once more, the British triumphed, and two-thirds of India passed to the Crown of Britain. English literature did much towards arousing India from her lethargy, but her own literature, largely rediscovered, has done more. She realises her own mighty past, her ancient discussions and experiments in political systems while Europe, save for Greece and Rome, was largely a howling wilderness, forests, swamps, young populations, virile, strong, evolving powerful manhood and womanhood. Pride has awakened, patriotism is aroused, Indians realise the greatness of their past, and are resolved to build a future which shall be worthy of it. The "fundamental unity of India" is rooted in her ancient religion, which recognised Bharatavarsha[1] as one; the thousand years of Islamic habitation have enriched the Indian culture, and its result is wrought into the fibre of the Indian Nation. The Musalman[2] is not a foreigner, but is bone of India's bone, flesh of her flesh.[3] Every Nation is builded of many elements, originally foreign but becoming national. Invaders who settle down, who live as part of the people, who cease to be conquerors and become comrades, these are children of the Homeland and not aliens. The claim of the Nation for its birthright comes alike from Hindu and from Muslim, for both are Indian.

1918

7. In the 1860s, Germany attacked Denmark and warred with Austria-Hungary; in 1870, France was defeated in the Franco-Prussian War.
8. Revelation 18:2.
9. The Indian Mutiny (1857–58), often considered the first war of Indian independence, was supposedly sparked by rumors that rifle cartridges were lubricated with fat from cows and pigs (offensive to Hindu and Muslim troops, respectively). As a result, soldiers revolted against their British offi-

cers. The British, for their part, used heavy force to quell the Mutiny, and to assume control of India from the British East India Company. In 1858 Queen Victoria issued a proclamation declaring India to be part of the British Empire.
1. Hindu name for India.
2. Muslim.
3. Paraphrase of Genesis 2:23: "And Adam said, This is now bone of my bone, and flesh of my flesh . . . ."

CULTURAL COORDINATES
A History of the Bra

Although early feminists are often characterized (or caricatured) as bra burners, the only actual instance of feminist bra burning was staged in Atlantic City to protest the 1968 Miss America pageant and was modeled on the burning of draft cards to protest the Vietnam War. What these feminists in 1968 were really protesting was the objectification of women's bodies symbolized by rituals like the Miss America contest. Women were expected to put up with a great deal of discomfort in the service of making themselves attractive and socially valuable, and the bra came to symbolize bodily restrictions. Ironically, bras were originally conceived of as a liberating form of undergarment, a more comfortable alternative to the corset.

1695

In France, towards the end of the 17th Century, corsages stuffed and pointed to the figure in front were outmoded by tightly fitting garments.

1945

The Gossard today is designed gently to mould the figure in the way it should go, give essential support, and prevent undue fatigue. Postwar Gossards will do all these things even better.

THE Gossard
LINE OF BEAUTY

Dress reformers stressed the damage that corsets did by "increasing friction" on the breasts and reducing lung capacity; corsets also restricted movement. Initially, bras were marketed to active women—working women, dancers, and athletes—but as increasing numbers of women went into the paid workforce in the early part of the twentieth century (by 1910, 18 percent were involved in paid labor), bras became more popular. Women wanted more flexible and comfortable alternatives to the corset, but they did not want to take on the "loose" appearance of prostitutes.

Bras were often designed and sold by women, and many of the technical innovations in bra design have been made by women. While the first proto-bra, which supported the breasts by lifting them from the shoulders with elastic straps, was designed by a man (Luman Chapman) in 1863, this undergarment did not become popular. A more successful corset alternative was offered in 1876 by Olivia Flynt, a dressmaker from Boston. The first sports bra was patented by Laura Lyon in 1904, and the word *brassiere* first appeared in 1905 in a patent application as the name for Gabrielle Poix's newest invention. In fact, about half of the 1,200 U.S. bra patents approved from the Civil War to the late 1960s were granted to women.

Since its invention, the bra has gone from being a garment that freed women from the torments of the corset to a symbol of what women put up with to avoid comment and achieve a desirable silhouette. From sports bra to Wonderbra, today's bra remains both a symbol of liberation and a symbol of women's sexuality.

The two women in the story that follows, "Roman Fever," come from "Old New York," the social world that Edith Newbold Jones Wharton was born into—a world of old money, gentility, and leisure. Although that world was to be the subject of much of her fiction, it was one from which she was increasingly distanced over the course of her life. Girls in her social circle were trained to be ornamental, marry wealth, and raise children. Wharton preferred reading in her father's voluminous home library and writing, publishing her first poems (one in the *Atlantic Monthly*) when she was just sixteen. Despite her literary predilections, she was also training for the life she was born to and at seventeen made her formal debut into New York high society.

She married thirty-six-year-old Edward (Teddy) Wharton when she was twenty-three, even though they seemed to have little in common aside from their social circle. He was an avid hunter, fisher, and gambler; she was interested in books, art, architecture, and fashion. Biographers disagree about the exact reasons they married, but apparently both were considered too old to continue being single and found the marriage convenient. It was not a happy marriage, by all accounts, at least in part because of a profound sexual incompatibility in addition to incompatibilities of interests. In a time of significant sexual prudery, Wharton grew up knowing little to nothing about sexuality; on her wedding day, when she asked her mother for information, her mother simply referred her to nude male statues and refused to tell her more. Biographers claim that the marriage went unconsummated for a long time because of Wharton's ignorance and anxiety.

Not surprisingly, during the late 1880s and early 1890s, frustrated both with her marriage and with the life a young, wealthy matron was expected to lead, Wharton suffered poor health—diagnosed as nerves—and was treated with the famous "rest cure" (see pp. 1170–71). During the "cure," Wharton returned to the writing that she had left off after her marriage, producing not only stories, novellas, and poems, but also books on decorating houses and gardening. The tremendous success of her early novel *The House of Mirth* (1905) established her as a major figure in American literature, bringing her both fame and a great deal of money (the novel sold more than 80,000 copies in its first few months of release). It also established many of the themes Wharton would address during her writing career: the damage done to young women by a system that teaches them little more than how to be decorative, the lack of options open to women besides traditional marriage, and the oftentimes bitter rivalries over men that such a lack of options lead women into.

In the early twentieth century, Wharton began spending more and more time in Paris, at least in part because life with Teddy was becoming increasingly difficult; he suffered from depression, drank heavily, and was accumulating gambling debts. She finally settled there permanently in 1909 (see pp. 1285–86). In Paris, Wharton finally experienced real love—both spiritual and sexual—with a journalist named Morton Fullerton. The affair lasted off and on for three years, between 1906 and 1909. Wharton had sued Teddy for divorce and hoped that she and

Fullerton could establish a life together when it was final (in 1913), but that was not to be. She lived the rest of her life in France, in close contact with a circle of friends, many of whom were artists, philosophers, and writers, including the novelist Henry James, who became a close friend and frequent traveling companion.

Wharton often wrote about the privileged world of New York high society, but she is also well known for works that explore the lives of women living in poverty, like *Ethan Frome* (1911). Known as a literary realist, she explored many of the social changes facing women during her lifetime, including divorce (in *Custom of the Country*, 1913, following her own divorce) and the restlessness facing the jazz generation (in *Twilight Sleep*, 1927). Wharton's list of works is extensive, despite the fact that she was almost forty before she began serious professional writing: she wrote fourteen novels, thirteen novellas, and eleven collections of short stories in addition to poetry, essays, and books about home decoration and travel. She was the first woman to win the Pulitzer Prize (in 1921, for her novel *The Age of Innocence*), the first woman to be awarded an honorary doctorate of letters from Yale University (in 1923), and the first woman to win the Gold Medal of the National Institute of Letters (in 1924).

"Roman Fever" reflects many of the themes that preoccupied Wharton: rivalry between women, the place of women in the world when their identities are defined by the men they marry, and the lives of wealthy Americans traveling in Europe. She explores the depths to which women will sink in their attempts to catch and keep the right man and contrasts their inner lives of turmoil to their outer appearances of comfort and wealth.

The novel *House of Mirth*, 1905, appears in full in the Library of Women's Literature.

Roman Fever

From the table at which they had been lunching two American ladies of ripe but well-cared-for middle age moved across the lofty terrace of the Roman restaurant and, leaning on its parapet, looked first at each other, and then down on the outspread glories of the Palatine and the Forum,[1] with the same expression of vague but benevolent approval.

As they leaned there a girlish voice echoed up gaily from the stairs leading to the court below. "Well, come along, then," it cried, not to them but to an invisible companion, "and let's leave the young things to their knitting"; and a voice as fresh laughed back: "Oh, look here, Babs, not actually *knitting*—" "Well, I mean figuratively," rejoined the first. "After all, we haven't left our poor parents much else to do. . . ." and at that point the turn of the stairs engulfed the dialogue.

The two ladies looked at each other again, this time with a tinge of smiling embarrassment, and the smaller and paler one shook her head and colored slightly.

"Barbara!" she murmured, sending an unheard rebuke after the mocking voice in the stairway.

1. Now an archeological site, the Forum was the political and economic center of Rome from 600 to 300 BCE and is located in a valley near the Palatine Hill (one of the seven hills of Rome).

The other lady, who was fuller, and higher in color, with a small determined nose supported by vigorous black eyebrows, gave a good-humored laugh. "That's what our daughters think of us!"

Her companion replied by a deprecating gesture. "Not of us individually. We must remember that. It's just the collective modern idea of Mothers. And you see——" Half-guiltily she drew from her handsomely mounted black handbag a twist of crimson silk run through by two fine knitting needles. "One never knows," she murmured. "The new system has certainly given us a good deal of time to kill; and sometimes I get tired just looking—even at this." Her gesture was now addressed to the stupendous scene at their feet.

The dark lady laughed again, and they both relapsed upon the view, contemplating it in silence, with a sort of diffused serenity which might have been borrowed from the spring effulgence of the Roman skies. The luncheon hour was long past, and the two had their end of the vast terrace to themselves. At its opposite extremity a few groups, detained by a lingering look at the outspread city, were gathering up guidebooks and fumbling for tips. The last of them scattered, and the two ladies were alone on the air-washed height.

"Well, I don't see why we shouldn't just stay here," said Mrs. Slade, the lady of the high color and energetic brows. Two derelict basket chairs stood near, and she pushed them into the angle of the parapet, and settled herself in one, her gaze upon the Palatine. "After all, it's still the most beautiful view in the world."

"It always will be, to me," assented her friend Mrs. Ansley, with so slight a stress on the "me" that Mrs. Slade, though she noticed it, wondered if it were not merely accidental, like the random underlinings of old-fashioned letter writers.

"Grace Ansley was always old-fashioned," she thought; and added aloud, with a retrospective smile: "It's a view we've both been familiar with for a good many years. When we first met here we were younger than our girls are now. You remember?"

"Oh, yes, I remember," murmured Mrs. Ansley, with the same undefinable stress. "There's that headwaiter wondering," she interpolated. She was evidently far less sure than her companion of herself and of her rights in the world.

"I'll cure him of wondering," said Mrs. Slade, stretching her hand toward a bag as discreetly opulent-looking as Mrs. Ansley's. Signing to the headwaiter, she explained that she and her friend were old lovers of Rome, and would like to spend the end of the afternoon looking down on the view—that is, if it did not disturb the service? The headwaiter, bowing over her gratuity, assured her that the ladies were most welcome, and would be still more so if they would condescend to remain for dinner. A full-moon night, they would remember. . . .

Mrs. Slade's black brows drew together, as though references to the moon were out of place and even unwelcome. But she smiled away her frown as the headwaiter retreated. "Well, why not? We might do worse. There's no knowing, I suppose, when the girls will be back. Do you even know back from *where*? I don't!"

Mrs. Ansley again colored slightly. "I think those young Italian aviators we met at the Embassy invited them to fly to Tarquinia for tea. I suppose they'll want to wait and fly back by moonlight."

"Moonlight—moonlight! What a part it still plays. Do you suppose they're as sentimental as we were?"

"I've come to the conclusion that I don't in the least know what they are," said Mrs. Ansley. "And perhaps we didn't know much more about each other."

"No; perhaps we didn't."

Her friend gave her a shy glance. "I never should have supposed you were sentimental, Alida."

"Well, perhaps I wasn't." Mrs. Slade drew her lids together in retrospect; and for a few moments the two ladies, who had been intimate since childhood, reflected how little they knew each other. Each one, of course, had a label ready to attach to the other's name; Mrs. Delphin Slade, for instance, would have told herself, or anyone who asked her, that Mrs. Horace Ansley, twenty-five years ago, had been exquisitely lovely—no, you wouldn't believe it, would you? . . . though, of course, still charming, distinguished. . . . Well, as a girl she had been exquisite; far more beautiful than her daughter Barbara, though certainly Babs, according to the new standards at any rate, was more effective—had more *edge*, as they say. Funny where she got it, with those two nullities as parents. Yes; Horace Ansley was—well, just the duplicate of his wife. Museum specimens of old New York. Good-looking, irreproachable, exemplary. Mrs. Slade and Mrs. Ansley had lived opposite each other—actually as well as figuratively—for years. When the drawing-room curtains in No. 20 East 73rd Street were renewed, No. 23, across the way, was always aware of it. And of all the movings, buyings, travels, anniversaries, illnesses—the tame chronicle of an estimable pair. Little of it escaped Mrs. Slade. But she had grown bored with it by the time her husband made his big *coup* in Wall Street, and when they bought in upper Park Avenue had already begun to think: "I'd rather live opposite a speakeasy for a change; at least one might see it raided." The idea of seeing Grace raided was so amusing that (before the move) she launched it at a woman's lunch. It made a hit, and went the rounds—she sometimes wondered if it had crossed the street, and reached Mrs. Ansley. She hoped not, but didn't much mind. Those were the days when respectability was at a discount, and it did the irreproachable no harm to laugh at them a little.

A few years later, and not many months apart, both ladies lost their husbands. There was an appropriate exchange of wreaths and condolences, and a brief renewal of intimacy in the half-shadow of their mourning; and now, after another interval, they had run across each other in Rome, at the same hotel, each of them the modest appendage of a salient daughter. The similarity of their lot had again drawn them together, lending itself to mild jokes, and the mutual confession that, if in old days it must have been tiring to "keep up" with daughters, it was now, at times, a little dull not to.

No doubt, Mrs. Slade reflected, she felt her unemployment more than poor Grace ever would. It was a big drop from being the wife of Delphin Slade to being his widow. She had always regarded herself (with a certain conjugal pride) as his equal in social gifts, as contributing her full share to the making of the exceptional couple they were: but the difference after his death was irremediable. As the wife of the famous corporation lawyer, always with an international case or two on hand, every day brought its exciting and unexpected obligation: the impromptu entertaining of eminent colleagues from abroad, the hurried dashes on legal business to London, Paris or Rome, where the entertaining was so handsomely reciprocated; the amusement of hearing in her wake: "What, that handsome woman with the good clothes and the eyes is Mrs. Slade—*the* Slade's wife? Really? Generally the wives of celebrities are such frumps."

Yes; being *the* Slade's widow was a dullish business after that. In living up to such a husband all her faculties had been engaged; now she had only her daughter to live up to, for the son who seemed to have inherited his father's gifts had died suddenly in boyhood. She had fought through that agony because her husband was there, to be helped and to help; now, after the father's death, the thought of the boy had become unbearable. There was nothing left but to mother her daughter; and dear Jenny was such a perfect daughter that she needed no excessive mothering. "Now with Babs Ansley I don't know that I *should* be so quiet," Mrs. Slade sometimes half-enviously reflected; but Jenny, who was younger than her brilliant friend, was that rare accident, an extremely pretty girl who somehow made youth and prettiness seem as safe as their absence. It was all perplexing—and to Mrs. Slade a little boring. She wished that Jenny would fall in love—with the wrong man, even; that she might have to be watched, out-maneuvered, rescued. And instead, it was Jenny who watched her mother, kept her out of drafts, made sure that she had taken her tonic. . . .

Mrs. Ansley was much less articulate than her friend, and her mental portrait of Mrs. Slade was slighter, and drawn with fainter touches. "Alida Slade's awfully brilliant; but not as brilliant as she thinks," would have summed it up; though she would have added, for the enlightenment of strangers, that Mrs. Slade had been an extremely dashing girl; much more so than her daughter, who was pretty, of course, and clever in a way, but had none of her mother's—well, "vividness," someone had once called it. Mrs. Ansley would take up current words like this, and cite them in quotation marks, as unheard-of audacities. No; Jenny was not like her mother. Sometimes Mrs. Ansley thought Alida Slade was disappointed; on the whole she had had a sad life. Full of failures and mistakes; Mrs. Ansley had always been rather sorry for her. . . .

So these two ladies visualized each other, each through the wrong end of her little telescope.

II

For a long time they continued to sit side by side without speaking. It seemed as though, to both, there was a relief in laying down their somewhat futile activities in the presence of the vast Memento Mori which faced them. Mrs. Slade sat quite still, her eyes fixed on the golden slope of the Palace of the Caesars,[2] and after a while Mrs. Ansley ceased to fidget with her bag, and she too sank into meditation. Like many intimate friends, the two ladies had never before had occasion to be silent together, and Mrs. Ansley was slightly embarrassed by what seemed, after so many years, a new stage in their intimacy, and one with which she did not yet know how to deal.

Suddenly the air was full of that deep clangor of bells which periodically covers Rome with a roof of silver. Mrs. Slade glanced at her wristwatch. "Five o'clock already," she said, as though surprised.

Mrs. Ansley suggested interrogatively: "There's bridge at the Embassy at five." For a long time Mrs. Slade did not answer. She appeared to be lost in contemplation, and Mrs. Ansley thought the remark had escaped her. But after a while she said, as if speaking out of a dream: "Bridge, did you say? Not unless you want to. . . . But I don't think I will, you know."

"Oh, no," Mrs. Ansley hastened to assure her. "I don't care to at all. It's so lovely here; and so full of old memories, as you say." She settled herself in her

2. Memento mori: reminder of death (Latin); Palace of the Caesars: a series of palaces built over   many years by the emperors of Rome on Palatine Hill.

chair, and almost furtively drew forth her knitting. Mrs. Slade took sideway note of this activity, but her own beautifully cared-for hands remained motionless on her knee.

"I was just thinking," she said slowly, "what different things Rome stands for to each generation of travelers. To our grandmothers, Roman fever;[3] to our mothers, sentimental dangers—how we used to be guarded!—to our daughters, no more dangers than the middle of Main Street. They don't know it—but how much they're missing!"

The long golden light was beginning to pale, and Mrs. Ansley lifted her knitting a little closer to her eyes. "Yes; how we were guarded!"

"I always used to think," Mrs. Slade continued, "that our mothers had a much more difficult job than our grandmothers. When Roman fever stalked the streets it must have been comparatively easy to gather in the girls at the danger hour; but when you and I were young, with such beauty calling us, and the spice of disobedience thrown in, and no worse risk than catching cold during the cool hour after sunset, the mothers used to be put to it to keep us in—didn't they?"

She turned again toward Mrs. Ansley, but the latter had reached a delicate point in her knitting. "One, two, three—slip two; yes, they must have been," she assented, without looking up.

Mrs. Slade's eyes rested on her with a deepened attention. "She can knit—in the face of *this!* How like her. . . ."

Mrs. Slade leaned back, brooding, her eyes ranging from the ruins which faced her to the long green hollow of the Forum, the fading flow of the church fronts beyond it, and the outlying immensity of the Colosseum. Suddenly she thought: It's all very well to say that our girls have done away with sentiment and moonlight. But if Babs Ansley isn't out to catch that young aviator—the one who's a Marchese—then I don't know anything. And Jenny has no chance beside her. I know that too. I wonder if that's why Grace Ansley likes the two girls to go everywhere together? My poor Jenny as a foil—!" Mrs. Slade gave a hardly audible laugh, and at the sound Mrs. Ansley dropped her knitting.

"Yes—?"

"I—oh, nothing. I was only thinking how your Babs carries everything before her. That Campolieri boy is one of the best matches in Rome. Don't look so innocent, my dear—you know he is. And I was wondering, ever so respectfully, you understand . . . . wondering how two such exemplary characters as you and Horace had managed to produce anything quite so dynamic." Mrs. Slade laughed again, with a touch of asperity.

Mrs. Ansley's hands lay inert across her needles. She looked straight out at the great accumulated wreckage of passion and splendor at her feet. But her small profile was almost expressionless. At length she said: "I think you overrate Babs, my dear."

Mrs. Slade's tone grew easier. "No; I don't. I appreciate her. And perhaps envy you. Oh, my girl's perfect; if I were a chronic invalid I'd—well, I think I'd rather be in Jenny's hands. There must be times . . . but there! I always wanted a brilliant daughter . . . and never quite understood why I got an angel instead."

Mrs. Ansley echoed her laugh in a faint murmur. "Babs is an angel too."

3. Roman fever is the common name for the fal-   the disease, formerly prevalent in Rome and the
ciparum strain of malaria, the deadliest form of   countryside around Rome.

"Of course—of course! But she's got rainbow wings. Well, they're wandering by the sea with their young men; and here we sit . . . and it all brings back the past a little too acutely."

Mrs. Ansley had resumed her knitting. One might almost have imagined (if one had known her less well, Mrs. Slade reflected) that, for her also, too many memories rose from the lengthening shadows of those august ruins. But no; she was simply absorbed in her work. What was there for her to worry about? She knew that Babs would almost certainly come back engaged to the extremely eligible Campolieri. "And she'll sell the New York house, and settle down near them in Rome, and never be in their way . . . she's much too tactful. But she'll have an excellent cook, and just the right people in for bridge and cocktails . . . and a perfectly peaceful old age among her grandchildren."

Mrs. Slade broke off this prophetic flight with a recoil of self-disgust. There was no one of whom she had less right to think unkindly than of Grace Ansley. Would she never cure herself of envying her? Perhaps she had begun too long ago.

She stood up and leaned against the parapet, filling her troubled eyes with the tranquilizing magic of the hour. But instead of tranquilizing her the sight seemed to increase her exasperation. Her gaze turned toward the Colosseum. Already its golden flank was downed in purple shadow, and above it the sky curved crystal clear, without light or color. It was the moment when afternoon and evening hang balanced in midheaven.

Mrs. Slade turned back and laid her hand on her friend's arm. The gesture was so abrupt that Mrs. Ansley looked up, startled.

"The sun's set. You're not afraid, my dear?"

"Afraid—?"

"Of Roman fever or pneumonia? I remember how ill you were that winter. As a girl you had a very delicate throat, hadn't you?"

"Oh, we're all right up here. Down below, in the Forum, it does get deathly cold, all of a sudden . . . but not here."

"Ah, of course you know because you had to be so careful." Mrs. Slade turned back to the parapet. She thought: "I must make one more effort not to hate her." Aloud she said: "Whenever I look at the Forum from up here, I remember that story about a great-aunt of yours, wasn't she? A dreadfully wicked great-aunt?"

"Oh, yes; great-aunt Harriet. The one who was supposed to have sent her young sister out to the Forum after sunset to gather a nightblooming flower for her album. All our great-aunts and grandmothers used to have albums of dried flowers."

Mrs. Slade nodded. "But she really sent her because they were in love with the same man—"

"Well, that was the family tradition. They said Aunt Harriet confessed it years afterward. At any rate, the poor little sister caught the fever and died. Mother used to frighten us with the story when we were children."

"And you frightened *me* with it, that winter when you and I were here as girls. The winter I was engaged to Delphin."

Mrs. Ansley gave a faint laugh. "Oh, did I? Really frightened you? I don't believe you're easily frightened."

"Not often; but I was then. I was easily frightened because I was too happy. I wonder if you know what that means?"

"I—yes . . ." Mrs. Ansley faltered.

"Well, I suppose that was why the story of your wicked aunt made such an impression on me. And I thought: 'There's no more Roman fever, but the Forum is deathly cold after sunset—especially after a hot day. And the Colosseum's even colder and damper.' "

"The Colosseum—?"

"Yes. It wasn't easy to get in, after the gates were locked for the night. Far from easy. Still, in those days it could be managed; it *was* managed, often. Lovers met there who couldn't meet elsewhere. You knew that?"

"I—I dare say. I don't remember."

"You don't remember? You don't remember going to visit some ruins or other one evening, just after dark, and catching a bad chill? You were supposed to have gone to see the moon rise. People always said that expedition was what caused your illness."

There was a moment's silence; then Mrs. Ansley rejoined: "Did they? It was all so long ago."

"Yes. And you got well again—so it didn't matter. But I suppose it struck your friends—the reason given for your illness, I mean—because everybody knew you were so prudent on account of your throat, and your mother took such care of you. . . . You *had* been out late sight-seeing, hadn't you, that night?"

"Perhaps I had. The most prudent girls aren't always prudent. What made you think of it now?"

Mrs. Slade seemed to have no answer ready. But after a moment she broke out: "Because I simply can't bear it any longer—!"

Mrs. Ansley lifted her head quickly. Her eyes were wide and very pale. "Can't bear what?"

"Why—your not knowing that I've always known why you went."

"Why I went—?"

"Yes. You think I'm bluffing, don't you? Well, you went to meet the man I was engaged to—and I can repeat every word of the letter that took you there."

While Mrs. Slade spoke Mrs. Ansley had risen unsteadily to her feet. Her bag, her knitting and gloves, slid in a panic-stricken heap to the ground. She looked at Mrs. Slade as though she were looking at a ghost.

"No, no—don't," she faltered out.

"Why not? Listen, if you don't believe me. 'My one darling, things can't go on like this. I must see you alone. Come to the Colosseum immediately after dark tomorrow. There will be somebody to let you in. No one whom you need fear will suspect'—but perhaps you've forgotten what the letter said?"

Mrs. Ansley met the challenge with an unexpected composure. Steadying herself against the chair she looked at her friend, and replied: "No; I know it by heart too."

"And the signature? 'Only *your* D.S.' Was that it? I'm right, am I? That was the letter that took you out that evening after dark?"

Mrs. Ansley was still looking at her. It seemed to Mrs. Slade that a slow struggle was going on behind the voluntarily controlled mask of her small quiet face. "I shouldn't have thought she had herself so well in hand," Mrs. Slade reflected, almost resentfully. But at this moment Mrs. Ansley spoke. "I don't know how you knew. I burnt the letter at once."

"Yes; you would, naturally—you're so prudent!" The sneer was open now. "And if you burnt the letter you're wondering how on earth I know what was in it. That's it, isn't it?"

Mrs. Slade waited, but Mrs. Ansley did not speak.

"Well, my dear, I know what was in that letter because I wrote it!"

"You wrote it?"

"Yes."

The two women stood for a minute staring at each other in the last golden light. Then Mrs. Ansley dropped back into her chair. "Oh," she murmured, and covered her face with her hands.

Mrs. Slade waited nervously for another word or movement. None came, and at length she broke out: "I horrify you."

Mrs. Ansley's hands dropped to her knee. The face they uncovered was streaked with tears. "I wasn't thinking of you. I was thinking—it was the only letter I ever had from him!"

"And I wrote it. Yes; I wrote it! But I was the girl he was engaged to. Did you happen to remember that?"

Mrs. Ansley's head drooped again. "I'm not trying to excuse myself . . . I remembered. . . ."

"And still you went?"

"Still I went."

Mrs. Slade stood looking down on the small bowed figure at her side. The flame of her wrath had already sunk, and she wondered why she had ever thought there would be any satisfaction in inflicting so purposeless a wound on her friend. But she had to justify herself.

"You do understand? I'd found out—and I hated you, hated you. I knew you were in love with Delphin—and I was afraid; afraid of you, of your quiet ways, your sweetness . . . your . . . well, I wanted you out of the way, that's all. Just for a few weeks; just till I was sure of him. So in a blind fury I wrote that letter . . . I don't know why I'm telling you now."

"I suppose," said Mrs. Ansley slowly, "it's because you've always gone on hating me."

"Perhaps. Or because I wanted to get the whole thing off my mind." She paused. "I'm glad you destroyed the letter. Of course I never thought you'd die."

Mrs. Ansley relapsed into silence, and Mrs. Slade, leaning above her, was conscious of a strange sense of isolation, of being cut off from the warm current of human communion. "You think me a monster!"

"I don't know. . . . It was the only letter I had, and you say he didn't write it?"

"Ah, how you care for him still!"

"I cared for that memory," said Mrs. Ansley.

Mrs. Slade continued to look down on her. She seemed physically reduced by the blow—as if, when she got up, the wind might scatter her like a puff of dust. Mrs. Slade's jealousy suddenly leapt up again at the sight. All these years the woman had been living on that letter. How she must have loved him, to treasure the mere memory of its ashes! The letter of the man her friend was engaged to. Wasn't it she who was the monster?

"You tried your best to get him away from me, didn't you? But you failed; and I kept him. That's all."

"Yes. That's all."

"I wish now I hadn't told you. I'd no idea you'd feel about it as you do; I thought you'd be amused. It all happened so long ago, as you say; and you must do me the justice to remember that I had no reason to think you'd ever taken it seriously. How could I, when you were married to Horace Ansley two months afterward? As soon as you could get out of bed your mother rushed you off to Florence and married you. People were rather surprised—they wondered at its being done so quickly; but I thought I knew. I had an idea you did it out of *pique*—to be able to say you'd got ahead of Delphin and me. Girls have such silly reasons for doing the most serious things. And your marrying so soon convinced me that you'd never really cared."

"Yes. I suppose it would," Mrs. Ansley assented.

The clear heaven overhead was emptied of all its gold. Dusk spread over it, abruptly darkening the Seven Hills.[4] Here and there lights began to twinkle through the foliage at their feet. Steps were coming and going on the deserted terrace—waiters looking out of the doorway at the head of the stairs, then reappearing with trays and napkins and flasks of wine. Tables were moved, chairs straightened. A feeble string of electric lights flickered out. Some vases of faded flowers were carried away, and brought back replenished. A stout lady in a dust coat suddenly appeared, asking in broken Italian if anyone had seen the elastic band which held together her tattered Baedeker.[5] She poked with her stick under the table at which she had lunched, the waiters assisting.

The corner where Mrs. Slade and Mrs. Ansley sat was still shadowy and deserted. For a long time neither of them spoke. At length Mrs. Slade began again: "I suppose I did it as a sort of joke—"

"A joke?"

"Well, girls are ferocious sometimes, you know. Girls in love especially. And I remember laughing to myself all that evening at the idea that you were waiting around there in the dark, dodging out of sight, listening for every sound, trying to get in—of course I was upset when I heard you were so ill afterward."

Mrs. Ansley had not moved for a long time. But now she turned slowly toward her companion. "But I didn't wait. He'd arranged everything. He was there. We were let in at once," she said.

Mrs. Slade sprang up from her leaning position. "Delphin there? They let you in?—Ah, now you're lying!" she burst out with violence.

Mrs. Ansley's voice grew clearer, and full of surprise. "But of course he was there. Naturally he came—"

"Came? How did he know he'd find you there? You must be raving!"

Mrs. Ansley hesitated, as though reflecting. "But I answered the letter. I told him I'd be there. So he came."

Mrs. Slade flung her hands up to her face. "Oh, God—you answered! I never thought of your answering. . . ."

"It's odd you never thought of it, if you wrote the letter."

"Yes. I was blind with rage."

Mrs. Ansley rose, and drew her fur scarf about her. "It is cold here. We'd better go . . . I'm sorry for you," she said, as she clasped the fur about her throat.

The unexpected words sent a pang through Mrs. Slade. "Yes; we'd better go." She gathered up her bag and cloak. "I don't know why you should be sorry for me," she muttered.

---

4. Traditionally, Rome is said to have been built on seven hills, though not all are discernible today.
5. Guidebook in a series inaugurated by German publisher Karl Baedecker (1801–59) in 1828, the first to include detailed information about lodging and transportation.

Mrs. Ansley stood looking away from her toward the dusky secret mass of the Colosseum. "Well—because I didn't have to wait that night."

Mrs. Slade gave an unquiet laugh. "Yes; I was beaten there. But I oughtn't to begrudge it to you, I suppose. At the end of all these years. After all, I had everything; I had him for twenty-five years. And you had nothing but that one letter that he didn't write."

Mrs. Ansley was again silent. At length she turned toward the door of the terrace. She took a step, and turned back, facing her companion.

"I had Barbara," she said, and began to move ahead of Mrs. Slade toward the stairway.

1936

◆━◆ EDITH MAUD EATON (SUI SIN FAR) ━◆━◆
1865–1914

Born to a Chinese mother and English father in England, Edith Maud Eaton (who published under the pseudonym Sui Sin Far) moved to upstate New York when she was a child and then to Montreal, Quebec; as an adult, she lived in Jamaica, San Francisco, Seattle, and Boston before returning to Montreal when her health failed. Although she is often called the first Chinese American writer, her life is more a reflection of the international spread of English in the twentieth century as well as the history of colonialism and migration in the early part of the century.

Eaton was the second of fourteen children and ended her formal education at age eleven to help care for her younger siblings (one of whom, Winnifred, was a novelist who published as Onoto Watanna). When she was eighteen, she went to work as a typesetter for a Montreal newspaper; she soon began a journalism career. She lived for a year as a reporter in Jamaica, where she contracted malaria, which weakened her health for the rest of her life. She then moved to the west coast of the United States, where she worked full-time as a newspaper writer while also publishing short stories, essays, and poetry.

Although she could have passed for white, Eaton embraced her Chinese heritage and championed the cause of Chinese immigrants in the United States. During the early part of the twentieth century, Chinese Americans were seen as profoundly alien and were subjected to intense prejudice and discrimination. Even though Chinese workers were enticed to come to the American West in order to work on railroads and in mining operations, there were strict immigration quotas that limited the number of Chinese people who would be allowed into the country, and people of Chinese heritage were not allowed to become U.S. citizens until 1943 (see pp. 1236–37). Cities often enforced housing restrictions that forced Chinese people to live in segregated neighborhoods (the origins of many contemporary "Chinatown" districts). In this climate of fear and hatred, Eaton took up the cause of introducing Americans to the lives of real Asians, rather than the stereotypical opium-eaters that lived in the popular imagination.

In the collection of stories from which the selection here is taken, *Mrs. Spring Fragrance* (1912), Eaton takes her readers inside the Chinatowns of San Francisco and Seattle. While Lae Choo, the mother in "In the Land of the Free," may seem a rather ordinary maternal figure from the early twentieth century, she would have been a revolutionary figure for Eaton's readers. Chinese women were rarely represented in American culture or literature at the time; when they were, they usually appeared as prostitutes or opium addicts, not as mothers who cared profoundly for their children. Chinese men were allowed in to work, but immigration laws made it difficult for women to gain entry to prevent the Chinese from building families and settling here permanently. Eaton takes her readers inside the experience of these laws to show the effects on a type of character who, despite her ethnicity, would seem familiar to American readers. In doing so, she hoped to open American minds.

In the Land of the Free

I

"See, Little One—the hills in the morning sun. There is thy home for years to come. It is very beautiful and thou wilt be very happy there."

The Little One looked up into his mother's face in perfect faith. He was engaged in the pleasant occupation of sucking a sweetmeat; but that did not prevent him from gurgling responsively.

"Yes, my olive bud; there is where thy father is making a fortune for thee. Thy father! Oh, wilt thou not be glad to behold his dear face. 'Twas for thee I left him."

The Little One ducked his chin sympathetically against his mother's knee. She lifted him on to her lap. He was two years old, a round, dimple-cheeked boy with bright brown eyes and a sturdy little frame.

"Ah! Ah! Ah! Ooh! Ooh! Ooh!" puffed he, mocking a tugboat steaming by.

San Francisco's waterfront was lined with ships and steamers, while other craft, large and small, including a couple of white transports from the Philippines, lay at anchor here and there off shore. It was some time before the *Eastern Queen* could get docked, and even after that was accomplished, a lone Chinaman who had been waiting on the wharf for an hour was detained that much longer by men with the initials U.S.C.[1] on their caps, before he could board the steamer and welcome his wife and child.

"This is thy son," announced the happy Lae Choo.

Hom Hing lifted the child, felt of his little body and limbs, gazed into his face with proud and joyous eyes; then turned inquiringly to a customs officer at his elbow.

"That's a fine boy you have there," said the man. "Where was he born?"

"In China," answered Hom Hing, swinging the Little One on his right shoulder, preparatory to leading his wife off the steamer.

"Ever been to America before?"

"No, not he," answered the father with a happy laugh.

The customs officer beckoned to another.

1. United States Customs.

"This little fellow," said he, "is visiting America for the first time."

The other customs officer stroked his chin reflectively.

"Good day," said Hom Hing.

"Wait!" commanded one of the officers. "You cannot go just yet."

"What more now?" asked Hom Hing.

"I'm afraid," said the first customs officer, "that we cannot allow the boy to go ashore. There is nothing in the papers that you have shown us—your wife's papers and your own—having any bearing upon the child."

"There was no child when the papers were made out," returned Hom Hing. He spoke calmly; but there was apprehension in his eyes and in his tightening grip on his son.

"What is it? What is it?" quavered Lae Choo, who understood a little English.

The second customs officer regarded her pityingly.

"I don't like this part of the business," he muttered.

The first officer turned to Hom Hing and in an official tone of voice, said:

"Seeing that the boy has no certificate entitling him to admission to this country you will have to leave him with us."

"Leave my boy!" exclaimed Hom Hing.

"Yes; he will be well taken care of, and just as soon as we can hear from Washington he will be handed over to you."

"But," protested Hom Hing, "he is my son."

"We have no proof," answered the man with a shrug of his shoulders; "and even if so we cannot let him pass without orders from the Government."

"He is my son," reiterated Hom Hing, slowly and solemnly. "I am a Chinese merchant and have been in business in San Francisco for many years. When my wife told to me one morning that she dreamed of a green tree with spreading branches and one beautiful red flower growing thereon, I answered her that I wished my son to be born in our country, and for her to prepare to go to China. My wife complied with my wish. After my son was born my mother fell sick and my wife nursed and cared for her; then my father, too, fell sick, and my wife also nursed and cared for him. For twenty moons my wife care for and nurse the old people, and when they die they bless her and my son, and I send for her to return to me. I had no fear of trouble. I was a Chinese merchant and my son was my son."

"Very good, Hom Hing," replied the first officer. "Nevertheless, we take your son."

"No, you not take him; he my son too."

It was Lae Choo. Snatching the child from his father's arms she held and covered him with her own.

The officers conferred together for a few moments; then one drew Hom Hing aside and spoke in his ear.

Resignedly Hom Hing bowed his head, then approached his wife. "'Tis the law," said he, speaking in Chinese, "and 'twill be but for a little while—until tomorrow's sun arises."

"You, too," reproached Lae Choo in a voice eloquent with pain. But accustomed to obedience she yielded the boy to her husband, who in turn delivered him to the first officer. The Little One protested lustily against the transfer; but his mother covered her face with her sleeve and his father silently led her away. Thus was the law of the land complied with.

II

Day was breaking. Lae Choo, who had been awake all night, dressed herself, then awoke her husband.

"'Tis the morn," she cried. "Go, bring our son."

The man rubbed his eyes and arose upon his elbow so that he could see out of the window. A pale star was visible in the sky. The petals of a lily in a bowl on the windowsill were unfurled.

"'Tis not yet time," said he, laying his head down again.

"Not yet time. Ah, all the time that I lived before yesterday is not so much as the time that has been since my little one was taken from me."

The mother threw herself down beside the bed and covered her face.

Hom Hing turned on the light, and touching his wife's bowed head with a sympathetic hand inquired if she had slept.

"Slept!" she echoed, weepingly. "Ah, how could I close my eyes with my arms empty of the little body that has filled them every night for more than twenty moons! You do not know—man—what it is to miss the feel of the little fingers and the little toes and the soft round limbs of your little one. Even in the darkness his darling eyes used to shine up to mine, and often have I fallen into slumber with his pretty babble at my ear. And now, I see him not; I touch him not; I hear him not. My baby, my little fat one!"

"Now! Now! Now!" consoled Hom Hing, patting his wife's shoulder reassuringly; "there is no need to grieve so; he will soon gladden you again. There cannot be any law that would keep a child from its mother!"

Lae Choo dried her tears.

"You are right, my husband," she meekly murmured. She arose and stepped about the apartment, setting things to rights. The box of presents she had brought for her California friends had been opened the evening before; and silks, embroideries, carved ivories, ornamental lacquer-ware, brasses, camphorwood boxes, fans, and chinaware were scattered around in confused heaps. In the midst of unpacking the thought of her child in the hands of strangers had overpowered her, and she had left everything to crawl into bed and weep.

Having arranged her gifts in order she stepped out on to the deep balcony.

The star had faded from view and there were bright streaks in the western sky. Lae Choo looked down the street and around. Beneath the flat occupied by her and her husband were quarters for a number of bachelor Chinamen, and she could hear them from where she stood, taking their early morning breakfast. Below their dining-room was her husband's grocery store. Across the way was a large restaurant. Last night it had been resplendent with gay colored lanterns and the sound of music. The rejoicings over "the completion of the moon,"[2] by Quong Sum's first-born, had been long and loud, and had caused her to tie a handkerchief over her ears. She, a bereaved mother, had it not in her heart to rejoice with other parents. This morning the place was more in accord with her mood. It was still and quiet. The revellers had dispersed or were asleep.

A roly-poly woman in black sateen, with long pendant earrings in her ears, looked up from the street below and waved her a smiling greeting. It was her old neighbor, Kuie Hoe, the wife of the gold embosser, Mark Sing. With her was a

---

2. A traditional celebration to give thanks for an infant boy's surviving his first month.

little boy in yellow jacket and lavender pantaloons. Lae Choo remembered him as a baby. She used to like to play with him in those days when she had no child of her own. What a long time ago that seemed! She caught her breath in a sigh, and laughed instead.

"Why are you so merry?" called her husband from within.

"Because my Little One is coming home," answered Lae Choo. "I am a happy mother—a happy mother."

She pattered into the room with a smile on her face.

The noon hour had arrived. The rice was steaming in the bowls and a fragrant dish of chicken and bamboo shoots was awaiting Hom Hing. Not for one moment had Lae Choo paused to rest during the morning hours; her activity had been ceaseless. Every now and again, however, she had raised her eyes to the gilded clock on the curiously carved mantelpiece. Once, she had exclaimed:

"Why so long, oh! why so long?" Then apostrophizing herself: "Lae Choo, be happy. The Little One is coming! The Little One is coming!" Several times she burst into tears and several times she laughed aloud.

Hom Hing entered the room; his arms hung down by his side.

"The Little One!" shrieked Lae Choo.

"They bid me call tomorrow."

With a moan the mother sank to the floor.

The noon hour passed. The dinner remained on the table.

III

The winter rains were over: the spring had come to California, flushing the hills with green and causing an ever-changing pageant of flowers to pass over them. But there was no spring in Lae Choo's heart, for the Little One remained away from her arms. He was being kept in a mission. White women were caring for him, and though for one full moon he had pined for his mother and refused to be comforted he was now apparently happy and contented. Five moons or five months had gone by since the day he had passed with Lae Choo through the Golden Gate; but the great Government at Washington still delayed sending the answer which would return him to his parents.

Hom Hing was disconsolately rolling up and down the balls in his abacus box when a keen-faced young man stepped into his store.

"What news?" asked the Chinese merchant.

"This!" The young man brought forth a typewritten letter. Hom Hing read the words:

"Re Chinese child, alleged to be the son of Hom Hing, Chinese merchant, doing business at 425 Clay street, San Francisco.

"Same will have attention as soon as possible."

Hom Hing returned the letter, and without a word continued his manipulation of the counting machine.

"Have you anything to say?" asked the young man.

"Nothing. They have sent the same letter fifteen times before. Have you not yourself showed it to me?"

"True!" The young man eyed the Chinese merchant furtively. He had a proposition to make and he was pondering whether or not the time was opportune.

"How is your wife?" he inquired solicitously—and diplomatically.

Hom Hing shook his head mournfully.

"She seems less every day," he replied. "Her food she takes only when I bid her and her tears fall continually. She finds no pleasure in dress or flowers and cares not to see her friends. Her eyes stare all night. I think before another moon she will pass into the land of spirits."

"No!" exclaimed the young man, genuinely startled.

"If the boy not come home I lose my wife sure," continued Hom Hing with bitter sadness.

"It's not right," cried the young man indignantly. Then he made his proposition. The Chinese father's eyes brightened exceedingly.

"Will I like you to go to Washington and make them give you the paper to restore my son?" cried he. "How can you ask when you know my heart's desire?"

"Then," said the young fellow, "I will start next week. I am anxious to see this thing through if only for the sake of your wife's peace of mind."

"I will call her. To hear what you think to do will make her glad," said Hom Hing.

He called a message to Lae Choo upstairs through a tube in the wall.

In a few moments she appeared, listless, wan, and hollow-eyed; but when her husband told her the young lawyer's suggestion she became as one electrified; her form straightened, her eyes glistened; the color flushed to her cheeks.

"Oh," she cried, turning to James Clancy, "You are a hundred man good!"

The young man felt somewhat embarrassed; his eyes shifted a little under the intense gaze of the Chinese mother.

"Well, we must get your boy for you," he responded. "Of course"—turning to Hom Hing—"it will cost a little money. You can't get fellows to hurry the Government for you without gold in your pocket."

Hom Hing stared blankly for a moment. Then: "How much do you want, Mr. Clancy?" he asked quietly.

"Well, I will need at least five hundred to start with."

Hom Hing cleared his throat.

"I think I told to you the time I last paid you for writing letters for me and seeing the Custom boss here that nearly all I had was gone!"

"Oh, well then we won't talk about it, old fellow. It won't harm the boy to stay where he is, and your wife may get over it all right."

"What that you say?" quavered Lae Choo.

James Clancy looked out of the window.

"He says," explained Hom Hing in English, "that to get our boy we have to have much money."

"Money! Oh, yes."

Lae Choo nodded her head.

"I have not got the money to give him."

For a moment Lae Choo gazed wonderingly from one face to the other; then, comprehension dawning upon her, with swift anger, pointing to the lawyer, she cried: "You not one hundred man good; you just common white man."

"Yes, ma'am," returned James Clancy, bowing and smiling ironically.

Hom Hing pushed his wife behind him and addressed the lawyer again: "I might try," said he, "to raise something; but five hundred—it is not possible."

"What about four?"

"I tell you I have next to nothing left and my friends are not rich."

"Very well!"

The lawyer moved leisurely toward the door, pausing on its threshold to light a cigarette.

"Stop, white man; white man, stop!"

Lae Choo, panting and terrified, had started forward and now stood beside him, clutching his sleeve excitedly.

"You say you can go to get paper to bring my Little One to me if Hom Hing give you five hundred dollars?"

The lawyer nodded carelessly; his eyes were intent upon the cigarette which would not take the fire from the match.

"Then you go get paper. If Hom Hing not can give you five hundred dollars— I give you perhaps what more that much."

She slipped a heavy gold bracelet from her wrist and held it out to the man. Mechanically he took it.

"I go get more!"

She scurried away, disappearing behind the door through which she had come.

"Oh, look here, I can't accept this," said James Clancy, walking back to Hom Hing and laying down the bracelet before him.

"It's all right," said Hom Hing, seriously, "pure China gold. My wife's parent give it to her when we married."

"But I can't take it anyway," protested the young man.

"It is all same as money. And you want money to go to Washington," replied Hom Hing in a matter of fact manner.

"See, my jade earrings—my gold buttons—my hairpins—my comb of pearl and my rings—one, two, three, four, five rings; very good—very good—all same much money. I give them all to you. You take and bring me paper for my Little One."

Lae Choo piled up her jewels before the lawyer.

Hom Hing laid a restraining hand upon her shoulder. "Not all, my wife," he said in Chinese. He selected a ring—his gift to Lae Choo when she dreamed of the tree with the red flower. The rest of the jewels he pushed toward the white man.

"Take them and sell them," said he. "They will pay your fare to Washington and bring you back with the paper."

For one moment James Clancy hesitated. He was not a sentimental man; but something within him arose against accepting such payment for his services.

"They are good, good," pleadingly asserted Lae Choo, seeing his hesitation.

Whereupon he seized the jewels, thrust them into his coat pocket, and walked rapidly away from the store.

IV

Lae Choo followed after the missionary woman through the mission nursery school. Her heart was beating so high with happiness that she could scarcely breathe. The paper had come at last—the precious paper which gave Hom Hing and his wife the right to the possession of their own child. It was ten months now since he had been taken from them—ten months since the sun had ceased to shine for Lae Choo.

The room was filled with children—most of them wee tots, but none so wee as her own. The mission woman talked as she walked. She told Lae Choo that little Kim, as he had been named by the school, was the pet of the place, and that his little tricks and ways amused and delighted every one. He had been rather difficult to manage at first and had cried much for his mother; "but children so soon forget, and after a month he seemed quite at home and played around as bright and happy as a bird."

"Yes," responded Lae Choo. "Oh, yes, yes!"

But she did not hear what was said to her. She was walking in a maze of anticipatory joy.

"Wait here, please," said the mission woman, placing Lae Choo in a chair. "The very youngest ones are having their breakfast."

She withdrew for a moment—it seemed like an hour to the mother—then she reappeared leading by the hand a little boy dressed in blue cotton overalls and white-soled shoes. The little boy's face was round and dimpled and his eyes were very bright.

"Little One, ah, my Little One!" cried Lae Choo.

She fell on her knees and stretched her hungry arms toward her son.

But the Little One shrunk from her and tried to hide himself in the folds of the white woman's skirt.

"Go'way, go'way!" he bade his mother.

1914

CULTURAL COORDINATES
Chinese American Women and Immigration

When Lae Choo arrives at Angel Island in Sui Sin Far's "In the Land of the Free," she would have been a relative rarity; very few Chinese women were actually allowed to enter the United States before 1943. In the story, the U.S. Customs Service questions her right to bring in her child; most women, however, would have faced fierce questioning when they arrived at the immigrant screening station in San Francisco Bay and then would have been detained and deported back to China. Although it may seem like immigration restrictions are a new issue in the United States today, immigration laws targeting specific ethnic groups were frequently passed during the late nineteenth century and the early twentieth century. The United States began restricting Chinese immigration with the Page Act of 1875, aimed specifically at preventing Chinese women from entering the country; the first major U.S. immigration law, the Chinese Exclusion Act of 1882, barred both Chinese men and women from immigration and was directed against the tide of workers who were entering the western states.

Chinese woman immigrant. Until 1943, when the ban was lifted, few Chinese women were allowed to immigrate; the intention was to discourage Chinese men from settling permanently in the United States by not allowing them to send for their families.

Even before the laws were passed, most Chinese immigrants to the United States were men; in 1882, about 95 percent of the Chinese population in America was male. Historians estimate that by the turn of the century, as much as 25 percent of California's workforce was Chinese. Chinese culture held that it was more important for a daughter-in-law to serve her husband's parents than to stay with her husband, so many women remained in China when their husbands left to work in the United States in the gold mines, on farms, in factories, in laundries, and building railroads. But cultural preferences do not adequately explain the gender imbalance in Chinese immigration. For that, we need to examine the laws aimed at Chinese women, laws that derived from fears, misconceptions, and outright racism.

Despite its history as a land of immigrants, the United States feared an influx of non-European immigrants.

Keeping Chinese women out of the United States meant that the Chinese population could be more easily controlled: male workers without families could be housed more easily, would require fewer government services (like education for children), would be less likely to press for decent wages, and would be more likely to return to China (especially since it was illegal for them to marry non-Chinese women).

One fear that had some basis in reality was an anxiety about prostitution among Chinese women immigrants. In 1870, according to historian Huping Ling, of the 3,536 adult Chinese women in California, 2,157 were listed as prostitutes. Many of these women were brought to the United States under false pretenses—they believed they were coming as wives, having been sent away by families devastated by a series of famines in China—and were sold into virtual slavery as prostitutes. To some extent, the Page Act was aimed at protecting these women. Concerns about prostitution and human trafficking does not fully explain the motives for the Page Act, though; as historian George Anthony Peffer has recently shown, it also reflected fears white Protestant women had of Asian women's supposed exotic beauty and sexuality. The Page Act prevented the immigration of virtually all Chinese women, except for a few wives of wealthy merchants; many women who were eligible to immigrate were nonetheless deported by immigration officials who used racist stereotypes when evaluating the women's claims.

New laws excluding both men and women from China were passed and old ones were renewed until 1943, when the United States lifted much of its ban on Chinese immigration as a result of China's pro–United States position during World War II. Although we now celebrate the contributions of Chinese Americans, including several noted women writers—among them Maxine Hong Kingston (pp. 1712–21) and Marilyn Chin (pp. 1944–48)—there was a time when the United States did not welcome their families to our shores.

CORNELIA SORABJI

1866–1954

Cornelia Sorabji was born in Nasik, about 125 miles northeast of Bombay (now Mumbai), India, into a reform-minded family committed to the education of girls. Although they were of Parsi origin—Parsis are followers of the ancient Persian religion of Zoroastrianism—and retained many Parsi cultural traits, Sorabji's family had converted to Christianity. Encouraged by her family to pursue an education, Sorabji did so with zeal, becoming the first woman to graduate from Deccan College, Poona. She also read extensively in classics and philosophy, subjects that formed part of the traditional curriculum for an educated man but that were hardly typical studies for a woman at the time.

Although Sorabji's outstanding academic achievements made her eligible for a scholarship to Oxford, she was disqualified from applying because of her sex. Undeterred, she took a job at a coeducational college as the principal—a position that women in England would have been barred from assuming at that time—and saved the money needed to pursue a law degree in England. Although it was highly unusual for an Indian woman to travel to England alone, she did just that, attending Oxford University from 1889 to 1891 and becoming the first woman—Indian or English—to take the bachelor of civil law examination.

In England, women were not admitted to the bar until 1922, so Sorabji was unable to practice law in the country where she received her degree. She returned to India in 1894 and worked to provide legal assistance to *purdahnashins,* Muslim and Hindu women in India who lived in seclusion (or *purdah*). Frequently the legal rights of *purdahnashins* were violated in the name of tradition and orthodoxy, so Sorabji worked to protect their property rights and to secure medical care and educational opportunities for these women. This struggle is recorded in her 1901 monograph, *Love and Life behind the Purdah.* From 1904 to 1923 Sorabji worked as special legal advisor to the Crown, a position she helped create. Finally, after more than three decades in India, she returned to England in 1929, where she remained until her death.

Throughout her many years of work in education, politics, and law, Sorabji also produced a great deal of writing. In addition to *Love and Life behind the Purdah,* she wrote short-story collections—*Sun Babies* (1904) and *Between the Twilight* (1908)—as well as two autobiographies—*India Calling* (1934) and *India Recalled* (1935)—written after her permanent return to England.

Sorabji's personality and politics were complex. To many, she was a committed Anglophile; nevertheless, while living in the heart of imperial England, she stayed close to her traditional Parsi roots. She rejected Western clothes, favoring saris worn in the traditional Parsi way—looped over the right ear and behind the left—and her letters expressed a distaste for English fashions. Her position as a feminist figure is also complex: she did not advocate the abolition of purdah and, in fact, criticized many of the women's movements of her time, yet she remained committed to the rights of Indian women in purdah. Perhaps Sorabji's paradoxical positions can be attributed to her diasporic condition—Parsi-Christian in India and Indian in England. In the following selection from her memoir *India Calling,*

Sorabji records her memories of Victorian life in England from 1889 to 1894, as well as her work on behalf of Indian women in India.

From India Calling: The Memories of Cornelia Sorabji, India's First Woman Barrister

Chapter 2
Preparation and Equipment: In India and England

The education I got as a girl, I owed to my Family—to my Father and my elder sisters, helped out by masters and mistresses for languages, mathematics, music and drawing. After passing my Matriculation I was still too young for admission to a College in England.

To exhaust possibilities in India seemed the only course. There were no Colleges for women in my Presidency,[1] but the Parents had ascertained that I could be admitted to the Men's College in our Town. I could live at home and drive the five miles out and back daily.

They put the problem to me. Would I care to do this?

That was how it came to pass that I became a member of the Deccan College, Poona. I will not say that I was not scared of the hundreds of Hindus and Moslems in the big lecture-rooms; but there was home, when it rang to Evensong.[2]

To my surprise I topped the Presidency in the final Degree Examination, and automatically obtained the Government of India Scholarship for a course at an English University—a handsome scholarship, including travelling and other expenses. In spite, however, of the University Constitution declaring that women were as men, I was not allowed to hold my scholarship. The test had been the same, and all conditions were fulfilled; but the Authorities said, "No!"—it was in fact impertinent of any woman to produce circumstances which were not in the mind of the Authorities as a possibility when they dangled a gilded prize before eyes that should have been male eyes alone!

The attitude of the Parents was a cheerful—"Hard luck! but the goal is still there. A way will open!"

And it did. A Men's College in Guzerat[3] was deprived of its English Principal. I was offered a short term Fellowship in English Literature—to cover his duties in this direction, till arrangements could be made to replace him.

I decided to take it, and so help towards replacement of my lost scholarship.

A professorship at eighteen, in a Male College, was solitary and (inwardly) terrifying; but the students and the professors—Parsees, Hindus, Moslems—were kind. And it was quite good fun from the point of view of hard work, and of absurd authority—of dealing with ragging, and making quick decisions.

There is only one story of this period which I will tell, and that, because Jowett of Balliol[4] loved it, and because it is illustrative of the atmosphere in which I worked.

---

1. British rule in India established three presidencies—Bombay, Madras, and Calcutta—for purposes of administration; Sorabji refers to the Bombay Presidency, which was spread over today's states of Gujarat, western Maharashtra, Karnataka, and Sind (in present-day Pakistan).
2. Poona: the city where Sorabji went to college,

part of the Bombay Presidency; evensong: evening prayer.
3. Present-day state of Gujarat.
4. Benjamin Jowett (1817–93), scholar, theologian, and master of Balliol College, University of Oxford.

There was then no communal feeling, as we now know it, in India; but Undergraduates were more insistent upon observance of Religion than they are now.

It was recess, and I was in my room glancing at my notes for an afternoon lecture.

Two students asked to see me—a Parsee and a Hindu. The Parsee told his story. He was a resident student: a mad dog had got into his room, and he had told one of the College messengers to remove it. The Hindu lived next door, and had objected. —"Consider," said he, "the Soul of my Ancestor might be in that dog. It's an indignity." Would I please settle their dispute?

I said that the beliefs of all students must of course be respected. That it was surprising that the Hindu should claim that the soul of his ancestor could inhabit a *mad* dog. But that at any rate, in that belief, filial obligation was not the Parsee's. The dog must be out of the compound before the afternoon session. The students must deal with their problem themselves.

Looking out of my window, ten minutes later, I saw the dog at the end of a long rope being led out of the compound by a College messenger!

By the time that my "locum" job came to an end, friends in England and Somerville College, Oxford (Lord and Lady Hobhouse and Miss Madeleine Shaw Lefevre being the ringleaders in this conspiracy of kindness),[5] had offered me a "substituted scholarship" which, with what we could add to it, made the English adventure immediately possible.

Of my time at College I do not propose to write in detail. I can never forget Oxford, seen for the first time in the October term with the reds and russets and tawny greens of the virginian creeper against the grey worn stone: nor can I forget the kindness of everyone, from the Somerville student—A. M. Bruce—who "adopted" me as her special Fresher, and taught me the ropes, to the Heads of Houses themselves.[6]

Through the Hobhouses, Jowett, then Master of Balliol, kindly came to call on me immediately.

When he went, the Warden[7] took me in her arms and said, "My child, this is a great honour." And in my ignorance I wondered if that were a traditional Oxford custom when aged cherubs with white hair were polite to foreigners. I was not long in realizing what she meant; and the Master of Balliol added to his marvellous kindnesses to the end of his life. He used to take me for walks, when my chief difficulty lay in matching my steps to his little ones. Happily, I did not realize that I ought to be awed—I chatted as I would to any companion. And he gave me staccato wisdom—in words that were unforgettable.

During his week-end parties, the kind Master always found room for me at the Lodge[8] dinner-table.

* * * The Master had a genius for bringing together opposing forces in thought and action, and giving them the opportunity of finding common ground. From all I met, I breathed in what was of infinite value. They led me to an observation point, as it were—from which, in the fullness of time, I was enabled to study

5. "Locum": temporary; Lord and Lady Hobhouse: patrons of Sorabji who helped support her education at Oxford; Miss Madeleine Shaw Lefevre: principal (1879–89) of Somerville College, Oxford, founded in 1879 as among the first colleges for women at the university.

6. Fresher: first-year student; heads of Houses: college principals.

7. Administrative officer.

8. Official residence of the master (head of college).

English politics, and the then new comradely attitude towards the East End;[9] the freedom of thought as to Religion, together with the loyalty to standards of rectitude inspired by Religion—so characteristic of the moment; the growing recognition of the rights of women; the definition of Culture and its changing interpretation from just "breed" alone, to what an old friend of mine used to call "breed and feed"[1] —though I knew also that Breed must ever prevail over Feed . . . (in India we knew about Breed but nothing whatsoever about Feed). Best of all, I learnt that difference of opinion need not affect friendship or personal appreciation; and that one could be a zealot and yet open-minded . . . could gain in breadth without losing in intensity. In short, I was hearing good talk, and getting England into my bones, without realizing how much I was learning, or how greatly I was privileged. I know now that it was this last fact which prevented self consciousness, and helped me to savour my experience at its best.

* * *

I remember too how the Undergraduates who had come in to coffee * * * would sit trembling at the end of a sofa when Jowett tried to set them at their ease. One day he said to me, of one such, "I am far more shy of him than *he* could ever be of me."

I had asked to read Law when I went up—and was told that no woman might read Law. Whereupon I said it was indifferent to me what I read, and our Warden was directing me to the then most popular School for a nondescript, when the Master asked me why I wished to read Law. I told him—and my programme of work was immediately changed. I was sent to lectures in Law, chiefly to Sir William Markby's, attended by both the Junior and Senior Indian Civil Service men up at Oxford; and to Professor Bryce on Jurisprudence.[2]

The Warden only laughed when I asked her questions about my mysterious course—and I was too happy to want to dig deeper.

Mystery thickened when I was told that I would do the Term's "Collections" in the Warden's room, supervised by herself. She produced a sealed envelope, and Sir William Markby called to retrieve my Papers.

I said how jolly it was of them to give me the feeling of a real examination over these "pretend" terminal tests, and thought no more about the matter—till the day when I was sent for to the Warden's Room. Dear old "Marker" was there, looking benevolent and happy, and he said, "You may read for the Honour School of Jurisprudence next Term. Ilbert[3] has marked your papers very high."

I knew the Ilberts at the House of Commons, but could not imagine what Sir Courtney had to do with Somerville Collections. The Warden explained that they had made me do the I.C.S. Law course and examination papers as a test. And it had been successful.

I won't try to say what I felt. It was such amazing luck.

* * *

9. Sorabji might be referring to the Settlement movement, founded to encourage university students to engage in social work in the East End slums, with the goal of helping to alleviate poverty and misery.
1. Heritage and education alongside material nourishment.
2. Sir William Markby: English judge and legal writer (1829–1914) specializing in Indian law

who served as judge of the Calcutta High Court 1866–78 and later taught Indian law at Oxford; Professor Bryce: jurist and statesman (1838–1922) who taught civil law at Oxford 1870–93.
3. Ilbert: Courtenay Ilbert (1841–1924), lawyer and administrator, associated with the controversial Ilbert Bill (1884), which would have allowed Indian magistrates to preside over cases involving Europeans.

The week before the final Examination I was dining quietly with the Master, and he said to me, "Would it make any difference to you if you did the B.C.L. papers sitting at your College, supervised by Miss Maitland" (the Warden)? I said, "Indeed it would. It would not feel like a regular University Examination; and some day when women are allowed to take degrees mine might be withheld because I had not sat in the Schools with the men. Why may I not sit with them?"

He said, "Because the London Examiner for the B.C.L. Examination refuses to examine a woman. But if you feel like that, we must get the University to pass a decree that you are allowed to sit for the Examination."

And, being Vice-Chancellor, he took the necessary steps.

It was an exhausting experience waiting for the verdict. And the kind V.C. said he would send me instant news from the meeting which was held on the eve of the opening Examination day. M.A.s had been cited to vote on the proposition:

"That Cornelia Sorabji be allowed to sit for the B.C.L. Examination."

The Master's letters to me were always written on minute paper in his minute, incisive hand.

"Congregation grants you your decree," was what his letter said. I received it at about 4 p.m. Soon after, my Roman Law Tutor was to be seen walking up the drive towards the West Building where I lived. He was greatly excited, his red beard shone in the sunlight and his red hair was flying in the wind; he carried his hat in one hand and a badly-rolled umbrella in the other. I was in the garden with my special College friends, who were rejoicing with me at the conclusion of an anxiety which they had shared, and I remember wincing, as at a false note in music, at the colour of Dr Grueber's hair against the pink spirals of the chestnut trees—a terrible disharmony.

"Miss Sorabyi" (as he always called me), said he, "you need not sit for that Examination."

"But why?"

"You have your decree. That is enough for a life-time. You need go no further. The University of Oxford" (and the thrill in his voice was awesome) "to pass a decree *like that!* . . ."

To whatever cause it was due that the result of my finals did not "copy fair the past"—it was, in fact, very bad indeed—it was not due to any lack on the part of others. I had overwhelming excuse for doing better in the teaching and opportunity given me. I had far more knowledge than I'd had for any of the examinations in which I had gained Alpha-pluses. But there it was!

And I pushed my disappointment in myself away. For, whatever my label, I'd got my equipment, and had had my fun! The lure and the delight of reading for a School which branched out in so many directions was that one was always going off the beaten track, pursuing enticing scents. Balliol and All Souls, as I have said, were the Colleges I attended for my lectures, and the Warden of All Souls, Sir William Anson, had kindly made me free of the Codrington Library, that exclusively male preserve. It was there that I spent my days between lectures in the little Ante-Room where Ethlinger, the Librarian, who was afterwards translated to Lincoln's Inn Library, supplied me with books on the nail, and seemed to think that I must always be cold. The kind man used to have a rug for my knees, which he pressed upon me even in the Summer: and on the closest of days he would call to the boy in attendance as I entered the Library—"Pile on more coals, Horsley!"

Long years after I had gone down, I was revisiting Oxford and met Sir George Trevelyan. A Life of Sir William Anson was in preparation and Sir George told me, teasingly, that there was going to be just one joke in it.

"Did Sir William Anson ever jest?"

"No! he winked only once in his lifetime. He winked at Miss Sorabji!"

The basis of this was the fact that when, after my time, History Student from Somerville asked to be allowed to read at the Codrington, Sir William would solemnly reply, "Certainly: if you can prove that you are Miss Sorabji!"

It was in June 1892 that I did my B.C.L. Examination. It was not till after the War that women were admitted to degrees. I took my degree of B.C.L., formally, in the Convocation of 1922—the earliest moment at which I could get back from my work in India to take it.

It was a good life, being up. Kindness and spoiling, feeling after one's powers, meeting people who thought, and people who talked clever nonsense: and finding companionship outside my family for the first time.

My College friends * * * and those others passed beyond sight, whose names are written in my heart and whose ideals are still my standard of conduct—were all utterly and undeservedly good to me. Then Oxford itself in every mood, how I loved it: if not perhaps as later I learned to love London. Oxford is to me the place in which to get ready for life; not, unless your work lies there, in which to live it. But Oxford had and has its very own niche in one's being—the river, the Towers, the Meadows, College gardens, ghostly Long Wall Street (down which a Welsh Professor was said to slink when he wanted to invite the right mood in which to write about Machiavelli).[4] College chapels—Magdalen and its music ("Like *that!*" said Farmer of Balliol. "Why, it's only a soul shampoo!"): the Sunday afternoon Services at the Cathedral—Oh! a hundred memories, from which one must turn with firmness, or one would never end fingering the sweet-scented rosemary.

Of Jowett, however, I must record one more memory, before I turn to the world outside Oxford. When living in London I often went back on visits to Oxford: and the Master would ask me to *tête-à-tête* breakfasts or lunches at the Lodge. He had given me an introduction to Miss Florence Nightingale,[5] and had asked me to write and tell him about my visit. And I wrote, no doubt garrulously, of the little old lady with rosy cheeks in a frilled nightcap whom I saw in bed, surrounded with flowers, her birds singing their hearts out in the aviary by the windows.

When I lunched with him after this visit, he said suddenly, indicating the only picture of a woman in his study—it hung on the wall, a girlish figure in a short-waisted dress standing beside a pedestal on which sat the figure of an owl—"Would you recognize that for the little old lady in a frilled night-cap whom you saw last week?"

I was silent, not knowing what to say, and Jowett continued:

"When she was like that, I asked her to marry me."

Needless to say, I was struck dumb; one had never thought of the Master in human terms, as having had a mother or sisters, for instance, or as dressing like other folk, or having been at any other age or in any circumstance save that at and wherein one knew him.

---

4. Italian philosopher and statesman (1469–1527), author of *The Prince*, which favored realistic and pragmatic views of political power.
5. Reformer of the nursing profession (see pp.

883–84); a biography of Nightingale (*Life of Florence Nightingale* by Sir Edward Cook) was published in 1913.

Jowett spoke again, elliptically—in his small abrupt voice: "It was better so."

When the *Life of Florence Nightingale* was published, a cousin of hers showed me an entry in F.N.'s Diary, which was surely a reference to this episode:

Benjamin Jowett came to see me. Disastrous!

Nothing more.

Life at Somerville was much as it is to-day. The College was about half its present size. There were only two residential buildings—the Old Hall and West Buildings. I lived in the latter, over which Miss Clara Pater, Classical Tutor, presided. Her brother, Walter Pater,[6] often came to see her, rushing through the garden "for fear of the petticoats," as he explained to Miss Pater, or sneaking in at the Woodstock entrance. When in her room he would sit for an hour at a time without speaking, his head between his hands. A pretty Irish student threatened to break in on this séance to see what would happen. She did, too—making some flippant remark. All Walter Pater said was, "What was that noise!"

* * *

What next? was the question with which I was faced. Lord and Lady Hobhouse, in whose special and beloved care I'd been since my arrival in England, suggested that I ought to try and get some training in the practice of the Law; and during the Long this suggestion moved towards reality. I was staying with the Aberdares, the parents of my College friend, Alice Bruce, at Duffryn in South Wales: and hearing of Lord Hobhouse's advice—"I have a Solicitor son-in-law, and a Barrister son-in-law," said kind Lord Aberdare—"at which end will you begin?" One of the partners of Lee & Pemberton's, the firm of Solicitors to which he had referred, was staying in the neighbourhood and rode over one morning to see me and ask why I wanted to acquire a profession not open to women. I told him.

In due course I heard from the firm offering to take me on as a pupil. I was not allowed to sit for the Solicitors' examination, but should get what apprenticeship offered, and if this would be any use to me, the firm would give me a Certificate at the end of my training. This Lee & Pemberton's nobly did. I had practice galore in draftsmanship and conveyancing; I attended the Courts with the partner in charge of litigation; I learnt how estates were administered; and how clients should be interviewed. As a rule the clients took me without comment. But two old ladies, in before-the-Flood garments, who drove in from the country once a year in an ancient barouche to see their solicitors, regarded me with bated breath. When the "Chief" was not looking, they bent forward—"Are you," they said, "a New Woman?"

My special "Chief" is still in the firm, and I find each time that I run in to 44, Lincoln's Inn Fields, that the memories of long-ago kindnesses, received in that ancient building, are not only as alive as they were in 1893, but are burnished with gold, because I know now how sadly I should have failed many a *Purdah-nashin*[7] in India, but for this experience.

When I left Lee & Pemberton's, to my amazement my fees were returned. I had had the stupendous luck to detect a flaw in some title deeds I was examining; any pupil would have done the like, but the partners generously said I had saved the firm more money than the cost of my training.

Truly, the debt that I owed to the world was growing with every breath I took!

* * *

6. English critic of literature and art (1839–94) and early proponent of the Aesthetic movement.   7. Women in "purdah," the practice of veiling and seclusion (see pp. 1325–26).

But life in England was not all work—anything but! I was taken to Art Galleries, Plays and Concerts: to Ranelagh and Hurlingham: to sittings of the Privy Council, to hear debates in the Houses of Parliament, to tea on the Terrace.[8]

The House of Commons delighted me. Julia Peel[9] was acting hostess for her father at the time. I had met her and her brothers at Oxford; and she was wonderfully kind to me: would apprise me of exceptional debates; and I often lunched and dined at the Speaker's House in the thrilling days of the Irish Home Rule Controversy,[1] "tasting the whole of it." * * *

* * *

It is not in human nature to withhold the story I now tell.

One day at lunch at the Speaker's, Colonel Sanderson, the famous Unionist, who sat next to me, said, "Have you seen a row in the House?" I said I had, and instanced what had seemed to me terribly excited and unseemly behaviour on several occasions.

"Those are not rows. You must see a real one. I'll make it."

"How?"

"Oh, it's easy. You sit on the hat of a Member, or you abuse an Irish Priest."

And that afternoon he kept his word. He called an Irish Priest "a scoundrelly rascal," when referring to some Irish incident being discussed in the House. Instantly there was Bedlam.

"Withdraw!—Draw!—Draw!" shouted one side; and "Hear! Hear!" shouted the other.

Mr Gladstone and Mr Balfour[2] both tried to restore quiet, but failed. Then the Speaker, who as a Speaker was perfect—he looked like a Mme Tussaud waxwork, and seldom spoke except *in extremis*—asked that the expression used should be withdrawn. Colonel Sanderson immediately complied, with the charm in which he was an expert:

"I withdraw the words 'scoundrelly rascal,' " said he. "I substitute for them 'excited politician'!"

In a minute the House was rocking with laughter.

I love that, about the House of Commons, more evident perhaps in the eighteen-nineties than now:—its youth and sudden changes, its quick jumps from anger to mirth, from division to unity.

My presentation at Court was a thrill of a different kind. Queen Victoria sent me a gracious message to the effect that "one of my 'pretty colours' (not white) would be permitted": and I wore an azalea *sari* something in colour between pink and yellow. I was given private *entrée*. The Queen said she was "glad to see me there" when she gave me her hand to kiss, and the long sequence of curtseys ended

8. Ranelagh: public garden in Chelsea, London, famous for the annual Chelsea flower show; Hurlingham: clubhouse; Privy Council: advisory body to the monarch that also functioned as an appeals court for British courts overseas; tea on the Terrace: traditional English tea on the terrace of the House of Commons.
9. Daughter of Sir Robert Peel, Conservative prime minister of Britain 1841–46.
1. Controversy surrounding the House of Lords' rejection of a bill to grant Ireland home rule (limited autonomy in decisions affecting its own territory); a home rule bill had also been rejected by the House of Lords in 1886.
2. Mr Gladstone: William Gladstone (1809–98), four-time Liberal Party prime minister (total of 14 years) between 1868 and 1894; Mr Balfour: Arthur Balfour (1848–1930): Conservative Party prime minister 1902–5, who authored the 1917 declaration that paved the way for the establishment of a Jewish homeland in Palestine.

(we did several, in those days, slithering past bunches of Serene Highnesses), I stood beside Lady (Gerald) Fitzgerald, who had presented me, watching others through their ordeal.

* * *

* * * In 1890 *The Times* had a brisk correspondence about "Jessie of Lucknow," and the incident commemorated in the song, "The Campbells are coming."

The story was, it will be remembered (everyone believed it to be history), that Jessie, a Scotch girl, had sensed the approach of the relief, by her gift of second sight, and encouraged the besieged garrison to hold on—thus saving the situation. *The Times* correspondents were wrangling over "Jessie"—some saying she was alive and claiming her as a maid: others equally claiming her, but saying she was dead.

I was staying in London at the time with Miss Adelaide Manning[3] (the daughter of Sergeant Manning), who said, "This is very funny—there's only one person who knows who Jessie was: and she has not written to *The Times*. Would you like to see her and hear her story?" I said that I should love to do that. So we made an expedition to a suburb of London, and found a dear old lady sitting by the window in her charming room. She had pink cheeks and wore her snow-white hair in curls under a lace cap. She looked very French, but was English, the widow of one of Talleyrand's secretaries.[4]

Miss Manning said, "Writers to *The Times* are quarrelling over 'Jessie of Lucknow'"—and told her about the correspondence. She flushed with delight. "My Jessie," she said, "still alive?" "Will you tell my Indian friend her story?" She complied at once and with evident pleasure. She said that her sister was married to a Colonel in the Indian Army: that the Colonel and his wife were both with the besieged garrison at Lucknow in 1857. That when the little force was at the very end of its strength, Lucknow was relieved by a Highland Detachment. Mme X——was in Paris when her sister's letter arrived, telling her all this. She was thrilled and sent the story (enlarging it, and inventing "Jessie" to make the tale more picturesque), in the form of a letter purporting to have come from India, to a Paris paper. How she chuckled over the true and honourable women who claimed to have pensioned or buried this fictitious person!

"Do write the truth to *The Times*," said Miss Manning. "Never!" said the delicious old lady. "My Jessie is alive—has lived all these years. How can you expect me to say that she was never born!" I believe *The Times* had traced the tale to the French paper in question: but could get no information from the then control about the writer of the letter.

* * *

It was a great moment when I was asked to write an Indian play for George Alexander—Mrs Patrick Campbell[5] to have the chief role. I said that I could not write a play, but would put into suitable form for the English stage a Sanskrit play, reputed as of the second century. (The original took a fortnight to act, and was staged by the roadside, the audience travelling with the players to succeeding scenes, arranged to punctuate the journey!)

---

3. Social reformer (1828–1905).
4. Secretary to Charles Maurice de Talleyrand-Périgord (1754–1838), the most influential French diplomat of the nineteenth century.

5. George Alexander: actor and producer (1858–1918), especially of Oscar Wilde's plays; Mrs. Patrick Campbell: celebrated British stage actress (1865–1940).

In due course this was done, and submitted to George Alexander's critic, who passed it, but said it must be put into blank verse—a fearful essay, but also passed. And then I was asked to stay at Graham Robertson's house at Witley.[6] He would do the illustrations to the play, and I was to read it to Mrs. Patrick Campbell, who was to be of the party.

We read it in the Early English cottage in the garden after dinner—Mrs Pat lying full-length on the hearthrug. Her comments were characteristic. The play portrays an aged and childless Brahmin wife who urges her husband to marry again, choosing a bride for him herself, a young and lovely girl. Mrs Pat was to play the young girl. "But this is immoral!" said Mrs Pat. "I could not bear the old woman to be nice to me. Make it Za-Za, a third-personal situation."

It was no use pointing out that that would be French, not Indian.

Then again:

"But you know I can never play happily unless I am the only important person in the play. Now the Brahmin man is as important as I am. You must change that."

I told our little group that night that I was afraid it was no good. The changes could not be made. The play was not mine, and its value lay in keeping it as close as possible to the original. Mrs Pat was flatteringly regretful. "Do change it. I long to play in Indian draperies. Do I not remind you of an Indian dream?" I was young and did not know how to frame a polite answer. Evasion she would not allow.

"No."

"Of what do I remind you? You must say. It is something Indian, I am sure." I admitted that it was. "What is it?" Pressed beyond power of extrication, I said, "Of a snake—you move so sinuously, do you not?" To my relief she was delighted.

"I long to be a snake. I always try to imagine myself a snake."

But about the play I was inexorable. Unless she entered into the spirit of it, it was no use. The changes she wanted could not be made.

It was interesting meeting Mrs Pat. I'd seen her only once before, at an artist's studio on Show Sunday, when she came in rustling—it was in the days of the rustling underskirt—Herr Zwintscher was playing lovely Eighteenth-Century music on a spinet, and Phillip Burne-Jones[7] said:

"Who's that hissing with her feet?"

She could say clever and original things—as, for instance, this: "I always tell a woman's age by her throat. First it's all right: then there's a pleat: then there's a gusset!"

After we left Witley a friend sent the play to Bernard Shaw.[8] It came back with the remark that it would be very expensive to stage; but was worth a trial. There was only one addition which he begged me to make. "Introduce," said he, "the incident of the Ninth Lancers and the Durbar!"[9] (Curzon's Durbar, and a contemporaneous Army incident.) I thought that he was laughing at me, even though he sent me a message asking if the change had been made. And I threw the

6. Graham Robertson: painter, illustrator, and costume designer (1866–1948) who drew portraits of famous actresses; Witley: village in Surrey, England.
7. Herr Zwintscher: German artist (1870–1916); Phillip Burne-Jones: English painter (1861–1926).
8. Social critic and playwright (1856–1950) whose works include *Pygmalion, Arms and the Man,* and *Major Barbara.*
9. Lord Curzon (1859–1936), then viceroy of India, received a chilly reception at the 1903 Delhi durbar (ceremonial gathering), a result of his unpopular punishment of officers of the Ninth Lancers, a cavalry regiment of the British army.

play into a corner of my room. I have since realized that the coupling of the centuries is a Shavian habit: and have always regretted my ignorance and silly touchiness. I might have asked him to do it himself!

Bernard Shaw, in the flesh, I have met only once lately at a House Party in Worcestershire. He greeted me with: "Why are you not in prison?" which helped me to retort that it was clear with what kind of Indian alone he was acquainted.

I did enjoy that meeting. How kindly he is and how gentle, and full of the fun which has no sting in its tail. But—whether deliberately or not (he will forgive me), he makes you feel that he is sitting for his photograph every moment of his life—in public, at any rate.

My brother and I paid a thrilling visit to the Tennysons[1] in September 1892, not long before the Laureate's last illness. After swearing us to secrecy, he read us *Akhbar,* then unpublished. We sat in the garden, he wore the big hat ("the boys in the street say they can see my legs dangling out of it") and cloak with which pictures had familiarized us; and every now and again his son gave him a spoonful of glycerine to moisten his throat. He talked of Gladstone, of Buddhism and of Alfred Lyall. With Lady Tennyson I fell in love at first sight. She looked like an abbess in her lace veil. Her wonderful recovery, after a lifetime on her back, she used in collecting material from her diaries for the Life of Alfred Tennyson.

English country-house visits really need a book to themselves. Life was good to me and I had ample opportunities of realizing what made the Englishmen of the Services what they are, at their best. Through the hospitality of friends I learnt to know many counties in England: I also visited Scotland, Ireland and Wales.

At Easter a beloved friend, Mrs Augustus Darling, used to take me abroad—to the Riviera, North Italy and Switzerland. She was sister-in-law to our "pretend" Grandmother, Lady Ford, after whom I was named. But Lady Ford was too ailing when I was in England to look after me, and Mrs Darling did it for her. She gave me the loveliest times, bless her! She was exquisite to look at, and we both loved books and flowers and the countryside: also, the same things made us laugh—perhaps, this last, the closer bond of all. My "English Mother" she called herself, and her wisdom, as I recognized later, lay not in reproof and denial, but in giving in. Monte Carlo was one instance. I had read about Monte Carlo, and when we were at Mentone,[2] I said, "I should like to go to Monte Carlo—to the Tables, I mean." She said, "My dear Child!"—I knew she hated the thought. And, I must have been more odious than even my memory of myself, for I kept saying, "I *do* want to go!"

She said, smiling, "You always get what you want from me." And I grinned back, "That is why I go on telling you that I still want it!"

Next morning she said to me, "We are going to drive in to Monte Carlo this afternoon. You will love the view, Mentone looking like a great amethyst in the distance. And we will go into the Casino. I've arranged for someone to take us round who understands about the play there: and (shyly), "I'd like my Birthday present to you to be some money to throw away."

Was anyone ever like her?

---

1. Emily Sellwood (1813–96) and her husband, Alfred, Lord Tennyson (1809–92), who was made poet laureate in 1850; "Akhbar" was a poem composed by Tennyson in the early 1890s.
2. Town on the French Riviera, northeast of Monte Carlo, Monaco, with its famous casino.

It was I who at the end of the afternoon said, "Let's get out of this, to the fresh air"; the faces of the women who played for gold only, in a room apart, had pricked the bubble of excitement.

I had played myself—and won; but I never want to go to Monte Carlo again.

From Mentone that year, we went to San Remo, driving through Ventimiglia, in a little *fiacre* (no motors in those days);[3] Mrs Darling's man and maid followed in another with the baggage. At the frontier Customs Office, the maid came to us distraught. "They will not pass Mamselle's clothes. They say they are silks being taken to Italy for sale."

"Explain to them, Rose," said Mrs Darling. "You've often seen Mademoiselle dress."

"I have done that; they only shrug their shoulders."

"Bring them to me," said my friend, and she explained in French, and in Italian, that what was in my boxes was exactly like what I was wearing.

"Ask us to believe that!" was their reply, emphasized with movements of hands, shoulders, eyebrows.

"You'll have to undress and dress before them," said Mrs Darling.

I was young—"Nothing would induce me," said I.

"Tell us what to pay," said she to the Officers.

"Impossible!" was the reply. It seemed both French and Italian Customs were involved, and we must wait till nine o'clock next morning, when the goods would be examined by a joint board.

Of course, I could not allow that: and very sulkily, I have no doubt, I said I would demonstrate.

We went into the Customs shed—one pull and my draperies were at my feet. The Officers stood in a circle round us, and how we laughed at their faces! But it was still difficult to drive on, not because they wanted to charge us duty—oh, no!—"everything was free," and they were most apologetic. But they wanted to see how it was done. "Do it again!" they kept saying, as if they were Alice in Wonderland or Peter Pan.

In these days when hundreds of Indian women of all races visit England and the Continent so frequently, a scene like this is hard to visualize. My sisters had preceded me to England, and Miss Adelaide Manning, that generous friend of Indians, had spoken of the visits of the late Dowager Maharani of Cooch Behar—but I believe this made the complete tale of us. Indian boys and men had long been coming in respectable numbers. But their clothes had not the same allure or suggestion of foreignness. Dear old ladies were always trying to convert me—for instance—the heathen at their gates. And they would talk to one very loudly in pidgin-English—"Calcutta Come?" "Bombay Come?" Only once did I try to undeceive a proselytizing old lady. She regarded me reproachfully, "But you *look* so very heathen!"

One more tale of "lingerie." "The Widow Green"—as the widow of the Historian[4] was known at Oxford—asked me one day to tea to meet some "African Chiefs" whom she had picked up somewhere. "I want them to make their women adopt your dress."

3. San Remo, Ventimiglia: towns in Liguria, Italy;   4. John Richard Green (1837–83): English
fiacre: small carriage.   historian.

I had my doubts, but I went: and the conversation turned instantly on clothes. "This," I said, indicating my *sari*, "is six yards long—how many yards of material go to the dress of an African lady in your part of the country?" The "Chief" said shortly—"Beads, and—this—" producing a handkerchief!

My only other "African" story is perhaps best told here, though it happened years later during the Boer War. I was back in England temporarily, and occupied a flat in Chelsea. I dropped into a nearby Church one Sunday for Service, being too late for my usual objective. To this accident I attribute what followed.

On Monday afternoon I got home to hear at the door that an English cleric from this Church had been waiting an hour to see me. I hurried to him, apologetic. I supposed that it was a parochial visit.

He advanced with both hands outstretched.

"It's so good to see you," he said. "So like Home!"

I'd never seen the man before, and said:

"Do you know India?"

"No."

"Or my People?"

"No! But it's *so* like Home to see you. I've been working among the Coolies[5] in South Africa!"

In 1894 I returned to India for the first time. The to-and-froings since are more than I can remember: and there have been many Continental visits—Italy, France, Belgium, Spain, Austria.

1934

◄◄ KATHERINE MAYO ►►
1867–1940

In the winter of 1925, American journalist Katherine Mayo spent three months in India. Her interest in the country had been awakened by a Senate bill on Indian citizenship rights, as well as by the British parliamentary debate on the Simon Commission, which had been formed to investigate political reform in India, in response to nationalist agitation. At the end of her stay, Mayo wrote *Mother India*, a blistering criticism of Indian society, particularly the position of women in it. In the book, she argued that, considering the conditions that Indian women faced, Indian men were unfit to take charge of the government.

Published in 1927, the book became a best seller and created a major controversy in India. The renowned Indian nationalist Mohandas (Mahatma) Gandhi likened it to a "drain inspector's report." The text was widely seen as the work of an imperialist's mind, since it seemed to attribute Indian women's degradation to the inferiority of the Indian race. While some credited her criticism of oppressive customs such as child marriage and superstitious approaches to motherhood, many rejected her presentation of Indian women as passive victims of Indian patriarchy.

The issues raised by *Mother India* still reverberate in contemporary discussions of Indian feminism. It could be argued that the controversy over this book not only facilitated a prompt passage of the Child Marriage Restraint Act in 1929

---

5. Derogatory term for indentured laborers from India and China.

but also contributed, due to the outraged response of Indian women, to the emergence of a modern and more inclusive Indian nationalism. The selection that follows is a chapter from *Mother India*. In it, Mayo excoriates the system of midwifery as dangerous and unscientific.

From Mother India
Chapter VIII
Mother India

Row upon row of girl children—little tots all, four, five, six, even seven years old, sitting cross-legged on the floor, facing the brazen goddess. Before each one, laid straight and tidy, certain treasures—a flower, a bead or two, a piece of fruit—precious things brought from their homes as sacrificial offerings. For this is a sort of day school of piety. These babies are learning texts—"mantrims" to use in worship—learning the rites that belong to the various ceremonies incumbent upon Hindu women. And that is all they are learning; that is all they need to know. Now in unison they pray.

"What are they praying for?" one asks the teacher, a grave-faced Hindu lady.

"What should a woman-child pray for? A husband, if she is not married; or, if she is, then for a better husband at her next re-birth."

Women pray first as to husbands; then, to bear sons. Men must have sons to save their souls.

Already we have seen some evidence of the general attitude of the Hindu toward this, the greatest of all his concerns, in its prenatal aspect. But another cardinal point that, in any practical survey of Indian competency, can be neither contested nor suppressed, is the manner in which the Hindu of all classes permits his much-coveted son to be ushered into the light of day.

We have spoken of women's hospitals in various parts of India. These are doing excellent work, mostly gynecological. But they are few, relatively to the work to be done, nor could the vast majority of Indian women, in their present state of development, be induced to use a hospital, were it at their very door.

What the typical Indian woman wants in her hour of trial is the thing to which she is historically used—the midwife—the *dhai*. And the *dhai* is a creature that must indeed be seen to be credited.

According to the Hindu code, a woman in childbirth and in convalescence therefrom is ceremonially unclean, contaminating all that she touches. Therefore only those become *dhais* who are themselves of the unclean, "untouchable" class, the class whose filthy habits will be adduced by the orthodox Hindu as his good and sufficient reason for barring them from contact with himself. Again according to the Hindu code, a woman in childbirth, like the new-born child itself, is peculiarly susceptible to the "evil eye." Therefore no woman whose child has died, no one who has had an abortion, may, in many parts of India, serve as *dhai*, because of the malice or jealousy that may secretly inspire her. Neither may any widow so serve, being herself a thing of evil omen. Not all of these disqualifications obtain everywhere. But each holds in large sections.

Further, no sort of training is held necessary for the work. As a calling, it descends in families. At the death of a *dhai*, her daughter or daughter-in-law may adopt it, beginning at once to practice even though she has never seen a confinement[1] in all her life. But other women, outside the line of descent, may also take on the work and, if they are properly beyond the lines of the taboos, will find ready employment without any sort of preparation and for the mere asking.

Therefore, in total, you have the half-blind, the aged, the crippled, the palsied and the diseased, drawn from the dirtiest poor, as sole ministrants to the women of India in the most delicate, the most dangerous and the most important hour of their existence.

The expectant mother makes no preparations for the baby's coming—such as the getting ready of little garments. This would be taking dangerously for granted the favor of the gods. But she may and does toss into a shed or into a small dark chamber whatever soiled and disreputable rags, incapable of further use, fall from the hands of the household during the year.

And it is into this evil-smelling rubbish-hole that the young wife creeps when her hour is come upon her. "Unclean" she is, in her pain—unclean whatever she touches, and fit thereafter only to be destroyed. In the name of thrift, therefore, give her about her only the unclean and the worthless, whether human or inanimate. If there be a broken-legged, ragged string-cot, let her have that to lie upon; it can be saved in that same black chamber for the next to need it. Otherwise, make her a little support of cow-dung or of stones, on the bare earthen floor. And let no one waste effort in sweeping or dusting or washing the place till this occasion be over.

When the pains begin, send for the *dhai*. If the *dhai,* when the call reaches her, chances to be wearing decent clothes, she will stop, whatever the haste, to change into the rags she keeps for the purpose, infected and re-infected from the succession of diseased cases that have come into her practice. And so, at her dirtiest, a bearer of multiple contagions, she shuts herself in with her victim.

If there be an air-hole in the room, she stops it up with straw and refuse; fresh air is bad in confinements—it gives fever. If there be rags sufficient to make curtains, she cobbles them together, strings them across a corner and puts the patient within, against the wall, still farther to keep away the air. Then, to make darkness darker, she lights the tiniest glim—a bit of cord in a bit of oil, or a little kerosene lamp without a chimney, smoking villainously. Next, she makes a small charcoal fire in a pan beneath the bed or close by the patient's side, whence it joins its poisonous breath to the serried stenches.

The first *dhai* that I saw in action tossed upon this coal-pot, as I entered the room, a handful of some special vile-smelling stuff to ward off the evil eye—my evil eye. The smoke of it rose thick—also a tongue of flame. By that light one saw her Witch-of-Endor[2] face through its vermin-infested elf-locks, her hanging rags, her dirty claws, as she peered with festered and almost sightless eyes out over the stink-cloud she had raised. But it was not she who ran to quench the flame that caught in the bed and went writhing up the body of her unconscious patient. She was too blind—too dull of sense to see or to feel it.

If the delivery is at all delayed, the *dhai* is expected to explore for the reason of the delay. She thrusts her long-unwashed hand, loaded with dirty rings and bracelets and encrusted with untold living contaminations, into the patient's body, pulling and twisting at what she finds there. If the delivery is long delayed and difficult, a second or a third *dhai* may be called in, if the husband of the patient will

---

1. Childbirth.   2. A sorceress (see 1 Samuel 28:3–25).

sanction the expense, and the child may be dragged forth in detached sections— a leg or an arm torn off at a time.

Again to quote from a medical woman:

One often sees in cases of contracted pelvis due to osteomalacia, if there seems no chance of the head passing down [that the *dhai*] attempts to draw on the limbs, and, if possible, breaks them off. She prefers to extract the child *by main force,* and the patient in such cases is badly torn, often into her bladder, with the resulting large vesico-vaginal fistulae so common in Indian women, and which cause them so much misery.

Such labor may last three, four, five, even six days. During all this period the woman is given no nourishment whatever—such is the code—and the *dhai* resorts to all her traditions. She kneads the patient with her fists; stands her against the wall and butts her with her head; props her upright on the bare ground, seizes her hands and shoves against her thighs with gruesome bare feet, until, so the doctors state, the patient's flesh is often torn to ribbons by the *dhai's* long, ragged toe-nails. Or, she lays the woman flat and walks up and down her body, like one treading grapes. Also, she makes balls of strange substances, such as hollyhock roots, or dirty string, or rags full of quince-seeds; or earth, or earth mixed with cloves, butter and marigold flowers; or nuts, or spices—any irritant—and thrusts them into the uterus, to hasten the event. In some parts of the country, goats' hair, scorpions' stings, monkey-skulls, and snake-skins are considered valuable applications.

These insertions and the wounds they occasion commonly result in partial or complete permanent closing of the passage.

If the afterbirth be over five minutes in appearing, again the filthy, ringed and bracelet-loaded hand and wrist are thrust in, and the placenta is ripped loose and dragged away.

No clean clothes are provided for use in the confinement, and no hot water. Fresh cow-dung or goats' droppings, or hot ashes, however, often serve as heating agents when the patient's body begins to turn cold.

In Benares, sacred among cities, citadel of orthodox Hinduism, the sweepers, all of whom are "Untouchables," are divided into seven grades. From the first come the *dhais;* from the last and lowest come the "cord-cutters." To cut the umbilical cord is considered a task so degrading that in the Holy City even a sweep will not undertake it, unless she be at the bottom of her kind. Therefore the unspeakable *dhai* brings with her a still more unspeakable servant to wreak her quality upon the mother and the child in birth.

Sometimes it is a split bamboo that they use; sometimes a bit of an old tin can, or a rusty nail, or a potsherd or a fragment of broken glass. Sometimes, having no tool of their own and having found nothing sharp-edged lying about, they go out to the neighbors to borrow. I shall not soon forget the cry: "Hi, there, inside! Bring me back that knife! I hadn't finished paring my vegetables for dinner."

The end of the cut cord, at best, is left undressed, to take care of itself. In more careful and less happy cases, it is treated with a handful of earth, or with charcoal, or with several other substances, including cow-dung. Needless to add, a heavy per cent of such children as survive the strain of birth, die of lock-jaw or of erysipelas.[3]

---

3. Lock-jaw: tetanus, a bacterial infection that causes rigidity of the muscles and prolonged, painful muscle spasms; erysipelas: severe skin infection.

As the child is taken from the mother, it is commonly laid upon the bare floor, uncovered and unattended, until the *dhai* is ready to take it up. If it be a girl child, many simple rules have been handed down through the ages for discontinuing the unwelcome life then and there.

* * *

Evidence is in hand of educated, traveled and well-born Indians, themselves holders of European university degrees, who permit their wives to undergo this same inheritance of darkness. The case may be cited of an Indian medical man, holding an English University's Ph.D. and M.D. degrees, considered to be exceptionally able and brilliant and now actually in charge of a government center for the training of *dhais* in modern midwifery. His own young wife being recently confined, he yielded to the pressure of the elder women of his family and called in an old-school *dhai*, dirty and ignorant as the rest, to attend her. The wife died of puerperal fever;[4] the child died in the birth. "When we have the spectacle of even educated Indians with English degrees allowing their wives and children to be killed off like flies by ignorant midwives," says Doctor Vaughan again, "we can faintly imagine the sufferings of their humbler sisters."

But the question of station or of worldly goods has small part in the matter. To this the admirable sisterhood of English and American women doctors unites to testify.

Dr. Marion A. Wylie's words are:

These conditions are by no means confined to the poorest or most ignorant classes. I have attended the families of Rajahs, where many of these practices were carried out, and met with strenuous opposition when I introduced ventilation and aseptic measures.

A fractional percentage of the young wives are now found ready to accept modern medical help. But it is from the elder women of the household that resistance both determined and effective comes.

Says Dr. Agnes C. Scott, M.B., B.S., of the Punjab, one of the most distinguished of the many British medical women today giving their lives to India:

An educated man may desire a better-trained woman to attend on his wife, but he is helpless against the stone wall of ignorance and prejudice built and kept up by the older women of the *zenana*[5] who are the real rulers of the house.

Dr. K. O. Vaughan says upon this point:

The women are their own greatest enemies, and if any one can devise a system of education and enlightenment for grandmother, great-grandmother and great-great-grandmother which will persuade them not to employ the ignorant, dirty Bazaar *dhai*, they will deserve well of the Indian nation. In my opinion that is an impossible task.

And another woman surgeon adds:

Usually a mother-in-law or some ancient dame superintends the confinement, who is herself used to the old traditions and insists on their observance. . . . It has been the immemorial custom that the management of a confinement is the province of the leading woman of the house, and the men are powerless to interfere.

---

4. An infection of the lining of the uterus following childbirth, usually caused by unhygienic conditions and medical practice; also called "childbed fever."

5. Separate living quarters for women (Persian).

Thus arises a curious picture—the picture of the man who has since time immemorial enslaved his wife, and whose most vital need in all life, present and to come, is the getting of a son; and of this man, by means none other than the will of his willing slave, balked in his heart's desire! He has thought it good that she be kept ignorant; that she forever suppress her natural spirit and inclinations, walking ceremonially, in stiff harness, before him, her "earthly god." She has so walked, obedient from infancy to death, through untold centuries of merciless discipline, while he, from infancy to death, through untold centuries, has given himself no discipline at all. And now their harvests ripen in kind: hers a death-grip on the rock of the old law, making her dead-weight negative to any change, however merciful; his, a weakness of will and purpose, a fatigue of nerve and spirit, that deliver him in his own house, beaten, into the hands of his slave.

Of Indian babies born alive about 2,000,000 die each year. "Available statistics show," says the latest Census of India, "that over forty per cent. of the deaths of infants occur in the first week after birth, and over sixty per cent. in the first month."

The number of still births is heavy. Syphilis and gonorrhea[6] are among its main causes, to which must be added the sheer inability of the child to bear the strain of coming into the world.

Vital statistics are weak in India, for they must largely depend upon illiterate villagers as collectors. If a baby dies, the mother's wail trails down the darkness of a night or two. But if the village be near a river, the little body may just be tossed into the stream, without waste of a rag for a shroud. Kites and the turtles finish its brief history. And it is more than probable that no one in the village will think it worth while to report either the birth or the death. Statistics as to babies must therefore be taken as at best approximate.

It is probable, however, in view of existing conditions, that the actual figures of infant mortality, were it possible to know them, would surprise the western mind rather by their smallness than by their height. "I used to think," said one of the American medical women, "that a baby was a delicate creature. But experience here is forcing me to believe it the toughest fabric ever made, since it ever survives."

1927

6. Sexually transmitted infections.

CULTURAL COORDINATES
The Memsahib

> "Here as there [in England] the end object is not merely personal comfort but the formation of . . . that unit of civilisation where father and children, master and servant, employer and employed can learn their several duties. . . . An Indian household can no more be governed peacefully, without dignity and prestige, than an Indian Empire."
> —Flora Annie Steele and G. Gardiner,
> *The Complete Indian Housekeeper and Cook* (1902)

In colonial India, membsahib (akin to "mistress") was used as a form of address for a European or white woman. The memsahibs, who were typically British women, had been present since the arrival of the British East India Company but began arriving in India in noticeable numbers only after the establishment of direct colonial rule in 1857, following the Indian Mutiny (what some consider the country's first war of independence). The influx of British women to India coincided with the British government's efforts to pacify the country by taking direct political control, increasing the number of British bureaucrats, and enlarging the British army on the ground. With this increase in the number of British men in the colony came an increase in the number of British women, especially following the opening of the Suez Canal in 1869, when the voyage to India was considerably shortened. British women came out in numbers to join husbands, visit male relatives, and look for suitable husbands from among the civil servants, planters, and army officers stationed there. (The latter group of women was known derogatorily as "the fishing fleet.")

British women came out in numbers to join husbands, visit male relatives, and look for suitable husbands. . . .

The arrival in large numbers of memsahibs to the colony coincided with a radical shift in social relationships between British men and Indians. During the time of the East India Company's control, British men were known to socialize with Indians, invite them to their homes, and enter into romantic relationships with Indian women, even taking some as wives. After the British government's establishment of direct rule, and with increasing numbers of British women on the scene, the British created a more inward-looking and insular society, closely guarding their homes in what they considered an alien and hostile land. Indians increasingly came to be looked upon as social inferiors, and social interaction with them became taboo.

Natives often considered the memsahibs to be overbearing and arrogant. Many of the women, few of whom had experience with a large staff in their home country, were now surrounded by whole retinues of Indian servants, made possible by the colonial offices occupied by their husbands and male relatives. They led lives of trivial pursuit—throwing parties and engaging in social competition with other memsahibs—in a sea of poverty and deprivation. They closed ranks against native society, their acts of exclusion becoming assertions of a British femininity that, if not equal to the masculine task of running an empire, could at least contribute to it by maintaining a stable home front and breeding children. Ironically, they also transmitted Indian culture—curries, Kashmiri shawls, and jewelry—to Europe, as their diaries, letters, recipe books, and household manuals reveal.

The Young Lady's Toilet (1842) by Joseph Bouvier. Although this picture predates direct British rule by some years, it accurately depicts the lavish lifestyle of a European woman in British India.

Ellen Glasgow was raised to be a genteel southern lady but early on rebelled against the strictures of both her southern heritage and the expectations of the day for women. Deeply shocked by the discovery of her strict, religious father's longtime affair with a woman of color, she rejected his beliefs when she was a young woman and turned to contemporary philosophy, especially the ideas of Charles Darwin, Herbert Spencer, and John Stuart Mill. In becoming a writer, she defied her society's idea of what a wealthy young woman should be and do, but then she went even further by renouncing a notion of southern literature popular at the time that romanticized the "old South" with its belles, chivalrous gentlemen, and happy slaves. Her fiction sought to portray realistically strong individuals struggling against an often hostile world.

Born as the seventh of eight children to a wealthy Richmond, Virginia, family, Ellen Anderson Gholson Glasgow was educated at home in part because she was a delicate child. She would always suffer from poor health and in her adulthood developed severe hearing loss. She began her writing career in 1897 with the anonymous publication of *The Descendant,* a novel about a social outcast who is a radical journalist. She went on to publish nineteen more novels, among them many best sellers and one Pulitzer Prize winner, over the course of her forty-seven-year career; she also published a collection of poetry, a volume of short stories, and a book of literary criticism. Glasgow never married but revealed in her posthumous autobiography, *The Woman Within,* that she had had a long affair with a married man who lived in New York. During the early years of the twentieth century, she traveled extensively in Europe, making the liaison with him easier. The travel also allowed her to meet many of the best-known realist novelists, including Thomas Hardy, Joseph Conrad, and Henry James.

As she grew older, Glasgow came to believe that writing and romance were mutually exclusive. Her affair ended around 1906 when her lover died, and while she became engaged just before World War I, she broke off the engagement. Many of her novels from the 1910s and 1920s reflect her resolve to celebrate the hard work and strength of women instead of their involvement in romance. One of her best-known works, *Barren Ground* (1925), concerns a poor woman whose wealthy lover deserts her to marry his social peer, leaving her pregnant, alone, and with nowhere to turn. Although many novels of the time might have depicted the woman's death as the most fitting resolution to such a situation, for Glasgow, there is much more to the story. Instead of giving up, Dorinda Oakley (the heroine of the novel) keeps her child, returns after her father's death to save the family farm, and becomes the wealthiest farmer in her county. Her former lover, Jason, succumbs to alcoholism and tuberculosis. Glasgow celebrates an ideal of womanly strength that many readers find difficult because it is often joyless and does not include romantic love. But it provides quite a change from the depictions of the swooning belles of earlier southern fiction.

"Jordan's End," the story that appears below, seems at first to belong to the genre of gothic fiction: A doctor makes his way through a strange forest along an abandoned road to a rundown ancestral house where he finds a man suffering from hereditary insanity. It has all the hallmarks of a story by Edgar Allan Poe (another Virginia writer), and when the young doctor meets the beautiful but faded young wife and the three weird aunts, we expect a ghost story. But Glasgow has a different idea in mind: the story takes a surprising turn toward realism, and the twist that follows may be more shocking for the reader than a conventional gothic twist might be. Like many of Glasgow's other works, "Jordan's End" offers us a female figure of surprising resolve but offers little hope for a romantic solution to real problems.

Jordan's End

At the fork of the road there was the dead tree where buzzards were roosting, and through its boughs I saw the last flare of the sunset. On either side the November woods were flung in broken masses against the sky. When I stopped they appeared to move closer and surround me with vague, glimmering shapes. It seemed to me that I had been driving for hours; yet the ancient negro who brought the message had told me to follow the Old Stage Road till I came to Buzzard's Tree at the fork. "F'om dar on hit's moughty nigh ter Marse Jur'dn's place," the old man had assured me, adding tremulously, "en young Miss she sez you mus' come jes' ez quick ez you kin." I was young then (that was more than thirty years ago), and I was just beginning the practice of medicine in one of the more remote counties of Virginia.

My mare stopped, and leaning out, I gazed down each winding road, where it branched off, under half bared boughs, into the autumnal haze of the distance. In a little while the red would fade from the sky, and the chill night would find me still hesitating between those dubious ways which seemed to stretch into an immense solitude. While I waited uncertainly there was a stir in the boughs overhead, and a buzzard's feather floated down and settled slowly on the robe over my knees. In the effort to drive off depression, I laughed aloud and addressed my mare in a jocular tone:

"We'll choose the most God-forsaken of the two, and see where it leads us."

To my surprise the words brought an answer from the trees at my back. "If you're goin' to Isham's store, keep on the Old Stage Road," piped a voice from the underbrush.

Turning quickly, I saw the dwarfed figure of a very old man, with a hunched back, who was dragging a load of pine knots out of the woods. Though he was so stooped that his head reached scarcely higher than my wheel, he appeared to possess unusual vigour for one of his age and infirmities. He was dressed in a rough overcoat of some wood brown shade, beneath which I could see his overalls of blue jeans. Under a thatch of grizzled hair his shrewd little eyes twinkled cunningly, and his bristly chin jutted so far forward that it barely escaped the descending curve of his nose. I remember thinking that he could not be far from a hundred; his skin was so wrinkled and weather-beaten that, at a distance, I had mistaken him for a negro.

I bowed politely. "Thank you, but I am going to Jordan's End," I replied.

He cackled softly. "Then you take the bad road. Thar's Jur'dn's turnout." He pointed to the sunken trail, deep in mud, on the right. "An' if you ain't objectin' to a little comp'ny, I'd be obleeged if you'd give me a lift. I'm bound thar on my own o' count, an' it's a long ways to tote these here lightwood knots."

While I drew back my robe and made room for him, I watched him heave the load of resinous pine into the buggy, and then scramble with agility to his place at my side.

"My name is Peterkin," he remarked by way of introduction. "They call me Father Peterkin along o' the gran'child'en." He was a garrulous soul, I suspected, and would not be averse to imparting the information I wanted.

"There's not much travel this way," I began, as we turned out of the cleared space into the deep tunnel of the trees. Immediately the twilight enveloped us, though now and then the dusky glow in the sky was still visible. The air was sharp with the tang of autumn; with the effluvium of rotting leaves, the drift of wood smoke, the ripe flavour of crushed apples.

"Thar's nary a stranger, thoughten he was a doctor, been to Jur'dn's End as fur back as I kin recollect. Ain't you the new doctor?"

"Yes, I am the doctor." I glanced down at the gnomelike shape in the wood brown overcoat. "Is it much farther?"

"Naw, suh, we're all but thar jest as soon as we come out of Whitten woods."

"If the road is so little travelled, how do you happen to be going there?"

Without turning his head, the old man wagged his crescent shaped profile. "Oh, I live on the place. My son Tony works a slice of the farm on shares, and I manage to lend a hand at the harvest or corn shuckin', and, now-and-agen, with the cider. The old gentleman used to run the place that away afore he went deranged, an' now that the young one is laid up, thar ain't nobody to look arter the farm but Miss Judith. Them old ladies don't count. Thar's three of 'em, but they're all addle-brained an' look as if the buzzards had picked 'em. I reckon that comes from bein' shut up with crazy folks in that thar old tumbledown house. The roof ain't been patched fur so long that the shingles have most rotted away, an' thar's times, Tony says, when you kin skearcely hear yo' years fur the rumpus the wrens an' rats are makin' overhead."

"What is the trouble with them—the Jordans, I mean?"

"Jest run to seed, suh, I reckon."

"Is there no man of the family left?"

For a minute Father Peterkin made no reply. Then he shifted the bundle of pine knots, and responded warily. "Young Alan, he's still livin' on the old place, but I hear he's been took now, an' is goin' the way of all the rest of 'em. 'Tis a hard trial for Miss Judith, po' young thing, an' with a boy nine year old that's the very spit an' image of his pa. Wall, wall, I kin recollect away back yonder when old Mr. Timothy Jur'dn was the proudest man anywhar aroun' in these parts; but arter the War things sorter begun to go down hill with him, and he was obleeged to draw in his horns."

"Is he still living?"

The old man shook his head. "Mebbe he is, an' mebbe he ain't. Nobody knows but the Jur'dn's, an' they ain't tellin' fur the axin'."

"I suppose it was this Miss Judith who sent for me?"

"'Twould most likely be she, suh. She was one of the Yardlys that lived over yonder at Yardly's Field; an' when young Mr. Alan begun to take notice of her, 'twas the first time sence way back that one of the Jur'dn's had gone courtin' outside the family. That's the reason the blood went bad like it did, I reckon. Thar's a sayin' down aroun' here that Jur'dn an' Jur'dn won't mix." The name was invariably called Jurdin by all classes; but I had already discovered that names are rarely pronounced as they are spelled in Virginia.

"Have they been married long?"

"Ten years or so, suh. I remember as well as if 'twas yestiddy the day young Alan brought her home as a bride, an' thar warn't a soul besides the three daft old ladies to welcome her. They drove over in my son Tony's old buggy, though 'twas spick an' span then. I was goin' to the house on an arrant, an' I was standin' right down thar at the ice pond when they come by. She hadn't been much in these parts, an' none of us had ever seed her afore. When she looked up at young Alan her face was pink all over and her eyes war shinin' bright as the moon. Then the front do' opened an' them old ladies, as black as crows, flocked out on the po'ch. Thar never was anybody as peart-lookin' as Miss Judith was when she come here; but soon arterwards she begun to peak an' pine, though she never lost her sperits an' went mopin roun' like all the other women folks at Jur'dn's End. They married sudden, an' folks do say she didn't know nothin' about the family, an' young Alan didn't know much mo' than she did. The old ladies had kep' the secret away from him, sorter believin' that what you don't know cyarn' hurt you. Anyways they never let it leak out tell arter his chile was born. Thar ain't never been but that one, an' old Aunt Jerusly declars he was born with a caul over his face, so mebbe things will be all right fur him in the long run."

"But who are the old ladies? Are their husbands living?"

When Father Peterkin answered the question he had dropped his voice to a hoarse murmur. "Deranged. All gone deranged," he replied.

I shivered, for a chill expression seemed to emanate from the November woods. As we drove on, I remembered grim tales of enchanted forests filled with evil faces and whispering voices. The scents of wood earth and rotting leaves invaded my brain like a magic spell. On either side the forest was as still as death. Not a leaf quivered, not a bird moved, not a small wild creature stirred in the underbrush. Only the glossy leaves and the scarlet berries of the holly appeared alive amid the bare interlacing branches of the trees. I began to long for an autumn clearing and the red light of the afterglow.

"Are they living or dead?" I asked presently.

"I've hearn strange tattle," answered the old man nervously, "but nobody kin tell. Folks do say as young Alan's pa is shut up in a padded place, and that his gran'pa died thar arter thirty years. His uncles went crazy too, an' the daftness is beginnin' to crop out in the women. Up tell now it has been mostly the men. One time I remember old Mr. Peter Jur'dn tryin' to burn down the place in the dead of the night. Thar's the end of the wood, suh. If you'll jest let me down here, I'll be gittin' along home across the old-field, an' thanky too."

At last the woods ended abruptly on the edge of an abandoned field which was thickly sown with scrub pine and broomsedge. The glow in the sky had faded now to a thin yellow-green, and a melancholy twilight pervaded the landscape. In this twilight I looked over the few sheep huddled together on the rugged lawn, and saw the old brick house crumbling beneath its rank growth of ivy. As I drew nearer I had the feeling that the surrounding desolation brooded there like some sinister influence.

Forlorn as it appeared at this first approach, I surmised that Jordan's End must have possessed once charm as well as distinction. The proportions of the Georgian front were impressive, and there was beauty of design in the quaint doorway, and in the steps of rounded stone which were brocaded now with a pattern of emerald moss. But the whole place was badly in need of repair. Looking up, as I stopped, I saw that the eaves were falling away, that crumbled shutters were sagging from loosened hinges, that odd scraps of hemp sacking or oil cloth were stuffed into windows where panes were missing. When I stepped on the floor of the porch, I felt the rotting boards give way under my feet.

After thundering vainly on the door, I descended the steps, and followed the beaten path that led round the west wing of the house. When I had passed an old boxwood tree at the corner, I saw a woman and a boy of nine years or so come out of a shed, which I took to be the smokehouse, and begin to gather chips from the woodpile. The woman carried a basket made of splits on her arm, and while she stooped to fill this, she talked to the child in a soft musical voice. Then, at a sound that I made, she put the basket aside, and rising to her feet, faced me in the pallid light from the sky. Her head was thrown back, and over her dress of some dark calico, a tattered gray shawl clung to her figure. That was thirty years ago; I am not young any longer; I have been in many countries since then, and looked on many women; but her face, with that wan light on it, is the last one I shall forget in my life. Beauty! Why, that woman will be beautiful when she is a skeleton, was the thought that flashed into my mind.

She was very tall, and so thin that her flesh seemed faintly luminous, as if an inward light pierced the transparent substance. It was the beauty, not of earth, but of triumphant spirit. Perfection, I suppose, is the rarest thing we achieve in this world of incessant compromise with inferior forms; yet the woman who stood there in that ruined place appeared to me to have stepped straight out of legend or allegory. The contour of her face was Italian in its pure oval; her hair swept in wings of dusk above her clear forehead; and, from the faintly shadowed hollows beneath her brows, the eyes that looked at me were purple-black, like dark pansies.

"I had given you up," she began in a low voice, as if she were afraid of being overheard. "You are the doctor?"

"Yes, I am the doctor. I took the wrong road and lost my way. Are you Mrs. Jordan?"

She bowed her head. "Mrs. Alan Jordan. There are three Mrs. Jordans besides myself. My husband's grandmother and the wives of his two uncles."

"And it is your husband who is ill?"

"My husband, yes. I wrote a few days ago to Doctor Carstairs." (Thirty years ago Carstairs, of Baltimore, was the leading alienist[1] in the country.) "He is coming to-morrow morning; but last night my husband was so restless that I sent for you to-day." Her rich voice, vibrating with suppressed feeling, made me think of stained glass windows and low organ music.

"Before we go in," I asked, "will you tell me as much as you can?"

Instead of replying to my request, she turned and laid her hand on the boy's shoulder. "Take the chips to Aunt Agatha, Benjamin," she said, "and tell her that the doctor has come."

While the child picked up the basket and ran up the sunken steps to the door, she watched him with breathless anxiety. Not until he had disappeared into the hall did she lift her eyes to my face again. Then, without answering my question, she murmured, with a sigh which was like the voice of that autumn evening, "We were once happy here." She was trying, I realized, to steel her heart against the despair that threatened it.

---

1. A psychiatrist.

My gaze swept the obscure horizon, and returned to the mouldering wood-pile where we were standing. The yellow-green had faded from the sky, and the only light came from the house where a few scattered lamps were burning. Through the open door I could see the hall, as bare as if the house were empty, and the spiral staircase which crawled to the upper story. A fine old place once, but repulsive now in its abject decay, like some young blood of former days who has grown senile.

"Have you managed to wring a living out of the land?" I asked, because I could think of no words that were less compassionate.

"At first a poor one," she answered slowly. "We worked hard, harder than any negro in the fields, to keep things together, but we were happy. Then three years ago this illness came, and after that everything went against us. In the beginning it was simply brooding, a kind of melancholy, and we tried to ward it off by pretending that it was not real, that we imagined it. Only of late, when it became so much worse, have we admitted the truth, have we faced the reality—"

This passionate murmur, which had almost the effect of a chant rising out of the loneliness, was addressed, not to me, but to some abstract and implacable power. While she uttered it her composure was like the tranquillity of the dead. She did not lift her hand to hold her shawl, which was slipping unnoticed from her shoulders, and her eyes, so like dark flowers in their softness, did not leave my face.

"If you will tell me all, perhaps I may be able to help you," I said.

"But you know our story," she responded. "You must have heard it."

"Then it is true? Heredity, intermarriage, insanity?"

She did not wince at the bluntness of my speech. "My husband's grandfather is in an asylum, still living after almost thirty years. His father—my husband's, I mean—died there a few years ago. Two of his uncles are there. When it began I don't know, or how far back it reaches. We have never talked of it. We have tried always to forget it—Even now I cannot put the thing into words—My husband's mother died of a broken heart, but the grandmother and the two others are still living. You will see them when you go into the house. They are old women now, and they feel nothing."

"And there have been other cases?"

"I do not know. Are not four enough?"

"Do you know if it has assumed always the same form?" I was trying to be as brief as I could.

She flinched, and I saw that her unnatural calm was shaken at last. "The same, I believe. In the beginning there is melancholy, moping, Grandmother calls it, and then—" She flung out her arms with a despairing gesture, and I was reminded again of some tragic figure of legend.

"I know, I know," I was young, and in spite of my pride, my voice trembled. "Has there been in any case partial recovery, recurring at intervals?"

"In his grandfather's case, yes. In the others none. With them it has been hopeless from the beginning."

"And Carstairs is coming?"

"In the morning. I should have waited, but last night—" Her voice broke, and she drew the tattered shawl about her with a shiver. "Last night something happened. Something happened," she repeated, and could not go on. Then, collecting her strength with an effort which made her tremble like a blade of grass in the wind, she continued more quietly, "To-day he has been better. For the first time he has slept, and I have been able to leave him. Two of the hands from the fields are in the room." Her tone changed suddenly, and a note of energy passed into it. Some obscure resolution brought a tinge of colour to her pale cheek. "I must know," she added. "if this is as hopeless as all the others."

I took a step toward the house. "Carstairs's opinion is worth as much as that of any man living," I answered.

"But will he tell me the truth?"

I shook my head. "He will tell you what he thinks. No man's judgment is infallible."

Turning away from me, she moved with an energetic step to the house. As I followed her into the hall the threshold creaked under my tread, and I was visited by an apprehension, or, if you prefer, by a superstitious dread of the floor above. Oh, I got over that kind of thing before I was many years older; though in the end I gave up medicine, you know, and turned to literature as a safer outlet for a suppressed imagination.

But the dread was there at that moment, and it was not lessened by the glimpse I caught, at the foot of the spiral staircase, of a scantily furnished room, where three lean black-robed figures, as impassive as the Fates, were grouped in front of a wood fire. They were doing something with their hands. Knitting, crocheting, or plaiting straw?

At the head of the stairs the woman stopped and looked back at me. The light from the kerosene lamp on the wall fell over her, and I was struck afresh not only by the alien splendour of her beauty, but even more by the look of consecration, of impassioned fidelity that illumined her face.

"He is very strong," she said in a whisper. "Until this trouble came on him he had never had a day's illness in his life. We hoped that hard work, not having time to brood, might save us; but it has only brought the thing we feared sooner."

There was a question in her eyes, and I responded in the same subdued tone. "His health, you say, is good?" What else was there for me to ask when I understood everything?

A shudder ran through her frame. "We used to think that a blessing, but now—" She broke off and then added in a lifeless voice, "We keep two field hands in the room day and night, lest one should forget to watch the fire, or fall asleep."

A sound came from a room at the end of the hall, and, without finishing her sentence, she moved swiftly toward the closed door. The apprehension, the dread, or whatever you choose to call it, was so strong upon me, that I was seized by an impulse to turn and retreat down the spiral staircase. Yes, I know why some men turn cowards in battle.

"I have come back, Alan," she said in a voice that wrung my heartstrings.

The room was dimly lighted; and for a minute after I entered, I could see nothing clearly except the ruddy glow of the wood fire in front of which two negroes were seated on low wooden stools. They had kindly faces, these men; there was a primitive humanity in their features, which might have been modelled out of the dark earth of the fields.

Looking round the next minute, I saw that a young man was sitting away from the fire, huddled over in a cretonne-covered chair with a high back and deep wings. At our entrance the negroes glanced up with surprise; but the man in the winged chair neither lifted his head nor turned his eyes in our direction. He sat there, lost within the impenetrable wilderness of the insane, as remote from us and from the sound of our voices as if he were the inhabitant of an invisible world. His head was sunk forward; his eyes were staring fixedly at some image we could not see; his fingers, moving restlessly, were plaiting and unplaiting the fringe of a plaid shawl. Distraught as he was, he still possessed the dignity of mere physical perfection. At his full height he must have measured not under six feet three; his hair was the colour of ripe wheat, and his eyes, in spite of their fixed gaze, were as blue as the sky after rain. And this was only the beginning, I realized. With that constitution, that physical frame, he might live to be ninety.

"Alan!" breathed his wife again in her pleading murmur.

If he heard her voice, he gave no sign of it. Only when she crossed the room and bent over his chair, he put out his hand, with a gesture of irritation, and pushed her away, as if she were a veil of smoke which came between him and the object at which he was looking. Then his hand fell back to its old place, and he resumed his mechanical plaiting of the fringe.

The woman lifted her eyes to mine. "His father did that for twenty years," she said in a whisper that was scarcely more than a sigh of anguish.

When I had made my brief examination, we left the room as we had come, and descended the stairs together. The three old women were still sitting in front of the wood fire. I do not think they had moved since we went upstairs; but, as we reached the hall below, one of them, the youngest, I imagine, rose from her chair, and came out to join us. She was crocheting something soft and small, an infant's sacque, I perceived as she approached, of pink wool. The ball had rolled from her lap as she stood up, and it trailed after her now, like a woolen rose, on the bare floor. When the skein pulled at her, she turned back and stooped to pick up the ball, which she rewound with caressing fingers. Good God, an infant's sacque in that house!

"Is it the same thing?" she asked.

"Hush!" responded the younger woman kindly. Turning to me she added, "We cannot talk here," and opening the door, passed out on the porch. Not until we had reached the lawn, and walked in silence to where my buggy stood beneath an old locust tree, did she speak again.

Then she said only, "You know now?"

"Yes, I know," I replied, averting my eyes from her face while I gave my directions as briefly as I could. "I will leave an opiate," I said. "To-morrow, if Carstairs should not come, send for me again. If he does come," I added, "I will talk to him and see you afterward."

"Thank you," she answered gently; and taking the bottle from my hand, she turned away and walked quickly back to the house.

I watched her as long as I could; and then getting into my buggy, I turned my mare's head toward the woods, and drove by moonlight, past Buzzard's Tree and over the Old Stage Road, to my home. "I will see Carstairs to-morrow," was my last thought that night before I slept.

But, after all, I saw Carstairs only for a minute as he was taking the train. Life at its beginning and its end had filled my morning; and when at last I reached the little station, Carstairs had paid his visit, and was waiting on the platform for the approaching express. At first he showed a disposition to question me about the shooting, but as soon as I was able to make my errand clear, his jovial face clouded.

"So you've been there?" he said. "They didn't tell me. An interesting case, if it were not for that poor woman. Incurable, I'm afraid, when you consider the predisposing causes. The race is pretty well deteriorated, I suppose. God! what isolation! I've advised her to send him away. There are three others, they tell me, at Staunton."

The train came; he jumped on it, and was whisked away while I gazed after him. After all, I was none the wiser because of the great reputation of Carstairs.

All that day I heard nothing more from Jordan's End; and then, early next morning, the same decrepit negro brought me a message.

"Young Miss, she tole me ter ax you ter come along wid me jes' ez soon ez you kin git ready."

"I'll start at once, Uncle, and I'll take you with me."

My mare and buggy stood at the door. All I needed to do was to put on my overcoat, pick up my hat, and leave word, for a possible patient, that I should return before noon. I knew the road now, and I told myself, as I set out, that I would make as quick a trip as I could. For two nights I had been haunted by the memory of that man in the armchair, plaiting and unplaiting the fringe of the plaid shawl. And his father had done that, the woman had told me, for twenty years!

It was a brown autumn morning, raw, windless, with an overcast sky and a peculiar illusion of nearness about the distance. A high wind had blown all night, but at dawn it had dropped suddenly, and now there was not so much as a ripple in the broomsedge. Over the fields when we came out of the woods, the thin trails of blue smoke were as motionless as cobwebs. The lawn surrounding the house looked smaller than it had appeared to me in the twilight, as if the barren fields had drawn closer since my last visit. Under the trees, where the few sheep were browsing, the piles of leaves lay in windrifts along the sunken walk and against the wings of the house.

When I knocked the door was opened immediately by one of the old women, who held a streamer of black cloth or rusty crape in her hands.

"You may go straight upstairs," she croaked; and, without waiting for an explanation, I entered the hall quickly, and ran up the stairs.

The door of the room was closed, and I opened it noiselessly, and stepped over the threshold. My first sensation, as I entered, was one of cold. Then I saw that the windows were wide open, and that the room seemed to be full of people, though, as I made out presently, there was no one there except Alan Jordan's wife, her little son, the two old aunts, and an aged crone of a negress. On the bed there was something under a yellowed sheet of fine linen (what the negroes call "a burial sheet," I suppose), which had been handed down from some more affluent generation.

When I went over, after a minute, and turned down one corner of the covering, I saw that my patient of the other evening was dead. Not a line of pain marred his features, not a thread of gray dimmed the wheaten gold of his hair. So he must have looked, I thought, when she first loved him. He had gone from life, not old, enfeebled and repulsive, but enveloped still in the romantic illusion of their passion.

As I entered, the two old women, who had been fussing about the bed, drew back to make way for me, but the witch of a negress did not pause in the weird chant, an incantation of some sort, which she was mumbling. From the rag carpet in front of the empty fireplace, the boy, with his father's hair and his mother's eyes, gazed at me silently, broodingly, as if I were trespassing; and by the open window, with her eyes on the ashen November day, the young wife stood as motionless as a statue. While I looked at her a redbird flew out of the boughs of a cedar, and she followed it with her eyes.

"You sent for me?" I said to her.

She did not turn. She was beyond the reach of my voice, of any voice, I imagine; but one of the palsied old women answered my question.

"He was like this when we found him this morning," she said. "He had a bad night, and Judith and the two hands were up with him until daybreak. Then he seemed to fall asleep, and Judith sent the hands, turn about, to get their breakfast."

While she spoke my eyes were on the bottle I had left there. Two nights ago it had been full, and now it stood empty, without a cork, on the mantelpiece. They had not even thrown it away. It was typical of the pervading inertia of the place that the bottle should still be standing there awaiting my visit.

For an instant the shock held me speechless; when at last I found my voice it was to ask mechanically.

"When did it happen?"

The old woman who had spoken took up the story. "Nobody knows. We have not touched him. No one but Judith has gone near him." Her words trailed off into unintelligible muttering. If she had ever had her wits about her, I dare-say fifty years at Jordan's End had unsettled them completely.

I turned to the woman at the window. Against the gray sky and the black intersecting branches of the cedar, her head, with its austere perfection, was surrounded by that visionary air of legend. So Antigone might have looked on the day of her sacrifice, I reflected. I had never seen a creature who appeared so withdrawn, so detached, from all human associations. It was as if some spiritual isolation divided her from her kind.

"I can do nothing," I said.

For the first time she looked at me, and her eyes were unfathomable. "No, you can do nothing," she answered. "He is safely dead."

The negress was still crooning on; the other old women were fussing helplessly. It was impossible in their presence, I felt, to put in words the thing I had to say.

"Will you come downstairs with me?" I asked. "Outside of this house?"

Turning quietly, she spoke to the boy. "Run out and play, dear. He would have wished it."

Then, without a glance toward the bed, or the old women gathered about it, she followed me over the threshold, down the stairs, and out on the deserted lawn. The ashen day could not touch her, I saw then. She was either so remote from it, or so completely a part of it, that she was impervious to its sadness. Her white face did not become more pallid as the light struck it; her tragic eyes did not grow deeper; her frail figure under the thin shawl did not shiver in the raw air. She felt nothing, I realized suddenly.

Wrapped in that silence as in a cloak, she walked across the windrifts of leaves to where my mare was waiting. Her step was so slow, so unhurried, that I remember thinking she moved like one who had all eternity before her. Oh, one has strange impressions, you know, at such moments!

In the middle of the lawn, where the trees had been stripped bare in the night, and the leaves were piled in long mounds like double graves, she stopped and looked in my face. The air was so still that the whole place might have been in a trance or asleep. Not a branch moved, not a leaf rustled on the ground, not a sparrow twittered in the ivy; and even the few sheep stood motionless, as if they were under a spell. Farther away, beyond the sea of broomsedge, where no wind stirred, I saw the flat desolation of the landscape. Nothing moved on the earth, but high above, under the leaden clouds, a buzzard was sailing.

I moistened my lips before I spoke. "God knows I want to help you!" At the back of my brain a hideous question was drumming. How had it happened? Could she have killed him? Had that delicate creature nerved her will to the unspeakable act? It was incredible. It was inconceivable. And yet. . . .

"The worst is over," she answered quietly, with that tearless agony which is so much more terrible than any outburst of grief. "Whatever happens, I can never go through the worst again. Once in the beginning he wanted to die. His great fear was that he might live too long, until it was too late to save himself. I made him wait then. I held him back by a promise."

So she had killed him, I thought. Then she went on steadily, after a minute, and I doubted again.

"Thank God, it was easier for him than he feared it would be," she murmured.

No, it was not conceivable. He must have bribed one of the negroes. But who had stood by and watched without intercepting? Who had been in the room? Well, either way! "I will do all I can to help you," I said.

Her gaze did not waver. "There is so little that any one can do now," she responded, as if she had not understood what I meant. Suddenly, without the warning of a sob, a cry of despair went out of her, as if it were torn from her breast. "He was my life," she cried, "and I must go on!"

So full of agony was the sound that it seemed to pass like a gust of wind over the broomsedge. I waited until the emptiness had opened and closed over it. Then I asked as quietly as I could:

"What will you do now?"

She collected herself with a shudder of pain. "As long as the old people live, I am tied here. I must bear it out to the end. When they die, I shall go away and find work. I am sending my boy to school. Doctor Carstairs will look after him, and he will help me when the time comes. While my boy needs me, there is no release."

While I listened to her, I knew that the question on my lips would never be uttered. I should always remain ignorant of the truth. The thing I feared most, standing there alone with her, was that some accident might solve the mystery before I could escape. My eyes left her face and wandered over the dead leaves at our feet. No, I had nothing to ask her.

"Shall I come again?" That was all.

She shook her head. "Not unless I send for you. If I need you, I will send for you," she answered; but in my heart I knew that she would never send for me.

I held out my hand, but she did not take it; and I felt that she meant me to understand, by her refusal, that she was beyond all consolation and all companionship. She was nearer to the bleak sky and the deserted fields than she was to her kind.

As she turned away, the shawl slipped from her shoulders to the dead leaves over which she was walking; but she did not stoop to recover it, nor did I make a movement to follow her. Long after she had entered the house I stood there, gazing down on the garment that she had dropped. Then climbing into my buggy, I drove slowly across the field and into the woods.

1923

◦◄ WILLA CATHER ►◦
1873–1947

Although best known for her writings about the American Midwest and West, Willa Cather actually lived most of her life in the urban East. She was born in Virginia and moved to rural Nebraska when she was ten and then into the town of Red Cloud a year later. She graduated from the University of Nebraska in Lincoln in 1895 and moved to Pittsburgh, where she worked as an editor for a women's magazine and taught English and Latin. In 1906, she moved to New York City to work for *McClure's Magazine* and lived there the rest of her life. The tension this suggests between her love of and respect for a rural way of life and her choice to stay in the city is just one of the complexities inherent in Cather's life and work. Her work often focuses on strong women, but she never accepted the label of feminist; she celebrated sophistication and the arts but mourned the loss of a simpler way of life.

Cather was an intensely private person—she burned as many of her letters as she could and left instructions that none of her remaining letters could be published—so some things we do not know about her life for a certainty. What we do know is that she was uncomfortable with the feminine role as it was prescribed during her youth. For four years, from age fifteen to nineteen, she cut her hair short, wore masculine clothing, and signed her name "William Cather." We also know that from 1901 to 1906 she lived with the McClung family and shared a room with Isabelle McClung, who was to be her lifelong friend. According to her biographer, Sharon O'Brien, McClung was the love of Cather's life, even though Cather was to live with her companion, Edith Lewis, from 1908 until her death. Critics have argued that Cather's work, especially her fascination with strong female characters, reveals a lesbian sensibility; others point to the importance of heterosexual love relationships in her work.

Whatever Cather's love life, we know that from an early age a good deal of her emotional energy was given to art, literature, music, and theater. She began writing reviews while she was still a college student and worked for many years in magazine publishing before she turned to writing full-time. Among her twelve novels are American classics like *O Pioneers!* (1913) and *My Ántonia* (1918), and she published short fiction, essays, and poetry as well. Her literary career was successful, though she was never entirely satisfied with it.

"A Wagner Matinee," though it appeared early in Cather's career, typifies many of the themes of her later work, especially the contrast between the life of the city—with its art, music, and comparative wealth—and the life of the prairie—full of hardship, brutal labor, long hours, and poverty. Hers is not an unbalanced view of this contrast; she sees the beauty of both ways of life. Like many of her finest novels, the story delves into the character of the narrator and uses differences between the city and the country to reveal his personality. Everything in the story is filtered through what he imagines his Aunt Georgiana is feeling and what he remembers about the time he spent during his childhood on the farm with her. We see Cather's use of a first-person male narrator, a technique she would use in *My Ántonia,* and perhaps a suggestion of how constricting she found the feminine role. Finally, we see Cather trying to capture the sense of how powerful a force art can be in a person's life, how it can call up something profound in us, even if our external life seems tremendously remote from the aesthetic world.

A Wagner[1] Matinee

I received one morning a letter, written in pale ink on glassy, blue-lined note-paper, and bearing the postmark of a little Nebraska village. This communication, worn and rubbed, looking as though it had been carried for some days in a coat pocket that was none too clean, was from my uncle Howard and informed me that his wife had been left a small legacy by a bachelor relative who had recently died, and that it would be necessary for her to go to Boston to attend the settling of the estate. He requested me to meet her at the station and render her whatever services might be necessary. On examining the date indicated as that of her arrival, I found it no later than tomorrow. He had characteristically delayed writing until, had I been away from home for a day, I must have missed the good woman altogether.

The name of my Aunt Georgiana called up not alone her own figure, at once pathetic and grotesque, but opened before my feet a gulf of recollection so wide and deep that, as the letter dropped from my hand, I felt suddenly a stranger to all the present conditions of my existence, wholly ill at ease and out of place amid the familiar surroundings of my study. I became, in short, the gangling farmer-boy my aunt had known, scourged with chilblains and bashfulness, my hands cracked and sore from the corn husking. I felt the knuckles of my thumb tentatively, as though they were raw again. I sat again before her parlour organ, fumbling the scales with my stiff, red hands, while she, beside me, made canvas mittens for the huskers.

The next morning, after preparing my landlady somewhat, I set out for the station. When the train arrived I had some difficulty in finding my aunt. She was the last of the passengers to alight, and it was not until I got her into the carriage that she seemed really to recognize me. She had come all the way in a day coach; her linen duster had become black with soot and her black bonnet grey with dust during the journey. When we arrived at my boarding-house the landlady put her to bed at once and I did not see her again until the next morning.

Whatever shock Mrs. Springer experienced at my aunt's appearance, she considerately concealed. As for myself, I saw my aunt's misshapen figure with that feeling of awe and respect for which we behold explorers who have left their ears and fingers north of Franz Josef Land, or their health somewhere along the Upper Congo.[2] My Aunt Georgiana had been a music teacher at the Boston Conservatory, somewhere back in the latter sixties. One summer, while visiting the little village among the Green Mountains where her ancestors had dwelt for generations, she had kindled the callow fancy of the most idle and shiftless of all the village lads, and had conceived for this Howard Carpenter one of those extravagant passions which a handsome country boy of twenty-one sometimes inspires in an angular, spectacled woman of thirty. When she returned to her duties in Boston, Howard followed her, and the upshot of this inexplicable infatuation was that she eloped with him, eluding the reproaches of her family and the criticisms of her friends by

1. German composer Richard Wagner (1813–83).
2. Franz Josef Land: an archipelago in the Arctic Ocean, north of Russia; Upper Congo: a river in central Africa, in what is now the Democratic Republic of the Congo, whose rugged terrain and malarial pools withstood Western efforts at exploration until the American journalist Henry Morton Stanley (1840–1904) partially explored the river in 1867.

going with him to the Nebraska frontier. Carpenter, who, of course, had no money, had taken a homestead in Red Willow County, fifty miles from the railroad. There they had measured off their quarter section themselves by driving across the prairie in a wagon, to the wheel of which they had tied a red cotton handkerchief, and counting off its revolutions. They built a dugout in the red hillside, one of those cave dwellings whose inmates so often reverted to primitive conditions. Their water they got from the lagoons where the buffalo drank, and their slender stock of provisions was always at the mercy of bands of roving Indians. For thirty years my aunt had not been farther than fifty miles from the homestead.

But Mrs. Springer knew nothing of all this, and must have been considerably shocked at what was left of my kinswoman. Beneath the soiled linen duster which, on her arrival, was the most conspicuous feature of her costume, she wore a black stuff dress, whose ornamentation showed that she had surrendered herself unquestioningly into the hands of a country dressmaker. My poor aunt's figure, however, would have presented astonishing difficulties to any dressmaker. Originally stooped, her shoulders were now almost bent together over her sunken chest. She wore no stays, and her gown, which trailed unevenly behind, rose in a sort of peak over her abdomen. She wore ill-fitting false teeth, and her skin was as yellow as a Mongolian's from constant exposure to a pitiless wind and to the alkaline water which hardens the most transparent cuticle into a sort of flexible leather.

I owed to this woman most of the good that ever came my way in my boyhood, and had a reverential affection for her. During the years when I was riding herd for my uncle, my aunt, after cooking the three meals—the first of which was ready at six o'clock in the morning—and putting the six children to bed, would often stand until midnight at her ironing-board, with me at the kitchen table beside her, hearing me recite Latin declensions and conjugations, gently shaking me when my drowsy head sank down over a page of irregular verbs. It was to her, at her ironing or mending, that I read my first Shakespere, and her old text-book on mythology was the first that ever came into my empty hands. She taught me my scales and exercises, too—on the little parlour organ which her husband had bought her after fifteen years, during which she had not so much as seen any instrument, but an accordion that belonged to one of the Norwegian farm-hands. She would sit beside me by the hour, darning and counting, while I struggled with the "Joyous Farmer," but she seldom talked to me about music, and I understood why. She was a pious woman; she had the consolations of religion and, to her at least, her martyrdom was not wholly sordid. Once when I had been doggedly beating out some easy passages from an old score of *Euryanthe*[3] I had found among her music books, she came up to me and, putting her hands over my eyes, gently drew my head back upon her shoulder, saying tremulously, "Don't love it so well, Clark, or it may be taken from you. Oh! dear boy, pray that whatever your sacrifice may be, it be not that."

When my aunt appeared on the morning after her arrival, she was still in a semi-somnambulant state. She seemed not to realize that she was in the city where she had spent her youth, the place longed for hungrily half a lifetime. She had been so wretchedly train-sick throughout the journey that she had no recollection of anything but her discomfort, and, to all intents and purposes, there were but a few hours of nightmare between the farm in Red Willow County and my study on

3. An 1823 opera by German composer Carl Maria von Weber (1786–1826).

Newbury Street. I had planned a little pleasure for her that afternoon, to repay her for some of the glorious moments she had given me when we used to milk together in the strawthatched cowshed and she, because I was more than usually tired, or because her husband had spoken sharply to me, would tell me of the splendid performance of the *Huguenots*[4] she had seen in Paris, in her youth. At two o'clock the Symphony Orchestra was to give a Wagner programme, and I intended to take my aunt; though, as I conversed with her, I grew doubtful about her enjoyment of it. Indeed, for her own sake, I could only wish her taste for such things quite dead, and the long struggle mercifully ended at last. I suggested our visiting the Conservatory and the Common before lunch, but she seemed altogether too timid to wish to venture out. She questioned me absently about various changes in the city, but she was chiefly concerned that she had forgotten to leave instructions about feeding half-skimmed milk to a certain weakling calf, "old Maggie's calf, you know, Clark," she explained, evidently having forgotten how long I had been away. She was further troubled because she had neglected to tell her daughter about the freshly-opened kit of mackerel in the cellar, which would spoil if it were not used directly.

I asked her whether she had ever heard any of the Wagnerian operas, and found that she had not, though she was perfectly familiar with their respective situations, and had once possessed the piano score of *The Flying Dutchman*.[5] I began to think it would have been best to get her back to Red Willow County without waking her, and regretted having suggested the concert.

From the time we entered the concert hall, however, she was a trifle less passive and inert, and for the first time seemed to perceive her surroundings. I had felt some trepidation lest she might become aware of the absurdities of her attire, or might experience some painful embarrassment at stepping suddenly into the world to which she had been dead for more than a quarter of a century. But, again, I found how superficially I had judged her. She sat looking about her with eyes as impersonal, almost as stony, as those with which the granite Rameses[6] in a museum watches the froth and fret that ebbs and flows about his pedestal—separated from it by the lonely stretch of centuries. I have seen this same aloofness in old miners who drift into the Brown Hotel at Denver, their pockets full of bullion, their linen soiled, their haggard faces unshaven; standing in the thronged corridors as solitary as though they were still in a frozen camp on the Yukon, conscious that certain experiences have isolated them from their fellows by a gulf no haberdasher could bridge.

We sat at the extreme left of the first balcony, facing the arc of our own and the balcony above us, veritable hanging gardens, brilliant as tulip beds. The matinée audience was made up chiefly of women. One lost the contour of faces and figures, indeed any effect of line whatever, and there was only the colour of bodices past counting, the shimmer of fabrics soft and firm, silky and sheer; red, mauve, pink, blue, lilac, purple, ecru, rose, yellow, cream, and white, all the colours that an impressionist finds in a sunlit landscape, with here and there the dead shadow of a frock coat. My Aunt Georgiana regarded them as though they had been so many daubs of tube-paint on a palette.

---

4. An 1836 opera by German composer Giacomo
Meyerbeer (1791–1864).
5. An 1843 opera by Richard Wagner.

6. Statue of the Egyptian pharaoh Ramses, from
the twelfth century BCE.

When the musicians came out and took their places, she gave a little stir of anticipation, and looked with quickening interest down over the rail at that invariable grouping, perhaps the first wholly familiar thing that had greeted her eye since she had left old Maggie and her weakling calf. I could feel how all those details sank into her soul, for I had not forgotten how they had sunk into mine when I came fresh from ploughing forever and forever between green aisles of corn, where, as in a treadmill, one might walk from daybreak to dusk without perceiving a shadow of change. The clean profiles of the musicians, the gloss of their linen, the dull black of their coats, the beloved shapes of the instruments, the patches of yellow light thrown by the green shaded lamps on the smooth, varnished bellies of the 'cellos and the bass viols in the rear, the restless, wind-tossed forest of fiddle necks and bows—I recalled how, in the first orchestra I had ever heard, those long bow strokes seemed to draw the heart out of me, as a conjurer's stick reels out yards of paper ribbon from a hat.

The first number was the *Tannhäuser*[7] overture. When the horns drew out the first strain of the Pilgrim's chorus, my Aunt Georgiana clutched my coat sleeve. Then it was I first realized that for her this broke a silence of thirty years; the inconceivable silence of the plains. With the battle between the two motives, with the frenzy of the Venusberg theme and its ripping of strings, there came to me an overwhelming sense of the waste and wear we are so powerless to combat; and I saw again the tall, naked house on the prairie, black and grim as a wooden fortress; the black pond where I had learned to swim, its margin pitted with sun-dried cattle tracks; the rain gullied clay banks about the naked house, the four dwarf ash seedlings where the dish-cloths were always hung to dry before the kitchen door. The world there was the flat world of the ancients; to the east, a cornfield that stretched to daybreak; to the west, a corral that reached to sunset; between, the conquests of peace, dearer bought than those of war.

The overture closed, my aunt released my coat sleeve, but she said nothing. She sat staring at the orchestra through a dullness of thirty years, through the films made little by little by each of the three hundred and sixty-five days in every one of them. What, I wondered, did she get from it? She had been a good pianist in her day I knew, and her musical education had been broader than that of most music teachers of a quarter of a century ago. She had often told me of Mozart's operas and Meyerbeer's, and I could remember hearing her sing, years ago, certain melodies of Verdi's.[8] When I had fallen ill with a fever in her house she used to sit by my cot in the evening—when the cool, night wind blew in through the faded mosquito netting tacked over the window and I lay watching a certain bright star that burned red above the cornfield—and sing "Home to our mountains, O, let us return!" in a way fit to break the heart of a Vermont boy near dead of homesickness already.

I watched her closely through the prelude to *Tristan and Isolde*,[9] trying vainly to conjecture what that seething turmoil of strings and winds might mean to her, but she sat mutely staring at the violin bows that drove obliquely downward, like the pelting streaks of rain in a summer shower. Had this music any message for her? Had she enough left to at all comprehend this power which had kindled the

---

7. An 1845 opera by Richard Wagner.
8. Mozart: Austrian composer Wolfgang Amadeus Mozart (1756–91); Meyerbeer: German composer Giacomo Meyerbeer (1791–1864); Verdi: Italian composer Giuseppe Verdi (1813–1901).
9. An 1865 opera by Richard Wagner.

world since she had left it? I was in a fever of curiosity, but Aunt Georgiana sat silent upon her peak in Darien.[1] She preserved this utter immobility throughout the number from *The Flying Dutchman,* though her fingers worked mechanically upon her black dress, as though, of themselves, they were recalling the piano score they had once played. Poor old hands! They had been stretched and twisted into mere tentacles to hold and lift and knead with; the palm, unduly swollen, the fingers bent and knotted—on one of them a thin, worn band that had once been a wedding ring. As I pressed and gently quieted one of those groping hands, I remembered with quivering eyelids their services for me in other days.

Soon after the tenor began the "Prize Song," I heard a quick drawn breath and turned to my aunt. Her eyes were closed, but the tears were glistening on her cheeks, and I think, in a moment more, they were in my eyes as well. It never really died, then—the soul that can suffer so excruciatingly and so interminably; it withers to the outward eye only; like that strange moss which can lie on a dusty shelf half a century and yet, if placed in water, grows green again. She wept so throughout the development and elaboration of the melody.

During the intermission before the second half of the concert, I questioned my aunt and found that the "Prize Song" was not new to her. Some years before there had drifted to the farm in Red Willow County a young German, a tramp cow-puncher, who had sung in the chorus at Bayreuth,[2] when he was a boy, along with the other peasant boys and girls. Of a Sunday morning he used to sit on his gingham-sheeted bed in the hands' bedroom which opened off the kitchen, cleaning the leather of his boots and saddle, singing the "Prize Song," while my aunt went about her work in the kitchen. She had hovered about him until she had prevailed upon him to join the country church, though his sole fitness for this step, in so far as I could gather, lay in his boyish face and his possession of this divine melody. Shortly afterward he had gone to town on the Fourth of July, been drunk for several days, lost his money at a faro table, ridden a saddled Texas steer on a bet, and disappeared with a fractured collarbone. All this my aunt told me huskily, wanderingly, as though she were talking in the weak lapses of illness.

"Well, we have come to better things than the old *Trovatore*[3] at any rate, Aunt Georgie?" I queried, with a well meant effort at jocularity.

Her lip quivered and she hastily put her handkerchief up to her mouth. From behind it she murmured, "And you have been hearing this ever since you left me, Clark?" Her question was the gentlest and saddest of reproaches.

The second half of the programme consisted of four numbers from the *Ring,* and closed with Siegfried's funeral march.[4] My aunt wept quietly, but almost continuously, as a shallow vessel overflows in a rainstorm. From time to time her dim eyes looked up at the lights which studded the ceiling, burning softly under their dull glass globes; doubtless they were stars in truth to her. I was still perplexed as to what measure of musical comprehension was left to her, she who had heard nothing but the singing of Gospel Hymns at Methodist services in the square frame schoolhouse on Section Thirteen[5] for so many years. I was wholly unable to gauge

---

1. An allusion to Keats's (1795–1821) "On First Looking into Chapman's Homer"; it means that she is awestruck.
2. Town in Bavaria, site since 1876 of an annual Wagner music festival.
3. *Il Trovatore* (The Troubadour), 1853 opera by Verdi.

4. *Der Ring des Nibelungen,* a series of four ambitious operas by Richard Wagner; Siegfried: a character from the Ring Cycle of operas.
5. Refers to the federal system for surveying and defining locations, established in 1812. Townships are divided into thirty-six numbered sections, each one mile square.

how much of it had been dissolved in soapsuds, or worked into bread, or milked into the bottom of a pail.

The deluge of sound poured on and on; I never knew what she found in the shining current of it; I never knew how far it bore her, or past what happy islands. From the trembling of her face I could well believe that before the last numbers she had been carried out where the myriad graves are, into the grey, nameless burying grounds of the sea; or into some world of death vaster yet, where, from the beginning of the world, hope has lain down with hope and dream with dream and, renouncing, slept.

The concert was over; the people filed out of the hall chattering and laughing, glad to relax and find the living level again, but my kinswoman made no effort to rise. The harpist slipped its green felt cover over his instrument; the flute-players shook the water from their mouthpieces; the men of the orchestra went out one by one, leaving the stage to the chairs and music stands, empty as a winter cornfield.

I spoke to my aunt. She burst into tears and sobbed pleadingly. "I don't want to go, Clark. I don't want to go!"

I understood. For her, just outside the door of the concert hall, lay the black pond with the cattle-tracked bluffs; the tall, unpainted house, with weather-curled boards; naked as a tower, the crook-backed ash seedlings where the dish-cloths hung to dry; the gaunt, moulting turkeys picking up refuse about the kitchen door.

1905

◄ GERTRUDE STEIN ►
1874–1946

One of the most original writers of the twentieth century, and one of the founders of literary modernism (see pp. 1193–97), Gertrude Stein is often better known for her connections to other artists or for famous quotations than for her work. In part, this may be because of the difficulty of that writing—she was interested in bold experimentation that pushed the limits of representation and in theories of art and psychology that challenged conventional ideas about perception.

Gertrude Stein was born into a second-generation American German-Jewish family in Allegheny, Pennsylvania; she lived her early years in Austria and Paris before her parents moved to Oakland, California (the subject of one of her most famous quotations: "There is no *there* there") in 1879. Orphaned as a teenager, she lived with her brother Leo for many years thereafter. She went with him when he attended Harvard and was admitted into the school that would become Radcliffe College. She studied with philosophers William James and George Santayana, among others, and graduated magna cum laude with a degree in philosophy. When Leo went to Johns Hopkins, she did too, and studied medicine there from 1897 to 1899. When she left medical school, she followed Leo to Europe. They settled in Paris in 1903, began collecting avant-garde art, and she began writing (see pp. 1285–86).

Before long, the Steins' apartment became a center for cultural and artistic life in Paris. Picasso, Cézanne, Matisse, and Stieglitz were among the visual artists who visited her salon, and later writers like novelists Ernest Hemingway, F. Scott Fitzgerald, and Natalie Barney; poet H.D. (pp. 1363–73), and story writers Sherwood Anderson and Thornton Wilder would become her friends. In 1907 or thereabouts, Stein met another California expatriate, Alice B. Toklas; the two soon became lovers and were lifelong companions. Toklas worked as Stein's proof-reader, editor, secretary, housekeeper, and publisher. They also worked together as ambulance drivers during World War I, and their home was a haven for American servicemen during both world wars. Stein's most popular work, *The Autobiography of Alice B. Toklas* (1933), is written in Toklas's voice, and one of our selections here, "Ada," is a stripped-down biography of Alice. Toklas outlived Stein by twenty-one years and continued to publish Stein's manuscripts for many of those.

Stein was intensely interested in modernist ideas of art and psychology, and she wanted to find ways that such ideas could take form in literature. She combined William James's theory that people experience reality as a series of present moments with cubist painters' attempts to capture multiple dimensions of an object in a two-dimensional plane and futurist artists' attempts to capture movement in a static medium to come up with a theory of literature that presents "reality" in a mode that is not at all realistic. Instead, the literature she wrote from this perspective tries to capture a sense of the eternal present of the moment and the *experience* of perception rather than the object being perceived. Her much-quoted "A rose is a rose is a rose" is an attempt to get at this ever-changing eternal present.

Much of her work is an experiment to see whether language can be used in the way that paint is used in an abstract painting, that is, not as a representation, but as a thing itself. Therefore, much of her writing plays with sound, repetition, imagery, and rhythm; she pares down description in order to get at sensation. "Preciosilla" and "Susie Asado" are "portraits" of a Spanish dancer and a Spanish singer that attempt to get at the experience of the women rather than provide a description of them. "Patriarchal Poetry" is hard to classify; it works as an essay, as poetry, and as neither of those. One Stein scholar, Marianne DeKoven, argues that it "defies interpretation." That anti-interpretive stance may be its point; DeKoven also tells us that Stein's work aims to present an "order of meaning [that is] genuinely oppositional—that is, antipatriarchal and antilogocentric."

Gertrude Stein was a prolific writer who worked in almost every genre, including fiction, essay, autobiography, biography, history, poetry, and drama. Her work has even been adapted into opera. Readers who would like to encounter a more accessible Stein should turn to her early work *Three Lives* (1909) or her late work, including her play about Susan B. Anthony, *The Mother of Us All* (1945–46).

Ada

Barnes Colhard did not say he would not do it but he did not do it. He did at it and then he did not do at it, he did not ever think about it. He just thought some time he might do something.

His father Mr. Abram Colhard spoke about it to every one and very many of them spoke to Barnes Colhard about it and he always listened to them.

Then Barnes fell in love with a very nice girl and she would not marry him. He cried then, his father Mr. Abram Colhard comforted him and they took a trip and Barnes promised he would do what his father wanted him to be doing. He did not do the thing, he thought he would do another thing, he did not do the other thing, his father Mr. Colhard did not want him to do the other thing. He really did not do anything then. When he was a good deal older he married a very rich girl. He had thought perhaps he would not propose to her but his sister wrote to him that it would be a good thing. He married the rich girl and she thought he was the most wonderful man and one who knew everything. Barnes never spent more than the income of the fortune he and his wife had then, that is to say they did not spend more than the income and this was a surprise to very many who knew about him and about his marrying the girl who had such a large fortune. He had a happy life while he was living and after he was dead his wife and children remembered him.

He had a sister who also was successful enough in being one being living. His sister was one who came to be happier than most people come to be in living. She came to be a completely happy one. She was twice as old as her brother. She had been a very good daughter to her mother. She and her mother had always told very pretty stories to each other. Many old men loved to hear her tell these stories to her mother. Every one who ever knew her mother liked her mother. Many were sorry later that not every one liked the daughter. Many did like the daughter but not every one as every one had liked the mother. The daughter was charming inside in her, it did not show outside in her to every one, it certainly did to some. She did sometimes think her mother would be pleased with a story that did not please her mother. When her mother later was sicker the daughter knew that there were some stories she could tell her that would not please her mother. Her mother died and really mostly altogether the mother and the daughter had told each other stories very happily together.

The daughter then kept house for her father and took care of her brother. There were many relations who lived with them. The daughter did not like them to live with them and she did not like them to die with them. The daughter, Ada they had called her after her grandmother who had delightful ways of smelling flowers and eating dates and sugar, did not like it at all then as she did not like so much dying and she did not like any of the living she was doing then. Every now and then some old gentlemen told delightful stories to her. Mostly then there were not nice stories told by any one then in her living. She told her father Mr. Abram Colhard that she did not like it at all being one being living then. He never said anything. She was afraid then, she was one needing charming stories and happy telling of them and not having that thing she was always trembling. Then every one who could live with them were dead and there were then the father and the son a young man then and the daughter coming to be that one then. Her grandfather had left some money to them each one of them. Ada said she was going to use it to go away from them. The father said nothing then, then he said something and she said nothing then, then they both said nothing and then it was that she went away from them. The father was quite tender then, she was his daughter then. He wrote her tender letters then, she wrote him tender letters then, she never went back to live with him. He wanted her to come and she wrote him tender letters then. He liked the tender letters she wrote to him. He wanted her to live with him. She answered him by writing tender letters to him and telling very nice stories indeed in them. He wrote nothing and then he wrote again and there was some waiting and then he wrote tender letters again and again.

She came to be happier than anybody else who was living then. It is easy to believe this thing. She was telling some one, who was loving every story that was charming. Some one who was living was almost always listening. Some one who was loving was almost always listening. That one who was loving was almost always listening. That one who was loving was telling about being one then listening.

That one being loving was then telling stories having a beginning and a middle and an ending. That one was then one always completely listening. Ada was then one and all her living then one completely telling stories that were charming, completely listening to stories having a beginning and a middle and an ending. Trembling was all living, living was all loving, some one was then the other one. Certainly this one was loving this Ada then. And certainly Ada all her living then was happier in living than any one else who ever could, who was, who is, who ever will be living.

1910   1922

◆━◆

Preciosilla

Cousin to Clare washing.

In the win all the band beagles which have cousin lime sign and arrange a weeding match to presume a certain point to exstate to exstate a certain pass lint to exstate a lean sap prime lo and shut shut is life.

Bait, bait tore, tore her clothes, toward it, toward a bit, to ward a sit, sit down in, in vacant surely lots, a single mingle, bait and wet; wet a single establishment that has a l i l y lily grow. Come to the pen come in the stem, come in the grass grown water.

Lily wet lily wet while. This is so pink so pink in stammer, a long bean which shows bows is collected by a single curly shady, shady get, get set wet bet.

It is a snuff a snuff to be told and have can wither, can is it and sleep sleeps knot, it is a lily scarf the pink and blue yellow, not blue not odor sun, nobles are bleeding bleeding two seats two seats on end. Why is grief. Grief is strange black. Sugar is melting. We will not swim.

Preciosilla.

Please be please be get, please get wet, wet naturally, naturally in weather. Could it be fire more firier. Could it be so in ate struck. Could it be gold up, gold up stringing, in it while while which is hanging, hanging in dingling, dingling in pinning, not so. Not so dots large dressed dots, big sizes, less laced, less laced diamonds, diamonds white, diamonds bright, diamonds in the in the light, diamonds light diamonds door diamonds hanging to be four, two four all before, this bean, lessly, all most, a best, willow, vest, a green guest, guest, go go go go go go, go. Go go. Not guessed. Go go.

Toasted susie is my ice-cream.

1913   1922

◆━◆

Susie Asado

Sweet sweet sweet sweet sweet tea.
Susie Asado.
Sweet sweet sweet sweet sweet tea.
Susie Asado.

Susie Asado which is a told tray sure.

A lean on the shoe this means slips slips hers.

When the ancient light grey is clean it is yellow, it is a silver seller.

This is a please this is a please there are the saids to jelly. These are the wets these say the sets to leave a crown to Incy.

Incy is short for incubus.

A pot. A pot is a beginning of a rare bit of trees. Trees tremble, the old vats are in bobbles, bobbles which shade and shove and render clean, render clean must.

　　　Drink pups.

Drink pups drink pups lease a sash hold, see it shine and a bobolink has pins. It shows a nail.

What is a nail. A nail is unison.

Sweet sweet sweet sweet sweet tea.

1913   1922

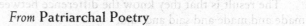

From Patriarchal Poetry

[*Their Origin and Their History*]

* * *

Their origin and their history patriarchal poetry their origin and their history patriarchal poetry their origin and their history.

Patriarchal Poetry.

Their origin and their history.

Patriarchal Poetry their origin and their history their history patriarchal poetry their origin patriarchal poetry their history their origin patriarchal poetry their history patriarchal poetry their origin patriarchal poetry their history their origin.

That is one case.

Able sweet and in a seat.

Patriarchal poetry their origin their history their origin. Patriarchal poetry their history their origin.

Two makes it do three make it five four make it more five make it arrive and sundries.

Letters and leaves tables and plainly restive and recover and bide away, away to say regularly.

Never to mention patriarchal poetry altogether.

Two two two occasionally two two as you say two two two not in their explanation two two must you be very well apprised that it had had such an effect that only one out of a great many and there were a great many believe in three relatively and moreover were you aware of the fact that interchangeable and interchangeable was it while they were if not avoided. She knew that is to say she had really informed herself. Patriarchal poetry makes no mistake.

Never to have followed farther there and knitting, is knitting knitting if it is only what is described as called that they should not come to say and how do you do every new year Saturday. Every new year Saturday is likely to bring pleasure is likely to give pleasure is likely to bring pleasure every new year Saturday is likely to bring pleasure.

Day which is what is which is what is day which is what is day which is which is what is which is what is day.

I double you, of course you do. You double me, very likely to be. You double I double I double you double. I double you double me I double you you double me.

When this you see remarkably.

Patriarchal poetry needs rectification and there about it.

Come to a distance and it still bears their name.

Prosperity and theirs prosperity left to it.

To be told to be harsh to be told to be harsh to be to them.

One.

To be told to be harsh to be told to be harsh to them.

None.

To be told to be harsh to be told to be harsh to them.

When.

To be told to be harsh to be told to be harsh to them.

Then.

What is the result.

The result is that they know the difference between instead and instead and made and made and said and said.

The result is that they might be as very well two and as soon three and to be sure, four and which is why they might not be.

Elegant replaced by delicate and tender, delicate and tender replaced by one four there instead of five four there, there is not there this is what has happened evidently.

Why while while why while why why identity identity why while while why. Why while while while while identity.

Patriarchal Poetry is the same as patriarchal poetry is the same as patriarchal poetry is the same as patriarchal poetry is the same as patriarchal poetry is the same.

Patriarchal poetry is the same.

If in in crossing there is a if in crossing if in in crossing nearly there is a distance if in crossing there is a distance between measurement and exact if in in crossing if in in crossing there is a measurement between and in in exact she says I must be careful and I will.

If in in crossing there is an opportunity not only but also and in in looking in looking in regarding if in in looking if in in regarding if in in regarding there is an opportunity if in in looking there is an opportunity if in in regarding there is an opportunity to verify verify sometimes as more sometimes as more sometimes as more.

Fish eggs commonly fish eggs. Architects commonly fortunately indicatively architects indicatively architects. Elaborated at a time with it with it at a time with it at a time attentively to-day.

Does she know how to ask her brother is there any difference between turning it again again and again and again or turning it again and again. In resembling two brothers.

That makes patriarchal poetry apart.

Intermediate or patriarchal poetry.

If at once sixty-five have come one by one if at once sixty five have come one by one if at once sixty-five have come one by one. This took two and two have been added to by Jenny. Never to name Jenny. Have been added to by two. Never have named Helen Jenny never have named Agnes Helen never have named Helen Jenny. There is no difference between having been born in Brittany and having been born in Algeria.

These words containing as they do neither reproaches nor satisfaction may be finally very nearly rearranged and why, because they mean to be partly left alone. Patriarchal poetry and kindly, it would be very kind in him in him of him of him to be as much obliged as that. Patriarchal poetry. It would be as plainly an advantage if not only but altogether repeatedly it should be left not only to them but for them but for them. Explain to them by for them. Explain shall it be explain will it be explain can it be explain as it is to be explain letting it be had as if he had had more than wishes. More than wishes.

Patriarchal poetry more than wishes.

Assigned to Patriarchal Poetry.

Assigned to patriarchal poetry too sue sue sue sue shall sue sell and magnificent can as coming let the same shall shall shall shall let it share is share is share shall shall shall shall shell shell shall share is share shell can shell be shell be shell moving in in in inner moving move inner in in inner in meant meant might might may collect collected recollected to refuse what it is is it.

Having started at once at once.

Put it with it with it and it and it come to ten.

Put it with it with it and it and it for it for it made to be extra.

With it put it put it prepare it prepare it add it add it or it or it would it would it and make it all at once.

Put it with it with it and it and it in it in it add it add it at it at it with it with it put it put it to this to understand.

Put it with it with it add it add it at it at it or it or it to be placed intend.

Put it with it with it in it in it at it at it add it add it or it or it letting it be while it is left as it might could do their danger.

Could it with it with it put it put it place it place it stand it stand it two doors or two doors two tables or two tables two let two let two let two to be sure.

Put it with it with it and it and it in it in it add it add it or it or it to it to be added to it.

There is no doubt about it.

Actually.

To be sure.

Left to the rest if to be sure that to be sent come to be had in to be known or to be liked and to be to be to be to be to be mine.

It always can be one two three it can be always can can always be one two three. It can always be one two three.

It is very trying to have him have it have it have him have it as she said the last was very very much and very much to very much to distance to distance them.

Every time there is a wish wish it. Every time there is a wish wish it. Every time there is a wish wish it.

Every time there is a wish wish it.

Dedicated to all the way through. Dedicated to all the way through.

Dedicated too all the way through. Dedicated too all the way through.

Apples and fishes day-light and wishes apples and fishes day-light and wishes day-light at seven.

All the way through dedicated to you.

Day-light and wishes apples and fishes, dedicated to you all the way through day-light and fishes apples and wishes dedicated to all the way through dedicated to you dedicated to you all the way through day-light and fishes apples and fishes day-light and wishes apples and fishes dedicated to you all the way through day-light and fishes apples and wishes apples and fishes day-light and wishes dedicated to dedicated through all the way through dedicated to.

Not at once Tuesday.

They might be finally their name name same came came came came or share sharer article entreat coming in letting this be there letting this be there.

Patriarchal poetry come too.

When with patriarchal poetry when with patriarchal poetry come too.

There must be more french in France there must be more French in France patriarchal poetry come too.

Patriarchal poetry come too there must be more french in France patriarchal come too there must be more french in France.

Patriarchal Poetry come to.

There must be more french in France.

Helen greatly relieves Alice patriarchal poetry come too there must be patriarchal poetry come too.

In a way second first in a way first second in a way in a way first second in a way.

Rearrangement is nearly rearrangement. Finally nearly rearrangement is finally nearly rearrangement nearly not now finally nearly nearly finally rearrangement nearly rearrangement and not now how nearly finally rearrangement. If two tables are near together finally nearly not now.

Finally nearly not now.

Able able nearly nearly nearly nearly able able finally nearly able nearly not now finally finally nearly able.

They make it be very well three or nearly three at a time.

Splendid confidence in the one addressed and equal distrust of the one who has done everything that is necessary. Finally nearly able not now able finally nearly not now.

Rearrangement is a rearrangement a rearrangement is widely known a rearrangement is widely known. A rearrangement is widely known. As a rearrangement is widely known.

As a rearrangement is widely known.

So can a rearrangement which is widely known be a rearrangement which is widely known which is widely known.

Let her be to be to be to be to be let her be to be to be to be let her to be let her to be let her be to be when is it that they are shy.

Very well to try.

Let her be that is to be let her be that is to be let her be let her try.

Let her be let her be let her be to be to be to be shy let her be to be let her be to be let her try.

Let her try.

Let her be let her be let her be let her be to be to be let her be let her try.

To be shy.

Let her be.
Let her try.
Let her be let her let her let her be let her be let her be let her be shy let her be
let her be let her try.
Let her try.
Let her be.
Let her be shy.
Let her be.
Let her be let her be let her let her try.
Let her try to be let her try to be let her be shy let her try to be let her try to
be let her be let her be let her try.
Let her be shy.
Let her try.
Let her try.
Let her be
Let her let her be shy.
Let her try.
Let her be.
Let her let her be shy.
Let her be let her let her be shy
Let her let her let her let her try.
Let her try.
Let her try.
Let her try.
Let her be.
Let her be let her
Let her try.
Let her be let her.
Let her be let her let her try.
Let her try.
Let her
Let her try.
Let her be shy.
Let her
Let her
Let her be.
Let her be shy.
Let her be let her try.
Let her try.
Let her try.
Let her try.
Let her let her try
Let her be shy.
Let her try
Let her let her try to be let her try.
Let her try.
Just let her try.
Let her try.

Never to be what he said.
Never to be what he said.
Never to be what he said.
Let her to be what he said.
Let her to be what he said.
Not to let her to be what he said not to let her to be what he said.

Never to be let her to be never let her to be what he said. Never let her to be what he said.

Never to let her to be what he said. Never to let her to be let her to be let her to be let her what he said.

* * *

1927   1953

CULTURAL COORDINATES
Two Women Writers in Paris, Never Meeting

Edith Wharton and Gertrude Stein were both expatriate American writers living on the Seine's Left Bank in Paris (only later an avant-garde colony), less than a mile apart. They both held literary and artistic salons, both undertook extensive relief work during World War I, and both were honored by the French government for that work. They both had left the United States for Paris in hopes of finding a world where their ambitions, interests, and writing would be better nurtured and where they could live outside the strictures of womanhood that dominated American culture. Yet they never met. Their similarities and differences tell us a great deal about both literary modernism (see pp. 1193–97) and about expatriate women writers in Paris in the early part of the twentieth century, a group that included H.D. (pp. 1363–64), Djuna Barnes (pp. 1424–25), and Jean Rhys

Since Edith Wharton (left, in 1908) was a carryover from the nineteenth century and Gertrude Stein (right, in 1934) was a harbinger of the experimentalism to come in the twentieth century, it is no surprise that these writers who lived within a mile of each other never met.

(pp. 1382–83) as well as Anaïs Nin, Natalie Barney, Mina Loy, Collette, Kay Boyle, and Jessie Redmon Fauset.

Stein settled in Paris in 1903; Wharton in 1906, though she had been a frequent visitor since 1893. Stein was middle-class, Jewish, and lesbian and moved in the world of the avante-garde, becoming friends with and an advocate for cubist artists whose work shocked the world; she collected paintings by Pablo Picasso, Henri Matisse, and Georges Braque, and the writers Ernest Hemingway, F. Scott Fitzgerald, and Sherwood Anderson were frequent guests at her house. Wharton was descended from old money and moved in the world of gentility; her literary and artistic friends included Paul Bourget, Jacques-Émile Blanche, Anna de Noailles, André Gide, and Henry James. Wharton's tastes ran to elegance; Stein's to the new and experimental. Oddly enough, even though both Wharton and Stein are now hailed as pioneering feminist writers, most of their intellectual and artistic companions were men.

As Shari Benstock explains in her extensive discussion of women artists in Paris, *Women of the Left Bank: Paris, 1900–1940,* the differences between Wharton and Stein were based on more than just class, sexual orientation, and taste. Wharton was essentially a nineteenth-century woman, even though she would live in the twentieth century for thirty-seven years, but Stein was a twentieth-century figure, through and through. Wharton chafed at the restrictions on women of her class and time, urging more freedoms for women (to divorce, to have careers, to pursue their own interests), but she did so in traditional narrative forms; she also held on to ideas of elegance and beauty, writing extensively on fashion and decorating houses. Stein, however, embraced the new; her narratives, poetry, and plays boldly experiment with syntax, style, and subject material. She cared little for fashion, insisting instead on comfort. Wharton belongs to the literary period of realism, even though she wrote well into the 1930s; Stein is one of the originators of literary modernism, which calls into question the whole idea of representing the world "realistically" in language. But as Benstock argues, both women found in Paris just the right blend of stimulation and isolation that they needed to be a writer and just the right distance from American society to be able to represent both its beauties and its faults. And though Wharton and Stein never met, it might be interesting to imagine such an encounter!

ALICE DUNBAR-NELSON
1875–1935

Alice Dunbar-Nelson is often described as a writer of the Harlem Renaissance (a period of creative activity in the African American arts during the 1910s to 1930s), and her association during the 1920s with African American writers like Georgia Douglas Johnson, Anne Spencer, and Angelina Weld Grimké, as well as her journalism and political activism during those years, supports such a claim. Her earlier short fiction, however, suggests we read her as a local color writer (an American regionalist), along with Kate Chopin and Sarah Orne Jewett.

Alice Ruth Moore was born in New Orleans, the multiracial daughter of a seamstress and a merchant marine. She was light-skinned, which meant that she was accepted into the higher echelons of African American society. She graduated from a two-year teacher-training program after high school and began a career as a teacher; she also was able to publish her first volume of poetry and fiction, *Violets and Other Tales* (1895), when she was only twenty. When her photograph and one of her poems appeared in a popular African American literary magazine, Paul Laurence Dunbar, one of the best-known black writers of his day, began writing to her; after a courtship carried on by letter, they were married in 1898. Although the marriage afforded Dunbar-Nelson the opportunity to devote more time to writing (her collection of stories *The Goodness of St. Roque* appeared in 1899), it was not a happy one, and the couple divorced in 1902. Alice Dunbar-Nelson moved to Wilmington, Delaware, where she taught English at Howard High School for eighteen years, until she was fired for engaging in political activism.

She had married the publisher of a prominent civil rights newspaper, Robert Nelson, in 1916, four years before her dismissal, and after she left teaching devoted her energies to writing and political activism. She worked for feminist causes, for civil rights (especially for anti-lynching laws), and for world peace (she was the executive secretary of the American Interracial Peace Committee 1928–31). During the 1910s and 1920s, she published political columns in newspapers as well as short stories, plays, and poetry, and she edited two collections of African American literature. She also kept a diary (which was edited and published by scholar Gloria T. Hull in 1984), which offers insights into her work and illuminates the intimate relationships she had with several women.

The two selections here reflect the range of Dunbar-Nelson's work. "Sister Josepha" is the story of a young woman of indeterminate race and background and serves as a meditation on the dangers facing a young woman at the turn of the century, as well as the racial politics of New Orleans. Camille's brown hands, dark eyes, and "tropical" appearance, along with her uncertain heritage, would have made her an object of sexual predators. "I Sit and Sew," written during the First World War, offers an interestingly feminine take on the problems of war and international peace.

Sister Josepha

Sister Josepha told her beads[1] mechanically, her fingers numb with the accustomed exercise. The little organ creaked a dismal "O Salutaris,"[2] and she still knelt on the floor, her white-bonneted head nodding suspiciously. The Mother Superior gave a sharp glance at the tired figure; then, as a sudden lurch forward brought the little sister back to consciousness, Mother's eyes relaxed into a genuine smile.

The bell tolled the end of vespers, and the sombre-robed nuns filed out of the chapel to go about their evening duties. Little Sister Josepha's work was to attend to the household lamps, but there must have been as much oil spilled upon the table tonight as was put in the vessels. The small brown hands trembled so that most of the wicks were trimmed with points at one corner which caused them to smoke that night.

"Oh, cher Seigneur,"[3] she sighed, giving an impatient polish to a refractory chimney, "it is wicked and sinful, I know, but I am so tired. I can't be happy and sing any more. It doesn't seem right for le bon Dieu[4] to have me all cooped up here with nothing to see but stray visitors, and always the same old work, teaching those mean little girls to sew, and washing and filling the same old lamps. Pah!" And she polished the chimney with a sudden vigorous jerk which threatened destruction.

They were rebellious prayers that the red mouth murmured that night, and a restless figure that tossed on the hard dormitory bed. Sister Dominica called from her couch to know if Sister Josepha were ill.

"No," was the somewhat short response; then a muttered, "Why can't they let me alone for a minute? That pale-eyed Sister Dominica never sleeps; that's why she is so ugly."

About fifteen years before this night some one had brought to the orphan asylum connected with this convent, du Sacre Coeur, a round, dimpled bit of three-year-old humanity, who regarded the world from a pair of gravely twinkling black eyes, and only took a chubby thumb out of a rosy mouth long enough to answer in monosyllabic French. It was a child without an identity; there was but one name that any one seemed to know, and that, too, was vague,—Camille.

She grew up with the rest of the waifs; scraps of French and American civilization thrown together to develop a seemingly inconsistent miniature world. Mademoiselle Camille was a queen among them, a pretty little tyrant who ruled the children and dominated the more timid sisters in charge.

One day an awakening came. When she was fifteen, and almost fully ripened into a glorious tropical beauty of the type that matures early, some visitors to the convent were fascinated by her and asked the Mother Superior to give the girl into their keeping.

Camille fled like a frightened fawn into the yard, and was only unearthed with some difficulty from behind a group of palms. Sulky and pouting, she was led into the parlour, picking at her blue pinafore like a spoiled infant.

"The lady and gentleman wish you to go home with them, Camille," said the Mother Superior, in the language of the convent. Her voice was kind and gentle apparently; but the child, accustomed to its various inflections, detected a steely ring behind its softness, like the proverbial iron hand in the velvet glove.

1. Rosary, beads used by Catholics to count out a
sequence of prayers.
2. "Oh Saving Host" (Latin).

3. Dear Lord (French).
4. The good God (French).

"You must understand, madame," continued Mother, in stilted English, "that we never force children from us. We are ever glad to place them in comfortable—how you say that?—quarters—maisons—homes—bien! But we will not make them go if they do not wish."

Camille stole a glance at her would-be guardians, and decided instantly, impulsively, finally. The woman suited her; but the man! It was doubtless intuition of the quick, vivacious sort which belonged to her blood that served her. Untutored in worldly knowledge, she could not divine the meaning of the pronounced leers and admiration of her physical charms which gleamed in the man's face, but she knew it made her feel creepy, and stoutly refused to go.

Next day Camille was summoned from a task to the Mother Superior's parlour. The other girls gazed with envy upon her as she dashed down the courtyard with impetuous movement. Camille, they decided crossly, received too much notice. It was Camille this, Camille that; she was pretty, it was to be expected. Even Father Ray lingered longer in his blessing when his hands pressed her silky black hair.

As she entered the parlour, a strange chill swept over the girl. The room was not an unaccustomed one, for she had swept it many times, but to-day the stiff black chairs, the dismal crucifixes, the gleaming whiteness of the walls, even the cheap lithograph of the Madonna which Camille had always regarded as a perfect specimen of art, seemed cold and mean.

"Camille, ma chere,"[5] said Mother, "I am extremely displeased with you. Why did you not wish to go with Monsieur and Madame Lafaye yesterday?"

The girl uncrossed her hands from her bosom, and spread them out in a deprecating gesture.

"Mais, ma mere,[6] I was afraid."

Mother's face grew stern. "No foolishness now," she exclaimed.

"It is not foolishness, ma mere; I could not help it, but that man looked at me so funny, I felt all cold chills down my back. Oh, dear Mother, I love the convent and the sisters so, I just want to stay and be a sister too, may I?"

And thus it was that Camille took the white veil at sixteen years. Now that the period of noviliate was over, it was just beginning to dawn upon her that she had made a mistake.

"Maybe it would have been better had I gone with the funny-looking lady and gentleman," she mused bitterly one night. "Oh, Seigneur, I'm so tired and impatient; it's so dull here, and, dear God, I'm so young."

There was no help for it. One must arise in the morning, and help in the refectory with the stupid Sister Francesca, and go about one's duties with a prayerful mien, and not even let a sigh escape when one's head ached with the eternal telling of beads.

A great fete day was coming, and an atmosphere of preparation and mild excitement pervaded the brown walls of the convent like a delicate aroma. The old Cathedral around the corner had stood a hundred years, and all the city was rising to do honour to its age and time-softened beauty. There would be a service, oh, but such a one! with two Cardinals, and Archbishops and Bishops, and all the accompanying glitter of soldiers and orchestras. The little sisters of the Convent du Sacre Coeur clasped their hands in anticipation of the holy joy. Sister Josepha curled her lip, she was so tired of churchly pleasures.

5. My dear (French).   6. But, Mother (French).

The day came, a gold and blue spring day, when the air hung heavy with the scent of roses and magnolias, and the sunbeams fairly laughed as they kissed the houses. The old Cathedral stood gray and solemn, and the flowers in Jackson Square smiled cheery birthday greetings across the way. The crowd around the door surged and pressed and pushed in its eagerness to get within. Ribbons stretched across the banquette were of no avail to repress it, and important ushers with cardinal colours could do little more.

The Sacred Heart sisters filed slowly in at the side door, creating a momentary flutter as they paced reverently to their seats, guarding the blue-bonnetted orphans. Sister Josepha, determined to see as much of the world as she could, kept her big black eyes opened wide, as the church rapidly filled with the fashionably dressed, perfumed, rustling, and self-conscious throng.

Her heart beat quickly. The rebellious thoughts that will arise in the most philosophical of us surged in her small heavily gowned bosom. For her were the gray things, the neutral tinted skies, the ugly garb, the coarse meats; for them the rainbow, the ethereal airiness of earthly joys, the bonbons and glacés of the world. Sister Josepha did not know that the rainbow is elusive, and its colours but the illumination of tears; she had never been told that earthly ethereality is necessarily ephemeral, nor that bonbons and glacés, whether of the palate or of the soul, nauseate and pall upon the taste. Dear God, forgive her, for she bent with contrite tears over her worn rosary, and glanced no more at the worldly glitter of femininity.

The sunbeams streamed through the high windows in purple and crimson lights upon a veritable fugue of colour. Within the seats, crush upon crush of spring millinery; within the aisles erect lines of gold-braided, gold-buttoned military. Upon the altar, broad sweeps of golden robes, great dashes of crimson skirts, mitres and gleaming crosses, the soft neutral hue of rich lace vestments; the tender heads of childhood in picturesque attire; the proud, golden magnificence of the domed altar with its weighting mass of lilies and wide-eyed roses, and the long candles that sparkled their yellow star points above the reverent throng within the altar rails.

The soft baritone of the Cardinal intoned a single phrase in the suspended silence. The censer took up the note in its delicate clink clink, as it swung to and fro in the hands of a fair-haired child. Then the organ, pausing an instant in a deep, mellow, long-drawn note, burst suddenly into a magnificent strain, and the choir sang forth, "Kyrie Eleison, Christe Eleison."[7] One voice, flute-like, piercing, sweet, rang high over the rest. Sister Josepha heard and trembled, as she buried her face in her hands, and let her tears fall, like other beads, through her rosary.

It was when the final word of the service had been intoned, the last peal of the exit march had died away, that she looked up meekly, to encounter a pair of youthful brown eyes gazing pityingly upon her. That was all she remembered for a moment, that the eyes were youthful and handsome and tender. Later, she saw that they were placed in a rather beautiful boyish face, surmounted by waves of brown hair, curling and soft, and that the head was set on a pair of shoulders decked in military uniform. Then the brown eyes marched away with the rest of the rear guard, and the white-bonnetted sisters filed out the side door, through the narrow court, back into the brown convent.

That night Sister Josepha tossed more than usual on her hard bed, and clasped her fingers often in prayer to quell the wickedness in her heart. Turn where she would, pray as she might, there was ever a pair of tender, pitying brown eyes,

7. Lord have mercy, Christ have mercy (Latin).

haunting her persistently. The squeaky organ at vespers intoned the clank of military accoutrements to her ears, the white bonnets of the sisters about her faded into mists of curling brown hair. Briefly, Sister Josepha was in love.

The days went on pretty much as before, save for the one little heart that beat rebelliously now and then, though it tried so hard to be submissive. There was the morning work in the refectory, the stupid little girls to teach sewing, and the insatiable lamps that were so greedy for oil. And always the tender, boyish brown eyes, that looked so sorrowfully at the fragile, beautiful little sister, haunting, following, pleading.

Perchance, had Sister Josepha been in the world, the eyes would have been an incident. But in this home of self-repression and retrospection, it was a life-story. The eyes had gone their way, doubtless forgetting the little sister they pitied; but the little sister?

The days glided into weeks, the weeks into months. Thoughts of escape had come to Sister Josepha, to flee into the world, to merge in the great city where recognition was impossible, and working her way like the rest of humanity, perchance encounter the eyes again.

It was all planned and ready. She would wait until some morning when the little band of black-robed sisters wended their way to mass at the Cathedral. When it was time to file out the side-door into the courtway, she would linger at prayers, then slip out another door, and unseen glide up Chartres Street to Canal, and once there, mingle in the throng that filled the wide thoroughfare. Beyond this first plan she could think no further. Penniless, garbed, and shaven though she would be, other difficulties never presented themselves to her. She would rely on the mercies of the world to help her escape from this torturing life of inertia. It seemed easy now that the first step of decision had been taken.

The Saturday night before the final day had come, and she lay feverishly nervous in her narrow little bed, wondering with wide-eyed fear at the morrow. Pale-eyed Sister Dominica and Sister Francesca were whispering together in the dark silence, and Sister Josepha's ears pricked up as she heard her name.

"She is not well, poor child," said Francesca, "I fear the life is too confining."

"It is best for her," was the reply. "You know, sister, how hard it would be for her in the world, with no name but Camille, no friends, and her beauty; and then—"

Sister Josepha heard no more, for her heart beating tumultuously in her bosom drowned the rest. Like the rush of the bitter salt tide over a drowning man clinging to a spar, came the complete submerging of her hopes of another life. No name but Camille, that was true; no nationality, for she could never tell from whom or whence she came; no friends, and a beauty that not even an ungainly bonnet and shaven head could hide. In a flash she realised the deception of the life she would lead, and the cruel self-torture of wonder at her own identity. Already, as if in anticipation of the world's questionings, she was asking herself, "Who am I? What am I?"

The next morning the sisters du Sacre Coeur filed into the Cathedral at High Mass, and bent devout knees at the general confession. "Confiteor Deo omnipotenti," murmured the priest; and tremblingly one little sister followed the words, "Je confesse a Dieu, tout puissant—que j'ai beaucoup peche par pensees—c'est ma faute—c'est ma faute, c'est ma tres grande faute."[8]

---

8. Du Sacre Coeur: of the sacred heart (French); Confiteor Deo omnipotenti: I confess to God Almighty (Latin); Je confesse . . . faute: I confess to God—that I have gravely sinned in thought—it is my fault—it is my fault—it is my most grievous fault (French).

The organ pealed forth as mass ended, the throng slowly filed out, and the sisters paced through the courtway back into the brown convent walls. One paused at the entrance, and gazed with swift longing eyes in the direction of narrow, squalid Chartres Street, then, with a gulping sob, followed the rest, and vanished behind the heavy door.

1899

I Sit and Sew

I sit and sew—a useless task it seems,
My hands grown tired, my head weighed down with dreams—
The panoply of war, the martial tred of men,
Grim-faced, stern-eyed, gazing beyond the ken
Of lesser souls, whose eyes have not seen Death,   5
Nor learned to hold their lives but as a breath—
But—I must sit and sew.

I sit and sew—my heart aches with desire—
That pageant terrible, that fiercely pouring fire
On wasted fields, and writhing grotesque things   10
Once men. My soul in pity flings
Appealing cries, yearning only to go
There in that holocaust of hell, those fields of woe—
But—I must sit and sew.

The little useless seam, the idle patch;   15
Why dream I here beneath my homely thatch,
When there they lie in sodden mud and rain,
Pitifully calling me, the quick ones and the slain?
You need me, Christ! It is no roseate dream
That beckons me—this pretty futile seam   20
It stifles me—God, must I sit and sew?

1920

SUSAN GLASPELL
1876–1948

Although she wrote over fifty short stories, nine novels, eleven plays, and one biography, won the Pulitzer Prize for Drama, and cofounded one of the most successful small theaters in the United States, Susan Glaspell is best known as the author of our selection here, the classic feminist play *Trifles* (1916), which she later rewrote as the short story "A Jury of Her Peers."

Glaspell was born in Davenport, Iowa, and after graduating from Drake University, she became a reporter for the *Des Moines Daily News* (where she covered the murder on which *Trifles* was based). After having some success at placing short fiction in magazines, Glaspell moved back to Davenport to devote herself full-time to writing and wrote two successful novels. There she met the socialist (and twice-divorced) George Cram Cook, whom she later married. They moved to Greenwich Village, where they quickly met like-minded intellectuals and artists, and eventually they settled in Provincetown, Massachusetts, on Cape Cod. They founded the Playwright's Theatre (which would come to be known as the Provincetown Players) in order to provide a stage for experimental and innovative drama written by Americans. Cook produced and directed plays, and Glaspell wrote and starred in many of them. Eugene O'Neill, Edna St. Vincent Millay (pp. 1421–24), and Djuna Barnes (pp. 1424–28) were among other playwrights who found a forum for their work there. In 1916, Glaspell and Cook moved the company to New York, continuing to produce plays until 1922, when they both grew disillusioned by their own success and by the pettiness of the theater world. They moved to Greece, where they took up a simple life as shepherds. After Cook's death in 1924, Glaspell returned to Provincetown, where she lived until her death in 1948 and continued to write both plays and fiction. Her 1928 novel, *Brook Evans,* was a best seller and was made into a movie by Paramount Pictures (titled *The Right to Love*), and her 1930 play, *Alison's House,* loosely based on Emily Dickinson's life, won the Pulitzer Prize in 1931.

Most of Glaspell's work focuses on independent women trying to make their way in a repressive society that insists on conformity. Her material often examines her own midwestern background: it looks at the pressures on women in rural and small town settings wrought by the demands of being a wife and mother. Her early work (including *Trifles*) tends to be quite realistic, but throughout the 1920s her writing grew experimental, seeking to combine ideas from expressionism and the symbolist movement with realism. A contemporary British reviewer compared her "feminine" style to that of Virginia Woolf (pp. 1330–51). The selection included here reflects Glaspell's interest in women, in lives lived under repressive circumstances, and her attention to the importance of symbolism. "Well, women are used to worrying over trifles," one of the male characters comments, and the rest of the play shows that a difference in what one considers "trifling" can make all the difference, even in cases of life and death. Glaspell shows how men's dismissal of the value of women's lives can blind them to the very thing they seek. She also explores the complex world of women's sympathies, examining how even women who do not know each other, or do not know each other well, may establish a significant bond.

Trifles

SCENE. *The kitchen in the now abandoned farmhouse of* JOHN WRIGHT, *a gloomy kitchen, and left without having been put in order—unwashed pans under the sink, a loaf of bread outside the bread-box, a dish-towel on the table—other signs of incompleted work. At the rear the outer door opens and the* SHERIFF *comes in followed by the* COUNTY ATTORNEY *and* HALE. *The* SHERIFF *and* HALE *are men in middle life, the* COUNTY ATTORNEY *is a young man; all are much bundled up and go at once to the stove. They are followed by the two women—the* SHERIFF's *wife first; she is a slight wiry woman, a thin nervous face.* MRS. HALE *is larger and would ordinarily be called more comfortable looking, but she is disturbed now and looks fearfully about as she enters. The women have come in slowly, and stand close together near the door.*

COUNTY ATTORNEY. [*Rubbing his hands.*] This feels good. Come up to the fire, ladies.

MRS. PETERS. [*After taking a step forward.*] I'm not—cold.

SHERIFF. [*Unbuttoning his overcoat and stepping away from the stove as if to mark the beginning of official business.*] Now, Mr. Hale, before we move things about, you explain to Mr. Henderson just what you saw when you came here yesterday morning.

COUNTY ATTORNEY. By the way, has anything been moved? Are things just as you left them yesterday?

SHERIFF. [*Looking about.*] It's just the same. When it dropped below zero last night I thought I'd better send Frank out this morning to make a fire for us—no use getting pneumonia with a big case on, but I told him not to touch anything except the stove—and you know Frank.

COUNTY ATTORNEY. Somebody should have been left here yesterday.

SHERIFF. Oh—yesterday. When I had to send Frank to Morris Center for that man who went crazy—I want you to know I had my hands full yesterday. I knew you could get back from Omaha by today and as long as I went over everything here myself—

COUNTY ATTORNEY. Well, Mr. Hale, tell just what happened when you came here yesterday morning.

HALE. Harry and I had started to town with a load of potatoes. We came along the road from my place and as I got here I said, "I'm going to see if I can't get John Wright to go in with me on a party telephone." I spoke to Wright about it once before and he put me off, saying folks talked too much anyway, and all he asked was peace and quiet—I guess you know about how much he talked himself; but I thought maybe if I went to the house and talked about it before his wife, though I said to Harry that I didn't know as what his wife wanted made much difference to John—

COUNTY ATTORNEY. Let's talk about that later, Mr. Hale. I do want to talk about that, but tell now just what happened when you got to the house.

HALE. I didn't hear or see anything; I knocked at the door, and still it was all quiet inside. I knew they must be up, it was past eight o'clock. So I knocked again, and I thought I heard somebody say, "Come in." I wasn't sure, I'm not sure yet, but I opened the door—this door [*indicating the door by which the two women are still standing*] and there in that rocker—[*pointing to it*] sat Mrs. Wright.

[*They all look at the rocker.*]

COUNTY ATTORNEY. What—was she doing?

HALE. She was rockin' back and forth. She had her apron in her hand and was kind of—pleating it.

COUNTY ATTORNEY. And how did she—look?

HALE. Well, she looked queer.

COUNTY ATTORNEY. How do you mean—queer?

HALE. Well, as if she didn't know what she was going to do next. And kind of done up.

COUNTY ATTORNEY. How did she seem to feel about your coming?

HALE. Why, I don't think she minded—one way or other. She didn't pay much attention. I said, "How do, Mrs. Wright, it's cold, ain't it?" And she said, "Is it?"—and went on kind of pleating at her apron. Well, I was surprised; she didn't ask me to come up to the stove, or to set down, but just sat there, not even looking at me, so I said, "I want to see John." And then she—laughed. I guess you would call it a laugh. I thought of Harry and the team outside, so I said a little sharp: "Can't I see John?" "No," she says, kind o' dull like. "Ain't he home?" says I. "Yes," says she, "he's home." "Then why can't I see him?" I asked her, out of patience. "'Cause he's dead," says she. "*Dead?*" says I. She just nodded her head, not getting a bit excited, but rockin' back and forth. "Why—where is he?" says I, not knowing what to say. She just pointed upstairs—like that [*himself pointing to the room above*]. I got up, with the idea of going up there. I walked from there to here—then I says, "Why, what did he die of?" "He died of a rope round his neck," says she, and just went on pleatin' at her apron. Well, I went out and called Harry. I thought I might—need help. We went upstairs and there he was lyin'—

COUNTY ATTORNEY. I think I'd rather have you go into that upstairs, where you can point it all out. Just go on now with the rest of the story.

HALE. Well, my first thought was to get that rope off. It looked . . . [*Stops, his face twitches*] . . . but Harry, he went up to him, and he said, "No, he's dead all right, and we'd better not touch anything." So we went back downstairs. She was still sitting that same way. "Has anybody been notified?" I asked. "No," says she, unconcerned. "Who did this, Mrs. Wright?" said Harry. He said it business-like—and she stopped pleatin' of her apron. "I don't know," she says. "You don't *know?*" says Harry. "No," says she. "Weren't you sleepin' in the bed with him?" says Harry. "Yes," says she, "but I was on the inside." "Somebody slipped a rope round his neck and strangled him and you didn't wake up?" says Harry. "I didn't wake up," she said after him. We must 'a looked as if we didn't see how that could be, for after a minute she said, "I sleep sound." Harry was going to ask her more questions but I said maybe we ought to let her tell her story first to the coroner, or the sheriff, so Harry went fast as he could to Rivers' place, where there's a telephone.

COUNTY ATTORNEY. And what did Mrs. Wright do when she knew that you had gone for the coroner?

HALE. She moved from that chair to this one over here [*Pointing to a small chair in the corner*] and just sat there with her hands held together and looking down. I got a feeling that I ought to make some conversation, so I said I had come in to see if John wanted to put in a telephone, and at that she started to laugh, and then she stopped and looked at me—scared. [*The* COUNTY ATTORNEY, *who has had his notebook out, makes a note.*] I dunno, maybe it wasn't scared. I wouldn't like to say it was. Soon Harry got back, and then Dr. Lloyd came, and you, Mr. Peters, and so I guess that's all I know that you don't.

COUNTY ATTORNEY. [*Looking around.*] I guess we'll go upstairs first—and then out to the barn and around there. [*To the* SHERIFF.] You're convinced that there was nothing important here—nothing that would point to any motive.

SHERIFF. Nothing here but kitchen things.

[*The* COUNTY ATTORNEY, *after again looking around the kitchen, opens the door of a cupboard closet. He gets up on a chair and looks on a shelf. Pulls his hand away, sticky.*]

COUNTY ATTORNEY. Here's a nice mess.

[*The women draw nearer.*]

MRS. PETERS. [*To the other woman.*] Oh, her fruit; it did freeze. [*To the* LAWYER.] She worried about that when it turned so cold. She said the fire'd go out and her jars would break.

SHERIFF. Well, can you beat the women! Held for murder and worryin' about her preserves.

COUNTY ATTORNEY. I guess before we're through she may have something more serious than preserves to worry about.

HALE. Well, women are used to worrying over trifles.

[The two women move a little closer together.]

COUNTY ATTORNEY. [With the gallantry of a young politician.] And yet, for all their worries, what would we do without the ladies? [The women do not unbend. He goes to the sink, takes a dipperful of water from the pail and pouring it into a basin, washes his hands. Starts to wipe them on the roller-towel, turns it for a cleaner place.] Dirty towels! [Kicks his foot against the pans under the sink.] Not much of a housekeeper, would you say, ladies?

MRS. HALE. [Stiffly.] There's a great deal of work to be done on a farm.

COUNTY ATTORNEY. To be sure. And yet [With a little bow to her] I know there are some Dickson county farmhouses which do not have such roller towels.

[He gives it a pull to expose its full length again.]

MRS. HALE. Those towels get dirty awful quick. Men's hands aren't always as clean as they might be.

COUNTY ATTORNEY. Ah, loyal to your sex, I see. But you and Mrs. Wright were neighbors. I suppose you were friends, too.

MRS. HALE. [Shaking her head.] I've not seen much of her of late years. I've not been in this house—it's more than a year.

COUNTY ATTORNEY. And why was that? You didn't like her?

MRS. HALE. I liked her all well enough. Farmers' wives have their hands full, Mr. Henderson. And then—

COUNTY ATTORNEY. Yes—?

MRS. HALE. [Looking about.] It never seemed a very cheerful place.

COUNTY ATTORNEY. No—it's not cheerful. I shouldn't say she had the home-making instinct.

MRS. HALE. Well, I don't know as Wright had, either.

COUNTY ATTORNEY. You mean that they didn't get on very well?

MRS. HALE. No, I don't mean anything. But I don't think a place'd be any cheerfuller for John Wright's being in it.

COUNTY ATTORNEY. I'd like to talk more of that a little later. I want to get the lay of things upstairs now.

[He goes to the left, where three steps lead to a stair door.]

SHERIFF. I suppose anything Mrs. Peters does'll be all right. She was to take in some clothes for her, you know, and a few little things. We left in such a hurry yesterday.

COUNTY ATTORNEY. Yes, but I would like to see what you take, Mrs. Peters, and keep an eye out for anything that might be of use to us.

MRS. PETERS. Yes, Mr. Henderson.

[The women listen to the men's steps on the stairs, then look about the kitchen.]

MRS. HALE. I'd hate to have men coming into my kitchen, snooping around and criticising.

[*She arranges the pans under sink which the* LAWYER *had shoved out of place.*]

MRS. PETERS. Of course it's no more than their duty.

MRS. HALE. Duty's all right, but I guess that deputy sheriff that came out to make the fire might have got a little of this on. [*Gives the roller towel a pull.*] Wish I'd thought of that sooner. Seems mean to talk about her for not having things slicked up when she had to come away in such a hurry.

MRS. PETERS. [*Who has gone to a small table in the left rear corner of the room, and lifted one end of a towel that covers a pan.*] She had bread set.

[*Stands still.*]

MRS. HALE. [*Eyes fixed on a loaf of bread beside the breadbox, which is on a low shelf at the other side of the room. Moves slowly toward it.*] She was going to put this in there. [*Picks up loaf, then abruptly drops it. In a manner of returning to familiar things.*] It's a shame about her fruit. I wonder if it's all gone. [*Gets up on the chair and looks.*] I think there's some here that's all right, Mrs. Peters. Yes— here; [*Holding it toward the window*] this is cherries, too. [*Looking again.*] I declare I believe that's the only one. [*Gets down, bottle in her hand. Goes to the sink and wipes it off on the outside.*] She'll feel awful bad after all her hard work in the hot weather. I remember the afternoon I put up my cherries last summer.

[*She puts the bottle on the big kitchen table, center of the room. With a sigh, is about to sit down in the rocking-chair. Before she is seated realizes what chair it is; with a slow look at it, steps back. The chair which she has touched rocks back and forth.*]

MRS. PETERS. Well, I must get those things from the front room closet. [*She goes to the door at the right, but after looking into the other room, steps back.*] You coming with me, Mrs. Hale? You could help me carry them.

[*They go in the other room; reappear,* MRS. PETERS *carrying a dress and skirt,* MRS. HALE *following with a pair of shoes.*]

MRS. PETERS. My, it's cold in there.

[*She puts the clothes on the big table, and hurries to the stove.*]

MRS. HALE. [*Examining the skirt.*] Wright was close. I think maybe that's why she kept so much to herself. She didn't even belong to the Ladies Aid.[1] I suppose she felt she couldn't do her part, and then you don't enjoy things when you feel shabby. She used to wear pretty clothes and be lively, when she was Minnie Foster, one of the town girls singing in the choir. But that—oh, that was thirty years ago. This all you was to take in?

MRS. PETERS. She said she wanted an apron. Funny thing to want, for there isn't much to get you dirty in jail, goodness knows. But I suppose just to make her

---

1. Ladies Aid Sewing Circle and Rescue Society, founded in 1893 to quilt and do charitable work, also worked for women's suffrage, women's prop- erty rights, and prohibition; the group disbanded in 1931.

feel more natural. She said they was in the top drawer in this cupboard. Yes, here. And then her little shawl that always hung behind the door. [*Opens stair door and looks.*] Yes, here it is.

[*Quickly shuts door leading upstairs.*]

MRS. HALE. [*Abruptly moving toward her.*] Mrs. Peters?

MRS. PETERS. Yes, Mrs. Hale?

MRS. HALE. Do you think she did it?

MRS. PETERS. [*In a frightened voice.*] Oh, I don't know.

MRS. HALE. Well, I don't think she did. Asking for an apron and her little shawl. Worrying about her fruit.

MRS. PETERS. [*Starts to speak, glances up, where footsteps are heard in the room above. In a low voice.*] Mr. Peters says it looks bad for her. Mr. Henderson is awful sarcastic in a speech and he'll make fun of her sayin' she didn't wake up.

MRS. HALE. Well, I guess John Wright didn't wake when they was slipping that rope under his neck.

MRS. PETERS. No, it's strange. It must have been done awful crafty and still. They say it was such a—funny way to kill a man, rigging it all up like that.

MRS. HALE. That's just what Mr. Hale said. There was a gun in the house. He says that's what he can't understand.

MRS. PETERS. Mr. Henderson said coming out that what was needed for the case was a motive; something to show anger, or—sudden feeling.

MRS. HALE. [*Who is standing by the table.*] Well, I don't see any signs of anger around here. [*She puts her hand on the dish towel which lies on the table, stands looking down at table, one half of which is clean, the other half messy.*] It's wiped to here. [*Makes a move as if to finish work, then turns and looks at loaf of bread outside the breadbox. Drops towel. In that voice of coming back to familiar things.*] Wonder how they are finding things upstairs. I hope she had it a little more red-up[2] up there. You know, it seems kind of *sneaking.* Locking her up in town and then coming out here and trying to get her own house to turn against her!

MRS. PETERS. But Mrs. Hale, the law is the law.

MRS. HALE. I s'pose 'tis. [*Unbuttoning her coat.*] Better loosen up your things, Mrs. Peters. You won't feel them when you go out.

[MRS. PETERS *takes off her fur tippet, goes to hang it on hook at back of room, stands looking at the under part of the small corner table.*]

MRS. PETERS. She was piecing a quilt.

[*She brings the large sewing basket and they look at the bright pieces.*]

MRS. HALE. It's log cabin pattern. Pretty, isn't it? I wonder if she was goin' to quilt it or just knot it?[3]

[*Footsteps have been heard coming down the stairs. The* SHERIFF *enters followed by* HALE *and the* COUNTY ATTORNEY.]

2. Made ready.
3. Two methods of finishing a quilt: quilting involves stitching an intricate pattern, knotting

involves simply securing all layers with a series of knots.

SHERIFF. They wonder if she was going to quilt it or just knot it!

[The men laugh, the women look abashed.]

COUNTY ATTORNEY. *[Rubbing his hands over the stove.]* Frank's fire didn't do much up there, did it? Well, let's go out to the barn and get that cleared up.

[The men go outside.]

MRS. HALE. *[Resentfully.]* I don't know as there's anything so strange, our takin' up our time with little things while we're waiting for them to get the evidence. *[She sits down at the big table smoothing out a block with decision.]* I don't see as it's anything to laugh about.

MRS. PETERS. *[Apologetically.]* Of course they've got awful important things on their minds.

[Pulls up a chair and joins MRS. HALE *at the table.]*

MRS. HALE. *[Examining another block.]* Mrs. Peters, look at this one. Here, this is the one she was working on, and look at the sewing! All the rest of it has been so nice and even. And look at this! It's all over the place! Why, it looks as if she didn't know what she was about!

*[After she had said this they look at each other, then start to glance
back at the door. After an instant* MRS. HALE *has pulled at a knot
and ripped the sewing.]*

MRS. PETERS. Oh, what are you doing, Mrs. Hale?

MRS. HALE. *[Mildly.]* Just pulling out a stitch or two that's not sewed very good. *[Threading a needle.]* Bad sewing always made me fidgety.

MRS. PETERS. *[Nervously.]* I don't think we ought to touch things.

MRS. HALE. I'll just finish up this end. *[Suddenly stopping and leaning forward.]* Mrs. Peters?

MRS. PETERS Yes, Mrs. Hale?

MRS. HALE. What do you suppose she was so nervous about?

MRS. PETERS. Oh—I don't know. I don't know as she was nervous. I sometimes sew awful queer when I'm just tired. *[*MRS. HALE *starts to say something, looks at* MRS. PETERS, *then goes on sewing.]* Well I must get these things wrapped up. They may be through sooner than we think. *[Putting apron and other things together.]* I wonder where I can find a piece of paper, and string.

MRS. HALE. In that cupboard, maybe.

MRS. PETERS. *[Looking in cupboard.]* Why, here's a bird-cage. *[Holds it up.]* Did she have a bird, Mrs. Hale?

MRS. HALE. Why, I don't know whether she did or not—I've not been here for so long. There was a man around last year selling canaries cheap, but I don't know as she took one; maybe she did. She used to sing real pretty herself.

MRS. PETERS. *[Glancing around.]* Seems funny to think of a bird here. But she must have had one, or why would she have a cage? I wonder what happened to it.

MRS. HALE. I s'pose maybe the cat got it.

MRS. PETERS. No, she didn't have a cat. She's got that feeling some people have about cats—being afraid of them. My cat got in her room and she was real upset and asked me to take it out.

MRS. HALE. My sister Bessie was like that. Queer, ain't it?

MRS. PETERS. [*Examining the cage.*] Why, look at this door. It's broke. One hinge is pulled apart.

MRS. HALE. [*Looking too.*] Looks as if someone must have been rough with it.

MRS. PETERS. Why, yes.

[She brings the cage forward and puts it on the table.]

MRS. HALE. I wish if they're going to find any evidence they'd be about it. I don't like this place.

MRS. PETERS. But I'm awful glad you came with me, Mrs. Hale. It would be lonesome for me sitting here alone.

MRS. HALE. It would, wouldn't it? [*Dropping her sewing.*] But I tell you what I do wish, Mrs. Peters. I wish I had come over sometimes when *she* was here. I— [*Looking around the room*]—wish I had.

MRS. PETERS. But of course you were awful busy, Mrs. Hale—your house and your children.

MRS. HALE. I could've come. I stayed away because it weren't cheerful—and that's why I ought to have come. I—I've never liked this place. Maybe because it's down in a hollow and you don't see the road. I dunno what it is, but it's a lonesome place and always was. I wish I had come over to see Minnie Foster sometimes. I can see now—

[Shakes her head.]

MRS. PETERS. Well, you mustn't reproach yourself, Mrs. Hale. Somehow we just don't see how it is with other folks until—something comes up.

MRS. HALE. Not having children makes less work—but it makes a quiet house, and Wright out to work all day, and no company when he did come in. Did you know John Wright, Mrs. Peters?

MRS. PETERS. Not to know him; I've seen him in town. They say he was a good man.

MRS. HALE. Yes—good; he didn't drink, and kept his word as well as most, I guess, and paid his debts. But he was a hard man, Mrs. Peters. Just to pass the time of day with him—[*Shivers.*] Like a raw wind that gets to the bone. [*Pauses, her eye falling on the cage.*] I should think she would 'a wanted a bird. But what do you suppose went with it?

MRS. PETERS. I don't know, unless it got sick and died.

*[She reaches over and swings the broken door, swings it again,
both women watch it.]*

MRS. HALE. You weren't raised round here, were you? [MRS. PETERS *shakes her head.*] You didn't know—her?

MRS. PETERS. Not till they brought her yesterday.

MRS. HALE. She—come to think of it, she was kind of like a bird herself—real sweet and pretty, but kind of timid and—fluttery. How—she—did—change. [*Silence; then as if struck by a happy thought and relieved to get back to every day things.*] Tell you what, Mrs. Peters, why don't you take the quilt in with you? It might take up her mind.

MRS. PETERS. Why, I think that's a real nice idea, Mrs. Hale. There couldn't possibly be any objection to it, could there? Now, just what would I take? I wonder if her patches are in here—and her things.

[*They look in the sewing basket.*]

MRS. HALE. Here's some red. I expect this has got sewing things in it. [*Brings out a fancy box.*] What a pretty box. Looks like something somebody would give you. Maybe her scissors are in here. [*Opens box. Suddenly puts her hand to her nose.*] Why—[MRS. PETERS *bends nearer, then turns her face away.*] There's something wrapped up in this piece of silk.

MRS. PETERS. Why, this isn't her scissors.

MRS. HALE. [*Lifting the silk.*] Oh, Mrs. Peters—it's—

[MRS. PETERS *bends closer.*]

MRS. PETERS. It's the bird.

MRS. HALE. [*Jumping up.*] But, Mrs. Peters—look at it! Its neck! Look at its neck! It's all—other side *to.*

MRS. PETERS. Somebody—wrung—its—neck.

[*Their eyes meet. A look of growing comprehension, of horror. Steps are heard outside.* MRS. HALE *slips box under quilt pieces, and sinks into her chair. Enter* SHERIFF *and* COUNTY ATTORNEY. MRS. PETERS *rises.*]

COUNTY ATTORNEY. [*As one turning from serious things to little pleasantries.*] Well, ladies, have you decided whether she was going to quilt it or knot it?

MRS. PETERS. We think she was going to—knot it.

COUNTY ATTORNEY. Well, that's interesting, I'm sure. [*Seeing the birdcage.*] Has the bird flown?

MRS. HALE. [*Putting more quilt pieces over the box.*] We think the—cat got it.

COUNTY ATTORNEY. [*Preoccupied.*] Is there a cat?

[MRS. HALE *glances in a quick covert way at* MRS. PETERS.]

MRS. PETERS. Well, not *now.* They're superstitious, you know. They leave.

COUNTY ATTORNEY. [*To* SHERIFF PETERS, *continuing an interrupted conversation.*] No sign at all of anyone having come from the outside. Their own rope. Now let's go up again and go over it piece by piece. [*They start upstairs.*] It would have to have been someone who knew just the—

[MRS. PETERS *sits down. The two women sit there not looking at one another, but as if peering into something and at the same time holding back. When they talk now it is in the manner of feeling their way over strange ground, as if afraid of what they are saying, but as if they can not help saying it.*]

MRS. HALE. She liked the bird. She was going to bury it in that pretty box.

MRS. PETERS. [*In a whisper.*] When I was a girl—my kitten—there was a boy took a hatchet, and before my eyes—and before I could get there—[*Covers her face an instant.*] If they hadn't held me back I would have—[*Catches herself, looks upstairs where the steps are heard, falters weakly*]—hurt him.

These two images, both taken by the prominent photographer Gertrude Kasebier in 1898, reflect the schism in Zitkala Sa's (Gertrude Bonnin's) life between American Indian and European American cultures.

From there, she went on to Earlham College and the Boston Conservatory, both on scholarship. A talented violinist, she became a music teacher and concert soloist for the Carlisle Indian School but was fired from that post for publishing auto-biographical essays that questioned the school's aim of erasing all evidence of American Indian ethnicity from its students (see pp. 1309–10).

Gertrude Simmons Bonnin's life reflects both her connection to her traditional roots and her inculcation in European American ways. In 1902 she married Raymond Talesfase Bonnin, a Sioux man she had known since childhood, and they moved to Uintah and Ouray Reservation in Utah, where he worked for the federal Indian Service. She was involved in political advocacy from that point on, eventually moving to Washington, D.C., to serve as the secretary for the Society of the American Indian—the first exclusively native-run advocacy organization of its kind—and to edit its journal, *The American Indian Magazine*. She also co-wrote (with William Hanson) *Sun Dance,* the first American Indian–authored opera, published a collection of traditional Sioux narratives, and co-authored *Oklahoma's Poor Rich Indians: An Orgy of Graft and Exploitation of the Five Civilized Tribes*. During the 1920s, she founded the National Council of American Indians to promote pan-tribal American Indian rights and served as its president until her death. She traveled extensively giving lectures on Indian rights and worked for American Indian citizenship and enfranchisement, the abolition of the Bureau of Indian Affairs, and tribal land-policy reforms. She used her linguistic abilities in English to promote the preservation of her tribal heritage and her knowledge of American culture to educate white Americans about the value of native culture.

Zitkala Sa's essays in *Harper's* and the *Atlantic Monthly,* from which our selections below are drawn, stand in contrast to most of the writings published by and about American Indians at the turn of the twentieth century. The typical narrative published for white audiences about Native Americans depicted them as savages or as grateful for being "saved" by white educators and Christian missionaries. Zitkala Sa wrote instead about the loss of culture, about an idyllic childhood before the tortures of school, about devotion to her traditional religion, and about the pain of being torn between two cultures. "The Cutting of My Long Hair" deals with the loss, not just of her hair, but of its cultural significance; losing her hair comes to stand for a loss of her earlier way of life. "Why I Am a Pagan" illustrates not only her respect for her traditions but also her respect for differences among people and her acceptance of change even while trying to preserve her own faith.

From School Days of an Indian Girl

The Cutting of My Long Hair

The first day in the land of apples[1] was a bitter-cold one; for the snow still covered the ground, and the trees were bare. A large bell rang for breakfast, its loud metallic voice crashing through the belfry overhead and into our sensitive ears. The annoying clatter of shoes on bare floors gave us no peace. The constant clash of harsh noises, with an undercurrent of many voices murmuring an unknown tongue, made a bedlam within which I was securely tied. And though my spirit tore itself in struggling for its lost freedom, all was useless.

A paleface woman, with white hair, came up after us. We were placed in a line of girls who were marching into the dining room. These were Indian girls, in stiff shoes and closely clinging dresses. The small girls wore sleeved aprons and shingled[2] hair. As I walked noiselessly in my soft moccasins, I felt like sinking to the floor, for my blanket had been stripped from my shoulders. I looked hard at the Indian girls, who seemed not to care that they were even more immodestly dressed than I, in their tightly fitting clothes. While we marched in, the boys entered at an opposite door. I watched for the three young braves who came in our party. I spied them in the rear ranks, looking as uncomfortable as I felt.

A small bell was tapped, and each of the pupils drew a chair from under the table. Supposing this act meant they were to be seated, I pulled out mine and at once slipped into it from one side. But when I turned my head, I saw that I was the only one seated, and all the rest at our table remained standing. Just as I began to rise, looking shyly around to see how chairs were to be used, a second bell was sounded. All were seated at last, and I had to crawl back into my chair again. I heard a man's voice at one end of the hall, and I looked around to see him. But all the others hung their heads over their plates. As I glanced at the long chain of tables, I caught the eyes of a paleface woman upon me. Immediately I dropped my eyes, wondering why I was so keenly watched by the strange woman. The man ceased his mutterings, and then a third bell was tapped. Every one picked up his knife and fork and began eating. I began crying instead, for by this time I was afraid to venture anything more.

---

1. In an earlier chapter, she explains that the children were enticed into attending school with the promise of apples; she uses this as a metaphor for

a fall from innocence.
2. Cut short and close to the head.

But this eating by formula was not the hardest trial in that first day. Late in the morning, my friend Judéwin gave me a terrible warning. Judéwin knew a few words of English; and she had overheard the paleface woman talk about cutting our long, heavy hair. Our mothers had taught us that only unskilled warriors who were captured had their hair shingled by the enemy. Among our people, short hair was worn by mourners, and shingled hair by cowards!

We discussed our fate some moments, and when Judéwin said, "We have to submit, because they are strong," I rebelled.

"No, I will not submit! I will struggle first!" I answered.

I watched my chance, and when no one noticed I disappeared. I crept up the stairs as quietly as I could in my squeaking shoes,—my moccasins had been exchanged for shoes. Along the hall I passed, without knowing whither I was going. Turning aside to an open door, I found a large room with three white beds in it. The windows were covered with dark green curtains, which made the room very dim. Thankful that no one was there, I directed my steps toward the corner farthest from the door. On my hands and knees I crawled under the bed, and cuddled myself in the dark corner.

From my hiding place I peered out, shuddering with fear whenever I heard footsteps near by. Though in the hall loud voices were calling my name, and I knew that even Judéwin was searching for me, I did not open my mouth to answer. Then the steps were quickened and the voices became excited. The sounds came nearer and nearer. Women and girls entered the room. I held my breath, and watched them open closet doors and peep behind large trunks. Some one threw up the curtains, and the room was filled with sudden light. What caused them to stoop and look under the bed I do not know. I remember being dragged out, though I resisted by kicking and scratching wildly. In spite of myself, I was carried downstairs and tied fast in a chair.

I cried aloud, shaking my head all the while until I felt the cold blades of the scissors against my neck, and heard them gnaw off one of my thick braids. Then I lost my spirit. Since the day I was taken from my mother I had suffered extreme indignities. People had stared at me. I had been tossed about in the air like a wooden puppet. And now my long hair was shingled like a coward's! In my anguish I moaned for my mother, but no one came to comfort me. Not a soul reasoned quietly with me, as my own mother used to do: for now I was only one of many little animals driven by a herder.

1900

Why I Am a Pagan

When the spirit swells my breast I love to roam leisurely among the green hills; or sometimes, sitting on the brink of the murmuring Missouri, I marvel at the great blue overhead. With half closed eyes I watch the huge cloud shadows in their noise-less play upon the high bluffs opposite me, while into my ear ripple the sweet, soft cadences of the river's song. Folded hands lie in my lap, for the time forgot. My heart and I lie small upon the earth like a grain of throbbing sand. Drifting clouds and tinkling waters, together with the warmth of a genial summer day, bespeak with eloquence the loving Mystery round about us. During the idle while I sat upon the sunny river brink, I grew somewhat, though my response be not so clearly manifest as in the green grass fringing the edge of the high bluff back of me.

At length retracing the uncertain footpath scaling the precipitous embankment, I seek the level lands where grow the wild prairie flowers. And they, the lovely little folk, soothe my soul with their perfumed breath.

Their quaint round faces of varied hue convince the heart which leaps with glad surprise that they, too, are living symbols of omnipotent thought. With a child's eager eye I drink in the myriad star shapes wrought in luxuriant color upon the green. Beautiful is the spiritual essence they embody.

I leave them nodding in the breeze, but take along with me their impress upon my heart. I pause to rest me upon a rock embedded on the side of a foothill facing the low river bottom. Here the Stone-Boy,[3] of whom the American aborigine tells, frolics about, shooting his baby arrows and shouting aloud with glee at the tiny shafts of lightning that flash from the flying arrow-beaks.[4] What an ideal warrior he became, baffling the siege of the pests of all the land till he triumphed over their united attack. And here he lay,—Inyan our great-great-grandfather, older than the hill he rested on, older than the race of men who love to tell of his wonderful career.

Interwoven with the thread of this Indian legend of the rock, I fain would trace a subtle knowledge of the native folk which enabled them to recognize a kinship to any and all parts of this vast universe. By the leading of an ancient trail I move toward the Indian village.

With the strong, happy sense that both great and small are so surely enfolded in His magnitude that, without a miss, each has his allotted individual ground of opportunities, I am buoyant with good nature.

Yellow Breast, swaying upon the slender stem of a wild sunflower, warbles a sweet assurance of this as I pass near by. Breaking off the clear crystal song, he turns his wee head from side to side eyeing me wisely as slowly I plod with moccasined feet. Then again he yields himself to his song of joy. Flit, flit hither and yon, he fills the summer sky with his swift, sweet melody. And truly does it seem his vigorous freedom lies more in his little spirit than in his wing.

With these thoughts I reach the log cabin whither I am strongly drawn by the tie of a child to an aged mother. Out bounds my four-footed friend to meet me, frisking about my path with unmistakable delight. Chän is a black shaggy dog, "a thorough bred little mongrel" of whom I am very fond. Chän seems to understand many words in Sioux, and will go to her mat even when I whisper the word, though generally I think she is guided by the tone of the voice. Often she tries to imitate the sliding inflection and long drawn out voice to the amusement of our guests, but her articulation is quite beyond my ear. In both my hands I hold her shaggy head and gaze into her large brown eyes. At once the dilated pupils contract into tiny black dots, as if the roguish spirit within would evade my questioning.

Finally resuming the chair at my desk I feel in keen sympathy with my fellow creatures, for I seem to see clearly again that all are akin.

The racial lines, which once were bitterly real, now serve nothing more than marking out a living mosaic of human beings. And even here men of the same color are like the ivory keys of one instrument where each resembles all the rest,

3. Inyanhoksila, a popular figure in Dakota Sioux lore, was born from a stone and known for his abilities with a bow and arrow.
4. arrow-beaks: arrowheads.

yet varies from them in pitch and quality of voice. And those creatures who are for a time mere echoes of another's note are not unlike the fable of the thin sick man whose distorted shadow, dressed like a real creature, came to the old master to make him follow as a shadow. Thus with a compassion for all echoes in human guise, I greet the solemn-faced "native preacher" whom I find awaiting me. I listen with respect for God's creature, though he mouth most strangely the jangling phrases of a bigoted creed.

As our tribe is one large family, where every person is related to all the others, he addressed me:—

"Cousin, I came from the morning church service to talk with you."

"Yes?" I said interrogatively, as he paused for some word from me.

Shifting uneasily about in the straight-backed chair he sat upon, he began: "Every holy day (Sunday) I look about our little God's house, and not seeing you there, I am disappointed. This is why I come to-day. Cousin, as I watch you from afar, I see no unbecoming behavior and hear only good reports of you, which all the more burns me with the wish that you were a church member. Cousin, I was taught long years ago by kind missionaries to read the holy book. These godly men taught me also the folly of our old beliefs.

"There is one God who gives reward or punishment to the race of dead men. In the upper region the Christian dead are gathered in unceasing song and prayer. In the deep pit below, the sinful ones dance in torturing flames.

"Think upon these things, my cousin, and choose now to avoid the after-doom of hell fire!" Then followed a long silence in which he clasped tighter and unclasped again his interlocked fingers.

Like instantaneous lightning flashes came pictures of my own mother's making, for she, too, is now a follower of the new superstition.

"Knocking out the chinking of our log cabin, some evil hand thrust in a burning taper of braided dry grass, but failed of his intent, for the fire died out and the half burned brand fell inward to the floor. Directly above it, on a shelf, lay the holy book. This is what we found after our return from a several days' visit. Surely some great power is hid in the sacred book!"

Brushing away from my eyes many like pictures, I offered midday meal to the converted Indian sitting wordless and with downcast face. No sooner had he risen from the table with "Cousin, I have relished it," than the church bell rang.

Thither he hurried forth with his afternoon sermon. I watched him as he hastened along, his eyes bent fast upon the dusty road till he disappeared at the end of a quarter of a mile.

The little incident recalled to mind the copy of a missionary paper brought to my notice a few days ago, in which a "Christian" pugilist commented upon a recent article of mine, grossly perverting the spirit of my pen. Still I would not forget that the pale-faced missionary and the hoodooed aborigine are both God's creatures, though small indeed their own conceptions of Infinite Love. A wee child toddling in a wonder world, I prefer to their dogma my excursions into the natural gardens where the voice of the Great Spirit is heard in the twittering of birds, the rippling of mighty waters, and the sweet breathing of flowers. If this is Paganism, then at present, at least, I am a Pagan.

1902

CULTURAL COORDINATES
Indian Boarding Schools

References to Indian boarding schools appear throughout this book—Zitkala Sa (pp. 1303–8) and Mourning Dove (pp. 1327–30) both were sent to them, Marianne Moore (pp. 1373–78) taught in one, and Louise Erdrich (pp. 1930–40) and Leslie Marmon Silko (pp. 1827–36), in her novel *Gardens in the Dunes*, have both written about them. Although today we still have a pattern of largely segregated education for American Indians, the phenomenon of the boarding school is an important part of American Indian history, especially in its relation to women writing in English.

By the late nineteenth century, millions of people from the First Nations (American Indians) had died from disease, wars, famines, and exploitation that were the result of the European settlement of North America, and the United States and Canada had removed most tribes from their traditional lands and settled them on reservations in areas then considered wastelands. Reformers were beginning to argue against open warfare and for education and assimilation to "civilize" the natives and make them part of U.S. and Canadian societies. There was no movement at the time to respect and preserve native cultures, languages, and knowledge; the goal from the beginning was to train young men and women to speak English, learn European ways, and leave behind their "Indian-ness."

These young Indian children from Spokane were sent across the state of Washington and south to an Indian boarding school in Portland, Oregon.

At first, missionaries tried day schools on reservations and then boarding schools near the reservations, but since students were able to remain in contact with their families, the goal of eradicating Indian languages, religions, and ways was not met. As Colonel Richard H. Pratt, the founder of the Carlisle Indian Industrial School (where both Zitkala Sa and Marianne Moore taught for a time), put it: "I believe that the system of removing them from their tribes and placing them under continuous training in the midst of civilization is far better than any other method. . . . The end to be gained . . . [is for] the Indian to lose his identity as such. . . . The sooner all tribal relations are broken up, the sooner the Indian loses all his Indian ways, even his language, the better it will be for him and for the government." The policies of the United States and Canada generally followed this line of thinking, and many residential schools, which children were compelled to attend, were established. Children were sometimes rounded up by the military, but more often they and their families were subjected to severe punishments, including starvation, if they refused.

As we see in Zitkala Sa's account of her experience, at the schools students were forbidden to speak their languages, use their real names (they were assigned European names), or practice their religions. Their appearance was forcibly Europeanized: their hair was cut, they were required to wear European clothing, and their clothing from home was burned. While Zitkala Sa was trained in music and oratory, most students were only minimally educated in academic or artistic subjects and were instead given vocational training that would prepare them for menial service. Many students reported physical, psychological, and sexual abuse. By the late 1920s and 1930s, it was becoming clear that the Indian schools were not working to anyone's benefit; students were not becoming assimilated but were returning from the schools alienated from both Indian and white culture. American Indian reformers were able to organize protests against the loss of native languages and cultures and were able to publicize the problems with the schools, which were gradually closed in favor of reservation schools, where children were able to remain with their families and tribes.

As readers of contemporary American Indian women writers, we stand in an odd relation to these schools. American literature has benefited enormously from the talent, history, and worldviews of native women writers, and we might not have benefited from their contributions today were it not for the education they and their forerunners received in English. But we also have to recognize that the very fact of their having to write in English is the result of a history of conquest and cultural destruction.

◄ MARGARET COUSINS ►
1878–1954

Margaret Cousins grew up in rural Ireland, the oldest daughter of a middle-class Unionist legal officer. While studying at the Royal Irish Academy of Music in Dublin, she became interested in Irish cultural nationalism; soon she became involved in the movement, particularly as an advocate for women's suffrage. Together with her husband, James Cousins, a like-minded radical thinker and writer, she founded the Irish Women's Franchise League (IWFL) in 1908. For several years, Cousins was a prominent leader in the IWFL, which was the most militant of the various Irish suffragist groups. Her activism twice led to her imprisonment.

In 1913, she and her husband emigrated to India, where they worked with the Theosophical Society in Madras in southern India. Still committed to the cause of women's suffrage, Cousins founded the Indian Women's Association in 1914. After becoming the first female magistrate in India in 1922, she agitated to include the rights of women in the drive for Indian independence, founding the first All-India Women's conference in 1928. In 1932, while serving as magistrate, Cousins was jailed again; she received a one-year sentence for protesting the curtailing of free speech in India. Following her release, she was elected president of the All-India Women's conference. She continued to work for women's rights in India until her death.

Central to Cousins's contributions to the women's movement are the connections she made in her writings between British imperialism in Ireland and India and the global struggle for women's rights. In the following excerpt from *The Awakening of Asian Womanhood* (1922), Cousins writes about the potential of Indian women to play a full and equal role in the formation of a free nation.

From The Awakening of Asian Womanhood

Chapter 2
Indian Womanhood: A National Asset

No movement for national, moral, or social progress can attain its true and maximum success if it studies the well-being and works through the agency of one sex only or primarily. Usually however the welfare of women is considered of such secondary importance that it is either overlooked, or left to the future for enquiry, or taken for granted as being so satisfactory as to need no improvement. Yet a little thought enables one to trace many of the problems needing solution back to the failure to recognise the vital importance to India of the service which can be rendered to her only by her women—problems that have arisen because of conditions in women's life which urgently need remedying in order that the gifts brought by them, in common with the women of all nations, to their motherland may be as valuable as nature has intended them to be.

The Creator of the universe has entrusted to women the supreme honour of creating in detail and bringing into being every human unit in the nation. Women are the supreme nation-builders in the physical sense. Their function of motherhood, with its pains, responsibilities, recompenses, sorrows and joys, is an international bond of union among women all the world over. The service given by women to the nation in the bearing of children is invaluable, a service paid for by their very lives in only too many cases, alas! since in India 232 more women than men die out of every 1,000 between the ages of 15 and 30. Women constantly face their own battlefield without any pomp, glory, proper equipment or due appreciation; and in their person is the struggle often fought to a finish between the forces of Life and Death. They are as much national heroes as any khaki-clad soldier in the European War.[1] Part of this great service of building bodies consists in the immense work of feeding, clothing, and cleaning the community. The work of the world would go on badly, and the temper of the men suffer seriously, but for the amount of cooking alone done by women! Men rarely realise that women's work is a great deal more than sitting at home. Women themselves rarely appreciate their own work at its proper and proportionate value. In reality Indian women are doing as great a part of the work of the country in building up the human bodies as men are doing in building up the National Constitution or in doing any other work that belongs to them.

* * *

* * * Turning to another side of women's influence on the national life, it is not sufficiently realised that women naturally demand and appreciate beauty in their surroundings. Their desire for lovely colours and fine textures in their clothes, for pretty ornaments and jewelry, for flower-decked hair and perfumes, have a much deeper root than vanity. It is an evidence of their inherent love of beauty, and it is an invaluable asset to the Nation since it draws forth the arts and crafts that are the pride of India. It is no harm for girls to have a love of really beautiful things. Far from being a weakness, it is a strength, so long as it is not used only for selfish enjoyment, but cultivated with a view also to adding to the beauty of their country. Let them be encouraged to bring all the loveliness they desire into their homes, their gardens, and their country. Thus will they enrich sordid human conditions. This same inherent love of beauty shows itself in the talent girls have for learning poetry, for acting (when they get the chance), for music. They have natural gifts of imagination and sensitive emotion which at present are largely wasted for want of the education which alone can make permanent the fleeting inspirations of the artistic soul. Who does not remember with pride such poetesses as Mira Bai, Mukta Bai, Toru Dutt and Sarojini Naidu?[2] There is a wealth of art-life hidden and dormant in Indian women waiting for educational opportunity to manifest itself. Oh, the tragedy of it that only one girl out of every hundred, or only thirteen out of every thousand, gets any education in India! The disgrace of this state of affairs is appalling, nay, criminal, when one thinks how in the West 90 girls out of every 100 get a good, free and compulsory education lasting at least eight years. In addition there is the insult shown to the feminine side in the fact that for every 13 girls educated there are 138 boys provided with schooling, that is, over ten times as much attention is paid to boys in India in one of the most vital points of the Nation's life than is paid to girls—a suicidal policy indeed! for the result is that of every 100 boys who wish to march forward, 90 will be held back by the illiteracy of their untaught girl-wives.

* * *

1. World War I.
2. Mira Bai: a sixteenth-century poet who wrote devotional verses dedicated to Lord Krishna; Mukta Bai: a thirteenth-century poet-saint who wrote devotional poetry; Toru Dutt: the first Indian woman (1856–78) to write poetry in English; Sarojini Naidu: also an Indian woman poet and nationalist (1879–1949; see pp. 1313–16).

Not only do common-sense and common science demonstrate the desirability, nay, the absolute necessity of greater education and greater freedom of body and soul for women, but all the Indian religions support this ideal of the equal comradeship of the masculine and the feminine. Time was in India when she could boast of her daughters as women of individuality, power and capability, women who were no mere shadows of men, but sturdy human souls, equaling men, with full freedom for self-expression. Indian women to-day must follow their example, nerving themselves to face and fight all forms of national evil, such as selfishness, intemperance, and immorality; emulating their self-reliance; thinking for themselves, ashamed to be hung any longer like mill-stones round the necks of their male relations, but, instead, offering their own free services to their Motherland with their own distinctive views concerning the solution of national problems. The Nation is but the larger household. The motherhood-spirit is wanted in its administration. Men are not mothers and fathers combined! Let them not arrogate all public service to themselves, but leave opportunities for public service as well as private service open to women. Now, when schemes of self-government are being developed, let no artificial man-made barriers and restrictions be placed in the way of woman's free entry into the political, religious and social life of the country. She may not be ready yet for it, but the path must not be in a state of blockade and of vested sex-prejudice when she reaches the point at which her spirit and influence of motherhood overflows from the private life to the mothering of the national family. God alone may put bounds to the progress of the human soul whether it functions in a male or female body. Let neither sex arrogate to itself that Divine right of restriction, but let *freedom* and *equal opportunity, mutual encouragement, respect* and *recognition* form the foundations of a new era of comradeship of men and women in the land sacred with the memory of heroes and heroines. Then only will India realise the value of the gifts her women can bring to her altar, and the impoverishment of her national life that is now taking place owing to the false conditions under which they have to live—conditions so bad that instinctively no man wants to be reborn a woman; and woman herself depreciates or is ignorant of her own value, acquiesces in wrong ideas of herself as "temptress," "unclean" and secondary, instead of realising the honour and responsibility that are given to her by the Creator.

It will not always be so, and those who work for the day of her coming into her full kingdom are amongst the blessed pioneers of humanity.

1922

◄ SAROJINI NAIDU ►
1879–1949

Sarojini Naidu, "the Nightingale of India," published three poetry collections— *The Golden Threshold* (1905), *The Bird of Time* (1912), and *The Broken Wing* (1912)—to critical acclaim; all attracted a wide readership in both India and England, and she was elected to the Royal Society of Literature in 1914. But under the influence of figures like Mohandas Gandhi, Naidu gave up poetry writing and became a passionate activist for Indian independence. She was the first elected governor of Uttar Pradesh, a large province in north India, at the time of her death.

The oldest of eight children, Naidu was born to an upper-caste (Brahmin) family. Her father was principal and founder of Nizam's College at Hyderabad (a princely state); her mother was a Bengali poet. A precocious student, she topped the matriculation examination at Madras University at the age of twelve; and at sixteen, she earned a scholarship to study in England, first at King's College, London, and later at Girton, the newly founded women's college at Cambridge University. Naidu found life at Cambridge spiritless and rigid, and her delicate health forced her to give up formal higher education; for a time, she remained in Europe, traveling, reading art books, and writing poetry. But she returned to India in 1898 to marry Govindarajulu Naidu, a non-Brahmin doctor. Their intercaste marriage scandalized conservative circles, but the couple led a happy married life.

In political spheres, Naidu gained a reputation as an activist and leader. She presided over the annual session of the Indian National Congress at Kanpur in 1925 and played a major role in the famous Dandi March, led by Gandhi against the British colonial policy of taxing salt. She also devoted herself to the emancipation of women, serving as president of the National Women's Conference for many years and to the cause of Hindu-Muslim unity. Naidu renounced the wearing of silks and other luxury fabrics in favor of the handspun *khadi*, a material that came to symbolize simplicity and self-reliance during the freedom struggle.

Accompanying Gandhi to England, Naidu played a key role in mobilizing support for Indian independence abroad. In 1928, she traveled to the United States to promote Gandhi's nonviolence movement and to counter the misrepresentations of Indian women propagated by Katherine Mayo's *Mother India* (see pp. 1251–55).

Naidu loved the British romantic poets, especially Percy Bysshe Shelley (1792–1822), and she was influenced by Alfred, Lord Tennyson (1809–92), and Elizabeth Barrett Browning (1806–61; see pp. 650–52). Her own poetry treats traditionally romantic themes such as love, death, and longing for an ideal past. The following poems, selected from *The Sceptered Flute* (1928), a collection of her previously published poems, represent the lyrical verse so characteristic of Naidu— reminiscent of English romanticism, they evoke a uniquely Indian landscape.

The Gift of India

Is there aught you need that my hands withhold,
Rich gifts of raiment or grain or gold?
Lo! I have flung to the East and West
Priceless treasures torn from my breast,
And yielded the sons of my stricken womb
To the drum-beats of duty, the sabres of doom.

Gathered like pearls in their alien graves
Silent they sleep by the Persian waves,
Scattered like shells on Egyptian sands,
They lie with pale brows and brave, broken hands,
They are strewn like blossoms mown down by chance
On the blood-brown meadows of Flanders and France.

Can ye measure the grief of the tears I weep
Or compass the woe of the watch I keep?
Or the pride that thrills thro' my heart's despair

5

10

And the hope that comforts the anguish of prayer? 15
And the far sad glorious vision I see
Of the torn red banners of Victory?

When the terror and tumult of hate shall cease
And life be refashioned on anvils of peace,
And your love shall offer memorial thanks 20
To the comrades who fought in your dauntless ranks,
And you honour the deeds of the deathless ones,
Remember the blood of my martyred sons!

1915

The Indian Gipsy

In tattered robes that hoard a glittering trace
Of bygone colours, broidered to the knee,
Behold her, daughter of a wandering race,
Tameless, with the bold falcon's agile grace,
And the lithe tiger's sinuous majesty. 5

With frugal skill her simple wants she tends,
She folds her tawny heifers and her sheep
On lonely meadows when the daylight ends,
Ere the quick night upon her flock descends
Like a black panther from the caves of sleep. 10

Time's river winds in foaming centuries
Its changing, swift, irrevocable course
To far off and incalculable seas;
She is twin-born with primal mysteries,
And drinks of life at Time's forgotten source.

1916

Bangle-Sellers

Bangle-sellers are we who bear
Our shining loads to the temple fair. . . .
Who will buy these delicate, bright
Rainbow-tinted circles of light?
Lustrous tokens of radiant lives,
For happy daughters and happy wives. 5

Some are meet for a maiden's wrist,
Silver and blue as the mountain-mist,
Some are flushed like the buds that dream
On the tranquil brow of a woodland stream;
Some are aglow with the bloom that cleaves 10
To the limpid glory of new-born leaves.

Some are like fields of sunlit corn,
Meet for a bride on her bridal morn,
Some, like the flame of her marriage fire,

Or rich with the hue of her heart's desire,   15
Tinkling, luminous, tender, and clear,
Like her bridal laughter and bridal tear.

Some are purple and gold-flecked grey,
For her who has journeyed through life midway,
Whose hands have cherished, whose love has blest   20
And cradled fair sons on her faithful breast,
Who serves her household in fruitful pride,
And worships the gods at her husband's side.

                                                                  1916

◦◄ ROKEYA SAKHAWAT HOSSAIN ►◦
1880–1932

Rokeya Sakhawat Hossain was born to an upper-class Muslim family in Paira-
band, a small village in what today is Bangladesh. Her father was a well-educated
and influential landowner whose massive estate was a stronghold for traditional
life in the region; her mother practiced *purdah*—the seclusion or veiling of women
(see pp. 1325–26)—and was the first of her father's four wives. As well-to-do traditional Muslims, Hossain's brothers attended St. Xavier's College, one of Calcutta's most prestigious institutions of higher education, while Hossain and her
sisters were educated at home. As was typical in elite Muslim families, the girls
studied Arabic so that they could read the Koran and learned Urdu so that they
could read popular books on feminine conduct. They were prevented from learning Bengali or English in order to "protect" them from Hindu and British society.
Breaking with tradition, Hossain's oldest brother, Ibrahim, secretly taught Rokeya
and her sister English and Bengali; both sisters became writers.

In 1896, Ibrahim arranged for sixteen-year-old Rokeya to marry Syed
Sakhawat Hossain, a distinguished, London-educated widower in his late thirties.
Syed was the district magistrate of the Bihar region of the Bengal Presidency, and
Ibrahim was impressed by his progressive outlook. After their marriage, Syed encouraged Hossain's writing, and in 1903–4, she started publishing articles on
women's subjugation in patriarchal society in various Calcutta journals. She wrote
mostly in Bengali, using humor and irony to reach ordinary Muslim women and
to raise consciousness about the oppressive social customs imposed upon women
in the name of religion or tradition.

When Syed died in 1909, Hossain started a school for Muslim women in her
husband's memory. A year later, a family feud over property forced her to close
the school and to abandon her house in Bhagalpur. Hossain moved to Calcutta,
where she started the Sakhawat Memorial Girls' School in 1911. The school flourished, and by 1930, it had attained the status of a high school.

Throughout her life, Hossain advocated, through writing and activism, for
women's rights. In 1916, she founded the Bengali Women's Association. In 1932,
she died while presiding over a session of the Indian Women's Conference. She left
an unfinished essay titled "Narir Adhikar," or "The Rights of Women."

The story that follows, "Sultana's Dream" (1905), is one of the earliest pieces of utopian literature written by a woman. (It precedes the American writer Charlotte Perkins Gilman's *Herland* by nearly a decade.) It anticipates future technologies such as solar power, while questioning the conventions of the present day. In particular, the author imagines a world in which *purdah* has been reversed, with men wearing veils and sequestered from public life and the ruling women ushering in an era of peace and prosperity

Sultana's Dream

One evening I was lounging in an easy chair in my bedroom and thinking lazily of the condition of Indian womanhood. I am not sure whether I dozed off or not. But, as far as I remember, I was wide awake. I saw the moonlit sky sparkling with thousands of diamondlike stars, very distinctly.

All on a sudden a lady stood before me; how she came in, I do not know. I took her for my friend, Sister Sara.

"Good morning," said Sister Sara. I smiled inwardly as I knew it was not morning, but starry night. However, I replied to her, saying, "How do you do?"

"I am all right, thank you. Will you please come out and have a look at our garden?"

I looked again at the moon through the open window, and thought there was no harm in going out at that time. The menservants outside were fast asleep just then, and I could have a pleasant walk with Sister Sara.

I used to have my walks with Sister Sara, when we were at Darjeeling. Many a time did we walk hand in hand and talk lightheartedly in the botanical gardens there. I fancied Sister Sara had probably come to take me to some such garden, and I readily accepted her offer and went out with her.

When walking I found to my surprise that it was a fine morning. The town was fully awake and the streets alive with bustling crowds. I was feeling very shy, thinking I was walking in the street in broad daylight, but there was not a single man visible.

Some of the passersby made jokes at me. Though I could not understand their language, yet I felt sure they were joking. I asked my friend, "What do they say?"

"The women say you look very mannish."

"Mannish?" said I. "What do they mean by that?"

"They mean that you are shy and timid like men."

"Shy and timid like men?" It was really a joke. I became very nervous when I found that my companion was not Sister Sara, but a stranger. Oh, what a fool had I been to mistake this lady for my dear old friend Sister Sara.

She felt my fingers tremble in her hand, as we were walking hand in hand.

"What is the matter, dear, dear?" she said affectionately.

"I feel somewhat awkward," I said, in a rather apologizing tone, "as being a purdahnishin[1] woman I am not accustomed to walking about unveiled."

"You need not be afraid of coming across a man here. This is Ladyland, free from sin and harm. Virtue herself reigns here."

---

1. A veiled woman (see pp. 1325–26).

By and by I was enjoying the scenery. Really it was very grand. I mistook a patch of green grass for a velvet cushion. Feeling as if I were walking on a soft carpet, I looked down and found the path covered with moss and flowers.

"How nice it is," said I.

"Do you like it?" asked Sister Sara. (I continued calling her "Sister Sara," and she kept calling me by my name.)

"Yes, very much; but I do not like to tread on the tender and sweet flowers."

"Never mind, dear Sultana. Your treading will not harm them; they are street flowers."

"The whole place looks like a garden," said I admiringly. "You have arranged every plant so skillfully."

"Your Calcutta could become a nicer garden than this, if only your countrymen wanted to make it so."

"They would think it useless to give so much attention to horticulture, while they have so many other things to do."

"They could not find a better excuse," said she with [a] smile.

I became very curious to know where the men were. I met more than a hundred women while walking there, but not a single man.

"Where are the men?" I asked her.

"In their proper places, where they ought to be."

"Pray let me know what you mean by 'their proper places.'"

"Oh, I see my mistake, you cannot know our customs, as you were never here before. We shut our men indoors."

"Just as we are kept in the zenana?"[2]

"Exactly so."

"How funny." I burst into a laugh. Sister Sara laughed too.

"But, dear Sultana, how unfair it is to shut in the harmless women and let loose the men."

"Why? It is not safe for us to come out of the zenana, as we are naturally weak."

"Yes, it is not safe so long as there are men about the streets, nor is it so when a wild animal enters a marketplace."

"Of course not."

"Suppose some lunatics escape from the asylum and begin to do all sorts of mischief to men, horses, and other creatures: in that case what will your countrymen do?"

"They will try to capture them and put them back into their asylum."

"Thank you! And you do not think it wise to keep sane people inside an asylum and let loose the insane?"

"Of course not!" said I, laughing lightly.

"As a matter of fact, in your country this very thing is done! Men, who do or at least are capable of doing no end of mischief, are let loose and the innocent women shut up in the zenana! How can you trust those untrained men out of doors?"

"We have no hand or voice in the management of our social affairs. In India man is lord and master. He has taken to himself all powers and privileges and shut up the women in the zenana."

"Why do you allow yourselves to be shut up?"

"Because it cannot be helped as they are stronger than women."

2. Women's living quarters (often secluded from the male sections of the household) (Persian).

"A lion is stronger than a man, but it does not enable him to dominate the human race. You have neglected the duty you owe to yourselves, and you have lost your natural rights by shutting your eyes to your own interests."

"But my dear Sister Sara, if we do everything by ourselves, what will the men do then?"

"They should not do anything, excuse me; they are fit for nothing. Only catch them and put them into the zenana."

"But would it be very easy to catch and put them inside the four walls?" said I. "And even if this were done, would all their business—political and commercial—also go with them into the zenana?"

Sister Sara made no reply. She only smiled sweetly. Perhaps she thought it was useless to argue with one who was no better than a frog in a well.

By this time we reached Sister Sara's house. It was situated in a beautiful heart-shaped garden. It was a bungalow with a corrugated iron roof. It was cooler and nicer than any of our rich buildings. I cannot describe how neat and nicely furnished and how tastefully decorated it was.

We sat side by side. She brought out of the parlor a piece of embroidery work and began putting on a fresh design.

"Do you know knitting and needlework?"

"Yes; we have nothing else to do in our zenana."

"But we do not trust our zenana members with embroidery!" she said laughing, "as a man has not patience enough to pass thread through a needlehole even!"

"Have you done all this work yourself?" I asked her, pointing to the various pieces of embroidered teapoy cloths.

"Yes."

"How can you find time to do all these? You have to do the office work as well? Have you not?"

"Yes. I do not stick to the laboratory all day long. I finish my work in two hours."

"In two hours! How do you manage? In our land the officers, magistrates, for instance, work seven hours daily."

"I have seen some of them doing their work. Do you think they work all the seven hours?"

"Certainly they do!"

"No, dear Sultana, they do not. They dawdle away their time in smoking. Some smoke two or three choroots during the office time. They talk much about their work, but do little. Suppose one choroot takes half an hour to burn off, and a man smokes twelve choroots daily; then, you see, he wastes six hours every day in sheer smoking."

We talked on various subjects; and I learned that they were not subject to any kind of epidemic disease, nor did they suffer from mosquito bites as we do. I was very much astonished to hear that in Ladyland no one died in youth except by rare accident.

"Will you care to see our kitchen?" she asked me.

"With pleasure," said I, and we went to see it. Of course the men had been asked to clear off when I was going there. The kitchen was situated in a beautiful vegetable garden. Every creeper, every tomato plant, was itself an ornament. I found no smoke, nor any chimney either in the kitchen—it was clean and bright; the windows were decorated with flower garlands. There was no sign of coal or fire.

"How do you cook?" I asked.

"With solar heat," she said, at the same time showing me the pipe, through which passed the concentrated sunlight and heat. And she cooked something then and there to show me the process.

"How did you manage to gather and store up the sun heat?" I asked her in amazement.

"Let me tell you a little of our past history, then. Thirty years ago, when our present Queen was thirteen years old, she inherited the throne. She was Queen in name only, the Prime Minister really ruling the country.

"Our good Queen liked science very much. She circulated an order that all the women in her country should be educated. Accordingly a number of girls' schools were founded and supported by the Government. Education was spread far and wide among women. And early marriage also was stopped. No woman was to be allowed to marry before she was twenty-one. I must tell you that, before this change, we had been kept in strict purdah."

"How the tables are turned," I interposed with a laugh.

"But the seclusion is the same," she said. "In a few years we had separate universities, where no men were admitted.

"In the capital, where our Queen lives, there are two universities. One of these invented a wonderful balloon, to which they attached a number of pipes. By means of this captive balloon, which they managed to keep afloat above the cloudland, they could draw as much water from the atmosphere as they pleased. As the water was incessantly being drawn by the university people, no cloud gathered and the ingenious Lady Principal stopped rain and storms thereby."

"Really! Now I understand why there is no mud here!" said I. But I could not understand how it was possible to accumulate water in the pipes. She explained to me how it was done; but I was unable to understand her, as my scientific knowledge was very limited. However, she went on:

"When the other university came to know of this, they became exceedingly jealous and tried to do something more extraordinary still. They invented an instrument by which they could collect as much sun heat as they wanted. And they kept the heat stored up to be distributed among others as required.

"While the women were engaged in scientific researches, the men of this country were busy increasing their military power. When they came to know that the female universities were able to draw water from the atmosphere and collect heat from the sun, they only laughed at the members of the universities and called the whole thing 'a sentimental nightmare'!"

"Your achievements are very wonderful indeed! But tell me how you managed to put the men of your country into the zenana. Did you entrap them first?"

"No."

"It is not likely that they would surrender their free and open air life of their own accord and confine themselves within the four walls of the zenana! They must have been overpowered."

"Yes, they have been!"

"By whom?—by some lady warriors, I suppose?"

"No, not by arms."

"Yes, it cannot be so. Men's arms are stronger than women's. Then?"

"By brain."

"Even their brains are bigger and heavier than women's. Are they not?"

"Yes, but what of that? An elephant also has got a bigger and heavier brain than a man has. Yet man can enchain elephants and employ them, according to his own wishes."

"Well said, but tell me, please, how it all actually happened. I am dying to know it!"

"Women's brains are somewhat quicker than men's. Ten years ago, when the military officers called our scientific discoveries 'a sentimental nightmare,' some of the young ladies wanted to say something in reply to those remarks. But both the Lady Principals restrained them and said they should reply not by word but by deed, if ever they got the opportunity. And they had not long to wait for that opportunity."

"How marvelous!" I heartily clapped my hands.

"And now the proud gentlemen are dreaming sentimental dreams themselves.

"Soon afterward certain persons came from a neighboring country and took shelter in ours. They were in trouble, having committed some political offense. The King, who cared more for power than for good government, asked our kindhearted Queen to hand them over to his officers. She refused, as it was against her principle to turn out refugees. For this refusal the king declared war against our country.

"Our military officers sprang to their feet at once and marched out to meet the enemy.

"The enemy, however, was too strong for them. Our soldiers fought bravely, no doubt. But in spite of all their bravery the foreign army advanced step by step to invade our country.

"Nearly all the men had gone out to fight; even a boy of sixteen was not left home. Most of our warriors were killed, the rest driven back, and the enemy came within twenty-five miles of the capital.

"A meeting of a number of wise ladies was held at the Queen's palace to advise [as] to what should be done to save the land.

"Some proposed to fight like soldiers; others objected and said that women were not trained to fight with swords and guns, nor were they accustomed to fighting with any weapons. A third party regretfully remarked that they were hopelessly weak of body.

"If you cannot save your country for lack of physical strength, said the Queen, try to do so by brain power.

"There was a dead silence for a few minutes. Her Royal Highness said again, 'I must commit suicide if the land and my honor are lost.'

"Then the Lady Principal of the second university (who had collected sun heat), who had been silently thinking during the consultation, remarked that they were all but lost; and there was little hope left for them. There was, however, one plan [that] she would like to try, and this would be her first and last effort; if she failed in this, there would be nothing left but to commit suicide. All present solemnly vowed that they would never allow themselves to be enslaved, no matter what happened.

"The Queen thanked them heartily, and asked the Lady Principal to try her plan.

"The Lady Principal rose again and said, 'Before we go out the men must enter the zenanas. I make this prayer for the sake of purdah.' 'Yes, of course,' replied Her Royal Highness.

"On the following day the Queen called upon all men to retire into zenanas for the sake of honor and liberty.

"Wounded and tired as they were, they took that order rather for a boon! They bowed low and entered the zenanas without uttering a single word of protest. They were sure that there was no hope for this country at all.

"Then the Lady Principal with her two thousand students marched to the battlefield, and arriving there directed all the rays of the concentrated sun light and heat toward the enemy.

"The heat and light were too much for them to bear. They all ran away panic-stricken, not knowing in their bewilderment how to counteract that scorching heat. When they fled away leaving their guns and other ammunitions of war, they were burned down by means of the same sun heat.

"Since then no one has tried to invade our country any more."

"And since then your countrymen never tried to come out of the zenana?"

"Yes, they wanted to be free. Some of the Police Commissioners and District Magistrates sent word to the Queen to the effect that the Military Officers certainly deserved to be imprisoned for their failure; but they [had] never neglected their duty and therefore they should not be punished, and they prayed to be restored to their respective offices.

"Her Royal Highness sent them a circular letter, intimating to them that if their services should ever be needed they would be sent for, and that in the meanwhile they should remain where they were.

"Now that they are accustomed to the purdah system and have ceased to grumble at their seclusion, we call the system *mardana*[3] instead of zenana."

"But how do you manage," I asked Sister Sara, "to do without the police or magistrates in case of theft or murder?"

"Since the mardana system has been established, there has been no more crime or sin; therefore we do not require a policeman to find out a culprit, nor do we want a magistrate to try a criminal case."

"That is very good, indeed. I suppose if there were any dishonest person, you could very easily chastise her. As you gained a decisive victory without shedding a single drop of blood, you could drive off crime and criminals too without much difficulty!"

"Now, dear Sultana, will you sit here or come to my parlor?" she asked me.

"Your kitchen is not inferior to a queen's boudoir!" I replied with a pleasant smile, "but we must leave it now; for the gentlemen may be cursing me for keeping them away from their duties in the kitchen so long." We both laughed heartily.

"How my friends at home will be amused and amazed, when I go back and tell them that in the far-off Ladyland, ladies rule over the country and control all social matters, while gentlemen are kept in the mardanas to mind babies, to cook, and to do all sorts of domestic work; and that cooking is so easy a thing that it is simply a pleasure to cook!"

"Yes, tell them about all that you see here."

"Please let me know how you carry on land cultivation and how you plow the land and do other hard manual work."

---

3. Men's quarters.

"Our fields are tilled by means of electricity, which supplies motive power for other hard work as well, and we employ it for our aerial conveyances too. We have no railroad nor any paved streets here."

"Therefore neither street nor railway accidents occur here," said I. "Do not you ever suffer from want of rainwater?" I asked.

"Never since the 'water balloon' has been set up. You see the big balloon and pipes attached thereto. By their aid we can draw as much rainwater as we require. Nor do we ever suffer from flood or thunderstorms. We are all very busy making nature yield as much as she can. We do not find time to quarrel with one another as we never sit idle. Our noble Queen is exceedingly fond of botany; it is her ambition to convert the whole country into one grand garden."

"The idea is excellent. What is your chief food?"

"Fruits."

"How do you keep your country cool in hot weather? We regard the rainfall in summer as a blessing from heaven."

"When the heat becomes unbearable, we sprinkle the ground with plentiful showers drawn from the artificial fountains. And in cold weather we keep our rooms warm with sun heat."

She showed me her bathroom, the roof of which was removable. She could enjoy a shower [or] bath whenever she liked, by simply removing the roof (which was like the lid of a box) and turning on the tap of the shower pipe.

"You are a lucky people!" ejaculated I. "You know no want. What is your religion, may I ask?"

"Our religion is based on Love and Truth. It is our religious duty to love one another and to be absolutely truthful. If any person lies, she or he is . . ."

"Punished with death?"

"No, not with death. We do not take pleasure in killing a creature of God— especially a human being. The liar is asked to leave this land for good and never to come to it again."

"Is an offender never forgiven?"

"Yes, if that person repents sincerely."

"Are you not allowed to see any man, except your own relations?"

"No one except sacred relations."

"Our circle of sacred relations is very limited, even first cousins are not sacred."

"But ours is very large; a distant cousin is as sacred as a brother."

"That is very good. I see Purity itself reigns over your land. I should like to see the good Queen, who is so sagacious and farsighted and who has made all these rules."

"All right," said Sister Sara.

Then she screwed a couple of seats on to a square piece of plank. To this plank she attached two smooth and well-polished balls. When I asked her what the balls were for, she said they were hydrogen balls and they were used to overcome the force of gravity. The balls were of different capacities, to be used according to the different weights desired to be overcome. She then fastened to the air-car two winglike blades, which, she said, were worked by electricity. After we were comfortably seated she touched a knob and the blades began to whirl, moving faster and faster every moment. At first we were raised to the height of about six or seven feet and then off we flew. And before I could realize that we had commenced moving, we reached the garden of the Queen.

My friend lowered the air-car by reversing the action of the machine, and when the car touched the ground the machine was stopped and we got out.

I had seen from the air-car the Queen walking on a garden path with her little daughter (who was four years old) and her maids of honor.

"Halloo! you here!" cried the Queen, addressing Sister Sara. I was introduced to Her Royal Highness and was received by her cordially without any ceremony.

I was very much delighted to make her acquaintance. In [the] course of the conversation I had with her, the Queen told me that she had no objection to permitting her subjects to trade with other countries. "But," she continued, "no trade was possible with countries where the women were kept in the zenanas and so unable to come and trade with us. Men, we find, are rather of lower morals and so we do not like dealing with them. We do not covet other people's land, we do not fight for a piece of diamond though it may be a thousandfold brighter than the Koh-i-Noor, nor do we grudge a ruler his Peacock Throne.[4] We dive deep into the ocean of knowledge and try to find out the precious gems [that] Nature has kept in store for us. We enjoy Nature's gifts as much as we can."

After taking leave of the Queen, I visited the famous universities, and was shown over some of their factories, laboratories, and observatories.

After visiting the above places of interest, we got again into the air-car, but as soon as it began moving I somehow slipped down and the fall startled me out of my dream. And on opening my eyes, I found myself in my own bedroom still lounging in the easy chair!

1905

---

4. Koh-i-Noor: "Mountain of Light" (Persian), name of a famous diamond belonging to the Mughal rulers of India (sixteenth to nineteenth centuries) and appropriated to make part of the British crown jewels (still on view in the Tower of London); Peacock Throne: legendary jewel-encrusted throne that belonged to the Mughal emperor Shah Jahan (builder of the famous Taj Mahal) and carried away from Delhi by the Persian invader Nadir Shah in 1739.

CULTURAL COORDINATES
Purdah

Purdah is the practice of secluding women from public life by veiling their faces and heads and covering their bodies or by segregating them within the home. Although mainly practiced by Muslims, purdah is also practiced by some Hindus in India. In fact, the word *purdah* means "curtain" in Hindi and Urdu (the languages spoken in Pakistan and in north India).

The practice of purdah likely began in Persia (now Iran) and was absorbed by Muslims in the seventh century when they conquered that region. The practice expanded with the spread of Islam, coming to the subcontinent of India with the Muslim rulers who conquered large parts of India and ruled from the thirteenth to the nineteenth century. Hindus, especially well-to-do Hindus, also absorbed the practice at this time.

Today, purdah in some form or another is practiced by Muslims around the world. In Western countries the practice is voluntary and is frequently limited to wearing a scarf to cover the hair. (Orthodox Jews observe a similar practice, with married women covering their own hair with a scarf or wig; until the mid-1960s, Catholic women were expected to cover their heads before entering a church.) More extreme forms of purdah are practiced where fundamentalist Islam is the state religion. In Afghanistan under the Taliban, women were forbidden to appear in public with any part of their bodies showing—even their eyes. In Iran, police chastise, arrest, and even beat women for wearing burqas (loose, hooded cloaks) that do not sufficiently disguise their bodies. Today, women in Iraq sometimes adopt the burqa to avoid being assaulted. But in many other places and contexts, Muslim women can choose either to wear the veil or not.

Some feminist scholars, like Fatima Mernissi, argue that purdah has nothing to do with religion and everything to do with patriarchal control of women. Many twentieth-century women's movements in Iran and Egypt decry purdah as having primarily negative effects on women's lives. Others, however, mostly believers in Islam, contend that purdah is a respectful practice that liberates women from the objectifying gaze of men, in line with other Islamic practices such as equal rights in matters of property and inheritance that exalt the status of

An Afghani woman wearing a burqa.

women. Some Muslim feminists have also argued that the practice of seclusion provides women with their own autonomous spaces, away from male control.

The issue of purdah has become central to the politics of multiculturalism and cultural difference in the Western world. In 2005, the French government decided to prohibit schoolgirls from wearing headscarves to public schools, causing a huge outcry and leading critics to claim that a hidden racism was behind such legislation. Despite all the controversy surrounding it, purdah remains an integral part of the everyday lives of people in the Middle East, India, Pakistan, and even Europe and the United States. In the practice of and resistance to purdah, the issues of women's rights and personal choice remain at the forefront.

MOURNING DOVE
(HUMISHUMA/CHRISTINE QUINTASKET)
1882?–1936

The first American Indian woman to publish a full-length novel, Mourning Dove was born in a canoe on the Kootenay River in Idaho. Her mother was a member of the Colville tribe and her father was Okanogan; she grew up among her extended family, the Salishans of eastern Washington, along the Kettle River. She attended several American Indian schools between 1895 and 1899 and again for a few years after the turn of the century, but she is said to have learned to read English—and to have read a good number of popular western novels—from an Irish American boy her family adopted. Many critics cite these novels as having had an influence on her novel, *Cogewea,* excerpted below.

Mourning Dove's life was not an easy one. She married twice, both times to men who either were or became alcoholics. Her first husband was abusive and put her in the hospital while she was pregnant, and either the abuse or the subsequent miscarriage left her unable to have more children. Although she worked for a time as a teacher, her main occupation was as a migrant farm laborer; she wrote at night in various farmworkers' lodgings. By the 1930s, she was also working as a lecturer and political rights activist; she died from chronic overexertion. Mourning Dove's work does not come to us exactly as she wrote it; in the early 1910s, she met Lucullus McWhorter, an anthropologist who helped her get her work published but who also edited it heavily. In addition to writing *Cogewea,* she also recorded and interpreted many traditional Salishan tales, published as *Coyote Stories* in 1933. In 1990, scholar Jay Miller collected and edited the papers she had left behind at her death as *Mourning Dove: A Salishan Autobiography.*

Our selection from *Cogewea* focuses on a traditional dance ceremony. The novel as a whole describes the difficulties of being a mixed-blood woman in both native and U.S. cultures, and it follows the lives of three sisters as they find different ways to make their way through the world—one chooses the white world, one attempts to live the traditions of her grandmother, and one, Cogewea, wants to combine them. The novel also attempts to describe American Indian life to a white audience, to repudiate negative stereotypes of Indians, and to explain the value and meaning of traditions. As we see in this selection, ceremonies are presented not as curiosities or savagery but as important and thoughtful components of a fully formed and sophisticated culture.

From Cogewea, the Half-Blood

[The Indian Dancers]

* * *

With the bucking contest over, many now hurried to the big brush shed where the Indians were to dance. Jim and Bob worked their way through the crowd to the center space set aside for the performances. The music, discordant and monotonous to the whites, is all rhythm to the Indian ear. The sudden break in time and pitch has a significance well understood by the initiated. The musicians are usually trained professionals and are held in high regard by their tribesmen. Sacred and emanating from the Great Spirit—giver of all life—no sacrilege is permissible at either the spirit or the war dance. The great drum, placed on an outspread blanket on the ground, is surrounded by the players, sitting in a cordon about it. These strike the instrument in perfect unison with single batons or sticks, terminating with elongated knobs of cloth or soft buckskin. The women contingent sits in an exclusive circle adjacent to the drummers, their voices blending harmoniously with those of the men.

All is ready; and "attention" bursts from the drum, to be echoed by the leader in animated song; decorously taken up by the other singers. The music swells in stirring cadence, but the dancers, enveloped in blankets crouching about the edges of the cleared arena, remain statued and immobile. They must not show haste or impatience. Suddenly a tall, grizzled old warrior stands up, and lifting high his ceremonial elkhorn club and whip combined, gives signal that the dance begin. The recumbent figures arise. Stripped of blankets, they appear dazzling and resplendent with feathers, wampum and native finery; with here and there the naked body of a bronze athlete glistening with symbolic emblems done in brilliant paint. The dancers must not lag or remain inactive after the signal to proceed. If they do, the leader is privileged to use the whip with no uncertain vigor, nor must the laggard resent such chastisement!

Watch the dancers! There is that aged battle scarred warrior whose movements denote the gliding serpent—the crouching panther—the stalking cougar—the leaping mountain-cat—the on-rushing swoop of the aerial eagle. Mark that visiting, stately Nez Perce![1] Although facing the sunset, decadence shows not on his sinewy form. A nephew of the immortal Chief Joseph,[2] he was young, when, in 1877, he fought and scouted over that thousand mile trail in a mad dash for the Canadian border, a dash unprecedented for brilliancy of achievement, throughout the annals of American warfare. That warclub he so exultingly holds aloft, still retains the sanguine stains of mortal combat. His step is that of the conqueror rather than that of the vanquished and fallen.

See those young men! Their slouchy *traipsing* tells of contact with the meaningless "waltz" and suggestive "hugs" and "trots" of the higher civilization—a vulgarity—a sacrilegious burlesque on an ancient and religiously instituted ceremony. Like other of his tribal cultures, the Indian's dance is suffering in modifications not always to be desired as morally beneficial.

There! that youth a mere lad! He has attained to the age when he is making his debut, as it were, declaring his intention of taking up the role of man and warrior in his tribe. For this privilege his parents or friends must give liberally in goods and horses, to be distributed among the assemblage at a later hour.

Not the least interesting is the dropping of a solitary feather from his regalia by an unfortunate young dancer. This trophy must not be recovered by the one losing it, but for his carelessness he will be required to pay such fine as the chief in charge

1. The Numiipu people, who lived in the region of the Snake River, in present-day Idaho, Washington, and Oregon, before the coming of Europeans; their lands were reduced to 7.5 million acres (1855), then 750,000 acres (1863), and finally 75,000 acres (1893).

2. A Nez Perce who resisted the confiscation of land and who, with others of his tribe, led people north, across the Rockies, during a four-month continuous battle with the U.S. Cavalry. He was eventually surrounded, and he surrendered, fearing that his people would starve.

may impose. No one touches the object until the conclusion of that particular dance, when the bravest or most noted warrior—the Nez Perce—calling upon his secret protective spirit-powers, proceeds to take it up. This is accomplished only after one or more seemingly futile attempts, amid the excited *ki-yiahs* of his dancing companions. The feather is retained by the Nez Perce, who then recites some thrilling incident of personal prowess in battle. For this honor, he donates a blanket to the general distribution fund, while the loser of the feather atones for his disgrace by contributing a saddle-pony.

There is a lull in the wild, circling war dance, which is ever measured by many breaks and rests. The old warrior in charge announces a change, which an interpreter renders in English.

"*La-siah* has spoken. The men will now take women for the final dance. For the benefit of those who do not understand, we will explain the custom, which has come down to us from our ancestors of other snows.

"Every man has this privilege. He can choose any woman from the assemblage to dance with him while the drummers sing the song of good-will. But he must pay her something; any thing he may see fit, as her value. If he likes his partner, he will pay well; but less if he does not care much for her. The woman has the same privilege of choosing and paying. As you circle in this dance, the position of the hand and arm of the man will make known how his heart and mind runs out to the woman. If he wants a maiden for wife, we will know it. If he wants to rob another man of his wife, we will know it. He must not do crazy things nor speak the lie with sign-actions. He must do the truth towards the woman. A married man may dance with a maiden for friendship, and the young man may dance with a married woman for friendship. This is a ceremony of friendly good will; where all the distant tribes may meet in harmony; a peace to be regarded well. All may dance, but it must not be mockery. It must be from the heart which should always be true. La-siah has shown you his mind."

The Chief of the Pend d'Oreille[3] came into the dance space with Cogewea. His warbonnet of eagle feathers was the best, a great billowy mass of swaying plumes. The floating tail piece, extending down his back in long undulating waves, just brushed the ground. His moccasins were decorated with bead work done in symbol, representing many suns of labor by his patient squaw. His broad chest was emblazoned with native wampum, as well as ornaments and beads highly prized. These last, his grandfather had purchased with beaver skins from the Hudson's Bay Company[4] nearly a hundred snows before. In his hand he carried his *te-kee-sten,*[5] with feathers and strips of fur attached.

The dancing was immediate, with other couples joining the ever lengthening, and widening circle. Moving to the left, the short measured side-step was a unit, with emphasis on the advanced foot. The music at the drum had changed to a softer melody, suggestive of love-passion, peace and good-will. Unlike the fierce, stirring notes of war, thrilling with the thunder's shock of death, there was the murmur of rippling water over pebbly mountain beds; the soughing of summer breezes through leafy groves the glad carolling of birds at the mating season. And

---

3. The Kalispel people, who originally lived in what is now Montana, Idaho, and Washington; now part of the confederated Salish and Kootenai tribes who live on the Flathead Reservation in Montana.
4. A Canadian fur-trading company chartered in 1670 and extending coast to coast by 1820.
5. Medicine cane.

over all was visioned the halo of an ancient glory, when the protective spirits dwelt more near the tribes.

The song died to a note like an echo from the canyon's clitty depths. The dancers stopped, holding their places. La-siah and his *Caller* came forward to name the presents. The Pend d'Oreille Chief spoke in a low, dignified tone, to be interrupted by the Caller.

"To this maiden of another tribe, I give, as a token of my good will to her and her people, one of my best horses. It is the *pinto*, ridden by my wife and which took second prize in today's race. My gift!"

Cogewea's heart bounded with gladness but Indian etiquette forbade any outward demonstration of gratitude. It was for her to reciprocate in a subsequent friendship dance.

The Nez Perce Chief, who danced with the "shy girl," took from his shoulder a splendid "King George" blanket and passing it to the gift-exchanger, through him spoke:

"Members of the different tribes meet here and are no longer strangers. This robe, which has sheltered me from the winter storms, carries with it the warmth of the Nez Perce's heart for this girl and her people. It is good to be friends!"

Jim gave to Stemteemä a blanket of rare design, which he had purchased from another Indian for that purpose, and from whom he had secured a dancing costume. At that moment he ingratiated himself in the old heart, far more than he ever realized. That gift, received in stoic silence, was bread cast in the van[6] of a fast gathering flood destined to break, dark and turbulent on the border shores of both their lives.

* * *

1927

◄ VIRGINIA WOOLF ►
1882–1941

Virginia Woolf is one of the most important writers in the history of English literature. The author of nine novels, several volumes of short stories, biographies, and more than five hundred published essays, she is also known for her private writings, including many posthumously published volumes of letters and diaries. She worked for feminist causes—including suffrage and working-women's rights—and in her literary life concerned herself with women's writing. Many of her essays examine the history of women's literature or raise questions about the ways that literature reflects a masculine viewpoint and style. Woolf herself is best known for her experimental style, one that reflects what she saw as a more feminine experience of the world—not linear, but focused on texture, on internal and private encounters not just with other people but with one's memories and sensory input. She led such a fascinating intellectual and emotional life that the brilliance of her writing is sometimes overshadowed by her biography.

Virginia Woolf was born the daughter of Leslie Stephen, an intellectual whose circle of friends included great figures of Victorian literature such as Henry James

---

6. Vanguard; in front of.

and George Eliot, and Julia Duckworth, whose family owned a publishing house. Woolf was never formally schooled but was given complete freedom in the family's extensive library to read widely. She was sexually molested by two older half-brothers for a number of years and suffered her first mental breakdown after first her mother and then her older sister died while she was still in her teens. She moved, with her sister Vanessa and brothers Adrian and Thoby, to the bohemian Bloomsbury neighborhood of London and began her publishing career in 1905, writing essays for the *Times Literary Supplement*. The Stephens soon became central figures in a circle of artists, writers, and philosophers that would come to be known as the Bloomsbury Group. Virginia married another member of the group, Leonard Woolf, in 1912. She and Leonard founded an important publishing house of their own, the Hogarth Press, around 1917, and published many of Virginia Woolf's novels, as well as many important texts of literary modernism, including works by T. S. Eliot, H. G. Wells, E. M. Forster, and the English translations of Sigmund Freud. Over the years, they both continued writing and kept up a lively social and intellectual life both in London and at their country home in Sussex, including several intimate relationships between Virginia and other women. Despite being known as a brilliant, funny, and charming conversationalist, she suffered several serious breakdowns and depressions during her life. Finally, worried that she was losing her mind and deeply distressed over World War II, Virginia Woolf committed suicide in 1941.

The intricacies of Woolf's life are only hinted at here by the basic outline of her biography. As critic Molly Hite has argued, "'biographical' critics have stressed different aspects of her life as defining features . . . [and] the result has been a number of Virginia Woolfs, each grounded in some part of the available information and each possessing a seductive completeness that resists more than superficial elaboration. The problem is really that we know far too many things about Virginia Woolf to wrap her up in [an] elegant package." And while we know "far too many things" about her, there are many things that we do not know for certain and about which scholars continue to debate: Was she actually raped by her half-brothers? Was her relationship with Leonard platonic or sexual? Were her lesbian relationships flirtations or serious love affairs? Did she suffer from mental illness or was she struggling against cultural restrictions?

We can, however, still study the astonishing body of work she left us. As we see in the three stories included here, Woolf often concerns herself less with plot than with character, less with what happens in a story than with feeling. "Kew Gardens" (1919), for instance, is organized around a flower bed and concerns itself less with a conventional story line than with small groups of people (and one snail) who pass by or through it. We are allowed to peek inside each group for a moment but must then move on. The result is a representation of how we experience the world as we move through it—small flashes of someone else's reality appear to us and are then gone. "A Haunted House" (1943) suggests, from its title, that we are about to encounter some conventional ghost story, and to some degree we do—there are ghosts who affect the current occupant's life—but the ghosts here remain ineffable and friendly, evidence of Woolf's own interest in history and the past and her own inner life. In "Mrs. Dalloway in Bond Street" (1923), a story that forms the kernel of Woolf's later novel *Mrs. Dalloway* (1925), the plot involves a woman walking down a London street to buy a pair of gloves. The action, however, is hardly important; instead, we spend time inside Clarissa Dalloway's consciousness (what will come to be called the stream-of-consciousness technique of narrative), registering what she's thinking about, how one detail makes her think of something else, how the sights and sounds of London form an interior landscape of awareness.

Although she writes in her book-length essay *A Room of One's Own* (1929), a portion of which appears here, that "it is fatal for any one who writes to think of their sex," Woolf spent a great deal of time thinking about the difference that sex might make to writing and questioning whether this was a difference of circumstances or a result of something "natural." She concludes that a great deal depends on material circumstances and argues that to be a fine writer one needs £500 a year (about $40,000 today) and a room to oneself, an independence that few women had ever had. *A Room of One's Own* investigates not just the history of women writers but also the history of women and serves as a call to young women to rewrite history, to look for the women whose stories and contributions have been hidden in (or by) history.

Kew Gardens

From the oval-shaped flower-bed there rose perhaps a hundred stalks spreading into heart-shaped or tongue-shaped leaves half-way up and unfurling at the tip red or blue or yellow petals marked with spots of colour raised upon the surface; and from the red, blue or yellow gloom of the throat emerged a straight bar, rough with gold dust and slightly clubbed at the end. The petals were voluminous enough to be stirred by the summer breeze, and when they moved, the red, blue and yellow lights passed one over the other, staining an inch of the brown earth beneath with a spot of the most intricate colour. The light fell either upon the smooth, grey back of a pebble, or, the shell of a snail with its brown, circular veins, or falling into a raindrop, it expanded with such intensity of red, blue and yellow the thin walls of water that one expected them to burst and disappear. Instead, the drop was left in a second silver grey once more, and the light now settled upon the flesh of a leaf, revealing the branching thread of fibre beneath the surface, and again it moved on and spread its illumination in the vast green spaces beneath the dome of the heart-shaped and tongue-shaped leaves. Then the breeze stirred rather more briskly overhead and the colour was flashed into the air above, into the eyes of the men and women who walk in Kew Gardens[1] in July.

The figures of these men and women straggled past the flower-bed with a curiously irregular movement not unlike that of the white and blue butterflies who crossed the turf in zig-zag flights from bed to bed. The man was about six inches in front of the woman, strolling carelessly, while she bore on with greater purpose, only turning her head now and then to see that the children were not too far behind. The man kept this distance in front of the woman purposely, though perhaps unconsciously, for he wished to go on with his thoughts.

"Fifteen years ago I came here with Lily," he thought. "We sat somewhere over there by a lake and I begged her to marry me all through the hot afternoon. How the dragonfly kept circling round us: how clearly I see the dragonfly and her shoe with the square silver buckle at the toe. All the time I spoke I saw her shoe and when it moved impatiently I knew without looking up what she was going to

1. The Royal Botanic Gardens in London, England.

say: the whole of her seemed to be in her shoe. And my love, my desire, were in the dragonfly; for some reason I thought that if it settled there, on that leaf, the broad one with the red flower in the middle of it, if the dragonfly settled on the leaf she would say 'Yes' at once. But the dragonfly went round and round: it never settled anywhere—of course not, happily not, or I shouldn't be walking here with Eleanor and the children. Tell me, Eleanor. D'you ever think of the past?"

"Why do you ask, Simon?"

"Because I've been thinking of the past. I've been thinking of Lily, the woman I might have married. . . . Well, why are you silent? Do you mind my thinking of the past?"

"Why should I mind, Simon? Doesn't one always think of the past, in a garden with men and women lying under the trees? Aren't they one's past, all that remains of it, those men and women, those ghosts lying under the trees, . . . one's happiness, one's reality?"

"For me, a square silver shoe buckle and a dragonfly—"

"For me, a kiss. Imagine six little girls sitting before their easels twenty years ago, down by the side of a lake, painting the water-lilies, the first red water-lilies I'd ever seen. And suddenly a kiss, there on the back of my neck. And my hand shook all the afternoon so that I couldn't paint. I took out my watch and marked the hour when I would allow myself to think of the kiss for five minutes only—it was so precious—the kiss of an old grey-haired woman with a wart on her nose, the mother of all my kisses all my life. Come, Caroline, come, Hubert."

They walked on past the flower-bed, now walking four abreast, and soon diminished in size among the trees and looked half transparent as the sunlight and shade swam over their backs in large trembling irregular patches.

In the oval flower-bed the snail, whose shell had been stained red, blue and yellow for the space of two minutes or so, now appeared to be moving very slightly in its shell, and next began to labour over the crumbs of loose earth which broke away and rolled down as it passed over them. It appeared to have a definite goal in front of it, differing in this respect from the singular high stepping angular green insect who attempted to cross in front of it, and waited for a second with its antennae trembling as if in deliberation, and then stepped off as rapidly and strangely in the opposite direction. Brown cliffs with deep green lakes in the hollows, flat, blade-like trees that waved from root to tip, round boulders of grey stone, vast crumpled surfaces of a thin crackling texture—all these objects lay across the snail's progress between one stalk and another to his goal. Before he had decided whether to circumvent the arched tent of a dead leaf or to breast it there came past the bed the feet of other human beings.

This time they were both men. The younger of the two wore an expression of perhaps unnatural calm; he raised his eyes and fixed them very steadily in front of him while his companion spoke, and directly his companion had done speaking he looked on the ground again and sometimes opened his lips only after a long pause and sometimes did not open them at all. The elder man had a curiously uneven and shaky method of walking, jerking his hand forward and throwing up his head abruptly, rather in the manner of an impatient carriage horse tired of waiting outside a house; but in the man these gestures were irresolute and pointless. He talked almost incessantly; he smiled to himself and again began to talk, as if the smile had been an answer. He was talking about spirits—the spirits of the dead, who, according to him, were even now telling him all sorts of odd things about their experiences in Heaven.

"Heaven was known to the ancients as Thessaly, William, and now, with this war, the spirit matter is rolling between the hills like thunder."[2] He paused, seemed to listen, smiled, jerked his head and continued:

"You have a small electric battery and a piece of rubber to insulate the wire—isolate?—insulate?—well, we'll skip the details, no good going into details that wouldn't be understood—and in short the little machine stands in any convenient position by the head of the bed, we will say, on a neat mahogany stand. All arrangements being properly fixed by workmen under my direction, the widow applies her ear and summons the spirit by sign as agreed. Women! Widows! Women in black—"

Here he seemed to have caught sight of a woman's dress in the distance, which in the shade looked a purple black. He took off his hat, placed his hand upon his heart, and hurried towards her muttering and gesticulating feverishly. But William caught him by the sleeve and touched a flower with the tip of his walking-stick in order to divert the old man's attention. After looking at it for a moment in some confusion the old man bent his ear to it and seemed to answer a voice speaking from it, for he began talking about the forests of Uruguay which he had visited hundreds of years ago in company with the most beautiful young woman in Europe. He could be heard murmuring about forests of Uruguay blanketed with the wax petals of tropical roses, nightingales, sea beaches, mermaids, and women drowned at sea, as he suffered himself to be moved on by William, upon whose face the look of stoical patience grew slowly deeper and deeper.

Following his steps so closely as to be slightly puzzled by his gestures came two elderly women of the lower middle class, one stout and ponderous, the other rosy cheeked and nimble. Like most people of their station they were frankly fascinated by any signs of eccentricity betokening a disordered brain, especially in the well-to-do; but they were too far off to be certain whether the gestures were merely eccentric or genuinely mad. After they had scrutinized the old man's back in silence for a moment and given each other a queer, sly look, they went on energetically piecing together their very complicated dialogue:

"Nell, Bert, Lot, Cess, Phil, Pa, he says, I says, she says, I says, I says—"

"My Bert, Sis, Bill, Grandad, the old man, sugar,
Sugar, flour, kippers, greens,
Sugar, sugar, sugar."

The ponderous woman looked though the pattern of falling words at the flowers standing cool, firm, and upright in the earth, with a curious expression. She saw them as a sleeper waking from a heavy sleep sees a brass candlestick reflecting the light in an unfamiliar way, and closes his eyes and opens them, and seeing the brass candlestick again, finally starts broad awake and stares at the candlestick with all his powers. So the heavy woman came to a standstill opposite the oval-shaped flower-bed, and ceased even to pretend to listen to what the other woman was saying. She stood there letting the words fall over her, swaying the top part of her body slowly backwards and forwards, looking at the flowers. Then she suggested that they should find a seat and have their tea.

2. Thessaly: northeastern part of Greece (on the   World War I.
Aegean Sea) and part of ancient Greece; this war:

The snail had now considered every possible method of reaching his goal without going round the dead leaf or climbing over it. Let alone the effort needed for climbing a leaf, he was doubtful whether the thin texture which vibrated with such an alarming crackle when touched even by the tips of his horns would bear his weight; and this determined him finally to creep beneath it, for there was a point where the leaf curved high enough from the ground to admit him. He had just inserted his head in the opening and was taking stock of the high brown roof and was getting used to the cool brown light when two other people came past outside on the turf. This time they were both young, a young man and a young woman. They were both in the prime of youth, or even in that season which precedes the prime of youth, the season before the smooth pink folds of the flower have burst their gummy case, when the wings of the butterfly, though fully grown, are motionless in the sun.

"Lucky it isn't Friday," he observed.

"Why? D'you believe in luck?"

"They make you pay sixpence[3] on Friday."

"What's sixpence anyway? Isn't it worth sixpence?"

"What's 'it'—what do you mean by 'it'?"

"O, anything—I mean—you know what I mean."

Long pauses came between each of these remarks; they were uttered in toneless and monotonous voices. The couple stood still on the edge of the flower-bed, and together pressed the end of her parasol deep down into the soft earth. The action and the fact that his hand rested on the top of hers expressed their feelings in a strange way, as these short insignificant words also expressed something, words with short wings for their heavy body of meaning, inadequate to carry them far and thus alighting awkwardly upon the very common objects that surrounded them, and were to their inexperienced touch so massive; but who knows (so they thought as they pressed the parasol into the earth) what precipices aren't concealed in them, or what slopes of ice don't shine in the sun on the other side? Who knows? Who has ever seen this before? Even when she wondered what sort of tea they gave you at Kew, he felt that something loomed up behind her words, and stood vast and solid behind them; and the mist very slowly rose and uncovered— O, Heavens, what were those shapes?—little white tables, and waitresses who looked first at her and then at him; and there was a bill that he would pay with a real two shilling piece,[4] and it was real, all real, he assured himself, fingering the coin in his pocket, real to everyone except to him and to her; even to him it began to seem real; and then—but it was too exciting to stand and think any longer, and he pulled the parasol out of the earth with a jerk and was impatient to find the place where one had tea with other people, like other people.

"Come along, Trissie; it's time we had our tea."

"Wherever *does* one have one's tea?" she asked with the oddest thrill of excitement in her voice, looking vaguely round and letting herself be drawn on down the grass path, trailing her parasol; turning her head this way and that way forgetting her tea, wishing to go down there and then down there, remembering orchids and cranes among wild flowers, a Chinese pagoda and a crimson crested bird; but he bore her on.

3. About $1.50 today.   4. About $6.00 today.

Thus one couple after another with much the same irregular and aimless movement passed the flower bed and were enveloped in layer after layer of green blue vapour, in which at first their bodies had substance and a dash of colour, but later both substance and color dissolved in the green-blue atmosphere. How hot it was! So hot that even the thrush chose to hop, like a mechanical bird, in the shadow of the flowers, with long pauses between one movement and the next; instead of rambling vaguely the white butterflies danced one above another, making with their white shifting flakes the outline of a shattered marble column above the tallest flowers; the glass roofs of the palm house shone as if a whole market full of shiny green umbrellas had opened in the sun; and in the drone of the aeroplane the voice of the summer sky murmured its fierce soul. Yellow and black, pink and snow white, shapes of all these colours, men, women, and children were spotted for a second upon the horizon, and then, seeing the breadth of yellow that lay upon the grass, they wavered and sought shade beneath the trees, dissolving like drops of water in the yellow and green atmosphere, staining it faintly with red and blue. It seemed as if all gross and heavy bodies had sunk down in the heat motionless and lay huddled upon the ground, but their voices went wavering from them as if they were flames lolling from the thick waxen bodies of candles. Voices. Yes, voices. Wordless voices, breaking the silence suddenly with such depth of contentment, such passion of desire, or, in the voices of children, such freshness of surprise; breaking the silence? But there was no silence; all the time the motor omnibuses were turning their wheels and changing their gear; like a vast nest of Chinese boxes all of wrought steel turning ceaselessly one within another the city murmured; on the top of which the voices cried aloud and the petals of myriads of flowers flashed their colours into the air.

1919

Mrs. Dalloway in Bond Street[5]

Mrs. Dalloway said she would buy the gloves herself. Big Ben was striking as she stepped out into the street. It was eleven o'clock and the unused hour was fresh as if issued to children on a beach. But there was something solemn in the deliberate swing of the repeated strokes; something stirring in the murmur of wheels and the shuffle of footsteps.

No doubt they were not all bound on errands of happiness. There is much more to be said about us than that we walk the streets of Westminster. Big Ben too is nothing but steel rods consumed by rust were it not for the care of H.M.'s Office of Works.[6] Only for Mrs. Dalloway the moment was complete; for Mrs. Dalloway June was fresh. A happy childhood—and it was not to his daughters only that Justin Parry had seemed a fine fellow (weak of course on the Beach); flowers at evening, smoke rising; the caw of rooks falling from ever so high, down down

5. A major and fashionable shopping district in London's West End.
6. Westminster: a district in London where the palace of Westminster, Parliament, and the clock

atop the Parliament building (Big Ben) are located; H.M.'s: His Majesty's—in 1923, George V (Elizabeth II's grandfather) was king.

through the October air—there is nothing to take the place of childhood. A leaf of mint brings it back: or a cup with a blue ring.

Poor little wretches, she sighed, and pressed forward. Oh, right under the horses' noses, you little demon! and there she was left on the kerb stretching her hand out, while Jimmy Dawes grinned on the further side.

A charming woman, poised, eager, strangely white-haired for her pink cheeks, so Scope Purvis, C.B.,[7] saw her as he hurried to his office. She stiffened a little, waiting for Durtnall's van to pass. Big Ben struck the tenth; struck the eleventh stroke. The leaden circles dissolved in the air. Pride held her erect, inheriting, handing on, acquainted with discipline and with suffering. How people suffered, how they suffered, she thought, thinking of Mrs. Foxcroft at the Embassy last night decked with jewels, eating her heart out, because that nice boy was dead, and now the old Manor House (Durtnall's van passed) must go to a cousin.

"Good morning to you," said Hugh Whitbread raising his hat rather extravagantly by the china shop, for they had known each other as children. "Where are you off to?"

"I love walking in London," said Mrs. Dalloway. "Really it's better than walking in the country!"

"We've just come up," said Hugh Whitbread. "Unfortunately to see doctors."

"Milly?" said Mrs. Dalloway, instantly compassionate.

"Out of sorts," said Hugh Whitbread. "That sort of thing. Dick all right?"

"First rate!" said Clarissa.

Of course, she thought, walking on, Milly is about my age—fifty—fifty-two. So it is probably that. Hugh's manner had said so, said it perfectly—dear old Hugh, thought Mrs. Dalloway, remembering with amusement, with gratitude, with emotion, how shy, like a brother—one would rather die than speak to one's brother—Hugh had always been, when he was at Oxford, and came over, and perhaps one of them (drat the thing!) couldn't ride. How then could women sit in Parliament? How could they do things with men? For there is this extraordinarily deep instinct, something inside one; you can't get over it; it's no use trying; and men like Hugh respect it without our saying it, which is what one loves, thought Clarissa, in dear old Hugh.

She had passed through the Admiralty Arch and saw at the end of the empty road with its thin trees Victoria's white mound, Victoria's billowing motherliness, amplitude and homeliness, always ridiculous, yet how sublime thought Mrs. Dalloway, remembering Kensington Gardens and the old lady in horn spectacles and being told by Nanny to stop dead still and bow to the Queen.[8] The flag flew above the Palace. The King and Queen were back then. Dick had met her at lunch the other day—a thoroughly nice woman. It matters so much to the poor, thought Clarissa, and to the soldiers. A man in bronze stood heroically on a pedestal with a gun on her left hand side—the South African war. It matters, thought Mrs. Dalloway walking towards Buckingham Palace. There it stood four-square, in the broad sunshine, uncompromising, plain. But it was character she thought; something

7. "Companion" in the Order of the Bath, an honor principally awarded to officers of the armed services, as well as to a small number of civil servants.
8. Admiralty Arch: a large office building in London, commissioned by King Edward VII in mem-ory of his mother, Queen Victoria; Victoria's white mound: the Victoria Memorial, a large white marble statue erected in 1911 in front of Buckingham Palace, in London; Kensington Gardens: one of the royal parks in London, located mostly in Westminster.

inborn in the race; what Indians respected. The Queen went to hospitals, opened bazaars—the Queen of England, thought Clarissa, looking at the Palace. Already at this hour a motor car passed out at the gates; soldiers saluted; the gates were shut. And Clarissa, crossing the road, entered the Park, holding herself upright.

June had drawn out every leaf on the trees. The mothers of Westminster with mottled breasts gave suck to their young. Quite respectable girls lay stretched on the grass. An elderly man, stooping very stiffly, picked up a crumpled paper, spread it out flat and flung it away. How horrible! Last night at the Embassy Sir Dighton had said, "If I want a fellow to hold my horse, I have only to put up my hand." But the religious question is far more serious than the economic, Sir Dighton had said, which she thought extraordinarily interesting, from a man like Sir Dighton, "Oh, the country will never know what it has lost," he had said, talking, of his own accord, about dear Jack Stewart.

She mounted the little hill lightly. The air stirred with energy. Messages were passing from the Fleet to the Admiralty. Piccadilly and Arlington Street and the Mall seemed to chafe the very air in the Park and lift its leaves hotly, brilliantly, upon waves of that divine vitality which Clarissa loved. To ride; to dance; she had adored all that. Or going on long walks in the country, talking, about books, what to do with one's life, for young people were amazingly priggish—oh, the things one had said! But one had conviction. Middle age is the devil. People like Jack'll never know that, she thought; for he never once thought of death, never, they said, knew he was dying. And now can never mourn—how did it go?—a head grown grey . . . From the contagion of the world's slow stain . . . Have drunk their cup a round or two before . . . . From the contagion of the world's slow stain! She held herself upright.

But how Jack would have shouted! Quoting Shelley, in Piccadilly![9] "You want a pin," he would have said. He hated frumps. "My God Clarissa! My God Clarissa!"—she could hear him now at the Devonshire House[1] party, about poor Sylvia Hunt in her amber necklace and that dowdy old silk. Clarissa held herself upright for she had spoken aloud and now she was in Piccadilly, passing the house with the slender green columns, and the balconies; passing club windows full of newspapers; passing old Lady Burdett Coutt's house where the glazed white parrot used to hang; and Devonshire House, without its gilt leopards; and Claridge's, where she must remember Dick wanted her to leave a card on Mrs. Jepson or she would be gone. Rich Americans can be very charming. There was St. James's Palace;[2] like a child's game with bricks; and now—she had passed Bond Street— she was by Hatchard's book shop. The stream was endless—endless—endless. Lords, Ascot, Hurlingham—what was it? What a duck, she thought, looking at the frontispiece of some book of memoirs spread wide in the bow window, Sir Joshua perhaps or Romney; arch, bright, demure; the sort of girl—like her own Elizabeth—the only real sort of girl. And there was that absurd book, *Soapy Sponge*, which Jim used to quote by the yard; and Shakespeare's Sonnets. She knew them by heart. Phil and she had argued all day about the Dark Lady, and Dick had said straight out at dinner that night that he had never heard of her. Really, she had married him for that! He had never read Shakespeare! There must be

9. Shelley: English poet Percy Bysshe Shelley (1792–1822), the author of "Adonais" (1821), an elegy of mourning for a young man, from which Mrs. Dalloway repeats phrases throughout the story; Piccadilly: a neighborhood in London's West End.
1. A London mansion, home to the Dukes of Devonshire, demolished in the 1920s.
2. Red-brick palace built by Henry VIII, just to the north of St. James Park.

some little cheap book she could buy for Milly—*Cranford*[3] of course! Was there ever anything so enchanting as the cow in petticoats? If only people had that sort of humour, that sort of self-respect now, thought Clarissa, for she remembered the broad pages; the sentences ending; the characters—how one talked about them as if they were real. For all the great things one must go to the past, she thought. From the contagion of the world's slow stain . . . Fear no more the heat o' the sun . . . And now can never mourn, she repeated, her eyes straying over the window; for it ran in her head; the test of great poetry; the moderns had never written any-thing one wanted to read about death, she thought; and turned.

Omnibuses joined motor cars; motor cars vans; vans taxicabs; taxicabs motor cars—here was an open motor car with a girl, alone. Up till four, her feet tingling, I know, thought Clarissa, for the girl looked washed out, half asleep, in the corner of the car after the dance. And another car came; and another. No! No! No! Clarissa smiled good-naturedly. The fat lady had taken every sort of trouble, but diamonds! orchids! at this hour of the morning! No! No! No! The excellent policeman would, when the time came, hold up his hand. Another motor car passed. How utterly unattractive! Why should a girl of that age paint black around her eyes? And a young man with a girl, at this hour, when the country— The ad-mirable policeman raised his hand and Clarissa acknowledging his sway, taking her time, crossed, walked towards Bond Street; saw the narrow crooked street, the yellow banners; the thick notched telegraph wires stretched across the sky.

A hundred years ago her great-great-grandfather, Seymour Parry, who ran away with Conway's daughter, had walked down Bond Street. Down Bond Street the Parrys had walked for a hundred years, and might have met the Dalloways (Leighs on the mother's side) going up. Her father got his clothes from Hill's. There was a roll of cloth in the window, and here just one jar on a black table, in-credibly expensive; like the thick pink salmon on the ice block at the fishmonger's. The jewels were exquisite—pink and orange stars, paste, Spanish, she thought, and chains of old gold; starry buckles, little brooches which had been worn on a sea-green satin by ladies with high head-dresses. But no looking! One must economise. She must go on past the picture dealer's where one of the odd French pictures hung, as if people had thrown confetti—pink and blue—for a joke. If you had lived with pictures (and it's the same with books and music) thought Clarissa, passing the Aeolian Hall, you can't be taken in by a joke.

The river of Bond Street was clogged. There, like a queen at a tournament, raised, regal, was Lady Bexborough. She sat in her carriage, upright, alone, look-ing through her glasses. The white glove was loose at her wrist. She was in black, quite shabby, yet, thought Clarissa, how extraordinarily it tells, breeding, self-respect, never saying a word too much or letting people gossip; an astonishing friend; no one can pick a hole in her after all these years, and now, there she is, thought Clarissa, passing the Countess who waited powdered, perfectly still, and Clarissa would have given anything to be like that, the mistress of Clarefield, talk-ing politics, like a man. But she never goes anywhere, thought Clarissa, and it's quite useless to ask her, and the carriage went on and Lady Bexborough was borne past like a queen at a tournament, though she had nothing to live for and the old man is failing and they say she is sick of it all, thought Clarissa and the tears actu-ally rose to her eyes as she entered the shop.

3. Novel published in 1851 by Elizabeth Gaskell (1810–65)

"Good morning," said Clarissa in her charming voice. "Gloves," she said with her exquisite friendliness and putting her bag on the counter began, very slowly, to undo the buttons. "White gloves," she said. "Above the elbow," and she looked straight into the shopwoman's face—but this was not the girl she remembered? She looked quite old. "These really don't fit," said Clarissa. The shop-girl looked at them. "Madame wears bracelets?" Clarissa spread out her fingers. "Perhaps it's my rings." And the girl took the gray gloves with her to the end of the counter.

Yes, thought Clarissa, it's the girl I remember, she's twenty years older. . . . There was only one other customer, sitting sideways at the counter, her elbow poised, her bare hand drooping vacant; like a figure on a Japanese fan, thought Clarissa, too vacant perhaps, yet some men would adore her. The lady shook her head sadly. Again the gloves were too large. She turned round the glass. "Above the wrist," she reproached the grey-headed woman, who looked and agreed.

They waited; a clock ticked; Bond Street hummed, dulled, distant; the woman went away holding gloves. "Above the wrist," said the lady, mournfully, raising her voice. And she would have to order chairs, ices, flowers, and cloak-room tickets, thought Clarissa. The people she didn't want would come; the others wouldn't. She would stand by the door. They sold stockings—silk stockings. A lady is known by her gloves and her shoes, old Uncle William used to say. And through the hanging silk stockings, quivering silver she looked at the lady, sloping shouldered, her hand drooping, her bag slipping, her eyes vacantly on the floor. It would be intolerable if dowdy women came to her party! Would one have liked Keats if he had worn red socks? Oh, at last—she drew into the counter and it flashed into her mind:

"Do you remember before the war you had gloves with pearl buttons?"

"French gloves, Madame?"

"Yes, they were French," said Clarissa. The other lady rose very sadly and took her bag, and looked at the gloves on the counter. But they were all too large—always too large at the wrist.

"With pearl buttons," said the shop-girl, who looked ever so much older. She split the lengths of tissue paper apart on the counter. With pearl buttons, thought Clarissa, perfectly simple—how French!

"Madame's hands are so slender," said the shop-girl, drawing the glove firmly, smoothly, down over her rings. And Clarissa looked at her arm in the looking-glass. The glove hardly came to the elbow. Were there others half an inch longer? Still it seemed tiresome to bother her—perhaps the one day in the month, thought Clarissa, when it's an agony to stand. "Oh, don't bother," she said. But the gloves were brought.

"Don't you get fearfully tired," she said in her charming voice, "standing? When d'you get your holiday?"

"In September, Madame, when we're not so busy."

When we're in the country thought Clarissa. Or shooting. She has a fortnight at Brighton.[4] In some stuffy lodging. The landlady takes the sugar. Nothing would be easier than to send her to Mrs. Lumley's right in the country (and it was on the tip of her tongue). But then she remembered how on their honeymoon Dick had shown her the folly of giving impulsively. It was much more important, he said, to get trade with China. Of course he was right. And she could feel the girl wouldn't like to be given things. There she was in her place. So was Dick. Selling gloves was her job. She had her own sorrows quite separate, "and now can never mourn, can

---

4. A seaside resort on the south coast of England.

never mourn," the words ran in her head, "From the contagion of the world's slow stain," thought Clarissa holding her arm stiff, for there are moments when it seems utterly futile (the glove was drawn off leaving her arm flecked with powder)—simply one doesn't believe, thought Clarissa, any more in God.

The traffic suddenly roared; the silk stockings brightened. A customer came in.

"White gloves," she said, with some ring in her voice that Clarissa remembered.

It used, thought Clarissa, to be so simple. Down, down through the air came the caw of the rooks. When Sylvia died, hundreds of years ago, the yew hedges looked so lovely with the diamond webs in the mist before early church. But if Dick were to die to-morrow? As for believing in God—no, she would let the children choose, but for herself, like Lady Bexborough, who opened the bazaar, they say, with the telegram in her hand—Roden, her favourite, killed—she would go on. But why, if one doesn't believe? For the sake of others, she thought taking the glove in her hand. The girl would be much more unhappy if she didn't believe.

"Thirty shillings,"[5] said the shop-woman. "No, pardon me Madame, thirty-five. The French gloves are more."

For one doesn't live for oneself, thought Clarissa.

And then the other customer took a glove, tugged it, and it split.

"There!" she exclaimed.

"A fault of the skin," said the grey-headed woman hurriedly. "Sometimes a drop of acid in tanning. Try this pair, Madame."

"But it's an awful swindle to ask two pound ten!"[6]

Clarissa looked at the lady; the lady looked at Clarissa.

"Gloves have never been quite so reliable since the war," said the shop-girl, apologising, to Clarissa.

But where had she seen the other lady?—elderly, with a frill under her chin; wearing a black ribbon for gold eyeglasses; sensual, clever, like a Sargent[7] drawing. How one can tell from a voice when people are in the habit, thought Clarissa, of making other people—"It's a shade too tight," she said—obey. The shop-woman went off again. Clarissa was left waiting. Fear no more she repeated, playing her finger on the counter. Fear no more the heat o' the sun. Fear no more she repeated. There were little brown spots on her arm. And the girl crawled like a snail. Thou thy wordly task hast done. Thousands of young men had died that things might go on. At last! Half an inch above the elbow; pearl buttons; five and a quarter. My dear slowcoach, thought Clarissa, do you think I can sit here the whole morning? Now you'll take twenty-five minutes to bring me my change!

There was a violent explosion in the street outside. The shop-women cowered behind the counters. But Clarissa, sitting very upright, smiled at the other lady. "Miss Anstruther!" she exclaimed.

1923

The novel *Mrs. Dalloway*, 1925, appears in full in the Library of Women's Literature.

---

5. A British coin worth one-twentieth of a pound; in today's currency, 30 shillings would be worth over $100.

6. Almost $200 in today's currency.

7. John Singer Sargent, American portrait painter (1865–1925).

From **A Room of One's Own**

[*Shakespeare's Sister*]

It was disappointing not to have brought back in the evening some important statement, some authentic fact. Women are poorer than men because—this or that. Perhaps now it would be better to give up seeking for the truth, and receiving on one's head an avalanche of opinion hot as lava, discoloured as dish-water. It would be better to draw the curtains; to shut out distractions; to light the lamp; to narrow the enquiry and to ask the historian, who records not opinions but facts, to describe under what conditions women lived, not throughout the ages, but in England, say in the time of Elizabeth.[8]

For it is a perennial puzzle why no woman wrote a word of that extraordinary literature when every other man, it seemed, was capable of song or sonnet. What were the conditions in which women lived, I asked myself; for fiction, imaginative work that is, is not dropped like a pebble upon the ground, as science may be; fiction is like a spider's web, attached ever so lightly perhaps, but still attached to life at all four corners. Often the attachment is scarcely perceptible; Shakespeare's plays, for instance, seem to hang there complete by themselves. But when the web is pulled askew, hooked up at the edge, torn in the middle, one remembers that these webs are not spun in midair by incorporeal creatures, but are the work of suffering human beings, and are attached to grossly material things, like health and money and the houses we live in.

I went, therefore, to the shelf where the histories stand and took down one of the latest, Professor Trevelyan's *History of England*. Once more I looked up Women, found "position of," and turned to the pages indicated. "Wife-beating," I read, "was a recognised right of man, and was practised without shame by high as well as low. . . . Similarly," the historian goes on, "the daughter who refused to marry the gentleman of her parents' choice was liable to be locked up, beaten and flung about the room, without any shock being inflicted on public opinion. Marriage was not an affair of personal affection, but of family avarice, particularly in the 'chivalrous' upper classes. . . ." * * * Indeed, if woman had no existence save in the fiction written by men, one would imagine her a person of the utmost importance; very various; heroic and mean; splendid and sordid; infinitely beautiful and hideous in the extreme; as great as a man, some think even greater.[9] But this is woman in fiction. In fact, as Professor Trevelyan points out, she was locked up, beaten and flung about the room.

---

8. Elizabeth I (1533–1603), queen of England (1558–1603).

9. "It remains a strange and almost inexplicable fact that in Athena's city, where women were kept in almost Oriental suppression as odalisques or drudges, the stage should yet have produced figures like Clytemnestra and Cassandra, Atossa and Antigone, Phèdre and Medea, and all the other heroines who dominate play after play of the "misogynist" Euripides. But the paradox of this world where in real life a respectable woman could hardly show her face alone in the street, and yet on the stage woman equals or surpasses man, has never been satisfactorily explained. In modern tragedy the same predominance exists. At all events, a very cursory survey of Shakespeare's work (similarly with Webster, though not with Marlowe or Jonson) suffices to reveal how this dominance, this initiative of women, persists from Rosalind to Lady Macbeth. So too in Racine; six of his tragedies bear their heroines' names; and what male characters of his shall we set against Hermione and Andromaque, Bérénice and Roxane, Phèdre and Athalie? So again with Ibsen; what men shall we match with Solveig and Nora, Hedda and Hilda Wangel and Rebecca West?"— F. L. Lucas, *Tragedy*, pp. 114–15. [Woolf's note]

A very queer, composite being thus emerges. Imaginatively she is of the highest importance; practically she is completely insignificant. She pervades poetry from cover to cover; she is all but absent from history. She dominates the lives of kings and conquerors in fiction; in fact she was the slave of any boy whose parents forced a ring upon her finger. Some of the most inspired words, some of the most profound thoughts in literature fall from her lips; in real life she could hardly read, could scarcely spell, and was the property of her husband.

* * *

* * * But what I find deplorable, I continued, looking about the bookshelves again, is that nothing is known about women before the eighteenth century. I have no model in my mind to turn about this way and that. Here am I asking why women did not write poetry in the Elizabethan age, and I am not sure how they were educated; whether they were taught to write; whether they had sitting-rooms to themselves; how many women had children before they were twenty-one; what, in short, they did from eight in the morning till eight at night. They had no money evidently; according to Professor Trevelyan they were married whether they liked it or not before they were out of the nursery, at fifteen or sixteen very likely. It would have been extremely odd, even upon this showing, had one of them suddenly written the plays of Shakespeare, I concluded, and I thought of that old gentleman, who is dead now, but was a bishop, I think, who declared that it was impossible for any woman, past, present, or to come, to have the genius of Shakespeare. He wrote to the papers about it. He also told a lady who applied to him for information that cats do not as a matter of fact go to heaven, though they have, he added, souls of a sort. How much thinking those old gentlemen used to save one! How the borders of ignorance shrank back at their approach! Cats do not go to heaven. Women cannot write the plays of Shakespeare.

Be that as it may, I could not help thinking, as I looked at the works of Shakespeare on the shelf, that the bishop was right at least in this; it would have been impossible, completely and entirely, for any woman to have written the plays of Shakespeare in the age of Shakespeare. Let me imagine, since facts are so hard to come by, what would have happened had Shakespeare had a wonderfully gifted sister, called Judith, let us say. Shakespeare himself went, very probably—his mother was an heiress—to the grammar school, where he may have learnt Latin— Ovid, Virgil and Horace[1]—and the elements of grammar and logic. He was, it is well known, a wild boy who poached rabbits, perhaps shot a deer, and had, rather sooner than he should have done, to marry a woman in the neighbourhood, who bore him a child rather quicker than was right. That escapade sent him to seek his fortune in London. He had, it seemed, a taste for the theatre; he began by holding horses at the stage door. Very soon he got work in the theatre, became a successful actor, and lived at the hub of the universe, meeting everybody, knowing everybody, practising his art on the boards,[2] exercising his wits in the streets, and even getting access to the palace of the queen. Meanwhile his extraordinarily gifted sister, let us suppose, remained at home. She was as adventurous, as imaginative, as agog to see the world as he was. But she was not sent to school. She had no chance of learning grammar and logic, let alone of reading Horace and Virgil. She picked

---

1. Three poets of Latin literature: Ovid (43 BCE– 17 CE) is best known for *The Metamorphoses*; Virgil (70 BCE–19 BCE) for his epic poem *The* *Aeneid*; and Horace (65 BCE–8 BCE) for his lyric poems (or odes).
2. Stage.

up a book now and then, one of her brother's perhaps, and read a few pages. But then her parents came in and told her to mend the stockings or mind the stew and not moon about with books and papers. They would have spoken sharply but kindly, for they were substantial people who knew the conditions of life for a woman and loved their daughter—indeed, more likely than not she was the apple of her father's eye. Perhaps she scribbled some pages up in an apple loft on the sly, but was careful to hide them or set fire to them. Soon, however, before she was out of her teens, she was to be betrothed to the son of a neighbouring wool-stapler.[3] She cried out that marriage was hateful to her, and for that she was se-verely beaten by her father. Then he ceased to scold her. He begged her instead not to hurt him, not to shame him in this matter of her marriage. He would give her a chain of beads or a fine petticoat, he said; and there were tears in his eyes. How could she disobey him? How could she break his heart? The force of her own gift alone drove her to it. She made up a small parcel of her belongings, let herself down by a rope one summer's night and took the road to London. She was not seventeen. The birds that sang in the hedge were not more musical than she was. She had the quickest fancy, a gift like her brother's, for the tune of words. Like him, she had a taste for the theatre. She stood at the stage door; she wanted to act, she said. Men laughed in her face. The manager—a fat, loose-lipped man—guf-fawed. He bellowed something about poodles dancing and women acting—no woman, he said, could possibly be an actress. He hinted—you can imagine what. She could get no training in her craft. Could she even seek her dinner in a tavern or roam the streets at midnight? Yet her genius was for fiction and lusted to feed abundantly upon the lives of men and women and the study of their ways. At last—for she was very young, oddly like Shakespeare the poet in her face, with the same grey eyes and rounded brows—at last Nick Greene the actor-manager took pity on her; she found herself with child by that gentleman and so—who shall measure the heat and violence of the poet's heart when caught and tangled in a woman's body?—killed herself one winter's night and lies buried at some cross-roads where the omnibuses now stop outside the Elephant and Castle.[4]

That, more or less, is how the story would run, I think, if a woman in Shake-speare's day had had Shakespeare's genius. But for my part, I agree with the de-ceased bishop, if such he was—it is unthinkable that any woman in Shakespeare's day should have had Shakespeare's genius. For genius like Shakespeare's is not born among labouring, uneducated, servile people. It was not born in England among the Saxons and the Britons. It is not born today among the working classes. How, then, could it have been born among women whose work began, according to Professor Trevelyan, almost before they were out of the nursery, who were forced to it by their parents and held to it by all the power of law and custom? Yet genius of a sort must have existed among women as it must have existed among the working classes. Now and again an Emily Brontë or a Robert Burns blazes out and proves its presence.[5] But certainly it never got itself on to paper. When, how-ever, one reads of a witch being ducked, of a woman possessed by devils, of a wise woman selling herbs, or even of a very remarkable man who had a mother, then I think we are on the track of a lost novelist, a suppressed poet, of some mute and

---

3. A wool merchant.
4. An intersection in south London near a pub (or public house) of the same name.

5. Emily Brontë: English writer (1818–48; pp. 836–42), author of *Wuthering Heights;* Robert Burns: Scottish poet and songwriter (1759–96).

inglorious Jane Austen, some Emily Brontë who dashed her brains out on the moor or mopped and mowed about the highways crazed with the torture that her gift had put her to. Indeed, I would venture to guess that Anon, who wrote so many poems without signing them, was often a woman. It was a woman Edward Fitzgerald, I think, suggested who made the ballads and the folk-songs, crooning them to her children, beguiling her spinning with them, or the length of the winter's night.[6]

This may be true or it may be false—who can say?—but what is true in it, so it seemed to me, reviewing the story of Shakespeare's sister as I had made it, is that any woman born with a great gift in the sixteenth century would certainly have gone crazed, shot herself, or ended her days in some lonely cottage outside the village, half witch, half wizard, feared and mocked at. For it needs little skill in psychology to be sure that a highly gifted girl who had tried to use her gift for poetry would have been so thwarted and hindered by other people, so tortured and pulled asunder by her own contrary instincts, that she must have lost her health and sanity to a certainty. No girl could have walked to London and stood at a stage door and forced her way into the presence of actor-managers without doing herself a violence and suffering an anguish which may have been irrational—for chastity may be a fetish invented by certain societies for unknown reasons—but were none the less inevitable. Chastity had then, it has even now, a religious importance in a woman's life, and has so wrapped itself round with nerves and instincts that to cut it free and bring it to the light of day demands courage of the rarest. To have lived a free life in London in the sixteenth century would have meant for a woman who was poet and playwright a nervous stress and dilemma which might well have killed her. Had she survived, whatever she had written would have been twisted and deformed, issuing from a strained and morbid imagination. And undoubtedly, I thought, looking at the shelf where there are no plays by women, her work would have gone unsigned. That refuge she would have sought certainly. It was the relic of the sense of chastity that dictated anonymity to women even so late as the nineteenth century. Currer Bell, George Eliot, George Sand,[7] all the victims of inner strife as their writings prove, sought ineffectively to veil themselves by using the name of a man. Thus they did homage to the convention, which if not implanted by the other sex was liberally encouraged by them (the chief glory of a woman is not to be talked of, said Pericles,[8] himself a much-talked-of man), that publicity in women is detestable. Anonymity runs in their blood. The desire to be veiled still possesses them. They are not even now as concerned about the health of their fame as men are, and, speaking generally, will pass a tombstone or a signpost without feeling an irresistible desire to cut their names on it, as Alf, Bert or Chas. must do in obedience to their instinct, which murmurs if it sees a fine woman go by, or even a dog, Ce chien est à moi.[9] And, of course, it may not be a dog, I thought, remembering Parliament Square, the Sieges Allee and other avenues; it may be a piece of land or a man with curly

---

6. Jane Austen: English novelist (1775–1817; pp. 545–47); Anon: anonymous; Edward Fitzgerald: English poet and translator of *The Rubáiyát of Omar Khayyám*.
7. Currer Bell: pen name of English novelist Charlotte Brontë (1816–55; pp. 826–33); George Eliot:

pen name of English novelist Mary Anne (or Marian) Evans (1819–80; pp. 862–80); George Sand: pen name of French novelist Amantine-Lucile-Aurore Dupin (1804–76).
8. Ancient Greek statesman (495 BCE–429 BCE).
9. That dog is mine (French).

black hair. It is one of the great advantages of being a woman that one can pass
even a very fine negress without wishing to make an Englishwoman of her.

That woman, then, who was born with a gift of poetry in the sixteenth century, was an unhappy woman, a woman at strife against herself. All the conditions of her life, all her own instincts, were hostile to the state of mind which is
needed to set free whatever is in the brain. But what is the state of mind that is
most propitious to the act of creation, I asked. Can one come by any notion of the
state that furthers and makes possible that strange activity? * * *

And one gathers from this enormous modern literature of confession and self-
analysis that to write a work of genius is almost always a feat of prodigious difficulty. Everything is against the likelihood that it will come from the writer's mind
whole and entire. Generally material circumstances are against it. Dogs will bark;
people will interrupt; money must be made; health will break down. Further, ac-
centuating all these difficulties and making them harder to bear is the world's notorious indifference. It does not ask people to write poems and novels and
histories; it does not need them. * * * A curse, a cry of agony, rises from those
books of analysis and confession. "Mighty poets in their misery dead"—that is
the burden of their song. If anything comes through in spite of all this, it is a miracle, and probably no book is born entire and uncrippled as it was conceived.

But for women, I thought, looking at the empty shelves, these difficulties were
infinitely more formidable. In the first place, to have a room of her own, let alone
a quiet room or a sound-proof room, was out of the question, unless her parents
were exceptionally rich or very noble, even up to the beginning of the nineteenth
century. Since her pin money, which depended on the good will of her father, was
only enough to keep her clothed, she was debarred from such alleviations as came
even to Keats or Tennyson or Carlyle,[1] all poor men, from a walking tour, a little
journey to France, from the separate lodging which, even if it were miserable
enough, sheltered them from the claims and tyrannies of their families. Such material difficulties were formidable; but much worse were the immaterial. The indifference of the world which Keats and Flaubert[2] and other men of genius have
found so hard to bear was in her case not indifference but hostility. The world did
not say to her as it said to them, Write if you choose; it makes no difference to me.
The world said with a guffaw, Write? What's the good of your writing?

[Peroration: Women Write!]

* * * Intellectual freedom depends upon material things. Poetry depends upon
intellectual freedom. And women have always been poor, not for two hundred years
merely, but from the beginning of time. Women have had less intellectual freedom
than the sons of Athenian slaves. Women, then, have not had a dog's chance of
writing poetry. That is why I have laid so much stress on money and a room
of one's own. However, thanks to the toils of those obscure women in the past, of
whom I wish we knew more, thanks, curiously enough, to two wars, the Crimean
which let Florence Nightingale out of her drawing-room, and the European War

1. English romantic poet John Keats (1795–1821);   (1795–1881).
English Victorian poet Alfred, Lord Tennyson   2. French novelist Gustave Flaubert (1821–80).
(1809–92); Scottish essayist Thomas Carlyle

which opened the doors to the average woman some sixty years later, these evils are in the way to be bettered.[3] Otherwise you would not be here tonight, and your chance of earning five hundred pounds a year,[4] precarious as I am afraid that it still is, would be minute in the extreme.

Still, you may object, why do you attach so much importance to this writing of books by women when, according to you, it requires so much effort, leads perhaps to the murder of one's aunts, will make one almost certainly late for luncheon, and may bring one into very grave disputes with certain very good fellows? My motives, let me admit, are partly selfish. Like most uneducated Englishwomen, I like reading—I like reading books in the bulk. Lately my diet has become a trifle monotonous; history is too much about wars; biography too much about great men; poetry has shown, I think, a tendency to sterility, and fiction—but I have sufficiently exposed my disabilities as a critic of modern fiction and will say no more about it. Therefore I would ask you to write all kinds of books, hesitating at no subject however trivial or however vast. By hook or by crook, I hope that you will possess yourselves of money enough to travel and to idle, to contemplate the future or the past of the world, to dream over books and loiter at street corners and let the line of thought dip deep into the stream. For I am by no means confining you to fiction. If you would please me—and there are thousands like me—you would write books of travel and adventure, and research and scholarship, and history and biography, and criticism and philosophy and science. By so doing you will certainly profit the art of fiction. For books have a way of influencing each other. Fiction will be much the better for standing cheek by jowl with poetry and philosophy. Moreover, if you consider any great figure of the past, like Sappho, like the Lady Murasaki, like Emily Brontë,[5] you will find that she is an inheritor as well as an originator, and has come into existence because women have come to have the habit of writing naturally; so that even as a prelude to poetry such activity on your part would be invaluable.

But when I look back through these notes and criticise my own train of thought as I made them, I find that my motives were not altogether selfish. There runs through these comments and discursions the conviction—or is it the instinct?—that good books are desirable and that good writers, even if they show every variety of human depravity, are still good human beings. Thus when I ask you to write more books I am urging you to do what will be for your good and for the good of the world at large. How to justify this instinct or belief I do not know, for philosophic words, if one has not been educated at a university, are apt to play one false. What is meant by "reality"? It would seem to be something very erratic, very undependable—now to be found in a dusty road, now in a scrap of newspaper in the street, now in a daffodil in the sun. It lights up a group in a room and stamps some casual saying. It overwhelms one walking home beneath the stars and makes the silent world more real than the world of speech—and then there it is again in an omnibus in the uproar of Piccadilly. Sometimes, too, it seems to dwell in shapes too far away for us to discern what their nature is. But whatever it touches, it fixes and makes permanent. That is what remains over when the

3. Florence Nightingale: pioneer of modern nursing (1820–1910), who served in the Crimean War (1853–56); European War: World War I.
4. About $40,000 in today's currency.
5. Sappho: ancient Greek female poet, said to

have been born on the island of Lesbos (c. 630 BCE–570 BCE); Lady Murasaki: Murasaki Shikibu (973–1014?), a Japanese woman writer and servant of the imperial court.

skin of the day has been cast into the hedge; that is what is left of past time and of our loves and hates. Now the writer, as I think, has the chance to live more than other people in the presence of this reality. It is his business to find it and collect it and communicate it to the rest of us. So at least I infer from reading *Lear* or *Emma* or *La Recherche du Temps Perdu.*[6] For the reading of these books seems to perform a curious couching operation on the senses; one sees more intensely afterwards; the world seems bared of its covering and given an intenser life. Those are the enviable people who live at enmity with unreality; and those are the pitiable who are knocked on the head by the thing done without knowing or caring. So that when I ask you to earn money and have a room of your own, I am asking you to live in the presence of reality, an invigorating life, it would appear, whether one can impart it or not.

Here I would stop, but the pressure of convention decrees that every speech must end with a peroration. And a peroration addressed to women should have something, you will agree, particularly exalting and ennobling about it. I should implore you to remember your responsibilities, to be higher, more spiritual; I should remind you how much depends upon you, and what an influence you can exert upon the future. But those exhortations can safely, I think, be left to the other sex, who will put them, and indeed have put them, with far greater eloquence than I can compass. When I rummage in my own mind I find no noble sentiments about being companions and equals and influencing the world to higher ends. I find myself saying briefly and prosaically that it is much more important to be oneself than anything else. Do not dream of influencing other people, I would say, if I knew how to make it sound exalted. Think of things in themselves.

And again I am reminded by dipping into newspapers and novels and biographies that when a woman speaks to women she should have something very unpleasant up her sleeve. Women are hard on women. Women dislike women. Women—but are you not sick to death of the word? I can assure you that I am. Let us agree, then, that a paper read by a woman to women should end with something particularly disagreeable.

But how does it go? What can I think of? The truth is, I often like women. I like their unconventionality. I like their subtlety. I like their anonymity. I like—but I must not run on in this way. That cupboard there,—you say it holds clean table-napkins only; but what if Sir Archibald Bodkin[7] were concealed among them? Let me then adopt a sterner tone. Have I, in the preceding words, conveyed to you sufficiently the warnings and reprobation of mankind? I have told you the very low opinion in which you were held by Mr. Oscar Browning. I have indicated what Napoleon once thought of you and what Mussolini thinks now.[8] Then, in case any of you aspire to fiction, I have copied out for your benefit the advice of the critic about courageously acknowledging the limitations of your sex. I have referred to Professor X and given prominence to his statement that women are intellectually, morally and physically inferior to men. I have handed on all that has

---

6. *King Lear:* 1605 play by William Shakespeare; *Emma:* 1816 novel by Jane Austen; *La Recherche du Temps Perdu: Remembrance of Things Past,* a seven-volume work by French novelist Marcel Proust (1871–1922).
7. Appointed director of public prosecutions in England in 1920, Bodkin was responsible for ban-

ning books, including James Joyce's *Ulysses* (1922) and Radclyffe Hall's *Well of Loneliness* (1928), for obscenity.
8. Oscar Browning: British historian (1837–1923); Napoleon: emperor of France (1769–1821); Benito Mussolini: Fascist leader of Italy before and during World War II (1883–1945).

come my way without going in search of it, and here is a final warning—from Mr. John Langdon Davies.[9] Mr. John Langdon Davies warns women "that when children cease to be altogether desirable, women cease to be altogether necessary." I hope you will make a note of it.

How can I further encourage you to go about the business of life? Young women, I would say, and please attend, for the peroration is beginning, you are, in my opinion, disgracefully ignorant. You have never made a discovery of any sort of importance. You have never shaken an empire or led an army into battle. The plays of Shakespeare are not by you, and you have never introduced a barbarous race to the blessings of civilisation. What is your excuse? It is all very well for you to say, pointing to the streets and squares and forests of the globe swarming with black and white and coffee-coloured inhabitants, all busily engaged in traffic and enterprise and love-making, we have had other work on our hands. Without our doing, those seas would be unsailed and those fertile lands a desert. We have borne and bred and washed and taught, perhaps to the age of six or seven years, the one thousand six hundred and twenty-three million human beings who are, according to statistics, at present in existence, and that, allowing that some had help, takes time.

There is truth in what you say—I will not deny it. But at the same time may I remind you that there have been at least two colleges for women in existence in England since the year 1866; that after the year 1880 a married woman was allowed by law to possess her own property; and that in 1919—which is a whole nine years ago—she was given a vote? May I also remind you that the most of the professions have been open to you for close on ten years now? When you reflect upon these immense privileges and the length of time during which they have been enjoyed, and the fact that there must be at this moment some two thousand women capable of earning over five hundred a year in one way or another, you will agree that the excuse of lack of opportunity, training, encouragement, leisure and money no longer holds good. Moreover, the economists are telling us that Mrs. Seton has had too many children. You must, of course, go on bearing children, but, so they say, in twos and threes, not in tens and twelves.

Thus, with some time on your hands and with some book learning in your brains—you have had enough of the other kind, and are sent to college partly, I suspect, to be uneducated—surely you should embark upon another stage of your very long, very laborious and highly obscure career. A thousand pens are ready to suggest what you should do and what effect you will have. My own suggestion is a little fantastic, I admit; I prefer, therefore, to put it in the form of fiction.

I told you in the course of this paper that Shakespeare had a sister; but do not look for her in Sir Sidney Lee's[1] life of the poet. She died young—alas, she never wrote a word. She lies buried where the omnibuses now stop, opposite the Elephant and Castle. Now my belief is that this poet who never wrote a word and was buried at the crossroads still lives. She lives in you and in me, and in many other women who are not here tonight, for they are washing up the dishes and putting the children to bed. But she lives; for great poets do not die; they are continuing presences; they need only the opportunity to walk among us in the flesh. This opportunity, as I think, it is now coming within your power to give her. For my belief

9. John Langdon Davies' *A Short History of Women* (1927). [Woolf's note]
1. Author of *A Life of Shakespeare* (1898) and successor to Woolf's father as editor of the *Dictionary of National Biography* in 1891.

is that if we live another century or so—I am talking of the common life which is
the real life and not of the little separate lives which we live as individuals—and
have five hundred a year each of us and rooms of our own; if we have the habit of
freedom and the courage to write exactly what we think; if we escape a little from
the common sitting-room and see human beings not always in their relation to
each other but in relation to reality; and the sky, too, and the trees or whatever it
may be in themselves; if we look past Milton's[2] bogey, for no human being should
shut out the view; if we face the fact, for it is a fact, that there is no arm to cling to,
but that we go alone and that our relation is to the world of reality and not only to
the world of men and women, then the opportunity will come and the dead poet
who was Shakespeare's sister will put on the body which she has so often laid down.
Drawing her life from the lives of the unknown who were her forerunners, as her
brother did before her, she will be born. As for her coming without that preparation, without that effort on our part, without that determination that when she is
born again she shall find it possible to live and write her poetry, that we cannot expect, for that would be impossible. But I maintain that she would come if we
worked for her, and that so to work, even in poverty and obscurity, is worth while.

1929

◄——╼▶

A Haunted House

Whatever hour you woke there was a door shutting. From room to room they
went, hand in hand, lifting here, opening there, making sure—a ghostly couple.

"Here we left it," she said. And he added, "Oh, but here too!" "It's upstairs,"
she murmured. "And in the garden," he whispered. "Quietly," they said, "or we
shall wake them."

But it wasn't that you woke us. Oh, no. "They're looking for it; they're drawing the curtain," one might say, and so read on a page or two. "Now they've found
it," one would be certain, stopping the pencil on the margin. And then, tired of
reading, one might rise and see for oneself, the house all empty, the doors standing open, only the wood pigeons bubbling with content and the hum of the threshing machine sounding from the farm. "What did I come in here for? What did I
want to find?" My hands were empty. "Perhaps it's upstairs then?" The apples
were in the loft. And so down again, the garden still as ever, only the book had
slipped into the grass.

But they had found it in the drawing-room. Not that one could ever see them.
The window panes reflected apples, reflected roses; all the leaves were green in the
glass. If they moved in the drawing-room, the apple only turned its yellow side.
Yet, the moment after, if the door was opened, spread about the floor, hung upon
the walls, pendant from the ceiling—what? My hands were empty. The shadow of
a thrush crossed the carpet; from the deepest wells of silence the wood pigeon
drew its bubble of sound. "Safe, safe, safe," the pulse of the house beat softly.
"The treasure buried; the room . . ." the pulse stopped short. Oh, was that the
buried treasure?

---

2. John Milton (1608–74), English poet, author of *Paradise Lost* (1667).

A moment later the light had faded. Out in the garden then? But the trees spun darkness for a wandering beam of sun. So fine, so rare, coolly sunk beneath the surface the beam I sought always burnt behind the glass. Death was the glass; death was between us; coming to the woman first, hundreds of years ago, leaving the house, sealing all the windows; the rooms were darkened. He left it, left her, went North, went East, saw the stars turned in the Southern sky; sought the house, found it dropped beneath the Downs. "Safe, safe, safe," the pulse of the house beat gladly. "The Treasure yours."

The wind roars up the avenue. Trees stoop and bend this way and that. Moonbeams splash and spill wildly in the rain. But the beam of the lamp falls straight from the window. The candle burns stiff and still. Wandering through the house, opening the windows, whispering not to wake us, the ghostly couple seek their joy.

"Here we slept," she says. And he adds, "Kisses without number." "Waking in the morning—" "Silver between the trees—" "Upstairs—" "In the garden—" "When summer came—" "In winter snowtime—" The doors go shutting far in the distance, gently knocking like the pulse of a heart.

Nearer they come; cease at the doorway. The wind falls, the rain slides silver down the glass. Our eyes darken; we hear no steps beside us; we see no lady spread her ghostly cloak. His hands shield the lantern. "Look," he breathes. "Sound asleep. Love upon their lips."

Stooping, holding their silver lamp above us, long they look and deeply. Long they pause. The wind drives straightly; the flame stoops slightly. Wild beams of moonlight cross both floor and wall, and, meeting, stain the faces bent; the faces pondering; the faces that search the sleepers and seek their hidden joy.

"Safe, safe, safe," the heart of the house beats proudly. "Long years—" he sighs. "Again you found me." "Here," she murmurs, "sleeping; in the garden reading; laughing, rolling apples in the loft. Here we left our treasure—" Stooping, their light lifts the lids upon my eyes. "Safe! safe! safe!" the pulse of the house beats wildly. Waking, I cry "Oh, is this *your* buried treasure? The light in the heart."

1943

◄ ANZIA YEZIERSKA ►
c. 1885–1970

Having fled the violent pogroms against Jews in her hometown, Plotsk, near Warsaw, Poland, Anzia Yezierska came to America at age fifteen with her siblings and parents, Bernard and Pearl Yeziersky. The Yiddish-speaking family settled in a tenement apartment in the Jewish ghetto of New York City's Lower East Side; it presented a strong contrast to the earthen-floored hut where she had been born, but it (and the city where it was located) also presented some challenges of its own. Her father was a Talmudic scholar and her mother a menial worker, and as a teenager Yezierska herself worked long hours as a domestic servant or in sweatshops (see pp. 1357–58) making clothes, attending school at night to learn English. After briefly pursuing a dream of becoming an actress by attending the American Academy of Dramatic Arts, at age eighteen she received a scholarship from Columbia University, where she studied domestic science (later called home economics) in preparation for becoming a teacher. Soon after graduating she learned that teaching did not suit her. Nor did married life: she was married twice—first, briefly, to a lawyer and then to a teacher, with whom she had a daughter. When she divorced her second husband, she turned over full custody of her daughter to him. In her thirties, Yezierska met and became romantically involved with the American philosopher John Dewey, about twenty years her senior, but that relationship ended after about a year. As shown by the biography her daughter, Louise Levitas Henriksen, published in 1988, the focus of Yezierska's energies was not love and marriage, but writing.

Yezierska's short stories and novels describe social, cultural, and religious aspects of Jewish ghetto life at the turn of the twentieth century. Her protagonists are often young or middle-aged women who struggle against the patriarchal structure and old-world values of the Jewish family of that era, while trying to find a place in an American society that does not welcome their differentness. Often drawing on her own feelings and experiences, Yezierska wrote only fiction, leaving no autobiographical record. She is best remembered for her novel *Bread Givers* (1925), which is loosely based on her own experience fighting poverty, lack of education, and parental control. Her first publishing success came with a collection of short stories, *Hungry Hearts* (1920), in which "Soap and Water," included here, first appeared. The collection was so popular that Hollywood producer Samuel Goldwyn bought the film rights to the stories and brought Yezierska to California to write for the movies. While living in Hollywood, and later in New Hampshire, Yezierska found that she needed to be in New York's Lower East Side in order to write productively about her chosen subject. Her work is doubly important to American literary history because it represents a woman's perspective on Jewish experience as well as a working-class Jewish contribution to women's writing.

"Soap and Water" illuminates the alienation of the immigrant woman that is a prevalent theme for Yezierska. As the story shows, cultural differences and class prejudice go beyond matters of language and custom, to the level of such profoundly personal matters as the care of one's body and clothing.

Soap and Water

What I so greatly feared, happened! Miss Whiteside, the dean of our college, withheld my diploma. When I came to her office, and asked her why she did not pass me, she said that she could not recommend me as a teacher because of my personal appearance.

She told me that my skin looked oily, my hair unkempt, and my finger-nails sadly neglected. She told me that I was utterly unmindful of the little niceties of the well-groomed lady. She pointed out that my collar did not set evenly, my belt was awry, and there was a lack of freshness in my dress. And she ended with: "Soap and water are cheap. Anyone can be clean."

In those four years while I was under her supervision, I was always timid and diffident. I shrank and trembled when I had to come near her. When I had to say something to her, I mumbled and stuttered, and grew red and white in the face with fear.

Every time I had to come to the dean's office for a private conference, I prepared for the ordeal of her cold scrutiny, as a patient prepares for a surgical operation. I watched her gimlet[1] eyes searching for a stray pin, for a spot on my dress,

---

1. A small hand tool for boring holes.

for my unpolished shoes, for my uncared-for finger-nails, as one strapped on the operating table watches the surgeon approaching with his tray of sterilized knives.

She never looked into my eyes. She never perceived that I had a soul. She did not see how I longed for beauty and cleanliness. How I strained and struggled to lift myself from the dead toil and exhaustion that weighed me down. She could see nothing in people like me, except the dirt and the stains on the outside.

But this last time when she threatened to withhold my diploma, because of my appearance, this last time when she reminded me that "Soap and water are cheap. Anyone can be clean," this last time, something burst within me.

I felt the suppressed wrath of all the unwashed of the earth break loose within me. My eyes blazed fire. I didn't care for myself, nor the dean, nor the whole laundered world. I had suffered the cruelty of their cleanliness and the tyranny of their culture to the breaking point. I was too frenzied to know what I said or did. But I saw clean, immaculate, spotless Miss Whiteside shrivel and tremble and cower before me, as I had shriveled and trembled and cowered before her for so many years.

Why did she give me my diploma? Was it pity? Or can it be that in my outburst of fury, at the climax of indignities that I had suffered, the barriers broke, and she saw into the world below from where I came?

Miss Whiteside had no particular reason for hounding and persecuting me. Personally, she didn't give a hang if I was clean or dirty. She was merely one of the agents of clean society, delegated to judge who is fit and who is unfit to teach.

While they condemned me as unfit to be a teacher, because of my appearance, I was slaving to keep them clean. I was slaving in a laundry from five to eight in the morning, before going to college, and from six to eleven at night, after coming from college. Eight hours of work a day, outside my studies. Where was the time and the strength for the "little niceties of the well-groomed lady"?

At the time when they rose and took their morning bath, and put on their fresh-laundered linen that somebody had made ready for them, when they were being served with their breakfast, I had already toiled for three hours in a laundry.

When the college hours were over, they went for a walk in the fresh air. They had time to rest, and bathe again, and put on fresh clothes for dinner. But I, after college hours, had only time to bolt a soggy meal, and rush back to the grind of the laundry till eleven at night.

At the hour when they came from the theater or musicale, I came from the laundry. But I was so bathed in the sweat of exhaustion that I could not think of a bath of soap and water. I had only strength to drag myself home, and fall down on the bed and sleep. Even if I had had the desire and the energy to take a bath, there were no such things as bathtubs in the house where I lived.

Often as I stood at my board at the laundry, I thought of Miss Whiteside, and her clean world, clothed in the snowy shirtwaists I had ironed. I was thinking— I, soaking in the foul vapors of the steaming laundry, I, with my dirty, tired hands, I am ironing the clean, immaculate shirtwaists of clean, immaculate society. I, the unclean one, am actually fashioning the pedestal of their cleanliness, from which they reach down, hoping to lift me to the height that I have created for them.

I look back at my sweatshop childhood. One day, when I was about sixteen, someone gave me Rosenfeld's poem "The Machine,"[2] to read. Like a spark thrown among oil rags, it set my whole being aflame with longing for self-expression. But I was dumb. I had nothing but blind, aching feeling. For days I went about with

2. Jewish poet Morris Rosenfeld (1862–1923), wrote in English, Yiddish, and German.

agonies of feeling, yet utterly at sea how to fathom and voice those feelings—birth throes of infinite worlds, and yet dumb.

Suddenly, there came upon me this inspiration. I can go to college! There I shall learn to express myself, to voice my thoughts. But I was not prepared to go to college. The girl in the cigar factory, in the next block, had gone first to a preparatory school. Why shouldn't I find a way, too?

Going to college seemed as impossible for me, at that time, as for an ignorant Russian shop-girl to attempt to write poetry in English. But I was sixteen then, and the impossible was a magnet to draw the dreams that had no outlet. Besides, the actual was so barren, so narrow, so strangling, that the dream of the unattainable was the only air in which the soul could survive.

The idea of going to college was like the birth of a new religion in my soul. It put new fire in my eyes, and new strength in my tired arms and fingers.

For six years I worked daytimes and went at night to a preparatory school. For six years I went about nursing the illusion that college was a place where I should find self-expression, and vague, pent-up feelings could live as thoughts and grow as ideas.

At last I came to college. I rushed for it with the outstretched arms of youth's aching hunger to give and take of life's deepest and highest, and I came against the solid wall of the well-fed, well-dressed world—the frigid whitewashed wall of cleanliness.

Until I came to college I had been unconscious of my clothes. Suddenly I felt people looking at me at arm's length, as if I were crooked or crippled, as if I had come to a place where I didn't belong, and would never be taken in.

How I pinched, and scraped, and starved myself, to save enough to come to college! Every cent of the tuition fee I paid was drops of sweat and blood from underpaid laundry work. And what did I get for it? A crushed spirit, a broken heart, a stinging sense of poverty that I never felt before.

The courses of study I had to swallow to get my diploma were utterly barren of interest to me. I didn't come to college to get dull learning from dead books. I didn't come for that dry, inanimate stuff that can be hammered out in lectures. I came because I longed for the larger life, for the stimulus of intellectual associations. I came because my whole being clamored for more vision, more light. But everywhere I went I saw big fences put up against me, with the brutal signs: "No trespassing. Get off the grass."

I experienced at college the same feeling of years ago when I came to this country, when after months of shut-in-ness, in dark tenements and stifling sweatshops, I had come to Central Park for the first time. Like a bird just out from a cage, I stretched out my arms, and then flung myself in ecstatic abandon on the grass. Just as I began to breathe in the fresh-smelling earth, and lift up my eyes to the sky, a big, fat policeman with a club in his hand, seized me, with: "Can't you read the sign? Get off the grass!" Miss Whiteside, the dean of the college, the representative of the clean, the educated world, for all her external refinement, was to me like that big, brutal policeman, with the club in his hand, that drove me off the grass.

The death-blows to all aspiration began when I graduated from college and tried to get a start at the work for which I had struggled so hard to fit myself. I soon found other agents of clean society, who had the power of giving or withholding the positions I sought, judging me as Miss Whiteside judged me. One glance at my shabby clothes, the desperate anguish that glazed and dulled my eyes and I felt myself condemned by them before I opened my lips to speak.

Starvation forced me to accept the lowest-paid substitute position. And because my wages were so low and so unsteady, I could never get the money for the clothes to make an appearance to secure a position with better pay. I was tricked and foiled. I was considered unfit to get decent pay for my work because of my appearance, and it was to the advantage of those who used me that my appearance should damn me, so as to get me to work for the low wages I was forced to accept. It seemed to me the whole vicious circle of society's injustices was thrust like a noose around my neck to strangle me.

The insults and injuries I had suffered at college had so eaten into my flesh that I could not bear to get near it. I shuddered with horror whenever I had to pass the place blocks away. The hate which I felt for Miss Whiteside spread like poison inside my soul, into hate for all clean society. The whole clean world was massed against me. Whenever I met a well-dressed person, I felt the secret stab of a hidden enemy.

I was so obsessed and consumed with my grievances that I could not get away from myself and think things out in the light. I was in the grip of that blinding, destructive, terrible thing—righteous indignation. I could not rest. I wanted the whole world to know that the college was against democracy in education, that clothes form the basis of class distinctions, that after graduation the opportunities for the best positions are passed out to those who are best-dressed, and the students too poor to put up a front are pigeon-holed and marked unfit and abandoned to the mercy of the wind.

A wild desire raged in the corner of my brain. I knew that the dean gave dinners to the faculty at regular intervals. I longed to burst in at one of those feasts, in the midst of their grand speech-making, and tear down the fine clothes from these well-groomed ladies and gentlemen, and trample them under my feet, and scream like a lunatic: "Soap and water are cheap! Soap and water are cheap! Look at me! See how cheap it is!"

There seemed but three avenues of escape to the torments of my wasted life, madness, suicide, or a heart-to-heart confession to someone who understood. I had not energy enough for suicide. Besides, in my darkest moments of despair, hope clamored loudest. Oh, I longed so to live, to dream my way up on the heights, above the unreal realities that ground me and dragged me down to earth.

Inside the ruin of my thwarted life, the *unlived* visionary immigrant hungered and thirsted for America. I had come a refugee from the Russian pogroms,[3] aflame with dreams of America. I did not find America in the sweatshops, much less in the schools and colleges. But for hundreds of years the persecuted races all over the world were nurtured on hopes of America. When a little baby in my mother's arms, before I was old enough to speak, I saw all around me weary faces light up with thrilling tales of the far-off "golden country." And so, though my faith in this so-called America was shattered, yet underneath, in the sap and roots of my soul, burned the deathless faith that America is, must be, somehow, somewhere. In the midst of my bitterest hates and rebellions, visions of America rose over me, like songs of freedom of an oppressed people.

My body was worn to the bone from overwork, my footsteps dragged with exhaustion, but my eyes still sought the sky, praying, ceaselessly praying, the

3. Organized massacres and persecutions of Jews in Russia.

dumb, inarticulate prayer of the lost immigrant: "America! Ach,[4] America! Where is America?"

It seemed to me if I could only find some human being to whom I could unburden my heart, I would have new strength to begin again my insatiable search for America.

But to whom could I speak? The people in the laundry? They never understood me. They had a grudge against me because I left them when I tried to work myself up. Could I speak to the college people? What did these icebergs of convention know about the vital things of the heart?

And yet, I remembered, in the freshman year, in one of the courses in chemistry, there was an instructor, a woman, who drew me strangely. I felt she was the only real teacher among all the teachers and professors I met. I didn't care for the chemistry, but I liked to look at her. She gave me life, air, the unconscious emanation of her beautiful spirit. I had not spoken a word to her, outside the experiments in chemistry, but I knew her more than the people around her who were of her own class. I felt in the throb of her voice, in the subtle shading around the corner of her eyes, the color and texture of her dreams.

Often in the midst of our work in chemistry I felt like crying out to her: "Oh, please be my friend. I'm so lonely." But something choked me. I couldn't speak. The very intensity of my longing for her friendship made me run away from her in confusion the minute she approached me. I was so conscious of my shabbiness that I was afraid maybe she was only trying to be kind. I couldn't bear kindness. I wanted from her love, understanding, or nothing.

About ten years after I left college, as I walked the streets bowed and beaten with the shame of having to go around begging for work, I met Miss Van Ness. She not only recognized me, but stopped to ask how I was, and what I was doing.

I had begun to think that my only comrades in this world were the homeless and abandoned cats and dogs of the street, whom everybody gives another kick, as they slam the door on them. And here was one from the clean world human enough to be friendly. Here was one of the well-dressed, with a look in her eyes and a sound in her voice that was like healing oil over the bruises of my soul. The mere touch of that woman's hand in mine so overwhelmed me, that I burst out crying in the street.

The next morning I came to Miss Van Ness at her office. In those ten years she had risen to a professorship. But I was not in the least intimidated by her high office. I felt as natural in her presence as if she were my own sister. I heard myself telling her the whole story of my life, but I felt that even if I had not said a word she would have understood all I had to say as if I had spoken. It was all so unutterable, to find one from the other side of the world who was so simply and naturally that miraculous thing—a friend. Just as contact with Miss Whiteside had tied and bound all my thinking processes, so Miss Van Ness unbound and freed me and suffused me with light.

I felt the joy of one breathing on the mountain-tops for the first time. I looked down at the world below. I was changed and the world was changed. My past was the forgotten night. Sunrise was all around me.

I went out from Miss Van Ness's office, singing a song of new life: "America! I found America."

1920

4. German or Yiddish for "Oh!"

CULTURAL COORDINATES
Sweatshops

Working her way through teachers' college at a laundry, the protagonist of Anzia Yezierska's "Soap and Water" thinks back to her "sweatshop childhood." At the turn of the twentieth century, when Yezierska was young, the U.S. garment industry relied heavily on immigrant workers to do "homework"—that is, to work by hand on pieces of clothing carried to and from the home. "Home" for many Russian-Jewish immigrants meant crowded urban tenements, with little space and few amenities. Many of these apartments contained "sweatshops," or small rooms where workers gathered to sew and press the latest fashions. They got their name from the sweat workers shed as they labored endlessly in these upper-story rooms.

While some sweatshops involved single families working long hours together at home, most were run by contractors who took on assignments from clothing manufacturers and retailers. The contractors paid low wages to men, women, and children who often worked seven days a week for twelve hours and longer. Clothing manufacturers on New York's Lower East Side would distribute bolts of cloth or cut-out pieces to contractors, who hired sweatshop workers to baste, stitch,

The Termine family sewed garments in their front room; thirteen-year-old Catina finished the garments and carried them back and forth to the supplier. (Photograph by Lewis Hine, 1912)

finish, and press them. Working conditions were crowded, and breaks or vacations (paid or otherwise) were unheard of.

Sweatshops are still common outside the United States, as multinational corporations use low-wage labor in developing countries to manufacture clothing they sell to American consumers at a high markup. In the United States, too, sweatshops still exist: according to the Lower East Side Tenement Museum, in 2000 about 60 percent of the shops that house New York City's 93,000 garment workers "could be deemed sweatshops in the sense that their operators abused and disregarded laws designed to ensure that workers were treated decently." Generations of immigrants have repeated Yezierska's youthful experience of American life.

ISAK DINESEN (KAREN BLIXEN)
1885–1962

Born and educated in Denmark, Isak Dinesen nevertheless wrote in English, the language she used when telling stories to her English lover in Africa. Perhaps best known for her memoir, *Out of Africa* (made into an Oscar-winning film in 1985), Dinesen was the author of several volumes of short stories, a novel, and a collection of essays but did not begin her writing career until she was in her forties. Her first collection was called *Seven Gothic Tales;* and there is, in most of her writing, an emphasis both on the gothic—the strange and wonderful tinged with the erotic—and on storytelling. The narrator of our selection here calls herself a storyteller, a title Dinesen herself claimed, stressing the oral, traditional nature of that role.

Karen Dinesen was born in Rungstedlund, Denmark, to a well-to-do family, and early on showed artistic inclinations. After being educated at home and at a finishing school in Switzerland, she went on to study art at the Royal Academy of Fine Arts, where she began writing, and published some fiction in a Danish journal under a pseudonym. She fell in love with a distant cousin but ended up marrying his twin brother, Baron Bror Blixen-Finecke. In 1913, they moved to Nairobi, where they had purchased several hundred acres of land, intending to run a coffee plantation, ignorant of the fact that the land was unsuitable for that purpose. Despite the difficulties of farming, Dinesen fell in love with Africa, with being an aristocratic landowner, and with the dignity and beauty of the African people. Her marriage with Bror quickly deteriorated, but not before he infected her with syphilis. In 1918, she met a British aristocrat, Denys Finch-Hatton, who was a pilot and safari leader, and the two became lovers, though she did not divorce until 1921. After her divorce, she ran the farm alone, through droughts, fires, and terrible harvests; she also suffered two miscarriages between 1926 and 1931. After Finch-Hatton's death in a plane crash, in 1931, facing both disastrous health problems (the result of syphilis) and bankruptcy, Dinesen returned to her mother's house in Denmark and took up writing, using the pseudonym "Isak," which means "the one who laughs."

Dinesen's outlook was decidedly aristocratic, and many of her tales focus on elaborate fantasies of aristocratic European life of the eighteenth and nineteenth centuries. Her work was critically acclaimed in England and the United States but much less well received in Denmark. By the 1950s, she was occasionally mentioned for the Nobel Prize in Literature (Ernest Hemingway, for instance, claimed she should have won it the year he did), but she never won the prize, and she wrote very little after the mid-1950s. She continued to travel, though her health was deteriorating; she eventually died of malnutrition in 1962.

"The Blank Page," which appears here, is one of Dinesen's best-known stories and has been described by feminist critic Susan Gubar as a kind of parable of female creativity. With its focus on women's work, women's bodies, and the mystery of the untold story, it stands as a kind of meditation on the unknown history of women as well as a celebration of the possibilities of storytelling. Like many of Dinesen's other tales, it evokes a bygone time and celebrates storytelling as a vital part of life; the old narrator hints at the beginning that she is Scheherezade, the teller of *The Thousand and One Tales of the Arabian Nights*, a woman whose life depended on her storytelling abilities. "The Blank Page" beautifully blends the tale told with the ones that remain untold and is an excellent example of Dinesen's preoccupation with both the aristocratic and the mysterious.

The Blank Page

By the ancient city gate sat an old coffee-brown, black-veiled woman who made her living by telling stories.

She said:

"You want a tale, sweet lady and gentleman? Indeed I have told many tales, one more than a thousand,[1] since that time when I first let young men tell me, myself, tales of a red rose, two smooth lily buds, and four silky, supple, deadly entwining snakes. It was my mother's mother, the black-eyed dancer, the often-embraced, who in the end—wrinkled like a winter apple and crouching beneath the mercy of the veil—took upon herself to teach me the art of story-telling. Her own mother's mother had taught it to her, and both were better story-tellers than I am. But that, by now, is of no consequence, since to the people they and I have become one, and I am most highly honored because I have told stories for two hundred years."

Now if she is well paid and in good spirits, she will go on.

"With my grandmother," she said, "I went through a hard school. 'Be loyal to the story,' the old hag would say to me. 'Be eternally and unswervingly loyal to the story.' 'Why must I be that, Grandmother?' I asked her. 'Am I to furnish you with reasons, baggage?' she cried. 'And you mean to be a story-teller! Why, you are to become a story-teller, and I shall give you my reasons! Hear then: Where the story-teller is loyal, eternally and unswervingly loyal to the story, there, in the end, silence will speak. Where the story has been betrayed, silence is but emptiness. But we, the faithful, when we have spoken our last word, will hear the voice of silence. Whether a small snotty lass understands it or not.'

"Who then," she continues, "tells a finer tale than any of us? Silence does. And where does one read a deeper tale than upon the most perfectly printed page of the most precious book? Upon the blank page. When a royal and gallant pen, in the moment of its highest inspiration, has written down its tale with the rarest ink of all—where, then, may one read a still deeper, sweeter, merrier and more cruel tale than that? Upon the blank page."

The old beldame for a while says nothing, only giggles a little and munches with her toothless mouth.

"We," she says at last, "the old women who tell stories, we know the story of the blank page. But we are somewhat averse to telling it, for it might well, among the uninitiated, weaken our own credit. All the same, I am going to make an exception with you, my sweet and pretty lady and gentleman of the generous hearts. I shall tell it to you."

High up in the blue mountains of Portugal there stands an old convent for sisters of the Carmelite order, which is an illustrious and austere order. In ancient

---

1. Scheherezade, narrator of *The Thousand and One Tales of the Arabian Nights*, told her mur-   derous husband a cliff-hanging tale each night— 1,001 of them—to stave off her execution.

times the convent was rich, the sisters were all noble ladies, and miracles took place there. But during the centuries highborn ladies grew less keen on fasting and prayer, the great dowries flowed scantily into the treasury of the convent, and today the few portionless and humble sisters live in but one wing of the vast crumbling structure, which looks as if it longed to become one with the gray rock itself. Yet they are still a blithe and active sisterhood. They take much pleasure in their holy meditations, and will busy themselves joyfully with that one particular task which did once, long, long ago, obtain for the convent a unique and strange privilege: they grow the finest flax and manufacture the most exquisite linen of Portugal.

The long field below the convent is plowed with gentle-eyed, milk-white bullocks, and the seed is skillfully sown out by labor-hardened virginal hands with mold under the nails. At the time when the flax field flowers, the whole valley becomes air-blue, the very color of the apron which the blessed virgin put on to go out and collect eggs within St. Anne's poultry yard, the moment before the Archangel Gabriel[2] in mighty wing-strokes lowered himself onto the threshold of the house, and while high, high up a dove, neck-feathers raised and wings vibrating, stood like a small clear silver star in the sky. During this month the villagers many miles round raise their eyes to the flax field and ask one another: "Has the convent been lifted into heaven? Or have our good little sisters succeeded in pulling down heaven to them?"

Later in due course the flax is pulled, scutched and hackled;[3] thereafter the delicate thread is spun, and the linen woven, and at the very end the fabric is laid out on the grass to bleach, and is watered time after time, until one may believe that snow has fallen round the convent walls. All this work is gone through with precision and piety and with such sprinklings and litanies as are the secret of the convent. For these reasons the linen, baled high on the backs of small gray donkeys and sent out through the convent gate, downwards and ever downwards to the towns, is as flower-white, smooth and dainty as was my own little foot when, fourteen years old, I had washed it in the brook to go to a dance in the village.

Diligence, dear Master and Mistress, is a good thing, and religion is a good thing, but the very first germ of a story will come from some mystical place outside the story itself. Thus does the linen of the Convento Velho draw its true virtue from the fact that the very first linseed was brought home from the Holy Land itself by a crusader.

In the Bible, people who can read may learn about the lands of Lecha and Maresha, where flax is grown.[4] I myself cannot read, and have never seen this book of which so much is spoken. But my grandmother's grandmother as a little girl was the pet of an old Jewish rabbi, and the learning she received from him has been kept and passed on in our family. So you will read, in the book of Joshua, of how Achsah the daughter of Caleb lighted from her ass and cried unto her father: "Give me a blessing! For thou hast now given me land; give me also the blessing of springs of water!" And he gave her the upper springs and the nether springs. And in the fields of Lecha and Maresha lived, later on, the families of them that wrought the finest linen of all. Our Portuguese crusader, whose own ancestors had once

2. St. Anne: the Virgin Mary's mother; Archangel Gabriel: God's messenger, he informs Mary that she is to give birth to Jesus, and, through the annunciation, she becomes pregnant.

3. Scutched: brushed; hackled: combed.
4. See Joshua 15:17–19; lands in what is now the Negev, the southern region of Israel.

been great linen weavers of Tomar,[5] as he rode through these same fields was struck by the quality of the flax, and so tied a bag of seeds to the pommel of his saddle.

From this circumstance originated the first privilege of the convent, which was to procure bridal sheets for all the young princesses of the royal house.

I will inform you, dear lady and gentleman, that in the country of Portugal in very old and noble families a venerable custom has been observed. On the morning after the wedding of a daughter of the house, and before the morning gift had yet been handed over, the Chamberlain or High Steward from a balcony of the palace would hang out the sheet of the night and would solemnly proclaim: *Virginem eam tenemus*—"we declare her to have been a virgin." Such a sheet was never afterwards washed or again lain on.

This time-honored custom was nowhere more strictly upheld than within the royal house itself, and it has there subsisted till within living memory.

Now for many hundred years the convent in the mountains, in appreciation of the excellent quality of the linen delivered, has held its second high privilege: that of receiving back that central piece of the snow-white sheet which bore witness to the honor of a royal bride.

In the tall main wing of the convent, which overlooks an immense landscape of hills and valleys, there is a long gallery with a black-and-white marble floor. On the walls of the gallery, side by side, hangs a long row of heavy, gilt frames, each of them adorned with a coroneted plate of pure gold, on which is engraved the name of a princess: Donna Christina, Donna Ines, Donna Jacintha Lenora, Donna Maria. And each of these frames encloses a square cut from a royal wedding sheet.

Within the faded markings of the canvases people of some imagination and sensibility may read all the signs of the zodiac: the Scales, the Scorpion, the Lion, the Twins. Or they may there find pictures from their own world of ideas: a rose, a heart, a sword—or even a heart pierced through with a sword.

In days of old it would occur that a long, stately, richly colored procession wound its way through the stone-gray mountain scenery, upwards to the convent. Princesses of Portugal, who were now queens or queen dowagers of foreign countries, Archduchesses, or Electresses, with their splendid retinue, proceeded here on a pilgrimage which was by nature both sacred and secretly gay. From the flax field upwards the road rises steeply; the royal-lady would have to descend from her coach to be carried this last bit of the way in a palanquin presented to the convent for the very same purpose.

Later on, up to our own day, it has come to pass—as it comes to pass when a sheet of paper is being burnt, that after all other sparks have run along the edge and died away, one last clear little spark will appear and hurry along after them— that a very old highborn spinster undertakes the journey to Convento Velho. She has once, a long long time ago, been playmate, friend and maid-of-honor to a young princess of Portugal. As she makes her way to the convent she looks round to see the view widen to all sides. Within the building a sister conducts her to the gallery and to the plate bearing the name of the princess she has once served, and there takes leave of her, aware of her wish to be alone.

---

5. Our Portuguese crusader: Henry the Navigator (1394–1460), Portuguese prince and Grand Master of the Order of Christ, a Christian crusading military organization, successor to the Knights Templar; Tomar: a region in central Portugal and home to the Knights Templar.

Slowly, slowly a row of recollections passes through the small venerable skull-like head under its mantilla of black lace, and it nods to them in amicable recognition. The loyal friend and confidante looks back upon the young bride's elevated married life with the elected royal consort. She takes stock of happy events and disappointments—coronations and jubilees, court intrigues and wars, the birth of heirs to the throne, the alliances of younger generations of princes and princesses, the rise or decline of dynasties. The old lady will remember how once, from the markings on the canvas, omens were drawn; now she will be able to compare the fulfillment to the omen, sighing a little and smiling a little. Each separate canvas with its coroneted name-plate has a story to tell, and each has been set up in loyalty to the story.

But in the midst of the long row there hangs a canvas which differs from the others. The frame of it is as fine and as heavy as any, and as proudly as any carries the golden plate with the royal crown. But on this one plate no name is inscribed, and the linen within the frame is snow-white from corner to corner, a blank page.

I beg of you, you good people who want to hear stories told: look at this page, and recognize the wisdom of my grandmother and of all old story-telling women!

For with what eternal and unswerving loyalty has not this canvas been inserted in the row! The story-tellers themselves before it draw their veils over their faces and are dumb. Because the royal papa and mama who once ordered this canvas to be framed and hung up, had they not had the tradition of loyalty in their blood, might have left it out.

It is in front of this piece of pure white linen that the old princesses of Portugal—worldly wise, dutiful, long-suffering queens, wives and mothers—and their noble old playmates, bridesmaids and maids-of-honor have most often stood still.

It is in front of the blank page that old and young nuns, with the Mother Abbess herself, sink into deepest thought.

1957

◄ H.D. (HILDA DOOLITTLE) ►
1886–1961

H.D. was in many ways at the heart of literary modernism: she was engaged for a time to Ezra Pound; was friends with the writers Frieda and D. H. Lawrence, Marianne Moore (pp. 1373–78), William Carlos Williams, Djuna Barnes (pp. 1424–28), Gertrude Stein (pp. 1275–84), and Amy Lowell, among others; starred in a film with Paul Robeson; and was analyzed by Sigmund Freud. Like many of her contemporaries, she was deeply affected by the two world wars. And like Pound and T. S. Eliot (poets with whom she is often compared), she was interested in using classical literature as a touchstone for her work. Unlike the work of the male modernists, however, H.D.'s poetry alludes to a particularly feminine pantheon of goddesses as a way of finding hope.

Hilda Doolittle was born in Pennsylvania, the daughter of a musician and an astronomer. She attended Bryn Mawr to study classical Greek literature but left after three semesters. She traveled to England in 1911 with her first love, Frances Josepha Gregg, and was to live most of her life from then on as an expatriate. Pound introduced her to the literary circles of London, and she began writing

imagist poetry: minimalist works that aim at capturing a precise feeling or moment with common language and in poetic rhythms more like natural speech.
Most of her poetry through the 1930s—six volumes in all—followed the ideals of
imagism. H.D. married the poet Richard Aldington in 1913, but they separated in
1918 after he had taken a mistress and she became pregnant by another man. In
1919, while still pregnant, she became seriously ill with pneumonia. Annie Winnifred Ellerman, a twenty-four-year-old heiress better known by her pen name
Bryher, took care of H.D. during that time and became H.D.'s lifelong partner,
helping her raise her daughter, Perdita. Although Bryher married twice, once to
help finance a publishing venture and once to H.D.'s lover, the filmmaker Kenneth
MacPherson, she and H.D. maintained both an intimate relationship and their independence for the rest of H.D.'s life. H.D. also wrote several novels (many of
them autobiographical) that deal with being a woman poet and that explore the
attractions of heterosexual and lesbian love.

H.D. and Bryher remained in London during the bombing raids of World
War II. Despite, or perhaps because of, the tremendous strain of that life, H.D.
began a period of intense poetic creativity that represents something of a break
with her earlier imagist poetics. In a series of poems that would become *Trilogy*
(from which our selections below are drawn), H.D. began to explore both poetic
and spiritual mythologies of regeneration. Often described as epic poetry, the
works in *The Walls Do Not Fall* (1944), *Tribute to the Angels* (1945), and *The
Flowering of the Rod* (1946) connect Judeo-Christian spirituality to Egyptian,
Greek, and Roman religious beliefs and focus on female creativity and life force.
In these poems, she places herself in the war-torn geography and history of London but imagines that world within a larger cycle of destruction and rebirth, a
cycle that is particularly affected by the use of language. After the war, H.D. had
a nervous breakdown, but she continued writing until her death. Among her late
works is a second epic poem, *Helen in Egypt,* and a memoir of her analysis with
Freud. Just before her death, in 1960, she received the American Academy of
Arts and Letters medal.

From The Walls Do Not Fall

* * *

[9]

Thoth, Hermes,[1] the stylus,
the palette, the pen, the quill endure,

though our books are a floor
of smouldering ash under our feet;

though the burning of the books remains   5
the most perverse gesture

and the meanest
of man's mean nature,

---

1. Thoth: an Egyptian god of creation, credited
with inventing language (and therefore the god of
scribes), geometry, astronomy, and medicine. Hermes: Greek messenger to the gods; also the god of
oratory, literature, and weights and measures, he
was a minor patron of poetry.

yet give us, they still cry,
give us books,   10

folio, manuscript, old parchment
will do for cartridge cases;

irony is bitter truth
wrapped up in a little joke,

and Hatshepsut's[2] name is still circled   15
with what they call the *cartouche*.[3]

[10]

But we fight for life,
we fight, they say, for breath,

so what good are your scribblings?
this—we take them with us   20

beyond death; Mercury,[4] Hermes, Thoth
invented the script, letters, palette;

the indicated flute or lyre-notes
on papyrus or parchment

are magic, indelibly stamped   25
on the atmosphere somewhere,

forever; remember, O Sword,
you are the younger brother, the latter-born,

your Triumph, however exultant,
must one day be over,   30

*in the beginning
was the Word.*[5]

* * *

1944

◄——►

From Tribute to the Angels

* * *

[8]

Now polish the crucible
and in the bowl distill

2. The first woman to reign in Egypt as pharaoh,
fifteenth century BCE.
3. Gun cartridge (French); refers to the design
drawn around the name of a pharaoh.

4. Roman messenger of the gods; god of trade
and profit; Roman name for Hermes.
5. John 1:1.

a word most bitter, *marah,*[6]
a word bitterer still, *mar,*[7]

sea, brine, breaker, seducer,   5
giver of life, giver of tears;

Now polish the crucible
and set the jet of flame

under, till *marah-mar*
are melted, fuse and join   10

and change and alter,
mer, mere, mère, mater, Maia, Mary,[8]

Star of the Sea,
Mother.

[9]

Bitter, bitter jewel   15
in the heart of the bowl,

what is your colour?
what do you offer

to us who rebel?
what were we had you loved other?   20

what is this mother-father
to tear at our entrails?

what is this unsatisfied duality
which you can not satisfy?

*   *   *

[11]

O swiftly, re-light the flame
before the substance cool,

for suddenly we saw your name
desecrated; knaves and fools

                                                                 5
have done you impious wrong,
Venus,[9] for venery stands for impurity

and Venus as desire
is venereous, lascivious,

---

6. Bitterness: a fountain at which the Israelites
stopped during the Exodus, whose waters were so
bitter that they could not drink from it.
7. Bitter (Hebrew); refers to the herb myrrh.
8. "mer, mere, mère, mater, Maia, Mary": respectively, French words for sea, small pond, and
mother; Latin for mother; eldest of the Pleides and
mother of Hermes; the name of the mother of
Jesus and a reference to Mary Magdalene.
9. Roman name for Aphrodite, goddess of love
and beauty.

while the very root of the word shrieks
like a mandrake when foul witches pull   10

its stem at midnight,
and rare mandragora itself

is full, they say, of poison,
food for the witches' den.

[12]

Swiftly re-light the flame,   15
Aphrodite,[1] holy name,

Astarte,[2] hull and spar
of wrecked ships lost your star,

forgot the light at dusk,
forgot the prayer at dawn;   20

return, O holiest one,
Venus whose name is kin

to venerate,
venerator.

[13]

"What is the jewel colour?"   25
green-white, opalescent,

with under-layer of changing blue,
with rose-vein; a white agate

with a pulse uncooled that beats yet,
faint blue-violet;   30

it lives, it breathes,
it gives off—fragrance?

I do not know what it gives,
a vibration that we can not name

for there is no name for it;   35
my patron said, "name it";

I said, I can not name it,
there is no name;

he said,
"invent it".   40

* * *

1. Greek goddess of love and beauty.   and war.
2. Egyptian goddess of fertility, beauty, love,

[19]

We see her visible and actual,
beauty incarnate,

as no high-priest of Astoroth[3]
could compel her

with incense   5
and potent spell;

we asked for no sign
but she gave a sign unto us;

sealed with the seal of death,
we thought not to entreat her   10

but prepared us for burial;
then she set a charred tree before us,

burnt and stricken to the heart;
was it may-tree or apple?

[20]

Invisible, indivisible Spirit,   15
how is it you come so near,

how is it that we dare
approach the high-altar?

we crossed the charred portico,
passed through a frame—doorless—   20

entered a shrine; like a ghost,
we entered a house through a wall;

then still not knowing
whether (like the wall)

we were there or not-there,   25
we saw the tree flowering;

it was an ordinary tree
in an old garden-square.

[21]

This is no rune nor riddle,
it is happening everywhere;   30

what I mean is—it is so simple
yet no trick of the pen or brush

3. Hebrew name for Astarte, seen as a demonic figure associated with lasciviousness.

could capture that impression;
music could do nothing with it,

nothing whatever; what I mean is—   35
but you have seen for yourself

that burnt-out wood crumbling . . .
you have seen for yourself.

* * *

[23]

We are part of it;
we admit the transubstantiation,

not God merely in bread
but God in the other-half of the tree

that looked dead—   5
did I bow my head?

did I weep? my eyes saw,
it was not a dream

yet it was vision,   10
It was a sign,

it was *the Angel which redeemed me,*
it was the Holy Ghost—

a half-burnt-out apple-tree
blossoming;

this is the flowering of the rood,   15
this is the flowering of the wood

where Annael,[4] we pause to give
thanks that we rise again from death and live.

* * *

[28]

I had been thinking of Gabriel,[5]
of the moon-cycle, of the moon-shell,

of the moon-crescent
and the moon at full: 5

I had been thinking of Gabriel,
the moon-regent, the Angel,

and I had intended to recall him
in the sequence of candle and fire

---

4. Usually spelled "Anael," traditionally one of the seven archangels (or angels of creation), associated with sexuality; H.D. attributes female aspects to Annael, whom she calls the "Peace of God."
5. One of the two chief archangels, the angel of mercy, resurrection, vengeance, death, and revelation, and a primary messenger of God.

and the law of the seven;
I had not forgotten   10

his special attribute
of annunciator; I had thought

to address him as I had the others,
Uriel,[6] Annael;

how could I imagine   15
the Lady herself would come instead?

* * *

[35]

So she must have been pleased with us,
who did not forgo our heritage

at the grave-edge;
she must have been pleased

with the straggling company of the brush and quill   5
who did not deny their birthright;

she must have been pleased with us,
for she looked so kindly at us

under her drift of veils,
and she carried a book.   10

[36]

Ah (you say), this is Holy Wisdom,
Santa Sophia, the SS of the *Sanctus Spiritus,*[7]

so by facile reasoning, logically
the incarnate symbol of the Holy Ghost;

your Holy Ghost was an apple-tree   15
smouldering—or rather now bourgeoning

with flowers; the fruit of the Tree?
this is the new Eve who comes

clearly to return, to retrieve
what she lost the race,   20

given over to sin, to death;
she brings the Book of Life, obviously.

* * *

6. One of the seven archangels; H.D. attributes
male characteristics to Uriel, whom she calls the
"Fire of God."
7. Santa Sophia: *sophia* is Greek for "wisdom";

Saint Sophia was the mother of the virgin martyrs
Faith, Hope, and Charity, in the early second century; Sanctus Spiritus: Holy Spirit (Latin).

[39]

But nearer than Guardian Angel
or good Daemon,

she is the counter-coin-side
of primitive terror;

she is not-fear, she is not-war,   5
but she is no symbolic figure

of peace, charity, chastity, goodness,
faith, hope, reward;

she is not Justice with eyes
blindfolded like Love's;   10

I grant you the dove's symbolic purity,
I grant you her face was innocent

and immaculate and her veils
like the Lamb's Bride,[8]

but the Lamb was not with her,   15
either as Bridegroom or Child;

her attention is undivided,
we are her bridegroom and lamb;

her book is our book; written
or unwritten, its pages will reveal   20

a tale of a Fisherman,[9]
a tale of a jar or jars,

the same—different—the same attributes,
different yet the same as before,

                                                                   1945

◆—◆

From The Flowering of the Rod

[5]

Satisfied, unsatisfied,
satiated or numb with hunger,

this is the eternal urge,
this is the despair, the desire to equilibrate

8. In Revelation 21:9, the city of Jerusalem, as re-   9. A common metaphor for Jesus.
vealed by one of the seven angels.

the eternal variant;   5
you understand that insistent calling,

that demand of a given moment,
the will to enjoy, the will to live,

not merely the will to endure,
the will to flight, the will to achievement,   10

the will to rest after long flight;
but who knows the desperate urge

of those others—actual or perhaps now
mythical birds—who seek but find no rest

till they drop from the highest point of the spiral   15
or fall from the innermost centre of the ever-narrowing circle?

for they remember, they remember, as they sway and hover,
what once was—they remember, they remember—

they will not swerve—they have known bliss,
the fruit that satisfies—they have come back—   20

what if the islands are lost? what if the waters
cover the Hesperides? they would rather remember—

remember the golden apple-trees;[1]
O, do not pity them, as you watch them drop one by one,

for they fall exhausted, numb, blind   25
but in certain ecstasy,

for theirs is the hunger
for Paradise.

[6]

So I would rather drown, remembering—
than bask on tropic atolls   30

in the coral-seas; I would rather drown
remembering—than rest on pine or fir-branch

where great stars pour down
their generating strength, Arcturus

or the sapphires of the Northern Crown;[2]   35
I would rather beat in the wind, crying to these others:

---

1. In Greek mythology, the Hesperides are nymphs of the evening who tend a splendid garden, in which grow golden apple trees, a gift from Gaia (the earth goddess) to Hera and Zeus for their wedding; "Hesperides" also refers to what the ancient world sometimes called the Fortunate Isles or Islands of the Blest, islands to the west of the then-known world, believed to be a paradise.

2. Arcturus: the fourth-brightest star in the sky; the name means "Bear Watcher." Northern Crown: the Corona Borealis, a constellation visible in the Northern Hemisphere in spring and summer; Greek mythology describes it as a crown given to Ariadne (daughter of King Minos) in honor of her assistance to Theseus in defeating the Minotaur.

yours is the more foolish circling,
yours is the senseless wheeling

round and round—yours has no reason—
I am seeking heaven;   40

yours has no vision,
I see what is beneath me, what is above me,

what men say is—not—I remember,
I remember, I remember—you have forgot:

you think, even before it is half-over,   45
that your cycle is at an end,

but you repeat your foolish circling—again, again, again;
again, the steel sharpened on the stone;

again, the pyramid of skulls;
I gave pity to the dead,   50

O blasphemy, pity is a stone for bread,
only love is holy and love's ecstasy

that turns and turns and turns about one centre,
reckless, regardless, blind to reality,

that knows the Islands of the Blest[3] are there,   55
for *many waters can not quench love's fire.*
                                                              1946

◄═══ MARIANNE MOORE ═══►
1887–1972

Known as a "poet's poet" during her lifetime, Marianne Moore is often regarded
as difficult to read but worth the effort. She is recognized as one of the central figures of literary modernism (pp. 1193–97), and is hailed for her precise crafting of
language, her use of intricate detail, and her keen observations. She also presents
something of a conundrum, in that she was often represented as a prim spinster
with almost Victorian values but at the same time was at the forefront of the literary avant-garde; she was a shy and private person but also an eccentric figure in
what became a rather public life of celebrity.

Moore was born in Kirkwood, Missouri, and never knew her father, an inventor who suffered a mental breakdown and was hospitalized before she was
born. Her mother, Mary Warner, raised her in Kirkwood and in Carlisle, Pennsylvania; Moore and her mother remained close and lived together until Warner's
death in 1947. Moore graduated from Bryn Mawr College in 1909 and later took
secretarial courses at Carlisle Commercial College after being advised to get secretarial skills if she wanted to be able to support herself. She then taught bookkeeping,

---

3. In the ancient world, islands to the west of the   the Hesperides.
known world, thought to be a paradise; also called

stenography, and business law for several years at the U.S. Industrial Indian School at Carlisle. In 1915, Moore left teaching and moved with her mother to New Jersey to keep house for her brother, a divinity student. When her brother became a Navy chaplain in 1918, Moore and her mother moved to Manhattan, where Moore began to work part-time at the New York Public Library; she would live in New York the rest of her life.

Moore had begun publishing poetry in the Bryn Mawr literary magazine during her undergraduate years, but her professional career began in earnest during the 1910s, when she was published in several of the leading modernist literary journals, including the *Egoist,* a magazine edited by her contemporary H.D. (pp. 1363–73). (In 1921, H.D. and her partner Bryher published Moore's first volume of poetry without letting Moore know first.) In 1924, Moore won a prestigious $2,000 prize from the literary magazine *The Dial* and from 1925 to 1929 was that journal's editor. During the 1930s and 1940s, she published several volumes of poetry, and recognition of her work by other poets grew steadily; she was friends with, and praised by, many of the leading figures of modernism: T. S. Eliot, Ezra Pound, Wallace Stevens, William Carlos Williams, and W. H. Auden were all among her admirers. She became a lifelong friend of and literary mentor to Elizabeth Bishop, a younger poet who had sought Moore out in the early 1930s. In 1951, she published *Collected Poems,* for which she won the National Book Award, the Pulitzer Prize, and the Bollingen Prize. By the 1960s, she had become a literary celebrity, known for her quick and intelligent conversation, her love of baseball, and her odd attire—in public she wore a specially made three-cornered hat and black cape modeled on a painting of George Washington crossing the Delaware. She was featured in such popular magazines as *Life* and the *New Yorker* and even threw out the opening pitch at a Brooklyn Dodgers' game in 1968.

Moore's poetry is often described as "mathematical" and "precise." She took enormous care in her language choices and in the metrical and rhyme schemes of her poems; most of her work falls into lines made up of equal numbers of syllables, often with intricate patterns of internal rhyme. Her descriptions are vivid and almost scientifically accurate, and yet she aims at images that project a deeper meaning. For instance, in "The Fish," one should look for the mathematical symmetry of the stanzas but also at the connections the poem draws between rich description and metaphysical insight. Similarly, in "Paper Nautilus," a poem she wrote for Elizabeth Bishop after Bishop gave her a nautilus shell, although she offers a meticulous picture of a nautilus's birth process, she does so against a backdrop of "authorities," "mercenaries," "writers entrapped by / teatime fame," and "commuters," all figures quite remote from the natural setting of a marine creature's protection and freeing of her eggs. While some people may aim at transitory comfort, she suggests, the nautilus constructs something beautiful and lasting, outside the demands of profit or power. Moore herself followed her own advice; her poetry is crafted to endure, and readers who take the time to appreciate it will find lasting beauty.

The Fish

wade
through black jade.
Of the crow-blue mussel shells, one keeps

      adjusting the ash heaps;
         opening and shutting itself like   5
an
injured fan.
      The barnacles which encrust the side
      of the wave, cannot hide
         there for the submerged shafts of the   10
sun,
split like spun
      glass, move themselves with spotlight swiftness
      into the crevices—
         in and out, illuminating   15
the
turquoise sea
      of bodies. The water drives a wedge
      of iron through the iron edge
         of the cliff; whereupon the stars,   20
pink
rice-grains, ink-
      bespattered jellyfish, crabs like green
      lilies, and submarine
         toadstools, slide each on the other.   25
All
external
      marks of abuse are present on this
      defiant edifice—
         all the physical features of   30
ac-
cident—lack
      of cornice, dynamite grooves, burns, and
      hatchet strokes, these things stand
         out on it; the chasm side is   35
dead.
Repeated
      evidence has proved that it can live
      on what can not revive
         its youth. The sea grows old in it.   40

                        1921

The Paper Nautilus

    For authorities whose hopes
      are shaped by mercenaries?
    Writers entrapped by
      teatime fame and by

    commuters' comforts? Not for these   5
        the paper nautilus
        constructs her thin glass shell.

      Giving her perishable
    souvenir of hope, a dull
        white outside and smooth-   10
        edged inner surface
    glossy as the sea, the watchful
        maker of it guards it
        day and night; she scarcely

        eats until the eggs are hatched.   15
    Buried eightfold in her eight
        arms, for she is in
        a sense a devil-
    fish, her glass ram's-horn-cradled freight
        is hid but is not crushed;   20
        as Hercules,[1] bitten

        by a crab loyal to the hydra,[2]
    was hindered to succeed,
        the intensively
        watched eggs coming from   25
    the shell free it when they are freed—
        leaving its wasp-nest flaws
        of white on white, and close-

        laid Ionic chiton-folds[3]
    like the lines in the mane of   30
        a Parthenon horse,[4]
        round which the arms had
    wound themselves as if they knew love
        is the only fortress
        strong enough to trust to.   35

                            1940

In Distrust of Merits

Strengthened to live, strengthened to die for
    medals and positioned victories?
They're fighting, fighting, fighting the blind
    man who thinks he sees—
who cannot see that the enslaver is   5

1. Latin name in Roman mythology for the hero who corresponds to the Greek hero Heracles, a paragon of masculine strength, courage, and appetites.
2. A mythical many-headed serpentine water beast; killing it was one of Hercules' twelve mythical tasks.
3. A form of Greek clothing worn during the Ar-

chaic period (800–500 BCE), two rectangles of fabric, up to ten feet wide, that were draped from shoulder to ankle and secured at the shoulders by jewelry, and at the torso by a belt.
4. The Parthenon, a major temple in Athens, Greece, featured several friezes celebrating the beauty of the horse; the friezes are housed at the British Museum in London.

enslaved; the hater, harmed. O shining O
    firm star, O tumultuous
        ocean lashed till small things go
  as they will, the mountainous
      wave makes us who look, know   10

depth. Lost at sea before they fought! O
    star of David, star of Bethlehem,
O black imperial lion
    of the Lord—emblem
of a risen world—be joined at last, be   15
joined. There is hate's crown beneath which all is
    death; there's love's without which none
        is king; the blessed deeds bless
    the halo. As contagion
      of sickness makes sickness,   20

contagion of trust can make trust. They're
    fighting in deserts and caves, one by
one, in battalions and squadrons;
    they're fighting that I
may yet recover from the disease, My   25
Self; some have it lightly; some will die. "Man's
    wolf to man" and we devour
        ourselves. The enemy could not
    have made a greater breach in our
    defenses. One pilot-   30

ing a blind man can escape him, but
    Job[5] disheartened by false comfort knew
that nothing can be so defeating
    as a blind man who
can see. O alive who are dead, who are   35
proud not to see, O small dust of the earth
    that walks so arrogantly,
        trust begets power and faith is
    an affectionate thing. We
    vow, we make this promise   40

to the fighting—it's a promise—"We'll
    never hate black, white, red, yellow, Jew,
Gentile, Untouchable." We are
    not competent to
make our vows. With set jaw they are fighting,   45
fighting, fighting—some we love whom we know,
    some we love but know not—that

---

5. Job's sufferings are described in the Old Testament book of Job; a righteous and rich man, Job has his faith tested by Satan, with God's permission. Satan robs Job of his wealth, kills his ten children, and afflicts him with leprosy. When Job refuses to curse God, his wealth and health are restored, and he has ten more children.

hearts may feel and not be numb.
It cures me; or am I what
    I can't believe in? Some   50

in snow, some on crags, some in quicksands,
    little by little, much by much, they
are fighting fighting fighting that where
    there was death there may
be life. "When a man is prey to anger,   55
he is moved by outside things; when he holds
    his ground in patience patience
        patience, that is action or
    beauty," the soldier's defense
        and hardest armor for   60

the fight. The world's an orphans' home. Shall
    we never have peace without sorrow?
without pleas of the dying for
    help that won't come? O
quiet form upon the dust, I cannot   65
look and yet I must. If these great patient
    dyings—all these agonies
        and wound-bearings and bloodshed—
    can teach us how to live, these
        dyings were not wasted.   70

Hate-hardened heart, O heart of iron,
    iron is iron till it is rust.
There never was a war that was
    not inward; I must
fight till I have conquered in myself what   75
causes war, but I would not believe it.
    I inwardly did nothing.
        O Iscariot-like crime![6]
    Beauty is everlasting
        and dust is for a time.   80
                                                                   1944

<hr />

WILLA MUIR
1890–1970

Born Wilhelmina Anderson in the Shetland Islands off the north coast of Scotland, Willa Muir became a prolific translator, a sociological essayist, and a novelist. In 1910, she was one of the first women to graduate from the University of St. Andrews in Scotland, earning a first-class degree in classics. She became vice principal

6. Judas Iscariot, the disciple who betrayed Jesus.

at the Gipsy Hill Training College in London, where she had been teaching, but she was forced to resign her position when she married an atheist, the Scottish writer Edwin Muir. She and Muir traveled extensively before returning to live in Scotland and were immersed in the literary culture of early-twentieth-century Europe. Edwin became a central figure in the "Scottish Renaissance" of the 1920s and 1930s; Willa Muir is only just now being acknowledged for her role in that movement, in large part because she devoted herself to translations to provide the family with an income, rather than pursuing her own literary ambitions. She also notes, in a memoir of her life with Edwin Muir, that while he worked upstairs in a spare, clean study, her work space was downstairs and cluttered with toys and laundry.

Willa Muir's sociological analysis, *Women: An Inquiry* (published in 1925 by Virginia Woolf's Hogarth Press), examines the strictures faced by women in Britain. Having been raised in a small conservative town in Scotland, Muir understood only too well the barriers women faced. In her novel *Imagined Corners,* from which the selection here comes, she focuses on two families, the Shands and the Murrays, who must cope with the narrow social and religious ideas of the small Scottish town they live in. Much of the novel focuses on two women who are related by marriage and are both named Elizabeth Shand; one is conventional, the other more outspoken. In our selection, the more conventional Elizabeth tries to come to terms with her identity as a wife; by the end of the novel, she will have to become more like her freer relative to gain self-knowledge. The novel draws on Muir's training in Freudian and Jungian psychology and employs the literary trope (or figure) of the "double," both in the two Elizabeths and in two male counterparts. Like her other novel, *Mrs. Ritchie* (1936), *Imagined Corners* contributes both to our knowledge of Scottish literature and to our understanding of women's literary rebellion against confining gender roles in the early twentieth century.

From Imagined Corners

Chapter 3
[Elizabeth Ramsay and Elizabeth Shand]

Elizabeth was still lying on her bed when Hector came home. She could see a patch of the night sky through the window. She had long stopped sobbing, and in the centre of the black cloud which encompassed her world a nucleus of calm weather was forming. She stared at the patch of sky; there was enough moonlight to illumine it faintly; clouds seemed to be marching over it to an unheard processional music, punctuated now and then by a star. What a fool she was, she thought. The love between Hector and herself was as enduring as those stars behind the fugitive clouds.

Her heart leapt as she heard him come in. He had not stayed at the Club, then; he had come back to her. She half turned, listening; his feet seemed to be mounting the stairs into her very bosom.

"Elizabeth!" he said, opening the door. His voice was humble. She sat up and held out her arms in the darkness.

"My darling, my darling," she said.

With inarticulate murmurs they caressed each other. The bliss of relaxation began to steal over Elizabeth, the peace of reunion, but Hector was still clutching her tight and pressing his face against her. She stroked his cheek.

"How could you do it, my love?" she asked.

"I was just mad with jealousy," said Hector, still clinging. "Jealous of that damned snivelling sky-pilot. I couldn't help it, Elizabeth; it just came over me, and I felt mad."

She kissed him on the forehead.

"But you *know*, don't you, that you needn't feel jealous of anybody?"

He shook his head vehemently.

"But you *do* know," she insisted. "You're a part of myself. I simply couldn't fall in love with anybody else."

"I'm always afraid of losing you," said Hector, his voice muffled in her dress. "I'm no highbrow; I can't talk about books and things; and some day you'll turn me down. . . . I deserve it," he went on, lifting his head. "When I think of all the girls I've turned down I feel that you're going to be my punishment for the lot."

Elizabeth's spirits were rapidly rising; she shook him a little and said: "Oh, you silly ass!" Then she kissed him full on the mouth. They lay for some time without speaking.

"All the same," said Elizabeth at last, "I'm glad you didn't stay at the Club drinking yourself dottier."

"I didn't go to the Club," said Hector, twisting and untwisting a piece of her hair. "I—you won't forgive me if I tell you, but I must tell you."

Elizabeth drew away a little. She had forgiven him; she didn't want confessions; she was beginning vaguely to dislike Hector's insistence on lengthy confessions.

"What does it matter?" she said. "The only thing that matters is *this*."

"It does matter." Hector's voice was sombre. "You don't know what an out-and-out rotter I can be. I went down the back lane with Mabel, and I was feeling so mad, and she was jawing at me about behaving myself better, and I knew what a little bitch she was, and her arm was always coming up against mine, and—well, I just took hold of her and kissed her as hard as I could."

"What?" said Elizabeth incredulously. "Mabel? Did she let you?"

"She liked it all right, you bet your life! She pretended she didn't. But I was— Oh, hell, when I'm in that state, I *know*, I tell you, and I just knew she was itching for it."

"Well," said Elizabeth, "is that all?"

Her voice was quite cool.

"That's about all," said Hector.

He was beginning to feel relieved. Elizabeth wasn't going to cut up rough after all.

"I swore I'd paint the town sky-blue scarlet unless she asked me in for a drink, and I gave her a lot of slosh about her influence over me and all that, until she nearly purred. So I went in with her and had a drink, and we danced a bit—"

"Have you been there all this time?"

Hector stopped in surprise at the sudden sharpness of the question.

"It's not so very late," he said. "John—"

Elizabeth pushed him away and sat up sobbing:

"That's all you care, is it? That's all you care. You go out leaving me heart-broken, and then you go fooling with Mabel for hours and hours, leaving me—leaving me—"

All the rage and self-pity that had apparently vanished was closing over her again.

"I had to tell you, don't you see?" Hector kept on repeating. "I *have* to be sure you won't turn me down."

He felt rather helpless; he had not expected her to be quite so jealous. He said so.

"I'm not jealous!" shrieked Elizabeth. "It would never come into my head to be jealous of anybody, let alone Mabel. I think jealousy is idiotic. I'm simply *angry,* because you could go out and enjoy yourself after hurting me so much."

"The hell you are!" Hector began to feel angry too. Damned unreasonable, he thought.

Elizabeth slapped the hand he was trying to caress her with.

He got off the bed.

"I might as well go and get roaring drunk," he said, making for the door.

Elizabeth sprang after him. "If you do," she said, "I'll come and get drunk too."

Her threat sounded like mere bravado even to herself. A sense of weakness came over her.

"Don't go," she said. "I can't do without you."

The reconciliation made them very happy. It also blinded them to the real issue between them which had obtruded itself nakedly enough in their quarrel, and as they sat cheek by cheek agreeing together what fools they had been their unanimity was more apparent than real. Elizabeth meant that she had been a fool to be miserable at all, since their love could never die, while Hector meant that he had been a fool to be jealous of a half-man like the minister. Elizabeth was now ready to regard Hector's sojourn with Mabel merely as an attempt to distract himself from his unhappiness, and Hector was ready to look on Elizabeth's friendliness to the minister as the polite amiability of a hostess; but they did not recognize that in so construing each other's actions they had each left out a good deal of the truth.

"We need a change of some kind," said Elizabeth finally, after turning over in her mind the various circumstances preceding the outburst. She was glad to lay the blame of it on Calderwick. "Let's take a day off to-morrow."

But perhaps it was an obscure sense of some change in herself that prompted her to use these words, for in the small hours she awoke with an anguished feeling that she was lost and no longer knew who she was. She had been dreaming that she was at home, but now the window, faintly perceptible, was in the wrong place, and she knew without seeing it that she would collide with unfamiliar furniture were she to get out of bed. There was sweat on her brow and her heart was thumping; the world stretched out on all sides into dark impersonal nothingness and she herself was a terrifying anonymity. She took refuge in a device of her childhood. I'm me, she thought; me, me; here behind my eyes. Mechanically she moved her arm and crooked her little finger as she had often done before. It's me making the finger move; I am behind my eyes, but I'm in the finger too. . . . But the clue she was striving to grasp still eluded her, and if she could not seize it she would be lost for ever. When she was almost rigid with terror the name "Elizabeth Ramsay" rose into her mind, and the nightmare vanished. Her body relaxed, but her mind with incredible swiftness rearranged the disordered puzzle of her identity. She was Elizabeth Ramsay but she was also Elizabeth Shand. Hector was there. She put out her hand and gently touched the mass of his body under the coverings on the neighbouring bed.

Elizabeth Ramsay she was, but also Elizabeth Shand, and the more years she traversed the more inalterably would she become Elizabeth Shand. Those years of the future stretched endlessly before her; with that queer lucidity which is seldom found in daytime thinking she could see them as a perspective of fields, each one separated by a fence from its neighbour. Over you go, said a voice, and over she went, then into the next and the next and the next. But this was no longer time or space, it was eternity; there was no end, no goal; perhaps a higher fence marked the boundary between life and death, but in the fields beyond it she was still Elizabeth Shand. She was beginning to be terrified again, and opened her eyes. Mrs Shand, she said to herself. It was appalling, and she had never realized it before.

Hector's quiet breathing rose and fell like an almost imperceptible ripple of sound. He was sunk beneath the waves of sleep, she thought, flying as usual from metaphor to metaphor; he was gathered up within himself like a tightly shut bud, remote, solitary, indifferent. He was stripped of everything that made companionship possible; he was now simply himself. You are a part of myself, she had told him, but was that true? When she had first emerged from sleep she had had no consciousness of him. In the ultimate resort she too was simply herself.

She was now wide awake, and she lay staring into the darkness seeing the separateness of all human beings. But as if they had gone round an immense circle her thoughts came back to the question of her own identity. Elizabeth Ramsay she was, but also Elizabeth Shand, and she herself, that essential self which awoke from sleep, had felt lost because she had forgotten that fact.

Elizabeth liked to find significance in facts, but she confused significance with mystery. The more mysterious anything appeared to her the more she was convinced of its significance. The change in her name which she had hitherto lightly accepted now seemed to her of overwhelming importance.

Hector, separate as he is, she argued, would not be sleeping so quietly if he and I were not in harmony. So even in sleep, that last refuge of the separate personality, there must be some communion between us. He rests in me and I in him. In a sense therefore it is true that we are part of each other.

She sat up in bed and bent half over him. He was curled up on his side, facing her, and she could just discern the outline of his cheek beneath the darker hair. A great tenderness towards him flowed through her. She could not live without him. She was not only herself: she was herself-and-Hector.

Their quarrel had ended, she remembered, when she had abandoned her pride and told him she could not do without him. Pride is the stalk, she said to herself, but love is the flower. Give up the old Elizabeth Ramsay, she told herself, emotion sweeping her away, and became Elizabeth Shand.

She lay down again. She must learn to be a wife. Was that what Aunt Janet was driving at?

It was a long time before she fell asleep. But she fell asleep smiling.

                                                                    1931

JEAN RHYS
1890–1979

Her father a Welsh doctor named Rhys Williams and her mother a Creole woman named Minna Lockhart, Ella Gwendolen Rhys Williams was considered "colored" by the elite white society of Roseau, Dominica, her Caribbean home. As her memoirs reveal, however, she identified herself as white though she was strongly attracted to the black culture that suffused her childhood. Her ability to shift her identity between dominant and oppressed groups was to surface in her fiction. It is especially evident in her important 1966 novel, *Wide Sargasso Sea,* a rewriting of Charlotte Brontë's *Jane Eyre* that incorporates the perspective of Mr. Rochester's incarcerated Creole wife, the "madwoman in the attic."

Having spent her childhood in Roseau, Rhys moved as a teenager to live with an aunt in Cambridge, England, where she attended school. At age eighteen she enrolled in the Royal Academy of Dramatic Art; she embarked the next year on a theatrical career, working as a chorus girl in traveling musical productions. In 1919, she married the dashing and mysterious Jean Lenglet, a former French Legionnaire who had fought on the western front in World War I and served as a secret agent for France. They had a son that same year, but the boy died three weeks after birth. The couple lived in Vienna, Budapest, Prague, and Brussels before settling in Paris with their daughter, born in 1922. They were not financially prosperous, so Rhys sought work as a model; to make matters worse, Lenglet was accused of trafficking in stolen art and went to jail in 1923–24. Rhys turned to new friends for help, moving in with British novelist Ford Madox Ford and the woman he was living with at the time, Stella Bowen. Ford became Rhys's literary mentor, and she became his mistress, which led to an uncomfortable situation that formed the material for her first novel, *Quartet* (1928), first published as *Postures*. When her husband was released from prison in 1924 he could not forgive her affair, and they eventually divorced in 1932. Around that time she met Leslie Tilden Smith, a literary agent who became her second husband in 1934. He died in 1945, and she met his cousin, attorney Max Hamer, at the funeral. Two years later they were married, and they lived in England until her death in 1979.

In novels such as *After Leaving Mr. Mackenzie* (1931), *Voyage in the Dark* (1934), and *Good Morning, Midnight* (1935), Rhy focuses on the lives of undereducated women with few resources and no ambitions who find themselves dependent on domineering and dismissive men. Although she was writing between the two world wars, her novels do not address the political situation in Europe; instead, she brings to life the psychological state of individual women whose gender and class position doom them to social failure. Hers is another kind of politics, a gender politics, which was not popular among readers at the time.

After publishing *Good Morning, Midnight,* Rhys did not write for many years, but in 1949 a dramatic adaptation of that novel gained some critical and popular success. During the 1950s Rhys began to work on *Wide Sargasso Sea,* a novel whose sympathetic portrayal of Mr. Rochester's mad wife was forever to alter readers' reception of *Jane Eyre.* She published it to much acclaim in 1966. She was working on *Smile, Please,* the incomplete autobiography from which our selections are drawn, when she died in 1979.

These three autobiographical selections show Rhys's modern style to advantage: her writing is clear, clipped, and minimal, yet evocative of the complicated culture in which she grew up. In an impressionistic style resembling Ford's, she follows the stream of her own thought, sprinkling her narrative with fragments of songs and other half-remembered utterances. Her unsentimental description of her relationship with her mother, her dryly humorous observation of her parents' attitudes toward the blacks among whom they lived, and her ambivalent portrayal of the attractions and terrors the black community held for her typify Rhys's way of seeing the world.

The novel *Wide Sargasso Sea,* 1966, appears in full in the Library of Women's Literature.

From Smile, Please

My Mother

I once came on a photograph of my mother on horseback which must have been taken before she was married. Young, slim and pretty. I hated it. I don't know whether I was jealous or whether I resented knowing that she had once been very different from the plump, dark and only sometimes comfortable woman I knew. I didn't dare tear it up but I pushed it away to the back of the drawer. What wouldn't I give to have it now? Yet wasn't there a time when I remembered her pretty and young?

That must have been when I was the baby, sleeping in the crib. They were going out somewhere, for she was wearing a low-cut evening dress. She had come to say "Good night, sleep well." She smelled so sweet as she leaned over and kissed me.

She loved babies, any babies. Once I heard her say that black babies were prettier than white ones. Was this the reason why I prayed so ardently to be black, and would run to the looking glass in the morning to see if the miracle had happened? And though it never had, I tried again. Dear God, let me be black.

Even after the new baby was born there must have been an interval before she seemed to find me a nuisance and I grew to dread her. Another interval and she was middle-aged and plump and uninterested in me.

Yes, she drifted away from me and when I tried to interest her, she was indifferent.

One day, thinking to please her (this must have been long afterwards), I said, "I'm so glad that you make our jam and we don't get it from England."

"Why?" she said, unsmiling.

"Because I've just read an article about a jam factory in London. It was written by a girl who dressed up as a working girl and got a job there. She said that carrots, scrapings off the floor, all sorts of filthy things were put into the jam."

"And you believed that?" my mother said.

"Yes, I do believe it, she saw it."

"Well, I wouldn't believe a word a girl like that said. Dressing up to spy and then make money out of what you pretend you've seen. Disgusting behaviour!"

I said, "Well, it wasn't so easy. She wrote that when she was dressed as a working girl men were very rude to her."

"Serve her right," said my mother.

One of her friends was a coloured woman called Mrs. Campbell. Her husband was a white man now retired from his business. Mrs. Campbell was kind, fat and smiling and I was very fond of her.

They lived some way out of Roseau.[1] On this particular afternoon her husband wasn't there, and she took us for tea and cakes to a summerhouse which they'd built in the garden. There were no walls, only posts, and on these she'd hung sweet oranges (and our oranges certainly were sweet) cut in two and sugared. What seemed to me dozens of hummingbirds flew in and out as we sat there, their wings quivering as they hovered, sipping with their long beaks, then flying away again. I'd never seen so many. Mrs. Campbell was smiling at them when my

---

1. The capital of Dominica, an island in the Caribbean.

mother began to cry. I had never seen her cry. I couldn't imagine such a thing. I stared at her more in wonder than in pity but I did eventually gather that she was crying about money.

"How could it stretch? What am I to do?" This is what I vaguely remember she said between sobs. I wondered if it was really money she was crying about.

Mrs. Campbell said, "I have lived long and now I am old, yet never have I seen the righteous forsaken or his seed begging their bread."

After a while my mother stopped crying and as we drove home in the trap[2] she was her usual self-contained, withdrawn self. As I looked at her I could hardly believe what had happened. But this was the end of my comfortable certainty that we were not people who had to worry about expenses. For the first time I vaguely wondered if my father's reckless, throwaway attitude to money wasn't a cover-up for anxiety.

On certain mornings a procession of old men, no women, would come to the house and for some reason my father insisted that I must stand on the pantry steps and hand out the loaf of bread and small sum of money, sixpence or a shilling, I can't quite remember, that was given to each one. My mother objected strongly, she said they were old and often not very well, it wasn't a thing I should be expected to do. Truth to tell I wasn't fond of doing it.

One of them was very different from the others. He bowed, then walked away through the garden and out of the gate at the other end with the loaf under his arm, so straight and proud, I couldn't forget him afterwards.

Il y avait une fois
Un pauvre[3] gars. . . .

My mother didn't argue any more but she arranged that we would leave Roseau two or three weeks earlier than usual. When we came back the bread and money had either been forgotten or someone else did it. There were no more arguments or processions of what the nuns called "God's poor."

Another memory. Sitting on the staircase looking through the bannisters, I watched her packing a trunk with blankets and warm things. One of the neighbouring islands had been hit by a bad hurricane and I don't suppose she was the only one to send all the help she could. I wonder if this happens now? I rather doubt it. I remember the expression on her face as she packed, careful and a little worried.

Just before I left Dominica she was ill and unable to come downstairs for some time. I went up to see her but walked softly and she didn't hear me. She didn't look up, she was sitting gazing out of the window, not reading, not crocheting or doing any of the things she usually did.

Behind her silence she looked lonely, a stranger in a strange house. But how could she be lonely when she was never alone? All the same she looked lonely, patient and resigned. Also obstinate. "You haven't seen what I've seen, haven't heard what I've heard." From across the room I knew she was like someone else I remembered. I couldn't think who it was, at first. She was like the old man walking out of the gate with a loaf of bread under his arm, patient, dignified.

2. A small horse-drawn vehicle.   (French).
3. Once upon a time, there was a poor guy . . .

I wanted to run across the room and kiss her but I was too shy so it was the usual peck. Next day she was well enough to come downstairs and life went on as before.

I think that she was happier when her twin sister left Geneva and came to live in Roseau. Though she didn't live with us, she was often at the house. It was impossible not to know that there was some link between them. One felt what the other was feeling without words. They would look at each other and both laugh quietly. This was often after one of my father's speeches about English politics.

He'd say, "Oh, I do like to see them laugh like that."

But I, watching, was uneasy. Could they possibly be laughing at me?

My mother was more silent but not so serene. Auntie B never lost her temper, my mother often did. My mother sewed beautifully but she could not cut out a dress. Slash, slash went Auntie B's scissors with a certainty and out of the material would appear a dress that fitted.

My mother could make pastry light as a feather.

Auntie B mixed famous punch.

Gradually I came to wonder about my mother less and less until at last she was almost a stranger and I stopped imagining what she felt or what she thought.

Black/White

I remember the Riot as if it were yesterday. I must have been about twelve. One night my mother came into the bedroom I shared with my baby sister, woke us up, told us to put on dressing gown and slippers and to come downstairs. We followed her half asleep. When we got into the sitting room my father said: "Why do you want to wake the children up at this time of night? It's ridiculous."

I heard far away a strange noise like animals howling but I knew it wasn't animals, it was people, and the noise came nearer and nearer.

My father said: "They're perfectly harmless."

"That's what you think," my mother said.

I half realised that we had dressed to run away from the ugly noise, but run where? We could run as far as Mr. Steadman's house on the bay but long before we got there they'd kill us.

Kill us! This strange idea didn't frighten me but excited me.

They surged past the window, howling, but they didn't throw stones. As the noise grew faint my mother said: "You can go up to bed again now."

My father said: "It was nonsense waking them up."

My mother didn't answer, she only tightened her mouth in a way that meant "You think one thing, I think another."

Upstairs I didn't sleep for a long time. He thinks one thing, she thinks another. Who is right?

This particular riot was aimed at the editor of the local paper. His house was near ours. He had written an article attacking the power of the Catholic priests in Dominica. The crowd was some of the faithful who intended to stone his house, frighten him and prevent him ever writing about religion again.

However, I could not forget the howling sound and there's no doubt that a certain wariness did creep in when I thought about the black people who surrounded me.

The black people whom I knew well were different, individuals whom I liked or disliked. If I hated Meta, I admired the groom, liked the housemaid Victoria. She came from one of the "English Islands," Antigua I think, and was an ardent Methodist. As she washed up she would sing hymns in a low voice ("Steal away, steal away, steal away to Jesus"). She was sad and unsmiling and I was vaguely sorry for her and wished she was happier.

Josephine the cook was a Dominican. A tall, good-looking woman who kept herself very much to herself. I was rather afraid of her and so, I am sure, was my mother, who never went to the kitchen. They met in the pantry—neutral ground— and there she'd be given money to go to the market and buy food: fish, vegetables, fruit, sometimes meat. The fishing boats went out then, very early. Fresh bread was delivered by women carrying laden trays on their heads.

Josephine liked to be talked to in patois.[4] Luckily my mother knew patois well. She was, in her way, a good cook. Her fish dishes were delicious, she made good curries, and often gave us crapeaux (frogs), crayfish, or stuffed crab. But I never liked her soup and she refused to make puddings.[5] All the sweets from float-ing island to Christmas pudding were made by my mother.

I once peeped into the kitchen. It was very smoky and Josephine scowled at me. There were several people there that I didn't know so I never ventured again.

But it was the others I was wary of, the others I didn't know. Did they like us as much as all that? Did they like us at all?

The next thing that shook me happened at the convent. I was young and shy and I was sitting next to a girl much older than myself. She was so tall and so pretty, and she spoke in such a confident way, that she quite awed me. She had aquiline features, large flashing eyes and a great deal of not too frizzy hair which she wore in a loose, becoming way. She didn't look coloured but I knew at once that she was. This did not prevent me from admiring her and longing to be friendly.

My father was not a prejudiced man or he would never have allowed me to go to the convent, for white girls were very much in the minority. If my mother was prejudiced she never talked about it so I tried, shyly at first, then more boldly, to talk to my beautiful neighbour.

Finally, without speaking, she turned and looked at me. I knew irritation, bad temper, the "Oh, go away" look; this was different. This was hatred—impersonal, implacable hatred. I recognised it at once and if you think a child cannot recog-nise hatred and remember it for life you are most damnably mistaken.

I never tried to be friendly with any of the coloured girls again. I was polite and that was all.

They hate us. We are hated.

Not possible.

Yet it is possible and it is so.

My few intimates at the convent were white, among them three sisters from a South American country whom I greatly admired. I still connect them with angos-tura bitters[6] through I'm sure their name wasn't Angostura. Their father was a papal count[7] and this impressed me. I had no idea where he lived: Martinique,

---

4. French dialect specific to a given region.
5. Desserts of any kind.
6. Aromatic bitters from Trinidad.

7. A noble title granted by the pope as head of state of the Vatican.

Paris, London? He was a tall, handsome man with a carefully trimmed beard, but his visits to his daughters were very few and far between. Once he came accompanied by a very pretty young white girl who he said was his adopted daughter. They used to drive about the Botanical Gardens in a smart trap and inevitably they were known as Svengali and Trilby.[8] There was a burglary scare in Roseau and he bought two large dogs; they were called "the count's Cuban bloodhounds."

His visit over, the count would depart and from Europe postcards would arrive. I saw one: "Study well, your loving Papa." When Mother Mount Calvary talked about the girls or their father she always looked worried. I can't help wondering now if money arrived any more regularly than the count did.

Side by side with my growing wariness of black people there was envy. I decided that they had a better time than we did; they laughed a lot though they seldom smiled. They were stronger than we were, they could walk a long way without getting tired. Carry heavy weights with ease.

Every night someone gave a dance; you could hear the drums. We had few dances. They were more alive, more a part of the place than we were.

The nuns said that Time didn't matter, only Eternity matters. Wouldn't black people have a better chance in Eternity? They were Catholics and I envied their faith, for I was much attracted by what I saw of Catholicism.

The Corpus Christi procession passed our house and I watched eagerly through the jalousies.[9] First came the priest, carrying the Host, then a procession of red-robed acolytes swinging censers. All along the way devout Negro women would erect little booths; sometimes they were very pretty to look at and the street outside was strewn with flower petals. At each of the booths the priest would stop and go in with his Host and the acolytes. What did he do in there, I wondered. What was it all about? I longed to know but never asked.

I would also watch through the jalousies as they passed the house on their way to Mass. They were dressed in their best, sweeping trains, heavy gold earrings and necklaces and colourful turbans. If the petticoat beneath the dress didn't make the desired frou-frou noise, they'd sew paper in the hems.

> Frou-frou, frou-frou
> Par son jupon la femme
> . . . . surtout
> Par son gentil frou-frou.[1]

Also there wasn't for them, as there was for us, what I thought of as the worry of getting married. In those days a girl was supposed to marry, it was your mission in life, you were a failure if you didn't. It was a terrible thing to be an old maid, on the shelf as they put it. The fact that I knew several old maids who seemed perfectly happy, indeed happier and livelier than the married women, didn't affect the question at all. I dreaded growing up. I dreaded the time when I would have to worry about how many proposals I had, what if I didn't have a proposal? This was never told me but it was in every book I read, in people's faces and the way they talked.

8. In George du Maurier's 1894 serial novel, *Trilby,* the hypnotist Svengali manipulates the heroine's singing talents for his own purposes.
9. Window blinds.

1. Remembered fragments of a song about women augmenting their "nice" petticoats with "frou-frou," elaborate ornamentation.

Black girls on the contrary seemed to be perfectly free. Children swarmed but Negro marriages that I knew of were comparatively rare. Marriage didn't seem a duty with them as it was with us.

All this perhaps was part of my envy, which rose to a fever pitch at carnival time.

Carnival

The three days before Lent were carnival in Roseau. We couldn't dress up or join in but we could watch from the open window and not through the jalousies. There were gaily masked crowds with a band. Listening, I would think that I would give anything, anything to be able to dance like that. The life surged up to us sitting stiff and well behaved, looking on. As usual my feelings were mixed, because I was very afraid of the masks.

Once when a friend of Victoria's came to visit her I was in the pantry. I was terrified of the way the visitor talked in a strange artificial voice with much rolling of the *r*'s. I was terrified of her mask. It was quite useless telling me, "Don't be silly, it's only Regina dressed up." I ran away crying.

Some of the men painted themselves either red or black and wore only loin-cloths. They would run along waving long sticks above their heads and jumping very high. They called themselves the Darkees or the Red Ochres. I used to think that if I met a mob of either Darkees or Red Ochres as I was going back to school after lunch, I would die of fright, but it never happened.

The only mask which I was not afraid of was called the Bois-Bois. He was not in a crowd but by himself, and he walked on high stilts and looked immensely tall. Before our house he would stop and do a formal little dance on the stilts and then I was sent out with sixpence or a shilling to give him. He would take the money, duck his head in a little bow, then stalk away to the next house to perform his little dance again.

I have watched carnivals on television. They are doubtless very colourful but it seems to me that it is all planned and made up compared to the carnival I remember, when I used to long so fiercely to be black and to dance, too, in the sun, to that music. The carnival I knew has vanished.

1979

◄ KATHERINE ANNE PORTER ►
1890–1980

From the perspective of the twenty-first century, Katherine Anne Porter's life appears tumultuous—she survived tuberculosis and a deadly influenza epidemic, took part in the Mexican Revolution, and met Hermann Göring, Hitler's second in command, in Berlin during Hitler's rise to power; she married and divorced four times and suffered many miscarriages and one stillbirth; she became a celebrated author at forty and won the National Book Award and the Pulitzer Prize; and she was a frequent dinner guest at the Johnson White House. From such personal tumult, perhaps, may come Porter's sensitive portrayals of everyday life and her ability to represent the mythical dimensions of the mundane.

She was born Callie Russell Porter in Indian Creek, Texas, but took on a version of her paternal grandmother's name after her first divorce. Porter had lived with her grandmother after her mother died in 1892. After her grandmother's death in 1901, Porter moved around a great deal with her father and siblings and, despite very little formal schooling, helped support the family by teaching and performing onstage from a young age. She married for the first time at sixteen but left her abusive husband after several years to attempt a career first in film and then as a singer. She earned her living as a journalist in the 1920s and began writing children's stories and working as a ghost writer. She also began to travel between Mexico and New York and to write stories inspired by her experiences. Her first volume of stories appeared in 1930; although it was not a popular success, it was extremely well received critically, and Porter became known as one of the best short-story writers of her generation. Even so, she was not able to earn her living as a writer until her only novel, *Ship of Fools,* became a best seller in 1962. She supported herself as a journalist and later by teaching at various universities in the United States and Europe.

Katherine Anne Porter was known during her lifetime as a consummate prose stylist and championed as a southern writer. More recently, she has been read for her thoughtful representations of women and politics. Many of the stories and novellas she wrote during the 1930s and 1940s are loosely autobiographical and focus on issues of balancing familial obligations with personal freedoms, especially for women. The selection here, "Virgin Violeta" (1923) is one of the earliest stories Porter published. It reveals some of her experience of Mexican culture and hints at both her conversion to Catholicism (during her first marriage) and her later disenchantment with religion. It reveals much of Porter's ability to capture both setting and character through deftly handled, spare prose, but it also shows her interest in focusing on the dilemmas faced by women: How do you balance your desire for an exciting life with your obligation to your family to be a "good girl"? How do you draw the line between a fantasy life and your real life? The story also shows us a girl as she begins to become a young woman and reveals much about the psychology of that transformation.

Virgin Violeta

Violeta, nearly fifteen years old, sat on a hassock, hugging her knees and watching Carlos, her cousin, and her sister Blanca, who were reading poetry aloud by turns at the long table.

Occasionally she glanced down at her own feet, clad in thick-soled brown sandals, the toes turned in a trifle. Their ugliness distressed her, and she pulled her short skirt over them until the beltline sagged under her loose, dark blue woolen blouse. Then she straightened up, with a full, silent breath, uncovering the sandals again. Each time her eyes moved under shy lids to Carlos, to see if he had noticed; he never did notice. Disappointed, a little troubled, Violeta would sit very still for a while, listening and watching.

> " 'This torment of love which is in my heart:
> I know that I suffer it, but I do not know why.' "

Blanca's voice was thin, with a whisper in it. She seemed anxious to keep the poetry all for Carlos and herself. Her shawl, embroidered in yellow on gray silk, slipped from her shoulders whenever she inclined toward the lamp. Carlos would lift the tassel of fringe nearest him between finger and thumb and toss it deftly into place. Blanca's nod, her smile, were the perfection of amiable indifference. But her voice wavered, caught on the word. She had always to begin again the line she was reading.

Carlos would slant his pale eyes at Blanca; then he would resume his pose, gaze fixed on a small painting on the white-paneled wall over Violeta's head. "Pious Interview between the Most Holy Virgin Queen of Heaven and Her Faithful Servant St. Ignatius Loyola," read the thin metal plate on the carved and gilded frame. The Virgin, with enameled face set in a detached simper, forehead bald of eyebrows, extended one hand remotely over the tonsured head of the saint, who groveled in a wooden posture of ecstasy. Very ugly and old-fashioned, thought Violeta, but a perfectly proper picture; there was nothing to stare at. But Carlos kept squinting his eyelids at it mysteriously, and never moved his eyes from it save to glance at Blanca. His furry, golden eyebrows were knotted sternly, resembling a tangle of crochet wool. He never seemed to be interested except when it was his turn to read. He read in a thrilling voice. Violeta thought his mouth and chin were very beautiful. A tiny spot of light on his slightly moistened underlip disturbed her, she did not know why.

Blanca stopped reading, bowed her head and sighed lightly, her mouth half open. It was one of her habits. As the sound of voices had lulled Mamacita to sleep beside her sewing basket, now the silence roused her. She looked about her with a vivacious smile on her whole face, except her eyes, which were drowsed and weary.

"Go on with your reading, dear children. I heard every word. Violeta, don't fidget, please, sweet little daughter. Carlos, what is the hour?"

Mamacita liked being chaperon to Blanca. Violeta wondered why Mamacita considered Blanca so very attractive, but she did. She was always saying to Papacito, "Blanquita blooms like a lily!" And Papacito would say, "It is better if she conducts herself like one!" And Mamacita said once to Carlos, "Even if you are my nephew, still you must go home at a reasonable hour!"

"The hour is early, Doña Paz." St. Anthony himself could not have exceeded in respect the pose of Carlos' head toward his aunt. She smiled and relapsed into a shallow nap, as a cat rises from the rug, turns and lies down again.

Violeta did not move, or answer Mamacita. She had the silence and watchfulness of a young wild animal, but no native wisdom. She was at home from the convent in Tacubaya for the first time in almost a year. There they taught her modesty, chastity, silence, obedience, with a little French and music and some arithmetic. She did as she was told, but it was all very confusing, because she could not understand why the things that happen outside of people were so different from what she felt inside of her. Everybody went about doing the same things every day, precisely as if there were nothing else going to happen, ever; and all the time she was certain there was something simply tremendously exciting waiting for her outside the convent. Life was going to unroll itself like a long, gay carpet for her to walk upon. She saw herself wearing a long veil, and it would trail and flutter over this carpet as she came out of church. There would be six flower girls and two pages, the way there had been at Cousin Sancha's wedding.

Of course she didn't mean a wedding. Silly! Cousin Sancha had been quite old, almost twenty-four, and Violeta meant for life to begin at once—next year, anyway. It would be more like a festival. She wanted to wear red poppies in her hair and dance. Life would always be very gay, with no one about telling you that almost everything you said and did was wrong. She would be free to read poetry, too, and stories about love, without having to hide them in her copybooks. Even Carlos did not know that she had learned nearly all his poems by heart. She had for a year been cutting them from magazines, keeping them in the pages of her books, in order to read them during study hours.

Several shorter ones were concealed in her missal, and the thrilling music of strange words drowned the chorus of bell and choir. There was one about the ghosts of nuns returning to the old square before their ruined convent, dancing in the moonlight with the shades of lovers forbidden them in life, treading with bared feet on broken glass as a penance for their loves. Violeta would shake all over when she read this, and lift swimming eyes to the delicate spears of candlelight on the altar.

She was certain she would be like those nuns someday. She would dance for joy over shards of broken glass. But where begin? She had sat here in this room, on this very hassock, comfortably near Mamacita, through the summer evenings of vacation, ever since she could remember. Sometimes it was a happiness to be assured that nothing was expected of her but to follow Mamacita about and be a good girl. It gave her time to dream about life—that is, the future. For of course everything beautiful and unexpected would happen later on, when she grew as tall as Blanca and was allowed to come home from the convent for good and all. She would then be miraculously lovely—Blanca would look perfectly dull beside her— and she would dance with fascinating young men like those who rode by on Sunday mornings, making their horses prance in the bright, shallow street on their way to the *paseo*[1] in Chapultepec Park. She would appear on the balcony above, wearing a blue dress, and everyone would ask who that enchanting girl could be. And Carlos, Carlos! He would understand at last that she had read and loved his poems always.

> *"The nuns are dancing with bare feet*
> *On broken glass in the cobbled street."*

That one above all the rest. She felt it had been written for her. She was even one of the nuns, the youngest and best-loved one, ghostly silent, dancing forever and ever under the moonlight to the shivering tune of old violins.

Mamacita moved her knee uneasily, so that Violeta's head slipped from it, and she almost lost her balance. She sat up, prickling all over with shyness for fear the others would know why she had hidden her face on Mamacita's lap. But no one saw. Mamacita was always lecturing her about things. At such moments it was hard to believe that Blanca was not the favorite child. "You must not run through the house so." "You must brush your hair more smoothly." "And what is this I hear about your using your sister's face powder?"

Blanca, listening, would eye her with superior calm and say nothing. It was really very hard, knowing that Blanca was nicer only because she was allowed to powder and perfume herself and still gave herself such airs about it. Carlos, who used to bring her sugared limes and long strips of dried *membrillo*[2] from the markets, calling her his dear, amusing, modest Violeta, now simply did not know she was present. There were times when Violeta wished to cry, passionately, so every-

---

1. The evening promenade.   2. Dried quince, a pear-shaped fruit.

one could hear her. But what about? And how explain to Mamacita? She would say, "What have you to cry for? And besides, consider the feelings of others in this house and control your moods."

Papacito would say, "What you need is a good renovating." That was his word for a spanking. He would say sternly to Mamacita, "I think her moral nature needs repairment." He and Mamacita seemed to have some mysterious understanding about things. Mamacita's eyes were always perfectly clear when she looked at Papacito, and she would answer: "You are right. I will look after this." Then she would be very severe with Violeta. Papacito always said to the girls: "It is your fault without exception when Mamacita is annoyed with you. So be careful."

But Mamacita never stayed annoyed for long, and afterward it was beautiful to curl up near her, snuggling into her shoulder, and smell the nice, crinkled, perfumed hair at the nape of her neck. But when she was angry her eyes had a considering expression, as if one were a stranger, and she would say, "You are the greatest of my problems." Violeta had often been a problem and it was very humiliating.

¡Ay de mi![3] Violeta gave a sharp sigh and sat up straight. She wanted to stretch her arms up and yawn, not because she was sleepy but because something inside her felt as if it were enclosed in a cage too small for it, and she could not breathe. Like those poor parrots in the markets, stuffed into tiny wicker cages so that they bulged through the withes, gasping and panting, waiting for someone to come and rescue them.

Church was a terrible, huge cage, but it seemed too small. "Oh, my, I always laugh, to keep from crying!" A silly verse Carlos used to say. Through her eyelashes his face looked suddenly pale and soft, as if he might have tears on his cheeks. Oh, Carlos! But of course he would never cry for anything. She was frightened to find that her own eyes were steeped in tears; they were going to run down her face; she couldn't stop them. Her head bowed over and her chin seemed to be curling up. Where on earth was her handkerchief? A huge, clean, white linen one, almost like a boy's handkerchief. How horrid! The folded corner scratched her eyelids. Sometimes she cried in church when the music wailed terribly and the girls sat in veiled rows, all silent except for the clinking of their beads slipping through their fingers. They were all strangers to her then; what if they knew her thoughts? Suppose she should say aloud, "I love Carlos!" The idea made her blush all over, until her forehead perspired and her hands turned red. She would begin praying frantically, "Oh, Mary! Oh, Mary! Queen Mother of mercy!" while deep underneath her words her thoughts were rushing along in a kind of trance: Oh, dear God, that's my secret; that's a secret between You and me. I should die if anybody knew!

She turned her eyes again to the pair at the long table just in time to see once more the shawl beginning to slip, ever so little, from Blanca's shoulder. A tight shudder of drawn threads played along Violeta's skin, and grew quite intolerable when Carlos reached out to take the fringe in his long fingers. His wrist turned with a delicate toss, the shawl settled into place, Blanca smiled and stammered and bit her lip.

Violeta could not bear to see it. No, no. She wanted to hold her hands over her heart tightly, to quell the slow, burning ache. It felt like a little jar filled with

3. "Oh!" or "Oh, my" (Spanish).

flames, which she could not smother down. It was cruel of Blanca and Carlos to sit there and read and be so pleased with each other without once thinking of her! Yet what could she say if they noticed her? They never did notice.

Blanca rose.

"I am tired of the old poetry. It is all too sad. What else shall we read?"

"Let's have a great deal of gay, modern poetry," suggested Carlos, whose own verses were considered extremely gay and modern. Violeta was always shocked when he called them amusing. He couldn't mean it. It was only his way of pretending he wasn't sad when he wrote them.

"Read me all your new ones again." Blanca was always appreciating Carlos. You could hear it in her voice underneath, like a little trickle of sugar. And Carlos let her do it. He seemed always to be condescending to Blanca a little. But Blanca could never see it, because she really didn't think of anything but the way she had her hair fixed or whether people thought she was pretty. Violeta longed to make a naughty face at Blanca, who posed ridiculously, leaning over the table.

Above the red silk lamp shade her face was not sallow as usual. The thin nose and small lips cast shadows on her cheek. She hated being pale, and had the habit, while reading, of smoothing her cheeks round and round with two fingers, first one cheek and then the other, until deep red spots would burn in them for a long while. Violeta wished to shriek after watching Blanca do this for hours at a time. Why did not Mamacita speak to her about it? It was the worst sort of fidgeting.

"I haven't the new ones with me," said Carlos.

"Then let it be the old ones," agreed Blanca gaily.

She moved to the bookshelves, Carlos beside her. They could not find his book. Their hands touched as fingers sought titles. Something in the intimate murmur of their voices wounded Violeta acutely. Sharing some delightful secret, they were purposely shutting her out. She spoke.

"If you want your book, Carlos, I can find it." At the sound of her own voice she felt calm and firm and equal to anything. By her tone she tried to shut Blanca out.

They turned and regarded her without interest.

"And where may it be, infant?" Carlos' voice always had that chilling edge on it when he was not reading aloud, and his eyes explored. With a glance he seemed to see all one's faults. Violeta remembered her feet and drew down her skirts. The sight of Blanca's narrow, gray satin slippers was hateful.

"I have it. I have had it for a whole week." She eyed the tip of Blanca's nose, hoping they would understand she wished to say, "You see, I have treasured it!"

She got up, feeling a little clumsy, and walked away with a curious imitation of Blanca's grown-up gait. It made her dreadfully aware of her long, straight legs in their ribbed stockings.

"I will help you search," called Carlos, as if he had thought of something interesting, and he followed. Over his suddenly near shoulder she saw Blanca's face. It looked very vague and faraway, like a distressed doll's. Carlos' eyes were enormous, and he smiled steadily. She wished to run away. He said something in a low voice. She could not understand him at all, and it was impossible to find the lamp cord in the narrow, dark hallway. She was frightened at the soft *pad-pad* of his rubber heels so close behind her as they went without speaking through the chill dining room, full of the odor of fruit that has been all day in a closed place. When they entered the small, open sunroom over the entrance of the patio, the moonlight seemed almost warm, it was so radiant after the shadows of the house. Violeta turned over a huddle of books on the small table, but she did not see them clearly; and her hand shook so, she could not take hold of anything.

Carlos' hand came up in a curve, settled upon hers and held fast. His roundish, smooth cheek and blond eyebrows hovered, swooped. His mouth touched hers and made a tiny smacking sound. She felt herself wrench and twist away as if a hand pushed her violently. And in that second his hand was over her mouth, soft and warm, and his eyes were staring at her, fearfully close. Violeta opened her eyes wide also and peered up at him. She expected to sink into a look warm and gentle, like the touch of his palm. Instead, she felt suddenly, sharply hurt, as if she had collided with a chair in the dark. His eyes were bright and shallow, almost like the eyes of Pepe, the macaw. His pale, fluffy eyebrows were arched; his mouth smiled tightly. A sick thumping began in the pit of her stomach, as it always did when she was called up to explain things to Mother Superior. Something was terribly wrong. Her heart pounded until she seemed about to smother. She was angry with all her might, and turned her head aside in a hard jerk.

"Keep your hand off my mouth!"

"Then be quiet, you silly child!" The words were astounding, but the way he said them was more astounding still, as if they were allies in some shameful secret. Her teeth rattled with chill.

"I will tell my mother! Shame on you for kissing me!"

"I did not kiss you except a little brotherly kiss, Violeta, precisely as I kiss Blanca. Don't be absurd!"

"You do not kiss Blanca. I heard her tell my mother she has never been kissed by a man!"

"But I do kiss her—as a cousin, nothing more. It does not count. We are relatives just the same. What did you think?"

Oh, she had made a hideous mistake. She knew she was blushing until her forehead throbbed. Her breath was gone, but she must explain. "I thought—a kiss—meant—meant—" She could not finish.

"Ah, you're so young, like a little newborn calf," said Carlos. His voice trembled in a strange way. "You smell like a nice baby, freshly washed with white soap! Imagine such a baby being angry at a kiss from her cousin! Shame on you, Violeta!"

He was loathsome. She saw herself before him, almost as if his face were a mirror. Her mouth was too large; her face was simply a moon; her hair was ugly in the tight convent braids.

"Oh, I'm so sorry!" she whispered.

"For what?" His voice had the cutting edge again. "Come, where is the book?"

"I don't know," she said, trying not to cry.

"Well, then, let us go back, or Mamacita will scold you."

"Oh, no, no. I can't go in there. Blanca will see—Mamacita will ask questions. I want to stay here. I want to run away—to kill myself!"

"Nonsense!" said Carlos. "Come with me this minute. What did you expect when you came out here alone with me?"

He turned and started away. She was shamefully, incredibly in the wrong. She had behaved like an immodest girl. It was all bitterly real and unbelievable, like a nightmare that went on and on and no one heard you calling to be waked up. She followed, trying to hold up her head.

Mamacita nodded, shining, crinkled hair stiffly arranged, chin on white collar. Blanca sat like a stone in her deep chair, holding a small gray-and-gold book in her lap. Her angry eyes threw out a look that coiled back upon itself like a whiplash, and the pupils became suddenly blank and bright on Carlos' hair.

Violeta folded down on her hassock and gathered up her knees. She stared at the carpet to hide her reddened eyes, for it terrified her to see the way eyes could give away such cruel stories about people.

"I found the book here, where it belonged," said Blanca. "I am tired now. It is very late. We shall not read."

Violeta wished to cry in real earnest now. It was the last blow that Blanca should have found the book. A kiss meant nothing at all, and Carlos had walked away as if he had forgotten her. It was all mixed up with the white rivers of moonlight and the smell of warm fruit and a cold dampness on her lips that made a tiny, smacking sound. She trembled and leaned over until her forehead touched Mamacita's lap. She could not look up, ever, ever again.

The low voices sounded contentious; thin metal wires twanged in the air around them.

"But I do not care to read any more, I tell you."

"Very well, I shall go at once. But I am leaving for Paris on Wednesday, and shall not see you again until the fall."

"It would be like you to go without even stopping in to say good-by."

Even when they were angry they still talked to each other like two grown-up people wrapped together in a secret. The sound of his soft, padding rubber heels came near.

"Good night, my dearest Doña Paz. I have had an enchanting evening."

Mamacita's knees moved; she meant to rise.

"What—asleep, Violeta? Well, let us hear often from you, my dear nephew. Your little cousins and I will miss you greatly."

Mamacita was wide-awake and smiling, holding Carlos' hands. They kissed. Carlos turned to Blanca and bent to kiss her. She swept him into the folds of the gray shawl, but turned her cheek for his salute. Violeta rose, her knees trembling. She turned her head from side to side to close out the sight of the macaw eyes coming closer and closer, the tight, smiling mouth ready to swoop. When he touched her, she wavered for a moment, then slid up and back against the wall. She heard herself screaming uncontrollably.

Mamacita sat upon the side of the bed and patted Violeta's cheek. Her curved hand was warm and gentle and so were her eyes. Violeta choked a little and turned her face away.

"I have explained to Papacito that you quarreled with your cousin Carlos and were very rude to him. Papacito says you need a good renovating." Mamacita's voice was soft and reassuring. Violeta lay without a pillow, the ruffled collar of her nightgown standing up about her chin. She did not answer. Even to whisper hurt her.

"We are going to the country this week and you shall live in the garden all summer. Then you won't be so nervous. You are quite a young lady now, and you must learn to control your nerves."

"Yes, Mamacita." The look on Mamacita's face was very hard to bear. She seemed to be asking questions about very hidden thoughts—those thoughts that were not true at all and could never be talked about with anyone. Everything she could remember in her whole life seemed to have melted together in a confusion and misery that could not be explained because it was all changed and uncertain.

She wanted to sit up, take Mamacita around the neck and say, "Something dreadful happened to me—I don't know what," but her heart closed up hard and aching, and she sighed with all her breath. Even Mamacita's breast had become a cold, strange place. Her blood ran back and forth in her, crying terribly, but when the sound came up to her lips it was only a small whimper, like a puppy's.

"You must not cry any more," said Mamacita after a long pause. Then: "Good night, my poor child. This impression will pass." Mamacita's kiss felt cold on Violeta's cheek.

Whether the impression passed or not, no word of it was spoken again. Violeta and the family spent the summer in the country. She refused to read Carlos' poetry, though Mamacita encouraged her to do so. She would not even listen to his letters from Paris. She quarreled on more equal terms with her sister Blanca, feeling that there was no longer so great a difference of experience to separate them. A painful unhappiness possessed her at times, because she could not settle the questions brooding in her mind. Sometimes she amused herself making ugly caricatures of Carlos.

In the early autumn she returned to school, weeping and complaining to her mother that she hated the convent. There was, she declared as she watched her boxes being tied up, nothing to be learned there.

1923

◄ AFRICAN AMERICAN WOMEN'S BLUES ►

What do you do when your man has left you or is treating you bad, the landlord has evicted you, and you can't get a job or any liquor? If there's nothing you can do to change the situation, you can at least feel better about it by singing the blues. The blues is one of the few distinctly American art forms, and like its close relation, jazz, it originated in the African American community. There are many sub-genres of the blues, but they all have in common the same central impulse: if you are feeling blue, singing about what is getting you down and making it humorous (or raucous) will make you feel better. Typically, the blues express longings for a better life and are very much a working-class art form, but they can also express powerful political outrage at injustice and prejudice. The blues are forthright about sexuality, a characteristic that made them perfect for the "Roaring Twenties." They also played an important part in launching the Harlem Renaissance, an explosion of African American cultural forms—music, art, and literature—in the 1910s, 1920s, and 1930s.

While most histories of the blues available in the United States today are devoted to male singers and performers, you would get a very different impression of the genre by looking at blues recordings from the 1920s. The earliest blues recordings were of female singers; in fact, record labels did not really believe that male vocalists would sell during the 1920s and did not begin to sign them to contracts until the 1930s. Once they did, female vocalists increasingly had trouble getting recorded, and the blues became the male-dominated genre that is now represented in the history books.

The selections here represent the work of three performers—Gertrude "Ma" Rainey, Bessie Smith, and and Alberta Hunter—from the "classic" age of women's blues, but many other women performed in theaters, clubs, and speakeasies and on records, including artists like Ethel Waters, Sippie Wallace, Ida Cox, Lucille Hegamin, Trixie Smith, and Rosa Henderson. The three here are among the best known and most influential early blues singers. Despite their immense popularity, these women rarely made adequate livings from their royalties, even though the recording companies often made huge profits from them, a common occurrence for African American recording artists in the twentieth century. Our selections here are not as extensive as we would like because of the high cost of permissions fees for reprinting the lyrics in a book for sale. Scholars can, however, get access to more of this important body of women's writing on the World Wide Web.

Although women performers often sang male-authored songs (sometimes putting their own twists on them), they also wrote their own lyrics, many of which reflect a distinctly female take on what it means to have the blues. There is, of course, an important component missing when we study lyrics without the music; a song is not the same as a poem, and in the blues, we're missing the oftentimes rollicking fun of the music behind the words that outline troubles. Technically, the blues is defined by musicologists as a I-IV-V chord progression laid over a twelve-bar framework or as music inflected by "blue notes," or flatted thirds and sevenths, but that definition is not very useful when you are studying the substance of the lyrics. According to Angela Davis, whose *Blues Legacies and Black Feminism* (1999) is one of the best studies of women's blues, although the lyrics rarely express a recognizable feminism directly, they do establish an African American female independence, lay the groundwork for community, articulate a specifically black female aesthetic, and, especially, reject the dominant culture's notion of female frailty and purity. Blues women were lusty, strong, sometimes violent and vengeful, and forthright about a sexuality that wasn't bounded by marriage. Davis also points out that blues women were often overtly political and used their music to protest racism, poverty, and injustice. Recordings of all these lyrics are available (many on the Internet) and are well worth listening to as well as studying.

◄ GERTRUDE "MA" RAINEY ►
1886–1939

Gertrude Rainey was known as "the Mother of the Blues." She was born into a vaudeville family in Georgia and began a career on the stage in 1900 in the variety shows of that era. She married "Pa" Rainey in 1904, and together they began touring the South, performing vaudeville and minstrel shows, but primarily singing the blues. In 1923, she began recording for Paramount Records. Although, like most other African American performers of the era, she did not reap great financial success from her recordings, she essentially established the label as a major force in the industry. One of the freedoms that came with being a blues artist was a frankness about sexuality, and Ma Rainey made little secret of her bisexuality: she was photographed wearing a man's suit and flirting with two women to advertise "Prove It on Me," and she was arrested in 1925 for hosting an "indecent party" of women. She retired from performing in 1935 and returned to Georgia, where she ran two theaters and became active in the Baptist Church. When she died, her obituary listed her as a housekeeper, but she remains popular today.

"Ma" Rainey was inducted into the Rock and Roll Hall of Fame and has appeared on a U.S. postage stamp.

Louisiana Hoodoo Blues

Going to Louisiana bottom to get me a hoodoo[1] hand
Going to Louisiana bottom to get me a hoodoo hand
Gotta stop these women from taking my man

Down in Algiers[2] where the hoodoos live in their den
Down in Algiers where the hoodoos live in their den
Their chief occupation is separating women from men

The hoodoo told me to get me a black cat bone
The hoodoo told me to get me a black cat bone
And shake it over their heads, they'll leave your man alone

Twenty years in the bottom, that ain't long to stay
Twenty years in the bottom, that ain't long to stay
If I can keep these tush-hog[3] women from taking my man away

So I'm bound for New Orleans, down in goofer dust[4] land
So I'm bound for New Orleans, down in goofer dust land
Down where the hoodoo folks can fix it for you with your man.

1925

Prove It on Me Blues

Went out last night, had a great big fight
Everything seemed to go on wrong
I looked up, to my surprise
The gal I was with was gone

Where she went, I don't know
I mean to follow everywhere she goes
Folks say I'm crooked, I didn't know where she took it
I want the whole world to know

They said I do it, ain't nobody caught me
Sure got to prove it on me
Went out last night with a crowd of my friends
They must've been women, 'cause I don't like no men

It's true I wear a collar and a tie
Make the wind blow all the while
'Cause they say I do it, ain't nobody caught me
They sure got to prove it on me

---

1. A magical practice including a mixture of voodoo, African spirituality, European and Native American herbalism, and Christianity.
2. A community within New Orleans.
3. An aggressive wild boar; in blues symbolism, it refers to a man having an affair with someone else's wife.
4. A mix of graveyard dirt, rattlesnake skin, sulfur, and herbs used as a jinx.

Say I do it, ain't nobody caught me
Sure got to prove it on me
I went out last night with a crowd of my friends
They must've been women, 'cause I don't like no men

Wear my clothes just like a fan
Talk to the gals just like any old man
'Cause they say I do it, ain't nobody caught me
Sure got to prove it on me.

1928

►◄ ALBERTA HUNTER ►◄
1895–1984

Alberta Hunter left her home in Memphis when she was still a teenager (some biographies claim she was just twelve years old) to try to make her living singing in Chicago. At first, she had gigs only in brothels, but she slowly made her way up from cheap saloons to clubs and finally to the popular Dreamland Café, where she was the star. She moved her mother to Chicago during this time to support her and married briefly (though it is rumored that she never consummated the marriage); she also met Lottie Taylor, who would be her companion for many years. By the 1920s, she had moved to New York, was recording for several different labels (often under pseudonyms to get around exclusive contracts), and was performing in high-profile revues in Harlem with many of the most famous jazz musicians of her time. During the 1930s and 1940s, she toured in Europe, where she was a sensation in Paris, London, and Copenhagen; she continued to tour Europe as part of the USO, entertaining troops during World War II. After the war, with bookings increasingly hard to find, she returned to New York to care for her mother. After her mother's death, Hunter went back to school at age fifty-nine to become a nurse and pursued this career until the hospital discovered she'd hidden her actual age and forced her to retire at eighty-one. Rather than just retire, however, Hunter returned to music, composing, performing, and recording new material until her death.

I Got Myself a Workin' Man

A lot of these chicks are cryin' murder, but I ain't moved my hand,
I say, a lot of these chicks are cryin' hard luck, but me, I ain't moved
    my hand,
I got myself a little apartment, dog and a cat, and a workin' man.

He couldn't win no beauty contest, goodness knows he don't dress fine
But he's healthy and ambitious, and he lays it on the line
He'd never win no beauty contest, and goodness knows he don't
    dress fine
Yes, he's healthy and ambitious, and he lays it on the line.

When some people see us out together, honey they kinda laugh and
   turn away
Ah, but they do, but the joke's on them
I say, when they see us out together, they kinda laugh and turn away
Ah, but the joke is on them, baby, 'cause I'm eatin' three square meals
   a day.

Now I don't like those hepster[1] lovers, they've got larceny in their eyes
They got a hand full of gimme, and a mouth full of much obliged.
I can't stand those hepster lovers 'cause they've got larceny in their eyes
They got a hand full of gimme, and a mouth full of much obliged.

So I say, let these chicks keep cryin' murder, me, I don't have to move my
   hand, ah, but I don't
So I say, let these chicks keep cryin' murder, me, I don't have to move
   my hand

I got myself a little apartment, a cat, and a workin' man.
1920s(?)   1961

You Gotta Reap What You Sow

You can boast about your riches, your every wish someone's command,
You can go around cheatin' people, by some trickery or plan,
You can tell lies on your neighbor, and think no one will ever know,
But as sure as you are livin', you got to reap just what you sow.

You got to reap just what you sow, yes, you got to reap just what you sow.
On a mountain, or in a valley, you got to reap just what you sow.

Yes, you can inconvenience others, you can make things easy for yourself,
You can steal some poor man's idea and accumulate great wealth.
But here's one thing that will happen, it's been tried and proved before,
All the wrong that you are doing, you got to reap just what you sow.

You got to reap just what you sow, yes, you got to reap just what you sow.
On a mountain, or in a valley, you got to reap just what you sow.

Yes, you can take every advantage of a fellow man that's down,
You can take somebody's heartstring and drag it on the ground,
High-hat[2] other people just because you're having luck
Even double-cross your best friend, and then try to pass the buck,
But there's one thing that will happen, makes no difference where you go,
Just before your final curtain, you got to reap just what you sow.

You got to reap just what you sow, yes, you got to reap just what you sow.
On a mountain, or in a valley, you got to reap just what you sow.

1923

---

1. Hipster; fashionable, up-to-date.   2. Snub.

◄ BESSIE SMITH ►
1898?–1937

Bessie Smith, 1936. (Photograph by Carl Van Vechten)

Known as "The Empress of the Blues," Bessie Smith was a hard-living, hard-drinking, exuberant woman who was probably the most influential singer of the blues era. She was a big woman—reputedly over six feet tall—and had a big voice that was also known for its subtlety. She was the highest-paid African American performer during the 1920s, making as much as $1,500 per week (almost $20,000 in today's dollars) and touring in a custom-made railroad car. Orphaned at nine, she rose to fame quickly; she began singing while still a child and was discovered and mentored by Ma Rainey when she was twelve or fifteen. Smith started recording for Columbia Records (in their "Race Records" series), producing 160 "sides" (one side of a record album), for which she was paid between $125 and $200 each. During the early 1930s, though, her career began to falter, partly because of changing musical tastes and partly because of her alcoholism. She was working on a comeback when she was killed in an automobile accident in Mississippi. Legend has it that she died after she was denied care at a whites-only hospital (in 1959, American author Edward Albee wrote a play based on this story, *The Death of Bessie Smith*), but recent research reveals that she was admitted to a black hospital with wounds too severe to survive. Even though as many as 10,000 people attended her lavish funeral, she was buried in an unmarked grave. In 1970, Janis Joplin found her grave and erected a headstone that reads "The Greatest Blues Singer in the World Will Never Stop Singing."

Preachin' the Blues

Down in Atlanta GA under the viaduct every day
Drinkin' corn[1] and hollerin' hooray, pianos playin' 'til the break of day
But as I turned my head I loudly said
Preach them blues, sing them blues, they certainly sound good to me
I been in love for the last six months and ain't done worryin' yet
Moan them blues, holler them blues, let me convert your soul
'Cause just a little spirit of the blues tonight
Let me tell you, girls, if your man ain't treatin' you right

---

1. Liquor distilled from corn, moonshine.

Let me tell you, I don't mean no wrong
I will learn you something if you listen to this song
I ain't here to try to save your soul
Just want to teach you how to save your good jelly roll[2]
Goin' on down the line a little further now, there's a many poor woman
    down
Read on down to chapter nine, women must learn how to take their time
Read on down to chapter ten, takin' other women men you are doin'
    a sin
Sing 'em, sing 'em, sing them blues, let me convert your soul
Lord, one old sister by the name of Sister Green
Jumped up and done a shimmy you ain't never seen
Sing 'em, sing 'em, sing them blues, let me convert your soul.

1927

Poor Man's Blues

Mister rich man, rich man, open up your heart and mind
Mister rich man, rich man, open up your heart and mind
Give the poor man a chance, help stop these hard, hard times

While you're livin' in your mansion, you don't know what hard times
    means
While you're livin' in your mansion, you don't know what hard times
    means
Poor working man's wife is starvin', your wife's livin' like a queen

Please, listen to my pleading, 'cause I can't stand these hard times long
Oh, listen to my pleading, can't stand these hard times long
They'll make an honest man do things that you know is wrong

Poor man fought all the battles, poor man would fight again today
Poor man fought all the battles, poor man would fight again today
He would do anything you ask him in the name of the U.S.A.

Now the war is over, poor man must live the same as you
Now the war is over, poor man must live the same as you
If it wasn't for the poor man, mister rich man, what would you do?

1928

---

2. Female genitalia.

CULTURAL COORDINATES
A Blues Life: Billie Holiday

Though the facts about her early years are hotly debated, it is clear that more than any other performer of her generation, Billie Holiday (1915–1959) lived the blues. Born Eleanora Fagan (or Harris or Gough) to a thirteen-year-old mother and a traveling guitarist named Holiday, her early life was chaotic and impoverished. We know that she was remanded to a reformatory when she was eleven, after admitting that she had been raped. She then ran away and moved with her mother to New York, where she worked as a domestic and moonlighted as a prostitute. She and her mother were arrested for prostitution in 1929 and served one hundred days at a workhouse. At about the same time, she began singing in bars and clubs under the name Billie Holiday, and by 1933, her unique voice, emotional singing style, and phrasing were earning praise from many experienced musicians. She became one of the most famous singers in the blues and jazz world, performing with big-name jazz bands. Working with Artie Shaw, she became the first African American singer to appear with a white orchestra, a gig that lasted less than a year because Jim Crow laws kept her from performing in many venues throughout the South. When she and the band were subjected to severe racism, she quit in disgust and became a solo artist. Between 1933 and 1944, Holiday recorded over 200 "sides" but was never paid any royalties; she made her living performing in clubs. During this time, she developed, with Lewis Allen and Sonny White, the song that would become her signature, "Strange Fruit," a forthright protest against lynching and racism. She also developed a drug habit, moving from alcohol and marijuana to opium and heroin. At first, her performances were unaffected by her addiction (although she was rumored to be spending half of her $1,000 weekly salary on heroin), but she became increasingly unreliable. When she was arrested for possession in 1947, she lost her cabaret card (her license to perform), could no longer perform in nightclubs, and so had to rely on her very small recording income. Through the 1950s, her voice began to show the effects of hard living, but she continued to record and to perform in Europe; in 1956, she published a popular autobiography, *Lady Sings the Blues* (later made into a film starring Diana Ross). In 1959, at the age of just forty-four, she collapsed of heart and liver failure, brought on by drug abuse.

Billie Holliday in the 1950s (© Bettman/Corbis).

ZORA NEALE HURSTON
1891–1960

One of the most important American writers of the twentieth century, Zora Neale Hurston nevertheless died almost unknown and forgotten. During her lifetime, she authored seven books, published widely in periodicals, wrote and produced plays, and did extensive anthropological fieldwork, but she also worked as a maid, a librarian, and a teacher. She had been at the center of a major artistic movement—the Harlem Renaissance—and had spent years with common working folk; she was both loved and reviled by many in the African American community. She was indeed a contradictory figure.

Hurston grew up in an all-black community, Eatonville, Florida, where her father was a three-term mayor of the town. After her mother's death in 1904, Hurston's formal schooling ended when her father and his new wife rejected her, and she went to work as a maid. She eventually moved north, where she was able to go back to school in Baltimore. When she enrolled at Howard University (which she paid for by working as a manicurist), she met prominent African American intellectuals and artists and began writing. In 1925, she won a literary award for her first short story, "Spunk." On the strength of this publication, Hurston moved to New York to settle in Harlem just when African American arts were beginning to flourish there.

In New York, Hurston continued to write and studied at both Barnard College and Columbia. Her talent for representing the lives, stories, and language of southern blacks caught the attention of the most prominent folklorist of the time, Franz Boas, who helped her to understand the value of preserving African American culture. Hurston undertook serious field research, eventually publishing books on oral traditions and voodoo in the South and the Caribbean, as well as writing and producing plays and revues that featured the tales and songs she had collected. While working as a folklorist, Hurston was also writing fiction, including the work for which she is best known, *Their Eyes Were Watching God* (1937). This novel focuses on a woman's search for a fulfilling life in African American Florida. *Their Eyes* is valuable not only for its representation of the struggles of a woman to make her way in the world but also for its vivid evocation of black culture. In its time, however, its reception was mixed: while many recognized the high quality of the narrative, others rejected its representation of black people as relatively untouched by white prejudice. Some also feared that the novel's use of folklore depicted African Americans as ignorant and superstitious.

Like much of *Their Eyes Were Watching God,* the selection below, "Sweat," is set in Eatonville and features rich language and storytelling as it focuses on the story of an unsuccessful marriage. Some readers may resent the depiction of the husband as so evil, but one can see the men on the front porch of the store as a counterpoint, something that distinguishes between the abusive Sykes and men in general. The men on the porch function like a classical chorus, commenting on the action of the narrative. The story also evokes biblical imagery, gothic tales, and stories about the strength of working women; it stands as one of Hurston's most successful pieces of short fiction.

In 1948, Hurston was falsely accused of sexually abusing a young boy, and despite being completely exonerated, she was never able to recover from the public scandal. She returned to Florida, where she worked as a librarian, teacher, and, eventually, once again, maid. She died of a stroke, alone in a welfare home. She was largely forgotten until the 1970s, when scholar Robert Hemenway and novelist Alice Walker began to reclaim her place in literary history. Walker found Hurston's grave site and erected a tombstone, claiming her as "A Genius of the South / Novelist, Folklorist, Anthropologist."

Sweat

It was eleven o'clock of a Spring night in Florida. It was Sunday. Any other night, Delia Jones would have been in bed for two hours by this time. But she was a washwoman, and Monday morning meant a great deal to her. So she collected the soiled clothes on Saturday when she returned the clean things. Sunday night after church, she sorted them and put the white things to soak. It saved her almost a half day's start. A great hamper in the bedroom held the clothes that she brought home. It was so much neater than a number of bundles lying around.

She squatted in the kitchen floor beside the great pile of clothes, sorting them into small heaps according to color, and humming a song in a mournful key, but wondering through it all where Sykes, her husband, had gone with her horse and buckboard.

Just then something long, round, limp and black fell upon her shoulders and slithered to the floor beside her. A great terror took hold of her. It softened her knees and dried her mouth so that it was a full minute before she could cry out or move. Then she saw that it was the big bull whip her husband liked to carry when he drove.

She lifted her eyes to the door and saw him standing there bent over with laughter at her fright. She screamed at him.

"Sykes, what you throw dat whip on me like dat? You know it would skeer me—looks just like a snake, an' you knows how skeered Ah is of snakes."

"Course Ah knowed it! That's how come Ah done it." He slapped his leg with his hand and almost rolled on the ground in his mirth. "If you such a big fool dat you got to have a fit over a earth worm or a string, Ah don't keer how bad Ah skeer you."

"You ain't got no business doing it. Gawd knows it's a sin. Some day Ah'm gointuh drop dead from some of yo' foolishness. 'Nother thing, where you been wid mah rig? Ah feeds dat pony. He aint fuh you to be drivin' wid no bull whip."

"You sho is one aggravatin' nigger woman!" he declared and stepped into the room. She resumed her work and did not answer him at once. "Ah done tole you time and again to keep them white folks' clothes outa dis house."

He picked up the whip and glared down at her. Delia went on with her work. She went out into the yard and returned with a galvanized tub and sat it on the washbench. She saw that Sykes had kicked all of the clothes together again, and now stood in her way truculently, his whole manner hoping, *praying,* for an argument. But she walked calmly around him and commenced to re-sort the things.

"Next time, Ah'm gointer kick 'em outdoors," he threatened as he struck a match along the leg of his corduroy breeches.

Delia never looked up from her work, and her thin, stooped shoulders sagged further.

"Ah aint for no fuss t'night, Sykes. Ah just come from taking sacrament at the church house."

He snorted scornfully. "Yeah, you just come from de church house on a Sunday night, but heah you is gone to work on them clothes. You ain't nothing but a hypocrite. One of them amen-corner Christians—sing, whoop, and shout, then come home and wash white folks clothes on the Sabbath."

He stepped roughly upon the whitest pile of things, kicking them helter-skelter as he crossed the room. His wife gave a little scream of dismay, and quickly gathered them together again.

"Sykes, you quit grindin' dirt into these clothes! How can Ah git through by Sat'day if Ah don't start on Sunday?"

"Ah don't keer if you never git through. Anyhow, Ah done promised Gawd and a couple of other men, Ah aint gointer have it in mah house. Don't gimme no lip neither, else Ah'll throw 'em out and put mah fist up side yo' head to boot."

Delia's habitual meekness seemed to slip from her shoulders like a blown scarf. She was on her feet; her poor little body, her bare knuckly hands bravely defying the strapping hulk before her.

"Look heah, Sykes, you done gone too fur. Ah been married to you fur fifteen years, and Ah been takin' in washin' fur fifteen years. Sweat, sweat, sweat! Work and sweat, cry and sweat, pray and sweat!"

"What's that got to do with me?" he asked brutally.

"What's it got to do with you, Sykes! Mah tub of suds is filled yo' belly with vittles more times than yo' hands is filled it. Mah sweat is done paid for this house and Ah reckon Ah kin keep on sweatin' in it."

She seized the iron skillet from the stove and struck a defensive pose, which act surprised him greatly, coming from her. It cowed him and he did not strike her as he usually did.

"Naw you won't," she panted, "that ole snaggle-toothed black woman you runnin' with aint comin' heah to pile up on *mah* sweat and blood. You aint paid for nothin' on this place, and Ah'm gointer stay right heah till Ah'm toted out foot foremost."

"Well, you better quit gittin' me riled up, else they'll be totin' you out sooner than you expect. Ah'm so tired of you Ah don't know whut to do. Gawd! How Ah hates skinny wimmen!"

A little awed by this new Delia, he sidled out of the door and slammed the back gate after him. He did not say where he had gone, but she knew too well. She knew very well that he would not return until nearly daybreak also. Her work over, she went on to bed but not to sleep at once. Things had come to a pretty pass!

She lay awake, gazing upon the debris that cluttered their matrimonial trail. Not an image left standing along the way. Anything like flowers had long ago been drowned in the salty stream that had been pressed from her heart. Her tears, her sweat, her blood. She had brought love to the union and he had brought a longing after the flesh. Two months after the wedding, he had given her the first brutal beating. She had the memory of his numerous trips to Orlando with all of his wages when he had returned to her penniless, even before the first year had passed. She was young and soft then, but now she thought of her knotty, muscled limbs, her harsh knuckly hands, and drew herself up into an unhappy little ball in the middle of the big feather bed. Too late now to hope for love, even if it were not Bertha it would be someone else. This case differed from the others only in that she was bolder than the others. Too late for everything except her little home. She had built it for her old days, and planted one by one the trees and flowers there. It was lovely to her, lovely.

Somehow, before sleep came, she found herself saying aloud: "Oh well, whatever goes over the Devil's back, is got to come under his belly. Sometime or ruther, Sykes, like everybody else, is gointer reap his sowing." After that she was able to build a spiritual earthworks against her husband. His shells could no longer reach her. *Amen*. She went to sleep and slept until he announced his presence in bed by kicking her feet and rudely snatching the cover away.

"Gimme some kivah heah, an' git yo' damn foots over on yo' own side! Ah oughter mash you in yo' mouf fuh drawing dat skillet on me."

Delia went clear to the rail without answering him. A triumphant indifference to all that he was or did.

The week was as full of work for Delia as all other weeks, and Saturday found her behind her little pony, collecting and delivering clothes.

It was a hot, hot day near the end of July. The village men on Joe Clarke's porch even chewed cane listlessly. They did not hurl the cane-knots as usual. They let them dribble over the edge of the porch. Even conversation had collapsed under the heat.

"Heah come Delia Jones," Jim Merchant said, as the shaggy pony came 'round the bend of the road toward them. The rusty buckboard was heaped with baskets of crisp, clean laundry.

"Yep," Joe Lindsay agreed. "Hot or col', rain or shine, jes ez reg'lar ez de weeks roll roun' Delia carries 'em an' fetches 'em on Sat'day."

"She better if she wanter eat," said Moss. "Sykes Jones aint wuth de shot an' powder hit would tek tuh kill 'em. Not to *huh* he aint."

"He sho' aint," Walter Thomas chimed in. "It's too bad, too, cause she wuz a right pritty li'l trick when he got huh. Ah'd uh mah'ied huh mahseff if he hadnter beat me to it."

Delia nodded briefly at the men as she drove past.

"Too much knockin' will ruin *any* 'oman. He done beat huh 'nough tuh kill three women, let 'lone change they looks," said Elijah Moseley. "How Sykes kin stommuck dat big black greasy Mogul he's layin' roun' wid, gits me. Ah swear dat eight-rock[1] couldn't kiss a sardine can Ah done thowed out de back do' 'way las' yeah."

"Aw, she's fat, thass how come. He's allus been crazy 'bout fat women," put in Merchant. "He'd a' been tied up wid one long time ago if he could a' found one tuh have him. Did Ah tell yuh 'bout him come sidlin' roun' *mah* wife—bringin' her a basket uh pee-cans outa his yard fuh a present? Yessir, mah wife! She tol' him tuh take 'em right straight back home, cause Delia works so hard ovah dat washtub she reckon everything on de place taste lak sweat an' soapsuds. Ah jus' wisht Ah'd a' caught 'im 'roun' dere! Ah'd a' made his hips ketch on fiah down dat shell road."

"Ah know he done it, too. Ah sees 'im grinnin' at every 'oman dat passes," Walter Thomas said. "But even so, he useter eat some mighty big hunks uh humble pie tuh git dat lil' 'oman he got. She wuz ez pretty ez a speckled pup! Dat wuz

1. Mogul: a great personage; eight-rock: blue-   of coal mines.
black color of the coal found at the deepest level

fifteen yeahs ago. He useter be so skeered un losin' huh, she could make him do some parts of a husband's duty. Dey never wuz de same in de mind."

"There oughter be a law about him," said Lindsay. "He aint fit tuh carry guts tuh a bear."

Clarke spoke for the first time. "Taint no law on earth dat kin make a man be decent if it aint in 'im. There's plenty men dat takes a wife lak dey do a joint uh sugar-cane. It's round, juicy an' sweet when dey gits it. But dey squeeze an' grind, squeeze an' grind an' wring tell dey wring every drop uh pleasure dat's in 'em out. When dey's satisfied dat dey is wrung dry, dey treats 'em jes lak dey do a cane-chew. Dey thows 'em away. Dey knows whut dey is doin' while dey is at it, an' hates theirselves fuh it but they keeps on hangin' after huh tell she's empty. Den dey hates huh fuh bein' a cane-chew an' in de way."

"We oughter take Sykes an' dat stray 'oman uh his'n down in Lake Howell swamp an' lay on de rawhide till they cain't say 'Lawd a' mussy.' He allus wuz uh ovahbearin' niggah, but since dat white 'oman from up north done teached 'im how to run a automobile, he done got too biggety to live—an' we oughter kill 'im," Old Man Anderson advised.

A grunt of approval went around the porch. But the heat was melting their civic virtue and Elijah Moseley began to bait Joe Clarke.

"Come on, Joe, git a melon outa dere an' slice it up for yo' customers. We'se all sufferin' wid de heat. De bear's done got *me*!"

"Thass right, Joe, a watermelon is jes' whut Ah needs tuh cure de eppizu-dicks."[2] Walter Thomas joined forces with Moseley. "Come on dere, Joe. We all is steady customers an' you aint set us up in a long time. Ah chooses dat long, bow-legged Floridy favorite."

"A god, an' be dough. You all gimme twenty cents and slice away," Clarke retorted. "Ah needs a col' slice m'self. Heah, everybody chip in. Ah'll lend y'all mah meat knife."

The money was quickly subscribed and the huge melon brought forth. At that moment, Sykes and Bertha arrived. A determined silence fell on the porch and the melon was put away again.

Merchant snapped down the blade of his jack-knife and moved toward the store door.

"Come on in, Joe, an' gimme a slab uh sow belly an' uh pound un coffee—almost fuhgot 'twas Sat'day. Got to git on home." Most of the men left also.

Just then Delia drove past on her way home, as Sykes was ordering magnificently for Bertha. It pleased him for Delia to see.

"Git whutsoever yo' heart desires, Honey. Wait a minute, Joe. Give huh two botles uh strawberry soda-water, uh quart uh parched ground-peas, and a block uh chewin' gum."

With all this they left the store, with Sykes reminding Bertha that this was his town and she could have it if she wanted it.

The men returned soon after they left, and held their watermelon feast.

"Where did Sykes Jones git dat 'oman from nohow?" Lindsay asked.

"Ovah Apopka. Guess dey musta been cleanin' out de town when she lef'. She don't look lak a thing but a hunk uh liver wid hair on it."

2. *A rapidly spreading epidemic among animals* (Greek: *epi*, "on," "upon," "at"; *zoo*, "living being," "animal").

"Well, she sho' kin squall," Dave Carter contributed. "When she gits ready tuh laff, she jes' opens huh mouf an' latches it back tuh de las' notch. No ole grandpa alligator down in Lake Bell aint got nothin' on huh."

Bertha had been in town three months now. Sykes was still paying her room rent at Della Lewis'—the only house in town that would have taken her in. Sykes took her frequently to Winter Park to "stomps." He still assured her that he was the swellest man in the state.

"Sho' you kin have dat lil' ole house soon's Ah kin git dat 'oman outa dere. Everything b'longs tuh me an' you sho' kin have it. Ah sho' 'bominates uh skinny 'oman. Lawdy, you sho' is got one portly shape on you! You kin git *anything* you wants. Dis is *mah* town an' you sho' kin have it."

Delia's work-worn knees crawled over the earth in Gethsemane and up the rocks of Calvary many, many times during these months.[3] She avoided the villagers and meeting places in her efforts to be blind and deaf. But Bertha nullified this to a degree, by coming to Delia's house to call Sykes out to her at the gate.

Delia and Sykes fought all the time now with no peaceful interludes. They slept and ate in silence. Two or three times Delia had attempted a timid friendliness, but she was repulsed each time. It was plain that the breaches must remain agape.

The sun had burned July to August. The heat streamed down like a million hot arrows, smiting all things living upon the earth. Grass withered, leaves browned, snakes went blind in shedding and men and dogs went mad. Dog days!

Delia came home one day and found Sykes there before her. She wondered, but started to go on into the house without speaking, even though he was standing in the kitchen door and she must either stoop under his arm or ask him to move. He made no room for her. She noticed a soap box beside the steps, but paid no particular attention to it, knowing that he must have brought it there. As she was stooping to pass under his outstretched arm, he suddenly pushed her backward, laughingly.

"Look in de box dere Delia, Ah done brung yuh somethin'!"

She nearly fell upon the box in her stumbling, and when she saw what it held, she all but fainted outright.

"Sykes! Sykes, mah Gawd! You take dat rattlesnake 'way from heah! You *gottuh*. Oh, Jesus, have mussy!"

"Ah aint gut tuh do nuthin' uh de kin'—fact is Ah aint got tuh do nothin' but die. Taint no use uh you puttin' on airs makin' out lak you skeered uh dat snake—he's gointer stay right heah tell he die. He wouldn't bite me cause Ah knows how tuh handle 'im. Nohow he wouldn't risk breakin' out his fangs 'gin yo' skinny laigs."

"Naw, now Sykes, don't keep dat thing 'roun' heah tuh skeer me tuh death. You knows Ah'm even feared uh earth worms. Thass de biggest snake Ah evah did see. Kill 'im Sykes, please."

3. Gethsemane: the garden in which Jesus prayed before his crucifixion; Calvary: the name (in English) of the hill on which Jesus was crucified.

"Doan ast me tuh do nothin' fuh yuh. Goin' 'roun' tryin' tuh be so damn astorperious. Naw, Ah aint gonna kill it. Ah think uh damn sight mo' uh him dan you! Dat's a nice snake an' anybody doan lak 'im kin jes' hit de grit."[4]

The village soon heard that Sykes had the snake, and came to see and ask questions.

"How de hen-fire did you ketch dat six-foot rattler, Sykes?" Thomas asked.

"He's full uh frogs so he caint hardly move, thass how Ah eased up on 'm. But Ah'm a snake charmer an' knows how tuh handle 'em. Shux, dat aint nothin'. Ah could ketch one eve'y day if Ah so wanted tuh."

"Whut he needs is a heavy hick'ry club leaned real heavy on his head. Dat's de bes' way tuh charm a rattlesnake."

"Naw, Walt, y'all jes' don't understand dese diamon' backs lak Ah do," said Sykes in a superior tone of voice.

The village agreed with Walter, but the snake stayed on. His box remained by the kitchen door with its screen wire covering. Two or three days later it had digested its meal of frogs and literally came to life. It rattled at every movement in the kitchen or the yard. One day as Delia came down the kitchen steps she saw his chalky-white fangs curved like scimitars hung in the wire meshes. This time she did not run away with averted eyes as usual. She stood for a long time in the doorway in a red fury that grew bloodier for every second that she regarded the creature that was her torment.

That night she broached the subject as soon as Sykes sat down to the table.

"Sykes, Ah wants you tuh take dat snake 'way fum heah. You done starved me an' Ah put up widcher, you done beat me an Ah took dat, but you done kilt all mah insides bringin' dat varmint heah."

Sykes poured out a saucer full of coffee and drank it deliberately before he answered her.

"A whole lot Ah keer 'bout how you feels inside uh out. Dat snake aint goin' no damn wheah till Ah gits ready fuh 'im tuh go. So fur as beatin' is concerned, yuh aint took near all dat you gointer take ef yuh stay 'roun' me."

Delia pushed back her plate and got up from the table. "Ah hates you, Sykes," she said calmly. "Ah hates you tuh de same degree dat Ah useter love yuh. Ah done took an' took till mah belly is full up tuh mah neck. Dat's de reason Ah got mah letter fum de church an' moved mah membership tuh Woodbridge—so Ah don't haftuh take no sacrament wid yuh. Ah don't wantuh see yuh 'roun' me a-tall. Lay 'roun' wid dat 'oman all yuh wants tuh, but gwan 'way fum me an' mah house. Ah hates yuh lak uh suck-egg dog."

Sykes almost let the huge wad of corn bread and collard greens he was chewing fall out of his mouth in amazement. He had a hard time whipping himself up to the proper fury to try to answer Delia.

"Well, Ah'm glad you does hate me. Ah'm sho' tiahed uh you hangin' ontuh me. Ah don't want yuh. Look at yuh stringey ole neck! Yo' rawbony laigs an' arms is enough tuh cut uh man tuh death. You looks jes' lak de devvul's doll-baby tuh me. You cain't hate me no worse dan Ah hates you. Ah been hatin' you fuh years."

4. Astorperious: arrogant, perhaps coined by   hit the road, leave.
Hurston or used in black social circles; hit de grit:

"Yo' ole black hide don't look lak nothin' tuh me, but uh passel uh wrinkled up rubber, wid yo' big ole yeahs flappin' on each side lak uh paih uh buzzard wings. Don't think Ah'm gointuh be run 'way fum mah house neither. Ah'm goin' tuh de white folks bout *you,* mah young man, de very nex' time you lay yo' han's on me. Mah cup is done run ovah." Delia said this with no signs of fear and Sykes departed from the house, threatening her, but made not the slightest move to carry out any of them.

That night he did not return at all, and the next day being Sunday, Delia was glad that she did not have to quarrel before she hitched up her pony and drove the four miles to Woodbridge.

She stayed to the night service—"love feast"—which was very warm and full of spirit. In the emotional winds her domestic trials were borne far and wide so that she sang as she drove homeward,

> Jurden[5] water, black an' col'
> Chills de body, not de soul
> An' Ah wantah cross Jurden in uh calm time.

She came from the barn to the kitchen door and stopped.

"What's de mattah, ol' satan, you aint kickin' up yo' racket?" She addressed the snake's box. Complete silence. She went on into the house with a new hope in its birth struggles. Perhaps her threat to go the white folks had frightened Sykes! Perhaps he was sorry! Fifteen years of misery and suppression had brought Delia to the place where she would hope *anything* that looked towards a way over or through her wall of inhibitions.

She felt in the match safe behind the stove at once for a match. There was only one there.

"Dat niggah wouldn't fetch nothin' heah tuh save his rotten neck, but he kin run thew whut Ah brings quick enough. Now he done toted off nigh on tuh haff uh box uh matches. He done had dat 'oman heah in mah house, too."

Nobody but a woman could tell how she knew this even before she struck the match. But she did and it put her into a new fury.

Presently she brought in the tubs to put the white things to soak. This time she decided she need not bring the hamper out of the bedroom; she would go in there and do the sorting. She picked up the pot-bellied lamp and went in. The room was small and the hamper stood hard by the foot of the white iron bed. She could sit and reach through the bedposts—resting as she worked.

"Ah wantah cross Jurden in uh calm time." She was singing again. The mood of the "love feast" had returned. She threw back the lid of the basket almost gaily. Then, moved by both horror and terror, she sprung back toward the door. *There lay the snake in the basket!* He moved sluggishly at first, but even as she turned round and round, jumped up and down in an insanity of fear, he began to stir vigorously. She saw him pouring his awful beauty from the basket upon the bed, then she seized the lamp and ran as fast as she could to the kitchen. The wind from the open door blew out the light and the darkness added to her terror. She sped to the darkness of the yard, slamming the door after her before she thought to set down the lamp. She did not feel safe even on the ground, so she climbed up in the hay barn.

5. Jordan, a river in what is now Israel, in which St. John the Baptist baptized Jesus.

There for an hour or more she lay sprawled upon the hay a gibbering wreck.

Finally she grew quiet, and after that, coherent thought. With this, stalked through her a cold, bloody rage. Hours of this. A period of introspection, a space of retrospection, then a mixture of both. Out of this an awful calm.

"Well, Ah done de bes' Ah could. If things aint right, Gawd knows taint mah fault."

She went to sleep—a twitchy sleep—and woke up to a faint gray sky. There was a loud hollow sound below. She peered out. Sykes was at the wood-pile, demolishing a wire-covered box.

He hurried to the kitchen door, but hung outside there some minutes before he entered, and stood some minutes more inside before he closed it after him.

The gray in the sky was spreading. Delia descended without fear now, and crouched beneath the low bedroom window. The drawn shade shut out the dawn, shut in the night. But the thin walls held back no sound.

"Dat ol' scratch is woke up now!" She mused at the tremendous whirr inside, which every woodsman knows, is one of the sound illusions. The rattler is a ventriloquist. His whirr sounds to the right, to the left, straight ahead, behind, close under foot—everywhere but where it is. Woe to him who guesses wrong unless he is prepared to hold up his end of the argument! Sometimes he strikes without rattling at all.

Inside, Sykes heard nothing until he knocked a pot lid off the stove while trying to reach the match safe in the dark. He had emptied his pockets at Bertha's.

The snake seemed to wake up under the stove and Sykes made a quick leap into the bedroom. In spite of the gin he had had, his head was clearing now.

"Mah Gawd!" he chattered, "ef Ah could on'y strack uh light!"

The rattling ceased for a moment as he stood paralyzed. He waited. It seemed that the snake waited also.

"Oh fuh de light! Ah thought he'd be too sick"—Sykes was muttering to himself when the whirr began again, closer, right underfoot this time. Long before this, Sykes' ability to think had been flattened down to primitive instinct and he leaped—onto the bed.

Outside Delia heard a cry that might have come from a maddened chimpanzee, a stricken gorilla. All the terror, all the horror, all the rage that man possibly could express, without a recognizable human sound.

A tremendous stir inside there, another series of animal screams, the intermittent whirr of the reptile. The shade torn violently down from the window, letting in the red dawn, a huge brown hand seizing the window stick, great dull blows upon the wooden floor punctuating the gibberish of sound long after the rattle of the snake had abruptly subsided. All this Delia could see and hear from her place beneath the window, and it made her ill. She crept over to the four-o'clocks and stretched herself on the cool earth to recover.

She lay there. "Delia, Delia!" She could hear Sykes calling in a most despairing tone as one who expected no answer. The sun crept on up, and he called. Delia could not move—her legs were gone flabby. She never moved, he called, and the sun kept rising.

"Mah Gawd!" she heard him moan. "Mah Gawd fum Heben!" She heard him stumbling about and got up from her flower-bed. The sun was growing warm. As she approached the door she heard him call out hopefully, "Delia, is dat you Ah heah?"

She saw him on his hands and knees as soon as she reached the door. He crept an inch or two toward her—all that he was able, and she saw his horribly swollen neck and his one open eye shining with hope. A surge of pity too strong to support bore her away from that eye that must, could not, fail to see the tubs. He would see the lamp. Orlando with its doctors was too far. She could scarcely reach the Chinaberry tree, where she waited in the growing heat while inside she knew the cold river was creeping up and up to extinguish that eye which must know by now that she knew.

1926

◄ NELLA LARSEN ►
1891–1964

Although she was for a time considered the leading African American woman of letters and was the first African American woman to be awarded a Guggenheim fellowship, Nella Larsen lived most of her last thirty years in obscurity, her work largely forgotten. During the 1920s, she was a major figure in the Harlem Renaissance, including among her friends the writers W. E. B. DuBois, James Weldon Johnson, and Jessie Fauset. After two successful novels, *Quicksand* (1928) and *Passing* (1929), her literary future looked bright. But when she returned from a fellowship year in Europe, she came home to charges of plagiarism (which were later disproven), to rejection of her new work, and to a divorce from her husband of fourteen years. She resumed her previous profession as a nurse and died alone in her apartment in Manhattan.

Nella Larsen was the daughter of a Danish woman and a man who is usually described as West Indian, but sometimes as African American. When she was a small child, her mother married a white man, who, it appears, rejected Nella because of her color (when Larsen died, her estate went to her half-sister, who claimed not even to have known she had a sister). She studied at Fisk University and at the University of Copenhagen and took a degree in nursing from Lincoln Hospital School of Nursing in New York City in 1915. She worked for a time at the Tuskegee Institute before returning to New York to work in the hospital where she had studied. By 1921, she had left nursing and taken a job working as a librarian, and it was during this period that she began writing, publishing short stories and some young-adult stories under pseudonyms. When her health began to suffer, Larsen quit working and took up writing full-time, producing her two major works of fiction. *Quicksand* and *Passing* focus on the difficulties African American women faced in early-twentieth-century America when trying to find their way in the world. Her heroines are by turns too dark or too light to fit comfortably in black culture but do not fit in a racist white culture, either. They are cultured and sophisticated but cannot find a role that takes advantage of their talents. Her works are indeed "novel" in their treatment of then-forbidden topics for women writers: illegitimacy, mixed-race heritage, and the frustrations of living in a racist society.

The story included here—"Sanctuary"—appeared in the journal *Forum* in 1930 and was her last published work. Raising the issue of race loyalty, it addresses questions of race from a different perspective than do her novels. When a

young man confesses a murder to Annie Poole, she agrees to hide him from the
authorities, despite her disdain for him, only because he is poor and black and the
men coming after him are white. Written in an era when lynching was a major
issue for African American activists and writers, "Sanctuary" can be read as a
warning against the lawlessness of white Americans (see pp. 1419–20). Read in
the context of her novels, it can be seen as another representation of the complex
problems facing early-twentieth-century African American women.

Sanctuary

1

On the Southern coast, between Merton and Shawboro, there is a strip of desolation some half a mile wide and nearly ten miles long between the sea and old fields
of ruined plantations. Skirting the edge of this narrow jungle is a partly grown-
over road which still shows traces of furrows made by the wheels of wagons that
have long since rotted away or been cut into firewood. This road is little used,
now that the state has built its new highway a bit to the west and wagons are less
numerous than automobiles.

In the forsaken road a man was walking swiftly. But in spite of his hurry, at
every step he set down his feet with infinite care, for the night was windless and
the heavy silence intensified each sound; even the breaking of a twig could be
plainly heard. And the man had need of caution as well as haste.

Before a lonely cottage that shrank timidly back from the road the man hesitated a moment, then struck out across the patch of green in front of it. Stepping
behind a clump of bushes close to the house, he looked in through the lighted window at Annie Poole, standing at her kitchen table mixing the supper biscuits.

He was a big, black man with pale brown eyes in which there was an odd
mixture of fear and amazement. The light showed streaks of gray soil on his heavy,
sweating face and great hands, and on his torn clothes. In his woolly hair clung
bits of dried leaves and dead grass.

He made a gesture as if to tap on the window, but turned away to the door
instead. Without knocking he opened it and went in.

2

The woman's brown gaze was immediately on him, though she did not move. She
said, "You ain't in no hurry, is you, Jim Hammer?" It wasn't, however, entirely
a question.

"Ah's in trubble, Mis' Poole," the man explained, his voice shaking, his fingers twitching.

"W'at you done done now?"

"Shot a man, Mis' Poole."

"Trufe?" The woman seemed calm. But the word was spat out.

"Yas'm. Shot 'im." In the man's tone was something of wonder, as if he himself could not quite believe that he had really done this thing which he affirmed.

"Daid?"

"Dunno, Mis' Poole. Dunno."

"White man o' niggah?"

"Cain't say, Mis' Poole. White man, Ah reckons."

Annie Poole looked at him with cold contempt. She was a tiny, withered woman—fifty perhaps—with a wrinkled face the color of old copper, framed by a crinkly mass of white hair. But about her small figure was some quality of hardness that belied her appearance of frailty. At last she spoke, boring her sharp little eyes into those of the anxious creature before her.

"An' w'at am you lookin' foh me to do 'bout et?"

"Jes' lemme stop till dey's gone by. Hide me till dey passes. Reckon dey ain't fur off now." His begging voice changed to a frightened whimper. "Foh de Lawd's sake, Mis' Poole, lemme stop."

And why, the woman inquired caustically, should she run the dangerous risk of hiding him?

"Obadiah, he'd lemme stop if he was to home," the man whined.

Annie Poole sighed. "Yas," she admitted slowly, reluctantly, "Ah spec' he would. Obadiah, he's too good to youall no 'count trash." Her slight shoulders lifted in a hopeless shrug. "Yas, Ah reckon he'd do it. Emspecial' seein' how he allus set such a heap o' store by you. Cain't see w'at foh, mahse'f. Ah shuah don' see nuffin' in you but a heap o' dirt."

But a look of irony, of cunning, of complicity passed over her face. She went on, "Still, 'siderin' all an' all, how Obadiah's right fon' o' you, an' how white folks is white folks, Ah'm a-gwine hide you dis one time."

Crossing the kitchen, she opened a door leading into a small bedroom, saying, "Git yo'se'f in dat dere feather baid an' Ah'm a-gwine put de clo's on de top. Don' reckon dey'll fin' you ef dey does look foh you in mah house. An Ah don' spec' dey'll go foh to do dat. Not lessen you been keerless an' let 'em smell you out gittin' hyah." She turned on him a withering look. "But you allus been triflin'. Can't do nuffin' propah. An' Ah'm a-tellin' you ef dey warn't white folks an' you a po' niggah, Ah shuah wouldn't be lettin' you mess up mah feather baid dis ebenin', 'cose Ah jes' plain don' want you hyah. Ah done kep' mahse'f outen trubble all mah life. So's Obadiah."

"Ah's powahful 'bliged to you, Mis' Poole. You shuah am one good 'oman. De Lawd'll mos' suttinly—"

Annie Pool cut him off. "Dis ain't no time foh all dat kin' o' fiddle-de-roll. Ah does mah duty as Ah sees et 'thout no thanks from you. Ef de Lawd had gib you a white face 'stead o' dat dere black one, Ah shuah would turn you out. Now hush yo' mouf an' git yo'se'f in. An' don' git movin' and scrunchin' undah dose covahs and git yo'se'f kotched in mah house."

Without further comment the man did as he was told. After he had laid his soiled body and grimy garments between her snowy sheets, Annie Poole carefully rearranged the covering and placed piles of freshly laundered linen on top. Then she gave a pat here and there, eyed the result, and, finding it satisfactory, went back to her cooking.

3

Jim Hammer settled down to the racking business of waiting until the approaching danger should have passed him by. Soon savory odors seeped in to him and he realized that he was hungry. He wished that Annie Poole would bring him something to eat. Just one biscuit. But she wouldn't, he knew. Not she. She was a hard one, Obadiah's mother.

By and by he fell into a sleep from which he was dragged back by the rumbling sound of wheels in the road outside. For a second fear clutched so tightly at him that he almost leaped from the suffocating shelter of the bed in order to make some active attempt to escape the horror that his capture meant. There was a spasm at his heart, a pain so sharp, so slashing, that he had to suppress an impulse to cry out. He felt himself falling. Down, down, down . . . Everything grew dim and very distant in his memory. . . . Vanished . . . Came rushing back.

Outside there was silence. He strained his ears. Nothing. No footsteps. No voices. They had gone on then. Gone without even stopping to ask Annie Poole if she had seen him pass that way. A sigh of relief slipped from him. His thick lips curled in an ugly, cunning smile. It had been smart of him to think of coming to Obadiah's mother's to hide. She was an old demon, but he was safe in her house.

He lay a short while longer, listening intently, and, hearing nothing, started to get up. But immediately he stopped, his yellow eyes glowing like pale flames. He had heard the unmistakable sound of men coming toward the house. Swiftly he slid back into the heavy, hot stuffiness of the bed and lay listening fearfully.

The terrifying sounds drew nearer. Slowly. Heavily. Just for a moment he thought they were not coming in—they took so long. But there was a light knock and the noise of a door being opened. His whole body went taut. His feet felt frozen, his hands clammy, his tongue like a weighted, dying thing. His pounding heart made it hard for his straining ears to hear what they were saying out there.

"Ebenin', Mistah Lowndes." Annie Poole's voice sounded as it always did, sharp and dry.

There was no answer. Or had he missed it? With slow care he shifted his position, bringing his head nearer the edge of the bed. Still he heard nothing. What were they waiting for? Why didn't they ask about him?

Annie Poole, it seemed, was of the same mind. "Ah don' reckon youall done traipsed way out hyah jes' foh yo' healf," she hinted.

"There's bad news for you, Annie, I'm 'fraid." The sheriff's voice was low and queer.

Jim Hammer visualized him standing out there—a tall, stooped man, his white tobacco-stained mustache drooping limply at the ends, his nose hooked and sharp, his eyes blue and cold. Bill Lowndes was a hard one too. And white.

"W'atall bad news, Mistah Lowndes?" The woman put the question quietly, directly.

"Obadiah—" the sheriff began—hesitated—began again. "Obadiah—ah—er—he's outside, Annie. I'm 'fraid—"

"Shucks! You done missed. Obadiah, he ain't done nuffin', Mistah Lowndes. Obadiah!" she called stridently, "Obadiah! Git hyah an' splain yo'se'f."

But Obadiah didn't answer, didn't come in. Other men came in. Came in with steps that dragged and halted. No one spoke. Not even Annie Poole. Something was laid carefully upon the floor.

"Obadiah, chile," his mother said softly, "Obadiah, chile." Then, with sudden alarm, "He ain't daid, is he? Mistah Lowndes! Obadiah, he ain't daid?"

Jim Hammer didn't catch the answer to that pleading question. A new fear was stealing over him.

"There was a to-do, Annie," Bill Lowndes explained gently, "at the garage back o' the factory. Fellow tryin' to steal tires. Obadiah heerd a noise an' run out with two or three others. Scared the rascal all right. Fired off his gun an' run. We allow et to he Jim Hammer. Picked up his cap back there. Never was no 'count. Thievin' and sly. But we'll get 'im, Annie. We'll get 'im."

The man huddled in the feather bed prayed silently. "Oh, Lawd! Ah didn't go to do et. Not Obadiah, Lawd. You knows dat. You knows et." And into his frenzied brain came the thought that it would be better for him to get up and go out to them before Annie Poole gave him away. For he was lost now. With all his great strength he tried to get himself out of the bed. But he couldn't.

"Oh, Lawd!" he moaned. " Oh, Lawd!" His thoughts were bitter and they ran through his mind like panic. He knew that it had come to pass as it said somewhere in the Bible about the wicked. The Lord had stretched out his hand and smitten him. He was paralyzed. He couldn't move hand or foot. He moaned again. It was all there was left for him to do. For in the terror of this new calamity that had come upon him he had forgotten the waiting danger which was so near out there in the kitchen.

His hunters, however, didn't hear him. Bill Lowndes was saying, "We been a-lookin' for Jim out along the old road. Figured he'd make tracks for Shawboro. You ain't noticed anybody pass this evening', Annie?"

The reply came promptly, unwaveringly. "No, Ah ain't sees nobody pass. Not yet."

4

Jim Hammer caught his breath.

"Well," the sheriff concluded, "we'll be gittin' along. Obadiah was a mighty fine boy. Ef they was all like him—I'm sorry, Annie. Anything I c'n do, let me know."

"Thank you, Mistah Lowndes."

With the sound of the door closing on the departing men, power to move came back to the man in the bedroom. He pushed his dirt-caked feet out from the covers and rose up, but crouched down again. He wasn't cold now, but hot all over and burning. Almost he wished that Bill Lowndes and his men had taken him with them.

Annie Poole had come into the room.

It seemed a long time before Obadiah's mother spoke. When she did there were no tears, no reproaches; but there was a raging fury in her voice as she lashed out, "Git outer mah feather baid, Jim Hammer, an' outen mah house, an' don' nevah stop thankin' yo' Jesus he done gib you dat black face."

1930

CULTURAL COORDINATES
Anti-Lynching Campaigns

African American women were at the forefront of the protest against the hate crime known as lynching. Billie Holiday helped write the anti-lynching anthem "Strange Fruit" and then made it her signature song; in it, she describes the "strange and bitter crop" of "black bodies swinging in the southern breeze." At the end of Nella Larsen's "Sanctuary," Annie Poole ends up protecting her own son's murderer from a lynching, telling him, "don' nevah stop thankin' yo' Jesus he done giv you dat black face," thus declaring racial solidarity in the face of mob violence. Lynching was not aimed exclusively at African Americans, but they were by far the majority of its victims: between 1892 and 1940, there were over 3,000 recorded cases of lynching in the United States; of that number, more than 2,600 were of African Americans. While there were many people who worked to stop lynching in the United States—including many organizations of African American men and white women—few were more active in the struggle than were African American women. Among those activists, few were as instrumental in bringing this injustice to light as Ida B. Wells.

Wells was an extraordinary woman. Her parents died when she was still a teenager, and to raise her five younger siblings in the segregated South, she quit school, made herself look older, and got a job teaching. In 1884, when a train conductor attempted to force her into the Jim Crow car (the segregated black car), she fought back and later sued for having been forcibly ejected from the train. After she lost her lawsuit, she began writing editorials; within a few years, she was the co-owner of a newspaper and a nationally syndicated columnist, all before the age of thirty. When three of her friends—black co-owners of a grocery store that was competing with a white-owned business—were lynched in 1892, Wells realized what a national scandal lynching had become. She wrote an editorial that condemned not only the lynching itself but also the pretexts for it. As a result, she received so many death threats that she had to leave Tennessee to live in the North for the next thirty years.

> . . . *lynching was not an enforcement of law but a systematic campaign of terror.*

Lynch mobs often claimed that their victims had broken laws, sometimes falsely claiming that African American men had assaulted white women. Wells became what we would now call an investigative reporter, exposing the claims against the victims of lynching as unfounded, revealing that lynching was not an enforcement of law but a systematic campaign of terror. She pointed out the racial and regional natures of the crimes and showed that victims were often not guilty of any crime beyond things like "insolence," being a successful business owner, or exercising the right to vote. She showed how often women and even children were being lynched—fifty African American women were lynched between 1889 and 1918. In her three major anti-lynching works, *Southern Horrors: Lynch Law in All Its Phases* (1892), *A Red Record* (1895), and *Mob Rule in New Orleans*

(1900), she called the United States to task for its claims to support democracy in the world while tolerating mob rule and terrorism at home.

Wells would eventually become one of two African American women to help establish the National Association for the Advancement of Colored People (NAACP) and would found an organization to promote African American women's right to vote. The NAACP and several other organizations would carry on the fight against lynching. In 1922, Mary Talbert, the president of the National Association of Colored Women, worked with the NAACP to form a group of women known as the Anti-Lynching Crusaders, who tried to establish the country's first anti-lynching law, the Dyer Bill, which passed in the House of Representatives in 1922 but failed to be enacted due to a filibuster in the Senate. It was not until 1946 that the federal government would be able to successfully prosecute someone for lynching.

Lest we think that the phenomenon of lynching is purely a matter of history, poet Joy Harjo dedicates her poem "Strange Fruit" (an echo of the Billie Holiday song) to the memory of an NAACP activist who was lynched in 1986 in California for her work protesting the 1985 lynching of a young African American man (see pp. 1845–46).

EDNA ST. VINCENT MILLAY

1892–1950

Though she fell into critical disfavor after her death, Vincent Millay (she was called Vincent rather than Edna) was one of the most popular and important American poets of the first half of the twentieth century and is being rediscovered by a new generation of readers and critics. She wrote most often in traditional verse forms but infused them with rebellious—and feminist—perspectives. She lived an unconventional life, and her work, too, challenges ideas about women and women writers in the 1910s and 1920s.

Millay's unconventionality began in her childhood: when she was a small girl, her mother divorced her father for financial instability and raised Vincent and her sisters by herself, supporting them by working as a nurse. Millay began writing poetry and plays while she was still in high school, and she gained national attention as a poet at the age of twenty. She won the Pulitzer Prize for poetry when she was just thirty-one. She also wrote, directed, and starred in several plays, working with the Provincetown Players, a theater company co-founded by Susan Glaspell (pp. 1292–1303). During her career, she published seventeen volumes of poetry, four plays, an opera libretto, and a translation of Baudelaire; she also spoke and read widely.

Her personal life was almost as well known as her publishing life: an acknowledged bisexual, Millay was described as "intoxicating" and had numerous affairs with both men and women. She eventually married a man a good deal older than she who was a self-proclaimed feminist. He took care of her and managed her career while accepting her insistence on an "open" marriage. Millay was also politically active, working for several communist causes and against fascism; as she grew older, her poetry became increasingly political. She suffered a nervous breakdown in 1944, at least in part from the strain of World War II, and never fully regained her health. She died of heart failure a year after her husband's death, alone at her estate in upstate New York.

Our brief selection of poems here represents Millay's challenges to traditional notions of the sonnet—usually reserved for poems that extol the virtues of true love. In Millay's hands, the sonnet becomes more charged: in the poem "I, being born," it celebrates lust without love; in the case of "Sonnets from an Ungrafted Tree," it explores the experiences of a woman watching at the deathbed of a husband she does not love; in the case of sonnets from *Fatal Interview,* a failed affair. We also have a sample of her political poetry, written to protest the execution of the anarchists Sacco and Vanzetti, who were convicted of murder in 1927. Many people believed they were framed because of their political beliefs, including Millay, who was arrested for her part in a "death watch" protest. Millay was known for her technical and lyrical expertise during her lifetime but may well be remembered now more as a feminist and political poet.

[I, being born a woman and distressed]

I, being born a woman and distressed
By all the needs and notions of my kind,
Am urged by your propinquity to find

Your person fair, and feel a certain zest
To bear your body's weight upon my breast: 5
So subtly is the fume of life designed,
To clarify the pulse and cloud the mind,
And leave me once again undone, possessed.
Think not for this, however, the poor treason
Of my stout blood against my staggering brain,   10
I shall remember you with love, or season
My scorn with pity,—let me make it plain:
I find this frenzy insufficient reason
For conversation when we meet again.

1923

From Sonnets from an Ungrafted Tree

I [So she came back into his house again]

So she came back into his house again
And watched beside his bed until he died,
Loving him not at all. The winter rain
Splashed in the painted butter-tub outside,
Where once her red geraniums had stood,   5
Where still their rotted stalks were to be seen;
The thin log snapped; and she went out for wood,
Bareheaded, running the few steps between
The house and shed; there, from the sodden eaves
Blown back and forth on ragged ends of twine,   10
Saw the dejected creeping-jinny vine,
(And one, big-aproned, blithe, with stiff blue sleeves
Rolled to the shoulder that warm day in spring,
Who planted seeds, musing ahead to their far blossoming).

* * *

X [She had forgotten how the August night]

She had forgotten how the August night
Was level as a lake beneath the moon,
In which she swam a little, losing sight
Of shore; and how the boy, who was at noon
Simple enough, not different from the rest,   5
Wore now a pleasant mystery as he went,
Which seemed to her an honest enough test
Whether she loved him, and she was content.
So loud, so loud the million crickets' choir . . .
So sweet the night, so long-drawn-out and late . . .   10
And if the man were not her spirit's mate,
Why was her body sluggish with desire?
Stark on the open field the moonlight fell,
But the oak tree's shadow was deep and black and secret as a well.

1923

Justice Denied in Massachusetts[1]

Let us abandon then our gardens and go home
And sit in the sitting-room.
Shall the larkspur blossom or the corn grow under this cloud?
Sour to the fruitful seed
Is the cold earth under this cloud,   5
Fostering quack and weed, we have marched upon but cannot conquer;
We have bent the blades of our hoes against the stalks of them.

Let us go home, and sit in the sitting-room.
Not in our day
Shall the cloud go over and the sun rise as before,   10
Beneficent upon us
Out of the glittering bay,
And the warm winds be blown inward from the sea
Moving the blades of corn
With a peaceful sound.   15
Forlorn, forlorn,
Stands the blue hay rack by the empty mow.
And the petals drop to the ground,
Leaving the tree unfruited.
The sun that warmed our stooping backs and withered the weed uprooted— 20
We shall not feel it again.
We shall die in darkness, and be buried in the rain.

What from the splendid dead
We have inherited—
Furrows sweet to the grain, and the weed subdued—   25
See now the slug and the mildew plunder.
Evil does overwhelm
The larkspur and the corn;
We have seen them go under.

Let us sit here, sit still,   30
Here in the sitting-room until we die;
At the step of Death on the walk, rise and go;
Leaving to our children's children this beautiful doorway,
And this elm,
And a blighted earth to till   35
With a broken hoe.

1927

1. Written to protest the executions of Nicola Sacco (1891–1927) and Bartolomeo Vanzetti (1888–1927), who were convicted of the 1920 murder of a paymaster and a payroll guard at a shoe factory; widely believed to be a miscarriage of justice based on the two men's anarchist political beliefs—both had alibis for the murders—the trial and execution became a cause célèbre for many intellectuals in the 1920s.

From **Fatal Interview**

XX [Think not, nor for a moment let your mind]

Think not, nor for a moment let your mind,
Wearied with thinking, doze upon the thought
That the work's done and the long day behind,
And beauty, since 'tis paid for, can be bought.
If in the moonlight from the silent bough   5
Suddenly with precision speak your name
The nightingale, be not assured that now
His wing is limed and his wild virtue tame.
Beauty beyond all feathers that have flown
Is free; you shall not hood her to your wrist,[2]   10
Nor sting her eyes, nor have her for your own
In any fashion; beauty billed and kissed
Is not your turtle; tread her like a dove—
She loves you not; she never heard of love.

* * *

XXVI [Women have loved before as I love now]

Women have loved before as I love now;
At least, in lively chronicles of the past—
Of Irish waters by a Cornish prow
Or Trojan waters by a Spartan mast
Much to their cost invaded—here and there,   5
Hunting the amorous line, skimming the rest,
I find some woman bearing as I bear
Love like a burning city in the breast.
I think however that of all alive
I only in such utter, ancient way   10
Do suffer love; in me alone survive
The unregenerate passions of a day
When treacherous queens, with death upon the tread,
Heedless and wilful, took their knights to bed.

1931

◄ DJUNA BARNES ►
1892–1982

One of the key innovators of literary modernism (pp. 1194–97), Djuna Barnes was
born in Cornwall-on-Hudson, a pastoral suburb of New York City, to a complicated family comprising her father, her mother, her father's mistress, her full siblings, and her half-siblings, all of whom lived together under the leadership of her
grandmother Zadel Barnes. But it was not a happy family. Besides the infidelity of

---

2. Reference to falconry: hunting falcons (hawks)   suit of prey.
are hooded to keep them docile when not in pur-

her father (which her grandmother sanctioned, though her mother did not), violence and incest created an undercurrent of almost gothic betrayal in the home. Nevertheless, the family's modest wealth allowed the children to be educated at home, where their natural proclivities were encouraged; its idiosyncrasy encouraged the children to spurn convention. For Djuna Barnes this meant that she received the kind of artistic training and encouragement she needed to enter the Pratt Institute and to join the Art Students League of Manhattan. In the exciting world of bohemian Manhattan in the 1910s, Barnes's wit, talent, and bisexuality assured her a place, even as a teen, in the avant-garde of artists and personalities who were trying to overturn what they felt were the stifling legacies of the nineteenth century in order to invent an adequate way to express the realities of the new century. This new aesthetic, exemplified in the short story included here, came to be known as modernism.

It was only after moving to Europe in the 1920s that Barnes began to develop seriously as a writer. Over the course of the twenties and thirties, she lived in Paris, Berlin, and London, where she became friends with other literary modernists, such as T. S. Eliot, Mina Loy, Samuel Beckett, and James Joyce. She also fell in love with the sculptor Thelma Wood, with whom she had a long relationship, fictionalized in her most famous novel, *Nightwood* (1936). Returning to New York City at the beginning of World War II, Barnes radically changed her life by withdrawing from the front lines (the avant-garde) of art and society to live almost as a recluse. Never having made significant money from her writing, Barnes lived the last forty years of her life in poor health, writing and seeing only a few friends.

An experimental writer, Barnes wrote in a variety of genres—the novel, the essay, the lyric poem, and the short story—and in a variety of moods—comic, satiric, and elegiac. But Barnes always pushes language to express the modern condition adequately. Often, as in her short story "Mother," which appears here, Barnes explores the subjectivity of the alienated and the alienating (the grotesque), while at the same time interrogating and challenging simple accounts of sexuality and desire.

Mother

A feeble light flickered in the pawn shop at Twenty-nine. Usually, in the back of this shop, reading by this light—a rickety lamp with a common green cover—sat Lydia Passova, the mistress.

Her long heavy head was divided by straight bound hair. Her high firm bust was made still higher and still firmer by German corsets. She was excessively tall, due to extraordinarily long legs. Her eyes were small, and not well focused. The left was slightly distended from the long use of a magnifying glass.

She was middle-aged, and very slow in movement, though well balanced. She wore coral in her ears, a coral necklace, and many coral finger rings.

There was about her jewelry some of the tragedy of all articles that find themselves in pawn, and she moved among the trays like the guardians of cemetery grounds, who carry about with them some of the lugubrious stillness of the earth on which they have been standing.

She dealt, in most part, in cameos, garnets, and a great many inlaid bracelets and cuff-links. There were a few watches, however, and silver vessels and fishing tackle and faded slippers—and when, at night, she lit the lamp, these and the trays of precious and semi-precious stones, and the little ivory crucifixes, one on either side of the window, seemed to be leading a swift furtive life of their own, conscious of the slow pacing woman who was known to the street as Lydia Passova.

No one knew her, not even her lover—a little nervous fellow, an Englishman quick in speech with a marked accent, a round-faced youth with a deep soft cleft in his chin, on which grew two separate tufts of yellow hair. His eyes were wide and pale, and his eye-teeth prominent.

He dressed in tweeds, walked with the toes in, seemed sorrowful when not talking, laughed a great deal and was nearly always to be found in the café about four of an afternoon.

When he spoke it was quick and jerky. He had spent a great deal of his time in Europe, especially the watering places—and had managed to get himself in trouble in St. Moritz, it was said, with a well-connected family.

He liked to seem a little eccentric and managed it simply enough while in America. He wore no hat, and liked to be found reading the *London Times,* under a park lamp at three in the morning.

Lydia Passova was never seen with him. She seldom left her shop; however, she was always pleased when he wanted to go anywhere: "Go," she would say, kissing his hand, "and when you are tired come back."

Sometimes she would make him cry. Turning around she would look at him a little surprised, with lowered lids, and a light tightening of the mouth.

"Yes," he would say, "I know I'm trivial—well, then, here I go, I will leave you, not disturb you any longer!" and darting for the door he would somehow end by weeping with his head buried in her lap.

She would say, "There, there why are you so nervous?"

And he would laugh again: "My father was a nervous man, and my mother was high-strung, and as for me—" He would not finish.

Sometimes he would talk to her for long hours, she seldom answering, occupied with her magnifying glass and her rings, but in the end she was sure to send him out with: "That's all very true, I have no doubt; now go out by yourself and think it over"—and he would go, with something like relief, embracing her large hips with his small strong arms.

They had known each other a very short time, three or four months. He had gone in to pawn his little gold ring, he was always in financial straits, though his mother sent him five pounds a week; and examining the ring, Lydia Passova had been so quiet, inevitable, necessary, that it seemed as if he must have known her forever—"at some time," as he said.

Yet they had never grown together. They remained detached, and on her part, quiet, preoccupied.

He never knew how much she liked him. She never told him; if he asked she would look at him in that surprised manner, drawing her mouth together.

In the beginning he had asked her a great many times, clinging to her, and she moved about arranging her trays with a slight smile, and in the end lowered her hand and stroked him gently.

He immediately became excited. "Let us dance," he cried, "I have a great capacity for happiness."

"Yes, you are very happy," she said.

"You understand, don't you?" he asked abruptly.

"What?"

"That my tears are nothing, have no significance, they are just a protective fluid—when I see anything happening that is about to affect my happiness I cry, that's all."

"Yes," Lydia Passova said, "I understand." She turned around, reaching up to some shelves, and over her shoulder she asked, "Does it hurt?"

"No, it only frightens me. You never cry, do you?"

"No, I never cry."

That was all. He never knew where she had come from, what her life had been, if she had or had not been married, if she had or had not known lovers; all that she would say was, "Well, you are with me, does that tell you nothing?" and he had to answer, "No, it tells me nothing."

When he was sitting in the café he often thought to himself, "There's a great woman"—and he was a little puzzled why he thought this because his need of her was so entirely different from any need he seemed to remember having possessed before.

There was no swagger in him about her, the swagger he had always felt for his conquests with women. Yet there was not a trace of shame—he was neither proud nor shy about Lydia Passova, he was something entirely different. He could not have said himself what his feeling was—but it was in no way disturbing.

People had, it is true, begun to tease him:

"You're a devil with the ladies."

Where this had made him proud, now it made him uneasy.

"Now, there's a certain Lydia Passova, for instance, who would ever have thought—"

Furious he would rise.

"So, you do feel—"

He would walk away, stumbling a little among the chairs, putting his hand on the back of every one on the way to the door.

Yet he could see that, in her time, Lydia Passova had been a "perverse" woman—there was, about everything she did, an economy that must once have been a very sensitive and a very sensuous impatience, and because of this every one who saw her felt a personal loss.

Sometimes, tormented, he would come running to her, stopping abruptly, putting it to her this way:

"Somebody has said something to me."

"When—where?"

"Now, in the café."

"What?"

"I don't know, a reproach—"

She would say:

"We are all, unfortunately, only what we are." She had a large and beautiful angora cat, it used to sit in the tray of amethysts and opals and stare at her from very bright cold eyes. One day it died, and calling her lover to her she said:

"Take her out and bury her." And when he had buried her he came back, his lips twitching.

"You loved that cat—this will be a great loss."

"Have I a memory?" she inquired.

"Yes," he answered.

"Well," she said quietly, fixing her magnifying glass firmly in her eye. "We have looked at each other, that is enough."

And then one day she died.

The caretaker of the furnace came to him, where he was sipping his liqueur as he talked to his cousin, a pretty little blonde girl, who had a boring and comfortably provincial life, and who was beginning to chafe.

He got up, trembling, pale, and hurried out.

The police were there, and said they thought it had been heart failure.

She lay on the couch in the inner room. She was fully dressed, even to her coral ornaments; her shoes were neatly tied—large bows of a ribbed silk.

He looked down. Her small eyes were slightly open, the left, that had used the magnifying glass, was slightly wider than the other. For a minute she seemed quite natural. She had the look of one who is about to say: "Sit beside me."

Then he felt the change. It was in the peculiar heaviness of the head—sensed through despair and not touch. The high breasts looked very still, the hands were half closed, a little helpless, as in life—hands that were too proud to "hold." The drawn-up limb exposed a black petticoat and a yellow stocking. It seemed that she had become hard—set, as in a mold—that she rejected everything now, but in rejecting had bruised him with a last terrible pressure. He moved and knelt down. He shivered. He put his closed hands to his eyes. He could not weep.

She was an old woman, he could see that. The ceasing of that one thing that she could still have for any one made it simple and direct.

Something oppressed him, weighed him down, bent his shoulders, closed his throat. He felt as one feels who has become conscious of passion for the first time, in the presence of a relative.

He flung himself on his face, like a child.

That night, however, he wept, lying in bed, his knees drawn up.

1920

◄ DOROTHY PARKER ►
1893–1967

Dorothy Parker is best known for her wit and sarcasm; she goes down in history as one of the great conversationalists and is remarkably quotable. Often described as a woman ahead of her time, in some ways Dorothy Parker exemplified the changing roles of women in the twentieth century: a self-supporting, independent woman who drank, had lovers, and was active in politics but who was full of self-doubt and attempted suicide three times. She wrote for *Vogue, Vanity Fair,* and the *New Yorker,* including a long-running and influential book-review column, "The Constant Reader." She published three volumes of best-selling poetry, three collections of short stories, and co-authored three plays. She won the prestigious O. Henry Award for the best short story of 1929 and an Oscar for screenwriting. Despite this success, she always considered her work to be inadequate. In fact, she claimed, "I'm never going to be famous. I don't do anything, not one single thing. I used to bite my nails, but I don't even do that anymore."

She was born the daughter of a Scottish mother and a Jewish father. Her mother died when she was four, and her father remarried a Catholic woman, but

Parker did not get along with either her father or her stepmother. She was sent to Catholic schools but, in one of her famous comments, claimed that she was expelled for insisting that the Immaculate Conception was spontaneous combustion. Her love life was always tempestuous; she had numerous extramarital affairs and at least one abortion (in 1923, after which she attempted suicide). She married a Wall Street businessman in 1917, but they separated after less than a year. Later, she married a writer eleven years her junior, divorced him, and remarried him; they separated again and then reunited until his death. Parker always considered herself an outsider and aligned herself politically with the poor and disadvantaged. (When she died, she left her estate to Martin Luther King's foundation, and it passed on to the NAACP after his death.) Many of her witty comments were aimed at privilege, such as: "If you want to know what God thinks of money, just look at the people he gave it to." She was politically active throughout her career, joining the Communist Party in 1934 and working against fascism during the Spanish Civil War (1936–39). In the 1950s, she was called to testify before Joseph McCarthy's House Un-American Activities Committee and refused to "name names," for which she was blacklisted in Hollywood. She is remembered as a pivotal member of the Algonquin Round Table, a group of writers and intellectuals who met for lunch at New York's Algonquin Hotel (where Parker lived) and whose conversations were widely repeated in the press (often for their unkindness). She has been the subject of a film (*Mrs. Parker and the Vicious Circle*) and a play (*Vitriol and Violets*).

Parker's work is sometimes dismissed because it relies heavily on humor and satire, which are often overlooked as "serious" literature, especially in literature by women writers. But as we can see in our selection here, "Lady with a Lamp," humor can be a cover for very serious intentions, in this case, addressing issues of women's friendships, the roles of women, and the then-illegal and very much secret abortion (see pp. 1435–36). The selection is also typical of her work stylistically, as it shows Parker's mastery of dialogue and realistic storytelling as well as her tendency toward cynicism.

Lady with a Lamp[1]

Well, Mona! Well, you poor sick thing, you! Ah, you look so little and white and *little,* you do, lying there in that great big bed. That's what you do—go and look so childlike and pitiful nobody'd have the heart to scold you. And I ought to scold you, Mona. Oh, yes, I should so, too. Never letting me know you were ill. Never a word to your oldest friend. Darling, you might have known I'd understand, no matter what you did. What do I mean? Well, what do you *mean* what do I mean, Mona? Of course, if you'd rather not talk about—Not even to your oldest friend. All I wanted to say was you might have known that I'm always for you, no matter what happens. I do admit, sometimes it's a little hard for me to understand how on earth you ever got into such—well. Goodness knows I don't want to nag you now, when you're so sick.

All right, Mona, then you're *not* sick. If that's what you want to say, even to me, why, all right, my dear. People who aren't sick have to stay in bed for nearly

1. Henry Wadsworth Longfellow (1807–82) called Florence Nightingale the "lady with the lamp" in a poem; Nightingale was the icon for "nurse" and the founder of modern nursing (see pp. 883–92).

two weeks, I suppose; I suppose people who aren't sick look the way you do. Just your nerves? You were simply all tired out? I see. It's just your nerves. You were simply tired. Yes. Oh, Mona, Mona, why don't you feel you can trust me?

Well—if that's the way you want to be to me, that's the way you want to be. I won't say anything more about it. Only I do think you might have let me know that you had—well, that you were so *tired*, if that's what you want me to say. Why, I'd never have known a word about it if I hadn't run bang into Alice Patterson and she told me she'd called you up and that maid of yours said you had been sick in bed for ten days. Of course, I'd thought it rather funny I hadn't heard from you, but you know how you are—you simply let people go, and weeks can go by like, well, like *weeks*, and never a sign from you. Why, I could have been dead over and over again, for all you'd know. Twenty times over. Now, I'm not going to scold you when you're sick, but frankly and honestly, Mona, I said to myself this time, "Well, she'll have a good wait before I call her up. I've given in often enough, goodness knows. Now she can just call me first." Frankly and honestly, that's what I said!

And then I saw Alice, and I did feel mean, I really did. And now to see you lying there—well, I feel like a complete *dog*. That's what you do to people even when you're in the wrong the way you always are, you wicked little thing, you! Ah, the poor dear! Feels just so awful, doesn't it?

Oh, don't keep trying to be brave, child. Not with me. Just give in—it helps so much. Just tell me all about it. You know I'll never say a word. Or at least you ought to know. When Alice told me that maid of yours said you were all tired out and your nerves had gone bad, I naturally never said anything, but I thought to myself, "Well, maybe that's the only thing Mona could say was the matter. That's probably about the best excuse she could think of." And of course I'll never deny it—but perhaps it might have been better to have said you had influenza or ptomaine poisoning. After all, people don't stay in bed for ten whole days just because they're nervous. All right, Mona, then they *do*. Then they do. Yes, dear.

Ah, to think of you going through all this and crawling off here all alone like a little wounded animal or something. And with only that colored Edie to take care of you. Darling, oughtn't you have a trained nurse, I mean really oughtn't you? There must be so many things that have to be done for you. Why, Mona! Mona, please! Dear, you don't have to get so excited. Very well, my dear, it's just as you say—there isn't a single thing to be done. I was mistaken, that's all. I simply thought that after—Oh, now, you don't have to do that. You never have to say you're sorry, to *me*. I understand. As a matter of fact, I was glad to hear you lose your temper. It's a good sign when sick people are cross. It means they're on the way to getting better. Oh, I know! You go right ahead and be cross all you want to.

Look, where shall I sit? I want to sit some place where you won't have to turn around, so you can talk to me. You stay right the way you're lying, and I'll— Because you shouldn't move around, I'm sure. It must be terribly bad for you. All right, dear, you can move around all you want to. All right, I must be crazy. I'm crazy, then. We'll leave it like that. Only please, please don't excite yourself that way.

I'll just get this chair and put it over—oops, I'm sorry I joggled the bed—put it over here, where you can see me. There. But first I want to fix your pillows before I get settled. Well, they certainly are *not* all right, Mona. After the way you've been twisting them and pulling them, these last few minutes. Now look, honey, I'll help you raise yourself ve-ry, ve-ry, slo-o-ow-ly. Oh. Of course you can sit up by yourself, dear. Of course you can. Nobody ever said you couldn't. Nobody ever thought of such a thing. There now, your pillows are all smooth and lovely, and you lie right down again, before you hurt yourself. Now, isn't that better? Well, I should think it was!

Just a minute, till I get my sewing. Oh, yes, I brought it along, so we'd be all cozy. Do you honestly, frankly and honestly, think it's pretty? I'm so glad. It's nothing but a tray-cloth, you know. But you simply can't have too many. They're a lot of fun to make, too, doing this edge—it goes so quickly. Oh, Mona dear, so often I think if you just had a home of your own, and could be all busy, making pretty little things like this for it, it would do so *much* for you. I worry so about you, living in a little furnished apartment, with nothing that belongs to you, no roots, no nothing. It's not right for a woman. It's all wrong for a woman like you. Oh, I wish you'd get over that Garry McVicker! If you could just meet some nice, sweet, considerate man, and get married to him, and have your own lovely place—and with your *taste,* Mona!—and maybe have a couple of children. You're so simply adorable with children. Why, Mona Morrison, are you crying? Oh, you've got a cold? You've got a cold, *too*? I thought you were crying, there for a second. Don't you want my handkerchief, lamb? Oh, you have yours. Wouldn't you have a pink chiffon handkerchief, you nut! Why on earth don't you use cleansing tissues, just lying there in bed with no one to see you? You little idiot, you! Extravagant little fool!

No, but really, I'm serious. I've said to Fred so often, "Oh, if we could just get Mona married!" Honestly, you don't know the feeling it gives you, just to be all secure and safe with your own sweet home and your own blessed children, and your own nice husband coming back to you every night. That's a woman's *life,* Mona. What you've been doing is really horrible. Just drifting along, that's all. What's going to happen to you, dear, whatever is going to become of you? But no—you don't even think of it. You go, and go falling in love with that Garry. Well, my dear, you've got to give me credit—I said from the very first, "He'll never marry her." You know that. What? There was never any thought of marriage, with you and Garry? Oh, Mona, now listen! Every woman on earth thinks of marriage as soon as she's in love with a man. Every woman, I don't care who she is.

Oh, if you were only married! It would be all the difference in the world. I think a child would do everything for you, Mona. Goodness knows, I just can't speak *decently* to that Garry, after the way he's treated you—well, you know perfectly well, *none* of your friends can—but I can frankly and honestly say, if he married you, I'd absolutely let bygones be bygones, and I'd be just as happy as happy, for you. If he's what you want. And I will say, what with your lovely looks and what with good-looking as he is, you ought to have simply *gorgeous* children. Mona, baby, you really have got a rotten cold, haven't you? Don't you want me to get you another handkerchief? Really?

I'm simply sick that I didn't bring you any flowers. But I thought the place would be full of them. Well, I'll stop on the way home and send you some. It looks too dreary here, without a flower in the room. Didn't Garry send you any? Oh, he didn't know you were sick. Well, doesn't he send you flowers anyway? Listen, hasn't he called up, all this time, and found out whether you were sick or not? Not in ten days? Well, then, haven't you called him and told him? Ah, now, Mona, there *is* such a thing as being too much of a heroine. Let him worry a little, dear. It would be a very good thing for him. Maybe that's the trouble—you've always taken all the worry for both of you. Hasn't sent any flowers! Hasn't even telephoned! Well, I'd just like to talk to that young man for a few minutes. After all, this is all *his* responsibility.

He's away! He's *what*? Oh, he went to Chicago two weeks ago. Well, it seems to me I'd always heard that there were telephone wires running between here and Chicago, but of course—And you'd think since he's been back, the least he could do would be to do something. He's not back yet? He's not *back* yet? Mona, what are you trying to tell me? Why, just night before last—Said he'd let you know the minute he got home? Of all the rotten, low things I ever heard in my life, this is really the—Mona, dear, please lie down. Please. Why, I didn't mean anything. I don't know what I was going to say, honestly I don't, it couldn't have been anything. For goodness' sake, let's talk about something else.

Let's see. Oh, you really ought to see Julia Post's living-room, the way she's done it now. She has brown walls—not beige, you know, or tan or anything, but brown—and these cream-colored taffeta curtains and—Mona, I tell you I absolutely don't know what I was going to say, before. It's gone completely out of my head. So you see how unimportant it must have been. Dear, please just lie quiet and try to relax. Please forget about that man for a few minutes, anyway. No man's worth getting that worked up about. Catch me doing it! You know you can't expect to get well quickly, if you get yourself so excited. You know that.

What doctor did you have, darling? Or don't you want to say? Your own? Your own Doctor Britton? You don't mean it! Well, I certainly never thought he'd do a thing like—Yes, dear, of course he's a nerve specialist. Yes, dear. Yes, dear. Yes, dear, of course you have perfect confidence in him. I only wish you would in me, once in a while; after we went to school together and everything. You might know I absolutely sympathize with you. I don't see how you could possibly have done anything else. I know you've always talked about how you'd give anything to have a baby, but it would have been so terribly unfair to the child to bring it into the world without being married. You'd have had to go live abroad and never see anybody and—And even then, somebody would have been sure to have told it sometime. They always do. You did the only possible thing, *I* think. Mona, for heaven's sake! Don't scream like that. I'm not deaf, you know. All right, dear, all right, all right, all right. All right, of course I believe you. Naturally I take your word for anything. Anything you say. Only please do try to be quiet. Just lie back and rest, and have a nice talk.

Ah, now don't keep harping on that. I've told you a hundred times, if I've told you once, I wasn't going to say anything at all. I tell you I don't remember *what* I was going to say. "Night before last"? When did I mention "night before last"? I never said any such—Well. Maybe it's better this way, Mona. The more I think of it, the more I think it's much better for you to hear it from me. Because somebody's bound to tell you. These things always come out. And I know you'd rather hear it from your oldest friend, wouldn't you? And the good Lord knows, anything I could do to make you see what that man really is! Only do relax, darling. Just for me. Dear, Garry isn't in Chicago. Fred and I saw him night before last at the Comet Club, dancing. And Alice saw him Tuesday night at El Rhumba. And I don't know how many people have said they've seen him around at the theater and night clubs and things. Why, he couldn't have stayed in Chicago more than a day or so—if he went at all.

Well, he was with *her* when we saw him, honey. Apparently he's with her all the time; nobody ever sees him with anyone else. You really must make up your mind to it, dear; it's the only thing to do. I hear all over that he's just simply *pleading* with her to marry him, but I don't know how true that is. I'm sure I can't see why he'd want to, but then you never can tell what a man like that will do. It would be just good enough *for* him if he got her, that's what *I* say. Then he'd see. She'd never stand for any of his nonsense. She'd make him toe the mark. She's a smart woman.

But, oh, so *ordinary*. I thought, when we saw them the other night, "Well, she just looks cheap, that's all she looks." That must be what he likes, I suppose. I must admit he looked very well. I never saw him look better. Of course you know what I think of him, but I always had to say he's one of the handsomest men I ever saw in my life. I can understand how any woman would be attracted to him— at first. Until they found out what he's really like. Oh, if you could have seen him with that awful, common creature, never once taking his eyes off her, and hanging on every word she said, as if it was pearls! It made me just——

Mona, angel, are you *crying*? Now, darling, that's just plain silly. That man's not worth another thought. You've thought about him entirely too much, that's the trouble. Three years! Three of the best years of your life you've given him, and all the time he's been deceiving you with that woman. Just think back over what you've been through—all the times and times and times he promised you he'd give her up; and you, you poor little idiot, you'd believe him, and then he'd go right back to her again. And *everybody* knew about it. Think of that, and then try telling me that man's worth crying over! Really, Mona! I'd have more pride.

You know, I'm just glad this thing happened. I'm just glad you found out. This is a little too much, this time. In Chicago, indeed! Let you know the minute he came home! The kindest thing a person could possibly have done was to tell you, and bring you to your senses at last. I'm not sorry I did it, for a second. When I think of him out having the time of his life and you lying here deathly sick all on account of him, I could just—Yes, it is on account of him. Even if you didn't have an—well, even if I was mistaken about what I naturally thought was the matter with you when you made such a secret of your illness, he's driven you into a nervous breakdown, and that's plenty bad enough. All for that man! The skunk! You just put him right out of your head.

Why, of course you can, Mona. All you need to do is to pull yourself together, child. Simply say to yourself, "Well, I've wasted three years of my life, and that's that." Never worry about *him* any more. The Lord knows, darling, he's not worrying about you.

It's just because you're weak and sick that you're worked up like this, dear. I know. But you're going to be all right. You can make something of your life. You've got to, Mona, you know. Because after all—well, of course, you never looked sweeter, I don't mean that; but you're—well, you're not getting any younger. And here you've been throwing away your time, never seeing your friends, never going out, never meeting anybody new, just sitting here waiting for Garry to telephone, or Garry to come in—if he didn't have anything better to do. For three years, you've never had a thought in your head but that man. Now you just forget him.

Ah, baby, it isn't good for you to cry like that. Please don't. He's not even worth talking about. Look at the woman he's in love with, and you'll see what kind he is. You were much too good for him. You were much too sweet to him. You gave in too easily. The minute he had you, he didn't want you any more. That's what he's like. Why, he no more loved you than——

Mona, don't! Mona, stop it! Please, Mona! You mustn't talk like that, you mustn't say such things. You've got to stop crying, you'll be terribly sick. Stop, oh, stop it, oh, please stop! Oh, what am I going to do with her? Mona, dear—Mona! Oh, where in heaven's name is that fool maid?

Edie. Oh, Edie! Edie. I think you'd better get Dr. Britton on the telephone, and tell him to come down and give Miss Morrison something to quiet her. I'm afraid she's got herself a little bit upset.

1932

CULTURAL COORDINATES
Margaret Sanger, Abortion, and Birth Control

Dorothy Parker's "Lady with a Lamp" never uses the word "abortion," but the story makes clear that the main character is recovering from one. At the time the story was published, not only was abortion illegal, but so was birth control, even mailing or publishing information about birth control. If we have a specific woman to thank for the current availability of birth control, it is the controversial Margaret Sanger (1879–1966), the founder of the American Birth Control League, the forerunner of today's Planned Parenthood.

Although birth control and abortion have been practiced in every culture throughout history (with varying success and safety), the Comstock Law of 1873 (named for a postal inspector who formed an anti-vice league) made it illegal to mail or distribute any information about birth control in the United States. The law was not officially repealed until 1936. Margaret Sanger defied this law numerous times and was eventually convicted and served time in a penitentiary.

Sanger's mother went through eighteen pregnancies (with eleven live births); Sanger herself had three children, despite suffering from tuberculosis (two of her children died in childhood). She came through these experiences convinced that women should have more control over their reproductive lives. Sanger had trained as a nurse, went to work in clinics in the slums of Manhattan, and began publishing a column, "What Every Girl Should Know," designed to provide information on the reproductive cycle and birth control for poor women. She opened the first family-planning and birth control clinic in the United States in 1916 and organized the first World Population Conference. Eventually, she saw the repeal of the Comstock Law and, in 1966, a Supreme Court decision (*Griswold v. Connecticut*) that effectively made birth control legal for married couples.

The Fight for
BIRTH CONTROL

Margaret Sanger

Cover of a 1916 pamphlet promoting a lecture tour by Margaret Sanger. It was not until 1966 that the Supreme Court's decision in *Griswold v. Connecticut* effectively made birth control legal for married couples. In 1916, not only was it illegal to distribute birth control, but it was also considered obscene (and therefore illegal) even to discuss it or write about it.

Sanger is a controversial figure because some of her writings have been interpreted as racist and eugenicist (that is, advocating a program of birth control and sterilization for "lesser" races and promoting births among the "superior"). Certainly, Sanger grew up in a culture that was deeply racist, and eugenics was widely supported by many middle-class white Americans during the 1920s and 1930s (before its real logic became apparent in Nazi Germany). However, she was also hailed by many African American civil rights leaders, including W. E. B. DuBois and Martin Luther King Jr., for her work in helping poor and African American women gain access to health care, especially reproductive health care. Sanger is sometimes hailed or blamed, too, for promoting abortion. While it is true that hers was the pioneering voice asserting women's right to control their own bodies, she was not an advocate of abortion, if only because during most of her lifetime the procedure was not particularly safe for women.

Abortion started becoming illegal in various states after the 1820s and by 1965 was illegal in all fifty states, with a few exceptions to save the life of the mother or in cases of rape or incest. The Supreme Court's landmark *Roe v. Wade* decision (1973) declared limits on first-trimester abortions unconstitutional, though since that time courts have begun to allow limitations. It is worth noting, however, that in the 1890s, a time when abortions were illegal, it is estimated that there were 2 million abortions per year in the United States (from a population of about 63 million people), compared to 1.3 million per year today (from a population of more than 280 million).

During her long career, Meridel LeSueur wrote novels, short stories, poetry, political essays, newspaper and magazine articles, and children's literature and was a stalwart advocate for poor, working-class, and marginalized women. She left school at sixteen to become a political activist, working on behalf of socialist and anarchist causes. For a while she lived in New York with the feminist anarchist Emma Goldman (1869–1940), and for a while in California, where she acted in several movies. By the 1930s, she had moved back to her native Midwest (she was born in Iowa) with her labor-organizer husband and two daughters and had won several awards for her stories and political journalism. Like many other leftist writers during the 1950s, she was informally blacklisted and found it difficult to publish, so she turned to working for American Indian rights and writing children's histories. With the burgeoning study of women writers, however, her work was rediscovered by feminist scholars and her career was revived during the 1970s. She continued writing until her death.

Much of LeSueur's early writing focuses on the lives of working-class and poor women during the Depression, detailing the ways that sexual abuse, pregnancy, and motherhood make women's experience of poverty different from men's. Her writing attends to the material conditions of marginalized lives but develops a kind of mythology to understand the power of those lives. While her early work often includes compelling symbolism focused on motherhood, her later work shows influences from American Indian lives and mythologies. In our selection, "Rites of Ancient Ripening," we can see both the mystical celebration of motherhood and a respect for and use of American Indian traditions of regeneration and rebirth.

Rites of Ancient Ripening

I am luminous with age
In my lap I hold the valley.
I see on the horizon what has been taken
What is gone   lies prone   fleshless.
In my breast I hold the middle valley   5
The corn kernels cry to me in the fields
        Take us home.
Like corn I cry in the last sunset
Gleam like plums.
        My bones shine in fever   10
Smoked with the fires of age.
Herbal, I contain the final juice,
Shadow, I crouch in the ash
        never breaking to fire.
Winter iron bough   15
        unseen my buds,
Hanging close I live in the beloved bone
Speaking in the marrow
        alive in green memory.

The light was brighter then.   20
Now spiders creep at my eyes' edge.
I peek between my fingers
                at my fathers' dust.
The old stones have been taken away
                there is no path.   25
The fathering fields are gone.
The wind is stronger than it used to be.
My stone feet far below me grip the dust.
I run and crouch in corners with thin dogs.
I tie myself to the children like a kite.   30
I fall and burst beneath the sacred human tree.
Release my seed and let me fall.
Toward the shadow of the great earth
                let me fall.
Without child or man   35
                I turn   I fall.
Into shadows,
                the dancers are gone.
My salted pelt stirs at the final warmth
Pound me death   40
                stretch and tan me death
Hang me up, ancestral shield
                against the dark.
Burn and bright and take me quick.
Pod and light me into dark.   45
Are those flies or bats or mother eagles?
I shrink   I cringe
Trees tilt upon me like young men.
The bowl I made I cannot lift.
All is running past me.   50
The earth tilts and turns over me.
I am shrinking
                and lean against the warm walls of old summers.
With knees and chin I grip the dark
Swim out the shores of night in old meadows.   55
Remember   buffalo hunts
Great hunters returning
Councils of the fathers to be fed
Round sacred fires.
The faces of profound deer who   60
                gave themselves for food.
We faced the east the golden pollened
                sacrifice of brothers.
The little seeds of my children
                with faces of mothers and fathers   65
Fold in my flesh
                in future summers.
My body a canoe turning to stone

Moves among the bursting flowers of men.
Through the meadows of flowers and food,
I float and wave to my grandchildren in the   70
    Tepis[1] of many fires
          In the winter of the many slain
I hear the moaning.
I ground my corn daily   75
In my pestle many children
Summer grasses in my daughters
Strength and fathers in my sons
All was ground in the bodies bowl
    corn died to bread   80
    woman to child
    deer to the hunters.
Sires of our people
Wombs of mothering night
Guardian mothers of the corn   85
Hill borne torrents of the plains
Sing all grinding songs
    of healing herbs
Many tasselled summers
    Flower in my old bones   90
        Now.
Ceremonials of water and fire
Lodge me in the deep earth
    grind my harvested seed.
The rites of ancient ripening   95
Make my flesh plume
And summer winds stir in my smoked bowl.
Do not look for me till I return
    rot of greater summers
Struck from fire and dark,   100
Mother struck to future child.
Unbud me now
Unfurl me now
Flesh and fire
    burn   105
        requicken
            Death.

                                                    1986

◄ EUDORA WELTY ►
1909–2001

Eudora Welty lived almost her whole life in her parents' house in Jackson, Mississippi. In her autobiography, *One Writer's Beginnings*, she described hers as a "sheltered life," given the relative narrowness of her experience of the world, but

---

1. Tepees.

she also saw it as "daring," in terms of her intellectual engagement with the issues of her times. She was a keen observer of the world around her and transformed her observations into the world of her fiction. In *The Eye of the Story*, she claimed that "the writer's mind and heart, where all this exterior is continually becoming something—the moral, the passionate, the poetic, hence the shaping idea—can't be mapped and plotted."

On some levels, Welty lived a very public life. In addition to publishing nineteen books of fiction (both novels and stories), numerous volumes of essays, criticism, and an autobiography, and two collections of her photographs, she had a busy schedule of lectures and readings. At the same time, she was intensely private about her relationships. But she also lived a very private life. Her unauthorized biographer, Anne Waldrup, was repeatedly rebuffed when she tried to interview people about Welty, finding that Welty had asked them not to talk about her personal life. Before her death, Welty repeatedly told critics and reviewers not to look to her biography to explain her stories; she insisted that there is "no explanation outside fiction."

Nevertheless, readers are interested in what has gone into shaping a writer. Welty was born to parents who had moved to Mississippi from Ohio and West Virginia, so although she was born in the South, she was still something of an outsider, since she was not southern by heritage. She left home for three years in the late 1920s to earn a degree from the University of Wisconsin and to attend Columbia Business School for a year. When her father died, though, she left school and returned to Jackson for good. She worked for a radio station and as a publicity agent for the Works Progress Administration; this latter job required her to travel around the state and allowed her to pursue her interest in photography. She began writing around this time and published her first story in 1936; her first collection of stories, *A Curtain of Green*, appeared in 1941. She continued to publish fiction for another forty years and won the Pulitzer Prize in 1973.

Welty's fiction has been influential for a new generation of southern writers. She is often described by critics as being particularly acute in her perceptions of both people and their surroundings and skillful at using detail to "show" the point of her stories. Readers often see the influence of photography on her fiction. But Welty was also a careful reader of fiction, and much of her work can be read as a kind of dialogue with other writers, both her predecessors and her contemporaries. Her work has been compared to Virginia Woolf's, for its experiments with narrative, point of view, and challenges to masculine modes of storytelling, and to William Faulkner's and her close friend Katherine Anne Porter's (pp. 1389–97), both for its evocation of the South during times of great change and for its construction of a southern mythos. Much of her fiction draws its themes from classical mythology and fairy tales. If an earlier southern literature was seen as "local color" or "regional," Welty was central in changing that critical perception by depicting the landscape, people, and culture of the South as simultaneously specific and legendary.

The selection included here, "A Still Moment," exhibits many of the preoccupations of Welty's fiction. The characters and landscape are in many ways very specific to a time and a place; the three main characters are based on real historical figures (though the three probably never met). At the same time, its implications are mythic; the heron takes on symbolic importance and the narrative turns on philosophical questions about single-minded pursuit. The story may allude to Sarah Orne Jewett's "A White Heron" (pp. 1042–48), in which a white heron comes to represent an embodied spirit of nature. Welty's story offers us three very different ways of seeing the heron, depending on the man who is looking at it. Each man, preoccupied with his own sense of calling, sees the heron as it relates to him. We then get a fourth perspective, that of the intersection of the three others, a view that is both specific to a moment in time and mythical in its implications.

A Still Moment

Lorenzo Dow rode the Old Natchez Trace[1] at top speed upon a race horse, and the cry of the itinerant Man of God, "I must have souls! And souls I must have!" rang in his own windy ears. He rode as if never to stop, toward his night's appointment.

It was the hour of sunset. All the souls that he had saved and all those he had not took dusky shapes in the mist that hung between the high banks, and seemed by their great number and density to block his way, and showed no signs of melting or changing back into mist, so that he feared his passage was to be difficult forever. The poor souls that were not saved were darker and more pitiful than those that were, and still there was not any of the radiance he would have hoped to see in such a congregation.

"Light up, in God's name!" he called, in the pain of his disappointment.

Then a whole swarm of fireflies instantly flickered all around him, up and down, back and forth, first one golden light and then another, flashing without any of the weariness that had held back the souls. These were the signs sent from God that he had not seen the accumulated radiance of saved souls because he was not able, and that his eyes were more able to see the fireflies of the Lord than His blessed souls.

"Lord, give me the strength to see the angels when I am in Paradise," he said. "Do not let my eyes remain in this failing proportion to my loving heart always."

He gasped and held on. It was that day's complexity of horse-trading that had left him in the end with a Spanish race horse for which he was bound to send money in November from Georgia. Riding faster on the beast and still faster until he felt as if he were flying he sent thoughts of love with matching speed to his wife Peggy in Massachusetts. He found it effortless to love at a distance. He could look at the flowering trees and love Peggy in fullness, just as he could see his visions and love God. And Peggy, to whom he had not spoken until he could speak fateful words ("Would she accept of such an object as him?"), Peggy, the bride, with whom he had spent a few hours of time, showing of herself a small round handwriting, declared all in one letter, her first, that she felt the same as he, and that the fear was never of separation, but only of death.

Lorenzo well knew that it was Death that opened underfoot, that rippled by at night, that was the silence the birds did their singing in. He was close to death, closer than any animal or bird. On the back of one horse after another, winding them all, he was always riding toward it or away from it, and the Lord sent him directions with protection in His mind.

1. Lorenzo Dow: a famous eccentric itinerant preacher (1777–1834) central to the early nineteenth-century religious movement known as the Second Great Awakening; he was not allowed in most conventional churches because of his wild preaching style and so spoke in open-air forums, often to crowds as large as 10,000; a rabid anti-Catholic, in 1799 he tried unsuccessfully to convert Ireland to Protestantism. Natchez Trace: one of the oldest roads in the United States, it began as an animal trail, was used by Native Americans, and later became a road for commercial and military purposes.

Just then he rode into a thicket of Indians taking aim with their new guns. One stepped out and took the horse by the bridle, it stopped at a touch, and the rest made a closing circle. The guns pointed.

"Incline!" The inner voice spoke sternly and with its customary lightning-quickness.

Lorenzo inclined all the way forward and put his head to the horse's silky mane, his body to its body, until a bullet meant for him would endanger the horse and make his death of no value. Prone he rode out through the circle of Indians, his obedience to the voice leaving him almost fearless, almost careless with joy.

But as he straightened and pressed ahead, care caught up with him again. Turning half-beast and half-divine, dividing himself like a heathen Centaur,[2] he had escaped his death once more. But was it to be always by some metamorphosis of himself that he escaped, some humiliation of his faith, some admission to strength and argumentation and not frailty? Each time when he acted so it was at the command of an instinct that he took at once as the word of an angel, until too late, when he knew it was the word of the Devil. He had roared like a tiger at Indians, he had submerged himself in water blowing the savage bubbles of the alligator, and they skirted him by. He had prostrated himself to appear dead, and deceived bears. But all the time God would have protected him in His own way, less hurried, more divine.

Even now he saw a serpent crossing the Trace, giving out knowing glances.

He cried, "I know you now!," and the serpent gave him one look out of which all the fire had been taken, and went away in two darts into the tangle.

He rode on, all expectation, and the voices in the throats of the wild beasts went, almost without his noticing when, into words. "Praise God," they said. "Deliver us from one another." Birds especially sang of divine love which was the one ceaseless protection. "Peace, in peace," were their words so many times when they spoke from the briars, in a courteous sort of inflection, and he turned his countenance toward all perched creatures with a benevolence striving to match their own.

He rode on past the little intersecting trails, letting himself be guided by voices and by lights. It was battlesounds he heard most, sending him on, but sometimes ocean sounds, that long beat of waves that would make his heart pound and retreat as heavily as they, and he despaired again in his failure in Ireland when he took a voyage and persuaded with the Catholics with his back against the door, and then ran away to their cries of "Mind the white hat!" But when he heard singing it was not the militant and sharp sound of Wesley's hymns,[3] but a soft, tireless and tender air that had no beginning and no end, and the softness of distance, and he had pleaded with the Lord to find out if all this meant that it was wicked, but no answer had come.

Soon night would descend, and a camp-meeting ground ahead would fill with its sinners like the sky with its stars. How he hungered for them! He looked in prescience with a longing of love over the throng that waited while the flames of the torches threw change, change, change over their faces. How could he bring

2. In Greek mythology, a race of creatures half horse, half man.
3. John Wesley (1703–91) founded the Methodist Church, and his brother Charles (1707–88) com-
posed hymns, many of which were based on familiar drinking tunes. Dow was officially a Methodist, though distant from its practices.

them enough, if it were not divine love and sufficient warning of all that could threaten them? He rode on faster. He was a filler of appointments, and he filled more and more, until his journeys up and down creation were nothing but a shuttle, driving back and forth upon the rich expanse of his vision. He was homeless by his own choice, he must be everywhere at some time, and somewhere soon. There hastening in the wilderness on his flying horse he gave the night's torch-lit crowd a premature benediction, he could not wait. He spread his arms out, one at a time for safety, and he wished, when they would all be gathered in by his tin horn blasts and the inspired words would go out over their heads, to brood above the entire and passionate life of the wide world, to become its rightful part.

He peered ahead. "Inhabitants of Time! The wilderness is your souls on earth!" he shouted ahead into the treetops. "Look about you, if you would view the conditions of your spirit, put here by the good Lord to show you and afright you. These wild places and these trails of awesome loneliness lie nowhere, nowhere, but in your heart."

A dark man, who was James Murrell[4] the outlaw, rode his horse out of a cane brake and began going along beside Lorenzo without looking at him. He had the alternately proud and aggrieved look of a man believing himself to be an instrument in the hands of a power, and when he was young he said at once to strangers that he was being used by Evil, or sometimes he stopped a traveler by shouting, "Stop! I'm the Devil!" He rode along now talking and drawing out his talk, by some deep control of the voice gradually slowing the speed of Lorenzo's horse down until both the horses were softly trotting. He would have wondered that nothing he said was heard, not knowing that Lorenzo listened only to voices of whose heavenly origin he was more certain.

Murrell riding along with his victim-to-be, Murrell riding, was Murrell talking. He told away at his long tales, with always a distance and a long length of time flowing through them, and all centered about a silent man. In each the silent man would have done a piece of evil, a robbery or a murder, in a place of long ago, and it was all made for the revelation in the end that the silent man was Murrell himself, and the long story had happened yesterday, and the place *here*—the Natchez Trace. It would only take one dawning look for the victim to see that all of this was another story and he himself had listened his way into it, and that he too was about to recede in time (to where the dread was forgotten) for some listener and to live for a listener in the long ago. Destroy the present!—that must have been the first thing that was whispered in Murrell's heart—the living moment and the man that lives in it must die before you can go on. It was his habit to bring the journey—which might even take days—to a close with a kind of ceremony. Turning his face at last into the face of the victim, for he had never seen him before now, he would tower up with the sudden height of a man no longer the tale teller but the speechless protagonist, silent at last, one degree nearer the hero. Then he would murder the man.

4. An infamous bandit (c. 1791–1845) operating around Natchez, about whom much information is in dispute; he was part of the outlaw gang known as the Mystic Clan and served time in prison for horse thieving (the "H.T." branded on his thumb later in the story); he was known as a "bushwhacker" (one who preyed on abolitionists) and as one who plotted slave rebellions (in order to loot during the disorder); he was caught plotting the "Mystic Rebellion," a slave uprising that would have simultaneously targeted New Orleans, Natchez, and Memphis.

But it would always start over. This man going forward was going backward with talk. He saw nothing, observed no world at all. The two ends of his journey pulled at him always and held him in a nowhere, half asleep, smiling and witty, dangling his predicament. He was a murderer whose final stroke was over-long postponed, who had to bring himself through the greatest tedium to act, as if the whole wilderness, where he was born, were his impediment. But behind him and before him he kept in sight a victim, he saw a man fixed and stayed at the point of death—no matter how the man's eyes denied it, a victim, hands spreading to reach as if for the first time for life. Contempt! That is what Murrell gave that man.

Lorenzo might have understood, if he had not been in haste, that Murrell in laying hold of a man meant to solve his mystery of being. It was as if other men, all but himself, would lighten their hold on the secret, upon assault, and let it fly free at death. In his violence he was only treating of enigma. The violence shook his own body first, like a force gathering, and now he turned in the saddle.

Lorenzo's despair had to be kindled as well as his ecstasy, and could not come without that kindling. Before the awe-filled moment when the faces were turned up under the flares, as though an angel hand tipped their chins, he had no way of telling whether he would enter the sermon by sorrow or by joy. But at this moment the face of Murrell was turned toward him, turning at last, all solitary, in its full, and Lorenzo would have seized the man at once by his black coat and shaken him like prey for a lost soul, so instantly was he certain that the false fire was in his heart instead of the true fire. But Murrell, quick when he was quick, had put his own hand out, a restraining hand, and laid it on the wavelike flesh of the Spanish race horse, which quivered and shuddered at the touch.

They had come to a great live-oak tree at the edge of a low marshland. The burning sun hung low, like a head lowered on folded arms, and over the long reaches of violet trees the evening seemed still with thought. Lorenzo knew the place from having seen it among many in dreams, and he stopped readily and willingly. He drew rein, and Murrell drew rein, he dismounted and Murrell dismounted, he took a step, and Murrell was there too; and Lorenzo was not surprised at the closeness, how Murrell in his long dark coat and over it his dark face darkening still, stood beside him like a brother seeking light.

But in that moment instead of two men coming to stop by the great forked tree, there were three.

From far away, a student, Audubon,[5] had been approaching lightly on the wilderness floor, disturbing nothing in his lightness. The long day of beauty had led him this certain distance. A flock of purple finches that he tried for the first moment to count went over his head. He made a spelling of the soft *pet* of the ivory-billed woodpecker. He told himself always: remember.

Coming upon the Trace, he looked at the high cedars, azure and still as distant smoke overhead, with their silver roots trailing down on either side like the veins of deepness in this place, and he noted some fact to his memory—this earth that wears but will not crumble or slide or turn to dust, they say it exists in one other spot in the world, Egypt—and then forgot it. He walked quietly. All life used this Trace, and he liked to see the animals move along it in direct, oblivious

---

5. John James Audubon (1785–1851), preeminent American ornithologist and artist, who shot birds, had them stuffed and mounted, and then painted them in exquisite detail.

journeys, for they had begun it and made it, the buffalo and deer and the small running creatures before man ever knew where he wanted to go, and birds flew a great mirrored course above. Walking beneath them Audubon remembered how in the cities he had seen these very birds in his imagination, calling them up whenever he wished, even in the hard and glittering outer parlors where if an artist were humble enough to wait, some idle hand held up promised money. He walked lightly and he went as carefully as he had started at two that morning, crayon and paper, a gun, and a small bottle of spirits disposed about his body. *(Note: "The mocking birds so gentle that they would scarcely move out of the way.")* He looked with care; great abundance had ceased to startle him, and he could see things one by one. In Natchez they had told him of many strange and marvelous birds that were to be found here. Their descriptions had been exact, complete, and wildly varying, and he took them for inventions and believed that like all the worldly things that came out of Natchez, they would be disposed of and shamed by any man's excursion into the reality of Nature.

In the valley he appeared under the tree, a sure man, very sure and tender, as if the touch of all the earth rubbed upon him and the stains of the flowery swamp had made him so.

Lorenzo welcomed him and turned fond eyes upon him. To transmute a man into an angel was the hope that drove him all over the world and never let him flinch from a meeting or withhold good-byes for long. This hope insistently divided his life into only two parts, journey and rest. There could be no night and day and love and despair and longing and satisfaction to make partitions in the single ecstasy of this alternation. All things were speech.

"God created the world," said Lorenzo, "and it exists to give testimony. Life is the tongue: speak."

But instead of speech there happened a moment of deepest silence.

Audubon said nothing because he had gone without speaking a word for days. He did not regard his thoughts for the birds and animals as susceptible, in their first change, to words. His long playing on the flute was not in its origin a talking to himself. Rather than speak to order or describe, he would always draw a deer with a stroke across it to communicate his need of venison to an Indian. He had only found words when he discovered that there is much otherwise lost that can be noted down each item in its own day, and he wrote often now in a journal, not wanting anything to be lost the way it had been, all the past, and he would write about a day, "Only sorry that the Sun Sets."

Murrell, his cheated hand hiding the gun, could only continue to smile at Lorenzo, but he remembered in malice that he had disguised himself once as an Evangelist, and his final words to his victim would have been, "One of my disguises was what you are."

Then in Murrell Audubon saw what he thought of as "acquired sorrow"— that cumbrousness and darkness from which the naked Indian, coming just as he was made from God's hand, was so lightly free. He noted the eyes—the dark kind that loved to look through chinks, and saw neither closeness nor distance, light nor shade, wonder nor familiarity. They were narrowed to contract the heart, narrowed to make an averting plan. Audubon knew the finest-drawn tendons of the body and the working of their power, for he had touched them, and he supposed then that in man the enlargement of the eye to see started a motion in the hands to make or do, and that the narrowing of the eye stopped the hand and contracted the heart. Now Murrell's eyes followed an ant on a blade of grass, up the blade and down, many times in the single moment. Audubon had examined the Cave-In Rock[6] where one robber had lived his hiding life, and the air in the cave was the cavelike air that enclosed this man, the same odor, flinty and dark. O secret life, he thought—is it true that the secret is withdrawn from the true disclosure, that man is a cave man, and that the openness I see, the ways through forests, the rivers brimming light, the wide arches where the birds fly, are dreams of freedom? If my origin is withheld from me, is my end to be unknown too? Is the radiance I see closed into an interval between two darks, or can it not illuminate them both and discover at last, though it cannot be spoken, what was thought hidden and lost?

In that quiet moment a solitary snowy heron flew down not far away and began to feed beside the marsh water.

At the single streak of flight, the ears of the race horse lifted, and the eyes of both horses filled with the soft lights of sunset, which in the next instant were reflected in the eyes of the men too as they all looked into the west toward the heron, and all eyes seemed infused with a sort of wildness.

Lorenzo gave the bird a triumphant look, such as a man may bestow upon his own vision, and thought, Nearness is near, lighted in a marshland, feeding at sunset. Praise God, His love has come visible.

Murrell, in suspicion pursuing all glances, blinking into a haze, saw only whiteness ensconced in darkness, as if it were a little luminous shell that drew in and held the eyesight. When he shaded his eyes, the brand "H.T." on his thumb thrust itself into his own vision, and he looked at the bird with the whole plan of the Mystic Rebellion darting from him as if in rays of the bright reflected light, and he stood looking proudly, leader as he was bound to become of the slaves, the brigands and outcasts of the entire Natchez country, with plans, dates, maps burning like a brand into his brain, and he saw himself proudly in a moment of prophecy going down rank after rank of successively bowing slaves to unroll and flaunt an awesome great picture of the Devil colored on a banner.

Audubon's eyes embraced the object in the distance and he could see it as carefully as if he held it in his hand. It was a snowy heron alone out of its flock. He watched it steadily, in his care noting the exact inevitable things. When it feeds it muddies the water with its foot. . . . It was as if each detail about the heron happened slowly in time, and only once. He felt again the old stab of wonder—what structure of life bridged the reptile's scale and the heron's feather? That knowledge too had been lost. He watched without moving. The bird was defenseless in the world except for the intensity of its life, and he wondered, how can heat of blood and speed of heart defend it? Then he thought, as always as if it were new and unbelievable, it has nothing in space or time to prevent its flight. And he waited, knowing that some birds will wait for a sense of their presence to travel to men before they will fly away from them.

Fixed in its pure white profile it stood in the precipitous moment, a plumicorn on its head, its breeding dress extended in rays, eating steadily the little water creatures. There was a little space between each man and the others, where they stood overwhelmed. No one could say the three had ever met, or that this mo-

---

6. A fifty-five-foot-wide cave in southern Illinois, used in the late eighteenth and early nineteenth centuries as a lair by robbers, who would lure their prey toward the cave, where they would be robbed and often murdered.

ment of intersection had ever come in their lives, or its promise had been fulfilled. But before them the white heron rested in the grasses with the evening all around it, lighter and more serene than the evening, flight closed in its body, the circuit of its beauty closed, a bird seen and a bird still, its motion calm as if it were offered: Take my flight. . . .

What each of them had wanted was simply *all*. To save all souls, to destroy all men, to see and to record all life that filled this world—all, all—but now a single frail yearning seemed to go out of the three of them for a moment and to stretch toward this one snowy, shy bird in the marshes. It was as if three whirlwinds had drawn together at some center, to find there feeding in peace a snowy heron. Its own slow spiral of flight could take it away in its own time, but for a little it held them still, it laid quiet over them, and they stood for a moment unburdened. . . .

Murrell wore no mask, for his face was that, a face that was aware while he was somnolent, a face that watched for him, and listened for him, alert and nearly brutal, the guard of a planner. He was quick without that he might be slow within, he staved off time, he wandered and plotted, and yet his whole desire mounted in him toward the end (was this the end—the sight of a bird feeding at dusk?), toward the instant of confession. His incessant deeds were thick in his heart now, and flinging himself to the ground he thought wearily, when all these trees are cut down, and the Trace lost, then my Conspiracy that is yet to spread itself will be disclosed, and all the stone-loaded bodies of murdered men will be pulled up, and all everywhere will know poor Murrell. His look pressed upon Lorenzo, who stared upward, and Audubon, who was taking out his gun, and his eyes squinted up to them in pleading, as if to say, "How soon may I speak, and how soon will you pity me?" Then he looked back to the bird, and he thought if it would look at him a dread penetration would fill and gratify his heart.

Audubon in each act of life was aware of the mysterious origin he half-concealed and half-sought for. People along the way asked him in their kindness or their rudeness if it were true, that he was born a prince, and was the Lost Dauphin,[7] and some said it was his secret, and some said that that was what he wished to find out before he died. But if it was his identity that he wished to discover, or if it was what a man had to seize beyond that, the way for him was by endless examination; by the care for every bird that flew in his path and every serpent that shone underfoot. Not one was enough; he looked deeper and deeper, on and on, as if for a particular beast or some legendary bird. Some men's eyes persisted in looking outward when they opened to look inward, and to their delight, there outflung was the astonishing world under the sky. When a man at last brought himself to face some mirror-surface he still saw the world looking back at him, and if he continued to look, to look closer and closer, what then? The gaze that looks outward must be trained without rest, to be indomitable. It must see as slowly as Murrell's ant in the grass, as exhaustively as Lorenzo's angel of God, and then, Audubon dreamed, with his mind going to his pointed brush, it must see like this, and he tightened his hand on the trigger of the gun and pulled it, and his eyes went closed. In memory the heron was all its solitude, its total beauty. All

---

7. Louis XVII (1785–95), imprisoned in 1792 during the French Revolution; it was rumored   (falsely) that another boy was executed in his stead and that the prince was spirited out of France.

its whiteness could be seen from all sides at once, its pure feathers were as if counted and known and their array one upon the other would never be lost. But it was not from that memory that he could paint.

His opening eyes met Lorenzo's, close and flashing, and it was on seeing horror deep in them, like fires in abysses, that he recognized it for the first time. He had never seen horror in its purity and clarity until now, in bright blue eyes. He went and picked up the bird. He had thought it to be a female, just as one sees the moon as female; and so it was. He put it in his bag, and started away. But Lorenzo had already gone on, leaning a-tilt on the horse which went slowly.

Murrell was left behind, but he was proud of the dispersal, as if he had done it, as if he had always known that three men in simply being together and doing a thing can, by their obstinacy, take the pride out of one another. Each must go away alone, each send the others away alone. He himself had purposely kept to the wildest country in the world, and would have sought it out, the loneliest road. He looked about with satisfaction, and hid. Travelers were forever innocent, he believed: that was his faith. He lay in wait; his faith was in innocence and his knowledge was of ruin; and had these things been shaken? Now, what could possibly be outside his grasp? Churning all about him like a cloud about the sun was the great folding descent of his thought. Plans of deeds made his thoughts, and they rolled and mingled about his ears as if he heard a dark voice that rose up to overcome the wilderness voice, or was one with it. The night would soon come; and he had gone through the day.

Audubon, splattered and wet, turned back into the wilderness with the heron warm under his hand, his head still light in a kind of trance. It was undeniable, on some Sunday mornings, when he turned over and over his drawings they seemed beautiful to him, through what was dramatic in the conflict of life, or what was exact. What he would draw, and what he had seen, became for a moment one to him then. Yet soon enough, and it seemed to come in that same moment, like Lorenzo's horror and the gun's firing, he knew that even the sight of the heron which surely he alone had appreciated, had not been all his belonging, and that never could any vision, even any simple sight, belong to him or to any man. He knew that the best he could make would be, after it was apart from his hand, a dead thing and not a live thing, never the essence, only a sum of parts; and that it would always meet with a stranger's sight, and never be one with the beauty in any other man's head in the world. As he had seen the bird most purely at its moment of death, in some fatal way, in his care for looking outward, he saw his long labor most revealingly at the point where it met its limit. Still carefully, for he was trained to see well in the dark, he walked on into the deeper woods, noting all sights, all sounds, and was gentler than they as he went.

In the woods that echoed yet in his ears, Lorenzo riding slowly looked back. The hair rose on his head and his hands began to shake with cold, and suddenly it seemed to him that God Himself, just now, thought of the Idea of Separateness. For surely He had never thought of it before, when the little white heron was flying down to feed. He could understand God's giving Separateness first and then giving Love to follow and heal in its wonder; but God had reversed this, and given Love first and then Separateness, as though it did not matter to Him which came first. Perhaps it was that God never counted the moments of Time, Lorenzo did that, among his tasks of love. Time did not occur to God. Therefore—did He even know of it? How to explain Time and Separateness back to God, Who had never thought of them, Who could let the whole world come to grief in a scattering moment?

Lorenzo brought his cold hands together in a clasp and stared through the distance at the place where the bird had been as if he saw it still; as if nothing could really take away what had happened to him, the beautiful little vision of the feeding bird. Its beauty had been greater than he could account for. The sweat of rapture poured down from his forehead, and then he shouted into the marshes.

"Tempter!"

He whirled forward in the saddle and began to hurry the horse to its high speed. His camp ground was far away still, though even now they must be lighting the torches and gathering in the multitudes, so that at the appointed time he would duly appear in their midst, to deliver his address on the subject of "In that day when all hearts shall be disclosed."

Then the sun dropped below the trees, and the new moon, slender and white, hung shyly in the west.

1943

◄ TILLIE OLSEN ►
1912–2007

Tillie Lerner Olsen exemplified the life she discusses in "Silences," the selection included here. Although she thought of herself as a writer for many years and worked on her craft as avidly as she could, she also had to support herself and her family, and she did not become a widely published writer until she was in her forties. Although her body of work remains relatively small, it is distinguished by its high quality and the high esteem in which it—and she—are held by writers and critics alike.

Olsen was born in Nebraska, the child of Russian Jewish immigrants who had fought in the failed 1905 revolution in Russia. Like her parents, she would become involved in Socialist and Communist Party activism, and her interests in helping the working poor are reflected in most of her writing. She left high school before graduating in order to work in a variety of blue-collar jobs—she has said that public libraries were her college—and participated in political activism that led to her being jailed twice. During this time she began writing polemical essays and poems, some of which were published, and working on her novel *Yonnondio*, which would remain unpublished until the 1970s. She had her first daughter at age nineteen, and in the early 1930s, she moved to northern California and became involved with her political compatriot Jack Olsen, with whom she would have three more daughters and whom she would eventually marry. She struggled during the 1930s and 1940s to combine her work outside the home with raising her four children, but she was able to do little writing.

In the 1950s, when her youngest child went to school, Olsen began writing again, taking creative writing courses at Stanford and San Francisco State Universities. She produced a group of stories that would be published together under the title *Tell Me a Riddle;* the title story won the O. Henry award in 1961 for the best short story of the year. These stories focus on lives lived under poverty and racism and examine in particular the world of women's work—both inside and outside the home—as well as the strains of family life. Her interest in family life, especially the mother-daughter bond, was reflected in two collections she edited during the 1980s, *Mother to Daughter, Daughter to Mother* and *Mothers and Daughters:*

That Special Quality. During the last two decades of her life, Olsen received numerous awards, grants, and honorary degrees; taught at universities all over the United States and abroad; and frequently gave lectures and readings.

"Silences" appeared first in 1965 but came to prominence with the publication of her book by the same title in 1978, (a book that also included Rebecca Harding Davis's story *Life in the Iron-Mills* (pp. 967–92), which Olsen rediscovered and brought to prominence). In the essay, she discusses the writer's life when it is lived without the "room of one's own" that Virginia Woolf (pp. 1342–50) describes as necessary to the craft. What has the world missed, what viewpoints have we systematically missed, she asks, because so many people—workers, the poor, women—have had so little time to create art based on their life experiences? Olsen calls attention to the relation between art and material existence here and has helped open the way for us to reclaim many of the formerly forgotten writers included in this anthology.

Silences

Literary history and the present are dark with silences: some the silences for years by our acknowledged great; some silences hidden; some the ceasing to publish after one work appears; some the never coming to book form at all.

What is it that happens with the creator, to the creative process, in that time? What *are* creation's needs for full functioning? Without intention of or pretension to literary scholarship, I have had special need to learn all I could of this over the years, myself so nearly remaining mute and having to let writing die over and over again in me.

These are not *natural* silences—what Keats[1] called *agonie ennuyeuse* (the tedious agony)—that necessary time for renewal, lying fallow, gestation, in the natural cycle of creation. The silences I speak of here are unnatural: the unnatural thwarting of what struggles to come into being, but cannot. In the old, the obvious parallels: when the seed strikes stone; the soil will not sustain; the spring is false; the time is drought or blight or infestation; the frost comes premature.

The great in achievement have known such silences—Thomas Hardy, Melville, Rimbaud, Gerard Manley Hopkins.[2] They tell us little as to why or how the creative working atrophied and died in them—if ever it did.

"Less and less shrink the visions then vast in me," writes Thomas Hardy in his thirty-year ceasing from novels after the Victorian vileness to his *Jude the Obscure.* ("So ended his prose contributions to literature, his experiences having killed all his interest in this form"—the official explanation.) But the great poetry he wrote to the end of his life was not sufficient to hold, to develop the vast visions which for twenty-five years had had expression in novel after novel. People, situations, interrelationships, landscape—they cry for this larger life in poem after poem.

It was not visions shrinking with Hopkins, but a different torment. For seven years he kept his religious vow to refrain from writing poetry, but the poet's eye he could not shut, nor win "elected silence to beat upon [his] whorled ear." "I had

---

1. John Keats: English romantic poet (1795–1821).
2. Thomas Hardy: English novelist and poet (1840–1928); Melville: Herman Melville, American novelist and short-story writer (1819–91);

Rimbaud: Jean Nicolas Arthur Rimbaud, French poet (1854–91); Gerard Manley Hopkins: English poet (1844–89); all stopped writing for some significant period during their careers.

long had haunting my ear the echo of a poem which now I realised on paper," he writes of the first poem permitted to end the seven years' silence. But poetry ("to hoard unheard; be heard, unheeded") could be only the least and last of his heavy priestly responsibilities. Nineteen poems were all he could produce in his last nine years—fullness to us, but torment pitched past grief to him, who felt himself "time's eunuch, never to beget."

Silence surrounds Rimbaud's silence. Was there torment of the unwritten; haunting of rhythm, of visions; anguish at dying powers, the seventeen years after he abandoned the unendurable literary world? We know only that the need to write continued into his first years of vagabondage; that he wrote:

Had I not once a youth pleasant, heroic, fabulous enough to write on leaves of gold: too much luck. Through what crime, what error, have I earned my present weakness? You who maintain that some animals sob sorrowfully, that the dead have dreams, try to tell the story of my downfall and my slumber. I no longer know how to speak.[3]

That on his deathbed, he spoke again like a poet-visionary.

Melville's stages to his thirty-year prose silence are clearest. The presage is in his famous letter to Hawthorne, as he had to hurry *Moby Dick* to an end:

I am so pulled hither and thither by circumstances. The calm, the coolness, the silent grass-growing mood in which a man ought always to compose,—that, I fear, can seldom be mine. Dollars damn me. . . . What I feel most moved to write, that is banned,—it will not pay. Yet, altogether, write the *other* way I cannot. So the product is a final hash . . .

Reiterated in *Pierre,* writing "that book whose unfathomable cravings drink his blood . . . when at last the idea obtruded that the wiser and profounder he should grow, the more and the more he lessened his chances for bread."

To be possessed; to have to try final hash; to have one's work met by "drear ignoring"; to be damned by dollars into a Customs House job; to have only weary evenings and Sundays left for writing—

How bitterly did unreplying Pierre feel in his heart that to most of the great works of humanity, their authors had given not weeks and months, not years and years, but their wholly surrendered and dedicated lives.

Is it not understandable why Melville began to burn work, then ceased to write it, "immolating [it] . . . sealing in a fate subdued"? And turned to occasional poetry, manageable in a time sense, "to nurse through night the ethereal spark." A thirty-year night. He was nearly seventy before he could quit the customs dock and again have full time for writing, start back to prose. "Age, dull tranquilizer," and devastation of "arid years that filed before" to work through. Three years of tryings before he felt capable of beginning *Billy Budd* (the kernel waiting half a century); three years more to his last days (he who had been so fluent), the slow, painful, never satisfied writing and re-writing of it.[4]

Kin to these years-long silences are the *hidden* silences; work aborted, deferred, denied—hidden by the work which does come to fruition. Hopkins rightfully belongs here; almost certainly William Blake; Jane Austen, Olive Schreiner,

---

3. *A Season in Hell.* [Olsen's note]

4. "Entering my eighth decade [I come] into possession of unobstructed leisure . . . just as, in the course of nature, my vigor sensibly declines. What little of it is left, I husband for certain matters as yet incomplete and which indeed may never be completed." *Billy Budd* never was completed; it was edited from drafts found after Melville's death. [Olsen's note]

Theodore Dreiser, Willa Cather, Franz Kafka; Katherine Anne Porter,[5] many other contemporary writers.

Censorship silences. Deletions, omissions, abandonment of the medium (as with Hardy); paralyzing of capacity (as Dreiser's ten-year stasis on *Jennie Gerhardt* after the storm against *Sister Carrie*). Publishers' censorship, refusing subject matter or treatment as "not suitable" or "no market for." Self-censorship. Religious, political censorship—sometimes spurring inventiveness—most often (read Dostoyevsky's[6] letters) a wearing attrition.

The extreme of this: those writers physically silenced by governments. Isaac Babel, the years of imprisonment, what took place in him with what wanted to be written? Or in Oscar Wilde, who was not permitted even a pencil until the last months of his imprisonment?[7]

Other silences. The truly memorable poem, story, or book, then the writer ceasing to be published.[8] Was one work all the writers had in them (life too thin for pressure of material, renewal) and the respect for literature too great to repeat themselves? Was it "the knife of the perfectionist attitude in art and life" at their throat? Were the conditions not present for establishing the habits of creativity (a young Colette[9] who lacked a Willy to lock her in her room each day)? or—as instanced over and over—other claims, other responsibilities so writing could not be first? (The writer of a class, sex, color still marginal in literature, and whose coming to written voice at all against complex odds is exhausting achievement.) It is an eloquent commentary that this one-book silence has been true of most black writers; only eleven in the hundred years since 1850 have published novels more than twice.[1]

There is a prevalent silence I pass by quickly, the absence of creativity where it once had been; the ceasing to create literature, though the books may keep coming out year after year. That suicide of the creative process Hemingway describes so accurately in "The Snows of Kilimanjaro":

He had destroyed his talent himself—by not using it, by betrayals of himself and what he believed in, by drinking so much that he blunted the edge of his perceptions, by laziness, by sloth, by snobbery, by hook and by crook; selling vitality, trading it for security, for comfort.

No, not Scott Fitzgerald.[2] His not a death of creativity, not silence, but what happens when (his words) there is "the sacrifice of talent, in pieces, to preserve its essential value."

5. William Blake (English poet, 1757–1827), Jane Austen (English novelist, 1775–1817), Olive Schreiner (South African short-story writer, 1855–1920), Theodore Dreiser (American novelist, 1871–1945), Willa Cather (American novelist, 1873–1947), Franz Kafka (Bohemian/German novelist and short-story writer, 1883–1924), and Katherine Anne Porter (American novelist and short-story writer, 1890–1980) were all writers known to have faced obstacles both in writing and in getting their work published; Dreiser and Kafka both faced considerable critical controversies about their work during their lifetimes. For more information about Austen, Cather, and Porter, and selections of their work, see pp. 545–51, 1269–75, and 1389–97 in this volume.
6. Fyodor Dostoyevsky (1821–81), Russian writer.
7. Isaac Babel (1894–1940) was shot in a Russian

prison, allegedly for espionage, but in actuality for publishing work critical of the Soviet Union under Stalin; Oscar Wilde (1854–1900) was imprisoned in England for "gross indecency" (because he was homosexual and homosexuality was illegal at that time).
8. As Jean Toomer (*Cane*); Henry Roth (*Call It Sleep*); Edith Summers Kelley (*Weeds*). [Olsen's note]
9. Collette: French novelist (1873–1954); her first husband, Henri Gauthier-Villars, used "Willy" as a pen name.
1. Robert Bone, *The Negro Novel in America*, 1958. [Olsen's note]
2. Hemingway: Ernest Hemingway (1899–1961), American novelist and short-story writer; Scott Fitzgerald: F. Scott Fitzgerald (1896–1940), American novelist and short-story writer.

Almost unnoted are the foreground silences, *before* the achievement. (Remember when Emerson hailed Whitman's genius, he guessed correctly: "which yet must have had a long *foreground* for such a start.") George Eliot, Joseph Conrad, Isak Dinesen, Sherwood Anderson, Dorothy Richardson, Elizabeth Madox Roberts, A.E. Coppard, Angus Wilson, Joyce Cary—all close to, or in their forties before they became published writers; Lampedusa, Maria Dermout (*The Ten Thousand Things*), Laura Ingalls Wilder, the "children's writer," in their sixties.[3] Their capacity evident early in the "being one on whom nothing is lost"; in other writers' spons. Not all struggling and anguished, like Anderson, the foreground years; cumstances the immobilization of long illness or loss, or the sudden lifting of re- writer-daughter's in writing necessary, make writing possible; others waiting circ- gement (George Eliot, her Henry Lewes; Laura Wilder, a

Very close to this last that she transmute her storytelling gift onto paper). writing. Among these, the mut┄g are the silences where the lives never came to are all struggle for existence; the barelous Miltons:[4] those whose waking hours lence the silence of centuries as to how life╌ated; the illiterate; women. Their si- of their making, of course, in folk song, lullaby, tales, language itself, jokes, max- ims, superstitions—but we know nothing of the creators or how it was with them. In the fantasy of Shakespeare born in deepest Africa (as at least one Shakespeare must have been), was the ritual, the oral storytelling a fulfillment? Or was there restlessness, indefinable yearning, a sense of restriction? Was it as Virginia Woolf in *A Room of One's Own* guesses—about women?[5]

Genius of a sort must have existed among them, as it existed among the working classes,[6] but certainly it never got itself onto paper. When, however, one reads of a woman possessed by the devils, of a wise woman selling herbs, or even a remarkable man who had a remark- able mother, then I think we are on the track of a lost novelist, a suppressed poet, or some Emily Brontë who dashed her brains out on the moor, crazed with the torture her gift had put her to.

Rebecca Harding Davis[7] whose work sleeps in the forgotten (herself as a woman of a century ago so close to remaining mute), also guessed about the silent in that time of the twelve-hour-a-day, six-day work week. She writes of the illiter- ate ironworker in *Life in the Iron Mills* who sculptured great shapes in the slag:

3. Some other foreground silences: Elizabeth (Mrs.) Gaskell, Kate Chopin, Cora Sandel, Cyrus Colter, Hortense Calisher. [Olsen's note] Other writers mentioned in this paragraph: Ralph Waldo Emerson (American essayist, 1803–82), Walt Whitman (American poet, 1819–92), George Eliot (English novelist, 1819–80), Joseph Conrad (Po- lish novelist, 1857–1924), Isak Dinesen (Danish short-story writer, 1885–1962), Sherwood Ander- son (American short-story writer, 1876–1941), Dorothy Richardson (English novelist, 1873– 1957), Elizabeth Madox Roberts (American poet, short-story writer, and novelist, 1881–1941), A. E. Coppard (English poet and short-story writer, 1878–1941), Angus Wilson (British short-story writer and novelist, 1913–91), Joyce Cary (Irish novelist, 1888–1957), Giuseppe Tomasi di Lampe- dusa (Italian novelist, 1896–1957), Maria Der- mout (Indonesian novelist, 1888–1962), Laura

Ingalls Wilder (American novelist, 1867–1957). For more information about Gaskell, Chopin, Eliot, and Dinesen, and a selection of their work, see pp. 713–32, 1048–1135, 862–80, and 1359–63. Henry Lewes (1817–78) was George Eliot's life partner. [Editor's note]
4. In "Elegy Written in a Country Churchyard," English poet Thomas Gray (1716–71) muses on the dead who may never have had the chance to write, calling them "mute inglorious Miltons," re- ferring to the English poet John Milton (1608–74).
5. For more information about Woolf and a se- lection from *A Room of One's Own,* see pp. 1342–50.
6. Half of the working classes *are* women. [Olsen's note]
7. For more information about Davis and the text of *Life in the Iron-Mills,* see pp. 967–92.

"his fierce thirst for beauty, to know it, to create it, to *be* something other than he is—a passion of pain"; Margret Howth in the textile mill:

There were things in the world, that like herself, were marred, did not understand, were hungry to know. . . . Her eyes quicker to see than ours, delicate or grand lines in the homeliest things. . . . Everything she saw or touched, nearer, more human than to you or me. These sights and sounds did not come to her common; she never got used to living as other people do.

She never got used to living as other people do. Was that one of the ways it was? So some of the silences, incomplete listing of the incomplete, where the need and capacity to create were of a high order.

Now, what *is* the work of creation and the circumstances it dem___ ___ functioning—as told in the journals, letters, notes, of the practit___, Valéry's *Course* Henry James, Katherine Mansfield, André Gide, Virgin___ ___, Flaubert, Rilke, Joseph Conrad; Thomas Wolfe's *Stor___* *in Poetics.*[8] What do they explain of the silence___ says (and demonstrated) Balzac:

"Constant toil is the law of art, as it is

To pass from conception to exe___ ___, to produce, to bring the idea to birth, to raise the child laboriously from infancy, to put it nightly to sleep surfeited, to kiss it in the mornings with the hungry heart of a mother, to clean it, to clothe it fifty times over in new garments which it tears and casts away, and yet not revolt against the trials of this agitated life—this unwearying maternal love, this habit of creation—this is execution and its toils.

"Without duties, almost without external communication," Rilke specifies, "unconfined solitude which takes every day like a life, a spaciousness which puts no limit to vision and in the midst of which infinities surround."

Unconfined solitude as Joseph Conrad experienced it:

For twenty months I wrestled with the Lord for my creation . . . mind and will and conscience engaged to the full, hour after hour, day after day . . . a lonely struggle in a great isolation from the world. I suppose I slept and ate the food put before me and talked connectedly on suitable occasions, but I was never aware of the even flow of daily life, made easy and noiseless for me by a silent, watchful, tireless affection.

So there is a homely underpinning for it all, the even flow of daily life made easy and noiseless.

"The terrible law of the artist"—says Henry James—"the law of fructification, of fertilization. The old, old lesson of the art of meditation. To woo combinations and inspirations into being by a depth and continuity of attention and meditation."

"That load, that weight, that gnawing conscience," writes Thomas Mann—

That sea which to drink up, that frightful task . . . The will, the discipline and self-control to shape a sentence or follow out a hard train of thought. From the first rhythmical urge of the inward creative force towards the material, towards casting in shape and form, from that to the thought, the image, the word, the line, what a struggle, what Gethsemane.[9]

8. Writers mentioned in this paragraph and the next: Henry James (American novelist, 1843–1916), Katherine Mansfield (New Zealand short-story writer, 1888–1923), André Gide (French novelist, 1869–1941), Gustave Flaubert (French novelist, 1821–80), Rainer Maria Rilke (Czech/German poet, 1875–1926), Thomas Wolfe (Amer-

ican novelist, 1900–1938), Paul Valéry (French poet, 1871–1945), and Honoré de Balzac (French novelist, 1799–1850).
9. Thomas Mann: German novelist (1875–1955); Gethsemane: garden in which Jesus spent the might before his crucifixion.

Does it become very clear what Melville's Pierre so bitterly remarked on, and what literary history bears out—why most of the great works of humanity have come from lives (able to be) wholly surrendered and dedicated? How else sustain the constant toil, the frightful task, the terrible law, the continuity? Full self: this means full time as and when needed for the work. (That time for which Emily Dickinson[1] withdrew from the world.)

But what if there is not that fullness of time, let alone totality of self? What if the writers, as in some of these silences, must work regularly at something besides their own work—as do nearly all in the arts in the United States today.

I know the theory (kin to "starving in the garret makes great art") that it is this very circumstance which feeds creativity. I know, too, that for the beginning young, for some who have such need, the job can be valuable access to life they would not otherwise know. A few (I think of the doctors, the incomparables: Chekhov and William Carlos Williams)[2] for special reasons sometimes manage both. But the actuality testifies: substantial creative work demands time, and with rare exceptions only full-time workers have achieved it. Where the claims of creation cannot be primary, the results are atrophy; unfinished work; minor effort and accomplishment; silences. (Desperation which accounts for the mountains of applications to the foundations for grants—undivided time—in the strange breadline system we have worked out for our artists.)

Twenty years went by on the writing of *Ship of Fools*, while Katherine Anne Porter, who needed only two, was "trying to get to that table, to that typewriter, away from my jobs of teaching and trooping this country and of keeping house." "Your subconscious needed that time to grow the layers of pearl," she was told. Perhaps, perhaps, but I doubt it. Subterranean forces can make you wait, but they are very finicky about the kind of waiting it has to be. Before they will feed the creator back, they must be fed, passionately fed, what needs to be worked on. "We hold up our desire as one places a magnet over a composite dust from which the particle of iron will suddenly jump up," says Paul Valéry. A receptive waiting, that means, not demands which prevent "an undistracted center of being." And when the response comes, availability to work must be immediate. If not used at once, all may vanish as a dream; worse, future creation be endangered—for only the removal and development of the material frees the forces for further work.

There is a life in which all this is documented: Franz Kafka's. For every one entry from his diaries here, there are fifty others that testify as unbearably to the driven stratagems for time, the work lost (to us), the damage to the creative powers (and the body) of having to deny, interrupt, postpone, put aside, let work die.

"I cannot devote myself completely to my writing," Kafka explains (in 1911). "I could not live by literature if only, to begin with, because of the slow maturing of my work and its special character." So he worked as an official in a state insurance agency, and wrote when he could.

These two can never be reconciled. . . . If I have written something one evening, I am afire the next day in the office and can bring nothing to completion. Outwardly I fulfill my office duties satisfactorily, not my inner duties however, and every unfulfilled inner duty becomes a misfortune that never leaves. What strength it will necessarily drain me of.

1. For more information on Dickinson and a selection of her work, see pp. 938–51 in this volume.
2. Chekhov: Anton Chekhov, Russian playwright and short-story writer (1860–1904); William Carlos Williams, American poet (1883–1963)—both physicians.

1911

No matter how little the time or how badly I write, I feel approaching the imminent possibility of great moments which could make me capable of anything. But my being does not have sufficient strength to hold this to the next writing time. During the day the visible world helps me; during the night it cuts me to pieces unhindered. . . . In the evening and in the morning, my consciousness of the creative abilities in me then I can encompass. I feel shaken to the core of my being. Calling forth such powers which are then not permitted to function.

. . . which are then not permitted to function . . .

1911

I finish nothing, because I have no time, and it presses so within me.

1912

When I begin to write after such a long interval, I draw the words as if out of the empty air. If I capture one, then I have just this one alone, and all the toil must begin anew.

1914

Yesterday for the first time in months, an indisputable ability to do good work. And yet wrote only the first page. Again I realize that everything written down bit by bit rather than all at once in the course of the larger part is inferior, and that the circumstances of my life condemn me to this inferiority.

1915

My constant attempt by sleeping before dinner to make it possible to continue working [writing] late into the night, senseless. Then at one o'clock can no longer fall asleep at all, the next day at work insupportable, and so I destroy myself.

1917

Distractedness, weak memory, stupidity. Days passed in futility, powers wasted away in waiting. . . . Always this one principal anguish—if I had gone away in 1911 in full possession of all my powers. Not eaten by the strain of keeping down living forces.

Eaten into tuberculosis. By the time he won through to himself and time for writing, his body could live no more. He was forty-one.

I think of Rilke who said, "If I have any responsibility, I mean and desire it to be responsibility for the deepest and innermost essence of the loved reality [writing] to which I am inseparably bound"; and who also said, "Anything alive that makes demands, arouses in me an infinite capacity to give it its due, the consequences of which completely use me up." These were true with Kafka, too, yet how different their lives. When Rilke wrote that about responsibility, he is explaining why he will not take a job to support his wife and baby, nor live with them (years later will not come to his daughter's wedding nor permit a two-hour honeymoon visit lest it break his solitude where he awaits poetry). The "infinite capacity" is his explanation as to why he cannot even bear to have a dog. Extreme—and justified. He protected his creative powers.

Kafka's, Rilke's "infinite capacity," and all else that has been said here of the needs of creation, illuminate women's silence of centuries. I will not repeat what is in

Virginia Woolf's *A Room of One's Own*, but talk of this last century and a half in which women have begun to have voice in literature. (It has been less than that time in Eastern Europe, and not yet, in many parts of the world.)

In the last century, of the women whose achievements endure for us in one way or another,[3] nearly all never married (Jane Austen, Emily Brontë, Christina Rossetti, Emily Dickinson, Louisa May Alcott, Sarah Orne Jewett) or married late in their thirties (George Eliot, Elizabeth Barrett Browning, Charlotte Brontë, Olive Schreiner). I can think of only four (George Sand, Harriet Beecher Stowe, Helen Hunt Jackson, and Elizabeth Gaskell) who married and had children as young women.[4] All had servants.

In our century, until very recently, it has not been so different. Most did not marry (Selma Lagerlof, Willa Cather, Ellen Glasgow, Gertrude Stein, Gabriela Mistral, Elizabeth Madox Roberts, Charlotte Mew, Eudora Welty, Marianne Moore) or, if married, have been childless (Edith Wharton, Virginia Woolf, Katherine Mansfield, Dorothy Richardson, H. H. Richardson, Elizabeth Bowen, Isak Dinesen, Katherine Anne Porter, Lillian Hellman, Dorothy Parker). Colette had one child (when she was forty). If I include Sigrid Undset, Kay Boyle, Pearl Buck, Dorothy Canfield Fisher, that will make a small group who had more than one child.[5] All had household help or other special circumstances.

Am I resaying the moldy theory that women have no need, some say no capacity, to create art, because they can "create" babies? And the additional proof is precisely that the few women who have created it are nearly all childless? No.

The power and the need to create, over and beyond reproduction, is native in both women and men. Where the gifted among women (*and men*) have remained mute, or have never attained full capacity, it is because of circumstances, inner or outer, which oppose the needs of creation.

Wholly surrendered and dedicated lives; time as needed for the work; totality of self. But women are traditionally trained to place others' needs first, to feel

3. "One Out of Twelve" has a more extensive roll of women writers of achievement. [Olsen's note]
4. I would now add a fifth—Kate Chopin—also a foreground silence. [Olsen's note] Other writers mentioned in this paragraph: Emily Brontë (English poet and novelist, 1818–48), Christina Rossetti (English poet, 1830–94), Louisa May Alcott (American short-story writer and novelist, 1832–88), Sarah Orne Jewett (American short-story writer, 1849–1909), Elizabeth Barrett Browning (English poet, 1806–61), Charlotte Brontë (English novelist, 1818–55), George Sand (French novelist, 1804–76), Harriet Beecher Stowe (American novelist, 1811–96), Helen Hunt Jackson (American novelist, 1830–85). For more information and a selection of their works, see pp. 836–42 for Emily Brontë; pp. 951–66 for Rossetti; pp. 999–1013 for Alcott; pp. 1041–48 for Jewett; pp. 650–80 for Browning; pp. 826–33 for Charlotte Brontë; pp. 732–78 for Stowe; and pp. 935–38 for Jackson.
5. Writers mentioned in this paragraph: Selma Lagerlof (Swedish novelist, 1858–1940), Willa Cather (American novelist, 1873–1945), Ellen Glasgow (American novelist, 1873–1945), Gertrude Stein (American poet, 1874–1946), Gabriela Mistral (Chilean poet, 1889–1957), Charlotte Mew (English poet, 1868–1928), Eudora Welty (American short-story writer, 1909–2001), Marianne Moore (American poet, 1887–1972), Edith Wharton (American novelist, 1862–1937), Henry Handel (Henrietta) Richardson (Australian short-story writer and novelist, 1870–1946), Elizabeth Bowen (Anglo-Irish short-story writer and novelist, 1879–1973), Lillian Hellman (American playwright, 1905–84), Dorothy Parker (American poet and short-story writer, 1893–1967), Sigrid Undset (Norwegian novelist, 1882–1949), Kay Boyle (American poet, short-story writer, and novelist, 1902–92), Pearl Buck (American novelist, 1892–1973), Dorothy Canfield Fisher (American short-story writer and novelist, 1879–1958). Lagerlof, Mistral, and Undset all won the Nobel Prize for Literature. For more information and a selection of their works, see pp. 1269–75 for Cather; pp. 1258–68 for Glasgow; pp. 1439–49 for Welty; pp. 1373–78 for Moore; pp. 1218–28 for Wharton; and pp. 1428–34 for Parker.

these needs as their own (the "infinite capacity"), their sphere, their satisfaction to be in making it possible for others to use their abilities. This is what Virginia Woolf meant when, already a writer of achievement, she wrote in her diary:

Father's birthday. He would have been 96, 96, yes, today; and could have been 96, like other people one has known; but mercifully was not. His life would have entirely ended mine. What would have happened? No writing, no books;—inconceivable.

It took family deaths to free more than one woman writer into her own development.[6] Emily Dickinson freed herself, denying all the duties expected of a woman of her social position except the closest family ones, and she was fortunate to have a sister, and servants, to share those. How much is revealed of the differing circumstances and fate of their own as-great capacities, in the diaries (and lives) of those female bloodkin of great writers: Dorothy Wordsworth, Alice James, Aunt Mary Moody Emerson.[7]

And where there is no servant or relation to assume the responsibilities of daily living? Listen to Katherine Mansfield in the early days of her relationship with John Middleton Murry, when they both dreamed of becoming great writers:[8]

The house seems to take up so much time. . . . I mean when I have to clean up twice over or wash up extra unnecessary things, I get frightfully impatient and want to be working [writing]. So often this week you and Gordon have been talking while I washed dishes. Well someone's got to wash dishes and get food. Otherwise "there's nothing in the house but eggs to eat." And after you have gone I walk about with a mind full of ghosts of saucepans and primus stoves and "will there be enough to go around?" And you calling, whatever I am doing, writing, "Tig, isn't there going to be tea? It's five o'clock."

I loathe myself today. This woman who superintends you and rushes about slamming doors and slopping water and shouts "You might at least empty the pail and wash out the tea leaves." . . . O Jack, I wish that you would take me in your arms and kiss my hands and my face and every bit of me and say, "It's all right, you darling thing, I understand."

A long way from Conrad's favorable circumstances for creation: the flow of daily life made easy and noiseless.

And, if in addition to the infinite capacity, to the daily responsibilities, there are children?

Balzac, you remember, described creation in terms of motherhood. Yes, in intelligent passionate motherhood there are similarities, and in more than the toil and patience. The calling upon total capacities; the reliving and new using of the

---

6. Among them: George Eliot, Helen Hunt Jackson, Mrs. Gaskell, Kate Chopin, Lady Gregory, Isak Dinesen. Ivy Compton-Burnett finds this the grim reason for the emergence of British women novelists after World War I: ". . . The men were dead, you see, and the women didn't marry so much because there was no one for them to marry, and so they had leisure, and I think, in a good many cases they had money because their brothers were dead, and all that would tend to writing, wouldn't it, being single, and having some money, and having the time—having no men, you see." [Olsen's note] Augusta, Lady Gregory (Irish writer, 1852–1932); Ivy Compton-Burnett (En-

glish novelist, 1884–1969).
7. Dorothy Wordsworth (English, 1771–1855, sister of poet William Wordsworth; see pp. 402–6); Alice James (American, 1848–92, sister of Henry and William James); Mary Moody Emerson (American, 1774–1863, aunt who raised Ralph Waldo Emerson).
8. Already in that changed time when servants were not necessarily a part of the furnishings of almost anyone well educated enough to be making literature. [Olsen's note] John Middleton Murry (English writer, 1889–1957), Mansfield's second husband.